The American Directory of

Writer's Guidelines

The American Directory of

Writer's Guidelines

A Compilation of Information for Freelancers From More Than 1,300 Magazine Editors and Book Publishers

2nd Edition

Compiled and Edited by John C. Mutchler

Quill
Driver
Books

Clovis, California

Published by
Quill Driver Books/Word Dancer Press, Inc.
8386 N. Madsen Avenue
Clovis, CA 93611
(559) 322-5917
FAX (559) 322-5967

Printed in The United States of America

Quill Driver Books/Word Dancer Press books may be purchased
at special prices for educational, fund-raising, business
or promotional use. Please contact:

Special Markets
Quill Driver Books\Word Dancer Press, Inc.
8386 N. Madsen Avenue
Clovis, CA 93611
1-800-497-4909

**To order an additional copy of this book
please call 1-800-497-4909**

ISBN 1-884956-08-4

Quill Driver Books/Word Dancer Press, Inc.
Project Cadre:

Gina-Marie Cheeseman
Doris Hall
Stephen Blake Mettee
Linda Kay Weber

The American directory of writer's guidelines : a compilation of
information for freelancers from more than 1,300 magazine editors
and book publishers / compiled and edited by John C. Mutchler.
    p.   cm.
    Includes index.
    ISBN 1-884956-08-4 (trade paper)
    1. Authorship--Handbooks, manuals, etc. 2. Journalism-
-Authorship--Handbooks, manuals, etc.   I. Mutchler, John C.,
1945-
    .
PN147. A479   1999
070.5'02573--DC21   97-4266
                                                         CIP

THIS BOOK IS DEDICATED TO EVERYONE WHO BEARS THE BURDEN OF THE TITLE "EDITOR," "PUBLISHER" OR ANY VARIANT THEREOF.

Contents

Periodicals

Book Publishers

Acknowledgments

THE CONCEPT BEHIND THIS BOOK—that writers, editors, and publishers will benefit from an extensive collection of writer's guidelines in a single reference work—is proving to be true if only because so many editors and publishers thought it worthwhile to participate.

No book has ever been placed on a shelf in a library or bookstore unless many folks worked very hard behind the scenes to help get it there. My wife, Susan, pitched in and spent many hours doing what had to be done to help build the manuscript. I am indebted to my publisher, Stephen Blake Mettee, and to the professionals on his staff who know how to take manuscripts submitted to them and turn them into something better. Writers, editors, and publishers everywhere will be better off as a result of your combined "pre-press" efforts. Thank you one and all.

Introduction

Dear Writer,

THE AMERICAN DIRECTORY OF WRITER'S GUIDELINES exists to provide you with the information you need to become published time and again.

Editors at the hundreds of magazine and book publishers included here have written these guidelines to explain what they hope to receive from freelance writers. They do this to make the process easier for you, the writer, but they also do it to make it easier on themselves in that submissions from writers who have read their guidelines are likely to be more on target. Less of the editor's time will be wasted culling the hits from the misses and less time will be spent repairing the near hits.

What editors are hoping for can be boiled down to two points: professionalism in the business end of things, including queries and manuscript format and—most important— good writing properly slanted toward the interests of those who read their publications or purchase their books.

For many writers it comes as bad news that the successfully published writer is also a successful marketer. In essence, the information in this directory is about what the market needs—and will buy. Whether you get published extensively is a function of how often and how well you supply *exactly* what the markets need. Writer's guidelines are recipes: Follow the instructions they contain, always write your best and you will be pleasantly surprised with the results!

Best wishes for your marketing and writing success,

— John Mutchler

P.S. If you have questions or comments about the material contained in this book—or about any aspect of marketing your work—send me an e-mail (JMutchler @worldnet.att.net). I'll be happy to send you a quick response.

How to Use This Book

- Publications and publishing houses are arranged alphabetically by name: periodicals beginning on page 7 and book publishers on page 545. Contact information for submissions is shown at the end of each set of guidelines.

- The Topic Index beginning on page 697 lists areas of interest such as agriculture, science fiction or woodworking. Names of the publishers interested in seeing material on or relating to these subjects are listed below each topic.

When You Already Have an Idea...

If you have a certain subject you wish to write about, consult the Topic Index. Periodical publishers are *italicized*, book publishers are set in roman type.

To Develop New Ideas...

Brainstorm for article, short story and book ideas by browsing both the guidelines themselves and the Topic Index.

Keep Track of Your Submissions...

Photocopy the Submission Tracking Sheet on page 2 to track your submissions.

A Couple of Notes...

The publishers selected the topics under which they are listed from a list supplied to them and added their own subjects when appropriate. The guidelines have been left much as they came in but were edited to avoid repeating *basic* manuscript preparation and submission requirements. You'll find this information in "A Word About Submissions" on page 3 and "Standard Manuscript Format," page 6. Some publishers have special requirements, so be sure to check individual guidelines carefully before submitting.

Submission Tracking Sheet

Photocopy this page for each item submitted

Title: _____

Notes:

① Publisher: _____ Editor: _____ Phone: _____

Address: _____ Date submitted: _____ Multiple Submission? No Yes

Date to follow up: _____ Date followed up: _____ Follow up note: _____

Date accepted: _____ Pub date: _____ Payment due date: _____ Payment amount: _____ Clips received: _____ Rejected date: _____

② Publisher: _____ Editor: _____ Phone: _____

Address: _____ Date submitted: _____ Multiple Submission? No Yes

Date to follow up: _____ Date followed up: _____ Follow up note: _____

Date accepted: _____ Pub date: _____ Payment due date: _____ Payment amount: _____ Clips received: _____ Rejected date: _____

③ Publisher: _____ Editor: _____ Phone: _____

Address: _____ Date submitted: _____ Multiple Submission? No Yes

Date to follow up: _____ Date followed up: _____ Follow up note: _____

Date accepted: _____ Pub date: _____ Payment due date: _____ Payment amount: _____ Clips received: _____ Rejected date: _____

④ Publisher: _____ Editor: _____ Phone: _____

Address: _____ Date submitted: _____ Multiple Submission? No Yes

Date to follow up: _____ Date followed up: _____ Follow up note: _____

Date accepted: _____ Pub date: _____ Payment due date: _____ Payment amount: _____ Clips received: _____ Rejected date: _____

⑤ Publisher: _____ Editor: _____ Phone: _____

Address: _____ Date submitted: _____ Multiple Submission? No Yes

Date to follow up: _____ Date followed up: _____ Follow up note: _____

Date accepted: _____ Pub date: _____ Payment due date: _____ Payment amount: _____ Clips received: _____ Rejected date: _____

A Word About Submissions

A HIGH-PROFILE MAGAZINE MAY RECEIVE HUNDREDS OF SUBMISSIONS each month, yet publish fewer than twenty articles or stories per issue. Likewise, many book publishers receive hundreds or thousands of submissions each year, but—without regard for the quality of the submissions—can only publish a small percentage.

For argument's sake, and because it'll be pretty close to the truth in many instances, let's say a publisher's acceptance-to-rejection ratio represents a one-in-fifty chance of any individual submission being published. While these are good odds compared with those offered by any of the various state lotteries, one-in-fifty still represents a highly competitive market.

How can you shave these odds? By making certain your submission fits the editor's needs and that your writing, including grammar, spelling and punctuation—along with its physical presentation in the form of your query letter, proposal or manuscript—adheres to professional standards.

A good place to start on this professional course is by studying the guidelines of the publisher you're targeting. Guidelines offer a wealth of information, and the smart—the professional—writer checks them out before submitting.

Making It Past the First Cut

The stack of unsolicited submissions—in publishing jargon called the "slush pile"—is so tall on the desks of many editors that they have developed methods similar to ones used by individuals in other industries who must deal with a heavy volume of incoming mail.

For example, if a personnel manager advertises to fill a vacancy, she may receive dozens of resumes in response. She may approach the task of evaluating the resumes by sorting them into two piles, those which exhibit a professional appearance and those that do not. This is a "first cut," and the sloppiest of the resumes will not survive it. She assumes those who submitted sloppy resumes will, if hired, do a sloppy job. And it's a good bet she's right.

Editors are not unlike our make-believe personnel manager. Here are some things you can do to assure your submission makes it past the first cut:

- Use 20- to 24-pound, good quality, letter-sized white paper for manuscripts and book proposals. Query letters and cover letters may be on your letterhead. If you use fanfold computer paper, separate the pages and tear off the line holes.
- Type or print on only one side of a page.
- Avoid difficult-to-read copy. Editors prefer clean, dark type. Photocopies should be top quality. Handwritten copy is almost always the kiss of death. Check individual guidelines to see if dot-matrix submis-

sions are acceptable.

• Unless a publisher's guidelines call for something different, follow a standard manuscript format such as the one shown on page 6. Cover letters and query letters are single spaced.

• Include your name, address and daytime telephone number (including area code) on all letters and on the first page of all manuscripts.

• Include an SASE (self-addressed, stamped envelope). Most editors won't acknowledge receipt of or reply to—and some report they don't even read—an unsolicited submission unless it is accompanied by an SASE.

This can be a large envelope for the return of all the material you submitted or a business-sized envelope for return of your cover or query letter and, perhaps, one or two sheets from the publisher. If you do not wish any part of the material you submitted returned to you, you may mark the outside of your submission "recycle if rejected." If you would like to know that the submission arrived, include a self-addressed, stamped postcard with the details of the submission written on it for an editor or staff member to return. If you submit to a foreign publisher, include International Reply Coupons for the return postage. Never include metered postage, coins, currency, checks or stamps in lieu of affixing the correct postage.

Other Things You Can Do

Focus your submissions to the right publishers. Don't send book proposals on woodcarving to publishers of political commentaries or an article on vegetarian cooking to business magazines. Look through the guidelines for publishers who have a history of publishing material similar to what you plan to submit, then familiarize yourself with exactly what they publish. This is particularly true with periodicals. It is best to read at least the last four or five issues.

Always address your submission to the appropriate editor by name. Editors change jobs and publishers change addresses. It is wise to invest in a phone call for the current information before submitting.

Consider submitting to the less glamourous markets. The large, highly-visible publishers are inundated with submissions and may choose authors with name recognition over others. Search for smaller publishers that specialize in the topic you're writing about or those that don't yet have vast distribution. After you have a few articles or stories published and/or a book or two under your belt, the heavily sought-after publishers are likely to be more receptive to your proposals.

Always submit your highest quality work. This means that you will have double-checked spelling and grammar. It also means that you will have checked your facts.

Keep a copy of everything you send to a publisher and never send original photos or artwork until requested to do so.

How Long Shall I Wait?

Most editors don't have time to spend on the phone with authors calling to see if the editor has read a query letter or book proposal. If five or six weeks have gone by and you haven't heard anything, it's OK to drop the editor a self-addressed, stamped postcard with a note asking about the status of your submission. If you still don't hear anything, chances are the editor is a louse and you should simply move on.

Query Letters

Editors often want to see query letters instead of finished articles, book proposals or complete manuscripts. (Short story editors usually prefer to see the finished manuscript.) A query letter is simply a one-page, single-spaced letter, addressed to a specific editor by name, asking if he or she would be interested in seeing an article, a novel's synopsis or a book proposal.

Query letters need to come right to the point. Begin with a sentence that will capture the attention of the editor, then, in four or five paragraphs, outline what you are proposing and why you are qualified to write it. Since this letter runs the chance of being the only example of your writing the editor is going to see, it needs to be your best. This is no place for extra words or thoughts. Write your query letters crisply and succinctly.

Book Proposals

With novels, a writer without a successful track record will nearly always need to submit a finished manuscript before a contract is signed, but nonfiction books are often presented and sold to editors—even by first time book authors—before they are written. This is done with an outline called a book proposal. A typical book proposal, about ten to thirty double-spaced pages, consists of an overview that includes a summary of the book, where and to whom the book will sell, an approximation of how many words it will have, what illustrations, if any, will be included, why the author is qualified to write the book and all other pertinent information that may convince the editor to commit to the project. It also includes a table of contents and one or two sample chapters.

Precise instructions for writing a book proposal are contained in the chapter by agent-author Michael Larsen titled "Sell Your Book Before You Write It" in *The Portable Writers' Conference: How to Get and Stay Published. The Portable Writers' Conference* is available at libraries or bookstores or by calling 1-800-497-4909.

Electronic Submissions

When your material is accepted for publication most publishers will want the manuscript on a computer disk as well as in hard copy. This saves the publisher the expense of re-keyboarding the manuscript and removes the chances of a typist introducing new errors.

Consult the publisher's guidelines or check with them about which formats are acceptable. If you find you need to convert your files to a format your software can't handle, DataViz, Inc. (55 Corporate Drive Trumbull, CT 06011, 1-800-733-0030) makes a useful utility called Conversions Plus which not only converts format to format for most popular software programs, but will do so across the Macintosh and PC platforms.

Standard Manuscript Format

There is no single correct page format for a manuscript, but following common format conventions, as shown here, is a good way to say to an editor: "I am a professional." Always use letter-sized, white paper. Always be sure the print is dark and legible. Paper clip sheets together or use a manuscript box; never staple. Be sure to check individual guidelines for special requirements.

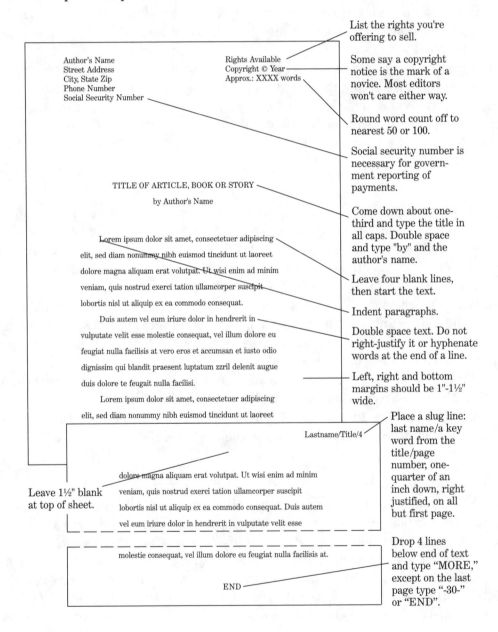

List the rights you're offering to sell.

Some say a copyright notice is the mark of a novice. Most editors won't care either way.

Round word count off to nearest 50 or 100.

Social security number is necessary for government reporting of payments.

Come down about one-third and type the title in all caps. Double space and type "by" and the author's name.

Leave four blank lines, then start the text.

Indent paragraphs.

Double space text. Do not right-justify it or hyphenate words at the end of a line.

Left, right and bottom margins should be 1"-1½" wide.

Place a slug line: last name/a key word from the title/page number, one-quarter of an inch down, right justified, on all but first page.

Drop 4 lines below end of text and type "MORE," except on the last page type "-30-" or "END".

Leave 1½" blank at top of sheet.

Periodicals

Periodicals
A-D

Above The Bridge Magazine

Word count must be included [on manuscript]. Indicate whether piece is fiction or nonfiction. Computer-printed submissions accepted. Letter quality preferred: dot matrix acceptable. Disk submissions accepted. IBM format or ASCII. Still supply hardcopy. We are on-line so electronic submissions are possible.

Important Note: All artwork and photographs will be returned if return postage is included. Keep negatives of your work. All types of photography accepted. Make prints no larger than 8"x10". *If postage is not included, you will not hear from us!*

Articles and short stories not longer than 2,000 words. 1,000 to 1,500 or short shorts are well received.

Above The Bridge is a family magazine published in Michigan's Upper Peninsula. Local writers are given preference, and all material *must be related to the area.* Specific needs include feature and current events, history, nostalgia, profiles of area personalities, and unique businesses. We are on-line now and we are looking for current feature pieces that we can put on our web pages. We are publishing some different things on-line than we are in the printed version and we are accepting things into the printed version that aren't on-line.

Send seasonal material at least 6 months in advance. Holding time of a year or more is not unusual. This is a bimonthly magazine so please be patient. If you haven't heard from us it's a good sign, but anytime you wish to check on the status of a piece, we will respond. Approximately four pages per issue devoted to poetry and children's stories.

Payment upon publication. 2 cents per word for articles and fiction. $5.00 for poems. photos and artwork. *No additional payment is made for photos that accompany articles, but can enhance chances of acceptance.*

Sample copy: $4.50 (includes postage). Published bimonthly. Annual subscription rate is $18.00.

Categories: Fiction—Nonfiction—Culture—Family—Outdoors—Poetry—Regional (Upper Michigan)—Travel

Name: Mikel B. Classen, Publisher and Editor
Material: All except poetry
Name: Sean MacManus, Poetry Editor
Material: Poetry
Address: PO BOX 416
City/State/ZIP: MARQUETTE MI 49855
Telephone: 906-484-2458
E-mail: classen@mail.portup.com
Internet: www.portup.com/above

Absolute Magnitude

Editor: Warren Lapine

Absolute Magnitude is a full-sized, quarterly science fiction magazine. We do not use fantasy, horror satire, or funny science fiction. We're looking for character-driven action/adventure based Technical Science Fiction stories from 1,000-25,000 words. We want tightly plotted stories with memorable characters. Characters should be the driving force behind the action of the story; and should not be thrown in as an afterthought. We need to see both plot development and character growth. Stories which are resolved without action on the protagonist's part do not work for us; characters should not be spectators in situations completely beyond their control or immune to their influence.

Payment: 1 to 5 cents per word on publication for first English language serial rights. All rights revert to the author upon publication.

Form: Standard manuscript form. We are very interested in working with new writers-we know how hard it can be to break in. We will consider simultaneous submissions. Writer-friendliness is a priority here.

Sample Copies $5.00 post paid. Subscriptions: 1 yr. $16; 2 yrs. $27. Please make check or money order payable to DNA Publications. Credit card charges will appear as Space-Crime Continuum.

Categories: Science Fiction

Name: Warren Lapine, Editor
Material: All
Address: PO BOX 910
City/State/ZIP: GREENFIELD MA 01302
Telephone: 413-772-0725
E-mail: AbsMag@shaysnet.com

ACCENT On Living

Over 21,000 disabled individuals throughout the U.S. and several foreign countries now receive *ACCENT On Living*. ACCENT was started in 1956 to provide information about new devices and easier ways to do things so people with physical disabilities can enjoy a better and more satisfying lifestyle.

Issued quarterly. Market is physically disabled persons, parents of handicapped children and specialists and counselors in the field of rehabilitation. Copyrighted. Buys one-time rights unless otherwise specified. Pays on publication. Reports in two weeks. We will send a sample copy for $3.50.

NONFICTION ARTICLES

Product Information that would be helpful to individuals with limited physical mobility. (Devices can be made commercially or homemade.) Questions to be answered in such articles include how the device can make a disabled person more independent, if device is commercially available where can you get it, and comments from users, if appropriate.

Examples of recent articles:
• Communication devices for people who cannot talk
• Special boots that help paraplegics walk
• A scooter guide to help individuals select the best one for them.

Good photos are important.

Intelligent discussion articles about physically disabled persons in *"normal"* living situations.

Popular subjects include:
• Relationships within a family situation and between partners when one or both are disabled
• Housing—different options for independent living and how to get money for such
• Jobs—how the ADA law will affect those with hidden disabilities
• Medical concerns of disabled persons such as is it possible to get too little salt?
• Travel—how accessible are specific destinations?

These are just a few examples—query with ideas.

How-to articles concerning everyday living. Recent how-to articles include "Working on Your Image": tips on improving your appearance, "Two Ideas for Showering Independently": how to remodel an existing bathroom, "Alternative to an RV": an individual's solution to getting gas mileage and comfort when traveling. These articles should give specific information about where to buy necessary items and how to carry out the idea. A good practice when submitting how-to articles, or any other, is to have someone who isn't familiar with the subject read the article for clarity.

Up-to-date news articles. Examples are "Down Under," A South Sea adventure for handicapped scuba divers; "Discounted Wheelchairs," the pros and cons of buying a chair through a catalog.

Disabled personalities. Recent interviews have been with Ron Kovic, whose story was the basis for the motion picture, *Born on the Fourth of July;* and Ellen Stohl-the first paraplegic to pose in *Playboy.*

Good strong interviews. Please submit a query first with the name of the person, his/her accomplishments, and a list of proposed questions. We may be able to help you with the slant of the article before you make an appointment for the interview.

Other areas of interest. These include architectural barriers (and new developments in overcoming them), vacations, accessible places to go, sports, organizations, humorous incidents, self improvements, and sexual or personal judgement.

GENERAL INFORMATION

ACCENT readers prefer an informal rather than an academic approach. We want to show individuals with disabilities getting involved in all aspects of life. Effective organization of ideas is important. The successful writer must be willing to cut, polish, check, rewrite and condense. An important element of most articles is good photos or illustrations.

Before preparing material for ACCENT you might like to inquire about interest in the subject. However, an expression of interest on our part does not constitute an assignment or a guarantee that the article will be purchased. Each submission will be accepted or rejected on its merits and editorial value to ACCENT. When ACCENT gives a definite assignment to a freelancer, the terms will be clearly stated in writing.

Length—Short, tightly written. 250 to 1,000 words. May be submitted on hard copy or via 3.5" floppy disk using DOS text, WordPerfect or QuarkXpress formats.

Rate of pay—10¢ a word and up, paid upon publication. Length of article, after editing and condensing, as it appears in the magazine will determine the payment for an article.

PHOTOS

Can use black and white or color. Need clear prints with captions. May be submitted as Photoshop TIFF file (Mac format) on floppy disk.

Rate of pay—$5 and up. $50 and up for cover (color) photo. Amount will depend on quality of photos and subject matter. Paid upon publication.

CARTOONS

Interested in humorous incidents encountered by physically disabled individuals in everyday living. A person in a wheelchair is typical and should be depicted in humorous but normal situations.

Rate of pay—$20 paid on acceptance.

Categories: Disabilities

Name: Betty Garee, Editor
Material: All
Address: PO BOX 700
City/State/ZIP: BLOOMINGTON IL 61702
Telephone: 309-378-2961
Fax: 309-378-4420
E-mail: acntlvg@aol.com

a journal of the Western Sierra

the ACORN
A New Journal for the Western Sierra

the ACORN will consider fiction, poetry, essays and nonfiction. No porn, erotica or articles of prejudice. Our focus is the western slope of the Sierra Nevada—its land, its people, its history, and its rural lifestyle—but other material will be considered. Length: 1,500 words maximum for prose; poems to 30 lines (shorter poems preferred). Deadlines are February 1 (spring issue), May 1 (summer), August 1 (autumn) and November 1 (winter).

Submissions should include your name and address on each page and a 50-word bio.

Subscriptions: One year $12.00

Individual copies: $4.00 (CA residents add $0.25 tax.)

Categories: Fiction—Nonfiction—Adventure—Biography—Fantasy—General Interest—History—Humor—Outdoors—Poetry—Rural America—Science Fiction—Short Stories

Name: Submissions Editor
Material: All
Address: PO BOX 1266
City/State/ZIP: EL DORADO CA 95623
Telephone: 916-621-1833
Fax: 916-621-3939
E-mail: jalapep@innercite.com

Ad Astra
The Magazine of the National Space Society

Ad Astra is the bimonthly magazine of the National Space Society, a non-profit organization dedicated to promoting space exploration and the establishment of a spacefaring civilization. The magazine is circulated to more than 27,000 members of our grassroots organization and to members of Congress and key personnel at the White House and NASA.

Approximately 50% of the articles in **Ad Astra** are submitted by freelance writers and we are always looking for new sources and fresh ideas. The articles are generally non-technical and cover a wide range of space-related topics.

Feature articles should be between 1,500-3,000 words and focus on any issue concerning space or space exploration. Articles with an emphasis on our future in space are of greater relevance to **Ad Astra** than historical accounts. Please query our editorial office prior to submitting any feature article. Unsolicited manuscripts will not be returned. **Ad Astra** pays $150-$250 for feature articles.

Several single-page departments are open to freelance writers. Most of these articles are donated, though in some cases **Ad Astra** will pay up to $75. These submissions are limited to 750 words and include reviews, editorials and pieces oriented toward education.

All writers should follow the guidelines of the *Associated Press Stylebook*. We prefer to receive submissions on a 3½" Word disc (Mac or PC). Disks should include author's name, address and phone number. When necessary, we will accept typewritten articles.

We are always looking for exciting and original space-related art. We prefer to receive 35mm slides, 3"x5" transparencies or prints of artwork or photography. Black and white submissions should be prints or originals. Please label each piece of art submitted with the artist's name, address and phone number for crediting purposes.

Categories: Nonfiction—Engineering—Science—Space—Technology—Travel

Name: Pat Dasch, Editor-in-Chief
Material: All
Address: 600 PENNSYLVANIA AVE SE STE 201
City/State/ZIP: WASHINGTON DC 20003-4316
Telephone: 202-543-1900
Fax: 202-546-4189
E-mail: adastraed@aol.com

Adolescence

Adolescence (ISSN 0001-8449) is published quarterly. Issues are dated Spring, Summer, Fall, Winter.

GENERAL POLICY: *Adolescence* is not dominated by a single point of view and wishes to present as many views as possible. It relies for its contents mainly on solicited material, but ideas and suggestions will be welcomed by the editor. Authors should not submit manuscripts; they should write to us about them and furnish short abstracts first.

MANUSCRIPTS, REFERENCES, AND REPRINTS: Manuscripts must be typewritten in duplicate. Footnotes, charts, tables, graphs, etc., should be kept to a *minimum* and submitted in the original, camera-ready copy. (We prefer that when practical, the information contained in this material be incorporated into the text instead.) References to books and articles should appear at the end of the manuscript under the heading "References," with items listed alphabetically by name of author, and following APA style.

Authors will be furnished galley proofs which must be returned to the editor within two *days*. Corrections should be kept to a minimum. A schedule of reprint costs and order blanks for reprints will be sent with galley proofs.

BOOK REVIEWS: *Adolescence* contains a substantial book review section. In each issue, a large number of books will be described in abstract form. More space may be devoted to some books deemed to warrant extensive review, but this will not be done at the expense of the larger number of brief reviews. Publishers are invited to send copies of books they would like us to review. Naturally, we cannot promise that all books submitted will be reviewed. Book reviews appear in alphabetical order by names of authors.

INDEXED in Psychological Abstracts; Abstracts for Social Workers; Exceptional Child Education Abstracts; Current Contents/Behavioral, Social and Educational Sciences; Social Sciences Citation Index; Community Mental Health Review; Sage Family Studies Abstracts; Chicorel Abstracts to Reading and Learning Disabilities; Women Studies Abstracts; Criminal Justice Abstracts; MEDLINE; Index Medicus; AGRICOLA (Agricultural Online Access); Social Work Research and Abstracts. In England, Sociology of Education Abstracts and Multicultural Education Abstracts.

MICROFORM EDITIONS: For information regarding microform editions, write to University Microfilms, Ann Arbor, Michigan 48106.

SUBSCRIPTIONS: All business communications, including subscriptions, renewals, and remittances should be addressed to Libra Publishers, Inc., at the address shown below.

Individual rates: U.S.A.: $71 (one year), $140 (two years), $209 (three years). All other countries: $75 (one year), $148 (two years), $221 (three years). These rates are applicable only to subscriptions paid by personal check for personal use.

Institutional rates (libraries, schools, governmental agencies, organizations): U.S.A.: $97 (one year), $192 (two years), $287 (three years). All other countries: $103 (one year), $204 (two years), $305 (three years). Copies of current or back issues are available at $22 each from Libra Publishers.

Categories: Nonfiction—Disabilities—Education (exceptional child)—Family (studies)—Health (mental)—Psychology—Social and Educational Sciences

Name: Submissions Editor
Material: All
Address: 3089C CLAIREMONT DR STE 383
City/State/ZIP: SAN DIEGO CA 92117
Telephone: 619-571-1414

Adventure Journal

Formerly *Adventure West*

Adventure Journal features insightful, informative articles about travel that goes beyond the norm. We aim to inspire readers to forgo the passive travel experience for a more exciting, stirring journey through locations around the world or even next door. *Adventure Journal* publishes both high-risk, "extreme" adventures of a lifetime and more feasible "soft" adventures that can be fulfilled in a week or a weekend.

We accept both query letters and unsolicited manuscripts, both of which should be accompanied by clips of previously published articles (unless submitting for shorter departments such as First Person) and your social security or taxpayer ID number. Manuscripts must be typed and double-spaced. If you'd like your materials returned, include a self-addressed stamped envelope with enough postage to get your materials safely back to you. Mail to: Submissions Editor, *Adventure Journal*, 650 S. Orcas St., Suite 103, Seattle, WA 98108. We will respond to written queries or manuscripts within eight weeks. We do not accept phone queries.

First North American serial rights to published stories shall remain with *Adventure Journal* for a period of six (6) months. Additionally, the author grants the nonexclusive rights to *Adventure Journal* to reproduce the work in electronic media.

Departments

Features (2,500 - 3,500 words) Whether national or international, this department includes stories that range from "adventures of a lifetime" that may change the course of your life, to weeklong journeys that offer a high degree of thrill and discovery. Feature stories must have a hook and must excite and entertain the reader.

First Person (150 - 300 words) These accounts may be humorous, thought-provoking, heroic or convey a sense of discovery about a personal travel experience.

Compass Points (Various lengths) Up-to-the-minute international and national travel news. Deals with environmental issues, new governmental policies on travel, wildlife information, archeological discoveries, anything of special interest to adventure travelers.

Protocol (700-1200 words) How-to pieces and practical advice for the international adventure traveler.

Discoveries Profiles those international and national hideaways that every adventurer longs to discover. This section is comprised of several subsections as follows:

Destinations (700 - 1,200 words) Features a region of a state or foreign country, a small island, etc. For example: the northern coast of California or a little-known island in the Caribbean.

Quick Getaways (500 - 700 words) Many travelers are foregoing longer vacations for more frequent, two-to-four-day vacations throughout the year. Quick Getaways features accessible destinations in Canada, the United States and Mexico, including information about where to stay and what to do.

Inns, lodges, resorts or structured trips that feature campsites provided by an outfitter (300 - 600 words). Must be unique in some way, or offer a base from which to take part in a multitude of activities.

Far from the crowds (500 - 600 words). Features a wilderness area, stretch of beach, etc., where a traveler can enjoy a fair degree of solitude.

Time Travel (700 - 1,400 words) Putting a historical context on a travel destination.

The Adventurer's Palate (600 - 750 words) Ask any adventurer about the highlights of a trip and he is certain to mention that "wonderful little restaurant we discovered." This column celebrates food all over the world.

Profile (750 words) Features people whose lives embody the spirit of adventure travel.

Photography Rates

Photographs must be itemized on a separate submission sheet that includes your name, address, telephone number and social security number. This will be used as your receipt. If you do not include an itemized breakdown of the slides you sent, we cannot be responsible for claims of lost slides.

Up to: 1/4 page	$50
1 / 2 page	$100
Full page	$150
1 & 1 / 2 page	$225
2 full pages	$325
Cover	$400

All photographs will be returned after the publication is printed; photographs not selected for use will be returned as soon as possible after an initial selection has been made.

Categories: Adventure—History—Nonfiction—Outdoors—Photograpy—Sports/Recreation—Travel

Name: Editor
Material: All
Address: 650 South Orcas Street, Suite 103
City/State/ZIP: Seattle, WA 98108
Telephone: 206-762-1922
Fax: 206-762-1886

Affaire De Coeur

1. AFFAIRE DE COEUR will accept short stories of two thousand words maximum. Short stories must be stories of romance with the following guidelines:

a. There are no limitations with regard to setting. Time of setting may be historical, contemporary or futuristic.

b. Plots may be general romance or may include suspense, mystery or intrigue.

c. There are no age restrictions on the couple. Romances can range from young adult romances to twilight romances. There are no restrictions on previous relationship.

d. There are no racial or ethnic restrictions on the couple. We welcome diversity as long as the portrayal of the race or ethnic groups are realistic and non-stereotypical.

e. Because of the short length of the story, we discourage a love scene unless it is vital to the story.

f. The story should end on a positive note. That does not necessarily mean that the couple ends up together and lives happily ever after. It may mean that the heroine realizes she is better off without the hero or vice versa.

g. In order to avoid the feel of a true confession we encourage the author to write the story in the third person. However, if he/she does write it in the first person and it works, it may be accepted.

2. AFFAIRE will not accept previously printed short stories. We require a contract to the effect that the work submitted is original.

3. AFFAIRE pays up to $35.00 per published short story depending on the length. Payment is made at the end of the quarter in which the story appears.

4. AFFAIRE reserves the right to edit all short stories. While it is not our intent to change the context or complexion of a story, we will alter it for the purposes of length and correct spelling or grammar.

5. Short stories printed in AFFAIRE become the property of AFFAIRE DE COEUR magazine and may not be reprinted without the expressed written permission of AFFAIRE DE COEUR.

6. Stories that are accepted must be resubmitted on computer disk, IBM compatible in ASCII or WordPerfect format. Disks will be returned.

Categories: Fiction—African-American—Reference—Romance—Women's Fiction—Writing

Name: Submissions Editor
Material: All
Address: 3976 OAK HILL RD
City/State/ZIP: OAKLAND CA 94605
Telephone: 510-569-5675
Fax: 510-632-8868
E-mail: SSEVEN@msn.com

Afterimage
The Journal of Media Arts and Cultural Criticism

GENERAL DESCRIPTION

Afterimage is a nonprofit journal of media arts and cultural criticism. The media arts includes independent photography and film, visual books, electronic imaging and on-line communications. We focus on artists and issues that do not receive adequate coverage in either mainstream art magazines or conventional academic periodicals. Our readership, which is international in scope, includes artists, critics, curators, students, educators and other members of the media arts community.

VITAL STATISTICS

Afterimage is a 10½"x17" tabloid, usually 28 pages in length, with approximately 25-30 illustrations per issue. It is published bimonthly (July/August; September/October; November/December; January/February; March/April; May/June) by the Visual Studies Workshop. *Afterimage* is supported in part by grants from the National Endowment for the Arts and the New York State Council on the Arts.

FORM, CONTENT, TONE, ETC.

Afterimage is neither a news magazine nor an academic journal; rather, it is a hybrid combining (ideally) the best of journalism and scholarship. We are interested in work and writing that crosses or stretches the boundaries of genre, medium, discipline and audience. Articles that simply describe one subject from one perspective, and fail to consider counter examples and alternative explanations, are discouraged. We are more interested in writing that constructively engages with work rather than uniformly praises or criticizes it, unless the criticizing contributes productively to a larger debate.

Afterimage articles should address a reader who is intelligent and reasonably well-informed, yet impatient with jargon. Most articles in *Afterimage* discuss contemporary phenomena (i.e., events, exhibitions, publications, discourses, institutions), although historical writing that introduces and develops new approaches is welcome. While our coverage may include international figures and issues, for funding reasons we emphasize work produced/distributed in the U.S.

Finally, for the sake of scholarly objectivity, *Afterimage* discourages submissions about a writer's own work or the work of his or her associates. We recognize that sometimes such connections are inevitable, even productive. Nevertheless, please be forthcoming about them during your initial contact with us.

SECTIONS

FEATURES—Ranging from 4,000-8,000 words, feature articles may be original investigative reporting or scholarly research; they may be biographies of important media artists or critics; they may use an event, exhibition, book, video, etc. as a jumping-off point for a discussion of larger economic, political and cultural issues. Use of endnotes is expected but not strictly required.

REVIEWS—Reviews are generally 1,000-1,500 words. They may cover individual or group exhibitions, installations, screenings and performances; or they may examine one or more media arts publications. References should be placed within the text, though endnotes are permitted.

ESSAYS—Like the feature in terms of prominence and scope, but more like the review in terms of timeliness and length (they range from 1,500-3,000 words), an essay may be written in a more "subjective" voice and may be on or about virtually any subject in the domain of media arts and cultural criticism. Most essays are written on commission, though *Afterimage* will consider unsolicited manuscripts. Endnotes are explicitly discouraged.

REPORTS—This section includes articles (1,000-1,500 words) about particular conferences, symposia, film and video festivals and other formal gatherings. A good report will provide both an account and an analysis of the event. Endnotes are discouraged.

NEWS—*Afterimage* publishes news stories on funding, legislation, activism and institutional restructuring, as well as obituaries and other topics of importance to our readership. Although most news items are written by *Afterimage* staff, longer news articles (1,500-4,000 words) are actively solicited from outside writers. References should be placed within the text, though endnotes are permitted in longer news articles.

RECEIVED AND NOTED—Much shorter than a review (generally no more than 300 words), a note is a concise yet critical description of a single book, exhibition catalog or periodical.

PAYMENT

Afterimage pays five cents a word, up to a maximum of $100 for news, reports and reviews; $150 for essays; $300 for feature articles. Payment is made after publication, not acceptance; checks may take several months to process. Feature writers receive 10 free copies of the issue; reviews, reports, essay and news writers, five. Writers also receive a half-price subscription voucher. To publicize *Afterimage* articles, we send tearsheets to galleries, publishers, distributors and event sponsors.

SUBMISSIONS

Afterimage accepts both commissioned and unsolicited manuscripts. With unsolicited manuscripts include writing samples. All writers are encouraged to discuss article ideas with the Editor before submitting finished articles. We do not reprint previously published pieces. Articles published in *Afterimage*—in both printed and electronic versions of the journal—are automatically copyright of the Visual Studies Workshop. Reprint is only by written permission.

Articles must be formatted in Microsoft Word, version 5.0, and submitted on a standard 3½" disk for Macintosh. Always include a double-spaced hard copy as well. Editorial changes will be made on the hard copy; when you add revisions to the article

during the editorial process we ask that you make them on the hard copy only. Please include a one-sentence author bio at the end of your article.

STYLE GUIDELINES

Refer to the *Chicago Manual of Style* and *Webster's 19th Collegiate Dictionary* for style and spelling. Use open punctuation: i.e., the minimum of commas, quotation marks, and other punctuation necessary for clear understanding of the writing, as well as a minimum of italics and capitalization and no underlining. Please double-check dates, titles, spellings of names, etc. Include makers' names and year dates of all works mentioned. All titles of works and publications should be in italics, and series should be in quotations; all exhibition titles should be in quotations. In features give full endnote references, not footnotes, for all writings quoted or referred to more than cursorily, including the volume and number references for scholarly journals.

Any article, including features, that reviews a particular work or event must include separately the following information: (1) *exhibitions:* title; name of artist if it is a solo show; name and city of venue; opening and closing dates; name, city, and dates of all venues to which the show has traveled or will travel; (2) *books and catalogs:* title, author/editor, publisher (with address if not well known), number of pages, price for hardback and softback copies; (3) *films/videos* not shown in a formal exhibition: title, artist, distributor(s) (with address if not well known), rental format and price; (4) *festivals/conferences:* title, location, sponsor, dates.

We make formatting and style revisions to documents according to publishing standards. However, it is greatly appreciated if you can incorporate such standards in the copy you submit. The best guide to these standards is *The Mac is not a Typewriter* by Robin Williams.

Categories: Nonfiction—Arts—Culture—Film/Video—Photography

Name: Karen vanMeenen, Managing Editor
Material: All
Address: 31 PRINCE ST
City/State/ZIP: ROCHESTER NY 14607
Telephone: 716-442-8676
Fax: 716-442-1992
E-mail: afterimg@servtech.com

AIM
America's Intercultural Magazine

SHORT STORY WRITERS:

Once a year AIM Magazine sponsors a short fiction award of $100 for a previously unpublished story that embodies our goals of furthering the brotherhood of man through the written word.

The contest is open particularly to new writers. We're looking for compelling well-written stories with lasting social significance, proving that people from different backgrounds are more alike than they are different. The story should not moralize.

Maximum length is 4,000 words. Winner is published every year in the fall issue. Deadline each year is August 15. Send typewritten entry to address below.

We also solicit essays, articles that deal with racial problems.

Categories: Fiction—Nonfiction—Essays—Multicultural—Short Stories

Name: Ruth Apilado, Associate Editor
Material: All
Address: 7308 S EBERHART
City/State/ZIP: CHICAGO IL 60619
Telephone: 773-874-6184
Fax: 206-543-2746

Air Force Times

Please refer to *Times News Service*

Alabama Living

Alabama Living
*A Publication of the Alabama
Rural Electric
Association of Cooperatives*

We are looking for readable articles of between 500-800 words on well-researched but little-known historical events in Alabama history. We also can use well-written rural Alabama nostalgia pieces.

Categories: Agriculture—Consumer—Energy—General Interest—Regional—Rural America

Name: Darryl Gates, Editor
Material: All
Name: Angela Mann, Recipe Editor
Material: Cooking
Address: PO BOX 244014
City/State/ZIP: MONTGOMERY AL 36116
Telephone: 334-215-2732
Fax: 334-215-2733
E-mail: area@mindspring.com

Alaska Quarterly Review
University of Alaska Anchorage

Alaska Quarterly Review, a journal devoted to contemporary literary art, and published by the College of Arts and Sciences, University of Alaska Anchorage, invites submissions in the following areas:

FICTION: Short stories and novel excerpts in traditional and experimental styles (generally not exceeding 50 pages).

POETRY: Poems in traditional and experimental styles but no light verse (up to 20 pages).

PROSE: Literary nonfiction in traditional and experimental styles (generally not exceeding 50 pages).

DRAMA: Short plays in traditional and experimental styles (generally not exceeding 40 pages).

No cover letter is necessary. Your submission will be judged on its own merits. If you do send a letter, please include your publication credits. You may submit a legible photocopy. Unless a SASE is enclosed with your submission, you will not hear from us unless we are interested in publishing your manuscript. We try to reply within 4 to 12 weeks. Unsolicited manuscripts are welcome between August 15 and May 15.

Rates for individuals: $8.00 (1 yr.); $15.00 (2 yrs.); $21.00 (3 yrs.)

Rates for institutions: $10.00 (1 yr.); $20.00 (2 yrs.); $30.00 (3 yrs.)

Note: Add $2.00 per year for subscriptions outside of the USA.

Sample copies: $5.00 (Outside the USA add $1.00)

Prices for back issues and special issues available upon request. Please make checks payable to: *Alaska Quarterly Review*.

Categories: Fiction—Nonfiction—Poetry

Name: Editor
Material: All
Address: UNIVERSITY OF ALASKA ANCHORAGE
Address: 3211 PROVIDENCE DR
City/State/ZIP: ANCHORAGE AK 99508
Telephone: 907-786-4775
Fax: 907-786-4775

Alfred Hitchcock Mystery Magazine
Dell Magazines

Thank you for your request for these Writers' Guidelines. Finding new authors is a great pleasure for all of us here, and we look forward to reading the fiction you send us. Since we do read all submissions, there is no need to query first; please send the entire story. You don't need an agent.

Content. Because this is a mystery magazine, the stories we buy must fall into that genre in some sense or another. We are interested in nearly every kind of mystery, however: stories of detection of the classic kind, police procedurals, private eye tales, suspense, courtroom dramas, stories of espionage, and so on. We ask only that the story be about a crime (or the threat or fear of one). We sometimes accept ghost stories or supernatural tales, but those also should involve a crime.

You might find it useful to read one or more issues of AHMM; that should give you an idea of the kind of fiction we buy. For a sample copy, send a check made out to AHMM for $4.00 to the address below.

Style. We prefer that stories not be longer than 14,000 words; most of the stories in the magazine are considerably shorter than that. They should, of course, be well-written. We are looking for stories that have not been previously published elsewhere, and among them for those that are fresh, well-told, and absorbing. They should be entirely fiction: please do not send us stories based on actual crimes, for instance, or other real-life events.

Manuscript preparation. Manuscripts should be typed with your name and address at the top of the first page. The title of the story as well as the byline you want to use should be on the first page of the story also. (We prefer that there not be a separate title page.) If you use a word processor, please do not justify the right-hand margin. Every page of the story should be numbered, preferably in the upper right-hand corner. If you number the pages by hand, be sure before you start that no page has been omitted. Do not use the italic, large-size, or boldface characters some computers are capable of generating. Underline words to indicate italics.

Indent for each paragraph. Do not leave one-line spaces between paragraphs. The number of lines per page should be uniform, or mostly so.

Stories should be mailed to us flat, with the pages bound together by a paper clip only—not stapled or enclosed in a binder. A cover letter isn't necessary. If you have sent us a photocopy and do not want it back, please advise us of that and enclose a smaller SASE for our response.

Revisions. Revised versions of a story should be submitted only on our request, as a rule. At the very least, tell us in a cover letter that the story has been submitted before but has been revised, and explain how.

NOTE: Stories submitted to AHMM are not also considered by or for *Ellery Queen's Mystery Magazine*, though we share the same address. Submissions to EQMM must be made separately.

We do not accept simultaneous submissions.

Categories: Fiction—Crime—Mystery—Short Stories

Name: Submissions Editor
Material: All
Address: 1270 AVENUE OF THE AMERICA
City/State/ZIP: NEW YORK NY 10020

Alive!
A Magazine for Christian Senior Adults

Alive! A Magazine for Christian Senior Adults is currently published bimonthly. Editor is J. David Lang; Office Editor is A. June Lang. Our office is in our home at 1452 Waycross Road, Cincinnati, OH 45240. Please send all communication to the address below.

FORMAT: 2 colors, 12 pages 8½"x11". Letter quality computer print-outs acceptable (no matrix, please). No fax please. Length may vary from 600 to 1,200 words.

MARKET: Christian senior adults approximately 55 years of age or older. Timely articles about Christian seniors in vital and productive lifestyles, travel, or ministries. The character of the magazine is upbeat and activity oriented rather than nostalgic. We can use fiction, jokes, articles about needs and interests of seniors, appropriate cartoons, and biographical sketches of active Christian senior adults.

RIGHTS: Prefer first rights, but will consider second rights and simultaneous submissions.

SUBMISSIONS: Prefer complete manuscripts rather than queries. Request for samples should include $1.00 for mailing and handling.

RATES: 3-5 cents per word. Payment on publication.

PHOTOS: A limited number of freelance black and white photos will be accepted. Photos with articles are welcomed, and will be paid for at our rates according to the quality.

Categories: Fiction—Nonfiction—Christian Interests—Health—Humor—Relationships—Senior Citizens—Short Stories—Spiritual—Travel

Name: A. June Lang, Office Editor
Material: All
Address: PO BOX 46464
City/State/ZIP: CINCINNATI OH 45246
Telephone: 513-825-3301

ALOHA
The Magazine of Hawai'i and the Pacific

ALOHA, The Magazine of Hawai'i is a bimonthly regional magazine of international interest. The majority of this publication's audience is outside the state of Hawai'i, although most readers have been to the Islands at least once. Even given this fact, the magazine is directed primarily to residents of Hawai'i in the belief that presenting material to an immediate critical audience will result in a true and accurate presentation that can be appreciated by everyone.

EDITORIAL CONTENT

ALOHA offers a wide variety of subject matter, all of which is Hawai'i-related. Categories generally covered in each issue and open to freelance writers are the arts, business, people, sports, destinations, food, interiors, history, Hawaiiana, fiction and poetry. All material with historical background must be thoroughly researched with a bibliography provided. Words in the Hawaiian language must be accurately spelled and correctly used. Dialect is not generally appreciated. Neither do we want vivid word pictures of romantic sunsets and swaying palms. Fiction depicting a tourist's adventures in Waikiki is not what we're looking for. As a general statement, we welcome material reflecting the true Hawaiian experience.

LENGTH

Depending on the depth of the story material, manuscripts can run to 4,000 words, with 2,000 to 3,000 being the average length.

PROCEDURE

We prefer to receive queries on all proposed submissions, with the exception of fiction and poetry. Both queries and completed manuscripts should be mailed to the address below. Upon acceptance, a letter confirming the assignment will be mailed.

MANUSCRIPTS

The University of Chicago's *Manual of Style* is our accepted book of style. Hawaiian language words are not italicized, although all other non-English words are. Where the word "Island" is used to replace the word "Hawaiian," it is capitalized. Do not hyphenate words at the end of a typed line. We appreciate receiving a copy on a disc, in Macintosh Microsoft Word format.

RATES

Payment for stories ranges between $150 and $400. Payment for poetry is $30. Payment is made within 30 days after publication. ALOHA purchases first North American serial rights and requires a signed contract, including the writer's social security number and General Excise Tax number, before payment can be made. If accepted for publication, the original manuscript will not be returned.

PHOTOGRAPHY GUIDELINES

ALOHA features one photo essay in each issue, "Beautiful Hawai'i," which is a collection of photographs illustrating that theme. A second photo essay by a sole photographer on a specific theme is featured on occasion. Queries are essential for the sole photographer essay. Decisions concerning photography for Beautiful Hawai'i are made during the first week of every other month, beginning January 10. Transparencies must be properly captioned and submitted in clear plastic slide sheets. All photographs are returned after use.

SIZE

Minimum size for black-and-white prints is 5"x7", with 8"x10" preferred. Minimum size for transparencies is 35mm. Color prints are rarely used.

All prints must bear the photographer's name, address and brief caption information. Even though caption sheets might accompany photographs, key location words on the photographs are very helpful. Caution: do not use paper clips to attach photo information as they may damage the slides.

RATES

ALOHA buys one-time rights to most photos used. Standard rates are:

• $25 each for black-and-white photographs
• $75 each for color photos used inside the magazine (less than full page)
• $100 each for photos used as a full-page
• $125 each for photos used as a double-page spread
• $250 for photographs selected for an ALOHA cover, model releases are required for identifiable people in a cover shot
• Assignments: Some assignment work is available on a flat fee basis.

ALOHA assumes liability for loss or damage of up to $500 for each original transparency accepted (maximum of $5,000). Liability for duplicate transparencies is limited to the cost of replacement.

SAMPLE COPIES

One sample copy of ALOHA is available at $2.95 plus $3.20 postage.

Categories: Culture—Travel

Name: Cheryl Chee Tsutsumi, Editorial Director
Material: All
Address: PO BOX 3260
City/State/ZIP: HONOLULU HI 96801
Telephone: 808-593-1191
Fax: 808-593-1327
E-mail: alohamag@aol.com

AMELIA

Amelia Press

The best guideline to any magazine's particular needs is, of course, a copy of the magazine itself. Single copies of AMELIA are available for $9.95 ppd. Single copies of CICADA or SPSM&H are $4.95 ppd. Annual subscriptions of AMELIA are $30.00 one year, $56.00 two years, $80.00 three years. Annual subscriptions to CICADA or SPSM&H are each $14.00 one year, $24.00 two years, $33.00 three years. We also offer a combination subscription to all three for $48.00 per year.

Writer's Guidelines

Amelia uses perhaps more traditional fiction and poetry than any other small press magazine published today, but we also look for the fresh and innovative as well. And neatness *does* count.

FICTION

Amelia: We look for depth of plot and strong characterization in stories of any type to 4,500 words. A piece would have to be exceptional to exceed that length. We use science fiction, westerns, romance and Gothic horror as well as mainstream. We like to have a feeling of "the whole world" in storylines. Payment of $35 on acceptance, plus two contributor copies, for stories over 2,000 words; less for shorter pieces.

Cicada: We use stories with an emphasis on the oriental, especially Japanese, though we have used stories set in China and other Asian locales. All types are welcome to 2,000 words maximum. Payment: $10 on publication, plus one copy.

SPSM&H: We use stories with romantic or Gothic themes, to 2,000 words maximum. Especially welcomed are tales which somehow incorporate the sonnet. Payment: $10 on publication, plus one copy.

POETRY

Amelia: We look for a strong sense of kinship with the reader, a feeling of importance and worth, stance and control in our poetry, any form to 100 lines. We use very short poems often as filler to break up long stretches of narrative. One-liners and aphorisms also are welcomed. Payment: $2 to $25 on acceptance, plus two contributor copies, except one-liners and aphorisms for which payment is one copy of the issue containing the piece.

Cicada: We use only poetry with oriental emphasis, primarily Japanese, though occasionally we have used Chinese and Korean forms. We especially look for excellent tankas, rengas, haibun and haiku sequences. From time to time we have featured other forms of poetry which explore elements of Asian cultures. Payment: three "Best of Issue" poets each receive $10 on publication, plus one copy; there is no other payment.

SPSM&H: We use only sonnets and sonnet sequences, experimental or traditional (SPSM&H *stands for Shakespeare, Petrarch, Sidney, Milton & Hopkins.*) See John Updike's "Love Sonnet" in *Midpoint* as an example of the limit to which experimentation is acceptable within the form. Payment: Two "Best of Issue" poets each receive $14 on publication, plus one copy; there is no other payment.

BELLES LETTRES

We also like to use one *belle lettre* in each issue, any topic including fictional vignettes, to 2,000 words. See the works of Joan Frank or Ruth Shigezawa as a good example. Payment $10 plus two copies.

TRANSLATIONS

We use translations of excellent quality of both fiction and poetry in above lengths. Copies or photocopies of the original works must accompany each piece, along with a biographical sketch of both the author and translator. Payment in most cases, the same as for similar categories above, plus two copies.

CRITICISM

We use one critical essay in every issue, approximately 2,500 words. Essays may evolve from any discipline but must be related to literature, and preferably to literature as it affects small press. Submissions may be included in theses or dissertations not yet complete for degree consideration, but none may have been previously published. Payment $10 plus two copies.

BOOK REVIEWS

We welcome review copies of small press books. We do consider tightly written reviews of important works from the small press on a speculative basis. Payment: Two copies.

ILLUSTRATIONS

We also use many b/w spot drawings, more fully realized b/w illustrations (fine pen and ink or line), sophisticated cartoons, and b/w photos with or without captions. We pay $5 to $25 on assignment to a particular issue, depending on use, size and relationship to editorial content. See *The Artist's Market* for a more complete description of our needs and rates.

OTHER

We like to be surprised. Give me something excellent which I haven't touched on above and I'll take it too. For instance, we frequently use prose poems. Though we do not wish to see the pornographic, we do use well-made erotica. We do not shy away from strong language, but we are not a gutter either. Do not try to shock us for shock's sake, in all likelihood it already has been done.

It is important that you read at least one issue of any magazine for which you would like to write. When you succeed with us, we are as delighted as you are. Now, let us see some of your work.

Frederick A. Raborg, Jr., Editor

CONTEST DEADLINES & GUIDELINES

All of our competitions are annuals. They may be entered at any time with the understanding that decisions are made 8-10 weeks following deadline date. All deadline dates are postmarks. Any number may be entered. Include an SASE with all entries—one for *each* category entered—if return is desired. If no SASE is included, non-winning entries will be destroyed following announcement of winners. AMELIA nor its staff can be responsible for materials lost in the mails. Except for the quarterly Encore Awards, first North American serial rights are required of all winners, otherwise the entry will be disqualified. Be sure that name, address and social security number appear on each entry. Telephone numbers also may be helpful.

JANUARY 2 DEADLINES

The Anna B. Janzen Romantic Poetry Award: $100 is offered for best romantic poem, any type to 100 lines. *Entry Fee: $4 each.*

The Bernice Jennings Poetry Award: $100 is offered for best poem, any type to 100 lines. *Entry Fee: $4 each.*

The Lester R. Cash Short Poem Awards: Six awards of $50, $30, $20 plus three HMs of $5 each are offered for best short poems, any form to 14 lines. *Entry Fee: $4 each.*

Marguerette Cummins Quarterly Broadside Award: $50 or 100 copies for best poem, any type to 500 lines. Winner will be distributed free to all *Amelia* subscribers. *Entry Fee: $5 each.*

The Charles Katzman Award: $50 is offered for best poem with social issues as theme to 50 lines. *Entry Fee: $4 each.*

FEBRUARY 1 DEADLINES

The *Amelia* Mystery/Horror Fiction Award: $100 is offered for best mystery or horror fiction to 3,000 words. *Entry Fee: $5 each.*

The Kate Smith Award: $50 is offered for best poem, any form to 50 lines, on a patriotic or Americana theme. *Entry Fee: $4 each.*

The *Amelia* One-Liner Awards: Six awards of $35, *$15,* $10 plus three $3 HMs are offered for best one-liners, including haiku. *Entry Fee: $2 each.*

New & Unpublished Writer's Award: A writer's library valued at $250 approximately is offered for best poem to 200 lines or best short story to 3,500 words by a writer who has not yet published in a magazine with a circulation larger than 1,000. *Entry Fee: $10 each.*

FEBRUARY 15 DEADLINES

The Patrick T. T. Bradshaw Fiction Award: $200 offered for best short story or novella, any genre to 25,000 words. Any number may be entered. *Entry Fee: $10 each.*

The Dak Rambo Gay/Lesbian Poetry Award: $50 offered for best poem, any form to 100 lines. *Entry Fee: $5 each.*

MARCH 1 DEADLINES

The Georgie Starbuck Galbraith Light/Humorous Verse Awards: Six awards of $100, $50, $25 plus three $5 HMs are offered for best light or humorous verse, any form to 39 lines. *Entry Fee: $4 each.*

Ardis Walker Haiku Award: $50 is offered for best haiku or haiku sequence. *Entry Fee: $4 each.*

***Amelia* Encore Award:** $50 is offered for best poem, any form to 50 lines, for which *second* rights are available. Include acknowledgment. *Entry Fee: $5 each.*

The *Amelia* Native American Poetry Award: Beautiful Native American artwork is offered for best Native American poem or poem with Native American theme, including Chicano(a). Length to 100 lines. *Entry Fee: $5 each.*

APRIL 1 DEADLINES

The Willie Lee Martin Short Story Award: $200 is offered for best short story, any type to 4,500 words. *Entry Fee: $7.50 each.*

The Lucille Sandberg Haiku Award: Six awards of $50, $30, $20 plus three $5 HMs are offered for best haiku, traditional or experimental. Sequences are eligible only if each haiku is entered separately; however, should any one haiku in the sequence win, the entire sequence will be published. *Entry Fee: $3 each.*

The Charles William Duke Longpoem Award: $150 or 100 copies offered for best longpoem, unlimited length, any form. Any number may be entered. Winning longpoem will be published in most appropriate format (Usually in chapbook form) *Entry Fee $10 each.*

Marguerette Cummins Quarterly Broadside Award: $50

or 100 copies for best poem, any type to 500 lines. Will be published in broadside format—flat or folded as appropriate—and distributed free to all *Amelia* subscribers. *Entry Fee $5 each.*

MAY 1 DEADLINES

The *Amelia* Erotic Poetry Award: $100 is offered for best erotic poem, any form to 100 lines. *Entry Fee: $5 each.*

The Grace Hines Narrative Poetry Prize: $100 is offered for best narrative poem any form to 100 lines. *Entry Fee: $4 each.*

The *Amelia* Short-Short Fiction Award: $50 is offered for best short-short fiction, any type to 500 words. *Entry Fee: $4 each.*

The Al Stanley Lyric Poetry Award: $50 is offered for best lyric poem to 50 lines. *Entry Fee: $3 each.*

MAY 15 DEADLINE

The Frank McClure One-Act Play Award: $150 is offered for best one-act play to 45 minutes running time. Winner will be published in *Amelia* and the playwright will receive 10 free copies. Play may have been produced (include acknowledgments) but not published. *Entry Fee: $15 each.* (Include $9.95 if copy of issue with winning play is desired when published).

JUNE 1 DEADLINES

The Cassie Wade Short Fiction Award: $200 is offered for best short story, any type to 5,000 words. *Entry Fee: $7.50 each.*

The Joe Logan Short Humor Awards: Six awards of $30, $20, $15 plus three $3 HMs are offered for best short humor, poem or prose, to 500 words. *Entry Fee: $4 each.*

The *Amelia* New Form/Avant Garde Poetry Prize: $50 is offered for best new form or avant garde form, any form to 100 lines (now is your chance to create *your own* new forms). Avant garde poems may relate to such matters as alternative life-styles etc. *Entry Fee: $4 each.*

The *Amelia* Encore Award: $50 is offered for best poem, any form to 50 lines, for which *second* rights are available. Include acknowledgment. *Entry Fee: $5 each.*

The *Cicada* Award: A beautiful crystal valued at approximately $100 is offered for best haiku sequence, renga, tanka, haibun, etc. Winner will be featured in *Cicada*. *Entry Fee: $5 each.*

JULY 1 DEADLINES

The *Amelia* Chapbook Award: $250 plus 10 copies are offered for best chapbook to 48 pp. (no more than 35 lines per page). Include acknowledgment. Winner will be published in chapbook form. Any number of manuscripts may be entered. *Entry Fee: $15.* (Include $9.95 if copy of winning chapbook is desired when published.)

The Johanna B. Bourgoyne Poetry Prize: Six awards of $100, $50, $25 plus three $5 HMs are offered for best poems, any form to 50 lines. *Entry Fee: $4 each.*

The *Amelia* Erotic Fiction Award: $150 is offered for best short story, any type to 3,000 words, with an erotic theme. *Entry Fee: $7.50 each.*

Marguerette Cummins Quarterly Broadside Award: $50 or 100 copies for best poem, any type to 500 lines. Winner will be published in broadside format—flat or folded as appropriate—and distributed to all *Amelia* subscribers. *Entry Fee: $5 each.*

AUGUST 1 DEADLINES

The Earl Stine Short Fiction Award: $100 is offered for best story, any type to 1,500 words. *Entry Fee: $5 each.*

The Nova Trembley Ashley Short Poem Prizes: Six awards of $50, $30, $20 plus three $5 HMs are offered for best short poems. Any form to 10 lines. *Entry Fee: $4 each.*

The Douglas Manning Smith Epic/Heroic Poetry Prize: $100 is offered for best epic/heroic poem, traditional or experimental, to 200 lines. *Entry Fee: $5 each.*

The Bernard Ashton Raborg Essay Award: A handsome engraved plaque is offered for best essay, including opinion and criticism, to 2,500 words. *Entry Fee: $7.50 each.*

A-D

The Richard Hugo Poetry Award: $100 is offered for best poem, any type to 100 lines. (It is always helpful to read a few of Richard Hugo's poems, which are available in any library.) *Entry Fee: $4 each.*

AUGUST 15 DEADLINES

The Stella Wade Children's Story Award: $125 is offered for best story to 1,500 words. Illustrations may be included, but they will be considered only after announcement of winner. Entries from children under age 17 must be signed by parent. teacher or guardian verifying originality. *Entry Fee: $7.50 each.*

The Annie Louis Raborg Poetry Award: $50 is offered for best poem dealing with handicaps and other traumatic conditions such as AIDS, MS, MD, etc., any form to 50 lines. *Entry Fee: $3 each.*

SEPTEMBER 1 DEADLINES

The Reed Smith Prize for Fiction: $200 is offered for best short story to 3,000 words. any type. *Entry Fee: $7.50 each.*

The Hildegarde Janzen Prizes for Oriental Poetry: Six awards of $50, $30, $20 plus three $5 HMs are offered for best Asian poetry including Indian and South Pacific (indicate form attempted on manuscript). *Entry Fee: $4 each.*

The Florence Balsom Poetry Award: $50 is offered for best poem any form, to 50 lines. *Entry Fee: $3 each.*

The Jaye Giammarino Poetry Award: $50 is offered for best poem, any form to 20 lines. *Entry Fee: $3 each.*

The *Amelia* Encore Award: $50 is offered for best poem, any type to 50 lines, for which *second* rights are available, Include acknowledgment. *Entry Fee: $5 each.*

The *Cicada* Award: A beautiful crystal valued at approximately $100 is offered for best haiku sequence, renga, tanka or haibun, etc. *Entry Fee: $5 each.*

OCTOBER 1 DEADLINES

The Charlie Henning Fiction Award: $100 is offered for best story, any type to 1,500 words. *Entry Fee: $5 each.*

The Eugene Smith Sonnet Prizes: Six awards of $100, $50, $25 plus three $5 HMs are offered for best sonnets, traditional or experimental. Sequences are eligible only if each sonnet is entered separately; however, if any sonnet from the sequence wins, the entire sequence will be published. *Entry Fee: $4 each.*

The Alice Mackenzie Swaim Poetry Award: $50 is offered for best poem, any form to 50 lines. *Entry Fee: $3 each.*

The Marcus Smith Poetry Award: $50 is offered for best poem, any form to 50 lines. *Entry Fee: $3 each.*

The A & C Limerick Contest: Six awards of $50, $30, $20 plus three $5 HMs are offered best limericks. *Entry Fee: $4 each.*

The Anne Passel Romantic Fiction Award: $100 is offered for best romantic or Gothic story to 2,000 words. *Entry Fee: $5 each.*

The Marguerette Cummins Quarterly Broadside Award: $50 or 100 copies is offered for best poem, any type to 500 lines. Winner will be published in broadside format—flat or folded—and distributed free to all *Amelia* subscribers. *Entry Fee: $5 each.*

NOVEMBER 1 DEADLINES

The Ruby Doyle Rice Short-Short Fiction Award: $100 is offered for best short-short fiction, any type, to 1,500 words. *Entry Fee: $5 each.*

The Leslie Edward Raborg Poetry Award: $50 is offered for best poem, any form to 50 lines. *Entry Fee: $3 each.*

The Mme. Eva LeFevre Award: $100 is offered for best French-form poem (villanelle, sestina, etc.), traditional or experimental. *Entry Fee: $4 each.*

The Richard Armour Humorous Verse Award: $50 is offered for best humorous poem, any form, to 10 lines. *Entry Fee: $3 each.*

The Montegue Wade Poetry Award: $100 is offered for best poem, any type, to 100 lines. *Entry Fee: $4 each.*

DECEMBER 1 DEADLINES

The *Amelia* Awards: Six awards of $200, $100, $50, plus three $10 HMs are offered for best poems, any form to 100 lines. First prize winner also receives plaque. *Entry Fee: $10 each.*

The Erin Patrick Raborg Children's Poetry Award: $50 is offered for best poem, any form to 50 lines, with children as its theme. *Entry Fee: $3 each.*

The *Cicada* Award: A beautiful crystal valued at approximately $100 is offered for best haiku sequence, renga, tanka, haibun, etc. Winner will be featured in *Cicada*. *Entry Fee: $5 each.*

The *Cicada* Chapbook Award: Publication plus 50 copies are offered for best haiku chapbook, to 16 pp. Include acknowledgments. Any number of scripts may be entered. *Entry Fee: $10 each.*

The *Amelia* Encore Award: $50 is offered for best poem, any type, to 50 lines, for which *second* rights are available. Include acknowledgment. *Entry Fee: $4 each.*

DECEMBER 15 DEADLINES

The *Amelia* Science Fiction/Fantasy Award: $100 is offered for best science fiction or fantasy to 3,000 words. *Entry Fee: $5 each.*

The Ardis Walker Poetry Award: $100 is offered for best poem, any type, to 50 lines. *Entry Fee: $4 each.*

The William Walker Cover Award: $100 is offered for best photo, cartoon or illustration, color or b/w. Winner will be published on *Amelia* cover. *Entry Fee: $10 for) to Sentries.*

SPECIAL DEADLINE (MAY 15)

THE AMELIA STUDENT AWARDS: $200 is offered for best poem to 100 lines or short story to 1,500 lines words by a high school student. One entry per student, and each entry must be signed by a parent, teacher or guardian verifying originality. No entries will be returned. *Entry Fee: none.* **For guidelines and sample, SASE & $3 handling.**

Categories: Fiction—Nonfiction—Adventure—African-American—Antiques—Arts—Asian-American—Biography—Cartoons—College—Comedy—Culture—Dance—Drama—Entertainment—Erotica—Ethnic—Family—Fantasy—Feminism—Film/Video—Gay/Lesbian—General Interest—Hispanic—History—Horror—Humor—Inspirational—Interview—Jewish Interests—Language—Lifestyles—Literature—Men's Fiction—Men's Issues—Multicultural—Music—Mystery—Native American—New Age—Outdoors—Philosophy—Photography—Poetry—Politics—Psychology—Reference—Regional—Romance—Rural America—Science Fiction—Senior Citizens—Sexuality—Short Stories—Society—Sports—Television/Radio—Theatre—Travel—Western—Women's Fiction—Women's Issues—Writing—Young Adult

Name: Frederick A, Raborg, Jr., Editor
Material: All
Address: 329 E ST
City/State/ZIP: BAKERSFIELD CA 93304-2031
Telephone: 805-323-4064
E-mail: Amelia@lightspeed.net

American Brewer

Mission Statement: *Buy a man a beer, and he wastes an hour. Teach a man to brew, and he wastes a lifetime.*

American Brewer, the Business of Beer, focuses on brewpubs and microbreweries. Topics include industry trends, events, personalities, and the trials and tribulations of brewing and selling beer in America. Informative and fun to read! Published since 1986, the circulation is 20,000 and growing.

Publisher's Statement: In 1983, I founded one of the first brewpubs in the nation, Buffalo Bill's Brewery. As a journalist-turned-brewer-turned-journalist, I know the beer business. I make few assignments and rely on writers to submit great story ideas on everything from the brewing to the consumption of beer.

Article Submissions: Fax query letters. No unsolicited manuscripts. After arranging with publisher, please submit your article via e-mail (preferably as an attachment) or on disk. Either way, *be sure to mail or fax us a hard copy of the article*. We prefer Mac diskettes; otherwise, please submit your article in ASCII file format.

Payment: On publication. Byline: Always given.

Rights: We purchase all rights, unless otherwise agreed upon.

Length: 1,000 to 3,500 words for feature articles.

Pay: $50 to $300 ($.10 per word) for features.

Perks: Attending beer festivals, brewpub openings and other events related to the brewing and drinking of beer.

Categories: Business—Food and Drink

Name: Bill Owen, Publisher/Brewmaster
Material: All
Address: PO BOX 510
City/State/ZIP: HAYWARD CA 94543-0510
Telephone: 510-538-9500
  (direct line—we answer our phones!)
Fax: 510-538-7644 (please fax your ideas before phoning)
E-mail: owens@ambrew.com
Internet: www.ambrew.com

American Business Review
University of New Haven

The *American Business Review* welcomes both empirical and theoretical articles that can be applied or be pertinent to current business issues and practices or contribute to academic research in finance and business.

Authors' articles should not exceed 25 double-spaced typewritten pages, and footnotes should appear on a separate page and follow A.P.A. style. The author should send three copies of his manuscript plus a short biography. Include also an abstract of not more than 75 words summarizing the paper.

All articles are anonymously reviewed by the editorial board entirely in terms of scholarly content.

Previously published articles cannot be accepted.

Categories: Business

Name: Editor
Material: All
Address: UNIVERSITY OF NEW HAVEN
Address: 300 ORANGE AVE
City/State/ZIP: WEST HAVEN CT 06516
Telephone: 203-932-7118
Fax: 203-931-6084
E-mail: mharvey@charger.newhaven.edu

American Careers

American Careers magazine is published three times during the school year for middle school, junior high school, high school and vocational-technical school students. Each issue contains up-to-date information on emerging careers, self-assessment questionnaires, how-to articles and other stories designed to promote career awareness, exploration and education.

Assignment Procedures

1. Many of our stories are provided at no charge by authors in business, education and government. Career Communications, Inc., sometimes makes work-for-hire assignments or buys all rights.

2. We assign stories by phone or letter detailing the story idea and focus, possible contacts, deadline, etc. We may ask you to include photographs, or suggest sources for photographs or other art to illustrate your article.

3. A signed contract must be on file before any payment is made.

4. We accept late copy only if you consult with us first. Writers who do not meet deadlines may not receive future assignments.

5. You may submit story ideas. Please query in writing.

Payment Rule

1. Payment rate varies with assignment.

2. Payment is made within 30 days of receipt of assigned work.

3. Reasonable expenses, approved in advance and documented, will be reimbursed within 30 days.

Copy Requirements

1. We request a hard copy of your manuscript along with a Macintosh-compatible diskette (Quark, Microsoft Word or WordPerfect programs preferred).

2. Use 1" margins, double-space your copy and use a head and page number on each page.

3. When possible we would appreciate photographs complementing your article, particularly photos of specific people addressed in your story.

4. Submit permission slips and release forms from all people photographed and all photographers. Also submit a list of all resources and a list of all names, addresses and phone numbers of your interviewees with each article.

5. Also submit one sentence of biographical information with your story.

Style

1. Reading Level/Story Length. Articles should be written at a seventh-grade reading level, or they will be returned for rewrite. Articles in *American Careers* usually run from 300-750 words. Some topics may require additional space for impact or clarity. These topics are discussed on an individual basis. Sometimes we run half-page or single-page items on topics such as recent career news or people who have been successful climbing the career ladder.

2. Style. Use the *Associated Press Stylebook* as a guide for style.

3. Names. First reference to students should include complete name, age (where relevant), class (e.g., freshman), school attended, location (city and state) and major (if possible). First reference to teachers and other adults should include complete name, position, school or company and location. Use first names in subsequent references to students. Use last names in subsequent references to teachers and other adults.

4. Focus. Stories should exhibit a balanced national focus, unless the assignment covers only one region or school.

5. Other style maters. Style matters particular to *American Careers* will be handled in editing. Career Communications, Inc. reserves the right to edit and revise all materials for publication.

Deadline and Issue Dates

COPY DEADLINE ISSUE DATE

Fall Issue June 15 Sept. 15

Winter Issue Oct. 15 Jan. 15

Spring Issue Jan. 15 April 15
Categories: Nonfiction—Careers—Education

Name: Submissions Editor
Material: All
Address: 6701 W 64TH ST
City/State/ZIP: OVERLAND PARK KS 66202
Telephone: 913-362-7788
Fax: 913-362-4864
E-mail: ccinfo@carcom.com

The American Cottage Gardener

Query & Submission

Step 1: Inquire before submitting. Send a one-page letter describing your topic, why it excites you, why you think it will interest our readers, and your qualifications to write about it. Include a short sample of your published or unpublished writing; it may be on any topic, not just gardening. Remember to give us your name, address, and phone number. Please do not submit unsolicited manuscripts; they will not be read or returned.

We will consider most topics related to cottage and folk gardening, with the following exceptions. We do not currently accept articles about medicinal uses of plants (though you may mention medicinal uses in a historic context if source quotations are provided). We tend to avoid articles centering on children and pets. We are not currently accepting poetry.

Just so you know: We define a cottage garden as a personal, informal, exuberant, usually lush garden, in which a wide mixture of plants (annuals, perennials, herbs, shrubs, vegetables, etc.) are grown. Cottage gardening appears all over the world; like language, it changes and evolves with time and place. It is a style, not a list of plants.

We avoid the use of the term "organic", preferring to use the word "safe". We are firmly committed to safe gardening practices, and will print no advice that we consider unsafe for gardeners, their families, their pets, benign wildlife, the ecosystem, and us.

Step 2: Study our magazine. If your query interests us, we'll send you copy of our magazine to study. This will help you understand our preferred style. We strive to publish clear, concise articles that combine horticultural knowledge with relevant personal anecdote. Please see **Style**, below.

Step 3: Prepare a first draft. We commit at this point to read and consider for publication what you send us. We will likely have editing changes to suggest. **We promise to change nothing in your article without your permission.** We feel that you have a right to say what is published under your name. In the unlikely event that you and we cannot agree on the changes we propose, we reserve the right not to publish your piece.

Step 4: Sign our contract. When we accept your piece for publication, we'll send you a contract and a statement of work. The contract outlines your rights and ours; it is a general statement of our relationship. (Our cover letter explains the contract in simple English.) The statement of work concerns the particular piece of writing; it is a specific statement with due-dates, title, and so on. We use this system so that writers who work with us often need only sign a brief statement of work for each article, rather than a new contract every time. See **Payment**, below. Please note that we usually ask *only* for first publishing rights.

Style

We like to hear our writers' voices, and make great efforts to leave those voices in the articles we print. The writing we like best is accurate but not pedantic, and informal but not folksy. We favor experience, memories, passion, and enthusiasm, but discourage cloying nostalgia and sentiment.

Write what you know. Write from your own experience, mistakes and all. We see too many "how-to" articles smelling only of the research library, not the compost heap. A certain amount of book research is appropriate, but the writing should not be based on it. All our writers are gardeners and grow the plants they write about.

Be specific. E. B. White counseled, "Don't write about Man. Write about a man." We'd rather you were too specific than too general. Tell us exactly what variety you like, and why. Tell us exactly which bug is a problem, and what you do about it (not just what "they" recommend). If you give instructions, make them concise and complete. Make sure the reader will be able to do what you did.

Be accurate. We love common names and encourage their use, but also require botanic names. Never make up names or guess; if you're uncertain, say so. We have a large reference library and may be able to help.

Be complete. "How-to" articles and plant portraits must contain enough information for the reader to grow the plant successfully. Include height and spread at maturity; attractive features and their timing; planting or sowing instructions; light, water, and soil needs; USDA hardiness zone information; heat, humidity, and drought tolerance; pest and disease information; and anything else you can think of. Please also list any mail order sources that you recommend—US or Canada for plants; anywhere for seeds.

Avoid jargon and trite phrases. All editors have a list of forbidden words or phrases. At the ACG we call them Horribles. "Riot of color" and "plant material" head our Horrible list. Other offenders include "user-friendly" and "richly varied tapestry." Just say what you mean in your own words. Quotations can be valuable additions, but if you quote, give us the exact source: author, title, and date published. Avoid references that will date quickly, such as those drawn from TV, the movies, or currently popular songs.

Be passionate. Along with facts, we want to know your feelings, prejudices, and opinions about your topic. Write, in your own clear voice, what *you* want to say.

Payment

Note: This is a guideline only and does not constitute a legal agreement. Contributors will be asked to sign a contract and a statement of work.

Writers, new material: We pay $25 per published page. Our pages run about 750 words, depending on the size of the illustration. Less than half of a published page is rounded down; half a page or more is rounded up. Writers also get three contributor's copies of the issue in which their work appears, and the option to buy up to 10 more at our cost. Writers grant us first publishing rights only. (We are asked occasionally for photocopy reprints and would appreciate permission to make them. We would request this as needed.) We register the copyright of the magazine as a whole, but if contributors wish it, we will transfer the copyright (of the writer's contribution) to the writer at a cost of $20 (which is what the Library of Congress charges to transfer copyright). Alternatively, we are always willing to grant written permission for the work to be reprinted wherever the writer wishes.

Writers, reprinted material: We very rarely accept material previously published elsewhere. The writer receives three contributor's copies and the chance to buy up to 10 more at cost.

Interviews: For Q & A type interviews, we offer the interviewees three contributor's copies plus the chance to buy up to 10 more at cost. They may also elect to have their company name and address (a small ad, in effect) printed in a biographical paragraph at the end of the article. So far, all interviews published have been done in-house, though we would consider others. See **Query & Submission**, above.

Ghost-written articles: Ghost-writing is done strictly in-house, from a taped interview. The interviewee, whose name appears on the byline, may request transfer of copyright (for $20) or permission to reprint, which we will gladly grant. This person receives three contributor's copies and the option to buy up to 10 more at cost, and may also use the biographical paragraph to advertise his or her business.

Categories: Nonfiction—Agriculture—Associations—Education—Gardening—Hobbies—Rural America

Name: Rand B. Lee, Acquisitions Editor
Material: All (Queries only)
Address: PO BOX 22232
City/State/ZIP: SANTA FE NM 87502-2232
Telephone: 505-438-7038
E-mail: randbear@nets.com

American Demographics

American Demographics is a magazine for marketers, advertisers, strategic planners, and other business leaders who need information about American consumers.

Feature articles typically explore one or more key areas of consumer markets: their size and characteristics (demographic and social characteristics); people's needs and wants (attitudes and values); their ability to pay (income and spending); and how to reach them (media). Articles also nearly always include specific examples of how companies market to consumers.

If you are interested in submitting an article to *American Demographics*, first write with a story idea and outline. You should get a response to your query within a few weeks.

If we decide to proceed with your proposal, an editor will call you about specifics regarding content, schedule, and payment. Short articles average 1,500 words, while longer ones average 2,500 words. Please submit a hard copy; an electronic file is also helpful, but not necessary. You should also submit draft versions of tables and/or charts to accompany your article; our art department will create finished versions. We also appreciate suggestions or submissions of photos and/or other illustrations for our consideration, although our art director is final arbiter on these matters.

Because *American Demographics* is a data-driven publication with a reputation for accuracy, authors must provide full back-up for our fact-checker. This includes data tables, copies of articles or other printed material, and interview notes including sources' names and phone numbers.

Upon publication, *American Demographics* owns copyright on all articles. At the time your article is received and accepted by the editors, you will receive a copyright agreement to sign and return. We retain the right to sell reprints of your article with no further financial obligation. However, if we grant permission to reprint the article in another publication, you will receive 50 percent of the proceeds.

Thank you for your interest in *American Demographics*. We hope to hear from you.

Categories: Nonfiction—Business—Consumer—Culture—Ethnic—Food/Drink—Health—Hobbies—Lifestyles—Marketing—Recreation—Regional

Name: Diane Crispell, Executive Editor
Material: All
Address: PO BOX 68
City/State/ZIP: ITHACA NY 14818
Telephone: 607-273-6343
Fax: 607-273-3196

American Fitness

American Fitness welcomes unsolicited and queried manuscripts for publication on the subjects of health, fitness, aerobic exercise, sports nutrition, sports medicine, innovations and trends in aerobic sports, fitness marketing, tips on teaching exercise and humorous accounts of fitness motivation, physiology and women's health and fitness issues (pregnancy, family, pre- and post-natal, menopause and eating disorders). Profiles and biographical accounts of fitness leaders are also used. Query with published clips or send complete manuscript. Length: 800-1,200 words. Pays $140-180.

American Fitness also accepts material for its columns and departments: "Adventure" (treks, trails and global challenges), "Strength" (the latest breakthroughs in weight training), "Clubscene" (profiles and highlights of the fitness club industry), "Food" (low-fat/non-fat, high-flavor dishes), "Homescene" (home workout alternatives) and "Clip 'n' Post" (concise exercise research to post in health clubs, offices or refrigerators). Query with published clips or send complete manuscript. Length: 800-1,000 words. Pays $100-140.

Review: All manuscripts are reviewed, refereed and edited according to the editors' discretion. Solicited manuscripts receive referee notification within three to four months. Only accurate, scientifically valid and well-documented material is accepted for educational articles. Manuscripts that deal with lighter, non academic material are not processed through the editorial review board.

Preparation: Manuscripts should be typed, double-spaced, with 1.25-inch margins. Due to our scanning capabilities, dot matrix submissions are now unacceptable. Manuscripts must be submitted on pure white paper with no last-minute, penciled notations. All italic type must be indicated with an underline. Electronic submissions on Macintosh compatible disks in Microsoft Word are welcome. SASE must be enclosed. Every attempt will be made to return artwork, line drawings, photographs and slides. However, neither the editors nor AFAA are responsible for lost or damaged submissions.

Exclusivity: It is understood that accepted manuscripts are not being considered for publication in any other magazine or journal.

Categories: Nonfiction—Adventure—Alternate Lifestyles—Children—Consumer—Food/Drink—Health—History—Inspirational—Interview—Physical Fitness—Senior Citizens—Sports—Recreation—Travel—Nutrition—Women's Issues—Pregnancy—Eating Disorders—Medicine—Humor—Nostalgia—Personal Experience—Home

Name: Peg Jordan, Editor-at-large
Material: All
Address: 15250 VENTURA BLVD., SUITE 200
City/State/ZIP: SHERMAN OAKS, CA 91403
Telephone: 818-905-0040
Fax: 818-990-5468

American Forests

American Forests—the magazine of trees and forests for those interested in *all* facets of forestry—is the nation's oldest conservation magazine, having begun regular publication in 1894. It emphasizes the trends, issues, policies, management, and enjoyment of America's forest resources, including trees in and around communities. The best way to get an idea of the kind of articles and photographs we commission and buy is to study the magazine. A sample copy will be sent to those who send a self-addressed, magazine-size envelope with $1.70 in postage.

ARTICLES

FORMAT: We're looking for factual articles that are well written, well illustrated, and will inform, entertain, and perhaps inspire. Most of our articles are now assigned, but we welcome informative news stories on controversial or current topics, as long as they are well documented and present the issue fairly. We do not, at this time, accept fiction or poetry. Articles should be neither too elementary nor too technical. About 80 percent of our readers have had college training, and about 30 percent have either a Master's or a Ph.D. degree.

Written queries are required, and we work four to 12 months in advance of an issue.

Most of our published manuscripts come to us on disc. Because the magazine is produced on Macintosh computers, we prefer Microsoft Word, but we can accept WordPerfect saved as ASCII text (DOS). Your disc must be accompanied by a paper manuscript. We can also accept articles via e-mail [or mailed] to the address below.

Although we are always willing to consider a submission, the acceptance of an article for review in no way constitutes a contract for publication. All submissions and queries are reviewed by the editors, and the author is informed of our decision within eight weeks.

PAY RATES: Payment for full-length articles—with photo or other illustrative support—ranges from $250 to $800, and is authorized upon acceptance.

PHOTOGRAPHS

FORMAT: Many of the photos used in *American Forests* are sent by the authors to illustrate their articles. These photographs should be related to the article and must be clear and sharp. A caption sheet, keyed to numbers on the photos, should describe each shot and name any people shown.

In black-and-white photos, we prefer 8"x10" glossies. In color, we need original—not duplicate—transparencies; 35mm is the most common, although 4"x5" or 5"x7" transparencies are good choices for cover shots. Fuji Velvia and Kodachrome 64 are two of the best color films for our purposes.

PAY RATE: Payment for cover photos is $300. For photos submitted with articles, payment is included in a check to the author. Inside shots not submitted with an article are paid for at a rate that depends on size, quality and placement in the magazine.

SUBMITTING ARTICLES AND/OR PHOTOGRAPHS

All material will be returned, provided a self-addressed, stamped envelope of suitable size accompanies your submission. Send submissions to the address below.

ADDITIONAL INFORMATION FOR PHOTOGRAPHERS

American Forests has long been noted for its coffee table—quality covers and inside photographs, and we intend to improve upon that reputation. We strive for the photos in our magazine to be more than simply a record of a place or event, but rather a creative interpretation that's pleasing to the eye and evokes an understanding of what is happening in the scene and/or a longing to be in that particular place, usually outdoors. Some detailed guidelines on outdoor photography follow for the semi-pros and nonprofessionals among our contributors.

FILM TYPE: For optimum reproduction, film should be a smooth-grained type such as Fuji Velvia or Kodachrome 64. Because of the relatively slow ASA speed of such films, there are times when a higher-speed film is needed—low-light conditions, for example. Under those conditions, the first option would be to use a longer exposure time with a camera mounted on a tripod. If the subject is stationary, shoot at 1/60th or 1/30th of a second. If that's not possible, the other alternative is to shoot high-speed Ektachrome with an ASA of 400. It's better to have a grainy photo than none at all.

BEST TIME OF DAY: The ideal time to photograph is when the sun is low on the horizon—from sunrise until about 10:30 and from 3:30 until sunset. A low sun lights a person's face or any vertical object, so that you can distinguish detail. When the sun is directly overhead, all the features are in dark shadows. Also, the light of a low sun is warmer, because it is passing through more atmosphere on its slanted approach.

Obviously, there are situations when the time of day cannot be prearranged and photographs must be taken when the opportunity arises.

POSING YOUR SUBJECTS: When working with people in your photos, it's best to have them doing their "thing," whatever that may be, rather than looking at the camera. If they are scientists, for example, they should appear to be studying some object that relates to the article. Posed shots usually are undesirable; when taking a portrait, strive for a more relaxed shot.

CAMERA EQUIPMENT: Because we are trying to portray a three-dimensional subject in two-dimensional form without the help of other senses, you should portray nature not exactly the way it appears, but a bit larger than life. To accomplish this, most photographers use lenses other than the "normal" 50mm lens that comes on most cameras. The lenses used most by professional photographers are wide-angle—either 35mm or 28mm—or short telephotos of 75mm or 135mm. These lenses produce a slightly exaggerated view of nature and appear fresh to the reader, who with the unaided eye has never seen nature quite that way.

It's impossible to provide detailed advice about camera selection here, but it pays to use the best you can buy or borrow. Even the newer point-and-shoot cam-eras, if they have a quality lens, can produce reproduction-quality photographs.

Packages to be handled by Federal Express, UPS, or other fast-delivery services should be sent to our street address—516 P St. NW, Washington, DC 20005.

Categories: Environment—Public Policy

Name: Michelle Robbins, Editor
Material: All
Address: PO BOX 2000
City/State/ZIP: WASHINGTON DC 20013
Telephone: 202-955-4500
Fax: 202-955-4588
E-mail: mrobbins@amfor.org
Internet: www.amfor.org

The American Gardener
Connecting People to Gardens

THE AMERICAN GARDENER is the official publication of the American Horticultural Society (AHS), a national, nonprofit, membership organization for gardeners founded in 1922. AHS is dedicated to promoting the art and science of horticulture in America through its publications and programs.

Readers of THE AMERICAN GARDENER include the approximately 20,000 members of the American Horticultural Society. Another 6,000 are sold on newsstands.

Editorial Content

The magazine is primarily freelance written, and its content differs considerably from that of other gardening publications. We run very few how-to articles. Our readers are advanced, sophisticated amateur gardeners; about 20 percent are horticultural professionals. Our articles are intended to bring this knowledgeable group new information, ranging from the latest scientific findings that affect plants, to the history of gardening and gardens in America. We introduce readers to unusual plants, personalities, and issues that will enrich what we assume is already a passionate commitment to gardening.

Among the topics of particular interest to us are profiles of prominent horticulturists whose work has a regional or national impact; plant research and plant hunting; plant conservation, biodiversity, and heirloom gardening; events or personalities in horticultural history; people-plant relationships (horticultural therapy, ethnobotany, and community gardening); "appropriate gardening" (choosing plants suited to one's region, using native plants, conserving water); plant lore and literature; the political issues affecting horticulture.

We stress environmentally-responsible gardening: minimal use of synthetic pesticides and water, not collecting plants from the wild, and avoiding plants that could escape and damage natural ecosystems. Proposals for articles on specific plants or plant families, public or private gardens, or design should stress a unique approach to the topic.

We prefer that authors query us before developing a manuscript. Queries must be accompanied by a self-addressed stamped envelope. We do not accept phone or fax queries. Queries should include a description of the proposed topic and an explanation of why it is of interest to a national audience of knowledgeable gardeners, as well as an outline of the major points to be covered in the manuscript.

When querying for the first time, authors should submit writing samples, and explain why they believe they are qualified to write on the subject they are proposing. We look for writers with a knowledge of plants, but also an ability to write in a strong journalistic style, complete with lively quotes from interviews or written sources.

Acceptance of an idea outlined in a query does not constitute acceptance of an article. All manuscripts are written on speculation only. While ideas for articles are evaluated separately from photographs or artwork, it is helpful to the evaluation process for submissions to include information on possible photo or illustration sources.

Maximum length for feature articles is 2,000 words.

Departments

THE AMERICAN GARDENER has a number of departments for which we accept freelance submissions.

• **Offshoots**. This is our essay department and the one exception to our "query first" rule. Topics can be humorous, sentimental, or express an unusual viewpoint. The average length is 1,200 words. Illustrated by an artist.

• **Conservationist's Notebook**. Articles about individuals or organizations attempting to save endangered species or protect natural areas. Runs 750 words.

• **Natural Connections**. Explains a natural phenomenon-plant and pollinator relationships, plant and fungus relationships, parasites that may be observed in nature or in the garden. Runs 750 words.

• **Urban Gardener**. Looks at a successful small space garden—indoor, patio, less than a quarter-acre; a program that successfully brings plants to city streets or public spaces; or a problem of particular concern to city dwellers. Runs 750-1,500 words.

• **Planting the Future**. This department recognizes innovative children and youth gardening programs around the country. Runs 750 words.

• **Plants and Your Health**. This department looks at all aspects of gardening and health, from sunburn, poison ivy, and strained backs to herbal medicines. Articles on herbal medicines need to reflect new, scientifically controlled studies. Runs 750 words.

• **Regional Happenings**. These reflect events that directly affect gardeners only in one area, but are of interest to others: an expansion of a botanical garden, a serious new garden pest, the launching of a regional flower show, a hot new gardening trend. Runs 250-500 words.

Policies

We make every effort to report back to the author within 90 days of receiving a query. Articles accepted are scheduled and published at the discretion of the editorial staff

We do not knowingly consider simultaneous manuscripts, and we retain the right to return at any time manuscripts that appear or have appeared as a whole or in part in another publication, regardless of whether the manuscripts have already been accepted or scheduled.

The staff of THE AMERICAN GARDENER retains the right to edit manuscripts as it deems necessary, for clarity, style, length, and accuracy. We do not as a matter of policy provide authors with revised manuscripts prior to publication. However, this can sometimes be negotiated at the time that an article is accepted.

Payment

Payment for feature articles ranges from $100 to $400 upon publication, depending on the article's length and complexity, and the author's horticultural background and publishing experience. Reimbursement for travel and other expenses can sometimes be negotiated. Contributors receive three complimentary copies of the issue in which their work is published. Additional copies are available at a reduced rate of $1 each.

Payment for departments is $150 for Offshoots; $100 for most other departments; and $50 for Regional Happenings. Payment for use of photographs used with articles is an additional $50 each.

The American Horticultural Society buys first North American serial rights. Although the Society copyrights each entire issue of THE AMERICAN GARDENER, the individual contributors retain the rights to their own unedited work.

We may occasionally wish to use a brief excerpt on the Internet for promotional purposes for a limited period only. Any objection to this use should be stated prior to publication of the article in THE AMERICAN GARDENER.

Very rarely we may wish to reproduce an entire article on the Internet. The rights to do so are negotiated separately.

We pay a 25 percent kill fee in those instances where an author has completed revisions of the text requested by our editorial staff and the article is still for any reason considered unacceptable.

Mechanical Requirements

• Submit material typewritten. If you are not using a computer, retain one copy for your files.

• Accompany the article with a brief biography plus your name, address, social security number, and telephone number.

• After a manuscript has been accepted, it is a great help to us to receive manuscripts on computer disks. Our system can use either Microsoft Word 6.0 or WordPerfect 5.1. If authors have other word-processing systems, they should use an ASCII (text only) format or consult with us before sending disks. All computer disks should be accompanied by a hard copy of the manuscript. In preparing a computer document, please do not underline or highlight words or indent paragraphs.

• Limit the article, whenever possible, to eight to 10 double-spaced, typewritten pages, excluding bibliography or sidebars.

• Avoid using footnotes. Incorporate citations or attributions in the body of the text. To assist us in editing, authors should include a bibliography of reference books or previously published articles used for background, and addresses and telephone numbers of individuals interviewed.

• For articles relating to particular plants or types of plant, we appreciate a list of retail mail-order sources, including the names, addresses, and phone numbers, and whether the nurseries charge for their plant lists or catalogs.

• Authors who are submitting photographs or illustrations to accompany an article should request a copy of our Photographers' Guidelines before doing so. Authors writing about specific plants should request a copy of our "Rules for Botanical Nomenclature."

Categories: Gardening

Name: Kathleen Fisher, Editor
Material: All
Address: 7931 E BOULEVARD DR
City/State/ZIP: ALEXANDRIA VA 22308
Telephone: 703-768-5700

American Health for Women

Dear Friend,

American Health for Women is always looking for stories that are new, authoritative, helpful and inspirational to female readers, ages to 35 to 55. We cover both the scientific and lifestyle aspects of women's health, nutrition and fitness. In each issue we run several feature articles of 1,000 to 2,500 words.

Ideas for feature articles are generated by editors at the magazines as well as proposals from experienced journalists.

The best way to help us decide about a story suggestion is with a written query. You should submit ideas in a few paragraphs, offering the best possible sample of your writing style and approach to the material as well as describing the value of the story and its basic facts. Please include several writing clips.

Currently, we are looking for real-life medical dramas, stories that track women's experiences with serious medical health conditions and how they were managed by their doctors and themselves.

We also read completed manuscripts sent to us on speculation. While we will make every effort to return your manuscript to you in the self-addressed, stamped envelope you will thoughtfully have provided, we recommend that you NOT send us an original. Things do get lost.

Categories: Consumer—Health—Fitness—Nutrition—Women's Issues/Studies

Name: Editorial
Material: All queries and/or complete submissions
Address: 28 West 23rd Street
City/State/ZIP: New York, NY 10010.
Telephone: 212-366-8900
Fax: 212-627-3833

American Hunter

American Hunter, an official journal of the National Rifle Association, is one of the most popular hunting magazines in the nation. Approximately 1.3 million NRA members receive *American Hunter* each month. For most issues, *American Hunter* buys out 50 percent or more of its editorial material and photos. The following information is intended to reduce confusion during the query, submission, and publication process and to inform contributors of our editorial needs and policies.

Feature Articles: An *American Hunter* feature story typically runs 1,800-2,000 words; however, the editors are more concerned with content than length. If an article is short (1,000-1,500 words) but good, we'll buy it.

Subject matter for feature articles falls into five general categories that run in each issue: deer, upland birds, waterfowl, big game and varmints/small game. Features may be written in a number of prose styles, including expository how-to, where-to, and general interest pieces; humor; personal narratives; and semi-technical articles on firearms, wildlife management, or hunting.

American Hunter does not buy poetry or articles on firearms legislation.

Story angles should be narrow, but coverage must have depth. How-to articles are popular with readers and might range from methods for hunting to techniques on making gear used on successful hunts. Where-to articles should contain contacts and information needed to arrange a similar hunt.

All submissions are judged on three criteria: story angle (it should be fresh, interesting, and informative); quality of writing (clear and lively - capable of holding the readers attention throughout); and quality and quantity of accompanying photos (sharpness, reproducibility, and connection to text are most important.)

Departments: We solicit material for one monthly department—"Hunting Guns." Contributors should study back issues for appropriate subject matter and style for this column. Copy length should be 1,200-1,500 words.

Photographs: Photo requirements are demanding. We reject more articles because of poor photo support than for any other reason. We use both color transparencies and black and white prints to illustrate features. The editors prefer article packages that contain both a good selection of color slides and a varied assortment of black and white glossy prints. We will accept black and white negatives with contact sheets. Captions should be detailed and should explain how the photo relates to the text. Photos should be given an identifying code to correspond to the caption sheet, and the name of the photographer should appear on every print or slide. Color slides should be protected in plastic. If a submitted photograph has been published previously, photographers are required to advise the editor of the title and date of publication.

American Hunter rates for photographs submitted and purchased separately and not as part of a photo package supporting a manuscript are:

Cover- $300
Centerspread or two-page spread- $225
Inside color (full page)- $175
Inside color (part page)- $50-$100
Black and white- $25

Query Letters: Although unsolicited manuscripts are welcomed, detailed query letters outlining the proposed topic and approach are appreciated and will save both writers and editors a considerable amount of time. If we like your story idea, you will be contacted by mail or phone and given direction on how we'd like the topic covered. NRA Publications accept all manuscripts and photographs for consideration on a speculation basis only. On those rare occasions when an advance assignment is made, it will be done in writing and valid only if signed by the Editor or the Executive Director of Publications.

Payment: We pay for articles on acceptance and for freelance-submitted photos on publication. We purchase first North American serial rights plus the subsequent reprint rights for NRA Publications. *American Hunter* currently pays up to $500 for full-length feature articles with complete photo packages. Payment may be reduced if we have to supplement your photo package or if your manuscript requires extensive clean-up or rewrite. Payment for departments ranges from $300-$350. Upon publication, all photographs and other material will be returned to the contributor. NRA Publications do not pay kill fees.

Specifications: All manuscripts must be typed double-spaced. No photocopied or hand-written submissions will be accepted; simultaneous submissions will not receive consideration. Please avoid script typefaces. Manuscripts should be submitted flat with a stamped, self-addressed return envelope. Manuscripts may be submitted on 5 1/4" floppy disk, IBM compatible operating system; manuscripts accepted in WordPerfect 4.2, 5.0, or 5.1, or other convertible word processors (Microsoft Word, Display Write, Multimate, Word Star), or in ASCII format along with a legible printout. Disks will be returned after publication or upon decline of purchase.

Replies: *American Hunter* receives more than a thousand queries and manuscripts a year, and although the editors try to respond within three weeks, it may take a month or more for an author to receive a reply. The editors are not responsible for unsolicited manuscripts or photos.

Categories: Nonfiction—Animals—General Interest—Law—Outdoors—Politics—Sports—Recreation—Hunting—Firearms—How-to—Humor—Personal Experience—Fishing—Camping

Name: Bill Rooney, Managing Editor
Material: All
Address: 11250 WAPLES MILL RD.
City/State/ZIP: FAIRFAX, VA 22030-9400
Telephone: 703-267-1316
Fax: 703-267-3971

American Indian Art Magazine

American Indian Art Magazine is a quarterly art journal that presents the art of the American Indian through articles and illustrations appealing to both lay people and professionals. We prefer articles that utilize the magazine's illustrated format—in other words, articles that tie the illustrations to the text. Our readers are collectors, dealers, scholars, students and other interested individuals. Some of our readers are knowledgeable about the field and some know very little; *American Indian Art Magazine* seeks articles which offer something to both groups.

Manuscript Review

Any article, whether solicited or volunteered, is subject to review by members of the magazine's Editorial Advisory Board and/or other authorities in the field. These readers may suggest revisions to be made by authors or may recommend additional material and illustrations. Manuscripts will be returned to the author for any substantive changes. An article must be approved by members of the Editorial Advisory Board before it is published in the magazine. Articles reflecting original research and expressing new hypotheses are preferred over summaries and reviews of previously discussed material. Acceptance of an article for publication does not guarantee its appearance in the next issue of the magazine.

In addition to research articles, the magazine publishes museum collection and exhibition features that are designed to give readers a sense of the overall strengths and weaknesses of the collection, in addition to answering questions about collection history, quality or problems of documentation and the like.

Style

Manuscripts published in the magazine generally run between twelve and eighteen pages in typescript form, exclusive of bibliography, captions and footnotes. We prefer to receive manuscripts on computer disc (Macintosh Microsoft Word) with a hard copy.

We would like an article to be as detailed and specific as possible; try to limit the article to a particular subject, small geographical area, particular object(s) or selected design style. For example, if the subject is Plains Indian shields, try to limit the article to one group or one type of shield or design. In an article discussing changes in style with time, try to explain how to date the changes, and what other contemporaneous styles were. Authors should discuss aesthetics as well as the anthropological context of a subject, if possible.

An article usually requires between eight and fifteen photographs, with a choice from both black and white and color. It is often a good idea to shoot all the subjects in both ways so that the article can be adapted to the technical limitations of the printing process. Please send photographs in individual sleeves with figure numbers clearly marked.

In obtaining photographs, make certain the photographer and processor know that the photographs will be used for reproduction in a magazine. Black-and-white photographs should be glossy 8"x10" prints. Color photographs should be transparencies and 35mm slides are acceptable. Use plain backdrops.

As a matter of policy, we prefer to illustrate material from public collections, avoiding items in private collections unless comparable material is not available elsewhere.

Other Illustrations

Occasionally an article will require a diagrammatic drawing to illustrate a particular manufacturing method. If the author provides a clear sketch or a standard reference source, the magazine will prepare a reproducible line drawing.

Permission

American Indian Art Magazine needs permission in writing to use illustrations which belong to other publications, historical societies, institutions, and private individuals. Sometimes it is necessary to obtain permission separately from the owner of the object in the picture, as well as from the owner of the photograph and/or photographer. With contemporary objects it is also necessary to obtain permission from the artist. Obtaining such permission is the responsibility of the author.

The magazine can supply copies of the printed article to the person or institution allowing use of the photograph; this is frequently a condition for receiving permission. Make certain any special phrases—e.g., "used by permission of"—stipulated by the permission-giver are included in the photograph caption.

Photograph Usage and Fees

American Indian Art Magazine buys onetime publication rights to photographs and returns the originals after the magazine has been printed. Fee schedules and reimbursable expenses are arranged for single photographs and for multiple photograph assignments; the magazine and the author jointly decide on these arrangements.

Conclusion

The Editor and staff of *American Indian Art Magazine* make every effort to help authors in preparing manuscripts, obtaining illustrations and permission, and generally assisting in article preparation. Authors are encouraged to make preliminary contact with the magazine before committing many long hours to work on the article: proposals and draft outlines will be reviewed if an author requests.

Style

Note: In preparing accepted manuscripts for publication, the editorial staff of the magazine attempts to conform to standard spelling and usage procedures. Reference works consulted include *Webster's Ninth Collegiate Dictionary* (Merriam-Webster Inc., Springfield, Massachusetts, 1985); *A Manual of Style* (University of Chicago Press, 1969, twelfth edition, revised); and *Ethnographic Bibliography of North America* by George Peter Murdock and Timothy J. O'Leary (Human Relations Area Files Press, New Haven, 1975, fourth edition).

Categories: Nonfiction—Arts—Native American

Name: Roanne Goldfein, Editor
Material: All
Address: 7314 E OSBORN DR
City/State/ZIP: SCOTTSDALE AZ
Telephone: 602-994-5445

American Kennel Club Gazette

Editorial Profile: The GAZETTE is the official publication of the American Kennel Club. It is read by breeders and exhibitors of pure-bred dogs, by dog show judges, by individuals who compete in obedience and field trials, hunting and tracking tests and other events, and by other individuals with a serious interest in the sport of dogs. The GAZETTE publishes articles on a wide range of subjects, including veterinary medicine, nutrition and health, care and training and living with dogs: their behavior and temperament, exhibition, handling and conditioning. The common denominator in all GAZETTE editorial is that it acknowledges the reader's sophistication and seriousness about the subject matter and is never condescending.

The GAZETTE gives highest priority to the breeds that are recognized by the American Kennel Club and to activities that are sanctioned by the AKC. A smaller amount of space is devoted to non-AKC activities that nevertheless are of interest to fanciers. The magazine strives to keep readers informed on issues affecting dogs and dog owners in society today.

Freelance Opportunities: We are looking for authoritative pieces that explore a subject of general interest or that report on specific events or activities. Because of its affiliation with the American Kennel Club, the GAZETTE cannot accept stories that appear to promote individual dogs, judges, handlers, breeders or kennels; nor that appear to rate or endorse specific products. (Exceptions are when a story has news value.)

Articles should be factual rather than opinion, except for monthly Point of View essays (see below). Whatever the subject, writers should be knowledgeable and credible and should be able to quote several expert sources. Veterinary articles are written by or with a veterinarian. Most unsolicited material rejected by the editors consists of "true life" accounts, in memoriam pieces, or other related material pertaining to one's own pet. Unless a work contains a timely, topical or newsworthy story of general interest to the dog fancy, the GAZETTE generally can't use it.

Fiction: Except for an annual short fiction contest (rules are published June through September, or are available on request with an SASE), the GAZETTE doesn't publish fiction.

Poetry, Puzzles, Cartoons: The GAZETTE does not publish poetry or puzzles. Cartoons are commissioned by the art director, and freelancers should not submit unsolicited cartoons.

Profiles: Profiles of individuals are published regularly, but should always be queried first in writing to the editor.

Clippings: These are never used.

Photography: The GAZETTE sponsors an annual photography contest (rules published September through December, or are available on request with an SASE). In addition, it welcomes candid photos of show-quality dogs in either color or black and white, and event-specific or relevant photography to accompany feature articles.

Illustrations: Professional illustrators interested in working with the GAZETTE should contact the art director. All art is commissioned. Illustrators should be able to accurately depict pure-bred dogs.

Point of View: The monthly Point of View column invites 800 word essays on important subjects facing the sport or the fancy. These are first-person opinion pieces and are published with a photograph of the author.

Specifications: Length: 1,000-3,000 words; payment: $200-$400. High-quality photos in either color or black and white are a definite plus; payment for photos is separate and is based on number and size used in magazine, ranging from $25 to $100 apiece.

Simultaneous submissions or previously published material will be considered, but author must advise in query letter.

Send query letter, proposal or complete manuscript. Reports in three weeks. Payment on acceptance for manuscripts; on publication for photography. Buys first North American serial rights, onetime use. All contributors retain copyright and reprint requests will be forwarded to them.

Categories: Animals—Hobbies—Pets—Sports

Name: Mark Roland, Features Editor
Material: Feature-length stories
Name: Josh Adams, Associate Editor
Material: News, new products, humor, reviews
Address: 51 MADISON AVE

City/State/ZIP: NEW YORK NY 10010-1603
Telephone: 212-696-8200
Fax: 212-696-8272

The American Legion Magazine

The American Legion Magazine - the 19th largest magazine in the U.S.- is an award-winning leader among national general-interest publications. It is published monthly by The American Legion for its nearly 3 million members, and is also widely read by members of the Washington establishment and other policy makers. Working through 15,000 community-level posts, the honorably discharged wartime veterans of The American Legion dedicate themselves to God, country and traditional American values. They believe in a strong defense; adequate and compassionate care for veterans and their families; community service; and the wholesome development of our nation's youth. We publish articles that reflect these values. We inform our readers and their families of significant trends and issues affecting our nation, the world and the way we live. Our major features focus on national security, foreign affairs, business trends, social issues, health, education, ethics and the arts. We also publish selected general feature articles, articles of special interest to veterans, and question-and-answer interviews with prominent national and world figures. We place a premium on accuracy, fairness and good taste. We are (generally) open to almost any form of article, essay or expose; the only absolute thematic taboo is an article promoting a partisan political agenda (e.g., "Why the Democrats Have the Right Idea on Health Care," etc.) The analysis should be of the causes themselves, not the men, women or parties advancing those causes. The distinction is often subtle, but it must be there.

Format and Style: If it works, it works. Ideally, issues should be covered in human terms, but expository articles should also include current facts, vivid examples and expert opinions needed to (a) tell the story, and (b) make the writer's case. Use a compelling lead and an engaging writing style.

Sources: We will not accept just a warmed-over compilation of quotes and background material taken from other publications (with or without attribution). Our authors must be willing to undertake firsthand research.

Query Required: We make all assignments based on a one or two-page query letter. It should show the general thrust of the article, outline its basic structure and content, and demonstrate the writer's firm understanding of the proposed topic. The best query clearly states the article's angle or point, explains why readers will want to read about this subject, and begins with an enticing proposed title for the article. Writers should include sample clips and list relevant experience or background.

Documentation: Completed articles must include appropriate documentation of facts and citations verifying all quotations and statements from sources. This is especially important when quoting people whose professional reputations could be damaged through improper quoting. All material published in The American Legion Magazine must first survive a legal reading by the Legion's in-house counsel

Rights: We purchase First North American serial rights, unless otherwise negotiated.

Payment, Length, Queries: Payment is individually negotiated depending on complexity of subject matter and current needs. Kill fees and reimbursement of expenses are available to writers working on assignment. Manuscript length varies from 600 words to about 2,200; most features are in the 1,200- to 1,700-word range. We report on queries within six to eight weeks. We will consider unsolicited manuscripts in two categories: (1) humor, and (2) wartime memoirs written by veterans themselves. All other unsolicited manuscripts will be returned unread. Telephone queries are not accepted. Queries, manuscripts and art must be accompanied by a self-addressed, stamped envelope (SASE) if the writer desires that they be returned. We will not return submissions without a SASE. We cannot assume any financial liability for the loss of any submissions.

Sample Magazines: The best way to get a feel for our type of article is to read several issues of the magazine. For a sample copy, send $3.50 to the address below.

Categories: Nonfiction—Arts—Business—Children—Family—Health—Military—Politics—Society—Religion—Education—Morality

Name: Joe Stuteville, Editor
Material: All
Address: P.O. BOX 1055
City/Stat/ZIP: INDIANAPOLIS, IN 46206-1055
Telephone: 317-630-1200
Fax: 317-630-1280
Internet: www.legion.org

American Libraries

American Libraries is ALA's [American Library Association] four-color monthly magazine and the primary perquisite of membership in the Association. Each issue features articles on professional concerns and developments, along with news of the Association, library-related legislation, and libraries around the country and the world. Expression of diverse viewpoints and critical interpretation of professional issues make the magazine the premier forum for the exchange of ideas crucial to the fulfillment of ALA Goal 200. Annual subscriptions are available to institutions at $60, $70 foreign.

STYLE: Informal, but informative. Factual article must be inviting and readable, with all statements backed by responsible research and interviews. The *Chicago Manual of Style* may be used in styling articles for publication, but extensive footnoting is discouraged.

FORMAT: Letter- or near-letter quality. One copy suffices.

SUBMISSIONS BY E-MAIL: In addition to considering manuscripts submitted by surface mail, *American Libraries* considers manuscripts sent e-mail. When e-mailing a submission, please include your surface-mail address to expedite our sending a contributor's contract if your submission is accepted for publication.

WORD PROCESSING REQUIREMENTS: Manuscripts should be submitted on a 3½" diskette (high density, 1.44 megabytes in size) and accompanied by a paper printout of the text. While *American Libraries* is capable of handling a wide range of word processing programs in both the PC and Mac formats, we prefer that manuscripts be in Word 6.x for Windows. When submitting a manuscript, indicate the word processing program used.

LENGTH: 600-2,000 words.

PAYMENT: Honoraria of $100 to $250 are offered for most articles, paid upon receipt of an acceptable manuscript.

EXCLUSIVE SUBMISSION: It is assumed that no other publisher is or will be simultaneously considering a manuscript submitted to *American Libraries* until that manuscript is returned or written permission is provided by the *American Libraries* editors.

RIGHTS: According to the contract provided to authors, exclusive North American rights are retained until three months after publication, unless another arrangement is made in writing. *American Libraries* retains rights to have the published material reproduced, distributed, and sold in microform or electronic text.

REPRINT POLICY: No reprints can be provided, but permission is usually granted for authors to reproduce their contributions as published in *American Libraries*. Others wishing to republish the text of an article are referred to the author for permission and fee information. A reasonable number of copies are sent to each author. Special arrangements may be necessary to reproduce illustrations.

ACKNOWLEDGEMENT: Unsolicited manuscripts are acknowledged when received.

REPORTS: The editors try to report on manuscripts within 4-8 weeks. Written reminders from the author after this period are welcome, and usually result in a prompt reply.

PUBLICATION DATE: On acceptance, an estimated date of publication may be provided to the author. Usually manuscripts can be published no sooner than two months after receipt.

EDITING: On accepted manuscripts, the editors reserve the right to make editorial revisions, deletions, or additions which, in their opinion, support the author's intent. When changes are substantial, every effort is made to work with the author.

GALLEYS: Galleys are not provided to the author.

PHOTOGRAPHS: Color prints, taken in natural light, are preferred for use with manuscripts or as picture stories. Transparencies and black-and-white prints are also considered for possible use. Payment is negotiated.

CARTOONS: Cartoons of the highest professional quality that relate to library interests and avoid librarian stereotypes will be considered. Average payment $50.

ILLUSTRATIONS: Illustrations are commissioned for certain articles and features.

Categories: Libraries

Name: Submissions Editor
Material: All
Address: 50 E HURON
City/State/ZIP: CHICAGO IL 60611
Telephone: 312-280-4216
Fax: 312-440-0901
E-mail: americanlibraries@ala.org
Internet: www.ala.org

American Medical News

American Medical News is the nation's most widely circulated newspaper focusing on socioeconomic issues in medicine. Published weekly by the American Medical Association, AMN covers the full spectrum of non-clinical news affecting physicians' practices. Our primary readers are about 320,000 physicians, most of whom receive the publication free as part of their AMA membership. Readers also include administrators of health-care organizations, government health-care policymakers and others with a professional interest in physicians and the U.S. health-care system.

AMN contracts with a relatively small group of freelance writers for news and feature articles that focus on policy development, legislation, regulation, economic trends, and physician-impact coverage in the categories that follow. We also seek articles about innovative efforts by individuals or groups to improve health-system functioning or physician practice in these areas.

Population health & related trends

• Health promotion and disease prevention: tobacco, alcohol and drug use; family and community violence; maternal and child health, including immunization; clinical preventive services

• Infectious diseases: AIDS; tuberculosis

• Treatment issues: health of targeted groups, including minorities, women, children, adolescents elderly and disabled; access to care for homeless, medically indigent and rural residents; organ transplantation

• Health protection: environmental and occupational health; accident prevention; food and drug safety

• Impact of health care market trends and policy developments on patients and population health

• How doctors are helping to implement public health goals

• Physician health, well-being and job satisfaction

• Physician-patient relationships

• Consumerism and patients' rights

Topic Editor: Wayne Hearn

Professional issues

• Medical education and training, including undergraduate, graduate and continuing medical education, specialty training, certification, credentialing and physician supply issues

• Medical-legal matters, including professional liability, antitrust, fraud, abuse and related questions

• Quality assurance, including licensure, discipline, professional regulation, peer review, outcomes measurement and practice standards

• Professional and clinical ethics

• Technology, medical informatics, the pharmaceutical industry and related biomedical research

• The institution of organized medicine

Health system structure and finance

• Developments in public policy and the private marketplace that affect the structure of the health care industry and determine the conditions, quality and financial rewards of the practice of medicine

• Physician services financing issues, including Medicare, Medicaid, other government payers, Blue Cross and Blue Shield, commercial insurers and managed care; physician pay

• Physician relations with health care delivery systems, including HMOs, PPOs, group practices, hospitals and integrated hospital/physician networks

• Workforce issues: supply of physicians, the mix between specialists and generalists, relations between physicians and other health professions

• Federal and state health system reform efforts

Business

• Practice management, including general small-business issues (i.e. taxes, employment policies, salary and benefits), small-business issues unique to medical practices (i.e. CPT coding, relations with other physicians and third-party payers), contracting with insurers, strategic planning, raising capital, integrating new technology in practice settings, forming partnerships and managing groups

Please submit written queries of about one typewritten page, containing a detailed account of what you intend to cover and beginning with a lead you consider suitable for a finished article. Alternatively, you may submit the story to us on speculation.

Categories: Health—Medicine

Name: Kathryn Trombatore, Editor
Material: All
Address: 515 N STATE ST
City/State/ZIP: CHICAGO IL 60610
Telephone: 312-464-4429
Fax: 312-464-4445

American Motorcyclist

American Motorcyclist magazine covers every facet of motorcycling. Each monthly issue details the people, places and events—from road rallies to road races—that make up the American Motorcycling experience. Plus, you'll find the most in-depth stories on the legislative issues that affect your right to ride, and the most comprehensive schedule of both road-riding and competition events anywhere.

Categories: Nonfiction—Motorcycling

Name: Bill Wood, Managing Editor
Material: All
Address: 33 COLLEGEVIEW RD
City/State/ZIP: WESTERVILLE OH 43081-1484
Telephone: 614-891-2425
Fax: 614-891-5012
E-mail: AMA@ama-cycle.org
Internet: www.ama-cycle.org

The American Poetry Review

The American Poetry Review publishes original poetry, literary criticism, interviews, essays and social commentary. Please use the following guidelines when sending material for publication:

1. Manuscripts should be typewritten.

2. Manuscripts should be addressed to "The Editors." Do not address unsolicited manuscripts to an individual editor.

3. Submissions must be accompanied by a self-addressed envelope. *No reply will be made to submissions not accompanied by sufficient return postage.*

4. Do not send previously published material or material that is currently under consideration by another magazine or periodical. Do not send work that is under consideration by APR to another magazine or periodical.

5. Our reporting time is approximately ten weeks. We will inform you of acceptance or return your manuscript. Please do not inquire about the status of your manuscript during the ten-week reporting period.

6. All work submitted to APR is considered for publication in *The American Poetry Review* only.

Copyright: APR holds first serial rights for material that we publish. The copyright automatically reverts to the author upon publication. We do not require that material be copyrighted prior to submission.

Contests: APR does *not* conduct a poetry contest. All work submitted to APR is considered for publication in *The American Poetry Review* only.

Prizes: **The Jerome J. Shestack Poetry Prizes** of $1,000 are awarded annually to each of two poets whose work has appeared in APR during the preceding calendar year.

The Jessica Nobel-Maxwell Memorial Poetry Prize of $2,000 is awarded annually to a younger poet whose work has appeared in APR during the preceding calendar year.

The S. J. Marks Memorial Poetry Prize of $500 is awarded annually for a writer's first appearance in APR during the preceding calendar year.

Thank you and best wishes.

The Editors

Categories: Poetry

Name: The Editors
Material: All
Address: 1721 WALNUT ST
City/State/ZIP: PHILADELPHIA PA 19103
Telephone: 215-496-0439

American Rifleman

The Publications Division of the National Rifle Association, which prepares both the *American Rifleman* and the *American Hunter* magazines, regularly purchases material submitted by freelancers. While we buy only a small portion of the material submitted, we do pay upon acceptance. Articles are received on speculation only, and NRA does not pay kill fees. Assignments are made only on written approval of the editor or the executive director of the Publications Division. The editors are not responsible for unsolicited manuscripts and/or photographs.

WHAT WE ARE LOOKING FOR: We want fresh material on all aspects of firearms and shooting. These can include gunsmithing, handloading, gun collecting, law enforcement training, competitive shooting, blackpowder, handguns, rifles and shotguns. Personality and firearms industry-related feature articles are also considered.

WHAT WE DON'T NEED: We can use equipment-related articles that involve hunting, but not straight hunting pieces. Consider sending those to the *American Hunter* at the same address. Nor can we use verse, fiction, essays and articles on gun legislation. We occasionally purchase pieces on the gun control issue, but the circumstances must be compelling or the material a new scholarly contribution to the literature.

NRA DOES NOT BUY GUN TESTS: Tests of new firearms and related equipment are conducted exclusively by the NRA Technical Staff or our Contributing Editors.

ILLUSTRATION: Pictures sell articles. We need good quality color and black and white photographs or slides. We want clarity and contrast. Weak, fuzzy photos get articles rejected. We often supplement photo packages, but we give first consideration to articles that have good photo support. We're not fussy about format: a good 4"x5" print is acceptable, and we like to receive negatives and proof sheets. We may be able to get more out of them than your local processor did. We return illustrative material three months after publication.

ARTICLE PREPARATION: Articles may range in length from five to perhaps 20 pages. We're not arbitrary about length. Manuscripts may be submitted on 5¼" or 3½" disks, IBM compatible operating system; articles accepted in WordPerfect Version 4.2, 5.0, 5.1 or 6.0 or in other convertible word processors (Microsoft Word, Display Write, MultiMate, Word Star) or in ASCII format along with a legible printout. Disks will be returned after publication or upon decline of purchase.

REPLIES: We generally purchase or reject manuscripts within about a month of receipt. Occasionally, this process may take a little longer.

WRITING FOR US: Aspiring writers should study carefully the content of past issues of the magazine to get an understanding of the type of material we publish. Inexperienced writers might consider first submitting an "In My Experience" article for publication. While NRA does not currently pay for these pieces, they generally represent good, concise writing and provide an opportunity for new writers to "test the water."

COPYRIGHT: The Copyright Law Revision of January, 1978, provides that, unless otherwise stipulated, a publisher purchases first publication rights only. The purpose of this notice is to include in addition to first publication rights, the NRA's right to reprint any manuscript or illustrative material purchased by the NRA, in future publications of the NRA. The right to offer this material to publishers other than the NRA remains with the author.

Categories: Firearms—Shooting

Name: Mark A. Keefe, IV, Managing Editor
Material: All
Address: 11250 WAPLES MILL RD
City/State/ZIP: FAIRFAX VA 22030-9400
Telephone: 703-267-1300
Fax: 703-267-3971

American Salesman

The *American Salesman* is a monthly magazine for sales professionals. Its primary objective is to provide informative articles which develop the attitudes, skills, personal and professional qualities of the sales representative, enabling them to use more of their potential to increase their productivity and achieve goals.

CONTENT: *The American Salesman* contains seven feature articles each month. Most of the articles are contributed by people with practical experience in sales. No advertising is used in this publication. Articles involving successful and innovative sales trends or case histories are considered.

NEEDS: We are interested in articles addressing the following: improving sales productivity, reviewing sales fundamentals, motivating sales staff, determining customer needs, customer service, knowing and analyzing competition, making sales presentations, handling objections, closing sales, following up, telephone selling, managing sales territory, planning, goal setting, time management and new innovative sales concepts.

SUBMISSION OF ARTICLES: We work in advance. Therefore, articles may be retained up to six months before tentative scheduling. Finished articles should contain from 900 to 1,200 words. A sample is mailed to the copy originator.

Manuscripts should be high-quality typed (suitable for scanning—do not submit articles on a low quality dot matrix printer). The *Associated Press Stylebook* is followed for editing. The author should indicate address, current byline containing background employment, company affiliation and educational degrees listing alma mater. Send a black-and-white glossy author photo to accompany credit line upon acceptance. Submissions must include a stamped, self-addressed return envelope.

Your experience and your ideas are valuable. We are always happy to receive inquiries from potential writers.

Categories: Business—Careers—Economics—Money/Finance—Sales

Name: George Eckley, Editor
Material: All
Address: National Research Bureau
Address: 320 VALLEY ST
City/State/ZIP: BURLINGTON IA 52601-5513
Telephone: 319-752-5415
Fax: 319-752-3421

The American Scholar
Phi Beta Kappa

Articles

The *Scholar* is a quarterly journal published by Phi Beta Kappa for general circulation. Our intent is to have articles by scholars and experts but written in non-technical language for an intelligent audience. The material that appears in the magazine covers a wide range of subject matter in the arts, sciences, current affairs, history, and literature. We prefer articles between 3,500 and 4,000 words, and we pay up to $500. To be accepted for publication, a manuscript must receive the affirmative votes of the editor and at least two members of the editorial board.

Poetry

Poems for submission to the *Scholar* should be typewritten, on one side of the paper, and each sheet of paper should bear the name and address of the author and the name of the poem. We have no special requirements of length, form, or content for original poetry. A look at several recent issues of the *Scholar* should give a good idea of the kind of poetry we publish and the way poems look on our pages. We suggest, too, that, from the author's point of view, it is probably most effective if not more than three or four poems are submitted at any one time. We pay $50.00 for each accepted poem.

We do not have arrangements for sending sample copies of the *Scholar* to prospective contributors. It would be possible, of course, for you to purchase the latest issue for the regular price of $6.95. If you do not care to purchase a copy, your library would probably have copies you could see.

Categories: Nonfiction—Arts—General Interest—History—Literature

Name: Submissions Editor
Material: All
Address: 1811 Q ST NW
City/State/ZIP: WASHINGTON DC 20009
Telephone: 202-265-3808

American Survival Guide
The Magazine of Self Reliance

American Survival Guide is for independent, self reliant people concerned with the protection of individual life, liberty, and property, and the preservation of the United States of America as a sovereign and independent nation.

Readers are interested in learning about human and natural forces posing threats in day-to-day life as well as possible threats in the future: crime, terrorism, riots, government tyranny, conventional and nuclear/biological/chemical warfare, disease, accidental injury, toxic wastes and other pollution, earthquakes, tornadoes, floods, hurricanes and other environmental disasters, poisonous plants and animals, etc.

Readers want to acquire the "how-to" of survival to enable them to succeed through knowledge of self defense, medicine and health, communications, transportation, and other aspects of survival.

American Survival Guide presents the knowledge, technology, hardware, tactics, strategies, attitudes, and philosophy for survival in a wide range of situations and scenarios.

Subject matter of high interest to readers includes: identification of threats, all forms of preparedness, instruction in self reliance, food production and storage, self defense and weapons, gun control and the Second Amendment, electronics and alarms systems, retreats, shelters, caches, field medicine, health and fitness, home and group defensive tactics, communications, and mental well being. Survival during natural and manmade disasters such as earthquakes, hurricanes, civil strife and urban violence, conventional, nuclear/biological/chemical warfare, and pollution dangers are also subjects of interest.

Submission Policy

Each submission to *American Survival Guide* should be a complete package. That is, text and photos or other illustrations should be present as a unit. Editors *will not accept text without photos or other illustrations*, and vise versa.

Articles should be submitted on computer floppy disk, either 3½" or 5¼" floppy with hard copy included. Microsoft Word files are preferred but other software text files will work such as WordPerfect.

Editors require either black and white photographs (minimum 4"x5") or color transparencies (35mm slides or larger), or color prints, *not color negative film*. Please include captions with each photo. The best and most exciting photos usually show people in action. Photo model releases are *mandatory* for all persons appearing in all photos submitted. Photos involving copyrighted material must be accompanied by written permission from their copyright holder.

Professional quality line drawings, charts, graphs, engineering drawings, and sketches are highly acceptable. Pen and ink drawings are preferred.

Query first by letter or telephone with regard to possible articles. Preferred article length is 1,500 to 2,000 words. Shorter, tighter articles of interest are also purchased. A good selection of artwork is desired. *American Survival Guide* buys exclusive first

time rights to text and illustrations for publications. Authors may request release and reassignment authorization. Payment is $80 per page in the magazine, on publication. Special rates may apply.

Categories: Nonfiction—Self Reliance—American Sovereignty—Survival

Name: Submissions Editor
Material: All
Address: Y-Visionary Publishing LP
Address: 265 S ANITA DR STE 120
City/State/ZIP: ORANGE CA 92868-3310
Telephone: 714-939-9991 ext. 203, 204
Fax: 714-939-9909
E-mail: jim4asg@aol.com, scott4asg@aol.com

American Visions

What kind of magazine is *American Visions*?

American Visions is the official magazine of the African-American Museums Association. It was launched in 1986 as the official publication of the Martin Luther King, Jr. national holiday. The magazine focuses on the "culturally active" African-American adult with editorial on culture, art, history, theater, music, dance, film, travel and technology from a unique cultural perspective. Its mission-in line with that of the American Visions Society is to promote an appreciation of black culture. Each issue also contains a cultural calendar of major local and regional events throughout the country.

Who reads *American Visions*?

Some 125,000 members of the American Visions Society and the general public read *American Visions*. Each issue is passed along to an average of 5 additional readers, for a total readership of more than 625,000.

What kind of articles does *American Visions* look for?

American Visions is interested in stories that present the elegant, sophisticated side of African-American culture in a pop-scholarly fashion. Topics covered include the arts, history, literature, cuisine, genealogy and travel-all filtered through the prism of the African-American experience. We frequently include a historical perspective on a topic, but we are not a scholarly publication. The magazine is reportorial, current and objective rather than academic or polemical. Departments include: *Arts Scene, Books, Calendar, Computers & Technology, Cuisine, Film, Genealogy, Music Notes and Travel. Special Supplements*, covering specific geographic areas and topics, are featured throughout the year as well.

When submitting material to *American Visions*...

Propose your *ideas* by letter or e-mail. Be specific: What will you write about the subject? Why will readers of *American Visions* find your story interesting?

Once we agree on a subject and an approach, we will work out length and scheduling details. Authors must provide good four-color or black-and-white illustrations where appropriate and must obtain permission from photographers and illustrators for the use of copyrighted materials. Editorial and word processing specifications are available upon request.

Writer's and Word Processing Guidelines

American Visions is the only magazine of its kind, in that it presents the elegant, sophisticated side of the African-American culture in a pop-scholarly fashion. Its scope includes the arts, history, literature, cuisine, genealogy and travel-all filtered through the prism of the African-American experience. Though we frequently include a historical perspective on a topic, we are not a scholarly publication.

Article Submissions

Manuscripts submitted for consideration should adhere to the following:

Feature Articles: 10 pages.

Department Articles: 4 to 6 pages.

Length is ultimately determined by subject matter and illustration possibilities.

Submission Essentials:

• Manuscripts should be submitted on 3½" high-density or double-density diskette with a hard copy whenever possible. Microsoft Word 2.0 is the preferred format, but other word processing formats are acceptable. They are listed below.

• A brief (one or two sentence) biographical sketch of the author(s) should follow the body of the manuscript.

• Graphics are almost always essential. All graphic materials (photographs, maps, slides, illustrations, etc.) should be submitted with the manuscript.

Format

• The following word processing formats (in preferential order) are also accepted: ASCII, WordPerfect 5.0, 5.1, WordStar 3.3, 3.4, 4.0, 5.0 and Word for Macintosh 4.0, 5.0. (When using WordStar, turn off the Vari-Tab feature.)

Please Do:

• Use your word processor as a text entry vehicle only.

• Mark titles of books, reports, etc., by underlining or italicizing.

• Press the space bar only once after a period or colon.

Please Don't:

• Use tabs.

• Right-justify text.

• Use boldface or different fonts.

If you have not written for *American Visions* before, we suggest that you familiarize yourself with the magazine before querying us. Also take note of the following:

1.) Make query suggestions *in writing* of no more than one page, or submit a manuscript on speculation.

2.) Send three (3) samples of your writing.

3.) Send material(s) that you do *not* wish to have returned.

4.) Allow two to three (2-3) months for review.

Departments

Arts Scene

A potpourri of articles on current events in the realms of theater, film, television, dance, music, visual arts, literature and more.

Books/Recent & Relevant

Reviews of recent releases and their social relevance, as well as profiles of writers and suggested reading lists. Capsule book reviews.

Calendar

A vibrant section listing major cultural events of particular interest to the black community.

Computers & Technology

A section aimed at informing the African-American community of innovations, resources and advantages of computer use and available technology-with news on software, the information superhighway and the like.

Cuisine

A column devoted to defining an African-American cuisine, sometimes discussing specific foods, sometimes offering profiles of black chefs and restaurateurs, nearly always including a recipe or two.

Film

Articles on the film industry, ranging from profiles of actors, producers, directors and technicians to reviews of theatrical releases.

Genealogy

Essays that encourage readers to explore their ancestry by recommending ideas and strategies, and by relating the adventures of others.

Music Notes/Earworthy

Interviews with musicians, as well as essays on the genres and literature of black music. Capsule reviews of newly released recordings.

Travel

A historical and pleasure guide to areas of particular interest to African Americans.

Categories: Culture—Ethnic

Name: Eric T. Vinson, Jr., Managing Editor
Material: All
Address: 1156 15TH ST NW STE 615
City/State/ZIP: WASHINGTON DC 20005
Telephone: 202-496-9593
Fax: 202-496-9851

American Woman Motorscene

American Woman Motorscene is a bi-monthly, national automotive publication geared towards working and family women of all ages and descriptions who are purchasing more than 50% of all new vehicles, 48% of all used vehicles and influencing 80% of all sales. New car sales to women equal $81 billion per year. Features include, but are not limited to: automotive interests related to cars, trucks, mini-vans, sport utility vehicles and motorcycling. As a bi-monthly magazine and monthly website, AWM accepts approximately 250 freelance manuscripts per year for review. Payment is always on publication, with an average 6 month holding period. The *American Woman Motorscene* reader is typically career and/or family oriented, independent, and adventurous. She demands literate, entertaining and useful information from a magazine enabling her to make educated buying decisions. Below are some specific suggestions to follow before submitting your manuscript:

Articles or evaluations on vehicles should be written in an educational as well as entertaining format. AWM educates women on such things as purchasing, leasing, renting, repairs and maintenance in a language she understands, can relate to and learn from. A glossary of terms should accompany each road test review.

Personality Profiles:

These interview-format articles focus on inspiring success on women of accomplishment breaking the traditional rules in a once male-dominated industry. She is active in the industry as either a professional making her way to the top, or an adventuress who ultimately serves as a positive rolemodel to other women that "they can do it too." One of her many interesting qualities is her thirst for knowledge to "do it herself" and passion and support for women pursuing their dreams. AWM is not a buff book for women. It is not about engines, 0-60 and gear ratios. While we include technical information in road test reviews for buying decisions, the bulk of the articles are more educational, entertaining and inspiring.

Please use quotes and humor whenever possible. We like to hear about women who have endured, challenged and overcome hardships, beat the odds, etc. Be sure to include other hobbies and sports she's involved in and add details about her career and family.

Travel and Safety:

Submit articles relative to professional and recreational travel ie: places to go, things to do, good deals on airlines, rentals, cruises, etc. Articles on keeping women safe on the road encouraged, supporting statistics appreciated. Touring articles must be accompanied by decent, clear black and white photos.* Also, submit particularly female-friendly restaurants, hotels, campgrounds, etc.

Columns:

Commentaries are always welcome. Road humor is best. Tell us your views about your respective automotive, motorcycle or motorsport experience, about non-enthusiasts, about anything that relates. Views on women adventurers need an unusual slant to be valuable and interesting. Bimbo stories are not welcome.

Buyers Guides:

Buyers guides which fit our format will be accepted if they contain knowledgeable and diverse information about the product and industry. Guides which do not fit our format will be returned upon request with SASE only. A separate payment schedule will be arranged upon acceptance due to the research and length of buyers guides usually require. Writers are contacted upon acceptance. Buyers guides are prearranged with editor-in-chief only.

Feature articles should be approx. 1500 words. Columns should be approx. 750 words.

Submissions should be type-written (dot matrix O.K.), use a 55 character width and be double spaced. They should be submitted via Email whenever possible or on 3" disk for Macintosh, saved in text. Typed articles reduces fee considerably.

Payment fluctuates between by-line only to $250.00 depending on quality, not length. Special features will be negotiated with the publisher.

• Photo submissions: Only high quality photos are accepted. Photos must be B&W 5X7 or 8X10. We prefer glossy without borders. For color, we prefer slides, either Kodachrome or Fujichrome. Color prints must be accompanied by negatives/slides. To be sure of your photo's safe return, send a stamped, self-addressed envelope with your submission.

Please call to confirm appropriate E-mail before sending any articles. AWM website: www.americanwomanmag.com

Categories: Automobiles—Women's Issues/Studies

Name: Editor
Material: All
Address: 1510 11th Street, Suite 201B,
City/State/ZIP: Santa Monica, CA 90401
Telephone: 310-260-0192
Fax: 310-260-0175

American Woodworker

AMERICAN WOODWORKER motivates, entertains, and challenges woodworking enthusiasts with accessible, in-depth information that will help them improve their skills.

Our writers are all woodworkers—amateur and pros—who want to share what they know with other craftsmen.

WHAT TO WRITE ABOUT

AMERICAN WOODWORKER buys original articles on any subject that relates to small-shop woodworking-amateur or professional. This includes technical articles about woodworking tools, techniques, materials, and design as well as plans for original woodworking projects and period-furniture reproductions. We also buy anecdotal stories and human-interest stories that have a woodworking theme.

The best place to look for article ideas is in your own workshop. Maybe you've developed a new technique or designed a clever jig. Maybe you've figured out a better way of doing something. Perhaps you've designed a project that other woodworkers would like to build. Maybe you want to reach others about a skill you're especially good at or share what you've learned about design, finishing, shop layout, etc.

Technique Articles

We're always in need of instructional articles that teach woodworking skills such as joinery, sharpening, safety, machine techniques, machine maintenance, veneering, carving, turning, wood drying, etc. We're especially interested in articles that teach the basic principles of furniture design and construction.

Projects

We're interested in good-looking, well-built original woodworking projects and period reproductions. Projects may range in difficulty from the very simple to the very challenging, from toys to tools to highboys. We'll consider any style of furniture, from period designs to ultra-modern.

Our readers want to know how you built your project. What tools. Techniques, and materials did you use, and why? What jigs or fixtures did you use in the process? Do you have any anecdotes or historical background on the project that would interest other woodworkers?

HOW TO GET STARTED

1. Get your hands on a recent issue of AMERICAN WOODWORKER and read it. Get a feel for the magazine; the types of articles; the style of writing; and the way that text, drawings, and photos work together and make instructions clear. Find an article that's similar to the article you want to write, and use it as a model when you write.

2. Write us a letter. Describe your article idea or project and be sure to include photos and drawings, if appropriate, to give us a clear idea of what you've got in mind. While you're at it, tell us about yourself. What kind of woodworker are you? What sort of things do you make? Do you have any writing experience? Do you have any drafting or photography skills?

After receiving your letter, we will contact you by mail or by phone within a month and let you know if we can use your idea. If we're interested in your project or article, we'll assign an editor to work with you and you'll receive further instructions. If we can't use your idea, we'll return your materials.

While we will consider unsolicited manuscripts, you stand a much better chance of being published if you send us a query letter first.

WHAT TO SEND ALONG

When you submit an article, be sure to include the following:

• A manuscript with your name, address, daytime telephone number, and social security number. Computer disks are also acceptable in either MS—DOS or Apple format. Please indicate word-processing format and version (e.g., WordPerfect 3.2).

• Drawings or sketches that explain processes, jigs and/or construction details with dimensions.

• Color slides of the finished project (if applicable) and/or key steps in the process you're describing. (See PHOTOGRAPHS.)

• Sources for any unusual hardware, tools, finishing materials, etc. mentioned in your article.

PHOTOGRAPHS

Photos for publication must be color slides (transparencies) in 35mm or larger format. Color prints or black-and-white prints are acceptable with a query letter.

If you know how to use a 35mm camera, we encourage you to try taking your own photographs.

For indoor shots without professional flash equipment, we recommend Kodak Ektachrome 160T tungsten slide film. Light your work with two or three 150-watt incandescent lights. Eliminate all daylight, fluorescent light, and flash when using tungsten film.

For outdoor daylight photography, use Ektachrome or Fujichrome slide film. If for some reason you can't supply publishable photos, we can arrange to have a photographer visit your workshop.

DRAWINGS

We don't expect you to draw like Michelangelo. What we're looking for are drawings or sketches that are clear enough to provide our illustrators with the information needed to produce final art. Just do the best you can to illustrate the important points of your article (jigs, tool setups, etc.) or the construction details of your project.

DEPARTMENTS

If you're interested in writing for AMERICAN WOOD-WORKER Departments, here's what you need to know:

Letters to the Editor—Reader letters on topics of interest to woodworkers. We do not pay for Letters to the Editor.

Offcuts—Woodworking news items and anecdotal pieces with a woodworking theme. A maximum of 1,000 words. Minimum payment $50.

Q & A—Woodworking experts answer questions from our readers. This service is free to our readers and we do not pay for questions.

Tech Tips—Woodworkers share their original tips and tricks for doing a job better, faster , and easier. We pay $50 for each item we publish and $200 for the best tip of the issue. Submissions must include a short description along with a photo (color prints are OK) or sketch for our illustrator to work from. Sorry, "Tech Tip" submissions cannot be returned.

Gallery—Photos of current work in wood. Submissions must include a description of the piece and a publishable-quality color slide in 35mm format or larger. Enclose a self-addressed envelope for return of slides. We pay $35 for each photo we publish.

Shop Solutions—Versatile jigs, fixtures, or shop accessories that can be explained in one drawing and up to 250 words. If we publish your "Shop Solution," you'll win a valuable prize. (See most recent issue for details.)

PAYMENTS AND RIGHTS

AMERICAN WOODWORKER pays upon publication unless special arrangements have been made in advance. Our standard rate for new authors is $150 per published magazine page. We buy the right to publish the article in AMERICAN WOOD-WORKER magazine and the option to republish the article in all other media for an additional payment for each use. Freelance photo and illustration rates upon request.

Thanks for your interest in AMERICAN WOODWORKER.

AMERICAN WOODWORKER is a how-to magazine for the woodworking enthusiast, whether amateur or professional. It provides readers with useful, accurate woodworking information in a style that's informal, entertaining, and easy to understand.

AMERICAN WOODWORKER is a reader-written magazine. The articles are written by amateur and professional woodworkers who want to share what they know. You don't need to be an accomplished woodworker to be published in AMERICAN WOODWORKER. Our editors are woodworkers, and they can help you put your ideas into words.

If you'd like to write for AMERICAN WOODWORKER, these guidelines will help you get started. Photographers and illustrators will also find the guidelines helpful.

Categories: Crafts—Hobbies

Name: Submissions Editor
Material: All
Address: 33 E MINOR ST
City/State/ZIP: EMMAUS PA 18098
Telephone: 610-967-5141
Fax: 610-967-7692
E-mail: awverne@aol.com

America's Civil War

Please refer to Cowles Enthusiast Media, Inc.

The Americas Review

The Americas Review is a tri-quarterly journal published by Arte Público Press at the University of Houston. The journal is dedicated to the publication of short fiction, poetry and criticism by or about U.S. Hispanic writers.

It is the policy of Arte Público Press that a subscription accompany submissions to *The Americas Review.* If you are not a subscriber, please remit a $15.00 subscription to *The Americas Review* at the University of Houston, Houston, TX 77204-2090.

Categories: Fiction—Hispanic—Poetry

Name: Lauro Flores
Material: All
Address: UNIVERSITY OF WASHINGTON ROMANCE LANGUAGES
Address: BOX 354360
City/State/ZIP: SEATTLE WA 98195-43660

Analog Science Fiction and Fact

Analog will consider material submitted by any writer, and consider it solely on the basis of merit. We are definitely eager to find and develop new, capable writers.

We have no hard-and-fast editorial guidelines, because science fiction is such a broad field that I don't want to inhibit a new writer's thinking by imposing Thou Shalt Nots. Besides, a really good story can make an editor swallow his preconceived taboos.

Basically, we publish science fiction stories. That is, stories in which some aspect of future science or technology is so integral to the plot that, if that aspect were removed, the story would collapse. Try to picture Mary Shelley's *Frankenstein* without the science and you'll see what I mean. No story!

The science can be physical, sociological, psychological. The technology can be anything from electronic engineering to biogenetic engineering. But the stories must be strong and realistic, with believable people (who needn't be human) doing believable things-no matter how fantastic the background might be.

Author's name and address should be on the first page of the manuscript. Indent paragraphs but do not leave extra space between them. Please do not put manuscripts in binders or folders.

Analog pays 6—8 cents per word for short stories up to 7,500 words, $450—600 for stories between 7,500 and 10,000 words, and 5—6 cents per word for longer material. We prefer lengths between 2,000 and 7,000 words for shorts, 10,000-20,000 words for novelettes, and 40,000—80,000 for serials.

Please query first on serials only. A complete manuscript is strongly preferred for all shorter lengths.

The entire contents of each issue is copyrighted at the time of publication. Payment is on acceptance.

Good luck!
Stanley Schmidt
Editor

Categories: Science—Science Fiction
Name: Stanley Schmidt, Editor
Material: All
Address: 1270 AVENUE OF THE AMERICAS
City/State/ZIP: NEW YORK NY 10020
Telephone: 212-698-1313

Angels on Earth

Angels on Earth publishes true stories about God's messengers at work in today's world. We are interested in stories of heavenly angels and stories involving humans who have played angelic roles in daily life. The best stories are those where the narrator has been positively affected in some distinct way. Look for unusual situations; we have a surplus of stories about illness and car accidents. We are also especially on the lookout for recent stories.

A typical *Angels on Earth* story is a first-person narrative written in dramatic style, with a spiritual point that the reader can "take away" and apply to his or her own life. It may be your own or someone else's story. Observe the following as you write:

1. The emphasis should be on one person, and is usually told from the vantage point of the individual most deeply affected by the angelic experience. But don't try to tell an entire life story; focus on one specific life event. Bring only as many people as needed to tell the story so the reader's interest stays with the dominant character.

2. Decide what your spiritual point will be. We like to see a positive and specific change in the narrator as a result of the angelic experience. Don't forget: We want our readers to take away a message or insight they can use in their own lives. Everything in the story should be tied in with this specific and inspiring theme.

3. Don't leave unanswered questions. Give all the relevant facts so the reader can clearly understand what took place. Let the reader feel as if he or she were there, seeing the characters, hearing them talk, feeling what they felt. Use dialogue, set scenes, build tension - dramatize the story. Show how the narrator becomes a new, or different, person.

The best rule of all: Study the Magazine!

Payment for full-length stories (1,500 words) usually ranges from $100-$400, and is made when the story is approved and scheduled for publication.

We are always looking for quotes, anecdotes to use as fillers, and material for our short features (50-250 words): —"Messages": brief, mysterious happenings, or letters describing how a specific *Angels on Earth* article helped you. Payment is usually $25. —"Earning Their Wings": unusual stories of good deeds worth imitating. Payment is usually $50. —"Only Human?": short narratives in which the angelic character may or may not have been a human being. The narrator is pleasantly unsure and so is the reader. Payment is usually $100.

Please do not send essays, sermons or fiction. We rarely use poetry and we do not evaluate book-length material. Manuscripts must be typed, double-spaced, and accompanied by a self-addressed stamped envelope. Allow three months for reply.

Categories: Nonfiction—Inspirational—Psychology—Self-Help—Society—Religion—Personal Experience

Name: **Colleen Hughes, Managing Editor**
Material: All
Address: 16 E. 34TH ST.
City/State/ZIP: NEW YORK, NY 10016
Telephone: 212-251-8100
Fax: 212-684-0679
E-mail: angelsedtr@guideposts.org

Animal People
News for People Who Care About Animals

ANIMAL PEOPLE welcomes freelance submissions of articles, informed guest opinion columns, original art, and photography, subject to the following terms and conditions:

• Material submitted for our consideration must not be simultaneously submitted to any other animal-related publication of national distribution. We must be informed if an item is simultaneously submitted to or has previously been published by some other type of publication, e.g. a local humane society newsletter or a general circulation magazine or newspaper.

• All submissions of writing will be either accepted or rejected within two weeks of receipt. Our usual turn-around time is less than one day.

• We buy either first North American serial rights or one-time reprint rights, depending on whether or not the material has been previously published, including the right of publication in both our newsprint and electronic editions. All other rights remain with the author.

• Because we are a nonprofit publication, we prefer to receive freelance materials as donations. However, recognizing that many contributors need to earn their livings by their work, we do pay the following honorariums: $25 per assigned book review, $15 per photograph or drawing, 10¢ a word for profiles and features. Payment is upon acceptance. We do not pay for guest opinion columns.

• Assignments will be made (or confirmed) in writing only, and only to contributors whose work we have previously published. Please do not query by telephone.

• We do not assign spot news coverage to freelancers.

• Profile submissions are particularly welcome, especially if accompanied by photographs. Although we may occasionally be receptive to a profile of a well-known subject, or a subject who has engineered a uniquely effective protest, our preference is to salute seldom recognized individuals of unique and outstanding positive accomplishment, in any capacity that benefits animals or illustrates the intrinsic value of other species. We are also particularly interested in those individuals who combine active concern for animals with active concern for fellow human beings.

• Profiles of organizations should be accompanied by a copy of the organization's most recent IRS Form 990 (unless we already have it on file.)

• We require independent verification of the animal care conditions at facilities whose reputations and administrations are unknown to us.

• We prefer to consider photography and art submissions on a portfolio basis. Query first, with examples of your work. If we think we might be able to use your material with reasonable frequency, we will invite you to send us prints of photos that might be appropriate, as you take them, identified with your name on the back of each. We will file them according to subject (aardvark to zebra mussel), and use them and pay you for them as our need to illustrate news items requires.

• We do not publish fiction or poetry.

• We are not interested in atrocity stories, essays on why animals have rights, or material that promotes or defends animal abuse, including hunting, fishing, trapping, and slaughter.

• We prefer to receive manuscript submissions by e-mail and/or in hard copy format.

Categories: Animals—Animal Protection

Name: Submissions Editor
Material: All
Address: PO BOX 960
City/State/ZIP: CLINTON WA 98236-0960
Telephone: 360-579-2505
Fax: 360-579-2575
E-mail: anmlpepl@whidbey.com
Internet: www.animalpepl.org

Animals

Overview:

Animals is a full-color, bimonthly magazine written and edited to deliver timely, reliable, and provocative coverage of wildlife issues, pet-care topics, and animal-protection concerns. It also publishes natural-history pieces that educate readers about animals' needs and behaviors.

The magazine circulates to a national audience (around 100,000), consisting mostly of direct subscribers, but also of newsstand consumers and some members of the Massachusetts Society for the Prevention of Cruelty to Animals and the American Humane Education Society, its publishers.

What We Publish From Freelance Sources:

About 90 percent of our editorial coverage is from freelance sources.

Feature Stories: Well-researched articles (1,200 to 2,000 words) on national and international wildlife, domestic animals, wildlife/conservation issues, controversies involving animals and/or their use, animal-protection issues, pet health, and pet care. Articles must engage readers who are interested in knowing more about a variety of creatures as well as those who consider themselves animal protectionists.

Reviews: Newly released books and videos on animals, animal-related issues, and the environment. These reviews run from 300 to 500 words and are for our Books column.

Profiles: Short pieces on individuals at work to save both domestic and wild animals, to make conditions better for animals, or on others whose interactions with animals makes them of interest to a wide-ranging audience. These reviews run about 800 words and are published in our ProFiles column.

What We Pay:

Because payment depends on the length of the article and the amount of research necessary to complete it, payment varies. Our range for short features usually starts at $350, plus reasonable and agreed-upon expenses such as telephone and fax fees.

How to Query:

Please query by letter and allow four to six weeks for a response. Query letters should include:

• a pointed summary describing the article's focus, purpose, approximate length, and finish date;

• a list of sources that you plan to contact or have already contacted. When dealing with controversies, sources should be from both sides of the issue;

• writing samples, preferably of comparable pieces;

• information on when and where you may have published, or plan to publish, a similar story, if applicable.

Additional Information:

For a sample copy of *Animals* Magazine, please send a check in the amount of $3.95, payable to *Animals* Magazine, to the address below.

For a copy of *Animals* Magazine's photography guidelines, please send a stamped, self-addressed envelope to the address below.

Thank you for your interest in *Animals* magazine.

Categories: Animals

Name: Joni Praded, Editor
Material: Wildlife queries
Name: Paula Abend, Managing Editor
Material: Pet/Domestic animal queries
Address: 350 S HUNTINGTON AVE
City/State/ZIP: BOSTON MA 02130
Telephone: 617-522-7400
Fax: 617-522-4885

The Animals' Agenda
Helping People Help Animals

The Animals' Agenda is a bimonthly magazine that seeks to inspire action for animals by informing people about animal rights and cruelty-free living. *Agenda* is committed to serving —and fostering cooperation among—all animal advocates from the grassroots to the national levels. The magazine is published by The Animal Rights Network Inc., an IRS 501(c)(3) federal tax-exempt, not-for-profit organization founded in 1979.

Submissions

The Animals' Agenda does not accept unsolicited manuscripts.

Article proposals or outlines, as well as letters to the editor, should be sent to *The Animals' Agenda* mailing address (see below). Once an article has been commissioned, we prefer it to be submitted via e-mail or on a 3.5" computer disk saved in standard ASCII format (with hard copy attached). Typed copy may also be faxed (letters to the editor may be neatly handwritten). Articles are due two months preceding the month of publication, and may be edited for space or clarity. *Agenda* reprints articles infrequently. Please indicate if an article is being submitted to other publications in addition to *Agenda*. We generally welcome other periodicals' reprinting articles from *Agenda* if those articles are credited properly. *Agenda generally does not offer payment for articles.*

Contents

• Letters to the editor allow readers to comment on articles or letters that have appeared in previous issues of *Agenda*, to voice opinions about matters of concern to animal advocates, and to offer advice on solving animal-abuse problems. Maximum length: 300 words.

• "Bulletin Board" is a collection of concise and late-breaking news briefs relating to animals and their well-being. These items may be obtained from magazines, newspapers, newsletters, or computer forums. Contributors should identify the sources of the "Bulletin Board" items they submit. Maximum length: 100 words.

• "Making a Difference" highlights victories and successes on behalf of animals, and is similar in style and format to "Bulletin Board."

• "Happy Endings" briefly recounts the true story of an animal(s) who was rescued from abusive, exploitative, or dangerous conditions, and who now lives a comfortable and secure life. Must include a photo of the animal(s). Maximum length: 400 words.

• "News" is a compilation of brief reports that describe animal abuse or exploitation practices, organizational campaigns for animals, recent pertinent developments, etc. A report should include information on how readers can help and a contact organization (if applicable), and may be accompanied by a photo. Maximum length: text, 400 words; photo with caption, 100 words.

• "Unsung Heroes" profiles individuals who work diligently, without major recognition, to protect the well-being and/or rights of animals—whether through direct hands-on assistance or other ongoing advocacy efforts. The individual should reflect a "regular" activist, not movement leaders or other professional advocates. Must include a photo of the activist. Maximum length: 500 words.

• "Investigations" are based on investigative reporting. They present considerable detail about a major source of animal exploitation or about a campaign to reduce or eliminate that exploitation. Must include photographs and material for "Your Agenda," outlining action readers can take to help. Maximum length: 1,200 words.

• "Analysis" serves a variety of functions: discussing strategies to reduce or to end animal exploitation, reviewing in detail a book or movie about animals or animal liberation, presenting a historical analysis of some facet of animal abuse, discussing the status of animals in society, etc. Must include photographs and material for "Your Agenda." Maximum length: 1,200 words.

• The cover feature presents in-depth and extensively detailed coverage of a major news story or development concerning the treatment or status of animals. Must include photographs, at least one sidebar, and material for "Your Agenda." Maximum length: 2,500 words.

• "Resources" presents brief reviews describing recently produced materials including books, computer software, CDs, campaign matter, videos, etc. that are intended to serve as educational or activist tools. Maximum length: 100 words.

• Reviews, while generally devoted to books about animal liberation or abuse, also may discuss the latest movies or CDs that treat these subjects. Must include the dust jacket or cover of the work reviewed. Maximum length: 800 words.

• "Commentary," provides a forum for guest columnists to offer a perspective on important issues and developments affecting the animal rights movement. Must include a photo of the author. Maximum length: 700 words.

• "Toward Kinship," an essay in which an author is free to consider any aspect of animal rights, should approach its subject in a personal, expansive, even offbeat manner. Whenever appropriate, submit a photograph or other image to illustrate the text. Maximum length: 1,200 words.

• "Activities" lists forthcoming conferences, demonstrations, protests, seminars, and other events of interest to animal advocates. Must include the name of a person and/or organization to contact about the listed event, as well as the address and phone number of that individual or organization. Maximum length: 50 words.

Categories: Animal Rights

Name: Kirsten Rosenberg, Managing Editor
Material: All
Address: PO BOX 25881
City/State/ZIP: BALTIMORE MD 21224
Telephone: 410-675-4566
Fax: 410-675-0066
E-mail: office@animalsagenda.org
Internet: www.animalsagenda.org

Annals of Improbable Research (AIR)
The Journal of Record for Inflated Research and Personalities

The *Annals of Improbable Research (AIR)* publishes original articles, data, effluvia and news of improbable research. The material is intended to be humorous and/or educational, and sometimes is. We look forward to receiving your manuscripts, photographs, x-rays, drawings, etc. Please do not send biological samples. Photos should be black & white if possible. Reports of research *results*, modest or otherwise, are preferred to speculative proposals.

Keep it short, please. Articles are typically 500-2,000 words in length. (Items intended for mini-AIR* should be much, much, much shorter.) Please send two neatly printed copies. Alternatively, you may submit via e-mail, in ASCII format.

Please don't spend a lot of efforting in elaborate text formatting. If the article is accepted for publication we will take care of that.

Sincerely and improbably,
Marc Abrahams
Editor
*For info about how to receive mini-AIR, our free monthly electronic newsletter, send e-mail to info@improb.com

Categories: Humor—Internet—Interview—Science

Name: Submissions Editor
Material: All
Address: PO BOX 380853
City/State/ZIP: CAMBRIDGE MA 02238
Telephone: 617-491-4437
E-mail: AIR@improb.com
Internet: www.improb.com

The Antioch Review

The best answer we can give on inquiries relating to what kind of material the ANTIOCH REVIEW uses is, "read the magazine." Look through a few representative issues for an idea of subjects, treatment, lengths of articles, and stories we have used; it will be far more rewarding than any theories we might try to formulate.

Unfortunately, we cannot honor requests for free sample copies. The REVIEW is expensive to produce and operates on a precarious financial margin. If copies are not available at your local newsstand or library, we will be happy to send you a back issue for $6.00, which includes postage and handling.

ARTICLES

Our audience is made up of educated citizens, often professional people, who are interested in matters beyond their fields of special activity. With few exceptions, our subjects cover most of the range of social science and humanities. Our approach tries to steer a middle course between scholars speaking exclusively to other scholars in their field, and workaday journalists appealing to a broad popular audience; both these approaches have their own journals and audiences. We try for the interpretive essay on a topic of current importance, drawing on scholarly materials for its substance and appealing to the intellectual and social concerns of our readers. We are also interested in reviving the moribund art of literary journalism.

FICTION

We seldom publish more than three short stories in each issue. Although the new writer as well as the previously published author is welcome, it is the story that counts, a story worthy of the serious attention of the intelligent reader, a story that is compelling, written with distinction. Only rarely do we publish translations of well known or new foreign writers; a chapter of a novel is welcome only if it can be read complete in itself as a short story.

POETRY

Like fiction, we get far more poetry than we can possibly accept, and the competition is keen. Here, where form and content are so inseparable and reaction is so personal, it is difficult to state requirements or limitations. Studying recent issues of the REVIEW should be helpful. No "light" or inspirational verse. Any poetry received without a self addressed stamped envelope will be discarded if rejected and no notice will be sent. No need to enclose a post card for the purpose of acknowledging receipt of a submission. Do not mix poetry and prose in the same envelope. Please submit three to six poems at one time. We *do not* read poetry manuscripts in the summer (May 1 to September 1).

REVIEWS

We do not publish unsolicited book reviews and very seldom do we publish essays on literary problems or the canons of significant contemporary writers. The editors and their associates regularly prepare a section of short book evaluations, selectively treating recent publications.

STYLE, LENGTHS, PAYMENT, ETC.

Our literary standards are as high as we can enforce them; we do not have the staff to engage in major editorial rewriting, except on rare occasions when the content justifies the effort.

Actually, we have no rigid expectations of length, preferring the content and treatment to determine size. Rarely, however, do we use articles or stories over 5,000 words - and 8,000 at the outside limit.

We prefer manuscripts to be mailed flat, fastened by paper clip only, and one at a time (does not apply for poetry). Do not mix prose and poetry in the same envelope, please.

We try to report on manuscripts within five weeks, but because material that interests us is occasionally read by several members of our staff, the process can sometimes take up to six or eight weeks.

Payment is upon printed publication at the rate of $10.00 per printed page (about 425 words) plus 2 copies of the issue. Authors may buy additional copies at an authors' discount of 40% off the cover price.

All material sent to the ANTIOCH REVIEW is read and considered, although we cannot comment on each rejection. However, we do *not* read simultaneous submissions.

Categories: Fiction—Nonfiction—Literature—Poetry

Name: Robert Fogarty, Editor
Material: Fiction, Nonfiction
Name: Judith Hall, Poetry Editor
Material: Poetry
Address: PO BOX 148
City/State/ZIP: YELLOW SPRINGS OH 45387
Telephone: 937-767-6389

Antique Trader Weekly

We're looking for authoritative and well-researched articles of 1,000-2,000 words on all types of antiques and collectibles (you can submit a query letter, instead of a complete mss.). Send four to 12 photos (color photos, slides or B&W) with cutlines. In addition to the hardcopy, you can also submit the article on a computer disk, ASCII, either Mac or IBM. We pay anywhere from $50 to $250 for feature articles, depending on the length and quality of writing and photos. Longer, more in-depth articles with good, sharp photos, are worth more to us.

The article should contain (if applicable):
• Lead paragraph that makes the reader want to continue reading the story
• Short history of item(s)
• What type of item(s) there are to collect
• How collectors collect the item(s)
• Advice for collectors (i.e., where to find the items, condition factors, fakes and repros, how to display collection and so on)
• List of prices for items. List as many prices and items as you can (25-100).
• List of related clubs, publications and books

In a nutshell, write a story-after which-someone who knew nothing about the collectible would have a general understanding of the collectible.

Most articles are used on a "space available" basis; publication is anywhere from one month to up to a year; though most are within six months. Payment is made one to four weeks after publication.

Photos will be returned after use. We reserve the right to edit any manuscript to fit our editorial needs.

We are not interested in any additional show or auction reports at this time.

Categories: Nonfiction—Antiques—Collectibles

Name: Kyle Husfloen, Editor
Material: All
Address: PO BOX 1050
City/State/ZIP: DUBUQUE IA 52004
Telephone: 319-588-2073 ext.121
Fax: 800-531-0880

ANVIL
MAGAZINE

ANVIL Magazine
The Voice of the Farrier and Blacksmith

For the past 21 years, *ANVIL Magazine* has been *The Voice of the Farrier and Blacksmith*. This international monthly is distributed throughout the United States and in over 20 foreign countries and enjoys a readership of over 10,000 per issue.

Our staff is always interested in your submission. We read and consider every contribution forwarded, as we sincerely believe that the responsibility of a good editor is to listen to many voices and to encourage writers to grow. We appreciate the efforts of our contributors, and when editing is necessary, we attempt to offer comment that promotes clarity. We reserve the right to edit in the interests of available space and clarity.

Contribution Categories
Feature/Pictorial

Events, personal profiles, question-and-answer interviews, local color, points of interest (e.g., museums, schools)

Blacksmithing

How-To-Do-It articles—illustrated step-by-step smithing processes. Metallurgy, history, craft hints, tools and techniques

Farriery

How-To-Do-It articles—illustrated step-by-step shoeing processes. Craft hints and techniques, shoeing experience with horses.

Veterinary/Technical

Research, studies, documented reports by professional individuals.

Equine Training Information

Reports, studies and personal experiences related to handling, training and locomotion of the horse.

Humor

As it pertains to the farrier and blacksmith.

Safety/Health/Psychology

Personal aspects of the industry: individual experiences, shop safety tips, exercise and nutrition information, psychology of working with horses.

Book Reviews on books of interest to the industry.

Business articles for the farrier and equine industry.

Guest Editorial

Personal opinion or consideration of an existing condition within the industry. Individual's name must be included with submission.

Horse Owner Information

Equine hoof, nutrition and handling, pertaining to farriery, written to inform the horse owner.

Submission Format and Requirements

Text: Formats listed in order of preference.

1. Commitment of material to a 5¼" or 3½" floppy disk with one (1) hard copy representation (printout, typewritten text, photocopy) of each submission. Computer files must be IBM compatible and utilize either WordPerfect, Word or ASCII text files. Hard copies are required, should there be complications involved in disk submission retrieval.

2. Computer printout or photocopy of typewritten material.

3. Handwritten articles.

All submissions must be legible and must include the name, address and phone number of author. If previously published material, full credit information of prior publication and written release to reprint are required. In the case of technical, historical or controversial submissions, the reference sources, bibliography or verification may be requested. Illustrations in the form of original art work and photographs enhance the literature. Contributors are encouraged to illustrate articles whenever possible.

Photography: Formats listed in order of preference.

1. High-contrast, high-clarity black-and-white 5"x7" photographs, labeled on backs for article reference.

2. Black-and-white proof sheets with negatives.

3. High-contrast color photographs.

4. Color slides.

All photo submissions must be clearly identified and must include photographer's name, address and phone number. Each individual photo should be clearly marked, preferably with paper label on the back with reference to the article. Names of subjects, dates and places or reference numbers to written sheet of captions are required. If previously published material, include full credit information of prior publication and written release to reprint.

Cartoons, Graphics, Illustrations: Must be original and the work of the artist of submission. Submissions must be clearly marked with name, address and phone number of the artist. In the case of illustration to text referrals, illustrations must be clearly marked in sequence. Black-and-white material is pre-

ferred. Computer files (TIFF or other formats) of art work are welcomed.

Submission Dates

Material targeted for a particular issue must be in our editorial offices two months prior to the first day of the month of issue. In case of important events, special arrangements can be made to accommodate time-sensitive material.

Publishing Policy

ANVIL Magazine publishes first-run material and reprints of previously published articles. We reserve the right to reject material and to professionally edit any first-run works submitted.

ANVIL Magazine reserves the right to offer articles for reprints, which are available at cost.

In addition, **ANVIL Magazine** reserves the right to place articles on the **ANVIL Magazine** World Wide Web Page. These articles will carry the copyright of the author, e.g., "© John Smith." The **ANVIL Magazine** Web Page is an information resource.

Material Appearance Policy

First-run material under contract to **ANVIL Magazine** may not appear in another publication prior to its appearance in **ANVIL Magazine.**

No material will be accepted for publication prior to review. No material will be considered in part, but must be forwarded in its entirety for editorial review.

Tear sheets of article/graphic appearance and a complimentary copy of the issue in which it appears are forwarded directly to author within 30 days of publication.

Disclaimer

ANVIL Magazine and its staff do not manufacture, test, warrant, guarantee or endorse any of the tools, materials, instructions or products contained in any articles published. **ANVIL Magazine** disclaims any responsibility or liability for damages or injuries as a result of the use or application of any information published in **ANVIL Magazine.**

Payment for Contributions

Payment for submissions is made directly to the author within 30 days of material acceptance. Rate of payment is determined on each individual submission and is based upon, but not limited to, article length, quality, complexity, timeliness and number of photos or graphics. **ANVIL Magazine** payments range from $25.00 to $250.00.

Categories: Blacksmithing—Ferriery—Veterinary

Name: Bob Edwards, Publisher/Editor
Material: All
Address: PO BOX 1810
City/State/ZIP: GEORGETOWN CA 95634
Telephone: 916-333-2142
Fax: 916-333-2906
E-mail: anvil@anvilmag.com
Internet: www.anvilmag.com

Archaeology

ARCHAEOLOGY is the official "public voice" of the Archaeological Institute of America. We reach more than 200,000 nonspecialist readers interested in art, science, history, and culture. Our reports, regional commentaries, and feature-length articles introduce readers to recent developments in archaeology worldwide.

Communicating your scholarly experience to the general public requires deft writing. Please keep the following in mind as you prepare your manuscript:

1. Keep technical terms to a minimum and explain those that you do use.

2. Assume a fairly minimal knowledge of your subject on the

readers' part, but don't talk down to them.

3. Be interesting and entertaining, with a strong opening that hooks readers and leads them into your main discussion; avoid the dramatic lead that slips into a site report by page two.

4. Keep in mind that certain articles require a broad historical framework if the reader is to comprehend the importance of the archaeological work.

5. Keep it personal, without being egocentric. Readers are interested in what you do, why you do it, what you have learned, and why they should be interested. They should be led through your material in a way that creates for them the same sense of awe that you have felt about your work.

6. In some form or another, a finished manuscript should contain an EXPOSITION (Guess what?), DEVELOPMENT (Here's what), and a CONCLUSION (So what?).

7. You should discuss your story idea with an editor before submitting a manuscript. A brief outline, accompanied by samples of available slides or photographs, is helpful.

Other Requirements

• No footnotes

• Separate captions

• Color photographs should be in the form of 35mm original slides or 4"x5" transparencies. Please supply captions and photo credits.

• Maps can be sketchy, but must show locations accurately. Our art director will make up a final map.

• Permission for reproducing published material must be obtained by the author directly from the publisher.

• Include a brief biographical statement.

• Include a brief, annotated bibliography (up to seven entries). In your bibliography, include remarks on the significance and quality of the references. Categorize and list entries in alphabetical order at the end of your article under the heading "Further Reading." Be sure to include publishers, date, and city of publication as well as title and author.

Examples:

Junius B. Bird, "Treasures from the Land of Gold," *Arts in Virginia* 24 (1969), pp. 23-33. An uneven but useful review of Peruvian gold.

Samuel K. Lothrop, *Inca Treasures as Depicted by Spanish Historians* (Los Angeles: University of California Press, 1938). An authoritative, specialized study, 40 years old but still the most complete treatment of breastplates.

• Measurements must be in miles and feet. While archaeologists usually use the metric system, our readers are most comfortable using English measurements.

Categories: Nonfiction—Science—Archaeology

Name: Peter A. Young, Editor-in-Chief
Material: All
Address: 135 WILLIAM ST 8TH FLOOR
City/State/ZIP: NEW YORK NY 10038
Telephone: 212-732-5154
Fax: 212-732-5707
E-mail: edit@archaeology.org
Internet: www.archaeology.org

Area Development

Area Development is an economic development publication. It has consistently maintained a quality of editorial unmatched by any other magazine in this field. Writers for *Area Development* should have an understanding of its advertising market and readership to avoid submission of unsuitable material.

Area Development's advertising market consists of countries, states, provinces, counties, cities, utilities, railroads, industrial and business parks, industrial real estate firms, port authorities, foreign-trade zones, enterprise zones, and location specialists/ consultants. These advertisers are in *Area Development* because they want to attract industry to their areas. However, editorial in *Area Development* is not directed towards its advertisers.

Editorial in *Area Development* is directed to corporate decision-makers responsible for selecting sites and planning facilities for their companies. The magazine's more than 40,000 readers are primarily chief executives of industrial corporations. Feature articles must be useful to them in making decisions involving expansion or relocation. A basic guideline for editorial is stated in the magazine's masthead: "sites and facility planning." This broad statement covers various factors including the following:

• Labor availability and costs • Availability of raw materials

• Infrastructure (highways, rail service, airports, ocean ports, inland ports and waterways) • Proximity to (and association with) colleges and universities

• Utilities (electricity and gas availability and costs) • Financing and incentives

• Training of employees • Taxes

• Quality-of-life factors (schools, housing, cultural opportunities, recreational facilities) • Availability of land and facilities for future expansion

• Community acceptance and relations • Government requirements and controls

• Telecommunications requirements and services • Access to markets

• Security (crime prevention, fire protection) • Support services for constructing and maintaining plants and equipment

• Pollution controls and environmental regulations • Legislation affecting economic development

• Working with architects, construction companies, and construction management firms • Technical equipment (such as robotics and CAD/CAM) when it is a factor in site selection and facility planning.

• Start-up and operating costs

When writing feature articles for *Area Development*, it is necessary to avoid blatant promotional or "puff" material. It is also necessary to avoid negative comments about any areas or comparisons of areas. With a few exceptions, *Area Development* does not publish case studies or information specifically about any area.

If there are any questions about the suitability of feature material for Area Development, please call the editor.

Categories: Business—Site & Facility Planning

Name: Geraldine Gambale, Editor
Material: All
Address: 400 POST AVE
City/State/ZIP: WESTBURY NY 11590
Telephone: 516-338-0900
Fax: 516-338-0100
E-mail: areadev@area-development.com
Internet: www.area-development.com

Arkansas Review
A Journal of Delta Studies

Arkansas Review: A Journal of Delta Studies focuses on the seven-state Mississippi River Delta. Interdisciplinary in scope, we welcome contributions from all the humanities and social sciences, including anthropology, art history, folklore studies, history, literature, musicology, political science, and sociology. Articles should be aimed at a general academic audience and follow the format specified in the *Chicago Manual of Style*, 14th edition. Submit articles in hard copy and on disk to the General Editor.

Photographs and other visual materials to accompany articles are encouraged. Do not submit originals until after the article has been accepted. When submitted, photographs should be black-and-white prints no larger that 8"x10" in either glossy or matte finish.

Arkansas Review also publishes creative material, especially fiction, poetry, essays, and visual art that evoke or respond to the Delta cultural and natural experience.

All material sent to the *Arkansas Review* will be refereed by the relevant editor and at least one other reviewer—in the case of articles, a specialist in the field of the article. We will attempt to respond to submissions within four months.

Contributors may also want to submit proposals for special issues of the *Review*, ones dealing with specific Delta topics. Such proposals should be sent to the General Editor.

Contributors will receive five copies of the issue of the *Arkansas Review* in which their work appears.

Categories: Fiction—Nonfiction—African-American—Arts—Culture—History—Literature—Multicultural—Music—Poetry—Regional—Short Stories

Name: General Editor
Material: As indicated in guidelines
Name: Creative Materials Editor
Material: Fiction, Poetry, Essays
Name: Art Editor
Material: Visual Art
Address: PO BOX 1890
City/State/ZIP: STATE UNIVERSITY AR 72467-1890
Telephone: 870-972-3043
Fax: 870-972-2795
E-mail: delta@toltec.astate.edu
Internet: www.clt.astate.edu/arkreview

Army Magazine

Length

Features are usually 1,000 to 1,500 words long. Shorter articles such as sidebars to features or photo essays are from 250 to 500 words.

Include a brief explanation of why your submission (if it is a feature article) is timely, innovative or important.

Book reviews, guest columns (such as "Sounding Off") and articles for "Front & Center" are preferably 500 to 1,000 words long. (We do not accept unsolicited book reviews. If you are interested in book reviewing, write us regarding your areas of interest and expertise. Send writing samples also.)

Format

Please send your article on a floppy disk, indicating the type of software used, and also send a triple- or double-spaced hard copy.

Photographs and Other Artwork

We are interested in seeing photographs or artwork that may enhance your article. We can use black and white or color prints as well as color slides. Please include caption and credit information with each photograph.

Headlines

We take your suggestions for headlines seriously. Please send headline suggestions with your article.

Author Biographies

Biographical information should be submitted with the text of the article. Include as much information as possible, preferably a vita.

Submissions

Please do not send us articles that have been submitted or published elsewhere. We do not accept simultaneous submissions.

Categories: Military
Name: Editor

Material: All
Adress: Box 1560
City/State/ZIP: Arlington, VA 22210-0860

Army Times

Please refer to *Times News Service*

ART PAPERS

Art Papers

Thank you for your interest in *Art Papers*. We hope to expand the number of cities covered and are specifically seeking writers to whom the editors can assign reviews. Any writer who has an idea for a review should contact the editors in advance.

Art Papers is primarily interested in reviews of contemporary and experimental artists' exhibitions and presentations, either group or solo, and especially those that take place outside conventional exhibition venues or deal with broader definitions about what constitutes contemporary art. We coincidentally cover more events occurring within the southeastern region of the United States than outside, but we are interested in any writing about art that is interesting and pertinent to our readers regardless of the artist's or exhibition's location. We are less interested in historical shows, unless the work or the writer's point of view are of particular relevance to contemporary art and artists. Because of space limitation, we no longer accept reviews of large juried exhibition or faculty shows, unless extraordinary circumstances warrant their coverage.

We have the advantage of welcoming a range of writing styles in our pages; you don't have to be a professional writer, but you do have to have a point of view and the ability to express it clearly in a personal voice. Remember, writing is an art, too—treat it that way. Here are some guidelines:

Content

Any review in any style should make its point clearly and concisely. You can assume that most readers have not seen the exhibition you are reviewing; therefore the writer must clearly evoke the art being reviewed, providing the reader a sense of the physical presence of the work and what the work was about. You should describe at least one of the works in vivid detail. Give some sense of an exhibition's physical layout; include number of works and the medium.

You should not, however, limit the review to descriptions of the works and the artist's biographical information. Rather, discuss the art in terms of the issues it raises or explores. Consider this exhibition in the context of the artist's *oeuvre*—is this a new direction for the artist? What are the historical precedents? Within what contemporary vernacular would you place this work? Why did the artist choose a specific medium? Are there sociological or epistemological issues raised?

Finally, you should be making judgments about whether or not the work is good—does it, in fact, succeed—and you should be providing a basis for those judgments in your writing? What is the point of this work? Does it succeed in making that point? Why or why not? When dealing with curated exhibitions, pay the same scrutiny to the curatorial choices. Question the programming decisions of museums and other art institutions.

Do not quote the artist's statement (which you probably want to read *after* you have seen the work and formed an independent opinion about it). Do not quote other reference materials or (especially) press releases and catalogue essays; we expect original thought and writing from you pursuant to your motivations and intuitions as well as your life experience and education. Do not, however, write about yourself unless your experience is necessary to understand the work.

Style

Write the way you speak. Write in plain English.

Correct spelling and grammar are the writer's responsibility. Do not use footnotes.

The editors of *Art Papers* do not believe that a review must accommodate a particular house style, and we occasionally publish "guerrilla" reviews in unconventional styles and formats.

Indent paragraphs. Titles of exhibitions are in quotes; titles of works are italicized, followed by the date of each work in parentheses. Enter only one space between sentences. The header includes the name of the artist, the venue, and the city and state; do not include the title of the exhibition (incorporate it into your body copy) unless it is a group exhibition. The footer is your name and the city and state in which you live; also include a one-line bio (such as "has written recently for *Art in America, The New York Times,* and other publications").

Technical Stuff

We encourage e-mail submissions. Also encouraged are submissions on computer disk, but you *must* check your disk for viruses before submitting. (We are tempted to refuse future articles from anyone submitting a disk with a virus!) Call to make sure we can translate the program you're using, and submit as text only.

Do not fax text; disk, e-mail, and hard copy are the only methods we find it feasible to use. Only photographs accompanied by a stamped, self-addressed envelope will be returned. Each photograph *must* be labeled with the artist's name, the work's title, date, medium, and dimensions, and your name. Original black and white or color photographs are our first choice, as they will reproduce the best in the magazine; color slides, a very distant second (the resulting reproduction will *not* be of good quality). Do not send transparencies or reproductions from catalogues. The quality of the photograph you submit will reflect directly on your review; it is your advantage to submit the best possible quality photographs.

Art Papers reviews are 800-1,000 words, or approximately 3-4 typed, double-spaced pages. We make rare exceptions for shorter or longer reviews. We also occasionally publish a review that covers several exhibitions, but the writer should check with the Editors first. Our writers' payments are currently $40 per review and are subject to change. If the writer needs to be reimbursed for any expenses, approval from the editors must be secured in advance. We request that whenever possible the writer arrange for the gallery to send directly to *Art Papers* a black and white photograph and a list of works or catalogue (we need the photograph for publication and the list or catalogue to check spellings, dates, etc.).

The deadline for reviews is the middle of the third month prior to the cover date of the magazine:

October 15 for the January/February issue
December 15 for the March/April issue
February 15 for the May/June issue
April 15 for the July/August issue
June 17 for the September/October issue
August 12 for the November/December issue

Conflicts of Interest

Be aware of conflicts of interest that will prevent *Art Papers* from being able to publish your article. If you have a relationship with the venue or the artist being reviewed—whether personal or professional—you must indicate to us the exact nature of that relationship so we can determine whether or not a conflict exists. For example, if the writer is married to the artist, or if the writer is employed by the gallery in which the exhibition is mounted,

that's a conflict. If you're not sure whether your relationship to the artist presents a conflict or not (i.e., you're good friends, or you used to be lovers but haven't slept together for a year), contact the editors *before* writing the article.

Features

With rare (if not memorable) exceptions, all feature articles and interviews are assigned by the editors. A writer who has an idea for a feature should contact the editors in advance. Our features are usually 2,500-10,000 words, with exceptions as appropriate. Proposed features should deal with issues pertinent and of interest to the regional, national and international arts audience, although we occasionally run special issues on themes pertinent to narrower segments of the arts community. In all cases, please check with the editors.

Features due dates:

November 1 for the January/February issue
January 1 for the March/April issue
March 1 for the May/June issue
May 1 for the July/August issue
July 1 for the September/October issue
September 1 for the November/December issue

Postscripts

Art Papers is expanding its news coverage of the arts community (in all disciplines, not just visual arts—performing, media, dance, etc., are encouraged). We are interested in short news items of general interest pertaining to the artists, arts institutions, and arts issues in all regions of the United States. In keeping with our origins as an arts advocacy newsletter, we are particularly seeking news and information related to political and legislative actions that bear directly on the arts community. The writer should submit the information in as concise and direct a manner as possible.

Letters

Art Papers prints all letters pertinent to the arts community, local and abroad, or to *Art Papers* itself. Please keep the letters brief and to issues of interest and importance to the readership. Please include your name, address, and telephone number with your communications; anonymous letters will not be printed.

Categories: Arts

Name: Ruth Resnicow, Editor-inChief
Material: All
Address: PO BOX 77348
City/State/ZIP: ATLANTA GA 30357
Telephone: 404-588-1837
Fax: 404-588-1836
E-mail: ruth@pd.org

Art Times

WRITER'S GUIDELINES FOR FIRST SERIAL RIGHTS
FICTION: Short Stories up to 1,500 words. All subjects but no excessive sex, violence or racist themes. Our prime requisite is high literary quality and professional presentation. Pay $25 upon publication, six extra copies of issue in which work appears and one year's complimentary subscription beginning with that issue. *We do not publish reprints.*

POETRY: Up to 20 lines. All topics; all forms. Same requisite high quality as above. Pay is six extra copies of issue in which work appears and one year's complimentary subscription beginning with that issue. *We do not publish reprints*. We do not encourage simultaneous submissions of poetry.

(Note: We are usually on about a *36-month* lead for fiction; *12-month* lead for poetry.)

Readers of ART TIMES are generally over 40, literate and arts conscious. Our distribution is heaviest in New York State (along the "Hudson River Corridor" from Albany into Manhattan). We are sold by subscription, newsstand; copies may be obtained free at selected art galleries. Subscription copies are mailed across the US and abroad. In addition to short fiction and poetry, feature essays on the arts make up the bulk of our editorial. (Note: Articles and Essays are not solicited).

Sample copy: $1.75 plus 9"x12" SASE with 3 first class stamps.

Categories: Arts—Crafts—Culture—Dance—Drama—Entertainment—Film/Video—Literature—Multicultural—Music—Poetry—Short Stories—Theatre

Name: Submissions Editor
Material: All
Address: PO BOX 730
City/State/ZIP: MT MARION NY 12456
Telephone: 914-246-6944
Fax: 914-246-6944
E-mail: ARTTIMES@mhv.net

ARTFUL DODGE

Artful Dodge
The College of Wooster

Dear Writer,
Thank you for your interest in *Artful Dodge*. Our guidelines are fairly straightforward: typed manuscripts; no simultaneous submissions or previously published material; allow one week to six months for response. Please send no more than 30 pages of prose or six poems, though long poems are encouraged. We pay in copies, plus $5 per page.

Translations should be submitted with original texts. We also prefer that you indicate you have copyright clearance and/or author permission.

Subscriptions: $10 for two double issues ($16 institutional); $5 for one double issue.
The Editors
Categories: Fiction—Poetry

Name: Daniel Bourne, Editor
Material: All
Address: DEPT OF ENGLISH
Address: THE COLLEGE OF WOOSTER
City/State/ZIP: WOOSTER OH 44691
Telephone: 330-263-2577

Arthritis Today

Arthritis Today is a national consumer health magazine published by the Arthritis Foundation. It is written for the nearly 40 million Americans who have arthritis or an arthritis-related condition as well as for the millions of other people whose lives are touched by these conditions. The magazine is a comprehensive and authoritative source of information about arthritis research, treatment, self-care and emotional coping.

Our magazine has a diverse audience because there are more than 100 arthritis-related conditions, including osteoarthritis, rheumatoid arthritis, fibromyalgia and lupus. These conditions, can affect anyone of any age, from children and young adults to middle-aged and older people. Our magazine speaks to all of these groups.

The editorial content of Arthritis Today is designed to empower people with arthritis to live healthier lives overall, emphasizing upbeat, informative articles that provide practical advice and inspiration. Feature articles of approximately 1,000 to 4,000 words focus on treatment options, research advances, ways of coping with physical and emotional challenges, empowerment, and exercise. Our Research Spotlight section reports on research advances in the understanding and treatment of arthritis, based on studies from respected medical journals and scientific meetings. The magazine also includes shorter items that address the whole person, such as brief items of 50 to 200 words on general health and medical topics, travel, nutrition, hobbies, leisure and relationships. We also include personal, inspirational essays of 500 to 1,200 words written by people who have arthritis-related conditions. Each issue is extensively reviewed by our medical editor who is the Arthritis Foundation's senior vice president for medical affairs, as well as by individual experts on our medical advisory board.

The articles in *Arthritis Today* are written by professional writers with experience writing for other consumer magazines. Writers interested in writing for *Arthritis Today* should provide nonreturnable clips of articles they've written that have been published in other consumer magazines. We also ask writers to send us their article ideas in writing. Queries should be typewritten and should include the following information: a general synopsis of the idea and the specific angle to be addressed in the article; research or other material you plan to cite to support the article; experts, such as researchers, health professionals or "real people," whom you plan to interview and quote in the article. We prefer not to receive unsolicited manuscripts. After reviewing your query, the editors will respond within six to eight weeks. At that time, we may ask for more details or request the manuscript on speculation.

Please include a self-addressed stamped envelope with your query. This will help speed up our response time.
Categories: Consumer—Health—Nonfiction

Name: Shelly Morrow, Associate Editor
Material: All
Address: 1330 West Peachtree St.
City/State/Zip: Atlanta, GA 30309
Telephone: 404-872-7100
Fax: 404-872-9559

The Artist's Magazine

The Artist's Magazine is a monthly publication written by artists for artists. Unlike coffee-table magazines for art collectors, *The Artist's Magazine is a* nuts-and-bolts, instructional resource for the artist in search of artistic and professional success. We show how artists deal with various issues—painting techniques, media and materials, design and composition, specific subjects, special effects, marketing and also other business-related topics.

Opportunities for professional artists and writers to work with *The Artist's Magazine* lie basically with feature articles and with our Swipe File and Drawing Board columns. Freelance writers must have the ability to write from the artist's viewpoint using the language of art.
Where to Start

Writers should query in advance rather than send unsolicited manuscripts. Queries should include:

• A brief outline giving us a clear picture of the subject, how—to angle and purpose of the proposed article (including a possible title and subtitle).

• The artist's resumé, credits and approximately 8-12 slides or larger transparencies of his or her work. (NOTE: All slides should be in protective plastic slide sleeves.)

• The writer's resumé, credits and photocopies of no more than two clips (if different than the artist).

Let your query demonstrate that you know where you want to go and how to get there. If we like your idea, we'll do one of two things: 1) ask for a comprehensive, detailed outline or 2) assign the piece to you. We'll try to respond to your query within three months.

All About Features

Our most consistent need is for instructional articles written in the artist's voice, rather than in newspaper-style reporting or Q&A interview styles. All features should emphasize the how-to: how you (or the artist) work with a medium, solve problems and conduct business. You're talking to artists, so techniques and methods must be specifically explained and demonstrated. Try to avoid cliches and concentrate on basic, practical, step-by-step instruction with a friendly, conversational tone. The goal is for the reader to be able to pick up a brush (or some other tool) and duplicate the described process or technique after reading the article.

Feature themes will generally fall into the following categories:

• Genres of art, including basic, new or unusual techniques of still life, landscape, portraiture or wildlife painting. Example: 10 ways to arrange a still life.

• Specific objects, such as flowers, animals, trees-objects commonly found in paintings and drawings. Example: How to paint basic flower shapes.

• Basic application techniques and how they're used with different media. Examples: Color mixing in watercolors, drybrushing with acrylics.

• Special effects, covering new or time-tested techniques in any one medium. Example: Using stencils with water-based media.

• Introduction to unusual media, including the necessary tools, materials and basic techniques of mastering the medium. Examples: How to work with encaustics, caseins or paper collage.

• Techniques of the masters-how a great artist created his or her works and how to emulate it. Example: How to paint like Monet.

• New markets for art sales, including the scope and potential of market categories, and how an artist can break in. Examples: Painting for the religious card market or romance book cover market.

• Business articles on any subject that the beginning artist needs to master to become a professional. Examples: Tips on recordkeeping, selling, portfolio building, etc.

Tips: *The Artist's Magazine* typically deals with realistic and semi-realistic painting; we *rarely* feature non-representational art. Therefore, we suggest that you peruse recent copies of the magazine and compare them to the work of the artist you have in mind before you send in your submission. Also, we're no longer accepting poetry, games/puzzles or strictly inspirational pieces, unless they include a how-to angle.

Feature articles typically range from 1,000 to 1,800 words. Pay can range from $200 to $350, depending upon the quality of the work, the length of the article and the completeness of the total package submitted by the writer. Articles are generally used within one year of acceptance.

If your manuscript is accepted, it should be submitted as typed hard copy and on a 3½" disk if possible, and should include captions, author bio and artist bio. The artwork package should contain at least 8-12 slides or larger transparencies of the artist's work for use in illustrating the article. It should also include at least one step-by-step progressive demonstration—a series of slides that shows how a painting is developed from concept to finish; include at least four distinct steps per set.

The slides/transparencies should be professionally shot, either by yourself or by *a* photographer; poorly shot artwork will not be reproduced. *All* slides should be correctly labeled with the artist's name, address, medium, dimensions, title and indication of top and front. For more information on correctly shooting slides of artwork, please see our Photography Guidelines.) A complete set of writer's guidelines will be provided upon acceptance of query. Slides and transparencies will be returned after publication of the article.

More Writing Opportunities

The Swipe File is a collection of tips and suggestions from our readers. Examples include everything from how to make a caddy for your art supplies to how to use packing foam to blend your pastels. Submissions can be sent directly to the Swipe File Editor without querying first. Photos and illustrations are welcome, and payment is dependent on the size and complexity of the tip and/or artwork.

Drawing Board is a monthly column that covers basic art or drawing skills, for example, improving your sketching techniques, using grids to improve composition, filling your landscapes with realistic trees and grass, painting textural hair and fur. Query first with illustrations. Word count is 1,200 words; payment is $250 and up.

For More Information

Sample copies can be ordered by sending $3 per copy to: Back Issue Manager, The Artist's Magazine, 1507 Dana Ave., Cincinnati OH 45207.

Categories: Arts

Name: Sandra Carpenter, Editor
Material: All
Address: 1507 DANA AVE
City/State/ZIP: CINCINNATI OH 45207
Telephone: 513-531-2690
Fax: 513-531-2902
E-mail: TAMEDIT@aol.com

The Asian Pacific American Journal

More stuff than the average mind can handle.

[Editor's note: the guidelines below solicit material for an issue of *The Asian Pacific American Journal* that will have gone to press by the time this book is published. The guidelines are included here for informational purposes; contact TAPAJ for information related to editorial needs and deadlines for future issues.]

The Asian Pacific American Journal New Voices issue will be edited by the staff and will be out in Spring 1998.

Age, experience or previous publication in other journals won't be factors in choosing contributors for this issue—only *exceptional literary merit*.

We are looking for **poets & fiction writers** who have not yet published in *The Asian Pacific American Journal*, for a special section devoted to **New Voices**.

SUBMISSION GUIDELINES

Poetry: no more than 10 pages: one poem per page

Fiction and creative nonfiction: one story/essay, double-spaced, per submission deadline.

Name, address and phone number on each submission.

Four (4) copies of each poetry submission.
Three (3) copies of each prose submission.
Send copies as *The APA Journal* will not return manuscripts.
Cover letter preferred with a brief biography.
We do not take submissions by e-mail.
The Asian Pacific American Journal
37 St. Marks Place #B New York, N.Y. 10003
Categories: Asian-American

Name: Eileen Tabios, Editor
Material: All
Address: 37 ST MARKS PL STE B
City/State/ZIP: NEW YORK NY 10025
Telephone: 212-228-6718
Fax: 212-228-7718
E-mail: AAWW@panix.com

Asimov's Science Fiction
Dell Magazines

Asimov's Science Fiction magazine is an established market for science fiction stories. We pay on acceptance, and beginners get 6.0 cents a word to 7,500 words, 5.0 cents a word for stories longer than 12,500 words, and $450 for stories between those lengths. We seldom buy stories longer than 15,000 words, and we don't serialize novels. We pay $1 a line for poetry, which should not exceed 40 lines. We buy first North American serial rights plus certain non-exclusive rights explained in our contract. We do not publish reprints, and we do not accept "simultaneous submissions," (stories sent at the same time to a publication other than *Asimov's*). *Asimov's* will consider material submitted by any writer, previously published or not. We've bought some of our best stories from people who have never sold a story before.

In general, we're looking for "character oriented" stories, those in which the characters, rather than the science, provide the main focus for the reader's interest. Serious, thoughtful, yet accessible fiction will constitute the majority of our purchases, but there's always room for the humorous as well. Borderline fantasy is fine, but no Sword & Sorcery, please. Neither are we interested in explicit sex or violence. A good overview would be to consider that all fiction is written to examine or illuminate some aspect of human existence, but that in science fiction the backdrop you work against is the size of the Universe.

Any ms. longer than 5 pages should be mailed to us flat. Dot matrix printouts are acceptable only if they are easily readable. Please do NOT send us submissions on disk. The ms. should include the title, your name and address, and the number of words in your story. Enclose a cover letter if you like. If you wish to save on postage, you may submit a clear copy of your story along with a standard (#10) envelope, also self-addressed and stamped. Mark your ms. "DISPOSABLE," and you will receive our reply only. We do not suggest that you have us dispose of your original typescript.

Finally, we regret that it's become necessary for us to use form letters for rejecting manuscripts, but time limitations are such that we have no choice. Unfortunately, we are unable to provide specific criticism of each story. Our response time runs about five weeks. If you have not heard from us within three months from the day you mailed your ms., you can assume it was lost in the mail, and are welcome to resubmit it to us.

Thanks for your interest in *Asimov's* and good luck!
Categories: Fiction—Fantasy—Science Fiction

Name: Gardner Dozois, Editor
Material: All
Address: 1270 AVENUE OF THE AMERICAS
City/State/ZIP: NEW YORK NY 10020
Telephone: 212-698-1313
Fax: 212-698-1198
E-mail: 71154.622@compuserve.com (correspondence only)

Aspen Magazine

Aspen Magazine is published six times a year for Aspenites everywhere—locals, second-home owners, former and would-be Aspen residents, visitors. We demand professionalism and work of the highest quality from all our contributors.

The best way to find out what kind of story we are likely to publish is to take a look at a few recent issues and get a feel for the style, content, and tone of the articles.

Our procedure is to evaluate written query letters. We consider all ideas. The best ideas, combined with the best visual presentations, are selected.

We are looking for well-written, original articles with a clear Aspen connection. If your story is a general feature about Aspen ("local chefs" or "the music festival"), we're not interested. We need that extra angle—a twist, a compelling reason that *Aspen Magazine* readers would be interested in what you have to say.

In evaluating ideas, these are the questions we ask: Is it fresh, exciting, innovative, timely? Is it well thought-out and meticulously researched?

We also publish *Travelers Guide for Aspen, Snowmass, and the Roaring Fork Valley*. Its travelogue format gives the reader a lyrical and inspiring look at a particular experience; for example: hiking, going to the Music Festival. Each article is accompanied by a "box" listing how the reader can participate in those activities-hours, details, phone numbers. Remember, *Travelers Guide* offers reader service, geared for travelers. Keep the difference between the traveling audience and our *Aspen Magazine* audience in mind when you are writing for either publication.

For both magazines, we require solid research, detailed reporting, good quotes, telling anecdotes, active verbs, and clean prose.

When we agree to assign a story, we will draw up an assignment letter and a contract. First-time assignments are usually "on spec."

QUERIES AND AGREEMENTS
We require a written query before considering any story idea. A query should be a straightforward outlining of your story idea, addressing these points:

- A fresh, well-focused idea (an *angle*, not a *topic*)
- A reason why you should write it
- Evidence of your research and writing ability
- Some indication you've read our publication
- Perfect, typo-free copy with flawless spelling

Rarely do we ask a writer to supply photographs; our art director will assign a photographer or other artist to illustrate your story. If you have any photo suggestions, we're happy to hear them-preferably in writing when you submit your query. First-time queries should include writing samples.

PROCEDURAL POINTS
Once you have an assignment, take notes or use a tape re-

corder. The accuracy of your article is ultimately your responsibility. *Never* promise your sources they will be able to read the story before publication.

Before any article is published, we must verify that it is factually accurate, fair and free of legal problems. Sometimes we will ask to see your notes or tapes. This fact-checking process protects the credibility of both the writer and the magazine and is standard magazine practice.

Type all manuscripts, or submit the story on a computer disk compatible with our apple Macintosh system. Include your name, address, phone number, and social security number on the first page. For style questions, consult the *Associated Press Style Manual* or *A Manual of Style* from the University of Chicago Press.

We reimburse some expenses, but only if they are cleared first by an editor. Keep receipts.

We pay within 30 days of publication. We are currently negotiating our rates on a per-article basis, depending not only on the length of the piece, but on your individual qualifications, the complexity of the assignment, the amount of research, time, and effort involved, and the shape the article is in when it reaches our office.

Categories: Nonfiction—Diet—Gardening—Health—Outdoors

Name: Melissa Coleman, Managing Editor
Material: All
Address: BOX G-3
City/State/ZIP: ASPEN CO 81612
Telephone: 970-920-4040
Fax: 970-920-4044
E-mail: aspenmag@rof.net

ASU Travel Guide
The Guide for Airline Employee Discounts

The *ASU Travel Guide* is published quarterly: January (winter issue); April (spring issue); July (summer issue); and October (fall issue). The publication comprises two sections. The first section contains four travel articles and other pertinent editorial matter. The second section, which is the bulk of the publication, is a directory of discounts available only to airline employees, their families, parents of airline employees and retired airline employees. Articles must be aimed at this well-traveled audience.

Style:

Clean and simple; use active verbs. You may use whatever narrative you deem best. Focus on what is unique about a destination: do not write descriptions that could apply to any tourist destination.

Photographs:

We do not buy photos. They are mostly obtained from tourist and convention bureaus.

Payment:

$200 upon acceptance-including one rewrite if needed—for 1,800-word articles.

Tips:

• Reader surveys indicate that most of our subscribers are interested in how to visit a destination inexpensively, so please include some cost-cutting hints.

• If you have information indirectly related to the article, such as a side trip, it is best presented as a sidebar.

• Send us a sample of your published travel writing and a list of destinations about which you can write. A list of recent articles is shown below. Be aware that we publish travel destination articles only (i.e., do not submit pieces on luggage or currency tips).

• Be patient. The next year's editorial calendar is made each

April, so an idea may not be acted upon immediately. We answer all mail as long as a self-addressed, stamped envelope is enclosed. To receive a sample copy of the publication, please submit a 6"x9" envelope (minimum) with $1.41 postage affixed.

Categories: Airline—Travel

Name: Christopher Gil, Managing Editor
Material: All
Address: 1525 FRANCISCO BLVD E
City/State/ZIP: SAN RAFAEL CA 94901
Telephone: 415-459-0300

Atlanta Parent
Atlanta Baby

Atlanta Parent is aimed at parents with children from birth to 16 years old. *Atlanta Parent* is published monthly.

Atlanta Baby is aimed at parents from when they find out they are pregnant until the baby is 2 years old. *Atlanta Baby* is published 6 times a year.

Article lengths typically run from 600 to 1,200 words.

• For publication in our magazines, please put only one space after a period at the end of a sentence—not two. Please indent paragraphs with a tab and indicate the approximate number of words.

• Authors should include their name, address and phone number at the top of the first page, along with the word count. On the rest of the pages, please print at least your name—top pages frequently get detached from the rest of the manuscript.

• Articles should address the parent, not the child.

• All of our articles are very down-to-earth—we print no philosophical or theoretical articles. Most are third person—we do VERY little first person. We publish no short stories or poetry.

• If writing about a problem of children or families, give parents the symptoms or signs of the problem and then the solutions or where they should turn to for help. We encourage you to include national resources and/or brochures that can be sent away for.

• We will not accept articles that have quotes from experts located in only one region of the country. For us to use it, the article needs to include either quotes from local experts or experts from around the country.

• Our readers also want to read articles that are activity-based. Keep the instructions short and to the point. Do the activity yourself or ask another person to follow the directions to make sure they are accurate.

• Replies on articles usually take 3-4 months.

• All articles sent are submitted on speculation unless specifically assigned in advance.

• Our normal procedure, if we like your article but have no immediate plans to use it, is to keep your article on file for possible future publication.

• If your article is accepted, we'll request a disk. We work on an IBM-compatible system and prefer 3½" disks. Disks are returned upon publication. On the disk, indicate the program used and file name including extensions.

• Photos and illustrations may be submitted with a story. Nominal payment is offered, if used.

• Payment is on publication.

Categories: Nonfiction—Children—Family

Name: Peggy Middendorf, Editor
Material: All
Address: 5330 GEORGETOWN SQ II STE 506
City/State/ZIP: ATLANTA GA 30338

Telephone: 770-454-7599
Fax: 770-454-7699
E-mail: atlparnt@family.com

Atlanta Singles Magazine

Dear Contributor:

Thank you for your interest in *Atlanta Singles Magazine*. Below are the guidelines you requested. We Welcome any submissions you might have for our magazine.

Who We Are: *Atlanta Singles Magazine is geared to the* single person in Atlanta who wants *to* meet new people. The magazine appeals to a broad range of singles. Features and articles are of general interest—dating, travel, activities, relationships, humor. Readers of the magazine are a specific market, interested in getting the most out of being single.

What We Need: We look *for* articles of interest to single men and women. We want creative, interesting, serious, incisive or humorous pieces. We do not publish fiction. We also consider gags and photographs for publication.

What We Pay: Payment for one-time rights to submissions range from $25 to $200 per article, $10-$20 per cartoon or gag filler. Photographs for cover art can be submitted on a per-photo basis.

Sincerely,

Shannon V. McClintock

Editor

Categories: Nonfiction—Comedy—Cooking—Entertainment—General Interest—Marriage—Men's issues—Romance—Sexuality—Society—Travel—Women's Issues

Name: Ms. Shannon V. McClintock, Editor
Material: All
Address: 180 ALLEN RD STE 304N
City/State/ZIP: ATLANTA GA 30328
Telephone: 404-256-9411
Fax: 404-256-9719

Attain

St. John's University Publications

Below are the writer's guidelines for our publication, ATTAIN. Our previous publications, MINISTER'S TIPS and GUIDE LINES, were combined with ATTAIN at the beginning of 1997 to form what we now publish as ATTAIN.

The editor reserves the right to accept or reject my article or advertisement submitted for publication.

All editorial copy should be addressed to Dr. E. Arthur Winkler in care of ATTAIN. Articles for *Attain, Minister's Tips* or *Guide Lines* should be original nonfiction manuscripts and include a bibliography of any references quoted or alluded to in the article. Preferred length is 1,000 words or less. ATTAIN retains the right to make editorial corrections and cannot assume responsibility for error or loss.

ATTAIN does not endorse the merits of any product or service advertised or included in any article.

Categories: Business—Children—Christian Interests—College—Comedy—Cooking—Crime—Disabilities—Economics—Education—Family—Games—General Interest—Health—Humor—Inspirational—Law Enforcement—Marriage—New Age—Paranormal—Physical Fitness—Psychology—Relationships—Religion—Sermons—Society—Spiritual—Sports—Teen

Name: E. Arthur Winkler, Th.D., Ph.D., Editor
Material: All
Address: 31916 UNIVERSITY CIRCLE

City/State/ZIP: SPRINGFIELD LA 70462-8243
Telephone: 504-294-2129
Fax: 504-294-2157
E-mail: stjohns@i-55.com

Audio Amateur Corporation

You can make our job a lot easier if you submit your manuscript in an organized fashion. Taking special care with your submission helps speed processing and eliminates errors.

Before You Write

It's always a good idea to query us before submitting an article. If you have an idea, draw up a brief outline of what you plan to do. If the idea is something we can use, we will give you the go-ahead. If, however, someone is working on a similar project or we do not foresee a need for such an article, we will let you know so that you won't waste time preparing a full-fledged manuscript.

Tone

Many technical writers use a highly impersonal style of writing, relying heavily on the passive voice and avoiding all personal pronouns. We want you to write as though you were talking to your best friend. Use "I" rather than the editorial "we" and don't be afraid to address the reader as you instead of the objective "one." Avoid constructions such as "It was found that…" and instead tell us who found what and how: "I found that this design worked better because…"

Organization

Writing in a personal style does not mean dashing off your article in longhand or not taking the time to correct typing errors. We strongly suggest you generate your manuscript on computer disk and include a neat printout. Make sure you keep a copy of the article in case we misplace ours or you have any questions about our editing. Every manuscript page, including labels, parts lists and artwork, should carry your name and the article title.

Be concise, but explain all technical terms. The first time an abbreviation or acronym appears, spell out the full term for which it stands. Do not assume that the reader will know what you are talking about. Our readers are at different levels of technical expertise, and we don't want to lose any of them with obscure writing.

Your lead paragraph should state the problem at hand and how you solved it. Then you can go on to explain any background material and design concepts. If your article involves construction, tell the reader how you designed (briefly) and built the equipment. Include a clear description of how the unit works, and be prepared to submit your prototype for verification and testing. (Transport and insurance will be at our expense.)

Sometimes you can convey material better in a table or diagram. Tables should be self-explanatory and should supplement, not duplicate, the text. Submit each table and its title on a separate sheet of paper, but remember to reference at the appropriate spot in the text. Parts lists and specifications should also be printed on separate sheets. Make sure you double-check them against text references and figures.

Pages should be numbered consecutively. Number your diagrams and photos in the order in which you refer to them in the text. Supply captions for all photographs and artwork. Include caption information on a separate sheet, and make sure each piece of art is labeled with the appropriate number, your name, and the article title.

Artwork

Make all drawings large and clear, giving all component designators (R1, R2, etc.) and parts values on the drawing. They need not be inked art, as we will redraw them for publication. If you can do acceptable reproduction drawings, we will pay an extra fee for their use. Please include pinouts for all ICs and solid-state devices on your schematics. Specify top or bottom view. Diagrams are usually set up with the input on the left and the signal or control moving to the output on the right, where possible. Use connector dots where crossing lines are connected, and "run arounds" for those crossing lines which are not connected. Use the traditional ground sign for power ground, and the other one for chassis ground. Schematics parts designators should include a part number as well as the value, capacitor and diode max voltages, and polarity signs. Do not include tolerances on the schematic. Much of our schematic capture is now done with OrCAD SDT, a fine software package which is easy to use, flexible, and customizable. If you have access to a drafting package, be sure to tell us what you used.

Please make a separate parts list to accompany schematics. In your parts list(s), be sure to include all wattages of resistors, type and voltage ratings of capacitors, and current ratings of transformers, chokes and diodes. List PIV (peak inverse voltage) ratings of rectifiers—even if you list a "1N" number as well. If tolerances are important, state them. If you use special or surplus parts, give the reader a readily available replacement and name the supplier and their address.

Schematic Conventions (others and our own)

1. Number parts with designators R1, C1) on all construction schematics from input to output, top to bottom. This gives readers a handle for asking about any particular component in a design.

2. Put part details beyond designator, value, and rating in your parts list. Keep special notes to a minimum by putting such information in the caption, or in the parts list.

3. Arrange your drawing of a schematic from input on the left side to output on the right side of the sheet.

4. Capacitor values. We prefer to use the standard nano- prefix for fractional farads as follows:

micro(F) * nano(n) * pico(p)

1.000 .000 FARADS; thus

Examples:

1F

l00n (nanofarads) = 0.1F

1n (nanofarads), NOT 1,000pF or 0.00lFF

l00pF, NOT 0.0001FF

(NOTE: micro = millionth, nano = billionth, and pico = trillionth. Thanks a lot, Michael Faraday.)

5. We believe it is safer to use the quantity unit to replace the decimal in many fractional values of capacitance and resistance to avoid confusion or to avoid the risk of the decimal disappearing on the fifth copy of the schematic.

5R4 vs. 5.4W (R is used in values below 10)

6K8 vs. 6.8K

6p8 vs. 6.8p This technique works best for small values of capacitance.

6. Please do not use lowercase "m" as an abbreviation for the micro- prefix. The "m" is reserved to represent the prefix "milli-" as in -amperes, -henries, -seconds, -volts, and so on. If you cannot access the Greek letter "F" (Alt + 109 on the keypad from the Symbol font in most word processors), use the Roman lowercase letter "u."

If you use perforated or etched boards for construction, please include component layout diagrams. (As with other drawings, put designators on your layout diagrams, and values on your part list.) If you use an etched board, submit a black and white film of the foil pattern, negative or positive, same size or 2x.

Photos should be clear, black and white, or color, at least 3"x5", but if you prefer to submit negatives and contact prints, we will be glad to consider these, even in 35mm form.

[You may wish to] consider Seattle FilmWorks, PO Box 34056, Seattle WA 98124 who will send you two rolls of free film on re-

quest. They offer to put your photos on a 3.5" disk and supply the software, PC or MAC, for viewing. These files can be submitted to us with articles on a 3.5" disk. These may also be downloaded from their website: http://www.filmworks.com. This is the very best way we know of to get your photos into your article.

The most important consideration in photographing equipment is light. The best results I've ever achieved in black and white resulted when I took photos against a neutral background, outside, on an overcast day, placing the equipment on it and shooting three frames: bracketing the exposure, one stop above, one at, and one below the computed exposure value. Halogen-type lights are becoming much more common and cheaper. These pointed at a light colored, reflecting surface, rather than directly at the object, give excellent results. Do not locate them close to flammable materials, however.

We welcome your photos for covers and will pay $50 each for those accepted—on acceptance.

We have a reprint of an article on how to photograph your work, which is an excellent source of information. If you'd like to receive it, just send us a SASE with enough postage to cover 2 oz. (outside the US, two postal coupons).

Do not write on your photographs. Use pencil to write on adhesive labels, then affix them to the photo. Don't use felt tip pens on photos. We pay from $5 to $7 per picture, depending on its quality.

References

If you quote others or refer to material published elsewhere, give full reference information, preferably within the text. Alternatively, you may number each reference and list them all at the end of the article. References should include the author's name, full title of the publication, place and date of publication, volume number (if applicable), and page number. Oblique references to so-and-so's design are not acceptable. Readers want to know where they can find additional information about that design, and authors should be given full credit for their work. If you use a long quote or copyright material, you must secure the owner's permission. Fees for such usage are subject to negotiation. Audio Amateur Corporation assumes no responsibility for this type of material unless fees are agreed to in writing.

Final Considerations

We will acknowledge your submission upon receipt, then either accept or reject it (or ask for an extension) within six weeks. It is helpful if you submit a short biographical sketch with your article.

We hope that you will consider submitting articles to one or all of our publications, and that you will be as attentive to detail as we try to be. After all, we both want the same thing: to let other hobbyists in on the latest in audio design.

Communications

If you need to communicate with us quickly, our fax machine is open 24 hours a day. Please do not fax manuscripts—only correspondence and corrections will be accepted via fax. Our [voice] line is switched to an answering machine at 4:15 p.m. every day, M-F, and is operative on weekends around the clock. You can also e-mail submissions.

About Letters

We have always made it a policy to safeguard the privacy of all authors. We do not give your address or telephone number to readers. Audiophiles like to talk and would love it if you were willing to redesign their systems or recommend the best choice of equipment. (If you mention in your ms. that readers can contact you, we will, of course, publish your address.)

When we receive a letter from a reader about your article, it may or may not be for publication. If we indicate it is not, you are entirely free to decide whether you wish to take the time to answer. If the question is frivolous or asking for too much of your time, you need not answer. It will help if you return the author's letter in the envelope we have provided with a polite refusal.

If the letter is marked for publication, we will have kept a copy of the reader's letter. Please send your reply to the author directly in the envelope he supplies, and a copy of your reply to us. We'll provide an envelope for returning the copy to us.

It helps a lot if we can have the text on a disk. When providing us with a stamped envelope, please include loose stamps (i.e., not glued to the envelope). This is especially important for overseas mail.

We do not ask you to answer letters which we aren't going to use. But it does happen that some letters inevitably get left behind and are finally killed. We regret that, but can't think of any way to avoid it

It would be difficult to overestimate the value of published correspondence. I try to keep it centered on the subject and to edit personal acrimony. If you think the reader or another author is being excessively personal, please indicate your opinion and I'll be certain to cut or temper the respondent's terminology if I agree with you.

Computers

We receive manuscripts (and letter replies if possible) on 5¼" 360K disks in any of the IBM formats and on 3¼" 1.4M and 720K types. We are also able to translate directly from Macintosh disks. We can now also manage almost any IBM word processor which you may be using. We can translate 32 word processor formats to and from each other. We have recently abandoned our practice of returning author disks, since the cost of return postage approaches today's cost for disks.

Please do not apply any fancy formatting to your text in an effort to duplicate our style. Text should be flush left (no indented left margins), with one space between paragraphs, no proportional spacing, and only a *single* spacebar between sentences. Also, please indicate clearly not only *which* word processor you are using but also which *version*. If you are submitting computer-generated figures, do not embed them into the text file—create a separate file for figures only.

We now have WordPerfect 5.2 and Microsoft Word

6.0 (both for Windows) for direct use of your disks. Those of you who use computers are probably aware of how much help spreadsheet packages can provide in your writing and designing. If you haven't discovered them yet, these programs are well worth the effort of learning. Our new favorite is MS Excel 4. The graphical capabilities of this program, along with its total compatibility with Lotus 1-2-3, is outstanding. These are fine tools and can enhance any technical writer's capabilities significantly. We highly recommend MS Excel for data presentation in graphical form, although Quattro Pro and Lotus perform graphical charts as well. Excel is also fine for drawings.

Categories: Audio

Name: Submissions Editor
Material: All
Address: PO BOX 176
City/State/ZIP: PETERBOROUGH NH 03458
Telephone: 603-924-9464
Fax: 603-924-9467
E-mail: audio@top.monad.net

Audubon

Audubon articles deal with the natural and human environment. They cover the remote as well as the familiar. What they all have in common, however, is that they have a story to tell, one that will not only interest *Audubon* readers, but that will interest everyone with a concern for the affairs of humans and nature.

We want good solid journalism. We want stories of people and places, good news and bad; humans and nature in conflict, humans and nature working together, humans attempting to comprehend, restore and renew the natural world.

We are looking for new voices and fresh ideas. Read the magazine, both features and departments before sending queries. Every story suggestion should be submitted in a brief query letter, accompanied by a stamped, self-addressed envelope; no telephone or FAX queries please. Be sure the query not only outlines the subject matter, but also indicates the approach you would take and how you would handle the material. Please estimate how many words you would need to cover the subject. Also, if we don't know your work, include some samples of your writing.

Among the types of stories we seek: profiles of individuals whose life and work illuminate some issues relating to natural history, the environment, conservation, etc.; balanced reporting on environmental issues and events here in North America and abroad; analyses of events, policies, and issues from fresh points of view. We do not publish fiction or poetry. We're not seeking first person meditations on "nature," or accounts of wild animal rescue or taming. Articles on birdwatching ought to be directed to another National Audubon Society publication, Field Notes.

Manuscripts should be accompanied by a stamped, self-addressed envelope of sufficient size. If you are submitting photographs with a manuscript, be sure your submission includes the stiffeners, sufficient postage, and instructions we need to return the photos the way you want them returned.

Author identification should be included; name, address, telephone number, fax number, social security number. Computer printouts and photocopies are acceptable though we will not consider simultaneous submissions. *Audubon* is vigorously fact-checked. Once an article is accepted, the author must be prepared to submit source materials that back up the text and enable us to verify all facts. Hard copy should be accompanied by a computer diskette (either 5 1/4" floppy or 3 1/2") on a standard IBM PC or Macintosh compatible program. Or, manuscripts can be transmitted via modem; telephone us for instructions.

We pay for articles on acceptance, and our rates vary according to length, the amount of work and thought required. Our lengths vary from 500-word text blocks accompanying photo essays to long articles. Generally we are looking for articles that will run to less than 4,000 words.

Thanks for your interest in writing for *Audubon*.

Categories: Nonfiction—Book Reviews—Conservation—Ecology—Environment—History—Interview—Outdoors—Nature—Essay—Humor—Opinion

Name: Lisa Gusselin, Editor
Material: All
Address: 700 BROADWAY
City/State/ZIP: NEW YORK, NY 10003-9501
Telephone: 212-979-3128
Fax: 212-477-9069
E-mail: editor@audubon.org
Internet: magazine.audubon.org

Automobile Quarterly

Automobile Quarterly is a hard-bound, advertising-free, 112-page journal of automotive history.

We accept queries regarding historical stories about automakers, individual automobile models, historical figures, past competition, automotive art and collectibles as well as automotive technology. Queries need to address available sources of information and illustrative materials.

Although we do review unsolicited manuscripts, queries are preferred.

Automobile Quarterly expects its stories to be based on original and primary research sources and to be accurate and well-written. Previously published sources must be used sparingly and be carefully documented. The magazine does not accept repackaged stories that have already been published in English.

Feature stories range from 1,500 to about 7,500 words. Payment will be negotiated, but generally ranges between $500 and $2,000 per story. We often rely on authors to assist in locating and supplying historical photos.

Writer/photographers are sometimes used to provide a complete package of words and color pictures. Fees will be negotiated.

Submissions should be made by hard-copy and on 3½" disc. Although we prefer WordPerfect for Windows (any version up to 6.1), we can convert most recent word processing programs, including Mac.

Queries should be directed to Karla A. Rosenbusch or Jonathan A. Stein.

Categories: Nonfiction—Automobiles—Consumer

Name: Jonathan A. Stein, Publishing Director
Material: Any
Name: Karla Rosenbusch, Managing Editor
Material: Any
Name: Stuart Wells, Assistant Editor
Material: Any
Address: PO BOX 348
City/State/ZIP: KUTZTOWN PA 19606-0348
Telephone: 610-683-3169
Fax: 610-683-3287

Avenues

Thank you for your interest in writing for *Avenues*, a bimonthly consumer magazine published by the Automobile Club of Southern California. *Avenues* feature coverage focuses on Southern California consumer issues, automotive topics, and local, domestic, and international travel.

Avenues editorial content is divided into three sections:

Directions: A section covering local news and information about transportation, car buying, community affairs, and automotive safety.

"Crack-Ups:" is a regular 350-word freelance contribution ($350) that tells a humorous story relating to cars, drives, car travel, etc. Apart from Crack-Ups, in general writers need to be familiar with Southern California to contribute to Directions.

Feature Articles: *Avenues* publishes three or four feature articles of between 1,500 and 3,000 words in each issue. Feature article rates are $1 per word. Generally, the cover feature focuses on a consumer issue of regional interest such as earthquake preparedness, fire safety, or recycling; a second feature has an automotive theme, such as parking, car washes, or automotive design; the third feature is travel related - for example, a service-oriented description of a popular destination, advice for travelers, or a roundup of a particular type of travel (for example, guided tours or little-known state parks).

*Passport to...*A series of short, travel-related pieces (this is the section most open to freelancers).

Ship's Log focuses on a specific experience during a cruise; it does not recount the cruise itinerary. Examples: tobogganing on Madeira, a Balinese beach party, a day on Pitcairn Island. Approach this piece as a page out of your trip diary. 600 words, $600.

Did You Know? introduces readers to an intriguing subject such as Galapagos turtles, a French church organist who plays a 17th-century organ on request, and songbird contests in Singapore. 450 words, $450.

Day-Tripping profiles a community or location in Southern California that makes a convenient one-day or two-day trip for residents or visitors. The L.A. County Arboretum, the San Pedro waterfront, Ojai, and Catalina are examples of places that have been profiled. 650 words, $650.

Great Stays spotlights a single hotel, resort, or inn in the Western U.S. or Mexico that is ideal for a short getaway. 650 words, $650.

On Location explores one destination from a special-interest angle and consists of three related short pieces. For a "Hawaii with kids" theme, for example, the three could be on the Kona Village Resort (350 words), a local guide who customizes tours for families (200 words), and a kid-friendly restaurant (150 words). $700.

Avenues encourages writers to submit concise queries outlining one or more feature article ideas. For Crack-Ups, you may submit spec manuscripts. In both cases, include samples of previously published work. Do not send feature proposals without writing samples. We do not accept proposals over the phone. We look for established writers with strong backgrounds of published stories for our feature articles. Writers with less experience are encouraged to submit queries for Crack-Ups and Passport to....

Always include a self-addressed, stamped envelope with your proposal to guarantee return of the material. We usually respond to queries within eight to 10 weeks.

Avenues purchases first North American rights, and our lead time is approximately six months. Seasonal material should be submitted at least eight months prior to publication. Contributors receive five copies of the magazine in which their article is published.

We look forward to reading your proposal.

Categories: Nonfiction—Arts—Automobiles—Biography—Consumer—Entertainment—Humor—Recreational Vehicles—Regional—Travel—Celebrities

Name: Laura Fisher, Editor-in-chief
Material: All
Address: 950 THIRD AVE.
City/State/ZIP: NEW YORK, NY 10022
Telephone: 212-758-9516
Fax: 212-758-7395

Aviation History

Please refer to Cowles Enthusiast Media, Inc.

BaBY Magazine

BaBY Magazine is a bimonthly publication geared towards women in the last trimester of pregnancy and the first year of baby's life. Our focus is on mom first, baby second. We're the chatty, down-to-earth girlfriend every new mom needs. We emphasize the experience and knowledge base of moms.

We focus on the lighter side of parenthood; humorous stories and personal essays are welcome. We like "how-to" stories designed to smooth the transition from pregnancy to parenthood. All articles are relatively brief and to the point, with personal experiences and quotes from moms weaved in.

Topics we've covered include: Going back to work after maternity leave; coping tips for mom when both she and baby are cranky; how to involve dad in the birthing process, and starting baby on solid foods. We look for articles that will make life easier for the new mom (and dad). We regularly run stories that address the changes a new baby brings to relationships with your spouse, family, and friends. Also, we frequently publish quizzes that are easy and quick to take and score.

We do *not* include stories about toilet-training, preschool, or anything related to children over *age one*. Feature stories generally run about 1,000 words (sidebars and photos are a plus). Quizzes run one page complete with scoring box. Payment is on acceptance for first North American serial rights.

Phone queries are *not* accepted. You can e-mail queries along with writer's credentials. We also suggest you review recent issues of the magazine. Feel free to call for a sample copy.

Categories: Parenting

Name: Jeanne Muchnick, Editor
Material: All
Address: 124 E 40ᵀᴴ ST STE 1101
City/State/ZIP: NEW YORK NY 10016
Telephone: 212-986-1422
Fax: 212-338-9011
E-mail: TheBaBYMag@aol.com

Babybug

In November 1994, The Cricket Magazine Group launched BABYBUG, a listening and looking magazine for infants and toddlers ages six to twenty-four months.

BABYBUG publishes simple stories and poems, words and concepts, illustrated in full color by the best children's artists from around the world.

BABYBUG measures 6¼"x7", contains 24 pages, and is printed in large (26-point) type on high-quality cardboard stock with rounded corners and no staples.

We hope that the following information will be useful to prospective contributors:

Editor-in-Chief: Marianne Carus
Editor: Paula Morrow
Senior Art Director: Ron McCutchan
Art Director: Suzanne Beck
Assistant to Editors: Julie Peterson
Published: by subscription at six-week intervals
Price: $32.97 for nine issues (1-year subscription)
Manuscripts
Stories: **very simple and concrete; 4 to 6 short sentences maximum**
Poems: **rhythmic, rhyming; 8 lines maximum**
Nonfiction: **very basic words and concepts; 10 words maximum parent/child**
Activities: **interaction; 8 lines maximum**
Rates vary; $25 minimum
Payment upon publication
We purchase first publication rights with reprint option; in some cases we purchase all rights.
Art

• By assignment only. Artists should submit review samples of artwork to be kept in our illustrator files. We prefer to see tearsheets or photo prints/photocopies of art.

• If you wish to send an original art portfolio for review, package it carefully, insure the package, and be sure to include return packing materials and postage.

• Author/illustrators may submit a complete manuscript with art samples. The manuscript will be evaluated for quality of concept and text before the art is considered.

• BABYBUG would like to reach as many children's authors and artists as possible for original contributions, but our standards are very high, and we will accept only top-quality material. Before attempting to write for BABYBUG, be sure to familiarize yourself with this age child.

• Please do not query first.

• We will consider any manuscripts or art samples sent on speculation. Submissions without a SASE will be discarded.

• Please allow 6 to 8 weeks response time for manuscripts, 12 weeks for art samples.

• We do not distribute theme lists for upcoming issues.

For a sample issue, please send $5.00 to Babybug Sample Copy.

Note: Sample copy requests from foreign countries must be accompanied by IRCs valued at US$5.00. Please do not send check or money order.

Categories: Fiction—Nonfiction—Children—Literature—Poetry—Short Stories

Name: Submissions Editor
Material: Manuscripts
Name: Suzanne Beck, Art Director
Material: Art Samples
Name: Mary Ann Hocking, Permissions Coordinator
Material: Questions about rights.
Address: PO BOX 300
City/State/ZIP: PERU IL 61354

Back Home In Kentucky

BACK HOME IN KENTUCKY is a beautiful, four-color, statewide publication-the "coffee table magazine of choice" in Kentucky homes. BACK HOME IN KENTUCKY offers a bimonthly glimpse of the state Kentuckians love—whether it's a drive down a country lane or a day spent in one of the state's cosmopolitan cities. Each time they browse through the publication, they'll find history, scenic beauty, the wildlife and natural history, as well as the "character" of the Commonwealth's people. Articles are designed to amuse, educate, and illustrate the Commonwealth, connecting the Highlands with the Purchase, the Pennyroyal with the Bluegrass.

GENERAL FEATURES

Fairs & Festivals—This is an abbreviated listing of events taking place across the state over the two-month period of a particular issue. Color photos and slides are welcomed, as is listing information. Deadline: two months prior to issue date.

*Pursuits—This department features interviews with Kentuckians involved with interesting hobbies and avocations, as well as professional craftsmen and artisans. Past features have included a look at men and women involved in woodworking, quilting, metalworking, basketmaking, photography, and crop dusting. Publication quality color images required (slides or prints). Submissions encouraged.

Cooking—This department focuses on interesting dishes for entertaining and family fare, tying each issue's feature to seasonal or other themes. Recipes are contributed from readers and reprinted from cookbooks offered by various civic organizations. (Individual recipes accepted, as are civic group's cookbooks, from which we may reprint recipes in exchange for purchase information about the cookbook.)

Wildlife/Natural History—These regular departments focus on flora and fauna native to the state of Kentucky as well as other aspects of the Commonwealth's natural history. From the mystery of a heronry to the stunning beauty of Pine Mountain, readers will find an interesting slice of Kentucky here.

*County Lines—A regular feature, the county salute covers a county's history, offers a present picture of the county and its communities, recreational opportunities, etc. We are actively seeking writers for county salutes in a variety of areas. Writers must provide photography to accompany the salute article (may be chamber or tourism furnished). Query first.

HISTORY

* Memories—This department features nostalgic writings offering the flavor of a slower, more friendly time submitted by our readers. Must be Kentucky-related. Black & white photos may accompany the submission. Images sent with submission enhance the chance of publication.

* Chronicle—A glimpse at the history of the state, this department explores some aspect of the Commonwealth's past in some depth. Themes have included: Kentucky women, Sports in Kentucky, Kentucky Inventors, Kentucky & World War II, Kentucky Medicine, etc. Queries encouraged.

* Profiles—This department captures the personality and characteristics of interesting Kentuckians who are no longer living. We feature well-known and lesser-known Kentucky men and women who have figured in the state's past. Queries and submissions encouraged.

*Departments for which submissions are most encouraged.

Writer's Guidelines

BACK HOME IN KENTUCKY is a regional hearth-and-home magazine reflecting a dynamic and contemporary Kentucky, yet one that is rich in history, hospitality, and natural beauty. BACK HOME fosters interest and pride in Kentucky, entertaining and educating the reader. The magazine covers the state's more obvious stories and sparks the interest with the lesser-known. Each issue focuses on one or more themes, which are outlined in the editorial calendar. We emphasizes the scenic beauty of the Commonwealth, as well as her wild creatures, natural history, and colorful characters.

We welcome queries and manuscripts on speculation that fall in these general areas: Kentucky history, Kentucky profiles, Kentucky nostalgia, county features, Kentucky crafts and craftspeople, and county features. Most articles must be accompanied by attractive, well-focused photographs. We have regular writers contributing features on wildlife, natural history, and cooking.

We particularly encourage submissions in these areas:

County Lines Assignments: These are chosen about a year in advance, although the calendar is flexible. These features should be 2,000 to 3,000 words in length and feature interesting aspects of the county—history, famous natives, interesting historical sites, tourist spots, geographical information, and anything else of interest. Color photos are required, although these may be obtained from local tourism commissions, chambers of commerce, state parks, etc. (slides or prints).

Memories: Submissions should be 500 to 900 words in length, written in first person. Stories should be of an anecdotal, "I remember when" style. Old family photos or photos pertaining to the story are greatly welcomed. Must be Kentucky related.

Pursuits: These features can be from 1,000 to 2,500 words in length and should feature a Kentuckian with an interesting hobby or avocation. Publication-quality color images required (slides or prints).

Chronicle: Perhaps our most popular feature, the Chronicle department in each issue covers a broad-based topic such as the history of medicine or aviation in Kentucky, Kentucky inventors, Kentucky women, etc. Feature length is 2,500 to 4,000 words. Submission of related historic images is encouraged.

Profiles: Features about little-known or well-known deceased figures in the Commonwealth's history, with a focus on what makes them so interesting. Length is 1,000 to 3,000 words and a historic image of the person must be available.

Special Assignments: There is always room for quality writing on a variety of Kentucky-related topics. Feel free to query the editor about any story ideas you think are feasible.

Payment: Payment for all materials is upon publication, unless otherwise negotiated. Payment is for first-time North American rights, unless otherwise negotiated. Writers receive a byline and three copies of the magazine containing their work. Material is placed in the magazine as content merits and space allows. The editor determines the suitability of material for inclusion in BACK HOME, as well as in which issue material appears. Payment for

articles varies and is negotiable with the editor. Generally, pay ranges from $15-100, depending on department.

Photographs: Photos accompanying articles are paid for as part of the manuscript purchase. Photo essay submissions are welcome. BACK HOME welcomes submissions of color transparencies for cover consideration and color feature photos. We use about 25 photos/issue, less than 10% on assignment. Do not submit any photo without identifying it, and photos will be returned only if a stamped, self-addressed envelope is enclosed with the materials. Transparencies (35mm and larger format) and prints are accepted. Payment for these is individually negotiated. No payment is made for photos submitted for the Fairs & Festivals section, as it is assumed their publication benefits the event. For complete photo guidelines, contact the editor.

Deadlines: BACK HOME editorial content is planned several months in advance. If an author wishes his/her work to appear in a particular month, he/she should work closely with the editor. Material should be in the editor's hands no later than ten weeks prior to the month of issue (that is, we need May/June material by February 15, and so forth).

Don't Forget: All submissions should include the writer's/photographer's phone number for the editor's convenience if questions arise. A word count is required. We accept diskettes of articles in a variety of software—call to see if yours is compatible. Single issue copies available for $3.

Categories: Nonfiction—Animals—Antiques—Architecture—Arts—Biography—Civil War—Collectibles—Cooking—Crafts—History—Regional (Kentucky-related only)—Rural America—Travel

Name: Nanci Gregg, Managing Editor
Material: All
Address: PO BOX 681629
City/State/ZIP: FRANKLIN TN 37068-1629
Telephone: 615-794-4338
Fax: 615-790-6188
E-mail: greg@edge.net

Backwoodsman Magazine
America's #1 Woodsrunning Publication

Subjects: Muzzleloading guns, muzzleloading hunting, 19th century woodslore, early cartridge guns, primitive survival, craft items from yesteryear, American history, grass roots gardening, leather crafting projects, homesteading, log cabin construction, mountain men, Indians, Indian bow & arrow construction, building primitive weapons, etc.

We are not particularly interested in fictional stories, or material that has the tone of a novel. Any material of this type submitted to *Backwoodsman Magazine* will be sent back. It is important that any material submitted also have illustration or photo, many times this is the determining factor whether an article is published. Pen and ink drawings, or b/w and color pictures will reproduce. No pencil drawings. Length of material is left up to the author, but lengthy material that covers a subject in depth is always favored over a short piece. We do not count words at *Backwoodsman*, only the depth by which a subject is covered.

Pay: *Backwoodsman Magazine* is not a paying magazine. In the near future it's possible that we can become a paying magazine, but at this time we can't afford to pay. We are willing to trade a 1/24 page display ad (value $55) for each article submitted and accepted. Several of our regular writers who have something to sell have chosen this route. In the event you don't have anything to sell in the buckskinning field we are willing to trade a subscription for an article accepted. We want writers who care about a special publication, not writers who care more for the money they might earn. If you can gain satisfaction from submitting subject material of importance to our BWM family of readers, then you are our type of people.

Misc.: We do not deal in world affairs, personal vendettas, or bad mouthing products. Our whole basis is yesteryear. This is not to say that you can't speak your mind. We also do not publish racially motivated material of any type. We don't need a law suit.

If you desire correspondence with us, please send a SASE.

Categories: Buckskinning—Crafts—Fur Trade—Historical (how-to)—History—Hobbies—Native American—Primitive Archery—Western

Name: Submissions Editor
Material: All
Address: PO BOX 627
City/State/ZIP: WESTCLIFFE CO 81252
Telephone: 719-783-9028
Fax: 719-783-9028

Balloon Life

Articles should be 1,000 to 1,500 words. Shorter articles in the 300 to 500 word range will be considered. Longer articles may be submitted, but are generally reserved for more technical or historical subjects. In addition, the writer may wish to present additional information as a separate item for use as a sidebar to the article.

Types of articles considered for publication:

Balloon events/rallies: May be written on events that have recently taken place. Post-event articles should be submitted as soon as possible after the completion of the event. Types of information to include would be: the event's name, its history, its organizers, participating balloonists, other attractions in the area (famous restaurants, river raft trips, shopping, etc.), value of the event to the community, etc. Short articles (±300 words) will be accepted for our Logbook section, which deals with an event that has recently taken place.

Safety seminars: Because this is an educational event, the article should be written as an educational piece that can be used by the readers to further their knowledge. If not written by the presenter whose information is being used, you must secure his/her permission.

Balloon clubs/organizations: Tell us the history of the organization, what they do, meetings, events, projects, activities, etc. How the club helps to promote the sport of ballooning and handles public relations.

General interest stories: Can be interviews or biographies of people that have made a contribution to the sport of hot air ballooning, or other general interest items.

Crew Quarters: A regular column devoted to some aspect of crewing. May be educational, tell as story of a crew experience, or share some other aspect of the sport. 900 words preferred.

The above contributions should include pictures (color and black & white) with captions (pictures should be able to tell the story), charts, maps, or additional information that would be helpful in conveying the story to the readers.

All material submitted will be on a speculation basis only. The writer will be notified in writing within two weeks of receipt of the material whether it is being considered for publication. BALLOON LIFE will only consider articles for publication which have not previously been published. BALLOON LIFE will pay

$50 for the first time North American rights of articles selected for publication and $20 for short article (our Logbook Section) balloon events that have recently taken place. Payment schedule for pictures is $15 inside and $50 for the cover.

Freelance pictures that are submitted will be considered for publication but generally only if they are of an unusual nature or used for the cover photo. See photo guidelines below for more information.

Those individuals who are interested in writing on a specific, technical topic may contact the editor to discuss subject areas, deadlines, and needs of the magazine. For these topics BALLOON LIFE will pay $100-200 for article(s) used on a specific subject, and provide assistance in researching the subject.

Photo Guidelines

BALLOON LIFE is a 4-color monthly magazine dedicated to the sport of hot air ballooning. Only photographs of the highest quality are considered. Photos should be of sharp exposure, good contrast and with excellent color saturation. The use of photos in the magazine is editorially driven; all photos, including the cover, must relate directly to inside editorial.

Submissions should be 35mm color transparencies. Color or black & white prints may also be acceptable. All photographs should be originals. (Duplicate transparencies will be considered but should be so identified.) Copyright must rest with photographer or written permission must be secured from third-party owners. Captions and model releases are preferred. Unless specific written assignment is made, all photos are accepted on a speculation basis only. Photographs will not be returned unless accompanied by a self-addressed, stamped envelope. The photographer generally will be notified within two weeks to confirm receipt of submissions. Simultaneous submissions and previously published work is okay.

Stock Needs: BALLOON LIFE rarely buys stock photography. As mentioned above, the magazine is editorially driven. Occasionally we are interested in "stock subjects" such as winter flying, mountain flying, commercial balloons, special shape balloons, etc. Photographers should query first for information on these anticipated needs. Please include an indication of the contents of your files.

Event Coverage: BALLOON LIFE targets a variety of balloon events for coverage each year and freelance photographs are often used with these articles. Photo coverage should include not only balloons, but other shots which help the reader to capture the true spirit of the event. For example, celebrities, scenics (with and without balloons) faces in the crowd, related events (arts & crafts fairs, chili cook-offs, polo games), etc. Photographers are welcome to query the magazine for interest if they will be attending an upcoming balloon event.

Assignments: Occasionally assignments are made to shoot either specific events, flights, or subjects. In these cases, BALLOON LIFE will provide the photographer with specific direction, contacts and other assistance. Assignment rates are negotiable.

Rates: BALLOON LIFE buys first North American serial rights. Payment schedule is $50 for the cover and $15 for inside color or B&W. Photos are returned and payment is made upon publication.

Categories: Nonfiction—Aviation—Outdoors—Sports

Name: Submissions Editor
Material: All
Address: 2336 47TH AVE SW
City/State/ZIP: SEATTLE WA 98116-2331
Telephone: 206-935-3649
Fax: 206-935-3326
E-mail: TOM@balloonlife.com
Internet: www.balloonlife.com

Baltimore Magazine

As a regional magazine serving the Baltimore metropolitan area, we're almost obsessive in our focus on local people, events, trends, and ideas. We sometimes write about national issues, but only those of immediate interest to our readers in Baltimore and surrounding counties. About 80 percent of our magazine is written by staff members.

We seek feature stories that are rich with character and drama, or that provide new insight into local events. These stories range from 2,000 to 4,500 words. To propose one, send a query letter and clips.

Unless you've already got a great set of feature clips and a powerful idea, though, the best way to break into *Baltimore* is through the shorter stories that run before and after the feature well, in departments such as "Sports" and "Body & Soul." These stories range from 1,000 to 1,500 words. To propose one, send a query letter and clips.

Another possible space for writers unknown to us is the personal essay, which requires a strong voice and a risky new take on local life. We're looking for bravery, background research, and, above all, original thought. These essays are 800 to 1,500 words. To submit one, send a query with several of your published essays in the same style, or else a cover letter with a completed draft.

We generally develop story ideas ourselves and sometimes assign them to freelancers. To be considered for such assignments, send clips and a letter about your specialties.

Throughout the magazine we need originality, so don't propose anything that you've seen in the *Sun*, the *Baltimore Business Journal*, or other local media, unless you offer a fresh perspective or important new information. Because of our two-month lead time, we can't do much with breaking news.

You're most likely to impress us with writing that demonstrates how well you handle character, dramatic narrative, and factual analysis. We also admire inspired reporting and a clear, surprising style.

Your query should fit on one page. If you want a response, you *must* include a stamped, self-addressed envelope with your submission.

Thank you for your interest.

Categories: Baltimore—General Interest—Maryland—Nonfiction—Regional

Name: Editor
Material: All
Address: 1000 Lancaster Street, Suite 400
City/State/Zip: Baltimore, MD 21202
Telephone: 410- 752-4200
Fax: 410-625-0280
E-mail: bmag@abs.net
Internet: www.baltimoremag.com

The Baltimore Review

The Baltimore Review is a biannual (winter and summer) literary journal featuring the short stories and poetry of writers from the Baltimore area and beyond. The BR is sponsored by the Baltimore Writers' Alliance, an organization founded in 1980 to foster the professional growth of writers in the Greater Baltimore area.

Submissions: Submit 1-5 poems or 1 story. Traditional and experimental forms welcome. Length and subject matter are open. No previously published work. Send a self-addressed, stamped business envelope for a response. Responds in 1-3 months. Pays 2 contributor copies, additional copies at a reduced rate.

We welcome your comments and suggestions.
Retail price: $7.95 (total with Maryland sales tax: $8.35)
Subscription:
One year (2 issues) $14.00
Two year (4 issues) $26.00
Address correspondence regarding *The Baltimore Review* or the Baltimore Writers Alliance to the address below.
Categories: Poetry—Short Stories

Name: Submissions Editor
Material: All
Address: PO BOX 410
City/State/ZIP: RIDERWOOD MD 21139
Telephone: 410-377-5265
Fax: 410-377-4325
E-mail: hdiehl@mail.bcpl.lib.md.us

Bass West
A Magazine for Western Bass Anglers

Our goal is to make BASS WEST the most authoritative reference guide in the West. As western water problems continue to grow and fisheries budgets suffer more cutbacks, bass will become even more important to the western fishing scene. With your expertise, we can make BASS WEST a major resource for bass anglers in the West. BASS WEST magazine focuses on western techniques for the deep, clear water and tough fishing conditions found in the West. Each issue has three main sections:

1. Columns by western bass pros such as Mike Folkestad, Don Iovino, Jay Yelas, and Dub LaShot.

2. In-depth features of 2,000 to 3,000 words on western techniques, strategies, issues, etc. Additional standard-length articles of 750 to 1,800 words about projects, tips or other items of interest to western bass anglers.

3. Serious reports on the West's best bass destinations. Up to 4,500 words.

EDITORIAL REQUIREMENTS
• Content geared to both the serious western bass angler and occasional western tournament angler
• Lots of quotes from other authorities on the subject-guides, manufacturers, and biologists
• Specific lures and equipment and identification of manufacturers
• Articles based on current scientific research—western-based biological data
• New facts, not rehashed or outdated opinions
SPECIFICATIONS
• **FEATURE ARTICLES:** In-depth. hands-on western bass information including seasonal and regional variations-Southwest, Northwest and Intermountain may vary. Educational content is important, as are practical solutions to tough fishing problems. Subjects: techniques, biology, technology, seasonal conditions, etc. Include any slides, photos, charts, maps or illustrations you may have. We also like to clarify subjects with sidebar explanations, illustrations and charts or graphs.
• **STANDARD ARTICLES:** Unique projects, tidbits, short technical pieces, innovative projects, etc. If helpful, use quotes from experts. Include slides, diagrams, etc.
• **DESTINATIONS ARTICLES:** We want to know the nuts and bolts-why, where, how. Include information on seasonal variations, good detailed maps and interviews with experts-guides, biologists, and major tournament anglers. List lodges, guides and camping areas with phone numbers.
• **PHOTOS AND ILLUSTRATIONS:** We require 35mm color slides. We strongly encourage fishing action shots and pho-

tos showing tackle, techniques, rigging, lures, locations (especially western scenic locations) and some big fish photos. Please send photo captions with names, places and pertinent information.

- **HUMOR/REAL LIFE ADVENTURES:** Creative entertainment.
- **PHOTOS:** Cover shot must include angler; bass, western scenery, and action in one shot.

RATES

Rates are based upon how well the article is written and how closely the author follows the writers' guidelines. Payment for articles and photographs payable 30 to 45 days after publication.

- Feature articles: 2,000 to 3,000 words—$200 to $500.
- Standard articles: 750 to 1,800 words—$75 to $300.
- Destinations articles: 2,000 to 4,500 words—$200 to $500.
- Humor/real life adventure: 750 to 1,000 words—$75 to $250.
- Photos: Independent inside use—$25 to $75. Cover shot-angler, bass, western scenery, and action—Up to $400.

Categories: Fishing

Name: Debra Brua Biser, Managing Editor
Material: Any
Name: Randy Brudnicki, Executive Editor
Material: Any
Address: 350 E CENTER ST STE 201
City/State/ZIP: PROVO UT 84606
Telephone: 801-377-7111
Fax: 801-377-7196

Bay Area Baby

Please refer to Bay Area Publishing Group, Inc.

Bay Area Parent of Teens

Please refer to Bay Area Publishing Group, Inc.

Bay Area Parent

Please refer to Bay Area Publishing Group, Inc.

Bay Area Publishing Group, Inc.

Bay Area Publishing Group, Inc., a 14-year-old company formerly known as Kids Kids Kids Publications, Inc., publishes these periodicals:

- **Bay Area Parent Magazine** is a regional monthly parenting magazine with distribution of 77,000 copies in Santa Clara, San Mateo and southern Alameda counties.
- **Valley Parent Magazine** is a regional monthly parenting magazine with distribution of 57,000 copies in central Contra Costa County and the Tri-Valley area of Alameda County.
- **Bay Area Baby** is published three times a year, with distribution of 60,000 copies to new and expectant parents all over the Greater San Francisco Bay Area.
- **Bay Area Parent of Teens** is a magazine for parents of adolescents ages 11-17 in the Greater San Francisco Bay Area.

Bay Area Publishing Group also publishes two annual magazines: **Education & Enrichment Guide** in September and Childcare & **Preschool Finder** in April.

To receive a free copy of one of these magazines, please send a self-addressed envelope (at least 8½"x11") stamped with ten stamps (**Bay Area Parent**); five stamps (*Valley Parent*); or four stamps (**Bay Area Baby, Education & Enrichment Guide** *or* **Childcare & Preschool Finder**). Indicate which publication you want to receive.

Most of the editorial for these publications is written by freelance writers on assignment. A few unsolicited articles are run. The information we are most likely to use is local, well-researched and geared to our readers, who are primarily parents of children ages birth to early teens. We do not publish poetry or fiction. Timeliness is critical, e.g., swimming in June and snow skiing in December. We plan editorial content months ahead, so articles pertinent to a particular season should be submitted well in advance.

We appreciate submission of appropriate photographs with a story. Payment is $10 to $15 per picture.

We pay upon publication. Payment is 6 cents per word if an article is used in one of our magazines, 9 cents a word if it is used in two magazines.

Categories: Parenting

Name: Mary Brence Martin, Managing Editor
Material: All
Address: 401 ALBERTO WAY STE A
City/State/ZIP: LOS GATOS CA 95032
Telephone: 408-358-1414
Fax: 408-356-4903
E-mail: BAPG@best.com

Belletrist Review

1. We accept adventure, contemporary, tasteful erotica, horror (psychological), humor/satire, literary, mainstream, suspense/mystery. We do not accept fantasy, juvenile, western, overblown horror, or confessional pieces. We rarely publish poetry.

2. Manuscripts should be 2,500–5,000 words. Please include word count in the upper right hand corner of the first page of the manuscript.

3. Manuscripts should [have] 1¼" space on all sides.

4. Do not send more than one manuscript at a time.

5. The first page of your story should include your name, address, and phone number in the upper left hand corner. Center the title and by-line one-third of the page down. Three lines after that, begin the body of your work.

6. We prefer [a SASE] large enough to accommodate your 8½"x11" format without having to fold it. It is not necessary to send your story by certified mail.

7. Please include a cover letter listing past publications, if any, and note if your manuscript is a simultaneous submission.

Categories: Fiction—Adventure—Crime—Culture—Erotica—Ethnic—General Interest—Humor—Literature—Mystery—Short Stories

Name: Marlene Dube, Editor
Material: All
Address: PO BOX 596
City/State/ZIP: PLAINVILLE CT 06062
Telephone: 860-747-2058

Bellingham Review
Western Washington University

The Bellingham Review is a nonprofit literary arts magazine published in Bellingham, Washington, by Western Washington University. The Bellingham Review is 120 pages, perfect bound, and published twice each year—in the spring and fall. Sample copies are available for $5.00 each. The Bellingham Review also sponsors three awards: the 49th Parallel Poetry Award (fall), the Tobias Wolff Award for Fiction (winter), and the Annie Dillard Award for Nonfiction (spring). Please send a self-addressed stamped envelope for complete details of the awards.

Subscription rates, as of January 1st, 1996:
$10.00 for one year (2 issues)
$19.00 for two years (4 issues)
$25.00 for three years (6 issues)
Subscriptions to foreign addresses are $1.00 a year extra. Institutional subscriptions are $12.00 for two issues. Please make checks payable to The Western Foundation/Bellingham Review.

Our submission period is from October 1st through May 1st. Manuscripts arriving between May 2 and September 30th will be returned unread. The editors welcome submissions of poems, stories, essays, reviews, plays, and photographs. There are no limitations on form or subject matter. Prose must be under 10,000 words. The editors prefer poetry submissions of 3-5 poems. Please indicate the approximate word count on prose pieces.

Simultaneous submissions are considered, as long as *The Bellingham Review* is notified immediately if the work is accepted elsewhere. All submissions must be previously unpublished in North America.

Reporting time normally varies from one week to four months, depending on whether the work is being considered for publication. All contributors receive one copy of the magazine in which their work appears, as well as a complimentary one-year subscription.

Categories: Fiction—Nonfiction—Poetry

Name: Submissions Editor
Material: All
Address: WESTERN WASHINGTON UNIVERSITY
MS 9053
City/State/ZIP: BELLINGHAM WA 98225

Bellowing Ark

We began publishing *Bellowing Ark* in 1984 because no market existed for the kind of literature that we wanted to read and wanted to see published; we set out to create such a market, and, by example, encourage others to do the same. We believe that there is more to art than the desire to shock and the glib and facile expression of nihilism and despair. We are also convinced that artists, particularly literary, have a responsibility to their audience and are required to present the world as meaningful, for, if the world has no meaning, how can life? The material we publish is the best expression of that responsibility that we can command.

We feel *Bellowing Ark* stands solidly in the Romantic tradition which passes from Blake and Wordsworth through the American Transcendentalists to Whitman, Frost, Roethke and Nelson Bentley then on to current writers Natalie Reciputi, Marshall Pipkin, L.L. Ollivier, Muriel Karr, Teresa Noelle Roberts and others. While we are in the Romantic tradition, we also take pride in being one of the most eclectic magazines ever published. There are essentially no restrictions on genre, length, or style.

We have published plays, serialized novels, short stories, poems, long-poems, epic poems (Nelson Bentley's *Tracking the Transcendental Moose* ran to 20,000 lines, published in 14 books, serialized sequentially), essays, memoirs, drawings, photographs, all forms of self expression, in fact, that we consider to meet our single, and sufficient criterion: everything that we publish demonstrates, to our satisfaction, that life is both meaningful and worth living. We are biased toward the narrative, both in poetry and fiction; that is, stories should have a plot, characterization, a beginning, a middle, and an end.

We have not, in our years of publication, ever published a *fiction*, nor anything pointlessly minimalist or surrealist—it seems to us that practitioners of those elegantly academic artforms have deliberately cut themselves off from an audience. We are interested in audience, since we believe art must be shared to be art.

We do ask that material submitted to *Bellowing Ark* be carefully presented. Please double-space prose, single space poetry, one poem per page. If you use a dot-matrix printer please make sure the print is dark enough to be legible: we read hundreds of submissions every month and eyestrain is always a danger. And, always submit a stamped, self-addressed envelope with every submission. Note: we do not consider simultaneous submissions.

Payment is in copies of the issue containing the artist's work, that is, on publication. Sample copies, and it never hurts to read a magazine to see if your work fits, are $3.00, postpaid from the address below.

Thank you for your interest in *Bellowing Ark*; we do hope to hear from you again.

Robert R. Ward, Editor
Categories: Fiction—Literature—Poetry

Name: Submissions Editor
Material: All
Address: PO BOX 45637
City/State/ZIP: SEATTLE WA 98145
Telephone: 206-545-8302

The Beloit Poetry Journal

How to submit poems—to us or to most literary magazines.
The *Beloit Poetry Journal* is a quarterly, established in 1950, published by The Beloit Poetry Journal Foundation, Inc. We seek only unpublished poems or translations of poems not already available in English. The reviews are by the Editor. The magazine is copyrighted, with rights reverting to the poet on publication.

Much as we appreciate the frustration of slow responses from editors, we consider it unethical for a poet to simultaneously submit the same work to more than one publisher (see #8 below).

We receive as many as 20 envelopes of poetry a day and reject most on the day they arrive. About two percent have some chance of ultimate acceptance; these we keep for up to four months, circulating them among the editors and continuing to winnow. At quarterly meetings of the Editorial Board we read aloud the surviving poems and put together an issue of the best.

We have no particular forms or lengths or subjects that we prefer. We accept what our judgement tells us is the best we receive. We are always watching for new poets, fresh insights, live forms and language. Our occasional chapbooks are special collections of categories of poems we don't usually receive. (Example: new poems from the People's Republic of China.) Our chapbooks are almost never the work of a single poet. The Chad Walsh Poetry Award ($3,000 in 1994) goes to the poem or group of poems judged by the editors to be the strongest published in each year.

1. Be familiar with any publication before you submit. Half of the poems we get are from poets who have obviously never seen an issue. Hundreds of libraries subscribe. A sample copy is $4. Poet's Market (in most libraries) gives essential details.

2. Type no more than one poem to a page, single-spaced. Put your name and address at the top of every sheet.

3. Don't send your life's work: what will go for one first-class stamp—about three pages, unless it's a long poem or a sequence of related poems.

4. Keep perfect copies of your work in case the originals are lost. We are seeing more and more loss in the mails. Still, Special Delivery or other special mailing services are not worth the expense and bother.

5. Use regular business envelopes (4"x9"). Don't worry about creases. Wasteful manila envelopes with excess postage just make us sad.

6. No covering note is necessary, unless you have something to say to us. (But many other editors do like them.) We use no contributors' notes. The emphasis is on the poem.

7. Keep a record of when and where you mail every poem. Never send a poem to two places at once. If you have no reply after four months, send a query. If after a month you still hear nothing, send a card announcing that you are withdrawing the poems.

8. Don't expect any comment on your work. Editors read as a labor of love, in spare moments, and if they fall behind they may have to read several hundred poems in a day. Sorry.

9. Don't be discouraged by rejections. Just keep writing and mailing—and reading what is being published.

Categories: Poetry

Name: Marion K. Stocking, Editor
Material: All
Address: RFD 2 BOX 154
City/State/ZIP: ELLSWORTH ME 04605
Telephone: 207-667-5598
Internet: www.zinnia.umfacad.maine.edu/~sharkey/bpj

Better Homes and Gardens

Only about ten percent of our editorial material comes from freelance writers, artists, and photographers; the rest is produced by staff.

We read all freelance articles submitted, but much prefer to see a letter of query than a finished manuscript. The query should be directed to the department where the story line is the strongest. See appropriate editor and department below.

A freelancer's best chance lies in the areas of travel, health, parenting and education. We do not deal with political subjects or with areas not connected with the home, community, and family. We use no poetry, beauty, or fiction. The best way to find out what we do use, and to get some idea of our style, is to study several of our most recent issues.

We buy all rights and pay on acceptance. Rates are based on our estimate of the length, quality, and importance of the published article.

Categories: Automobiles—Computers—Cooking—Decorating—Environment—Family—Gardening—Health—Money/Finance—Nonfiction—Parenting—Physical Fitness—Remodeling—Software—Travel

Name: Joan McCloskey
Material: Building and Remodeling
Name: Nancy Byal
Material: Food and Nutrition
Name: Sandra Sona
Material: Furnishings and Decorating
Name: Mark Kane
Material: Garden
Name: Lamont Olson
Material: Money Management, Automotive

Name: Nina Elder
Material: Travel
Name: Steve Mumford
Material: Environment
Name: Martha Miller
Material: Health/Fitness and Cartoons
Name: Richard Sowienski
Material: Education and Parenting, BH&G Kids
Address: 1716 Locust Stree
City/State/ZIP: Des Moines, IA 50309-3023
Telephone: 515-284-3000

Bicycling

Bicycling magazine is eager to work with freelance writers and photographers who understand cycling and can convey helpful information and passion for the sport. If you want to write or take photos for us, please study several issues of the magazine. It is the best guide to what we are looking for.

We are an 11-issue-per-year how-to magazine that covers the entire world of cycling. Our focus centers on technique and training advice for both road and off-road riding, fitness and nutrition information related to cycling, bicycle advocacy, and racing and other competitive events.

Sold by subscription and on the newsstand, we are the world's largest cycling publication with a circulation of more than 300,000 and a worldwide readership of more than 2 million. Most of these readers are at least intermediate-level cyclists - experienced recreational or fitness riders, or racers - knowledgeable and well-informed about the sport. They look to *Bicycling* for the latest information and definitive opinions on new equipment or training techniques.

But we don't snub novices. *Bicycling* is friendly, helpful, and never elitist. We are the best resource for new riders, and every issue contains material suitable for beginners. Even this material, however, is written from an experienced and expert point of view. We rarely publish novice-eye-view stories such as "My First Tour" or "How I lost 30 pounds by Taking up Cycling at 40."

Our readership is well educated (38.9% are college graduates), and the majority 55.1% are between the ages of 18-34. The median age is 33.4. Although about 80 percent of our readers are male, we value our female readers and never ignore them.

Here's how our subscribers use their bicycles. (Because of multiple answers to our survey, the total adds up to more than 100 percent.)

Fitness	85.8%
Fast rec. riding	72.5%
Weight Control	50.9%
Day-long tours	37.8%
Rec. offroad riding	36.6%
Century/club rides	32.6%

We look for stories with broad appeal, because the magazine serves all 50 states, Canada, and thousands of foreign readers. Information about a local cycling personality in Massachusetts probably wouldn't interest a reader in California, so we rarely publish articles with narrow regional appeal.

We do not use fiction or poetry. We do not pay for newsclippings.

Manuscript: Feature articles should be 850 (one magazine page) to 2,000 (three or four magazine pages) words in length.

Paper submissions should be typed in double-space on one side of 8½"x11" paper, with 1½" margins. A title, subtitle, and your name should appear at the top of the first manuscript page. Include a cover letter containing your name, address, and home and work phone numbers. We will not reply unless SASE is included.

We accept fax submissions fulfilling the same requirements,

but will not reply unless the answer is positive.

We accept E-mail submissions in text-only format, accompanied with the requested contact information. Again, however, we will only reply if the answer is positive. Address stories to DWBicMagra@aol.com.

Unless we have previously worked together or you have significant cycling or writing credentials, do not send queries. When working with new writers we prefer to see the entire manuscript.

We buy all rights to published text and/or photographs, including the right to reuse them in other Rodale Press publications or media. We also purchase the right to grant reprint permission, unless otherwise negotiated before publication. Payment is made on acceptance. For information on fees, see the current copy of Writer's Yearbook (F&W Publications).

Keep our lead time in mind when submitting articles. Each issue is prepared four to five months in advance of its publication date. For instance, a story on spring training submitted in March or even February will be too late and have no chance of acceptance.

Like many magazines, *Bicycling* turns down a majority of freelance submissions. Do not be discouraged by form rejections or several rejections in a row. If you know the sport and study the magazine, you are ahead of most writers in the submission pile.

Types of Articles: *Articles for Novices.* We publish at least one article each issue directed at the person just getting into cycling. Such articles are likely to include basic tips for training or touring. As noted, however, they must not be written from a novice point-of-view. Length is about 1,000 words. For examples, see "The 10 Simplest Things You Can Do to Improve Your Fitness" (Nov. '94) or "We Dare You to Ride 100 Miles in 1 Day" (Aug. '94).

Touring Features. We publish 8-10 touring stories each year, several written by freelancers. These must be heavily supported by good photographs that show cyclists (wearing helmets when riding). The story should give readers a sense of what it's like to cycle in the area (including terrain and weather), local color, expense, a dose of history, and solid information and contacts for planning a similar trip.

We generally avoid "road-map" stories, although detailed information about a classic route has a chance of acceptance. For an example, see "The Best Bike Tour in France" (April '94).

We favor adventure stories or articles that border on epics. These are often about places most of our readers will never ride but enjoy reading about. For an example, see "So Close to Infinity" (Dec. '94).

Length is 1,000 to 2,000 words. We encourage you to submit 35mm color slides of your tour, since photo availability often determines an article's potential to be printed.

Fitness and Training Articles. Most of these are written by our staff of expert cyclists. But we're always looking for good writers with a background in cycling physiology, sports medicine, nutrition, racing, or coaching. Tips for fast recreational riding, short-distance touring, racing for beginners, and endurance riding are the most popular topics. Submissions must be well substantiated by experience and research. We prefer stories accompanied by proven workouts, schedules, or training charts. Length is 750 to 1,250 words. For examples see "Training for Real People" (April '95), "Ultimate Fitness" (Jan. '95), and "The Caffeine Questions" (Jan. '94).

Riding Techniques. These how-to articles discuss efficiency and skill on the bike. Even when aimed at less-experienced riders, these stories must contain information that helps longtime cyclists fine-tune their ability. We also do advanced technique stories. Length is 1,000 to 1,250 words. For examples see any issue containing the columns Road Scholar or Dirt Degree, or "Singletrack U" (March '95).

Profiles and Interviews. Each year we publish 4-8 interviews with famous cyclists, coaches, or cycling personalities. These must

be "working" interviews filled with plenty of how-to information as well as color. Most of these are staff-written, but we're willing to look at submissions from writers who have access to someone our readers will be interested in and can learn from. Length is 1,200 to 2,000 words. For examples see "Jeanne Golay" (May '95), or "Trying to Find the One That Breaks Me" (June '95).

Advocacy, Political, or Cycling Issues. These important issues are often hard to report with liveliness because they involve so many legal details, and because there may be new developments before we publish the story. A story on the events or concerns of both road and off-road bicycle activism is worth national attention if it's precedent-setting or has some general-interest appeal. You should know the subject well enough to write with authority about the conclusions that can and can't be drawn from the issue. You may have to explain the importance of the issue for our readers. Length is 750 to 1,250 words. For examples see "Death of a Bike Shop" (Nov. '94), or "Good Company" (Dec. '94).

Personal Essays. We publish one "Off the Back" personal essay each issue. These are mainly staff-written. but the column is also open to freelance submissions. Acceptable essays tell humorous or thought-provoking stories based on the writer's riding experiences. Do not send "My First Bike," "My Worst Wreck." or other predictable topics. Length is 800 words. For examples, see "Off the Back" in any issue.

We also publish one *Women's Cycling* column in each issue. These freelance essays are written by famous riders, women involved in the cycling industry, and readers. Topics range from personal essays on cycling written from a female perspective to solid, how-to pieces. Length is 850 words. For examples, see Women's Cycling in any issue.

Short News Items. Our Bike Shorts department contains 50- to 500- word pieces on new technology, upcoming events, cycling games and activities, odd products, books, videos, art, tours, personalities, and other subjects. This section is an ideal place for a new writer to break in with the magazine. If you're in doubt your idea will work in Bike Shorts, read several issues.

Equipment Articles. This is handled in-house. We accept proposals from knowledgeable technical writers who have access to a laboratory or other testing equipment. Repair and maintenance features are handled by our staff.

Cycling Events. Bicycling is not a race magazine, but we cover major events such as the Tour de France, Tour DuPont, and mountain bike World Championships. These stories are written by our staff. Mass-participation rides such as the New York City Five-Boro Bike Tour might be mentioned in our Bike Shorts department.

Photography: Content: Exciting, inspiring photography is essential to us. All of our features and departments are illustrated with photographs (or illustrations). Riding photos should capture the energy and skill of cycling in a way that motivates readers to go out and ride. We like action shots of experienced cyclists. We prefer models to be real riders using up to date bikes, gear, and clothing—it doesn't need to be brand new but it should reflect current trends. An example would be no "cereal bowl" helmets. We strive to depict female and male cyclists of all races and age groups. Landscape photos with cyclists should leave our readers thinking: Wow, I would love to ride there.

Refer to writer's guidelines and a copies of *Bicycling* for more on content.

Technical Considerations: Most of our pictures are color but black and white photography receives equal consideration. We also consider computer or processing manipulated photos. There are no limitations on the type of film that can be submitted. There are many excellent professional films from Kodak, Fuji, Agfa, Ilford, etc. We rely on the photographer to pick a film that suits his/her purpose. If you need help, a professional camera shop can make recommendations based on what and how you will be shooting. Transparencies should be presented in easy to view plastic pages. Negatives must be accompanied by contact sheets (11"x14" preferred) or working prints.

Please Note: *Bicycling* requires a certain standard, poorly exposed photography is returned immediately.

Assignments: All product shooting and many feature stories and department photos are assigned by the Photography Director. In most cases, portfolios or samples are a prerequisite for receiving an assignment. Portfolios should be submitted with return "postage" via courier.

Stock: Stock submissions are welcome on a speculative basis. We encourage photographers to submit photos that meet our guidelines. Our stock rates are: 1/4 page $100.00, 1/2 page $125.00, full page $150.00, 2 page spread $300.00 and cover $500.00.

Submission Procedure: Photos should be securely packaged but do not over tape when sealing them up. Cutting through excess tape can damage material inside. We recommend that a courier be used. We use UPS with an acknowledgment of delivery (AOD) to return all photos. If we decide to hold photos you will be sent a tracking sheet that identifies the number we are holding and potential story uses. There is no need to call before sending. Once we receive your film, it will be handled by professionals who know how to take good care of it, but be advised that we will not be responsible for speculative submissions that are lost or damaged in transit. All photography is returned.

Note: We encourage you to provide caption information.

Covers: Most of our covers are assigned, but occasionally a cover will come from stock. The cover image(s) need to accommodate the logo and sell lines. If you are framing in a rectangular (35mm, 6x7, etc.) vertical format works best for a single image. Models should be skilled riders with cover charisma. See Tech. Considerations for gear and clothing specs.

Vista: "Vista" is our new photography feature. It is a two-page spread that opens the magazine. The theme of "Vista" is cycling that is rarely viewed. This section seeks to surprise, inform, amaze and/or delight our readers with a view of cycling that they have never seen before. We want the unusual cycling image worthy of a two page spread with *Bicycling*'s name affixed. We encourage photographers to keep this section in mind whenever they are shooting.

Graphics: The use, slant, and intended impact of editorial illustration is discussed with the editor, art director, and artist before sketches are begun. Several roughs are prepared by the artist to explore a variety of approaches to the article. Editorial illustration is often commissioned under tight deadline.

Payment is negotiated between the artist and art director and depends on several factors: the type of work required; the complexity of the illustration; the work's intended use; the artist's credentials.

Review issues of the magazine for content and to see whether your ideas and style are appropriate. Send us samples or tear sheets of your best work. All submitted work will be routed to Rodale Press's Sports Group art directors for review.

Categories: Nonfiction—Biking—Consumer—Health—Physical Fitness—Sports—Recreation—Travel—Technology—How-to—Nutrition—Humor

Name: Stan Zukowski, Managing Editor
Material: All
Address: 33 E. MINOR ST.
City/State/ZIP: EMMAUS, PA 18098
Telephone: 610-967-5171
Fax: 610-967-8960
E-mail: bicmag@aol.com
Internet: www.bicyclingmagazine.com

The Big Apple Parents' Paper
New York's Award Winning Parenting Magazine

Circulation:
Family Communications, Inc. publishes two monthly newspapers for New York City parents—the *Big Apple Parents' Paper* (circulation 62,000) and the *Queens Parents' Paper* (circulation 40,000).

Readership:
Readership for both papers ranges from expectant parents, to parents of children, newborn through teen.

Big Apple Parents' Paper: BAPP readers live in high-rise Manhattan apartments; it is an educated, upscale audience. Often both parents are working full-time in professional occupations. Child care help tends to be one-on-one, in the home. Kids attend private schools for the most part.

Queens Parents' Paper: While not quite a suburban approach, some of our QPP readers do have backyards (though most live in high-rise apartments). It is a more middle-class audience in Queens. More kids are in day care centers; majority of kids are in public schools.

Coverage:
We have a very local focus; our aim is to present articles our readers cannot find in national publications. To that end, news stories and human interest pieces must focus on New York and New Yorkers. Child-raising articles must include quotes from New York-based experts/sources. To work in QPP, we must have Queens sources.

Submissions:
We are happy to read queries or manuscripts. You do not have to write long, detailed cover letters. We don't require clips or other published work. Our bottom line is very simple: the piece will either work for us or it won't.

Simultaneous submissions are fine. Send us a disk if you wish (Mac or IBM), or at least tell us the piece is available on disk. If we buy it, we'll contact you to send us the disk.

Payment:
We pay $35-$50 per article, at the end of the month following publication. Kill rate fee on assigned articles is 50%. We will always send you a copy of the issue in which your article appears.

Photos are generally paid at the rate of $20 per.

We use reprints, and pay at the same rates as first-usage pieces.

Rights:
We buy first New York area rights, which revert automatically to the author upon publication. We reserve the right to publish an article in either or both the Manhattan and Queens editions; and online.

Sample issues:
Sample issue(s) available on request.

Our current needs:
We are always looking for news and newsy pieces; we keep on top of current events, frequently giving issues that may relate to parenting a local focus so that the idea will work for us as well.

What's new in family health and in education are areas that are always of interest to us.

We are *never* interested in ideas for regular columns.

Currently, we do not need: personal parenting essays, humor, cartoons, or family travel. And we never publish "filler."

Tips for freelancers:
Most of our publication(s) is freelance-written. While, like everyone else, we do have writers we use regularly, we are always open to using new people and to considering new ideas. Just make sure your idea/piece is directly targeted to *parents*.

Except for the summer months, we will reply to you in one to two weeks.

Categories: Men's Issues—Parenting—Women's Issues

Name: Submissions Editor
Material: All
Address: 36 E 12TH ST
City/State/ZIP: NEW YORK NY 10003
Telephone: 212-533-2277
Fax: 212-475-6186
E-mail: parentspaper@family.com

Big World Magazine

Big World began publishing bimonthly beginning in February, 1995 as a magazine for people who like their travel on the cheap and down-to-earth. And not necessarily because they have to—but because they want to. For people who prefer to spend their travelling time responsibly discovering, exploring, and learning, in touch with local people and their traditions, and in harmony with their environment.

Take a look at the fluffy travel mags in the bookstore. They're not what we're about. With no incessant cheerleading, no big-name advertisers, and no apologies for traveling on a budget, *Big World* is breezy, laid-back, intelligent, and active—just like our 3,000 readers.

Travel, after all, (to us, anyway) isn't about Intercontinental Hotels, $45 dinners, sight-seeing in an air-conditioned bus, or stuffy beach resorts. To us, travel is meeting people and learning new customs, exploring new environments, experiencing different ways of living, and finding adventure wherever you are (maybe only in the next town) in a responsible, down-to-earth way. Consider us somewhere between the excellent "Lonely Planet" and "Let's Go" guidebook philosophies.

Articles we're looking for would include laid-back, practical, how-to guides for the traveler, tips on getting the best transportation buys for the dollar, adventuring hints, or tales of a visit to an unusual, "off the beaten path" locale. Advice on working or studying overseas, humorous anecdotes, first-person experiences with unfamiliar cultures, or helpful travel resource informational pieces are also appreciated in any length from 500 to 4,000 words—more or less if need be.

Practical sidebars (best times to visit, extra reference material, etc.) are also very much appreciated. Style? Friendly, fresh and breezy. Laid back. Intelligent but not snooty. In a word, we want our readers to experience your destination the way you did. But how you do that is up to you. You may first want to send for a sample copy ($3) or subscribe ($14 for six issues) to see what other writers have done.

We don't care if you're a first-time writer or an old pro—as long as your story is factually correct, helpful to the potential traveler, and successfully captures the spirit or adventure or whimsy of travel, we would love to take a look at it. Submissions on 3.5" disc (DOS/Windows-readable, please) or paper are welcomed, and slides, photos, or illustration submissions are also encouraged but not at all necessary. Electronic submissions are especially welcome.

We will gladly accept previously-published articles, and all rights following publication remain with the author.

Payment is on publication, and frankly, it's pretty low. Big World is not a big operation and we can only pay between $10 and $25 (plus copies) for feature stories. If that doesn't scare you off, and you find yourself somewhat in agreement with our philosophy of travel, we would love to work with you.

Lastly, we're always open to your ideas and your suggestions. And thank you for your interest!

Categories: Nonfiction—Biking—Camping—Outdoors—Travel

Name: Jim Fortney, Editor
Material: All
Address: PO BOX 8743-F
City/State/ZIP: LANCASTER PA 17604
Fax: 717-569-0217
E-mail: Bigworld@paonline.com

Bike Magazine

Greetings and thanks for your interest in BIKE Magazine. What follows are our photographer's guidelines, but we'd also like to suggest that you refer to previous issues of BIKE or our sister publications—POWDER, SNOWBOARDER, and SURFER—for an idea of the type of photos we buy. In short, however, we'll tell you that we're looking for bold and exciting photography, images that capture the energy and passion of hard-core mountain biking.

As with POWDER, SNOWBOARDER, and SURFER, we are looking for expert action, scenics, exquisite light, and humor. We are looking for the people, places, and things that truly define the sport. Black & white, cross-processing, high grain, and any other creative approach is more than welcome. With your help, we intend to bring a fresh and inspiring publication to the world of mountain biking.

Guidelines

1. Put film in the camera.
2. Take the lens cap off.
3. Shoot everything and anything related to hard-core mountain biking. Shoot all riders, all conditions, all terrain, all weather. Try to capture the excitement, thrill, speed, and adventure of mountain biking. Try to say something about the sport.
4. Shoot things we don't see enough of: women riders, exciting singletrack, before and after riding, and anything that illustrates mountain bike culture.
5. Avoid the cliches of mountain biking, or at the very least present them in ways never seen: sunset silhouettes, pan blurs, strobed racing action in the woods, and grindy, thrashy air.
6. Avoid bad light. Even the prettiest scene—even Moab—can be rendered ugly by the harsh midday sun.
7. Shoot funny things, even if they're in bad taste. Especially if they're in bad taste.
8. Send 35mm originals or black & white prints by registered or certified mail.

Categories: Nonfiction—Adventure—Recreation

Name: Rob Story, Managing Editor
Material: All
Address: PO BOX 1028
City/State/ZIP: DANA POINT CA 92629
Fax: 714-496-7849
E-mail: Bikemag@aol.com

Birds & Blooms Magazine

Birds & Blooms is all about "beauty in your own backyard"—and our editorial matter reflects this life-style, with relaxed, conversational writing and top-quality photographs of birds, blooms and other backyard scenes. We showcase the beauty and detail of feathers and petals across North America and share insights from folks drawing on their personal experiences.

The magazine is full-color throughout, printed on high-quality coated paper, with an extra-heavy varnished cover. Published six times a year, it contains no paid advertising and is available primarily by subscription.

Each editorial and photographic sub-mission is reviewed thoroughly. The ideal time for freelance submissions is 4 months before the issue date. Unless a specific assignment is made, all freelance material will be considered on a speculative basis.

Photography: We welcome submissions. See separate Reiman Publications Photo Guidelines for payment schedule.

Features: We don't publish fiction—and we use very little poetry. Instead, we invite people to tell their own stories. We encourage our contributors to share personal observations and experiences with wild birds, flowers, gardening, landscaping, etc. Our goal is to present people enjoying the wonders of backyard living.

Payment, on acceptance, varies according to length, quality of photos, and amount of editing required to make it fit the format and style of *Birds & Blooms*. In most cases, payment is $100-200 per page published in the magazine, depending on length of the article.

"Backyard Banter" and other shorter articles: We also use shorter articles about people and backyards. Payment, upon acceptance, ranges from $75-$100, depending on length and quality.

We prefer transparencies for all color work (including photos submitted along with feature articles). Color prints are acceptable if they are of high quality. Be sure every image is identified for proper return.

Potential contributors are encouraged to obtain samples of *Birds & Blooms* to learn about our needs. With high production costs and our no-advertising policy—we're solely supported by subscriptions—we regret that we can't give away samples.

Issues are $2 plus a 9"x12" envelope with $1.93 in postage. Freelancers may subscribe at a special rate of $10.98 per year (regularly $16.98). Contributors receive a complimentary copy of the issue in which their work appears.

Categories: Animals—Family—Gardening—Hobbies

Name: Jeff Nowak, Managing Editor
Material: All
Address: 5925 COUNTRY LN
City/State/ZIP: GREENDALE WI 53129

BPR

Birmingham Poetry Review
University of Alabama—Birmingham

Birmingham Poetry Review publishes poetry of any length (within reason), form, style, or subject matter. We subscribe to no trend or school and look for quality work from both new and established poets. We do not play favorites. It's great to print work by someone we've heard of before, but even better to come across good work by a new voice. Our goal is to print the best we receive, regardless of whether it comes from local, regional, national, or international writers.

No more than five poems per submission, please, with SASE. No cover letters. Poet's name and address should appear on each page. Poetry only, no reviews or articles. We prefer not to receive photocopies and will not consider simultaneous or multiple submissions. We do consider translations.

Sample copies are $2.00.

Subscriptions are $4.00 for one year, $7.00 for two. BPR welcomes patrons, who, for a tax-deductible minimum of $10.00 receive a two-year subscription and are listed on our patrons' page, which appears in every issue.

Categories: Poetry

Name: Robert Collins, Editor
Material: Any
Name: Randy Blythe, Editor
Material: Any
Address: ENGLISH DEPARTMENT
Address: UNIVERSITY OF ALABAMA—BIRMINGHAM
City/State/ZIP: BIRMINGHAM AL 35294
Telephone: 205-934-4250

Birth Gazette

BIRTH GAZETTE is a quarterly magazine for midwives, physicians, nurses, childbirth educators, interested parents and policy makers. BIRTH GAZETTE had its beginning at a national midwifery conference in 1977, starting out as an eight page newsletter entitled THE PRACTICING MIDWIFE. It's aim was, and is, to facilitate the reawakening of midwifery, and to promote safe and healthy care for mothers and babies.

Since 1977, THE PRACTICING MIDWIFE/BIRTH GAZETTE has served a new and growing network of people who wish to safeguard the birth process by promoting midwifery and sensible birthing practices in a society which tends to worship high technology even when there are better routes available.

Articles must be computer [printed] or typewritten. Articles can be anywhere from 700 to 3,500 words. Include your name, address and telephone number on the first page of your article.

Please include a short biographical statement along with submissions of full length articles. You may use a pen-name or be anonymous if you wish.

THE BIRTH GAZETTE is published in January, April, July, and October. Submissions should be made two months before publication dates. Authors of full-length articles will receive [a] one year subscription as payment for their work.

We are looking for articles which fit the following categories:

INTERVIEWS WITH FASCINATING MIDWIVES. Each issue of BIRTH GAZETTE features a contemporary midwife. Sometimes she is a practicing midwife, but sometimes she is noteworthy because she is not able to practice, despite her training and other qualifications. We need 3"x5" or 5"x7" photos, with captions, and identification of those pictured. Black and white photos are best but good clear color photos are fine too. If other people than yourself are pictured, we need a signed release giving us permission to reprint the photo. Send along a self addressed stamped envelope if you want photos returned.

YOUR OPINION. Here is your chance to register your opinion on any subject relating to childbirth. You may have strong ideas about licensing vs. certification of midwives or about legislative or public relations strategies. If you are brief, your opinions will be printed in the regular feature, "Your Letters." If your submission is 750-1,000 words, it may be published as a full-length article.

MIDWIFERY LORE. This feature includes articles which focus on the type of knowledge that has largely been ignored by the medical establishment of the twentieth century. Here we are interested in ways you have found to help mothers having difficult labors, to prevent lacerations or cesareans, to deal with shoulder dystocia, to help fathers know what to do during pregnancy and labor—all the skills and knowledge that are invaluable but not widely known.

PEOPLE WHO DON'T CARE. Unfortunately in the U.S. of the 1980s, there is a growing number of people who "fall between the cracks " of the U.S. healthcare system. We feel that it is one of our obligations to document who and where these people are, in order that we may help to find ways that such families may find better treatment in our society. Articles dealing with such issues must be adequately researched and documented to fit our editorial standards.

MIDWIFERY ABROAD. We are interested in what is going on with midwifery at regional, state, provincial, national and international levels. Let us know if you have legislation pending in your state which needs national support. Maybe your state association did something remarkable lately. Send us a paragraph or two on what is happening in your area. We especially want to know about incidents of arrests or harassment. Not only that, we want to hear about new practices, new birth centers or good publicity you've gotten.

ABSTRACTS. Several of our readers have requested that we include abstracts of scientific articles which relate to childbirth in some way. Abstracts are synopses of full length articles. If you contribute abstracts, please give accurate information as to source, original publication date and author.

CASE HISTORIES. We are interested in publishing case histories of births which can teach something. For instance, those of us who serve women who are usually considered too young or too old for natural childbirth may have some important experience to share with our colleagues who serve a more restricted group of women. Be sure to include all information pertinent to the mother whose childbirth you describe, including age, parity, number of previous births, miscarriages and abortions. Write down everything that you are trying to teach. Use a fictitious name for mother. We are particularly interested in anything you might have learned along the way.

WHAT WOULD YOU DO? This feature presents a situation that might occur in pregnancy or in labor and asks our subscribers to submit essays on what they would have done if faced with that situation in real life. Maybe you dealt with a problem in a certain way and later wondered if you did the right thing. Write up the situation and see what our other readers have to say about what they would have done.

BOOKS, VIDEOS, AND FILM REVIEWS. We welcome your reviews of written, videotaped or filmed materials which pertain to pregnancy, childbirth or breastfeeding. Because there is now so much material of this kind available, our readers have come to appreciate intelligent reviews of works which you have found especially helpful or significant. Be sure to include title, author, publisher, price, and publication date for books, and title, producer or distributor, length, and price of videos or films.

PHOTOS AND ARTWORK. We are interested in photos, cartoons, poems, humor and artwork. Photos should be 3"x5" or 5"x7" and black and white or clear color with good contrast. Other work should be done in black ink on white paper. Get written permission if you submit something that is other than your own work. We need written releases from the subjects of all photographs, so please provide these.

Thank you and we are looking forward to hearing from you.

Categories: Nonfiction—African-American—Asian-American—Cartoons—Diet—Education—Family—Health—Hispanic—Humor—Lifestyles—Midwifery—Midwives—Native American—Nursing—Sexuality—Women's Issues

Name: Ina May Gaskin, Editor

Material: Midwifery and Childcare
Name: Pamela Hunt, Assistant Editor
Material: Midwifery and Childcare
Address: 42 THE FARM
City/State/ZIP: SUMMERTOWN TN 38483
Telephone: 615-964-3798
Fax: 615-964-3798

The Birthkit

Please refer to *Midwifery Today*.

Black Belt

Publishers of *Black Belt*, *Karate/Kung Fu Illustrated* and *M.A. Training* Magazines

Thank you for your interest in writing for *Black Belt*, the oldest martial arts publications in the United States. The magazine's subjects include martial arts styles and techniques, training methods, historical pieces, health and fitness articles, and interviews with prominent martial artists.

Before mailing a completed manuscript to BB, we advise you to send a query letter. It will save your time and ours. Describe your proposed article, including a sample lead or story outline. If the subject attracts our interest and has not been covered too recently, we may request to see the article on a speculation basis. *Please enclose a self-addressed stamped envelope if you want your materials returned.*

Articles must address an area of specific interest or concern for the serious martial artist. The vast majority are educational; they either teach technical and strategic skills, or enlighten the reader interest with a strong lead, then hold it with information that is exact, concrete and focused around a strong central theme. All quotes and anecdotes should pertain to that theme.

BB seldom uses first-person accounts, because most are of interest only to the author and his or her friends. In addition, while many instructors are dedicated and high-ranking, the magazine rarely requests personality profiles. (If you do choose to write about an individual, your article should prove that your subject is unique or particularly significant.) Remember: if you have a chance to meet or train with a great martial artist and want to write an article afterward, discuss what that person knows rather than how his or her life has unfolded.

All statements and quotes must be accurate and verifiable. Use authoritative sources and cross-check your information. Be certain of all spellings—especially names and foreign words—and define foreign terms in parentheses after first usage only.

Manuscripts should be 1,000 to 3,000 words long, typed and double-spaced. If you use a computer, please output to a laser or ink jet printer. Because we electronically scan freelance submissions, we require quality printouts. Please include black-and-white lead and technique photos *and negatives* with plain, contrasting backgrounds. If absolutely necessary, we can use color photographs with sharp contrast and high definition. Feature articles receive $150 to $200, and we pay upon publication. Simultaneous or previously published submissions must be identified as such.

Categories: Martial Arts

Name: Robert Young, Executive Editor
Material: All
Address: Rainbow Pubications, Inc.
 24715 Ave. Rockefeller, P.O. Box 918,
City/State/ZIP: Santa Clarita, California 91380-9018
Telephone: 805- 257-4066
Fax: 805-257-3028

Black Child

Please refer to Interrace Publications.
Categories: Nonfiction—African-American—Children—Ethnic—Family—Parenting

Name: Candy Mills, Editor
Material: All
Address: PO BOX 12048
City/State/ZIP: ATLANTA GA 30355
Telephone: 404-350-7877
Fax: 404-350-0819

Black Lace

Black Lace is a lifestyle magazine for African-American lesbians. Published quarterly, its content ranges from erotic imagery to political commentary. About 60 to 80 percent of the magazine is freelance-written. Every year we utilize 10-25 full-length articles.

Subjects

The best way to determine our needs is to read and study several recent issues.

Here is a partial list of our needs:

• Full-length erotic fiction of 2,000-4,000 words detailing the exploits of black lesbians.

• Politically-focused articles on lesbians and the African-American community as a whole.

• Nostalgia and humor pieces are welcome if they are black, lesbian and erotic. We also publish historical articles and first-person accounts that meet these criteria.

• Where-to articles that include details on where black lesbians congregate. These can range from the latest local bar to out-of-the-way resorts. Thoroughness and accuracy are the keys to acceptance of these articles.

• Shorts. We use articles of 400 to 700 words with one to two photos for one-pagers. Subjects include fresh, sharply focused erotic ideas.

• We publish several poems in each issue.

• We do not solicit product reviews, games or puzzles.

• Subjects considered inappropriate include stories which refer to minors, illegal drugs, bestiality, water sports and scat.

Black Lace seeks erotic material of the highest quality, but it need not be written by professional writers. The most important thing is that the work be erotic and that it feature black lesbians or themes. We are not interested in stories that demean black lesbians or place them in stereotypical situations.

Erotic fiction can range from descriptions of idealized women having idealized sex, to depictions of typical women in plausible encounters, to unconsummated hints at sex. We are partial to the latter two categories.

We want to publish concise, well-organized articles, so material must be tightly written. We reserve the right to edit submissions and to change titles as necessary.

Study the magazine to see what we do and how we do it.

Some fiction is very romantic, other is highly sexual.

Most articles in *Black Lace* cater to black lesbians between these two extremes.

Articles should be typewritten with at least 1½" margins on all sides of each page. Such pages contain about 250 words. Most material we publish is 250 to 3,000 words.

Include your name and address on the title page as well as your pseudonym, if you intend to use one.

We encourage contributors to send their submissions on floppy disk in either IBM-compatible or Macintosh format. (Be sure to send hard copy as well.) Indicate which program was used; we can read most. *Black Lace* is also available via modem. Contact us for information.

Deadlines

Submit seasonal material six months in advance. For instance, a piece about Kwanzaa in December must be received in June, and an April piece about Easter must be in our hands in October.

We prefer queries to completed manuscripts, but completed manuscripts are also welcomed, especially for material of 1,000 words or less. In this way we can better plan issues and avoid duplication of authors' ideas. Articles written from queries stand a better chance of acceptance than unsolicited manuscripts. Query at least eight months in advance.

Payment and Rights

If your work is accepted, we secure first rights and the right to anthologize. If the material you are submitting has appeared elsewhere, tell us when you submit it.

You will receive two copies of the issue in which your work appears as payment.

Acceptance is by letter. After a manuscript or illustration has been accepted, the author must provide a written statement attesting that the work has not been previously published and that it is not under consideration by any other publication.

If the work you submit to us is being submitted to others as well, please let us know.

Correspondence

All materials—queries, manuscripts, and artwork—are reviewed on speculation. When you submit anything to *Black Lace*, please include a self-addressed, stamped envelope. We report on queries within two weeks, and on manuscripts in four to six weeks.

These are guidelines, not a contract, and they are subject to change without notice.

One final word. Because you're reading these guidelines, you're one step closer to having us accept your work than are many others. We want to hear from you by way of a tantalizing query, a top-notch completed manuscript, or an article we can't resist featuring on the cover. Every year we work with a few unpublished writers, and in our pages you can also find the bylines and credits of established professionals. To us it doesn't matter if you're a pro or a novice—if the material meets our needs and standards, we use it.

Categories: African-American—Gay/Lesbian

Name: Submissions Editor
Material: All
Address: PO BOX 83912
City/State/ZIP: LOS ANGELES CA 90083-0912
Telephone: 310-410-0808
Fax: 310-410-9250
E-mail: newsroom@blk.com
Internet: www.blk.com

Black Mountain Review
"American Authors"

Articles should be well-researched and footnoted, with a bibliography. Length 500-2,000 words. Payment is 1¢ per word plus 2 copies.

Fiction must relate to the author/theme, and can be on the author's life, writing style, or similar work. Typical length is 500-1,500 words. Payment is 1¢ per word plus 2 copies.

Poetry must be on the author/theme. Length and style are open. Payment is 2¢ per word plus 2 copies.

Art and photos are welcome, and some payment will be made, plus copies.

Literary classifieds are at 10¢ per word, for books, periodicals & related services. BMR reserves the right to refuse inappropriate ads.

Categories: Fiction—Nonfiction—Literature—Poetry

Name: David A. Wilson, Editor
Material: All
Address: PO BOX 1112
City/State/ZIP: BLACK MOUNTAIN NC 28711-1112

Blackfire

Blackfire, published bimonthly, features the erotic images, experiences and fantasies of black gay and bisexual men. About 60 to 80 percent of the magazine is freelance-written. Every year we utilize 30-50 full-length articles.

Subjects

The best way to determine our needs is to read and study several recent issues.

Here is a partial list of our needs:

• Full-length erotic fiction of 2,000-4,000 words detailing the exploits of black gay men.

• Parody articles in the style of well-known writings for "Fantasy Re-Rights of History." These add black gay men (and erotica) to situations where they were originally absent.

• Nostalgia and humor pieces are welcome if they are black, gay and erotic. We also publish historical articles and first-person accounts that meet these criteria.

• Where-to articles that include details on where black gay men congregate. These can range from the latest local bar to out-of-the-way resorts. Thoroughness and accuracy are the keys to acceptance of these articles.

• Shorts. We use articles of 400 to 700 words with one to two photos for one-pagers. Subjects include fresh, sharply focused erotic ideas.

• We publish several poems in each issue.

• We do not solicit product reviews, games or puzzles.

• Subjects considered inappropriate include stories which refer to minors, illegal drugs, bestiality, water sports and scat.

Writing Style

Blackfire seeks erotic material of the highest quality, but it need not be written by professional writers. The most important thing is that the work be erotic and that it feature black gay men or themes. We are not interested in stories that demean black men or place them in stereotypical situations.

Erotic fiction can range from descriptions of idealized men having idealized sex to depictions of typical men in plausible encounters to unconsummated hints at sex. We are partial to the latter two categories.

We want to publish concise, well-organized articles, so material must be tightly written. We reserve the right to edit submissions and to change titles as necessary.

Study the magazine to see what we do and how we do it. Some fiction is very romantic, other is highly sexual. Most articles in *Blackfire* cater to black gay men between these two extremes.

Articles should be typewritten with at least 1½" margins on all sides of each page. Such pages contain about 250 words. Most material we publish is 250 to 3,000 words.

Include your name and address on the title page as well as your pseudonym, if you intend to use one.

We encourage contributors to send their submissions on floppy disk in either IBM-compatible or Macintosh format. (Be sure to send hard copy as well.) Indicate which program was used; we can read most. *Blackfire* is also available via modem. Contact us for information.

Deadlines

Submit seasonal material six months in advance. For instance, a piece about Kwanzaa in December must be received in June, and an April piece about Easter must be in our hands in October.

We prefer queries to completed manuscripts, but completed manuscripts are also welcomed, especially for material of 1,000 words or less. In this way we can better plan issues and avoid duplication of authors' ideas. Articles written from queries stand a better chance of acceptance than unsolicited manuscripts. Query at least eight months in advance.

Written queries are welcome, and can be sent by fax.

Payment and Rights

Rights purchased vary. For most material we prefer to buy first rights and the right to anthologize. If the material you're submitting has appeared elsewhere, tell us when you submit it. Payment for articles varies from $20 to $100. This payment is based on quality of the material, research required to complete the piece, length of the copy, and how badly we want the story.

Be sure to include your social security number with your manuscript or photo submission.

Acceptance is by letter. After a manuscript has been accepted, the author must provide an invoice stating the title of the story, the author's name, address, social security number and amount stipulated, along with a written statement attesting that the story or article has not been previously published and that it is not under consideration by any other publication. Payment is made approximately 30 days after the issue is released.

If the work you submit to us is being submitted to others as well, please let us know.

Correspondence

All materials—queries, manuscripts, and artwork—are reviewed on speculation. When you submit anything to *Blackfire*, please include a self-addressed, stamped envelope. We report on queries within two weeks, and on manuscripts in four to six weeks.

These are guidelines, not a contract, and they are subject to change without notice.

One final word. Because you're reading these guidelines, you're one step closer to having us accept your work than are many others. We want to hear from you by way of a tantalizing query, a top-notch completed manuscript, or a article we can't resist featuring on the cover. Every year we work with a few unpublished writers, and in our pages you can also find the bylines and credits of established professionals. To us it doesn't matter if you're a pro or a novice—if the material meets our needs and standards, we use it.

Categories: African-American—Gay/Lesbian

Name: Submissions Editor
Material: All
Address: PO BOX 83912
City/State/ZIP: LOS ANGELES CA 90083-0912
Telephone: 310-410-0808
Fax: 310-410—9250
E-mail: newsroom@blk.com
Internet: www.blk.com

bleach

Bleach Magazine

Briefs:
(short points of interest; products, oddities, etc.) 80-150
Upfronts:
(short features including celebrity interviews/short essays)
600-1,200
Fiction:
(Writers are given carte blanche but should keep in mind young, alternative audience) 1,500-2,000
Feature Stories:
(cover stories and researched pieces) 1,200-1,800
Word & Image:
(short poetic observation pieces) 40-150
Video Reviews:
(4-6 videos) 80-120 per
CD Reviews:
80-120 per
Music Q&As:
800-1,000
Music Features:
1,100-1,500
Unsigned Bands:
(Interviews with bands who have yet to get signed) 800-1,000
• No story/article shall be printed in any other publication within six months time of *Bleach*'s publishing.
• Entertainment-related pieces should have a largely independent slant.
• All copy should be saved as a "text only" file.
• Story ideas should first be pitched to editors by way of fax, mail or e-mail.
Categories: Arts—Comedy—Entertainment—Film/Video—Humor—Interview—Lifestyles—Literature—Music—Photography—Short Stories—Travel—Writing—Young Adult

Name: Dave Carpenter, Senior Editor
Material: All Editorial
Name: Alex Leon, Jr., Music Editor
Material: Music Editorial
Address: 2060 PLACENTIA AVE STE C3
City/State/ZIP: COSTA MESA CA 92627
Telephone: 714-574-7500
Fax: 714-574-7980
Internet: bleachmagazine.net

BLK

BLK is the national magazine of the black lesbian and gay community. Issued monthly in traditional newsmagazine format, it includes dispatches and information from across the nation organized by category. Because of its breadth, BLK has become the black lesbian and gay community's publication of record. About 50 percent of the magazine is freelance-written. Every year we utilize articles varying from several paragraphs to full length features.

Subjects
The best way to determine our needs is to read and study several recent issues. BLK does not publish fiction or poetry.

News
Our first priority is *news* (just the facts, ma'am) of interest to the community. This can be advance word of things about to happen or reports on things that have already happened.

We are interested in news as modest as the election of officers of a local black gay organization, or as significant as a national demonstration. And if you can secure photographs, all the better.

A number of people keep us informed on news events by simply sending us clippings from their local gay or straight newspapers. That's perfectly appropriate. If you do this, be sure to let us know the name of the publication in which the article appeared and the date it ran.

Features
We are interested in *fact-based* features and personality pieces. Although we are less interested in "editorials" per se (someone's opinion on some subject), we are extremely interested in comprehensive pieces which include and analyze the dominant thinking on some subject before coming to a conclusion, making or proposal or stating a proposition. Although BLK has no editorial page, we do publish short non-fact-based opinion pieces commenting on something that has appeared in BLK as non-paid "letters to the editor." Currently, BLK has no place for long opinion pieces except as they are fully researched, fact-based articles as described above.

Arts
Subjects covered in our arts section include movies, books, television, dance, music, art, photography and theater. BLK runs two kinds of stories in this section: reviews which are evaluative and offer opinion; and background or news pieces provide information about a cultural event or personality. All of these pieces tend to be short. Longer pieces become features, as described above.

Reviews: It is not enough simply to have an opinion for a review to be accepted into the pages of BLK. It must be an informed opinion. The writer must demonstrate sufficient knowledge of the subject matter to provide a perceptive evaluation. That doesn't mean we require a college degree in dance to be a dance critic. But it does mean that simply saying "I liked it," "I didn't like it," "It was powerful and moving" isn't sufficient. We need to know *why* it was "powerful and moving." If it was "the best you've seen" we need to know that you've seen enough to make that statement.

Although some categories such as movies and music are covered by regular critics, we will occasionally run reviews by other persons if the regular reviewer in that category declines to offer a piece. Other categories such as books regularly require many reviews from a variety of reviewers.

Unsolicited reviews of a specific work are not accepted.

Background or news: Stories in this category are much like news except for the subject matter. We also run regular columns which are compilations of short news items.

Images
As words are important, so are images. BLK can use illustrators, graphics artists and photographers to bring a writer's words to life, or to portray what words cannot do.

BLK also needs female and male models in various age ranges and body types.

Writing Style
Although BLK seeks material of the highest quality, it need not be written by professional writers. The most important thing is that the work be written according to traditional journalistic standards and that it have the black lesbian or gay community as its theme or subject.

As we want to publish concise, well-organized articles, the material must be tightly written. We reserve the right to edit submissions and to change titles as necessary.

Articles should be typewritten with at least 1¼" margins on all sides of each page. Such pages contain about 250 words. Most material we publish is 250 to 3,000 words.

Include your name and address on the title page as well as your pseudonym, if you intend to use one.

We encourage contributors to send their submissions on floppy disk in either IBM-compatible or Macintosh format. (Be sure to send hard copy as well.) Indicate which program was used; we can read most. You can also e-mail us your submissions.

Deadlines

Submit seasonal material three months in advance. For instance, a piece about Kwanzaa in December must be received in September, and an April piece about Easter must be in our hands in January.

If you're not sure an idea (or your approach to an idea) is appropriate for BLK, contact us outlining what you have in mind. Articles written from queries stand a better chance of acceptance than unsolicited manuscripts. Also, feel free to submit story ideas to us even if you have no interest in doing the piece. Or tell us of interesting people you think are appropriate for profiles or the "BLK Interview."

If your work is accepted, we secure first rights and the right to anthologize. If the material you are submitting has appeared elsewhere, tell us when you submit it.

You will receive two copies of the issue in which your work appears as payment.

Acceptance is by letter. After a manuscript or illustration has been accepted, the author must provide a written statement attesting that the work has not been previously published and that it is not under consideration by any other publication.

Correspondence

All materials—queries, manuscripts, and artwork—are reviewed on speculation. When you submit anything to BLK, please include a self-addressed, stamped envelope. We report on queries within two weeks, and on manuscripts in four to six weeks.

These are guidelines, not a contract, and they are subject to change without notice.

One final word. Because you're reading these guidelines, you're one step closer to having us accept your work than are many others. We want to hear from you by way of a tantalizing query, a top-notch completed manuscript, or a article we can't resist featuring on the cover. Every year we work with a few unpublished writers, and in our pages you can also find the bylines and credits of established professionals. To us it doesn't matter if you're a pro or a novice—if the material meets our needs and standards, we use it.

Categories: African-American—Gay/Lesbian

Name: Submissions Editor
Material: All
Address: PO BOX 83912
City/State/ZIP: LOS ANGELES CA 90083-0912
Telephone: 310-410-0808
Fax: 310-410-9250
E-mail: newsroom@blk.com
Internet: www.blk.com

BlueRidge Country

BLUE RIDGE COUNTRY is a bimonthly, full-color magazine embracing the feel and the spirit of the Blue Ridge region—the traditions and recipes, the outdoor recreation and travel opportunities, the country stores and bed-and-breakfast inns, the things to visit and learn about. In short, it is everything that will allow and encourage the reader to "take a trip home for the weekend" even if he or she has never lived in the region.

Our territory extends from Western Maryland south through Virginia's Shenandoah Valley of Virginia down into northern Georgia and including all territory within about a half day's drive of the parkway. It includes the mountain regions of Virginia, North Carolina, West Virginia, Tennessee, Maryland, Georgia, South Carolina, and Kentucky.

MAIN PIECES (750 - 2,000 WORDS)
PLACES

Everything there is to find out and tell about a great Blue Ridge town, city, or locale. The history, the current economic status, the quaint spots and characters, the best places to eat. A profile so complete our readers can make hard decisions on going to spend a weekend or even moving there.

HISTORY & LEGENDS

From people and events to unexplained occurrences or phenomena, the magazine prints fascinating tales of past and present.

THE BLUE RIDGE PARKWAY AND THE APPALACHIAN TRAIL

There's a wealth of wildlife, beauty, history and future plans involving the parkway and the trail and the areas immediately surrounding each. We bring our readers a new piece of America's favorite scenes highway and favorite footpath in each issue.

GENERAL ARTICLES

Anything that is well-researched, well-written and brings us some of the flavor of the region will get strong consideration. We'll be looking for at-home kinds of things—recipes and craft articles, natural history and wildlife, and especially pieces that embrace the whole of the region. Plus humor, first-person adventure or discovery and the "bests" of the region.

DEPARTMENTS

Very much like the main pieces, but in shorter versions; places to see, things to do, recipes to try, great people doing great things, new books, etc.—anything and everything that contributes to the sense of the place.

RIGHTS

We buy exclusive first North American serial rights until the off-sale date of the issue in which material is published, as well as exclusive rights to the work for promotional and reprint use.

PAY

We pay from $25 (for department shorts) up to about $250 for major pieces. Payment is upon publication. Manuscripts not supplied on disk are paid 20% under the above rates.

Sample copies of the magazine are available. Send $3.00 and a magazine-size SASE.

PHOTOGRAPHY

We use primarily color slides, and pay $25 to $50 for exclusive first North American serial rights until the off-sale date of the issue in which material is published, as well as exclusive rights to the work for promotional and reprint use.

Categories: Consumer, General Interest, Outdoors, Regional, Travel

Name: Editor
Material: All
Address: P.O. Box 21535
City/State/ZIP: Roanoke, VA 24018
Telephone: (540) 989-6138

BorderLines

BorderLines

BorderLines is a monthly bulletin devoted to the progressive, bi-national analysis of issues and themes related to the U.S.-Mexico border area. We require that articles, no matter what the topic, be relevant to the border region, however, in certain cases (as in the case of cross-border labor organizing, for example) geographic boundaries can blur or disappear. Our special emphasis is environmental issues, but we welcome stories about labor issues, human rights, immigration, politics, economic alternatives, NAFTA, sustainable development, international solidarity, narcotrafficking, indigenous cultures, cultural interplay, etc. We also review books related to these themes.

Part of *BorderLines'* mission is to bridge the gaps which so often exist between activists, academics, and officials. If asked, we'd place ourselves on the activist side of most issues, but sincerely believe dialogue between different sectors can generate the best solutions to many borderlands problems. Accordingly, articles that not only chronicle problems but offer solutions are especially welcome, as are those which focus on the positive side of the borderland's multicultural, multifaceted reality.

We're hoping to widen our contact with Mexican, Latino, and Native American writers. Average story length is 1,200 words, although we can go longer in certain circumstances.

Subscriptions

BorderLines, published monthly (11 times per year), is available to individuals and institutions in the U.S. for $20/year. Outside the U.S., subscriptions are $25/year. Back issues are available for $3/copy.

Categories: Nonfiction—Border Issues—Conservation—Culture—Development—Ecology—Economics—Education—Environment—Ethnic—Feminism—Government—Health—Hispanic—Labor—Latino Issues—Law Enforcement—Maquiladora—Mexico—Multicultural—Native American—Politics—Regional

Name: George Kourous, Editor
Material: All
Address: PO BOX 2178
City/State/ZIP: SILVER CITY NM 88062
Telephone: 505-388-0802
Fax: 505-388-0619
E-mail: irc1@zianet.com

The Boston Review
Massachusetts Institute of Technology

Boston Review is a bimonthly magazine of cultural and political analysis, reviews, fiction, and poetry. The editors are committed to a society and culture that foster human diversity and a democracy in which we seek common grounds of principle amidst our many differences. In the hope of advancing these ideals, the *Review* acts as a forum that seeks to enrich the language of public debate.

The best way to get a sense of the kind of material the *Review* is looking for is to read the magazine (sample copies are available for $4.50). Recent issues have featured articles by Stephen Lerner on rebuilding American unions, Sven Birkerts on the decline of reading, and Atilio Boron on prospects for Latin American democracy. Also poetry by Robert Pinsky, Charles Simic, and Jorie Graham, fiction by Tom Paine, Patricia Traxler, and Elizabeth Graver, and criticism by Richard Howard, Raphael Campo, and Marjorie Perloff.

FICTION: From Jodi Daynard, fiction editor: "I'm looking for stories that are emotionally and intellectually substantive and also interesting on the level of language. Things that are shocking, dark, lewd, comic, or even insane are fine so long as the fiction is *controlled* and purposeful in a masterly way. Subtlety, delicacy and lyricism are attractive too." Work should be polished—clearly revised, grammatical, proofread. Length should be no less than 1,200 and no more than 5,000 words.

NONFICTION: Please query with clips before devoting time to an article or essay. Also realize that the editors plan issues well in advance, and the Review's bimonthly publication schedule often cannot accommodate topical or especially timebound material.

REVIEWS: We do not accept unsolicited book reviews: if you would like to be considered for review assignments, please send your resume along with several published clips.

GENERAL: *Boston Review* acquires first serial rights on accepted pieces; copyright reverts to the author after publication. We do not consider previously published material. Simultaneous submissions are fine as long as we are notified of the fact; however, we do not accept electronic submissions. Payment varies. Response time is generally 6-8 weeks. A self-addressed stamped envelope must accompany all submissions.

Thank you for your interest in *Boston Review*.

Categories: Fiction—Nonfiction—Arts—Economics—General Interest—Law—Literature—Poetry—Politics—Public Policy—Short Stories—Writing

Name: Jodi Daynard, Fiction Editor
Material: Short Stories
Name: Mary Jo Bang, Poetry Editor
Material: Poetry
Name: Matthew Howard, Managing Editor
Material: Nonfiction Submissions
Address: E53-407; MIT
Address: 30 WADSWORTH ST
City/State/ZIP: CAMBRIDGE MA 02139
Telephone: 617-253-3642
Fax: 617-252-1549
E-mail: bostonreview@mit.edu

Bowling Magazine

When making submissions to *Bowling Magazine*, please follow these general guidelines. These general policies will greatly assist us in editing, filing and following up on any matters related to your submission:

MANUSCRIPTS

1. Leave at least two-inch margins on both sides of your copy.

2. Number each page at the top.

3. On your first page, start typing 3-4 inches from the top of the page. Include the following in order:

a. HEADLINE: your suggested headline.

b. SUBHEADLINE: directly below major headline, a very brief subheading related to your story.

c. BYLINE: By _____(your credit line, typed in upper\lower case)

d. Start your copy.

4. On each subsequent page, include a "slug name" in the upper left-hand corner with page number in upper-right hand corner.

5. At the close of your story, double-double space and then include an "editor's note" explaining who you are. Example: Editor's note—Joe Smith is a sportswriter with the *Argon Daily News.*

6. Finally, at the bottom of the final page, include your mailing address, a telephone number where you normally reached during weekday business hours, and your social security number.

PHOTOGRAPHS

1. B&W: 5"x7" or 8"x10" photos are acceptable.

2. Color: 35mm or larger transparencies, or 5"x7" or 8"x10" color prints are acceptable (note: for specific assignments, color print negatives may be submitted and we will make prints if detailed caption/photo identifications are included with film). NOTE: *Our preference is color negative film* in all cases unless specifically agreed upon otherwise. We are better able to archive negatives and make additional prints when situations arise.

3. QUALITY IS CRITICAL: *Bowling Magazine* is striving for the highest quality graphics possible, in content as well as in color accuracy and detail.

4. DARE TO BE DIFFERENT: Make certain you first cover the subject matter using traditional journalistic values, but then try something new or different or unique. Our artists are exceptional; we have no fear of trying something different if it works…

5. PRINTS (color or B&W):

a. Either attach a photo caption to each print, or write a "code" on each print to accompany a corresponding sheet of captions so we can clearly identify photos.

b. Send prints in an envelope stiffly backed with cardboard and marked "photos" on the front, to protect from shipping damage.

6. COLOR TRANSPARENCIES:

a. Ship all slide/transparencies in plastic sleeves so they are fully protected (in sheet-style holders preferred; please do not ship transparencies loose in plastic boxes!)

b. Make certain every slide is identified with a code or number. If possible, write your last name (at least) on the slide border in permanent ink.

c. Include a complete caption sheet with slides, corresponding to number, or code on each slide.

7. Include with all photos a separate cover letter including your name, mailing address, a telephone number where you can normally be reached during weekday business hours, and your social security number.

ORIGINAL ARTWORK

Inquire first. We almost never purchase unsolicited, unassigned art work. We do not publish cartoons. Otherwise, follow guidelines under "Photographs" when making submissions.

GENERAL FREELANCE SUBMISSION POLICIES

1. *Bowling Magazine* pays upon acceptance of submissions. You will normally receive payment within 14 days of the acceptance of your materials.

2. Rates paid for written or photographic submissions vary depending upon the nature of the subject, its importance, quality and other factors.

3. All photographs submitted to, and paid for by, *Bowling Magazine* for assigned stories or features become the property of the American Bowling Congress and will not be returned un-less specific agreement has been reached regarding the return of unused/unpublished materials.

4. Submission deadlines for assigned stories/photos will be rigidly enforced. Failure to meet deadlines may result in the cancellation of publication of the assigned materials.

5. *Bowling Magazine* retains the full and complete right to edit manuscripts for style, accuracy, length and (if necessary) content and context. We will assume you accept that policy when you submit materials.

6. Manuscripts may be submitted on 3.5" floppy disk in DOS formats: Word, WordPerfect or ASCII, accompanied by a hard copy of the material in case there is a problem.

Categories: Bowling—Recreation—Sports

Name: Bill Vint, Editor
Material: All
Address: 5301 S 76TH ST
City/State/ZIP: GREENDALE WI 53129
Telephone: 414-423-3232
Fax: 414-421-7977

Boxoffice Magazine
The Business Magazine of the Motion Picture Industry

Articles run 700-3,000 words and relate directly to the film industry as a business. Our readers are executives in the exhibition, distribution and allied industries. Query first; pay is 10¢ per word.

Categories: Nonfiction—Entertainment—Film/Video—Film Exhibition and Distribution

Name: Ray Greene, Editor-in-Chief
Material: All
Address: 6640 SUNSET BLVD STE 100
City/State/ZIP: HOLLYWOOD CA 90028
Telephone: 213-465-1186
Fax: 213-465-5049
E-mail: boxoffice@earthlink.net

BOYS' LIFE®

Boys' Life

Boys' Life is a general interest, four-color monthly, circulation 1.3 million, published by the Boy Scouts of America [BSA] since 1911. We buy first-time rights for original, unpublished material.

NONFICTION. Major articles run 500 to 1,500 words; payment is $400 to $1,500. Subject matter is broad. We cover everything from professional sports to American history to how to pack a canoe. A look at a current list of the BSA's more than 100 merit badge pamphlets gives an idea of the wide range of subjects possible. Even better, look at a year's worth of recent issues. We are found in libraries and BSA council offices.

Columns run 300 to 750 words; payment is $150 to $400. Column headings are science, nature, earth, health, sports, space and aviation, cars, computers, entertainment pets, history, music and others. Each issue uses seven columns, on average. We also have back-of-the-book how-to features that bring $250 to $300.

FICTION. Fiction runs 1,000 to 1,500 words. Payment is $750 and up. All stories feature a boy or boys. We use humor, mystery, science fiction and adventure. We use one short story per issue.

Articles for *Boys' Life* must interest and entertain boys ages 8 to 18. Write for a boy you know who is 12. Our readers demand crisp, punchy writing in relatively short, straightforward sentences. The editors demand well-reported articles that demonstrate high standards of journalism. We follow The New York Times manual of style and usage.

We receive approximately 100 queries and unsolicited manuscripts and 75 fiction manuscripts per week. Unsolicited nonfiction manuscripts are returned unread.

Please query by mail, not by phone.

Thank you for your interest in *Boys' Life.*

Categories: Fiction—Nonfiction—Adventure—Animals—Automobiles—Aviation—Careers—Cartoons—Children—Computers—Conservation—Crafts—Ecology—Education—Electronics—Entertainment—Environment—Fishing—Games—General Interest—Health—Histories—Hobbies—Humor—Juvenile—Outdoors—Science—Science Fiction—Short Stories—Sports—Technology

Name: Shannon Lowry, Associate Editor
Material: Fiction Manuscripts
Name: Mike Goldman, Articles Editor
Material: Nonfiction Queries (NO mss.)
Address: 1325 W WALNUT HILL LN
Address: PO BOX 152079
City/State/ZIP: IRVING TX 75015-2079
Telephone: 972-580-2366

Boys' Quest
A Word At The Outset

Every BOYS' QUEST contributor must remember we publish only six issues a year, which means our editorial needs are extremely limited.

It is obvious that we must reject far more contributions that we accept, no matter how outstanding they may seem to you or to us.

With that said, we would point out that BOYS' QUEST is a magazine created for boys from 6 to 13 years, with youngsters 8, 9, and 10 the specific target age.

Our point of view is that every young boy deserves the right to be a young boy for a number of years before he becomes a young adult.

As a result, BOYS' QUEST looks for articles, fiction, nonfiction, and poetry that deal with timeless topics, such as pets, nature, hobbies, science, games, sports, careers, simple cooking, and anything else likely to interest a young boy.

Writers

We are looking for lively writing, most of it from a young boy's point of view—with the boy or boys directly involved in an activity that is both wholesome and unusual. We need nonfiction with photos and fiction stories—around 500 words—puzzle, poems, cooking, carpentry projects, jokes, and riddles.

Nonfiction pieces that are accompanied by black and white photos are far more likely to be accepted than those that need illustrations.

The ideal length of a BOYS' QUEST piece—nonfiction or fiction—is 500 words.

We will entertain simultaneous submissions as long as that fact is noted on the manuscript. Computer printouts are welcome.

BOYS' QUEST prefers to receive complete manuscripts with cover letters, although we do not rule out query letters. We do not answer submissions sent in by fax.

All submissions must be accompanied by a self-addressed, stamped envelope, with sufficient postage.

We will pay a minimum of five cents a word for both fiction and nonfiction, with additional payment given if the piece is accompanied by appropriate photos or art. We will pay a minimum of $10 per poem or puzzle, with variable rates offered for games, carpentry projects, etc.

BOYS' QUEST buys first American serial rights and pays upon publication. It welcomes the contributions of both published and unpublished writers.

Sample copies are available for $3.00 within the US and $4.00 outside the US. All payment must be in US funds. A complimentary copy will be sent to each writer who has contributed to a given issue.

Photographers

We use a number of black and white photos inside the magazine, most in support of articles used. Payment is $5-10 per photo used, depending on the quality and $5 for color slides.

Artists

Most art will be by assignment, in support of features used. The magazine is anxious to find artists capable of illustrating stories and features and welcomes copies of sample work, which will remain on file. Our work inside is pen and ink. We pay $35 for a full page and $25 for a partial page.

There's one more thing

BOYS' QUEST, as a new publication, is aware that its rates of payment are modest at this time. But we pledge to increase those rewards in direct proportion to our success. Meanwhile, we will strive to treat our contributors and their work with respect and fairness. That treatment, incidentally, will include quick decisions on all submissions.

Categories: Fiction—Nonfiction—Animals—Cartoons—Children

Name: Marilyn Edwards, Editor
Material: All
Address: PO BOX 227
City/State/ZIP: BLUFFTON OH 45817
Telephone: 419-358-4610

Bride's Magazine

Bride's magazine is written for the first- and second-time bride, the groom, their families, and their friends. The editorial goal is to help the couple plan their wedding and adjust to married life. *Bride's* does not publish fiction or poetry. Submit all travel queries directly to the Travel Department. Payment starts at $.50 per word.

Choosing a Topic:

1) Personal essays on wedding planning aspects of weddings or marriage. 800 words. Written by brides, grooms, attendants, family members, friends, in the first person. The writer's unique experience qualifies them to tell this story.

2) Articles on specific relationship and lifestyle issues. 800 words. Select a specialized topic in the areas of relationships, religion, in-laws, second marriage, finances, careers, health, fitness, nutrition, sex, decorating, or entertaining. Written either by experts (attorneys, doctors, financial planners, marriage counselors, etc.) or freelancers who interview and quote experts and real couples.

3) In-depth explorations of relationship and lifestyle issues. 2,000-3,000 words. Well researched articles on finances, health, sex, wedding and marriage trends. Should include statistics,

quotes from experts and real couples, a resolution of the issues raised by each couple.

Preparing an Article: First, familiarize yourself with the magazine by reading several of the most recent issues (also check the masthead; if you're writing to a specific editor, make sure she is still here). Next, send a detailed outline or query explaining how you would research and organize the piece, along with a self-addressed, stamped legal-size envelope and clippings of your previously published work. You should receive a response within eight weeks. Please do not call to check on your query's status; each submission will be read and carefully considered.

Enrich your article with couple anecdotes and quotes from experts. Attribute all statistics to organizations or agencies. Include experts' full names, academic degrees and affiliations, cities and states; couples' first names, ages, occupations, cities and states. Do not cite secondary sources; use other magazine articles and books as background reading only (you may interview the authors of these sources).

Categories: Nonfiction—Family—Gardening—Marriage—Parenting—Relationships—Beauty—Home

Name: Millie Martini-Bratten
Material: All except travel
Name: Travel Department
Material: Travel
Address: 140 EAST 45TH STREET
City/State/ZIP: NEW YORK, NEW YORK 10017
Telephone: 212-880-8800
Fax: 212-880-8331

The Bridge

The Bridge is a lively, literary magazine that brings well-known and brand-new writers to its readers. Our first issue featured New Yorker writers Celia Gilbert, James Reiss, William Matthews, and Phyllis Janowitz—and rising newcomer, Karen Rile. National writers X.J. Kennedy, Kathleen Spivack, Ruth Whitman and talented newcomers, Laurie Conde, Elizabeth Moore, and Tom Sime, have appeared in our pages. We have a Michigan contingent, Gay Rubin, Patricia Hooper, Steven Tudor, Stephen Dunning, and Henrietta Epstein. Recent contributors include David R. Slavitt, Nora Roberts, and Carol Kaplan.

Above all we believe in quality and eclecticism, in finish, spirit, and a fusion of content and style. We mean to keep an American flavor, an openness to quality, wherever its origin, but remain open to all fine English writing wherever it comes from. The Bridge has received an award from the Council of Literary Magazines and Presses (an agency of the N.E.A.). A *Library Journal* review has recommended us to all libraries.

Poetry to 200 lines. Fiction to 20 double-spaced pages. Mainstream. Some book reviews.

Subscriptions are $8 a year (two issues), $12 for two years (four issues), $5 for a single issue. Donations are tax exempt to the full extent of the law: tax I.D. 38-3005104.

Categories: Fiction—Literature—Poetry

Name: Jack Zucker, Editor
Material: Any
Name: Helen Zucker, Fiction Editor
Material: Fiction Submissions
Name: Mitzi Alvin, Poetry Editor
Material: Poetry Submissions
Address: 14050 VERNON ST
City/State/ZIP: OAK PARK MI 48237
E-mail: HZucker@oakland.edu

British Car™ A-D
M A G A Z I N E

British Car Magazine

BRITISH CAR MAGAZINE is the only American magazine devoted exclusively to British automobiles. Our intention is to assist the active enthusiast in buying, using, maintaining, and enjoying his or her British car.

In each issue, readers find a spectrum of articles on all facets of the cars and their hobby.

Classic profiles, providing historical information about a marque and model and a close-up of a specific car that typifies the marque being profiled are very popular, and we publish two to three in each issue.

Technical articles are intended to help readers understand basic technical principles, carry out general maintenance, and undertake restoration projects.

Historical articles provide readers with nostalgia and information on the cars and their development.

Articles about individual enthusiasts and their activities, such as long-distance tours, restoration projects, and unique personal histories also make entertaining reading, providing vicarious enjoyment.

Overall, the magazine is "the next best thing to driving your car."

FEATURES/PROFILES

Classic marque features including factual information and driving impressions are the core of the magazine, but should only be attempted by those with a good knowledge of the vehicles in question. All articles pertaining to a particular model or marque should be extremely well researched, compiled, and composed in such a way as to not sound like something that's been said many times before. A detailed article based around photographs of an excellent example of the model and marque and full of supporting facts and figures, current resources and historical background makes a desirable feature.

Articles can run from 1,500-4,000 words, depending on depth and scope, and should include a comprehensive set of pictures, preferable shot as slides, including front, back, sides, interior, engine compartment, trunk, and detail close-ups, plus attractive posed or driving shots.

TECHNICAL/HOW-TO ARTICLES

These articles must be well-researched. The author should have past hands-on experience and be considered an expert in the subject chosen. A query with a complete outline and introduction is acceptable for discussion prior to a completed manuscript. Step-by-step photos are, in most cases, required to illustrate the manuscript.

RESTORATION ARTICLES

British Car is always on the lookout for articles documenting complete restorations. These articles should provide a combination of specific tips on restoration of a particular model and marque, and general advice on how other readers can restore their own cars. Clear pictures documenting each step in the restoration, as well as attractive pictures of the final result are a critical element of these articles. Articles may be complete in one issue, or spread over two to three issues if they are very detailed.

ENTHUSIAST ACTIVITIES

Long tours, scenic drives, vintage races, and other organized or individual activities where the cars are put to active use are also desirable. These articles normally emphasize photography and use only a minimum of explanatory text to explain the event or activity.

"DESPATCHES"

Articles about specific field meets or events must be newsworthy, accurate, timely and well-written, accompanied preferably with one or two photos. Length should be one-half to one page, typed double-spaced. Contributors receive a small gift in return for their submission

YOUR CARS

This regular department features readers' personal cars owned by them now or in the past. Submissions should include clear photos of the car and from one to four pages typed manuscript, including history, technical information, anecdotes, funny stories, or other related information about the car Please include a SASE if you want photos returned. Upon publication a one-year subscription or renewal to British Car will be entered. No additional payments are made for "Your Car" articles.

SUBMISSION OF MANUSCRIPTS

Manuscripts should be submitted on computer disc, in either PC or MAC format, stored in MS Word or ASCII text and accompanied by typed hardcopy. Please do not fax manuscripts.

SUBMISSION OF PHOTOS

Well-focused, composed, and uncluttered photos are the best choice. For black and white reproduction, color prints with good contrast but without dark shadows are preferred, at least 4"x6" in size. For features, color transparencies (slides) are best. Slides should be submitted in plastic sheet slide protectors. All photos should be accompanied by captions detailing the pictures, including names of individuals pictured and identification of cars. Do not write on the backs of photos. Instead, please provide a typed manuscript sheet of captions, keyed to photo numbers.

PAYMENT

Standard payments are $75 to $100 per equivalent published page, including both text and photos, unless previous written agreement has been made, and is paid upon publication. For reprinted, previously published work, or work that requires extensive editing, the rate is $50 per equivalent page. *British Car* buys exclusive first North American publication rights as well as non-exclusive worldwide rights for manuscripts published, and any accompanying photos and artwork, including the non-exclusive right to reprint or republish the material in other electronic formats, unless other arrangements are made. The editorial staff reserves the right to edit for clarity and space without review or approval of the author.

ARRANGEMENTS AND CONSIDERATION

Before preparing material for submission, potential contributors are strongly encouraged to review several recent issues of the magazine to acquaint themselves with the approach, coverage, and format of editorial material.

Contributors wishing to have material considered for publication in *British Car* are encouraged to submit finished articles and/or photos for consideration. The staff will make every effort to acknowledge receipt of material that is not immediately returned, but can not make commitments as to publication potential.

Individuals who have had material published in other periodicals may submit proposals for specific articles if accompanied by samples of previously published work. Because of time constraints, the editorial staff can not respond by telephone or in writing to concepts or proposals for articles by individuals who do not have previous publication credits.

Categories: Automobiles

Name: Gary Anderson, Editor and Publisher
Material: All
Address: 343 SECOND ST STE H
City/State/ZIP: LOS ALTOS CA 94022-3639
Telephone: 415-949-9680
Fax: 415-949-9685
E-mail: britcarmag@aol.com

Buffalo Spree Magazine

BUFFALO SPREE MAGAZINE is a high-quality, consumer-oriented, quarterly magazine mailed to a literate audience of approximately 21,000 above-average-income residents of metropolitan Buffalo. We publish fiction, nonfiction, and poetry. Except for a few regular features, our editorial is derived solely from unsolicited submissions.

FICTION: We are looking for well-written stories with strong conflicts and well-developed characters. Dramatic and literary as well as light and humorous pieces are welcome. We do not consider pornographic works.

NONFICTION: We are interested in articles of interest to residents of Western New York as well as poignant or humorous commentaries and essays.

Ideal length for fiction and nonfiction pieces is 1,000-2,000 words.

Payment is upon publication.

We accept but do not encourage simultaneous submissions.

Estimated response time is 1-3 months.

Thank you for your interest.

We look forward to receiving your submissions.

Categories: Fiction—Nonfiction—Poetry—Short Stories

Name: Johanna VanDe Mark, Editor
Material: Fiction and Nonfiction
Name: Janet Goldenberg, Poetry Editor
Material: Poetry
Address: PO BOX 38
Address: 4511 HARLEM RD
City/State/ZIP: BUFFALO NY 14226
Telephone: 716-839-3405
Fax: 716-839-4384

Bugle
Journal of Elk and the Hunt

Dear Writer,

The BUGLE editorial staff is always looking for high-quality manuscripts depicting the world of elk. We accept fiction, nonfiction and scientific articles geared to the layman. We encourage query letters, but also accept unsolicited manuscripts. Stories may range from 1,500-4,500 words (1,000 to 3,000 words for departments like "Women in the Outdoors" or "Situation Ethics"), but we have no set length requirements.

Please send us a copy of your story on an IBM-formatted disk—saved in WordPerfect or an ASCII text file—and enclose a hard copy, along with an appropriately sized self-addressed, stamped envelope (SASE). When you submit an article, you will receive a receipt acknowledging its arrival. We will evaluate your story based on content, writing quality and our needs for the coming year. If we decide not to publish it, the story will be returned in your SASE with a letter to that effect.

By familiarizing yourself with BUGLE prior to submitting (it's available on the newsstand), you will have a better sense of the kinds of stories we might publish. Thoughtful hunting stories, elk-related human interest stories, and new material for "Situation Ethics," "Thoughts and Theories" and "Women in the Outdoors" are always high on our needs list. However, we do not publish "how-to" articles.

The Elk Foundation is a nonprofit conservation organization committed to putting membership dollars into elk habitat, management and research. So we appreciate, and still receive, donated manuscripts. However, if you would like to be paid for your work, please say so in your cover letter. We pay 20 cents per word. In either case, should your story appear in BUGLE, you will receive three complimentary copies.

Please feel free to inquire into the status of your manuscript at any time.

Sincerely,
Lee A. Cromrich
Editorial Assistant

Categories: Fiction—Nonfiction—Adventure—Animals—Conservation—Ecology—Environment—History (elk-related)—Humor (elk-related)—Hunting—Outdoors—Photography—Public Policy (hunting only)—Recreation—Science (in relation to hunting)—Short Stories (elk or hunting only)—Sports (Hunting only)—Technology (in relation to hunting)—Western (elk, wildlife, hunting)—Women's Fiction (elk, wildlife, hunting only)—Women's Issues (elk, wildlife, hunting only)

Name: Don Burgess, Hunting Editor
Material: Elk/Hunting
Name: David Stalling, Conservation Editor
Material: Elk/Conservation/Natural History
Name: Jan Brocci, Managing Editor
Material: Elk/Women Hunting
Address: PO BOX 8249
City/State/ZIP: MISSOULA MT 59807-8249
Telephone: 406-523-4568
Fax: 406-523-4550

Business Start-Ups Magazine

Thanks for your interest in *Business Start-Ups* magazine, the fastest-growing small-business magazine in North America. We've designed these guidelines to help you help us. Read them carefully and design your query to appeal to our ultimate boss—our reader.

First Things First

Business Start-Ups pays $100 for briefs, between $200 and $400 for departments, and between $400 and $600 for features. For information about our payment process, see "Acceptance and Payment" below.

The BSU Reader

We're looking for articles that will appeal to two distinct groups: 1) people eager to launch their own companies, and 2) people who run new or very small-but growing-companies.

BSU's 220,000 monthly readers are:
• Fairly young (median age: 42 years old).
• Well-educated (75 percent attended or graduated college; 20 percent have grad school experience).
• Managers, executives or professionals interested in launching a service or retail company (almost two-thirds of our readers).
• Solidly middle-class (median income about $44K), but with very little capital to invest ($7,700 median).

What They Want

• **New Business Ideas.** Hence our almost constant theme, "A Bazillion New Businesses To Start."
• **How-to Articles About Business Start-Up.** We're looking for precision: articles that focus on one element of the start-up process—marketing, PR, business plan writing, taxes, financing, selling, low-cost advertising and the like.

BSU Articles Should Be:
• Lessons-oriented. Get right to the point and tell our readers how to operate their businesses better.
• Intelligent. Be specific and use real world examples of entrepreneurs who are successfully using the techniques you are suggesting in your article.

• Concrete. Stay away from abstract management theory. Our readers want to know the three things they must do before they hire their first employee, not a rundown on Total Quality Management.
• Written with self-reliance in mind. Don't tell our readers to hire someone to write their business plan. Tell them how they can do it themselves. Provide the names, addresses and phone numbers of appropriate trade associations. Suggest some good books (including complete titles, authors' names, publishing companies, and toll-free ordering numbers) that further illustrate your suggestions.

Writing & Submission: A Checklist

• Proofread your article. *Check all facts for accuracy before submission.* Get full corporate or organization names (and find out if "The" is part of the name). If a name is an acronym, find out what it stands for. Check the exact spelling of the source's name, his or her age, and the month and year the business was started. What does the business do? Where is it based? Ask for financial indicators about the business-where it is now (sales figures!) and where it is going (industry-wide trends)?
• Once your query is accepted, submit your copy on disk or by modem, accompanied by a typed manuscript. You may also e-mail your article to us. Be sure you include a complete list of all contact sources, addresses and telephone numbers. If you send your story on disk, we need 3½" or 5¼" disks with the text in ASCII, XyWrite or Microsoft Word format.
• If you wish to modem the article to us, dial (714) 261-9020. Covert your file to ASCII text and send it as a binary file. At the password prompt, type in "Guest." Your filenames must be shorter than eight letters.
• Include a signed writer's contract, which you'll receive when your story is accepted and assigned.
• Include an invoice with your work. On it, include your name, address, day and evening phone and fax numbers, social security number, description of assignment, and date of invoice.
• If you have any questions, please don't hesitate to call us.

Acceptance & Payment

BSU pays on acceptance. To eliminate false expectations, here's how the process works:

Your manuscript arrives with your invoice. The story is reviewed, usually within two weeks. If the manuscript requires a rewrite, we'll let you know why. We offer one shot at rewrites; if we're still not satisfied, we'll offer you a 20 percent kill fee.

If we like the manuscript, we'll let you know it's been accepted. We'll ship your invoice to our accounting department and begin the (roughly) 60-day payment process, which should get the check to you about the same time the magazine hits the stands. While we'll work assiduously to move your invoice through the system, there may be delays. We hope you'll calculate your cash flow appropriately.

Categories: Business

Name: Donna Clapp, Editor-in-Chief
Material: Queries for stories
Address: 2392 MORSE AVE
City/State/ZIP: IRVINE CA 92614
Telephone: 714-261-2083
Fax: 714-755-4211

Business97

Please refer to Group IV Communications, Inc.

ByLine

We believe Erskine Caldwell was right when he said, "Publication of early work is what a writer needs most of all in life." Tenacity is essential to success in writing, but while success as a writer is a great achievement, considerable merit attaches to the effort itself. As in athletics, training is the struggle; victory is merely the affirmation of that struggle.

Our message to writers is a simple one:

Believe in yourself and keep trying.

Since its founding in 1981, *ByLine* has published the first work of hundreds of fiction writers, poets and nonfiction writers. We encourage and advise novice writers; we publish the work of beginners and veterans alike. Every month we publish articles on the craft or business of writing, including regular columns on writing poetry, fiction, nonfiction, and children's literature. We also publish short fiction and poetry, and a special feature for student writers.

ByLine sponsors monthly contests with cash prizes, designed to motivate writers by providing deadlines and competition against which to match their skills. In addition, we sponsor the annual ByLine Literary Awards as a gesture of appreciation to our subscribers. This contest carries a November first deadline and a cash prize of $250 in each of two categories, short story and poetry. Unlike the monthly contests, which are open to anyone, the Literary Awards are open to subscribers only. Winners of the *ByLine* Literary Awards are published in the magazine along with brief stories about the authors. Marcia Preston is editor & publisher.

WRITER'S GUIDELINES

Manuscripts without SASE will not be read or returned. Do not submit computer diskettes unless requested.

FICTION-general short fiction, mainstream, literary or genre; 2,000 to 4,000 words. Good writing is the main criterion. Payment is $100 on acceptance.

FEATURES-Instructive or motivational articles that could be of genuine help to writers, especially how-to-write or how-to-sell to specific market areas. Length 1,500 to 1,800 words; query or submit full manuscript. We also solicit interviews with editors of freelancer-friendly publications for our Inside Information feature. Query with editor's name and sample of his publication; we'll provide specific guidelines. Payment is $50 on acceptance for all features.

END PIECE-A strong, thoughtful, first-person essay of 700-750 words, related to writing. May be humorous, motivational or philosophical. Read several back issues as examples. Payment is $35 on acceptance.

DEPARTMENTS-Read the magazine for examples. **First Sale** carries 250 to 300-word accounts of a writer's first sale. Payment is $20 on acceptance. Writing-related humor of 100 to 600 words needed for **Only When I Laugh.** Pays $15 to $25 on acceptance. **Great American Bookstores!** features outstanding independent bookstores in 500-600 words and pays $30 ($40 with photo).

POETRY-Our poetry also deals with the subject of writing. We lean toward free verse but will accept skillful rhyme if it is not predictable. We get an abundance of short, humorous verse but seek good-quality, serious poetry about the writing experience. Poems about writer's block, "the muse," and inspiration that comes in the middle of the night have been overdone. Payment is $10 for poems of more than five lines, $5 for five lines and under.

We purchase first North American rights only; no reprints. Submissions must follow standard manuscript format. (Send SASE if you need guidance on format.) List your full name, address, and telephone in upper left corner of first page and an accurate word count (line count for poetry) in upper right corner. Send a #10-sized SASE or larger.

Categories: Writing

Name: Kathryn Fanning, Managing Editor
Material: All Nonfiction and Fiction
Name: Betty Shipley, Poetry Editor
Material: Poetry
Address: PO BOX 130596
City/State/ZIP: EDMOND OK 73013-0001
Telephone: 405-348-5591
E-mail: ByLineMP@aol.com

Byte

Byte provides detailed, in-depth coverage of new computer products and technologies to technically sophisticated readers. The *Byte* audience wants to know not only how a technology functions, but why it's important, and how to integrate it with existing hardware and software. Our readers look to us for advice on which technologies to implement now, and several years from now. If you have an idea for a product review, full-length feature, or short news item that fulfills the above criteria, please query an editor following the instructions below.

Byte editors prefer a query letter rather than a complete manuscript. Your letter should include an outline and sample paragraph(s) of the proposed article, and your credentials for writing it. You may address your query by e-mail, fax, or traditional mail. In the case of the latter, please include an SASE. For a list of specific editors, see *Byte* Editorial Contacts.

Acceptance: If your article proposal is accepted you will be contacted by an editor, who will send you a signed contract that stipulates the approximate length of the piece and the rate. You must sign the contract and return it to *Byte*. Rates vary, depending on the type of article. *Byte* generally buys all rights (including electronic) to the articles it publishes. In most cases, *Byte* pays on acceptance, and payment arrive 4-6 weeks after that (if we have received your signed contract). Please note that not all article assignments are fee-eligible.

Submission: *Byte* strongly encourages you to submit manuscripts electronically through the Internet or a variety of commercial on-line services. Mailing a floppy is also acceptable. Arrange the submission medium and word processor format with your editor before you send the manuscript. Authors must also submit figures (charts, schematics, etc.) along with the manuscript. YOU MUST CITE SOURCES FOR FIGURES AND CHARTS. Again, contact your editor for the proper format for figures and charts. In any case, please submit a hard copy as well to help us verify that transmission was complete and accurate. *Byte* makes every effort to provide proofs of manuscript layouts to each author. Due to publishing deadlines, we are not always able to provide these in time for authors to make changes.

***Byte* Does Not Cover the Following Types of Stories:** New Web sites (unless they involve ground-breaking technological implementation). Calendar items such as announcements of upcoming shows, promotions. Industry personalities. Reviews of office equipment and non-computer related items. Business stories such as mergers, acquisitions, channel partnerships, or executive promotions.

Ethics: We require potential authors to disclose any business or professional ties to companies or products discussed in their articles. *Byte* strives to avoid even the appearance of a conflict of interest. All articles written for *Byte* must be exclusive (not previously published) unless the author has made a special agreement with *Byte* prior to publication.

With certain exceptions, *Byte* does not accept contributed articles from the vendor community. You may contact the appropriate editor and suggest an interview with someone representing a vendor, but *Byte* will accept, reject, or edit such input according to its standards. There are two exceptions to this policy: *Byte* reserves the right to publish non-promotional technical articles by experts in the vendor community; and *Byte* also reserves the right to publish bylined articles by acknowledged world leaders in computer technology.

Whom Do I Address? Please address your letters/manuscripts to the appropriate Senior Editor.

Categories: Nonfiction—Book Reviews—Computers—Consumer—Software—Technology

Name: Dave Essex: dave.essex@byte.com
Material: Product Reviews
Name: Rich Friedman: rich.friedman@byte.com
Material: CD-ROM, Book Reviews, International
Name: John Montgomery: john.montgomery@byte.com
Material: Features
Name: Tom Thompson: tom_thompson@byte.com
Material: Core Technologies columns
Address: 24 HARTWELL AVENUE
City/State/ZIP: LEXINGTON, MA 02173
Telephone: 617-860-6336
Fax: 617-860-6522
MCI Mail: 250-0135 *Byte* Magazine

Cafe Eighties Magazine

The Perfect Blend of Yesterday's Grinds And What's Brewing in Your Mind Today

Cafe Eighties Magazine is created by and for the mini-generation that "came of age" in the early-to-mid 1980s. We want our stories to be told. We want *Cafe Eighties* to serve as a forum, a scrapbook, a storybook, an historical reference and an all-encompassing diary of who we are and the events and trends that lead us into today. We will consider expressions of these uniquely identifiable images, ideas and stories in a variety of forms.

The Basics of Submitting to *Cafe Eighties:*

• Each and every submission *must* include a cover letter

• *Cafe Eighties* will consider **simultaneous submissions** and **previously published** works, but you *must* state in your cover letter if either applies.

• Payment for publication is in one copy of the issue in which your work appears.

• Because of the unique nature of *Cafe Eighties*, we highly recommend purchasing a sample copy before submitting. This will prevent you from wasting your time and postage by submitting inappropriate work. To order, send a check for $5.00 to the address below.

What We Publish:

• **FICTION:** *Cafe Eighties* will not be reading any more fiction until further notice. However, we will be sending out postcards to our mailing list of fiction writers when we are ready to read again. If you'd like to be notified, please write and ask to be added to the mailing list.

• **POETRY:** Poems must not exceed one page each. Always include your name, address and phone number on each page.

• **MUSIC REVIEWS:** Send a letter of interest with a writing sample. Your sample does not have to be published work. It can be a CD review, or another piece of nonfiction writing, like an essay or an article.

• **BOOK REVIEWS:** Send a letter of interest, a list of the types of books you like to read, and any kind of writing sample, published or unpublished.

• **ESSAYS:** Send your manuscript or query with an idea.

• **MEMOIRS:** Send your manuscript or query with an idea.

• **COLUMN PROPOSALS:** Query with your idea and enclose a writing sample.

• **HUMOR PIECES:** Send your piece or query with an idea.

• **ILLUSTRATIONS:** *Cafe Eighties* uses illustrations to accompany short stories, articles and other magazine features. You can obtain a list of subjects for which we need illustrations by sending a self-addressed stamped envelope and requesting "Illustrator's List." You may have stock art that matches our needs, or you may want to draw something to our specifications and submit it for consideration. If you wish, you may send a sample of your work when requesting our Illustrator's List. If your style suits a particular project, we may request a specific assignment from you.

• **COMIC STRIPS:** *Cafe Eighties* is currently looking for a comic strip to feature regularly in the magazine. If you are interested. please write to us with samples of your artwork. High quality photocopies are acceptable.

• **PHOTOS:** *Cafe Eighties* uses photos to accompany magazine features. We also need photographers to participate in celebrity interviews. You can obtain a list of subjects for which we need photos by sending a self-addressed stamped envelope and requesting "Photographer's List." You may have stock photos that match our needs, or you may want to shoot something to our specifications and submit it for consideration. If you wish, you may send a sample of your work when requesting our Photographer's List. If your style suits a particular project, we may request a specific assignment from you. If you'd like to photograph celebrities during interviews, please write to us and let us know to which major cities you are able and willing to travel and what kind of transportation you have, if any.

• **CELEBRITY INTERVIEWS:** Please query with your interest. There is a special need for interviews with early 1980s celebrities, however, we will consider interviews with more current celebrities. *Cafe Eighties* will assist you in obtaining interviews if necessary.

• **ARTICLES (TRAVEL, HOW-TO, ETC.):** Send manuscript or query with an informal proposal. Include writing samples if possible.

We Look Forward To Seeing You In The Cafe!

Kimberly Brittingham, Publisher/Editor-in-Chief

Categories: Fiction—Nonfiction—Entertainment—Humor—Interview—Music—Poetry—Short Stories

Name: Submissions Editor
Material: All
Address: 1562 FIRST AVE STE 180
City/State/ZIP: NEW YORK NY 10028
Telephone: 212-802-4528

California Explorer

Editorial Guidelines

Thank you for your interest in writing for California Explorer. We accept free-lance manuscripts and photography on approval for each of the following departments. Please query with ideas before sending material. Writers having three articles published in the previous six issues will be listed as Contributing Writers in the inside cover masthead.

Features:

These are expanded articles designed to be in-depth studies of the location/activity. Subjects chosen for Features must have one or more special aspect which lifts it above a "scenic walk in the woods," e.g., interesting history, unique geology, flora or fauna; current topical interest, or a "peak experience" for the author. This last item points to a major highlight of Features—author involvement.

While the articles should be written in an informative style, Features are meant to be a showcase for your writing as well. Give us the Where, What, Why, When, and How of the subject, but throw in the "Feel" of it too! All articles should be written from a well-researched point-of-view, not a "I went here, and I did this" style. Be informative, be descriptive, be interesting, and check your facts, (and spelling of proper names!). Include a short biography to be included at the end of your article—a sentence or two telling the readers who you are.

Details:

Articles should be 1200 to 1500 words. Submissions should include one black and white photo or color transparency. The fee paid for a Feature article and photograph is $125. Author gets a by-line and a copy of the magazine in which it is published, for one-time, non-exclusive use of the article and photograph. Make sure your manuscript is identified with your name, etc., including your social security number.

Escapes:

These are designed to be shorter, more informative pieces. They can be very localized or specific activities. Escapes should be 90 percent information—the Why, Where, and How of a particular journey/location.

Details:

Articles should be 500 to 750 words. Submissions should include a black and white photo or color transparency. The fee paid for an Escape article is $75 with by-line and one copy of the magazine in which it is published, for one-time, non-exclusive use of the article and photograph.

Photography:

Color transparency or black and white photographs may be submitted for consideration as possible covers. Photos must be accompanied by notes or specifications on the shooting of the photograph(s). Cover photos must be vertical with area suitable for masthead graphic.

Details:

Fee paid is $50 and a copy of the issue, for one-time, non-exclusive use. The photographer will be credited.

Notes for putting together your articles:

" Each article must be accompanied by information necessary for the sidebar Getting There.

Please see attached sample to guide you. Be sure to include appropriate phone numbers and/or addresses of agencies having jurisdiction in the area covered by your story. Be as helpful as possible to make the reader's trip effortless and pleasant.

" Identify all photographs with your name. If your photos are identified as copyrighted material, include a release to publish. This is especially important if you submit color slides which will need to have an inter-neg made. (Regular contributors may submit a blanket release to have on file.) Suggested photo captions should accompany the photographs and are greatly appreciated!

" We gladly accept manuscripts on computer disk—but Macintosh only. Hard copies should be identified with your name, address, phone numbers, and social security number.

" In choosing subjects for your article, we prefer articles that get people out of their cars and involved in the activity. Remember, our roots are as a hiking and backpacking journal. Our readers are all ages and abilities, which gives a broad range to possible activities. Also, one of the most stringent goals is to showcase lesser-known locations. Admittedly, this is getting increasingly difficult as the population of California relentlessly expands. We are looking for pockets of solitude, off the beaten path. Review articles in past issues to "get a feel" for the style and content that characterizes California Explorer articles.

" All articles should have an introductory paragraph that clearly lets the reader know what activity the article features—hike, bike ride, car trip, rafting—within the first two paragraphs! Also, the general characteristics should be worked in, e.g., overnight hike, week-long backpack, afternoon walk in the woods. The introduction should let the reader know what they will be reading about, and hopefully doing, and there should always be a one or two sentence conclusion.

" California Explorer attempts to use articles appropriate to the season. Winter articles generally feature lower elevations and move up to high elevations during summer months. Be sure to let the reader know the best times to visit the destination you are writing about.

" A tip: Most of the time the Forest Service can be a big help in putting together information for articles. The national forests often have a historian or archeologist on staff. Cultivate this relationship—they can be a great source of information. I have found that Forest Service personnel are most accommodating and often are willing to review stories I have written for accuracy and comment. We want our readers to be able to rely on our information as timely and accurate.

If you have any questions, please don't hesitate to call. Please direct queries to:

Kay Graves, Editor
California Explorer
Drawer 1300
Carnelian Bay, Ca 96140
530/ 583-6541 - voice
530/ 583-5522 - fax
calexplore@aol.com - e-mail

California Journal
Independent Analysis of Politics and Government

Thank you for your interest in *California Journal.*

The *Journal* is a non-partisan monthly magazine that reports on California government and politics. Article submissions should be news-oriented and should focus on issues or personalities of statewide interest. The *Journal* puts a premium on lively, well-written articles that feature strong and original reporting. The editors usually assign stories on topics that are receiving widespread press coverage to *Journal* staff members, so these should be avoided unless some new, unreported angle is involved. Payment for stories is negotiated on an individual basis and ranges from $150 to $1,000, depending on the complexity of the story and the qualifications of the writer. Lengths vary according to subject. The *Journal* buys all rights to stories.

It is best to query a proposed article with the editor by phone, letter, or e-mail, and writers should establish their credentials on a given subject at the time an inquiry is made. Final submissions should be submitted on IBM-PC compatible disks or sent via fax or modem. Normally, the *Journal* does not pay a kill fee or expenses; however, these are negotiable. Payment for stories is normally made within two weeks after publication.

Categories: Government—Politics—Public Policy—Reference

Name: A.G. Block, Editor
Material: Any
Name: Steve Scott, Managing Editor
Material: Any
Address: 2101 K ST

City/State/ZIP: SACRAMENTO CA 95816
Telephone: 916-444-2840
Fax: 916-444-2339
E-mail: editor@statenet.com

California Wild
California Academy of Sciences

CALIFORNIA WILD "Natural Sciences for Thinking Animals" (formerly *Pacific Discovery*) is a quarterly magazine published by the California Academy of Sciences, the research facility, natural history museum, and aquarium in San Francisco's Golden Gate Park. Circulation is approximately 30,000.

California Wild's readers are well-educated, and most are residents of California. They are concerned about environmental issues and are committed to informing themselves and others about the natural world. Our readers' interests range widely, from ecology to geology, from endangered species to anthropology, from field identification of plants and birds to an armchair understanding of complex scientific issues.

Articles should avoid a textbook style. It is not enough for a topic to be interesting scientifically, articles must also tell a story and illuminate for our readers the greater significance and timeliness of a topic. New information, new theories, new research should be featured prominently. Where there is controversy it is fine to take a stance, but opposing arguments should be aired. We prefer to emphasize possible solutions to conservation and environmental issues, rather than list problems. We're primarily looking for stories within our geographic region, which includes California and adjacent seas and regions, but almost every issue contains something farther afield.

Departments: *Skywatcher:* An account of recent research in a field of astronomy: 2,000-3,000 words. *Wild Lives:* A description of unusual behavior in a particular species or genus: 1,000 words plus excellent photos. *Trail Less Traveled:* A 1,000-word description of the fauna and flora seen along a little known, but not too strenuous, hike.

We purchase first North American serial rights and we also request electronic rights, as a version *of California Wild* is available through the Internet. Payment is 25 cents per word, two weeks prior to publication. Articles range in length from 1,000 to 3,000 words. Most authors are asked to submit on speculation; few assignments are given.

Authors of articles typically are well-informed professional writers or authoritative scientists with experience writing for popular audiences. Authors should interview and quote specialists and other authorities. There can be a primary source but use more than one source. Some first-hand experience with the subject is also appreciated.

Query letters: A proposal should take the form of the proposed story's opening paragraphs, followed by a description or outline of the remaining text. Faxed queries are fine, but we don't encourage e-mail queries.

Style of articles should be friendly, anecdotal, and thorough. We prefer to avoid technical language and to define specialized terms only when the words themselves and the concepts they embody are appropriate to the story. Regardless of the complexity of the subject matter, authors should try to write simply, using short sentences and paragraphs of not more than four or five sentences. Colloquial usages are fine as long as they're not carried to extremes. Stories should include fleshed out personalities, these may be scientists, environmentalists, or historical figures.

Manuscripts should be neat, with margins of not less than one and one-quarter inches all around. The author, abbreviated title, and page number should be typed in the upper right corner of every page. The first page must include the author's name, address, telephone number, social security number, and a close estimate of the number of words in the article. Once a manuscript is accepted, we will request a computer disk, if one is available. The story should be saved in ASCII or "text only."

Style Tips: Include scientific names in parentheses after common names of species. Spell out numbers from one to twelve and use numerals for measurements. Refer to *The Chicago Manual of Style.*

Source Documentation must be available for every manuscript. Authors should be prepared to provide a list including complete information about publications consulted and interviews conducted, including the name, title, address and telephone number of each source.

Photography

Photographs should be submitted in the form of original color transparencies or reproduction—quality dupes. Color slides must be mounted in flexible, page-size sleeves and must also be protected with individual slide protectors. Each transparency must be clearly marked on the cardboard mount itself with: the photographer's name and address, a sequencing number, and information describing the content of the photograph. Enclose a stamped, self-addressed envelope, return mailing instructions, and sufficient postage to cover safe return, including insurance if you wish. Our current photo needs are published in the Guilfoyle Report (Call 212-929-0959 for information).

Most articles are illustrated. If an author has no direct access to photographs (the author's own or others), referrals to photographers with professional-quality material are appreciated. We rarely use photographs without an accompanying text. But the right photos might inspire us to find one. We also use photographs which "tell a story" of a sequential event.

We purchase one-time publication rights to images. Payment ranges from $75 to $175 inside, and $200 for a cover. We may also use images as part of pages in promotional material. In the unlikely event that an original transparency is lost or damaged, the Academy's liability is limited to fair market value, and we are not bound by any arbitrary valuations.

Captions, typed on separate pages, must be numbered to correlate with numbers on the photographs. Captions should be written as complete sentences, providing both primary and secondary information about the subject of the photograph. If the photographs include people, their names must be noted with correct spelling. Plants and animals should be carefully identified.

For a sample copy, send a self-addressed, stamped envelope with postage-$1.75.

Categories: Ecology—Environment—Science

Name: Keith Howell, Editor
Material: California Natural History/Traditional Cultures
Address: GOLDEN GATE PARK
City/State/ZIP: SAN FRANCISCO CA 94118-4599
Telephone: 415-750-7116
Fax: 415-221-4853

Calliope
World History for Young People

General Information: CALLIOPE covers world history (East/West)—and lively, original approaches to the subject are the primary concerns of the editors in choosing material. Writers are encouraged to study recent back issues for content and style. (Sample issue is available at $4.50. Send 7½"x10½" (or larger) self-addressed stamped ($2.00) envelope.) *All material must relate to the theme of a specific upcoming issue in order to be con-*

sidered. CALLIOPE purchases all rights to material.

Procedure: A query must consist of all of the following to be considered: a brief cover letter stating the subject and word length of the proposed article; a detailed one-page outline explaining the information to be presented in the article; an extensive bibliography of materials the author intends to use in preparing the article; a self-addressed stamped envelope. (Authors are urged to use primary resources and up-to-date scholarly resources in their bibliography.) Writers new to CALLIOPE should send a writing sample with the query. If you would like to know if your query has been received, please also include a stamped postcard that requests acknowledgment of receipt.

A writer may send as many queries for one issue as he or she wishes, but each query must have a separate cover letter, outline, bibliography, and SASE. Telephone queries are not accepted. Handwritten queries will not be considered.

Articles must be submitted on disk using a word processing program (preferably Microsoft Word-Mac). Text should be saved as ASCII text (in MS Word as "text only"). Disks should be either Mac- (preferred) or DOS-compatible 3½".

Guidelines

Feature articles, 700-800 words. Includes in-depth nonfiction, plays, and biographies. Pays $.20-$.25 per printed word.

Supplemental nonfiction, 300-600 words. Includes subjects directly and indirectly related to the theme. Editors like little-known information but encourage writers not to overlook the obvious. Pays $.20-$.25 per printed word.

Fiction, up to 800 words. Authentic historical and biographical fiction, adventure, retold legends, etc., relating to the theme. Pays $.20-$.25 per printed word.

Activities, up to 700 words. Includes crafts, recipes, woodworking projects, etc., that can be done either by children alone or with adult supervision. Query should be accompanied by sketches and description of how activity relates to the theme. Pays on an individual basis.

Poetry, up to 100 lines. Clear, objective imagery. Serious and light verse considered. Pays on an individual basis. Must relate to theme.

Puzzles and Games (no word finds). Crossword and other word puzzles using the vocabulary of the issue's theme. Mazes and picture puzzles that relate to the theme. Pays on an individual basis.

Photo Guidelines

To be considered for publication, photographs must relate to a specific theme. Writers are encouraged to submit available photos with their query or article. We buy one-time use.

Our suggested fee range for professional quality photographs* follows:

    1/4 page to full page
    b/w $15 to $100
    color $25 to $100

*Please note that fees for non-professional quality photographs are negotiated.

Cover fees are set on an individual basis for one-time use, plus promotional use. All cover images are color.

Color transparencies, slides, and color prints can be submitted for inside black/white use since they can be scanned at the printer.

Prices set by museums, societies, stock photography houses, etc., are paid or negotiated. Photographs that are promotional in nature (e.g., from tourist agencies, organizations, special events, etc.) are usually submitted at no charge.

If you have photographs pertaining to any upcoming theme, please contact the editor by mail or fax, or send them with your query. You may also send images on speculation.

Note: Queries may be submitted at any time, but queries sent well in advance of deadline *may not be answered for several months.* Go-aheads requesting material proposed in queries are usually sent five months prior to publication date. Unused queries will be returned approximately three to four months prior to publication date.

Categories: Children—History—Juvenile—World History—Young Adult

Name: Rosalie Baker, Editor
Material: World History for Kids 8-14
Address: 7 SCHOOL ST
City/State/ZIP: PETERBOROUGH NH 03458
Telephone: 603-924-7209
Fax: 603-924-7380

Calyx Journal
A Journal of Art and Literature by Women

Thank you for your interest in CALYX. *CALYX Journal* accepts submissions of poetry, short fiction, visual art, essays, reviews, and interviews. The writer's/artist's guidelines are as follows:

Prose (includes essays) should not exceed 5,000 words.

Poetry submissions are limited to 6 poems.

Reviews should not exceed 1,000 words. If you are interested in reviewing books, please send a resume, published samples of writing, and an SASE. After reviewing these, you will be contacted about the book review list.

Interviews should be limited to 2,500 words.

Visual Art should be submitted on 35mm slides or 8"x10" or 5"x7" black and white glossy photographs (limit 6 slides or photos). All art media are considered. Please label all slides and photos with your name, titles, media, dimensions, and date. Also mark the top of the work. **Do not write on photos!** Attach all necessary information on a label. Include a brief biographical statement and a separate 50-word statement about your artwork. **CALYX is always open for art submissions.**

Black and white reproductions are used inside the *Journal*, so consider how well your work will look in black and white. Color is only used on the covers.

Submit art separately from prose and poetry.

All submissions should include author's name on each page and be accompanied by a brief (50-word or less) biographical statement, a self-addressed, stamped envelope (SASE), and a phone number. Even if you indicate that it is unnecessary to return submission(s), enclose an SASE for your notification. **Prose and poetry should be submitted separately with separate SASEs for each submission category.**

CALYX assumes no responsibility for submissions received without adequate return postage, packaging, or proper identification labels. Every effort is made to respond to submissions in a timely manner, but CALYX receives a large number of submissions when open, and it may take up to six to nine months to read and review everything received. Simultaneous submissions are accepted.

PLEASE NOTE: *CALYX Journal* is only open for submissions for prose and poetry at special times—March 1-April 15 and October 1-November 15.

Sample copies of CALYX *are* available for $9.50 plus $2.00 postage and handling.

Thank you for your interest in CALYX.

We look forward to reviewing your work.

Categories: Fiction—Nonfiction—African-American—Asian-American—Feminism—Gay/Lesbian—General Interest—Hispanic—Literature—Multicultural—Native American—Poetry—Short Stories—Textbooks—Women's Fiction—Women's Issues

Name: Micki Reaman, Managing Editor
Material: Any
Name: Beverly McFarland, Senior Editor
Material: Any
Address: PO BOX B
City/State/ZIP: CORVALLIS OR 97330
Telephone: 541-753-9384
Fax: 541-753-0515
E-mail: calyx@proaxis.com

Camping Today

We appreciate your interest. *Camping Today* is a 32 page, ten times per year magazine which serves the 20,000 member families of the Family Campers & RVers (founded as NCHA, National Campers & Hikers Association). The July/August and January/February issues are combined. Because organization news is a priority we can only buy one or two articles a month. We print on a two month lead time.

75% of our readers are over age 55 and most are owners of recreational vehicles such as travel trailers, fifth wheels, and motorhomes. They enjoy reading nonfiction articles around 1,500 words on interesting places to visit by RV, how-to-do-it features related to camping, and topics of general interest to campers.

Payment is in the range of $35 to $125 depending on the type of article and photographs. We prefer b&w prints, but sharp, clear color prints will work. We can use slides (vertical preferred) for covers. Please send the photos with the article. We buy one time rights and will consider previously published articles (at minimum rates). We can't use poems or essays on "our first or worst campout."

Allow 60 days for a response.
Categories: RV/Camping

Name: DeWayne Johnston, Editor
Material: RV Travel
Address: 126 HERMITAGE RD
City/State/ZIP: BUTLER PA 16001
Telephone: 412-283-7401

Canoe & Kayak Magazine

Thank you for your interest in *Canoe & Kayak* Magazine! If you haven't already done so, we suggest you review a recent issue of our magazine so you can see what kinds of stories and photos we are using. You'll find *Canoe & Kayak* Magazine at many bookstores, large newsstands, and paddlesports retail shops. If you have trouble finding a copy, we'll send you a sample if you send us a self-addressed, 9"x12" envelope with seven first-class stamps. Subscriptions are $17.97 per year.

Our readers include flatwater and whitewater canoeists and kayakers of all skill levels. We provide comprehensive information on destinations, technique, and equipment. Beyond that, we cover a variety of subjects of interest to our readers including canoe and kayak camping, safety, the environment, and the history of boats and sport. We publish a limited number of personal-ity pieces (must be someone one of at least national importance).

Most issues contain at least three feature articles of 2,000 to 2,500 words each. These features cover the range of subjects appropriate for our audience and are distinguished from departments by more in-depth coverage in the story and more liberal use of accompanying photographs. Regular departments, of 1,200 to 1,500 words, cover specific subjects such as techniques, destinations, new equipment, and boat reviews. **Take Out,** our back-page department, is devoted to reflective, personal essays on paddling.

The **Put-In** section uses short (500 words or less), newsy pieces that cover conservation, interesting people, and events. Keep in mind that you are writing for a national audience.

Our **Destinations'** articles emphasize canoeing and kayaking trips that take no more than a few days to complete. Submissions should be no more than 1,400 words in length and include a map of the area, showing the put-in, take-out, towns, tributaries, and features mentioned in the article, and copies of materials we may need to check facts (name spelling, phone numbers, prices, etc. that confirms mentions in an article), a selection of color slides with captions; a sidebar giving driving directions to the put-in from the nearest town; trip-length; seasonal information; permit requirements for paddling and camping; whitewater classification and hazards; recommended guidebooks (author, title, publishing information); and phone numbers of local sources.

Submissions

You may either query or submit material on speculation. If querying, give a brief outline of the proposed article. Allow at least six weeks for a response. We prefer submissions in both hard copy and on disk. Please note whether your files are in Mac or IBM format on your disk and please *do not* double-space electronic copy or set tabs. We can accept most popular word processing formats, but to be safe, please save a copy of the file in text format as well. Hard copies should be [printed] on laser, daisy-wheel, or NLQ dot matrix printers.

We follow the *AP Stylebook* and *Chicago Manual of Style*. Preference will be given to writers who can supply color photographs with articles (see photo guidelines below). This is especially true for destination pieces.

Payment and Rights

Our base rate is 12.5¢ per published word, or about $250 for a 2,000-word article. Payment is made on publication. Rate for assigned articles may vary. We purchase first international rights, which includes first anthology rights and electronic rights.

Photo Submissions

Canoe & Kayak Magazine is always looking for strong images appropriate for the magazine in 35mm, 2¼"x2¼" or 4"x5" slide formats. We prefer duplicates for selection purposes provided they are of good quality. We require a model release when the subject of the photo is easily identifiable.

We prefer unpublished images and do not use images that show a lack of common sense, lack of knowledge about paddlesports, or disregard for safety or the environment. People are usually wearing life preservers in photos we select. We do not use images of people in sailboats, rowing craft, or powerboats.

Canoe & Kayak Magazine pays on publication and purchases onetime or international serial rights. Rates are based on the published size and use (color or b/w) of the image:

Color Black and White
$300 for a cover
$100 for a full page or larger
$175 for a half to full page
$75 for a half page to a full page
$75 for a quarter to a half page
$50 for a quarter to a half page
$50 for less than a quarter page
$25 for less than a quarter page

Place your name, address, and phone number on each image. *Canoe & Kayak* Magazine will handle each submission with due care, but we assume no liability for unsolicited original or duplicate slides, prints, or transparencies. Include a self-addressed envelope with proper postage for the return of your material. We normally reply to unsolicited material within six weeks.

Photo submissions should be addressed to our Art Director.

Categories: Nonfiction—Adventure—Boating—Consumer—Family—Outdoors—Recreation—Sports

Name: Jan Nesset, Editor
Material: Canoeing and Kayaking
Address: PO BOX 3146
City/State/ZIP: KIRKLAND WA 98033
Telephone: 206-827-6363
Fax: 206-827-1893

Car and Driver

We do not accept unsolicited manuscripts, but story ideas in writing are accepted.

Categories: Nonfiction—Automobiles—History—Satire—Sports—Recreation—Humor—Nostalgia

Name: Csaba Csere, Editor-in-Chief
Material: All
Address: 2002 HOGBACK ROAD
City/State/ZIP: ANN ARBOR, MI 48105-9736
Telephone: 734-971-3600
Fax: 734-971-9188
E-mail: editors@caranddriver.com
Internet: www.caranddriver.com

The Magazine For Those Who PLAY TO WIN!

Card Player

As a columnist or writer for *Card Player*, you are required to know not only how to use a dictionary and the *AP Stylebook and Libel Manual*, but also what *Card Player* style guidelines are when differing from *AP Style* or, more frequently, in reference to gaming terms and gaming usage.

These guidelines are being provided to assist you in the submission of articles that meet the criteria provided here. If you think that anything has been left out of these guidelines, please inform *Card Player* (preferably in writing), and we will give all suggestions serious consideration.

All material submitted for publication must be the writer's original work-submissions containing material from other written sources must be duly and totally credited.

All material submitted to *Card Player* for publication should adhere to the following guidelines:

• Fax copies are not accepted, nor are handwritten articles, without prior approval of the publisher.

• Normal article length is three typed pages, double-spaced.
Card Player STYLE

• No *underlines*, **bold**, or CAPS for emphasis; use *italics*.

• When typing a letter to the editor, always include who it is from and where the writer is from, in italics, after an em dash (shift option dash). Example: -*Shelly Kornhandler, Beverly Hills, CA*

Also, letters to the editor always have some sort of headline,

no "Dear Linda" or "Dear *Card Player.*"

Responses are handled similarly. Example: W. Lawrence Hill Responds (as a headline to the response).

• When denoting seat position or referring to anything in numerical order, use No. 1, not #1 or number one.

• Don't use "etc.," use "and so on." Don't use e.g., use "for example."

• Sports scores are as follows: 43-32. Odds are 43-to-32. Also, when talking about points or pointspreads in sports, use figures. Example: The Bengals were ahead by 3 points.

• Spell out city and state names. (There are exceptions, as with letters to the editor and tournament results.)

• A comma goes after *all* items in a list. Example: We ate turkey, dressing, salad, and pie.

• 50-cent piece, not fifty-cent piece. Also, "50 cents" is correct; "50¢" and "fifty cents" are incorrect.

• Spell out twenty, nickel, and dollar when used in casual reference or a quote. "He dropped a twenty at the table."

• Downtown and the Strip are always capitalized in reference to Las Vegas. No double quotes or italics in headlines.

• No italics in captions, but double quotes are OK.

• Ellipses are made with the option semicolon key, not three periods in a row. There is always a space between the ellipses and copy, and between quote marks and ellipses. Same with em dashes. Example: He could not - would not - do it. He could not ... would not ... do it.

• Capitalize the first word after a colon only if it is the first word of an independent clause; that is, if it could stand on its own as a sentence, capitalize. Example: "My first question was: Should you call here with the remainder of your chips?"

• Spell out percent, don't use the % sign, except in tables.

• In a news story, after first reference, refer to someone by last name only.

• A casino, hotel, or any other inanimate object is not a "who" or a "their," it is an "it." For example: The Mirage is training *its* employees in *its* new in-house training program.

• Commas and periods always go inside quotation marks. "No way," he said.

• That and which: follow *AP Style*.

• Numerals: follow *AP Style* (except in sports references).

• If a writer has an opinion about something, he thinks or believes it but he doesn't feel it. You feel something with your fingers. Example: "I feel there are too many rules in poker." No, you think there are too many rules in poker.

• When pluralizing years, do not use an apostrophe "s." Example: 1930s (not 1930's) and '30s (not '30's).

• Attribution usually works best in the middle of a quote. Example: "I won the tournament because I'm a good player," said Nilly Premrajh. "I just want to be respected as such, that's all."

• OK, not Okay, o.k., or O.k.
TERMINOLOGY GUIDELINES

A-game, ace high (noun), ace-high (adjective), aces, aces full (singular), aces up (singular), ace-to-five draw, add-on (noun), all in (adverbial phrase), all-in (adjective), backdoor, bad beat (noun), bad-beat (adjective), boardcard, bookmaker/bookie, bring-in (noun), bring in (verb), rushperson, burn card, buy-in (noun), buy in (verb), card counter, card counting, card playing, cardroom, center pot, check-raise, chip runner, come bet, cut card, day shift, dead spread, decision-making (adjective), deuce-to-seven draw, doorcard, double-suited, downcard, drawout (noun), draw out (verb), eight-or-better facecard, facedown, faceup, 52-card deck, five-card stud, flat bet (noun), flat-bet (verb), floorperson, flush draw, four-flush, four-straight, fourth street (noun), fourth-street (adjective), freeroll, freezeout, full house, future book, graveyard shift, gutshot, handicapper, heads-up (adjective), heads up (adverb), high card (noun), high-carded (verb), high-low split, high-limit (adjective), high limit (noun), high roller, highest-ranking (adjective), high stakes (noun), high-stakes (adjective), hold'em, holecard, horse racing, jackpot, jacks, jacks or better, kill pot, kings, kings full, laydown, live one, lowball, low card (noun), low-card (adjective), low roller, low stakes (noun), low-stakes (adjective), main pot, minisatellite, multihanded, multiway, ninehanded, no-brainer, nut-nut, no-limit, oddsmaker, odds-on (adjective), offsuit, Omaha, open-end, open-end straight draw, outdraw, overcard, overkill, pai gow poker, panguingue, parimutuel payoff/payout, pointspread, poker face, poker room, pot-limit, preflop, queens, racehook, racetrack, rebuy, reraise, rip-off (noun), rip off (verb), ring game, river card, rolled up, rulebook, runner-runner, sandbag, scare card, semi bluff, setup (noun), seven-card stud, shorthanded game, side action, side bet, side pot, slow play (noun), slow-play (verb), slow roll, soft-play (verb), split pot (noun), split-pot (adjective), spot card, sportsbook, string bet (noun), string-bet (verb), stripped deck (noun), stripped-deck (adjective), supersatellite, swing shift, three of a kind, two pair, turn card, undercard, underpair, upcard, underdog, wheel card, wild card, wraparound

Categories: Poker—Gaming

Name: Steve Radulovich, Managing Editor
Material: All
Address: 3140 S POLARIS STE 8
City/State/ZIP: LAS VEGAS NV 89102
Telephone: 702-871-1720
Fax: 702-871-2674
E-mail: cardplay@wizard.com

Career Focus

Please refer to Communications Publishing Group, Inc.
Categories: Nonfiction—African-American—Arts—Associations—Business—Careers—College—Computers—Consumer—Culture—Diet—Economics—Education—Engineering—Entertainment—Ethnic—Government—Health—Hispanic—Internet—Law—law Enforcement—Lifestyles—Money/Finance—Multicultural—Native American—Nursing—Technology

Name: Amy Schiska, Associate Editor
Material: All
Address: 660 PENN TOWER
Address: 3100 BROADWAY
City/State/ZIP: KANSAS CITY MO 64111-2413
Telephone: 816-960-1988
Fax: 816-960-1989

Careers and Majors

Please refer to Oxendine Publishing, Inc.
Categories: Education

Name: Kay Quinn, Managing Editor
Name: Teresa Beard, Assistant Editor
Material: Any
Address: PO BOX 14081
City/State/ZIP: GAINESVILLE FL 32601
Telephone: 352-373-6907
Fax: 352-373-8120
E-mail: oxendine@compuserve.com

The *CareFREE*
ENTERPRISE

"Arizona's Second-Oldest" **Magazine**

Carefree Enterprise

What is the *Carefree Enterprise* and who reads it?

The *Carefree Enterprise* magazine is a general interest publication that is produced 11 times annually (the July/August issue is combined). The *Enterprise*, Arizona's second-oldest magazine, offers "good news" and positive articles. Entertaining and informative, a variety of subjects are provided in each issue. Topics in this family-oriented publication include Arizona history, travel (state/nation/world), cooking/recipes, desert flora and fauna, health care, interior design, and enjoying the outdoors (bicycling, fishing, hiking, birdwatching, camping, RVing, etc.). The youngest regular columnist, a 12-year-old, writes from a kid's perspective.

CONTRIBUTOR'S GUIDELINES

• We accept freelance materials on speculation; we prefer queries but either will work.

• Features (with color or black & white prints) may run from 800 to 1,500 words, depending on the topic, but this would need to be assigned before you invest the time and energy into producing a piece that we may or may not be interested in using. We prefer query letters; no phone calls please. Shorter pieces pay $5 and up, depending on length, and a copy of the magazine.

• Handwritten articles will be returned unread. Disks (PC) in WordPerfect, Microsoft Word or ASCII text format are OK, but send hard copy, too, in case we have a problem reading your diskette. Preference: 3½" diskettes.

• We distribute through subscription, newsstands and special arrangements with Chamber of Commerce locations, real estate offices and resorts.

• Readership is 20,000 per issue and worldwide. The *Enterprise* is considered to be a "coffee table" edition.

• Primary service areas are Carefree, Cave Creek, Pinnacle Peak, Tonto Hills, North Scottsdale, Rio Verde, Fountain Hills, New River, Desert Hills and Northeast Phoenix. "Local" pieces can include any of these areas.

• We reach an upwardly mobile audience...college educated, with degrees. In addition to loyal subscribers, many doctors/professionals subscribe for their waiting rooms.

• Any/all Arizona history and statewide travel is welcomed. We prefer destination pieces with photo support. We use seasonal, reflective, thought-provoking and inspirational pieces. We do not publish anything that is not suitable for families. Some poetry is used (sparingly). We prefer articles with a local slant, except for nationwide/worldwide travel. We give assignments once we are familiar with a writer's work.

• Photos must be identified. Subject matter, captions with names of persons included in photos; name of article photos are accompanying; name, address and phone number of photographer; and model releases (model releases *must* be enclosed or the photos will not run).

• Nearly any human interest story with a positive upbeat slant works for us—i.e., local residents, Arizona residents...anyone with an extremely interesting story. (A feature we ran on a young, autistic, local artist was very well received and was consequently picked up by television and newspapers, statewide.) Our youngest columnist is 12 years old and we enjoy pieces that appeal to a younger audience on occasion.

• The *Enterprise* is a "Pollyanna-ish" publication. Only "good news" items have a chance. We do not publish negative or contro-versial stories. The **Enterprise** *is not* in "the newspaper busi-ness"—we don't cover the news.

• As writers, we have the opportunity to influence others in a positive way. This is our "gift" to our readers.

• Our pay scale is $5 to $50 and a copy of the magazine when your article is published. Payment is usually made 30-60 days after publication, and in some instances, 60-90 days.

• **Sample** copy $4.00; *or* $2.00 and a 12"x15" SASE with first class postage affixed ($2.16, 1997 rates).

DEADLINE:

Editorial material must be received no later than the fifth of the month preceding the month of publication. We would appre-ciate receiving editorial and photographs as early as possible for timely events, and up to four months in advance of issue date for regular features (assigned or on spec.). If we receive materials late, chances are they won't run. Your adherence to deadline dates will be greatly appreciated.

PLEASE NOTE—DEADLINE FOR HOLIDAYS:

• **Holiday months**, (May, Sept., Nov., Dec., & Jan.) all mate-rials are due by the 15th of the month *two months prior to the month of publication*, (i.e. two weeks earlier than usual. We lose one week or more of production time during holiday months. Your cooperation is appreciated!)

• Editorial may be supplied on disk; either size. We can con-vert WordPerfect 5.1 or 5.2 for DOS or WP 5.1 to 6.2 for Win-dows.

• **Diskettes:** All editorial disks must be submitted with NO commands or style sheets entered. (i.e., *don't* center, tab, capital-ize words inside sentences; no italics, etc. in text. We cannot con-vert it successfully.) Special formatting has to be stripped out by our staff before typesetting, anyway.

• All editorial disks must be submitted with a hardcopy of the text. Disks must be labeled with writer's name/address/phone and article title. *No exceptions!*

• We prefer 12 point Helvetica or similar sans serif type for text that must be scanned. (Most PCs come loaded with Times Roman as a default font. Please switch your font to Helvetica or Arial. Thanks.

• Send queries or submissions with clips.

Categories: Nonfiction—Arts—Consumer—Cooking—En-vironment—Family—Fishing—Food/Drink—General Interest—Health—Inspirational—Lifestyles—Outdoors—Physical Fit-ness—Recreation—Travel

Name: Fran Barbano, Editor
Name: Laura Hadley, Assistant Editor
Name: Steve Strine, Graphic Design
Material: Any
Address: PO BOX 1145
City/State/ZIP: CAREFREE AZ 85377
Telephone: 602-488-3098
E-mail: FB1CEM@aol.com

The Carolina Quarterly
University of North Carolina

History

Since 1948 *The Carolina Quarterly* has served as a forum for the best work by writers with established reputations and by writers at the very beginnings of their careers. Among the many fine writers whose work has appeared in *The Carolina Quarterly* are Conrad Aiken, Wendell Berry, Anthony Burgess, Raymond Carver, Don DeLillo, Annie Dillard, Louise Erdrich, Lawrence Ferlinghetti, Paul Green, Michael S. Harper, Archibald MacLeish, Joyce Carol Oates, Reynolds Price, Kenneth Rexroth, and Tho-mas Wolfe. Among contributors to recent issues are Mark Doty, Stephen Dunn, Clyde Edgerton, George Garrett, Barry Hannah, William Harmon, X. J. Kennedy, James Laughlin, Denise Levertov, Robert Morgan, and Gregory Orr.

Guidelines for Writers

The editorial board of *The Carolina Quarterly* welcomes sub-missions of fiction, poetry, reviews, nonfiction, and graphic art. Prose and poetry in all styles and on all subjects are of interest. The board also considers translations of work originally written in languages other than English. Black-and-white graphic art is used to illustrate prose in each issue and to decorate each cover.

Despite its name, *The Carolina Quarterly* goes to press three times a year, so manuscripts and artwork may be kept under se-rious consideration for four months or more. The editorial board considers unpublished work only and does not consider simulta-neous submissions. All correspondence may be sent to the edito-rial board at the address below. Writers and artists should send only clear *copies* of their work.

Contributors of writing and art receive four copies of the is-sue in which their work appears and a 50% discount on additional copies. *The Carolina Quarterly* acquires first-publication rights to each work accepted for publication; subsequent to publication, rights revert to the author. Writers without major publication credits are eligible for the yearly Charles B. Wood Award for Distinguished Writing, a $500 prize for the best poem or story by an unestablished writer published in each volume.

Sample Copies and Subscriptions

Writers and artists may find it helpful to look at a sample copy of *The Carolina Quarterly*. A sample copy of a recent issue costs $5 (including shipping and handling). Yearly subscriptions to *The Carolina Quarterly* are just $10 to individuals. Interna-tional subscriptions to individuals are $12.

Categories: Fiction—Nonfiction—African-American—Drama—Gay/Lesbian—Interview—Literature—Men's Fic-tion—Men's Issues—Multicultural—Native American—Poetry—Reviews—Short Stories—Women's Fiction—Women's issues—Writing

Name: Fiction Editor
Name: Poetry Editor
Address: EDITORIAL BOARD CB 3520 GREENLAW HALL
Address: UNIVERSITY OF NORTH CAROLINA
City/State/ZIP: CHAPEL HILL NC 27599-3520
Telephone: 919-962-0244
Fax: 919-962-3520

Cartoonist and Comic Artist Magazine

Magazine (8½"x11"). Provides industry news and features for the aspiring cartoonist. Circulation: 2,500+

Needs: Articles should focus on news and trends in the busi-ness. Interviews with prominent cartoonists and comic artists must include information about how they produce their art, and hoe they became successful. 500-2,000 words. Mail or e-mail com-plete manuscript.

Reports in two weeks.

Payment: Varies, usually ranges from $50 to $100.

Advice: Our magazine is for people interested in cartooning, so it is very visual. We need art and photographs for our features.

Categories: Cartoons

Name: Steve Pastis, Publisher/Editor
Material: All
Address: 2747 N GRAND AVE STE 250

City/State/ZIP: SANTA ANA CA 92705
Telephone: 714-550-9933
Fax: 714-550-9933
E-mail: cartoonmag@aol.com

Cascades East Magazine
Central Oregon's Quarterly Magazine
—Since 1976

Two types of articles offer limited opportunities for freelancers:

First-Person Accounts of Outdoor Activities

First-person accounts, with black & white or color photos, of outdoor activities in Central Oregon (Deschutes, Jefferson & Crook counties) are of particular need. Activities can include fishing, hunting, camping, hiking, backpacking, spelunking, etc. These would be strong narratives although treatment can be dramatic, factual or humorous. No "travel folder" tours. Queries are considered, however finished articles of 1,000 to 2,000 words are preferred.

Historical Features

Each issue includes a "Little Known Tales from Oregon History" feature. Query letters are preferred along with a statement of the availability of black & white photos. Length from 1,000 to 2,000 words.

Payment for the Above

5 to 10 cents a word with additional payment for photos. Payment is made upon publication.

Color Photos

Horizontal, color transparencies of superior quality are needed, on a limited basis, for the magazine cover.

Editing

Any material accepted is subject to such revision necessary in our sole discretion to meet the requirements of CASCADES EAST.

Categories: Nonfiction—History—Outdoors—Recreation—Regional

Name: Kim Hogue, Editor
Material: All
Address: PO BOX 5784
City/State/ZIP: BEND OR 97708
Telephone: 541-382-0127
Fax: 541-382-7057
E-mail: Sunpub@sun-pub.com

Cat Fancy

Writing for *Cat Fancy*:

Thank you for your interest in *Cat Fancy*, a consumer magazine directed to the general cat-owning population and dedicated to improving the lives of cats worldwide. We have listed below some of the publication requirements of our magazine.

Before you get started, we suggest that you read past issues of the magazine to acquaint yourself with the type of material we use. Past issues are available at many public libraries, or you may order a sample issue by sending $5.50 to the address on the back.

Unsolicited Manuscripts: *Cat Fancy* does not read or accept unsolicited manuscripts; however, the editors are happy to consider article queries. Unsolicited manuscripts sent with a self-addressed, stamped envelope are returned unread. Those without an SASE are discarded. Please query if you have an article idea in mind.

Feature Articles: While 90 percent of the feature articles that appear in *Cat Fancy* are assigned to writers we work with regularly, we do occasionally accept a feature or feature sidebar from a new contributor.

Each month, we try to provide our readers a mix of informative articles dealing with feline health, nutrition, grooming, behavior and training, as well as a fun feature or two on cat-related events, hobbies, etc. Breed profiles, run nearly every month, are usually assigned to a breeder or cat show judge. Occasionally, we run exceptional pieces of fiction or photo essays. We rarely use stories in which the cat speaks as if it were human.

While we assign most medical and behavior pieces to certified experts in the particular field, we will consider well-researched pieces by freelancers it experts are consulted. While there is no substitute for good writing, experts add credibility.

Department Articles: With few exceptions, our departments are written by regular columnists or by the editors. We occasionally accept articles of less than 1,000 words for our Cat Newsline column. Such articles should cover news items of national interest to cat lovers. Possible subjects include new legislation affecting cat owners, medical breakthroughs and trends in cat care.

We also use short stories, how-to pieces, word puzzles, quizzes and craft projects in our Kids for Cats column, a section aimed at our readers between 10 and 16 years old. Good-quality photographs are essential to craft projects.

The Feline Friends department is a column written by readers about their special cats. We accept Feline Friends submissions for consideration only once or twice a year. Check the end of the Feline Friends column in a current issue of the magazine for an announcement of when we will be accepting manuscripts again and for submission specifications. If no announcement appears, we are not currently accepting submissions.

Poetry: Poetry is the one exception to our query-first policy. The editors are happy to consider short, cat-related poems, which are used primarily as filler in the back of the magazine. We put no limit on the number of poems you may submit, but be sure to include a self-addressed, stamped envelope large enough for their return.

In general, we're looking for straightforward poems that capture the essence of the cat or of what owning a cat means to our readers. We rarely go for esoteric poems with deep hidden meanings. To get a feel for our readers, read back issues of the magazine.

The Query: Following are a few points to consider when querying:

When possible, limit your query to one typewritten page.

We will be judging your writing ability on your query letter—put as much effort into your letter as you plan to put into your manuscript.

Research, research, research. Before sending a query, know the subject and be sure your letter reflects this knowledge. If you wish to write on a medical or behavioral subject in which you are not a certified expert, plan to interview an expert or two for your story. Include that information in your query.

Read back issues to find out whether we've recently covered your planned topic and to familiarize yourself with our style and readership.

If available, include one or two previously published writing samples.

Excellent-quality color photographs are essential to considering stories on regional events or cat-related attractions.

Please be patient. We'll make every effort to respond to your query within eight weeks. Occasionally, however, this simply isn't possible.

We do not consider fax, telephone or e-mail queries.

Submission Specifications: We only assign articles to writers with whom we work regularly; all others will be asked to submit work on speculation. After assignment or a go-ahead to send an article on speculation, your manuscript should be typewritten and double-spaced. Send both a hard copy and an electronic file in ASCII or text-only format on a 3.5 inch disk.

We prefer that articles be accompanied by appropriate art in the form of professional-quality transparencies or professional illustrations. We rarely use black-and-white photos. For more information, send for our photo guidelines, photo needs list and/ or artist's guidelines.

With every submission, include a self-addressed, stamped envelope large enough to accommodate return of your materials.

Payment: *Cat Fancy* pays on publication. Article fees are based on the quality of the article and the experience of the author. We pay more for manuscripts accompanied by good-quality photographs.

You can expect payment to arrive in the latter part of the cover month in which the article appears (for example, if your piece appears in the November issue, your check should arrive in the latter part of November). We buy first North American Serial Rights on an exclusive basis; the nonexclusive right to use the article and/or artwork in electronic media; and the nonexclusive right to use the article and/or artwork as well as your name, image and biographical data in advertising and promotion.

Responsibility: We cannot assume responsibility for materials you submit, but we assure you that we will take all reasonable care in handling your work.

Miscellaneous:

Inquiries should be in writing. While it may seem quicker to call, interruptions throughout the day will lead to a longer turnaround time for manuscripts and queries in the long run.

Additional guidelines are available for artists and photographers. Send an SASE with your request.

You must include a self-addressed, stamped envelope with every query or submission. We cannot respond to or acknowledge any correspondence or submission that does not include an SASE.

If you've been assigned an article and must send it via an express delivery service to meet your deadline, call our offices to get the street address. Please do not fax materials unless requested to do so by the editors.

Categories: Fiction—Nonfiction—Animals—Children—Crafts—Games—Health—History—Hobbies—Poetry—Short Stories—Pets—How-to—Humor—Personal Experience—News

Name: Debbie Phillips-Donaldson, Editor
Material: All
Address: P.O. BOX 6050
City/State/ZIP: MISSION VIEJO, CA 92690
Telephone: 714-855-8822
Fax: 714-855-3045
Internet: www.petchannel.com

Catholic Digest

What material *Catholic Digest* uses

Nonfiction articles: 1,000-3,500 words on almost any topic. Our readers have a wide range of interests — religion, family, science, health, human relationships, nostalgia, good works, and more.

Catholic Digest article rates: $100 for reprints, $200-$400 for originals. For re-use in electronic form, we pay half of all traceable revenue derived from use to owner/author. Online-only articles receive $100, plus half of any traceable revenue from electronic use. A copy of the issue is included with payment if published in *Catholic Digest.* Finders' fees are $15 per article published.

If submitting by mail, enclose a self-addressed, stamped envelope (SASE).

Fillers: *Catholic Digest* features four regular fillers each month plus a variety of other fillers.

1) OPEN DOOR — Statements of true incidents through which people are brought into the Catholic faith, or recover the Catholic faith they had lost. (200-500 words)

2) SIGNS OF THE TIMES — Amusing or significant signs. Give exact source.

3) IN OUR PARISH — Stories of parish life. (50-300 words)

4) One of the following:

PEOPLE ARE LIKE THAT — Original accounts of true incidents that illustrate the instinctive goodness of human nature. (200-500 words)

PERFECT ASSIST — Original accounts of gracious or tactful remarks or actions. (200-500 words)

HEARTS ARE TRUMPS — Original accounts of true cases of unseeking kindness. (200-500 words)

Other fillers: jokes, short anecdotes, quizzes, and informational paragraphs. (one-liners to 500 words)

Catholic Digest filler rates: To authors, we pay $2 per published line (full-page width) upon publication. For this payment, your filler may be published in any *Catholic Digest* publication, including but not limited to *Catholic Digest, Catholic Digest Reader* Large Print, and HEAVEN, our online Web site (http://www.CatholicDigest.org). A copy of the issue is included with payment if published in *Catholic Digest.* Finders' fees are $5 or $10, depending on length.

If submitting by mail, enclose a self-addressed, stamped envelope (SASE).

Tips on selling a manuscript to *Catholic Digest*

Before you submit a manuscript, study a copy of *Catholic Digest* for article tone and style, or check HEAVEN (http://www.CatholicDigest.org).

We favor the anecdotal approach. Stories submitted must be strongly focused on a definitive topic. This topic is to be illustrated for the reader by way of a well-developed series of true-life, interconnected vignettes.

Most articles we use are reprinted — they have appeared in another periodical or newspaper. But we also consider original submissions.

Don't query. Send the article itself.

We don't consider fiction, poetry, or submissions simultaneously sent to other publications.

Include your name, address, and telephone number on each submitted page.

If you are submitting an article for reprint consideration, you must include the name, address, and editor of the original publication source, the copyright line from the original source, and the page number and date of the original publication.

If you are submitting an original manuscript by mail, please send a double-spaced, typewritten photocopy and, if possible, an ASCII text file saved on a 3.5" diskette. E-mail submissions should be included in the text of your message rather than as an attached file.

Categories: Catholic Church—Nonfiction

Name: Articles Editor
Material: Articles:
Name: Fillers Editor
Material: Fillers
Address: P.O. Box 64090
City/State/ZIP: St. Paul, MN 55164
E-mail to: Cdigest@stthomas.edu.

Catholic Near East

Catholic Near East magazine strives to educate its readers about the culture, faith, history, issues and people who form the Eastern Christian churches.

Established in 1974 by Catholic Near East Welfare Association, this bimonthly publication also attempts to inform its readers of the presence and work of the Association and its sister agency, the Pontifical Mission, in those nations that many Eastern Christians call home.

The goal of *Catholic Near East* is to inform, but its contents should not be academic. People, details of contemporary life, history and "local color" should be woven together. Eastern Christians—Catholic and Orthodox—are frequently depicted as relics of the past. Our goal is to portray these communities as living bodies of men, women and children living and coping in a confused and often troubled world.

Catholic Near East is also a tool of ecumenical and interreligious dialogue. Eastern forms of Christianity, Catholic and Orthodox, should be highlighted. However, the Jewish, Hindu and Muslim communities should not be ignored.

The most successful articles are written by those in the field. Stringers in each PM city and in other CNEWA countries offer the most objective, accurate and sensitive portraits of their subjects. Articles should not exceed 1,500 words. This stipulation allows for the lavish use of color photographs.

Photographers, if they are not writers as well, should work with the respective author (the editor should coordinate these efforts). Photographs must illustrate what is described in the article—people, places, festival, etc. General or thematic illustrations are exceptions.

Categories: Christian Interests—Religion

Name: Michael La Civita, Executive Editor
Material: All
Address: 1011 FIRST AVE
City/State/ZIP: NEW YORK NY 10022-4195
Telephone: 212-826-1480
Fax: 212-826-8979

Catsumer Report™
The Consumer Newsletter for Cat Owners!

Please refer to *Good Dog!*
Categories: Nonfiction—Animals

Name: Judi Becker, Managing Editor
Material: All
Address: PO BOX 10069
City/State/ZIP: AUSTIN TX 78766-1069
Telephone: 512-454-6090
Fax: 512-454-3420
E-mail: gooddogmag@aol.com

The Centennial Review
Michigan State University

The Centennial Review is committed to reflection on intellectual work, particularly as set in the University and its environment. While University professionals come from many specializations, models of disciplinary research, or even typical modes of work and production, they usually share at least the idea of the University as a community or a crucial site of cultural production. One of CR's particular commitments is to seek out work that writes to and from the community of University experience.

CR's editors look for certain qualities in most of the essays we publish (there are always exceptions), and these follow from the way in which we imagine our audience, which we think of as a general intellectual audience. We aren't aiming to publish very specialized disciplinary work (though the essays we publish may very well *begin* from the experience of specialized research), nor are we aiming for a popular audience. While a **CR** essay should proceed discursively, relating its materials to a general audience, there should be no sense of 'writing down.' It may be necessary occasionally to use some specialized vocabulary, but it ought to be either explained or so built into the discursive structures that its significance is clear to the general reader.

We are looking for argument, discursive narrative, critical review: neither overly theoretical on the one hand nor simply a presentation of the results of specialized research on the other. However, an essay which addresses new technological developments, or the transformation of research areas, may require the 'presentation' of data, techniques, or emerging models that characterize a developing area which is becoming generally important to university experience. While we welcome polemical essays and anticipate that some of the best contributions will have distinctive arguments to offer, we don't require that our essays develop such arguments: there's always room for articles that are relatively dispassionate in their exposition.

In questions of style and documentation, contributors should consult *The Chicago Manual of Style* or the *MLA Handbook*. Two copies of all submissions must be furnished to the Editor. When work has been accepted for publication we will request that authors send a final manuscript copy on computer disk.

Categories: Nonfiction—African-American—Agriculture—Architecture—Arts—Biography—Careers—College—Culture—Drama—Ecology—Economics—Education—Electronics—Engineering—Feminism—Government—History—Language—Law—Literature—Multicultural—Philosophy—Politics—Psychology—Public Policy—Society—Technology—Theatre

Name: R.K. Meiners, Editor
Material: All
Address: MICHIGAN STATE UNIVERSITY
Address: 312 LINTON HALL
City/State/ZIP: E LANSING MI 48824-1044
Telephone: 517-355-1905
Fax: 517-432-1858
E-mail: CENREV@pilot.msu.edu

Challenges

Challenges
America's Recovery Communications Network

Challenges has been in continuous publication since March of 1992, sharing vital information with those who are determined to help themselves. Because *Challenges* is not affiliated with any 12 step program or organization, it is in a unique position to recognize the work of those in the recovery field. Several times a year, as appropriate, a specific group or individual is chosen to receive *Challenge*'s Outstanding Service Award.

Think of *Challenges* as a clearinghouse that, every month, pulls together the best of timely information from many different sources. While *Challenges* is not a substitute for professional counseling or participation in a reputable recovery program, it often serves as a welcome adjunct.

To submit written material:

Make sure that your name and address appear on every page. Type or write clearly. Submissions must relate to recovery from abuse, addiction, codependency, eating disorders, obsessive/compulsive behaviors, loss, physical problems, et cetera.

Subscription information:

Order a one-year subscription to timeless wisdom! You'll receive a printed copy of the 40-page bimonthly (Challenges is published every other month, six times per year) mailed to your home address. Using US funds, mail your check or money order for $25 (USA addresses) or $31 (Canada addresses) or $40 (all other addresses) to the address below.

Categories: Nonfiction—Family—Health—Inspirational—Marriage—Mental Health—Psychology—Recovery (from anything)—Relationships—Self-Help—Spiritual

Name: Submissions Editor
Material: All
Address: 2050 PARKER ST
City/State/ZIP: SPRINGFIELD MA 01128-1255
Telephone: 413-796-7826
Fax: 413-796-7802
E-mail: publisher@challenges.com
Internet: www.challenges.com

Champion BASS Magazine

Our goal is to make *Champion BASS* the most authoritative reference guide for bass tournament anglers. The focus of the magazine deals with the mental and physical preparation to fish bass tournaments. It is not only about "how" to fish, but also about the "whys" and adapting to seasonal changes. Biological information is very important.

Each issue has three main sections:

1. Columns by bass pros such as Jay Yelas, Gary Klein, Kevin VanDam, Shaw Grigsby, Guido Hibdon, Ken Cook, and David Fritts

2. In-depth features of 1,500 to 3,000 words on strategies, issues, etc. Additional standard-length articles of 750 to 1,800 words about projects, tips or other items of interest to tournament anglers.

3. Serious reports on the top bass tournament waters like Sam Rayburn, Minnetonka, and 1,000 Islands. Up to 4,500 words.

EDITORIAL REQUIREMENTS

• Content geared to the serious and occasional tournament angler

• Quotes from authorities on the subject—pros, guides, manufacturers and biologists

• Specific lures and equipment and identification of manufacturers

• Articles based on current scientific research and biological data

• Very important—new facts, not rehashed or outdated opinions

SPECIFICATIONS

• **FEATURE ARTICLES:** In-depth, hands-on bass information including seasonal and regional variations—southern, northern and western strategies may vary. Educational content is important, as are practical solutions to tough fishing problems. Subjects: techniques, biology, technology, seasonal conditions, etc. Include slides, photos, charts, maps and/or illustrations. We also like to clarify subjects with sidebar explanations.

• **STANDARD ARTICLES:** Unique projects, tidbits, short technical pieces, innovative projects, etc. If helpful, use quotes from experts. Include slides, diagrams, etc.

• **TOURNAMENT DESTINATIONS ARTICLES:** We want to know the nuts and bolts-why, where, how. Include information on seasonal, variations, good detailed maps and interviews with experts-guides, biologists, and major tournament anglers. List lodges, guides and camping areas with phone numbers.

• **PHOTOS AND ILLUSTRATIONS:** We require 35mm color slides. We strongly encourage fishing action shots and photos showing tackle, techniques, rigging, lures, locations and some big fish photos. Please send photo captions with names, places and pertinent information.

• **HUMOR/REAL LIFE ADVENTURES:** Creative entertainment. (Not used in every issue, but creative efforts are needed.)

• **PHOTOS:** Cover shot must include angler bass, scenery, and action in one shot.

RATES

Rates are based upon how well the article is written, photo support or illustrations and how closely the author follows the writer's guidelines. Payment for articles and photographs payable 30 to 45 days after publication.

• Feature articles: 1,500 to 3,000 words-$200 to $500.
• Standard articles: 750 to 1,800 words-$75 to $200.
• Destinations articles: 2,000 to 4,500 words-$200 to $500.
• Humor/real life adventure: 750 to 1,000 words-$75 to $250.
• Photos: Independent Inside use $25 to $75.
• Cover shot (angler, bass, scenery, and action)-Up to $400.
Categories: Fishing

Name: Randy Brudnicki, Executive Editor
Material: Any
Name: Debra Brua Biser, Managing Editor
Material: Any
Address: 350 E CENTER ST STE 201
City/State/ZIP: PROVO UT 84606
Telephone: 801-377-7111
Fax: 801-377-7196

Change
The Magazine of Higher Learning

Change is an opinion magazine dealing with contemporary issues in higher learning. It is intended to stimulate the thoughts of reflective practitioners in colleges, universities, corporations, government, and elsewhere. Using a magazine style and format, rather than that of an academic journal, *Change* seeks to spotlight trends, provide new insights and ideas, and analyze the implications of educational programs and practices.

The editorial focus of *Change* includes articles and profiles on trend-setting institutions and individuals, innovative teaching methods, economics and finance, administrative practice and governance, public policy, professional development, curriculum, the changing needs of students, educational philosophy, and the social role of higher education.

The editors encourage well-founded discussion of controversial policy issues, whether brief expressions of a point of view-

750 to 1,500 words-or more extended articles ranging from 2,500 to 5,000 words long.

Audience

Change, which is published six times a year, is intended for individuals responsible for higher learning in college, university, and other settings, including faculty, administrators, trustees, state and federal officials, students, and corporation, union, and foundation officers.

Manuscripts

• All manuscripts should be submitted in duplicate. If the article is accepted, at that time we will request a disk of the article in either Microsoft Word 5.0 (or higher) or WordPerfect 5.1.

• Because **Change** is a magazine rather than a journal, footnotes should not be included. References can be worked into the text or given parenthetically when necessary. Lists of "Related Readings" or "Resources" can be provided with the article where appropriate.

• A separate title page should provide short biographical information (up to four or five lines), and contact information including the complete address, telephone, and fax number of the author(s). The first-named author of a multi-authored article will receive the notification of acceptance, rejection, or need for revision.

Review Process

When we receive your manuscript, you will be sent a postcard verifying that your article has entered the review process. All manuscripts will be critically read by a consulting editor and an executive editor, a process that takes from three to four months to complete. (Should the manuscript be held for consideration longer than usual, you will be notified at the end of four months and offered the option of withdrawing the manuscript from consideration.)

If the article is accepted, you will be contacted to discuss editing procedures and the production schedule for the issue of the magazine in which your article will appear. Each author receives six complimentary copies of the issue in which the article is included. Authors may also order additional copies or reprints (minimum order of 100). We do not usually pay for unsolicited manuscripts.

Manuscripts should be submitted exclusively to this publication.

EDITORIAL
CONTRIBUTING TO CHANGE

Twelve years ago, when AAHE assumed editorial responsibility for **Change,** we faced a problem of a depleted author pool. In response, we worked energetically to identify topics and commission articles, hoping thereby to set a new expectancy for **Change** among readers and writers alike.

Happily, **Change** did gain in stature; today, good writers bring their best work to us. Yes, we still commission articles, especially for issues with cover themes. But we're pleased that today's **Change** can be less prescribed and editor-driven, and more a vehicle for independent voices-including, perhaps, your own.

Should you be writing for **Change**? Let me encourage the thought by telling you how we operate and what we're looking for.

Owned by Heldref Publications, a division of the nonprofit Helen Dwight Reid Education Foundation here in Washington, **Change** is one of the 44 education-related journals and magazines published by Heldref. The magazine staff at Heldref includes a full-time managing editor, Nanette Wiese, and an associate editor, Lorraine Brincka. It is to Heldref that you direct all manuscripts, letters to the editor, and queries about guidelines for writers, as well as questions regarding advertising and subscriptions. (See the masthead for relevant contact information.)

By agreement with Heldref, AAHE is responsible for all editorial judgments about the magazine—its themes, articles, and editorial voice. We exercise that judgment through a team of three executive editors-Zelda F. Gamson, Art Levine, and me. I devote two days a week to **Change** as AAHE's in-house "lead editor." When the executive editors meet as a group, we're joined by Nanette Wiese and AAHE President Russell Edgerton.

Our manuscript review process works like this. Nanette Wiese receives and acknowledges all submissions. She and I then read and make an initial judgment about each manuscript's aptness for **Change**. If the chances look poor, we try to let authors know within six weeks so they can pursue placement elsewhere.

After the initial screening, Lorraine Brincka sends all remaining manuscripts off for review to one or more consulting editors (these are listed on the masthead). **Change** doesn't claim to be "refereed" in the sense of a journal, but its articles are indeed evaluated for accuracy, argument, style, and interest to the readership.

Manuscripts and reviewer comments are then read by the executive editors, with the concurrence of at least two editors needed to accept or reject. Even the best manuscripts compete at this point for limited space: we publish just six times a year and can use but 20 or so of the hundreds of manuscripts submitted. We dislike acceptance "for future use" and try to hold only those we can use soon. Our goal is to get final word to authors within three months of submission.

What accounts for acceptance or rejection? In my experience, few manuscripts fail for general ignorance or poor writing. More typically, they turn up on topics that have been done to death (the culture wars) or that are too broad (the history of universities in 2,000 words or less) or too specific for our broad, generalist audience (preventing dormitory theft). Or they're written in the style of a journal-heavy on jargon and footnotes, light on analysis and point of view.

This last criterion is important. **Change** is a *magazine,* and the magazine *article* is a genre unto itself. What characterizes that genre? There's no formula, but a good article compels attention to an important matter. It shows a mind at work, one that reaches judgment and takes a stance. It is necessarily personal: it has a voice that speaks to the reader. It is credible: it knows its subject and the context. And it is concrete: it names people, places, dates, specific statements, and events-these to convey feeling for the subject and for life as it is lived, not as abstracted from an armchair. For models, I look to the *Atlantic Monthly.*

Change doesn't start with an ideological predisposition; we court good ideas from all sides, plus voices that remind us that change isn't the same as improvement. But tracts, broadsides, and grand plans seldom impress reviewers (or readers), who prefer real, usable ideas that someone has actually tried out and evaluated.

Most writers who submit manuscripts do so with a main feature article in mind (2,500 to 5,000 words), which is fine. But the magazine has a continuing need, too, for shorter pieces-a column (700 words), a profile, even humor. Another department to consider is our front-of-the-book Forum, for which we're after a shorter statement (700 to 2,000 words) on a controversial topic, in which you put yourself on the line.

Beyond writing *for* **Change,** let me encourage you to write *to* the magazine, or to me or one of the other executive editors. Feedback is not plentiful in the magazine business; I assure you that any reader comment gets full attention. Feedback helps your editors make **Change** better and more valuable for all of us.

Categories: College—Education

Name: Submissions Editor
Material: All
Address: 1319 18TH ST NW
City/State/ZIP: WASHINGTON DC 20036

Telephone: 202-296-6267
Fax: 202-296-5149
E-mail: ch@heldref.org
Internet: www.heldref.org
Nota bene: *Change* is a magazine for professors and administrators at colleges and universities.

Charleston

Charleston Magazine has been a Lowcountry institution for over six years, distilling the essence of Charleston and her outlying districts into a lively, informative, entertaining, and sophisticated resource for both residents and visitors. Each bimonthly issue brings to readers 68 pages of editorial and artistic excellence, tapping into the pulse of the Lowcountry and bringing its audience closer to what's going on in South Carolina's most vivacious city. The editorial mission of *Charleston* Magazine is simple: To be the single most indispensable resource in the Charleston area for comprehensive coverage of entertainment, arts and culture, leisure pursuits, personalities, and issues in a manner characterized by originality, thoroughness, and an artistic and journalistic excellence unmatchable by any other medium in the city.

Charleston, although a city with a formidable history, is a vibrant, modern community with no shortage of newsworthy subjects. Consequently, this is the Charleston we wish to present, not the Charleston of hundreds of years ago. Our goal is to be read, not to provide colorful decoration for coffee tables. We are normally uninterested in gratuitous history articles (at least those lacking a timely relevance) and articles that brim over with teary-eyed nostalgia for "the South" in general. We want to cultivate an editorial identity that is cutting-edge, urbane, sophisticated, witty, and completely contemporary.

Editorial categories we are especially interested in soliciting queries and manuscripts for include the following:

Features

Features are the strongest element of the magazine; we generally include either three or four per issue. They are characterized by thorough reporting on issues and concerns facing Lowcountry residents today (although features are by no means limited to "issues"). *Charleston* Magazine is in the singular position of being able to cover most subjects with a thoroughness unapproachable by any other medium in the city. We take advantage of that position whenever possible with articles that run anywhere from 1,500-3,500 words.

Channel Markers

Channel Markers is a two- to four-page department featuring short articles that highlight timely items of interest with a clever or witty twist and lively writing that snaps. Many of these brief items are written in-house, but we freely assign articles for Channel Markers if a query sounds worthwhile. (50-400 words)

Spotlight

Short profiles of entertaining, unusual, provocative, and influential personalities in the area. Spotlight profiles rarely run more than 300 words. In them, we do not attempt to encapsulate the subject's life in 300 words; rather, we give only as much background as is necessary to explain why the person is worth mentioning in the present context. (250-300 words)

20 Questions

20 Questions affords *Charleston* the opportunity to present a notable Charleston personality in a question- and-answer format. The questions may either range across a wide spectrum of subjects or focus in on a more narrow, contextually relevant theme. (2,200-3,000 words)

The Sporting Life

Humorous, adventurous or informative essays on Lowcountry pastimes such as sportfishing, golf, hunting, and racing, as well as modern adventure tales about the outdoors experience in general. (750-1,200 words)

The Arts

The Arts provides a forum for discussion of what's interesting in theater, dance, art, and music in Charleston and her surrounding communities. Usually two to three pages, with discussions of a given genre confined to a page each. (700 words each)

The Home Front

The Home Front is a venue for articles about homes, gardens, architecture, and interiors. Editorial ranges from stylish ways to use window boxes to renovation projects and interior design. (1,000-1,200 words)

The Marketplace

Profiles an exceptional local business for originality, greater-than-average success in a competitive market, community service, or some other significant quality. The Marketplace is often part of a larger advertising effort, and so is usually predetermined in-house. Even so, we willingly accept queries. (1,000-1,200 words)

The Good Fight

The Good Fight focuses on worthwhile battles being fought locally and statewide. Whether in the courts or on a homeowner's front lawn, The Good Fight highlights struggles that may not garner a big presence in other news media, and by its nature tends toward campaigns where there is a clear underdog readers can identify with. (1,000-1,200 words)

On the Road

On the Road considers travel opportunities and destinations in the Carolinas—especially those within weekend driving distance of Charleston. (1,000-1,200 words)

To Your Health

To Your Health is an umbrella department for discussing current issues in medicine, nutrition, healthcare, and exercise. (1,000-1,200 words)

Lowcountry Look

Lowcountry Look often acts as a catch-all department for those subjects of relevance to Charleston and of editorial merit that don't necessarily fit neatly into another department. (1,000-1,200 words)

Good Tastes

In Good Tastes, we discuss dining in the city and regional culinary trends. Ideally, we illustrate any such trend or dish with one or more examples from Charleston's bounty of restaurants. We do not limit ourselves to the finest restaurants in town; in fact, we encourage a wide range of culinary discussions. (1,000-1,200 words)

Southern View

This page is reserved for readers and writers with original thoughts to share about life in Charleston, with an emphasis on personal experience and individual perspective. Articles usually tend toward the short essay format, although masterful, succinct writing of any sort is welcomed. (750 words)

Categories: Nonfiction—Architecture—Arts—General Interest—Lifestyles—Regional

Name: Louise Chase Dettman, Editor
Material: All
Address: PO BOX 1794
City/State/ZIP: MT PLEASANT SC 29465-1794
Telephone: 803-971-9811
Fax: 803-971-0121
E-mail: LDettman@awod.com

The Chattahoochee Review
DeKalb College

The Chattahoochee Review pays $20.00 per *Chattahoochee* page for fiction, $15.00 per *Chattahoochee* page for essays, $100 per omnibook review, $25.00 per review of a single book, $100.00 per interview, and $50.00 per poem.

The aim of *The Chattahoochee Review* is to encourage unacknowledged writers and to provide printing space for published authors, striking a balance between the two. We are open to poetry and prose, both fiction and nonfiction. *The Chattahoochee Review* is copyrighted in its entirety. However, we are happy to grant reprint rights upon written request; we require only that the *Review* receive printed acknowledgement as first publisher.

All manuscripts should be typed. Prose should be double-spaced, and poetry should be single-spaced within stanzas, and double-spaced between stanzas. One poem to a page, please. Send originals or clear photocopies. The author's *name, address, telephone numbers* (including fax number, and e-mail address if available) should appear on the first page of each poem or prose piece. Send no more than one short story or nonfiction piece and no more than five (5) poems per submission. Your cover letter should provide sufficient information for us to compile a two- to three-sentence biography for our "Notes on Contributors" page, should the work be accepted. Do not send any work that is being simultaneously submitted to other publishers. Submit only work that has not been previously published.

Reviews: We usually review the categories that we publish: collections of poems or short stories. If you are submitting an omnibook review, please submit more of an essay than just a review-a piece that reflects the writer's other books and other relevant information. Please give the review a title inclusive of the book's title and provide the following bibliographic information: title of piece, author, title of book, publisher, date, number of pages, price.

Interviews: We are interested in a wide range of subjects, but favor interviews with notable Southern authors. If you wish to interview a writer for *The Chattahoochee Review,* please contact the nonfiction editor.

Essays: We prefer literary essays that focus on aesthetics, essays that are intelligent, insightful, and artful. We also welcome essays that address literary trends and activities. Submissions of personal essays should reveal human truths in evocative styles; essays in the traditions of Thoreau, Monette, and Rodriguez-masters of the personal essay. The human experience is powerful, especially if shared with beautiful language, honest reflection, and clear prose.

Subscriptions: $16.00 per year, $30.00 for two years, $5.00 per copy.

Categories: Fiction—Nonfiction—Literature—Poetry—Short Stories—Writing

Name: Lawrence Hetrick, Editor
Material: Any
Name: Jo Ann Yeager Adkins, Managing Editor
Material: Any
Name: Collie Owens, Poetry Editor
Material: Poetry
Address: 2101 WOMACK RD
City/State/ZIP: DUNWOODY GA 30338
Telephone: 770-551-3019
Fax: 770-551-7471

Chelsea
Awards for Poetry and Short Fiction

About the Awards

Chelsea, a nonprofit literary magazine founded in 1958 and appearing twice a year, awards two annual prizes of $750, for the best work of short fiction and for the best group of poems selected by the editors in anonymous competitions. Winning entries are published in *Chelsea*, and all work entered is considered for publication. The magazine has been funded in part by the National Endowment for the Arts and the New York State Council on the Arts as well as private foundations.

Manuscript Requirements

All manuscripts must be typed. Fiction must be double-spaced with standard margins; poetry may be single-spaced. The writer's name should not appear on the manuscript itself. Instead, include a single, separate cover sheet with title(s), name, address, and telephone number. Only previously unpublished work is eligible, and the manuscript should not be under consideration elsewhere or scheduled for book publication within six months of the competition deadline. *Manuscripts cannot be returned.*

For the poetry competition: Submit four to six poems. The entire entry should not exceed 500 lines. The editors look for overall excellence; it is not necessary that the poems be related thematically.

For the fiction competition: Send only one story. The manuscript should not exceed 30 typed pages or about 7,500 words. The editors welcome both traditional and experimental fiction.

Entry Fee

An entry fee of $10 is required, for which entrants will receive a subscription to *Chelsea.* Please make checks payable to Chelsea Associates, Inc. The fee will be waived for individuals who are current subscribers at the time of deadline and identify themselves as such. (N.B.: Be sure to notify the editors promptly of any changes of address since the post office will not automatically forward copies of the magazine.)

Annual Deadlines

June 15 for fiction; December 15 for poetry. Winners will be announced about two months after each deadline. Include a self-addressed, stamped envelope for notification of competition results.

Categories: Fiction—Nonfiction—Book Reviews—Literature—Poetry—Short Stories—Translations

Material: Chelsea Award Competition
Address: PO BOX 1040
City/State/ZIP: YORK BEACH ME 03910
Name: Richard Foerster, Editor
Material: General Submissions
Address: PO BOX 773 COOPER STATION
City/State/ZIP: NEW YORK NY 10276-0773
Telephone: 212-989-3083
Fax: 212-989-3083
Nota bene: Entry fee required for non-subscribers.

Chicago

A major magazine that covers a wide metropolitan area with a limited number of articles each month has to be highly selective about what it prints. Naturally, articles written with our readers in mind will interest us most. Our typical readers live along the lakefront or in other affluent communities, mainly in the suburbs. They have had more than four years of college and hold unusually high-paying jobs, often professional or managerial. Many are parents. They are well read and are interested in the arts and social issues. They go out several times a week to the city's theatres, music halls, and restaurants. They travel widely.

Procedures. Usually we assign or buy articles only after they have been discussed in editorial conferences, so put your queries in writing and send us samples of your best published work. In your query, tell us why you think your idea would interest our particular readers and why you are especially well qualified to write it.

Should we assign the story, you will be contacted by an articles editor, who will negotiate deadline and payment and outline the main features of the article we expect to receive. We will then send you a contract to sign and return.

Payment is on acceptance. What we pay depends on the length of your manuscript, the extent and nature of your research, and the importance we attach to the subject. You will be reimbursed for all reasonable expenses. Although we have paid both more and less, the following ranges will give you an idea of our rates:

Feature articles (including sidebars) $350-$1,500
Supplemental sidebars $150- $250
Short articles (columns) $275- $600

Standards. These are not hard-and-fast rules, and they don't apply to every article. If you have questions, discuss them with your articles editor.

1. A well-organized story usually answers a single question-often a very simple one. You may not know what it is at first, but after a little research you and your articles editor should be able to formulate one, and the answer ought to be the core of your story.

2. Your research should help you support a point of view. Your story is less likely to be successful if you merely present all sides of an issue and hope that the reader will discern the truth, or if you force a point of view that is not substantiated by your research, or if you tailor your research to validate a preconception.

3. A good magazine story is a good *story*. It doesn't just describe a state of affairs. It tells how and why the situation came about, who was instrumental in making it happen, what it means to the reader, and what the future holds. Often, novelistic devices can be effective: description, narrative, anecdote, dialogue, sensory detail. But if the situation in the story is not intrinsically interesting or does not have consequences that affect our readers, it might not be appropriate for us.

4. A good story usually focuses on individuals. Although institutions take action, it is ultimately individuals who make them act and whose lives are affected. A writer can make almost any story more vivid, and even more truthful, by concentrating on the people involved-their personalities, backgrounds, and motives-on what they stood to gain and lose, and on how they fared.

5. Good stories are rewritten stories. Our readers' time is limited; your manuscript should be a distilled version of your original draft. Remember: We don't pay by the word.

6. Above all, a good magazine story is believable and fair. Any person or institution whose character or actions have been impugned by the author or by anyone quoted in the article has a right to rebut those charges within your article. If that person or institution declines comment, say so in your story. *Chicago*

magazine's libel insurance does not cover free-lance writers.

Chicago magazine does not publish fiction, poetry or cartoons.

Categories: City/Regional
Name: Submissions Editor
Material: All
Address: 500 N DEARBORN STE 1200
City/State/ZIP: CHICAGO IL 60610
Telephone: 312-222-8999
Fax: 312-222-0699
E-mail: ChiMag@aol.com
Chicago Review
University of Chicago

Thank you for your interest in *Chicago Review*. Since 1946, *Chicago Review* has published innovative fiction, poetry, and essays, including work by John Ashbery, Leslie Silko, Joyce Carol Oates, William Burroughs, Susan Sontag, Thom Gunn, Robert Pinsky, Nikki Giovanni, Charles Simic, and many others. Recent special issues have focused on the literatures of India and the North Pacific Rim, the relation between poetry and mass culture, and new writing in Chicago. A 50th Anniversary retrospective issue was published in summer, 1996. A special issue on contemporary poetry and poetics was published in autumn, 1997.

Chicago Review welcomes both solicited and unsolicited manuscripts. The editors have established the following guidelines for contributors:

Simultaneous submissions are discouraged. If work is accepted elsewhere, please notify the *Chicago Review* office at once.

Chicago Review's staff tries to read and respond to all manuscripts promptly. However, turnaround time varies depending on how much unsolicited work is received. Also, work that is being seriously considered may be held longer. Please feel free to query by mail about the status of your manuscript.

There are no strict length requirements. The poetry editor prefers 3-7 pages of poetry. Fiction and nonfiction submissions average about 20 pages. Nonfiction should follow guidelines in *The Chicago Manual of Style*.

Contributors receive three copies of the issue in which their work appears, plus a one-volume subscription.

Potential contributors are encouraged to read a copy of the magazine. *Chicago Review* is carried by many universities, public libraries, and bookstores. Or, a sample issue can be ordered directly ($6 domestic, $11 overseas).

Categories: Fiction—Nonfiction—Literature—Poetry—Short Stories—Writing

Name: John Roberts, Fiction Editor
Material: Short Stories
Name: Devin Johnston, Poetry Editor
Material: Poetry
Name: Andrew Rathmann, Editor
Material: Nonfiction
Address: 5801 S KENWOOD AVE
City/State/ZIP: CHICAGO IL 60637
Telephone: 773-702-0887
Fax: 773-702-0887
E-mail: chicago_review@uchicago.edu

Child

Child magazine is published 10 times a year, with combined issues in June/July and December/January.

Child provides parents of children from birth to age 12 with the newest thinking, information, and advice they need to raise their families in a constantly changing, time-pressed world.

Freelance writers are invited to submit query letters only, on the following topics:

• children's health,

- parenting and marital relationship issues,
- child behavior and development, and
- personal essays pertaining to family life

Child purchases first-time rights for articles and pays upon acceptance. Fees vary depending on length and positioning of articles.

Writers must include clips of previously published work and a stamped, self-addressed envelope (SASE) with their queries. Please allow 8 weeks for a reply.

Categories: Children—Consumer—Parenting

Name: Submissions Editor
Material: All
Address: 375 LEXINGTON AVE
City/State/ZIP: NEW YORK NY 10017
Telephone: 212-499-2000
E-mail: childmag@aol.com

Childcare & Preschool Finder

Please refer to Bay Area Publishing Group, Inc.

Child Life

Please refer to Children's Better Health Institute

Children's Better Health Institute

We at the Children's Better Health Institute have a constant need for high-quality stories, articles, and activities with health-related themes. "Health" is a broad topic that includes exercise, nutrition, safety, hygiene, and drug education.

Health information can be presented in a variety of formats: fiction, nonfiction, poems, and puzzles. Fiction stories with a health message need not have health as the primary subject, but they should include it in some way in the course of events. Characters in fiction should adhere to good health practices, unless failure to do so is necessary to a story's plot.

Remember that characters in realistic stories should be up-to-date. Many of our readers have working mothers and/or come from single-parent homes. We need more stories that reflect these changing times but at the same time communicate good, wholesome values.

We are especially interested in material concerning sports and fitness, including profiles of famous amateur and professional athletes; "average" athletes (especially children) who have overcome obstacles to excel in their areas; and new or unusual sports, particularly those in which children can participate.

Nonfiction articles dealing with health subjects should be fresh and creative. Avoid an encyclopedic or "preachy" approach. We try to present our health material in a positive manner, incorporating humor and a light approach wherever possible without minimizing the seriousness of what we are saying.

Word and math puzzles, games, and other activities can also successfully convey health messages if they are enjoyable to young people and are age-appropriate.

We also welcome recipes that children can make on their own with minimal adult supervision. Ingredients should be helpful, so avoid using fats, sugar, salt, chocolate, and red meat. In all material submitted, please avoid references to eating sugary foods, such as candy, cakes, cookies, and soft drinks.

Although our emphasis is on health, we certainly use material with more general themes. We would especially like to see more holiday stories, articles, and activities. Please send seasonal material at least eight months in advance.

Caution: Reading our editorial guidelines is not enough! Care-ful study of current issues will acquaint writers with each title's "personality," various departments, and regular features, nearly all of which are open to freelancers. Sample copies are $1.75 each (U.S. currency) from the address below.

Turtle Magazine for Preschool Kids (ages 2-5)
Humpty Dumpty's Magazine (ages 4-6)

Turtle and *Humpty Dumpty* use stories and poems, as well as some creative nonfiction. Because these two magazines are designed to be read to children who are not yet reading independently, the editors look for submissions with a good "read-aloud" quality.

Games and crafts should require a minimum of adult guidance. They should also have clear, brief instructions, and use readily available materials. *Turtle* uses simple science experiments; *Humpty Dumpty* features healthful recipes requiring little or no use of kitchen appliances. Nonfiction, which editors always have a need for, must be narrow and specific in focus.

Children's Playmate (ages 6-8)
Jack And Jill (ages 7-10)

Children's Playmate uses easy-to-read fiction for beginning readers, as well as poems, rhyming stories, and nonfiction. *Jack And Jill* is edited for somewhat more accomplished readers; stories and articles are written at about a second- or third-grade reading level.

Both titles are heavy on fiction, using realistic, adventure, mystery, and fantasy. Humorous stories are especially needed. Nonfiction material may deal with sports, science, nature—even historical and biographical articles. Most nonfiction features touch in some way on health and fitness.

Child Life (ages 9-11)
Children's Digest (preteen)

Child Life editors encourage the submission of interesting nonfiction, especially profiles of kids or adults in sports, or active hobbies. Nonfiction articles should be accompanied by professional quality photographs or transparencies; no "snapshots," please. *Child Life* is a good market for offbeat or "slightly wacky" fiction, adventure, or science fiction.

Children's Digest readers want stories that are a little longer and "meatier." Fiction is especially needed: adventure, mystery, science fiction, and humorous stories. Some fiction may have a subtle health message, but this magazine, too, uses factual health features to educate about good health. Games, puzzles, crafts, and hobbies are also welcome, as are nonfiction articles about sports, nature, and the environment.

Manuscript Format

Manuscripts must be typewritten and double- or triple-spaced. The author's name, address, telephone number, date of submission, and the approximate word count of the material should appear on the first page of the manuscript. Title pages are not necessary. Please submit to a special magazine, not just to CBHI.

Please send the entire manuscript. All work is on speculation only; queries are not accepted, nor are stories assigned. The editors cannot criticize, offer suggestions, or enter into correspondence with an author concerning manuscripts that are not accepted, nor can they suggest other markets for material that is not published.

Photos and Illustrations

We do not purchase single photographs. We do purchase short photo features (up to 6 or 8 pictures) or photos that accompany articles and help illustrate editorial material. (please include captions and model releases.) Suggestions for illustrations are not necessary but are permissible. Please do not send drawings or other artwork. We prefer to work with professional illustrators of our own choosing.

Review Time

About three months are required to review manuscripts properly. Please wait three months before sending status inquiries. If a manuscript is returned, it should not be submitted to a different youth publication at this address. Each manuscript is carefully considered for possible use in all magazines, not only the one to which it was originally addressed.

Rates and Payment Policies

Turtle and *Humpty Dumpty*, up to 22¢ a word
        Fiction/nonfiction—up to 500 words
Children's Playmate, up to 17¢ a word
        Fiction/nonfiction—300 to 700 words
Jack And Jill, up to 17¢ a word
        Fiction/nonfiction—500 to 800 words
Child Life, minimum 12¢ a word
        Fiction/nonfiction—500 to 800 words
Children's Digest, minimum 12¢ a word
        Fiction—500 to 1,500 words
        Nonfiction—500 to 1,000 words
        Poetry—$15.00 minimum
        Photos—$15.00 minimum
        Puzzles and games—no fixed rates (Send SASE to receive separate guidelines for activities.)

Payment is made upon publication. Each author receives ten complimentary copies of the issue in which his or her material is published.

Rights

We purchase all rights to manuscripts. We buy one-time rights to photos. Simultaneous submissions are discouraged. One-time book rights may be returned when the author has found an interested publisher and can provide us with an approximate date of publication.

Children's Contributions

Except for items that are used in children's columns, the editors do not encourage submissions from children. Even highly talented young people are not usually experienced enough to compete on a professional level with adult authors. There is no payment for children's contributions.

CBHI also publishes *U.S. Kids, A Weekly Reader Magazine*, for readers 5-10. Although unsolicited manuscripts are welcome, editorial content is largely assigned. For more information, send for separate *U. S.Kids* guidelines—free with SASE—at the address below. Sample copies are $2.95 each.

Categories: Fitness—Health—Nonfiction

Name: Editor, (Magazine Name)
Material: All
Address: 100 Waterway Boulevard
        Box 567
City/Stete/ZIP: Indianapolis, IN 46206
Telephone: 317-636-8881

Children's Digest

Please refer to Children's Better Health Institute

Children's Playmate

Please refer to Children's Better Health Institute

Chiron Review

Chiron Review presents the widest possible range of contemporary creative writing—fiction and nonfiction, traditional and off-beat—in an attractive, professional tabloid format, including artwork and photographs of featured writers.

All submissions are invited. No taboos. Send five poems typed or printed legibly. Photocopies are okay. *We do not consider simultaneous submissions or previously published material.* We recommend writers see a sample copy before submitting. Report in 2-6 weeks. Pays 1 copy. CR is copyrighted; writers retain all rights to their work.

Deadlines: Winter, Nov. 1; Spring, Feb. 1; Summer, May 1; Autumn, Aug. 1.

About a quarter of each issue is devoted to news, views, and reviews of interest to writers and the literary community. We are always on the lookout for intelligent nonfiction, as well as talented reviewers who wish to write in-depth, analytical reviews of literary books and magazines (300-1,000 words).

Past contributors include Charles Bukowski, William Stafford, Marge Piercy, Gavin Dillard, Edward Field, Antler, Robert Peters, Miriam Sagan, Joan Jobe Smith, Fred Voss, Janice Eidus, Virginia Love Long, Lyn Lifshin, Will Inman, Richard Kostelanetz, Lorri Jackson, Susan Sheppard, and a host of others, well-known and new.

Sample copy: $4. Foreign: $8. 1-year subscription (4 issues): $12. Foreign: $24. Institutions: $28.

Categories: Arts—Gay/Lesbian—Literature—Poetry

Name: Michael Hathaway, Editor
Material: All
Address: 522 E SOUTH AVE
City/State/ZIP: ST JOHN KS 67576-2212
Telephone: 316-549-3933

Chitra Publications

We offer complete directions and diagrams for completing quilt projects, as well as interesting and instructional articles concerning all aspects of quilting. Articles should be informative to quilters, presenting new ideas or techniques. Upon submission of your manuscript, please allow six to eight weeks for a response. Articles are scheduled for publication up to a year in advance. Publication hinges on the quality of photos or the availability of quilts for photography.

SUBMISSIONS

We seek articles with one or two magazine pages of text and quilts that illustrate the content. (Each page of text is approximately 750 words, 6,500 characters, or three double-spaced typewritten pages.) Ideas need to be logical, sequential and fully developed. We may ask you to revise or clarify your manuscript to make it publishable.

We prefer original material accompanied by 35mm slides or 2¼" transparencies. Please include detailed photo captions and photo credits. You may send suggestions for a one-line subhead after the title, a pull quote and a cover line of three or four words if you wish, but these are generally written by our editors. Send the names and addresses of your subjects in case we need to contact them for more information.

Please include the following information in the upper right-hand corner of the first page: your name, address, telephone number, social security number and the estimated number of words in your article.

Magazines are published six times per year. Specific guidelines for each magazine follow:

Traditional Quiltworks is a pattern magazine offering a variety of instructional features and directions for up to a dozen full-size projects. "What If...Design Challenge" is a regular column which encourages quilters to creatively use one pattern in many different ways. "Featured Teacher" is a profile about a quilting teacher accompanied by photos of her/his work. It is followed by "Private Workshop" which contains the teacher's instructions for completing a specific project. We occasionally feature one-page human interest/personality profiles accompanied by quilt slides/photos.

Quilting Today offers feature articles on quilt history, techniques, tools and quilters sharing their knowledge with readers. Articles are accompanied by color slides/photos and sidebars containing helpful tips. The pattern section offers six quilt patterns. Patterns are written according to the established magazine format. Other features include book and product reviews, a calendar of quilt events, a guest editorial and "The Sampler," a news column. Fictional pieces are rarely accepted.

Miniature Quilts offers dozens of patterns for small quilts with block sizes 5" or less. Also included are how-to articles, profile articles about quilters who make small quilts and photo features about noteworthy miniature quilts or exhibits.

EDITING

We reserve the right to edit and/or rewrite for style, clarity, length and adherence to format. When an article is ready for publication, a pre-press copy is provided as a courtesy to ensure that all facts are accurate.

PHOTOS

Clear 35mm slides or 2¼" or larger transparencies can be used. Photos should be professional quality. Quilts should be shot straight-on so they do not appear distorted. Include your name and address on all photos. Write "TOP" on all slides. Include the photographer's name for the photo credit if required. Send photos in plastic sleeves or cardboard to protect them.

PAYMENT

Upon preparation of your manuscript for publication, you will be asked to sign a contract stating that your submission is not an infringement on the rights of others. Payment is made approximately 6 weeks after the on-sale date. Payment varies, depending upon the amount of work required to prepare the article and whether or not the article promotes your business. Payment averages $75 per 800 published words, without photos. If your photo is used for a feature article or a pattern quilt, payment is $20. Payment varies for multiple photos. No payment will be made to you for quilts photographed by Chitra Publications. No payment is made for photos shown in the "letters" columns in any of the magazines.

RETURN OF MATERIALS

Please enclose a self-addressed envelope with the appropriate amount of return postage affixed with all submissions. The return of your materials cannot be guaranteed without it.

REGULAR COLUMNS

If you would like us to consider your idea for a regular column, please use the following guidelines:

• Submit a description of the proposed feature, indicating its philosophy or goals and indicating why readers would benefit from reading it in sequential issues.

• Submit an autobiography of about 100 words, with an emphasis on quiltmaking, along with a professional-quality photo.

• Submit an outline of one year's columns (six).

• Submit two sample columns, including snapshots of projects or to-scale diagrams, if applicable. Patterns must be written to our format.

Upon acceptance of a feature, we require submission of one year's worth of manuscripts (six) before publication of the first installment. Upon receipt of the installments, we will edit the material and issue a contract. Payment for each installment is made approximately six weeks after the on-sale date. Should we desire the column to continue, a new contract will be issued at the proper time.

Categories: Crafts—Quilts/Quilting

Name: Editorial Team
Material: All
Address: CHITRA PUBLICATIONS
Address: 2 PUBLIC AVE
City/State/ZIP: MONTROSE PA 18820
Telephone: 717-278-1984
Fax: 717-278-2223

CHRISTIAN HOME & SCHOOL

Christian Home & School
Christian Schools International

Manuscripts can range from 750 to 2,000 words and should be typed with the author's name and address at the top of the first page. Include a sentence or two about yourself for us to use as a contributor's note; this could include humor.

Christian Home & School has a circulation of 60,000 and is designed for parents in the United States and Canada who send their children to Christian schools and are concerned about the challenges facing Christian families today. These readers expect a mature, biblical perspective in the articles, not just a Bible verse tacked onto the end. Use an informal, easy-to-read style rather than a philosophical, academic tone. Try to incorporate vivid imagery and concrete, practical examples from real life.

The style of our articles varies from a reflective or humorous first-person account of a single incident relating to a topic to a more comprehensive, more objective discussion of a topic in general. A sidebar that contains further suggestions or resources related to your subject is often helpful.

Suggested topics are listed below, but don't limit yourself to these ideas. (The first 9 topics are new to the list) We are interested in articles that deal with timely issues that confront Christian parents (no poetry, please). Also of interest are articles about Christian schooling and the relationship of parents to Christian schools. Each year we also include seasonal articles dealing with such topics as the beginning of the school year, Christmas, Easter, end of the school year, graduation, summer activities, and vacations.

We pay $125-$200 upon publication, depending upon the length of the laid-out article, and prefer to buy first rights only.

If you would like a sample copy of our magazine, please send us a 9"x12" self-addressed manila envelope with four first class stamps affixed. For more information, contact Roger W. Schmurr, senior editor.

Christian Home & School Schedule
Issue/Author's Deadline
Sept./June 1
Oct./Nov. July 1
Dec./Aug. 1
Jan./Feb. Oct. 1
Mar./Apr. Dec. 1
May/June Feb. 1

Some possible topics for future issues of *Christian Home & School*:

How to raise polite kids in a rude world

Puppy love: how should parents respond to a child's romantic notions?

Learning disabilities: when and how to ask for an evaluation of your child

What's wrong with being average?

Teaching children to respect the views of people with whom they disagree

How to help your child handle conflict and anger

Competition: what should you teach your child about winning and losing?

Maintaining a good relationship with your spouse while raising kids

Should your kids attend summer camp?

What do you do when your child uses bad language?

Helping the gifted child

Cliques: how preteens deal with them

Teaching kids about diversity

Preparing your child for independence

Raising world citizens: helping children develop an international perspective

What music, movies, TV shows, etc. are influencing teens now?

Teaching your child patience

Rewards for good behavior: Are they bribes?

How can the extended family help me in my parenting responsibilities?

How can you open the world to your kids and yet fend off unwelcome influences?

Sex education at home, church, and school

Co-parenting after divorce

Resolving sibling rivalry

How parents can help their children succeed in school

How to avoid nagging

Blending two families after remarriage

Teaching children about money: allowances, spending, saving, giving, family budget, etc.

The role of fantasy and imagination in the development of children

How to talk to your child about bad things: e.g. drugs, AIDS, and violence

Sexual abuse of children: recognizing and dealing with it

Raising secure children: helping children feel spiritually, physically, and emotionally safe

When parents fail: living with the mistakes we've made

The danger of living through your children: parents and their children's achievements

Too much too soon? Pushing early childhood development

Kids and work: from household chores to their first paid job

Nurturing creativity in children

Dealing with family crises: death, divorce, serious illness, unemployment

Learning styles: recognizing and responding to them

Categories: Education—Family—Marriage

Name: Roger W. Schmurr, Senior Editor
Material: All
Address: 3350 E PARIS AVE SE
City/State/ZIP: GRAND RAPIDS MI 49512
Telephone: 616-957-1070 ext. 239

Christian Living

STATEMENT OF PURPOSE

Christian Living seeks to help readers:

• Learn about people, both nearby and around the world.

• Put faith into practice in everyday life.

• Deepen relationships with friends, family members, and God.

GUIDELINES FOR WRITERS

The magazine publishes articles (700-1,800 words) and short fiction (700-1,200 words), as well as occasional poems (24 lines maximum). We're interested in material related to community, family, and spiritual growth. More specifically, we're looking for pieces that have a cross-cultural dimension, connect the arts to one of these areas, simply tell a good story or give insights on a difficult issue.

To increase your chances of acceptance:

• Write concisely.

• Focus on one topic per article.

• Include lots of anecdotes and examples.

• Use everyday language, avoiding jargon or "churchspeak."

• Emphasize what readers *can* do, rather than what they *should* or shouldn't do.

• Type the manuscript. If you prefer, you may submit a 3½" or 5¼" disk in a major word processing format, such as WordPerfect.

We prefer that you send finished manuscripts, rather than queries. Good illustrations, especially black and white photos, will help place your material with us. Color prints are acceptable if the contrast is good. Artwork is also welcome with good contrast.

We pay on a sliding scale with a base of five cents a word for prose and fiction, up to $2 a line for poetry, and up to $35 for photos, depending on quality and content. We will occasionally cover expenses, if prior arrangements are made.

Steve Kriss

Editor

Categories: Nonfiction—Biography—Careers—Christian Interests—Conservation—Disabilities—Ecology—Environment—Ethnic—Family—Men's Issues—Multicultural—Poetry—Recreation—Relationships—Society—Spiritual—Women's Issues—Young Adult

Name: Steve Kriss, Editor
Material: All
Address: 616 WALNUT AVE
City/State/ZIP: SCOTTDALE PA 15683
Telephone: 412-887-8500
Fax: 412-887-3111

Christian*New Age Quarterly
A Bridge Supporting Dialogue

Thank you for your interest in writing for *Christian*New Age Quarterly*. We welcome your creativity and insights, focused upon some facet of the Christian-New Age relationship.

C*NAQ is a forum for clear, respectful dialog between Christians and New Agers. Here we entertain, but do not assume, an underlying compatibility of the two. While we allow for the possibility of irreconcilable ideological differences, we have yet to see a single reason which precludes honest, mutually supportive communication. Moreover, we have discovered many reasons why such genuine communication is warranted, even crucial.

Our readership is comprised of Christians and New Agers, as well as those exploring other avenues of spiritual expression. While extraordinarily diverse, our readers also tend to be keenly observant, intelligent and in touch with spirituality. Consequently, we do not accept material marked by either a patronizing style, which assumes the reader needs to be taught some self-evident spiritual insight, or self-circular reasoning, which confuses subjective truth with observable fact.

As you select words for your insight or observation, aim for vital, flowing, yet precise language. **C*NAQ** especially looks for a certain caliber of vantage that surprises us with a slant we've yet to consider. Take a look at a topic, then wrestle with it, contemplatively and vigorously. Capture and submit it in simple style and fine polish.

If yours is a controversial theme, we would be pleased to consider it—as long as you have thought it through with research and sensitivity. Here, you needn't be wary of words considered taboo in other journals; "church," "Savior," "feminism" and "Goddess" are all functional terms in **C*NAQ**. But pieces that put forth an exclusivistic stance would best be submitted to one of the more singularly Christian or New Age periodicals which abound.

Besides staff-composed columns and "The Letters Library," we publish 2-3 articles per issue. Recommended word length is 400-1,500 words. The more peripheral the content is to our main focus, the shorter it needs to be. Articles with content especially pertinent may aim for the upper end of the range. Still, if you have composed an outstanding piece that exceeds length recommendations, we might consider it. We do try to be flexible when it comes to truly noteworthy pieces.

We do not accept poetry, photos, trendy pieces, channeled wisdom or fiction. We do, however, welcome original line drawings and cartoons. If you are in doubt regarding the propriety of an intended subject, feel free to query prior to investing your energies in its composition.

As to blind submissions, we at **C*NAQ** find it presumptuous when authors submit work with no knowledge of our periodical's focus. If one is drawn to Christian-New Age dialog to the extent that one would write on the subject, it would seem reasonable to expect interest in at least examining **C*NAQ**. Doing so provides the opportunity not only to explore our stylistic preferences, but also to learn from the views of other writers who are published here. Though our acceptances are not prejudiced by whether or not a writer reads **C*NAQ**, those who have familiarized themselves with our work are far more likely to create the kind of piece we seek to publish. If you are not currently a subscriber, you may obtain a sample by sending your check or money order, payable to **Christian*New Age Quarterly,** in the amount of $3.50.

C*NAQ rarely accepts material offered on a basis other than "first rights." Please indicate "first rights" on your manuscript or detail, in your cover letter, why first rights are not available. *Never do we consider simultaneous submissions;* don't send them here. We require a note of assurance, accompanying your submission, that we are the sole periodical considering the piece. After your work has been published in **C*NAQ**, you are free to submit it elsewhere.

We reserve the right to edit. Although **C*NAQ** honors the personal style of our authors, editing may be necessary for clarity or length. If you are opposed to revising your manuscript yourself or allowing us to do so, clearly state this in your cover letter. Our preliminary evaluation of submissions often is based on their "editability." Rest assured that we would not print a piece requiring substantial editing without first obtaining the author's approval on necessary changes.

The request of a revision does not ensure eventual acceptance. It does means we are seriously interested. But acceptance depends upon our approval of your final copy.

For accepted articles, you'll receive, as payment, a one-year complimentary subscription or an extension to your current subscription. For each drawing or cartoon, you'll receive one copy of the issue in which your work appears.

Our decisions are commitments. If we accept a piece for publication, you may rest assured that it will be published. Although we try to publish accepted material as soon as possible, we work carefully to achieve a balance of content in each issue. Therefore, we may wait upon an appropriate issue to include accepted articles.

Please enclose an SASE with sufficient postage in all correspondence. We are not responsible for returning manuscripts, advising you of our decision, or answering inquiries which arrive without SASEs. Please help us to be responsive to you!

C*NAQ's Editor, Catherine Groves—as well as our readers—will look forward to the opportunity to explore your thoughts.

Categories: Nonfiction—Christian Interests—Interfaith—New Age—Religion—Spiritual

Name: Catherine Groves, Editor
Material: All
Address: PO BOX 276
City/State/ZIP: CLIFTON NJ 07011-0276

Christian Parenting Today

So you want to write for CPT? That's good news!

We're always looking for writers who can provide our readers with helpful information and keep us editors supplied with chocolate. But it will take more than a box of Godiva's finest to get your articles published in our pages. So we need to tell you a few things about CPT, our readers, and us ever-picky editors.

WHAT YOU ABSOLUTELY, POSITIVELY NEED TO KNOW

Our goal is to assist parents in the *discipleship* of their children ages birth to 12. CPT readers are striving to "train up" their children by helping them internalize Christian values and high moral standards, and by lovingly molding their children's character to reflect the life of Christ. We seek to help parents accomplish these goals in four ways:

1. By showing them how to lay foundations for godly living via instructing their children in spiritual matters. For example:

• instilling *godly character* such as compassion, mercy and humility

• nurturing *spiritual disciplines* such as a personal commitment to Christ, a prayer life and an attitude of worship

• teaching *biblical literacy* such as the Easter story, the life of Christ, and Bible heroes

2. By guiding them through circumstances of spiritual/moral significance faced by them and their children. For example:

• *relationship issues* such as coping with peer pressure, sibling rivalry and racism

• *educational issues* such as countering non-Christian values, "standing alone" for Christ, and respecting authorities

• *behavioral issues* such as disciplining the child who lies, steals, is rebellious or disobedient

• *family lifestyle issues* such as weighing work/career options, wants vs. needs, or child-care issues

3. By equipping them to model and teach Christian values or life application of those values within the context of family life. For example:

• nurturing the *parents personal spiritual health* through inspirational stories that have practical application

• creating *opportunities* for *family activities* that lead to the "teaching" or handing down of spiritual truths

4. By strengthening the marriages of readers who want their marriage to be the spiritual foundation of their homes. For example:

• deepening their *intimacy* on spiritual, emotional, physical and intellectual levels

• holding together during *crises* such as financial hardship, personal tragedy or spiritual attack

• honing their effectiveness as *partners in parenting* through skill-building, communication, teamwork and support

CPT readers belong to the Buster, Xer, Survivor, call-them-what-you-will generation. Strengthening family bonds, transferring Christian values to their children, and protecting their kids from an unkind world are among their top priorities—a vivid reaction to the difficult latchkey-kid childhoods many of them had. They've had primarily middle-class-American life experiences. Most own their own home (or hope to soon); most have dual incomes, often out of necessity. They are generous, educated pragmatists who take an experiential approach to life. They are "computer babies" who are comfortable with technology and who look at both present and future with attitudes of blunt realism. Their homes are "safe places," retreats from a harsh society where they can look for meaningful tradition. Their Christian churches provide them with friendly communities that give direction on strengthening their faith, families and marriages. Most are married mothers—around 30 years old—who have two young children. What does such a parent want? Stability. Direction. A strong Christian family. Realistic help raising godly kids. And to do a better job at "family making" than their parents did.

OK, so don't bother sending chocolate. What we really crave are writers who demonstrate:

• a desire to assist our readers on both the spiritual and in-the-flesh levels of parenting

• an understanding of our readers and an ability to identify with them on a personal level

• experiential expertise relevant to the topic

• a willingness to work with demanding editors

That's not all. Your manuscript needs to demonstrate a few things too. Please be sure it:

• has a distinctly Christian perspective

• has a strong parenting angle

• applies fresh ideas to familiar issues

• anticipates readers' questions

• contains practical, doable, vividly explained suggestions

• doesn't condescend or sermonize

• is authoritative, based on current research from respected and reliable sources

• is brought to life by "real people" (the voices of everyday parents and kids)

• is personal, speaking to the reader in a one-on-one, chat-over-latte style

If you've read this far, you must really want to write for us. So we willingly offer a few more tips:

• Tell it like it is. CPT readers have a "get real" attitude that demands a down-to-earth, pragmatic take on topics. Don't waffle. Don't fabricate sincerity. Don't pretend that the inside of a dirty diaper doesn't smell bad.

• If *you've* "been there," say so. Transparency is OK. The first-person, used appropriately, is OK. Our readers trust people who have walked in their Doc Martens.

• If *appropriate*, give your article a developmental spin. Some topics work best when they focus on the needs of certain-age children. We typically work within five developmental brackets: Babies (birth to 2), Toddlers (2 to 3), Preschoolers (3 to 5), Early Elementary Schoolers (5 to 8), and Late Elementary Schoolers (8 to 12).

• Cut out the "four areas" mentioned earlier; highlight them, paste them on neon paper, and tape them to your bathroom mirror next to your Scripture of the day. Ask yourself, Does my manuscript specifically address one of these areas? If the answer is no, chances are ours will be too.

NOW FOR THE TECHNICAL STUFF

We prefer queries, but complete manuscripts are OK. *We accept submissions sent via fax or e-mail: however, we won't respond to them unless we're interested.* Please allow eight weeks for us to respond. If we turn out to be no more on time than Alice's rabbit, please drop us a gentle *whatintheworldhaveyoudonewith myarticle!* inquiry.

In addition to features, the following departments are open to free-lance writers:

• **TRAIN THEM UP:** articles of about 700 words that address the spiritual development and character building of children in five age brackets: Babies, Toddlers, Preschoolers, Early Elementary and Late Elementary. Send query or manuscript. Pays $125.

• **HEALTHY & SAFE:** practical "how-to" articles of 400-450 words that speak to parents' desire to provide their kids with an emotionally and physically safe environment at home and away. Send query or manuscript. Pays $50—$75.

• **THE LIGHTER SIDE:** a humorous look at everyday family life. 600-700 words. Send manuscript. Pays $125.

Submissions to Life In Our House and Parent Exchange are not acknowledged or returned. No SASE required.

• **LIFE IN OUR HOUSE:** an insightful anecdote of 25-100 words about something funny that happened at home. Pays $30.

• **PARENT EXCHANGE:** a tried-and-true parenting idea of 25-100 words. Pays $30.

The technically perfect query includes:

• your name, address and rights offered (we buy first [North American serial] and reprint)

• a working title for our reference

• a detailed but tentative outline

• a SASE

• anticipated length of proposed article

When submitting manuscripts, please:

• include your name, address, social security number and rights offered

• limit your manuscript to 2,000 words (most features published are 600 to 1,800 words)

• outline your qualifications for writing the article

• do not send photos, slides or artwork (except to Parent Exchange)

• do not send fiction, poetry, diatribes, essays, profiles, interviews, report cards, or Grandma's treasured nut-bread recipe

And finally:

• We occasionally accept reprints from non-competing magazines. Send a fresh manuscript, a photocopy of the published piece, and the name and date of the publication in which it appeared.

• Unless specified by the editor, manuscripts requested via query aren't assignments, but are requested on speculation.

• Submit seasonal material at least eight months in advance. The earlier the better.

• For a sample copy of our magazine, please send a 9"x12" SASE bearing $3 postage.

• Sorry, we don't have editorial calendars or theme lists available.

• Usually, payment (15 to 25 cents per published word, or a pre-stated flat rate), is on acceptance of completed manuscript for assigned articles; on publication for unsolicited manuscripts that we have accepted.

"Acceptance" is a loaded word around our offices. It means we've put you through the mill, if necessary, on rewrites and revisions—and we don't apologize for working you hard to meet our readers' needs. Please remember that we love writers, but at the bottom line we love our readers more and will go to (you'll believe) unthinkable lengths to serve them. CPT's best writers are dependable, committed professionals who not only agree with this but join us in commitment to it!

Our Staff: Erin Healy, Editor • Kathy Davis, Associate Editor • Colin Miller, Art Director • Sherry Dixon-Leonard, Editorial Assistant

Categories: Christian Interests—Parenting

Name: Kathy Davis, Associate Editor
Material: All
Address: 4050 LEE VANCE VIEW
City/State/ZIP: COLORADO SPRINGS CO 80918
Telephone: 719-531-7776
Fax: 719-535-0172
E-mail: CPTmag@aol.com

Christian Social Action

Christian Social Action

Dear Writer:

In response to your request for editorial guidelines, we are sending you the following information for potential freelance writers.

Published by the General Board of Church and Society of The United Methodist Church, *Christian Social Action* offers an analysis of social issues from the perspective of the Christian faith and positions of the United Methodist Church. *Christian Social Action* gives you:

• **Feature articles.** Subjects ranging from concern for children, homosexuality, racial justice, mental illness, health care, poverty and many more.

• **Special issues.** Racial justice. Children's issues. Upcoming elections.

• **From the Word.** Provides biblical reflections and insight on a wide range of social issues.

• **Talking.** A column for readers to publish their concerns about and positions on social issues.

• **Media reviews.**

• **How to Use this CSA.** Offers ideas on how to use the magazine effectively as a resource for study and action.

• **Empower.** Suggestions for United Methodists to carry out justice ministries in their local communities.

• **Word from Washington.** This eight-page newsletter insert includes:

• Updates on legislation and policy changes affecting social issues on which you may be working.

• Information on Church and society programs, activities, initiatives and resources.

• Action alerts on what you can do to create social change.

• Tips for social justice advocates.

Articles for *Christian Social Action* should be 1,500-2,000 words in length, discussing a current social issue, and should reflect a thorough knowledge of the subject. We are primarily concerned with content, and we only consider well-written articles which deal with social concerns. For example we carry only articles on: war and peace issues, race relations, environmental concerns, international relations, economic and labor issues, ethnic concerns, women's rights, health and welfare concerns.

The *Social Principles of the United Methodist Church* shows the range of issues with which we work. Copies of this pamphlet are available from the Service Department of the General Board of Church and Society (800-967-0880).

If you have articles that fit these criteria, we would be happy to consider them.

Thank you.

THE EDITORS
Categories: Christian Interests—Public Policy—Religion—Social Issues

Name: Lee Ranck, Editor
Material: All
Address: 100 MARYLAND AVE NE
City/State/ZIP: WASHINGTON DC 20002
Telephone: 202-488-5621
Fax: 202-488-1617
E-mail: Lranck@igc.org

Christianity and the Arts
America's Guide to Christian Expression

Mission: To celebrate the revelation of God through the arts and to encourage excellent Christian artistic expression.

Christianity and the Arts is a quarterly publication. We publish: February, May, August, and November.

Do you publish freelance articles?

We are interested in publishing as many talented writers as possible. Query or send the article. We prefer articles less than 2,000 words. Because of the high cost of printing and postage, it is expensive to print long articles. Also, unfortunately, we live in a time when everyone has a short attention span. Say it well and concisely.

The following categories of articles have worked well with us:

• **Interviews**: We have published a number of interviews with artists, writers, musicians, dancers, and actors. We especially like interviews that probe deep. Too many interviews read like public relations releases.

• **Advice articles**: These articles give straightforward information, i.e., "How to Stage a Drama Ministry," "Everything You Need to Know about Handbells." Think how such an article will benefit the reader.

• **Think pieces**: We would like to publish more essays that raise interesting questions about literature, music, or art. Reflect on how you can capture a reader's attention. Too many essays that are sent to us are boring.

Do we pay?

Unfortunately, *Christianity and the Arts* is staffed by volunteers and managed by a nonprofit corporation. We are a new magazine struggling to find a market niche. We simply can't afford to pay contributors and continue to produce a magazine. Solution? Subscribe and tell your friends. As soon as we can secure a financial base, we will pay contributors. A one-year subscription is $21. A two-year subscription is $36.

What are your themes?

We like to work with themes. We feel the world is juxtapositioned enough without yet another magazine that offers disconnected ideas. We try to relate the articles to each other. Recent themes: Resurrection, February 1998, Women Mystical Saints, May 1998, and Fools for Christ, August 1998. In addition to the themed articles, we publish independent articles and columns as space is available.

Who is your audience?

We reach Protestant, Catholic, and Orthodox readers throughout the United States and Canada. Our readers tend to be upscale and well-educated, with an interest in several disciplines, such as music and the visual arts. Because we have a national audience, we've had to reject some articles because they only have a local approach.

Do you accept poetry and fiction?

We have published poetry since our first issue in February 1994. We wish to support the efforts of Christian poets, however we get more poetry than any other type of writing. We can't publish everyone's wonderful efforts but we do try to include as many poems, as possible, especially when the poems concern our themes. Many submissions read more like prayers than poems. We are looking for quality verse. Please submit poetry directly to Robert Klein Engler, c/o Richard J. Daly College, 7500 S. Pulaski, Chicago, Illinois 60652.

Fiction is difficult for us to publish at this time. Fiction—in order to do it properly—needs space, and we just haven't had the financial resources to commit to extra pages at this time. That doesn't mean that if we didn't find the right short story, we won't change our mind. Try us and be patient. Please submit fiction directly to Terrence Neal Brown, P.O. Box 381528, Germantown, Tennessee 38183.

Do you publish photographs?

In almost every issue, we devote the back page to a feature entitled, "Parting Shot." We publish black-and-white photographs that relate to the themes in the issue.

Color photographs are expensive for us. It costs $400 for separation of the colors, plus $45 per image. We reserve our color to show artists' works.

How do you help writers, artists, musicians, and others who are working in the area of Christian expression?

We are helping people in the creative fields in two ways: a calendar and features. The quarterly calendar lists events and artists' showings that will attract audiences and patrons. There is no charge for subscribers to list events (as space is available). Secondly, we focus on numerous people in the area of Christian expression, always listing their addresses and/or phone numbers so that people can directly contact them. We are proud that our articles have generated commissions for artists.

How can I reach the audience of Christianity and the Arts if your editorial space is filled?

For as little as $125 for a quarter page, you can take out an ad. A full page is $400; a half page is $250. We circulate to 5,000 people—both subscribers and bookstores. Please contact the publisher if you are interested in placing an ad.

If my idea is rejected, should I give up?

Just because one idea doesn't work for us doesn't mean another might not work. We want to include as many people as possible in *Christianity and the Arts.* Yet, at the same time, our first commitment is to our audience. If we can't produce articles that are of an interest to readers, we won't have an audience base to help anyone.

We are committed to excellence. We want to produce the best magazine possible that will glorify the Creator.

What is our wish list?

We would like more articles on:
• Well-known personalities.
• Minorities.
• Dance, film, and drama.
• Articles that will appeal to a national audience. (Get beyond the local angle.)
• Submissions from professional, published writers.
• Good photos for our "Parting Shot" page.
• Literary criticism with a flare.

Do you believe in what we are doing and would like to help? We need lists of people who would like to read and subscribe to *Christianity and the Arts.* We also need the names of people who would like to advertise.

Thank you for your interest in *Christianity and the Arts.*

Categories: Fiction—Nonfiction—Architecture—Arts—Culture—Dance—Drama—Film/Video—Literature—Music—Poetry—Religion

Name: Marci Whitney-Schenck, Publisher and Editor
Material: All, except as noted in guidelines

Address: PO BOX 118088
City/State/ZIP: CHICAGO IL 60611
Telephone: 312-642-8606
Fax: 312-266-7719
E-mail: chrnarts@aol.com

CHRISTIANITY TODAY

Christianity Today

WHAT WE LOOK FOR IN CHRISTIANITY TODAY ARTICLES:

A. *Good Ideas.*
    1. fresh, creative ideas that plow up new ground
    2. that fit the purpose and stance of CHRISTIANITY TODAY
    3. that are useful to the reader; that answer the question: "Good for what?"
    4. that contain new insights, wisdom, judgment, analysis, interpretation
    5. that are interesting to CHRISTIANITY TODAY readers

B. *Evidence of Hard Work.*
    1. not superficial generalities
    2. strong supporting evidence for the article's major proposition
    3. careful diagnosis and solutions
    4. related to the real world
    a. not limited to academic research
    b. related to real problems and needs
    5. correlation with and applications of Christian values and principles

C. *A Strong Logical Case*
    1. point-by-point, with transitions
    2. shows the reader where you are going and why
    3. makes clear what you are trying to prove

D. *Compelling Opening and Conclusion*
    1. introductory paragraphs that hold attention
    2. an ending that summarizes and provokes thought

E. *Careful Craftsmanship*
    1. high regard for language and style, words, punctuation, grammar, etc
    2. colorful, vivid, moving language
    3. simplicity, clarity, readability
    4. no technical jargon or professional academic language
    5. adherence to our word limits, usually 1,500 to 3,000 words. The Speaking Out columns use 800-word articles. Book reviews are usually commissioned. Letters of inquiry are requested before these are sent out.
    6. We prefer exclusive original submissions. If you have sent your manuscript to another magazine, please advise. Word processor printouts, as long as they are clear, are acceptable. We prefer these to be on 8½"x11" sheets.

CHRISTIANITY TODAY expects query letters before manuscripts are sent.

    1. Material should not be submitted without first becoming thoroughly familiar with the magazine's content over a period of time.
    2. Outline your article proposal. State your subject, theme, proposition and your main points.
    3. Outline your research, experience, qualifications.
    4. Tell us something about yourself. Why are you qualified to

write this particular article?

Payment: Essays purchased at $75.00 and up for columns, and $100.00 and up for articles. Reimbursement upon acceptance. CT is *not* a market for fiction or poetry.

Categories: Christian Interests—Religion

Name: Carol R. Thiessen, Administrative Editor
Material: All
Address: 465 GUNDERSEN DR
City/State/ZIP: CAROL STREAM IL 60188
Telephone: 630-260-6200
Fax: 630-260-0114
E-mail: ctedit@aol.com

Chronicles
A Magazine of American Culture

CHRONICLES is a monthly magazine of ideas devoted to discussions of first principles in all branches of humane learning. It is not an academic journal. Our special concern is with the intersection of arts and letters with social and political issues. While our editorial policy can be described as traditionalist or conservative, our pages are open to a broad spectrum of opinions.

The ideal contributor to CHRONICLES is a writer or scholar who can express his ideas clearly enough to reach the general reader. We try to avoid both ideological polemics and academic jargon in favor of liveliness and clarity.

"VIEWS": Two or three essays are commissioned for each CHRONICLES issue and are usually devoted to some aspect of the issue's theme. These pieces run anywhere from 1,500-3,000 words long.

"OPINIONS": These are our longer review essays of about 1,500 words on a theme derived from a current book or number of books. The subject of the essay is not just the books themselves but a topic suggested by the books. The main part of the essay should be devoted to developing the writer's own ideas.

"REVIEWS": These are our shorter reviews in 500-1,200 words, reviewers are asked to identify the primary themes of a book and put them into perspective. In the case of fiction, please resist the temptation to summarize the plot.

"VITAL SIGNS": This is our cultural section, in which we run movie, theater, and art reviews. This is also the place for reportage on subjects such as legal cases, academic issues, and the like.

"CORRESPONDENCE": Our "Letters From…" fall into this section, which has the loosest criteria. In the past we have run reportage, personal essays, and more philosophical pieces.

When reviewing books, please be sure to include all book review information: title, author (or editor), publisher, city, state, price, and page number.

To assist us in fact-checking, please include at the end of the article sources of any quotations used within the text.

We will need you to provide us with a short bio, one or two sentences long.

CHRONICLES does not accept unsolicited fiction.

Categories: Christian Interests—Culture—Education—Environment—Government—Literature—Poetry—Politics—Regional

Name: Theodore Pappas, Managing Editor
Material: All

Address: 934 N MAIN ST
City/State/ZIP: ROCKFORD IL 61103
Telephone: 815-964-5054

 *THE CHRYSALIS READER*

The Chrysalis Reader
Journal of the Swedenborg Foundation

WHAT IS THE CHRYSALIS READER?

Chrysalis, originally a journal issued three times per year, has evolved into an engaging book format to explore contemporary questions on spirituality. Each *Chrysalis Reader* seeks to give fresh perspectives on a theme through articles and art from many traditions, including spiritual insights of Emanuel Swedenborg (1688-1772)—scientist, inventor, civil engineer, government official, and mystic, who used his rational and scientific orientation to explore the world of spirit.

WRITER'S GUIDELINES

Articles, fiction, and poetry should focus on one of the *Chrysalis Reader*'s upcoming themes, expanding upon it, and adding subjective new dimensions of experience or a logically expressed thesis. In editing, our primary goal is maintaining the integrity of the author's style and point of view. Editing is designed not to unify perspectives but to clarify focus and keep the writing in the *Chrysalis Reader* vigorous and interesting.

The Chrysalis Reader does not accept material that has been published previously, nor do we publish simultaneously. A list of upcoming themes and copy deadlines is available upon request.

The *Chrysalis Reader* style follows the *The Chicago Manual of Style* (14th ed.). We request an outline prior to submission of the manuscript itself. Manuscripts should be no shorter than 1,500 words. The final copy of an accepted manuscript should be submitted in hard copy and on computer disk using preferably WordPerfect 5.0 or 6.0 (IBM/DOS format).

The interval between submission of the accepted manuscript and the final draft involves extensive communication between author, reviewers, and editors. Our schedule is designed to allow flexibility and a liberal amount of time for each communication. If you have missed the date for an outline but feel you have a solid idea for a piece, simply send the outline to us as quickly as possible, and we will try to respond immediately. We look forward to your contribution. Previously issued titles are $10 each.

THE CHRYSALIS READER AUDIENCE

Chrysalis readers are thoughtful, well-read men and women interested in stretching their inner resources; many of them work in psychology, education, religion, the arts, or one of the helping professions. *The Chrysalis Reader* audience includes people from many faiths and spiritual traditions. Our readers come from all walks in life and share a common interest in growing spiritually.

Example Themes and Copy Deadlines
The Good Life

Everyone wants to be "good," but what constitutes a "good life"? Is it a matter of integrity and purity? of purposefulness and clarity of values? Is a good life necessarily a happy life? Is it balanced, and if so, what are the ingredients of the balance? Can I make life good for someone else, or only for myself? How do I go about doing so? Is a creative, imaginative life a good one? Does a good life depend on health? wealth? Does it result from faith and the practice of religion? What makes your life of value? And what is the shadow side of a good life?

Symbols: Beyond Seeing

Symbols can be gateways to the soul and are said to emerge

from the collective unconscious. Have you ever tried to tap the unconscious to create a symbol—a logo, a design for a shirt, a garden—to represent or express what you treasure? What did you discover as you looked deeply into nature to distill its essence and express it in a form? What symbols have special meanings for you-a flag? a rose? a traffic light? a horse? What are those meanings, and how did you come to realize their significance? Did someone suggest the meanings for you, or did you discover them yourself? Symbols, correspondences, representations-what revealing indicators of the magical! What windows into the transcendental! How do they quicken our spirits and help us? What do they do for us as they kindle our imaginations and move us beyond seeing toward understanding? What ultimate realities do they manifest, so humans can respond to their beauty and power? For Swedenborg "the whole visible world is a theater that portrays the spiritual world" (*Arcana Coelestia*, paragraph 5173.2). His extensive descriptions of correspondences between objects in nature and the spiritual realities they represent have inspired many people, including artists who, as Coleridge recognized, seek to "imitate that which is *within* the thing."

Choices

Choices depend on seeing alternatives, on envisioning possibilities in what seems likely to be happening tomorrow, next week, next year—soon or far in the future. Sometimes we must take the bull by the horns and *not* go with the flow, at those times we direct the flow in tune with our own principles or whatever may be our own ideals and values. Sometimes we may be faced with Hobson's Choice, in other words have no choice. Swedenborg, the mystic, emphasizes that we have been provided with freedom of choice and live in a space between heaven and hell, with our daily choices moving us closer to one or the other.

Education

Education has been described as the process of leading knowledge out of a pupil and as leading the pupil out of ignorance into knowledge. It has been called training in the perception of relationships or patterns and also as two persons sitting on a log-with a willing student at one end and master teacher at the other. Swedenborg saw education as initiating a person into the kind of knowing that is possible when the best intentions are joined with the truest discernment.

Categories: Fiction—Nonfiction—Arts—Literature—Poetry—Philosophy—Spiritual

Name: Carol S. Lawson, Editor
Material: All
Address: RT 1 BOX 184
City/State/ZIP: DILLWYN VA 23936
Telephone: 804-983-3021
Fax: 804-983-1074
E-mail: LAWSON@ABA.ORG

Cicada

Please refer to Amelia Press.

Cimarron Review
Oklahoma State University

Thank you for your interest in *Cimarron Review.*

Cimarron Review seeks short fiction, poetry, and essays of serious literary quality; we welcome submissions from all writers, often published, seldom published, unpublished. We are not interested in juvenile or genre material nor in any of the current literary "isms" in, coming in, or fading from fashion.

We have no bias with respect to subject matter, form (traditional to radically experimental), or theme. Reviews are assigned, and some material is solicited. We prefer to consider only one fiction or essay manuscript or one set of three to six poems per submission. No simultaneous submissions. We copyright all material we publish.

Thank you again for your interest in *Cimarron.*

We look forward to hearing from you at any time.

Best regards.

Categories: Fiction—Nonfiction—Culture—Literature—Native American—Poetry—Short Stories—Writing

Name: E.P. Walkiewicz, Editor
Material: All
Address: OKLAHOMA STATE UNIVERSITY
Address: 205 MORRILL HALL
City/State/ZIP: STILLWATER OK 74078-4069
Telephone: 405-744-9476
Fax: 405-744-6326

Cineaste

Published quarterly, and appearing regularly since 1967, *Cineaste is* today internationally recognized as one of America's foremost film magazines. An independent publication, with no financial ties to the film industry or academic institutions, *Cineaste* features contributions from many of America's most articulate and outspoken writers, critics, and scholars. Focusing on both the art and politics of the cinema, and always stressing a popular, readable style displayed in an attractive, lavishly illustrated format, *Cineaste* offers colorful and thought-provoking coverage of the entire world of cinema, including:

• Probing and informative interviews with directors, screenwriters, performers and other creative and technical film production personnel.

• Feature articles on topical issues and contemporary film trends

• In-depth reviews of the latest Hollywood movies, independent productions and foreign films

• Regular coverage of films from developing nations in the Third world

• Critical symposiums and debates on such controversial films as *JFK, Do the Right Thing, Thelma & Louise, Boyz N the Hood,* and *Malcolm X*

• Special supplements on such subjects as Central and Eastern European Cinema, The Arab Image in American Cinema, The Restoration of *Spartacus,* and Sound and Music in the Movies

• A continuing series on "Race in Contemporary American Cinema"

• Regular columns such as "Book Reviews," "Homevideo," "A Second Look," "Festivals," and "Short Takes"

Guidelines for Writers

Cineaste offers a social, political and esthetic perspective on the cinema. We are not affiliated with any organization or institution. We are interested in all areas of the cinema, including Hollywood films (old and new), American independents, quality European films, and the cinema of the Third World. Familiarity with our editorial policies is a must for authors. The most frequent reason we reject material is that the potential contributor has sent material which, because of length or style or orientation, is clearly out of place in our pages.

STYLE: Our target audience is the intelligent general public, a public that is fairly sophisticated about both art and politics. No matter how complex the ideas or arguments advanced, we demand readability. We think it is the job of the writer to clarify his or her thoughts and not for the reader to decipher clumsy formulations. We dislike academic jargon, obtuse Marxist terminology, film buff trivia, trendy 'buzz' phrases, and show biz references. We do not want our writers to speak of how they have 'read' or 'decoded' a film, but to view, analyze and interpret same. The author's processes and quirks should be secondary to the interests of the reader. Warning the reader of problems with specific films is more important to us than artificially 'puffing' a film because its producers or politics are agreeable.

FEATURE ARTICLES: Articles should discuss the subject (a film, film genre, a career, a theory, a movement, etc.) in depth. The author should detail the particular sociopolitical and artistic content. When appropriate, provide documentation or quotes on the producer's intentions rather than your speculations. Be aware of the political implications of the work and its social perspectives, whatever the actual plot or genre. Whenever possible, sources should be incorporated into the text rather than footnoted. Preferred length for feature articles is 3,000-4,000 words. Send a letter of inquiry on a feature idea or provide an outline. *Do not* call the office to speak to an editor about article ideas. We want to see your proposal *in writing.*

One article format we encourage is an omnibus review of several current films, preferably those not reviewed in a previous issue. Such an article would focus on films that perhaps share a certain political perspective, subject matter, or generic concerns (e.g., films on suburban life, or urban violence, or revisionist Westerns). Like individual Film Reviews, these articles should incorporate a very brief synopsis of plots for those who haven't seen the films. The main focus, however, should be on the social issues manifested in each film and how it may reflect something about the current political/social/esthetic climate.

INTERVIEWS: Interviews may be with directors, performers, writers, composers, producers, distributors, technicians, or anyone else involved in the creative or business side of filmmaking. We expect the interview to be hard hitting in that challenging (not necessarily hostile) questions are posed and difficult or controversial points pursued. Our experience is that most interviewees respect a well-prepared interviewer who takes their work seriously enough to ask demanding questions. 'Puff' pieces are boring. We are interested in 1) In-depth career interviews with major personalities; 2) Medium-length interviews usually on a current production or issue; and 3) Very short interviews of a few questions which can be used as a sidebar interview with a review.

An interview is more than a transcript of questions and answers. Transcripts must be edited, condensed, and, if necessary, rearranged to bring major themes into focus. The interviewee should see this material for approval before submission to us. It is helpful, but not necessary, to provide a brief, straightforward introduction and a suggested title. Photos are also appreciated. We wish to emphasize that the focus of the interview is the interviewee, not the interviewer. A typical sign of a poor interview is the inordinate length of the questions which are as long, or even longer, than the answers.

FILM REVIEWS: We prefer reviews that focus on one current film. The review should tell what is of merit and what is not in the film under discussion. It should incorporate a very brief synopsis or description of the plot for those who haven't seen the film. Your review should not be a long plot outline with appended evaluations. We are concerned with esthetics as well as content, with how cinematic techniques affect a film's impact. Preferred length is about 1,500 words for feature reviews

BOOK REVIEWS: Book reviews should deal with newly published books, although recent books as much as two years old may be covered depending on the work's importance. Reviewers may focus on one title or cover several related ones. We encourage review-essays in which the discussion serves as a vehicle for a broader treatment of ideas or issues; but, to be fair to authors, their works deserve to be treated seriously rather than merely as launching pads for general essays. Preferred length for fea-

ture reviews is 1,000-2,000 words; capsule reviews are 300-400 words. Provide *complete* publication information (e.g., publisher, year of publication, number of pages, illus., etc.), following the format used in the "Book Reviews" section. In general, writers should query the Book Review Editor before submitting book reviews.

COLUMNS: "Homevideo" articles (1,000-1,500 words) should deal with topics of general interest or a related group of films; individual title reviews should be 300-500 words. "A Second Look" articles (1,000-1,500 words) should offer a new interpretation of a film classic or a reevaluation of an unjustly neglected release of more recent vintage. "Lost and Found" articles (1,000-1,500 words) should discuss a film that may or may not be released or otherwise seen in the U.S. but which is important enough to be brought to the attention of our readers. "Festivals" columns (1,000-1,500 words) should focus on film festivals of particular political importance, providing as much broader social and artistic context as possible for the specific films discussed since many of the latter may not be released or otherwise screened in the U.S.

SUBMISSIONS: We assume that all manuscripts are not reworked versions of previously published or simultaneously submitted material. Manuscripts will be responded to in from 2-4 weeks. Unsolicited material will be given serious consideration, but it is best to query first in case the film, book, or topic has already been assigned. No term papers, please! Do not call the office about submissions unless more than a month has elapsed since making your submission. Long distance phone calls will be returned collect.

REVISIONS: If we feel the material needs further work, we will either 1) Return the material to you with suggestions for changes, or 2) Make changes and submit the revised manuscript for your approval before publication. A Writer's Agreement Form will be sent for all manuscripts accepted for publication.

PAYMENT: We currently pay a minimum of $20 for film reviews and other short pieces, $12 for book or video reviews (the author also gets to retain the book or video reviewed), and a minimum of $25-$30 for feature material, on publication. Contributors also receive three copies of the issue for short pieces and six copies for feature material. We hope to raise these rates, knowing that good writing merits adequate compensation. Kill fees (50% of the above rates) may be paid for material originally solicited by the editors. Royalties from subsequent publication in foreign journals or anthologies will be split 50/50 with the author. Our percentage will be waived when the book is a collection of the author's work or is edited by the author.

All material submitted will be carefully read. Although we have published some of the best known writers on film, we have also been the first place of publication for many writers. All the editors are themselves writers and are aware of the curt treatment writers so often receive from indifferent editors. The least you can expect from us is a thoughtful reading of your work, even though we may not be able to write you with detailed comments.

Categories: Film/Video

Name: Submissions Editor
Material: All
Address: 200 PARK AVE S STE 1601
City/State/ZIP: NEW YORK NY 10003
Telephone: 212-982-1241
Fax: 212-982-1241
E-mail: CINEASTE@cineaste.com
Internet: www.cineaste.com

Circle K

Thank you for your interest in *CIRCLE K* magazine.

CIRCLE K is a sixteen-page collegiate publication distributed five times during each academic year (October, November/December, January/February, March, and April) to the 10,000 members of Circle K International, as well as additional subscribers.

Circle K International is the world's largest collegiate service organization, and its members are above-average college students, primarily residing in the United States and Canada, who are committed to community service and leadership development.

Articles published in CIRCLE K are of two types: serious and light nonfiction. Most articles purchased for publication in CIRCLE K address broad areas of interest to *all* college students but specifically to service-minded individuals, such as current trends (social, collegiate, etc.), leadership and career development, self-help, and community involvement. No fiction, short humor, or travel pieces are accepted. Also, we do not publish historical or philosophical pieces, nor do we accept profiles.

CIRCLE K articles average between 1,500 and 2,000 words (six to eight pages, typed double-spaced); payment is "on acceptance" and ranges from $150 to $400, depending on depth of treatment, appeal to our special audience, and other factors. Query letters are preferred to finished manuscripts.

Proposed articles are tested against two major criteria: They should (1) cover a broad subject rather than an individual person, place, or event; and (2) be applicable to the lives and concerns of today's college students.

Some of our recently published articles include "Student Legal Woes," "Mum's the Word" (political correctness), "The Black and White of How to Get a Job," "Cultural Diversity 101," "Television's College Cult," "Crossing the Student/Mentor Line," "When Children and Collegians Click," "The Graduate School Climb," "Last Call for Alcohol," and "Students of Divorce."

In all articles, treatment must be objective and in-depth, and each major point should be substantiated by illustrative examples and quotes from expert sources. Authors are required to base their stories on interviews and research rather than on personal insights and experiences, and serious articles should avoid intrusions of writers' views. Single-source articles and essays are quickly rejected.

Writing style should be smooth, personable, and to the point, with strong narration, anecdotes, and use of descriptive detail where appropriate. An article's lead must be strong, capturing the readers' attention and setting the tone of the piece. It should be followed by a clear thesis statement of the article's central point. The reader should know quickly what he or she is going to read about and why.

Treatment of light subjects must be as authoritative as serious subjects, but humorous examples and comparisons, as well as a lighter writing style, also are valued when appropriate.

Writers should be aware that CIRCLE K is not exclusively a US publication but has readers in Canada and the Caribbean as well. Avoid terms such as "our nation" and "our president," and strive for some quotes and examples from non-US sources, if practical.

Photographs (color and/or black-and-white) are not essential but are when they are of high quality and add substantially to the impact of article. Photos and artwork are purchased as part of the manuscript with consideration given to the extra time and expense of the author.

Mail or fax query letters.

Categories: Nonfiction—African-American—Asian-American—Associations—Business—Careers—Children—College—Computers—Culture—Disabilities—Education—General Interest—Jewish Interests—Leadership—Lifestyles—Multi-cultural—Native American—Student Service—Young Adult

Name: Nicholas K. Drake, Executive Editor
Material: All
Address: 3636 WOODVIEW TRACE
City/State/ZIP: INDIANAPOLIS IN 46268-3196
Telephone: 317-875-8755
Fax: 317-879-0204
E-mail: circleK@iquest.net

The Circle

Our submission guidelines are very flexible—it's quality, not word count, that is most important to the editors of *The Circle*.

Poetry—Any genre, any subject, 60 lines or less (preferably).

Short Stories—Any subject, we prefer less than 2,000 words but will consider longer stories.

Feature Articles—If interested in submitting a feature article, please e-mail us first for guidelines.

Categories: Fiction—Nonfiction—Comedy—Culture—Humor—Interview—Literature—Music—Paranormal—Philosophy—Poetry—Science—Science Fiction—Short Stories—Writing

Name: Penny Talbert, Editor
Name: Christopher Layser, Editor
Name: Christopher Talbert, Editor
Material: Any
Address: PO BOX 104
City/State/ZIP: WERNERSVILLE PA 19565
Telephone: 610-927-0917
Fax: 610-670-7017
E-mail: Circlemag@aol.com

City Primeval

Thank you for your interest in CITY PRIMEVAL, the first journal to feature Urban narrative as originally defined by Robert R Ward, the editor of *Bellowing Ark*:

"We are particularly interested in a genre of fiction that has evolved in the last thirty-five or forty years. The **Urban** novel developed from two subgenera: the western and the hard-boiled or NOIR detective novel. As the Western was set in the untamed lands, the Urban novel is set in the now uncivilized and barbaric "big-city" environment. The hero, and he is hero and not protagonist or antihero, moves into, and through, this dark (though in some cases, particularly the later novels of Donald Westlake, comic) environment, encountering and contending with the destructive elements that threaten society's moral cohesion. As with the hero of the Western, the Urban hero moves alone, through a basically hostile environment, seeking self-knowledge and resolution: the basics of the epic quest."

Robert R. Ward, *Bellowing Ark*
Volume 8, # 6 (Nov/Dec 1992)

CITY PRIMEVAL seeks narrative work-fiction or poetry-that addresses the nature and movement of men and women contending in, and with, the evolving urban environment: the breaking down of social structures and their recreation, the continuing redefinition of male and female roles, family structure and the individual's responsibilities to those structures. These characters will be marginalized in some way-those who accept the strictures and conventions of the "city" are largely indifferent to heroic action—but ultimately find satisfaction and meaning in their contention. Consider the possibility of a new tribalism, or of wealth seized and transformed; didn't Europe finally become civilized at the hands of men whose immediate ancestors were brigands and bandits? Consider that all law depends upon raw power; he who has the biggest weapons rules. No? Ask Randy Weaver, Sacco and Vanzetti, the Black Panthers, or the Branch Davidians. We are interested in writing that addresses a new way of looking at the possibilities of civilization: how that concept is changing and what that change means.

A familiarity with the work of Elmore Leonard, Margery Allingham, Richard Stark, Louis L'Amour, Elizabeth Linnington, Micky Spillane, Thomas Perry, and James Lee Burke will be of value.

We are only interested in literate writing; we intend to publish what will be the literature of the future. We leave it up to you, though we warn you, *fictions* need not apply. We will comment on work which seems to us promising.

For the present, we prefer stories of 15,000 words or less and poems under 150 lines. We are also interested in line drawings of suitable tenor and black and white photographs. Fiction typed, doubled spaced, poetry single spaced. Good clear photocopies are quite acceptable but *no* simultaneous submissions. Payment, at present, will be in copies.

Quarterly publication. Subscriptions $13/year, $4 per copy. We look forward to hearing from you.

David Ross, Editor

Categories: Fiction—Crime—General Interest—Literature—Men's Fiction

Name: Submissions Editor
Material: All
Address: PO BOX 30064
City/State/ZIP: SEATTLE WA 98103-0064
Telephone: 206-545-8302

Classic Home

Please refer to Colonial Homes

Clockwatch Review
Illinois Wesleyan University

About *Clockwatch Review*
• *Clockwatch Review* is a true independent, not-for-profit journal of the arts founded in 1983 by current editor James Plath. Though based at Illinois Wesleyan University, money to publish comes largely from subscriptions, single copy sales, individual patronage, and fundraising events.
• In 1990, *Clockwatch Review* was one of five magazines in the United States to receive an Editors Award for "editorial excellence and vision" from the Council of Literary Magazines & Presses.
• Internationally syndicated columnist Bob Greene devoted an entire column to *Clockwatch Review* in September, 1994, and Chicago Bulls coach Phil Jackson had a copy of *Clockwatch Review* in an ad promoting America's literary magazines featured in the June 1995 *Harper's Magazine*.
• The only American literary magazine to spotlight an ongoing series of interviews with artists, *musicians*, and other creative people besides writers, *Clockwatch Review* has featured

exclusive in-depth interviews with such talents as Vincent Price, Buddy Guy, Suzanne Vega, Arlo Guthrie, Dawn Upshaw, "Gatemouth" Brown, Dik "Hagar the Horrible" Browne, Romare Bearden, Jack Levine, Friz "Bugs Bunny" Freleng, Bob Newhart, Maria Tallchief, and David "Airplane!" Zucker.
• Two years after the magazine was founded, the Mark Twain Sesquicentennial Commission of Hannibal, Missouri chose *Clockwatch* to sponsor a fiction contest and to serve as the official literary magazine for the 1985 Twain celebration.
• *Clockwatch* has had a number of "firsts," including the first short story dealing with AIDS as a central issue to be published by a small press magazine; previously unpublished poetry by Salvador Dali; and, more recently, what we're told may be the first comic-style treatment of a serious literary short story. Like other literary magazines, *Clockwatch* features previously undiscovered and unpublished writers alongside such prize-winning authors as Rita Dove, James Dickey, Howard Nemerov, and Bob Shacochis. "Outsiders" are also represented, with past issues featuring poems by prisoners, the homeless, and Skid Row residents.

In poems, we look for:
Literary quality; a strong, mature, natural voice; control of language; fresh images and word choices; an awareness of the world beyond self; poems which *say* something, not just stylistic exercises or emotional exorcisms; poems 32 lines or less, since extremely long or extremely short poems are difficult to pull off; poems on any subject, except for religious poetry or poetry which is obscene/erotic without apparent need. We are not a market for self-involved or brooding verse.

In fiction, we look for:
Upbeat, offbeat plots-more than a single chronological strand; engaging and well-integrated sideplots, scenes that come alive; stories other than relationship-gone-down-the-toilet tales (of which we see too many); memorable/believable characters with meat on their bones; dialogue which rings true-not small talk; fresh, controlled language; a mature and distinctive narrative voice; fiction to 4,000 words (we'll make an exception if the work is exceptional).

In a genre piece (sci-fi, fantasy, western, mystery, etc.) the story must break the mold—it must move beyond the genre in some significant way

Essays/Criticism/Interviews:
• We seek thoughtful essays/articles on aspects of society and human behavior, ala H.L. Mencken, E.B. White, James Thurber. Query first or submit complete essay.
• For literary criticism, use MLA style documentation. We are less impressed by jargon than by substance and the author's sensitivity to the material. Best bet: query to find out what artists, musicians, topics, and literary figures will be featured in future issues, and submit a related critical essay.
• Most interviews with writers, artists and musicians are staff-written, in-depth discussions of an artist's work, not personal life. Read the magazine for style. We'll consider freelance work if the writer has access to someone we don't, or brings someone to our attention who deserves a wider national audience.

Submission Guidelines:
• Submit year-round, but be advised that we usually can't keep up with mss. volume in July. We receive 15-60 unsolicited mss. daily, depending upon the season. Sometimes we get swamped. Please be patient. We try to report within four months.
• No electronic submissions accepted at this time.
• Send 3-6 poems or 1 short story (2, if short-shorts).
• No arm-long vitas, please, but a 3-sentence contributor's note is helpful.
• Send us your *best* work—we publish the best magazine that we can, and fair is fair.
• Believing that it's in the best interests of our writers, we buy first North American and electronic rights and retain the

copyright so that we can grant permission for reprints through the Copyright Clearance Center, which handles academic (classroom) requests, and make current and back issues available on the worldwide web. Authors who wish to have the copyright reassigned to them need only request that in writing, and we will immediately reassign the rights. Our only interest is in being able to get copies of *Clockwatch* via reprints into the classroom and on the web, and thus increase public awareness of the magazine and the authors we publish. No previously published or simultaneously submitted material is generally accepted. Payment is currently $25 for fiction, $5 per poem.

Categories: Fiction—Arts—Literature—Music—Poetry—Short Stories

Name: Submissions Editor
Material: All
Address: DEPARTMENT OF ENGLISH
Address: ILLINOIS WESLEYAN UNIVERSITY
City/State/ZIP: BLOOMINGTON IL 61702-2900
Telephone: 309-556-3352
Fax: 309-556-3411
E-mail: jplath@titan.iwu.edu

Club Connection

What is *Club Connection*?

Club Connection is an exciting new magazine especially for girls and Missionettes leaders. The magazine appeals to all girls of any age. *Club Connection* includes crafts, games, skits, songs, and snack ideas for girls to do at home or in the Missionettes club meetings. Girls will also enjoy the devotional, fun facts and news, music and book reviews, missions facts and trivia, the write-in question-and-answer column, and other great features. The salvation message will be presented in each issue.

Did we forget about Leaders?

Of course not! *Club Connection* will provide the same great tips, plans, and ideas found in *Memos*, but in a newly energized format. The crafts and activities can be used straight from the girls' pages. Leaders can also refer to the special eight-page leader's section for leadership resources, discipleship materials, write-in questions and answers from the national office, fund-raising ideas, crowning ideas, the latest information on important current issues, and missions lesson plans that correspond with the girls' pages.

What type of articles does *Club Connection* use?

Club Connection

Girls Edition *Club Connection*

Leader Edition
• Personal Experience of Missionettes • Club meeting ideas
• Devotionals • Personal experiences of sponsors
• Memorization helps • Social awards, presentations
• Nature, camping, pets • Field trips
• Club journal • Assisting girls with special needs
• Sports • Honor Star crowning ceremonies
• Science • Missionettes and outreach ministries
• How to...Witness • Discipline in the clubroom
Draw • Leadership development
Stay in shape • Spiritual growth

etc. • Discipleship

How are manuscripts submitted for Club Connection?
Club Connection writers should...
• Make theologically correct statements
• Confirm illustrations
• Check Scripture references; identify versions
• Confirm all facts (history, nature, etc.)
• Indicate...
• if the manuscript is gratis
• if the article has been submitted to another publisher
• if the article has been printed before
• Include...
• name, address, and social security number on manuscript
• photos relevant to manuscript (see photo guidelines)
What happens next to the manuscript?

Each manuscript is read and evaluated, then either returned or held in a planning file for further evaluation and possible use. Since *Club Connection* is a quarterly publication, this process may take several months. If your material is published, you will be notified and/or receive payment upon acceptance. You wil also receive two complimentary copies of the issue in which your article is published.

Enjoy writing!

Club Connection connects girls to Jesus, their local churches, to other girls, and to their Missionette leaders. *Club Connection* connects Missionette leaders with resources, ideas, information, encouragement, and inspiration.

Categories: Nonfiction—Children—Christian Interests—Girls—Inspirational

Name: Kerry Clarensau, Editor/Missionettes Coordinator
Material: All
Address: 1445 BOONVILLE AVE
City/State/ZIP: SPRINGFIELD MO 65802-1894
Telephone: 417-862-2781

Coal People Magazine
A Monthly Publication Dedicated to Coal People!

THEME:
• History of a coal town or special event related to coal mining
• Focus on people in different facets of the coal mining industry
• Old coal mining pictures

Please note: story ideas related to coal mining will be reviewed, however special assignments must be approved by the editors of COAL PEOPLE MAGAZINE.*
• Payment upon publication only
• All submissions must be typed.
• Computer disc acceptance (PC or Mac) in Word format
Please allow 3 months after date of submission.
Short Stories: $35.00 (1,500 words or under)
Regular Features: $60.00 (under 5,000 words)
Features: $75.00 (5,000 words or more)
Poems/Puzzles/Cartoons/Fillers: $15.00
Pictures: Cost, plus 15%
*Special assignment payments will be determined.
Categories: Fiction—Nonfiction—Coal Mining

Name: Submissions Editor
Material: All
Address: PO BOX 6247
City/State/ZIP: CHARLESTON WV 25362
Telephone: 304-342-4129
Fax: 304-343-3124

Coast to Coast

Coast to Coast Magazine

As the membership publication for Coast to Coast Resorts, *Coast to Coast* is mailed to 250,000 readers eight times a year. Coast to Coast Resorts unites nearly 500 private camping and resort clubs across North America. A portion of the magazine is devoted to news about the Coast to Coast network: its programs, products and services, and, of course, its members. The remainder of the magazine focuses on travel, recreation and good times. *Coast to Coast* strives to be a fun, unpretentious but well-written and informative publication that offers a balanced mix of articles on things to do, places to visit, people to meet and ways to ensure a safe and happy trip.

Destination features in *Coast to Coast* should focus on a city or region of North America and should strive to convey the spirit of the place. The most readable place pieces go beyond typical tourist stops to interview locals and synthesize anecdotes and first-person observations in a way that is useful, entertaining and enlightening. Keep in mind that *Coast to Coast*'s readers already have more than 500 camping resorts at which to stay, so reporting on accommodations is almost always beside the point.

Activity or recreation features should introduce readers to or rekindle their interest in a sport, hobby or other diversion. As with the general public, most of our audience can be assumed to possess a basic knowledge of, say, golf or bicycling, but few have experienced rock climbing or skydiving. Nor would they care to, for the most part.

Many of our readers own recreational vehicles, so we feature the RV lifestyle in at least one article per issue. This is where lively, concise writing is especially in demand. If the writing is dry, the article will be, at best, unappealing; at worst, deadly. What's essential in these features is that readers identify with the situations they're reading about, that they pick up new information and at the same time are engaged and entertained.

The editors of *Coast to Coast* encourage queries and manuscripts. If you possess the requisite professional ability and have a lively writing style, please summarize your story idea, supplement it with a few opening paragraphs and forward it to our editorial offices with a selection of your best published clips or other writing samples. The editors are also pleased to review completed manuscripts.

Coast to Coast publishes first North American serial rights; articles must not appear in other publications for 90 days after they are first published in *Coast to Coast*. In accepting an assignment from *Coast to Coast*, writers agree to submit stories on or before the stated deadline and agree to rewrite them, if required, in a timely fashion. Assigned stories should be submitted electronically, either on disk or via e-mail, with an accompanying hard copy. Payment is made upon acceptance.

Categories: Recreational Vehicles—Travel

Name: Valerie Law, Editor
Material: All
Address: 2572 VISTA DEL MAR DR
City/State/ZIP: VENTURA CA 93001
Telephone: 805-667-4100

Cobblestone
American History for Kids

"Wherever possible, events should be seen through the eyes of participants such as explorers, American Indians, colonists, free blacks and slaves, children, or pioneers."
—California U.S. History Curriculum, Grade 5

General Information: Historical accuracy and lively, original approaches to the subject are the primary concerns of the editors in choosing material. Writers are encouraged to study recent back issues for content and style. (Sample issue is available at $4.50. Send 7½"x10½" (or larger) self-addressed stamped ($2.00) envelope.) *All material must relate to the theme of a specific upcoming issue in order to be considered.* To avoid repetition, it is a good idea to review COBBLESTONE's index (available at $9.95 plus $3.00 shipping) for a listing of subjects covered in back issues. COBBLESTONE purchases all rights to material.

Procedure: A query must consist of all of the following to be considered: a brief cover letter stating the subject and word length of the proposed article; a detailed one-page outline explaining the information to be presented in the article; an extensive bibliography of materials the author intends to use in preparing the article; a self-addressed stamped envelope. (Authors are urged to use primary resources and up-to-date scholarly resources in their bibliography.) Writers new to COBBLESTONE should send a writing sample with the query.

A writer may send as many queries for one issue as he or she wishes, but each query must have a separate cover letter, outline, bibliography, and SASE. Telephone queries are not accepted. Handwritten queries will not be considered.

Articles must be submitted on disk using a word processing program (preferably Microsoft Word—Mac). Text should be saved as ASCII text (in MS Word as "text only"). Disks should be either Mac- (preferred) or DOS-compatible 3½".

Guidelines

Feature articles, 700-800 words. Includes in-depth nonfiction, plays, first-person accounts, and biographies. Pays $.20-$.25 per printed word.

Supplemental nonfiction, 300-600 words. Includes subjects directly and indirectly related to the theme. Editors like little-known information but encourage writers not to overlook the obvious. Pays $.20-$.25 per printed word.

Fiction, up to 800 words. Authentic historical and biographical fiction, adventure, retold legends, etc., relating to the theme. Pays $.20-$.25 per printed word.

Activities, up to 700 words. Includes crafts, recipes, woodworking projects, etc., that can be done either by children alone or with adult supervision. Query should be accompanied by sketches and description of how activity relates to theme. Pays on an individual basis.

Poetry, up to 100 lines. Clear, objective imagery. Serious and light verse considered. Pays on an individual basis. Must relate to theme.

Puzzles and Games (no word finds). Crossword and other word puzzles using the vocabulary of the issue's theme. Mazes and picture puzzles that relate to the theme. Pays on an individual basis.

PHOTO GUIDELINES

To be considered for publication, photographs must relate to a specific theme. Writers are encouraged to submit available photos with their query or article. We buy one-time use.

Our suggested fee range for professional quality photographs* follows:

1/4 page to full page
b/w $15 to $100
color $25 to $100

*Please note that fees for non-professional quality photographs are negotiated.

Cover fees are set on an individual basis for one-time use, plus promotional use. All cover images are color. Text images are primarily four-color.

Color transparencies, slides, and color prints can be submitted for inside black/white use since they can be scanned at the printer.

Prices set by museums, societies, stock photography houses, etc., are paid or negotiated. Photographs that are promotional in nature (e.g., from tourist agencies, organizations, special events, etc.) are usually submitted at no charge.

If you have photographs pertaining to any upcoming theme, please contact the editor by mail or fax, or send them with your query. You may also send images on speculation.

Note: Queries may be submitted at any time, but queries sent well in advance of deadline *may not be answered for several months*. Go-aheads requesting material proposed in queries are usually sent five months prior to publication date. Unused queries will be returned approximately four to five months prior to publication date.

Categories: American History—Children—Juvenile—Young Adult

Name: Meg Chorlian, Editor
Material: American History for kids 8-14
Address: 7 SCHOOL ST
City/State/ZIP: PETERBOROUGH NH 03458
Telephone: 603-924-7209
Fax: 603-924-7380

Collecting Toys

Thanks for your interest in writing for COLLECTING TOYS. As the premier magazine of the toy collecting hobby, we're always looking for superior material. Before you submit an article to us, we recommend you write to let us know exactly what you have in mind. We can then tell you if your proposed article fits our needs or if we'd like a different approach than what you have in mind.

We publish articles on all aspects of toy collecting. Our editorial focus is predominantly on toys from the post-World War II era, but we are interested in material covering all eras of toy production. Again, it's best to contact the editor before you begin. If you have an idea on a subject you haven't seen us cover, write and ask. Here's a general list of our requirements:

TEXT: Present your subject simply and directly in plain English. Keep it as brief as you can while still covering the subject; the key is to limit your topic to a manageable size. Our payment is based upon the length of the *published* article, not the length of the *submitted* article, so there's no advantage to writing more material than necessary. It would help us estimate manuscript length if you would set your typewriter or printer margins for 75 characters (e.g., 5 and 80) and double-space. Type exactly 25 lines per page. If you use a computer, use a new ribbon and separate the printout into individual sheets. Include a caption for every photo you submit, and number all illustrations and photos in the text with corresponding consecutive figure numbers.

PHOTOGRAPHS: Since at least half of COLLECTING TOYS editorial space is photo-graphs, superior photography is critical. We can improve your text, but we can't do much with weak photos. Part of the toy collecting hobby's appeal is the color and look of the toys, so we prefer color, except in cases where color doesn't enhance your message. We prefer original 35 mm (or larger) color transparencies (slides). However, we can also use glossy color prints 5"x7" or larger.

If you do shoot print film, send the negatives with the prints; if you wish, we can return the negatives after the article has been published.

In general, the minimum requirements for submitting publishable photos are that you shoot with a 35mm SLR and put *plenty* of light on the subject.

We prefer you use one of the following film types when taking color photos *indoors* for publication in COLLECTING TOYS:

Fujichrome 64 T, code RTP, made by Fuji Photo
Ektachrome 64 Tungsten, code EPY, made by Kodak

These are "professional" films, which means that they are available from better camera stores. Fujichrome and Ektachrome are color-balanced for 3200K tungsten lighting, and take E6 processing, which allows quick turnaround from local film labs. Both films are available in 35mm cassettes, 120 (2¼"-square) rolls, and larger-format sheet sizes.

Ektachrome EPY has an ISO rating of 50, while Fujichrome RTP has a rating of 64. Some photographers find that an ISO of 40 is closer to the actual performance of Fujichrome RTP, but if you make adequate bracket exposures you can get good results with a meter setting of either 64 or 40.

PAYMENT: We pay upon acceptance at the rate of $25 per typeset column. Our contract specifies the purchase of *all rights* to your material; if you prefer to retain rights, payment is reduced. If the article runs longer than estimated, we'll make up the difference at the standard rate.

Send everything for one article at one time and in one package. Include a cover letter with your name, address; and daytime phone number. Address your package "To the Editor, COLLECTING TOYS" and mark it "MANUSCRIPT ENCLOSED." We'll send you a card acknowledging receipt of the article and will review your material within 60 days. We'll return articles we can't use if you include return postage.

Thanks for your interest in contributing to COLLECTING TOYS.

Photo Guidelines

Attractive photography has made COLLECTING TOYS rise above its competitors. To maintain the quality of photography we publish, we have produced these guidelines to help you take the best possible pictures to contribute to an attractive, creative layout. It is our policy to return only the pictures that are not used in the magazine.

Film

1. We can use glossy color prints, but we *prefer color slides* (35mm or larger formats) because they reproduce better than prints. Send duplicates if you want your own complete set.

Background

1. Use a *smooth*, seamless paper or cloth backdrop.

2. Do *not* use backgrounds that have a texture that will detract from the toy (i.e., carpet).

3. Use a solid, light-colored backdrop, such as tan, light blue, white, or light gray.

4. Use the same color backdrop for all the pictures.

5. Be sure the backdrop is big enough to fill the frame of the picture so you don't see the edge or area beyond the backdrop when looking through the camera.

Technical info

1. Avoid shadows. For best results, place lights slightly above the object.

2. Get the entire object in focus. If you have a point-and-shoot camera, read the manual to see how close you can get to an object and have it remain in focus. Experiment and take a number of pictures at varying distances and exposure lengths.

3. If you have a more advanced camera, use a 55mm close-up lens. It will produce the best results. To get the entire toy in focus, use the smallest F-stop possible (i.e., F-32 or smaller).

4. Use a tripod and cable release, if possible.

Viewpoint

1. At least one picture of each toy should be taken straight on from the front. To do this, place the camera at the level of the toy or just slightly above it.

2. Shoot toys from a variety of angles.

3. If the toy has a "nose"(like a car, boat, or action figure), also take angle shots, one with the toy angled left and one with it angled right.

Frame

1. Get close to the toy, but be sure the *entire* toy is inside the frame of the picture and not touching the edge of the picture. For example, if a toy has a tail or antenna, be sure it is also well within the frame.

2. When taking pictures of flat things (like posters, instruction sheets, or illustrations) photograph them straight on (from above, looking down at them).

3. Group shots are fine if they aren't cluttered and every item is completely in the frame.

4. If you take a group shot, also take individual pictures of each item in the group shot. (Exceptions to this apply to toys like playsets. We don't need individual shots of playset figures unless they are rare or unusual.)

Categories: Antiques—Collectibles—Games—Hobbies

Name: Ton Hammel, Editor
Material: Collectible Toys (Post-War boys' toys)
Address: 21027 CROSSROADS CIRCLE
City/State/ZIP: WAUKESHA WI 53187
Telephone: 414-798-6470
Fax: 414-796-1142
E-mail: thammel@toysmag.com
Internet: www.toysmag.com

Collector Editions

COLLECTOR EDITIONS, published seven times a year, is the leading consumer magazine covering limited-edition decorative collectibles: ceramic, glass and metal figurines; collector plates; prints and canvas transfers; dolls; cottages and lighted buildings; and ornaments. We publish well-researched, professionally written articles that are illustrated with color and/or black-and-white photographs of high quality.

Length of articles varies with subject matter, but ranges from 800 to 1,500 words, with the majority of articles published being about 1,000 words. Articles submitted should be authoritative, with a strong collecting angle, and of interest to a national audience. They should include substantiated values or suggested retail prices for all artworks discussed, and information on availability of the pieces. Our readers are knowledgeable collectors of limited-edition art, and they want hard facts, information about trends and help in identifying pieces. Wide-ranging surveys in any of our areas of interest are not desirable.

We specialize in contemporary collectibles, but publish occasional articles about antiques if they are generally available or are being reproduced today. We publish profiles of the artists and companies that create limited-edition collectibles, as well as roundups on subjects such as artworks depicting ballerinas, angels, Santa Claus or dragons.

We are also interested in profiles of celebrity collectors, if the celebrity is a household name throughout the country and collects pieces relevant to our publication. COLLECTOR EDITIONS is a consumer magazine, so we do not publish articles on retail shops or businesses. We have regular columnists who cover the auction houses and are experts on antiques, stamps, coins and sports memorabilia, so are not interested in additional articles on these subjects.

Queries submitted with sample photographs (color transparencies or black-and-white prints) will be given top consideration. Queries without photographs will also be considered. Querying by telephone is not acceptable. If the subject is of interest, writers new to the magazine should expect to be asked to submit the article on speculation. Unsolicited manuscripts will be considered, too. With rare exception, we expect our writers to supply photographs. If submitting an unsolicited manuscript without photographs, please indicate what illustrative material is available.

We will respond within six weeks and regret that we cannot offer individual comments on any submissions. Rates for accepted material vary, but rarely exceed $350 (including expenses). We purchase first North American rights only, and will return (after publication) all color transparencies submitted with material; black-and-white prints will not be returned. Payment is made within six weeks of acceptance. Writers are strongly advised to study an issue of COLLECTOR EDITIONS before submitting any material. Sample copies are available by request (one per writer) for $5.

Categories: Collectibles

Name: Joan Pursley, Editor
Material: All
Address: 170 FIFTH AVE 12TH FLOOR
City/State/ZIP: NEW YORK NY 10010
Telephone: 212-989-8700
Fax: 212-645-8976

Collectors News
Written With Collectors in Mind

SUBJECT MATTER: Freelance article topics sought—

1. Articles about individuals & their collections, emphasizing personal insights.

2. Informational articles on antiques and collectibles: Farm-Country-Rural memorabilia, Care and/or Display of specific types of antiques and collectibles, Furniture, Glass, China, Music and related topics, Art, Transportation, Bottles, Timepieces, Jewelry, Lamps, Nostalgia, Political items, Western items, Textiles, and any 20th-century collectibles and timely subjects.

CONTENT:

• Collecting tips on how to collect, where to locate items, and brief histories with information that will enhance the collecting process are encouraged in copy whenever appropriate.

• It is preferred that current values of your subject matter are included, either within copy or as a sidebar. Be sure to credit sources for the prices.

• Sidebars containing Reproduction Alerts and/or topical resources (books, clubs, etc.) also are recommended.

PHOTOS: Articles accompanied by photographs are given first consideration. Quality color or black-and-white prints are best for newsprint reproduction. Sharply focused pictures of individual items with an uncluttered background work best. When appropriate, photos including collectors and/or a grouping of collectibles add interest to an article. A selection of 2 to 8 prints is suggested.

FRONT PAGE PHOTOS: Articles are eligible for full-color front page consideration when accompanied by quality color prints, color slides, and/or color transparencies. Only one article is highlighted on the cover per month.

LENGTH: Shorter articles of 900 words or less are preferred; longer articles sometimes must await space availability or may be published in a serial.

COPY: Manuscripts are accepted as typed copy by mail or by fax. Specifics are available upon request.

PAYMENT: Basic payment is $1.00 per column inch, including space for published photos. Any article providing a color photo selected for front page use receives an additional $25.00. Payment is routinely sent upon publication.

Basis of Purchase of Editorial Material by *Collectors News*

All news articles and related editorial materials purchased by *Collectors News* are purchased on the basis of exclusive, first serial rights, unless otherwise stipulated by the author and agreed to by *Collector News* at the time of the submission and/or acceptance.

Categories: Nonfiction—Antiques—Collectibles—Hobbies

Name: Linda Kruger, Managing Editor
Material: All
Address: 506 2ND ST
Address: PO BOX 156
City/State/ZIP: GRUNDY CENTER IA 50638
Telephone: 319-824-6981
Fax: 319-824-3414
E-mail: collectors@collectors-news.com
Internet: www.collectors-news.com

College Bound Magazine

College Bound Magazine is designed to provide high school students with a view of college life from the inside. College students from around the country (and those young at heart), are welcome to serve as correspondents to provide our teen readership with **personal accounts on all aspects of college**. Give us your expertise on everything from living with a roommate, choosing a major, and joining a fraternity or sorority to college dating, interesting course offerings on your campus, how to beat the financial aid headache and other college-application nightmares.

College Bound Magazine is published six times throughout the academic year with an Annual National Edition published in January. We're also on-line with a World Wide Web site. In cyberspace, the writing opportunities are endless! Keep in mind that the **tone** of our articles is very light-hearted and informative. Imagine you're relating your experiences to a younger sibling or friend. You want to tell them "how it *really* is" and give them helpful pointers to make the transition between high school and college easier to handle.

College Bound Magazine is comprised of both **regular departments and full feature articles**. We typically pay $15 to $50 for department inclusions and $50 to $75 for feature articles; our rates depend upon length of story, topic, and research involved. Departments run approximately 500-1,000 words in length. Features are usually 1,200-1,500 words. We usually buy first rights to a piece. We will consider buying second rights if your published piece has not appeared in a high school-oriented publication, or any other magazine written primarily for college-bound teenagers. For all departments and features, you will receive payment upon publication.

WE RECOMMEND THAT YOU QUERY US BY STRUCTURING AN ARTICLE PROPOSAL IN THE FOLLOWING MANNER:

• Begin with the lead you expect to put on the article. Make it catchy-**grab our attention!**

• Write a **summary** of your intended areas of coverage.

• Give specifics about who you plan to interview, what types of real-life anecdotes you'll include, which resource you plan to utilize, and what **conclusion** the story might reach.

We would also like to get an idea of how well you report, write, and interpret stories. With your query; send us two or three **samples of your writing** from your college newspaper, composition class, etc. Photocopies are a good idea, as we cannot guarantee the safe return of all clips.

Familiarize yourself with *College Bound Magazine* before you submit ideas!

Get to know our style and what kinds of articles we love. Here's some help…

Departments:

• **CLIP NOTES**—Includes informative college admissions facts and advice as well as interesting tidbits on teenage "happenings" related to junior and senior students' lifestyles.

• **BOOKS**—In every issue, we review books and guides that make college life and preparation easy. If reviewing is your thing and you can be objective and add style and flair, this may be the department for you!

• **TRADITIONS**—In an effort to give our high school readership an inside look at college life, this department offers you the opportunity to write about events on college campuses that are timeless and entertaining. Some examples: "Mini Lollapalooza" at the University of Maryland; Casino Night at Bay Path College, MA; etc.

• **FOCUS**—This department provides an in-depth profile of a community organization, student-funded group, or other college and high school-related group of interest.

• **TECHIE TRENDS**—Presents exciting news in the world of technology and cyberspace, from interesting Internet and Web related news; techno-homework helpers, software reviews, etc.

• **APPLAUSE!**—All about academic accolades, schools that have won awards, big scholarship winners, etc.

• **THAT'S LIFE**—Covers a variety of topics ranging from Money Tips, Current Events, Social Commentaries, etc. Have a suggestion? Let us know!

• **CLASS CUT-UP**—Make us laugh! This department features reader-submitted comics, jokes, one-liners, etc.

• **INTERVIEW**—Gives readers an inside look at the college application process, presenting a profile of various college administrators, deans, teachers, career advisors, etc.

Features:

We look for original thought-provoking ideas—**be creative!**

Or, give us your "spin" on some topics we're interested in covering in future issues…

• "Your social life (as you know it) is about to change…. How you can make a smooth transition!"

• Overview of interesting and wacky college course offerings

• Profiles of teens who go "above and beyond…"

• Electronic Classrooms: Learning in Cyberspace

• How to impress your professors

• Tokens, trains, & tickets: Tips that make commuting a cinch!

• On Your Own-All about on- and off-campus housing

• Don't get testy! The ultimate guide to SAT success!

• Don't go into a financial aid frenzy-how you can survive!

• Where will you be in 10 years? A look at emerging new careers

• Get "in" on-line. Internet applications made easy

• The pressure's on! How to keep stress in check

• Student Activism: The new '70s.

• Spring Break: What students who *aren't* at the beach are doing!

• "If only I knew then what I know now!" One struggling student's story

• The hunt is on! The search for a summer job begins now!

• Studying Abroad

Please note that our response time to queries is approximately five weeks. Although we assign quick-quick-quick for a stupendously great story, our normal editorial lead time is four months!

Good luck, and thanks again for your interest!

Categories: Education—Young Adult

Name: Gina LaGuardia, Editor-in-Chief
Material: All queries and clips
Address: 2071 CLOVE RD STE 206
City/State/ZIP: STATEN ISLAND NY 10304
Telephone: 718-273-5700
Fax: 718-273-2539
E-mail: ramholtz@intercall.com

College Preview

Please refer to Communications Publishing Group, Inc.

Colonial Homes

Colonial Homes

Thank you for your interest in writing for *Colonial Homes* and *Classic Home*.

Our readers are generally married, college educated, and employed men and women who have a passion for history and design. The magazine offers its readers a celebration of America's spirit with articles featuring art, architecture, interior design, travel, and profiles of historical figures. We balance past and present, culture and history, and style and design.

1) If you have not already done so, study a few issues of the magazine to familiarize yourself with our tone, style, and content. We aim to be informative as well as entertaining.

2) Most of our articles run about 1,000 to 1,500 words.

3) Generally, articles are by assignment only. We usually commission photographers to photograph a site before a writer is assigned to the story. For this reason, we do not accept unsolicited manuscripts. We will, however, consider queries. We regret that materials sent to us will not be returned unless you provide us with a self-addressed stamped envelope.

4) We will not accept phone queries or faxed queries.

5) With your query, be certain to include a resume, as well as some representative clips of your published work.

6) All materials should be labeled with your name and address. For materials exceeding one page, label individual pages.

7) We pay upon acceptance of the manuscript. If an article is not accepted for publication, we generally pay a 25% kill fee.

8) Kindly allow four weeks for a response.

9) *Colonial Homes* and *Classic Home* do not publish fiction. We are looking forward to hearing from you!

Categories: Nonfiction—Architecture—Culture—Gardening—History—Travel—Home—Profiles—Interior Decorating

Name: Roberta Dell'Aquilo, Chief Copy Editor
Material: All
Address: 1790 BROADWAY, 14TH FLOOR
City/State/ZIP: NEW YORK, NY 10019
Telephone: 212-830-2900
Fax: 212-586-3455
E-mail: ashanley@hearst.com

Colorado Business Magazine

KEY POINTS:

1.) We plan editorial content at least four months in advance.

2.) Be proactive. Queries (phone or written) are welcome. Most of our news hole will be filled by editorial calendar items and departments, but we also welcome queries for other stories.

The departments are *Turning Point* (about an individual who has made, or is making changes, in his/her life and business) and *On Target* (an advice column for business owners and entrepreneurs). Both are 900 words.

Our features focus on the big picture, on trends and overviews in Colorado business; we rarely write about only one company. We try to include businesses from around the state, not just the Front Range. They run about 1,500 words, including sidebars. Charts and graphs are welcome.

We also run the occasional personality profile.

3.) Our readership is a high-end audience, with average salaries of $142,000. Many are CEOs, business owners, or high-ranking executives or managers. Our readership is 75 percent male, but our female readership includes many successful women business owners and operators.

They seek information on any business development that's new, interesting and useful to their business life or personal life. They want to read about trends, and interesting individuals and businesses, in the state.

4.) Stories are due two months in advance, i.e., Sept. 1 for the November issue. Stories can be sent by e-mail or submitted on a 3½" disk, PC format (Microsoft Word is our preference). We can convert Mac disks into our format.

Your submission should include the disk, a hard copy of the story, your invoice (including a social security number), phone numbers of people quoted, a photo suggestion list, and separate backing for statistics. We fact-check, so be prepared to be questioned. If you send by e-mail, forget the disk and hard copy.

Pay is on acceptance, which we define as the day the magazine goes to the printer, and averages 22 cents per word. In addition, we will add $25 to feature story payments to cover anticipated revenue from electronic pickups.

5.) If you are also a public relations consultant, you can't write about your clients for *Colorado Business*.

Categories: Business

Name: Bruce Goldberg, Editor
Material: All
Address: 7009 S POTOMAC ST
City/State/ZIP: ENGLEWOOD CO 80112
Telephone: 303-397-7600
Fax: 303-397-7619
E-mail: bgold@winc.usa.com

Columbiad
A Quarterly Review of the War Between the States

SUBJECT and TONE

The entire American Civil War and anything related to it form the legitimate subject matter of *Columbiad*. Articles should not have been published elsewhere; if an article has been published previously, the author must note this in the query or cover letter. Talks and papers delivered verbally may, however, be submitted as articles, but the author should note when and where the speech was given. Articles should represent substantial research in primary and appropriate secondary source materials, and should embody a well-reasoned, documented inner logic. Graceful, clear writing is crucial. Examine a copy or two of *Columbiad* for examples of what the editors are looking for.

METHODS OF SUBMISSION

Queries are preferred, but unsolicited manuscripts will be considered. A cover letter should be attached to each manuscript. Allow at least eight weeks for answers on queries and manuscripts.

DOCUMENTATION

All articles should be annotated. Footnotes or margin notes in the manuscript are preferred. Notes should contain complete information about sources; in the case of books, they should include the author's entire name, the exact title, place of publication, publisher, year of publication, and pages cited. In the case of reprinted books, the original year of publication should be noted, followed by the publication information relating to the reprint. Informational notes are acceptable and may be used to include parenthetical material of interest.

LENGTH

Articles may range from about 5,000 words (approximately twenty double-spaced letter-sized pages with standard margins) to 10,000 words (approximately forty pages), not counting annotations.

FORMAT

The editors prefer that articles be submitted both as hard copy and as word processing files on a 3½" floppy disk. Articles submitted only as hard copy will be considered nonetheless.

STYLE

In general, *Columbiad* follows the most current edition of *A Manual of Style* from the University of Chicago Press. The dictionary used by *Columbiad's* editors is the third edition of *The American Heritage Dictionary of the English Language*.

PAYMENT

Columbiad pays authors upon acceptance. Article prices are negotiated individually, and are generally based on the article's quality of information and writing, the originality of the article's content, and the author's reputation.

Sample copies are available for $10/ea.

Categories: Civil War

Name: Jim Kushlan, Editor
Material: All
Address: 6405 FLANK DR
City/State/ZIP: HARRISBURG PA 17112
Telephone: 717-657-9555
Fax: 717-657-9552
E-mail: CWT@cowles.com
Internet: www.cowles.com

The Comedy Magazine

To Our Friends in the Very Serious Business of Comedy:

Thank you for your recent inquiry [regarding] submissions and contributions to the *Comedy Magazine*. We need quality writers, illustrators, cartoonist and joke writers, so we are glad to hear from you.

As far as guidelines for submissions go, we are young and carefree enough that we aren't very rigid. Because a sense of humor is a unique personal preference, and because we like to reach as broad a range of readers as possible, we try not limit our contributors in terms of what topics to cover or what style to use. The main concerns we have are these:

1.) Keep it short. Few, if any written pieces longer than about one page will be considered.

2.) Keep it simple. If your area of expertise is so narrow that no one has any clue what you're referring to, it won't be funny.

3.) Make it affordable. No matter how much we love your work, we can't print it if we can't afford it. You have a better chance of being published if you make us an offer we can't refuse—we'll

return the favor someday, we promise.)

4.) Be creative! Show us something we haven't seen before. Make us chuckle out loud. As a matter of fact, go for the belly laugh.

5.) If you have any questions or you want some feedback, just ask us. We will be happy to discuss your ideas with you and help develop them. Direct faxes to Nancy Rothlein.

We hope to hear from you soon—good luck. And have fun.
Sincerely,
The Comedy Magazine editorial staff
Categories: Cartoons—Comedy—Entertainment—General Interest—Humor

Name: Submissions Editor
Material: All
Address: 5290 OVERPASS RD STE 128
City/State/ZIP: SANTA BARBARA CA 93111
Telephone: 805-964-7841
Fax: 805-964-1073
E-mail: comedy@silcom.com

Commercial Investment Real Estate Journal

Selecting a Topic

CIREJ readers are interested in how-to, trend, and forecast articles on a variety of topics, including taxes, development, brokerage, leasing, financing, property management, technology, and investment. Submit a detailed outline on a topic at least one month in advance of the manuscript. Call to discuss a topic with the editor.

Preparing the Manuscript

Submit articles on an IBM-compatible disk, along with a printed copy on 8½"x11" paper. Microsoft Word or ASCII files are preferred. Article length should be 8 to 12 double-spaced, typed pages—about 2,000 to 3,000 words.

Supply a brief professional biography, including present title, designations, place of employment, published articles, and expertise in the subject about which you are writing.

Graphics

Include charts, graphs, photographs, and illustrations when possible to emphasize and clarify points in your article. All hand-drawn graphics should be suitable for reproduction (camera-ready) as submitted.

Style

Aim for clear, concise, and lively writing, even if your topic is technical. CIREJ follows the *Chicago Manual of Style*, 14th edition, as a style guide. When appropriate, include case studies.

Promotional material is not acceptable and editors will remove it from your article.

The Review Process

All articles are reviewed by the editorial board, which is composed of commercial investment real estate professionals. The board determines whether an article is appropriate for publication in CIREJ.

A manuscript approved by the editorial board "with revisions" may be returned to the author with specific recommendations for further information or clarification. After the editor receives the revised article, the editor and author will discuss a publication date.

Copyright

CIREJ is seeking original, unpublished material, and it owns the copyright for all of its contents. If your manuscript has been published elsewhere, please provide us with full information about the publication in which it appeared. Please inform us if your manuscript is currently under consideration or scheduled for publication elsewhere.

The Benefits of Writing

Share your knowledge and receive national recognition in your field by joining the ranks of well-respected CIREJ authors. Authors receive five complimentary copies of the issue in which their article appears. In addition, article reprints are available at a minimal cost and make excellent handouts to current and potential clients.

Categories: Associations—Real Estate

Name: Catherine Simpson, Editor & Publisher
Material: All
Address: 430 N MICHIGAN AVE STE 800
City/State/ZIP: CHICAGO IL 60611-4092
Telephone: 312-321-4460
Fax: 312-321-4530
E-mail: csimpson@cirei.com
Internet: www.cirei.com

COMMON BOUNDARY

EXPLORING PSYCHOLOGY, SPIRITUALITY & CREATIVITY

Common Boundary
Exploring Psychology, Spirituality & Creativity

Common Boundary is a bimonthly magazine directed to mental health professionals, pastoral counselors, spiritual directors, as well as lay readers interested in the relationship among psychology, spirituality, and creativity. We accept manuscripts for feature articles, essays, and book reviews. Major features run from 12 to 16 pages (3,000 to 4,000 words), and shorter articles for departments such as "In Your Own Words," "Trends," "Innovations," and "Into Practice" run between 6 and 7 pages (1,500 to 1,800 words). Small news items can be submitted to our "Network News" section and should run roughly 500 words.

Our audience is highly educated and well read, but *Common Boundary* is not a scholarly journal. Manuscripts submitted for consideration should be written as magazine articles, not as research papers or lectures, nor as newspaper reports. By the same token, although we publish personal essays and some articles that draw on the authors' experiences, in general we are looking for writing that is applicable to our readers' lives and brings them information on emerging issues in an objective, unbiased manner. We shy away from navel-gazing as well as ivory-tower musings. Rather than simply promoting a specific therapy or healing method for its own sake, we step back and look at trends and developments in the psycho-spiritual field, the ways in which various approaches respond to and influence one another. Finally, if you're proposing an interview, it should be timely or newsworthy in some way—for example, the interviewee has a new book out.

Take some time to see what has been written on your chosen subject before—particularly what has been written on it in *Common Boundary*. Keep in mind that a topic that is new to you may be something we've already covered. The best way to know how to write a *Common Boundary* article is to read the magazine. Prior to submitting a manuscript, it is wise to send a query letter describing the piece—its thrust, major points, and why it would be of interest to our readers. Writing samples are also useful. Because of the volume of manuscripts we receive, we will not accept telephone calls regarding stories and manuscripts. Please allow 6 to 8 weeks for a response.

Categories: Nonfiction—Psychology—Religion—Spiritual

Name: Manuscript Editor
Material: All
Address: 5272 RIVER RD STE 650
City/State/ZIP: BETHESDA MD 20816
Fax: 301-652-0579
E-mail: connect@commonboundary.org
Internet: www.commonboundary.org

COMMONWEAL
FOUNDED 1924

Commonweal

COMMONWEAL is a biweekly journal of opinion edited by Catholic lay people. Founded in 1924, the magazine welcomes original manuscripts dealing with topical issues of the day on culture, religion, politics, and the arts. We look for articles that are timely, accurate, and well-written. Articles fall into three categories:

1. "Upfronts," running between 750-1,000 words, are brief, "newsy" reportorials, giving facts, information, and some interpretation behind the "headlines of the day."

2. Longer articles, running between 2,000-3,000 words, are more reflective and detailed, bringing new information or a different point of view to a subject, raising questions, and/or proposing solutions to the dilemmas facing the world, nation, church, or individual.

3. "Last Word" column, a 750-word reflection, usually of a personal nature, on some aspect of the human condition: spiritual, individual, political, or social.

Please send a query with outline and resume. We do not consider simultaneous submissions.

Articles should be written for a general but well-educated audience. While religious articles are always topical, we are less interested in devotional and churchy pieces than in articles which examine the links between "worldly" concerns and religious beliefs.

Notes and footnotes are discouraged. Please allow 3-4 weeks for an editorial decision.

Those with MS-DOS or Macintosh systems are encouraged to send the article on a diskette, along with hard copy. The diskette will be returned. Payment for articles is generally made on publication.

Poetry: We publish about thirty high quality poems a year.

Categories: Nonfiction—Culture—Literature—Politics—Public Policy—Regional

Name: Patrick Jordan, Managing Editor
Material: All
Address: 475 RIVERSIDE DR STE 405
City/State/ZIP: NEW YORK NY 10115
Telephone: 212-662-4200

Communications Publishing Group

Communications Publishing Group provides publications designed to inform and motivate minority youth and young adults (16-49) on higher education, career preparation and challenging opportunities. All publications are nationally distributed by subscriptions, direct and bulk mail.

Publications & Audiences

CAREER FOCUS. "The Briefcase Mentor" designed for today's rising Black and Hispanic professionals provides information on job search techniques, career development and skills for advancement. By profiling successful Black and Hispanic professionals in different fields, **CAREER FOCUS** provides insider secrets about career prospects for these recent graduates and aspiring executives. This unique magazine highlights corporate promotions, outstanding achievement, and career success. Published bimonthly.

COLLEGE PREVIEW. A resource guide for Black and Hispanic junior and senior high school students, this magazine offers helpful tips and advice on college preparation, financial aid, admissions and career planning. Published four times a year in January/February, March/April, September/October, and November/December.

DIRECT AIM. For the Black and Hispanic college students at traditional, non-traditional, vocational and technical institutions. This magazine informs students about college survival skills and planning for a future in the professional world. Published four times a year in January/February, March/April, September/October, and November/December.

FIRST OPPORTUNITY. Designed for Black and Hispanic high schoolers, this magazine prepares students for higher education and careers in vocational, technical, math and science fields. Published four times a year in January/February, March/April, September/October, and November/December.

VISIONS. A resource guide for Native-American high school and college students offering helpful tips and advice on college preparation, financial aid, admissions and career planning. Published semi-annually in March and September

FOCUS Kansas City. Published for the regional Kansas City area minority business and professional minded. Focuses on entrepreneurship, professional development, personal growth, and life management skills.

Editorial Topics

Profiles of outstanding, successful students, business people or corporate professionals who serve as positive role models to our audiences. Persons profiled must be Black, Hispanic, Asian American or Native American, preferably ages 16-35. Color photographs or slides must accompany manuscript.

For college graduates and rising professionals: hot career prospects, resume writing tips, interviewing techniques, office politics, managerial styles, career advancement, higher education, entrepreneurship and resource lists.

For high school juniors, seniors and college students: college preparation and selection, financial aid information, money management, study methods, campus living, extracurricular activities, higher education, hot career prospects.

For all audiences: news items from college campuses, current events, fads and trends, politics, fashion, sports, technology, entertainment, multi-cultural information, and minority business development.

Style and Tone

Articles should be informative and motivating, yet entertaining and easy-to-read. Format should take a who, what, where, when, and why approach to achieving goals. Providing tips or a checklist as a sidebar is acceptable. For example, "10 Tips on Money Management" could follow an article on "Financial Planning in the 90s."

Second or third person preferred in features and short stories; first person accepted in an essay of widespread interest.

Taboos

Assuming readers are totally unsophisticated; overly ponderous or "cute" writing styles; preaching; or casual mention of drug and alcohol abuse or sex. However, drug, drinking or sex may be treated responsibly in a short story or feature.

Article Length

Features: 1,000 to 2,000 words.

Profiles: 500 to 800 words. Subjects must be Black, Hispanic, Asian-American, or Native-American and a suitable role model for youth. Must include color photos, slides or B&W glossies. Snapshots are unacceptable.

News Briefs: 100 to 500 words. Timely information that will be of widespread interest.

Fillers: 25 to 100 words. Tasteful quotes, cartoons, poems and jokes relevant to college or professional life.

Announcements: 25-200 words for Promotions or other noteworthy achievement.

Professionals & Students on the Rise: 100 to 500 words.

Manuscripts

All first-time writers with CPG must submit full-length manuscripts, resume and other published work in order to be considered by CPG editors. Manuscripts will not be returned unless specifically requested. Address to a particular magazine and direct to the attention of the editor.

Submissions

Submitting manuscript along with disk (PC—WordPerfect or ASCII file or Word/Mac) will enhance your acceptability. CPG pays additional for disk. All manuscripts must include the following on first page: name, address, telephone number, social security number, word count, and title. Number and staple pages together.

Queries

Queries are reserved for writers who have had at least two articles published by CPG. Queries should detail the topic, how the writer plans to approach it, and how it will benefit our readership. Telephone calls are not accepted for queries.

Hold Status

After reviewing a submitted manuscript, CPG may decide to hold it for further consideration for an upcoming issue. A manuscript may be held up to six months as some articles are timeless and appropriate for any CPG publications. Notice of this hold status will be mailed to you. However, hold status **does not** constitute an acceptance. If these conditions are unacceptable or if the manuscript has been accepted by another publication, please notify our editorial staff immediately.

Acceptance

All articles are reviewed by our editorial staff who make recommendations for publications. As all CPG publications are published as a series of editions, all accepted articles can be utilized in one or more editions in the same series. For example, any articles on college preparation may appear in the spring editions of *College Preview, First Opportunity* and/or *Visions*. It will not appear in the fall editions. Therefore, CPG purchases one-time rights for use in our series of magazines.

Bylines and brief biographies of author are given generously at the discretion of the editor.

CPG reserves the right to edit all editorial for clarity and length.

Please allow eight to twelve weeks for a follow-up on queries and manuscripts. **Acceptance is upon publication.**

Payment

Notification of acceptance will be mailed along with payment. Pay rate is 10 cents per word, not to exceed $400.00 for a full-length feature. Pay rate is $10-$25 each for accepted poems, puzzles, jokes, cartoons; $25.00 each for color photos/slides; $20.00 each for B&W photos. CPG does not pay for photos supplied by public relations agencies or other entity seeking public service promotion.

$10 for each disk. If multiple submission, place all articles on one disk.

Art Submission

Art or suggestions for art to accompany a submitted manuscript are encouraged, but not mandatory. However, manuscripts submitted with color photos and/or illustrations have a greater chance of acceptance.

B&W Photos: Glossies, 5"x7" or 8"x10"; transparencies, no snapshots.

Color Photos: Transparencies preferred, glossies accepted; no instant photos.

Categories: Nonfiction—African-American—Arts—Associations—Business—Careers—College—Computers—Consumer—Culture—Diet—Economics—Education—Engineering—Entertainment—Ethnic—Government—Health—Hispanic—Internet—Law—Law Enforcement—Lifestyles—Money/Finance—multicultural—Native American—Nursing—Technology

Name: Amy Schiska, Associate Editor
Material: All
Address: 660 PENN TOWER
Address: 3100 BROADWAY
City/State/ZIP: KANSAS CITY MO 64111-2413
Telephone: 816-960-1988
Fax: 816-960-1989

Complete Woman

Thank you for your interest in submitting material to *Complete Woman.* We welcome all manuscripts and cartoons or illustrations that address the concerns of today's woman. Topics may vary over a range, including positive approaches to home, family, career, health, relationships, and self-improvement. Subject matter is limited only by your imagination and understanding of what it means to be a complete woman in today's society.

Manuscripts should be between 1,000 and 2,200 words in length, including any sidebar or supplementary material. Because all materials are received on speculation only, we suggest you query us with clips before sending your articles.

Complete Woman is published bimonthly. We pay upon publication (during the month of the cover, and after publication).

We look forward to seeing your work.

Sincerely,

Bonnie L. Krueger

Editor-in-Chief

Categories: Business—Careers—General Interest—Inspirational—Marriage—Relationships—Sexuality—Women's Issues

Name: Bonnie L. Krueger, Editor-in-Chief
Name: Lora M. Wintz, Associate Editor
Material: All
Address: 875 N MICHIGAN AVE STE 3434
City/State/ZIP: CHICAGO IL 60611-1901
Telephone: 312-266-8680

Compressed Air

Compressed Air Magazine

First off, don't let our name mislead you. We are not just a trade journal about compressed air and gases. *Compressed Air* is published by Ingersoll-Rand Company for its customers, and includes articles on all of the worldwide markets served by Ingersoll-Rand, including agriculture, architectural door hardware, assembly/manufacturing, automotive, construction (general, highway, and bridge), energy, food, landscaping, mining, and much more. We also publish articles on general technology, hobbies, the arts, management, nature, and history.

Compressed Air is looking for articles that inform our readers of technological innovations in the workplace and at home, enhance our readers' ability to manage their professional lives, and increase our readers' awareness of their surroundings and history. Potential authors should be guided by the fact that we prefer articles that tell our readers "why," instead of "how-to."

If, after reviewing sample issues, you are interested in writing for *Compressed Air,* send a one-paragraph story outline to my attention. Writing examples/clippings and references also should be included. If we commission an article, we pay upon acceptance. We generally ask for 2,000-word manuscripts, and they should be accompanied by color photography and captions.

Categories: Technology

Name: Tom McAloon, Editor
Material: All
Address: 253 E WASHINGTON AVE
City/State/ZIP: WASHINGTON NJ 07882
Telephone: 908-850-7840
Fax: 908-689-3095
E-mail: camag@ingersoll-rand.com
Internet: www.ingersoll-rand.com

Computing Today
A Christian Guide to Software, Web, Online and Multimedia Resources

COMPUTING TODAY is looking for articles that are both informative and engaging. Articles should entertain the reader by displaying the writer's personality. Good use of humor is a plus. Treat the readers as a confidant; interjections and peripheral or parenthetical comments are welcome.

Our audience are computer users with a distinctly Christian world view. Many are church leaders interested in church or Bible study applications. But all of our readers should be interested in home applications that will benefit the Christian family.

We aim to avoid technical jargon. Write in a style similar to PC NOVICE or FAMILY PC magazines. If you must use computer acronyms or technical terms, be sure to provide a definition or explanation. Many Christian computer users are fairly new to the field and stand at the beginning of the learning curve. It's your job as a writer to help them navigate the subject without overwhelming them.

Most of our articles are assigned, though we welcome queries suggesting article ideas. Articles usually range from 1,000 to 1,300 words. First-time submissions are paid approximately 15 cents per word upon acceptance. Articles may be sent via e-mail (preferred), or a hard copy and floppy disk.

Please write for an editorial calendar of planned topics.

Categories: Computers—Education—Family—Internet

Name: Submissions Editor
Material: All
Address: 465 GUNDERSEN DR
City/State/ZIP: CAROL STREAM IL 60188
Telephone: 630-260-6200
Fax: 630-260-0114
E-mail: ComputingT@aol.com

ComputorEdge®
San Diego's Computer Magazine

What is *ComputorEdge*?

ComputorEdge is the nation's largest regional computer weekly, with editions in Southern California and Colorado. The magazine provides non-technical, entertaining articles on all aspects of computer hardware and software, including productivity, advice, personal experience and an occasional piece of computer-related fiction. While focusing on novice and intermediate computer users and shoppers, our well-educated readers also include experts.

Who writes for *ComputorEdge*?

Our writers are clear and conversational. They share their technical expertise in a relaxed, personable manner without unnecessary technical jargon. This is a rare combination of talents.

We want writers with flawless accuracy, new angles, interesting solutions and real wit. We don't want forced humor, flowery wordiness and 10-year-old concepts. Don't be condescending; instead, write as if you're talking to a friend who's intelligent, but not a computer expert.

Don't send single-product reviews. We prefer a goal-oriented, problem-solving approach evaluating several solutions. Our issues have themes, but we're looking for more than just articles fitting the issue subject; our issues have two or three different treatments of the cover theme, rounded out by inside articles and columns on a variety of topics, including online systems, the Internet, multimedia, Macintosh hardware and software, alternate operating systems and answers to common computer problems.

Freelance writers contribute to most sections of the magazine. We pay $100 per feature article, 30 days after publication—if an article runs in both the California and Colorado editions, we pay $150. We buy first North American serial rights, as well as subsequent electronic publishing rights. Feature articles should be approximately 1,000 words in length. Shorter pieces (between 500 and 800 words) accepted for our Beyond Personal Computing section earn $50 ($75 for both editions).

The columns Mac Madness and I Don't Do Windows (alternate operating systems such as Amiga, Linux, OS/2, etc.) are open to freelancers. Columns pay $75 each, and $100 if run in both editions. Columns should be from 750 to 900 words.

What's the best way to proceed?

Be familiar with the magazine. Read several issues, understand the editorial focus. Know why we cover a topic and what level of knowledge is imparted. Understand what we're doing with our columns and departments. If you send us a catalog-size envelope with seven first-class stamps, we'll be happy to send you a sample issue or two. Or you can read the current issue on our Web site.

If you have an idea for an article, you can either submit a query letter or the completed piece with a cover letter. In either case, your letter should state the following:

• The problem, technique, profile, event, or products you wish to cover.

• Why *ComputorEdge* readers would be interested in your story.

• Specific solutions and/or conclusions you've found.

• Why you should be the writer covering this story.

• Whether the proposed story has a regional angle, or is of general interest.

If we accept an article or want to discuss a query, we'll contact you—please provide an e-mail address and day/evening phone numbers in addition to your mailing address. Don't call us about the status of your story; if in doubt, send us a "reminder" postcard or e-mail.

If product reviews are proposed as part of a story, we can arrange for product delivery. When the article is completed, we'll need it in ASCII or WordPerfect format (6.0 for DOS/Windows or 3.1 for Mac)—on diskette or e-mailed to the magazine's editor (please do not e-mail unsolicited manuscripts or queries).

Acceptance of a piece does not guarantee its immediate publication. If we've rejected a piece and you've included a SASE, we'll notify you by mail. We cannot guarantee the return of any unsolicited manuscript, diskette, photograph, or other materials. If we do reject your article, try again.

Thanks for your interest in *ComputorEdge*.

Categories: Computers

Name: John San Filippo, Editor
Material: All
Address: PO BOX 83086
City/State/ZIP: SAN DIEGO CA 92138
Telephone: 619-573-0315
Fax: 619-573-0205
E-mail: editor@computoredge.com
Internet: www.computoredge.com

Construction Marketing Today

Construction Marketing Today is a business news tabloid that covers company and marketing news for manufacturers serving the construction industry. *Construction Marketing Today* also publishes news and features providing how-to information for marketers, as well as information on construction markets and conditions. The audience is marketing and upper level executives at construction equipment and materials manufacturers.

Construction Marketing Today will review unsolicited manuscripts, and consider publication if they meet the audience's needs. For a reasonably prompt reply, include a self-addressed, stamped envelope or postcard. Fees are negotiated upon acceptance.

Construction Marketing Today makes freelance assignments to writers with business writing experience. Assignments typically require two-to-three-week turnaround, and often require follow-up work. Fees depend on the assignment, but generally starting at $200. Payment is made upon publication, unless other terms are negotiated. To be considered, please send relevant clips.

Categories: Business

Name: Ross Brown, Managing Editor
Material: All
Address: 426 S WESTGATE ST
City/State/ZIP: ADDISON IL 60101
Telephone: 800-837-0870
Fax: 630-543-3112
E-mail: Rbrown@wocnet.com

Consumers Digest

Consumers Digest is written "for people who demand value." This means we try to help our readers make lifestyle, purchasing, investment and personal financial decisions that directly benefit their daily lives. To do this, we evaluate a wide range of products and services, identifying products by brand name and evaluating them thoroughly and objectively. In most product articles, we tell our readers which specific products are Best Buys, where to buy recommended products (particularly discount sources) and how much they should expect to pay. In addition, every issue includes a special tear-out Buying Guide section including Best Buys and purchasing information for a range of related products (automobiles, electronics or household appliances, for example) with List and Best Prices available on a national basis.

The editorial concept of *Consumers Digest*, however, goes

beyond product-purchasing advice. We show our readers how to obtain the best value for the services they need: doctors, lawyers, hospitals, financial advisers, and so on. We tell our readers about recent advances in medicine, medica technology, nutrition and health care and how the reader can access these new developments. "Quality of Life" is an important consideration in most articles, which also applies to occasional articles about travel and leisure activities, such as entertainment. Throughout the magazine, the underlying theme is reinforced—telling the readers how they can get the most at the lowest possible cost. And on occasion, we run articles on developing trends—warranties as marketing tools that benefit consumers, for example—and speculative pieces about what the future may hold in important consumer areas. However, the core of *CD*'s identity remains Best Buys in a broad sense: Best Buys in products and Best Buys in services. Top value for the dollars spent forms the base for a majority of our editorial.

The median age of the *Consumer Digest* readership is about 46; 58% of the audience is aged between 18 and 49. Median income is about $45,000 and 42% of the audience has a household income above $50,000. The majority of our readers own their homes; 67% are married; 63% are employed at full or part time jobs; 64% completed or attended college. The male/female division is fairly even (51%/49%). *CD* readers, in other words, are intelligent and mature, with disposable income that they want to spend wisely. They are frequent and well-informed purchasers of all consumer goods.

Consumers Digest is published six times a year on a bimonthly schedule beginning with January/February. Articles are usually assigned four to six months in advance of publication. Articles must be thoroughly researched, well-documented (Best Buy documentation to be intensely scrutinized). We make frequent use of charts, graphs and sidebars. Writers should be well acquainted with the product or service they are evaluating and be prepared to render opinions concerning value and reliability. For articles including Best Buys, additional guidelines are provided. Just as important, articles must be lively; every *CD* article should be enjoyable reading, regardless of subject matter.

Article lengths generally range between 1,000 and 3,000 words. First time contributors should query with clips, if available, and a stamped, self-addressed envelope. All queries should be comprehensive enough to give a realistic idea of how the subject would be handled, including an overview of the treatment and an outline. All articles are produced on an assignment basis; editorial assignment contracts, detailing payment terms and deadline, are signed for each article. Base payment for all rights is 35-50 cents per assigned word, paid on acceptance of the manuscript. The kill fee for a rejected article is 50% of the assigned payment.

Categories: Nonfiction—Automobiles—Computers—Consumer—Electronics—General Interest—Health—Law—Money/Finance—Physical Fitness—Recreational Vehicles—Reference—Travel—How-to

Name: John Manos, Editor-in-Chief
Material: All
Address: 8001 N. LINCOLN AVE.
City/State/ZIP: SKOKIE, IL 60077
Telephone: 847-763-9200
Fax: 847-763-0200
E-mail: Jmanos@consumersdigest.com
Internet: www.consumersdigest.com

Remember: Editors change jobs and publishers change addresses. It is wise to invest in a phone call for the current information before submitting.

Continuum
Defining Excellence for Administrators in Skilled Nursing, Assisted Living and Subacute Care

SUBMISSIONS
Academic or technical manuscripts are subject to blind review by at least two members of the Editorial Advisory Board and occasionally one or more experts in the field. Manuscripts are accepted for consideration with the understanding that they are not under simultaneous consideration by any other publication and have not been published.

Authors must convey copyright ownership to The American College of Health Care Administrators (ACHCA) by submitting a transferal letter signed and dated by all authors which contains the following language: "In consideration of *Continuum* taking action in reviewing and editing [title of submission], the author(s) undersigned hereby transfers, assigns or otherwise conveys all copyright ownership to the American College of Health Care Administrators."

Articles and essays that offer advice, opinion or analysis are not necessarily subject to review by the Editorial Advisory Board, but the aforementioned copyright restrictions do apply.

PREPARATION
Manuscripts must be limited to 12 pages, including references, tables and legends. Use typefaces of good letter quality. Organize the manuscript in the order of text, references and tables. On a separate page, give a brief biographical sketch of the author(s), including full name, post-graduate academic degrees, title of current position, institutional affiliation and address.

References should follow *The Chicago Manual of Style* and be typed, double-spaced and arranged alphabetically by author. Tables and illustrations should enhance understanding of the manuscript and not summarize or repeat information given in the text. Obtain written permission from the copyright holder for the use of tables or illustrations previously published and copyrighted.

Illustrative photos and camera-ready art are welcome. Please identify persons or situations in each photo. Materials will be returned upon request.

Submit all manuscripts and articles with a letter of transmittal giving the name, address and telephone number of the corresponding author. Accepted submissions become the permanent property of ACHCA and may not be published elsewhere without written permission from the editor.

Categories: Health—Nursing—Senior Citizens

Name: Kelley Sheahan, Publications Specialist
Material: All
Address: 325 S PATRICK ST
City/State/ZIP: ALEXANDRIA VA 22314-3571
Telephone: 703-739-7900
Fax: 703-739-7901
E-mail: info@achca.org
Internet: www.achca.org

Cooking Light

Cooking Light, the Magazine of Food and Fitness, is the recipe for healthy living. Nearly 85% of our 5.2 million readers are women, most between the ages of 30 and 60. Our readers are affluent, sophisticated, well-educated, professional, and interested in living holistically healthy life styles. They come first to the magazine for our recipes, but the lively writing as well as health and fitness coverage help keep them coming back issue after issue. Here's what the editors of *Cooking Light* look for when assigning articles:

Knowledge of the Magazines: You can now find *Cooking Light* — the nation's largest epicurean magazine — at just about any supermarket or newsstand.

Lead Time: For food articles, it's anywhere from six months to a year, due largely to seasonality and the extensive work our Test Kitchens must do on every recipe. For healthy life styles articles, it's anywhere from three to eight months.

Story Ideas: Those lead times acquire that our stories be seasonal, long-range, or forward-looking. A trend of today can be old news in a six months, so please keep that in mind when developing queries. We're looking for fresh, innovative stories that yield worthwhile information for our readers — a cooking tip, a trend, a suggestion of how they can use a particular recipe, nutritional information that may not be common knowledge, reassurance about their lifestyle or health concerns, etc.

Food Queries: Cooking Light strives to offer new ideas and information than help readers make informed meal-planning, food-purchasing, and food-preparation decisions for a healthier way of eating — with more starch, dietary fiber, and water, but less fat, sodium, sugar, and alcohol. Our principles involve replacing the old, adapting the traditional, and creating the new. We expect our writers to adhere to the ethical standards set by the national Association of Food Journalists to keep our stories free of any commercial bias.

Submitting Queries: All story ideas must be submitted in writing. Please enclose a paragraph or two about each idea, your resume, and some sample clips. Because of the volume of mail we receive, we guarantee a response only if you include a self-addressed, stamped envelope with your query. We'll get back to you, even if by form letter, within about a month.

Our street address (for overnight services) is 2100 Lakeshore Drive, Birmingham, AL 35209.

Categories: Nonfiction—Cooking—Food/Drink—Health—Physical Fitness—Travel—Diet

Name: Jill Melton, Senior Food Editor
Material: Food
Name: Lisa Delaney, Senior Fitness Editor
Material: Fitness
Address: P.O. BOX 1748
City/State/ZIP: BIRMINGHAM, AL 35201
Telephone: 205-877-6000
Internet: cookinglight.com

Cornerstone

These are the writers' guidelines for *Cornerstone* magazine. Our purpose is to communicate doctrinal truth based on Scripture and to break the "normal Christian" mold with a stance that has cultural relevancy. We appreciate your interest and hope you will find these guidelines helpful.

Articles

The kind of article we are looking for is the well-documented piece dealing with contemporary issues. This kind of writing takes time to prepare, i.e., research, interviews. We may use one unsolicited manuscript per year with up to 4,000 words maximum and pay 8-10 cents per word.

Opinion Pieces/Reviews/Cartoons

We welcome various opinion pieces, personal testimonies, cartoons, and reviews. These items should be between 500 and 1,000 words, and, again, we pay 8-10 cents per word. We also publish book and music reviews. These should feature a recent publication or artist focusing on the work and/or the artist's worldview and value system.

Fiction

We are looking for high quality fiction with skillful characterization, plot development, and imaginative symbolism. We welcome material which touches on current social and theological issues. We are open to all types of fiction from the traditional to experimental pieces. Manuscripts should be from 250 to 4,000 words, though this can be negotiated. We, again, pay after publication 8-10 cents per word.

Poetry

We accept avant-garde, free verse, haiku, light verse-though we have no room for epic poetry. We usually print 5-6 poems per issue at $10.00 per 1-15 line poem, $25.00 per 16+ line poem. We are looking for good use of imagery, words that elicit a sensory response in the reader, a poem that has memorable quality.

Response Policy

Due to the volume of material we receive, we cannot return your work, so never send us your only copy because we discard those manuscripts that we do not wish to hold. We will contact you only if we would like to hold your work because it might fit well in a future Issue of *Cornerstone*, so please do not send a SASE. Our response time is generally three to six months.

Mark your envelope "Attn: Joyce Paskewich, Submissions Editor" or for poetry, "Attn: Tammy Perlmutter, Poetry Editor." (You are also welcome to fax your submission.) Because *Cornerstone* publishes only 3-4 issues a year, we use very few of the freelance manuscripts submitted, but rest assured, all material sent to *Cornerstone* is read and considered.

We look forward to hearing from you soon.

Sincerely,

Joyce Paskewich

Categories: Christian Interests

Name: Joyce Paskewich, Submissions Editor
Material: Short Fiction, Articles
Name: Tammy Perlmutter, Poetry Editor
Material: Poetry
Address: 939 W WILSON AVE
City/State/ZIP: CHICAGO IL 60640
Telephone: 773-561-2450
Fax: 773-989-2076

Corporate Legal Times

Corporate Legal Times is a monthly business and management magazine for general counsel and other attorneys who work in the legal departments of corporations. We purchase stories that examine, discuss and analyze the actions and/or decisions of corporate legal departments. We do not purchase stories that discuss substantive legal issues.

Potential story ideas must be presented in a query letter to the managing editor, Jennifer King, before investing a lot of time in reporting and writing. Query letters should be one page or less, and include the pertinent background on the story, a list of sources and anticipated length of the story. We do NOT accept simultaneous submissions.

We want to give our audience useful information and practical advice. Any time you can supply concrete examples or case studies that explain the issue, it is far preferable to hypothetical cases. Our audience wants to read about how their counterparts solve problems, develop creative procedures, make tough decisions, etc.

While law firm attorneys can serve as good sources and are helpful for giving background information, we will not purchase stories that rely solely on law firm lawyers as sources. All stories must present the in-house counsel's point of view. In general, the higher up the ladder, the better, i.e. the general counsel is better than an assistant general counsel, but the assistant is better than a staff attorney, if that's who will call you back. However, for a story that focuses on a particular case, sometimes the environmental attorney or patent attorney with direct responsibility for the matter will know more about it than the general counsel. Consultants, too, should be used mainly for background and direction. Quote consultants only when they say something you can't get an in-house attorney to say.

The following information/material must be included with your story:

• A suggested headline

• Fact-checking material. Include copies of business cards or letterhead that will allow us to check the spelling of individuals and companies. You must also include the phone number and address of every person quoted. Any items such as press releases, newspaper clippings or court papers used to prepare the article must also be included.

• Since virtually every story needs some type of picture or graphic, please include a note that gives art and/or graphics suggestions. If your research turned up an appropriate list or chart, please include it (along with where you found the info).

• A hard-copy print out of your article.

All stories must be submitted by mail on 3½" disk (PC preferred) or by e-mail as an attached file. Copy deadlines are approximately two months before the cover date. Writer's compensation will be determined at the time of the assignment. We pay on the 15th of the month the story is published.

If you have any questions regarding these guidelines or any aspect of the article you are writing, please do not hesitate to call.

Categories: Nonfiction—Business—Law—Management

Name: Jennifer King, Managing Editor
Material: All
Address: 3 E HURON ST
City/State/ZIP: CHICAGO IL 60611
Telephone: 312-654-3500
Fax: 312-654-3525
E-mail: jking@gsteps.com
Internet: www.gsteps.com

Corrections Today

Please refer to American Correctional Association.

Cosmopolitan

Non-Fiction: Catherine Romano, Executive Editor

Cosmopolitan is a monthly magazine for young career women. All nonfiction should tell readers how to improve and better enjoy their lives. Within this sphere, articles range from serious women's issues to relationship advice and humor. Crisp, incisive, entertaining writing is a must, with a heavy emphasis on reader involvement. Full-length articles should be no more than 2,500 words, front-of-book pieces from 800-1200 words. Payment is commensurate with quality of work.

Fiction: *Cosmopolitan* does not accept unsolicited fiction submissions. Novels and short stories will be considered only if they are submitted by a publisher or agent. Payment is open to negotiation with the author's publisher or agent.

PLEASE ENCLOSE A SELF-ADDRESSED, STAMPED ENVELOPE OR YOUR SUBMISSION CANNOT BE RETURNED.

Categories: Fiction—Nonfiction—Book Reviews—Careers—Entertainment—Fashion—Health—Money/Finance—Physical Fitness—Relationships—Self-Help—Sexuality—Travel—Beauty—Personal Development—Nutrition—Home—Lifestyles—Women's Issues—Romance—Essay—Interior Decorating—Celebrities—How-to—Humor—Opinion—Personal Experience

Name: Catherine Romano, Executive Editor
Material: All
Address: 224 W. 57TH ST.
City/State/ZIP: NEW YORK, NY 10019
Telephone: 212-649-2000
Fax: 212-956-3268

Council for Indian Education

We are now receiving more than 200 manuscripts per year, from which we publish about six, usually five fiction, one nonfiction, and possibly one poetry anthology. We are only interested in *high quality material which accurately interprets Native American life, culture, and ideals. We publish nothing else.*

What kind of material can we use?

These are our preferences, in the order listed:

Fiction - High interest stories for any age, preschool through high school. (See Fiction Guidelines that follow.) This fiction may be:

Contemporary Indian life - Exciting stories that could happen to Native American children now. (Be sure the children act like present-day Indians, not like some other culture.)

Stories of the old days - Authentically portrayed. Be specific about who, where, and when.

How-to - Indian arts, crafts, and activities. We currently have only two of these books, one on canoeing, and one on tracking. We need others.

Biography - Native Americans past and present.

Folk stories and legends - High interest, expressing Indian traditions and values. Name the specific tribe.

Beginning Reading - Our beginning reader series gives beginning readers of any age reading material which will interest them, and make them want to read, while it teaches a basic sight vocabulary and builds reading skills.

Poetry - possibly - if it is positive, upbeat, and expresses real Indian ideals.

Instructional materials and methods for teachers teaching Native American children.

For whom are you writing?

Our books are for children - kindergarten through high school. Half of our readers, or more, are Indian, largely on reservations. Our books give these Native American children reading materials which are relevant to their backgrounds and authentic in their interpretation of Indian ways, and also give them pride in their culture. They should also help the other half of our readers gain a better understanding of their Indian neighbors.

What should you send?

For manuscript up to 75 pages, submit in its entirety. For longer manuscripts, you may prefer to send only the first two and the last chapters with a synopsis of the remainder. *Send photocopies only, book rate.* Never let the original out of your hands. Include photocopies of photographs or other illustrations if you have them. We use only black and white illustrations but can sometimes get black and white prints from color photos. We assume you are sending your material to other publishers also. **Do not send any manuscripts between June 1st and October 1st.**

How long do you wait?

All manuscripts must be read by our Intertribal Indian Editorial Board, who make the final selection. This usually takes four to nine months because our editors and board members are all volunteers with many responsibilities. None are paid. This Board makes sure the material is true to the Indian way of life and is the kind of material they want their children to read. We try to meet three times per year to make final decisions. Publication is usually one to two years after acceptance.

What is the rate of pay?

For novels, a royalty of 10% (ten percent) of wholesale price as the books are sold-no advances. Short stories to be included with others-$0.02 per word. Poetry-copies only.

Artists: We need illustrations for only about two books per year. We use only black and white. If you want to be considered, state in your letter that you will illustrate a book for our standard price of $5.00 per illustration.

FICTION GUIDELINES

Before you send your manuscript to us, answer the ten questions that follow. These are the questions our Intertribal Indian Editorial Board will answer when they decide whether or not to publish your material. If the answers to these questions are "NO", don't send the manuscript-you would be wasting your effort, your postage, and our time.

1. Interest: Is it so interesting that children will read it rather than watch TV? If you were buying a book for an Indian child, would you buy this book in preference to most of the books in the store? If the story is based on someone's actual experience, is it a real story, or are you so concerned about recording a real incident that only your own family will be interested? If so, give it to your children. Don't send it to us.

2. Cultural authenticity: Does it portray Indian characters acting as Indian children really act? If it is a contemporary story, do they act and speak the language of the 1990s? If it is of the past, do they live the part of Cheyenne children of the 1870s, or whatever the particular time, place, and culture you have chosen? *Know* the culture and the values thoroughly. Make sure this is a true portrayal of the people about whom you write.

3. Freedom from prejudice: Are you downgrading any group of people? Of course, you have to have a problem for your main character to solve. The problem may be people, nature, or situations, but if the problem is one or more people, no matter how evil, it should not be implied that they are typical of their race or their culture. There are good and bad people in every race and every group. Don't imply that any race, nationality, or culture is superior or less worthy than another. Never imply that any person is bad because he belongs to any cultural or racial group. Have you eliminated the use of any words such as *squaw, massacre, gook*, that might offend some readers?

4. Quick start, fast action: Children's stories must be quick starting and fast action. Have you hooked the reader on the first page of your novel, or, if it is a short story, the first two paragraphs? If in that space there is not something that makes the child eager to read on to find out what is going to happen, he will lay the book down and choose a different one. So will your editor! If your first pages are a description of the Indian boy on his horse, what he looks like, the beautiful romantic setting, tear them up and throw them in the rubbish. However, if your first pages are building background which is *essential* to your story, remove them, and work the information unobtrusively into your second or later chapters. No matter how important your subject, how valuable the information, or how important the moral you teach-it is all worthless if nobody reads it. If it has a slow start, children won't read it, so there would be no point in our publishing it.

5. Plot: Is there a well-developed, on-going plot that will keep the reader wanting to read on?

6. Characterization: Are your characters fully developed? Is character demonstrated through action rather than description? By the end of the first two to three pages, does the reader feel that he really knows and cares about the main character? Unless it is a one-character story, the reader should truly know at least one other character by the end of the first chapter. Are the characters realistic? No one is completely bad, and good people do make mistakes. In fact, mistakes are often the instigation for the plot.

7. Positive attitude: Does your story portray a cheerful, positive, upbeat and hopeful attitude? Are you complaining? "Oh, we poor Indians, look what you terrible people did to us!" If that's

what you write, we will not publish it, and we hope nobody else will.

8. Self-concept builder: Will it build the self-esteem of the Indian child who reads it, and give the non-Indian reader a better understanding of his Indian neighbors?

9. Focus on children: How intrusive are the adults? If the child gets into a problem (your plot) and an adult solves it for him, this is *not* a children's story. Sure, he can remember his grandfather's teaching, but grandfather can't tell him what to do, or do it for him. The child has to solve the problem *himself* through *his own* thinking and his own action.

10. Ending: Is there a satisfying ending that makes the reader end up feeling good about the book and the characters it portrays?

If the answers to 9 out of these 10 questions are "YES," submit your story to:

Categories: Fiction—Nonfiction—Adventure—Biography—Children—Education—Ethnic—History—Juvenile—Language—Multicultural—Native American—Outdoors—Poetry—Teen—Textbooks—Western—Young Adult

Name: Hap Gilliland, Editor
Material: All
Address: 2032 WOODY DR
City/State/ZIP: BILLINGS MT 59102-2852
Telephone: 406-652-7598
E-mail: cieclague@mcn.net
Internet: www.mcn.net/~cieclague

Country America

CIRCULATION: 900,000
PUBLICATION SCHEDULE: 6 times annually
EDITORIAL PHILOSOPHY: *Country America* reflects and upholds the values, traditions, activities, and interests of country people who love country music.

COUNTRY AMERICA READERS: Mainstream America whose values include freedom, honesty, patriotism, individuality and loyalty. They are people who consider themselves down-to-earth, straightforward, neighborly, hard-working and honorable.

What makes a good *Country America* article?

The ideal *Country America* article will be tightly written with potential for several color photographs. Think visually. The magazine serves the needs and interests of people who live in the country or identify with traditional country values and lifestyles found throughout the nation. *Country America* provides feature stories on country music and country entertainers, travel, cooking, recreation, crafts, traditions, and people.

WRITING SUGGESTIONS:

1.) Remember to keep a national audience in mind. Don't narrow the articles so much that they only interest a small segment of our audience. Country is not only a location but a state of mind.

2.) Write in a conversational, easy-going manner to make for enjoyable reading. Many of our readers are do-it-yourselfers; "how-to" sidebars are desirable.

3.) Make it easy for the readers to take action by providing addresses and phone numbers telling them where to get more information.

FACT CHECKING: All articles must be checked back and cleared with the sources before submission to *Country America* to ensure the accuracy of information. It is also highly recommended that the reputations of sources be checked in the community.

RIGHTS: Articles written for *Country America* are lifetime—we buy all rights. We very rarely reprint an article.

QUERIES: It is strongly recommended that freelance writers first query *Country America* with their story ideas before writing. Keep in mind that an original article is more valuable than one assigned by the editorial department. The respective editors are:

SAMPLE COPIES: For a sample copy, send $4.95.

PAYMENT TERMS: Country America pays between $.35 and $1 per word and buys lifetime rights on acceptance within three weeks. All freelance *contributors* must sign a standard freelance contract form and provide social security number or tax ID number before payment can be made.

PHOTOS: Color transparencies are required. Rates start at $75 for color photos and $50 for black and white. Photographers are required to obtain signed photo releases of all subjects before payment can be authorized.

Categories: Nonfiction—Antiques—Collectibles—Cooking—Crafts—Entertainment—General Interest—Lifestyles—Music (Country)—Rural America—Travel—Western

Name: Bill Eftink, Managing Editor
Material: All
Address: 1716 LOCUST ST
City/State/ZIP: DES MOINES IA 50309
Telephone: 515-284-3787
Fax: 515-284-3035

Country Connections
"Seeking The Good Life— For The Common Good"

We encourage submissions of articles, column ideas, essays, poems, short stories and book reviews. Word count for articles generally does not exceed 2,500. Please query us before submitting a feature, article, book review or new column. All other material may be submitted directly for consideration.

Because of the unique nature of our publication, it is important that contributors read the journal and become familiar with our direction. (Sample copies are available for $4.00. Subscriptions are $22 per year.) We look for a strong, personal point of view, original thinking, and focused, accomplished execution. Humor is also appreciated.

All non-art submissions should include a word count, and the writer's name, address, and telephone number on the top right of the first page and the writer's name and telephone number on the top right of all subsequent pages. We have listed below in order of preference the methods for submission of written material:

1. Include submission as part of message to our e-mail address.

2. Attach Microsoft Word for Mac file and send to our e-mail address. (We will respond via e-mail for 1 and 2.)

3. Mail typed or printed copy to the address below.

Categories: Animals—Culture—Diet—Ecology—Environment—Feminism—Poetry—Progressive Politics—Social Activism

Name: Submissions Editor
Material: All
Address: 14431 VENTURA BLVD STE 407
City/State/ZIP: SHERMAN OAKS CA 91423
Telephone: 818-501-1896
Fax: 818-501-1897
E-mail: countryink@countryink.com
Internet: www.countryink.com

Country Home

Does not accept unsolicited submissions.

Country Living

Thank you for writing *Country Living* and for requesting our writer's guidelines.

While we do not commission work based on query letters, we are happy to review completed manuscripts.

Manuscripts should be triple-spaced, allowing wide margins on both sides, as well as at the top and bottom of the page. Please use white bond paper only.

Our fees vary depending on the nature of the work and on the inclusion of supplemental photos and/or art work.

All manuscripts should be sent to our Features Editor, Ms. Marjorie Gage, at the address below.

Sincerely,

For the Editors

Categories: Nonfiction—Antiques—Collectibles—Conservation—Cooking—Crafts—Entertainment—Family—Food/Drink—Gardening—Hobbies—Marriage—Real Estate—Travel—Home—Interior Decorating—Nature

Name: Ms. Marjorie Gage, Features Editor
Material: All
Address: 224 W. 57TH ST.
City/State/ZIP: NEW YORK, NY 10019
Telephone: 212-649-3509
Fax: 212-956-3857

Country Woman Magazine

Country Woman is a 68-page, full-color, bimonthly magazine for women who live in or long for the country. It is a positive, upbeat, entertaining publication that reflects the many interests and roles of its readers through short, photo-illustrated personality profiles of rural women...antiques and gardening articles...nostalgic photos and reader remembrances.

Freelance material to be considered for publication should have a rural theme and be of specific interest to women who live on a farm or ranch, or women who live in a small town or country home, and/or simply have an interest in country-oriented topics.

Many of the stories, columns, anecdotes and photos in CW come directly from its readers. But we count on free-lancers such as you for the balance of each issue. Here are some of our regular features that free-lancers help us with:

Features/Profile stories...in each issue, we feature about half a dozen profile pieces, stories about ordinary country women doing interesting and extraordinary things. Stories must be told in a light, entertaining, conversational style with plenty of direct quotes from the featured country woman. This is her story; let her tell it. Stories should have a strong, readily identifiable "angle," and must be focused throughout. Stories must be country related, and the "why" behind what the woman is doing must be clearly explained.

Many of our profile pieces focus on cottage industries or small businesses women have started themselves. Recent issues have included profile pieces on: a farm woman who has become a wool spinner and whose husband has begun to make spinning wheels as a result of her craft; a country woman who makes rag rugs out of scraps of old cloth; a grade school teacher who takes the chicks she raises on her farm into her grade school classroom and uses them as "teaching aids." These profile pieces are not limited to farm women, however; features on women who live on a country place or in a small town are also acceptable. We are not interested, however, in recent "transplants" to the country or in upscale "yuppie country" operations.

Bright and beautiful color photos must accompany all profile pieces. We prefer to work with 35mm or 2¼" Kodachrome transparencies, but have had remarkable luck with bright, clear color prints, as well. CW is looking for top-quality color, focus, and lighting in all photos. Profile pieces are most often rejected because of poor quality photos! Take good action, not posed, shots of your featured country woman in her natural environment-at work on the ranch, cutting out Christmas cookies, stitching a quilt, or doing whatever it is that you are focusing on in your story.

While your subject should be colorfully dressed, she should not be wearing much makeup—we prefer the "natural," wholesome look. Manuscript length should be about 1,000 words, accompanied by a good variety of photos-give us lots to choose from, please! Payment for photo-feature package, on acceptance: $100-$225. Generally, payment is in the $150 range, except for regular contributors, who are paid at the higher end of the scale.

Cover shots. We are always in the market for strong cover photos! Cover shots must be strong verticals, with bright and vibrant colors. Focus must be razor-sharp—no soft-focus shots will be accepted. No hot spots either! Use fill-in lighting where necessary to avoid hulking shadows. We have found that Kodachrome film generally provides the best color saturation, although other brands in the hands of skilled photographers have also met our high standards. We can work from either 35mm or 2¼" transparencies, but prefer the larger-format photos.

Photos must focus on a close-up shot of a country woman in her natural surroundings. Subject should be attractive, but in a natural, wholesome way. She should not look "made up" or "modelish" or too dressed up. She must be a true country woman, preferably with a "traditional" family life. Prefer subjects in their 30s to mid-40s, although attractive older women are acceptable, as well. It is our cover lady's "job" to invite the reader into the magazine. Subject should look as if she's just stopped whatever she was doing for a moment to glance up and smile warmly out at the reader. Try for as spontaneous a look as possible.

While the magazine's logo does not overprint the cover photo, several small lines of type do—so try to plan a small solid area somewhere in the background to accommodate. When possible, covers should portray a strong, seasonal look, as well. Occasionally, we make cover assignments. More often, we find an acceptable shot from a standard feature/profile submission (see above). We always need at least one additional pose for the inside cover story. Cover prices are somewhat negotiable, but generally range around $300, depending on quality. Inside shot: $50-$75, depending on quality and size at which it's used.

Service Features. These must relate specifically to the lives of country women. Some "how-to" articles we've bought recently include: how to start your own at-home business; how to market your crafts; how to sell your work to publishers; how to preserve old family photos; a listing of mail-order sources for holiday baking. Maximum length: 500-600 words. Color photos: where appropriate. Rate: $50-$75.

Country Crafts. Sewing. Needlework: emphasizing quick, easy and inexpensive country crafts. Prefer items that are utilitarian as well as pretty. Include a list of all materials needed, detailed patterns, instructions and illustrations. Actual item must be enclosed so we can check it against instructions. Rate: $35-$75, depending on quality and degree of difficulty.

Also welcome features on contemporary sewing methods, ideas for "remakes," quilting tips, practical wardrobe planning, etc. Good color photos where appropriate. Rate: $35-$75.

Decorating. We're always looking for features on home improvements along with before and after photos, short tips on decorating and exciting features on how to accomplish that "country look." Again, good quality color transparencies are a must. Rate: $50-$125.

Nostalgia. We're looking for well-written nostalgic pieces that fall into three categories: "I Remember When" is a country woman's recollection of a past event that the vast majority of read-

ers can identify with; "I'll Never Forget" is a more personal recollection describing an event unique to the writer; general nostalgia captured in fiction and poetry. Length: 750-1,000 words. Rate: $50-$75.

Inspirational. Material should reflect the positive way in which the country enhances your own life. Length: about 750 words. Rate: $50-$75.

Poetry. Must have a rural theme and be positive and upbeat. Always looking for good, seasonal poetry. We accept only traditional styles-poems must have rhythm and rhyme! Poems should be 4 to 25 lines in length, with some exceptions. Rate: $10-$25.

Fiction. Well-written short fiction is a continuing need. The subjects should center on life in the country, its problems and joys, as experienced by women, and contain a positive, upbeat message. The main character *must* be a country woman. Length: 1,000 words. Rate: $90-$125.

Unless a specific assignment is made, all freelance material will be considered *on a speculative basis*. CW is published 6 times per year. The ideal deadline for freelance material is 6 months before the date of the issue.

For craft submissions, send return postage in the form of a check or money order. Submissions without adequate return postage will not be returned.

Country Woman reserves the right to rewrite any and all material it buys to comply with our very particular in-house style. If you are not willing to have your material rewritten, do not submit it!

A decision on free-lance material is generally made within 2-3 months after receipt of the article. Payment is upon acceptance. If querying first (and do query on all feature/profile pieces), please enclose a stamped, self-addressed envelope.

If you are notified that your manuscript is being held for future publication and later on you [wish to inquire] about its status, please enclose a self-addressed return envelope. Be sure to remind us of the subject matter of the article in your letter—don't just give the title. This will help us locate it in our files. Of course, articles we hold are not available for resale until we've notified you of publication. *We sometimes hold articles several years or longer before publishing.*

Contributors are strongly urged to study the magazine carefully before querying or submitting. CW is generally not available on the newsstand. Freelancers may subscribe at a special rate of $10.98 per year (regularly $16.98). To obtain a sample copy, send $2.00 plus a 9"x12" envelope with $1.93 in postage to the address below.

Categories: Consumer—Cooking—Crafts—Family—Lifestyles—Rural America

Name: Kathy Pohl, Managing Editor
Material: All
Address: 5400 S 60TH ST
City/State/ZIP: GREENDALE WI 53129

Cowles Enthusiast Media, Inc.
History Group

MILITARY HISTORY   VIETNAM
WORLD WAR II   AVIATION HISTORY
WILD WEST   AMERICA'S CIVIL WAR

Cowles History Group, a division of Cowles Enthusiast Media, Inc., in Leesburg, Va., publishes six bimonthly historical magazines: *America's Civil War, Aviation History, Military History, Vietnam, Wild West,* and *World War II*. Prospective contributors should be familiar with the individual magazines before querying. *America's Civil War, World War II,* and *Vietnam* cover strategy, tactics, personalities, arms and equipment for the applicable period. *Military History* deals with war throughout human history. *Aviation History* covers military and civilian aviation from man's first attempts at flight to the jet age. *Wild West* covers the American frontier, from earliest times through its westward expansion.

Historical accuracy is imperative. We do not use fiction or poetry. We do not publish reprints.

STYLE: The two paramount considerations in all Cowles History Group publications are absolute accuracy and highly readable style. Give proper attribution in the manuscript when using another author's work and cite your major sources for our review. We like to see action and quotes where possible to heighten reader interest.

QUERY: Submit a short, self-explanatory query summarizing the story and its highlights. Also state your sources and expertise. Cite any color and black-and-white illustrations and primary sources of illustrations (museums, historical societies, private collections, etc.) you can provide. Please put complete name on *every* photo submitted. Photocopies of suggested illustrations are extremely helpful. Illustration ideas are an *absolute must*. The likelihood that articles can be effectively illustrated *often determines the ultimate fate of manuscripts*. Many otherwise excellent articles have been rejected due to a lack of suitable art. *All submissions are on speculation and must be accompanied by an SASE.*

FORMAT: We strongly urge authors to submit with manuscripts computer disks that are IBM or Macintosh compatible. The disk will be returned to the sender. Name, address, telephone number and social security number must be on the first page [of manuscript]. Indicate sources and suggested further reading at the end of your manuscript. Include a 1-2 paragraph autobiography.

LENGTH: Feature articles should be 3,500-4,000 words in length and should include a 500-word sidebar. Departments should be 2,000 words or less. Cowles History Group retains the right to edit, condense or rewrite for style.

PAYMENT: Payment, which is made 30 days after publication, varies by magazine and ranges from $200 for *World War II* features to $400 for *Military History* features (including sidebar) and $100 to $200 for departments. We also use book reviews, payable at a per-published-word rate, with a minimum payment of $30. Cowles History Group buys exclusive worldwide publication rights, and the right to reprint the article in all languages, in hard copy or through electronic means, at no additional cost. Payment for Web site article usage is set at 50% of the applicable magazine rate. For previously run magazine articles that are reprinted on our Web site, we pay 10% of our original payment or $25, whichever is more.

REPORTING TIME: Please allow six months' response time for queries and manuscripts. If you want immediate verification that a submission has been received and is being considered, please enclose a stamped, self-addressed postcard containing the title of your submission. Be forewarned that in some cases we have a 2-year backlog of scheduled manuscripts.

COWLES HISTORY GROUP EDITORIAL PHILOSOPHY

Cowles History Group is committed to creating accurate, entertaining. and informative magazines, books, and products. It is our responsibility to ensure the loyalty and confidence of our customers by maintaining the highest editorial standards. To this end, our editorial content is never used as a sounding board for political partisanship, religious points of view, or social agendas. Our mission is to present an undistorted view of history and to encourage understanding and appreciation for the events, personalities. and artifacts of the past.

Just as writer's guidelines provide the mechanical requirements for submission of a manuscript, the following tips are intended to provide more subjective guidance for the preparation of copy that is editorially "clean" and enjoyable to read.

• Please give the reader a little excitement, some sense of being there, with lively-but always factual-anecdotes. Lead with one of these, if possible, to foster the reader's interest in seeing more of your story and to let him or her know that here is an article that is worth reading.

• Know what the reader expects from the publication in terms of subject matter and style of writing. Be very careful to keep technical terminology in the proper context.

• Start most paragraphs with a simple, active sentence-so many begin with As, When, Because, After, or other passive openers. Active writing keeps readers' eyes open. Our aim is to bring life to history, not to use it as a bedtime soporific. The same goes for "…ing" verbs; use them sparingly, as you do sleeping pills, to which their effects are related.

• Provide each paragraph with more than one sentence, except to make an occasional emphatic point. Break a paragraph before it runs on and takes up half a page.

• Keep to your story, and tell one story at a time. If there is a related aside, put it into a sidebar rather than break the flow of the main story.

• Maintain a smooth flow of information. It's fine to begin with an attention-getting action lead and a flashback, but from then on proceed straight through the story rather than jump around chronologically. If you make it difficult for the reader to follow your story, he will desert you; if you do that to the editor, he will protect his readers from a similar experience.

• Watch your spelling and grammar. You may be an expert in your subject, but your credibility can be shattered by sloppy copy.

• When you-either in exhaustion or exultation-finish the last keystroke, never, never rush the manuscript into the mail in an I'm-so-glad-to-be-finished dismissal. Put the manuscript aside and out of your mind at least overnight; then get back to it in a day or two and play editor. Go through the entire manuscript slowly, thoroughly and critically and correct all spelling errors. **Question the spelling of every name-person, thing, company—all of them.**

• Make sure you have included full name and rank/title for every person mentioned. Read through the manuscript as if you were the reader who has never seen it before and does not know what you are trying to get across. Does it flow smoothly? Does it say what you want it to say? Does it proceed logically through a basic beginning, middle and end? Is it simple and clear rather than flowery and hobbled by descriptive adjectives? **Are your facts straight?** Check how presentable the final, assembled package is. Make it professional, not pretty. Do not dress it in fancy folders or tie it with ribbons. Keep your manuscript straight, neat and clean.

• What you are doing here is just what the editor will do when he receives your material. His job is to select quality material that will hold the interest of his readers. If your submission is unprofessional, it may be returned unread with a standard rejection letter. A professional presentation of a well written and researched manuscript has a better chance of being reviewed and seriously considered. From then on, the appropriateness of the subject, the writing and the facts will influence whether the editor believes your manuscript will please the reader-and will determine its acceptance.

• **Keep your facts straight.**

Categories: Aviation (*Aviation History*)—Civil War (*America's Civil War*)—History (All magazines)—Military (*Military History, Vietnam, World War II*)—Western (*Wild West*)

Name: Jon Guttman, Editor
Material: *Military History* Submissions
Name: Art Sanfelici, Editor

Material: *Aviation History* Submissions
Name: Greg Lalire, Editor
Material: *Wild West* Submissions
Name: Roy Morris, Jr., Editor
Material: *America's Civil War* Submissions
Name: Harry Summers, Jr., Editor
Material: *Vietnam* Submissions
Name: Mike Haskew, Editor
Material: *World War II* Submissions
Address: 741 MILLER DR SE STE D-2
City/State/ZIP: LEESBURG VA 20175
Telephone: 703-771-9400
Fax: 703-779-8345
E-mail: cheryls@cowles.com
Internet: www.thehistorynet.com

Crayola Kids Magazine

In April 1994, Meredith Publishing Services and Binney & Smith, the makers of Crayola, launched *Crayola Kids*, a magazine for 3-to-8-year-olds. The mission of *Crayola Kids* magazine is to excite young children about the magic of reading and the joy of creativity - and, in so doing, help parents encourage successful learning. *Crayola Kids* is a brightly colored, fun-filled magazine that presents top-quality children's literature and related coloring, drawing, crafting and fact-based activities as a creative and intellectual springboard for prereaders and early readers. Each bimonthly issue focuses on a single theme and features a full-length reprint of a previously published picture book (trade book) and related puzzles, crafts, and activities. Issue themes are carefully selected for how vitally linked they are to the needs and interests of all children in the audience. Activities must be fresh, exciting, and challenging to children in the magazine's target age range (3 to 8 years). In addition to the material aimed directly at young children, *Crayola Kids* offers a Family section with activities that involve a small degree of parental involvement, such as food preparation or a craft requiring minimal adult assistance. Our family section also will occasionally feature material that is better suited for small groups than for an individual reader.

How to query: We do not publish theme lists for upcoming issues. However, we are interested in highly creative multicultural, nonsexist activities, visual puzzles, games, and craft ideas. We also publish brief interviews with children's book authors and illustrators. Tell us your story or activity idea and what's unique and fun about it. Convince us that kids will love reading it, doing it, or making it. Please include a resume and sample copies of your work and a self-addressed stamped envelope. At this time we do not accept original, unpublished fiction or poetry (unless you are between the ages of 3 and 8). Please allow four weeks to receive a reply.

Articles/Activities: Please be accurate. Double-check all of your facts and send photocopies of documentary source material you might have used. Please provide the names, addresses, and phone numbers of sources you talked to or used. If you are providing an activity or craft idea, please kid-test the project with a child in our magazine's target age range and share his/her comments with us. Include clear step-by-step directions for every craft activity. Provide simple sketches or Polaroid shots (not to be used for publication but to assist the editors in understanding the steps involved).

Length: Features: 150-250 words. Crafts/Activities: one to four pages.

Rates: 550-$250 (may vary)

Crayola Kids normally purchases the following rights:

1. For stories and activities previously unpublished, Meredith Corporation purchases the material outright. The work becomes the property of Meredith Corporation, and it is copyrighted in the name of Meredith Corporation. Payment is made upon acceptance.

2. For material previously published, Meredith Corporation purchases non-exclusive, second-serial publication rights. Fees vary. Payment is made upon acceptance. With the exception of our feature books, we have a strong preference for material that has not been previously published. At the present time we are purchasing rights for our feature books only from established publishers of children's books.

Format for submission: *Crayola Kids* is on a Macintosh system that uses WordPerfect. You can send your story on a disk. If you use other software on your Macintosh, or if you use an IBM computer, you can also send your material by disk, and we can convert it. Of course, we'll take your work the old-fashioned way - printed on paper, too! Use double spacing, please.

For a sample copy, please send $2.95 to:

Crayola Kids Sample Copy, Meredith Publishing Services, at the address below.

Categories: Nonfiction—Animals—Children's Picture Books—Crafts—Family—Games—Hobbies—How-to—Interviews—Nature—Puzzles

Name: Editor
Material: All
Address: 1912 GRAND AVE.
City/State/ZIP: DES MOINES, IA 50309-3379
Telephone: 515-284-2390
Fax: 515-284-2064

The Cream City Review
University of Wisconsin—Milwaukee

The Cream City Review, founded in 1975, is a non-profit literary magazine operated entirely by students and published semi-annually in association with the creative writing concentration of the English Department of the University of Wisconsin—Milwaukee.

Our review takes its name from the "City of Cream-colored Bricks" or "Cream City," as Milwaukee was once known. The first "cream" brick was made in 1835. Pale yellow, the bricks proved more durable and aesthetically pleasing than the traditional red bricks produced by East Coast kilns. Popular throughout the 1800s, cream city bricks were used for ornamental architecture in the United States and Europe.

Our magazine is perfect bound in the standard magazine format of 5½"x8½" inches, with a four-color cover, averaging 250 pages. It is distributed to major university and public libraries and independent bookstores throughout the United States. We are indexed by *The American Humanities Index*, the *Index of American Periodical Verse*, and the *Annual Index to Poetry in Periodicals*, and are members of CLMP and COSMEP.

Submissions

Of course the best way to figure out what we really want is to read the magazine. Check out the samples and the preview of issue 19.2 or just go ahead and subscribe.

Submission Guidelines

First of all, we are sorry to say that we cannot accept electronic submissions at this time. We just don't yet have a reliable way of distributing an electronic manuscript among our various editors. So until further notice, you must rely on the US Postal Service.

Author's name and address should appear on the first page of the manuscript or on each individual piece of art work. Address submissions to the editors of the appropriate genre followed by our full address. Simultaneous submissions are acceptable as long as TCCR is notified at the time of submissions and in the event that work is accepted elsewhere. Submissions which do not include an SASE will not be read or returned.

We seek to publish all forms of writing, from traditional to experimental. We strive to produce issues which are challenging, diverse, and of lasting quality. We are not interested in sexist, homophobic, racist, or formulaic writings.

Please include a few lines about your publication history and other information you think of interest. TCCR seeks to publish not only a broad range of writing but a broad range of writers with diverse backgrounds as well. Both beginning and well established writers are welcome.

Reporting time is at least eight weeks. We do not read from May 1-Sept. 1. Contributors are given a one-year subscription to TCCR beginning with the issue in which their work appears. Copyright automatically reverts to the author upon publication, although TCCR retains the right to republish in future issues of the magazine.

Genres

Fiction: Preferably under thirty pages, although we occasionally consider longer material. Please submit no more than one story at a time.

Poetry: No length restrictions. Please submit no more than five poems at a time.

Nonfiction: We are interested in reviews (one to ten pages), interviews, and personal essays.

Art: We are interested in camera-ready black-and-white artwork and photography. Please submit prints or slides. We use approximately twelve pieces of art per issue. As with text, we can accept submissions only through the mail. Keep an eye out, however, for a call for art specifically for our web page.

Categories: Fiction—Nonfiction—Arts—Literature—Poetry—Short Stories—Writing

Name: **Staci Leigh O'Brien**
Material: **Any**
Name: **Laura Micciche or Karen Howland**
Material: **Poetry Editors**
Name: **Geoff Carter or Christopher Grimes**
Material: **Fiction Editors**
Name: **Nancy Gaynor or John Allen**
Material: **Nonfiction Editors**
Address: **UW-MILWAUKEE ENGLISH DEPT**
Address: **PO BOX 413**
City/State/ZIP: **MILWAUKEE WI 53066**

Creation Spirituality Network Magazine

Creation Spirituality Network Magazine (Matthew Fox, Editor-in-Chief) is a voice of the creation spirituality movement, which integrates the wisdom of Western spirituality and the global indigenous cultures with the emerging scientific understanding of the universe and the passionate creativity of art. It is the earliest tradition of the Hebrew Bible and was celebrated by the mystics of medieval Europe.

On the individual level, creation spirituality recognizes the artist, mystic, and prophet in each person by honoring the experiences of awe and gratitude; suffering, darkness, silence, and mystery; imagination, creativity, renewal, and rebirth; and justice-making and celebration.

On the community level, creation spirituality provides a solid foundation and holistic perspective from which to address the critical issues of our times, including the revitalization of education, religion, work and culture; the honoring of women's wisdom; the restoration and celebration of hope in today's youth; and the promotion of social and ecological justice.

On a cosmological level, creation spirituality advocates the telling of the universe story, and our active participation in that story, through art, education, and ritual.

Because we are a small non-profit publication with an even smaller staff, we request that a proposal be submitted prior to a full-length article. The proposal should summarize the intended article in approximately 500 words, and it should be double-spaced. We request that all proposals be typed. Please include a SASE if you would like your proposal returned, or if you would like a reply other than confirmation of receipt. We regret that we are unable to enter into correspondence about editorial decisions.

We like getting artwork and proposals from women, from visible and non-visible minorities, from animals and plants and rocks and water. We like it when writers and artists look beyond the human circle and include the rest of the planet and the universe. We like writing that is clear, concise, and comprehensible to people who don't have the background that the writer does. We like articles that move beyond theory and tell us how to put concepts into practice. We like work that recognizes that we are a diverse group of people: country bumpkins and city slickers, nineteen and ninety, comfortable and struggling, monotheistic and pantheistic, and everything in between.

We look forward to hearing from you, to reading your proposals and your poetry, to seeing your artwork, to hearing your music.

Authors and artists will receive three copies of the issue in which their work appears.

CSN reserves the right to edit all material if approved by the editors for publication.

Categories: Nonfiction—Ecology—Religion—Spiritual

Name: **Rémi Tremblay, Editor**
Material: **All**
Address: **PO BOX 20369**
City/State/ZIP: **OAKLAND CA 94620**
Telephone: **510-836-4392**
Fax: **510-835-0564**
E-mail: **csmag@hooked.net**

Creative Nonfiction

"Now that you have established this journal called *Creative Nonfiction*," people ask, "what does it mean?"

It's surprising how many writers (and readers) don't understand, exactly, the elements of the form in which they are writing. Some are attracted by the word "creative" and think that because their prose is unusual or distinctive and because the stories they are telling are true, they are writing "creative nonfiction."

Others, usually people with a journalistic background, are put off by the word "creative," maintaining that if it is creative, it certainly can't be accurate, believable, or ethical, which are the essence and anchor of nonfiction prose.

But there is no conflict between being a good "reporter" and a good writer, creative in technique and approach. The essays published in each issue of *Creative Nonfiction* are models of the truest forms of creative nonfiction, in that they simultaneously "showcase" or "frame" fact in creative context.

"Truth"—which should not be confused with the factual or informational aspects of the genre—is another important element of the "classic" creative nonfiction form-and often a more personal one. A writer's concept of the truth may not be universally accepted and may even conflict with the facts as others understand or remember them. Good creative nonfiction does not deny personal opinion: to the contrary, it welcomes the subjective voice.

Take, for example, Hilary Masters' essay, "Son of Spoon River," in our summer, 1996 "Five Fathers" issue. Masters discusses the ways in which the media and the publishing industry tend to brand or categorize people for their own comfort and pleasure, despite the personal and professional damage such "public" judgments may cause. Masters is the son of Edgar Lee Masters, of *Spoon River Anthology* fame; he and his father were the victims about whom he writes. The writer's message is often called the "theme" or "main point of focus."

As it was in Masters' piece, it is often the writer's personal depiction of the message that makes the work unique. Presenting the theme with a personal take makes the writer's work creative. But there are other ways in which writers can go about making their nonfiction creative.

Fiction techniques often capture a subject and add a distinctive feel that conventional journalism may not. Action-oriented scenes contain dialogue and evocative description with great specificity and detail. Fiction techniques include the use of dialogue, characterization, description, and point of view. But using the devices of fiction does not give the creative nonfiction writer a license to fabricate. John McPhee once noted that creative nonfiction is "an attempt to recognize that a piece of writing can be creative while using factual materials,that creative work can respect fact."

Writers must always respect fact-as distinguished from universal truth-in their work. Writers for *Creative Nonfiction* must present their personal interpretation of the truth without becoming overly experimental or egocentric. Though we encourage the subjective voice and encourage a unique approach, writers are still bound to the fundamental duty of journalism: to inform or teach the reader.

An essay from our third issue, "Emerging Women Writers," serves as a good example of a highly subjective voice that adheres to the principle of accuracy. The author, Lauren Slater, a practicing psychologist, used her skills as a fiction writer to give her readers insight into her struggles as a professional counselor and her own recovery from a debilitating mental illness. The reader feels close to Slater as she describes how she was assigned to counsel a patient in a hospital in which she herself had once been a patient. Every aspect of her essay was true, though she used scene and dialogue to embellish the facts into a larger and more universal truth.

There are no length requirements, although we are always searching for writers who can communicate a strong idea with drama and humor in a few pages. Payment is $10 per published page. We report in two months. Query for author profiles only.

Points to Remember When Submitting to *Creative Nonfiction*:
- Strong reportage.
- Well-written prose, attentive to language, rich with detail and distinctive voice.
- An informational quality or "teaching element" offering the reader something to learn-for example, an idea, concept, collection of facts-strengthened with insight, reflection, interpretation.
- A compelling, focused, sustained narrative that's well-structured, makes sense, and conveys a meaning.
- Manuscripts will not be accepted via fax.

Categories: Nonfiction—General Interest—Literature—Writing

Name: Submissions Editor
Material: All
Address: 5501 WALNUT ST STE 202
City/State/ZIP: PITTSBURGH PA 15232
Telephone: 412-688-0304
Fax: 412-683-9173
E-mail: lgut@pitt.edu

Creative With Words Publications

1. **Focus:** CWW furthers a) folkloristic matter; b) creative writing in children (poetry, prose, language and computer art); c) creative writing by all ages. Please state age of child and verify authenticity of writing; d) creative writing in special interest groups, senior citizens (state age), disabled (state why), shut-ins of any kind (state why).

2. **Language:** English only; will accept translations by a native English speaker from another language. All manuscripts will be edited by the CWW project editor.

3. **Manuscripts:** Typed or legibly written, double-spaced (prose), one poem per page, 1½" margin on all sides; name, home address, age (if child, up to 19) top left on every page; pages numbered. Do not fax manuscripts.

4. **Length:** *Poetry*: 20 lines or less, no more than 46 characters across any line; *Prose*: maximum 1,500 words, excluding title. *Note*: Shorter poems/prose have a better chance, if of quality. Our staff readers do count the words.

5. **Format:** Title poems (except haikus); do not indent each line differently, nor put a single word on a separate line, unless it is a language-art piece and poem is a graphic depiction. Title prose, use standard font.

6. **Style:** *Poetry*: any, unless otherwise stated by CWW on theme list. *Folkloristic tales and such*: any. *Folkloristic research*: use latest *MLA Handbook for Writers of Research Papers, Theses, and Dissertations. Prose*: Quality writing. Do not include brand names, names of companies, movies, television shows, etc., in stories and poems. CWW is not their sponsor.

7. **Content:** CWW publishes according to set themes. Poetry or prose containing violence of any nature, over-preoccupation with death, racial slurs or preferences, pornographic material, or current sensationalisms will not be accepted.

8. **Cover Letter:** Manuscripts must be accompanied by cover letter or CWW submittal form, stating name of project submitted to. Name of author, home address, child's age (up to 19), senior/disabled/shut-in status, must be given on each page and officially verified by a responsible adult.

9. **Multiple Submissions:** Are not accepted.

10. **Previously-Published Manuscripts:** Are not accepted. If of folkloristic nature, will only be accepted if permission of reprint is enclosed.

11. **SASE (with sufficient postage plus 2 oz. postage for CWW material):** Must accompany all manuscripts and correspondence. Rule: No SASE, very delayed to no response. Manuscripts and correspondence submitted without SASE are generally destroyed at end of month submitted.

12. **Query:** Is preferred. CWW does not publish self-contained books. CWW publishes anthologies according to themes set twice a year and according to specific length (see there).

13. **Copyright:** CWW Publications, After publication, rights revert back to author for submission elsewhere. CWW requests a credit line be given to CWW for having published the item first. Content and graphics submitted must be copyright-free or a copyright-clearance statement must be included.

14. Evaluation: Manuscripts are read by CWW staff or guest readers. Folkloristic items are read by guest scholars of folklore. CWW editors take the readers' and scholars' suggestions into consideration when further evaluating manuscripts. All manuscripts are subject to be edited to reflect the standards of CWW. CWW offers suggestions how to improve the story/poem.

15. Reading Time: One to two months after deadline of theme. Tentative deadlines are set twice a year. Therefore, first notice might come one year after submitting to a specific theme. It is the writer's responsibility to notify CWW of any changes.

16. Payment: Writers published by CWW receive a 20% discount on every copy purchased of issue containing the writing; on orders of ten copies or more, there is an additional 10% discount. Note: A poet or writer does not have to order a copy to get published. There are no tear sheets nor free copies. Manuscripts and graphics accepted are not returned. (Byline— name of writer/poet, age (if child/senior), city and state— given with poem/prose.) **Best of the Month** writer receives one free copy (general anthologies) or US$10 (*The Eclectics*).

17. Contract: No contract is issued. A statement of publishing intent is forwarded with acceptance notification, at which time a writer/poet may withdraw manuscript within a given time.

18. Publications per Annum: 11-12 written by all ages; 2 anthologies containing the writing and language/computer-art work by children only (must be written by children, up to 19 years of age, not by well-meaning adults); 2 *The Eclectics* for adults only.

19. Market/Readership: Family, schools, libraries, universities, editors, physicians, political and religious leaders, shut-ins. CWW publications are evaluated at trade fairs and trade conferences and are presented at book fairs.

20. Editors/Advisors: *Editor-in-Chief/Publisher*: Brigitta Geltrich; *Visiting Editor*: Bert Hower; *Advisor*: D.G. Spencer Ludgate.

21. Cost of Issues: *Single*: US $9-12 ($9 for 50-60 pp.; $11.50 for 61-80 pp.; $12 for 81+ pp.). *Special*: US $15-20; *Back Issues*: US $6 (CWW determines when an issue becomes a back issue). *Subscription*: 12 issues for US $60; 6 issues for US $36; 3 issues for US $21 (Inform whether to include the two children-only issues or the two adults-only issues). Credit card orders are not accepted at this time. Libraries and schools receive a 10% discount. Back-order status of an issue is set by CWW according to specific specifications.

22. Reading Fees: Are reasonable and available. Write with SASE to CWW for information and fee.

23. Check: Make check payable to: Brigitta Ludgate. Thank you!

Categories: Fiction—Adventure—Animals—Children—Comedy—Culture—Education—Family—Folklore—Gardening—History—Humor—Juvenile—Nature—Outdoors—Poetry—Relationships—Senior Citizens—Short Stories—Teen—Travel—Writing—Young Adult

Name: Brigitta Geltrich, Editor/Publisher
Material: All
Address: PO BOX 223226
City/State/ZIP: CARMEL CA 93922
Fax: 408-655-8627
E-mail: CWWPUB@USA.NET

Cricket

In September, 1973 the Open Court Publishing Company started publication of CRICKET, a literary magazine for young people. CRICKET is now published by Carus Publishing Company.

CRICKET, for ages 9-14, publishes original stories, poems, and articles written by the world's best authors for children and young adults. In some cases, CRICKET purchases rights for excerpts from books yet to be published. Each issue also includes several reprints of high-quality selections.

CRICKET measures 8"x10", contains 64 pages, has a full-color cover, and is staple-bound. Full-color and black-and-white illustrations of the highest quality appear throughout the magazine.

We hope the following information will be useful to prospective contributors:

Editor-in-Chief: Marianne Carus Published: 12 months a year
Editor: Deborah Vetter Price: $32.97 for 1-year subscription
Senior Art Director: Ron McCutchan (12 issues)
Comments:

CRICKET would like to reach as many illustrators and authors as possible for original contributions, but our standards are very high, and we will accept only top-quality material. PLEASE DO NOT QUERY FIRST. CRICKET will consider any manuscripts or art samples sent on speculation and *accompanied by a self-addressed, stamped envelope*. For art, please send tearsheets or photoprints/photocopies. *Do not* send original artwork either as art samples or with a manuscript submission. Please be sure that each sample is marked with your name, address, and phone number. Allow 12 weeks for a reply.

Themes:

CRICKET does not publish an advance list of themes. Submissions on all appropriate topics will be considered at any time during the year.

CRICKET normally purchases the following rights for works appearing in the magazine:

1. For stories and poems previously unpublished, CRICKET purchases first publication rights in the English language. Payment is made upon publication. CRICKET also requests the right to reprint the work in any volume or anthology published by Carus Publishing Company upon payment of half the original fee.

2. For stories and poems previously published, CRICKET purchases second North American publication rights. Fees vary, but are generally less than fees for first publication rights. Payment is made upon publication. Same applies to accompanying art.

3. For recurring features, CRICKET purchases the material outright. The work becomes the property of CRICKET, and it is copyrighted in the name of Carus Publishing Company. A flat fee per feature is usually negotiated. Payment is made upon publication.

4. First publication rights plus promotional rights (promotions, advertising, or any other form not offered for sale) for commissioned artwork, subject to the terms outlined below:

(a) Physical art remains the property of the illustrator.

(b) Payment is made within 45 days of acceptance.

(c) CRICKET retains the additional, *nonexclusive* right to reprint the work in any volume or anthology published by CRICKET subject to pro-rata share of 7% royalty of net sales.

Art Submissions:

CRICKET commissions all art separately from the text. Any review samples of artwork will be considered. Samples of both color *and* black-and-white work (where applicable) are appreciated. It is especially helpful to see pieces showing young people, animals, action scenes, and several scenes from a narrative (i.e., story) showing a character in different situations and emotional states.

CRICKET accepts work in a number of different styles and media, including pencil, pen and ink, watercolor, acrylic, oil, pastels, scratchboard, and woodcut. While we need humorous illustration, we cannot use work that is overly caricatured or "cartoony." We are always looking for strong realism. Many assignments will require artist's research into a particular scientific field, world culture, or historical period.

Types of work in CRICKET

Fiction: realistic, contemporary, historical, humor, mysteries, fantasy, science fiction, folk tales, fairy tales, legends, myths

Nonfiction: biography, history, science, technology, natural history, social science, geography, foreign culture, travel, adventure, sports (A bibliography is required for *all* nonfiction articles.)

Poetry: serious, humorous, nonsense rhymes

Other: math puzzles, challenging mazes, crossword puzzles, crafts, recipes, plays, music, art

Length: stories-200 to 2,000 words (2 to 8 pages); articles-200 to 1,200 words (2 to 6 pages); poems-not longer than 50 lines (1 page, 2 pages maximum)

An exact word count should be noted on each manuscript submitted. Word count includes every word, but does not include the title of the manuscript or the author's name.

Rates: Stories and articles: up to 25¢ per word (2,000 words maximum) Poems: up to $3.00 per line. Payment upon publication.

For a sample issue of CRICKET, please send $4.00 to the address below. NOTE: Sample copy requests from foreign countries must be accompanied by International Postal Reply Coupons (IRCs) valued at US $4.00. Please do *not* send a check or money order.

Categories: Fiction—Nonfiction—Children—Literature—Poetry—Short Stories

Name: Submissions Editor
Material: Manuscript Submissions
Name: Ron McCutchan, Senior Art Director
Material: Art Samples
Name: Mary Ann Hocking, Permissions Coordinator
Material: Rights and Permissions
Address: PO BOX 300
City/State/ZIP: PERU IL 61354
Telephone: 815-223-2520
Fax: 815-224-6675

Critical Review

Critical Review was founded in 1986 by Jeffrey Friedman, a libertarian graduate student who was having grave doubts about his political creed. Unhappy with the isolation of libertarian thought from mainstream scholarship, he envisioned a journal that would bring the most intense criticism to bear on libertarian and free-market ideas in order to see which of these ideas, if any, would withstand scrutiny and contribute to our understanding of the world.

After several years of pursuing this plan, it became apparent that the emancipatory aspirations of libertarian philosophy were better expressed by liberal and radical thought than by libertarianism, and that these aspirations actually conflicted with free-market empirical claims rather than buttressing them, as libertarians hold (see Friedman's essays in vol. 3, nos. 3-4 and vol. 4. no. 4, and the debate in vol. 6, no. 1). Accordingly, *Critical Review* began to pursue a "postlibertarian" agenda in which libertarian philosophical doctrines were separated from free-market economics and considered independently (see Introduction to vol. 8, no. 4).

While *Critical Review* remains committed to inquiring open-mindedly into whether laissez-faire capitalism is conducive to human welfare, its agenda is now much broader. We now seek to draw on all of the social sciences in examining the effects on human well-being—not just on material prosperity—of not only laissez-faire capitalism and the alternatives to it, but of all other conceivable forms of social life. For instance, we are interested not only in publishing research on the politics and economics of

the interventionist and redistributive state, and on the economic effects of capitalism, but anthropological research on the effects of modernity on human happiness; studies of the influence of capitalism on art; historical work on the origins of the modern state and its nationalist-liberal development; historical and political-economy studies of whether that state is a necessary concomitant of modernity, or is instead the product of popular or intellectual misapprehensions about the failings of capitalism; political science research on public opinion formation, public ignorance, and the real-world nature of mass democracy and state bureaucracy; cultural studies of the dynamics of human desires under capitalism and democracy; and sociological work informed by (or critical of) state theory as well as classic sociological theory.

Call For Papers

Submit appropriate papers not under consideration elsewhere to the address below. Please be prepared to make your article conform to our style guidelines, described below, if it should be accepted.

Fax queries about the appropriateness of an article or the need for a review essay on a book. Please do not fax manuscripts.

N.B. *Critical Review does* not publish policy advocacy or critical examinations of proposed public policies. All articles are restricted to the examination of past or present policies' or social systems' effects, theories about these effects, or philosophical reflection on the desirability of these effects.

Critical Review also does not publish either empirical or philosophical papers that take the desirability of capitalism, liberalism, or freedom for granted, or that equate capitalism or liberalism with freedom. All of these issues are held open to question and debate in our pages.

For more information about the type of articles that are most appropriate for *Critical Review,* please see our Internet site devoted to the journal's history and purpose.

Style Guidelines

1. Please note that all articles in *Critical Review* should avoid policy advocacy, policy recommendations, and criticism of proposed policies. That is, all articles should address themselves to the causes and consequences of past conditions and policies, not directly to what should be done in the future. Please leave it to our readers to infer what policies or reforms they should favor based on your analysis of their past effects or politics.

2. Controversial assumptions about the desirability of capitalism, liberalism, or freedom, or the equivalence of capitalism or liberalism with freedom, should be avoided. These are some of the issues that the journal is designed to debate, rather than take for granted.

3. *Critical Review* publishes (i) research papers, (ii) review essays, (iii) articles, (iv) symposia, and (v) replies and rejoinders to previous papers. *All research papers, articles, and review essays, unsolicited or invited, may be subject to editorial and peer review prior to acceptance.* Therefore, they should not contain indications of your identity in the text or notes. Peer review is undertaken at the discretion of the editor and is anonymous; authors receive copies of the reviewers' comments. Symposium contributions, replies, and rejoinders are not usually subject to peer review, although they may be rejected as inappropriate and the editor may, as with all articles, suggest revisions.

4. All articles in *Critical Review,* including review essays, are expected to be substantial and serious contributions to scholarly discussion. We do not publish "opinion pieces" or short book reviews. Book reviewers and symposium participants, like all contributors, are expected to set forth the relevant aspects of their topic in detail before providing their own rigorously argued, evidentially supported response.

5. *Audience*: *Critical Review*'s readers are scholars and advanced students accustomed to reading scholarly works in their own disciplines and, like readers of *The New York Review of Books,*

willing to pursue complex issues in other disciplines as well. However, specialization makes the most technical aspects of some disciplines inaccessible to nonspecialists. Technical jargon, topics of interest only to experts, and visual displays that merely re-express ideas presented verbally should be avoided.

6. *Tone*: Although *Critical Review* is not a specialized research organ, it is a scholarly journal that attempts to foster the dispassionate exploration of political and cultural issues. It seeks to consider alternative points of view respectfully and sympathetically. Ideological and personal polemics have no place in its pages.

7. *Review essays*: The purpose of *Critical Review*'s review essays is neither to recommend books to our readers nor to pan them. Rather, their aim is to allow our writers the opportunity to confront important issues discussed in the books under review. A book's ideas and arguments, not its organization, style, or physical appearance, should be the reviewer's main concern.

8. *Article length*: 4,000 words (@20 typed, double-spaced pages) is usually the minimum required to explore a topic in appropriate depth. We can accommodate longer manuscripts if necessary.

9. *Format*: Manuscripts should be paginated and double-spaced throughout, including the notes and references. In review essays, the first mention of a book should include parenthetically: (city: publisher, year). Subsequent page references need not include the book's author, unless more than one book is being reviewed.

10. *Title, subheads*: Please suggest a title for your paper or review essay and brief, underlined (not capitalized) subheads every four or five pages. Only very long articles should use numbered subheadings; please use Roman numerals for such enumeration.

11. *Abstract*: A 100-word-maximum abstract should appear at the beginning of all essays, review essays, and research papers. It should be in the form of a direct summary statement of the substance of your argument rather than a description of the issues discussed or the methods used to investigate them. Please consult back issues for sample abstracts.

12. *Biographical note*: On a separate page please provide a three- or four-line double-spaced biographical note for us to publish with your paper. Include your name; academic affiliation; mailing address; telephone and fax numbers; the titles, publishers, and years of any recent books; and any acknowledgements.

13. *Page citations* should be written as in these examples: "10-12," "101-2," "213-14," "252-53." Do not use the abbreviation "p." or "pp."

14. *Gender-neutral language* is preferred; alternating he and she is acceptable.

15. *Quotation marks*: Please follow standard American literary usage. Double quotation marks should surround quotations, with commas and periods enclosed. Single quotation marks should surround quotations within quotations. Single words or phrases take double quotation marks.

16. *Citations and references* should follow the "author-date" system described in the *American Political Science Assn. Style Manual*, copies of which are available from the Business Office (e-mail requests, including your mailing address). When the text directly refers to a work, omit parentheses: "As Tversky 1990 shows...." When referring directly to the author of a work, include parentheses: "Tversky (1990) is among those who argue...." When making the first direct mention of an author, use his or her first name: "Amos Tversky (1990) is among those who...." Classic works that have appeared in many editions with a universal section-numbering system may be cited like this: Aristotle N.E. X.iv.1175a13. Please do not use postal acronyms for the states of publishers (i.e., write "Cambridge, Mass.," not "Cambridge, MA"). Do always put a space between the colon following journal volume numbers and page numbers. Do not abbreviate authors'

names with initials (e.g., J. Q. rather than James Q. Wilson) unless this is how the name appears in the cited work.

17. *Explanatory notes* should be in the form of end notes, not footnotes.

18. Please use *underlining* for emphasis; no bold or italic type.

19. Please do not right-justify your *margins;* leave them ragged.

20. When initially *submitting your manuscript*, please send 4 copies to the address below. *Please do not fax manuscripts.* Within three months of the submission of an unsolicited manuscript, you will receive either a notice that the manuscript is inappropriate or, should the paper be accepted, editing suggestions and referee comments. Authors are asked to provide a computer disk (if possible) of the final draft of papers accepted for publication. Any program is acceptable.

Categories: Critical Essays—Review Essays—Public Policy

Name: Submissions Editor
Material: All
Address: PO BOX 10
City/State/ZIP: NEWTOWN CT 06470-0010
Telephone: 203-270-8103
Fax: 203-270-8105
E-mail: info@criticalreview.com
Internet: www.sevenbridges.com

Critique
The Magazine of Graphic Design Thinking

Critique, the magazine of graphic design thinking, is a critical quarterly in graphic design. Where other design journals publish how-to tips, personality profiles, and academic essays, *Critique* publishes articles on critical thinking for practitioners who want to raise the level of their own work, this week.

A *Critique* article may be about intercultural symbolism, concepting, audience psychology, enriching the meanings of images, historical typography, perception, marketing strategies, cyclical trends in the profession, or narrative structures in Web sites. We speak of design by referring to aesthetic principles and elements, instead using vague emotional language. We illustrate articles with examples of design from all eras, instead of just what's hot this year.

We're also very interested in quantifying as much as can be quantified about visual communication—and since we aren't experts in psychometrics, we could use a lot of help. What does the audience see? What do they prefer? How do they respond?

At the same time, if design doesn't have that magic, that aesthetic beauty, who needs it? What are the elements of that beauty? How can a designer tap in to the magical part of their mind? How can they analyze their own work to make it better, purer, and deeper?

The *Critique* style is based on Strunk and White's "Elements of Style." Your writing should never sacrifice clarity for sophistication: we feel the two are the same. As you write, consider the fact that your audience thinks visually. Choose illustrations while doing research, use visually descriptive examples in your text, and consider how your text can be structured, visually, in the final layout.

For examples of past *Critique* articles, visit our Web site. We're hoping to find new writers who can write ever sharper, deeper, more informative pieces. A list of our upcoming themes follows:

Thanks for your interest. Incidentally, we pay $1,000.00 for a 1,500—word piece, especially if you help us find pictures.

Categories: Nonfiction—Arts—Graphic Design—Marketing—Marketing Communications

Name: Nancy E. Bernard, Managing Editor
Material: All
Address: 120 HAWTHORNE AVE STE 102
City/State/ZIP: PALO ALTO CA 94301
Telephone: 650-323-7225
Fax: 650-323-3298
E-mail: editor@critiquemag.com
Internet: www.critiquemag.com

Crochet World

I am pleased to review and consider crochet designs for publication in *Crochet World* which is published by the House of White Birches, publishers of 18 internationally distributed women's magazines. The company also produces special issues and pattern sets relating to many crafts, including crochet, which are sold through their catalogs.

• *Crochet World* is a bimonthly publication which features a wide variety of crochet designs geared to the beginner to intermediate crocheter with very few advanced designed offered. Designs include afghans, toys, clothing, household items, baby items, gift and bazaar items and more.

WHAT I WANT

Only, original, never-before-published crochet designs for which we can buy all rights.

SUBMISSION GUIDELINES

• **Preparation:** Typewritten or printed via a computer, double spaced on white paper. Or, you can submit a 3½" floppy disk provided you use WriteNow 4.0 for Macintosh or Microsoft Word 4.0 programs. Include your name, address (including a UPS street address),telephone number and social security number on the top of the first page and your name and address on the top of additional pages. Leave 3 inches at the top of the first page and 1 inch at the top of all additional pages. Use only one side of each sheet and number each page. Indent paragraphs five spaces.

• **Introduction:** Describe your design. List its specific qualities, why you decided to create it and how the reader can best use it for personal use, home decor, gift giving or bazaar selling.

• **Directions:** Indicate the skill level needed for a crocheter to make your design-easy, intermediate or advanced.

• **Size:** When designing clothing, such as a sweater, please offer a size range (such as S,M, L), **not just one size.** Clothing submissions offering just one size will be returned. What is the finished size of your **model** design? We need to know this in order to line up the correct size model.

• **Materials:** List all supplies and materials necessary to complete your design. List the hook size(s), amount, size, color etc. needed. Use readily available yarns and threads and list the company name you chose and the color numbers. Make sure that your design uses current materials which will still be part of a company's line when the article is published, not discontinued yarns and threads.

• **Gauge:** A stitch gauge is mandatory. (Example: With crochet hook size F, 4 sc = 1 inch; 5 sc rows = 1 inch.)

• **Instructions:** Please familiarize yourself with our format of direction writing and use the standard crochet abbreviations as indicated in the "Stitch Guide" which appears in each issue.

• **Diagrams:** Provide diagrams only when absolutely necessary to make the instructions clear. They should be done on white paper in black ink, separate from the typewritten copy. Label accurately as Diagram A or Diagram B, making sure the labels correspond to your instructions. Add easily understood cutlines, such as "fold line" or "cut here."

• **Graphs:** Use a two square border of graph paper around the design. Please be legible! We prefer symbols to colored squares. Make sure you **keep a copy** for your files!

• **Photography:** House of White Birches will be responsible for all photography.

GENERAL INFORMATION

• **Multiple Submissions:** We *do not* accept patterns you are submitting to other publications at the same time.

• **Electronic Submissions:** Must be on a 3½" diskette using WriteNow 4.0 for Macintosh. Actual item must accompany the diskette.

• **Send Item:** Instructions should accompany the **actual crocheted item** itself. Be sure your sample is of top quality workmanship. In the case of heavy, bulky items such as afghans, you may send a good, clear color photo as a query. If accepted, you will have to send the actual item.

• **Shipping:** Send UPS or first class mail. *Include return postage!*

• **Labeling:** Make sure each item is **tagged** with a stringed tag that includes your name and address on one side of the tag; name of design on the other. In the event of multiple pieces, make sure each piece is tagged with above information.

• **Proofread:** Proofread your pattern several times to eliminate possible errors. Suggestion: Have a crocheting friend read over your pattern to help spot errors or hard-to-follow sections.

• **Keep in Mind:** Each set of instructions must stand alone. When writing instructions, you must assume that this is the first project of its kind the reader has ever done.

• **Copies:** Be sure to **keep a copy** of the pattern for your file!

• **Payment:** We pay competitive rates for original, top-quality designs.

Categories: Needlework

Name: Submissions Editor
Material: All
Address: PO BOX 776
City/State/ZIP: HENNIKER NH 03242-0776
Telephone: 603-428-7289
Fax: 603-428-7289

CRONE CHRONICLES®
A Journal of Conscious Aging

Crone Chronicles
A Journal of Conscious Aging

Crone Chronicles is a quarterly magazine by and for women who wish to move through the aging process in a *conscious* manner. "Crone" is identified as the third aspect of the ancient Triple Goddess: Maiden/Mother/Crone. Crone symbolizes the wisdom present in a woman of any age, but which usually becomes stronger as she grows older.

The patriarchal culture's valuation of the female is based on the youthful beauty of her bodily appearance, her "image." By this measure, the older a woman becomes, the less she is valued. Rather than accepting our culture's devaluation of women as they age, *Crone Chronicles* was founded to transform our way of understanding the aging process altogether.

To understand the Crone stage of life *consciously* is to look beyond appearances to reality, the reality of a long full life, through which much learning has been gleaned. To evaluate the Crone stage of life *consciously* is to see this phase as the crowning glory, the time when a woman enters into her full maturity, inside and out. By this new (and very ancient) measure, the Crone is the most revered stage of life, rather than the least; she is the most honored, not the most ignored. Distilling wisdom from experience, her words, attitudes and actions can now serve as examples to others.

Our readers are women (and a few men!) from their early 30s to 100, the majority of them from 40 to 80. Some come from New Age backgrounds, others are much more traditional. What we all have in common is a commitment to conscious aging, which includes transforming the derogatory meaning of the word "Crone". If you feel this kind of commitment yourself, then we welcome your contributions to the *Crone Chronicles.* Most of each issue is created from readers' contributions, so your willingness to share is vital to this journal!

Crone Chronicles is geared mainly towards women. However, we do not wish to limit our readers to women, nor to assume that men are excluded from the wisdom of Crone. Indeed, on an archetypal level, we assume that as each woman includes male and female elders within her, so does each man. With that understanding, both men and women are welcome to submit to this journal for possible publication.

The following guidelines may help you gear your submission to the context of *Crone* Chronicles.

Subject Matter

All submissions—whether written or artistic—should focus in some way on issues relating to the aging process itself or to perceptions of any subject which are altered or filtered through the process of "growing older". What we are looking for is the expression of "one's own unique Crone point of view". In other words, we wish to publish the wisdom *you* have gained from *your* experience, and strongly prefer submissions which are either written entirely from a personal point of view, or at least include personal experience as an example of what is being talked about. Thus, most of what we publish is nonfiction. Fiction and myth will be considered, but only as they are particularly relevant to Crone.

Written Submissions

All written submissions should be the original work of the author. We prefer double-spaced manuscripts but will also accept neatly handwritten pieces. We are also able to accept computer disks. If you work on a computer, please send both the disk and a written copy of the manuscript. We are Macintosh-based and will accept 3.5" disks with text in either text or Microsoft Word 4 formats. We can also read 3.5" IBM-compatible disks in ASCII (.txt) format.

We publish articles ranging from 100 to 6,000 words; please keep in mind that very long manuscripts are less likely to be published, due to space limits. Please include the author's name, address and phone number on each page. Please be clear about the name under which you wish us to publish your material if we decide to use it.

We do edit for clarity, grammar, and sometimes for length—sometimes at the last minute before publication. If you do not want your article edited in any way, please write "Do not edit" on the manuscript clearly and in large letters. We will respect your wishes; however you should be aware that manuscripts so marked are far less likely to see publication in our pages.

Writers: here is your chance to tell *your* stories! Personal essays, reviews, journal entries, dreams, jokes, cartoons, asides— all are welcome. *Crone Chronicles* is here to help document and report on the Crone archetype as she resurrects Herself within the ashes of the patriarchal culture.

If you have something to say, and would rather talk about it than write it down, you are welcome to send us a tape for us to transcribe. If you know any older women who can serve as mod-els for the rest of us, we will also transcribe your interviews of these tapes. Besides the magazine, we are also collecting interviews of interesting crone women for possible inclusion in a book.

We receive lots of poetry, all of which goes in a file for possible use in some future issue.

Graphic Art

All graphic art submissions should be the original work of the artist. Clear, black and white drawings are best, but penciled or colored works are sometimes acceptable. Please be aware that all artwork will be reproduced in black and white only except for pieces used on the outside cover. Our covers are usually commissioned works, but feel free to submit color photocopies or slides of your color work for possible use on the cover. Please send us clean copies of your artwork only—we cannot be responsible for original artwork.

We are always looking for new artists. If you have a portfolio of your work, feel free to send it; when doing so, please let us know if any of the pieces have been previously published or are not available for publication. We keep files of artwork, by artist, and when an issue is in production we find the pieces of artwork on file that fit each article, and then inform the artist that we will be publishing that piece of work. This means that art work is on file for months, even years—and may, sooner or later, still be published. Please let us know if this does not work for you, and we will make other arrangements.

Photography

All photographic submissions should be the original work of the photographer. If persons other than the photographer are shown, a signed release from said person(s) must be included in order for us to publish the photo. Please send standard prints. We cannot publish from negatives or slides. Photographs may be in black and white or color—but please be aware that all photographs will be reproduced in black and white only, unless the photo is selected for the cover. We are especially interested in photos of old women whose beauty of character shows in their faces and bodies; also in subject matter which is reminds us in some way of Crone. (For example, old trees, plants in their winter appearance, crossroads, gateways, etc.)

Special Note to Artists and Photographers

Crone Chronicles is one arm of the Crone Corporation. The other arm is Crone Art (formerly known as Crone Creations) which is seeking images of Crone for a fill line of Crone greeting cards. Images can be either in color or black and white. Color is preferred. Contact Claudia Kimball, Box 2344, Vashon Island, WA 98070.

General Information

If you do not wish your submission returned, please write "Do not return" on it, and send a SASE or stamped postcard for us to respond.

If we are interested in using your material in some future issue, you will be notified. Otherwise, you will not be notified unless you have sent us an SASE for that purpose. Please realize that we cannot guarantee publication of anything, and that even when we have decided to use your piece, it may or may not get into any particular issue, as there are sometimes enormous changes at the last minute. Remember also, that poetry, art work, and photos are filed, sometimes for years, before being used. If you do not wish us to keep your work on file, please let us know, and we can make other arrangements.

We prefer material which has not been previously seen or published—please inform us of multiple submissions or previous publication.

Crone Chronicles is published quarterly.

Compensation and Rights

At this time, *Crone Chronicles* is unable to offer cash compensation for unsolicited artwork, photography or written work. Given our growing circulation, we assume this will change in the future. At this point, funds left over from printing, postage, rent, utilities and supplies all go into marketing efforts to support increased circulation, as well as beginning to pay staff salaries.

If your material is accepted, you will receive a free copy of the issue in which your work appears; if you are a subscriber this will be in addition to the copy you receive as part of your subscription.

Copyright for all work reverts to authors and artists upon publication. However, we may also wish to reprint it in future *Crone Chronicles* collections. Please let us know if that is not possible.

If there are any questions which these guidelines do not cover, please feel free to call or write for more information, or simply to try out your ideas on us! Please leave a message if we are not here to receive your call.

Thanks for your interest in Crone Chronicles.

I look forward to hearing from you soon.

Blessings,

Ann Kreilkamp

Please realize that your contributions to the *Crone Chronicles* need not be limited to the theme of any issue. Though one section of each issue is theme-based, there is room for other contributions as well. Seasonal topics and articles on any aspect of the emergence of Crone in any form are always welcome.

Categories: Nonfiction—Biography—Culture—Feminism—Health—Inspirational—Interview—Lifestyles—New Age—Paranormal—Philosophy—Poetry—Psychology—Relationships—Religion—Senior Citizens—Sexuality—Spiritual—Women's Issues

Name: Ann Kreilkamp, Editor
Material: All
Address: PO BOX 81
City/State/ZIP: KELLY WY 83011
Telephone: 307-733-5409
Fax: 307-733-8639
E-mail: AKCrone@aol.com

Cross & Quill
The Christian Writers Newsletter

Cross & Quill serves an audience of writers, speakers, editors, conference directors, group leaders, researchers, and agents involved in the Christian publishing industry. Please keep that in mind when submitting.

Our purpose is to inform, instruct, and equip writers to produce writing of the highest biblical and professional standards.

Our needs are as follows:

Meet the Pro: Assigned. Front page features one of our professional members.

This Side of the Desk: Written in-house.

Writing Rainbows!: 500 to 600 word devotional thought including Scripture and prayer that comes from your writing experience. Give Bible translation.

Writers Helping Writers: 200 to 800 words. More instructional and how-to articles, fewer personal experiences. Need more articles directed to the veteran, rather than the beginning writer. (Feature Article)

Tots, Teens, & InBetweens: 200 to 800 word how-to and informational articles on writing for the juvenile marketplace. (Feature Article)

Editor's RoundTable: 200 to 800 word interviews with editors on current needs of the publication or publishing house. Ask questions that help writers understand the joys, frustrations, and challenges of editorial work. Find out what the editor has often

wanted to tell writers to make the editor's and the writer's jobs easier, more productive, and more profitable. Professional quality B&W glossy of editor improves chances of acceptance. (Feature Article)

Computer Wise: Assigned. Kay Hall, Contributing Editor. http://www.computermom.com

Business Wise: 200 to 800 how-to and informational articles on the business side of writing such as tax information, recordkeeping, and other related topics. (Feature Article)

LegalEase: 200 to 800 words on various legalities in the writing profession: contracts, copyright, etc. (Feature Article)

Connecting Points: 200 to 800 word how-to and informational articles on leading and attending writers groups. Especially want articles on how to critique various kinds of writing such as nonfiction, fiction, poetry, and various others.

The Conference Circuit: Assigned.

Poetry: 1 to 8 line poems on helpful and inspirational topics, limit 3 per envelope. Currently overstocked on poetry.

Fillers: 25 to 100 word helpful hints, newsbreaks, tips, cartoons. Book and other writing product reviews, 100 to 300 words.

Submissions: Prefer complete manuscript. Accept computer and electronic submissions, but query first for specs. No simultaneous submissions.

Rights: Buy first, one-time, or reprint rights. If manuscript is a reprint, state when and where the piece has been used.

Payment: Small honorarium on publication for features as indicated above. For all others, payment in 3 contributors copies.

Sample copy available for $2 and SASE.

Categories: Nonfiction—Arts—Associations—Careers—Christian Interests—Education—Internet—Language—Literature—Poetry—Religion—Writing

Name: Sandy Brooks, Editor/Publisher
Material: All
Address: CHRISTIAN WRITERS FELLOWSHIP
INTERNATIONAL
Address: RT 3 BOX 1635 JEFFERSON DAVIS RD
City/State/ZIP: CLINTON SC 29325
Telephone: 864-697-6035
E-mail: CWFI@aol.com

Crusader
A Magazine for Cadets and Their Friends

ABOUT THE MAGAZINE

The *Crusader* is a Christian-oriented magazine for boys aged 9-14. It circulates among 13,000 boys in the United States and Canada who are members of a Christian youth organization known as the Calvinist Cadet Corps. Boys from several Protestant denominations make up *Crusader's* audience.

Although the **Crusader** is the official publication of the Cadet Corps, it publishes material designed to appeal to every pre-adolescent boy.

Generally speaking, **Crusader** boys are active, inquisitive, and imaginative. They imitate "heroes" they see in the world around them, and they love adventure. They are sociable and form gangs easily. Many of them make decisions for Christ that affect them the rest of their lives.

• **Crafts and hobby articles**

Stimulating with clear, accurate instructions. Made with easily accessible materials. Our artists can illustrate.

• **Sports articles**

Coaching tips, articles about athletes, articles about developing Christian character through sports-up to 1,500 words. Black and white photos appreciated. Be original.

• **Camping and nature**

Camping skills, nature study, survival exercises. Practical "how to do it" approach works best. "God in nature" themes also appreciated, if done without "preachiness."

• **Fiction**

Fast moving stories of 1,000-1,300 words that appeal to a boy's sense of adventure or sense of humor are welcomed. Avoid "preachiness" and simplistic answers to complicated problems. Avoid long dialog and little action.

• **Cartoons**

Boy oriented, of course.

• **Miscellaneous**

Nothing is too strange to be read and considered.

SUBMISSIONS

• **Copy**

Name and address in upper left corner, along with number of words, statement regarding terms of sale (all rights, first right, or second rights.)

• **Second rights**

We have no qualms about purchasing rights to articles that have been printed elsewhere, providing the audiences do not overlap.

• **Cartoons**

Single gags, panels, and full-page cartoons. Send finished cartoons.

• **Editing and rejections**

The *Crusader* staff reserves the right to edit any accepted manuscript or cartoon. Rejected submissions will be put in the mail within one week of the final decision.

PAYMENT

• **Rate of payment**

Payment is made upon final acceptance of the material, occasionally varying according to the amount of editing required. The current rates:

Manuscripts 3¢ per word and up (first rights with no major editing). **Cartoons** $5.00 and up for single gags; $15.00 and up for full page panels. **Puzzles** rates vary. **Photos** $5.00 for each photo used with an article.

THEMES

Each issue of *Crusader* deals with a specific theme or topic. The themes are selected each year in January, and most purchasing is completed for the coming editorial season sometime in April. Thus, the best time to submit fiction is between January and April.

A writer desiring to sell fiction to *Crusader* should request a list of themes.

Categories: Fiction—Nonfiction—Adventure—Boys—Christian Interests—Comedy—Family—Juvenile—Religion—Sports—Young Adult

Name: G. Richard Broene, Editor
Material: All
Address: PO BOX 7259
City/State/ZIP: GRAND RAPIDS MI 49510
Telephone: 616-241-5616
Fax: 616-241-5558
E-mail: Cadets@aol.com

*Curriculum*Vitae

Curriculum Vitae
Curriculum Vitae Literary Supplement

Curriculum Vitae is an eclectic environment. We like everything: creative nonfiction, theory, cartoons, interviews, reviews, and especially personal essays. **CV** is a thematic zine, but quality work is always welcome whether or not it applies to our current theme. Please send complete manuscripts with a short cover letter. Sample copies are $4 ppd. Four issue subscriptions can be ordered for $6. Payment consists of two contributor copies and a years subscription. We Will accept electronic submissions.

Recent Themes:
Autumn 1997 (September, October, November)—**Movies**
Winter 1997 (December, January, February)—**Love**
Spring 1998 (March, April, May)—**Food**
Curriculum Vitae Literary Supplement

The **CVLS** is published two times a year concurrent with the Summer and Winter issues of **CV**. The **CVLS** is open to any kind of submissions, including but not limited to: poetry, fiction, reviews, and novel excerpts. The **CVLS'** focus is on emerging writers. Submissions should include a short cover letter to give us an idea of who you are. Electronic submissions are accepted.

Chapbook and Poetry Postcards:
Prose and poetry to be considered for chapbook publication should include a manuscript. We publish a very small number of chapbooks per year. In addition we are currently looking for poets who would like to be part of our Poetry Postcard series. Interested writers should query to The **CVLS** Poetry Postcard Project for more information.

Categories: Fiction—Nonfiction—Arts—Cartoons—Culture—Literature—Multicultural—Music—Philosophy—Poetry—Politics—Short Stories—Travel—Writing

Name: Michael Dittman, Editor
Material: Essays and Articles for CV
Name: Amy Kleinfelder, Editor
Material: Poetry, Fiction and Review Material for CVLS
Address: GROVE CITY FACTORY STORES
Address: PO BOX 1309
City/State/ZIP: GROVE CITY PA 16127
Telephone: 814-671-1361
E-mail: SimPub@hotmail.com

CutBank
University of Montana

• We accept submissions from August 15 until March 15. Deadline for the fall issue is November 15; deadline for the spring issue is March 15.

• Please address all submissions to the appropriate editor-poetry, fiction, or art.

• You must include a stamped, self-addressed envelope with each submission.

• Manuscripts must be typed or letter quality printout, double-spaced, and paginated. To avoid possible loss or confusion, your name should appear on each page.

• Fiction writers should submit only one story at a time, no longer than 40 pages.

• Poets may submit up to 5 poems at one time.

• Artists and photographers may submit up to 5 works at one time. Do not send original art.

• If a piece has been submitted simultaneously to another publication, please let us know.

CutBank is interested in art, poetry, and fiction of high quality and serious intent. We regularly print work by both well-known and previously unpublished artists. All manuscripts are considered for the Richard Hugo Memorial Poetry Award and the A. B. Guthrie, Jr. Short Fiction Award.

Categories: Fiction—Nonfiction—Poetry—Short Stories

Name: Poetry Editors

Material: Poetry
Name: Fiction Editors
Material: Fiction/Nonfiction
Address: DEPARTMENT OF ENGLISH
Address: UNIVERSITY OF MONTANA
City/State/ZIP: MISSOULA MT 59812
Telephone: 406-243-6156
Fax: 406-243-4076

Dagger of the Mind

Like the title, *Dagger of the Mind*, implies, I want fiction and poetry that'll leave a sharp, vivid, lingering impression upon the souls of my readers. Do your best and send in *only the finest*. Take note of what I'm looking for.

FICTION: I will consider Lovecraftian stories from both realms of fiction: Dunsanian and the Cthulhu Mythos. From Gothic, Poe-influenced works to contemporary horror I will also consider. I'll also accept science fiction, heroic fantasy, high fantasy, dark fantasy, swords and sorcery, mystery, adventure and Gothic romance—so long as there's an element of horror in it.

Work with your own style or the style which you feel the most comfortable with. And if you are working in the Lovecraftian vein, come up with **new and original** settings for your stories. Be creative; invent your own pantheon and characters. Originality and intelligence are the main keys to being accepted into this market. However, if you decide to use established Lovecraftian characters, e.g., Hastur, Yog-Sothoth, Ubbo Sathla and even mighty Cthulhu himself, **make sure you place them in your own storyline.** I'm going to be looking for material that haunts me long after I've read it. Impress me. I want material that will change the way people look at and perceive the universe and life itself. Give me something that will shake up the views of the common man. I'm not concerned with entertainment for its own sake. **I want quality fiction whose primary function is to teach— not preach.** I want to educate the readers or at least open their eyes a little more to the problems facing our world and society. One of the best examples that I can give of this is The Twilight Zone. That's what I'll be looking for and this is my primary concern as an editor and publisher. I'm more concerned with the "fable" aspect than I am with all the bloody rot of horror. And please, **don't** come right out and tell me what the theme is, **show it** through plot and dialogue.

NONFICTION: I'm looking for articles dealing with new breakthroughs in all fields of science. Physics, archeology and medicine, just to name a few, are some of the fields I'm currently looking at. I'm seeking articles dealing with the Unified Field Theory and electromagnetic fields as well as the discovery of a fifth dimension. I'm also seeking human interest pieces. **Before you submit, query first.** Include tearsheets and a detailed background listing of your credits. I want to know where you got your sources from and how you obtained them. I have a strong background in science so I know what to look for. I'm able to separate fact from fiction, be thorough and accurate. I also publish articles on all aspects of the occult and unknown. If you have an idea for a column or feature article, drop me an outline of your proposal. I'm always in need of scholarly works. I'm usually very receptive to new columns and articles.

POETRY: Length and style are open. Bear in mind the guidelines. I'm always in need of Lovecraftian poetry. Keep that in mind.

ART: I'll be looking for very little in the way of art for story illustrations. My art department will be handling this. From time to time I feature artists in the ART GALLERY. If you would like for your work to be considered for a centerfold spread, please send me sample copies of your work. I am very, very selective in this field. But if you have something that you think might fit in well with what I'm doing with *Dagger of the Mind*, by all means,

please submit to this market.

WHAT I DON'T WANT TO SEE: Read this thoroughly and carefully. Keep every word in mind. I *do not* want to see anything sexist/racist, vulgar, pornographic, gruesome, blasphemous, humorous and generally sick. I don't object to dark humor—but I do mind sitcom humor and slapstick. Humor irritates me and I have no care for it. I too, frown greatly upon stories whose sole purpose is gore for the sake of gore. The same dynamics apply equally for those stories whose sole purpose is the glorification of violence. And if there's anything else I hate more than all of the above are weak, exploited women stories. To ensure that these points are clear, I'll elaborate on some of the finer aspects for you. I have Christian values and morals and I don't want to see anything profane against Christian Doctrine, I don't care if it's only *hinted* at. **That includes using the word damn or damit after the word God.** I don't want to see anything which involves acts or suggested acts of fornication between Good and Evil and I certainly don't want to see anything involving bestiality. Along similar lines, I don't want to see any demon lover stories. This brings me up the next point. This is not a smut publication. There are plenty of them out there. I especially don't want to see any gay or lesbian sex scenes or even heterosexual love scenes for that matter because these are usually thrown in for cheap thrills. **I do not publish fictional vampire, werewolf, zombie and ghost stories.** I also don't want to see any stories which have a *witty* one line punch-line which is supposed to carry the full weight of the story.

LENGTH: Open. I'll read anything from short-short to novelette to longer works.

PAYMENT: 1/2 a cent per word on publication plus 1 contributor's copy. I purchase **all** first time publishing rights. Second Editions and other reprints will be negotiated with the author.

TURNAROUND: I receive more than 250 submissions per month; some of the submissions are lengthy. I need time to read the book mss. as well. Response time is now six to eight weeks.

OTHER TIDBITS: Be sure to submit a brief bio with your cover letter which should also include a history of all your published credits. Depending upon background and knowledge of the contributor, I will sometimes ask for nonfiction works. Anything marked POSTAGE DUE will be returned. I sometimes receive postage and no response envelope or the envelope without the postage. Either case guarantees that the contributor will not receive a response from K'yi-Lih Productions and his or her work will go unread. I encourage you to read a copy of *Dagger of the Mind* **before** submitting to this market.

This is not an easy market to break into. I strongly advise you to take heed and familiarize yourself with this market so you can see what the guidelines mean translated into black and white. Don't let these guidelines scare you off. Actually, I happen to be a very open minded person. You would do best though to *see* instead of just read what I'm talking about, this way there's no lingering doubt. If you have a manuscript and are still uncertain if this market is right for your work, **send me a detailed query before submitting.** If you are ordering a copy of *Dagger of the Mind*, please make all checks and or money orders out to **me alone:** Arthur William Lloyd Breach. Single orders are $3.50 plus five postage stamps on a large SASE. Texas residents must include tax on all orders at 8¼%.

Categories: Fiction—Nonfiction—Adventure—Crime— Fantasy—Horror—Paranormal—Poetry—Reviews—Science— Science Fiction

Name: Arthur William Lloyd Breach, Executive Editor
Material: All
Address: 1317 HOOKRIDGE DR
City/State/ZIP: EL PASO TX 79925-7808

Dakota Outdoors
Premier Outdoor Magazine of the Dakotas

Dakota Outdoors is a regional, monthly (12 issues per year) outdoor publication for and about the Dakotas. *Dakota Outdoors* contains feature articles about fishing, hunting and other outdoor pursuits. *Dakota Outdoors* focuses on how- and where-to articles, written by local sportsmen, that provide a local perspective on outdoor life in the Dakotas that you cannot get elsewhere. We also cover legislative, governmental and regulatory concerns, as well as product information, hints and tips, personalities, and humor relative to our Dakota Outdoors. Articles from writers outside our region are welcome, so long as they cover topics of concern to Dakotans.

Articles submitted should be applicable to the outdoor life in the Dakotas.

Topics: Topics should center on fishing and hunting experiences and advice. Other topics, such as boating, camping, hiking, environmental concerns and general nature, will be considered as well.

Rights: Exclusive rights to an article are not mandatory, but we would like to have exclusive rights in our area. Please inform us if the article has been, or will be, published elsewhere.

Deadlines: Timely articles are important. Typically, copy deadline is the 10th of the month prior to the month of publication.

Photos: Photos will also be considered for publication. Either color or black and white prints or negatives (not slides unless requested) are acceptable. If prints, a 5"x7" size is preferable, but larger or smaller sizes are acceptable. If submitted with an article, the photo should be pertinent to the article. All photos should be identified with the photographer's name and address as well as the name and address of the subject(s). The location where the photo was taken should be included as well. Photos will be returned with SASE.

Format: Articles should be submitted in typewritten form, double spaced. A headline and byline should be included on the submission. Articles will be accepted on computer disk in one of two forms. Either a 5.25" disk in an IBM compatible format with ASCII text or a 3.5" disk in an Apple Macintosh format will be acceptable. Computer disks will be returned after use. Please inquire for other formats. If submitting on disk, please let us know what format the file is in. Submissions will also be accepted on CompuServe at the address shown below.

Rates: Rates are negotiable and depend upon the quality of the article and the amount of work necessary to put it into final form. Rates typically run from $5 to $40 per article. If a specific rate is requested, the price should be negotiated prior to publication.

Kids Korner: Dakota Outdoors publishes a kids outdoors column each month. We look for articles addressing kids from 12 to 16 years of age, from 50 to 500 words in length. Payment will generally range for $5 to $15.

Shorts & Fillers: Dakota Outdoors accepts shorts and fillers and uses them on an as needed basis. There is generally no payment for these items. If you submit a short of filler item and require payment, please notify us in advance.

Payment: Payment will be made for articles and photos after the issue is published, unless other arrangements are made.

Categories: Fishing—Hunting

Name: Rachel Engbrecht, Managing Editor
Material: All
Address: PO BOX 669
City/State/ZIP: PIERRE SD 57501-0669
Telephone: 605-224-7301

Fax: 605-224-9210
E-mail: 73613.3456@compuserve.com

An Association of Marketing Students®

DECA Dimensions

DECA is...
The national association of marketing education students—ambitious, talented students eager to explore their career interests in marketing, merchandising, and entrepreneurship.

A nonprofit educational association, DECA has 150,000 members in all 50 states, Guam, Puerto Rico and Canada. The majority of members are of high school age, 15-19, while those in the post-secondary division, Delta Epsilon Chi, are 18 and older.

For 50 years, DECA has provided a program of leadership and professional development designed to merge with the marketing education curriculum. *DECA is not extracurricular, but is a part of classroom instruction.*

Working hand-in-hand with the education and business communities, DECA utilizes on-the-job experience, chapter projects and an outstanding program of competency based competitive events in specific occupational areas including sales, advertising, finance, retailing, wholesaling, fashion merchandising, restaurant management, tourism and hospitality among others.

Formerly known as the Distributive Education Clubs of America, National DECA is governed by a board of directors and guided by councils of educators, as well as two advisory boards—the National Advisory Board (NAB) consists of representatives from more than 60 of America's major businesses and corporations; the Congressional Advisory Board (CAB) is made up of select members of the United States Congress.

DECA helps its members develop a "career success kit" to carry with them from school to work.

Dimensions is...
the journal magazine for DECA's membership. Published four times a year during the school year, i.e., September/October, November/December, January/February and March/April, *Dimensions* reaches 150,000 young people and the adults who support their goals. It is a glossy publication, 8¼"x10¾", printed in two- and four-color. Its audience is primarily high school students ages 15-19.

Because it is an education journal with a unique audience, *Dimensions* is a publication of substance but with the appeal of a commercial magazine for young adults. It's approach is direct and conversational—not academic.

Advertising and freelance articles are accepted. Topics covered include general business—corporate and small business; management and marketing—domestic and international; leadership development; entrepreneurship; fashion merchandising and trends; sales; business technology; personal and business finance; advertising and visual display; security; tourism and hospitality industries; food service-quick and full-serve; the retail food industry; career opportunities; employment and academic tips and helps; job skills; school-to-work incentives; current issues of interest to the association or audience, including school and peer issues.

Dimensions feature articles are approximately 1,000 words; columns approximately 500 words. A short bio statement should accompany bylined articles. Submissions on Mac disk along with hard copy are preferred. Photos, black and white or four-color,

A-D

and/or illustrations are accepted. Small honorariums may be paid upon use.

Preparing to Write

Writing a column, a feature piece or a book is an experience that can be satisfying for you and rewarding for your reader. Producing a well-written, accurate work clearly conveys your knowledge and expertise to the audience. Each author has his own style and editors try diligently to maintain that flavor in the finished piece. However, once your writing has been submitted to the publisher, it is assumed that editorial changes can and will be made as needed without consultation. Most often this will be done to accommodate available publication space.

To minimize editorial changes to your work, you will want to observe the following points:

• Keep in mind the audience you are trying to reach. The readers may be young, but they are knowledgeable in their areas and accustomed to a professional presentation. They will expect valuable, timely information that they can learn from or practice.

• Don't talk down to your reader, but at the same time don't use wordy or jargon-filled language. Whatever style you adopt, casual or formal, stay consistent throughout.

• Avoid language or content that could be interpreted as humiliating or slighting to any minority group or specific segment.

• The use of specific examples or stories to explain concepts is always a good idea.

• Laws governing what may or may not be used from another source are very complex and often difficult to interpret. **You, as the author, are legally responsible for obtaining permissions, whether for text or illustration.** Permission must be obtained not only for the directly quoted material but also for significant material that has been paraphrased or condensed. It is best to get permissions in writing and submit copies of them for our files along with your article. Sources must be acknowledged in the text or in a credit line.

Categories: Associations—Business—Careers—Education—Teen—Young Adult

Name: Carol Lund, Managing Editor
Material: All
Address: 1908 ASSOCIATION DR
City/State/ZIP: RESTON VA 20191
Telephone: 703-860-5000
Fax: 703-860-4013
E-mail: Carol_Lund@deca.org
Internet: www.deca.org

Decorative Artist's Workbook

Decorative Artist's Workbook (DAW) is a bimonthly publication *for* decorative painters of all skill levels. The magazine covers a wide range of decorative painting subjects, including folk art (such as rosemaling), stroke work, stenciling, fabric painting and faux finishing methods, just to name a few. Paintings are done in acrylics, oils, alkyds and watercolors on such surfaces as tin, wood, canvas, fabric and glass. Whatever the medium or surface, we're seeking the new, the unique and the traditional presented in a fresh way

FEATURES

Our most consistent need is for instructional articles. We use between six and 10 features per issue, and all features should emphasize the how-to: the step-by-step process used to complete a project or master a technique. These features range from 1,000 to 2,000 words in length, but we certainly welcome short features on quick projects that can be explained in one or two pages.

Articles that introduce a traditional folk art style, for instance, or new technique, are usually combined with a finished project.

This type of article explains how a style or technique originated, the history of the technique (if applicable), the materials used, and how it can be completed.

Pay for all features ranges from $200 to $300, and is, of course, dependent upon the complexity of the artwork, the writing, the article's length and the total package submitted by the writer. To submit a feature idea, see "How to Query" below.

COLUMNS

Opportunities with DAW lie primarily with feature articles. Most of the columns are written by our staff, contributing editors or editorial board members. We will, however, accept queries for "Stenciling," "By Design" (which covers the principles of design), "Home Decor" (decorative painting for the home), "Creative Painting" (new ideas, techniques and trends in decorative painting), and "Artist of the Issue" (profiles of up-and-coming artists).

Submissions for columns should follow the same format as for features. Pay varies depending on the length and content. To submit a column idea, see "How to Query" below.

OTHER NEEDS

"Ask the Masters" is a column that offers expert answers to your painting questions from the country's top decorative painters. To participate, send your questions to "Ask the Masters," *Decorative Artist's Workbook.* (See address below.)

In "Brush Talk," we share our reader mall-projects, creative ideas, painting solutions and opinions-that were inspired by the pages of *Decorative Artist's Workbook.* To participate, send your letters to "Brush Talk" at the address below.

ORIGINALITY AND RIGHTS

All material submitted must be original and unpublished. If accepted, DAW purchases First North American Serial Rights for one-time use in the magazine and all rights for use of the article (text and illustration/art) in any F&W promotional material/product or reprint.

You always retain copyright of your work and are free to use it in any way you wish after it appears in the magazine. We ask, however, that you do not publish this same material for at least six months from the time it appears in our publication.

HOW TO QUERY

Please query in advance rather than send unsolicited manuscripts and artwork. You may query with more than one idea at a time. Your query should include:

• A brief outline of the proposed article, telling us the skill level, medium and surface used, and anything else about the project that makes it special or unique.

• A color photo or slide of the project/s.

• A short biographical sketch. Include your accomplishments, address and a daytime phone number.

MANUSCRIPT SUBMISSION

Once your article query has been given the go-ahead, here's what you'll need to send next:

1. **The Manuscript:** This should be typed. If you have a computer, you may submit the article on a 3½" inch disk along with the printed copy. Check with an editor for details.) Place your full name, address and phone number on the first page. Your manuscript should include the following.

• *Title*

• *Introduction*

Describe an important point about your project or subject. What made you develop the idea or design for it? You might note an unusual technique, surface or medium, how it can be used, or why it's one of your favorites.

• *Preparation*

Explain any necessary pre-painting steps such as sanding, sealing, etc.

• *Painting Instructions*

Writing in a conversational style, go step-by-step through

the painting process, explaining each point clearly and concisely, as if a beginning painter were looking over your shoulder. Make sure you include every detail (such as the brush size and pigment being used). Spell out the full names of paint colors, and please don't shorten terms (e.g., P.G. for Paynes Gray).

• *Finishing*

Give complete instructions on how to finish the painted project (varnishing, sanding, heat setting, etc.).

• *Closing*

Close your article with a brief statement that ties everything together. Also, if you can, add an estimate of the approximate time needed to complete the project.

• *Materials*

Please provide a complete list of the materials used to complete the project. We ask that you include the following with the assumption that any product mentioned carries your endorsement for quality.

• Palette: paint brand, medium and colors (be sure these are spelled correctly).

• Brushes: brand name, type and size.

• Surface: size (if applicable), supplier's name, address, phone number and the price of the surface (including shipping charges).

• Miscellaneous: Note every other item used, from pencils to glue and spray.

• *About the Artist*

This sidebar runs with every feature. Tell us about yourself, including the following information:

• How long have you been painting and how did you get "hooked"?

• Have you won any awards?

• Have you published any painting books or pattern packets?

• If you teach, give the what, when and how.

• Any anecdotes about painting.

• Your philosophy regarding decorative art.

• Your advice for beginners.

• Include a photo of yourself.

2. **Visual Aids:** Visual aids are an important part of instruction and are essential for project articles, so remember to submit quality painted worksheets of key painting steps for each element of the design (such as petals, leaves, and flower center).These worksheets should show the painting progression, corresponding as much as possible with the written instructions. For example, if the first step is base coating, the first illustration would show only that. If the second step is adding the shading, the second illustration would show that, and so on. (Please note: If adding written instructions on the illustrations, do not do so directly on the art. Instead, place them on a tracing piper overlay and we'll compile the information into captions.)

Also include on the worksheets paint swatches for the paint mixtures used for the project.

Step-by-step worksheets should be painted on canvas, canvasette or sturdy paper, and should be neat and easy to see with plenty of contrast between the painted step and the background color. Also, keep plenty of blank space around each step as we may have to cut out illustrations for art purposes.

3. **Sidebars:** If a certain technique is important in the project, such as dry brushing or cross blending, make a suggestion for a special "sidebar" explaining that technique. Tips and hints to ensure success also make good sidebars.

4. **Alternate Instructions:** Whenever possible, we like to provide instructions for painting a project in an alternate medium. So if you've painted your project in Oils, for instance, and are able to translate those instructions or suggest tips for acrylic painters, please include them in your package.

5. **The Pattern:** Include a "drawn-to-scale" line drawing of the pattern (neatly drawn with a technical pen) for inclusion in the pull-out pattern section of the magazine.

6. **The Project:** Please send the completed project, ready to be photographed. (If the project is on canvas or watercolor paper, please frame it.) All artwork, photos and drawings will be returned after publication.

Categories: Arts—Crafts—Hobbies

Name: Submissions Editor
Material: All
Address: 1507 DANA AVE
City/State/ZIP: CINCINNATI OH 45207
Telephone: 513-531-2690
Fax: 513-531-2902
E-mail: DAWEDIT@aol.com

Defenders

DEFENDERS magazine is published quarterly for the membership of Defenders of Wildlife, a national nonprofit organization devoted to wildlife conservation. DEFENDERS has a paid circulation of about 130,000. Content reflects the organization's focus on endangered species, national wildlife refuges, habitat and biodiversity conservation, the international wildlife trade and similar subjects. Most issues contain several sizable features, as well as departments and wildlife issue reports. Most content deals with North American wildlife, although we print international articles from time to time. Study an issue of the magazine and query before submitting any material.

Manuscripts

Query first. Include a brief description of your background and qualifications. Most articles are assigned after a query.

We do not accept fiction or poetry. Essays are accepted rarely.
Length and Format
Usual length: 2,000 words and up.

Manuscripts must be typed with unjustified lines. Each page should be numbered at top center and should have sufficient margins to allow editing. Photocopies are not acceptable. Computer printouts and WordPerfect disks are acceptable.

Proposals and manuscripts submitted simultaneously to other publications are not acceptable, nor is previously published work.

The content is directed to a general audience, but scientific accuracy is essential. We do not want encyclopedia extracts or other second-hand natural history descriptions. We emphasize threats to wild species and habitat, worthwhile action to save wildlife, and informed discussions of government programs and policies. We seek to maintain a high literary, reportorial and graphic standard.

Amount of payment depends partly on length, time and effort required and subject matter. Payment follows publication.

All book reviews are assigned.

Be patient; evaluating submissions takes time.

Categories: Animals—Conservation—Environment

Name: Submissions Editor
Material: All
Address: 1101 14TH ST NW STE 1400
City/State/ZIP: WASHINGTON DC 20005
Telephone: 202-682-9400
Fax: 202-682-1331
E-mail: JDEANE@defenders.org
Internet: www.defenders.org

Dermascope

As a trade publisher to the aesthetics and body therapy and spa industries, our subscribers have come to depend on *Dermascope* as their source of clear educational information. All articles submitted that are to be considered for publication must meet the following criteria:

Style: Written from an aesthetic educator's point of view, articles must be educational, comprehensive, and positive. Whenever, practical, alternative options and techniques should be mentioned. Overall, articles must remain generic in nature. Therefore, manuscripts cannot promote particular products, procedures, or people. Instead, press releases, new products, industry profiles, news items, etc., will be considered for inclusion within courtesy sections: Worth A look, News & Events, and Names & Faces—depending on space availability and other editorial criteria.

Furthermore, articles must not be slanted against a particular segment of the trade. Support your hypothesis based on documented facts about your subject; theory must be able to stand on its own merits, without referring negatively to other industry services, procedures or products. Please include research and other reference materials that support your claim.

Topics/Length: How-to, body therapy, diet, nutrition, spa, equipment, medical procedures, make-up and business articles should be approximately 700-2,500 words. Feature stories are usually between 1,000-2,500 words. Stories that are more than 2,500 may be printed in part and run in concurrent issues of the magazine.

Acceptance Policy: No simultaneous submissions, please. Reprints are rarely accepted. Computer disk submission of materials is preferred. We utilize Mac platforms, but will accept PC format as well.

Articles should include quality photographs or recommendations for photos, graphics, charts or other illustrations that would enhance the article. Transparencies or slides are preferred, but very good prints *may* be acceptable. Photo credits, model releases, and identification of subjects or techniques shown in photos are required. Sidebars are a plus.

Authors are requested to supply their biographies, limited to a maximum of 100 words. A professional color headshot is also needed to accompany the bio. The photo will be returned if requested.

Dermascope acquires all rights and a signed release form is required. *Dermascope* pays between $50-250 for manuscripts up to allotted yearly budget. We publish manuscripts on an average of four to six months after acceptance and reserve the right to final edit of all materials, kill an article, or reschedule its publication date.

Categories: Aesthetics—Health

Name: Jeanie Reiber, Managing Editor
Name: Saundra Wallens, Editor
Material: Any
Address: 3939 E HWY 80 STE 408
City/State/ZIP: MESQUITE TX 75150-3355
Telephone: 972-682-9510
Fax: 972-686-5901
E-mail: dermascope@aol.com

Diabetes Self-Management

Diabetes Self-Management is written for the growing number of people with diabetes who want to know more about controlling and managing their diabetes. Our readers need up-to-date and authoritative information on nutrition, pharmacology, exercise, medical advances, self-help, and a host of other how-to subjects. We address the day-to-day and long-term concerns of our readers in a positive and upbeat manner and enable them to make informed choices about managing their diabetes.

The rule of thumb for any article we publish is that it must be clear, concise, interesting, useful, and instructive, and must have immediate application to the day-to-day life of our readers. For that reason, we do not publish personal experiences, personality profiles, exposés, or research breakthroughs.

Our audience ranges from the newly diagnosed diabetic—who has little knowledge of diabetes—to people who have been intimately involved in their own treatment for many years and often know more about diabetes than well-informed health writers. We do not assume knowledge of our audience, but we do assume intelligence and are careful not to write down to our readers.

Most articles range between 1,500 and 2,500 words. We do not accept previously published material. While we buy all rights, we are extremely generous regarding permission to republish. Articles are published with bylines and payment is made on publication. Payment rates vary depending on the quality of the material and the skill and effort required of the writer. Kill fees are 20%.

Tips

Use plain English; avoid medical jargon, but where appropriate for understanding, explain technical terms in simple, easily understood language. Writing style should be simple, upbeat, and leavened with tasteful humor where possible. Information should be accurate, up-to-date, and from reliable sources. References from lay publications are not acceptable.

Tables, charts, drawings, and sidebars are particularly useful when they are concise, illustrative, and help explain the text. Photographs are generally not accepted. Authors are required to include with their article a list of suggested reading to be published as a sidebar to the article.

Query with a one-page rationale and outline, and include writing samples. Reports will be made within six weeks. If your query is accepted, expect heavy editorial supervision. We use computers when editing, and we appreciate receiving article manuscripts on computer disk.

Categories: Diet—Health

Name: James Hazlett, Editor
Name: Ingrid Strauch, Senior Assistant Editor
Name: Melissa Glim, Associate Editor
Material: Any
Address: 150 W 22ND ST
City/State/ZIP: NEW YORK NY 10011
Telephone: 212-989-0200
Fax: 212-989-4786

Dialogue

Blindskills, Inc. welcomes the submission of freelance material from visually impaired authors for possible publication. The best way to get an idea of the kind of material we publish is to purchase a sample copy and review it.

Current Needs: Interviews of interest or assistance to newly blind and other visually impaired persons, examples of career and leisure experiences, fiction, humor, and poetry

Material that is religious, controversial, political, or contains explicit sex, is not acceptable.

Payments: Since DIALOGUE is entirely dependent upon public contributions for its support, payment is necessarily low. We think we offer an unusual opportunity for beginning writers. We send an explanatory letter along with each returned manuscript. A copy of the large-print edition of the magazine will be sent to each article contributor. Payments for fiction or nonfiction articles will be made at the rate of $15 to $50. Payment for poetry will be $10 to $15. All payments for articles used in a given issue will be made after all formats of DIALOGUE have been shipped

Rules: 1) No simultaneous submissions to other publications are allowed while being considered by DIALOGUE.

2) We reserve the right to do minor editing.

3) Manuscripts must be the original work of the writer, and, in most cases, must not have been previously published. If material has been previously published, state where and when.

Rights: We buy all rights with a generous reprint policy.

Deadlines: For publication in the Spring issue, material must be received by January 1; for the Summer issue—April 1; for the Fall issue—July 1; and for the Winter issue—October 1.

SPECIFIC GUIDELINES

Nonfiction: Though the freelance portion of any issue is generally representative of the kind of material we are buying, freelance pieces on subjects now being staff-written are always welcome. Currently, we are especially interested in first-person accounts of travel experience, articles about participation in sports, information on new products useful to the blind, features on homemaking, and descriptions of feelings and methods experienced by those losing vision or recently blind.

Fiction: Fiction pieces that promote the purposes of DIALOGUE will be printed. We are interested in well-written stories of many types: mystery, suspense, humor, adventure, romance, fantasy, science fiction, and mainstream. We prefer contemporary problem stories in which the protagonist solves his or her own problem. We are looking for strongly-plotted stories with definite beginnings, climaxes and endings. Characters may be blind, sighted, or visually in-between. Because we want to encourage any writer who shows promise, we may return a story for revision when necessary. Fiction pieces should not exceed 1,800 words.

Poetry: We are eager to find new poets. Our readers enjoy traditional forms of poetry such as blank verse and free verse. Submit one poem, complete with title, date, and name and address of author to a page. Poems should not exceed twenty (20) lines in length. Poems may mention a supreme being, but will not be accepted if their theme or nature is religious. Submit no more than five poems at a time.

Recorded Interviews: Taped interviews should be recorded on a cassette recorder of very good quality at 1-7/8 inches per second. The interview should be professionally conducted and should not be over twenty (20) minutes in length unless the subject or the guest has outstanding significance. The taping session should be preceded by careful research, and at least some of the questions should be prepared in advance. Where possible, submit the original tape. Tapes which are not accepted will be returned as promptly as possible. Each tape interview submitted will be evaluated on the basis of timeliness, content, and technical quality.

Short Items/Fillers: Specify what department the item is for— "ABAPITA," "Connie's Kitchen," "Classified," "Resources, New and In Review," "Department K-9," etc.

Manuscripts: Material should be submitted on a low-density IBM compatible disk in WordPerfect format. Include a hardcopy and a SASE if you would like your disk returned. If you do not have a computer, material may also be submitted in typed, brailled, or recorded form.

On the first page be sure to type your name, complete address, and date of submission in the top left-hand corner. Type the title of the article below these identifying data, preferably in the center of the page. On all subsequent pages, be sure to include your name and the title of your submission in the top left corner and the page number in the top right corner. Edit material on tape as carefully as you would a typed manuscript, making certain that each word is exactly as you intend it to appear in print. Spell any unusual words and proper nouns whose spelling is unclear or variable.

Length: Due to space limitations necessitated by quarterly publication, shorter lengths are preferred both for fiction and nonfiction. Stories and articles of more than 1,800 words are rarely used. We do occasionally run long nonfiction articles if the importance of the topic or nature of the material warrants it. In these cases we divide articles into two or three parts and carry them over from issue to issue.

Time Needed For Reply: At least one month.

Categories: Disabilities—Health—Lifestyles

Name: Carol M. McCarl, President
Material: All
Address: PO BOX 5181
City/State/ZIP: SALEM OR 97304-0181
Telephone: 800-860-4224
Fax: 503-581-0178
E-mail: blindskl@teleport.com

Diamond Insight
Penetrating the Multifaceted World of Diamonds

Diamond Insight, winner of the APEX Award for Publication Excellence in 1995, 1996 and 1997, solicits timely information and vital intelligence about:

• The global diamond market;

• The world's important stones;

• Key individuals behind the trends;

• Events in the mining, manufacturing, wholesale and retail sectors;

• De Beers and CSO activities;

• Interviews, letters, comments and analyses by leading experts.

Categories: Diamonds—Jewelry

Name: Guido Giovannini-Torelli, Editor
Material: All
Address: 790 MADISON AVE
City/State/ZIP: NEW YORK NY 10021
Telephone: 212-570-4180
Fax: 212-772-1286

DINOSAURUS

Dinosaurus

Make It Fun

Fun is an essential part of *Dinosaurus*. We welcome word play that kids will understand, and the approach to subject matter can be equally playful. For example, in "Prehistoric Poop," we conveyed what scientists can learn from coprolites, or fossilized feces, in a playful fashion. In a story on mini-dinosaurs, we compared individuals' sizes to cats, dogs, even pepperoni pizzas!

Accuracy and Timeliness

With a scientific subject, accuracy is essential. Our advisory board of the country's most notable paleontologists reviews all our text, but writers need to do their homework and present material they believe is correct to the best of their knowledge. Information taken from encyclopedias, however current, may already be outdated.

Speaking directly with scientists is essential. We will check quotes and fact-check all manuscripts. Please provide a list of all the people whom you interviewed, with their professional affiliations, addresses, and phone numbers for fact-checking purposes. Also provide copies of any other articles you relied upon.

Don't assume the subjects of *Dinosaurus* are long-dead—paleontologists are constantly revising theories and making new discoveries that modify old beliefs. *Dinosaurus* attempts to respond to such changes. We are far more likely to cover a specific dinosaur if there is a news hook to hang the story on. For example, recent and numerous discoveries of dinosaurs in China and Mongolia have unearthed new species and new theories about the relationship of dinosaurs to birds. Or, how do scientists use computers to do work that was previously impossible?

Length

Dinosaurus is very graphically driven; whatever can be said visually minimizes the length of copy. Most features run no longer than 750 words, as befitting the attention span of the age group. Most articles are in the 500-600 word range, and some are even shorter, particularly in some departments. In general, we like to break up stories so that some material is contained in easy-to-grasp sidebars and boxes.

Format

Manuscripts must be submitted on disk. We use Macintosh with Quark Express software, but we can convert from PC disks and most popular software programs. Also submit a hard copy. We expect to be able to receive e-mail shortly.

Rights and payment

Dinosaurus buys first-time North American rights for use in the magazine and to reproduce the same article (or part of it) on our Web site. We will pay an additional fee for any other uses. Articles assigned and accepted by *Dinosaurus* are not to be published elsewhere within a year from original publication. In the event of syndication, the author will receive credit and 50 percent of the syndication fee.

Dinosaurus pays on acceptance of manuscripts. Please submit your bill with your manuscript. Those deemed unacceptable will receive a kill fee equal to 20 percent of the assignment fee. Payment will be made within 45 days of receiving the bill, assuming the manuscript is acceptable.

We will reimburse you for phone calls upon submission of your phone bill. Other expenses need to be cleared in advance.

We will send you three copies of the issue in which your article is published.

Sample copies will be sent upon receipt of a 9"x12" envelope with postage of $1.70.

Categories: Children—Education—Science

Name: Olivia Bell Buehl, Editor-in-Chief
Material: All
Address: 826 BROADWAY 4TH FLOOR
City/State/ZIP: NEW YORK NY 10003
Telephone: 212-979-1333
Fax: 212-979-6555
Internet: www.dinosaurus.com

Direct Aim

Please refer to Communications Publishing Group, Inc.

Discipleship Journal

OUR PURPOSE

Discipleship Journal strives
• to help believers develop a deeper relationship with Jesus Christ, and
• to provide practical help in understanding the Scriptures and applying them to daily life and ministry.

CONTENT

Most of the articles we publish fall into one of three categories:

• **Teaching on a Scripture** passage, such as a study of an Old Testament character or a short section of an episode, explaining the meaning and showing how to apply it to daily life
• **Teaching on a topic,** such as what Scripture says about forgiveness or materialism
• **How-to,** such as tips on deepening your devotional life or witnessing in the workplace

We **do not** publish testimonies, devotionals, purely theological material, book reviews, news articles, or articles about Christian organizations. We occasionally use profiles of lay people who exemplify a quality treated in a theme section.

TOPICS

About half of each issue is devoted to a theme section, which explores in-depth a subject such as time pressures, evangelism, or leadership. Send a self-addressed, stamped envelope (SASE) to request a theme list. Theme articles require queries at least three months before the issue deadline.

We encourage first-time writers to write non-theme articles, which can touch on any aspect of living as a disciple of Christ. Recent issues have dealt with subjects such as rekindling passion for God, judging others, stages of development in personal discipling, overcoming bitterness, and Jesus' principles for small group leadership.

We'd like to see more articles that (1) encourage involvement in world missions, (2) help readers in personal evangelism, follow-up, and Christian leadership, or (3) show how to develop a real relationship with Jesus.

OUR READERS

Be sure to consider our audience as you choose a topic and approach:
• Slightly more than half are women.
• Median age is 42.
• Most are professionals with at least some college education.
• Nearly all have regular personal devotions.
• About half lead a small group Bible study.
• More than half meet individually with younger Christians to help them grow.
• Many consider busyness the greatest obstacle to their spiritual growth.

TIPS FOR SUCCESSFUL ARTICLES

• **Derive your main principles from a thorough study of Scripture.** You will probably want to include some personal experience and quotes from others, but these should not form the basis of your article. You need not always quote a verse or reference, but you should be able to support your assertions from the Bible.

• **Illustrate** each principle. Use analogies, examples, and illustrations to help the reader gain understanding.

• **Show how to put each principle into practice.** Show the reader what applying this principle would "look like" in everyday life.

• **Be vulnerable.** Show the reader that you have wrestled with the subject matter in your own life. Write from the perspective of a fellow pilgrim, not someone who has "arrived."

HOW TO SUBMIT AN ARTICLE

Due to an increasing volume of submissions, **we can no longer accept unsolicited manuscripts.** Please send a query letter first.

Queries. Please include (1) the working title (2) a clear statement of purpose, (3) a tentative outline, (4) some indication of the style and approach you plan to use, (5) the prospective length, (6) a short description of your qualifications to write the article. If possible, include a few samples of your published work.

Phone queries are discouraged.

Manuscripts. (Submit a manuscript only after receiving a positive response to a query.) Dot matrix submissions are acceptable. On the first page, in the upper left-hand corner, type your name, address, phone number, and social security number. At top right, indicate an approximate word count and rights offered (first or reprint). We prefer Bible quotes from the *New International Version.*

Length should be from 500 to 3,000 words; most articles are between 1,500 and 2,500 words. **Response time** is usually within four weeks. Feel free to drop us a note if you haven't heard from us after two months; some manuscripts do get lost in the mail. Payment of 20 cents per word for first rights or 5 cents per word for reprints is made on acceptance. Reprints from non-competing publications are acceptable; be sure to indicate the publication in which the article originally appeared and the date of publication. Simultaneous submissions are discouraged.

Before you submit an article, be sure to study several recent issues of *Discipleship Journal.* Look at the types of articles we publish, common writing styles, and the way our writers approach their topics. To obtain a sample copy, send a self-addressed 9"x12" envelope with $2.24 in postage to Diane Sevcik at the address shown below. If you have other questions, write to editors Susan Maycinik or Jonathan Graf at the same address.

Categories: Nonfiction—Christian Interests—Inspirational—Spiritual

Name: Adam Holz, Associate Editor
Material: All
Address: PO BOX 35004
City/State/ZIP: COLORADO SPRINGS CO 80919
Telephone: 719-548-9222
Fax: 719-598-7128

Discover Magazine

Thank you very much for writing to *Discover.*

While we do not publish a formal list of guidelines for writers, we suggest that you look at the features that appear in the magazine and shape your outlined proposal to match them.

Also, include samples of previously published work and a brief biography.

We do not accept proposals for Breakthroughs or Watches.

Because of the large volume of mail we receive, please allow six to eight weeks for a response.

The Editors
Categories: Nonfiction

Name: Josie Glausiusz, Researcher/Reporter
Material: All
Address: 114 Fifth Avenue
City/State/ZIP: New York, NY 10011

The Divorced Parents X-Change

Type: 8—12 page b&w newsletter. Established 1993.
Payment: 1 cent a word or writer's copies
Focus: DPX primary focus is to educate parents on legal is-sues. Secondary focus is to advocate co-parenting and cooperation. Third—a support network.

Objective: DPX publishes positive, informative articles and stories about co-parenting, mediation, healing after divorce, divorce itself, children of divorce, step-parenting, grandparents, legal updates, parental rights, non-custodial parents, information about parents in courtroom situations (and sometimes how to avoid them), stories where parents overcame obstacles, anecdotes, letters, powerful/true stories, getting life organized after a divorce, protecting your rights and interviews of authors, legal professionals, counselors, parents, etc.

Submission: Lead articles should be 900-1,300 words. All other articles, stories, etc. should be 100-750 words. All material must be typewritten or neatly handwritten. *Need to have word count!* Editor has the right to edit all material. Include researched citations. Buys onetime rights. Reprints are okay.

Categories: Nonfiction

Name: Terri J. Andrews, Editor
Material: All
Address: PO BOX 1127
City/State/ZIP: ATHENS OH 45701-1127
Telephone: 614-664-3030

DogGone
The Newsletter About Fun Places To Go and Cool Stuff To Do With Your Dog

DogGone™ is a bimonthly newsletter about fun places to go and cool stuff to do with your dog. The editorial focus is split between travel pieces and activity articles. Popular vacation spots, resorts, hotels, campgrounds and weekend getaways are profiled. Also highlighted are fun activities such as flyball, jogging with your dog, lure coursing and obedience trials. In short, it's a travel and activity newsletter for dog owners.

DogGone readers range in age from young singles to families to retired seniors. All are dog owners, many with multiple dogs (up to 5 or 6!). Breeds range from miniature dachshunds to pit bulls to dogs with doubtful ancestry. Our own "roving reporter" is a beagle. *DogGone* readers are typically active folks who like to travel and wouldn't dream of leaving the canine member of their family behind. Many are outdoor types, enjoying hiking, wilderness camping, roller blading and other activities, though some subscribers are physically impaired. Some readers prefer luxury accommodations, some are looking for moderate and budget lodgings and others RV it.

What We're Looking For

DogGone is looking for lively, entertaining, intelligently written pieces on travel and dogs-allowed activities. A sampling of travel features includes resort destinations, bed & breakfasts, camping, and air travel tips - all written from a dog angle. Activities features can be dog sports, like agility, or people activities to enjoy with your dog, like roller blading or antiquing.

For travel pieces, resorts and inns which are especially dog-friendly (perhaps even offering a Pampered Pooch Package) warrant a profile. Other accommodations that welcome dogs can be can be incorporated into a theme article (i.e., fall foliage destinations, ski resorts or suite hotels).

For destination articles (such as "Boston With Terrier" or "Viszlas in Vegas"), it's important to find fun activities in the area for owners to take their pets - nearby parks, hiking trails, pet-friendly tourist attractions, yearly festivals where dogs are allowed, gardens or zoos that permit pets, things of this nature. Our readers aren't bringing their dogs on vacation just to leave them in a hotel room! Destination features should include lodging recommendations. Lodgings should allow any size pets, although particularly nice accommodations with "small pets only" rules may be part of a longer list. Contact phone numbers and addresses should be included, along with rates, number of dogs permitted in room and any pet fees or deposits.

Combination travel/activity articles include themes such as dogs-allowed beaches in the U.S., pet-friendly hiking trails, cross-country ski trails that permit dogs, etc.

Transportation articles could include international travel documentation requirements, railroads which permit pets, rating the airlines on their treatment of pet passengers, sailboat or houseboat travel with your dog, etc.

Activity features will introduce readers to new hobbies to enjoy with their pooch. Dog-related sports such as agility, field trials, skijoring, obedience trials and pet therapy are possibilities. How to include your dog in your present spare-time activities, such as backpacking, rockhounding cross-country skiing or birdwatching, are of interest.

Short submissions are accepted for *DogGone's* regular departments: "Beyond Fetch" offers creative suggestions for games to play with your pooch and "Parks Department" features pet-friendly national, state, regional or local parks, forests and recreation areas. Photos welcome.

Style

Upbeat, humorous and easy-to-read are the main criteria for *DogGone's* style. AP style is loosely adhered to, however, we prefer articles to sound colloquial. Therefore, a sentence does not necessarily have to be "complete" in a conversational style article.

Addresses and phone numbers of destinations and accommodations can be included in the text, if possible, or can appear as a sidebar or blurb at the end of an article. All information should be fact-checked personally; chamber of commerce and other published info is often outdated. For activity articles, it is important to include contacts for further information, as we will only be able to introduce readers to the sports.

Articles can be anywhere from 300 to 900 words. An approximate word count will be agreed upon at acceptance so we plan the rest of the newsletter accordingly.

Articles may be submitted on diskette (3.5" preferred) in word processing (text only) or ASCII format. Scannable hard copy is acceptable. Manuscripts are also be accepted via e-mail, with photos sent via USPS.

Artwork

Destination articles *must* include photographs. Location photographs of guests with their dogs are preferred. Line art may be interspersed with photography, but cannot be the sole graphics for a destination feature. Color prints are preferred, but B&W prints or color slides are acceptable.

Activity articles may be accompanied by a photograph of a dog and owner participating in the featured activity. Line art is acceptable as well. Or, our illustrator can provide graphics.

Pay Rate

Depends on article. No more than $100 per feature with photos supplied, with $34 the usual for a 300-word story and $67 for 600-900 words. A one-year *DogGone* subscription can be partial payment for the first published article. Two- to four-paragraph "tips" on pet-friendly places or events pay $15.

Queries

If you have an article you feel would fit into *DogGone's* editorial format, submit a query or the actual article (include word count) in writing. Response time is usually 2-4 weeks.

Categories: Animals—Outdoors—Recreation—Senior Citizens—Travel

Name: Wendy Ballard, Editor/Publisher
Material: All
Address: PO BOX 651155
City/State/ZIP: VERO BEACH FL 32965-1155
Telephone: 561-569-8434
Fax: 561-569-1124
E-mail: doggonenl@aol.com

Dogwood Tales Magazine
For The Fiction Lover In All Of Us

Dogwood Tales Magazine is a literary magazine published bimonthly and distributed throughout the United States and internationally to people who love to read. Each issue consists of 8-12 fictional short stories (52 pages) in all genres except pornography, religious and children's stories. Each issue is 5½"x8" printed on 20 lb. paper and bound with 67 lb. cardstock.

The magazine is distributed through yearly subscriptions and single copy orders. *Dogwood Tales* ranked 19th in *Writer's Digest* Fiction 50 Best Short Story Markets—1996.

Writer's Guidelines

Manuscripts are carefully reviewed by the editorial staff. Previously unpublished and reprint fictional stories are accepted. *Dogwood Tales* is published 6 times a year with 8-10 stories in each issue.

Send complete manuscript with cover letter listing previous publications. We do accept first time authors and encourage their submissions. Please submit only one (1) story at a time.

Manuscript copies and computer printouts in letter quality are ok. No dot-matrix. Please put your name, complete address, and average word count on your manuscript, along with your name and story title on all following pages. Send in above manuscript format only-do not send us published clips as a submission.

Only fiction done in good taste is accepted. We choose good clean stories suited for the general public. We will consider any genre at this time except religious, pornography, X-rated, nonfiction and stories written for small children. Strong offensive language or subject matter will be an automatic rejection. Each issue will include a special feature story with a southern theme, person or place from any genre. Seasonal material should be submitted at least 6 months in advance.

Pays 1/4¢ to 1/2¢ per word on acceptance plus 1 contributor copy containing story. Authors can purchase extra copies of the issue which contains his/her story at a reduced rate.

Length—4,500 words maximum. A story of 3,000 words or less is preferred and has a better chance of acceptance.

Rights—First time rights and reprint rights. All rights revert back to author upon publication of their work.

Response time—Our average response time is 14 weeks but allow up to 10 weeks before contacting us concerning your submission.

Send us your best short story. We select those that are fresh and action moving. We like strong endings. If we reject your manuscript, don't be discouraged. Try us again with another story. Send the one we rejected to another magazine. It might not have been what we're looking for but it might be perfect for another publisher.

Check out our Web pages for up-to-the-minute info.

Happy writing! We hope to hear from you soon!!

Categories: Fiction—Entertainment—Humor—Men's Fiction—Mystery—Romance—Short Stories—Women's Fiction

Name: P. Carman, Fiction Editor
Material: All
Address: PO BOX 172068
City/State/ZIP: MEMPHIS TN 38115
E-mail: Write2Me@aol.com

The Dollar Stretcher

Thanks for asking for *The Dollar Stretcher* guidelines. If you have any questions I can be reached by email or phone. To insure proper payment please label all correspondence as a **"Hard Copy Submission."**

Who we are:

The Dollar Stretcher is a monthly newsletter dedicated to "Living Better...for Less." The goal is to provide readers with ways to help them save time and money. Occasionally we will also include material on ways to make money at home.

The newsletter's first issue was February, '98. It follows in the footsteps of an online newsletter (circulation 22,000) and web site <www.stretcher.com> created in the April, 1996.

Compensation:

Payment is at the rate of $0.05 per published word. Payment is made at the time of publication and will be sent to the address provided. Payment will be by check in US$. At present we are only able to pay for material that appears in the monthly hardcopy version of the newsletter.

Rights:

We are purchasing first time rights including reprint rights. Reprints will be provided free of charge to non-profit organizations and may also be used for promotional purposes. Non-profits may be asked to cover the cost of production and shipping. Any sale of reprints will be negotiated separately with the author.

Writer's Qualifications:

You need not be a professional in the area being discussed. But you must be knowledgeable. Knowledge is more important than literary skill. Personal, hands-on, experience is valued. Unpublished authors are welcome.

Article Length:

We are interested in articles up to 1,500 words in length. The majority of articles that will be used will be in the 500 to 750 word range.

Type of Material Used:

• how-to articles based on personal or professional experience
• profiles of people who are successfully living the frugal lifestyle
• time and space saving techniques
• creative ways to save on food, housing, auto and clothing
• stage-of-life material for babies, children, teens, college students, singles, couples, the divorced, single parents, empty nesters and retirees.
• Material targeting different levels of experience with frugal living is welcome. We are looking for articles for the newcomer as well as the experienced tightwad.
• material on dealing with non-frugal partner, children or significant others

Interviews:

We are also interested in interviews with people who have successfully found ways to save time and money. An emphasis is put on those who have found new and creative ways to accomplish the frugal lifestyle and who can share ideas that can be imitated by our readers.

Columns:

A series of two or more articles on a theme.

Possible themes include (but aren't limited to):
• how we became a one income family
• home repair projects you can do yourself
• simple solutions from the Depression Era
Please send a proposal before submitting columns.

Finding "regulars" who can act as a professional in an area will be a priority for us. We will also be looking for people who can respond to readers' questions in print.

Book Reviews:

Book reviews should be limited to 500 words.
When reviewing a book, include:
• book title in capitals
• author, publishing company, year of publication, soft or hard cover, number of pages and price
• suggestions for discussion
• general description
• who would it appeal to
• author's goal in writing the book
• author's qualifications
• merits of the book
• any weaknesses of the book
• quality of indexes, recipes or financial aids

Your Article:

The article should be submitted either as an e-mail attachment or on 3.5" diskette in ASCII text file format. We cannot be responsible for returning diskettes. If you're mailing your submission and want to include a printed copy of the article, that's ok. But please don't forget to include the diskette. Our typist is too busy already! Please make sure that your e-mail and postal addresses, as well as your daytime phone number, are included in the e-mail or on the disk label.

Please include a brief one or two sentence bio statement with your text, and any title suggestions that you may have.

If your article includes resources, please make sure that you provide the necessary addresses and phone numbers, and that they are correct!

Please make sure that your lead "hooks" the reader. In a newsletter dedicated to saving time and money our readers are very quick to skip to the next article.

How to Submit:

• E-mail as an attachment. Please indicate hardcopy submission in the subject of the email. We also publish material in the online newsletter without paying the writers. Neither one of us would be happy if your work was used without payment!
• By regular mail to the address below.

Categories: Children—Consumer—Ecology—Education—Environment—Family—Marriage—Money/Finance

Name: Gary Foreman, Publisher
Material: All
Address: PO BOX 23758
City/State/ZIP: FORT LAUDERDALE FL 33307
Telephone: 954-772-1696
Fax: 954-772-1678
E-mail: Gary@stretcher.com
Internet: www.stretcher.com

The Door

The easiest way to get into *The Door* is to write something funny. Not funny ha ha. But funny HA HA HA. Laugh-out-loud-funny. We're not looking to mildly amuse here.

So what do we consider funny? Whatever makes us laugh. The best way to determine that is to read several issues of *The Door*. If you'll do that ahead of time, you'll realize that we no longer accept poetry, first-person essays, sermonettes, and articles that won't make any sense unless you grew up in the Church. Second, our thrust has always been to use humor and satire to point out the absurdities of people who either use religion to enrich their own savings accounts or use religion to convince/brainwash others into following *their* peculiar agendas. This means *any* kind of religion. We're not particular.

(Exception #1: If your article is funny enough, forget the above couple of paragraphs. Humor *rules.*)

Here is an important point: we don't want to be exclusive. The new owners are *serious* about making fun of pomposity and self-righteousness *wherever* it is found, including all other religions, faiths, and credos. (That includes the New Age, Wicca, Druidism, Buddhism, Zoroastrianism, and any other *-ism* you can think of.)

And that means your articles have to be funny to both someone with only a vague, nodding acquaintance with religion in general and to a born again/Sunday School/Training Union/Bible Sword Drill/Youth Choir/Southern Baptist Deacon. *The Door* is a religious jargon-free zone.

(Exception #2: If your article is funny enough, forget the above paragraph.)

If you've got an article that qualifies, send it to the address below. If you're computer-empowered, e-mail it. If not, we currently use WordPerfect 5.1 for DOS, running on IBM machines on Double Density (DD) disks—*not* High Density (HD) disks.

If you can't do either of those things, go ahead and send it on hard copy. But be forewarned: it won't be very long before we're going to have to accept stuff electronically—*exclusively.*

If your piece meets the above requirements, just send it our way. It's hard to tell from a query letter if an article is *Door* funny.

Also: put your name, address, social security number, and telephone number on both your cover letter and the first page of your manuscript, no matter how short or long it is.

Oh yeah—grab a copy of *The AP Style Book* at your local used book store. That's the stylebook we'll be using from now on.

We're simply getting too much stuff to return articles, disks, photographs, drawings, or whatever without return postage attached.

Speaking of drawings, we *love* single panel gag cartoons. No need to send originals—good quality photocopies will do. Just write "Please Do Not Fold—Artwork Enclosed" on the outside of your oversized envelope.

A couple of final tips: we don't commission articles or interviews. We like 'em, we buy 'em. We don't, we send 'em back.

Payment and author's copies are sent within a couple of weeks after publication.

We generally try to respond to submissions within a month or so. Robert Darden screens all articles. Ones he likes he takes before the Star Chamber/Trinity Editorial Board, which is generally comprised of Ole Anthony, Skippy R., and whoever doesn't have kitchen duty that night. The board hashes 'em out, argues over 'em, consults chicken entrails, casts lots, and eventually comes to a consensus. These articles go into our "accepted" pile where they are considered with each upcoming issue of The *Door.* Articles that don't survive the process are returned to their authors.

In other words, the entire process is completely arbitrary. Just because we didn't buy your article this time doesn't mean we won't go scalded ape *crazy* over your next one and practically *throw* money at you.

So fire away. We're looking forward to hearing from you. *The Door* is 90% freelance written and proud of it.

Categories: Humor—Religion

Name: Robert Darden, Editor
Material: Religious Humor & Satire
Address: PO BOX 1444

City/State/ZIP: WACO TX 76703-1444
E-mail: 103361.23@compuserve.com

Dovetail
A Journal by and for Jewish/Christian Families

Dovetail is always looking for articles and essays written by people with experience with interfaith families. Most of our articles are written by partners in Jewish/Christian marriages, children of interfaith families, clergy who work with intermarried couples, and lay experts such as therapists and social workers. A large percentage of our authors have little or no previous writing experience, and we are happy to work closely with authors to help develop a style compatible with Dovetail's editorial content. For *Dovetail,* what you have to say is much more important than how well you say it.

Articles, whether solicited or unsolicited, should follow this format:

• 800 to 1,000 words, typewritten or submitted on diskette (either Mac or IBM word-processing programs acceptable) or via e-mail. If you submit a diskette, please enclose as well a hard copy of your article.

• written in first or third person, in clear, accessible language.

• accompanied whenever possible by a photo of the subject of the article or of the author (and family, if desired).

• accompanied by a two- or three-sentence biographical sketch of the author.

We encourage potential authors to familiarize themselves with back issues of *Dovetail*, in order to match our topic interests and our style.

Dovetail also considers the following types of material, as long as the topic relates to interfaith families:

• cartoons
• humor
• photographs

We accept submissions via mail, e-mail, and fax.

We look forward to hearing from you!

Categories: Family—Parenting—Relationships—Religion

Name: Submissions Editor
Material: All
Address: PO BOX 19945
City/State/ZIP: KALAMAZOO MI 49019
Telephone: 616-342-2900
Fax: 616-342-1012
E-mail: dovetail@mich.com

Downstate Story

Downstate Story is published annually. We decide what to use in the fall. Deadline for the 1999 issue is June 30, 1999.

We aim to present a variety of work so every reader who looks at *Downstate Story* will find something fascinating.

Meanwhile we also promote *Downstate Story*, as well as the reading of fiction in general. We hold readings, and our writers have read and been interviewed on radio and TV. We have 500 copies printed, and now *Downstate Story* has its own Web page on the Internet, making the work of its contributors available internationally. The Internet address is listed below.

As a not-for-profit venture, our goal is to break even financially through sales, so that *Downstate Story* can support itself and need not depend on subsidies, grants or advertising—though we're flexible, and not ruling out these entirely. People can help by mentioning *Downstate Story* to friends, encouraging libraries to order copies, or by buying copies for themselves and friends. We encourage writers to buy a copy so they will be familiar with our publication.

Story guidelines, in general: short fiction or narrative written to the standards of fiction, under 2,000 words, never published before. Shorter is better. We prefer some connection with Illinois or the Midwest. Anyone can submit work.

I am interested in stories with political implications, and also humor. Both are in short supply in the submissions we receive. We get too many stories from the point of view of children, and many pieces on suicide. We publish 10 stories per issue. We also need illustrators.

All contributors are paid $50 on acceptance for their work. We buy first rights only.

We prefer disposable manuscripts, as well as Internet correspondence. But we need a hard copy of the manuscript itself, NOT submission via e-mail or disk.

Back issues (Vol. I, II, III, IV) are available for $6 each. Vol. V is $8.00. Order all five issues for $30.00. Enclose check or money order. Add more names and addresses if necessary. *Downstate Story* makes a terrific gift. We pay postage in the USA.

Categories: Fiction—Short Stories

Name: Submissions Editor
Material: All
Address: 1825 MAPLE RIDGE
City/State/ZIP: PEORIA IL 61614
Internet: www.ecnet.net/users/mfgeh/dss/

DRAMATICS
The magazine for students and teachers of theatre

Dramatics
The Magazine for Students and Teachers of Theatre

THE MAGAZINE AND ITS READERS

Dramatics is an educational theatre magazine published since 1929 by the International Thespian Society, a non-profit honorary organization dedicated to the advancement of secondary school theatre. (In the '80s ETA was formed to oversee the Society as well as a distinct professional association for teachers.) *Dramatics* is published nine times a year, September through May. It has a circulation of about 35,000.

Approximately 80 percent of its readers are high school theatre students; about 10 percent are high school theatre teachers. Other subscribers include libraries, college theatre students and teachers, and others interested in educational theatre.

The primary editorial objectives of the magazine are: to provide serious, committed young theatre students and their teachers with the skills and knowledge they need to make better theatre; to be a resource that will help high school juniors and seniors make an informed decision about whether to pursue a career in theatre, and about how to prepare for a theatre career; and to prepare high school students to be knowledgeable, appreciative audience members for the rest of their lives.

OPPORTUNITIES FOR CONTRIBUTORS

We buy four to eight articles for each issue, general length 800 to 4,000 words. Articles are accepted on any area of the performing arts, including film and dance. A typical issue might include an interview with someone who has made a significant contribution to the theatre; an article describing some innovative approach to blocking, costume design, or set construction; a survey of leading theatre schools describing what they look for in students; and a photo spread, with copy, on some ground-breaking performer or theatre group. Short news items, book reviews, and humor pieces (if they're funny) are also part of the mix.

The test we apply, in deciding whether to accept an article, is whether it would engage an above-average high school theatre student and deepen his or her understanding and appreciation of the performing arts. We also look for pieces a theatre teacher might use in the classroom, studio, or rehearsal hall, although articles of this kind are more likely to be published in our quarterly journal *Teaching Theatre* ([request] separate guidelines).

PLAYS

We print at least five one-act and full-length plays a year. We do reprint plays, but prefer that they be unpublished. Plays should be performable in high schools, which places some restrictions on language and subject matter; however, we tend not to publish children's theatre pieces, teen angst dramas, and overly didactic "message" plays.

We buy one-time, non-exclusive publication rights to plays. The playwright retains all other rights.

GRAPHICS

Photos and illustrations to accompany articles are welcomed, and when available, should be submitted at the same time as the manuscript. Acceptable forms: color transparencies, 35mm or larger; black and white prints, 5"x7" or larger; line art (generally used to illustrate technical articles). Unless other arrangements are made, payment for articles includes payment for photos and illustrations. We occasionally buy photo essays.

RIGHTS AND RETURNS

We buy first publication rights (unless we make other arrangements with an author), pay on acceptance, report in six weeks (or notify authors if a longer period is needed for review), and return all material that is accompanied by a self-addressed stamped envelope.

QUERIES AND SAMPLE COPIES

We prefer to see a finished manuscript but will respond to query letters. Phone and e-mail queries are discouraged. Sample copies of the magazine cost $2.50. Subscriptions cost $18 a year.

PAYMENT

Honorariums of $25 to $400 are paid for accepted work. Payment is based on quality of work, amount of editing or rewriting needed, length of work, and inclusion of photos or graphics. Contributors also receive five free copies of the issue in which their piece appears and may obtain additional copies at a minimal charge.

MS. SPECIFICATIONS

We edit manuscripts to conform to the *Chicago Manual of Style*. Manuscripts should be typed double-spaced on a sixty-character line. Photocopies are acceptable as long as they are clearly legible.

Once articles are accepted, authors can score big points with the editorial staff by supplying their work electronically via e-mail or on IBM-compatible diskettes.

All submissions are subject to editing, and we try to involve authors in that process as much as possible. Whenever time allows, we send galley proofs to authors for review—usually by fax.

A CONTRIBUTOR'S CHEAT SHEET: WHAT MAKES US CRANKY

• Writers who are too lazy or careless to do basic reporting and research. Very few articles are complete with only one quoted source.

• Writers who misrepresent themselves as experts, or are not up front about if and where a piece has been previously published.

• Submissions that ignore or misunderstand our audience; articles that either talk down to our readers or are way over their heads. (If a piece has footnotes, it's probably too academic for us.)

• Contributors who create an impression of conflict of interest by writing about an organization in which they themselves are involved—although we do sometimes publish first-person accounts.

• Would-be playwrights who do not understand the basic conventions of playscript format, or even the basic conventions of the stage.

• Writers who are impossible to get a hold of, or who do not return messages.

WHAT MAKES US HAPPY

• Writers who really understand our audience.

• Writers who bring lots of strong, specific article ideas to the table, and keep abreast of topics recently covered by the magazine.

• Contributors who submit written queries or complete articles, rather than interrupting our work to make a sales pitch by phone.

• Writers who understand the need for editorial input, and can make and/or accept necessary changes gracefully.

• Writers who can provide publishable photography to go along with their pieces (snapshots are not publishable). Illustration ideas are also appreciated.

• Writers who include student voices in their pieces when appropriate, as well as a variety of other sources.

• Writers whose work is well organized, factual, and clean.

• And if nothing else: Writers willing to work for what we can afford to pay.

Categories: Acting—Careers—Drama—Entertainment—Film/Video—Playscripts—Theatre Education

Name: Sunmissions Editor
Material: All
Address: 3368 CENTRAL PKWY
City/State/ZIP: CINCINNATI OH 45225
Telephone: 513-559-1996
Fax: 513-559-0012
E-mail: Pubs@one.net

Dream Network
A Quarterly Journal Exploring
Dreams & Myth Since 1982

The *Dream Network* invites articles, interviews, news items, photographs and artwork which will, in some way, inspire, inform or otherwise encourage our readers to value their dreams. Recommended are dream and myth related **experiential articles, accounts of a personal/transformative nature and/or educational information** that will empower readers in learning to understand the symbolic and metaphoric language of dreams and mythology. Our writers and readers consist of lay persons, students & professional dreamworkers. It is our goal to unite individuals who respect their dreams, to demystify dream work and to integrate dreamsharing into our culture. We also publish a few short poems in each issue.

Strictly promotional material is discouraged, since this is best addressed through advertising, also available in the Journal. (Send for publicity packet.)

Articles which attack, demean, or otherwise negate other people, organizations, philosophies, or systems are not accepted. Intelligently written articles which analyze or disagree with issues are welcomed as such material helps us understand one another better.

One section in each issue revolves around questions that were asked in the previous issue, i.e., our theme. Please contact us directly, by phone or mail, if you wish to be made aware of upcoming questions/themes. Other special sections are *The Art of Dreamsharing* and *The Mythic Connection*.

If you are not familiar with *Dream Network*, we ask that you avail yourself of several back issues so as to experience the texture and purpose of our mission.

LENGTH OF ARTICLES & FORMAT

If you enter your submission on a personal computer, **please send copy of the article on computer disk,** ideally with complementary illustrations and/or photographs. Include a one-sentence biographical statement and address at the end of each article submitted.

A page consists of approximately 900 words with room for title and a 2-5/8"x2-5/8" illustration and/or photograph of yourself. Preferred length, 2 to 3 pages, including photos &/or illustrations. **Maximum length of articles,** 1,800 words or approximately 3/4 pages, **including illustrations/photos.**

Please indicate copyright preference and date on submissions. DNJ reserves the right to edit all materials submitted for publication.

ART MATERIAL & PHOTOGRAPHS

Reproducible black and white original artwork and photographs are preferred. We use one color (black and white) graphics of many types—line drawings with washes, and photographs. Graphics need to be of high quality and camera ready.

TIMING

Once an article is accepted for publication, we do our best to publish it in the next available issue. However we are routinely blessed with more material than we can publish. If you do not see your article in print immediately, please be patient. If you want us to consider your material for a specific issue, please indicate and/or advise us. We should be in receipt of the article no later than six weeks prior to the publication "Lifeline" and preferably much sooner. We do not promise any particular publication date for articles.

PAYMENT

In appreciation, we offer a free one year subscription and several complimentary copies of the issue in which your submission appears.

We do not pay money for articles nor do we give free advertising in exchange. If you are in business, we will also print a brief (no more than 40 words) statement of who you are and how people can reach you.

The reason we do not pay for articles is based on philosophical as well as financial considerations. The *Dream Network* exists to provide a community forum in which we learn from one another as well as a place for us to dialogue with one another. Once acceptance of articles is based upon financial remuneration, a certain segment of the population is denied access. Those denied such access would be those whose ability to express themselves well enough in writing is not such that they can earn a fee, i.e., only professional writers would be heard. Obviously, we encourage well-written articles and professional writers do write for us out of a desire to share with the dream community.

Approximate 'Lifelines' (formerly 'deadlines'):
All Saints Day/Halloween (Winter); Valentine Day (Spring);

Memorial Day (Summer) Labor Day (Autumn)

Approximate Distribution Dates: January (Winter); April (Spring); July (Summer); October (Autumn)

Thank you for your interest in dreams & the *Dream Network*.

Categories: Dreams

Name: Submissions Editor
Material: All
Address: PO BOX 1026
City/State/ZIP: MOAB UT 84532
Telephone: 801-259-5936

Dreams of Decadence
Vampire Poetry and Fiction

Editor: *Angela Kessler*

Dreams of Decadence is a quarterly digest devoted to vampire poetry and fiction.

Fiction: Looking for atmospheric, well-written stories, 1,000—7,000 words. The emphasis is on dark fantasy rather than horror. Vampires may be either protagonists or villains, but in either case characters should be well-developed. We want to see original ideas and story concepts, not rehashes. I like stories that take the traditional concept of the vampire into new territory, or offer a new perspective.

The following are not stories; please do not send them to me: *Someone becomes a vampire; Vampire feeds; Vampire gets laid; Vampire gets staked.* If that is all that happens in your story, this is *not* the market for it. It is okay for any of those things to happen in a story, but none of those is a sufficient plot. "Vampire feeds" is equivalent to "Someone eats a hamburger": It happens all the time, but it doesn't make much of a story. I like elegantly-crafted, poetic prose with a Gothic feel, but remember: stories do need well-developed characters and plot no matter how lovely the writing style may be.

Payment: 1 to 5 cents per word for original fiction. In general, reprints will be considered on a for-copy basis and only if last published at least two years ago.

Poetry: Looking for all forms; however, the less horrific and the more explicitly vampiric a poem is, the more likely it is to be accepted. I believe that "horror poetry" is an oxymoron, at least within *my* editorial worldview, and do not buy it.

Payment: contributor's copy.

Form: Standard manuscript form. We are very interested in working with new writers-we know how hard it can be to break in. We will consider simultaneous submissions. Writer-friendliness is a priority here.

Sample Copies $5.00 post paid. Subscriptions: 1 yr. $16; 2 yrs. $27. Please make check or money order payable to DNA Publications. Credit card charges will appear as Space-Crime Continuum.

Categories: Fiction—Fantasy—Poetry

Name: Angela Kessler, Editor
Material: All
Address: PO BOX 910
City/State/ZIP: GREENFIELD MA 01302
Telephone: 413-772-0725

Remember: Editors change jobs and publishers change addresses. It is wise to invest in a phone call for the current information before submitting.

Drum Business

Drum Business is designed exclusively for individuals involved in the sale of acoustic and electronic percussion and related equipment. The primary objective is to help the dealer run his operation more effectively by delivering relevant information on other successful operations. Other editorial will consist of manufacturer profiles, industry news, and in-depth coverage on new product information. While it is not crucial that all of our writers have worked in a drum shop or drum department, it is necessary that they know enough about drums, drum retailing, and retailing in general to be able to write about managing, merchandising, advertising, sales tips, and other topics associated with running a retail establishment

Additionally, DB is looking for journalists who can present information in an objective manner so as to avoid making value judgments. Therefore, keep all articles as objective as possible. We are interested in how and why a particular store owner or manager operates a certain way; readers can make their own decisions about whether or not they can adapt it for use in their own store.

Before you attempt to write an article for *Drum Business*, you should ask yourself the following questions: Will this article help a substantial number of retailers improve their operations? Will it enlighten them on a particular phase of retailing? Will it save time, money, or effort? Is the topic interesting enough to attract a large number of readers? Will the article help them arrive at a decision or draw a conclusion? Will the article help retailers do their jobs better or run their stores more efficiently? Not every article will do all of those things, but if the article does not do any of them, then DB will probably not be interested in it.

Please query us on lengthy material before you begin writing. This helps us avoid receiving articles we cannot use, and it will help you avoid having your articles returned. Send us a brief outline of the subject matter and your angle on the story. The editors will then be able to guide you in tailoring the material to the exact needs of the magazine. Also, if your idea has already been assigned or covered, we can notify you before you begin working. If you are writing for DB for the first time, or if your idea is somewhat out of the ordinary, you will be asked to submit your piece on speculation.

The above information should guide you in submitting material to *Drum Business*. If you need any further information, please write to us. We are always interested in acquiring good editorial material and in finding talented, competent writers.

PAYMENT

Drum Business pays upon publication. Rates vary depending upon the length of the story after editing, whether the article will be used as a feature article or column, and, to some extent, the length of the writer's association with *Drum Business*.

General Rates:

Feature article: $250 - $350. Buys all rights.

Column: $100 - $200. Buys all rights.

(Receipt of payment generally occurs three to six weeks after publication.)

OPEN COLUMNS

Retailing Columns—Column material can be technical, conceptual, or philosophical in nature. Topics should be very specific, and we encourage the use of drawings, photos, or illustrations where applicable. (750-1000 words)

Progressive Management: Insightful management techniques for everything from computer usage to hiring and firing.

Effective Merchandising: Tips and practical ideas on merchandising drum and related equipment, store layout, displays, etc.

Sales Seminar: Tips on retail sales techniques.

A-D

Advertising Guideposts: How to run cost-effective ad campaigns.

Studio Insights: Setting and running a teaching program.

Manuscripts are edited to conform with style policies, as well as for consistency and readability. This may involve condensing, rearranging, retitling, and, to some extent, rewording the article. Please refer to the DB Style sheet below for specific style preferences. Final decisions regarding style, grammar, and presentation are the right of the editorial staff of *Drum Business* magazine.

DB STYLESHEET

I. MANUSCRIPT LAYOUT

A. Margins

1. First page—three-inch margin at top, one-inch margin at bottom and sides.

2. Subsequent pages—one-inch top, bottom, and sides.

B. Type specs

1. Pica preferred, elite acceptable, no script.

2. For those using computers or word processors, manuscripts should look as much like typewritten manuscripts as possible, i.e., margins as specified above, common typeface.

3. For those submitting articles on disk: Modern Drummer Publications, Inc. utilizes Microsoft Word 5.1a for Macintosh. If using DOS based word processing software, save your file as a text file, and please specify on the label what software was used. If we are unable to read files submitted on disk, they will be returned to author. Use 3½" disks only. If submitting article on disk, please provide hard copy as well.

C. Page Numbering—consecutive

D. Paper

1. Original manuscript or clear photocopy.

E. Bylines

1. Top of first page under title—at left margin—"by" (lower case) followed by name of author, and underlined.

2. Author's address and phone number should also appear on manuscript.

II. COPY LENGTHS

A. Feature material should range from 2,500 to 3,000 words.

B. Column material should range from 750 to 1,000 words.

III. PUNCTUATION

A. Album, film, and book titles, as well as periodicals, should be underlined. Trademarks and model names should also be underlined, e.g., Tama *Titan* hardware, Paiste *Rude* crash cymbal, Remo *Pinstripe* head, Pro-Mark *5A* drumsticks, Ludwig *Black Beauty* snare drum.

B. Do not hyphenate words at the end of lines.

C. Dashes should be typed as a double hyphen with a space before and after (—).

D. The Initial letter of each word in album, film, and book titles, and in the names of periodicals, should be capitalized.

IV. GEOGRAPHIC TERMS

A. Specific locations should be capitalized, e.g., Midwest, East Coast, West Coast.

B. General directions should be in lowercase, e.g., east, west, north, south.

V. MUSICAL GENRES

A. Capitalize Gospel, Latin, and Dixieland. All other musical genres should be lowercase, e.g., rock, jazz, etc.

B. R&B or rhythm & blues; C&W or country & western; rock 'n' roll.

VI. STYLE NOTES

A. Use words for numbers most of the time, except in a list of measurements or specific scientific measurements.

B. '70s, '80s, '90s when dealing with decades.

C. Forties, fifties, and sixties when dealing with age.

D. LP (LPs), 45 (45s) CD (CDs)

VII. PARAGRAPHING

The first paragraph of an article should be aligned entirely with the left margin. The first line of subsequent paragraphs should be indented one tab when using a word processing device (or five spaces on manual typewriters), with subsequent lines aligning with the left margin. Do not insert line spaces between paragraphs.

VIII. INTERVIEWS

A. For question and answer format, introduction should follow paragraph format described in VII above. Uppercase initials of interviewer (followed by a colon) should precede questions, and initials of interviewee (also followed by a colon) should precede responses.

B. Interviews that follow narrative format should follow paragraph rules outlined in VII above.

IX. PREFERRED SPELLINGS

A. Okay

B. Alright

C. Tom-tom

D. Hi-hat

E. Drumset

F. Drumkit

G. Drumhead

H. Drumsticks

I. Mic' (microphone) (noun) plural—mic's, e.g., I use three mic's.

J. Miking, miked, mike (verb), e.g., I mike my sound room.

K. Setup (noun), e.g., The article describes my store setup.

L. Set up (verb), e.g., I will set up the new display.

M. "(inch), e.g., 2"

N. x(by), e.g., 5x4

X. LANGUAGE

A. Do not use gonna for going to, gotta for got to, or 'cause for because. In general, stay away from contracting verbs by omitting the ending "g," e.g., sayin' or playin'.

B. Language should be reasonably "clean." Obscenities should be kept to a minimum, or avoided, if possible.

Categories: Business—Money/Finance

Name: Kevin W. Kearns, Associate Publisher/Editor
Material: All
Address: 12 OLD BRIDGE RD
City/State/ZIP: CEDAR GROVE NJ 07936
Telephone: 973-239-4140
Fax: 973-239-7139
E-mail: MDINFO@moderndrummr.com
Internet: www.moderndrummr.com

Periodicals
E - L

THE ENVIRONMENTAL MAGAZINE

E Magazine

As the largest independent environmental magazine on the newsstand today, with a circulation of 70,000, E serves an important role as the voice for the environmental movement and as a vital information source on national and international coverage of environmental issues. Founded in 1990, E is sponsored by Earth Action network, a nonprofit organization located in Norwalk, CT. In an attempt to stay consistent with our values and goals, we print our magazine on recycled paper and screen our advertisers carefully.

1. We request that writers send a written query when first contacting E with a story idea. Please indicate approximate article length and which section of the magazine you are targeting, allowing a three-month lead time. We will contact you on acceptance of an article. Please include writing samples with your submission.

2. Payment: E pays $0.20/word upon publication. We do not pay for product or book reviews.

3. Articles should be submitted on deadline with an approximate word count indicated on the printout. Fax and e-mail transmissions are acceptable. We request that articles be sent on an IBM-compatible disk when possible. Please include a few sentences about who you are for the brief "author bio" we include at the end of most articles.

4. Articles for E should be written in a journalistic style in order to be easily understood by those not immersed in the environmental movement. Unfamiliar terms, scientific language and jargon should be avoided or explained for the benefit of the lay reader. We are not interested in strident, opinionated writing. We want a balanced tone that will not alienate the casual reader; E is an "advocacy" magazine that aims to broaden the base of the environmental movement, not to preach to the converted.

5. We are interested in articles dealing with environmental issues, currents of environmental thoughts and action and the dynamics of the movement (see "Section Guidelines" below). We are also interested in articles that explore the connections between environmental and other social change/humanitarian issues. We like articles which suggest ways to become involved and include places to write letters of support or protest, contact names and addresses, resources to tap, etc.

6. If photos and/or artwork are available, please indicate so in your query. *Please do not send any art materials unless they are requested.* Rates are negotiable.

7. We reserve the right to edit for brevity, clarity and tone. We prefer gender-neutral phrasing—i.e., "humankind" instead of "mankind."

8. We do not publish poetry, fiction, nature writing or first-person accounts.

9. E's newest section, "Green Living," features regular departments: Your Health, Eco Home, Going Green, Money Matters and Consumer News. These articles individualize the environmental movement and discuss ways readers can implement environmental practices into their homes and family lifestyles.

Section Guidelines

Features In-depth articles on key national environmental issues; often broadly themed (i.e., population, transportation, energy). Length: 2,400 to 4,000 words.

Conversations

Question-and-answer interviews with environmental "movers and shakers," usually people involved with cover story topic. Length: 2,000 words. Previous personalities: Jacques Cousteau; Richard Leakey.

Currents

News stories. Length: 1,000 words; four per issue. Previous topics: Garbage in Orbit; Exxon's Mining; A Last Chance for Endangered Species.

Green Business

Stories about personal finance with an environmental focus. Length: 800 words. Previous topic: Making Sense of Corporate Environmental Reports.

Eco-Travel

A new section about the fast-growing vacation option of ecotourism. Length: 800 words. Previous location: Hawaii, the Ecotraveler's Paradise.

Consumer News

Examines consumer products and services and what industries are doing in response to growing environmental concerns such as recycled paper, natural cosmetics, energy-efficient appliances, etc. Length: 1,400 words. Previous articles: Rethinking Hemp; Paper or Plastic Bags.

Eco-Home

A new section introducing services and products beneficial in the creation of a green home. Length: 800 words. Previous topic: Compact Fluorescents.

Health

Explores environmental aspects of personal health. Length: 1,000 to 1,200 words. Previous topic: Chemical "Endocrine Disruptors."

New Product Reviews

Quick mentions of new products, books and publications. Length: 100 words; unpaid. Previous products: *Blueprint for a Green School* by Jayni Chase; Nature's Way Feline Pine Litter

Updates

News on changes and developments in previous *E* stories. Length: 150 words; three per issue. Previous topics: Brazil's Yanomami in Peril; The CIA's Environmental Mission.

Categories: Animals—Conservation—Consumer—Ecology—Environment—Politics—Science

Name: Jim Motavalli, Editor
Material: All
Address: 28 KNIGHT ST
City/State/ZIP: NORWALK CT 06851
Telephone: 203-854-5559 ext. 107
Fax: 203-866-0602
E-mail: emagazine@prodigy.com

Early American Homes

Early American Homes is a bimonthly magazine about the details of the American domestic past. Our time period ranges from the Pilgrim Century to 1850 and extends later if the subject warrants.

Our readers are interested in material and social history. They value what this information adds to their own lives and surroundings. They want to know more, in-depth, about the history inherent in objects—houses, gardens, textiles, painted decoration, furniture, pottery, food—indeed every element that was commonplace to early America. They like to see, and read about, the details.

This magazine is about reproductions as well as antiques. Fine craftsmanship—the work of someone who lived and worked at a certain time in a particular place—is integral to the value of objects past and present. We feature new houses, textiles, furniture, ceramics and other decorative objects and techniques made with attention to their historic precedents. Projects our readers can try themselves are also appealing, provided they, too, have an early American background.

We're receptive to articles that explore travel to historic places, discuss preservation issues, the antiques and reproductions market, journals, diaries, and inventories. We are always interested in articles that examine the human dimensions of American history; in the regular department called Early American Life we explore what went on day to day in a particular place in a certain period. Academic writing and images of past grandeur do not appeal.

Photographs accompanying article queries are helpful to us; their quality need not be professional, just informational. We do return them. We pay for articles on acceptance.

Mimi Handler

Editor

Categories: Antiques—Architecture—Arts—Biography—Collectibles—Gardening—History

Name: Mimi Handler, Editor
Material: American life, social history, and arts before 1850
Address: 6405 FLANK DR
City/State/ZIP: HARRISBURG PA 17112

East Bay Monthly

The Monthly, as you might have guessed, is a magazine published monthly and distributed throughout the East Bay (Oakland, Berkeley and environs). *The Monthly*'s circulation—95,000—is the largest in the East Bay.

The Monthly's editors welcome queries from freelance writers. You should know that our first commitment is to fine writing. We appreciate the passionate essay, the deft parody, the tale well-told, first-person narratives, historical pieces, interviews, as well as carefully reported features and in-depth investigative articles. Just about the only genres we are *not* interested in are poetry and fiction.

We aim to be a forum for distinctive, intelligent, individual voices on every conceivable topic of interest to our audience. We like stories about local people and issues, but we also accept ideas for articles about topics that range beyond the East Bay's borders or have little or nothing to do with the region. We suggest you spend some time looking over recent issues of *The Monthly* to get a sense of what we publish and what might appeal to us.

To propose an article, send us some recent writing samples, a self-addressed stamped envelope and a cover letter with the following information: What your story idea is, how you will approach it, your point of view, proposed length and why you think your story will make our readers sit up and take notice.

Expect to receive a reply from us in four to six weeks. Please note that if you do not send us an SASE, we are not responsible for the fate of your submission.

The Editors

Categories: Culture—Lifestyles

Name: Tim Devaney, Editor
Name: John Sens, Associate Editor

Material: Any
Address: 1301 59TH ST
City/State/ZIP: EMERYVILLE CA 94608
Telephone: 510-658-9811
E-mail: THE MONTHLY@aol.com

East Texas Historical Journal
Stephen F. Austin State University

The *East Texas Historical Journal* is published in the Spring and Fall of each year. It includes articles and reviews of recently published books, mainly on Texas history, especially East Texas history. Submission must be on disk (3.5") compatible with Macintosh 636 in Microsoft Word and hard copy other than dot matrix for editing. Notes should be placed at the end. Articles that do not exceed twenty-five to thirty pages, notes included, are easier to place, but exceptions are made for exceptional articles. We also welcome new book reviews.

Categories: Nonfiction—History

Name: Archie P. McDonald, Director and Editor
Material: All
Address: BOX 6223
Address: STEPHEN F AUSTIN STATE UNIVERSITY
City/State/ZIP: NACOGDOCHES TX 75961
Telephone: 409-468-2407
Fax: 409-468-2190
E-mail: AmcDonald@sfasu.edu

Ebany

Does not accept unsolicited submissions.

Echoes Magazine

Publication: *Echoes* is a quarterly magazine which is dedicated entirely to the classic styles and designs of the 20th century. Particular emphasis is placed on the 1930s, 1940s, 1950s, and 1960s eras. *Echoes* readers are interested in learning more about the design movements, icons, architects, culture, and collectibles of these eras, and the vintage market which trades in the objects they seek.

Tips: We are looking for feature stories written by knowledgeable individuals in the field of mid-20th century collecting. Especially sought are submissions on furniture designers/styles; influential architects of the period; new related events and promotions; museum and gallery showings of 20th century works; new/exceptional restaurants, hotels, and businesses with 1930s—'60s themes; 20th century textiles and clothing; collecting trends within the 20th century market; reproductions of 20th century items; and advice on repairing/restoring vintage pieces.

Guidelines: Articles should not exceed 2,000 words in length. Please include *word count* with submission information. *Submissions on disk are preferred,* in Mac WordPerfect or basic text format. If not submitted on disk, submissions must be typed and photographs (professional color or black and white images. preferably submitted as slides or transparencies) which accompany the article must be included. If the article submitted has been published previously, or if you plan to submit the same article to other publications in the future, that information must be disclosed with the submission. Publication is not guaranteed. Deco Echoes reserves the right to edit submissions.

Payment: Deco Echoes payment rate is 15 cents per published word. Payment is rendered once submitted article has been published.

Deadlines: Deco Echoes typically schedules articles two to three issues in advance. Articles submitted according to the following deadlines may or may not be included in that particular issue. depending on scheduling:

Spring issue deadline: January 9
Summer issue deadline: April 10
Fall issue deadline: July 10
Winter issue deadline: October 9

Categories: Nonfiction—Antiques—Architecture—Collectibles (all mid-century modern)

Name: Suzanne Cheverie, Editor
Material: All
Address: PO BOX 2321
City/State/ZIP: MASHPEE MA 02649
Telephone: 508-428-2324
Fax: 508-428-0077
E-mail: ney@deco-echoes.com
Internet: www.deco-echoes.com

Eclectic Rainbows
Committed To Making A Positive Difference

WHO WE ARE

The motto for this annual magazine is "Committed To Making A Positive Difference." Dedicated to covering the people, places and things that make a positive difference in our lives and in the universe in which we live, we actively seek writers who wish to utilize this unique forum to share their own informational "pots of gold."

We are "eclectic" because we all have different sources of inspiration in our lives. We are "rainbows" because we could think of no other image that so beautifully and accurately evokes our hopes, dreams, goals and aspirations. No two individuals are inspired by quite the same people, places, things and ideas. By sharing, we expand our horizons.

We are not Pollyanna. The world is in a precarious state. So are many individuals. The problems we face are often complicated and overwhelming, on both a personal and global scale. Yet, there *are* solutions. Never before has the power of just one person to affect many others and effect change been so enormous. We believe that each problem inherently contains within it the seeds to its own solution, and we are dedicated to find those solutions.

Our readership is intelligent, informed and well-educated—there is no need to ever "write down" to this audience. The demographics are as eclectic as our contents: about 50/50 male-female, moderately upscale, predominantly professional, mostly baby-boomers. Many readers work in the creative arts and/or are self-employed.

This publication is not available on newsstands. Circulation is currently 5,000.

WHAT WE WANT

Anything and everything that can be tied in, however tangentially, to the above. If it fascinates you, perhaps it will fascinate us. We're partial to the environment, world affairs, politics, celebrities, humor, astrology and other "New Age" topics, and anything else that piques your interest. You should always express a strong and well-articulated point of view, preferably your own.

Read the magazine to get a "fix" on what we're looking for, but don't be restricted by it. We are very suggestible and intend to be a reader/writer driven publication.

Specific ongoing needs are for:

• Essays: 1,000 words minimum—3,000 words maximum, depending upon the subject's complexity and the depth in which it is pursued. Factual back-up/foundation for your stand/approach is essential.

• Personal opinion/experience: 1,500 words maximum. Please, *no autobiographical nostalgic ramblings* of what it was like when you were young, or the so-called positive lessons you learned when your mother/father/friend/cat/dog/etc. died. We are looking for issue-oriented stands and observations in this area.

• Humor/satire: 1,500 words maximum, or whenever you run out of hilarity.

• Interviews

• Celebrities and non-celebrities: 1,500-3,000 words. (Note: The "Spotlight On" feature is devoted to a journalist/writer, and for the moment, is written only by this editor.) For other profile/interview subjects, we want individuals who are making a difference in their chosen field. Choose someone who has inspired you and/or made a difference in your life. National recognition factor a "plus." Photos (b/w or color prints only) are essential; those furnished by your subject are acceptable, since we cannot, at this time, offer additional payment for photos.

• Reviews of books, films, music, videos: Keep our twice-yearly schedule in mind and be as timeless as possible in your choice of subjects.

• Short Stories: 4,000 words maximum. Please, absolutely NO science fiction or horror. (They give your editor nightmares.) Also, no literary "artsy-fartsy" pieces that require an interpreter. Give us strong characters and a strong plot. Romance, mystery or a combination thereof would be ideal.

• Poetry: 30 lines or less. Your poems should not be totally obscure. Readers want to understand what you are saying with your word pictures. Any subject is acceptable. You may submit up to five poems for consideration at any one time. Please type them in the format in which you would want to see them printed.

PAYMENT AND TERMS

Payment is upon publication. Payment is up to $25 for each piece, depending on its length, complexity, amount of research, etc. We purchase one-time rights. Yes, we consider reprints, provided you give us clear proof (at the time of submission) that the reprint rights are yours to sell. Payment for poetry is in contributor's copies only.

All writers receive the following: byline, masthead listing in that issue as "contributing writer", brief bio note at end of article, and one copy.

We try to edit with a light hand, so do the ruthless editing yourself. Should we find it necessary to edit heavily, you will receive an advance copy of the edited piece for your approval.

HOW TO APPROACH US WITH YOUR IDEAS

In writing, please. The staff is minuscule—the quickest way to a definite "no" and a grouchy editor is to inundate the office with phone calls. Expect a response within four weeks; we'll try to make it faster when possible.

For articles that require research or someone else's cooperation (like interviews), please query first. Try to keep it to two pages, less if possible. A query should contain your idea, angle or focus, and a tentative outline of the eventual article.

Include some published clips if you have them, and some BRIEF information about who you are personally—why should you write this story? (Try to make the clips relevant to our magazine - we have purchased more than a few reprints this way—we *do* read those clips!) If you are good and professional, the lack of prior publication will not handicap your chances in any way. Quality is the key to publication in this magazine.

If the article's already written, and you've read our magazine and feel it's a "match," send the completed property. Always submit the entire manuscript for short stories and poetry.

Always include a self-addressed, stamped envelope with sufficient postage to accommodate your work if you wish its return. Otherwise, a #10 SASE will suffice, and we'll recycle the paper.

If you are able to submit material on computer diskette, let us know that in your initial query/cover letter. Do not send the diskette until we ask for it.

A FINAL TIP...

If you can easily think of a half-dozen other markets that would be a likely "fit" for your idea/article—by all means, send it to them instead! They can probably pay you more and faster. What we want is the stuff that is really, really well-written—but just doesn't quite "fit" into any other publication that you know of. We look forward to hearing from you and reading your work.

Sample copies are available for $5.00, including postage. We strongly suggest you familiarize yourself with us prior to making any submissions.

Categories: Nonfiction—Ecology—Entertainment—Environment—General Interest—Interview—Native American—New Age—Philosophy—Poetry—Psychology—Relationships—Short Stories—Spiritual—Travel

Name: Linda T. Dennison, Editor
Material: All
Address: 1538 TENNESSEE WALKER DR
City/State/ZIP: ROSWELL GA 30075-3152
Telephone: 770-587-5711

The Educated Traveler®

General Format and Length for Submissions

Longer Articles (Learning Vacations, Cover Feature—Travel Program Profile, An ET Find)

Approximately 800 words, including sidebar with contact information. Articles should reach the point (i.e. providing detailed information) quickly. The first two to three paragraphs, however, are crucial in setting the scene, whetting the appetite for the particular type of specialty travel or destination being discussed and making readers want to participate in such a travel experience and learn how to do it. The personal experience perspective (either your own or citing an interview source) as an introduction (and woven throughout the article) is important as readers will want to know "what it's like" in order to motivate them to read further. We will have armchair travelers who want to enjoy the experience through your perspective as well as travelers who want to take what you've done and use it in their own travels.

An ET Find is something relatively obscure that may not be adequately publicized but is a delightful, upscale, in-depth travel experience. Travel Program Profiles require a chart as sidebar, detailing different types of programs/tours available (contact information, tour size, price, typical destinations and dates, leadership, amenities, etc.).

For Shorter Articles (Theme Tours, Inside Knowledge)

Approximately 250-300 words. Theme Tours focuses on one particular type of tour (in one specific destination or area of the world usually). A few paragraphs describe the type of tour or why that type of tour is particularly suited for that destination. The main purpose of the column, however, is to list operators (with addresses and phone numbers) that serve that market, so that readers can request, and compare, itineraries.

Inside Knowledge asks one specific question (of interest to readers) of an insider in the travel industry (for example, asking Lars Lindblad, the travel pioneer, what is the next destination he expects to open up to U.S. travelers).

Fillers (Discoveries)

Approximately 50-60 words. See examples in the representative issue listing. All information must be up to date and verified by you and, preferably, written to format.

For All Articles

Never lose sight of the principle purpose of this newsletter, to collect and provide information that is:

• not readily available
• must be ferreted out through research and insider contacts
• unique, reeking of personal entree, and, therefore, worth the price of a subscription

All articles/short articles should have titles—short, pithy, in keeping with the newsletter format.

NOTE: For now, the newsletter is using material on international destinations only. Also, no how-to articles or cost-saving pieces are required.

Ongoing Columns

A Guide's Guide and Literate Travels are being written on assignment by specific writers. The Editor will write most of the Discoveries section and, in most issues, the Inside Knowledge column.

Fee Schedule

Payment is on publication only. Writer's fees are for first-time rights only.

Articles of 800 words, with information sidebars $100
Articles of 250-400 words (1/3 to 1/2 page) $ 50
Fillers, short takes, current information $ 15
(we pay for ideas that we rewrite, too)

Categories: Travel

Name: Joanne Cosker, Assistant Editor
Material: All
Address: PO BOX 220822
City/State/ZIP: CHANTILLY VA 20153
Telephone: 703-471-1063
Fax: 703-471-4807
E-mail: edtrav@aol.com

Education & Enrichment Guide

Please refer to Bay Area Publishing Group, Inc.

Education in Focus

Education in Focus is a 6-page newsletter that enlightens readers to urgent concerns in education in a fundamental way. All material must maintain a humane premise, rationally defended, and be *suitably documented*. Length is limited to about 3,000 words (more in exceptional cases). Please don't submit articles that support the failures of the education system or that lack sensible solutions to *urgent* problems. Payment is modest. Comp copy available (provide SASE—#10, one stamp).

Categories: Education

Name: Submissions Editor
Material: All
Address: PO BOX 2
City/State/ZIP: ALEXANDRIA VA 22313
Telephone: 703-548-0457
E-mail: Staff@bfat.com
Internet: www.bfat.com

Educational Leadership

Educational Leadership is the official journal of the Association for Supervision and Curriculum Development (ASCD). Its contents are intended for all persons interested in curriculum, instruction, supervision, and leadership in education. Each issue contains articles by leading educators, reports of effective programs and practices, interpretations of research, book reviews, and columns.

Issues are organized around themes. In general, the more

appropriate your article is for a theme issue, the more likely we will be able to publish it. We also accept articles on "Special Topics" if the subject is of great interest but not related to a theme. In addition, we invite international contributions all year long, but especially for those three to four issues designated as having an International Section.

Other important information: ASCD offers no remuneration for articles by professional educators.

Decisions regarding publication are made by the Editor and the editorial staff. ASCD reserves the right to reject material, whether solicited or otherwise, if it is considered lacking in quality or timeliness.

WHAT WE LOOK FOR...

The editors look for brief (1,500-2,500 words) manuscripts that are helpful to practicing K-12 educators. We are not looking for term papers or reviews of literature, and we rarely publish conventional research reports. We prefer articles in which the writer speaks directly to the reader in an informal, conversational style. The treatment of the topic should be interesting, insightful, and based on the writer's experiences. Practical examples should be used to illustrate key points. When reporting their own research, writers should emphasize explanation and interpretation of the results, rather than the methodology. We usually don't find query letters helpful; we prefer to read the manuscript.

HOW TO PREPARE YOUR MANUSCRIPT...

To prepare your manuscript, number *all* pages and show your name, address, phone number, fax number, and e-mail address on the cover sheet only. We prefer manuscripts that look like manuscripts, not like typeset articles from desktop publishing. On page one, just above the title, *please* indicate the number of words in the manuscript, including references, figures, and the like.

Cite references in the text like this (Jones 1988), and list them in bibliographic form at the end of the article; or use citations in the form of numbered endnotes. See a recent issue of *Educational Leadership* for examples of citations. Authors bear full responsibility for the accuracy of citations, quotations, figures, and the like.

For other matters of style, refer to *The Chicago Manual of Style* and *Webster's Collegiate Dictionary.*

HOW TO SUBMIT YOUR MANUSCRIPT...

Send two copies. It is not necessary to send unsolicited manuscripts by overnight mail-our deadlines are target dates, not factors in selection. You can expect to receive a postcard telling you that the manuscript has arrived; a response from an editor should arrive within eight weeks.

If you discover a small error after mailing your manuscript, please do not send a correction; small errors can be corrected in the editing process.

WHAT HAPPENS NEXT...

If your manuscript is accepted, even provisionally, we will ask you to send a computer disk or a letter-quality original of your article. Then your manuscript enters the pool of manuscripts on hand for a particular theme issue (or for use in "Special Topics"). When the editors assemble a particular issue, they review all manuscripts to make selections for the table of contents. All manuscript selections are tentative until we go to press.

When we select articles for each issue, we consider many factors, such as the balance of perspectives, locations, grade levels, and topics. If your manuscript becomes a contender for the final table of contents, you will be notified, and we'll ask you to send a computer disk or a letter-quality original. During the editing and layout process, however, we may have to make last minute adjustments, with resultant disappointments to authors.

WHAT TO DO ABOUT COMPUTER DISKS...

We edit on computer, so we'd like you to submit your manuscript on disk as well as on paper. We can use IBM-compatible or Mac disks but *not* Apple. Write on the disk both the kind of computer and the name of the word processing program you used-and be specific: include version numbers where applicable. If your disk has been formatted high-density, indicate this, too. And please indicate on the disk your last name and the file name of your manuscript.

If you cannot send a disk, we will use an electronic scanner to transfer your manuscript to a disk. We can only scan it, however, if it's a high-quality (clear and sharp) typewritten text or print-out.

We will also accept articles scheduled for *publication* sent to us via the Internet. Our e-mail address is shown below.

HOW TO SURVIVE THE EDITING PROCESS...

If your manuscript becomes a contender for the issue's table of contents, it is assigned to a staff editor, who shepherds it through all the editing and layout processes. Once your manuscript is edited, you will receive an edited version for your review, correction, and approval. At this time you will have a chance to correct errors, answer our queries, and update any outdated information. The style requirements of *Educational Leadership—as* well as space limitations—dictate heavy editing, and we appreciate collaboration with the authors in the process.

One more word about correcting your edited manuscript:

Please do *not* retype it! Just mark your corrections directly on the manuscript, and mail or fax it back to us. If you have insertions, please type or write them on separate pieces of paper; and indicate on the manuscript where they are to be inserted.

When you receive the edited version of your manuscript, you should also receive a transfer of copyright form, which includes permission to record your article (in case the editors select it for *EL on Tape),* and permission to use your article online. Please indicate your preferences on these forms, and return them by first-class mail or fax as soon as possible.

ABOUT ARTWORK AND PHOTOGRAPHS...

The editors like to have photographs and artwork related to the manuscripts, but these do not influence editorial selection. We appreciate having the opportunity to see your artwork-photos (black and white or color) or slides, and student papers and artwork. Send artwork when you are notified that your manuscript has been accepted or when the editors request it. Send photos to us by overnight mail.

Authors are responsible for ensuring that all persons in each photograph have given their permission for the photograph to be published; they are also responsible for ensuring that they have permission to use all other artwork, such as student work. Please include the name of the photographer or the source so that we may give proper credit; and, on the back of each item, tape a small piece of paper with your name and address. (Do not write directly on the back of the photo.) And please add a note to explain what's happening in each photo, including the name and location of the school, or a note to explain the artwork. This information helps us when it's time to write captions.

WHEN YOUR ARTICLE COMES OUT...

As soon as the issue is off press-about the first of each month of issue-we'll send your complimentary copies. Article authors receive five copies; column authors, two copies; book reviewers, one copy. We'll also send an "Author's Feedback Form" to gather your comments about our work. Fill that out quickly, and it's time to arrange your autograph party.

[Themes from previous issues of *Educational Leadership*:]

September, 1997: Teaching for Multiple Intelligences

October, 1997: Schools as Safe Havens

November, 1997: Integrating Technology Into Teaching and Learning

December, 1997/January, 1998: The Equity Gap

February, 1998: Strengthening the Teaching Profession

March, 1998: What Is Basic?

April, 1998 Rethinking School Leadership
May, 1998: Engaging Parents and Community in the Schools
Categories: Nonfiction—Education

Name: Marge Scherer, Editor
Material: All
Address: ASCD
Address: 1250 N PITT ST
City/State/ZIP: ALEXANDRIA VA 22314-1453
E-mail: el@ascd.org
Internet: www.ascd.org

EEO BiMonthly
Opportunities for Diversity

Dear Writer:

We would like to see samples of your work before we can assign or accept articles for publication. When submitting ideas for our consideration, they must be sent both on disk and in hard copy.

Sincerely,
Robert Shannon
Senior Editor

Categories: Nonfiction—African-American—Careers—Hispanic—Internet (careers)—Money/Finance

Name: Robert Shannon, Senior Editor
Material: All
Address: 1800 SHERMAN AVE STE 300
City/State/ZIP: EVANSTON IL 60201
Telephone: 847-475-8800
Fax: 847-475-8807
E-mail: casspubs@casscom.com
Internet: www.casscom.com

1812
An Alternative Webzine of the Arts

We are looking for stories, poems, plays, other forms, and use artwork. We are looking for the unusual—in other words, no stories that start with the character waking, none that end with the character waking, none with writers as characters, no stories about people dying of cancer, and none that begin in the setting of a funeral.

We want snail mail submissions with SASE. (E-mail submissions must be included in the text of the e-mail, and will not be accepted as attachments.) Include a *short* cover letter, listing previous publications if any.

The electronic version of our magazine gives examples of the type of work we are looking for, and can be found at the URL shown below.

Categories: Stories—Poems—Plays

Name: Richard Lynch, Editor
Material: All
Address: PO BOX 1812
City/State/ZIP: AMHERST NY 14226
E-mail: NewWriting@aol.com *or* Box 1812@aol.com
Internet: www.1812.simplenet.com/

> **Remember: Editors change jobs and publishers change addresses. It is wise to invest in a phone call for the current information before submitting.**

The Electron
Cleveland Institute of Electronics and World College

How to write for *The Electron*

Articles in *The Electron* have "news value." We cover recent developments and trends in electronics and high technology. Because The Electron is published every other month, the editors and writers can't report breakthrough immediately when they occur. However, any items covered must be timely to justify its publication in our newspaper.

Cover Stories

The Electron's front page features must be written in the journalistic style, have news value, and contain quotes based on interviews with one or more sources.

Other elements the editors look for are strong lead paragraphs, a good angle, descriptive language and general readability.

You may use news releases as source material, but a manuscript that reads like a sales pitch will be rejected. Avoid an obvious slant toward a particular product or company. (An exception to this would be a "corporate profile," in which activities of a company in the forefront of electronics technology are examined. AT&T Bell Laboratories is a good example of one organization we have covered.)

You should have the ability to write about electronics/high technology in a manner the layperson can understand. Define terminology with a brief line of explanation set off with dashes or parentheses, or with a concise one or two line paragraph. Practical examples are helpful:

"Requirement at startup will be 75 kilowatts—enough to power a small radio station..."

Acronyms or terms common in everyday usage—IC, LCD, semiconductor, solid-state—do not require an explanation.

Suggested length for a cover story is 800 words.

The above guidelines also apply to articles written for **The Electron**'s various departments. However, we do not necessarily require that you interview sources or include quotes. If you are well-versed in an area (computers, broadcasting, avionics, etc.), you may rely upon your knowledge of, or expertise in that field to write your article.

Main Features

The Electron's main (photo) feature covers in depth a broad area in electronics/high technology. Examples of topic areas we have already covered include: Artificial Intelligence; Medical Electronics; Robotics; and Telecommunications.

The main feature, run on a semi-regular basis, reflects that issue's editorial theme. Other articles in the issue will relate to the main feature, particularly the cover stories.

You should follow the cover story guidelines for style, content and readability. Remember, this is a photo feature. Ask about the availability of photographs when interviewing sources for facts and quotes.

Due to the length of the main feature (2,000 words), we recommend that you take the following approach. Break down the topic area by writing a main/overview article and one sidebar. In the main article, review trends and developments relating to the general topic. For the sidebar, you may write a retrospective of the technology, or interview a prominent person in the field.

We will consider your suggestions for alternative approaches to the main feature.

Technical Features

The Electron's technical articles focus on a timely topic in technology. The preferred writing style here is "tutorial" (essay form is best). Thus, technical articles in **The Electron** have news and educational value.

Most of your readers will be the students of The Cleveland Institute of Electronics and World College. Knowledge of electronics in relation to **The Electron**'s readers range from an electronics technician (associate degree level) to an electronics engineer (bachelor's degree level.) As a technical writer for **The Electron,** you are a teacher. Help the readers understand difficult points and concepts by providing illustrations. Supplement text discussion with tables and figures. These may be submitted as clean freehand drawings or sketches.

Your choice of topic should relate to the issue's editorial theme, if possible. Suggested length for a technical feature is 1,000 words.

Categories: Education—Electronics

Name: Ted Sheroke, Advertising Manager
Material: All
Address: 1776 E 17TH ST
City/State/ZIP: CLEVELAND OH 44136
Telephone: 216-781-9400
Fax: 216-781-0331

Electronic Servicing & Technology

These writers' guidelines describe the kinds of articles published in *Electronic Servicing & Technology*, give some idea of the recommended length, and suggest a format for manuscripts.

Also included is a list of possible article subjects as well as a list of vocabulary words that we would like to define in depth in the magazine. These are meant as idea starters, and are not intended to exclude from consideration subjects that are not on the lists.

Also included are specific guidelines for preparing materials for publication in the SYMCURE and Troubleshooting Tips departments.

Sincerely,
Conrad Persson
Editor

Electronic Servicing & Technology is written primarily for servicing technicians who sell, install, and service home electronics equipment.

Articles for *Electronic Servicing & Technology* should be technical in nature and be about an electronics or electronics-related subject. Articles published in ES&T ordinarily fall into the following general categories:

• Specific servicing procedures for specific electronic products.
• General troubleshooting/servicing procedures.
• Theory/operation of specific items of test equipment.
• Reports of new electronics technology of interest to electronic servicing technicians.
• Tutorial articles on electronics theory.
• Symptom/cure type brief articles.
• Troubleshooting tips.
• Articles on business, as related to consumer electronics servicing.

ES&T article coverage is not limited to these subject areas, however, and we welcome inquiries from prospective authors.

We use drawings, schematics, and photos, both B&W and color. For color photos, we prefer transparencies, although we can work from prints. We have access to artists who can create finished art, so don't be hesitant to include rough hand drawings. We can put them in final form.

We especially welcome articles that are on computer disk. We use IBM format, and can accept either 3½" or 5¼" disks. Preferred format is ASCII, but we can usually accept output from any word processor. Please be sure to include information that tells us what word processor you used to create the document.

Article length for a feature article should ordinarily be between three and fifteen typewritten pages. That's just a rough guide, though, not a hard and fast rule. Articles should be as long as they have to be to cover the subject thoroughly. Other manuscripts like Symcure, Troubleshooting Tips and others may be very brief.

It might be to the writer's advantage to submit a query beforehand, outlining a proposed article. That would allow the editors to comment specifically on whether an article is appropriate and/or needed, as well as to suggest to the writer information that should be included.

In any case, do not hesitate to write or call the editors to request comments and guidance on writing for ES&T.

Symcure

The term Symcure is a contraction of the two words: Symptom/cure. Problems that are published in ES&T in the Symcure department are those that have occurred more than once.

This is the kind of problem that you can solve without even a second thought because you've already seen so many of that particular brand and model of set with those symptoms and in almost every case it was the same component that had failed, or the same solder joint that had opened.

Because of the manner in which we publish Symcure, submissions, if they are to be considered, must follow these rules:

1. Each submission must consist of *seven* individual symptom/cure units on a single brand and model of television set. Seven are requested so we may choose the most appropriate for publication.

2. We must have the following information about the set:
• Manufacturer's name
• Model and chassis number or ID
• Sams Photofact number if you know it
• A rough sketch of the schematic where the fault was found. Each sketch should contain a major component such as a transformer, a tube, a transistor or an IC to provide a landmark for the ES&T staff.

3. Because the very nature of Symcure is based on schematics, if for any reason there is no Sams Photofact on the unit, we cannot accept the submission.

Troubleshooting Tips

A troubleshooting tip is a description of the procedure used by a servicing technician to diagnose, isolate and correct an actual instance of a specific problem in a specific piece of electronic equipment. Its value to readers, however, lies in the general methods described rather than its applicability to the repair of the specific piece of electronic equipment.

A good, useful troubleshooting tip has the following elements:
• A brief but complete, accurate and concrete description of the problem symptoms.
• A complete identification of the set, including manufacturer's name, model and chassis number and the Sams Photofact number, if known.
• A rough, simplified, schematic sketch of the area where the trouble occurred. Include some major component such as a transformer, tube or transistor, to serve as a landmark to the ES&T staff.
• A detailed step-by-step description of the procedure used to track down the cause of the problem. This should include the thinking process used—for example, "the absence of B+ voltage led me to believe...etc."

• A mention of any symptoms that misled you and perhaps caused you to follow false trails.

• A narrative telling why the defect was suspected and how it was determined to be the cause of the problem (e.g., tested open, shorted, etc.).

• A description of how the repair was performed, including any precautions about possibility of damage to the set or injury to the servicing technician, if applicable.

The characteristics of a good candidate for troubleshooting tips are as follows:

1. The cause of the problem should be relatively uncommon.

2. The diagnosis and repair should not be obvious, and preferably should present something of a challenge to a competent servicing technician.

Article Ideas

This is a list of ideas for articles for *Electronic Servicing & Technology* that readers have suggested, and that the editorial staff has added to. It is not meant to limit articles in *Electronic Servicing & Technology* to these subjects, merely to serve as a list of possible articles and idea starters.

• One type of article that many readers have requested is the article, or more usually a series of articles, that examines a relatively new model of TV set from end to end, describing all of the circuitry, and especially dwelling on any new type of circuitry.

Other article subjects:
• Power conditioning
• Troubleshooting HV and LV circuits and how they work
• Understanding and servicing TV shutdown circuits
• Understanding TV startup circuits
• Understanding TV voltage regulator circuits
• Troubleshooting horizontal circuits
• Troubleshooting vertical circuits
• Troubleshooting TV power supply circuits
• Servicing cellular telephones
• Specific troubleshooting procedures for specific brands and models of TV
• Dealing with newer, more exotic TV
• Understanding the NTSC waveform
• Preventive maintenance for printers
• Understanding electronic tuners and tuning
• DC motor control
• Servicing two-way radio
• IBM PC computer servicing
• The personal computer as a servicing tool
• Servicing CB radio
• Personal computer servicing: general and product specific
• Servicing compact disc players
• Servicing VCRs
• Understanding and servicing VCR control systems
• Servicing TVRO: downconverters, LNAs, actuators
• Understanding new circuitry: SAW filters, phase-lock loops, comb filters
• Using a spectrum analyzer in troubleshooting
• Fundamentals of electronics
• Fundamentals of electronic servicing
• Servicing projection TV
• Servicing video cameras/camcorders
• Test equipment use and operation
• Do-it-yourself circuit construction
• Diagnosing antenna problems
• Servicing consumer electronic instruments: keyboards, organs, etc.
• Troubleshooting older TVs
• Servicing microwave ovens
• Servicing, repair and calibration of test equipment
• Inexpensive test equipment/accessories
• Testing methodology

• Suggested general troubleshooting techniques/tips/hints
• Servicing audio equipment
• Detailed descriptions of how circuits work
• New methods of soldering/desoldering for new soldering technology
• Suggestions on finding/tailoring general replacements when exact replacements are no longer offered by manufacturer
• Lightning and surge protection
• TV tuner repair
• Understanding digital circuit design and operation
• Troubleshooting/repairing digital circuits
• Signal injection/signal tracing
• CIB calculations for MATV
• Identifying sources of TV interference and correcting problems
• Electronics in home appliances: what they are, how to fix
• Test equipment for personal computers
• Servicing mechanical components
• Understanding wire and cable
• Sources of replacement parts
• Description of the evolution of consumer electronic servicing
• The new multistandard TVs
• A step-by-step approach to troubleshooting: using the senses, what's the next step, etc.
• Equipping a test bench
• Troubleshooting logic circuits with logic probes, pulsers, etc.
• Training/studying
• Multichannel TV sound
• Understanding digital circuit test equipment
• Component testing: resistors, capacitors, inductors, diodes, transistors, ICs
• How switching power supplies work, and are there a lot of TVs or other consumer electronics with switchers in them
• Something like SYMCURE and Troubleshooting Tips for computers/VCR
• Information on electronics societies, organizations
• ESD protection
• Servicing the new Sanyo power supplies
• What is "HQ" circuitry in VCRs

One reader would like to see a shop hints department showing better ways to make repairs faster in the shop.

How about a mini course in relay and control logic for such purposes as microwave oven controls?

Here's an idea I've toyed with from time to time: Would it be possible to start with a bare bones TV receiver and add colored overlays showing how TV has evolved from its inception to today?

• Troubleshooting using an oscilloscope
• Understanding electronics math
• Logs, R/C time constants, Kirchhoff's laws, Trigonometric functions, math primer
• Finding schematics is a problem, but is it possible in some instances to recreate the schematic by tracing the wiring and doing your own drawing?
• How does detection actually work?
• Math Cad review
• Remote control cable converters
• How does AGC work?
• How does AFC work?
• How does a VCO work?
• Discuss filters: high pass, low pass, band pass, active. And how about the word "filter"? Is it really a good word? In one sense, a filter is used to pass a band of frequencies while rejecting others. In another it is used to "smooth" a pulsating dc after rectifying an ac waveform. How should a tech think about filters?

• Why do we use Q to identify a transistor, CR or Y to identify a diode, etc.?

• What does sampling rate mean when we're talking about, for example, a digitizing oscilloscope?

• Why not a primer on transistors, explaining, among other things, why the base, emitter and collector are so called, why use a and ß for amplification, getting into PNP and NPN to a certain degree. That, then, gets into another interesting question: should bipolar transistors and FETs in fact be both called transistors? What are the similarities that get them both the name "transistor" (transfer/resistor), and what are the differences?

• Modulation: among other things, we call the modulating waveform the "carrier", when in fact it can be suppressed before transmitting the signal. It seems like it's a poor choice of terminology.

• An article on antique radio, phono, etc. What the rewards are. What the equipment is. What people, organizations, companies are involved, etc.

• The organizations that ES&T readers belong to, or that might be able to help readers: NESDA, ETA, FIA, etc. What is a CET from the point of view of NESDA and ETA, etc.

• What is a "waveform analyzer"? Is it simply an oscilloscope with some other features like a built in DMM, etc.?

• How about an article on reading manufacturers model numbers: do the numbers mean anything?

• Correcting VCR loading problems

• Correcting VCR speed selection circuit problems

• One thing I'd like to do if possible is to track and publish information on companies that seem to disappear: like Symphonette, Bohsei, etc. I'd welcome any thoughts on how to do that.

• An article that looks at herringbone on screen, and describes what problem causes it and examines the circuits involved and the mechanics of the problem.

• We frequently talk about a two-port or three-port device. How about an explanation of what we mean by that?

• Ways to deal with intermittent problems

• Sorting out all of the transistor and IC part numbers

• How about an article on closed-captioning circuitry for TVs for the hearing impaired?

• What is an "eye" pattern on an oscilloscope? What is it used to measure and how is it used?

• What is a parametric amplifier and where is it used?

• What do ferrite beads do, what are they made of, when were they introduced, etc.?

• What books, catalogs, etc. are essential to a servicing technician's library?

• Warranties, manufacturer's and extended

• Satellite TV scrambling and descrambling

• Such things as active high, active low, Vdd, Vss, etc.

• Charge pump?

• Swallow counter

• Prescaler

• How to go about estimating a job

• Reading a schematic diagram

• Technical support from manufacturers. Tech help phone lines and price and availability of service literature.

• Frequency synthesis and frequency division—what do we mean by these?

• What are servos used for and how do they work?

• On a digital multimeter, why is there a 1/2-digit, and what does "an accuracy of "2% + 2 digits (or whatever) mean?

• Bar-code scanners. Bar codes are now being used to program VCRs

• This one was suggested by a reader who sent in a Reader Service card. An article on a complete sales/service center management software package.

• I'd like to see us do an article on transformers. Describe line isolation transformers, variable transformers, autotransformers, variable isolation transformers, discuss trademarks like Variac, step up, step down, coupling.

• How about a rundown of the safety related components in a consumer electronics product? What are their special characteristics, and why can't they be replaced with universal replacements.

Vocabulary

Here are some words that we would like to define in the magazine at some convenient time. One possible way would be for a writer to write an article on a subject to which several of the words relate, and define the terms in the article. Most vocabularies or glossaries provide just a brief definition of the word. I would like to include in-depth definitions.

Something to keep in mind, is that where the term is not particularly apt, this should be pointed out. For example, I'm not sure that the terms "active" and "passive" are really descriptive of the characteristic they describe, although they come fairly close. Another example is the term "carrier" in regard to electromagnetic transmission. If you can transmit without the "carrier", then it really isn't a carrier, is it?

• Here's another term I have a hard time with - Injection, as of a signal or a voltage? What does "injection" mean, and is it apt?

• Slew rate

• Synchronous/asynchronous

• Prescaler

• Preemphasis

• PWM

• How about an article on abbreviations concerning computers, like MS-DOS, etc.

• Ramp up

• Bio of Lord Kelvin

• Why do we use U followed by a number to designate an IC?

• Scan-derived

• It would be interesting to delve into why the elements of a transistor: base, emitter and collector are so called.

• Why do we call certain portions of a TV circuit a driver?

• A to D and D to A conversion

• What is heat sink grease made of?

• In cable TV, what is meant by head end?

• What is a balun?

• What is meant by the term "leaky" in conjunction with electronic components? For example, transistors can be leaky, or capacitors. Anything else?

• Piecrusting

• Motorboating

• Barkhausen lines

• Turbo (in connection with computers)

• Servo

• WWV

• Alignment: TV, FM, VCR, Disc drive, other?

• Bias (There's forward and reverse bias on semiconductor junctions, and a bias used on magnetic tape). Any others?

• What do we mean by sampling rate when it comes to A to D conversion?

• Where does the term "capacitor" come from.

• What does "peak reading" mean when it comes to capacitors?

• Why not do a simple article to reveal the difference between "linear" and "nonlinear"? You could use actual resistors and diodes to do the research and suggest the readers do the same experimentation to find out what's going on.

• What is meant by "dynamic range"?

• There seems to be more than one meaning of "saturation":

one, for example when talking about a circuit current condition, and one when talking about tape recording. What do they mean? Are there other meanings?

- Describe modulation: AM and FM. Come to think of it, why not include PCM, and any other Ms that come to mind?
- Define "harmonics".
- Dropout
- Retrace: Is this a good term, or is it misleading?
- Damper
- Keystoning
- Explain abbreviations like BNC, DIN, etc.
- Active filters
- Data communications "protocol"
- algorithm
- excursion
- Why is the supply voltage (in some cases the "scan derived" voltage) called a B+ voltage
- The term "flyback" would be one worth exploring at some time.
- Coupling, decoupling
- Neutralization as regards transistor amplifiers
- Countdown, as in TV output circuits
- Parasitic, as in parasitic oscillations.

It saves us a great deal of time, not to mention typographical errors, if writers who submit articles to ES&T are able to submit a floppy disk containing the text along with the manuscript. All of the computers used by the ES&T editorial staff are IBM compatible, and we can handle either to 5¼" or 3½" floppy disks formatted at any density.

Our preferred formats for articles that are submitted on disk are ASCII, or Word Star format, but we can work with files created on most word processors. If you submit an article on disk in any format other than pure ASCII, please include information that tells us what word processor you used to create the file.

There really are few stringent requirements for preparation of manuscripts for ES&T, but here are a few suggestions for writers who submit manuscripts on computer disc, that will make it easier for the editors.

1. If you feel that a term, or some kind of description requires emphasis, make a note of it on the manuscript, with your suggestion of the type of emphasis: italic, boldface, etc. Please don't include such things as underline or all caps, because we don't do that kind of emphasis in the magazine. And don't include that kind of emphasis in your document if you're submitting it on disc, because we would have to eliminate those imbedded commands and change to our typesetting codes for that emphasis.

2. Don't leave large open spaces in the text to show where figures go. Simply refer to the art in the text, for example "see Figure 1." The art department will try to put the art in the right place.

3. Don't put the caption at the point in the article text where the art goes. At the end of the article type in the word Captions, leave a couple of line spaces, and type in the captions, like this:

Figure 1. Connect the probe of the oscilloscope to

4. If you're submitting hand drawn art to be prepared in final form by the ES&T artist, it would be very helpful to the editors if you could type the callouts for all of the art on a separate sheet of paper, as well as writing them in on the hand drawn diagram, in all capitals. This has to be done by someone before the callouts can be sent to the typesetter.

Categories: Electronics—Technology

Name: Conrad Persson, Editor
Material: All
Address: PO BOX 12487
City/State/ZIP: OVERLAND PARK KS 66282-2487
Telephone: 913-492-4857

Fax: 913-492-4857
E-mail: cpersedit@aol.com

Electronics Now

Dear Author:

If you have an electronics-related story, I want to see it. If I like it, I'll buy it and use it in *Electronics Now.*

What kind of articles is *Electronics Now* looking for? The kind we've always sought: first-rate stories on communications, computers, test equipment, components, video, and audio.

I am always willing to review completed manuscripts. If you have an idea for an article but haven't yet completed a manuscript, send a query letter to my attention, including a description of the article you would like to write and a proposed outline. If the article idea shows promise, I'll give you a go-ahead to complete it. I cannot accept an article for publication until I see the complete manuscript.

The feature articles I buy usually fall into one of the following categories: Construction, Tutorial, Technology, and How-to articles.

CONSTRUCTION ARTICLES should show readers how to build electronic gadgets and projects. The devices should be of practical use in the field of electronics, in hobby pursuits, or around the house or car. It shouldn't cost more to build the project than it does to buy a similar device that's commercially available. The best construction articles describe products that are not available elsewhere.

I look for different types of construction articles, ranging from those for neophytes to those for experienced builders and experimenters. A premium goes to the story that tells how to build a complex project very easily.

Manuscripts for construction articles need special care. Schematics, parts list, parts-placement diagrams and text must be in 100% agreement.

The text should include an introduction stating the justification for building the project, the project's difficulty, and its cost.

Important construction details should be included as well. Let the reader benefit from your experience and from what you learned as you designed and built your project.

Don't forget calibration and adjustment instructions! Where special equipment is required, be specific. Do not merely say "quad NAND gate" if the logic family and speed of the device is critical. Give type and number of all mechanical components and tell why they were chosen and how they can be adjusted. Failure to do this may mean that some reader won't be able to make the project work and will blame the magazine or author.

Place critical voltages on schematics; these help the builder check his equipment. Include debugging information: How long did it take to get the device working? To build it? The reader may have some of the same difficulties.

Send a complete list of parts, with brands and type numbers. Make sure the list agrees with the identification codes given in the text and on schematics. Avoid hard-to-get items or those that are one-of-a-kind. There should be two sources for every part. Where values are not critical, say so and give approximate tolerances. Also include a table listing the specifications of your project.

Do not dismantle equipment or make changes after sending us your manuscript. If the article is accepted, we will need to examine the device.

If a project requires software of any kind, I must obtain a copy that I can post on our FTP site. Such software includes the contents of any EPROMs, software for microcontrollers, or executable computer files.

TUTORIAL or general report-type feature articles are popular among our readers. The prime requirement is authenticity. Make sure you have your facts straight and complete. Our editors should not have to do your research job. If you aren't in a position to research it thoroughly and document the facts, you shouldn't write the story in the first place. Be thorough and accurate.

ARTICLES ON NEW TECHNOLOGY and the theory behind new devices are always valuable and make for interesting reading. If you're involved with the development of some new semiconductor device, you can put together an excellent article on how it works and what it can be used for.

A HOW-TO-DO-IT feature article is one of the most interesting articles you can write. Show a reader ten new ways to use his scope or sweep generator or an easy way to make PC boards, and you'll have a friend for life. Include methods that haven't been tried before or are not common knowledge.

GENERAL SUGGESTIONS:

Finish the job. Don't send half-done manuscripts. "Photos to come" or "material to be added here" are flags of incompleteness. I can't judge the manuscript without seeing all of it. Don't expect *Electronics Now* editors to find material for you. It's your manuscript; take pride in doing the whole job. Stories with no illustrations or those without enough text to hold the illustrations together show poor preparation and are not acceptable.

Although *Electronics Now* does not require that article text be submitted on floppy disk, I do greatly encourage it. I can not, however, accept submissions that do not include hard copy. PC-compatible diskettes are preferred. Macintosh-compatible disks must be in the 1.44 megabyte high-density format. Although we can convert from many popular word processing programs, we prefer to receive text files in the ASCII file format. Do not include illustrations in the text files.

If a disk does not accompany your manuscript, you must double-space between lines. Make sure your name and address appears somewhere on each page. Also be sure to include the telephone number where you can be reached during the day in case our editors have a question that requires immediate attention.

Diagrams must be clearly drawn and readable. Except for printed-circuit foil patterns, artwork need not be camera-ready; we redraw all art to *Electronics Now* style. Draw each diagram on a separate page. Drawings must be accurate. Check each one carefully; it is almost impossible for our editors to catch some errors as we may consider them part of your design. Photographs should be 3"x5" or larger, black-and-white glossy prints, in good focus all over. All details should be easy to see, not hidden in dark areas or "whited out" in overexposed or too-bright areas. Don't write on prints! You'll simply spoil them for reproduction. If you need to identify components, put a piece of tracing paper over the print and make the identification lightly on it, or else send an extra print.

If any of your illustrations are smaller than 8"x10", fasten them to standard-size sheets; a 2"x3" scrap of paper can be lost too easily, especially if we're not looking for it.

Put an asterisk or the figure number in the margin of your text when you refer to an illustration or figure. Try to scatter illustrations throughout the story so they're not all bunched. If you have page-layout ideas for your article, include them with the manuscript.

Do not send photocopies of the manuscript or illustrations. Send the original and keep the copy for your files.

RATES OF PAYMENT:

Our payment calculations are not based on a simple page rate. We consider such variables as reader interest, illustrations vs. text, charts and tables, photography, how much editing our staff will have to do, accuracy of research and originality of approach.

The rate for a feature article can vary from $150 to $400 or more. Manuscripts that need practically no editing, that hit pre-cisely the slant we want and do it completely, that are written in the easy-reading style we strive for in *Electronics Now*, and that are thoughtfully and imaginatively illustrated—these command the highest rate.

Our staff members are trained in writing, researching, and editing. As you are developing a story, we will gladly work with you. After we buy your manuscript, your help is often needed to track down odd part numbers, fill gaps in your story, check a doubtful connection on a schematic, etc. We take every step and precaution to make sure your article is authoritative, easy-to-read, and interesting.

I look forward to reviewing your manuscripts.
Sincerely,
Carl Laron, Editor
Categories: Nonfiction—Electronics

Name: Carl Laron, Editor
Material: All
Address: 500 BI-COUNTY BLVD
City/State/ZIP: FARMINGDALE NY 11735
Telephone: 516-293-3000
Fax: 516-293-3115

Elegant Bride Magazine

Now in its tenth year of publication, *Elegant Bride* is a national magazine published four times per year for the upscale bride who is in the midst of planning a ceremony steeped in elegance and tradition. Our reader tends to be a bit older and better educated, and willing to spend money to make her wedding day dreams come true.

We accept submissions that would be of interest to the upscale market, and focus on actual wedding planning, as well as fashion, the newlyweds' first home and honeymoon travel, and touch on life after the wedding with a regular "Perspective" column and occasional relationship-oriented features. We typically do not feature new products or health-related issues. Again, our approach is traditional.

Categories: Bridal—Marriage—Wedding Planning—Women's Issues

Name: Martie Emory, Managing Editor
Material: General
Name: Debra Janin, Travel Director
Material: Travel
Address: 1301 CAROLINA ST
City/State/ZIP: GREENSBORO NC 27401
Telephone: 336-378-6065
Telephone: 212-683-7284 (Debra Janin, NY-based)
Fax: 336-378-8261

The Elks Magazine

The Elks Magazine is published 10 times a year for the 1.3 million members of the BPOE. Editorially it is a general-interest magazine. Articles should be fresh, provocative, thought-provoking, well-researched and documented. A thumbnail profile of the average reader would be a person over 40, with some college and

E-L

an above-average income, living in a town of 500,000 or less.

Our regular columns deal with medicine, business and travel. Articles on these topics are acceptable (except travel), but the angle must differ appreciably.

NOT NEEDED: Fiction, travel, political or religious articles, humor, fillers and poetry. We do not accept first-person pieces.

WHAT WE CAN USE: Informative, entertaining articles on a variety of subjects, including technology, science, medicine, information, problems and situations in contemporary life, self-help, sports, history and nostalgia. Articles should be authoritative (please include sources), tightly written and geared toward the lay person. Articles should run between 1,500 and 3,000 words.

EDITORIAL REQUIREMENTS

• **Query:** *Yes.* Do not send an article without a written query first. Do not phone.

• **Rights:** First North American serial rights.

• **Photos:** Purchased as part of a manuscript package only. Will be returned after publication upon request.

• **Rates:** We pay 15 to 20 cents a word, on acceptance. We request most articles on speculation but will occasionally assign articles (based on a query) to writers with whom we have established a relationship. Include your social security number with your manuscript.

• **Format:** Articles should be typewritten in a 12-point type size. If possible, please send a disk (we prefer IBM-compatible, but we can also convert Macintosh) or transmit the article as the text of an e-mail message, in addition to a hard copy.

For a sample copy, please send 9"x12", self-addressed envelope with $1.01 postage.

Categories: Nonfiction—General Interest—History—Rural America— Science—Sports

> **Name:** Anna L. Idol, Managing Editor
> **Material:** All
> **Address:** 425 W DIVERSEY PKWY
> **City/State/ZIP:** CHICAGO IL 60614-6196
> **Telephone:** 773-528-0433
> **E-mail:** ELKSMAG@elks.org
> **Internet:** www.elks.org

Ellery Queen's Mystery Magazine
The World's Leading Mystery Magazine

Ellery Queen's Mystery Magazine is always in the market for the best detective, crime, and mystery stories being written today—by new writers as well as by "name" writers. We have no editorial taboos except those of bad taste. We publish every kind of mystery: the suspense story, the psychological study, the deductive puzzle—the gamut of crime and detection from the realistic (including the policeman's lot and stories of police procedure) to the more imaginative (including "locked rooms" and "impossible crimes"). We need private-eye stories, but do not want sex, sadism, or sensationalism-for-the-sake-of-sensationalism. We especially are interested in "first" stories—by authors who have never published fiction professionally before—and have published more than 600 first stories since EQMM's inception.

Ellery Queen's Mystery Magazine has been published continuously since 1941, and critics agree it is the world's leading mystery magazine. From the beginning there have been three criteria—quality of writing, originality of plot, and professional craftsmanship. These criteria still hold and always will. The most practical way to find out what EQMM wants is to read EQMM: Every issue will tell you all you need to know of our standards and of our diversified approach. To receive a sample copy send a check or money order for $2.95 and a 6"x9" self-addressed stamped envelope.

We use stories of almost every length. 4,000-6,000 is the preferred range, but we occasionally use stories up to 10,000 words and feature one or two short novels (up to 20,000 words) each year. Short-shorts of 1,500-2,000 words are also welcome. Our rates for original stories are from 3 to 8¢ a word, occasionally higher for established authors.

We urge you to support the high standards of EQMM by writing the best mystery stories of our time, and by giving EQMM first chance to publish them. Note to beginners: It is not necessary to query us as to subject matter or to ask permission to submit a story. We do not want fact-detective cases or true stories; this is a fiction magazine. Please mark Department of First Stories. We cannot provide criticism on stories. Response time is three months. Please do not call the editorial offices.

Categories: Literature—Mystery—Short Stories

> **Name:** Janet Hutchings, Editor
> **Material:** Mystery Fiction
> **Address:** 1270 AVENUE OF THE AMERICAS
> **City/State/ZIP:** NEW YORK NY 10020
> **Telephone:** 212-698-1313

BLACK AMERICA'S NEWSMAGAZINE
emerge

Emerge Magazine
Black America's Newsmagazine

Thank you for your interest in **Emerge.** Since the magazine's premiere in October 1989, readers have begun looking to us for fresh insights into the issues and events affecting African-Americans. We believe **Emerge** is a primary source of thoughtful, sophisticated commentary and in-depth reporting about African-American life in the 1990s.

While we have several freelance contributors, we are always interested in new writing talent. These guidelines are designed to give potential contributors an understanding of the type of material we are most interested in and the best way to present story ideas.

Although we will consider completed manuscripts, we prefer query letters detailing your ideas for an article, accompanied by samples of your published work and a brief bio or resume.

When submitting story ideas, keep in mind that our three-month lead time is necessary for meeting a monthly magazine deadline.

We usually respond in six to eight weeks after receipt of a query. We respond sooner if an idea is time sensitive and it meets our editorial needs. Because of the large volume of our mail and small size of our staff, however, it sometimes takes longer. Please allow ample time before writing or calling to inquire about status of submission. Also, please be sure to include a self-addressed, stamped envelope if you would like a written reply. Queries by fax and e-mail also are accepted.

Emerge buys exclusive first-time North American rights to all articles printed. Our fees start at 50 cents a word for a first assignment. Payment is made upon acceptance of an article, and it generally takes six to eight weeks for checks to be mailed.

FEATURE ARTICLES

Our feature articles can range in length but are usually 1,800 to 3,000 words, with a focus on current issues, ideas or news personalities that are of interest to successful, well-informed African-Americans who are our target audience.

The hallmark of an **Emerge** story is a sophisticated journalistic approach. Under **Emerge's** new design, an even greater emphasis is put on detailed features that are tightly-written and amiable to the use of photos, charts and/or graphics. Our readers expect fresh and detailed information that only original, diligent reporting can provide. While point of view need not be absent, we feel pure polemics are a poor substitute for real information.

Emerge also runs feature-length interviews with notable news figures. These interviews, which appear in the editorial as well in a Q & A format with a 200-word introduction, must present the essence of the individual's work and ideas and their distinctive impact on or contribution to the African-American community and/or the world in general. Occasionally, *Emerge* assigns shorter-format interviews to run in one of the magazine's departments, described below.

DEPARTMENTS

Various departments provide the remaining copy in each month's *Emerge*. Lengths range from 650-750 words, unless noted otherwise. Writers should be able to suggest photos or graphics ideas with queries. Included are:

COVER TO COVER: Reviews and provides news on new books or magazines. All reviews must coincide with the book's publication date

DESTINATIONS: *Emerge*'s travel section showcases experiences, culture and adventure in far-off places or unique approaches to familiar destinations. We prefer travel pieces that would be of particular interest to the African-American traveler and/or highlight African heritage.

DIALOGUE: A short-formed Q & A with African-American newsmakers and scholar. This feature is usually about 2,000 words, with a 200-word introduction.

DIASPORA WATCH: This one-page department is staff written and focuses on events and people in Africa and other nations with significant African heritage.

EDUCATION: Contains news and trends on teaching and academics as they impact African-Americans.

ETCETERA: Stories or insights—often humorous—that do not fit into an existing category. Usually, this department runs about 750 words on one page.

FILM: What's new and of interest to African-American movie-goers and home videos. In addition to criticism, this column offers behind-the-scenes reporting on the film industry. We are not interested in dated material or interviews with celebrities. Can run from 750 words to 1,800 words.

GALLERY: A critical perspective and news about visual arts and artist.

INTERNATIONAL: Covers all corners of the globe from an Afrocentric perspective, taking a special interest in the Third World and African Diaspora. Length: 650-1,200 words, although occasionally can be feature length.

MEDIA: Television and radio shows, their stars and creators are the central characters in this department. Behind the scenes insight is essential.

PERSPECTIVE: This department offers writers a chance to include personal thought and experience in column form. Articles may examine a current news topic or in-depth reflection on a topic of the author's choosing. The emphasis must be on analysis and can be from 1,200-2,000 words in length.

RELIGION: This department examines the church and the role it plays in the African-American community.

SPEAKING VOLUMES: Interview with new authors or publishers; usually as part of the 'Cover to Cover' department

THEATRE: Spotlight on the world of theatre and dance.

TAKE NOTE: A look at musical artists, new releases and trends in the music industry.

THE LAST WORD: A full page opinion piece, usually written by ordinary readers, that can be on any topic the author chooses.

COLUMNS

Veteran African-American journalists each month contribute an examination of issues, thoughtful commentary and their unique insights into their specialty areas:

CAPITOL SCENE: Written by Washington editor Kevin Merida, this column examines how activity in our nation's capitol affects the African-American population.

FILM SCREENING: Dwight Brown, a professional film critic, provides capsule reviews of films that feature African-American stars or themes.

FRIENDLY FIRE: This column offers humorous or satirical commentary on newsmakers and current events, written in a personal editorial tone by contributing editor Lauren Adams DeLeon.

JUST JAZZ: Written by Gene Seymour, the column interprets - for the novice or the aficionado - developments on the jazz music scene and talks to the people who make the music.

MINDING OUR BUSINESS: Highlights stories on African-American enterprises and entrepreneurs, unique start-up business or established businesses that have broken new ground. Also contains Ernest Holsendolph's monthly business column.

RACE MATTERS: Camilla Gilbert compiles news items from around the nation about the plight of African-Americans.

TECHNOLOGY: Nathaniel Sheppard Jr. writes about the information superhighway and technology's impact on the Black community.

VITAL SIGNS: Harriet Washington spotlights health issues.

Xs & Os: Kelly Carter and others examine sports beyond the traditional personality profile, as it effects and impacts the African-American community.

A look at recent issues of *Emerge* will illustrate the range of material that can be accommodated in our editorial format. We encourage you to send us your article ideas. Remember to enclose a self-addressed, stamped envelope to receive a written response. Submissions also are accepted by fax; e-mail can be sent to either address below. Please note, however, that because of the volume of mail and queries we receive, we are not able to respond to fax and e-mail correspondence.

Thank you for your interest in *Emerge: Black America's Newsmagazine.*

Categories: Nonfiction—African-American—General Interest—News

Name: Query Editor
Material: All
Address: 1900 W PLACE NE
City/State/ZIP: WASHINGTON DC 20018
Telephone: 202-608-2100
Fax: 202-608-2598
E-mail: EmergeMag@compuserve.com

Employee Benefits Digest

Since 1954 the International Foundation of Employee Benefit Plans has been recognized as the foremost educational association in the employee benefits field. The International Foundation is a nonprofit organization offering educational programs, publications, information services, the Certified Employee Benefit Specialist (CEBS) Program and a student intern program.

The International Foundation continuously examines the latest issues and trends in the employee benefits field, and publishes in—depth reports, studies, survey results, periodicals and books for both the benefits professional and the general consumer.

The International Foundation of Employee Benefit Plans has two publications that welcome article submissions. *Employee Benefits Digest* is a monthly newsletter for members, and *Employee Benefits Journal* is a quarterly journal for members and other subscribers. Both publications include articles on subjects directly or indirectly related to the employee benefits field. Articles covering new or developing areas of employee benefits are particularly appropriate. We welcome queries or outlines of proposed articles, and the editors of the respective publications will respond promptly.

We assume that all material submitted to the publications is the original work of the listed authors and has not been accepted for publication elsewhere. In the event of any potential conflict, it is the author's responsibility to notify the editor prior to publication. We will ask you to sign a publication agreement.

Articles for the *Employee Benefits Journal* may range in length from about 1,000 words to approximately 7,500 words. Those used in the *Digest* are shorter, generally not more than 2,500 words.

You will be notified whether your article has been accepted within about four weeks.

Writing the article

Organize your article carefully. Avoid overly specialized jargon.

Format

Please submit your manuscript on diskette along with a hard copy. The diskette should be 3.5". If using a word processing system other than WordPerfect, please save as text on a high density disk.

Style

Follow a general style manual, such as the *Chicago Manual of Style* or *A Manual for Writers* by Kate L. Turabian.

Endnotes and References

Please use endnotes rather than footnotes. Number them consecutively and be sure there is a reference to each endnote in the text. Accuracy and adequacy of the references are the responsibility of the author. It is the author's responsibility to obtain any necessary permissions for the use of lengthy quotations or other material (charts, surveys, etc.) originally prepared by others.

Headings

Please provide headings and subheadings that are succinct and that include words useful for information retrieval.

Tables and Figures

Construct tables and figures so they are completely understandable on their own, without further reference to the text. Tables and figures should be labeled correctly in the text.

Author Note

Write a brief biographical note, including present position title and address, as well as educational background, professional affiliations, etc.

Author Copies and Reprints

Authors will receive ten copies of the issue containing their material. Reprints are available for a nominal charge.

Categories: Nonfiction—Employee Benefits

Name: Dee Birschel, Senior Director of Publications
Material: All
Address: INTERNATIONAL FOUNDATION OF EMPLOYEE BENEFIT PLANS
Address: PO BOX 69
City/State/ZIP: BROOKFIELD WI 53008-0069
Telephone: 414-786-6710 ext. 8240
Fax: 414-786-2990
E-mail: books@ifebp.org
Internet: www.ifebp.org

Employee Benefits Journal

Please refer to Employee Benefits Digest.

Endless Vacation

Endless Vacation is a magazine for vacation travelers. It is not for business travelers or armchair travelers. *Endless Vacation* shows readers where to go and what to do on vacation, and perhaps most important, why. *Endless Vacation* also addresses the issues of timeshare ownership and timeshare exchange and offers travel information geared to increasing the enjoyment of our readers who own a timeshare condominium.

Freelance writers contribute three to five features of 1,200 to 2,200 words in each issue. In addition, there are several departments of 800 to 1,000 words each.

Our features focus primarily on domestic vacation travel, with some mainstream international vacation articles. Features should cover new and interesting vacation options and should have a solid angle. Topics range from Colorado resorts in the fall to Civil War steamboating. Although limited, the international features cover easily accessed areas of Europe, South America, Africa, and the Pacific. We are not looking for Nepalese mountain treks or hiking the wilds of Vietnam-however, the romantic towns of Bavaria or shopping in Singapore might turn our heads.

Department topics for which *Endless Vacation* accepts some freelance contributions include weekend travel destinations, health and safety on the road, short travel service and news-oriented pieces, and hot news tips and trends in travel.

Before You Write Your Manuscript or Query

1. The editors strongly suggest that you read the magazine thoroughly to get an understanding of our style and approach. Reading the magazine may also prevent you from querying us on a topic that has recently been covered.

2. Because our readers are doers, not dreamers, your article should cover destinations they can visit and activities in which they can participate.

3. Features should have a narrow focus but not be so limited as to have a parochial appeal. An article on the renaissance of a city is good; an article on a common event or festival in a city usually is not.

4. Articles should provide a fast read, packed with anecdotes, examples, and mini-stories. We are not looking for guidebook material, but finely written, well-constructed travel stories. Personal observations and experiences, interviews with other vacationers or local guides, and solid facts are elements we look for. Many, many publications are competing for our readers' time. Brevity, clarity, and conciseness should be hallmarks of your article.

5. Audience (based on 1994 demographic study by MRI)
• Sex: 42 percent male; 58 percent female
• Median age: 42.3
• College graduates: 32 percent
• Married: 65 percent
• Income: $57,000 median
• In addition, other research shows that 99 percent own a timeshare condominium and rank their most important activities while on vacation (in descending order) as: leisure time, visiting local tourist attractions, dining, shopping, swimming, sports activities, cultural activities, and entertaining.

For more information, *Endless Vacation*'s media kit, which includes a copy of the magazine and an 18-page demographic profile of readers, is available for $10. Single copies of the magazine are $5 each, and subscriptions are available to freelance writers for $33.50 (standard subscription rate is $67). Please mail requests to the attention of Myra Bibert.

How to Submit Manuscripts and Queries

Our editorial calendar is booked many months in advance, and currently we have extremely limited space for freelance submissions. We will review manuscripts on speculation, and for a writer who is unfamiliar to us, this may be the best entrée to our publication. The lead is crucial. If the first sentence does not catch our attention, we may never get to the second one.

If you are Interested in submitting a query for a specific issue, please submit your query as early as possible. A year in advance is suggested.

Query letters should include three to four concise paragraphs indicating the focus and tone of the proposed article. Please include samples of your travel writing so that we may give your query full consideration. Materials will be returned if you include a self-addressed, stamped envelope. We generally respond to queries by letter in 30 days.

Please do not telephone us with your query. It is necessary for us to have queries in written form.

Photography

Photographers should submit a stock list and printed samples to the photo editor. (We cannot guarantee the return of unsolicited slides and transparencies.) The photo editor will contact you if your portfolio matches our needs.

If you are asked to submit materials, please make sure that your name and some form of ID number are on each 35mm slide and color transparency. Photos must be identified on the slide mount or with a caption sheet.

Payment for photos generally ranges between $100 and $500 per photo used, depending on size. Cover photos earn more.

Model releases are required.

If a writer submits slides with a story, they will be considered by the photo editor, and if selected, payment will be negotiated separately from the article. We do not, however, encourage writers to submit photos.

Manuscript Payment

Payment is negotiated upon assignment and tendered upon acceptance. The following ranges will give you an idea of our rates:
- **Feature articles** (including sidebars): $500 to $1,000
- **Departments**: $300 to $800
- **News Briefs**: $75 to $100

Expenses are not guaranteed and are negotiated individually.

If you are assigned an article, you will be sent a contract with a brief description of the topic, terms, and payment. Sign the contract and return it immediately. We cannot send payment without a signed contract on file.

Assigned deadlines are absolute. Failure to meet them may result in the cancellation of the assignment.

Categories: Travel

Name: Jami Stall, Senior Editor
Material: Manuscripts
Name: Julie Piatt, Associate Editor
Material: Marketing, PR Releases
Address: 3502 WOODVIEW TRACE
City/State/ZIP: INDIANAPOLIS IN 46268
Telephone: 317-871-9500
Fax: 317-871-9507
E-mail: EVMAIL@aol.com

Entre Nous
A Journal of Fiction and Poetry

A thematic journal. Type for which theme submitting on first page of mss.

SHORT STORY: *No children's stories.* General Fiction 2,000 word limit; no minimum. Foreign submissions send SASE & 2 int'l postage coupons.

POETRY: Any style (traditional or contemporary; rhymed or unrhymed). Line limit 40. Shorter poems get preference but will not be accepted based on length alone.

ART WORK & PHOTOGRAPHY: Pen & ink drawings or black & white photography. Clear, sharp images that scan well. Art work and photography returned only it SASE with proper postage is included.

Entre Nous does not pay in money or in copy.

INCLUDE SHORT BIOGRAPHY. Include prior publications, awards, or other writing accomplishments, education, interests, hobbies, or anything you wish to share with the reader. Submit 45 days prior to date of journal. *Indicate for which theme you are submitting.*

Sample copies $2.50 + 6½"x9" envelope with $1.24 postage
GUIDELINES FOR *Entre Nous* WRITING CONTEST

Contest submissions are separate and apart from general submissions. No mss. returned. We read April through January. Winners announced in March of each year, but contest winners **are not** published. No previously published works will be considered. Any style, any subject acceptable.

Poetry: $50 first place; $25 second place; Honorable Mentions receive a copy of *Entre Nous* journal of poetry and short fiction with announcement of winners. Line limit 50. Submit up to 6 poems. Reading fee $3/poem.

Short Fiction: $50 first place; $25 second place; Honorable Mentions receive a copy of *Entre Nous* journal of poetry and short fiction with announcement of winners. Word limit 3,600. Submit up to 3 stories. Reading fee $5/story. For acknowledgement of manuscript, send SAS postcard. For winners' list send SASE. All payment in US dollars.

Categories: Fiction—Literature—Poetry

Name: Manda Russell, Editor
Material: All
Address: 1824 NACOGDOCHES STE 191
City/State/ZIP: SAN ANTONIO TX 78209-2216
E-mail: stonflower@aol.com
Nota bene: Entry fees required for writing contest.

Entrepreneur Magazine

Focus

Entrepreneur readers already run their own businesses and are seeking innovative methods and strategies to improve their business operations. They're also interested in new business ideas and opportunities.

Entrepreneurial Woman is no longer being published.

Types of Articles
- Profiles of entrepreneurs with unique businesses and stories to tell.
- Articles offering how-to advice for running a business or explaining how a current business issue, such as the health insurance crisis, affects the operation/management of a business.
- Psychological topics such as coping with stress or how personality affects management style.
- Industry round-ups covering the state of a particular industry and the future trends of that industry.
- Columns *are not* open to freelancers.

Where to start
- You must read the magazine before attempting to query an article.
- Submit queries only. Full-length manuscripts are discouraged.
- Submit all queries in writing to the attention of the editor.
- Queries should describe the topic clearly and succinctly.
- Allow a minimum of 6-8 weeks for a response. No phone calls please.

• Include a return address and both day and evening phone numbers on all correspondence.

• Entrepreneur Group buys first worldwide rights and pays upon acceptance.

Entrepreneur International

Entrepreneur International is published quarterly and distributed to international businesspeople in 85 countries. Its focus is on trends in franchising and business opportunities. Before sending queries, writers should keep in mind that the magazine is written for an international audience *only*.

Categories: Business

Name: Editor
Material: All
Address: 2392 MORSE AVE
City/State/ZIP: IRVINE CA 92614
Telephone: 714-261-2325
Fax: 714-755-4211
E-mail: 104074.3477@compuserve.com

Environment

Environment welcomes manuscripts and proposals that make an original contribution to the public's understanding of global and regional environmental issues. The award-winning magazine, now in its 39th year of publication, has a broad audience that includes world-renowned scientists, researchers, and policymakers; college and university professors and high school teachers (who read the magazine for themselves as well as assign it to their students); and concerned citizens. Those readers expect thought-provoking articles that provide balanced, authoritative analyses written in an accessible way.

Like a policy "white paper," the goal is for those interested in—but not necessarily familiar with—the topic to be able to easily grasp the key science and policy issues without wading through jargon or overly technical material. The magazine offers readers extended articles on key environmental problems, shorter articles that explore parts of such problems, reviews of major governmental and institutional reports, commentaries that provide different points of view than those in the articles, book recommendations, pointers to the best environmental Web sites and other digital media, and staff-written news briefs.

Our executive editors review all submissions and may request other experts, including contributing editors, to review manuscripts and proposals. The executive editors may accept the piece as submitted, accept it pending revision, or reject the manuscript. Final publication decisions rest with them on the five types of manuscripts:

• Main article submissions (between 2,500 and 4,000 words in length) should expose readers to the major scientific and policy issues surrounding a significant topic. Articles must be concise, objective, technically accurate but free of jargon, and factually supported. They should also give appropriate weight to alternative points of view. We encourage authors to include endnotes that offer readers suggestions for further reading and document more technical information or controversial points (30 references is an appropriate number). We also encourage the use of maps, tables, graphs, and sidebar boxes to illustrate key points in the manuscript, describe relevant case studies, or provide background information for readers unfamiliar with the topic discussed.

The concluding section is especially important. The conclusions must follow logically from the facts and analyses presented, must give the reader an idea of what is likely to happen in the future, and must indicate the implications for both policy and future research. This section is more detailed that the typical magazine or journal article. Recent article topics include risk management; rights to biodiversity; shrimp aquaculture; environmental problems in the Czech Republic; environmental taxes; plutonium production in the United States and the former Soviet Union; critical environmental zones; sustainable agriculture; and alternative markets for forest resources.

• Manuscripts for Departments (which focus on special topics such as education, energy, economics, and public opinion) should be between 1,000 and 1,700 words in length and should elucidate a small portion of a larger problem. Though not as comprehensive in coverage as the main articles, these manuscripts should also be objective, free of jargon, factually supported, technically accurate, and well referenced. As examples of the appropriate scope, one piece presented a geographic breakdown of U.S. membership in environmental organizations while another explored the environmental implications of local currencies.

• The "Report on Reports" section provides lengthy reviews (1,500 to 2,000 words) of institutional and governmental reports. The reviews subject new research reports produced by government agencies and private institutions to the same scholarly scrutiny usually given to an individually authored book or monograph. Recently reviewed report topics include soil conservation programs; urban habitats; improvements in automotive technology; climate change and world food supply; and the greening of national accounts systems.

• "Commentary" (maximum of 750 words) seeks to broaden the debate on various topics by providing thoughtful, alternative points of view to those expressed elsewhere in the magazine.

• The "Books of Note" section provides short (100 to 150 words) notices of recent print publications with the aim of calling readers' attention to a wide range of important books rather than providing detailed critical evaluations. Reviewers and books to be reviewed are selected by the magazine's contributing editors, executive editors, and managing editor on the basis of a volume's relevance to the general themes of *Environment* and of their accessibility to a non-specialist audience.

More detailed guidelines for these sections are available from the editorial offices.

Editing and Style References

Once a manuscript is accepted for publication, it is edited thoroughly by the editorial staff for style, substance, and clarity. We assume that, although our readers have a keen interest in the topic, they are unlikely to be familiar with the details that the article covers.

Because we bring complex and technical analyses to a broad audience, we edit more extensively than do most journals or magazines. Articles that exceed the specified length may be shortened. We compose titles and subheads without consultation. We query authors concerning any substantive editorial changes.

We offer rapid publication of timely material, so when we send authors typescripts of the edited manuscript, we require a rapid turnaround to our queries. The staff works closely with authors to ensure a mutually satisfying product.

Environment follows the 14th edition of *The Chicago Manual of Style* by the University of Chicago Press. For spelling, we refer to The *American Heritage Dictionary.*

Manuscript Submission and Technical Requirements

1. Send *three* clean copies of your manuscript to Barbara T. Richman, Managing Editor, *Environment*, Heldref Publications, 1319 Eighteenth Street, N.W., Washington, DC 20036-1802. Legible photocopies are acceptable.

2. *Double space everything, including endnotes and tables.* Use 1-inch or greater margins and confine the page length to 10 inches or fewer. Manuscripts that are not double spaced will be automatically returned to the authors. Graphs, tables, and figures *must* be on separate pages at the end of the manuscript; do not imbed graphs, tables, or figures within the text.

3. Authors' names, positions, titles, places of employment,

mailing addresses, and telephone numbers must appear on the cover page. Fax numbers and e-mail addresses are also useful.

4. Quotations of more than two lines should be indented, underlined, and double spaced, and quotation marks should be omitted.

5. Authors are encouraged to submit photographs and original artwork of professional quality to accompany the text. Authors are responsible for obtaining permission to use such materials. Captions and a credit line identifying the photographer must accompany each photograph. The editorial and graphics staff determines use of all photographs based on relevance, aesthetic value, and space availability. Maps and figures are also useful and are usually redrafted to match *Environment*'s style. In some cases, maps and figures can be prepared from raw data, but authors must send very clear material from which to work.

6. Authors should submit manuscripts on disk as well as in hard copy once a manuscript has been accepted for publication. The preferred formats are Microsoft Word 5.1 for Mac or WordPerfect 5.1 for DOS. Although most word processing programs are also acceptable, we *cannot* read documents in WordPerfect 6.0. Please label the disk with format information, file name(s), and author(s) names. Use 1-inch or greater margins; do not exceed 65 characters per line. Use the endnote—not footnote—function in the word processing program; endnotes must be double spaced. In addition, if manuscripts include figures, it is extremely helpful if they are submitted on disk using Illustrator or Freehand software (Mac versions). Tiff or EPS files are also acceptable.

7. Authors are responsible for the accuracy of endnotes, and all references and quotations must be checked against the original sources. Permission to use material quoted from copyrighted publications must be obtained by the author.

8. All endnotes must be typed double spaced and placed at the end of the article. In the text, place the endnote number above or at the end of the sentence, following the quoted material. *Do not use endnotes in headlines or author affiliations.* Provide enough information to allow the reader to retrieve the referenced material from the most available source. Use the author's name as it appears on the referenced work, and include the title, date, place of publication, and the publisher. *Environment* uses the following style:

Book:
1. E. Eckholm, *Losing Ground: Environmental Stress and World Food Prospects* (New York: W. W. Norton, 1976), 87-89.

Book with more than five authors:
1. A. B. Pittock et al., *Physical and Atmospheric Effects*, vol.1 of *Environmental Consequences of Nuclear War: SCOPE 28* (Chichester, England, and New York: John Wiley & Sons, 1985).

Chapter in a book:
1. J. E. Dooley, "The Management of Nuclear Risk in Five Countries: Political Cultures and Institutional Settings," in R. E. Kasperson and J. X. Kasperson, eds., *Nuclear Risk Analysis in Comparative Perspective* (Boston, Mass.: Allen & Unwin, 1987), 136.

Scholarly journal:
1. F. Shaumberg, "Critical Path for Environmental Management in Developing Countries of Latin America," *Journal of Environmental Systems* 9, no.1 (1979): 89-98.

Magazine:
1. W. Fulton, "Selling the Right To Pollute," *Governing*, March 1992, 40.

Newspaper or regular newsletter:
1. P. P. Passel, "Curing the Greenhouse Effect Could Run Into the Trillions," *New York Times*, 19 November 1989, A1.

Interview or personal communication:
1. Robin L. Rivett, attorney, Pacific Legal Foundation, letter to Robert Burford, director, Bureau of Land Management, 2 February 1993.

2. Maurice F. Strong, secretary-general of the United Nations Conference on Environment and Development, Washington, D.C., personal communication with the author, 12 December 1993.

Additional references to a previous note:
5. Graves, note 1 above, page 7.

For another reference to a note immediately preceding:
6. Ibid., page 17.

Government report:
1. U.S. Environmental Protection Agency, *Evaluation of the Potential Carcinogenicity of Electromagnetic Fields: External Review Draft*, EPA-600-6-90-005B (Washington, D.C., October 1990), table 3.

International treaty:
1. "Protocol on Substances That Deplete the Ozone Layer," Montreal, 1987, in *International Legal Materials* 26 (1987): 1550.

U.S. federal law:
1. *Endangered Species Act of 1973, U.S. Code*, vol.16, sec. 1531(1973).

Congressional bill where title of bill appears in the text:
1. H.R. *3055*, 94th *Cong.*, 2nd sess., *Congressional Record*, 122, no.5, daily ed. (15 July 1976): H16,870.

Congressional bill where title of bill does not appear in the text:
1. *Food Security Act of 1985*, 99th Cong., 1st sess., H.R. 2100, *Congressional Record*, 131, no.132, daily ed. (8 October 1985): H8461-66.

Press release:
1. National Center for Atmospheric Research, "Scientists to Test New Weather Monitoring Systems," press release (Boulder, Colo.; 22 January 1992).

Unpublished discussion papers:
1. V. Norberg-Bohm, "Potential for Carbon Dioxide Emission Reductions in Buildings"(discussion paper for the Global Environment Policy Project, John F. Kennedy School of Government, Harvard University, Cambridge, Mass., March 1990).

For other types of notes, refer to the 14th edition of the *Chicago Manual of Style* or to a recent issue of *Environment*.

For subscription information, contact the Customer Service Department, Heldref Publications, 1319 Eighteenth Street, N.W., Washington, DC 20036-1802 (1-800-365-9753).

Categories: Nonfiction—Agriculture—Animals—Ecology—Energy—Environment—Environmental Science & Policy—Science

Name: Barbara T. Richman, Managing Editor
Material: All
Address: 1319 18TH ST NW
City/State/ZIP: WASHINGTON DC 20036-1802
Telephone: 202-296-6267
Fax: 202-296-5149
E-mail: env@heldref.org
Internet: www.heldref.org

Equal Opportunity Publications

Thank you for your interest in writing for our career-guidance magazines which provide college-level and professional women, minorities, and people with disabilities with information on how to find employment and develop their career potential.

CAREERS & the disABLED: Published four times a year with Fall, Winter, Expo, and Spring editions. It is devoted to promoting the personal and professional growth of individuals with disabilities.

EQUAL OPPORTUNITY: Published three times a year with

Fall, Winter, and Spring editions. It is dedicated to advancing the professional interests of blacks, Hispanics, Asian Americans, and Native Americans.

MINORITY ENGINEER: Published three times a year with Fall, Winter, and Spring editions. it is focused on advancing the careers of minority engineering students and professional engineers.

WOMAN ENGINEER: Published three times a year with Fall, Winter, and Spring editions. It is aimed at advancing the careers of women engineering students and professional engineers.

WD-WORKFORCE DIVERSITY: Published quarterly with Fall, Winter, Spring, and Summer editions. It addresses professional women, minorities, and people with disabilities about how they can succeed as part of a diversified work force.

•First North American serial rights are owned by Equal Opportunity Publications. Previously published articles are also acceptable.

•The rate for articles is ten cents per word paid within six weeks after publication. The rate for each photograph used is $15; cartoons, $25. All manuscripts are submitted on speculation.

•Articles are best submitted on disk (Microsoft Word or ASCII), with printed version that includes your telephone and social security numbers. E-mail address is also available.

Categories: Nonfiction—African-American—Asian-American—Associations—Careers—College—Disabilities—Education—Engineering—Ethnic—Health—Hispanic—Multicultural—Native American—Technology—Women's Issues

Name: Anne Kelly, Editor
Material: Women
Name: James Schneider, Editor
Material: Minorities, Disabilities
Address: 1160 E JERICHO TPK STE 200
City/State/ZIP: HUNTINGTON NY 11743
Telephone: 516-421-9421
Fax: 516-421-0359
E-mail: EOPub@aol.com

Erosion Control
The Journal for Erosion and Sediment Control Professionals

Erosion Control's audience is composed of planning, engineering, construction, development, operations, and regulatory professionals employed in activities involving erosion and/or sediment control. As the audience is made up entirely of working professionals in the field, you should assume a high level of expertise and familiarity with your subject matter.

The bulk of interviews, the preponderance of ascriptions and quotes, as well as the prevailing perspective should belong to direct participants in erosion or sediment control activities. If you find yourself writing about non-participants, take another look at the assignment and see if you're headed in the right direction. To paraphrase a naval axiom, "no writer can go far wrong by asking a working professional what he or she thinks...then putting the answer in quotes."

ASSIGNMENT OF ARTICLES
Erosion Control assigns articles to benefit its readership. The initial assignment sheet will specify substantive aspects of the article such as working title, subject, approach, significance, and length. Additionally, administrative aspects such as due date, remuneration, and reimbursements will be detailed at the time of article assignment.

PUBLISHER'S POLICY ON COMPENSATION AND PUBLICATION RIGHTS

1. Author grants to Forester Communications, Inc. all rights for publication in any of its products. All rights to the submitted material are the sole property of Forester Communications, Inc., including copyright to the material as it appears in Forester Communications, Inc. products.

2. Copyright permission for previously printed material is the responsibility of the author. On submission, we assume that such permission, where required, has been granted. (Note: Many of our authors now find that the best way to avoid copyright problems is for them to copyright the materials they present at conferences. Then they can grant permission to any publication they wish.)

3. Agreed-upon remuneration will be due and payable within 30 days of publication. Approved expenses will be reimbursed upon verification of a detailed expense report/phone bill.

4. The writer is in no way considered as an employee of Forester Communications, Inc. The writer is considered a subcontractor and is therefore responsible for all taxes applicable to remuneration where appropriate.

5. Articles that have been published elsewhere or have been submitted concurrently to other publications are generally not acceptable. However, there are exceptions such as foreign publications, conference proceedings, obscure journals, or significantly different exposure which may mitigate our policy. We are striving to have the best possible material and will, therefore, be flexible. Notify us in writing if it has been submitted elsewhere.

HOW MATERIAL SHOULD BE PREPARED FOR SUBMISSION

1. All materials must arrive at Forester Communications' editorial offices no later than close of business on the agreed upon due date. These include:

a. MS-DOS readable diskette (3.5" or 5.25" single or double-density) using any standard PC-compatible word processor formatting (Microsoft Word preferred). Under special circumstances, and subject to prior arrangement, the electronic submission may be accomplished by modem.

b. Double-spaced, hard copy original for reference and validation.

c. Graphics materials, properly identified and fully annotated and accompanied by a signed release or other proper authorization for their use.

Do not write on the back of a photo with a ballpoint pen or felt tip marker. Instead, type the caption copy on a separate sheet of paper and glue or tape it to the back of the photo, or simply number your photographs and provide a separate sheet with caption copy for each appropriate photo.

High-quality transparencies, slides, or glossy finish B&W or color prints are acceptable, but not photos taken with instant print or similar low image quality cameras.

Drawings, charts, and diagrams must always be accurate and suitable for reproduction. When submitting an article, please include the original artwork or high-quality photostats of the originals. If color will clarify a drawing's effectiveness, include it on a copy of the original, but do not use screens, self-adhesive tints, or patterns on originals.

If you have any questions or are in doubt concerning the use of visuals in your article, please contact the editorial department for advice.

d. Appropriately labeled tape recordings of interviews (for legal and accuracy reasons).

2. Forester Communications requires a signed copy of this document (Author's Guidelines) for its files.

3. The invoice for editorial services you've provided must include your social security number or federal [taxpayer] identification number.

GENERAL GUIDELINES
Think like your audience. Put yourself in an erosion control

professional's boots. What makes this subject important enough that you would take time out from your busy schedule to stop and read the article? Where's the hook? How best to bait it, cast it, troll it, and sink it? When you've satisfied yourself on those scores, you're ready to write.

Probably you've developed a style that feels comfortable to you, so that's a good starting point. But keep in mind your audience and the subject matter at hand. While a breezy, vernacular approach may work in some cases, you may find it misapplied in presenting highly technical detail. Similarly, a terse, didactic treatment of narrative materials is likely to put your audience to sleep no matter how serious and important the subject matter might be. Use your best judgment, try stating your thoughts aloud and see how they sound, or if you're really in doubt call and discuss the situation with us.

Engage your reader. Leave no doubt in anyone's mind who your audience is and why what you have to say is important. Rivet your full attention on your readers and drag them into the middle of your subject, address them directly and personally. For instance, instead of saying, "sediment can be kept out of the water-course in a number of ways," you might say, "If you want to keep sediment out of the streambed, here are some things you can do."

Here's a good example from one of our recent articles:

You must control surface water before it gets into the slope's sub-surface, but when you do that, you're likely to concentrate the flow which can cause surface erosion. You can use roots to help anchor the soil in place while leaves, stems, and branches help dissipate the impact of rain and slow the velocity of surface flows.

Since the audience is composed of working professionals, aim high in your expectations of their knowledge and expertise. While there's no reason to be pedantic or arcane, you should avoid simplifications as well. You have no need to explain or define the things professionals should know. Assume also that your readers know and appreciate superior use of language and grammar, though not to the point that it becomes stilted or contrived.

Don't shy away from technical aspects of your subject. Make the less educated or less technically proficient readers "reach," but do not "write down" to your readers. If the article is too simple or basic, we can't use it.

As far as rules are concerned, follow the latest *Chicago Manual of Style*. We have a set of conventions of our own (e.g. NPDES, EPA, NRCS, USDA), however, we'll apply them as appropriate leaving you to concentrate on more important matters. Use acronyms where appropriate but only where there will be multiple callouts or (rarely) where the acronym is in such common usage that the full name might not be familiar to readers. There are some usage matters having to do with dimensions, quantities, and measures we'd like you to observe:

Primary measures should be metric succeeded immediately by their English equivalents in parentheses [cm, m, l, mg/l, etc. and (in., ft., cu. ft., gal., etc.).

The numbers one through nine should be spelled out, but 10 and up should be presented in Arabic numeral form except at the beginning of a sentence.

When used at the beginning of a sentence, numbers and their accompanying attributes (i.e. inches, percent, degrees) are spelled out, otherwise percentages and degrees should be presented numerically accompanied by the appropriate symbol (% or °).

Identify yourself as a writer on assignment for *Erosion Control* and conduct yourself and the interview in an open, friendly manner. Please refrain from confrontational behavior because of its reflection on the magazine and the questionable service it provides to the informational value at hand.

Think about the article's appearance as you do your interviewing. How might graphics help sell an important point, or what will entice a browser to take the plunge? Get as much graphic material as possible (photos, charts, illustrations, etc.). The more options our art director has, the better.

Verify all titles of those whom you interview as well as the spelling of all names, jurisdictions, companies, equipment, and products if applicable. Please contact people from different geographic regions across the country so it won't be an article about just one specific region (this is a national publication). The majority of your interviews should be with practicing professionals (not manufacturers or suppliers). Do not interview and do not include quotes from public relations firms or their employees. The first quote/reference in any article should be from someone in the trenches.

Please include a cover page indicating the author's (or authors') name, title, affiliation, address, and phone number. State whether or not the material is being sent exclusively to *Erosion Control*.

The above guide has general applicability to *MSW Management* and *Remediation Management* magazines as well.

Categories: Environment

Name: John Trotti, Editor
Material: All
Address: 5638 HOLLISTER AVE STE 301
City/State/ZIP: SANTA BARBARA CA 93117
Telephone: 805-681-1300
Fax: 805-681-1312
E-mail: erosion@ix.netcom.com

Esquire

In all correspondence with us:

1. Please consult a recent issue of the magazine for content and style and consider carefully before making your submission.

2. Materials sometimes get lost in the mail or in the great wave of submissions we receive daily. We cannot track down wayward or unanswered manuscripts.

For fiction:

1. It is best to send the finished manuscript. We will consider short stories only; please do not send full-length novels.

2. We do not accept query letters for fiction.

3. Please send one story at a time; we will not read entire collections.

4. We do not publish pornography, science fiction, poetry or "true romance" stories.

5. We receive so many manuscripts that it is impossible for us to comment individually on them.

For nonfiction:

1. While we rarely publish unsolicited manuscripts, all submissions are read and answered within four to six weeks

2. We prefer receiving a query letter together with some published feature samples, rather than receiving a finished manuscript.

3. Suggested length for nonfiction manuscripts is 1,500 to 4,000 words.

4. Fees vary. We pay upon acceptance of an article.

Categories: Men's Issues

Name: Erika Mansourian
Material: Fiction
Name: David Granger

Material: Nonfiction
Address: 250 W 55TH ST
City/State/ZIP: NEW YORK NY 10019

Essence

Thank you for your interest in writing for ESSENCE Magazine. ESSENCE publishes provocative feature-length articles for African-American women, on subjects that are important to our personal development and empowerment. We are interested in well-written self-help articles as well as celebrity profiles and essays on personal, political and social issues. We are looking for how-to articles on careers, money, health and fitness, electronics, computers and cars. We also run freelance-written short gazette items on health, work, money, parenting, computers, people in the arts and community activists. Word length is given upon assignment.

Please send a query letter rather than submitting a completed manuscript. If we have recently done a story on your topic, if we would like you to approach the topic from another angle, or if we cannot use your story idea, a query letter will save you the time and effort of preparing a manuscript. The only exceptions are for Interiors, Windows, Brothers and Back Talk columns; essays submitted for these pages should run no longer than 1,000 words and should be clearly addressed to the editor of the column.

Be sure to include in your query your name, address and daytime phone number. Give us a clear and concise outline of your story; one page is sufficient. It will help if you include a brief bio that describes your writing experience. Clippings are welcome.

If you wish to submit more than one idea to us, write a separate query for each topic and send each one to the appropriate editor. Check our masthead in the current issue to learn which areas each editor covers.

If we feel your subject will be of interest to our readers and you are a writer new to ESSENCE, you will be asked to submit the completed manuscript on speculation. Manuscripts are then read and a decision is made by our editors. Payment for articles is made upon acceptance for publication. Please allow six weeks for review.

We look forward to hearing from you.

Categories: Fiction—Nonfiction—African-American—General Interest—Health—Relationships—Self-Help

Name: The Editors
Material: All
Address: 1500 BROADWAY
City/State/ZIP: NEW YORK NY 10036
Telephone: 212-642-0600
Fax: 212-921-5173

Et Cetera
A Review of General Semantics

The International Society for General Semantics, founded in 1943, publishes articles, essays, fiction, and correspondence related to general semantics. Our publications include a quarterly journal, *ETC: A Review of General Semantics*, and numerous books and anthologies.

General semantics, a science-oriented, educational discipline first formulated by Alfred Korzybski, applies to a wide range of human activities: communication, evaluating, perception, problem-solving, inference-making, critical thinking, to name a few.

As a writer, you communicate. You communicate your view of the world, based on your assumptions, observations, inferences, and conclusions. General semantics offers a wealth of material for the writer because it helps you understand some of the processes underlying thinking, evaluating, and communicating.

Our publishing covers many areas, including:

- Humor
- Multi-Media
- Effective Writing
- Comment
- How to Apply General Semantics
- Book Reviews
- Self-Esteem
- Fiction
- Language & Behavior
- Education
- Research Results
- Self-improvement Through General Semantics
- Metaphor
- The Media
- Problem-Solving with General Semantics
- Popular Culture
- Critical Thinking
- Communication
- Science & Language
- The Press
- Psychology
- Folklore
- History of Thought
- Computers & Networks

We produce books on using and teaching general semantics, including a number of anthologies of original material and reprints from *ETC: A Review of General Semantics*. We use material from published and unpublished writers.

Preparing to Write

Read about general semantics. Before making submissions, study *ETC: A Review of General Semantics* in order to familiarize yourself with content and style.

Read some of the recent general semantics books, such as *Thinking and Living Skills: General Semantics for Critical Thinking, To Be or Not: An E-Prime Anthology*, and *More E-Prime: To Be or Not II*. The latter two books have examples of general semantics fiction.

Our anthologies now in print also include: *Classroom Exercises in General Semantics, Bridging Worlds Through General Semantics, Teaching General Semantics, Enriching Professional Skills Through General Semantics*.

Manuscripts Needed

We need material for a forthcoming anthology of general semantics-related fiction. We also need submissions for *ETC: A Review of General Semantics*. As we have done in the past, we may select material from *ETC: A Review of General Semantics* for reprinting in future anthologies. We will select some articles to put on our computer Bulletin Board System.

The Society, a nonprofit educational organization which exists to disseminate information related to general semantics, pays for publication with contributor's copies.

You may have noticed that we wrote these guidelines without *to be* verbs: *is, was, am, were, be, being, been*, etc. We call this variant of English *E-Prime*. Perhaps you heard about E-Prime on National Public Radio's *All Things Considered* or read about it in The *Atlantic Monthly* (February 1992). You may wish to find out how E-Prime can help improve your writing.

Preparing Submissions

When submitting your manuscript, please use standard ms. preparation: Submit two copies. We cannot accept handwritten submissions. Put your name, address, and phone number on the first page at top left. Keep length of ms. below 4,000 words. Include a biography of up to thirty words. For reference style, see copies of *ETC: A Review of General Semantics*. Please advise us if you have a word processing disk available.

If you would like a sample copy of *ETC: A Review of General Semantics,* please let us know.

Meanwhile, do the important thing—keep on writing!

Categories: Education—General Interest—Language—Literature—Psychology—Writing

Name: Jeremy Klein, Editor-in-Chief
Name: Paul D. Johnston, Managing Editor
Address: PO BOX 728
City/State/ZIP: CONCORD CA 94522
Telephone: 510-798-0311
Fax: 510-798-0312
E-mail: isgs@a.crl.com

Eternity Magazine Online
The Online Journal of the Speculative Imagination

Please refer to Eternity Press.

Eternity Press

PULP ETERNITY: [SF/F/H] Themed Issues, FNASR, Fiction under 2,500 words, firm. Pays 3 cents/word on publication. Quarterly full size magazine 48-64 pages, black and white. 2,000+ print run. Themes:

Pulp Eternity Volume 1
Time...A Retrospective
Short fiction only, no longer than 2,500 words.

The stories must adhere to the following format: Either the protagonist or antagonist must be an historic figure. The historic figure can be a politician, artist, writer, sports figure, entertainer, scientist, etc. They do not necessarily have to be the time traveler. Their actions, appearance and reactions must be consistent with the historical data about them. They must be an active participant in the story but *do not* have to be the point of view character. Short fiction only, no poetry or essays.

See below for manuscript submission details. Deadline for entries was March 1, 1998. The magazine premiered at Dragon*Con '98.

Pulp Eternity Volume 2
I Am Dragon

Short fiction must be under 2,500 words and be told from the point of view of a dragon. Other kinds of characters may appear in your stories, but a dragon must be the point of view character. The stories can be any flavor of the fantastic, and are not limited to traditional fantasy. Be creative, have fun, but research dragon lore for accuracy. Cybernetic dragons OK.

No nonfiction, poetry or essays. Deadline for entries was June 1, 1998, and the issue will be published in January of 1999.

Pulp Eternity Volume 3
Alternatives I

Eternity Press will dedicate every fourth issue to presenting the panorama of alternative sexuality in speculative fiction. To this end, stories for Alternatives I must contain at least one major character of alternative sexuality. The character or characters must be more than token additions to fit the guidelines. The sexuality issue must be at the heart of the conflict and resolution process. Stories dealing with the following types of characters and issues will be considered: Homosexual, bisexual, transgender, multi-gender or, perhaps, a new sexuality of your creation. You are not limited by genre here. Anything from hard science fiction to gothic to traditional fantasy will be considered. This is your chance to explore and create a new vision. Short fic-

tion must be under 2,500 words. No nonfiction, poetry or essays. Deadline for entries will be October 1, 1998, and will be published in May of 1999.

Pulp Eternity Volume 4
The Price of Magic

Short fiction must deal with the price paid for the use of magic, the more tragic and high the stakes, the better. Stories where the characters simply tire when they use their magic will have little chance for selection. Also, find new costs rather than limbs falling off or characters aging unless you can put a new spin on the familiar. Stories again must be under 2,500 words. No poetry or nonfiction will be considered for this issue. Deadline for entries will be January 10, 1999, and will be published August 1999.

Eternity, The Online Journal Of The Speculative Imagination

Eternity Magazine Online pays for quality works of fiction and verse from published and unpublished authors. All manner of speculative fiction considered. When in doubt, submit. We buy stories not names. 20,000 words maximum, under 5,000 words preferred.

Payment: *Eternity Online* pays from $2-30 for short stories. Each featured short story will also be eligible for our story of the year contest voted on by our readers. Our twelve monthly winners compete for publication of the winning story in Pulp Eternity ($50 payment), our sister print magazine. They will also be featured in our online publication and receive an invitation to contribute an original piece (subject to editing) to the *Pulp Eternity* issue of their choice.

Poetry: Short and epic poems of all types considered. Freeverse, rhyming. haiku, etc. with speculative themes are welcome. We also consider personal essays dealing with the fantastic, bizarre, paranormal, UFOs, witchcraft, the vampire lifestyle and fetish subjects.

Payment: $1 minimum, $5 maximum for poetry, shorts and essays.

Manuscripts

Standard manuscript format. Always include a cover letter. No handwritten manuscripts. Send SASE for reply. We prefer disposable manuscripts.

Electronic Submissions: You must include your real name, address, telephone number, and pen name, if you use one. You *must* include a cover letter. We are very open to new and established writers.

You can cut-and-paste electronic submissions into the body of an e-mail (preferred) or attach them as a separate ASCII text, rich text format, Works, WordPerfect, or Word file. One submission per e-mail, please. All other formats are not acceptable. You may also send your submission on disk to the snail mail address.

Due to the growing number of submissions, please submit only one fiction manuscript or no more than three poems at one time. Wait until a decision is made on your submission before sending another.

Acceptances and Rejections

Reading time varies. Current reading time is 30 days for the online publication, 60 for the print magazine. Because of the long lead times on some issues, response times will vary. We will try to report back within 90 days, if at all possible. Be patient, we'll be back with you as soon as we can. We will comment on every manuscript received. We hope that this criticism is constructive. We never attack the writer. Sometimes we will offer suggestions and ask for a rewrite. We will never send a form letter. You are too important to us.

Simultaneous and Reprints

We *do not* accept simultaneous submissions, and no longer accept reprints.

Categories: Fiction—Nonfiction—Fantasy—Gay/Lesbian—Horror—Poetry—Romance—Science Fiction—Short Stories

Name: Steve Algieri, Editor
Material: All
Address: PO BOX 930068
City/State/ZIP: NORCROSS GA 30003
Telephone: 770-934-6598
E-mail: eternityol@aol.com

Evangel

Evangel is a weekly publication of Light and Life Communications that is geared toward adults. All submissions should reflect the needs, interests, and struggles of adults striving to maintain a vital relationship with Christ in the midst of everyday experiences—or seeking to know Christ in these same experiences. (In general, stories should be aimed at young to middle-aged adults.)

We accept both fiction and nonfiction work. Material can range from first person stories to Christian growth and living articles to devotional articles. Material should not be preachy or overly predictable. First-time rights are preferred, although second rights and reprints will be considered.

Materials should be limited to 1,200 words or less. We can use a larger quantity of short articles compared to long ones.

Short anecdotes and humor articles are welcome, although use is less frequent. Poetry is used on a very limited basis.

SUBMISSIONS

In the *upper left-hand corner* of the first page, include your name, address, phone number and social security number. In the *upper right-hand corner*, specify the number of words in the manuscript, what rights you are offering and if the piece is fiction or nonfiction. One-third of the way down the page, give the manuscript title and your name. All subsequent material must be double-spaced, with one-inch margins. Number your pages.

Always include a word count, and a cover letter which introduces yourself and your work.

If you produce your material on computer please indicate what program and platform IBM/Mac) you use. If we accept your article, we may ask you to provide a computer disk. When preparing computer manuscripts:

- Do not justify margins.
- Use single spaces after periods and colons.
- Use tabs to begin paragraphs (not 5 spaces).

Allow six to eight weeks for response. Send seasonal material at least 9-12 months in advance.

PAYMENT

Rate of pay is four cents per word as published. Minimum payment is $10.00. Your check and complimentary copy are sent on publication.

PHOTOGRAPHY

Good-quality black-and-white or color photographs relating to your article are welcome. Rate of pay is $10.00 per selected photo. Include photo credit.

COMPLIMENTARY

If you would like to examine the style and content of *Evangel*, sample issues are available when [requests are] accompanied by a self-addressed, stamped envelope (business size).

MISSION STATEMENT

The *Evangel*, a weekly adult publication, seeks to increase the reader's understanding of the nature and character of God and the nature of a life lived under the lordship of Christ. Devotional in character, it directly and unashamedly lifts up Christ as the Source of salvation and hope.

Hints:

- *Evangel* is limited in space.
- Don't ramble, *stick* to your thesis or theme.
- Don't be *unnecessarily* redundant.

- Brevity and simplicity of content makes for a more readable piece.
- Material not accompanied by a self-addressed stamped envelope is not returned and may not receive a reply.
- Rhyming poetry is seldom seriously considered.
- Failure to include your social security number results in delayed payment of published piece.

Categories: Fiction—Nonfiction—Christian Interests—Inspirational

Name: Julie Innes, Editor
Material: All
Address: PO BOX 535002
City/State/ZIP: INDIANAPOLIS, IN 46254-5002
Telephone: 317-297-4131

Evergreen Chronicles

Evergreen Chronicles is a tri-annual literary journal, dedicated to presenting quality lesbian, gay, bisexual, and transgender literary and visual artists. What is revealed are the unique perspectives and sensibilities of GLBT communities as seen through their respective artistic creations: short stories and plays, journal work, poetry, experimental writing, pen and ink drawings, and black & white photographs. *Evergreen Chronicles* is published in April, July, and October.

SUBMISSION INFORMATION

We are interested in works by gay, lesbian, bisexual, and transgender artists in a wide variety of genres. We publish poetry, fiction, plays or performance art pieces, creative nonfiction, memoir, essays, book reviews, and experimental writing. *Evergreen* is off-set printed and perfect bound at 5-3/8"x8-3/8".

Writers and Artists Guidelines:

Please send **four copies** of your work.

Short stories or plays—send up to 25-page stories, with a limit of three stories.

Poetry—send up to ten pages total.

Artwork—submit clean copies up to 8½"x11". **Do not send originals. Artwork cannot be returned.**

Evergreen buys one-time rights. We pay a $50 honorarium and one copy upon publication. Editors read twice a year in January and July. Notification follows six weeks after deadline.

Deadlines for submissions are:

Spring issue-January 1

Fall issue-July 1

Special novella issue-September 30

Send a self-addressed stamped postcard for notification of receipt of manuscript. Send another SASE for decision notification and a short biographical paragraph describing yourself and your work.

SUBSCRIPTION INFORMATION

Individual Subscription
One year-$20 Two year-$38
International Subscription (outside USA)
One year-$25 Two year-$45
Institutional Subscription
One year-$40 Two year-$75
Single issues & back issues
$7.95 ($5.00 pre-l990) plus $3.00 shipping and handling.
Send check or money order payable to *Evergreen Chronicles*.

Categories: Arts—Gay/Lesbian—Literature—Poetry

Name: Louisa Castner, Managing Editor
Material: All Entries, Manuscripts
Address: PO BOX 8939
City/State/ZIP: MINNEAPOLIS MN 55408-0939
Telephone: 612-823-6638
Fax: 612-722-9005
E-mail: evgrnchron@aol.com

Evolving Woman

Evolving Woman

Dear Writer:

Thank you for your interest in *Evolving Woman*. We are a monthly magazine published in the Kansas City area for women who are on an inner journey toward wholeness. We publish articles on spirituality, psychology, inner growth and self-actualization.

We are always seeking articles from interested free-lance writers and welcome your submission. In addition to feature articles, we encourage you to send submissions for our departments. Departments include Body, Mind & Soul which covers issues such as health, fitness and relaxation; Reflections, a back-page department that usually focuses on peace and serenity and is intended to give the reader a final thought to ponder; Journaling and Meditations.

Although *Evolving Woman* can afford to pay its freelance writers only a token fee of $10, there are many benefits to writing for this new magazine. In addition to the small fee, you will receive a byline, a bioline and credit in the masthead. We provide an excellent opportunity for inexperienced writers to gain valuable experience, get published and to get the all-important clips portfolio built. In addition, we offer some freelancers the opportunity to contribute regularly through assignments.

Below you will find a list of guidelines and style for the magazine. Please do not hesitate to send any manuscript that you feel would benefit our readers. If you have any questions or desire additional information please write us.

We look forward to working with you.

Sincerely,

Jill Borders, Publisher

Guidelines & Style Sheet for Submissions

Guidelines:

• Double space all manuscripts. Include your name, address and phone number in the top left of the first page.

• On subsequent pages type your last name, page number and slug in the upper left corner.

• Do not staple pages.

• Feature articles should run 1,200-2,000 words. (There may be exceptions with prior editorial approval.)

• Department articles should run approximately 500-800 words.

• You may write your own titles and subheads. However, these are also subject to editing.

• Please include your bioline. (Example: "Jane Doe is a freelance writer from New York city.")

• All feature articles must have, as a minimum, three to five (3-5) live sources. There may be fewer (with prior editorial approval) for department pieces.

• We do not accept simultaneous submissions.

• All work will be returned for re-writes if necessary and the final submission will be edited.

• We reserve the right to edit all material.

• All submissions (unsolicited and assigned) must include a list of sources as follows: Live sources include: source's name, address, phone number and date and mode (telephone, live, etc.) of interview. Written sources include: title, author, publisher (or publication) and publication date.

Style:

• We prefer anecdotal leads, however, this is not an absolute necessity.

• First name on second reference except when referring to an expert or professional. (Example: "Susan says..." but "Dr. Jones says...")

• When introducing a quote use present tense "says."

• In all other matters follow AP style.

Categories: New Age—Psychology—Spiritual—Women's Issues

Name: Submissions Editor
Material: All
Address: PO BOX 73
City/State/ZIP: GARDNER KS 66030
Telephone: 913-856-7491

Eye

Frequency: Bimonthly

EYE is both a vital information trove and a hot-wired pop-culture joyride. EYE juxtaposes an exposé of the pet food industry with a fond look back at '70s bug movies. The Federal Reserve conspiracy with *Scooby Doo* revisionism. A dissenting view of Mother Teresa with Jack Chick's kooky Christian comics.

EYE appeals to everyone who wants useful information in a fun, dynamic package. EYE examines pop culture, industry scams, music, technology, retro TV, fringe culture, B-movies, toys, bizarre science, and unspoken histories.

Articles on the following topics are of interest to us...

conspiracies

technology

drugs

retro TV and vintage film

sciences

fringe culture

animals

atrocities

cults/religions/paranormalities

medicine

kitsch

myths/fairy tales/lore

STYLE AND TONE: Sharp, hip, fast-paced, and succinct: tight writing that's highly readable and appealing. Needless repetitive, repetitive repetition and redundant redundancy causes ZZzzzz. (Some caustic humor now and then is never bad, either).

LENGTH: 1,500 to 2,000 words is usually optimal.

LEGAL STUFF: EYE reserves the right to edit and shorten works if necessary. Writers retain all rights to his or her piece.

ART: Black-and-white photos are *always* needed and appreciated. Let us know if you need them back. Provide proper credits and any information that should be included in captions.

RESOURCES: Please provide resources such as books, magazines, web sites, etc. where EYE's readers can learn more about the topics that you write about.

PAY: EYE pays $150 to $200, depending on the piece. We pay upon publication and send three copies. Submissions via e-mail or diskette (either Mac or IBM) are *extremely* appreciated.

We strongly suggest that you actually see an issue of EYE before contacting us. Sample copies are available at your local newsstand or directly from EYE for US$3.95.

If you are interested in writing for EYE, please do not phone. Instead, submit a query via e-mail or regular mail with a SASE and we will respond promptly.

Lisa Crosby
Editor/Publisher
Categories: Nonfiction—Culture—Entertainment—Film/
Video—General Interest—Internet—Lifestyles—Paranormal—
Psychology—Science—Society—Technology—Television/Radio

Name: Submissions Editor
Material: All
Address: 301 S ELM ST
City/State/ZIP: GREENSBORO NC 27401-2636
Telephone: 910-370-1702
Fax: 910-370-1603
E-mail: eye@nr.infi.net

Faces
The Magazine About People

General Information: Lively, original approaches to the subject are the primary concerns of the editors in choosing material. Writers are encouraged to study recent back issues for content and style. (Sample issue is available at $4.50. Send 7½"x10½" (or larger) self-addressed stamped ($2.00) envelope.) **All material must relate to the theme of a specific upcoming issue in order to be considered.** FACES purchases all rights to material.

Procedure: A query must consist of all of the following to be considered: a brief cover letter stating the subject and word length of the proposed article; a detailed one-page outline explaining the information to be presented in the article; an extensive bibliography of materials the author intends to use in preparing the article (if appropriate); a self-addressed stamped envelope. Writers new to FACES should send a writing sample with the query. Manuscripts should include final word count. Authors are requested to supply a 2- to 3-line biographical sketch.

Articles must be submitted on disk using a word processing program (preferably Microsoft Word-Mac). Text should be saved as ASCII text (in MS Word as "text only"). Disks should be either Mac- (preferred) or DOS-compatible 3½".

Guidelines
• *Feature articles*, about 800 words. Includes in-depth nonfiction and personal accounts. Pays $.20-$.25 per printed word.
• *Supplemental nonfiction*, 300-600 words. Includes subjects directly and indirectly related to the theme. Editors like little-known information but encourage writers not to overlook the obvious. Pays $.20-$.25 per printed word.
• *Fiction*, up to 800 words. Retold legends, folktales, stories from around the world, etc., relating to the theme. Pays $.20-$.25 per printed word.
• *Activities*, up to 700 words. Includes crafts, games, recipes, projects, etc., that can be done either by children alone or with adult supervision. Should be accompanied by sketches and description of how activity relates to the theme. Pays on an individual basis.
• *Poetry*, up to 100 lines. Clear, objective imagery. Serious and light verse considered. Pays on an individual basis. Must relate to theme.
• *Puzzles and Games (no word finds)*. Crossword and other word puzzles using the vocabulary of the issue's theme. Mazes and picture puzzles that relate to the theme. Pays on an individual basis.

PHOTO GUIDELINES
To be considered for publication, photographs must relate to a specific theme. Writers are encouraged to submit available photos with their query or article. We buy one-time use.

Our suggested fee range for professional quality photographs* follows:

1/4 page to full page
b/w $15 to $100
color $25 to $100
*Please note that fees for non-professional quality photographs are negotiated.
• Cover fees are set on an individual basis for one-time use, plus promotional use. All cover images are color.
• Color transparencies, slides, and color prints can be submitted for inside black/white use since they can be scanned at the printer.
• Prices set by museums, societies, stock photography houses, etc., are paid or negotiated. Photographs that are promotional in nature (e.g., from tourist agencies, organizations, special events, etc.) are usually submitted at no charge.
• If you have photographs pertaining to any upcoming theme, please contact the editor by mail or fax, or send them with your query. You may also send images on speculation.
Note: Queries may be submitted at any time, but queries sent well in advance of deadline **may not be answered for several months.** Go-aheads requesting material proposed in queries are usually sent five months prior to publication date. Unused queries will be returned approximately three to four months prior to publication date.
Categories: Children—Culture—Juvenile—Multicultural—Young Adult

Name: Lynn Sloneker, Editor
Material: World Cultures for Kids 8-14
Address: 7 SCHOOL ST
City/State/ZIP: PETERBOROUGH NH 03458
Telephone: 603-924-7209
Fax: 603-924-7380

Family Circle

Dear Reader:

Writers are sometimes surprised to find out that most of the articles FAMILY CIRCLE publishes are written by freelance writers. We are always looking for new contributors.

If you want to submit an article proposal to **FAMILY CIRCLE,** please pay careful attention to the following points:

1. Take a close look at **FAMILY CIRCLE** for some knowledge of format and an understanding of subjects we have tackled in the past, remembering that we are a general interest women's magazine which focuses on the family. We are looking for family-oriented stories with strong plot lines and characters with whom an audience composed primarily of women would identify. We are especially interested in women who make a difference in their community, news and information on health, childcare, relationships, finances and other matters of concern to today's family, and dramatic personal experiences.

2. Submit a detailed outline first, and include a brief cover letter describing your publishing history with two representative clips. Remember to consider our lead time (usually three months) when proposing articles; for example, we finish our back-to-school issue in June and our Christmas issue in September.

3. Maximum length for articles is 2,500 words.

4. Though we try to review queries quickly, please be patient. We receive thousands of proposals per year and we consider them all very carefully before making decisions.

Query individual category editors listed on masthead.

Thank you for your interest.

Sincerely,
THE EDITORS
Categories: Childcare—Personal Experiences—Family—General Interest (women)—Health—Money/Finance—Relationships

Name: Appropriate Editor From Masthead
Material: As appropriate
Address: 375 LEXINGTON AVE
City/State/ZIP: NEW YORK NY 10017-5514
Telephone: 212-499-2000

The Family Digest

Thank you for your interest in our bimonthly publication. This writer's guidelines is yours to keep in your writer's portfolio. It outlines our editorial needs and requirements for this parish-oriented publication.

Types of articles we're looking for:

The Family Digest is dedicated to the joy and fulfillment of Catholic family life. *The Family Digest* is looking for articles of interest to the Catholic family, particularly in its relationship to the Catholic parish. We are especially looking for upbeat articles which affirm the simple ways in which the Catholic faith is expressed in daily life.

Article topics include:

• Family life
• Seasonal
• Parish life
• Prayer
• Spiritual life
• Inspiration
• Church traditions
• How-to

Word length and seasonal articles:

Writers are encouraged to submit articles between 700 to 1,200 words in length. *The Family Digest* prefers to purchase and publish previously unpublished articles, but will consider previously published pieces. Please include the publication history with your article submission. Articles on seasonal or holiday themes should be submitted seven months prior to date of issue. *The Family Digest* does NOT publish poetry or fiction.

Rates of payment:
• Articles: 5 cents per word
• Cartoons: $20.00
• Humorous anecdotes: $10.00 for exclusive, unusual stories drawn from personal experiences (25 to 125 words)

The Family Digests pays for accepted articles, cartoons and anecdotes within one month of acceptance.

Response time:

Writers can expect to hear back on submitted articles within four to eight weeks. Due to the sheer volume of manuscripts received, personalized replies are not possible.

Reading the articles published in *The Family Digest* will give you the best sense of the types of articles *The Family Digest* accepts.

Best wishes in your writing efforts!

Categories: Nonfiction—Cartoons—Catholic Parish Life—Catholic Traditions—Christian Interests—Family—Inspirational—Marriage—Parenting—Religion

Name: Corine B. Erlandson, Editor
Material: All
Address: PO BOX 40137
City/State/ZIP: FORT WAYNE IN 46804

Remember: Editors change jobs and publishers change addresses. It is wise to invest in a phone call for the current information before submitting.

FamilyFun

E-L

FamilyFun

Thank you for inquiring about freelance opportunities at *FamilyFun*. We are a national service magazine for parents of children ages three to twelve and we cover all the great things families can do together: educational projects, holiday celebrations, crafts, travel, cooking, and more. Our goal is to provide our readers with all of the practical information, plus related books and contact phone numbers, they need to carry out ideas for having fun together with their own resources. Issues are scheduled and assigned several months in advance of their cover date.

Queries should describe the content, structure, and tone of the article. Since we receive many queries on the same topics, please be as specific as possible about what makes your idea unique. With each query, please enclose two or three relevant clips for our review. We're sorry, but we no longer accept unsolicited manuscripts for feature stories. We will continue to accept manuscripts for the following departments: Traveler, Almanac, Family Ties and My Great Idea (Please note department on envelope). We generally take four to eight weeks to respond and regret that we cannot, under any circumstance, consider queries over the telephone.

FEATURES:

We look for stories that are fun for the whole family, inexpensive, and easy to plan. Topics that we cover include travel, food, crafts, activities, games, and educational projects. *FamilyFun*'s style is upbeat and straightforward with an emphasis on play. Features generally run 850 to 3,000 words and pay $1 per word.

DEPARTMENTS

FAMILY ALMANAC provide readers with simple, quick, practical, inexpensive ideas and projects (outings, crafts, games, nature activities, learning projects, and cooking with children). It is direct and cheerful in tone and is seldom written in the first person. We read both freelance manuscripts and queries for **FAMILY ALMANAC**. Pieces are assigned from 200 to 600 words at $.50 per word. We also pay $75 for ideas in the event that we decide to use a staff writer.

FAMILY TRAVELER consists of brief, newsy items about family travel—what's new, what's great, and especially, what's a good deal. This section is informative and direct in tone and covers very specific topics (e.g. a new program at one hotel, rather than a round-up of hotels around the country). We cover resort news, festivals, museum exhibits, outdoor outfitters, specialized travel agencies, educational trips and programs. Because we are budget-conscious, we rarely cover international travel or expensive American resorts or programs. We read freelance manuscripts for **FAMILY TRAVELER** and pay $100 for 100 to 125-word pieces. We also pay $50 for ideas in the event that we decide to use a staff writer.

FAMILY TIES is a first-person column that spotlights some aspect of family life that is humorous, inspirational, or interesting. At the heart of each essay is the emotional relationship between the writer and his or her children. This is a chance for the magazine to get personal and to provide an editorial pause in the magazine otherwise packed with ideas. **FAMILY TIES** runs 1,500 words and pays $1,500.

MY GREAT IDEA explains fun and inventive ideas that have worked for a writer's own family. Examples from previous issues include a game that gets children excited about visiting art museums, a fourth grade letter-writing project that teaches writing skills, and a kid's home lab that ignites interest in learning about science. The simpler and more clever the idea, the better. The column runs 800 to 1,000 words, and pays $750 upon acceptance. We consider ideas in query, letter or manuscript form.

In addition, we publish the best letters from writers and readers following the column. **MY GREAT IDEA LETTERS** run 100 to 150 words and pay $25 upon publication. Please address your submissions to **MY GREAT IDEAS** Editor.

We will announce in the magazine any invitations for photographic submissions. If you would like to send copies of slides that you think we should consider publishing, please direct them to Dave Kendrick, Art Director. Do not send any slides or photographs that you wish to have returned.

If you would like to receive a sample copy ($3 per copy) or to order a subscription for *FamilyFun* Magazine (a 1-year subscription costs $14.95), please call 1-800-289-4849 or write to the address below.

Categories: Family

Name: Clare Ellis, Editor
Material: General
Name: Deborah Geigis Berry, Travel Editor
Material: Travel
Name: Cindy Littlefield, Associate Editor
Address: 244 MAIN ST
City/State/ZIP: NORTHAMPTON MA 01060
Telephone: 413-585-0444
Fax: 413-586-5724
E-mail: Letters@familyfun.com
Internet: www.familyfun.com

Family Life

Thank you for your interest in writing for *Family Life*.

Our readers are parents of children ages 3-12 who are interested in raising their kids in the most educational, innovative environment available today. Most are college educated and work hard at a full-time job. We want fresh articles dealing with the day-to-day issues that these families face, with personal insight and professional opinion on how to handle them.

Our "Family Matters" section in the front of the book consists of newsy shorts on noteworthy individuals, new educational programs, cool travel destinations and the latest on health issues; pieces run from 150-250 words.

Individual columns run from 1,000-1,500 words, and are divided accordingly: "First Thoughts" is our first-person essay about life with children. "A Child's Eye" discusses the personal issues children face while growing up; "Family Affairs" deals with those issues which crop up in a couple's relationship as parents. "School Smart" discusses today's educational issues. "Family Strategist" deals with family financing. "House Calls" is our health column and "Chip Chat" addresses the latest in family computing.

Features run from 2,000-3,500 words. We prefer a written proposal of your idea, accompanied with several previously published clips and a self-addressed, stamped envelope for our response.

The Children's Hour reviews books, videos, TV, movies, music, software and other entertainment for children or parents. Please send information or review items to the attention of The Children's Hour editor.

We appreciate you interest in *Family Life*.
Categories: Nonfiction—Children—Parenting

Name: Peter Herbst, Editor-in-Chief

Material: All
Address: 1633 BROADWAY
City/State/ZIP: NEW YORK NY 10019
Telephone: 212-767-4918
Fax: 212-489-4561
E-mail: familylife@aol.com

Family Safety and Health

Writing Style
• Keep your writing positive, upbeat and simple. Write at a 9th-grade reading level and be creative. We would rather have to tone down your writing than spice it up.
• Write creative lead paragraphs to draw readers into the article. Stick to your word count. Write tight, clear sentences.
• Write in the active voice with present-tense attribution. (Passive example: Skin cancer can be treated easily if caught early, Smith said. Better: It's easy to treat skin cancer if you catch it early, Smith says.)
• Minimize gerunds and participles. An overuse of these -ing words usually occurs when action is taking place in the writing without any actor. When no actors perform the action, less concrete writing results and readers lose interest. Example: "Keeping a healthy and safe home is not an easy initiative." Better: "It isn't always easy to keep your home healthy and safe."
• Avoid sexist language. Usually, you can avoid the "he or she" problem if you structure the sentence to use the plural "their."
• Use the *Associated Press Stylebook* for journalistic style.
• If you refer to somebody and don't refer to them again for at least four paragraphs, re-reference that person. Example: "Healthy Medical College's Smith says that...."
• Put parentheses around area codes in phone numbers. Example: (630) 775-2286 or (800) 775-2286.
• It's the National Safety Council on first reference and the Council on second reference. (Unless it's four paragraphs away or more.)
• Capitalize people's titles only when you put them before their name. Examples: National Safety Council President John Smith. Or, John Smith, National Safety Council president.
• Use commas in a series only in complicated phrases. Simple-series example: I like dogs, cats and all animals. Complicated-series example: I like dogs who chew on grass that people grow, cats that grew up on the city's south side, and all types of animals that come from small rural towns.
• Italicize the names of books, journals, magazines and other publications.
• We send all articles and departments to in-house or outside experts for technical review. We might ask you to follow up on technical-review questions or concerns.
• Refer to doctors on second reference by their last names only. First reference example: Dr. John Smith of Healthy Medical College. Second reference: Smith. If the two references are four paragraphs away or more, re-identify the person on second reference.
Sources
• Interview expert sources and non-experts with varying views, such as real people who have experience with a certain topic. This offers different perspectives and helps create a multidimensional article.
• Source review: Our policy is to allow sources to review their quotes before publication if they so request. You don't need to volunteer that service if a source doesn't request it.
• Document all statistics. Use National Safety Council statistics when possible.
Use of Quotations
• Try not to overquote a single source. Rule of thumb: More

than two or three direct quotes from one source is usually too much.

• Make indirect quotations of statements that are not truly quoteworthy. For example, it would not be quoteworthy to state: She said, "I don't agree." Better: She said she didn't agree.

Library Resources

• Feel free to contact the National Safety Council Library at (630) *775-2199*. Let them know you are writing an article for FAMILY SAFETY AND HEALTH. The librarians can do a computer search of background information and send you a printout.

• After you receive the printout, you can ask the librarians to send you copies of the articles listed, within reason.

Format

• Please supply three headlines with your article.

• To add variety to the magazine, FAMILY SAFETY AND HEALTH offers readers a variety of article formats. Follow the format outlined in your assignment letter.

• Include catchy subheads within the text body to draw readers in. Use verbs in your subheads when possible.

• When you write a sidebar, assume that readers might not read the main article. Therefore, refer to all sources with their full titles. Insert "boiler" paragraphs to explain terms or concepts that appear in the main article.

• Provide a list of addresses for sources quoted in the article. That way, we can send all sources a copy of the published article.

• Please don't indent your paragraphs—this confuses our computer program. Separate each paragraph with an extra return. Single space between lines. Use only one space after periods.

• Submit work on an IBM-compatible disk in WordPerfect (any version) or in ASCII. If you use a Macintosh, please save your file in ASCII. Or you can e-mail to the address below.

Artwork

• Solicit free art or photography from sources. Ask sources for color transparencies, slides or high-quality prints. We will add $50 to your final payment for each photo or other artwork you provide that is printed with the article.

Invoice Procedures

• Payment is made on acceptance. Typically, it takes approximately 60 days for our Accounting Department to process your payment.

• Please send an invoice directly to the editor who assigned you the article. Provide an invoice number, the issue the article is for (e.g., Fall 1997 FAMILY SAFETY AND HEALTH), the purchase-order number and the date that you turned in your article.

• Bill us for the minimum amount for the article. Articles must be on time and be of superior quality (as determined by the editors) to be eligible for an incentive.

• We reimburse writers for reasonable phone and fax expenses. Include this amount to your total bill. If your expenses exceed $50, submit your phone bill to your editor as documentation. We will determine if the excess is reasonable and make payment accordingly.

If you have any questions, please give us a call.

And good luck with your article!

Categories: Health

Name: Sharon R. Lewis, Associate Editor
Name: Laura Coyne, Editor
Material: Any
Address: 1121 SPRING LAKE DR
City/State/ZIP: ITASCA IL 60143
Telephone: 800-621-7615
Fax: 630-775-2285

Family Therapy
The Journal of the California Graduate School of Family Psychology

The editor welcomes succinct, well-written papers within the broad field of family and marital therapy. Clinical articles devoted to techniques, and richly endowed with illustrative dialogue, are most highly regarded.

MANUSCRIPTS, REFERENCES AND REPRINTS: Manuscripts must be type-written in duplicate. All manuscripts must include an abstract of 100-150 words and typed on a separate sheet of paper. Footnotes, charts, tables, graphs, etc. should be kept to a minimum and submitted in the original, camera-ready copy. (We prefer that, when practical, the information contained in this material be incorporated into the text instead.) References to books and articles should appear at the end of the manuscript under the heading "References," with items listed alphabetically by name of author.

Authors will be furnished galley proofs which must be returned to the editor within two days. Corrections should be kept to a minimum. A schedule of reprint costs and an order blank for reprints will be sent with galley proofs.

SUBSCRIPTIONS: All business communications, including subscriptions, renewals, and remittances should be addressed to:
Libra Publishers, Inc.
3089C Clairemont Dr., Suite 383
San Diego, CA 92117
SUBSCRIPTION RATES
Individuals-U.S.A.: One year $62; Two years $122; Three years $182 Other countries: One year $69; Two years $136; Three years $203
Institutions-U.S.A.: One year $70; Two years $138; Three years $206 Other countries: One year $75; Two years $148; Three years $221
Copies of current or back issues are available at $22.00 each from Libra Publishers.

Categories: Family and Marital Therapy

Name: Martin G. Blinder, M.D., Editor
Material: All
Address: 50 IDALIA RD
City/State/ZIP: SAN ANSELMO CA 94960

Fan
A Baseball Literary Magazine

FAN Magazine is a quarterly collection of writings and drawings that celebrate the game of baseball. Each issue includes selected essays, poetry, short fiction and original Illustrations. Some issues carry specific themes or reflect a particular season of the year.

In selecting material for FAN, we are drawn to that which reveals something about the contributor's own connection to baseball. We like work that evokes memories, that somehow conveys a personal view of baseball's timeless qualities. We prefer polished material, of course, but sometimes we will work with a rougher piece if it promises a credible story rooted in emotional authenticity.

Some specific requirements:

• Prose pieces should contain fewer that 1,500 words.

• Poetry should be brief; 30 lines is a suggested maximum length.

• Very brief musings and untitled poems are collected for Mudville Diary. Each piece contains fewer than 300 words. Many are excerpted from longer submissions.

• Artwork should be line art (as opposed to half-tone), one color, and of a size to fit easily within the size of the magazine. (5½"x8½")

• All written material should be typed, and all excepting poetry should be double-spaced. Prose pieces should include a word count. All sub-missions should include a brief biographical note.

As payment, contributors will receive copies of FAN.

Thanks for your interest in FAN.

The Editors.

Categories: Fiction—Nonfiction—Family—General Interest—History—Inspirational—Literature—Poetry—Relationships—Short Stories—Sports

Name: Mike Schacht, Publisher/Editor
Material: All
Address: 145 15TH ST NE STE 805
City/State/ZIP: ATLANTA GA 30361
Telephone: 404-607-9489

Fast and Healthy Magazine

Fast and Healthy Magazine is a family-oriented food magazine with healthful recipes for active people. Its emphasis is on Monday through Friday cooking. All recipes can be prepared in about 30 minutes or less and meet the U.S. Dietary Guidelines for healthful eating. *Fast and Healthy Magazine*'s editorial reinforces the health and convenience aspects of the recipes.

If you are interested in proposing an article for *Fast and Healthy*, please consider the following:

• CONTENT - *Fast and Healthy* is a mainstream magazine about everyday healthful cooking; it is not a diet magazine or a gourmet cooking magazine. The majority of *Fast and Healthy*'s features and departments are comprised of recipes with supporting editorial. The editorial is consumer-oriented with news and tips about quick and healthy cooking. We occasionally include non-recipe articles that also focus on quick meat preparation and healthy cooking and lifestyles. Article length can range from 200 to 1,500 words, but most often the editorial is short and is divided into smaller blocks of information, with frequent use of sidebars and charts.

• STYLE - Our editorial voice is upbeat, friendly, straight-forward and consumer-oriented.

• STORY IDEAS - While feature ideas are generated by the editors, we are open to proposals from experienced writers or writer/recipe developers. Please do not send completed manuscripts. Instead, present your idea in a concise paragraph or two and accompany it with a resume and representative clips. If you are experienced in recipe development and are proposing recipe ideas, please keep in mind that recipes must meet our nutrition and time criteria to be accepted. (Detailed information is pro-

vided to those given an assignment.)

• RIGHTS/PAYMENT - We buy all rights to editorial material and recipes. We pay upon acceptance. Rates vary depending on length and difficulty of the assignment. A kill fee of 20% is offered.

• SAMPLE COPIES - A sample copy is available for $3 from the address below. (Fast and Healthy Magazine also is available on newsstands.)

Thank you for your interest in *Fast and Healthy Magazine*.

Categories: Cooking—Food/Drink—Health—Nonfiction

Name: Editor
Material: All
Address: 200 S. 6th St., M.S. 28M7
City/State/ZIP: Minneapolis, MN 55402
Telephone: 612-330-4475
Fax: 612- 330-4875

Farmer's Market
Elgin Community College

1. Writers may submit up to 30 pages of prose, 6 poems.

2. Copy should be clean: typewritten or letter-quality printout. Photocopies are acceptable. Double space prose. If your manuscript is selected for publication, we can also use computer files: Macintosh 3.5" disk, most word processing programs; or ASCII from DOS.

3. A SASE must be enclosed for notification or return of manuscript.

4. Previously published materials will not be considered. We strongly discourage simultaneous submissions.

5. The editors suggest reading the magazine to determine the appropriateness of submissions. We are not a market for sentimental pastorals, nor are we limited in scope to rural stories or poems about tractors and livestock.

6. Payment is in two copies of the magazine in which the writer's or artist's work is published and a one-year subscription. Additional copies of the issue may be purchased at a reduced rate by contributors.

7. Our reading period is from March-May for our Fall/Winter issue; from September-November for our Spring/Summer issue. Writers whose work has been accepted for publication will be notified no later than two weeks following the conclusion of the reading period.

8. Artwork should be black-and-white; vertical format preferred.

Categories: Fiction—Literature—Poetry—Short Stories

Name: Joanne Lowery, Poetry Editor
Material: Poetry
Name: Rachael Tecza, Fiction Editor
Material: All Prose Fiction
Address: ELGIN COMMUNITY COLLEGE
Address: 1700 SPARTAN DR
City/State/ZIP: ELGIN IL 60123-7193
Telephone: 847-697-1000 ext. 7265
Fax: 847-888-7995

FATE

FATE
True Reports of the Strange & Unknown

Thank you for your interest in writing for FATE. We've prepared these guidelines to show you what we look for and to help you submit manuscripts that are likely to be considered for publication. Please be aware than we cannot accept every good article we receive; we simply don't have enough pages.

Submit your article along with the attached author information form. Because of the volume of submissions we receive, you can expect to wait one to several months for a response.

FATE magazine does not publish book-length manuscripts, but our parent company does. If you want to submit a book, please [refer to Llewellyn Publications, elsewhere in this book].

QUERIES

If you plan to submit a full-length feature article, we encourage you to query us first. This will save both of us time if your article is not on a topic we currently seek. Queries are not necessary for briefs, fillers, or items for "My Proof of Survival" and "True Mystic Experiences."

TOPICS

FATE magazine reports a wide variety of strange and unknown phenomena. We are open to receiving any well-written, well—documented article. (FATE does not publish poetry or fiction, however.) Our readers especially like reports of current investigations, experiments, theories, and experiences. Here is a partial list of typical FATE subjects:

• **Psychic Phenomena** Dreams, prophecies, telekinesis.

• **Recent Fortean Phenomena** Strange creatures, mysterious events, unexplained coincidences.

• **Life After Death** Near—death experiences, mediumship, spirit contact, reincarnation, astral travel, and other proof of life after death.

• **Healing** Alternative healing systems and experiences, including acupuncture, herbalism, and psychic techniques.

• **Ghosts and Hauntings** Experiences and investigations of ghosts, hauntings, and poltergeists.

• **Scientific Breakthroughs** Including free energy, new discoveries about matter, lost continents, ley lines, and mind machines.

• **Recent UFO Occurrences** UFO sightings, encounters, abductions, activity, investigations, and disclosures.

• **How-To** Healing, divination, mediumship, dowsing, ghost hunting, spiritual growth. Practical applications of astrology, dream analysis, graphology, visualization, and the like.

• **Sacred, Mystic, and Historic Sites** Modern archaeological discoveries and reinterpretations of old ones, the true stories behind myths and folklore, and ancient religions and cultures.

• **Spirituality** Alternative forms of spirituality.

DEPARTMENTS

True Mystic Experiences and My Proof of Survival

Articles for "True Mystic Experiences" and "My Proof of Survival" departments should be fewer than 500 words.

These should recount personal mystic or psychic experiences of the writer, or the writer's experience that proves survival after death, such as an encounter with a dead relative. All the details described must be true. If your account is accepted for publication, you will be required to send a notarized affidavit attesting that the incident described is true.

"True Mystic Experiences" and "My Proof of Survival" con-tributors should include a photo of themselves. Photos should be at least 3"x5", either color or black and white. We will return photos unharmed after publication.

Many photos we receive are poor quality. They are too small, too dark, or have other problems that make them difficult to reproduce in the magazine. Make sure your picture has good contrast and detail. A plain background is best. Make sure your face shows and is not shadowed by hats or trees, and that glasses don't create a glare. Photocopies, pictures cut from larger photos, large group shots in which you are one tiny face among many, and I.D. cards are not acceptable. If you hove a photo that contains other people, send the whole photo, but clearly indicate which person is you. Do not use scissors to trim the photo; our graphics designer will "cut you out" electronically. If you have no photo of yourself, you might find a friend with a camera to take one or two snapshots of you, preferably against a plain background. You could also go to one of the inexpensive photo booths often found in drugstores.

Payment for "True Mystic Experiences" and "My Proof of Survival" is $25, including the use of the photograph.

PHOTOS AND ARTWORK

We want FATE to be as visually appealing as possible. Articles with accompanying photographs and illustrations are more likely to be accepted and published faster.

• Articles, illustrations, and photos must be legally reproducible. If you are using illustrations, photos, or text from other published sources, they may fall under copyright law. You are responsible for obtaining permissions for use from either the publisher or copyright holder before the manuscript is accepted for publication. We cannot assume items are in the public domain unless you tell us so and give the source and year of publication.

• We prefer quality black and white or color photos.

• Attach a slip of paper to the back of photos and illustrations, with your name, the story title, and captions.

• Keep copies in case of loss.

STYLE

Write to Entertain and Inform

Articles should be lively, personal, and informative. They should play up the wonder of the subject matter and/or develop practical benefits. Avoid academic-style writing, and please be aware that we rarely publish theoretical articles.

Although FATE publishes relatively brief articles, we look for depth of content. We rarely want round-ups that merely list a variety of sightings or events. In general, it is best to focus on one event or type of event, or one time period, and provide convincing detail. Let the reader feel what it was like to be at the event.

LENGTH

• Feature articles should run 1,500 to 3,000 words.

• Briefs are 500 to 1,000 words.

• Fillers are less than 500 words and are used when a tidbit is needed to fill the page. Short fillers of 150 words or less are particularly welcome.

TRUTHFULNESS

FATE is nonfiction. All articles should be documented in these ways:

• Personal experience articles should include full details of names, dates, times, and places. Although some of this material may be withheld from publication if you specifically request it, we must have it all correctly documented for our files.

• You may be asked to provide contact information for all participants if you have not included it with the article. You may be asked for a sworn and notarized statement from yourself and other participants or witnesses verifying facts described. You will be reimbursed for this cost after publication if you provide a copy of your receipt.

• Sources for quotes and unusual information must be footnoted or be given in the body of your manuscript, although we may choose not to use this information in the published article.

• Articles that are not based on personal experience should include a bibliography. References should include author, title, publisher, and place and date of publication. If sources are other than published works (i.e. personal research or interviews), this too should be detailed.

FORMAT

• Include the author information form [below] with your submission.

• We encourage e-mail submissions or submissions on 3½" Macintosh or PC disks. Label disks with your name, article title, whether the disk is Macintosh or PC, and the word processing program used. If you are using an unusual word processing program, save it as a plain text or ASCII file. Include a printed copy of the article.

• On the first page, include your full name, address, and phone number.

• Place identification at the top of each page. Include your name, the article's title, and page numbers.

• Faxed articles are not acceptable unless we specifically ask you to fax a piece.

• If return postage is not included and your submission is not accepted, you will receive notification but your article will be discarded.

PAYMENT

• The standard rate of pay for feature articles is 10 cents per word in U.S. currency, payable after publication. FATE does not pay kill fees if an article is not used, except for contracted, assigned articles where an arrangement has been specified, in writing, in advance.

• Payment for "*True* Mystic Experiences" and "My Proof of Survival" is $25, including the use of the photograph, which will be returned.

• Photos and illustrations that accompany news and feature articles will be paid for after publication, at a rate of $10 per item. (We do not pay for the use of contributor's photos in True Mystic Experiences and My Proof of Survival.) Photo use will be determined by the graphics designer and will depend in part on space availability and quality of the photos or illustrations.

• We will send you three copies of the issue in which your feature article appears, with a coupon enabling you to buy additional copies at a discount price.

POLICIES

• FATE normally purchases the right to assign copyright and all rights, literary, electronic, and otherwise, to all articles and photos we accept. FATE generally retains all rights to the articles, illustrations, and photographs that we publish. This entitles FATE to use the article again, in print or in any other media, including but not limited to radio, film, and electronic media. It does not prevent you from sending a substantially different article on the same subject to another publication.

• We like to see our writers published! If you are having a book published that includes material from an article you have published in FATE, write to us, giving details, and we will send you written authorization to use the article at no charge as long as FATE is credited as the original source (month and year of issue).

• If you have questions about this policy or about re-selling your work elsewhere, please write to us with your specific question and we will send a detailed reply.

• Original manuscripts, photographs, illustrations, documentation, etc., that are published will remain the property of FATE.

FATE looks for new writers and encourages them. We hope that your inquiry is the beginning of a long and mutually beneficial relationship!

Terry O'Neill

Editor-in-Chief

FATE AUTHOR INFORMATION

True Reports of the Strange & Unknown

Please type or print all information clearly. If article is co-written by more than one author, include information for all authors.

You may photocopy this form.

Writer's legal name as used in contracts

Writer's legal address as used in contracts

Writer's preferred mailing address if different from above

Writer's name as it should appear on the article: preferred style, pen name, etc., if different from legal name

Writer's social security number, or similar number for tax reporting purposes if resident of nation other than the U.S. (Note: although we do not deduct taxes from payments, we may have to report them according to IRS rules.) If more than one author, please indicate how payment is to be made—i.e., to which author. Be sure his/her social security number is listed.

Daytime Telephone Evening Telephone

Fax E-mail Address

Citizenship

Birthplace Date of Birth

Current Occupation

Write a brief biography of yourself that we may choose to adapt to use with your article. Include such things as honors, college degrees, recent books or articles you've had published and who published them, field(s) in which you are an expert and what makes you an expert, any other information that you would like to include, particularly items relating to this article. Use the back of the page if necessary.

Categories: Adventure—Consumer—Culture—Entertainment—General Interest—Paranormal—Spiritual

Name: Editors
Material: All
Address: PO BOX 64383
City/State/ZIP: ST PAUL MN 55164-0383
Telephone: 612-291-1970
Fax: 612-291-1908
E-mail: LWLPc@fatemag.com
Internet: www.fatemag.com

FBI Law Enforcement Bulletin

GENERAL INFORMATION

The *FBI Law Enforcement Bulletin* is an official publication of the Federal Bureau of Investigation and the U.S. Department of Justice.

Frequency of Publication: Monthly

Purpose: To provide a forum for the exchange of information on law enforcement-related topics.

Audience: Criminal justice professionals, primarily law enforcement managers.

MANUSCRIPT SPECIFICATIONS

Length: Feature article submissions should be 2,000 to 3,500 words (8 to 14 pages, double-spaced). Submissions for specialized departments, such as Police Practice, Case Study, and Sound Off, should be 1,200 to 2,000 words (5 to 8 pages, double-spaced).

Format: All pages should be numbered, and three copies should be submitted for review purposes. When possible, an electronic version of the article saved on computer disk should accompany the typed manuscript.

References should be used when quoting a source exactly, when citing or paraphrasing another person's work or ideas, or when referring to information that generally is not well known. Authors should refer to *A Manual for Writers of Term Papers, Theses, and Dissertations*, 6th ed., by Kate L. Turabian, for proper footnote citation format.

Research papers, reports, and studies should be revised to reflect the editorial needs of the *Bulletin*. Subheadings and lists should be used to break up the text and provide direction to readers.

Writing Style and Grammar: Articles generally should be written in the third person. (Point of View and Sound Off submissions are exceptions.) The *Bulletin* follows *The New York Public Library Writer's Guide to Style and Usage*. Potential authors should study several issues of the magazine to ensure that their writing style meets the *Bulletin's* requirements.

PHOTOGRAPHS AND GRAPHICS

A photograph of the author(s) should accompany the manuscript. Other suitable photos and illustrations that support the text and enhance reader comprehension also should be furnished. Black-and-white glossy prints of a moderate size (3"x5" to 5"x7") reproduce best. Prints are preferred over negatives or slides.

PUBLICATION

Basis for Judging Manuscripts: Material that has been published previously or that is under consideration by other magazines will be returned to the author. Submissions will be judged on the following points: Relevance to audience, factual accuracy, analysis of information, structure and logical flow, style and ease of reading, and length. Generally, articles on similar topics are not published within a 12-month period. Because the *Bulletin* is a government publication, favorable consideration cannot be given to articles that advertise a product or service.

Query Letters: Authors may submit a query letter along with a detailed 1- to 2-page outline before writing an article. Editorial staff members will review the query to determine suitability of topic. This is intended to help authors but does not guarantee acceptance of any article.

Author Notification: Receipt of manuscript will be confirmed. Notification of acceptance or rejection will follow review. Articles accepted for publication cannot be guaranteed a publication date.

Editing: The *Bulletin* reserves the right to edit all manuscripts for length, clarity, format, and style.

Categories: Computers—Crime—Government—Law—Law Enforcement—Technology

Name: Editor
Material: All
Address: MADISON BLDG RM 206
Address: FBI ACADEMY
City/State/ZIP: QUANTICO VA 22135
Telephone: 703-640-8666
Fax: 703-640-1474
E-mail: LEB@fbi.gov
Internet: www.fbi.gov

Feed-Lot

Feed-Lot is published 6 times per year. Circulation is approximately 11,000. A subscription costs $25.00 (foreign $30).

Feed-Lot is a trade publication for large feedlots and their related cow and calf operations and 500-plus head and stocker operations. The magazine covers all phases of production from breeding, genetics, animal health, nutrition, equipment design, research through finishing fat cattle-serious articles with information readers can use. Writers need to have knowledge of the industry and good sources of information for research.

Editorial content is reviewed by the Editor.
Categories: Agriculture—Cattle Feeding

Name: Robert Strong, Editor
Material: All
Address: PO BOX 850
City/State/ZIP: DIGHTON KS 67839
Telephone: 316-397-2838
Fax: 316-397-2839

Fellowship
A Magazine of Peacemaking

Fellowship is published six times a year: January/February, March/April, May/June, July/August, September/October, November/December.

Deadline:
For articles and reviews deadline is two months prior to the first day of the first month of the issue. Accompanying photographs and graphics six weeks prior.

Maximum length:
For articles, 2,000 words (1,000 preferred in most cases).
For book reviews, 500 words.

Format:
Typed copy must be *clean* (free of italics, corrections, white-out, pen or pencil markings). **Late changes may be indicated on another copy—we will incorporate.** Since we scan our hard copy submissions into the computer for editing and layout, we regret that we cannot accept faxes or dot-matrix printouts except as queries.

Computer diskettes are preferred for submissions. We are pleased to receive 3½" diskettes in either PC or Mac format, and documents written in any of the major word processing programs, or saved as ASCII ("Text") files. As is standard with editorial offices, we cannot be responsible for returning your diskettes. If you send a diskette, please also send a hard copy and include your address and author note.

Required Information:
For all submissions, two lines of biographical information to serve as an author note. For **book reviews,** full **title and subtitle** of the book; full **author** listing; full **publisher's address; year** of publication; number of **pages.** Please note whether the book is **paperback or hardcover,** or both, and the **prices** in either case.

This information must be listed at the top of your review.
(example):
The Challenge of Shalom: The Jewish Tradition of Peace and Justice
Murray Polner and Naomi Goodman, editors.
1994, 278 pages, $18.95 (paper). New Society Publishers, 4722 Baltimore Avenue, Philadelphia, PA 19143.

Categories: Peace—Justice—Nonviolence

Name: Submissions Editor
Material: All
Address: PO BOX 271
City/State/ZIP: NYACK NY 10960
Telephone: 914-358-4601
Fax: 914-358-4924
E-mail: fellowship@igc.apc.org

Feminist Studies
University of Maryland

FEMINIST STUDIES publishes serious writing of a critical, scholarly, speculative, and political nature; creative work, particularly poetry and art; and reports from the women's movement, such as manifestos, position papers, and strategies for change.

We solicit manuscripts not presently under consideration for publication elsewhere. Three (3) copies should be submitted along with an abstract of no more than 200 words that will be used for editorial routing. Since manuscripts will not be returned, authors should retain a copy of their work. In order to protect anonymity, the author's name should appear only on a separate title page. Please consult a recent copy of *The Chicago Manual of Style* for proper manuscript form.

Creative writing manuscripts will be reviewed twice a year; in May and December. The deadlines for these submissions will be May 1 and December 1. Authors will receive notice of the board's decision by June 30 and January 31. Please send one (1) copy of your work.

For submission of art work, good black and white glossy photographs made directly from the work to be reproduced are essential. Do not send original works of art. Photographs will be retained indefinitely in our files for future consideration.

MANUSCRIPT REVIEW PROCEDURE

Manuscripts submitted to FEMINIST STUDIES are sent to one member of the editorial board chosen to take charge of the review process because of her area of interest and/or her current editorial workload. She, in turn, sends the manuscript to one or more referees. Only the editor is aware of the author's identity. Within three to four months the editor in charge of the manuscript reviews the referees' reports and determines whether the manuscript should be held for further consideration by the editorial board as a whole, or returned to the author for further work or submission elsewhere. Referees offer written comments in a form which would be helpful to the author; these comments are either summarized in the managing editor's report to the author or included separately.

FEMINIST STUDIES editors represent a broad range of disciplines, and all editors participate in final publication decision. This assures that each manuscript, individually, and all manuscripts, collectively, reflect and compliment the varied interest of our multi-disciplinary readership. Fine examples of current scholarly interest to specialists are oftentimes deemed inappropriate for publication for this reason.

If a manuscript is selected for publication in FEMINIST STUDIES, one editor works with the author to make changes that the editors and referees have required. The author's willingness to cooperate with the editor and to meet deadlines is essential. Copyediting and proofreading are handled from the managing editor's office. The author will have the opportunity to review the copyeditor's changes to ensure that there are no unintended alterations to the substance of the work. The author also proofreads her own typeset galleys.

All FEMINIST STUDIES editors and referees serve the journal without reimbursement for their time or the various charges incurred in the course of their work. Editors and referees work for FEMINIST STUDIES in addition to other full-time pursuits. We regret that this inevitably results in a lengthy review process of up to four months.

Categories: African-American—Culture—Feminism—Gay/Lesbian—History—Literature—Women's Fiction—Women's Issues

Name: Submissions Editor

Material: All
Address: C/O DEPT OF WOMEN'S STUDIES
Address: UNIVERSITY OF MARYLAND
City/State/ZIP: COLLEGE PARK MD 20742
Telephone: 301-405-7415
Fax: 301-314-9190
E-mail: femstud@umail.umd.edu

FIBERARTS Magazine

Dear Friend:

Our readers are interested in a broad range of textile-related subjects. Among these are contemporary trends in fiber sculpture, weaving, surface design, quilting, stitchery, papermaking, basketry, felting, wearable art, and mixed textile techniques. Historical and ethnic textiles, technical information, dyeing, fashion, and eccentric tidbits are all of interest.

The readers are professional artists, textile students, fashion designers, museum curators, gallery owners, and nonprofessional fiber aficionados. While the professional is essential to the editorial depth of FIBERARTS, and must find timely information in the pages of the magazine, this is not our greatest audience. Our editorial philosophy is that the magazine must provide the non-professional textile enthusiast with the inspiration, support, useful information, and direction to keep her or him excited, interested, and committed.

Regarding submissions, I prefer to begin with an initial look at color transparencies (35mm slides or larger formats acceptable) or black-and-white photos that represent the subject, along with a brief outline *and* a prose synopsis of the proposed article. If interested, I will be back in touch with you to arrange specifics such as word length and fee, and to schedule the article's appearance.

I cannot guarantee publication of an unsolicited manuscript, but I will be happy to carefully consider the submission.

Cordially,

Ann Batchelder, Editor

Editorial Policy Regarding Submissions

1. Submissions should be in the form of an outline and a prose synopsis of the proposed article. All proposals must be accompanied by good quality 35mm slides or black & white photos, representative of the subject of the article. (We prefer publication quality 2"x2" or 4"x5" transparencies.)

2. All articles must be cleanly typed or computer printed, double-spaced, with one-inch margins and 25 lines per page (in this format, there are approximately 250 words per page). Please include a short bioline. An additional photocopy would be helpful.

3. Writers are responsible for accuracy of fact and correct spelling of names, places, and titles of works. We do not have the resources to check all of this information, so we must be able to depend on the writer's accuracy.

4. Unless other arrangements are made with the editor, authors are responsible for collecting all visual material to illustrate their article, and for providing all caption information on a separate number keyed sheet. Complete caption information includes artist's name, title of work, dimensions, materials and techniques used, year of execution, in whose collection and where, name of photographer, and designation for top of work shown. Authors must also provide appropriate names and addresses of artists and/or photo sources, for correct return of visuals.

5. The editor may request revisions of the article, and final editing of the material is at the editor's discretion. Writers are responsible for abiding by the word limit established for the article; manuscripts that substantially exceed the word count will be returned to the writer for shortening.

6. Deadlines are serious. All manuscripts, illustrations, and

caption information are due by the date indicated, unless specifically discussed with the editor prior to that time. The editor reserves the right to kill any piece that is not submitted on time.

7. No kill fee will be paid if the material is not acceptable and if, in the editor's opinion, revisions will not make it so.

8. Payment for articles is made after publication. The signed author's agreement is confirmation of total amount due. Additional expenses must be discussed with the editor prior to submission of the completed manuscript.

Content for Feature Articles

We are seeking feature-length articles of approximately 2,000 words that communicate in an informal tone the work and personality of an artist or a concept. The latest work of a celebrated artist is appropriate for a feature-length article, as is that of a promising new talent. Also appropriate are articles that compare the work of two or three artists, discuss the work and workings of a group, present an important technique, explore textile history, or present ethnic textiles. Articles might also focus on a promising-but-lesser-known artist, a particular aspect of an artist's work, a folk artist, an innovative organization, a visionary collector, or a personal technique.

Bear in mind that the readers have a fairly sophisticated knowledge of the field. At the same time, please be clear in your writing and explain specific techniques. Payment: $300-$400.

Content for Swatches, Profile, and Review Articles

Swatches cover such topics as new ideas for fiber, unusual or off-beat subjects, work spaces, resources, and marketing. In addition, we are looking for articles on technique, materials, equipment, design, and trends. These articles are typically 300-400 words in length. Payment: $75-$100.

A Profile article focuses on one artist and is 400 words in length. The article and one photo must fit on one page. Payment: $100.

Review articles are 400 words in length and include three to five photos. Payment: $100.

Photos

Visuals *must* accompany every article. A feature includes four to eight photos. Send a selection of 35mm slides (larger formats are preferable). The more photos to choose from, the better; all will be returned. We depend on *quality* visuals to complement your writing and to present the subject as attractively as possible.

Full photo captions are essential. *Please include a separate, number-keyed* caption sheet. The names and addresses of those mentioned in the article or to whom the visuals are to be returned are necessary.

Proposals

We cannot commit to an article proposal on the telephone. Please see the cover letter regarding submissions.

Manuscripts

Refer to the *Chicago Manual of Style* or *The New York Times Style Manual*. A one-sentence author's bioline should be included at the end of the manuscript, together with address and telephone/FAX numbers.

Our philosophy is to preserve the author's voice, while still monitoring clarity, grammar, usage, etc. Minor revisions are made at the editor's discretion; major revisions are made in conference with the author.

Call if you have questions.

Exhibition Reviews

What to Include

In no more than 350-400 words, you should provide a summary of the overall quality, significance, focus, and atmosphere of the show, and then evaluate selected pieces. The choice of what to select might be based on what is most outstanding, unusual, trend-setting, and/or appealing to you. Aesthetic quality, content, and technique are all valid criteria for evaluation. Not all work

deserves praise; we prefer honest and thought-provoking criticism.

Bear in mind that we have an international readership. Because many of the artists you will be presenting may be known only on a local or regional level, brief biographical information or pertinent quotes within the review might be necessary.

What to Avoid

The "who's who" approach (a list of artists' names, titles of work, and short descriptive phrases) is inadequate. Also, we find that a list of award winners has little value. A review which has appeared, or is going to appear in another publication is unacceptable. In addition, *you are not eligible to review a show in which you have participated as an artist, organizer, curator, or juror.*

Photographs

Publication quality visuals must accompany the review. We require 35mm slides (larger format transparencies are preferable) or black-and-white glossy photos, 5"x7" or 8"x10" inches. Visuals must be clear and sharply focused to be acceptable. Often visuals are available from the show organizers, or even the artists themselves.

Do not cite works for which visuals are not available. A number-keyed caption sheet with the following information must accompany the visuals: artist's name, title of work, dimensions, materials and techniques, year of execution, in whose collection, name of photographer, and *Top* designated.

Format

Include a working title and sub-title [on all ms.]. Be sure to list title, show dates, gallery, city and state, and touring schedule. Please send the show's catalog.

On a separate sheet, include addresses and phone numbers of artists whose visuals accompany the review.

Categories: Arts—Crafts

Name: Ann Batchelder, Editor
Material: All
Address: 50 COLLEGE ST
City/State/ZIP: ASHEVILLE NC 28801
Telephone: 704-253-0467
Fax: 704-253-7952
E-mail: fiberarts@larkbooks.com

Fiction Writer's Guideline

The Fiction Writers Connection (FWC) is a membership organization providing practical assistance and information to writers pursuing the craft of fiction. Among the benefits to members is a monthly newsletter, *Fiction Writer's Guideline*.

TOPICS: How-to Articles offering practical advice on the craft of writing fiction and practical tips and advice on getting published.; **Success Stories; Interviews with Authors, Agents, and Editors.** No personal essays. (See below for required and suggested questions).

RATES: *Fiction Writer's Guideline* is a fledgling publication. As circulation increases, so will writers fees. Fees currently range from $1 to $25, depending upon length and subject matter. Payment is within two weeks after publication.

RIGHTS: One-time rights or reprint rights.

WORD COUNT: From 250 to 1,200 words.

MANUSCRIPT SUBMISSION: All articles will be considered "on spec." Please submit complete manuscript. All manuscripts must have the exact word count typed in the upper right hand corner of the first page. Be sure to include your name, address, and telephone number. An SASE must accompany all submissions.

AUTHOR INTERVIEWS: You are free to choose the authors you interview. The only requirements are that he or she is an author of fiction and has been at least moderately successful. Ask each author how he or she became interested in writing as a profession and detail how he or she got started. How did they get their first book published—did they go through an agent—or submit to editors themselves? How many places did they submit their manuscript to until it was accepted—any interesting anecdotes/feedback/comments in the process? How were they notified of their first sale—phone/mail etc? How much did they get paid—advance/royalty % for their first sale. For the latest sale? Advice to aspiring writers. Next project in the works?

AGENT INTERVIEWS: Agents interviewed must handle fiction, be open to new writers, have room to add new clients to their list, and must not charge a reading fee. The following information must be obtained during your interview: genres they are most interested in; how they prefer to be approached, i.e. telephone, query; what they want to see, i.e. synopses, the first 3 chapters/50 pages, etc.; response time; recent sales (if available); commission charged; any photocopying/fax fees, etc.; advice to FWC members.

EDITOR INTERVIEWS: Editors interviewed must handle fiction and be willing to accept unagented submissions. The following information must be obtained during your interview: genres they are interested in; how they want to be approached initially, response time, submission do's and don'ts, advances, royalties, advice, etc.

Categories: Nonfiction—Writing

Name: Blythe Camenson, Director
Material: All
Address: PO BOX 4065
City/State/ZIP: DEERFIELD BEACH FL 33442
Telephone: 954-426-4705
E-mail: BCamenson@aol.com

Field & Stream®

FIELD & STREAM is a tightly focused magazine. All material is related to hunting and fishing, with the articles ranging from basic how-it's-done pieces to carefully crafted features with a philosophical edge. The magazine introduced a Continuous edit format in the December 1996 issue which has created more opportunities for freelancers, including:

• Short pieces (500 to 750 words) on hunting and fishing tactics and techniques, natural history relating to hunting and fishing, and DIY [Do-It-Yourself] projects with a hunting/fishing slant.

• Longer how-to features (1,500 words maximum) on hunting and fishing.

Freelancers can also score in categories like humor, mood, nostalgia (see "Guest Shot," in particular), and Sportsman's Projects—word count is flexible, but shorter is better. We are also looking for personal essays suitable for the "Finally..." department on the last page of the magazine (750 to 800 words). We also buy material for the Regional Sections (see guidelines below).

Another good new market for freelancers is our new four-page "Up Front" section, which first appeared in the January 1997 issue. We're interested in short pieces that run the FIELD & STREAM gamut, from natural history to conservation news, anecdotal humor, short tips, and carefully crafted opinion pieces (word length: 25 to 400).

Writers are encouraged to submit queries on article ideas.

These should be no more than a page, and should include a summary of the idea, including the angle you will hang the story on, and a sense of what makes this piece different from all others on the same or a similar subject. Many queries are turned down because we have no idea what the writer is getting at. Be sure that your letter is absolutely clear. We've found that if you can't sum up the point of the article in a sentence or two, the article doesn't have a point.

Pieces that depend on writing style, such as humor, mood, and nostalgia or essays often can't be queried and may be submitted in manuscript form. The same is true of short tips. All submissions to FIELD & STREAM are on an on-spec basis.

Before submitting anything, however, we encourage you to *study*, not simply read, the magazine. Many pieces are rejected because they do not fit the tone or style of the magazine, or fail to match the subject of the article with the overall subject matter of FIELD & STREAM. *Above all, study the magazine before submitting anything.*

FIELD & STREAM does not pay by the word. Payment ranges from $100 to as much as several thousand dollars, depending on the quality of the work, the experience of the author, and the difficulty of obtaining the story.

All queries and completed manuscripts submitted to FIELD & STREAM must be typed and double spaced. The magazine also accepts 3.5" disks, but does not accept e-mail or fax submissions.

FIELD & STREAM needs an accurate word count for *every* submission. Estimates based on the old system of 250 words per page have proven inaccurate. Please make your word counts accurate and include them at the top of the first page of every submission.

REGIONAL EDITIONS

FIELD & STREAM includes one of four regional sections in each issue. These sections carry short articles geared to the hunting and fishing scene in one of four U.S. regions: East, Midwest, South, or West. Regional stories range from a maximum of 600 words to as few as 100 words or less. Primary emphasis is on regional where-to and how-to material, although sections may also contain state- or region-specific conservation articles, personality profiles, and short news items related to the outdoors.

Potential contributors should limit where-to article ideas to specific locations to the greatest extent practical without endangering a resource. For example, one or a few bodies of water instead of a state-or region-wide lake survey; a single watershed or river section rather than multiple rivers; a single national forest or in-state region rather than a state- or region-wide hunting report.

Regional how-to is just what the term implies: hunting and/or fishing tactics/techniques that are region-specific or locally hot. Generic bass-fishing tips, for example, aren't regional. But the latest in jigging tactics for walleyes in a well-known Wisconsin lake could be a perfect regional fit.

Payment (on acceptance) for regional material ranges from a minimum of $100 for 100 words or fewer, on up to $400 for a maximum of 600 words.

Assignments are made five to six months in advance of publication. For where-to and how-to material, time your query/submission to fit what you believe to be the best month/season for a particular activity. Mistimed queries will be returned with a note asking the contributor to resubmit at the appropriate time. Non-seasonal queries, such as profiles, should arrive on or before the first of each month.

Queries should tell the best timing for the idea and why it deserves mention at all. Specify locations, access, and species as appropriate. Also mention the availability of maps, photos, charts or other illustration ideas that would suitably accompany your article. We accept hard-copy manuscripts, but prefer electronic copy delivered on disk or sent by modem.

Telephone and e-mail queries are not acceptable from first-time contributors.

There are four regional sections:

EAST: Connecticut, Delaware, Maine, Maryland, Massachusetts, New Hampshire, New Jersey, New York, Pennsylvania, Rhode Island, West Virginia, Vermont, New Brunswick, Quebec, Maritime Provinces.

MIDWEST: Illinois, Indiana, Iowa, Kansas, Michigan, Minnesota, Missouri, Nebraska, North Dakota, Ohio, Oklahoma, South Dakota, Wisconsin, Manitoba, Ontario, Saskatchewan, Northwest Territory.

SOUTH: Alabama, Arkansas, Florida, Georgia, Kentucky, Louisiana, Mississippi, North Carolina, South Carolina, Tennessee, Texas (eastern), Virginia.

WEST: Alaska, Arizona, California, Colorado, Hawaii, Idaho, Montana, Nevada, New Mexico, Oregon, Texas (western), Utah, Washington, Wyoming, Alberta, British Columbia.

Categories: Nonfiction—Fishing—Hunting—Outdoors

Name: The Editor
Material: All Non-Regional Material
Name: The Regional Desk
Material: Regional Pieces
Address: 2 PARK AVE
City/State/ZIP: NEW YORK NY 10016-5295
Telephone: 212-779-5000
Fax: 212-725-3836
E-mail: FSMAGAZINE@aol.com

Field
Oberlin College Press

FIELD, the semi-annual journal of contemporary poetry and poetics, emphasizes the best in contemporary poetry, poetry in translation, and essays by poets on the craft. Please include proof of permission to translate, when appropriate. We read submissions year-round, usually responding within six weeks.

Categories: Poetry

Name: Submissions Editor
Material: All
Address: RICE HALL #17
Address: OBERLIN COLLEGE
City/State/ZIP: OBERLIN OH 44074
Telephone: 216-775-8408
Fax: 216-775-8124
E-mail: oc.press@oberlin.edu

Film Comment

Dear Writer:

Thank you for your inquiry. We have no writer's guidelines, but maybe the following remarks will serve.

We make no formal demands regarding the state of manuscripts; if we can read it without eyestrain and without getting our hands dirty, we are content. It is not necessary to send articles on disk, though if anyone cared to, we speak WordPerfect 5.1 and Microsoft Word 6.0 (which can convert a lot of formats).

Files can be attached to e-mail sent to the address shown below.

As a glance at any issue will discover, we print a wide range of articles, on films new and old, foreign and domestic; on directors, performers, writers, cinematographers; on studios, national cinemas, genres; opinion pieces, history pieces. We are more or less impervious to "hooks," don't worry a whole lot about who's hot and who's not" or tying in with next fall's surefire big hit (we think people should write about films they've seen, not films that haven't even been finished). We appreciate good writing (writing, not journalism) on subjects in which the writer has some personal investment and about which he or she has something noteworthy to say.

We read and consider anything sent to us; few issues have lacked for a piece, or pieces, that just "came in over the transom" and seemed worthwhile—occasionally terrific—and found a home in our pages. We almost never *commission* pieces from writers with whom we have not established a relationship (can't afford to), so the query process is somewhat limited in utility. We can save the writer and ourselves some bother by saying "That doesn't sound like something we'd be interested in" or "That sounds like something we'd be interested in—in fact, we already have two articles about it in the forthcoming issue." We may say, "We're interested and we think you ought to play up this aspect and play down that one—but you'll still be writing on spec."

I hope this is at least approximately what you wanted.

Best of luck.

Yours truly,

Richard T. Jameson, Editor

Categories: Film/Video

Name: Richard T. Jameson, Editor
Material: All
Address: 70 LINCOLN CENTER PLAZA
City/State/ZIP: NEW YORK NY 10023
Telephone: 212-875-5614
Fax: 212-875-5636
E-mail: RTJFC@aol.com

Film Quarterly
University of California Press

In preparing material for submission to *Film Quarterly,* keep in mind that while many of our contributors are academics, only a fraction of our readers are.

By the standards of the commercial magazine world, FQ is quite specialized and its circulation is small—about 7,000, which means perhaps 8,000 to 10,000 readers, since library copies have multiple readers. But by the standards of the narrower academic journals, this is very large.

Since its inception in 1958, *Film Quarterly*'s mission has been to bring intelligent film thought to as large a readership as possible (including film-makers, incidentally). The magazine is sold about two-thirds by subscription and one-third by retail sales in bookstores—which are located in cities, university towns, and (yes!) even suburban shopping malls. We also have numerous subscribers scattered throughout the world.

The English-language film journal universe includes several publications whose contents are aimed primarily at scholars, such as *Cinema Journal, Quarterly Review of Film and Video, Screen, The Journal of Film and Video,* and to some degree *Wide Angle* and *Camera Obscura.* Popular magazines, such as *Film Comment* and *Premiere* aim at a wide audience of moviegoers. *Cineaste* and *Jump Cut,* like *Film Quarterly* and *Sight and Sound,* occupy a middle ground, hoping to make specialized ideas familiar to literate and "cinemate" readers and to promote discussion of films which, for various reasons, do not get treated by general-audience publications.

We aim at the whole community of educated readers seriously concerned with film (and, to an increasing degree, video) in much the same way that a literary magazine aims at the whole community of people interested in literature. An issue may be taken for granted within the community of film scholars but it is still necessary to make clear to our larger readership why it is important to them.

You should familiarize yourself with the full range of film periodicals so that you can judge for which ones your work is likely to be most appropriate and so that you can be guided in preparing it in a way likely to lead to acceptance. Careful study of back issues is imperative for new writers hoping to have contributions accepted by *Film Quarterly*. (If your library does not subscribe, you might wish to call the magazine to the attention of the periodicals librarian.)

We like to surprise our readers with unusual material, but we have certain emphases and do not publish certain kinds of writing. We never use personality or reportage pieces, for instance, nor do we cover festivals. We are interested in important theoretical developments, but when we run theoretical articles they must include treatments of real films and thus demonstrate a connection between theory and practice.

Our basic concern has traditionally been with current films; thus, in the past, we have generally run articles on "classic" or older films only when the author provided a novel reassessment or reinterpretation. But we are now using more pieces on important older films that are readily available on videocassette, and more wide-ranging historical articles.

Generally, we run an interview in each issue—mostly with directors but occasionally with writers, directors of photography, etc. Interviews are best done by writers who know the interviewee's work thoroughly, can obtain the time and attention for an extended conversation, and can prepare a solid introduction.

You should always submit the completed article, since the Editor and the Board read and assess all submissions and cannot accept anything on the basis of a query or an outline. You can, of course, check with the Editor to make sure your idea or film review is not already in the FQ pipeline. (Book reviews are assigned separately; if you are interested in doing a review of a particular book, check with the Book Review Editor.)

Our working rule of thumb for article length is that it should not exceed 25 double-spaced manuscript pages, or about 6,250 words, although we occasionally run longer pieces and can certainly consider shorter ones. If you contemplate a really long manuscript, it may be helpful to query the Editor before setting to work.

Film reviews ideally amount to around six pages, but we do run longer pieces if the issues involved seem sufficiently substantial.

We seek reviews with analytic treatments that:

1.) give readers (who may not have seen the film) a clear idea of what it is like, in stylistic as well as plot-precis terms;

2.) provide some implicit or explicit "theory" to account for what the film seems to be trying to do—structurally, emotionally, politically, etc.; and

3.) give an estimate of its success and general quality. We are more impressed with analytic power than by vehemence or charm of opinions, and we are always searching for that elusive ideal, the "definitive" review which treats a film so intelligently and subtly that the review will remain readable in ten years.

In writing book reviews, remember that we are trying to give at least brief coverage to as many English-language film books as possible, mostly but not entirely in our Summer and Fall book roundup issues. The comprehensiveness of our coverage is a much appreciated feature of the magazine, but this scope means that most individual reviews must be kept as compact as possible. We try to review books of major importance in five manuscript pages, while books of less weight may be assigned three manuscript pages; books of lower quality or ones likely to interest only a small portion of our audience are given short annotations.

Writing a brief but convincing review is a challenging intellectual and stylistic task that many would-be reviewers seriously underestimate. A review should describe the book succinctly (it is not necessary or desirable to recapitulate its contents), evaluate it without indulging in nitpicking, and sometimes comment on how the book compares to closely related important works in its area.

Guidelines on Book Reviews are available from either the Editor or the Book Review Editor—Stephen Prince, Virginia Tech, Dept. of Communication Studies, 11 Agnew Hall, Blacksburg, VA 24061-0311.

Miscellaneous technical matters: Professional writers always type their name, address, phone number, and social security number at the top of a manuscript, since the envelope it comes in will be discarded and a cover letter will be separated from it during editing and typesetting. A brief biographical description should be placed at the end of the article or review. Keep a copy of your manuscript, since we cannot be guarantors of its safety.

If you happen to possess stills relevant to your manuscript, please mention the fact but do not send stills along with the manuscript; they will be asked for at a later time. Everything in the manuscript should be double-spaced, including notes, so that there is enough room for editorial and typographic markings, and ample margins should be provided. If you need guidance on detailed points of manuscript preparation, you should follow the *Chicago Manual of Style*.

Editors and typesetters dislike dot-matrix printouts intensely; submitting one is like giving yourself a grade-point handicap, unless the printout is near-letter quality. We cannot use discs at first submission, but if your manuscript is accepted, getting it on disc as well as on hard copy is highly encouraged, since it helps us keep production costs down.

We can deal with several different types of files-IBM, Mac, and usually UNIX—as long as they are on 3½" disks, and in a commonly used word processing program such as (but not necessarily limited to) Microsoft Word, WordPerfect, or UNIX (nroff, troff) format. In case we can't read your disk, it is always best that you provide a clean, first-generation hard copy (not photocopied or faxed), so that we can scan it.

Manuscripts are discussed by our Editorial Board at quarterly meetings (usually at the end of January, April, and October, and at the beginning of August—deadlines are one month before the meetings). Decisions about submissions can take about a month to reach the writer. We always have a backlog of manuscripts, and you should count it taking about a year from acceptance to publication. Payment for a published manuscript is slightly above the magnificent sum of two cents per word, plus two gratis copies.

We welcome communications and submissions from writers. There is no closed "club" of contributors to the magazine and many now well-known writers published their first articles or reviews with us. We are eager to find innovative approaches deployed with energy, and we relish making unknown or esoteric films accessible to American audiences; we pay considerable attention to non-Western cinema, avant-garde cinema, and documentary. We also welcome commentary and critiques on the magazine and particulars of its contents; some such letters are published in our Controversy & Correspondence section if they seem to us to have sufficient general interest.

Ann Martin
Editor
Categories: Film/Video—Television

Name: Ann Martin, Editor
Material: All
Address: 2120 BERKELEY WAY
City/State/ZIP: BERKELEY CA 94720
Telephone: 510-601-9070
Fax: 510-601-9036

Financial Freedom Report Quarterly

Thank you for your interest in writing for our publication. Our publication is geared towards the individual investor—specializing in real estate investments. Each quarter we cover many aspects of real estate ownership—purchasing, landlording, fix up, finance, etc.

We have also branched out slightly to include topics on business management, again treating your real estate investments as a business. We've had articles on setting up your own business, advertising for your business, hiring employees, compensation for those employees, etc.

Articles run between 1,500-2,500 words, typewritten, double spaced or on computer disk with an accompanying hard copy. The deadline is the 10th of May for the Summer Quarterly; 10th of August for the Fall Quarterly; 10th of November for the Winter Quarterly and 10th of February for Spring Quarterly. Pictures or graphs are appreciated when applicable. Payment is at the rate of 10¢ per published word and payment is upon publication.

After reading through our publication if you have some ideas for stories that you feel might fit our reading audience, please feel free to give me a call. We can go over your ideas and I can give you some further guidance.

Carolyn Tice
Managing Editor
Categories: Business—Money/Finance—Real Estate—Rental Property
Name: Carolyn Tice, Managing Editor
Material: All
Address: 4505 S WASATCH BLVD STE 140
City/State/ZIP: SALT LAKE CITY UT 84124
Telephone: 801-273-2335
Fax: 801-273-2399
E-mail: carolyn@homebusiness.com

Fine Gardening

Fine Gardening is a bimonthly magazine for enthusiastic landscape and ornamental gardeners. Filled with practical information and innovative ideas, *Fine Gardening* seeks to inform, assist, and inspire gardeners of all skill levels. What makes *Fine Gardening* unique is that all articles are written by home gardeners, horticulturists, or landscape professionals based on their own experience and knowledge-whether it be about a plant, gardening technique, design approach, or project.

Style

All of our stories are written in first person, based on firsthand experience. The tone should be friendly, yet informative. The style should be casual—that of one gardener sharing information with another as they walk through the garden together.

Features

Fine Gardening features ornamental plants and home landscaping ideas. Most of our feature stories fall into the following categories: design, techniques, plants, or garden structures. Most stories are how-to or instructional in nature; many are projects. We often include other related stories, such as those on tools or garden pests and diseases. While we do not publish general gar-

den profiles, we illustrate most stories with photographs taken in our authors' gardens. Content should appeal to both beginning and experienced gardeners. Accurate botanical names, USDA Hardiness Zones, and cultural information must be provided for all plant profiles.

Departments

Tips, Q&A, Reader's Exchange, and Letters to the Editor are all reader-written departments. Of these, we pay for published tips. Praiseworthy Plants, Basics, Reviews, and Container Gardening are most often assigned to horticulture professionals, but we welcome queries. Last Word features gardening essays—humorous, insightful, or sentimental—that are selected from among unsolicited manuscripts.

Most of the photography in *Fine Gardening* is taken by our editors. We occasionally use professional photographers or accept photography supplied by the author. Additional fees are paid for any published photographs not taken by staff members.

Copyright and Payment

At *Fine* Gardening, we generally purchase the following rights:
- The right to be the first magazine to publish the article.
- The right to reprint the article in one or more of our anthology books.
- The right to use portions of the article in materials promoting *Fine Gardening* or The Taunton Press.
- The right to publish the article on our *Fine Gardening* web page.

We pay for all stories on a project basis. Payment runs from $200 - $1,000 per story, depending upon its length and complexity. A portion of this fee is paid upon acceptance of a publishable manuscript and signed copyright agreement. The balance is paid upon publication. Please note that by signing a copyright agreement with you, we do not guarantee publication of your article. We reserve the right to decide later not to publish it. This doesn't happen often, but if it does, you are entitled to keep your advance as a kill fee.

We pay $35 - $50 per published tip. For individual photographs, we pay $25 - $200 per published photograph, depending upon size and use. For assignment photography, we pay day rates, plus reasonable expenses.

Submitting a Query

If you would like to propose a story, please send a brief query explaining why the subject would be of interest to our readers. Be sure to highlight key points that would be covered in the story, and enclose any snapshots, sketches, or other materials that will help us evaluate story potential. With the exception of Last Word, we prefer that a proposal precede the development of any manuscript.

All queries, tips, and reader contributions should be sent to the address below. Please submit only one story idea per query and allow 4-6 weeks for a response. If your proposal is accepted, an editor will be assigned to work with you. If at any time you have a question regarding the status of your proposal or story, please contact our editorial secretary at 800-926-8776, ext. 509.

Categories: Gardening

Name: Lee Anne White, Editor
Material: All Features
Name: Virginia Small, Associate Editor
Material: Last Word
Name: Steve Silk, Associate Editor
Material: Praiseworthy Plants
Address: PO BOX 5506
City/State/ZIP: NEWTOWN CT 06470
Telephone: 203-426-8171
Fax: 203-426-3434
E-mail: fg@taunton.com

Internet: www.taunton.com

FineScale Modeler

How to Prepare Your Article for *FineScale Modeler* magazine:

Go ahead—it's easier than you think!

Who can contribute

Most FSM articles are contributed by modelers, not professional writers. This means that if you have a modeling story to tell, you can be an FSM author! In evaluating manuscripts we look first at the quality of your photos and illustrations, second at how you present your how-to information, and only third at writing style.

If you have a modeling technique that FSM readers would like to learn about, our editors can rework your writing to the magazine's format and style.

What FSM needs

FSM feature articles concern how-to-do-it technique: How to build a kit into a more accurate or more representative model; how to make parts you can't buy or parts that are better than what you can buy; how to paint a model or how to paint a particular color scheme; how to build a display or diorama; and so on. Virtually every how-to aspect of modeling, including hints, tips, and workshop techniques, is a worthwhile subject for an FSM article.

By far, the best way to learn what FSM needs is to study how stories are presented in current issues.

Typing your manuscript

Set up your typewriter or word processor for a column 38 to 42 characters wide and 25 lines long. This leaves room to indicate where photos and sketches should be placed relative to the text.

If you have a computer word processor, send the printout. Set up the printer for large type (8, 9, or 10 characters per inch). Our computer text-editing system can accept input from Macintosh and IBM-compatible computers. If you can provide your text on a 3½" or 5¼" floppy disk for one of those computers, tell us in your cover letter, but always include a printout. If possible, format your disk document in ASCII for easy conversion.

In the upper right corner of the first page of your text, type your name, address, home and work telephone numbers, and the date you submit the article.

In addition to the main text, provide captions for all photos you submit. Provide these on a separate sheet, double spaced (width doesn't matter), and make sure you describe everything shown in each photo.

Writing style

Keep your writing simple and direct, but give lots of detail. Our readers need a clear description of what you did to the model, how you did it, and what tools and materials you used. Be specific. Did you use sheet or tube styrene? Tell us the sizes. What brands and colors of paint—exactly—did you use? What sort of putty—epoxy, acrylic—did you use? Don't simply say "I scratchbuilt the transmission from sheet, tube, and rod styrene." Tell us how you did it, step by step.

The best way to do this is to write as if you were telling a friend how to duplicate your modeling project. The best method for organizing your text is in chronological order, from the start of the project to its completion.

Be sure to provide a complete list of materials you used and a list of references, if applicable (use the formats shown in the magazine).

Length

Articles should be brief; most range from 750 to 3,000 words. While big features such as "How I Scratchbuilt the Hughes Spruce Goose in 1/24 scale" are used occasionally, FSM has a greater need for short articles. Such reports usually cover only a single aspect of a project—perhaps, how to paint a model, or how to modify or re-detail a kit without describing how to paint it. Your best chance for breaking into print is to contribute a short article that focuses on a single modeling technique.

Photos

Photography makes or breaks most FSM articles, and by far our most common reason for rejecting a story is poor photos.

We need color slides or prints from 35mm or larger film. Black-and-white photos usually are acceptable if color is not available, such as with historical photos. How-to shots should be taken against a plain background.

Obtaining quality black-and-white prints can be a problem, but if you send snapshot-quality prints and your negatives we can make reproduction-quality prints in our photo lab. Please include the negatives regardless of the quality of your prints.

In-progress, how-to-do-it photos are especially important for selling your article to FSM. We often have to reject excellent material simply because it does not include photos taken while the model was being built. Showing the model before painting tells a lot about what you did to it.

Scale drawings and how-to illustrations

You don't have to be a professional draftsman to include sketches, patterns, templates, or plans with your article. Our artists can work from rough sketches. Draw the roughs as carefully and neatly as you can. If you can furnish reproduction quality artwork your article will qualify for higher rates of payment.

We often include arrows, circles, and words in photos to point out what's going on. You can suggest such pointers by attaching a tracing-paper flap to your photo and writing on the flap.

Other items

For first-time FSM contributors, we often run a "meet the author" box with a three- or four-paragraph biography (please concentrate on your modeling interests) and a photo showing you engaged in some modeling or research activity. Please include these with your first article.

Submitting your article

First, don't send pieces—send the whole package at once! We can't evaluate your article unless it's 100-percent complete, so don't send it to us with a note that more photos will follow or that you're still working on the drawings.

Package your article in a sturdy envelope with cardboard stiffeners to protect photos and drawings. Write "article manuscript" on the lower left corner of the envelope. Be sure your name and return address appear on the envelope and inside as well.

Prepare a cover letter listing all the items in your manuscript package. If you are submitting more than one article, send each in a separate package with its own cover letter.

We'll send a postcard receipt when your article arrives at FSM, and we'll review it as soon as time permits. Be prepared, however, to wait for one or two months for an answer on your manuscript.

We don't consider articles which are submitted simultaneously to other modeling publications.

FSM pays for feature articles upon acceptance-when we accept a complete feature for publication, you get a check. We normally purchase all rights to the material. The minimum editorial rate, per published page, is $40. That means that if your article fills five pages in the magazine, and includes only material that you provided, you can expect to be paid a minimum of $200. If we underestimate the space your article requires, we issue a second payment upon publication.

We up the per-page rate substantially when an author does a particularly good job, or when the material is especially timely or interesting. Articles that include camera-ready scale drawings or how-to artwork also qualify for special rates.

Returning your materials

Rejected articles will be sent back to you if you provide return postage and packaging materials. For articles that are used, we return unused photos and negatives promptly after the magazine is printed.

Article inquiries

We strongly recommend that you send a written inquiry describing your proposed article, and ask for comments or interest before preparing a complete article package. We prefer letters or e-mail, but occasionally can clear up our requirements in a brief phone call.

FSM needs you! Remember, FSM readers, not professional writers, contribute almost 100 percent of what we present in each issue. Your chances for breaking into print in FSM are excellent—so get to work on that article!

Please let us know if you have any questions or if there's any way we can assist you.
Bob Hayden, Editor
Categories: Hobbies

Name: Bob Hayden, Editor
Name: Dick McNally, Managing Editor
Material: Any
Address: 21027 CROSSROADS CIRCLE
City/State/ZIP: WAUKESHA WI 53187
Telephone: 414-796-8776
Fax: 414-796-1383
E-mail: RMCNALLY@finescale.com
Internet: www.finescale.com

FIRE CHIEF®

Fire Chief

FIRE CHIEF is the management magazine of the fire service, so our readers are predominantly chief officers, especially chiefs of department. We're potentially interested in any article that can help fire chiefs and fire officers do their jobs better, whether that's as incident commanders, financial managers, supervisors, leaders, trainers, planners, or ambassadors to municipal officials or the public.

Our authors are usually fire chiefs, although our contributors over the last several years have included other fire officers, firefighters, civilians and academics.

Article ideas

Unless you're quite sure your article will work for us, it's a good idea to query us first. Even if we like your idea, we can often fine-tune it before you actually write the article, saving both you and ourselves some work in the long run. Your best way to estimate what we're likely to publish is to review some back issues.

The most common reason we reject a manuscript or ask the author to rewrite it is a lack of focus. Writers often tackle too large a topic, with the result that the article winds up too shallow and basic. Narrower and deeper is usually the way to go. Remember that many of our readers are highly experienced officers, often with college degrees and/or training at the National Fire Academy.

Someone recently asked why, since we're the fire service's management magazine, we don't publish more articles on management theory. The answer is that we don't get many good management-related articles. It's easy to string together some quotes from books by people like Peter Drucker or Stephen Covey (or from "Reinventing Government") along with some general ob-

servations about how they relate to the fire service, but our readers won't get much from the resulting article,

On the other hand, if your department has made some changes in its structure, budget, mission or organizational culture (or really did reinvent itself in a serious way), an account of that process, including the mistakes made and lessons learned, could be a winner. Similarly, if you've observed certain things that fire departments typically could do a lot better and you think you have the solution, let us know.

One possible source for article ideas is to ask yourself what your department is really good at. What does your department have a solid reputation for? What does your department do that other departments don't, but possibly should?

One caution in regards to that last point. Often, someone will call or write us to propose an article about a new program his or her department has just put into operation. In such cases, we almost always ask the prospective author to contact us again in six months or so. Napoleon once said that no battle plan survives the first contact with the enemy intact, and similarly, new fire department programs almost invariably go through a phase of fine-tuning once they're up and running. Once you've made those mid-course corrections, you'll be in much better shape to tell our readers how to carry off a similar program.

Another suggestion for article ideas is any courses you might have taught, or any presentations you might have given at a fire service (or similar) conference.

We *do not* publish fiction, poetry or historical articles.

We also aren't interested in straightforward accounts of fires or other incidents, unless there is a specific lesson to be drawn from a particular incident, especially a lesson that's applicable to a large number of departments. If you want to write an article like this for us, be prepared to discuss what went wrong and how it will be handled differently next time.

Feature articles

For features, length is highly flexible. We've run features shorter than 1,000 words and longer than 10,000, though most fall between 2,000 and 3,000 words.

Some of the features we have published started out as Executive Fire Officer papers, master's degree theses or similar academic writing. While the content in these is often good, they usually need extensive rewriting to change the academic tone to one that's more appropriate to a magazine article. Normally we ask the author to take the first shot at this. Also, in anything adapted from academic writing, we ask our authors to keep footnotes to a minimum or avoid them entirely. When they are needed, we reformat them as endnotes.

One of the most common problems with academic papers is a lack of specific examples to illustrate the theoretical points. One way to organize a feature article is by roughly alternating important, interesting, important, interesting," which can also he thought of as "theory, example, theory, practice." All theory makes for a dull, arid article, while all examples can come off as a disjointed series of war stories. Combine them intelligently for the best results.

Columns

Most of our regular columns are written by standing columnists, although three, "Training Perspectives," "EMS Viewpoints" and "Sound Off" are open to outside writers. Typical length is 1,200 to 1,000 words.

If you have a proposal for a training column, contact the editor or Gary Wilson, University of Kansas Fire Service Training, 913-064-4467, (gwilson@falcon.cc.ukans.edu).

If you're interested in writing an EMS column, contact the editor or Kevin Brame, Orange County CA Fire Department, 909-371-3335.

In our guest editorial, "Sound Off," which runs on an occasional basis, a point of view is important, but we also look for columns that go beyond merely opinion and constructively address some issue in the fire service.

Editing

Your article will he edited by one of our staff editors, who will contact you about any areas that need to be clarified or expanded. If your article is typical, you'll probably notice that after editing it's shorter than it was, yet still contains 90% to 100% of the original information.

Time permitting, when an article has gone through heavy editing, or the author has requested it, we will fax a copy of the completed edit (but before final proofreading) to the author. It will be the author's responsibility to get back to us promptly with any final changes or questions.

Artwork

Authors are normally responsible for supplying any art to illustrate their articles, especially photos.

Charts and graphs will be redrawn by our art director or staff artist, and tables will be typeset by someone on our editorial staff.

If there are no photos to go with an article, we will sometimes arrange to have a staff or freelance artist do an illustration in black-and-white or color to go with the article. We encourage authors to work with us in developing ideas for this kind of artwork, but we reserve the final decision as to the form and appropriateness of editorial illustrations.

Copyrights

When your article has been accepted for publication, you'll receive a copyright release form, which you should sign and return to us promptly.

If you have any questions about the form, or if its specific wording might cause any problems, please call us. Although the specific terms of copyright release can sometimes be altered, we must have a signed copyright release on file before we print your article.

One problem prospective authors should be aware of, but often aren't, is when they send the same article or query to more than one publication at a time. In the magazine business, this is called simultaneous submission, and it's a real no-no. The best approach is to decide which publication is the one you most want to submit your article to, and stick with them until they decide whether to publish it.

Scheduling

If you haven't heard from us within 60 days of sending your query or manuscript, please call, fax or e-mail us to follow up. We have a small staff and we sometimes fall behind in reviewing queries and articles.

Articles are sometimes accepted with our intent to publish them in a specific issue or with one or more other articles as part of a specific editorial package. In other cases, an article on an "evergreen topic" will be accepted with our intent to use it in the next suitable issue. (In case planned articles fall through at the last minute, we try to always have several edited articles in reserve, ready to go.)

In either case, circumstances beyond our control can delay an article's publication, sometimes for several months. Combined with deadline pressures, this can lead to the "Hurry up and wait" situation familiar to military veterans, but we ask authors to please understand. An author whose article has been accepted for publication is always welcome to call us and ask for the current schedule on his or her article.

Submissions

We prefer article submissions on a 3.5" diskette with a hard copy, but can make other arrangements. Queries and article submissions can also be e-mailed via ICHIEFS (<FIRECHFMAG>) or the Internet.

Categories: Nonfiction—Emergency Services—Fire Services—Government

Name: Scott Baltic, Editor
Material: All
Address: 35 E WACKER DR STE 700
City/State/ZIP: CHICAGO IL 60601
Telephone: 312-726-7277
Fax: 312-726-0241
E-mail: Firechfmag@connectinc.com

Firehouse Magazine

Firehouse is the world's largest publication devoted exclusively to the fire service. Our primary editorial objectives are to educate, inform and entertain our audience of 1.5 million career and volunteer firefighters and thousands of fire buffs.

Generally, we are interested in all incidents, innovations, controversies and trends that affect the fire service world. Specifically, we concentrate on the following areas:

MAJOR FIRES AND DISASTERS: detailed accounts and technical analyses of firefighting operations at major incidents (see "On the Job" specifications).

APPARATUS AND EQUIPMENT: innovations in fire apparatus and other equipment (including protective gear), advice on purchasing, new and best uses of equipment, converting and repairing equipment, analysis/critique of equipment.

COMMUNILATIONS: equipment, dispatch systems and dispatchers, command centers, fireground communications systems.

TRAINING: methods and tools; new, successful courses; training simulations.

HAZARDOUS MATERIALS: incidents, training, equipment, command, protective equipment.

ARSON: investigation, prevention, analysis. trends.

LAW: fire-related legislation at local and national levels.

FIRESAFETY: new, and successful ways of educating the public.

MEDICINE: health concerns, fitness of firefighters.

LEADERSHIP: improving command skills and systems on the fireground interviews with high-ranking fire service personnel (commissioners and chiefs of major fire departments).

RESCUE: unusual incidents, successful methods and tools.

EMS: major events involving EMTs, concerns of medical technology in the fire service.

FIREFIGHTING HISTORY: great fires of the past, collectibles and memorabilia, fire museums, old-time equipment.

HEALTH AND SAFETY: issues pertaining to firefighter health and safety.

PUBLIC RELATIONS: improving relations with the community, fund raising.

HUMAN INTEREST: lifestyles, profiles of firefighters with unusual hobbies and interests.

Query us first, so we can give you more specific guidance, required length of the manuscript and deadlines. *Firehouse* does not accept multiple submissions; that is, the material submitted must be an exclusive to *Firehouse*. The writer must verify, in writing, that the material submitted is his *original* work, it has not been published previously and that it is not under consideration at another publication.

We would appreciate receiving manuscripts that are submitted on computer disk accompanied by a printed copy. *Firehouse* uses Macintosh computer systems. However, we can convert almost any format and application. Please indicate the system (MS-DOS, Macintosh, etc.), program used (WordPerfect, MS Word, etc.) and how it was saved (ASCII, text, etc.). Please use a Courier 10-point typeface (the standard issue of typewriters) or comparable with one-inch margins throughout the document. Do not hand write corrections on typewritten copy, as our electronic scanning equipment cannot read it. Handwritten, dot matrix printed (without floppy disk) or photocopied manuscripts will be returned.

Please keep in mind that you are writing a magazine article. Most magazine readers, including those of *Firehouse*, want to be able to learn the important aspects of a given topic without having to read through numerous paragraphs of background information. The average length of each article in *Firehouse* is between two and three pages including visuals. In the past we have received manuscripts that would be suitable for the first chapter of a book. Making these stories fit in the allocated space requires a great deal of editing on our part. More importantly, we may be cutting material that you would rather have included. A good rule of thumb is that one typeset page in *Firehouse* is equal to about four double-spaced, typewritten pages.

Firehouse is a visually-oriented publication. Please include photographs (color preferred), illustrations, charts or diagrams that support your manuscript. The highest priority is given to those submissions that are received as a complete package.

Please include a daytime telephone number and fax number if you have one. If we have any questions regarding copy or additional information is needed, we will contact you directly. If you have any stories ready to send prior to deadline dates, please send them along. We appreciate early arrivals.

Firehouse makes payment only upon publication of written and photographic material. Please include your social security number so that payment is not delayed.

If you have any story ideas, questions, hints, tips, etc., please do not hesitate to call. We appreciate and thank you for your assistance, enthusiasm and promptness.

Categories: Fire-related

Name: Submissions Editor
Material: All
Address: PTN PUBLISHING/FIREHOUSE MAGAZINE
Address: 445 BROAD HOLLOW RD
City/State/ZIP: MELVILLE NY 11747
Telephone: 516-845-2700
Fax: 516-845-7109
E-mail: ptnpub@idt.net

First Opportunity

Please refer to Communications Publishing Group, Inc.

First Things
A Monthly Journal of Religion and Public Life

FIRST THINGS does not accept unsolicited manuscripts. Guidelines are as follows:

Opinions: 800-1,500 words. Honorarium of $125.

Articles: 4,000-6,000 words. Honorarium of $450.

Book Reviews: 800-1,500 words. Honorarium of $125.

Review Essays: 4,000-6,000 words. Honorarium of $450.

Categories: Nonfiction—Christian Interests—Culture—Education—General Interest—Government—Jewish Interests—Law—Philosophy—Politics—Public Policy—Religion—Spiritual

Name: James Nuechlerlein, Editor
Material: All
Address: 156 FIFTH AVE STE 400
City/State/ZIP: NEW YORK NY 10010
Telephone: 212-627-1985, -2288
Fax: 212-627-2184

Fitness Magazine

Stories in *Fitness* should appeal to an educated, nationwide audience of women (median age: 30) who are interested in their health, fitness and general well-being. Front-of-the book short features cover news items, health and fitness trends, new products and workout videos. Articles cover a range of topics, including exercise (for mind, body and/or spirit),sports, trend and news-driven special reports, beauty, fashion, sex and relationships, health, nutrition, food, first person profiles and *Fitness* makeovers.

It would be helpful to look at a copy of the magazine before submitting a query. Sample copies are available from our offices for $3.50 or may be purchased at supermarkets and newsstands.

Query letters should give a sample of the style of the proposed article, tell us your angle or perspective on the subject, and specify what material you would like to cover. Please include samples of published writing, preferably consumer-magazine work, and an appropriate-size, self-addressed, stamped envelope with all submissions. *Fitness* assumes no responsibility for unsolicited material.

Acceptance and Payment: If we assign an article, you will be notified of our decision to accept it within six weeks. We do not commit to a publishing date.

We pay within 60 days of acceptance of a completed manuscript. The fee is negotiated when an assignment is made. A written agreement must be signed before payment can be made. We pay a 20% kill fee for assigned manuscripts that are not acceptable for publication.

Categories: Nonfiction—Consumer—Fashion—Food/Drink—Health—Physical Fitness—Psychology—Relationships—Sexuality—Sports—Recreation—Beauty—Diet—Profiles

Name: Jennifer Cook, Executive Editor
Material: All
Address: 375 LEXINGTON AVE.
City/State/ZIP: NEW YORK, NY 10017-5514
Telephone: 212-499-2000
Fax: 212-499-1568

Fitness Management
Issues and Solutions to Fitness Services

FITNESS MANAGEMENT is a popularly written and designed business and professional magazine for decision makers in private-sector adult physical fitness enterprises. Its readers are more than 25,000 owners, managers and program directors of a wide variety of fitness facilities from health clubs to sports medicine centers to corporate fitness nationwide.

Article submissions: We seek articles that are authoritative, timely, clear and brief, that readers can apply to benefit their indoor fitness-service enterprises. Major emphases are on professional fitness leadership and profitable management. Related topics include program leadership, center management, exercise testing and prescription, injury prevention and first aid, applied exercise physiology, diet and nutrition, legal and financial management, marketing, advertising and promotion, retail sales, franchising, auxiliary revenue sources, facility design and equipment, instructor training, client motivation, social director of the center, medically supervised rehabilitation, joint ventures, computer use in management and programs. Articles should solve the problems or meet the opportunities which are specific to our selected readers. An article that would suit the needs of most newsstand fitness magazines probably is not focussed on the particular interests of our readers.

Articles should not promote one company's product to the exclusion of others. (We ask you to state any gainful relationship you have to a company you write about.) Articles should be based on scientifically sound professional knowledge. Editors follow the positions and opinions of the American College of Sports Medicine and check questionable statements with our professional advisors in sports medicine, management and other fields. We do not believe in instant diets, "cellulite," the use of tanning lights, miracle vitamins and little-known cures, for example.

News reports on research and events in health and fitness are used. News must be written succinctly, but interpretively, indicating its application or importance to the reader. Care must be exercised in interpretation; readers should not be led to accept a single research finding as "proof," but should be given at least a hint of the study's meaning in the context of mainstream research in the field. Product news is staff written. It is wise to query at once on new ideas; the staff reads the major journals and will begin to write important news in-house if an author has not expressed early interest. A fresh quote from a researcher makes the piece more desirable than a bare summary of the reported research.

Photo submissions: We buy photographs to accompany articles. We prefer black-and-white and color glossy prints, but accept some sharp 35mm or larger color transparencies. No halftones are accepted. We like to illustrate most pieces. Please indicate your ability to provide photos or illustrations, or state your ideas for illustrating your piece when you query. Payment is $10 per published photo submitted with manuscript.

Article length: 1,000 to 2,500 words for feature articles (about 2,000 preferred). Consider using sidebars, tables or graphs to limit the length of main text. News reports run from 100 to 750 words.

Payment rates: The standard rate is 8 cents per word. Industry professionals who stand to gain exposure from a published piece will not be compensated. Freelance writers whose living depends on fees from articles are paid at the rate of 12 cents per word. Agreed-upon fees are payable on publication. Following the receipt of a query, manuscripts are invited on speculation unless otherwise stated in assignment letter or contract. Firm assignments may be made to proven freelancers, and may specify payment of expenses and a kill fee.

Rights: We buy all rights.

Manuscript mechanics: Standard format should be followed. If in doubt, refer to the guide at the front of this book. Computer printouts are OK (dot-matrix print should be run in double density). Please provide us with submissions on Macintosh or IBM-compatible 3½" diskettes, if possible.

Obtaining an assignment: Send a query letter of two or three paragraphs describing your story idea, indicating your access to authoritative information, and demonstrating the writing style you will apply. A sample of your published writing and a resume may be included. We do not invite unsolicited manuscripts, and may not have time to read them.

Categories: Fitness—Health

Name: Ronale Tucker, Editor
Material: Feature Articles
Name: Christina Gandolfo, Senior Editor
Material: New Products, Press Releases
Address: 215 S HWY 101 STE 110
Address: PO BOX 1198
City/State/ZIP: SOLANA BEACH CA 92075
Telephone: 619-481-4155
Fax: 619-481-4228
E-mail: fitmgt@cts.com

Florida Hotel & Motel Journal

Market: Our magazine is a reference tool for managers and owners of Florida's hotels, motels and resorts—circulation 7,000. The magazine is mailed on the first of each month, except January and August.

Editorial content: Nonfiction only. Preference is given to articles that include references to member properties and general managers affiliated with the Florida Hotel and Motel Association. Since the association acquires new members weekly, queries may be made prior to the scheduling of interviews. This does not preclude the use of materials or ideas based on non-member properties, but member property sources are preferable.

Approach: Queries are encouraged. Articles submitted for an issue with a specific theme must be received two months in advance of the publication date.

Format: Length is determined by nature and import of subject matter, not to exceed 2,500 words unless specified by the editor. Shorter articles with accompanying sidebars are preferred.

Attributions: All opinions, quotations and statements used should be attributable to a creditable source, i.e., a person in the lodging industry, a footnoted quotation from texts or clearly identified as the personal viewpoint of the author.

Writing and editing: *Clarity and organization of content are essential.* The editor reserves the right to edit for grammar, punctuation and simplification of subject matter, as necessary, without changing the author's intent.

Photos and Artwork: Submissions accompanying an article should be of professional quality and authorized in advance by the editor. Color slides and/or black and white glossy prints are acceptable.

Rates and Rights: Payment is $.10 per word upon publication for first U.S.A. rights. Travel and/or telephone expenses must have the editor's advance approval. Three complimentary copies of the issue in which a commissioned article appears will be mailed to the author. Additional copies may be purchased.

Categories: Nonfiction—Associations—Business—Regional—Hotel/Motel Management

Name: Janet Litherland, Associate Editor
Material: All
Address: 200 W COLLEGE AVE
City/State/ZIP: TALLAHASSEE FL 32301
Telephone: 850-224-2888
Fax: 850-222-3462

Florida Keys Magazine

Please refer to *Gibbons—Humms Guide*.
Categories: Consumer—Lifestyles

Name: Submissions Editor
Material: All
Address: PO BOX 6524
City/State/ZIP: KEY WEST FL 33040
Telephone: 305-296-7300
Fax: 305-296-7414

Florida Leader
For College Students

Please refer to Oxendine Publishing, Inc.
Categories: Education

Name: Kay Quinn, Managing Editor
Name: Teresa Beard, Assistant Editor
Material: Any
Address: PO BOX 14081
City/State/ZIP: GAINESVILLE FL 32601
Telephone: 352-373-6907
Fax: 352-373-8120
E-mail: oxendine@compuserve.com

Florida Leader
For High School Students

Please refer to Oxendine Publishing, Inc.
Categories: Teen

Name: Kay Quinn, Managing Editor
Name: Teresa Beard, Assistant Editor
Material: Any
Address: PO BOX 14081
City/State/ZIP: GAINESVILLE FL 32601
Telephone: 352-373-6907
Fax: 352-373-8120
E-mail: oxendine@compuserve.com

Florida Wildlife

FLORIDA WILDLIFE magazine is interested in reviewing articles and photographs on the following topics:
ARTICLES
• Fishing—any freshwater fishing
• Hunting—any Florida game species (prefer not to show graphic scenes), hunters wearing "hunter orange" safety clothing
• Distinctive natural areas in Florida and how to enjoy them
• "How-to" articles for outdoor-related activities—canoeing, camping, hiking, projects, etc.
• Natural history of interesting but little-known Florida animals and plants
• Interesting "Vanishing Florida" stories relating to early Florida's natural history (from a personal perspective)
PHOTOGRAPHS
• Florida natural areas, wildlife preserves and parks
• Florida conservation activities—including individuals working with wildlife officers or wildlife education groups
• How environmental changes affect wildlife-inland or coastal (cause and effect of industry, suburban sprawl, agriculture or litter on wildlife and the environment
• Photo-essay—20 or more quality slides on natural history subjects, preferably with short, narrative text; can be seasonal selections
• Florida plant life—especially rare or endangered plants
• Game birds of Florida—including ducks, quail, turkey, dove

• Florida mammals—game and non-game species, threatened and endangered species
• Freshwater fish—game fish, especially bass, bream and speckled perch, people fishing
• Endangered and rare freshwater fish
• Outdoor activities—hiking, camping, camp cooking, bird watching, outdoor photography, boating, etc.
• Florida reptiles and insects
• **Note:** We have more water bird slides than anything else. Please be selective when sending these. Hard to find photos include black bears, wild boars, rare and endangered mammals, birds, reptiles, fish and migratory birds.

Please put your name on all slides. Identify slides and put subjects/locations on a separate sheet. Include a model release form in scenes where people are featured. Include your mailing address, telephone and social security number. When submitting slides for our freelance files, be aware that we have many files and the magazine is published bimonthly. It may take months before we use your slides. You may call or write us to have your slides returned to you.

Writer's Guidelines

THE LEAD—The lead is the bait you use to lure readers into getting hooked on your story. Write and rewrite ones that grab your readers and pull them into your tale.

THE MIDDLE—This holds the vital innards of your story. This is where you supply the payoff for the reader.

THE END—Wrap up everything here and give the reader a glimpse of the probable future or futures, or point out the value to the reader of what he or she has read.

COVER ALL YOUR BASES—Be sure to answer the questions of: who?, what?, when?, where?, why? and how?, in your stories.

STYLE—Use *The Associated Press Stylebook and Libel Manual* for questions over word usage, grammar, punctuation and so on.

We want bright, crisp copy. If you want to write well, you've got to read excellent material to fuel your brain. Devour *National Geographic* and other well-written magazines.

VOICE—Write in the active voice, not passive. Instead of, "It is possible to have, perhaps, been in error," get to the point and say, "We goofed." (See active and passive voice suggestions below.) Shoot action into your story telling. Good writing takes your reader along on a verbal amusement ride. Use action verbs like those you read in sports stories, when appropriate, such as, hit, smash, pound.

FOCUS—Stay tightly focused on your subject. Tight is right. Look for words or sentences to cut.

RESEARCH—Use at least four sources. Single-source, first-person narratives can frequently be fascinating to the writer and far less so to the reader.

Do lots of research for your story and let the reader know it. Pulling in a wide range of perspectives gives your story and FLORIDA WILDLIFE integrity, breadth, depth and balance. By making your writing reflect comprehensive research, you get closer to reflecting the truth of the situation you're investigating.

Use a broad spectrum of sources, such as magazines, newspapers, brochures, leaflets, news letters, books, encyclopedias, other reference hooks, press releases, interviews with sources, personal experience and whatever it takes to hammer out a good story.

When you use sources other than interviews and personal experience, either paraphrase them in your uniquely clever fashion, or use short quotes, and attribute them accurately. Sometimes it pays to paraphrase nimbly from a piece of writing and attribute it to the source.

FLOW—Keep things flowing—at a quick, smooth pace.

COLOR—A healthy sprinkling of anecdotes breathes colorful life into your stories. Find them and use them.

CONFLICT—Recall your high school English classes and conflict, a crucial element in human story telling. Stories without it are like picnics without ants: something's missing.

COMPLICATIONS—Another pivotal part of story telling is complication and resolution. This builds suspense, makes the reader hunger for more of your deathless prose.

You see complications all the time in TV and movies. The heroine is running from some horrible beast with huge fangs and you wonder if she's going to survive, or become lunch (conflict). She sees a car with the keys in it, jumps in and tries to start it. She keeps trying, the car doesn't start and she appears doomed (complication). She hits the dashboard in disgust, the car starts and she escapes (resolution).

Look for complications in your nonfiction stories. When you start looking for them, you'll see them where you've never seen them before.

PARAGRAPHS—Avoid long paragraphs. Long unbroken chains of words are boring.

PLAGIARISM—Never plagiarize. The first time any one does that for FLORIDA WILDLIFE will be the last.

VARIETY—Vary words that build your story. Elegant variation is a key that unlocks reader interest. Kick out redundancies.

Active Voice vs. Passive Voice

Passive: A good time was had by all.

Active: All had a good time.

Passive: Three suspects were arrested by wildlife officers.

Active: Wildlife officers arrested three suspects.

Passive: One hundred deer were taken by hunters.

Active: Hunters took 100 deer.

Passive: The data was input into the computer by operators.

Active: Operators fed the data into the computer.

Always use the active voice unless there is a reason not too.

Rules of Grammar Often Violated

1. The subject and verb must agree in number.

WRONG: A can of worms are good bait.

RIGHT: A can of worms is good bait.

2. The subject of your sentence can't be singular and plural at the same time.

WRONG: The Commission will consider the proposal at their next meeting.

RIGHT: The Commission will consider the proposal at its next meeting.

3. May and can don't mean the same thing.*

WRONG: Sportsmen may obtain more information by calling the regional office.

RIGHT: Sportsmen can obtain more information by calling the regional office.

WRONG: Hunters can take raccoons at night.

RIGHT: Hunters may take raccoons at night.

"May" involves permission. "Can" involves ability to do something.

HOW TO SUBMIT MANUSCRIPTS

FLORIDA WILDLIFE is a noncommercial, bimonthly conservation magazine published by the Florida Game and Fresh Water Fish Commission to promote hunting, freshwater fishing, outdoor ethics and conservation of Florida's natural resources. Our readership varies from schoolchildren to senior citizens, and a large number of subscribers reside in urban areas and in all 50 states.

Submissions are welcome on all aspects of Florida wildlife, including hunting, freshwater fishing and conservation. Potential contributors are encouraged to study back issues (available at many public libraries) for examples of subjects and style. Well-written Florida fishing and hunting stories which emphasize more than the harvest are welcomed. We use stories on outdoor ethics, nature appreciation, natural history, boating, hiking, camping,

ecology, how-to topics, as well as wildlife photography.

Articles that advertise or promote businesses, refer to alcohol or tobacco products, or use profanity are not accepted. All brand names should be omitted if possible. We also prefer not to show bloody scenes.

We prefer submissions to include text and slides. However, we may be able to provide photographs or art to illustrate outstanding articles, or write text to accompany exceptional slides. Submissions are acknowledged upon arrival.

Submissions are on speculation. FLORIDA WILDLIFE reserves the right to use all or part of your submission. Proper credit is given to authors, artists and photographers. Because we have such a small editorial staff, we review submitted manuscripts rather than answer query letters.

We normally purchase one-time rights to manuscripts and photographs. If submissions are being considered by other magazines, please tell us. We sometimes use photographs and text submitted by different contributors. Contributions are purchased with the understanding that we will edit to suit our style. Separate credits and payments are given in these cases.

PREPARATION OF MANUSCRIPTS: Manuscripts of 800 to 1,200 words may be submitted. IBM compatible 3½" or 5¼" disks created in WordPerfect 5.0 or ASCII can accompany manuscripts. Submit accurate and original (or properly attributed) material. FLORIDA WILDLIFE uses the *Associated Press Stylebook* as a guide and submissions should conform. The first page should include the writer's name, address, social security number and telephone number.

Thank you for considering FLORIDA WILDLIFE.

Categories: Animals—Bass Fishing—Boating—Conservation—Ecology—Environment—Habitat—History—Native American—Outdoors—Recreation—Travel—Wildlife

Name: Richard Sublette, Editor
Material: All
Address: 620 S MERIDIAN ST
City/State/ZIP: TALLAHASSEE FL 32399-1600
Telephone: 850-488-5563
Fax: 850-488-1961
E-mail: subleld@mail.fl.us

Flower and Garden Magazine

Subject Matter: Articles in *Flower & Garden* must specifically relate to the topic of home gardening. This includes, but is not limited to, information on enhancing the homeowner's outdoor living areas. All stories must focus primarily on ideas that can be applied to the home garden and outdoor environs. How-to articles are the best way to approach topics, although historical and background articles are considered if a specific adaptation can be obviously related to home gardening. Story ideas that do not fit into the category described will not automatically be eliminated, but it is always best to query first. *Flower & Garden* is a national magazine with a circulation of over 650,000 subscribers, so articles must have a broad-based appeal.

Queries & Manuscripts: Queries should include 1) a statement of the article's purpose, 2) an outline of the proposed article and 3) suggestions for illustrations or photography and an indication of graphics to be provided for consideration. Whenever we deem it necessary, alternate means may be found to illustrate an article if we feel submitted graphics do not adequately illustrate the message conveyed. *Flower & Garden* is published six times a year and stories are generally scheduled one to two years in advance of publication. Because of the long lead time, you are advised to query before submitting finished manuscripts so we may make suggestions to enhance the chances of your material being accepted. Completed manuscripts should include a short, succinct author bio suitable for publication. Good quality slides/transparencies increase your chances of acceptance. When applicable, source lists or charts of detailed information make for a better article. We are able to professionally finish any rough drawings you may supply and appreciate seeing some type of graphic with your completed manuscript.

Although all submissions are handled with care, safe return of unsolicited materials is not guaranteed. Please include a self-addressed stamped envelope (SASE). Allow us six to eight weeks to report on submissions.

Photographs: We prefer to receive photographs that accompany a related manuscript rather than unsolicited photos with no text. Black-and-white prints are used occasionally, but for the most part, flowers, gardens and plants look most appealing in color. Photos should be sharp, clear, evenly exposed and of top quality. An accurate packing list must accompany all submissions. Work must be labeled with the photographer's name, including address if possible. Individual slides should be numbered with a corresponding description sheet including Latin botanical and common names. Accurate identification is extremely important. In shots of individual flowers or plants, clearly indicate which end is up on each photo. Although all submissions are handled with care, safe return of unsolicited materials is not guaranteed. Please include a SASE (with adequate return postage) with all submissions. We will make every attempt to be prompt in notifying you of our interest or in returning your submission. Please allow us three to four weeks for consideration. It is our policy to pay for photos upon publication, so be aware that there is often a considerable delay in returning accepted photos. Duplicate slides or transparencies do not provide reproduction suitable to our standards, so please do not submit duplicates or ask us to make duplicates and return your originals immediately. If our photograph policy is unacceptable to you. please write and explain your special circumstances and we will attempt to make alternate arrangements.

Pay Rates: Rate of pay varies with use, required editing and quality of material. It is our policy to pay for manuscripts on acceptance and photos separately upon publication.

Article Type, Word length, Payment: Featurette, 500 words, $200 ($250 for story and one usable color photograph). Feature article, 1,000 words, $350-$500 (depending on the technical nature of the material, required editing and author's credentials).

Photo Rates, Size used, Payment: Color slides or transparencies preferred.
1/4 page, $100
1/2 page, $150
Full page, $200

Note: Cover photos must be submitted as transparencies 2-1/4" or larger. 35mm slides or color prints are not suitable for covers.

Sample copies are available for $4.50. Make check or money order payable to *Flower & Garden*.

Categories: Nonfiction—Environment—Gardening—History—How-to—Landscaping—Home

Name: Editorial Department
Material: All
Address: 700 W. 47TH ST., SUITE 310
City/State/ZIP: KANSAS CITY, MO 64112
Telephone: 816-531-5730
Fax: 816-531-3873

Flyfisher

We're looking for writing and photography that help us reinforce our mission to 'conserve, restore and educate through fly fishing.'

Founded in 1965, the Federation of Fly Fishers (FFF) is the nation's largest, oldest and most influential fly-fishing organization. The *Flyfisher*, first published in 1968, is the Federation's flagship publication and this country's oldest fly-fishing magazine.

Circulation of each issue is a minimum of 12,500 copies. More than 10,000 copies are delivered by mail to FFF members. The balance is distributed by the FFF to its nearly 200 affiliated local fly-fishing clubs around the country, to retail fly shops, at fly-fishing shows and expositions and in FFF promotions.

Mirroring the FFF's mission to "conserve, restore and educate through fly fishing," each issue of the *Flyfisher* takes a hard look at resource issues affecting cold-water, warm-water and salt-water game fish and their habitats.

The magazine also serves as an educational tool for the FFF and its International Fly Fishing Center, providing practical information focusing on fly fishing techniques—including emphasis on fly tying, which many FFF members enjoy. *Flyfisher* editorial also aims to attract and support new constituencies for the sport, particularly women and youths.

Feature stories

We carry features that have been the hallmark of the *Flyfisher* for nearly 30 years. We're particularly interested in how-to and technique features, fly-fishing history and tradition, personality profiles and interviews, personal narratives, fly-fishing trends, conservation profiles, fly tying and, on rare occasions, fiction. We'll run occasional where-to-fish stories that feature a fishing destination, but feel these types of stories predominate in the for-profit magazines and are less reflective of the FFF mission. Length should be from 750 to 1,500 words. Payment: $50 to $150.

Conservation stories

We run conservation-oriented stories as short news stories of not more than 400 words, or as longer stand-alone features not exceeding 1,500 words. At various times the *Flyfisher* will also feature a longer story or package of stories focusing on a conservation issue of national concern that impacts the quality of freshwater or saltwater fishery habitats or resources. We're looking for top-notch environmental journalism that 1) gets *Flyfisher* readers interested in the topic and concretely demonstrates how it affects the sport of fly fishing; and 2) provides easily assimilated information that will further reader knowledge. Length should be from 750 to 1,500 words for an individual story, or up to 2,500 words for a package of stories. If querying a conservation package idea, please suggest possible sidebar subjects and visual support. Payment: $20 to $40 for short conservation stories; $50 to $150 for stand-alone feature stories; or $150 to $250 for a package of stories.

Photography

We're always interested in photography to accompany writing, and good photos make a story more attractive to us. Although we assign very little photography, we use several stock images per issue. We encourage interested photographers to submit a list of subjects in stock and a resume of credits. If you wish to submit photos for consideration, the *Flyfisher* staff responds within one month of receiving materials with an Acknowledgment of Receipt and will hold materials with potential for use for up to 90 days.

Solicited material will be returned via Postal Service certified mail.

We use black-and-white photos which should be submitted

as 5"x7" or 8"x10" prints, or as negatives with proof sheets. For color, we use 35mm or larger format transparencies. We may wish to reproduce a color photograph in black-and-white; if you object to this, please specify when submitting. Payment: $10 to $25 for black-and-white usage, $15 to $50 for color, $100 for cover. Credit line is given on all photographs. Model release is required when subject is easily identifiable and potential for litigation exists.

General guidelines

Although we'll look at unsolicited manuscripts, we encourage writers to submit query letters. If you are simultaneously submitting your story or photos elsewhere, please specify this. We also like to see one or two clips or writing samples from authors with whom we are unfamiliar.

Accuracy is of paramount importance. Writers are responsible for the accuracy of their stories, and for ensuring names and proper nouns are correctly spelled. For some subjects we may require writers to send us background material and a source list to help us perform fact checking.

Keep the length of your story within the guidelines set forth above. We strongly favor concisely written stories. Also, remember the *Flyfisher* is published in February, April, July and November; bear in mind our seasonal needs and query at least 120 days prior to the season for which your story is appropriate.

The first page [of your manuscript] should include your name, address, phone number and social security number. We use a Macintosh computer system and welcome submissions on disk in any word processing program. If you write on an IBM compatible, simply save in ASCII (text only) format on a 3.5" floppy. If you do send a disk, be sure to send along a hard copy, too.

We may also receive your story via e-mail. At this time, however, we prefer that queries be sent by regular U.S. mail, rather than as e-mail.

The *Flyfisher* buys first North American serial rights, and payment is made on publication. Writing is done on speculation unless a kill fee is agreed to in advance.

Categories: Fishing

Name: Richard Wentz, Managing Editor
Material: All
Address: PO BOX 1722
City/State/ZIP: SANDPOINT ID 83860
Telephone: 208-263-3573
Fax: 208-263-4045
E-mail: Flyfisher@keokee.com

Fly Fisherman

Fly Fisherman is the nation's first and largest consumer magazine devoted solely to the sport of fly fishing. Most other national outdoor magazines give coverage to hunting, camping, boating and other sports or, in the case of general fishing publications, give coverage to other types of fishing in addition to fly fishing.

We don't assume that all of our readers are expert fly fishermen, nor do we assume that they are all novices. We select material for publication that, overall, provides stimulation to the accomplished, instruction to the beginner, and even an invitation to non-fly fishermen. Similarly, we provide geographic coverage that meets our responsibility as an international publication.

Almost all of our contributors are avid readers of the magazine, and their submissions reflect a familiarity with the style and content of material used in the magazine. Potential contributors should likewise familiarize themselves with the kind of material *Fly Fisherman* uses by looking over recent issues.

Eighty percent of *Fly Fisherman*'s readers are college educated, and nine out of ten of them are male. However, the magazine is regularly read by other members of the household-including non-fly fishermen. Our readers fish for almost any species of fish that will take a fly in fresh or salt water.

Editorial Format

The general types of articles that we normally publish include:

1. Main features of 2,000-3,000 words, illustrated with black-and-white prints or color transparencies (slides) or both. These articles embrace a wide variety of subjects, including major destinations—where to fish; instruction about fishing techniques, and how to tie flies; Fiction, humor and personality profiles are used infrequently and represent a very small portion of the articles we purchase each year.

2. Short features of about 750-1,500 words usually illustrated in black-and-white or color. These articles highlight a specific aspect of the sport; most are short destination or how-to-do-it stories. The short feature is an important component of our magazine. It allows us to present a wide variety of information and topics to our readers.

3. Technical feature articles of about 2,000 words, illustrated in black-and-white or color, deal with subjects that lend themselves to presentation in the "Fly Tier's Bench"; or "Tips From The Experts," departments. Sometimes these are used in the main feature section of the magazine. The text usually includes step-by-step instructions (such as fly-tying instructions), and if such instructions are included, appropriate photos, illustrations, or diagrams should accompany the text.

4. Mini-articles of 100-800 words, concentrate on a very specific experience or aspect of the sport. These stories are illustrated in black-and-white (if they are illustrated at all) and may deal with a range of topics similar to those mentioned under short feature articles; but the mini-article is much more crisp and to the point in its presentation of information.

All submissions to *Fly Fisherman* containing factual information must be thoroughly and carefully documented. Double-check stream or lake locations and names (especially spelling); if you're unsure of any factual detail and can't document it, leave it out. When referring to insects or fish by their Latin names, consult a standard college text for correct spelling and nomenclature.

Photographs and Artwork

We can't overemphasize the importance of quality illustrations to accompany submissions. Color photographs should be in the form of 35mm slides or 2¼" x 2¼" transparencies, as color prints do not reproduce satisfactorily. The preferred format for black-and-white photographs is 8"x10" glossy prints. Articles are best accompanied by both black-and-white and color, giving us the option of using one or the other or both to illustrate your work.

If you don't have photos, send the article anyway—we may have the appropriate illustrations on file. However, good photos often sell an article that is less than the ultimate coverage of a topic.

Quality color or black-and-white art is always welcome. Often we request permission to keep a selection of such submissions on file here so that we can draw from them to illustrate appropriate stories.

All photographic submissions should be accompanied by a caption sheet. Such sheets should identify each slide (or black-and-white print) and include an appropriate credit line and the names of the water, fish species, insect species, etc., that are pictured. A credit line and general location information should be written on the border of each slide or on the back of each black-and-white print.

If we request permission to hold your photos on file here, payment is not made until publication. Naturally, if you request any or all submissions on file to be returned, we will do so promptly.

If you wish to submit color photographs for consideration as covers, they must be of exceptional quality and must be appropriate for vertical format.

Maps and diagrams should be submitted with articles when called for by the text. When submitting fly-tying articles, drawings or black-and-white prints showing tying steps should be included when appropriate.

Submissions of cartoons are welcome.

Preparation of Material and Submission Procedures

We do not accept photocopies of original manuscripts. Computer printouts are acceptable. We also accept manuscripts on computer disk. Manuscripts on 3½" disks in Microsoft Word can be accepted directly. Other files on disk must be in the ASCII or Text format. The name, address and phone number of the author should be on the first page of the manuscript. The name of the story, the name of the author and the page number should be on each ensuing page of the manuscript. The author's name and credit line (if different) should be on each piece of photographic material or artwork submitted, and care should be taken to package all material properly before mailing.

We strongly recommend that you query us in advance on a specific article or article idea. A query allows us to suggest a slant on the article, or at least to inform you in advance of our interest in your proposed story idea

Reporting on the status of submissions adheres to the following schedule. Upon receipt of a submission we'll send an acknowledgement; within six to eight weeks after receipt, material will either be returned, purchased or we'll ask for permission to retain it pending further consideration. Article queries will be answered within four weeks, and queries concerning the status of submissions (after our reply deadline of six to eight weeks) will be answered immediately.

Payment

Payment is made within 30 days of publication or acceptance of material. *Fly Fisherman* buys first-time North American rights. *Fly Fisherman* does not accept simultaneous submissions or previously published material. Shortly after publication, all photos, illustrations, diagrams, maps, etc. will be returned. Original manuscripts will be kept here on file. (Writers who regularly make submissions to any publication should familiarize themselves with the current copyright laws.)

Fees to contributors vary according to the manuscript's professional level, frequency of accepted contributions, and length of article. The same applies to photographs and artwork. Fees range from $300 to $500 for main features, from $100 to $250 for short features, from $200 to $300 for technical features and from $50 to $100 for mini-articles.

Fees are paid for complete packages, which include manuscript, artwork, and photographs. Payment for photographs and artwork purchased without manuscripts is determined by the size and use inside the magazine and ranges from $35 to $200. We pay $500 for a photograph used on the cover of the magazine.

Publication Schedule

Fly Fisherman magazine is published six times per year. The editor usually purchases manuscripts one year in advance.

Months of Issue: February, March, May, July, September, December

Style Guide for Potential Contributors

1. Indent the first line of each paragraph.

2. Show the end of a story by writing End, The End, 30, #, or similar mark.

3. Use standard scientific nomenclature when referring to insects: Consult standard references, such as "Mayflies of North and Central America," Edmunds et al, for correct spellings.

4. The common names of insects are lower case, the proper names of fly patterns are capitalized: The black gnats were a nuisance that night, but I caught four trout on a Black Gnat dry fly.

5. The common names of fish are lower case unless the name includes a proper noun: I like to fish for coho salmon, Chinook salmon, Atlantic salmon and brown trout.

6. Some preferred spellings: caddisfly, drys (dry flies), fish-for-fun, fly-fishing, fly-fishing-only, fly rod, fly-rodder, fly tier, fly-tying, Matuka, marabou, mayfly, mylar, no-kill, Opening Day, snowmelt, snowpack, stonefly, whip-finish.

An excellent, concise and handy guide to style is *The Elements of Style* by William Strunk, Jr. and E.B. White (2nd ed., Macmillan Publishing Co., New York, 1972, $1.95) and we recommend it highly.

Please advise us of any change in your address or telephone number so that we may keep our files up to date and ensure that your submissions are returned safely. Include both home and office phone numbers as well as any seasonal addresses.

Categories: Fishing

Name: Editor
Material: Fly Fishing
Address: 6405 FLANK DR
City/State/ZIP: HARRISBURG PA 17112

Fly Fishing in Salt Waters

Thanks for your interest in *Fly Fishing in Salt Waters* magazine. If you would like to write for **FFSW** please send us a query letter first with a clear, succinct outline of the article you propose. We will respond as quickly as possible.

About the Magazine: FFSW is a highly designed, graphic-oriented magazine serving a diverse world-wide audience of saltwater fly fishers ranging from beginners to experts. Contributors need not be experts themselves, but they should have a thorough knowledge of their subject and plenty of fly-fishing experience to back it up. We are interested in thoughtful, provocative articles about saltwater fly fishing anywhere in the world, especially articles that blaze new trails—for example, stories about new fly-rod species, new places to fish, new techniques, or new methods. The best advice we can give potential contributors is to study the magazine carefully to see what type of content we prefer.

FFSW is a copyrighted magazine published six times a year (December/January, February/March, April/May, June/July, August/September, October/November). Articles aimed at a specific issue should be submitted *at least* 90 days in advance of publication.

FFSW buys first North American serial publication rights plus the right of storage and retrieval through electronic media. Reporting time usually is four to eight weeks.

FFSW buys five or six feature articles per issue, plus additional material for regular departments. Requirements are as follows:

Feature Articles: These range up to 2,000 words. Text and photos (35mm color transparencies) usually are purchased together as a package (if a photo submitted along with an article is chosen for use on the cover, the author will receive additional payment). We prefer thoughtful, well-researched articles with a major emphasis on new developments in saltwater fly fishing—destinations, species, techniques, etc. Writers are encouraged to rely on personal experience, when appropriate, and provide a full description of the environment in which they do their fishing.

Pay starts at $300 for a first sale and ranges up to $500 or more for experienced writers, depending on the quality and importance of the article and the amount of work necessary to prepare the article for publication (for example, we will pay more for an article submitted on a computer disk that does not require scanning or rekeying for typesetting).

Fiction: FFSW buys occasional high-quality fiction related to saltwater fly fishing. These pieces can range up to 2,500 words. Pay is up to $500.

Departments: Most department material is staff-written, but several departments are open to free-lancers. These include:

• **Fly Tier's Bench:** Articles up to 1,200 words about saltwater fly patterns and how to tie them. Each article should focus on a single pattern. This may be a new pattern or a variation of a traditional pattern, so long as its use and effectiveness is well documented. The article should tell something about the fly's history and use, provide a list of necessary materials and clear step-by-step instructions on how to tie it. These instructions must be accompanied by clear, genuinely illustrative close-up photos (35mm color transparencies) that show each key step in the tying process. The photos should be shot against a neutral-colored background (*not* black) providing enough contrast to clearly display the materials used to tie the fly. Pay is $400-$500.

• **FFSW Budget:** Articles up to 1,200 words describing "budget" saltwater fly-fishing trips. These should include a brief description of the area and its fishing, necessary tackle and fly patterns, plus lists of nearby accommodations and restaurants (including addresses, phone numbers and price ranges), fly shops, guides, and similar services. Obviously the costs described in the article should support the "budget" theme. Only one or two photos are necessary to illustrate these articles, but the editors prefer to see a wider selection. Pay varies.

• **Tackle & Technique:** Articles up to 1,500 words describing new or unusual items of saltwater fly-fishing tackle or proven new techniques. This should include a brief description of how the item or technique was developed and by whom, plus anecdotes concerning its use, if appropriate. Clear, concise descriptions of techniques are essential, as are photos and/or illustrations. Pay is $400-$500.

• **Resource:** Articles up to 1,500 words describing a resource or conservation issue of key importance to saltwater fly fishers. These articles must be carefully researched and documented and authors should not shy away from taking a strong point of view, if justified. Photos are not required for this type of article, although they are welcome if they help illustrate the point of the article. A query letter is especially important for articles aimed at this department. Pay is $400-$500.

• **Legends and Reminiscences:** Profiles of famous, legendary or pioneer saltwater fly fishers, guides, fishing clubs, etc., or personal reminiscences of saltwater fly fishing in bygone days. Preferred length up to 2,000 words, with photos. Again, a query is essential. Pay is $400-$500.

• **New Products:** This department normally is staff-written, but freelance contributions may occasionally be accepted. Articles should cover new products aimed at saltwater fly fishers, such as tackle, boating accessories, sunscreens or other skincare preparations, eyewear, clothing, etc. Articles should carefully describe the new product and provide such information as sizes, colors, prices, etc. They should be brief—no longer than 500 words—illustrated with appropriate photos. Pay varies. Again, be sure to query first.

• **Salt Spray:** Short (100-300 words) news items of interest or to saltwater fly fishers. Examples: Tournament results, the sale of an important lodge, new saltwater fly-rod records, awards, oddities, humorous experiences, etc. Pay is $25-$50 for items accepted. No query necessary.

• **Saltwater 101:** This department is aimed at helping newcomers to saltwater fly fishing. Articles should deal with basic saltwater fly-fishing techniques and tackle, with emphasis on teaching. Preferred length 1,500 words, plus photos or illustrations. Pay up to $500. A query is essential.

*M*anuscript Submission Requirements: Text should be submitted in printed form (letter-quality type) *and* on a 3½" computer disk (IBM-compatible ASCII format preferred). The first page of the manuscript should include the author's name, address and telephone number. Also *be sure to include your social security number*. Manuscripts should be accompanied by color transparencies and maps or other illustrations, if appropriate, in a single package (see photo submission requirements, below).

FFSW does not publish poetry.

Photo Submission Requirements: We accept 35mm (or larger) color transparencies only. *Captions must accompany transparencies in every case*. Each transparency also should be clearly labeled with the name and address of the photographer.

Color prints or black-and-white photos will be considered only if they are of historical significance and necessary to illustrate an article that is historical in nature (for example, the Legends series). Photos of dead fish are NOT accepted.

FFSW buys stand-alone photos for covers or to augment illustration of articles inside the magazine. Again, *captions are necessary in every case*. Payment for cover photos is on publication and ranges up to $500. Payment for photos used inside the magazine also is on publication and varies according to the number and size of photos used.

Maps and Other Illustrations: Maps and other artwork needed to illustrate articles should be submitted with manuscripts. These may be in rough form for finishing by **FFSW** artists, or in a form suitable for scanning into a computer, or as graphic files on a computer disk. Ordinarily such illustrations will be purchased as part of a package along with an article and photos.

Categories: Fishing

Name: R. P. Van Gytenbeek, Editor and Publisher
Material: All
Address: 2001 WESTERN AVE STE 210
City/State/ZIP: SEATTLE WA 98121
Telephone: 206-443-3273
Fax: 206-443-3293
Internet: www.flyfishinsalt.com

Flying Horse

Flying Horse, an alternative literary journal published semi-annually, features short fiction, poetry, essays, black-and-white photographs and art work. We seek heterogeneity of voice. Circumstance, class, and formal education are not weighed. Nor do we count writing credits. What moves us to say *yes* is the authority of a submitted work, its conviction and originality of expression.

• We accept submissions throughout the year.
• Fiction and essays should be limited to 7,500 words or less.
• Poets may submit up to 10 poems at one time.
• Artists and photographers are encouraged to submit work. Please do not send original art.
• We accept simultaneous submissions.

Although *Flying Horse* welcomes contributions from all talented artists, we particularly hope to give voice to those often excluded from the dominant media. For example, we actively solicit inner city learning centers, community and public colleges, prisons, homeless shelters, social service agencies, unions, the military, hospitals, clinics or group homes, Indian reservations and minority studies programs for contributors. Please allow two months for a response. *Flying Horse* will pay each successful contributor $10 to $25 for one-time publication rights plus two journal copies.

Single Issue: $4.00 Subscription: $7.00 a year

Categories: Fiction—Nonfiction Essays—Poetry—Short Stories

Name: Dennis Must, Editor
Material: All

Address: PO BOX 445
City/State/ZIP: MARBLEHEAD MA 01945

FOCUS Kansas City

Please refer to Communications Publishing Group, Inc.

The Food Channel

The Food Channel is an Internet resource site and bimonthly food trendletter created by Noble & Associates, a food-marketing agency. It provides the latest information, and promotes new thinking, on the trends and issues facing the food industry today.

The Food Channel is the food industry's only interactive resource to provide readers with top line news and trends on topics affecting all aspects of the food industry. Its analysis of new products, consumer preferences and opportunities, as well as insight into the future are *The Food Channel*'s most appealing attributes. Our editorial board is always in search of new material that will extend the depth and range of food knowledge among subscribers. They are particularly interested in:

- Culinary Trends
- Eating Trends
- Foodservice Trends
- Packaged-Good Trends
- New Product Development
- Consumer Issues Related to Food
- New Products (Food)
- Food Science and Technology
- Beverage Trends
- Nutrition Issues
- Government Regulations Pertaining to Food
- International and Domestic Food Show Coverage

The director maintains close contact with writers throughout all stages of article development to ensure the integrity and quality of articles published. Copies of research used in story development are maintained on file with the editor. Prospective authors should send a resume and copies of recent work to the editor at the address shown below.

Notes for Contributors

Copyright Infringement: Authors submitting articles for publication warrant that the work is not an infringement of any existing copyright and will indemnify the publisher against any breach of such warranty.

Electronic Publishing: *The Food Channel* is made available electronically via the Internet, with plans to expand to other electronic formats in the future. All articles written for, and published by, *The Food Channel* become its property.

Preparation of Articles: Length should be determined with editor before article is submitted.

Typing: Articles should be submitted on an IBM or Macintosh compatible disk, double spaced, with one-inch margins.

Headings: Every 250 words (approximately), initial caps only without underlining.

Payment: Amount of payment determined by the editor.

About the Publication

Frequency: Biweekly

Distribution Base: 2,500

Price: $195/year (24 issues); $245/year foreign rate

Categories: Business—Food/Drink

Name: Joshua Isenberg, Editor
Material: All
Address: 515 N STATE ST 29TH FLOOR
City/State/ZIP: CHICAGO IL 60610
Telephone: 312-644-4600

Fax: 312-644-0493
E-mail: webmaster@foodchannel.com
Internet: www.foodchannel.com

Food & Service

Food & Service is a four-color magazine published 7 times a year for restaurant owners and managers by the Texas Restaurant Association. Each issue includes four or five feature articles, but *Food & Service* is not a magazine filled with sumptuous pictures of food. Its purpose is to inform restaurateurs of wise business practices, trends, legislative issues and actions, employee concerns, new products and Association and chapter activities. Circulation is approximately 5,500.

The magazine has been included in *Print's Regional Design Annual*, has won the Press Club of Dallas' award for best special interest magazine, has won Best of Austin awards in the categories of Best Four-Color Magazine and Best Design/Four-Color Magazines and is listed in *Artist's Market*.

Food & Service's editor is Olivia Carmichael Solis. Its art director is Gina Wilson.

WRITER'S GUIDELINES

Before your assignment

- Query: Do not submit unsolicited manuscripts.
- Send clips with your query.
- You should be experienced in writing about business.
- Ask for a copy of the Food & Service editorial calendar. Topics are tentative and suggested. Choose one, or use the topics to create a related one of your own.
- Do not propose human interest stories, restaurant reviews, recipe stories or wine articles.

Your article

- Sources must be members of the Texas Restaurant Association. Articles about nonmembers will be returned. Call the editor to determine what companies or restaurants are members.
- Features should be four to seven double-spaced typed pages, 12-pitch (about 10 point).
- Submit manuscript on 5.25" diskette for IBM PC compatibles in Microsoft Word Version 6.0 or less, or in ASCII. (Macintosh diskette in Microsoft Word or ASCII is acceptable, but not preferred.)
- Write informally, but don't use jargon, trendy '90s cant, journalese, legalese or computerese.
- Use quotations freely.
- If a sidebar seems natural for a feature, write it. Think in terms of tips, numbers, dos and don'ts, lists, testimonials, how-to.
- Do not take photographs unless you want to. Do not hire a photographer to take photographs. If we need them, we will assign a photographer.

Normal turnaround time for articles

Usually one month, and seldom less than three weeks.

Rates for articles

Determined for each article. Cover feature pays approximately $500, and other features pay approximately $250 to $350, depending on length.

Publishing rights

TRA buys first-time rights unless otherwise stipulated.

Copies of published article

You will receive two copies of the issue in which your article appears.

Categories: Texas Restaurants

Name: Olivia Carmichael Solis, Editor
Material: Restaurants & Food Service
Address: 1400 LAVACA ST

Address: PO BOX 1429
City/State/ZIP: AUSTIN TX 78767-1429
Telephone: 512-472-3666
Fax: 512-472-2777
E-mail: osolis@tramail.org
Internet: www.txrestaurant.org

Fourteen Hills: The SFSU Review
San Francisco State University

Fourteen Hills: The SFSU Review is a literary journal dedicated to high quality innovative work. Writers published in recent issues include Amiri Baraka, Ron Carlson, Paul Hoover, Bernadette Mayer, Aaron Shurin, and CD Wright.

Fourteen Hills accepts submissions of fiction, poetry, short plays and creative nonfiction. To be considered for the fall issue, your submission must be received by September 15; the deadline for the spring issue is February 15. No more than one submission of fiction (three maximum if short-shorts) and five submissions of poetry per writer, please.

Sample issue/Back issue: $5.00
Single issue/Current issue: $7.00
One year subscription (Two issues): $12.00
Two year subscription (Four issues): $21.00

Prices include shipping and handling. Please enclose a check payable to *Fourteen Hills: The SFSU Review.*

Categories: Drama—Gay/Lesbian—Literature—Poetry—Short Stories—Women's Fiction

Name: Submissions Editor
Material: All
Address: DEPT OF CREATIVE WRITING, SFSU
Address: 1600 HOLLOWAY AVE
City/State/ZIP: SAN FRANCISCO CA 94117
E-mail: hills@sfsu.edu

The Fractal

The Fractal publishes literary science fiction, fantasy and horror genre short stories, poetry, nonfiction essays and line art. Experimental forms and ideas are encouraged. Rejections are accompanied by editors' comments and suggestions.

Fiction and Poetry
• Name and address should appear in the upper right corner of the first page. Name, the title and the page number should appear on all subsequent pages.
• *The Fractal* pays $25 for accepted fiction submissions and $5 for accepted poetry submissions.

Nonfiction
• *The Fractal* publishes academic nonfiction, interviews, and reviews of academic work.
• *The Fractal* pays $50 for accepted nonfiction submissions.
• Name and address should appear in the upper right corner of the first page. Name, the title and the page number should appear on all subsequent pages.

The Fractal reserves first publication rights to accepted work. Subsequent rights revert to the author/artist.

The Fractal accepts fiction, poetry and art based on original characters and situations only; please do not submit media-based stories.

If Hemingway were to have written science fiction, if Lawrence were to have written fantasy, if Faulkner were to have written horror, *this would be the work we are seeking.*

Art
• *The Fractal* uses black and white line art, and a small number of halftone pieces.
• *The Fractal* pays $25 for cover illustrations, and $5 for interior art.
• Art submissions should be pen and ink. Query first for charcoal or pencil art or photography.
• For art submissions, the name should appear in pencil on the backs of all submissions.

The Fractal is published semiannually in a digest sized (8.5"x5.5"), black and white, 60 page publication.

Single copies/sample issues are five dollars U.S. each.

One year/two issue subscriptions are eight dollars U.S.

The Fractal is available for classroom use. Universities, colleges, and instructors should contact *The Fractal* for further information.

Distributors and bookstores interested in carrying *The Fractal* should contact our offices directly.

The Fractal back issues are five dollars U.S. each. Available issues include:
• Fall 1993 (Limited numbers available)
• Spring 1994
• Fall 1994
• Spring 1995
• Fall/Winter 1995

The Fractal is copyrighted by Fractal Ink Press.

Categories: Fiction—Nonfiction—Horror—Literature—Poetry—Science Fiction—Short Stories

Name: Lisa Jirousek, Fiction Editor
Material: All Fiction
Name: Scott Deck, Nonfiction Editor
Material: All Nonfiction
Name: Malia Miller, Poetry Editor
Material: Poetry
Address: 4400 UNIVERSITY DR MS 206
City/State/ZIP: FAIRFAX VA 22030
Telephone: 703-933-2904
E-mail: FRACTAL@gmu.edu

THE FREEMAN
IDEAS ON LIBERTY

The Freeman
Ideas on Liberty

An Invitation to Authors

We welcome the opportunity to consider thoughtful articles exploring the principles underlying a free society: private property, the rule of law, voluntary exchange, individual morality and responsibility, and limited government. We publish both scholarly and popularly written articles; we prefer nonfiction.

Though a necessary part of the literature of freedom is the analysis of collectivist errors, we emphasize the positive case for freedom. We advocate the methodology of freedom; self-improvement rather than compulsory reform of others. We try to avoid name-calling, and we believe satire is of little use as an educational device. We do not advocate political action as a cure for problems caused by government intervention.

Manuscript Preparation
- Manuscripts should be typed, and accompanied by a letter including the author's name, address, telephone number, social security number, and a sentence or two that we may use to identify the author to our readers.
- Suggested manuscript length: 1,500-3,000 words. (Manuscripts should not exceed 5,000 words; we welcome shorter articles and book reviews.) Book reviews are accepted for books published during the present and the preceding year.
- Please send your manuscript on both paper and computer disk. We prefer WordPerfect 6.0 or 5.1 on a 3.5" disk.
- Facts and quotations must be fully documented.
- We prefer to purchase full rights to an article, but we will withhold reprint rights at the author's request. We prefer original manuscripts. By submitting an article, the author is warranting that he has unencumbered rights to the article. We pay our authors when their articles are published.

Categories: Economics—Education—Government—History—Philosophy

Name: Submissions Editor
Material: All
Address: 30 S BROADWAY
City/State/ZIP: IRVINGTON NY 10533
Fax: 914-591-8910
E-mail: freeman@westnet.com

Fresh Cut
The Magazine for Value-Added Produce

Editorial Focus: *Fresh Cut* magazine is written for people in the food business who manufacture, sell, use or distribute packaged salads or cut and packaged fresh fruits and vegetables. Articles can be written for actual produce processors as well as retail grocers, restaurant or foodservice operators, and others who handle or distribute these products.

Article Length: No more than 1,200 to 1,500 words, 1,000 words for guest opinion.

Suitable Articles

Feature stories: Again, fresh-cut processors can be the focus of such articles, but retailers who have had success with specific items or with their fresh-cut section in general and foodservice operators who use fresh-cut products successfully can also be feature material.

New Technology: Articles can include new equipment, packaging, supplies, processes or other advances which make the world a better place for processors or users of fresh-cut products.

Eating Trends: Time is the commodity of the 90s and articles illustrating how consumers are turning to convenient, healthful fresh-cut produce items are meat for *Fresh Cut* magazine. Any new and exciting fresh-cut product is fair game. Reports on health and nutrition as they relate to fresh fruits and vegetables and the 5 A Day Program are also of interest. Even information from other magazines can be reported or quoted in *Fresh Cut.*

Meeting Reports: Speakers who address topics related to fresh-cut produce often relate important news for our readers. Reporting their messages makes excellent copy.

Food Safety: Articles could include sanitation techniques, sanitary plant and equipment design and even keeping the "cold chain" intact to assure optimum product shelf life.

Categories: Nonfiction—Food/Drink—Produce & Processing—Technology

Name: Submissions Editor
Material: All

Address: PO BOX 9036
City/State/ZIP: YAKIMA WA 98909-0036
Telephone: 509-248-2452
Fax: 509-248-4056
E-mail: Ken@freshcut.com
Internet: www.freshcut.com

Frontiers
Washington State University Press

Frontiers is published three times a year at Washington State University, Pullman, Washington, under the editorship of Sue Armitage and the Frontiers Editorial Collective, which includes Shelli Booth Fowler, Jo Hockenhull, Maria Montes de Oca Ricks, Camille Roman, Marian Sciachitano, Noël Sturgeon, and Amy Wharton. The Collective is joined by a distinguished roster of contributing editors. *Frontiers* has published feminist scholarship and literary works since 1975.

Frontiers: A Journal of Women Studies is a juried publication committed to the discussion of the full variety of women's lives *as* they are shaped, for example, by such factors *as* gender, race, class, and sexual orientation. We seek papers that explore this variety through interdisciplinary scholarly work as well as literary and artistic contributions. We encourage unsolicited submissions.

All textual submissions must be word processed, unstapled, and accompanied by a title page with the author's name. No other page in the manuscript should identify the author. Two copies of the text should accompany the original. One set of visual materials is sufficient and slides are preferred. Art should be identified only by title, medium, and number. A list of all work sent, which includes the artist's name and address, should accompany the submission. Artists are responsible for insuring work, and only copies of originals (35mm slides or black and white photos) should be submitted for editorial review. Most published work will be in black and white.

Scholarly articles must follow *The Chicago Manual of Style,* 14th edition, for text and endnotes. Permissions are the responsibility of the author.

Manuscripts are judged by the members of the Editorial Collective and by readers who have competence in the applicable field(s). This initial process usually requires three months. If the article is accepted for publication, we reserve the right to edit and/or revise it, in consultation with the author, in accordance with our space limitations and editorial guidelines. Contributors receive two copies of the issue in which their work appears.

Copyright for published material belongs to the Frontiers Editorial Collective, Inc. We do not consider previously published material or work under consideration by other journals.

Subscriptions and orders for back/sample issues should be addressed to Frontiers, Washington State University Press, 99164-5910. Personal Subscription: $24; Single Issue: $9. All orders must be prepaid. Make checks (US funds) payable to *Frontiers: A Journal of Women Studies.* Visa and MasterCard accepted.

Categories: Feminism—Gay/Lesbian—Hispanic—History—Multicultural—Women's Fiction—Women's Issues—Scholarly

Name: Managing Editor
Material: All
Address: WILSON 12
Address: WASHINGTON STATE UNIVERSITY
City/State/ZIP: PULLMAN WA 99164-4007
Telephone: 509-335-7268
Fax: 509-335-4377

E-mail: frontier@wsu.edu

Funny Times

Dear Writer/Cartoonist Person,

Thanks for your interest in the *Funny Times*. We are currently looking for material and welcome your submissions. We are especially interested in written humor columns, interviews, book reviews, stories, and 1-2 page comics.

Here are some guidelines:

• Your submissions should be funny. If it isn't funny, don't bother sending it to us.

• Most of our material is reprinted from other sources or syndicated. We welcome submission of previously published material.

• Our pay rates vary, but in all cases are pitifully small. We pay upon publication. Figure about $20 for a single panel cartoon and $50 for a humor essay.

• We buy one-time rights; all other rights stay with the copyright holder.

• Send copies only, no originals. We cannot promise you will ever receive back anything you send us.

• Include a SASE; if not, you can simply assume you've been rejected unless we call or write you.

• There are only two of us reading these, and sometimes it takes a long time to get through it all. Don't expect a lightning-fast response and don't bug us.

• Send only complete work. No query letters.

Now get to work! Make us laugh!

Sincerely,

Raymond Lesser and Susan Wolpert

Co-editors

Categories: Humor

Name: Submissions Editor
Material: All
Address: 2176 LEE RD
City/State/ZIP: CLEVELAND HTS OH 44118
Telephone: 800-811-5267
Fax: 216-371-8696
E-mail: FT@funnytimes.com
Internet: www.funnytimes.com

FUTURIFIC

Futurific Magazine

Futurific Inc., **Foundation for Optimism,** is a not-for-profit research and educational organization reporting its findings every month in *Futurific Magazine*. We highlight positive developments in all subject areas—everything from international affairs, science, technology, and finance, to all aspects of human interest. *Emphasis is on accurately forecasting the future*. Material submitted, text and/or graphics, should provide realistic forecasts and/or analysis of what the future *will* be.

FUTURIFIC welcomes book, software, CD-ROM, hardware, magazine, movie, theater, or other reviews, short stories, interviews and poetry providing they follow the guidelines listed above. Copy should be appropriate to the subject. Art work accompanying the submission, graphics, cartoons and illustrations are all useful.

Typically, writers retain full rights to their work and receive a number of copies of the issue in which their work appears un-

der their byline. Based on the importance of their story, writers occasionally receive payment for their expenses. These conditions are negotiable.

FUTURIFIC accepts no responsibility for unsolicited queries, articles, photographs, short stories or poetry.

Submissions accepted on 3½" or 5¼" diskettes, DOS compatible format.

Categories: Nonfiction—Agriculture—Architecture—Automobiles—Aviation—Business—Computers—Economics—Education—Electronics—Energy—Engineering—General Interest—Internet—Military—Money/Finance—New Age—Politics—Public Policy—Science—Society—Technology—Television/Radio

Name: Submissions Editor
Material: All
Address: 305 MADISON AVE
City/State/ZIP: NEW YORK NY 10165
Telephone: 212-297-0502
Fax: 212-297-0502
E-mail: KEY TO NYC@aol.com

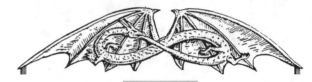

The Gate

Thank you for your interest in writing for THE GATE.

THE GATE does not accept fiction or poetry. It only accepts factual articles that deal with some aspect of the paranormal. If you have a topic that you'd care to research and write about then please drop me a quick note and let me know what it's about. This way we can avoid any duplication of manuscripts. If you can't seem to come up with a topic, then feel free to choose one I have listed below. Once you decide, I again ask that you contact me and tell me which one you have chosen.

Sea serpents
Alchemy
Lake monsters/swamp creatures
Strange footprints
Surviving dinosaurs
Animal oddities
Fortean falls (blobs, fish, etc.)
Mysterious places
Spontaneous human combustion
Secret societies
Ley lines and unknown energies
Poltergeist activity
Out-of-place animals
Unexplained sounds
Fairies, gnomes and giants
Astronomical Strange haloes and fireballs in the sky
 Ancient technology
Mysteries
Big birds (pterodactyls, thunderbirds, etc.)
Unusual artifacts found in diggings
Events preceding earthquakes
Ancient astronauts
Pre-Columbian visitors to America
Invisible assailants
Archeological anomalies
Synchronicity
Prophecies
 I also suggest a trip to the library. Most large libraries have

adequate paranormal and Fortean books available that will list numerous and exciting topics.

Article length is 1,500 words or less. Payment is one contributor's copy and reporting time on submissions is immediately. Accepted articles are published on a first come, first served basis. No deadlines are available. If you have any further questions, please write.

Sincerely,
Beth Robbins
Editor

Categories: Nonfiction—Paranormal

Name: Beth Robbins, Editor
Material: All
Address: PO BOX 43516
City/State/ZIP: RICHMOND HTS OH 44143

Gateway Heritage

Thank you for your interest in *Gateway Heritage*, the quarterly magazine of the Missouri Historical Society. Please send one copy of your manuscript to the address below. A Macintosh or PC disk with your manuscript and the name of the word processing program you used to prepare it is also requested. Though the magazine no longer publishes endnotes, if notes are necessary they should be supplied and prepared in accordance with the *Chicago Manual of Style*, as we keep them on file and in our library for those who are interested.

Gateway Heritage publishes articles on St. Louis and Missouri cultural, social, and political issues, both historical and contemporary. Submissions for full-length essays ideally run 3,500 to 5,000 words (not including notes). *Gateway* also publishes shorter essays in its departments. Submissions for these departments should run approximately 1,500 to 2,500 words.

The Missouri Biographies department features essays focusing on individual Missourians. Submissions to this department often can not (and should not) cover a subject's entire life. Some of the most successful biographical sketches choose one particular aspect of their subject on which to focus.

Literary Landmarks includes sketches of literary figures with a Missouri background.

Our Gateway Album department features excerpts from diaries and journals from the Missouri Historical Society's collections and other collections.

Missouri Memories highlights firsthand accounts of Missouri's historical personalities and events.

In the Collections focuses on the Missouri Historical Society's artifacts.

Finally, At the Society spotlights events and the work of the staff at the Missouri Historical Society.

Not all articles submitted to *Gateway Heritage* are subject to a referee process, but some articles may be sent to scholars or other experts for advice and guidance. In addition, if you are affiliated with a university or college that requires your article be submitted for peer review, such review will be arranged. In any case, you will be notified if your article will be sent out for review.

In general, the editor will let you know within four weeks from the date your submission is received in the office if it will be accepted for publication; if there will be a delay longer than four weeks, you will be notified. Should you have any other questions on our submissions policy, feel free to contact us by mail or by telephone.

Categories: History—Regional

Name: Tim Fox, Editor
Material: All
Address: PO BOX 11940

City/State/ZIP: ST LOUIS MO 63112-0040
Telephone: 314-746-4557
Fax: 314-746-4548

George & Mertie's Place

GMP is published monthly, except January. Samples are $2.00.

GMP uses stories, essays, poetry, tidbits with a twist, jeremiads, and polemicals...you name it! Subject matter, style open. Our goal is to create an entertaining sometimes informative, monthly literary *canape*.

GMP pays a penny a word, plus a copy of issue. Minimum of $2.00 for anything we use. **GMP** also **awards a $10 best of issue prize** each month.

GMP is a micro-magazine (4 to 8 unbound pages, 8½"x11", on colored stock paper). Our limited space means we cannot publish everything we would like to. Maximum prose length would be 2,500 words. 1,000-1,500 is best.

We purchase **first serial rights** and the right to republish your work in any future anthology of exclusively **GMP** work (such as a 10 year retrospective). All other rights return to creator.

Include a cover letter with biographical notes. We are not seeking a long list of publication credits but for biographical details which will personalize your entry if published.

Turn-around in 30 to 60 days.

Categories: Fiction—Nonfiction—General Interest—Poetry—Politics

Name: Submissions Editor
Material: All
Address: PO BOX 10335
City/State/ZIP: SPOKANE WA 99209-1335
Telephone: 509-325-3738

Georgia Journal

Articles are assigned on speculation and only on the basis of a query letter. **We do not accept unsolicited manuscripts and queries by phone**. Allow up to six months for a response to a query.

Georgia Journal accepts only nonfiction articles with **authoritative, well-defined points of view**. We are interested in all aspects of Georgia's human and natural history, including the roles historic personalities played in shaping our state, important yet sometimes overlooked historical/political events, archaeological discoveries, unsolved mysteries (both natural and human), flora and fauna, and historic preservation. We encourage sidebars, such as interesting marginalia and reading lists.

We also accept adventures that explore the Georgia landscape. These may range from strenuous activities such as biking, boating, rafting, back-packing, rock climbing and caving, to weekend antique hunting, camping, walking tours, arts & crafts festivals and driving trips. Adventures should be told through the author's personal experience and point of view, include a historical perspective on the locale explored, and be accompanied by detailed map data and other pertinent location information, such as tips on access, lodging and camping.

Georgia Journal is looking for authoritative topical articles as well. Subjects may include Georgia's environment, lifestyle and social trends, mysteries, and profiles of Georgia authors, adventurers, artisans, artists, sports figures and other personalities.

We pay 10 cents a word, upon publication. Feature articles may range up to 5,000 words, including sidebars. The Back Porch essay and other departments should be no longer than 750 words. Articles for the Pure Georgia section may range up to 500 words. **No article will be accepted unless accompanied by a list of sources.** These must include reference books, newspaper or magazine articles, and the names, addresses and phone numbers of the people the author interviewed to obtain information, however insignificant.

Georgia Journal publishes a limited amount of fiction and poetry, but while it encourages promising new writers, it is not looking for first-time or unpublished authors. Optimum length for short stories is 4,000 words. **Stories and poems must have a Georgia theme and a Georgia setting.** Payment varies, depending on publishing history; poems are paid with copies of the magazine.

Because *Georgia Journal* is in many homes, libraries and schools, articles, short stories, poems and photographs must be appropriate for the general reader.

All manuscripts must include name, address and Tax ID number of the author on the title page. **No article will be accepted unless also on 3.5" IBM-formatted computer disk in either WordPerfect the ASCII generic format.** Please do not double-space the article on disk. We follow the *Associated Press Stylebook* for punctuation, spelling and general style.

Georgia Journal is published bimonthly. Publication dates are: Jan/Feb, Dec. 15; March/April, Feb. 15; May/June, April 15; July/Aug, June 15; Sept/Oct, Aug 15; Nov/Dec, Oct. 15. Send $5.00 for sample copy. Editorial deadlines generally are two months before publication dates.

Mail queries and submissions to the address below. Mail poetry submissions to Janice Moore, Poetry Editor, PO Box 144, Young Harris, GA 30582.

Categories: Nonfiction—Adventure—Agriculture—Antiques—Biography—Civil War—Ecology—Environment—Gardening—Outdoors—Poetry—Regional

Name: David R. Osier, Publisher & Editor
Material: General
Name: Janice Moore, Poetry Editor
Material: Poetry
Address: PO BOX 1604
City/State/ZIP: DECATUR GA 30031
Fax: 404-377-1820

German Life

German Life is a bimonthly, written for all interested in the diversity of German culture, past and present, and in the various ways that the United States has been shaped by its German element. The magazine is dedicated to solid reporting on cultural, historical, social, and political events.

Writers/Reporters

Starting Out—To suggest a story send us a query letter with backup clips. Refrain from sending us a lengthy, wordy proposal. Three or four concise paragraphs should be enough to pitch your idea. Keep in mind that we receive numerous solicited and unsolicited manuscripts. The more directly and quickly your proposal stands out, the better your chances to be recognized.

Timing is Everything—Each issue of *German Life* is bound by our editorial calendar and seasonal events. For example, a summer travel piece would likely find its way into the April/May issue, which typically covers topics for summer but also fall travelers; our October/ November issue is dedicated to Oktoberfest. Depending on your interests, plan accordingly! Given scheduling restraints, we prefer that you submit your work several months prior to the appropriate issue.

Manuscript Mechanics—Your manuscript should not exceed 2,000 words. Longer pieces will be considered solely at the Editor's discretion. Manuscripts considered too lengthy will be immediately returned for revision. Smaller tidbits fit for a sidebar or one of the magazine's anecdotal departments should range between 30-800 words. Book reviews average 25-350 words.

Due Credit and Accuracy—Please ensure that we are the sole recipients of your manuscript. If the piece is being considered by other publishers or has already been published, we will return it to you. Moreover, please guarantee your work's originality. Give proper credit for any other author's ideas that you may use. If your article recounts only firsthand experiences, references are seldom necessary. In all other cases, cite the direct source on a separate sheet of paper, following *The Chicago Manual of Style*. Check the accuracy of your items carefully!

Submission—On the title page, include each author's name, current position, mailing address, daytime telephone, and fax number.

Please submit manuscript **both** on disk and as hard copy. We accept IBM-compatible 3.5" or 5.25" high density disks. Both manuscript versions must be double spaced. Submit the original(s) (including photos, slides, and/or illustrations), along with a SASE.

Photographers/Illustrators

Starting Out—With or without manuscript, feel free to submit photographs, transparencies, or illustrations that are in accordance with the magazine's direction and style. We look for pictures that capture and/or detail the diversity of German(-American) life and culture, including images of everyday life, landscapes, people, architecture, art, festivals, and so on.

Timing is Everything—Please read carefully the notes on timing in the Writers' section of these guidelines.

Photo/Illustration Mechanics—Photos should be black-and-white or color glossy prints, 5"x7" or large, with excellent focus, fine grain, and clear contrasts. Tape an identifying label to the back of each photo. Do not write on back of photos-ink stamp or paper clip labels to them.

Transparencies are the most frequently purchased photographic material without manuscripts. 35mm slides are acceptable. For best reproduction on press, slides should be perfectly exposed or slightly underexposed. Identify slides by writing your name, the location, and the subject on the margins.

For illustrations, any medium is acceptable. With four-color art, please send 35mm transparencies. Computer illustrators may submit four-color laser printouts of their work (e.g., maps, charts, and graphs) for consideration. In the case of black-and-white art, we prefer to first see photocopies. However, unless you are (have) a professional artist (available), submit only rough sketches for figures and diagrams. Type captions on separate sheet of paper, along with any credit lines.

Due Credit—Please note that any photograph or illustration with an article must be credited and a photograph release form must be included. A release must also be signed by the person or party responsible for object(s) not open to public photography (e.g., special museum items). In addition, to avoid legal complications and embarrassing situations, please alert us to any purchase of your work by other publications.

Submission—Include with each submission all relevant contact information, such as the artist's name, current position, mailing address, daytime telephone, and fax number if available.

For each photograph, submit on separate piece of paper a description and photo credit. Please do not submit more than 25 glossies at a time. The same goes for transparencies. On separate sheet of paper, include a description and photo credit for each. Place slides in individual plastic protectors and in a plastic slide sleeve fit for 20 slides. Limit your submission to 80 slides or four slide sheets at a time.

With your permission, we will keep visual materials of appropriate quality and interest for our files. Photographs, slides, illustrations, and sketches are returned only upon request.

The Editorial Process

Acknowledgment—Expect acknowledgment of your submission within one to two weeks from the date of receipt. The editorial staff considers all manuscripts, solicited and unsolicited, without obligation for publication. Within four to six weeks of acknowledgment, the Editor will notify you of the decision on your submission-revision request, acceptance, or rejection. Manuscripts requiring revision are either returned in original form or first edited and then sent to the author for approval.

Acceptance—If your submission is accepted, you will receive notice within one week of our decision. *German Life* purchases over 60 manuscripts annually. Most manuscripts are published from three months to one year after acceptance. Publication of photographs/illustrations depends on need and topic.

Please be advised that all manuscripts at the acceptance stage, including solicited works, are considered on speculation. You will be duly alerted when your accepted manuscript/photo/illustration has been scheduled into an upcoming issue.

Payment is upon publication and ranges from $300 to $500 for feature articles, from $100 to $130 for reviews and short pieces, and to $80 for fillers. In exchange for remuneration, *German Life* retains first English/German language serial rights.

Final Status—All manuscripts are edited for style, consistency, and clarity. The editorial staff will send you a copy of the edited manuscript for approval shortly before publication. The final title of the published article, subheads, captions, photographs and illustrations, and other elements that attract attention to an article or contribute to the tone and appearance of the magazine are the Editor's prerogative.

The Publisher reserves the right to change these policies at any time.

Categories: Special Interest (German)

Name: Heidi L. Whitesell, Editor
Material: All
Address: 1 CORPORATE DR
City/State/ZIP: GRANTSVILLE MD 21536
Telephone: 301-895-3859
Fax: 301-895-5029
E-mail: GWWC14A@prodigy.com

Gibbons-Humms Guide
to the Florida Keys and Key West

Dear Author:

Thank you for your interest in Gibbons Publishing, Inc. Our guidelines for FLORIDA KEYS MAGAZINE, the *GIBBONS-HUMMS GUIDE to the Florida Keys and Key West*, and ADVENTURE FLORIDA are:

• We accept queries or manuscripts on subjects pertaining to the Florida Keys, including people, history, humor, wildlife, ecology, sports, events, etc. Material should be broad and informative, with several quotes.

• All submissions should be on a 5¼" or 3½" WordPerfect floppy diskette (versions 5.0, 5.1, and 5.2 are acceptable, as well as most IBM compatible software), or clearly typed.

• No submission should exceed 2,000 words.

• Photos may be submitted with manuscripts, but there is no additional payment.

• Payment is $2.00 per printed column inch, with a maximum of $50.00, and will be paid on publication. Gibbons Publishing, Inc. does not offer a kill fee for returned or rejected articles.

• All submissions are subject to review by the Editorial Committee. Gibbons Publishing, Inc. reserves the right to accept or reject any article submitted (whether submitted on spec, unsolicited, or by assignment) without giving a reason, based on the committee's collective opinion.

Please feel free to contact us if you have any further questions or wish to discuss article ideas.

Again, thank you for your interest in our magazines, and good luck with your writing.

Sincerely,
GIBBONS PUBLISHING, INC.
Tara Valdez
Editorial Assistant

Categories: Consumer—Reference—Tourist Guide

Name: Submissions Editor
Material: All
Address: PO BOX 6524
City/State/ZIP: KEY WEST FL 33041
Telephone: 305-296-7300; 800-273-1026 (South Florida)
Fax: 305-296-7414

Girlfriends MAGAZINE

Girlfriends Magazine

Girlfriends Magazine is America's fastest-growing lesbian magazine. Our mission is to provide its readers with intelligent, entertaining, and visually pleasing coverage of culture, politics, and sexuality—all from an informed and critical lesbian perspective.

The sections for which we encourage freelance submissions are:

Parenting: 600 words from a first-person perspective. Anecdotal, controversial, and challenging pieces encouraged. Tell us what is different about your parenting experiences, your children, or your family structure. Give us examples. Must include two or more photos of you and your child(ren)/family.

Travel: 800 words in main text; 180 word sidebar on "best-of" the profiled area. You must tell us something unique about the area; tell us something no one else could tell us.

Fiction: 1,300 words maximum. All styles considered.

Humor: 800 words; must have some relevance to lesbian readers.

Sports: 800 words; action-oriented profile of a particular athlete, team or group involved in a sport that has some interest among lesbians. Tell us what is unique about this particular athlete.

Spirituality: 600 words; profile-oriented piece on a religious leader or activist that has some relevance to lesbians. Profiles of unusual or underrepresented religions also encouraged if they have some particular meaning for lesbians.

Health: 600 words; essay or how-to article on socio-political health issue (is Prozac good?) or on a particular ailment that affects lesbian women (breast cancer; yeast infections).

Authors are encouraged to query the editorial staff via letter or e-mail before they submit unsolicited material. Please make sure you study the magazine's style and previous articles before you send us unsolicited work. (Note: some book, video, movie, music & multimedia reviews may also be written on assignment; query with clips of work.)

Fees: *Girlfriends* magazine pays ten cents per word for all written contributions.

Please keep in mind that we use the *Chicago Manual of Style* in considering the editorial clarity of our contributions. It is strongly encouraged that you read an issue of the magazine before you send material in for consideration.

For editorial submissions, we would like copy to arrive on floppy disc, formatted in Microsoft Word for the Macintosh. Traditional and express mail are acceptable. Please allow six to eight weeks for a response.

Categories: Nonfiction—Culture—Entertainment—Feminism—Gay/Lesbian—Politics—Sexuality

Name: Donna Han, Editorial Assistant
Material: All
Address: 3415 CESAR CHAVEZ STE 101
City/State/ZIP: SAN FRANCISCO CA 94110
Telephone: 415-648-9464
Fax: 415-648-4705
E-mail: staff@gfriends.com
Internet: www.gfriends.com

Girls' Life ™
The New Magazine for Girls

1. Girls' Life does not accept unpublished fiction or poetry from adults.

2. Girls' Life accepts unsolicited manuscripts on a speculative basis only. Send query letters with descriptive story ideas. Please include a detailed resume and published writing samples.

3. All stories will be assigned by the editors. Once assigned, a memorandum of agreement is to be executed by both parties before payment is made.

4. Every story should have a headline, by-line, introduction, lead, body and conclusion. Author's full name and address must be provided. Referrals for art sources are appreciated.

5. Girls' Life conforms to The *Associated Press Stylebook and Libel Manual*. Please submit in MS Word 5.1 or similar program on disk.

6. All research must rely on primary sources. Manuscripts must be accompanied by a complete list of sources, telephone numbers and reference materials.

7. Queries are responded to within 90 days if submitted with a self-addressed stamped envelope. If material is not returned in due time, it has been placed in a file for possible future consideration.

Categories: Fiction—Animals—Children—Cooking—Crafts—Ecology—Entertainment—Environment—Fashion—Film/Video—Food/Drink—General Interest—Interview—Money/Finance—Music—Outdoors—Poetry—Relationships—Sports—Technology—Travel—Young Adult

Name: Kelly White, Senior Editor
Material: General
Name: Kim Childress, Associate Editor
Material: Books
Name: Anne Gregor, Associate Editor
Material: Computers
Address: 4517 HARFORD RD
City/State/ZIP: BALTIMORE MD 21214
Telephone: 410-254-9200
Fax: 410-254-0991

Glimmer Train Stories

The mechanics of writing can be taught, the basic rules and tools and guidelines, but as in any art, all the rest comes from doing and doing and doing. The most important part of the process is learning to trust one's own vision, to work hard at developing one's own style and voice, and then having the confidence to follow where it goes.

-Mary McGarry Morris

GUIDELINES FOR STANDARD SUBMISSIONS
• 1,200 - 7,500 word limit, typed and double-spaced.
• Our issues have no themes. Please, no poetry, children's stories, or nonfiction.
• Simultaneous submissions are okay.
• Send your stories during the months of January, April, July, and October.
• We pay $500 for first publication and nonexclusive anthology rights. Payment is made upon acceptance.
• Please include a self-addressed sufficiently stamped envelope for the return of your manuscript, or a single-stamped envelope if you would prefer we send a response only.
• Single issues available for $9 in most bookshops or directly from us payable by check.

SHORT STORY AWARD FOR NEW WRITERS
• Open to any writer whose fiction hasn't appeared in a nationally-distributed publication with a circulation over 5,000.
• Story length: 1,200 - 7,500 words. Must be typed, double-spaced, and not previously published.
• Our issues have no themes, but please, no poetry or children's stories.
• **First-place winner receives $1,200, publication in *Glimmer Train Stories*,** and twenty copies of that issue. Second- and third-place winners receive $500/$300, respectively.
• **Please staple all pages together.** Cover letter is optional. First page of story to include your name, address, and phone. No need for SASE, as materials will not be returned.
• **$11 check covers reading fee** for up to two stories sent together in same envelope. Please be sure the address on your check is correct: we will mail results to all entrants.
• **Please write "Short-Story Award"** on the envelope.
• **Contest opens December 1 and ends March 31.** Entry must be postmarked between these dates.

VERY SHORT FICTION AWARD
• Open to all writers, published and unpublished.
• Story length **must not exceed 2,000 words.** (Word count needs to appear on first page of story.) Must be Typed, double-spaced, and not previously published.
• Our issues have no themes, but please, no poetry or children's stories.
• **First-place winner receives $1,200** and possible publication in *Glimmer Train Stories*. Second- and third-place winners receive $500/$300, respectively.
• **Please staple all pages together.** Cover letter is optional. First page of story to include word count and your name, address, and phone. No need for SASE, as materials will not be returned.
• **Reading fee is $10 per story.** Please be sure the check address is correct. We will mail results to all entrants.
• **Please write "Very Short Fiction Award"** on the envelope.
• **Contest opens April 1 and ends July 31.** Entry must be postmarked between these dates.

Since winning the Short-Story Award for New Writers, numerous agents have contacted me, and that story has been picked up by two anthologies. Clearly, Glimmer Train has a meaningful readership.

-Steve Adams

Categories: Fiction—Literature—Short Stories

Name: Submissions Editor
Material: All
Address: 710 SW MADISON ST STE 504
City/State/ZIP: PORTLAND OR 97205
Telephone: 503-221-0836
Fax: 503-221-0837
Nota bene: Reading fee required for AWARD entries.

Glamour

Thank you for your request for guidelines.

Most of our readers are women between the ages of eighteen and thirty-five, and articles that are slanted to our older readers must work for the younger ones as well. We do not publish short stories or poems, and although we want timely articles, we steer away from subject matter that will seem dated by the time of publication.

We do review manuscripts; however, we usually prefer to see a proposal first, as we may already have assigned or published an article on the same subject.

"Viewpoint," our opinion page, is approximately 1,000 words, for which we pay $500-$1,000. As the name implies, "Viewpoint" works best when the writer has a strong point to make about a newsworthy subject. Our "Bridges" column is also approximately 1,000 words, for which we pay up to $1,000. "Bridges" essays attempt to span racial, religious, sexual and experiential gaps of all kinds. For articles of 2,000 or more words, we pay $1,500 and up. Manuscripts should be typed and double-spaced, and a self-addressed, stamped envelope should be enclosed.

We appreciate your interest in *Glamour*.

Sincerely,

Pamela Erens, Articles Editor

Categories: Nonfiction—Book Reviews—Careers—Cooking—Entertainment—Fashion—Food/Drink—Health—Physical Fitness—Psychology—Relationships—Society—Travel—Beauty—How-to—Lifestyles—Women's Issues

Name: Pamela Erens, Articles Editor
Material: All
Address: CONDÉ NAST 350 MADISON AVE.
Street/State/ZIP: NEW YORK, NY 10017
Telephone: 212-880-8800
Fax: 212-880-6922
E-mail: glamourmag@aol.com

Gnosis

A Journal of the Western Inner Traditions

GNOSIS welcomes the submission of material dealing with all aspects of the esoteric and mystical traditions of the West. In order to make our efforts compatible, please keep the following guidelines in mind.

• We prefer that manuscripts be typewritten (or computer-printed), with your name, address, and phone number in the upper right-hand corner of the first page. Please leave generous margins on each page. If you write on an Apple Macintosh, it would be helpful if you could send a disk containing your article, in the event we accept it, so that we don't have to retype it. (If you use an IBM-compatible computer, we request articles in ASCII or MS Word format on a 3½" disk.)

• It is OK to send us a photocopy or printout of your manuscript; be sure to indicate if you do not need it returned and if it has also been submitted elsewhere. We prefer that submissions not be made simultaneously to several publications at once.

• We try to respond promptly to all submissions. At most we try to take no more than two months to respond. Please be patient and allow up to ten weeks before expecting to hear from us. Our response to submissions may be delayed during production the five weeks before each issue's publication.

• Though we work to maintain a high level of scholarship, GNOSIS isn't an academic journal per se. Our goal is to bring the discussion of the esoteric and mystical traditions to an interested general public. Accordingly, you are encouraged to write in an accessible, informal manner, as if you are talking to an intelligent, interested friend. Displays of enthusiasm, emotion, or subjective opinion are not taboo, though you should keep in mind that GNOSIS is more interested in exploring points of agreement or clarifying differences between traditions and paths than in sponsoring wrestling matches. Since space is always at a premium, we prefer writing that is concise, to the point, and engaging. It is very helpful if you familiarize yourself with the kind and style of material that we publish before submitting your own.

We are looking for the following kinds of material:

• first and foremost, articles that fit within the themes of upcoming issues (see list below); articles on esoteric traditions and practices, past and present (up to 5,000 words);

• news items relating to current events in esoteric spirituality (up to 1,000 words);

• book reviews of new spiritual and occult books rarely reviewed elsewhere (up to 1,000 words); interviews with spiritual teachers, authors, and scholars (varying lengths);

• letters to the editor (up to 250 words). We do not pay for letters.

All lengths indicated are approximate.

• If you have a topic you would like to pursue, we encourage you to send us a short query letter—well ahead of the deadline date before you begin writing. If possible, include a clipping or photocopy of writing you've done, if you think we may not be already familiar with your style. All published contributors receive contributors' copies, and a complimentary four-issue subscription. In addition, we are presently paying $100-$250 per article, depending on length, editing requirements, and other considerations. Book reviews receive $50 per book reviewed. Please note: we cannot pay "kill fees." All submissions are "on spec." Payment is upon publication.

• We reserve the right to copy-edit material for style, grammar, and conciseness. If major rewriting or editing are called for, we will try to contact the author before publishing. We generally try to avoid cuteness, recycling of material available elsewhere, or story ideas more appropriate to other focused publications such as *Yoga Journal* or *Shaman's Drum*.

• GNOSIS buys first-use rights and nonexclusive reprint rights. Contributors reserve other rights. We reserve the right to post selected articles and reviews on-line through the GNOSIS conference on The WELL (Whole Earth 'Lectronic Link), our gopher site on the Well and on the World Wide Web. Our contributors retain their own copyrights.

Sample copies of GNOSIS are available for $7 (plus $2 postage) from the address below. Subscriptions are $20 per year in the U.S., $25 per year for foreign readers. GNOSIS is published quarterly.

We appreciate your interest and look forward to hearing from you.

Categories: Paranormal—Philosophy—Religion

Name: Richard Smoley, Editor
Material: All Submissions and Inquiries
Address: PO BOX 14217
City/State/ZIP: SAN FRANCISCO CA 94114-0217
Telephone: 415-974-0600
Fax: 415-974-0366
E-mail: smoley@well.com

GOLD and TREASURE HUNTER

Gold and Treasure Hunter

Writers' & Photographers' Guidelines

Written Material

The editorial staff of *Gold & Treasure Hunter* is looking for how-to articles on gold mining and treasure hunting, fiction and nonfiction stories about mining and treasure hunting experiences, or about experiences in the great outdoors. Fiction material must be labeled as such. We also publish interesting profiles about people within our industry. Since we are a membership organization dedicated to preserving our rights to mine gold and recover treasure, we are also interested in articles concerning our legal rights, politics and issues. We publish some historical articles and routinely review products on new equipment within the industry.

Important: We do not print stories or articles which are primarily oriented toward the promotion of a product or service. However, we do not object to the author mentioning the type of equipment used during a gold find or treasure discovery or who to contact for more information about locations to visit or other services written about in an article.

Preferred Material

Our general readership is comprised mostly of individuals who are actively involved in gold mining or treasure hunting, or people who are interested in reading about others who are active and successful in the field. True stories of actual discoveries, along with good color photos—particularly of gold—are preferred. Also, valuable how-to information on new and workable field techniques, preferably accompanied by supporting illustrations and/or photos.

Rate of Pay

We purchase your material for three cents per published word, $10 for each black and white photo used, $10 to $25 for each illustration/cartoon used, $25 for each color photo used, and $50 for the main cover photo if used alone or as a full bleed. Payment is made upon publication, along with a copy of the magazine. Please include your social security number along with your submission if you wish to receive payment.

Internet Publishing and Rates

We reserve the right to republish any of our previously published and paid for material inside our Internet publication, *Wonderful World of Gold and Treasure Hunting*. Any material which we publish on the Internet that has not yet been printed in our magazine will be paid at the rate of $.02 per word and $10 per photo used, with the balance of magazine rates to be paid if and when the same material, or a portion of it, is published in the printed magazine.

Photographs

Since our magazine is very much a graphically oriented publication, good quality photographs are vitally important. Probably more manuscripts are rejected for poor illustrations or poor quality photography than for any other reason. All photos should be sharp with good composition and include captions. **Please do not write or mark on front or back of photos!** We prefer good quality prints rather than negatives—although we can work with the negative if you are sending us a print that is damaged or poorly developed. We also work with 35mm color slides.

General Copy Requirements and Length

IBM compatible 5¼" or 3½" disks along with computer print-out are also acceptable. We also work with Macintosh formatted 3½" disks. All disks will be returned once we are finished with them. Copy should be as sharp and clear as possible in order that our scanning equipment will be able to read it with minimum error. Please send original printed matter. Manuscripts can be up to 2,000 words in length, but 1,500 words or less is ideal (include number of words on manuscript). Do not submit previously published material or material which has subsequently been submitted to any other publication.

Acceptance

Manuscripts submitted are considered "accepted" when published. All editorial material being held for future issues is subject to change or rejection right up until the time of printing. All material is subject to light editing according to the needs of our publication. It is understood that any material submitted is original, free and clear of all copyrights, and does not infringe upon previously published works. All material must be submitted with the agreement that upon publication, either in our printed magazine or our Internet publication, we are buying all rights to the material and photos published, without exception. The author, in submitting material, acknowledges this agreement.

Categories: Fiction—Nonfiction—Adventure—Entertainment—Family—History—Hobbies—Lifestyles—Outdoors—Recreation—Senior Citizens—Travel

Name: Marcie Stumpe, Managing Editor
Material: All
Address: PO BOX 47
City/State/ZIP: HAPPY CAMP CA 96039
E-mail: goldgold@snowcrest.net

Golf Digest

Rarely accepts unsolicited manuscripts.
Categories: Nonfiction—Physical Fitness—Sports—Recreation—Golf

Name: Michael O'Malley, Managing Editor
Material: All
Address: P.O. BOX 395
City/State/ZIP: TRUMBULL, CT 06611
Telephone: 203-373-7240
Fax: 203-371-2162

The Golfer

These departments are open to freelance contributions:

Sports Fitness: Written with an authority on some aspect of fitness. These stories are usually written with the "we" voice (i.e. We should avoid dehydration.), mixed with references to "players" or "athletes" and maybe the very occasional "you." The goal of this section is to inform, hopefully about something "cutting edge" while trying to avoid making things sound dry and scientific. Usually about 1,400 words.

Chip Shots: Personal experiences are great, but beware the fact that at one time or another most golf writers believe that they have written the first story about someone who has a **real passion** for the game. Look for the offbeat.

Destinations: First-person travel stories. Approximately

1,000 to 2,000 words.

Categories: Health—Physical Fitness—Sports—Travel

Name: Allison Roarty, Managing Editor
Material: All
Address: 21 E 40TH ST 13TH FLOOR
City/State/ZIP: NEW YORK NY 10016
Telephone: 212-696-2484
Fax: 212-696-1678

Golf Journal Magazine

We appreciate your interest in *Golf Journal*, the official publication of the United States Golf Association. We purchase articles from freelance writers on a wide variety of subjects: history, players of the game (both past and present), course architecture, the environment, equipment (of a historic nature), profiles and humor. We do not generally publish instruction or equipment (new product) stories, nor can we publish any stories that could be construed as an endorsement by the USGA, one of the game's governing bodies. Fictional stories are also considered.

Articles and stories should range from 1,200 to 2,800 words. Payment is negotiated on an individual basis at the editors' discretion and we generally purchase first time rights.

All manuscripts are submitted on speculation at the author's risk. We accept no responsibility for unsolicited manuscripts, but will make every effort to return them. Stories must be typewritten and accompanied by a stamped, self-addressed envelope large enough to hold the manuscript. Queries should also include a stamped, self-addressed envelope. Manuscripts are usually read and processed within three to four weeks, although processing can take slightly longer during our busy championship season (summer months). If desired, writers may first send inquiries as to the suitability of their subject and approach.

Categories: Sports—Golf

Name: Brett Avery, Editor
Name: Rich Skyzinski, Managing Editor
Material: Any
Address: GOLF HOUSE
Address: PO BOX 708
City/State/ZIP: FAR HILLS NJ 07931-0708
Telephone: 908-234-2300
Fax: 908-781-1112
E-mail: golfjournal@usga.org
Internet: www.usga.org

Good Dog!®
The Consumer Magazine for Dog Owners

These guidelines also apply to *Catsumer Report*™ magazine and *Sneeze the Day!*™

Please read several issues of *Good Dog!* and analyze our style. Note our distinctive voice. Please try to write in this style: informative, talkative, friendly, expert, fun.

Write in third person, unless first person is more appropriate as with a humor or opinion piece.

Every article needs a beginning, a middle and an end. The thoughts must flow in a logical sequence, carrying the reader through from the beginning to the end.

Each paragraph must have a topic sentence which states the main thought of the paragraph. Other sentences should support the topic sentences.

Your writing must be interesting and tightly written, with your personality showing through. If you write about a dog, let the dog's personality come through, too.

Use anecdotes and occasional quotes to liven things up. Storytelling techniques will humanize your piece.

Back up your statements with quotes from an expert to give your story credibility.

Use contractions: "I wouldn't" as opposed to "I would not." Always keep in mind that we want a conversational style.

We reserve the right to edit or rewrite your work.

We do not accept material "written" by the dog or cat.
We do not accept fiction or poetry.

We cannot run stories that have been printed (or will be printed) in Dog World, Dog Fancy, or the AKC Gazette. We *will* reprint articles from breed and obedience club newsletters and from regional dog publications or other regional publications with written permission of the author and of the publication.

We prefer submissions to be on Macintosh or IBM (ASCII) 3.5" disks. Please provide hard copy along with the disk.

We can also accept articles sent via modem, CompuServe, America On-Line or Internet. Call for details.

Submissions may also be typed or computer printed. **Please type your name, address, daytime and night-time phone numbers on your manuscript and *print* this information on any photos, slides and transparencies that you send or that we request.**

Currently, our budget only allows us to pay a minimal amount for articles. We will discuss fees if we decide to publish one of your articles.

If you don't hear from us within a reasonable time, give us a call. We are phone-friendly.

We appreciate your interest in *Good Dog!* Please call if you have any questions.

Thank you,
Judi Becker,
Editor
Categories: Nonfiction—Animals

Name: Judi Becker, Managing Editor
Material: All
Address: PO BOX 10069
City/State/ZIP: AUSTIN TX 78766-1069
Telephone: 512-454-6090
Fax: 512-454-3420
E-mail: gooddogmag@aol.com

Good Housekeeping

Good Housekeeping addresses 24 million married women, most of whom have children (anywhere from newborn to college age) and who work outside the home.

Areas of interest covered include consumer issues, human interest, social issues, health, nutrition, relationships, psychology and work/career.

Several sections are especially well suited to freelancers: Better Way, which is comprised of 300 to 500 word how-to pieces; Profiles, 400 to 600 word features on people involved in inspiring, heroic or fascinating pursuits; and "My Problem and How I Solved It," a first person or as-told-to format, in which a woman (using her real name) relays how she overcame an especially difficult impasse in her life.

It's best to familiarize yourself with the tone and content of *Good Housekeeping* before you query us. (Back issues will likely be available at your local library.) The most successful queries or manuscripts are those that are timely, appropriately researched, engagingly written, freshly angled, and tailored to *Good Housekeeping* readers in particular.

Manuscripts and queries submitted on speculation should be typed, and when possible, should have clips of previously published articles attached. Please allow 2 to 3 months for a response due to the large volume of unsolicited queries we get.

Categories: Fiction—Crime—Diet—Family—General Interest—Health—Human Interest (dramatic narratives)—Humor—Lifestyles—Marriage—Profiles (inspirational, real people)—Short Stories—Women's Fiction—Women's Issues

Name: Diane Salvatore, Deputy Editor
Material: All
Address: 959 8TH AVE
City/State/ZIP: NEW YORK NY 10019
Telephone: 212-649-2260
Fax: 212-265-3307

The Good Red Road

Publisher: Turquoise Butterfly Press
Format: 12-page bimonthly newsletter. Established in 1997.
Focus: The goal of the *Good Red Road* is to act as a study guide to the life, legends, teachings, beliefs, traditions, medicines, recipes, parenting, history, tribal differences, language, leaders, games, etc., of the Native American people from yesterday and today.

Submissions: Lead articles should be 900-1,500 words. All other articles and stories should be 100-900 words. Pays in copies. All material must be typed or neatly handwritten. *Include a word count!* Editor has the right to edit material. Photos or artwork may be sent with submission. Include research citations. Buys one-time rights. Reprints okay. Pays upon publication. Sample copy $3.50

Categories: Native American

Name: Terri J. Andrews, Editor
Material: All
Address: PO BOX 1127
City/State/ZIP: ATHENS OH 45701-1127
Telephone: 614-664-3030

Good Times
The Lifestyle Magazine For Mature Pennsylvanians

Good Times, the lifestyle magazine for mature Pennsylvanians which is published monthly except January and August, provides general interest information to people who have retired or are contemplating retirement. Articles focus on legal and financial rights, health and medical issues and news, lifestyle and relationships, cuisine, travel, fashion, celebrities, hobbies and leisure activities, gardening and more.

Writing for Good Times
There are five steps to writing for *Good Times*:

1. Submit a query letter, together with your resume and a few writing samples.
2. If we are interested in your article, we will discuss it with you.
3. Or, we may ask you to write an article on another topic that suits your experience as well as our audience.
4. When we agree on topic, article length and compensation, we will send you a letter, setting forth the terms, for you to sign and return.
5. Submit your article by the predetermined date, and send us an invoice, including your social security number, for your payment.

Topic Selection
Your article should focus on topics of interest to retired persons and persons planning retirement. Your article should address the concerns of the readership and offer practical advice, recommendations and solutions to the readers. As appropriate, your article should offer readers sources for additional information.

Writing Style
Your writing should be clear and concise, using terms that are easily understood by the reader. Spell out all acronyms and abbreviations on first reference. After you have completed your article, review it for places where you can eliminate wordiness.

Graphics
Diagrams, tables and photographs can add impact to your article. Include appropriate graphics when you submit your article. Reference all graphics in the text, indicate the source if appropriate, and include a caption. We can also accept sketches if they are complete and accurate. Our design and production department will convert your sketches into color graphics. We can accept photographs as transparencies, slides or prints, in that order of preference. We prefer four-color photographs to black-and-white, and we cannot accept negatives.

Submitting Your Article
Submit your article as a standard word processing document on a Mac or IBM 3½" floppy disk. When formatting disks on a DOS computer, always format standard double-sided disks in the 720K format; always format high-density disks in the 1440K format.

Categories: Lifestyles—Seniors—Mature Adults

Name: Karen Detwiler, Editor-in-Chief
Material: All
Address: ROBERT MORRIS BLDG 9TH FLOOR
Address: 100 N 17TH ST
City/State/ZIP: PHILADELPHIA PA 19103
Telephone: 215-246-3433
Fax: 215-665-5723

Gothic Journal
Keeping you in romantic suspense!

Gothic Journal

The *Gothic Journal* is published bimonthly (June/July, Aug/Sept, etc.) Audience: readers, authors, aspiring authors, booksellers, librarians, agents, editors, and publishers of romantic suspense, romantic mystery, gothic romance, supernatural romance, and woman-in-jeopardy romance novels. Submissions are welcome in the following categories. Buys all or first serial rights.

ARTICLES Articles are welcome on topics related to the genres we cover, such as the best locales, what makes a believable hero and/or heroine, the history of gothics, the future of romantic suspense, paranormal vs. supernatural, when should the bedroom door close, how to locate older titles, etc. Length: approximately 1,000-2,000 words. Payment: $20.00 and 3 contributors copies, upon publication.

AUTHOR PROFILES Profiles of popular (actively-writing or out-of-print) authors of books in our genres should include a biographical sketch and information about how the writer works, what personal interests contribute to his or her writing, plans for future works, etc. Information should include more than that available in library biographical references, if possible. Basis on an interview or direct contact with the author is preferred. A list of published works (in order by first year published, with years listed) must be included along with brief, unrated descriptions, cover blurbs and/or excerpts from at least three of the author's novels. Include a black and white photo of the author, if possible. Query regarding suitability of author before submitting profile. Length: 3,000-4,000 words. Payment: $30.00 and 3 contributors copies, upon publication.

AUTHOR NOTES Authors who wish to be included in the Author Notes section are encouraged to write for a copy of the Gothic Journal's Author Questionnaire. Their response plus any additional comments submitted, will be used by the Gothic Journal staff to write an Author Note to be published in the issue in which a review of the author's book appears. An author will be featured in an Author Note only once per year. A black and white photo of the author and a list of the author's published works (in order by first year published, with years listed) should accompany the completed author questionnaire. The photo will not be returned. Author Notes are written by a Contributing Editor, so please submit them at least 2 weeks prior to our editorial deadline. Payment: 3 contributors copies.

INDUSTRY FIGURE PROFILES Agents, editors, publicists, etc., who wish to be profiled are encouraged to write for an appropriate Gothic Journal questionnaire. The response to the questionnaire, plus any additional comments submitted, will be used by the Gothic Journal staff to write a profile. From 1-3 candid photos of subject in work and/or home life setting should be included. Black and white photos are preferred, but color photos are acceptable. Photos will be returned. Payment: 3 contributors copies.

BOOK REVIEWS Potential reviewers should contact the Editor for a reviewer questionnaire and trial book assignment. Detailed stylebook is provided. Length: approximately 500 words. Must be at least 50% commentary. Payment: $5-10 per issue plus complimentary subscription after one year; manuscripts, galleys, and/or review copies of books are provided, when available; they may be kept by the reviewer. If *Gothic Journal* cannot provide a review copy, reviewers must obtain the book to be reviewed.

LETTERS The Letters column provides an open forum for readers, writers, and publishers to communicate their opinions, needs, and concerns about novels in our genres, and their readers, writers, and publishers. Letters to the editor are very much encouraged. Letters may be edited or only portions of letters may be printed, as appropriate and due to space limitations, but the meaning and intent of the writer will be preserved. Payment: byline only.

READER COMMENTS Readers are encouraged to submit short comments about the books in each upcoming titles list for inclusion in the Reader Comments column in the next issue. Payment: byline; if three or more by the same reader are published in one issue, payment is a Gothic Grab Bag.

MARKET NEWS Submissions of market news are encouraged for inclusion in the "Reading Between the Lines" column. Please provide source of information. Payment: contributor copy sent to market source at "contact" address.

ARTWORK Drawings and/or floor plans of the exteriors and/or interiors of houses/settings used in novels (or houses/settings which would be excellent for gothic novels) are needed for the magazine cover. Drawings may also be considered for article illustration and filler art. Hidden picture puzzles also wanted. Submissions should be suitable for black and white reproduction. Rights revert to artist upon publication. Payment: $10-50 per drawing (and floor plan combination, if included), upon publication.

MANUSCRIPT PREPARATION Ideally, submissions should be submitted as word processing files (single-spaced) on 3.5" IBM PC format floppy disk, double-sided, double density (DSDD) or high density (HD). Computer text files should preferably be in Microsoft Word or ASCII text format; other formats are usable (inquire first). Photocopied submissions are acceptable. Fax or disk submissions are preferred. Letters, reader comments, questionnaires, and reviews will not be returned. Editorial deadlines are the 1st of the month prior to issue month (e.g., March 1 for April/May issue). Usually reports within 3 weeks from receipt of submission. Please be patient if there is a delay during deadline periods.

Sample copies: $4.00 plus $2.00 postage and handling (add $1.50 for rush delivery)

Subscriptions: $24.00/year (6 issues) US, $30/year Canada, $36/year foreign

Categories: Nonfiction—Book Reviews—Literature—Mystery—Romance—Writing

Name: Kristi Lyn Glass, Publisher
Material: All
Address: PO BOX 6340
City/State/ZIP: ELKO NV 89802-6340
Telephone: 702-738-3520
Fax: 702-738-3524
E-mail: kglass@gothicjournal.com
Internet: www.gothicjournal.com/romance/

Government Executive

Government Executive, a publication of National Journal Inc., a subsidiary of Times Mirror Co., is a monthly business magazine serving executives and managers in the federal government. Our 60,000 subscribers are high-ranking civilian and military officials who carry out the laws that define the government's role in our economy and society.

Government Executive aspires to serve the people who manage these huge agencies and programs much in the way that *Fortune*, *Forbes* and *Business Week* serve private-sector managers. Editorial goals include:

• Covering news and trends about the organization and management of the executive branch;

• Helping federal executives improve the quality of their agencies' services by reporting on management innovations;

• Explaining government problems and failures in ways that offer lessons about pitfalls to avoid;

• Creating a greater sense of community along the elite corps of public servants to whom the magazine circulates;

• Improving the image of the public service by teaching our non-government readers about the challenges federal officials confront.

Government Executive has twice won the Gerald R. Ford Prize for Distinguished Reporting on National Defense, in 1990 and 1995.

TYPES OF ARTICLES WE PUBLISH
Feature Stories

These usually range in length from 1,500 to 4,000 words. Any sidebars must be figured into the total word count. Feature stories fall into these general categories:

Management issues. These focus on topics of broad interest and include reporting from several agencies. Topics could include downsizing of agencies; reinventing government; recruitment and retention; ensuring that computers succeed in improving productivity; and upgrading training.

Agencies. These stories often focus on one agency with an eye toward finding generally applicable lessons for federal managers. For example, one story assessed the change in NASA's culture as the agency handed off operation of the space shuttle to a private firm.

Government people. Some articles are organized around certain professions within government. For example, we've written about the influence of economists on policy-making, how to make the best use of agency lawyers, and how to recruit and retain a good clerical work force.

Civil service issues. These include articles about pay, executive training, ethics, politicization of the civil service and the impact of technology on the workplace.

Guest Columns

Our **Management and Viewpoint** columns are good forums for members of our audience to share an opinion or their experiences. Management columns should include advice that would be useful to managers in a variety of fields. Viewpoint columns express opinions on issues relevant to civil servants. These columns are usually about 1,000 words long.

Other Departments

These are usually 1,000 words or 1,700 words, except as noted. Monthly departments for which we sometimes use freelance contributions include:

Executive Memo: A series of short news items, 100-200 words each.

Travel: On government/business travel.

Information Technology: government applications of computer technologies.

OUR CONTRIBUTORS

Following are some guidelines for different categories of would-be contributors:

Professional journalists. These may be full-time freelance writers or employees of other publications. We look for people who have expertise in civil service issues or the management of federal agencies.

Current or former federal employees. We publish personal reflections on the problems and opportunities of public service, as well as analytical articles on the causes and solutions of real-life agency problems. However, we often prefer to assign stories suggested by government officials to writers outside of government. We think independent reporting and analysis often lends credibility to an article.

Consultants corporate executives public relations representatives. We shy away from articles that seem to be aimed at promoting the fortunes of any individual, product, or program. We almost never publish articles submitted by or on behalf of companies or trade associations.

HOW TO GET AN ASSIGNMENT

We prefer to receive queries about possible assignments in the form of a one- or two-page letter that lays out the subject you want to write about, the angle you will take and the sources you will interview. The letter should also detail any relevant experience you have. If you do send us a completed manuscript, be warned that deadline pressure often prevents us from considering or returning unsolicited manuscripts in a timely manner. We do not object if you submit a piece to other publications simultaneously. We do not return unsolicited manuscripts.

STORY SUBMISSION CHECKLIST

Stories may be submitted via e-mail or on floppy disk. Along with your manuscript, please include:

Art memo. Your written list of ideas for graphics may include portraits of your major sources, other photographs, cartoons and illustrations. We especially like to run charts, tables and graphs, so keep any eye out for information relevant to your story that could be presented that way. Please provide us with the contacts we need to arrange to shoot or obtain photographs.

Author bio. At the end of the story, please include a one to two sentence description of your professional background.

Contract. The first time you write for us, you must sign a contract stating that you will pay income taxes on your fees. If you have never signed such a contract, please request one when you submit your story.

WHAT HAPPENS NEXT?

Rewriting. We may ask for a second draft of a story, particularly if you haven't written for us before.

Accuracy checks. We expect you to check all names, titles, dates and facts for accuracy before your story is submitted. However, we always send an edited version of the story back to you so that you may check that no errors have crept in during the editing process.

Payment. We pay upon acceptance, which means after you have completed any requested rewriting or additional research to our satisfaction. Please submit an invoice for the amount agreed upon at the time the story was assigned.

Copyright. *Government Executive* holds all rights for publication (including publication on the World Wide Web) and all reprint rights.

Categories: Government

Name: Timothy Clark, Editor and Publisher
Material: All
Address: 1501 M ST NW STE 300
City/State/ZIP: WASHINGTON DC 20005
Telephone: 202-739-8500
Fax: 202-739-8511
E-mail: govexec@govexec.com
Internet: www.govexec.com

Gray Areas

We do not print fiction, poetry or short stories. We have no word count limits and prefer depth to fluff.

We explore gray areas of law and morality in the fields of law, music, technology, sociology and popular culture.

We print all points of view and run articles by active criminals, academics, victims, law enforcement, psychiatrists and ordinary citizens.

We also review books, movies, computer software, video games, concerts, comics, catalogs, music CDs, small press magazines and more.

Categories: Computers—Culture—Film/Video—Internet—Law—Music—Society

Name: Netta Gilboa, Publisher
Material: All
Address: PO BOX 808
City/State/ZIP: BROOMALL PA 19008

The Green Hills Literary Lantern
North Central Missouri College

Fiction

The Green Hills Literary Lantern is published annually, each summer, by North Central Missouri College and the North Central Missouri Writer's Guild. It includes poetry as well as fiction. The publication runs about 160 pages, consisting of one half fiction (6-7 stories), one half poetry. It is printed on good quality paper with a glossy cover. For the past 4 issues, it has received grants from the Missouri Arts Council.

We respond to work in 3-4 months. When submitting manuscripts, please send a short bio listing publications (50-100 words). We accept simultaneous submissions but discourage multiple submissions, though 2-3 "short shorts" are acceptable. Please send an SASE for return of manuscript or for reply only. Please include a phone number on manuscript where we can reach you.

This magazine is open to the work of new writers as well as more established writers. We are interested in stories that demonstrate a strong working knowledge of the craft. Avoid genre fiction or mainstream religious fiction. Otherwise, we are open to short stories of various settings, character conflicts, and styles, including experimental.

Above all, we demand that work be "striking." Language should be complex, with depths, through analogy, metaphor, simile, understatement, irony, etc.—but all this must not be overwrought, or self-consciously literary. This does not mean that in rare cases, style itself cannot be center stage, but if so, it must be interesting and provocative enough for the reader to focus on style alone. "Overdone" writing surely is not either.

We tend to be interested in stories with strong character, with conflicts that matter (where the stakes are fairly high), and with stories that do not have simple resolutions. Stories that go nowhere, that get blurred in focus, or that seem thin in idea have little chance of being accepted for publication.

We accept short stories, short shorts, and excerpts from novels. Our maximum length is 5,000 words. There is no absolute minimum.

If work is accepted, author will receive prepublication galleys. Publication is copyrighted. We purchase one-time rights.

Poetry

Submit 3-7 poems, typed, one poem per page. There are no restrictions on subject matter, though pornography and gratuitous violence will not be accepted. Obscurity for its own sake is also frowned upon. Both free and formal verse forms are fine, though we publish more free verse overall. Poems of under six lines or over two pages are unlikely to be published. A genuine attempt is made to publish the best poems available, no matter who the writer. First time poets, well-established poets, and those in-between, all can and have found a place in the GHLL. A cover letter is appreciated but not required. We try to respond within 3-4 months, if not sooner. We try to supply feedback, particularly to those we seek to encourage.

Categories: Fiction—Poetry

Name: Sara King, Fiction Editor
Material: All Fiction
Name: Joe Benevento, Poetry Editor
Material: All Poetry
Address: PO BOX 375
City/State/ZIP: TRENTON MO 64683
Telephone: 660-359-3948 ext. 324
Fax: 660-359-2211
E-mail: JSmith@ncmc.cc.mo.us

Green Mountains Review
Johnson State College

The GREEN MOUNTAINS REVIEW is an international journal publishing poems, stories, and creative nonfiction by both well-known authors and promising newcomers. The magazine also features interviews, literary criticism, and book reviews.

The editors are open to a wide range of styles and subject matter as is apparent from a look at the short list of writers who have published in its pages: Julia Alvarez, Hayden Carruth, Stephen Dobyns, Mark Doty, Stephen Dunn, Carol Emshwiller,

Linda Gregg, Donald Hall, Maxine Kumin, Denise Levertov, Larry Levis, Phillip Lopate, Dionisio D. Martinez, William Matthews, Naomi Shihab Nye, Lynne Sharon Schwartz, Ntozake Shange, Reginald Shepard, Alix Kates Shulman, David St. John, Walter Wetherell, and Meredith Sue Willis.

Past issues have included interviews with writers such as Galway Kinnell, Grace Paley, and Derek Walcott, as well as literary essays such as David Wojahn's on the stylistics of memory narrative and David Mura's on the heteroglossia of multicultural writing.

There have been several special issues: one devoted to Vermont fiction writers, a second called "Women, Community, and Narrative Voice" featuring short stories by women, a third filled with new writing from the People's Republic of China, and another devoted to multicultural writing in America.

The editors read manuscripts between September 1 and May 1. During that period they will make every attempt to respond within three months. Manuscripts received during the summer months will be returned unread.

Categories: Fiction—Nonfiction—Literature—Poetry

Name: Neil Shepard, General Editor
Material: Poetry, Essays, Interviews
Name: Tony Whedon, Fiction Editor
Material: Fiction
Address: JOHNSON STATE COLLEGE
City/State/ZIP: JOHNSON VT 05656
Telephone: 802-635-1350

GREENPRINTS
"THE WEEDER'S DIGEST"

GreenPrints
The Weeder's Digest

Thanks for your interest! GREENPRINTS lives because people like you *care* about gardening—and about *sharing* with other gardeners. Without your contributions, the magazine simply would not exist. Still, it almost feels like a contradiction in terms to offer writer's guidelines for GREENPRINTS (after all, what we want is special, exciting, provocative, sparkling, unordinary writing—and how do you prescribe that?). But people do ask, so I better be a good fellow and come up with something! To wit:

1.) We want the best, **personal** (key word, that) garden writing we can find. Expressive, thoughtful, humorous, angry, contrite, flippant, searching, witty, observant, sad, inviting-whatever! We focus on the human, not the how-to side of gardening. On the people as well as the plants. After all, gardening is a relationship, not a recipe. GREENPRINTS explores that relationship, not by instructing, preaching, or lecturing about it. Instead, we celebrate it...by *sharing* the stories and experiences we all have trying (and sometimes failing) to get along with plants.

I can put what we want in one word: *Storytelling*. Or maybe storyshowing. The most common shortcoming I see is people who forget the old high school English class dictum: *Show, don't tell*. Take us through the experiences with trenchant details and descriptions. *Don't* tell us how profound or funny or beautiful it was: *make us experience* the feeling.

2.) We're not opposed to essays, but the good ones a) evolve *directly* from personal experience and b) offer new insights or at least new ways of expressing old insights. We're not opposed to fiction, either, but don't you agree that it should offer something special that the nonfiction stories we get wouldn't? (i.e., don't just imitate reality).

3.) One thing for sure, we don't want sappy, gooey writing. Tender, moving, poignant is *wonderful*. But *syrupy* is the biggest trap GREENPRINTS has to avoid. (Trap #2: preachy. We can all read lectures and sermons plenty of other places, *nest-ce pas?*)

4.) Length? I don't know. Since we're digest-sized, most of our pieces have been no more than 2,000 words. But write what you have to. If it's good, we'll work out length problems.

5.) Payment? Did you have to ask? We pay miserably; top payment right now is $100 and we often pay less. (No payment for "Cuttings," for instance.) I apologize. You deserve more. When GREENPRINTS starts making money, I intend to share it. Right now, I'm working for peanuts and hanging in there until this different little gardening gem takes off. We pay on acceptance; buy first North American serial rights (unless you've already published it somewhere else first; we're happy to reprint pieces— long as they're good!).

6.) Poetry: Well, we run about 1 poem per issue. That's 4 per year (in contrast to 50 or more prose pieces), so let's admit there's not much chance I can accept your poem. The ones I do take tend to be a) not too hard to follow, b) not too saccharine, but most of all c) clever. Innovative. Offering well-expressed, detail-dressed new twists or outlooks on this magazine's very old topic. Pay: $10.

7.) One last thing: Are you a subscriber? If not, would you please consider becoming one for $17.97 a yr.? Not only does it get you a wonderful little magazine and the best possible feel for the type of writing we run, it also helps us survive so we can run *your* writing!

Thanks again.

Best to you with prose and plants—and the rest of life, too.

Pat Stone, Editor

P.S. Oh, one more thing: Often I can't find time to read submissions until after an issue deadline: Nov., Feb., May, & Aug. Sorry.

Categories: Gardening

Name: Pat Stone, Editor
Material: All
Address: PO BOX 1355
City/State/ZIP: FAIRVIEW NC 28730
Telephone: 784-628-1902

The Greensboro Review
University of North Carolina—Greensboro

• No previously published works, works accepted for publication, or dual submissions are eligible.

• Poetry may be any length; maximum length for fiction is 7,500 words.

• All manuscripts must be typed and accompanied by a self-addressed, stamped envelope for return.

• All manuscripts must arrive by September 15 to be considered for the Winter issue (acceptances in December) and February 15 to be considered for the Summer issue (acceptances in May). Manuscripts arriving after those dates will be held for the next consideration.

Categories: Fiction—Poetry

Name: Poetry Editor
Material: Poetry
Name: Fiction Editor
Material: Fiction
Address: UNCG ENGLISH DEPARTMENT
City/State/ZIP: GREENSBORO NC 27412-5001

Telephone: 910-334-5459
Fax: 910-334-3281
E-mail: clark;@fagan.uncg.edu

GRIT Magazine
American Life & Traditions

WHO WE ARE

GRIT, America's family magazine since 1882, is dedicated to bringing its readers good news. We publish items about ordinary people doing extraordinary things, accounts of interesting places or events and tips on how to make your life just a little better.

We tailor our magazine to provide an informative yet entertaining look at life in America, past and present. GRIT explores values, lifestyles and traditions important to those concerned about themselves, their families and their communities.

GRIT focuses not on age or abilities, but on attitude—taking a positive approach to life. GRIT celebrates our readers' courage, dedication and determination to make a difference.

GRIT gladly accepts reader contributions and freelance materials appropriate for publication. We encourage freelance writers and photographers to become familiar with recent issues. Copies are available by subscription, or by requesting a sample copy directly from GRIT Guidelines at the address shown below. Please include $4 for postage and handling, plus a self-addressed 9"x12" envelope when requesting a sample copy.

FEATURES

GRIT publishes feature-length articles (1,200-1,500 words) about topics important to today's families—American values and quality of life; outstanding people and interesting places; parenting and grandparenting; home and garden; arts and crafts; American history; traditions and cultures; family lifestyles; community involvement or service; family-oriented media and movies; Americana and nostalgia; and collectibles and antiques. Submit manuscripts on speculation for review with black-and-white or color photos (original negatives and slides preferred) to illustrate the article. Provide Photo releases of subjects.

DEPARTMENTS

Each issue of GRIT offers a variety of departments. Submit manuscript and photos on speculation for review.

• **Readers' True Stories**—First-person account with a lesson learned or message of life woven into a favorite memory; event or situation; 800 to 1,200 words.

• **Looking Back**—Short personal reflection of America's past in a 50- to 250-word submission.

• **Readers' Travels**—Experiences of readers traveling the backroads or to out-of-the-way places; 800 to 1,200 words.

• **Readers' Hometowns**—Historical and personality stories about small towns; 800 to 1,200 words.

• **Outdoor Life**—Hobbies, activities and events that use nature as their backdrop; 800 to 1,200 words.

• **Pet Tales**—Humorous and/or heartwarming stories about people and their pets; 800 to 1,200 words.

• **Preserving Our Heritage**—Portrayal of those who keep history alive by restoring buildings or promoting old-time professions and hobbies; 800 to 1,200 words.

• **Today's Family**—The many issues affecting parents, grandparents and children; 800 to 1,000 words.

• **Crafters' Corner**—Original craft ideas: sewing projects, woodworking designs, dried floral crafts, ribbon embroidery; jewelry making, wheat weaving or doll making. Send step-by-step instructions and photos; 800 to 1,000 words.

- **Home Life**—lifestyle pieces, including decorating, remodeling, gardening, crafting and entertaining; 800 to 1,000 words.
- **Profile**—Character profiles of individuals who demonstrate strength of character, or who reflect a positive or unusual aspect of American life; 800 to 1,000 words.

FICTION & POETRY

GRIT regularly publishes historical, mystery, Western and romance serials (15,000 or more words in 1,000-word chapters with cliff-hangers) and short fiction (1,000-2,000 words). Stories should emphasize the positive aspects of American life. 22 cents per word paid on publication.

GRIT publishes free verse, light verse, traditional, nature and inspirational poems that are easy to read, with down-to-earth themes. Limit submissions to batches of five or less, length 4-16 lines each. $2 per line, $30 maximum on publication.

PHOTOS

GRIT expects professional quality color and black-and-white negatives, slides, transparencies or prints. Original negatives and slides are preferred but allowances may be made for nostalgia photos. Be sure to label each submission with your name, address and telephone number and include caption information.

SUBMISSIONS & PAYMENT

Submissions are evaluated within 90 days of receipt; seasonal and topical materials may be held longer. GRIT assumes no responsibility for any material that is not returned or is lost or damaged.

Generally the standard rate of payment for nonfiction is upon publication at 22 cents per published word and $50 per original published photograph. Crafters' Corner contributors are paid a flat $50 for the article and photos. Looking Back contributors are paid a flat $25 for the article and photos.

TIPS FOR CONTRIBUTORS

See recent issues for types of stories we use, and GRIT style.

Include the names and telephone numbers of all sources for fact-checking. Identify sources fully, including their credentials, titles or reasons they are qualified to comment, and provide full references for any publications used as sources.

Articles should have national appeal. Information in sidebar or graph form is appropriate for many stories: lists of tips, resources or questions to help readers better understand the subject. For travel stories, include tips such as prices, how to get there, where to stay, etc.

HOW DO I SUBMIT SOMETHING TO GRIT?

- Include your full name, address, telephone number, social security number and submission title on each page. Also send a brief synopsis of your submission or proposal, and a paragraph-long personal biography in your dated cover letter.
- Submit typed manuscripts. If possible, submit the same material on a 3.5" Macintosh disk. Send only completed, proofread manuscripts. GRIT does not accept submissions made simultaneously to other publications.
- Include a return envelope with adequate postage for acceptance/rejection correspondence.
- No calls, please. A follow-up letter or fax is acceptable.

Categories: Fiction—Nonfiction—Animals—Children—Christian Interests—Collectibles—Cooking—Crafts—Family—Gardening—General Interest—History—Inspirational—Poetry—Rural America—Senior Citizens

Name: Donna J. Doyle, Editor-in-Chief
Material: All
Address: 1502 SW 42ND ST
City/State/ZIP: TOPEKA KS 66609
Telephone: 913-274-4300
Fax: 913-274-4305

Group IV Communications, Inc.

Independent Business and *Business97* are national magazines for and about small business in America. With a combined circulation of more than 1.2 million, they rank among the nation's largest business magazines. Virtually all readers of *Independent Business* and *Business97* own and manage their own small businesses—retail, service and manufacturing.

Independent Business is distributed to the entire membership of the National Federation of Independent Business (NFIB), the nation's oldest and largest small business organization.

Business97 is distributed to the best small business customers of a network of major banks coast to coast, including NationsBank and Wells Fargo Bank. Please note, however, that editorial content (including the small business owners mentioned in the magazine) is in no way limited to NFIB members or customers of the various banks.

Independent Business and *Business97* cover only topics of interest to the small (and we mean small) business owner. The average reader's business has $1 million in annual revenues, employs fewer than 20 people and has been in business 13 years. These are *not* start-ups. Nor are they big mature companies. They are established, small companies.

Our editorial emphasis in both magazines is on providing practical, "how-to" information our readers can use in operating a small business and to do it better than any other publication in the country.

Regular department and column topics include marketing, advertising, management, computing, taxation, banking and finance, among others.

Departments run 1,200 to 1,800 words; features run 1,500 to 2,500 words in length.

Our editorial approach: We get right to the point. We spell it out in plain English. All articles are tightly written; tightly edited. *Independent Business* and *Business97* contain no high-brow economic theory or PR puffery. No wading through text about giant corporations to find a few small business nuggets.

Writers must use real small business examples (no "XYZ Company" examples) to illustrate points being made. This is a key component of all *Independent Business* and *Business97* stories.

Don't use first-person. Address readers as "you," in familiar terms. Be conversational. Don't be afraid to have a sense of style—and a sense of humor—in your writing. Make it lively.

Avoid academic-type "introductions" and repetitive "conclusions." Use *active verbs*. Avoid passive constructions.

To keep articles short and interesting, *Independent Business* and *Business97* use liberal doses of sidebars. We consider these part of the story; writers are responsible for supplying sidebars. All *Independent Business* and *Business97* articles have one to three such sidebars in addition to either a "Follow-Up File," or "Action File" which includes names, addresses and phone numbers on how to find more information on the article subject. Study the magazine for further guidance. Make use of checklists and bulleted lists within articles.

Writers are required to conduct their own fact checking. *You* are responsible for accuracy. Please provide a complete list of all sources mentioned in your article, including names, current addresses and phone numbers.

We handle all photos and illustrations; this is not a responsibility of our writers.

Independent Business and *Business97* pay writers on acceptance for first North American serial rights and non-exclusive reprint rights. We pay reasonable, documented expenses. Our kill fee is 25%. Writers always receive bylines and bio tags.

Articles *must* be *submitted* either on computer disk or via modem. Writers are responsible for checking in advance about

E-L

appropriate computer formats and disk/software compatibility. A writer's invoice should be submitted with the article, along with receipts for expenses.

Article queries on subjects appropriate to *Independent Business* and *Business97* are always welcome; however, unsolicited manuscripts are not. All articles are assigned.

For a sample issue, mail a check for $6 to IB L.P. or Business90s L.P., depending on the magazine you want. Send it to the attention of Kim Pisapia, along with a brief note outlining which issue you would like to receive.

Categories: Business—Running a Small Business

Name: Maryann Hammers, Managing Editor
Material: All
Address: 125 AUBURN CT STE 100
City/State/ZIP: THOUSAND OAKS CA 91362
Telephone: 805-496-6156
Fax: 805-496-5469
E-mail: GoSmallBiz@aol.com

gryphon
house inc.

Gryphon Publications

Dear Contributor,

Thank you for letting me get a chance to see your work. Until now I've usually commented on each and every manuscript sent to me, anything from a few encouraging words to a one-page letter. I know how important it is to get feedback on your work. However, lately, the volume of manuscripts has reached critical mass, and it has become impossible to comment on an individual manuscript any longer. I hope this short letter will help you get a better understanding of what my needs are for various Gryphon Publications.

Please read carefully before sending anything.

HARDBOILED: I'm looking for very hard, cutting-edge crime fiction, usually under 3,000 words (longer would have to be extraordinary) and with *impact*. The kind of story that stays with a reader, that might just *change* that reader. The competition is rough, you're up against some of the best of the Pros, so only send me your best, but there is always room for newcomers. Each issue of HARDBOILED is 100+ pages, typeset, with *color* covers, and has many stories by unknown and first-time writers. Your work is what's important, not your name. Payment is in two free copies of the issue you appear in and a nominal cash payment by contract upon publication.

Sample copies and all back issues are $7 each; subscriptions 6 quarterly issues @ $35 by third class; outside USA $8 each and 6/$42 surface mail.

PAPERBACK PARADE needs all types of nonfiction, articles, essays, book lists, interviews, etc. about collectible paperbacks, authors, artists, publishers, etc. This is a magazine for book lovers, published since 1986, with 42 issues so far, 100+ pages, typeset, with *color* covers! A great place to showcase work, but only the best and most detailed bibliographical material are needed. Query first with SASE.

Sample copies and back issues $7 each; subscriptions: 6 bimonthly issues $35 third class; Outside USA, $8 each, 6/$42 surface mail.

OTHER WORLDS is an annual paperback magazine, per-

fect-bound, 100+ pages. I'm looking for short, hard SF shockers, stories with impact, usually under 3,000 words. Science Fiction or Science Fiction Fantasy, also some SF horror. No outright fantasy, horror or supernatural at all. Payment in one free copy of the issue you appear in.

Sample copies of #1-4 @$4 each; #5 and #6 are 100pp perfect-bound paperback issues @$9.95.

GRYPHON DOUBLES showcase two longer works, back-to-back like the old Ace Doubles. A cover for each story. I need only extraordinary longer works. Only quality material. All types of work here, 10,000 to about 20,000 words. *Do not send ms.* Send only a one-page letter about the work with an SASE.

Samples of Doubles are $9.95 each, subscriptions: 5 issues as they appear for $45.

GRYPHON BOOKS: I also publish, from time to time, hardcover and paperback (trade size) books on certain special subjects. *Do not send ms.* Send only a one-page letter about the book with an SASE.

The best way to break into writing for a publisher is to be familiar with that publisher's product. I suggest you try a recent copy of HARDBOILED or PAPERBACK PARADE, or try a GRYPHON DOUBLE. See what they're about. The stories in HARDBOILED are all interesting and may open your eyes to a new and better way to say what you want to say in your own work. The articles in PAPERBACK PARADE will give you an added perspective too few writers wanting to break into the field have today. To their disadvantage. Some of the best work being done today is appearing in these publications, it's just plain good writing, good reading, and fun stuff.

Categories: Fiction—Crime

Name: Submissions Editor
Material: All
Address: PO BOX 209
City/State/ZIP: BROOKLYN NY 11228

Guideposts®
A Practical Guide to Successful Living®

Guideposts® magazine, A Practical Guide to Successful Living®, is a monthly inspirational, interfaith, nonprofit publication written by people from all walks of life. Its articles present tested methods for developing courage, strength and positive attitudes through faith in God. Our writers express viewpoints from a variety of Protestant, Catholic and Jewish faith experiences.

A typical *Guideposts* story is a first-person narrative written in simple, dramatic, anecdotal style with a spiritual point that the reader can "take away" and apply to his or her own life. The story may be the writer's own or one written in the first person for someone else. Even our short features, such as "His Mysterious Ways," "What Prayer Can Do," "Angels Among Us" and "The Divine Touch" use this format. Writing a short feature is often the easiest way of making a sale to *Guideposts*.

Please observe the following in writing your *Guideposts* story:

• Don't try to tell an entire life story in a few pages. Focus on *one* specific happening in a person's life. The emphasis should be on *one* individual. Bring in as few people as possible so that the reader's interest stays with the dominant character.

• Decide what your spiritual point, or "takeaway," will be. Everything in the story should be tied in with this specific theme.

• Don't leave unanswered questions. Give enough facts so that the reader will know what happened. Use description and dialogue to let the reader feel as if he were there, seeing the characters, hearing them talk. Dramatize the situation, conflicts and struggle, and then tell how the person was changed for the better or the problem was solved.

• Most important: Study the magazine.

Payments:

• Full-length manuscripts (750-1,500 words): $250-$500, occasionally higher.

• Shorter manuscripts (25-750 words): $ 100-$250.

• Short features and fillers (under 250 words): $25-$l00. These include "What Prayer Can Do" and heavenly encounters such as "His Mysterious Ways," "Angels Among Us" and "The Divine Touch"

We do not use fiction, essays or sermons, and we rarely present stories about deceased or professional religious people. We do not evaluate book-length material.

Manuscripts must be typed and accompanied by a self-addressed, stamped envelope. We receive thousands of unsolicited manuscripts each month, so allow two months for a reply.

Categories: Inspirational—Religion

Name: Submissions Editor
Material: All
Address: 16 E 34TH ST
City/State/ZIP: NEW YORK NY 10016
Telephone: 212-257-8100

Guideposts for Kids

About Our Magazine—*Guideposts for Kids* is published bimonthly by Guideposts Associates, Inc. for kids 7-12 years old (emphasis on upper end of that age bracket). It is a 32-page, four-color, value-centered direct mail magazine that is *fun* to read. It is *not* a miniature *Guideposts*. (Sample issue available; send $3.25 to Guideposts; 39 Seminary Hill Road; Carmel, NY 10512 Attn: Special Handling.)

About Your Manuscript—Make it good. Relevant, playful. No preachy stories about Bible-toting children. *Guideposts for Kids* is not a beginner's market. Some areas of interest to freelancers:

FEATURE STORIES—One each issue. 1,500 words, including sidebar(s). Tough, issue-oriented, controversial, thought-provoking. Something kids not only *need* to know, but *want* to know as well. Recent features include "No Place Like Home" (homeless kids), "All God's Creatures" (animal rights), ADventure (what you buy and why). *Query*

SECONDARY FEATURES—One each issue. 700 words including sidebar(s). More playful. Possible photo essay. Recently included "Bright Ideas" (stories behind the invention of Band-Aids, ear muffs, the safety pin) and "Chocolate: How Sweet It Is." *Query*

ONE-PAGERS—Poetry, trivia "Did-you-know-that..." 300 words or less. Anything that will grab the attention of a real-live 10-year-old.

FEATURING KIDS!—Profiles of kids doing interesting and unusual things. Winners. Overcomers. Creators. Also interested in stories of kids from other cultures, foreign and domestic. 200-500 words. "Finder's Fee" for clippings used. Query with lead/slant.

FICTION—1,300 words maximum. Stories featuring conflicts our readers will respect, resolutions our readers will accept. Problematic. Tight. Filled with realistic dialogue and sharp imagery. No stories about "good" children always making the "right" decision. If present at all, adults are minor characters and *do not* solve kids' problems for them. Especially interested in mystery and historical. Always interested in *short* short stories—500-700 words.

About the Money—There is some. Features range in payment from $250 to $350; fiction from $175 to $350. We pay higher rates for stories exceptionally well-written or well-researched.

Regular contributors get bigger bucks, too. Buys all rights.

Closing Comments and Parting Advice—Study our magazine. (Sure, you've heard that before-but it's *necessary!*) Neatness *does* count. So do creativity and professionalism. SASE essential.

Now, a word from our Editor—

Know Who We Are

We do not view ourselves as a religious publication. We are a value-centered, FUN magazine for kids. We do not feature Bible puzzles or stories about sermonic children. Instead, we deal with issues that concern and affect kids. *How can I find my way through the advertising that's all around me? Do animals have rights? What can I do to help homeless kids? Is it okay if my family fights? Does being afraid make me "chicken"? Will anyone ever live on Mars? What if I buckle under peer pressure? Is it ever right to end someone's life?* Tough questions for tough times.

We strive to give kids a Biblical perspective on today's problems—to teach them *how* to think rather than *what* to think. Basic values like kindness, patience, self-discipline, and honesty run through the magazine like arteries. They are shown, not told.

Know How to Do It

We're fresh and bold and professional. Don't try to write for us unless you:

• invest in a sample copy

• respect kids' problems

• spend time listening to kids talking

• believe in fun

• are willing to rewrite (and rewrite)

• want to do something of lasting importance.

Do your homework. Keep your eyes open. Think. And go easy on the animal pieces. The co-editor of *Guideposts for Kids* is a turtle named Wally, and he's very selective about that sort of thing.

FICTION GUIDELINES

We're looking for the good stuff. Fast-paced, well-crafted stories aimed at kids 8-12 years of age. Stories should reflect strong traditional values and run between 700 and 1,300 words. Each fiction piece gets a two or four-page, four-color spread, supported by strong, memorable graphics and eye-catching tease lines. And since we publish between six and eight stories per year, we only buy the best.

The following information is intended to help you, the writer, structure your fiction to the specific needs of our market. These guidelines are *not* a substitute for studying our magazine. Never read our fiction? Then write for sample copies of our magazine.

Here's how to write the **GUIDEPOSTS FOR KIDS** story:

Don't preach. This is not a Sunday School handout, but a good solid piece of fiction that reflects traditional values and morality. Build your story around a solid principle and let the reader gain insight by inference.

Don't let adults solve problems. While adults can appear in stories, they can't give the characters life's answers. Don't make your kid protagonist grateful and awed by sage, adult advice. (How many of *you* did what adults told you to do when you were growing up?)

Be original. We want a good mix of fiction-contemporary, historical, fantasy, sci-fi, mystery-centered around things that interest and concern kids. A kid reader should be able to identify with the characters strongly enough to think, "*I know just how he feels!*"

Create a plot with believable characters. Here's how it works: the story must tell what happens when someone the reader likes (character) reaches an important goal (climax) by overcoming obstacles (conflict). Let kids be kids. Your dialogue (and use plenty of it!) should reflect how the kids sound, think and feel. Avoid slang, but listen to how real kids talk before you try and write for them. Give your characters feelings and actions suitable for the 4th to 6th grader.

Make tension work for you. Is the character's goal worth fighting for? Is there doubt that the character will get what he wants? What might happen if he *doesn't* get what he wants? Have a satisfying ending. Kids are astute, and if a problem is solved too easily then it's not enough of a problem to sustain a story. Give predictable endings a new twist by using unexpected or surprising details.

Be professional. All the rules of short story writing, grammar, spelling and punctuation apply. Keep verbs active, not passive. **Show** your reader what's happening, don't **tell** him. Keep a tight time frame. You can't follow a character through an entire year of school in 1,300 words. Focus on a single event to make a single strong impact on the reader.

Finally, about the money. There is some. We pay competitive rates ($175-$350) upon **acceptance**. Well-written stories get more $$$. So do your homework and give us a try. We're bright and bold and eager to acquire innovative (**creative, imaginative, ingenious, inventive, original, resourceful, untraditional**) writers.

Categories: Fiction—Nonfiction—Children—Christian Interests

Name: Submissions Editor
Material: All
Address: PO BOX 638
City/State/ZIP: CHESTERTON IN 46304
Telephone: 219-929-4429

Guitar Player

Our goal is to enable readers to become better guitarists, more successful musicians and more informed equipment buyers. If you write for us, this is your goal too.

The essential question: *What can the reader take away from a story to become a better player?* This can include insights into an artist's technique, equipment use and recording tricks, and general information like creative philosophy, career tips and influences. The article must be detailed and accurate.

Guitar Player is about music, not pop culture. Merely recounting a player's or band's background or latest CD is inadequate. Artist interviews should include comprehensive information about technique and equipment, including model names and numbers for all gear mentioned. Readers should learn how the artist uses the gear, not just what's used. For longer features, musical examples-scales, modes, chord diagrams, whole pieces-should be included when possible.

We address a variety of topics on guitarists and instruments. In addition to interviews with guitarists in all styles, we run historical and analytical pieces, how-to articles about musical technique and equipment, and profiles of instrument makers, composers, and teachers important to guitarists. A story must appeal to dedicated musicians, but that's no excuse for dry writing. A colorfully written story is preferable to a dull one—if it meets all other requirements.

Verify the spellings of all names and other proper nouns. Include correct titles and labels of record albums mentioned, and provide the address of lesser-known independent labels. Style: album title in italic, song title in quotation marks, record label in brackets—"Beck's Bolero" from *Truth* [Epic].

Do not submit a story if any part has been previously pub-

lished or if any part has been submitted to any other publisher.

Send us the address and phone number of the person interviewed so we can follow up if necessary and send tearsheets. Let us know if you have leads for photos.

Payment is generally $250 for Intros, $350 for Profiles, and $450 and up for Features. *GP* buys first-time and reprint rights. Payment is on acceptance. We can provide freelancers copies of issues in which their features appear.

Article categories and approximate lengths:
- Intro, 1,600-2,000 characters (250-300 words).
- Profile, 3,500-6,000 characters (550-1,000 words).
- Feature, 7,000 characters (1,100 words) and up.
- Lesson, usually 20-40 measures of examples with explanatory text.

The preferred form for submission is Microsoft Word for Macintosh, though we can translate PC files and other text programs. Files may be sent by modem, e-mail or mailed on disc along with a hard-copy version. Printed manuscripts should be double-spaced and can be faxed. Submissions should be accompanied by an invoice that includes your social security number.

Article ideas should first be submitted in writing. DO NOT contact artists in *GP's* behalf before a story has been assigned. Submissions will be responded to as soon as possible.

Categories: Music

Name: Submissions Editor
Material: All
Address: 411 BOREL AVE STE 100
City/State/ZIP: SAN MATEO CA 94402
Telephone: 415-358-9500
Fax: 415-358-9216
E-mail: guitplyr@mfi.com

Guns & Ammo

The leading magazine in its field, *Guns & Ammo* has a monthly worldwide circulation in excess of 575,000 copies. A technical yet entertaining special-interest publication, *G&A* covers the full firearms spectrum - from guns and ammunition to ancillary gear and accessories of interest to all firearms hobbyists be they serious shooters or inquiring beginners. Be advised that the best "style guide" is a copy of *G&A* itself; you'll notice our heavy use of graphic elements include high-quality photography, informative charts and graphs and reference directories. Our writing style is to the point - informative and entertaining - even when imparting technical information. These are the elements we are looking for - these are the elements you must include to make a sale to *G&A*.

Manuscripts: Feature article length should not exceed 2,500 words. Featurettes should run 800 to 1,200 words. Proof House articles pertaining to firearms should run to 1,200 words in length, while ancillary product Proof Houses should not exceed 800 words. Manuscripts must be typed/printed, double-spaced, on plain white paper with the author's name, story title and page number appearing on each page. We reserve the right to edit any manuscript accepted. Petersen Publishing's policy is to purchase "all rights." Subject matter should be technical in nature, dealing specifically with firearms, ammo, reloading and products only. *G&A* does not accept "hunting" stories, although evaluating an applicable firearm, load or product "in the field" is acceptable.

Computers: With the advent of computer-assisted production and design, we are asking all authors using IBM-compatible computers to submit a printout of their story as well as a floppy-disk containing the manuscript, graphs, charts, captions, directories, etc., so that we can download the story to our computers for editing. Please note the filename and software program and version you are using on the disk.

We request that all manuscripts be sent in "raw" format form (straight ASCII files without formatting or macros). Modem copy can also be sent and accepted. Please call ahead and we will make arrangements to receive your files. Those who are using Apple equipment (Macintosh) may also send diskettes.

Graphics: All manuscripts must be accompanied by high-quality (sharp, uniformly lighted and full range of tones) black & white glossy prints, no smaller than 5x7 inches. Color transparencies 35mm or larger and good quality prints are also acceptable. Bear in mind that photo packages that accompany a story should be able to tell the story photographically.

In addition to photographs, *G&A* is also interested in receiving additional graphic elements, to include graphs, charts and line drawings that assist in illustrating your story.

Captions: All photo submissions must be keyed to a numbered caption sheet. Captions should be detailed enough to require little or no rewriting by in-house editorial staff (again, for *G&A* caption style, please see a copy of the magazine.) People in photographs should be identified and model releases submitted with your package. All bullet and cartridge lineups should also be accompanied by callouts for easy identification.

Payment: Rate of pay varies upon quality and length of material, interest level of subject matter, quality of supportive graphics package etc. Professional writers should be advised that we expect manuscripts to be well written, proofed by the authors for spelling and grammatical errors, neat and organized.

Deadlines: Strict adherence to deadlines is essential to a continuing working relationship.

Should you have further questions or would like to direct queries, please call or fax me.

Best regards,

Kevin E. Steele, Editor

Categories: Nonfiction—Consumer—History—Hobbies—Outdoors—Sports—Recreation—Firearms—Hunting—Shooting—Profiles—Opinion

Name: Kevin E. Steele, Editor
Material: All
Address: 6420 WILSHIRE BLVD.
City/State/ZIP: LOS ANGELES, CA 90048
Telephone: 213-782-2160
Fax: 213-782-2477

Hadrosaur Tales

Hadrosaur Tales is a literary journal published by **Hadrosaur Productions**. We are looking for well written, thought provoking speculative fiction. We accept short stories, poetry, and artwork.

Certain hadrosaurs (better known as duck-billed dinosaurs) had tall head crests and resembled the unicorns of fantasy. To us, this merging of creature of science and creature of fiction seemed the perfect symbol for a magazine of literary science fiction.

Manuscripts must be legible. The story should not be longer than the equivalent of 25 typewritten, double-spaced pages. We will consider longer stories, but they risk being rejected due to lack of space. Please send only complete manuscripts.

Currently, the plan is to publish the *Hadrosaur Tales* approximately every six months. As circulation grows, we hope to publish more frequently.

Each author whose story appears in *Hadrosaur Tales* will receive (2) copies of the journal. Additional copies may be purchased at a 20% discount. Standard payment is $6.00 for short stories and $2.00 for poetry in addition to the copies. In our opinion, a skillfully told 5-page story has as much merit as a 25-page story.

When we accept a story for publication, we request one-time rights. After publication, all rights revert to the author. We reserve the right to correct typos, punctuation, and grammar. Major revisions will be done by the author. We copyright each issue of *Hadrosaur Tales.*

Tips: Let your imagination soar and write down the result. Our only restrictions are no graphic horror and no use of previously copyrighted characters (unless you own the copyright!).

Sample copies may be ordered for $6.00.

Categories: Fiction—Fantasy—Literature—Poetry—Science Fiction

Name: David L. Summers, Editor
Material: All
Address: PO BOX 8468
City/State/ZIP: LAS CRUCES NM 88006-8468
Telephone: 505-527-4163
E-mail: Billosaur@aol.com

Handcraft Illustrated

About Our Readers

Our audience is primarily made up of college-educated women in their late 30s or older. They read *Handcraft Illustrated* for ideas on how to personalize their home with relatively quick, hands-on projects. As they complete each project, they're also learning basic handcraft skills. When writing your article, you should assume that the reader has no previous experience with the project or technique at hand, nor a great deal of time to complete the process. Any terms, tools, or processes specific to your area of expertise should be defined and explained.

Basic Requirements

1. Manuscripts should be submitted on disk. We prefer files stored as Microsoft Word documents in Macintosh format, but we also accept PC (DOS or Windows) disks with files saved in ASCII (.txt) format. If you have questions, phone Barbara Bourassa. When sending articles on disk, be sure to include a printed copy of the piece.

If you do not have access to a personal computer, we will accept articles that have been typed. We do not accept handwritten articles.

If sending sketches or diagrams, please make them as clear as possible, mark important references and include all captions.

2. All articles should be accompanied by the following items, unless otherwise noted in the assignment process:

a.) A photograph of the project, or the project itself.

b.) A complete list of materials. Every tool, supply, or material used in the project should be listed in the order in which it will be needed. Give as much detail as possible when listing the materials—i.e., 1 quart latex paint, 1 ½ yard fabric of choice, etc.

c.) Step-by-step instructions. The instructions should be written strictly in order, and should take the reader through the entire project, from laying down newspaper to protect the work surface, for instance, to tying the finishing bow.

d.) Mail-order sources. Every article should be accompanied by a list of mail-order sources for each tool, supply, or material used in the project.

Payment

We pay authors 60 days from final acceptance of an article or receipt of invoice, whichever comes later.

Sending Your Manuscript

All completed articles, projects, photographs, and diagrams should be sent to the attention of Barbara Bourassa at the address shown below.

A Few Simple Suggestions

1. Your writing should be personal, but remember to keep the focus on the project, not on yourself. Be friendly to the read-

ers and try to make them feel at ease. They should feel like this project is something they can do. Otherwise what's the point in you writing about it?

2. Write in a way that comes naturally. Write as you would speak, in common, everyday language. Don't try to adopt a "literary" style. Don't use a long word where a short one will do. Keep your sentences simple and clear.

3. Define every term the reader might be unfamiliar with. If you define the term the first time you use it, that will give the reader a sense of confidence, not only in his or her ability to do the project, but also a sense of confidence that you know what you're doing.

4. Do everything in order. Many readers won't read all the way through the instructions before they start, so be sure that every material and every instruction is given in exactly the order needed.

5. Be careful with prepositions and words like "top" and "bottom." They are the words most likely to be misinterpreted. UP means away from the pull of gravity; the TOP is the surface facing UP. If the project involves, for instance, a piece of paper which has been laid out on the table, do not refer to the top of the paper unless you mean the surface of the paper facing away from the table. If you mean the end of the paper away from you (or the reader), say so.

6. Be consistent. If you call a spade a spade in the first part of the article, don't start calling it a shovel in the latter part. Pick words that mean what you want them to mean, then define them (if necessary), and stick with them. You'll be doing your readers a service.

7. When you have written your article, reread it trying to put yourself in the position of an inexperienced reader. See if there's a way to misinterpret anything you've written. If there is, correct it. The true measure of your own expertise is in how well the reader can complete the project using your instructions.

Categories: Crafts

Name: Barbara Bourassa, Executive Editor
Material: All
Address: 17 Station Street, P.O. Box 509
City/State/ZIP: Brookline Village, MA 02147
Telephone: 617-232-1000

The Happy Times Monthly
The Good News Newspaper

The Happy Times Monthly, the good-news newspaper, is a forum to spread positive ideas everywhere, and contains what people **like you** send us or tell us about. It provides the community with education, humor, wisdom, inspiration, and awareness of what's good in the news, and highlights people, businesses, social groups and events that can give a positive lift to our readers.

Does one of these categories bring a *Happy Times* story to mind?

What I'm thankful for • Random Acts of Kindness • Tribute to an amazing friend • Successful people in business, life, health, or love • People who care • Good deed stories • Positive events • Everyday heroes • People helping people • Tragedy turned positive • Outstanding students/teachers • Funniest thing that ever happened to you • The best time of your life • Gratitude and thank you's • Nature & environment stories • Un-

usual, funny or cute pet or animal stories • Humorous relative stories • Someone that really inspired you!

Write about the person and the experience and send in *one or two photos* with it

Seeks 150 to 500 word articles with 1 or 2 photos (place name and address on back of photos). Encourages human interest, feature-type articles about people, organizations, or animals on a good news theme. **Stories need to be expressed from the heart.** For more writer guidelines/information or suggestions on articles, go to our Web Site. Pays in copy. SASE for sample issues. Subscriptions $20.

Categories: Nonfiction—Adventure—Animals—Business—Careers—Cartoons—Children—Comedy—Cooking—Entertainment—Environment—Family—Fishing—Games—Gardening—General Interest—Good Deeds—Good News—Heartfelt—Hobbies—Humor—Inspirational—Lifestyles—Marriage—Men's Issues—Outdoors—Parenting—Philosophy—Photography—Physical Fitness—Positive—Recreation—Relationships—Romance—Senior Citizens—Short Stories—Teen—Writing

Name: Brigitte Lang, Publisher
Material: Human Interest, Heartfelt Articles, etc.
Address: PO BOX 7253
City/State/ZIP: BOCA RATON FL 33431
Telephone: 561-394-7466
Fax: 561-395-1313
E-mail: BrLang@aol.com
Internet: www.thehappytimes.com

Hardboiled

Please refer to Gryphon Publications.

Harper's Magazine

Thank you for requesting our submission guidelines. If you have not already done so, we suggest that before sending us a manuscript or a query you read a few issues of the magazine to ensure *Harper's* is the appropriate place for your work.

Harper's only rarely publishes unsolicited work, but we will consider submissions that fall within the following guidelines:

1) No submissions of any kind will be considered or returned without a self-addressed, stamped envelope (SASE) with proper postage. A SASE is required for a response, even if the writer does not want the manuscript returned.

2) We do not consider or read multiple submissions: articles or stories sent simultaneously to more than one magazine. This policy is necessary to ensure that the originality of each piece is protected.

3) Correspondence will be expedited if it is addressed to the appropriate editor or to his or her assistant. Submissions that are sent priority or express mail cannot receive attention faster than other submissions.

4) Please do not send original manuscripts or documents.

5) **Non-Fiction:** *Harper's* does not accept non-fiction articles without a preceding query letter. The letter should explain the style, tone, and argument of the proposed article, include an indication of sources, and explain why the author is best suited to write the piece. The query can be accompanied by clips of previous work, a resume, and a list of places previously published.

6) **Memoirs:** Memoirs, too, should be preceded by a query. The memoirs we publish generally use the writer's own experiences to elucidate some larger societal issue.

7) **Fiction:** Many story submissions, though well-written and memorable, are simply unsuited to *Harper's*. Most writers ready to be published in a national magazine such as *Harper's* have been

previously published in literary journals, or have published novels, etc. We cannot consider manuscripts over 30 pages.

8) **Poetry:** We no longer consider or return unsolicited poetry.

9) **Faxes:** *Harper's* does not accept faxed submissions.

10) **Readings:** We reprint recent, previously published articles, speeches, brochures, etc. We welcome suggestions and clips from readers. Unfortunately, we cannot pay readers for their efforts.

11) We do not publish the following:
Interviews
Profiles
Historical non-fiction
Children's fiction
Lifestyle pieces
Society or gossip items
Book, movie, travel, or music reviews
Fashion articles
Consumer articles

Our staff receives many hundreds of unsolicited submissions each week. It generally takes between four to six weeks to guarantee a manuscript or query has been read. After that period of time, a follow-up call is acceptable.

The Editors

Categories: Fiction—Nonfiction—Arts—Business—Crime—Culture—Literature—Poetry—Politics—Science—Society—News—Essay—International Affairs—Humor—Humanities—Memoirs

Name: Lewis H. Lapham, Editor
Material: All
Address: 666 BROADWAY, 11TH FLOOR
City/State/ZIP: NEW YORK, NY 10012
Telephone: 212-614-6500
Fax: 212-228-5889

Hawaii Review
University of Hawaii

Thank you for inquiring about *Hawaii Review*'s guidelines/requirements.

Hawaii Review publishes fiction, poetry, creative nonfiction, essays and translations.

We have no specific length, subject-matter, or style requirements. To get an idea of what we're looking for, we recommend reading a sample copy of the *Hawaii Review.* To order a sample copy, please send a check for $10 made payable to *Hawaii Review* to the address below.

Hawaii Review looks for original work from both new and published authors. Our issues are open-themed and we welcome submissions year round. Please send no more than one story at a time, and no more than six poems per packet. We do not accept handwritten or badly photocopied submissions.

Hawaii Review is published three times a year, spring, fall and winter. Please allow six weeks for a reply on poetry manuscripts and translations, and ten weeks for a reply on fiction manuscripts. Replies on summer submissions may take a little longer.

If you have any further questions, just drop us a note. We try to respond promptly.

Categories: Fiction—Nonfiction—Poetry

Name: Submissions Editor
Material: All
Address: UNIVERSITY OF HAWAII-MANOA DEPT OF ENGLISH
Address: 1733 DONAGHHO RD

City/State/ZIP: HONOLULU HI 96822
Telephone: 808-956-3030
Fax: 808-956-9962

Hayden's Ferry Review
Arizona State University

Hayden's Ferry Review is a nationally distributed magazine publishing quality literary and visual art. Produced twice a year at Arizona State University, HFR promotes the work of emerging and established visual artists and writers of fiction, poetry and creative nonfiction. Writers are urged to read the magazine before submitting. Editors serve for two issues (Fall/Winter, Spring/Summer).

Deadlines (postmark): Fall/Winter, February 28; Spring/Summer, September 30.

Submissions received after the deadline will be held for the next issue. Response time is 8—12 weeks after the deadline. Payment is two copies. No fee. Authors/artists receive page proofs for review prior to publication.

Manuscripts must be typed or letter-quality printed; clean photocopies are acceptable. Send poetry and prose separately, limiting submissions to six poems or one story or essay per submission. Please send one manuscript per genre at a time, and wait for response before you submit additional work. We do not respond to manuscripts unless they are accompanied by an SASE. Art submissions can be in slides or prints. Please limit your submission to ten. HFR publishes eight pages of art in black and white and one in color for the cover.

Sample issues are $6.00. Yearly subscriptions are $10.00 (two issues).

Categories: Fiction—Poetry

Name: Fiction Editor
Material: All Fiction
Name: Poetry Editor
Material: All Poetry
Address: ARIZONA STATE UNIVERSITY
Address: PO BOX 871502
City/State/ZIP: TEMPE AZ 85287-1502
Telephone: 602-965-1243
Fax: 602-965-8484
E-mail: HFR@asuvm.inre.asu.edu

Headway Magazine

Headway (formerly *National Minority Politics*), a monthly opinion and news magazine, is the magazine for today's political leaders. Unlike most publications which include commentaries from members of minority groups our magazine takes a moderate to conservative approach to political issues. We also do not limit ourselves to matters concerning race and civil rights; rather, we believe Americans who happen to be from minority groups do and should discuss issues which affect the entire nation.

We are looking for:
• Insightful commentary and opinion on current issues
• Well-written essays or features, supported by facts and/or statistics
• Well-reasoned, expert analysis.
We are not looking for:
• Approaches which assert racism as the reason for all or most of the problems facing African Americans, Hispanics and others
• Ax-grinding or venting tirades

Articles should be 750 to 1,000 words in length. All finished manuscripts must be accompanied by a cover letter containing your name, address, day and evening phones, social security number and credentials, i.e., your qualifications to write on the particular subject. Mail articles to the address below. Once manuscripts are accepted for publication, a 3½" floppy disk in WordPerfect format must be forwarded by first-class mail to *Headway* or the manuscript must be forwarded via e-mail to the address below.

Fax submissions are accepted. If you submit by fax, please provide a return fax number, and you will be notified by fax if possible (otherwise, you will be notified by mail).

We cannot accept telephone queries. If we accept your article for publication, you will be notified by phone or mail, before the article is published.

Writer's Fees: *Headway* purchases first rights for 90 days. Fees are: $100.00 for opinion pieces. $150.00 for interviews and profiles. Fees for feature articles/analysis range from $100.00 to $250.00. All interviews/profiles and feature articles are assigned. All writers receive a copy of the issue in which their article appeared.

Types of Material

We accept articles for the following sections of the magazine:

Featured Politico: An in-depth interview with a minority politician of national prominence.

Speaking Out: Opinion piece of a personal nature on an issue of concern to the writer.

Book Review: Analysis of a recently published political book.

The Nation: Commentaries on National Issues: Strong opinion concerning a current issue of national debate.

DEADLINES: Deadlines are the 28th of each month, two months prior to publication date. For example, the deadline for the February issue is December 28; the deadline for the June issue is April 28; etc.

Categories: African-American—Politics

Name: Gwen Richardson, Editor
Material: All
Address: 13555 BAMMEL N HOUSTON STE 227
City/State/ZIP: HOUSTON TX 77066
Telephone: 281-444-4265
Fax: 281-583-9534
E-mail: grichardson@ghgcorp.com

Health

Health's focus is not on illness, but rather on ideas, events, and people. Our stories are written to inform decisions and compel action—in effect, giving readers more control over their own health. Each issue of the magazine presents some of the most important developments that health specialists are following in their journals, but in readable stories written with warmth, wit, and authority.

For our readers, health is a topic as varied as people are, with unexpected connections to all sorts of concerns and curiosities. Our stories must not only inform readers but surprise and entertain them as well. We scan the nation's newspapers for notable events that exemplify larger trends or concerns. And in considering story proposals, we look especially for well-articulated ideas that have the same kind of narrow focus and broad appeal.

The audience for *Health* is predominantly college-educated women who, by reason of their intellectual curiosity or practical interest, want both a dependable source of useful health information and a perspective on the rapidly changing face of American health care.

Health is published seven times a year, with a nationwide circulation of approximately 900,000. The magazine relies heavily on staff writers and contributing editors. We buy 30 to 35 freelance

manuscripts - including long features and short departments - each year. We usually assign features to regular contributors or to experienced writers whose work we know - and only after extensive discussion. Departments are more open to freelance writers new to us. Practical, service-oriented ideas are more likely to receive consideration. First-time contributors should propose stories for our Food, Relationships, Great Escapes, Mind, Smart Buys, Remedies, Vanities, and Fitness departments. (Vital Signs, Body Work, and Healthy Cooking are closed to freelancers.)

Departments usually run about 1,200 words and the standard fee is $1,800. Fees are paid on acceptance. We pay research and travel expenses that have been agreed upon with the assigning editor. In all cases, accepted stories are returned to the writer for revision after editorial review.

How to Query: All writers must submit written proposals before sending manuscripts, regardless of the planned length or nature of the story.

Proposals should be no more than one or two double-spaced pages in length, sharply focused, with the style and sources clearly defined. Send proposals, along with a #10 self-addressed stamped envelope, resume, and copies of no more than two published stories.

We'll try to reply within two months.

Categories: Nonfiction—Cooking—Family—Food/Drink—Health—Marriage—Physical Fitness—Psychology—Relationships—Self-Help—Diet—Medicine

Name: Paula Motte, Editorial Assistant
Material: All
Address: 301 HOWARD ST., 18TH FLOOR
City/State/ZIP: SAN FRANCISCO, CA 94105
Telephone: 415-512-9100

HealthQuest
The Publication of Black Wellness

WHO

HealthQuest is looking for writers who have a strong interest in the well-being of black people. Experienced writers are preferred, but we have a history of working with new writers whose work exhibits style, skill and promise. So that we can get a sense of what your writing is like, and how your mind works, send us samples of your nonfiction writing along with a query letter that outlines your story idea(s).

WHAT

In each issue, our Focus Section comprises several stories and sidebars related to a single health issue. Features and departments cover fitness, nutrition, image, travel, spirituality, disease and other issues that affect black health. If you have an idea that fits our editorial goals, send us a query letter. We prefer a query to articles that are sent "on spec," but we will review and consider unpublished manuscripts. We cannot promise to return your unsolicited manuscript, but you can be sure that we won't print your story without contacting you first. If you haven't heard from us about the status of your story, contact the Editor.

WHEN

We plan Focus Sections at least one year in advance of publication and other features and departments as much as six to eight months out. If you're assigned a story, your deadline will he approximately 3 months before the magazine is published. Keep this schedule in mind if you are querying us about a story that has a seasonal slant. Writers are paid in full within 30 days after publication. If, for any reason, we are not able to run a story we have assigned, we will either pay you a kill fee as agreed upon in the contract, or we will arrange to hold the story to run in a future issue.

WHY

When you write for *HealthQuest* you will he associated with a top-quality publication. We are the only nationally distributed, black-owned magazine that covers African-American health issues—and our concern for black health shows in the depth and quality of the articles we publish. Writing for us puts you in league with Dr. Joycelyn Elders, Iyanla Vanzant, Pearl Cleage and others who have written for us. Good writers make for a good publication—so we value strong skills and we pay competitively.

HOW

We emphasize strong reporting and creative writing. Our writers take a conversational, reader-friendly tone without being too colloquial. We encourage writers to he as creative as possible—taking into consideration the nature of the story. Don't feel repressed; your writing should be interested and interesting. Dig-in reporting covers all sides of an issue—often health issues are not black and white, hut all shades of brown. And we take a holistic approach to the way we look at specific treatments and health in general—emphasizing the importance of physical, mental, emotional, spiritual and social wellness.

WHERE

If you want to get to know *HealthQuest* a little better you can find us distributed in newspapers throughout fifteen major cities nationwide. When you're ready, send samples and queries.

Categories: Nonfiction—African-American—Diet—Ethnic—Health

Name: Tamara Jeffries, Editor
Material: All
Address: 200 HIGHPOINT DR STE 215
City/State/ZIP: PHILADELPHIA PA 18914
Telephone: 215-822-7935
Fax: 215-997-9582

Heartland Boating
Mid America's Premier Boating Magazine

Readership description: *HeartLand Boating* magazine is devoted to both power and sail boating enthusiasts throughout middle America. Primary geographic readership areas include Tennessee, Kentucky, Alabama, Mississippi, Illinois, Missouri, Georgia, Arkansas, Indiana, Iowa, Ohio, Louisiana, Michigan, Wisconsin, Pennsylvania, Kansas, Minnesota, Nebraska, Florida, South Carolina and North Carolina.

Publication description: *HeartLand Boating* is the official magazine for the boater who isn't going around the world. The content is both informative and humorous-describing boating life as the heartland boater knows it. We aren't pretentious. But, we are boating and enjoying the outdoor, water oriented way of life. The content reflects the challenge, joy and excitement of our way of life afloat.

Freelance Submissions: *HeartLand Boating* welcomes submissions of photographic and written material for possible publication. Our focus is on the freshwater inland rivers and lakes of

the Heartland...primarily the waters of the Tennessee, Cumberland, Ohio and Mississippi rivers, the Tennessee-Tombigbee Waterway and the lakes among these rivers. The magazine caters to all kinds of boating: sail, houseboats, cruisers, runabouts, pontoons, etc.

No Great Lakes or salt water material will be considered unless it applies in some way to our area. Example: "What the fresh water boater should know about salt water cruising."

Writers not familiar with *HeartLand Boating*'s style should write for a sample issue. Enclose $5.00.

We are looking for materials with a fresh "snap." Don't be afraid to let your personality show.

Please be Correct, Concise, Clear and Colorful.

Regular features open to freelance writers:

• *Marina Profile:* A regular feature highlighting a marina in the area already described. Writers should provide comprehensive information about marina facilities, restaurants, services, things to do, etc...the kind of information traveling boaters want to know about marinas they might visit. Articles should be accompanied with a good selection of sharply focused color and b/w photos. 1,000-1,200 words.

• *Near the Water:* A regular department featuring shore based, close-to-the water places of interest to boaters. Places that are near, but not necessarily on the water. (Guard against a "touristy tone.") Article should be accompanied with a good selection of sharply focused color and b/w photos. 1,000-1,500 words

• *Books Aboard:* Reviews on nautical books. Book reviews don't have to be dry and boring. Prove it. 600 – 800 words.

• *Maintenance/Nuts and bolts (boats)* articles: Technical articles on boat maintenance/repair. Supply charts/graphics. 500-1,000 words.

• *Environment/Ecology:* An aid to education of boaters on how to do our part in keeping our waters clean for boating *and* swimming. (Tear-out sheet that might be posted on a marina bulletin board.) 600-800 words.

• *Electronics:* Technical articles. 300-1,000 words with art if possible.

• *Miscellaneous:* Anything not already mentioned which would be of interest to boating enthusiasts. Query first.

Manuscript specifications: We prefer that prospective contributors query an idea first rather than submit an unsolicited manuscript. However, if sending an unsolicited manuscript, it must be accompanied with a SASE to insure return of the material.

Manuscripts must be typed. *Please indicate the approximate number of words* and mark all sheets with the page number, feature title and author's name. Those using Macintosh personal computers are asked to submit a Macintosh computer disk (MacWrite or Word OK or indicate what application you used) along with the hard copy. For IBM DOS-save as text file.

Freelance photographers: *HeartLand Boating* buys a limited number of photographs each issue. Freelance photographers query first with sample of your work.

Black and white photos: 8"X10" glossy prints preferred. High quality with moderate contrast and sharp focus. Contact sheets can be submitted for consideration.

Color: Good quality transparencies are acceptable for editorial use. Color prints are preferred if submitted with negatives. Consideration will be given to 35mm for possible use as covers, but large format transparencies are preferred. Photo essays are very occasionally awarded to an artistically outstanding series centered on a single facet of boating in our editorial area.

General: *HeartLand Boating* pays for all contributions upon publication. We are specifically looking for a core of freelancers who are also boating in the inland waters of middle America.

Categories: Adventure—Boating—Hobbies—Outdoors—Recreation—Travel

Name: Molly Blom, Editor
Material: All
Address: PO BOX 1067
City/State/ZIP: MARTIN TN 38237
Telephone: 901-587-6791
Fax: 901-587-6893

Heartland USA

HEARTLAND USA is a general-interest, bimonthly magazine with a circulation of over 750,000 and a readership exceeding 2.3 million. Targeted primarily at blue-collar working men, the publication regularly includes an eclectic mix of short, easy-to-read articles on spectator sports (motorsports, football, basketball and baseball), hunting, fishing, how-to, travel, music (both C&W and soft rock), gardening, wildlife, and the environment.

Articles focus on *interesting*, positive aspects of life in these United States. Quality photography and entertaining cartoons are an integral part of the overall mix.

Please keep in mind that our average reader is a working person with a high school education. We have consciously chosen not to "write down" to our readers, but rather to pursue an editorial voice that reflects a relaxed, jocular, street-smart familiarity, with just a hint of attitude. The liberal use of anecdote or compelling quotations—anything to breathe some life into a piece—is looked upon favorably.

The target length for feature articles is 1,200 words, with payment varying from $250 to $950. Feature-length pieces must lend themselves to strong photographic support.

Department-length articles (generally 550 - 1,200 words) pay from $140 to $950.

We pay on final acceptance (i.e. when we're certain the piece will appear in an upcoming issue), offer a 20% kill fee on assigned work, purchase the first or second North American serial rights, and copyright our publication. Hard-copy submissions must be sharp and legible. Simultaneous, photocopied, and reprint submissions are okay. Enclose a SASE with any query or submission. Response will usually be within 4-6 weeks. A free sample copy is available on request. Clips of published work should accompany hard-copy queries.

E-mail queries may be sent to the address below.

Categories: Nonfiction—Adventure—Animals—Automobile—Aviation—Biography—Boating—Cartoons—Civil War—Conservation—Crime—Disabilities—Ecology—Environment—Fishing—Gardening—General Interest—Hunting—Inspirational—Martial Arts—Men's Issues—Military—Music—Outdoors—Recreation—Rural America—Sports—Technology

Name: Brad Pearson, Editor
Material: All
Address: 1 SOUND SHORE DR
City/State/ZIP: GREENWICH CT 06830
Telephone: 203-622-3456
Fax: 203-863-5393
E-mail: HUSAEDIT@aol.com

Heaven Bone

Poetry

We love the work of Rainer Maria Rilke and how he had the capability of being able to articulate rare and nearly inexpressible thoughts and images. He showed that disciplined work can be simple and carry great emotional impact. Although the basic tone of our magazine is surreal, sensual and spiritual, we are not traditionally religious, not homophobic, and generally dislike all forms of bustle in the name of the holy. That includes blind theocratic rants for or against one deity or another.

We have Buddhist tendencies, however, and you are welcome to exploit that in your submission strategy. Our bottom line is inspiration, bringing something of the gods down into the flesh and bone of our normal, spectacularly ordinary experiences. Bridging with the mind toward a realm of muse and music. Our biannual chapbook contest is open to all poets. Additional guidelines available upon request. There is a cash prize and publication of the winning manuscript. We have an impressive backlist.

Prose

As with poetry, the editor feels fiction ought to not only inspire the reader to put the magazine down and go out and live, but that the text have citizenship on other planets as well. Again, we recommend seeing our earlier issues, notably our latest, since it's most likely the only ones we have left.

If a bias in subject matter could be said to exist, it might tend toward the so called alternative-cultural, post-beat, and yogic/anti-paranoiac. Keep to under 5,000 words. Book and magazine reviews, particularly of work that would be relevant to our readership, are welcome within a range of 250-2,500 words. We are also accepting essays on various surrealist, futurist, dada, ecological, social, artistic and esoteric topics reflecting literary excellence and attention to scope and detail. Please query first with synopsis. We shun sensationalism but not controversy and we enjoy writing that displays a keen attention to nature.

Art, Graphics, Photographs, Collages & Cartoons

Send prints, slides, veloxes or anything else which actually represents your best work. Consider the comments above and always include an SASE. Our production values are being enhanced with each issue, as the desktop publishing technologies advance and we welcome submissions of electronic artwork in any format. Again, our tastes are eclectic; our minds probably more open than you'd think.

Considerations

Perhaps it needn't be said again, but for the record: without including a self addressed stamped envelope, it's unlikely anything will happen. Payment is always in contributor's copies unless other arrangements are made in advance. We report in three to thirty-eight weeks (we are a biannual publication). If it takes much longer, it is likely that your work is being considered favorably, and we're just trying to see if and how we can fit it in to the next issue.

Unlike many other small presses, we believe that, if you took the time to inquire about us, we want to put you into our database and respond personally. So have a heart. Please don't swamp us with large submissions every few weeks. Let's put it this way: submissions accompanied by a check for a publication, a sample issue, or better yet a subscription, are greeted very happily indeed. ($16.95 for 4 issues or single copy at $6.00)

Since we think we're covering ground no one else is, we'd like to develop all the friends to the press we can. We rely on the support of our readers and contributors for our creative survival. We receive no other financial support from any state or federal agency. Paid advertising is accepted and rates are available upon request.

Categories: Fiction—Nonfiction—Arts—Fine Art—Poetry—Reviews—Writing

Name: Submissions Editor
Material: All
Address: PO BOX 486
City/State/ZIP: CHESTER NY 10918

Telephone: 914-469-9018
Fax: 914-469-7880
E-mail: POETSTEVE@compuserve.com

The Hellenic Calendar

Tabloid newspaper (17"x11") presenting news and features of special interest to the Greek-Americans of Southern California and the Great Southwest. Circulation 10,000.

Needs: Articles on prominent Americans of Greek descent, also on trends or issues of special interest to Greek-Americans. 500-2,000 words. We're not interested in a story about your trip to Greece or the best gyro you ever ate. Mail or e-mail complete manuscript.

Reports in two weeks.

Payment: Varies, usually ranges from $25 to $75.

Categories: Ethnic

Name: Steve Pastis, Publisher/Editor
Material: All
Address: 2747 N GRAND AVE STE 250
City/State/ZIP: SANTA ANA CA 92705
Telephone: 714-550-9933
Fax: 714-550-9933
E-mail: greekpaper@aol.com

HerbalGram

HerbalGram is a publication of the American Botanical Council and the Herb Research Foundation. ABC and HRF are non-profit, educational and research organizations which focus on herb and medicinal plant research, regulatory issues, market conditions, native plant conservation, and other general interest aspects of herb use.

All articles published in *HerbalGram* are peer reviewed by some of the leading authorities in the field of phytopharmaceutical research, including James A. Duke, Ph.D., U.S. Department of Agriculture, retired; Varro Tyler, Ph.D., Lilly Distinguished Professor of Pharmacognosy, Purdue University; Norman Farnsworth, Ph.D., Professor of Pharmacognosy, University of Illinois Medical School, and Dennis V. C. Awang, Ph.D., MediPlant, Ottawa, Canada.

We welcome proposals and finished manuscripts in hard copy form, preferably accompanied by a computer disk. We prefer Microsoft Word for Macintosh, but can interpret from Word for Windows. If neither of these programs are possible, then please save your text in rich text format (.rtf), a universal style which retains any italics or other individual formatting. *Do not* send manuscripts formatted in WordPerfect. If you have any questions about rich text format, please contact the editorial office at the number below. You may also send articles to our e-mail address.

We also prefer that you send straight text, with little or no formatting except when necessary for presentation of charts or diagrams. The common name of all botanicals mentioned *must* be followed by the Latin binomial. References *must be complete*, with title of the article cited as well as author/s names, publication, pages, and dates. [Example—Smith, Maurice I., and E. Elvove, with the cooperation of P.J. Valaer, Jr., William H. Frazier and G. E. Mallory, "Pharmacological and Chemical Studies of the Cause of So-Called Ginger Paralysis: A Preliminary Report," *Pub. Health Rep.*, 45 (1930): 1703-1716 (especially p.1704).]

Our stylistic authority is the *Chicago Manual of Style* and our botanical reference is *The Plant Book* by D. J. Mabberly.

If you have *excellent quality* color or black and white slides or photographs to illustrate your article we are interested in seeing them and will, of course, return them to you. Please include a proper description of such materials and label your photos/slides with your name and the name of the subject.

We do not pay for manuscripts, but will send you six copies of the issue in which your material appears.

We strongly suggest that you obtain a sample copy of at least one of the latest issues in order to familiarize yourself with our subject matter, journalistic style, and general focus.

If you have any questions, please contact Barbara Johnston, Managing Editor.

Categories: Nonfiction—General Interest—Health—Herbal Medicine—Herbs—Medicinal Plants

Name: Barbara Johnston, Managing Editor
Material: All
Address: PO BOX 201660
City/State/ZIP: AUSTIN TX 78750
Telephone: 512-451-4820
Fax: 512-451-3897
E-mail: BJ@herbalgram.org
Internet: www.herbalgram.org

The Higginsville Reader

Published by the Higginsville Writers, *The Higginsville Reader* seeks submissions of original writing and artwork.

The Higginsville Reader seeks poetry, and short (less than 3,500 words) fiction and essays. For art submissions, line drawings reproduce most accurately with our production methods. We also accept photographs and other continuous tone works which we digitally enhance for pleasing, if not completely accurate, reproduction.

Although not mandatory, it is preferable that submissions be typewritten. Handwritten material is more prone than typewritten to developing errors in format and content when it is typeset.

Payment to the author upon publication of a submitted work(s) is one copy of the issue(s) in which the work(s) is (are) published.

All rights revert to the author upon publication.

Subscriptions & Discounts

A 1 year subscription (4 issues) to *The Higginsville Reader* is $5.00 ($8.00 to foreign addresses). Single issues are $1.50 (plus $0.75 foreign postage). Single copy discount: 8 copies for $10.00, 20 copies for $20.00 (foreign postage extra). Please make checks payable to The Higginsville Writers.

Categories: Fiction—Literary Essay—Poetry—Short Stories

Name: Eileen Fisher, Editor
Name: Frank Magalhaes, Editor
Name: Kathe Palka, Editor
Material: Any
Address: PO BOX 141
City/State/ZIP: THREE BRIDGES NJ 08887
Telephone: 609-924-2842
E-mail: fmag@eclipse.net

The Highlander
The Magazine of Scottish Heritage

• Fiction and poetry are not accepted.

• Articles should be related to Scotland in a time span of roughly 1300 to 1900, although there is some flexibility in the time. We are not concerned with modern Scotland or with current problems or issues in Scotland.

• Articles should be related to some incident in Scottish history, to Scottish clans or families, or have some relationship to Scottish heritage. Focus should be fairly specific, not general. Articles must be historically accurate.

• Articles should be interesting, not pedantic. Length is generally 2,000 to 3,000 words, although there is some flexibility here also, as shorter pieces are often accepted. The article should be long enough to tell the story.

• Articles should be typed. If possible, please submit a disk (preferably for PC, Microsoft Word 5.0 or 6.0) along with the hard copy.

• The article may have appeared elsewhere, but we must know where and when, and who owns the copyright. Please include photographs (in color, if possible), transparencies, maps, and/or line or historical drawings to illustrate your work. These will be returned to you after publication, along with a copy of the issue in which your story appears.

• We purchase first North American rights and second reprint rights. Payment will be made on acceptance of story.

Categories: Nonfiction—Ethnic—History—Scottish Heritage

Name: Crennan Wade, Editor
Material: All
Address: PO BOX 22307
City/State/ZIP: KANSAS CITY MO 64113-2307
Telephone: 816-523-4141
Fax: 816-523-7474
E-mail: HILANDER@gvi.net

Highlights for Children

We appreciate your interest in Highlights for Children. Highlights is published monthly for children 2 to 12. Circulation is nearly 3 million.

Please note:

• We do not pay persons under age 15 for contributions.

• We buy all rights, including copyright, and do not consider material previously published.

• We prefer to see a manuscript rather than a query.

• All material is paid for on acceptance.

• We accept material year round, including seasonal material.

FICTION should have an engaging plot, strong characterization, and lively language. Stories for younger readers (ages 3-7) should be 400 words or less. Stories for older readers (8-12) should be 900 words or less and be appealing to younger readers if read aloud.

• We prefer stories that teach by positive example, rather than by preaching.

• Suggestions of crime and violence are taboo.

• Frequent needs include humor, mystery, sports, and adventure stories; retellings of traditional tales; stories in urban settings; and stories that feature world cultures.

• We seldom buy rhyming stories.

Payment: $100 and up.

REBUS STORIES are a monthly feature for beginning readers, featuring a variety of familiar words that can easily be shown as pictures. Rebuses should be 125 words or less.

Payment: $75 and up.

NONFICTION includes biography, autobiography, and various approaches to the arts, science, history, sports, and world cultures. All articles should be 800 words or less.

• Focused articles are more successful than broad factual surveys.

• We prefer research based on consultation with experts or firsthand experience.

• Writers with an extensive background in a particular field are encouraged to share their experiences and personal research.

• Articles about cultural traditions and ways of life should reflect a deep understanding of the subject.

• Biographies of individuals who have made significant artistic, scientific, or humanitarian contributions are strengthened by the inclusion of formative childhood experiences. We prefer biographies that are rich in anecdotes and place the subject in a historical and cultural context.

• Nonfiction articles geared to our younger readers (ages 3-7) are especially welcome. These should not exceed 400 words.

• References or sources of information must be included with submissions.

• Color 35mm slides, photos, or art reference materials are helpful and sometimes crucial in evaluating submissions.

Payment: $100 and up.

CRAFTS should appeal to a wide age range, with clear, numbered directions, typically not more than five steps.

• A well-made sample should be submitted with each craft idea.

• Projects must require only common household items or inexpensive, easy-to-obtain materials.

• Projects should result in attractive, useful gift items, decorations, toys, and games.

• Crafts that celebrate holidays or religious traditions are welcome. Crafts from world cultures are a current need.

Payment: $25 and up.

FINGER PLAYS/ACTION RHYMES should have plenty of action and minimal text. They must be easy for very young children to act out, step-by-step, with hands, fingers, and body movements.

Payment: $25 and up.

PARTY PLANS should give clever, original party ideas organized around a single theme, clearly described in 300 to 700 words. Plans should include invitations, favors, decorations, refreshments, and a mix of quiet and active games. Materials used should be inexpensive. Include drawings or samples of items.

Payment: $50 and up.

VERSE is purchased sparingly. It is rarely longer than 16 lines and should be meaningful for young readers.

Payment: $25 and up.

Categories: Children

Name: Beth Troop, Manuscript Coordinator
Material: All
Address: 803 CHURCH ST
City/State/ZIP: HONESDALE PA 18431
Telephone: 717-253-1080
Fax: 717-253-1079
E-mail: Highlights@ezaccess.net

High Technology Careers

High Technology Careers serves a readership of technical professionals. The magazine's circulation of 135,000 is mainly throughout the San Francisco Bay Area's Silicon Valley. HTC is mailed directly to the homes of 80,000 readers. It is distributed via racks and newsstands, bookstores, computer stores, libraries, universities, career resource centers, technical training schools, outplacement centers, and minority organizations.

The publication's audience consists of three groups of readers:

• those in search of a job because they have relocated to the Bay Area, are entering the work force for the first time, or are reentering the work force

• those presently employed but wanting to make a vertical or lateral career move, change jobs or careers

• those employed but interested in remaining career conscious and aware of job opportunities, salaries, positions, and trends

Advertising content is employment-related.

ARTICLES

We buy **three regular features that examine cutting-edge or futuristic developments in high technology** and their effects on our planet, our civilization, our careers, and/or our lifestyle. Technology articles should be 1,200 to 1,500 words, include up to three short sidebars, and provide a nonacademic and lively treatment of developments in computers, science, aerospace, and biotechnology, etc., for a general but professional audience. We also like pie-charts, graphs, stills, and other types of visual aids to accompany features. Features may have up to three sidebars (300 to 500 words).

COLUMNS

Columns are sought for the following categories: employment-related how-to, on-the-job strategies, the next step in a job or career change, and ethics in the workplace. In addition, we use columns about health and fitness, new innovations and on-line job search strategies.

Column content covers the following:

• **How-To**—Information on how to write resumes, improve interviewing skills, conduct a job search, etc.

• **On-the-Job Strategies**—Topics for the reader currently employed or newly hired, including such subjects as job retention, setting realistic career goals, company politics, and advancement from within.

• **The Next Step**—Topics for the reader who has decided to change jobs or make a career change, including such subjects as risk-taking, salary negotiation, job hunting while still employed, starting your own company, and consulting.

• **Ethics**—Articles that cover ethics and integrity and that examine the reader's actions in relation to ethical beliefs and the daily work situations that require decisions with ethical implications. Topics include sexual harassment, dishonesty, padding expense accounts, equal employment opportunity hiring, etc.

• **Innovations**—Articles that cover new hardware, software, and emerging technologies.

• **Lifestyle**—Covers lifestyle issues and choices affecting high-tech professionals.

• **Manager's Corner**—Provides information for managers on such topics as conflict resolution, listening skills, and techniques for leadership.

• **Online Job Search Strategies**—Provides tips and strategies for searching online for a job.

• **Health & Fitness**—Provides information, tips, strategies, and techniques to maintain good health while leading an active professional life.

• **Valley News**—staff written

Columns must have a career tie-in and should be written in a positive, straightforward manner that stresses the benefits and applications of the topic covered. All columns should be of a timely, serious, and informative nature. Humorous or satirical pieces are not accepted.

Length

Column length is 750 words. We reserve the right to edit all manuscripts accepted for publication.

Payment

Payment for original articles begins at 17.5 cents per word, based on the final, edited word count, and is administered through Writers Connection with final approval from the publisher. Payment is made upon publication.

High Technology Careers buys all rights. The entire magazine is placed in a virtual library, which can be accessed at *http://www.vjf.com.* Authors may market reprints of articles six (6) months after their *High Technology Careers* publication date. Any reprint must contain the following notice: "© *High Technology Careers Magazine* (1997 or year the article was first published), Santa Clara, California." Please inform HTC and send a copy of the reprinted article to HTC.

We do not guarantee publication of assigned articles, and publication may be advanced or delayed for space or editorial considerations.

The publication pays a 25 percent kill fee for assigned articles that are not used. No kill fee will be paid if articles are delivered after deadline or if the author fails to comply with requests for revisions or additional research.

Style

Please avoid the following:

• first person point of view

• negative personal opinions

• social injustice or public impropriety issues

• profanity (except when quoting a source)

• gender-specific pronouns (he or she) in general statements

The following additional guidelines are suggested:

• The article should contain a strong lead, an article body that develops and delivers on the lead, and a definitive conclusion.

• Quotes, facts, statistics, and anecdotes that illustrate the point should be included and presented in an interesting way.

• Please seek out recognized experts in their respective fields for quotes and interviews.

• While objective articles are preferred, stress on the positive aspects of the subject matter is preferred to a negatively slanted article.

Manuscript Preparation

For submissions on disk, IBM-compatible format is required. Microsoft Word or ASCII are preferred, but other formats are acceptable. If you use a printer, please submit letter-quality material only.

Format for the title page is as follows: writer's name, address, and telephone number in the upper left corner; word count in the upper right corner; and article title with writer's byline centered in the middle of the page. Subsequent pages should have a running head in the upper right corner consisting of the following: writer's last name/article title (use a key word from the title instead of complete title if the title is lengthy), and page number.

Underline the following for emphasis: italicized words or phrases, foreign words, and titles.

Manuscripts should be free of errors and corrections. Minor corrections should be clearly printed and held to a minimum.

Queries and Submissions

For columns or feature articles, query or send completed manuscripts. Query with or without published clips. Each query should include the primary focus of the proposed article, the main points of discussion, and a list of any authorities who would be described or interviewed in the article. Absolutely **no phone calls,** please.

Writers should familiarize themselves with the publications' style and format prior to submitting a query. Copies of *High Technology Careers* are available without charge at various Silicon Valley locations where newspapers or computer-related publications are dispensed. Or send $2.90 in stamps with your sample-copy request to Writers Connection (see address below). Always include a one-paragraph author's bio note with your article or column.

Categories: Business—Careers—Electronics—Engineering—High Technology Careers—Science—Technology

Name: Ms. Meera Lester, Managing Editor
Material: All
Address: WRITERS CONNECTION
Address: PO BOX 24770
City/State/ZIP: SAN JOSE CA 95154-4770
Telephone: 408-445-3600
Fax: 408-445-3609
E-mail: Writerscxn@aol.com

Highways

Thank you for your interest in *Highways*, the official publication of the Good Sam Club. *Highways* is published 11 times a year by TL Enterprises, Inc. and is a sister publication of *Trailer Life* and *MotorHome*.

Highways is a specialty magazine for RV enthusiasts and has a circulation of more than 900,000. We suggest that potential writers study recent issues before sending us queries or manuscripts. All manuscripts must be submitted on a 3.5" diskette (most word processing programs are acceptable) and typed. Photocopy submissions are OK. Please allow eight weeks for replies on unsolicited submissions.

Payment is on acceptance for publication. However, we reserve the right to hold sidebars and other related material until the feature layout is designed. Sidebar fees are negotiated by the editorial staff on an individual basis. *Highways* buys first North American serial rights and electronic rights. The editors reserve the right to edit and even rewrite any article in order to make it suit the theme or space limitations of a specific issue. Major alterations will be discussed with the author when possible.

TRAVEL FEATURES:

The easiest way to sell your work to *Highways* is to write an interesting and tightly focused RV travel story. Please do not send us 500-word descriptions of cross-country RV trips. We need features that evoke the sights, sounds, smells and even tastes of specific travel destinations. Consequently, we'd much rather have a tight 2,000 words on traveling to Anchorage in the spring than on all of Alaska. The maximum length for travel features, unless cleared by the editorial staff, is 2,500 words. We accept queries, not manuscripts, via e-mail.

Highways' stories are usually in color, although some run in black and white. All stories (excluding humor) should be accompanied by a comprehensive selection of clear, color transparencies with captions. When possible, the transparencies should feature RVs against a scenic backdrop. Think cover shot (vertical) when taking these photos and remember lighting is crucial to the overall effect. Focus your photography on scenic or panoramic views for the opening layout and points of interest, local color and activity shots for the carryover pages. Fees for full-length travel features with photos start at $300. Higher fees are negotiable. Short travel features start at $150 and max out at $300.

MAINTENANCE AND TECHNICAL:

Highways publishes several types of technical stories.

• Maintenance: RV maintenance stories should be 1,800 to 2,500 words long and written so that they are of interest to both the novice and the veteran RVer. Color transparencies showing the maintenance procedure are essential.

• How-to: These features for handy RVers should be 1,500 to 2,500 words and include step-by-step instructions, diagrams and transparencies.

• RV Safety: An example of this type of a story includes a look at extension-cord use by RVers. Stories should be 1,400 to 2,000 words and be accompanied by a selection of transparencies.

• RV Accessory Overviews: If you know a lot about RV air conditioners, tires, batteries, and/or generators, you may be able to create this kind of feature. However, it is guaranteed to be a tough sale. Overview features tend to be lengthy (1,500 to 2,500 words) and should be as comprehensive as possible. An example of this is the holding tanks story in our January, 1995 issue. Before writing a technical story of this type, it is best to send a query letter to the editor. Be sure to include clips of similar published features.

• Product Evaluations: All product evaluations are assigned by the editorial staff. If you are interested in writing such a story, query the editor and include published clips of similar work. Product evaluations must be fair and unbiased. Queries by any representative of the product's manufacturer or distributor will be rejected and all product claims must be independently substantiated. No writer is to contact a manufacturer or distributor as a representative of *Highways* without explicit permission of the editorial staff.

If you are assigned a story by the editorial staff, please keep in mind that you now represent *Highways*. Be conscious that if you receive information or materials about the subject/area you are covering, you must still write an ethical, objective story.

VEHICLE TESTS:

Highways does not publish vehicle tests.

All technical copy is reviewed by the technical editor of *Highways* for accuracy. Payment for technical stories ranges from $250 to $600, depending on complexity of the story and quality of the manuscript.

SPECIAL INTEREST:

Highways' editorial focus can be expanded to include hobbies, crafts and other recreational activities that are popular among RVers. Recent stories have covered vintage vehicles, the Iditarod Trail Sled Dog Race, computers and other hobbies. Special interest features should be 1,500 to 2,500 words and pay $275 to $450.

RV HUMOR:

In each issue of *Highways*, we try to include a humorous vignette on some aspect of the RV lifestyle. Humor stories should be directly related to the RV experience. Maximum length for humor stories is 1,500 words; minimum, 800 words. Do not send photographs. All humor stories are illustrated by line drawings. Fees start at $200. Higher fees are negotiable.

COLUMNS:

All *Highways* columns are assigned. If you have a column idea and wish to discuss it with us, write us several sample columns and we will consider them. Columns are a tough sale and we do not foresee a need to add any new columns to the magazine in the near future.

HUMAN INTEREST:

Highways generally does not publish personality features.

POETRY AND FICTION:

Highways does not publish poetry or fiction.

PHOTO REQUIREMENTS:

Travel features should be accompanied by a minimum of 15 color transparencies, all originals. All transparencies should be numbered with an accompanying caption sheet identifying each subject. Photos and slides supplied by someone other than the manuscript author should be clearly identified for photo credit. All photos and slides will be returned after publication when possible. Please include a self-addressed, stamped envelope for this purpose.

Categories: General Interest—Lifestyles—Outdoors—Recreation—RV—Senior Citizens—Travel

Name: Ronald H. Epstein, Editor
Material: Travel, Humor

Address: 2575 VISTA DEL MAR DR
City/State/ZIP: VENTURA CA 93001
Telephone: 805-667-4100
Fax: 805-667-4454

Historic Traveler

Historic Traveler magazine is an invaluable resource of useful and accurate information on historic destinations. Topics might include battlefields, museums, antique shows, events, hotels, inns, transportation, reenactments, preserved communities, and architectural wonders. In short, the places where history was made and the stories behind them. Our focus is primarily domestic, but we do cover international destinations too.

We particularly like pieces that are informative and entertaining to travelers of all ages. Articles should be written with an active voice and be short on adjectives. We are not interested in "scholarly" writing. A strong destination is important. It helps to include people—historical or modern—and we like to hear them in their own words, so use quotes. At the destination, writers should attempt to go "behind the scenes" to find information and material the ordinary visitor would not normally have. Whenever possible, talk to curators, historians or other people involved with the site. A sense of humor is helpful. It is *very* important to verify historic facts relating to the article. We also ask writers to prepare a sidebar of service information—how to get there, hours of operation, addresses and phone numbers, where to dine and lodge in the area and other useful facts.

HT features range in length from 1,500 to 3,000 words. All original material published is strictly nonfiction. No original poetry, fiction, or cartoons are ever accepted. Payment to authors is on acceptance. Rates for original material vary on how each article is used within the magazine's format. Departments run somewhat shorter and include "Superior Stays" (historic lodging places), "All-American Towns," "Great Conveyances" (historic transportation), "The Grand Tour" (great trips from history, i.e. Dickens' lecture tour of the U.S.), and "Museum Watch" (covering a specific institution).

Query us before writing an article for HT. We may have covered your story before or have something similar already assigned to another writer. Written queries only—no telephone queries. A good query should contain a sample lead and follow-up paragraphs and an outline indicating where your story will follow from that point. Emphasize what angle makes your story unique, details as to why you are an authority on the subject, and your qualifications for writing the piece. Provide a list of your research sources. Clips of your previously published work are helpful.

Only typewritten or computer-generated manuscripts are acceptable.

We strongly suggest that before submitting a query, you review *Historic Traveler* to get an idea of the tone, style, and subject matter we use. If copies are unavailable in your area, they may be obtained by sending $5 to this office for each one ordered.

Categories: History—Travel

Name: Submissions Editor
Material: All
Address: 6405 FLANK DR
City/State/ZIP: HARRISBURG PA 17112
Telephone: 717-657-9555
Fax: 717-657-9552
E-mail: HistoricTraveler@compuserve.com

HOCKEY PLAYER®

Hockey Player Magazine
The Magazine of Winning Hockey

From ice rinks to inline arenas, *Hockey Player Magazine* is edited exclusively for players of the world's fastest team sport. The monthly publication is devoted to helping players, coaches and parents get the most out of every game and practice. Each issue reflects the unique balance of what being a player is all about: improving skills, staying informed on the game's best players and leagues—and checking out all that gear. *Hockey Player* is the game's most in-depth instruction and equipment magazine.

Categories: Sports

Name: Submissions Editor
Material: All
Address: PO BOX 1007
City/State/ZIP: OKEMOS MI 48805
Telephone: 517-347-1172
Fax: 517-347-0686
E-mail: hockeymag@aol.com

The Hollins Critic
Hollins College

Poetry submitted to *The Hollins Critic* should be typed or word processed. Poems should be fairly short. There are no rules about style or subject.

The *Critic* pays $25.00 per poem, upon publication. All rights revert to the author following publication, but if the poem is reprinted elsewhere, the *Critic* should be credited.

Besides poetry, the *Critic* publishes an essay on a contemporary author in each issue, and book reviews as space permits. The *Critic* does not accept unsolicited essays. Rarely do we accept unsolicited book reviews. When a review is published, the author receives a copy of the issue, and two copies are sent to the book's publisher.

Thank you for your interest in *The Hollins Critic*.
Amanda Cockrell
Managing Editor
Categories: Nonfiction—Literature—Poetry

Name: Cathryn Hankla, Poetry Editor
Material: Poetry
Address: HOLLINS COLLEGE
Address: PO BOX 9538
City/State/ZIP: ROANOKE VA 24020
Telephone: 540-362-6275
Fax: 540-362-6642
E-mail: acockrell@hollins.edu

Home Business News
America's Leader in Moving Business Home™

Thank you for your interest in writing for our publication, *Home Business News*. Our publication is geared towards those individuals who are interested in starting their own businesses—and running the business from the comfort of their own home.

Each quarter we will cover a variety of topics from the nuts and bolts of running your own business to what type of furniture you need in a home office.

Articles run between 1,200 to 1,500 words, typewritten, double spaced or on computer disk with an accompanying hard copy. The deadline is May 10 for the Summer Quarterly issue, August 10 for the Fall Quarterly issue; November 10 for the Winter Quarterly issue and February 10 for the Spring Quarterly issue. Photos or graphs are appreciated when applicable (color photos are preferred). Payment is at the rate of 10¢ per published word and payment is upon publication.

If you have some ideas for stories that you feel might fit our reading audience, please feel free to give me a call. We can go over your ideas and I can give you some further guidance.

Carolyn Tice
Executive Editor
Categories: Nonfiction—Business—Money/Finance

Name: Carolyn Tice, Executive Editor
Material: All
Address: 4505 S WASATCH BLVD STE 140
City/State/ZIP: SALT LAKE CITY UT 84124
Telephone: 800-664-2422
Fax: 801-273-2399
E-mail: carolyn@homebusiness.com
Internet: www.homebusiness.com

Home Education Magazine

Dear HEM Contributors,

The HEM Letter is a free bimonthly e-mail newsletter for HEM columnists, contributors, and other interested persons. The HEM Letter is usually e-mailed the first week after each issue is mailed. We'll be happy to add your name to our e-mailing list upon request.

Home Education Magazine is for families who enjoy living and learning together. If you're not familiar with homeschooling please study our publication before submitting.

TOPICS

Any topic of interest to homeschooling families will be considered. Please be aware that we have the most widely diverse readership in the homeschooling community, and our content reflects that diversity.

We do not utilize an editorial calendar when planning our issues. We select articles on the basis of their interest and information for our readership, and each issue contains articles on a wide variety of topics. If you'd like to submit an article on any aspect of homeschooling, simply send it to my attention any time, and, if accepted, it will run in the next available issue.

SUBMISSIONS

Our computers are Macintoshes, but we have many filters and we can read most submissions on disk. Please send your work as an ASCII file (text only), and please always send a hard copy of your article. Submissions via e-mail are also welcome. And of course we still accept handwritten articles.

Please include a 40-60 word credit with your submission.

PHOTOS

We always need sharp, clear photos for inside editorial use. Regular B/W print sizes work fine for inside use; for covers, color enlargements are best. We prefer photos showing children and families doing everyday things, not necessarily posed educational-type shots. We advise studying our magazine before attempting photo submissions. Please include information about the photo, including names of anyone in the pictures, and the name of the photographer.

RIGHTS

Home Education Magazine buys one-time electronic and print rights to all articles, columns, and photos. We are studying the possibility of making HEM available in CD-ROM format, and rights purchased would include our right to reproduce your article in that format as well as in other formats of *Home Education Magazine*.

AMERICA ONLINE/WWW

Home Education Magazine has a forum on America Online, and we upload selected articles and columns from each issue approximately two weeks after an issue is mailed to subscribers. We also have a site on the World Wide Web, and we upload selected articles, columns, and cover photos to that site as well.

PAYMENT

Feature articles—$25.00 to $50.00 each, depending upon subject, length, and other factors. We occasionally pay more for articles we've requested, or which require special expenses or considerations. Photos for inside use $10.00 each. Cover photos $50.00 each. We pay for all work upon publication, and contributors always receive a copy of the issue in which their work appears.

For subscription problems or non-submission related questions please e-mail home edu@televar.com.

Categories: Education—Homeschooling

Name: Helen Hegener, Managing Editor
Material: All
Address: PO BOX 1083
City/State/ZIP: TONASKET WA 98855-1083
E-mail: HomeEdMag@aol.com
Internet: www.home-ed-press.com/

Home Furnishings Executive

Home Furnishings Executive is a monthly business journal for home furnishings executives—that is, owners of retail furniture stores-nationwide. We use concise, well-researched articles on topics that interest informed retail and manufacturing executives. Copy should be in the present tense and in the active voice.

We follow *The Associated Press Stylebook* and recommend that our writers refer to *The Elements of Style* (William Strunk Jr. and E.B. White) for general guidance.

We expect writers to double-check facts and to confirm spelling on all proper names. We require more than one source for most stories and require a source list with telephone numbers upon submission.

Topics chosen for *Home Furnishings Executive* cover business and product trends that are shaping the home furnishings industry. Examples include:
• Advertising and Marketing
• Consumer and Industry Research
• Business Profiles
• Product Trends
• Technology
• Quality Improvement

But our readers also need good, solid advice on managing their businesses—and particularly their employees—more effectively, and they rely on *Home Furnishings Executive* for such advice.

Writers should include writing samples with initial inquiries. We buy first North American serial rights and pay upon acceptance. Feature rates start at $250.

Categories: Business—Home Furnishings

Name: Trisha McBride, Editor
Material: All
Address: PO BOX 2396
City/State/ZIP: HIGH POINT NC 27261
Telephone: 910-883-1650
Fax: 910-883-1195

Home Furniture

We gladly accept submissions for *Home Furniture*. If you'd like to write an article, start by sending us a proposal. Summarize your topic and point of view in a paragraph or so and include an informal outline of the material you plan to cover in the article. Include a paragraph about yourself and your woodworking background. You'll hear from us again when we've decided whether we want you to go ahead with the article. If we do, a staff editor will be assigned to work with you.

Submitting a furniture project for possible publication is even easier. Just send us a snapshot of the piece you've built and a very brief description of what you were trying to accomplish with the design. If we accept it for publication, we'll arrange for photos and ask you for more information.

What makes *Home Furniture* special is that most of our articles are written by people who actually do the work they write about. We're more interested in your experiences, point of view and technical expertise than in your writing style or ability to provide grammar-perfect English. It's best to adopt an easy, conversational style, as if you were describing something to a friend in a letter. Don't hesitate to use a drawing. Sketches should be clear, but they don't have to be works of art. Please type your manuscript if possible. Include snapshots or photos if you have them to illustrate your points. Don't worry about photo quality too much now. We can reshoot photos later.

Payments and copyrights

Our basic rate is $150 per published magazine page. We'll also reimburse you for out-of-pocket expenses, such as for film purchases and photo processing (only if we approve the project before you begin shooting). We'll also reimburse you for shipping or courier charges and for materials purchased for making samples or building projects specifically for the article. Any other reimbursements must be cleared with us in advance. All requests for reimbursement must be accompanied by a *photocopy* of your dated receipts (the IRS says you should keep the originals).

Once your editor has a manuscript that's ready for editing, we'll send you a copyright agreement to sign. The agreement constitutes our acceptance of the article for publication. Once you sign the copyright agreement and return the original to us, we'll send you an advance of $150. We'll pay the balance at time of publication. We'll also send you two complimentary copies of the issue in which your article appears.

Please note that by signing a copyright agreement with you, we do not *guarantee* publication of your article. Even if we schedule the article for a specific issue, our editorial needs and direction sometimes change. Therefore, we reserve the right to decide later not to publish your article. That rarely happens. If it does, the advance will serve as a kill fee. The material would be returned, releasing you from the copyright agreement and freeing you to sell it to another magazine.

Editing and author corrections

Your editor may ask you to supply additional information, or ask you to rewrite or revise sections of your manuscript. The editor will try to be sensitive to your individual writing style and retain as much of the character of the original writing as possible. If any major changes are warranted or if we have any doubts about changes we're considering during the editing process, your editor will call you to discuss the matter. After your manuscript has been edited, we'll mail you a galley—an edited version of the text—so that you'll have a chance to review it for accuracy before it goes to press.

Questions?

If you have any further questions, feel free to call us. Ask for the *Home Furniture* editorial department.

Categories: Nonfiction—Woodworking

Name: Submissions Editor
Material: All
Address: 63 S MAIN ST
Address: PO BOX 5506
City/State/ZIP: NEWTOWN CT 06470-5506
Telephone: 800-283-7252

HOME*improver* MAGAZINE

Home Improver Magazine
The Guide to All Your Home Improvement Needs

STYLE & POLICY GUIDELINES

The goal of *Home Improver* is to provide readers with concise information reported in a responsible manner. Individual style is encouraged, but not at the cost of good journalism techniques, proper word usage and grammar. Our purpose is to be informative, educational and entertaining.

It is strongly recommended that all writers read and consult Strunk & White's *Elements of Style* with particular regard for those sections detailing punctuation and sentence structure. Originally published in 1935, this small text is neither outdated nor a fundamental primer. Its contents are the foundation of skillful written communication. A writer's personal style develops from the proper creative use of the basic writing tools. It's inexpensive, a quick read and an invaluable writer's companion.

FREELANCE SUBMISSIONS

We want our editors to be known throughout the Home Improvement Industry and *Home Improver* encourages you to submit articles for publication in other periodicals. The only exceptions, of course, are submissions to our direct competitors. If possible, try to include your title of Contributing Editor, *Home Improver* as byline information.

FAX TRANSMISSIONS

Please double space all copy transmitted by fax service. Our fax machine is open 24 hours, 7 days a week.

As a backup, please have a printed copy available so it can be resent if possible.

E-MAIL TRANSMISSIONS

Files must be transmitted in ASCII.txt format. They should be sent to LouKojak@aol.com

FRACTIONS

You may write fractions in either decimal (1.75 pounds) or fraction (1 3/4 pounds) format. For modem transmissions only, please prefix fractions with a hyphen (-) as in 1 - 3/4 pounds. As with italic notations, this cues our computer to alter the printing style.

NUMBERS

Unless the reference is to a weight or measure (as above) numbers from zero to ninety-nine should be written. Numbers of 100 and above should be numerical.

JARGON

We face the use of slang and colloquialisms everywhere in the home improvement industry and we face the urge to emphasize such jargon words with quotes and italics. To do so tends to exclude the reader and makes it appear as if the reader is on the outside of a clique that knows better. Avoid emphasizing jargon words whenever possible.

PROPER NAMES

There are many ways individuals choose to spell their names and many ways to spell various location place names around our region. Without exception, we will defer to the spelling that you provide so double-check your copy.

BLOCK THAT METAPHOR

Be judicial in your use of metaphors and in your use of words that may be offensive to readers. When in doubt, don't write it.

©Home Improver Publications, Inc., 1998

Categories: Nonfiction—Architecture—Consumer—Gardening—Home Improvement—Lifestyles—Remodeling

Name: Susan Luft, Editor
Material: All
Address: 11 VIRGINIA RD
City/State/ZIP: WHITE PLAINS NY 10603
Telephone: 914-328-1992
Fax: 914-328-1993
E-mail: HImprove@aol.com

Home Times

Home Times is a monthly tabloid newspaper, distributed locally and nationally by U.S. Mail to paid subscribers and requestors, covering world & national news & views, home & family, arts & entertainment, and religion, all with a Biblical worldview. It is pro-Christian and pro-Jewish—but not religious.

We are a NEWSpaper, so content is generally keyed to current events and hot issues of the day. It is aimed squarely at the general public and written for them, though it receives most of its support from Christian readers. The news articles are often what we call "virtual exclusives," stories unpublished or underpublished in the regular news media, often reporting on trends months, even years before they find their way into the regular press. Features on family, education, parenting, entertainment (movies, books, TV, videos) are practical, not preachy, related to issues and values.

Home Times is non-denominational and non-doctrinal, free of religious cliches or churchy or preachy perspectives. It tries not to moralize but to just be positive and Biblical in perspective. Our goal is to publish godly viewpoints in the marketplace, and to counteract the culturally elite of media and politics who reject Judeo-Christian values, traditional American values, true history, and faith in God.

Home Times is different from all other "Christian" publications—we strongly suggest you read these guidelines AND sample issues. Once you understand our slant, and if this is your kind of writing—you'll enjoy writing for *Home Times*!

We make it easy for you to "test ride" *Home Times*: send $3 to receive the next 3 issues when published (no SASE). Or as a freelance writer, subscribe at $9 (regular $12) for 12 issues ("Writer's Sub").

We encourage new writers at HOME TIMES. We do not pay much—but it is a great opportunity for writers, especially new writers, to hone their skills. The editor has even written a l2-chapter report for new writers entitled "101 Reasons Why I Reject Your Mss"—which is an effective training course for new freelancers, easy to understand and written with lots of humor.

General Requirements: We want complete manuscripts—no queries please. Photos and illustrations may enhance a story if appropriate. No slides, negatives, computer disks, faxes or e-mail please. Pay is upon publication and ranges from $0 to $25 ($0 to $10 for reprints—which are accepted). PHOTOS if used are paid at $5 each. SEASONAL materials: 4-6 weeks in advance. LENGTH: as brief as possible, 500-750 words. Major stories up to 900 words are accepted but not as readily. We reserve the right to shorten your story and edit it somewhat to fit our slant and style. REPLIES: we're understaffed and overworked so sometimes we get back to you in a few days, sometimes in a month. Holler if you don't hear in six weeks.

Special Opportunities: We want personal features in these categories: **Human Heroes**, true-to-life stories 500-750 words with photo(s), generally about ordinary people who do extraordinary things, or about the goodness of God in our lives; **Light One Candle**: little people who do something to change our world for the better; **Sports Essays**, brief (300-600 words) on the values or issues side of sports. These pay the usual rate.

Local Opportunities: Local People Stories, local events; local calendar, local issues and news events of importance to the family; usually with a slant that is of interest to families everywhere. These kinds of stories are often assigned, or suggested to the editor by phone if you are local; not available if you are not local (SE Florida). Quite frankly, we need some volunteers in this area too.

Some Non-Cash Opportunities: We generally pay for the following with a six-issue subscription: We want **Briefs** of all sorts, **Anecdotes** in various categories such as: **Family Life** (funny stories from Parents & Kids), **Tales Out Of School** (funny incidents from teachers & students, all grades through college), **In The Pew** (funny things that happened in church or synagogue), **First Grade Jokes** (clean corny kid stuff), **America!** (funny stories about Americans), and **Good News Only** sharing faith in God and Jesus Christ; ALSO: **Great Shots!** (photos of babies, kids, family, pets, action, news events that are cute, funny or unusual); and **Letters to the Editor** (to 200 words) and OpEds (to 400 words).

Some Do's & Don'ts:
- Don't preach. No devotionals.
- We do accept **poetry** (traditional or light verse to 16 lines) and **short fiction** (up to 750 words) but it's best to read "HT" samples to see what we like.
- The **Religion section** is more spiritual and wants articles on prayer, unity, revival and harvest
- We run **Special Emphases** but they are usually tied into current events and rarely planned ahead.
- **Internships/volunteers**: We will talk to students interested in a career in our kind of journalism, about summer or school-year internships. We also have a small corps of volunteers who help with writing, layout, distribution, mailings, phone work, etc. "HT" is more than a business—it is a ministry to our nation, seeking to restore our godly roots—please call if interested!

Categories: Fiction—Nonfiction—Adventure—African-American—Arts—Business—Careers—Cartoons—Christian Interests—Conservative Issues—Cooking—Culture—Diet—Economics—Education—Entertainment—Family—Film/Video—Gardening—General Interest—Government—Health—History—Hobbies—Humor—Inspirational—Interview—Jewish Interests—Literature—Marriage—Men's issues—Money/Finance—Parenting—Philosophy—Poetry—Politics—Public Policy—Recreation—Relationships—Religion—Rural America—Science—Senior Citizens—Short Stories—Spiritual—Sports—Teen—Television/Radio—Travel—Writing

Name: Dennis Lombard, Editor & Publisher
Material: All
Address: 3676 COLLIN DR STE 12
City/State/ZIP: W PALM BEACH FL 33406
Telephone: 561-439-3509
E-mail: hometimes@aol.com

Hope Magazine
Humanity Making a Difference

Editorial Mission Statement

Hope magazine is edited to inspire a sense of hope among readers: that the world can be made a better place, and that we can better know our place within it. The editorial and photography focuses on individuals, businesses, and organizations working hard to make a difference, especially the ordinary and un-sung who are doing extraordinary and inspiring things, yet whose stories are rarely heard. It reports on individuals helping others in myriad ways, individuals overcoming adversity of varying nature and degree, and businesses and organizations acting to make a difference in their communities and their world. It also seeks to share, with an unblinking, yet compassionate eye, the dignity in those human beings whose stories we are so often inclined to over-look: individuals who have not yet found their *place* in the world, or whose place we cannot easily comprehend from the vantage of our own lives. And yet, even in this darker and more challenging focus, *Hope* seeks to provide a much-needed balance and depth to the unrelenting bad news that abounds from nations to neigh-borhoods.

A magazine without religious, political, or new age affilia-tion, *Hope* strives unabashedly to explore and celebrate the most enduring human values, and to help us glimpse our common bonds as we move together toward the 21st century, worried about our elderly, worried about our youth, and worried about ourselves. It hopes to awaken the impulse we all have—however hidden or distant—to make our world a little better, to make ourselves more responsive to it, and to better understand our place and purpose here. Without proselytizing, preaching, or asking certain action of us, *Hope* reacquaints us with much more of humanity, even in its flawed beauty, than we find in the mass media. It is not about the trappings of wealth and glamour, nor the powerful and influ-ential. It is about *us*. The *real* us. And though the picture will not always be pretty, it will endeavor to be compelling.

Carefully designed to be attractive, inviting, and accessible, *Hope* is an intimate magazine which goes directly to the heart while engaging the mind; a welcome antidote to the fast-paced, de-personalizing way of life in which so many of us find ourselves immersed.

Published for a readership of diverse ages and interests, *Hope* appeals to the curious and the concerned, the thoughtful and the educated, the active and impassioned among us, from idealistic teens to mindful septuagenarians. There is no magazine quite like it, and yet elements of others will be found here: *Hope* as-pires to the intellectual ideals of *Atlantic Monthly*, *Harper's*, and *The New Yorker*, as well as the emotional instincts of *The Reader's Digest*, *People*, and *Life*. It will be as surprising and unpredict-able as *The Utne Reader*, *Vanity Fair*, and *Colors*, and yet thor-oughly inviting and embracing in style and content. It will be as timeless, as honest, and compelling as the once-ubiquitous book *The Family of Man*.

Hope is a magazine whose mission is to gently alter the ways in which its readers see the world by honoring values worth pur-suing, traditions worth preserving, and futures worth changing for the better. It will touch our hearts and inspire our minds, and given time, it could change the way we see the world and our-selves; given time, it could change the way we respond to the world and each other. Given time, it could help us change the world.

Guidelines for Writers and Photographers

These guidelines should combine with *Hope* magazine's edi-torial mission statement to provide insight for writers and pho-tographers whose work might advance or enlighten its mission, and we welcome queries.

The myriad good news/bad news agendas of *Hope* might seem at first glance to be in contradistinction to one another, and to the objective of inspiring a sense of hope among readers. Why, after all, would such a magazine publish articles on the volatile and violent subculture of the inner city? Or the haunted world of the homeless mentally ill? Or the unfathomed mind of the rapist and murderer? On the other hand, why is a magazine determined to avoid the *institutions* of religion so interested in individuals whose lives are *inspired* by it? What are we doing saluting the efforts of those working to change political systems while steering clear of politics itself? Where, exactly, is our focus? The short answer is that our focus is broad.

Hope will be consistent only in its intention to awaken, in-form, educate, and entertain, and in its determination to avoid cynicism as an overarching form. Beyond that, it is a magazine searching all corners, all surfaces—the dark and the light—for aspects of humanity too precious to avoid or ignore. Its mission is to convey good news—hopeful and inspiring news—but it is also to convey perspectives on overwhelming negative truths, and on the shifting realities that weave lives through the margins of good and bad, of failure and success. These are domains where hope itself often fades and fails, and where inspiration and action must be catalyzed. Our responsibility is to find these stories, and to reflect an honest light upon their most intricate elements.

If *Hope* is to be an effective magazine, it must foil precon-ception. It must be different from the journalistic norm, ever un-predictable, and yet embracing and respectful of readers. To some extent, it must seduce the wary and cynical beyond the title, for its mission is to be a catalyst for individual change by touching readers as directly and deeply as possible. So it must surprise, engage, inform, unnerve, and inspire with fine and honest writ-ing and compelling photography and illustration. It must find exciting and artful ways of sharing good news, for we can be eas-ily bored without intellectual and emotional tension, without a recognition of the *fragility* of individual goodness. It must weave humor into its sensitivity, for *Hope* cannot become melancholy.

In the darker subjects, our writing must be no less artful, and it will require courage to look into the maw, imagination to uncover the detail, and compassion to honor that which deserves it. We may struggle with the line between empathy and sympa-thy, but our objective is empathy: the sense we need most to in-crease our awareness, and to become, as it were, *allies* of one another, even as we preserve our individualism. We may also struggle, in the writing and the photojournalism, with the fine line between what is relevant to our missions, and what is pruri-ent or exploitative.

We are not here to shock our readers, but we *must* be com-mitted to awakening them to largely unheard cries, largely un-seen faces, and largely unknown realities. We may, in fact, be searching for new definitions of terms as we attempt to share stories that *move*, rather than *lull* us. We're in this together; the world needs work, as do we all, and humor, tolerance, and opti-mism will be as critical to the context of our missions as unblink-ing honesty. The more voices heard, the more visions shared, the more effective *Hope* can be. *Empathy* is our ultimate objective. All the writing, all the photography, and all the illustration should create, sustain, or inform our empathy in some way, no matter what the subject.

Our occasional essays on varied subjects run from 1,000 to 3,000 words in length. Our features run from 3,000 to 8,000 words, depending on subject, and we're happy to integrate sidebar ma-terial where it adds substance. In addition to the core features, we run regular departments, in which different aspects and ex-pressions of hope are included and explored:

Signs of Hope: notes and dispatches, generally ranging from 300 to 1,500 words, in which good and great works and ideas are reported.

Aspirations: 1,500-word reports on individuals or groups in their teens—or younger—who are engaged in works worthy of our recognition.

Possible Dreams: 3,000-word candid, personal essays on the grand and grim realities of our culture's innumerable professions and occupations.

Networking: A guide to resources and opportunities in ad-ventures, causes, studies, and projects of worth around the coun-try and the world.

The Arts of Hope: Reviews of music, art, and literature, in which a sense of hope is inspired or somehow conveyed.

Book Reviews: Devoted primarily to nonfiction works in widely diverse subject areas relevant to struggle and triumph, and to hope in general.

Last Hope: Ways in which individuals have given special meaning to their last moments on Earth—for themselves or for others.

Hope is a strongly visual magazine. While our covers are printed in color, our editorial photography and illustration is printed in high-quality black & white. Our sensitivity to the technical and aesthetic aspects of the illustrative material is very keen, and we are *always* interested in seeing examples of photographers' and illustrators' works. We obtain the best results in color by utilizing transparencies, but we can work from reflective art, as well. Black & white images may arrive for examination in contact-sheet form, as long as they're accompanied by a couple of 5"x7" prints from the sheet, which allow us to better appreciate focus and contrast in the images.

We tend to favor prints that are rich in detail and balanced in contrast—in short, very readable, very detailed. As for content, we seek to evoke a sense of access and intimacy, of art and honesty. The closer the photographer can bring us to the reality of the human being, or to the experience and the circumstance, the better we like it. Uninhibited emotion, from joy to contentment, from rage to despair, from loneliness to love, is what we want to share and convey. In this regard, we're also very interested in feature-length photo essays.

We invite and welcome samples and portfolios, asking only that return postage accompany unsolicited material. All materials furnished for publication by photographers and illustrators will be returned upon publication of the issue in which they're used.

We purchase serial rights for one-time use of text and images, except in cases of prior agreement by the parties, and all published material is protected under the umbrella copyright of *Hope* magazine. Our rates of payment are rather modest at this formative stage, and we look forward to the time when we can raise them, for it will mean that *Hope* is succeeding as a venture. For the time being, however, we are limited, and can only offer the following by way of inspiration and rationalization:

"Beyond their pride in being a part of *The New Yorker,* about the only thing the magazine's fiction and nonfiction writers had in common, at least for the first fifteen or twenty years, was dissatisfaction with their pay, which ranged from the merely inadequate to the execrable. In its later years, *The New Yorker*'s rates would become among the highest in the business, but through adolescence its penury was almost a point of pride."

—From **Genius in Disguise: Harold Ross of *The New Yorker*** by Thomas Kunkel (Random House, 1995)

There is no pride in low rates for us, but we couldn't resist sharing this passage, under the circumstances. Our basic rates are:

Currently $300 per 1,000 words of text.

Cover (color) rate: $500.

Editorial (B&W) $300/full page and down.

We welcome queries via fax, e-mail, and U.S. Mail. We prefer responding to brief descriptions and detailed outlines, which tend to receive more careful attention. Manuscripts should be accompanied by diskettes whenever possible. We use Microsoft Word for Windows 6.0, although we are usually able to open and work with other DOS and Mac systems.

We look forward to hearing from you.

With best wishes,

Jon Wilson, Editor & Publisher
jon@hopemag.com

Kimberly Ridley, Associate Editor
kimr@hopemag.com

Categories: Nonfiction—Arts—Associations—Disabilities—Education—Family—General Interest—Human Insight/Interest/Spirit

Name: Adrienne C. Bassler, Editorial Assistant
Material: All
Address: PO BOX 10
City/State/ZIP: BROOKLIN ME 04316
Telephone: 207-359-4651
Fax: 207-359-8920
E-mail: Hope@hopemag.com
Internet: www.hopemag.com

Hopscotch for Girls

A Word At The Outset

Every HOPSCOTCH contributor must remember we publish only six issues a year, which means our editorial needs are extremely limited. An annual total, for instance, will include some 30 to 36 nonfiction pieces, 9 or 10 short stories, 18 or so poems, six cover illustrations, and a smattering of puzzles, crafts, and the like.

It is obvious that we must reject far more contributions than we accept, no matter how outstanding they may seem to you or to us.

With that said, we would point out that HOPSCOTCH is a magazine created for girls from 6 to 12 years, with youngsters 8, 9, and 10 the specific target age.

Our point of view is that every young girl deserves the right to be a young girl for a number of years before she becomes a young adult.

As a result, HOPSCOTCH looks for articles, fiction, nonfiction, and poetry that deal with timeless topics, such as pets, nature, hobbies, science, games, sports, careers, simple cooking, and anything else likely to interest a young girl. We leave dating, romance, human sexuality, cosmetics, fashion, and the like to other publications.

Writers

We are looking for lively writing, most of it from a young girl's point of view—with the girl or girls directly involved in an activity that is both wholesome and unusual. Examples have included girls in a sheep to shawl contest, girls raising puppies that are destined to guide the blind, and girls who take summer ballet lessons from members of the New York City Ballet.

While on the subject of nonfiction—remembering that we use it 3 to 1 over fiction—those pieces that are accompanied by black and white photos are far more likely to be accepted that those that need illustrations.

The ideal length of a HOPSCOTCH nonfiction piece is 500 words or less, although we are not about to turn down a truly exceptional piece if it is slightly longer than the ideal. We prefer fiction to not run over 1,000 words.

We will entertain simultaneous submissions as long as that fact is noted on the manuscript. Computer printouts are welcome if they are (as all submissions should be) double-spaced.

HOPSCOTCH prefers to receive complete manuscripts with cover letters, although we do not rule out query letters. We do not answer submissions sent in by fax.

We will pay a minimum of 5 cents a word or both fiction and nonfiction, with additional payment given if the piece is accompanied by appropriate photos or art. We will pay a minimum of $10 per poem or puzzle, with variable rates offered for games, crafts, cartoons, and the like.

HOPSCOTCH buys first American serial rights and pays upon publication. It welcomes the contributions of both published and unpublished writers.

Sample copies are available for $3.00 within the US & $4.00 outside the US. All payment must he in US. funds. A complimentary copy will be sent each writer who has contributed to a given issue.

Photographers

We use a number of black and white photos inside the magazine, most in support of articles used. Payment is $5-10 per photo, depending on the quality and $5 for color slides.

Artists

Most art will be by assignment, in support of features used. The magazine is anxious to find artists capable of illustrating stories and features and welcomes copies of sample work, which will remain on file. Payment is $25 for partial illustrations and $35 for full-page illustrations.

Incidentally

Although we are working far into the future, we occasionally have room for one or two pages.

One More Thing

We are always in need of cute and clever recipes, well-written and illustrated crafts, riddles, and jokes.

Categories: Fiction—Nonfiction—Animals—Cartoons—Children

Name: Marilyn Edwards, Editor
Material: All
Address: PO BOX 164
City/State/ZIP: BLUFFTON OH 45817
Telephone: 419-358-4610

Horticulture
The Art of American Gardening

Published: 10 times per year
Circulation: 320,000
Query response time: 8 to 10 weeks
Number of articles purchased: About 25 a year from the approximately 400 unsolicited queries and manuscripts received
Rights purchased: One-time, first North American serial; all rights purchased for some departments
Expenses: Reasonable expenses paid if previously arranged with editor
Kill fee: Depends on final fee
Rates:

Type of article	Word length	Payment
Features	1,500-3,000	$600-$1,000
Departments	200-1,500	$50-$600

The Magazine

Horticulture, the country's oldest gardening magazine, is designed for active amateur gardeners. Our goal is to offer a blend of text, photographs, and illustrations that will both instruct and inspire readers. While we place great emphasis on good writing, we also believe that every article must offer ideas or illustrate principles that our readers can apply in their own gardens. No matter what the subject, we want articles to help our readers become better, more creative gardeners.

We assume that our writers have an interest in and some experience with gardening. We look for and encourage personal experience, anecdote, and opinion. At the same time, an article should place its subject, to whatever degree appropriate, in the broader context of horticulture.

Query Letters

Tell us why—as succinctly as possible—you think your idea belongs in *Horticulture* and give us the general outline of your piece. Please let us know your personal involvement with the subject. If the article will require research or reporting, give us a brief description of the work you'll need to do.

We appreciate receiving any background material you may have that will help us assess the appropriateness of your idea. Proposals for garden profiles, in particular, should be accompanied by photographs or transparencies. We would also like to see a sample of your writing.

Queries with a seasonal angle should be submitted at least ten months in advance of the proposed publication date.

Manuscript Submissions

We prefer that a query precede any manuscript. Manuscripts should be neatly typed and accompanied whenever possible by a computer disk. Include your name at the top of each page.

Categories: Nonfiction—Gardening

Name: Thomas Fischer, Executive Editor
Material: All
Address: 98 N WASHINGTON ST
City/State/ZIP: BOSTON MA 02114
Telephone: 617-742-5600
Fax: 617-637-6364
E-mail: Hortmag@aol.com

Hot Calaloo

Hot Calaloo welcomes on a non-paying basis prose or poetry on issues pertaining to both the Caribbean region and residents from the Caribbean living in North America. Please limit articles to less than 500 words.

Categories: Ethnic—Caribbean

Name: Michael Phillips, Publisher
Material: All
Address: PO BOX 429
City/State/ZIP: RIDERWOOD MD 21139
E-mail: Hcal@dclink.com

THE FAMILY MAGAZINE FOR AMERICAN HOUSEBOATERS

HOUSEBOAT

Houseboat

Houseboat is a family oriented publication for pontoon and deck boat users across the United States and Canada. Readers of *Houseboat* include families, couples, retired couples, renters, manufacturers, other boaters, water-sport enthusiasts, fishermen, travel enthusiasts and so on.

Within our pages, readers will find manufacturer reviews, test reports, destination pieces, new product reviews, a calendar of events and boat shows, how-to, service tips, fishing, secondary water sports, buying guides, special events and more. If a topic can be tied into pontoon or deck boating, there may be a place for it in our publication.

QUERIES: Query first with story ideas. Include one or two paragraphs that briefly outline your idea and tell us why your story is timely, unique, new or of special interest. What qualifies you to write the story? Do you have good? visual support?

MANUSCRIPTS: Features should run between 1,800 and 2,000 words. In addition, we like to run sidebars with features when appropriate. Fillers and Mini Features can range from 500

E-L

to 1,500 words.

All submitted material should be consistent with the Associated Press Style Guide. Pay particular attention to the use of numerals and measurements. For example, write *6 inches*, not *six inches* or *6"*—unless you are compiling technical information for use in a table or graph.

In general, avoid "symbol shortcuts" like %, &, @ etc. Also, use AP abbreviations—not postal ones—when following a city with a state (Ex: *Panama City, Fla.*, not *FL)*. And remember, some major cities such as New York, Chicago and Los Angeles stand without reference to the state at all. Postal abbreviations should only be used when listing an address.

The AP Style Guide is available from The Associated Press at Stylebook, AP Newsfeatures, 50 Rockefeller Plaza, New York, NY 10020.

Manuscripts must be typed using double-spacing for hard copy and single-spacing for electronic submissions. Include author's name, address and phone number on lead page. Pages should be numbered. Harris Publishing reserves the right to edit submitted material as required.

We use IBM compatible software and Microsoft Word 8.0. If possible, submit a 3.5-inch floppy disc with your typed manuscript. Documents converted to ASCII text are usually acceptable. Text files can also be sent by e-mail.

PHOTOS: We work with color transparencies only. We prefer E100SW by Kodak, or Velvia by Fuji. Good contrast and sharp focus are a must. Submit 10 to 15 different photos to illustrate a feature thoroughly.

Get people involved in every photo possible. Show action and movement and attempt to do so from a fresh perspective. Utilize dawn and dusk lighting for dramatic photos.

**If you submit photos that belong to another person, you are responsible for splitting payment with him/her. We purchase manuscripts and photos as one package and pay only one fee.

CAPTIONS: All photo submissions must be keyed to a numbered caption sheet. Captions should be detailed enough to require little or no rewriting by our editorial staff.

Please identify people in your photos. Obtain a signed, model release if necessary and submit with the photos. Your name and address should be on each photo or transparency for proper credits, payment and photo returns.

PAYMENT: Rates vary according to several factors including length, quality of the material, quality of the photos, and how much editing or rewriting is required.

We work with professionals to maintain a certain level of quality for our readers. Therefore, we expect copy and photos to be of high quality.

Payment for features (including photos) range from $150 to $300. Columns, departments, mini-features and fillers (including photos) are worth $50 to $175.

Houseboat buys first North American serial rights to manuscripts and photos. Payments are made after publication.

Make every effort to educate and entertain readers. We want our readers to feel they can sit back, put their feet up and enjoy reading *Houseboat* from cover to cover. When they're finished, they should know of new places to travel, where to find services, how to better maintain and handle their own pontoon or deck boat and so on. If you can make it educational and "fun" to read at the same time, so much the better.

Categories: Nonfiction—Boating—Fishing—Lifestyles—Recreation

Name: Steve Smede, Editor
Material: All
Address: 520 PARK AVE
City/State/ZIP: IDAHO FALLS ID 83402
Telephone: 208-524-7000

Fax: 208-522-5241
E-mail: hbmag@srv.net

House, Home and Garden

House, Home and Garden, a bimonthly publication, publishes articles related to the home, gardening, cooking and entertainment. We reach a diverse audience whose interests include various aspects of home life. We would like to see more submissions with informational, new product, decorating and pet themes.

About three quarters of what we publish is written by non-staff writers (approximately 50 manuscripts per year). If you are new to us, please send for a sample copy of our magazine before submitting your work ($1.50 and 9"x12" SASE with four first class stamps). Doing so will help you to better understand our style and content requirements.

We will accept queries or complete manuscripts. Computer printouts are fine.

Word length varies for both articles and department/columns. When thinking about an article for us, think about real estate, practical decorating ideas, house and home, antiques, travel, leisure and crafts. For departments/columns, think about home management, beauty, new products and travel.

We will negotiate rights and pay $0.03 per word on publication, plus one contributor's copy.

Thank you for your interest in writing for *House, Home and Garden*. We look forward to hearing from you.

Categories: Adventure—Animals (Pets)—Antiques—Architecture—Arts—Children—Collectibles—Computers—Cooking—Crafts—Diet—Electronics—Entertainment—Family—Fashion—Feminism—Food/Drink—Gardening—Health—Hobbies—Money/Finance—Short Stories—Travel

Name: Submissions Editor
Material: All
Address: 809 VIRGINIA AVE
City/State/ZIP: MARTINSBURG WV 25401-2131
Telephone: 304-267-2673
Fax: 304-262-4585

Humpty Dumpty

Please refer to Children's Better Health Institute

Hurricane Alice
Rhode Island College

We want every issue of *Hurricane Alice* to reflect the variety of women's lives and works. We welcome all feminist work, and are especially interested in work by women of color, lesbians, working class women, older women, disabled women, and young women. We will not publish work that we think demeans women.

In general, it takes about three months from date of submission to date of response, and about three more months from acceptance to publication. We do not consider work already published. Simultaneous submissions should be clearly marked as such, and should be sent with the understanding that the editorial board will consider them only as time allows.

Send at least a first-class SASE for our correspondence to you even if you do not want the entire manuscript returned, as we operate on a tiny budget. We cannot accept electronic submissions.

If you would like a sample copy of *Hurricane Alice* send $2.50 to the address below.

Guidelines for Writers

• Submit manuscripts clearly labeled with your name and address on the first page, and your name and page number on each succeeding page.

• After the title, identify the genre of the piece so that it gets sent to the appropriate review committee.

• Fiction and nonfiction should be a maximum of 3,500 words.

• Please submit no more than three pieces at one time.

• We do not accept unsolicited book reviews; if you are interested in reviewing books, contact Meg Carroll at the address below for reviewers' guidelines.

• We do accept unsolicited reviews of other cultural productions, including films, television programs, and the like.

Guidelines for Artists and Photographers

• Label drawings and photographs on the back with title, your name, and your address.

• We will accept photocopies rather than originals, but need originals if your work is accepted.

• All photographs should be black and white, 5"x7" or 8"x10".

Categories: Fiction—Nonfiction—Culture—Feminism—Gay/Lesbian—Literature—Multicultural—Short Stories—Women's Fiction—Women's Issues

Name: Joan Dagle, Submissions Manager
Material: All
Address: DEPT OF ENGLISH
Address: RHODE ISLAND COLLEGE
City/State/ZIP: PROVIDENCE RI 02908
Telephone: 401-456-8377

The Iconoclast

Mission: To serve readers stranded between the low intellectual level of commercial publishing and the arcana printed by the universities. To have a sense of humor. Not to have an agenda, save for the exploration of thought and emotion in the hope of reflection, leading to wisdom, personal accountability, and sheer delight.

Appearance: 32-40 8½"x5½" white pages double stapled, professionally photocopied.

Needs: Poetry and Prose from writers more interested in the sharing and transmission of ideas, imaginings, and experiences than in career advancement or self-recognition. Impress us with clarity and sincerity of thought, not lists of credits.

PROSE: To 2,500 words. Subject matter and style completely open within the dictates of public taste—ask yourself: Would I read this aloud to my parents or teenaged children?

No zealotry, militancy, cruelty, or intolerance—unless in the service of fiction—and then there'd better be a positive revelation. Needless profanity is annoying.

We like work to have a point (or more). We don't care for the 'slice of life' type of story, which remind us of virtual reality, which, aside from technical applications, is a poor substitute for the original. Entertainment (as in humor, lovable characters, and unusual virtuosities) can, when done well, be a point in itself. Sensationalism or the gross cannot.

Please don't send preliminary drafts. Or work which leaves the writer indifferent.

One submission a month is quite adequate. Simultaneous/reprint submissions are o.k. But be honest. We don't want to publish anything within at least a year of anyone else. Only one time publication rights are desired at present. Reports: 1 day to 1 month.

Other indications of professionalism and social gracefulness are appreciated.

POETRY: To 2 pages. Everything above applies. Try for originality; if not in thought, than expression. No greeting card verse or noble religious sentiments. Look for the unusual in the usual, parallels in opposites, the capturing of what is unique or often unnoticed in an ordinary, or extraordinary moment. What makes us human—and the resultant glories and agonies.

ART: Drawing is a lost craft among the populace. Maybe people just don't have the time or patience for sketching as a self-entertainment or communication skill. As a result, we're always starved for decent line art: simple black and white drawings to use as features, illustrations, cartoons, or fillers.

Payment: Generally—PROSE, 2 copies. ART and POETRY, 1 copy. 40% discount for additional copies. Monetary payment will begin six months after we've gone into the black.

Reality Check: People who buy, read, and subscribe to The ICONOCLAST keep it alive and available to those who seek publication. This is not a government program, but an abstract community of folks interested in a freewheeling approach to life. No interest, no zine. If The ICONOCLAST is good enough to send your work to, is it good enough to buy?

Single copy: $2.00

Subscription: $12.00 for 8 issues (1 year); $24.50 for 16 issues (2 years)

Categories: Fiction—Nonfiction—Adventure—Arts—Biography—Cartoons—Culture—Drama—General Interest—Humor—Interview—Literature—Poetry—Short Stories

Name: Submissions Editor
Material: All
Address: 1675 AMAZON RD
City/State/ZIP: MOHEGAN LAKE NY 10547-1804

ID Systems
The Magazine of Automated
Data Collection

Thank you for your interest in writing for ID Systems magazine. ID Systems readers are buyers, specifiers, and users of automated data collection products. Our editorial mission is to provide them with authoritative and accurate information on that technology. Coverage includes bar code, magnetic stripe, OCR/OMR, radio frequency data communications (RF/DC), radio frequency identification (RF/ID), smart cards, touchscreen, and voice.

Feel free to contact us with your article ideas or for further assistance. Please submit your application/case history ideas on our ID Systems "Article Proposal" forms.

Following is a description of the areas in which ID Systems welcomes submissions:

APPLICATION FEATURES/CASE HISTORIES (approximately 1,500 words) profile automated data collection systems in use, and detail their benefits. Please include resources—listing name, address, and phone number of hardware and software vendors, as well as the systems integrator or VAR if appropriate.

TUTORIALS (1,500 to 2,000 words) address the educational needs of both novice and veteran end users by presenting overviews on current and emerging technologies. If possible, a roundup of available products, along with manufacturers' names and addresses, should be included.

READERS' SUCCESS STORIES (1,500 to 2,000 words) present first-person accounts by end users on installing automated data collection systems in their companies. (Please include photo of author.)

OPINION PIECES (500 to 700 words) offer issue-oriented viewpoints on technologies, industry trends, and events that are shaping the automated data collection marketplace. (Please include photo of author.)

Writer's Guidelines

Here are some style notes to help you write your article once your idea has been accepted:

• For application features and case histories, include the following:—Briefly describe company implementing the system, including annual sales or size.

• What problem was solved?

• Get details on how the technology was chosen, what its advantages are, and what technology or manual system it replaced.

• What system was selected (include details on computer system, printers, etc.) and why? Include the manufacturer, name, address, and phone number for all equipment used.

• What bar code symbologies and scanners are used?—To what computer is the system interfaced?

• How was the system set up, designed, and installed? Were there problems encountered during installation? How were they solved?

• What, if any, national or international bar code labeling or EDI standards apply?

• Has the system achieved payback? Anticipated payback? What were the gains in accuracy and productivity?

• What would the company do differently?

• Focus on the application, not the company.

• Look for attention-getting lead paragraphs and quotations from your information source.

• Obtain photos of the system in use—black and white or color prints or transparencies.

Important: Names, addresses, and phone numbers of everyone quoted in the article or contacted for the article should accompany your manuscript.

Additional Instructions:

1. Articles should be submitted on 3.5-inch disks (Mac format preferred), with data stored in straight ASCII or Microsoft Word, accompanied by printed manuscripts.

2. Color photos or transparencies (2¼-inch format minimum) related to feature articles may be submitted as possible cover candidates, but consult with the editor first. Submissions should be professionally generated. Format should be 2¼-inch or 4- by 5-inch transparencies. Photo submission does not guarantee acceptance.

3. Figures accompanying articles must be camera ready.

4. Submit a short bio of author.

5. Acceptance of article does not guarantee publication.

6. Helmers Publishing, Inc., requires transferal of all rights to accepted material.

Categories: Nonfiction—Automated Data Collection—Bar Codes

Name: Robert Bell, Editor
Material: All

Address: 174 Concord Street
City/State/ZIP: Peterborough, NH 03458
Telephone: 603-924-9631
Fax: 603-924-7408

IIE Solutions
Institute of Industrial Engineers

IIE Solutions welcomes feature articles and letters to the editor. Please use the following guidelines to help you develop your article.

Feature Articles

Try to focus on the most current industrial engineering issues, problems, and solutions, or recent developments and research that may have a significant and positive impact on today's industrial engineer. While every submission will be considered for publication, emphasis will be placed on the article's practical value and analytical approach. Highly theoretical or statistical articles are discouraged. Articles based on experience and actual "hands-on" operating situations, or those that have valuable applications in a working environment will be favored. Authors are encouraged to include supporting graphics and/or color photographs with articles.

Submission

Articles submitted to *IIE Solutions* should be offered on an exclusive basis and limited to 3,500 words or less. *In addition to printed copy, please include a Microsoft Word or ASCII version of the article on a PC-compatible or Macintosh disk.* Charts, graphs, and other non-photo artwork should be sent separately or included as individual files (BMP, JPEG, or TIFF) on the same disk. Articles are subject to normal review and editing procedures by the editor.

Additional Tips

The following hints may also assist in preparing an article for publication:

• Number each page.

• Photographs: High-quality transparencies/slides or prints are best. Provide identification and caption material with all photos, and do not attach with paper clips or staples. Also, please don't write on the back of photos. Specify whether the photo should be returned.

• Include a short biographical paragraph about the author and co-authors of the article.

IIE Solutions holds the copyright of all published articles. For permission to use the article for personal or educational purposes, please contact the Permissions Department at the Institute of Industrial Engineers (IIE).

Categories: Ergonomics—Facilities Planning—Industrial Engineering—Logistics—Production & Inventory Control—Technology—Warehousing

Name: Kathy Boggs, Editor
Material: All
Address: 25 TECHNOLOGY PARK/ATLANTA
City/State/ZIP: NORCROSS GA 30092
Telephone: 770-449-0461
Fax: 770-263-8532

Iliad Press

ILIAD LITERARY AWARDS
Quarterly open-style competition
Four $1,000 grand prizes and 396 other prizes annually
The Iliad Literary Awards Program is the "flagship" competition of Iliad Press. The awards program is an open competition; poems and essays of any style of family—reading subject

are acceptable. Poems are limited to 30 lines and essays to 300 words. No purchase or entry fee is required for the first two (2) entries in any quarterly competition. Entries must be accompanied by a #10 (business size) self-addressed, stamped envelope. If you send more than two entries in any quarterly contest, there is a reading fee of $2 for each additional entry. Contest deadlines: March 31, June 30, September 30, and December 31. Late entries will automatically be enrolled into the next competition.

YOUTH AWARDS PROGRAM
Quarterly open-style competition
Four $200 First Prizes; Four $100 Second Prizes;
Four $50 Third Prizes

The Youth Awards Program is designed for writers under twenty-one (21) to encourage writing among our youth. It is part of the Iliad Literary Awards Program and all contestants that enter the Youth Awards Program will automatically be enrolled in the Iliad Literary Awards Program providing that you are under 21 and write your age on the entry form. Submit poetry (30 line limit) and Prose (300 word limit) by March 31, June 30, September 30, and December 31. No entry fees for the first (2) entries, $2 for each additional entry.

General Guidelines
• When you mail your entries mark the *competition name* on the outside of the envelope in which you mail your entries and on the top left-hand corner of each entry.

• Be sure to include your name and address on each entry. You may enter as many times as you wish, provided you enclose the appropriate reading/entry fee.

• Use a separate entry form for each contest you enter. Entry forms can be reproduced.

• To receive a Winner's List for any contest, please send a #10 SASE (long, business-size) for *each* Winner's List you wish to receive. Please mark the words "WINNER'S LIST" and the contest name on the lower left-hand corner on the front of the envelope. Lists will be mailed within six months of the end of the competition.

• No entries will be returned. Void where prohibited. All contest entries are eligible for consideration in the National Authors Registry President's Awards for Literary Excellence.

Categories: Fiction—Literature—Poetry—Writing

Name: Sharon Derderian, Executive Editor
Material: Poetry, Prose, Short Stories, Articles
Address: 36915 RYAN RD STE WG
City/State/ZIP: STERLING HTS MI 48310
Telephone: 810-795-3635
Fax: 810-795-9875
Nota bene: Entry fee required for third and subsequent submissions.

Illinois Entertainer

We are a monthly free music magazine focusing alternative local and national bands.

Categories: Arts—Culture—Drama—Electronics—Entertainment—Film/Video—Interview—Lifestyles—Music—Society—Technology—Television/Radio—Theatre

Name: Michael C. Harris, Editor
Name: Ben Kim, Associate Editor
Material: Music
Address: 124 W POLK STE 103
City/State/ZIP: CHICAGO IL 60605
Telephone: 312-922-9333
Fax: 312-922-9369
E-mail: ieeditors@aol.com

Independent Business

Please refer to Group IV Communications, Inc.

Industrial Management

Industrial Management welcomes feature articles, critical reader comment, and brief notes of interest. Please use the following guidelines before sending contributions.

Feature Articles
Try to focus on the most current managerial problems and solutions, or recent developments and research that may have a significant and positive impact on today's operating manager. While every submission will be considered for publication, emphasis will be placed on the article's practical value and accessibility. Highly theoretical or statistical articles are discouraged. Articles based on experience and actual "hands-on" operating situations, or those that have valuable applications in a working environment will be favored. Authors are encouraged to include supporting graphics and/or photographs with articles.

Perspective
Opinions, comments, or constructive criticism of a particular subject or previously published article are welcomed.

Submission
Articles submitted to *Industrial Management* should be offered on an exclusive basis and limited to 3,500 words or less. In addition to printed copy, please include a Microsoft Word or ASCII version of the article on a 3.5" PC-compatible or Macintosh disk. Charts, graphs, and other non-photo artwork should be sent separately or included as individual files on the same disk.

Upon the request of an author, articles may be peer-reviewed. Articles will still be subject to review and editing procedures by the editor. Furthermore, the editor makes the final decision about whether to accept or reject the article.

Additional Tips
These following hints may also assist in preparing an article for publication:
• Number each page
• Photographs: High-quality transparencies/slides or prints are best. Provide identification and caption material with all photos, and do not attach with paper clips or staples. Please do not write on the back of photos. Specify if the photo should be returned.
• Include a short biographical paragraph about the author and co-authors of the article.

Industrial Management holds the copyright of all published articles. For permission to use the article for personal or educational purposes, please contact the Permissions Department at the Institute of Industrial Engineers (IIE).

Categories: Technology—Industrial Engineering

Name: Kathy Boggs, Editor
Material: All
Address: 25 TECHNOLOGY PARK/ATLANTA
City/State/ZIP: ATLANTA GA 30092-2988
Telephone: 770-449-0461
Fax: 770-263-8532
E-mail: kboggs@iienet.org
Internet: www.iienet.org

Industry Week

Executive Level Audience
IW readers are primarily executives—people with the title of vice president, executive vice president, senior vice president, chief executive officer, chief financial officer, chief information

officer, chairman, managing director, and president. Your article should be targeted accordingly.

Global Focus

IW's executive readers oversee global corporations. While IW's primary target audience a senior executive in a U.S. firm, your story should provide information that any executive anywhere in the world can use.

Company Size

IW executive readers manage companies that employ 100 or more employees. While most of your sources should be chosen from among mid- to large-sized corporations, you may write about a smaller manufacturing company or a CEO of a smaller manufacturing company if you can demonstrate that the IW reader will learn something by reading that story.

Industries Served

IW's executive readers manage companies in manufacturing and manufacturing-related industries (insurance, transportation, construction, utilities, telecommunications services). However, many of the stories you tell should be useful to executives of companies in any industry.

Executive Profiles

IW is particularly looking for profiles of executives who have a unique management style or philosophy that has helped them create more profitable, more competitive, more effective, and more humane companies.

Educational

All stories should be entertaining to read, yet carry with them something that the executive reader can take away—ideas about new strategies, processes, and technologies that will help that executive manage more profitably, more competitively, more effectively, and more humanely.

Best Practices

The core of our articles are those about best practices—stories describing how one or more companies have solved a problem or addressed a specific strategic management issue.

Urgency

Our readers are busy people. To capture their attention, you must include a clear, concise statement early in your article that shows the executive reader why he *must* read this story *now*; it should show how he will benefit or what he will learn by reading the article.

General

Industry Week does not allow anyone outside the magazine to review editorial material prior *to* publication.

Contributions Policy

Industry Week reviews and, when appropriate, solicits [contributions] that will help IW better serve readers, and achieve its mission and vision.

IW compensates contributors according to a uniform schedule which is available upon request. It also reserves the right to negotiate a fee with an individual contributor to arrive at mutually satisfactory compensation. This fee schedule covers written material only.

IW expects contributors to submit photography and illustrations to accompany their story. Most contributors fulfill this requirement by directing the company(ies) with whom they are working to forward the photographs and illustrations. Photography and illustrations produced by the contributor and used in IW are compensated separately. All photographs and illustrations will be returned only upon request, which should be confirmed in writing at the time of submission.

IW will reimburse contributors for routine expenses incurred in the preparation of articles. It will not reimburse long-distance travel expenses, except those expressly approved in advance.

IW pays contributors upon acceptance in Cleveland, and upon receipt of an invoice and Publication Agreement [available upon request] that includes a social security or federal employer [tax]

identification number. Two types of Publication Agreements are available: The first, "Editorial Correspondent Agreement," is usually signed by a contributor who wishes to establish a continuing relationship with IW. The second, "Granting of Certain Publication Rights," can be signed by a writer who plans to write for IW only once or intermittently.

IW reviews outside contributions periodically, and its decisions are final. It assumes no responsibility for unsolicited contributions, but makes every attempt to return those it cannot use.

IW prefers that manuscripts be sent via e-mail, in ASCII text ("text-only") format. Manuscripts submitted by post should be double-spaced, with pages numbered and the word count noted in the upper right corner.

Except by special arrangement, IW does not accept any article which previously has appeared in other publications, or will appear in other publications prior to appearing in IW.

Queries may be submitted in writing via post or e-mail. If you are a new contributor to IW, please include three or four clips and a complete resume that includes the publications for which you are currently writing.

Categories: Business

Name: Patricia Panchak, Managing Editor
Material: Queries
Address: 1100 SUPERIOR AVE
City/State/ZIP: CLEVELAND OH 44114
Telephone: 216-931-9887
Fax: 216-696-7670
E-mail: ppanchak@industryweek.com
Internet: www.industryweek.com

INK Literary Review

INK Literary Review

Submission Policy/Submission Fee

INK will *only* accept original works that have not been published before. Strongly favored works include poetry, short stories, reviews of current books, fresh interpretations of the classics or popular texts, literary essays, personal anecdotes related to the writing profession, interviews and calendar of literary, artistic or scholarly events.

INK does not require submission fee for contributors.

INK is a non-paying publication.

Style

For poems: each poem should not exceed 50 verses.

For short essays and book reviews: between 500 to 600 words. Must follow the guidelines set by the *MLA (Modern Language Association) Handbook for Writers of Research Papers*, by Joseph Gibaldi and Walter S. Achtert.

For short stories: between 500 to 2,000 words.

For short plays: at most, 2 pages (single space).

Editorial Standards

INK Literary Review will not publish works that contain unnecessary or irrelevant obscene, pornographic or distasteful expressions, severe grammatical and syntactical errors, and gross misspellings. We also require submissions to follow the style guidelines.

Submissions, letters to the editor, subscription requests, inquiries regarding advertisements or advertorials, donations and other types of correspondence may be sent via regular mail or e-mail.

Categories: Fiction—Nonfiction—Adventure—Arts—Biography—Culture—Drama—Ethnic—Fantasy—Gay/Lesbian—General Interest—Humor—Inspirational—Language—Literature—Men's Fiction—Multicultural—Poetry—Romance—Short Stories—Theatre—Women's Fiction

Name: R.R. Delfin, Editor
Material: All
Address: 11 SPRING HILL TERRACE
City/State/ZIP: SOMERVILLE MA 02143
Telephone: 617-629-0855
E-mail: INKLITT@aol.com

Inside Sports

Inside Sports accepts freelance contributions and queries for both its features section and various departments in the magazine. Prospective articles and queries should be typed and submitted with the author's address and phone number and a self-addressed, stamped envelope for reply to the editor's attention at the address below. Please make queries in writing and not by phone.

Inside Sports accepts freelance feature articles and queries on a variety of sports-related topics, such as personalities and trends in the world of sports. The magazine concentrates on feature coverage and previews (as opposed to event coverage) of major sports. Most articles are 500-4,000 words in length. *Inside Sports* most often features articles on the following sports: baseball, pro and college football, pro and college basketball, hockey, boxing, and auto racing. *Inside Sports* also accepts submissions and queries for the following departments: The Insider, Media, Pro & Con, Inside Interview, Numbers, and The Fan.

Please do not query us on obvious ideas; please limit submissions and queries to exclusive (i.e., not mass-mailed to other publications) and unique ideas. Please allow approximately four weeks for a response to a submission or query. Fees upon acceptance of an article are negotiable.

Categories: Nonfiction—Interview—Sports—Recreation—Profiles

Name: Ken Leiker, Editor
Material: All
Address: 990 GROVE ST.
City/State/ZIP: EVANSTON, IL 60201
Telephone: 847-491-6440
Fax: 847-491-0867
Internet: www.insidesports.com

Inside Texas Running
The Tabloid Magazine That Runs Texas

INSIDE TEXAS RUNNING is a tabloid magazine issued monthly, except June and August, and is published primarily for Texas runners. Each issue averages 32-40 pages and includes race reports, a "Texas Roundup" of news from around the State, in-house columns on sports medicine and nutrition, the over-40 runner ("Concerning Masters") and articles on unusual running events, training, etc. All but the columns require freelance input.

We also are seeking good photos. General guidelines are as follows:

ARTICLES: We need profiles, travel tips, unusual races, historic pieces or almost anything that would interest our readers. If you are not sure about a subject, try us anyway—especially if it's Texas-related. General topics about running are usually handled by our columnists. Unique slants are wanted.

Our audience includes beginning runners as well as veteran marathoners and triathletes, so the subject matter may reflect the varying abilities of our readers. Since ability varies so widely, we might be interested in a five-hour marathoner, for example, if there is something unique about that marathoner that would inspire or intrigue. Controversy is welcomed, but not faddish or dangerous nutritional or training pieces; observing the common sense rules of running, etc. is necessary. Training articles should be written by or with the help of experts such as reputable coaches (always state experience and background) and elite athletes.

Anecdotes, examples and quotes are very much appreciated.

Payment ranges from $25 for fillers of less than 500 words up to $75 for 1,000 to 1,500 words. Higher fees are available for established writers. Byline is provided.

RACE REPORTS: We contact race directors from around the state for race reports and results and cover many major races. Any unusual happening (odd weather, lost runners, unique course layout, etc.), along with a brief account of the race, will find eager acceptance here. Results listing the top finishers (minimum top 10 overall male and female, top 3 age division winners) should accompany the write-up. The report should include the proper name of the race, the date, the distance, weather conditions, number of participants, and, if possible, quotes from participants reacting to some aspect of the race. Payment: $25 for report, one usable photo and results. **Length:** 100-250 words max.

CORRESPONDENTS: We are looking for regular correspondents from around the state to cover races, do interviews, report races, take photos and keep us informed of upcoming races. These regulars will be listed on the masthead of the publication and receive the publication complimentary.

FICTION: Sorry, but we no longer publish fiction.

BEST WAY TO BREAK IN: Our Texas Roundup Section includes short items of one to several paragraphs long that include news about races-unusual themes, celebrity runners, prize money, and other information above and beyond its basic calendar listing-as well as human interest, records set, and miscellaneous tidbits. We are looking for items across the state, particularly outside the Houston area.

PHOTOS: Only prints (either B&W or color) may be considered. Please don't send snapshots of runners where features are undefinable and figures are miles away.

Human interest subject matter is desired, as well as our always necessary race photos. Articles profiling runners should be accompanied by photos of the subject training, at work, with his family or whatever else will illustrate the piece appropriately. Similarly, travel pieces might have figures running past recognizable landmarks. Payment: $10 per photo, $25 for color photo on cover. More for outstanding shots.

CARTOONS: Like everything else in INSIDE TEXAS RUNNING, cartoons are about runners, etc., but the subject matter might overlap into medical concerns, diet, non-running spouse, general fitness. Payment: $10.

ON SUBMISSIONS: Complete manuscripts only; no queries. Please do not send photo negatives. We will pay on acceptance and will report on all submissions received as above within several weeks. Please indicate whether ms is simultaneous submission.

THANK YOU FOR YOUR INTEREST IN INSIDE TEXAS RUNNING.

Joanne Schmidt

Publisher Editor
Categories: Outdoors—Physical Fitness—Recreation—Regional—Sports

Name: Joanne Schmidt, Publisher/Editor
Material: All
Address: 9514 BRISTLEBROOK DR
City/State/ZIP: HOUSTON TX 77083
Telephone: 281-498-3208
Fax: 281-879-9980
E-mail: ITRJCS@aol.com

INsider Magazine

Dear Writer,

Thank you for your interest in *INsider* magazine. Enclosed are the writer's guidelines that you requested, as well as a copy of our Editorial Guidelines. In addition, we may have included a list of article ideas. If any of these interest you, please let us know via the most convenient method. Our e-mail address is listed below. We accept unsolicited manuscripts as well and are always interested in any story ideas you might have. We encourage you to send your proposals in the form of a query letter and we'll get back to you either way with a response. Once again, we thank you for your interest in writing for our publication and look forward to hearing from you. Please sign, date and provide all information on the editorial contract and then either fax or mail it to us. We must have your contract on file before we may consider reviewing any of your submissions.

Before you turn in your writing there are a number of steps you must take:

1. Please type your piece(s) on Microsoft Word for Macintosh and turn it in on a floppy disk. Also, send us a hard copy back-up of your work along with the floppy, just in case of mishap. if you are unfortunately using a PC program then save your copy as *text*.

2. Put your name, address, phone number, social security number, and birth date in the upper left-hand corner above the piece.

3. Below the personal information, you must include a title headline (25 characters) and subtitle (50 characters) relating to your piece.

4. All dashes should be made using the "shift-option-dash" command. The dash should look larger than a regular hyphen. Make ellipses by pressing "option-colon".

5. Always use soft returns.

6. Use single spacing for lines and between sentences.

7. Use smart quotes. (under preferences)

8. List all your sources so we can call for more information.

9. Check your story for AP style. Italicize all titles rather than putting them in quotes.

Please call if you have any questions.

Sincerely,

Tim Plamondon

Associate Publisher

Editorial Guidelines

Publication Definition:

INsider magazine is a national general interest publication published 5 times per year. *INsider* has a minimum circulation of 200,000 and over 8 million readers. It is distributed directly to 445 colleges and direct mailed to over 1,500 college newspapers and 600 college radio stations. There are over 15 individualized local editions of the magazine targeting various campuses and metropolitan markets. Our target audience is 18 to 34 year olds. *INsider* is also available as a national publication at many major newsstands including Borders Books and Barnes & Noble Bookstores.

INsider's Readers:

INsider magazine is a publication designed and written by twentysomethings from all over America. We have graduated, per se, from focusing on the college market and our stories should reflect this new readership. It is important when writing to appeal above the college level, not at it.

Monthly surveys conducted in the magazine show that 18 to 34 year olds have tremendously varied habits and interests. In general, they love music and buy numerous CDs. They are concerned about their health and appearance. They are very active socially, going to nightclubs, bars and concerts several times a month and are constantly pursuing relationships and meeting new people. They love to see movies both at the theater and at home on video tape. They are very aware of current events, actively vote in major elections and are very active as volunteers for causes dealing with the environment, political issues, etc. A majority have credit cards that they use on a regular basis.

INsider entertains our readers' interests while developing a unique editorial impression that celebrates the exclusivity of being a young adult today. One thing is true for all college-age consumers; they do NOT like to be referred or spoken to as college students. We want to emphasize what is unique about this demographic without exposing its limitations (i.e., their age, where they are in their careers). Any quantitative observation makes students recoil from fear of being labeled a "member of the pack."

Themes:

Each issue of *INsider* revolves around a theme. Consider these themes when submitting.

September: Computer Software/College Football Preview
October: Annual Ski and Winter Sports Issue
November: Annual Travel Guide/Spring Break Issue
March: Auto Issue/March Madness Preview/Extreme Sports
May: Outdoor and Adventure Issue

Guest Editor:

Each issue of *INsider* magazine is hosted by a guest editor that interacts with several of the on-going featured columns. Guest editors are featured on the cover of the magazine; there is a two page interview with the guest editor; we note their birthday on the horoscope page; the guest editor also assists in reviewing music and products in the issue. The guest editor is generally a notable actor; actress or musician.

DEPARTMENT DESCRIPTIONS:

Sports, Travel, Activities & Product Reviews:

IN Fashion—These five to seven page spreads are usually related to the theme of each month. Other fashion features have been on nightclub fashion or back-to-school clothes. The fashion editor solicits the clothes and writes all copy for the section.

IN Product—This section features the newest products on the market appealing to *INsider's* readership. From mountain bikes to backpacks to beers, this section previews the latest trends. *INsider* is a key source of information for readers looking to buy the best products for the most reasonable price. *INsider* reviews the latest products on the market for quality, versatility and affordability. The top selections are given the *INsider* Choice Award. Anywhere from four to eight products are previewed with graphics and accompanying descriptions including any outstanding qualities, where they can be found and the cost. Product review sections should be between 750 and 1,500 words and should reflect a number of related products.

IN Sports—This section features stories on participatory sports popular with our readership like ultimate Frisbee or rugby as well as profiles of professional or amateur athletes. Stories and profiles should be 750 to 1,500 words.

IN Picks *(I Beat Bernie)*—This section portrays five notable sports casters and their choices as to who wins the league to who is the best player from football to basketball. All commentary is in two to three sentence answers.

IN Travel—This section includes stories on destinations popular with our readership, but focuses more on more distant, international travel. *INsider* will also consider humorous travel stones, travel tips and travel round-ups. Stories should be 500 to 1,500 words, often with accompanying sidebar.

Entertainment:

IN Books—*INsider* attracts a highly literate audience. They enjoy engaging stories about a wide and diverse range of authors. and writers. Profiles should be 750 to 1,500 words. Short reviews on books of interest to our readers, from fiction to career and travel guides should be 200-300 words.

IN Film—*INsider* focuses on up-and-coming actors and directors as well as established stars who appeal directly to our readership. Recent profiles include new faces such as Kevin Smith (the director of *Clerks*) and Michael Rapaport (star of *Kiss of Death*) as well as Hollywood fixtures like Sara Jessica Parker and Ethan Hawke. *INsider* probes the celebrities to tell about their lives, careers and details of upcoming movies. In-depth articles, usually featuring personality profiles or interviews, should be 1,500 to 2,400 words. These are often the cover story. Movie reviews and guides featuring upcoming releases should be 200 to 300 words.

IN Music—This section examines the hottest music and trends throughout the musical spectrum. From Funkadelic to R.E.M. to Phish to Garth Brooks, readers look to *INsider* first to find out what they should be listening to. In-depth features and interviews from the music industry should be from 750 to 1,500 words. These may be considered for cover stories. Shorter profile pieces, concert reviews *(IN Bin)* or band reviews should be between 200 to 300 words. CD reviews (Spin Cycle) should be no more than 300 words. The IN Retro column focuses on music revivals and re-releases. IN Traxs are short 30 word reviews of new releases.

IN Techno—Here we review the latest CD-ROMs, computer software and computer hardware. Software reviews should be 200 to 400 words.

INterActive—This section features the latest in happenings and issues on the info superhighway. Stories and profiles should be 750 to 1,500 words. Individual web site reviews should be no longer than 300 words. Each issue of *INsider* features a page of web site reviews related to that issue's theme.

IN Town—Each local edition contains its own 8-32 page signature featuring editorial, advertising and the local calendar for that particular city (i.e. Chicago, Austin, San Francisco) which highlights cool events and places around town. There are bimonthly spotlights featuring restaurant picks, local musical acts, bar and night club reviews and live theatre reviews. Spotlights should be no longer than 750 words and no shorter than 700 words. Please supply photographs related to specific review(s).

INTV—INTV features interviews of notable television stars md reviews of hip new television shows. People turn on their television for both information and entertainment, and we want to find the alternative venues, programming and stars that spark ideas in our readers - not programs that only spark channel-surfing. Stories and profiles should be 750 to 1,500 words.

IN Video—IN Video is a round-up of the latest videos for rent. Readers look to *INsider* for the newest releases and the greatest classics on the market. Video reviews and features should be 150 to 300 words. IN Video also includes a column called *"If the Walls could Talk"* which is a monthly movie-industry buzz column that details soon to be released movies and the actors who star in them.

Issues:

IN Careers—*INsider* gives our readers an edge on how to get ahead, from writing their résumé to tips on how to interview. Past features have included advice from recent graduates, job and salary demographics and the do's and dont's of job interviews. This department also features articles related to the magazine's theme for that month. Informative/resource articles pertaining to job or career issues should be 400 to 750 words with a national slant.

IN Forum—This section portrays notable thinkers, educators, journalists and leaders answering questions involving social, political, and economic issues of America. Debates will focus on mainstream solutions involving: education, labor and job creation, urban renewal, transportation and welfare. All commentary is in two to three sentence answers.

IN Issues—*INsider* brings readers the latest information about what is happening in the world and how it directly affects their lives. Bimonthly, *INsider* offers one to two pages of national features covering current issues such as alcohol/drug use, AIDS and sex in the '90s and environmental issues. Features are 750 to 2,100 words, often with accompanying sidebar.

IN Money—The IN Money section consists of a one to two page article on financial information pertinent to *INsider*'s demographics. Example are how to invest, buying your first home and how to negotiate your first lease. Stories and profiles should be 750 to 1,500 words.

IN Party—IN Party describes non-mainstream political movements in America including the following: Natural Law Party, Henry Georgists, New Party, Green Party, and the Socialist Party. Stories and profiles should be 750 words.

IN Politics—These articles explore political issues in depth. In-depth analysis of America's economic policies effecting our society including spotlights on NAFTA: Protectionism or Free Trade; Social Security - Argument for privatization; Debt and America; and Capitalism in America. Stories should be 750 to 1,500 words.

IN Site—This section describes and analyzes web sites encompassing political, economic, and social issues. Topics of such sites will include education, political action committees, political magazines, environmental and employment sites. Individual web site reviews should be no longer than 300 words.

IN Spire—This section focuses on metaphysical and spiritual philosophies and trends. Examples of articles would focus on WICCA, Buddhism, Teachings of Don Juan, occult, etc. Stories and profiles should be 750 words.

Our Editorial Creed

Informative, entertaining, progressive, cutting edge.

The individualist's forum for the '90s.

Our Editorial Philosophy

INsider magazine, a publication written by twentysomethings for twentysomethings.

INsider magazine reflects every aspect of our readers' lives. They are faced with making important decisions concerning who they are, where they fit and what they want. We directly speak to their needs and deliver what is important to them: adventure, technology, careers, education, sports, social issues, entertainment, and outstanding quality and value in products and services.

INsider magazine stands out as an honest resource of genuine quality and integrity in today's varied scope of journalism.

INsider magazine speaks for our readers and the world in which they live. Insider magazine. When reaching our generation means getting INside.

INsider's editorial caters to the proactive attitudes of our readers. The people we want to attract are outgoing, conscientious individuals who are interested in bettering themselves and the world around them. These people, by nature, are active participants in many outdoor activities and we want to have an underlying theme in each issue that relates to this extreme sports mind set.

Our target audience are rollerbladers, mountain bikers, triathletes, and skiers. By promoting and featuring a variety of outdoor activities, we can tie into our annual college sports (football, basketball) and outdoor/adventure issues to provide a magazine that hip and vibrant young adults will want to be part of. Being active is the key to our editorial raison d'etre. Focusing on participatory sports and activities gives *INsider* the feel of a lifestyle magazine because we feature things that our readers care about and participate in. There are plenty of publications aimed at the college couch-potato; *INsider* is not one of them.

Beyond those categories mentioned above, we are constantly seeking out the most interesting and stimulating stories for, our readership from the diverse arenas of sports, travel, relationships, lifestyles and so on. Our editorial policy is simple: since the entire editorial staff, we feel, represents a good cross section of our readership, if a story idea appeals to us, it should appeal to our readers. We are constantly seeking well written and researched stories that our readers will find both entertaining and informative. Our goal is to stay a step ahead of the mainstream by finding the ideas, issues and personalities that are and will be shaping our world.

Format and Style Guidelines

Submissions—Articles must be submitted on Macintosh disk with Microsoft Word 6.0 or an earlier version. If this is not possible, then e-mail the article. If you are unfortunately using a PC program, then save the file as text and submit it on disk. Always submit a hard copy of the article with your disks. Fax or e-mail story ideas or queries.

Compensation

There are several classes of writers and each is compensated differently. The Associate publisher and Senior Editor are in charge of all class promotions.

Contributing writer 1¢ per word
Senior Writer 2¢ per word
Senior Writer 3¢ per word
Featured Columnist To Be Negotiated

Costs of article are included in payment. Any other costs associated with the production of an article must be approved in advance by the Publisher. You will not receive payment if the article is not submitted by deadline.

Assignments

Most stories are by assignment, however suitable submissions are considered. Queries and story ideas are strongly encouraged. There is no guarantee that unsolicited articles will be returned, even with SASE. If interested in writing, please send a resume, a completed contract and writing samples (published or otherwise) with any story ideas or area of interest to the address below.

Freelance Writer's Contract

All freelance writers are hired on a per-assignment basis. There is no guarantee that the assigned article will be published. Payment for articles is on publication only. *INsider* will not guarantee a kill fee, or payment of any kind, should the assigned article not be published.

Upon publication, payment will be based upon the rates noted in the Editorial Guidelines or unless agreed otherwise. Higher honorariums are paid to the regular writers, columnists and for articles that require a great deal of research. Checks are cut every two weeks, and payment is only made if the article is submitted to *INsider* by deadline.

All writers are allowed to publish their works in other publications for additional moneys only after *INsider* has had first right to publication. Any situation that may arise that is affected by this policy should be made aware to the publisher. There are no exceptions.

INsider reserves the rights to publish submitted articles in any of *INsider*'s affiliate publications, electronic publications, websites and syndication services without the permission of the writer to reprint said article. All payment for articles will be made payable to the undersigned writer.

Guidelines for submissions:

All copy should be laid out based upon the following specifications noted in the Editorial Guidelines: Saved on a Macintosh disk using Microsoft Word version 5.0 or higher; spell checked; typeset in Helvetica 12 Pt ragged right; and, most importantly, written according to the AP Stylebook. Working titles should appear on the first line, not exceeding 25 characters, with a subtitle not to exceed 50 characters, followed with the byline. Do not slug article with identifying page numbers or end of copy (#,-30). Do not indent paragraphs, and always use one space between sentences.

Deadlines: Unless otherwise stated, all editorial copy is due by 5 p.m. on the 7th of each month, two months prior to publication date.

Categories: Nonfiction—Adventure—Arts—Automobiles—Careers—College—Computers—Conservation—Consumer—Culture—Economics—Entertainment—Environment—Feminism—Film/Video—Food/Drink—General Interest—Government—Internet—Interview—Law—Men's Issues—Music—Outdoors—Politics—Public Policy—Regional—Relationships—Sexuality—Society—Sports—Technology—Theatre—Travel—Women's Issues

Name: Debra Eckerling, Senior Editor
Material: Entertainment
Name: Rita Cook, Senior Editor
Material: Theme
Name: Adam Monroe, Senior Editor
Material: Issues
Address: 4124 W OAKTON
City/State/ZIP: SKOKIE IL 60076-3267
Telephone: 847-673-3703
Fax: 847-329-0358
E-mail: insideread@aol.com

INSIGHT

INSIGHT is a weekly Christian magazine for teenagers. Here are some things to keep in mind as you write for it:

1. We print mostly true stories with a teen's point of view.

2. We look for good story—telling elements such as a dramatic beginning, realistic dialogue, and believable, alive characters.

3. We prefer stories that take a Christ-centered, positive approach to topics of teen interest in simple, current language.

4. We buy articles and stories that fit into the following categories:

On the Edge. True "drama in real life" stories. Can be written in *third person* (someone else's story) or *first person* (your own). 800-1,500 words. Please include real photos of the people and incident if possible. Payment: $75-$125.

It Happened to Me. Personal experience stories written in *first person*. Should tell about an unusual experience that taught a lesson or had a lasting impact. Please include a photo of the author if possible. Word count: 600-900 words. Payment: $50-$100.

So I Said... True short stories or opinion pieces written in *first person*. Focuses on common, everyday events and experiences that taught the writer something edifying. If it's a story, it must include dialogue, in which the writer states what he/she has learned. This is an opinion piece, preferably communicated through narrative. 300-500 words. Payment: $40-60.

How I Became Friends With God. True, *first-person* accounts describing how the writer became friends with God. Might define one dramatic incident causing a spiritual change, or describe a gradual process. Should help readers see the importance and need of a friendship with God. Include a sidebar with a few specific recommendations for finding and growing closer to God. Should focus on the teen years. Please include an author photo. Length: 600-900 words, including sidebar. Payment: $50-$100.

Please include your name, address, phone number, and social security number (necessary for payment) with all submissions.

Submission to us constitutes permission to edit as necessary.
Categories: Nonfiction—Christian Interests—Religion—Teen

Name: Editor
Material: All
Address: 55 W OAK RIDGE DR
City/State/ZIP: HAGERSTOWN MD 21740
Telephone: 301-791-7000
Fax: 301-790-9734
E-mail: insight@rhpa.org

Instructor

There's no better way to establish yourself as a teacher-writer than to write for *Instructor* magazine. *Instructor* publishes more teachers' bylines each issue than any other educational magazine. We would love to hear from you!
SECTIONS OF THE MAGAZINE TO TARGET
Features: 1,000 to 2,500-word articles that address a timely issue in elementary education in a practical manner or report effective teaching strategies in science, math, social studies, language arts, technology, and other subject areas. Please send us a query letter (a brief letter in which you describe the article you'd like to write) before writing the article. To give you an idea of the type of articles we publish, here are examples from past issues:
• **Multimedia on a Shoestring**
• **Classroom Design that Works Every Time!**
• **Ten Ways to Improve Your Theme Teaching**
• **Inclusion: 12 Secrets to Making It Work in Your Classroom**
• **Student-Led Parent Conferences**
• **Find the Funds for Your Great Ideas**
Payment for features: $250-$500.
Idea Notebook: "When you need a good idea overnight"—brief practical ideas for all grades, from cross-curricular activities and management tips to seasonal craft and bulletin board ideas. 250-word maximum; color snapshots or samples of students' work that clarify your ideas are helpful. Payment: $25-$50
General Tips
• Read the magazine so you're familiar with our style and our needs.
• As you write, think: How can I make this article most *useful* for teachers? Write in your natural voice; we shy away from wordy, academic prose.
• Let us know what grade/subject you teach and name and location of school.
• Send seasonal material at least six months in advance.
• Send only one copy of your manuscript.
• Print name and address on manuscript and on all photos and samples.
• Enclose a large self-addressed stamped envelope and include your phone number.
• Expect a reply from us within 8-12 weeks.
Categories: Nonfiction—Education

Name: Manuscript Editor
Material: All
Address: 555 BROADWAY
City/State/ZIP: NEW YORK NY 10012
Telephone: 212-505-4965

International Midwife

Please refer to *Midwifery Today*.

The International Railway Traveler

The International Railway Traveler (IRT) is the official newsletter of The Society of International Railway Travelers, an international organization of sophisticated travelers who prefer going by rail. IRT provides exclusive and up-to-date information on rail travel world-wide for both prospective and armchair railway travelers.

Information about international rail-travel possibilities geared to the general traveler, as opposed to the train fan, is available from no other single source.

While IRT concentrates on Europe and North America, it also covers more exotic rail-travel destinations. IRT conveys both the romance of rail travel as well as practical information vital to making successful rail trips.

IRT's full-length features and other articles are referenced to the world-famous *Thomas Cook European and Overseas Timetables*, making trip-planning easy.

IRT is not limited to inter-city passenger trains. It covers regional passenger trains, suburban passenger trains, mountain trains, as well as trams and "light rail." In short, if it runs on rails, IRT is interested in it.

In the almost 15 years of its existence, IRT has become recognized as the leading publication on international railway travel.
WRITERS
In general, IRT needs reports that are timely, detailed, and, above all, scrupulously accurate. All story submissions should include appropriate photos and/or graphics (i.e., items with a railroad's logo, etc.)

IRT seeks the following kinds of reports:
1.) News Shorts no more than 100 words long. These appear in the regularly featured column "Sidetrack."
2.) Short Features of around 250-500 words in length. These stories report on new equipment, services, routes, fares, package deals, dining and sleeping car services, stations, and anything else of interest to the railway traveler.
3.) Travel Features consist of the main story and a detailed, informational ("If You Go...") sidebar, which together should run no more than 1,400 words. (Lengthier submissions will be returned.)
Main Story
IRT's travel features should convey the romance, wonder and excitement of rail travel for the newsletter's sophisticated, well-traveled readership. The stories should be lively, personal and, above all, not dull. Also, where it is appropriate, they should be opinionated. Writers are encouraged to dwell on any aspect of their journey that appeals to them: unusual food in the dining car, interesting people met, unusual places visited, etc.
Sidebar
The following information must be included in a separate sidebar (except where otherwise noted) if the story is to be considered for publication. Stories will be returned if this information is not included:
a) Prices for major portions of trip described, such as air and rail fares, hotel, restaurant, public transit, major attractions, etc.
b) Specific advice on amenities from the *rail traveler's* point

of view. That is, hotels, restaurants, museums, etc., accessible to the main railroad station or public transit, or those facilities which cater specifically to the rail traveler through special packages, promotions and/or fares.

c) Phone, fax, Internet address, Web page URL and mailing addresses of travel providers/attractions mentioned in story as well as contact information for the national tourism office in the U.S. of the country or countries described. *The writer is responsible for the accuracy of this information. Please double-check these numbers and addresses.*

d) Any other pertinent traveler's information, such as visa requirements, health news, political updates, etc.

e) Relevant *Thomas Cook Timetable* numbers.

f) Date the trip was taken.

4.) Spotlight Features cover the following topics on an occasional basis:

a) **STATIONS**—A detailed look at railway stations around the world from the point of view of facilities and services of interest to the railway traveler (i.e., restaurants, shops, information booths, hotels, access to city center and public transport, etc.). These stories also give something of the "aesthetics" of the station-its architecture, denizens, and overall "mood."

b) **DINERS**—This is an appreciation of dining cars from around the world, with an emphasis on the type of food served, prices, method and quality of service, as well as a physical description of the dining car, both inside and out.

c) **SLEEPERS**—As with "Diners," "Sleepers" stories feature a detailed description of the cars' physical appearance/quality of service, comfort, amenities, etc., as well as their overall character.

d) **DESTINATIONS**—As the term implies, these are short descriptions of places of aesthetic, cultural or historical interest which can be reached by train and which are of special interest to the enthusiastic railway traveler (railway museums, for example). Please include directions for reaching these places by public transport.

PHOTOGRAPHERS

Trains may be fascinating to look at and a joy to ride. But pictures of them tend towards monotony if they are taken from the same dull perspective (i.e., on the station platform, with the train describing an oblique, diminishing line). Include people with train shots wherever possible.

Also, IRT likes train photographs which include something of the country's native scenery, photographs which emphasize the word "international" in IRT's name. (The Japanese "Shinkansen" racing past Mt. Fuji is the classic example.)

Photos should be black-and-white glossy, high contrast, and in focus, preferably 8"x10", although 5"x7" will be accepted. IRT uses no color.

PAYMENT

IRT pays for stories and photos on publication. IRT buys first North American serial rights and all electronic publishing rights to stories and photos.

In the event a story requested or accepted by IRT is unsuitable for publication, IRT will pay its author a 25 percent "kill fee."

Payment is $.04 per word plus $10 for each 8"x10" or 5"x7" black-and-white glossy photo used ($20, if the photo is the main page-one art). Payment is in U.S. dollars. To receive full payment, photos should be submitted camera-ready (8"x10" or 5"x7" black-and-white glossy prints.) Costs associated with converting photographic material to camera-ready form are deducted from payment.

Sample copies of *The International Railway Traveler* cost $6 each.

SUBMISSIONS

IRT encourages submissions by e-mail or on computer disk (3½" disks for IBM or compatibles with WordPerfect preferred; those for Macintosh computers acceptable. Use ASCII file format if WordPerfect not available. Disks will be returned if SASE is enclosed.)

IRT welcomes the submission of unsolicited material. Query letters with published clips are strongly encouraged.

Categories: Nonfiction—Travel—Rail Travel

Name: Gena Holle, Editor
Material: Rail Travel
Address: PO BOX 3747
City/State/ZIP: SAN DIEGO CA 92163
Telephone: 619-260-1332
Fax: 619-296-4220
E-mail: irt.trs@worldnet.att.net

International Sports Journal
University of New Haven

The *International Sports Journal* welcomes both empirical and theoretical articles that can be applied or be pertinent to current sports issues and practices or contribute to academic research in the international sports community.

Authors' articles should not exceed 25 double-spaced typewritten pages, and footnotes should appear on a separate page and follow A.P.A. style. References should be listed separately corresponding to the body of the manuscript. The author should send three copies of his/her manuscript plus a short biography. Include also an abstract of not more than 100 words summarizing the paper.

All articles are anonymously reviewed by the editorial board entirely in terms of scholarly content. Previously published articles cannot be accepted.

Categories: Sports

Name: Thomas Katsaros, Ph.D., Editor
Material: All
Address: UNIVERSITY OF NEW HAVEN
Address: 300 ORANGE AVE
City/State/ZIP: WEST HAVEN CT 06516
Telephone: 203-932-7118
Fax: 203-931-6084
E-mail: mharvey@charger.newhaven.edu

Interrace Publications

INTERRACE (founded November 1989; circulation 25,000; bimonthly) focuses on issues concerning interracial, intercultural, interethnic couples—married or dating-families, and multiethnic people.

CHILD OF COLORS (founded January 1996) is a child care magazine for parents of interracial or transracially adopted children. Formerly *Biracial Child;* now incorporated into every issue of INTERRACE.

BLACK CHILD (founded September 1995; circulation 50,000; bimonthly) is a parenting/child care magazine for parents of African American children.

For **INTERRACE**, submissions...

1.) must have an interracial, intercultural or interethnic theme.

2.) can be nonfiction, news event, commentary, success story, research/study, personal account, expose', historical, entertainment, music, art, literature, love interest, friendship, race relations, interview, poetry. **Fiction not accepted** at this time.

3.) are not limited to black/white issues. Interaction between blacks, whites, Asians, Latinos, Native Americans, etc. is also desired.

4.) should be original. Previously published work acceptable.

LENGTH: Articles-800-plus words; Fillers accepted

PAY RATE: Subscriber-supported; *No payment*; national exposure; can supply up to 3 complimentary copies and/or free one-year subscription upon request

For **CHILD OF COLORS**, follow guidelines above except submissions...

1.) must have an interracial parenting or child care theme.

For **BLACK CHILD**, submissions...

1.) must have a (black) parenting or child care theme; interracial parenting themes also acceptable

2.) 2) can be nonfiction, news event, commentary, success story, research/study, personal account, expose', black history, multimedia reviews, race relations, interview. **Fiction not accepted** at this time.

3.) should be original. Previously published work acceptable.

LENGTH: Articles-800-plus words; Fillers accepted

PAY RATE: 4¢ PER WORD ($40 per 1,000 words)

PLEASE NOTE:

1.) Our staff is very limited, so please be very patient.

2.) Sample copies are $2 each.

3.) Include name, address, and phone number on submitted material.

4.) No vulgar or sexually explicit material considered for publication.

Categories: Nonfiction—Ethnic—Multicultural

Name: Submissions Editor
Material: All
Address: PO BOX 12048
City/State/ZIP: ATLANTA GA 30355
Telephone: 404-350-7877
Fax: 404-350-0819
E-mail: intrace@aol.com

IN TOUCH

In Touch/Indulge

GENERAL INFO: Emphasis is on the light-hearted, romantic, erotic, provocative and entertaining. No limits on sexual content or explicitness in fiction, **although safer sex must be depicted.** Please refrain from submitting stories involving fantastical characters (i.e. vampires, ghosts, Tarzan).

All individuals must be 18 years of age or older whether they are models or characters in fiction. All submissions are subject to editing.

Sample issue is $5.95/postage paid.

EROTIC FICTION & ARTICLES: 3,000 to 3,500 words; fiction or nonfiction; may be submitted on Mac Computer disk or via modem (please call for details); Fee Paid: $75

FEATURE ARTICLES: 2,500 to 3,500 words; *must be pre-approved by editor*; Fee Paid: $100

SHORT ARTICLES & CARTOONS: Under 2,500 words, size variable, short items, etc. Fee Paid: $25-$50

NON-MODEL PHOTOGRAPHY: Color or B&W prints acceptable; slides or transparencies preferred; no Polaroid or Instamatic, please; Fee Paid: $25—$35 per shot; submissions for Touch & Go are not compensated, unless prior arrangements are made.

MODEL PHOTOGRAPHY: Call or write for Photographer guidelines.

Fees listed are for one-time usage, first North American rights, paid upon acceptance (photographs/illustrations) or publication (stories/articles/cartoons).

Thank you.

Categories: Fiction—Erotica—Gay/Lesbian—Men's Fiction

Name: Alan W. Mills, Editor
Material: All
Address: 13122 SATICOY ST
City/State/ZIP: N HOLLYWOOD CA 91605
Telephone: 818-764-2288
Fax: 818-764-2307
E-mail: alan@intouchformen.com
Internet: www.intouchformen.com

Intuition Magazine
A Magazine for the
Higher Potential of the Mind

Intuition is a magazine dedicated to exploring and furthering the higher potential of the human mind. Although we deal with topics such as intuition, creativity, and spiritual development, we try to appeal to a broad readership, since it is our belief that everyone can relate to these issues in their lives. Specifically, we aim at exploring ways in which these areas of human experience can improve the quality of life in all areas of human endeavor, including: business; education; the arts; physical, mental, and emotional health; and personal growth.

Articles range in length from 750-5,000 words, depending upon the topic, and payment ranges from $25 for book reviews to $1,200 for feature-length cover stories.

Feature articles deal with a wide range of topics, including ways in which intuition is used in various areas of life, theories of creativity and the creative process, and different approaches to spiritual growth. We try to avoid journal-style articles that are overly academic in tone. We prefer pieces that are well-reported and include real-life examples of how intuition and creativity are used. In addition, articles should include good, solid documentation by a broad spectrum of experts in the field.

In addition to articles that detail groundbreaking research or cutting-edge approaches to fostering intuition and creativity, we prefer stories that contain information that readers can use to develop their own creative and intuitive abilities either through example or by direct experience.

Interviews: In each issue, we generally run one feature-length interview with a significant personality. These interviews include intuition and creativity trainers, researchers and thinkers in the fields of creativity and consciousness, futurists, spiritual leaders, and sometimes artists, writers, or musicians.

Departments usually run 750-2,000 words. They include:

Profiles of intuition trainers, creativity researchers, writers, artists, poets, musicians, and healers, as well as creators of tools (or games) for fostering intuition and creativity.

Intuition at Work: Real-life stories of people who have benefited from using their intuitive or creative skills in the workplace.

Frontier Science: Articles highlighting breakthroughs in science or ongoing research pertaining to consciousness, the mind-body connection, parapsychology, and creativity.

Intuitive Tools: Articles focusing on the history and application of a traditional approach to accessing intuitive information. Examples include: Tarot, the *I Ching*, shamanism, mysticism, alchemy, etc.

Book Reviews: We welcome reviews of books, audio and video tapes, and new oracular or divinatory tools (such as Tarot decks). Before sending complete reviews, please query us to check that we have not already reviewed the work you are considering (250-400 words).

First Person: A short personal essay recounting a firsthand experience of intuitive insight, synchronicity, or a paranormal occurrence. (approx. 750 words).

Submissions:

We welcome unsolicited ideas from freelancers. Submissions should be in the form of a query letter outlining in as much detail as possible the article idea, approximate length, and possible interviewees or contacts. Also, please include a brief bio, along with published writing samples and a SASE. Please do not call, and do not send full-length manuscripts. The one exception is essays for First Person, which should be submitted in their final form.

We will try to respond to all queries within four to six weeks. Sample issues are available upon request for $6.

Categories: New Age

Name: Submissions Editor
Material: All
Address: PO BOX 460773
City/State/ZIP: SAN FRANCISCO CA 94146
Telephone: 415-949-4240
Fax: 415-917-8905
E-mail: INTUITMAG@aol.com

IRIS

A Journal About Women
University of Virginia

IRIS: A Journal About Women offers feature stories, fiction, art and photography, poetry, book reviews, news, and personal essays focusing on women's issues. We reach a varied audience of both sexes that appreciates fine writing and cogent analysis of important issues of the day. We are a non-profit organization, staffed by volunteers. The magazine appears twice yearly, in November and April.

Please submit two typed, clean copies of all material and use language inclusive of differences in gender, sexual orientation, and race. Follow the parenthetical MLA format for citations.

Features should be no less than 2,500 and no more than 4,500 words. We're looking for timely, well-written pieces on topics such as cultural representation, race/ethnicity, spirituality, the politics of aging, international affairs, gay/lesbian issues, the arts, health, education, the law, and so on.

Personal essays may run up to 2,500 words. We are interested in all varieties of personal experience, but we are not interested in trite, sentimental language.

Book reviews should run around 900 words for a single book and 1,500 words for a combined review. Write to request the current book list.

Forerunners should run around 2,500 words. We are interested in in-depth analyses of the lives and works of women whose contributions in prior generations laid the groundwork for the concerns and emphases of modern feminist and women's liberation movements.

News items should run 500 to 1,000 words. We seek issues not generally covered in the mass media. Please keep in mind our twice yearly publishing cycle.

Fiction submissions should run between 2,500 and 8,000 words. We prefer a woman's slant or point of view. We're seeking a special "something" that sets the stories apart from those that appear in mainstream publications.

Poetry is selected with a view toward presenting a variety of women's voices and experiences. We seek poems that take risks and have a freshness of particularity and style. Send no more than three poems. Please be patient as turnaround times can be up to six months.

We also accept **cinema and music reviews**. And we are always looking for art & photography—especially with a good story behind them.

Upon acceptance, please submit a copy of your piece on a Macintosh-formatted computer diskette, Microsoft Word 5.0 and higher or ASCII (text) format. We also require a brief biography (two or three sentences).

IRIS acquires one—time rights to the work we publish. If in the future you sell the piece to a reprint publication, remind the editors to forward a standard permission form to us and acknowledge that the piece first appeared here.

You will be paid a one—year subscription including the magazine in which your work appears. Additional copies are available to contributing authors for $3.00 each.

Thank you for sending your work to us.

We look forward to having it appear in our magazine.

Categories: Fiction—Nonfiction—Arts—Feminism—Gay/Lesbian—Multicultural—Photography—Poetry—Short Stories—Women's Fiction—Women's Issues

Name: Susan Brady, Editor-in-Chief
Material: Personal Essays/Art, Book Reviews (Art, Movies, Music)
Name: Margaret Muirhead, Fiction Editor
Material: Fiction
Name: Margo Figgins, Poetry Editor
Material: Poetry
Name: Jenny Koster, Features Editor
Material: Nonfiction Features
Address: THE WOMEN'S CENTER, BOX 323 HSC
Address: UNIVERSITY OF VIRGINIA
City/State/ZIP: CHARLOTTESVILLE VA 22908
Telephone: 804-924-4500
Fax: 804-982-2901

It's Your Choice Magazine
Journal of Ethics and Morality

Regular Features

Editorials—Staff written; Columns by special assignment.

Feature Articles—Open to freelancers

Short Stories—Open to freelancers

Op-Ed Commentaries—Open to freelancers, payment: 5 copies

Personal Experience—Open to freelancers, payment: 5 copies

"Bottom Line" Fillers—50 words max., payment $5

Letters to the Editor—Open to the general public, no payment

Manuscripts must be:

1.) Typed (Courier 10-pitch only). Computer printouts acceptable if legible.

2.) No more than 1,000 words (four pages), *Do not overwrite.*

3.) Original mss. only, no clips

4.) One manuscript at a time

MANUSCRIPT REVIEW POLICY. Newly arrived manuscripts are reviewed at least once a month. Those not meeting our guidelines are rejected immediately. If your manuscript is not returned within four weeks, it is because it merits further consideration by our editors. It will be returned as soon as a final decision is reached. Feel free to submit elsewhere in the meantime.

Queries: We do not respond to queries concerning mss. to be submitted. Send complete manuscript. To follow-up on retained mss., send SASE.

Payment varies from copies to $1 per word. If we would like to publish your article or story, we'll make an offer of payment by sending you a "Publication Agreement." When we receive your written acceptance (signed copy) of our offer, payment will be authorized within 24 hours, unless otherwise stipulated in the offer. You should receive a check or money order within ten days.

IMPORTANT: All articles/stories must be related to ethics/morality issues in an essential way. "Tacking on" a couple of statements about ethics/morality to a story you have already written will not do. We regard ethics as the scientific study of the rightness or wrongness of human behavior in any context, which opens the field to a wide variety of articles. You might write about the larger social issues such as abortion, murder, capital punishment, war, greed; or about personal actions such as your son's hiding his report card because he got an F in "playing."

CURRENT TOPICS OF INTEREST: Crime, capital punishment, abortion, euthanasia, learning behavior, religious behavior, self-destructiveness, honesty/dishonesty, cheating, behavior/decision-making by government officials, personal responsibility (concept of duty, etc.), self-development, concern for others, sexual behavior, lifestyles, environment, schooling, criminal justice, you name it.

We look forward to receiving your submission.

Subscription $9.84. Sample copy $2.00.

Categories: Fiction—Nonfiction—Adventure—African-American—Asian-American—Children—Crime—Culture—Diet—Education—Environment—Ethics—Family—Feminism—Gay/Lesbian—Government—Health—Inspirational—Juvenile—Lifestyles—Marriage—Morality—New Age—Parenting—Philosophy—Politics—Psychology—Public Policy—Relationships—Religion—Senior Citizens—Sexuality—Short Stories—Society—Spiritual—Teen—True Crime—Women's Fiction—Women's Issues—Young Adult

Name: Editor
Material: All
Address: PO BOX 7135
City/State/ZIP: RICHMOND VA 23221-0135

Jack and Jill

Please refer to Children's Better Health Institute

Jam Rag

Jam Rag's editorial coverage is primarily related to the Michigan/Toledo area independent music scene—interviews, reviews, etc. of independent musicians. We are also interested in stories about politics, the environment and so on, but especially from a social activism point of view. Our current focus is on the corporate entertainment state (label and broadcaster consortiums) which dominates the public airwaves.

We're looking for feisty material, but heavy on facts and light on opinion. No assignments given; our writers set the editorial direction of the paper, at least within the prescribed topic range. Nor do we solicit a certain style, or care much for good grammar for that matter. We want our contributors' unique personalities to survive the editing, and that ever-evolving blend is what makes *Jam Rag*. Call, or send your stuff. Oh yeah, we do pay—but not much and not too quickly!

Categories: Entertainment—Music—Politics—Society

Name: Submissions Editor
Material: All
Address: PO BOX 20076
City/State/ZIP: FERNDALE MI 48220
Telephone: 248-542-8090

Jewish Action

Thank you for expressing an interest in our publication.

Submissions should cover topics of interest to an international Orthodox Jewish audience. Articles related to current ongoing issues of Jewish life and experience, human interest features, poetry, art, music and book reviews, historical pieces and humor are all acceptable. Because the magazine is a quarterly, we do not generally publish articles which concern specific timely events. Authors must be thoroughly familiar with Orthodox beliefs and lifestyle!

Articles should average 1,000-3,000 words, including foot-notes. If used, foot-notes should follow the article. The author's name, address and daytime telephone number should be enclosed with the article.

Authors will be informed of a decision within six—eight weeks of submission.

Jewish Action is published by the Orthodox Union. The editor is Charlotte Friedland.

Categories: Jewish Interests

Name: Submissions Editor
Material: All
Address: 333 7TH AVE
City/State/ZIP: NEW YORK NY 10001
Telephone: 212-613-8146
Fax: 212-613-8333

Jewish Currents

JEWISH CURRENTS prints articles, reviews, fiction and poetry pertaining to Jewish subjects or presenting a Jewish point of view on an issue of interest. Pieces submitted should ideally be 3-4 magazine pages in length, but in any case, should not exceed 5 such pages. (A magazine page contains approximately 600 words.) Submissions must be typed and accompanied by a SASE and a brief biographical note including the author's publishing history. We do not accept simultaneous submissions, nor do we reprint material already published elsewhere.

Finally, JEWISH CURRENTS is unable to pay its contributors beyond a year's free subscription plus six copies of the issue in which they appear.

Categories: Jewish Interests
Name: Morris U. Schappes, Editor
Material: All

Address: 22 E 17TH ST STE 601
City/State/ZIP: NEW YORK NY 10003
Telephone: 212-924-5740
Fax: 212-924-5740

Jewish News of Western Massachusetts

The *Jewish News* is a biweekly publication of news and features serving the Jewish communities of Western Massachusetts. Writers are encouraged to submit unsolicited manuscripts whose content is of interest to an exclusively Jewish readership.

Manuscripts should be between 500 and 1,000 words. Accompanying photographs and illustrations may also be submitted. We prefer black and white or line drawings, but color artwork can be used.

The *Jewish News* purchases one-time publication rights to manuscripts. Writers will be paid within one month of publication at a rate of $15-$35 per story and $5 per published photograph.

We have an ongoing need for original, creative writing on Jewish life-cycle events and Jewish holidays. The following is a list of special promotional sections published annually in our paper:

- Jewish Weddings (2)
- Bar and Bat Mitzvah Guide (2)
- Focus on Jewish Business
- Health (monthly)
- Senior Living (monthly)
- Holiday Guides
- Book Reviews
- Jewish Kitchens

Other Publications

Annual Guide to Jewish Living in Western New England
EMEK—A Jewish Literary Review for Western Massachusetts

Do not send queries.

Categories: Jewish Interests

Name: Kenneth White, Editor
Material: All
Address: PO BOX 269
City/State/ZIP: NORTHAMPTON MA 01061
Telephone: 413-582-9870
Fax: 413-582-9847
E-mail: JWNews@aol.com

Joiners' Quarterly

Dear Author,

Thank you for thinking of *Joiners' Quarterly*. While our basic interest lies in timber framing, we also pursue several topics that are relevant to natural and traditional building. We look for new enclosure systems such as straw bales, straw/clay and wood chips/clay, rammed earth, wheat straw panels, or any other new products that would be suitable for enclosing a timber frame.

We also look for articles on mechanical systems such as heating, air conditioning, solar, plumbing and electrical and how they can be applied to timber frame structures, whether it is an article about new innovations, historical uses, or simply installation techniques and precautions. We're always looking for articles on joinery techniques, timber frame design, CAD programs compatible with timber framing, engineering aspects whether modern or historical. Natural house building and whole house building systems also appeal to us.

Other topics: historical building techniques (especially if they are still viable today), hand-hewing, thatch, historic paints, barns, outbuildings, boats, innovative projects, new materials or equipment that would pertain to any of the above, green building. We also desire book and video reviews on any of the above subjects. The more relevant your articles are to timber framing and sustainable construction, the more likely we are to be interested in publishing them.

Payment is generally $50 per published page including photos and/or diagrams.

Manuscripts should be typewritten. Each page should have a page number, title of article, and author's name. Photos should be developed "glossy" and should be labeled with a suggested caption and ID info on back. We do not pay for cover photos.

Diskettes need to be Mac formatted in Microsoft Word.

Call for e-mail submissions.

Thank you,

Editorial Staff at JQ

Steve Chappell, Laurie LaMountain, Jim Marks, and Janot Mendler

Categories: Nonfiction—Architecture—Engineering—Environment—Sustainable Building—Technology—Timber Framing

Name: Jim Marks, Editorial Assistant
Material: All
Address: PO BOX 249
City/State/ZIP: BROWNFIELD ME 04010
Telephone: 207-935-3720
Fax: 207-935-4575
E-mail: foxmaple@nxi.com

The Journal of Adventist Education

The Journal of Adventist Education is the professional publication of Seventh-day Adventist teachers and administrators, and should address topics of interest to that group.

The target audience may be elementary, secondary, college, or university. Writers should define their target group precisely and address its concerns in a specific manner.

Articles may deal with educational theory or practice, although the *Journal* seeks to emphasize the practical. Articles dealing with the creative and effective use of methods to enhance teaching skills or learning in the classroom are especially welcome. Whether theoretical or practical, such essays should demonstrate the skillful integration of Seventh-day Adventist faith/values and learning.

The *Journal*'s constituency is international, a fact writers should keep in mind as they explore the implications or applications of a given topic. Special attention, where applicable, should be given to the concerns of minorities.

Periodically, issues will deal extensively with a single topic or issue. Articles representing various approaches or the in-depth discussion of aspects of the issue will be welcome.

Types of articles with broad audience appeal acceptable to the *Journal* are the following: new methods and educational approaches, effective administration and supervision, classroom control, reviews of recent books of interest to educators, how-to articles, short inspirational or personal-experience articles, poetry, news notes, and brief reports of recent events or special programs at schools. Clear, sharp, black-and-white photographs and appropriate charts and graphs are a welcome adjunct.

When sending materials to the *Journal*, include the following information: your position as an educator, or status if a student; social security number and home address if employed in the United States.

The following manuscript form is preferred: Articles should be six to eight pages long, with a maximum of ten pages in length, including references. Two-part articles will be considered. Material should be printed using a 70-character line and standard paragraph indention. Subheads should be inserted at appropriate intervals.

Quotations of more than five lines should be single-spaced and indented five spaces from the margin. Please follow the instructions in the *Chicago Manual of Style* for bibliography and footnotes. Endnotes, in numerical order, should include complete bibliographic information (author, title of work, volume and number if applicable, city of publication, publisher, date, and page number). *Please enclose photocopied pages to verify facts and quotations. The information to be photocopied is as follows: the page(s) on which the fact or quotation occurs, the title page of the book or journal, and copyright information.* Authors should obtain permission for reprints of charts, graphs, and photos.

The Journal of Adventist Education is published five times yearly, with approximately eight articles appearing in each issue. Due to space limitations, many articles will not be published immediately. Articles should be submitted at least five months before publication date. The editorial staff reserves the right to edit all manuscripts as they deem necessary.

Categories: Nonfiction—Christian Interests—Education

Name: Submissions Editor
Material: All
Address: 12501 OLD COLUMBIA PIKE
City/State/ZIP: SILVER SPRING MD 20904-6600
Telephone: 301-680-5075
Fax: 301-622-9627
E-mail: 74617.1231@compuserve.com

Journal of Asian Martial Arts

MESSAGE FROM THE EDITOR

There are more aspects related to Asian martial arts than commonly meet the eye. Most publications have focused on this subject only to satisfy the interests of the mass market, while other scholarly writings limit themselves to a highly specialized audience. Our journal spans both types of readership. How? Although the journal treats the subject with academic accuracy, we believe that writing styles need not lose the reader! The *Journal of Asian Martial Arts* offers a mature, well-rounded view of this uniquely fascinating subject, attracting a readership that has a close affinity to Asian history and culture.

Our journal logo stylizes the tips of a sword and pen—symbolic of the martial and the cultured. Entwined, they represent an embodiment of balanced characteristics that is necessary for individual and social welfare. Viewed in this perspective, the field of Asian martial arts offers a broad range of interrelated material to cover. Therefore, being both general and specific, our journal offers a unique display case for works by artists and writers. We appreciate your interest and thank you for considering our journal as a medium for your work. Feel free to contact me personally, the editor, regarding any aspect of the journal.

EDITORIAL POLICY

The *Journal of Asian Martial Arts* is a cover perfect bound 8.5"x11" quarterly journal. We publish three types of materials: (1) scholarly articles based on primary research in recognized scholarly disciplines, e.g., cultural anthropology, comparative religions, psychology, film theory, and criticism, etc.; (2) more informal, but nevertheless substantial interviews (with scholars, master practitioners, etc.) and reports on particular genres, techniques, etc.; and (3) reviews of books and audiovisual materials on the martial arts. These three types of materials are organized in separate sections of the journal.

In order to ensure the quality of all submissions in terms of scholarship as well as writing, each submission will be reviewed by at least two members of our editorial board. We look forward to making the journal accessible to all readers while establishing and maintaining a high quality of scholarship, writing, and graphics.

Editorial content:
- interview/profile • art/aesthetics • philosophic
- technique • scientific • legal
- announcements • cross-cultural • translation
- weaponry • reports • social
- media reviews • comparative • geographic
- historical • literary • health

Article length: 2,000 to 10,000 words for feature articles.
Review length: 1,000 or less for news items, reviews and reports.
Buys: First world rights with reprint rights.
Pays: For articles, $150-500 on publication; plus 2 copies. Payment in copies for reviews.
Audience: Although the journal is targeted for college-level readers, it is distributed to persons of varied backgrounds, ages and occupations. For this reason, articles are written in a clear style for those who may not be totally familiar with the subject and its particular vocabulary. Internationally distributed: practitioners, scholars, schools, libraries, bookstores, and institutes.
Reports: 2-4 weeks on queries; 1-2 months on manuscripts.
Bionote: Given. Include a short summary of your background and credentials (academic and martial) in your cover letter.

STYLE DETAILS FOR WRITERS

Writers should have at least some martial arts experience and a great familiarity with Asian culture. Query letters should tell of the writer's qualifications, provide a clear outline of the intended article, and state if illustrations are available. We pull our hair out when submissions arrive that simply rehash old material or are geared to the wrong audience! Articles are published for knowledgeable readers and must offer special information and insights not available elsewhere.

It is not necessary to provide clips. We like to work with writers and are happy to provide suggestions on how to improve any materials that do not meet all criteria the first time through our office door. If you decide to submit a manuscript, have a martial artist and/or Asian scholar critique it first. Of course, the best guide for suitability is the journal itself.

Reviews all articles on speculation. Typed manuscripts or letter-quality computer printout acceptable. If possible, also provide text on computer disk in any basic word processing program (Macintosh formats preferred). Articles must be historically and technically accurate with a list of references at the end. Keep footnotes at a minimum.

Romanization: Provide Chinese and Japanese characters when possible for important names, terms, and places mentioned in the article. Give personal names in the Asian order with family name first. We use Pinyin Romanization for Chinese.

DETAILS FOR PHOTOGRAPHERS & ARTISTS

We expect the quality of article illustrations to be of equally high quality as the articles we publish. The talents of a professional photographer should be utilized in order to meet the proper standards for printing. Most photographs and other illustrations should emphasize what is important to the text.

Special note must be taken when photographs are used to illustrate technical aspects of a martial art. Please do not include distracting backgrounds, such as school insignia or busy geometric patterns! A simple, plain background works best in these cases. We want to view the martial art, not studio decor or geographic scenery. However, we do encourage photographers to be creative whenever appropriate. Photos showing movement, a mood enhancing environment, or a particular social aspect are welcome whenever they portray a significant insight, feeling, or thought that relates to martial arts.

Material Requirements: We will only consider good quality black-&-white glossy prints, negatives, and color transparencies. Color photography is reproduced in black-&-white inside the journal, but full color if used on the cover. Contact sheets and photocopies of hand art can be submitted for preliminary review purposes.

Acceptance & Payment: Reviews art work on speculation. In the case of computer generated art, we prefer Macintosh formats, such as QuarkXpress, Adobe Illustrator, or PhotoShop. Rates vary, but are competitive with other publications of similar standards.

Model Releases: Photo model releases and captions are required for all photos.

Categories: Asian-American—Culture—Health—History—Martial Arts—Military—Physical Fitness—Sports

Name: Michael A. DeMarco, Editor-in-Chief
Material: All
Address: 821 W 24TH ST
City/State/ZIP: ERIE PA 16502
Telephone: 814-455-9517
Fax: 814-838-7811
E-mail: viamedia@ncinter.net

JCN

Journal of Christian Nursing

The *Journal of Christian Nursing* strives to help Christian nurses view nursing practice through the eyes of faith. It is a professional journal by and for nurses. Topics covered include Christian concepts in nursing, professional issues, spiritual care, ethics, values, healing and wholeness, psychology and religion, personal and professional life, patient/client experiences which include a faith dimension (including case studies), and stories of nurses who have stepped out in faith to care for others in new or unusual ways in the U.S. or overseas. Articles must be relevant to Christian nursing and consistent with the purposes and statement of faith of Nurses Christian Fellowship (available on request). *Priority will be given to nurse authors, although some articles by non-nurses will be considered.*

Preparing Your Manuscript

1. **Style.** Scan a recent copy of JCN. You will see that the style is popular, not academic. Articles should be written to communicate clearly to staff nurses. Avoid (or define) technical jargon and abbreviations (these may differ in other clinical settings). Use lively illustrations. Give practical examples. Share; don't preach. Academic papers may have some good content which JCN readers would appreciate, but they must be rewritten in article format. See "Avoiding the 'School Paper Style' Rejection," by Suzanne Hall Johnson, *Nurse Author & Editor*, Summer 1991, for help in revising an academic paper. Style is governed by *The Chicago Manual of Style*, 13th edition (Chicago/London: University of Chicago Press, 1982).

2. **References.** Limit your references to only those necessary to document your point. Avoid presenting a review of the literature. As the author of the article *you* are the expert. Endnotes must contain the full name of authors (not just initials of first name) and be listed as they appear in article, not alphabetically. Be sure to include page numbers. See back issues of JCN for examples. You are responsible for accuracy in citation and interpretation of resources. Check spelling of authors' names carefully. If a reference has more than one author, list them in the correct order.

3. **Length.** Most articles range from 6 to 12 double-spaced, typewritten pages. Essays on "Why I Love Nursing" should be about 750 to 900 words. Use one-inch margins.

4. Number your pages and put your name on each page.
Submitting Your Manuscript

1. **Query letter.** If your article fits these guidelines, we prefer to receive the manuscript without a query letter. However, if you are uncertain about the suitability of your topic, please query either by letter or phone. *Most articles by non-nurse freelance authors are rejected unless they have outstanding insights valuable to nurses.* We will work with nurses who have significant information to communicate but need help with writing style.

2. **Manuscript.** Send one copy, typed, to the address below. If your manuscript is accepted, we prefer to have a copy on disk.

3. **Review process.** Manuscripts with significant professional content will be sent to several review panel members for evaluation. If your manuscript is reviewed you will receive copies of the reviewers' comments. We may ask you to revise an article based on reviewers' suggestions. Names of authors and reviewers are kept confidential in the review process.

4. **Illustrations.** Good candid photos can bring an article to life. We can use diagrams and illustrations. Photos and illustrations will be used at the discretion of the editorial staff and art director. Do not write on photos or use paper clips. Include captions or explanatory material with each illustration. Place it in a labeled envelope and clip envelope to manuscript.

Note: Identify all persons in photos and include a signed, written release for each. Suggested release format: *I hereby give (author's name) permission to submit this photo of (subject's name) for possible use in the Journal of Christian Nursing.*

5. **About the Author.** Give a brief description of yourself including your nursing credentials, where you work, your church and community involvement, and any other information you think readers might like to know—especially anything that would enhance your credibility in the topic covered in your article.

6. **Remuneration.** Ranges from $0 to $80. We do not pay for book reviews, but reviewers may keep the book reviewed.

7. **Rights.** JCN usually buys first rights. We occasionally purchase reprint rights. If your article has been published before, please indicate where and when. *Never submit an article to two publications at the same time.* We retain the right to grant permission to photocopy articles for educational purposes.

8. **Poetry.** JCN no longer accepts poetry.

Categories: (All categories only as they pertain to Christian nurses!) Nonfiction—Children—Christian Interests—Disabilities—Education—Family—Feminism—General Interest—Health—History—Humor—Inspirational—Interview—Multicultural—Music—Nursing—Physical Fitness—Psychology—Relationships—Religion—Spiritual—Women's Issues

Name: Melodee Yohe, Managing Editor
Material: All
Address: PO BOX 1650
City/State/ZIP: DOWNERS GROVE IL 60515
Telephone: 630-887-2500
Fax: 630-887-2520
E-mail: jcn@ivpress.com

Journal of Information Ethics
St. Cloud State University

Manuscripts dealing with any aspect of information ethics

are welcome. The *Journal of Information Ethics* deals with ethics in all areas of information or knowledge production and dissemination. This includes, but is not limited to, library and information science, education for these professions, technology, government publication and legislation, graphic display, computer security, database management, disinformation, peer review, privacy, censorship, cyberspace, and information liability approached from sociological, philosophical, theoretical, and applied perspectives. The *Journal of Information Ethics* publishes letters to the editor, brief notes (4-6 pages), essays (10-25 pages), and book or topical journal issue reviews. Upon publication, authors will receive an honorarium and two copies of the issue.

General Instructions: When preparing a manuscript, please avoid right-hand justification and number pages consecutively. Two copies of the manuscript are sufficient. If a computer disk is available, please enclose it. Include your name, affiliation, address (which will be printed with your article), and phone number. On a separate sheet of paper, provide a biographical statement of 75 words or fewer, which will be edited and published in the "About the Contributors" section.

Content: All submissions must deal with some aspect of information ethics. Scholarship does not have to be mind-numbing, tedious, or pedantic; try to create stimulating, controversial, and enticing pieces.

Style: This is a scholarly journal. Therefore, develop paragraphs fully; neither contractions nor first or second person pronouns; avoid repetition, jargon, sexist language, and awkward syntactical constructions; do use a limited number of succinct headings and subheadings; and underline or italicize when required.

Carefully honed, mellifluous prose is as important as substantive content. A good way to achieve these objectives is to show the manuscript to a colleague whose writing you respect. All accepted material is subject to editorial emendation.

Documentation: Use current APA (American Psychological Association) style. Do not number references. Avoid footnotes. Follow the style manual *carefully;* attend to the details of order, punctuation, inversions, upper and lower cases, and the precise method of parenthetical documentation.

Please include a self-addressed, stamped envelope.
Query or send manuscripts directly to the editor.
Thank you.

Categories: Nonfiction—Ethics—Information Science—Internet—Library Science—Philosophy—Public Policy—Technology

Name: Robert Hauptman, Editor
Material: All
Address: LEARNING RESOURCES SERVICES
Address: 720 4TH AVE S
Address: ST CLOUD STATE UNIVERSITY
City/State/ZIP: ST CLOUD MN 56301
Telephone: 320-255-4822
Fax: 320-255-4778

Journal of Modern Literature
Temple University

The editors of the *Journal of Modern Literature* welcome submissions of research-based studies of modern literature as well as critical studies based on scholarship. Work based upon examination of manuscripts, correspondence, and the like is particularly welcome.

Essays should conform to the JML House Style, which varies somewhat from the 1977 *MLA Style Sheet*. Please see recent issues for typical documentation style.

We usually send acknowledgements within a week of receipt of the article. Since the JML is a fully juried journal, the review process usually takes 8-10 weeks, although during the summer and Christmas vacations the delay may be slightly longer.

If the article is accepted, we ask that the writer send us a copy on a WordPerfect 5.1 diskette. A list of specific requirements will accompany the letter of acceptance.

All articles published in the JML receive a Foundation for Modern Literature copyright.

Our editor's introduction in Volume 20, number 2, should be of interest to prospective contributors regarding articles most likely to be accepted:

JML remains a scholarly journal in the traditional sense of that term. That is, we are interested especially in manuscript, historical, biographical, and related forms of archival studies and in the new critical light which they can sometimes throw on authors and texts. We continue to publish only those exceptional critical readings which are strong enough to demand publication.

Categories: Academic—Literature

Name: Dr. Morton Levitt, Editor-in-Chief
Material: All
Address: ANDERSON HALL RM 921
Address: TEMPLE UNIVERSITY
City/State/ZIP: PHILADELPHIA PA 19122
Telephone: 215-204-8505
Fax: 215-204-9620

Kaleidoscope
International Magazine of Literature, Fine Arts, and Disability

KALEIDOSCOPE Magazine has a creative focus that examines the experiences of disability through literature and the fine arts. Unique to the field of disability studies, this award-winning publication is not an advocacy or rehabilitation journal. Rather, KALEIDOSCOPE expresses the experiences of disability from the perspective of individuals, families, healthcare professionals, and society as a whole. The material chosen for KALEIDOSCOPE avoids stereotypical, patronizing, and sentimental attitudes about disability. Although the content always focuses on a particular aspect of disability, writers with and without disabilities are welcome to submit their work

The criteria for good writing apply: effective technique, thought-provoking subject matter, and in general, a mature grasp of the art of story-telling. Works should not use stereotyping, patronizing, or offending language about disability ("uses a wheelchair" not "confined to a wheelchair" or "wheelchair bound"). KALEIDOSCOPE uses person-first language ("person who has cerebral palsy" not "cerebral palsied').

KALEIDOSCOPE is published twice a year, in January with a submission deadline of August 1, and in July with a submission deadline of March 1.

KALEIDOSCOPE accepts:

Nonfiction—Articles relating to the arts, both literary and visual, interviews, or personal accounts.

Fiction—Short stories with a well-crafted plot and engaging characters—5,000 words maximum.

Poetry—Poems that have strong imagery, evocative language—six poems maximum.

Book reviews—Reviews that are substantive, timely, powerful works about publications in the field of disability and/or the arts. The writer's opinion of the work being reviewed should be clear. The review should be a literary work in its own right.

Visual arts—Art of all media, from watercolor and charcoals to collage and sculpture; three to six works maximum. We accept art in 5"x7" or 8"x10" black and white glossy photos or 35mm slides, or color photos. The photos should have minimal background with the art as the main focus. Include captions on the photos stating the size, medium, and title of work.

Publishing information
- Considers unsolicited material
- Accepts simultaneous submissions
- Publishes previously published work
- Acknowledges receipt in two weeks
- Rejects or accepts within six months
- Accepts photographs or illustrations complementing work
- Reserves right to minor editing without author's approval; substantive editing with approval

Payment information
- Payment is made upon publication, and varies from $10 to $125.
- Contributors receive two complimentary copies of the magazine.
- Copyright reverts to author upon publication.

Subscription rates:
 Individual—$9 per year
 Institutional—$14 per year
 Sample copy—$4, prepaid
 Single copy—$5
Add $8 for international, $5 for Canadian (U.S. funds only) for postage and handling.

Categories: Arts—Disabilities—Literature

Name: Gail Willmot, Senior Editor
Material: All
Address: 701 S MAIN ST
City/State/ZIP: AKRON OH 44311
Telephone: 330-762-9755
Fax: 330-762-0912

ꝃKalliope

Kalliope
A Journal of Women's Art

Kalliope is recognized as one of the *best* women's literary journals in the U.S.A. 1998 marks *Kalliope*'s twentieth anniversary, which makes us one of the oldest feminist literary journals in the U.S.! Please support *Kalliope* in our effort to ensure that women's works will continue to be seen and heard.

Kalliope publishes poetry, short fiction, interviews, reviews, and visual art by women. We are open to experimental forms. Please submit poems in groups of 3-5; submit short fiction under 3,500 words.

Visual art should be sent in groups of 4-10 works. We require B&W professional quality glossy prints made from negatives. Please supply photo credits, date of work, title, medium, and size on the back of each photo submitted. Include artist's resume and model releases where applicable. We welcome an artist's statement of 50-75 words.

Please include SASE and a short contributor's note with *all* submissions. Foreign contributors must send U.S. postage or International Reply Coupons. Manuscripts without SASE will be neither read nor returned. Payment is usually in copies; a grant sometimes permits a small stipend. Copyright reverts to the author upon request. Because each submission is reviewed by several member of the *Kalliope* Writers' Collective, response time may be 3-6 months.

Thank you, in advance, for your patience.

Categories: Fiction—Arts—Biography—Literature—Poetry—Women's Fiction—Women's Issues—Writing

Name: Submissions Editor
Material: All
Address: 3939 ROOSEVELT BLVD
City/State/ZIP: JACKSONVILLE FL 32205

Karate/Kung Fu Illustrated

Thank you for your interest in writing for KKI, one of the oldest martial arts publications in the United States. The magazine's subjects include martial arts styles and techniques, training methods, historical pieces, health and fitness articles, and interviews with prominent martial artists.

Before mailing a completed manuscript to KKI, we advise you to send a query letter. It will save your time and ours. Describe your proposed article, including a sample lead or story outline. If the subject attracts our interest and has not been covered too recently, we may request to see the article on a speculation basis.

Articles must address an area of specific interest or concern for the serious martial artist. The vast majority are educational; they either teach technical and strategic skills, or enlighten the reader about historical and philosophical matters. Writing should capture reader interest with a strong lead, then hold it with information that is exact, concrete and focused around a strong central theme. All quotes and anecdotes should pertain to that theme.

KKI seldom uses first-person accounts, because most are of interest only to the author and his or her friends. In addition, while many instructors are dedicated and high-ranking, the magazine rarely requests personality profiles. (If you do choose to write about an individual, your article should prove that your subject is unique or particularly significant.) Remember: if you have a chance to meet or train with a great martial artist and want to write an article afterward, discuss what that person knows rather than how his or her life has unfolded.

All statements and quotes must be accurate and verifiable. Use authoritative sources and cross-check your information. Be certain of all spellings—especially names and foreign words-and define foreign terms in parentheses after first usage only.

Manuscripts should be 1,000 to 3,000 words long, and typed. If you use a computer, please output to a laser or ink jet printer. Because we electronically scan freelance submissions, we require quality printouts. Please include black-and-white lead and technique photos *and negatives* with plain, contrasting backgrounds. If absolutely necessary, we can use color photographs with sharp contrast and high definition. Feature articles receive $100 to $150, and we pay upon publication. Simultaneous or previously published submissions must be identified as such.

Robert Young
Executive Editor
Categories: Martial Arts

Name: Submissions Editor
Material: All
Address: PO BOX 918
City/State/ZIP: SANTA CLARITA CA 91380
Telephone: 805-257-4066
Fax: 805-257-3028

The Kenyon Review

The Kenyon Review
Kenyon College

SUBMISSIONS: Material offered for first publication only is considered. Simultaneous submissions are not accepted We consider short fiction and essays (up to 7,500 words), poetry (up to 10 pages), plays (up to 35 pages), excerpts (up to 35 pages) from larger works and translations of poetry and short prose. The original-language work must accompany the translation and the translator is responsible for author permission. We do not consider unsolicited reviews or interviews. We do not accept electronic submissions.

Unsolicited manuscripts are read September-November and February-March. Review of submissions takes up to four months. We generally follow *The Chicago Manual of Style* and *Webster's Ninth New Collegiate Dictionary*. Authors planning to use end notes and/or citations should send a stamped, self-addressed envelope for our citation style guide before submitting manuscripts.

WRITING PROGRAMS: Each summer *The Kenyon Review*, in association with Kenyon College, conducts two residential writing programs. Distinguished visiting writers and instructors lead the select groups of participants. College and non-degree graduate credits may be earned in the ten-day WRITERS WORKSHOP, and financial assistance is available for the two-week YOUNG WRITERS AT KENYON program. Applications for both programs are accepted through March. Call or write for information.

SUBSCRIPTIONS: Individuals—one year $22, two years $40, three years $60. libraries and institutions—$30/year. Add $8 per year for foreign addresses. Agency discount, foreign and domestic, 15%. Claims for missing issues will be honored only within a four-month period following publication (six months for foreign subscribers).

Single copies: $8 single issue, $11 double issue (Summer/Fall), includes postage and handling.

Classroom discounts: 40% discount and free teaching copy for orders of 10 or more non-returnable copies for classroom use. Copies of available Old Series back issues priced higher. **Microfilm** versions are available from University Microfilms International, 300 North Zeeb Road, Ann Arbor, MI 48106 (800-521-0600). Selected works from recent issues are available on **Audio tapes.** Call or write *The Kenyon Review* for information.

Indexed/Abstracted in *Abstracts of English Studies, American Humanities Index, Annual Bibliography of English Language and Literature, An Index to Book Reviews in the Humanities* and *MLA International Bibliography.*

PERMISSIONS: Authors in the New Series (beginning in 1979) hold the rights to their individual works and should be contacted directly. *The Kenyon Review* may be able to help in locating these authors. Permission for republishing works from the Old Series (through 1970) should be requested in writing by mail, fax, or e-mail.

Categories: Fiction—Nonfiction—Arts—Drama—General Interest—Language—Literature—Multicultural—Poetry—Short Stories—Writing

Name: Submissions Editor
Material: All
Address: KENYON COLLEGE
City/State/ZIP: GAMBIER OH 43022
Telephone: 614-427-5208
Fax: 614-427-5417
E-mail: kenyonreview@kenyon.edu

Kinesis

Kinesis *suff.* 1. Motion.

There's quite a relaxed atmosphere here at our editorial offices. One of our editors is cranking away at his computer every morning by 7:30 a.m., another doesn't even show up until noon. There's usually a dog asleep under a desk somewhere. We like to listen to music while we work, and we put away endless pots of coffee. We don't have too many rules, but we have a philosophy—*If it moves, print it!* We don't have any "types" of writing that we will or won't print. We judge everything on whether it moves. *It has to move!*

What does that mean? It means we don't like inquiries. We'd rather see the piece. Inquiries don't convey movement. Only the actual words you've chosen can do that. It means you shouldn't be afraid to send us anything. Whether fiction, poetry, essays, book or movie reviews, illustrations or photography, we judge it all by the same criteria: Movement! Remember, the words you use, how you use them, is infinitely more important than what your piece is about. Please do include a cover letter with your submission. We like to know a little about you, it makes our day more interesting.

We realize this isn't all that helpful. You wanted guidelines and we're giving you philosophy and mumbo jumbo. What might be helpful is reading the magazine. That's the best way to learn what we're all about. Subscriptions are $20 for one year-12 monthly issues. Sample copies are available for $4.

We generally print 2-3 short stories, 6-8 poems, 2-3 essays and 2-3 book reviews each issue. In addition we have 4 columnists who write for us each month. We respond to submissions within 6 weeks, usually a lot sooner. Don't worry about length. If it moves, we'll make room.

We have a readership of more than 7,000 and we're distributed by subscription and sold in bookstores, art galleries and coffee houses. We're in stores large and small, including urban centers like Seattle, Portland, San Francisco and Manhattan; places like Spokane, Missoula, Sausalito and New Hope, and in many University bookstores.

Payment—One year's subscription and 5 copies.

We hope to hear from you soon!

Categories: Fiction—Nonfiction—Book Reviews—Food/Drink—Literature—Movie Reviews—Music Reviews—Poetry—Short Stories—Writing

Name: Leif Peterson, Editor
Material: All
Address: PO BOX 4007
City/State/ZIP: WHITEFISH MT 59937
Telephone: 406-756-1193

Kitchen Garden

Kitchen Garden is a bimonthly magazine for home gardeners who love to grow their own vegetables, fruits, and herbs and use them in cooking. We are a how-to magazine that provides solid, useful information in an engaging, entertaining style. About 70% of our content is devoted to gardening and the other 30% to cooking. Most of our readers have some gardening and cooking experience, and a number of them are advanced in both areas. We incorporate material that is credible and informative to the expert but is accessible and instructive to the novice.

We run six types of feature articles: (1) Plant Profiles, (2) Garden Profiles, (3) Techniques, (4) Design, (5) Projects, and (6) Cooking. A word of explanation about each category:

• **Plant Profiles** cover a vegetable, fruit, or herb in depth, including information ranging from planting to harvesting. These profiles are accompanied by big "sidebars" called "Kitchen Talk," which may be written by a different author, that focus on using the subject of the profile in the kitchen. "Kitchen Talk" always includes from one to three original recipes featuring the subject of the profile.

• **Garden Profiles** are articles that take the reader on a tour of a strikingly beautiful, unusual, or successful kitchen garden. The primary focus of these profiles is to spark ideas about how readers might want to shape their own gardens.

• **Techniques** come in two types: basic and advanced. Basic techniques are practices or general gardening information every gardener needs to know about, such as soil improvement and mulching. Advanced techniques, such as seed-saving and hydroponics, probably will be of interest to only a subset of our readers.

• **Design** articles focus on helping readers make their gardens beautiful as well as productive. They may be about specific gardens, garden elements (e.g., structures, paths, plant combinations), or environmental considerations in design (e.g., shade, water conservation). Without being overtly didactic, these are intended to foster the use of good design principles in the kitchen garden and to promote the idea that kitchen gardens can be an ornamental part of the landscape.

• **Projects** include things to build (e.g., trellises, raised beds) and things to do (e.g., dry herbs, grow tomatoes in containers). These articles include sufficient detail that the reader has step-by-step guidance in all phases of the project.

• **Cooking** articles, as distinct from the "Kitchen Talk" sidebars discussed above, focus entirely on cooking, not growing, but the primary ingredient(s) must be from the kitchen garden. They include two to three original recipes.

We also run substantive sidebars (in addition to "Kitchen Talk") ranging in length from one-half column to two columns. These sidebars are intended to add depth, breadth, or an imaginative angle to the main article (e.g., a sidebar on designing with rhubarb to accompany a profile of rhubarb).

How We Work

Our articles are written in the first-person, by people with first-hand experience, who have something of substance to say. While we are happy to find accomplished writers who also have significant gardening or cooking expertise, the expertise is more important than the writing skills. Our editors work very closely with authors throughout the process of generating a story, and they are very good at working with words, as well as with gardeners, so first-time authors should not be deterred.

We maintain a story list of ideas we want to pursue in each of the six categories outlined above, and in most cases, we search until we find the right author for the pieces we want to do.

However, we also welcome submissions of ideas from potential authors, which may be in the form of letters, phone calls, or e-mail. We need enough detail to get a good idea of what you'd like to do, but we discourage you from developing full proposals just for *Kitchen Garden* until an editor has contacted you. Potential authors have no way of knowing what stories are already working and may waste time in developing proposals on topics already assigned to someone else. However, if you have a proposal you have already developed, by all means send it to us. We make every effort to reply to unsolicited ideas within four weeks.

In most cases, an editor visits the author before an article is definitely assigned. This is so scouting photographs can be taken and the editor can get to know the author, which facilitates developing an outline and then the story. It is important that our authors grow the plants about which they write, and that their gardens be suitable for photographing for the magazine. Once we have made the decision to proceed with a story, the editor and author collaborate on a brief outline that guides the development of the manuscript. Also at this time, we send a letter summarizing verbal agreement on payments and deadlines.

Payments and Copyrights

In general, no payment is made and no copyright agreement is executed until we have received an acceptable manuscript, at which point we send a copyright agreement to the author. When it has been signed, a percentage of the total fee is paid. In the case of cooking articles or "Kitchen Talk" pieces, "acceptable manuscript" means that we have tested the recipes and found them suitable for publication. The remaining payment is made when the author has approved the galley for the article.

In deciding payments, we try to gauge the amount of work that will be required from the author and the amount of work that will be required from us to make the manuscript publishable and arrive at a reasonable price that way. In addition to producing a manuscript, authors are asked to review and correct the galley before publication of the article and to permit a photographer, in most cases, to take pictures to accompany the text. We reimburse authors for any out-of-pocket expenses associated with producing the manuscript, but such expenses must be approved by the editor before they are incurred.

In order to get the right editorial mix for a given issue, and because so much of our work must be done during the growing season to allow for photography, considerable time may elapse between a manuscript's acceptance and its eventual publication. Acceptance of a manuscript and execution of a copyright agreement are not a guarantee of publication. They are an indication of our intent to publish the manuscript. If we do not publish it, all rights you granted to us revert to you.

The only exclusive right given to The Taunton Press in the copyright agreement is for first publication of the material. You may republish the material 90 days after our first publication date. We also ask for various republication rights in other forms and for promotional uses. Authors who are under consideration for a manuscript are welcome to review the standard copyright agreement on request prior to committing to produce a manuscript. We reserve the right to edit, revise, or adapt manuscripts prior to publication in ways that will make them more understandable and enjoyable to our readers.

Categories: Nonfiction—Cooking—Gardening

Name: Kitchen Garden Editorial
Material: All
Address: 63 S MAIN ST
City/State/ZIP: NEWTOWN CT 06470
Telephone: 203-426-8171
Fax: 203-426-3434
E-mail: KG@taunton.com
Internet: www.taunton.com

Kite Lines

We are always delighted by people who know and love kites—especially if they want to write about them. By following these guidelines and acquainting yourself with our magazine you can make both of us happy. *Kite Lines* will receive relevant, quality material, and you will receive recognition and respect for your work and for your knowledge of kites.

Readers

Our readers are educated, active, sophisticated and longtime kite fliers. Most have flown kites for at least two years and many have been at it for over 20! They already have some kite books in their libraries; they want new information beyond the basics that connects them to kite events, people and achievements worldwide.

Kite Lines is also considered a trade magazine for the kite industry because our advertising reaches those with a business interest in kiting. Editorially, however, our magazine is directed at kite consumers.

Our diverse readership is united by an intense interest in kites and demanding standards regarding them. These kiters want good information intelligently presented.

Subject Matter

We strive for variety, from objective technical papers to gossipy news, from high arts to spontaneous inventions, from inspirational profiles to straightforward how-to. We cover trends, innovations and events both national and international.

We publish complete kitemaking plans, historic studies, techniques and reviews of new kites, books and accessories.

We select articles by importance, timeliness, interest, balance of contents and quality of writing. Availability of illustrations (drawings and/or photographs) may affect acceptability of material.

Be advised: we are a magazine about kites. We are not interested in hang gliding, balloons, airplanes, boomerangs, windmills or Frisbees. Fiction, poetry and puzzles are not considered for publication. Cartoons are rarely considered. We do not accept articles about commercial activity, such as a story on a new kite shop simply because it opened.

Our greatest needs are for plans for new kite designs and coverage of kite activities in places where we presently lack correspondents.

If you're writing about kite events, include the following: official name of event; site; date; which annual; whether competitive and the prizes and awards; entry fee; and sponsor.

We are not interested in kite events open only to children.

Also, in writing about competitions, do not merely recite the winners without describing their kites. Better still, the stories behind the kites should be given. In *Kite Lines* it is almost impossible to overdescribe a kite.

Style

We like a fresh, lively, honest, objective outlook. We adhere to the basic tenets of good writing: be specific; be concise; use the active voice; avoid qualifiers, fancy and foreign words; don't overstate. Be willing to rewrite, edit and polish. Some articles go back and forth many times in this process.

The winning trait for an article is when the writer has brought something to the subject from his or her own perceptions, lending depth or an element of surprise to the work.

Our specific requirements are:

• ACCURACY—Use only the most reliable sources and crosscheck all facts. Support superlatives. Use direct quotations in personal interviews. Present all sides fairly if reporting on a controversy.

• CLARITY—Make technical material as understandable as possible to the widest range of readers. Define uncommon terms.

• COMPLETENESS—Always answer the basics: *who, what, where, when* and *why.* In the case of kites, include *how.*

To better study the style of *Kite Lines,* you may order a sample copy for $5.50 postpaid.

Format

We do not specify a length for any article. Write as much as you must to tell your story. Some of our articles are no more than

a photograph and a long caption; others are many pages. Yet we do appreciate compression since space is limited.

If computer printed, submit a hard copy first. If accepted, we will ask for a diskette or transmission by modem or e-mail. We use QuarkXpress on a Macintosh system, but usually we can "translate" other formats. Photocopied or dot-matrix-printed material is acceptable if legible.

At the end of the manuscript, add brief biographical information-your age, occupation, other writings, history with kites, etc.

Slides or negatives used are always returned after publication; prints are returned on request.

Please follow our format for construction plans for kites and/ or accessories:

• Brief introduction—give the background of the kite, its general characteristics, how difficult it is to make and how much time it takes to make it. Give the range of sizes to which the plans can be scaled up or down. Note the cost, especially if high or low.

• Materials required—Give exact quantities and sizes.

• Tools used—List any beyond scissors, pencil, etc.

• Steps In construction—Break down into as many steps as is logical, using a careful sequence.

• Set of complete kite drawings—Provide front, side and top or bottom views. At least one photograph of the kite in flight is required.

• Instructions for flying the kite—Describe a normal performance, the wind conditions needed, portability aspects, visual effects, etc.

Lead Time

Before beginning an article, query us first, since we may have a similar work pending or already at hand. We may want to direct your research elsewhere or suggest another slant. We prefer written queries; please do not telephone us with ideas. Usually we work on articles far in advance, but we try to be flexible to accommodate late-breaking news. Good stories that arrive too late may be held for publication as long as a year.

We do not consider simultaneous submissions. You must state that the material you submitted has not been given to another kite publication, even a newsletter.

Photos & Drawings

Articles often depend on photographs or drawings or both. Text and illustrations should work together. Our interest in a photo is based on whether it pertains to news or an article.

We like to see new kites, story-related kites and outstanding kites (having innovation, graphic quality, craftsmanship). We are not interested in commercial kites, ordinary kites (sleds, Eddys), cluttered festival scenes and gratuitous kids, dogs, posed groups or trophies.

We prefer photos of excellent technical quality. Use a good camera, preferably with a zoom lens, to capture fast-climbing kites. We prefer slide film, since it's much finer and can be enlarged without as much loss of quality. We like black-and-white photos and use them in the magazine, but any color photo can be converted to black and white if need be. If you've taken color prints instead of slides, go to a good color lab for processing and get 4"x6" or larger glossy prints. This will maximize your results in this format.

Some hints for taking pictures:

• GOOD LIGHT—Photos taken in early morning light or late day can give depth and shading that the harsh, glaring midday sun can't provide.

• BACKGROUNDS—Above all, make sure of the absence of negatives, such as cars, motels, distracted spectators and especially overhead wires. Establish the scene by trying to include landmarks or the atmosphere of the location. Try for blue skies, especially with big, white chunky clouds. Include people as much as possible, preferably in action and candid rather than posed.

You may need to resort to the usual compromise picture of the flier holding the kite.

• **COMPOSITION**—Photograph kites at representative angles of flight. Get the whole kite in the picture, leaving at least a bit of sky on all sides. Never bump the nose of a flying kite against the edge of the picture. Get the whole tail, but if it's very long you may take alternate shots that crop out some tail in order to get a good close-up of the body. Close-ups of details may be important to get for some well-finished kites. Avoid "arty" shots of strange angles and pieces of kite—they will frustrate our readers who want to see the whole kite.

• **QUANTITY**—Take and submit plenty of pictures and many views of the kites you've selected as worthwhile subjects.

• **CAPTION**—Always identify the kite, its maker, its flier (if different from its maker), people prominent in the photo, the event, location, date and photographer. Number slides in their sleeves and enclose a separate sheet with the captions keyed to the corresponding numbers. For prints, do not write on the back—attach paper flaps, so there will be no damage or interference with reproducibility. Don't use paper clips or staples on photos.

Model releases are required only when recognizable persons are photographed in a nonpublic place. Photos taken at public events present no release problems.

Drawings should be neat and clean, in black line on white paper. Do not use color, grays, faint lines or graph paper. Drawings done on computer (for example, using Adobe Illustrator for the Macintosh) should be submitted in hard copy first. If accepted, we will discuss our standards with you and ask for a diskette or transmission by modem or e-mail.

Agreements

We occasionally give definite assignments to writers, but most material is submitted on speculation, with no guarantee of publication until the article is accepted for a specific issue. Prospective contributors in the field should not give the impression they represent *Kite Lines*. Explain you are on a freelance basis.

Material submitted is open to editing. It must be original and clear of all copyrights, in no way infringing on previous work.

Kite Lines is copyrighted and this will protect your work. We acquire first world serial rights and do not claim ownership (or buy all rights) to any work other than that which is staff-produced. The copyright notice in the magazine alerts publishers to obtain magazine and author permission for possible reprinting. When publishers make such requests through *Kite Lines*, we become the author's temporary agent. We ask that a specified line crediting *Kite Lines* as well as the writer appear in the reprint. We retain the right to reprint all contributions in subsequent issues of *Kite Lines*. Other reuses are separately agreed upon.

Pay Rates

As a small journal, our pay is modest:

• Short articles and tips—$16 to $50, depending on published length and levels of editing required.

• Longer articles-$50 to $200, depending on published length and levels of editing required.

• Color slides/photos—$30 to $50, depending on published size and quality.

• Black-and-white photos—$20 to $40, depending on published size and quality.

• Drawings—$40 to $100 depending on published size, complexity, quantity of elements and levels of editing required.

We occasionally arrange special assignments in advance, pay to be negotiated, considered in combination with expenses. Time of payment varies and may be upon acceptance or to as late as time of publication.

Upon publication, we send you a copy of the magazine you contributed to by first class mail.

We offer a high-quality environment for writers to showcase their work. Our design, printing and editing are top—notch and our national and international readership will help build your reputation as a writer and kite authority.

Categories: Nonfiction—Arts—Hobbies—Kites—Recreation

Name: Submissions Editor
Material: All
Address: PO BOX 466
City/State/ZIP: RANDALLSTOWN MD 21133-0466
Telephone: 410-922-1212
Fax: 410-922-4262
E-mail: KITELINES@compuserve.com

THE **KIWANIS** MAGAZINE

Kiwanis
A Magazine for Community Leaders

KIWANIS magazine is a monthly publication, except for combined June/July and November/December issues. It is distributed to the 275,000-plus members of Kiwanis clubs in North America, as well as to clubs in more than seventy overseas nations. Though KIWANIS is the official magazine of Kiwanis International and is responsible for reporting organizational news, each issue also includes five or more feature articles geared to other interests of Kiwanians and their families and friends.

Kiwanis club members are business and professional persons who are actively involved in community service.

Freelance written materials submitted to KIWANIS may deal with almost any topic of interest to an intelligent readership. Editorial need primarily is for articles on current business, international, social, humanitarian, self-improvement, and community-related topics. Other subjects of continuing appeal include health and fitness, family relations, young children's needs, sports, recreation, consumer trends, education, and transportation.

The magazine has a special need for articles on business and professional topics that will directly assist readers in their own businesses and careers.

Some of KIWANIS magazine's recent titles have included: "Operation Zero-Defect Marketing," "Shots for Tots," "The Downsizing Myth," "Withstanding the Coastal Crunch," "One's Quest for Self-Renewal," "Farming Fields of Dreams," "Preventing Lead's Poisonous Legacy," and "Organ Donations: A Thin Harvest."

DEMOGRAPHICS

To help you identify the audience to which you are writing, here are some statistics on KIWANIS magazine readers:

• **Median age** 56
• **Graduated high school** 98%
• **Attended/graduated college** 87%
• **Post-graduate degree** 29%
• **Median household income** $57,100
• **Married** 90%
• **Manager** 61%
• **Professional** 29%
• **Owner/Partner** 15%
• **Own a home** 88%
• **Market value of home** $142,000
• **Median size of company/business employees** 26

Articles published in KIWANIS magazine are of two general types: serious and light nonfiction. (No fiction, poetry, filler items, jokes, opinions, or first-person accounts are used.) Manuscripts should be between 2,000 and 3,000 words in length (eight to twelve pages, typed double-spaced). Payment is on acceptance, ranging from $400 to $1,000 depending on current editorial need, depth of treatment, appeal to the magazine's readership, and other factors. Queries are preferred to manuscript submissions.

Proposed articles are tested against two major criteria: (1) be about an overall subject rather than an individual person, place, event, or organization, and (2) have applicability in the lives and concerns of KIWANIS magazine's readership.

In addition, an article, when feasible, should be international in scope, providing information from various world regions. Writers should be aware that KIWANIS magazine is not an exclusively US magazine; it has readers in Canada, Europe, Central and South America, Australia, Africa, and Asia as well. Terms such as "our nation" and "our president" must be avoided. Articles on global topics, particularly if they have a strong bearing on current US developments, could be ideally suited for KIWANIS magazine.

In all manuscripts, a writer's treatment of a subject must be objective and in depth, and each major point should be substantiated by illustrated examples and quotes from persons involved in the subject or qualified to speak on it. The question "why?" should be as important as "what?" and perceptive analysis and balanced treatment are valued highly. Serious articles should not contain intrusions of the writer's views. Writing style should not be pedantic but rather smooth, personable, and to the point, with anecdotes, descriptions, and human detail where appropriate.

Treatment of light subjects must be as authoritative as serious topics, but humorous examples and comparisons and a lighter writing style are valued where needed.

An article's lead must be strong, drawing the reader's attention and setting the tone of the piece. It should be followed by a clear statement of the article's central thesis: Readers quickly should know what they are going to read about and why.

Manuscripts also should contain pertinent background and historic information, as well as a balanced presentation of issues. Firsthand interviews as well as research of published sources are essential. All information should be the most current available on the subject. And the article's conclusion should summarize the consequences of what has been said.

Photos are not essential, but they are desirable when they are high quality and add substantially to the impact of the text. Black-and-white photos should be 8"x10" glossy prints; color transparencies and color slides also are used. All photos should be captioned and are purchased as part of the manuscript package.

Writers are encouraged to study a recent issue of KIWANIS magazine for a better understanding of the writing styles and story subjects used in this publication. To receive a sample copy, send a self-addressed, stamped (five first-class stamps) large envelope to the address shown below.

Your interest in KIWANIS magazine as a market for your work is appreciated.

Categories: Associations

Name: Submissions Editor
Material: All
Address: 3636 WOODVIEW TRACE
City/State/ZIP: INDIANAPOLIS IN 46268
Telephone: 317-875-8755
Fax: 317-879-0204
E-mail: Kiwanismail@www.kiwanis.org
Internet: www.kiwanis.org

Knives Illustrated™
The Premier Cutlery Magazine

KNIVES ILLUSTRATED™, the world's premier cutlery magazine, is respected worldwide for its superior editorial mix and high quality articles. We feature the full range of custom and high tech production knives, from miniatures to swords, leaving nothing untouched. We're also known for our outstanding how-to articles and technical features on equipment, materials and knife making supplies.

We do not feature knife maker profiles as such, although we do spotlight some makers by featuring a variety of their knives and insight into their background and philosophy. We also feature articles on various knife maker's shops, under the "Shop Tour" heading. With only six issues per year at this time, and more than 900 knife maker's work (photos) on file, we are naturally swamped with material to choose from. Therefore, we can often compliment freelancer's articles with good photos. We do seek to concentrate on people who produce quality and/or inspirational work.

If you are interested in submitting work to **KNIVES ILLUSTRATED** magazine, it is suggested you analyze at least two or three different editions to get a feel for the magazine. It is also recommended that you call or mail in your query to determine if we are interested in the topic you have in mind. While verbal or written approval may be given, all articles are still received on a speculation basis. We cannot approve any article until we have it in hand, whereupon we will make a final decision as to its suitability for our use. Bear in mind we do not suggest you go to the trouble to write an article if there is doubt we can use it promptly.

We use IBM compatible PCs and prefer text on 3½" discs in Microsoft Word. If you send in a disc, send a printed copy of the text with it. Relative to captions, number the photos and/or slides and write numbered captions. Don't write on the back of the photos or on slide mounts.

We use more black & white than color, but you can submit good color prints of everything if B&Ws cost you more money. Relative to color, we prefer color transparencies (slides) but good color prints will sometimes do.

Payment is made upon publication, but in reality you get paid before the mag hits the newsstands. Payment amount depends on the article involved. I can tell you the amount when the article is accepted for use. Send your social security number with your first submission.

Categories: Fishing—Hunting—Outdoors

Name: Bud Lang, Editor
Material: All
Address: 265 S ANITA DR STE 120
City/State/ZIP: ORANGE CA 92868
Telephone: 714-939-9991
Fax: 714-939-9909
E-mail: budlang@pacbell.net

Kuumba

KUUMBA, published twice a year, is a journal of poetry dedicated to the celebration of the lives and culture of black lesbians and gay men. Although many poems are submitted to us, we publish about 35 in each issue. Each issue also includes several illustrations. We do not publish photographs.

Poetry

KUUMBA seeks verse of the highest quality, but it need not be written by professional writers. The most important thing is that the work be well-written and that it feature themes that are relevant to the black lesbian or gay experience.

All poetry should be typed with line and stanza breaks clearly delineated. Include your name and mailing address in the upper left corner of each page of your submission. If you use a pseudonym, include it on each page as well.

Send no more than five poems at a time, and please no more than one poem per page. Send only your best work.

Illustrations

KUUMBA seeks line-art illustrations related to black lesbians or gay men. These are typically images of two women or two men, but we are open to other possibilities.

Acceptable media include pen-and-ink, pencil line, linoleum cut, woodcut and computer-generated or digital illustration that mimic these styles. We are less interested in illustrations that include tonal graduations such as watercolor, airbrush, charcoal, shaded pencil or acrylics. Black and white illustrations are preferred. Color images will be judged, in part, on the quality of their reproducibility in black and white.

Do not send originals. Clear photocopies are perfectly acceptable.

We seek submissions on all subjects reflecting experiences within the black lesbian and gay community. Typical areas of interest are: coming out, involvement with family, interactions with surrounding communities, substance abuse, the arts, political activism, oral histories, AIDS and intimate relationships. Writers and illustrators, however, are not limited to these subjects.

Payment and Rights

If your work is accepted, we secure first North American rights and the right to anthologize. If the material you are submitting has appeared elsewhere, tell us when you submit it.

You will receive two copies of the issue in which your work appears as payment.

Acceptance is by letter. After a manuscript or illustration has been accepted, the author must provide a written statement attesting that the work as not been previously published and that it is not under consideration by any other publication.

If the work you submit to us is being submitting to others as well, please let us know.

Correspondence

All poems and illustrations are reviewed on speculation. We respond within four to six weeks.

These are guidelines, not a contract, and they are subject to change without notice.

Categories: African-American—Gay/Lesbian

Name: Submissions Editor
Material: All
Address: PO BOX 83912
City/State/ZIP: LOS ANGELES CA 90083-0912
Telephone: 310-410-0808
Fax: 310-410-9250
E-mail: newsroom@blk.com
Internet: www.blk.com

L.A. Parent

Thank you for your interest in our parenting publications.

For a sample copy, send $2 to L.A. Parent magazine at the address below.

L.A. Parent, Parenting (Orange County) and **San Diego Parent** are city magazines with a strong service-to-parent slant.

Always query first, to save your time and the editor's. Phone calls are difficult due to an editor's tight production schedule. A letter allows more time for valid decision-making.

Include one or two clips of previously guiblished work. An unpublished manuscript will be considered but may take longer for evaluation. Even though your query may be rejected, you may be matched up with future assignments.

Recent titles published include: Is My Kid a Klutz? The Too Precious Child, The Public School Crisis, Bed and Breakfasts that Welcome Children, Nurturing a Creative Youngster, Evaluating Test Scores and Weird Places to Take Your Kids. The Woman's Pages section focuses on issues affecting women from home to the workplace. Family Health is a quarterly section devoted to children's and parents' well-being.

When dealing with generic parenting articles we often quote regional and national sources. Balanced reporting is a must. Local writers should quote San Diego and Orange County sources when appropriate.

Payment

Unless otherwise indicated, we pay 20 cents a word (see below for special circumstances). We will cover some expenses (phone calls, mileage at 25 cents per mile in excess of 20 miles, etc.), but these must be pre-approved by your assigning editor. Unless otherwise indicated, when we make an assignment it is with the understanding that it is for first-time use in all our editions (currently, **L.A. Parent, Parenting** and **San Diego Parent** magazines).

Feature Articles

The average length for a feature article is 1,100 words. We pay $300 for these stories. We reserve the right to assign a sidebar if, upon reading your manuscript, the editor decides the story would be incomplete without one. This is considered part of your assignment and is included in the flat $300 rate.

Flash Facts

From childcare advice on the Internet to the Daddy Saddle, Flash Facts covers what's new on the world of parenting. Writers should aim for a tight and breezy style.

• We pay $25 for straightforward product reviews; average length is 100 to 150 words.

• For more involved assignments (those that require field work or interviews), our rate is $50. Word count is between 150 and 300 words.

• Occasionally, we run lengthier articles (up to 500 words) on topics requiring more extensive research (Aromatherapy for Kids, Parents on the Net). For those assignments we pay our standard rate of 20 cents per word.

Entertainment Pages

This column includes movie, video, audio, theater and multimedia reviews. We generally do not cover mileage and parking expenses for these assignments.

Parenting People

These 200 to 500 word interviews profile individuals with something significant to say about the challenges of parenting. Typical candidates are experts and celebrities with a provocative and/or novel viewpoint. Bear in mind that we generally like to set up a photo session with the person you're interviewing (this can be tricky if that individual is a Big Star or resides in Tahiti). We pay $50 ($60 if you come up with the idea).

Other Columns

Freelance writers are rarely used for Kids Cuisine, HealthNotes, etc. When we do assign out a story, we pay our standard rates.

Artwork/Photographic

We generally pay $50 plus processing expenses (not to exceed $12) for black and white photos. For inside color, our standard rate is $75. The cover is $300, expenses included. Stock photos used on the cover are paid at $150. Four-color fashion spreads are reimbursed at the rate of $350, expenses included.

Artwork/Illustration

For spot art we pay $50, $75 for more detailed line art.

Is the Check in the Mail?

You will generally receive payment 30 days after acceptance

of the manuscript or artwork. We require that you submit an invoice stating your name, address, phone number, social security number and assignment to process your request. Failure to do so may delay payment.

Categories: Nonfiction—Children—Cooking—Crafts—Education—Family—Feminism—Health—Parenting—Regional—Women's Issues

Name: David Jamieson, Managing Editor
Material: General
Name: Janis Hashe
Material: Entertainment
Name: Christina Elston
Material: Women's Issues, Health
Address: PO BOX 3204
City/State/ZIP: BURBANK CA 91504
Telephone: 818-846-0400

Lacunae

Lacunae publishes comics, fiction, poetry, prose, reviews of independent music, film, fiction, comics and web sites. We are always open to new ideas and pride ourselves on versatility.

Please pay attention to the guidelines. They are important. And, if you are not familiar with the publication, take the time to read a copy to see if your work suits our needs.

Lacunae offers some of the writing and comics industry's best information, art, reviews and fiction. *Lacunae* is a great market for professional and never-before-published writers and artists. Published bimonthly by CFD Productions, *Lacunae* is distributed internationally, features full color covers and at least 32 interior b/w pages. Standard cover price is $2.50 USA.

Lacunae is for **mature readers** (*not* adults only). We don't publish full nudity, but we do present some mature themes. There is no requirement to submit mature or provocative manuscripts or illustrations.

SUBMISSIONS

Short stories, poems, columns, reviews, comics, illustrations, photography, among other forms of work are generally considered for publication year-round.

Fiction and poetry may be almost any genre (humor, horror, sci-fi, etc.), except **no romance**. Lengths vary upon submission and space availability. Generally, the cap on word count is 3,500. *Please Note: Lacunae* is overwhelmed with poetry submissions and is cutting down on the amount of poetry featured each issue.

Illustrative submissions should consist of a clean photocopy, and should be mailed, not e-mailed.

Reviews (of old and new media) must always include price, ordering address (if applicable), ISBN or other identification and other standard information (page count, media type...)

Submissions must be typed in a serif font (preferably Courier). Usual response time is 3-6 weeks, but this time may vary during certain seasons, depending on the influx of submissions. If you have not received a response in 12 weeks, feel free to alert us.

When making a submission, be sure to include full name and address on the first page of any manuscript, name on subsequent pages; full name and address on each page of poetry or artwork. A cover letter is required. When making an e-mail submission, include text as an e-mail message. *Lacunae* does not accept uploads of submissions.

PAYMENT

Lacunae pays in copies according to work (usually 5 to 25 copies) and great recognition in the comics and writing markets. Copies of each issue are sent to major publishers and agents in the industries. Writers and artists retain all rights to their work

and *Lacunae* contracts allow for creators to republish their work in other publications after such works appear in *Lacunae*. Previously published works are OK, provided there is no buying of second rights on *Lacunae's* part. No work may be published in *Lacunae* without a contract (provided by *Lacunae).*

REVIEWS

Lacunae accepts other publications—magazines, comics, books, albums, videos, etc. for review. These will not be returned, but offered as giveaways to our readers. The creators or publishers of reviewed works will receive a tearsheet, but will be required to purchase an entire issue at a discount cost if desired.

COPIES

If there are questions as to whether your work(s) meet our specifications, we, as all publishers, recommend you review a copy of our latest issue. Those requesting guidelines may purchase the latest issue at $3.25 (standard cost, includes postage).

Anyone published in *Lacunae* requesting additional copies will be able to purchase them at a discounted rate.

QUESTIONS?

Just ask!

THE CFD E-MAIL LIST

CFD Productions periodically notifies those interested of upcoming projects, calls for submissions and publishing schedules. To be included on the CFD e-mail list, send us your e-mail address.

Categories: Fiction—Entertainment—Horror—Interview—Music—Mystery—Writing

Name: Pamela Hazelton, Editor
Material: All
Address: PO BOX 827
City/State/ZIP: CLIFTON PARK NY 12065
E-mail: lacunaemag@aol.com

Ladies' Home Journal

Thank you for your interest in writing for the *Journal*. While we do not have specific guidelines about subject matter or writing style, we do offer these suggestions:

Read Back Issues: We do not publish an editorial calendar, so familiarizing yourself with our editorial content and style will help you decide if your work fits our needs. Back issues can be found in the periodicals section of your library or purchased from our customer service department for $3 each (Call 800-678-2699). Do not send payment to our editorial offices.

We Have a Four Month Lead Time and seasonal material is usually assigned six months in advance.

Submit Queries Rather than Manuscripts: Keep your query brief - one to two pages - citing your lead and describing how you will research and develop your story. Be specific, and always direct your query to the appropriate editor, as listed on the masthead of the magazine. If you have been published before, send clips, your credits and a resume.

Always Include a Self-Addressed, Stamped Envelope: We will not respond unless an SASE is enclosed (with adequate postage for return of the manuscript, if so desired). We are not responsible for returning unsolicited material, so do not send original copies or photographs.

Payment, Story Length and Deadlines are discussed upon assignment and writers are paid upon acceptance. Average story length is 2,000 words.

We particularly welcome reader submissions for the following column: "A Woman Today": Submissions should be approximately 1,500 words, written in the first person and typed double spaced. These must be true, personal stories about dramatic events. Enclose a self-addressed, stamped envelope and mail to:

Ladies' Home Journal, BOX WT at our New York address. We will pay $750 for accepted stories.

Submit Fiction Only Through a Literary Agent

We Do Not Accept Poetry of Any Kind

Please Do Not Call to Query or Follow up on a Submission: We read every query carefully, and do our best to respond as promptly as we can. It may take up to three months to receive a response.

We Cannot Provide Comments on Unaccepted Material: Due to the large volume of manuscripts we receive, we are unable to evaluate each writer's work personally.

Categories: Fiction—Nonfiction—Arts—Biography—Children—Consumer—Cooking—Crafts—Entertainment—Family—Fashion—Food/Drink—Gardening—Health—Hobbies—Marriage—Parenting—Psychology—Relationships—Self-Help—Sexuality—Society—Travel—Beauty—Nutrition—Medicine—Interior Decorating—Celebrities—Education—How-to—Women's Issues

Name: Editor
Material: All
Address: 125 PARK AVE., 20TH FLOOR
City/State/ZIP: NEW YORK, NY 10017-5516
Telephone: 212-557-6600
Fax: 212-455-1333

Ladybug
The Magazine for Young Children

In September 1990, the Magazine Division of Carus Publishing Company launched LADYBUG, a magazine for young children ages 2 to 6.

LADYBUG publishes original stories and poems written by the world's best children's authors. In some cases, LADYBUG purchases rights for excerpts from books yet to be published. Each issue also includes several reprints of high-quality selections.

LADYBUG measures 8"x10", is full-color, contains 36 pages and a 4-page activity pullout, and is staple-bound.

We hope that the following information will be useful to prospective contributors:

Editor-in-Chief: Marianne Carus Published: 12 months a year

Editor: Paula Morrow Price: $32.97 for 1-year subscription

Senior Art Director: Ron McCutchan (12 issues)

Art Director: Suzanne Beck

Categories

Fiction: fantasy, read-aloud stories, picture stories, folk and fairy tales

Poetry: serious, humorous, rhymes, lullabies

Other: crafts, learning activities for 2-3 and 4-6 year olds, games, songs, and finger games

Length

Stories: 300 to 850 words

Poems: not longer than 20 lines

Crafts/Activities/Games: one to four pages

An exact word count should be noted on each manuscript submitted. Word count includes *every* word, but does not include the title of the manuscript or the author's name.

Rates

Stories and articles: up to 25¢ per word (850 words maximum)

Poems: up to $3.00 per line

Payment upon publication.

Art

Any review samples of artwork will be considered. If you are sending an original art portfolio, package it carefully and insure the package. Make sure to include return packing materials and postage.

LADYBUG would like to reach as many children's authors and artists as possible for original contributions, but our standards are very high and we will accept only top-quality material. *Please do not query first.*

LADYBUG will consider any manuscripts or art samples sent on speculation and accompanied by a self-addressed stamped envelope. Although LADYBUG prefers to see tearsheets or photo prints/photocopies of art, if you are sending original art as part of a portfolio, package it carefully and insure the package. Please allow 1-2 weeks to receive a reply.

We do not distribute theme lists for upcoming issues.

LADYBUG purchases material with the understanding that the work will appear in both the regular and the classroom edition of the magazine. LADYBUG normally purchases the following rights:

1. For stories and poems previously unpublished, LADYBUG purchases first publication rights in the English language. Payment is made upon publication. LADYBUG also requests the right to reprint the work in any volume or anthology published by Carus Publishing Company upon payment of half the original fee.

2. For stories and poems previously published, LADYBUG purchases second North American publication rights. Fees vary, but are generally less than fees for first serial rights. Payment is made upon publication. Same applies to accompanying art.

3. For recurring features, LADYBUG purchases the material outright. The work becomes the property of LADYBUG, and it is copyrighted in the name of Carus Publishing Company. A flat fee per feature is usually negotiated. Payment is made upon publication.

4. For commissioned art assigned by LADYBUG's art director, LADYBUG normally purchases first publication rights subject to the terms outlined below:

(a) physical art remains the property of the illustrator

(b) payment is made within 45 days of acceptance

For a sample copy of LADYBUG, please send $4.00 to Ladybug Sample Copy. Note: Sample copy requests from foreign countries must be accompanied by International Postal Reply Coupons (IRCs) valued at US $4.00. Please do *not* send a check or money order.

Categories: Fiction—Children—Crafts—Fantasy—Poetry—Stories

Name: Marianne Carus, Submissions Editor
Material: Manuscripts
Name: Suzanne Beck, Art Director
Material: Art Samples
Name: Mary Ann Hocking, Permissions Coordinator
Material: Questions about rights.
Address: PO BOX 300
City/State/ZIP: PERU IL 61354

Lansing City Limits

Lansing City Limits is a full-color monthly magazine covering people, places and goings-on in the Lansing and surrounding areas. We normally run 2 to 4 feature pieces per issue as well as our 'regular' columns and articles. Past features have included such things as "The Return of the 1970s," "Basement Beer Brewing," "Area Bed and Breakfasts" and "The Local Music Scene." Obviously, all subjects must have a strong Lansing-area slant.

We are always on the lookout for good writers to submit feature ideas. A one-page query outlining subject matter and approach (and maybe even a possible lead paragraph) is preferred to manuscripts. New writers may want to include samples of previously published writing (photocopies, please, no tearsheets). All features should be in third person unless specified otherwise. Tone can be anything from humorous to serious.

'Regular' columns and features (such as Day in the Life, Restaurant Review and Home Tour) are generally assigned. Please query with ideas for specific 'regular' columns.

Deadline for all writing is normally two months before date of target issue. Payment is upon publication.

Writers should familiarize themselves with the magazine. Current issues, available in most bookstores, cost $3.50. Back issues, available in our office, are $5.

Attention all queries to 'Editor.'

Categories: Nonfiction—Regional

Name: Editor
Material: All
Address: 325-B N CLIPPERT ST
City/State/ZIP: LANSING MI 48912
Telephone: 517-333-0333
Fax: 517-332-3837

Law and Order Magazine
The Magazine for Police Management

All material is submitted on speculation. Editor will attempt to evaluate material within 45 days and reply. Articles should be aimed at our primary audience—the administrators of law enforcement agencies (chiefs, sheriffs, commanders, supervisors and managers). While each issue has a specific focus topic, articles pertaining to other subjects are also included. Editorial emphasis is on the application of new ideas, methods/systems and products that readers can apply to their own operations.

Submissions must include a hard copy and, if possible, a PC disk. Please include the author's name on the disk label. The paper hard copy must be printed sufficiently dark so that it can be processed by an image scanner if necessary. Courier typeface or any style with distinct serifs is preferred. Copy must be clean, no hand editing after typing. Typos will be caught by our spell checker.

Our copy format is one space after a period, not two. Write in the past tense (e.g. he said, *not* he says). We use the *Associated Press Style Book*. Authors should include a brief biographical sketch (no photo).

We pay $.10 per printed word and $25.00 for each photograph or series of photographs used. Color slides and both color and black & white prints are acceptable. Color is preferred. Standard payment for a color cover photograph is $300.00.

Law and Order purchases worldwide print and electronic rights and the right to reprint, republish and distribute the material. Material submitted must be exclusive to this publication. Material accepted becomes Hendon Company property.

Categories: Law Enforcement

Name: Bruce Cameron, Editorial Director
Material: All
Address: 1000 SKOKIE BLVD STE 500
City/State/ZIP: WILMETTE IL 60091
Telephone: 847-256-8555
Fax: 847-256-8574
E-mail: laworder@cris.com

The Ledge Magazine

1. Submit 3-5 poems with SASE.

2. Because we carefully consider each submission, we ask that you allow as long as four months for a response.

3. Do not submit between July 1 and August 15. Manuscripts (except chapbook contest entries) postmarked during that period will be returned unread.

4. We encourage you to read a copy of *The Ledge* before sending us your work. The current issue is $7 postpaid. Better yet, a subscription is $12 for 2 issues, $22 for 4 issues.

5. We accept all types of poems. We believe that the best poems appeal to the widest audience and consider poetry a truly democratic medium in that regard. We seek poems with purpose, poems we can empathize with, powerful poems. Excellence is the ultimate criterion.

6. We consider simultaneous submissions but not previously published poems.

7. Contributing poets receive two copies of any issue in which their work appears. We always send galley proofs of all poems to poets before we go to press.

Categories: Poetry

Name: Timothy Monaghan, Editor and Publisher
Material: All
Address: 78-08 83RD ST
City/State/ZIP: GLENDALE NY 11385

Left Curve

Editorial Statement:

Left Curve is an artist-produced critical journal that addresses the problem(s) of cultural forms, emerging from the crisis of modernity, that strive to be independent from the control of dominant institutions, and free from the shackles of instrumental rationality. In general we are interested in any form of work that can be readily reproduced within a 7"x9" format. We encourage open, critical, defetishized work that attempts to unravel, reveal contemporary (inner/outer) reality.

Articles:

We publish fiction (traditional or experimental) and nonfiction texts (critical social, cultural, historical, philosophical essays, as well as reviews, interviews, journalistic pieces, etc.) that are concerned with issues that deal with our general editorial thrust. Length can be roughly up to 5,000 words, though most are about 2,500. Illustrations to accompany texts (photos, graphics, etc.) are welcomed.

Poetry:

Most of our published poems are one page length, though we have published longer poems of up to 8 pages. We will look at any form of poetry, from experimental to traditional.

Visuals:

We are interested in any form of visual work (reproducible painting, line drawings, traditional as well as electronic graphics, photography, visual/verbal art, etc.) that fit into our general editorial thrust.

Other Information:

We make a serious attempt to personally respond to all submissions. Please allow at least 3 months response time. Our issues are published irregularly. For accepted work, we will let you individually know when to expect the work to appear. In general, payment for published work will be 5 copies of the issue in which the work appears for longer pieces, 3 copies for short works. In the event that we receive funding specifically for honorariums (which has happened once so far), payments will be determined on an individual basis depending on available funds. Sample copies of the current issue are $10, $8 for back issues. A list of published issues will be sent upon request with a SASE.

For accepted longer work we prefer submission of final draft on a Macintosh compatible disk. E-mail submissions are also acceptable.

Categories: Arts—Cultural Critique—Culture—Literature—Poetry—Politics

Name: Csaba Polony, Editor/Publisher
Material: Any
Name: Jack Hirschman, Associate Editor
Material: Poetry
Address: PO BOX 472
City/State/ZIP: OAKLAND CA 94604
Telephone: 510-763-7193
Fax: Leftcurv@wco.com

Lessons On Life

Publisher: Turquoise Butterfly Press
Format: Bimonthly 12-page newsletter. Established in 1997.
Focus: Inspirational, uplifting, optimistic, positive, and beautiful stories, poetry, articles, interviews, and artwork. Focus on lessons learned through experiences and how the reader can relate. Reflect on successful parenting, simplicity, love, compassion, healing, friendship and relationships. Find solutions to problems.
Submissions: Lead articles should be 900-1,500 words. All other articles and stories should be 100-900 words. Pays in copies. All material must be typed or neatly handwritten. *Include a word count*! Editor has the right to edit material. Photos or artwork may be sent with submission. Include research citations. Buys one-time rights. Reprints okay. Pays upon publication. Sample copy $4.50
Categories: Nonfiction—Inspirational—Parenting—Poetry

Name: Terri J. Andrews, Editor
Material: All
Address: PO BOX 1127
City/State/ZIP: ATHENS OH 45701-1127
Telephone: 614-664-3030

Letter Arts Review

Letter Arts Review

Letter Arts Review magazine (formerly *Calligraphy Review*) began publication in 1982 as a focal point for the exchange of calligraphic information. Published quarterly, LETTER ARTS REVIEW has evolved into its current status as the primary international publication of record for the lettering arts. As such, LETTER ARTS REVIEW actively encourages and welcomes submissions from practicing calligraphers, graphic designers, and lettering artists, as well as from professional writers, photographers and others with an interest in the related arts.

Audience

LETTER ARTS REVIEW readers include calligraphers, lettering artists, graphic designers, teachers, students and individuals who appreciate the best in lettering.

Objectives

The only magazine in the field, **LETTER ARTS REVIEW**'s objective is to serve the lettering community on many levels: **LETTER ARTS REVIEW** offers the amateur and the professional informative articles on topics ranging from historical manuscripts to contemporary trends; **LETTER ARTS REVIEW** presents thought-provoking viewpoints which stimulate inquiry into related topics; as well as quality reproductions which provide the serious student and the art lover with a valuable visual resource.

Format

Each 64 page issue (except for the *Annual Review*) has 4-6 feature articles plus up to 4 other columns.

Feature articles should be between 1,500 and 3,500 words unless otherwise agreed upon. Contents should be of lettering interest or related in nature. For instance, many of the book arts would be of interest to practicing calligraphers. Practical and conceptual treatments are welcomed, as are learning and teaching experiences. Third person is preferred, however first person will be considered if appropriate. Contributors should read current issues of **LETTER ARTS REVIEW** prior to submitting queries or materials.

Topics of particular interest to our readers include

Profiles of past and present leaders in the field-this can be written in interview form, or third person. Several examples of the artist's work should be included;

Manuscripts-reproductions of both contemporary and historical manuscripts appear in this section. Advanced and beginning calligraphers should be able to refer to this section as a resource. Color reproductions are often used;

Creative process pieces;

Ethical issues of specific interest to the lettering audience.

Columns should generally be between 500 and 1,000 words. Topics include:

Viewpoints: this department contains feedback from readers as well as input of new ideas and personal opinions on all aspects of lettering.

Reviews: Reviews of books, exhibitions, or new type designs. Some reviews can be in-depth, others can be noteworthy.

Other topics and new ideas will gladly be considered.

Guidelines for submitting work to be reproduced in full color in LETTER ARTS REVIEW:

1. For best lighting and color-and to avoid the "Keystone" effect that usually results from using standard lenses and equipment—have your work shot by a professional.

2. When interviewing a photographer, look for one who is skilled not only in lighting and technology, but who also understands the limitations of printing. Look at their **printed** portfolio, not just their transparencies and color prints.

3. Whenever possible, submit transparencies (slide format, 2¼", 4"x5", etc.).

4. When shooting 35mm, use Kodachrome rather than Ektachrome for sharpness and color quality. When possible, use Kodachrome 25 because of its absence of grain.

5. When shooting 2¼" or 4"x5", use as low a speed Ektachrome film as possible—or Fujichrome films.

6. Open up dark shadow areas (even when shooting outdoors) by using fill-in flash.

7. Shoot at the correct exposure—as well as one f-stop underexposed and one-half and one f-stop overexposed. Indicate the one which best represents the color as you see it-but submit all transparencies to provide for the best reproduction at the separation and print stages.

Submission Requirements

Queries for all submissions are preferred. Unsolicited manuscripts and artwork will be considered.

Photography and artwork: Photographs and artwork/illustrations are an integral part of each issue. Considerable space is devoted to illustrative material. Black and white photographs, and color transparencies are preferred. Good quality 35mm slides are acceptable. Please arrange with our editor as to what would be required specifically. Captions indicating artist, title, medium, size and date must be included for each piece.

Payment: Manuscript rates range from $100-250 for feature articles depending on length and quality. Review rates are $50. Photography and artwork rates must be agreed upon.

All payments are mutually agreed upon in advance of commitment to publish. *Payments are made upon publication.*

Assignments: Assignments are made by written agreement. If for any reason **LETTER ARTS REVIEW** does not accept an assigned feature after completion and submission on deadline, the contributor will be paid a "kill fee" of 25% of the mutually agreed upon payment. All materials will be returned to the contributor with all rights. When schedules permit, contributors will be given an opportunity to resubmit.

Sample Copies: A sample copy of **LETTER ARTS REVIEW** is available upon request accompanied by a self-addressed 9"x12" mailing envelope with seven first class postage stamps.

Categories: Arts—Calligraphy—Lettering

Name: Karyn L. Gilman, Publisher
Material: All
Address: 1624 24TH AVE SW
City/State/ZIP: NORMAN OK 73072-5709
Telephone: 405-364-8794
Fax: 405-364-8914
E-mail: letterarts@netplus.net

LIBIDO
The Journal of Sex and Sensibility

Libido
The Journal of Sex and Sensibility

Dear Contributor:

To paraphrase Oscar Wilde, LIBIDO is a literary answer to a horizontal urge. It is a journal of the erotic arts and uses fiction, wordplay, photography, poetry, fine arts, essays, interviews and reviews dealing in sex and sensibility.

LIBIDO's guidelines are purposely simple and loose. All sexual orientations are appreciated. The only taboos are exploitative and violent sex.

Stories should be in the range of 1,000 to 3,000 words, with a maximum of 5,000 words. We accept submissions on disks compatible with Macintosh and Microsoft Word.

Poetry of all styles. (You should know, however, that **LIBIDO** uses *very little* poetry.)

Essays should be 1,000 to 2,000 words.

Reviews of current books, films, and music should be 400 to 800 words.

Black and white photos. We prefer 8"x10", B&W prints, but 5"x7" is OK. We will look at slides, contact sheets, and portfolios. All photos taken after July 5, 1995 require a photo ID as well as model release, per federal requirements.

So send us your work! We'll use your name or we'll let you use a pseudonym. In return, we'll promote you, shower you with untold honor and glory, and send you two copies of your issue—along with lunch money.

Sincerely,
Marianna Beck & Jack Hafferkamp
Co-Publishers/Editors

Categories: Erotica—Feminism—Gay/Lesbian—Literature—Men's Fiction—Men's Issues—Photography—Relationships—Sexuality—Short Stories—Women's Fiction—Women's Issues—Writing

Name: M. Brenengen, Story Editor
Material: All
Address: PO BOX 146721
City/State/ZIP: CHICAGO IL 60614
Telephone: 773-275-0842
Fax: 773-275-0752

THE LiBRARY iMAGiNATiON PAPER!

The Library Imagination Paper

Please do not embrace the stereotypical image of the librarian—spinster, bun, "sh-h-h," etc. This is a lively, intelligent readership needing the same in articles they read. Experience in the field of Library Public Relations—school or public—is helpful.

Front Page piece: 650 words/payment upon acceptance $25
Back Page piece: 2,000 words/payment upon acceptance $50
50-word author bio/credits needed
$5 for every photo used
Supplementary materials to support piece appreciated.
Since this publication emphasizes public relations, special focus upon publicity plans, ideas & materials is required.

Categories: Clip Art—Education—Library—Library Public Relations—Public Relations

Name: Carol Bryan, Editor-Publisher
Material: All
Address: 1000 BYUS DR
City/State/ZIP: CHARLESTON WV 25311

Life

No guidelines but accepts unsolicited manuscripts.

Categories: Nonfiction—Arts—Biography—Business—General Interest—Celebrities—Lifestyle—Human Interest—News

Name: Isolde Motley, Managing Editor
Material: All
Address: TIME & LIFE BLDG.
ROCKEFELLER CENTER
City/State/ZIP: NEW YORK, NY 10020
Telephone: 212-522-1212
Fax: 212-522-0304

Light
A Quarterly of Light and Occasional Verse, Squibs, Satire, Puns, and Word Play

LIGHT is the only magazine available in this country devoted exclusively to light verse, satire, cartoons, parodies, and word-play. Published quarterly, each issue contains thirty-two pages of the best of well-known and new writers. (Our contributors include John Updike, William Stafford, Donald Hall, Michael Benedikt, J.F. Nims, Tom Disch, W.D. Snodgrass, and William Matthews, among others.)

• What's unique in this magazine is that it prints not only funny, topical, satiric and witty verse (both free-form and metrical), but that this verse is understandable by a literate reader, and enjoyable as well. Its pages are accessible, with large typefaces and elegant graphics. It also features light and literate essays and articles, gossip, prose satire and letters, and puzzles that are guaranteed to sharpen your mind and blunt your pencil.

• You're invited to discover (in X.J. Kennedy's words) "the one place in America that regularly prints new work by the best unserious poets alive."

> A FAIRY TALE ROMANCE
> Lady Di, so chaste and shy,
> Of late has made us wince:
> She didn't turn into a frog
> Until she kissed a prince.
> —PAT D'AMICO

> JARRING NEWS
> The price of pots in Athens!
> It really made me burn
> when the potter told me just how much
> I owed on a Grecian urn.
> —JACK LITTLE

Guidelines for contributors:

NO HALLMARKS—unless stamped out of the same aery yet durable material as that of Rochester, Swift, Pope, Calverley, Byron, Praed, W.S. Gilbert, Beerbohm, Belloc, Shaw, Chesterton, Benchley, Coward, Dorothy Parker, Ogden Nash.

LIGHT seeks to continue the tradition established by the *Punch* of the eighteen-nineties, the *Vanity Fair* of the twenties, and the *New Yorker* of Ross and Shawn, of De Vries and Nabokov, of Thurber and E.B. White. Slang and superciliousness, epigrams and aphorisms, parodies and satire, cartoons and line drawings, nonsense and spoonerisms and absurdist clippings from the daily press: If it has wit, point, edge or barb, it will find a home here.

Verse written for an *occasion*, private or public, is particularly welcome.

Reviews and essays are encouraged, in the spirit (if not the words) of Stevenson, Beerbohm, Chesterton. Any topic, from Light Verse or its antecedents to ephemeral or everyday objects, may suit; in lengths from brief *apéritifs* to lengthy meditations. Write with proposals or for further details.

Please be neat, submit letter-quality typescripts or clean photocopies, and a stamped self-addressed business (#10) or manila-sized envelope (no post cards). There should be only one poem on each page, and each page should have your name and address on it. Works that extend over several pages should be numbered. Submissions of more than one page should be folded once; that is, do not fold each sheet of paper separately. Payment is in copies (two for domestic contributors, one for foreign) of the issue your original contribution appears in. Foreign submissions should include sufficient U.S. postage for their return.

Cartoons and line drawings are also solicited, from those solicitous of the honorable and corrosive tradition laid down by Rowlandson, Daumier, Hogarth, Lear, Steinberg, Beerbohm, and Thurber; or continued in the acid-dropping work of Trudeau, Larsen, L.J. Barry, R. Crumb, Robt. Williams, and S. Clay Wilson. The dimensions of your work should normally be no larger than 3.75"x6". This is so that they can be scanned into the computer. Once scanned, the size can be adjusted to be larger or smaller. *Line drawings only; no washes or half-tones.* Send only clean photocopies on good heavy-weight white paper. Submissions should be in black and white.

If you wish to connect with a vital tradition, subscribe to the magazine USA TODAY described as "...much like *The New Yorker* without the annoying hubris." Subscriptions are $16/yr. (four issues), $28/2 yrs. (eight issues), $24 International; single copies $5, and back issues/sample copies $4. For domestic First Class postage, add $2.00 per copy. Send checks (drawn on a U.S. bank) to the address below. Or call toll-free (VISA or MASTERCARD): 1-800-285-4448.

If you're not completely satisfied for any reason, we'll be happy to give you a full refund.

Categories: Fiction—Nonfiction—Cartoons—Comedy—Humor—Literature—Poetry—Short Stories—Writing

Name: Submissions Editor
Material: All
Address: PO BOX 7500
City/State/ZIP: CHICAGO IL 60680

Light of Consciousness
A Journal of Spiritual Awakening

We welcome articles of inspiration and spiritual awakening, preferably with a universal approach, meaning or message. These range from personal accounts to epic passages and include fiction and poetry as well as nonfiction and "how-to." The criteria would be: reader friendly (non-academic), uplifting (not derogatory), and of genuine interest to the seeker in today's world.

Please send clean documents (spell-punctuation checked), 1,000-4,500 words, if possible on a 3½" disk, MAC format (though DOS is ok, too). Photographs and artwork are also welcome.

Currently, LIGHT OF CONSCIOUSNESS prints 6,000 copies and is nationally distributed. Our readers are interested in spiritual unfoldment, meditation, personal growth, music, books/magazines, healing, environment, nature, the arts and travel.

LIGHT OF CONSCIOUSNESS is offered as a not-for-profit service; we make no profit on it nor do any of us take salaries. As such, we rely upon and are deeply grateful for the generosity of contributors and artists; full credit to the contributor is published with the article.

Categories: Fiction—Nonfiction (all ages)—Biography—Healing—Native American—New Age—Poetry—Religion—Spiritual

Name: Submissions Editor
Material: All
Address: DESERT ASHRAM
Address: 3403 W SWEETWATER DR
City/State/ZIP: TUCSON AZ 85745-9301
Telephone: 520-743-8821

Liguorian

LIGUORIAN *is a leading Catholic magazine written and edited for Catholics of all ages. Our purpose is to lead our readers to a fuller Christian life by helping them to better understand the teachings of the gospel and the Church, and by illustrating how these teachings apply to life and the problems confronting them as members of families, the Church, and society.*

1. Articles and stories should not exceed 2,000 words. Style and vocabulary should be popular and readable. Use an interest-grabbing opening, state Wily the subject is important to readers, use examples, quotes, anecdotes, make practical applications, and end strongly.

2. LIGUORIAN does not consider simultaneous submissions or articles previously accepted or published.

3. Topical articles should be submitted six months in advance.

4. Manuscripts should be typewritten, double spaced, and should include name, address, and *social security number*. (No check may be issued without a SS#.)

5. Please allow six to eight weeks for our response.

6. We pay 10 to 12 cents a published word on acceptance.

7. Authors are advised to read and study several issues of LIGUORIAN before submitting articles.

8. LIGUORIAN receives over two hundred manuscripts each month. Your manuscript stands a better chance of acceptance if it is neatly presented, carefully polished, and on a topic of special interest to our readers.

Good luck and we hope to be hearing from you soon.

The editors of *Liguorian*

Categories: Christian Interests—Family—General Interest—Parenting—Relationships—Religion—Senior Citizens—Spiritual—Young Adult

Name: Allan Weinert, C.SS.R., Editor-in-Chief
Material: All
Address: ONE LIGUORI DR
City/State/ZIP: LIGUORI MO 63057
Telephone: 314-464-2500
Fax: 314-464-8449

Lilith
The Independent Jewish Women's Magazine

LILITH, the independent Jewish women's magazine, published since 1976, welcomes high quality, lively writing: nonfiction on people, issues and developments of interest and concern to Jewish women as well as fiction, poetry, and drama. We encourage you to read our magazine to judge whether LILITH is the appropriate vehicle for your work. Examples of topics we have covered are given below. You may order a sample copy of LILITH by sending a check for $5.00 (includes postage) to our office.

Content:

• **Nonfiction** can include: autobiography (testimony, letters, journals, memoirs); biography of women living or dead, whether known or unknown; interviews; analysis of issues and events of importance to Jewish women of a legal, literary, political or historical nature, or concerning the lives, lifestyles, decisions, work, health, culture and struggles of Jewish women; sociological research; historical research (written or oral history); literary criticism, book reviews and essays, film, television, recordings, music and art reviews; investigative reporting; coverage of local, national and international events, trends and developments of concern to Jewish women; reports on relevant conferences and grass roots projects; opinion pieces.

• In addition to these general overall features categories, LILITH also welcomes Letters to the Editor, and submissions to Kol Ishah (news pages) and Tsena-Rena (resource listings).

• **New Ceremonies and Rituals** should relate to the lives of Jewish women.

• **Poetry, Fiction and Drama** should also relate to lives of Jewish women.

(NOTE: Poetry submissions will be read by the poetry editor twice each year. Submit by March 1 or September 1 for each cycle.)

Editorial Specifications:

• **Length:** 1,000-3,000 words for features. Author should indicate "possible cuts" in the left margin.

• **Author's bio:** one to two sentences, written in the third person, should accompany the manuscript.

• **Footnotes:** Our style does not include footnotes. Sources should be incorporated into the story, in parentheses if necessary. Larger digressionary remarks or information should be submitted on separate pages for use as possible "boxes" or "sidebars" (companion pieces to the main feature).

• **Translations:** All non-English (including Hebrew or Yiddish) words or phrases must be followed by English translation the first time they are used in a nonfiction piece and should appear in italics.

• **Form:** All manuscripts should be typed double-spaced. Clear photocopies are acceptable. The author's name, address and phone number should be on the first page.

Procedures:

Editorial decisions are usually made within twelve weeks. The editors will notify the author if major revisions are required. All artwork and photographs accompanying articles that need to be returned should be so labeled (lightly on the back). Letters to the Editor cannot be acknowledged or returned and must include the writer's name and address, though these can be withheld at the writer's request.

Topics We Have Covered:
Eat, eat! DIET, DIET!
Abortion Foes Are Bad News for Jews
Letty Cottin Pogrebin
"A Letter to Harvey Milk"
Meet the Matriarchs
Beyond "J.A.P." Baiting
Healing After Abuse in Jewish Families
Women's Holocaust Memoirs
The New Face of Women's Philanthropy
Bris Anxiety?
Ritual Junkies Unite!
Breast Cancer
Jewish Hair!
Creating Sacred Space
Gender-Bending in Yiddish Film
Altruistic Acts
A Feminist Curriculum for Hebrew School
Twentysomething
Orthodox Feminists?
We've Waited 3,000 Years
The New Minority: Jews Who Choose Jews
Teen Girl Angst
Single Moms by Choice
Jewish Women's Music

Categories: Fiction—Nonfiction—Biography—Drama—Film/Video—Jewish Interests—Lifestyles—Music—Poetry—Women's Issues

Name: Submissions Editor
Material: All
Address: 250 W 57TH ST
City/State/ZIP: NEW YORK NY 10107-0172
Telephone: 212-757-0818
Fax: 212-757-5705
E-mail: lilithmag@aol.com

Linn's Stamp News

Our goal at *Linn's* is to create a weekly publication that is indispensable to stamp collectors. Everything we do, from the broadest editorial policy to the most trivial stylistic idiosyncrasy, is thought out in the light of this one overriding goal.

We try to achieve indispensability in various ways:

Every collector, from the beginner to the most sophisticated, wants to know the news. Our aim is to provide all the news, as conveniently and as accessibly as we can. In this regard, we feel we are the *New York Times* of philately.

In stamp collecting, the news is not just club and show announcements, new issues and auction realizations.

New discoveries are constantly being made, sometimes involving material that is decades or even centuries old. We cover this news too, relying on the worldwide network of columnists and correspondents who contribute to our pages.

Of course, we rely on these contributors for much more than hard news. Many of the feature items in *Linn's*, which make up the bulk of our editorial content, originate with freelance contributors in the collector community.

Here *Linn's* performs an important educational function, by bringing to the attention of more than 70,000 subscribers (and hundreds of thousands of readers) a diverse selection of facts, thoughts and observations about stamps, postal markings, covers and stamp-related subjects.

Writing in *Linn's*, the freelance contributor has the opportunity to share his specialized knowledge with the largest stamp collector audience of any periodical in the world.

It should go without saying, then, that *Linn's* features are aimed at a broad group of relatively novice collectors, whose average level of sophistication, on any given subject, is less than that of the specialist author.

Linn's writers should *keep* this general interest level of the audience uppermost in mind. Advanced or more sophisticated collectors, as many of our columnists tend to be, must also avoid writing down to the reader.

The goal in writing *for* the *Linn's* audience is to provide information that makes stamp collecting more interesting to more people. Ideally, every feature we run promotes the hobby.

A *Linn's* article is not the appropriate place to showcase everything the author knows, nor is it a lofty podium from which to speak over people's heads.

The *Linn's* writer must strive to reach out and embrace the reader, to invite him in, even to hold his hand along the path. This attitude of friendliness and openness in one's prose is difficult to articulate, but it's extremely important. It is very much a part of our desire to make *Linn's* accessible to all collectors, and to help them grow as philatelists.

Without condescending, the *Linn's* writer should assume that the reader knows little or nothing about the specific subject at hand. Complicated terms or unfamiliar words should be defined, even if they might be familiar to the more advanced philatelist.

The *Wall Street Journal* is a good model here: Every time the editors use the phrase "short sale," they define what it is. *Linn's* strives to be similarly introductory in its approach to the jargon of philately.

The ideal *Linn's* feature would contain enough new (or newly presented) information to instruct even the specialist in the field, written in a way to capture the attention (and hold the interest) of the beginning collector.

While the scope of our editorial interest ranges as widely as philately itself, many of our features focus on U.S. and U.S.-related material. No matter what his collecting specialty, the *Linn's* reader still maintains an interest in the stamps and postal history of his own country. Week after week, *Linn's* offers the most complete coverage of the U.S. philatelic scene available anywhere.

This is not to say that we ignore the philately of the rest of the world—quite the contrary. We have regular columns in many non-U.S. areas; we record and notice the new issues of the entire world; and our feature writers routinely range the globe, writing on subjects from classic to contemporary.

Linn's is also big enough to accommodate a wide range of writing styles. Many of our columnists have individual voices, and we don't discourage this. We will always try to preserve a writer's style, assuming that he is a writer and has a style.

TERMS

We purchase first worldwide periodical rights plus a non-exclusive right to anthologize or otherwise reuse on a proportion-

ate royalty basis.

In other words, we want to be the first periodical to publish the work. The author is subsequently free to resell the work elsewhere, 60 days after we've published it; but here we'd like to be credited. We reserve the right to reuse all works published in *Linn's* (in our almanac or in an anthology, for instance), and we will pay an appropriate royalty for such reuses.

The specific legal details of our purchase are spelled out in the "Standard terms governing acceptance of original material" section of this pamphlet.

Articles submitted should be exclusive to *Linn's*. We are not interested in material that is simultaneously submitted to other publications (except press releases, of course, which are not part of this discussion). Thus, we want to see original type scripts, and we tend to look unfavorably on photocopies and carbon or fax copies.

We reserve the right to edit, cut or reject anything submitted.

Articles accepted may not appear immediately. Please be patient. The rejection process is fairly quick (three weeks at most), but accepted pieces sometimes sit for months before publication.

Payment for features and columns is made upon publication. Checks are mailed monthly, shortly after the 5th of the month. Thus, in the ordinary course of events, writers should have received, by the middle of the month, our check for whatever of their works was published in the issues of *Linn's* cover-dated the previous month.

Rates vary, generally between $20 and $50 per feature. We do strive to pay every contributor who produces original work for us. This is more by way of saying "thank you" than providing a livelihood, since the economics of newspaper publishing don't sustain magazine rates.

Payment varies according to quality, craft, degree of difficulty, previous work done for *Linn's*, number and quality of visuals, and length.

We do *not* pay by the word. Longer is not necessarily better. In fact, the longer a feature, the less likely we'll have room for it.

We usually have a large inventory of half- to full-page features (over 750 words) and a screaming need for shorter items (200-500 words).

ILLUSTRATIONS

Include illustrations wherever possible: stamps, covers, postmarks or whatever other visual material supports your text.

Many would-be contributors seem to break down here. For *Linn's*, a picture is indeed worth, if not 1,000 words, at least 250. More frequently than we would prefer, we find ourselves returning otherwise publishable work because it lacks the necessary visual support.

As a general rule, the best way to write an article on almost any philatelic subject is to have the photos in front of you before you begin. That way you are sure to properly illustrate your subject, and your text is fairly certain to explain what's in its pictures.

Conversely, an easy way to get into trouble is to write an article with no visual support, in the expectation of finding a photo after the article is done. Nine times out of ten, the result is a text that lacks illustrations or doesn't connect to them.

On the other hand, bear in mind that in final page make-up there must be a balance between illustrations and text. Too many illustrations can overpower a skimpy text and make it difficult (sometimes impossible) for us to lay out the words.

We prefer crisp, sharp-focus, high-contrast glossy black and white photos. A few items that have no tonal gradations, postmarks or surcharges for instance, can be reproduced adequately from photocopies. Stamps and covers cannot.

If you can't provide decent photos, send us the material and we'll make the photos here. (Clear this with us first if the value is substantial.)

Please don't expect us to seek out your visuals for you; we don't have the time or the resources.

Our typical purchase includes the acquisition of the illustrations. If you want your photos returned, we should discuss this beforehand. Include your name and full address on the reverse of each photo.

Along with illustrations, we expect you to provide captions. Please provide captions on a separate sheet of paper, not imbedded within your manuscript. The ideal caption should explain what the picture shows and make the reader want to read the accompanying text. At the very least, a caption should explain what's in the picture. Identify all people and everything else that would provoke reader curiosity. "Figure 1" with no explanation is not an acceptable caption.

Don't paste visuals or captions onto your manuscript. Keep them separate.

COPY PREPARATION

Put your name and the page number in the upper right corner of each page.

Avoid typewritten strikeovers, especially with figures. Better to cross it out and say it again. Clarity is more important than neatness, because everything we publish must be retyped on a personal computer anyway.

Footnotes and bibliographies are not appropriate to our newspaper style. If attribution or citation is essential, then it's important enough to be worked into the text.

Refer to illustrations as Figure 1, Figure 2, etc. Avoid eye directions such as above and below, which might be contradicted by page make up.

For similar reasons, charts in the text should be avoided. They typically run wider than one column width, and cause difficult (sometimes impossible) make-up problems. If you must include a chart, prepare and discuss it separately, as if it were a photo.

STYLE: GENERAL

Linn's is a weekly magazine in newspaper format. Our editorial style is designed to communicate information as quickly and as clearly as possible. Stylistic quirks that hinder rapid communication are discouraged. Our basic reference in matters of editorial style is *The Associated Press Stylebook,* available from AP at 50 Rockefeller Plaza, New York, N.Y. 10020.

Even though your subject might be specialized, write it understandably. Always explain terms. Remember that *Linn's* is read by tens of thousands of readers who don't know your subject as well as you do. Reach out and help them.

Avoid lengthy paragraphs. One typewritten line makes two lines of type in *Linn's.* Our newspaper style calls for very short paragraphing. This also aids readership.

Don't use lengthy sentences. Two or three short sentences are easier to read than one long one. Never use parentheses or dashes when commas or separate sentences will serve the same end. Never use a comma when a period will do. That saves ink.

Avoid cliches. Don't try to be cute. Re-read your sentences to see if you can express the same thoughts in fewer words.

Check and double check all facts, especially names, addresses, catalog numbers and other critical bits of information. We rely on you for the accuracy of your prose.

Don't be afraid of the first person. We'll be publishing your work under your name. "We" or "this writer" are pedantic and often confusing. Say "I" if it's appropriate.

Use a dictionary or a spelling guide. Frequent misspellings suggest a lack of attention to detail that is inappropriate to the craft of journalism. The back pages of Webster are useful regarding punctuation and grammar.

Avoid jarring repetition of the same words or phrase. There are many ways to say the same thing.

STYLE: LINN'S

Never refer to a stamp by Scott number only. Describe it first and then add the Scott number if needed. As an example: "The U.S. 10¢ 1869 stamp (Scott 116)..." In a series, it's Scott 51-58; 233-37.

Spell out numerals one through nine, then use figures for 10 and higher. Don't use decimals after an even number of dollars (i.e., we say $20, not $20.00). For large numbers, insert the comma beginning with 1,000. Generally, figures are used in ages; always in percentages.

No comma after a month without a day (March 1983); adding the day requires the comma (March 13, 1983). The reverse "13 March 1983" takes no comma, but is difficult to read and should be avoided.

We abbreviate months when used with days (Aug. 12, 1869) but not without days (August 1869). We never abbreviate the five short months: March, April, May, June, July.

We never use italics or quotation marks for emphasis. If you want to emphasize a word or a point, write emphatically. Don't use quotation marks to indicate anything other than a quotation. Periods and commas go inside the quotation marks; semicolons go outside.

Abbreviations: In text, we use the old-style state abbreviations. We don't abbreviate Alaska, Hawaii, Idaho, Iowa, Maine, Ohio, Texas, Utah. Two-word states are abbreviated with no space: W.Va.

Mr. is used only with Mrs. or when the man is dead. Mrs. and Miss are generally unnecessary. We never use Ms.

We don't use periods with most well-known organizations: USS, HMS, UPU, USPS, UNPA, APS, APO, GPO, etc. However, we do use periods with country initials: U.S., U.N., U.S.S.R.

Postal administrations and other organizations take the singular: APS will stage its spring meeting, UNPA will announce its 1984 stamps.

Note the punctuation and separation of the following:

Citizens' Stamp Advisory Committee, bank note, price list. The following are all one word: mailcoach, handcancel, handstamp, datestamp, semipostal, multicolor, steamship.

Our general style is lowercase. When in doubt over whether a word should be capitalized, leave it down.

STANDARD TERMS GOVERNING ACCEPTANCE OF ORIGINAL MATERIAL

Linn's Stamp News, a division of Amos Press Inc. (the publisher), accepts original copy and/or artwork subject to the following terms and conditions:

1. First Worldwide Periodical Rights. The contributor grants to publisher the exclusive right to be the first to publish the article and supporting artwork in whole or edited fashion (sometimes referred to collectively as the "work") in *Linn's Stamp News* and to use said work in advertising and/or promotion.

2. Subsequent Use. The contributor retains the right to sell the work elsewhere provided such subsequent sale occurs no sooner than sixty (60) days after publication by *Linn's Stamp News.* The contributor agrees that any subsequent reprint will appropriately reference *Linn's Stamp News* copyright. The contributor grants to publisher a right to reuse said work in any publication of the publisher, subject to publisher's payment of an appropriate fee to the contributor.

3. Copyright. The contributor grants to the publisher the right to obtain copyright on the work in the publisher's name in the United States and any other country, subject to the contributor's retained non-exclusive right to reuse as set forth above.

4. Indemnity. The contributor warrants and guarantees that he is the sole proprietor of the work; that said work violates no existing copyright, in whole or part, that it contains no libelous or otherwise injurious matter; that the work has not heretofore been published; that he is the sole and exclusive owner of the rights granted herein to the publisher; and that he has not heretofore assigned, pledged, or otherwise encumbered said work. At his own expense, the contributor will protect and defend said work from any adverse claim of copyright infringement, and shall indemnify, defend and hold the publisher harmless from asserted claims of whatever nature, damages, costs and expenses which the publisher may incur as a result of the publication of said work and/or subsequent reuse.

5. Payment. The contributor accepts such amount as is tendered by separate check from the publisher as payment in full for the rights in the work granted herein to the publisher; provided, however, that it is agreed that additional monies may be due only as a result of subsequent reuse as set forth in paragraph 2 hereof.

6. Rights Reserved. All rights in the work not specifically granted to the publisher are expressly reserved to the contributor.

7. Applicable Law. The agreement between the contributor and publisher shall be governed by the law of Ohio and shall be deemed to have been entered into at Sidney, Ohio, as of the date of the issuance of publisher's check in payment of the amount due to the contributor pursuant to paragraph 5.

8. Arbitration. Any claim, dispute or controversy arising out of or in connection with the agreement between the contributor and publisher or any breach thereof, shall be arbitrated by the parties before the American Arbitration Association under the rules then applicable of that association. The arbitration shall be held in the city of Sidney, Ohio.

9. Successors and Assigns. The agreement of the contributor and publisher shall be binding upon, and inure to the benefit of each of their respective heirs, successors, administrators, and assigns.

10. Entire Agreement. It is understood by the contributor and publisher that these Standard Terms And Conditions and publisher's check tendered in payment in accordance with paragraph 5 sets forth the parties' entire agreement regarding this work and may not be varied except by an additional writing signed by the contributor and the publisher.

Categories: Hobbies (stamp collecting only)

Name: Elaine Boughner, Managing Editor
Material: All
Address: PO BOX 29
City/State/ZIP: SIDNEY OH 45365
Telephone: 937-498-0801
Fax: 800-340-9501
E-mail: linns@linns.com
Internet: www.linns.com

The Lion Magazine

THE LION Magazine welcomes freelance article and photo submissions that depict the service goals and projects of Lions clubs on the local, national and international level.

Contributors may also submit general interest articles that reflect the humanitarian, community betterment and service activism ideals of the worldwide association or family-oriented, humorous essays.

Lions Clubs International is the world's largest service club organization, with a membership composed of more than 1.4 million men and women in 178 countries and geographical areas. Lions are recognized globally for their commitment to projects that benefit the blind, visually handicapped and people in need.

The Headquarters Edition of THE LION Magazine, produced in Oak Brook, Illinois, is published 10 times yearly; December/January and July/August are combined issues. The circulation of the Headquarters Edition reaches approximately 600,000 readers.

Article length should not exceed 2,000 words, and is subject to editing. *No gags, fillers, quizzes or poems are accepted.* Photos should be at least 5"x7" glossies; color prints are preferred. THE LION Magazine pays upon acceptance of material.

Advance queries save your time and ours.
Categories: Nonfiction—Associations

Name: Robert Kleinfelder, Senior Editor
Material: All
Address: 300 22ND ST
City/State/ZIP: OAK BROOK IL 60523
Telephone: 630-571-5466

Liquid Ohio

Our format is 8.5"x11", 26-30 pages, b&w.
Poetry—try not to go over 60 lines, but a good epic is fine.
Short stories—between 2,000-3,000 words.
Photography/artwork—color or b/w, but they will appear in b&w.

All written work sent in via e-mail should either be pasted into the letter itself or in ClarisWorks for Mac format.

Photography or artwork should be sent via postal mail for clarity. If you would like your work returned, please indicate this with your submission.

Our deadlines for submission are:
June 1st
September 1st
December 1st
March 1st
Sample copies are available for $3.00.
Subscription rates are $12.00/year for 4 issues.
Please make checks payable to Amber Goddard Publications.
Categories: Fiction—Arts—Cartoons—College—Feminism—General Interest—Photography—Poetry

Name: Submissions Editor
Material: All
Address: PO BOX 60265
City/State/ZIP: BAKERSFIELD CA 93386
Telephone: 805-871-0586
E-mail: liquidohio@aol.com
Internet: www.macgyvergraphics.com/liquidohio/

Literal Latté
Mind Stimulating Prose, Poetry & Art

Send unpublished stories, personal essays or poems up to 6,000 words or art—from cover art to literary cartoons, photographs, paintings, drawings in black & white or color (slides or copies, not originals).

Styles range from classical to experimental from the shortest short to the nearly epic.

Include biography and self addressed stamped envelope for response/return of work. For poetry & fiction awards information—send SASE (or subscribe!!!).

Simultaneous submissions welcome, let us know if a piece is accepted elsewhere.

REMEMBER

The best way to learn what we like is to read the magazine.

1 year/6 issue subscription only $11 ($25 international), sample issue, $4

Categories: Fiction—Nonfiction—Literature—Poetry

Name: Jenine Gordon Bockman, Fiction Editor
Material: Fiction and Essays
Name: Jeff Bockman, Editor
Material: Poetry
Address: 61 E 8TH ST STE 240
City/State/ZIP: NEW YORK NY 10003
Telephone: 212-260-5532
E-mail: litlatte@aol.com

Literary Magazine Review
The University of Northern Iowa

Literary Magazine Review is devoted to providing critical appraisals of the specific contents of small, predominantly literary periodicals for the benefit of readers and writers. We print reviews of about 1,500 words which comment on the magazines' physical characteristics, on particular articles, stories, and poems featured, and on editorial preferences as evidenced in the selections.

Manuscripts accepted for publication become the property of LMR unless otherwise indicated. The views reflected in the articles are those of the writers, not the editors or sponsors.

Please query before sending manuscripts.

Yearly subscriptions (four issues) are available for $13.50, as are single issues for $4.00 (and double numbers for $6.50).

Categories: Literature

Name: Grant Tracey, Editor
Material: All
Address: THE UNIVERSITY OF NORTHERN IOWA
Address: DEPT OF ENGLISH & LITERATURE 115 BAKER HALL
City/State/ZIP: CEDAR FALLS IA 50613
Telephone: 319-273-2821
Fax: 319-273-5807
E-mail: grant.tracey@uni.edu

The Literary Review
Fairleigh Dickinson University

MAJOR INTERESTS: TLR has an international focus and welcomes work in translation.

CONTENT: Original poetry, fiction, work in translation, essays, review essays on contemporary writers and literary issues. Review-essays should include a group of works of common interest rather than a single title.

LENGTH: We have no length restrictions for fiction or poetry; however, long works must meet an exceptionally high standard of excellence. In general, essays should be under 5,000 words and reviews from 1,500 to 2,500 words.

STYLE: We accept work in any format or style, ranging from traditional to experimental. We expect our contributors to have a strong understanding of technique and a wide familiarity of contemporary writing, but editorial decisions are based on quality alone.

NUMBER: We read only one story, essay, or review-essay by an author at one time, and no more than six poems.

PRESENTATION: Clear photocopies and dot-matrix printouts are permissible.

TIME: We try to advise of our decision within 8 to 12 weeks of receiving a manuscript. Accepted manuscripts usually appear within 18—24 months, often sooner, depending upon our commitment to special issues.

COMPENSATION: Contributors receive two copies of the issue in which their work appears and are eligible to compete in our annual Charles Angoff cash award.

COPYRIGHT: All material appearing in TLR is copyrighted. Authors are granted reprint rights as TLR only holds one-time rights to their work.

SAMPLES: Sample copies are available for $5.00 U.S., $6.00 foreign, prepaid.

Categories: Fiction—Nonfiction—Literature—Poetry—Short Stories—Writing

Name: Submissions Editor
Material: All
Address: 285 MADISON AVE
City/State/ZIP: MADISON NJ 07940
Telephone: 201-443-8564
Fax: 201-443-8564
E-mail: tlr@fdu.edu

Literary Sketches

Literary Sketches publishes articles and fillers under 750 words on books and authors. Biographical material should concern human interest information not found in general knowledge or encyclopedia entries.

Although the readers have a strong background in literature, the tone should be informal rather than scholarly.

Information must be documented. Sources may not be published but will be kept on file.

Send original manuscripts, not photocopies.

Payment is 1/2¢ word, and five author copies, on publication.

Categories: Nonfiction—Biography—Language—Literature

Name: Submissions Editor
Material: All
Address: PO BOX 810571
City/State/ZIP: DALLAS TX 75381-0571
Telephone: 972-243-8776

LIVING WITH Teenagers

Living With Teenagers

Living With Teenagers is a Christian monthly magazine for parents of teenagers. It focuses on the practical aspects of parenting, as well as informs, educates, and inspires parents to be aware of issues and understand their teenagers as they grow into responsible young adults.

Content: The editorial staff will evaluate articles dealing with any subject of interest to parents of teenagers.

Preparation: Cover page should include suggested title and blurb, by-line, author's full name, address, social security number, and rights offered (all, first, one-time reprint).

Submit manuscripts 600-1,200 words in length.

Queries with writing sample are preferred.

Disk submissions must be accompanied by a hard copy. Prefer disk on a Macintosh word processing program, but can convert most IBM programs.

Writing Tips: Quoted material must be properly documented (publisher, location, date, and page numbers), along with permission verification.

Include Bible references and thoughts when appropriate.

Remember readers are parents of teenagers.

Use brief, clear sentences.

Construct paragraphs logically.

Sidebars helpful.

Payment: Payment is negotiable and on acceptance.

Publication: Writers will receive, without cost, 3 advance copies of the issue in which their manuscripts are published. Extra copies can be ordered from the Customer Service Center (MSN 113 at address below, or 800-458-BSSB).

• For a sample copy, send a 9"x12" manila envelope with your address and return postage.

Categories: Parenting

Name: Editor
Material: All
Address: 127 NINTH AVE N
City/State/ZIP: NASHVILLE TN 37234-0140
Telephone: 615-251-2229
Fax: 615-251-5008
E-mail: lwt@bssb.com

Llamas

1) *Llamas* is written for camelid owners and enthusiasts everywhere. The magazine encompasses all aspects of camelids, but the emphasis is on llamas.

2) Practically any subject of interest to the readership is appropriate for the magazine (medicine, nutrition, behavior, packing, marketing, wool, legal questions, etc.) as long as the manuscript is well written.

3) *Llamas* is dedicated to accurate information. If there are serious mistakes in reporting fact, an article will be rejected. Likewise, writers should be able to verify sources and factual information in any manuscript that is considered for publication.

4) *Llamas* will provide a place for personal opinions that address subjects of general interest in the department, **In My Opinion.** *Llamas* will make it clear, that though the space is provided for divergent views, *Llamas* does not necessarily agree with the views expressed.

5) *Llamas* will seek to inform, interpret and explain all pertinent information affecting camelids and their owners.

6) In most instances, we prefer clear, interesting, lively narrative form writing. A little color and description to bring the reader into the world you're talking about helps. Quotes from others help a little more. Redundancy, long involved sentences and abstract detail are to be avoided. Most of all, a manuscript should maintain focus on a clearly defined subject and rely on clear, direct sentence structure. Transitions should carry readers smoothly from one idea to the next in a story that is a continuous, uninterrupted train of thought.

7) Articles should also display a balanced and accurate treatment of the subject. Check your facts with an 'expert' before submitting your manuscript for review.

8) Articles should be subject oriented and not reflect negatively on specific individuals.

Categories: Llamas

Name: Cheryl Dal Porto, Editor
Material: All
Address: 46 MAIN ST
City/State/ZIP: JACKSON CA 95638
Telephone: 209-223-0469
Fax: 209-296-2672
E-mail: claypress@aol.com

Log Home Living

Description

Log Home Living is a bimonthly magazine for people who own or are planning to build contemporary log homes. It is devoted almost exclusively to modern manufactured and handcrafted kit log homes. Our interest in historical or nostalgic stories of very old log cabins, reconstructed log homes, or one-of-a-kind owner-built homes is secondary and should be queried first.

Readership

Our audience comprises primarily married couples between 30 and 45 years old. They are generally well-educated and very individualistic do-it-yourselfers.

Specifications

Log Home Living welcomes new talent and strives to develop long-term relationships with those contributors who consistently deliver quality work. We buy two to four bylined feature articles of 1,000 to 2,000 words per issue. These articles should reflect readers lifestyles and interest in log homes as follows:

• **Log Home Owner Profiles.** Articles about people who have built modern log homes from manufactured or handcrafted kits. In a conversational tone, describe the home as it is and tell how it came to be. Emphasize the elements that make this home special-intent, design, solutions to unique problems, features, furnishings, interior design and landscaping. Every story must include feature photos. Floorplans of the completed home, construction costs and schedules are a plus.

• **Design & Decor Features.** Photo stories on various architectural features of log homes. Stories can focus on a particular home or the same architectural feature on different homes.

• **Historical Features.** Articles about historical log structures in North America or abroad and restorations of same. As mentioned before, we have a limited need for this material.

• **Technical Articles.** How-to advice about specific aspects of log home construction or pre-construction. Examples are scheduling a construction project, selecting wood preservatives, installing flooring, decorating log homes, dealing with subcontractors and innovative financing programs. Writers of these articles should be experts or able to interview experts and convey the information for a lay audience.

Submissions

Computer printouts are acceptable, but we prefer they be unjustified (ragged right) and letter quality. We will read unsolicited manuscripts but prefer an outline or a detailed query letter first. Enclose a SASE.

Photos

Stories must be accompanied by extensive professional-quality color photographs of log home interiors, exteriors or construction shots as appropriate. See our **Photographers Guidelines** for specific requirements. If you are not a professional photographer, advise us in your query. Also tell us if you know a professional photographer who can work with you on an assignment; otherwise, we will locate one to accompany you.

Payment & Rights

Payment for features ranges from $250 to $500 (without and with photos), depending on their length, the nature of the work and the amount of editing required. We acknowledge receipt of submissions immediately and try to provide an editor's response within thirty days. Payment is made within 30 days of acceptance.

Cancellations

If we determine that a submitted article requires substantial rewriting, we will pay a $100 research fee for the information supplied. If we decide not to use an assigned accepted article, we will pay a $100 kill fee.

Rights & Conditions

Log Home Living buys first North American rights and non-exclusive reprint rights. Upon publication, authors will receive two complimentary copies of the issue with their work.

We cannot accept responsibility for the personal safety or property of any freelancer while on assignment for the magazine. Writers and photographers are urged to have their own insurance in place while on assignment.

We assume that all contributed manuscripts are original and that all facts and quotes have been verified. Articles that have been published or submitted elsewhere must be so identified; in such cases, the author is responsible for obtaining permission to reprint previously published materials prior to submission to ***Log Home Living.***

Expenses

Reasonable expenses will be covered, provided that travel plans and all anticipated costs are discussed beforehand with the editor. A complete expense report, including receipts for all claims, should accompany the contributor's work. Expense reimbursement is made with payment for an accepted article.

Sample Copy

If you would like a sample copy of ***Log Home Living*** magazine, please send your check or money order for $4.00 to HBPI, Attn: Sample Copy, at the address below.

Categories: Nonfiction—Shelter (Custom Homes)

Name: Janice Brewster, Executive Editor
Material: All
Address: PO BOX 220039
City/State/ZIP: CHANTILLY VA 20153
Telephone: 703-222-9411
Fax: 703-222-3209

Long Island Parenting News

Long Island Parenting News is published monthly. 54,500 copies are circulated *free* throughout Nassau & Suffolk counties at schools, libraries, hospitals, doctors' offices, after-school programs, banks, museums, mothers' centers, children's theaters, toy stores, bookshops, childrenswear and maternity boutiques, movie theaters, and other retail outlets.

Long Island Parenting News is dedicated to educate, inform and inspire parents of young children (from pregnancy to teens) in the development of their understanding, appreciation, and celebration of their families.

Regular Columns

On The Island—Local, national and international NEWS of interest to parents.

Off The Shelf—Reviews and previews of children's BOOKS. Also author profiles.

Fun & Games—Reviews of GAMES, TOYS and HOBBIES.

The Beat—Reviews and previews of MUSIC for children. Also artist profiles.

Kid Vid—Reviews and previews of children's VIDEOS and TELEVISION. Also artist profiles.

Words Worth—Reviews and previews of STORYTELLING audio and video. Also artist profiles.

The Big Picture—Previews and reviews of FILMS for children.

Also artist profiles.

Monitor—Reviews and previews of COMPUTER SOFTWARE for children.

Getaway—Reports and reviews about FAMILY VACATIONS and recreational activities.

Soon Come—Reports and stories of special interest to EXPECTANT PARENTS.

Educaring—Reports and stories about PARENTING.

Growing Up—Reports on HEALTH and SAFETY.

On The Ball—Reports on SPORTS, FITNESS and martial arts for children.

Something Special—Reports of interest to parents of CHILDREN WITH SPECIAL NEEDS.

Family Matters—Views (often humorous) of FAMILY LIFE, parenthood and children.

Teen Time—Reports of interest to parents of teenagers.

Special Features

JANUARY: Schools, Sleepaway Camps, Family Safety

FEBRUARY: Camps, Family Health, Kids' Rooms

MARCH: Sports & Fitness Programs

APRIL: Swing Sets, Party Planning, Sports & Camping, Pets

MAY: Summer Programs & Camps, Summer Vacations

JUNE: Maternity & Birthing, Childcare

AUGUST: Schools & Fall Programs, Continuing Education, Special Needs

SEPTEMBER: Dance, Music & Arts programs, Party Planning, Children's Health

OCTOBER: Women's Health, Childcare, Halloween

NOVEMBER: Winter Vacations, Special Needs

DECEMBER: Winter & Spring Programs, Home Entertainment, Continuing Education

Manuscripts

• Please include suggested headlines, subheads, and a brief biography, if desired (to appear at end of article).

• Include any photographs or artwork (preferably black & white) that may enhance the presentation of your article.

• Include your name, address, and telephone number.

• Allow 6 to 10 weeks for a response.

Deadlines

First day of the month preceding publication. (i.e.—February issue deadline is January 1.

Rights

Long Island Parenting News buys one-time rights to articles that will not appear in other publications in the Long Island and New York City area within one year of publication.

Rates

1/3 page: 400-500 words $30

1/2 page: 500-750 words $40

2/3 page: 700-1,000 words $50

3/4/ page: 750-1,200 words $60

Full page: 1,000-1,500 words $70

Payment

Payment will be mailed within 30 days of publication.

Categories: Children—Family—Lifestyles—Parenting—Women's Issues

Name: Patrice Simms-Elias, Editorial Director
Material: All
Address: PO BOX 214

City/State/ZIP: ISLAND PARK NY 11558
Telephone: 516-889-5510
Fax: 516-889-5513
E-mail: LIParent@family.com

Long Island Update

Update is open to new and exciting ideas for feature pieces. Unsolicited manuscripts will be acknowledged.

All manuscript pages should be numbered consecutively.

All articles must be original, unpublished work. Authors must submit articles with the understanding that they cannot be submitted for publication elsewhere.

Once a completed and/or revised manuscript has been reviewed and accepted, it will be scheduled for production. Please keep in mind that production situations change quickly, making it difficult to know for certain which article will appear in a given issue. Once an article has been prepared for publication, however, every effort will be made to publish it in as timely a manner as possible.

Update pays between $25 and $100 for articles, depending on the circumstances and length. Payment is usually 30 days subsequent to publication.

Categories: Arts—Computers—Consumer—Entertainment—General Interest—Health—Lifestyles—Regional

Name: Cheryl A. Meglio, Editor-in-Chief
Material: All
Address: 990 MOTOR PKWY
City/State/ZIP: CENTRAL ISLIP NY 11735
Telephone: 516-435-8890
Fax: 516-435-8925

THE LONG TERM VIEW

The Long Term View
Massachusetts School of Law

Editorial Philosophy

The Long Term View is a public policy journal which devotes each issue to a balanced discussion of a single topic or question. We provide a forum where academics, professionals, and other knowledgeable persons can make their information available to lay persons m a direct and readable manner.

To achieve this objective, we welcome submissions in many forms, including essays and analytical articles. Whatever the format, we want unambiguous, economical prose. We discourage the extensive use of footnotes: main points should be made in the text. Authors are responsible for the accuracy of all citations and data.

Manuscripts will be edited for clarity, brevity, and style. Topics for future issues of LTV are printed at the end of each issue.

Manuscript Guidelines

Authors are asked to include a disk copy of their manuscript (along with the name and version number of the software package).

Any footnotes should appear at the end of the manuscript.

Except where content and style suggest otherwise, *The Long Term View* follows guidelines set forth in the *Chicago Manual of Style* (14th ed., 1993).

Please include a separate cover page with your name, affiliation, title of manuscript, and a brief biographical note.

Categories: Nonfiction—Government—Law—Politics

Name: Nancy Bernhard, Editor
Material: All
Address: 500 FEDERAL ST
City/State/ZIP: ANDOVER MA 01810
Telephone: 508-681-0800
Fax: 508-681-6330
E-mail: NEBERNHARD@aol.com

The Lookout
For Today's Growing Christian

Our Magazine

THE LOOKOUT is a 16-page, full-color weekly magazine from Standard Publishing with a circulation of more than 105,000.

THE LOOKOUT is written and designed to provide Christian adults with true-to-the-Bible teaching and current information that will help them fulfill their desire to mature as individual believers, develop godly homes, and live in the world as faithful witnesses of Christ. In short, we want to help our readers understand and respond to the world from a biblically based viewpoint.

THE LOOKOUT publishes from a theologically conservative, nondenominational, and noncharismatic perspective. It is a member of the Evangelical Press Association.

Our Readers

We have a diverse audience, but our main readership can be readily described:

• We have readers in every adult age group, but we aim primarily for those aged 35 to 55.

• Most readers are married and have older elementary to young adult children. But a large number come from other home situations as well.

• Our emphasis is on the needs of ordinary Christians who want to grow in their faith, rather than on trained theologians or church leaders.

Our Needs

As a Christian general-interest magazine, we cover a wide variety of topics—from individual discipleship to family concerns to social involvement. We value well-informed articles that offer lively and clear writing as well as strong application. We often address tough issues and seek to explore fresh ideas or recent developments affecting today's Christians.

A list of major upcoming themes is available on request (send a SASE). *Please query for theme-related articles.* You may send complete manuscripts for non-theme articles.

We usually publish five kinds of nonfiction articles:

• *Teaching articles* (500-1,800 words): Help readers practically apply Scripture to present-day needs or show them fresh ways to grow in their Christian walk. Your article should provide either solid principles to help readers better understand your subject or skills to help them effectively respond.

• *Informational and journalistic articles* (500-1,800 words): We are looking for timely, well-researched articles, interviews, profiles, or essays dealing with topics of current concern. (List sources when applicable.)

• *Human-interest stories* (400-1,800 words): Let your unique experiences and observations help our readers see God at work in the world. Better yet, show us the experiences of others. Become a reporter and tell our readers about Christian individuals or families with extraordinary stories. Humor and brief inspirational articles are welcome.

• *"Outlook"* (350-800 words): We publish reader-written opinion essays addressing current issues that concern Christians. Address your submission to "Outlook."

• *"Salt & Light"* (500-800 words): This column informs our

readers about fresh, creative ways Christians are reaching out to their communities and to the world. We're looking for exciting true stories about people who are making a positive difference.

Your Submission

• Please query at least six months in advance for theme-related articles. Your query letter should concisely describe the article you propose to write. Enclose a legal size, self-addressed, stamped envelope. If we are interested, we will ask for the article "on speculation," which means we are willing to examine the article, but cannot promise to publish it.

• You may send complete manuscripts for non-theme articles.

• Enclose a legal size, self-addressed, stamped envelope. (Self-addressed, stamped reply postcards are also acceptable.) Do not send more than one manuscript per SASE.

• Fax transmissions are acceptable, but remember we cannot guarantee a reply.

• We do not accept unsolicited electronic submissions (diskettes, e-mail).

• With your submission, please provide your name, address, daytime telephone number, social security number, and approximate word count.

• Allow up to 10 weeks for reply.

• Submit seasonal material six to nine months in advance.

• THE LOOKOUT pays up to nine cents per word for first rights on unsolicited articles; up to fifteen cents per word for assigned articles (first rights); up to six cents per word for onetime or second (reprint) rights. We pay on acceptance.

• Simultaneous submissions to non-competing markets are acceptable.

• THE LOOKOUT does not accept unsolicited poetry or fiction.

• To receive a sample issue, please send 75¢ and your mailing address with your request.

Categories: Nonfiction—Christian Interests—Family

Name: Andrea Ritze, Managing Editor
Material: All
Address: 8121 HAMILTON AVE
City/State/ZIP: CINCINNATI OH 45231
Telephone: 513-931-4050
Fax: 513-931-0950

Lost Treasure

Lost Treasure, Inc. reviews manuscript submissions for two treasure magazines as follows: 1) *Lost Treasure, a* monthly publication, accepts lost treasure, folklore, personal adventure stories; legends; and how-to articles. 2) *Treasure Cache*, an annual publication, accepts only documented treasure cache stories with a sidebar from the author telling the reader how-to search for the cache highlighted in the story. Additional tips and guidelines on writing for *Treasure Cache* are sent on request (be sure to include an SASE).

SUBMISSIONS

1. **Original Stories with photos, maps, and documentation are what we want!** No rehashes of well known treasure stories.

2. **Queries:** *Lost Treasure*—not required. *Treasure Cache*—required. Queries should be typed, one page or less, and may be faxed or mailed. Queries are answered as quickly as possible, usually 2-4 weeks.

3. **Source Documentation:** *Lost Treasure* and *Treasure Cache*—require source documentation. Articles dealing primarily with personal how-to information does not require source documentation unless the author makes reference to information outside of the realm of his/her personal experience. Then

documentation is required. For source documentation requirements, see **Source Documentation, #15.**

4. **Format, Disk:** Manuscripts must be typed, caps and lower case (not all capital letters) and accompanied by a readable 3½" floppy disk in ASCII or Microsoft Word. If a disk is not available, typewriter copy must be of scannable quality (clean, clear, sharp black ribbon). See #8 below.

5. **Page Identification:** Your name, address, telephone number (including area code) and social security number should appear on each manuscript page in the upper right hand corner, and on the backs of all slides, photos, maps, or other accompanying material. Photos should also be numbered on the back (see # 9 below).

NOTE: Do not rubber stamp nor write information on the backs of photos, maps, etc., as damage may result making them unusable.

TIP: Type information on a sticky back label and affix or, type on a piece of paper and tape to the back of the photo.

6. **Word Count:** An approximate word count should appear in the upper right hand corner on the first page of your manuscript.

7. **Page Numbering:** Manuscript pages should be page numbered.

8. **Sequence:** Manuscripts should be typed in the following sequence: 1) Article. 2) Sources. 3) Captions (photo, map, art) and should appear on your disk as well as hard copy.

9. **Identification—Photos and Captions:** All photos should be assigned an identification number (i.e., 1, 2, 3, etc.). Accompanying captions should be typed and numbered to correspond to photo I.D. numbers and, appear at the end of the article. If you are submitting a computer disk, captions must appear on the computer disk at the end of the article.

10. **All or Nothing:** All photos, maps, documentation, other pertinent information and floppy disk (if available) should accompany your manuscript at the time of submission.

11. **Article Lengths:** *Lost Treasure*—500-1,500 words. *Treasure Cache*—1,000-2,000 words. Occasionally two-part articles are published. These are accepted by query only.

12. **Issue Themes:** *Lost Treasure* articles should coordinate with an issue's theme if possible (editorial calendar available on request. Send SASE with [one first class stamp]). Stories deviating from the theme are always considered and used whenever possible. How-to articles are used in each issue. *Treasure Cache* is documented stories.

13. **Caution:** Stories should not read like ads for particular products. It is acceptable to name products in your story, but refrain from consistently repeating the detector's name or the name of other equipment unless you are submitting a field test story or the product did something unusual.

14. **Don't Fold Them:** Submissions should be mailed *unfolded* in 9"x12" (or larger) envelopes.

15. **SOURCE DOCUMENTATION:** At least two sources (preferably more) are required with each submission. Exception: personal experience stories.

Newspapers: List newspaper name, issue date, article title. If newspaper clippings have no identification or date, note this fact in your sources.

Magazines: List magazine title, publication date (month and year), article title, article's author.

Books: List by author, title, publisher, publication date.

National Archives, Library of Congress, etc.: List title, document number.

Historical Societies, Museum Files, etc.: List organization name, location (city, state), and other identifying information as applicable.

Personal experience stories:

Yours: Identify yourself as the source, telling this is a personal experience, where it happened and when.

Others: Identify whose experience it is, where it happened and when. Tell how you learned of the experience (examples: interview, letters, other).

TIP: Write down source information as you work. This insures accuracy and eliminates the necessity of backtracking.

16. **PHOTOS:** (Remember to identify them. See #'s 5 and 9 above.)

Cover Photos: Accepted with or without accompanying story. Only 35mm color slides (vertical shots) are accepted.

Article Photos: Black and white or color photos, any size smaller than 5"x7" accepted. No Polaroid shots. All photos must have sharp focus with good contrast.

17. **MAPS:** May be hand drawn or copied. They should indicate where the lost treasure is located and contain specific directions to lost treasure sites. (Remember to identify them. See #'s 5 and 9 above.)

18. **PICTURES, BLACK AND WHITE LINE ART (not created by you):** May be used only if you have received permission to do so and, credit is given to the source (museum, Library of Congress, illustrator's name, etc.). Exception: Newspapers—permission is not required but, credit must be given to the newspaper if a picture is copied. (Remember to identify them. See #'s 5 and 9 above.)

19. **CARTOONS:** As a rule we do not use cartoons in our magazines. Occasionally a cartoon accompanying a story is used.

20. **SAMPLE ISSUES OF OUR MAGAZINE:** Available on request. Write to: Managing Editor, Lost Treasure, Inc., at the address shown below. Enclose SASE with $1.47 postage.

21. **NON ACCEPTANCE:** We do not accept foreign manuscripts. Writers must reside in the U.S.A.

22. **CONTRACT:** We required a signed contract (our Magazine Rights Agreement form) from each writer giving us ALL rights to all material used (manuscripts, photos, art, etc.). No exceptions.

23. **PAYMENT:** Cover shots—$100.00. Articles—4¢ per word. Photos, hand-drawn maps, artwork—$5.00 each used. Payment is made on publication, not acceptance.

We appreciate your interest and hope to receive a submission from you soon.

Patsy Beyerl
Managing Editor
Categories: Treasure Hunting

Name: Patsy Beyerl, Managing Editor
Material: Metal Detecting/Treasure Hunting
Address: PO BOX 451589
City/State/ZIP: GROVE OK 74344
Telephone: 918-786-2182
Fax: 918-786-2192
E-mail: managingeditor@losttreasure.com

Lucidity Poetry Journal
A Quarterly Journal of Verse

Lucidity exists to provide a showcase for poets who create verse which has something to say in clear and comprehensible English and it serves as a protest against stringing together groups of unrelated words for no apparent reason, sprinkling in some vulgarity and calling it poetry.

We dedicate our journal to publishing the poets who express their thoughts, feelings and impressions about the human scene with clarity and substance. We are open to poetry dealing with the good, bad and ugly.. if done with finesse and style.

Submitting to *Lucidity*

1. Poems may be on any subject, any style but not to exceed 38 lines including all spaces. Please notice the maximum line length is about 75 characters.

2. Submit 1 legible copy of poems with your name and address at top in right hand corner. Do not send more than 5 poems in each category.

3. Please—no poems about birds, bees, butterflies, sunrise, sunset, politics, philosophy or your religious persuasion. We seek poetry dealing with daily human encounters and relationships...interactions of people whether present or past.

4. Since *Lucidity* is an on-going publication we have no entry deadlines. If poems arrive when one issue is already filled, your entries will be held for consideration in the next edition. Depending on when a poem arrives in our publication cycle, response time may vary from 1 to 5 months. If you're in a big hurry, please do not submit. It takes time to assemble, select, typeset, format, print, bind, trim and mail.

5. We have 3 categories of recognition. *Lucidity* publication is made possible by the nominal reading fees and faithful subscribers, which are our sole sources of revenue. Our volunteer staff is unpaid.

A. **JURIED SUBMISSIONS** (Fee $1.00 per poem entered) Poets chosen are paid $1 cash plus one free copy.

B. **CASH AWARD SUBMISSIONS** (Fee $2.00 per poem) Top 3 poets chosen are paid $15/$10/$5 plus a copy of *Lucidity*. Others selected receive $1 plus copy.

C. **SUCCINCT SUBMISSIONS** (No fee if sent with other entries) Poems of 12 lines or less/Sorry, no pay.

Categories: Poetry

Name: Ted O. Badger, Editor
Material: Poetry
Address: 398 MUNDELL RD
City/State/ZIP: EUREKA SPRINGS AR 72631
Telephone: 501-253-9351
E-mail: tbadger@ipa.net

The Lutheran Digest

The Lutheran Digest, published quarterly, accepts a limited number of original manuscripts. Approximately 70 percent of the magazine's content is reprinted from other publications. *The Digest's* goal is twofold: To entertain and encourage believers and to subtly persuade non-believers to embrace the Christian faith. Distribution is free through participating Lutheran churches.

ARTICLES: Articles should be no more than 7,500 characters in length. Articles of less than 3,000 characters are encouraged. Stories frequently reflect a Lutheran Christian perspective, but are not intended to be "lecturing" sermonettes. Popular stories show how God has intervened in a person's life to help solve a problem. Also needed are seasonal and special interest stories and stories reflecting God's presence in nature. Payment is $15-$25 on acceptance, plus a complimentary copy upon publication.

POETRY: *The Digest* accepts a limited number of *short* poems each issue. We're most likely to accept poems of one or two stanzas that will fit into a single column of the magazine. Only two full-page poems are used each issue. Subject matter is open. There is no payment for poetry, however a complimentary copy is sent when the poem is used. Please do not submit more than three poems at a time. Each poem should be typewritten on a separate sheet of 8½"x11" paper.

FILLERS: Items such as "Recipes Lutherans Digest" and original hymn verses may be submitted. A complimentary copy of the magazine will be sent on publication.

REPRINTS: Authors may submit previously published articles for which they have retained reprint rights. Content should be similar to that described in "Articles" above. Payment is $15-$25 on acceptance plus a complimentary copy upon publication. **Note:** As a professional courtesy, the last publication to feature the article will be acknowledged via a credit line. Be sure to include the name and publication date of that publication.

TIPS FOR SUBMITTING MANUSCRIPTS: Carefully study several issues of *The Lutheran Digest* to see the type of things we publish. Upbeat articles that can be read in one sitting are preferred. For seasonal items, keep in mind that we work two to three issues ahead.

BIBLICAL QUOTATIONS: Scripture references, which should be included for any Biblical quotations, should be inside the final quotation mark. (Example: "God so loved...life (John 3:16).") Also, the first letter of all pronoun references to God and/or Jesus should be capitalized.

MANUSCRIPT MECHANICS: Front page-In the upper-left corner include your correct full name, address, phone number and social security number. In the upper-right corner note the character count (not word count). Title should be centered and printed in upper- and lowercase lettering, 1/3 down the page followed by your byline. Manuscripts should be typed with paragraph indentations and spacing between paragraphs. A short, one-line description of the author should follow the article. Please do not submit more than three items at a time. Simultaneous submissions will be considered, but please notify us if that's what you're doing.

RIGHTS PURCHASED: *The Lutheran Digest* buys one-time rights for original material or one-time reprint rights for previously published items. We also ask that authors allow us to grant limited reprint permission to individual churches for use in their congregations. (Commercial inquiries are referred to the author.)

Categories: Nonfiction—Animals—Cartoons—Children—Christian Interests (area of primary interest)—Confession—Conservation—Consumer—Diet—Family (area of primary interest)—Gardening—General Interest—Health—Hobbies—Humor—Inspirational (area of primary interest)—Marriage—Money/Finance—Outdoors—Parenting—Recreation—Relationships—Religion (area of primary interest)—Rural America—Senior Citizens—Spiritual (area of primary interest)

Name: David L. Tank, Editor
Material: All
Address: PO BOX 4250
City/State/ZIP: HOPKINS MN 55343
Telephone: 612-933-2820
Fax: 612-933-5708

Lynx Eye

LYNX EYE is a quarterly literary magazine of short stories, poetry, essays, social commentary, and black-and-white art. "Lynx-eyed" means sharp-sighted, and each issue showcases the work of visionary writers and artists. Familiar formats are combined with the experimental; experienced contributors appear alongside new voices. The opening feature, *Presenting*, introduces a previously unpublished artist.

The pages of LYNX EYE take you on imaginative journeys in the company of colorful characters. You may visit a Baltimore diner, the Indiana state fair, or a Tuscan village. Meet the world's greatest fishing dog, a forgetful vampire, and the queen of jingle junk. From pastoral odes to biting commentary, each issue of LYNX EYE offers thoughtful and thought-provoking reading.

Along with the pleasure of the written word, visual treats are plentiful. Original cover art invitingly presented—occasionally in eye-opening color—greets the LYNX EYE reader. Graphic designs, pen-and-ink drawings, and astute cartoons are scattered throughout the publication.

LYNX EYE is a journal-sized magazine; average page count is 120. It is published every February, May, August, and November. With a steadily growing readership, the lynx has been spotted worldwide: Paris, Kharkov, Bangkok...and Whidbey Island. Shouldn't your address be listed too?

In the U.S.
• One-year subscription (4 issues): $20.00
• Two-year subscription (8 issues): $38.00
Outside the U.S.
• One-year subscription (4 issues): $24.00
• Two-year subscription (8 issues): $48.00

Please make checks payable to ScribbleFest Literary Group.

ScribbleFest Literary Group is a nonprofit organization dedicated to the promotion and development of the literary arts. With a mission to encourage excellence in writers and artists, founders Pam McCully and Kathryn Morrison began publishing LYNX EYE in November, 1994. ScribbleFest plans to expand its activities by sponsoring special events, readings, and support services vital to the development of the literary arts.

"From our humble beginnings over tepid cappuccino in a Westwood coffeehouse, our love of literature compelled us to provide a forum for uncommon ideas and unheard voices."

—Pam and Kathryn

Writer's Guidelines

Each issue of LYNX EYE includes fiction, essays, poetry and black-and-white artwork. Prose should be between 500 and 5,000 words, Poetry should be 30 lines or less. Our format is journal size; artwork should be 6"x4" (or something that will reduce to that size). If you have an excellent piece of work that falls outside of our requirements, send it.

Each issue opens with the feature, *Presenting*, in which a writer or artist makes his or her print debut.

LYNX EYE accepts never-before-published work only. We acquire first North American serial rights to your work. All other rights remain with you. We pay $10 per piece upon acceptance. You also receive three complimentary copies of the publication.

Manuscripts must be typed. Artwork should be camera-ready. We will respond within eight to twelve weeks.

Creativity is the antithesis of prejudice: having an open mind in the most complete sense of the word-non-judgmental, open to possibilities, open to new ideas, open to one's own feelings, open to others' feelings and needs.

Creativity is not-stopping too soon. How many creative ideas are squelched, and how many creative possibilities are never approached because someone gave up? But the creative person has to know when to "change gears": on arriving at an idea you really believe in, determination becomes necessary to follow through with it and to not be discouraged by others. Creative people work hard.

—From Cognition to Creativity
LYNX EYE

We are committed to the written word and anxiously await reading yours.

Categories: Essays—Poetry—Short Stories—Social Commentary

Name: Pam McCully, Co-editor
Material: All
Address: 1880 HILL DR
City/State/ZIP: LOS ANGELES CA 90041

Remember: Editors change jobs and publishers change addresses. It is wise to invest in a phone call for the current information before submitting.

Periodicals
M-R

The MacGuffin

The MacGuffin publishes the best poetry, fiction, and creative nonfiction submitted. Except for special issue call for manuscripts, we rarely publish drama, haiku, light verse, concrete poetry, genre fiction, and academic articles. We do not publish reviews.

FOR ALL SUBMISSIONS
• Simultaneous submissions are discouraged.
• Allow eight to twelve weeks for evaluation. At that time, you will be notified of the acceptance of your work, your work will be returned, or you will be notified that your work is still under consideration.
• If your work is accepted we request brief biographical information.
• If your work is accepted and it is possible, we appreciate if you can send it to us on disk in any standard PC or Macintosh format. This will reduce typesetting costs and increase accuracy.
• You may withdraw manuscripts until issues enter the typesetting process. The dates when typesetting begins for each issue are: January 20, for spring issues; March 15, for special issues; and September 1, for fall issues.
• *The MacGuffin* is copyrighted. However, upon publication all rights revert to authors. We appreciate acknowledgment as first place of publication.
• At this time, payment is limited to two contributor's copies plus reduced price offers.

POETRY
• We consider all forms of poetry whether traditional, formal, free verse, experimental. Poems can be up to 400 lines. There are no subject biases. Please do not submit more than five poems at a time.

FICTION and NONFICTION
• We consider the best fiction and nonfiction. There are no subject biases. Maximum length is 5,000 words. If you submit portions of longer works, please include a synopsis.
Categories: Fiction—Nonfiction—Literature—Poetry—Short Stories—Writing

Name: Submissions Editor
Material: All
Address: 18600 HAGGERTY RD
City/State/ZIP: LIVONIA MI 48152
Telephone: 313-462-4400 ext. 5292
Fax: 313-462-4558

Mademoiselle

We look for quality **nonfiction**. The subject matter should be of interest to single, working women between the ages of 18 and 31. We run reporting pieces, essays, first person accounts and humor. The topics we cover include work, health, relationships, and trends that affect women in their twenties.

Writers should submit proposals or final manuscripts and published clips. Proposals should be about one page long. Articles generally run from 1,000 to 2,000 words.
Categories: Nonfiction—Careers—Entertainment—Fashion—Film/Video—Lifestyles—Physical Fitness—Relationships—Sexuality—Spiritual—Television/Radio—Women's Issues

Name: Kathy Brown Weissman, Executive Editor
Name: Faye Haun, Managing Editor
Material: Any
Address: 350 MADISON AVE
City/State/ZIP: NEW YORK NY 10017
Telephone: 212-880-8627
Fax: 212-880-8248
E-mail: MlleMag@aol.com

Maelstrom

1. *Maelstrom* accepts submissions of poetry, short fiction, black and white art, cartoons and humor. Simultaneous submissions and previously published material are o.k.

2. There are no specifications in regards to genre, length or forms. *Maelstrom* does not accept pornographic materials.

3. Submissions are accepted by e-mail in the body of the text with the exception of art submissions which may be sent in attached files.

4. Submission of poetry—submit no more than 4 poems at a time

5. Submissions of short fiction—please do not submit more than one piece of short fiction and please keep short fiction selections to a 5 typed page maximum.

6. Book reviews—we also review books, published and unpublished—authors should send queries first.

7. Editor responds to submissions within 1 month. Pay for accepted work is 1 copy.

8. *Maelstrom* is 8½"x7" saddle stitched, published bimonthly and circulating between 500 and 1,000 copies per issue. Subscriptions are $15.00 for one full year and single copies are $3.00. Contributors may purchase additional copies for a discounted price of $2.00.

Categories: Fiction—Book Reviews—B/W Art—Cartoons—Humor—Poetry

Name: Christine L. Reed, Editor
Material: Poetry, Short Fiction, Book Reviews
Name: Mike Safferthwaite, Art Editor
Material: B/W Art, Cartoons
Address: PO BOX 7
City/State/ZIP: TRANQUILITY NJ 07879
E-mail: IMaelstrom@aol.com

The Magazine of Fantasy & Science Fiction

We have no formula for fiction. We are looking for stories that will appeal to science fiction and fantasy readers. The SF element may be slight, but it should be present. We prefer character-oriented stories. We receive a lot of fantasy fiction, but never enough science fiction or humor. Do not query for fiction; send the entire manuscript. We publish fiction up to 25,000 words in length. Please read the magazine before submitting. A sample copy is available for $5.

We do not accept simultaneous or electronic submissions. Please type your manuscript. Put your name on each page. Manuscripts received without return postage will be discarded.

Our columns and nonfiction articles are assigned in house. We do not accept freelance submissions in those areas.

Payment is 5-8 cents per word on acceptance. We buy first North American and foreign serial rights and an option on anthology rights. All other rights are retained by the author.

Allow 8 weeks for a response. Please write if you have any questions.

Cartoon and art queries as well as orders for sample copies should be sent to Ed Ferman, 143 Cream Hill, West Cornwall, CT 06796.

Categories: Fiction—Fantasy—Horror—Science Fiction

Name: Gordon Van Gelder, Editor
Material: All
Address: PO BOX 1806
City/State/ZIP: NEW YORK NY 10159-1806
Fax: 212-982-2676
E-mail: GordonFSF@aol.com

The Magazine of La Cucina Italiana
Good Food for Good Living

The Magazine of La Cucina Italiana is unique in its authoritative approach to Italian cuisine, travel, wine, and culture. Readers rely on our publication to provide them with in-depth, accurate information concerning Italian regional foods, dining establishments, places and people of interest, and Italian specialty food shops in Italy and around the world. We are the only Italian magazine in North America, and our editorial mission is to educate the public about the many pleasures of Italian gastronomy, tradition, and tourism.

When assigning articles, we look for authors whose knowledge of Italy (whether wide-ranging or specific) is sufficiently deep to educate our readers. Some of our writers are experts on Italian wines or liqueurs; others are chefs or restaurateurs whose experience makes them a reliable source for restaurant reviews; and others still are authorities on specific regions or cities of Italy. All articles must be based on a solid foundation of accurate information, and personal opinion should be indicated as such.

Articles should be pleasurable to read as well as informative, and while our editors may bring minor or major changes to your manuscript to suit our readership, we do prefer writers whose prose flows and whose ideas are expressed coherently and appealingly. The writing style we favor varies from piece to piece, with some articles taking a lighter tone and others a more scholarly approach depending on their content. Yet the magazine's aim is primarily to enlighten our readers in the most pleasant way possible: the well of solid, reliable information that we supply is what ultimately distinguishes us from other publications.

We ask that any article or feature idea be submitted to our editors in writing along with sample clips of your writing if you have any. When submitting a query, you may send us the entire manuscript if you wish, although we prefer a short outline of your proposal. Seasonal material should be submitted six to eight months ahead. Mention the availability of photographs in your proposal.

When querying, send along some information about yourself: who you are, what you do, and how you acquired your knowledge. If you want to be certain of a response, enclose a self-addressed stamped envelope, and keep in mind that it will take between 8 and 12 weeks to receive a response to your query.

Categories: Food/Drink

Name: Micol Negrin, Editor
Material: All
Address: 230 FIFTH AVE STE 1111
City/State/ZIP: NEW YORK NY 10001
Telephone: 212-725-8764
Fax: 212-889-3907
E-mail: piacere@earthlink.net

The Magazine of Speculative Poetry

MSP was founded in 1984 by Mark Rich and Roger Dutcher. Mark published one the first speculative poetry magazines, "Treaders of Starlight." Roger published "Uranus," another speculative poetry magazine. Finding themselves in the same city, they naturally founded a new magazine. MSP went 13 issues with both as editors when Mark, having moved and found success in his writing, decided to "move on." MSP has been edited by Roger since then. Mark will continue as a contributing editor, providing reviews, essays and, hopefully, cover art. David Memmott will continue ass contributing editor, he began with issue V4#1.

Basics:

3 cents a word, $3.00 minimum, $25.00 maximum on acceptance.

First North American rights.

All rights revert to the author(s) upon publication, except for permission to reprint in any "Best of" or compilation volume. Payment will be made for such publication.

Poets receive a copy of the issue in which their poem(s) appears.

Return time of 1 to 8 weeks. Usually 1 to 2 weeks.

No simultaneous submissions; we do not use reprints.

What MSP wants:

I want more than just images. I want a poem to take me someplace I haven't been before. Have a fresh look at an old trope. I am more concerned with a good poem first, then a speculative poem.

Speculative poetry: Speculative poetry may be described as the equivalent in poetry to speculative fiction, that interesting confluence of post modernism and science fiction in the late sixties and early seventies of Britain and America. Authors associated with this movement include: J.G. Ballard, James Sallis, Pamela Zoline, Keith Roberts, Brian Aldiss, Samuel Delaney, Thomas Disch, and the poets George MacBeth and D.M. Thomas.

Speculative poetry can result from several approaches. One might be called projection: we imagine ourselves viewing from other perspectives than our own or simply being another being—for instance, we might be a tree, an alien sentience, perhaps ourselves five years from now. A second approach is simply that of the extended metaphor: science fiction has created a rich vocabulary of images and ideas, many of which might be utilized in generating poetry. Other approaches may be used and the poems themselves may range from the meditative to the narrative to the lyric. What is most important to remember is that speculative poetry is a species of imaginative literature, and that it is a new species. Each poem in part defines the field as it is written.

I will leave it to others (or to another place) to argue whether speculative poetry is separate from or inclusive of, yet more than, science fiction poetry and the other identifiers we use, fantasy and horror. "Slipstream" seems to be a term that is similar. Literary has been used to describe the type of poetry we use.

Science fiction poetry: The bulk of what we publish, based on science (soft or hard) and speculating on or exploring that science for an outcome we, in our current world, have not discovered yet. How do we react to, manage in, the world you have constructed. Was it Ray Bradbury who said SF doesn't predict the future, it tries to prevent it.

Science poetry: Read Diane Ackerman and Loren Eisley for

an idea. The poem should still convey a sense of wonder. Not just nature poetry. Astronomical poetry with an edge perhaps. Speculation on contemporary science perhaps.

Fantasy poetry: I don't see enough fantasy poetry. What does MSP want? Fantasy from the realm of myth, fairy tales, and contemporary fantasy like Tolkien, Susan Cooper's "Dark is Rising" series, Le Guin's "Earthsea", McKillip's "Riddle Master" series, etc. Jim Dorr "Flight From the Tower" in a previous MSP fits the bill. I don't mean horror, dark fantasy or sword & sorcery. Once in awhile MSP sees Beowulf "like" poems, usually epic in length, no, I don't mean these, either, and not just because of the length. Just because there is an elf doesn't make it fantasy. I don't particularly like elf with motorcycles and assault weapons fantasy. In contemporary settings I enjoy the prose of James Blaylock and prose and poetry of Charles de Lint.

Horror or Dark Fantasy poetry: I am hard to please in this area. There is a lot of poetry written in this area. There are a lot of markets in this area. It is going to take a poem that grabs me to be accepted. It is not likely to be a vampire, werewolf or zombie poem. I do seem to have a penchant for mummies. It is most likely to be psychological horror that I will look at more closely. I am not likely so take a "splatter" poem.

Concrete or prose poetry: OK, I have not seen a lot of concrete poetry I have liked that was speculative, but then again, it seems the field should be able to produce some interesting visions. I would probably ask for a disc copy of any poem I might accept.

I won't try to define prose poetry. Shorter will be better. Have more than images.

Not much help? If you feel it is a good poem and you want to spring for the postage, try me out. MSP would publish good poems in any of the areas above. I would rather read, enjoy and accept a poem than not have it sent because of any strictures inferred or implied above.

I have sent back good poems that are: mainstream, love, nature or political in content, but are not speculative. I have taken some I have liked because they are "on the edge."

Length, style, etc.:

A number of editors are very strict about how they want everything. You should pay attention to those details if you are submitting to them. Although we have always been pretty easy going, there are some general guidelines that make it easier for me.

We are a small magazine, we can't print epics, yet they still arrive now and again. We have printed some poems that run two or three pages, but it is rare to do anything longer. If you have something you feel is your best and it is longer, go ahead and send it.

No simultaneous submissions. We do not use reprints.

I am not persnickety about the number of poems you send. Send as many as you want to spring for postage on. Your acceptance is based on your poem, not on the number. Be reasonable though, not twenty or thirty. There does seem to be a correlation between a poet sending large numbers and my not liking the poetry, but that could be illusion. But, it seems a waste to send one, unless it is long, so send what you want. Three to five seems to be the most common number.

I have read poems that are hand written (usually prisoners or young people), single-spaced, double-spaced, with a regular font, with hard to read fonts, etc. I am not persnickety here either, but double-spaced (on smaller poems) is better, and a "regular old font" is best. I don't recall ever accepting a poem that was handwritten, in a hard to read font or something out of the ordinary. Not because of the handwriting but because of the poem; again, there seems to be a correlation. My eyes do seem to require more focusing of late, so double-spacing is best.

Cover letters: I like 'em. But they aren't necessary. If you do include a cover letter, make it more than "here are my poems, I hope you like them." A practical matter is to include the names of the poems you are submitting, if the poems get separated from your cover letter, then it helps to find them. Tell me where you have been published before (you don't have to have been) if you want, it may help trigger a memory of a poem you have done. You don't need to send a complete list of every poem you have ever published, just some high spots. Tell us where you have heard of us, it helps us know which market sources produce the best results. You can tell me a bit about yourself if you like.

Your name and your address should appear somewhere on each poem, your name on each page if it is a longer poem. This is practicality, if your poems get separated from your cover letter or return envelope, I am not likely to recall whose they are. Including the number of lines/words in each poem, usually in the corner opposite your name and address, is useful as well.

Postage: You should include an appropriate amount of postage for the return of your mss., if it cost you 78 cents to mail them to me it is going to cost you 78 cents to mail them back. If you are submitting from a country other than the US, remember, I can only use US stamps. Send loose US stamps (see USPS website for current rates to your country) or an IRC. I have yet to meet a USPS employee who has treated an IRC the same as another. Most of the time I have good luck with them. However they do require you and me to stand in line and to have the employee figure out what to do with them. If you can arrange a stamp swap with someone, that is nice. In the case of non-US poets *only*, if you don't want your mss. returned, send me your e-mail address and I will let you know. My e-mail address is a work address and seriously limited re: non-work related mail.

If you send me your poems in an 8"x10" envelope and a #10 envelope for their return, I am going to stuff them all in the #10 envelope. This can result in an envelope which is overweight for the postage on it. I don't put on extra postage, you are liable to get a postage due return.

If you don't want your mss. returned, please state this clearly in your cover letter and/or on the mss. itself. If you don't, you will get your poems back in whatever envelope you send me.

If your submission comes to me postage due you are very likely to get it returned to you as "refused."

Submissions without an SASE or postage/IRC are held for about 2 to 3 months. If I haven't received an SASE in that time the poems are recycled.

Electronic submissions: Yes, it is the world of the Internet and e-mail, no, I don't have a computer (believe it or not.) I do have an e-mail address but it is for work and I *have* to limit the amount of non-work e-mail I receive. I am not open to electronic submissions. With the exception of non-US poets noted above, I can not e-mail a poet about their submission.

At the moment I am not requiring or requesting submissions on disk.

MSP does not want:

Prose. Plays. Art work.

Nature poetry, animal/pet poetry, religious poetry, love poetry unless they have some correlation to one of the genres we publish. We get a fair amount of the type of poetry completely unrelated to speculative poetry, some of it is good, most of it bad, but none of it accepted.

Essays or reviews unless you query first with general idea/outline.

An Organization of interest:

Science Fiction Poetry Association, now in its 21st year. Send $15 to John Nichols, 6075 Bellevue Dr, North Olmsted, OH, 44070. The SFPA publishes *Star*Line*, a newsletter, six times a year and the association administers the Rhysling Award for best science fiction poems of the year. You also receive the *Rhysling Anthology*, which publishes the nominated poems, with your membership.

Categories: Fantasy—Horror—Poetry

Name: Roger Dutcher, Editor
Material: All
Address: PO BOX 564
City/State/ZIP: BELOIT WI 53512

Magical Blend Magazine

Thank you for your interest in *Magical Blend.* We are always interested in reviewing focused, well-written articles and interviews. The best way of assessing our style is to look at copies of our magazine. You could also examine our anthology of best articles, *Magical Universe* (Swan Raven, 1996), or find us on our Website. The following information can give you some of the distinctions we use in selecting work for publication.

SUBJECT MATTER:

We do not respond to query letters. We only consider final products. We are no longer publishing fiction or poetry. Purely personal essays, sermons, prophecies and opinions are strongly discouraged. Almost all of our feature articles are interviews with, or articles about, leadership and innovations in the field of global transformation.

Readers of *Magical Blend* are primarily interested in personal and planetary growth and change, with an emphasis on spiritual and social subjects that are intellectually challenging and well-researched. They respond to significant discoveries and research into cultural mythologies and spiritual disciplines. They want innovative techniques for living life more fully. They want to be related to themselves, their families, cultures, technologies and the environment. They are curious about alternative health technologies and the significance of the Internet. Their musical tastes range from world beat to contemporary funk.

Artistic, cultural, extra-terrestrial, health, musical, psychic, psychological, spiritual and technology-oriented material is requested. Light-hearted pieces with a point to make about the human condition are welcome. We are more likely to publish constructive approaches to social change rather than assaults on the status quo. We do not grind political axes, but encourage articles which can inform readers about conditions which shed light on the process of global transformation.

FORMAT:

While size matters less than content, feature articles range in length from 1,000-3,500 words. That's between four and eleven pages of 1.5 line-spaced twelve point Palatino type using Word 5.1 for Macintosh. Be concise yet informative enough to support your topic. We have always generously edited manuscripts for length and conciseness, but prepared work is appreciated. We also welcome for our Culture Watch section 200-450 word current events articles which are to the point and have a punch.

NOTIFICATION:

Let us know if you have photographs to support your article, and if it is available on diskette or by e-mail. Do not send photographs or diskettes with your unsolicited manuscripts. Do not fax us long articles; they are difficult to read on our fax paper.

Payment is usually in copies; we infrequently pay money for unsolicited work. Pay rates vary from zero to $200, and are considered on an individual basis.

Categories: Nonfiction—Culture—Ecology—Energy—Feminism—Health—History—Inspirational—Interview—Lifestyles—Men's Issues—Multicultural—Native American—New Age—Philosophy—Psychology—Relationships—Religion—Science—Spiritual—Technology—Women's Issues

Name: Jerry Snider, Publisher/Editor
Material: All
Address: 133½ BROADWAY

City/State/ZIP: CHICO CA 95928
Telephone: 916-893-9037
Fax: 916-893-9076
E-mail: magical@crl.com
Internet: www.magicalblend.com

Mail Call Journal
Where the Spirit of the Civil War Soldier Lives

Dear Writer,

Profile. MAIL CALL JOURNAL...*Where the Spirit of the Civil War Soldier Lives* is published six times a year by Distant Frontier Press with subscribers throughout the United States. Readers are interested in the social aspects of the war...the events (well-known or little known) that happened to or occurred because there was an individual behind it. MAIL CALL JOURNAL was first published in April 1990.

What MAIL CALL JOURNAL Is. This publication focuses on the time period of the Civil War. Although the subject matter varies, all submissions should somehow be related to the Civil War—either about the Civil War, taking place between 1861 and 1865, having an effect that led to the war, information about a place or person that played a role in the Civil War but discussing something that happened to the place or person after the war, looking back to that time period, pretending to be of that time period, or making comparisons of that time period to another.

Topics. The subjects are endless—from the war (battle strategies, camp anecdotes, long marches, etc.) and its many players (officers, privates, physicians, orderlies, nurses, local citizens near battlefields, civilians far away, those in foreign countries, etc.) to issues and topics (the economy, the future, politics, farming, education, health, etc.) as well as impressions excerpts from diaries, letters, period publications, etc.) to your own feelings about the time period or one of the above issues.

Best Submissions. Write from your heart for an audience that is looking to be touched and amazed. All subjects are acceptable unless there is absolutely no connection with the Civil War or that time period.

Editorial Policy. Due to the limited number of pages, we do reserve the right to edit all submissions. If you would like to see how we will edit your submission before publication, you must include a SASE, then if you approve of the edited version, you must return it to us. Headlines are subject to change and/or editing without notice.

Compensation. All those whose submissions are accepted will receive two free complimentary copies of that issue. Additional copies will be sent if you request them up front. No other payment is available. This is a hobbyist newsletter and readers submit material as well as writers.

Who Retains Ownership. Each issue is copyrighted as to format. However, your work (in its original form) remains your own. However, we do retain the right to reprint material published in **MAIL CALL JOURNAL** for advertising purposes; as part of our future Web site; and to give permission for other publications to reprint your article with full credit given to you and citing **MAIL CALL JOURNAL** as the source. You will receive copies of these reprints which appear in other publications that we are aware of.

Deadlines. We accept submissions throughout the year. However, we try to keep seasonal topics in season. For example, submissions pertaining to a winter during the war will usually appear in our Christmas or February issues. You may submit material at any time of year, however, and we will keep it on file. Submissions that do not pertain to any particular time of year will be considered for publication for all issues throughout the year.

Multiple Submissions. Please note whether your material has been published, will be published, or has been submitted to other publishers: this will *not* disqualify your submission! We need to know the copyright information on it however—whether it was, is, or will be copyrighted in your name or that of the publisher as we prefer to include this information so that interested readers doing research can go back to the original source. If it has already been published, please include the name of the other publication or book, publisher's name and address, and copyright information (date and owner).

Cover Letters. Cover letters are not required. But you may include one if you need to explain your submission or some other point requested of you in these guidelines. Hard copy submissions in any form (handwritten, typed, or computer printout) are accepted as long as they are clearly legible. Do not send submissions on computer disks.

Reporting Time. Material will be kept on file if we feel it may be appropriate for a future issue. If accepted, you will be notified of a likely publication date. Inappropriate material will be sent back as soon as possible. If you wish to know the status of your submission, please send a self-addressed reply card with a 20¢ stamp for a quick reply either with your original submission or at a later date.

What's Acceptable. Acceptable submissions include poems, articles, stories, think pieces, your personal journal entries, reviews of historical sites, song lyric parodies, fillers, etc. Fiction as well as nonfiction are acceptable as long as you specify which it is. For nonfiction, please indicate sources.

Bylines. Your name, city and state (street address if you wish) will be included in a byline. Credentials may or may not appear. They need to be evaluated and decided how appropriate they are to our publication.

Descendants of Those Who Fought. If you are related to anyone who fought or lived during the time period, we will be most delighted to publish this information. So please include as much information as possible about this person and your relationship. You may even include a quote about how you feel being related to this person (this might even be the essence of your whole submission).

Queries. Queries are not necessary. We evaluate all submissions equally and fairly.

Length. 500 to 1,000 words is preferred. If your submission runs longer and we feel it deserves the space, we may continue it in the succeeding issue. If not, we will edit it and note any missing passages by ellipses.

Issues. MAIL CALL JOURNAL is published six times a year. Issues are mailed in February, April, June, August, October, and December. Single, sample, and back issues are sold for $5.00 each with a discounted annual subscription rate of $24.95. Checks are payable to Distant Frontier Press.

Writing Tips. In **MAIL CALL JOURNAL**, you'll find everything from death and dying to humorous stories and interesting quotes. Do not worry about the tone of your submission, most everything will be considered.

Categories: Fiction—Nonfiction—Arts—Biography—Civil War—Education—Entertainment—History—Hobbies—Inspirational—Literature—Military—Poetry—Recreation—Reference—Short Stories—Writing

Name: Anna Pansini, Managing Editor
Material: All
Address: PO BOX 5031 DEPT P6
City/State/ZIP: SOUTH HACKENSACK NJ 07606
Telephone: 201-296-0419
E-mail: mcj@historyonline.net
Internet: www.historyonline.net

Mama's Little Helper Newsletter

Publisher: Turquoise Butterfly Press
Format: 12-page bimonthly newsletter.
Focus: Primary goal is to support and assist parents of hyperactive, ADHD, spirited and energetic children with guidance, information, tried and tested tips and medical information. Topics include: Ritalin, does diet help?, positive discipline, stressbusting, car trips and restaurant, dealing with schools, siblings, recipes, ADHD history—and much more!
Submission: Lead articles should be 900-1,500 words. All other articles, personal stories, interviews, humorous pieces etc., should be 100-900 words. All material must be typewritten or neatly handwritten. *Include a word count!* Artwork and photos may accompany piece. Editor has the right to edit material. Buys one-time rights. Buys reprints. Include researched citations. Pays in copies. Sample copy is $3.50.
Categories: Children—Parenting

Name: Terri J. Andrews, Editor
Material: All
Address: PO BOX 1127
City/State/ZIP: ATHENS OH 45701-1127
Telephone: 614-664-3030

Managed Care

Our mission
MANAGED CARE is a magazine about the ever-changing health care marketplace. Our articles are written in accessible, conversational prose rather than the formal language of academic monographs. They cover trends in the managed care industry and how they affect primary care physicians and managed care administrators.

Topics include physician payment mechanisms, risk arrangements, contracting issues, quality measurement, public and purchaser perceptions of managed care, practice guidelines, outcomes management, legal and antitrust matters, ethical dilemmas, practice style and pertinent legislation and regulation. We also welcome firsthand accounts of how individual physicians or HMO administrators have met particular managed care challenges. Most feature articles are commissioned, but we consider both ideas and article manuscripts submitted by freelancers.

Recent articles by doctors and lawyers include:
• **What To Tell Patients About Managed Care,** Alan L. Hillman, M.D., MBA, health economist at the University of Pennsylvania, Philadelphia
• **Lessons America Should Learn From a Land of 'Free' Health Care,** Eric C. Anderson, M.D., a San Diego-based family physician
• **Will Health Plans Keep Their ERISA Shield?,** David L. Coleman, J.D.
• **Three New Kinds of Liability Stalk Managed Care,** Mike Folio, J.D.
• **Managed Care Has No Place For Unscientific 'Therapies',** Stephen Barrett, M.D., an Allentown, Pa.-based psychiatrist

Recent articles by freelance writers include:
• **Are Physicians Really Listening to Patients?**
• **Making Sure Patients Get Their Test Results**
• **Can One Physician's Campaign End Payment by Capitation?**
• **The Most Satisfying HMO: What It's Doing Right**
• **Why Managed Care is Getting a Bad Rap**

Only original manuscripts that have not been published and are not under consideration by other publications will be considered. Authors should list their academic degrees above bachelor's and provide a biography (2-3 sentences), including current job affiliation or relevant past experience. If submitted electronically, manuscript files should be either Microsoft Word or standard text format.

Categories: Nonfiction—Business—Health

Name: Timothy Kelley, Editor
Material: All
Address: 301 OXFORD VALLEY RD STE 1105A
City/State/ZIP: YARDLEY PA 19067
Telephone: 215-321-6663
Fax: 215-321-6670
E-mail: editors@managedcaremag.com
Internet: www.managedcaremag.com

Managing Office Technology

CONCEPT: *Managing Office Technology* is a controlled-circulation trade magazine that serves executives responsible for efficient management of white-collar personnel, business information processing, and the science of design and furnishing of working environments.

READERS: Circulation of 61,661 subscribers and a total audience of more than 300,000 includes individuals involved in planning, evaluating, specifying, authorizing, implementing and/or managing procedures and systems, products, and services used in offices.

CONTENT: A typical issue contains two features and six sections from the following: Management and Human Resources, Facilities/Ergonomics, Information Technology (which includes Office Applications Software, Office Computing, Document Management, Business Communications, Office Equipment, and Office Supplies. Ninety percent of the feature articles and sections are staff-written, and all are staff-edited and produced.

The editors will consider material for:

FEATURES: Full-length features (usually no longer than 2,500 words) on such topics as new concepts, management techniques, technologies, applications, or any topics consistent with MOT's editorial charter. Illustrations such as charts, graphs, art, photos, and the like should be included with the article. Four-color preferred.

SECTIONS: Trend articles, topical articles, case studies average 600-750 words. Again, include photos and illustrations. Four-color preferred.

COVERS: We are always happy to review exceptional cover photographs depicting any of the technologies or management areas we cover. We are also looking for quality conceptual covers. Photos must be high-quality color originals on 4"x5" or larger vertical format.

FORMAT: Published monthly. Average length: 60 folio pages. Typical ad/copy ratio is 60/40. Saddle stitched, printed web stock. Trim size 8-1/8"x11-1/16". Body copy is 10/11 Sabon.

MECHANICAL: Hard-copy manuscripts must be typed double-spaced on white bond paper. Dry photocopies only. The author's name, address, and phone number should appear on the first page with an approximate word count. Photo captions should be typed on a separate page. Include a working headline.

Submissions on diskette should be in either ASCII and Microsoft Word or ASCII and WordPerfect formats. Include hard copy printout of file.

PHOTOS: Color transparencies may be 35mm or larger. Color prints and black and white glossies accepted. Please identify products or people in each photo.

TERMS: Available on request. The editors reserve the right to edit, revise, or otherwise alter manuscripts and to crop or retouch photos so long as such changes do not alter the theme or intent of the work. (This does not apply to photographs which will be credited but used at the discretion of the editors).

Notification of acceptance or rejection will be within eight weeks.

Copy of editorial calendar sent upon request.

Deliver by mail at least 12 weeks prior to targeted issue date (certified mail for safety of original photos) to:

Categories: Communications—Computers—Management—Office

Name: Submissions Editor
Material: All
Address: 1100 SUPERIOR AVE
City/State/ZIP: CLEVELAND OH 44114
Telephone: 216-696-7000
Fax: 216-931-9769
E-mail: lromei@penton.com
Internet: www.penton.com

Manoa
A Pacific Journal of International Writing
University of Hawai'i

Thank you for inquiring about Manoa's guidelines/requirements.

MANOA publishes fiction, poetry, and translations; natural-history essays; occasional articles of current literary or cultural interest; and short reviews.

Fiction, poetry, and essays need not be related to Asia, the Pacific or Hawai'i in particular, nor be by writers from the region. We're as interested in Tennessee or Toronto as a locale for a story as we are in Tonga. Ordinarily, we are not interested in genre or formalist writing for its own sake, or Pacific exotica and picturesque impressions of the region. We also prefer to see five or six poems at a time, depending upon the length.

Translations are usually commissioned by a guest editor who is responsible for a portion of the issue; and that portion of the issue usually features writings from one country. The rest of the issue is usually reserved for North American writings. We may occasionally run translations other than the guest editor's, but you might want to query us first.

We do not have specific length, subject-matter, or style requirements; like most literary magazines, we suggest reading a copy of the magazine to get an idea of what we like to publish. A sample copy is $15 (including postage); to order one, please send a check to the address shown below.

Reviews are on recent books in the arts, humanities, or natural sciences; usually, these books are related to Asia, the Pacific, or Hawai'i, or are published in these places. Separate guidelines are available for reviews.

MANOA is published twice a year, summer and winter, and accepts submissions throughout the year. Submissions should be originals or good photocopies; handwritten manuscripts, dot-matrix printouts, and originals typed on onion-skin sheets are not acceptable. Please allow about four weeks for reply on poetry manuscripts, essays, and reviews, and about eight weeks for reply on fiction manuscripts.

If you have further questions, we'll be glad to answer them. Just drop us a note. We try to reply promptly.

Categories: Fiction—Nonfiction—Asian-American—Literature—Multicultural—Poetry—Short Stories

Name: Ian MacMillan, Fiction Editor
Material: Fiction

Name: Frank Stewart, Poetry Editor
Material: Poetry, Essays, Nonfiction
Address: UNIVERSITY OF HAWAII ENGLISH DEPT
Address: 1733 DONAGHHO RD
City/State/ZIP: HONOLULU HI 96822
Telephone: 808-956-3070
Fax: 808-956-3083
E-mail: mjournal@hawaii.edu

MARINE CORPS GAZETTE

Marine Corps Gazette
The Professional Journal of Marines Since 1916

Our basic policy is to fulfill the stated purpose of the *Marine Corps Gazette* by providing a forum for open discussion and a free exchange of ideas relating to the U.S. Marine Corps and military capabilities.

The Board of Governors of the Marine Corps Association has given authority to approve manuscripts for publication to the editorial board and editor. Editorial board members are listed on the *Gazette*'s masthead in each issue. The board, which normally meets once a month, represents a cross section of Marines by professional interest, experience, age, rank, and gender. The board reads and votes on each manuscript submitted as a feature article. A simple majority rules in its decisions. Other material submitted for publication is accepted or rejected based on the assessment of the editor. The *Gazette* welcomes material in the following categories:

• **Commentary on Published Material:** Submit promptly. Comments normally appear as letters (see below) 3 months after published material. *Be brief.*

• **Feature Articles:** Normally 2,500 to 5,000 words, dealing with topics of major significance. Ideas must be backed up by hard facts. Evidence must be presented to support logical conclusions. In the case of articles that criticize, constructive suggestions are sought. Footnotes are not necessary, but a list of any source materials used is helpful.

• **Ideas and Issues:** Short articles, normally 500 to 2,000 words. This section can include the full gamut of professional topics so long as treatment of the subject is brief and concise.

• **Letters:** Limit to 300 words or less and *double-spaced.* As in most magazines, letters to the editor are an important clue as to how well or poorly ideas are being received. Letters are an excellent way to correct factual mistakes, reinforce ideas, outline opposing points of view, identify problems, and suggest factors or important considerations that have been overlooked in previous *Gazette* articles. The best letters are sharply focused on one or two specific points.

• **Book Reviews:** Prefer 300 to 750 words. It is a good idea to check with the editor in advance to determine if a review is desired. Please be sure to include the book's author, publisher (including city), year of publication, number of pages, and cost of the book.

The best advice is to write the way you talk. Organize your thoughts. Cut out excess words. Short is better than long. Submissions should include one copy of the manuscript and, if possible, a disk in ASCII Text format and author's name clearly indicated. All electronic correspondence can be sent to our Internet address. Any queries may be directed to the editorial staff by calling 800-336-0291, extension 306/309.

Note: Honorariums are no longer paid for articles. Exceptions are made for enlisted personnel on active duty and in some cases for students and faculty at designated military schools. Consult editor for details.

Categories: Military

Name: Col. John E. Greenwood, USMC (Ret.), Editor
Material: All
Address: PO BOX 1775
City/State/ZIP: QUANTICO VA 22134
Telephone: 703-640-6161
Fax: 703-640-0823
E-mail: gazette@illuminet.net

Marion Zimmer Bradley's Fantasy Magazine

Marion Zimmer Bradley's Fantasy Magazine buys well-plotted short stories, up to 5,500 words (yes, this *is* a firm limit). We prefer 3,500 to 4,000 words, but we also buy short-shorts (under 1,000 words). Stories longer than 5,500 words are bought by commission only.

We buy original fantasy (*not* sex fantasies) with no particular objection to modern settings, but we do want action and adventure. The primary purpose of your story should be to entertain the reader; and although any good story has a central point behind the plot, the reader should be able to deduce it rather than having it thrust upon him. Fantasy content should start on the first page and must appear within the first three pages. We prefer strong female characters, and we will reject stories in which we find objectionable sexism. We also reject stories with bad grammar or spelling. We do not favor strong language because, although we *are not* a magazine aimed at children or young adults, we do have many young readers.

Nonfiction should be queried; it is done on commission only.

Please read a few issues before submitting so that you can see the kind of thing we do buy. For a sample copy, send $4.00 and a 9"x12" self-addressed envelope.

Please *do not* **submit:** Poetry, serials, novel excerpts, children's stories, shared world stories, science fiction, hard technology, occult, horror, re-written fairy tales, radical feminism, romances (in which love, romance and marriage are the main motivations), surrealism, or avant-garde stories, stories written in the present tense, or stories about God, the Devil, or "hearth-witches."

Beware of: "dime-a-dozen" subjects such as dragons, elves, unicorns, wizards, vampires, writers, sea creatures, brute warriors, ghosts, adventuring sorcerers/sorceresses, thieves/assassins, or final exams for wizards. We get dozens of these kinds of stories every week, and we reject all but the *truly* unusual and well-written ones.

GENERAL INFORMATION:

• We do not accept simultaneous submissions or reprints (no matter how obscure the original). Do NOT resubmit a story unless we specifically request it. This applies also to stories submitted to MZB for any other market, such as SWORD AND SORCERESS. Since MZB reads everything herself, each story is considered for all the projects she's working on unless the author requests otherwise.

• All manuscripts must be typewritten or printed with a letter quality printer. Manuscripts must follow the format given in the enclosed Manuscript Preparation Guidelines. MZB can not read small, dim or dot-matrix printing, and if she can't read it, she can't buy it. Type must be at least 12 point, and we prefer Courier 12 typeface. This is Courier 12. Do not justify the right margin. Underline any phrases in the manuscript which should appear in italics; do not actually use italics. Please do not tell or explain your story in your cover letter.

• Care will be taken, but we cannot assume responsibility for unsolicited stories. *Each* manuscript *must* be accompanied by a SASE (Self-addressed Stamped Envelope): #10 with one stamp (or two IRCs) if your manuscript is disposable (which is what we prefer), or large with sufficient postage if you want your manuscript returned. Manuscripts without a SASE will be *thrown out unread*. If you want to know that we received your story, enclose a self-addressed stamped postal card. If your manuscript is rejected, it will be returned as soon as possible. If we do not return it within 4 months, we are probably holding it for possible use and will write to you as soon as we can.

• *Do not* use Certified, Express or Registered mail; we haven't time to stand in line and sign for them.

We buy only first magazine rights. Rates are professionally competitive, and we pay on acceptance.

MANUSCRIPT PREPARATION GUIDELINES

APPEARANCE:

• Your manuscript must be typed, or printed on a letter-quality printer.

• If you use a computer, print your manuscript on a *letter quality printer*, preferably a laser printer. *Do not* use dot matrix, or any printer that does not produce clear, sharp, black letters.

• *Do not* send stories on disk unless you are specifically requested to do so.

• Use a *plain typeface* with a size of at least 12 point. we prefer courier 12, but other editors may have different preferences.

• *Do not* use bold or italic type at all; underline any words or phrases you want to emphasize.

• Do not use a fancy typeface for the title; the editor wants to see your writing, not your graphic design skills.

• Use a *paper clip* to hold the manuscript together, *not* staples, folders, or binders.

FORMAT:

• A cover letter is not necessary; if you must have one, make it short and professional (see the section on THE SUBMISSION PACKAGE, below). *Never* tell or explain the story in your cover letter.

• Margins should leave adequate room for editorial remarks. Use 1½" at the top and left, 1" at the bottom and right. Do not hyphenate words in a manuscript. Do not justify the right margin.

• On the first page of your story:

• Put your real name, mailing address, telephone number, and social security number in the top left corner, single-spaced. If desired, your e-mail address goes here.

• Put the number of words, rounded to the nearest 100, in the right top corner.

• About halfway down the page, type the name of the story.

• Beneath the title, type your name or pen name.

• Leave a space beneath your name, and begin typing the story.

• *Indent* the beginning of each paragraph 1/2 inch; do not put three blank lines between them.

• Put the page number, and your last name, at the top of *each page*.

• At the end of the story, type "THE END" (not "-30-" or "-00-") so the editor will not wonder if she is missing the last page.

• *Proofread* your manuscript! Spelling and grammar *are* important, and that includes punctuation. Note that spell checking won't catch a spelling error if the mistake is a legitimate word (for example, if you type 'pair' instead of 'lair')

CONTENTS:

• Be sure your story conforms to the writer's guidelines for a particular market. A cover letter that begins "I know this doesn't fit your guidelines, but..." is a really good way to annoy an editor—almost as good as "I've never read your magazine or your guidelines, but I'm sure my story is perfect for it."

• Make sure your stated word count is credible. A page of manuscript is about 300 words, so a 26-page manuscript claiming to be 5,000 words long is going to be regarded with suspicion.

SUBMISSION DOs and DON'Ts:

• Do not send simultaneous submissions! (That is, don't submit the same story to two markets simultaneously.)

• If you send more than one story at once, include a separate SASE for each story. If you don't, rejection for one story will strongly encourage rejection for them all.

• Do not send artwork with your story.

• Keep a log of where you send your stories, so you don't send the same story to the same market or editor twice.

THE SUBMISSION PACKAGE:

• Use a 9"x12" envelope to send manuscripts longer than 4 pages. For manuscripts of up to 4 pages, a #10 business envelope is adequate. Make certain there is enough postage on your package; editors don't want to pay Postage Due on the slush pile.

• Do not include a cover letter unless you have explicit instructions for the disposition of your manuscript, or unless you want your story considered for only one market. A chatty personal letter or synopsis of your story wastes the editor's time. *If she buys your story, then* she'll ask for your biography!

• Send manuscripts by first class mail. *Do not* use certified, registered, or express mail; no one wants to wait in line at the post office to sign for them.

• If you don't need your manuscript returned, include a #10 SASE in your submission package, and indicate that your manuscript is disposable.

GENERAL ADVICE:

• A good-looking manuscript never sold a rotten story; but I am convinced that if an editor has two marginally acceptable manuscripts on hand, he or she will keep the one that is easiest to read. A professionally presented manuscript encourages the editor to regard *you* as a professional and to take your story seriously—and you can't ask for more than that!

MZB

Categories: Fiction—Fantasy

Name: Mrs. Marion Z. Bradley, Editor
Material: All
Address: PO BOX 249
City/State/ZIP: BERKELEY CA 94701-0249
Telephone: 510-644-9222

Marlin
The International Sportfishing Magazine

1. Marlin accepts freelance-written articles on a query basis for both features and departments. Please send written queries for any articles you may have for *Marlin* with your name, address, phone number, social security number and an SASE. Queries should be concise and pertain to *offshore* fishing, destinations, personalities and related topics only. For detailed information regarding *Marlin*'s scope, direction and editorial needs, call editor David Ritchie.

2. All features will be edited as necessary, usually to a length of 1,500 to 2,500 words. If an assigned article is unacceptable as submitted, the author may be given one opportunity at a rewrite. If an article is accepted by the editor, but is not used for reasons out of the author's control, a one-third kill fee will be paid to author.

3. Marlin gladly accepts "over the transom" submissions, but accepts no responsibility for the return of such materials. In all cases, though, the editors will attempt to respond to such materials in a timely fashion.

4. Very often, one of the key determining factors in our decision-making process regarding submitted queries and manuscripts is the amount and quality of available photography on the subject in question.

5. One of the easiest ways to begin publishing your material in *Marlin* is by contributing to the smaller departments:

• Send short news items which directly relate to offshore fishing, fishery regulations, the boating industry or other related topics to the attention of **"Blue Water Currents."** Keep the items short and to the point, and provide photography or illustration support when possible.

• The **"Tips & Techniques"** section is the place for you to submit short briefs on offshore fishing techniques, tackle innovations, boat handling advice, etc. Keep the items under 250 words, and provide photo or illustration support.

• **"The Rip Line"** is *Marlin*'s section for tournament reports. Call editor David Ritchie to discuss possible event coverage. Keep "over the transom" reports short, make sure all names and boats are spelled correctly, detail the "Keys to Victory" that led to the winning catch, and provide a photo of the winners when possible. No hanging fish photos, please.

PHOTOGRAPHER'S GUIDELINES

Marlin continues to emphasize the finest saltwater fishing photography to be found in any magazine. Most of that comes from freelance professionals. *Marlin* provides bona fide international exposure for photographers' best work. [Editor's Note: See also "Guide for Submitting Photos to *Sportfishing* and *Marlin*" under the "Sportfishing" listing.]

POLICIES

RETURN POLICY: It remains our fundamental goal to review and send out images not selected within a few days of receipt. We do NOT ordinarily hold photos at all unless we have a projected possible use. A tracking sheet will be included with images returned showing which slides are being kept and for what purpose.

SHIPPING: If we call and request photography quickly, we'll pay shipping. Otherwise, the photographer pays to ship. We'll take care of returns, usually via Certified Mail unless otherwise specified.

OVER-THE-TRANSOM SUBMISSIONS: When in doubt, ship it out. We're always happy to review images, whether solicited or unsolicited (and since we won't hold those for which we see no specific, possible use, there's little to lose and much to gain).

WHAT TO SEND

FILM TYPE: We prefer Fujichrome 100 (or Velvia 50 for nonaction shots in bright light) or Kodachrome-64 and Lumiere; High shutter speeds for moving fish (1/1000+); Bracket where possible and try for both horizontals and verticals; Compose to keep fish main focus of most shots and to avoid extraneous objects in frame (also avoid clothing with nasty/racist/sexist inferences).

DUPES OR ORIGINALS?: We run originals, not dupes. You may send in duplicate slides for review purposes, but only if the originals are available. Also, there is always a better chance of selection for an original slide simply because it offers better definition and color than subsequent generations.

SUGGESTIONS

DON'T SEND US FUZZY SHOTS!!!

Instead, give us photos that are, by any measure, "tack sharp." Every day I see otherwise great shots precluded from use by being too "soft." There's just not much point in sending any images that are not crystal clear.

AVOID INANIMATE "GRIN & GRAB" SHOTS.

Send us images of people animated as they hold fresh (preferably lively) but not bloody fish. Counteract the dreaded Zombie Stare Syndrome. Have subject interacting with someone else if available. (Have 'em hold fish together and look at/talk to each other—while forgetting the camera even exists—anything to get subject loose, happy, natural.) If subject alone, suggest interaction with the fish—hook removal, lifting from deck, even admiring it (looking at it, not you). Avoid dead fish in such photos—take 'em quick when the fish is in the boat and lively, before it's clubbed or languishes to a pale, glassy-eyed state of rigor mortis.

Finally, do keep the angler's tackle in the shot!

AVOID KILL SHOTS OF BILLFISH AND BLUEWATER SHARKS!

Send us exciting, in-focus shots of leaping, tailwalking, greyhounding fish; of fish being wired for tagging or being released or admired at the boat. Skip the traditional dead stuff—hanging at the dock, draped over the transom, bleeding on deck—or anything with a gaff in it.

"Kill" shots of other, food fish okay if—you should pardon the expression—tasteful. Sport, not carnage, is what we're after.

AVOID SHADOW-DARKENED SHOTS.

Give us shots liberal with use of fill flash under high sun or backlit conditions.

DON'T LIMIT SUBMISSIONS TO FISH/FISHING ALONE.

Have an eye to all things related to fish/fishing, viz.: rigging, technique (gear/action), baits, lures, equipment, diving birds, weather, water (color/rips/ weedlines), feeding schools, schools of baitfish (and catching them), other boats fishing/running, Bimini starts, etc, etc. Also, don't hesitate to photograph any/all nearshore/offshore species, gamefish or others, including those that are unusual.

COVERS

Marlin covers emphasize fish, boats and fish action—fish leaping, underwater, at the surface, on a line out of the water and so on. That may include anglers interacting with fish—fighting fish, releasing or tagging fish and the like. Other offshore pelagic gamefish may occasionally qualify. Remember: 35mm focus must be laser-sharp to retain its quality when enlarged 1,200 percent. The dominant image must fill most of the frame to minimize blow-up necessary (e.g. a jumping fish that's a dot on the horizon won't make it).

WHEN PACKAGING SUBMISSIONS

1. Make sure that every image has—at the very least!—your name on it. Otherwise, return can't be guaranteed. Words of description (area, species, etc.) written right on the slide can be of great help.

2. If sending slides/other images in one package targeting two or more articles, please places slides in a separate sheet (or sheets) for each different article and mark the sheet accordingly.

3. If brief captions are written on each image, a page with extended captions is helpful; if no information is written on images, a sheet of captions is essential.

4. Make sure your social security number is included somewhere, unless you are certain we have it (or unless you have no interest in remuneration.)

5. Payment will be issued to the first name on the slide (stock agency or photographer) unless other payment arrangements are specified.

COMMUNICATIONS

Don't hesitate to call anytime you have any general or specific questions about photo needs, submissions or payments.

Categories: Nonfiction—Adventure—Boating—Conservation—Consumer—Fishing—Outdoors—Recreation—Sports

Name: David Ritchie, Editor
Material: All
Address: PO BOX 2456

City/State/ZIP: WINTER PARK FL 32790
Telephone: 407-628-4802
Fax: 407-628-7061
E-mail: Marlin@worldzine.com

Martha Stewart Living

No guidelines, but does accept unsolicited manuscripts.
Categories: Nonfiction—Collectibles—Cooking—Crafts—Entertainment—Food/Drink—Gardening—Hobbies—Travel—Home

Name: Editor
Material: All
Address: 20 W. 43RD STREET, 25TH FLOOR
City/State/ZIP: NEW YORK, NY 10036
Telephone: 212-827-8000
Fax: 212-522-1715

Martial Arts Training

Dear Writer,

Thank you for your interest in *M.A. Training*, the leading magazine covering physical and mental training in the martial arts. About 90 percent of the magazine is written by freelancers, so your innovative ideas and dazzling prose are much needed and appreciated.

Before sending a complete article to *M.A. Training*, however, it is advisable to send a query letter, outlining your proposed topic. If the subject fits our format, and has not been covered too recently, you may then be asked to send the complete manuscript with photos.

What is the magazine's format? MAT does not deal with self-defense techniques. Instead, we focus on the conditioning that allows a martial artist to execute those techniques to their fullest. This includes training drills, exercise tips, workouts with new or home-built training tools and advice on injury prevention, etc.

Articles focusing on drills for increased speed, strength, agility, power, etc., are the most likely to be accepted right now. The content ratio should be 4/5 (or more) drill how-to and no more than 1/5 telling the importance of the drills, physiological explanations or quotes. Do not include self-defense techniques except if *necessary* to **briefly** explain how the exercises are applicable. Also, do not identify the exercises as being from, or for, a specific martial art. *M.A. Training's* articles are meant to be for martial artists of all styles.

Articles should be about 2,000 words long or slightly shorter if many photos accompany the piece. Because our manuscripts are scanned electronically, do not send dot-matrix submissions. Articles should not be written in first person ("I train this way. This happened to me", etc.) Do, however, include a short "about the author" to run after the article.

Though you may initially send a manuscript without photos for consideration, photos must be provided for final acceptance. (Usually, photos are not purchased without a manuscript.) The photos, which may be black and white or color, should be clear, **well-lit and in focus.** The subject should contrast with the background. Photos should illustrate the training techniques in the story and should include a general lead shot. Model release forms should accompany the photos. We will gladly send a copy of our model release form if requested.

Payment for an article and accompanying photos is approximately $125-175 for all rights. If you have further questions about *M.A. Training*, please feel welcome to write or call.

Sincerely,
Douglas Jeffrey

Executive Editor
Categories: Martial Arts

Name: Submissions Editor
Material: All
Address: 24715 AVE ROCKEFELLER
City/State/ZIP: VALENCIA CA 91355
Telephone: 805-257-4066
Fax: 805-257-3028

Masonia Roundup

The *Masonia Roundup* is a quarterly personal magazine containing articles of general interest written by real people, about what has happened to them, their thoughts and ideas, or anything else they wish to share with the world, published in January, April, July, and October. Let us know what is happening in your part of the world. Tell us what's on your mind.

Our readers are mostly U.S. college educated adults with families, ranging from 20 to 75 years of age.

The ***Roundup*** is looking for stories, poems and articles. Please send complete manuscripts. No queries. Manuscripts should be tightly written. Please include SASE with all correspondence. Byline given, sometimes a brief bio included. Disk submissions welcome: Macintosh format or DOS text files only.

Nonfiction Features: This is our major area of interest. We are looking for news about your adventures. Tell us what you have been up to. Done something weird lately? Have an idea or opinion? Don't like what's happening in Philadelphia? Here is your forum. Editorials welcome. Circa 500 words.

Poems: We are looking for a limited number of all types of poetry. Iamb on down to the mailbox and send us your best. We love to laugh. We are willing to cry. Circa 30 lines. (Exceptions will be made for exceptional works.)

Fiction: While we are not really a fiction forum, we will consider well written short pieces, any genre, though we are especially interested in science fiction and mysteries. Humor is always welcome. Circa 500 words.

Puzzles: If you have a mental challenge, we are not particularly interested in trying to solve it, but if you submit it with the solution, we will present it to our readers. We are looking for puzzles for people of all ages.

PAYMENT: The ***Roundup*** will pay two complimentary issues for all published manuscripts. Additional issues may be purchased for $1 each.

Non paying departments:

Brag Corner: Have some news to share? Want to wish someone happy birthday? Do something spectacular lately? Send your notices to Brag Corner.

Letters-to-the-Editor: Want to tell us how we did on the last issue? Send compliments or complaints to Letters-to-the-Editor.

Fillers: If you have any thoughts, jokes, notes, hints, tips, personal ads, or observations, please feel free to send them. Circa 15 words.

Sample issues: $1.50 and SASE.
Categories: Nonfiction—Family—General Interest

Name: Dan or Ardis Mason, Editors
Material: All
Address: 1996 S COOLWELL RD
City/State/ZIP: MADISON HTS VA 24572
Fax: 804-929-7601

> **Remember: Editors change jobs and publishers change addresses. It is wise to invest in a phone call for the current information before submitting.**

The Massachusetts Review
University of Massachusetts

Thank you for your interest in *The Massachusetts Review*, a quarterly of literature, the arts and public affairs. We represent no stylistic or ideological coterie. The Editors seek a balance between established writers and artists and promising new ones, and material of variety and vitality relevant to the intellectual and aesthetic life of our time. We aspire to have a broad appeal; our commitment, in part regional, is not provincial.

"Inspired pages are not written to fill a space, but for inevitable utterance; and to such our journal is freely and solicitously open." (Emerson)

ARTICLES & ESSAYS of breadth and depth are considered, as well as discussions of leading writers; of art, music, and drama; analyses of trends in literature, science, philosophy, and public affairs. No reviews of single books.

FICTION: We consider one short story per submission, usually up to 25-30 pp.

POETRY: A poetry submission may consist of up to six poems. There are no restrictions in terms of length, but generally our poems are less than 100 lines. Please write your name on every page.

Fiction and Poetry manuscripts should be submitted separately.

No mixed submissions, *please*.

MR no longer considers plays for publication.

In addition:

Please include your name and address on first page of manuscript.

Please do not send mss. from June 1st through October 1st.

Please do read a copy of MR before sending work.

The Massachusetts Review is a nonprofit journal and it is impossible for us to acknowledge receipt of the many manuscripts we receive, or to honor requests made for sample copies. You may order an issue for $7.00 (incl. Postage) or begin a subscription. Subscription rates:

Individuals, USA: 1 year, $18; 2 years, $30; 3 years, $40
Outside USA: 1 year, $30
Libraries: 1 year, $24
Categories: Fiction—Essays/Articles—Memoirs—Poetry

Name: Paul Jenkins or Anne Haley, Editors
Material: Poetry
Name: Robert Dow or Ella Kusnetz, Editors
Material: Fiction
Address: SOUTH COLLEGE
Address: UNIVERSITY OF MASSACHUSETTS
City/State/ZIP: AMHERST MA 01003
Telephone: 413-545-2689

Massage Magazine

Thank you for requesting a copy of *Massage Magazine*'s writer's guidelines. We are interested in articles on many aspects of the massage profession and related healing arts. Listed below are some of our requirements to assist you in preparing submissions.

ARTICLES

We are looking for articles based on solid information, with an emphasis on investigative, technique-oriented, "how-to" pieces. In-depth profiles of innovative and exceptional bodywork professionals are a high priority. We also publish massage-related articles in the areas of business, politics, law, health care, insurance, cultural exchange and travel. Short news items (include source reference), fillers, poetry and humor are always welcome.

FORMAT

Manuscripts should be typewritten, preferably on a Macintosh-compatible disk in Microsoft Word. Articles may also be submitted by attaching a file to e-mail sent to the address below. Reference lists (required on technical pieces) should include the author, title, publisher, city of publication and publication date of works cited. Please include a 20- to 100-word author's biography at the end of your article.

LENGTH

Article length runs from 250-4,000 words, depending on the subject matter and category. For example, 250-500 words for news brief items; 1,000-1,500 words for short articles; and 2,000+ words for in-depth feature or technique articles.

PAYMENT

Payment ranges from $50 to $300, depending on the article's technicality, length and quality of writing. Payment offered increases proportionately for longer and more weighty articles. Payment is made 30 days after the publication date of the issue in which the material appears, along with two complimentary copies of the issue. We generally request first North American rights and electronic rights. Reprints will be considered.

GRAPHICS/ARTWORK/PHOTOGRAPHS

Massage Magazine is always interested high-quality artwork or photography to support your written work. Artwork should be in the form of photographs, slides or professional illustrations. Color is preferred. Prints should have a gloss rather than linen finish.

Client and therapist clothing should be appropriate; client should not be shown in underwear (use a drape).

Select appropriate color clothing: no plaids, bright colors or patterns. Black should not be worn. When possible, coordinate subjects' clothing colors and background as appropriate.

Be aware of lighting and avoid harsh shadows.

Please include photo attribution and the photographer's name, address and phone number.

RESPONSE/PUBLICATION

Response to your submission is made as soon as it has been circulated in the editorial department, generally within two months. If we decide to publish your work, a publishing agreement will be sent to you.

Massage Magazine is a bimonthly publication. The length of time between acceptance and publication can vary from two to 10 months or more.

We look forward to considering your work.

Categories: Nonfiction—General Interest—Health

Name: Karen Menehan, Editor
Material: All
Address: 200 7TH AVE STE 240
City/State/ZIP: SANTA CRUZ CA 95062
Telephone: 408-477-1176
Fax: 408-477-2918
E-mail: edit@massagemag.com
Internet: www.massagemag.com

Mature Years

So You Want to Write for *Mature Years*

Mature Years magazine is published by Abingdon Press. The audience comprises persons of retirement age and beyond (55 plus), and the magazine's purpose is to help persons understand and use the resources of the Christian faith in dealing with specific opportunities and problems related to aging.

We publish quarterly with 112 pages, trim size 8.5"x11", four-color, 14 point Century Old Style typeface. Circulation is approximately 70,000. The magazine is mailed throughout the United States, and through the Protestant Church-Owned Publisher's

Association, it is available in some military base chapels around the world.

Writers are not restricted to older adults.

Reader Description

Our readers like to see themselves in what they read. Writers should acknowledge the reader's maturity and use illustrations that reflect older adult lifestyles which are varied. Some older adults are employed; some are retired. Some of our readers are active; some are not. Some are married while others are widowed or never married. Housing arrangements may be in their own homes, living with adult children, or in congregate housing of varied types.

Most older adults are in good health, but many are ill. They have a variety of educational backgrounds, but writers should assume that they are intelligent and not treat them as forgetful, mindless individuals. Financial status is also greatly varied among our readers.

Mature Years magazine readers do not want *to* see only older adults in their stories, poems, and articles. They are fearful of being shut up in an "older adult ghetto." Intergenerational pieces rate high with our audience.

Guidelines for General Editorial Content

When we review manuscripts we look for the following:

Appropriate Subjects—Popular articles address current health issues in aging; including health and fitness, housing, financial conditions, social and emotional needs, personal security, family life, self-help, and so on. Articles should provide practical aids for older adults: what to do, how to, when to, where to. Especially important are opportunities for older adults to read about service, adventure, fulfillment, and fun. Items of entertainment, like hobbies and crafts, are also popular.

Positive Viewpoint—Articles should be upbeat, picturing older adults who are enjoying this period of their lives. When articles are about the problems of living as an older adult, they should demonstrate the power of faith for difficult times and offer possible solutions and/or sympathy and comfort.

Active Subjects—Persons featured in articles should be active, creative, involved with their family, church, community, nation, and world. While many of our readers are inactive, they do not want to read about people sitting and doing nothing with their lives.

Variety of Approaches—Articles can be serious or humorous. They may be based on memories or current experiences. Fiction may be for the purpose of pure entertainment, or stories may explore a social justice issue or concern of aging.

Christian Orientation—Articles should demonstrate faith in God as a resource for life in all circumstances, both good and bad. Persons featured should be older adults with a vital lifestyle. For instance, when they travel it will be for educational purposes or to engage in ministry or service to others. Articles should reflect the joy of living out one's Christian faith.

Absence of Stereotypes—Older adults should be freed from the stereotypes of age, gender, nationality, and race. Examples of aging stereotypes are frailty, memory loss, illness, sedentary lifestyle. Be supportive of persons and groups rather than poking fun at them.

Guidelines for Specific Features

Cartoons—Cartoons may either have a religious theme or relate to aging as outlined in the "Guidelines for General Editorial Content" above. While bringing some humor to older adult situations, cartoons should never trivialize circumstances and should never demean anyone or their circumstance.

Photographs—If photographs accompany articles, color prints or transparencies are required. If photos are historical, black and white prints or negatives are acceptable. Publication always begins with an article, story, or poem, never with art or photography. Do not submit photos without accompanying text.

Poetry—Poems are limited to not more than sixteen lines of up to fifty characters. Content should conform to the "Guidelines for General Editorial Content" detailed above. Free verse is accepted. When using rhyme and meter, be sure they are accurate. Seasonal poems are accepted according to the Submission Schedule below.

Guidelines for Departments

Book Source—This department is not open to unsolicited submissions.

Fragments of Life—This department uses short glimpses of everyday life (cuddling with grandchildren, a humorous moment at church, a sweet memory) to inspire and to illustrate the joys, sorrows, and poignancy of living. It may or may not overtly mention God, but it never preaches. (250 to 600 words)

Going Places—Travel articles must:

a) feature some location or travel aspect particularly appropriate to older adults, such as special activities or facilities planned for the age group. Seniors hiking or snorkeling are examples. Tours for grandparents and grandchildren is another example.

b) reflect the predominantly Christian character of the magazine by taking our readers to Bible lands or on a pilgrimage, discuss the historic sites of Christian believers, or show the countryside or towns of different Christian groups. Typical articles might feature the cathedrals of Europe, monasteries or retreat centers in the United States, Amish communities, or Roman Christian catacombs. (1,000 to 1,500 words)

Health Hints—Health problems and fitness opportunities for older adults are found in this department. Description of health problems and solutions for alleviating or eliminating conditions should be discussed. Other articles might tell about exercises and activities designed to help older adults keep fit. (900 to 1,200 words)

Merry-Go-Round—This page features cartoons, jokes, and 4-6 line humorous verses. The subjects of all these items must conform to the "Guidelines for General Editorial Content" or for "Cartoons" printed above. We publish two cartoons in each issue.

Modern Revelations—Overtly religious and inspirational, this department deals with contemporary understanding of the Christian faith. While it is often an essay relating the Bible to modern life and quotes Scripture, it is not a classical Bible study. It may give advice for spiritual living as an older adult. (900 to 1,100 words)

Money Matters—All economic issues of importance to older adults are acceptable; including banking, investing, wise purchasing, savings instruments, cost of health care, and insurance. All articles must be written with a personal finance point of view. (1,200 to 1,800 words)

Puzzle Time—Many different forms of puzzles and quizzes are published; including crosswords, word finds, anagrams, and unique formats. Subjects must either have biblical or religious themes or have older adults interest such as great dance bands, grandparenting, or reminiscence. Puzzles and quizzes should be challenging.

Social Security Questions and Answers—This department is not open to unsolicited submissions.

Seasonal Purchasing Schedule

Mature Years magazine closes manuscript purchases for individual issues approximately one year before publication. We are looking for seasonal articles and poems in the following time frames:

Spring during December, January, February
Summer during March, April, May
Fall during June, July, August
Winter during September, October, November

Because *Mature Years* magazine has such a long lead time, we are not able to publish hard news or anything with specific upcoming dates. The exception to this rule is annual events.

M-R

Guidelines for Manuscript Preparation

Maximum Word Limits—Specific department lengths are printed above. For all other articles no more than 2,000 words are published.

Format—Do not send computer disks.

Quoted Material—You **must** include photocopies of any material quoted from other sources and give a complete citation.

Subheads—You may include subheads in your text. The editor may or may not use them. If there are multiple levels of subheads, be sure that they are plainly distinguishable.

Photo Captions—Be sure that captions are clearly matched with photographs to guarantee proper placement with the photographs.

Submission—Send manuscripts printed with your name, address, telephone number, and social security number along with a **required** SASE to the address below.

Rights

Mature Years requests a variety of rights depending upon the material offered. Our most common request is for one-time North American serial rights. For work-for-hire we normally require All Rights.

Payment Schedule

Payment is made upon acceptance of any text or cartoon. We pay 5 cents per word for articles and $1.00 per line of poetry. Verses and fillers used in the Merry-Go-Round department are paid a flat $5.00.

Payment for photos accompanying stories are paid $20.00 for each one published internally. Covers pay more. Payment for photos follows selection in the design stage. The price paid for professional quality photography is negotiable.

Miscellaneous

Response Time—Replies to unsolicited manuscript submissions come within eight weeks of receipt. We do not acknowledge receipt of manuscripts at the time they are received. Because of the tremendous volume of submissions, it is not possible to make comments in the replies.

Letters of Inquiry—Inquiries are permissible with a **required** SASE. Responses come within two weeks of receipt. Acceptance only indicates *consideration* for publication.

Samples—Sample copies are available for $4.50 each including shipping and handling.

Columns—*Mature Years* magazine is not interested in adding regular columns.

Categories: Cartoons—Christian Interests—Health—Poetry—Religion—Senior Citizens—Spiritual—Travel

Name: Marvin W. Cropsey, Editor
Material: All
Address: 201 EIGHTH AVE S
City/State/ZIP: NASHVILLE TN 37202
Telephone: 615-749-6292
Fax: 615-749-6512

The Maverick Press
Southwest Poets' Series

There are several quirks and biases on the parts of the editors. Please examine them to see where your submission fits.

All correspondence requires a business size envelope or larger, and all submissions *require a 9"x6" or larger document envelope*. Staple upper left corner with SASE on the bottom. Name and address on every page (cover letter included) are a must. Business size SASE if you do not wish documents returned. Submissions without SASE must be discarded unread.

I feel about rhyming poetry like the little old Baptist teetotaler who, when reminded that Christ drank wine, said, "Yes, but I wish he hadn't!"

We do not accept any previously published material or:
• Short stories over 5 pages/1,500 words
• mss. Written from the young child's point of view with ten syllable words and philosophic observations that do not show what the adult has gleaned from the youthful recall
• gothic or horror themes
• pieces that do not fit the theme of this particular issue, though not all issues have themes. April is always open.
• concrete or shaped poetry
• political posturings
• diatribes on current events
• non-literary/non-soaring/"mainstream" pieces
• poems or stories rife with cliches, pedestrian adjectives or hackneyed adverbs—(in fact, avoid adverbs that qualify, weaken or cripple your verbs; use stronger verb or an original metaphor instead.)

New policy: TMP, in an attempt to modernize our views and conform to the realities of current writing, encourages multiple submissions **with notification up front and a prompt phone call if ms. is accepted elsewhere and must be removed from our consideration.**

We recommend, but certainly do not require, that *Southwest Poet Series* entrants and *The Maverick Press Journal* submitters examine a copy of *Alacrán*, or 1996 SPS winner *Blues in a Red Eye Glass* by Jo LeCoeur to have a clearer idea of what the editors are looking for in terms of strong, uncluttered figurative language here in this maverick desert.

Golden Apples of the Sun, Silver Apples of the Moon

What the editor looks for in selecting a poem for The Maverick Press
• Originality—fresh perspectives
• Fresh vocabularies—both personal and geographic (Poems should arise from Place.)
• Play of syntax that can lead me on a dance through the beauty of English
• Skill or craft—voice.
• Attention to consistent vocabulary, mood, tone
• No flaws in the logic established within the piece
• Uncluttered figurative language—metaphor and analog
• Accessibility at some level, but at this same time mystery, so that I may come back for more than one reading
• Layers of meaning, unstated implications: "a riddle wrapped in a mystery inside an enigma." I like poems that can be read more than one way or that are, possibly, ambiguous without being vague.
• No preaching or didacticism. I am a pagan and get tired of proselytizers.
• Literary allusions, mythopoeic allusions, especially from outside the mainstream of Western Civ., but also have a fondness for Greek allusions if they aren't too dense. By no means does every poem have to have mythic references, but even if the myth is an unfamiliar one it provokes a tone of magical realism.
• Unmodified nouns and verbs—no adverbs, or, at least, relatively few!
• Magic, the "Wyrd" in the Anglo axon sense—not to be confused with the topic of superstition, sorcery, witchcraft, or occult (which does not interest me), but Magic in the sense of text that leaves me enchanted, spellbound, hypnotized, seduced.

• Unsentimental, stark beauty that has a slight edge—not to be confused with "in your face" poetry.

• Longer, fully developed poems. I think in 4 years I've maybe picked only 5-8 poems under 10 lines and *prefer about 24-36*: poems longer than this must be rich, complex and going somewhere. Poets cannot be expected to write toward a particular length—when the poem is finished it's finished, and beating a dead horse never gets us across the creek. I have also published a few 4-pagers and welcome the occasional treatment over 100 lines.

• Poems that stir the imagination, ignite the intellect, burn in the darkness of my three pound universe.

FICTION GUIDELINES

Preferences: Sudden or Flash Fiction. "Prose poem" quality for short-shorts.

• 1,200 words—5 pages **maximum** per story

• Send no more than three stories at a time.

• Bio and cover letter a must.

• I prefer not to return ms., so a **business size** letter is sufficient for my response.

• Submit all ms. In a 9"x6" envelope, minimum—prefer 9"x12".

• Staple each story of more than one page in upper left corner.

• Type full name and address at top of each and every page—right corner works best for me. This includes the cover letter and bio pages.

Major Considerations

• Originality—fresh perspectives

• Fresh vocabularies—both personal and geographic

• Skill or craft

• Attention to consistent vocabulary, mood, tone.

• Prefer *en media res* with little "back talk," i.e., expository writing.

• We are looking for literature, NOT genre fiction:

• NO love stories, horror, fantasy, juvenile, etc.

This editor hates stories about children—yes, that includes *Tom Sawyer*, etc.—send them elsewhere.

Fond of Raymond Carver & Charles Bukowski, but not to the exclusion of other styles.

In all honesty The Maverick Press is primarily interested in poetry and runs only 2 to 4 fiction pieces an issue, so competition for those few slots can be fierce with shorter pieces that have something to say winning hands down.

One other editorial quirk: I'm suspicious of texts that load up on adverbs—choose a figure of speech or stronger verb.

Thanks!

Carol Cullar, Editor

Categories: Fiction—Poetry—Short Shorts—Sudden Fiction

Name: Carol Cullar, Editor
Material: Poetry, Short Fiction
Address: RT 2 BOX 4915
City/State/ZIP: EAGLE PASS TX 78852-9605
Telephone: 830-773-1836
Fax: 830-773-8877
E-mail: mavpress@admin.hilconet.com

Meat Whistle Quarterly

A quarterly magazine of verse & fiction dedicated to publishing quality literature, regardless of names or styles. All forms of poetry & prose are welcomed, although we especially encourage experimental works & free verse by new & established writers.

Our guidelines are limited to: single submissions within a manuscript should not exceed 8 pages typed & double-spaced, however, manuscripts can be of any length. We reserve the right to serialize any works longer than our guidelines permit.

Response time is within a month. We pay with two contributor's copies.

Sample copies $2.50. Current issue $3.

A sample of what we are looking for:

rivers of suggestion

some nights
the poems
will just not come.

lost
somewhere
in the fingers.

they will fester,
teetering
on madness,

these fingers
which could
just as easily
murder men
or pull flowers
from the earth.

these soft white
fingers
heavy as stone,

holding back
rivers
of
suggestion.

Categories: Fiction—Nonfiction—Arts—Literature—Poetry

Name: Submissions Editor
Material: All
Address: 12916 HERITAGE DR STE 204
City/State/ZIP: PLYMOUTH MI 48170
Telephone: 313-414-0476
E-mail: LulaSunday@aol.com

ME Magazine

ME Magazine is an outrageously idiosyncratic publication (since 1980), concerned with the subject of ME, mail art or correspondence art, cutting edge figurative oil painting, messages to the worldwide artist community (33 countries), and outlandish poetry suitable to the above subjects.

Please do not bother ME otherwise.

All other pertinent queries, etc., returned when accompanied with a SASE.

Categories: Arts—Painting—Poetry

Address: ME MAGAZINE
City/State/ZIP: ME 04008-0182

Medical Device & Diagnostic Industry

Scope of Magazine

Medical Device & Diagnostic Industry is a monthly magazine written exclusively for original equipment manufacturers of medical devices and in vitro diagnostic products. The goal of MD&DI is to help industry professionals develop, design, and manufacture medical products that comply with complex and demanding regulations and market requirements.

Readers are professional personnel in product R&D, design, manufacturing, quality assurance, regulatory affairs, and corporate management. Worldwide circulation is approximately 40,000.

Subjects covered include:
Business & Marketing
Legal Affairs
Research & Development
Clean Manufacturing
Manufacturing/Production
Site Selection
Design
Materials
Software
Diagnostics
New Technologies
Standards
Drug Delivery
Packaging
Sterilization
Electronics
Plastics
Testing(Validation
Human Factors
Quality Control/Assurance
Training
Labeling
Regulatory Affairs
Requirements for Publication

The publishability of a manuscript in MD&DI is determined by a variety of factors. Manuscripts must be clearly directed to MD&DI's readership, must not repeat recent coverage of the same topic, must be sharply focused on a well-defined thesis, and must meet the standards of peer reviewers. When possible, authors should consult with editorial staff before beginning manuscripts. Query letters, summaries, and outlines are welcome.

Manuscript Format

References and bibliographies are acceptable (see below for format); abstracts and footnotes to the text are not.

The appropriate length of submitted manuscripts varies with subject matter and audience. In general, manuscripts addressing topics of broad interest to a wide variety of MD&DI readers range from 2,500 to 5,000 words long; topics appealing to narrower audiences, such as one specific job category or type of manufacturer, typically do not exceed 3,000 words. Guest Editorials, however, should be no longer than 1,500 words.

Whenever possible, please submit manuscripts on a 3½", IBM-compatible disk as well as on paper, in either Microsoft Word for Windows, WordPerfect, or ASCII format.

Review Process

All manuscripts are subjected to double-blind peer review to ensure the quality and relevance of the materials. Manuscripts are also subject to copyediting. Authors are given the opportunity to review and approve or alter the edited draft before publication. On average, submissions require four to six weeks for review and one to three months for publication following review.

Conditions

1. Manuscripts are accepted for consideration with the understanding that they are unpublished and are not under review elsewhere.

2. While MD&DI does not discourage vendors or others engaged in the sale of products or services to our readers from submitting articles for publication, we do ask that authors disclose any financial interest in the material presented and strive to discuss it in a balanced, objective way.

3. No promotion of a specific brand or source of products or services is acceptable. Similarly, efforts to steer readers toward products or services offered by authors must be avoided.

4. Canon Communications, Inc., assumes the copyright to published manuscripts.

5. Canon Communications, Inc. assumes no responsibility for unsolicited manuscripts or artwork, although they are accepted for review.

Tables

1. Tables should be typed on separate, standard-size pages and must not be included in manuscript copy.

2. Tables should contain only words and common mathematical and technical symbols; art (arrows, etc.) should not be included.

3. Tables should be numbered Roman numerals) in order of mention and clearly identified on the back.

4. Each must have a brief title or legend; additional information may appear as footnotes to the table or as discussion in text.

5. Tables should be limited to one per four manuscript pages.

Figures and Illustrations

1. Artwork must be provided on separate pages, must not be included in the manuscript copy and must correspond exactly to the text explanation.

2. Line art, graphs and photographs should be camera-ready. One set of originals is sufficient.

3. Figures should be numbered (Arabic numerals) in order of mention and clearly identified on the back.

4. Each must have a brief title or legend; additional information should appear as discussion in text.

5. Lettering and symbols should be large enough to remain legible after reduction.

6. Figures or illustrations should be limited to one per four manuscript pages.

7. Artwork will returned on request.

References and Bibliographies

1. References should be typed double-spaced on a separate page, should be numbered in the order in which they are mentioned, and should be indicated in text by superscript Arabic numerals.

2. Bibliographies (i.e., suggested readings) are unnumbered and should be organized alphabetically.

3. Use the following styles:

Article in journal—

Culver DH, Horan T, Gaynes RP, et al., "Surgical Wound Infection Rates by Wound Class, Operative Procedure, and Patient Risk Index," *Am J Med*, 91:1525-1575, 1991.

Placencia AM, Arin ML, Peeler JT, et al., "Physical Tests Are Not Enough," Med Dev & Diag *Indust* 11(9):72-78, 1988. (Issue number [9] needed because journal not consecutively paginated.)

Book and book chapter—

Putz-Anderson V, *Cumulative Trauma Disorders*, New York, Taylor & Francis, 1988.

Small A, "Design for Older People," in *Handbook of Human Factors*, Salvendy G (ed), New York, John Wiley, pp 499-500, 1987.

Standards and reports—

Selected ASTM Standards on Packaging, 2nd ed., Philadelphia, American Society for Testing and Materials, 1987.

Human Factors Engineering Guidelines and Preferred Practices for the Design of Medical Devices, AAMI HE-1988, Arlington, VA, Association for the Advancement of Medical Instrumentation, 1988.

Proceedings and meeting abstracts—

Hernandez J, Klein K, Learned V, et al., "Isokinetic Wrist Strength of Females with Carpal Tunnel Syndrome," in *Proceedings of the Human Factors Society 34th Annual Meeting*, Santa

Monica, CA, Human Factors Society, p 795, 1990.

Margolis WE and Finniman F, "What Quality Means to the Drug Industry," presented to the American Society for Microbiology at the 78th Annual Meeting, Dallas, May 1980. (For unpublished proceedings, give city and date of meeting where presentation was made, not the city of the organization's office.)

Legal citations—
Federal Register, 57 *FR*:10702
21 USC 551(4)
Community Nutrition Institute v. *Young,* 818 F2d, 943 (DC Cir 1987).
SMDA, Section 16, amending FD&C Act, Section 503.
Categories: Health—Medical Devices

Name: Sherrie Steward, Senior Editor
Material: All
Address: 3340 OCEAN PARK BLVD STE 1000
City/State/ZIP: SANTA MONICA CA 97405
Telephone: 310-392-5509
Fax: 310-392-4920
E-mail: mddi@cancom.com

MEDIPHORS

Mediphors
A Literary Journal of the Health Professions

DESCRIPTION: *Mediphors* is a semiannual literary magazine publishing broad work in medicine and health. The writing is of special interest to health care professionals, but because of a unique perspective, *Mediphors* has received much enthusiasm from general readers interested in high quality creative writing in medicine. Types of work include short story, poetry and humor. Nonfiction works include essay, commentary and opinion. Photography, cartoons and artwork are also published.

SUBMISSIONS: *Mediphors* encourages unsolicited material. We do not pay in monetary form; however, an honorarium of two publication copies is given (one for Misc Mediphors page). Our goal is to place in print as many new voices as possible. We encourage submissions from authors both within and outside the health field. Previously unpublished work is preferred without simultaneous submission.

Topics of work should have some relation to medicine and health, but may be quite broad. Acceptable examples range from short story or historical fiction through current healthcare criticisms and beyond to science fiction. Well written personal essays are welcome. Please note that *Mediphors* is not a technical scientific journal. We have no scientific peer review and do not publish research or review articles, except of a historical nature.

Please enclose two manuscript copies that we can keep and a stamped self-addressed envelope. We try to return manuscripts if sufficient postage included. **Do not** send books, chapbooks, parts of novels, or more than 6 poems at one time. Because our editors strive to read all submissions thoroughly, there may be delays in response of up to 4 months. **Do not** send corrections to work being reviewed. There are no deadlines.

If accepted, the author will be required to sign an authenticity of authorship statement and copyright agreement (first NA serial rights). There are no reading or other fees. *Upon acceptance* interested authors are encouraged to submit original artwork or photographs to complement their written work.

MAXIMUM LENGTH OF WORK:
Lead Story—to 2,500 words by arrangement.

Fiction/Nonfiction stories—to about 4,500 words.
Essay—to about 2,000 words.
Poetry—to 30 lines preferred.
Commentary/Opinion/Criticism—to 1,500 words.

ART & PHOTOGRAPHY: Please note that payment is two (2) publication copies. We hope that exposure in a nationally distributed magazine will be of additional value. Submitting a title and signing of work is encouraged. Artists/photographers are credited on the contributor's page of the issue. If an artist is interested in illustration of a short story or prose work, we can make advance assignments.

Submissions should be related to health and medicine, but may be broadly interpreted. Examples of previously published photographic subjects: scenes of a Mexican clinic, emergency room, abandoned nursing home, a hospital, medical helicopter, abandoned doctor's house, etc. It is preferred that any person seen in the work should not be identifiable (or a signed release would be required).

Mediphors standard guidelines apply regarding copyright and simultaneous submission (see *Mediphors* guidelines, above). Work may be submitted in black & white or color, but publication is black & white only. What has worked well is a group submission with a single copy (photocopy or extra print) of each item in 4"x5" or 5"x7". The collection is reviewed and if an item is accepted, the copy may be used or a higher quality copy or original can be forwarded. All work can be returned upon a request that includes SASE. Particularly interesting photos will be considered for the magazine cover. Turnaround time for review is usually one month or less.

Consider ordering a sample copy of *Mediphors* to get an idea of the publication style.

SUBSCRIPTIONS: One year $15. Two years $25. Three years $35. (PA residents add 6% sales tax). Foreign: $20/30/40 US. We strive to keep our fees affordable to everyone. The more subscribers, the more authors we can place into print. Please notify us 6 weeks in advance if you are moving. Provide old and new addresses. Sample copy $6.00. Additional author copies $5. Back issues $6 subject to supply.

PROBLEM? If there is a problem in mailing, whether a damaged or lost issue, please drop us a note. It will be replaced free. Contact us if any error arises concerning your subscription. Our most important goal is placing *Mediphors* into the hands of our readers.

TAX-DEDUCTIBLE DONATIONS: *Mediphors* is a non-profit corporation under IRS 501(c)(3). We welcome individual or corporate contributions to help with production costs. For more details, please write us.

MEDIPHORS (ISSN1068-9745) is published twice yearly by Mediphors, Inc., a private, non-profit organization composed of medical professionals combined with nationally published writers and poets. With the exception of possible tax-deductible donations, we are not affiliated with any pharmaceutical, product marketing, or other corporation. Ideas expressed are those of the authors and do not necessarily reflect the opinion of our staff. We enjoy reading comments or suggestions from readers and authors. Correspondence is answered promptly when accompanied by a SASE. We do not accept phone calls.

Categories: Fiction—Nonfiction—Cartoons—Health—Humor—Literature—Medicine—Photography—Poetry—Short Stories

Name: Eugene D. Radice, MD, Editor
Material: All
Address: PO BOX 327
City/State/ZIP: BLOOMSBURG PA 17815

Medusa's Hairdo Magazine

1. The scope of the magazine

Modern mythology is the mythology of our generation—a description of our time as you perceive it, *not* a retelling of classical mythology. We print stories, shorts, poetry and artwork of any genre, inclining towards the literary. However, we do not handle sexual, violent, or profane material. We also do not print humorous poetry.

2. The specifications for fiction & poetry submissions

4,000 word maximum; no minimum. Informal cover letter required. Electronic submissions preferred, but disposable paper submissions also accepted. Simultaneous submissions are OK if so noted; multiple submissions are acceptable up to ten poems or three stories.

3. The specifications for art submissions

Send a representative sample of your artwork to us, along with a description of your preferred subject matter, and we will contact you when we need a story illustrated. Alternatively, you may submit a particular piece of artwork for consideration, but please be sure to specify that in a cover letter.

4. Reading period & response times

Reading periods are as follows:

May 15-August 15

November 22-30

March 1-March 31

Submissions exceeding these periods by more than a couple of days will be shelved until the next reading period arrives, without notification. We often respond personally and in detail, so be prepared for a constructive appraisal of your work. Queries and guideline requests may be made year round, with a 2-wk RT.

5. If accepted

All accepted non-electronic submissions over 1,000 words must be remitted on a 3.5" IBM-formatted diskette. The file should be saved in both ASCII (text) format and a word processing format (I use WP-8.) Lead time averages one year. Some stories may be illustrated at the discretion of the editor. Grammatical and minor stylistic changes may be made. Payment is one contributor's copy only, except for solicited artwork, which is $2-$5 flat fee plus one contributor's copy.

6. Subscriptions

Due to the unusual scope of the magazine, it is highly recommended to at least try a sample copy, or, ideally, to subscribe for a year. Sample copies are $4.50; back issues of MH 1-3 are $4. Subscriptions are discounted at $8.70/year/2 issues. Bulk rates are also available, and ad trades are welcomed.

Categories: Fiction—Fantasy—Horror—Literature—Poetry—Science Fiction—Short Stories

Name: Submissions Editor
Material: All
Address: PO BOX 358
City/State/ZIP: CATLETTSBURG KY 41129
Telephone: bymoor0@pop.uky.edu

Men's Fitness

Men's Fitness magazine is a total-service publication for healthy, active men. It contains a wide range of features and monthly departments devoted to all areas of health, fitness and an overall active lifestyle.

Editorial fulfills two functions: entertainment and information, with special attention paid to accuracy.

Manuscript tone: The editorial voice must be friendly, speaking directly to the healthy, active man. Academic-journal composition is not acceptable. Please read the magazine for an under-standing of its style.

Manuscript length: 1,000 to 1,250 words for departments; 1,500 to 1,800 words for features.

Response time: Four to six weeks.

Writers' contracts/kill fees: Contracts are required for all work. Kill fees (paid if we find the work unacceptable for any reason after a contract is signed) are 1/3 the original payment amount.

Payment rates: $500 (or less) for departments; $1,000 (or less) for features. All fees are negotiated individually. Payment made within six weeks of final acceptance.

Fact checking: Accuracy is the responsibility of the author. Manuscripts should be accompanied by the telephone numbers of sources quoted within the article, so editors can verify their names, titles and educational credentials. Products or services mentioned in the articles should also be accompanied with contract names and phone numbers. Books should be cited by complete title, publisher and price. Include photocopies of both covers and the title page in the article's backup. Include a copy of the abstract of any studies cited. If the information cited comes from a secondary source, include a copy of the newspaper or magazine article.

Queries: One-page summary of idea or ideas. Send recent clips with bylines. Please send only clips that reflect your own writing style along with a SASE.

Unsolicited manuscripts: We prefer queries. Please do not send manuscripts.

Sample copies: Unfortunately, we cannot offer sample issues.

Categories: Nonfiction—Consumer—Health—Inspirational—Physical Fitness—Psychology—Science—Self-Help—Sexuality—Nutrition

Name: Dean Brierly, Managing Editor
Material: All
Address: 21100 ERWIN STREET
City/State/ZIP: WOODLAND HILLS, CA 91367
Telephone: 818-884-6800
Fax: 818-704-5734

Men's Health

It's not easy to break into *Men's Health*. Don't even try if you haven't been published in a major magazine. Still with us? Okay, study a back issue or two, then consider the following: Most unsolicited queries fail because they don't address the *Men's Health* reader.

The *Men's Health* Reader: Our circulation is 1,400,000+; 85 percent of our readers are men. Our average reader is 35 years old and is a well-educated urban or suburban professional. He's active in a number of sports and exercise pursuits.

What We Cover: As you'll see, we're an authoritative source of information on all aspects of men's physical and emotional health. We rely on writers to seek out the right experts, and to either tell a story from a first-person vantage or to get good anecdotes. We carefully fact-check all quotes and health information contained in the magazine.

Tone: Most of our articles have the tone of a peer who happens to have spoken to a few authorities on the issue at hand. Imagine you're relating that information to the reader, one on one, over a beer or at dinner.

Length, Payment, Rights: The best place to break into the magazine is "Malegrams" or one of our one-page columns. For "Malegrams," we seek submissions of about 200 words. We pay $25 to $50 upon completion of fact-checking. Other than that:

Departments run 1,500 words and pay $500-$2,000

Features run 1,200-4,000 words and pay $1,000-$5,000

We usually buy all rights, but this is negotiated on an individual basis. We will consider buying second rights, if your published piece has not appeared in another national magazine, in another health magazine, or in another magazine written primarily for men. When we pay: For departments and features, following acceptance, upon completion of the fact-checking process.

The Departments:

Malegrams: Short takes relevant to men. Clinical and research advances in health, medicine, psychology, sports performance, work and relationship issues, the offbeat.

Training: We cover what's tried and needs to be tried again (i.e., calisthenics revisited), as well as the trends.

Nutrition: What to eat and when.

Working: How to succeed. How to fail. How to know the difference.

Couples: New takes on major relationship issues.

Self-Care: What to do so that you don't have to call a doctor.

Looks: Practical and health aspects of grooming, dressing, etc.

Man-to-Man: Simple, well-told stories about manhood, manliness, machismo, momentary lapses. The wiser you are, the more of a wiseguy you can be.

Mind/Body: The psychology of men, and how that relates to health, exercise, performance.

Clips: We don't assign anything without seeing published clips. Photocopies are a good idea, as we may not return clips. Send your best. One or two will do. They don't all have to be about health or medicine. We want to see how well you report, write and interpret stories.

How to Query *Men's Health*: Structure an article proposal this way:

Start with the lead you expect to put on the piece.

Write a summary of where you'll go from there.

Give specifics on whom you plan to interview, what types of real-life anecdotes you'll include, what research sources you plan to go to and what conclusion the story might reach. Queries shouldn't run longer than one page, single-spaced. We'll get back to you in two-four weeks. (Be sure to enclose a SASE.)

Manuscripts: If you send a manuscript, it must be typed double- or triple-spaced, with margins of at least 1 inch. Send a copy of your original, just in case. We report on manuscripts in four to eight weeks.

Back Issues: Send a check payable to *Men's Health* for $5 per issue requested (no more than two) and enclose a 9X12 SASE.

The Editors

Categories: Nonfiction—Careers—Fashion—Health—Physical Fitness—Relationships—Sports—Recreation—Travel—Nutrition

Name: Peter Moore, Managing Editor
Material: All
Address: 33 E. MINOR ST.
City/State/ZIP: EMMAUS, PA 18098
Telephone: 610-967-5171
Fax: 610-967-8963

Men's Journal

Men's Journal is a men's lifestyle magazine for 25- to 49-year-old active men. Its editorial emphasis is on travel, fitness, adventure and participatory sports, but it is also open to a wide range of topics of interest to contemporary American men.

Front-of-the-book articles cover a wide range of general interest topics and news, and are between 400-1,200 words. Feature articles and profiles run between 2,000-7,000 words. Articles for the equipment and fitness sections are 400-1,800 words. These are service-oriented articles meant to provide sporting and leisure reviews for the active man.

One-page queries, accompanied by one or two applicable clips, should be sent to:

Categories: Adventure—General Interest—Men's Issues—Physical Fitness—Sports—Travel

Name: Submissions Editor
Material: All
Address: 1290 AVENUE OF THE AMERICAS
City/State/ZIP: NEW YORK NY 10104
Telephone: 212-484-1690
Fax: 212-767-8204

Mentor & Protege
Accelerating Professional and Personal Development Through the Art and Practice of Mentoring

Thank you for requesting information about writing for MENTOR & PROTEGE. Guidelines are simple: The subject is mentoring and only mentoring, wherever that occurs and however it occurs (for example, as coaching, role modeling, parenting, or traditional mentoring). Articles, book and movie reviews, and short stories are accepted. Length is generally 700-1,200 words. Although longer treatments can be considered as a series, and shorter items are acceptable for the news section, "Worth Repeating," or as filler.

The main focus of MENTOR & PROTEGE is the mentoring relationship. How does it work? What do the mentor and protege do? What are the problems within a mentoring relationship and how have mentors and proteges solved them? How do mentors become mentors; what is the process? How do proteges find mentors; what do they do if they can't find them? etc.

If your manuscript is accepted for publication, there are three payment options for regular manuscript submissions: 1) a subscription to MENTOR & PROTEGE ($30.00 value) plus 2 contributor's copies; 2) waiver of $5.00 entry fee in MENTOR AWARD-this offers the chance to win the $100.00 Grand Prize awarded yearly in January; 3) 3 cents per word. MENTOR & PROTEGE is a good opportunity for new writers as the editor is willing to work with you to produce an article that will help you hone your skills and produce an article suitable for publishing.

Or you simply may choose to enter The Mentor Award. The contest was conceived as a way to promote mentoring, to enlighten those who may not know about mentoring, and to encourage mentors and their proteges to keep up the good work they have begun. There are at least 7,000 mentoring programs across the country, 13.5 million at-risk youth, but only 340,000 actual mentoring relationships, so there are plenty of possibilities for stories. In addition, between 30% and 50% of all corporations have some type of mentoring activity going on.

The Mentor Award focuses on *unpublished** essays, articles, and short stories written by professional or aspiring writers age 16 or over. The contest deadlines occur quarterly: March 31, June 30, September 30, and December 31. An entry form is required. Entry fee is $5, and entries cannot be returned. Winners of the quarterly contests receive an award certificate, plus their winning entry may be published in MENTOR. All quarterly winners are eligible for The Grand Prize of $100 which is awarded every January for the one best submission from the previous year.

1997 winners of The Mentor Award include Tonya Evetts Weimer for her essay "My Mother Is a Rodeo Queen." 1996 winners include John Jurley for his movie review of "Dead Man Walking," Melissa Anthony for her newspaper article "Program Turns Writer Into Tutor," and Charline McCord for her essay "In the Kitchen with Thelma" (1996 Grand Prize winner). Other recent winners include Lynn Stearns (two- time winner of the annual

Grand Prize) for her essay "Grandmother's Jar of Buttons" and her short story "Raymond's Role Model." Each winner received a certificate; some of the winning entries were published in MENTOR.

A sample issue of the newsletter is available for only $3. Or for $5 you may wish to order "What is Mentoring," a collection of *Mentor* reprints (including some Mentor Award winners) that shows a wide range of articles, essays, and short stories from past issues of the newsletter.

If you belong to a writers group, please share news about The Mentor Award with your peers.

*SPECIAL NOTE: The Athena Award is a sister competition. It accepts professional submissions that include mentoring-related articles, academic papers, books, magazines, training materials, and videos *published, presented, or distributed* after January 1, 1993. Annual deadline is January 31. A plaque is awarded but no monetary reward. The Athena Award Winners publication is available for $5.00.

Categories: Nonfiction—Business—Careers—Education—Mentoring

Name: Submissions Editor
Material: All
Address: PO BOX 4382
City/State/ZIP: OVERLAND PARK KS 66204
Telephone: 913-362-7889
Nota bene: Mentor Award may require entry fee.

Mercury

Mercury
The Journal of the
Astronomical Society of the Pacific

Thank you for agreeing to write for *Mercury*, the Journal of the Astronomical Society of the Pacific. In its original incarnation, *Mercury* was first published by the ASP in 1925. It is now read by 5,200 ASP members and at 800 academic libraries, observatories, and other institutions in 71 countries. The ASP is the largest general astronomy society in the world. Our members include professional astronomers, amateurs, educators, and motivated lay people.

Fees
Alas, because the ASP is nonprofit and impoverished, we are unable to pay for submissions. Writing for *Mercury* is a labor of love and good exposure for your ideas. We do have a limited capacity to reimburse expenses, such as postage or photo reproduction. We send four free copies to all contributors and can provide more, within reason.

Queries
We are unequipped to review unsolicited manuscripts; if you have article ideas, please write or e-mail the editor. In your letter, please discuss the basic idea for the article, its general content, its relevance to our readership, and the relationship of the prospective writer to the subject matter. The editor tries to respond to all correspondence within two weeks, although it may take somewhat longer or shorter depending on other deadlines we must meet.

Level of Articles
We encourage writers to read past issues to get a sense of our style. *Mercury* assumes that its readers are motivated and informed about basic astronomy. In our 1994 survey of readers,

49 percent of the respondents said they were involved in amateur astronomy, 29 percent in astronomical research, and 86 percent in astronomy education at some level. *Mercury* articles are roughly at the same level as *The Sciences:* between a mass-market science magazine such as *Discover* and a more scholarly magazine such as *Scientific American.*

We think of *Mercury* as the *Atlantic Monthly* of astronomy, giving informed perspectives on salient issues in research, education, history, and public policy. An article should not focus solely on the research or history of any particular individual, unless it is of unusual importance. Articles should appeal to readers' personal experiences and draw broader conclusions about how science is conducted. We encourage writers to be innovative and forceful, to devise clever metaphors, to go out onto a limb. The ASP does not endorse anything our contributors say, but we believe in challenging readers and making *Mercury* a vigorous part of the marketplace of ideas.

Length of Articles
Regular departments are one magazine page, or 1,000 words. Book reviews are two pages, 2,000 words. The standard feature is four magazine pages, 3,000 words plus illustrations and a sidebar.

Rights
The ASP asks that contributors transfer their copyright to the ASP in order to facilitate electronic distribution and academic photocopying, which we allow free of charge. In return, we grant writers the non-exclusive right to reuse any part or all of their work. We have found that this arrangement avoids hassles, but if contributors prefer to retain copyright, we have no problem with that. Our concern is simply to protect ourselves legally. The minimum we can accept is worldwide first appearance, non-exclusive print and electronic rights.

Submission
To avoid transcription errors, we require electronic submission. We prefer rich text, (.rtf) or Microsoft Word 5.1 format, but will accept plain-text, MacWrite, or WordPerfect formats. You can e-mail the document to the address below or send us a 3½" low-density Macintosh diskette. If you send a plain text file, we ask that you fax or mail a formatted version as well.

Deadlines
First drafts are due 10 weeks before the cover date; final drafts, eight weeks before.

Editing
Mercury rarely rejects a manuscript. When you submit an article, we assume that you agree to work with the editor in preparing it for publication. The *Mercury* editor is an active one who enjoys bouncing ideas back and forth and who takes pain to ensure readability and interest. Most writers realize that every manuscript benefits from careful, respectful critiquing.

Editing occurs in two stages. First, the editor reads the submitted draft and makes suggestions for a revised draft. On occasion, the editor may ask an anonymous outside reviewer for advice. Typical issues include: making sure readers know where the article is heading and why they should be reading it; making sure that the article does not present readers with too much information too quickly; checking that concepts are defined as naturally as possible; identifying and highlighting particularly enlightening ideas; and anticipating and addressing readers' questions.

Second, the editor copy-edits the revised draft for grammar, spelling, flow, style, and so forth. We make every reasonable effort to show writers the final version of their articles while there is time to make changes. There is one exception: During layout, the editor sometimes must condense in order to fine-tune length, eliminate widows, or correct errors noticed at the last minute. Usually such changes are vanishingly minor. We cannot inform writers of such changes.

Titles, abstracts, subheads, and captions are our domain, although we generally work from writers' suggestions and include these elements in the drafts we return for writers' approval.

House Style

Mercury is somewhere between a magazine and an academic journal. In most cases, it adheres to *Associated Press* style, with concessions to *Chicago* style. Exceptions are detailed in the *Mercury* stylebook and are routinely made during copy-editing.

Mercury does not have footnotes or formal bibliographies. If acknowledgment has to be given, work it into the body of the article or the biography. Articles should not include a bibliography unless it is interesting in itself. Such bibliographies should be short and annotated.

Mercury uses SI units, with English equivalents given in parentheses. Spell out the names of measurement units. Take care not to overstate precision. Normally, two significant figures suffice.

Acronyms intimidate readers. Use only abbreviations likely to be recognized outside a specialty. Do not define an abbreviation in parentheses on first reference: If the abbreviation is not obvious enough to be recognized on second reference, it shouldn't be used to begin with.

Biography

Following every article is a one-paragraph biography of the writer, written in third-person, including research interests, a personal anecdote or factoid, and an e-mail address.

Illustrations

We ask the writer to obtain, help to obtain, or at least suggest illustrations. This ensures that the illustrations are what the writer intends; in any event, most writers have better access to illustrations than we do. We prefer photographs in print form and can reimburse reproduction expenses. We can also accept GIF, JPEG, and TIFF files. *Mercury* is published in two colors.

Categories: Education—Science

Name: Submissions Editor
Material: All
Address: 390 ASHTON AVE
City/State/ZIP: SAN FRANCISCO CA 94112
Telephone: 415-337-1100
Fax: 415-337-5205
E-mail: gmusser@stars.sfsu.edu

MESSAGE Magazine

Thank you for your interest in MESSAGE Magazine. MESSAGE is the oldest and most widely circulated religious journal addressing ethnic issues in the USA. We work hard to preserve our unique role interpreting current events through a Black, Christian perspective. We're happy you want to be a part of this powerful ministry.

Get to know MESSAGE

• *Published:* Bimonthly, in a 32-page format, by The Review and Herald® Publishing Association. Sponsored by the Seventh-Day Adventist Church.

• *Audience:* Predominantly Black and Seventh-Day Adventist. *Message* is, however, a missionary journal geared for the unchurched.

• *Lead time:* When submitting seasonal material, remember our production schedule requires us to work four to six months ahead.

• *Payments: Message* pays upon acceptance.

• *Rights: Message* purchases first rights to all articles. Each article should carry a credit line for *Message* when reprinted elsewhere.

WHAT TO WRITE

• *Message publishes:* informational, devotional, inspirational, doctrinal, profile, interview and self-help articles that have wide appeal to people of many backgrounds.

• *Message does not accept:* sermons, outlines, poetry, reprints, or anything that is not in an article format.

• *Topics include:* biblical exposition, celebrity and humanitarian profiles, family, health, education, worship, news and current events, religious freedom and racial reconciliation. Often our writers query us by phone about article ideas. Feel free to call and bounce an idea off the editors.

Departments

• *Message*—also accepts freelance material for the following departments:

• *Healthspan*—This 700 word column covers a variety of health topics of interest to our audience. It is typically accompanied by a sidebar or chart.

• *Message Jr*—Our column reserved for children, ages 5 to 8, is no longer than 500 words. We prefer biblical stories, but stories with a clear-cut moral are also accepted.

HOW TO GET PUBLISHED:
Nine Ways to Woo Our Editors

1. Make sure your article is biblically sound and offers spiritual perspective and insight.

2. Support your material with facts, statistics and quotes from experts.

3. Invite the reader to reads your whole story by writing an interesting lead.

4. Sharpen your focus. Sometimes writing a title, subtitles and subheadings helps.

5. Use interesting, fresh, insightful angles to old topics. Say something new.

6. Take a position, make a point, stick to the point, then cut to the chase.

7. Write about timely topics and events.

8. Answer the underlying, heartfelt questions a reader may have about your topic.

9. Be a good storyteller. Make people and places come alive by expressing details.

How to submit a manuscript

• Submit articles no longer than five pages.

• Enclose your name, address, and social security number.

• Enclose a line about yourself.

• We greatly appreciate manuscripts on computer disk with a WordPerfect (PC) format, along with the hard copy.

• You will be notified by postcard that we have received your manuscript. If your article is accepted, you will be notified within six to eight weeks.

Categories: Fiction—African-American—Christian Interests—Consumer—Inspirational—Religion—Spiritual

Name: Stephen P. Ruff, Editor
Material: All
Address: 55 W OAK RIDGE DR
City/State/ZIP: HAGERSTOWN MD 21740
Telephone: 301-791-7000 ext. 2565
Fax: 301-714-1753
E-mail: 74617.3047@compuserve.com

METROPOLIS

Metropolis

We recommend that a writer considering submittal of a query letter examine at least the last couple of issue of the magazine before submission. Send query letters-not completed manuscripts-describing the particulars of your story idea and why it would be good for *Metropolis*. Be as concise, specific, and clear as possible, describing the issues that surround the event, building, person, firm, or process that is the nugget of your story idea.

Keep in mind that at *Metropolis*, a firm's new work isn't a story-but the critical issues that their work brings to light might be a story. We do not cover conferences or seminars, though if such events offer new perspectives on contemporary issues in the world of art, architecture, design, graphics, urbanism, development, planning, or preservation, then an article could be framed that way.

The ideal *Metropolis* story will be based on strong reporting skills, include a knowledgeable examination of current critical issues, and will be written in a clear essay style. We are a special-interest consumer publication, and our audience is made up of designers, architects, planners, and others who are interested in those topics. It is not a professional-only audience, so technical jargon is to be avoided.

When possible, include a couple of recent clips of your stories. Ideally, we would like to see clips that relate to the kind of topic you are proposing for us, but anything that reveals your writing skills is helpful.

If you would like to submit an idea for the Insites section, send your query to Noel Millea, Assistant Editor. If you have an idea for the By Design section, send your idea to Janet Rumble, Senior Editor. If your idea is for the Visible City section, send it to Kira Gould, Managing Editor, and if it's for the Metropolis Observed section, send it to David Brown, Associate Editor. Feature ideas can go to Marisa Bartolucci, Executive Editor, or Susan Szenasy, Editor in Chief, or any of the other editors.

Generally, ideas about furniture, graphic design, or the process of design should go to Janet Rumble or Noel Millea; architecture ideas or European topics should go to Marisa Bartolucci, and urban, development, political/social, and planning ideas should go to Kira Gould or David Brown. Our book review section, In Print (queries for which can be addressed to any editor), tends to run about 2,500-3,000 words, and typically focuses on the issues covered in a group (two to four) of books.

Queries can be mailed, faxed, or submitted electronically. If you have other questions about submissions, call Kira Gould at 212-360-3316, or e-mail her at the address below.

Categories: Nonfiction—Architecture—Arts—Consumer—Culture—Environment—General Interest

Name: Refer to Guidelines
Address: 177 E 87TH ST
City/State/ZIP: NEW YORK NY 10128
Telephone: 212-722-5050
Fax: 212-427-1938
E-mail: edit@metropolismag.com (Queries)
E-mail: kira@metropolismag.com (Submission Questions)

Michigan Historical Review
Central Michigan University

The *Michigan Historical Review* publishes articles on Michigan's political, economic, social, and cultural history, and those on American, Canadian, and Midwestern history that explore important themes related to Michigan's past. All manuscript submissions receive a double-blind peer review, but final decisions about publication rest with the editorial staff. The MHR does not accept manuscripts under consideration elsewhere.

Prospective authors are requested to use the following guidelines:

1. Manuscripts should not exceed 7,000 words; endnotes must be used and are to be double spaced.

2. Authors should submit three paper copies of the manuscript and a copy on an IBM-compatible diskette (preferably in WordPerfect). To permit anonymous reviewing, the author's name should appear on a separate title page.

3. The *Chicago Manual of Style*, 14th edition, should be followed in matters of style and for endnote format. The MHR uses open punctuation and standardizes spelling of Native American tribal names.

4. Authors are requested to use bias-free language that is sensitive to race, ethnicity, gender, religion, age, ability, and sexual orientation. We recommend *Guidelines for Bias-Free Writing*, by Marilyn Schwartz and the Task Force on Bias-Free Language of the Association of American University Presses (Bloomington: Indiana University Press, 1995).

5. We encourage the inclusion of photographs, illustrations, and graphs within articles. Photographs should be in 8"x10" black-and-white glossy format. It is the author's responsibility to secure permission to publish when necessary.

6. For additional information, please contact the editorial staff via telephone or e-mail.

Categories: History

Name: Editor
Material: All
Address: CLARKE HISTORICAL LIBRARY, CMU
City/State/ZIP: MT PLEASANT MI 48859
Telephone: 517-774-6567
Fax: 517-774-2179
E-mail: MIHISREV@cmuvm.csv.cmich.edu

MICROpendium
Covering the TI99/4A and Geneve 9640

Thank you for your interest in writing for *MICROpendium*. *MICROpendium* is a magazine for the advanced or sophisticated T199/4A user and for the Geneve 9640 user. We are interested in all phases of these computers and are open to games, utilities, hardware projects and programming hints, as well as reviews of available products.

We feel that TI's manuals are the right place for the beginner to learn. We do not usually print "beginner" type articles, because we feel that this is a repetition of material that our readers can find elsewhere.

In terms of product reviews, be fair. Remember that evening and weekend hackers are the source of most new products for this "orphan" now. Don't compare them to Microsoft.

We prefer reasonably short submissions, though articles on hardware projects of sufficient interest may appear as a series. We prefer text submissions on DV/80 files along with a printout, although we will consider printed or typed copy alone. Submit programs on disk, if possible, along with a printout.

User notes are always welcome.

Categories: Nonfiction—Computers

Name: Submissions Editor
Material: All
Address: PO BOX 1343
City/State/ZIP: ROUND ROCK TX 78680
Telephone: 512-255-1512
Fax: 512-255-1512
E-mail: jkoloen@io.com

Mid-American Review
Bowling Green State University

Stories, poems, and articles will generally be returned or accepted within one to four months. Sample copies $5.00, current issue $7.00, rare back issues $10.00. Payment is $10.00 per page (pending funding) for fiction, poetry, translations and nonfiction with a maximum payment of $50.00; contributing authors receive two complimentary copies. All rights revert to the author upon publication. Manuscripts are not read from June through August. MAR does not consider simultaneous submissions, nor work which has previously appeared elsewhere.

Poetry

Poems should emanate from textured, evocative images, use language with an awareness of how words sound and mean, and have a definite sense of voice. Each line should help carry the poem, and an individual vision must be evident. We encourage new as well as established writers. There is no length limit on individual poems, but please send no more than six poems.

Translations

All submissions must include the original as well as the translated work. Chapbooks (approx. 10-15 poems) are designed to provide readers with an introduction to a single contemporary poet or a group of poets. An introductory essay of 300-500 words outlining the historical context of the poetry is encouraged. Translations of contemporary fiction are also welcome and should follow these guidelines as well as those listed under Fiction.

Nonfiction

The *Mid-American Review* seeks essays and critical articles which focus on contemporary authors and topics of current literary interest. Contributions should generally not exceed 15-20 pages and should follow standard MLA style. We also seek short (500-1,000 words) book reviews of current works of poetry, fiction, and nonfiction prose, published within the last one to two years. Address book reviews to the Nonfiction Editor.

Fiction

Mid-American Review prefers quality fiction which is both character- and language-oriented; we are open to experimental work, but discourage juvenilia and genre-type fiction. Do not submit more than one story at a time. The *Mid-American Review* usually prints stories 10-20 pages in length; authors submitting manuscripts of over 30 pages should query first with SASE.

Categories: Fiction—Nonfiction—Book Reviews—Poetry—Translations

Name: Michael Czyzniejewski, Fiction Editor
Name: David Hawkins, Poetry Editor
Name: Amy Withrow, Translation Editor
Material: As Appropriate
Address: DEPT OF ENGLISH
Address: BOWLING GREEN STATE UNIVERSITY
City/State/ZIP: BOWLING GREEN OH 43403
Telephone: 419-372-2725

Mid-Atlantic Country

Mid-Atlantic Country is a travel and lifestyle publication that covers New York, New Jersey, Pennsylvania, Delaware, Maryland, Washington, D.C., Virginia, West Virginia, and North Carolina.

We do not publish formal writer's guidelines because most stories in the magazine are assigned by the editors. We are, however, happy to consider individual queries, which must have a strong regional focus.

Categories: Nonfiction—Lifestyles—Recreation—Regional—Travel

Name: Lois Perschetz, Editor-in-Chief
Material: Queries
Address: 250 S PRESIDENT ST LEVEL 1-S
City/State/ZIP: BALTIMORE MD 21202
Telephone: 410-539-0005
Fax: 410-539-5828
E-mail: MACoMagaol.com

The Midwest Motorist

The Midwest Motorist is published bimonthly by the AAA Auto Club of Missouri and is sent to almost 420,000 AAA households in Missouri, Arkansas and portions of Illinois and Kansas. Readership is almost 800,000.

The magazine's goal is to provide members with a variety of useful information on travel, auto safety, and other topics that appeal to the motoring public. The magazine carries on average six articles per issue and buys 20-30 manuscripts per year.

How to contact us: Send queries rather than finished manuscripts. In addition, please send a list of credits or published clips when you query us for the first time. We will not take phone queries and prefer not to see a laundry list of story ideas. In general, we try to reply within four weeks of receipt. We will consider a previously published article if it appeared in a non-competing publication. Simultaneous queries are acceptable, but tell us the idea is being considered elsewhere.

Assignments: We work from an editorial schedule and assignments are usually made at least six months in advance. Sometimes the calendar is assigned by July for the following year. Usually purchase first North American rights. A story assignment is always made by letter. The writer signs an outline-agreement and returns one copy to the editor. We do not pay any expenses in conjunction with the article (travel expenses, phone bills, etc.). Payment for an article is made upon acceptance. Our rates range from $50 to $350. It helps to send photos/slides (color only) with manuscripts. While we do not pay for photos, we consider it in payment for the manuscript. To assist with fact-checking, please send copies of materials used to research the article.

Style: We use the *AP Stylebook*. Third-person voice usually works best, but in some cases first-person description is appropriate. A copy of a current magazine will be sent with assignment so our editing style can be observed. A story will not be drastically changed without discussing this with the writer. Send the manuscript on floppy disk, saved either in Microsoft Word 5.1 or a lower version, or as an ASCII text file. Always include hard copy with the disk.

Taboos: Humor, satire, fiction, poetry, cartoons. Technical and safety articles usually are written by staff. Departments (e.g. "Travel Treasures, Day Tours") also are written by staff.

Sincerely,
Michael J. Right
Editor

Categories: Associations—Automobiles—Consumer—Travel

Name: Deborah Klein, Managing Editor
Material: All
Address: 12901 N FORTY DR
City/State/ZIP: ST LOUIS MO 63141
Telephone: 314-523-7350
Fax: 314-523-6982
E-mail: aaadmk@ibm.net

Midwest Poetry Review

OUR PLEDGE: *Midwest Poetry Review* is a quarterly committed to quality, *accessible* poetry. If we don't understand your poem, we'll ask you to share it with another publication. We publish no fiction or other prose. We do our best to deliver a knowledgeable, friendly, and inspiring book which will encourage you to produce more and better poetry. We are not a vanity market. You must have talent to get in, but we're open to new poets. If you don't write poetry, we hope to give you new insight on life.

INCOME: Primary sources: subscriptions and contest entry fees. We need, and depend on, our subscribers' loyalty. We know we have to earn it. We don't publish glitzy anthologies. We won't try to sell you anything whether or not we accept your work.

POLICY: In selecting poetry, we give the edge to our subscribers, but we welcome work from others. We choose on the basis of quality (as we subjectively define it). Your subscription doesn't guarantee publication.

LINE LIMIT: 40 lines (except in contests whose rules specify a shorter length).

SUBMISSION: Send no more than five poems a month. Please put your name and address (legibly) on each poem. One poem to the page. We prefer #10 business envelope. If you want your work read, or a response, enclose SASE. No bios or credit lists. We'll try to judge each poem on its own merit, independent of what you've done before.

CONTEST ENTRANTS: One contest in each issue is open to anyone; others are restricted to subscribers. Send *two* copies of each poem. Your name and address and name of contest on one; name of contest only on second (for judge). Name of contest on outside of #10 business envelope.

PAYMENT: Currently, we pay $5 for each poem accepted. Contest awards range from $10 to $150. Each issue has one contest paying a total of $250.

ORIGINALITY: We publish only work that has not appeared elsewhere. We accept no second printings, simultaneous submissions, or anything that isn't your own work. Your sending a manuscript for consideration implies that it is your own work, that you own all rights to it, or are licensed to submit it for publication. Violate these simple requirements and you severely compromise your chances of being considered again. Ever.

RESPECT FOR PRIVACY: By submitting work for consideration, you guarantee us that you have not libeled any person or violated the privacy or publicity rights of anyone.

RIGHTS: We buy the right of first publication. After appearing in *Midwest Poetry Review*, all rights revert to you. Your work is still your property. You're free to send it elsewhere, in any form, after we use it.

CRITIQUE: Our critique panel will review your work. Maximum: 10 poems at a time. Fee of $10 and SASE must accompany critique request.

DEADLINES: First of the month prior to issues published in January, April, July, and October.

SUBSCRIPTION: US $20 annually for four issues. Sample copy: US $5.78. Back issues (when available) US $5.78 each.

Categories: Poetry

Name: Submissions Editor
Material: All
Address: PO BOX 20236
City/State/ZIP: ATLANTA GA 30325-0236
Telephone: 404-350-0714
Fax: 404-352-8417

Midwest Streams & Trails

Midwest Streams & Trails is published five times annually in Waverly, Iowa. The goal of this publication is to explore the abundance of outdoor experiences available in our region. There are endless low-cost excursions that do not require a lot of money or extensive travel. From hiking to canoeing, biking, camping, and more, there are many economical ways for Midwesterners to enjoy their own region.

The area of coverage is primarily the upper Mississippi Valley—Iowa, Minnesota, Wisconsin, Illinois, and Missouri. We will also feature destinations in Michigan, Nebraska, North and South Dakota, Kansas, Indiana and Ohio. The magazine is published in February April, July, September, and November. Our target audience consists of families and couples who enjoy outdoor recreation in the Midwest.

Content of Articles

The focus of *Midwest Streams & Trails* is on trails and Class I, II and III rivers, campgrounds and state parks in the Midwest. Only occasionally will the magazine feature Class IV, V and VI rivers. Sidebars or infographics highlight unique places families might enjoy visiting as a side-trip en route to the streams and trails featured in the magazine. *Midwest Streams & Trails* runs profiles of interesting canoeists, hikers, bikers and environmentalists in the Midwest. Articles will vary in length. The average article will be about 1,500 words long. We will not publish product reviews or fiction.

Style

All articles are printed in Associated Press Style. We are looking for both first-person and third-person accounts of canoeing, biking, hiking, camping, or related outdoor activities in the Midwest. All articles written in third-person should include plenty of quotes to add personality to the story. Articles written in first-person should tell a story rather than "review" a river or a trail.

Departments

Each issue of *Midwest Streams & Trails* will contain 10 to 12 features, mostly written by freelancers. The magazine will start out with five regular departments. A **Common Sense in the Outdoors** column will appear in each issue to provide safety tips to readers. The Last Mile will be the one-page final column in each issue. This column will not necessarily be written by the same person for each issue. **The Gallery** department will be a four-page section of photographic images. A third department will update readers on environmental quality and relevant proposed legislation. The **Personal Profiles** department will have profiles on interesting outdoors people.

Queries

Although we prefer queries, we will accept unsolicited materials. The act of contributing any material constitutes an express warranty that the material does not infringe on the rights of others. If we have already published your work and are familiar with your style of writing, you may call Maribeth Witzel to discuss additional articles you would like to write.

Submissions

Please submit your articles typed in Associated Press Style. Include a paragraph or two about yourself to be placed at the end of the article if space permits. Indicate how you would like your name to appear in the byline. Please include where we can reach you and the best time to do so. Deadlines are determined with freelancers on an individual basis. Typically, articles for the February issue are due in early November, articles for the April issue are due mid-January articles for the July issue are due mid-April, articles for the September issue are due at the end of May, and articles for the November issue are due mid-August.

Photos

Photos submitted should be accompanied by captions and photo model releases for all persons in photos. For more detailed information on our photo policies, call Matt Cure.

Publication and Payment

We reserve the right to use material at our discretion and to edit material to meet our editorial requirements. We will try to notify you should any significant changes be made to your material. Payment for one-time publication rights is submitted upon publication. Payment arrangements are determined on an individual basis and are determined by the length of an article, the number of accompanying photos, and other factors. Payments generally range from $100 to $400 for an article.

Tearsheets

You will be sent three tearsheets of your work as it appears in the magazine.

For More Information

If you have any questions, please feel free to write or call. We are very excited about the possibilities here in the Midwest and look forward to working with you in the near future.

Categories: Nonfiction—Outdoors—Recreation—Regional—Travel

Name: Maribeth Witzel, Co-editor
Material: Manuscripts and Queries
Name: Matt Cure, Co-editor
Material: Photographs
Address: PO BOX 209
City/State/ZIP: WAVERLY IA 50677
Telephone: 319-352-2030
Fax: 319-352-2232
E-mail: mst@pitnet.net

Midwifery Today
and Childbirth Education

Our Mission

Through networking and education, *Midwifery Today*'s mission is to return midwifery care to its rightful position in the family; to make midwifery care the norm throughout the world; and to redefine midwifery as a vital partnership with women.

Please consider writing for our new publication, *International Midwife*. We would really like to hear from birth practitioners in other countries. Send in your birth stories, news items, information about herbs and customs and more!

Midwifery Today, *International Midwife* and *The Birthkit* are quarterly publications for birth practitioners, childbirth educators, and parents-to-be. We emphasize natural childbirth, breastfeeding, networking and education. Our aim is to foster communication between practitioners and families, and to promote responsible midwifery and childbirth education around the world.

We seek a balance between scientific or technical material and "softer" personal and/or philosophical articles, including birth-related art, poetry and humor. We consider submissions on all aspects of pregnancy and childbirth. The professional and business aspects of midwifery and childbirth education are also of interest to our readers.

We will not consider multiple submissions or previously published articles for publication in *Midwifery Today*, *The Birthkit* or *International Midwife*. We also reserve the right to publish articles in other forms, such as themed booklets, and electronic sources including World Wide Web pages.

Concise material which clearly expresses your knowledge, experience, feelings or findings will receive consideration. If you are submitting an instructive article aimed at midwifery procedure or practice, please be accurate and factual. Identify and credit your sources of information. Proofread your material. We reserve the right to edit for clarity, content, and length.

We prefer articles that are typewritten and double-spaced, although neatly written articles are also accepted. Include your name, address and telephone number, as well as your fax number and e-mail address (if applicable) on the opening page. Your name, article title, and page number should appear on each following page. Please include a biographical sketch of no more than 40 words. If you wish to withhold your name, please indicate this; instruct us whether you prefer an anonymous citing, your initials, or a pseudonym.

Photographs and artwork are welcome. You may submit any style of photograph—of authors, mothers, babies, birth, midwives, educators, and families—either in connection with an article, or to be used at our discretion. Photographs should be black and white; color is acceptable only if the photograph is particularly clear. Captions, model releases (if subject is other than yourself or your immediate family) and identification of subjects are required. Submit several photographs, if possible. Clearly state the name of the photographer for proper photo credit. Never send your original photographs; we generally do not return photos. Artwork should be done in black ink on white paper. Clearly state the name of the artist.

Please Note:

1. All submissions are reviewed by the editors and are considered for the upcoming editorial year.

2. Send a self-addressed stamped envelope with all submissions.

3. We cannot guarantee return of material submitted. Submit high quality copies of your work; retain a copy of your article, photography, or artwork.

4. *Midwifery Today*, *International Midwife* and *The Birthkit* are non-paying markets. Contributors receive two copies, and authors of full-length feature articles receive a complimentary one-year subscription to either *Midwifery Today*, *International Midwife* or *The* Birthkit, depending on placement.

Columns and Features

Full Length Articles: All pregnancy, birth and postpartum subjects, directed toward midwives, childbirth educators or their clients. Technical, objective (or journalistic reporting), or instructive, as well as personal experience. References encouraged where appropriate. Photographs, charts, diagrams, other graphics useful. May reflect the quarterly theme.

Quarterly themes are useful for our editorial plan, but please do not feel constrained by them. In addition to columns on computers, breastfeeding and nutrition, we welcome additional contributions to any of the following columns:

Abstracts: Synopses of full-length scientific articles or manuscripts. Accuracy is essential; restricted to objective review of scientific reports or studies. Give full credit to source, and include name(s) of original author(s), date, title of piece, name of journal/book/magazine it appeared in, page numbers, volume/issue numbers.

Birth Insights: Birth stories told in a way to share insights or information.

Formulary: Mixing and measuring and down-to-earth chemistry. Submit recipes for tinctures, hotpacks, herbal treatments, salves, teas, as well as nutrition-packed recipes for pregnancy and labor. Use accurate measurements where applicable. Explain why a treatment works. A similar column called "Remedies" is published in *The Birthkit* and in *International Midwife.*

Global Midwifery: Living and working around the world. Describe your experience with another country's birth practices, options, birth consciousness, customs, herbal remedies or legal issues. Whether it is your home country or not, we are interested in reaching out to midwives around the world. Photos are encouraged.

Herstory (His and Kids', too): Birth stories that are powerful, poignant, challenging, entertaining and educational, related by mothers or other family members, with the specific intent of helping birth practitioners gain insight. Photos encouraged.

Improving Your Practice: Specific information, systems, and suggestions to help midwives and childbirth educators improve their practices. How have you maintained a good library for clients, or developed charting systems? How do you work with apprentices? Collect money? Charts, forms, or handouts useful.

In My Opinion: A chance for readers to comment on technology, laws, and more. Back your opinions with fact.

It's Only Hearsay: An ongoing column in *The Birthkit* for comical birth stories, interesting news items, anecdotes, remedies and more. Review past issues of *The Birthkit* for style information.

Media Reviews: Each publication features media reviews. Be sure to include the following information: authors/editors, name of book/video/cassette, cost, pages/length, format, publisher/producer name, address, phone. Keep in mind the item should be useful to birth practitioners or parents; explain why it is or isn't helpful and give readers a feel for what the product is like. Topics covered? Clearly covered? References included? Photos or illustrations included?

Meet the Practitioner: An autobiographical or biographical portrait. How and why did you enter the birthing field; your training, practice(s), goals, family, non-birthing interests and insights. Let us get to know you! Photos especially welcomed. (Must be written in article, rather than interview, format.)

Midwife's Journal: Share some of your journal entries with *Birthkit* readers. Your article could be pages from "a day in the life" to several days or a week in the life of a midwife. See past issues of *The Birthkit* for more information about this column.

Midwifery and the Law: News, litigation, information and advice, pending legislation, insurance issues concerning the practice of midwifery. In-depth article treatment or networking contacts for those forced to practice without official sanction of state or country. Submit names and addresses of contact persons, politicians, lobbyists supportive of midwifery.

Networking: The loom where the fabric of communication is woven. Air formal and informal comments and opinions, share news, ask questions, critique articles in past issues, and give technical advice or spiritual support. Two to five paragraphs, or in letter form.

Question of the Quarter: Reader's insights, comments, arguments, instruction in response to a query posed in each issue. Questions are published two issues in advance.

There Oughta Be: An ongoing column in *The Birthkit*. This is your chance to ask questions and wonder why things are or aren't a certain way. Past columns have covered the lack of midwifery listings in career guides for young people, the lack of a defense organization for midwives, and a suggestion for a new designation for due dates.

Tricks of the Trade: Information you won't find in a textbook. Share practical wisdom and helpful hints from your practice.

Categories: Childbirth—Midwifery—Nursing—Women's Issues

Name: Jan Tritten, Editor
Material: All
Address: POB 2672
City/State/ZIP: EUGENE OR 97402
Telephone: 541-344-7438
Fax: 541-344-1422
E-mail: Midwifery@aol.com

Military History

Please refer to Cowles Enthusiast Media, Inc.

Military Images
Photographic History of the U.S.

Soldier and Sailor in the 19th Century

Published since 1979, MI is a unique magazine devoted to the study of the American soldier & sailor of the years 1839-1900, as seen in period photos; at least three-quarters of the articles published deal with the Civil War era. Major subject categories include:

1. Analyses of period photos: unique content, subject, background, etc.

2. Analyses of uniforms, equipment & insignia as seen in photos.

3. Biographies emphasizing the common soldier (enlisted men and junior officers), usually published as short vignettes of one or two pages with photo(s) of the subject at time of service. We prefer subjects in combat units as opposed to hospital stewards, quartermasters, reservists, etc. Generally we do not cover post-war veterans organizations and related photos.

4. Unit histories: company, regimental and brigade level. Combat narratives should emphasize tactics, action, and human interest details. Some relevant photos are a must. Sidebars cover issued weapons, T.O. & E., casualty statistics, etc. *We do not publish* broad brush accounts of generals and campaigns, nor do we cover modern reenactments.

5. Photo-surveys of image collections, usually, but not necessarily, on a theme: cavalry, naval, zouaves, blacks, weapons, humor, etc.

6. Letters & diaries if accompanied by photo(s) of writer in uniform.

7. Technical articles on 19th century photography: techniques, preservation, restoration, acquisition, etc.

PAYMENT is an honorarium, usually $15 to $25 per article, paid upon publication. Most articles are written by photo collectors for photo collectors; unless you are already engrossed in our very narrow realm of interest, you will not find it easy to be published in our pages.

RIGHTS: We buy first North American serial rights only. All revert to author after publication.

REQUIREMENTS: 1,000 to 12,000 words. Most of our articles are written by collectors and buffs, not professional authors. We maintain the right to edit and rewrite substantially. If you have an IBM-compatible PC, we prefer your manuscript on disk, with paper copy; most word processing programs (or ASCII format) are acceptable, as are files sent via e-mail.

PHOTOS: Clear black-and-white prints (or the originals) are required for publication, but good photocopies will suffice with initial submission. We cannot use color prints or slides. If ferrotypes or ambrotypes are in brass mats, please include the entire mat in your copy. Do not crop ovals.

Queries Preferred.

Categories: Civil War—History—Military—Photography

Name: Submissions Editor
Material: All
Address: RR 1 BOX 99-A
City/State/ZIP: HENRYVILLE PA 18332
E-mail: milimage@csrlink.net

Millennium Science Fiction & Fantasy

We are always on the lookout for new material. Below you will find some areas that we are currently taking submissions for or, in which we are compiling new information for future endeavors.

MILLENNIUM SCIENCE FICTION & FANTASY MAGAZINE

Short SF & F stories approximately 2,500 words with twist endings.

Payment: $10.00 Plus one complimentary hard copy.

Christian SF & F short stories. Read C. S. Lewis.

Payment: $10.00 Plus one complimentary hard copy.

CONTINUING SAGAS

The best way for new writers to break into our magazine is by being an active contributor to one or more of our sagas.

Payment: One free "Full E-mail" subscription for the month that your section appears.

MOVIE/BOOK Review

Tell us in 500 words or less, a book or movie that you love/hate.

Payment: One free "Full E-mail" subscription for the month that your section appears.

MIRACLES

Non fiction pieces, 500 words on an inspirational miracle that has happened to you. Payment: $5.00

WRITER'S FIRSTS

Short nonfiction articles, 500 words on how you made your first sale. Payment: $5.00

101 COVER LETTERS

Feedback on how it helped and/or how we can make it better. Payment: N/A

Categories: Science Fiction

Name: L.D. Van Valkenburg, Executive Editor
Material: Fiction
Name: Dietmar Trommeshauser
Material: Movie/Book Reviews
Address: 3507 TULLY RD STE E2-130
City/State/ZIP: MODESTO CA 95356
E-mail: Millennium@gnp1.com
Internet: www.gnp1.com (Free sample)

Remember: Editors change jobs and publishers change addresses. It is wise to invest in a phone call for the current information before submitting.

Milwaukee MAGAZINE

Milwaukee Magazine

Dear Writer:

Thank you for your interest in *Milwaukee Magazine*. Here are some guidelines that will help you in submitting material:

WHO WE ARE

1. *Milwaukee Magazine* is a monthly magazine covering the people, issues and places of Milwaukee and southeastern Wisconsin. Total circulation is approximately 42,000.

2. Get to know our publication by reading it. Sample copies may be bought on newsstands throughout the area ($3) or requested by mail ($5). One-year subscriptions are $18.

WHAT WE WANT

1. We are interested in timely stories about current issues, local personalities, area business, sports, healthcare, Wisconsin travel, education, politics, arts and culture, architecture and urban life, history; food, shopping, music and nightlife, recreation and the environment.

We are particularly looking for writers who can deliver brightly written, well-researched service articles, but are also interested in investigative stories from qualified reporters. Full-length feature stories run 2,500-7,000 words; if your query leads to an assignment, we'll specify what length we're looking for. We pay $400-$1,000.

2. We are also in the market for two-page "breaker" stories, which are often short on copy (less than 1,800 words) and long on visuals. For example, we've run shorts on eavesdropping, tourist traps and apartment living. As with other features, query first. Payment is $150-$400.

3. Stories for our front-of-book Insider section range from exposés to amusing slices of local life to interesting people profiles. We're looking for stories you won't find in other local publications and unconventional angles on the current scene. Freelance writers often begin their association with *Milwaukee Magazine* here. These stories usually run no more than 500 words and pay $25-$150. Query Stephen Filmanowicz, senior editor. Mini-reviews for our City Slants page are assigned by Bruce Murphy, senior editor. Mini-reviews run no longer than 125 words and pay $35.

We also look for story ideas for our monthly arts and entertainment insert, *M Magazine*. Profiles on local bands, visual and performing artists, musicians, etc., as well as city architecture, are topics that have been covered.

WHAT WE DON'T WANT

1. As you'll see by studying the magazine, we focus very closely on Milwaukee and the surrounding area. *Milwaukee Magazine* is simply not in the market for articles that are not about the people, places and issues of our region. Nor are we much interested in stories about former Milwaukeeans or national subjects that touch our region only tangentially.

2. Many of our columns are written by regular contributors, but occasionally we publish freelance submissions.

HOW TO PITCH US

1. Your best bet is to query with samples of your previously published work. Tell us why your idea is right for our magazine and why you're the right one to write it.

2. Include a self-addressed, stamped envelope for our reply. Please allow four to six weeks for a response.

THE DETAILS

1. Completed manuscripts should be accompanied by a computer disk, either Macintosh (Microsoft Word preferred) or PC.

M-R

2. For all stories, *Milwaukee Magazine* buys first rights and pays on publication, unless otherwise indicated. Pre-approved out-of-pocket expenses will be reimbursed with proper documentation.

OTHER CONSIDERATIONS

1. When contacting sources, you may state that "I'm writing an article for *Milwaukee Magazine*" if the article has been specifically assigned, in writing, by the editor of *Milwaukee Magazine*. You may not represent yourself as anything other than an independent contractor on assignment for *Milwaukee Magazine*.

2. If you or a close relative or friend are related in any way (e.g., board memberships, employment, volunteer work) to a story you wish to work on, this relationship must be disclosed to the editor prior to accepting the assignment.

3. Under no circumstances are writers allowed to accept gifts, gratuities, free tickets or other special privileges in connection with an assignment for *Milwaukee Magazine*.

We are actively seeking freelance writers who can deliver lively well-researched stories that help our readers make the most out of the Milwaukee area. We respect writers who can deliver copy on deadline that fits the specifications of our assignment. If you fit this description, we'd love to work with you.

Thanks for your interest in *Milwaukee Magazine*.

Sincerely,

John Fennell

Editor

Categories: General Interest

Name: John Fennell, Editor
Material: All
Address: 312 E BUFFALO
City/State/ZIP: MILWAUKEE WI 53202
Telephone: 414-273-1101
Fax: 414-273-0016
E-mail: milmag@qgraph.com

Mind Fire

Here are our submission guidelines to *Mind Fire*. We are pretty much open to all styles of *poetry*. As we said, we are here to set the imagination ablaze...Can you?

• You may submit up to three poems (any style, any length, within reason), for consideration in upcoming issues of *Mind Fire*. No more than three submissions per two-week period unless otherwise specified, please. If we take an extraordinary time in answering you, do not hesitate to write. You must have an e-mail account to send submissions and receive correspondence.

• Notification of acceptance or non-acceptance will occur via e-mail. If you ask for comments, by either myself or Thomas you will most likely get them: otherwise, you may or may not. This publication is here to let others view your work, we are not here to discourage you or hinder your creative juices. If you have any more questions, please let us know. We will try and respond as soon as humanly possible.

• Obviously, the author grants *Mind Fire* the rights to print any and all work submitted in *Mind Fire*. Writers retain copyrights of material submitted. We will be offering back issues in the future.

• In submitting any work to *Mind Fire*, you are attesting the work is entirely yours, your original creation. Simultaneous submissions and previously published material okay, if so specified. Please provide past or current relevant data with submission.

• There is currently no monetary compensation for work published in *Mind Fire*. (Frankly, we are starving artists, ourselves.)

Thank you very much,

Gina & Thomas

Editors

Include this with your submission: Please read carefully!

• **Please** put "Submission" in the subject heading. Or there might be a chance it might not be read right away.

• **Include your full name or alias,** or how you want it to appear in *Mind Fire*.

• **Author's Bios:** Any other pertinent information on you, your writing and or web site. To be used in our "Author's Bio's" section. 50 words or less, please. ex: name, age, e-mail address, inspiration, web address, description.

• **Inspiration**: What is your inspiration for writing. Limit it to one sentence or so. You will only be asked once for this, failure to include this in your submission will result in it not being added as part of your bio in the "Author's Bio" section.

• **Complete e-mail address.** (Any false e-mail accounts will be rejected.)

• **Do not attach any files** to your submissions. Attached files will not be read.

• **Deadline** for all submissions is the 10th of every month. We so to print on the 13th. Submissions without the above information will be rejected.

Categories: Poetry

Name: Thomas Fortenberry, Co-editor
Name: Gina Denlinger, Co-editor
Material: Poetry
Address: PO BOX 28335
City/State/ZIP: BALTIMORE MD 21234
E-mail: Kurvanas@aol.com
Internet: http://members.aol.com/cireanig2

Miniature Quilts

Please refer to Chitra Publications.

---

the minnesota review

the minnesota review
University of Missouri, Columbia

Regarding your query concerning submission guidelines for *the minnesota review*, please note the following:

We have a long tradition of publishing politically engaged work, whether it be marxist, socialist, feminist, etc. Our aim now is to publish the work of committed younger writers.

Many of our future issues will be organized around a special topic. Our next four issues target "The Institution of Literature," which specifically include fields and theories, literature and culture, institutional structures, and the politics of publishing, respectively. After the "Institution" series, we are planning an issue which explores the concept of "whiteness."

We will continue to publish poetry and fiction on a variety of topics that do not necessarily adhere to our special topics. In each issue our editor's aim is to present vanguard writing that is stylistically and conceptually daring.

A journal of committed writing, we have a long tradition of publishing marxist and politically engaged work (from a range of people, including Fredric Jameson, Pierre Macherey, Mark Poster, Gayatri Spivak, Jean Franco, John Berger, and others). Our aim now is to publish the work of engaged younger critics and writers, such as Bruce Robbins, Michael Berube, and Barbara Foley in criticism; Jim Daniels, Kathleen Spivak, and Martin Espada in poetry; and Joan Frank, Harold Jaffe, and Lynda Schor in fiction. Many of our future issues will be organized around a special topic, such as our Spring 1997 issue on "Whiteness" and our Spring 1998 issue on "Academostars." In each issue, our aim is to present writing that dares to encroach bounds, whether they be stylistic or conceptual. Theory's a good word here.

As for technical matters, we ask that articles, essays, reviews, and manuscripts be submitted in duplicate. Upon acceptance, a computer disk (preferably 3.5" Mac OS formatted) will be requested. Essays and reviews should adhere to the form specified in the *MLA Handbook*. Clear photocopies are okay. Simultaneous submissions are welcome.

Thank you for your interest in our journal.

Best of luck with your pursuits.

Sincerely,

Jessica Gutliph

Editorial Assistant

Categories: Fiction—Nonfiction—Criticism—Culture—Feminism—Film/Video—Gay/Lesbian—Literature—Multicultural—Philosophy—Poetry—Politics—Public Policy—Short Stories

Name: Jeffrey Williams, Editor
Material: All
Address: UNIVERSITY OF MISSOURI, COLUMBIA
Address: 107 TATE HALL
City/State/ZIP: COLUMBIA, MO 65211
Telephone: 573-882-6421

The Mississippi Rag

The Mississippi Rag
The Voice of Traditional Jazz and Ragtime

The RAG staff consists of only one full-time person (the editor/publisher) and three part-timers (responsible for handling circulation, listings, and billing). All writers and photographers are freelancers, most located outside of the Minneapolis area. If you need a fast response, don't wait for a letter-call. There is simply too heavy a workload for the editor to guarantee a quick answer by mail, especially the third week of the month when the RAG is in the production phase.

The RAG has been in existence for more than 23 years, so we have covered a tremendous range of topics and personalities. We try very hard not to repeat subjects, so editor should be consulted before a writer launches into a feature. Even if we haven't run a feature on a particular artist, one of our regular writers may be working on just such a story and he/she would have first claim on RAG space.

Most of our readers are career musicians, Jazz writers, researchers, or knowledgeable jazz and ragtime enthusiasts. Don't write an article for the RAG if you aren't well acquainted with the traditional (classic) Jazz world.

Almost all record reviews are assigned, so don't send reviews on speculation. We don't use articles on modern jazz, poetry, fillers, cartoons, or jokes.

Features may run from 2,500 words to 6,500 words, depending upon the topic and amount of artwork available to run with the story. Editor must be consulted regarding length.

A few basic rules: In the body copy, song titles are in quotes, book, movie and album titles are italicized (if you have that capability on your word processor). We don't run footnotes; incorporate them into the story. Use -30- at the end of story. If you can save to a disk in ASCII, send the disk and a hard copy. We'll return the disk. If you can't send a disk, send clean copy, using a good printer ribbon so the story can be scanned.

No simultaneous submissions accepted. We also do not run material that has been previously published in another publication. We buy all rights unless other arrangements have been made prior to publication. Payment is on publication, with checks being sent by the end of the publication month. The rate is 2 cents per word, $5 per photo for photos we can keep (black and white glossies preferred).

Thank you for your interest in THE MISSISSIPPI RAG. We have a tried and true staff of freelancers who've been with us for many years, but we are always willing to consider work from a new (to us) writer.

(Ms.) Leslie Johnson, Editor/Publisher

Categories: Music

Name: Leslie Johnson, Editor/Publisher
Material: All
Address: 1401 W 76TH ST STE 250
City/State/ZIP: MINNEAPOLIS MN 55423
Telephone: 612-861-2446
Fax: 612-861-4621
E-mail: lesliemrag@aol.com

Mississippi Review
University of Southern Mississippi

Mississippi Review is a national literary magazine founded in 1970 and published, in its print version, twice yearly by the Center for Writers at The University of Southern Mississippi. The *Mississippi Review* online is a Web-specific version of the magazine, a separate publication, which is an outlet for online fiction, poetry, essays, graphics, sound, video, and similar. It is published monthly except August by the Center for Writers.

Submissions are invited. Works should be sent via e-mail in ASCII with double-spaced paragraphs, or as attachments in WordPerfect or Word for Windows format. Other formats are discouraged. There are no limitations on length or content, though we suggest you get acquainted with the magazine before you submit your work.

For information about subscriptions or back issues of *Mississippi Review* please write or e-mail Rie Fortenberry. Other online correspondence may be addressed to the editor.

Categories: Fiction—Essays—Poetry—Regional

Name: Frederick Barthelme, Editor
Material: Fiction
Name: Angela Ball, Poetry Editor
Material: Poetry
Address: USM BOX 5144
City/State/ZIP: HATTIESBURG MS 39406-5144
Telephone: 601-266-4321
Fax: 601-266-5757
E-mail: fb@netdoor.com

Model Railroader

Thanks for your interest in contributing to MODEL RAILROADER. Before you prepare and submit any article, you should write us a short letter of inquiry describing what you want to do. We can then tell you if it fits our needs and save you from working on something we won't want.

We publish articles on all aspects of model railroading and on prototype (real) railroading as a subject for modeling. Here's a general list of our requirements:

TEXT: Present your subject simply and directly in plain English. Keep it brief-most of our articles are one-third text and two-thirds illustrations-and type it as described on the "Typing manuscripts" sheet below. If you use a word processor, it's okay to print your text on a dot-matrix printer that prints no more than 10 characters per inch. You're welcome to send text files on diskette in Microsoft Word or ASCII format without carriage returns, but please do not omit the printed "hard copy."

PHOTOGRAPHS: For color we need original 35mm slides or larger transparencies; or glossy color prints 5"x7" or larger. Step-by-step photos should be in color if color will enhance the article's value. Examples would be scenery or car-painting techniques. Otherwise black and white photos are preferable. For black-and-white photos we want glossy prints 5"x7" or larger. Usually it's best to send the negatives too, but never send just negatives. Be sure to include a caption for every photo.

Photography makes or breaks most of the articles we see, so here are six pointers on color photography:

1. Load your 35mm (or larger format) camera with slow-speed indoor color film such as Fujichrome 64T (RTP) or Kodak Ektachrome 64T (EPY).

2. Use at least three photo floods matched to your color film. Floodlights rated for 3200K match the Fuji RTP and Kodak EPY films.

3. Stop your camera down as far as it goes; f22 is good for a 35mm camera, f32 is best. Mount your camera on a tripod so you can make long exposures.

4. Position your lights for even lighting with no harsh shadows. Always light the background first, then the foreground.

5. Bracket your exposures by time, and make lots of bracket exposures over a wide range. You're bound to get a couple of good exposures.

6. Select what you think is the best exposure for each shot, along with one lighter and one darker for insurance. The best exposure for magazine reproduction is the "perfect" exposure.

DRAWINGS: Clean, neat pencil drawings are fine for how-to illustrations, electrical schematics, track plans, and maps-these will be redrawn by our art staff for publication. Track plans must be to scale. If you are a draftsman and want to contribute prototype drawings, write for information on our style and standards.

Send everything for one article at one time, if possible all in one package, and with your name and address on every item. Address your package to "TO THE EDITOR, MODEL RAILROADER MAGAZINE," and mark it "MANUSCRIPT ENCLOSED." We'll send you a card acknowledging receipt of your article, and try to review it within 60 to 90 days. We'll return articles that we can't use if you include return postage.

If we can use your article, we'll pay you for it upon acceptance. Our standard rate is $30 per column, or $90 per page, including drawings and photos. Our standard acceptance agreement specifies that we are buying all rights to the article.

The soonest an article can appear in MODEL RAILROADER is usually four months after acceptance, and we try to use most articles within a year. Our initial payment will be based on a space and color estimate, and we'll make an additional payment upon publication if the article exceeds our estimate. We'll return photos and other material that we don't publish, but we usually keep everything that is used in MODEL RAILROADER.

Thanks for your interest in MODEL RAILROADER.

How-to checklist

The how-to article you send to MODEL RAILROADER should include the following items:

1. TEXT: Tell how you did the project, or tell the reader how to do it, in simple, clear, and direct language. Keep it as brief as possible-most MODEL RAILROADER stories are no longer than six magazine pages. (See "Typing Manuscripts for MODEL RAILROADER" below for tips on estimating length.) Use photos and drawings extensively, and put details, dimensions, and part numbers in the illustrations. Use active description or in-

struction, such as "I painted the roof black" or "Paint the roof black," and avoid the passive, "The roof was painted black."

2. LEAD PHOTOGRAPH: Show the model or project at its best, to get the reader's attention and encourage him to read and follow the article. The lead photo should be in color. Usually it's best to show the subject of the article in a finished model scene, with the photo composed so the article subject is the dominant element. Alternately, show the subject against a plain, untextured backdrop of a neutral color-seamless photo backdrop paper is ideal.

3. HOW-TO ILLUSTRATIONS: Use drawings and photos to show the project under construction. Number each as a figure, i.e., fig. 3, and refer to them by the corresponding number in the text. Neat, legible pencil drawings are adequate, as our art staff will prepare finished ink drawings for publication. Drawings need not be to scale unless scale is important, as with exact-size templates, for example. How-to photos should be black-and-white unless color is required or helpful, and generally they should be taken against plain backgrounds. You may include callouts-labels with pointers-in a black-and-white photo: make a photocopy of the print and write and draw on the copy.

4. BILL OF MATERIALS: Give a detailed list of items needed to build the project. Include manufacturers' names, part numbers, part names or descriptions, and quantities required. Be sure your information is current. Explain if the reader will have to substitute for items which are no longer available. If you doubt that the reader will know where to find some item, include the manufacturer's address.

5. PROTOTYPE INFORMATION (where applicable): Use photos and/or drawings to show the reader the prototype you followed. Photos may be color, black-and-white, or both. If you have drafting skills and would like to prepare prototype drawings, write for information about our requirements.

Typing Manuscripts for *Model Railroader*

Set your margins for a column 37 characters wide. Don't split words at the end of a line; stop short or run over. Type double-spaced, 23 lines per page, to help estimate how much you've written.

Indent three character spaces at the start of each paragraph. Identify each page as follows:

Short title—your name—page number.

Identify illustrations mentioned in text by figure number, i.e., fig. 2. Lump photos and drawings together and number consecutively.

MR uses columns 71 lines long, 3 to a page. To estimate length, figure that 9 typed pages of 23 lines each = 1 typeset page.

Another rough estimation for how-to articles is that one third of the article will be text and the rest illustration. Twelve typed pages make a four-page article.

Basic Model Railroad Photography

Jeff Wilson, Associate Editor, MODEL RAILROADER Magazine

Camera: The best general-purpose camera for model photography is the 35mm SLR (single lens reflex). The 35mm film has a large enough image area that photos can be enlarged without losing sharpness or showing grain, and the SLR feature allows you to see in the viewfinder the exact image that your camera is shooting. Most fixed-focus non-SLR 35mm cameras (point-and-shoot snapshot-type cameras) aren't suitable, as the optics don't provide a sharp enough image and the aperture is generally not adjustable.

Cameras that use film sizes smaller than 35mm aren't suitable, as the resulting images are too small to be enlarged without showing film grain. Larger format cameras provide excellent images, but the equipment is very expensive and can be bulky and difficult to use.

To get started in photography, consider buying a used camera body and lens. Many photography stores sell used equipment with limited warranties (which generally allow a few weeks for testing). Used cameras and lenses are much less expensive than new, and by sticking with name brands (Canon, Minolta, Nikon, Pentax) you'll generally get quality equipment. Avoid unfamiliar brand names, as the quality of optics is often poor.

Aperture and shutter speed: Cameras should be capable of full manual or aperture-priority automatic control. To achieve maximum depth of field (depth of focus) the aperture should be set to the smallest opening possible (f22 or f32). The shutter speed should then be adjusted to set the proper exposure.

Lenses: 50mm, 55mm, and 60mm Macro lenses are excellent for most model photography. The Macro feature allows focusing very close to the subject, and most Macro lenses stop down to f32, which provides good depth of field. Macro lenses are also much more expensive than standard lenses. Standard (non-Macro) 50 to 60mm lenses work well, but generally focus a minimum of 24 to 30 inches from the subject, making them difficult to use for close-up shots. Wide-angle lenses (especially Macros) are handy, especially when working in tight quarters. Telephoto lenses have limited use in model photography, but can be used to create some nice special effects.

Close-up filters are available in +1, +2, and +4 powers. These screw on the front of the lens and enable the camera to get very close to the subject, but they also reduce the depth of field.

Pinhole lenses are standard lenses that have been modified with a very small opening (usually around f90). The major benefit of these is that the depth of field extends from just beyond the lens face to infinity. The disadvantage is that the image will be soft in focus overall compared to a standard lens. All pinholes are not created equal: The quality and sharpness of the image depends on the quality of the lens optics and the skill of the person who modified the lens. In general, pinhole lenses are good for photos where a foreground object is a few inches away from the lens—otherwise, a Macro is usually the best choice.

Film: Slide film is preferred for photos intended for publication for two reasons: 1.) The fine grain of ISO 64 film yields a sharp image, and the film grain won't be visible when the image is enlarged; and 2.) slides are first-generation images (the final image is the film that was in the camera), so images will be sharper and colors more accurate than prints. Color prints are second-generation images—the prints are made from the film. Each generation softens the image and introduces potential color shifts. Slides are also very versatile—good-quality prints can be made from them.

For model photography using photo floodlights, use Fujichrome 64T (RTP} Tungsten film if possible; substitute Ektachrome 64T (EPY) Tungsten if necessary. Don't use Ektachrome 160T—the film grain is coarse and becomes quite noticeable when the image is enlarged. For photography outdoors or with strobe (flash) lighting, use Kodachrome 64 Daylight or other low-speed daylight film. Avoid using any film with an ISO greater than 100.

Lighting: It's critical to match the type of lighting to the film being used. Floodlights rated at 3200°K match tungsten films. Strobe units are rated at 5500°K to match daylight films. Failing to match the lighting results in poor color rendition: Using daylight film with floodlights or other incandescent lighting results in a reddish/yellowish cast on photos, using tungsten film outdoors or with a flash will result in a bluish cast on the photos, and fluorescent lighting will leave a green cast in photos.

It's best to avoid shooting under fluorescent light. Various types of tubes render colors differently. If you must shoot with fluorescents, daylight film with a 30M (magenta) filter will generally provide the best results.

Scenes should be lighted evenly. This usually takes at least two light sources: a key (or main) light, and a fill light to soften shadows. It's generally wise to soften the fill light with a bounce umbrella or diffusion screen (which helps avoid multiple shadows). On large scenes a third light is often necessary to light the background.

Camera-mounted flashes don't work well for models. The resulting image usually has a hot (overexposed) area at the center, as well as harsh shadows and dark background. Since a low f-stop is also required, depth of field becomes a problem. If you must use a flash, take it off of the camera. Mount the camera on a tripod, keep the shutter open, and fire the hand-held flash from the same angles you'd use for floodlights. Multiple flashes are usually required (because the f-stop should be set at its smallest opening), which means this technique takes a lot of experimentation. Using a hand-held camera meter can remove some of the guesswork.

Be sure details in shadow areas can be seen. If necessary, use a white card to bounce light into dark areas such as locomotive running gear. Weathering models also helps (you can use gray powdered chalk as a temporary fix).

Composition: Here are a few tips to keep in mind when taking photos:

• **Quality of modeling.** Remember that the camera sees everything. Crooked decals, sloppy painting, buildings not "planted," unpainted rail, glossy plastic surfaces, figures with plastic bases, and other faults will be amplified - especially in close-up views. The better the modeling is, the better the photo will be.

• **Have a focal point.** Keep the camera focused on what's important. Have a locomotive, structure, figures, or specific scene as the key of the photo.

• **Tell a story with the photo.** This ties with the focal point: Use figures and other details to show life and action.

• **Limit distracting elements.** Keep items such as telegraph poles and signs in the background. For example, if you're taking a photo of a locomotive, be sure you can see the *whole* locomotive—keep telegraph poles, trees, and other objects out of its way.

• **Use realistic photo angles.** Overall shots taken from high angles can be good for recording scenes, but the most dramatic views are those taken from low angles—what your scale people would see from their vantage point.

• **Be sure models are clean.** Bright photo lights will highlight dust, fuzz, stray ground foam, and other distracting items. Use a soft brush to dust off locomotives, cars, buildings, and streets. Clean and polish water surfaces—few things look more unrealistic than dusty water.

• **Add as much detail as possible.** Avoid barren areas, such as storefronts with no signs or window detail. Add figures and detail items whenever possible. Locomotives with bare number boards and unpainted or missing handrails are distracting, especially if they're featured prominently.

Try, try again: Don't give up if your first photography efforts aren't what you hoped for. As with any activity, photography takes some practice. Take a critical look at your efforts and work to improve both your photography and your modeling—many veteran modelers credit the camera with helping to improve their modeling.

Categories: Hobbies

Name: Submissions Editor
Material: All
Address: PO BOX 1612
City/State/ZIP: WAUKESHA WI 53187-1612
Telephone: 414-796-8776
Fax: 414-796-0126
E-mail: mrmag@mrmag.com
Internet: www.mrmag.com

Modern Bride

1. We are a consumer bridal publication. All articles must be of direct interest to the engaged or newly married couple.

2. Send query letter with a brief outline of areas to be covered or complete manuscript. Enclose a stamped self-addressed envelope for response or return of material.

3. If you are a published author, send two clips with your query.

4. Queries usually are answered within four weeks of receipt.

5. Article lengths range from short features, 500 to 800 words, to main features, 1,500 to 2,000 words.

6. Prefer typed, double-spaced manuscript or computer letter-quality print-out. Dot-matrix and multiple submissions not acceptable.

7. Assignments may be made on speculation or with a 25 percent kill fee provision depending on circumstances.

8. Purchase first periodical publishing rights. Payment on acceptance.

Categories: Nonfiction—Book Reviews—Consumer—Crafts—Family—Fashion—General Interest—Health—Hobbies—Marriage—Money/Finance—Physical Fitness—Psychology—Relationships—Self-Help—Travel—Home—Beauty—How-to—Personal Experience

Name: Mary Ann Cavlin, Executive Editor
Material: All
Address: 249 W. 17TH ST.
City/State/ZIP: NEW YORK, NY 10011
Telephone: 212-337-7096
Fax: 212-367-8342
Internet: www.modernbride.com

Moderna®
The Latina Magazine

MODERNA magazine is a fashion, health and beauty, bilingual, quarterly publication with a circulation of 150,000 and a readership of 500,000. Our scope is national, and our typical reader is an 18- to 44-year-old college educated Latina with an average household income of $35,000. Most of our readers are second and third generation Latinas who were born in the U.S. and speak English as their primary language.

We publish newsworthy, fashion related articles, profiles of Latina personalities, and entertaining stories about health and fitness, relationships, parenting, food and recipes, travel, film and book reviews, and any other aspect of U.S. society that affects Latinas. We do not run articles on people, places, or businesses simply because they are Hispanic. We publish poetry and fiction from well-known authors or excerpts from books as space allows. We do not publish late-breaking news, since we work on an issue two months before it hits the newsstand (for example; stories for December are assigned in September). MODERNA is a bilingual magazine with 1/3 of its articles published in Spanish. There are English translations of all Spanish articles published in the back section of MODERNA.

Story Types and Rates

Features range from 2 to 4 magazine pages (1,200 to 3,000 words) in length. Each month we include a feature covering: fashion, beauty, health, money management and special features on relationships; The average payment for features is $200 for short articles, $300 for longer stories.

Departments are one-page stories covering the topics of Money, Leisure Travel, Cars, Health, Beauty, Fashion, Food, Personal Narrative and a Man's Perspective. The average payment for departments is $100.

Short pieces are published in the Hotline section, as boxes in ¿Qué pasa? or Moda, Belleza and Salud. The average payment for a short piece is $50.

All story payments will be agreed upon in advance with the assigning editor and will be included on the contract.

Manuscript Submission

Submit all ideas in writing in the form of a query letter or full manuscript.

Queries are preferred, and are acceptable by fax. The author's full name, address, and phone number(s) should appear on the first page of manuscripts. We are not staffed to return manuscripts or photos; so, please do not send us your only copy.

Before you submit a query, read the magazine carefully so as to be aware of the topics we have recently covered and to get a clear idea of our target audience. We prefer a tone that does not over-explain the Hispanic perspective (such as not explaining Hispanic symbolism or translating Spanish words to English). The tone should be inclusive: the point of view should be "we" rather than "they."

Acceptance

We will contact you if we want you to develop your query into a story for MODERNA. If we decide to use your submitted manuscript, we will contact you and issue a contract, which we will send to you for your signature. The contract specifies the rights, resale, length, due date, and payment amount for the story. Please send the accepted story on diskette if possible (in either Macintosh Microsoft Word or PC text only/ASCII format).

All facts in the article (whether from an interview with a person or a written source) will be checked by our staff. Therefore, if we accept your story, you must provide phone numbers for all people and organizations mentioned and all people used for background information. Also, provide a photocopy of every document from which you got information or data. If available include photos or photo sources.

Deadlines

If the story is not in our office by the deadline specified in the contract, the piece may be canceled or moved to a later issue.

Payment

Payment is upon publication, unless otherwise specified. Reimbursement for expenses is made on a case-by-case basis and must be discussed before work commences on the story. Additional expenses incurred by the author but not discussed with the assigning editor will not be reimbursed.

A kill fee will be paid only if the accepted article is not published within six months of the issue date specified by assigning editor and if it cannot be rescheduled for a future issue. In that event, we will compensate the writer 25 percent of the total amount specified on the contract.

Rights

MODERNA buys all rights to articles, unless otherwise specified.

Categories: Consumer—Fashion—Health—Hispanic—Lifestyles—Women's issues

Name: Christine Granados, Editor
Material: All
Address: 98 SAN JACINTO BLVD STE 1150
City/State/ZIP: AUSTIN TX 78701
Telephone: 512-476-5599
Fax: 512-320-1943
E-mail: moderna@hisp.com

Modern Drummer

Modern Drummer is dedicated to helping drummers in all areas of music, and at every level of ability. It is important to understand that MD is not a "fan magazine" for people who like drummers; it is a professional magazine for drummers themselves. In fact, many of our columns are written by top professional drummers and drum teachers.

While it is not crucial that all of our writers actually be drummers, it *is* necessary that they know enough about drums and drumming to be able to write about such topics as technique, equipment, style, and musical philosophies. A certain amount of biographical information is good, as long as it serves to provide background or put things in perspective. But remember: There are any number of magazines providing biographical and life-style information; MD is read by people who want information about drumming, so do not get too far away from our main focus.

Additionally, MD is looking for music journalists rather than music critics. Our aim is to provide information, not to make value judgements. Therefore, keep all articles as objective as possible. We are interested in how and why a drummer plays a certain way; the readers can make their own decisions about whether or not they like it.

Before you attempt to write an article for *Modern Drummer*, make sure you are very familiar with the magazine. You should have read at least three recent issues to acquaint yourself with our general style and tone. (Sample copies are available upon request at $3.50 apiece.)

In addition, when considering an article, you might ask yourself the following questions: Will this article help a substantial group of drummers improve their abilities? Will it enlighten them on a particular phase of drumming? Will it save the reader time, money, or effort? Is the topic interesting enough to attract a large number of readers? Will the article help the reader arrive at a decision or draw a conclusion? Will the article help drummers do their jobs better? Not every article will do all of those things, but if the article does not do any of them, then MD will probably not be interested in it.

Please query us on lengthy material before you begin writing. This helps us avoid receiving articles we cannot use, and it will help you avoid having your article returned. Send us a brief outline of the subject matter and your angle on the story. The editors will then be able to guide you in tailoring the material to the exact needs of the magazine. Also, if your idea has already been assigned or covered, we can notify you before you begin working.

If you are writing for MD for the first time, or if your idea is somewhat out of the ordinary, you will be asked to submit your piece on speculation.

The above information should guide you in submitting material to *Modern Drummer*. If you need any further information, please write to us. We are always interested in acquiring good editorial material, and in finding talented, competent writers.

PAYMENT

Modern Drummer pays upon publication. Rates vary depending upon length of the story after editing, whether the article will be used as a feature article or column, and, to some extent, the length of the writer's association with *Modern Drummer*.

General Rates

Feature article: $200-$500. Buys all rights.

Column: $50-$150. Buys all rights.

(Receipt of payment generally occurs

three to six weeks after publication.)

OPEN COLUMNS

Music Columns: Column material can be technical, conceptual, or philosophical in nature. Topics should be very specific, and we encourage the use of musical examples, where appropriate, as well as photos or illustrations. (If using music, request our Music Guidelines.)

Rock Perspectives: Mainstream or commercial rock

Rock 'N' Jazz Clinic: Progressive rock and fusion

Jazz Drummers' Workshop: Mainstream, bebop, or avant-garde jazz

Driver's Seat: Big band

Strictly Technique: Technical studies that could be applied to any area of drumming

Shop Talk: How-to's concerning maintaining, customizing, and restoring drums

Latin Symposium: Latin and reggae rhythms as applied to drumset

Teachers' Forum: Articles dealing with teaching and education

The Jobbing Drummer: Freelance drumming casuals, weddings, etc.

In The studio: All facets of recording

Show Drummers' Seminar: Broadway, Vegas, theater, resorts, circus, ice shows, etc.

Profile Columns: These columns are similar to feature interviews, but shorter in length (2,500-3,000 words).

Portraits: Drummers from all areas of music

Up & Coming: Drummers who have recently come to national attention

From The Past: Historical drummers from all areas of music

EDITORIAL POLICY

Manuscripts are edited to conform with style policies, as well as for consistency and readability. This may involve condensing, rearranging, retitling, and, to some extent, rewording the article. Please refer to the MD Stylesheet for specific style preferences. Final decisions regarding style, grammar, and presentation are the right of the editorial staff of *Modern Drummer*.

Excerpts From the MD Stylesheet

Bylines: Top of first page under title-at left margin-"by" (lowercase) followed by name of author, and underlined. 2. Author's address, phone number, and social security numbers hould also appear on manuscript.

Copy Lengths: Feature material should range from 4,000 to 6,500 words. Column material should range from 500 to 2,500 words.

Punctuation: Album titles, film titles, books, and periodicals should be underlined. Trademarks and model names should also be underlined, e.g., Tama *Titan* hardware, Paiste *Rude* crash cymbal, Remo *Pinstripe* head, Pro-Mark *5A* drumsticks, Ludwig *Black Beauty* snare drum. Dashes should be typed as a double hyphen with a space before and after.

Musical Genres: Capitalize Latin and Dixieland. All other musical genres should be lowercase, e.g., rock, jazz, etc. R&B or rythym & blues; C&W or country & western; rock 'n' roll

Style notes: The first paragraph of an article should be aligned entirely with the left margin. The first line of subsequent paragraphs should be indented five spaces with subsequent lines aligning with the left margin.

Preferred Spellings: Okay; alright; onstage (when used as an adjective); offstage (when used as an adjective); tom-tom; hi-hat; drumsets; drumkit; drumhead; drumsticks; Mic' (microphone, noun; plural mic's, i.e., I use three mikes.); miking; miked; mike (verb, i.e., I miked my drumset.); setup (noun, i.e., The article describes my drum setup.); set up (verb, i.e, I will set up my equipment.); " (inch, i.e., 2"); x (by, i.e., 5 x 4)

Language: Do not use gonna for going to, gotta for got to, or 'cause for because. In general, stay away from contracting verbs by omitting the ending "g," i.e., sayin' or playin'. Language should be kept reasonably "clean." Profanities should be kept to a minimum; obscenities should be avoided.

Categories: Music

Name: Submissions Editor
Material: All

Address: 12 OLD BRIDGE RD
City/State/ZIP: CEDAR GROVE NJ 07009
Telephone: 201-239-4140
Fax: 201-239-7139

Modern Haiku

Modern Haiku is a journal devoted to English-language haiku, book reviews and articles on haiku. Publication is three times a year: February, June and October. It has an international circulation and is widely subscribed to by university, school and public libraries. *Modern Haiku* has been cited by the International Division of the Museum or Haiku Literature in Tokyo as: "The best haiku magazine in North America." Issues have from 90 to 180 pages.

Material submitted to *Modern Haiku* should meet these guidelines:

1. Haiku should by typed or clearly printed. They may all be on one sheet of paper or may be on separate sheets of any size, but each sheet must contain the contributor's name and full address in the upper left corner.

2. A self-addressed, stamped envelope must accompany each submission of material.

3. It is advisable to submit several haiku at a time.

4. All material submitted to *Modern Haiku* must be the original, previously unpublished work of the contributor, and no material must be currently under consideration by any other publication.

Normally, contributors will receive a report on their material in two weeks.

Modern Haiku does not give copies of the magazine to contributors whose work has been accepted, as it pays $1 for each haiku that is accepted and $5 a page for articles and essays.

Since *Modern Haiku* refrains from carrying advertising and depends on subscriptions to meet publication, mailing, payments and all other costs, we would sincerely appreciate your subscription. If you enter a gift subscription a card in your name will be sent at your request to the recipient with the first issue.

A one-year subscription (3 issues) is currently $17.25. Payment should be made in U. S. currency. A single copy is $6.00.

Thank you for your support of *Modern Haiku*,
Robert Spiess, Editor
Categories: Haiku—Poetry

Name: Robert Spiess, Editor
Material: All
Address: PO BOX 1752
City/State/ZIP: MADISON WI 53701-1752
Telephone: 608-233-2738

Modern Maturity

General Editorial

Most *Modern Maturity* features are assigned to writers whose work is known to us and who have an established reputation in journalism. We rarely assign a major feature as the result of an unsolicited query.

The magazine does, however, encourage query letters for specific features and departments. These should be one-page in length and accompanied by recent writing samples. We expect proposers to be familiar with the magazine and its departments.

Modern Maturity discourages the submission of unsolicited manuscripts and assumes no responsibility for their return.

Features and departments cover the following categories:

Finance, investments, legal matters

Health

Food (including recipes; emphasis on healthy eating)

Items of regional interest - 150 to 300 words

Travel (domestic and international)

Consumerism (practical information and advice)

General interest (new thinking, research, information on timely topics, etc.)

Rate of Payment: *Modern Maturity* pays on acceptance at the minimum rate of $1.00 per contracted word. A kill fee of 25% will be paid for assigned articles that are not accepted for publication.

Categories: Nonfiction—Careers—Cooking—Food/Drink—Health—Relationships—Senior Citizens—Society—Travel—Money/Finances—Retirement—Medicine

Name: J. Henry Fenwick, Editor
Material: All
Address: 601 E ST., NW
City/State/ZIP: WASHINGTON, DC 20049
Telephone: 310-496-2277
Fax: 310-496-4124

Modern Romances

Dear Writer:

Thank you for your interest in *Modern Romances* magazine. We would like to see your work. However, we do not issue official guidelines. As an alternative, we suggest that you read several issues of the magazine for an idea of the style of stories we print.

Manuscripts should be typed, and between 2,500 and 12,000 words. Only those stories offering us all rights, and written in the first person will be considered.

Subject matter can be anything from light romance to current social concerns that would be of interest to our readers. Our current rate of pay is 5 cents per word.

Each manuscript we receive will be considered, and a reply will be sent to you between 3-9 months after we receive your work. We do not acknowledge receipt of manuscripts.

We also accept light, romantic poetry, such as love poems, or poems with seasonal/holiday themes. The maximum length should be about 24 lines. Payment is based on merit.

We look forward to reading your story. Best of Luck!!

Categories: Romance

Name: Colleen M. Murphy, Editor-in-Chief
Material: All
Address: 233 PARK AVE S
City/State/ZIP: NEW YORK NY 10003
Telephone: 212-979-4894
Fax: 212-979-7342

Mom Guess What Newspaper

CONTENT: General and Political News, Book, Film, Restaurant, Theater Reviews, Entertainment, Interviews, Art Profiles, Advertising, Sports, Features, and Financial.

AUDIENCE: A newspaper for gay men, lesbians and their straight friends in the State Capitol and the Sacramento Valley area. Founded In 1978. First and oldest gay newspaper in Sacramento.

FORMAT: Deadlines: 10th and 25th. 60%, 40% advertising. Tabloid, 34". Newsprint. Trim size 17"x11¼". Body copy is 9/10 points. 85 line screen photographs. Free and/or 50¢ donation. Published every 2 weeks since 1978. 8,000 copies. $25 subscription. Sample issue $1.00. 32+ pages each issue.

NEEDS: Freelance articles on People, Politics, Trendsetters, Features, Health, Artists, Photography, Artwork. Material is not limited to the gay & lesbian lifestyle. 1,500-2,500 words.

TERMS: MGW is published primarily from volunteers. With some freelancers payment is made. Put requirements in your cover letter. Byline appears with each published article; photos credited. Editors reserve right to edit, crop, touchup, revise, or otherwise alter manuscripts, and photos, but not to change theme or intent of the work. Enclose SASE postcard for acceptance or rejection.

MECHANICAL

REQUIREMENTS: Author's name, address, phone should appear on first page with approximate word count. Photo captions should be typed on a separate page. Black & white glossy preferred. 5"x7" or 8"x10". No negatives or slides. Label all photos.

DISKS: Label each diskette with:
1. Headline/Filename
2. Your name
3. Program and version you used
4. Type of computer: PC-IBM compatible or Macintosh
5. Date you're submitting the disk
6. Your phone number

Send printed copy with disk. We use IBM + Mac, PageMaker, WordPerfect, Word for Windows, and CorelDraw.

CARTOONS: Pen & Ink. High contrast. PMT/stats, velox preferred. Do not send originals.

Categories: Feminism—Gay/Lesbian—Lifestyles—Men's issues—Relationships—Sexuality

Name: Submissions Editor
Material: All
Address: 1725 L ST
City/State/ZIP: SACRAMENTO CA 95814
Telephone: 916-441-6397
Internet: www.mgwnews.com

Money

Does not accept unsolicited submissions.

Montana
The Magazine of Western History

Montana The Magazine of Western History, published quarterly by the Montana Historical Society, welcomes authentic articles on the history of Montana and the American and Canadian west.

Montana is a scholarly journal, which means that articles are submitted to peer review and must show evidence of original research, through footnotes or bibliography, on significant facets of history or provide a new interpretation of historical events that changes the way we view a particular historical topic. A rewriting of standard incidents generally available in other sources will not be accepted.

Manuscript length should run between 3,500 and 6,500 words, or about 14 to 25 double-spaced pages, plus endnotes. Because we are an illustrated journal, photographs of acceptable quality assist in our judgments.

In reviewing articles, if your article is judged appropriate for *Montana,* we will submit it to anonymous review; that is, a blind copy of your manuscript will be sent out-of-house for evaluation, usually to two experts in the field. Upon receiving their comments, we will forward a summary of the readers' reports to you with our determination. The process usually takes six to eight weeks.

The best guide to style for *Montana* is a recent issue of our magazine, but generally we follow the latest revised edition of *The Chicago Manual of Style.*

We prefer receiving two copies of your manuscript for review and end notes instead of footnotes. No computer disk is necessary at first, although we will request to have your manuscript on computer disk if accepted. At that time, endnotes should be made a separate document from the text. We prefer 3.5" disks and use WordPerfect for Mac 3.0, although we can convert most programs.

Categories: Nonfiction—History—Regional—Western History

Name: Charles E. Rankin, Editor
Material: All Western History
Address: 225 N ROBERTS ST
Address: PO BOX 201201
City/State/ZIP: HELENA MT 59620-1201
Telephone: 406-444-4708
Fax: 406-444-2696
Internet: www.his.mt.gov

The Montana Catholic

The Montana Catholic newspaper serves the Roman Catholic community residing in western Montana. Tabloid in format, it is published 16 times per year—usually every three weeks—and is mailed directly to some 9,200 homes for an estimated readership of 21,000. Some parishes and institutions make free copies available on their literature stands. Total printed circulation is 9,400.

Nearly all recipients of *The Montana Catholic* are paid subscribers. All contributors to the Diocesan Offertory Program—the annual appeal of the Catholic Diocese of Helena—receive a one-year subscription to the newspaper as part of their contribution. Individuals who do not contribute to the DOP may subscribe separately. Provision is made for free subscriptions for persons who wish to receive the paper but cannot afford it.

Our predominant editorial focus is to report news and develop feature stories which relate directly to the activities and concerns of the Catholic community in western Montana.

News and Feature Articles

We buy a limited number of news and feature articles from freelance writers. The majority of these are articles which originate with or are assigned to established freelance writers who reside in western Montana. However, several articles each year are purchased from freelance writers outside the area who write more general feature stories relating to seasonal or special supplement topics.

Seasonal topics include Thanksgiving, Advent, Christmas, Lent, and Easter. Supplement topics have been scaled back recently, but two that will remain will be Religious Vocations (January and early Spring) and Respect Life (October).

Submissions are also welcome for an ongoing series on the coming of the Third Millennium.

In general, however, our emphasis is on the local church; therefore, we look primarily for Catholic-oriented material with a tie-in to western Montana.

We buy one-time rights; reprint rights and simultaneous submissions are accepted. We prefer full disclosure of where else submitted or previously printed.

Commentaries

At present, our only regular columns are by local writers. However, we often allow space for occasional commentary by other local, non-local, or syndicated writers. Thoughtful commentaries on issues of current or seasonal concern to the Catholic church are welcome.

Photos/Illustrations

Original photos and illustrations which help highlight news

and feature stories are encouraged. All pertinent subjects appearing in the photo must be identified and, where necessary, permission for use must be granted.

Poetry

Please do not submit poetry. We have published perhaps three poems in the last eight years, only one of which was written by a freelance writer.

Length

News and feature articles can range from 400 to 1,200 words, although most successful writers keep their work in the 600- to 900-word range. We reserve the right to edit all manuscripts accepted for publication.

Payment

For original news and feature articles assigned to local freelance writers, we pay up to $0.10 per word based on the final, edited word count, up to the maximum word count assigned.

For other news, features and commentaries, we generally pay $0.05 per word, based on the final, edited word count.

Rarely, a different fee or rate can be negotiated for first rights on a particularly outstanding piece.

We do not guarantee publication of assigned articles, and publication may be advanced or delayed for space or editorial reasons.

Kill fee on assigned articles is 50%. If writer has been informed that article is "accepted for publication" but the article is later killed, kill fee is 25%. No kill fee will be paid if articles are delivered after deadline or if the author fails to comply with requests for revisions or additional research.

Payment for photos varies from $5 to $20 per photo published.

Style

Please observe the following writing guidelines:

Although there are exceptions, avoid writing in the first person, except perhaps for commentary pieces.

Maintain a positive, uplifting tone—but avoid Pollyannaism.

Avoid "preachiness," including excessive quotation of scripture or other church documents. When scripture citation is appropriate, use the New American Bible or the Revised Standard Version.

Check all facts and quotations. One error will cast suspicion upon the accuracy of the entire manuscript.

Also check spelling and grammar carefully; leaving fundamental writing errors is the fastest way to make an editor lose interest in a writer.

Do not inject subjective language into news pieces; limit its use in feature stories.

We value strong leads, a body of the article which develops and delivers on the lead, and a definitive conclusion.

Manuscript Preparation

Please do not use a dot-matrix printer. For submissions on disk, IBM-compatible format is required, preferably using Microsoft Word or ASCII. Use a standard indent for paragraphs and a one-inch margin on every page.

Title page should include writer's name, address, and telephone number in the upper left corner; word count in the upper right corner; and article title with writer's byline centered in the middle of the page. Subsequent pages should have a running head in the upper right corner with the writer's surname, article title (abbreviated if necessary), and page number.

Underline titles, italicized words or phrases, and foreign words for emphasis.

Handwritten corrections and changes should be few and legible.

Queries and Submissions

For news and feature stories pertinent to the Catholic community in western Montana, query or send completed manuscripts. Writers should familiarize themselves with our style and format prior to submitting a query. Each query should include the primary focus of the proposed article, the main point of discussion, and a list of any authorities who would be consulted in the article. No phone calls except from freelance writers in western Montana who have an established relationship with us.

Categories: Catholic—Montana—Regional—Religion—Rural America

Name: Gerald M. Korson, Editor
Material: All
Address: DIOCESE OF HELENA
Address: PO BOX 1729
City/State/ZIP: HELENA MT 59624
Telephone: 406-442-5820
Fax: 406-442-5191

Montana Magazine

Thank you for your interest in submitting articles to *Montana Magazine*.

Montana Magazine is published bimonthly, in January, March, May, July, September, and November. Please read our publication so you have a good grasp of our style and content. Back issues are available for $5. Subscriptions cost $21 per year.

We assign work, and also consider freelance material. **Please query in writing.** We read every query and try to respond within two months.

Overview

Montana Magazine varies from 100 pages to 132 pages. We are noted for excellent photographs and entertaining, informative writing about Montana.

The magazine contains about five feature articles of 2,000 to 3,500 words, and four to six departments of 800 to 1,500 words. The issues vary from about half four-color and half black & white to four-color throughout.

Focus

Montana Magazine subscribers include lifelong Montanans, first-time visitors, and "wanna-be" Montanans from around the nation and the world. Readership is estimated at 120,000.

We look for articles on recreation, people, natural history, cities, small towns, humor, wildlife, nostalgia, geography, history, places to dine and sleep, byways and infrequently-explored countryside, made-in-Montana products, local businesses, environment, and contemporary issues—in short, anything that will inform and entertain our readers. We avoid commonly-known topics so Montanans won't ho-hum through more of what they already know. If it's time to revisit a topic, we look for a unique slant.

We are strictly a Montana-oriented magazine. Articles of generic Western flavor will not make it. We're ill-disposed toward stories of wild-animal trapping, gory hunting tales, or "me & Joe" adventures. No poetry or fiction, please.

Queries

We prefer written queries over unsolicited manuscripts, but all submissions are reviewed. Telephone queries are heartily discouraged.

If we like your proposal, we may ask to see it on speculation. Acceptance for review does not imply that the article will be published.

Queries should include a thorough outline of the proposed article. Start with the lead, then write a short summary of content, including specifics on whom you plan to interview, research sources, highlights, anecdotal information, and conclusion.

Provide several samples of your writing if we are unfamiliar with your style.

Rates

Montana Magazine's basic rate is approximately 15¢ per published word for features and columns. Higher payment for assignments involving extra expenses may be arranged before publication.

Payment, returnable materials, and a complimentary copy of the magazine are sent to each author within 30 days of publication.

Other Details

Most material is purchased on a one-time-rights basis, which does not require the written exchange of copyright.

We reserve the right to edit and rewrite to comply with our style. Author proofs are not generally provided.

Categories: Regional

Name: Beverly Magley, Editor
Material: Queries
Address: PO BOX 5630
City/State/ZIP: HELENA MT 59604
Telephone: 406-443-2842
Fax: 406-443-5480

Moody Magazine

OUR PURPOSE: Published six times a year, MOODY magazine exists to encourage and equip Christians to live biblically in a secular culture. That process involves articles that focus on our application of God's Word for doctrine, reproof as needed, correction, and instruction in righteousness.

OUR READERS: MOODY readership encompasses more than 250,000 conservative evangelicals each issue (circulation 112,000) focused in the United States and Canada. The average reader is married, a college graduate, and active in his church. Less than 20 percent are pastors. The male-female ratio is 41-59.

OUR CONTENTS: MOODY primarily seeks practical, popular-level articles that show the application of scriptural principles in daily life. Articles must be contemporary and relevant, showing the human condition and biblical principles at work. Other articles report on current events and issues from a scriptural perspective.

WRITING FOR MOODY: Because we assign each issue's package of cover articles—and because we seek to present a variety of topics in each issue—we do not offer an editorial theme list. Instead, we look for freelancers to query us about individual article proposals.

FEATURE ARTICLES cover a broad range of topics, but have one common goal: to foster application—by a broad readership—of specific scriptural principles. While many of our authors use a personal narrative style, we are also open to articles that take an anecdotal reporting approach. Length: 1,200 to 2,200 words.

DO'S AND DON'TS:

• *How-to*: Rather than directive how-to, we prefer articles that show how you (or other believers) have learned to approach a situation scripturally and the difference that has made.

• *Exhortations*: Similarly, we do not seek articles declaring a certain issue is a problem Christians should address. We prefer a journalistic approach that shows examples of believers who are already taking a positive, scripturally based response.

• *Inspirationals*: Our goal for narratives is not simply to describe a dramatic or inspirational event, but to show the process of one seeing the need to apply the truth of God's Word to an aspect of everyday life—and then following through with that application.

• *Profiles*: We prefer not to spotlight individuals or the work of individual ministries. We would, however, consider a journalistic article that reports how several different people or ministries across the country are responding to a particular concern or need.

• *No biographies, historical articles, or studies of Bible figures.*

DEPARTMENTS:

We also invite freelancers to query us for three departments:

1. FIRST PERSON—This is our gospel tract, the only article written specifically for non-Christians.

A personal testimony (we also accept "as told to"), its objective is to tell a person's salvation testimony, primarily through anecdotes, in such a way that the reader will understand the gospel and consider trusting Christ as Savior. Avoid cliches and Christian jargon; they defeat the purpose of communicating to nonbelievers. We prefer no testimonies of entertainers, athletes, public figures, and new Christians (received Christ less than two years ago). Length: 800 to 1,000 words.

Essential points (devote about one-third to each):

1. *Conflict*. What kept this person from Christ?
2. *Conversion*. Must include (with verse references):
a. Christ's death for his sin.
b. Repentance from sin.
c. Faith in Christ alone for salvation.
3. *Change*. How is this person a new creation in Christ? This must relate to the introductory conflict. Show how Christ has resolved or is resolving the conflict.

2. JUST FOR PARENTS—These articles use narrative, first-person anecdotes to illustrate how a couple is taking a specific scripturally based approach to one aspect of their child-rearing that other parents can also relate to and apply. **Length:** 1,500 words.

3. NEWS FOCUS—An in-depth, thoroughly researched journalistic account of a current news event or trend. Query by fax or phone to the News Editor. **Length:** 1,000—1,400 words.

OUR PROCEDURE: MOODY does not accept unsolicited manuscripts—they will be returned unread with a form letter that explains our submission procedure. Writers must first write a query letter and secure permission to forward their manuscripts. Query response is usually in four to six weeks. Do not query by telephone or fax unless urgent subject matter requires an immediate editorial response.

QUERY LETTERS: In your letter, which should be only one page, include:

• a working title
• suggested length
• your article's topic, intended reader application, and scriptural basis
• a representative sample paragraph
• your qualifications to write on this subject
• your writing experience.

Please, no simultaneous or reprint queries.

DEADLINES: MOODY begins editing each issue five months prior to the date of publication and plans each issue several months in advance of that. For seasonal material, query nine months in advance.

POETRY AND FICTION: MOODY does not print poetry. Although we print little fiction, we will consider well-written contemporary stories that are directed, like our nonfiction, toward showing scriptural application. Dialogue, action, and descriptions must be crisp and believable. Avoid cliched salvation accounts, biblical fiction, parables, and allegories. **Length:** 1,200 to 2,200 words.

MANUSCRIPT FORMAT: Include a 3.5" floppy disk in any popular word processing format as well as text-only version.

Include on the first page the approximate article length, your name, address, day phone, and Social Security number. Return the Writer Information Sheet sent in response to your query.

PAYMENT AND RIGHTS: On acceptance, MOODY pays 15 cents a word for sharp, well-edited queried manuscripts. MOODY buys first North American serial rights. Once the work has been published in an issue of MOODY magazine, MOODY retains the non-exclusive right to re-publish that work in electronic form, without further compensation to the author. MOODY may authorize electronic "readers" worldwide to print a copy of the work for personal use; however all requests for commercial reprints shall be referred to the author. All other rights return to the author once the article has been published.

MANUSCRIPT POLICY: We examine all manuscripts on speculation. A positive response to a query does not guarantee purchase.

The author grants MOODY the right to edit and abridge the manuscript and warrants that it has not already appeared in print and that it has not been simultaneously submitted to other publications. Further, the author warrants that nothing in the article infringes the copyright ownership of any person, firm, or corporation, and that he is its sole and true author.

Categories: Evangelical Christianity—Religion

Name: Andrew J. Scheer, Managing Editor
Material: Queries
Address: 820 N LA SALLE BLVD
City/State/ZIP: CHICAGO IL 60610
Telephone: 312-329-2164
Fax: 312-329-2146

MoonRabbit Review
Asian Pacific American Voices

About the Review

MoonRabbit Review is a literary journal of Asian Pacific American voices. The *Review* features short fiction, poetry, reviews, and photography & artwork in a variety of media. The first issue debuted June 1, 1995.

The *MoonRabbit Review* is a nonprofit organization dedicated to creating a literary space for emerging Asian Pacific American writers. We are a biannual journal. To subscribe send a check for $17.00 ($7 for a sample copy) to the address below. We are also available through Small Press Distribution (800) 869-7553, the Asian American Booksellers (212) 228-6718 and Bernard DeBoer (201) 667-9300.

Submission Guidelines

Submissions must be typed. Photocopies, Macintosh or PC disks are also accepted (we prefer digital files on floppy disks if possible). Please include your **name, address, daytime phone number, and a SASE** with your manuscript.

We reserve one-time use of the first North American serial rights and non-exclusive anthology rights.

Artwork & Photos

Artwork must be submitted as B&W prints or PMTs. Photography must be in the form of 25mm slides, negatives, or prints. *Please note*: artists and photographers are encouraged to submit their works on Photo CDs, with low and high resolution scans. Do not send original art or photography. We assume no responsibility for lost or damaged work.

Contact Jack Hadley Design at (303) 516-9382 if you have further questions.

Categories: Asian-American—Ethnic—Literature—Poetry

Name: Jackie Lee, Editor
Material: Fiction/Poetry
Address: 2525 ARAPAHOE AVE STE E4-230
City/State/ZIP: BOULDER CO 80302
Telephone: 303-439-7285
Fax: 303-439-8362
E-mail: jhlee@ucsub.colorado.edu
Internet: www.spot.colorado.edu/~jangd/moonrabbit

MOTHERJONES
Mother Jones

WHO WE ARE

Mother Jones, with a paid circulation of 120,000 is one of the largest progressive publications in the country. The national bimonthly magazine is known for its investigative journalism and exposés, and its coverage of social issues, public affairs and popular culture. Most of the articles we print are written by freelancers.

WHAT WE'RE LOOKING FOR

• Hard-hitting, investigative reports exposing government cover-ups, corporate malfeasance, scientific myopia, institutional fraud or hypocrisy, etc.

• Thoughtful, provocative articles which challenge the conventional wisdom (on the right or the left) concerning issues of national importance.

• Timely, people-oriented stories on issues such as the environment, labor, the media, health care, consumer protection, and cultural trends.

HOW TO QUERY US

Send us a letter proposing your story idea(s). Explain what you plan to cover and how you will proceed with the reporting. The query should convey your approach, tone, and style, and should answer the following: What are your specific qualifications to write on this topic? What "ins" do you have with your sources? Can you provide full documentation so that your story can be fact-checked?

Keep in mind that our lead time is three months and submissions should not be so time-bound that they will appear dated. If we, or another publication, have run a similar story in the last few years, explain how your story will differ.

If you have not contributed to *Mother Jones* before, please send two or three photocopies of previously published articles along with your query. We do not accept unsolicited manuscripts or fiction. Please do not query us by phone or FAX.

Back issues are $6.00 and can be ordered through Reader Services at the address below.

Categories: African-American—Asian-American—Culture—Economics—Environment—Film/Video—General Interest—Government—Interview—Money and Finance—Multicultural—Nonfiction—Politics—Reporting, Investigative

Name: Editor
Material: All
Address: 731 Market Street, Suite 600
City/Stete/ZIP: San Francisco, CA 94103
Telephone: 415-665-6637
Fax: 415-665-6696
E-mail: last name@motherjones.com

The Mother is Me
Alternative Essays on the Motherhood Experience

The Mother is Me: Alternative Essays on the Motherhood Experience is a magazine which seeks to provide a forum for mothers who are currently defining their role in contemporary society. Unlike mainstream parenting publications, our intention is not to prescribe guidelines for childrearing; rather, we intend to explore the conflicting emotions and ideas implicit in the act of mothering. *The Mother is Me* is of a progressive, feminist nature. We accept personal essays, nonfiction articles, poetry, fiction, artwork, and reviews of relevant books. Sample copies of the magazine are available upon request.

We prefer that you submit your work in a typed format, accompanied by a cover letter detailing your name, address, phone number, and a brief biography. You may also submit your piece on computer disk, electronically via e-mail or by conventional mail to the address listed below. We do not specify length although we retain the right to edit your work as necessary. Book reviews should indicate title, author, publisher, number of pages, publisher's address, and book price.

If your work is accepted for publication, we will credit your work as well as send you two copies of the issue in which your article appears and a one year subscription to the magazine. We also pay $10 for accepted essays. Notices regarding women's resources and activities will be considered for publication free of charge. *The Mother is Me* is written by and for mothers, and we welcome your comments and questions. For further information, please visit our Website.

Categories: Family—Feminism—Parenting—Women's Issues

Name: Amy Condra-Peters, Editor
Material: All
Address: 3010 WOODLAWN AVE
City/State/ZIP: FALLS CHURCH VA 22042
Telephone: 800-693-6852
E-mail: TMIM@aol.com
Internet: www.members.aol.com/zoey455/index.html

Mountain Living

1. SUBJECT
Subject will be determined following discussion with editor, who will provide resource materials, contact names and suggestions for research when possible. Editor prefers written queries.

2. LENGTH
Department articles usually run 300-1,500 words. Feature articles run 1,200-2,000 words.

3. DEADLINES
All assignments are due on the morning of the date assigned. If an agreed-upon deadline can't be met, please contact the editor a minimum of two weeks beforehand to renegotiate an appropriate date.

4. SIDEBARS
As discussed with editor. Department articles may require a sidebar with information such as reference-book listing, ingredients, facts and figures, and addresses.

5. PHOTOGRAPHS
For all department articles and some features, we ask that you speak with your sources about obtaining photographs. Slides or transparencies are preferable. When possible, mail the photos with your completed article. Otherwise, include a list of photo resources. We will return all artwork after the issue has been published.

6. RESOURCE LIST
Each home feature must be accompanied by a list of interior designers, architects, landscape planners, contractors, builders, etc., who have contributed to the project, as well as their company names, addresses and phone numbers. Each feature must also be accompanied by a list of design resources, for *all* furnishings, fabrics and materials (available retail or wholesale) used in the project. Only antiques are excluded—custom pieces should be identified as such, with credit to the designer and manufacturer. The interior designer or other professionals who contributed to the project are usually willing to help put together this list.

7. COMPLIMENTARY COPIES
Include a list of photo, research and interview resources, their addresses and phone numbers, so we can send a complimentary copy of the magazine.

8. DELIVERY
Printed submissions should be accompanied by a disk. Speak with the editor about sending articles on-line.

9. PAYMENT
As discussed with the editor and stipulated in the contract. Checks are usually mailed two to three weeks after the material is accepted. A 15 percent kill fee is paid for unacceptable material.

Categories: Antiques—Architecture—Arts—Conservation—Cooking—Culture—Ecology—Entertainment—Environment—Fishing—Gardening—Health—History—Lifestyles—Travel

Name: Submissions Editor
Material: All
Address: 7009 S POTOMAC ST
City/State/ZIP: ENGLEWOOD CO 80112
Telephone: 303-397-7600
Fax: 303-397-7619
E-mail: rgriggs@winc.usa.com
Internet: www.winc.usa.com

Mountain Pilot

Subjects
As our name implies, we are a mountain flying performance magazine. We are interested in mountain and high-altitude flying, aircraft performance at high density altitudes, mountain hazards, mountain winds and weather, personal flying experience,

opportunities, challenges, and special places to visit in the mountains. We want first-hand, credible and knowledgeable accounts of unique or unusual flying experiences, excursions or creative perspectives of flying and ever-popular destinations.

We welcome unsolicited manuscripts, but a brief query with the editor will help determine if your manuscript proposal will fit current editorial requirements.

Queries are appreciated. Keep in mind that *Mountain Pilot* cannot afford to send writers on exotic assignments or reimburse expenses incurred on such trips. We need stories that you have garnered while performing a goal other than writing for our magazine.

Writing and essay styles

Mountain Pilot seeks all kinds of stories—News, features, columns and opinions, and humor. Acceptable essay forms include exposition, description, persuasion, and narration.

Presentation can be designed as chronological, cause-and-effect, comparison/contrast, definition, inverted pyramid, and problem-to-solution.

The manuscript should have a beginning (identifying the topic and what you want to say about it), a middle (containing descriptive details and explanations that support the topic) and an end (supporting the beginning with a logical wrap-up). Information is more credible when it is supported by facts and references. You are solely responsible for fact-checking your own article as our small *Mountain Pilot* staff has neither the time nor the resources to fact-check it for you. Please be sure to check all spellings, proper nouns, resources, companies, addresses and telephone numbers for correctness.

Our pages are not exclusively dedicated to well-published authors or high-time pilots. Experienced authors are a valuable resource, but previous publishing experience is not a requirement. We are interested in writers who can tell a story well—interesting to pilots—containing detail, accuracy and a sense of adventure. Naming airports, recommending people to contact, and offering tips to accommodate pilots are helpful. We encourage adventure through aviation by bringing it to the reader and, when possible, making it feasible for the pilots to duplicate such adventures.

Length

Per assignment by editor; however preferred length for articles is 1,000 to 2,000 words. Shorter vignettes of 100-1,000 words are also considered.

Deadlines

All assignments are due on the morning of the date assigned by the editor. If an agreed-upon deadline cannot be met, please contact the editor a minimum of two weeks prior to deadline to renegotiate an appropriate date. In all cases, however, deadlines should be met unless extremely unusual circumstances prevail.

Art

Visual aids are very important in our selection process. As you research a story, ask each interviewee whether they can provide you with related photos or, if not, where you might locate some. Collect photos and mail them with your completed article. (Please include a list of photo resources, in case photo quality is poor and we must secure alternatives.)

Photo requirements are as follows: 4-color transparencies (4"x5", 2¼" or 35mm formats) or b/w glossy prints. If you are unable to find any, then discuss with the editor about using color prints or slides, maps, charts or illustrations. The maps and illustration do not have to be professionally complete, but must convey the idea so our art department can create an acceptable copy.

Identify each person in photographs from left to right using complete names, titles, and affiliations. Include the date, location and photo credit. A signed release may be required from individuals who are identifiable in pictures.

Identify transparencies by carefully numbering each one on the upper right corner of the mount with the emulsion side up. Be sure your name is also on the transparencies.

Because we receive stories on speculation, duplicate visual aids are recommended. We will call for the originals if we decide to publish.

Packaging of the visual aids should be done by placing them between stiff pieces of cardboard with the cardboard pieces taped together. Always place photographs back-to-back, never together face-to-face. Transparencies should be placed in plastic sleeves before being placed between cardboard.

Captions are nearly as important as the story. They should be included with the manuscript, written with detail in complete sentences and taped to the photograph. Never write on the photograph itself. Label each caption with a number and put those numbers on the transparencies, pictures, slides or the back of the art. Provide a manuscript page titled "Captions," to provide corresponding numbers and captions for each of the transparencies.

Visual aids placement within the story is easier if notes in the margin tell which of the visual aids refer to that point in the text; for example, "Insert Figure 1 here."

If you find that photos are unavailable from any of your sources, please contact the editor one week prior to story deadline to discuss alternatives. This is important!

Photos are retained for archival files unless a request for their return is made in the cover letter. Include a self-addressed, stamped envelope.

Headlines/Deks

Although editorial usually creates these, it would be wonderful to receive two suggested heads and deks with your completed story. (Because it's your storyline, no one has a better feel for the headline than you.) It might be helpful for you to look thorough several past issues of *Mountain Pilot* or *Wings West* to get a sense of our headline/dek style, then try to match it.

Manuscripts

Include a cover letter with each manuscript. Unless you tell us otherwise, we assume the manuscript is original, that it has not been previously published, that it will not be presented to other periodicals for consideration if accepted by *Mountain Pilot*.

Changing a few words in another author's information does not relieve the borrower of identifying the passage and attributing the source. Identify such information with quotation marks and cite the quoted information accurately.

We occasionally consider articles previously published, however we pay less for them and we expect that they be tailored for our readership. To consider reprints (second serial "reprint" rights), we need the name of the publication(s) the article appeared in and the issue date.

If your manuscript has been copyrighted, a copyright transfer may be required before it will be published by *Mountain Pilot*.

Send one copy of the manuscript. Use 12-point typeface. Place two double-spaces between paragraphs.

Do not embellish your manuscript with such desktop features as bold-face, italics, centering, special indents or margins, any font but Times New Roman, field settings, or anything else that would need removed for typesetting. Such features make a manuscript look good, but creates extra work for the editor, who removes it.

Mountain Pilot reserves the right to edit all manuscripts. Editing is subjective and is built on specific rules of grammar and style. We strive to retain the accuracy and context of the original manuscript. If substantive changes are necessary, the author will be consulted. Editing is done to comply with the standards and styles in *The Associated Press Stylebook and Libel manual*. However, this stylebook neglects many commonly used aviation terms. When in doubt, spell it out. Do not use abbreviations or acronyms that the reader would not quickly recognize. Do not use idioms, slang, jargon or contractions. Spell the first use of all names, followed by the abbreviation or official acronym in parentheses.

Include your full name, address, social security number or business tax identification number, contact numbers (daytime and evening to clarify questions that may arise) and manuscript's estimated number of words on the upper right corner of the first page. On all pages after the first page, include your last name and the appropriate page number.

We mail each contributor one copy of the magazine. Additional copies may be purchased for $2.50 each.

Author's Bio and Photograph

Provide a listing of your current position, previous background, special accomplishments and education to lend credibility to the manuscript. Provide details of your aviation experience, including total flight time, certificates and ratings. Include a personal photograph.

Categories: Aviation

Name: Ed Huber, Editor
Material: Aviation
Address: 7009 S POTOMAC ST
City/State/ZIP: ENGLEWOOD CO 80112
Telephone: 303-397-7600
Fax: 303-397-7619
E-mail: Ehuber@winc.usa.com
Internet: www.winc.usa.com

MovieMaker Magazine

1. Submission Options: Send copy on 3.5" floppy disk or e-mail your copy with the copy as an attachment. Please do not fax more than three-page articles.

2. Spacing: Double-space hard copy between lines. Single-space between the period and the start of the new sentence.

3. Spelling: Triple-check all spellings, especially titles and names.

4. Photographs: Writers should attempt to source photographic material when applicable. If photos are unavailable, let editorial staff know as soon as possible and forward any leads or contacts for art sources.

5. Photographers: Photographers should submit black and white glossies (or 4"x5" color transparencies for possible cover use). No snapshots.

6. Designers: Illustrators and graphic artists should contact Art Designer with samples. Single-panel cartoons preferred.

7. Q&A: Follow *MovieMaker* format for question and answer interviews.

8. Personal Information: Contributors should include name, address, phone number and social security number on each submission.

9. Lengths: Features range between 1,500 and 3,500 words. Profiles have a 1,000 word average (always confirm with editor).

10. Attribution: Attribute all quotes.

11. Style: Italicize all titles; movies, books, songs. The style we use is compatible with the *Associated Press Stylebook*.

12. Rates: Flat fee $100-400 (cover) for features. $75-100 for profiles, columns. $25-50 for Reviews. *MovieMaker* reimburses no expense to writers or artists unless separate arrangements have been specifically authorized.

13. Deadlines: Art/Feature/Column deadlines are approximately the first of the month for the issue two months following (i.e., September first deadline for the November issue).

Categories: Film/Video

Name: Tim Rhys, Publisher/Editor
Material: Charles McEnerney, Managing Editor
Name: Any
Address: 750 S EUCLID AVE
City/State/ZIP: PASADENA CA 91106
Telephone: 626-584-6766
Fax: 626-584-5752
E-mail: Charlie@moviemaker.com
Internet: www.moviemaker.com

Ms. Magazine
The World of Women

Thank you for your interest in *Ms. Magazine*.

Writers wishing to submit to *Ms. Magazine* should be advised of the following:

1. Ms. does not accept, acknowledge, or return unsolicited poetry or fiction. *Ms.* considers only nonfiction manuscripts and queries.

2. In order for nonfiction submissions to be considered, we need the following to be included:

• Resumé
• Previously published clips

3. Submissions should be typewritten, and not longer than 2,000 words.

4. It is strongly encouraged that writers check several recent issues of the magazine, to find if your proposal is suitable for *Ms.* The most successful submissions are tightly-focused pieces which contain unique information with a feminist perspective. Generally, we do not cover beauty, fashion, fitness, travel or food stories. Film and book reviews are usually covered in house.

5. Our rates vary and are not discussed until acceptance of an article for publication.

6. Due to the shortage of staff and the enormous volume of material received, *Ms.* regrets that we cannot discuss queries or manuscripts over the phone. The *Ms.* staff will try to respond to queries within twelve weeks.

We do appreciate the time and effort it takes for you to submit to us.

Categories: Feminism—Women's Issues

Name: Manuscripts Editor
Material: All Manuscript Submissions
Name: Query
Material: All Queries
Address: 135 W 50TH ST 16TH FLOOR
City/State/ZIP: NEW YORK NY 10027
Telephone: 212-586-7441
E-mail: ms@echonyc.com (No submissions via e-mail.)

MSW Management

Now in its seventh year of publication, *MSW Management* has grown to become the preeminent journal focusing on public-sector municipal solid waste issues. It is well known throughout the industry and at all levels of government, looked upon by all as a fair and viable forum for ideas. Its departments and feature articles are informative, to the point, and readable...even when dealing with technical subjects.

About Our Audience

MSW Management's audience is composed of solid waste professionals employed by local municipal governments (city/county/township), regional solid waste management authorities, and their engineers (both outside, independent, consulting engineers and those employed by the municipality). Our readers are responsible for all aspects of integrated solid waste management (source reduction, composting, recycling, incineration, landfilling, etc.). Over 20% of our readers are engineers and since the audience is made up entirely of working professionals in the field, you must assume that they have a high level of expertise and familiarity with your subject matter.

For this reason the bulk of interviews, the preponderance of ascriptions and quotes, as well as the prevailing perspective should belong to *MSW* managers and staff. If you find yourself writing about non-municipal activities or people, take another look at the assignment and see if you're headed in the right direction. To paraphrase a naval axiom, "no writer can go far wrong by asking a public-sector MSW professional what he or she thinks...then putting the answer in quotes."

Assignment of Articles

MSW Management assigns articles to benefit its readership. The initial assignment sheet will specify substantive aspects of the article such as working title, subject, approach, significance, and length. Additionally, administrative aspects such as due date, remuneration, and reimbursements will be detailed at the time of article assignment.

Publisher's Policy on Compensation and Publication Rights

1. Author grants to Forester Communications, Inc. all rights for publication in any of its products. All rights to the submitted material are the sole property of Forester Communications, Inc., including copyright to the material as it appears in Forester Communications, Inc. products.

2. Copyright permission for previously printed material is the responsibility of the author. On submission, we assume that such permission, where required, has been granted. (Note: Many of our authors now find that the best way to avoid copyright problems is for them to copyright the materials they present at conferences. Then they can grant permission to any publication they wish.

3. Agreed-upon remuneration will be due and payable within 30 days of publication. Approved expenses will be reimbursed upon verification of a detailed expense report/phone bill.

4. The writer is in no way considered as an employee of Forester Communications, Inc. The writer is considered a subcontractor and is therefore responsible for all taxes applicable to remuneration where appropriate.

5. Articles that have been published elsewhere or have been submitted concurrently to other publications are generally not acceptable. However, there are exceptions such as foreign publications, conference proceedings, obscure journals, or significantly different exposure which may mitigate our policy. We are striving to have the best possible material and will, therefore, be flexible. Notify us in writing if it has been submitted elsewhere.

How Materials Should Be Prepared for Submission

1. All materials must arrive at Forester Communications' editorial offices no later than close of business on the agreed upon due date. These include:

a. MS-DOS readable diskette (3.5" or 5.25" single or double-density) using any standard PC-compatible word processor formatting (Microsoft Word). Under special circumstances and subject to prior arrangement, the electronic submission may be accomplished by modem or to our Internet address.

b. Hard copy original for reference and validation.

c. Graphics materials, properly identified and fully annotated and accompanied by a signed release or other proper authorization for their use.

Do not write on the back of a photo with a ballpoint pen or felt tip marker. Instead, type the caption copy on a separate sheet of paper and glue or tape it to the back of the photo, or simply number your photographs and provide a separate sheet with caption copy for each appropriate photo.

High-quality transparencies, slides, or glossy finish B&W or color prints are acceptable, but not photos taken with instant print or similar low image quality cameras.

Drawings, charts, and diagrams must always be accurate and suitable for reproduction. When submitting an article, please include the original artwork or high-quality Photostats of the originals. If color will clarify a drawing's effectiveness, include it on a copy of the original, but do not use screens, self-adhesive tints, or patterns on originals.

If you have any questions or are in doubt concerning the use of visuals in your article, please contact the editorial department for advice.

d. Appropriately labeled tape recordings of interviews (for legal and accuracy reasons).

2. Forester Communications requires a signed copy of this document (Author's Guidelines) for its files

3. The invoice for editorial services you've provided must include your social security number or Federal Taxpayer Identification Number.

General Guidelines

Think like your audience. Put yourself in an MSW manager's boots. What makes this subject important enough that you would take time out from your busy schedule to stop and read the article? Where's the hook? How best to bait it, cast it, troll it, and sink it? When you've satisfied yourself on those scores, you're ready to write.

Probably you've developed a style that feels comfortable to you, so that's a good starting point. But keep in mind your audience and the subject matter at hand. While a breezy, vernacular approach may work in some cases, you may find it misapplied in presenting highly technical detail. Similarly, a terse, didactic treatment of narrative materials is likely to put your audience to sleep no matter how serious and important the subject matter might be. Use your best judgment, try stating your thoughts aloud and see how they sound, or if you're really in doubt call and discuss the situation with us.

Engage your reader. Leave no doubt in anyone's mind who your audience is and why what you have to say is important. Rivet your fell attention on your readers and drag them into the middle of your subject, address them directly and personally. For instance, instead of saying, "hazardous waste can be kept out of the landfill in a number of ways," say, "If you don't want hazardous waste going into it, here are some things you can do."

Here's a good example from one of our recent articles:

Let's say that each week your crews are collecting newspaper, glass, aluminum, steel, and plastics at the curbside for recycling. You're also collecting brush and leaves for composting. Households are doing their part, and the amount of waste you're disposing of is decreasing—but not as much as you'd like. Tipping fees are still high, and you're having a hard time covering the costs of providing service. What alternatives do you have?

Since the audience is composed of working professionals, aim high in your expectations of their knowledge and expertise. While there's no reason to be pedantic or arcane, you should avoid simplifications as well. You have no need to explain or define the things MSW professionals should know. Assume also that your readers know and appreciate superior use of language and grammar, though not to the point that it becomes stilted or contrived.

Don't shy away from technical aspects of your subject. Make

the less educated or less technically proficient readers "reach," but do not "write down" to your readers. If the article is too simple or basic, we can't use it.

As far as rules are concerned, follow the latest *Chicago Manual of Style*. We have a set of conventions of our own (e.g. MSW, EPA, WTE, MRF), however, we'll apply them as appropriate, leaving you to concentrate on more important matters. Use acronyms where appropriate but only where there will be multiple callouts or (rarely) where the acronym is in such common usage that the full name might not be familiar to readers. There are some usage matters having to do with dimensions, quantities, and measures we'd like you to observe:

1. Primary measures should be English units [in., ft., cu. ft., gal., etc.] with their metric equivalents (if desired) in parentheses (cm, m, I, mg/l, etc.) If you're going to present conversions, please make sure of their accuracy.

2. The numbers one through nine should be spelled out, but 10 and up should be presented in Arabic numeral form except at the beginning of a sentence.

3. When used at the beginning of a sentence, numbers and their accompanying attributes (i.e. inches, percent, degrees) are spelled out, otherwise percentages and degrees should be presented numerically accompanied by the appropriate symbol (% or ?).

Identify yourself as a writer on assignment for *MSW Management* and conduct yourself and the interview in an open, friendly manner. Please refrain from confrontational behavior because of its reflection on the magazine and the questionable service it provides to the informational value at hand.

Think about the article's appearance as you do your interviewing. How might graphics help sell an important point, or what will entice a browser to take the plunge? Get as much graphic material as possible (photos, charts, illustrations, etc.). The more options our art director has, the better.

Verify all titles of those whom you interview as well as the spelling of all names, jurisdictions, companies, equipment, and products if applicable. Please contact people from different geographic regions across the country so it won't be an article about just one specific region (this is a national publication).

The majority of your interviews should be with public sector MSW managers and engineers (not manufacturers or private haulers). Do not interview and do not include quotes from public relations firms or their employees. The first quote/reference in any article should be that of an MSW manager.

Please include a cover page indicating the author's (or authors') name, title, affiliation, address, and phone number. State whether or not the material is being sent exclusively to *MSW Management.*

Categories: Environment

Name: John Trotti, Editor
Material: All
Address: 5638 HOLLISTER AVE STE 301
City/State/ZIP: SANTA BARBARA CA 93117
Telephone: 805-681-1300
Fax: 805-681-1312
E-mail: erosion@ix.netcom.com

Murderous Intent
A Magazine of Mystery & Suspense

MURDEROUS INTENT, A Magazine of Mystery & Suspense, is a quarterly magazine targeting the readers and writers of mystery/suspense who want not only to be entertained but challenged. The format is 8½"x11", saddle-stitched, approximately 68 pages with a two color glossy cover.

FICTION: Send only your best short stories, no longer than 5,000 words (prefer 2,000 to 4,000 words) (short shorts considered—200 to 400 word flash mysteries that have a beginning, middle, & twist ending). We will also consider cross-genre mysteries (i.e. horror, science fiction, romance) if the strongest emphasis is on the mystery/suspense. Give at least a hint of the mystery on the first page and keep suspense high. We publish what we feel are outstanding stories. Plot and character are of equal importance.

NONFICTION: We are looking for articles (no longer than 4,000 words) applicable to writing or reading mysteries. For example, articles covering forensics, police practices, district attorneys and how their offices operate, weaponry, crime scenes, medical examiners, private investigators, criminal defense lawyers, DNA testing, etc. We are open to anything pertaining to the mystery field BUT the articles must be authentic and you *must* include sources. No true crime.

FILLERS: Actively seeking mystery related cartoons, poetry, jokes, limericks, or very short mystery related nonfiction articles etc.

SUBMISSIONS: Please send a cover letter end brief publishing bio with submission. Send hardcopy now. Be prepared to supply a computer disk with your story, single spaced, on acceptance. We do not accept manuscripts for publication unless they are on a suitable 3½" floppy disk. Please observe all manuscript conventions and use 12 point Courier font.

NO gratuitous or explicit sex, violence, or language. No cannibal stories. Only one story and/or article per submission, please!

PAYMENT: Fiction or nonfiction, payment for first North American serial rights is $10 plus two free copies per story or article, on acceptance. The author will be expected to sign a contract stating that the work is original and that he or she is the author. Reprints seldom accepted. Fillers: related to mystery are needed. Pays $2. Subscriptions: $18 per year for four issues or $5.00 plus SASE (9"x12" envelope) with four first-class stamps attached or $6.24 & SASE (9"x12" envelope) for a sample copy.

You may e-mail me with questions (not manuscripts). E-mail me if you are interested in subscribing to the shortmystery-l-digest on the Internet. It's easy & it's free!

TIPS: No cannibal stories. Send us mysteries like the ones you love to read—as long as they fit within our guidelines. We love humorous mysteries, mysteries with exotic settings, go puzzles, all around good stories. Read the magazine before submitting.

Categories: Mystery

Name: Margo Power, Editor
Material: All
Address: PO BOX 5947
City/State/ZIP: VANCOUVER WA 98668-5947
Telephone: 360-695-9004
Fax: 360-693-3354
E-mail: Madison@teleport.com

Muscle & Fitness
For Super Fitness & Vigorous Health

Thank you for your interest in writing for *Muscle & Fitness.*
Of note, we generally don't assign articles to new freelancers but rather ask that you pitch us a detailed query. Please try and narrow in on a specific topic(s) of interest and the points you will bring up. If relevant, cite research, experts you will speak with and any pro bodybuilders that will help fill out the article. As we are a bodybuilding publication, M&F likes to include quotes from exercise/nutrition researchers and bodybuilders whenever possible to bring in an "in the trenches" perspective.

Please contact me if you have any further questions.

Sincerely,

Bill Geiger

Editor

Editorial Guidelines

MUSCLE & FITNESS is a bodybuilding and fitness publication for healthy, active men and women. It contains a wide range of features and monthly departments devoted to all areas of bodybuilding, health, fitness, injury prevention and treatment, and nutrition.

Editorial fulfills two functions: information and entertainment, with special attention to how-to advice and accuracy.

Assignments: All features and departments are written on assignment (including those written on speculation). Writers must be cognizant of deadlines, article length, outline approval and technical requirements. Writers should check assignment confirmation forms for details, and contact assigning editor if necessary.

Queries: Contact us in writing with your article ideas. Your query should be a short summary (one page or less) of your idea or ideas, along with potential sources and your own qualifications to write the article. Send recent clips with bylines. Please send only clips that reflect your own writing style.

Manuscript tone: The editorial voice must be friendly, speaking directly to the healthy, active man or woman. Academic journal composition is not acceptable. Please read the magazine for an understanding of its style.

Manuscript length: As specified with assignment. Generally 500-800 words for departments; 1,500-1,800 words for features.

Writer's contracts/kill fees: All manuscripts from first-time contributors are read on speculation only. Contracts specifying kill fees and author rights are available to repeat contributors.

Payment rates: $360 (or less) for departments; $400-800 (or less) for features. All fees are negotiated individually. Writer must sign M&F contract before any payment can be made.

Fact checking: Accuracy is the responsibility of the author. Manuscripts should be accompanied by the telephone numbers of sources quoted within the article, so editors can verify names and titles, professional associations and any related product prices. If a book is referred to in the article, you must include the author's name, the book publisher, year of publication and the book's price if it's still in print. For scientific journal citations, full references are required (and photocopies requested).

Unsolicited manuscripts: We require queries. Please do not send manuscripts.

8 STEPS TO WRITING A BETTER ARTICLE FOR M&F

The following guidelines are intended to remind all writers on those elements that make for great copy. They include:

1) Focus your article. What's your special angle? Why is it important to readers? What new do you have to add to the volumes already printed on the subject?

2) Be clear on where you are going. What questions will you answer? What controversies are there? What research supports the question? What relevant bodybuilders and experts can provide insight? Get an outline together and talk to your assigning editor about it.

3) Get quotes. Unless you are THE one and only expert, it's better to quote those who really are. This adds credibility. Dissenting quotes also offer balance. Quotes from bodybuilders are also good because these are the people who've done it "in the trenches."

When you quote a "doctor," like a physician, dentist, chiropractor or university professor, do not precede the name with "Dr.," but rather give their degree after the name (like MD, DC, PhD, etc.) Also affiliation if applicable (i.e., from the University of Pittsburgh School of Medicine) and its location.

When you introduce anecdotal persons, provide more than just name. Also include city, state, age, maybe profession.

4) Leave out filler. Too many articles come in over 3,000 words that must be returned to be cut. (Or would you rather have a copy editor unfamiliar with your material cut it for you?) Make your points succinctly and don't repeat yourself.

5) Pull the reader into the article. Know why the reader is going to be interested in reading your piece. What's she learning that she can use? Provide solutions and how-to information. How-to articles work well in the second person: for example, "Keep your arms by your sides at all times as you curl the weight."

6) Use subheads to break up long sections of copy and to organize ideas. Use sidebars for background that slows the flow of the main copy, like tangential but relevant topics, technical information, a summary of tips, relevant diagrams or charts, background information, or related information that doesn't insert into the text well but is important to the article.

7) Make sure you're on schedule. Talk to your editor in advance if you need an extension. Don't turn in a half-baked article just to meet deadline; it will be coming back to you for a rewrite.

8) Review your article. Double check the spelling of all names, titles and facts. Also do a spell check.

How to send: Completed manuscript should be e-mailed, sent via dial-in modem connection to M&F at 818-348-1195 (we use PC Plus, 9600 baud, settings are N,8,1). By mail, send 3.5" disk. We prefer IBM Microsoft Word for Windows 6.0 (saved as a document); other software users should save as ASCII text files. Don't forget a clean manuscript as well.

Categories: Diet—Health—Men's Issues—Physical Fitness

Name: Vince Scalisi, Editor
Material: All
Address: 21100 ERWIN ST
City/State/ZIP: WOODLAND HILLS CA 91367
Telephone: 818-884-6800
Fax: 818-595-0463
E-mail: vscalisi@earthlink.net

Mushing
The Magazine of Dog-Powered Sports

Mushing works with experienced freelance writers and photojournalists as well as first-time authors and photographers. These guidelines are intended to provide an idea of the kinds of submissions we are looking for as well as how our submission process works. Please feel free to contact us if you have questions or if you would like to discuss an idea for submission.

EDITORIAL PROFILE

Mushing is an international bimonthly magazine that covers all aspects of dog-powered sports. *Mushing* was founded in 1987 and strives to inform, educate and entertain readers by publishing articles on all aspects of the growing sports of dogsledding, skijoring, carting, dog packing and weight pulling. *Mushing* promotes responsible dog care through feature articles and up-dates on working animal health care, safety, nutrition and training.

Available by subscription and in retail outlets, *Mushing* is distributed in 49 states and 25 countries. Readers include both recreational and competitive mushers with a wide range of experience, from beginners to veterans. In addition, some readers are "armchair mushers," who enjoy reading about or watching the sport but are not mushers themselves.

We urge contributors to study the magazine before submitting material. Samples are $5 in the United States, $6 U.S. to Canada and $8 U.S. overseas.

SUBMISSIONS

We prefer detailed query letters but also consider unsolicited manuscripts. Please make proposal letters informative yet to the point and succinct. Spell out your qualifications for handling the topic. We like to see clips of previously published material, but we are eager to work with new and unpublished authors too.

Submissions should include your telephone number, social security number (for tax purposes), name(s), address and the article's approximate word count.

Mail all submissions to the address below. Queries (not manuscripts) may be sent by fax or by e-mail, but these may be responded to by regular mail, so please include complete contact information.

ARTICLE CONTENT

Each issue of *Mushing* includes a mix of information, features and columns. We consider articles on canine health and nutrition, sled dog behavior and training, musher profiles and interviews, equipment how-to, trail tips, expedition and race accounts, innovations, sled dog history, current issues, personal experiences and humor. We use primarily nonfiction but will consider well-written and relevant or timely fiction. We also consider cartoons and junior puzzles. See editorial calendar below for current special issue focuses.

All articles should be well researched, logically organized and readable. Appropriate photo support and/or illustrations are welcomed. (See "Images" below.)

STYLE AND LENGTH

We prefer clear, concise, straightforward writing. We generally follow Associated Press style, although we also have our own style guide and consult the *Chicago Manual of Style* on occasion. *We reserve the right to edit all submissions.*

Features generally run between 1,000 and 2,500 words. Longer articles are considered if well written and of particular interest. Columns and departments usually run from 500 to 1,000 words. Short news pieces run from 150 to 500 words.

ARTICLE FORMAT

Contributor phone number, social security number, names(s), address and the article's approximate word count should appear at the top of the first page. Please number all pages after the first. Also include an author's biography of three to four sentences.

Include a cover letter with the manuscript. Photocopied submissions are fine if the copy quality is good. Handwritten, very light or single-spaced copy may be returned unread.

Submissions on 3½" Macintosh or IBM-format computer disk are encouraged, but please include a complete hard copy to protect against disk errors. Please specify the type of computer hardware and software the document was created on.

PHOTOGRAPHS

Mushing uses both color and black-and-white photographs. All photos and slides to be considered must be clean, sharp and accurately exposed. Potential subjects include dogs working, playing and resting as well as expedition and racing events, recreational mushing, skijoring, winter camping freighting, mushing equipment and mushing personalities. We use a variety of horizontals and verticals.

We work at least three months ahead of each publication date, so we need summer photos beginning in February and winter photos in July. We are always looking for good cover photographs. These should be strong, sharp, vertical photographs with enough open area at the top for the *Mushing* banner.

Submitted black-and-white photos should ideally be 8"x10" glossy prints or negatives accompanied by a contact sheet. High-quality 8"x10" prints on semi-matte paper are acceptable but not preferred.

We prefer color photos in 35mm or 120mm Kodachrome transparencies but will consider other formats. Slides must be submitted in plastic slide sheets and accompanied by a detailed caption sheet. Every slide or print must be clearly marked with the photographer's name and address. If you are concerned about the safety of your slides, you may submit duplicate slides as long as originals are available for final printing. Please identify any duplicate slides.

Black-and-white images account for about 50 to 80 percent of the art in any given issue, so we welcome good black-and-white submissions. However, color submissions are often published as black-and-white images as well. *Contributors of color images agree to have their images published in the black-and-white format unless a specific written agreement is made with Mushing in advance of submission.*

ARTWORK

Mushing uses black-and-white illustrations and drawings on occasion. Mostly we use simple images of sled dogs doing something-running, howling, sleeping, eating, playing, etc.-although we are always open to other possibilities. We occasionally use color artwork on the cover. In addition, sled dog-related cartoons are considered. Some artists submit work (or good photocopies) that *Mushing* can keep on file and use as the need arises.

All photographs, slides and original artwork are returned after consideration or use unless other arrangements are specified.

RATES RIGHTS AND PAYMENT

We purchase first serial rights and second (reprint) rights. Article rates average $.09 per published word. Photograph and artwork payment rates average as follows:

Black and white: $20 to $40
Color: $35 to $50
Back cover: up to $85
Front cover: up to $165

We also purchase the right to publish articles and photos on our World Wide Web site for one year following the print publication date. An additional fee of $10 per photo and $20 per article is paid for this use.

We send payment within 60 days of publication. Unless a written agreement is made between *Mushing* and a writer or photographer, exact rate of payment for articles and photographs will be determined by the editorial staff of *Mushing*.

Unless otherwise notified in writing, all contributions are considered to be submitted on a speculation basis. An affirmative response to a query proposal does not necessarily mean the resulting article will be accepted.

All slides with a copyright notice on the slide cover should be accompanied by a signed release that gives *Mushing* the right to duplicate images for processing (i.e., to make a black-and-white interneg and print or color separation and proof).

EDITORIAL SCHEDULE

The following are the submission deadlines for the six bimonthly issues of *Mushing*. We welcome early submissions to allow ample time for questions and clarifications. Issue focuses are subject to change.

Issue Focus Deadline
Jan./Feb. Iditarod Issue Oct. 15
Mar./Apr. Expedition/peak of Season Dec. 15
May/Jun. Health & Nutrition Feb. 15
Jul./Aug. Meet the Mushers Apr. 15
Sep./Oct. Equipment Issue Jun. 15
Nov./Dec. Races & Places Aug. 15
Categories: Nonfiction—Animals—Recreation

Name: Todd Hoener, Editor-in-Chief
Material: All

Address: PO BOX 149
City/State/ZIP: ESTER AK 99725-0149
Telephone: 907-479-0454
Fax: 907-479-3137
E-mail: mushing@polarnet.com

Muzzle Blasts

Thank you for your interest in our magazine. Enclosed is a set of writing guidelines to help you prepare your manuscript. If you have any further questions, please don't hesitate to call.

SELECTED TOPIC INFORMATION

Many of our members are knowledgeable in various fields of our muzzleloading sport and the era we represent. Our magazine publishes articles with topics on the *history* of the muzzleloading era, on *hunting* with a muzzleloading rifle, and on *technical* aspects of muzzleloading firearms. If you would like to write an article on any given topic related to muzzleloading, the following will provide needed information in submitting your manuscript.

If your article deals with the *history* of the muzzleloading era or a muzzleloading firearm, please include detailed information about all references used in developing the article. Articles will not be accepted without proper source documentation in footnote or endnote form. If quoting from a book, please include the author's name, title of book, city and state of publication, publisher's name, year of publication, and page references. If periodicals (such as magazines) are sources, include the author's name, title of periodical, volume and issue numbers, cover date, and page references. If extensive quotations are used, submit photocopies of the pages from which the quotations came.

If *hunting* is your forte, precede your article with a short descriptive background of the hunting area so the reader can better envision the hunt. Give full details of the firearm used-include the manufacturer or gunmaker, bullet make and caliber, and powder type and load. (Beware of blackpowder overloads; do not exceed manufacturer's recommended maximums.) Pay attention to the details of the hunt, and try to relay humorous situations that occurred, or the imminent danger that was present.

If your article is *technical or instructional* ("how-to"), be sure to mention the equipment used and describe the procedures step-by-step. Relate the reasons why the subject matter works. Be especially accurate in measurements. Include all charts, photographs, and tables necessary to give a complete description of the process. Remember to include all relevant manufacturer information, especially if the article involves a product evaluation.

In whatever topic you are writing, do not be wordy. Simple and direct writing enhances your subject matter. On the other hand, be sure you provide all necessary information.

TO SUBMIT AN ARTICLE

First, *know your topic.* Know that the subject matter conforms to the standards of our association and that it has been researched thoroughly.

Be aware of *all safety measures* (see photo requirements) when writing technical, instructive, or hunting articles.

Present a manuscript on *DOS format computer diskette,* preferably in one of the WordPerfect™ formats, Microsoft™ Word©, Lotus™ Ami Pro©, or in ASCII. If that is not possible, please submit the typewritten manuscript.

Six to eight typewritten pages, double-spaced, provide the editor with an average-sized article. Longer manuscripts will be considered if the topic warrants the length. Please number manuscript pages.

All manuscripts accepted for publication are subject to editing. This will ensure that they conform to MUZZLE BLASTS' format, style, and space limitations.

Be sure your name, address, telephone number, *and social security number* are included in a cover letter accompanying your manuscript. Please note: We require your social security number for payment and taxation purposes only.

Manuscripts will be acknowledged upon receipt.

ILLUSTRATIONS

All submissions should include high-contrast black-and-white or color photographs and/or well-defined diagrams. Black-and-white or color prints are preferred and must be of good quality. Photos will be reviewed and selected by the editor. On the back of the photo(s) submitted, *print your name, address, and title of the article.* Use a very soft lead pencil or a typed label. Ink pens, especially felt pens, can bleed through the backing paper. Include a separate sheet of paper with captions, and key the captions to the photos.

All mechanical art, line drawings, and tables must be submitted in black and white. If necessary, ink the drawings for clean-cut reproduction. Submit on a separate sheet of paper. Mechanical art and line drawings produced on IBM-compatible computers can be submitted on a diskette in PCX or TIFF formats, among others. Contact the editor for more information.

REQUIREMENTS FOR PHOTOS AND MECHANICAL ILLUSTRATIONS

Photos should be 5"x7" or 8"x10". However, a good, sharply contrasting 3"x5" photograph is acceptable. All submissions should be black-and-white or color prints. The submission of color slides with a document may be the cause for its return.

Mechanical artwork, including charts, may be lettered in pencil; such text will be typeset and sized to fit the illustration. Identify the manuscript location of illustrative work on the back of the sheet.

When submitting cover art, recognize that 3"x5" transparencies are preferred; sharply-contrasting 35mm color slides are acceptable if the subject is unusual or exceptionally deserving of attention, but acceptance is *extremely* rare. Submissions for cover art must be in portrait (vertical) format.

BE AWARE OF SAFETY WHEN SUBMITTING PHOTOS

Do not submit photos that depict firearms used in an unsafe manner (such as with a blocked muzzle, pointed in an unsafe direction, cocked or half-cocked, and so forth). When submitting photos for technical articles, be aware of and demonstrate all safety measures; for example, if the topic is a review of a new rifle, all shooters who are photographed should be wearing hearing and eye protection.

WRITER/ARTIST RESPONSIBILITIES

Liability for copyright-law compliance of submitted materials (such as artwork or text), as well as the procurement of all model-release forms, is the responsibility of the submitter and not the NMLRA or its affiliates. When submitting materials that have been reproduced whole or in part from other sources, include with the materials copies of permission letters from the appropriate person or persons.

Upon receipt, articles will be reviewed for MUZZLE BLASTS publication by the editor, the publications committee, and technical advisors as deemed necessary. Payments will be made for articles that deal with muzzleloading firearms or firearms with historical value, and for those that provide good instructive subject matter. If there are questions on an accepted article, the editor will contact the writer.

ELECTRONIC RIGHTS

The National Muzzle Loading Rifle Association also publishes MUZZLE BLASTS ONLINE on the World Wide Web. This electronic magazine is focused primarily for a nonmember audience. From time to time the editor will contact a writer if he feels that a submission is appropriate for the Web publication. Writers and photographers are free to accept or reject this use of their work, and statements regarding this issue can be enclosed with your submission. Payments for electronic rights are made in addition to regular rates for the paper publication.

MUZZLE BLASTS Writers' Pay Schedule
(All payments made upon publication.)

Special-Purchase Photos
Black and white, up to $30 maximum
Four-color (for covers), *up* to $300 maximum

Product Reviews
All reviews, $100-$300, depending on the amount of research and tests necessary and the number of photos submitted.

Columns and Articles
All standing columns, $50-$150, depending on the amount of research and tests necessary and the number of photos or illustrations submitted (if any).

All features, $100-$400, depending on the amount of research and tests necessary and the number of photos or illustrations submitted.

Electronic Use
Standing columns, $50 paid in addition to standard scale above.

Feature articles, $100 paid in addition to standard scale above.
Categories: Associations—History—Hobbies

Name: **Terri Trowbridge, Director of Publications**
Name: **Eric A Bye, Editor**
Material: **Any**
Address: **PO BOX 67**
City/State/ZIP: **FRIENDSHIP IN 47021**
Telephone: **812-667-5131**
Fax: **812-667-5137**

My Legacy

My Legacy is for short stories only, and the guidelines are short and sweet. Just remember 2,500 words maximum (sometimes a bit longer is OK). Please submit work in good taste...with no bad language (think of a better way to say it). Stories on any subject are read but must catch my eye to be accepted. The "Editor's Choice Award" of $5 goes to my favorite story in each issue.

USA Rates for Subscription/Single Copy: $12/4 issues; $3.50 next issue only.
Categories: Fiction—Adventure—Animals—Children—Christian Interests—Civil War—Crime—Culture—Ethnic—Family—Fantasy—Inspirational—Mystery—Native American—New Age—Rural America—Science Fiction—Senior Citizens—Short Stories—Spiritual—Western—Writing

Name: **Kay Weems, Editor/Publisher**
Material: **All**
Address: **HCR-13 BOX 21AA**
City/State/ZIP: **ARTEMAS PA 17211-9405**
Telephone: **814-458-3102**

Na'amat Woman

Dear Writer:
Per your request, our writers' guidelines are as follows:

An article must be of particular interest to the Jewish community and/or on women's issues; fiction must have a Jewish theme. An article/story should be approximately 2,000 words in length. Payment is eight (8) cents a word upon publication.

If you have any questions, please do not hesitate to contact me.
Sincerely,
Judith A. Sokoloff
Editor

Categories: Jewish Interests—Women's Issues

Name: **Judith A. Sokoloff, Editor**
Name: **Gloria Gross, Assistant Editor**
Material: **Any**
Address: **200 MADISON AVE STE 2120**
City/State/ZIP: **NEW YORK NY 10016**
Telephone: **212-725-8010**

Nails Magazine
Advanced Education for Nail Professionals

If a query contains an idea that will provide something valuable to our readers, it will capture our attention. It should be easy to read, with the central idea in the first (short) paragraph. Further details should indicate where the writer will go for his or her information (interviews, books, self expertise, etc.) If the writer can provide photographs, it is a big plus.

Send no more than one or two of your best clips. Include other publications you've written for in your query letter. A SASE is nice, but not necessary. Writers may call if they haven't heard from us within six weeks of sending their query. Faxed queries are acceptable; e-mail is acceptable, but it is not monitored as frequently.

Writers who have some knowledge and/or experience in our industry will have an advantage. However, a newsworthy subject pitched by a good writer will certainly get serious consideration. We are not able to place stories immediately; consequently, the waiting period can sometimes be long. Be patient, but feel free to call if you want to make sure something arrived, or have additional ideas to add to your query.
Categories: Nonfiction—Beauty

Name: **Erika Kotite, Managing Editor**
Material: **All**
Address: **2512 ARTESIA BLVD**
City/State/ZIP: **REDONDO BEACH CA 90278-3295**
Telephone: **310-376-8788**
Fax: **310-376-9043**
E-mail: **nailsmag@bobit.com**

The Nation

Thank you for your interest in writing for *The Nation*. We are a journal of left/liberal political opinion—130 years old this year—covering national and international affairs. We publish weekly (summer biweekly).

We are looking both for reporting and for fresh analysis. On the domestic front, we are particularly interested in civil liberties; civil rights; labor, economics, environmental and feminist issues and the role and future of the Democratic Party. Because we have readers all over the country, it's important that stories with a local focus have real national significance. In our foreign affairs coverage we prefer pieces on international political, economic and social developments. As the magazine which published Ralph Nader's first piece (and there is a long list of Nation "firsts"), we are seeking new writers.

While detailed queries (a page or two) are preferred, we're happy to consider finished pieces on timely issues. Faxed manuscripts will only be acknowledged if accepted. Our full-length pieces run 1,500 to 2,000 words and (signed) editorials 500 to 750. Calvin Trillin has made us famous for paying in the high two- or very low three-figures—that is, from $75 for an editorial to $225-300 for a full-length piece. Deadlines are 10 days before the magazine goes to print for stories, 4 days for editorials. The magazine goes to print on Wednesdays.

The Nation publishes poems of outstanding aesthetic quality, by poets such as Emily Dickinson, William Butler Yeats, D.H. Lawrence, Marianne Moore, William Carlos Williams, Robert Lowell, Randall Jarrell, W.S. Merwin, Derek Walcott, Pablo Neruda, Mona Van Duyn, Joseph Brodaky. Payment: $1 a line not to exceed $35.

Let us hear from you.

The Editors

Categories: Nonfiction—Civil Liberties—Civil Rights—Economics—Environment—Feminism—Politics—Poetry—Public Policy

Name: Sue and John Leonard, Literary Editors
Material: Queries and Submissions, Books/Arts
Name: Grace Schulman, Poetry Editor
Material: Poems; Discovery-The *Nation* Contest (Unpublished Poets)
Address: 72 FIFTH AVE
City/State/ZIP: NEW YORK NY 10011
Telephone: 212-247-8400
Fax: 212-463-9712
E-mail: submissions@thenation.com
Internet: www.thenation.com

National Enquirer

An *Enquirer* story requires fast, extremely detailed, accurate work. It's not particularly complex, but it has to be done. On the other hand, *The Enquirer* pays enough money to make the work worthwhile. A number of freelancers are making better than $1,500 a week right now and there is room for twenty more like them.

You get $360 or $180 just for providing a story idea, plus source information, *even if you do nothing more on the story*. If you go ahead and cover the story, you get another $720 or $450. So that's either $1,080 or $630 a story—the difference being whether it's used as a "T" (top page) or a "D" (down page). You should aim for twenty leads and one or two stories each week and don't worry about the high attrition rate of story suggestions. Everyone faces the same situation and it's worth it if you can get one out of ten.

The lead fees and story rates I've just mentioned are the best in the country for newspaper stories. What do you have to do to get them? Well, you have to do a couple of things differently from the way they are done on most newspapers.

First, the writing: the difference here is that we want you to overwrite substantially. We want a basic magazine structure: lead, backup (with anecdotes), conclusion. But forget about stylistic tricks—everything is rewritten, you are supplying a basic file, like *Time* reporters do—and you write at least five to seven double-spaced pages. Just put on a straight introduction covering the points raised in the lead sheet and follow it mostly with quotes—the more that's in direct quotes the better, far more than you'll see in the finished story. And get this point clear in your

mind—even a small story has to start out this big. We need to cover all the bases.

Your report will be read for the quality of the reporting, not the writing. I know this is frustrating, but it is an essential part of the system and you will be highly regarded for doing it. I might add that, since you don't have to worry about tight writing, style and paraphrasing, an *Enquirer* piece tends to go a lot quicker than a magazine yarn.

Second, there will be questions and call backs. Please don't feel put down if I come back and ask for clarifications. There are three levels of people beyond me whose job it is to nitpick—we strive not just for accuracy but for proof of accuracy. So almost everyone gets called back, though not on every story, and has to check back sources. Just do a thorough reporting job and callbacks will be minimal. We know it is tedious. One of the reasons we pay more than other publications is to compensate you for this occasional necessity.

Here's how to avoid callbacks:

1. Don't state anything in your copy unless you have it in quotes or have other adequate proof that it is true. Don't leave any unanswered questions.

2. Each assignment will have a story number. Mark this number on your copy and add a '*contact sheet*' with names and phone numbers of interviewees (they won't be called back if you don't want it, but we need them for our files).

3. Get *backup* for any substantial claims from other reputable sources. A medical breakthrough, for instance, needs details of test results proving its efficacy, *plus* a statement by some other authority (often the original source will refer you to others in the file) that the discovery is valid and significant.

4. Avoid dull copy by including anecdotes where at all possible (and appropriate).

5. Follow the lead sheet exactly. If the lead says something is an incredible breakthrough, then you can't quote someone as saying it may be a breakthrough. *Enquirer* stories are black and white—there are no gray areas. We don't do balanced stories. If we decide to run a story, it's because we believe in it. Negative or questioning comments by anyone quoted—either in the file or in the tape recording of interview—will lead to the story being killed.

To ease the shock of all of this, think of this—you can get as much as $2,780 for one story in the *Enquirer*. That's $360 for the lead, $720 for the reporting—and $1,700 if your story makes Page 1. That bonus is paid twice every week and each week we use eighty to ninety stories about half from non-staffers.

Okay, so where do you get these stories? The basic starting points are the newspapers—all the newspapers. Next comes the TV and radio talk shows, then the magazines, general and special interest; then the trade papers and specialist journals, abstracts, and so on. Offbeat books also tend to be good sources. There are also your personal contacts in the various fields—show biz, the universities, hospitals, politics, newspapers and so forth. Also stories you have worked on, are now working on, often have aspects that make an *Enquirer* angle.

Here's how to recognize an *Enquirer* story and how to write a lead that'll grab us. First, you can pretty much rule out stories that have been picked up by the wire services, unless you find a completely fresh angle. Second, look for stories that have mass appeal to about half the population. Third, look for the significant things the daily press tends to miss—the story behind the story: a case in point was the disastrous Kentucky nightclub fire some years ago, where *Enquirer* reporters discovered that the reason so many people died was that the management was trying to collect customers' checks before opening the doors.

In writing your lead suggestion, try always to indicate a clear, fresh angle to the story. But be awfully careful you don't write anything in the lead that you can't back up. This is a major reason for stories being killed. In fact, it is a very good idea to do some investigation of your story before submitting it. This will enable you to spell it out with concise facts, figures and examples and give you a much better chance of getting it accepted.

Here's what happens to your idea when you submit it. If I like it, I send it to the Editor. He either okays the lead or kills it. He marks it a "T" or a "D" if approved. I have the approved ones typed on lead sheets. We then give it a story number and check the computer to see that we haven't already done the story in the last five years or that no one currently is working it. When I get the lead sheet back, I assign the story to you or someone else if you can't or don't want to do it.

When you send in your copy—always with the story number on it, I check that it's all there and then I send it to an evaluator. His job is to assess how big the story should finally run and he writes this opinion, along with a summary of your file for the writers to then re-write to the length decided. The written article then goes to the researchers, who check it. You can see that there are quite a few steps here and this is why it's important that your file be complete—otherwise any or all of these people will ask for clarification and this causes delays.

What kind of stories? Please read the paper. Browse through some back issues. They will tell you more than I could. The requirements haven't changed, except perhaps that stories pertaining directly to women are more popular now than before. A general test is—would this story interest 50% of our readers?

Here are some suggestions and reminders you should tape to the wall over your desk:

1. Scandals, big news breaks, exclusives of all kinds—especially untold angles on major stories.

2. Anything about major personalities, especially TV—romances, breakups, illnesses, interviews with them. Almost any interview is usable if the star is big enough but always look for a fresh angle.

3. Medical breakthroughs, especially concerning cancer, heart disease, arthritis, diabetes, and other maladies a broad spectrum of the public has or is worried about. Important scientific discoveries—especially involving common substances.

4. Interesting new diets.

5. Beauty ideas that people can use.

6. Dramatic new fashions, good news and self-help for women.

7. Success stories, people overcoming adversities.

8. Miracle escapes, great rescues, adventures, survival.

9. Ghosts, exorcisms, physics, ESP, UFOs.

10. New self-help ideas—five steps to a new you (especially getting smarter or more successful).

11. Great ripoffs.

12. New light on famous unsolved mysterious (e.g. Amelia Earhart, Bermuda Triangle, etc.)

13. The Kennedys, Reagans, Clintons—their fads, dirty linens, new interests, etc.

14. New information on major controversies—saccharine and cancer, butter and cholesterol, etc.

15. 'Fringe Medicine'—acupuncture, graphology, reflexology, healing—studies that appear to show they have scientific validity. Dreams that come true. But there must be good backup on all these offbeat claims.

16. Governmental misbehavior—officials ripping off funds, unnecessary trips, putting relations on payrolls, misuse of government plans, FDA keeping valuable drugs off the market, CAB keeping airlines unsafe, etc.—major sources are government auditors, congressional committee staffs and investigators (and equivalents on state and city levels) and ambitious 'out' politicians. Also good are consumer and special interest groups and wayout publications.

17. Sins against the community by other major power blocks—business lobbying and ripoffs, oil depletion, unions costing people their jobs by feather-bedding that kills the firm, stealing pension funds. Labor rackets like the wholesale organized stealing on waterfronts.

18. Public health—good and bad news—e.g., plague still a threat, cancer 'epidemic' in Rutherford, New Jersey, polio is dead.

19. Where are they now? Film star Betty Hutton is a cook in a rectory, etc.

20. New info, especially with pics, on childhoods of famous people or hidden episodes in their lives.

21. Delicately handled sex stories like 'How to Put New Life Into Your Marriage,' 'Why Husbands Lose Interest,' etc.

22. Stories of great wealth—like the custom-made aircraft of the rich.

23. Every kind of 'How To' story especially ten ways to variety.

24. Significant new gadgets and scientific devices, like attaching magnets to your fuel line to increase gas mileage 30 to 40%.

25. News about computers—especially development of artificial intelligence, computer crimes and means of combatting the privacy issue, 'the government has your number' sort of thing.

26. Wacky stunts, such as those of having an *Enquirer* reporter check the waiting time in hospital emergency rooms across the country or taking the Encyclopedia Britannica sales course and reporting all the sales tricks they teach.

27. Human interest. This can be anything that people like to read and talk about. But it's got be good. If it's a dying child who miraculously survives, I want quotes that make me cry, ones that will really touch my heart. If it's a handicapped man who's climbed Mount Everest, I want quotes in the story that will make me cheer. Human interest stories are obviously 'people' stories, but don't forget their pets too.

28. Any happening or development that will cause readers to exclaim, 'Gee Whiz!' or 'How Dare They?' or similar expressions of amazement, joy or anger.

29. There is one other story source—a most important one. It's what we refer to here as 'off the top of your head.' This source can be tapped single-handedly by sitting back, putting your feet on the desk and just thinking in headlines. Think of the sort of headline you've seen on the front page of the *Enquirer*, on the cover blurb of *Reader's Digest*, on the TV ads for this and other publications. Then mentally write a few yourself. All you have to do then is figure out where and how and from whom you can get a story that would fit such a headline. And there you have it—the $1,700 front page bonus. Joint assaults on the top of the head also work; sit around with some of your favorite friends and favorite substances and bounce a few 'what-ifs' around. You'll be amazed how they blossom in mid air. As often as not, this sort of process is the source of our big 'production numbers,' and they're the stories we like best and that will score best for you.

Samples of the sort of thing I mean.

What if there is one best diet?

How to find your roots

100 easy ways to save money

Harvard docs reveal simple plan to beat stress

Lose weight on fast food diet

TV shows that reduce stress

Simple no-drug headache cure

Live up to 20 years longer

Each one of these made a front-page banner headline. Of course, the slight catch to it is that the reporters who thought of those leads also came up with ideas on how to do them.

I am also sending along a couple of other idea ticklers: one is an alphabetical listing of *Enquirer*-type subjects, the other is a list of *Enquirer* 'category' stories.

You may choose to specialize in one or two of these areas; it can be a good strategy. But be aware of them all. There's money in every one. Good luck and stay in touch.

***Enquirer* Category Stories:**

Card & Letter Appeal: for the very sick/lonely/courageous.

Celebrity Fantasies: *The Enquirer* can make come true.

Contests: see those we publish to spark your imagination.

Court Watch: shocking examples of injustice.

Diet

Education

Enquirer Impact: how an *Enquirer* article has changed a reader's life for the better.

Escape From the Rat Race: focusing on somebody successful who's given it all up for a less stressful, preferably wayout, life.

Good Samaritan Award

Government Waste or Bureaucracy Run Wild: self-explanatory examples of red tape, incompetence, bureaucratic waste that will make our readers hot under the collar.

Hero Award: potential recipient must have risked own life.

Honest Person Award

How To: self-improvement, etc.

How To: improve your marriage.

How To: beat loneliness.

Incredible World of Animals: each feature concentrates on fascinating attributes of a particular creature.

Medical: general—breakthrough, new treatments, techniques, etc. We have sub-categories recognizing readers' special interests in cancer, arthritis and heart problems.

My Most Embarrassing Moment: (celeb)

My Most Frightening Moment: (celeb)

Occult

Rags to Riches: subjects must have started in straitened circumstances and now be verifiably wealthy.

Recipe for a Happy Marriage: (celeb)

Reveal Personality: interesting how mannerisms, habits, etc. show us what we're really like.

Success Without College: subject must be well-known or be associated with a well-known venture.

Woman at the Top: must be well known.

Women's Interest: fashion, beauty, etc.

Young Achiever: kids, preferably under 20, who've achieved fame or fortune through their own endeavor (not showbiz).

Quiz: relatively light—often psychological (such as "How Brave Are You?") or general knowledge ("How Much You Know About Such and Such?")

Categories: Nonfiction—Adventure—Alternate Lifestyles—Animals—Arts—Biography—Entertainment—Fashion—Government—Health—New Age—Physical Fitness—Relationships—Science—Self-Help—Sexuality—Celebrities—Astrology—Medicine—UFO experiences/research—How-to—Human Interest—Diet—Education—Women's Issues

Name: Charlie Montgomery, Articles Editor
Material: All
Address: 600 EAST COAST AVENUE
City/State/ZIP: LANTANA, FLORIDA 33464
Telephone: 800-628-5697 ext. 2216
Fax: 800-336-3973

National Geographic Magazine

Does not accept unsolicited submissions.

National Geographic Traveler

Thank you for your interest in contributing to *National Geographic Traveler*, which is a bimonthly publication of the National Geographic Society. *Traveler*'s purpose, like that of its parent organization, is to increase and diffuse geographic knowledge, and it does so by making the subject of travel more interesting, meaningful, and enjoyable for its readers.

What types of stories does *Traveler* publish?

Every issue contains several regular departments and five or six features, each presented with a mixture of text and photography. The majority of *Traveler* features are on U.S. subjects, but about 30 percent cover Canadian and other foreign destinations, particularly Europe. Generally, we are interested in places accessible to most travelers, not just the intrepid or wealthy.

Traveler features are usually narrow in scope; we do not cover whole states or countries, other than small nations. Subjects of particular interest to us are national and state parks, historic places, cities, museums, little-known or undiscovered places, train trips, cruises, and scenic drives. Service information is generally given separately at the end of each feature in a section that includes how to get to the destination, things to see and do there, and where to obtain more information. This section is prepared by the *Traveler* staff, although the writer is expected to send along as much service information as possible with the manuscript. We also publish nondestination service pieces on such subjects as money, health, regional food, recreation and educational vacations, ecotourism, travel bargains, and any other topics that will enlighten our readers about the world of travel and help them find ways to explore the world more easily and enjoyably.

What kinds of proposals is *Traveler* looking for?

We do not actively solicit proposals for feature articles, since nearly all ideas for features are generated by the *Traveler* staff and are assigned to freelance writers from our roster of regular contributors. We do assign features to new writers on occasion, but only to those whose published clips demonstrate the highest level of writing skill. We do not accept phone queries. And please do not send us unsolicited manuscripts for feature articles.

We do not accept freelance queries or manuscripts for the following departments, which are written by contributing editors: Bulletin, By the Way, Highlights, Learning Vacations, and Photography. We do accept freelance queries for these departments: Ecotouring, Foods of the Region, Journeys, Learning Vacations, Traveling Easy, Value Vacations, and Weekends. For Ecotouring we only seek proposals that incorporate ecology or an ecotourism issue; a simple nature-travel story is not enough. For Foods of the Region we are only interested in ideas from freelancers who have credentials as food writers. For Value Vacations we are looking for writers who have a feel for budget travel and who know a place or a subject well. We do not accept proposals about trips that are subsidized in any way.

How should an idea be proposed?

Proposals should be no more than two pages long, and should highlight why the piece would be of interest to *Traveler* readers, who are mostly middle-aged, well educated, and well traveled. Check the *Traveler* index, published each year in the January/February issue, to make sure we have not recently run a piece on the topic you are proposing. Include your credentials and relevant published clippings of travel writing that give clear evidence of your ability to write vividly. Prospective contributors doing preliminary research for a story must avoid giving the impression that they are representing the National Geographic Society or *Traveler*. They may use the name of the magazine only if they have a definite assignment. When *Traveler* gives an assignment to a writer or photographer, the terms are clearly stated in a written contract.

How long are *Traveler* feature stories and departments?

Most *Traveler* features range from 1,000 to 3,500 words, depending on the subject. *Traveler* departments generally run from 750 to 1,500 words. Payment is approximately $1 a word, upon acceptance. We buy all rights to manuscripts.

What does *Traveler* look for in writing style?

The best advice: Read and study the magazine. In general,

Traveler features avoid a guidebook approach. Although we do not wish to impose rigid restrictions on a writer's style, we have found that our most successful contributions share certain characteristics, notably a strong sense of the author's personality and experiences, vivid reporting, a high literary quality, and, in the case of service-oriented departments, meaty practical information. We want our articles to be strongly evocative of a place, as well as explain what's of interest to see and do there. We want our readers to finish reading each story with the feeling that they've shared in the experience of visiting the destination and learned something of value as well.

The Editors
National Geographic Traveler
Categories: Nonfiction—Consumer—Ecology—Economics—Food/Drink—Health—Money/Finance—Photography—Regional—Sports—Recreation—Travel—Education

Name: Richard Busch, Editor
Material: All
Address: NATIONAL GEOGRAPHIC SOCIETY
      17TH & M STS. NW
City/State/ZIP: WASHINGTON, DC 20036
Telephone: 202-775-6700
Fax: 202-828-6640
Internet: nationalgeographic.com/media/traveler

National Parks Magazine

The National Parks and Conservation Association (NPCA) is the nation's only private nonprofit citizen organization dedicated solely to protecting, preserving, and enhancing the U.S. National Park System. An association of "Citizens Protecting America's Parks," NPCA was founded in 1919, and today has more than 500,000 members.

Subject Matter: NPCA publishes articles about areas in the National Park System, proposed new areas, threats to parks or park wildlife, new trends in park use, legislative issues, and endangered species of plants or animals relevant to national parks.

Queries: *Query first*, enclosing samples/clips of your work. Include a brief outline of your idea(s) with submission.

Submissions: Material submitted for publication in *National Parks* is considered on speculation. We are not obligated to buy a manuscript, including stories we assign, until we have read it. We do, however, pay a 33-1/3 percent kill fee if we find an assigned story unacceptable.

We do not accept unsolicited manuscripts. Payment for articles is made upon acceptance and after all parties sign a purchase agreement. *National Parks* uses professional writers, but a meticulous writer who approaches the subject in a fresh, new manner has been known to catch our attention, even if new to the field.

Copyright: NPCA buys first North American serial rights and copyrights articles as part of the collective work, National *Parks.* Authors must warrant their manuscripts as original and unpublished. Articles published in our magazine must not be subsequently published elsewhere without our permission. (Policy on reprint permission is liberal, however, and permission may be negotiated.) Authors are responsible for obtaining any necessary permission to quote from other publications and to reproduce copyrighted photographs or artwork. Enclose permission letters with material submitted. Occasionally *National Parks* will consider excerpts from books by accomplished authors on relevant topics for use in the magazine.

Editing: Manuscripts accepted are subject to our editing; however, we send authors a copy of the edited script for their approval before publication. In case of disputes, we have final

word, but prefer to negotiate an agreement acceptable to everyone. NPCA does not guarantee publication of manuscripts, even if accepted.

Writing: Articles for *National Parks* should be directed to a largely nonscientific but well educated audience. Features run approximately 2,000 words. Articles should have an original slant or news hook and cover a limited subject, rather than attempt to treat a broad subject superficially. Specific examples, descriptive details, and quotes are always preferable to generalized information. The writer must be able to document factual claims, and statements should be clearly substantiated with evidence within the article. *National Parks* does not publish fiction, poetry, personal essays, or "My trip to..." stories.

Photographs: When submitting photographs, identify each with your name, subject, social security number, and credit requirements. Provide a caption sheet, typed, double-spaced, and keyed by number on photo. Query before sending photos to eliminate inconveniences. *National Parks* rarely uses unsolicited photos. We prefer that you send a stock list, biographical information, and samples we can keep, such as postcards, tear sheets, etc., first.

Color Transparencies: Do not send color prints or negatives. We prefer sharp, clear 35mm slides, 2¼", or 4"x5" positive color transparencies for best printing reproduction. Transparencies should be protected with cardboard or in rigid slide mailers. Do not send glass-covered slides unless absolutely necessary. These tend to crack and mar slides in transit. We must have original transparencies for printing. All originals will be returned by Federal Express.

Note: *National Parks* is color throughout.
Photography rates:
  Less than 1/2 page: $100 Full page plus: $175
  One-half or more: $125 Full spread: $200
  Full page: $150 Cover shot: $500

Photographers are paid within 30 days after publication. Please remember to include social security number. Three copies of the magazine will be sent after publication.

Subjects covered: We use scenics, historical structures, landform details, plants, animals, and actions shots of people that relate to the parks in the United States. We look for new subjects. A good mix for a general-interest park story would include close ups, scenics, mid-range shots, showing different times of day, a range of lighting situations, plus horizontals and verticals of the best scenics. We'd rather see more transparencies than fewer, but please be selective; send the best of the widest variety.

We use only photographs that can accompany articles in the magazine. Photographers should find out our current photo needs before submitting their work. A list of photo needs is available in the second week of even months.

As a nonprofit organization we are unable to pay research or holding fees.

We will send out sample copies upon receipt of a check in the amount of $3.00 and 8½"x11" or larger self-addressed envelope.

Categories: Associations—Conservation—Environment—Outdoors

Name: Linda Rancourt, Managing Editor
Material: All
Address: 1776 MASSACHUSETTS AVE NW STE 200
City/State/ZIP: WASHINGTON DC 20036
Telephone: 202-223-6722
Fax: 202-659-0650
E-mail: EditorNP@aol.com

M-R

National Review

NR isn't a likely place to break in; virtually all our contributors are established writers and/or experts in their fields. In our articles section we publish reports on aspects of the current political or socioeconomic scene—opinionated reporting, not pure opinion. We prefer articles of not more than 2,000 words, and we suggest writers new to NR try a shorter piece, from 900 to 1,500 words.

NR is different enough from other magazines that new writers generally need to read a few issues to understand what we're looking for. It's best to send the articles editor a query by mail before writing an article. (Queries about book reviews should be addressed to the literary editor.)

Categories: Nonfiction—Politics—Public Policy

Name: Andrew Oliver, Articles Editor
Material: All
Address: 215 LEXINGTON AVE
City/State/ZIP: NEW YORK NY 10016
Telephone: 212-679-7330

Natural Health

Writer's Guidelines: While it is *Natural Health*'s policy to read all unsolicited queries and manuscripts, we expect that writers interested in having their work published in *Natural Health* be familiar with the magazine and submit their work accordingly.

We are interested in service-oriented articles that will help readers derive the benefits of natural living. Our stories emphasize body, mind, and spirit self-care through vegan whole foods, supplements, body care, exercise, meditation, visualization, and natural products for the self and the home.

We do not review CDs or videos, publish fiction or poetry, reprint articles from other publications, run articles written by manufacturers, or cover events.

Please send a resume and clips with your detailed query or manuscript. An enclosed SASE will ensure a quicker response. We cannot accept telephone queries.

Categories: Nonfiction—Book Reviews—Conservation—Consumer—Cooking—Ecology—Family—Fashion—Food/Drink—Gardening—Health—Inspirational—New Age—Physical Fitness—Psychology—Self-Help—Spiritual—Nutrition—Holistic Health—How-to—Personal Experience—Education—Beauty—Home—Nature—Religion—Philosophy—Metaphysical—Alternate Lifestyles

Name: Elizabeth Cameron
Material: All
Address: 17 STATION ST., P.O. BOX 1200
City/State/ZIP: BROOKLINE VILLAGE, MA 02147
Telephone: 617-232-1000
Fax: 617-232-1572

NATURAL HISTORY

Natural History

We are a magazine of nature, science, and culture published monthly by the American Museum of Natural History. Articles for *Natural History* are written by scientists, scholars, and writers. We run articles on biological sciences, ecology, cultural and physical anthropology, archaeology, earth sciences, and astronomy.

What all of our writers have in common is a depth of knowledge and thorough understanding of their subject matter. Scientists may write about their own research findings or report upon new findings in their field. Writers may write on their own explorations of some subject of natural or cultural history, but are expected to "do their homework" and give our readers an intimate, insider's look. In every case, the highest standards of writing and research apply. All submissions are subject to review by experts in the field and rigorous fact-checking.

We are not interested in straight conservation or environmental stories. Our interest lies in research on the nature of the species or place that needs saving, or in an exploration of the chemistry or biology of disease or environmental contamination.

The most important thing to do before submitting a proposal to *Natural History* is to look closely at the magazine. We run a range of columns and features. While many are written by staff or regular contributors, we do welcome new submissions. Columns run from 800 to 1,500 words. Columns include: Journal, a short piece of reporting from the field on a timely subject of scientific interest or debate. Findings is a summary of new or ongoing research that poses some new questions, usually written by a scientist about his or her own work. Naturalist At Large is a report from a scientist in the field or a profile of a scientist in the field. The Living Museum is a story that relates to the American Museum of Natural History. We also publish essays, profiles, and commentaries on current events in science.

Features run from 1,500 to 3,500 words and occasionally longer. They are usually accompanied by photographs. Writers may submit photographs but most photography for *Natural History* is commissioned from professional photographers. Often, a photographer will be commissioned to work directly with a scientist or writer.

Discovery is a regular feature. It is the exploration of the natural or cultural history of a specific place where a scientist has done long term research or that a writer has an intimate knowledge of. It is not a travelogue. A Discovery article leads to some special understanding of a place's nature, culture, or the relationship between them.

Article proposals may be submitted at any time. Our article schedules are set at least six months in advance. Please consider this in proposing articles with a time-critical or seasonal connection. (We are glad to work with scientists who would like a general article on their research to appear in *Natural History* the same month their research paper appears in *Nature*, *Science*, or other peer review journal. We will develop the article ahead of time and, if necessary, hold it until the research paper appears.)

Article proposals should be brief. Scientists should accompany their proposals with samples of their published work in the field and/or in general publications. Writers should submit select writing samples from other magazines. Unless arranged beforehand, we do not accept proposals or submissions via fax. Editorial decisions are usually made within two to six weeks. Because of the number of submissions we receive it's not possible for us to comment on the reasons for rejection.

Payment for articles ranges from $500 to $2,500 depending upon length.

Bruce Stutz
Editor-in-Chief
Categories: Nonfiction—Anthropology—Environment—Natural History—Science

Name: Bruce Stutz, Editor-in-Chief
Material: All
Address: AMERICAN MUSEUM OF NATURAL

HISTORY
Address: 79TH ST AT CENTRAL PARK WEST
City/State/ZIP: NEW YORK NY 10024
Telephone: 212-769-5500
Fax: 212-769-5511
E-mail: NHMag@amnh.org
Internet: www.amnh.org

Natural Living Today

NATURAL LIVING TODAY is a contemporary bimonthly magazine geared towards women, 18-35, who are enthusiastic about a natural lifestyle. Our interests include nutrition, beauty, meditation, alternative fitness, holistic medicine, skin care, spas, homeopathic remedies, herbs, etc. We are seeking talented freelance *writers* and *reporters* to take on assignments and offer pitches.

Applicants should write with personality, show reportorial follow-through, and be able to get facts across without being too technical. We feature a creative, fun, upbeat style—informative and entertaining in equal parts. Prior work published in magazines is a plus, but bright beginners are welcome.

Payment varies from $100 to $200 per article. Details, and possible assignments and/or pitches, will be discussed after clips are reviewed.

To apply, please mail or e-mail resumé and writing samples.
Categories: Diet—Health—Lifestyles—Relationships—Sexuality—Women's Issues

Name: Emily Nussbaum, Senior Editor
Material: All
Address: 175 VARICK ST 10TH FLOOR
City/State/ZIP: NEW YORK NY 10014
Telephone: 212-924-1762
Fax: 212-691-7828
E-mail: Naturalliv@aol.com

Naturally

OVERVIEW:
For the average American, a vacation is a period of travel and relaxation when you take twice the clothes and half the money you need. And for nude vacationers? Well, the latter is still true, but the places where you spend that money are oh-so-different!

NATURALLY nude recreation looks at why millions of people believe that removing clothes in public is a good idea, and at places specifically created for that purpose-with good humor, but also in earnest. NATURALLY nude recreation takes you to places where your personal freedom is the only agenda, and to places where textile-free living is a serious commitment.

NATURALLY nude recreation invokes the philosophies of naturism and nudism, but also activities and beliefs in the mainstream that express themselves, barely: spiritual awareness, New Age customs, pagan and religious rites, alternative and fringe lifestyle beliefs, artistic expressions and many individual nude interests. Our higher purpose is simply to help restore our sense of self.

NATURALLY's parent company, Events Unlimited, is a marketing-publishing firm which came out of the naturist movement—a non-membership-based organization with efficient access to the public. Besides NATURALLY, Events Unlimited publishes and distributes educational materials about nude recreation; its attractive Internaturally catalog is known worldwide and will soon be interactive on the Worldwide Web.

NATURALLY showcases nude resorts, nude parks, and other nude service organizations, because their successes assure your future nude recreation vacations. We support public nude beaches, volunteer groups and even private nude homes, because their successes increase public participation. I was going to include "nude recreation in the workplace," but then the boss might not appreciate the part about "recreation."

It's obvious that nudity or nude activities are not philosophies in themselves, but rather products of certain philosophies and ideologies—some of which are deeply rooted in history and social ritual—like nude public bathing and skinny-dipping, meditation and celebration through dance. For most nudist and naturist organizations social nudity, and its benefits, is a serious philosophy and lifestyle commitment that is their main purpose for existence. Other alternative lifestyle groups include nudity ritually, peripherally, or spontaneously, as one of many ways to express cleansing, a celebration of life, and personal freedom.

Although the term "nude recreation" may, for some, conjure up visions of sexual frivolities inappropriate for youngsters—because that can also be technically true—these topics are outside the scope of NATURALLY magazine. Here the emphasis is on the many varieties of human beings, of all ages and backgrounds, recreating in their most natural state, at extraordinary places, their reasons for doing so, and the benefits they derive.

NATURALLY exists to explore these notions of higher personal freedom and recreational possibilities, worldwide. This is our purpose and your invitation to submit your story, articles and pictures.

PHOTOGRAPHY:
NATURALLY's photo policy is liberal We encourage photography at all clothes-free events by courteous and considerate photographers. Although NATURALLY publishes primarily the work of *nudist and naturist* (amateur and professional) photographers, we believe strongly that all who are interested in taking pictures at nude events should be free to do so without extraneous restrictions for purposes of protecting anonymity. Unreasonable photo restrictions connote shame and sabotage the depiction of genuine, open and sincere nude recreation. Of course, we do respect the rights of nudist and naturist clubs to set the rules as hosts. NATURALLY will honor imposed publishing restrictions placed upon some photos by a host.

Photographs taken on public land or in establishments open to the public, do not require photo releases unless intended for commercial use (e.g., in an advertisement, to sell something). However, common courtesy and consideration prevails. Photographs acquired by insensitive methods are not accepted for publication.

Photographs taken in closed private areas, not generally thought of as public, should have releases from all recognizable persons when the photo is not of a newsworthy situation. For a legitimate newsworthy photograph, NATURALLY magazine does not require photo releases, even when the picture is taken on private property. Again, common courtesy and consideration prevails, and photographs acquired by insensitive methods are not accepted for publication. Photo releases are the responsibility of the photographer.

Photographs may be submitted in color or b & w, as prints, negatives, or slides. Slides or negatives yield the highest reproduction quality.

Payment for published photographs include the value of the photo print or transparency. Prints or transparencies that are requested returned, a deduction of $10 per photo is made from payments, otherwise selected photos for publication are retained as file copies for possible future use. Unpublished photos are returned as a matter of procedure, unless there is a good chance for future publication in NATURALLY magazine or other books and magazines published by Events Unlimited.

ORGANIZATIONS:
We support most naturist and nudist groups and organiza-

tions in their endeavor to educate the mainstream about nude recreation. Toward this endeavor, we have chosen a less political and more lighthearted approach. However, articles and/or photos submitted by nudist/naturist organizations, to inform, to promote an event or political agenda, are accepted and appreciated.

Fund-raising appeals are accepted for publication from naturist and nudist organizations. Brevity is requested.

We accept event schedules for publication if open to all comers and dated sufficiently ahead (preferably 5-6 months) to be useful to our readers for at least up to one month after publication.

PAID PARTICIPATION (at time of publication):

All contributors receive copies of NATURALLY magazine in which their material appears.

NATURALLY pays $70 per published page (text and/or visuals). Fractional pages or fillers are pro-rated.

Frequent contributors and regular columnists, who develop a following through NATURALLY, are paid from the Frequent Contributors Budget. Payments increase on the basis of frequency of participation, and the budget is adjusted quarterly as NATURALLY grows.

We purchase news items that are creatively combined and submitted as one major news article. Blurbs or short news write-ups are graciously accepted as contributions to the cause (see unpaid participation).

UNPAID PARTICIPATION & CONTRIBUTIONS:

Published materials, submitted with a commercial agenda, such as product releases, news releases, resort news, etc. are not paid.

Published articles intended to promote a commercial entity, resort or nudist park, organization, group, etc. are not paid. It is generally understood that NATURALLY publishes this material as free promotional/publicity support.

Short news (current events) items and clippings are also appreciated as contributions to the cause of promoting the benefits of clothes-optional freedom.

Opinion pieces are accepted as contributions only when adequately researched.

EXCLUSIVITY:

We accept articles and photos that have been previously published elsewhere, when submitted by the original authors or photographers. However, the value of the material is diminished as a non-exclusive submission. We deduct 30% from previously published submissions if accepted for publication.

ASSIGNMENTS:

When all-expense-paid assignments are awarded, NATURALLY magazine will provide paid travel and accommodation expenses. Food and other routine daily living expenses are not paid for. Additional payments are made for the published article(s) and/or photo(s), based upon the above-stated "Paid Participation" criteria. Articles and photos resulting from assignments are for NATURALLY magazine's exclusive use.

Categories: Travel

Name: Submissions Editor
Material: All
Address: PO BOX 317
City/State/ZIP: NEWFOUNDLAND NJ 07435
Telephone: 201-697-3552
Fax: 201-697-8313
E-mail: naturally@nac.net

> **Remember: Editors change jobs and publishers change addresses. It is wise to invest in a phone call for the current information before submitting.**

NAVY TIMES

Navy Times

Thank you for your interest in *Navy Times*.

We publish an independent newspaper for Navy, Marine Corps and Coast Guard personnel, retirees and their families.

Our newspaper has a circulation of about 90,000 and an estimated readership of about a half million. We are part of the privately owned Army Times Publishing Co., which also publishes the *Army Times, Air Force Times, Federal Times, Defense News* and *Space News.*

WHAT TYPE OF ARTICLES WE WANT: *Navy Times* is interested in well-written freelance articles that are informative, entertaining or stimulating and deal with sea service life. We do not publish fiction or poetry. We do accept opinion and commentary pieces to a maximum of 800 words. We typically pay $75 for commentaries.

We are interested in good, colorful stories. They can highlight how some unit or ship in the Navy, Marine Corps or Coast Guard functions; what life is like on an installation in the United States or overseas; or how some regulation directly affects a service member or his or her family. The stories also can describe special military events; outstanding individual performance; inter- or intraservice sports; interesting characters or trends in sea service lifestyles. Stories should be written "off the news"— that is, they should have a timely reason for being written and reported.

Stories can range in length from 500 to 1,500 words. Payment varies from $125 to about $250. When you send us a query, we'll give you guidance concerning length.

PHOTOS: We are interested in good color photographs or slides, or B&W photographs, to illustrate story submissions. We do want identification of people and objects in the photographs and slides. We prefer receiving a selection to choose from and will pay up to $50 apiece for slides or photographs published.

Submissions should be sent, along with a stamped, self-addressed envelope, to the address below. We prefer to receive both a hard copy and an IBM-compatible 3½" floppy disk on which your submission has been saved in MS Word or "Text only" format. It is better to query us in advance.

If you want to buy a copy of the newspaper to see the kinds of material we use, please call our single copy sales department (800) 424-9335, ext. 7400. Feel free to write or call us to discuss your ideas.

Categories: Military

Name: Submissions Editor
Material: All
Address: 6883 COMMERCIAL DR
City/State/ZIP: SPRINGFIELD VA 22159
Telephone: 703-750-8636
Fax: 703-750-8622
E-mail: NAVYDESK@aol.com

NEBO
A Literary Journal
Arkansas Polytechnic University

Submissions are preferred from August through February.

Please enclose a cover letter with author's name and address, brief bio, a short list of published works, and a SASE. Indicate for return of manuscript if necessary, and use the required amount of postage.

We do not accept simultaneous submissions or previously published material.

Poetry: We accept blank verse, free verse, sonnets, dramatic monologues, etc. No more than five poems per submission.

Fiction: Short-short (up to 750 words) and short stories are the stuff of life and we appreciate all such submissions. Due to space restraints, please limit stories to 2,000 words.

All works must be typed (single-spaced for poetry is acceptable). Please include an approximate word count for short prose fiction.

Advice to Writers

We are interested in quality poetry and fiction by new and established writers. In fiction we are open to a wide range of styles, but ask that the length be kept to 2,000 words (750 for short-shorts). We seek poems whose content is convincing and whose rhythms are as compelling and memorable as their diction and images.

Thank you for your interest in our journal!
Categories: Fiction—Poetry

Name: Dr. Michael Karl Ritchie
Name: Karyn Trahan, Editor
Material: Any
Address: ENGLISH DEPT ARKANSAS TECH UNIVERSITY
City/State/ZIP: RUSSELLVILLE AR 72801-2222
Telephone: 501-968-0487
E-mail: egnebo@atuvm.atu.edu

The Nebraska Review
University of Nebraska-Omaha

Quality, well-crafted literary fiction and poetry. No restrictions on content, style, or length, although fiction generally should not exceed 7,500 words. Longer pieces of exceptional merit will be considered. Response in 3 to 6 months, sometimes sooner.

Please note these submissions deadlines:

Open submission of original fiction and poetry

January 1 - April 15

Fiction manuscripts should include the writer's name and address on the first page.

Poetry may be single-spaced, and should include the writer's name and address on each poem. Standard submission is three to six poems.

Subscriptions: $9.50 per year (2 issues); $18 for two years. Individual copies: $5. Back issues and sample copies: $3.50 when available.

Categories: Fiction—Nonfiction—Literature—Poetry—Short Stories—Writing

Name: Susan Aizenberg, Poetry Editor
Material: Poetry
Name: James Reed, Fiction Editor
Material: Fiction and Nonfiction
Address: PROGRAM IN CREATIVE WRITING
Address: UNIVERSITY OF NEBRASKA-OMAHA
City/State/ZIP: OMAHA NE 68182-0324
Telephone: 402-554-2880

NEBRASKAland Magazine

I. General Information

A. *NEBRASKAland Magazine* is published ten times yearly by the Nebraska Game and Parks Commission, 2200 North 3rd Street, Lincoln, Nebraska, 68503. Current circulation is about 50,000. Monthly issues are 52 pages including covers. Specials, typically published as combined January-February issues, are devoted to a single subject and range from 64 to 148 pages. All issues are illustrated with color and black-and-white photographs and color and monochrome art.

B. The magazine's content reflects its broad, general-interest audience and the specific concerns of its publisher, the Nebraska Game and Parks Commission. All articles have a strong Nebraska association. Subject matter includes all varieties of outdoor recreation including hunting, fishing, camping, canoeing and the like, Nebraska parks, wildlife, natural history, scenic areas, unique personalities, art, culture, history and personal reminiscence.

C. About 90 percent of the articles and photographs published in *NEBRASKAland* Magazine are produced by magazine staff writers and photographers. The magazine welcomes submissions from readers and freelance writers and photographers, but with rare exceptions, payment is in subscriptions and copies only.

II. Guidelines for Writers

A. *NEBRASKAland* welcomes high-quality articles with a Nebraska slant. Topics may include any of those listed above. Serious or light and humorous treatments are acceptable. "How-to" articles are welcome. Fiction and poetry are rarely used. Product promotions are not used. Queries are encouraged.

B. First person narratives ("Me and Joe" stories) are likely to be published only if they describe a unique experience, go beyond the simple details of a hunting or fishing trip or are uniquely reminiscent of Nebraska's past.

C. Submissions accompanied by appropriate illustration (photos or art) or appropriate suggestions for illustration stand a better chance of acceptance than does text alone. See photo guidelines for more information.

D. Stories average about 2,500 words, but lengths range from about 800 words to about 4,000 words.

E. Submit typed manuscripts. Computer print-outs are acceptable. Floppy disks (IBM compatible, WordPerfect or ASCII text files) are acceptable, but should be accompanied by a paper copy of the submission. The author's full address and telephone number must accompany every submission, and the author's name should appear on every manuscript page.

F. Seasonal material should be submitted at least six months before anticipated publication. Final acceptance is usually made only after full editorial staff review. It will usually be several weeks or more before authors will be notified concerning acceptance or rejection. Scheduling decisions are ordinarily made three times a year, and accepted material is often published on a "space available" basis; thus authors should be prepared to have accepted manuscripts held for a year or more.

G. The editor reserves the right to make any editorial modifications necessary. The editor regrets that a detailed evaluation of rejected work cannot be provided.

III. Guidelines for Photographers

A. An average issue of *NEBRASKAland* contains up to about 30 color photographs and up to 10 black-and-white photographs. More than 90 percent of the photos published are taken by staff photographers. *NEBRASKAland* welcomes the submission of high-quality color slides and black-and-white photographs that illustrate Nebraska's wildlife, parks and recreation areas, outdoor activities, scenery and history.

Photos must be razor sharp and properly exposed. We are unlikely to use "blood and guts" bag shots or scenes in which alcohol, cigarettes or blatant advertising are prominent. All hunting and fishing activity pictured must clearly conform to the appropriate legal regulations and to high ethical standards. All scenes must be from Nebraska. Model releases must be available upon request. Previously unpublished photos are preferred.

B. Single-subject or thematically related groups of photos stand a better chance of publication than do individual shots or unrelated groups. See past issues of *NEBRASKAland* for examples of the "color spread" photo essay.

C. Photos accompanied by appropriate text, or with suggestions for accompanying text, stand a better chance of publication than do unaccompanied photos.

D. Color: Only original transparencies (slides), 35mm and larger, will be considered for publication. Color prints are not acceptable. Clearly labeled duplicate transparencies are acceptable for review, but originals must be made available for publication. Transparencies should be submitted in protective slide pages. The photographer's name must appear on each slide mount or protective sleeve. Captions or descriptions keyed to each photo by number are encouraged.

E. Black-and-White: Submit 5"x7" or 8"x10" prints on glossy or matte-finish paper (no heavily textured specialty papers). Do not send negatives or contact sheets. The photographer's name and a photo caption or description should be attached to each photo.

F. If photos are accepted for publication, layout, photo cropping and placement of photo credits and captions will be at the designer's discretion. Caption content will be at the editor's discretion.

G. Seasonal material should be submitted at least six months before anticipated publication. A minimum four months lead-time is required. Scheduling decisions are ordinarily made three times a year, and photos accepted for publication might be held for six months or more.

H. *NEBRASKAland* cannot provide a detailed critique of rejected photographs.

Categories: Environment—Fishing—Hunting—Outdoors—Recreation—Regional—Travel

Name: Don Cunningham, Editor
Name: Tim Reigert, Art Director
Material: As Appropriate
Address: PO BOX 30370
City/State/ZIP: LINCOLN NE 68503
Telephone: 402-471-0641
Fax: 402-471-5528
E-mail: nebland@ngpsun.ngpc.stste.ne.us

Nedge
The Poetry Mission

NEDGE publishes primarily poetry, as well as some *short* fiction, essays, reviews, and black & white artwork. The magazine comes out irregularly, about twice each year. Circulation is small but growing. Payment, we are sorry to say, is minimal: 1 contributor's copy. Each issue is perfect-bound and runs roughly 75-100 pp. Sample copy: $6.00. Back issues (1-4) are available for the same price.

All submissions should be by snail mail (no e-mail) and include SASE. We read no simultaneous submissions. Response time is 1-2 months. We accept less than 5% of material submitted for publication.

NEDGE began in 1969 as HARBINGER; the name was changed in the mid-70s to NORTHEAST JOURNAL and in the late 1980's to NEDGE. The magazine has moved gradually from being a regional RI literary journal toward something more cosmopolitan and experimental. We are interested in original and authentic writing, and aim for an eclectic middle path between the past and the future. We are grateful for unsolicited manuscripts, and welcome "unknown" writers; however, we accept very

little for publication, and a rejection should not be an occasion for discouragement.

For more information on the content of issues 1-4, and other Poetry Mission publications, see our citation in the Electronic Poetry Center's literary magazine archive at the Internet address shown below.

Thank you for your interest in our magazine.
Sincerely,
The Editors
Categories: Poetry

Name: Henry Gould, Co-editor
Name: Janet Sullivan, Co-editor
Material: Any
Address: PO BOX 2321
City/State/ZIP: PROVIDENCE RI 02906
Internet: www.wings.buffalo.edu/epc/mags/nedge

Nevada Magazine

Nevada Magazine is constantly searching for stories and photographs that tell the story of Nevada.

Stories and photos are accepted on speculation. Recommended subjects include Nevada's people, history recreation, entertainment, events, towns, and scenery. If you have another Nevada topic you'd like to write about, we'd be happy to hear your suggestion. However, if your article is about a Nevada character in Europe, or a recreational article that takes place half the time in California, it probably won't work. Keep in mind that the magazine's purpose is to promote tourism in Nevada.

Payment is on publication and varies with article length and the size and quality of photographs. We encourage you to submit photos with your stories. Most stories range between 500 and 1,800 words. Fees range from $75 to $400 for words and $25 to $150 for photos and illustrations. The magazine buys first North American rights.

Manuscripts should be typed with a suggested title, byline, and writer's credit. Your name, address, phone(s), and social security number should be on the first page of the manuscript, and be sure to leave ample margins on the sides and bottom of each page.

If you use a Macintosh, IBM, or IBM compatible, you're welcome to submit your story on a disk. We use Macintoshes to produce the magazine. Our software program, Microsoft Word, can convert most Macintosh word processing programs, and IBM-type programs can be converted. Be sure to indicate which program has been used. Please include a hard copy. You also can e-mail queries to the address below.

For color photographs, we prefer transparencies (35mm slides and larger) to color prints, although good color prints can be used. With black-and-white photos, we prefer 8"x10" glossies. If you send 35mm slides, please present them in see-through sleeves. Write your name, address, and identification of the subject on each slide or photograph. With prints, make sure the ink you use won't show through the opposite side.

The editors reserve the right to edit all material and cannot guarantee against damage to, or loss of, any materials. However, we will make every effort to handle submissions as if they were our own, and to work with writers and photographers. You can help by sending a self-addressed, stamped envelope with your material to ensure its safe return. Please allow four or five weeks for reply.

I look forward to hearing from you.
Carolyn Graham
Associate Editor
Categories: Nonfiction—Regional—Travel
Name: Carolyn Graham, Associate Editor

Name: David Moore, Editor
Address: 1800 HWY 50 E STE 200
City/State/ZIP: CARSON CITY NV 89710
Telephone: 702-687-5416
Fax: 702-687-6159
E-mail: nevmag@aol.com

New Choices

Dear Writer: Thank you for your interest in *New Choices* for Retirement Living, a news and service magazine for active, mature adults in their pre-retirement and retirement years (median age: 60).

As you'll note from studying the magazine, our topics include planning for retirement, personal health and fitness, finance strategies, housing options, travel, profiles/interviews (celebrities and newsmakers), relationships, leisure pursuits and various other lifestyle/service subjects. Features generally run between 750 and 2,000 words.

We prefer queries to manuscripts, except for personal essays and humor articles, which may be submitted on spec. Queries should be accompanied by 2 or 3 relevant samples of your writing.

Your chances for getting an assignment will improve if you put some real work into the query (statistics/original quotes to make your case, names of experts you d speak to, etc.). Of course, you must specifically target our readers - the story you propose should be tailor-made for *New Choices* and no other magazine.

Queries and manuscripts should be sent to the attention of Allen J. Sheinman, articles editor, and must be accompanied by a self-addressed, stamped envelope if you want your materials returned. All manuscripts should be typed, double-spaced and easy to read. Do keep a copy for yourself of whatever you send us. (Do not send original slides and photographs that can't be replaced.) Replies to unsolicited material take from 4 to 8 weeks. We cannot accept telephone calls regarding receipt of or response to your material.

Thanks for your interest.

Categories: Nonfiction—Cooking—Food/Drink—Health—Interview—Money/Finance—Physical Fitness—Relationships—Sports—Recreation—Travel—Home—Retirement—Celebrities—Profiles—Essay—Taxes

Name: Allen J. Sheinman, Articles Editor
Material: All
Address: 28 W. 23RD ST.
City/State/ZIP: NEW YORK, NY 10010
Telephone: 212-366-8600
Fax: 212-366-8786
Internet: www.seniornews.com/new-choices/

New England Review
Middlebury College

New England Review is published four times a year: winter, spring, fall, and summer. However, our reading period is September 1 through May 31 (postmark dates) only. Any submissions that arrive during the summer will be returned unread.

We consider short fiction, including shorts, short-shorts, novellas, and self-contained extracts from novels. We consider a variety of general and literary, but not narrowly scholarly, nonfiction: long and short poems; speculative, interpretive, and personal essays; book reviews; screenplays; translations; critical reassessments; statements by artists working in various media; interviews; testimonies; and letters from abroad. We are committed to exploration of all forms of contemporary cultural expression in the United States and abroad. With few exceptions, we print only work not published previously elsewhere.

We suggest that you peruse a copy of NER to see what our standards and preferences are. The current issue is available for $7.00 from the better bookstores or post paid (add $2 for overseas surface delivery, $3 for air mail) from Subscription/Order Department, University Press of New England, 23 South Main Street, Hanover, NH 03755-2048.

Prose: maximum of thirty pages in length (except novellas, of course). Please send just one piece at a time, unless the pieces are very short.

Poems: send no more than six at once, please. Good photocopies are acceptable. Brief cover letters are useful.

Please do not send another submission until hearing about the first. We cannot accommodate changes, revisions, or forgotten SASEs. Additional manuscripts will be returned unread. We will consider submissions that have been offered simultaneously to other publications, as long as you withdraw your submission immediately upon acceptance elsewhere.

NER will respond to your submission within twelve weeks. After twelve weeks have passed, you may query as to the status of your submission by mail or phone, but we will respond by postcard only, in the order received. If you call, please wait until after 7:00 P.M. EST, and leave your name, address, phone number, and the postmark date of your submission on our voice mail.

A contract is sent on acceptance, and payment is ten dollars per page, twenty dollars minimum, plus two free copies of the issue your work appears in, upon publication. Authors receive pre-publication galleys. Copyright reverts to the author upon publication. *New England Review* retains the right under copyright law to reprint your work only as part of a whole volume—in a *New England Review* anthology or re-issue, for example—or in publicity materials.

LETTERS TO THE EDITOR

We invite your response to what we publish, and are open to reasoned expression of alternative points of view. For those who prefer e-mail, our address is shown below.

Categories: Fiction—Essays—Literature—Poetry

Name: Stephen Donadio, Editor
Material: Fiction, Poetry, Literary Essays
Address: MIDDLEBURY COLLEGE
City/State/ZIP: MIDDLEBURY VT 05753
Telephone: 802-443-5075
E-mail: NEREVIEW@mail.middlebury.edu.

New Home Life

New Home Life is a lifestyle magazine directed towards homeowners and new homebuyers. The publication is published every 60 days and focuses on quality living in Northeast Florida. Editorial copy is written by many of the best writers in the state. Photography is taken by some of the nation's most talented photographers. Articles cover the complete gamut of individual interest from moving into or purchasing a new home to decorating and recreational activities.

In Every Issue:
Local Builder and Business Profiles
Community Locator Map
Bed & Breakfast Inn Reviews
Categories: Nonfiction—Lifestyles—Outdoors—Physical Fitness—Recreation—Travel

Name: Lani Barna, Editor
Material: All
Address: 179 WELLS RD
City/State/ZIP: ORANGE PARK FL 32073

Telephone: 904-264-0008
Fax: 9041-269-9149

New Letters
University of Missouri-Kansas City

Dear Writer,

Thanks for your interest in *New Letters*. Although we do not have any formal writers' guidelines, here are a few suggestions:

• We prefer that you send no more than six poems or two short stories per submission.

• We prefer shorter stories to longer ones. An average length is 3,500 words.

• We have no rigid preferences as to subject, style or genre, although "commercial" efforts tend to put us off. Even so, our only fixed requirement is on *good* writing.

• We discourage multiple submissions, but appreciate knowing if you're sending your work to us and someone else simultaneously.

• Like most literary magazines, our staff is small, so our reporting time varies from 6-18 weeks. Sorry.

• We do not read submissions between May 15 and October 15.

Sample copies are available from this office for $5.50. We pay the postage if you prepay.

I hope this information is helpful.

Cordially,
James McKinley
Editor

Categories: Fiction—Literature—Poetry—Short Stories

Name: James McKinley, Editor
Material: All
Address: UNIVERSITY HOUSE
Address: 5101 ROCKHILL RD
City/State/ZIP: KANSAS CITY MO 64110
Telephone: 816-235-1168
Fax: 816-235-2611

New Mexico Magazine

New Mexico Magazine examines the people, culture, arts, history and landscape of New Mexico for an educated readership, two-thirds of whom live outside the state. Monthly magazine, 64 to 100 pages. Established 1923. Circulation: 125,000. Pays on acceptance for manuscripts, on publication for photos. Buys first North American serial or one-time rights for photos and artwork. Query first. Buys few manuscripts on speculation. Plans issues 6-12 months in advance. SASE. We reply in 4-6 weeks. Sample copy $2.95.

Articles: Profile, travel, historical (examining little-known facets of New Mexico history or shedding new light on major events and personalities of the past), humor, Southwest lifestyles (food, fashion, homes, gardens), arts and crafts, cultural topics (traditional ways of life, customs, unusual celebrations, social trends), photo features, offbeat science and business stories. Buys 7-10 manuscripts/issue. Send published writing samples with query. Length: 250-2,000 words. Pays $100-$600. (We do not publish poetry or fiction).

Style: Type name, address and phone number in the upper left corner of manuscript. Double- or triple-space text. Number pages. Typed manuscript or computer diskette. Include two or three sentences of biographical information about author at conclusion of story.

How to Break In: Send a superb short (250 to 500 words) manuscript on an unusual event, facet of history, person or place to see in New Mexico. Accurate research, strong writing, lively style, please.

Rejects: No generalized odes to the state or the Southwest. No sentimentalized, paternalistic views of Indians or Hispanics. No story ideas covered by the magazine in the past four years. Only topics relating to New Mexico and the Southwest.

Categories: Regional—Book Reviews—Travel—Western

Name: Jon Bowman, Editor
Material: Book Reviews, Features
Name: Emily Drabanski, Editor-in-Chief
Material: Features
Address: 495 OLD SANTA FE TRAIL
City/State/ZIP: SANTA FE NM 87501
Telephone: 505-827-7447
Fax: 505-827-6496

New Millennium Writings

Now accepting submissions for *New Millennium* Awards IV for Fiction, Poetry and Nonfiction $2,000 in Cash Prizes, Plus Publication ($1,000 for best story; $500 for best poem; $500 for best nonfiction).

Twenty-five runners-up received Certificates of Honorable Mention and were named in the Fall '97 Issue of NMW.

1. All winners and selected finalists will be published in the Fall issue, which will feature interviews, new and noteworthy writings, photographs and illustrations. **All contestants receive a copy.**

2. There are no restrictions as to style, content, format, or number of submissions. Keep entries to no more than 25 typed, double-spaced pages of prose or five pages of poetry (three poems). No previously published material accepted.

3. Deadlines are June 16 (postmarked by then) and January 16 (twice annually).

4. **Send a $10 check payable to NMW with each submission.**

5. Each piece of fiction or nonfiction prose (essay, article, interview, etc.) is counted as a separate submission. Each Poetry submission may include up to three poems. Simultaneous and/or multiple submissions welcomed.

6. Include name, phone number, address and category (Fiction, Poetry, or Nonfiction Prose) with each submission. Paper clips preferred, but staples O.K.

7. Manuscripts will not be returned except in hardship cases (printer broken? no computer? Include SASE in such instances). We do recycle. **Winners and finalists will be notified in August.** Enclose business-size SASE for list.

Judges and editorial advisors include: Novelists and short story writers Jon Manchip White and Allen Wier; Poets Lisa Coffman and Marilyn Kallet; Journalists and essayists Fred Brown, David Hunter and Don Williams, editor.

To subscribe only, send $14.95 to "Subscribe" at the address below. For pre-contest sample copy, send $8; Phone for more information.

Categories: Fiction—Nonfiction—Literature—New Age—Philosophy—Poetry—Science Fiction—Short Stories—Spiritual—Travel—Writing

Name: Dan Williams, Editor
Material: All
Address: NMW CONTEST ROOM 101
Address: PO BOX 2463
City/State/ZIP: KNOXVILLE TN 37901
Telephone: 423-428-0389
Nota bene: Contest entry fee required.

New Moon
The Magazine for Girls and Their Dreams

Objectives of *New Moon:*

New Moon portrays girls and women as powerful, active and in charge of their own lives—*not* as passive beings who are acted upon by others. *New Moon* celebrates girls and their accomplishments. *New Moon* supports girls' efforts to hold onto their voices, strengths and dreams as they move from being girls to becoming women. *New* Moon is a tool for a girl to use as she builds resilience and resistance to our sexist society, moving confidently out into the world, pursuing her unique path in life.

New Moon strives to

• be an international, multicultural magazine which connects girls and celebrates diversity by providing a place for girls to express themselves and communicate with other girls around the world.

• portray strong female role models of all ages, backgrounds, and cultures now and in the past.

• encourage pursuit of interests in which girls are often discouraged, e.g. math, science, and physical activity.

• acknowledge the difficulties and celebrate the joys of being female in the world.

• understand that respecting girls, attending to their needs and giving them voice and power means upsetting the fabric of society.

Therefore, we seek high-quality literary and artistic work which has a diversity of cultural and stylistic influences, and represents real connection with girls.

General Guidelines:

All material should be pro-girl and focus on girls, women, or female issues. *New Moon* was created by girls and women for girls who want their voices heard and their dreams taken seriously. It is edited by and for girls ages 8-14. *New Moon* takes girls very seriously; the publication is structured to give girls real power. The final product is a collaboration of girls and adults. An Editorial Board of girls aged 8-14 makes final decisions on *all* material appearing in the magazine.

1998 Themes

July/Aug. Astronomy, Astrology, and Mythology—January 1, 1998

Sept./Oct. Adventures and Mysteries—March 1, 1998
Nov./Dec. Animals May 1, 1998

1999 Themes

Jan./Feb. Coming of Age—July 1, 1998

Mar./Apr. Business, Power, and Money—September 1, 1998

May/June Writers and Writing—November 1, 1998

July/Aug. Humor and Happiness—January 1, 1999

Sept./Oct. Families—March 1, 1999

Nov./Dec. Preserving the Past and Foreseeing the Future—May 1, 1999

For All Submissions:

Please read a copy of *New Moon* to understand the style and philosophy of the magazine. Writers and artists who comprehend our goals and philosophy have the best chance of publication.

Include your name, address and phone number on the title page of each submitted work or query.

New Moon is not able to respond to queries about submissions over the telephone.

New Moon prints original works, except under special circumstances. If your work has been published previously, note the date and publication. If you are sending this work simultaneously to another publication, please let us know this, too.

For Writers:

New Moon edits manuscripts for style, length, clarity and philosophical considerations.

We prefer e-mail submissions. All other work must be typed, double spaced with one-inch margins. Your name and address should appear on each page. Submit only copies of your work, not originals. We are unable to return submissions.

Nonfiction articles are between 300 and 1,200 words. **Nonfiction profiles of women and girls are preferred.** Nonfiction has better chance for publication when accompanied by several good photographs (b&w preferred), focuses on one of our editorial themes (see above), and uses several quotes. We regularly publish adult nonfiction in our Herstory, Women's Work, and Earth to Girls sections.

New Moon considers only one or two serializations of longer fiction pieces each year, and such fiction must be readily convertible to serialized form. About three-six short fiction pieces (300-1,200 words) are published annually.

For Artists and Photographers:

New Moon has a four-color cover and two-color interior (inside colors change from issue to issue).

For cover guidelines, send us a SASE. Proposals for covers should be sent as drafts, and include examples of earlier, finished artwork. Several drafts may be required in the multi-step process by which the Girls Editorial Board chooses a cover.

Photographs and inside art should be submitted in black and white. Please send copies, or photos of art, since we cannot be responsible for unsolicited original works. **Do not send negatives or your only copy of a slide.**

Attach your name, address, phone number, media used and date of work to the back of the work. Please include clear, specific instructions (if needed) for reproduction, processing and layout of your work.

Categories: Fiction—Nonfiction—Children—Feminism—Teen—Women's Issues—Young Adult

Name: Barbara Stretchberry, Managing Editor
Material: All
Address: PO BOX 3620
City/State/ZIP: DULUTH MN 55803-3620
Telephone: 218-728-5507
Fax: 218-728-0314
E-mail: newmoon@computerpro.com

New Odyssey Review
Thomas Jefferson University Press

Submit up to ten poems, each on a separate page. If you're interested in reviewing books of poetry, please send a letter expressing your interest along with a curricula vita.

Please note: the first issue of the *Review* is planned for spring of 1999 or 2000.

Don't hesitate to contact New Odyssey Press for more information.

Categories: Poetry

Name: Timothy Rolands, Poetry Editor
Material: All
Address: 100 E NORMAL ST MC111L

City/State/ZIP: KIRKSVILLE MO 63501-4221
Telephone: 816-785-7299
Fax: 816-785-4181
E-mail: newodyssey@tjup.truman.edu
Internet: www.tjup.truman.edu/newodyssey

the new renaissance

At *the new renaissance* (*tnr*), we're looking for writing that has something to say, says it with style and grace, and, above all, speaks in a personal voice.

FICTION: Contemporary, literary, off-beat, translations, humor, satire, prose/poems and, occasionally, experimental fiction. We don't want to see popular or slick writing, overly academic or sentimental fiction, or strictly commercial pieces. Also, no pornography. One story per submission unless stories are four pages or less, then two stories are allowed.

We are especially interested in fiction that offers a revelation or illumination on the human condition. Although we stress substance, style is important, and we pay close attention to diction, phrasing, and personal vision.

Approximations in language are just not good enough. Since we accept only one ms out of every 125 submissions, we ask writers to read *tnr* closely and to send in stories that are at least as good, however different, as those we've been publishing. Mss. can be two to 36 pps. although we will occasionally accept a longer work. We are interested in translations (send originals). Allow 4-5 months for a decision.

POETRY: Contemporary, lyrical, narrative, humorous and satirical poems are OK, but we don't want pornography or obscenity. Eroticism will be considered. We are especially interested in poetic imagery ground in experience. No greeting card verse.

Mss. of 3-6 one-page poems, or 2-4 two-page poems are preferred, but we occasionally publish the long poem; only one long poem per submission, please. We are especially interested in translations (send originals). Allow 2-4 months for a decision.

SUBMITTING PERIODS: [1997] January through May; and September and October.

HOW TO SUBMIT: All fiction and poetry submissions are tied to our award programs: The Louise E. Reynolds Memorial Fiction Award and a poetry award. These awards have been established in order to honor *tnr*'s Founding Manager, Louise E. Reynolds, to reward *tnr*'s writers, and to promote quality writing. Only writers published in a three-issue volume are eligible.

Independent judges will determine winners. Winners from Vol. IX, Nos. 1-3 were announced in the Fall of 1996; Vol. X, Nos. 1-3, will be announced in the Spring of 1998. All published writers will receive our regular, nominal rates of payment as well as a copy of the issue containing their work. There are three awards in each category: *Fiction*: $500.00, $250.00, and $100.00. Honorable Mention $35.00. Poetry: $250.00, $125.00, and $50.00, with three honorable mentions for poetry ($20.00 each).

Current subscribers: Send ms. with SASE or IRC, and $10.00 entry fee ($11.50 foreign). Each discipline and each submission requires an entry fee. **You may extend your subscription or receive two back issues or a recent issue.**

All others: Send ms. with SASE or IRC, and $15.00 entry fee ($16.50 foreign). **You will receive two back issues or a recent issue.** Each discipline and each submission requires an entry fee.

Categories: Fiction—Nonfiction—Culture—Film/Video—General Interest—Interview—Literature—Multicultural—Music—Poetry—Politics—Short Stories—Television/Radio—Theatre

Name: Louise T. Reynolds, Editor-in-Chief
Material: All
Address: 26 HEATH RD STE 11

City/State/ZIP: ARLINGTON MA 02174-3645
Nota bene: Entry fee required.

Newsday

Dear Contributor,
Thank you for your interest in writing for *Newsday*.
We require that all manuscripts be submitted on spec providing that no trip has been subsidized in any way. Proof of payment will be required if story is accepted for publication.

If you have original slides, please do not include them with the manuscript. Duplicate slides or glossies are acceptable. Or indicate that photos are available. *Newsday* does not take responsibility for art submitted with unsolicited manuscripts.

Stories generally run about 1,200 words, plus 300 words for an If You Go box. Payment runs between $75 and $400, depending on usage. We pay extra for use of your photographs.

Please include self-addressed envelope with all submissions.
Looking forward to your manuscript,
Marjorie Robins
Travel Editor
Categories: Travel

Name: Marjorie Robins, Travel Editor
Material: Travel
Address: 235 PINELAWN RD
City/State/ZIP: MELVILLE NY 11747-4250
Telephone: 516-843-2980
Fax: 516-843-2065
E-mail: Travel@newsday.com
Internet: www.newsday.com

Newswaves
for Deaf and Hard-of-Hearing People

Welcome!
Thanks for your interest in writing for *Newswaves*. We aim to be the first real newspaper in the deaf and hard-of-hearing community. Instead of printing the same old press releases, newspaper clippings and "things people send in," we are building a staff of good writers who can produce fresh material on subjects in the news today.

We print the kind of stories that people want to read. We go beyond the press releases and find out the real story. We answer the questions our readers have on their minds. We emphasize short feature articles that are tightly focused and make every word count. And we emphasize photographs; it's a rare feature that will run without any illustrations.

What to write about
Before you approach us with a story idea, make sure you've seen at least one issue of *Newswaves* and understand the approach we are taking. You can request a sample issue for $2 postage paid.

There are two approaches you can take:
1. Hi, I'd like to write for *Newswaves*. What do you want me to write about?
2. Hi, I'd like to write for *Newswaves*. I know a deaf woman who just won a million dollars in the lottery. Want me to write about her?

The second approach is better. It isn't good for the editor to come up with all the story ideas. It's better for the writers to develop their own ideas.

Where do you get ideas? Get on the mailing lists of all the deaf and hard-of-hearing organizations in your area and scour their newsletters. Keep an eye open for interesting and unusual things you come across in your everyday life. Look at bulletin boards. Go to events and talk with people. Check out Websites related to deaf and hard-of-hearing people. Read a lot and think of ways in which current events affect the hearing impaired. Look for trends. Interview successful people. Interview people in the street.

Getting started

A query letter is the best way to get things started. Here's what it should contain:

1. A brief description of the article. What are you writing about? Why? What makes it timely and/or interesting? Do you have access to sources and information?

2. A projected word count (500 to 1,000 is the target for a feature).

3. How will it be illustrated? Can you borrow photos from your subjects? Can you take pictures yourself? Does the story lend itself to a pen-and-ink illustration? Think of how your story will look on the printed page.

4. Is there any possibility for a sidebar? Sidebars add visual interest and allow you to focus on a specific aspect of your story.

5. What month is this for? When will you complete the assignment? Keep in mind that the deadline is generally the 10th of the month preceding publication, but there is always some flexibility when we know a story is on its way.

6. Will there be any unusual expenses? We can reimburse for reasonable costs (postage, telephone) but anything out of the ordinary should be discussed up front.

Queries may be submitted via e-mail, fax or, when time is not a factor, by traditional mail. Please do not call unless absolutely necessary.

What happens next

Your story idea will either be accepted or declined. If accepted, we may suggest ideas to enhance the story. Details regarding payment, deadline, photos, etc., can then be agreed upon.

If things are going well and you expect to meet the deadline, you don't need to check in. But if problems develop that put your article in jeopardy, then please let us know as soon as possible. We'll be holding space for the article and if it's not going to come in as planned, we need to know.

Sending it in

When your article is done, you have several options to submit it:

1. E-mail. This works best as there is no scanning or typesetting involved. If possible, include your article in the body of your e-mail message rather than as an attachment, since there are sometimes problems with downloaded text if we don't have the program you used.

2. Fax. If you don't have access to e-mail and there isn't enough time to mail the article, you can fax it. But try to print out your article at 12 or 14 points so the type is easy to read. We scan articles into the computer with OCR software and sometimes a fax is not clear enough to scan when the type is small.

3. Mail. If time is not a big factor, you can send your article by traditional mail. There is no need to send a disk; a clear printed copy of the article is fine.

If you are e-mailing or faxing the article, you will still need to send any photos via traditional mail (or FedEx, UPS, etc.) If you know what you're doing, you can try sending scanned photos as files via e-mail.

Deadlines

In general, the deadline is the 10th of the month preceding publication (i.e. Jan. 10 for February issue). This does not mean we go to press on the 11th. Actually there is usually another week to 10 days before the paper is printed, which gives us time to include late-breaking news. But feature articles that have been assigned in advance should come in by the appointed deadline since there is a limit to the amount of last-minute material that can be handled.

Payment

As a new newspaper with a small but growing circulation, *Newswaves* can pay only a modest fee to writers at this time. As the newspaper grows, so will the fees. In general, we pay $25 for a short feature (around 500 words) and $50 for a longer feature (up to 1,000 words). A specific fee will be determined when assigning the article. Payment is made during the month in which the article appears. If you submit an article on time but it is held for a later issue, you will still be paid as if it had appeared as scheduled. It is rare for an assigned article to go unused, but if this should happen we will pay a kill fee of 50% of the agreed-upon payment. If you are taking pictures to accompany your article, we will pay $20 for the first picture used and $10 for any additional photographs from the same assignment.

Rights

We buy first North American serial rights. After an assigned article is published in *Newswaves*, all rights revert to the author. We ask that if you publish the article again in another publication, that you include a credit line stating that it first appeared in *Newswaves*. Any reprint requests that our office receives will be referred to the author. You do not need to check with us if you receive a reprint request directly but again, we'd appreciate a credit line mentioning *Newswaves*.

Headlines

You are welcome to suggest a headline for your story, although it is not required. We are looking for interesting headlines that capture the eye and make people want to read the article. Humor and puns are always welcome (except, of course, in obituaries and other serious articles). Headlines must be an appropriate length to match the article. A one-word headline would usually not work, for example, since it would have to appear in huge type to fill the space. Conversely, a long headline also would not work in most cases. Study a sample issue to get a better idea of the kinds of headlines we use and how long they should be.

Photographs

If you have photography skills, you are welcome to take pictures to accompany your articles. It is better to show people doing something rather than posing for a photograph. If someone is getting an award, show them doing what they did to get the award instead of just standing around holding the award. Always try to get close to your subjects and crop out unnecessary items. Look for unusual angles and interesting backgrounds. Put some thought into the pictures; don't just point and click.

Miscellaneous tips

1. We prefer not to run straight question-and-answer articles. This is the lazy writer's *modus operandi;* presenting the raw material rather than constructing it into an article. But Q&A's sometimes work well as a sidebar to the main article.

2. Always try to write a lively introduction. Be creative; give your readers a reason to keep reading.

3. First-person articles are frowned upon. Get out of the way and let your subjects be the focus of the story.

4. Use lots of quotes. It is not necessary to use exact quotes as long as the spirit of the quote is there. People tend to talk funny; there's nothing wrong with cleaning things up so their point is made concisely.

5. Paragraphs should almost never contain more than two or three sentences.

A few notes on *Newswaves* style

1. We do not capitalize "deaf" or "hard of hearing." We avoid saying "the deaf." We also avoid using the term "hearing impaired," although it can be used occasionally for variety.

2. Hyphenate "hard of hearing" when used before a noun (i.e., "hard-of-hearing people"). Don't hyphenate it when it stands alone ("people who are hard of hearing").

3. Use postal abbreviations for states only when giving a mailing address. Otherwise use traditional abbreviations (i.e., Wash., Mich., N.J.).

4. Do not use courtesy titles (Mr., Ms., Dr.). Use last names

for adults and first names for youth. Do not put credentials such as Ph.D. or M.S. after a person's name.

5. Do not capitalize job titles, departments or entities like "board of directors." The exception is when a job title comes right before a person's name (i.e., Gallaudet President I. King Jordan).

6. Use italics for book titles, names of TV shows, plays, etc. Do not use quotation marks. If you are unable to type in italics, use underlines and we will change it to italics.

7. Numbers from one to nine should be spelled out. From 10 and up they should appear as digits. The exception is when a number starts a sentence; then it is always spelled out.

8. Most articles begin with a dateline—put the city in capital letters followed by the state using traditional abbreviation. If it's a well-known city, it is not necessary to include the state.

9. Write phone numbers as follows: (800) 555-1234 (i.e., area code in parentheses, no "1" in the front. When necessary, put Voice, TTY or Voice/TTY as appropriate after the number (not in parentheses).

10. If you have spell check, please use it.

Categories: Nonfiction—Disabilities

Name: Tom Willard, Editor
Material: All
Address: 302 N GOODMAN ST STE 205-A
City/State/ZIP: ROCHESTER NY 14607
Telephone: 716-473-5240 (TTY)
Fax: 716-473-6328
E-mail: Newswaves@aol.com

Newsweek

My Turn Column

My Turn's are between 1,000 and 1,100 words. It must be original for *Newsweek* and not published elsewhere.

Include a phone number, day and evening, if it's different from your home address.

We will let you know, but it can take a couple of months. We get about 500 essays. It takes time to read them and make decisions.

If your piece is very timely, say a couple of weeks, then it's probably not for us. Otherwise, we will let you know, but it does take time.

Categories: Nonfiction—News—Opinion

Name: Owen Clark
Material: My Turn essays
Address: 251 W. 57TH STREET
City/State/ZIP: NEW YORK, NY 10019
Telephone: 212-445-4000
Fax: 212-445-5068

⊤HE NEW TIMES

The New Times
Enriching and Changing Lives Since 1985

We welcome your interest in contributing to *The New Times*, a grassroots forum for sharing ideas, information, philosophies, interviews, and opinions.

The New Times is a monthly newspaper, thoughtfully blending the mystical and the pragmatic, and focusing on personal growth, spirituality, and holistic approaches to wellness and our environment. Distributed free to 45,000 readers at more than 300 locations throughout the Pacific Northwest, it also boasts over 1,500 paid subscriptions in 49 states.

Here we provide a quick reference along with a more detailed explanation of our policies. Please read and follow these guidelines before submitting your article.

TYPES OF MATERIAL

We accept articles, interviews, news items, poetry, fiction, photographs, cartoons, and art which will, in some way, inspire, inform, or otherwise encourage our readers to create a more spiritually aware, happy, and healthy world in which all of us can live and grow. We accept articles which analyze or disagree with issues (as they help us understand one another better) but do not print articles which attack, demean, or negate other people, organizations, philosophies, or systems. We do not accept articles which are racist, sexist, ageist, homophobic, heterophobic, or otherwise hateful in nature. Unless the topic being discussed is gender specific, articles must be written in gender-inclusive language. We *do not* print material that is strictly promotional. We *do not* print press releases.

HOW WE DECIDE WHAT TO PRINT

We print material on a wide variety of topics, including some which may not align with our personal philosophies. We do not base our decisions on whether or not advertising is being placed, whether we like or dislike the author, whether someone is famous, or whether we agree with the material. Acceptance (or rejection) of an article submitted to *The New Times* is based on the answers to the following questions:

Will it benefit the readers? Will this article in some way provide our readers with new, unique, or relevant insights or information that will be useful to them?

Is the article original? It is a disservice to our readers to offer the same article seen in other publications. Most of our readers read publications from many geographical locations on a wide variety of topics and expect to see fresh material. For this reason, we do not accept articles that are excerpted, previously published, or simultaneously submitted. Again, this includes press releases or similar documents that amount to requests for free advertising.

Does the article stand alone? Will the readers benefit from this material whether or not they visit the author, interviewee, or organization discussed?

How well written is the article? We often accept articles which need to be edited for grammar and spelling, but if the article is very difficult to understand, we may return it (see section on editing).

DEADLINES, ACCEPTANCE AND TIMING

Articles are due the second Friday of each month if they are to be considered for inclusion in the following month's issue, and acceptance/rejection letters are sent out within a few days of deadline. Articles received after the second Friday of the month will be held for the following deadline.

Because we routinely receive more material thin we can print each month, we are not able to promise any particular publication date for articles accepted. Once an article is accepted for publication we do our best to publish it in the next available issue, but a few articles may be held over a month or two. Please be patient If we have accepted your article, it will appear as soon as possible.

We reserve the right to publish your article as a reprint in a different format (stand-alone reprints of popular articles). Some articles also appear in *The New Times* Internet Edition. We are also considering the possibility of producing an audio series. We assume that we have your permission to use accepted material in any or all of these forms unless you specifically let us know; at the time of your submittal, which you would like exempted.

PHONE CALLS

We do not discuss articles over the phone. If you have not heard back from us regarding your article (and it was to us by deadline with a self-addressed envelope bearing sufficient postage), drop us a postcard.

ORIGINALS AND RETURNS

Send us a copy and keep the original in a safe place. If you wish to have a photo or article returned, please enclose a self-addressed envelope bearing sufficient postage. If you fax or e-mail your article, you must also send a copy via the mail. We prefer submissions on IBM-PC compatible disk ("text" format preferred) and ask that you enclose a hard copy of your article with or without the disk. If you do not supply a disk, please make sure your paper copy will scan well. This means it should be free of markings except for text, and that a sans-serif font, eleven points in size or larger, should be used.

CHANGES

Any changes made to an article must be made in writing prior to the deadline date. Changes made after that date will make it necessary for us to hold the article until the next deadline. We do not take changes over the phone

EDITING

We edit every article for punctuation, spelling, grammar and readability (including capitalization and article title), that may result in some minor changes. However, we do not engage in substantial editing; if this has to be done we may return the article with some suggestion as to what is needed. We feel that the author is the best person to make extensive changes while maintaining the original intent of the article.

PHOTOS

We encourage writers to send photos with their articles to provide visuals for the readers. Photos must be 5x7 or smaller, glossy or matte, black-and-white or good quality color. Be sure to carefully label photos with identifying data as well as a photo credit, if desired. Do not halftone the photo before you send it We prefer photos that relate to the subject being discussed to portrait shots of the author. We are unable to use color or black-and-white photocopies of photos. Generally speaking the better the original looks, the better it will reproduce.

We also publish art-quality black-and-white photographs that are of an inspiring nature.

CARTOONS AND ARTWORK

We accept cartoons and artwork; they need to be black-and-white line art, not pencil, charcoal, or wash.

POETRY

We accept a limited amount of poetry. We prefer poetry that is less than a page long. Because of our column format, we may find it necessary to break long lines of poetry.

FICTION

We ask that your fiction piece is in keeping with the subject matter of *The New Times*. Length and submission format is the same as for nonfiction articles.

MULTIPLE SUBMISSIONS

We ask that you not submit more thin one article at a time. Space restrictions preclude us from running more than one article by any one writer at a time, *so* if we receive multiple articles, we will select only on

e for consideration. After your article has been accepted and appears in *The New Times*, then please feel free to submit again. Once more, reprints, excerpts, and material submitted to other publications *are not accepted.*

ARTICLES AND ADVERTISING

If you wish to place an ad after your article has been accepted, please do so knowing that the article is not guaranteed to run in a specific issue. We do not coordinate articles and advertising. The reason for this policy is that we customarily accept more articles than we can print (see section on deadlines). Coordinating articles and ads would put us in the position of having to run articles at a given time instead of making decisions based on what would be the best balance of articles in a particular issue. *The New Times* has a firm commitment to accepting articles on their merits, irrespective of advertising

COMMUNITY NEWS

A special section in *The New Times*, Community News is a place for announcements of new businesses, marriages, deaths and transitions, new hires, relocation of businesses or practices, etc. Events such as classes or seminars are not appropriate for this section. Please limit your submission to 300 words and send it to us in the format as above.

PAYMENT

You receive a free one-year subscription upon publication. We do not pay for articles nor do we give free advertising for them. If you wish, at the end of the article you may include a short (40-60 word) statement of who you are and how people can reach you. The reason we do not pay for articles is based on philosophical considerations.

The New Times exists to provide a community forum for us to learn from, and dialogue with, one another. If acceptance were based upon financial remuneration, those who cannot write well enough to earn their livings from writing would be denied a voice and only professional writers would be heard.

Obviously, we encourage well-written articles, and professional writers *do* submit to us out of a desire to share with the community. We may reject an article because of poor writing skills, but we also sometimes accept articles which, though not as well written, come from the heart of the writer and deserve to be shared with the rest of us.

A FINAL NOTE TO FIRST-TIME WRITERS

Writing an article doesn't have to be a chore. When it is experienced as a playful, insightful sharing process, the words seem to flow. Think about how you'd like to have someone share information with you and write from that perspective. Readers like articles that they don't have to wade through. Even though the concept you're writing about may be complex or challenging, try to convey it in language that is clear and simple. Try speaking your article out loud. If it sounds good, chances are it's a good read, too. If you have to explain or enlarge on something to a listener, you will probably have to do the same for a reader. Above all else, have fun, and happy writing!

AT A GLANCE

1. Your article must be original (reprints, excerpts, and material submitted to other publications are not accepted).

2. We prefer material to be submitted along with an electronic copy (PC "text" format disk).

3. All submissions must include a word processed, typed, or neatly written. All paper copies *not* accompanied by electronic ones should be free of marks, smears, and doodles, and should be printed in a sans-serif font 11 points or larger in size.

4. Pages must be numbered, with author's name, address, and phone number on first page.

5. Maximum length: 1,800 words (roughly no more than 8 pages).

6. Label all photos by affixing Post-It brand notes to the backs, giving photo credits if desired. Do not write on the front or back of photos.

7. A mailed copy of the article must follow faxed or e-mailed articles.

8. All communication must be in writing. (No phone calls.)

9. No changes can be made to your article once it is accepted.

10. The submission deadline is the second Friday of each month for consideration for publication in the following month's issue.

Categories: Nonfiction—Diet—Ecology—Environment—Feminism—Gay/Lesbian—Health—Inspirational—Interview—

Lifestyles—Men's Issues—Native American—New Age—Paranormal—Psychology—Religion—Spiritual—Women's Issues

Name: David A. Young, Editor
Material: All
Address: PO BOX 51186
City/State/ZIP: SEATTLE WA 98115
Telephone: 206-524-9071
Fax: 206-524-0052
E-mail: Dyoung@speakeasy.org

New Woman

Thank you for your query concerning our writer's guidelines. *New Woman* is interested in considering articles on relationships and psychology. The categories which make up our magazine are good guidelines to what we're looking for: e.g. Self-Discovery, Relationships, Successful Living, Love and Sex, and Career and Money. We're also interested in Travel Articles with a self-discovery angle.

We like articles that are based on solid research, as well as more personal essay-like pieces. In terms of style, we like a friendly, accessible, intimate approach. Our articles run anywhere from 800 to 2,500 words, depending on the subject matter and the category.

We pay on acceptance; between $500 and $2,500, depending on the length and "weight" of the article - and how long the writer has been working with us.

It's not necessary for you to have an agent to represent your work. You may submit either a query or a finished manuscript, but please include a self-addressed stamped envelope with enough postage for our reply or for the manuscript's return.

Please address your double-spaced, typed submission to *New Woman* Manuscripts and Proposals, at the address below.

We look forward to considering your work.

Please note that the magazine no longer accepts fiction or poetry submissions.

Categories: Nonfiction—Family—Health—Marriage—Physical Fitness—Psychology—Relationships—Self-Help—Beauty—Women's Issues

Name: *New Woman* Manuscripts and Proposals
Material: All
Address: 2 PARK AVE.
City/State/ZIP: NEW YORK, NY 10016
Telephone: 212-545-3600
Fax: 212-251-1590

New Writer's Magazine

NEW WRITER'S MAGAZINE (NW) is a bimonthly publication for aspiring writers and professional ones as well. NW serves as a "Meeting Place" where all writers are free to exchange thoughts, ideas, backgrounds and samples of their work. We are always seeking new and innovative writers with imagination and promise. And we are always looking for 'how-to' articles with a different slant. New trends in the publishing field and freelance writing is always welcomed, plus new trends on the Internet.

NONFICTION: An "Up Close and Personal" interview of a recognized or new author, preferably with photos, and all major "in depth" articles on writing and the writing life. All such articles must be original and previously unpublished. 700-1,000 words. Payment on publication: $10 up to $40.00.

FICTION: Will publish a good fiction piece that has some sort of tie-in with the world of the new writer. Open to all styles/forms of expression. 700-800 words. Payment on publication: $20-$40.00.

POETRY: Humorous slant on writing life especially welcomed. Free verse, light verse and traditional. Submit maximum 3 poems. Length 8-20 lines. Payment on publication: $5.00 each poem.

CARTOONS: Black & white line drawings. Humorous slant on writing life. Submit copies or originals. Payment on publication: $10.00 each.

FILLERS: Anecdotes, facts, and short humor. Length: 20-100 words. Payment on publication: $5 max.

TIPS: The old adage still is true: *Study the market (NW) first!* And always include an SASE, otherwise your submission may not be answered or otherwise be long delayed. No e-mail submissions.

AMERICA ONLINE (AOL): NW is a Content Provider to AOL. Visit NW in the Writers Club section under The Business of Writing, and then to New Writers Market News, which is updated monthly. Also visit our Poetry/Writing Contests section each month.

Sample copy is $3.00: Send check payable to Sarasota Bay Publishing or *New Writer's Magazine.*

SUBSCRIPTION INFORMATION:

One year (six issues) $15.00; Two years (twelve issues) $25.00; Canadian one year $20.00 (U.S. funds); International one year $35.00 (U.S. funds)

Categories: Fiction—Nonfiction—Cartoons—Poetry—Writing

Name: George J. Haborak, Editor/Publisher
Material: All
Address: PO BOX 5976
City/State/ZIP: SARASOTA FL 34277-5976
Telephone: 800-249-0658
E-mail: Newriters@aol.com

Nimrod

International Journal of Prose and Poetry
The University of Tulsa

Annual Sales: 4,000 copies

Subject: Quality poetry & short fiction & essays. Two issues annually. *Awards Issue* (fall publication)—no designated theme. Winners and finalists of yearly competition. *Thematic Issue* (spring publication): Previous themes have included the following: Writers of Age; American Indian; The City; and numerous issues devoted to emerging writers from several countries including China, India, Latin America, Russia, Canada, Australia, Eastern Europe.

Format: Each issue 160 pp.; perfect bound; 4-color cover.

Titles in print: 84

Alternate formats: Audio + portions on Web

Subscription: $17.50/1 year (outside USA $19); $30.00/2 years (outside USA $33)

Sample copies: $10.00 each

Publication: Always pays with two copies and when budget permits $5 per page ($25 maximum per manuscript).

Annual Contest: $2,000 First Prize; $1,000 Second Prize in poetry and fiction. Send SASE for contest guidelines. Deadline usually in April.

Categories: Fiction—Nonfiction—Arts—Culture—

Drama—Language—Literature—Philosophy—Photography—Poetry—Writing

Name: Francine Ringold, Editor-in-Chief
Material: Poetry, Fiction, Essays
Address: THE UNIVERSITY OF TULSA
Address: 600 S COLLEGE
City/State/ZIP: TULSA OK 74104-3189
Telephone: 918-631-3080
Fax: 918-631-3033
E-mail: ringoldfl@centum.uttulsa.edu
Internet: www.si.umich.edu/~jringold/nimrod/nimrod.html

Nineteenth Century

Nineteenth Century, members' magazine of THE VICTORIAN SOCIETY IN AMERICA, publishes scholarly articles related to the cultural and social history of America circa 1790-1917. We encourage features on personalities, material culture, architecture, gardens, interior design, fine and decorative arts, and photography. Submitted manuscripts are reviewed by an editorial board.

Length: Maximum 3,000 words, including notes. Send three printed copies, including photocopies of suggested illustrations.

Do *not* send a disk until the edited copies are returned to you.

Documentation: We use notes for documentation, with no additional bibliography. Follow the form suggested in the Modern Language Association *MLA Handbook for Writers of Research Papers*, fourth edition (1995) beginning on page 242. Please check your notes carefully for correct form and punctuation. Keep them short! Alternatively, you may submit an article without notes; include a listing of Sources Consulted.

Illustrations: A maximum of eight per article will be printed. You may send more for our consideration. Glossies should be professional quality 8"x10", black and white. Color prints generally will be considered only for the cover. All permissions to publish, and related costs, are the sole responsibility of the author.

Caption Form: Object or Subject, Date. Designer/Artist/Photographer, as appropriate. Publication and/or Place. Courtesy of _____. One sentence for clarification or description, if needed. Affix a permanent label to the reverse of each glossy. Indicate "top" and include your name and address. Supply a separate list of captions with the manuscript.

Author's Credit: Include two sentences of biographical information for the list of contributors.

Categories: Nonfiction—Antiques—Architecture—Collectibles—Culture—General Interest

Name: Sally Buchanan Kinsey, Editor
Material: All
Address: PO BOX 511
City/State/ZIP: DEWITT NY 13214-0511
Telephone: 315-446-8031
Fax: 315-446-8031

Nite-Writer's International
Literary Arts Journal

Nite-Writer's International is "dedicated to the emotional intellectual with a creative perception of life."

Nite-Writer's International Literary Arts Journal is a quarterly publication of today's most creative and inspiring poets, writers, and artists. It is 8.5"x11" with 30-50 pages, side stapled with sleeve and stock cover showcasing an artist's work.

We are open to beginners as well as professionals. Some of our past and present contributors: Ryan G, Van Cleave, Maury E. Shepard, Tony Davino, Chukwuemeka Osuagwu, Lyn Lifshin, Michael R. Lane, Ace Boggess, Carol Frith, Julie Sanders, Rob Rosenthal, Rose Marie Hunold, Sister Lou Ella Hickman, I.W.B.S., Jo Anne N. Gurda and Carol Frances Brown.

We want "**strong imagery**" in anything you write.

We accept:
• Poetry—All Forms
• Haiku/Senryu—3 per page
• Fiction/Nonfiction—up to 1,000 words
• Short Stories—up to 850 words
• Articles on writing—up to 850 words
• Art—B&W only, pen/pencil. Must be 1" border.
• Photographs—B&W only, 3"x5". (creative, scenic, nature)

All material must be double-spaced and include name and address in upper left corner. If sending art, may put name and address on back. Please note if material has been published elsewhere.

We are tax exempt and all donations or contributions over fifty dollars ($50.00) are tax deductible. Any person sending $50.00 or more will be the featured "writer" in an up-coming edition and will be listed as Honorary Contributor. All funds help foster literary achievements & literacy.

Anyone wishing a copy may do so by writing to the address below.

Categories: Literature

Name: Bree Ann Orner, Associate Editor
Material: Book Reviews
Address: 965 STREETS RUN RD STE 200
City/State/ZIP: PITTSBURGH PA 15236-2224
Telephone: 412-885-9119
E-mail: NiteWrite2@aol.com

Nocturnal Ecstasy

If you have a question or uncertainty about a submission, send a sample or inquiry. The best guideline is to simply send it in. All submissions should be vampire related, or related to the vampire lifestyle. (gloomy types of work, as well as twisted or evil material. Body piercing, music, suicide, s&m, torture, cults, death, religion, fetishes, anything of a gothic nature, fashion, other obsessions, castles, cemeteries, tattoos...you get the idea!)

I prefer submissions to be typed or on 3.5" IBM compatible disk. If you are hand writing a submission, please print.

At the present time we are unable to compensate contributors with payment. Our profits are a negative amount. However, the journal is distributed worldwide, and is seen by most of the other vampire publications as well as other editors and staffs of major publications. It is sent out to various record label employees as well as bands around the world.

We encourage our readers to send in comments on items published and will pass on any reviews that your material receives.

Nocturnal Ecstasy is a great place to get your work seen by others. Exposure is what we offer at the present time. Should you care to order an issue in which your work appears, we do offer sample copies at $6 each.

POETRY: All forms of poetry accepted (including free verse, haiku, cinquain).

SHORT STORIES: All fiction accepted, providing that characters are original. (No previously copyrighted characters, unless the character is a creation of your own. We want your version of a vampire, not Bram Stoker or Anne Rice's.) Erotica, power vampires, any twisted or unusual vampires, etc. Use your creativity. The more original, the better your chances of being published with *Nocturnal Ecstasy*. Keep in mind that we like stories that deal with sex. (All vampires have nympho tendencies.) Stories that are 3,000 words or less are preferred; although we have been known to accept stories that were up to 5,000 words. Like I said, it's best to send it in.

NONFICTION: All nonfiction accepted. Your own research, authors, artists, self proclaimed vampires and blood fetishists, as well as your own letters, observations, essays or debate.

ART: Black & white preferred. Ink, pen, or marker drawings as well as computer art or any other medium. Full dimensions are 8.5"x11". Small pieces of filler art and borders are also needed. Borders should be ¼" away from the edge of the paper and could be up to 1" wide. Larger borders needed for poetry pages. We are looking for artists to develop borders that will be used in every issue for our regular features. We also encourage cover drawings. Vampire erotica, bondage scenes encouraged. Nudity accepted as long as it is tasteful.

REVIEWS: All reviews should include title, year and publisher or movie/record label. If you have something of your own creation that you would like to see reviewed in NE, send it to Reviews, c/o NEVC. (books) All fiction and nonfiction reviews accepted, including children's stories, magazines, and comic books. (movies) all movie reviews accepted, including TV series, made for television, and cartoons. (music) all music reviews accepted. Vampire bands, as well as gothic, doom, industrial and punk encouraged. Full length recordings as well as one song reviews are accepted.

PHOTOGRAPHY: All photos are accepted, including member photos, people dressed up like vampires, gothic & bondage images, etc.

VAMPIRE NEWS: Anything vampire related that you think may be of interest to members.

INTERVIEWS: Interviews with bands, artists, vampire researchers, writers, zine editors, music industry people, etc. are encouraged. We prefer article format rather that Q&A, but both are accepted.

No rights are required for submissions, as all rights revert back to the respective contributors upon publication. By sending in a submission, you agree to our one time publishing rights.

Categories: Fiction—Nonfiction—Entertainment—Erotica—Fantasy—Gay/Lesbian—Goth Scene—Horror—Literature—Music—Poetry—Science Fiction—Sexuality—Spiritual—Underground—Vampires

Name: Darlene Daniels, Editor
Material: Art, Nonfiction, Interviews
Name: Tina Kern, Assistant Editor
Material: Fiction, Poetry
Address: PO BOX 147
City/State/ZIP: PALOS HTS IL 60463-0147
E-mail: VAMPIR4@juno.com

NOMMA Fabricator
Ornamental & Miscellaneous Metal

These guidelines provide general tips on producing high-quality, easy-to-read articles for Fabricator magazine and The Scroll newsletter.

Tip #1:

Articles should be written in a clear, concise, easy-to-read format. When writing, put yourself in the shoes of the reader and ask yourself such questions as, "Does this make sense?," "Is this interesting?," "Would I read this article if I were a *Fabricator* subscriber?"

Tip #2:

Make sure the "Five W's" are included in the story:

Who, What, When, Why, Where. Do not assume the reader knows what you're talking about. Explain highly technical terms in plain English.

Tip #3:

As a writer, remember your goal is to benefit the reader. Whether your article is to educate, entertain, or inspire, always keep your reader in mind.

Tip #4:

Place emphasis on things of special interest about your topic: Trivia, facts about the project's history, anecdotes, etc. Feel free to throw in humor and consider approaching your topic in a creative manner.

Tip #5:

Once you have received an assignment, give yourself a couple of days to think about how to approach the story and what to include. If you are excited about the article, and it flows out easily, then chances are you have a great story. If a story must be forced out, line for line, then you may want to take a step back and consider another angle.

Tip #6:

Always try to come up with artwork for a story—either drawings or photos. An illustrated article will catch the reader's eye, while a gray article will usually turn a reader off. If you can't find suitable artwork, then consider including a mug shot or photo of your business (all photos and artwork will be returned unharmed in about four weeks).

Tip #7:

If you are a supplier, *never* make your articles sound like an "advertorial" or free advertisement. The purpose of the article is to provide helpful and interesting information as a valuable industry service—not to be self-serving. No "puff" pieces, please.

All articles published must be original material (i.e. you must control the copyright). If you use published information, it must be done in accordance with U.S. copyright laws. The article should not infringe on any existing copyrights.

When writing the article, you must honor any agreements on publicity that may have been signed with owners, architects, primary contractors, or other fabricators. As a matter of fairness, please credit subcontractors, partners, or employees when credit is due.

Transmission Methods

1) **U.S. Mail**—All stories will be scanned into our computer. Thus, they should be printed in dark ink on plain white paper.

2) **Floppy Disk**—Any PC format, including ASCII, Microsoft Word, or WordPerfect. Either 3½" or 5¼" disk is OK.

3) **E-mail**—Either as e-mail or as an "attached file."

4) **Fax**—You can fax directly into our computer. When faxing, please set your machine on the highest-quality setting.

Editing:

All articles in *Fabricator* are subject to editing. Stories are typically edited for grammar, style, clarity, transition, voice, and length. If a story is edited, the editor will make every effort to preserve the author's original idea and intent. If a story requires complete rewriting, the editor will contact the writer. If a story is highly technical in nature, with lots of figures, the editor will likely send a proof after editing.

Statement of Purpose:

Fabricator's mission is to inform, educate, and inspire the industry. The magazine's long-term goal is to strengthen both the industry and NOMMA by fostering the free flow of information and knowledge.

For Freelance Writers:

Fabricator welcomes unsolicited articles and photos. As articles are written as a service to the industry, *Fabricator* normally does not pay for stories. However, exceptions are made for certain types of articles.

Categories: Metalworking

Name: Submissions Editor
Material: All
Address: 804 MAIN ST STE E
City/State/ZIP: FOREST PARK GA 30050
Telephone: 404-363-4009
Fax: 404-363-2857
E-mail: nomma2@aol.com

THE
NORTH AMERICAN
R E V I E W

The North American Review
University of Northern Iowa

A NOTE TO PROSPECTIVE CONTRIBUTORS

The NAR is the oldest literary magazine in America (founded in 1815) and one of the most respected; though we have no prejudices about the subject matter of material sent to us, our first concern is quality.

Poetry, fiction, and articles/essays should be sent to the address below. Do *not* submit book reviews.

The NAR pays fifty cents a line for poems (minimum payment is $20) and approximately $12 a published page for prose. We try to report on manuscripts within three months, but we have a very small staff to read some 4,000 submissions annually. If you haven't had a response within three months, you should ask us what the status of your work is. If we purchase work from you, note that we buy first North American serial rights only; copyright reverts to the author after publication.

Please note that we read fiction *only* between January 1st and April 1st. We read poetry and nonfiction year-round. Fiction received between April 1st and January 1st will be returned unread.

We do *not* consider material that is being submitted simultaneously to other markets, nor do we consider material that has been previously published, even if earlier publication is of small circulation.

Some trivia: Please don't mail your work to us in a Tyvek envelope; it defies letter-openers. Otherwise, our mechanical requirements are the usual ones. Material sent to us *must* be accompanied by a stamped, self-addressed envelope. If you don't supply postage, or if the envelope isn't large enough to contain the manuscript, we assume that you don't want your work sent back. If you submit photocopies, please be sure they're readable. Please don't send us work printed out in dot-matrix draft mode. *Please don't send diskettes; if we buy the work, we'll ask if it's available on diskette, or if it can be directly uploaded from your computer to ours.*

Do send us work you're proud of.

THE EDITORS

We hope you're already a reader, but if not, we invite you to subscribe at the special author's rate of $18 for six issues, or send us $5 for the current issue of THE NORTH AMERICAN REVIEW.

Categories: Fiction—Nonfiction—Short Stories—Theatre—Travel

Name: Peter Cooley, Poetry Editor
Material: Poetry
Name: Robley Wilson, Editor
Material: Fiction, Nonfiction

Address: UNIVERSITY OF NORTHERN IOWA
City/State/ZIP: CEDAR FALLS IA 50614
Telephone: 319-273-6455
Fax: 319-273-6455
E-mail: NAR@uni.edu

NORTH DAKOTA
horizons

M-R

North Dakota Horizons

Horizons is a quarterly, non-profit magazine with circulation in all 50 states and several foreign countries. The mission of *Horizons* is to discover and showcase North Dakota's resources and people. The magazine promotes North Dakota's many virtues: a clean environment, open spaces, friendly and creative people, and interesting things to see and do. Stories that encourage people to travel to North Dakota places and events are of prime importance.

Unsolicited contributions are welcome; however, telephone or written inquiries are encouraged. *Horizons* seeks short, non-fiction stories (1,000 to 1,500 words) and major in—depth feature articles (1,500 to 4,000 words).Whenever possible, manuscripts should be accompanied with illustrations, black and white photographs, color slides or color prints. Prints should be glossy finished. *Horizons* strives to be a visual publication. Sketches, maps, artwork or whatever illustration is available and appropriate should be submitted for ideas.

Work may be submitted on IBM compatible 5¼" or 3½" diskettes. On the disk, please indicate your word processing software. Your name, address and phone number should be clearly marked. Identifications for illustrations and photos should be clearly marked and as complete as possible.

Horizons reserves the right to edit all material submitted. We cannot provide proofs to authors or photographers prior to publication.

Payment: *Horizons* pays upon publication unless there are advance arrangements made with the editor. Short articles and essays average $50 to $100. Feature length articles average $125 to $300 depending on subject matter, timeliness and available illustrations.

Horizons also encourages the submission of photographs that relate to life in North Dakota, which may include people, places and events. Payment for front or back cover photos runs $50 to $100. Major layouts range from $125 to $300. Photos used in the annual calendar pay up to $100 per photo. Generally, photo rates are based on a one-time use. Photographs and original artwork are returned to the photographer or illustrator unless other arrangements are made by the editor in advance.

Payment for stories and photographs will be agreed upon in writing prior to publication.

Categories: Consumer—Regional—Rural America—Travel

Name: Lyle Halvorson, Editor
Material: All
Address: PO BOX 2639
City/State/ZIP: BISMARCK ND 58502
Telephone: 701-222-0929
Fax: 701-222-1611
E-mail: lhalvors@btigate.com

Northeast Corridor

Northeast Corridor
Beaver College

Northeast Corridor publishes fiction, poetry, personal and critical essays, and black and white line art/photographs. We search for excellence in every category.

Fiction: We seek finely-crafted short stories that meet several criteria. First, they must reveal a love of language (a good story line written in dull prose—passive voice, too much telling rather than showing, weak verbs, flimsy or absent metaphors—will probably be rejected). Secondly, stories need to have a point (a slice of life, a resonating moment, an interesting character sketch is not enough).

We seek stories that quickly reveal both character and conflict, and that move towards a resolution. Finally, because of space restraints, stories should be under fifteen pages. (Occasionally, there will be exceptions to this rule, but you have a much better shot at publication if you keep it short.) In general, we're not interested in science fiction or "romance" fiction.

Poetry: No restraints on form; we seek the best of its kind, whatever the kind. However, in terms of content, overly sentimental or simplistic poetry is not to our taste. We appreciate poetry that is rich and accessible to the intelligent reader. In general, submit in batches of five or less.

Critical Essays: Must be written for a literate but *not necessarily academic* audience. In other words, avoid tendentious prose and jargon. Avoid verbs like "valorize" and "privilege"; don't assume the reader just put down Fredric Jameson's *The Political Unconscious* or something similar. *Do* assume that your reader is interested in literature, history, and culture and would like to carry something meaningful away from your article. Again, attempt to keep it short: anything over fifteen pages will be hard to publish.

Personal Essays: Well-written, reflective essays with a clear and compelling "voice." Look at the "Hors" or the "About Men" columns in the *New York Times* Sunday magazine, or read the most recent edition of *Best American Essays*. We certainly appreciate wit, too, in addition to wisdom. Aim for essays that are five pages or less in length.

Art/Photographs: Send us copies *(not* originals) and let us *see* your work. The occasional tasteful cartoon would not be amiss, nor would good black & white border art, à la *The New Yorker.*

We appreciate your interest in *Northeast Corridor* and look forward to seeing your best work!

Categories: Fiction—Nonfiction—Biography—Drama—Interview—Literature—Poetry—Short Stories—Writing

Name: Susan Balée, Editor
Material: Fiction, Essays
Name: Janna King, Poetry Editor
Material: Poetry
Address: 450 S EASTON RD
City/State/ZIP: GLENSIDE PA 19038
Telephone: 215-572-2870
E-mail: balee@beaver.edu

Northeast Equine Journal

The *Northeast Equine Journal* welcomes freelance submissions. Following are the basic guidelines we suggest.

1. Most of our features run approximately 1,600-2,000 words in length. Occasionally, a topic is such that it can not be adequately covered within this range; two-part features are arranged in this instance.

2. Photographs, if available. are welcome. It is better to note their availability rather than enclose them.

3. An "Editorial Calendar" listing each month's primary topics is available.

Depending on length and complexity of the topic, features pay between $65-$100. Photographs used receive an additional $10/photo.

We do our best to respond to each submission. However, if after four to six weeks you have not heard back on an article you sent please follow up with a phone call to our editor.

Categories: Animals—Equestrian—Sports

Name: Janice Montgomery, Managing Editor
Material: Horses
Address: 312 MARLBORO ST
City/State/ZIP: KEENE NH 03431
Telephone: 603-357-4271
Fax: 603-357-7851
E-mail: neastequinejnl@tnonad.net

Northwest Regional Magazines

WRITERS:

We prefer a clear, crisp writing style. We publish family magazines-no four-letter words or off-color references. We do not want stories of limited interest or any that are exceedingly technical. We do not publish fiction or poetry.

Thoroughness, accuracy, and logical organization are crucial. We respond best to articles that are rich in anecdotes, quotations, and personal experiences. Be perceptive-but not flowery.

Writing must be accurate. Check and double-check spelling-especially proper names-and any numbers before submitting an article. Be wary of details that may change between writing and publication.

We cannot emphasize enough the importance of accuracy of all material submitted for publication. We subject manuscripts to a fact checking process, but it is the primary duty of the contributor to provide accurate, up-to-date information. Stories containing errors or out-of-date information may be returned, and stories that require excessive editing may receive less than the standard rate of pay.

Include current addresses and phone numbers of your key sources of information and photocopies of references to aid in editing and fact checking. Brochures are helpful.

Brief information, if applicable, should include how to get to a featured destination, places of interest nearby, opening and closing times of attractions, whether they are wheelchair-accessible, when roads are open and if they are suitable for RVs, and where to obtain more information.

In general we consider any article submitted to Northwest Regional Magazines for use in any of our magazines.

We buy first North American serial rights with an understanding that the article will not be offered to a similar publication for at least six months following its appearance in one of our magazines. Similar publications include *Cascades Fast, Western Living, Sunset, Travelin',* and *Beautiful* B.C.

We don't want stories written from travel brochures. Bring your story alive with quotes and anecdotes.

QUERY LETTERS

Please do not telephone us about story proposals. Send us a query letter, with clips of your work, that briefly outlines the ideas (no more than three at once) being proposed. If we like your idea, we will ask to see your story on speculation, set a story length, and give you a deadline. A go-ahead on spec does not constitute an assignment or guarantee publication.

We prefer *not* to receive queries or manuscripts via fax.

ARTICLES SUBMITTED ON SPEC

Features, usually supported by some black-and-white or color photos, maps, or art, from 1,250 to 2,000 words (5 to 9 double-spaced typed pages): $100 to $250 total.

Features of special interest requiring special research or with heavy photo or art content, from 1,250 to 2,000 words (5 to 9 double-spaced typed pages): $200 to $350 total.

Restaurant reviews (Oregon Coast) should be about 1,000 words and include prices of foods mentioned and a recipe (if possible). A menu, brochure, or something with the restaurant's name or logo should accompany the review. Payment for restaurant reviews is $125, and we do not reimburse for the meal.

Do not announce you are doing a review or do anything that would obligate you to give a favorable review or create an expectation in a proprietor's mind that a story will be published. Interview a restaurant owner, resort manager, or B&B proprietor after your meal or stay or make a follow-up phone call.

ASSIGNED ARTICLES

We occasionally assign an article. Payment will be agreed upon at the time of assignment. Such assignments will be made in writing. If an assigned story is not run for any reason, a kill fee of 1/3 the agreed upon price will be made.

EDITING

We reserve the right to edit all material submitted for publication.

PAYMENT SCHEDULE

Payment is made after publication, and the amount is dependent on quality, not length. Most photos supporting submitted articles will be considered part of the editorial package.

You must return a completed W-9 form to us. Your name as shown on the form must exactly match the name on your federal income tax return. We cannot issue payment without this form.

Typical news-release items, such as chamber of commerce reports of coming events or local club news, will be accepted on a no-fee basis. We are pleased to receive such articles and will publish as many as space permits.

DEADLINES

Copy and accompanying photographs should be in our office at least four to five months prior to desired date of publication. Stand-alone color photographs should arrive at least three months prior to publication.

PHOTOGRAPHERS (COLOR SUBMISSIONS)

We prefer to work with positive transparencies 35mm to 4"x5" but can use color negatives. It is sometimes necessary to cut negatives. If you object to this, please send duplicates.

We do not send out want lists but would be happy to review your work. Please send 20 to 40 seasonal scenic shots in mostly vertical format.

Payment for magazine cover photo, $325; for photos used in calendars (including the cover), $100; for full-page photos used inside the magazine, $75; for less than full-page $25-$55. Payment is for one-time rights, with the understanding that no pictures will be printed in any similar magazine within two months. We reserve the right to use photographs of the magazines and calendars in which your work has been published in our own promotional material. Unless we are informed otherwise, we reserve the right to use color photos in a black-and-white format to accompany editorial features.

We publish two annual four-color calendars. One calendar needs photos of the Oregon Coast and the other one needs photos of the Northwest. Submissions should be horizontal rather than vertical and be in slide or other transparency format. Any size up to 4"x5" is acceptable. Deadline for calendars is May 15.

We prefer scenic photos for calendar and full-page use. In *Oregon Outside* we prefer to show some human involvement in the stand-alone and cover photos. We will need model releases for cover photos. We also have a need for humorous, unusual, or animal photos for features in all three magazines.

We take every precaution with photographic submissions, but we cannot be responsible for damage in processing, loss in mailing, or normal wear. If a transparency is damaged beyond repair, we will pay up to three times our normal one-time use fee.

PLEASE NOTE: We do not sign personal delivery memos and agree only to the terms stated herein.

GENERAL INFORMATION

If your submission includes slides, negatives, or historical photos, add $1.10 [beyond the cost of postage] to cover cost of return by certified mail. We do not guarantee return of submissions unless you include return postage. Label all photographs with a number and your name and address.

Be sure to provide a complete caption and credit for each photo on a separate typed sheet. If your manuscript is on disk, include the captions on the disk also. Send slides or negatives in plastic sleeves or protectors, not loose or in plastic boxes. Check accuracy and spelling on captions. Advise us of any change in your address.

If art is needed for a story, send a photocopy. Usually color prints or slides are satisfactory.

We accept 5¼" or 3½" IBM-formatted diskettes in WordPerfect 5.1 or ASCII text. Enclose a hard copy. Leave at least 1½" margins on all sides of copy. Your manuscript should be typed or printed using 10- or 12-point type with name, address, and phone number on the first page. Allow one character space between sentences. Don't use tabs. Use hard returns at ends of paragraphs only.

Portions of our magazines may be used on the Internet at http://www.presys.com/highway. Before any writer's or photographer's work appears on the Internet, permission will be obtained. The fee will be negotiated and paid afterwards.

Oregon Coast and Northwest *Travel* magazines are published bimonthly. *Oregon Outside* is published quarterly.

Sample copies are available for $4.50, which includes shipping and handling.

Send all mail to the address below. The address for Federal Express and UPS is 1525 12th Street, Suite C.

OREGON COAST

Oregon Coast publishes articles of interest to residents, visitors, and anyone else who loves the coast. Some suggested topics to develop are:

- Historical items
- Beachcombing adventures
- Special happenings
- Backroads and byways
- Favorite camping and picnicking spots
- Nature and everyday science
- Popular one-day driving tours
- Community profiles
- Walking tours
- Restaurant reviews
- Profiles of notable coastal residents

NORTHWEST TRAVEL

Northwest Travel regularly covers Washington, Oregon, British Columbia, Idaho, and occasionally covers adjacent areas and Alaska.

Northwest Travel emphasizes places to visit. Some suggested topics to develop are:

- Special happenings in the Northwest
- Community profiles
- Popular one-day tours
- Profiles of notable Northwest residents
- Adventure stories

- Backroads and byways
- Restaurant features
- Weekend getaways
- Historical (prefer to have museum, park, or other present-day connection)
- Eye-catching photo (slide) and brief text (100 words) for back page (Include camera type and lens, film, and F/stop used.)
- B&Bs, country inns, or other small lodging establishments
- Photo essays
- Nature and wildlife stories (prefer to have travel connection)

The Worth a Stop department features bylined 300-500 word stories on unusual destinations that are worth a stop—$50 payment. Photos are occasionally used.

OREGON OUTSIDE

Oregon Outside publishes articles and photographs for Oregon residents and visitors interested in outside activities in Oregon. We will cover activities on land and water and in the air, but not involving sailplanes or airplanes. Don't plan on seeing hunting or golf stories either.

Some possible topics to develop are:
- Walking/hiking
- Camping/backpacking
- Bicycling/mountain biking
- Wildlife watching
- Outdoor excursions/field trips
- Scuba diving
- Boating/other water activities
- Rustic retreats
- Horseback riding/llama packing
- Hot air ballooning
- Hang gliding/parapenting
- Spelunking
- Rock climbing
- New equipment round-ups
- Skiing—downhill & cross-country/winter activities
- Profiles of special outdoor people
- Eye-catching photo (slide) and brief text (100 words) for back page (Include camera type and lens, film, and F/stop used.)

PROFILE FOR WRITERS AND PHOTOGRAPHERS

Please provide a 30- to 50- word summary of appropriate information. (Please note we reserve the right to edit.) See samples below for style.

Return of this form indicates that you have read and understood the writers and photographers guidelines.

Samples of typical profiles:
- Norman Hesseldahl is the Public Affairs Staff Officer for the Siuslaw National Forest. He and his family are regular visitors to the Oregon Coast, where they have discovered many special places.
- Melissa Livingston, a native Oregonian, has lived in France and traveled extensively throughout the United States. She returned to Oregon after living in New Jersey while attending Rutgers University. Currently she is writing a children's book.
- Karen Keltz is a nationally published poet, essayist, and freelance Writer-photographer. An English teacher at Tillamook High School, she has written a novel and accompanying writing textbook for the upper elementary grades.

Categories: Nonfiction—Outdoors—Regional—Travel

Name: Judy Fleagle, Co-Editor
Material: All
Address: PO BOX 18000
City/State/ZIP: FLORENCE OR 97439
Telephone: 800-997-9170
Fax: 541-997-1124

NORTHWEST REVIEW

Northwest Review
University of Oregon

NORTHWEST REVIEW is published tri-annually, and invites submissions of previously unpublished poetry, fiction, essays, interviews, book reviews and artwork. Artists are encouraged to query before sending their work. Manuscripts are considered year-round.

1. The only criterion for acceptance of material for publication is that of excellence.

2. No simultaneous submission will be considered.

3. If submitting both poetry and fiction, please send in separate envelopes.

4. There are no length restrictions.

5. The author's name and address should appear on *each* poem and on the cover page of *each* story submitted. The author's name should appear on each page of his or her story.

6. We try to respond within ten weeks. Payment (unless grant money comes available for this purpose) is in contributor's copies. Potential contributors are encouraged to subscribe to any magazine that they admire enough to want their work to appear therein. Magazines such as *Northwest Review* depend for their survival on subscriptions.

7. We encourage you to study a recent issue of *Northwest Review*. available to authors at the discounted price of $4.00.

Subscriptions:
One year (three issues) at $20.00.
Two years (six issues) at $38.00.
Three years (nine issues) at $53.00.
Students: $17.00/year; $31.00/two years.
Foreign subscribers please add $4.00/year for handling.
Special Bonus
Subscribe for two years and receive *free* our *30-Year Retrospective* issue, a $10.00 value.

Subscribe for three years and receive the *Retrospective* plus our six-color Morris *Graves/Northwest Review* poster, a $30.00 value.

Categories: Fiction—Arts—Literature—Poetry

Name: John Witte, General Editor
Material: Essays, Artwork, Interviews, Book Reviews
Name: John Witte, Poetry Editor
Material: Poetry
Name: Jan MacRae, Fiction Editor
Material: Fiction
Address: 369 PLC
Address: UNIVERSITY OF OREGON
City/State/ZIP: EUGENE OR 97403
Telephone: 541-346-3957
Fax: 541-346-1509

Northwest Travel

Please refer to Northwest Regional Magazines.

Northwoods Journal
A Magazine for Writers

As a small press publisher since 1963 I've learned that the most important thing to an author is to be paid.

The most important thing to a small press is to survive.

The answer to both of these things is readership.

We have addressed each of these problems with the **Northwoods Journal.**

During the decade of the 70s I published about 5,000 different writers in the *Northwoods Journal.* Few of them subscribed or supported the magazine in any way. It seems people who write poetry and literary type stuff don't actually read much, just their own. If they did, small presses would flourish.

To offset this known lack of support we could do several things. We could require a subscription. We could require a donation each time a piece is accepted. We might require membership in C.A.L [The Conservatory of American Letters]. We could require an author to buy enough copies to cover production costs.

We don't really like any of those choices. We don't want to have to make choices. We want to publish the best work submitted to us without any compromise. That's what we want, that's Utopia. Reality is somewhat different. We have to survive, and it costs approximately $25.00 per page to publish the *Northwoods Journal* The commercial press accepts works which are profitable, without regard to literary quality. We want to be different.

Our solution? A small reading fee, and a plea. For each poem submitted non-members of the **Conservatory of American Letters** will be required to include $1.50 per poem for a reading fee. Members will be required to include $.50 per poem, but only in multiples of even dollars.

For each piece of prose nonfiction submitted, the reading fee will be $5.00 for non members, $3.00 for members for each 2,500 words or any part.

Reading fees for poetry and nonfiction are waived on request if you join or renew your membership in the Conservatory ($24.00 per year) with submission. Each member gets one free read per year if the submission accompanies membership order. To make it one free read per year and not have it be concurrent would require record keeping and more hours of labor for which we must pay.

Fiction:

Fiction should be submitted to Ken Sieben, Fiction Editor, 253 Ocean Avenue, Sea Bright, NJ 07760. Reading fee for fiction is $3.00 for non members and $2.00 for members. Make checks payable to Ken Sieben. No free read for membership or renewal. (As you can surmise, C.A.L. gets none of the reading fee.)

Reviews:

Reviews and books for review should be sent to Elizabeth Klungness, Reviews Editor, *Northwoods Journal,* 2130 Sunset Dr. #47, Vista, CA 92083. For each book submitted, there will be a $2.00 fee for non members and a $1.00 fee for members. This fee makes your book eligible for review, and guarantees you a listing under *"Books Received."* The reviews section considers only small press and self-published books.

Reviews should be sent under the same terms as fiction, with a reading fee of $3.00 for non members and $2.00 for members. It is not necessary to submit the book when you submit a review. Authors are paid the same for reviews as anything else in the magazine.

When books or reviews are accepted for publication, authors or publishers will be notified in advance.

Make checks payable to Elizabeth Klungness. No freebie on membership or renewal. (As you can surmise, the company gets none of the reading fee.)

And the plea.

Please join the Conservatory when you submit ($24.00 annually), or subscribe to the *Northwoods Journal* ($12.00 annually, 4 issues), and prepare a list of people who might buy the magazine if you are featured. Put these names on pressure sensitive labels and be prepared to submit them when you are accepted. We send a no-pressure announcement telling them of your appearance in the magazine. For all sales we can attribute to your influence you earn a 10% royalty.

Payment:

Each author will be paid approximately $4.00 per page on acceptance. This payment is a non refundable advance against royalties on sales we can attribute to your presence in the magazine.

We buy first publication rights only. We do not consider previously published materials. No simultaneous submissions. Please do not fax any submissions to us unless requested to do so.

Schedule:

Published quarterly, the first day of each season. Deadline for the next issue is the first of the month following the first day of each season. Example, Summer issue is published June 21, deadline for fall is July 1.

Price:

Free to C. A. L. members. By subscription, $12.00 per year. By individual copy, $5.00 for next issue, $7.75 for current issue, $12.75 for back issue if available (most are not). Price is post paid in all cases. Extra singles to participants and members (and anyone else) ordering 10 or more are $3.00 each, plus regular shipping, $6.75 for 10 plus .25 each for all over 10.

Style:

See some of our back issues, or if none available, order a copy of the *Dan River Anthology,* $12.95 plus $2.75 shipping. No use wasting postage with versy stuff that rhymes or poetry about poetry/writing poetry.

Length:

Due to G.E.R (Grim Economic Reality) it is unlikely that we will accept anything of more than 2,500 words, fewer is better.

Production values:

Some say we do the nicest small press books and mags out there. That's nice to hear, but irrelevant to our purpose. We do try and provide high quality work.

Our purpose is basically the same as the Conservatory of American Letters' purpose. All non profit, tax exempt organizations must have a stated purpose and must show work toward that purpose.

C. A. L.'s purpose is:

To conserve and publish works of exceptional merit without regard to commercial potential.

To encourage and develop literary talent.

To provide the reading public with an alternative to modern mass marketing mediocrity.

If you agree with our purpose and don't particularly want to enrich the coffers of some company or entrepreneur with your work, won't you support us?

Donations are nice (and deductible on all tax forms), but we'd rather have your participation and readership.

Categories: Fiction—Nonfiction—Literature—Poetry—Textbooks—Writing

Name: Refer to guidelines for submission information.
Address: CONSERVATORY OF AMERICAN LETTERS
Address: PO BOX 298
City/State/ZIP: THOMASTON ME 04861
Telephone: 207-354-0998
Fax: 207-354-8953
E-mail: olrob@midcoast.com
Nota bene: Reading fees (and/or membership, and/or subscription) required.

Nor'westing

Nor'westing

Mission

Nor'westing aims to be the definitive journal of Pacific Northwest cruising. Our goal is to reflect the boater's experience afloat, and to describe the many reasons Pacific Northwest residents chose to ply our local waters. Our articles include experiences from the Oregon Coast to the Alaskan shores. Since our topics deal with cruising destinations and local boating characters, we serve both a power and sailboat audience.

We also enjoy delving into our area's rich maritime history, our boating artisans, and the local industry. We keep an eye on state and federal issues that affect boaters—including tax concerns and environmental action. We watch clubs for happenings, and highlight newsworthy action both on the water and in the clubhouse. Columnists cover galley tips, fishing, boating electronics, life on board, and local points of interest.

Because we are a family oriented magazine, we listen to our most important critic—the reader. *Nor'westing* is like a trusty ol' boat—constantly evolving (with the owner's love and care) to make the cruising experience as pleasurable as possible, while serving the one initial purpose—to get all boat enthusiasts out on the water.

In General:

• All queries and submitted material will be read and responded to. As we have a small editorial staff, this process sometimes takes up to eight weeks.

• Please allow us at least six weeks lead time; a summer cruising piece received in August has far less chance than the same article in April.

• Pleases send photos! These greatly enhance the story and increase its chances of being considered.

In Specific:

Cover Photos

We want high quality, high action, and high resolution photos in sharp focus, with varying contrast. Simple compositions work best, and vertical shots most easily fit the 8½"x11" format.

We look for photos that tell a story—or, as some of our photographers refer to as "slice of (boating) life" photography. We prefer slides to be duplicates and clearly identified with photographer's name, and a brief description of the image. Please send SASE with all submissions, we'll add insurance to the mailing cost.

Editorial Photos

We work most often with story/photo/graphics combinations. Feature work should be taken with black and white film (35mm or larger), close to subject matter, and uncluttered. We prefer action shots, people shots, and photos of the boats and areas featured in the story. Glossy prints are preferred, but contact sheets with negatives are accepted. Color prints are accepted in lieu of black and white. We encourage graphics and graphics ideas in any form.

Rights

Nor'westing generally buys first-time rights and onetime rights to all stories and photographs. We will consider reworked stories from non-competing publications. Information and a copy of the story or photo must be provided upon submission.

Queries

Mail a manuscript or query letter, rather than call. We ap-preciate the inclusion of published writing samples along with your letter. All queries will be responded to within eight weeks time.

Editing

All accepted stories are subject to editing. It's easier for us if your story comes to us on an IBM-formatted disk (along with the hard-copy), on any common word processing software.

Fees

Fees vary. Typically, a feature story will earn $100; a longer story with artwork, however, can earn $150. Columnists earn between $50-$75, depending on research put into the piece and the length of the article

Length

Features should be 1,500-3,000 words. Columns should be 700-900 words.

Categories: Boating—Hobbies—Northwest—Outdoors—Recreation

Name: Jennifer Oxley, Editor
Material: All
Address: PO BOX 70608
City/State/ZIP: SEATTLE WA 98107-0608
Telephone: 206-783-8939
Fax: 206-783-9011

Nostalgia
A Sentimental State of Mind

Submissions welcomed.

Poetry: Nostalgic content. Prefer modern prose, occasional rhyme.

Short stories: True personal experience, reflection, insight. Approximately 1,000—1,500 words.

Payment varies. (See Awards, below.)

Nostalgia appears spring & fall. Single copy $5.00 Year: $8.00
Nostalgia Poetry Award

$150 and publication for unpublished, nostalgic, modern prose poem.

Honorable Mentions: $25 & publication.

Deadlines: 6/30 and 12/31 each year.

Judges: Announced each issue & Connie L. Martin, Editor.

Rules:

1. Entry fee $5.00, covers 3 entries, reserves Fall Edition. Subscription extended accordingly.

2. Include name, address, phone number on each poem.

3. SASE announces winners. Manuscripts not returned.
Nostalgia Short Story Award

$150 and publication for unpublished, true personal experience, reflection, and insight. Try not to dwell on memories of relatives. Tell what's happened to you.

Approximately 1,000—1,500 words.

(Editing, with approval, may apply.)

Honorable mention: $25.00 & publication

Deadlines: 3/31 and 8/31 each year.

Judges: Announced each issue & Connie L. Martin, Editor.

Rules:

1. Entry fee $5.00, covers 3 entries, reserves Spring Edition. Subscription extended accordingly.

2. Include name, address, phone number on story.

3. SASE announces winners. Manuscripts not returned.

Categories: Nonfiction—Adventure—Comedy—Poetry—Religion

Name: Connie L. Martin, Editor
Material: All
Address: PO BOX 2224

City/State/ZIP: ORANGEBURG SC 29116
Nota bene: Entry fees required for all submissions.

Oatmeal & Poetry
Wholesome Nutrition From the Heart

STATEMENT OF PURPOSE

OATMEAL & POETRY, Wholesome Nutrition From The Heart, is the product of a dream; to keep alive the integrity and beauty of traditional, metric poetry as an art form. Along with poetry, we welcome stories and articles which allow one to see with the mind's eye-the picture of life's creation—the human spirit.

Voyager Publishing is homed in the plush, St. Croix River Valley, the birth place of Minnesota—Stillwater.

OATMEAL & POETRY is offered as a forum for new and seasoned poets and writers. Each submission is carefully considered for publication based on its own merit. Authors do not "compete for the privilege of publication." We will not consider any work which is of a violent, sexually explicit, or profane nature. This is a family magazine. Poems and stories by children as well as adults are encouraged.

About Our Journal

Now entering our fourth year of publication, OATMEAL & POETRY is a full-size (8.5"x11") literary journal, (44 pages) formatted on an IBM compatible computer, using Microsoft Publisher for Windows. "OPIE" is printed on 20 lb. white stock with a 60 lb. colored parchment cover, and saddle stapled. Whenever possible, we include biographies and/or photos of our poets and writers. We encourage submissions of original artwork as well as photographs (B&W) which may be suitable for accompanying a poem or story, or even for use as our cover. OATMEAL & POETRY is distributed to subscribers and contributing authors throughout the United States, Canada and overseas.

What We Publish

Haiku, Senryu, Tanka, Ballads, Limericks, Sonnets, Pastorals, etc. Form poetry is always welcomed. Free verse must be exceptional and meet our high standards of excellence. Stories should stir the imagination and have a positive message. They can be romantic, life-changing, spiritual, mysterious, humorous, adventurous...send us your best! In addition, our "Network Muse Market" section can get you in touch with other fine publications and informs you of nationwide contests offering top cash prizes.

Subscribers never pay a reading fee to have their submissions considered for publication in OATMEAL & POETRY but are required to submit the appropriate fees when entering all contests.

Editor's Choice Award

To encourage you to send us your very best submissions, we offer *Oatmeal & Poetry,* not only as a publication home for your writing, but as a quarterly, literary *contest* as well. Each time you submit your poem, story or article to us for consideration, it is entered into our Editor's Choice Award Contest. Submissions by subscribers are automatically entered.

A nominal reading fee is charged to *non-subscribers* which covers the cost of the awards. Two awards are presented per issue, one for prose and one for poetry. The monetary award is based on a percentage of all submissions for that quarter. The winners also receive a beautifully typeset certificate of excellence, suitable for framing. (Reading fees for non-subscribers are indicated below.)

SUBMISSION GUIDELINES

POETRY: Max 32 lines. Rhymed verse preferred. Free verse must be exceptional to be published. *$1.00 reading fee per poem.*

SHORT STORIES: 1,200 word max. *$2.00 reading fee per story.*

ARTICLES: 500 word max. *$2.00 reading fee per article.*

NOTE: Fees under $5.00, please send cash to avoid bank service charges.

CONTESTS: In addition to the Editor's Choice Award, four cash-prize contests are held throughout the year; two in poetry and two in prose. Guidelines for contests are available free of charge for a #10 SASE.

PAYMENT: All *unsolicited* manuscripts and/or poems accepted for publication are paid in one (1) contributor copy wherein your work is published. We request one-time rights. Copyright reverts to author upon publication.

SASE: A #10 self-addressed, stamped envelope MUST accompany all submissions. Canadian and overseas submissions—include IRC or U.S. Stamps. Sorry, no SASE, no response.

The best way to see what we like and what we publish is to send for a sample copy-only $5.50 post paid.

Manuscripts and poems are not returned.

Categories: Fiction—Nonfiction—Adventure—Animals—Biography—Cartoons—Culture—Environment—Ethnic—Family—Fantasy—Humor—Inspirational—Mystery—Poetry—Rural America—Short Stories—Women's Fiction

Name: Demitra Flanagan, Editor/Publisher
Material: Poetry, Short Stories
Name: Kerry Parsons, Markets Editor
Material: Market News
Name: Mark Gilbertson, Managing Editor
Material: Subscriptions
Address: PO BOX 2215
City/State/ZIP: STILLWATER MN 55082
Telephone: 612-578-9589
Nota bene: Reading fee required from non-subscribers.

Oblates

OBLATES is a bimonthly publication of the Missionary Association of Mary Immaculate—20 pages. Circulation 500,000. Two poems and two inspirational articles freelance per issue. All photos and features done in-house. No fiction, fillers, or book reviews.

AUDIENCE We write mainly for a mature adult Catholic audience. Our readers are looking for encouragement, comfort, and, most of all, a sense of positive Christian direction applicable to their lives.

EDITORIAL NEEDS We need poems and nonfiction articles which inspire, uplift, and motivate through expressions of positive Christian values as they relate to everyday life.

Nonfiction Articles 500-600 words. We use well-written, tightly edited articles with pertinent and well-developed themes. First person approach seems to work best. Keep tone positive. We do not use preachy, research, psychological, theological, or spiritual journey pieces. A Christian slant or Gospel message should be apparent, but subtle. Avoid topical and controversial issues.

Poems 16 line average. We use well-written, perceptive, inspirational verse. Avoid obscure imagery, allusions, and irreverent humor. Make sure rhyme and rhythm flow without strain.

PAYMENT $80 for articles; $30 for poems.

TERMS All manuscripts are submitted on speculation and must be the original work of the writer. We consider completed manuscripts only. **Do not query. No reprints** purchased. Simultaneous submissions accepted if so noted. Submit seasonal material 6 months in advance. Manuscripts must be typed, with a self-addressed, stamped envelope enclosed (2 FIRST CLASS STAMPS). Response within 6 weeks. Payment upon acceptance for first North American serial rights. Three complimentary copies sent on publication.

Categories: Christian Interests—Inspirational—Poetry—Religion

Name: Mary Mohrman, Manuscripts Editor
Material: All
Address: 9480 N DE MAZENOD DR
City/State/ZIP: BELLEVILLE IL 62223-1160
Telephone: 618-398-4848

Obsidian II
Black Literature in Review
North Carolina State University

OBSIDIAN II: Black Literature in Review is a biannual review for the study and cultivation of creative works in English by Black writers worldwide, with scholarly critical studies by all writers on Black literature in English.

All bibliographies and documented articles should follow the MLA *Handbook for Writers of Research Papers* (fourth edition, 1995). Manuscripts should, if possible, be submitted on a disk, along with two printed copies. Manuscripts may be submitted in a variety of word processor formats. Macintosh and IBM users are urged to submit files in Microsoft Word. Text files from other word processors may be used if the files are saved in ASCII format. All disks should be high density 1.40/1.44MB 3.5" floppies. If a disk file is not available, we are equipped to scan printed manuscripts produced on laser printers, daisy wheel printers, ink jet printers, dot matrix near-letter-quality printers, and typewriters. However, we cannot scan draft quality dot matrix print, or less-than-perfect photocopies. Therefore, to avoid technical difficulties and delays in processing your manuscript, send us the original rather than a copy.

OBSIDIAN II is created on a Power Macintosh© using Microsoft Word© 6.0a, and PageMaker6.0. Documents are scanned using the Hewlett Packard ScanJet IICX.

All manuscripts, whether typed or printed copies of material submitted on disks, should be double-spaced throughout, 30 pages maximum length), including quotations from prose and verse, with notes and works cited on separate pages at the end. All submissions (typed or printed copies), must be in duplicate.

Poetry submissions can be three to six poems, with one poem per page. Please submit critical essays with a cover sheet bearing author's name, address, and title of the article, so that the author's name does not appear on the manuscript. **Do not send simultaneous submissions or previously published material.** Submissions should include a short biographical sketch (maximum 50 words), and should include the author's name and address on each page in the upper right corner. Normally, two to three months is required before the submission can be returned.

One year subscription, $12.00; two years, $20.00. Single copies $6.00, double issues, $12.00. Checks and money orders payable to OBSIDIAN II. If you have questions, please call or e-mail Kelley Sassano.

Categories: Fiction—Nonfiction—African-American—Culture—Drama—Ethnic—Interview—Language—Literature—Men's Fiction—Multicultural—Poetry—Reference—Theatre—Short Stories—Women's Fiction—Writing

Name: Submissions Editor
Material: All
Address: DEPT OF ENGLISH BOX 8105
Address: NORTH CAROLINA STATE UNIVERSITY
City/State/ZIP: RALEIGH NC 27695-8105
Telephone: 919-515-4153

Fax: 919-515-6071
E-mail: Krsassan@unity.ncsu.edu

Odyssey
Adventures In Science

General Information: Scientific accuracy, lively approaches to the subject, and inclusion of primary research (interviews with scientists focusing on current research) are the primary concerns of the editors in choosing material. Writers are encouraged to study recent back issues for content and style. (Sample issue is available at $4.50. Send 10"x13" (or larger) self-addressed stamped ($2.00) envelope.) *All material must relate to the theme of a specific upcoming issue in order to be considered.* ODYSSEY purchases all rights to material.

Procedure: A query must consist of all of the following to be considered: a brief cover letter stating the subject and word length of the proposed article; a detailed one-page outline explaining the information to be presented in the article; a bibliography of sources (including interviews) the author intends to use in preparing the article; a self-addressed stamped envelope. Writers new to ODYSSEY should send a writing sample with the query. If you would like to know if your query has been received, please also include a stamped postcard that requests acknowledgment of receipt.

A writer may send as many queries for one issue as he or she wishes, but each query must have a separate cover letter, outline, bibliography, and SASE. Telephone queries are not accepted. Handwritten queries will not be considered.

Articles must be submitted on disk using a word processing program (preferably Microsoft Word-MAC). Text should be saved as ASCII text (in MS Word as "text only"). Disks should be either MAC- (preferred) or DOS-compatible 3½".

Guidelines

Feature articles: 750 words. Includes in-depth nonfiction articles (*Interactive approach a plus.*), Q&A interviews, plays, and biographies. Pays $.20-$.25 per printed word.

Supplemental nonfiction: 200-500 words. Includes subjects directly and indirectly related to the theme. Editors like little-known information but encourage writers not to overlook the obvious. Pays $.20-$.25 per printed word.

Fiction: up to 750 words. Science-related stories, poems, science fiction, retold legends, etc., relating to the theme. Pays $.20-$.25 per printed word.

Activities: up to 750 words. Includes models, science fair projects, astrophotography projects, etc., that can be done either by children alone, with adult supervision, or in a classroom setting (group activity). Query should be accompanied by sketches and description of how activity relates to the theme. Pays on an individual basis.

Department Features: "Far Out"; "Places, Media, People to Discover"; "First Person"; "Sideline Science"; 200-250 words. See back issues for direction of these departments that are also theme-related. Pays $.20-$.25 per printed word.

Puzzles and Games: No word finds. Crossword and other word puzzles using the vocabulary of the issue's theme. Mazes and picture puzzles that relate to the theme. Pays on an individual basis.

Note: Queries may be submitted at any time, but queries sent well in advance of deadline *may not be answered for several months*. Go-aheads requesting material proposed in queries are usually sent five months prior to publication date. Unused queries will be returned approximately three to four months prior to publication date.

PHOTO GUIDELINES
To be considered for publication, photographs must relate to

a specific theme. Writers are encouraged to submit available photos with their query or article. We buy one-time use.

Our suggested fee range for professional quality photographs* follows:

1/4 page to full page
b/w: $15 to $100
Color: $25 to $100

*Please note that fees for non-professional quality photographs are negotiated.

Cover fees are set on an individual basis for one-time use, plus promotional use. All cover images are color. Text images are primarily 4/color.

Color transparencies, slides, and color prints can be submitted for inside black/white use since they can be scanned at the printer.

Prices set by museums, societies, stock photography houses, etc., are paid or negotiated. Photographs that are promotional in nature (e.g., from tourist agencies, organizations, special events, etc.) are usually submitted at no charge.

If you have photographs pertaining to any upcoming theme, please contact the editor by mail or fax, or send them with your query. You may also send images on speculation.

Categories: Children—Juvenile—Physical Sciences—Science—Young Adult

Name: Beth Lindstrom, Editor
Material: Physical Sciences/Astronomy for kids 8-14
Address: 7 SCHOOL ST
City/State/ZIP: PETERBOROUGH NH 03458
Telephone: 603-924-7209
Fax: 603-924-7380

 # Office Number One

Office Number One

ONO is an 8.5"x11", 12 page zine set in 10 pt times, printed virtually randomly and distributed to approximately 1,800 of the most fortunate people on the planet. Sample copies are $2 & SASE. Subscriptions are $8.82/6 issues (note this is by the issue, not by the year).

Guidelines

Articles should be in the 200 word range *or less* (few exceptions). Stories should be no longer than 400 words. Poetry should be technically perfect. All should satisfy one or more of the following conditions:

Know who you are addressing and why. Writing should create a change in the person reading it. Be aware of the kind of change you create in who.

A Shock of Liberation: A very special shock can create freedom. The shock can be subtle. It can have a time fuse. No genre of writing is excluded. The shock is a paradox because it seems to come from elsewhere, yet it is here.

Satire: Satire should address something that should be changed intrinsically, not merely based on personal likes or dislikes. For example, many people protest violence, yet their solution is violent. They are prime targets for satire. Not because being passive or violent is politically correct, but because one of their aims must fail.

Provide an unusual angle, be up beat and humorous. Bear in mind, humor is a funny thing. It doesn't have to be funny to be humorous. "Up beat" means liberation for tortured souls.

Be short and to the point. No fair having the point be there is no point or some other non-sense. If your idea gets too long, break it into several short pieces each of which can stand on their own. Try to say it in 200 words or less.

Do not substitute slapstick absurdity, non-sequiturs or gimmicks for humor, satire or shock. If you don't enjoy the issue of ONO you received, then you'll probably have a hard time writing for it.

Articles should be written in one of the following styles:

News Report	Interview
Essay	Limerick (technically perfect)
Super Short Story	Haiku (5-7-5 or 3-5-3 only)
Quiz or Test	Quatrain (consistent rhyme & meter)
Review (Imaginary theater or book)	Cartoon

Of course, I'm open to something else if it works.
Carlos B. Dingus, Editor

Categories: Fiction—Horror—Humor—Paranormal—Philosophy—Poetry—Satire—Short Stories

Name: Carlos B. Dingus, Editor
Material: All
Address: 1708 S CONGRESS ST
City/State/ZIP: AUSTIN TX 78704
E-mail: ONOcDingus@aol.com

OHIO Magazine

Stories must appeal to an educated Ohio audience. We insist on solidly researched reporting that uncovers Ohio issues of public concern, reveals offbeat and previously unreported Ohio topics or uses a novel approach to familiar Ohio topics. Any issue of the magazine would be a helpful guide. We do not use fiction, poetry or cartoons.

A query letter should precede submission of the manuscript. The letter should provide a sample of the style of the proposed article, indicate a perspective and list material to be covered. A brief outline showing the direction and approach of the proposed article should accompany the letter. Clips demonstrating ability to write about similar topics or in a similar style are helpful. Telephone, e-mail and fax queries are strongly discouraged.

Acceptance: All materials should be considered submitted on speculation until formally accepted. A formal answer will be sent to you usually within six to eight weeks. If your manuscript is accepted, an editor will be assigned to you. By accepting your article, we make no commitment to a publishing date.

Preparation of copy: On the cover page of the manuscript the author should include his or her name, mailing address, social security number and telephone number where editors may call during the working day. At the end of the manuscript, include names and telephone numbers of contacts, as well as the names and numbers of any potential art/photo contacts. If possible, include a copy of the manuscript on 3.5" disk. Most word processing programs—Microsoft Word, Works, WordPerfect, MacWrite, etc., are acceptable. Please identify the program on the disk.

Editing: The editor's job is to make the magazine as readable and unimpeachable as possible. We consult with the author about editorial changes whenever possible. The author has the option to withdraw a story if agreement on points of editing cannot be reached.

Your editor will continue to work with you until the manuscript reaches its finished form. You might be contacted by a copy editor and a fact checker assigned to your story. After the editing process, you will receive a set of galleys of your story (features only).

Payment: Payment for a story is made on acceptance. The fee is negotiated and agreed upon when the writer is notified that the manuscript has been accepted or when an assignment is made.

Length: There are three categories of manuscripts: features, departments and upfront "Journal" stories. Features are generally 1,500 to 2,500 words in length, departments, 1,000 to 1,500

words and Journal stories, 500 to 1,000 words. Rates for features range from $800-$3,000; departments: $300-$500; Journal stories and other fillers: $50-$300.

Submitting the story or manuscript: Enclose an 8½"x11" SASE to receive one free sample issue.

Categories: Regional

Name: Jean P. Kelly, Editor
Material: All
Address: 62 E BROAD ST
City/State/ZIP: COLUMBUS OH 43215-3522

Ohio Writer

We are looking for nonfiction articles that deal with any area of writing, including how-to, profiles and interviews with Ohio writers, poets and journalists. *Ohio Writer* is read by both beginning and experienced writers and hopes to create a sense of community among writers of different genres, abilities and backgrounds. We want to hear a personal voice, one that engages the reader. We're looking for intelligent, literate prose that isn't stuffy.

Focus articles should be approximately 1,500 words. Payment: $25 on publication. Reprinted articles: $15 on publication.

Feature articles should be approximately 2,000 - 2,500 words. Payment: $50 on publication.

Reviews are accepted of any publication or book by an Ohio writer or Ohio press. Include title, author, press, city where published, year of publication, number of pages and price. Occasionally we use reviews of events: conferences, readings, bookstores, etc. Length: 400-600 words. Payment: $5-$10.

Include short biographical statement with all submissions. Unsolicited manuscripts and book reviews will be accepted. Reporting time: Four to six weeks.

We suggest writers unfamiliar with the magazine order a sample copy. Back issues are available for $2.00 plus 50 cents postage.

We buy one-time rights, plus the right to reprint. Any editing, except copy editing, will be done with author's approval.

We also accept announcements or notes concerning writing, writing opportunities, and the writing life in Ohio for publication in our **"Notes, Previews and Announcements"** column. Suitable calendar listings are published without charge.

Categories: Fiction—Nonfiction—Literature—Poetry—Short Stories—Writing

Name: Ron Antonucci, Editor
Material: All
Address: C/O Poets League of Greater Cleveland
Address: PO Box 91801
City/State/ZIP: Cleveland OH 44101
Telephone: 216-932-8444

Oildom Publishing

Writer's guidelines for
Underground Construction and *Pipeline & Gas Journal*
• Article rate includes basic telephone work. However, extensive long distance phone work and/or faxes, along with other relevant expenses may be paid by Oildom Publishing. Significant expenses (generally defined as over $25 per story) should be pre-approved. Payment upon final article approval by the magazines' editors. Always submit invoice with final story draft/disk.
• We prefer stories submitted on disk. Oildom Publishing is PC based. Sometimes stories written on a Mac can be imported via special programs we have; often times they can't. The word processing software we support for PC is WordPerfect Windows

7.0 (earlier formats are generally acceptable), Microsoft Word for Windows 6.0, XyWrite III+, or generally any program in ASCII or ANSI formats. To circumvent any software incompatibilities, a clean, clear hard copy should accompany all submissions. We can then scan the story into our system. For specific questions on formats and compatibility issues, contact Michael Speer, in the Houston office, (713) 558-6930, ext. 11.
• Whenever possible, all stories should be accompanied by artwork: Slides, color photographs and/or graphics. For specific graphic formats and compatibility inquiries, contact Lori Laxen-Brown for *Underground Construction*, (713) 558-6930, ext. 16, or Sheri Biscardi, (713) 558-6930, ext. 14 for *Pipeline & Gas Journal*.
• We like to break out all significant manufacturers, vendors and/or contractors with reader service numbers so interested readers can easily obtain information. Please include contact names, address, phone and fax numbers whenever possible.
• We buy exclusive rights. We prefer story queries, but cold submissions are considered. We generally will respond within 30 days.
• As a rule, we follow the *Associated Press Stylebook*. Exceptions include certain industry-accepted terms and abbreviations, and two-letter state abbreviations.
• Our readers tend to be management personnel from both contractors and owning companies. Technical material is acceptable only to a moderate level. Our readers are responsible for dollars. Always try to include economic considerations when applicable and practical.
• Kill fees are addressed on a case-by-case basis.

Categories: Underground Construction (gas, sewer, water, cable)

Name: Robert Carpenter, Editorial Director
Material: *Underground Construction*
Name: Jeff Share, Editor
Material: *Pipeline & Gas Journal*
Name: Rita Tubb, Managing Editor
Material: *Underground Construction/Pipeline & Gas Journal*
Address: PO BOX 219368
City/State/ZIP: HOUSTON TX 77218-9368
Telephone: 281-558-6930
Fax: 281-558-7029
E-mail: ginfo@undergroundinfo.com
Internet: www.undergroundinfo.com

OKLAHOMA TODAY

Oklahoma Today Magazine

Oklahoma Today is a regional bimonthly magazine with a circulation of 43,000. Stories, essays, columns, etc. deal with Oklahoma people, places, or topics. *Oklahoma Today* is considered a travel magazine by many, but we see ourselves more as a regional magazine, and we work hard to give readers a sense of what the state of Oklahoma is like and being an Oklahoman is all about. People figure strongly in *all* stories, because we believe the best way to write a story is not to tell it but to explore it through the anecdotes, quotes, and experiences of the people living or doing it.

The magazine prides itself on informing its reader about the staple leisure pursuits in Oklahoma as well as those off the beaten track. The criteria for choosing many subjects is, "Can the reader go see or participate in whatever the article describes?" or "Does the story expand the Oklahoma cultural vocabulary of the reader?" The criteria for approving stories is, "Does the writer answer the questions a reader might have about this subject and, more importantly, does he surprise the reader with unexpected insights and those wonderful quirky little details that let a reader (and an editor) know you've done your homework on a subject?"

Our readers like history and we believe the history or background of a person or place adds interest to a story and makes it easier for the reader to understand contemporary points being presented. We like our history woven into a story with a light hand, for the emphasis of the story should be on what can be seen or experienced today.

Topics in *Oklahoma Today* run the gamut. Successful stories from past issues have included a roundup of Oklahoma cowboy poets (and their poetry), a visit with two men who have been friends for forty years, a primer to the writings of Native American writer N. Scott Momaday, a guide to the state's best barbecue, and a glorious photo essay on the Tallgrass Prairie. We have files and files of topics—camping trips, biking tours, saddle makers, chamber groups—we'd like to see in *Oklahoma Today*, so most all of our stories are assigned to writers whose past work or present reputation indicates they can deliver a story up to our standards. However, we are *always* looking for new writers whose clips show talent. Hands down, the best way to hit pay dirt at *Oklahoma Today* is to submit a query that offers a fresh, clever, or intriguing angle on a new or old subject or person.

We expect our writers to read the magazine—regularly. It is the only way to keep abreast of what we're doing and how we do it. We have high standards for our writers. Most have journalism or creative writing degrees. By far the majority have worked in newspapers or magazines for more than ten years by the time they break into the ranks of our regular contributors. And our best writers keep working on their craft. Most read good magazines—*Texas Monthly*, *Vanity Fair*, *Outside*, *National Geographic*, *Yankee*, *Conde Nast's Traveler*, *The New Yorker*—*and* good books. They read newspapers and *Time*, *People*, or *Newsweek* to keep up with the world, and they offer us timely stories because they keep a finger on the pulse of Oklahoma and its residents.

Deadlines

1. *Oklahoma Today* is planned a year in advance, though certain departments of the magazine are designed to accommodate "breaking news," which in the magazine world still means three to four months advance notice.

2. *Oklahoma Today has* begun to publish poetry but we ask that it be regional in subject matter.

3. Photo essays, fiction, short stories., and essays are welcome but we ask that they be labeled as such. All should be regional in nature.

4. *Oklahoma Today* receives *volumes* of mail, telephone queries, etc.—please remember that we are a small magazine (editorial staff of 1 1/2) and it can take a few months for us to respond with anything more than an acknowledgment that a manuscript or query has arrived.

Story/Illustration Guidelines

1. Stories range from 1,000 words in one of our four regular departments (food, weekend trips, arts or Oklahoma Omnibus) to 3,000 words in a major feature.

2. We prefer to be queried in advance, but will review speculative submissions. Include clippings of past published material with query letter.

3. Speculative submission of high-quality color transparencies and black-and-white photographs with manuscripts are welcomed. We prefer scenic photographs or scenic photographs that include people in a tasteful manner. We reserve the right, however, to reject photographs submitted with a story, even if we accept the story itself.

Rates/Payment

1. We pay for quality not quantity.

2. We do not pay expenses, but do take into account the demands of a story assignment when negotiating payment.

3. Rates start at $25 to $50 for very short pieces or anecdotes; $75 and up for department and feature stories, $300 and up for major profiles or articles.

4. If a writer fails to meet an agreed upon deadline, payment will be docked $25 for each day it is late.

5. Payment is on publication, unless the writer and editor agree otherwise up front.

Policies & Procedures

1. Articles should be submitted on a 3" diskette in ASCII, with accompanying printout.

2. Include a stamped, self-addressed envelope with all material submitted. Rejected material generally will be returned within eight to twelve weeks.

3. Photographs or other materials sent with the manuscript will be returned after publication of the article.

4. Payment for articles includes any rewriting required; and if rewriting is necessary payment usually coincides with the publication of the magazine. Payment for polished manuscripts that fulfill their editorial objectives exactly may be made sooner.

5. Payment for photographs is on publication.

Categories: Consumer—History—Native American—Regional—Travel

Name: Jeanne Devlin, Editor-in-Chief
Material: All
Address: PO BOX 53384
City/State/ZIP: OKLAHOMA CITY OK 73152
Telephone: 405-521-2496
Fax: 405-522-4588

Old West

Please refer to Western Publications.

OMNIFIC

Are *you* guilty of storing your poetry in the closet? Do *you* say that contests are not for you because you would waste your money? Do deadlines make you nervous? If you answered "yes" to any of these questions, then this publication is for *you*.

Get those poems out of the closet and dust them off because OMNIFIC is now accepting 4 poems per person, per year, for publication in this well-known quarterly. Just think of it. Each issue could feature one of *your* poems. This is *your* chance to become published and stay published.

Poems are attractively displayed in alphabetical order according to *your* state, along with complete address of author. Readers vote on their favorites, and for now we have small prizes to be awarded. The top three entries receiving the most votes receive the next issue free. There is also an "Editor's Choice Award" of $5, and the poem(s) in the "Lucky No. 7" spot will receive a small award. As interest builds and subscriptions come in, prizes will be increased. (Not to mention the contact and awards furnished by some of our readers.)

Each author's complete name and address will be published with his/her poem. This encourages reader/writer contact, and also the awards given by our readers may be mailed directly to YOU. (However, if you wish your address to remain anonymous, I will accept your awards and forward them on to you. But YOU *must* let me know this at the time you send in your poetry, or upon receiving your acceptance letter.)

You will be proud to see your work published here and I can also promise that you will enjoy reading each issue, along with voting for your favorites. And the excitement builds from one issue to the next, because after reading OMNIFIC and casting your vote, you will want to know who the winners will be—and that information will be disclosed in the next issue.

OMNIFIC means "all creating" and as poets and writers, isn't that what we're doing?

COME...join our family today. Don't you be the one to miss out on the fun that's in store for everyone.

Wouldn't YOU like to be published in this exciting, fun-filled quarterly and have your poem appear in the *next* issue?

There is *no entry fee* and due to the weight involved, *no payment in copies*. Poetry to 40 lines (sometimes over), and in any style or format. Submission does not guarantee publication. Only work in good taste is accepted.

1 Year Subscription (4 issues) $16.00/Overseas $20 (US Funds)

Single issue—$4.50/Overseas $5.00 (US Funds). Payable to Weems Concepts.

This publication is habit-forming and good for your morale. Read at your own risk.

Categories: Poetry

Name: Kay Weems, Editor/Publisher
Material: Poetry
Address: HCR-13 BOX 21AA
City/State/ZIP: ARTEMAS PA 17211-9405
Telephone: 814-458-3102

On The Scene

• In print since 1979, *On The Scene* is a complimentary, monthly lifestyle and entertainment magazine with a 30,000+ circulation and a multi-generational readership. We use general interest articles and stories of an average of 600 words, but will consider manuscripts to 1,200 words. In style, we prefer the humorous and upbeat which entertains as well as informs. Reprints are accepted.

• On the first [manuscript] page, include your name, address and phone number along with article title and word count. The title and page number should appear on all other pages. If you have photos or artwork for the article, please indicate availability, but do not include at this time.

• We *do not* respond, nor do we return manuscripts, unless a SASE is provided. With a SASE, you will be notified in approximately 90 days whether your submission has been accepted, rejected, or needs revision in order to be considered.

• All manuscripts are accepted for *probable* future publication, based on timeliness and availability of space. Because our editorial needs are comparatively small and it may be several months before we can use an article, we encourage authors to make simultaneous submissions to other publications. If you wish to withdraw your article before we are able to publish it, send us a request to return or destroy.

• *On The Scene* reserves the right to edit any material accepted for publication.

• Payment for material ranges from $5 to $35, depending upon length and content (and, these days, budget restrictions, as well). Payment is mailed, together with tear sheet, approximately 45 days following publication.

• A sample copy of *On The Scene Magazine* is available at a cost of $3 for postage and handling, *or* send a 9"x12" self-addressed envelope with four first class stamps for each copy you wish sent.

Categories: Fiction—Nonfiction—Adventure—Animals—Children—Comedy—Family—Gardening—General Interest—Health—Humor—Inspirational—Lifestyles—Marriage—Music—Native American—New Age—Parenting—Recreation—Relationships—Romance—Short Stories—Singles

Name: Gail Skinner, Editor
Material: All
Address: 3507 WYOMING NE
City/State/ZIP: ALBUQUERQUE NM 87111
Telephone: 505-299-4401
Fax: 505-299-4403

Open Exchange Magazine
Tips for Administrators, Artists, Therapists & Professionals In Business

Use plain English! Good writing is easy to read and encourages the reader to become involved. Have fun! Let your enthusiasm for the topic shine through! Accompanying photos and artwork add interest and improve response.

Longer articles, 500-1,500 words, should be topical and of general interest, i.e., "How Psychotherapy Can Change Your Life." Would someone want to read this piece even if they were not about to attend *your* particular service or event? Break up longer articles with subtitles for organization.

Mini-articles, under 500 words, may be more personal, autobiographical, or commercial, i.e., "20 Years As A Therapist by Jane Smythe."

Open Exchange Magazine accepts articles only from paid advertisers. We publish the best articles we receive on a space available basis. We give priority to typeset quality printing with no strikeovers. Book excerpts are especially welcome. In practice we use about 75% of the articles submitted issue to issue. For listers who continue to advertise, chances approach 100% that we'll use your article within a six month period.

We do not pay for articles but (unlike some publications) we do not charge to run them either. We do not reprint phone numbers or addresses with articles, but we refer readers to the contributor's listings or ads in an editorial introduction. See you in print!

Categories: Nonficiton

Name: Submissions Editor
Material: All
Address: PO BOX 7880
City/State/ZIP: BERKELEY CA 94707
Telephone: 510-526-7190
Fax: 510-527-4273
E-mail: openex@aol.com
Nota bene: Publishes articles by paid advertisers only.

OPTOMETRIC ECONOMICS

Optometric Economics

The mission of *Optometric Economics* is to help optometrists build bigger, more successful practices, manage their practices more efficiently in today's rapidly changing health care environment, increase their business skills, and stay up-to-date on the latest trends in health care and the business world.

Optometric Economics draws on the knowledge of management experts within optometry and in other fields to make it the most detailed, best-written practice management resource in the profession. In addition, *Optometric Economics* is the only major optometric periodical to focus *exclusively* on practice management issues.

Optometric Economics is a direct outgrowth of AOA's [American Optometric Association] Professional Enhancement Program (PEP), and is solely devoted to practice management. Clinical submissions should be directed to the editor of the *Journal of the American Optometric Association*.

Style

Optometric Economics' style is light, direct, and conversational. Add color to your submissions with anecdotes and quotes.

Optometric Economics is a magazine, not a scholarly journal. Avoid footnotes, lists of references, and overly detailed discussions of research. If your article reports survey or study results, focus on the information's practical benefits to the reader, and illustrate it with interesting graphs and/or charts.

Some helpful hints:

• Choose subjects with appeal to a broad range of optometric practitioners, and write *for* optometrists. If you do not come from an eye care background, demonstrate that you have made the effort to understand optometry. Our readers are not ophthalmologists, opticians, or laypersons.

• Give specific "how-to" advice on how optometrists can build, improve, better manage, or enjoy their practices.

• Avoid overly general articles. For example, "The Top Ten Ways to Market Your Practice" covers too much ground. Better to focus on one or two marketing principles and cover them in detail.

• Introduce your main points early. Use short words, sentences, and paragraphs. Our readers are busy professionals and you must quickly show them why it is important that they read your article.

• Suggest a title for your article, and include subheadings for different sections.

Illustrations, Graphics, and Art

If possible, supply good-quality photos or other illustrations with your story. Color slides or black and white prints (8"x10" or larger) are preferred.

Tables and graphs are useful in articles including survey or study data. Tables and graphs need not be camera-ready; the editors will format tables and graphs to fit the magazine's design.

Photographs should be referred to as "Photo 1," "Photo 2," etc. if mentioned in your text. Tables graphs, illustrations, or diagrams should be referred to as "Figure 1," "Table 2," etc.

Cartoons featuring humor from the viewpoint of optometrists may be submitted.

How to Submit

Start by submitting a letter of inquiry and, if possible, an outline to the editor. If you're a freelance writer and you've never written for OE, please include clips and references. The editor, if interested in your idea, will usually offer guidelines and/or background information. Every effort will be made to ensure that writer and editor are on the same "wavelength" before the writing begins.

Articles are—with exceptions—usually in the range of 1,500 to 3,000 words.

If accepted, your article may require editing for organization, style, or length, but the editors will make every effort to preserve the author's individual style. Don't take criticism personally.

Please include a brief "author's blurb" indicating how you would like to be identified if your article is published.

Articles may be submitted as hard copy on diskettes, or via e-mail. Use a standard 3.5" diskette formatted for Macintosh or PC. Files may be sent in nearly any Macintosh, DOS, or Windows word processing format. If in doubt, put files in a "text-only" format. E-mail submissions should be sent to the Editor at the address below.

With all disk submissions, please include one hard copy of the article in case of damage to the diskette.

Clearly identify all enclosures.

Policy on Commercialism

AOA cannot promote any commercial product, service, or organization. Articles should therefore be generic in nature. Specific products, services, and organizations may be mentioned if needed to illustrate a point.

Scheduling

The deadline for submitting articles or illustrations is generally eight to 11 weeks before the issue date. For example, the deadline for a December issue will usually be in late September or early October. The editor will give you a specific deadline when an article is commissioned.

Depending on the backlog of manuscripts and your article's subject, the editors reserve the right to delay publication past the initial publication date.

Payment

Payment varies with the length and complexity of the story and will usually be determined when the article is commissioned. Upon acceptance of an article, a written agreement will be drawn up for your signature, indicating rights assigned and amount of payment. Generally, *Optometric Economics* purchases all rights to articles.

Suggested Topics of Interest

Professional marketing
Patient communication
Staff development and management
Eyewear features and marketing
Professional and consumer surveys
Modes of practice
Managed care
Personal and practice planning
Professional ethics
Legal and malpractice issues
Practice and personal finance
Office planning and remodeling
Coping with changing demographics
Optometric education and student issues
Billings and collections
Practice sale or purchase
Humorous anecdotes and observations

"Doctors of optometry are independent primary health care providers who examine, diagnose, treat and manage diseases and disorders of the visual system, the eye and associated structures as well as diagnose related systemic conditions." — *The official definition of an optometrist, adopted by the AOA Board of Trustees in September 1993.*

Categories: Nonfiction—Associations—Eye Care—Health—Optometry

Name: Gene Mitchell, Editor
Material: All
Address: C/O AOA 243 N LINDBERGH BLVD
City/State/ZIP: ST LOUIS MO 63141-7881
Telephone: 314-991-4100
Fax: 314-991-4101
E-mail: OptoEcon@aol.com

Oracle Poetry & Letters

Please refer to Rising Star Publishers.

Oracle Story & Letters

Please refer to Rising Star Publishers.

Orange Coast Magazine

Orange Coast Magazine and *Orange Coast Online* (www.orangecoast.com) are published for the educated and affluent residents of Orange County, California. Priority is given to well-told stories that have strong local interest, always with an emphasis on stylish writing and clear thinking.

GUIDELINES

To propose a story, writers should send a detailed query with published writing samples, or a completed manuscript. Proposals that arrive with a stamped, self-addressed envelope will be returned if the manuscript is not usable. Others will not be returned. Manuscripts should be saved in ASCII, or text-only, format and sent on a 3½" computer disc or by e-mail. A hardcopy of the manuscript should also be sent via mail or fax. Writers should include their name, address, phone number and social security number.

WRITING TIPS

1. Read previous issues of *Orange Coast* to gauge the range of story ideas and how they were handled.

2. Give stories a hard, narrow focus. Rather than a story about the Pacific Symphony Orchestra, tell us the story of the lead cellist who scoured the world for the perfect cello, then mortgaged his house in order to buy it.

3. Once the story is focused, broaden the perspective. A story focused on our cellist should raise much larger questions: Why would a musician take a huge financial risk to get an instrument that to an untrained ear sounds pretty much like any other cello? What does the musician hear that the rest of us don't?

4. Narrative stories work best, with scenes, characters and situations developed in the writer's own words. But the editors also encourage writers to experiment with style—there is no right formula. Ask yourself what's the best way to tell this particular story. The story should dictate the style and the style never should dominate or obscure the story.

5. Show, don't tell. Instead of telling readers the room was cold and drafty, give them the details that show the cold: a character puffing clouds of vapor, a flickering candle, the butler wearing mittens. Effective details let the reader see; useless details clutter the story.

6. Avoid newspaperese. In the economy of newspaper writing, a man who dedicated his life to police work, who built a career during weekends and midnight shifts and who faced countless dangers for inadequate pay becomes a "28-year police veteran." In magazine writing, you can create real characters for the reader. There is no need to boil the elements of a personality into such efficient language.

7. But don't overwrite. If the subject isn't compelling enough to carry the story without embellishment, the value of the story immediately comes into question.

8. When appropriate, draw conclusions and interpret what you have seen and learned. If the most powerful banker in town has a pencil-thin mustache and dresses in hand-painted Niagara Falls ties, white bucks and loud sports jackets, provide the reader with those details. Then, if you think he looks like a used-car salesman, you're certainly free to say so. Just make sure the image is precise and accurate.

9. Save your notes in case additional material is needed for the story.

10. Remember that you are writing for an audience that generally is literate, wealthy and sophisticated, but avoid dry intellectual discourse.

11. Write about real people in real situations; let their stories crystallize the broader issues.

RATES

• *Orange Coast* pays between $400 and $800 for main features, which generally range between 2,000 and 3,000 words. The amount of the payment ultimately depends on the amount of reporting involved and the quality of the writing, and it includes the writer's expenses. Secondary and department features pay between $100 and $200. Short Cut stories pay between $25 and $50.

• Payment is made after the editors accept and schedule the story for publication, which generally is three months prior to the magazine's issue date. Editorial payments are processed on the 20th of each month and checks are mailed out within one week. No additional payments are made for photographs or accompanying artwork

• For stories done on speculation, no kill fee is paid if the submission is unsuitable for use. For stories assigned by the editors, the kill fee will not exceed 20 percent of the agreed-upon publication price.

• *Orange Coast* buys one-time rights. If the submitted article has appeared elsewhere, writers should let the editors know when and where, and verify in writing that they have not relinquished their rights to it.

Categories: Lifestyles—Regional

Name: Martin J. Smith, Editor
Name: Sharon Chan, Managing Editor
Material: Any
Address: 3701 BIRCH ST STE 100
City/State/ZIP: NEWPORT BEACH CA 62660
Telephone: 714-862-1133
Fax: 714-862-0133
E-mail: ocmag@aol.com

Oregon Business
Helping Oregon Companies Grow

Dear Prospective Contributor:

Our purpose is to produce a useful, compelling and indispensable monthly magazine that will serve our business readers and help us earn our motto: "Helping Oregon companies grow." In addition we hope we can help you in your professional development. We understand that our contributors are the editorial engine of Oregon Business.

Kathy Dimond, Editor-in-Chief

Readership

Our subscribers include owners of small and medium-sized businesses, government agencies, professional staffs of banks, insurance companies, ad agencies, attorneys and other service providers. The typical reader earns an average of $87,000 a year, is college educated and owns a home. Circulation is 19,490, although readership reaches 46,000.

Coverage

About 30% of the magazine's content is written by freelancers, including standing section stories and cover features. Although freelancers most commonly pitch general profiles, we rarely cover a company just because it's there. An *Oregon Business* story must meet at least two of the following criteria:

• **Size and location:** The topic must be relevant to Northwest businesses. Companies (including franchises) must be based in Oregon or Southwest Washington with at least five employees and annual sales above $250,000.

• **Service:** Our sections (1,200 words) are reserved largely for service pieces focusing on finance, marketing, management or other general business topics. These stories are meant to be instructional, emphasizing problem-solving by example: "Building a Business Plan: Company X broke the rules and succeeded."

• **Trends:** These are sometimes covered in a section piece, or perhaps a feature story (2,000 to 4,000 words). We aim to be the state's leading business publication, so we want to be the first to spot trends that affect Oregon companies. If we can't be first, we'll be best. That means going deeper than the typical coverage, offering fresh perspectives and challenging assumptions: "Are Employee Incentives on Their Way Out?" "The New Oregonians: They came, they stayed, get used to it."

• **Exclusivity or strategy:** Usually a feature or cover story offering a insider's account of an event, whether it's a corporate merger, a dramatic turnaround, a marketing triumph or a PR disaster. The rare breaking news story will focus on the "what"; the more common piece analyzing strategy will talk about the whys and the hows: "Two CEOs. One Golf Game: How the courtship between U.S. Bank and West One led to marriage."

• **Compelling figures:** A personality profile of a business leader whose style or accomplishments merit an in-depth look. The subject must be interesting, complex, visionary or controversial: "High Volume, High Pressure. How Scott Thomason turned a single dealership into an auto empire."

Standards

Oregon Business adheres to the highest journalistic standards of fairness, diligence and accuracy and expects our contributors to do the same. Stories must be authoritative, which requires thorough reporting using several sources. They must be clearly organized with a well defined theme. And they must be illustrated with real—life examples, because, above all, business is composed of people.

We expect smart and elegant writing in the best of magazine traditions. This means telling—or more accurately, showing—the story from the players' perspectives: the executives who did the deal, the middle manager who got laid off, the line workers who changed the manufacturing process. Industry analysts and statistics are necessary to support a point, but they should be used sparingly.

Writers are responsible for making sure their submissions are error-free; this includes fact checking in final draft form. Editors will return for a rewrite stories that are sloppily put together or underreported. Poor rewrites requiring extensive editing may result in a fee reduction.

Submissions

We do not accept unsolicited material, but we're happy to receive query letters in writing (no phone calls). If we like your idea we'll give you a written assignment along with a word length and deadline, usually 45 days before publication.

• **Format.** Send material via e-mail or disk, filed under text-only format or ASCII. Always submit a hard copy by fax or snail mail.

• **Compensation.** We pay an average of $360 for a section story and between $400 and $1,000 for a feature story, depending on length and complexity. Submissions should include an invoice. Payment is shortly after publication.

• **Rights.** We buy first publication rights, which include the contributor's agreement not to sell the story or photo to another publisher within four months after publication in *Oregon Business*.

Photography

Oregon Business is recognized for its artful and unusual pictures. A successful contributor will have an eye for turning the mundane into the interesting and the drab into the colorful. We encourage creativity, which sometimes means puffing together elements from disparate locations or asking subjects to travel off site. The more our magazine's reputation grows, the more our subjects are willing to go along with the photographer's vision.

We like candid shots as much as portraits, so please include both to give us a variety. We do not accept grip-and-grin shots, gimmicky set ups or "class picture" poses. If we receive photos that do not meet our standards, we may request a reshoot at no extra charge.

• **Format:** Color slides, either 2¼" or 35mm. To avoid confusion, stamp each frame with your name, address and phone number and encase the slides in plastic sleeves. Attach the subject's business card and always include written caption information.

Although we like a variety of shots, one roll of film is usually enough and not more than two.

• **Compensation:** We pay $85 plus film and processing for photos inside the magazine and a flat $450 for covers. Include an invoice with your submission. We return the slides along with a copy of the issue on publication. Payment is sent shortly after publication.

• **Loss/damage.** We will not be liable for any lost or damaged slides, negatives or prints if the photo was assigned by the magazine. Photographers submitting stock photos must obtain written loss/damage protection in advance.

What you can expect from us

We will do our best to treat you fairly and professionally. If we need you to turn around work for us quickly, we will try to remember that you write or shoot for other publications, too. If your story requires substantive editing, we'll go over the changes with you before the piece goes to press.

We want to create steady, long-term relationships with our contributors. The best will be given frequent assignments and projects.

We look forward to working with you to make a good magazine even better.

Categories: Business—Regional

Name: Shirleen Holt, Managing Editor
Material: E-mail or Disk Query
Address: 610 SW BROADWAY STE 200
City/State/ZIP: PORTLAND OR 97205
Telephone: 503-223-0304
Fax: 503-221-6544
E-mail: Sholt@class.orednet.org

Oregon Coast

Please refer to Northwest Regional Magazines.

Oregon Outside

Please refer to Northwest Regional Magazines.

Oregon Quarterly
The Magazine of the University of Oregon

Oregon Quarterly is the successor to *Old Oregon*, the University of Oregon's alumni magazine founded in 1919. Although our 110,000 readers consist predominantly of UO alumni, our editorial approach has evolved in the past few years from a traditional alumni magazine to a regional magazine of ideas. To highlight this change, we now describe ourselves as "The Northwest Perspective from the University of Oregon."

Unlike a traditional alumni magazine, the majority of our features are not about the UO as such. Instead, we generally address topics of state and regional interest (ideas, issues and personalities) using the resources of UO faculty and alumni. The UO benefits from its *involvement* in these stories, not as their subject matter. Our goal is to reach a broad, well-educated regional audience, whether or not they have ties to the UO. As a magazine, we want to be recognized for the quality of our writing.

Good magazine stories should have shape and depth. They are closer in conception and execution to a thoughtful essay than to a newspaper feature. They should involve the reader, awaken the imagination. They require some effort to write, but they are much more a pleasure to read.

Although our departments are staff-written, most of our features and short subjects are contributed by free lancers. If the topic has a contemporary regional interest, and if UO involvement can be demonstrated (through faculty or alumni participation), we'd like to hear about it. We prefer brief query letters that show the flavor of the proposed article and your writing style. Submit clips that demonstrate your ability. If you don't have a story idea but would like to be considered for assignments, submit clips with a cover letter explaining your interests and experience.

We invite queries for features, which generally run 2,500-3,000 words. We pay 20 cents a word on acceptance (after requested revisions), plus reasonable expenses (with receipts), provided they are cleared by us in advance. For contracted stories we do not accept, we pay a kill fee of 20 percent the contracted amount. We generally follow the *Chicago Manual of Style*.

Recent Freelance Features

"Oregon's Miracle?" by Lisa Cohn (Winter 1995): What the boom of high-tech manufacturing in the region may mean to Oregon's future.

"New Voices" by Alice Evans (Autumn 1995): How the UO Creative Writing Program emerged from a period of turmoil to become nationally renown.

"The Resurrection of Knowles Creek" by Lucy Vinis (Summer 1995): How saving Oregon's salmon runs may involve not only hard work, but a close reading of Aristotle as well.

Categories: Nonfiction—College—Culture—Education—Regional

Name: Submissions Editor
Material: All
Address: 5228 UNIVERSITY OF OREGON
City/State/ZIP: EUGENE OR 97403
Telephone: 541-346-5048
Fax: 541-346-5578
E-mail: gmaynard@oregon.uoregon.edu

Other Voices
University of Illinois-Chicago

Fiction Guidelines

1. OV reads unpublished, unsolicited manuscripts between October 1 and April 1, only.

2. Short stories and self-contained novel excerpts only.

3. One story at a time, please!

4. 5,000 word maximum preferred, but not mandatory.

5. Writer's name on each page of mss.

6. Save a tree-the Editors suggest a letter-size SASE for reply only (and promise to recycle your mss.).

7. 10-12 week reply

8. No taboos, except ineptitude and murkiness.
Send Us Your Best Voice/Your Best Work/Your Best...
Categories: Fiction

Name: L. Hauselman, Executive Editor
Name: Tina Peano, Assistant Editor
Name: Ruth Canji, Assistant Editor
Material: Fiction
Address: UNIVERSITY OF ILLINOIS AT CHICAGO
Address: 601 S MORGAN
City/State/ZIP: CHICAGO IL 60607
Telephone: 312-413-2209

Out & About

Thank you for your interest in writing for *Out & About*.
We pay $50-$80 for City Briefs (1,300-1,400 words)
$100-$450 for features (800-3,000 words)
$50 for B&B reviews (400-450 words)
$50 for Traveler's Diary (250-350 words)

Our pay scale depends on how much additional reworking is necessary to match to our standard format for City Briefs, and completeness, accuracy and style of features. We envision the City Brief section as the kind of information you would give to a friend who was coming into town for three or four days. Throughout each section, we try to include more unusual, less well known establishments with a local flavor. Our restaurant selections should cover the gamut from cheap, quick food to the kind of place you would go if you were really splurging, especially if the latter is notable, new and trendy. For bars and clubs, we try to reduce a Damron's guide listing to what's hot right now, and where and when to find the best crowds.

Features should include a historical context, abbreviated travel logistics information, and coverage of areas and activities of general travel interest. Unless an assignment is specifically for the gay male or gay women's market, all submissions must include information for men and women, with a clear explanation of if and how venues are separate, and to the extent men or women dominate the scene.

We prefer submission on 3.5" disc or text file by AOL to screen name OUTndABOUT. Alternate submission can be arranged.

Note that we do not accept any editorial that has been previously published elsewhere.

Please call if you have any questions or concerns—we can be reached day and night. If we're out of the office, just leave a time and number to call you back.

Very truly yours,
Billy Kolber
Editor

EDITORIAL GUIDELINES

Out & About is not so much about gay travel as it is about the gay traveler. The emphasis is on travel for the purpose of cultural enrichment, environmental diversity and the sensory stimulation it provides. While our perspective is gay, the information we present is intended to facilitate and enhance the travel experience, not define it.

Features should highlight travel destinations and experiences that have both genuine travel interest, as well as specific interest for gay men and lesbians. City briefs should focus on highlights for the short term visitor. In addition to bars and clubs, great emphasis is put on hotel, dining, shopping and sightseeing recommendations, which are not limited to gay owned/operated or predominantly patronized. Best in town, best value and unique to their locale are our primary focus. Articles focus on the mechanics of travel, especially aspects that are different for gay and lesbian travelers.

Our mission is to enable gay and lesbian singles, couples and families to identify and choose travel experiences that are appropriate to their preferences and lifestyles.

Our tone is upbeat, sophisticated and very subjective, with an understanding that our readers will cross a broad spectrum of financial and social backgrounds. Without being judgmental, we will not cover bath houses, sex tours or provide information relating to paid sexual activities.

Sexual references will be encouraged to the extent that they enhance our sense of humor and broaden our appeal without compromising our professional image.

All destinations, hotels, restaurants and clubs mentioned must have been personally inspected by a reliable source, and if that source is not the author, we must be informed. Agency commission policies and credit card acceptance information must be obtained for each hotel and tour, in addition to name, address phone/fax numbers and the name of an owner/manager/contact.

All recommendations should be supported by one or two substantive feature descriptions. Recommendations against a specific hotel or vendor must be supported by a deficiency that would prove objectionable across the bulk of our subscriber base. Any hotels or travel products recommended that do not cater specifically to a gay clientele must have their procedures verified to insure that they are not gay-hostile.

Free travel may not be solicited by *Out & About* contributors, and articles based on free or junket travel must be approved in advance. Any supplier s offering discounted or gratis travel or accommodations must sign a disclaimer indicating that the discount was not requested, and that they understand that their product may receive no coverage, negative coverage or be compared unfavorably to a competitor who nay not have provided any consideration.

EVALUATION CRITERIA

Hotels:

Location: What is near? What is accessible within ten minute walk or drive? How accessible by public transportation? How far from airport/train?

Staff: Friendly? Offer assistance beyond minimum?

Furnishings: Cleanliness? Do they look like they're from Sears/Macys/Bloomingdales/custom designed? What is in a standard room besides the bed?

Ambiance: Who are the other guests? Are they primarily gay? Are there a lot of families? Conventions? Ask the staff about what the guest make-up is usually like. This is the most difficult and important aspect to assess.

Special Services: What additional services/benefits are included or are routinely arranged by the hotel staff (i.e.: Manager's cocktail party, or gym passes at hotels that don't have gym facilities.

We like to feature a range of hotels, with an emphasis on great value and interesting accommodations. At a minimum, selection must include: Best in town, gay owned/operated/patronized (if it exists and is not of poor quality or value), and a moderately priced selection.

Restaurants:

Food: What are the specialties? Is it local or ethnic cuisine? What is the average cost of an entree? What is the quality of the food and presentation?

Service: Is it efficient? Does the waiter tell you his name? Does the waiter tell you his name and life story? Is there enough of it, including busboys and host?

Atmosphere: Would you have a business meeting there? Would you propose marriage there? Is it the kind of place you want to linger over your food? Is there sawdust on the floor, or an ancient photo of the chef and Dean Martin on the Wall? Is the clientele primarily gay? Can you eat at the bar or a counter? Would you want to?

Details: Are reservations accepted/required/suggested? Do they serve breakfast, lunch, dinner, brunch? Which credit cards do they take?

We require a range of dining options including at least one of each: Haute cuisine, hip/trendy, fun/quick/cheap, ethnic (Asian, European or South American). Listings should include restaurants with a gay following, as long as they are noteworthy. Listing must mention the following when they apply: restaurant accepts no credit cards, reservations are difficult to get, dress code would require more than jeans and a clean shirt, clientele is perceptibly straight.

Clubs:

What type of crowd is it? Is the bar in an upswing in popularity or a downswing? What regular features are offered: gogo boyz, beer blast, wet jockey shorts, etc. Is it crowded on specific nights of the week? What is the best feature? (outdoor patio, lots of pool tables, hot guys, cheap beer). We do not need an exhaustive listing. We focus on where the action is centered. The most valuable information is where there is a progression from early crowd to after-hours, or certain nights of the week where one club is particularly hot. Information for lesbians is required in all assignments.

Gyms:

What are the facilities? Free weights? What kind of machines? Is there enough equipment? When is it busiest? When is it crusiest? Aerobics? Racquetball? Pool? Sauna? Steam room? How much is the daily fee? Legitimate gyms only; if the primary gay gym in a city is part of a bathhouse complex it may be included with full disclosure.

Shopping:

Unusual is the key here: stores which offer a unique environment or experience, or merchandise which is not widely available are preferred. Variety is much less important in this category; clothing and local handicrafts, if existent, should always be included.

Sightseeing:

One or two major tourist highlights, preferably with a hint as to how to best enjoy them, and one or two less known, off-beat or gay-oriented highlights.

Categories: Gay/Lesbian—Travel

Name: Billy Kolber-Stuart, Editor
Material: Gay/Lesbian Travel
Address: 8 W 19TH ST STE 401
City/State/ZIP: NEW YORK NY 10011
Telephone: 212-645-6922
Fax: 212-645-6785
E-mail: editor@outandabout.com
Internet: www.outandabout.com

Outdoor Life

Outdoor Life serves the active outdoor sportsman and his family. The magazine emphasizes hunting, fishing, outdoor adventures and game conservation.

If you are interested in writing for *Outdoor Life*, *study* the magazine. What we publish is your best guide to the kinds of material we seek. Whatever the subject, you must present it in a way that is interesting and honest.

We pay on acceptance. We use no fiction, and we use no poetry.

We accept very little unsolicited material. The best advice is to write a query letter first. Most of the material we buy originates this way. Our Compass and regional sections are two places for writers who have never worked with us before to break in.

Do you have something to offer the reader that will help him or her enjoy hunting and fishing more? How do you think it will help? How would you present it?

You are better off to be early—even considerably early—with a query than to be even a little late. We think at least a year ahead. Right now, we are concerned about what will be in *Outdoor Life* a year from now. Writers and photographers should be thinking the same way.

Though we have millions of readers, we never forget that we reach them one at a time. A reader who picks up a copy of *Outdoor Life* is asking, "What's in it for me?"

You are writing for an intelligent reader who is eager t learn more about the outdoors. Your job is to make it clear and interesting.

Preparing Manuscripts and Photos: Manuscripts must be typed, double-spaced or triple-spaced. Use a medium quality non-erasable 8½" X 11" paper (editing on erasable paper is murder). Number the page, and type your name and the story title at the top of every page. Leave wide margins. Do not staple or bind manuscript pages. Paper clips are fine. All submissions should include a copy of your manuscript on a 3½" floppy disk either in a Word document or MS-DOS file.

Black-and-white photos should be professional-quality 8" X 10" glossy prints (we may ask for negatives). Color photos should be the original positive transparencies and of 35mm size or larger. The best way to mount transparencies is in notebook-size plastic holders that hold 20 of the 35mm transparencies. Your name and address should be on the back of each black-and-white print and on the cardboard mount of each transparency. Every print and transparency should be clearly marked with a number. Submissions should number no more than 20 photographs and be keyed to a detailed caption sheet that goes beyond merely identifying people in the photos to teach the reader something new and interesting.

We take every possible precaution in handling unsolicited materials. However, we are not responsible for their damage or loss. Submissions not accompanied by a properly stamped, self-addressed envelope *will not* be returned.

Categories: Nonfiction—Adventure—Animals—Book Reviews—Conservation—Consumer—Cooking—Crafts—Ecology—Health—History—Hobbies—Interview—Outdoors—Photography—Physical Fitness—Regional—Sports—Recreation—Travel—Fishing—Hunting—How-to—Nostalgia—Essay—Personal Experience—Nature

Name: Todd W. Smith
Material: Editor
Address: TWO PARK AVENUE
City/State/ZIP: NEW YORK, NY 10016-5695
Telephone: 212-779-5000
Fax: 212-686-6877

OutLoud And Proud!!

Publisher: Turquoise Butterfly Press
Format: 8-page bimonthly newsletter. Established in 1998.
Focus: Our newsletter is a forum for self-expression. We publish essays, opinions, thoughts, and stories about everything and anything. Letting it all out and refusing to hold back is what works best. Get angry—get informed—be political—be bitchy—say it as it is!
Submission: Lead articles should be 900-1,500 words. All other articles, personal stories, interviews, humorous pieces etc., should be 100-900 words. All material must be typewritten or neatly handwritten. Include a word count! Artwork and photos may accompany piece. Editor has the right to edit material. Buys one-time rights. Buys reprints. Include researched citations. Pays in copies. Sample copy is $3.50.
Categories: Nonfiction—Essay—Opinion

Name: Terri Andrews, Editor
Material: All
Address: PO BOX 750
City/State/ZIP: ATHENS OH 45701-1127

Outside: Speculative and Dark Fiction

Who We Are: *Outside* is a paying professional magazine of SF and dark imaginative fiction, aimed at people who love to read well-plotted, character-driven genre fiction. We are interested in fiction that transcends the limitations and ventures outside the stereotypes of genre fiction.

What We Publish: short (1500-4000 words) science fiction, horror, and darkly imaginative fiction. We seek well-written, professionally executed fiction, with attention to basics - grammar, punctuation, usage. We do not accept sword & sorcery, pornography, or excessive violence and gore beyond the legitimate needs of a story. Also no derivative works (e.g., emulating TV shows and movies - no *Star Trek* stories, for example).

Our Goals: We strive to be both writer-friendly and reader-friendly. We eagerly look forward to receiving top quality, professional material from you.

Requirements: All stories must be typed double-spaced, on only one side of each sheet with sheets loose — no fasteners of any kind. The author's full name and address should appear in the upper left-hand corner of page one; an approximate word count should appear in the upper right-hand corner. Each page should be numbered and include the title and author's last name. We will accept letter quality 24-pin dot-matrix computer print—please separate the pages. If you choose to submit photocopies, they must be clear and readable. No simultaneous submissions, please.

Grammar, punctuation, spelling, and usage weigh heavily as we consider the story. You must master these essentials to be a professional writer. We expect that a professional writer owns, and regularly uses, a dictionary and at least one or two usage books (e.g. Strunk & White, Fowler). To be a successful writer, you should be a voracious but discriminating reader. Many books are available about the craft of writing — read them all for free through your public library. Join a writers' group. Write constantly to improve your craft — it's a tough discipline, as difficult and time consuming as learning to play symphony-quality violin or piano. Visit SharpWriter.Com for a comprehensive writer's resource. Finally, despite all these somewhat dire words, we wish you a passionate and successful love affair with writing.

We pay three cents per word upon acceptance of your manuscript for first serial rights for one year. Acceptance constitutes final editorial approval of content. We strive to pay as promptly as possible, but please allot a reasonable amount of time (6-8 weeks after acceptance) for your check to arrive.

Manuscripts must be sent by postal mail only. E-mail submissions will be deleted without being read. Please include an appropriately sized, self-addressed, stamped envelope (SASE). (Contributors residing outside the United States should use international reply coupons.) Even if you do not want your manuscript returned, we require a letter-size SASE for our response; manuscripts without an SASE will not be returned.

If you have an e-mail address, please furnish it on your hardcopy. Our e-mail address is outside@clocktowerfiction.com.

We usually respond within six weeks after receiving a submission. Depending on many variables, however, it can sometimes take longer. Please give us ample time before you begin writing to inquire about a submission's status. Please do not send us the only copy of your manuscript (accidents happen and mail gets lost). No simultaneous or previously published work.

Categories: Fiction—Science Fiction—Horror

Name: Brian Callohan and John Cullen, Editors
Material: All
Address: CLOCKTOWER FICTION,
        6549 MISSION GORGE ROAD, BOX 260
City/State/ZIP: SAN DIEGO, CA 92120
E-mail: outside@clocktowerfiction.com
Internet: www.clocktowerfiction.com/Outside

Overland Journal

The *Overland Journal* is always in need of articles, and all articles received are appreciated and given careful consideration. There are three general requirements for an *Overland Journal* article.

TOPIC

The focus of an article must be on some aspect of the emigrant trails or the overland migration in western America.

ORIGINAL RESEARCH

An article must reflect some form of original research or interpretation. It should not be just a compilation of information from modern authors' articles or books (i.e., secondary sources.) Original research would include any one or combination of the following:

1. articles that are based substantially on primary written source material, both published and unpublished, such as diaries, journals, reminiscences, letters, contemporary newspapers, government reports and other archival materials. It is understood that articles of original research can and usually will make use of and have reference to secondary sources, but the main supporting evidence should be taken from primary sources. An exception to this requirement would include articles that interpret, evaluate or analyze secondary sources and published primary sources of published emigrant trail literature.

2. articles that are based on non-literary evidence drawn from areas of archaeology, technology, geology, geography, cartography, field research, statistics or personal interviews.

3. articles that are themselves primary sources and are supported by primary and secondary sources, such as an unpublished emigrant diary edited and annotated especially for the *Overland Journal*.

The requirements on documentation and original research are not to imply that the *Overland Journal* is a scholarly publication primarily written for academic specialists. Quite the contrary, it is a history magazine primarily designed for the lay reader who is interested in the western overland trails and the migration experience. Nevertheless, even with this lay emphasis, there is a need for original ideas and interpretations that are convincingly documented.

Articles submitted for consideration must not be submitted to other publications concurrently.

DOCUMENTATION

All significant evidence, references, assertions, data and facts not commonly known must be well documented. The appropriate form of documentation will depend on the type of evidence used.

The *Overland Journal* uses endnotes rather than footnotes. Text and notes are based for the most part on *The Chicago Manual of Style*. However, the best reference to use when preparing a manuscript is a copy of the *Overland Journal* itself. If you do not have a copy of the *Journal*, please write to the Oregon-California Trails Association headquarters for a sample copy.

Endnotes should include author of publication cited, editor if appropriate, exact title (including unusual spelling, capitalization or punctuation), city and state of publisher, publisher's name, date of publication *of the source you used* and page numbers of text to which you have referred.

When quoting from a diary, please give the present location of the diary and whether it has been published. If it has been published, all of the above information about annotation of books would apply.

Below are examples of endnote styles. There may be exceptions to these, and in those cases the editor will determine the style to be used.

Merrill J. Mattes, *Great Platte River Road*, 2nd ed. (Lincoln, NE: Nebraska State Historical Society, 1969), p. 23.

Peter Tamony, "To See the Elephant," *Pacific Historian*, Vol. 12, 1968, p. 23.

Abigail Jane Scott Dunniway, trail diary (1852), [insert here if you are referring to one specific day only, i.e., 25 June 1852]. Manuscript #432 [if there is an access number for the manuscript], Oregon Historical Society, Portland, Oregon.

T. J. Able, letter to parents, 12 October 1857. Manuscript HM 16763, Huntington Library, San Marino, California.

U.S. War Department, *Annual Report of the Secretary of War* (Washington, D.C., 1852), p. 136-137.

Ibid.

Ibid., p. 82.

We do not use "op cit" when referring to a work cited previously. Instead, we use the last name of the author and a few key words from the title.

Lienhard, *From St. Louis*, p. 28. (Reference cited is shown below.)

Heinrich Lienhard, *From St. Louis to Sutter's Fort, 1846*, ed. Erwin G. and Elisabeth K. Gudde (Norman, OK: University of Oklahoma Press, 1961), p. 28-29.

War Department, *Annual Resort*, p. 156.

Scott, trail diary, 27 June 1852.

MANUSCRIPT

Manuscripts, both text and endnotes, should be typed and average approximately 35 double-spaced pages in length. We have published a few articles that were shorter and a few that were longer, but this is an average.

When directly quoting from another source, *please* triple check for exact accuracy of spelling, wording and punctuation as the author wrote it. Some sources are difficult for us to obtain for verification. This is of utmost importance when quoting from a diary. When a diarist has not bothered with punctuation, we use *four spaces* to indicate we *think* this is the end of a sentence. We do not improve upon spelling, punctuation, etc.

COMPUTER DISKETTES

We are, of course, always glad to receive a computer diskette if you have a computer and can use either 5¼" or 3½". We use WordPerfect 4.2, 5.0 or 5.1.

If you are working on a computer rather than a typewriter and are able to send a diskette, please use *as few codes as possible* as some codes do not transfer between programs. For example, if your computer has an endnote code which enables you to move back and forth from body copy to endnotes, *please do not use it*. It will not transfer into our desktop publishing program and causes us no end of trouble. Another example of a code that will not transfer is an automatic hyphenating program. It is best to use your computer as you would a typewriter, i.e., just use your indent and paragraph return. Nothing fancy!

BIOGRAPHY

Please include with your manuscript a brief biography, one to three sentences about yourself, that can be used to accompany your article.

Categories: Nonfiction—History—Western

Name: Marilyn Holt, Editor
Material: All

Address: 901 N BUCKEYE
City/State/ZIP: ABILENE KS 67410
Telephone: 785-263-1572

Over the BACK FENCE

Over the Back Fence

For written submissions used in *Over the Back Fence* or in other publications produced by *Back Fence Publishing, Inc.*, the following rates and guidelines apply:

Over the Back Fence is a regional magazine serving seventeen counties in Southern Ohio: Adams, Athens, Clinton, Fairfield, Fayette, Gallia, Greene, Highland, Hocking, Jackson, Lawrence, Meigs, Pickaway, Pike, Ross, Scioto and Vinton. We are adding Washington County in late 1996. Our approach can be equated to a friendly and informative conversation with a neighbor about interesting people, places and events.

Back Fence Publishing, Inc. purchases one-time North American print publication rights from freelance writers as well as makes assignments for specific articles. We reserve the right to reprint written submissions and will make payment for any additional usage—negotiable, but not to exceed original payment. If a submission has been previously published elsewhere, the date and name of the other publication must accompany text.

QUERIES: It is good to send queries or proposals for stories. This allows Back Fence Publishing, Inc. the opportunity to work with writers in developing the most appropriate stories for our publications. However, you may send samples of your writing style, or may send existing stories for consideration.

SUBMISSIONS: Your manuscript should include your name, address and daytime phone number on the top right corner of the first page. And your name must appear on every page thereafter. Submission on disk is appreciated, but not required for initial consideration.

If on disk, submissions should be saved in an ASCII text format or in a WordPerfect file. This disk should be labeled with your name, address, daytime phone number, name of format and name of file. Always send a cover letter with your name, address, daytime telephone number and a brief description of your submission.

Feature stories are usually 1,000 to 1,800 words after editing. A byline will appear in the publication for writers of published submissions, *except* in the case of paid advertisements, where it may or may not appear.

Our magazine is published quarterly—each February (spring issue), May (summer issue), August (fall issue) and November (winter issue). Please make submissions at least six months to one year before the intended issue. Please consider the season for which your work is submitted.

RATES: Rates begin at 10 cents per word, but may be negotiated depending upon experience. A minimum fee of $25 will be paid in the case of pieces shorter than 250 words. Payment is upon publication (net 15 days).

ASSIGNMENTS: Writers may be selected to complete writing assignments that match their writing styles, interests, specializations, or location and ability to travel to neighboring counties.

TEXT/PHOTO PACKAGES: For writers who want to supply photographs (or illustrations) along with their submissions, please request our Photographers' and Illustrators' Rates and Guidelines.

Rates and guidelines are subject to change without notice.

Sample copies of the magazine may be obtained by sending $2.95 and a self-addressed, postage paid envelope at least 10"x13". For questions or to obtain a subscription, call the number shown below or 800-718-5727

Categories: Family—General Interest—History—Regional—Rural America—Travel

Name: Ann Zalek, Editor-in-Chief
Material: General
Name: Barbara Jividen, Managing Editor
Material: Features, Poetry, Adventure
Name: Sarah Williamson, Senior Editor
Material: Features, History, Humorous
Address: PO BOX 756
City/State/ZIP: CHILLICOTHE OH 45601
Telephone: 614-772-2165
Fax: 614-773-7626
E-mail: backfenc@bright.net

Owen Wister Review
University of Wyoming

[Editor's note: The following guidelines contain a submission deadline that will have passed prior to the publication of this directory. Please solicit current guidelines from the publisher prior to submitting any work.]

The expanded, Spring 1998 edition of *Owen Wister Review* will be dedicated to art and literature of or about the western region. The "western region" to us means any state west of the Missouri River but east of the west coast. Art and literature "of or about the western region" to us means any work from artists living in the region, or work about the region from artists living elsewhere. In dedicating the magazine to this theme, we hope to provide an outlet for the many writers and artists working in the west, as well as for writers and artists working elsewhere in the world who feel a connection to our region.

Deadline for all submissions is December 1,1997.

Art: Please send 35mm slides, no more than 20 per artist, and no fewer than 5. Color or black and white work is accepted. Each slide should be labeled with your name, plus the media, the size, title, and date of the piece. Selections will be based on the quality and originality of the work. Please include a brief biographical sketch with your name, phone number and address.

Manuscripts: All submissions of poetry, art, or prose must be typed or printed by an inkjet or laser printer. Please include a cover letter including your name, address, phone number, and a brief biographical sketch; do NOT put your name on the manuscript.

Poetry: Please send no more than five poems.

Fiction/prose: Please send stories or nonfiction essays from 1,200 to 6,500 words in length.

Contributors to the *Owen Wister Review* receive a free copy of the magazine, plus a 10% discount on additional copies. All rights revert back to the contributor upon printing of the magazine. Please note that we accept only hard copy submissions: no electronic or faxed submissions. We will respond to submissions as soon as possible. We do not read manuscripts during the months of May, June, July, or August. Work received during these months will be returned, unopened.

• If you are a University of Wyoming Student and want to be considered for the Best of Show Competition, please indicate this on the outside of your submission.

Categories: Fiction—Arts—Literature—Western—Writing

Name: Submissions Editor
Material: All

Address: STUDENT PUBLICATIONS
Address: UNIVERSITY OF WYOMING
Address: PO BOX 3625
City/State/ZIP: LARAMIE WY 82071
Telephone: 307-766-6190
Fax: 307-766-4027

Oxendine Publishing, Inc.

Publisher/Editor-In-Chief: W. H. "Butch" Oxendine, Jr.
Managing Editor: Kay Quinn King
Assistant Editor: Teresa L. Beard
Art Director: Jeffrey L. Riemersma
THE PUBLICATIONS
Oxendine Publishing produces four publications for high school and college students, three of which are distributed in Florida and one nationally. The Florida publications are read by students at 70 colleges and more than 343 public high schools. In October 1993, Oxendine Publishing launched a national leadership magazine called *Student Leader* which is read by the top five percent of active students at more than 890 colleges and universities nationwide.

Florida Leader for college students is published in March, April, and September with a circulation of 20,000 per issue. The high school edition of *Florida Leader* is published in January, June, and August with a circulation of 25,000. *Careers and Majors* and *Transfer Student* each are published in January and June with respective circulations of 18,000 and 15,000 per issue.

Student Leader, a national leadership development magazine, is published in October and March with a circulation of 100,000 per issue. In addition to student readers, *Student Leader* and Oxendine's regional magazines are read by college and high school guidance counselors, career faculty, deans of students, directors of campus activities, college and corporate recruiters, and public relations directors.
EDITORIAL FOCUS
Both *Florida Leader* magazines feature academic-major and career articles, current financial aid and admissions information, and stories on other aspects of college life for current or prospective college students.

Careers and Majors targets graduating college seniors who are pursuing advanced degrees or beginning their careers. Articles include interview and job-search articles, up-to-date career profiles, and advice on how to choose and apply to graduate and professional schools.

Oxendine Publishing's national magazine, *Student Leader,* focuses on helping veteran and developing campus leaders become more effective and ethical campus decision-makers. Typical articles include advice on motivating and organizing students, recent leadership and management strategies, how to balance school, work and extracurricular activities, and news about service and fund-raising projects and achievements nationwide.
WRITER'S TIPS
Full-length articles (about 1,000 words) should include seven to 12 sources, quoting student and collegiate leaders, as well as appropriate sources. For the four Florida publications, primary sources, for the most part, should be from colleges, high schools and businesses within the state. For *Student Leader,* college and corporate sources should be varied geographically and demographically. Writers may query ideas for articles or discuss pos-

sible assignments already on the calendar. If possible, state availability of photos with query.

Copy should follow AP style. When students are mentioned by name, first reference should include year in school, institution they attend, and if relevant, their major. The full names, titles, addresses, and day-time phones of all interview subjects should be included separately with each submission. Articles may be edited for space and content.

Writers are responsible for the accuracy of all information in the article. Articles by first-time writers may be used, but only experienced writers will receive payment, which varies from $35 to $75 per piece for Florida publications and from $50 to $200 for *Student Leader.* Payment is made within 30 days after publication. All writers will receive at least one full-color copy of their article. Send a SASE envelope to receive query response, an editorial calendar, or $3.50 for a sample issue.
INTERNSHIPS
On-site or "remote" internships for students are available for one or more semesters.
Categories: Teen

Name: Kay Quinn, Managing Editor
Name: Teresa Beard, Assistant Editor
Material: Any
Address: PO BOX 14081
City/State/ZIP: GAINESVILLE FL 32601
Telephone: 352-373-6907
Fax: 352-373-8120
E-mail: oxendine@compuserve.com

Pacific Coast Journal

56 pages • paper w/paper cover • photocopied • $3.00 list price • $2.50 author's extra copies • quarterly • unaffiliated with any university or other institution • $12.00 for a five-issue subscription • $8.00 for a three-issue subscription

general focus: We have recently become interested in art on art. That is, writing and creative efforts about writing and the creative process. Otherwise, there is a tendency towards the western half of North America and the Pacific Rim.

short fiction: We usually don't print stories with more than 4,000 words. Average length of our stories is around 2,500 words. Erotica OK if it's really good. Sci-Fi is generally not accepted, but we do print some magical realism.

short short fiction: Fiction that is 500 words or less is always wanted. It approaches prose poetry and, in many cases, is indistinguishable from it.

essays: Papers with a general literary focus are appreciated. We don't print hard-core criticism, so please limit yourself to soft-crit.

poetry: Please limit submissions to 8 pages. Can be in any style, but we generally don't accept rhyming poetry—it better have a good reason to rhyme.

artwork: send in b/w drawings, collages, etc., with bold, obvious lines. Remember that this is a photocopied magazine so fine details may be lost.

photos: are not accepted for submission at this time.

Sometimes the editors write comments about a particularly comment-worthy ms., so please use a disposable copy of your ms. and always use a SASE. Indicate e-mail address if you have one, and whether or not you would like notification of acceptance by e-mail.

All work is copyrighted and rights revert to the author upon publication. We offer one-time rights only. This means that we occasionally do reprints if the material warrants it. Please provide credits where necessary.
Categories: Fiction—Poetry—Science Fiction

Name: Stillson Graham, Editor
Material: All except fiction
Name: Stephanie Kylkis, Fiction Editor
Material: Fiction
Address: PO BOX 23868
City/State/ZIP: SAN JOSE CA 95153
E-mail: paccoastj@juno.com

Pacific Currents Magazine

Pacific Currents Magazine is one of the original general interest "on-line" Internet magazines. As compared to the often "counter culture" fare found on the net, *Pacific Currents Magazine* offers stimulating, useful and decent "G" rated content, with a focus on the cultures, arts and natural treasures of the Northwest and the Pacific Rim, plus general articles on the issues that are affecting women and families today. Readers come to the site for the news and features they have grown to expect and enjoy.

Our target reader is as likely to be female as male, has a computer both at the office and at home, is part of a two car family, and plans a traveling vacation n the near future. Although the target audience is adult, *Pacific Currents Magazine* is a safe and rewarding on-line environment for younger viewers as well.

Submission Guidelines

Pacific Currents Magazine is 50% freelance written. Regular study of the magazine is the best way to learn what we want.

STYLE: Writers and cartoonists published in *Pacific Currents Magazine* have a style that starts fast, is fresh, bright, "hip", sometimes politically incorrect (but not juvenile) and "G" rated.

NEEDS: Query first. Book reviews, music reviews, movie reviews, articles on health issues, people, career, travel, arts, cultural, "event" articles; articles of exotic destinations whether in the Northwest or not, finances (if slant is unique), and features for children. Politics is not taboo, but focus must be on the event or person, not the political slant. One of our hottest needs is for articles of interest to women.

• Articles of from 600 to 1,500 words.
• We like a photograph with the article. Model release required.
• On occasion we publish book excerpts, or serializations, in trade for the exposure it gives.
• Cartoons may be in color or not. Submit electronically (.jpg or .gif file).
• Author assigns all rights to *Pacific Currents*. Our policy is to release secondary rights to the author upon written request. Author agrees that submitted work is original and agrees to indemnify *Pacific Currents Magazine* against any copyright infringement or breach of privacy suit.

PAYMENT: Pays up to $1,500 for original articles from "name" writers. Writers of reviews and articles are either paid in coupons* or to $25 and up where a paying sponsor makes payment possible.

*Coupons: Writers who have unpaid submissions published in *Pacific Currents Magazine* receive coupons called "Clam Bucks" with no cash value, but which can be applied once a year for discounts on purchases from our official and exclusive *"Prize Winning Writers"* catalog. Items in the catalog range from computer equipment and software to collectible Alaskana.

Bring your own sponsor: Once a writer becomes established with us as a regular contributor to a magazine feature our ability to pay usually goes up. "Established" in most cases means readership for the feature is growing and we have found a regular sponsor (advertiser) for a feature. We pay a bonus to writers who find their own sponsor (must be arranged in advance by contacting the editor of *Currents Magazine,* and sponsors must meet our "G" rated and other criteria).

SUBMISSIONS: Electronic submissions **required**. Submit as a standard text file attached to e-mail to the address below or mail the 3½" floppy disk (MS-DOS as a standard ASCII text file). US Postal submissions must be accompanied by SASE or you won't get your floppy disk back.

Categories: Travel—Children—Environment—Health—Wildlife—Women

Name: Editor
Material: All
Address: 10121 EVERGREEN WAY STE 152
City/State/ZIP: EVERETT WA 98204
Fax: 206-522-1027
E-mail: editor@go2net.org

PACK-o-FUN
Projects for Kids & Families

If you would like to submit a craft idea for possible publication, we ask that you follow these guidelines:

• Send us a photo of the item or items and a telephone number where you can be reached during the day.
• Write complete, accurate instructions (typed and double-spaced, please). Explain *everything* someone would need to know to complete the project. Use a current issue of the magazine as a guide.
• Include all patterns. Suggest any illustrations you feel necessary to make things clear. A quick line drawing may save many words of instruction.
• If drawing a cross-stitch or needlepoint chart, draw one symbol for each color, using a black grid and black ink. DO NOT color in chart squares.
• Please include a source for hard-to-find supplies. if a brand name is given, indicate whether a ™ or ® is used with the name. (Look on the packaging.)

We will contact you if we are interested in your project. If the design is accepted for publication, you will be asked to send the item to be photographed.

We are looking forward to seeing your original designs and hope that we will be able to work with you sometime soon!

POLICIES

Final Acceptance

• When you are notified that your design has been accepted for publication, you will be asked to send the completed design to us. We reserve the right to ask you to rework your design or the right to return it if we do not feel that your completed design meets our necessary standard for publication.

Contracts

• Contracts are sent to the designer on the Design-In date, provided the completed design and instructions are in our office. Check the schedule card. The design and instructions must be in our office before we send the contract.
• Payment will be sent 30 days after Design-In date, provided the signed contract is in our office by the due date stated on the contract. Otherwise, payment will be sent within 30 days of the date contract is received.
• You may send your completed design to us earlier than the Design-In date; however, the contract will not be sent until the Design-In date.

Design Fees

• The design fees we pay are based on quality, originality, craftsmanship, complexity, and appeal of the design. We also consider the accuracy and completeness of the instructions.
• All fees quoted are for all rights to the design. Fees are discounted 10% for first rights.
• Six complimentary copies of the issue in which your design appears will be sent to you shortly after the On-Sale date. Addi-

tional copies are available to designers at a discounted rate.

Rights

• We buy all rights to the design, which means that you grant us all rights to the design/article, including the right to publish the article in printed form and to publish video productions and other derivative works.

• If you would like to print your original article in another publication after we have purchased all rights, please let us know which publication and the publication date; we will be happy to grant you permission whenever possible.

• You must warrant that you are the sole owner of the design/article, that it is original and does not infringe upon the copyrights or rights of anyone else, and that it has never been published in any form.

• We will buy first rights upon special request, paying 10% less than the originally quoted design fee.

Issue of Publication

• When a design is accepted, we will notify you of the magazine issue in which your design is scheduled to appear. If we move your design to another issue before the Design-In date, we will let you know the new deadline. If we move your design after the Design-In date (after the contract has been signed and payment processed), we will let you know that it has been held-over for another issue, and we will keep you informed of its status.

Manufacturer/Product Names

• We will list manufacturers' names only when use of their specific products are vital to the successful completion of the design.

Completed Designs

• We ask that you send us your completed design so we can photograph it in our studio; the completed design also helps us edit instructions accurately. We will keep your design until the magazine is published. We will return the design to you shortly after the On-Sale date. If for some reason you need your design returned before then, please let us know in advance, and we will try our best to comply.

Categories: Children—Cooking—Crafts—Ecology—Education—Recreation

Name: Bill Stephani, Editor
Material: All
Address: 2400 DEVON STE 375
City/State/ZIP: DES PLAINES IL 60018
Telephone: 847-635-5800
Fax: 847-635-6311

Paddler Magazine
World's No. 1 Canoeing, Kayaking and Rafting Magazine

Paddler Magazine is published six times per year and is written by and for those knowledgeable about river running, canoeing and sea kayaking. Our core audience is the intermediate to advanced paddler, yet we strive to cover the entire range from beginners to experts.

Paddler represents a perfect opportunity for writers and photographers to bolster their portfolios with an established publication. Our editorial coverage is divided between whitewater rafting, kayaking, canoeing and sea kayaking. We strive for a balance between the eastern and western U.S. paddling scene and regularly cover international expeditions. Since one of the publications merged to form *Paddler* was *Canadian Paddler*, we also try to integrate the Canadian paddling scene into each publication.

Writer's Guidelines

We prefer to receive manuscripts on 3.5" Macintosh-compatible disks under Microsoft Word or Works programs. Please submit material on double-density disks instead of high density. Include typed hard copy with each submission. Dot matrix print-outs are acceptable; letter-quality is preferred. Please include name, address, telephone number and social security number in upper left-hand corner of title page. Place name and page number in upper left of each succeeding page.

We prefer queries, but will look at manuscripts on speculation. Most positive responses to queries are on spec, but based on experience, we will occasionally make assignments. Please allow six to eight weeks for a response.

Features and Departments:

Features: *Paddler* publishes at least three features per issue, trying to give equal representation to whitewater rafting, kayaking, sea kayaking and canoeing. One feature per issue is of general interest to all paddlers (i.e. *Riverborn Businesses, Top 10 Paddle Towns*, etc.).

Surprise us with unique ideas. We see entirely too many overwritten, "Me and Joe" destination manuscripts. Unless it's special, save destination-type stories for our destination section. All features should be between 2,000 and 3,000 words and accompanied by high quality transparencies.

Departments: *Paddler* has seven sections per issue. Each submission should include transparencies or black and white photographs.

• **"Profiles"** is about unique people involved in the sport. We include three profiles per issue: one canoeist, one sea kayaker and one whitewater rafter or kayaker. Each profile should be no longer than 600 words.

• **"Destinations"** is designed to inform paddlers of unique places to take their crafts. Submissions should include map and photo (800 words).

• **"Hotline"** concerns itself with timely news relating to the paddling industry. Ideas should be newsworthy (250-750 words).

• **"Gear"** is about equipment paddlers use, from boats and paddles to collapsible chairs and other accessories (250-800 words).

• **"Paddle Tales"** are short, humorous anecdotes from trips past, giving the reader a way to get involved with the magazine (75-250 words).

• **"Skills"** presents a forum for experts to share their tricks of the trade, from techniques to cooking in the backcountry (250-1,000 words).

• **"Environment"** covers issues related to the paddling environment, from dam updates to access issues and profiles (250-1,000 words).

Manuscript Payment

Paddler pays 10 cents per word upon publication, based upon the published column inch. This averages out to about $5 per column inch. To encourage brevity, we pay a maximum of $300 for features. Contributors to "Paddle Tales" will receive a subscription to *Paddler*. Letters to the Editor and press releases are unpaid. *Paddler* buys first North American serial rights. All subsequent rights revert back to the author.

PHOTOGRAPHY:

Photo submissions should be 35mm transparencies (Kodachrome or Fujichrome preferred) and/or black-and-white glossy prints. Dupes are acceptable if so marked and if originals are available for publication. Place name, address and phone number on each image. We give one photo credit per image and pay on publication. Photos for "Frames" tend to be scenic; photos for "Ender" are more off-the-wall. Payment is as follows:

Color Black and White

• $150 for cover; $50 for cover inset • $50 full page
• $75 for full page • $25 half to full page
• $50 for half page to full page • $20 quarter to half page
• $25 for a quarter page to half page • $15 less than

quarter page
- $20 for less than a quarter page

Address all submissions to appropriate department.

Categories: Nonfiction—Adventure—Associations—Boating—Conservation—Environment—Fishing—Lifestyles—Outdoors—Paddlesports—Physical Fitness—Recreation—Regional—Short Stories—Sports—Travel

Name: Eugene Buchanan, Editorial Director
Material: Features
Name: Aaron Bible, Assistant Editor
Material: Departments
Address: PO BOX 775450
City/State/ZIP: STEAMBOAT SPRINGS CO 80477
Telephone: 970-879-1450
Fax: 970-879-1450
E-mail: 104556.2251@compuserve.com

PanGaia
Living the Pagan Life

PanGaia is a magazine for all people who share a deep love and commitment to the Earth. This includes both religious Pagans (Wiccans, Neo-Pagans, Druids, etc.) as well as people on other spiritual paths. We are pleased to accept contributions of essays, fiction, poetry, ritual scripts, plays, interviews, editorial pieces, factual articles, cartoons and black and white art and photographs pertaining to the topics and themes of *PanGaia.*

Length Articles should be 500-3,000 words, reviews 300-500 words, poems one or two pages, including layout.

Topics include ecology, magic, personal development, shamanism, prayer, ritual, insight experiences, fiction (including fantasy), scholarly research, history, legends, mythology, God and Goddess lore, gardening, herbs, recipes, health, political concerns, celebrations of Nature, Love, Birth, Death and other transitions, humor, interpersonal relations, sexuality, interviews and profiles of individuals and groups.

Reviews *PanGaia* prints reviews of books, movies, videos, music and other relevant products. Unsolicited reviews are accepted and a list of items available for review may be obtained by sending an introductory note outlining your interests with a SASE.

Art At present, *PanGaia* is not seeking color art. Drawings should be clear, high quality copies on 8½"x11" white paper. Photos may be prints or electronic formats. Sending original art is strongly discouraged.

All submissions must be the original work of the author/artist.

Format Clearly labeled PC or Macintosh disks accompanied by hard copy with the contributor's name, address and phone number, are strongly preferred for lengthy written work. Clearly typed, double spaced manuscripts are acceptable for short pieces and poetry. The editor works in Microsoft Word. The editor will try to reply promptly to your submission.

Compensation *PanGaia* is able to offer a small monetary consideration for feature articles, art and photographs. Contributor's copies of the issue in which an article, poem, graphic piece or review appears will be sent to the writer or artist. Other exchanges, such as subscriptions or ad space, may be discussed.

Purpose *PanGaia* is dedicated to helping explore our spiritual and mundane worlds in a way which respects all persons, creatures, and the Earth, and which has immediate application to our everyday lives. We encourage folks of all paths to send their work, but our focus is on material which expresses an Earth-centered spirituality.

PanGaia will not publish material which demeans or in any way seeks to negate persons and practices. We do not publish personal attacks, gossip or diatribes. *PanGaia* is a tool, not a weapon.

Don't be shy if you are not a "professional" writer or artist-*PanGaia* depends upon the contributions of our readers to make this magazine a reflection of the earth-loving community as a whole.

Categories: Fiction—Nonfiction—Animals—Comedy—Conservation—Culture—Dance—Ecology—Environment—Ethnic—Family—Fantasy—Gardening—Health—History—Humor—Inspirational—Multicultural—Music—Native American—New Age—Outdoors—Pagan—Parenting—Philosophy—Poetry—Relationships—Religion—Science—Science Fiction—Sexuality—Short Stories—Spiritual

Name: D.C. Darling, Editor
Material: All
Address: PO BOX 641
City/State/ZIP: POINT ARENA CA 95418
Telephone: 707-882-2052
Fax: 707-882-2973
E-mail: dcdarling@zapcom.net

Pangolin Papers

PANGOLIN PAPERS is published tri-annually by Turtle Press.

1. We publish literary fiction from short-shorts up to 7,000 words, including novel extracts. We do not publish genre fiction such as science fiction and romance.

2. We generally respond within two months, or sooner.

3. Simultaneous submissions not considered, but please advise if your ms. has been previously accepted for publication.

4. We can only pay in copies for now. Turtle Press retains first North American serial rights. Copyright reverts to the author on publication.

5. We like crisp copy. Laser prints are fine. Stories on IBM-compatible PC disks using Microsoft Word™ or WordPerfect™ formats are acceptable. Disks can be returned on request.

6. We follow the *Chicago Manual of Style* and the *American Heritage Dictionary.*

PANGOLIN PAPERS is published summer, winter, and spring by Turtle Press.

Single copies $5.95 + $1.00 postage. Subscription rates one year $15.00, two years $25.00. Canadian subscribers add $5.00 per year in U.S. funds.

Categories: Fiction—Literature—Short Stories

Name: Submissions Editor
Material: All
Address: PO BOX 241
City/State/ZIP: NORDLAND WA 98358
Telephone: 360-385-3626

Papyrus

We welcome manuscripts from serious beginning writers. Manuscripts should, if possible, be submitted on a 3.5" disk, along with a printed copy. Macintosh users should submit files in ClarisWorks, Microsoft Word, WordPerfect or MacWrite II format. IBM users should submit files saved in ASCII or RTF format. All manuscripts, whether typed or printed copies of material submitted on disks, should be double-spaced, including quotations from prose or verse. Do not send simultaneous submissions or previously published materials. Payment is copies of the issue carrying your work, except for book reviews and craft articles, for which we pay $25.00. Copyright reverts to you upon publication.

PAPYRUS is in the market for material that interests black Americans:
- articles on the art of writing, up to 1,500 words
- book reviews of fiction and nonfiction, up to 3,200 words
- fiction, any subject matter, from 1,500 to 3,500 words
- nonfiction, any subject matter, from 1,500 to 3,200 words
- and poetry, not to exceed five manuscript pages per submission.

We welcome the opportunity to review your work in consideration for publication in our craftletter.

For a sample copy send $2.20. For a subscription, send $8.00 in check or money order to the address below.

Thank you for your interest.

Categories: Fiction—Nonfiction—African-American—Arts—Ethnic—Literature—Short Stories—Writing

Name: Ginger Whitaker, Editor
Material: All
Address: PO BOX 270797
City/State/ZIP: WEST HARTFORD CT 06127-0797
E-mail: gwhitaker@imagine.com

Parabola Magazine
The Magazine of Myth and Tradition

PARABOLA is a quarterly journal devoted to the exploration of the quest for meaning as it is expressed in the world's myths, symbols, and religious traditions. Particular emphasis is focused in the journal on the relationship between this vast store of wisdom and contemporary life.

Each Issue of PARABOLA is organized around a theme. Examples of themes we have explored in the past include Rites of Passage, Sacred Space, The Child, Ceremonies, Addiction, The Sense of Humor, Hospitality, The Hunter, and The Stranger.

TYPES OF SUBMISSIONS
Articles and Translations
PARABOLA welcomes original essays and translations. We look for lively, penetrating material unencumbered by jargon or academic argument. All articles must be directly related to the theme of an issue.

Poetry and Short Fiction
We rarely consider original fiction, and then only if directly related to the theme of an issue. We do not accept submissions of poetry.

Tangents
PARABOLA occasionally publishes extended reviews of books, movies, videos, performances, art exhibitions, and other current programs or events in a section called "Tangents." These reviews are intended as a bridge between the theme-related front half of the magazine and the reviews in the back. Tangents should bear some connection to the theme of the issue, although it does not have to be as direct as an article.

Book Reviews and Epicycles
Separate guidelines for book, video, and audio reviews and for retellings of traditional stories are available upon request.
1. Length
Articles run 1,000-3,000 words
Book Reviews run approximately 500 words
Retellings of traditional stories run 500-1,500 words
2. Query Letter

Please send us a one-page letter describing what you propose to write about and how it relates to a given theme. We will let you know if we are interested, or we may suggest a different approach or subject. If the idea fits into our editorial plans, you will be given a deadline to submit a finished manuscript. Assignment of a deadline does not guarantee acceptance or publication of the article; it only means that we are interested in your idea and would like to pursue it.

Brief queries may be sent via e-mail.
3. Preparation of copy
In the upper left-hand corner of the first page of your article, please type the following information:
1. Your name
2. Your address and telephone number
3. Your social security number
4. Word count

If endnotes are used, they should be as complete as possible: include the author's name, book or article title, translator or editor (if applicable), city of publication, name of publisher, date, and page numbers.
4. Electronic submissions
Articles may be submitted electronically only if prior arrangements have been made. Please state in your cover letter if you will be able to provide us with electronic copy on disk or by e-mail. We can accept 3.5" or 5.25" diskettes in most Macintosh and IBM-compatible applications; 3.5" is preferable.

Upon acceptance we will request your disk or transmission. *PARABOLA will not accept any articles via e-mail without a prior query.*

If you are sending us a disk copy, please try to keep the formatting as simple as possible. In particular, we prefer manual endnotes to automatic footers.
5. Biographical Information
On a separate page, include a brief (2-3 sentence) biographical description of yourself. Fit the description to the subject matter of the article, e.g., for an article on Tibetan Buddhism, "Smith spent three years travelling in Tibet." Or, a publication credit: "Smith is the author of *Pilgrimage in Tibet* (W. W. Norton, 1987)." Always include your publisher.
6. Rights
PARABOLA purchases the right to use an article in all substantially complete versions (including non-print versions) of a single issue of our journal. We also request the right to use the piece in the promotion of PARABOLA, and to authorize single-copy reproductions for academic purposes. All other rights are retained by the author.
7. Payment
Payment is made upon publication. Publication is not guaranteed.

Categories: Philosophy—Religion—Spiritual

Name: Editorial Department
Material: All
Address: 656 BROADWAY
City/State/ZIP: NEW YORK NY 10012
Telephone: 212-505-9037
Fax: 212-979-7325
E-mail: parabola@panix.com

Parade

Thank you for your interest in *Parade*. The following guidelines should help prospective writers tailor and present article ideas for editorial consideration.

Give us a unique perspective on the news.
Parade covers topics as diverse as the 81 million readers we reach each Sunday. Many stories involve news, social issues, com-

mon health concerns, sports, community problem-solving or extraordinary achievements of ordinary people. We seek unique angles on all topics-this is especially important for subjects that have already received national attention in newspapers and other media.

Topics must appeal to a broad audience.

• Your subject must have national scope or implications. For example, a story about first-year interns at a Dubuque hospital might have limited appeal, but the subject of job opportunities or work conditions in hospitals across the nation would be of widespread concern.

• Reporting must be authoritative and original, based on interviews that you conduct yourself. Health for example, should quote medical experts rather than simply relating a personal tale.

• Choose a topic that you care about deeply. If your story does not make you happy or sad, angry or elated, excited or curious, chances are that *Parade* readers won't care that much either.

Do not propose spot news, fiction or poetry, cartoons, regular columns, nostalgia or history, quizzes, puzzles or compilations of quotes or trivia. We almost never assign unsolicited technical-science queries or unsolicited queries for interviews with entertainment celebrities, politicians or sports figures.

You should be able to write your article concisely.

Parade has room to publish only the most tightly focused story. Topics that will be compelling and complete at 1,200 to 1,500 words are the only ones worth proposing.

How to submit your proposal to Parade:

Assignments are based on query letters of one page-three or four paragraphs should be sufficient

Propose only one topic per query. The query should include:

• Your central theme or point in no more than a few sentences. If you cannot state the theme in this way the article surely lacks focus.

• Your sources on all sides of the issue. Whom will you interview?

• The story's general trajectory. Briefly, how will you organize it?

• A summary of your most important writing credits.

Attach one or two writing samples and a self-addressed, stamped envelope and send to the address below.

Parade is not responsible for unsolicited materials. Do not send any valuable or irreplaceable items. Though many queries have merit, because of great volume we can only assign those few that precisely meet our needs and standards.

Again, thank you for your interest, and best of luck in your efforts.

Categories: General Interest

Name: Submissions Editor
Material: All
Address: 711 THIRD AVE
City/State/ZIP: NEW YORK NY 10017
Telephone: 212-450-7000
Fax: 212-450-7284

Parameters
U.S. Army War College Quarterly

SUBJECT: *Parameters* is a refereed journal of ideas and issues, providing a forum for mature professional thought on the art and science of land warfare, joint and combined matters, national and international security affairs, military strategy, military leadership and management, military history, military ethics, and other topics of significant and current interest to the U.S. Army and the Department of Defense. It serves as a vehicle for continuing the education and professional development of USAWC (U.S. Army War College) graduates and other senior military officers, as well as members of government and academia concerned with national security affairs.

STYLE: Clarity, directness, and economy of expression are the main traits of professional writing, and they should never be sacrificed in a misguided effort to appear scholarly. Avoid especially Pentagonese and bureaucratic jargon. Recall that humdrum dullness of style is not synonymous with learnedness; readers will appreciate such qualities as liveliness and verve. Theses, military studies, and academic course papers should be adapted to article form before submission. In the interest of economy, security, and conformity with the stylistic standards of *Parameters*, the editor reserves the right to edit all manuscripts; however, substantive changes will be made only with the author's consent.

LENGTH: Articles of 4,000-5,000 words (corresponding to 16-20 double-spaced, typewritten pages) are preferred.

CONCURRENT SUBMISSIONS: Do *not* submit your manuscript to *Parameters* while it is being considered elsewhere.

MANUSCRIPT: Should be carefully edited, and identified with the author's name, address, and phone number on the front sheet. Manuscripts may be transmitted as electronic files by attachment to an e-mail message or on a floppy disk. Identify the operating system and the word processing program used; we can convert Macintosh files only if they are on a high-density disk. Do not submit original material by fax.

DOCUMENTATION: Documentation is placed in endnotes; bibliography is not necessary. Indicate all quoted material by quotation marks or indentation. Reduce the number of endnotes to the *minimum* consistent with honest acknowledgment of indebtedness, consolidating notes where possible. Lengthy explanatory endnotes are discouraged. Endnotes must contain complete citation of publication data. *Parameters* uses the conventions prescribed in Kate L. Turabian, *A Manual for Writers*, 4th ed. (Chicago: Univ. of Chicago Press, 1973).

ILLUSTRATIONS: Charts and graphs should be used only if they are absolutely essential to clarify or amplify the text. Photos are seldom used, but illustrative black-and-white photos (preferably 5"x7") are considered.

BIOGRAPHICAL SKETCH: Include a brief biographical sketch of four to six lines, highlighting credentials.

CLEARANCE: Manuscripts by US military personnel on active duty and civilian employees of the Defense or service departments may require official clearance (see AR 360-5, ch. 4). *Parameters* will assist authors on request.

HONORARIA: Upon publication, *Parameters* extends a modest honorarium to eligible contributors.

AUTHOR'S ADDRESS: Include current telephone number (both office and residence), address, and an e-mail address if you have one. Please keep the *Parameters* office notified of any changes.

REVIEW PROCESS: We send acknowledgment to the author when the manuscript is received. Submissions are read by the editors within a couple of days. Submissions not forwarded to our editorial board for further consideration are generally returned to the author within two weeks. For submissions sent to our board, the review process can take from four to eight weeks from date of receipt. We try to respond as soon as possible.

OUR WEB SITE: To gain a better understanding of our current editorial scope, or to acquire our most recent author's guide, visit our Internet site at the address shown below.

Categories: Nonfiction—Military—Public Policy

Name: Col. John J. Madigan III (USA, Ret.), Editor
Material: All
Address: U.S. ARMY WAR COLLEGE
City/State/ZIP: CARLISLE BARRACKS PA 17013

Telephone: 717-245-4943
E-mail: AWCA-Parameters@@carlisle-emh2.army.mil

paramour

Paramour

All submissions should have erotic, sexual or sensual content; it need not be explicit. We publish a wide range of work from subtle/sensual to graphic/explicit. All styles of sexuality (gay, straight, bi, mono; leather, lace, appliance, vegetable…) are acceptable. If you have not seen the magazine and would like to see it, sample copies are available for $4.95 US ($6 overseas) by check or money order payable to *Paramour.*

All *work* should have your name, address and phone number on *every* page. **All** work submitted should be for publication; don't send samples of work which you don't intend for us to publish. If you send work that has been published before or has been multiply submitted, *please* tell us where (we're extremely peevish about this)! Also, *please* include a two or three sentence biography, suitable for use in our Contributors Notes. If we've already published your work, let us know if it needs to be updated. If your work is accepted we may want to use it on our (Internet) Web site. If you *don't* want your work on the net, please let us know.

WRITING SUBMISSIONS: Paramour accepts unsolicited **fiction**. We generally print one or two stories per issue of up to 4,000 words. We print a great many more stories of 1,000 - 2,000 words or even shorter. We're also interested in **essays, interviews, reviews** (film, video, performance, book, comic, and many other products) and column ideas, but strongly suggest you discuss your concept with us first. If we encourage you to pursue your concept, this does not guarantee your piece will be accepted. Interviews and reviews should be accompanied by imagery of the subject whenever possible.

Poetry: Please do not send more than 10 poems per quarter.

Please submit your work in hard copy. If possible, also submit it on a Mac disk, in Microsoft Word or ASCII file format. Or, you may e-mail submissions to the address below—please place the text within the e-mail message, unencoded.

Writing submissions will not be returned.

ARTWORK SUBMISSIONS: Paramour accepts photographs, illustrations, cartoons, collages and reproductions of larger media. Work may be submitted in hard copy or tiff files (300 dpi) on Mac disk. Please *do not* e-mail image files.

Photos: Slides are acceptable (please number them!), but we prefer prints, 4"x6" or larger if possible black and white are best; color work that has a lot of contrast is fine). Photos must be accompanied by copies of your model releases **and copies of models' driver's licenses or birth certificates.**

Drawings, Paintings, Cartoons, etc.: Please do not send your originals! If you get halftones, use a 150 line screen. If the reproductions you send are not adequate print quality, we'll contact you.

PAYMENT: Payment is 3 copies of the issue in which your work appears plus a one-year subscription to the magazine.

Please allow up to four months response time.

Deadlines: March 1 for Spring/Summer Issue; release date May 1

June 1 for Summer/Fall; release August 1
September 1 for Fall/Winter; release November 1
December 1 for Winter/Spring; release February 1

Please call or e-mail if you have questions.
Thank you for your interest.
Categories: Erotica

Name: Submissions Editor
Material: All
Address: PO BOX 949
City/State/ZIP: CAMBRIDGE MA 02140-0008
Telephone: 617-499-0069
E-mail: paramour@@paramour.com
Internet: www.paramour.com

Parent & Child

Parent & Child, published six times a year, is a magazine for parents of children from birth to age six.

We are distributed through early childhood programs, so our articles largely focus on issues that relate to young children's education and development. We are the learning link between home and school.

Our articles are short. Most of our pieces run between 600 and 900 words.

We are interested in well-written "conversational pieces submitted by people who are familiar with early childhood education. In particular, we look for articles that are activity-oriented or that highlight a program or initiative that can be easily replicated by parents in any community.

Since we are a small magazine, we do not accept many unsolicited manuscripts for publication. However, we still welcome your submission.

If you'd like us to return your manuscript, please enclose a SASE.

Categories: Nonfiction—Children—Family—Health—Parenting—Relationships—Education

Name: Article Submissions
Material: All
Address: 555 BROADWAY
City/State/ZIP: NEW YORK, NY 10012

ParentGuide News

Thank you for your interest in PARENTGUIDE, the New York Metropolitan area's largest and oldest parenting publication. We are a monthly, tabloid sized newspaper catering to the needs and interests of parents who have children under the age of 12. Our total circulation is 210,000.

PARENTGUIDE's monthly columns and feature articles cover health, education, child-rearing, current events, parenting issues, recreational activities and social events. We also run a complete calendar of local events.

We welcome articles from professional authors as well as never-before-published writers. Share your personal experiences, advice, humorous anecdotes, parental concerns, professional knowledge or newsworthy observations with us. Manuscripts can be written in either third or first person format. You are invited to send a query letter or finished manuscript. Allow for a three month lead time.

All manuscripts should be between 750 and 1,500 words in length. A brief bio should be included and, if possible, photos or any other artwork. PARENTGUIDE assumes no responsibility for the loss or damage of submitted materials. We do NOT offer financial payment to any of our freelance writers, but all contributors do receive masthead credit, a byline and a brief bio.

We appreciate your interest and look forward to working with you.

Thank you,
The Editors
Categories: Nonfiction—Children—Diet—Education—Family—Health—Marriage—Parenting

Name: Jenine Marie DeLuca, Editor-in-Chief
Material: All
Address: 419 PARK AVE S 13TH FLOOR
City/State/ZIP: NEW YORK NY 10016
Telephone: 212-213-8840
Fax: 212-447-7734

Parenting Magazine

Parenting addresses readers who are considering pregnancy or expecting a child, as well as parents of children from birth through age 12. The magazine covers both the psychological and practical aspects of parenting.

The magazine is largely freelance written. Fees for articles depend on length, degree of difficulty, and the writer's previous experience. Generally, articles run between 1,000 and 3,000 words in published form.

For writers new to *Parenting*, the best opportunities are the departments, which are comprised of pieces that range from 100 to 800 words. Queries for each of these departments should be addressed to the appropriate editor (such as Family Reporter Editor, or Ages & Stages Editor).

Put all queries in writing (no phone calls, please), and enclose a stamped, self-addressed envelope for a reply and the return of any materials you submit. Allow two months for a response, due to the large volume of unsolicited queries we receive. We will not consider simultaneous submissions. In addition, we do not publish poetry.

The best guide for writers is the magazine itself. Please familiarize yourself with it before submitting a query - read several issues if possible. The most successful queries and manuscripts are timely, appropriately researched, well-written, and geared to *Parenting* in particular.

Categories: Nonfiction—Book Reviews—Children—Consumer—Family—Folklore—Health—Marriage—Parenting—Physical Fitness—Psychology—Relationships—Humor—Personal Experience—Education

Name: Editor
Material: All
Address: 1325 AVENUE OF THE AMERICAS
27TH FLOOR
City/State/ZIP: NEW YORK, NY 10019
Telephone: 212-522-8989
Fax: 212-522-8699

ParentLife

ParentLife is a Christian monthly magazine for parents of children birth to twelve. It focuses on the practical aspects of parenting, as well as informs, educates, and inspires parents to be aware of issues and understand their children at each stage of development.

Content: The editorial staff will evaluate articles dealing with any subject of interest to parents of preschoolers and children.

Preparation: Cover page should include suggested title and blurb, by-line, author's full name, address, social security number, and rights offered (all, first, one-time reprint).

Submit manuscripts 600-1,200 words in length. Queries with writing sample are preferred.

Disk submissions must be accompanied by a hard copy. Prefer disk on a Macintosh word processing program, but can convert most IBM programs.

Writing Tips: Quoted material must be properly documented (publisher, location, date, and page numbers), along with permission verification.

Include Bible references and thoughts when appropriate. Remember readers are parents of preschoolers and children. Use brief, clear sentences. Construct paragraphs logically. Sidebars helpful.

Payment: Payment is negotiable and on acceptance.

Publication: Writers will receive, without cost, 3 advance copies of the issue in which their manuscripts are published. Extra copies can be ordered from the Customer Service Center (MSN 113 at address below, or (800) 458-BSSB).

For a sample copy, send a 9"x12" SASE.

Categories: Parenting

Name: Editor
Material: All
Address: 127 NINTH AVE N
City/State/ZIP: NASHVILLE TN 37234-0140
Telephone: 615-251-2229
Fax: 615-251-5008
E-mail: parentlife@bssb.com
Internet: www.bssb.com

Parents

We are interested in:

Articles which offer professional and/or personal insights into family and marriage relationships.

Articles that help women to cope with our rapidly changing world.

Well-documented articles on the problems and successes of preschool, school-age, and adolescent children—and their parents.

Good, practical guides to the routines of baby care.

Reports of new trends and significant research findings in education and in mental and physical health.

Articles encouraging informed citizen action on matters of social concern.

We prefer a warm, colloquial style of writing, one which avoids the extremes of either slanginess or technical jargon. Anecdotes and examples should be used to illustrate points which can then be summed up by straight exposition.

Articles vary in length from 1,500 to 3,000 words. Payment is on acceptance.

We recommend that writers query us about the article idea before submitting a completed manuscript. Manuscripts should be typed, double-spaced, and must be accompanied by a stamped, self-addressed envelope.

Please allow three to four weeks for a reply.

The Editors
Parents Magazine
Categories: Nonfiction—Children—Family—Fashion—Health—Marriage—Physical Fitness—Relationships—Beauty—Retirement—Women's Issues

Name: Wendy Schuman, Executive Editor
Material: All
Address: 375 LEXINGTON AVENUE
City/State/ZIP: NEW YORK, NY 10017
Telephone: 212-499-2000
Fax: 212-867-4583
Internet: www.parents.com

Parents' Press

Parents' Press is a monthly newspaper for parents and expectant parents in the San Francisco Bay Area counties of Alameda, Contra Costa, Marin, San Francisco and Solano. Our circulation is 75,000. The majority of our readers have children ranging from infancy to primary grade students.

What We Buy

Our focus is on practical, down-to-earth articles. We use very little academic, theoretical or personal-experience pieces. No political material, fiction or poetry. Please study the newspaper before submitting ideas. We do not mail out sample copies, but free copies are available at most Bay Area Safeway stores, libraries and children's stores. Back issues are available at some local libraries, or by mail from us for $3 per issue.

Writers

We use up to 3 freelance articles per issue. We prefer a detailed query letter with samples of published clips. We prefer letter-quality printouts. Dot-matrix is barely acceptable, provided you use high-contrast black ribbon. You may submit a story on disk, if you accompany it with a printout. If you are PC-based, we prefer files in Word. 6.0 or WordPerfect 5.0, 5.1 or 6.0. If you are Mac-based, we prefer files submitted in Word or ClarisWorks on a 1.4MB floppy. We do not currently accept electronic submissions.

Articles on health, education and child development are usually written by professionals in those fields. Good possibilities for non-specialist writers include interviews with well-known Bay Area figures who have young children; places to go with children; parent resources (e.g., crisis hotlines); "how-to" articles on everyday aspects of childrearing (e.g., giving a birthday party, buying play equipment, dealing with peer pressure). We're also very interested in stories dealing with issues that affect preteens and teens (children from 9 to 17). We seldom use articles that focus on a single organization. Round-up articles should cover the five counties named above.

Popular past articles by freelancers have included: "Skates and Blades: Bay Area Youths' Hot New Pastimes," "How To Set Up a Parent Co-op," "Air Travel with Children," "Choosing the Right School for Your Child" and "Are You Spoiling Your Child?"

Parents Press generally buys all rights (with certain rights assigned back to the author upon written request). Other rights we will purchase include first North American serial rights with a provision for perpetual exclusivity in Northern and Central California. This means that an article that appears in *Parents' Press* cannot be sold without our written permission to *any* publication whose primary circulation area is in Northern or Central California.

We will occasionally buy reprint rights or simultaneous submissions, but pay considerably less for such material and require the same territorial exclusivity. We do not buy material that has been simultaneously submitted to other Northern or Central California publications. You must accompany previously printed or syndicated submissions with a statement of their publishing history.

Payment

Payment ranges from $50 to $500, depending upon the complexity of the material, quality of writing, amount of research and length. Articles generally run from 300 to 1,500 words, occasionally up to 2,500 words. We usually pay within 45 days of publication. If we accept an article that we think may be delayed in getting published, we will pay on acceptance. If you accompany an article with photos, the fee we negotiate with you will include payment for them.

Photographers and Artists

We use 10 to 20 black-and-white photos of children per issue. Photos should be submitted as glossy, professional quality 5"x7" or 8"x10" prints (with borders for crop marks). We encourage the submission of photos of children of different ethnicities, abilities and ages. We require written parental permission for any child whose face is identifiable in a photo, as well as model releases for similarly identifiable adults.

Payment is $15 per photo, paid within 6 weeks of publication; one-time rights. Call Renee Benoit to show photos. (You may submit photos by mail, accompanied by an SASE, but we cannot guarantee a quick response.)

We occasionally use cover art created by outside contributors. Contact Renee Benoit to discuss rates and requirements.

Expenses

Parents' Press will pay certain expenses (mileage, phone, photocopies, film) within limits stated in writing at the time we commission an article.

Categories: Children—Parenting

Name: Patrick Totty, Managing Editor
Material: All
Address: 1454 SIXTH ST
City/State/ZIP: BERKELEY CA 94710
Telephone: 510-524-1602
Fax: 510-524-0912
E-mail: ParentsPrs@aol.com

Parent.TEEN

Parent.TEEN is a free bimonthly magazine for parents and families of teenagers (ages 13-19) in the San Francisco Bay Area counties of Alameda, Contra Costa, Marin, San Francisco, San Mateo and Santa Clara. Our circulation is 50,000.

What We Buy

Our focus is on practical, down-to-earth articles that deal with teen behavior, health, school, work and culture. We use very few academic, theoretical or personal-experience pieces. No political material, fiction or poetry. Please study the magazine before submitting ideas. We do not mail out free sample copies, but free copies are available at most Bay Area Safeway and Lucky stores, and libraries. Back issues are available at some local libraries, or by mail from us for $2 per issue at the address below; make checks payable to *Parents' Press*.

Writers

We use up to 5 freelance articles per issue. We prefer a detailed query letter with samples of published clips. We prefer letter-quality printouts. Dot-matrix is not acceptable. You may submit a story on disk, if you accompany it with a printout. If you are PC-based, we prefer files in Word 6.0 or WordPerfect 5.0, 5.1 or 6.0. If you are Mac-based, we prefer files submitted in Word or ClarisWorks on a 1.4MB floppy. You may also e-mail queries and stories to us.

While we are open to queries, most of our article ideas are generated in-house and assigned to freelance writers. Subjects include health, educational, financial, social and developmental issues that affect families with teens. Among the possibilities are profiles of unusual or little-known college programs, and short profiles of programs and activities affecting teens. We prefer heavy, careful research and tight writing, with sidebars. Most material should have a Bay Area focus and be written to appeal to both parents and teens. Round-up articles should cover the six counties named above.

Popular past articles by freelancers have included: "Inside Toughlove," "Is Your Middle School Safe?," "Teen Pregnancy: The Epidemic That Wasn't," "Our Car Insurance Is Going Up *How Much?*," "The High price of Perfect Skin," "Is Lacrosse 'The Next Soccer?'," and profiles of unusual colleges or internal college programs, such as the California State Maritime Academy in Vallejo.

M-R

Parent.TEEN generally buys all rights (with certain rights assigned back to the author upon written request). Other rights we will purchase include first North American serial rights with a provision for perpetual exclusivity in Northern and Central California. This means that an article that appears in *Parent.TEEN* cannot be sold without our written permission to *any* publication whose primary circulation area is in Northern or Central California.

We will occasionally buy reprint rights or simultaneous submissions, but pay considerably less for such material and require the same territorial exclusivity. We do not buy material that has been simultaneously submitted to other Northern or Central California publications. You *must* accompany previously printed or syndicated submissions with a statement of their publishing history.

Payment

Payment ranges from $50 to $500, depending upon the complexity of the material, quality of writing, amount of research and length. Articles generally run from 300 to 1,200 words, occasionally up to 1,500 words. We usually pay within 45 days of publication. If we accept an article that we think may be delayed in getting published, we will pay on acceptance. If you accompany an article with photos, the fee we negotiate with you will include payment for them.

Photographers and Artists

We use 8 to 12 black-and-white photos of teens or teen activities per issue. Photos should be submitted as glossy, professional quality 5"x7" or 8"x10" prints (with borders for crop marks). We encourage the submission of photos of teens of different ethnicities, abilities and ages. We require written parental permission for any child whose face is identifiable in a photo, as well as model releases for similarly identifiable adults.

Payment is $15 per photo, paid within 6 weeks of publication; one-time rights. Call Renee Benoit to show photos. (You may submit photos by mail, accompanied by an SASE, but we cannot guarantee a quick response.)

We occasionally use cover art created by outside contributors. Contact Renee Benoit to discuss rates and requirements.

Expenses

Parent.TEEN will pay certain expenses (mileage, phone, photocopies, film) within limits stated in writing at the time we commission an article.

Categories: Parenting—Teen

Name: Patrick Totty, Managing Editor
Material: All
Address: 1454 SIXTH ST
City/State/ZIP: BERKELEY CA 94710
Telephone: 510-524-1602
Fax: 510-524-0912
E-mail: ParentsPrs@aol.com

Parnassus Literary Journal

PARNASSUS LITERARY JOURNAL is proud to have been selected from the thousands of small journals around the country for the 1993 *Writer's Digest* Poetry 60. We are a triyearly (spring, summer, fall/winter) consisting of 84 pages of poetry book reviews, articles, and graphics. A subscription is currently $18.00 in the US and Canada and $25.00 overseas. Sample copies are $5.00 when available. (Please make checks or money orders payable to Denver Stull.)

We welcome well constructed poetry in any form, but ask that you keep it uplifting, and free of language that might be offensive to one of our readers. Our journal is copyrighted and, on publication, all rights return to the author. We have no regularly

scheduled contests, but contests are occasionally sponsored by subscribers.

Non-subscribers are welcome, but when two submissions of equal quality are received, the subscriber is given preference. A minimum number of non-subscribers are paid in copies; however, we remind all poets that without the small press, our chances of ever appearing in print would be greatly diminished. We receive no grants, we sell no advertising, and our editor is not independently wealthy. We solicit your support.

Please hold your poetry to 24 lines. Shorter would be better. It is also requested that you not submit anything that will not fit on a page in our journal (5½"x8½") otherwise, we will be forced to break lines where they were not intended to be broken.

Type your poems one to a single sheet of 8½"x11" bond (haiku excepted) and enter your name and address at the upper left corner of each page. Clear photocopies ok; simultaneous submissions and previously published work ok. Haiku should be submitted all on one page.

Do not submit poetry on half sheets, 3"x5" cards and never more than 3 poems. No prose unless solicited. Book reviews are done by our book reviewer.

Submit your work in a number 10 (business size) envelope. If you do not desire the return of your work please so state. There is nothing to be gained by wasting postage on oversize envelopes. They irritate the editor because they take up too much space. Three copies of manuscript and an SASE folded in thirds will usually go for one first class stamp.

IMPORTANT: I do not acknowledge submissions, requests for guidelines, or queries unless a SASE is included. Further, it is important that you type your name and address on each page of manuscript. Otherwise, your submission is in danger of becoming lost. I also do not accept work that arrives here with postage due.

Our last issue contained over 145 poets from the beginner to the well known, including Lynn Lifshin, BZ Niditch, TK Splake, and many others. Ours is one of the oldest and most respected literary journals in the business. We recommend you purchase a sample copy for your own verification. You will not be disappointed.

Categories: Poetry

Name: Submissions Editor
Material: All
Address: PO BOX 1384
City/State/ZIP: FOREST PARK GA 30298
Telephone: 404-366-3177

Parnassus
Poetry in Review

Thank you for your interest in *Parnassus*. We consider unsolicited poetry and prose year round, and usually respond within two months. However, you should know that virtually all our material is solicited; while we try to give unsolicited work close scrutiny, we almost never publish it. On poetry, we place few restrictions of length, form, or style. As for prose, though, we have no interest in reading academic or "theoretical" work, only criticism that is colorful, idiosyncratic, and written with verve.

Categories: Literature—Poetry

Name: Ben Downing, Managing Editor
Material: Poetry, Poetry Criticism
Address: 205 W 89TH ST APT 8F
City/State/ZIP: NEW YORK NY 10024-1835
Telephone: 212-362-3492
Fax: 212-875-0148

Passager

A Journal of Remembrance and Discovery
University of Baltimore

"...a fresh tongue to cut from the past thoughts and dreams unspoken for too many years."
Virginia Wilson

Passager publishes fiction, poetry, and interviews that give voice to human experience. We seek powerful images of remembrance and discovery from writers of all ages. One of our missions is to provide exposure for new older writers; another is to function as a literary community for writers across the country who are not connected to academic institutions or other organized groups. We encourage writers to take a look at a copy of *Passager* to fully understand our editorial interests.

FICTION: 4,000 words max.
POETRY: 30 lines max.
No reprints.
Sample copy: $4
Subscriptions:
$15 per year (4 issues)
$28 for two years
Send check or money order to address below.
Categories: Fiction—Poetry—Memoir

Name: Submissions Editor
Material: All
Address: UNIVERSITY OF BALTIMORE
Address: 1420 N CHARLES ST
City/State/ZIP: BALTIMORE MD 21201-5779

Passages North

Northern Michigan University

Passages North, a biannual literary journal, has been publishing since 1979. The journal features poetry, short fiction, creative nonfiction, and interviews.

General Guidelines
All work submitted should:
• Include your name and address on the top right corner of each page.
Additional Poetry Guidelines
• Poems need not be double-spaced.
• Please submit 3-6 poems only.
Additional Prose Guidelines
• We accept prose up to 5,000 words.
Hints for Writers
• Brief cover notes help.
• Editors review work only from the beginning of September through May.
• Simultaneous submissions cannot be considered.
• If you wish, please include your phone number and/or e-mail address.
• We seldom publish poems over 100 lines.
Payment for accepted work is one copy of **Passages North.**
Subscriptions
Passages North, a voice of the nation from the shores of the Great Lakes, publishes twice yearly in June and December. Like all literary journals, **Passages North** is entirely dependent upon its subscribers, occasional grants, and donations. We invite you to take this opportunity to subscribe or renew your subscription. Please make checks payable to **Passages North.**
2 years (4 issues): $25/US, $30/Foreign
1 year (2 issues): $13/US, $16/Foreign
Sample (current issue): $7/US, $9/Foreign

Back issue: $3/US, $5/Foreign
Categories: Fiction—Nonfiction—Arts—General Interest—Literature—Poetry—Short Stories—Writing

Name: Submissions Editor
Material: All
Address: DEPT OF ENGLISH NORTHERN MICHIGAN UNIVERSITY
Address: 1401 PRESQUE ISLE AVE
City/State/ZIP: MARQUETTE MI 49855-5363

PC World

What kind of magazine is PC World?
PC World is a monthly magazine providing real-world reviews, advice, feature stories, news, and how-to support to people who buy manage, and use IBM and compatible computer systems for professional productivity. It is geared to a consumer audience of business decision makers who are responsible for making their personal computers work on the job. *PC World's* circulation exceeds 1,000,000 copies per month.

Who Writes for PC World?
We look for writers who have a clear writing style and a degree of technical knowledge appropriate to a knowledgeable PC user audience. This combination of talents can make it difficult to break into our pages. Freelance writers contribute to all sections of the magazine.

We pay varying amounts depending on the author's experience, the quality of the writing, and the length of the piece. The fee is negotiated with a staff editor whose specialties include the subject area under consideration. At every stage of every article, editors work closely with writers to generate the best work possible.

Though most of our regular writers are people we're familiar with, we do welcome queries from those who are new to us. One way we discover new talent is by assigning short tips and how-to pieces.

What's the Best Way to Proceed?
Our first suggestion is to be familiar with the magazine. Read some issues, understand the editorial focus (why particular topics are covered, what level of knowledge is imparted), and learn what the magazine's sections are and what goes into each one.

Once you're familiar with *PC World*, you can write us a query letter if you have an idea for a review, how-to, news item, or feature. Your letter should answer the following questions as specifically and concisely as possible:
• What is the problem, technique, or product you want to discuss?
• Why will *PC World* readers be interested in it?
• Which section of the magazine do you think it best fits?
• What is the specific audience for the piece (e.g. database or LAN users, desktop publishers, and so on)?

PC World editors ask these questions when considering ideas for every piece in the magazine, and we expect you to do the same. So send us a letter with your ideas, but please do not send unsolicited manuscripts, clips, or any disks: We will not be able to return them. If we're interested in your query, we'll contact you for more information and proceed from there.

Thanks again for your interest in *PC World* magazine. We hope this information is useful. Feel free to write us.
Categories: Computers—Technology

Name: Proposals
Material: Queries
Address: 501 2ND ST
City/State/ZIP: SAN FRANCISCO CA 94107

Telephone: 415-243-0500
Fax: 415-442-1891

PEARL

Pearl
A Literary Magazine

PEARL appears three times a year and is supported entirely by patrons & subscribers. It is a 96 page, perfect-bound magazine featuring poetry, short fiction, and black & white artwork. We also sponsor the Pearl Poetry Prize, an annual chapbook contest, as well as a short story contest.

Our Spring and Fall/Winter issues are devoted primarily to poetry, though we often include two or three pieces of *very short* fiction. Our Summer fiction issue is devoted entirely to prose and includes "shorts" as well as some of the longer stories submitted to our contest.

Submissions are accepted September through May *only*. Manuscripts received in June, July or August will be returned unread. We report back in 6-8 weeks. Work accepted for publication appears 6-12 months from date of acceptance.

POETRY: Send 3-5 previously unpublished poems with cover letter and SASE. Simultaneous submissions must be acknowledged as such. We prefer poems no longer than 40 lines, though we occasionally consider longer ones. Our format and page size, however, will not accommodate lines of more than 10-12 words. So unless you're Walt Whitman or Allen Ginsberg, please consider your line breaks.

FICTION: Seed previously unpublished stories with cover letter and SASE. We only consider stories up to 1,200 words (about 5 manuscript pages). Longer stories (up to 4,000) words may be submitted to our short story contest *only*. All contest entries are considered for publication.

CONTESTS: The submission period for the Pearl Poetry Prize is May 1 - July 1; for the Pearl Short Story Contest, December 1 - March 15. Complete guidelines are available for SASE.

ARTWORK: Send camera-ready, black & white artwork (either photocopies or originals) and SASE. Accepted artwork is kept on file and used as needed.

PAYMENT: Contributors receive two free copies as payment.

SAMPLES: We recommend reading our magazine before submitting. For a sample copy, send $6 check or money order payable to *Pearl*. (If you wish to receive a copy of the all-fiction issue, please specify.) Subscriptions: $15/year (individuals); $10/year (students); $30/year (patrons).

Although we have no taboos stylistically or subject-wise, we are *not* interested in sentimental, obscure, predictable, abstract, or cliché-ridden poetry or fiction...

"Go in fear of abstractions...Don't be 'viewy'—leave that to the writer of pretty little philosophical essays..." —Ezra Pound

We are interested in accessible, humanistic poetry & fiction that communicates and is related to real life...

"Be electric, lusty...express the full-sized body, male and female...beautiful, lasting, commensurate with America...with the inimitable sympathies of having been boys and girls together." —Walt Whitman

Along with the ironic, serious, and intense, humor & wit are welcome. Just remember...

"There are no dull subjects. There are only dull writers."—H.L. Mencken

"No tears in the writer, no tears in the reader. No surprise for the writer, no surprise for the reader." —Robert Frost

"And let's not forget we're women. So the writing better make us weep, or at least curl our hair" —Joan Jobe Smith, Founding Editor

Categories: Fiction—Literature—Poetry—Short Stories

Name: Joan Jobe Smith or Barbara Hauk, Poetry Editors
Material: Poetry
Name: Marilyn Johnson, Fiction Editor
Material: Short Fiction
Address: 3030 E SECOND ST
City/State/ZIP: LONG BEACH CA 90803
Telephone: 562-434-4523

Pennsylvania Farmer
The Farm Business Magazine of Mid-Atlantic Agriculture

Article Requirements

Pennsylvania Farmer constantly seeks articles of interest to commercial farmers: dairy, live stock, poultry, field crop, machinery, or fruit-oriented. We prefer practical farm-based articles using multiple sources and written to help readers save time, make money, or in any way improve their farm enterprise. No poetry or gag material.

We publish once a month except in January, February, and March; two issues are published in each of these months. We have 63,000 subscribers in Pennsylvania, Delaware, Maryland, New Jersey and West Virginia. We place almost exclusive emphasis on articles written about and developed in our five-state area. Editors prefer stories derived from first-hand on-farm experience.

Article size is flexible. An average of 750 to 1,000 words typed would be good ballpark length. We also accept humorous or poignant short stories about Mid-Atlantic rural life happenings for our Country Air column. Suggested length is 250 to 300 words or 22 to 27 lines of type.

Artwork should be black and white unless color is agreed on by the editors. Photographs may be 4"x6" color prints, but slide transparencies are preferred. Diagrams, charts and the like should be drawn in black ink on white paper, one drawing per sheet.

Letters or telephone calls of inquiry are suggested. Manuscripts are accepted with the understanding they are subject to revision. Feature articles must be cleared for accuracy with the sources before submission.

Manuscripts must be submitted exclusively to *Pennsylvania Farmer* in our five-state area. Major revisions will be checked with authors. Include your social security number; payment for articles is made upon publication.

Thank you for your interest.
Categories: Agriculture

Name: John Vogel, Editor
Material: All
Address: PO BOX 4475
City/State/ZIP: GETTYSBURG PA 17325
Telephone: 717-334-4300
Fax: 717-334-3129

Pennsylvania Game News

Thanks for your interest in GAME NEWS.

PENNSYLVANIA GAME NEWS is the official voice of the Pennsylvania Game Commission. It is designed to promote hunting and other wildlife-related recreation in the state, and what the agency is doing to manage and enhance these opportunities. We consider nearly any outdoor subject except fishing and boating. Our primary feature subjects are hunting and hunting-related activities. We also run wildlife natural history accounts and conservation-related articles. All material must have a Pennsylvania locale or be of such a nature that location is not relevant.

We rarely use freelance material on technical subjects about guns and archery, as these are covered by our columnists. Likewise, most wildlife management issues and problems are better covered by agency specialists.

One of our goals is to teach and encourage young hunters to hunt in a safe and ethical manner. Stories must never show a person acting in an unsportsmanlike manner—unless, perhaps, he is a game law violator who ultimately is apprehended by a conservation officer. "How-to" or other informational articles should be factual, to the point and basically educational. Text should be cut to a minimum here, so long as nothing is left out.

Our features typically run from 1,500 to 2,500 words. Good black and white photos are a big help with all articles.

We usually reach a decision on material within six weeks. Payment is on acceptance, at a minimum rate of 6 cents per word and $15 per photo. With a few exceptions, we buy first North American serial rights.

Manuscripts should have your name and address on page 1. We welcome submissions on PC-formatted disks, preferably in WordPerfect format; be sure to include a hard copy, too.

Material is scheduled up to a year in advance; seasonal or timely subjects, such as spring gobbler hunting, should be submitted at least six months prior to appropriate season.

Feel free to contact us if you have any questions or comments. Again, thanks for your interest in GAME NEWS.
Cordially,
Bob Mitchell, Editor
Categories: Hunting—Wildlife

Name: Robert D'Angelo, Associate Editor
Material: All
Address: 2001 ELMERTON AVE
City/State/ZIP: HARRISBURG PA 17110-9797
Telephone: 717-787-3745
Fax: 717-772-2411

Pennsylvania Heritage

PURPOSE
Pennsylvania Heritage is a popularly styled, illustrated magazine published by the Pennsylvania Historical and Museum Commission (PHMC). The quarterly is intended to introduce readers to Pennsylvania's rich culture and historic legacy, to educate and sensitize them to the value of preserving that legacy, and to entertain and involve them in such a way as to ensure that Pennsylvania's past has a future.

CONTENT
Heritage strives to convey a sense of Pennsylvania and to connect its past with what the Commonwealth is today or what it is likely to become. The magazine seeks articles relating to Pennsylvania's history and culture which are intended for intelligent lay readers. Articles on such varied topics as fine and decorative arts, architecture, archaeology, oral history, exhibits, industry and technology, natural history, historic sites, travel and folklore, as well as state and local history, are all suitable.

Submissions must be written with an eye toward illustration and, when possible, should be accompanied by photographs, maps, drawings or other such material. Photographic essays are also invited.

STYLE
The style should be popular, readable and entertaining, but without fictionalization and extensive quotation (except in the case of oral history). Manuscripts must be concise, thoroughly researched and documented, well organized and accurate. Articles accepted will be edited according to guidelines recommended by *The Chicago Manual of Style.* Submissions should follow those guidelines.

MANUSCRIPT REQUIREMENTS
Manuscripts, ranging from 3,000 to 3,500 words, must be typewritten, with at least 1½" margins on all sides of each page, and submitted in duplicate. They should be accompanied by a suggested title and a brief biographical sketch of the author. Although footnotes are not required, a list of sources and suggested further readings is requested.

Queries, including a brief outline of the proposed contribution, should be sent prior to manuscript submission to avoid duplication, to assist in planning and to permit the editorial staff to make recommendations before writing actually begins. Hence, manuscripts prepared following queries are more likely to be accepted than those forwarded without prior consultation; completed manuscripts, however, will also be reviewed.

ILLUSTRATION REQUIREMENTS
Photographs and/or other illustrative material should be submitted with manuscripts for review and will greatly enhance the possibility of publication. When absolutely necessary, the photo editor will assist in the location of illustrations.

For black-and-white photographs, 8"x10" glossies with borders are preferred, but 5"x7" glossies are acceptable. For color, mounted slides or transparencies (35mm or larger), shot preferably with Ektachrome 200, are requested. Suggested caption and credit lines must accompany all illustrative material.

PAYMENT AND RIGHTS
The PHMC will pay authors upon acceptance of an article, according to a payment schedule which begins at $100. The payment schedule for photographers and artists is: $100 for covers, $25-50 for back covers, $25 for inside color photos or drawings, and $5-10 for black and white photos. Individuals requesting payment should include their social security numbers in their requisitions.

On acceptance, all rights are transferred to *Pennsylvania Heritage;* upon publication, rights may be reassigned to the author on written request.

CORRESPONDENCE
All submissions are reviewed on speculation and must be accompanied by a self-addressed, stamped envelope. Replies to queries are generally made within two to three weeks; to manuscripts within four to six weeks.

Categories: Antiques—Architecture—Arts—Biography—Civil War—Culture—Education—Ethnic—History—Multicultural—Native American—Pennsylvania—Photography—Regional—Rural America

Name: Michael J. O'Malley III, Editor
Material: All
Address: PO BOX 1026
City/State/ZIP: HARRISBURG PA 17108-1026
Telephone: 717-787-7522
Fax: 717-787-8312

Pennsylvania Magazine

WHO ARE WE? *Pennsylvania Magazine* is a privately owned, bimonthly publication produced by a team-our staff and people like you, the freelance contributors throughout the state who have contact with the topics that our subscribers will enjoy. Since our name is *Pennsylvania*, all topics we cover must have an obvious link to someone, something, or some event within our borders. And, since our subscribers live in all parts of the state, your topic must also have an interest to this widespread audience.

THE SUBSCRIBERS OF *Pennsylvania Magazine* expect the magazine to be a source of timely articles about interesting people, unique places, fun festivals, and fascinating history. When our readers exclaim, "I didn't know that about Pennsylvania," we have succeeded and they are likely to renew their subscription.

WE RELY ON FREELANCERS. Therefore, we've included more advice and comments in our guidelines than you may find in others'. We've found that when we begin with a contributor who knows how we work, much time is saved in queries, rewrites, photographs, and other aspects of the publishing routine. So please take the time to review these guidelines thoroughly.

Begin With a Query Letter

WE LIKE TO WORK FROM QUERIES. This simple letter that briefly explains your idea saves time and effort for both of us. Within four weeks of our receipt of your query, you'll receive one of the following responses:

1. **Go ahead with your idea.** Guidance as necessary for completion of your article will be provided.

2. **We need more information to make a decision.** You will be asked to supply illustration samples for your topic, provide more information about your topic, or supply something else so that we can determine if our subscribers will find your topic of interest.

3. **Send this idea to another publication.** This idea is not what our subscribers look for in our magazine. If possible, we will direct you to another publication that may be interested in your topic.

Hints for Your Query

1. If you are sending a multiple query, use a separate sheet of paper for each topic. This helps us respond faster.

2. Explain how you would cover the topic and give an estimated word count.

3. Consider these topics first:

• Historical events (past).

• Travel with a historical interest (specific theme, i.e. hex signs, steeples or geographic area-county, region).

• Vacation/weekend trip ideas within the state.

• People/family success stories-see Panorama.

• General interest subjects that are related to happenings in Pennsylvania.

• Statewide roundups of attractions, resources, happenings, etc.

4. We usually avoid these topics: Hunting, skiing, fashions, exposes and scandals, film and product reviews, government/church/borough/institution anniversary-related events.

Template for Your Query Letter to Pennsylvania Magazine

Today's date
Your name/address
City/State/Zip Department/Feature
Phone Number Estimated word count
If seasonal, when the article should run
RE: Article subject

Introduction paragraph—who you are, why you suggest this topic now to *Pennsylvania Magazine*, why the subject would be of interest to our readers.

Explain what types of photos you can supply to illustrate your subject. Enclose photocopies of existing illustrations for your topic, or of photos similar to the ones you will supply.

What is your expected timeline for completion? Is this a simultaneous submission? Has this been printed previously elsewhere? Have you seen coverage of this topic in other publications?

Your name
List any enclosures

Tips

1. In your query, send photocopies of available illustrations or tell how you will provide them.

2. Do not send original slides at any time.

3. Do not send originals or anything valued by you or the owner (such as an old photo or certificate). Send a photocopy when you query.

4. We want people-related photos. With few exceptions, we do not want photos of building/structures (such as, "This is the house William Penn built.") or rooms/an empty field/etc. as the only illustration.

5. We prefer to begin with a written query, but if you already have a ms, you can send us a photocopy (include how you will handle illustrations).

6. Tell us if your material has been printed or is being considered elsewhere.

7. Do not send samples of previously published work.

8. Send your ideas often. The wider the choice, the more likely of a go-ahead.

9. We strongly suggest you send for a sample copy ($2.95 prepaid) if you are not already familiar with the magazine.

When an Article Is Submitted

SUBMITTING MATERIALS Send your article and its illustrations together. Do not have an illustrator or photographer send illustrations to us under separate cover. We can wait for you to assemble all components of an article package before sending it to us. Provide names and addresses of photographers or artists whose work is used. You will need to supply written permission for our use of photos/illustrations from owners/copyright owners) and their names so we can provide credit.

EDITING All written materials submitted to us are subject to editing for style, clarity, flow, and organization. This editing is intended to keep a cohesive, familiar style for readers of the magazine.

STYLE NOTES We use the *Associated Press Stylebook*. Do not use the terms first, only, or unique unless you can prove it. Include a citation with your text.

Write in the active voice. Location of a person, place or event should usually be cited in the first paragraph and include the county-Terry Smith of Camp Hill in Cumberland County. Omit county references for the following: Erie, Harrisburg, Lancaster, Philadelphia, Pittsburgh, Scranton, Allentown, Bethlehem, and York.

DEADLINES We operate without rigid deadlines for most stories. If your item is appropriate for an upcoming issue, and we expect that you are able to complete it for that issue, we'll give you a deadline. Otherwise, articles are scheduled in the magazine when we have a suitable text/illustration package and the subject/geographical location fits a niche in the content of a specific issue.

ASSIGNMENTS When we respond favorably to a query from a potential contributor who has not worked with us before, this does not constitute an assignment (and we will not pay a kill fee if the materials are not acceptable).

A contributor new to us submits only on speculation.

Payment for accepted materials is usually made upon acceptance. It may sometimes follow editing if the writer has exceeded the word limit.

Unless we specify otherwise, we purchase first, one-time use rights of your original materials. We then own our edited, published version. You can resell your original copy elsewhere after our publication of your material.

Payment Information

RATES We pay 10 to 15 cents a word, depending on the amount of editing required. (Payment for reprinted articles is five cents per word.)

We pay $15 to $25 for each photo you take, depending on the number we use. For a cover, we pay up to $100. Photos you obtain from a subject's file: $5 each. We may suggest a flat package fee for an article with illustrations.

MINIMUM RATES We pay a minimum of $50 for each item (copy and one photo) appearing in the PANORAMA and MUSEUM departments-more if two photos and/or copy exceeding 350 words are used.

EXPENSES We seldom pay expenses. The only expense that we usually pay is for the reasonable fee for reproduction of a photo or illustration provided by a museum, library or historical society.

Quick Reference

CREDITS In the author credit at the end of the article, we like to mention your hometown, county, and any related interest you may have in the subject of your article.

COPIES Upon publication, we will return your materials with two copies of that issue. Additional copies can be purchased for $2.50 each, plus a shipping charge, prepaid.

COPYRIGHT We copyright each edition of the magazine with the Lbrary of Congress.

Specifics Regarding Content

Features ALMANAC AND GENERAL Usually range between 1,000 to 2,500 words in edited form and cover historical items (places, people, and events), travel with a people focus, and topics of current interest. GENERAL FEATURES must be illustrated with a majority of color photos; ALMANAC ITEMS should have period photos or appropriate illustrations. Published articles range from two to six pages.

Departments Usually range between 250 to 900 words.

PANORAMA items cover people and organizations involved in noteworthy projects/festivals, unusual activities, or significant achievement.

MUSEUM items usually cover collections in the state that are open to the general public on a regular (not appointment) basis.

AMERICANA PHOTO JOURNAL includes one to four interesting photos and a lengthy (250 words) caption about a single topic.

PHOTOGRAPHY ESSAY highlights our annual Photo Contest entries. The contest is announced in the first two issues of the year, and winners are announced/published in the fourth.

Details on Photography

WE ALWAYS ASK OUR CONTRIBUTORS TO supply photographs with articles. If you don't own or are not familiar/comfortable with a camera, we suggest that you join a photography club in your area to refine your skills. We believe that you will sell more material to us and other publications when you can supply the illustrations as a package.

We prefer people to be in photographs for articles and department items. This is for scale and personality. In close-up shots,

we should have people's names and addresses (if their photo is used, we'll send a copy of that magazine).

People should be doing something or talking to one another to give the photograph vitality. Objects important to the article can be in the foreground or background, and people can also be shown looking slightly off camera. The best way to show people in a natural setting is to ask them questions and shoot as they respond, remembering to direct their attention away from you and the camera. A flash on the camera should not be used unless the background wall is at least 10 feet away.

We do not want original slides and will not be responsible for them. We prefer color prints (4"x6" to 5"x7") and can use duplicate slides. We have found that Kodacolor, if shot in a contrasting setting (sunshine and dark areas in the same scene) will result in either over- or under-exposure. Seek shade or all sun in a scene. If faces are in shade or backlit, use flash for fill-in.

Articles about resorts, parks, etc. should have a people focus, with them in the fore- or background of shots. We don't need model releases. But if a person notices you taking a picture and objects, do not take or use it. Do not send us photos of Amish people. We need to identify people when appropriate. For example, staff in a museum or attraction photo.

We may hold your submission for some time, so do not send us your only copies of original illustrations. Make and send a copy.

Categories: History—Regional

Name: Matthew K. Holliday, Editor
Material: All
Address: PO BOX 576
City/State/ZIP: CAMP HILL PA 17001-0576
Telephone: 717-697-4660

Penthouse

1. The best way to discern the material *Penthouse* might be interested in is to look at the magazine. Articles are usually related to current affairs or topics that would appeal to our readers (predominately male, aged 18-49). Subjects might include celebrity or sports figure profiles, exposes on government or corporate affairs, and analyses of trends in lifestyle or sexuality. Interviews should be exclusive queries on personalities who are obviously of interest to a diverse audience.

2. Queries should include a detailed description of your article, who or what your sources will be, and how you plan to present the material. Queries should demonstrate an in-depth knowledge of the subject. Proposals for photo essays should be accompanied by slides or suggestions for sources of art.

3. Please submit any credits, clips or other examples of your published writings, if available. A stamped, self-addressed envelope is essential for a reply or return of material.

4. Features run 3500 to 5000 words and shorter articles for our "View From The Top" section are 600-700 words.

5. Writer's fees and expenses are negotiated when an assignment is made. Features pay from $2,500 to $5,000, depending on length and complexity of subject. Shorter pieces pay $250. Payment is made on acceptance. There is a 25% kill fee on assigned articles.

6. Forum letters should carry name and address, though these will be changed by the editor. All letters become the property of *Penthouse*. We do not pay for letters but your submissions are welcome.

7. All letters should be sent to address below. Designate Editorial Department and appropriate editor (i.e. - features, fiction, sports, forum).

Bedtime Stories, Women's Erotic Fiction Section Writer's Guidelines: Thank you for your interest in "Bedtime Stories," *Penthouse*'s women's erotic fiction section.

Stories for the column should be well-developed, well-plotted, erotic in nature, written by a woman, and between 2,000-2,500 words in length. The main character or voice should be female. We request that the stories contain no bondage/discipline, S/M, painful anal sex, fist fucking, excessive come on the face, or minors (which includes reflections on adolescence—no one even thinking about being younger than 19). We also request that the material be unpublished, and that it not be submitted to any of our associate publications during the time we are reviewing it. If it is being considered elsewhere, please make note of that in your cover letter.

The manuscript should be double spaced, with 1" margins, on white paper. Please make sure the pages are numbered, and that your name, address, phone number, and social security number appear on the first page. The fees vary per author and individual story. We do request that writers use their own names, not pseudonyms; if this is a problem for you, please consider it before submitting material.

We will return submissions which arrive with envelopes large enough to accommodate them. If not, they will be discarded.

We look forward to hearing from you soon.

Categories: Fiction—Nonfiction—Entertainment—Erotica—Fashion—Food/Drink—Interview—Sexuality—Society—Sports—Recreation—Humor—Government—Celebrities—Lifestyles—Profiles

Name: Lavada B. Nahon
Material: Bedtime Stories
Name: Designate Editorial Department
        and Appropriate Editor
Material: All
Address: 277 PARK AVE., 4TH FLOOR
City/State/ZIP: NEW YORK, NY 10172-0033
Telephone: 212-702-6000
Fax: 212-702-6279
Internet: www.penthousemag.com

AMHERST
WRITERS
& ARTISTS
PRESS

Peregrine

History and Background
of Amherst Writers and Artists

Amherst Writers & Artists is a fifteen year old arts organization, offering creative writing workshops, retreats and public readings for both established and beginning writers, and training in writing workshop leadership. Thousands of local writers and friends of writers have participated in AWA events, as leaders and as members of workshops, retreats and leadership trainings. Last year Pat Schneider, founder/director of AWA, was recognized by *The Massachusetts Review* as the originator of the Pioneer Valley's remarkable flowering of community writing workshops.

The history of Amherst Writers & Artists is a story of thousands of local writers, their stories wind poems, essays, plays and libretti. At the heart of our work is the conviction that every human person is endowed with genius, and that the best way to achieve work of genius is in a non-competitive, supportive environment of mutual support and encouragement.

Peregrine has provided a forum for national and international writers for more than 15 years, and is committed to finding exceptional work by new as well as established writers. Every manuscript is read by three or more readers. We publish what we love, knowing that all responses are subjective.

Peregrine is published annually. Our yearly deadline is February 28. Submissions received after the deadline are held for consideration in the following year.

The length of our journal makes it necessary for us to limit prose manuscripts to 4,200 words (short pieces have a better chance of publication; 1,000-2,500 words preferred). *Indicate word count on first page.*

We accept poetry manuscripts of 1-5 poems, each poem limited to 76 lines. *Indicate line count for each poem.*

We accept only original, unpublished work. We accept simultaneous submissions.

If you submit under a pseudonym, please also provide us with your legal name for mailing purposes.

Enclose a #10 SASE for our response to you. We recycle and encourage submission of disposable manuscripts.

If you wish to receive acknowledgement of manuscript receipt, you must also include a self-addressed stamped postcard, with "Peregrine Submission" written on it. Thank you.
Nancy Rose,
Managing Editor
Categories: Fiction—Poetry

Name: Nancy Rose, Managing Editor
Material: All
Address: PO BOX 1076
City/State/ZIP: AMHERST MA 01004
Telephone: 413-253-7764
Fax: 413-253-7764
E-mail: awapress@javanet.com

Permanent Buildings
& Foundations

PERMANENT BUILDINGS & FOUNDATIONS (PBF), published seven times per year, is written and edited for residential, commercial and industrial building contractors. Its circulation is 35,000 and growing. We generally pay 20 to 40 cents per printed word on publication for assigned submissions, less if extensive editing is required, more if travel is necessary. We buy one-time rights with byline given. Queries welcome, SASE preferred. Length from 250 to 2,000 words.

Articles should probe the whys of issues confronting the construction of residential, commercial and industrial buildings. No essays or opinions. Articles must be clear and well-defined. The magazine avoids writing features "about" places or products simply because they exist; there should be a thesis or subject that concerns our reader—techniques, designs, business management, news, equipment, for example.

Good articles must contain facts backed up by pertinent examples from first-hand sources. Please keep your style simple and direct. Try to make one major point at a time and support it with facts and examples or anecdotal evidence. We especially like pieces about people and how they solved a problem.

Article ideas may be suggested to the editor by a phone call, e-mail, query letter or outline. The usual approach is to call with a general idea and follow-up with a one-page letter describing what you propose to write and what our readers can learn from it. We'll let you know if we already have something similar in the works or we may suggest a different subject or approach. If the idea fits into our current or future editorial plans, you will be assigned a deadline by which to submit a finished manuscript. Assignment of a deadline does not guarantee acceptance or publication of an article. It only means we're interested in your idea and would like to pursue it.

The editorial staff reviews articles to determine whether manuscripts meet the criteria for publication. Authors are notified of the acceptance or rejection of their manuscript. They also may be asked to revise an article before it can receive further consideration for publication. When a manuscript requires extensive rewriting, it will be returned to the author.

Once a complete and/or revised article has been reviewed and accepted, it will be scheduled for production. Please keep in mind that production situations change quickly, making it difficult to know for certain which article will appear in given issue. Once an article is prepared for publication, however, every effort is made to publish it in as timely manner as possible.

Categories: Nonfiction—Business—Construction

Name: Roger W. Nielsen, Editor
Material: All
Address: PO BOX 11067
Address: 5245 N KENSINGTON
City/State/ZIP: KANSAS CITY MO 64119
Telephone: 816-453-0590
Fax: 816-453-0591
E-mail: rnielsen@kcnet.com

Personally Yours

Please refer to Christian Publications, Inc.

Perspective
Christ in Every Phase of Life

Perspective magazine, published three times a year by Pioneer Clubs, serves as an inspirational and idea resource for adult leaders of Pioneer Clubs. Pioneer Clubs include girls and boys age 2 through grade 12 and are sponsored by local churches in the United States and Canada.

The purpose of *Perspective* is to provide information that will aid lay leaders in developing leadership skills and relationship skills. It also serves as an organizational voice. (For a sample copy of *Perspective*, send $1.75 and a self-addressed stamped [four first class stamps] 9"x12" envelope.)

Most of our articles are done on assignment; consequently, we accept only a few of the freelance manuscripts submitted to us. We need articles, 1,000-1,500 words, that deal with subjects contributing to the purposes listed above. We also accept short "how to" pieces (100-200 words): ideas for special events, games, holiday celebrations, service projects, missions projects, and so on. Writing that reflects understanding and knowledge of *Perspective* and Pioneer Clubs is most likely to be purchased.

We usually buy first rights. Payment for articles ranges from $50-$90, depending on length, quality, and amount of editing required. Payment for "how to" pieces is from $7-$15, depending on length, completeness, and clarity. Payment is upon acceptance.

Allow four to eight weeks for consideration of your submission. Submit seasonal material nine months in advance.

Freelancers who are interested in working on assignment and have been involved with, or have access to, a Pioneer Clubs program may contact us.

Thank you for your inquiry.

The Editors

Categories: Christian Interests—Education—Religion

Name: Rebecca Powell Parat, Editor
Material: All
Address: PO BOX 788
City/State/ZIP: WHEATON IL 60189-0788
Telephone: 630-293-1600 ext. 340
Fax: 630-293-3053

Petersen's Bowhunting

Your interest in *Petersen's Bowhunting* is very much appreciated. In an effort to make your next submission the best it can be, please review this sheet.

1.) Feature articles must be supplied to *Petersen's Bowhunting* in either 5.25" IBM (or compatible) or 3.5" Macintosh floppy disks. Files should be saved as ASCII format using a popular word processing program. Hard copy must be included with all submissions. The author's name, address, telephone number, and social security number should be in the upper left-hand corner of the title page.

Featured works are approximately 2,000 words in length (no more than 14 double-spaced pages). With rare exceptions, no feature submissions will be accepted unless they are accompanied by a minimum of 30 color transparencies. Author-supplied captions are mandatory and charts, graphs, and line drawings are welcome.

It is the policy of Petersen Publishing Company to buy all rights to manuscripts accepted for publication. The editors reserve the right to edit and modify any manuscript to fit the magazine's format.

a) The rate of pay for features (including black and white photo usage) is $300 to $400. Author-supplied color photo usage pays an additional $50 to $250, depending on the number and size used. Payments for the written and black and white graphic portion of a feature package are made upon acceptance; color transparency usage pays upon publication.

2.) **Short success stories** (approximately 1,000 words) detailing how, when, and where an exceptional game animal has been bow bagged pay up to $250. These can be written in either first or second person and a minimum of one high-quality "success" photo must accompany the submission. The editors reserve the right to edit and modify any manuscript to fit the magazine's format.

3.) **Photography only submissions** will be reviewed and a selection will be kept on file for consideration. Those that won't be used in the near future will be returned within four to six weeks. It is the policy of Petersen Publishing Company to buy all rights to photographs used at the time of publication.

The photographer should mark each 35mm slide holder and the back of each black and white print with his or her name and address. Published transparencies will be returned; Petersen Publishing will retain all black and white prints used. With photography submissions, please include your complete address, telephone number, and social security number. All photographs on file will be returned upon request.

a) The rate of pay for published photographs is: $500 for covers; $50 to $250 (depending on the number and size) for color transparencies used inside the magazine; and $35 per black and white photo. Color transparencies converted to black and white will earn b/w rates. Payments for photographs are made upon publication.

Thank you again for your interest in *Petersen's Bowhunting.* Study the magazine for variations in theme that could make you one of its contributors. We look forward to reviewing your submissions detailing the tools, techniques, and adventures indigenous to hunting with the bow and arrow.

Categories: Hunting—Outdoors—Sports

Name: Jay Michael Strangis, Editor

Material: Bowhunting
Address: 6420 WILSHIRE BLVD
City/State/ZIP: LOS ANGELES CA 90048

Phic-Shun
An Anthology of Stories

• Each issue will have a central *theme.*
• Fiction only, but any genre is acceptable. Please, no poetry, children's stories, or nonfiction.
• Absolutely no pornography; otherwise no restriction on genre or content.
• 1,000-5,000 words limit.
• Must be available digitally (e-mail or disc) or arranged to become so.
• Simultaneous submissions and previously published material okay, if so specified. Please provide past or current relevant data with submission.
• Stories required at least two weeks *prior* to publication date in order to be considered.
• Please include a short bio (50 word limit) to be published with story and please *tell us* what genre it is. Though we can guess, we prefer you tell us under what genre you want your story listed.
• Please include a *web-page link and/or e-mail address* along with the bio.
• Writers retain copyrights of material submitted. Submission is for one time use only. (If we ever go to paper, we'll ask ya!)
• Issues *may* be available as "back issues."
Please submit your stories via e-mail in a text form.
Do not hesitate to ask any questions you may have!
Sincerely,
Roland Mann and Thomas Fortenberry, *co-editors*
Categories: Fiction

Name: Thomas Fortenberry, Co-editor
Material: Short Fiction
Name: Roland Mann, Co-editor
Material: Fiction
Address: PO BOX 28335
City/State/ZIP: BALTIMORE MD 21234
E-mail: rmann@ebicom.net *or* Kurvanas@aol.com

PHOEBE
A JOURNAL OF LITERARY ARTS

Phoebe
A Journal of Literary Arts
George Mason University

All submissions must be typed or printed. Address submissions to the editors of the appropriate genre (poetry or fiction).
Phoebe seeks to publish quality writing in all forms. Do not send formulaic writings, romance fiction, or greeting card poetry.
Reporting time is two to eight weeks. *Phoebe* does not read during June, July, and August.
Contributors are given two (2) copies of the magazine upon publication. Copyright automatically reverts to the author upon publication.
Subscriptions are $12 for one year (2 issues), $21 for two years (4 issues). Make checks payable to *Phoebe.*

Phoebe also sponsors a poetry and a short fiction contest each year. Please send a SASE for guidelines.
Categories: Fiction—Literature—Poetry—Writing

Name: Poetry Editor
Material: Fiction Editor
Name: As Appropriate
Address: GEORGE MASON UNIVERSITY MSN 2D6
Address: 4400 UNIVERSITY DR
City/State/ZIP: FAIRFAX VA 22030-4444
Telephone: 703-273-5668
E-mail: phoebe@gmu.edu

Pipeline & Gas Journal
Please refer to Oildom Publishing.

PITTSBURGH
Pittsburgh

It's your town. Make the most of it.
Mission: PITTSBURGH magazine is the monthly community publication for Western Pennsylvania, Eastern Ohio, Northern West Virginia and Western Maryland. PITTSBURGH presents issues, analyzes problems and strives to encourage a better understanding of today's community to more than 75,000 readers.
Style: Each issue features a mix of stories that includes a "people" profile, in-depth news and a service piece, plus feature and lifestyle stories for our target reader: primarily 30ish, professional, with children. Without exception-whether the topic is business, travel, the arts or lifestyle—each story is clearly oriented to Pittsburghers today and the greater Pittsburgh region of today. We have minimal interest in historical articles. PITTSBURGH does not publish fiction, poetry, advocacy pieces or personal reminiscences.
Scheduling: Seasonal story ideas should be submitted at least six months in advance. Each issue is fully scheduled at least four months in advance; feature ideas that do not fit that timeframe cannot be considered. Short (under 200 words) timely items for UpFront can be considered as late as six weeks before publication.
Payment & rights: Features vary from $300 up, depending upon length and complexity of story, and experience of writer. Feature fees are negotiated separately. UpFront items start at $50, up to $100 for Weekender (a local travel story of about 300 words, following a specific format; query first). Most feature stories and service pieces range from 1,200 to 4,000 words, in-depth news features up to 5,000. We purchase first North American serial rights; second rights, only when the article has not appeared in the same geographic market.
Submission: Address all queries to the managing editor. PITTSBURGH prefers to receive a brief query with a sample lead and one-page outline, not completed manuscripts. We will, however, review manuscripts on spec. Writers should enclose samples of their writing when submitting queries. We do not assign stories to new freelancers. All queries will be answered within six weeks. Manuscripts and other materials will be returned only if the writer includes a self-addressed stamped envelope, or can be picked up at the office. The writer guarantees that the piece is his or her own work and is not plagiarized.
After acceptance: Once a story is accepted, we will review

the first draft and, possibly, ask for changes and a second draft. The writer is responsible for completing all research deemed necessary by the editors. We prefer that the final draft be submitted on disk with no extraneous commands. (Call for electronic submission.) Delete line spaces, tabs, etc. We also want a hard copy, single-spaced on unmarked paper, with your name, address, phone number(s) and social security number, plus a list of sources and their phone numbers for fact-checking.

Categories: Regional

Name: Michelle Pilecki, Managing Editor
Material: All
Address: 4802 FIFTH AVE
City/State/ZIP: PITTSBURGH PA 15213-2918
Telephone: 412-622-1360
Fax: 412-622-7066
E-mail: editor@wqed.org

Plain Jane
Alpha Beat Press

Alpha Beat Press has been publishing Beat Generation, post-Beat independent and other modern writings since 1986. Alpha Beat had its beginnings in a Montreal flat with the idea of keeping the aesthetics and sensibilities of the Beat Generation alive—our first magazine, *Alpha Beat Soup*, was unique, being the only small press magazine publishing original and current Beat writings. In our new magazine, *Bouillabaisse*, and in our other poetry publications we have continued in that tradition, publishing a wide variety of writers and styles—from Bukowski to the lesser known poets. Alpha Beat Press is certainly the best of the small press!

PLAIN JANE is looking for homespun to risque poems—short stories derived from your life experiences—where you have been and where you are now and the people past and present in your lives—PLAIN JANE likes to have fun!

Sample $3.00

Categories: Beat Generation—Culture—Erotica—Literature

Name: Dave Christy, Editor/Publisher
Name: Ana Christy, Editor/Publisher
Material: Any
Address: 31 WATERLOO ST
City/State/ZIP: NEW HOPE PA 18938
Telephone: 215-862-0299

The Plain Truth

• **OUR PURPOSE**
The goal of *The Plain Truth* is to lead our readers to Jesus Christ and to help those who are already in Christ to enjoy a closer walk with him.

• **OUR READERS**
For over 60 years, *The Plain Truth* was published as a free magazine. In 1996, we became a paid subscription magazine. Circulation is currently 130,000 in the United States and Canada. The average reader is 54 years of age. The male-female ratio is 52-48.

• **WRITING FOR THE PT**
If you are interested in writing for us, here's what we look for in a standard article:

Personal interest: Material should offer biblical solutions to real life problems. Both first person and third person illustrations are encouraged.

Creative thinking: Articles should take a unique twist on a subject. Material must be insightful and practical for the Christian reader, moving him or her toward a closer relationship with Jesus.

Biblical accuracy: All articles must be well-researched and biblically accurate without becoming overly scholastic. We seek to make the Bible plain to our readers by bringing the Scriptures to life.

Compelling logic: Use convincing arguments to support your Christian platform. Make it clear to the reader where you are going, and make it difficult for him or her to turn down your invitation to follow.

Colorful personality: Use vivid word pictures, simple and compelling language, and avoid stuffy academic jargon.

• **DEPARTMENTS**
Christian People: These articles are testimonial interviews with Christian leaders or members of the community who have kept Christ first in their lives. Featured people should be actively involved in their church and their neighborhood, bringing the good news to the world. We are interested in both well-known Christian celebrities as well as lesser known Christian servants. Approximately 1,500 to 1,600 words.

Family: These articles are two-page features dealing with family relationships. Topics range from marriage and child-rearing, to dealing with aging parents or handling sibling rivalry. These articles should be full of warmth, love and practical Christianity. Approximately 1,500 words.

Query letters: *The Plain Truth* does not accept unsolicited manuscripts. Please first submit a query letter and secure permission to forward manuscript. A positive response to a query does not guarantee a purchase.

Your query letter should include the following information:
• Your specific subject and working title
• An outline of your ideas, punctuating your main points
• A profile of your experience and qualifications, as well as any other personal information that lets us know why you are the person to write this article

Manuscript format: Manuscripts are preferred on floppy disk in a WordPerfect format. If no disk is available, please send manuscripts on double spaced computer printout. Include your name, address, daytime phone and social security number in the upper left hand corner of the first page.

Payment and rights: *The Plain Truth* buys one-time non-exclusive rights. All manuscripts are examined on speculation. If you have submitted your material to another magazine before ours, please advise. We pay 25 cents a word on publication of an acceptable manuscript, 15 cents a word for reprint material.

The author grants *The Plain Truth* the right to edit and abridge the manuscript and warrants that he or she is the sole and true author of the submitted material.

Categories: Christian Interests—Inspirational—Religion

Name: Susan Stewart, Managing Editor
Material: All
Address: 300 W GREEN ST
City/State/ZIP: PASADENA CA 91129
Telephone: 626-304-6077

Fax: 626-795-0107
E-mail: Susan_Stewart@ptm.org
Internet: www.ptm.org

Planetary Connections
International Forum for Solution-Oriented News

Planetary Connections is an international newspaper. It features news about people and organizations that have a positive impact on the world.

Planetary Connections is a quarterly tabloid-size newspaper, printed in soy ink on recycled newsprint. There are four editions released during the year: Winter Issue (January), Spring Issue (April), Summer Issue (July), and Autumn Issue (October).

Circulation and distribution. This widely-respected publication is found in over 80 countries and in every state in the USA. Annual subscriptions are only $18. Individual issues are sold at bookstores, health food stores, churches, and various international meetings. They are also distributed through environmental and other organizations, as well as health practitioners.

Readers are self-motivated networkers. They are interested in personal health and well-being, the arts, spiritual unfoldment, and social and environmental issues. Planetary Connections provides a link that creates a supportive, wide-spread community of lightworkers.

Join the team—60,000 readers from 80 countries are waiting for news from you!

Planetary Connections is looking for both correspondents and writers.

Regional correspondents agree to submit quarterly news from their city, region, or nation. This includes original articles and clippings from other publications. Regional correspondents are recognized as volunteer staff members of the paper.

Writers submit single or occasional articles.

Please label all material with your name, address and phone number.

Submissions

We welcome contributions that are:
• news of positive planetary transformation
• reports on major conferences, meetings, and organizations around the globe
• interviews with people living with heart and purpose
• profiles of organizations making a social or environmental difference
• letters from readers

Clippings from other publications (with source and date) and photos are welcome. Submission does not guarantee publication. We reserve the right to edit all materials.

How to submit

Send submissions as text only (synonymous with ASCII or DOS file) or rich text files (indicate file type and name) on 3.5" floppy disk with printed copy. We also accept typed, and occasionally handwritten submissions.

Selection process: our criteria
• Does the article tell about people using positive, solutions-oriented approaches to solving problems?
• Is the topic about current, contemporary events which affect many people?
• Is the story complete, including participant's names, as well as locations and dates?
• Does the topic have broad enough appeal for our global audience?
• Is a good quality photo included?
• Is the content non-promotional in nature?
• Is the article the right length (500-1,000 words)?

Other considerations

Planetary Connections is a newspaper rather than a magazine. We print concise, objective and timely articles. With rare exceptions, we do not use self-help or how-to articles. We will consider analysis or commentary on issues of wide-spread concern.

We do not use press releases and articles that obviously promote products and services. Instead, we encourage you to purchase our reasonably priced and highly effective advertising space for such promotions. Contact Advertising Director Earle Belle at the number below.

Deadlines (livelines?)

Issue	Submit by
Winter	October 1
Spring	January 1
Summer	April 1
Autumn	July 1

Articles not used in a particular issue may be used in a subsequent one.

Photographs

Good black & white or color photos that show activity in progress, or individuals engaged in problem-solving discussions are welcome.

Please include the following:
• names and addresses of people in photo
• details of subject and date when picture was taken
• your name, address and phone number
• photographer's name, address and phone number (if known)

Payment

Planetary Connections does not currently offer payment for news or photos. However, a biographical sketch (three lines or less) is printed at the end of the article. Please include a brief statement about your profession, education, residence, or other networking information.

Exceptions: In some cases a small honorarium is awarded to authors of exceptional articles that originate in Eastern Europe, the Middle East, Africa, South America, or Asia.

Categories: Fiction—Nonfiction—Animals—Arts—Associations—Comedy—Culture—Diet—Ecology—Education—Environment—Esoteric—Ethnic—Film/Video—Government Cover-up—Health—Holistic—Humor—Inspirational—Internet—Inventions—Lifestyles—Literature—Multicultural—Music—Native American—New Age—Paranormal—Philosophy—Politics—Public Policy—Relationships—Religion—Science—Spiritual—Suppressed Information—Technology—UFO/ET

Name: Nancie Belle, Editor/Publisher
Material: All
Address: 305 W MAGNOLIA ST STE 348
City/State/ZIP: FORT COLLINS CO 80521
Telephone: 970-282-1797
Fax: 970-282-0091
E-mail: planetnews@aol.com

Playboy

Playboy regularly publishes nonfiction articles on a wide range of topics - sports, politics, music, topical humor, personality profiles, business and finance, science and technology - and other topics that have a bearing on our readers' lifestyles.

You can best determine what we're looking for by becoming familiar with the nonfiction we are currently publishing. We frequently reject ideas and articles - many of high quality - simply because they are inappropriate to our publication. We have a six-month lead time, so timing is very important.

Your brief query should outline your idea, explain why it's right for *Playboy* and tell us something about yourself. Handwritten submissions will be returned unread. Manuscripts should be typed, double-spaced and accompanied by a self-addressed, stamped envelope. Writers who submit manuscripts without a stamped, self-addressed return envelope will receive neither the manuscript nor a printed rejection.

The average length for nonfiction pieces is 4,000 to 5,000 words, and minimum payment for an article of this length is $3,000. We do not accept unsolicited poetry. *Playboy* buys first North American serial rights only - no second serial rights are considered. *Playboy* does not accept simultaneous submissions.

A bit of advice for writers: Please bear in mind that *Playboy* is not a venue where beginning writers should expect to be published. Nearly all of our writers have long publication histories, working their way up through newspapers and regional publications. Aspiring writers should gain experience, and an extensive file of by-lined features, before approaching *Playboy*. Please don't call our offices to ask how to submit a story or to explain a story. Don't ask for sample copies, a statement of editorial policy, a reaction to an idea for a story, or a detailed critique. We are unable to provide these, as we receive dozens of submissions daily. Our response time is approximately four weeks.

We appreciate your interest in *Playboy*. We hope these guidelines will assist you in submitting work that is suited to *Playboy's* high standards.

Categories: Nonfiction—Business—Culture—Entertainment—Fashion—General Interest—Interview—Money/Finance—Music—Politics—Science—Sexuality—Sports—Recreation—Humor—Profiles—Technology

Name: Articles Editor
Material: Nonfiction
Address: 680 NORTH LAKE SHORE DRIVE
City/State/ZIP: CHICAGO, IL 60611
Telephone: 312-751-8000
Fax: 312-751-2818
E-mail: articles@la.playboy.com
Internet: www.playboy.com

Playgirl

PLAYGIRL addresses the needs, interests and desires of women 18 years of age and older. We provide something no other American women's magazine can: an uninhibited approach to exploring sexuality and fantasy that empowers, enlightens and entertains.

We publish feature articles of all sorts: interviews with top celebrities; essays and humor pieces on sexually related topics; first-person accounts of sensual adventures; articles on the latest trends in sex, love, romance and dating; and how-to stories that give readers sexy news they can use. We also publish erotic fiction-from a women's perspective or from an empathic, sex-positive male point of view-and reader fantasies. The common thread-besides, of course, good, lively writing and scrupulous research-is a fresh, open-minded, inquisitive attitude.

Prospective writers should read a few issues before submitting ideas. Query letters with published clips are preferred, but completed, unsolicited manuscripts will be considered. Payment rates vary. No submission will receive response without a self-addressed stamped envelope.

NONFICTION FEATURES: These run 1,800 to 2,500 words. Send an outline of your idea and tell how you'd approach the topic. Include proposed sources of information.

CELEBRITY FEATURES: Mostly assigned in-house, but we'll consider pitches from reputable freelancers. 2,500-3,500 words. Must supply contacts you are working with, interview transcript and interview tape.

PLAYGIRL PUNCH LINE: A humorous look at a wide range of sexually related topics-from offbeat experiences to kinky explorations. 1,000 Words.

GUEST ROOM: First person essays on sex-positive, fun experiences from both male and female perspectives. 2,000 – 2,500 words.

GIRL TALK: Q&A and features of fabulously engaging women who in some way empower the evolution of female sensuality and pleasure. 2,000 – 3,000 words.

FANTASY FORUM: Our readers are major contributors to this creative column devoted to female pleasures of the flesh. This is the best place for new writers to break into the magazine. Fantasy of the month pays $100, while others are $25. Submissions should be sent to Fantasy Forum, c/o PLAYGIRL.

EROTIC FICTION: We consider ourselves the country's premier magazine outlet for erotica from a woman's perspective and encourage writers to submit complete manuscripts only. We look for well-written, well-structured prose of 3,000 – 4,000 words that includes sizzling sex scenes and storylines related to female sexual self-expression.

Categories: Fiction—Nonfiction—College—Confession—Consumer—Diet—Entertainment—Erotica—Fantasy—Fashion—Feminism—Film/Video—Interview—Lifestyles—Romance—Sexuality—Short Stories—Television/Radio—Women's Fiction—Women's Issues

Name: Patrice Baldwin, Managing Editor
Material: All
Address: 801 2ND AVE
City/State/ZIP: NEW YORK NY 10017
Telephone: 212-661-7878
Fax: 212-697-6343
Internet: www.playgirlmag.com

Pleiades
Central Missouri State University

PLEIADES is a semiannual, national journal of poetry and prose published by Pleiades Press at Central Missouri State University.

PLEIADES is open to unsolicited submissions of poetry, fiction, translations, essays, reviews, notes, and experimental prose from any writer. All submissions are assumed to be original, unpublished, and not under consideration from any other publisher.

Poetry: Submit no more than seven poems, typed, single spaced, with name and address in upper corner of page.

Fiction: Fiction should be typed, with name, address, and word count noted on the first page. Novel excerpts should be noted as such. Short stories and novel excerpts of over 8,000 words have little chance of being accepted for publication.

Essays: All essays should conform to the current *MLA* style. They should be typed, with name, address, and word count noted on the first page. Essays of over 8,000 words have little chance of being accepted for publication.

Reviews: PLEIADES reviews current poetry, fiction, or literary nonfiction with a special interest in books published by small or university presses. Reviews should be typed, with name, address, and word count noted on the first page. Please also include a copy of the book or pre-publication galleys under review. If you would like the book returned to you, enclose sufficient postage and envelope.

Enclose a stamped, self-addressed envelope for reply and return of manuscript. Sample back issues are available for $3.50. Current issues are $5.00 each.

The editors consider manuscripts year-round.

Categories: Fiction—Book Reviews—Drama—Literature—Personal Essays—Poetry

Name: Kevin Prufer, Co-Editor
Material: Poetry, Book Reviews
Name: R.M. Kinder, Editor
Material: Fiction, Essays
Address: DEPT OF ENGLISH
Address: CENTRAL MISSOURI STATE UNIVERSITY
City/State/ZIP: WARRENSBURG MO 64093
Telephone: 816-543-4425
Fax: 816-543-8544
E-mail: kdp8106@cmsu2.cmsu.edu

Ploughshares
Emerson College

Ploughshares welcomes unsolicited submissions of fiction and poetry. We consider manuscripts from August 1 to March 31 (postmark dates). All submissions sent from April to July are returned unread. We adhere very strictly to the postmark restrictions. Since we operate on a first-received, first-read basis, we cannot make exceptions or hold work.

Ploughshares is published three times a year: usually mixed issues of poetry and fiction in the spring and winter and a fiction issue in the Fall, with each guest-edited by a different writer.

In the past, guest editors often announced specific themes for issues, but we have revised our editorial policies and no longer restrict submissions to thematic topics. In general, if you believe your work is in keeping with our standards of literary quality and value, submit it at any time during our reading period.

We do not recommend trying to target specific guest editors unless you have a legitimate acquaintance with them. Our backlog is unpredictable, and staff editors ultimately have the responsibility of determining for which editor a work is most appropriate. If a manuscript is not suitable or timely for one issue, it might be considered for another. For your information, however, at the start of the next reading period, we will be screening work for the Spring 1998 fiction and poetry issue, guest-edited by Stuart Dybek and Jane Hirshfield.

Please send only one short story and/or one to three poems at a time (mail fiction and poetry separately). Poems should be individually typed either single- or double-spaced on one side. Prose should be typed and no longer than twenty-five pages. Although we look primarily for short stories, we occasionally publish personal essays and memoirs. Novel excerpts are acceptable if they are self-contained. We do not accept unsolicited book reviews or criticism, nor do we consider book-length manuscripts of any sort.

Please do not send multiple submissions of the same genre for different issues/editors, and do not send another manuscript until you hear about the first (no more than a total of three submissions per reading period, please). Additional submissions will be returned unread. Mail your manuscript in a page-size manila envelope, your full name and address written on the outside, to "Fiction Editor," "Poetry Editor," or "Nonfiction Editor." Unsolicited work sent directly to a guest editor's home or office will be

discarded. We suggest you enclose a business-size SASE with a [first class] stamp and ask for a reply only, with the manuscript to be recycled if unaccepted (photocopying is usually cheaper than return postage).

Expect three to five months for a decision (sometimes faster, depending on the backlog). We have a small staff and receive quite a number of submissions, but we are committed to considering each manuscript carefully. We cannot respond to queries regarding the status of a manuscript until five months have passed. To query at that time, please write to us, indicating the postmark date of the submission, instead of calling. Simultaneous submissions are amenable to us as long as they are indicated as such and we are notified immediately upon acceptance elsewhere.

We cannot accommodate revisions, changes of return address, or forgotten SASEs after the fact. We do not reprint previously published work. Translations are welcome if permission has been granted. Payment is upon publication: $25 a printed page, with a $50 minimum per title and a $250 maximum per issue, plus two copies of the issue and a one-year subscription.

More information about *Ploughshares* is available on the Web.

Sample copies are available to writers at a discount: $8 (regularly $9.95). Writers also receive a discounted subscription rate: $18 (regularly $21) for one-year (3 issues).

Thank you for your interest in *Ploughshares*.

Categories: Fiction—Nonfiction—Literature—Poetry

Name: Submissions Editor
Material: All
Address: 100 BEACON ST
Address: EMERSON COLLEGE
City/State/ZIP: BOSTON MA 02116
Telephone: 617-824-8753
E-mail: Pshares@emerson.edu
Internet: www.emerson.edu

Pockets
A Devotional Magazine for Children

The purpose of *Pockets* is to open up the fullness of the gospel of Jesus Christ to children. It is written and produced for children and designed to help children pray and be in relationship to God. The magazine emphasizes that we are loved by God and that God's grace calls us into community. It is through the community of God's people that we experience that love in our daily lives.

General Guidelines

Each issue is built around a specific theme with material that can be used by children in a variety of ways. Scripture stories, fiction, poetry, prayers, art, graphics, puzzles, and activities are included. Submissions do not need to be overtly religious. They should help children experience a Christian lifestyle that is not always a neatly wrapped moral package but is open to the continuing revelation of God's will. Seasonal material, both secular and liturgical, is appropriate. We welcome submissions from children.

Pockets is ecumenical, and our readers include persons of many cultures and ethnic backgrounds. These differences should be reflected in the references which are made to lifestyles, living environments (suburban, urban, rural, reservation), families (extended families, single-parent homes), and individual names. Stories should show appreciation of cultural differences and not leave the impression that one way is better than another.

Age Group

The magazine is for children six through eleven with a target reading age of eight through eleven. Though some may share it with their families, it is designed primarily for the personal use of children.

Format and Length

The magazine is published monthly except February and includes a wide variety of materials.

Fiction and scripture stories should be 600 to 1,500 words. We occasionally publish two-part stories of up to 2,600 words. Our primary interest is in stories that can help children deal with real-life situations. We prefer real-life settings, but we occasionally use fables. We do not accept stories about talking animals or inanimate objects. Fictional characters and some elaboration may be included in scripture stories, but the writer must remain faithful to the story.

Stories should contain lots of action, use believable dialogue, be simply written, and be relevant to the problems faced by this age group in everyday life. Children need to be able to see themselves in the pages of the magazine. It is important that the tone not be "preachy" or didactic. Use short sentences and paragraphs. When possible, use concrete words instead of abstractions. However, do not "write down" to children.

It is no longer common practice to use such terms as "man," "mankind," "men," in the familiar generic sense. Substitute nonsexist terms that are inclusive of everyone (e.g., "humankind," "persons," "human beings," "everyone").

Poems should be short, not more than 24 lines.

Nonfiction articles should be 400 to 1,000 words. These should be related to a particular theme which has been projected (a list of themes and due dates is available from the editorial office). We also seek biographical sketches of persons, famous or unknown, whose lives reflect their Christian commitments and values. These may be either short vignettes (a single incident) or longer and more complete biographies. Articles about various holidays and about other cultures are included.

We particularly desire articles about children involved in environmental, community, and peace/justice issues.

Style

We *do not accept manuscripts by fax.* Writers who wish to save postage and are concerned about paper conservation may send a SASE for notification of unaccepted manuscripts, and we will recycle the paper the submission is printed on. Please list the name of the submission(s) on the card.

Payment

Payment will be made at the time of acceptance. We will make an initial response within one month after receiving the manuscript. We often place manuscripts on long-term hold for specific issues. Authors are free to request that their manuscripts be returned to them at any time during the long-term hold. We purchase newspaper and periodical rights and accept one-time previously published material.

- Stories and articles: 14¢ a word
- Poetry: $2.00 per line; $25.00 minimum
- Activities, games: $15.00 and up

List of themes* will be sent free upon receipt of SASE. Sample copy with 7½"x10½" or larger SASE ($1.05 postage).

*Themes are set each year in December. Our published authors automatically receive our themes at that time. Others need to request themes and include an SASE.

Guidelines for POCKETS Fiction-Writing Contest

Guidelines for the contest are essentially the same as for regularly submitted material.

As you consider your submission, remember that **POCKETS**

is a devotional magazine published by the Upper Room and geared toward children in grades 1-6.

Submissions will be:
- received after March 1 and postmarked by August 15 of the current year;
- returned if accompanied by an SASE. Your SASE must include sufficient postage for your submission *plus* 2 pages—a letter of notification and writers' guidelines. If this totals 1-6 pages, send postage for 1 ounce. If 7-12 pages, send postage for two ounces, etc. *Please note*—if postage rates increase, postage on the return envelope will need to be increased accordingly.
- *Submissions should be:*
- 1,000 to 1,600 words - word count noted on the cover sheet (we do adhere to our word parameters);
- unpublished and not historical fiction;
- designated **Fiction Contest** on the envelope and on the cover sheet.

There are no specific themes for this contest. Use your imagination!

There is no entry fee. The winner, notified by the first of November, will receive a $1,000 award. Since the purpose of the contest is to discover new writers, previous winners are not eligible.

Thank you for your interest in the contest. We wish you well in your writing endeavors!

Categories: Children—Religion

Name: Lynn W. Gilliam, Associate Editor
Material: Fiction Writing Contest Submissions
Name: Janet R. Knight, Editor
Material: POCKETS Submissions
Address: PO BOX 189
City/State/ZIP: NASHVILLE TN 37202
Telephone: 615-340-7333
Fax: 615-340-7006
E-mail: pockets@upperroom.org
Internet: www.upperroom.org

Podiatry Management

Podiatry Management is the national practice management magazine for podiatrists.

A sample of the current issue is posted at the Internet address shown below.

We invite articles to be submitted via e-mail. Articles can also be mailed along with an IBM formatted disk to the address below.

You may telephone us.

Articles should be of interest to the practicing podiatrist. Articles which feature quotes from podiatrists or are about DPMs are preferred.

Categories: Nonfiction—Business—Health—Management—Podiatry

Name: Barry Block, Editor
Material: All
Address: PO BOX 750129
City/State/ZIP: FOREST HILLS NY 11375
Telephone: 718-897-9700
E-mail: bblock@prodigy.com;
copy to: bblock@prodigy.net
Internet: www.podiatrymgt.com

POEM
University of Alabama-Huntsville

An international magazine of poetry written in English,

POEM has been in continuous publication since 1967. Published in May and November of each year, POEM is dedicated to presenting quality poetry in a handsome format, without augmentation.

POEM encourages submissions from all serious poets, including established as well as less known and beginning poets. We are open to traditional as well as non-traditional forms; however, we prefer well-crafted free verse and do not normally publish light verse, "prose" poems, shaped verse, 'visual' or 'conceptual' poetry, or other forms of avant garde verse.

We have no bias as to subject matter or theme, although we do not publish religious verse and favor poems that are about inspired sentiments earned from within the poem itself. We favor poems that have a high degree of verbal and dramatic tension, and that transpire from the particular to the universal.

We do not accept translations, previously published works, simultaneous submissions, or prose.

POEM is a magazine of verse only. The poems and poets within its pages do not have to compete with distractions such as advertising or high-profile glitz-and-glamour production. Accordingly, while POEM is open about format or subject matter, it demands a high degree of verbal precision and poetic ability from its contributors. POEM's commitment to meaning and to poetry as a form of soul-to-soul communication emphasizes musicality and tradition as well as innovation. The extremes of experimental verse will not be found in POEM's pages, nor will poetry without a sense of history or community.

Editorial Staff: The editorial and the administrative staff work on a volunteer basis and are directly responsible to the Board of the Huntsville Literary Association, which appoints them and underwrites the publication of POEM. Editor Nancy Frey Dillard, a professor of English, and Associate Editor Susan Luther, a poet and independent scholar, have served on the editorial staff of POEM since 1975 and 1985, respectively.

Circulation: POEM's circulation of approximately 370 goes to all Huntsville Literary Association members, libraries throughout the USA and Canada, and individual subscribers from coast to coast.

Magazine description: 4-3/8"x7¼", perfect bound, colored matte cover. 68-72 pages of poetry per issue, professionally printed.

Content: Poetry only. Includes notes on contributors.

Contributors: New and established poets from across the USA and abroad such as R. T. Smith, Robert Cooperman, Ron Wallace, Nancy Westerfield, Margaret Holley, Kim Homer, Rick Bursky, Scott Ward, Mary Winters.

Submission requirements: We prefer to read submissions of 3-5 poems and routinely return submissions of fewer than three poems. We generally respond within a month, and publish about 3-4% of submissions received. Manuscripts are read year-round, although work may he returned when we have a backlog. In order to present the work of as many poets as possible, we normally wait several issues before republishing recent contributors.

Payment and copyright: POEM acquires first serial rights only. As payment, each contributor receives two copies of the magazine.

Subscriptions: Available to persons outside the Huntsville area for $15.00/year. Sample copies and back issues: $5.00. Write to Subscription Staff, POEM, c/o HLA, P.O. Box 919, Huntsville, AL 35804.

POEM is a member of CLMP and is indexed in the *Index of American Periodical Verse*.

Categories: Poetry

Name: Nancy Frey Dillard, Editor
Material: All
Address: DEPT OF ENGLISH

Address: UNIVERSITY OF ALABAMA HUNTSVILLE
City/State/ZIP: HUNTSVILLE AL 35899
Telephone: 205-890-6320

Poetic Realm

Poetic Realm is for poetry only. The guidelines are easy. Poems to 36 lines on any subject, in good taste. No reading fee...and my favorite poem in each issue will receive the "Editor's Choice Award" of $5.00.

Please help keep this publication afloat by either becoming a subscriber or purchasing the copy you are published in.

Thank you.

USA Rates for Subscription/Single Copy: $12/4 issues; $3.50 next issue only.

Categories: Poetry

Name: Kay Weems, Editor/Publisher
Material: All
Address: HCR-13 BOX 21AA
City/State/ZIP: ARTEMAS PA 17211-9405
Telephone: 814-458-3102

Poetry

POETRY has no special manuscript needs, no special requirements as to form or genre: we examine in turn all work received and accept that which seems best. We can accept nothing which has been previously published or accepted for publication, anywhere, in any form, either in this country or abroad. Nor can we consider poems scheduled for book publication within a year. We do not consider simultaneous submissions. We regret that the volume of submissions received and the small size of our staff do not permit us to give individual criticism.

Submissions should be limited to **four poems or fewer,** typed single spaced, not exceeding ten pages total. Manuscripts are usually reported on within 12 to 14 weeks from the day of receipt. All manuscripts must be accompanied by a stamped, self-addressed envelope. Stamps alone are not sufficient. Writers living abroad must enclose a self-addressed envelope together with enough postage in international reply coupons for at least sea mail return. Manuscripts should contain the author's name and address on every page. Avoid oversized envelopes. Please wait at least one year after our reply before submitting again. Do not send revisions unless they have been specifically requested by the editors. Inquiries about the status of a manuscript should be avoided, but when necessary must be made in writing.

Payment is made on publication at the rate of $2.00 per line. POETRY is copyrighted for the protection of its contributors. The author, the author's agents or heirs, and no one else, will be given transfer of copyright when they request it for purposes of republication in book form.

Several prizes, awarded annually, are announced each November for the best work printed in POETRY during the preceding year. *Only poems already published in the Magazine are eligible for consideration, and no formal application is necessary.* The Ruth Lilly Poetry Prize is also given each year to a poet whose published work merits special recognition. The selection is made by a panel of judges and no applications are accepted. Two Ruth Lilly Poetry Fellowships are awarded annually to students who have not yet received the M.A. or M.F.A. degree, based on work submitted. Students must be nominated by their program directors or department chairs.

Anyone contemplating a submission is encouraged to examine the Magazine before sending mss.

To that end, POETRY offers subscriptions to writers at a

professional discount. You can purchase a year-long subscription (12 monthly issues) at the special rate of $24.50 ($31.50 foreign). Sample copies cost $3.00 plus $1.50 for postage and handling. Checks should be made out to *Poetry*. Please allow 6 weeks for subscription to begin.

Categories: Poetry

Name: Submissions Editor
Material: All
Address: 60 W WALTON ST
City/State/ZIP: CHICAGO IL 60610

Poetry Motel

Send three to six pages of poetry or literary memoirs with a SASE and a brief bio.
Categories: Poetry

Name: Submissions Editor
Material: All
Address: 1410 ACRE STE 306
City/State/ZIP: DULUTH MN 55811

Poets'Paper

Poets' Paper
The Newspaper For Poets

Poets' Paper features the kinder, gentler poetry which was the hallmark of the original *Feelings Poetry Journal*/FPJ.

Submission requirements for *Poets' Paper* are simple:

1. Send no more than 3 poems, any style, any length (a good poem knows when to end).

2. Always send an SASE. Previously published poems and simultaneous submissions are *not* welcome; nor is harsh language or thought.

3. Sentimental poems are ok but do not send weepy, self-pity poems (the kind that say he/she left me and I'm so blue); cheerful, upbeat, life experience poems, poems with clear images and fresh thoughts will find ink in *Poets' Paper*.

4. Carole J. Heffley and Harriett Hunt are the editors and they enjoy **rhyme and meter as well as free verse**.

5. *Poems will not be read in the months of June and October.* Cost for the Poets' newspaper is $5 for a single copy and $9 for one year (2 issues: winter and fall).

There is no obligation to purchase any issue; your poem will be published regardless of whether you subscribe or not! That's fair; but don't ask for a free contributor copy, that's not fair.

Please: no submissions accepted by fax or e-mail. Use e-mail for questions only.

Categories: Poetry

Name: Carole J. Heffley, Executive Editor
Name: Harriett Hunt, Submissions Editor
Address: PO BOX 85
City/State/ZIP: EASTON PA 18044-0085
Telephone: 610-559-3887
Fax: 610-559-3927
E-mail: Irregular@silo.com

Police Times &
The Chief of Police Magazine
The Voice of Professional American Law Enforcement

Dear Writer/Photographer:

Thank you for your recent inquiry regarding guidelines for writers and photographers addressed to *Police Times*.

Police Times is the official journal of the American Federation of Police. We seek articles on speculation regarding all areas of law enforcement, with special emphasis on stories involving smaller police departments or individuals who have made a special place in law enforcement...past or present.

The newspaper is published bimonthly as is *The Chief of Police Magazine*, the official journal of the National Association of Chiefs of Police. For *The Chief of Police Magazine*, we seek articles that would be of particular interest to command-rank American law enforcement personnel. If accepted we may elect to publish a particularly interesting piece in both publications. Allow 90-180 days for publication, which is at the editor's discretion.

We pay one cent per word, $5 per photo or cartoon and $25 for photos used in the color format. Photos, however, may be submitted in b/w or color. Fillers and short articles are also considered and paid at the same rate. Length of articles may vary, but usually range up to 3,500 words For *Police Times*; 5,000 words For *The Chief of Police Magazine*. Payment is made upon acceptance. One complimentary copy of the issue in which the article appears is provided to the writer.

If you are using a personal computer for typing articles, please send them on IBM compatible 3½" disks as well as a hard copy.

Sample Copies: For *Police Times* $2.50, For *The Chief of Police Magazine* $3.00. Include SASE with all submissions.

Assigned Articles: Articles specifically assigned by the editors are paid at double scale. These are reserved for writers who we have previously published in our publications.

Faxed Proposals: Accepted by faxing short proposal to the number shown below. Allow ample time For reply.

Categories: Law Enforcement

Name: Jim Gordon, Executive Editor
Material: All
Address: 3801 BISCAYNE BLVD
City/State/ZIP: MIAMI FL 33137
Telephone: 305-573-0070
Fax: 305-573-9819

Politically Correct Magazine

Type: 20-28 page b&w (spot color cover) magazine. Debuted September, 1997.

Payment: 1 cent a word or writer's copies.

Focus: Primary focus is to educate teens/young adults about their rights as U.S. citizens. Second-to discuss current issues (interactively). Third-to give readers a voice, allowing them to be published and express opinions.

Objective: Offers an in-depth explanation of current events and political happenings to readers age 14-21. Educating young voters, helping them to make informed decisions, addressing problems such as drug abuse, pregnancy, career choices, AIDS, safesex, fads & trends, school, college, relationships, body images, parents, etc. Interviews with exceptional teens, history of the United States, government, volunteering profiles and general interest.

Submissions: Lead articles should be 900-2,400 words. All other writings should be 100-900 words. All material must be type-written or neatly hand-written. *Include word count!* Editor has the right to edit material. Include researched citations.

Tips: This is a new magazine. If your article is great-you have a higher than normal chance of getting published with us. We are looking for regular contributors also. *We want to see hard-hitting, controversial topics!*

Categories: Nonfiction—Government—Politics—Public Policy—Society—Teen—Young Adult

Name: Terri J. Andrews, Editor
Material: All
Address: PO BOX 750
City/State/ZIP: ATHENS OH 45701-0750
Telephone: 614-664-3030

Pontoon & Deck Boat

Pontoon & Deck Boat is a family oriented publication for pontoon and deck boat users across the United States and Canada. Readers of *Pontoon & Deck Boat* include families, couples, retired couples, renters, manufacturers, other boaters, water-sport enthusiasts, fishermen, travel enthusiasts and so on.

Within our pages, readers will find manufacturer reviews, test reports, destination pieces, new product reviews, a calendar of events and boat shows, how-to, service tips, fishing, secondary water sports, buying guides, special events and more. If a topic can be tied into pontoon or deck boating, there may be a place for it in our publication.

QUERIES: Query first with story ideas. Include one or two paragraphs that briefly outline your idea and tell us why your story is timely, unique, new or of special interest. What qualifies you to write the story? Do you have good visual support?

MANUSCRIPTS: Features should run between 1,800 and 2,000 words. In addition, we like to run sidebars with features when appropriate. Fillers and Mini Features can range from 500 to 1,500 words.

All submitted material should be consistent with the Associated Press style guide. Pay particular attention to the use of numerals and measurements. For example, write *6 inches*, not *six inches* or 6"—unless you are compiling technical information for use in a table or graph.

In general, avoid "symbol shortcuts" like %, &, @ etc. Also, use *AP* abbreviations—not postal ones—when following a city with a state (Ex: *Panama City, Fla.*, not *FL)*. And remember, some major cities such as New York, Chicago and Los Angeles stand without reference to the state at all. Postal abbreviations should only be used when listing an address.

The *AP* style guide is available from The Associated Press at Stylebook, AP Newsfeatures, 50 Rockefeller Plaza, New York, NY 10020.

Manuscripts must be typed using double-spacing for hard copy and single-spacing for electronic submissions. Include author's name, address and phone number on lead page. Pages should be numbered. Harris Publishing reserves the right to edit submitted material as required.

We use IBM compatible software and Microsoft Word 8.0. If possible, submit a 3.5" floppy disc with your typed manuscript. Documents converted to ASCII text are usually acceptable. Text files can also be sent by e-mail.

PHOTOS: We work with color transparencies only. We pre-fer E100SW by Kodak, or Velvia by Fuji. Good contrast and sharp focus are a must. Submit 10 to 15 different photos to illustrate a feature thoroughly.

Get people involved in every photo possible. Show action and movement and attempt to do so from a fresh perspective. Utilize dawn and dusk lighting for dramatic photos.

**If you submit photos that belong to another person, you are responsible for splitting payment with him/her. We purchase manuscripts and photos as one package and pay only one fee.

CAPTIONS: All photo submissions must be keyed to a numbered caption sheet. Captions should be detailed enough to require little or no rewriting by our editorial staff.

Please identify people in your photos. Obtain a signed model release if necessary and submit with the photos. Your name and address should be on each photo or transparency for proper credits, payment and photo returns.

PAYMENT: Rates vary according to several factors including length, quality of the material, quality of the photos, and how much editing or rewriting is required.

We work with professionals to maintain a certain level of quality for our readers. Therefore, we expect copy and photos to be of high quality.

Payment for features (including photos) range from $150 to $300. Columns, departments, mini-features and fillers (including photos) are worth $50 to $175.

Pontoon & Deck Boat buys first North American serial rights to manuscripts and photos. Payments are made after publication.

Make every effort to educate and entertain readers. We want our readers to feel they can sit back, put their feet up and enjoy reading *Pontoon & Deck Boat* from cover to cover. When they're finished, they should know of new places to travel, where to find services, how to better maintain and handle their own pontoon or deck boat and so on. If you can make it educational and "fun" to read at the same time, so much the better.

Categories: Nonfiction—Boating—Fishing—Lifestyles—Recreation

Name: Steve Smede, Editor
Material: All
Address: 520 PARK AVE
City/State/ZIP: IDAHO FALLS ID 83402
Telephone: 208-524-7000
Fax: 208-522-5241
E-mail: pontoon@srv.net

Popular Electronics

An open letter to authors who wish to be published in *Popular Electronics*

Dear Author:

If you have a story or a story idea centered around electronics, I'd like to have the chance to read it, and consider it for purchase and use in *Popular Electronics*. To improve the probability of your story being published, I have placed some suggestions in this guide to help you prepare your article.

What type of article is *Popular Electronics* seeking? I've always sought first-rate stories covering communications, computers, test equipment, audio, video and virtually every other electronics subject. Good construction, tutorial, informational, and how-to articles are always in demand. If they are timely, their appeal and chances of acceptance are further enhanced.

Articles about new technology or the theory behind new devices are particularly valuable and make for interesting reading. The key to writing such an article with authority is thorough research and accuracy. A poorly researched article can lose its author some respect among the editors, as well as lose the sale.

Make sure of your facts, and make them complete. The editors should not have to do your research job. If you aren't in a position to research thoroughly and document the facts, you shouldn't write the story in the first place.

How-to-do-it features are among the most interesting types of articles that you can write. Show a reader ten new ways to use his oscilloscope or sweep generator or an easy way to make printed-circuit boards, and your story will be enjoyed by our readers.

Troubleshooting and service manuscripts, on the other hand, require an experienced author. Nothing falls apart as thoroughly as a troubleshooting article written by someone who knows little about the subject. Technical inaccuracies in the manuscript quickly ruin its chances for acceptance.

Construction articles should show readers how to build electronic projects. The devices discussed must be of practical use in the field of electronics, in hobby pursuits, or around the house or in the car. The cost of parts is important; the cost of assembling a project should be justified by what it does. I seek construction stories at different levels, some for neophytes and some for those who have the training to carry out complex building instructions. In general, easier projects take preference, although a premium goes to the story that tells how to build some advanced project easily.

Construction manuscripts need special care. Schematics must be complete and detailed. Show all IC pinouts, power connections, bypass capacitors, parts designations and values, etc. If a printed-circuit board is used, a clear, reproducible, full-size foil pattern must be included. Parts-placement diagrams should be shown from the component side of the board and the parts should be identified by part number, not values. Completely describe all construction methods and techniques that are not common knowledge.

Include calibration and adjustment instructions in all construction articles that require them. Include debugging information: How long did it take to get the device working? To build it? The reader may experience some of the same difficulties. Place critical voltages on schematic diagrams; those help the project builder check the operation of the finished project.

Include a complete list of parts, manufacturers, type numbers, and electrical/electronic specifications and ratings where appropriate. Make sure that the list agrees with the information presented in the text and on schematic diagrams. Accuracy is absolutely necessary! Avoid hard-to-get items or those that are one-of-a-kind. If you must use an uncommon part, you must give two sources for that part. Where values are not critical, say so and give approximate tolerances. Where special parts are required, be precise in the Parts List by including all the specifications. Do not merely say "5,000-ohm relay" if contact spacing or armature tension is critical. Tell us (in the text) why a particular part is chosen over others like it. Failure to make the parts list complete may mean some reader can't make the project work and will blame the magazine or author.

Check and double check your work. Be sure that the schematic agrees with the Parts List, the parts-placement diagram, other illustrations, and the text. Our editors review every manuscript for accuracy, but it is impossible to catch all errors. Your reputation as an author, as well as the reputation of this magazine, can be damaged by inaccurate or sloppy work.

Commonly used abbreviations such as AC, DC, IC, Hz, etc., may be used freely. However, the use of less common abbreviations should be limited except when their use promotes clarity. All such abbreviations must be defined in the article the first time they are used.

Do not dismantle your equipment or change it after sending us your manuscript. If the article is accepted, the editors must compare it to its description to check for accuracy.

Finish the job! Don't send half-done manuscripts. "Photos to come" or "material to be added here" are flags of incompleteness. I can't judge the manuscript without seeing all of it. Incomplete articles will be rejected as they cannot be properly evaluated.

MECHANICS:

There are some things you should consider when writing any article; let's explore those things next. The best-written articles are useless if they can't be published. An article on high-voltage sources might be perfect; but if it requires five TV-receiver schematic diagrams, it will not be printed because the drawings alone would take up too much space in the magazine. Stories with no illustrations or those without enough text to hold the illustrations together show poor preparation and are not acceptable.

You must have your name and address in the top left corner of the first manuscript page; some authors use a rubber stamp to put their name and address on the back of each succeeding page. Also include a telephone number where you can be reached during the day in case my editors have a question that requires immediate attention.

If you are working on a computer, submit your story with text pages printed on a letter-quality or dot-matrix printer and include a floppy disk of the manuscript, in ASCII, readable by an IBM or compatible computer. Tell us what DOS version and word processor program you use. A disk of your article will save input time and eliminate typing errors at this end.

Mail the manuscript flat. Include a self-addressed envelope and return postage. Save a copy of your manuscript until you see it in print. It is often necessary for us to ask questions about it so having access to a copy is important. Furthermore, a copy helps protect your work should it get lost in the mail. Do not send photocopies of the manuscript or the illustrations. Send the original and keep the copy for your own files.

ILLUSTRATIONS:

If any of your illustrations are smaller than 8 by 10 inches, fasten them to standard-size sheet of paper.

Photographs should be 5"x7", or larger, black-and-white glossy prints, and in good focus all over. Avoid using color prints. All details should be easy to see, not hidden in dark areas or "washed out" in overexposed or too-bright areas. Don't mark or write on prints; you simply spoil them for reproduction. If you need to identify sections of a photograph, put a piece of tracing paper over the print

Put an asterisk or the figure number in the margin of your text when you refer to an illustration or figure. Try to scatter illustrations throughout the story so they're not all bunched.

Diagrams must be clearly drawn in pencil or ink, but need not be finished artwork, as all art is redrawn here in *Popular Electronics* style. To enhance accuracy, we request that you adopt *Popular Electronics* parts designations and symbol conventions where possible. Contact us for a sample issue if needed.

Draw each diagram on a separate page. Use standard-size paper or sheets that can be folded to standard size. Drawings must be accurate. Check each one carefully; it is almost impossible for the editors to catch all errors.

RATE OF PAYMENT:

My payment calculations are more complex than a simple page rate, since I consider such variables as reader interest, illustrations, text, photography, how much editing my staff will have to do, accuracy of research, and originality of approach.

The payment rate currently ranges from $100 to $500. Manuscripts that need practically no editing, are complete, that hit precisely the slant we want, that are written in the easy-reading style of *Popular Electronics*, and that are thoughtfully and imaginatively illustrated will command the highest payment rate.

The staff members are trained in writing, researching, and editing. As you are developing your story, I will gladly work with you. After I buy your manuscript, your help is often needed to fill gaps in your story, check a doubtful connection on a schematic diagram. etc. The editors take every possible step and precaution to make sure that your article is authoritative, easy-to-read, and interesting, but much of the responsibility must, of course, rest with the author.

I'll look forward to reviewing your manuscripts.

Julian S. Martin

Editor

Categories: Computers—Electronics—Hobbies—Science

Name: Editor-Popular Electronics
Material: All mss.
Address: 500 BI-COUNTY BLVD
City/State/ZIP: FARMINGDALE NY 11735
Telephone: 516-293-3000
Fax: 516-293-3115

Popular Mechanics

We are always in the market for good free-lance articles, and invite your queries. Because our magazine is divided into departments according to subject matter, you should direct editorial queries to the departmental editor m your area of interest. The editors are listed at the end of this guide. Since we do not print fiction, please don't submit any fiction articles. Because of the workload of our editors, queries are best handled by a short paragraph and perhaps a photo or drawing, via mail. Before you submit a query, do a little homework. Check with the Guide To Periodic Literature and/or our own indexes to editorial features. Chances are, we've already published an article similar to the one you are about to propose. Don't waste your time unless you can give us something new that we haven't run before. Our typical reader is male, about 37 years old, married with a couple of kids, owns his own home and several cars, makes a good salary and probably works in a technically oriented profession. Keep this in mind before proposing articles. In any article query, you should be specific as to what makes the development new, different, better, interesting or less expensive.

Submission Format: All articles must be submitted to us typewritten, double spaced on one side of the page only. All manuscripts must include a self-addressed, stamped envelope with sufficient return postage in case we do not accept your submission. All how-to articles must be accompanied by well-lit, clear, black-and-white photos or rough artwork that we can use to produce finished art for publication. Photos should be either 5x7 or 8x10 in size, glossy finish. If we like an idea, we may also ask you to supply color photos. These should be 35mm or larger transparencies. We pay anywhere from $300 to $1000 and more for features. We pay on acceptance and purchase all rights. If we pay for your submission, we are under no legal obligation to run the piece, but will make our best effort to get it into print. Material is subject to editing for length, style and format Here is some specific information from each of our areas of editorial interest:

Automotive: We do all of our own road testing and conduct our own owner surveys. Please don't query us about submitting driving reports on specific models, or articles about what it's like to own a specific car.

Home Improvement: We buy how-to-do-it articles on home improvement, home maintenance, energy-saving techniques, and shop and craft projects. These must be well illustrated with drawings and photos. Finished drawings suitable for publication are not necessary. Rough, but accurate, pencil drawings are adequate for artist's copy. Topnotch photos are a must, shot during construction of the project as well as after construction. Photos should be taken with a background that is not cluttered or distracting

from the main action.

Science/Technology/Aerospace: We are interested in long and short pieces that cover the latest developments in science, technology, aerospace, industry and discovery. We stress newsworthy items here. An old subject can be interesting if new facts have recently become known. Accuracy is paramount. Check your facts and sources before submitting queries. As a rule, we are not interested in machines or inventions applicable to a very limited field or industry, ordinary industrial processes, informative material without a news angle as found in textbooks or encyclopedias, or items that deal with accidents or freaks of nature. We publish articles on sport aviation, homebuilt aircraft, net commercial aircraft, new combat aircraft, etc. Also, we are interested in restoration projects on older collectible aircraft and other hands-on type articles that involve planes.

Boating/Outdoors: Testing of new boats, recreational vehicles or outdoor gear is conducted by our own staff. We publish articles on new equipment in the boating and outdoors areas, as well as articles on how to maintain and/or repair boats, boat engines, camping equipment, motorcycles, recreational vehicles, etc. We are interested in articles covering new types of outdoor recreational devices, such as paraplanes, balloons, all-terrain vehicles and campers.

Electronics/Photography/Telecommunications: We publish articles on new types of equipment in the audio, video, computer, telecommunications, photographic and optical fields, but our staff does most of these. We also publish technique articles, such as how to take trick photos, new developing techniques, how to hook up stereo equipment and telephones in the home, etc. Check some back issues for specific areas of our coverage.

General Interest Articles: We occasionally publish general interest articles. We look for pieces with a strong science, exploration or adventure emphasis.

Departmental Editors: If your query doesn't fit into any of the department, send it to the editor-in-chief.

Categories: Nonfiction—Automobiles—Aviation—Business—Computers—Consumer—Crafts—Engineering—Environment—Military—Outdoors—Photography—Science—Recreation—Home—Boating—Technology—How-to—Audio—Telecommunications—Electronics

Name: Don Chaikin
Material: Automotive
Name: Steven Willson
Material: Home Improvement
Name: Joe Oldham
Material: Electronics/Photography/Telecommunications
Name: Jim Wilson
Material: Science/Technology/Aerospace
Name: James Grant
Material: Boating/Outdoors
Name: Joe Oldham, Editor-In-Chief
Material: All other material
Address: 224 W. 57TH ST., 3RD FLOOR
City/State/ZIP: NEW YORK, NY 10019
Telephone: 212-649-2000
Fax: 212-586-5561
E-mail: popularmechanics@hearst.com
Internet: www.popularmechanics.com

Popular Science

Popular Science

Popular Science covers new and emerging technology in the areas of science, automobiles, the environment, recreation, electronics, the home, photography, aviation and space, and computers and software. Our mission is to provide service to our readers by reporting on how these technologies work and what difference they will make in our readers' lives. Our readers are well-educated professionals who are vitally interested in the technologies we cover.

We seek stories that are up-to-the-minute in information and accuracy. We expect the writer to interview all sources who are essential to the story, as well as experts who can provide analysis and perspective. If a hands-on approach is called for, the writer should visit critical sites to see the technology first-hand—including trying it out when appropriate.

We publish stories ranging from hands-on product reviews to investigative feature stories, on everything from black holes to black-budget airplanes. We expect submissions to be, above all else, well written: that is, distinguished by good story-telling, human interest, anecdotes, analogies, and humor, among other traits of good writing. Stories should be free of jargon, vague statements, and unconfirmed facts and figures.

We seek publishable stories written to an agreed-upon length, with text for agreed-upon components such as sidebars or how-to boxes. The writer is responsible for the factual content of the story and is expected to have made a systematic checking of facts. We require that the writer file with his story contact numbers for all important sources and subjects in the story.

We expect our authors to deliver a complete package. The Popular Science Art department requires illustrations, photographs, and diagrams/sketches pertaining to stories submitted. These may be in the form of copies, but we prefer camera-ready artwork. We accept the following formats: four-color or black and white photography, illustration and digital files (tiff or eps) We track and log all artwork and, if indicated on the original, we will return artwork. We also require more than one piece of reference material. This allows for more accurate and original artistic interpretations.

A story should come with a headline for each story element and captions for photos. The complete package will include background material and documentation used by the author.

Freelance contributions to Popular Science range from feature-length stories to shorter "newsfront pieces" and shorter-yet stories to accompany What's New products.

We respond promptly to queries, which should be a single page or less and include an SASE. The writer should submit a tight summary of the proposed article and provide some indication of the plan of execution. Samples of the writer's past work and clips concerning the emerging story are helpful.

Catagories: Automobiles—Aviation—Computers—Electronics—Environment—General Interest—Photography—Science—Technology, Home

Name: Editor
Material: All
Address: 2 Park Avenue
City/State/ZIP: New York, NY 10016
Telephone: 212-779-5000
Fax: 212-481-8062

Popular Woodworking

Popular Woodworking is a bimonthly magazine that invites woodworkers of all levels into a community of experts who share their hard-won shop experience through in-depth projects and technique articles, which helps the readers hone their existing skills and develop new ones. Related stories increase the readers' under-standing and enjoyment of their craft. Any project submitted must be aesthetically pleasing, of sound construction and offer a challenge to readers.

FEATURES

On the average, we use six to nine features per issue. Our primary needs are "how-to" articles on woodworking projects and instructional features dealing with woodworking tools and techniques. Our secondary need is for articles that will inspire discussion concerning woodworking. Tone of articles should be conversational and informal, as if the writer is speaking directly to the reader. Word length ranges from 1,200 to 2,500. Payment for features starts at $125 per published page, depending on the total package submitted, including its quality, and the writer's level of woodworking and writing experience.

COLUMNS

• **Tricks of the Trade.** This section shares one- to two-paragraph "tips" on how to make woodworking easier or safer. We pay $35 per printed submission.

• **Out of The Woodwork.** This one-page article, averaging about 500 words, reflects on the writer's thoughts about woodworking as a profession or hobby. The article can be either humorous or serious. Payment is $100.

• **Business End.** This column focuses on woodworking's professional side to offer helpful tips and insight.

QUERIES

All submissions, except Tricks of the Trade, need to be preceded by a query. We will accept unsolicited manuscripts and artwork, although they must be accompanied by a self-addressed stamped envelope to be returned.

Queries must include:

• A brief outline of the proposed article.

• A summary of the techniques used to complete the project. Include step-by-step illustrations.

• A short biographical sketch, including both your woodworking and writing experience and accomplishments. Also provide your address and daytime telephone number.

• A color photo or transparency of the completed project.

• A list of all materials needed (it's best to use materials that are easily available).

MANUSCRIPT SUBMISSIONS

Your manuscript must be typed, and we also highly prefer submissions on 3½" computer disc (save all manuscripts generically, preferably in ASCII). We also accept submissions through e-mail at the address below.

For project articles, include the following:

1. **Introduction:** Describe an important point about your project or subject. What made you develop or design it? Also note any unusual qualities.

2. **Preparation:** Explain any work needed to be done before staring the project.

3. **Instructions:** Go step-by-step through the process, ex-

plaining each point without including excessive detail. Include only necessary information, and write in a conversational style. When writing, keep in mind that there may be multiple ways to do any one step. Offering these options to the reader makes your manuscript more flexible and appealing. Clarify any technical words. NOTE: Brand names should only be included when they are critical to the construction or finishing process.

4. Finishing: Give complete instructions on how to finish the project.

5. Closing: Close your article with a brief paragraph that ties everything together.

6. Materials: Please provide the list of all materials used in the project, including types and sizes (thickness, width & length). Also, if materials are hard to find, include the supplier's address and telephone number (with the price of the product & shipping, if available).

7. About the Writer: Provide a brief biography on your experience and interests.

ILLUSTRATIONS

Visual aids are a vital part of instruction, and essential to both projects and articles. Whenever possible, PW prefers to show through photography and diagrams how a step is done rather than tell though text. Remember to submit well-lit photographs (clearly labeled color transparencies are preferred). Place any copy describing the process or technique on a piece of paper attached to the back of the illustration. Keep plenty of blank space around each step. We often have to crop illustrations for design purposes.

• If a complex technique is necessary for the project, make a suggestion for a special "sidebar" demonstrating it. Sidebars also can be used as an important source of additional information, such as suggesting alternative methods or tools.

• All artwork, photographs and drawings will be returned upon request.

ORIGINALITY AND RIGHTS

All material submitted must be original and unpublished. *Popular Woodworking* purchases first North American serial rights for one-time use in the magazine, and all rights for use of the article (both text and illustrations) in any F&W Publications, Inc. promotional material/product or reprint. You always retain the copyright to your work, and are free to use it in any way after it appears in the magazine. We request, however, that you do not publish the same material for at least six months from the time it appears in our publication.

POPULAR WOODWORKING'S GUIDE TO WRITING AND STYLE

Write as if you're standing beside the readers as they follow your instruction. Use second person (ex: Cut the wood size.). Only use first person when talking specifically about yourself (ex: I chose oak, but any wood will do.).

• Writing should be concise and straightforward.

• Watch redundancies and get rid of unnecessary words, such as *that, all, rather, in order, very,* etc.

• Avoid repeating the same word within the sentence or in the following one. For example: *The board should be sanded on the board's right side.* Include a pronoun instead: *The board should be sanded on its right side.* Don't be afraid to use pronouns, unless they hinder comprehension.

• Replace passive voice with active voice to avoid redundancies and increase clarity. Hint: Watch for words like *was, were, is* and *are*—they usually indicate passive voice. Passive: *The project was a success.* Active: *The project succeeded.*

• Possessive apostrophes also can cut back on your word count. For example, the side of the board can become the board's side. As a side note, remember *it's* is a contraction of *it is,* while *its* shows possession.

• For measurements, *Popular Woodworking*'s style is: 7" x 8", 7", 7"-thick board. Take note of the difference between measurements: The *7"-thick board should be cut 2" wide.* The hyphenated version is used as an adjective of *an* object, while no hyphen denotes a measurement itself.

• Commas, as a general rule, should be placed where a reader would pause naturally.

• Generally, a comma does not separate the last series member from a verb. For example: *You will need shellac, sandpaper and wood.* However, if the omission of commas becomes too confusing, leave them in: *You will need shellac and stain, sandpaper and steel, and pine and maple wood.*

• When using *and, but, so, nor, or,* remember the comma precedes them when it introduces a complete sentence. Never use the phrase *and then.* Only *then* is necessary.

• Parentheses should be used sparingly and only for information that needs understatement. For example, note the distinction between the use of dashes and parentheses in this sentence: *For ten hours - but only ten hours - let the glue dry (yellow carpenter's glue works best) so your project will not come apart while you are working.*

• Always have punctuation follow parentheses, unless a complete sentence is within it: *This book is excellent for beginners (zero to one year experience), but only a handy guide for more advanced levels. I cut the wood according to size. (I later found out I had used the wrong materials.)*

FINAL CHECKLIST

Although the following reminders are simple, they've been neglected by writers in the past. So make sure your manuscript meets these requirements when you read it over a final time:

• Sentences must have both a subject and a verb to be complete.

• If you have any doubts on a word's spelling, don't hesitate to look it up.

• Make sure you're getting your point across to the readers. Look at the article through their eyes - not your own experienced ones.

• Double check all measurements and facts to make sure they're correct. We don't want any unsuccessful projects!

• Watch the overuse of *you* and *I.* It does make the piece more personable, but use sparingly. Often you can get the same point across after omitting them.

• Make sure all punctuation is used correctly.

Categories: Hobbies

Name: Christopher M. Schwarz, Managing Editor
Material: All
Address: 1507 DANA AVE
City/State/ZIP: CINCINNATI OH 45207
Telephone: 513-531-2690
Fax: 513-531-7107
E-mail: popwood@earthlink.net

Potato Eyes
Literary Arts Journal

Poetry

• Submit 3-6 poems with short letter of introduction and #10 SASE with sufficient postage. Mail received without SASEs is destroyed. No electronic submissions, please.

• Our favorite form of poem is the narrative. Voice should not be self-conscious or exploitative of others' misfortune.

• Generally, we do not use rhymed verse or other formalist styles/devices, however, we have accepted a few over the years.

• We like to see a certain amount of word-courage and imagery, vitality, solid intensity, tension, strong enjambment, risk taking, thoughtful lineation with no diving boards.

• The poem has to be as good *read* as it is *on the page*. In other words, we do not generally accept poems with slack and unmusical lines.

• We do not use wide, blocky poems with over 70 characters per line.

• Don't send religious, Hallmarkian or cute poetry.

• Sex and erotica are OK, but no porn or man- or woman-hating stuff. Save that for the therapist.

• We believe that the best "guideline" is to read a recent issue. A current issue is $7.95; recent back-issue is $5.00.

• NOTE: Payment in copies (one for each poem) upon publication.

Fiction & Essay

• **Essays** should be acerbic, timely, and/or satirical. We like the "personal essay" when it is not self-conscious. Length: <5,000 words

• **Fiction**: <5,000 words, Micro-fiction OK.

• Strong opening and characterization. Keep the story focused!

• Forget boozy bums, ex-cons, druggies. We can read about them in newspapers.

• We like humor, satire, regional, urban/woodsy, experimental, gay/lesbian, feminist, and multicultural OK.

• Send a non-narcissistic cover letter & stories—flat!

• NOTE: Payment in copies (2) for each story upon publication.

Art

• Send us B/W art for covers and inside (photocopy OK). We maintain files for spot art and will contact you prior to use.

• *No* cartoons or computer-generated stuff. We want to see the artist's hand!

• NOTE: Payment upon publication $25 for *Potato Eyes* cover, more for Nightshade Press book covers. Payment in copies (variable) for spot art.

Categories: Fiction—Literature—Outdoors—Poetry—Short Stories

Name: Carolyn Page, Editor
Material: All
Address: PO BOX 76

City/State/ZIP: **TROY ME 04987**
Telephone: **207-948-3427**
Fax: **207-948-5088**
Internet: **www.maineguide.com/giftshop/potatoeyes**

Potluck Children's Literary Magazine

1. Material should be clean, typed, (1" margins), and **exactly** the way you would like it printed. **Always** double check your work. It is a good idea to have a parent or a teacher review it.

2. Your name, age, e-mail address, and word or line count should be in the upper left hand corner.

3. A self-addressed stamped envelope (SASE), is required for reply. E-mailed submissions will receive a response via e-mail.

4. Material without SASE will not be considered. Material without an e-mail address will not be considered.

5. All material must be original, not previously published, and not submitted elsewhere.

6. We do not accept works of a profane, sexual, or violent nature.

7. *Potluck CLM* acquires first rights. All rights revert back to author upon publication.

8. Payment is one copy in which work appears.

9. *Potluck CLM* responds within 4 weeks from deadline.

Poetry (line count) 30 line max.

Single-spaced with a double space between the stanzas. All forms. We want to see well-crafted poems which speak to the reader.

Short Stories (word count) 250 word max.

Double-spaced, subject matter is open.

Book Reviews (word count) 150 word max.

What made it worth the read? Why do you recommend it? How did it effect you? Most importantly, don't forget to tell us what it's about!

Submission fees

Subscribers may submit 3 articles each quarter.

Non-subscribers may submit one article.

Submissions beyond the above limits, $2 per article.

[Write with SASE for ongoing deadlines]

Subscription/unit cost

1 year (4 issues)costs $16; Single issues $4.50 prepaid

(All checks payable to the editor)

Categories: Children—Juvenile—Literature—Poetry—Short Stories—Teen—Writing

Name: Susan Napoli Picchietti, Editor
Material: All
Address: PO BOX 546
City/State/ZIP: DEERFIELD IL 60015-0546
Telephone: 847-948-1139
Fax: NAPPIC@aol.com

M-R

Potomac Review

- Poetry: up to three pages/five poems at a time.
- Fiction/nonfiction: up to 2,500 words, as a rule.
- Art: line art preferred, as a rule; best to inquire first.

Type manuscripts. If possible, provide IBM disk for a longer prose piece. Put name and address of author on each poem and prose ms. Simultaneous submissions acceptable. Include SASE and brief biographical note. Reporting time three months. Payment one copy, for first North American rights only.

A vivid, individual quality is sought. *Potomac Review* aims to inform, entertain and provide ethical depth. We strive to get at "the concealed side" of life.

We are open to good writing from all points, though our non-profit quarterly is regionally rooted in the Potomac River basin, which reaches from Virginia and West Virginia up through Maryland into Pennsylvania, with Washington, D.C., and Baltimore two polar sites.

"We want competence, but competence itself is deadly. What you want is the vision to go with it." —Flannery O'Connor

Have you seen *Potomac Review*? A copy of our latest issue is $5, including postage. A subscription is $15 (4 issues), two years $28 (8 issues).

"Writers are notorious for failing to support their own. How many writers buy or even read literary magazines, for example?" —Thomas E. Kennedy

Categories: Fiction—Nonfiction—Arts—Children—Culture—Ecology—Environment—Literature—Poetry—Regional—Short Stories—Writing

Name: Submissions Editor
Material: All
Address: PO BOX 354
City/State/ZIP: PORT TOBACCO MD 20677

Potpourri

GUIDELINES FOR CONTRIBUTORS

Potpourri, a quarterly magazine of the literary arts, accepts a broad genre including short stories, poetry, essays, and travel and original line art. No religious, confessional, racial, political, erotic, abusive, or sexual preference materials will be accepted unless fictional and necessary to plot or characterization.

PAYMENT

Payment is one copy when published. Writers also benefit from publication in *Potpourri*, an international publication, and from readership response. Authors may order at professional discount copies of issue containing their work. *Potpourri* offers annual $100 prizes for the David Ray Poetry Award and the Herman M. Swafford Fiction Award for best of volume and also the Council on National Literatures Award for the poem or short story (alternating years) which best expresses our multicultural diversity or historical background. Write for CNL Award guidelines.

SUBMISSIONS

Potpourri is copyrighted but not registered. The writer's work is protected by copyright of this publication. All prior rights and all rights to new material revert to the contributor after publication. Contributors must obtain and supply copyright permissions for any previously published material.

a) **NUMBER**: Submit your best original material but no more than one (1) work of prose, 3,500 words maximum, three (3) poems and ten (10) haiku. Send seasonal themes twelve months in advance.

b) **PROSE**: Submit neat, typewritten material, preferably 12 point type. Type your name, address, and telephone number at the upper left margin of your first page and the total number of words in your manuscript in the upper right hand corner. Type your last name and page number on each consecutive page. When prose is accepted, editors will request a copy on Macintosh or IBM 3½" disk in Word, WordPerfect, QuarkXpress, or PageMaker. We prefer that computer documents be sent in ASCII or text format, particularly if using word processing programs with a version number higher than 5 (e.g., Word 6, WordPerfect 6).

c) **POETRY**: Submit as in (b) except that poetry may be single spaced. Submit no more than one poem on a page with your name and address on each poem, length to 75 lines,—approximately 30 lines preferred.

d) **HAIKU**: May submit in traditional haiku form, 17 syllable poem in lines of 5, 7, 5 syllables. Western haiku, Tanka, Renga, and Senryu are accepted. Haibun submissions are accepted, but may be too long for publication due to space limitations. Traditional haiku should contain a seasonal reference as well as an "ah" moment. Prepositions and articles should be used sparingly. *Potpourri* prefers to publish haiku without titles. Haiku submissions are not returned.

e) **ILLUSTRATIONS**: Submit black and white line art work for cover and interior illustrations. Theme and tone should be appropriate for a literary magazine.

f) **SASE**: Include a stamped self-addressed #10 envelope with each submission to receive a response from *Potpourri*. Send no metered envelopes.

g) **SAMPLE COPY**: Send 9"x12" envelope and $4.95, shipping and handling included. For overseas, add $2.25 surface mail. Annual subscriptions of four issues are $15.

h) **E-MAIL**: Address is for correspondence only. Send all submissions via conventional mail.

Potpourri Publications Company is funded in part by the National Endowment for the Arts, a federal agency, the Kansas Arts Commission, the Missouri Arts Council, state agencies, and the Prairie Village, Kansas, Municipal Arts Council.

Categories: Fiction—Nonfiction—Adventure—Arts—Biography—Culture—Education—Literature—Multicultural—Poetry—Short Stories—Travel—Writing

Name: Terry Hoyland, Fiction Editor
Material: Poetry
Name: Fiction Editors
Material: Fiction
Address: PO BOX 8278
City/State/ZIP: PRAIRIE VILLAGE KS 66208
Telephone: 913-642-1503
Fax: 913-642-3128
E-mail: Potpourpub@aol.com

POWER & MOTORYACHT

Power & Motoryacht

Power & Motoryacht is edited and designed to meet the needs and pleasures of owners of powerboats 24 feet and larger, with special emphasis on the 35-foot-plus market. Launched in 1985, the magazine gives readers accurate advice on how to choose, operate, and maintain their boats as well as what electronics and gear will help them pursue their favorite pastime. In addition, since powerboating is truly a lifestyle and not just a hobby for these experienced readers, PMY reports on a host of other topics that affect their enjoyment of the water: chartering, cruising (day, weekend, and extended trips), sportfishing, and the environment.

Some of the regular feature themes are:
• **SEAMANSHIP**—Rules of the Road and boating protocol techniques
• **CRUISING**—places readers can take their own boats for a few days' enjoyment
• **MAINTENANCE**—tips on upkeep and repair
• **ENGINES**—innovations that improve efficiency and/or lessen environmental impact
• **SPORTFISHING**—fishing news and travel pieces
WRITING STYLE
Since PMY readers have an average of 28 years' experience boating, articles must be clear, concise, and authoritative; knowledge of the marine industry is mandatory. Include personal experience and information from marine industry experts where appropriate. Also include a list of the people and organizations (with phone numbers) contacted during your research.

All manuscripts must be sent on disk (WordPerfect, Microsoft Word, or another DOS-compatible format) and in hard-copy form, double spaced. Articles should run between 1,000 and 2,000 words. If a travel story is being submitted, 35mm color slides must accompany the manuscript.

PAYMENT POLICY
Depending on article length, compensation is between $500 and $1,000; this fee includes photography if it is part of an assignment. Payment is upon acceptance; if an assigned article does not meet with our guidelines, a one-third kill fee will be given.

SUBMISSIONS
Query first; unsolicited manuscripts and photography are *not* accepted and will not be returned. Send a one-page query with a self-addressed, stamped envelope.

Categories: Boating—Outdoors—Travel

Name: Diane M. Byrne, Managing Editor
Material: All
Address: 249 W 17TH ST
City/State/ZIP: NEW YORK NY 10011
Telephone: 212-462-3616
Fax: 212-367-8331
E-mail: pmy@panix.com

Power and Light

Power and Light is a full-color weekly story paper for preteens. It correlates with the WordAction Sunday School materials for 11 and 12 year olds.

Allow 8-12 weeks for a response. Four complimentary contributor issues available upon publication. Payment is made upon production. Projected publication/production dates supplied upon acceptance.

Fiction
• Written for preteens. 600-850 words. Show character building or scriptural application.
• Submit contemporary, true-to-life portrayals of preteens.
• Use active voice. Write in third person.
• Avoid fantasy, abnormally precocious children, and personification of animals.
• Avoid extensive cultural or holiday references. Write for an international audience.
• Themes and outcomes should conform to the theology of the Church of the Nazarene.
• Payment is 5¢ per word for multi-use rights. Power and Light reserves the right to reprint these manuscripts with no additional compensation.
• Updated theme list is available for a SASE.

Spotlight the Past Articles
• Written for preteens. 300-400 words. Archaeological background articles.
• Work for hire. Assigned themes. Send query. Payment is 5¢ per word.

Preteen Survival Guide Articles
• Written for preteens. Topics should be current and of importance to preteens (peer pressure).
• 500-700 words. Work for hire or freelance submissions accepted. Payment is 5¢ per word.

Puzzles
• Designed for preteens. Life application or Bible verse correlation. Theme list available.
• Concise design and instructions. Work for hire or freelance multi-use. $15 per puzzle.

Cartoons
• Spot or strip. Humor involving children. Correlate with lesson themes if possible.
• $15 per cartoon. Avoid child-related humor from an adult viewpoint.

Artwork/Photographs
• Work for hire or assignment only. Variety of styles. Payment varies. Submit query/portfolio.

Thank you for your interest!
We look forward to your submissions.
Categories: Fiction—Nonfiction—Adventure—African-American—Asian-American—Cartoons—Children—Christian Interests—Crafts—Family—Games—Humor—Jewish Interests—Juvenile—Multicultural—Mystery—Religion—Short Stories—Teen

Name: Beula Postlewait, Editor
Material: Preteen
Name: Melissa Hammer, Associate Editor
Material: Preteen
Address: 6401 THE PASEO
City/State/ZIP: KANSAS CITY KS 64131-1284
Telephone: 816-333-7000
Fax: 816-333-4439
E-mail: mhammer@nazarene.org
Internet: www.nazarene.org

Prairie Schooner
University of Nebraska Press

Thank you for your interest in our magazine. *Prairie Schooner* publishes short stories, poems, interviews, imaginative essays of general interest, and reviews of current books of poetry and fiction. Scholarly articles requiring footnote references should be submitted to journals of literary scholarship.

Prairie Schooner's intention is to publish the best writing available, both from beginning and established writers. In our seventy years of publication, we have printed the work of Eudora Welty, Octavio Pas, Tennesse Williams, Weldon Kees, Joyce Carol Oates, *and* Rita Dove, Richard Russo, Reynolds Price, Julia Alvarez, Sharon Olds, Cornelius Eady, plus scores of others.

All submissions to *Prairie Schooner* should be typed, double-spaced (except for poetry). Be sure to put your name on each page of the manuscript. A self-addressed envelope, with adequate return postage on it, must accompany the submission. For poetry, we prefer a selection of 5-7 poems; for fiction, essays, and reviews, we prefer you send only one selection at a time.

Please allow 3-4 months for a reply. *Prairie Schooner* does not read simultaneous submissions, and submissions must be received between September and May.

Writing prizes awarded by *Prairie Schooner*

Prairie Schooner offers the following writing prizes annually, based on availability of funds. *Only pieces published in Prairie Schooner are eligible for consideration.* Awards for the year *are* announced in the spring issue of the following year.

The Lawrence Foundation Award

$1,000 for the best short story published in *Prairie Schooner*. The Lawrence Foundation is a charitable trust located in New York City.

The Virginia Faulkner Award

$1,000 for fiction, nonfiction, poetry, or translations published during the previous year.

The Strousse Award

$500 for the best poem or group of poems published during the previous year.

The Bernice Slote Award

$500 for the best work by a beginning writer published during the previous year.

The Edward Stanley Award

$500 for poetry published during the previous year.

The Hugh J. Luke Award

*250 award open to any genre published during the previous year.

Prairie Schooner/Reader's Choice Awards

$250 each, awarded on a year to year basis to work published during the previous year. All genres of writing are eligible for these awards.

We encourage you to read *Prairie Schooner.* To subscribe or order a sample copy, send your check for the appropriate amount to the address below.

Sample copy $ 5.00
Current issue $ 7.25
1 year subscription $22.00
2 year subscription $38.00
3 year subscription $50.00
Categories: Fiction—Creative Nonfiction—Poetry

Name: Hilda Raz, Editor
Material: All
Address: 201 ANDREWS HALL
City/State/ZIP: LINCOLN NE 68588-0334
Telephone: 402-472-0911
Fax: 402-472-9771
E-mail: lrandolp@unlinfo2.unl.edu

The Preacher's Magazine
"...speaking the truth in love..."

Memo To: Freelance Writers
From: *The Preacher's Magazine* Editorial Staff
The Preacher's Magazine is a quarterly publication for Christian ministers. It reaches an international and interdenominational audience. It is Wesleyan-Arminian in theological persuasion, and it seeks to provide insights and resources for lifelong ministerial development [while] endeavoring to apply biblical theological truths to modern-day ministry. *The Preacher's Magazine* uses both scholarly and practical articles.

The magazine has two parts. The first part is divided into departments made up of articles on major sections such as: Church Administration, Church Growth, Pastoral Care, Evangelism, Theology, Multiple Staff Ministries, The Minister's Mate, Pastor's Personal Growth, Pastor's Professional Growth, Holiness Heritage, Preaching, Biblical Studies, Church Music, and Finance.

Articles should be 700 to 2,500 words in length. When thinking of manuscript length, please keep in mind, "less is better." Payment is $.035 per published word upon publication.

Payment will notify the writer of his acceptance.

All scripture quotations must be identified, including the version quoted. For example: (James 5:16, KJV). Only the New International Version need not be identified because it is covered throughout the magazine. The NIV example would be: (James 5:16).

Quotations should be identified by footnotes to give the source: author's name, title of book, city of publisher, publisher, date of publication, and page(s) quoted. For example: Randal E. Denny, In Jesus' Strong Hands (Kansas City, MO: Beacon Hill Press, 1989), p.2. The writer must obtain permission to use copyrighted material of more than 120 words. Permission letter should accompany the submitted manuscript.

Due to limited number of magazines printed, we are unable to send sample copies.
Categories: Religion

Name: Randal E. Denny, Editor
Material: All
Address: 10814 E BROADWAY
City/State/ZIP: SPOKANE WA 99206
Telephone: 509-226-3464
Fax: 509-926-8740

Presbyterians Today

Presbyterians Today is a magazine for members of the Presbyterian Church (U.S.A.). It is published 10 times a year, with combined January/February and July/August issues. Circulation is more than 90,000.

The target audience for *Presbyterians Today* is lay people.

Readers are quite diverse in age, sex, education, theological viewpoints, and involvement in the life of the church.

Presbyterians Today seeks to:

1. Stimulate interest *in* and provide a more complete awareness and support of the mission of the Presbyterian Church (U.S.A.).

2. Report in a balanced way the news and activities of the denomination as it performs its mission through its designated agencies, governing bodies and congregations.

3. Enhance and celebrate the common bonds of heritage and faith that bind the Presbyterian Church (U.S.A.) together as a community of believers, and to provide for an expression of the rich diversity within the denomination.

4. Provide information, inspiration and guidance for readers as they seek to live as Christians in all aspects of life.

5. Confess that Jesus Christ is Lord, to lead readers to strengthen their understanding of the meaning of Christ and commitment to him, and to reflect the resources available through the Christian community.

6. Portray in an informative and stimulating manner the interaction of the Presbyterian Church (U.S.A.) with other Christian bodies and to interpret theologically the world in which and for which it performs its mission.

7. Foster understanding of the oneness of the Christian Church.

FEATURE ARTICLES

Presbyterians Today welcomes contributions from free-lance writers. Stories vary in length (800-2,000 words; preferred, 1,000-1,500). Appropriate subjects: profiles of interesting Presbyterians and of Presbyterian programs and activities; issues of current concern to the church; ways in which individuals and families express their Christian faith in significant ways or relate their faith to the problems of society.

Most articles have some direct relevance to a Presbyterian audience; however, *Presbyterians Today* also seeks well informed articles written for a general audience that can help individuals and families cope with the stresses of daily living from a Christian perspective.

Presbyterians Today almost never uses fiction or short fillers, and poetry only occasionally. Original manuscripts are preferred. Reprints are occasionally used, but submission of reprints and multiple submissions are not encouraged.

Authors are asked to submit only one article at a time. Manuscripts are read by at least two editors, and a reply given normally within one month after receipt.

Presbyterians Today pays for articles upon acceptance. With the author's permission, the magazine may hold a manuscript for future consideration (which does not preclude the author from submitting the article elsewhere), and payment will be offered at the time the article is scheduled for publication-if publication rights are available to *Presbyterians Today* at that time. Authors receive complimentary copies of issues in which their articles appear.

SHORT FEATURES

Presbyterians Today also accepts short features (250-600 words) about interesting people, programs, events and congregations related to the Presbyterian Church (U.S.A.), for the "SpotLight" department. The editors may suggest that a full-length feature article, because of timeliness, space limitations or content, would be more appropriate as a "SpotLight" feature.

HUMOR

Presbyterians Today uses jokes or short humorous stories for the "LaughLines" department. Credit *will* be given to contributors, but the material should be in the public domain, not copyrighted. Preferred length: 150 words or less.

QUERIES

Queries are not required, but may save effort and postage if a subject proposed is dearly inappropriate or if similar articles have fairly recently been used or are currently in the works. Manuscripts are received on speculation.

SUBMISSIONS

Manuscripts should be typed. The author's name and address, including zip code, and social security number should be typed on the manuscript as well as the cover letter. Manuscripts may also be submitted by e-mail.

Photos accompanying a manuscript should be of good quality for reproduction. Black-and-white or color prints, transparencies, or contact sheets are acceptable. They should be identified as to content and credit line. Photos may be sent after an article is accepted, but it is helpful to know whether or not they are or could be available.

Facts, quotations and the spelling of proper names should always be checked for accuracy. *Presbyterians Today* normally uses the New Revised Standard Version for Biblical quotations; if another version of Scripture is used, this should be indicated. If copyrighted material is quoted, the author should secure permission in writing from the copyright holder and cite the work, author, publisher and date of copyright.

Writer's Digest has suggested 20 rules for good writing:

1. Prefer the plain word to the fancy.
2. Prefer the familiar word to the unfamiliar.
3. Prefer the Saxon word to the Romance.
4. Prefer nouns and verbs to adjectives and adverbs.
5. Prefer picture nouns and action verbs.
6. Never use a long word when a short one will do as well.
7. Master the simple declarative sentence.
8. Prefer the simple sentence to the complicated.
9. Vary the sentence length.
10. Put the word you want to emphasize at the beginning or end of your sentence.
11. Use the active voice.
12. Put the statements in a positive form.
13. Use short paragraphs.
14. Cut needless words, sentences and paragraphs.
15. Use plain, conversational language.
16. Avoid imitation. Write in your natural style.
17. Write dearly.
18. Avoid gobbledygook and jargon.
19. Write to be understood, not to impress.
20. Revise and rewrite. Improvement is always possible.

To these *Presbyterians Today* adds one more:

Reporting is preferred to reflection. Your chances of having your article accepted for publication increase to the extent that you write in the third person, not the first person. Most stories can be told better without the use of "I."

Before you begin to write, ask yourself: "What do I want to say?" "Why?" "To whom?" "How do I plan to say it?" If your article is geared to a Presbyterian audience, make sure it is clear how and why the subject relates to that audience. Assemble and organize your material. An outline may help. After you have written your first draft, it is good practice to leave it for a time. When you return to it, read it aloud, making sure its language flows freely and comfortably.

Categories: Religion

Name: Catherine Cottingham, Managing Editor
Material: All
Address: 100 WITHERSPOON ST
City/State/ZIP: LOUISVILLE KY 40202-1396
Telephone: 502-569-5637
Fax: 502-569-8632
E-mail: today@pcusa.org PresbyNet in-box: today

M-R

Presentations
Technology and Techniques for Effective Communication

To ensure your manuscript meets our specifications we require you to keep in mind the following guidelines. It will make your job, and ours, easier.

• Read the magazine for style, content and story selection.
• Use AP style guidelines.
• Stay away from special formatting other than bold, italic and underline.
• Put all attributions in present tense ("say" not "said").
• Use the familiar "you" when appropriate.
• Do not write in first person unless requested.
• Use active tense whenever possible.
• Never create situations or scenarios that did not happen unless you fully describe to the reader the event is fictional.
• Attempt to interview end users of technology when appropriate for a piece.
• Provide possible headlines and subheads.
• Provide a list of names and phone numbers for all sources referenced in your article.
• Provide a list with the exact company name, product name and phone number for all manufacturers and service providers referenced in your article.
• Provide captions for all images submitted with your article.
• Provide a biographical reference for any publications or reports referenced in your article.
• All articles should be submitted electronically, either by diskette, e-mail or modem. You may use the online addresses shown below. Please notify your assigning editor by phone when materials have been sent.
• Screen captures should be 640x480 [pixels resolution] in the highest color resolution possible. We can accept a variety of file formats, including JPEG, PICT, TIFF, PCX and BMP. They may be sent by diskette or e-mail. We can also accept art on CD-ROM or SyQuest [removable media disks]. High quality 35mm slides or 4"x5" transparencies are also acceptable.
• All materials should be sent to the attention of your assigning editor.

Categories: Business—Computers—Education—Government—Internet—Presentations—Technology

Name: Jean Cook, Managing Editor
Material: General Inquiries
Name: Jon Hanke, Associate Editor
Material: Product Reviews
Name: Mary Creswell, New Products Editor
Material: New Products
Address: 50 S NINTH ST
City/State/ZIP: MINNEAPOLIS MN 55402
Telephone: 612-333-0471
Fax: 612-333-6526
E-mail: sheimes@presentations.com, or jcook@presentations.com
Internet: www.presentations.com

Press

Press accepts Poetry and Short Fiction.

All submissions must be accompanied by a SASE and a short writer's biography.

3-5 poems should be sent to the attention of the Poetry Editor, should be typed and the author's name should appear on each page.

Short fiction (no more than 2 stories; each no longer than 25 pages) should be typed and double-spaced. All short fiction should be sent to the attention of the Fiction Editor and the author's name should appear on the first (or title) page.

For unsolicited poetry, *Press* pays a minimum of $50/accepted poem.

For unsolicited short fiction, *Press* pays a minimum of $100/accepted story.

No simultaneous submissions.

Press acquires first rights.

Artistic Guidelines

Poetry: All poems must make sense. That is, all complicated rhythms and fanciful word choices, all emotional and psychological gestures, must have a public value as well as a personal one.

We are looking for poems that are thematically and stylistically uniform: meaningful, balanced, and powerful. Loose abstraction, random alliteration, confusion (whether purposeful or not) and any other device or gesture that corrupts meaning is, simply, not for us.

Short Fiction: While almost all forms are acceptable, prose poems and more experimental writing (stories that don't actually tell a story) are discouraged.

We are looking for a strong and specific plot (where 'something' actually happens); one that makes a reader want to turn the page. We want stories where the author's style does not interfere with the plot, but strengthens the expression of that plot.

Categories: Fiction—Literature—Poetry—Short Stories

Name: Poetry Editor
Material: Poetry
Name: Fiction Editor
Material: Fiction
Address: SUITE 323, 2124 BROADWAY
City/State/ZIP: NEW YORK, NY 10023
E-mail: pressltd@aol.com

Prevention Magazine

Dear Writer:

Thank you for your recent request. Unfortunately, we do not have writers' guidelines to send you because we use very little freelance material. If you are interested in submitting material, we suggest sending a query with full details.

If the piece is already written, you may send a nonreturnable copy if you wish.

We appreciate your interest in our publication.

Best wishes!

Sincerely yours,

Readers' Service

Categories: Nonfiction—Cooking—Food/Drink—Health—Physical Fitness—Nutrition—Medicine

Name: Denise Foley, Features Editor
Material: All
Address: 33 E. MINOR ST.
City/State/ZIP: EMMAUS, PA 18098
Telephone: 610-967-5171
Fax: 610-967-7654

Primavera

IN GENERAL

Primavera publishes original fiction, poetry, and art that reflects the experiences of women. We interpret this theme as broadly as possible. We select works that encompass the lives of women of different ages, races, sexual orientations, social classes, and locations. We will consider work by male writers but it must not require a male perspective to be understood or enjoyed.

Address all submissions to the editors at the address below. All submissions without an SASE will be discarded—illustration or manuscript.

Primavera pays both writers and artists in contributors' copies: two for each published item. If your work is accepted, we will send you a form to assign us the first rights to its publication. After publication, the copyright reverts to you, and you may reprint your work as long as *Primavera* is credited with its initial publication.

Do not send previously published work or simultaneous submissions.

We are happy to offer artists and writers a special discount on copies of *Primavera!* Back issues, usually $7.00 each, are only $5.00 when you mention this offer; current issues, usually $9.00, cost only $7.00. We pay for shipping.

WRITING

Poetry should be single-spaced, with stanza and line breaks clearly indicated. Computer printouts are fine, as long as the type is legible.

Primavera is published by a small staff of volunteers who meet biweekly (less often in summer), and it often takes several weeks, even months, before a manuscript completes the review process. Please be patient with us! We will respond to you, although unfortunately our staff is too small, and the volume of manuscripts we receive too large, for us to comment on each submission.

We edit poetry and fiction. If your work is selected, we may write to you with proposed changes, or ask you to rewrite troublesome sections. We always send you the edited version for your approval before publication.

We are interested in all writers, published and unpublished. We judge each work on its merit and not on the author's reputation (or lack of one).

ART

Primavera publishes black-and-white art inside the magazine: line and continuous-tone drawings, paintings, and photographs. Infrequently, we publish color illustration. We accept submissions on approval and do not commission work. We review work by women artists only.

For review, please send slides or photocopies. If we select your work for publication, we will ask you to send us the original or a professional-quality transparency. Write us if you aren't sure of the best way to represent your work

Categories: Fiction—Poetry—Women's Fiction

Name: Board of Editors
Material: All
Address: PO BOX 37-7547
City/State/ZIP: CHICAGO IL 60637
Telephone: 773-324-5920

Prime Health & Fitness

Welcome to *Prime Health & Fitness.* We're pleased to have you on board as a freelancer. Please review our editorial guidelines and procedures, as well as the list of items you must have in your back-up file.

Guidelines

Accuracy

We're sticklers for accuracy. Please double-check all facts to make sure the information is correct.

Biographical Line

Include a biographical line about yourself, not more than one sentence in length, at the end of the article.

Originality

Always use primary sources. Unless using book quotations from a source whose quoted speech appears in the article, don't pass off as original reporting previously published quotes or writing in your article, no matter what the source. (Published source material, such as scientific or medical studies, of course, can be used as background information or as the seed idea for an article—such as a report in JAMA that represents a medical breakthrough and we then report on its significance and repercussions.)

Race

Don't include a source's ethnicity or race unless this information is relevant to the story.

Style

Follow *The Associated Press Stylebook and Libel Manual.*
Procedures for Manuscript Preparation

1. Use just one space after periods.

2. Adhere to the assigned length of the article. If you must write over, don't exceed 300 additional words. If you come across information you feel should be included in your piece, write it in a sidebar or include it on a separate page.

3. Use a wide right-hand margin to leave space for annotations.

4. The last page of your manuscript should be a numbered list of phone numbers of all your sources, including individuals, groups, government agencies, organizations and institutions.

5. Enclose a separate, annotated copy of your manuscript when you turn in your original work to your editor. Each annotation should refer the editor to the name of a source or an item in the back-up file. In news articles, all statements and claims must be substantiated by original information-gathering and interviews on your part. Information that is not attributed to a source must *be* readily verifiable by materials in the back-up file.

6. Submit your manuscript in both electronic and paper formats. Submit your document text-only on diskette:

• If you use WordPerfect, save the document in a text-only format in this way: while the article is on the screen,

• press Text In/Out (Ctrl-F5)

• select Save As (3)

• select Generic (1)

• If you use Microsoft Word, save as Word.

• If you have a Macintosh, save your document to the diskette in the usual way

• If you have a modem and would like to send your file via e-mail, you may do so at the e-mail address below. Call us to alert us that you intend to do this.

Back-up File

Send a comprehensive back-up file to your editor. If your article entails any of the following things, your back-up should include the items listed with them here:

1. Telephone numbers of lead researchers and others consulted for article

2. Copies of studies/research articles:
Abstract ____ OR
complete study or article (preferred) ____
Correspondence with sources or experts ____
Magazine articles used as background ____
Newspaper articles used as background ____
Book passages used as background ____

3. Excerpts from or adaptations of a book:
the actual book ____
permissions letter and contract ____

4. Mentioned books:
photocopies of title and copyright pages ____
phone number of publisher ____

5. Mentioned videos:
the actual video ____ OR
photocopies of box (front and back) ____

6. Products for R&D:
packaging ____
7. Products for R&D and Grooming articles:
Presskits ____
brand names ____
manufacturers' names/phone numbers
of company contacts ____
prices ____
Categories: Nonfiction (over-40 men)—Health—Nutrition—Men's Issues—Physical Fitness—Psychology—Relationships—Sexuality—Travel

Name: Bill Bush, Editor
Material: All
Address: 21100 ERWIN ST
City/State/ZIP: WOODLAND HILLS CA 91367
Telephone: 818-595-0442
Fax: 818-595-0463
E-mail: primefit1@aol.com

Professional Pilot Magazine

Professional Pilot is a monthly aviation trade magazine with an approximate qualified circulation of 33,500. The circulation is national and international and is composed primarily of regional airline pilots, corporate pilots and aviation managers. Annual subscriptions are available free of charge to qualified recipients. Revenue is derived solely from advertising.

The majority of the feature articles in the magazine are written on a freelance basis by professional pilots or people who have expertise in one particular aspect of aviation. Typical subjects include new aircraft design, new product reviews (especially avionics), pilot technique, profiles of regional airlines, fixed base operations, profiles of corporate flight departments and technological advances. In general, stories should appeal to pilots flying turbine-powered aircraft for a living and aviation managers.

The typical reader has a sophisticated grasp of piloting/aviation knowledge and is interested in articles that help him/her do the job better, or more efficiently.

Story ideas should first be queried in writing to the Managing Editor before sending an unsolicited manuscript. However, unsolicited manuscripts will be acknowledged and returned if accompanied by a self-addressed, stamped envelope with sufficient postage.

Typical article length is 750 to 2,000 words. A fee for the article will be established at the time of assignment. Writers are paid after the manuscript has been received and approved for publication; *Professional Pilot* buys exclusive publication rights. Manuscripts should be sent in hard copy and as an ASCII text file on a disk (IBM or Mac format).

It is expected that authors will also submit artwork relevant to the article. This may be photos and/or illustrations supplied by a manufacturer or directly by the author. First-generation color transparencies are preferred although color prints are acceptable. Photo credit will be given. Artwork will be returned if accompanied by a self-addressed, stamped envelope with sufficient postage.

Authors should indicate relevant aviation experience and pilot credentials (certificates, ratings and hours).

Pro Pilot does not publish articles that have appeared in other publications.
Categories: Aviation

Name: Chad Trautvetter, Managing Editor
Material: All
Address: 3014 COLVIN ST
City/State/ZIP: ALEXANDRIA VA 22314

Telephone: 703-370-0606
Fax: 703-370-7082
E-mail: propilot@flightdata.com

Progressive Engineer

What We're About

Progressive Engineer celebrates the accomplishments of engineers in North Carolina, Virginia, West Virginia, Maryland and discusses topics important to them. The four-color magazine is published bimonthly and distributed free to qualified engineers and contractors in the mid-Atlantic region. With a circulation of about 40,000, *Progressive Engineer* reaches engineers of all disciplines in all types of jobs.

How to Approach Us

We welcome contributions from freelance writers as well as engineers and other technical people. Read our brochure or a sample copy of the magazine and then send us a query letter outlining your idea with samples of your writing, if you have any. We review unsolicited manuscripts and field queries by phone, but we much prefer to work by letter. Our response time on queries and manuscripts runs about four weeks.

Types of Articles

Features: These consist of profiles of engineers or descriptions of projects in the region. Profiles detail major achievements made by engineers in the course of their jobs and careers and tell of engineers applying their skills in unusual and innovative ways. Besides describing the technology involved, we delve into the background and personal side of the engineer. What led to them to do what they did, and what motivates them?

Project features cover high-profile projects that entail large amounts of engineering with far-reaching implications and describe the technology used, profile the engineers involved, and tell about the contractors and suppliers providing services. Occasionally, such projects bring controversy and touch emotional hot buttons of citizens in surrounding areas; *Progressive Engineer* explains the pros and cons from a technical standpoint, so engineers can form intelligent opinions. Length: Approximately 2,000-2,500 words (including 500-word sidebar). Payment: $350.

Short Profiles: Describe engineers or inventors who accomplish something significant. These are usually average people who do something out of the ordinary either on the job or off. Length: 800-1,000 words. Payment: $150.

Issues: Focus on career development and explore avenues engineers can take in their careers. They also discuss issues, trends, and developments affecting the engineering profession and take a candid look at ethical and philosophical questions. Length: Approximately 1,500 words. Payment: $225.

Places to Visit: Describe sites engineers can visit to learn about technology and engineering while on vacation or out for a country drive. These showcase the heritage of our engineering past as well as the latest inventions. All lie within the mid-Atlantic region, or a short drive from it, and feature exhibits explaining the technology on display. Length: Approximately 1,000 words. Payment: $150.

Style

Progressive Engineer covers engineering in an easy-to-read style devoid of equations, jargon, and long words found in many technical journals. When applicable, we expect authors to use several sources in researching an article to maintain balance and objectivity. Obtain quotes from experts, principles involved in projects, and subjects of profiles. Feel free to use first person if appropriate. Features use sidebars (generally about 500 words) to complement the main body; those focusing on an engineer should have a sidebar on the technology involved, while project features should have a sidebar that profiles an engineer or group of engineers involved.

Manuscript Requirements

Include name, address, phone number, and social security number at the top of the first page of the manuscript. We can use submissions on diskette if formatted for Macintosh; always include hard copy with it.

Photos

When possible, supply photos (and diagrams, if helpful) with your manuscript or tell us where we can obtain them. We can use B&W and color prints and 35mm or larger transparencies—originals or duplicates. Do not send negatives. Slides should have your name and address on them. If you didn't take a photo you send us, tell us who did so we can give proper credit. Send a list of captions keyed to numbers on the photos. We accept photos from companies and PR firms but don't pay for them. Payment: $25 per photo used in an article, $100 for cover shots.

Rights and Payment

Progressive Engineer considers reprints and simultaneous submissions if the markets don't overlap or compete; payment is 50 percent of normal rates. In many cases, we can use previously published material modified for our slant, in which case we pay full rate. Payment for all work is on publication.

Categories: Nonfiction—Engineering—Regional—Technology

Name: Tom Gibson, Editor
Material: All
Address: PO BOX 20305
City/State/ZIP: ROANOKE VA 24018
Telephone: 540-772-2225

PROTOONER

For Both the Amateur and Professional Cartoonists & Gagwriters!
PROTOONER features:

• Magazine markets
• Cartooning tips & info
• Interesting articles
• Readers' letters
• Buys cover cartoons, inside spot cartoons and humor articles
• Freebies: Gives 3 free PT issues per each Cartoonist/ Gagwriter bio printed.
• More Freebies: Prints Cartoonist & Gagwriter business cards and promo sheets as a FREE service.
• Reports on folded/DU markets on a regular basis, to keep your market files updated.

CARTOON COVERS

Humorous, themed to cartooning, the cartoonist or gagwriter, rejections, acceptances.

Submit: Fresh material, roughs only. 7½"x8" B&W (with/ without captions). PT adds own coloration.

Avoid: Profanity, gender slandering, racial digs.

Pays: $20 on acceptance.

INSIDE SPOTS

3½"x3½" B&W. Prefers captionless. On assignment only.

Pays: $10 on acceptance.

SHORT HUMOR

500-2,000 words (with B&W illustration) typed.

Submit: Query letter with brief synopsis of article before submitting.

Avoid: How-to articles.

Pays: Negotiable payment upon publication.

SUBMISSION

1. Neatly print or type your name, address, phone and social security numbers on the back, upper right-hand corner of each submission.

2. SASE a must!

3. Sample copy is available for $5.00.

Categories: Cartoons—Comedy—Humor

Name: Ladd A. Miller, Art Director
Material: All
Address: PO BOX 2270
City/State/ZIP: DALY CITY CA 94015
Telephone: 415-755-4827
Fax: 415-755-3005

Psychology Today
MIND BODY SPIRIT

Psychology Today
Mind Body Spirit

Thanks for your interest in *Psychology Today!* As you know, PT explores every aspect of human behavior, from the cultural trends that shape the way we think and feel to the intricacies of modern neuroscience. Although many psychologists and mental health professionals read PT, most of our readers are simply intelligent and curious people interested in the psyche and the self. Think of us as a health magazine for the mind!

WHAT WE NEED: good, clearly articulated feature ideas-and writers with the talent to bring those ideas to life. Nearly any subject related to psychology is fair game. We value originality, insight, and good reporting; we're not interested in stories or topics that have already been covered *ad nauseam* by other magazines unless you can provide a fresh new twist and much more depth. Although our articles are aimed at an intelligent mainstream audience, rather than specifically at psychologists, the ideas and claims made in the stories should be backed up where appropriate by good, solid scientific research. We're not interested in simple-minded "pop psychology."

While our readership is two-thirds female and largely college-educated, it is also diverse. There is no typical PT reader-and no typical PT story.

HOW TO GET AN ASSIGNMENT: Please don't send us complete manuscripts-our desks are already overflowing with journals, faxes, books, and articles awaiting editing. Instead, send a one- to two-page query letter explaining:

• what you want to write,
• why you want to write it *now*, and
• why you should be the one to write it.

Tell us why and how your story will affect people's lives, if applicable, and mention sources you might contact. If your work has been published before, feel free to attach a clip or two. Address the query to executive editor Peter Doskoch or features editor Jill Neimark. We greatly appreciate an enclosed SASE.

We highly recommend that you read some recent back issues of the magazine to get a feel for what we publish and what topics we've covered lately. If we've written about topic X in a recent issue, chances are we won't want to run another feature on the subject for at least a year or two.

Most of the pieces in our News & Trends section are staff written, but we do run piece by freelancers. Also, the Style column-which discusses trends in style and fashion from a psychological angle-includes freelance contributions as well. Address your queries to news editor Annie Murphy Paul.

WE DON'T PUBLISH poems or short stories; nor do we consider first-person accounts of psychological illness or recovery (unless they are part of a well-researched, general interest story).

PLEASE NOTE that we receive a lot of queries, and sorting through all that mail takes time, particularly for a tiny staff. We usually answer queries within four to six weeks, but if your letter arrives as deadlines approach we may not get to it for awhile. Please be patient.

MISCELLANY: We pay on publication. Payment will be negotiated between the writer and editor, but in most cases we pay about 75 cents per word. We'll also reimburse you for minor necessary expenses (phone calls, yes; plane tickets, no). Of course you'll also receive some contributor's copies.

If your article has a seasonal or timely aspect, keep in mind our production schedule: our editorial deadline for an issue is nearly three months before the issue hits newsstands. Count on a five month lead time to get an assignment.

If you have any further questions, feel free to call Executive Editor Peter Doskoch (ext. 134).

Thanks again for your interest, and we look forward to hearing from you!

Categories: Nonfiction—Health—Psychology—Science

Name: Jill Neimark, Features Editor
Material: Features
Name: Peter Doskoch, Executive Editor
Material: Features
Name: Annie Murphy Paul, News Editor
Material: News
Address: 49 E 21ST ST 11TH FLOOR
City/State/ZIP: NEW YORK NY 10010
Telephone: 212-260-7210
Fax: 212-260-7445

Pulp, a newspaper
The Stuff That Matters

Think of PULP as a publication written for a young college student and you're probably on the right track. Our readers are both average and superior, male and female, urban and suburban; the goal is to interest everybody. Professional writing should be fresh, alive and free of cliches and "hip" teenage lingo. The single greatest way to turn off a teen reader is to talk down to him or her, or to try and sound "like them." Instead, seize on a topic that will make them stop and read. If it's a common subject (i.e. getting into college, job hunting, etc.) make the angle a new one. If it bores you—or a friend—in the slightest, it will certainly turn off our audience.

That said, blow us away. Show us a celebrity or band we want to know. Explore the unusual business, event or situation. Introduce us to a teenage gambling addict. Make an issue real. One hint: if the subject matter is hard to relate to, tell it through a person. For instance, rather than tell readers how scary the AIDS epidemic is, introduce them to some young people who've gotten the disease or a teen caring for an afflicted adult. Connect the abstraction to reality. Not every story need have a personal angle, PULP is also about vivid service journalism. Young people have the world before them and have yet to be exposed to many things.

ARTICLE BASICS

All mailed submissions should by typed with name, address, phone number in the upper left-hand corner. Please number any additional pages and indicate name or story title on each page.

To expedite matters, submissions made on deadline should be e-mailed or sent on disk along with hard copy. Since we long ago joined the digital age, we much prefer e-mail correspondence and writers equipped to handle this.

Be fastidious with research, but don't overload us with facts. And remember, we can't check every fact. You're our first line of defense.

PULP is a very broad-focused newspaper covering almost any subject matter pertaining to youth culture. That means news, issues, sports, controversy, music, film, computers, the web, games, comics, health, fitness, nutrition, advice, gossip, education, careers, colleges, and on and on. We are big fans of humor and irreverence, should it be appropriate. Pitch us an idea, however wild. We might just bite.

CASHOLA

Freelance writers on assignment will be paid according to experience, article length and research involved. Typical fees for features will range from $50 to $160 dollars, factored on a standard rate of $0.10/word—though, as stated, compensation is negotiated, particularly in instances involving great research or limited travel. Whenever possible, limit feature length articles to 1,200 words or less. The 600-900 word range is ideal.

Writers of columns and opinion pieces under 500 words will be paid up to $75. Some columns open to freelancers are:

• *On the Job:* A brief (400 words) profile of a young professional in an unusual job situation (white water guide, private investigator, etc.) that may not seem like a "typical" career.

• *Buy Products:* Either one extended (700 or less) piece on a new, highly unusual/useful/totally worthless product or service or a series of blurbs (100-200) focusing on a number of interesting products.

• *Filter:* Short current event or "news" related blurbs for the front of the book (typically 300 words or less), not unlike what you'd find in a number of publications. They should either be universally significant or of particular interest to young readers.

• *Jock Itch:* A short, opinionated (hopefully witty) rant about a recent sports occurrence that really "burns" you as a fan, spectator or human.

• *Fashion Victim:* Our style column. As with Buy Products, this could be one extended highlight or a series of blurbs. We prefer the latter.

***Check with an editor for updated columns, as they tend to evolve with somewhat annoying consistency.

UNSOLICITED MATERIAL

Unsolicited submissions should be addressed to "Submissions Editor," and must include stamped, self-addressed envelope if acknowledgment of consideration is requested.

WHERE TO REACH US

As stated earlier, email is our preferred method of communication. If you are deemed worthy, we will dispense personal e-mail accounts later. Please keep letterbombs to yourself. Fax works usually. The phone number—well—use this only as a last resort.

Categories: College—General Interest—Juvenile—Lifestyles—Teen

Name: Submissions Editor
Material: All
Address: PO BOX 638
City/State/ZIP: ORADELL NJ 07649
Telephone: 201-262-1501
Fax: 201-262-4938
E-mail: PulpNews@aol.com

Pulp Eternity

Please refer to Eternity Press.

Quarterly West
University of Utah

Dear Writer:

Thank you for your interest in our magazine. We do not have many formal guidelines *per se*, but you may wish to know the following information:

1) Quarterly West expects the standard format for fiction or essays. Poetry should be single-spaced.

2) We accept simultaneous submissions, but wish to be informed of that fact. If the manuscript is taken elsewhere, we expect to be notified.

3) We read manuscripts year round, trying to respond within four to six months.

4) Manuscripts accepted for publication should be submitted on computer disk, preferably in a Macintosh format.

5) Contributors receive two copies of the issue in which their work appears, as well as a small honorarium.

6) Quarterly West also sponsors a biennial novella competition. Entries for the 1996-97 competition were accepted between October 1 and December 31, 1996. Guidelines for the next competition were available in June, 1998. Send SASE for current guidelines.

Good luck in your writing. We look forward to reading your work.

The Editors

Categories: Fiction—Nonfiction—Interview—Literature—Poetry—Short Stories—Writing
Name: Fiction Editor
Name: Poetry Editor

Name: Nonfiction Editor
Material: As Appropriate
Address: UNIVERSITY OF UTAH
Address: 200 S CAMPUS CENTER DR RM 317
City/State/ZIP: SALT LAKE CITY UT 84112-9109
Telephone: 801-581-3938

The Queens Parents' Paper

Please refer to *The Big Apple Parents' Paper*.

Quilting Today

Please refer to Chitra Publications.

Remember: Editors change jobs and publishers change addresses. It is wise to invest in a phone call for the current information before submitting.

R-A-D-A-R

R-A-D-A-R

For Your Information

R-A-D-A-R is a weekly Sunday school take-home paper for children in grades three and four. Our goal is to reach these children with the truth of God's Word and to help them make it the guide of their lives.

R-A-D-A-R's features correlate with Standard Publishing's Middler Sunday school curriculum; therefore, we buy submissions to fit in with specific themes. A quarterly theme list is available on request. You may also request that your name be placed on our mailing list to receive the most current theme list four times a year.

Preparing Your Submission

• Use a 60-character line, double space, and leave generous margins.

• Place your name, address, social security number, and approximate number of words in your manuscript on the first page.

• Enclose an SASE with all submissions.

Payment and Perks

• Fiction/nonfiction-3-7 cents per word

• Puzzles-$15.00-$17.50

• Poetry-50¢ per line

• Cartoons-$15.00-$20.00

• R-A-D-A-R pays on acceptance.

• Contributors receive four copies of the issue in which their work appears.

• We purchase first rights and reprint rights.

Materials Accepted for Publication

Fiction-The hero of the story should be a nine or ten-year-old in a situation involving one or more of the following: mystery, animals, sports, adventure, school, travel, relationships (with parents, friends, and others). Stories should have believable plots. They should be wholesome and should teach Christian values. Make prayer, church attendance, and Bible reading a natural part of the story. Brief references to such actions throughout the story will do more than tacking a moral onto the end of the story.

Word length should be 900-1,000 words. Occasionally we use a two-part story of 2,000 words complete length. Please allow 3-4 weeks for consideration of submissions not written for a specific topic. Allow 1-2 weeks after the due date for consideration of materials submitted for a specific theme. (The due date is on the quarterly theme list.)

Nonfiction-We purchase articles of 400-500 words on hobbies, animals, nature, life in other lands, sports, science, etc. Articles should have a religious emphasis. Document your articles with the sources that you have used. Please allow 1-2 weeks after the due date for consideration of nonfiction submissions. (The due date is on the quarterly theme list.)

Puzzles-Our puzzles correlate with the quarterly theme list or with holidays and special occasions. Some types of puzzles we use are: word searches, acrostics, crosswords, fill-in-the-blanks, matching. Our official translation for puzzles is the *New International Version* of the Bible. Answers to all puzzles should be given. Puzzles should be challenging, but not too difficult, and they should not be longer than one printed page of R-A-D-A-R.

Cartoons

• Appeal to 8-10 year old children

• May or may not correlate with themes.

Poetry

• Biblical, or about nature
• May or may not correlate with themes.

Final Thoughts

Keep in mind that children today are different from the way they were when you were a child. Get to know children before you begin to write for them. Many manuscripts are returned simply because the plot or vocabulary is outdated for modern children.

Before you submit, get to know R-A-D-A-R. Sample issues are available on request (enclose SASE, please).

We are always looking for great ideas and fresh manuscripts. We hope to see your work soon!

Categories: Fiction—Nonfiction—Adventure—Animals—Cartoons—Children—Christian Interests—Inspirational—Short Stories

Name: Elaina Meyers, Editor
Material: All
Address: 8121 HAMILTON AVE
City/State/ZIP: CINCINNATI OH 45231

Radiance
The Magazine for Large Women

RADIANCE: The Magazine for Large Women, is a quarterly magazine now celebrating our second decade in print with more than 50,000 readers worldwide. Our target audience is the one woman in four who wears a size 16 or over-an estimated 30 million women in the United States alone.

RADIANCE brings a fresh, vital new voice to women all sizes of large with our positive images, profiles of dynamic large women from all walks of life, and our compelling articles on health, media, fashion and politics. We encourage women to feel good about themselves now-whatever their body size or shape. RADIANCE, one of the leading resources in the "Size Acceptance Movement," links large women to the network of products, services, and information just for them. RADIANCE documents and celebrates womens' growing body acceptance in the '90's.

DEPARTMENTS

Up Front & Personal Interviews or first-person accounts of women all sizes of large. We like strong, intimate, in-depth profiles about a person's life and philosophy.

Health & Well-Being Articles on health, fitness, and emotional well-being related to women in general and large women in particular. Also, profiles of healthcare professionals who are sensitive to size issues. Articles on "obesity" research.

Perspectives Cultural, historical, and social views on body size and female beauty.

Expressions Interviews with artists who are large themselves, or whose work features ample-bodied women.

Getaways Articles on vacation spots and world travel. Prefer if article includes ideas or tips for women of size.

On the Move Articles about large women and sports-physical activities of all kinds. Fitness video reviews.

Images Interviews with designers or manufacturers of large and supersize clothing and accessories. Also welcome-articles on color, style, wardrobe planning.

Children and Young Adults Articles on issues around children, weight, and self-esteem.

Book Reviews Books relating to women, body image, health, spirituality, eating and food, cooking, career, psychology, politics, media, fashion, cultural attitudes, self-esteem, travel, hobbies, leisure activities.

Short Stories & Poetry Stories and poetry on body image, relationships, health, well-being, food and eating, work, politics, fashion, cultural attitudes, spirituality, self-esteem, and accep-tance.

Home, Cooking, Gardening, Dining Out Articles on any of these.

Women and Mid-Life, Aging Articles on all important passages in a woman's life.

DEADLINES

Winter: June 15; Spring: September 15; Summer: December 15; Fall: March 15

We recommend that you read at least one issue of RADIANCE prior to writing for us. A sample copy for writers costs $3.50. Query us far in advance of the deadline if you want assurance that you article(s) will be considered for a particular issue. Our usual response time is about three to five months. We have a small staff and are committed to reading each submission carefully. Include your name, address and phone number and e-mail address (if you have one) on the title page and type your name and page number on subsequent pages. Be sure to enclose a SASE for a response and returned materials. Remember to indicate availability of photos, artwork or illustrations (or ideas for them) in your query or with your article. Pertinent, high quality photos or art can greatly enhance an article's desirability. If you do send photos, please make sure that they are marked with a caption and the photographer's name, phone number and address.

PAYMENT

At this time, payment is made on publication. As we grow, we will increase payment to writers, photographers and illustrators. We appreciate and value your interest in contributing to RADIANCE.

Book Reviews: $35+
Features: $50-$100
Short Stories: $20-$50
Poetry: $10-$15

Once we develop a good working relationship with the writer, artist or photographer and we can count on your professionalism, service, quality and reliability, and as our circulation grows, payment can increase. We will always send the contributor a copy of the magazine she/he is in. The contributor needs to send us an invoice after the work is completed with details of the service.

EDITORIAL STAFF

Alice Ansfield—Publisher/Editor
Catherine Taylor—Senior Editor
Katherine L. Kaiser—Copy Editor/Proofreader
Pam Polvi—Editorial Assistant
Mary Hower—Poetry Consultant

Categories: Fiction—Nonfiction—Adventure—African-American—Arts—Biography—Business—Careers—Cartoons—Children—Consumer—Cooking—Crafts—Culture—Dance—Diet—Disabilities—Education—Entertainment—Environment—Erotica—Ethnic—Family—Fashion—Feminism—Film/Video—Food/Drink—Gardening—Gay/Lesbian—General Interest—Health—History—Hobbies—Human—Inspirational—Internet—Lifestyles—Literature—Marriage—Multicultural—New Age—Parenting—Philosophy—Physical Fitness—Poetry—Politics—Psychology—Recreation—Reference—Relationships—Romance—Sexuality—Short Stories—Society—Spiritual—Sports—Television/Radio—Theatre—Women's Fiction—Women's Issues—Writing—Young Adult

Name: Alice Ansfield, Publisher
Material: All
Address: PO BOX 30246
City/State/ZIP: OAKLAND CA 94604
Telephone: 510-482-0680
Fax: 510-482-0680
E-mail: Radmag2@aol.com
Internet: www.radiancemagazine.com

Radio World

Why should I contribute to *Radio World*?

Radio World is the U.S. radio industry's best read newspaper, with almost 19,000 readers. Our readers are the people who own, manage and operate FM and AM radio stations, as well as the suppliers and other organizations that serve this audience. These readers are radio professionals: engineers, general managers, owners, production people, news reporters, show hosts, educators and more. We have a technical pedigree but have evolved into a publication covering a broad range of news and feature topics.

Your article will reach a nationwide audience of important radio people. Exposure in *Radio World* can increase your stature in the industry and help you build a valuable network in our business. In addition to the satisfaction they feel in taking part in this forum, many of our contributors benefit professionally from the exposure that their articles give them.

What topics does *Radio World* seek?

Our readers want to know about radio in the United States: how to use new technology, how to keep or find a job, what the latest management trends are. We write about books, education, industry news, public radio, the Internet and more. You can help them by bringing your expertise on a given topic to an article, or by writing about other people involved in these trends. Our sister publication, **Radio World International**, pursues a similar mission abroad.

RW is divided into several sections: *News, Features, Running Radio, Studio Sessions, Buyers Guide.*

News: Goal: to provide news and in-depth analysis. **RW** news articles are more in-depth than those found in other trade publications, many of which are not devoted strictly to radio. **RW** articles also address the important technical side of these issues, which is lacking in other trades. This section includes breaking industry developments, regulation, important technology, convention coverage, obituaries, format trends. The news section also contains Readers Forum letters to the editor and longer Guest Commentaries from industry figures.

Features: Goal: to provide a broad range of general-interest articles, including technical how-to tips, personality interviews, history of radio, unusual new programming, ideas on finding or keeping a job, product news, humor.

Running Radio: Goal: to help the radio manager understand our medium and make his or her station more profitable or successful at meeting its mission. Station promotional ideas, radio business trends, station profiles, advertiser profiles, station services.

Studio Sessions: Goal: to provide a resource for studio production personnel. Product reviews, how-to articles, profiles of successful production people and voice-over talent, humor.

Buyers Guide: Feature articles about technology trends in a given category, plus news of recent product introductions. Goal: to assist equipment buyers in making their decisions. Every other issue of **RW** contains a Buyers Guide category (e.g., Microphones, FM Transmitters, Live Assist and Automation).

• Your editor will specify the target story length (usually between 600 and 1,200 words).

• On questions of style, refer to the Associated Press Stylebook and Libel Manual published by The Associated Press, 50 Rockefeller Plaza, New York, N.Y. 10020. From time to time, **RW** will provide a list of industry-specific style points to complement the AP Stylebook.

• We prefer hard copy and photographs to be mailed so that they reach us by the deadline. If possible, please send a 3½" disk with the story saved as an ASCII file. We work in Microsoft WORD 6.0 for Windows; if you happen to be compatible, please save the file in that format.

• Text can also be sent to us via e-mail.

• Or you can fax the article to the attention of Radio World.

• Although headlines are frequently reworked to comply with our format and to fit the allotted space, please give your article a title.

• Include your name as you want it to appear in the byline. Include your title, address and phone number.

• RW often includes a brief bio at the end of stories, usually a sentence or two. ("The author is a freelance writer and former production manager for Smith Broadcasting. Reach her at (703) 998-7600 or via e-mail at carrot@aol.com.") Please let us know whether we can print your phone number for use by our readers.

Should I submit photographs? In what format?

• You are responsible for providing artwork to illustrate your articles. Please do not overlook this important part of your story. Visual elements help pull the reader into your story and make it more informative.

• Artwork can be a picture of a piece of equipment, a studio snapshot, a "headshot" photo of your subject, company logos, a copy of the book you are reviewing, charts and graphs, or any other visually interesting art that pertains to the story. Use your imagination! No one knows the topic like you do.

• We can accept a print, slide or electronic file of the image. **RW** publishes images in both color and black-and-white.

• If you wish to have artwork returned to you, please include a note to that effect with your article.

• Most **RW** writers find that they can obtain artwork for their stories at no cost. For example, if you are writing about AM antenna monitors, call one or two manufacturers of such equipment and request photos to illustrate your story. Most will be happy to oblige you and will ask only that you include a photo credit. If you are writing about a radio station group owner, ask for a headshot of the company president, a photo of their headquarters, a studio picture, a logo, a copy of the company's annual report, or any goofy photos from recent station events.

• If you expect to incur expenses related to artwork (for instance, if you plan to shoot your own pictures), please call your editor first to make arrangements.

• Call your editor with any questions. We would rather hear from you ahead of time, than discover later that we and you had different expectations about your article.

• Each section of our newspaper has its own demands and guidelines. If you are uncertain where your article would appear and would like help in targeting your article, don't hesitate to call your editor.

Thanks for writing for *Radio World*!

Categories: Engineering—Internet—Television/Radio

Name: Paul McLane, Managing Editor
Material: All
Address: PO BOX 1214
City/State/ZIP: FALLS CHURCH VA 22041
Telephone: 703-998-7600
Fax: 703-820-3245
E-mail: 74103.2435@compuserve.com

Rag Mag

Theme issues are filled and will be over with when Volume 15 #1 and 2 are published. Vol. 14 #1 and 2 are still available, the best issues yet according to readers. Talk your library or your local bookstore into subscribing or buying an issue—especially if you are in it. Give your librarian a flyer and show them your copy.

RAG MAG welcomes your poetry, prose, book reviews, plays, essays and art (photos, drawings, etc.) Include a post card for reply and I'll recycle your manuscript.

Poetry: Up to 8 pages of your best work. Please proofread

carefully before submitting. Poetry will be published as is. Name and address, title on each page. Indicate stanza breaks when continuing to next page.

Prose: No more than three submissions per issue. Please include publishing information and cost of book with reviews. Prose may be edited lightly for punctuation, spelling, clarity & length. Reviews must include samples of the work and as little display of the reviewers vast knowledge as possible.

Art Work: Up to 8 pieces. No originals. Camera-ready, not larger than 6"x9" unless you think it is cover material. B&W photo copies are usually used. Originals will be asked for when needed. I do not solicit or keep files of artwork (or writing) beyond the next issue.

All Manuscripts: Include a brief bio. Previously published works and simultaneous submissions are acceptable but please acknowledge both. All rights return to artist upon publication: first printing copyrights apply. Pays in copies (usually 1) on publication. **Not considering chapbooks or book-length manuscripts at all.**

Remember: RAG MAG, which is 112 pages, is published only twice a year (April and October, if I'm diligent and solvent) so number of poems, photos, etc. that can be used is limited. **RAG MAG** does not solicit but simply chooses from what comes in the mail from a formal submission. Files are not kept beyond what is needed for the next issue. Please limit submissions to once per issue. *Submissions will not be read during June, July and August*. All submissions will be returned unread during those months.

Marketing: most is done by mail. Not available in many bookstores. The best way to get a feel for it is to read an issue. $6 one issue-$10 for 2-issue subscription.

If this all sounds too complicated, just send up to 8 pages of your best work. Any and all materials eagerly read.

ANTHOLOGY

I am also looking for poems about HAIR-if that doesn't sound too strange-but hair. No rules, etc. Just good writing about hair. To print in 1999. Send to HMR, Box 12, Goodhue, MN 55027 with stamped, self-addressed post card. No manuscripts returned. Will notify on postcard and recycle submissions.

NOTE: Because of the great response to the Families issue, I am reading as it comes in. Due to financial conditions at the moment (taxes and all that), wanting to get my desk cleared (which will take through 1998), and also wanting to reclaim my life, I am cutting back, regrouping, so to speak. Until I get it sorted out, I am planning no more **RAG MAGs** beyond the Families issue, hence, I will be accepting no materials for the magazine in 1998. I will return everything that comes.

Thank you for your writing and support over the years.

Categories: Art—Literature—Photography—Poetry

Name: Submissions Editor
Material: All
Address: PO BOX 12
City/State/ZIP: GOODHUE MN 55027
Telephone: 612-923-4590

The Ragged Edge

1. Please do read the magazine before submitting material.

2. We prefer that all work submitted be typed, double-spaced if fiction, letter quality printer or typewriter.

3. We are seeking quality fiction and poetry about disability experiences by disabled and non-disabled writers. While we are open in terms of style and approach, we are not particularly drawn to sentimentalized accounts, "plucky cripples," or a story where the focus is a non-disabled person's realization that we are not sub-human.

4. We make every effort to respond very promptly to submissions. We ask, therefore, that you not simultaneously submit work under consideration by us. However, if six weeks have passed since sending your work, you may feel free to send it elsewhere.

Categories: Disabilities

Name: Mary Johnson, Editor
Material: General
Name: Anne Finger, Poetry/Fiction Editor
Material: Poetry and Fiction
Address: PO BOX 15
City/State/ZIP: LOUISVILLE KY 40201

Rail Classics

EDITORIAL POLICY

RAIL CLASSICS is edited to inform and entertain people who have an interest in trains. With extensive photographic coverage, RAIL CLASSICS describes railroading—equipment and operations, steam and diesel, passenger and freight, current and historical. Primary coverage is North America.

TYPE OF MATERIAL

Prospective contributors should read one or more back issues to understand our editorial style and scope. The Editorial Policy, above, outlines the type of material desired. Within these policy constraints, contributors are encouraged to be original, inventive, and stimulating. We want new ideas, rather than old material redecorated. Typical article length is 500 to 1,500 words, but articles may be longer or shorter.

MANUSCRIPTS

Each article should have a title sheet with your suggested title and subtitle typed about 1/3 of the page down from the top, followed by your by-line as you want it to appear. (For example, are you J.D., James, or Jim?)

COMPUTER DISK. It is recommended that manuscripts be submitted on an IBM compatible floppy disc, either 5¼" or 3½". When saving a file to disc for submittal to *Rail Classics*, use Save As (or equivalent in you particular word processor) and select Text.

Each of the many different computer word processors saves with its own set of unique codes. These codes are not useful to us and confuse our typesetters. We may not be able to read your file at all. Therefore, save your file as Text, sometimes called ASCII. A copy of the printed manuscript should be included in case of difficulty in reading the computer disc.

E-MAIL. Manuscripts may be sent in the body of e-mail messages. Do *not* send the manuscript as an attachment.

PAPER. If manuscript is typed on paper, it should have pages numbered and your name, address and phone number on the first page. Do not capitalize all letters or use script type.

When preparing a manuscript, it is more important to leave a clear record than to try to cover up the fact that a mistake was made. Corrections by erasure, correction liquid, or strikeover are often hard to read. It is desirable to retype pages with many corrections.

PHOTO CUTLINES (CAPTIONS)

If you are supplying prints, the identification of subject, date, and other data to be used in the cutline should be on the back of the print along with your name and address. It is usually easiest to type the information on a sheet of paper, then cut it to a size smaller than the print, and tape it to the back of the print.

Use of a rubber stamp or felt marker on the back of prints is *not* recommended unless you obtain special ink that will dry on photographic RC paper. One pen brand which does work is the "Sharpie" marker. In any event, be sure the ink is dry before you handle or stack the prints. It is usually best to stack prints face-to-face so that any wet ink will smudge only the back of the adjacent print.

If you are supplying color slides, write your name and address and a key number on the mount of each slide. If the slides are mounted in plastic, a "Sharpie" marker works best. Type the caption material for the slides on a separate sheet of paper using the key numbers for identification.

PHOTOGRAPHS

Color slides can be published in either color or black and white. Slides are better than color prints for color reproduction. The process for color publication requires that the slide be removed from the mount, but the slide is otherwise unharmed and can be remounted if desired. If you prefer to send prints, be sure they are sharp. Larger sizes such as 8"x10" are better than small. Glossy finish is best.

SUBMITTAL

All material is submitted at the sender's risk. Acceptable material will be held until used and will not be returned unless requested by sender. Unacceptable and excess material will be returned only if accompanied by a suitable return envelope and sufficient postage.

ORIGINALITY

All submitted material must be the original work of the sender or must include permission of the originator.

PAYMENT

Editorial material in RAIL CLASSICS is contributed without remuneration by rail enthusiasts who write the articles and take the photos as part of their enjoyment of the hobby.

WHAT MAKES THE EDITOR SMILE

What the editor likes best is a package with a computer disc and/or three to 12 pages of double-spaced text and five to 30 prints or slides, including two to four in vertical format for possible use on the cover.

He hopes your submittal contains an interesting, imaginative article with new approaches to the subject of trains.

QUERIES/QUESTIONS

Please write to the editor if you have any questions or wish to query on a specific idea.

Categories: Travel

Name: Submissions Editor
Material: All
Address: 7950 DEERING AVE
City/State/ZIP: CANOGA PARK CA 91304
Telephone: 818-887-0550 ext. 110
Fax: 818-884-1343
E-mail: mail@challengeweb.com
Internet: www.challengeweb.com

Ranger Rick

Subject Selection: Our audience ranges from ages six to twelve, though we aim the reading level of most materials at nine-year-olds or fourth graders.

Fiction and non-fiction articles may be written on any aspect of wildlife, nature, outdoor adventure and discovery, domestic animals with a "wild" connection (such as domestic pigs and wild boars), science, conservation, or related subjects. To find out what subjects have been covered recently, consult our annual indexes or the Children's Magazine Guide. These are available in many libraries.

The National Wildlife Federation (NWF) discourages the keeping of wildlife as pets, so the keeping of such pets should not be featured in your copy. We also do not accept pieces on wildlife rehabilitation, except for the rehabilitation of threatened or endangered species.

Except in rare cases, human qualities are attributed to animals only in our regular feature, "Adventures of Ranger Rick,"

which is staff written.

Avoid the stereotyping of any group. For instance, girls can enjoy nature and the outdoors as much as boys can, and mothers can be just as knowledgeable as fathers. Stories should reflect the ethnic and cultural diversity of our society.

The only way you can write successfully for *Ranger Rick* is to know the kinds of subjects and approaches we like. And the only way you can do that is to read the magazine. Recent issues can be found in most libraries or are available from our office. To obtain a copy from our office, please send $2.15 plus a 9x12 self-addressed, stamped envelope.

Submitting Materials: Send a query describing your intended subject, along with a lead or sample paragraph. Any special qualifications you may have to write on that subject would be worth mentioning If you are not an expert on the subject, please list your main references and names of experts you will contact, Please do not query by phone or fax. Include a self-addressed, stamped envelope with all queries.

Unless you are an expert in the field you are covering, or unless your information is clearly anecdotal or from personal experience, all facts within your copy must be supported by up-to-date, authoritative references.

New Policy: An index number must follow each fact and must refer to a footnote listed on a separate sheet. (See example below) Any manuscript not footnoted in this manner may be rejected and any agreement on a kill fee may be cancelled.

We strongly recommend that you consult with experts in the field when developing material and that one of them read the finished manuscript for accuracy before you submit it.

Footnoting Style: ...the spitting cobra rears up and sprays venom into the [6] face of any intruder...

(Separate sheet)

6. Living Snakes of the World, by J.M. Mehrtens (Sterling Press, 1987), page 254.

All submissions are made on speculation unless other arrangements have been made. Manuscripts are considered carefully and will be returned or accepted within one to two months. Our planning schedule is 10 months prior to cover date. Please do not submit your manuscript to other magazines simultaneously.

Except for letters on our "Dear Ranger Rick" pages, we do not publish material written directly by children. Articles with children's bylines have in fact been written "as told to" an adult, by an adult.

Payments: Payments range up to $575 for a Full-length feature (about 900 words), depending on quality of writing and research.

Upon acceptance of a manuscript, a transfer of rights form will be sent to you. NWF purchases exclusive first-time worldwide rights and non-exclusive worldwide rights thereafter. Payment checks will be processed after we receive the signed transfer of rights form. (To receive a sample form send a self-addressed, stamped envelope.) It is not necessary that illustrations or photographs accompany your materials. If we do use photographs you've included with your copy, these will be paid for separately at current market rates.

The NWF can take no responsibility for unsolicited submissions. However, we make every effort to return such materials if accompanied by a self-addressed, stamped envelope.

Guidelines—Addendum:

Fiction: Science fiction, mystery, fantasy, straight-forward fiction, plays, and fables (but no myths, please). Particularly interested in stories with minority or multicultural characters and stories that don't take place in the suburbs. Present-day stories need to be about today's kids (with working and/or single parents, day care, etc.). Stories must treat children respectfully (no wise old grandfather teaches dumb kid, please). All nature and environmental subjects OK, but no anthropomorphizing of wildlife. We publish fiction about four times per year; plays or fables every two years. About 900 words maximum.

Poetry: We are currently overloaded with poetry and not accepting new submissions.

Puzzles: No word searches, instantly visible dot-to-dots, or crossword puzzles. A puzzle should be nature-related, challenging, fun, creative, unlike schoolwork, and something an 8- to 10-year-old can finish without help. It should also offer the possibility of an attractive illustration. Please cite your source for each fact in the puzzle, unless the fact is very well known. Sending a photocopy of the source is especially helpful. We buy one or two freelance puzzles a year, but would like to buy more with fresh ideas.

Riddles: We aren't buying any these days. We're asking readers to send in their favorites and may occasionally get permission from a publisher to use a group of riddles from a book.

Categories: Fiction—Nonfiction—Animals—Children—Conservation—Crafts—Environment—Games—Hobbies—Multicultural—Mystery—Outdoors—Science—Science Fiction—Nature—Fantasy—Plays—How-to

Name: The Editors
Material: All
Address: 8925 Leesburg Pike
City/State/ZIP: Leesburg, VA 22184-0001
Internet: www.nwf.org/rrick/

Reader's Digest

Reader's Digest, headquartered in Pleasantville, N.Y., 45 minutes north of Manhattan, has been published monthly since February 1922. From that first issue, founders DeWitt Wallace and Lila Acheson Wallace built a mass-interest magazine that is now bought by more than 16 million people in the United States and nearly 31 million around the world—reaching 100 million readers every month.

What is the market for original material at *The Digest*? Roughly half the 30-odd articles we publish every month are reprinted from magazines, newspapers, books and other sources. The remaining 15 or so articles are original—most of them assigned, some submitted on speculation. While many of these are written by regular contributors—on salary or on contract—we're always looking for new talent and for offbeat subjects that help give our magazine variety, freshness and originality. Payment, on acceptance, is $3,000, plus reasonable expenses. For a "Drama in Real Life" or "Unforgettable Character," we pay $3,500. This rate covers all world-wide periodical rights—including condensation, adaptation, compilation and anthology rights—for all forms of print and electronic publishing media. *Reader's Digest* also reserves the right of first refusal on all remaining rights. For assigned articles that don't work out, our kill fee is $500. There's one other important market: fillers and short department items. We pay up to $400 for true, unpublished stories used in our departments; for original material that runs as a filler, we pay $30 per *Reader's Digest*, two-column line, with a minimum payment of $50. To the first contributor of an item we use from TV, radio or a published source, we pay $35. For more on this market, check the front of the magazine, where we solicit reader contributions each month.

How should an original article be proposed to *The Digest*? Don't send us unsolicited manuscripts. We no longer read them. Just send a letter to *The Digest*, briefly describing the article you'd like to do and, if you're new to us, listing your writing credits. If the idea sounds right for us, we'll check our article index, our assignment list and our inventory of original and reprint material for overlaps. If there are none, we'll ask to see a manuscript on speculation, or, if the idea is assignable, we'll request a

detailed outline—not a formal A-B-C outline, but a structured, reasonably polished piece of writing that sells not only the article but also you-the-writer and what you bring to your subject. In three or four double-spaced pages, give us a lead that could sit on top of your finished article, and show us where you plan to go from there. Above all, we want a sharp, crisp focus and viewpoint. Here is how Patricia Skalka opened a proposal about a flood that threatened Fort Wayne, Ind., and how Fort Wayne's children helped save the city:

"I can't feel my fingers anymore," the young girl sobbed. "Don't stop. Don't stop," the others cried. With hands bloody, backs sore and eyes bloodshot from exhaustion, they continued to pass bag after bag of heavy sand down the line. Nearby someone told a joke. In the distance, a rhythmic chant began. The lines of volunteers knew the words from days of marching with schools bands to victory, from evenings spent sitting around Scout camp fires. "One-two. Sound off. Three-four. Once more . . . ." Now in the eerie dark, rain-soaked from head to foot and mired ankle-deep in mud, they joined the chant.

Along a 32-mile network of water-logged earthen dams, they sang. They sang to keep going, to keep the sand bags moving. They sang for themselves, for their city. They sang to protect the lives and homes of total strangers. They sang because it is the nature of youth to face danger with bravado, innocence and good spirit. They sang to win one of the country's most awesome battles against the forces of nature. This is the story of Fort Wayne, Ind., and last month's "Great Flood," a disaster of such proportions that it literally threatened to destroy the city. Nearly one third of Fort Wayne's populace fought to save the city from the flood waters that poured over the banks of the St. Mary, St. Joseph and Maumee Rivers. Of the estimated 50,000 volunteers who joined in the effort, 30,000 were students. Some were as young as eight years old. Some were in college. Most of them were teenagers. When it was all over, their valor reduced Fort Wayne's mayor to tears and brought them credit for saving the city.

How soon, after assignment, does *The Digest* expect to see a completed manuscript? We seldom set deadlines, because our magazine is geared toward articles of lasting, rather than passing or topical, interest. Such material can usually run anytime. But as a rule, writers deliver two to three months after assignment.

How long should a manuscript run? Only as long as it take to tell your story. The average manuscript length on straight, reportorial journalism is 3,000 to 3,500 words. Some manuscripts run much longer, some shorter. Only after an article is purchased and scheduled do we start thinking about its final length in the magazine. So don't try to write to *The Digest* length—almost certainly, you'd exclude some top-notch material. Leave the condensation to us. This is a meticulous process in which article length is reduced by a third to a half or more—while preserving the style, flavor and integrity of the original manuscript and, more often than not, heightening the effect. The author, of course, reviews the edited version before publication.

How does a writer get his previously published material reprinted in *The Digest*? If your article has appeared in a major American magazine or newspaper, the chances are it's already been considered. In our search for article pickups, fillers and department items, our reading staff screens more than 140 publications each month, along with 2,000 books a year. If in doubt, simply submit tear sheets of your article. For reprinted articles, we pay $1,200 per *Reader's Digest* page for world periodical rights. This is split 50-50 between the original publication and the writer.

What kinds of articles is *The Digest* looking for? The best advice: read and study the magazine. You'll find our subject matter as varied as all human experience. Here are some titles from a single typical issue: "Beirut Under Siege," "Why Our Weather Is Going Wild," "Help Keep Your Teen-Age Driver Alive," "Are

You a Man or a Wimp?", "The Real 'Lessons of Vietnam,'" "The Day Jessica Was Born," "Troubled Waters for Our Coast Guard," "Dancing Ground of the Sun," "Top Secret: Is There Sex in Russia?", "Trapped in a Sunken Ship," "New Ways to Buy and Sell Houses," "From Cuba With Hate: The Crime Wave Castro Sent to America." The common thread that weaves through all these articles is reader involvement. When we deal with major concerns—child abuse, government waste, Mideast tensions, breast cancer—we want a constructive approach that goes beyond the problem itself and points the way toward solution or hope. In the same way, we want profiles that go beyond merely "interesting" or "successful" people; we want to celebrate those who inspire by their example. "Chi Chi Rodriguez: Golf's Ace with Heart" was typical. Here's how Jolee Edmondson opened her article:

It was another tournament town, another cardboard hotel room, another evening spent staring at the too blue, too orange TV images atop the Formica-covered bureau. Juan "Chi Chi" Rodriguez, vying for the lead at the 1967 Texas Open in San Antonio, was practicing putts on the carpet and thinking about the birdies that had got away that afternoon. The drone of the evening news suddenly riveted his attention: a reporter was interviewing a distraught woman whose home in Illinois had been destroyed by a tornado. All she had left were the clothes she had on. Rodriguez was so moved that he made a pact with himself. If he bagged the trophy the following day, he would send the tornado relief fund $5,000. The next day he won—and so did the tornado victims.

A prime article category is the personal happening or awakening. In "Lure of the Winter Beach," Jean George stumbled onto one of nature's many magical surprises and had an experience everyone can readily share and appreciate. She opened her article this way:

After a storm several winters ago, a friend asked me to check on her Long Island beach house. So one bright, windy day I bundled against the cold and drove out to the edge of the Atlantic Ocean. I imagined a dreary scene — an abandoned cottage set among pines, stirred by mournful winds. But the instant I climbed from my car my senses came awake. The air smelled clean as I looked out on a brilliant waterscape. The sea was a violet-blue, the sky turquoise, and the beach, which last summer had sloped gently, was no steep, scooped-out and luminous. Crabs scurried for burros and gulls spiraled down on them, like paper airplanes against the sky. At the water's edge, empty shells that whisper when summer waves turn them now made shrill, whistling sounds.

What does *The Digest* look for in writing? Clarity. Straight, simple sentences in simple, direct language. We also want the writer to show us, through solid example or anecdote—not just tell us—through general statements without anything to back them up. The best writing evokes an emotion and gets the reader to experience what the writer experienced—whether shock, affection, amusement. When he wrote his hard-hitting article on "Auto Theft Turns Pro," Thomas R. Brooks combined fact, viewpoint, emotion and anecdote in a deceptively simple, straightforward lead:

Every 28 seconds, somewhere in the United States, a car is stolen. That's 1.1 million vehicles a year. If your turn is next, chances are you will never get your car back. If you do, it possibly will have been stripped for parts. When Connecticut police showed a West Hartford owner his new Buick Riviera—minus fenders, hood, doors and wheels—he wept.

Above all, in the writing we publish, *The Digest* demands accuracy—down to the smallest detail. Our team of 83 researchers scattered through 19 cities around the world scrutinizes every line of type, checking every fact and examining every opinion. For an average issue, they will check 3,500 facts with 1500 sources. So watch your accuracy. There's nothing worse than having an article fall apart in our research checking because an au-

thor was a little careless with his reporting. We make this commitment routinely, as it guarantees that the millions of readers who believe something simply because they saw it in *Reader's Digest* have not misplaced their trust.

How to Submit Brief Anecdotes to *Reader's Digest:* Have you read—or heard—something interesting or amusing you would like to share? Although *Readers' Digest* does not read unsolicited article-length manuscripts, it welcomes short contributions. Payment is made on publication:

$400 for Life in These United States. Contributions must be true, unpublished stories from your own experience, revealing adult human nature and providing appealing or humorous sidelights on the American scene. Maximum length: 300 words. Address: Life in U.S. Editor.

$400 for true, unpublished stories used in Humor in Uniform (experiences in the armed services), Campus Comedy (life at college), Tales Out of School (highschool anecdotes), and All in a Day's Work (humor on the job). $35 to the first contributor of each item from a published source used in any of these departments. Maximum length: 300 words. Address: Humor in Uniform, Campus Comedy, Tales Out of School or All in a Day's Work Editor.

$50 for an original item for Toward More Picturesque Speech. $35 for the first contributor of a published item. Address: Picturesque Speech Editor.

For items used in Laughter, the Best Medicine, Notes From All Over, Personal Glimpses, Points to Ponder, Quotable Quotes and elsewhere: $35 to the first contributor of an item from print or electronic media; $30 per Reader's Digest two-column line for original material. Original poetry is not solicited. Address: Excerpt Editor.

Original contributions—which become our property upon acceptance and payment by *Reader's Digest*—should be typewritten. Previously published material must have the source's name, date and page number. Please address your submission to the appropriate features editor; for electronic mail, put feature name under Subject. Include your name, address, phone number and date; in e-mail, make this part of your Message.

Contributions Cannot Be Acknowledged or Returned.

Categories: Nonfiction—General Interest—Health—Physical Fitness—Society—Medicine—Humor—Human Interest—Education—Inspirational—Interview—Profiles—Opinion—Personal Experience

Name: (Appropriate Feature) Editor
Material: All
Address: READER'S DIGEST RD.
City/State/ZIP: PLEASANTVILLE, NY 10570-7000
Telephone: 914-238-1000
Fax: 914-238-6390
E-mail: readersdigest@notes.compuserve.com
Internet: www.readersdigest.com

Real People

Dear Friend:
Thank you for expressing an interest in writing for REAL PEOPLE Magazine.

We are interested in queries about articles that deal with men and women of significance.

Here are some tips for writers:

1. Length should be 500-1,500 words maximum unless otherwise requested.

2. We are mainly interested in articles/interviews with celebrities of national prominence (i.e. instantly recognizable personalities from television, film, society pages, some sports, etc.). Pro-

M-R

files of celebrities must be based on personal interviews. As a rule, profiles should be tough, revealing, exciting and entertaining. Please, no secondhand bios from sources already published in books, magazines, etc.

3. Q&A formats are not encouraged. Please check with editors before undertaking such a project.

4. All unsolicited and assigned manuscripts are on speculation only unless prior arrangement is made.

5. We only consider original unpublished material.

6. We do not consider simultaneous submissions.

7. Please, no fiction, poetry or cartoons.

8. Fees range from $100-$300. Payment is on publication.

9. If you own an IBM compatible PC, we would appreciate receiving both a print-out of the manuscript and a 5¼" diskette. Our system prefers WordPerfect 4.2 but can translate most other programs. Please specify.

10. Sample copies of the magazine are available for $4.00 per issue plus postage. Send check or money order to the address below.

Thank you for thinking of us at REAL PEOPLE.

Categories: Film/Video—General Interest—Television/Radio

Name: Submissions Editor
Material: All
Address: 450 SEVENTH AVE
City/State/ZIP: NEW YORK NY 10123
Telephone: 212-244-2351
Fax: 212-244-2367

Recreation News

About 80 percent of the feature articles In *Recreation News* comes from freelance writers or outside contractors. Although we have many fine writers whose work consistently appears on our pages, you can increase your chances of breaking Into the lineup if your story meets certain criteria. We offer the following guidelines to help you tilt the odds in your favor.

Your article must fit the publication. Our target readership is the more than 250,000 federal employees working in the Washington, D.C., metropolitan area. They want to know about relaxing or stimulating-but always interesting-ways to spend their leisure time. Your story must address that need. Most articles we flatly reject are turned down because they have nothing to do with recreation, fail to provide a logical Washington connection, or they offer little of interest to the typical government worker. We strongly suggest you browse several recent issues, if possible. If not, we will be glad to mail you a sample copy if you send to us a self-addressed 9"x12" envelope bearing $1.05 postage.

It's not essential that your story deal with a place or activity near Washington, D.C., but it helps. Most of our features cover subjects within a weekend drive of the capital area. Yes, our readers do travel out of the region, which is why we have a "Great Escape" column, a feature spotlighting more distant locales across the country. But most of our readers' leisure time is spent near home. We therefore don't cover foreign travel, except for an occasional story about Canada, Mexico or nearby islands.

Approach and style. For the most part, *Recreation News* strives for a lively, informal style. That doesn't mean wordiness or endless tangents. It does mean a conversational tone that's lean and brisk. Try to give your article a fresh point of view and, if at all possible, cover some out-of-the-ordinary subject matter. Your article must go beyond the self-serving listing of information doled out by visitors' bureaus, travel agents and PR firms. Work in quotes from visitors to the sites, or the participants in a particular activity, and let them express their thoughts about how they feel about a place or activity. If they happen to be federal employees and/or from around Washington-hooray! And particularly with destination pieces, comments from colorful locals also spice up a story. Remember, you'll catch our eye faster with a piece about a little-known location or activity rather than with one about a subject everyone already knows about. We basically follow the *Associated Press Stylebook* and *Webster's New World Dictionary, Second College Edition.*

If you're planning to submit a piece focusing solely on a favorite resort, hotel, inn, lodge or restaurant...please don't. You'll stand a much better chance of scoring with us by expanding your coverage to a wider scope. It's helpful to give passing mention to lodging and dining facilities available, but only as sidebar material. And remember, no blatant puffery, please.

How long should an article be? *Recreation News* stories are relatively short. Our longest pieces-those featured on our cover-seldom exceed 2,200 words. In addition to "Great Escape," cover stories are culled from our "Pursuits" column (sports or activities around the Washington, D.C. area) or "Weekend Away" destinations within a three-hour drive of Washington, D.C.). The "Weekend Away" and Pursuits" columns should run about 1,300-1,500 words. Stories intended for the "Day Off" column (activities or destinations around the Washington area) should run about 900 words. All stories should be accompanied by a sidebar, or information box, listing pertinent contact information, hours, rates, etc. *Recreation News* does not carry poetry or "reflection" type articles.

Our editorial calendar. We plan and assign articles anywhere from six months to a year in advance, so writers should plan accordingly. In other words, don't wait until the snow falls to query us about a skiing or ice-fishing piece.

Because of an unusually heavy upsurge in unsolicited manuscripts during the past year or so, our editorial cupboard is heavily stocked, particularly with "Great Escape" vacation-site stories outside the Washington area. Some manuscripts have been on hold for more than six months waiting for a spot to open, so be prepared for a wait. Stories aimed at "Day Off," "Pursuits," and "Weekend Away" are currently more in demand.

Acceptance and payment. If we accept your article, we will contact you and send an agreement spelling out your rights and the rights you sell to us. Specific questions you may have about the agreement should be directed to the editor at the address or phone number on the agreement.

Recreation News pays upon publication, with checks being mailed within a day or two of the 15th of the month of publication. Rates vary, depending on length, placement, previous publication and other factors negotiated between the author and the editors. As a general rule, rates range from $50 (reprint) to a ceiling of $300. All articles are submitted on speculation.

Photography. *Recreation News* welcomes photographs that illustrate your story. Photos must be of good quality and composition and should, as a rule of thumb, include people enjoying the location. Black-and-white prints are preferred, however, good sharp color prints and color slides are acceptable. Rates for original photographs are $25 for each published black-and-white print and $120 for a color print or slide used on the cover. We do not pay for photos supplied by PR firms and visitors' bureaus, although they are certainly welcome with your article. A well-written article, accompanied by good photography, has the best chance of being published in *Recreation News*.

Along with snail mail, we welcome queries via e-mail.

Thanks for thinking of *Recreation News*. Good luck on your submissions to us.

Categories: Nonfiction—Adventure—Recreation—Sports—Travel

Name: Rebecca Heaton, Editor
Material: All

Address: PO BOX 32335/CALVERT STATION
City/State/ZIP: WASHINGTON DC 20007-0635
Telephone: 202-965-6960
Fax: 202-965-6964
E-mail: Recreation_News@mcimail.com

Redbook

Redbook is targeted to young married women between 25 and 44 who define themselves as smart, capable and happy with their lives. Each issue is a provocative mix of features geared to entertain and inform them, including:

News stories on contemporary social issues that strike a universal chord and reveal the emotional ramifications

First person essays about dramatic pivotal moments in a woman's life

Marriage articles with an emphasis on strengthening the relationship

Short parenting features on how to deal with universal health and behavioral issues

Reporting exciting trends in women's lives

Writers are advised to read at least the last six issues of the magazine (available in most libraries) to get a better understanding of appropriate subject matter and treatment.

We prefer to see detailed queries, rather than completed manuscripts, and suggest that you provide us with some sources/experts. Please enclose two or more samples of your writing, as well as a stamped, self-addressed envelope.

The *Redbook* Short Story Contest has been discontinued, but we continue to welcome high quality, accessible short stories.

Writer's Guidelines for Fiction: Thank you for your interest in *Redbook*. We publish approximately 15 short stories a year, and we welcome unsolicited short story manuscripts. Our fiction has received such prestigious honors as the National Magazine Award for Fiction and inclusion in *Prize Stories/The O. Henry Awards* and *The Best American Short Stories*.

Redbook's target reader is a woman between the ages of 25 and 45 who is or was married, has children, and generally is employed outside the home. Because she's a bright, well-informed individual with varied interests, she's not solely concerned with fiction that reflects her own life—although most of our stories deal with topics of specific interest to women: relationships, marriage, parenthood, relatives, friendships, career situations, financial problems, and so forth.

All submissions should be typed and double-spaced and accompanied by a self-addressed, stamped envelope. (If you do not send an SASE, you will not hear from us unless we are interested in buying the story.) Our reply time is usually 8 to 10 weeks. We receive approximately thirty-five thousand submissions per year and take every care in handling them, but we cannot be responsible for the receipt or the condition of the manuscript. (In the interest of protecting the original manuscript, you may submit a legible photocopy.)

Redbook publishes short stories 25 manuscript pages or fewer; the average length is 15 pages. Payment for a short story begins at $1,000. *Redbook* buys First North American Serial Rights and pays on acceptance. Most stories are scheduled within a year of purchase, and prior to publication, short story galleys are sent to the author. Please note that we do not consider unsolicited poetry and novels.

Sorry, but we are unable to provide complimentary copies.

Categories: Fiction—Nonfiction—Arts—Biography—Book Reviews—Business—Children—Cooking—Crime—Entertainment—Fashion—Food/Drink—Health—Marriage—Money/Finance—Parenting—Psychology—Sexuality—Society—News—Celebrities—Beauty—Women's Issues

Name: Dawn Raffel, Fiction Editor
Material: Fiction
Name: Andrea Bauman, Health Editor
Material: Health
Name: Pamela Lister, Senior Editor
Material: All except fiction and health
Address: 224 W. 57TH ST.
City/State/ZIP: NEW YORK, NY 10019
Telephone: 212-649-3450
Fax: 212-581-8114

Referee

FOR OVER TWENTY YEARS, THE #1 SOURCE OF OFFICIATING INFORMATION

Referee is the only magazine in the world devoted exclusively to officials of all levels and all sports. As such, we are not interested in stories that often appear in the general sports media. To reach our readers, a story must include the insight and ability to address matters relating to officials—not every writer has that ability.

I suggest you look over the feature articles in the magazine. They are samples of the type of material we must have to grow and prosper. There are many angles available and an unlimited number of story ideas out there—we welcome, in fact cherish, your suggestions.

Most of our features run between 1,500 and 2,500 words. Fees for new authors start around 10 cents per *published* word. All contracted manuscripts are paid within 45 days of receipt of signed contract. Complimentary copies of each issue in which your story appears are provided.

As I said earlier, if you have specific ideas or thoughts, don't be shy about dropping me a line. We rely on freelance contributors and are anxious to develop new working relationships.

Thanks for your interest in *Referee*. I hope I'll hear from you soon...

Sincerely,
Scott Ehret
Editor

Categories: Nonfiction—Sports Officiating

Name: Andrew Greene, Features Editor
Material: All
Address: PO BOX 161
City/State/ZIP: FRANKSVILLE WI 53126
Telephone: 414-632-8855
Fax: 414-632-5460
E-mail: REFMAG@execpc.com

Remediation Management

About Our Audience

Remediation Management's audience is composed of planning, engineering, construction, development, operations, and regulatory professionals employed in activities involving isolation, stabilization, and remediation of contaminated sites. As the audience is made up entirely of working professionals in the field, you should assume a high level of expertise and familiarity with your subject matter.

The bulk of interviews, the preponderance of ascriptions and quotes, as well as the prevailing perspective should belong to di-

M-R

rect participants in remediation activities. If you find yourself writing about non-participants, take another look at the assignment and see if you're headed in the right direction. To paraphrase a naval axiom, "no writer can go far wrong by asking a working professional what he or she thinks... then putting the answer in quotes."

Assignment of Articles

Remediation Management assigns articles to benefit its readership. The initial assignment sheet will specify substantive aspects of the article such as working title, subject, approach, significance, and length. Additionally, administrative aspects such as due date, remuneration, and reimbursements will be detailed at the time of article assignment.

PUBLISHER'S POLICY ON COMPENSATION AND PUBLICATION RIGHTS

1. Author grants to Forester Communications, Inc. all rights for publication in any of its products. All rights to the submitted material are the sole property of Forester Communications, Inc., including copyright to the material as it appears in Forester Communications, Inc. products.

2. Copyright permission for previously printed material is the responsibility of the author. On submission, we assume that such permission, where required, has been granted. (Note: Many of our authors now find that the best way to avoid copyright problems is for them to copyright the materials they present at conferences. Then they can grant permission to any publication they wish.)

3. Agreed-upon remuneration will be due and payable within 30 days of publication. Approved expenses will be reimbursed upon verification of a detailed expense report/phone bill.

4. The writer is in no way considered as an employee of Forester Communications, Inc. The writer is considered a subcontractor and is therefore responsible for all taxes applicable to remuneration where appropriate.

5. Articles that have been published elsewhere or have been submitted concurrently to other publications are generally not acceptable. However, there are exceptions such as foreign publications, conference proceedings, obscure journals, or significantly different exposure which may mitigate our policy. We are striving to have the best possible material and will, therefore, be flexible. Notify us in writing if it has been submitted elsewhere.

How Materials Should Be Prepared for Submission

1. All materials must arrive at Forester Communications' editorial offices no later than close of business on the agreed upon due date. These include:

a. MS-DOS readable diskette (3.5" or 5.25" single or double-density) using any standard PC-compatible word processor formatting (Microsoft Word preferred). Under special circumstances and subject to prior arrangement, the electronic submission may be accomplished by modem or to our Internet address.

b. Graphics materials, properly identified and fully annotated and accompanied by a signed release or other proper authorization for their use. Do not write on the back of a photo with a ballpoint pen or felt tip marker. Instead, type the caption copy on a separate sheet of paper and glue or tape it to the back of the photo, or simply number your photographs and provide a separate sheet with caption copy for each appropriate photo.

High-quality transparencies, slides, or glossy finish B&W or color prints are acceptable, but not photos taken with instant print or similar low image quality cameras.

Drawings, charts, and diagrams must always be accurate and suitable for reproduction. When submitting an article, please include the original artwork or high-quality Photostats of the originals. If color will clarify a drawing's effectiveness, include it on a copy of the original, but do not use

screens, self-adhesive tints, or patterns on originals.

If you have any questions or are in doubt concerning the use of visuals in your article, please contact the editorial department for advice.

c. Appropriately labeled tape recordings of interviews (for legal and accuracy reasons).

2. If an materials are to be returned at the completion of production, they must be accompanied by an addressed, stamped envelope.

3. Forester Communications requires a signed copy of this document (Author's Guidelines) for its files.

4. The invoice for editorial services you've provided must include your social security number or federal [taxpayer] identification number.

General Guidelines

Think like your audience. Put yourself in a remediation professional's boots. What makes this subject important enough that you would take time-out from your busy schedule to stop and read the article? Where's the hook? How best to bait it, cast it, troll it, and sink it? When you've satisfied yourself on those scores, you're ready to write.

Probably you've developed a style that feels comfortable to you, so that's a good starting point. But keep in mind your audience and the subject matter at hand. While a breezy, vernacular approach may work in some cases, you may find it misapplied in presenting highly technical detail. Similarly, a terse, didactic treatment of narrative materials is likely to put your audience to sleep no matter how serious and important the subject matter might be. Use your best judgment, try stating your thoughts aloud and see how they sound, or if you're really in doubt call and discuss the situation with us.

Engage your reader. Leave no doubt in anyone's mind who your audience is and why what you have to say is important. Rivet your full attention on your readers and drag them into the middle of your subject, address them directly and personally. For instance, instead of saying, "sediment can be kept out of the watercourse in a number of ways," you might say, "If you want to keep sediment out of the streambed, here are some things you can do."

Since the audience is composed of working professionals, aim high in your expectations of their knowledge and expertise. While there's no reason to be pedantic or arcane, you should avoid simplifications as well. You have no need to explain or define the things professionals should know. Assume also that your readers know and appreciate superior use of language and grammar, though not to the point that it becomes stilted or contrived.

Don't shy away from technical aspects of your subject.. Make the less educated or less technically proficient readers "reach," but do not "write down" to your readers. If the article is too simple or basic, we can't use it.

If you're profiling a project, provide the audience with the information you'd like to know about someone else's project. As a basic guideline you might consider the following:

1. What was the situation that needed attention?
2. What alternatives did you consider?
3. What did you do?
4. What were the results?
5. What lessons did you learn?

As far as rules are concerned, follow the latest *Chicago Manual of Style*. We have a set of conventions of our own (e.g. NPDES, EPA, SCS, USDA), however, we'll apply them as appropriate leaving you to concentrate on more important matters. Use acronyms where appropriate but only where there will be multiple callouts or (rarely) where the acronym is in such common usage that the frill name might not be familiar to readers. There are some usage matters having to do with dimensions, quantities, and measures we'd like you to observe:

• Primary measures should be English succeeded immediately by their metric equivalents in parentheses: for instance, *in., ft., Cu. ft., gal.,* etc. *(cm, m, l, mg/l,* etc.).

• The numbers *one* through *nine* should be spelled out, but *10* and up should be presented in Arabic numeral form except at the beginning of a sentence.

• When used at the beginning of a sentence, numbers and their accompanying attributes (i.e. inches, percent, degrees) are spelled out, otherwise dimensions, percentages, and degrees should be presented numerically accompanied by the appropriate symbol (4° or 85%).

Identify yourself as a writer on assignment for *Remediation Management* and conduct yourself and the interview in an open, friendly manner. Please refrain from confrontational behavior because of its reflection on the magazine and the questionable service it provides to the informational value at hand.

Think about the article's appearance as you do your interviewing. How might graphics help sell an important point, or what will entice a browser to take the plunge? Get as much graphic material as possible (photos, charts, illustrations, etc.). The more options our art director has, the better.

Verify all titles of those whom you interview as well as the spelling of all names, jurisdictions, companies, equipment, and products if applicable. Please contact people from different geographic regions across the country so it won't be an article about just one specific region (this is a national publication). The majority of your interviews should be with practicing professionals (not manufacturers or suppliers). Do not interview and do not include quotes from public relations firms or their employees. The first quote/reference in any article should be from someone in the trenches.

Please include a cover page indicating the author's (or authors') name, title, affiliation, address, and phone number. State whether or not the material is being sent exclusively to *Remediation Management.*

Categories: Environment

Name: John Trotti, Editor
Material: All
Address: 5638 HOLLISTER AVE STE 301
City/State/ZIP: SANTA BARBARA CA 93117
Telephone: 805-681-1300
Fax: 805-681-1312
E-mail: erosion@ix.netcom.com

Renaissance Magazine

Founded in 1989, Phantom Press publishes *Renaissance Magazine, Next Phase,* a biannual literary magazine, as well as books, including *Illumined Black and Other Adventures* by Mac Tonnies.

Phantom Press accepts unsolicited manuscripts related to the Renaissance and Middle Ages, including but not limited to: historical articles, martial arts, recipes/culinary arts, travel, interviews with artisans, articles on the SCA and related re-enactment groups, etc. Before pursuing any topic, please query first to confirm our need for it.

Average article is approx. 3,000 words in length although longer work will be considered. Sidebar information is also encouraged, as well as graphics, including copyright-free logos, illustrations and photographs. *Renaissance Magazine* takes full North American serial rights on all work accepted.

Those interested in writing for *Renaissance Magazine* on a regular basis as a staff writer must query first, and include a brief bio/resume and sample article. If accepted, a writing contract will be mailed to that individual and this person will be expected to contribute articles on a regular basis.

All submissions should be set up in the standard manuscript format (title, name, address, phone number, approx. word count on title page, and every subsequent page fully numbered). Cover letter should include a brief bio and credits, where you heard of *Renaissance Magazine,* and any other pertinent information. An SASE must be included with your submission to be considered. We encourage writers to e-mail their articles directly, to save on mailing and paper costs. E-mail all queries and submissions to the address below.

Work may receive a written critique and editorial suggestions. All work will be edited to some degree, to match our editorial format. *No one need submit articles who is not willing to have their work edited.* Allow 3-6 weeks for a response.

Although all writers will be notified of acceptance within a few weeks of submission, we cannot guarantee a publication date. However when the article is scheduled for an upcoming issue, we will attempt to notify the writer before publication. We reserve the right to reject previously accepted work at any time and for any reason.

Book Reviews: We accept unsolicited reviews of Renaissance and Medieval-related books, including fiction and nonfiction (500 words max.). Please include the original cover of the book or a GOOD photocopy of the book jacket along with review. Authors of Renaissance and Medieval-related books (fiction or nonfiction) are encouraged to submit a review copy of their book to Kim Guarnaccia, Editor, at the address below.

Editorial Suggestions: We encourage all readers and writer to make suggestions on what kind of articles should be published in *Renaissance Magazine.* To do so, call, write or e-mail Kim Guarnaccia, Editor.

PAYMENT

Payment of $.03 per published word is made upon publication. Two (2) contributor copies will also be given to each contributor, and more copies are available upon request. Direct your queries to Kim Guarnaccia, Editor.

SAMPLE ISSUES

Sample issue: $3.95; 1 year subscription (4 issues) $14; 2 year subscription (8 issues) $25. To order, make checks payable to Phantom Press Publications and mail to the address below. US funds only. Overseas orders, please add an additional $4 per year to order. Back issues are available; please query first for prices.

Categories: History

Name: Kim Guarnaccia, Publisher/Editor
Material: As Above
Name: Isa Rosenbloom, Assistant Editor/Advertising Director
Material: Any
Address: 13 APPLETON RD
City/State/ZIP: NANTUCKET MA 02554
Telephone: 508-325-0411
Fax: 508-325-0056
E-mail: 76603.2224@compuserve.com

Reptile & Amphibian Magazine

Original articles from freelance authors are welcome. *Reptile & Amphibian Magazine* is directed to the devoted, advanced amateur herpetologist. Generally, our readers are college educated and familiar with the basics of herpetology. They enjoy articles on life cycles of various reptiles and amphibians; special behavioral characteristics of common species dealing with reproduction, feeding, adaptation to environmental changes, etc.; interrelationships with other species, including man; and captive care and breeding. Many of our articles are written from an ecological perspective, but we do not actively promote any special causes.

Manuscripts: Feature articles should be about 1,500-2,500 words in length, book reviews approximately 750 words. Submit tables and diagrams if they help clarify text (they must be self-explanatory and neatly presented; our graphics department can convert them to final form for printing). The use of generic names is preferred; a trade name, when necessary, must be verified as complete and accurate (correct spelling, capitalization, and hyphenation). If not well-known, include the full name and address of the manufacturer. *Authors should adopt a journalistic/text-book style, and avoid first-person narratives.* Data given in metric measurements it must be accompanied by English conversions. Submission on disk is encouraged (3.5", any popular word processing format can be translated), and should be accompanied by a hard copy as well.

Editorial Review: Controversial or unfamiliar subjects may be clarified by editorial commentary, and the editor reserves the right to make revisions when appropriate. Likewise, the cropping of photos and illustrations is at the editor's discretion.

Payment: We purchase first-time North American publishing rights, and *pay upon acceptance.* Feature articles are paid $100 each. Book reviews are paid $50 each. Authors receive a byline; authors, photographers, and artists receive credit on the masthead. Complimentary issues are provided to contributors. Purchased articles may be reproduced on *R&A Online* (http://petstation.com/repamp.html).

Before submitting a manuscript, the author is encouraged to query the editor to ensure that the topic chosen has not been covered by another writer. For a sample copy, send $5. To see what articles have been published, an index is available (send a SASE). The U.S. subscription rate is $20 per year (8 issues) or $35 for two years (16 issues).

PHOTOGRAPHER'S GUIDELINES

Submission of Photographs: *Reptile & Amphibian Magazine* publishes approximately 300 photographs per year. About 90% of these are full—color reproductions of 35mm slides submitted by freelance photographers. Each transparency received is examined on a light table. If it is considered to be a likely purchase in the near future (within 6—9 months), or if we have an article in the files in need of such an image, the slide is held on file. All originals we *do not need* are returned to the photographer, or agency, of origin, normally within two weeks. We also accept artwork, medium format transparencies, color prints, black and white prints, and 35mm color or B&W negatives. The above procedure is adapted to accommodate these other formats.

Payment: *Reptile & Amphibian Magazine* pays $25 per color photo or artwork, and $10 per black & white photo or artwork. If photos are included as part of a manuscript, or if they fill an immediate need, payment may be made upon selection. In all other cases, payment is upon publication. Payment is made each time a photo is used (i.e., if a picture, or a part of that picture is used in three issues, the photographer is paid three times). It is not our intention to purchase exclusive or first-time rights to any photograph. Photographers may submit previously published material and likewise sell material to other markets after the originals are returned, even before publication in *Reptile & Amphibian Magazine.* Also, it is not our intention to purchase copyright privileges, which remain with the photographer. Purchased photos may be reproduced on *R&A Online* (http://petstation.com/repamp.html).

Credit & Editorial Review: Controversial or unfamiliar subjects may be qualified by editorial commentary, and the Editor reserves the right to crop photos and illustrations. Photographers and artists are credited on the masthead and also receive complimentary copies of any issue in which their work appears. All species must be identified on the mount with common and scientific name. A clearly worded statement indicating that photos submitted are intended for use in *Reptile & Amphibian Magazine* must accompany all photographs. The photographer may also state any special conditions which affect publication of his/her pictures. A standard permission form (below) is included for this purpose, or photographers may write their own.

WRITER'S & PHOTOGRAPHER'S STATEMENT

I hereby give Ramus Publishing, Inc. and *Reptile & Amphibian Magazine* permission to copy my imprinted and/or copyrighted photographic material for use in *Reptile & Amphibian Magazine* and *R&A Online.* Articles may be reproduced on *R&A Online* as well.

Signed _____

Studio Name _____

Copyright or imprint sample as it appears on photographic material

Categories: Nonfiction—Animals—Biology—Conservation—Ecology—Herpetology—Reference—Science

Name: Erica Ramus, Editor/Publisher
Material: All
Address: 1168 RT 61 HWY S
City/State/ZIP: POTTSVILLE PA 17901
Telephone: 717-622-6050
Fax: 717-622-5858
E-mail: eramus@csrlink.net

Response
A Contemporary Jewish Review

An independent journal of Jewish expression, *Response* is an affiliate of the Jewish Student Press Service, a constituent member of the Committee on Independent Student Initiatives of Hillel: The Foundation for Jewish Campus Life, and a member of the Association of Jewish Libraries and the Council of Literary Magazines and Presses. Financial contributions are tax deductible. Students are encouraged to apply for semester-long and summer internships.

Call for Submissions and Art

Response seeks critical, unconventional material exploring Jewish identity, community, culture, and politics. Essays, artwork, short fiction, photography, interviews, cartoons, and poetry are welcome. Book reviewers should contact us.

Awards: To encourage and recognize excellence in the international Jewish student community, we will award $100 and a four-issue subscription to three top student essayists (graduate or undergraduate). Original thinking and original writing: We're looking for freshness, clarity, and grace—with an edge. Top poets and fiction writers will be nominated for Pushcart Prizes.

Topics that interest us include the "new Jewish cultural studies," Jewish feminism, Jews and American politics, and Jewish perspectives on technology and the digital age.

SUBSCRIPTIONS

In U.S., four issues: Students-$12; Individuals-$20; Institutions-$36. Canadian subscriptions add $2; subscriptions outside of North America add $4. Bulk and long-term discounts available. Students, please include proof of status with subscription order. Available back issues $3 each. Single copies $6.

SUBMISSIONS

Response welcomes articles, letters, fiction, poetry, reviews, artwork, and photography. Student submissions are given priority. Manuscripts sent for consideration should be approximately ten pages. Author's name, address, phone number, and short bio must be included on the first page of each manuscript. Nonfiction may be edited as necessary. Simultaneous submissions acceptable. Decisions take at least eight to ten weeks; accepted articles are published within approximately four to six months of acceptance. Authors should be prepared to forward accepted work on computer disk (IBM or Macintosh formats only; Macintosh Microsoft Word 5.0 and later preferred).

All contributions, correspondence, submissions, books for review, subscription orders, and advertising requests should be sent to the address below. Inquiries may also be made by phone or e-mail. To find us on the World Wide Web or to join our electronic mailing list of events, e-mail us.

Categories: Fiction—Nonfiction—Arts—Cartoons—College—Ethnic—Feminism—Gay/Lesbian—Jewish Interests—Literature—Philosophy—Religion—Sexuality—Society—Women's Issues

Name: David R. Adler, Editor
Material: All
Address: 114 W 26TH ST STE 1004
City/State/ZIP: NEW YORK NY 10001-6812
Telephone: 212-620-0350
E-mail: response@panix.com

Reunions Magazine

Dear Writer:

Thanks for your interest in *Reunions*. The writers' guidelines you requested is enclosed. As you develop your submission, please consider some of these additional suggestions.

Please address our readers

Our readers are people who organize family, class and military reunions; or who are searching for those and other reunions (adoptees and birthparents, lost loves, friends, ancestors).

What our readers want

Our readers want to learn about the details for organizing successful reunions. They want help, suggestions, smashingly fresh new ideas. They also want to be inspired and learn from other reunions. What's special about yours? Where was it and why? Who did you invite and why?

We highlight, delve into and examine ways to be a savvy reunion consumer. Point them in the direction of wonderful places to say, friendly, loving faces that like reunions as much as our readers do.

Ease the challenges they face. Answer questions they've not even figured out yet. Solve problems before they know they have them.

Our readers want ideas about how to get people engaged, involved, enchanted by the idea of being part of a special group—who together grew, played, worshipped, sang, danced, learned, fought, vacationed, gossiped, and enjoyed.

Family reunions—especially—want ways for entertaining kids. Not just theme parks and video games but active play, exploring, involving all generations, grounding them with family, history, pride, strength, and fun.

Titles

Please be a bit more creative than any of the following titles: *Reunion, Reunions, The Reunion, A Reunion, Our Reunion, My Reunion*. In fact anything with any of the foregoing titles is rarely read with eagerness.

Say it with humor, expertise, passion, perseverance, creativity, a fresh approach...

Comments

We appreciate constructive feedback. If you have a complaint, tell us. If you have praise, tell others—though we'd not mind hearing praise too!

INTRODUCTION

The mobility of Americans only intensifies a desire to return to a place or people left behind, to recapture what surely seems to be a simpler time the older we get. Reunions touch everyone. Reunions can be had with families, friends, classmates, associates, buddies, neighbors, survivors. For adult adoptees and their birthparents/families reunions are with persons who have no memory of meeting.

Reunions magazine is primarily for those actively involved with class, family and military reunions or ongoing adoptive or genealogical searches. Our readers refer to *Reunions* for practical ideas about searching and researching, planning, organizing and attending reunions, as well as for good stories.

Read *Reunions* magazine to discover what we like. We welcome your queries.

CONTENT GUIDES

Feature Articles

Features are written mainly by our readers and fall roughly into these categories:

• **How-to articles about organizing reunions, searching and researching** are usually limited in scope, addressing single issues of relevance to any one or many groups of people. Examples include early decisions, how to begin and how to follow through with a plan, how to use city directories in your search, documenting reunions.

• **Personal stories** are inspiring examples to encourage others initiating similar reunions. Articles which elaborate the process of organizing a reunion or search are preferred. We lean heavily toward stories of triumph. Many readers have similar stories to share, so those with a better chance at publication tell of unusual or heartwarming reunions or reveal unique aspects of universal insights. Story topics include adoptees reunited with birthparents, genealogical searches with surprising results, recollections of class, family and military reunions with humorous or poignant narratives, a group of military buddies returning to the scene, attempts at recapturing...

• **Profiles...people, organizations, events** are third-person accounts intended to acquaint readers with available resources—reunion planning services, innovative or new products, adoption organizations and key members, genealogists or family associations. Readers may also wish to write about interesting family members—for example—an influential clan matriarch on whose birthday an annual family reunion is held.

When appropriate, feature articles should include additional sources, including names and addresses of organizations, publication title, author, publisher, etc.

Departments

• **Reviews**

Reunion books, movies, TV programs, computer software or plays are reviewed. We're looking for professional reviewers with a proven level of expertise on the subject. A bio must accompany reviews. Materials with a request for review are welcome.

• **RSVP: Inviting Examples**

We share examples of interesting invitations used for class, family, military, group reunions. Include a sample invitation, its use, distribution and why it was effective.

• **Scrapbook.**

Readers are encouraged to clip and send newspaper and magazine articles about reunions. Sources and dates must be identified. Credit will be given to the first contributor.

• **Photos.**

Photo submissions are encouraged. They can accompany an article or be submitted independently with a caption. All pictures must be clearly identified with name, address, phone number of owner, names of persons in the picture and a signed release giving permission for publication.

• **Hot Spots.**

Tell us about exciting or unusual places to have reunions. You may have a particularly significant city park or room/building ideal for your purposes. Or, perhaps your family went to a resort. Tell us where, how to get there, what's special and why you'd go back.

• **Recipes, cartoons, fillers.**

Anything relating to reunions is welcome. Please provide source.

• **Regular columns**

Columns highlight single issues or current trends in genealogy, adoptive searches, class, family and military reunions. These columns are written by experts such as certified genealogists, independent search consultants or professional reunion planners. Submissions to this section are limited to 1,000 words and have a universal and timeless appeal.

SPECIFICATIONS

For feature articles, send query letter with outline. We will make suggestions and provide direction for you to tailor a story to our needs.

Readable dot matrix copy is acceptable. Indicate if your submission is available on 3.5" disks formatted for either PC or Macintosh. We will request a disk if your submission is accepted.

Replies in 12 to 15-weeks. Possible 12-month delay between acceptance and publication.

Categories: Nonfiction—Family

Name: Submissions Editor
Material: All
Address: PO BOX 11727
City/State/ZIP: MILWAUKEE WI 53211-0727

Rhino

The new editors of RHINO are looking for compelling poetry, short/shorts and *occasional* essays on poetry—all of which manifest the author's passion, originality and artistic conviction. Wisdom, wit, discovery, mystery, and a love affair with language are most welcome.

We are not interested in political or religious lessons or in writing that is superficial or deliberately abstruse.

We encourage regional talent while listening to voices from around the world.

Submit 3-5 poems, short/shorts or essay with SASE. No previously published submissions accepted. Simultaneous submissions are acceptable if we are told of them. We try to report in 3 months.

Sample copies are available at $6 plus $1.24 postage.
Categories: Fiction—Arts—Language—Literature—Poetry—Short Stories—Writing

Name: Alice George, Editor
Name: Deborah Nodler Rosen, Editor
Material: Any
Address: PO BOX 554
City/State/ZIP: WINNETKA IL 60093

Rider Magazine

INTRODUCTION

If you wish to contribute articles and photographs to *Rider Magazine*, here are some guidelines to help you succeed. Whether you're a writing pro or a reader with an idea that you feel would be fun to share, please keep the following in mind:

Rider is written to please the most mature, affluent and discerning readers in motorcycling. They are mostly experienced motorcycle enthusiasts. *Rider* readers are demanding critics; that's why many of the manuscripts we receive are rejected.

The articles we do buy often share the following characteristics:

1. The writer queried us in advance by regular mail (not by telephone or e-mail) to see if we needed or wanted the story.

2. The story was well written and of proper length.

3. The story had sharp, uncluttered photos taken with the proper film-*Rider* does not buy stories without photos.

Sound simple? It is if you have good, creative writing skills and the know-how to take sharp, well-composed photographs.

WHY THE IMPERSONAL REJECTION SLIP?

A rejection slip usually says something like, "Thank you for submitting your manuscript. Unfortunately, it does not meet our needs at this time." It means just that. It also means that we really don't have enough time to explain your rejection in a detailed personal letter. It doesn't mean that we didn't bother to read the manuscript or look at the photos. Most important, it doesn't mean that we don't like you, because we do! All manuscripts, even the unsolicited ones, are read by *Rider's* top staffers.

AIM BEFORE YOU SHOOT; QUERY BEFORE YOU WRITE!

It happens all the time. A *Rider* reader takes a great tour or has what he or she thinks is a unique story idea, bangs out a story the size of a small novel, develops the snapshots in worn-out chemicals at the local drugstore and sends the whole disorganized mess off to *Rider*. The package is certain to be rejected.

Your chances will improve if you query *Rider* in advance. Write us a short note explaining your story idea. While your idea may be good, we may have already accepted a similar story in which case we can't buy yours. In any event, it's better to know we're interested before you waste days preparing an article that *Rider* can't buy.

HOW TO SUBMIT MANUSCRIPTS

Rider agrees to review all stories on speculation unless other arrangements are made by the editor.

Stories must be submitted typed so that they are easily read and may be easily edited if they are accepted. Leave a margin of at least three quarters of an inch at the top and bottom of the page, and a right margin of at least 2-plus inches. Put your name, address, telephone number and social security number on the first page. Each page should be numbered, and identified with your name.

If you write on a word processor or computer and can submit a copy of the story on floppy disc along with the printed copy please do so. These days we can convert just about any file type, but it helps us if you save the file as text only (sometimes called ASCII).

Rider does not accept extremely long stories. Even fully developed travel stories should not be longer than 2,500 words, and most merit even less length than that.

HOW TO SUBMIT PHOTOGRAPHS

Rider rarely buys photographs that do not accompany an article and vice versa. All feature stories must be accompanied by 35mm color slides, though *Rider* will accept black-and-white prints for some articles. Good color slide film choices are Kodachrome 64, Fujichrome 50 or 100. Black-and-white photos should be submitted as at least 4"x5" prints of professional quality; best results are achieved with slower films such as Kodak Plus-X Pan. Please don't send us color prints, contact sheets or undeveloped film!

Photos should be properly exposed, neither light and washed-out looking nor so dark that detail is hard to make out. Each photo you send should have your name on it, and be sure to write a descriptive caption of 25 words or less for each photo on a separate sheet, numbered so that it keys to a number on the slide or print. The caption for each photo should tell who or what is in the picture, when (if appropriate, e.g., season, time of day, special event time), where the scene is (region, state, town, highway) and, if appropriate, why the photograph is relevant to the story. Be aware of the five Ws of journalism: who, what, when, where and why.

Protect slides for mailing by inserting them in flat glassine envelopes or transparent plastic slide pages. Protect black-and-white photographs by packing them between two pieces of light cardboard, or sending them in mailers designed to ship prints.

WHAT RIDER DOESN'T BUY

Rider prepares much of its own material. We do not buy road tests, riding impressions, product tests or motorcycle fix-ups, and *Rider's* monthly columns are assigned to our editors.

Rider does not buy improperly prepared materials. We do not accept handwritten manuscripts, single-spaced manuscripts, illegible typing or printing, faded photocopies or manuscripts with no margins, left, right, top or bottom. Handwritten manuscripts have to be returned unread.

Finally *Rider* does not buy general material or travel material that is not specially written for motorcyclists, with the needs and wants of motorcyclists in mind.

WHAT RIDER DOES BUY

FAVORITE RIDES

These are mini travel stories that require the use of a few good color or black-and-white photos, and about 700 to 1,000 words of copy They're a nice genre for *Rider* readers to try because they are short:

Your comments should focus on how the route, place or destination might be of interest to a motorcyclist. Short day trips near your own home are good sources for ideas. Don't forget the photo caption sheet! Payment on publication: $150.

FULL LENGTH TRAVEL FEATURES

This type of story offers a good opportunity for prospective contributors. Invariably the *Rider* travel feature requires the use of spectacular color slide photography and is given considerable emphasis in the magazine. Depending upon the way a travel feature is used and its quality payment (upon publication) varies from $250 to $700.

OTHER TOPICS

Almost anything in the world of motorcycling is fair game for *Rider*, but be sure to query first. Some examples: interesting old motorcycles, unusual museums or events, motorcycle achievers (like Malcolm Forbes, Dudley Perkins), stand-out motorcycle organizations.

DO'S AND DON'TS OF WRITING TRAVEL STORIES

Don't write blow-by-blow diaries filled with minute, personal details. Structure your story with an opening that makes the reader want to read more. Research your story before you write it. Think about what a fellow rider would want to know. Your article should include hotels or campgrounds in the area, key attractions and how to get to them, interesting places to eat or the dates of special regional events. You can get much of this information from state and city tourist bureaus. Make sure that all information is current, and include a map and fact sheet pertinent to your visit.

Stage some of your scenic photos so that they include motorcycles in them, both with and without rider(s). This may require taking a tripod along if you're traveling alone, but people in your bike/scenic photos are an important element.

PAYMENT AND RIGHTS

Payment for all articles and photos is upon publication, and varies from $150 to $700. *Rider* buys first North American serial and one-time publication rights; i.e., the article/photo has never been published elsewhere and is guaranteed exclusively to *Rider*. Please don't send us an article that has been simultaneously submitted to another publication! Finally we reserve the right to edit any material we accept.

Categories: Nonfiction—Adventure—Automobiles—Motorcycles

Name: Submissions Editor
Material: All
Address: 2575 VISTA DEL MAR
City/State/ZIP: VENTURA CA 93001

Rising Star Publishers

ORACLE POETRY & LETTERS and ORACLE STORY & LETTERS are quarterly publications by Rising Star Publishers. Association of African Writers is a subsidiary of Rising Star Publishers. ORACLE POETRY & LETTERS and ORACLE STORY & LETTERS are literary magazines of poems and short stories respectively.

Material submissions to these magazines must be original, well written and unpublished. Neophytes as well as established writers are encouraged to submit materials for editorial evaluation. Poems may be of any form. Well-made short stories are likely to be considered for publication. Scholarly articles and literary refereed articles should conform to the MLA documentation style or the APA documentation style. A sample copy is available for $5.00 plus $1.50 for shipping.

TERMS AND CONDITIONS: Rising Star Publishers will acquire first North American serial rights for any material it publishes.

MEMBERSHIP: Membership to the Association of African Writers is $20.00 (individual) and S30.00 (institution/library) for each magazine annually.

SUBMISSIONS: Members and nonmembers may submit manuscripts for consideration. Manuscripts must include name(s), address(es), and telephone number(s) at the top right-hand corner of each page. Supply on floppy disk in WordPerfect 5.1 format. Short stories to ORACLE STORY & LETTERS must not exceed 20 type—written pages. A SASE (or an international reply coupon) with enough postage to cover return of manuscript or to answer a query must accompany all submissions. Multiple or simultaneous submissions are unacceptable.

Receipt of manuscripts will be acknowledged in 4 to 6 weeks. Manuscripts will be published in 6 months to one year after acceptance. Query is unnecessary.

BENEFITS: Become a member of the Association of African Writers and receive copies of ORACLE POETRY & LETTERS and ORACLE STORY & LETTERS. For nonmembers, copies are available on subscription, $20.00 (individual) and $30.00 (institution/library) for each magazine, annually.

CONTRIBUTOR'S PAYMENT: Any contributor whose work is published gets a copy of that publication.

Categories: Fiction—Adventure—African-American—Biography—Children—Christian Interests—Comedy—Confession—Crime—Culture—Disabilities—Education—Ethnic—General Interest—Government—History—Hobbies—Horror—Humor—Inspirational—Juvenile—Language—Literature—Men's Fiction—Men's issues—Military—Philosophy—Poetry—Politics—Psychology—Public Policy—Romance—Short Stories—Teen—Textbooks—Travel—True Crime—Western—Women's Fiction—Women's Issues—Writing—Young Adult

Name: Obi Harrison Ekwonna, Publisher
Material: All
Address: 2105 AMHERST RD
City/State/ZIP: HYATTSVILLE MD 20783
Telephone: 301-422-2665
Fax: 301-422-2720

Remember: Editors change jobs and publishers change addresses. It is wise to invest in a phone call for the current information before submitting.

RIVER STYX

River Styx

Thank you for your interest in *River Styx*. We currently read submissions from May to November. All manuscripts sent from December to April will be returned unread. *River Styx* is published tri-annually.

As a multicultural journal of poetry, prose and graphic arts, *River Styx* publishes works of both new and established artists significant for their originality, quality, energy and craftsmanship. Please send three to five poems. In addition to poetry, we publish short fiction, essays, and interviews. Prose must be double-spaced and under 35 pages in length. All submissions must include an SASE. We prefer not to read simultaneous submissions but will if a note is enclosed with your work, and if we are notified immediately upon acceptance elsewhere.

Expect three to five months for a decision; do not query us until five months have passed. Please do not send us another manuscript until you hear about the first. We do not reprint previously published material. Translations are welcome if permission has been granted. We cannot be held responsible for delay, loss, or damage.

We invite you to subscribe to *River Styx*. Subscriptions are $20/3 issues, $35/six issues, $48/9 issues, or $7 for a single copy. Send checks to the address below.

Thanks again for considering *River Styx*.

The Editors

Categories: Fiction—Nonfiction—Arts—Essays—Interview—Literature—Multicultural—Poetry—Short Stories

Name: Richard Newman, Editor
Material: All
Address: 3207 WASHINGTON
City/State/ZIP: ST LOUIS MO 63103
Telephone: 314-533-4541

RiverSedge
The University of Texas-Pan American

RiverSedge is published twice yearly by the Journals Division of The University of Texas-Pan American Press, under the direction of Dr. Patricia De La Fuente, for the Department of English, The University of Texas-Pan American, Edinburg, Texas. The contents of the journal do not necessarily represent the viewpoints of the University.

RiverSedge welcomes submissions of art, photography, poetry, short stories and essays. Works may be submitted in either traditional or electronic media, but must be accompanied by postage and packaging if return is desired. Artwork should be reproducible in black and white. Please include telephone number. Payment is in copies. Rights revert to artists and writers.

Submission deadlines: Fall issue, November 15; Spring issue, April 15. Please remember to include a short bio with each submission. Address submissions to the address below or contact the editors by e-mail.

FICTION GUIDELINES

RiverSedge, a journal of arts & literature, seeks quality mainstream literary and experimental fiction, emphasizing that prose which has a regional Southwestern flavor or locale, but not excluding voices from other areas. Characters should be memorable and plots believable within the story's setting and context.

Our audience is educated and largely academic, but we are interested in work that transcends the campus and explores the real world in language and contexts accessible to lay readers.

Because of limited space, stories should not exceed 2,500 words. Payment is two copies upon publication. Short biographical sketch should accompany submission.

Submissions should be accompanied by SASE, or clear instructions not to return. Simultaneous submissions should be identified, although they are not prohibited. Computer disks in Macintosh format preferred.

Notification time is usually within 3 to 4 months, but may be sooner.

POETRY GUIDELINES

RiverSedge seeks quality mainstream literary and experimental poetry, emphasizing regional Southwestern flavor or locale, but not excluding voices from other areas. Any variety is welcomed, although most of the poetry we print is modern free verse. There are really no limitations on themes, topics, or language.

Our audience is educated and largely academic, but we are interested in work that transcends the campus and explores the real world in language and contexts accessible to lay readers. Poetry should be foolishly simple, but divinely insightful.

Because of limited space, poems of 25 or fewer lines are preferable, although longer ones are used on occasion, since quality and interest are more important than length.

Payment is two copies upon publication. Short biographical sketch should accompany submission.

Submissions should be accompanied by SASE, or clear instructions not to return. Simultaneous submissions should be identified, although they are not prohibited.

Notification time is usually within 3 to 4 months, but may be sooner.

Subscriptions: $12.00

Categories: Literature—Poetry—Short Stories

Name: Dr. Patricia De La Fuente, Director
Material: All
Address: THE UNIVERSITY OF TEXAS-PAN AMERICAN
Address: 1201 W UNIVERSITY DR CAS 266
City/State/ZIP: EDINBURG TX 78539
Telephone: 210-381-3638
Fax: 210-381-3697
E-mail: Bookworm@panam.edu

Riverside Quarterly

RQ issues no formal guideline but just asks each would-be contributor to inspect a copy or two of the magazine to see the type of story it prints. Fred Pohl once remarked that his magazine received 2,000 mss. per year that never would have been submitted had the writer bothered to read it—and a similar statement applies to RQ.

Preferred length is under 3,500 words, although longer stories are sometimes accepted. Send mss. directly to the fiction editor, David Rike.

Although RQ is not sold at news-stands you should have no trouble in finding copies, since it is taken by virtually all major American university and public libraries.

Finally, if the editor writes a criticism of your story, try to *learn* something from it: do not waste your time composing a letter saying the editor is "crushing down all rising talent" (a phrase quoted by the late Anthony Boucher) or proving that the editor rejected your story because he is too young, too old, too stupid, or too neurotic.

Categories: Fantasy—Science Fiction

Name: Sheryl Smith, Poetry Editor
Material: Poetry: 515 Saratoba #2, Santa Clara CA 95050
Name: David Rike, Fiction Editor
Material: Fiction: PO BOX 11 Crockett CA 94525
Name: Submissions Editor
Material: All but Fiction and Poetry
Address: PO BOX 12085
City/State/ZIP: SAN ANTONIO TX 78212
Telephone: 210-734-5424

ROCK & ICE

Rock & Ice
America's #1 Climbing Magazine

Rock & Ice covers rock climbing, ice climbing and mountain climbing. It is published six times a year, appearing by the first of January, March, May, July, September and November. Issue line-ups are finalized three to six months before the publication date. Please be aware of this scheduling if you are submitting seasonal material. A guide to a summer rock climbing area, for example, would have to be suggested by February 10 at the latest; it would be due March 10 for inclusion in our July issue.

We encourage you to query us first with your idea. Please include published writing samples with your query, as well as an SASE. Full manuscripts are also considered. In either case, please mention the availability of professional-quality transparencies or prints to illustrate your article.

If the query/manuscript is accepted, we will expect you to provide the work on disk and to carefully fact-check all your material. Please include your name, address, telephone number and social security number on every submission. Please be aware that while email submissions are accepted they must include all of the above-mentioned information, and because of the difficulty in reading long email transmissions, email query submissions are not recommended.

FEATURES

Features run from 1,500 to 5,000 words and generally fall into one of the following categories: profiles; issues; climbing adventure or climbing travel; surveys or guides to foreign and domestic climbing locations; humor, and fiction.

We are looking for profiles of articulate, interesting personalities—cutting-edge climbers, historical figures, or people who have combined climbing with their careers (expedition doctors, climbing rangers) are examples. Profiles should deal with the climber as a whole person—the emphasis should be on his or her climbing, but the personality must be rounded out for a fuller portrait. Quotes from people who know the climber and anecdotes of her or him climbing add an important perspective to profiles.

Issues deal with the more serious side of climbing. In one article, for example, we looked at mountain-guide certification and the politics behind guide concessions in Denali. Issues must be thoroughly researched and fact-checked with extreme care.

We primarily publish **climbing adventure travel** stories. We are looking for one of the following hooks: the place must either be exceptionally unusual or relatively unknown; something of particular interest or drama must have occurred during the trip; a well-known area must be looked at from a special angle (best in-

termediate routes; European sport tour). Climbing travel should be accompanied by top-notch photography and be extremely well-written (first-person, humor and/or drama are always good). Since this is our most competitive category, we are quite choosy.

Humor/Fiction articles are free-form. *Rock & Ice* is known for not shying away from the irreverent or the weird, and we don't plan to change that approach and attitude.

DEPARTMENTS

Except as otherwise indicated, department submissions should be 800 to 2,500 words. Write tightly and don't leave anything out.

Guides: Should be either to areas that have never been covered by guidebooks or to ones that have a number of new routes not previously covered. Please request our separate "Guidelines for Guides" sheet.

Performance: Clear, step-by-step instructions on how to do anything related to climbing, from building an indoor gym to sharpening ice tools.

Body Logic: This section covers anything to do with staying alive and healthy: nutrition, sports medicine, and wilderness first-aid are some examples. All articles must have a climbing angle.

Enviro: How climbing impacts the environment, and how environmental problems can be mitigated or prevented.

Goldline: An historical look at the people, places, climbs and equipment that make up the fabric of our climbing culture.

Rap Station: We're looking for especially eloquent writing for this one-page section. Express a point of view, or just wax lyrical. Please limit your story to 900 words.

Reviews: Critical reviews of new books, videos, or other commercially available art forms that apply to climbing and climbers. 100 to 400 words. Please call first to discuss your review ideas.

Excursions: Meant to inform about destinations, domestic or foreign, providing unique opportunities to climb. Use the same hooks, but keep it at around 1,000 words. Refer to our "Guidelines for Guides," and include compelling photographs.

Field Tests: Post-field experience critical reviews of new products that contribute to climbers' safety, performance and comfort. 100-200 words. Please call first to discuss your ideas.

Classics: These trade routes are *not* found in "50 Classic Climbs," yet they are or could be time-tested must-do's for generations of climbers. Write 900 words covering history and flavor. Refer to our "Guidelines for Guides" for providing beta on pre-trip preparation and travel.

Competitions: Competition reports should be 30~500 words on events of national importance, focusing more on human interest elements that occurred during the comp than on the traditional "and-then-he-lunged-for-the-next-jug" reporting, unless this can be written in a very engaging way. Query (phone or write) before submitting a comp report.

You should receive feedback from us within six to eight weeks of your submission.

Good luck, and thank you for your interest in contributing to *Rock & Ice*.

Categories: Sports—Rock Climbing

Name: DeAnne Musolf Crouch, Editor-in-Chief
Material: All
Address: 603 A S BROADWAY
City/State/ZIP: BOULDER CO 80303
Telephone: 303-499-8410
Fax: 303-499-4131
E-mail: editorial@rockandice.com
Internet: www.rockandice.com

Rockford Review

The Rockford Writers' Guild was formed originally in 1947 and now has over 100 members nationwide. A non-profit, tax-exempt corporation, the Rockford Writers' Guild exists to encourage, develop and nurture writers and good writing of all kinds and to promote the art of writing in the Rockford area.

The Guild provides an environment for writers to develop ideas, improve their craft, and share their writing experiences and marketing techniques. We seek to increase community interest, support and appreciation for the literary arts by providing a forum for discussion, conducting workshops and encouraging local talent.

Three times a year, we publish the *Rockford Review,* which has been praised for the quality of its content and its production values. Its poetry, short stories, essays, art and photography represent the best works submitted from all parts of the world.

The *Rockford Review* is a 50-page literary arts magazine published by the Rockford Writers' Guild each winter, spring, and fall. The spring issue is devoted to Guild members who are invited to publish any one piece of their choice.

Review seeks experimental or traditional poetry of up to 50 lines (shorter works are preferred). Short fiction, essays, and satire are welcome in the 250 to 1,300-word range. We also publish one-acts and other dramatic forms under 10 pages (1,300 words). *Review* prefers genuine or satirical human dilemmas with coping or non-coping outcomes that ring the reader's bell. We are always on the lookout for black and white illustrations and glossy photos in a vertical format.

If your work is accepted, you will receive an invitation to be a guest of honor at a Contributors' Reading & Reception in the spring and a complimentary copy of the *Review.* Your work also will be considered for the $25 Editor's Choice Prizes. We award six prizes each year.

Try us with up to three pieces of your best unpublished work at a time. We read year-round and try to report within six to eight weeks. There is no reading fee. Simultaneous submissions are okay.

Good luck!

Categories: Fiction—Drama—Poetry—Satire

Name: David R. Ross, Editor-in-Chief
Material: All
Address: PO BOX 858
City/State/ZIP: ROCKFORD IL 61105

Rosebud
The Magazine for People Who Enjoy Good Writing

Dear Writer:

Thank you for your interest in *Rosebud.* It's a magazine for people who enjoy good writing. I encourage you to submit material for our upcoming issues. We review material throughout the year.

How the process works:

After you send in your submission you will receive a postcard from *Rosebud* saying we have received it. Your submission will be read by the fiction or poetry editor. This part of the process can take from one to five months depending on the amount of submissions. Be patient and keep in mind three things: 1) all submissions are read by a person making final decisions, 2) it does not matter to Rosebud if a piece is published elsewhere, in fact, we encourage you to submit this work simultaneously to other publications, 3) we read pieces in the order they are received but we are dealing with thousands of submissions per month.

If your work is accepted you will get a phone call from the appropriate editor. If we cannot use it in the next two issues, you will receive a rejection letter. If you have received a postcard but do not hear from us in six months, assume your piece has been rejected.

What you need to keep in mind:

We publish *short* stories, articles, profiles and poetry—the ideal length for prose is 1,200 to 1,800 words. Send one to three of your strongest pieces. We like good storytelling, real emotion and authentic voice. Poetry should have clear imagery. We must sell magazines to stay in business; the departments listed later in these guidelines have proved popular with readers.

Don't worry about labeling your piece for a department—we will do the groupings—but before you send something that doesn't look like it fits within any of these areas, read an issue of the magazine to be sure it will be of interest to our readers. You'll be contacted when your piece is accepted and asked if you have any further revisions.

Rosebud purchases one-time rights for original or previously published pieces; this means you are free to sell that same piece to another publication. *Rosebud* pays $45 plus three extra copies for all pieces that are accepted. Payment is made shortly after publication. At the time of the Anniversary Issue, three awards of $150 are also made for the top three selections of the previous year.

What is important to Rosebud:

We must be able to easily contact you for acceptance by phone, e-mail or regular mail. Fiction and nonfiction submissions must be typed, double spaced; poetry must be typed, single spaced. Place the writer's name at the top of each page. Only send hardcopy; if your piece is accepted be prepared to send an electronic file by e-mail or on disk. We use *The Chicago Manual of Style* and *Webster's Collegiate Dictionary* (10th Edition) as editorial guides. We prefer to respond with an individualized letter (send an SASE for this) and recycle submitted manuscripts. We can only give detailed editorial feedback on pieces we are going to buy. As much as we would like to oblige (and encourage) new writers, our effort has to be directed toward producing a magazine.

Why we're in this together:

Rosebud is distributed nationally (50 states), in Canada and in Europe with subscribers in many other parts of the world. It is available through all major bookstore chains. As writers we're dependent upon magazines which publish our work. And these magazines depend upon us. If we don't buy, read and promote them, they cease to exist. This is particularly true of periodicals like *Rosebud* that are open to submissions from new voices. We are a non-profit organization with no outside affiliation, grants or subsidies. Send in your manuscripts, but also send in your subscription. Let us, together, create a new kind of writing-publishing success.

Sincerely,
John Lehman
Publisher
608-423-9609

***Rosebud* Departments include:**
1. City and Shadow *(urban settings)*
2. Songs of Suburbia (suburban themes)
3. These Green Hills (nature and nostalgia)
4. En Route (any type of travel)
5. Mothers, Daughters, Wives (family relationships)

6. Ulysses' Bow (challenges)
7. Paper, Scissors, Rock (childhood, middle age, old age)
8. The Jeweled Prize (concerning love)
9. Lost and Found (loss and discovery)
10. The Way It Was (the past)
11. Voices in Other Rooms (historic or cultural)
12. Overtime (involving work)
13. Dark Corner (noir)
14. Hooray for Hollywood (show business)
15. Wild Card (humor)
16. I Hear Music (music)
17. Season to Taste (food)
18. WordJazz (wordplay)
19. Apples to Oranges (miscellany, profiles)
20. Frame by Frame (examining a genre)
21. Sneak Preview (excerpts from longer pieces about to be published)

A 1-year subscription (4 issues) is $19; a 2-year subscription (8 issues) is $36 and includes a *Rosebud* coffee mug. Sample copies are $5.95 each, including postage.

For subscriptions, renewals, and sample copies contact:
Bill Lubing, *Rosebud* Circulation Manager
1889 E. Washington Avenue
Madison, WI 53704
608-244-9562
800-786-5669

Categories: Fiction—Nonfiction—Arts—Biography—Consumer—Drama—Erotica—Family—Fantasy—Feminism—General Interest—Humor—Language—Literature—Men's Fiction—Men's issues—Music—Mystery—Native American—New Age—Poetry—Rural America—Science Fiction—Short Stories—Theatre—Women's Fiction—Women's Issues—Writing

Name: Roderick Clark, Editor
Material: Fiction, Articles
Name: John Smelcer, Poetry Editor
Material: Poetry
Address: PO BOX 459
City/State/ZIP: CAMBRIDGE WI 53523
Telephone: 608-423-9609

The Rotarian

EDITORIAL PROFILE

THE ROTARIAN is the official magazine of Rotary International, a nonprofit world fellowship of more than one million business and professional leaders united in the ideal of "Service Above Self"; that is, betterment of business and professional ethics, community life, and international understanding and goodwill. THE ROTARIAN's editorial content reflects these aims.

CIRCULATION

More than 520,000 readers in some 150 countries subscribe to THE ROTARIAN. Therefore, our articles must be of interest to an international audience.

EDITORIAL PURPOSE

The chief aim of THE ROTARIAN is to report Rotary organizational news. Most of this information comes through Rotary channels and is staff-written or edited.

The best field for freelance articles is in the general interest category. These run the gamut from humor pieces and "how-to" stories to articles about such significant concerns as business management, world health, and the environment.

Generally, THE ROTARIAN publishes articles of 1,500 words or less. We look for topical 800-word articles for our *Manager's Memo, Executive Health, Executive Lifestyle, Trends,* and *Earth Diary* columns.

EDITORIAL EMPHASIS

Since THE ROTARIAN's establishment in 1911, the bylines of the likes of Albert Einstein, Thomas Mann, Helen Keller, Winston Churchill, Mahatma Gandhi, Betty Friedan, Luigi Barzini, Bill Moyers, Jacques Cousteau, and Jimmy Carter have appeared in our pages. Most of the work of this international array of authors has covered four major areas which complement Rotary's ideal of service.

1.) **Advancement of international understanding, goodwill, and peace, and discussion of global issues**

The United Nations, European unity, Pan-American relations, international assistance programs, world trade...all are topics THE ROTARIAN covers occasionally, such as "The Land Mine Crisis," by Boutros Boutros-Ghali, and "Global Television," by John M. Dunn. We have devoted the editorial contents of special issues to topics such as AIDS, drug abuse, world literacy, and endangered species.

2.) **Better vocational relationships**

Articles in this category encourage high standards in business and the professions, and explore new ideas in management and business technology. Our award-winning article "Strung Out on the Job" took a hard look at employees who abuse drugs and alcohol at work-and at what employers can do to help those workers. Other features have dealt with career counseling for young people, vocational education for high school dropouts, and business and professional ethics.

3.) **Better community life**

Such articles make readers aware of community concerns and problems and suggest solutions. In "Too Much Trash," THE ROTARIAN examined options for effective waste management, a problem that confronts industrialized and developing nations alike. We also run articles on urban affairs, crime prevention, alternative energy sources, and new educational methods.

4.) **Better human relationships**

Rotary is interested in improving the human condition and in promoting goodwill among all of the world's people. *THE ROTARIAN has presented special issues that focused on me*ntal health, illness, and old age. We tell about institutions that help the physically, mentally, and socially disabled. Since Rotary activities furnish us with a wealth of such material, we have little need for freelance submissions on these subjects. When we do accept freelance articles about community projects, we like them to have some Rotary connection-either with a Rotary club or an individual Rotarian.

Also, culture- and travel-related articles, particularly about the site of annual Rotary conventions, are very popular. General interest articles frequently appear in our pages, such as "Communities of the Mind" (exploring the Internet) and "Crossword Puzzles."

THE ROTARIAN IS NOT INTERESTED IN

• criticism and exposés, or articles with direct political and religious slants (except for ethical discussions). The magazine's rationale, mirroring that of the organization it serves, is one of hope and encouragement.

• articles that are solely "U.S." in subject matter and viewpoint.

• We do not buy fiction or poetry.

PAYMENT TERMS

We pay on acceptance, and our rates depend on the value of the material to us.

PHOTOGRAPHY AND ILLUSTRATIONS

Because photos and artwork accompany our articles, we encourage authors to include photos (slides preferred) with their manuscripts, or indicate sources of good images.

Both black-and-white and color images and illustrations are used in the body of the magazine, while our cover is always four-color. Cover illustrations are either photos or conceptual art, and we are particularly interested in easily identifiable landscapes (This is Japan...This is Brazil...) and lively shots of people.

CONTACT

We prefer written queries, though the editors do consider all submissions. We ask that a self-addressed envelope with adequate return postage accompany all proposals. Please furnish final manuscripts on 3.5" diskettes, preferably in a Word for Windows format.

We look forward to hearing from you.

Categories: General Interest & Rotary News

Name: Submissions Editor
Material: All
Address: 1560 SHERMAN AVE
City/State/ZIP: EVANSTON IL 60201
Telephone: 847-866-3000
E-mail: 75457.3577@compuserve.com

Rugby Magazine

Due to the increasing number of tournaments and our small staff, we have to rely upon you to provide us with an article and photos from your tournament in order for your event to be covered in *Rugby.*

To simplify the process, please limit your report to the following items:

• **TO BEGIN:** List the tournament name, place, date(s) and author of the article.

• **FIRST PARAGRAPH:** State the finalists, who won and what the score was.

• **SECOND PARAGRAPH:** Mention the number of teams, the number of divisions, major sponsors, crowd size, weather, etc.

• **PRELIMINARIES/SEMIFINALS:** List all opponents and match scores for the two finalists.

• **THE FINAL:** Characterize the final, with its flow of play, key scoring plays, and game-winning score, etc. Include the first and last names of all individuals mentioned in the report, and the lineup (including the ref) for both teams in the final.

• **ACKNOWLEDGMENTS:** Give credit to sponsors, officials, organizers and civic organizations/causes involved. Also, mention any facet of the event that furthers the image of rugby (i.e. donations to charities, etc.). Include the contact for next year's event.

• **AVOID:** Horror stories, drinking exploits, overly-clinical injury descriptions, etc.

• **PREPARING YOUR STORY:** If possible, please send your story on a computer disk along with the hard copy. (WordPerfect 5.0 or 4.2 and Microsoft Word 3.0 are the preferred word processing programs, but we can translate from most programs for the IBM or from a text-only file, but you must indicate on the disk what program was used).

• **PHOTOS:** Black-and-white photos are best, but color photos will also reproduce. Good action shots or team photos of the winners are preferred. If possible, please identify all players in the photos (write the captions on the back of the photos).

• **TEAM PHOTOS:** Team photos should be well-organized, i.e. proper/matching uniforms, with the back row's arms folded, the front row on a knee, all eyes forward, etc.

You will find it easier to compile the necessary details if you give the task to someone with no other tournament responsibilities.

Categories: Nonfiction—Rugby Football—Sports

Name: Michael Malone, Managing Editor
Material: All
Address: 2350 BROADWAY
City/State/ZIP: NEW YORK NY 10024
Telephone: 212-787-1160
Fax: 212-595-0934
E-mail: rugbymag@aol.com

Runner's World

Dear Freelance Writer,

We're providing the following information to help you tailor materials for publication in *Runner's World*. It should go without saying that the best way to understand *RW*, and what we're looking for from freelancers, is to read several recent issues of the magazine closely.

In addition, you should understand that most *RW* articles are written by staffers, senior writers or experts (podiatrists, nutritionists, etc.). In other words, it's not easy to be published in *Runner's World*. We don't need and won't publish general articles on the benefits of running, fitness and the like. We may agree with your sentiments and advice but that alone isn't enough to make an article publishable.

Our columns and departments offer the best opportunities for freelancers, in particular: Finish Line, Women's Running and Human Race. It's not necessary to query when contributing to these sections of the magazine; all submissions are on speculation.

Finish Line is our back-of-the-magazine essay. Topics defy descriptions, ranging from humor to life and death. Finish Line is about the running experience and all the variety it brings to our lives. The successful Finish Line essay should strongly identify you as a runner and at the same time relate an experience that other runners can identify with. No fiction. Approximately 750 words. Pays $300 on acceptance. Address all materials to "Finish Line".

Women's Running is an essay page written by and for women. There's no formula for success here, but the best essays tend to describe emotional experiences that have been colored by the writer's running. Pays $300 on acceptance. Address all materials to "Women's Running."

Human Race tells the everyday, inspirational and humorous stories of typical middle-of-the-pack runners. Almost anyone can be a Human Race story so long as you find out something interesting about the person's running or lifestyle. Pay's $50 plus a photo space rate. Photos essential. Address all materials to "Human Race."

Other Departments and Features: Other parts of the magazine are more difficult to break into. An exception is "Warmups" which mixes international running news with human interest stories. If you can send us a unique human interest story from your region, we'll give it serious consideration.

We receive hundreds of first-person stories every year, most from people describing how they ran their first marathon. These are never publishable unless they contain something highly unusual or emotional.

We are always looking for "Adventure Runs" from readers - runs in wild, remote, beautiful and interesting places. These are rarely race stories but more like backtracking/running adventures. Great color slides are crucial.

Photos. Nearly all our photos are taken by professionals. The exception would be the photo that you managed to capture that no one else in the world got, i.e., Madonna running in Central Park, a scenic wilderness photo, a photo of an elephant chasing a runner in India.

We hope the above answers many of your questions.
Happy writing and running.
The Editors
Categories: Nonfiction—Health—Physical Fitness—Sports—Recreation

Name: Claire Kowalchik, Managing Editor
Material: All
Address: 33 E. MINOR ST.
City/State/ZIP: EMMAUS, PA 18098
Telephone: 610-967-5171
Fax: 610-967-7725

RURAL HERITAGE

Rural Heritage

RURAL HERITAGE was established in 1975 as a link with the past, not for nostalgic reasons, but to help preserve a way of life for future generations. Our readers are commonsense country folks who enjoy doing things for themselves. Many of them have always farmed with horses, mules, or oxen; others are returning to the practice for economic and/or environmental reasons. Our editorial policy is guided by the philosophy that the past holds the key to the future.

Subjects: We publish hands-on how-to stories covering the broad spectrum of rural skills and creative problem solving, with emphasis on draft animals used in the field or wood lot. We are especially seeking technical details on specific pieces of horse-drawn equipment, how it was obtained/restored, how much it cost, how it's put together, how it works, problems encountered, and how they were solved. We do not publish religious material or non-relevant political or social topics.

Submission: If you are unknown to us, please either submit your material on speculation or else query (outline what you intend to cover and how you'll handle it) and if possible include clips of three previously published pieces. Be sure you know your subject—our savvy readers are quick to notice errors in terminology, breed identification, and similar details.

Format: We prefer submissions in standard manuscript format, accompanied by a diskette (either size and density) in WordPerfect 5.1 or ASCII. Please include a two or three sentence bionote describing your non-writing interests and qualifications for your subject.

Length: Minimum is 650 words with at least one illustration (850 words without illustration); features run 1,200 to 1,500 words; special subjects occasionally run longer.

Illustrations: Illustrations are not required, but we do feel the author is best qualified to provide appropriate photos or artwork. We will look at black and white glossy prints or color prints with good contrast (no snapshots). Please include detailed captions identifying breed(s), equipment, and visible people, and indicate the name of the photographer or artist to whom we should give credit. Put your name and address on the back of each piece and send a self-addressed stamped envelope for the return of your material.

Payment: Payment for first English language rights is 5 cents per published word and $10 per illustration, paid on publication, and two copies of the issue bearing your work.

Sample copy: If you are not familiar with RURAL HERITAGE and would like a sample issue, please send $6.00 (US $7.25 to Canada or US $8.00 overseas). Subscriptions to the bimonthly are $22.00 per year (US $26.20 to Canada, US $37.00 overseas).
Categories: Nonfiction—Draft Animals—Farming—Livestock—Logging—Rural America

Name: Gail Damerow, Editor
Material: All
Address: 281 DEAN RIDGE LN
City/State/ZIP: GAINESBORO TN 38562-5039
Telephone: 615-268-0655
E-mail: RuralHeritge@infoave.net

Russian Life

Russian Life (RL) has as its fundamental editorial mission telling the story of Russia. It is a primary looking glass into Russia for some 40,000+ Americans and covers Russian culture, travel, history, politics, art, business and society. As a monthly magazine, RL focuses on current issues and events facing Russia and Russians. This is not to say it is a newsmagazine. It is not. The majority of RL content is feature articles, most of which are not time-sensitive, but all of which are current.

A large portion of RL articles are written by freelance Russian journalists and writers. The role of contributions by freelance *Western* or *expatriate* writers is to provide a unique "outsider" perspective. While no one knows Russia like Russians, sometimes it takes the view of foreigners to help shape a message that resonates with foreign readers. In all cases, the freelance writer should, in the context of professional presentation, bring to bear some unique experiences or perspectives on a region or event in Russia, its history and life—something other readers will want to read. And RL has a very demanding, knowledgeable and responsive readership—the average subscriber reads 85% of the magazine each month.

RL's writing style is frank, terse, and incisive. The model is good, third-person American journalism style (and spelling) on the lines of the AP stylebook. We seek to provide coverage of Russia that is free of illusions (but not blemishes) and full of hope (but not ideology or agendas). Our job is to present a realistic, truthful and independent view that balances these realities, providing enjoyable, insightful reading. It is also helpful to remember that RL is a very visual magazine; few stories do not include photographs of professional caliber.

What we do not seek from freelance writers: stories about personal trips to Russia, travel diaries, etc.; editorials or personal viewpoints on developments in Russia; unsolicited travel photos; articles with a hidden or open intent to advertise the services of a company, non-profit organization or governmental agency; articles espousing the viewpoint of specific companies, organizations or governments.

Persons interested in either submitting articles (or photos) to RL or being assigned stringer work should first contact RL editorial offices (in Moscow: the best means is by e-mail—74754.3234@compuserve.com) to discuss the parameters of such work with our editors. While we welcome unsolicited manuscripts, we feel that it is most productive to work with writers ahead of time—to hone story ideas to fit the RL mold. Submissions may also be made electronically, with prior approval. Fees for freelance work are agreed upon on a individual basis, depending on the scope, difficulty and nature of the story being written. Payment is upon publication. Most stories will be between 1,000-2,000 words in length.

Categories: History—Travel

Name: Publisher's Office
Material: 89 Main Street, Suite 2, Montpelier, VT 05602
Name: Russia Editorial Office

Material: Pokrovsky bulvar 8, No. 305, Moscow, Russia 109817
Name: Subscription address
Material: PO Box 10665, Riverton, NJ 08076-0665
Telephone: 802-223-4955
Fax: 802-223-6105
E-mail: nsvt@compuserve.com

RV West® Magazine

STORY and PHOTO GUIDELINES & TERMS

• Stories are chosen for how they serve the RV traveler. The tone should be conversational and entertaining, and the stories should contain "meaty" information. Stories must mention RVs and must be accompanied by B&W prints or color slides and/or line art, unless other arrangements have been made. Submission of both B&W prints and color slides is preferred, since there may be use for both with a story. Publication-quality color slides that have RVs in them will be considered for cover art. High-quality photos can enhance the chance of acceptance of a story. RV photos also greatly increase the desirability of a story.

• Articles are accepted on speculation. Acceptance does not necessarily guarantee publication. Please submit complete articles with all photographs and art—no queries, please. Include phone number. fax number and social security number, as well as address, with submissions.

• All stories, whether destination, event or historical, must contain specific information in the article, or in a sidebar, that lists places for RVers to camp/park, including name, address, phone, fees, # of RV spaces, any RV length restrictions, amenities (pool, laundry, game room, sauna, spa, golf course nearby, boat rentals, fishing, etc.) and facilities (dump stations, hookups, handicapped access, etc.), and must also include the number and address of an appropriate tourism agency to call for more information.

• Please also include the name, address and phone of one or two places in the area where RVers could get their RVs repaired (make sure the places have done RV-specific repairs). And, for best chance of acceptance, be specific in your story. For example, if you say there is a winery tour, a fishing charter, a horseback ride, etc., give info such as name, fee, address, phone, hours if unusual, where/how far attraction is in relation to main location in story, and whether there is a place to park your RV. All stories should focus on activities and what to do in the area, with tips on making the visit an enjoyable and successful one.

• Send photocopies or letter-quality printouts. Microsoft Word (v. 4.0 or higher) submissions on 3½" disk for Macintosh, with backup hard copy, are preferred. We acquire exclusive first-time North American serial rights; full rights to historical/recap/reprint/archival *RV West*-related use; and full but non-exclusive rights for current or future electronic, digital or optical use, including on-line use. Original articles required vs. reprints. If you would like acknowledgement of delivery, send via certified mail, return receipt requested.

• For proper return of photo(s) and proper credit, every photo must be labeled with name and address of photographer, and place and date of photo. Cutline information for each photo must also be provided. Photo releases required for photos showing identifiable people or private property. Only photos will be returned unless your cover letter specifies return of the manuscript, as well, and there is sufficient postage for manuscript and photos. Postage for photos must allow for return by certified mail, return receipt requested. Failure to provide funds for photo return by certified mail will be your authorization for us to return photos by regular mail (if you have provided a regular mail SASE) and your acceptance of and sole responsibility for any risk therefrom, such as inability to track lost photos. Submissions submit-

ted without even sufficient regular postage/envelope for return will be held or tossed, at VPI's [Vernon Publications, Inc.] sole option. If no materials need to be returned, please specify in cover letter. If you want your materials returned by insured mail, you must so note, specify the amount of insurance desired, and include funds to cover its cost.

• Rates are as follows: $1.50 per published column inch (about .05/word), $5 for each published photo. Payment is made and checks are mailed the month following publication. Preferred length: minimum of 750 words and a maximum of 1,750 words for stories. Short items of interest may also be submitted, including tips, humorous anecdotes and jokes related to RV'ing. *RV West* reserves the right to edit all copy and crop all photos as *RV West* deems fit.

• Submissions, both article and photo, are reviewed as our schedule permits, and may be held for several months. We do not pay holding fees. If your photos are chosen for possible publication, they will be held through production for possible use, and then returned if an appropriate SASE has been provided.

• *RV West*/Vernon Publications Inc. are not responsible or liable for payment for photos, transparences (slides) or prints that are damaged or lost in the mail, while not in our possession, or through no fault of our own. With that in mind, package your materials carefully. Use plastic sleeves or clear vinyl pocket packages for prints and transparencies. Examine your slides for scratches and pinholes before submitting them. If your submitted slides should be lost or damaged by VPI while in our possession, however, VPI's liability shall be zero for color or B&W prints, negatives and color duplicates, and limited to $25 for each original color slide lost or damaged.

• By the act of submitting copy/photos, contributor warrants that the information and that the photos have not been used by and are not copyrighted or owned by, any other source, and agrees to hold *RV West*/VPI harmless, and defend RV West/VPI from any claims or problems arising from use of the information or photos.

• Submission of article(s)/photo(s) constitutes acceptance of the above guidelines. If these guidelines and terms are not acceptable to you and you have already submitted an article or photos, please notify VPI in writing within 5 days of your receipt of this information, and any materials submitted by you within the preceding 15 days will be returned to you by mail as long as you have provided an appropriate SASE. Lack of notification to VPI of an objection, or, a subsequent submission of an article or photo materials, will be considered your acceptance of these guidelines and terms. Acceptance and holding of photo submissions, including delivery memos, by RV West/VPI does NOT constitute acceptance of any terms contrary to those stated above. Article and/or photo contributor understands and agrees that these terms may not be altered unless agreed to in writing by VPI, and that no representations to the contrary are otherwise binding.

Destination Story

• Stories should focus on destinations within the 12 Western states, Alaska, western Canada or northern Mexico. Explain where the trip will take the traveler and approximate the destination's distance to major highways and a major city or landmark. Simple but clear map showing spot in relation to surrounding highways is desirable. Provide complete campground information for a sidebar. (You can write about the campgrounds in the story; the sidebar is for quick reference.)

• Answer questions such as these: Why would you go there? Is it the season of the year, an activity, the topography or what? What are the things to see and do at the place/in the area? What are these attractions like? What tips do you have to offer as someone who has been there?

• (For example: "1.5-mile hike up High Canyon is strenuous but well worth it; 360-degree view of valley and sound make it a must-see," or, "Bring Insect repellent.") Are walks/lookouts handi-capped accessible? Are there height, length, parking or other re-strictions at campsites or attractions that would affect RVers? Also be sure to indicate to the editor the best time of the year to run the story.

Event Story

• Tell us all about the event: background, dates, times. Ex-plain why the event would be of interest to RVers. Be sure to also include the kinds of information listed above. Best time for pub-lication of an event story is the month or two preceding the event.

Historical Story

• We use some historical stories, especially those that relate to the RVer in a tangible way (for instance, a historical event that is recreated in a place easily visited by RVers). Be sure to keep the RVer in mind rather than the historian, and be sure to include all the kinds of information listed under "Destination Story."

Activity Story or RV Humor

• Activity story: Quizzes or other entertaining activities RVers would enjoy while on the road. RV Humor: Short humorous an-ecdotes, jokes or limericks specific to traveling, specifically RVing. Must be in good taste.

Categories: Recreation—Senior Citizens—RVs—Travel

Name: Michelle Arab, Editor
Material: All
Address: 3000 NORTHUP WAY STE 200
Address: PO BOX 96043
City/State/ZIP: BELLEVUE WA 98009-9643
Telephone: 800-700-9372
Fax: 206-822-9372

Periodicals
S-Z

SAFARI Magazine

SAFARI Magazine was founded in 1971 as the official publication of Safari Club International. *SAFARI Magazine* is bi-monthly; is focused on big game hunting and conservation; and, includes editorials, feature stories and columns about SCI national, international and chapter activities, affiliated organizations and members' hunting reports from around the world. Circulation is 27,000-30,000, mailed nationally and internationally to the SCI membership list and to selected other individuals or organizations. Send submissions to SCI, at the address shown below.

EDITORIAL CONTENT

The magazine scope of interest is:

• Outdoor recreation with special emphasis on big game hunting around the world

• Ethnic and traditional hunts of particular regions around the world

• Current or historical hunting and conservation • Philosophy and heritage of hunting

• Background on a particular species • Conservation and environmental affairs relevant to big game or hunters

We buy first rights manuscripts. Queries prior to submissions are encouraged; no fiction or poetry accepted. Avoid sending simple hunting narratives that lack new approaches. Features run 2,000-2,500 words and should be informative, accurate, designed to appeal to sportsmen and women as well as others who enjoy out-of-doors. Rate for a full-length story with illustrations submitted by a professional writer is $300 *paid upon publication.* Short stories or non-pro contributions by SCI members rate an honorarium of $25. (Professional photographers are paid up to $100 for each color photo used, depending on size, up to $45 each B&W-all on if *published/when published* basis.)

News briefs are welcomed and will include bylines, but are not bought by SAFARI.

MANUSCRIPT PREPARATION

Submitted manuscripts should fit these specifications in order to be reviewed.

• **Original:** typed or laser jet printout, no photocopies. • Consecutive-number all manuscript pages.

• **Computer disks:** ASCII language accepted with hard copy. (Mac 3½" or IBM 5¼")

• Double-spaced or 1½-spaced text OK.

• **All pages:** 1½" left margin, 1" right and base.

• **Title page (first page):** Author name, address, telephone in upper right corner, title halfway down first page, followed by text. Author name on all pages following. • Pica-sized, sans-serif type preferred.

• Spell-check for proper names, animals, places.

• Do not staple manuscript pages.

• We have prepared an editorial style sheet for information and use on any manuscript.

PHOTOGRAPHY SUBMISSION

We are interested only in huntable big game subjects of trophy quality in a natural setting.

Color photographs, slides or transparencies are preferred. (Prints accepted for color or black-and-white uses. In all cases, use will depend on the reproduction quality of submitted materials.)

All photos must be captioned. Type caption information on a separate sheet of paper and number to match slide or print being described. We prefer to receive more photos than we may be able to use, in order to have a choice. Send SASE. All photos will be returned *following publication* unless otherwise directed.

• **Color Slides:** use plastic sheets to hold slides or transparencies; do not ship unprotected. Label each slide with name stamp or label.

• **Black-and-White:** 35mm contacts, glossy or semi-gloss prints; added minimum of ½" white border on four sides *preferred.*

• Slides or transparencies *preferred* for color and should be sharp and well-exposed. (Prints are OK, glossy preferred. If 35mm: double-sized, or 5"x7" or larger). • Print sizes 5"x7" or 8"x10" *preferred;* others considered based on quality and story needs.

• Do not write on prints. Attach label with pre-typed information or use grease-pencil only.

Categories: Conservation—Hunting—Outdoors

Name: Manuscripts Editor
Name: William R. Quimby, Director of Publications
Material: Any
Address: SAFARI CLUB INTERNATIONAL
City/State/ZIP: 4800 W GATES PASS RD
Telephone: TUCSON AZ 85742
Fax: 520-620-1220

SageWoman
Celebrating the Goddess in Every Woman

SageWoman is a quarterly magazine of women's spirituality. Our readers are people who identify positively with the term 'Goddess'. Our readership includes women of a variety of religious faiths, ranging from Roman Catholic to Lesbian Separatist Witch and everywhere in between.

What our readers have in common is summed up in the statement 'Celebrating the Goddess in Every Woman'. If you feel a connection with our subject matter, we welcome your contributions to our pages. The majority of every issue is created from the contributions of our readers, so your creativity and willingness to share is vital to *SageWoman*'s existence! We welcome material from women of all races, ages, sexual orientations, and socioeconomic backgrounds. Our editorial staff is English speaking only, so we ask that written contributions and letters to us be submitted in English, but we encourage submissions from non-American women and women for whom English may be a second language. We also *strongly* encourage contributions from women of color.

SageWoman offers the following guidelines to help you in submitting your work to us.

1. **Subject matter**

a. All submissions should focus on issues of concern to pagan and other spiritually minded women. We accept non-fiction prose related to women's spiritual experience. We accept very modest amounts of poetry, and receive far more poetry than we can publish. We also accept photographs and graphic artwork (drawings, painting, prints, etc.) suitable for publishing in a magazine format. We do not accept fiction, screenplays, or long narrative poems.

b. *SageWoman* is dedicated to helping women explore their spiritual, emotional, and mundane lives in a way which respects all persons, creatures, and the Earth. We encourage women of all spiritual paths to send writings and artwork, but our focus is on material which expresses an Earth-centered spirituality. Our editorial style focuses on personal experience; please write in the first person! Please don't limit yourself because you aren't a "professional" writer or artist—most of our published material is from previously unpublished writers. If you haven't seen a copy of *SageWoman*, please send for a sample copy ($7) or look at our sample articles at our web site before submitting material; this will enable you to understand the kind of material we publish, and will save both you and us a lot of time!

c. *SageWoman* accepts material created by women only. (Male contributors are encouraged to contact our brother publication *The* Green *Man*, at the same address.) The concerns of our sisters, of women, form the core of our editorial and design, and is, in fact, the reason that we gather in the Circle of *SageWoman*.

2. Written Submissions

a. All written submissions should be the original work of the author. We prefer receiving material via e-mail or on computer disk if possible (it saves us *valuable* typing time) accompanied by a paper manuscript. (Please don't just send the disk—sometimes compatibility problems prevent us from reading disks which are submitted to us, and without a manuscript, we won't be able to evaluate your submission!)

We are PC-based and prefer 3½" floppy disks, ASCII compatible, but we may be able to translate Macintosh based disks as well. Disks sent to us will not be returned unless you send us a SASE with adequate postage with the submission. If computer-based submission is not possible, typed, double-spaced manuscripts are also acceptable, as well as neatly handwritten pieces if no other method is possible. *Please* do not send us your only copy of your manuscript; accidents can happen and material sent to us is occasionally lost or damaged.

b. Articles should be between 200 and 5,000 words in length, and written manuscripts should contain the author's name, pen name (if appropriate), address and phone number on each page.

c. We are aware that you have worked hard on your writing, it is personal and special to you, and contains your unique voice. Nonetheless, we often find it necessary to edit for length, clarity and grammar, sometimes at the last minute before publication. Therefore, we *cannot* guarantee that your article will appear precisely as you submitted it. If you do not want your material edited in any way, please do not submit your writing to us. (Also, please inform us of deliberate uses of non-traditional spelling so the tone of your work will not be accidentally altered.)

3. Graphic Art

a. All graphic art submissions should be the original work of the artist. Clear, black and white drawings are best, but penciled or colored works may be acceptable in some cases. Please be aware that all artwork will be reproduced in black and white only except for pieces used on our outside covers. Our covers are usually commissioned works, but you may feel free to submit color photocopies or slides of your color work for possible use on the cover. Please send us clean copies of your artwork *only*—we cannot be responsible for your original artwork! We encourage the submission of artwork which celebrates the Goddess and women in all of our many guises; different skin colors, cultures, ages, sexual orientations, body types, sizes, and shapes, and levels of [ability].

b. We are always looking for new artists to share their creativity ill our pages. If you have a portfolio of your work, feel free to send it; when sending a body of work, please inform us if any of the pieces have been previously published or are not available for publication. We do commission special pieces of artwork for the magazine; however, the majority of artwork we publish has been sent by artists on spec.

We keep files of artwork, by artist, and when an issue is in production we find the pieces of artwork on file that fit each article, and then inform the artist in question that we have decided to publish their work. For this reason, your artwork may be on file for months, or years, without being used—if this is a problem for you, please inform us so we can work out other arrangements with you.

4. Photography

a. All photographic submissions should be the original work of the photographer. If persons other than the photographer are shown, a signed release from said person(s) must be included in order for us to publish the photo. Please send standard black and white or color prints—we cannot publish from negatives or slides. All photographs will be reproduced in black and white only. Our use of photography is similar to that of graphic art; please see guidelines above.

5. General Information

a. If you do not wish for your submission to be returned, please write 'Do not return' on it, and simply send us a SASE or stamped postcard for us to respond to your submission. Please put your name, address and phone number (with area code) on each page of your manuscript.

b. Your submission will be acknowledged when we receive your material; we cannot guarantee exact publishing dates but will attempt to keep you up-to-date on the status of your work. We prefer to accept material which has not been previously seen or published—please inform us of multiple submissions or previous publishings.

c. *SageWoman* publishes quarterly. All material should be sent to the attention of the Editor at the address shown below (either e-mail or US mail). Upcoming issue themes and deadlines are listed at the end of this letter.

6. Compensation and Rights

a. *SageWoman* offers modest cash payments for unsolicited artwork, photography, or articles. Articles are compensated at approximately $.03 per word for unsolicited material, with a minimum of $10.(No payment is made for Rattle letters or networking information printed in Weaving the Web) Artwork and photography are compensated on a piece-by-piece basis, depending on the size, complexity and usefulness of the piece. Artists and photographers are paid a minimum of $15 per piece for their work. We are often able to pay more in cases where the article, artwork, illustration or photograph is commissioned especially for *SageWoman*; please contact us if you are interested in working with us on commission.

We realize how very modest these payments are; we offer them not as full compensation for your creativity, but as a 'thank you' for sharing your gifts with us. Our ability to pay is limited by the nature of our publication; we operate primarily as a gift from and to the Goddess, not as a moneymaking venture, and our budget reflects this fact. If you are a business or craftsperson who would benefit from advertising in our pages, please inform us that you are interested in trading advertising for your contributions; we are able to be substantially more generous in trading for advertising space than we can be in our cash payments!

b. If your material is accepted, you will also receive a free copy of the issue in which your work appears; if you are a subscriber this will be in addition to the copy you receive as part of your subscription. Payment will be sent to you within 30 days of your return of our contributor's form, which is sent out to all contributors shortly after an issue goes to press. *SageWoman* prefers to acquire first North American serial rights, all rights for one year, and the right to reprint in future *SageWoman* collections and non-exclusive electronic rights (for use on the "sample" page of the *SageWoman* web site.) All remaining rights will revert to you. When you sub-

S-Z

mit work to us, we will assume your work is available for the purchase of these rights at the compensation level specified above, unless you state otherwise.

If there are any questions which these guidelines do not answer, please feel free to e-mail, call or write to us for more information, or simply to try out your ideas on us! Our usual office hours are 9-5 Pacific Time, Monday-Friday, but feel free to leave a message if you don't reach us. We will return your call!

Thanks again for your interest in *SageWoman*.

We look forward to hearing from you soon.

Categories: Feminism—Religion—Spiritual—Women's Issues

Name: Submissions Editor
Material: All
Address: PO BOX 641
City/State/ZIP: PT ARENA CA 95468-0641
Telephone: 707-882-2052
Fax: 707-882-2793
E-mail: info@sagewoman.com
Internet: www.sagewoman.com

Sailing Magazine

20% freelance. *Sailing Magazine* is for the sailor committed to the sport. All kinds of sailing are featured on big pages full of pictures and text complemented by technical articles. Welcomes new writers. Circ. 40K. Monthly.

Pays on publication. Publishes ms 6 months after acceptance. Buys one-time rights. Rarely accepts reprints. Responds 2 months. Sample for written request and $5. Subscription $28; $40 outside US. Guidelines by mail with SASE.

Needs: Features with pictures. Pays $250-500 for 800-2,500 words. Submit complete ms with cover letter by mail with SASE.

Photos/Art: Pays $50-800.

Categories: Nonfiction—History—Outdoors—Sports—Recreation—Boating

Name: Micca Hutchins, Editor
Material: All
Address: P.O. BOX 249, 125 E. MAIN STREET
City/State/ZIP: PORT WASHINGTON, WI 53074
Telephone: 414-284-3494
Fax: 414-284-7764
E-mail: 75553.3666@compuserve.com
Internet: www.sailnet.com/sailing

Sailing World
The Authority on Performance Sailing

Prospective contributors should study recent issues of the magazine to determine appropriate subject matter. The emphasis here is on performance sailing: keep in mind that the *Sailing World* readership is relatively educated about the sport. Unless you are dealing with a totally new aspect of sailing, you can and should discuss ideas on an advanced technical level; however, extensive formulae and graphs don't play well to our audience. When in doubt as to the suitability of an article or idea, submit a query before time and energy are misdirected.

All mss. should be typewritten. Unless specific arrangements have been made ahead of time with *Sailing World*, submissions must include all necessary artwork and photos. (See SW's Photographer's Guidelines.) Materials should bear the contributor's name, address and phone number.

Most writing for *Sailing World* falls into one of several cat-

egories. Articles on one-design or offshore sailing can be presented as any of the following:

1. Feature (B&W or color)
A. Instructional
B. Event-oriented
C. Personal Experience
2. Race Report
3. Finish Line

Cruising-oriented features may be either instructional or narrative; in the latter case, suitability for SW will be determined by the quality of writing and ideas, or by the value of lessons learned. "Gee-whiz" impressions from beginning sailors are generally not accepted.

Payment for article is upon publication, and varies with the type of article, its placement in the magazine, and the amount of editing required. Average payment is $50 per column of text.

Thank you for your interest in contributing to *Sailing World*.

The Editors

Categories: Boating—Outdoors—Sailing—Sports

Name: Kristan McClintock, Managing Editor
Material: All
Address: PO BOX 3400
City/State/ZIP: NEWPORT RI 02840
Telephone: 401-847-1588
Fax: 401-848-5048
E-mail: editor@sailingworld.com
Internet: www.sailingworld.com

St. Anthony Messenger

St. Anthony Messenger is a general-interest, family-oriented Catholic magazine. It is written and edited largely for people living in families or the family-like situations of Church and community. We want to help our readers better understand the teachings of the gospel and Catholic Church, and how they apply to life and the full range of problems confronting us as members of families, the Church and society.

Types and examples of the kinds of articles we publish:

1. Church and Religion: "The Church Against the Mafia," "Which Scripture Translation is Best," "Lessons from the Book of Genesis: An interview With Dianne Bergant," "Images of Jesus From Around the World," "I'd Like to Say: Wake Me Up When Mass is Over."

2. Marriage, Family and Parenting: "Toughing Out the Tough Times Together," "Long Distance Grandparenting," "Holy Families Aren't Always Perfect Families," "Stay At Home Dads."

3. Social: "The Death Penalty and the Catholics Conscience," "Sister Mary Howard Johnstone: Compassionate Attorney for Kids Who Need Protection," "A Job-training Program That Works," "HOPE House: A Place of New Beginnings."

4. Inspiration: "Prayers for Caregivers," "Veronica Wipes the Face of the World," "The Eucharist: Life, Love & Communion," "Eight Gifts of Motherhood."

5. Psychology: "Codependency: Killing Yourself With Kindness-to Others," "Forgiving Doesn't Mean Forgetting," "Making Retirement the Time of Your Life," "The Death of a Lie."

6. Profiles and Interviews: "Tim Russert: Feisty Host of *Meet the Press,*" "Skater Bonnie Blair and Her Gold-medal Attitude," "Chicago Remembers Mother Cabrini," "Father Solanus Casey: Saintliness of a 'Slow' Priest," "Pope John Paul II at 75."

7. Fiction: "The Bridge," "The Calling Card," "Legerdemain," "Paper Prayers."

The best way to know what we publish is to read and study several recent issues of *St. Anthony Messenger.*

GUIDELINES FOR WRITING, PREPARING AND SUBMITTING AN ARTICLE.

1. Query in advance. State proposed topic, sources, authorities and your qualifications to do the article. *Library research does not suffice.* Fresh sources and interviews with experts or people in the field will be necessary. Reporting articles are more needed than opinion pieces. Seasonal material (Mother's Day, Lent, Christmas, etc.) should be submitted six or more months in advance.

2. We do not publish filler material-anecdotes, jokes, thoughts to ponder.

3. We do not publish articles or stories in installments or serial form. And we very rarely reprint from other sources.

4. We do not use essays or personal reminiscences. Articles about historical events or people no longer living need a current news peg.

5. We do not consider articles submitted simultaneously to other magazines.

6. Mark your submission fact or fiction. Place your name, address, phone number and social security number on the first page. Number the pages. Address manuscript to Norman Perry, O.FM., editor, St. Anthony Messenger (see address below.)

7. Articles should not exceed 3,000 words. Oversize articles invite automatic rejection.

8. Keep the vocabulary simple. Avoid jargon, technical and theological language. Keep sentences short. Ask, "Would my grandmother understand this?"

9. An attention-getting introduction is important! Use anecdotes, examples, quotes from real people. Make practical applications. End strongly.

10. Please allow up to eight weeks for return or purchase of publication rights. Hardly any manuscript is published without review by eight or more staff members. Phoning the editor for a progress report invites aborting review process and returning the manuscript immediately to avoid more phone calls.

11. Payment for articles and fiction is 14 cents a published word-upon acceptance and return of signed author-publisher agreement form.

12. Payment for photos accompanying an article is $25 for each photo used. Photos should be documented with any necessary releases from photographers or persons in the photos. Payment for photos is made after photos have been selected and the issue laid out and printed.

13. Articles sent after a positive response to a query are received on a speculation basis.

14. If no article is received within two months after a positive response to a query, we feel free to consider a query on the same subject from another author.

INFORMATION FOR FICTION AUTHORS

Besides these guidelines, freelance authors submitting fiction pieces should read our general information sheet [above] for all freelance writers. Note the audience for whom we publish and the purpose of *St. Anthony Messenger.* Most of our readers live in families. The greater part are women between 40 and 70 years old.

1. Preferred word length for short stories is 2,500 to 3,000 words.

2. Please do not phone to ask if your manuscript has been received. Allow six to eight weeks for a response or return of your manuscript. Any story that is accepted will have had at least six or eight readers. And many that are returned may also have had as many readers.

3. We receive over 1,000 short story submissions a year. We publish 12 at the most-one an issue. Many stories must be returned-even stories that may be well-written and have merit.

4. In submitting a short story please clearly label it as fiction. Number the pages. Include a self-addressed, stamped envelope and your social security number (information we must supply the IRS when issuing a purchase check).

5. We pay 14 cents a word on acceptance for first North American serial rights and do not consider stories submitted to other publications at the same time or reprints.

6. We are interested in stories about family relationships, people struggling and coping with the same problems of life our readers face. Stories that show people triumphing in adversity, persevering in faith, overcoming doubt or despair, coming to spiritual insights. Stories about people that offer hope. Characters and resolutions must be real and believable. Sudden realizations, instant conversions and miracle solutions won't do.

7. Stories that sound more like essays or monologues, stories that are straight narratives with no dialogue or interaction on the part of characters will not succeed.

8. Dialogue should contribute to moving the story forward. It should sound real-the way people talk to each other in real life. Conversation should not be artificial or sound stilted.

9. We are not interested in retold Bible stories or stories overly sentimental or pietistic.

10. Seasonal stories (Christmas, Easter, etc.) should be submitted at least six months in advance.

INFORMATION FOR POETRY WRITERS

The poetry we publish attempts to reflect the philosophy stated above. Poetry is subjective, for the most part, but we do require that the poems we publish have most or all of these characteristics: 1) originality 2) creativity in word choice, images and overall thought/idea 3) each section of the poem fitting together well with other sections 4) subject matter somewhat universal in nature 5) a religious (in a broad sense, not theological) or family dimension.

Both rhyming and non-rhyming material are considered. We do not consider previously published poetry, or poetry submitted at the same time to other publications.

Each poetry submission should be typed, double-spaced on a separate piece of paper. Your name, address and social security number should be typed at the top.

Please do not submit poems longer than 20-25 lines—the shorter, the better. Due to space limitations, the poetry section does not appear every month. When space is available for it, there is room for only one page of poetry (four to five poems at the most). Therefore, *our poetry needs are very limited.*

As we like to give as many people as possible the chance to be published poets, we do not buy "collections" of poems for publication (that is the role of a poetry book publisher), nor do we usually buy more than a few works from each poet a year. And while we pay on acceptance, publication may not follow for a considerable length of time. When a poem is published the poet receives two complimentary copies of the issue it appears in.

We pay $2 (two dollars) per line for each poem purchased. We try to return poems not accepted within four to six weeks. Please do not write or phone to ask if your poem has been received until that amount of time has passed.

Due to the poetry editor's time constraints, poetry critiques will not be given. Thank you very much for your interest!

The best way to know what we publish is to read and study several recent issues of *St. Anthony Messenger* containing poetry.

Categories: Fiction—Nonfiction—Catholics (beliefs, prac-

S-Z

tices)—Family—Inspirational—Interviews—Profiles—Religion—Short Stories—

Name: Norman Perry, O.F.M., Editor
Material: Manuscripts
Name: Poetry Editor
Material: Poetry
Address: 1615 REPUBLIC ST
City/State/ZIP: CINCINNATI OH 45210
Telephone: 513-241-5615
Fax: 513-241-0399

Salt Water Sportsman

Salt Water Sportsman buys fact-feature articles, short fillers, and color transparencies(slides) dealing with marine sport fishing along the coast of the United States and Canada, the Caribbean, Central America, Bermuda, and occasionally South America and other overseas locations.

IMPORTANT!

In all cases, we suggest that you query us first with your story ideas. This will prevent wasted effort on your part. Contact the Editor in writing (no phone calls, please) and briefly outline the article you have in mind. Tell us what the story is about, what you intend to cover, when the peak season is for that type of fishing, and what you have available for photos and illustrations. We will get back to you within a week or two. This gives us the opportunity to cross-check your proposal against material we're currently holding in inventory or have out on assignment, and we're thus able to give you a better answer as to whether we think we can use your story.

We do not buy "blood and thunder," and we do not want overly romantic "remember when." We buy no poetry, fiction, or cartoons. Editorial advertising is strictly taboo. A popular lure or tackle item should be described if possible; however, a brand name and/or model number may be given if it's pertinent to the story and if it is the most concise way of describing the item to the reader.

Example:

Unacceptable: "We skimmed out into the bay in our soft-riding Whizzer Craft model 1802 powered by a reliable, smooth-running Gale 25-hp motor."

Acceptable: "In seven days of fishing, we found that red-headed, four-inch darting plugs, such as the MirrOlure 99-M, produced the most snook for us in that area of the river."

There is no taboo about naming charter skippers, lodges, airlines, guides, people, etc. However, we are not interested in celebrities per se—our celebrity is the marine angler. *Above all avoid promotion* simply *for the sake of promotion!*

Emphasis should be on the how-to, where-to, when-to of salt water fishing, not straight "Me & Joe" adventures.

We need specific semi-technical information that our average reader will understand. Articles dealing with fishing at a specific time of the year should be submitted about six months ahead of the optimum publication date and no less than four months. We rarely hold material for more than six months ahead of acceptance, except for the straight how-to piece that isn't roadblocked by a time element.

Preferred copy length for feature material is 800 to 1,200 words. We frown on manuscripts much over 1,500 words and we do not publish "Continued Next Month" serials.

Rates we pay vary, depending upon the overall quality of the photo/manuscript package. The average rate tends to run from $300 to $500, but may be more if copy is clean and photos are above average. Similarly, less will be paid if we must extensively rewrite and/or provide usable photos for your story. *Salt Water Sportsman* buys first American rights, and strives to report back within 30 days. We pay on acceptance. We try to work with our writers, and articles submitted on speculation are carefully considered. If they cannot be used, we attempt to tell the writer why.

Each submission should be accompanied by a stamped, self-addressed envelope or other means of return shipping unless the writer has previously sold material to this magazine. **All manuscripts and photos that are returned for any reason, including photos returned after an article has been published, will be sent via first class U.S. mail.** *Salt Water Sportsman* assumes no liability for loss or damage by the Postal Service. Contributors who would prefer a different method of return shipping must provide that means to *Salt Water Sportsman.*

All articles must be typed or computer-written. No faxes or photocopies of manuscripts will be considered. Binders are unnecessary. The manuscript should be paper-clipped together, not stapled, and mailed in an envelope stout enough to defeat the U.S. mail service. If a story has been written on computer, a floppy disk (either size 5.25" or 3.5") with the story on it and a note describing the software program it was written in (i.e., WordPerfect, Microsoft Word) and the version of the program (i.e., WordPerfect 5.1) should be submitted as part of the manuscript package. Disks will be returned with photos. When in doubt as to which computer programs are compatible with our system, don't hesitate to call.

The first page of your manuscript should include your name, address and social security number at top left. At top right, give us an estimate of word count. Space down at least three or four inches and center the title of your choice. Beneath the title, center your byline as you wish it to appear in print. Be advised that we may not use your title.

Fillers and Short Features

SWS is currently seeking short feature articles ranging from 500 to 1000 words. Subject can focus on regional hot spots, species, special rigs, fishing methods, etc. Payment will range from $200 to $500, depending on the quality of writing and accompanying photos. Please query first.

SWS also welcomes "over-the-transom" (no query necessary) submissions for our "Sportsman's Workbench" department. We're looking for 100- to 300-word how-to articles dealing with all phases of salt water fishing, tackle, boats, and related equipment. Emphasis is on building, repairing, or reconditioning specific items or gear. Rough or finished art work, samples, and/or black-and-white photos should accompany copy. All "Workbench" and short feature submissions should be sent to the attention of Tom Richardson, Managing Editor.

Photo and Illustration Guidelines

Salt Water Sportsman is asking that 35mm color transparencies (slides) be used to illustrate feature and department articles and for cover shot submissions.

Subject: Photos provided to illustrate an article should, first of all, tell the story. Try to include scenic shots with human interest, shots of the boat, water conditions, the lodge, close-ups of rods and reels used, lures, baits, flies, equipment, structure, fish being landed and released, and general how-to. Action is most important, and it should be right there on the scene, not back at the dock. Try to tell the story with the camera. Shoot early and late in the day for best light. Have your subject take off his or her hat, or use fill-flash to illuminate the face. Try shots of releasing fish or removing hooks. Leave lures or flies in fish's mouth to show what it was caught on. Watch out for shadows, crooked horizons, and rods, hands, or other distracting objects intruding into the frame. Make sure subject is in *sharp* focus.

By all means, include a picture of yourself in action if you want, but do not send us a great many photos of yourself or the same fishing companions. The is especially important if you are a fairly regular contributor—readers want to see new faces, and we want to give credit to a host of fine skippers, guides, and sportsmen out there, not just a select few.

We do not want photos of piles of dead fish. Large numbers of dead fish are unimportant and they offend conservation-minded readers. Stress quality in sport, not quantity.

Transparencies: Color transparencies should be 35mm slides. Give us a good selection of horizontals and verticals. All slides should be sent in a transparency sleeve, never loose in an envelope or box. Make sure your name, address, and phone number is labeled on every slide, and that each slide is numbered to correspond with the caption sheet (see below).

Captions: Caption information must accompany all photos. We prefer that photos be numbered and submitted with a separate caption sheet. Give us as much information as possible in the captions, such as model names, dates, places, fish species, sizes of fish, lures or baits used, boat names, and so forth. Even if these things aren't evident in the photo we'd rather have too much info than not enough.

Covers: We pay $1,000 for one-time use of cover transparencies. We're looking for 35mm vertical-format slides (or 2.25"x2.25") that are colorful, sharp, and show fishing action or mood. Be sure there is enough room (dead space) at the top for our logo. Think scenery, human interest, boats on the grounds, story-telling close-ups of anglers in action, and so forth. Make it "come alive"—and don't bother us with obviously posed "dead fish with fisherman" shots taken back at the dock.

We Cannot Use: snapshots, black & whites, Polaroid prints, color prints or matte prints of any kind. We will not accept negatives for any reason. Do not send contact sheets and negatives, asking us to indicate what we want to see and requesting that we return them to you for processing. Pick the shots you think are best and have them processed into prints before sending the package to us.

Computer-Altered or Enhanced Images: *Salt Water Sportsman* requires that any computer-manipulated image be identified as such.

Illustrations: Drawings, particularly those which depict a specific rig, tackle item, or how-to procedure are always welcome. These may be rough sketches, and should include appropriate labels so that we can produce the finished art work. Similarly, nautical chart segments and/or maps of fishing areas are very valuable in illustrating a story. We can use black-and-white photos or Polaroid prints as guidance for illustrations. Also, if appropriate, send us the actual lure, fly, rig or materials used to build it so we can use them as reference.

Payment: We pay between $50 and $400 for inside photos, depending on size used. We pay $1,000 for cover shots. Payment is made after publication of image.

Return of Photos: Rejected photos will be returned via the method provided for by the photographer. Otherwise they will be sent via U.S. mail. Most photos used in the magazine will be returned via UPS 3-Day service within a month after publication, unless special arrangements are made.

Categories: Fishing

Name: Barry Gibson, Editor
Material: All
Address: 77 FRANKLIN ST
City/State/ZIP: BOSTON MA 02110
Telephone: 617-338-2300
Fax: 617-338-2309
E-mail: swsfish@ultranet.com

San Diego Parent

Please refer to *L.A. Parent.*

San Francisco Peninsula Parent

OUR PURPOSE
San Francisco Peninsula Parent, established in 1984, is the only monthly parenting publication that exclusively serves families in San Francisco and on the Peninsula. Our aim is to provide the most up-to-date resource information that will enhance all aspects of parenting and family life for parents and parenting professionals who live in this area. *San Francisco Peninsula Parent* is distributed free at more than 1,000 locations.

OUR WRITERS
Most of our writers work for us on a freelance basis. Our staff writers are freelancers who write for us monthly. They are assigned stories and they also suggest topics to us. Many of our staff writers began by submitting manuscripts to us on an occasional basis. We accept work from other freelancers who send us a query or a manuscript on a topic of interest. Our features are typically 1,000 words in length on a variety of topics from home schooling to child safety to day trip outings. Features require careful research, thorough knowledge of our audience and well-developed interviewing skills.

OUR DEADLINES
Articles are generally due on the first of the month prior to publication. However, articles are scheduled three to four months in advance.

OUR PAYMENT
We pay $150 for first time rights, $25 to $50 for second rights, depending on the article. Payment is upon publication.

OUR ADVICE TO NEW WRITERS
First, read a few back issues of **San Francisco Peninsula Parent** to get a feel for what we publish. Then send a query letter in which you state two or three story proposals. We're most interested in articles that have a local focus although we do publish some general articles on parenting and child development issues. If you have writing samples, send a few along with your query. All articles are assigned on "spec" or speculation; that means, we'll buy the finished article if it meets our standards.

Don't be surprised if you don't hear from us for a month or so. Freelance submissions tend to fall to the bottom of the pile and get attention once our pressing deadlines have passed.

Categories: Parenting

Name: Lisa Rosenthal, Editor
Material: Parenting
Address: 1480 ROLLINS RD
City/State/ZIP: BURLINGAME CA 94010
Telephone: 415-342-9203
Fax: 415-342-9276
E-mail: SFPP@aol.com

San Francisco

We do not have formal writer's guidelines. We accept queries with attached clips.

Categories: Culture—General Interest—Lifestyles—Regional

Name: Melanie Haiken, Managing Editor
Material: All
Address: 243 VALLEJO ST
City/State/ZIP: SAN FRANCISCO CA 94111
Telephone: 415-398-2800

S-Z

Sandlapper
The Magazine of South Carolina

EDITORIAL PHILOSOPHY

Sandlapper is a quarterly magazine focusing on the positive aspects of South Carolina. We look for articles and photo-essays about South Carolina's interesting people, places, activities, heritage and cuisine. No political/controversial issues, except as they relate to history. *Sandlapper* is intended to be read at those times when people want to relax with an attractive, high-quality magazine that entertains and informs them about their state.

ARTICLE CONTENT & STYLE

We consider for publication nonfiction articles and photo-essays. No fiction or poetry, at this time. We occasionally buy reprints. Simultaneous submissions are not accepted; we presume an article submittal is for our exclusive consideration, subject to terms under the "Payment & Rights Acquisition" section, below.

The editors consider articles of variable length, from approximately one to six magazine pages (800-4,000 words). Any approach the author chooses to take—standard third-person, first-person, Q&A format, impressionistic, etc.—may be accepted, provided it works. We look for top-quality literature. Humor is encouraged. Profanity is discouraged. Good taste is a standard. Unique angles are critical for acceptance.

Dare to be bold. But not too bold. –Napolean, or whoever
Topics to avoid:
- Politics.
- Topical/controversial issues.
- R-rated subjects.
- Commercial enterprises.
- First-person nostalgia.

Articles should not be submitted incomplete or subject to change/correction/addition. Late changes can create major problems. If you elect to let your sources review your manuscript draft, then *you* deal with them; please complete all discourse with them before submitting the manuscript for publication.

The editors reserve the right to change the title of a submitted article and to alter, condense, expand and otherwise edit the text of the article without approval by the author.

PHOTOGRAPHS & ILLUSTRATIONS

Sandlapper buys black-and-white prints, color transparencies and art. Photographers should submit working cutlines for each photograph. Unused photos will be returned to the photographer if adequate return postage is provided. Photos accepted for publication will be retained permanently by *Sandlapper.* (The photographer will hold the copyright, however, and may submit copies for subsequent publication elsewhere at a later time. See "Payment & Rights Acquisition," below.)

QUERIES, ASSIGNMENTS & ARTICLE SUBMITTALS

Unsolicited manuscripts will be considered, but we strongly recommend that you query *in writing* with a brief description of the article topic you have in mind. Several ideas may be described in one query. (Please don't send further query letters until we have responded to your first one.) One or two (maximum) clips of your previously published work would be helpful.

Telephone queries are *discouraged;* we will not be able to give you an immediate decision on the phone, and we prefer that you submit your own typed description rather than make us scribble a description based on telephone notations.

Seasonal article ideas should be suggested at least six months in advance.

Article topics are discussed at regular editorial staff meetings. We try to report on queries within one month. If we like an idea, we will invite the author to submit the article *on speculation;* we will not guarantee purchase of an article in advance of submittal. No kill fees.

Article submittals on microcomputer diskette are encouraged but not required. Acceptable disk systems are PC/MS-DOS in WordPerfect (versions 4.2, 5.0 or 5.1) or generic (ASCII) word processing formats, disk size 5¼" only. The diskette should be accompanied by a print-out of the text. Submittal via computer/modern/phone is accepted only in tight deadline situations; electronic text transmittal must be conducted before or after regular business hours, at a time prearranged with the managing editor.

Do not submit an article that is incomplete, is pending approval or revision by your sources, or is otherwise subject to change before we go to press.

PAYMENT & RIGHTS ACQUISITION

Payment for articles and photographs varies, based on a freelance budget of approximately $50-100 per published magazine page (including combined text and photography/art). We typically pay $25-$75 per photograph and artwork; maximum $100 for a cover or centerspread photo.

Payment normally is made approximately one month after publication.

The author will retain the copyright. *Sandlapper* will acquire a) the right of first publication of the article, b) subsequent, multiple reprint rights and c) the right to grant access to the article, its title and other bibliographic citation material stored electronically in public databases, and to furnish printed copies thereof requested through such public databases. If the author subsequently grants reprint rights to another publication, *Sandlapper* requests but does not require that the subsequent publication include credit to *Sandlapper* as the original publisher. *Sandlapper* requires a current issue embargo on subsequent publication; the article must not appear in print elsewhere until after the dateline period of its *Sandlapper* appearance has ended.

By submitting an article, the author warrants and represents that a) the author has included no material in the article in violation of any rights of any person or entity, and b) the author has disclosed to *Sandlapper* all relationships of the author to any person or entity featured in the article, and all relationships to any person or entity producing or marketing any product or providing any service referred to in the article.

A NOTE ABOUT IDEA SUBMITTALS

Before the start-up of the magazine was announced formally, the editors began building a database of article ideas (several hundred, initially). Most of these were the editors' ideas; some came from prospective freelance writers. We immediately discovered many suggestions were duplicates—as many as five different writers suggested the same article topic almost simultaneously. In the ensuing weeks, as more freelancers got word of pending publication, the duplicity of certain article topics quickly became a *multiplicity.*

We try to be fair. Whenever we receive a good article suggestion, we enter a brief description of it in a computer database, noting the name of the original proposer. However, we make no pledges. If you suggest an article idea to us and you see an article on the subject published later in the magazine under another writer's byline, it probably will be because a) that writer submitted the idea first or b) we believed that writer had better credentials to prepare that particular article.

Thank you for your interest in *Sandlapper!* We wish you the best with your writing, photography and art, and we hope to work with you in the future.

Categories: Nonfiction—Arts—Cooking—Culture—Entertainment—Environment—Gardening—General Interest—History—Hobbies—Humor—Interview—Lifestyles—Outdoors—Photography—Recreation—Regional—Rural America—Sports—Travel

Name: Aïda Rogers, Assistant Editor
Material: All

Address: PO BOX 1108
City/State/ZIP: LEXINGTON SC 29071
Telephone: 803-359-9954
Fax: 803-957-8226
Internet: www.sandlapper.org

Scavenger's Newsletter

Scavenger's is a market newsletter for SF/Fantasy/Horror/Mystery writers and artists with an interest in the small press and as such is a limited market for writing and art, though most of the content is markets information. However, with 12 regularly scheduled issues a year, it is a market for some types of writing and art.

WRITING: Articles of specific interest to my readers who are writers/artists/small press editors. While I look at topics about the "basics," I'm always looking for unique subjects or treatments. 1,000 words max.

Short humor: emphasis on the bizarre as opposed to the whimsical or cute. Humor used only occasionally. 500-700 words.

Flash fiction: 700-1,200 words in the genres covered by SCAV. Looking for work that has great style and atmosphere and at least seems to say a great deal in the small space. No writing-related fiction unless it is spectacular.

Poetry: 10 lines and under, used as filler. Genres as above. Writing-related used if it is not of the "poor pitiful me as writer" school.

ART: Covers: half-legal size (8½"x7"). Genre themes. Inside art: small, usually no larger than 4"x4". Artwork may be expanded or reduced, but not to any great degree. Send clear photocopies, not originals.

PAYMENT: $4 articles, covers, fiction, $2 poems, humor, inside art. On acceptance + 1 contributor's copy.

TIME LAG: As with all small press magazines it can be awhile before your work sees print, but I try to have everything accepted in print within a year. That doesn't mean I always accomplish it, but it's my goal. If I'm holding something of yours and you're getting impatient, inquire politely and that sometimes speeds things up.

COPYRIGHT: Copyright not registered, but a notice appears on the contents page: Rights revert to creators upon publication. I buy only one-time rights. I use reprints and pay the same as for originals, however, I need to have copyright information on reprints so I can give credit for first publication.

FORMAT: You can send everything, with the exception of covers, in a #10 envelope. Unlike many editors, I'm willing to receive submissions without SASE under these conditions: If your submission is absolutely irresistible, I will accept it, and pop for the postage to send the check. If I cannot use the submission, there will be no response. If you haven't heard anything in a month from the postmark date, consider the ms. rejected. Of course, if you do send SASE, you will get a reply within a month.

I'm willing to look at any readable submission. Simultaneous submissions, dot matrix, photocopies okay. I will probably be asking if you can supply your ms on a disk, but having it available on disk has nothing to do with its acceptance or rejection. If I request a disk I will return it at my expense. If you send an unsolicited disk without SASE, I won't pay to return it. My computer is IBM compatible and can use either 3.5" or 5.25" disks. Now open to e-mail submissions. I don't usually get attachments. Short submissions probably best by this means. If I don't confirm receipt within a week I probably didn't get it.

SCAV is not a subscribers only publication but I hope you're realistic enough to know that without monetary support small press wouldn't exist. Sample copy $2.50 in US & Canada, $4 overseas. Subscription $17/yr (12 issues), $8.50/6 mo bulk mail. $21, $10.50 First Class, $20, $10 Canada, $26, $13 overseas (Air Mail).

Canada/Overseas orders in US currency, international money order in US funds, IRCs or US mint stamps.

CURRENT STATUS: Reading selectively due to backlog.

Categories: Fiction—Nonfiction—Fantasy—Horror—Science Fiction—Writing

Name: Janet Fox, Editor/Publisher
Material: All
Address: 519 ELLINWOOD
City/State/ZIP: OSAGE CITY KS 66523-1329
Telephone: 785-528-3538
E-mail: foxscavl@jc.net

Science of Mind
A Philosophy, a Faith, a Way of Life

Science of *Mind*® magazine accepts query letters only. Include a brief description/outline and word count. We publish several types of articles that teach, inspire, motivate, and inform. Editorial content addresses the concerns, interests, and problems of readers offering thoughtful perspectives on how they can experience greater self-acceptance, empowerment, and meaningful living. Achieving wholeness through applying Science of Mind principles is the primary focus.

The basic requirements of good, clear writing apply to all material used in the magazine. In addition, these special guidelines should also be noted:

First-Person Articles—These articles concern individuals who have experienced a significant, often dramatic, event in their lives. The theme of the article should inspire readers to make a similar change in their own lives. The article may also recount a deep spiritual experience or the way in which Science of Mind principles have been applied to create a positive inner change. **Queries only.** Length: 1,000-2,000 words. Payment: $25 per printed page.

Interview—Each month an interview with a notable spiritual leader is featured. These articles are usually assigned, but queries are welcome. Refer to previous issues of SCIENCE OF MIND for typical interview subjects and style to be followed. Bio, lead-in and photo required. Length: 3,500 words. Payment: $350.

Daily Guides—Inspirational meditative readings for each day of the month are based on SOM teachings and include a quotation from scripture as well as THE SCIENCE OF MIND by Ernest Holmes. A sample set of six Daily Guides may be submitted. These are usually written by Science of Mind ministers or practitioners, but not always. Refer to previous issues of SCIENCE OF MIND for length, style, and sample content. Payment: $250-$300.

Poetry—A limited number of poems are accepted and should be inspirational in theme and characterized by an appreciation for SOM principles. Average length: 8-12 lines. Max. length: 25-30 lines. (Not necessary to submit a query for poetry). Payment: $25.00.

Payable within 30 days of publication.

1. Carefully check punctuation, spelling, and sentence structure before submitting your article. ELEMENTS OF STYLE by William Strunk is an excellent source book for basic writing practices.

2. Make a concerted effort to use language that is inclusive and gender neutral.

3. All accepted articles should be typed and preferably accompanied by Macintosh or IBM disc.

4. Type the number of words in the upper right corner of the first page. Be sure to include your name, address, and telephone number.

REMINDERS

- Ensure quality printout.
- Double-space everything, including quotations.
- Do not try to imitate the typeset copy using different styles of type. Simply type everything normally using lower-case letters, capitalizing in accordance with standard practice.
- Represent the quotations accurately and be sure they are sourced correctly.
- Be sincere.

SOM Photo Guidelines

Images for use in *Science of Mind* magazine should reflect the contemporary, creative, and empowering message of the Science of Mind philosophy. From conceptual to artistically literal, photographic materials should convey a thoughtfulness and originality which will enhance editorial content.

SOM magazine accepts duplicate transparencies or prints only. Please do not send original images. All photographic material must have the photographer's name clearly printed on each image. Credit line is given. On acceptance, images will be filed in the *Science of Mind* Stock Library by subject matter. Upon usage, the photographer will be notified. *Always* include a 6"X9" SASE when submitting images for consideration.

Payment is $300 for cover, $100 inside. For other publications, i.e., books, brochures, flyers, advertising, product, etc., payment will be determined on a per project basis. Advertising usage is limited to the instance per advertisement and does not reflect the number of times the advertisement is run.

Payment will be made within 30 days of the masthead date. For example, photographs used in the June issue will be paid by June 30. We buy one-time rights unless otherwise specified. Simultaneous submissions and previously published work are accepted.

Include a SASE for safe return of images. Again, please send only duplicates.

Categories: Nonfiction—Inspirational—New Thought—Poetry—Religion—Spiritual

Name: Jim Shea, Assistant Editor
Material: Daily Guides, Articles, Queries
Name: Randall Friesen, Art Director
Material: Photographic Material, Artwork
Name: Sylvia Delgado, Poetry Editor
Material: Poetry
Address: PO BOX 75127
City/State/ZIP: LOS ANGELES CA 90075-0127
Telephone: 213-388-2181
Fax: 213-388-1926

Sci-Fi Invasion!
The Science Fiction Magazine

Thank you for your interest in *Sci-Fi Invasion!: The Science Fiction Magazine*.

Invasion! assigns articles from freelance writers on a broad range of subjects related to science fiction entertainment. We've done previews of upcoming movies such as "Alien Resurrection" and "Starship Troopers," episode guides on shows such as "X-Files" and "Babylon 5," Q&As and interviews with Anthony Daniels and J. Michael Straczynski, articles that examine potential "Star Wars" prequel and sequel plots, an analysis of women in sci-fi and a list of the top 25 aliens of all time, as well as other standard and humorous features and departments.

Story lengths generally range from 500 to 3,500 words. Please query first as to the suitability of your subject and approach. Because of our quarterly schedule, please consider timeliness when querying. Writers whose work has not appeared in *Invasion!*

should include tear sheets or published articles when submitting story proposals, as well as a letter detailing your knowledge base and industry contacts. **Introductory writers may be asked to write on speculation, with no guarantee of payment.**

Allow at least six weeks for consideration of a query or manuscript. No follow-up phone calls, please. Work that's assigned and contracted is paid upon publication.

The editors regret that they cannot accept unsolicited manuscripts or offer individual comments on submissions. Correspondence should include the writer's name, address, phone number with area code and e-mail address.

Categories: Nonfiction—Entertainment—Film/Video—Science Fiction—Television

Name: Matthew Saunders, Associate Editor
Material: All
Address: 151 WELLS AVE
City/State/ZIP: CONGERS NY 10920
Telephone: 914-268-2000
Fax: 914-268-0053
E-mail: SFIMatt@aol.com

SciTech Magazine

Thank you for your interest in *SciTech*, a quarterly magazine that motivates young adults about learning science, math, and technology. *SciTech Magazine* is an easy-to-read resource that teaches how everyday activities and events are related to science and technology.

SciTech helps teenagers make the "science and math connection" so that they can find it easier to learn and like these subjects. The quarterly contains articles dealing with everything from the physics of space travel to the life of a transplant surgeon.

Guidelines:

Articles must be written with a depth of knowledge and understanding of the subject matter suitable for young adults. We are always looking for new and fresh ideas, particularly about current events in science, nature, and technology. Most articles also refer readers to related web sites on the Internet to encourage them to become computer literate. *SciTech Magazine* is also a college preparatory package. Each issue focuses on a college-related issue such as finding college scholarships.

Approximately 70 percent of the articles in *SciTech Magazine* are written by freelance writers. The articles run anywhere from 400 to 1,200 words. They are usually accompanied by photographs, but there is no expectation that authors will submit photographs with the articles.

It is best to first submit a one-page proposal introducing the article you envision. Describe the approach, sources, and possibilities for illustration. Please suggest a length for the story and the proposed feature. Writers should include a list of their credits and tear sheets of published articles. We will consider simultaneous submissions.

There are several columns that a writer might consider writing for. A partial list includes: Science Mysteries, Science & Society, Medical Specialties, Alternative Careers (a section about a science or technology-related field), Technology/Computers, Cool Web sites and Puzzles.

Before submitting a proposal, the author is encouraged to study a recent issue of the magazine. A copy may be obtained by sending a check for $4.00 (includes postage).

Allow four to eight weeks for consideration of a proposal or a manuscript. Articles that are submitted must be accompanied by a 3.5" disk for use on a IBM-compatible computer. Electronic submissions are also accepted. References or sources of information must be included with submissions. Disks should include author's name, address, and daytime phone number.

We purchase first North American publishing rights and pay within 30 days of acceptance. Rates vary, depending on length and content, from $15 for puzzles to $40 to $100 for articles. Complimentary issues are provided to contributors. We are always looking for exciting and science-related original art. We prefer to receive 35mm slides or photographs. We pay photographers $40 to $100 per photo.

Send article ideas, manuscripts, and artwork. No follow-up phone calls, please.

We look forward to your ideas and stories.

Categories: Nonfiction—Careers—Computers—Internet (related web sites)—Medical—Puzzles—Science—Technology—Young Adults

Name: **Kim Magliore, Editor**
Material: **All Articles**
Name: **Illeny Maaza, Art Director**
Material: **Art**
Address: **1382 THIRD AVE STE 399**
City/State/ZIP: **NEW YORK NY 10021**
Telephone: **212-288-0914**
Fax: **212-439-9109**
E-mail: **km@interport.net**

The Scroll Newsletter

Please refer to *NOMMA Fabricator* magazine.

Sea Kayaker

Sea Kayaker is devoted solely to sea kayaks, their use, design, and history. Our feature articles, written by both amateur and professional writers, explore subjects in depth. Because we seek to inform, as well as entertain, we prefer contributions from experienced kayakers. Our ideal manuscript conveys interesting and useful information in clear, vivid terms.

Proposals and queries

If you have a story idea you think might interest us, phone us to get our immediate feedback. After we've had a chance to establish the story's suitability, we may ask you to follow up with a more detailed outline and samples of your work. If you have slides, photos or drawings that might help us in our evaluation, send those along. You are welcome to submit finished manuscripts, but you can often save a lot of work by consulting with us before you write.

Get familiar with the magazine

To gain a better understanding of the types of articles we tend to publish, look at a few back issues. We'll gladly sell those to you if they aren't available in your area. To order back issues give us a call at (206) 789-9536. Keep in mind, however, that we welcome new ideas and approaches. Our emphasis is on touring, though we occasionally look at other aspects of the sport such as surf kayaking, ocean kayak racing, or surf skiing.

Article topics

To submit a *Health, Safety, Technique*, or *Equipment* article, you must have some expertise on the subject about which you are writing. Similar guidelines apply to *History* pieces (traditional equipment and technique, journeys from long ago, ethnographic research, legends, etc.). We occasionally accept stories or poems about sea kayaking under our *Fiction* or *Poetry* headings. For travel narratives that often appear as color features, we look for well-crafted stories that convey a strong sense of place and adventure. *Destination* articles are straightforward descriptions of the paddling potential of areas that can accommodate lots of trips without becoming crowded. We look for familiarity with the area (local knowledge); one trip is not enough.

Under our *Technique* heading, we've published articles on bracing, surf entry and exit, and various Eskimo rolls. Kayaking with kids, military use of kayaks, and kite sailing are some of the topics we've covered in the *Alternatives* section. In *Pursuits*, we've looked at beachcombing, fishing, beach hiking, expedition planning, and team kayaking. Directions for a homemade spray skirt, Greenland paddle, kite, and kayak building projects have appeared in our *Do-It-Yourself* pages. We've run a few articles on kayak design, a subject that interests us a great deal. We have a significant *Environment* section in which we've published a series on marine invertebrates, a series on birds, and articles about pollution, geology, and bears. We also do *Essays*, and evocative *Impression* pieces, occasional profiles and book excerpts, and book reviews.

Submission requirements

Text: We need typed copy. Articles usually run from 1,000 to 3,000 words, depending on the subject. If you write on a word processor, please send a disk with your hard copy. Mark your disk with your name, the file name, and the program used. Enter plain text; any fancy formatting makes conversion to our system difficult. Do not submit manuscripts by mail unless requested.

When submitting a story with illustrations or photographs, include a list of captions or descriptions. Maps, if they are appropriate, should accompany your submission. Mark locations as they relate to the text.

Send a stamped, self-addressed envelope or enough money in the form of postal coupons to cover the cost of your material's return from Seattle. Keep a copy of your text on paper or on disk to refer to should we need to call with questions.

We will acknowledge receipt of your submission as soon as possible, but it may take us some time to evaluate it. Once we have accepted an article it will be at least three months before it is published.

Photographs

We work most often from color slides. If you send either black-and-white or color prints we may ask for negatives so we can make prints to meet our requirements. We prefer to work with original slides instead of duplicates.

Unusual, humorous, or spectacular photos suitable for our *Document* section (a "parting shot" photo) or for our cover artists pay around $45.

Mark all prints and slides with your name and address. Include a list of descriptions. If you mark your slides for copyright ©, please send us a signed letter authorizing us to have prints made from them.

Artwork

We use color cover artwork in any medium (oil, acrylic, watercolor, etc.), and especially artistic photographs. Contact us for details. We also commission artwork for inside pages.

Return of Materials

Discs and reference materials (maps, sketches, etc.) will be returned by first-class mail. Irreplaceable photographs and artwork should be sent via registered mail. We will return such materials by the same means (certified, registered, insured, etc.) in which we received them. We take great care in handling your materials but we cannot assume responsibility for damage or loss of your contributions.

Rates

Text: We pay about $120 per 1,000 words. Excellent writing and special projects may pay more.

Artwork: We pay a minimum of $250 for cover art, more for commissioned works. For other drawings and illustrations we pay between $25 and $250, depending upon size, colors and complexity.

Photographs:

	Color	B&W
Full page	$100	$75

¾ page	75	60
½ page	65	45
¼ page	45	30
Spot	25	15

We buy first North American rights, and occasionally consider second rights. You are welcome to submit your material on speculation. Simultaneous submissions or inquiries must be clearly identified as such. Freelance contributions are paid upon publication. We will send you a copy of the issue in which your contribution appears when it is available.

Thank you, and we hope to hear from you.

Christopher Cunningham
Managing Editor
Sample Issue: $5.75
Subscriptions (rates based on six issues a year):
$20.95 for US addresses
$24.00 US for Canadian addresses
$27.00 US for all other addresses
Washington State residents please include 8.6% sales tax
Categories: Sports—Kayaking—Sea Kayaking

Name: Karen Matthee, Editor
Material: Sea Kayaking Articles
Address: PO BOX 17170
City/State/ZIP: SEATTLE WA 98107-0870
Telephone: 206-789-1326
Fax: 206-781-1141
E-mail: seakayak@eskimo.com

Sea
The Magazine of Western Boating

ABOUT SEA

Sea is four-color, monthly publication for active West Coast boat owners. It was founded in 1908, and is published by the Duncan McIntosh Co. Circulation is approximately 50,000.

Sea is read by power boaters and sportfishing enthusiasts from Alaska to Mexico, and across the Pacific to Hawaii. *Sea* contains articles on Western cruising and fishing destinations, new boats and marine electronics, safety, navigation, seamanship, maintenance how-to, consumer guides to boating services, marine news and product buyer's guides.

Readers of *Sea* are experienced boaters: • 89.4% own a boat • 91.5% own a power boat • 58.8% have been boating 20+ years • 63% sportfish from their boat. —Source: Simmons Market Research

EDITORIAL FOCUS

Feature articles generally are between 1,000 and 1,200 words. Other articles range between 250 and 750 words. First-time contributors are encouraged to pitch articles on:

• West Coast cruising destinations—especially those in Baja California, Southern California, Puget Sound and British Columbia.

• Boating news from your Western home port.

• Western boating trends and issues.

• Seamanship (power boating only).

• Boat maintenance and repair.

Another good avenue for freelancers is *Sea*'s West Coast Focus section. It is comprised of brief news stories or isolated bits of information about Western boating and sportfishing. Focus stories are about 250 words each, and stand the best chance of running if they are accompanied by a color slide.

Focus story topics include: new marinas and boating projects; new fishing regulations; boat parades, festivals or owner rendezvous; and boating legislation updates. Preview stories are preferred over post-event reports, so readers who wish to partici-

pate may do so.

WHAT NOT TO SEND

Sea is not the market for stories about: boardsailing, canoeing, kayaking or surfing; power boat racing; wetlands restoration; party boat fishing; commercial fishing; boating accident reports; fiction; poetry; yacht club-oriented social activities; marine mammals; ferry boats, steamships, military ships, cruise ships, river boats or any boat or ship that is not a pleasureboat; and boating events on the East Coast of the United States or abroad.

SUBMISSION GUIDELINES

Submit written queries.

• Please allow 4 weeks for review of unsolicited manuscripts.

• Assigned stories should be sent on 3.5" computer disk, single spaced in ASCII format or Microsoft Word. Enclose a hard copy of the story with the disk.

• Include your address, daytime phone number and social security number on the first page of the manuscript.

• Sea buys first-time North American rights. Please notify us if your query or manuscript is a simultaneous submission or has been previously published.

PAYMENT

• Rates are based on length of the article, amount of research required and complexity of the assignment. A rate will be quoted by the assigning editor prior to commencement of work.

• Payment for articles and photographs used is made on publication. Checks are sent out in the first week of the issue month.

• Quoted rates may change if a story does not meet the criteria of the assignment. If major revisions are required, we will return the manuscript to the author to revise prior to final editing or rate adjustment.

• Some expenses, such as telephone calls or mileage, may be reimbursed by the assigning editor only if approval for such expenses is requested in advance. An invoice itemizing the expenses must be submitted within 10 days of the article.

• Approved overnight mail charges are reimbursed. We do not accept C.O.D. packages and do not have an account with a mailing service.

• Sea retains reprint rights via print and electronic media. The contributor retains all other rights for resale, re-publication, etc.

• It may be necessary to reschedule the publication date of the author's accepted work as editorial space dictates.

FOR MORE INFORMATION

Individual guidelines are available upon request for:

• West Coast Focus, SoCal Focus, Boat Reports and Cruising Destination Features.

Thank you for your interest.

Categories: Nonfiction—Boating—Recreation—Sports—Travel

Name: Bart Ortberg, Managing Editor
Name: Erin McNiff, Executive Editor
Material: Any
Address: 17782 COWAN STE C
City/State/ZIP: IRVINE CA 92614
Telephone: 714-660-6150
Fax: 714-660-6172

Seattle Magazine
The Magazine for the Pacific Northwest

Seattle, The Magazine for the Pacific Northwest, is the four-color glossy magazine serving the Seattle area-from North Bend to Vashon, from Edmonds to Tacoma-and the Pacific Northwest region. Articles for the magazine should be written with our readership in mind. Most of our readers live in Western Washington, though we also reach newcomers and visitors to the area. Active and well-educated, our readers, male and female, hold well-paying jobs, often professional or managerial. They are interested in the arts, social issues, their homes and gardens and in maintaining the region's high quality of life.

Our features cover these subjects as well as local personalities, history, education, real estate, fashion and seasonal events. Regular columns in *Seattle* include Dining, Nightlife, Neighborhood, Weekends, Style, Private Eye and Heroes. In each issue, our Weekends column contains a lead profile of a Pacific Northwest destination, as well as short reviews of the region's best bed and breakfasts or small hotels. Neighborhood columns are first-person looks at specific neighborhoods. Nightlife covers original entertainment to be found in the city.

Private Eye is a short one-page profile of a local personality that focuses on one of his or her private interests or passions, preferably something that has not already been covered extensively in the press. And Heroes profiles people who are making a difference in the community. Other columns cover local history, sports, arts and entertainment and nature. Our front section, Front Lines, features short articles, usually with pictures, on interesting local issues, people, events and companies.

Although the magazine is 80 percent freelance written, we have contributing editors who regularly write the home design features, compile the calendar and cover food and restaurants for our Dining column.

Procedures: All queries should be in writing. Short outlines of story ideas are preferred over fully written manuscripts. First-time writers should submit a resume and sample clips. We do not accept multiple submissions. Typical response time is three months.

Good queries generally suggest how and when the proposed article will best fit into the magazine, and compelling reasons why the story is right for *Seattle*. In addition, they should show that the writer has read the magazine and understands its content and readership.

Should we decide to assign the story, you will be contacted by an editor. Style and content, as well as deadline and payment, are negotiated when the assignment is made. The editor will then issue a contract to be signed by both writer and editor. Writers new to the magazine sometimes work on speculation.

Payment. Freelance writers are paid upon publication, receiving their checks in the middle of the month the story is published. Expenses-such as phone calls or mileage incurred during research-must be agreed upon in advance and will be paid on invoice. *Seattle, The Magazine for the Pacific Northwest*, purchases one-time rights. All editorial material is protected by copyright. Adams Publishing of the Pacific Northwest, Inc. retains the right to reprint editorial material for promotional or nonprofit use by this company only, with credit given.

Features: Word length: 1,000 to 2,500. Payment: $250 or more.
Columns: Word length: 600 to 1,400. Payment begins at $150.
Front Lines: Word length: 150 to 400. Payment: $50-$150.
Categories: Regional

Name: Giselle Smith, Editor
Material: Features, Travel, Profiles
Name: Shannon O'Leary, Associate Editor
Material: Short Features, Intern Info
Name: Ellen L. Boyer, Editorial Assistant
Material: Calendar of Events
Address: 701 DEXTER AVE N STE 101
City/State/ZIP: SEATTLE WA 98109
Telephone: 206-284-1750
Fax: 206-284-2550
Internet: www.seattlemag.com

The Secret Place
For every season, for every reason...

The Secret Place was begun over fifty years ago by a woman who wanted to provide a way to draw Christians closer to Christ and one another. It's now a quarterly devotional magazine with a worldwide readership of over 150,000 and editions in regular print, large print, Braille, and cassette. Produced primarily by Educational Ministries of the American Baptist Churches in the U.S.A., *The Secret Place* is published jointly by the American Baptist Churches in the U.S.A. and the Christian Church (Disciples of Christ), Christian Board of Publication.

The Secret Place is written by freelance writers, and anyone may submit original meditations. Each submission should be typed (if possible), and contain:
• your name, address, phone number, and social security number in the upper left corner.
• a title.
• a suggested Scripture reading of five to ten verses.
• a "Thought for Today," which is usually a Scripture quote (be sure to cite chapter, verses, and Bible version) but may also be a pertinent thought. We will use the New Revised Standard Version unless you specify otherwise.
• an original meditation of 100 to 175 words that relates to the suggested Scripture reading and "Thought for Today." (Do not quote another source unless you have obtained written permission and attached it to your submission.)
• a brief concluding prayer.

We are especially interested in devotional meditations that:
• are original, creative, and spiritually insightful.
• explore less familiar biblical passages.
• address urban/suburban as well as rural/nature experiences.
• appeal to young adults as well as older adults.
• encourage outreach, mission, and service.
• are concise and focused on one theme.
• are inclusive in their use of language.
• are racially and culturally diverse.

We retain the right to edit submissions as necessary for clarity, brevity, and inclusivity of language. Original one-page poems and clear, high-quality photographs (eight-by-ten-inch color prints for the cover, four-by-six-inch or larger black/white or color prints for inside) are also welcome. We pay $15 for each submission published and buy first rights to published materials. We work nine to twelve months ahead of schedule, so please plan your submissions accordingly and allow up to six months for response. Published material will not be returned.

Thank you for contributing to this ministry through your support, submissions, and prayers.

SAMPLE
Your Name
Your Street Address
Your City, State, and ZIP Code
Your Telephone Number
Your Social Security Number
Philippians 4:4-8   Saying Thanks
THOUGHT FOR TODAY: It is good to give thanks to the LORD. Psalm 92:1

Kristen's birthday party was over. Her many gifts were on the table, along with plates of partially eaten cake and ice cream. As her last friend left, Kristen remarked, "It was a nice party, but where's my puppy? I thought I was going to get what I wanted on my birthday!" I saw her mother's disappointed expression; she had spent days and considerable money to make this a happy day for Kristen. She needed some appreciation and thanks.

God must often feel like that. God gives us so many blessings, both in our physical world and in our individual lives. We think those are fine, but "I want" statements still prevail in our thoughts and prayers. The Bible speaks about the importance of being thankful. We can trust the One who knows everything about us, loves us, and cares for our every need. We deprive ourselves as well as God when we forget to be thankful.

PRAYER: Dear God, you are generous to me in so many ways. Forgive my shortsightedness and lack of appreciation. Today I simply give you thanks; in Jesus' name. Amen.

Your Name—City, State

Categories: Religion—Devotional

Name: Kathleen Hayes, Managing Editor
Material: All
Address: PO BOX 851
City/State/ZIP: VALLEY FORGE PA 19482-0851

Seek
the abundant life

For Your Information…

SEEK is a colorful, illustrated weekly take-home or pass-along paper designed to appeal to modern adults and older teens. SEEK first appeared in its present form in 1970, expanding a four-page Sunday school lesson leaflet, which was published for ninety-five years, into a new concept for personal spiritual enrichment. Its use ranges from the classroom of the Sunday morning Bible class to group discussion and light inspirational reading for individuals and the family.

Materials Accepted for Publication…

ARTICLES—400 to 1,200 words in length. Usual rate of payment is about 5¢ per word. Articles for publication in SEEK should be in one of the following categories:

1. Inspirational, devotional, personal, or human interest stories.

2. Controversial subject matter, timely religious issues of moral or ethical nature.

3. First-person testimonies of Christian life or experiences, true-to-life happenings, vignettes, emotional situations or problems, examples of answered prayer.

Articles should not be preachy or patronizing. They must be wholesome, alive, vibrant, current, relevant for today's reader, and have a title that demands the article be read. No poetry, please!

Articles are purchased for SEEK as early as one year before the date of publication. Complimentary copies of articles are mailed to writers immediately following publication.

PHOTOGRAPHS—Good human interest pictures of professional quality to accompany articles. We prefer 8"x10" glossy photos with sharp black-and-white contrast. Rate of payment is about $25.

May We Suggest…

Please type manuscripts on 8" paper. Write name, address, and social security number in upper left-hand corner of the first page. Also indicate approximate number of words in the manuscript at the upper right-hand corner of the first page. Number all pages in center top.

Because of the large volume of correspondence involved, we are unable to critique or offer suggestions in regard to contributions that are not acceptable. You may best determine our needs by a careful study of issues of the magazine. Write for free copies. Self-addressed stamped envelope appreciated.

Categories: Fiction—Nonfiction—Christian Interests—Inspirational—Religion—Short Stories

Name: Eileen Wilmoth, Editor
Material: All

Address: 8121 HAMILTON AVE
City/State/ZIP: CINCINNATI OH 45231-2396
Telephone: 513-931-4050

Self Employed Professional

Who We Are:

Self Employed Professional is the business owner's partner. We provide advice on how to meet the unique challenges of running a small company more efficiently and profitably, whether it's a firm of one or a company of 50. Our articles provide strategies and information in three main areas—finance, technology and marketing. Though our readers come from varying backgrounds, they share a passion for being self-employed, a passion which *SEP* strives to capture in each issue.

Our Editorial Focus:

Articles in *Self Employed Professional* should:

• *Have a small business focus.* You should *interpret* your material for the owner of a business with one to 50 employees. For instance, a marketing story could describe how to scale down effective big-company marketing ideas to a small-company budget. A story on investing in mutual funds would not only describe the funds but could suggest investment strategies for the small business owner who is likely to have an uneven cash flow and difficulty committing chunks of money for long periods of time.

• *Provide insider's information* from small business owners, for instance, guerrilla marketing ideas or ways to keep creditors at bay. You should provide "tricks from the trenches." Give your material an edge. At least some of your information should be new or recast. Otherwise reading your story will be like watching the TV reruns!

• *Include meat.* We need examples from actual small businesses around the country to illustrate all major points of your story. Whenever possible include dollars, percentages, and statistics.

• *Include negatives as well as positives.* You can often learn more from failures than from successes. Be sure to include some negative examples—some small-business failures and what they illustrate. When discussing strategies, always mention risks as well as benefits. *Self Employed Professional* is not the magazine of success but rather, the magazine of success in the making!

• *Provide hands-on, problem-solving information* whenever appropriate. A story on accounting, for example, could provide information that would help a small business owner decide whether to do his accounting in-house or to outsource some or all of it.

The Types of Articles We Publish:

Features (1,500-2,500 words): Feature articles are the showcase pieces of each issue and cover all themes pertinent to being self-employed. Feature writers use their expertise to explore topics in greater depth and to present them in a lively and informative manner. These stories may provide problem-solving tools (for instance, strategies for raising capital), give instructions (how to produce effective direct mail), provide inspiration (a profile of a successful small-business owner and how he or she reached the top) or provide comparative information (the pros and cons of venture capital vs. private investors).

Technology Articles (1,000-1,200 words): Our technology articles run under a separate banner and feature the latest hardware and software for small businesses. While the main purpose of these stories is to inform our readers of new products and their features, we avoid straight product descriptions. Instead, we prefer technology articles to be application driven.

Financial Articles (1,000-1,200 words): These articles also run under a separate banner and cover topics such as business cash flow (for instance, collection and cash management strategies) personal investing, retirement options and banking options. Many financial topics apply to businesses of any size. Be sure to explain the implications and risks for a self-employed professional.

Departments (700-1,200 words). Departments are short, meaty, informational or how-to articles on a variety of topics, again, interpreted for smaller businesses. Departments such as "Boss" (management), "Client Relations," "Marketing," "Marketing Mix," "Cost Cutter," "Employee Relations," "Insurance," "Lawyer," "Taxes," "Managing Technology," and "Up at Night" (last page) run on a rotating basis. Please read some departments in *Self Employed Professional* before you send us ideas.

Query Us:

We work on an assignment basis, so please don't send finished articles. Query us with a succinct outline or description of the proposed story contents and explain why the subject matter is particularly important to a small-business owner. It helps to include your resume, description of your background and a small number of clips pertinent to your query and our content. Query us by letter, fax, or e-mail. We suggest you follow up an electronic query with a hard copy via regular mail. We try to respond to queries within 60 days.

Rights and Payment

We buy all rights (print and electronic). We will not consider articles or article ideas submitted simultaneously to more than one publication. We publish original material, although occasionally we will consider stories or rewrites of stories previously published in small regional publications. We will also consider book chapters on a selective basis if the content is particularly appropriate.

We pay by the word; the rate varies depending on the qualifications of the writer and type of article. When we assign an article, we provide you with a brief that describes the article's content, and we ask you to sign a writer's agreement which specifies payment and terms. You will receive payment approximately 45 days after we accept your finished article.

Categories: Nonfiction—Business (firms of 1-50 employees: management, marketing, money/finance—technology issues)

Name: Carole Matthews, Senior Editor
Material: All
Address: 462 BOSTON ST
City/State/ZIP: TOPSFIELD MA 01983
Telephone: 978-887-7900
Fax: 978-887-6117
E-mail: sepedit@aol.com

Senior Living

About *Senior Living* Newspapers: *Senior Living* newspapers has a circulation of 50,000 plus. Papers are published monthly with distribution in Arkansas, Missouri, Kansas, & Oklahoma. Editorial slant is directed to mid-life and retirement lifestyles and offers a positive and upbeat look at the 50 + reader.

Senior Living readers are primarily well-educated and affluent retirees, homemakers, and career professionals—most of whom enjoy a very active lifestyle.

Topics: *Senior Living* publishes feature articles, personality profiles, and timely articles on travel, health, finance, relationships, nostalgia, consumer issues and retirement. We do very little poetry and no fiction. Staff writers and columnists do most of our writing, but we welcome queries and unsolicited manuscripts.

Query & Cover Letters: A query letter is not necessary, but should you choose to send one, make it short and to the point. Indicate the focus and tone of your proposed article. We prefer that you send a cover letter with your manuscript informing us about your experience or qualifications as a writer. If you don't

have any experience, tell us that too. Perhaps we will be able to help you get a much needed byline. No need to tell us what the article is about, we'll know that when we read it.

Manuscripts should be no longer than 800 words. Preferred length is 400-600 words. They should be typewritten and double-spaced on 8 1/2 X 11 inch paper, with 1 inch margins. Place name, address and Social Security number in upper left corner and word count in upper right corner. Computer discs are acceptable, but you still need to send hard copy. Absolutely no manuscripts or photographs will be returned without a SASE with ample postage to cover their return.

Style: Keep it clear, simple and to the point. Originality, concrete details, short paragraphs and strong words are essential. Avoid flowery prose in articles. Accuracy is a must.

All articles are submitted on a speculative basis unless assigned.

Payment of ($5 to $35) will be decided according to timeliness of article, content, clarity and neatness. Fillers and Poetry, if accepted pays $1 to $5. Checks are mailed 30-45 days post publication. Beginning writers who need a byline, may stand a chance with *Senior Living*. We welcome articles and poems that require no compensation. Please state if payment is, or is not required. Unpaid writers may obtain a paper containing their work by request.

Categories: Nonfiction—General Interest—Health—History—Inspirational—Physical Fitness—Poetry—Senior Citizens—Sports—Recreation—Retirement—Essay—Nostalgia—Personal Experience—Humor

Name: Joyce O'Neal, Managing Editor
Material: All
Address: 318 E. PERSHING
City/State/ZIP: SPRINGFIELD, MO 65806
Fax: 417-862-9079
Internet: www.seniorlivingnewspaper.org

Senior Magazine
If you're over 49 or plan to be!

Senior Magazine welcomes submissions from freelance writers.

Our ideal story or article length is 900—1,200 words.

We are interested in profiles of unusual or notable people, nostalgia, unique hobbies, men and women in second careers, health, physical fitness, humor (if handled deftly, not heavy-handed), travel and reviews of current books.

We pay $1.50 per published column inch and $10-$15 for photos we use with the article or story. We prefer black and white photos.

We receive many more submissions than we can publish. If you would like a query answered or an article returned if we can't use it, enclose a stamped, self-addressed envelope with the query or submission.

For a sample copy of the magazine send $1.50 in postage and a large self-addressed stamped envelope.

We try to respond to queries and submissions within two weeks after receiving them.

Categories: Nonfiction—Biography—Collectibles—Diet—Entertainment—Gardening—Health—Hobbies—Music—Televi-

S-Z

sion/Radio—Theatre—Travel

Name: Anne Stubbs, Health Editor
Material: Health & Fitness
Name: George Brand, Managing Editor
Material: All Other Submissions
Address: 3565 S HIGUERA
City/State/ZIP: SAN LUIS OBISPO CA 93401
Telephone: 805-544-8711
Fax: 805-544-4450

Senior World®
Newsmagazine

Senior World Newsmagazine

TO : Freelance Writers/Photographers
FROM : *Senior World* Editor
RE : Writer's Guidelines
AUDIENCE: *Senior World* is an award-winning monthly tabloid newspaper published for active older adults, 55-plus. Approximately 475,000 copies of *Senior World* are distributed free each month in the following Southern California counties: San Diego, Orange, Riverside, San Bernardino, and Los Angeles. Freelance material purchased by *Senior World* will be considered for use in all editions.

EDITORIAL PROHIBITIONS: *Senior World* will not consider stories that stereotype seniors or portray aging in a negative light. Submissions of poetry and nostalgia pieces are discouraged.

WHAT WE'RE LOOKING FOR: *Senior World* consists of four basic sections: 1) News-local, state and national; 2) Living-features about celebrities, remarkable seniors, consumer stories, finance and investment, housing, sports, hobbies, collectibles, trends, etc; 3) Health-stories on health and medicine emphasizing wellness and preventive care and the latest on medical research, and 4) Travel-stories on international, domestic and close-to-home travel destinations as well as "how-to" stories.

HOW TO SUBMIT YOUR WORK: We prefer a good query letter accompanied by a cover letter providing a synopsis of the submission. Simultaneous and photocopied submissions or a typewritten manuscript are OK.

PAYMENT: Average story length is between 700 and 1,100 words. Payment will be negotiated with each writer on an individual basis. Average payment ranges from $25 to $75. Stories have a better chance at acceptance if good photos/slides are available. Normally, *Senior World* does not pay separately for photos. Please provide captions and a model release (when appropriate).

RESPONSE TO SUBMISSIONS: Allow a minimum of two months. Payment will be made within 30 days of publication.

COLUMNS: Send query letter and sample of proposed column.

TIPS ON HOW TO GET PUBLISHED IN SENIOR WORLD: Read the publication to get an idea of format and style. Sample copies cost $4; an annual mail subscription costs $10 (USA only). Adhere to the above guidelines. Do not make telephone inquiries. Poor spelling and grammar and sloppy presentation will automatically disqualify a submission. Include your address and telephone number on all submissions and related correspondence.

We look forward to hearing from you.
Categories: Senior Citizens

Name: Laura Impastate, Executive Editor
Material: All

Address: 500 FESLER ST
Address: PO BOX 13560
City/State/ZIP: EL CAJON CA 92022
Telephone: 619-593-2910

Sensual Aspirations
The Journal for the Sexually Inspired

Thank you for your interest in submitting your material to Sensual Aspirations, The Journal for the Sexually Inspired.

Our intent is to give unpublished/new writers a chance to get their hard work out there, while providing a quality, theme oriented, journal of erotica.

All submissions are welcomed.
Writers Guidelines:
Fiction between 500 and 5,000 words. Subject matter pertaining mainly to bondage type scenarios. Includes Dom/sub, mind control, non-consensual/rape, FemDom, fantasy, M/M, F/F. Anything well written will be considered, but the main focus is bondage, and "the not so accepted" fantasies.
Poetry Guidelines:
Must be erotic in nature, b&d oriented a major plus, no depressing prose will be considered. Short, to the point, sexual, sensual, not necessarily "graphic." We are in need of more stories than poetry at the moment, so send no more than 5 at a time.
Illustrator Guidelines:
One caption scenes, either self explanatory, or with a one liner. Black and white only. Send a copy, never the original.
Payment:
As this is brand "spankin" new and funded totally by me, (funds? What are *those*!?), payment at this time consists of contributor copies, (up to four), and my sincere gratitude.
Miscellaneous:
Short jokes, (one liners), to use as fillers between stories. No "bathroom humor", must be amusing, b&d, or sexual in nature a plus, 15-25 words. *True tales,* a recount of a true to life, preferably real, sexual encounter, 500-2,000 words.
E-mail Submissions:
We accept submissions via e-mail—no file attachments (note: file attachments are fine as long as they are text based and not zipped). *No* submission will be published without a signed consent, so please include an address to snail mail the consent form.
Categories: Fiction—Erotica—Humor—Poetry—Short Stories

Name: S.A. Voishe, Managing Editor
Material: All
Address: PO BOX 8252
City/State/ZIP: BERLIN CT 06037
E-mail: Domn8me189@aol.com
or SensualAspirations@juno.com

Shape Magazine

When submitting a manuscript to Shape, please follow the guidelines below regarding format, style, fact-checking and backup information. For further information see a recent issue of the magazine. Any manuscript submitted without adequate information will be returned to you, which may result in a delay in publication. Shape is not responsible for unsolicited material. We reserve the right to edit any article as we see fit.

Manuscripts should be typed double-spaced, with numbered pages. Include your name, address, phone number and social security number on the first page. Use the Associated Press Stylebook and Libel Manual for style information, along with the information below.

Include professional degrees with experts' names, and a brief description of each person's position, i.e., Dr. James Brown should be James Brown, M.D., Ph.D., a cardiologist at University Hospital in Madison, Wisconsin.

If source information was reported in another article (newspaper, journal, bulletin, magazine), get original study or verification from author or publisher of original material.

Backup materials should be provided by the writer and should include:

* Correct spellings of names and reference institutions.

* Correct spellings of all brand names with attention to upper and lower case, hyphens and unusual spacing.

* Current addresses if mentioned (checked).

* Phone numbers: Authors should call the number noted to ask whether it is the correct number for the purpose and if we can print it. Please note on your manuscript the name and position of the person you talked to.

* Sources for items the readers may buy, including 800 numbers. If the 800 number is not good in Canada or in a particular state, provide a regular number as well, or an address for ordering.

* Correct spelling of all book titles and authors' names cited as:

Bookname, by Author, academic/professional degree (City, State: Publisher, year). Include a phone number for checking reprint rights as well, if necessary.

* Phone numbers we can use to check all of the above.

Provide a biography for yourself, in this form: Jane Doe, Ph.D., is a psychiatrist at State University, Dallas, Texas, and author of Writing for Dollars. (Include phone numbers for institutions listed in bio, for fact-checking.)

When we use recipes, we use the following abbreviations:

cup/cups
tsp/tsp
tbs/tbs
oz/oz
lb/lbs

• List all ingredients in the order in which they are used in the recipe.

• List topping or dressing ingredients under a subhead in the order in which they are used in the recipe.

• If it's possible to say "Combine the next live ingredients," instead of listing the ingredients, please do so.

• We list "Preheat the oven to XXX F" first, if the oven is used.

• List the number of servings or the yield of the recipe in italics under the recipe name.

• In a separate paragraph at the end of the recipe, list the calories per serving (if you listed yield instead of servings at the beginning, indicate a serving size) as follows: Per 6-ounce serving: 67 calories; 54-percent carbohydrate, 20-percent protein, 26-percent fat. Check that the percentage adds up to 100. If not, correct the figures.

• Recipes published in Shape must contain no more than 30-percent calories from fat.

• When listing brand-name items, include actual label for fact-checking.

Photos or slides should be submitted with the photographer's or institution's name as it is to appear in the credit printed on them. Include a description of the location if necessary and model releases for every identifiable person in the photo.

Categories: Nonfiction—Cooking—Fashion—Food/Drink—Health—Interview—Physical Fitness—Sports—Recreation—Travel—Nutrition—How-to—Profiles—Medicine—Beauty—Women's Issues—Diet

Name: Peg Moline, Editorial Director
Material: All
Address: 21100 ERWIN ST.
City/State/ZIP: WOODLAND HILLS, CA 91367
Telephone: 818-595-0593
Fax: 818-704-762
Internet: www.shapemag.com

Shofar Magazine

Managing Editor Gerald H. Grayson. For Jewish children 9-13. Reports in 6-8 weeks. Complete manuscripts preferred. Queries welcome. Pays on publication. $0.10/word plus five copies. Black/white, color prints purchased with mss. at additional fee.

Nonfiction, fiction (600-1,000 words), poetry, photos, puzzles, games, cartoons. (Artwork on assignment only.) **All material must be on a Jewish theme.** Special holiday issues. (Submit holiday theme pieces at least four months in advance.) Will consider photocopied and simultaneous submissions. Buys first North American serial rights or first serial rights. For free sample copy send a 9"x12" SASE with four first class stamps.

Categories: Jewish Children's Magazine

Name: Managing Editor
Material: All
Address: 43 NORTHCOTE DR
City/State/ZIP: MELVILLE NY 11747
Telephone: 516-643-4598
Fax: 516-643-4598

Shuttle Spindle & Dyepot
Handweavers Guild of America, Inc.

Published by the Handweavers Guild of America, Inc., *Shuttle Spindle & Dyepot* magazine features emerging artists and craftspeople, highlights innovative techniques and events, and honors established fiber artists and textile traditions. SS&D is a magazine for artists and craftspeople. As an international forum for weavers, spinners, dyers, basketmakers, and felters, it is a visually appealing, in-depth publication that promotes excellence in fiber art through articles that inform, enlighten, instruct, and inspire.

Articles:

We are interested in articles that present ideas and concepts related to textile arts, articles on textile history and preservation, artists' profiles and guild-related projects. We feature in-depth reviews of museum, gallery and textile shows as well as articles examining current issues relative to textiles.

Targeting all levels of experience, we look for articles on weaving, spinning, dyeing, felting, weaving with beads and basketmaking that examine a technique or tradition. Our emphasis is on developing design skills, understanding techniques, marketing and craftsmanship.

Manuscripts:

We invite written proposals that summarize the subject and point of view of the article. Complete articles, not exceeding 1,200 words, are also welcomed.

Please present your article or ideas in the following format:

• Type and double space.

• Provide a hard copy and a disk copy in an ASCII file, Microsoft Word* (saved as Word 2), or WordPerfect (saved as WP 5.1). Indicate IBM or Macintosh format.*

• Place your name and address and on the upper right hand corner of each page.

• Indent paragraphs.

• Use two-inch margins at the top and bottom and one inch

on the sides.

• If the article is unsolicited, please include a brief outline of the article, hard copy only (no longer than one page).

• Include the bibliography at the end of the manuscript on the hard copy and disk.

• Include photo captions on the hard copy and disk.

• Include a list (hard copy) of enclosed illustrations (photographs, slides, drawdowns, graphs, line drawings) with an accompanying descriptive note of each illustration.

• Include a brief autobiographical note.

Illustrations:

We use clear, good quality original slides, 4X5 transparencies and/or black and white glossy prints to illustrate articles.

All slides and photographs should be sharp and clear without background clutter. Photographs should be included on the list of illustrations with a brief description. All illustrations/photographs/ samples should be keyed to the text and captioned. Do not write on the back of photographs but tape a piece of paper on the back of the photo. People in the photograph should be identified.

All illustrations should be labeled with the following information:

• Name of artist and/or author

• Address of author (or artist if different)

• Name of piece, dimensions, fiber content and other pertinent information

• Name of photographer to be given photo credit

• How the piece is keyed to the text for example (*illustration 1*)

• An arrow on the right side indicating the top of the slide/ photograph!

When it is necessary for the author/artist to send in the actual piece for in-house photography, the item must be tagged with:

• Owner's name and shipping address

• Title of the piece

• An indication of the right side

• Insurance value

• The piece must be keyed to the text.

We will return the piece/s postage paid, insured via the same transport service used for delivery.

Drafts:

In order to keep drafts uniform all drafts will be redone on a computer software program to our specifications.

• Draw drafts on graph paper.

• Use numbers to mark the threading draft.

• For the rising shed (jack loom) tie-up draft, number the harnesses, with the highest number on top and the lowest on the bottom, and indicate it as a rising shed.

• For the sinking shed (counter balance) tie-up draft, use X.

• Use short vertical dashes for the treadling draft.

• For the drawdown, fill in the squares where appropriate.

• Be sure to label the threading and the treadling.

• Indicate tabby by using a and b.

The Publication Process

Once a manuscript is chosen for publication, the copy is read for content, clarity, conflicts and duplications. Then it is sent to the copy-editor.

The copy editor checks spelling, punctuation and grammar. This editor also corrects awkward sentence structure, then edits and checks to see that names and places are spelled correctly, whatever appears on the original copy from the author is considered correct. For example, if a person's last name is Smith and the author spells it Smythe, we have no way of knowing that it should be Smith.

The copy then goes to the typesetter for page layout. The typesetter places the copy in a three column format and prints a proof copy.

Author Proof:

A proof or draft copy is returned to the author for verification and author comments.

It is extremely important to check the spelling of names and places at this time. Everyone-authors, members and guilds-loves to see their name in print, especially in their national organization's magazine, but only if it is spelled correctly!

Check: Photo, illustration and diagram captions; author's biographical note, as well as Illustrations and diagrams.

Comments from the author should be forwarded (faxed, if possible) to the editor as quickly as possible with errors, misspelled names or misplaced diagrams noted on the returned copy.

Review by Consultants:

The manuscript will also be reviewed by a specialist. For example, an article that includes formulas for mixing dyes will be reviewed by a chemist. Once the consultant's and author's comments have been implemented the page layouts are designed.

Proofreader:

The proofreader inspects all final copy and photo captions.

Honoraria and Publication Agreement:

The Handweavers Guild of America, Inc., provides a small honorarium upon publication of an article. In exchange, the author agrees to convey first English Language publication rights and Anthology (reprint) rights to The Handweavers Guild of America, Inc./*Shuttle Spindle & Dyepot*. In addition, the author agrees not to sell, assign or transfer any remaining rights in and to the article until six months after publication in SS&D, unless otherwise agreed with the editor.

References:

All references must be documented.

Bibliography:

Please use this format for a book:

Atwater, Mary M. *The Shuttlecraft Book of American Hand-Weaving*. New York: Macmillan Publishers, 1928.

Use this format for a magazine article:

Guy, Sallie. "Twill 2-Double Width Afghans." *Shuttle Spindle & Dyepot*, Winter 1983, 34.

Citations:

Parenthetical references are used to clarify (in the body of the text) when documenting research, or when reference should be made to a particular book, page or section of a book.

For example: author, date method (Atwater 1928)

or author, date, page method (Atwater 1928, p.178)

For sample see: Duncan, Kate. "The Kutchin Baby Carrying Strap." *Shuttle Spindle & Dyepot*, Spring 1992, 38.

Book Review Guidelines:

Book reviews follow general manuscript instructions:

See page one (1) of Writer's Guidelines

Please begin your book review with this format:

BOOK TITLE IN CAPITALS, by (Author's Name). Publishing Company, Street, City, State, Zip. Year of Publication. Soft or hard Cover. Number of pages. Price.

Do not exceed 500 words.

Suggestions for discussion:

• general description

• to whom would it appeal

• author's purpose in writing the book

• author's qualifications

• merits of the book

• any weakness

• quality of illustrations and/or diagrams

• Reviewed by *Your Name City and State or Province*

Categories: Arts—Associations—Crafts—Culture—Education—Fashion—General Interest—Hobbies—Reference

Name: Submissions Editor
Material: All

Address: 3327 DULUTH HWY STE 201
City/State/ZIP: DULTUH GA 30096
Telephone: 770-495-7702
Fax: 770-495-7703
E-mail: 73744.202@compuserve.com

SIERRA

Sierra
The Magazine of the Sierra Club

Sierra is a bimonthly national magazine publishing writing, photography and art about the natural world. Our readers are environmentally concerned and politically diverse; most are active in the outdoors. We are looking for fine writing that will provoke, entertain, and enlighten this readership.

Though open to new writers, we find ourselves most often working with writers we have sought out or who have worked with us for some time. We ask writers who would like to publish in *Sierra* to submit written queries; phone calls are strongly discouraged. If you would like a reply to your query or need your manuscript returned to you, please include a self-addressed stamped envelope. Prospective *Sierra* writers should familiarize themselves with recent issues of the magazine; for a sample copy, send a self-addressed envelope and a check for $3 payable to *Sierra*.

Please be patient: Though the editors meet weekly to discuss recently received queries, a response time of from six to eight weeks is usual.

Please do not send slides, prints, or other art work. If photos or illustrations are required for your submission, we will request them when your work is accepted for publication.

Feature Articles
Sierra is looking for strong, well-researched, literate writing on significant environmental and conservation issues. Features often focus on aspects of the Sierra Club's national conservation work. For more information, contact our Information Center at 85 Second St., 2nd Floor, San Francisco, CA 94105. Writers should look for ways to cast new light on well-established issues. We look for stories of national or international significance; local issues, while sometimes useful as examples of broader trends, are seldom of interest in themselves. We are always looking for adventure travel pieces that weave events, discoveries and environmental insights into the narrative. Nonfiction essays on the natural world are welcome, too.

We do not want descriptive wildlife articles, unless larger conservation issues figure strongly in the story. We are not interested in editorials, general essays about environmentalism, or in highly technical writing. We do not publish unsolicited poetry or fiction; please do not submit works in either genre.

Recent feature articles that display the special qualities we look for are "Kaiparowits for Keeps" by Paul Rauber, (March/April 1997), "Among the Giants" by Rebecca Solnit (July/August 1997), and "Poison Pens" by David Helvarg (January/February 1997). Feature length ranges from 1,000 to 3,000 words; payment is from $800 to $2500, plus negotiated reimbursement for expenses.

Departments
Much of the material in *Sierra's* departments is written by staff editors and contributing writers. The following sections of the magazine, however, are open to freelancers. Articles range from 750 to 1,000 words in length; payment is $500 unless otherwise noted. Expenses up to $50 may be paid in some cases.

"Food for Thought" is concerned with what we eat and its connection to the environment. Topics range from drying food for backpacking to bovine growth hormones to the consequences of buying Southern Hemisphere produce. The column is oriented toward cooking and eating; submissions should include an appropriate recipe.

"Good Going" tells of an adventure journey or destination. We are not looking for descriptive itineraries, but rather for travel writing at its traditional best, with thoughtful observation of place and personality.

"Hearth & Home" offers information with advice on how we can live our environmental principles in our own homes; topics have ranged from composting with worms to building with straw to cooking with insects. Articles for this department should be accurate, lively, and helpful.

"Way to Go" travels to wild areas the Sierra Club is working to protect or has recently preserved, tells how to get there and how to help.

"Lay of the Land" focuses on environmental issues of national or international concern. Regional issues are considered when they have national implications. At 500 to 700 words, "Lay of the Land" articles are not sweeping surveys, but tightly focused, provocative, well-researched investigations of environmental issues. Payment varies according to length.

"Natural Resources" offers short (200-to-300 word) reviews of books on environmentalism and natural history. Payment is $50 per review.

Payment for all articles is on acceptance, which is contingent on a favorable review of the manuscript by our editorial staff, and by knowledgeable outside reviewers, where appropriate. Kill fees are negotiated when a story is assigned.
Categories: Conservation—Ecology—Environment—Travel

Name: Robert Schildgen, Managing Editor
Material: All
Address: 85 SECOND ST 2ND FLOOR
City/State/ZIP: SAN FRANCISCO CA 94105-3441
Telephone: 415-977-5572
Fax: 415-977-5794
E-mail: robert.schildgen@sierraclub.org
Internet: www.sierraclub.org

Signature Bride
Bridal Lifestyles for Today's Black Woman

The magazine publishes quarterly and works on monthly schedules. Assignments are generally assigned 4 to 5 months prior to deadline. The magazine follows AP style and *Webster's New World*.

The magazine is divided into various sections, with regular departments featured issue by issue.

Sections include: Bridal Planning, Health & Beauty, Finance, Food, Communication, Fashion, Art, Bridal Registry, Home Decor, Honeymoon and Men, The feature well covers anything and everything—from bridal to everyday life occurrences. Special features appear annually in certain issues (cakes, Signature Salutes, etc.).

Generally, departments run anywhere from 3-5 pages; features 4-6. Writers are responsible for submitting four-color when appropriate (travel, art, etc.).

To be considered, please submit a resume and samples (3-5) of writing—preferably different styles. If querying an idea, please submit in writing, along with above.

Editors will contact via writing or phone.
Categories: Bridal

Name: Submissions Editor

Material: All
Address: 101 W GRAND AVE STE 200
City/State/ZIP: CHICAGO IL 60610
Telephone: 312-527-6590
Fax: 312-527-6596
E-mail: SigBride@aol.com

SignCraft Magazine
The Magazine for the Sign Artist and Commercial Sign Shop

If you're interested in writing for *SignCraft*…

Like any trade or specialized publication, *SignCraft* needs material of direct benefit to its readers. The quality and value of the information is more important than style, length, or anything else. Experience or knowledge of the trade is a real asset, since it gives the writer a greater understanding of the reader's needs.

We welcome unsolicited manuscripts, but do suggest that you send a query first before you start on an article for *SignCraft*. If an article, such as a profile or a step-by-step, will include photographs, please send along a few with the query.

How long should an article be? Long enough to cover the subject, but as concise as possible. Most of the articles in *SignCraft* are between 500 and 2,500 words, but we certainly don't see length as a direct indication of quality or value.

We will gladly review articles from those who provide a product or a service to the industry or from those who handle public relations for those companies. But we do ask that the piece be written without an effort to directly promote or advertise a product or service. Readers are quick to pick up on this and it damages the credibility of both the article and the publication. At the same time, readers value accurate, high quality articles written with a genuine interest to inform. The by-line and mention of the author's situation in the industry at the end of the article both have tremendous value when an excellent article lies between them.

Here are a few notes that writers may find helpful:

1. To minimize trademark problems, avoid mentioning specific product names. Use a generic term instead. For example, we say, "transfer lettering" rather than "Prestype."

2. Don't attack other techniques, products, or procedures. There is usually more than one process that can be used to get satisfactory results. In the case of technique, if there is another way to do something, it should at least be mentioned.

3. If an article is not an original, unpublished work, or is submitted to another publication simultaneously, please mention this at the time of submission.

4. We edit copy to help the author to get his or her message across as effectively and efficiently as possible without affecting the style. The edited copy will be sent to the author for approval.

5. Remember to keep the article practical. Write in an active, down-to-earth style.

6. The type of photo—print, slide, etc.—is less important than its quality. We need photos that are in focus and properly exposed. 35mm color prints are fine, though we can work with most anything.

7. We try to respond to all submissions and answer all query letters within four weeks.

About sending photos to SignCraft…

One of the best things about putting *SignCraft* together is the opportunity to see photos of quality sign work from all over. From "routine" jobs and knockouts to masterpieces, we like to see 'em all. Though we have room to include a small portion of these photos in the magazine, it's a real help to see what *SignCraft*'s readers are turning out. So if you're in doubt about sending photos—send them! We really enjoy seeing them.

Here are a few notes that may answer some of the questions you have about sending photos to *SignCraft*:

1. **We can work with any type of photograph—print or slide, color or black and white.** In most cases, we prefer good color prints. Slides are fine, too, as are sharp black and whites. There is no need to send negatives when you are sending color prints. If we do need a negative for a particular photo, we can always contact you later.

Far more important than the type of photo is that it be properly exposed, and in focus. When photographing your work remember to keep this in mind. Make sure there is at least a little background around the sign, but try to avoid distracting backgrounds that may take away from your work. Of course if the quality of a photograph of a certain job is a little less than perfect, send it anyway. We like to see the work and we can always worry about photo quality later on.

2. **Yes, you'll get them all back.**

Since starting the magazine back in 1980 we haven't lost a photo yet. Though we can't be sure that it will never happen, we make every effort to take care of your photos as though they were our own. (If you do not want the photos returned, please be sure to make mention of that.)

3. **We are likely to trim photos that are used in the magazine unless told otherwise.**

When we use photographs in *SignCraft*, we frequently must trim a little foreground or background to fit our layout. (We never cut into the actual sign.) If you are sending photos that you do not want cut, just make a note—preferably on the back of the photo—that it should not be cut. We can sometimes use such photos by cutting a mask for them.

4. **If you write on the back of a photo, be careful what type of pen you use.**

Most felt tip pens will not dry properly on the back of a photo. Instead, they usually transfer to the front surface of the photo they are stacked on top of. The ink does dry on the photo's surface, which usually ruins it.

We have found that a standard ball-point pen with very light pressure works fine. Pressing too hard may "emboss" the photo causing damage to the front surface as well. It's best to use a light touch. If you're not sure about marking on the back of photos, test one first. Let it dry a few minutes and then see if it smears or transfers with your fingers. If it does, you can usually wipe it off with rubbing alcohol. Rubber stamp ink can cause the same problems as felt tip pens, so it's wise to test first.

5. **If the design for a particular sign came from another source, such as an advertising agency, please make note.** Unless told otherwise, we assume that all designs are the work of the sign artist. It's important for us to know where the design came from when the design was provided by another source.

6. **Package your photos carefully for shipment.**

Since traveling through the mail can be a rough journey for a package of photos, it's a good idea to take a little extra care when packing them. A piece of cardboard in the envelope will help prevent bending. If a thick stack of photos causes an envelope to bulge, it might be a good idea to reinforce the edges, or use a slightly heavier weight envelope so there is less risk of it tearing during postal handling. There's no need to get carried away and send a photo between two pieces of 1/2-inch plywood, but it helps to be a little more careful with them than you would a standard letter.

Perhaps the most important thing to remember is to send photos along- whether they're your own work, work of another sign artist you know, or just interesting signs that you have seen and photographed. If you don't have time to write an explanation when sending them along, that's no problem. Jot down your name and address and a sentence or two saying whose work it is, then get them in the mail.

Bill, Dennis, and I have worked in sign shops and had a few of our own, so we know just how busy you can be. That's why we doubly appreciate your taking the time to send such photos along. Thanks a million.

Thanks for your interest in *SignCraft*.
I hope these guidelines are of help to you.
Tom McIltrot, *Editor*
Categories: How-To—Interview—Profiles

Name: Tom McIltrot, Editor
Material: All
Address: PO BOX 60031
City/State/ZIP: FT MYERS FL 33906
Telephone: 941-939-4644
Fax: 941-939-0607
E-mail: signcraft@signcraft.com
Internet: www.signcraft.com

Signs of the Times

What is *Signs of the Times?*

Signs of the Times is an outreach magazine of the Seventh-day Adventist Church for North America, both the United States and Canada. It has been in continuous publication since 1874 and is thus one of the oldest religious magazines in North America. The mission of *Signs* is to share the gospel with those who are not of our faith, both Christians and non-Christians. *Signs* is a 32-page monthly magazine. A free sample copy is available on request. Include an 8½"x11" SASE with postage for two ounces.

Queries

We depend heavily on freelance articles. While some are assigned, many of those published are unsolicited. You may query us if you wish. However, we prefer to see the completed manuscript. We will consider simultaneous submissions, but request that you let us know you have submitted your manuscript to other publications.

Manuscript preparation

Authors submitting on speculation please send hardcopy only. Whenever possible, assigned articles should be submitted both on hardcopy and on disk. Disk submissions should be in any version of either MS Word or WordPerfect. We pay $25 less for articles that do not come in either of these formats.

Payment

Signs of the Times pays on acceptance. For first North American serial rights we pay 10 to 20 cents a word, half that for reprints. Since some articles are posted on our Web page, we request electronic rights as well. When accepting an article for publication, we send the author a contract specifying the rights we are purchasing and the amount of the payment.

Types of articles

Signs of the Times publishes articles in the following categories: Doctrine, gospel, prophecy, Christian lifestyle, and first-person stories. Also needed are one-page fillers of 600 to *650* words. Following are descriptions of what we are looking for in each of these articles.

Doctrinal

Doctrinal articles deal with the teachings of the Bible as understood by Seventh-day Adventists. These articles are entirely assigned. We are not open to queries or unsolicited manuscripts in this category. Also, almost without exception, our doctrinal articles are written by persons who are Seventh-day Adventists.

Gospel

Gospel articles deal with salvation and how to experience it. This includes articles on salvation by faith, how to cultivate a devotional life (Bible study, meditation, prayer), how to experience victory over temptation and sin, how to trust God in trial, etc. Stories that share what others have learned in these areas are also welcome. While most of our gospel articles are assigned or picked up from reprints, we do occasionally accept unsolicited manuscripts in this area. Gospel articles should be 1,000 to 1,200 words. We like sidebars that give additional information on the topic wherever possible. Sidebars should be included in the word count.

Prophecy

Prophecy articles are either staff written or assigned. We are not open to queries or unsolicited manuscripts in this category.

Christian lifestyle

Lifestyle articles deal with the practical problems of everyday life from a biblical and Christian perspective. Recently published titles in this category include "Taming the Strong-willed Child," "Emotional Abuse: What It Is and Why it Hurts," "When Kids Are Home Alone," and "How to Comfort a Grieving Friend." Lifestyle articles are typically 1,000 to 1,200 words. We request that authors include sidebars that give additional information on the topic wherever possible. Sidebars should be included in the word count.

First-person stories

These articles must be written in the first person. Authors who are writing about someone else's experience should use "as told to" in the by-line. First-person stories must illuminate a spiritual or moral truth that the individual in the story learned. We especially like stories that hold the reader in suspense or that have an unusual twist at the end. First-person stories are typically 600 to 1,000 words.

Short fillers

Often a one-page article is needed to fill an empty spot in a particular month's layout. These fillers can be inspirational/devotional, Christian lifestyle, stories, comments that illuminate a biblical text—in short, anything that might fit in a general Christian magazine. Fillers should be 500 to 600 words.

Suggestions for Writers

Audience

The audience for *Signs of the Times* includes both Christians and non-Christians of all ages. However, we recommend that our authors write with the non-Christian in mind, since most Christians can easily relate to articles that are written from a non-Christian perspective, whereas many non-Christians will have no interest in an article that is written from a Christian perspective. Also, writing for readers who are in the 25- to 45- year age span will probably attract adults of nearly all ages.

Religion versus spirituality

In today's world, "spiritual" is in and "religion" is out, as are also "church" and "denomination." Thus, unless religion, church, or denomination are an essential part of the article or story, we prefer that these be left out. While *Signs* is published by Seventh-day Adventists, we mention even our own denominational name in the magazine rather infrequently. The purpose is not to hide who we are but to make the magazine as attractive to non-Christian readers as possible. Also, please avoid denominational jargon and stained-glass piety. These are almost guaranteed to cause non-Christians to stop reading the magazine.

Solutions to problems

We are especially interested in articles that respond to the questions of everyday life that people are asking and the problems they are facing. Since these questions and problems nearly always have a spiritual component, articles that provide a biblical and spiritual response are especially welcome. A good rule of thumb is to write two words of solution for each word you write stating the question or problem. Write about benefits! What benefit will the reader get from reading your article?

Reprints

If you have written an article that you feel meets our criteria but that has already been published elsewhere, feel free to submit it to us with a notation that you are offering us second rights. Photocopies of previously published articles are acceptable. And, according to current U.S. copyright law, unless you sold all rights to the previous publisher, neither you nor we need to request the first publisher for permission to reprint. The copyright reverted to you once the article appeared in the previous publication.

Sidebars

Any time you can provide us with one or more sidebars that add information to the topic of your article, you enhance your chance of getting our attention. Sidebars can vary in length from a short paragraph to a column. Two kinds of sidebars seem to be especially popular with readers: Those that give information in lists, with each item in the list consisting of only a few words or at the most a sentence or two; and technical information or long explanations that in the main article might get the reader too bogged down in detail. Whatever their length, sidebars need to be part of the total word count of the article.

Introductions

We like the articles in *Signs of the Times* to have interest-grabbing introductions. One of the best ways to do this is with anecdotes, particularly those that have a bit of suspense or conflict. We find that it also helps to include one or two more anecdotes later in the article. Readers also like to know that someone who is an authority on the topic supports the author's point. Thus we encourage authors to do a bit of research to find some authorities they can quote in their article.

Quotations of a paragraph or two are considered to be "fair use," and you need not obtain permission from the original author. However, even a couple of lines from a song or poem can constitute such a large percentage of the total work as to violate copyright law. It is the author's responsibility to obtain any permissions that are required and to pay for those permissions where that is necessary.

Religious affiliation

It is not necessary to be a Seventh-day Adventist in order to be published in *Signs of the Times*. However, you may find it helpful to know something about our beliefs, which we will be glad to share with you in a booklet called *Let's Get Acquainted*, available free on request. Please include a 6¼"x9½" SASE with postage for two ounces.

Manuscript submission

If your article will include photos, send them with the manuscript.

Response can take up to two months.
Categories: Religion

Name: Marvin Moore, Editor
Material: All
Address: PO BOX 5353
City/State/ZIP: NAMPA ID 83653-5353
Telephone: 208-465-2579
Fax: 208-465-2531

The Silver Web
A Magazine of the Surreal

THE SILVER WEB is a semi-annual publication featuring fiction, poetry, art, and thought provoking articles. The Editor is looking for works ranging from speculative fiction to dark tales and all weirdness in between; specifically works of the surreal.

PAYMENT: Upon acceptance, unless another arrangement is made. Fiction: 2-3 cents a word, Nonfiction: negotiable, Poetry: $10-50, Art: $10-20 story illustrations, $25-50 cover, $5-10 filler. Also two copies of the issue in which the work appears (reduced rates to contributors for additional copies).

SUBSCRIPTION RATES: $12.00/year (2 issues) or $14.00 foreign and Canada; sample copy $5.95 +1.25 p&h ($2.00 p&h for Canada & overseas).

FICTION: Short stories of 8,000 words or less (don't send anything longer w/o a query first, or it will be returned unread). The Web is looking for well-written work that is unusual and original; stories that are too bizarre for mainstream publications but that do not fit the standard mold of genre. The preference is for stories that develop out of character rather than fiction based on ideas.

No traditional storylines; no vampires, werewolves, zombies, witches, fairies, elves, dragons, etc. No high fantasy, Sword & Sorcery or quest/adventure stories. And please, please, please no revenge stories. Open to submissions from January 1st through September 30th.

POETRY: Poems must use standard poetic conventions whether free verse or rhyming. As indicated for FICTION above, no genre cliches.

ART: Separate guidelines for artists available. Most artwork is assigned, although I do take some unsolicited filler art.

NONFICTION: Please query about specific articles. Interested in interviews with writers, poets, artists, etc. Satire and humor also invited and I love Letters to the Editor.

OTHER INFORMATION: All submissions must be in standard manuscript format; if not, they will be returned unread. Reprints considered, but query first with prior publication information. Simultaneous submissions accepted, but no multiple submissions. Cover letters are enjoyed but not essential. Provide an SASE with proper postage to ensure a response. You may use my e-mail address for queries, etc. but *not accepting electronic submissions, send hardcopy. The Silver Web* is not responsible for loss or damage to any unsolicited work. Allow 6-8 weeks response time. You may receive a form rejection, but I will do my best to give personal comments as time allows. All rights revert to contributors upon publication.

Thank you for your interest in *The Silver Web*.
Categories: Fiction—Arts—Poetry—Speculative Fiction

Name: Ann Kennedy, Publisher
Material: All
Address: PO BOX 38190
City/State/ZIP: TALLAHASSEE FL 32315
E-mail: annk19@mail.idt.net

Singles
A Newsmagazine

Singles Newsmagazine is published monthly for single/divorced men and women (ages 25-55) in Greater Cincinnati and Northern Kentucky. It focuses on lifestyle, entertainment, information & people. Circulation: newsstand, singles' events, and subscription.

Rate Schedule

Payment on publication.
• Reprint rights or first time rights, 800 words or less—$50
• Reprint rights/first rights, 800+ words—$100

• Commissioned feature—$150

Final manuscripts should be submitted in text-only computers files (either Mac or IBM formats) accompanied by a printed copy. Photographs or graphics are encouraged. Writers are invited to submit articles of any length. Absolutely no fiction or poetry. Submit by mail. Previously published articles are welcomed for reprint.

Editorial Goals

• serves as the definitive, local source of lifestyle information for single people and single parents between the ages of 25 and 49

• builds a sense of community among readers through information, activities and promotions

• is an advocate for the readers' interests

• assists the development of the singles' market into a recognized economic force bringing greater financial opportunities to its readers

Editorial Tone

Singles Newsmagazine uses bright graphics and colorful photography. The editorial content is written to be of interest to people from all walks of life, representing all races, creeds and socioeconomic brackets. All editorial should be approached from or easily edited to the single/divorced person's viewpoint. *Singles Newsmagazine* does not address alternative lifestyles.

Singles Newsmagazine takes a positive and proactive stand on the issues confronting its readers. The tone of the editorial is upbeat and direct, yet handled with respect and dignity. Readers should be able to read the entire magazine at work without fear of embarrassment from questionable advertising or content.

The target readers are characterized by emotional disenfranchisement—no sense of community or commonality. The primary goal in serving this group is to build a sense of community through a common source of information and shared experience. At its most basic level, the editorial should satisfy the readers' needs for socialization, human contact, support and information. Articles should encourage readers to make the best of this part of life.

Key Concepts

• Features and columns are short and a "fast read." Articles are not split into the back of the magazine.

• Supply visuals if they are available.

• Liberal use of testimonials, quotes and examples to support key concepts

• Prologues, epilogues, sidebars and strong lead paragraphs are encouraged.

• Supply readers with a source of follow-up information where they can find more information.

• Editorial is balanced to be of interest to both men and women.

Editorial Calendar

10 issues/year—For better newsstand distribution and placement, SN is *not* published on the first of the month.

Editorial Topics

The content is divided into four categories:

• Psychological Issues
• Lifestyle Issues
• Sociological Issues
• Physical Issues

Sociological Issues

Career

The focus of many single lives is work and career. Topics include education, retraining, entrepreneurism, career skills, and the elements of success. Sample topics:

• Career Self-sabotage
• Liberate Your Business Creativity
• Intuition: The Business Edge
• Corporate Creativity Camp
• Personal Productivity

• Jumping Off the Fast Track
• The Price of Success

Social Issues

Many of society's issues are of specific concern to single readers. For example, the tax code is administered by marital status as are many social programs. Issues of national and local concern will be examined editorially from the distinct perspective of single people.

• Credit Discrimination
• Legislation that Affects Single People
• Sexual Harassment

People

The heart and soul of *Singles Newsmagazine*'s editorial product is people. Every issue features profiles of interesting single people who are presented in a newsworthy, topic-centered context. This focus on people provides a sense of community and belonging.

• Single CEOs: Risk-Taking Has Its Cost
• Profile of a Single Parent
• Life on the "A" List
• Building a Support System
• Dating at Work: Asking for Trouble?
• Interviews with significant singles from the world of entertainment, sports, business and the media

Legal/Financial

Child support, custody, divorce, taxes, retirement and credit covered by experts in their respective areas of expertise. Legal and financial information will be specific to a single's lifestyle. Financial articles cover specific information on taxes, budgeting, investment, preparing for retirement, and caring for both parents and children on one income.

• Single Parent's College Fund
• 20 Ways to Cut Your Expenses
• Tax Deductions for Individuals
• Credit Card Catastrophes
• Retirement Planning

Lifestyle Issues

Food

This demographic group has very unique eating habits. They are the largest group of restaurant patrons eating out an average of four times a week (both for food and human contact). They rarely have a sit-down meal at home and prefer light, fast meals on the run. Fine cooking and food connoisseurship is, conversely, of great interest to this group, but reserved for entertaining.

• Fast and Fabulous Food for One
• Make-Ahead Meals
• Gourmet Salads
• Bringing Wine for Dinner
• Convenience Foods High in Nutrition
• Power Lunches
• Brain Food
• Business Meals: To Drink or Not

Home

Home is an important concept to single people. Home ownership is the ultimate status symbol of this demographic group. Editorial coverage explores all facets of this topic including financial aspects, home maintenance with only one income and one set of hands, products, and single-friendly neighborhoods. Topics might include:

• Qualifying for a Home of Your Own
• Look Inside The Ultimate Bachelor Pad
• The Perfect Home Office
• Patio Gardens in the City
• Faux Finishes Overhaul Used Furniture
• Living Large: Decorating with High Style
• Decorating Kids' Rooms: For Non-custodial Single Parents

Entertainment

The magazine recognizes the unique entertainment interests of its readers with full pre- and post-event coverage of activities, travel, and nightlife.

- Learning Vacations
- Spa Vacations
- Coffeehouses: Trendiest Place to Talk
- Photo Safari to Africa

Purchasing

Singles consume the same wide variety of products and services as the population at large. They are in their peak earning years and have more discretionary income than any other demographic group but they are value-conscious. They spend a lot of their free time shopping. Topics might include advertising, new trends, and product reviews.

- Advertisers Target the Singles Market
- Designer Furniture Knock-offs
- Auctions: Home Furnishings with History
- The Shopping Mall: Playground of the 90s
- Computer Budgeting Programs
- Buying a Car Online
- Why We Shop Too Much

Physical Issues

Fitness

Readers' active lifestyles incorporate regular exercise, fitness awareness, weight control and the use of health products. Sport and activities are an integral part of their lives. Sample topics include:

- Indoor Rock Climbing
- Sand Volleyball: Coed Team Fun
- Just How Much is That New Sport Going to Cost?
- Best Coed Sports

Health

Medical and psychiatric experts cover topics of specific interest to single people such as addiction/recovery, sports injuries, sexually-transmitted disease, plastic surgery, eating disorders, and mental and emotional problems.

- Adventure Injuries
- Colo-Rectal Cancer is Linked to Single Status
- Addiction: The Stigma Lingers After Recovery
- You Are What You Eat
- Why Does Everyone Seem to Have a Therapist?
- Hypnotherapy Changes Attitudes
- Adult Acne

Appearance

Careful attention to one's physical appearance is an integral part of the single's mindset. Features and short topics will keep readers up on the latest news regarding personal appearance.

- Body Image Reality Check: What Your Mind Sees
- Dressing for Comfort
- Casual Friday Caché
- Collagen for Lips
- Skin Salvation: Dermabrasion
- Hair Implants
- Body Language Signals

Psychological Issues

Attitudes and Interests

Research speaks frequently of a singles' mindset. Nowhere is this more apparent than in the attitudes and interests of this group—their priorities, self-image and goals. A wide range of interests entertains them in what little free time they have—music, media, career, collecting, hobbies, self-improvement and technology.

- Making It On Your Own
- The "EX" Syndrome—Getting on with Life
- Life Priorities
- Recovering Your Self-esteem After Divorce
- Nobody's Going to Take Care of You—Except You

- Male Bashing
- The Subculture of Boat Owners
- Bartending Classes
- Bookstores: The New Singles Spot
- Collections: Automobile Memorabilia

Relationships

Children, parents, colleagues and friends comprise the majority of relationships. Articles will encourage enjoying single life and making the best of this natural phase of life. Upbeat features provide insight into social skills and interpersonal relationships. Topics might include:

- How to Start a Conversation
- Old Friends and New Friends
- Spotting a Social Climber
- Marrying Later and Smarter
- Why Second Marriages Fail
- Guerrilla Dating Tactics
- Divorce: From Anger to Forgiveness
- You're Turning Into Your Parents
- How to Make the First Move

Single Parenting

The resources, shared experiences, and information by many of the readers are provided through frequent articles on shared parenting. The topics would range from simple care, education and food through complex issues of values and interpersonal relationships.

- Single Parents: Exhausted and Alone
- Instilling Values
- Grandparents' Rights
- Single Parent Support Groups
- Dad Cooks?
- Building Holiday Memories
- How Fathers Contribute to Self-esteem
- When A Mother Leaves a Family
- Rights of Fathers
- Something Besides Fast Food
- Deadbeat Parents

Singles Newsmagazine is a product of MultiFile Publishing Co. All rights reserved.

Categories: Nonfiction—Lifestyles

Name: Ellen Lytle, Publisher
Material: All
Address: MULTIFILE PUBLISHING CO.
Address: 111 E 13TH ST LOFT 4
City/State/ZIP: CINCINNATI OH 45210
Telephone: 513-621-3060
Fax: 513-723-9337
E-mail: CinSingles@aol.com

Skeptical Inquirer

Skeptical Inquirer
The Magazine for Science and Reason

SKEPTICAL INQUIRER critically examines claims of paranormal, fringe-science, and pseudoscientific phenomena from a responsible, scientific point of view and provides a forum for informed discussion of all relevant issues. Our subtitle is "The Magazine for Science and Reason." We encourage science and scientific inquiry, critical thinking, and the use of reason and the methods of science in examining important issues. The readership includes scholars and researchers in many fields and lay readers of diverse backgrounds.

Write clearly, interestingly, and simply. Avoid unnecessary technical terms. Maintain a factual, professional, and restrained tone. All submissions are judged on the basis of interest, clarity, significance, relevance, authority, and topicality

Direct critiques toward ideas and issues, not individuals. Be prepared to provide documentation of all factual assertions. A useful set of guidelines for those who seek to evaluate paranormal claims, titled "Proper Criticism" and written by Professor Ray Hyman, is available from the Editor. Among the guidelines: clarify your objectives, let the facts speak for themselves, be precise and careful with language, and avoid loaded words and sensationalism. State others' positions in a fair, objective, and nonemotional manner.

CATEGORIES OF CONTRIBUTIONS

Categories of contributions include: Articles, Book Reviews, News and Comment, Forum, Follow-Up, and Letters to the Editor.

Articles: Articles may be evaluative, investigative, or explanatory. They may examine specific claims or broader questions. Well-focused discussions on scientific, educational, or social issues of wide common interest are welcome. We especially seek articles that provide new information or bring fresh perspective to familiar subjects. Articles that help people find natural explanations of unusual personal experiences are useful. So are articles that portray the vigor and excitement of a particular scientific topic and help readers distinguish between scientific and pseudoscientific approaches. Well-balanced articles that report on and evaluate controversial scientific claims within science itself are also needed.

SKEPTICAL INQUIRER must be a source of authoritative, responsible scientific information and perspective. The Editor will usually send manuscripts dealing with technical or controversial matters to reviewers. The authors, however, are responsible for the accuracy of fact and perspective. It is good practice to have knowledgeable colleagues review drafts before submission. Reports of original research, especially highly technical experimental or statistical studies, are best submitted to a formal scientific journal; a non-technical summary may be submitted to SKEPTICAL INQUIRER. Studies based on small-scale tests or surveys of students will be considered only if they establish something new, provide a needed replication of some important earlier study, or test some new theoretical position.

Space is at a premium; there are always many accepted articles awaiting publication, and many submitted articles cannot be published. Articles are typically 2,000 to 3,500 words (about 8 to 12 double-spaced typewritten pages). We cannot publish treatises. Articles should be organized around one central point or theme. Be succinct. Remember, Watson and Crick's paper reporting the discovery of the structure of DNA took just over one page in *Nature*.

Articles should have a title page. Begin with a succinct, inviting title followed by a concise, 20- to 30-word statement of the article's main point or theme. This "abstract" will be published in display type on the first page of the printed article and used as a summary on the Contents page. The title page should also give the name of the author(s), full addresses, and the lead author's office and home telephone numbers, fax number, and e-mail address. At the end of the manuscript, include a suggested author note of one to three sentences that gives relevant affiliations and credentials and an address for correspondence. If you do not want your address included in the author note, please say so. The manuscript should be accompanied by a brief cover letter stating that the article has not been submitted elsewhere and providing any other essential background for the Editor.

Rook Reviews: Most book reviews are about 600 to 1,200 words. Both solicited and unsolicited reviews are used. Include publication data at the top of the review in this order: *Title. Au-*

thor: Publisher, city. *Year. ISBN. Number of pages. Hardcover or softcover (or both), price.* Include a suggested author note. If possible, include the cover of the book for illustration.

News and Comment: News articles from 250 to 1,000 words are welcome. They should involve timely events and issues and be written in interpretative journalistic style. Use third person. The news sections of *Nature, Science, New* Scientist, and *Science News* are excellent models. Balance, fairness, and perspective are important. In reporting on controversies, seek and include comment and perspective from the various opposing parties.

Forum: The Forum column consists of brief, lively, well-written columns of comment and opinion generally no more than 1,000 words. Space allows only one or two per issue.

Follow-Up: The Follow-Up column is for response from persons whose work or claims have been the subject of previous articles. The original authors may respond in the same or a later issue.

Letters to the Editor: Letters to the Editor are for views on matters raised in previous issues. Letters should be no more than 250 words. Due to the volume of letters received, they cannot be acknowledged, and not all can be published. Those selected may be edited for space and clarity. Authors whose articles are criticized in the letters column may be given the opportunity to respond in the same issue.

MECHANICAL REQUIREMENTS

Text: All manuscripts should be printed out double-spaced, including notes and references. Number all pages in sequence, including those for references, figures, and captions. For Articles, submit an original and two photocopies (for reviewers); for other categories, an original and one photocopy. In either case, we also request the document on a computer disk, which may be submitted at the same time or upon acceptance (see below).

References and Notes: SKEPTICAL INQUIRER uses the author-date system of documentation as found in *The Chicago Manual of Style*. Sources are cited in the text, usually in parentheses, by author's last name and year of publication: (Smith 1994). These text citations are amplified in a list of References (alphabetized by last name of author), which gives fill' bibliographic information. *Sample book* entry: Smith, John. 1994. *A Skeptical Book.* New York: Jones Press. *Sample journal-article entry:* Smith, John, and Jane Jones. 1994. A skeptical article. *The Journal* 5(1): 7-12. Use endnotes (not footnotes) for explaining or amplifying discussions in the text.

Illustrations: Figures and graphs should be in high-quality camera-ready form. Photos can be glossy or matte black-and-white. Color photos are also acceptable. Assign each illustration a Figure number and supply captions on a separate sheet. Suggestions for obtaining other illustrations are welcome.

Disks: For all contributions except letters and short items, we request a 3½" computer disk. Preferably, it should be submitted to the editor with the manuscript (to save time). Otherwise, it should be sent to our editorial production office at the following address once the manuscript is accepted:

Managing Editor
SKEPTICAL INQUIRER
PO BOX 703
AMHERST NY 14226

Any Macintosh or PC word processing format is acceptable, although a Macintosh format is preferred.

Proofs: Once the manuscript of an article, review, or column has been tentatively scheduled, copyedited, and typeset, we send proofs to the author. The proofs should be returned corrected within 72 hours.

Copyright: Unless otherwise agreed, copyright will be transferred to CSICOP upon publication.

Authors are sent several complimentary copies of the issue,

plus a form for ordering reprints.

The fax may be used for important messages and inquiries. It is generally not for submission of manuscripts, with the exception of short editorial items from abroad or other brief contributions known to be urgent.

Do not send manuscripts to CSICOP's headquarters in Amherst, N.Y. Do not use Certified mail; that only delays delivery. If you use overnight express (generally not necessary), please initial the signature-waiver requirement.

Categories: Nonfiction—Paranormal—Science

Name: Kendrick Frazier, Editor
Material: All
Address: 944 DEER DR NE
City/State/ZIP: ALBUQUERQUE NM 87122
Telephone: 716-636-1425
Fax: 716-636-1733
E-mail: skepticedt@aol.com

Ski Tripper
The Newsletter for Discerning Southeastern Skiers

What We're About

Ski Tripper brings inside information on downhill skiing to readers from Florida to southern Pennsylvania. Much of this is accomplished with trip reports on resorts within this region as well as destinations outside it. Regional resorts covered include Blue Knob, Liberty, Roundtop, Whitetail, Seven Springs, Hidden Valley, Wisp, Canaan Valley, Timberline, Snowshoe, Gatlinburg, Sugar Mountain, Beech Mountain, Hawksnest, Cataloochee, Wolf Laurel, Winterplace, Wintergreen, and Massanutten. We also use features on skiing issues and trends that have a bearing on the region—topics have included discount ski cards, ski clubs, rental cars, slope condition reports, and skiing information by computer. For any type of article idea, query first by letter and include clips if you're new to us.

Generally, long-distance trip reports are written by skiers traveling from the east coast, documenting the travel process along the way. However, we also welcome reviews from experts in other areas, particularly people who live near far-flung resorts and know them intimately. Long-distance trips include resorts in western U.S. and Canada as well as overseas in areas such as Europe, South America, and New Zealand. Much of our audience consists of upscale professionals such as doctors and lawyers, who don't mind spending a few bucks on a trip but look for value. We're especially receptive to ideas on trips with a unique twist to address this market segment such as heli-skiing, taking a train, skiing at a Club Med resort, taking a family, or skiing in conjunction with a professional seminar.

Our Unique Slant

Trip reports are unbiased critical reviews. We provide readers with information they won't get from resorts, other magazines, travel agents, chambers of commerce, or airlines. Our unbiased status is maintained by not accepting advertising. Your objectivity as a writer is maintained by not accepting favors from resorts or travel services and by never revealing that you're evaluating for publication. To them, you're just an average customer, not a writer.

Style

• Use first person

• Report on every facet of a trip that's pertinent to a regional audience. In addition to the resort, this includes travel agents, public agencies, restaurants, hotels, ski shops, airlines, airports, roads, and ground transportation services, if skiers in the region would likely use them.

• Feel free to use facts and figures to complement your observations and experiences and to use opinions of other people, both experts and consumers. Also, it's helpful to give background information on a resort such as its history, size, and unique characteristics. Often, an article will describe a resort's reputation and then tell whether it's true, based on personal observation.

• Report on anything out of the ordinary, giving details where possible. For example, if lift lines stretched around the lodge, mention it; if they were just average, don't.

• We cover regional resorts in a concise, newsy, and fact-filled style. On the other hand, we expect more lengthy and colorful descriptions in long-distance trip articles. Make readers feel like they're along on the trip by telling stories about funny or interesting things that happened.

Length

Regional day trip reports run approximately 500 words, regional weekend reports 750 words, long-distance reports 1,500 words, and features 1,000 words.

Payment

Regional day trip reports pay $75, regional weekend reports $115, long-distance trip reports $225, and features $150. Writers also receive a year's subscription to *Ski Tripper*. Payment is on acceptance.

Rights

Ski Tripper buys first as well as second and simultaneous rights. We can use material published in overlapping markets if modified for our slant and it meets our objectivity requirements.

Categories: Nonfiction—Outdoors—Recreation—Regional—Sports—Travel

Name: Tom Gibson, Editor
Material: All
Address: PO BOX 20305
City/State/ZIP: ROANOKE VA 24018
Telephone: 540-772-2225

Skiing
The Magazine of Winter Adventure

SKIING has established a new editorial direction over the past several years. This culminated in the adoption of "the magazine of winter adventure" theme. Every SKIING article addresses something that's special about skiing or, in selected cases, about winter adventures other than skiing.

Our articles take one of two tacks: entertainment or information. We describe great experiences and adventures at resorts and areas big and small. We capture the scene that gives these places their distinct character. We profile truly extraordinary and noteworthy people. (In fact, it's often easiest to write about an adventure through the experiences of other skiers. An adventure can be written in the third person or the first.) We'll spot and highlight new gear and trends. Any story that captures the passion, the thrill of discovery, the striving to meet a new challenge, the coolest new ideas or trends, or any other element of a great adventure, is a good candidate. We don't want you to force ancillary information into an adventure story. Sidebars were invented to carry that freight.

Since our regular contributors have already pitched us on the really fantastic stories (China, South America, New Zealand, Russia, Iran, Morocco, Antarctica, and every heli-skiing variation), consider less obvious subjects: smaller ski areas, specific local ski cultures, unknown aspects of popular resorts.

A few notable unlikely stories we've done in the past 3-4 seasons: biathlon, the Hood River ski/boardsailing culture, night racing, the ski/sports culture of Bend, Oregon, "underground" Vail, Holiday Valley (N.Y.), a brief history of sex and skiing.

Be expressive, not merely descriptive! We want readers to feel the adventure in your writing—to tingle with the excitement of skiing steep powder, of meeting intriguing people, of reaching new goals or achieving dramatic new insights. We want readers to have fun, to see the humor in and the lighter side of skiing and their fellow skiers.

We entertain ideas about adventures beyond skiing: on snowshoes, snowmobiles, ice skates, dogsled, sleighs, or toboggans. So long as the adventure is accessible and appeals to skiers, it's fair game.

And we don't really ignore the interests of the many skiers who crave information, either. Skiers want to spend money wisely, to get the best possible experience. Sometimes, they just want to know. We provide our readers with the most useful or sought-after information. We address the things that affect and bug skiers the most, via departments such as Travel Advisory, Health/Fitness, Gear Talk, and Trial Run. (Don't be shy about contributing to the departments. They need to be as smart and informed as our features. Consider the departments as a doorway into SKIING.) We'll gladly consider a service feature, too.

Categories: Adventure—Outdoors—Sports

Name: Rick Kahl, Editor-in-Chief
Material: All
Address: 929 PEARL ST STE 200
City/State/ZIP: BOULDER CO 80302
Telephone: 303-448-7600
Fax: 303-448-7676

Skin Inc.® Magazine
The Complete Business Guide for Face & Body Care

Manuscripts are considered for publication that contain original and new information in the general fields of skin care and makeup, dermatological, plastic and reconstructive surgical techniques. The subject may cover the science of skin, the business of skin care and makeup establishments or of an individual esthetician, or treatments performed by estheticians, dermatologists and plastic surgeons on healthy (i.e., non-diseased) skin. Subjects may also deal with raw materials, formulations and regulations governing claims for products and equipment.

A manuscript must be written exclusively for this publication, that is, not submitted to any other publication, and contain significant material not previously published elsewhere. Publication rights for reprints and other republication purposes is normally granted on request.

Acceptance for publication is in the hands of our Editorial Committee. A decision will be given to an author within one month.
TECHNICAL DETAILS

A manuscript must be submitted in English, although perfect grammar and style are not required. We reserve the right to edit all manuscripts accepted for publication. Any editing required will be done by our editorial staff. Whenever possible, please submit your manuscript to us on a 3½" DS/DD PC disk. Manuscript file must be submitted in *Microsoft Word* or ASCII format.

All product trade names for product lines, drugs, equipment, etc. must be credited to their manufacturers including the city and state of manufacture. All facts quoted or used in the manuscript text from other literature sources must be properly referenced. References must be submitted according to the style sheet below.

Illustrations should be provided as black and white glossy photographs. Original charts and graphs should be in black ink on white paper. They will be returned at the author's request. Photocopies of illustrations are most often not clear enough to be reproduced in a publication.

Two copies of the manuscript should be supplied.

The usual scheduling of manuscripts is done four to eight months in advance of publication. This will be the usual time between acceptance of a manuscript for publication and its appearance in the magazine. Galleys will be sent only to authors who request them, providing time permits before publication.

In the case of original material written exclusively for this magazine, an honorarium will paid to the author upon publication. This will be a cash payment unless the author requests one hundred reprints.

Style Sheet for References and Footnotes
REFERENCES
Magazines, Journals, and Periodicals
Please number the references. Start with the author's name(s), article title, journal or magazine name, volume number, issue number, starting page number, month and year of publication.

1. Science of beauty: High tech products: form meets function. *Elle IV* (2), 252 (October 1988)

2. C Duhe, Powder is back: The return of delicate dustings. *Elle IV* (2), 276 (October 1988)

Please note that the author's initials precede the surname, that there is very little punctuation, that only the *first letter* of the article title is capitalized, that the first number is the volume number, followed by the issue number, followed by the page numbers, followed by the year. *The page number and issue month and year must be included with each reference.*
Books
Start with the book's author(s), chapter name and number if appropriate, book name, editor's name(s) if any, publisher's city and state, publisher name, year of publication, and page number(s)

2. L Schorr and SM Sims, The need for skin care, Ch 6, in *Lia Schorr's Seasonal Skin Care*, New York, NY: Prentice Hall Press (1988) p 87
FOOTNOTES
Retin-A (Ortho Pharmaceutical Corporation, Raritan, NJ)

Please footnote all trade names (e.g. drugs, product lines) used in the text. Include the full name of the manufacturer, its city and state.

Please contact the editor if you have any questions on this style sheet.

Categories: Nonfiction—Business—Skin Care

Name: Melinda Taschetta-Millane, Managing Editor
Material: All
Address: 362 S SCHMALE RD
City/State/ZIP: CAROL STREAM IL 60188
Telephone: 630-653-2155
Fax: 630-653-2192
E-mail: skininc@allured.com

Skylark
Purdue University Calumet

Skylark, founded in 1972, is an award-winning literary arts annual from Purdue University Calumet. Just as the skylark rises in flight, we too want authors to rise to new heights in their writings.

Categories include: Short Stories, Poetry (up to 6 poems), Short Essays, Translations, Illustrations and Photographs. Each issue features a Special Section and a Young Writers Section. Special Section for 1998 is OLD AGE.

The author's name and address should appear in the upper left-hand corner of the first page. Young Writers should state age and the name of the school they are attending. Material from anyone under 18 should be accompanied by a note from teacher or parent verifying that the work is original. Manuscripts that are not proofread for correct grammar and punctuation will be returned unread. Note: We no longer accept material written by adults for the Young Writers Section.

All material must be original and not previously published; this fact must be stated on the manuscript (under author's name and address). After first publication in *Skylark*, all material reverts to the ownership of the author. If it should be republished, *Skylark* expects to be credited with first publication.

All submissions copyrighted by the author must be accompanied by an authorization for *Skylark* to publish them.

Manuscripts are read from October 15th to April 30th. Simultaneous submissions are not accepted.

All graphics and photographs must be black and white, with name and address on the back of each entry. Young illustrators should avoid pencil unless the pencil lines are dark enough to reproduce, and illustrations should not be done on lined paper.

All writers and artists published will receive one complimentary copy of *Skylark*. Additional copies may be ordered at reduced rates.

For each copy of *Skylark* you may wish to order, send $8.00 payable to Purdue University to *Skylark* at the address below. (Back issues are available for $6.00 each.)

Categories: Fiction—Poetry—Regional (Midwest)—Short Stories—Young Adult (written by them)

Name: Pamela Hunter, Editor-in-Chief
Material: Fiction, Poetry, Essays, Special Theme Material
Name: Shirley Jo Moritz, Young Writers Editor
Material: Young Writers Submissions
Address: 2200 169TH ST
City/State/ZIP: HAMMOND IN 46323
Telephone: 219-989-2262
Fax: 219-989-2581
E-mail: skylark@mwi.calumet.purdue.edu

SLAM

Pitch ideas in writing by mail, fax or e-mail. Story meetings are held once a month, at which point we'll decide what to assign and then get back to you. Do *not* pitch a story a day and expect immediate response.

Please include a cover letter with your name, address, phone number and social security number. We pay upon publication.

STYLE

Single-digit numbers (0-9) should be spelled out except when referring to a ranking or a player's number; then use No. X.

"With four returning freshmen, Columbia is ranked No. 233."

Numbers greater than nine should only be spelled out at the beginning of the sentence.

"Thirty-eight is a higher score than 33."

Age: The phrase "XX-year-old" is always hyphenated; the phrase "XX years old" is not.

"63-year-old point guard Sedale Threatt is 63 years old."

Height and weight: "7-1, 800-pound center Kevin Duckworth."

Positions can be expressed any way you please, as long as you use recognizable basketball terms.

Dates: drop the "19" when referring to the year; replace it with an apostrophe. Spell out the month.

"Yinka Dare had no assists in January '95. Hopefully, his '96-97 season will be more productive."

Refer to **states** by the two-letter postal abbreviation with no periods—NY, LA (Louisiana—L.A. is Los Angeles), DE...

Use the present **tense** (i.e. "says") for quotes unless the speaker is dead, the quote originally appeared somewhere else or you specify that the quote was given in the past ("in '95, disaster Shawn Bradley said...").

Changes to **quotes** that clarify the speaker's meaning—from "and then he yelled at us" to "and then [coach Huggins] yelled at us"—should be surrounded by brackets, not parentheses.

Additions that provide information—"that game against Boston *[in which Mourning sank the winning shot]* was the greatest"—should be surrounded by brackets and italicized.

Likewise descriptions of the speaker's actions, usually in a Q & A. "Jordan: I love this game *[laughs]*."

Spell out **"percent"**.

Titles of books, TV shows, movies and albums are italicized. Titles of chapters, episodes, articles and songs appear in quotes.

NBA (and ABA and ABL...): all caps, no periods.

The contracted form of **and** is 'n' or 'nd—an apostrophe for every missing letter. Use it and words ending in -in' (instead of -ing) sparingly. Very sparingly.

Spell check is there for a reason, but don't use it blindly. Nick Van Excel isn't a real player.

SUBSTANCE

Anecdotes. If you get a really good one, use it to start the story. We don't like the basic newspaper-style lead. Most of our readers don't read a lot of newspapers anyway.

When **profiling** a player, mention height, weight, age, position, team and (for pros) what college he/she attended.

Generally speaking, the more **stats,** the better, as long as they don't interrupt the flow *too* much.

Never refer to **Shawn Bradley** as a "project". He sucks.

Are a lot of **rhetorical questions** a good idea? No.

Too many sentences that end in "..." are annoying...

COMMON SENSE

Check your facts. Period. Don't assume someone went to a certain school, assume you know his ppg average or assume you can spell her name correctly.

Don't pitch us stuff we just did.

Find **lesser-known players** with interesting stories, players outside of NYC, L.A. and Chicago. An unknown in Nebraska or Mississippi will beat an over-exposed player in NYC most of the time. We already know about the Jordans, Kemps and Webbers of the world.

Categories: Basketball

Name: Anna K. Gebbie, Managing Editor
Material: All
Address: 1115 BROADWAY 8TH FLOOR
City/State/ZIP: NEW YORK NY 10010
Telephone: 212-462-9635
Fax: 212-620-7787
E-mail: annag@harris-pub.com

Sleuthhound Memorandum

Sleuthhound is an educational newsletter for writers and artists. We are looking for professional writing and drawing techniques, interviews with writers and artists, book reviews, a new experience that would be of interest to the writer or artist. Such as an interview with a beekeeper, or a mountain man who is doing things his way and enjoying it, and etc.

Pays 4 cents a word on publication, usually 3 to 6 months after acceptance. 50% freelance written. We consider all quality manuscripts. Send complete manuscript, length from 500 words to 2,500 words. Reports in eight to twelve weeks. Must be original, unpublished words.

Manuscript Requirements

Good clear computer printouts are acceptable. Include your name, address, and telephone number on upper left of first page.

Place approximate word count on upper right side of your first page. Center the title of your story 10 spaces from top. Put your name on upper left and number consecutively in upper right beside story title on each page thereafter. Submit a neat, clean, and well organized manuscript.

Whispering Willow Publications
Annual Contests for Writers and Artists

DAGGER
Mystery competition
Deadline March 10- Publication date July Edition
$200.00 plus publication. Illustration of winning story will be on the cover of this edition book. $5.00 reading fee for each entry.

TRAVEL
Mystery Competition
Deadline July 1 Publication October Edition
First place $200.00 plus publication and illustration of cover of book. Second place winner $150.00 plus publication.

$5.00 reading fee for each entry. Story must happen someplace away from home.

BOOKMARK
Mystery Contest
Deadline October 1 Publication date January Edition
First place $200.00 plus publication and illustration of cover. Picture illustrating story will be on the limited edition bookmark for the year.

$5.00 reading fee for each entry.

SLEUTH
Mystery Competition
Deadline December 31 Publication date April Edition
First place $200.00 plus publication and illustration of their story on cover. Second place $150.00 plus publication. Third place $125.00 plus publication. $10.00 reading fee for each entry. Story about an amateur sleuth.

Categories: Fiction—Nonfiction—Crime—Education—Literature—Mystery—Short Stories—Travel—True Crime—Writing

Name: Peggy D. Farris, Editor-in-Chief
Material: Writing-Art, Educational Interviews, Articles, Book Reviews
Address: PO BOX 890294
City/State/ZIP: OKLAHOMA CITY OK 73189-0294
Telephone: 405-239-2531
Fax: 405-232-3848
E-mail: wwillows@telepath.com
Nota bene: Contests require reading fee.

Slick Times

We're looking for humorous and satirical treatment of subjects relating to the Clinton Presidency. Its policies, the President himself, his past, his family, staff members, and friends are all fair game. (No ugly daughter pieces, please). Generally speaking, the more biting the better, however, your piece must be *funny* not bitter or angry. (If you have a non-humorous "message", call Western Union.) Outrageously hysterical, well-written satire and good-old-fashioned chain yanking are what we're looking for. Please note: The truth is often very funny. Comparing pre-election promises with Presidential performance can be comical if done in a humorous or ironic style.

Unless by special arrangement, stories should not exceed 2,000 words. Most will be substantially shorter.

On questions of style, refer to the *Chicago Manual of Style*. However, if you write your article as if you're writing to an intelligent friend, you'll do fine. We reserve the right to make minor stylistic changes and deletions to your manuscript. You will be informed of any substantive changes before publication. When making changes and deletions, we aim to be fair and restrained.

Payment is negotiated for each article based on a number of subjection criteria (not the least of which is general wonderfulness). Accompanying graphics increase the value of your submission. Payment in full is made within ten days of publication. A kill fee of 25% of the negotiated price will be paid for work in progress, if the work is cancelled at least 10 days before delivery date by publisher. (Story may just have been done elsewhere, premise is no longer relevant or appropriate, etc.) Bear in mind that work is rarely cancelled.

All submissions are purchased as work for hire. All articles purchased by *Slick Times* must be original, unpublished work. You must submit your article with the understanding that it cannot be submitted to other publications. We purchase all publication rights, which means we are purchasing the right to reprint the article in subsequent editions, republish it in book form (The Best of *Slick Times*), or make other use of the work in addition to publishing it in *Slick Times*. However, we can make other arrangements on request. For example, we may purchase all serial (i.e., magazine) publication rights, but not book publication rights or the rights to adapt the material for oral presentation. Again, we aim to be flexible and fair, and we pay reasonable rates for the rights we purchase.

Pay rates vary with your writing skills and experience as well as the value of the subject matter to our readers.

IMPORTANT: Manuscripts will be considered only when they are submitted on 3.5" diskette in ASCII/delimited format with hard copy. Each page should be numbered and carry the story title and author's name.

Categories: Cartoons—Comedy—Politics

Name: Submissions Editor
Material: All
Address: PO BOX 1710
City/State/ZIP: VALLEY CENTER CA 92082
Telephone: 760-633-3910
Fax: 760-633-3914

Slipstream Magazine

MAGAZINE: Submit poetry, short fiction under 15 pages, black & white photographs and graphics (recommend sending photocopies of artwork rather than originals). *Reading now for a theme issue on* Men's Room/Ladies Room (use your imagination). Like contemporary urban themes; shy away from pastoral, religious, and rhyming verse. Strong writing from the gut that is not afraid to bark or bite gets our attention. Pay in copies. If you do not include a SASE, do not expect a response. If you're unsure, the editors strongly recommend you sample a back or current issue—a mere five bucks. Submitting "blindly" to any magazine may result in wasting your time, money, and effort.

ANNUAL CHAPBOOK CONTEST: $500.00 prize plus 50 copies for winning poetry chapbook submitted. Send up to 40 pages of poetry—any style, format, theme (or no theme), plus a SASE with correct postage for return of your manuscript, and a $10.00 check, bank draft, or money order for reading fee. Simultaneous submissions are o.k. as long as you keep us informed of status. Previously published poems with acknowledgments and photocopies that are easy on the eyes are also acceptable. All entrants receive a copy of the winning chapbook and a one issue subscription of SLIPSTREAM. A winner is selected in March at which time all manuscripts are returned. Winner will be featured on the Grants & Awards page of *Poets & Writers Magazine* as well as on the SLIPSTREAM web site, and will also receive exposure in SLIPSTREAM catalogs, press releases, and promotional materials. Past winners have included Gerald Locklin, Richard Amidon, Robert Cooperman, Serena Fusek, Sherman Alexie, Kurt Nimmo, David Chorlton, Katharine Harer, Matt Buys, and Leslie Anne Mcilroy.

Categories: Fiction—Literature—Poetry—Short Stories

Name: Dan Sicoli, Co-Editor
Material: Poetry, Fiction
Address: PO BOX 2071
City/State/ZIP: NIAGARA FALLS NY 14301

Small Farm Today

Small Farm Today magazine is dedicated to preserving and promoting small farming, rural living, community and agripreneurship. We use a "can-do," upbeat, positive approach and all articles submitted should reflect this attitude.

We need "how-to" articles (how to grow, raise, market, build, etc.), as well as articles about small farmers who are experiencing success through diversification, specialty/alternative crops and livestock, and direct marketing. *Small Farm Today* is especially interested in articles that explain how to do something from start to finish citing specific examples involved in the process or operation being discussed. **It is important to include data on production costs, budgets, potential profits, etc.** See the list of topics at the end of these guidelines for ideas. We do not usually use fiction, poetry or political pieces.

REPRINTS: If your manuscript has been printed in another publication, please list the publications and dates published. We prefer to publish original articles.

WE PREFER:
• 1,400-2600+ word articles, typed or on a 3.5" disk in text format.
• Accompanying captioned photographs with SASE for photo return.
• The article should be "how-to", describing how to raise the crop or animal and how it is marketed. It should list the address of the farm examined or other resources to contact for more information.
• Please include data on production costs, budgets, profit information, and marketing methods.
• Articles which meet these preferences and the other standards listed herein (in the opinion of the editors) **will be paid a 1/2¢ bonus per word published.** Contact the Managing Editor for more information.

MANUSCRIPTS
We welcome both completed manuscripts and queries, but recommend you query your idea before sending in a manuscript.

Manuscripts submitted for consideration become the property of Missouri Farm Publishing, Inc. and will NOT be returned unless accompanied by a self-addressed, stamped envelope. Please type manuscripts, allowing at least 1/3 page at the top of the first page for editing notes. We also accept articles on disks compatible with a Macintosh computer. Length, depending on subject, should probably be between 800 and 3,000 words (we usually pre-

fer 1,200-2,600 words). **We prefer manuscripts with accompanying photos** (see *Photos*, below).

Because we use an image scanner to transfer most hard copies of manuscripts onto the computer, we would prefer an original copy of your manuscript or a very clean photocopy.

It is important to include the addresses and phone numbers of your primary sources/interviewees. We usually include this information at the end of the article so the readers can contact them for more information. Please specify if the source or interviewee does not wish to have their phone number or address listed at the end of the article.

If you have charts, diagrams or sources for additional information on your subject matter, we will try to use them as sidebars with the article.

ALTERATIONS
Small Farm Today reserves the right to alter your manuscript for readability or space considerations. There will be no deliberate changes in the meaning of the text. Although every effort is made to avoid error, *Small Farm Today* does limit its responsibility for any errors, inaccuracies, misprints, omissions, or other mistakes in the article content.

SPECIAL SECTION: *OUR PLACE*
Small Farm Today features a special section called *Our Place*. This section is written by farmers/landowners about their own property. We prefer it to be written in first person form (I, we, our). It should include a description of your farm and what you raise. Some "how-to" tips on what you have learned from dealing with your crops/livestock would be appreciated. Other things that can be mentioned are: how you got started, plans for the future, what makes your property unique, and marketing strategies you employ.

Several people have expressed concern about their writing abilities-don't worry. The story will be edited for publication, but will still contain your own unique voice. Payment for *Our Place* is a box of magazines of the issue featuring your story. You can pass it out to family, friend, and customers.

HOLDING POLICY
After the article is received, it is submitted to the editor for review. If approved, it will be slated for publication. There is a long waiting period for articles to be published, often close to a year. This is due to limited space (only 6 issues) and a multitude of interested writers. Please bear with our slow publishing times. If we have not published the issue after one year, we will return the story to you (if you included an SASE). If you would prefer not to have your story held, please send notification of this with your manuscript.

EDITORIAL CALENDAR & DEADLINES FOR ARTICLES
Deadlines for manuscripts are as follows:

ISSUE	EMPHASIS	DEADLINES
February	Wool & Fiber	December 5
April	Equipment	February 10
June	Livestock	April 10
August	Alternative & Rare Breeds	June 10
October	Draft Animals	August 10
December	Greenhouses & Gardening	October 10

PAYMENT
Unless otherwise arranged with the publisher, Missouri Farm Publishing, Inc. buys first serial rights and nonexclusive reprint rights (the right to reprint article in an anthology) for both manuscripts and photos. Missouri Farm Publishing, Inc. reserves the right to edit the story for publication. (See *Alterations*, page 2.) Rate of pay for reprints may be less than our standard rate of pay.

Payment for articles:
• 3.5¢ per word for each word *published* (See above paragraph.) for first serial rights and nonexclusive reprint rights.

• There is a 1/2¢ per word bonus for quality articles. (See *We Prefer*, above.)

• 2¢ per word for each word published for reprinted articles.

• We do not pay for book reviews

Payment for photos:

• $6.00 each for b&w or color prints

• $10.00 for photo used on cover

• $4.00 each for negatives or slides

Payment for line art, graphs, charts, and cartoons:

• $5.00 each

Payment is made 30-60 days after publication. Sorry, no exceptions.

PHOTOS, LINE ART, GRAPHS, CHARTS, & CARTOONS

Please send color or black and white prints of photos and **include information about each photo for use in captions.** Only color photos can be used on the cover. If you do not have prints, we can use negatives or slides. *All photos sent to us will be returned if you include a SASE for photo return.*

Cartoons, line art, graphs and charts are also welcome.

SUBJECT MATTER

Here is a list of some of the topics we cover regularly:

• Money-making alternatives for the small farm

• Exotic animals (ostriches, buffalo and elk are some we have covered)

• Minor breeds (Jacob sheep, Dexter cattle and red wattle hogs are some we have covered)

• Draft horses (Using them on a small farm; also other draft animals)

• Small stock (sheep, goats, rabbits, poultry)

• Direct marketing (farmers markets, subscription marketing, roadside stands, U-pick)

• Gardening

• Wool and other fibers (production, processing, and marketing)

• Specialty crops

• New uses for traditional crops (Ethanol and plastic from corn, for example)

• New sustainable farming methods

• Rural living (particularly how-to)

• Small fruits (grapes, berries, exotic new fruits)

• Tree fruits

• Sustainable agriculture (organic, reduced-input, agroecology)

• Horticulture (herbs, ornamentals, wild flowers, vegetables, other opportunities)

• Aquaculture (catfish, crawfish, fee fishing, tropical fish)

• Home-based business (crafts, food processing)

• Small-scale production of livestock (cattle, hogs, poultry)

• Equipment appropriate to small-scale acreage work

Be warned that stories may have a long lead time. As of this writing, we have 80 stories in stock. We do not limit ourselves to the topics on this list. If you have an idea for a story, drop us a note outlining your idea. If you are not familiar with *Small Farm Today*, we can send you a sample copy for $3.00.

Thank you for showing an interest in *Small Farm Today*! If you have any other questions, please write or call.

Categories: Nonfiction—Agriculture

Name: Paul Berg, Managing Editor
Material: All
Address: 3903 W RIDGE TRAIL RD
City/State/ZIP: CLARK MO 65243-9525
Telephone: 573-687-3525
Fax: 573-687-3148

Small Press Creative Explosion

SMALL PRESS CREATIVE EXPLOSION reaches 500-1,000 individuals each month who self-publish their own comics, comic books, music, films, radio plays, etc. They operate out of their homes on a shoestring budget, and there is usually only one individual behind any given publishing house. We are interested in articles that will help these people produce better products and market what they create more efficiently. Also, the practical aspects of running a home-based business, such as bookkeeping and tax obligations. 1,000—3,000 words. Payment in copies. Reply within 30 days.

Categories: Arts—Cartoons—Comedy—Comic Books—Comics—Humor—Music—Printing Methods—Short Stories—Writing

Name: Timothy R. Corrigan, Editor
Material: All
Address: PO BOX 25
City/State/ZIP: HOUGHTON NY 14744

Smithsonian Magazine

Thank you for inquiring about submitting articles to *Smithsonian Magazine*. We prefer a written proposal of one or two pages as a preliminary query. The proposal should convince us that we should cover the subject, offer descriptive information on how you, the writer, would treat the subject and offer us an opportunity to judge your writing ability. Background information and writing credentials and samples are helpful.

All unsolicited proposals are sent to us on speculation and you should receive a reply within eight weeks. Please include a self-addressed stamped envelope. We also accept proposals via electronic mail at siarticles@aol.com. If we decide to commission an article, the writer receives full payment on acceptance of the manuscript. If the article is found unsuitable, one-third of the payment serves as a kill fee.

Smithsonian is buying First North American Serial Rights only. Our article length ranges from a 1,000 word humor column to a 4,000 word full-length feature. We consider focused subjects that fall within the general range of Smithsonian Institution interests, such as: cultural history, physical science, art and natural history. We are always looking for offbeat subjects and profiles. We do not consider fiction, poetry, travel features, political and news events, or previously published articles. We have a two-month lead time.

Illustrations are not the responsibility of authors, but if you do have photographs or illustration materials, please include a selection of them with your submission. In general, 35mm color transparencies or black-and white prints are perfectly acceptable. Photographs published in the magazine are usually obtained through assignments, stock agencies or specialized sources. No photo library is maintained and photographs should be submitted only to accompany a specific article proposal.

Copies of the magazine may be obtained by sending your request and a check for $3.00 per copy for the current issue ($5.00 per copy for back issues) to the subscription office at the address below.

We publish only 12 issues a year, so it is difficult to place an article in *Smithsonian Magazine*, but please be assured that all proposals are considered.

I appreciate your interest in *Smithsonian*.

Marlane A. Liddell

Articles Editor

Categories: Nonfiction—Arts—Conservation—Culture—

Ecology—History—Science—Society—Travel—Nature—Technology—Archaeology

Name: Marlane A. Liddell, Articles Editor
Material: All
Address: 900 JEFFERSON DR.
City/State/ZIP: WASHINGTON, DC 20560
Telephone: 202-786-2900
Fax: 202-786-2564
E-mail: siarticles@aol.com
Internet: www.smithsonianmag.si.edu

Snake Nation Review

Snake Nation Review appears four times a year: two-contest issues and two non-contest issues:
Entry fees: $5 for stories and $1 for poems
$300, $200, $100 prizes for stories
$100, $75, $50 for poems
We welcome submissions throughout the year.
Include your name on title pages only!
Fiction: 5,000 word limit
Poetry: 60 line limit
Essays: 5,000 word limit
Art: pen & ink drawings, photographs,
Payment $100 for art
Subscriptions are $20; sample copy $6 (includes mailing)
Institutions $30
Subscription includes the contest poetry book.
All well-written submissions on any topic in any form will be considered.
Simultaneous submissions are allowed with prompt notification if the piece places elsewhere.
Payments are given for the non-contest issues.
Editors' Choice for the non-contest issues
wins $100 for each category.
Categories: Fiction—Arts—Culture—Poetry—Science Fiction—Sexuality—Writing

Name: Nancy Phillips, Editor
Material: Poetry
Name: Roberta George, Editor
Material: Fiction
Address: 110 #2 WEST FORCE
City/State/ZIP: VALDOSTA GA 31601
Telephone: 912-247-2787
Fax: 912-242-6690
Nota bene: Entry fee required for contest issues.

> **Remember: Editors change jobs and publishers change addresses. It is wise to invest in a phone call for the current information before submitting.**

Sneeze The Day!™

Please refer to *Good Dog!*
Categories: Nonfiction—Consumer—Health

Name: Judi Becker, Managing Editor
Material: All
Address: PO BOX 10069
City/State/ZIP: AUSTIN TX 78766-1069
Telephone: 512-454-6090
Fax: 512-454-3420
E-mail: gooddogmag@aol.com

SNOW COUNTRY

Snow Country
The Year-Round Magazine of Mountain Sports and Living

What is *Snow Country*?

Snow Country is subtitled "The Year-Round Magazine of Mountain Sports and Living," and the phrase perfectly describes our magazine. As more and more people move to the mountains or vacation there, *Snow Country* reflects both the reality and fantasy of life in the high country. Ours is a regional magazine based on geography: We cover those places defined by mountains and lofty elevations or cold climates, places where outdoor recreation is a way of life. Snow country stretches from the Sierra Nevadas of California and the Coast Mountains of British Columbia to the Adirondacks and the White Mountains of the East. It includes remote rural communities as cosmopolitan resort towns.

In six winter issues, we cover all of the snow sports: alpine skiing at resorts and in the backcountry; snowboarding, whether alpine carving or freestyle; nordic skiing, from skating to telemarking to touring. In two warm-weather issues, we cover the things people do in the mountains once the snow melts: mountain biking, hiking, whitewater rafting, camping, in-line skating, fly-fishing and more. And all year long, our editorial mix includes a wide range of lifestyle articles: profiles of people who live in the mountains or recently have moved there, analysis of important issues confronting the high country, tales of adventure and intriguing events.

Snow Country also covers the recreational equipment people use in the mountains, from skis and snowboards to bikes and hiking boots, and offers helpful instruction articles and fitness tips for skiing and other sports.

Recent issues, for example, have included articles on topics as varied as heli-skiing in British Columbia, the snowmobiling scene in Yellowstone, "bikepacking" on wilderness trails, adventure-sport summer schools, the death of two young rangers on Washington's Mount Rainier, how to use a skidded turn to improve your skiing, and efforts to control growth and development in Montana's Flathead County.

What kind of stories does *Snow Country* look for?

Snow Country looks for articles that educate, inform or entertain our readers. And if a single word can describe the writing style we hope to achieve, it's "lively." Whether in a first-person feature or a straightforward service article, we're interested in colorful quotes, unexpected anecdotes and engaging material that not only imparts information but also paints a colorful picture for readers.

In addition, it's critical that the article be carefully researched and accurate. We do not have a fact-checker to catch mistakes. With that in mind, we insist that writers verify their own work before submitting it. Our readers rely on us for accurate information, and writers who can't meet that standard will not work with us again.

Beyond that, it's difficult to describe the perfect *Snow Country* article. Often, we simply know it when we see it. So the best way to understand our magazine is to read it.

What kind of articles does *Snow Country* reject?

Every week, we receive dozens of queries that are variations on the same tired theme: "My Excellent Ski Trip to Fill-In-The-Blank Resort." Although there's nothing better than a great day on the slopes, these articles are the ski-magazine version of your great-aunt's slide show from her trip to Texas. Other common and cliched themes: How I Learned to Ski or Snowboard, How I Learned to Ski or Snowboard (And I'm Over 40!), Senior Citizens Who Ski, Teaching Your Kids to Ski, Why I don't Like Snowboarders, and How I Recovered from a Painful Knee Injury. If your story idea is along any of these lines, you're likely to get a rejection letter.

What areas of the magazine are open to freelancers?

A few sections of the magazine are developed by our staff and contributing editors, and generally are not written by freelancers. These include our annual equipment reviews Skis and boots, snowboards, hiking boots and cars), our fashion coverage (outdoor apparel and accessories) and two departments: Real Estate and Travel Watch. That said, we occasionally publish articles on these topics by outside writers. So if you think you have a good idea, send it.

In other areas, we rely heavily on freelance writers. Here's the editorial line-up:

Mountain Living is a magazine within a magazine. As the title suggests, the five-page department offers a wide-ranging slice of high-country life: news and gossip, people and points of view, anecdotes, trends and issues. Stories range in length from 100 to 700 words. In general, the short takes tend to be offbeat, pithy and lighthearted. The longer stories often deal with more serious topics. Recent issues have included pieces on a Steamboat rancher fighting to save his valley from real estate development and a proposed Montana gold mine that could threaten Yellowstone National park. Suggesting a good Mountain Living item is the best way for freelance writers to "break in" to *Snow Country*.

Datebook lets readers know about "can't-miss" events in the Mountains. World Cup races and athletic competitions, guided trips and outdoor adventures, ski clinics and outdoor sports camps, festivals and concerts and street fairs. In every issue, we select 12 events. Each item runs no longer than 120 words. Freelancers occasionally contribute to Datebook, and we also pay a nominal fee for great Datebook ideas.

Portfolio is a six-page photo essay. Normally, these essays focus on the work of one outstanding mountain photographer, and center around an unusual theme or central point in his work. The text is almost always written by our editors.

Featurettes are stories that aren't long enough to qualify for the feature well. These articles run in the front of the book, range from 1,000 to 2,000 words and usually fall into one of several broad categories: first-person adventure articles (dogsledding in Minnesota, toboggan racing in Maine, skiing the new alpine terrain parks); short travel articles (spending the holidays in Santa Fe, skiing the Swiss resorts of Klosters and Davos); service-oriented stories (best ski-town bars, great ridgeline hikes); profiles of interesting snow country residents (Gerald Hines of Aspen Highlands, a paraplegic ski patroller at Washington's Crystal

Mountain); and investigative or issue-oriented articles (ski-area liability laws, turmoil in the U.S. Skiing boardroom).

Features cover the same topics as featurettes, but deserve more space. Features generally occupy four or six ad-free pages, and can run as long as 4,000 words. The feature well is also where you'll find *Snow Country*'s annual Top 50 Resorts package (September), our major equipment reviews (October through December), and major-destination resort profiles.

Follow me is an instruction department that offers one easy-to-understand tip on each page. In winter, the tips cover alpine skiing, snowboarding, nordic skiing, snowshoeing and other snow sports. In summer, we turn to mountain biking, hiking, in-line skating and the like. Follow me is always written or ghost-written by highly qualified experts, such as members of the PSIA demonstration team or pro mountain-bike racers. High-quality photography is critical to the department and must be assigned and overseen by the Snow Country staff.

Architecture is a topic we try to cover as often as possible. Past articles have included a story on a house built atop Telluride Mountain, a two-page illustration by a leading architect who designed the ultimate ski house, and a piece on Janet's Cabin, a solar-powered backcountry lodge on Colorado's Tenth Mountain Trail.

Does it Work offers capsule reviews of new gear that people use in the mountains, excluding the equipment we cover in our annual packages (skis, boots, bindings and snowboards, hiking boots). Recent examples include an oversized ski bag, replacement liners for Sorel boots, a deluxe headlamp and an innovative water purifier.

Armchair Mountaineer reviews the latest books, videos, software and CD-ROMs that might be of interest to our readers. Each review runs no longer than 200 words.

Money and other details

Snow Country's basic pay rate is 80 cents per word, although it can vary, depending on circumstances. In general, rates reflect how much time and effort the story will take. Fees are negotiable in advance with the story editor, as are expenses. We generally reimburse writers for phone calls, and usually pay mileage, lodging, meals and other predetermined costs. The fee includes any rewrites and any additional reporting that may be required.

We pay on acceptance, which means when the editors agree that the article is ready to go. *Snow Country* buys first-time-all world rights, which includes the right to publish the article on our World Wide Web online site.

If we haven't worked with you before, your query must be accompanied by clips and a resume. We try to respond to all queries promptly. If the answer is "no," you'll probably hear from us within two weeks. If we're interested in your idea or your writing style, you'll be contacted by an editor, but it may take a bit longer. On rare occasions, if you're new to *Snow Country*, you may be asked to write the article on spec.

Thanks for your interest in *Snow Country*.

Categories: Nonfiction—Adventure—Consumer—Lifestyles—Outdoors—Recreation—Sports

Name: Submissions Editor
Material: All
Address: 5520 PARK AVE
City/State/ZIP: TRUMBULL CT 06611
Fax: 203-373-7111
E-mail: editor@snowcountry.com
Internet: www.snowcountry.com

S-Z

SNOWSHOER

The Snowshoer

The SNOWSHOER is published five times per season. It is a publication devoted to the promotion of snowshoeing, catering to a broad demographic from young families to older more adventuresome adults and recreational as well as competitive snowshoers. Each issue includes: calendar of events, destinations, fitness, personalities, new product reviews, humor, fiction, national & international race news. Circulation is by individual subscription, free distribution to qualified retailers, winter resorts, nature centers, shows and events.

Destinations

The magazine features locations in North America with an occasional piece on areas overseas.

Especially important in all destination pieces is the inclusion of pertinent information about facilities, location, and contact address and telephone, so readers can act on the Ideas presented. Feature articles accompanied by professional quality photos will receive priority consideration.

Short Trips, within 150 miles of metropolitan areas, are of special interest to snowshoers who take day trips throughout the season. 750 words.

Regular Columns

Columnists are selected for their expertise in a certain area. Prospective writers should query the editor.

How to Submit Material

• Word processed hard copy or computer generated on 3½" high density disks. Can be either PC or Macintosh, Mac is preferred. Word Processing programs: Microsoft Word/WordPerfect. If not Mac please send by modem or floppy in ASCII format. A hardcopy printout must be included with the disk. Double space between lines; do not double space between sentences. Helvetica or Times typefaces preferred.

• Send electronically to e-mail address below

• Destination and General Interest features: 1,000-1,500 words.

• Support pieces: 300-500 words.

• Professional quality photos, color/black & white/slides for story accompaniment—3"x5" or larger. Acceptance will be based on quality. Published photos returned only upon request and if accompanied by SASE.

Acceptance

• Writers will be notified of acceptance, pending acceptance, or rejection within one month of submission.

• Final acceptance will be made one month prior to publication, with the understanding by the writer that space limitations may force an article to be held until a later publication date.

• The SNOWSHOER reserves the right to edit all materials.

Pay

• Five cents per word

• Five dollars per photo

• Payment upon publication.

Deadlines

• Two months prior to cover date for columns and solicited material

• Unsolicited articles must be received three months in advance of cover date if they relate to a specific month or issue theme. For more information write/call:

Categories: Lifestyles—Outdoors—Physical Fitness—Recreation—Sports

Name: Jim Radtke, Executive Editor

Material: All
Address: PO BOX 458
City/State/ZIP: WASHBURN WI 54891
Telephone: 715-373-5556
Fax: 715-373-5003
E-mail: SNOSHU@win.bright.net

Southern Living

Thank you for your interest in submitting articles to Southern Living. However, with the exception of our Southern Journal column, the articles and photography are produced by members of our staff or our regular contributing editors.

For Southern Journal, we don't have a rigid set of guidelines; however, there are some characteristics of a typical Journal that you might find interesting. Above all, it must be Southern. We need comments on life in this region— written from the standpoint of a person who is intimately familiar with this part of the world. It's personal, almost always involving something that happened to the writer or someone he or she knows very well. Most of the articles submitted are reminiscences, but we take special note of stories that are contemporary in their point of view.

We require that the piece be original and not published. We need about 1,000 words, typed and double spaced. The writing must have an essay quality—as opposed to a reporting, interpretive, or editorial approach. Finally, it must be of exceptionally high quality.

We can't guarantee acceptance of any piece for publication, but if we do decide to use it, we require complete ownership rights. If interested, send your manuscript to Nancy Dorman Hickson, Associate Features Editor. If she is interested, she will contact you directly.

Again, thanks for considering Southern Living. Good luck in placing your work.

Sincerely,
Brenda Harris Administrative Assistant

Categories: Nonfiction—Book Reviews—Cooking—Food/Drink—Gardening—Regional—Travel—Nutrition—Home

Name: Nancy Dorman Hickson,
  Associate Features Editor
Material: All
Address: 2100 LAKESHORE DRIVE
City/State/ZIP: BIRMINGHAM, AL 35209
Telephone: 205-877-6000

South Florida History

South Florida History

Purpose of the Magazine

To engage readers in stories about our region's past in a manner that is both educational and entertaining and is illustrated with both historic and contemporary images.

Distribution

As of 6/1/97, 5,000 copies of the magazine are printed, reaching an estimated readership of 9,000, not including users in libraries and at other institutions receiving the magazine in their collections. Currently, members of seven institutions receive the magazine regularly with the majority of the circulation going to members of the Historical Museum of Southern Florida. Member associations include:

Boca Raton Historical Society (Boca Raton)
Clewiston Museum (Clewiston)

Collier County Museum (Naples)
Florida History Center and Museum (Jupiter)
Fort Myers Historical Museum (Fort Myers)
Historical Museum of Southern Florida (Miami)
The Museum of Florida's Art and Culture (Sebring)
Book stores in the South Florida area also distribute the magazine.

History

The Historical Association of Southern Florida began publication of the magazine in 1974 under the name *Update*. In 1988 the name was changed to **South Florida History Magazine**.

Presentation Style

Article should be suitable for general audiences with interest—but not necessarily with a great deal of background—in our region's history. The editors strive for variety and balance so that each issue contains at least one article of interest to each reader.

Style Authority

The *Associated Press Stylebook and Libel Manual* should be consulted on matters of style as this is the guide used by the editors of the magazine. *Webster's* first choice is used when multiple spellings of a word are acceptable. Exceptions are made when the presentation form warrants.

Content

Articles should recall, retell and explore historic events, people, places and themes pertaining to southern Florida and the Caribbean. The magazine covers Florida from about Lake Okeechobee on down, coast to coast, and all countries in the Caribbean. Articles are generally presented as non-annotated narratives in third person or first person, and can include quotations from historic records, diaries and other documents. Exceptions are made when material warrants. Bibliographies and footnotes will not be published.

Photographs

Photographic illustration is very important in *South Florida History Magazine;* authors are encouraged to identify available accompanying visual material whenever possible and provide copies of such images when submitting manuscripts. Original documents and photographs that must be returned to their owners will be copied by the historical Museum of Southern Florida and handled according to the highest level of curatorial standards. Materials will be returned via certified delivery systems after publication of the magazine.

Regular Features

The Visual Record. A pictorial account, usually historic photograph or objects, fitting the same content description as above. If owned by entities other than the author or Historical Association of Southern Florida, permission must be obtained to use images.

Book Reviews. Reviews are encouraged for publications relating to southern Florida and the Caribbean and to Florida generally. It is suggested that potential reviewers inquire about a specific book they would like to cover to see if a review is already in the works.

Around the Galleries. This section features upcoming exhibitions and events hosted by the magazine's member associations as listed previously and is prepared by the Historical Museum's editorial staff.

New Features Under Consideration for the Future

Family Histories
Company Histories
Submission of Articles

A typed manuscript is requested with accompanying computer disk copy of the article whenever possible (Preferred format is PC compatible 3.5" diskette, in Microsoft Word or WordPerfect; Macintosh is acceptable). Manuscripts are also accepted through e-mail. Photographs and other illustrative materials, if identified, should be submitted with the manuscript (cop-

ies acceptable). Scanned photographs and images may be sent electronically as well, but prints will be required upon acceptance of the article for production. Articles may be submitted at any time throughout the year and should be 500 to 2,500 words in length.

The editorial staff of *South Florida History Magazine* strives to respond to writers who have submitted manuscripts in a timely fashion. Writers are asked to call if a timely response has not been made. The first response back will generally be an indication of whether the material is of interest for the publication and whether any additional research or writing is requested. If acceptable, the article becomes part of the pool of material undergoing production steps to ready them for publication. Articles are pulled from the pool and assigned to specific issues on an ongoing basis. The Editors at the Historical Museum of Southern Florida maintain the right for flexibility in deciding publication dates as geographical, thematic and seasonal concerns are considered.

Payment to authors for articles used includes the Historical Museum of Southern Florida's most sincere appreciation and 10 copies of the magazine.

Standards

The editorial staff of *South Florida History Magazine* strives for the highest level of accuracy and fairness possible when presenting the past. Standard journalistic and research practices and principles should be adhered to at all times. Please refer to the *Associated Press Stylebook and Libel Manual* for any questions or doubt.

The Historical Association of Southern Florida disclaims any responsibility for errors in factual material or statements of opinions expressed by contributors.

A Word to Contributors

You are the **lifeblood** of *South Florida History Magazine*. Your time, energy and thoughtfulness in submitting a contribution are sincerely appreciated as we strive to spread interest in and understanding of our region's rich past. Thank you.

The Editors, *South Florida History Magazine*

Categories: Nonfiction—African-American—Arts—Asian-American—Biography—Conservation—Culture—Ethnic—Hispanic—History—Jewish Interests—Lifestyles—Multicultural—Native American—Regional

Name: Rebecca Eads, Editor
Name: Stuart McIver, Editor
Material: Any
Address: 101 W FLAGLER ST
City/State/ZIP: MIAMI FL 33130
Telephone: 305-375-1492
Fax: 305-375-1609
E-mail: hasf@ix.netcom.com

The Southern California Anthology
University of Southern California

We read all fiction and poetry that comes to us, whether traditional or non-traditional, and publish a variety of forms and styles. *The Southern California Anthology* selects manuscripts for publication using literary merit as the sole criteria.

All manuscripts should be typed. Poetry should be single-spaced within stanzas; double-spaced between stanzas.

Fiction submissions and interviews should be no longer than twenty-five pages. Please limit prose submissions to one.

Please limit poetry submissions to no more than five. Place only one poem per page.

We appreciate cover letters. They give us not only a sense of the writer, but are also helpful if they include sufficient information for the editors to compose a brief biography in the event of acceptance.

Categories: Fiction—Poetry

Name: Inga Kiderra, Fiction Editor
Name: Lisa Swanstrom, Poetry Editor
Name: Brian McCormick, Poetry Editor
Material: As Appropriate
Address: UNIVERSITY OF SOUTHERN CALIFORNIA WPH 404
City/State/ZIP: LOS ANGELES CA 90035
Telephone: 213-740-3252
Fax: 213-740-5775

SHR *Southern Humanities Review*

Southern Humanities Review
Auburn University

The *Southern Humanities Review* publishes fiction, poetry, critical essays, and book reviews on the arts, literature, philosophy, religion, and history. The journal is issued quarterly, in February, May, August, and November; approximately 750 copies, including contributors', exchange, and complimentary copies, are distributed. It is indexed in the *National Index of Literary Periodicals*, the *Bulletin of Research in the Humanities*, the *Humanities Index*, the *Book Review Index*, the *MHRA Bibliography*, and *Abstracts of English Studies*, and its contents are considered for *Best American Essays*, *The Art of the Essay* (forthcoming from Anchor/Doubleday), the *O. Henry Awards*, *Best American Poetry*, and *New Stories from the South*. The annual subscription rate is $15.00 in the United States, $20.00 foreign. Single copies are $5.00 US, $7.00 foreign. US funds only.

Submission Guidelines

General

Queries are welcome. Simultaneous submissions are NOT accepted. Submit poetry, fiction, and essays separately, as different editors will consider them. Do not submit a second manuscript if we already have one from you under consideration. With the exception of translations, we do not consider material that has been published elsewhere. Use at least a 10-pt. font. Payment is two contributors' copies; copyright reverts to author upon publication. Response time varies from two weeks to three months, depending on the editors' other responsibilities.

Poetry

Send three to five poems in a business-sized (#10) envelope, *not* a large manila envelope. It is wise to submit no more than four times per year unless the editors ask to see more of your work. We rarely print a poem longer than two pages. Translations are encouraged, but please include the original *and* written permission from the copyright holder for you to publish a translation.

Fiction

Send only one story per submission. Manuscripts should be between 3,500 and 15,000 words. It is wise to submit no more than four times per year unless the editors ask to see more of your work. Please do not assume from our name that we are interested in Southern literature only; any setting or subject matter is acceptable, but do avoid excessive vulgarity, profanity, and jargon (medical or military, for example). Translations are encouraged, but please include the original *and* written permission from the copyright holder for you to publish a translation.

Essays

Send only one essay per submission. Manuscripts should be between 3,500 and 15,000 words, double-spaced (including notes). Please do not assume from our name that we are interested in Southern topics only; any subject matter in the liberal arts is acceptable, but be sure to direct your essay to a general humanities audience, avoiding specialist jargon. Translations are encouraged, but please include the original *and* written permission from the copyright holder for you to publish a translation.

The Hoepfner Awards

The Hoepfner Awards were established to honor a colorful scholar of the Auburn University English Department in residence here from 1941 until his death in 1966. They are given each year to the best essay, story, and poem *published* in the previous volume. In other words, they are not a contest to be entered, but an award made for work already accepted and published through the regular submission process. They are announced in the Editors' Comments of Winter Issues.

Categories: Fiction—Nonfiction—Arts—Criticism—History—Humanities—Literature—Music—Philosophy—Poetry—Short Stories

Name: Editors
Material: All
Address: 9088 HALEY CENTER
City/State/ZIP: AUBURN UNIVERSITY AL 36849

Southern Lumberman
The Sawmill Magazine

The Magazine: SOUTHERN LUMBERMAN is The Sawmill Magazine and is edited for owners and managers of sawmills in North America. Articles explore sawmill equipment and management issues. Sawmill operations include primary breakdown of logs, production of lumber, dimension parts, treated wood, chips, pallets and boxes, and other wood by-products. Subjects featured include marketing, economics, kiln-drying, computerization, and processing of products.

In its 116th year, the magazine targets an average reader who is the owner or manager of a small- to medium-sized sawmill operation. Circulation is 14,500 and growing. An average issue presently is 48 pages. Regular features are: calendar, industry news, dateline news, new products, lumber market trends, species of the month, and value added opportunities. We also include at least one theme article each month, frequently an equipment-themed piece. Two features, Lumbermen and Installations, are particularly suitable for freelance writers' queries and submissions.

What We Want: We're interested primarily in articles about sawmill operations across the country—we're strongest east of the Mississippi, but we are a national publication. Articles might include: sawmill operations (or who is doing what better) and how-to or technical pieces dealing with the lumber industry. Sawmill operation stories should be about those that are doing something different—better marketing, venturing into a new market, installing new facilities to change or improve production, and so forth.

Sawmill operation stories should include information about the mill's history, the owner/manager's insights into changes in the industry, and of course what it is that is being done that is different/better than other mills. We're always interested in stories about sawmills branching out into value-added opportunities or success stories tied to installation of a particular piece or pieces of equipment. Stories should be 500-900 words long and accompanied by publication quality color photographs.

To Query or Not: We welcome queries or manuscripts. A query should describe author's qualifications, the article's focus and probable length, and describe pictures that will accompany the article. Writers will find the editor most helpful in giving direction to an article of interest to SOUTHERN LUMBERMAN's readers.

Payment: Payment, upon publication, is for first North American serial rights—$100-$150 for most stories. Color images to accompany stories are included in this price. Other color photographs may be considered for purchase (payment on publication) depending on subject matter (coverage of national lumber association meetings, for example) at $10 each. Slides and transparencies of attractive lumber-related scenes (woods, logging, sawmills, etc.), preferably tied to some event, are also welcome on a submission basis (enclose SASE for return). Payment is negotiable.

Don't Forget: *All manuscripts should include the writer's phone number* so the editor can contact the writer with whatever questions arise.

Categories: Sawmills

Name: Nanci P. Gregg, Managing Editor
Material: All
Address: PO BOX 681629
City/State/ZIP: FRANKLIN TN 37068-1629
Telephone: 615-791-1961
Fax: 615-790-6188
E-mail: grou@edge.net
Internet: www.lumberman.com/magazine

The Southern Review
Louisiana State University

The Southern Review publishes fiction, poetry, critical essays, interviews, book reviews, and excerpts from novels in progress, with emphasis on contemporary literature in the United States and abroad, and with special interest in southern culture and history. Poems and fiction are selected with careful attention to craftsmanship and technique and to the seriousness of the subject matter. Although willing to publish experimental writing that appears to have a valid artistic purpose, *The Southern Review* avoids extremism and sensationalism. Critical essays and book reviews exhibit a thoughtful and sometimes severe awareness of the necessity of literary standards in our time.

Minimum rates to contributors are twelve dollars a printed page for prose and twenty dollars a page for poetry. Payment is made on publication. Two complimentary copies of the issue in which the work appears are sent to each contributor; no reprints are available. Manuscripts must be typewritten. Manuscripts will not be returned without adequate return postage. Only previously unpublished works will be considered. Allow at least two months for editorial decisions.

Poetry lengths preferred are one to four pages; fiction, four to eight thousand words; essays, four to ten thousand words. All book reviews are on a commissioned basis. Do not send fillers, jokes, plays, feature articles, or artwork. Queries are not necessary. First American serial rights only are purchased.

Manuscripts will not be considered during the months of June, July, and August.

Sample copies are $6.00 payable in advance. For style information, see *A Manual of Style,* published by the University of Chicago Press. Use a minimum of footnotes. Send, on a separate sheet, citations for quotations used in essays. *The Southern Review* and Louisiana State University do not assume responsibility for views expressed by contributors.

Categories: Fiction—Nonfiction—Interview—Literature—Poetry—Short Stories

Name: James Olney, Editor

Name: Dave Smith, Editor
Name: Michael Griffith, Associate Editor
Address: 43 ALLEN HALL LOUISIANA STATE UNIVERSITY
City/State/ZIP: BATON ROUGE LA 70803-5005
Telephone: 504-388-5108
Fax: 504-388-5098
E-mail: bmacon@unixl.sncc.lsu.edu

Southwest Contractor

It is important to remember that as a freelance writer for *Southwest Contractor,* you will be writing for a trade publication, not a newspaper or news magazine; therefore, your article should be written for the contractor, not the general public.

During the interview and while writing the article, you need to remember to discuss details about the construction process. Although on occasion you should include general information within the body of the article, it should *not* be given high priority.

Reading our magazine carefully will give you an idea of the magazine's style and the information needed in a project story.

WHAT TO DO AFTER A STORY IS ASSIGNED

I. Immediately call your contact person with the general contractor to 1.) get a list of subcontractors and suppliers and 2.) schedule an appointment.

II. After getting a list of subs and suppliers, either fax it to my office or mail, depending on your deadline.

III. Points to remember during the interview:

a. Since you may be unfamiliar with much of the construction, the best approach is to ask the jobsite superintendent or project manager to "walk you" through the project chronologically, step-by-step. Ask specific questions about each phase, such as the duration of the phase, contractors involved, equipment involved, quantities, etc. Most important, *don't be afraid to ask questions*.

b. When talking about each project phase, ask him to highlight things which may be unique, innovative or unusual.

c. Specific information needed about construction process (this is just a brief overview and does not cover every aspect of the project):

1. Contract awarded when, dollar volume of project.
2. Site preparation
3. Foundation work. If it includes piles or grade beams, get the dimensions.
4. Ready-mix concrete, quantity in cubic yards.
5. Reinforcing steel quantity (tonnage) and suppliers. Where is reinforcing steel being installed?
6. Composition of main structure: Is it concrete and steel, poured-in-place concrete or precast concrete?
7. Dimensions of overall structure (square footage, height, number of floors, etc.)
8. Anything unique about the construction process, such as the scheduling, management structure, techniques used, etc.?
9. Number of crewmen.
10. Tonnage of structural steel within the structure. How is it being lifted (by lattice boom or hydraulic crane) and who is lifting it (is it a subcontractor?).
11. Is concrete poured in place or precast, or both? Any unique concrete placement techniques or mixes?
12. Any other major materials in structure that need mentioning?
13. Go through the list of subs and suppliers and ask for details about what each is doing or supplying.

IV. Within the body of the story:

a. Focus on an important aspect of the project in your lead. Try to zero in on the most interesting part of the project.

Much of the construction may be fairly common, so it is sometimes a challenge to uncover its unique or interesting aspects. Write the story so a contractor who reads it can learn something that will help him with his business or project.

b. Walk through the project step-by-step and point out interesting phases or processes.

c. Give important quantities, dimensions.

d. Provide plenty of quotes from the jobsite superintendent and important subcontractors (if a particular subcontractor is no available at the jobsite, you may want to contact him later by phone).

WHAT TO DO WHEN TAKING PHOTOGRAPHS AT THE JOBSITE

I. You will need two or three rolls of 200 speed, 35 millimeter color film, preferably Fuji or Kodak. Many places (Wal-Mart, K-Mart, Target) sell it in three-packs, which is cheaper. Keep your receipt for reimbursement.

II. Photographs need to be taken of the following:

a. Construction activity. We need *close-up* shots of construction crewmen performing various functions at the jobsite, such as pouring concrete, tying reinforcing steel, erecting structural steel, performing mechanical work (heating and air conditioning systems), performing interior work, laying bricks or concrete masonry units. *Take many pictures both inside and out; also get names of subcontractor companies in photographs.*

b. Overall picture of the project.

c. Face shots of jobsite superintendent, project manager, architect, (if applicable), engineer, important subcontractor foremen if they are at the site. These can be taken individually or as a group shot.

d. Construction equipment in operation.

III. As you take photos, get enough information about what is going on in the picture for cutlines.

IV. Develop film at Wal-Mart, Walgreens, K-Mart or Target, whichever is more convenient. Keep receipt for reimbursement.

V. Type photo cutlines (double-spaced) at the end of the story, then number the backs of the photographs *in pencil* to correspond with the cutlines.

WHAT TO DO AFTER YOUR STORY IS COMPLETE

I. Edit story, checking for "typos," grammatical areas, continuity, transition, missing information, etc.

II. Put the story on disk, if possible. We can easily accommodate WordPerfect and Microsoft Word programs. If you have another program, please check with the editor. Otherwise, type the story.

III. Mail photos and story together.

PAYSCALE:

Stories:

I. 750-1,150 words: $125

II. 1,150-1,900 words: $150

III. More than 1,900 words: $200

This pay scale is based on the length of an edited story as it is printed. Every word is counted, including "a", "an" and "the". The article should *never* be shorter than 750 words. Most of the time, we prefer stories to be in the 1,150-1,900 word range.

Photos:

I. $10 per photo or other art element you supply that is printed in the magazine, whether you took the photos or obtained the photos for us.

a. If you obtain photos through the contractor, make sure that the contractor has full editorial rights to the photos and make sure we receive the proper photo credit information. If a photo that the contractor provided is used on the cover, the rate is $10.

b. We will reimburse for photography costs, which shouldn't be more than the purchase cost and development

of three rolls of film.

II. $75 for a cover photo that you take. It should be vertical. I will notify you if one of your photos makes the cover.

INS AND OUTS OF OUR STYLE

I. For the most part, follow AP style.

II. Indent each paragraph with the tab key.

III. Use only one space between sentences.

Categories: Nonfiction—Construction

Name: Submissions Editor
Material: All
Address: 2050 E UNIVERSITY DR STE 1
City/State/ZIP: PHOENIX AZ 85034
Telephone: 602-258-1641
Fax: 602-495-9407
E-mail: Sweditor@aol.com

Southwest Review
Southern Methodist University

Articles published by the *Southwest Review* embrace almost every area of adult interest: contemporary affairs, history, folklore, fiction, poetry, literary criticism, art, music, and the theatre. Material should be presented in a fashion suited to a quarterly that is not journalistic and not terribly overloaded with academic apparatus or jargon. It should not be too specialized, after the manner of papers that appear in "learned journals" of different fields of study.

SHORT STORIES

In each issue the *Southwest Review* publishes two or three stories, which must be of high literary quality. We have published fiction in widely varying styles. We prefer stories of character development, of psychological penetration, to those depending chiefly on plot. We have no specific requirements as to subject matter. Some of our stories have a southwestern background, but even more are not regional. We prefer, however, that stories not be too strongly regional if the region with which they deal is not our own.

The preferred length for articles and fiction is 3,000 to 5,000 words.

POETRY

It is hard to describe the *Southwest Review's* preference in poetry in a few words. We always suggest that potential contributors read several issues of the magazine to see for themselves what we like. But some things may be said: We demand very high quality in our poems; we accept both traditional and experimental writing; we place no arbitrary limits on length; we have no specific limitations as to theme.

THE JOHN H. MCGINNIS MEMORIAL AWARD

The John H. McGinnis Memorial award is given to the best works of fiction and nonfiction that appeared in the magazine in the previous year. The two awards consist of cash prizes of $1,000 each. Robert F. Ritchie of Dallas established the award in 1960 to commemorate the man who edited the *Southwest Review* from 1927 to 1943.

THE ELIZABETH MATCHETT STOVER MEMORIAL AWARD

The Elizabeth Matchett Stover Memorial award was established in 1978 by Jerry S. Stover of Dallas in memory of his mother, who was for many years a key member of the Southwest *Review.* The award consists of a $150 cash prize and is given to the author of the best poem or group of poems published in the magazine during the preceding year.

Please note that manuscripts are submitted for publication, not for the prizes themselves.

N.B.: The *Southwest Review* prefers not to receive simultaneous submissions and does not consider work that has been published previously.

Because of the great number of submissions, manuscripts will not be read during the summer months, June, July, and August.

The *Southwest Review* is published quarterly. We make a nominal payment upon publication and we also send the author three gratis contributor's copies of the issue in which the work appears.

Categories: Fiction—Nonfiction—Arts—Culture—Essays—Interview—Literature—Multicultural—Poetry

Name: Submissions Editor
Material: All
Address: 307 FONDREN LIBRARY WEST
Address: SOUTHERN METHODIST UNIVERSITY
Address: PO BOX 750374
City/State/ZIP: DALLAS TX 75275-0374
Telephone: 214-768-1037
Fax: 214-768-1408
E-mail: SWR@mail.smu.edu

SPSM&H
(Shakespeare, Petrarch, Sidney, Milton & Hopkins)
Please refer to Amelia Press.

SPARE TIME

Spare Time Magazine

Our mission.
The editorial mission of SPARE TIME magazine is to provide our readers with the inspiration, information and advice they need to plant, grow and maintain their own spare-time businesses.

How we try to accomplish it.
First of all, we keep our readers in mind-average people who are more likely to be looking for a way to start their first business than to already have one. Most haven't much business experience or savvy and haven't the money (or the inclination to invest it) for high start-up costs or franchise fees. That means, among other things, that when they do get started, their spare-time business will most likely be one they can do out of their homes, and that will supplement their regular income rather than replace it (at least for the time being).

With such readers in mind, we cover such business basics as sales, production, marketing, customer service, management, taxes and legal issues. Again, recognizing their nature and needs, that means arming our readers with the skills, resources and techniques for things like setting up a home-based office, telephone sales, promotion through free publicity, direct marketing, personalized customer service, time management (just how do you find any "spare time" these days?), simple bookkeeping (both for the business and for the IRS), and a few legal issues like incorporation, contracts, government regulations, etc. We also try to cover the less tangible requirements of success-like attitude, self-improvement, healthy living, balancing work and family, how to pick the right venture (not only financially right, but personally as well).

What we look for
To reach our readers most effectively, we look for articles that:

Are unusual or unique—topics you don't often, or never, see in business opportunity literature, but are nonetheless relevant to our audience. Help give us an edge on the competition! Uncommon approaches to common topics will also catch our eye.

Include examples of successful people whose experiences illustrate the points you're trying to make, and inspire our readers with the hope that they, too, can succeed. Choose more than one, if possible (unless you're doing a profile)—the greater the variety of people and experiences, the greater the number of readers who can identify with your examples. Maximize your, and our, readership reach.

Quote experts rather than read like essays. If you're the expert, give some examples from your own experiences, but try to include comments from at least one other expert and one other person's real-life experiences. Don't make it just an anecdotal essay based primarily on your own personal experiences or opinions. Include your expert's (or your) credentials.

Add sidebars with checklists, to-dos, tips, examples or additional resources.

Are under 1,100 words (not including sidebars, pull-quotes or captions), unless you're doing a cover story (1,500 to 2,000 words), or an installment series (up to three parts of no more than 1,100 words each). This limit is not absolute, however (though not far from it). If the story's subject matter and your treatment merits it, we can stretch the limit to 1,500 words, tops. If you're doing a series, organize it around natural breakpoints between installments, and include a preview of the upcoming installment at the end of all but the final one, and a recap at the top of each installment subsequent to the first one.

Art and photos—especially action photos-to "dress up" your piece.

What we avoid
Spare Time is a business opportunities magazine, not a consumer publication; we do not print comparative or negative product reviews, as valuable as they may be in their own context. Nor do we represent any political, philosophical or religious viewpoint; we do not engage in controversy of any kind, however valuable such commentaries may be in their respective contexts.

Start by ordering a sample copy of *Spare Time*. Send $2.50, pre-paid, to the address below with your order. Then, before you start writing an article, query us in writing first, so you and our editor can develop a consensus between you as to the article's subject matter and your approach to it. Include any clips of your previous work, and any credentials or experience you may have on your proposed article's subject matter.

If you have an article you've already written, let us know if and where it's been published before; but don't send us any recent "reruns" from our competitors. Unsolicited manuscripts will be considered for publication, and we'll let you know if, and tentatively when, we plan to publish them.

If you compose your articles on a computer, please submit them on a 3.5" computer diskette, along with your hard copy. We can access almost any such disk, regardless of the kind of computer or word processing program you use. Please save your articles to the disk in your native word processing format, plus a second version in Microsoft Word for Macintosh 5 or earlier, or Interchange/Rich Text Format [.rtf], or plain ASCII text. You can also attach each version to an e-mail message. Either way, your articles will get into our production pipeline that much faster than if you only supplied them on paper.

Please also include a brief biographical paragraph about yourself, and a photograph to accompany it, for the "shirt-tail" we publish at the end of almost all of our articles.

Photos and art

Let us know in your query if any art, graphics or photographs will accompany your article. If they are not already available in final form, discuss with the editor what you have in mind, just as you would for the article itself. While we don't pay for photos provided by your subjects, we do pay fifteen dollars ($15) for each photo you take yourself which we publish.

Payment

Spare Time magazine Pays fifteen cents (15¢) per word upon publication for first-time serial rights (including online publication on our Web site for no more than one year) for *all* assigned articles and accepted submissions. Because of our policy of working with writers when making assignments or discussing queries, we print what we assign, and, so, do not offer a kill fee.

We will occasionally ask a writer to submit an article "on spec"—subject to an editorial review before a commitment to publish-and we always do so for a writer's first *Spare Time* assignment.

Photographs and artwork are negotiated individually. While we don't pay for photos supplied by your subjects or other third parties, we do pay fifteen dollars ($15) for each photo you take yourself that we publish.

Additional information

For queries, questions and comments, or to follow-up on previous communications, feel free to write, call, fax, or e-mail our editor.

Categories: Nonfiction—Business—Business Opportunities—Careers—Cartoons—Health—Marketing—Money/Finance—Selling—Taxes—Time Management—Vocational Education

Name: Peter Abbott, Editor
Material: All
Address: 5810 W OKLAHOMA AVE
City/State/ZIP: MILWAUKEE WI 53219-4300
Telephone: 414-543-8110
Fax: 414-543-9767
E-mail: editor@spare-time.com
Internet: www.spare-time.com

SPECIALTY TRAVEL INDEX

Specialty Travel Index

SPECIALTY TRAVEL INDEX (STI) is the number one magazine about worldwide adventure travel. We are predominantly a trade magazine, with a circulation of 50,000 (45,000 travel agents, 5,000 consumers).

The magazine is semi-annual, published in January (Spring/Summer issue) and August (Fall/Winter issue). In addition to a directory-type listing of over 600 adventure tour operators, the magazine runs approximately 12 special-interest travel stories per issue.

Our editorial requirements are:

Length: 1,250 words

Rate: $250.00 (payable upon publication)

Lead time: Six months

We consider both written queries (accompanied by published clips and writer bio) plus finished manuscripts *on spec. Absolutely no submissions by phone or fax.* Stories should deal with special-interest, adventure-type travel—from soft adventures (bicycling through French wine country) to daring exploits (an exploratory river-rafting run in Pakistan). A variety of styles work for us: first person, descriptive, etc. In general, STI does not like articles written in the present tense.

Articles should have a lively immediacy, not just relate facts that readers probably know already. Since the readership includes both travel agents and consumers, avoid using "you" in the articles:

"You'll walk through flower-filled meadows..."

Instead, say:

"Travelers (or trekkers or participants) walk through..."

For submission of accepted materials, we require:

Hard copy

5.25" or 3.5" disk—IBM Compatible (ASCII)

Color transparencies (no extra payment for photos)

Categories: Adventure—Specialty Travel

Name: Susan Kostrzewa, Managing Editor
Name: Risa Weinreb, Editor
Material: Any
Address: 305 SAN ANSELMO AVE STE 313
City/State/ZIP: SAN ANSELMO CA 94960
Telephone: 415-459-4900
Fax: 415-459-4974
E-mail: spectrav@ix.netcom.com

Spectacle
Life, Art, Passion...

SPECTACLE is a new semi-annual journal featuring essays, articles, interviews and reportage on a broad spectrum of lively and unusual themes, such as:

• **Women on Popular Culture,** the Summer '97 premiere issue, presented the writings of 26 women who reflected upon the power American popular culture has exerted on their lives. The essays—ranging from the personal to the academic—illuminate our understanding of the interplay between individual identity and mass culture. The issue dealt critically with a variety of topics including: Hollywood's portrayal of African Americans, manic consumerism, telethons, 1950s gender ethos, television and the Barbie phenomenon.

• **Madness and the Creative Imperative,** the Winter 97/98 issue, examined the link between mental illness and creativity in the lives and works of Poe, Woolf, Ginsberg, Sexton and others, and offered a renewed appreciation for and greater understanding of the complex and controversial relationship between "the perceptually different" and their art.

• **GEEK Love,** the Summer 1998 issue, posed the question: "In a hostile world, can GEEKS find friendship, love and happiness?"

This issue delved into the love life of GEEKS. We define GEEK as any person who as a result of some characteristic, attribute or condition is labeled as "different" or "weird" and therefore subjected to mistreatment, ridicule, and rejection from his/her peers. This individual may exhibit higher than average social awkwardness, which in turn makes the pursuit of intimate relationships and friendships especially challenging.

In addition to personal narratives, submissions exploring this theme in literature, theater, film, TV and other media were encouraged, as were accounts of GEEK love drawn from the enormous reservoir of published memoir and biography.

Topics also included: • GEEK alter egos • GEEK transformations • odd couples • GEEK stalkers and soulmates • GEEK dating and marriage • unrequited love • GEEK fantasies • GEEK revenge • über GEEKS, etc.

Example

News Junkie
Winter 1998

This issue explores the personal and collective obsession with news consumption. What drives this hunger for news? How do we sift through the barrage of competing sources? How do traditional and new-media outlets compare and compete? Who can you trust—the mainstream or alternative press? Is a radical restructuring of U.S. media necessary? What's the latest body count in the war between hard news and "infotainment." Can news and advertising coexist?

Other topics included: • merger mania and corporate conflict of interests • liberal vs. conservative bias • increasing "tabloidization" of TV news • the demise of small-town, family-owned newspapers • interviews/profiles of exceptional journalists and media innovators • censorship and news blackouts • the future of public radio/TV • profession vs. industry • comparison of U.S. and foreign journalism standards • Information Fatigue Syndrome case studies of controversial news stories, etc.

Age of Conspiracy
Summer 1999

This issue offered an interdisciplinary forum for the study of conspiracy culture. We sought insightful works that examined the relationship among public opinion and debate; official vs. "fringe" views; the role of media; the nature and dissemination of rumor, (dis)information and propaganda; the dynamics of public controversy; and how these work to create the conditions necessary for the conception, development and propagation of conspiracy beliefs.

As an interdisciplinary effort committed to presenting a diversity of methodological approaches and theoretical perspectives we encourage submissions from academics, journalists, media critics, conspiracy theorists, folklorists, independent scholars and researchers. We will consider panoramic overviews to focused case studies.

How to Submit

All submitted work should be informed, compelling and well-crafted writing. We prefer insightful, provocative, analytical pieces including essays, articles, critiques, reportage, interviews and case studies. Scholarly articles should be accessible to the layman. No poetry or fiction please. Manuscripts will be reviewed only during designated reading periods. All submissions should be original and unpublished. If in doubt about a topic or approach, query first.

Length can run a maximum of 5,000 words. Be sure to include your name, address, daytime phone, and word count on the first page and indicate the issue you're submitting to.

Please note: those submitting research papers should include an abstract of up to 150 words and provide fully referenced endnotes and/or bibliography on back pages in the format prescribed by the *MLA Handbook* (1995). The author(s) has/have responsibility for the accuracy of references, and for obtaining permissions to reproduce any artwork that is not their own or has been published elsewhere.

In your cover letter please include a brief bio. Also include a self-addressed, stamped postcard for quick acknowledgment that your submission has been received. Please send no more than three works. Also include a #10 SASE and a second SASE large enough to accommodate your manuscript if you want it returned. If you do not want it returned, please mark it "Disposable Copy." There is no reading fee involved.

Payment $30.00 upon publication and two copies of journal.
Sample Copies/Subscriptions
Single issue price is $9.00
Subscription rates for individuals is 1 yr./$12; 2 yrs./$22; institutions 1 yr./$15; 2 yrs./$25.

MA residents add 5% sales tax. Please make checks or money orders payable to Pachanga Press.

Categories: Nonfiction—Arts—Biography—Film/Video—History—Humor—Interview—Literature—Multicultural—Psychology—Television/Radio—Travel

Name: Richard Aguilar, Editor
Material: All
Address: 101 MIDDLESEX TURNPIKE STE 6-155
City/State/ZIP: BURLINGTON MA 01803

Spider
The Magazine for Children

In January, 1994 the Cricket Magazine Group of Carus Publishing Company launched SPIDER, a magazine for children ages 6 to 9.

SPIDER publishes original stories, poems, and articles written by the world's best children's authors. In some cases, SPIDER purchases rights for excerpts from books yet to be published. Each issue also includes several reprints of high-quality selections.

SPIDER is full-color, 8"x10", with 34 pages and a 4-page activity pullout. It is staple-bound. We hope that the following information will be useful to prospective contributors:

Editor-in-Chief: Marianne Carus
Senior Art Director: Ron McCutchan
Associate Editor: Christine Walske
Published: 12 months a year
Price: $32.97 for 1-year subscription (12 issues)

Categories

Fiction: realistic, easy-to-read stories, fantasy, folk and fairy tales, science fiction, fables, myths

Nonfiction: nature, animals, science, technology, environment, foreign culture, history (A short bibliography is required for *all* nonfiction articles.)

Poetry: serious, humorous, nonsense rhymes

Other: puzzles, mazes, hidden pictures, games, brainteasers, math and word activities

Length

Stories: 300 to 1,000 words
Articles: 300 to 800 words
Poems: not longer than 20 lines
Puzzles/Activities/Games: 1 to 4 pages

An exact word count should be noted on each manuscript submitted. Word count includes every word, but does not include the title of the manuscript.

Rates

Stories and articles: up to 25¢ per word (1,000 words maximum)

Poems: up to $3.00 per line
Payment upon publication

Themes

There is no theme list for upcoming issues. Submissions on all appropriate topics will be considered at any time during the year.

Comments

SPIDER would like to reach as many children's authors and artists as possible for original contributions, but our standards are very high and we will accept only top quality material. *Please do not query first.* SPIDER will consider any manuscripts or art samples sent on speculation and accompanied by a self-addressed, stamped envelope.

For art samples, it is especially helpful to see pieces showing children, animals, action scenes, and several scenes from a narrative showing a character in different situations. SPIDER prefers to see tear sheets or photoprints/photocopies of art.

SPIDER will also consider submissions of photography, either in the form of photo essays or as illustrations for specific nonfiction articles. Photographs should accompany the manuscript. Color photography is preferred, but black-and-white submissions will be considered depending on subject matter. Photocopies or prints may be submitted with the manuscript, but original transparencies for color or good quality black-and-white prints (preferably glossy finish) must be available upon acceptance.

Please allow 12 weeks to receive a reply to submissions. SPIDER normally purchases the following rights:

1. For stories and poems previously unpublished, SPIDER purchases first publication rights in the English language. Payment is made upon publication. SPIDER also requests the right to reprint the work in any volume or anthology published by Carus Publishing Company upon payment of half the original fee.

2. For stories and poems previously published, SPIDER purchases second North American publication rights. Fees vary, but are generally less than fees for first serial rights. Payment is made upon publication. Same applies to accompanying art.

3. For recurring features, SPIDER purchases the material outright. The work becomes the property of SPIDER and is copyrighted in the name of Carus Publishing Company. A flat fee per feature is usually negotiated. Payment is made upon publication.

4. First publication rights plus promotional rights (promotions, advertising, or in any other form not offered for sale to the general public without payment of an additional fee) for commissioned artwork, subject to the terms outlined below:

(a) Physical art remains the property of the illustrator.

(b) Payment is made within 45 days of acceptance.

(c) SPIDER retains the additional, nonexclusive right to reprint the work in any volume or anthology published by SPIDER subject to pro rata share of 7% royalty of net sales.

For a sample issue of SPIDER, please send $4.00 to the address below. NOTE: Sample copy requests from foreign countries must he accompanied by International Postal Reply Coupons (IRCs) valued at US $4.00. Please do *not* send a check or money order.

Categories: Fiction—Nonfiction—Children—Games—Poetry—Puzzles

Name: Submissions Editor
Material: Manuscripts
Name: Ron McCutchan, Art Director
Material: Art Samples
Name: Mary Ann Hocking, Permissions Coordinator
Material: Questions about rights.
Address: PO BOX 300
City/State/ZIP: PERU IL 61354

Spilled Candy
A BiMonthly Newsletter for Self-Promoting Writers

Editor/Publisher: Lorna Tedder

Established: 1995

Purpose: Bimonthly newsletter covering book promotion tips for the self-published, the subsidy-published, and the under-advertised author. Tone is informal and informative, a must for any author who hasn't yet hit the *NY Times* bestseller list.

Pays on acceptance.

Byline given as well as mention of writer's upcoming book. Complete manuscripts only. Reports in two months if SASE is included with manuscript.

Sample copy available for $5.

No fiction. Buys promotion tips: 25-100 words, pays $5-15 each tip, depending on length and merit.

Buys one "focus" article per issue: 250-500 words, pays $25-50 per article; will to go to 1,000 words and higher payment if subject is extremely valuable to readers; examples of focus articles include booksignings, quotes, advance review copies, press kits, and public speaking.

Helpful hints: *"We teach guerilla marketing techniques to new and established writers. We're a friendly but small business, so you really need to include SASE with your submission so that we can afford to pay our writers instead of our postman. Our newsletter has a unique tone and approach, so we encourage you to borrow a back issue from a friend or library, or order a sample copy. Concentrate on innovative but inexpensive ways to promote books."*

Check out our new web site—**under construction**—coming to the Internet address below.

Categories: Business—Careers—Interview—Writing

Name: Lorna Tedder, Editor
Name: Shannon Kyle, Assistant
Material: Book Promotion Tips
Address: PO BOX 5202
City/State/ZIP: NICEVILLE FL 32578-5202
E-mail: SPILLCANDY@aol.com
Internet: members.aol.com/spillcandy

The Spirit

The Spirit of Woman in the Moon is the literary newsmagazine of our publishing house, Woman in the Moon Publications. Across its pages, we report news, features and special events important to the Woman in the Moon mission: W.I.M and its authors' participation in literary and cultural happenings; coverage of Black feminist literary leaders; West coast (California) and national literary announcements; and our Open Letter Forum from our network of worldwide readers on topics ranging from women's politics to education.

This is all in addition to our regular columns, departments and features on short fiction, poetry, "Black History Square," profiles of current authors and books published by Woman in the Moon, along with book reviews, winning poems from our Poetry contests and awardees of the W.I.M. Writers' Grants and Literary Prizes. Each issue lists the Woman in the Moon current Call for Submissions for all our publications and annual book publishing list.

We are constantly seeking new writers, who can convey through their work the importance of semantics, the beauty of the English language with great writing. We prefer New Age topics and short to mid-length narrative poems.

The Spirit is published biannually: Winter (December/January issue), Summer (August/September), and Spring Special Issue (May/June. Circulation: 3,000 plus

Submission Requirements

The Spirit of Woman in the Moon is a 24-36 page, U.S. copyrighted literary newsmagazine printed with black and white photos. Freelance submissions, to be considered for publication, should be written on any topic cognizant of our stated interests. We are seeking well-written work that enlightens and inspires our readers. Previous publishing experience is not a requirement.

We are particularly interested in material on current New Age feminist topics; Black feminist literary news; local, national and international literary events pertaining to opportunities for women; coverage of young female writers; and stories, essays and poems on personal reflections on any of the topics above so long as they encompass the common good of our readers.

The Spirit is a positive, upbeat and informative publication. Our Woman in the Moon logo represents our belief in the new Age when the compassion, patience and understanding of human behavior, inherent in women, will become paramount for the duration of the Age of Aquarius. According to The Woman's Dictionary of Symbols and Sacred Objects, authored by Barbara G. Walker, the Age of Aquarius was called the Age of Gula the Goddess, by the Babylonians and the Romans named the two thousand year-era for the Goddess Juno, Queen of Heaven. We believe we are under the watch of Hathors of Venus, and Diana of Luna the Moon, and are truly on the threshold of a New Age. The writings published in *The Spirit* should reflect this.

We Need

Poetry, fiction, futuristic essays and nonfiction on prophetic reflection and New Age spirituality; metaphysical topics including angel lore and psychic phenomena; women's issues; African-American, feminist and lesbian themes; business; health; and the art of writing. Same topics for fillers. We are also looking for illustrations and cartoons on New Age topics.

Payment for accepted submissions is $20 for poetry, $30 for prose, $25 for illustrations and cartoons, plus two copies of the issue in which the work appears.

You may submit at any time before the next quarter. Please query on nonfiction articles, but send complete manuscripts for fiction and poetry. Always submit two copies of each item. Our limits are: poems-40 lines/prose-3,000 words. Poetry must use standard poetical conventions whether for free verse or rhyming. Please type or word process submissions in standard format.

To be considered, every submission must include the reading fee which includes the current issue of *The Spirit*: Poetry (3 poem packet)-$8.00; Fiction and Nonfiction-$12.00 up to five pages, $3.00 for each additional page.

If you want your work returned to you in the event it is rejected for publication, you must include a self-addressed envelope of sufficient size to accommodate your work with sufficient postage affixed to the envelope. At this time, we *do not* accept electronic submissions. Hardcopy only, but we'd appreciate it if you include the diskette with ASCII configuration of work submitted to facilitate editing and possible publication.

The Spirit reserves the right to edit *accepted* material for length and content. Please allow 6-8 weeks response time. You may receive a form rejection, but if time permits, we try to give personal comments.

All rights revert to contributors upon publication. Unless a specific assignment is given by the publisher/editor, all freelance material will be considered on a speculative basis. *The Spirit* is not responsible for loss or damage to any unsolicited work. Keep a copy of your manuscript, send us the original. We seriously recommend that all those wishing to submit work, study an issue of *The Spirit before* querying or submitting.

Categories: Fiction—Nonfiction—African-American—Business—Ethnic—Feminism—Gay/Lesbian—Health—Inspirational—Metaphysical Topics—Multicultural—New Age—Poetry—Women's Issues

Name: Submissions Editor
Material: All
Address: 1409 THE ALAMEDA
City/State/ZIP: SAN JOSE CA 95126
Telephone: 408-279-6626
Fax: 408-279-6636
E-mail: womaninmoon@earthlink.com
Nota bene: Reading fee required with submissions.

Sport Fishing

BACKGROUND

Sport Fishing is geared to serious saltwater fishing around North America. That means bluewater, reefs, inlets and inshore (bays, flats and backcountry). It is published nine times per year (monthly, January-June; bimonthly, July-December). Our readers, over 100,000 nationally, are generally well-educated and quite affluent. Nearly all are men who own boats, often both a large offshore boat and skiff as well.

EDITORIAL CONTENT

Material in *Sport Fishing* should provide useful information about saltwater fishing which is:

1.) new/fresh/different

2.) specific/in-depth and

3.) accurate.

Concepts behind all queries should meet these criteria.

Please don't submit an idea which has been written about by us and/or similar publications. *Find a fresh idea or a fresh angle to an old idea*; like most publications, we too are looking for subjects that will have our readers saying, "I never knew that!". Examples of material that would be of interest: a new, effective technique for a species or type of fishing that has wide applicability; an area recently opened up to sport fishing; or a new look at conservation concerns regarding a particular fishery or species/group. As with any magazine, our very specific needs are best understood by studying recent issues.

FEATURES

We strive for a mix of genres, including fishing how-to, fishing where-to and conservation. Remember that our readers are *not* beginners; they're seeking to advance their knowledge, not rehash basic saltwater fishing.

We cannot use material related to pier/jetty/surf fishing; a boat must be involved if an idea is to work for *Sport Fishing*.

DEPARTMENTS

We are always looking for good material for several departments, particularly: "Technique," "Rigging" and "Fish Tales." These usually run 800 to 1,200 words, though we are always looking for technique and rigging "shorts." Except for the humorous "Fish Tales" (for which a cartoonist draws art), these columns are illustrated. Clear photos or even a good hand sketch from you will do; we will have it professionally drawn for publication.

QUERIES

We will look at over-the-transom submissions, but your efforts are much more likely to bear fruit if you query us first. "Laundry list" written queries are a welcome initial step. While editors of most national publications prefer to avoid telephone queries, you may call and speak to an appropriate editor (see "*Sport Fishing* Editor/Responsibilities" below)to review an idea. We ask that you be brief and specific. If an idea is of initial interest, you will still be asked to submit a query in writing.

If a query warrants a speculative submission (as close to an "assignment" as **Sport Fishing**, like many magazines, gives freelance writers), *communication with the editor* becomes the key to making things work. The editor will send something in writing to reiterate exactly what we expect in terms of substance, slant, style, length, sidebars, maps/charts and of course deadlines and request a written/e-mailed response.

Most **Sport Fishing** editors now work from some sort of outline from the writer. Generally, this step is an invaluable way to (1) make sure the writer doesn't waste his/her time on something not right for us and (2) in general, maintain close communication between writer and editor to make sure what the writer *thinks* the editor wants is in fact what the editor really wants. Often the outline will be reworked, so when the writer actually begins writing the feature he'll be on the right road. Finally, if questions develop as you work, *give the editor a call to discuss it*.

We welcome the opportunity to work with new/unestablished writers who know their stuff-and how to say it.

SUBMITTING FEATURES/DEPARTMENTS

Most features, after editing as necessary, run 1,500 to 2,500 words including sidebars, rarely longer. Payment (see below) is for edited length. Please try to keep length of your features under 3,000 words; avoid submitting rambling 8,000-word manuscripts.

If extensive rewriting *is* necessary, we like to work with the writer to resubmit the feature rewritten to meet our needs. However, again, writer-editor communication before and during the time the feature's written should minimize the chances of any major rewrites.

TIPS FOR SPORT FISHING CONTRIBUTORS

1.) Meet or beat deadline dates. We like to work regularly with writers we can count on. Also, that gives us time to ask you to rewrite if necessary.

2.) Send photos. They may be yours or those of other photographers (remember: photo payment is *additional* to payment for manuscript).

3.) Get quotes from experts. When possible, interviewing one or more professionals (skippers, mates), tournament experts or the like gives a subject great credibility. Also, wherever appropriate, contact fishery managers/biologists regarding status of species/fisheries. (Often they can provide tables, graphs, charts, etc. to help illustrate a topic.

4.) Balance information with readability. Anecdotes can impart information while lending human interest. These are safest in third person but there are times when first-person narrative, if not overdone, is useful. Avoid talking down to our informed readership, but also avoid sounding ponderous or using ten-dollar words when five-cents' worth says it clearly.

5.) Include sidebars where appropriate. In any feature that has to do with a destination, include information on travel, lodging, charters/guides, etc. We also like to see a seasonal availability chart for species (a hand sketch is acceptable): see recent issues for examples of required format. If a feature has to do with a genre of product, include a sidebar listing manufacturers.

FORMAT FOR SUBMISSIONS

Unless prior arrangements with an editor are made, we expect all written material on a PC-compatible disk/diskette in WordPerfect, Microsoft Word or ASCII format and on a hardcopy manuscript—headed, in both cases, with your address, phone and social security number.

Any photos submitted should meet our photo submission guidelines below. Where appropriate, we'll expect to see maps, line art (which we can have professionally redrawn), charts/diagrams etc. in the package.

PAYMENT

Payment is initiated after the manuscript has been edited. All features and columns are submitted on speculation. For features, we pay $200 to $600 (the higher rates reflect the occasional request for an unusually long feature or the receipt of one exceptionally well-written, requiring little editing). On the other hand, a financial penalty may be warranted for work which is late and/or requires extensive editing. Keep in mind this is for manuscript and related materials only; you will be paid $50 to $300 for each of your photos used to illustrate a manuscript. Other payment schedules: Second-author sidebars-$100, Departments-$200 (less for short contributing items), Fish Tales-$150.

SPORT FISHING EDITORS/RESPONSIBILITIES

To help you direct inquiries most efficiently, editorial positions at **Sport Fishing:**

Doug Olander, Editor-in-Chief: Plans and executes editorial schedule and content; oversees each issue from start to finish. Also responsible for Fish Tales, Letters, Sportfishing News and Fly Fishing departments, editorials, and for writing many features throughout the year.

Dave Ferrell, Managing Editor. Guides magazine through production; responsible for New Products and International Hot Spots departments.

Albia Dugger, Senior Editor. Contributes many features throughout the year and responsible for Rigging/Techniques Tips and Fish Facts departments.

Jason Cannon, Assistant Editor. Contributes features and various editorial; works with photographers and writers and initiates payments.

Dean Clarke, Executive Editor. Contributes some features (including annual Boat Buyers Source Book); responsible for Boat Reviews and New Boats and Electronics departments.

GUIDE FOR SUBMITTING PHOTOS TO *SPORT FISHING* AND *MARLIN*

Sport Fishing and **Marlin** *continue to emphasize the finest saltwater fishing photography to be found in any magazine. Most of that comes from freelance professionals.* **Marlin** *provides bona fide international exposure for photographers' best work;* **Sport Fishing** *offers national readership of 150,000.*

POLICIES

RATES/PAYMENT: Sport Fishing pays $1,000 for covers. For inside use, *rates* for both magazines are: two-page spread—$300/200 (action or underwater/non-action shots), full page—$200/150, half-page—$150/100, more than 1/4 but less than 1/2 page—$100/75, 1/4 page or less—$75/50, sequences—$100 to $200, and for **Sport Fishing**'s annual calendar—$250. Payment is processed upon publication, based on published size of each magazine. Payment is normally issued to the photographer credited on the slide; if any other payment arrangement is to be honored, please mark on slide: "payment to: _____." Please note that **Sport Fishing** does *not* pay research or shipping fees without prior approval.

RETURN POLICY: It remains our fundamental goal to review and send out images not selected within a few days of receipt. We do NOT ordinarily hold photos at all unless we have a projected possible use. A tracking sheet will be included with images returned showing which slides are being kept and for what purpose.

SHIPPING: If we call and request photography quickly, we'll pay shipping. Otherwise, the photographer pays to ship. We'll take care of returns; USPS Certified is our default shipping method (we've had fine results) but we'll try to honor photographers' requests for other carriers.

OVER-THE-TRANSOM SUBMISSIONS: When in doubt ship it out. We're always happy to review images, whether solicited or unsolicited (and since we won't hold those for which we see no specific, possible use, there's little to lose and much to gain).

COMMUNICATE! Don't hesitate to call anytime you have any general or specific questions about photo needs, submissions or payment.

SUGGESTIONS

DON'T SEND US FUZZY SHOTS!

Instead, give *us* photos that are, by any measure, "tack sharp." Every day I *see* otherwise great shots precluded from *use* by being too "soft." There's just not much point in sending any images that are not crystal clear.

AVOID INANIMATE "GRIN & GRAB" SHOTS.

Send us images of people animated as they hold fresh (preferably lively) but not bloody fish. Counteract the dreaded Zombie Stare Syndrome. Have subject interacting with someone else if available. (Have them hold fish together and look at/talk to each other-while forgetting the camera even exists; suggest one tell the other a joke or "explain" about the fish—anything to get subject loose, happy, natural.) If subject alone, suggest interaction with the fish-hook removal, lifting from deck, even admiring it (looking at *it*, not you). Avoid dead fish in such photos-take them quick when the fish is in the boat and lively, before it's clubbed or languishes to a pale, glassy-eyed state of rigor mortis.

Finally, *do keep the angler's tackle in the shot!*

AVOID KILL SHOTS OF BILLFISH AND BLUEWATER SHARKS!

Send *us* exciting, *in-focus* shots of leaping, tailwalking, greyhounding fish; of fish being wired for tagging or being released or admired at the boat. Skip the traditional dead stuff—hanging at the dock, draped over the transom, bleeding on deck-or anything with a gaff in it.

"Kill" shots of other, food fish okay if-you should pardon the expression-tasteful. But that doesn't include piles of fish on deck or dock-sport, not carnage, is what we're after. Gaffs are not unacceptable, but generally not particularly desirable, either.

AVOID BLOODY SHOTS OF FISH AT/IN THE BOAT.

Send alive and lively fish but dip them or wipe them or shoot the "clean" side if they're dripping blood.

THINK BOATS.

Surveys show our national/international affluent readership owns and fishes from boats. Accordingly, we rarely have much interest in photos of fishing from piers, surf; jetties, etc.

AVOID SHADOW-DARKENED SHOTS.

Give us shots liberal with use of fill flash under high sun or backlit conditions.

DON'T LIMIT SUBMISSIONS TO FISH/FISHING ALONE.

Have an eye to all things related to fish/fishing, viz: rigging, technique (gear/action), baits, lures, equipment, diving birds, weather, water (color/rips/weedlines), feeding schools, schools of baitfish (and catching them), other boats fishing/running. Bimini starts etc, etc. Also, don't hesitate to photograph any/all nearshore/offshore species, gamefish or others, including those that are unusual.

COVERS

Sport Fishing covers emphasize fish-fish leaping, underwater, at the surface, on a line out of the water and so on. That may include anglers interacting with fish-fighting fish, releasing or tagging fish and the like. Most saltwater gamefish may qualify. 35mm focus must be laser-sharp to retain its quality when enlarged 1,200 percent. The dominant image must fill most of the frame to minimize blow-up necessary (e.g. a jumping fish that's a dot on the horizon won't make it). And of course there *must* be room at the top for the logo and along the left side (often shots may be flopped) for cover blurbs.

CALENDARS

Throughout the year, we're on the lookout for strong candidates for the slick *Sport Fishing* annual calendar. Horizontals particularly exciting/dramatic/colorful may qualify.

OTHER SUGGESTIONS

We prefer Fujichrome or Provia 100 (Velvia 50 for nonaction shots in bright light) or Kodachrome-64 and Lumiere; Shutter speeds for moving fish should be at least 1/1000-second; Bracket where possible and try for both horizontals and verticals; Compose to keep fish main focus of most shots and to avoid extraneous objects in frame (also avoid clothing with nasty/racist/sexist inferences).

DUPES OR ORIGINALS?

We run originals, not dupes. You may send in duplicate slides for review purposes, but only if the originals are available. However, originals permit us to accurately determine a shot's potential, with optional definition and color that subsequent generations always lack.

WHEN PACKAGING SUBMISSIONS:

1. Make sure that every image has—at the very least-your name on it. Words of description (area, species, etc.) written right on the slide can be of great help.

2. If sending slides/other images in one package targeting two or more articles, please place slides in a separate sheet (or sheets) for each different article and mark the sheet accordingly.

3. If brief captions are written on each image, a page with brief captions is helpful; if no information is written on images, a sheet of captions is essential.

4. Make sure your social security number is included somewhere, unless you are certain we have it (or unless you have no interest in remuneration).

5. Payment will be issued to the first name on the slide (stock agency or photographer) unless other payment arrangements are specified.

6. If any of the images submitted have appeared (or will appear) in any potentially competing publication, please make that clear. (This doesn't necessarily preclude us from choosing it, but it's good to know.)

COVER PHOTO TIPS—A QUICK CHECKLIST

During the fervor of campaigning in 1992, George Bush said, "We're enjoying sluggish times—and not enjoying them very much." The same might be said of many cover photo submissions we're receiving at *Sport Fishing* these days. Given the lack of quality of many shots we're seeing, I thought I'd offer a few reminders of what your shot needs to include for cover consideration for *Sport Fishing*. They're good criteria to keep in mind while shooting new photos as well as making selections from past shoots. While trying to meet these needs, keep in mind that I've raised the cover rate from $500 three years ago to $750 and last year to $1,000.

• **Format-Vertical!** Is the shot vertical or, if horizontal, croppable to a vertical format that will fit? (If you think a horizontal may be croppable to fit,* be aware of how much the image will need to be enlarged—if a great deal, too much grain will preclude its use.)

• **Format-space at the top!** Is there plenty of space at the top for both title and subtitle?

• **Format-space on the left!** Is there plenty of room along left side for cover blurbs (without covering up any essential part of image)?

• **Format-Image/Composition!** Does the image do a good job of filling the frame? (A distant, jumping fish on a 35-mm slide cannot be blown-up large enough for cover use without becoming a grainy mess.) Will the image fall in the right area? Mentally grid the cover in four equal rectangles; the focal point of the image will need to be roughly in upper left corner of the bottom right box (i.e. slightly down and to the right of center).* Note that your image *can* be flopped as long as nothing shows in the way of logos, boat names etc.

• **FOCUS!** Is it tack sharp? (That includes the entire image, not just part of it.) If not, sending the image is a waste of your time and money.

• **Background-Bright, monochromatic and uncluttered!** Is the background color bright? (Need bright blue sky, water—dull greys or browns won't make it.) Is the background monochromatic so lettering over it will "pop"? (Believe it or not, many otherwise great photos are rejected because the top of the page contains too much light/dark contrast—best example: rippled surface of water where bright white reflective patches alternate with dark water.) Is the background uncluttered? (Title can't be put over tackle, boat towers, etc.)

• **Subject-Right for our "look"!** Is the subject appropriate for the "*Sport Fishing*" look? (All the criteria above can be met perfectly, but the subject must fit our needs. Don't send us rainbow trout or jetty fishing or bloody fish, etc. Look at recent covers to see what *SF* looks for. If you're unsure, call and ask.)

* A good way to figure out yourself if an image works: Using an actual cover as a guide, cut a piece of white posterboard to size and sketch in with a black marker the title/subtitle and some blurbs; then project your image onto it (which will allow you to "crop" as you might feel optimal) to see how it fits.

Categories: Boating—Conservation—Fishing

Name: Dave Ferrell, Managing Editor
Material: All Queries
Name: As Above

Material: As Above
Address: 330 W CANTON
City/State/ZIP: WINTER PARK FL 32789
Telephone: 407-628-4802
Fax: 407-628-7061
E-mail: do1@worldzine.com

Sports Afield

Dear Outdoor Writer:

If you are interested in writing for *Sports Afield*, we recommend that you study the magazine closely. *Sports Afield* is a hunting and fishing magazine that encompasses affiliated backcountry subjects such as camping, survival, hiking, cross-country skiing, mountain biking and boating. We are interested in where-to-go and how-to articles as well as literary experience pieces. Features based on outdoor products are welcome if they have a fresh slant. We also publish fiction, humor and cartoons, but no poetry.

We prefer detailed queries first. This saves time and effort on your part as well as ours. If you are sending a finished manuscript, it should be double-spaced and a computer disk should be available if the story is accepted. If you are submitting photos, send only duplicates because there is always the chance that originals could be lost. Should we want original photos for publication, we will contact the photographer. *Sports Afield* is not responsible for any unsolicited photos or manuscripts.

Our features range from 500 to 2000 words. Almanac submissions should range from 200 to 300 words. More specific word count instructions can be obtained by querying first.

You must enclose a self-addressed, stamped business-size envelope with your manuscript and/or query in order to receive a response. We will try to respond within six weeks. If you would like your material returned to you, we ask that you enclose a self-addressed, stamped envelope large enough to accommodate your submission along with a request for the return of your material.

Thank you for your interest in *Sports Afield*.

The Editors

Sports Afield is a publication of Hearst Magazines, a division of the Hearst Corporation.

Categories: Fiction—Nonfiction—Adventure—Cartoons—Conservation—Consumer—Ecology—Environment—Outdoors—Sports—Recreation—Camping—Hunting—Hiking—Biking—Boating—Fishing—How-to—Humor—Nostalgia

Name: John Atwood, Editor-In-Chief
Material: All
Address: 250 WEST 55TH STREET
City/State/ZIP: NEW YORK, NY 10019
Telephone: 212-649-4300
Fax: 212-581-3923

spotlight

Spotlight

The tri-state area's only general interest publication, Spotlight focuses on the hot issues, the innovative trends, the people on the scene, what to do and where to go in New York, New Jersey and Connecticut. Departments focus on area people in the news, regional events, travel , gift ideas, restaurants and theater, health and fitness, among others.

Editorially, *Spotlight* tries to reflect the values of the strongest magazine journalism: objective reporting, lively writing and trenchant analysis. We are interested in the news of the area—the creative idea, happening, the important concern, the entertainment the unusual place or "find"—delivered in sophisticated, crisp and punchy fashion.

Spotlight accepts queries and clips from all writers. Manuscripts should be accompanied by a self-addressed stamped envelope, cover letter, resume and any applicable clips. The annual subscription rate for writers is $15, the professional rate.

Articles are accepted on speculation as well as assigned. Optimum length for articles is 2,000 words. If you have photographs relating to your story, please include them.

Thank you for your interest in our magazine.

Categories: Regional

Name: Dana B. Asher, Editor-in-Chief
Material: All
Address: 126 LIBRARY LN
City/State/ZIP: MAMARONECK NY 10543
Telephone: 914-381-4740
Fax: 914-381-4641

Sports Illustrated

Does not accept unsolicited submissions.

Sports Illustrated for Kids

Freelance writers may query *Sports Illustrated for Kids* with specific story ideas. Completed articles, submitted on the basis of speculation, will be read. But such articles are not encouraged. Be advised that most *Si for Kids* articles are staff written. Fewer than 20 freelance proposals are accepted each year.

Sports Illustrated for Kids reaches an audience whose median age is 11 years old. Articles should be written on a fifth-grade reading level. Remember that the magazine strives to be both fun and educational, and prefers ideas that can be illustrated with great photos or artwork.

The following are categories in which we might accept freelance material:

* Lead articles or profiles. Articles about athletes (either adults or children ages 8-13) or sport topics of interest to kids. 1,000-1,500 words. ($1,000 - $1,250). Editor: Amy Lennard Goehner.

* Short features. Articles of 500-600 words about an interesting young athlete or sports topic not worthy of a longer piece. ($500). Pro Athlete: Jon Scher. Stories about kids: Erin Egan.

* Departments. Please see reverse side for specific editors' beats.

* Puzzles & games ($500 - $1,000) Editor: Erin Egan.

* Fiction. We do NOT run general fiction stories.

* Poems & fillers. We do NOT run poems or fillers.

* Stories written by kids. We run short "What I Think" opinion pieces by children ages 14 and under in Sports Shorts (Editor: Bob Der).

Kids can submit letters, drawings or poems to *Si for Kids*

Do NOT send us anything that cannot be replaced, such as original photographs. If you would like your manuscript returned, you must enclose an 81/2 x 11, self-addressed envelope. Also, we do NOT have photo guidelines. For information, call the Photo Department at 212-522-4087.

Editors' Beats: Please send your query or submission to the appropriate editor in writing. DO NOT send photographs or other original materials unless specifically requested.

Beat Editor:
Book ideas: Cathy Wolf
Cards: Bob Der

Features: Amy Lennard Goehner
Hot Shots (kid athletes): Erin Egan
Inside Story: Amy Lennard Goehner
Kid Features: Erin Egan (kid writing or reporting)
Kids Ask: Bob Der
Letters, Poems & Artwork: Amy Lennard Goehner
Olympics: Erin Egan/Bob Der
Poster/Big Shot: Amy Lennard Goehner
Pro & Con: Amy Lennard Goehner
Pro Athletes: John Scher
Puzzles & Games: Erin Egan
Sports Parents: Cathy Wolf
Sports Shorts: Bob Der (unusual stories, special interest stories)
Tips From the Pros: Erin Egan
What's the Call?: Jon Scher
When I Was a Kid: Amy Lennard Goehner
Worst Day: Erin Egan
Categories: Nonfiction—Children—Games—General Interest—Inspirational—Interview—Sports—Recreation—How-to—Humor—Profiles

Name: Name of editor from above
Material: As appropriate
Address: TIME & LIFE BUILDING,
    1271 SIXTH AVE. 4th Floor
City/State/ZIP: NEW YORK, NY 10020
Telephone: 212-522-5437
Fax: 212-522-0120

Spy

Dear Potential Contributor,

Thank you for your interest in SPY Magazine. As you know, SPY is a bimonthly, satirical publication and every subject is fair game, particularly targets in Hollywood, Washington, and Wall Street. There are no sacred cows.

What we are looking for: Intelligent, funny, articulate feature, column, and Naked City ideas (i.e. possible pranks, celebrity dirt, politician dirt, dirt in general). The best way to get an idea about what we publish (and what we haven't already written about) is to take a look at some back issues.

How to get an assignment: This is a busy office. We do not have time to read complete manuscripts, so please send us a query letter explaining:

- what you want to write
- why you want to write it
- why you're qualified to write it

You may also want to include sources for your research and clips of past articles you have written (if any).

We don't have a large staff and we receive lots of queries. Going through all this mail takes a while, but we'll try to get back to you within six weeks. Please be patient.

Other stuff you may want to know: We pay on publication. Payment will be negotiated between the writer and the editor. As a special bonus you will get your very own contributor's copy. Keep in mind that we are bimonthly when submitting timely pieces.

That's pretty much it. Thanks again for your interest. We look forward to hearing from you soon.

Categories: Nonfiction—Comedy—Culture—Entertainment—Humor—Music—Politics—Satire
Name: Adam Lehner, Deputy Editor
Material: All
Address: 49 E 21ST ST 11TH FLOOR
City/State/ZIP: NEW YORK NY 10010
Telephone: 212-260-7210
Fax: 212-260-7445
E-mail: spymagaz@aol.com

Stage Directions

Readership. *Stage Directions,* founded in 1988, is a national publication whose readers are active in all aspects of regional, community, academic or youth theater.

Topics. Articles focus on solving problems or enhancing the reader's ability to deal with typical theatrical situations. Most are how—to pieces, stressing imaginative, low-cost solutions.. We do not publish reviews of theatrical performances. While we will consider articles on almost any theatrical topic, we are particularly interested in pieces on costuming, makeup, lighting, scenic design and decoration, props, special effects., fundraising, audience development and acting and directing techniques. In addition, we would like to see pieces on working with children, high school and college students, senior citizens and handicapped men and women—either as performers and technicians or as audiences.

Length. A feature article is 800-1,500 words, and can have artwork accompanying it. Short pieces of 400 to 500 words, which focus on one problem and its solution, are also welcome. Articles longer than 900 words may be split and printed in consecutive issues. We are always looking for short pieces, and these are a good way to approach us at first.

Style. Because of our how—to focus, articles are informal in style and make frequent use of the second-person pronoun. When the reader finishes an article he or she should be able to take action based on the information received. Please do not submit articles without first reading through several issues. This is the best way we know to understand the style, tone, length and level of technical difficulty we expect. Free guidelines, sample copy and index are available upon request with a 9"x12" SASE. ($1.25 postage).

Editing. All articles submitted are subject to editing for style and length. Stories also will be checked for accuracy. *Stage Directions* generally follows the style rules of the *Chicago Manual of Style,* 13th edition.

Submissions. You nay send a query letter or a completed article for consideration. Online submissions or submissions on IBM—compatible 5.25" or 3.5" disks—along with a printed copy—are preferred; disks must be clearly labeled with program (WordPerfect 4.2, 5.01 or 5.1 preferred) and complete film names. Otherwise, stories must be typed, with the author's name, address, telephone (and fax if appropriate) on the front page. Simultaneous submissions must be clearly indicated. Pre-publication drafts will be sent to the author and primary sources, so please provide names and addresses of persons quoted at length.

Photos/Illustrations. All photos or illustrations should be submitted with artist and caption clearly printed on an attached label. All art must be royalty-free or cleared for publication by the artist or holder of copyright. Payment for original art or photographs is negotiated directly with the artist or photographer. First generation slides, transparencies, or prints are acceptable, color or black and white. In general, the closer-up and fewer people in a photograph, the better. Action photos are better than static (posed).

Rights. *Stage Directions* purchases all rights in most cases. Other publication rights may be negotiated with the managing editor; in return, you agree not to market the story to any publications aimed at the same readership for six months from the date of acceptance. All articles are given full author credit unless you request otherwise.

Payment. Current rates are approximately 10 cents per word; payment is made upon publication. You will receive five complimentary copies of the issue in which each article appears. Additional copies may be purchased for a discounted price.

Categories: Nonfiction—Arts—Culture—Drama—Theatre

Name: Neil Offen, Editor
Material: All
Address: PO BOX 18869
City/State/ZIP: RALEIGH NC 27619
Telephone: 919-872-7888
Fax: 919-872-6888
E-mail: stagedir@aol.com

Standard

Thank you for considering *Standard* for your freelance submission.

Standard is published 52 times a year by Beacon Hill Press of Kansas City and has a circulation of more than 150,000. Based on biblical truth and the Wesleyan-Arminian tradition, *Standard* seeks to present quality Christian material for adults to read. *Standard* uses over 200 manuscripts and 100 poems per year.

Standard is read by a diversity of adults: college age through retirement age, single or married, widowed or divorced, parents and grandparents.

Standard publishes a variety of material, including:

- Short stories (fiction or true experience)
- Christian poetry
- Puzzles
- Cartoons

In *Standard* we want to show Christianity in action, and we prefer to do that through stories. We do not use Bible expositions, sermons, devotionals, or how-to articles, which are all published in other areas of WordAction Publishing. Our main interest is short stories which demonstrate Christians dealing with life's issues in ways that result in spiritual growth.

Standard purchases one-time rights, either first or reprint, and will respond within 90 days. Payment is made on acceptance as follows:

- First Rights: 3 ½ cents per word
- Reprint and simultaneous submissions: 2 cents per word
- Poetry: 25 cents per line

Material accepted for publication will appear in *Standard* approximately 18 months after acceptance. Contributors will also receive five complimentary copies at time of publication.

To save on rising costs of postage, please send a manuscript we do not need to return. Then your return envelope will only need one first-class stamp. Be sure to write the manuscript title on the return envelope, so you will know what manuscript is being referenced when it comes back. Or you can request that the first page of the manuscript be returned in your envelope.

Even though postage is getting higher, we still need a self-addressed, stamped envelope—not a postcard. If your manuscript is accepted, we need the envelope to correspond with you.

RIGHTS

Selling Your Rights

Your manuscript is your property. You own it and simply sell the publication the right to print it. These are the most common rights sold:

First Rights (Formerly, North America serial rights)
When you sell first rights, you give the magazine the opportunity to be the first publication to print your articles.

Reprint Rights (Second Rights)
When you've sold an article to one publication, you're free to sell it elsewhere. That's what Reprint Rights means—you're giving a publication the opportunity to reprint this article. You still maintain ownership.

Simultaneous Submissions

This is sending the same article, story, or poem to several publishers at the same time. Always indicate on the manuscript if you are doing this. *Standard* does not purchase first rights on simultaneous submissions. Due to our lead time, we assume that the story will appear elsewhere before *Standard* goes to press.

Above information courtesy of: *From Dreams to Dividends* ©1992 by Jeanette D. Gardner. For more information contact:

Jeanette D. Gardner Publication Services, 4708 Delmar, Roeland Park, KS 66205-1344, (913) 722-4601.

STYLE TIPS

- Stories should express biblical principles and a holiness lifestyle through action and dialogue. Avoid moralizing.
- Keep in mind the international audience of Standard with regard to scenarios, references, and holidays. We cannot use stories about cultural, national, or secular holidays.
- Do not mention specific church affiliations. Standard is read in a variety of denominations.
- Keep your writing crisp and entertaining by using action verbs, avoiding passive voice, and keeping sentences concise. Vary sentence length. Make the dialogue and characters believable. Always keep in mind the rules of good fiction writing.
- Avoid clichés—both secular and religious.
- Be conscientious in your use of Scripture. Don't overload your story with Scripture quotations. When you do quote Scripture, quote it exactly and cite your reference. (Standard will handle copyrights.)
- Except for quotations from the Bible, written permission for the use of any other copyrighted material is the responsibility of the writer.
- Do not send query letters. Since we accept unsolicited manuscripts, query letters are unnecessary. Submit only complete manuscripts.
- Articles should be no longer than 1,700 words.

MANUSCRIPT PREPARATION

Tear sheets are acceptable, if photocopied to 8½"x11" size. Seasonal material will be considered at any time. Do not submit any manuscript which has been submitted to or published in any of the following: *Vista, Wesleyan Advocate, Herald of Holiness, Preacher's Magazine, World Mission,* or various teen and children's publications produced by WordAction Publishing Company. These are overlapping markets.

Please follow the sample format shown below when submitting manuscripts to *Standard* for consideration.

SAMPLE
Your Name
Approximate Number of Words
Mailing Address
Simultaneous Submission?
City, State/Province, Zip
Fiction or True Experience?
Telephone Number
Rights Offered?
Social Security Number
If Reprint, Where Published?
Story Title
by YOUR NAME
Your story text should begin here, typed and double-spaced. Use a good ribbon on your typewriter or dot-matrix printer. Check

the toner in your laser printer. Dark copies are easier to read. Please don't justify the right margin. That sometimes makes manuscripts hard to read.

Do not staple the pages of the manuscript together. Please use paper clips. Please repeat your last name, the story title, and the page number in one line on page two and following. (Sometimes pages get separated.)

Proofread your manuscript. Check your grammar and punctuation. Neatness counts, too! Always include a SASE (a self-addressed, stamped envelope).

For *Standard* subscription information write:
Subscription Department
Beacon Hill Press of Kansas City
P.O. Box 419527
Kansas City, MO 64141
800-877-0700
May God bless you as you write!
Categories: Religion

Name: Everett Leadingham, Editor
Material: All
Address: 6401 THE PASEO
City/State/ZIP: KANSAS CITY MO 64131

The Star

Dear Reader:
Reading *Star* Magazine is the best guide to our requirements. *Star* Magazine is a weekly magazine which features celebrity news and upbeat human interest stories.

Payment on publication, varies, but usually falls within the $100 to $400 range for other than brief items.

Star is the largest newsstand selling, celebrity news-driven publication in America today.

It is a news magazine whose editorial product features an inside look at celebrity news and lifestyles. In addition, reader service editorial covering topics such as health and fitness, diet and food, and parenting is showcased.

Categories: Fiction—Nonfiction—Biography—Book Reviews—Consumer—Cooking—Family—Fashion—Food/Drink—Government—Health—Parenting—Physical Fitness—Psychology—Celebrities—Human Interest—Education—Women's Issues—How-to—Diet—Beauty—News

Name: Phil Bunton, Editor-in-Chief
Material: All
Address: 660 WHITE PLAINS RD.
City/State/ZIP: TARRYTOWN, NY 10591
Telephone: 914-332-5000
Fax: 914-332-5043

Stone Soup
the magazine by young writers and artists

Stone Soup

Strict Requirement: All submissions must be accompanied by a self-addressed stamped envelope large enough and with sufficient postage for the return of the submission. (Foreign contributors need not include return postage.) Unfortunately, we cannot send any response at all to contributors whose work is not accompanied by a self-addressed stamped envelope.

How to Submit Your Work: Mail your submission to the address shown below. Include your name, age, home address and phone number.

Reporting Time: If you have enclosed an SASE, you will hear from us within four weeks of the date we receive your submission. We usually publish work three months to a year after notification of acceptance.

General Information: *Stone Soup* is made up of stories, poems, book reviews, and art by children through age 13. We encourage you to send us your work! To get an idea of the kind of work we like, the best thing you can do is to read a couple of issues of *Stone Soup*. If it's not in your library, you can order a sample copy for $4.

Send us writing and art about the things you feel most strongly about! Whether your work is about imaginary situations or real ones, use your own experiences and observations to give your work depth and a sense of reality.

Writing need not be typed or copied over. We are happy to consider writing in languages other than English. Include a translation if possible. Art work may be any size, in color or black and white. Please don't send us work that you are also sending to other magazines. Send your work to one magazine at a time.

Illustrators: If you would like to illustrate for us, send us some samples of your art work, along with a letter saying what kind of story you would like to illustrate.

Book Reviewers: If you are interested in reviewing books for *Stone Soup*, write and tell us a little about yourself and what kinds of books you like to read. We'll write back with more information.

Payment: All contributors whose work is accepted for publication receive a certificate, two complimentary copies, and discounts on other purchases. In addition, contributors of stories, poems, and art work are paid $10 each, book reviewers are paid $15, illustrators are paid $8 per illustration, and the cover artist is paid $25.

Categories: Children

Name: Ms. Gerry Mandel, Editor
Material: All
Address: PO BOX 83
City/State/ZIP: SANTA CRUZ CA 95063
Telephone: 408-426-5557
Fax: 408-426-1161
E-mail: editor@stonesoup.com
Internet: www.stonesoup.com

Stoneflower Literary Journal

No dated meter return envelopes please. Foreign submissions send self-addressed envelope with 2 international postage coupons for response.

SHORT STORY: 2,500 word limit. *Will not consider longer fiction.* Pays $10/published story. **POETRY:** any style, any length, but shorter poems get preference. Poems will not, however, be accepted based on length alone. Pays $5/published poem. **INTERVIEWS:** of well-known writers, editors, publishers, agents, or others in writing field, artists, professional photographers. Query first, Pays $10/published interview. Submissions not returned. **ART AND PHOTOGRAPHY:** art submissions limited to ink drawings or quality black and white photography, not to exceed 8½"x11". Pays $8/art or photograph.

Include **A SHORT BIOGRAPHY** with all submissions. **FORMAT:** standard manuscript format. **DO NOT** use "Old English," italics, or other ornate type which does not scan well. Courier, Times, and Helvetica are acceptable. Type poem as you want it to appear on the page.

PROSE, POETRY AND PEN & INK DRAWINGS BY YOUTH: considered for up to age 16. Pays $2/published poem, $5/published prose and art work. Include age, gender, school attending, other writing accomplishments and interests/hobbies. Older youth's works will be considered along with those of adults. No children's stories or poems *written by adults* will be accepted.

Stoneflower reserves the right to proofread edit, copy-edit, or revise literary submissions and to crop art and photography. Will consider simultaneous submissions or previously published work *if notified at time of submission* with name, address, time, and volume of previous publisher.

All payment is in US dollars. Reporting time—up to 3 months. Sample copies $5 + $2 S&H

GUIDELINES FOR *Stoneflower* WRITING CONTEST

This competition is separate from general submissions for publication in *Stoneflower.*

POETRY: AWARDS—$50 first place; $10 second place; copy of journal to honorable mentions.

Poetry Reading fee $5 for first poem, $3 additional poems

SHORT STORY: AWARDS—$75 first place; $25 second place; copy of journal to honorable mentions.

Short Story Reading Fee $10 for first story, $8 additional stories

Winners announced in the spring edition of *Stoneflower. Winners are not published in the journal.*

For notification that your manuscript and entry fees have been received, include a self-addressed, stamped postcard. No manuscripts returned. For winners' list, send a SASE.

Absolutely no response to any correspondence without SASE.

No previously-published works or prior winners of previous Stoneflower literary contests will be considered.

Reading Period: May through March of each year. All payment is in US dollars.

Categories: Fiction—Interview—Poetry—Profiles

Name: Joy Lake, Poetry Coordinator
Material: Poetry
Name: Coley Scott, Fiction Coordinator
Material: Fiction
Name: Brenda Davidson-Shaddox, Editor
Material: Interview/Profile Inquiries; Works by Children
Address: 1824 NACOGDOCHES STE 191
City/State/ZIP: SAN ANTONIO TX 78209-2216
Nota bene: Reading fees required for contest entries.

Story

General Focus: *Story* publishes literary short stories on a quarterly basis for discerning readers of short fiction. We buy 10-12 stories for each issue, up to 8,000 words.

We publish fiction only—experimental to mainstream. We are not interested in genre fiction such as mystery or science fiction. We welcome novel excerpts though they must be self-contained. We do not publish poetry or non-fiction.

While we regularly showcase today's top writers, we also encourage young or unpublished writers to submit their work. In keeping with *Story*'s reputation as the magazine of discovery, we offer a careful and compassionate reading to everyone, though due to the volume of stories we receive, we cannot comment on individual manuscripts as often as we'd like. A form rejection letter doesn't mean your story hasn't received attention.

To obtain a sample issue of *Story*, send $6.95 plus postage ($2.40 for first class, $1.30 for third class) to: Circulation Secretary, *Story*, 1507 Dana Avenue, Cincinnati OH 45207.

How to Submit: Please submit typed manuscripts, double-spaced on 8½" x 11" white paper, one side only. Erasable paper is not acceptable. We prefer legible photocopies. Submissions must include your name, address, and daytime telephone number as well as a self-addressed, stamped envelope. Otherwise your manuscript will not be responded to or returned.

Please send only complete manuscripts. We cannot gauge the quality of your work from a query letter or synopsis of the story. Simultaneous submissions are acceptable, but please let us know that in your cover letter. We attempt to reply within one month of receiving a manuscript. We do not accept fax or electronic submissions.

Payment and General Terms: We pay $1,000 upon acceptance for short stories and $750 for short shorts (1,500 words or fewer). We buy first North American serial rights, one-time use only. Contributors also receive 5 copies of the issue in which their story appears.

Categories: Fiction—Literature—Short Stories

Name: Lois Rosenthal, Editor
Material: All
Address: F&W PUBLICATIONS, INC. 1507 DANA AVE.
City/State/ZIP: CINCINNATI, OH 45207-1005
Telephone: 513-531-2222
Fax: 513-531-1843

Straight

We're Always Looking for *Ideas*! . . .and maybe you have just the one we're looking for!

Straight is a weekly magazine for Christian teenagers, published quarterly by the Standard Publishing Company.

Straight is distributed through churches in the United States and other English-speaking countries. It's designed to correlate with Standard Publishing's Young Teen and High School curriculum.

Fiction must appeal to teenagers and have an interesting, well-constructed plot. The main characters should be contemporary teens who cope with modern-day problems using Christian principles. Stories should be uplifting, positive and character-building, but not preachy. Conflicts must be resolved realistically, with thought-provoking and honest endings. Accepted length is 1,100 to 1,500 words.

Nonfiction is accepted. We use articles on current issues from a Christian point of view, teen profiles, and humor. Nonfiction pieces should concern topics of interest to teens, including school, family life, recreation, friends, part-time jobs, dating and music.

Photos of professional quality are appreciated. Submit high contrast black and white glossy and color transparencies. We use photos of teens and teen activities, and those which accompany or illustrate articles. All photos should feature teens who are conservative in appearance, with no revealing clothing or outrageous hairstyles. Teens should have a natural, expressive appearance, not an artificial, posed, "too perfect" look.

Devotions and Art are done by assignment only. If you'd like to be considered for an assignment, please let us know.

Poetry is accepted from teens only. The author's birth date must accompany all poetry submitted.

What you can expect in payment

Payment is on acceptance. *Straight* pays 3-7¢ per word. We purchase first rights and reprint rights. Photos bring $50-75 for inside use. Color shots for cover use are $125. Rates for teen submissions vary.

Your *social security number* is required for payment if you live in the United States. Your birth date is required if you are under 20 years of age. Please include this information with all submissions.

Before you submit. . .please get to know us. Sample issues are available on request (enclose SASE, please).

Manuscripts are submitted on speculation. Type your name, address, and social security number on the first sheet, as well as the approximate word count. Due to the various types of software, we request that you contact us before submitting disks. We do not accept submissions by fax.

Expect to wait 4-8 weeks to hear from us.

These clues will help you.

To avoid a rejection, keep these things in mind:

• Teenagers today are different from the way they were when you were a teen, even if you are a young person. Get to know teens before you begin to write for them. Many manuscripts are rejected simply because the plot or vocabulary is outdated for modern teens.

• Some teenagers read no higher than sixth grade level. Don't write down to kids, but keep this in mind as you write. Words should be simple. Stories should be short and direct.

• A tacked-on moral does not make a religious story. Make your characters Christian, and the religious slant will take care of itself.

• We look for material to correlate with Bible school lessons, so each quarter we are considering specific topics. If you request it, we will put you on our mailing list to receive quarterly themes.

• We produce *Straight* long before its publication date. Send seasonal material 9-12 months in advance.

Categories: Fiction—Nonfiction—Religion—Teen

Name: Heather Wallace, Editor
Material: All
Address: 8121 HAMILTON AVE
City/State/ZIP: CINCINNATI OH 45231
Telephone: 513-931-4050
Fax: 513-931-0950

Strategic Health Care Marketing

Editorial Profile

Twelve-page monthly newsletter, covering all areas of marketing and business development in a wide range of health care settings—hospitals, medical group practices, home health services, HMOs. Editorial focus is on strategies and techniques employed within the health care field and on relevant applications from other service industries. No photos or artwork. Byline on longer articles.

Kinds of Articles/Style

News, interviews, profiles, opinion and commentary, advice and how-to. Preferred format for feature articles is the case history approach to solving marketing problems. Crisp, almost telegraphic style...most articles range from 500 to 2,000 words in length.

Reader Profile

Directors/Vice Presidents of Marketing, Public Relations, Planning in hospitals. Administrators in small hospitals, medical groups, and in other types of delivery systems. Marketing and advertising consultants and agencies serving the service sector of the health care industry. Pharmaceutical and medical device sectors are *not* represented.

Rights

All articles must represent original unpublished work. First North American serial rights; Publisher also retains rights to use work in subsequent editorial reprints, collections, advertising and promotion, and in any other Health Care Communications publications.

Payment

Upon publication. Payment runs $100-$400+, depending on complexity of assignment, length, and writer's credentials. Articles normally published within two months of manuscript acceptance. Two revisions if necessary.

Kill Fee

25% for specifically commissioned material.

Out-of-Pocket Expenses

For commissioned material will reimburse long-distance telephone and out-of-pocket travel expenses, provided documentation submitted. Prior approval required for expenses (individual or in total per article) that will exceed $50.

Query First!

Many articles are written by marketing authorities and practitioners in the health care field. You should be familiar with either marketing or the industry—preferably both.

Categories: Health Care Marketing

Name: Submissions Editor
Material: All
Address: 11 HERITAGE LN
City/State/ZIP: RYE NY 10580
Telephone: 914-967-6741
Fax: 914-967-3054
E-mail: healthcomm@aol.com

Student Leader

Please refer to Oxendine Publishing, Inc.
Categories: Education

Name: Kay Quinn, Managing Editor
Name: Teresa Beard, Assistant Editor
Material: Any
Address: PO BOX 14081
City/State/ZIP: GAINESVILLE FL 32601
Telephone: 352-373-6907
Fax: 352-373-8120
E-mail: oxendine@compuserve.com

Succeed Magazine
The Magazine for Continuing Education

SUCCEED Magazine is designed to provide its readers with information about postgraduate and continuing education programs. The magazine's editorial content includes information of interest to adults recommitting themselves to education and provides insight on making such a transition easier.

Published three times a year to coincide with the fall, spring, and summer academic semesters, *SUCCEED Magazine* is distributed to colleges and universities, career and planning centers, corporations, and public library branches throughout the New York, New Jersey, and Connecticut area.

SUCCEED Magazine is comprised of both regular departments and full-length feature articles. We typically pay $50 to $75 for department inclusions and $75 to $125 for feature articles. Departments run approximately 500-1,000 words. Features should be 1,000-1,500 words in length. We usually buy first rights to a piece. We will consider buying second rights if your published piece has not appeared in a national magazine, continuing education-oriented publication, or any other magazine written primarily for adults returning to the classroom. For all departments and features, you will receive payment upon publication.

Please query us by structuring an article proposal in the following manner:

• Begin with the lead you expect to put on the article—grab our attention!

• Write a summary of your intended areas of coverage.

• Give specifics about who you plan to interview, what types of real-life anecdotes you'll include, which resources you plan to utilize, and what conclusion the story might reach.

(With your query, please send us two or three published clips. Please send photocopies; we do not return writing samples.)

Familiarize yourself with *SUCCEED* Magazine. Get to know what kinds of articles interest our readership of over 155,000 professionals.

SUCCEED Magazine Departments

We're constantly developing new and innovative departments. Got any suggestions? Send them along, too!

• **Memo Pad**—Consists of short, newsworthy items filled with information, tidbits, and trends that relate to today's changing job market and continuing education. Some recent examples include Open House events at various colleges and universities; Salary information; Time management tips and solutions; Money management short courses; etc.

• **Books**—In every issue, we review books and guides that help advance one's career; offer guidance to educational transitions; present an overview on postgraduate programs; suggest ways to reduce stress; explore alternative career opportunities; etc.

• **Solo Success**—With today's proliferation of self-employment endeavors, home-business start-ups, and distance learning alternatives, more and more adults are focusing their attention on making their own "Solo Success. This department will include the important aspects of how to "do it on your own," as well as discuss economical forecasting affecting such pursuits; resources, books and software designed to effectively fulfill such aspirations; and more.

• **To Be**—This mini-profile section presents inside looks at two or three persons in various careers. What do they do? What skills are required for them to do their jobs? What are their likes and dislikes? What advice do they have to offer others interested in pursuing careers in their field?

• **Financial Fitness**—This section will show you how to keep your money in tip-top shape even *after* you sign your tuition check! It consists of tips, information, and current trends on how to financially afford returning to school. Resources utilized include the latest books offering such advice, financial consultant services, economic research findings, etc.

SUCCEED Magazine Features

Submit your intelligent, thought-provoking ideas. To us, a winning article presents useful information with creativity!

Here are some topics we're interested in covering in future issues…

• Finding A Career That Fits
• Strategies For Successful Retirement
• Ethics In The Business World...Do They Still Exist?
• Get A Jump Start On Your Return To School: It's All About Portfolio Assessment!

Keep in mind that our response time to manuscripts and queries is approximately four to five weeks.

Categories: Careers—Education

Name: Gina LaGuardia, Editor-in-Chief
Material: All
Address: 2071 CLOVE RD STE 206
City/State/ZIP: STATEN ISLAND NY 10304
Telephone: 718-273-5700
Fax: 718-273-2539
E-mail: ramholtz@intercall.com

Success Connection, Inc.

Publisher: Turquoise Butterfly Press
Format: 12-page bimonthly newsletter. Established in 1997.
Focus: To support self-employed hard-working parents who

struggle to balance working from home, caring for the house, and the children. Stress management, boosting business, budgeting, time management, and parenting skills are regular topics.

Submission: Lead articles should be 900-1,500 words. All other articles, personal stories, interviews, humorous pieces etc., should be 100-900 words. All material must be typewritten or neatly handwritten. *Include a word count!* Artwork and photos may accompany piece. Editor has the right to edit material. Buys one-time rights. Buys reprints. Include researched citations. Pays in copies. Sample copy is $3.50.

Categories: Nonfiction—Parenting—Self-Employment—Time Management

Name: Terri J. Andrews, Editor
Material: All
Address: PO BOX 1127
City/State/ZIP: ATHENS OH 45701-1127
Telephone: 614-664-3030

SUCCESSFUL Black Parenting

Successful Black Parenting

Successful Black Parenting Magazine is a parent-friendly bimonthly publication for those interested in raising the Black child. *Successful Black Parenting* explores the influence of historical events on child-rearing styles of today. It seeks to promote the healthy development of children, beginning with the prenatal period and continuing through late adolescence.

Successful Black Parenting's mission is to create a network of support for Black parents and to encourage positive, creative responses to the many aspects of parenting. Articles should be culturally responsive to the unique characteristics of the African American community and to the challenging role of parenting. Articles should have positive angle, emphasizing the strengths of the parent-child-family relationship and offering practical, sensitive advice.

Successful Black Parenting will consider submissions for the following areas:

Feature articles—800 to 1,500 words in length; refer to the editorial calendar for a listing of projected articles.

Department articles—500 to 800 words in length; departments are: On My Own (single parenting), Nubian Dad, Young'uns (for grandparents), Chelsea's Cupboard (nutritional recipes for children), We & Our PC (family computing).

Special columns—150 to 500 words in length; these are human interest stories, anecdotal tales and practical, no-nonsense parenting tips.

Please send a letter stating your interest in writing. Include any research that you may have already done on the topic. *Successful Black Parenting* does not return unsolicited articles. *Successful Black Parenting* has first time publication rights on those articles accepted for publication. Payment for articles is made after publication. Please allow six weeks for review. Please be advised that we have a 2-4 month lead time for articles; articles needed for Sept/Oct, for example, are reviewed as early as May.

We look forward to hearing from you soon.

The Editors!

Categories: Nonfiction—African-American—Parenting

Name: Marta Sanchez-Speer, Co-Publisher
Material: All
Address: PO BOX 6359

City/State/ZIP: PHILADELPHIA PA 19139-6359
Telephone: 215-476-7660
Fax: 215-476-1664
E-mail: BlkParent@aol.com

Sun Valley Magazine

• Articles should relate specifically to the Wood River Valley.
• Almost all stories are assigned to local authors.

We will consider articles of a more general nature as they relate to life in the mountains. Examples of articles we've purchased from freelancers:

• reviewing ski movies
• humor article on the plight of the salmon

Typically we pay $.10/ word, upon publication. Query with entire article (departments average 1,200-1,500 words), or fully developed idea (including opening paragraph, brief outline, and conclusion).

We begin developing our storyline a year in advance. Send SASE with $1.49 postage for sample copy of magazine.

For articles of a more general nature regarding Idaho, query Alan Minskoff, editor of another of our publications, *Boise Magazine*, 102 S. 17th Street, Suite 100, Boise, ID 83702.

Categories: Outdoors—Recreation—Regional—Sports

Name: Colleen Daly, Editor
Material: All
Address: PO BOX 697
City/State/ZIP: HAILEY ID 83333
Telephone: 208-788-0770
Fax: 208-788-3881

The Sun
A Magazine of Ideas

We're interested in essays, interviews, fiction, and poetry. While we tend to favor personal writing, we're open to just about anything—even experimental writing, if it doesn't make us feel stupid. Surprise us; we often don't know what we'll like until we read it.

We pay from $50 to $200 for poetry, from $300 to $500 for fiction, and from $300 to $750 for essays and interviews, the amount being determined by length and quality. We may pay less for very short works. For photographs we pay from $50 to $200, depending on placement. We'll consider photographs of any size, but we can use only black-and-white prints. For drawings and cartoons (which, be forewarned, we rarely publish), we pay up to $75. We also give contributors a complimentary one-year subscription to *The Sun*.

We're willing to read previously published works, though for reprints we pay only half our usual fee. We discourage simultaneous submissions. We rarely run anything longer than seven thousand words; there's no minimum word length. Don't bother with a query letter, except perhaps on interviews; the subject matter isn't as important to us as what you do with it.

We try to respond within three months. However, with more than seven hundred submissions a month, our backlog of unread manuscripts is often substantial. Don't let a longer wait surprise you.

Submissions should be typed. Your work will not be returned without sufficient postage, and we cannot respond unless a return envelope is provided.

Thanks for your interest in *The Sun*.
Sy Safransky
Editor
P.S. To save your time and ours, we suggest you take a look at *The Sun* before submitting. Sample issues are $3.50 each.

Categories: Fiction—Nonfiction—Interview—Literature—Photography—Poetry—Short Stories

Name: Sy Safransky, Editor
Material: All
Address: 107 N ROBERSON ST
City/State/ZIP: CHAPEL HILL NC 27516
Telephone: 919-942-5282

Sunset Magazine

Dear Freelance Writer or Photographer:

Please excuse our form letter as we try to answer some of your questions about writer and/or photographer guidelines for *Sunset* magazine.

Sunset is largely staff-written. Our writers work four to twelve months in advance of publication. Our editorial calendars undergo constant refinement, and we do not distribute them outside the company.

Travel items account for the vast majority of *Sunset*'s freelance assignments. We also contract out some short garden items. We have no formal guidelines for departments other than travel and garden. If you wish to submit a food, building or crafts idea, follow the procedures outlined for travel writers.

Most Sunset stories are illustrated by freelance or stock photography. Stories researched by our writers go through a lengthy planning process with story editors, photo editors, and art directors to determine specific color photo requirements. We then hire freelance photographers or search stock houses.

Freelance photographers are commissioned by our photo editors. These professional photographers are paid $350 per day plus agreed-upon expenses. We purchase one-time photo rights. Photo space rates range from $100 to $1,000; these are deducted from day rates and the money due is paid upon publication.

Our photo editor will be happy to review photography portfolios. Please drop off your material in our lobby or send it to us; we will return the material promptly. Unfortunately, we do not have time to give personal interviews after portfolio reviews.

Freelance Guidelines for Sunset's Home & Design Section
(*Sunset Magazine* circulation: 1,430,000)

Our target readers are active suburban families (women as well as men), in metropolitan areas of the Western thirteen states, from Colorado to Hawaii, with the majority of readers along the coast from Seattle to San Diego. They want help in making their often cramped or generic living spaces more personal, interesting, functional, and enjoyable. They seek "real life" solutions as well as inspiration.

The Home & Design section appears after the Main Editorial well and consists of mostly one- and two-page articles. To supplement a solid core of staff writing, we are looking for stories about fresh, imaginative, and practical home design ideas with wide reader appeal. An ideal such story would be one that inspires readers to act upon the advice and information given. To make Sunset a resource for goods as well as ideas, we are also expanding our coverage of products and furnishings.

We are a magazine for and about the West and so we are especially interested in regional aspects of home design. In judging a story proposal we often ask "What's Western about it?" by which we mean does it address or illuminate some aspect of living in the West. For example, we are always eager to see home furnishings (chairs, beds, mirrors, rugs, cookware, lighting fixtures, etc.) handcrafted by artisans living and working in the West.

As a visual magazine, *Sunset* considers photographs the key elements in a story. Scouting photographs are essential and must accompany queries. In reviewing queries, Sunset looks for such qualities as simplicity, informality, clarity, warmth, craftsmanship,

S-Z

an expressive use of natural materials, and a commitment to the highest standards of design. News value, evidence of a rising trend, relevance to a wide readership, and an engaging tale to tell are also important.

Though freelance queries on the spectrum of home and design subjects are welcome, two new monthly departments within the Home & Design section are specifically looking for freelance input at this time:

1. The **Before & After** page shows a vivid and appealing transformation; usually a small before photograph and a much larger after photo, with text describing the change. Over the course of 12 months, it should be a strong mix of interior and exterior ideas, one element of a room or a whole room, a chair or a bedroom suite. Text must include "highlights"—details on such things as: cost, time needed, major stumbling blocks, unusual materials used, color/brand of paint.

2. The **"I Did It"** column, runs a page or more (is more texty than Before and After) and describes a homeowner's adventure in remodeling, furnishing, or design, with tips and resources where appropriate. The story should emphasize the homeowner's involvement in the process, including major frustrations or surprises that occurred along the way. Geographic diversity is important.

Submission Procedures

No responsibility is assumed for unsolicited manuscripts. Writers must submit a query letter to the editor in advance. The query letter should explain and outline the proposed story idea(s), and suggest an appropriate month. Snapshots showing before and after transformations, reader accomplishments, products, objects, or interior designs should be submitted with the query letter whenever possible.

All Home & Design story ideas are presented at quarterly Home & Design planning meetings. Once an editor accepts a writer's idea, the editor and writer work up a synopsis that the editor will present at the planning meeting for discussion. If the story idea is approved at that meeting, the writer will be issued a Story Contract assigning an approximate word length and due date for the text. The contract specifies the terms of the agreement between the writer and Sunset Publishing Corporation.

Following submission of the text, the writer may be asked to revise the manuscript for publication or to supply further information or answer questions posed by the editor.

Word-length

One page stories usually run 300 to 500 words, depending on the number of photographs or illustrations.

Accuracy

Every *Sunset* article must be correct. *Sunset* is proud of its reputation for accuracy and dependability. Writers are urged to verify their information.

Style

Stories should be written using the active voice. The tone should be informative but friendly, intelligent but not intimidating. Write as if you are giving guidance to a friend or family member. Begin with an arresting lead that clearly establishes a reason for reading on. Separate source and price information, how-to-instructions, and additional tips from the running text so they can appear as lists or tint blocks for easy legibility.

Payment

Payment will be made upon acceptance of the text with the submission of an invoice in the amount specified in the contract.

Sunset Editorial Guidelines for Freelance Garden Writers

Sunset is Western America's largest-circulation regional magazine, with monthly issues devoted to four subject areas: travel and recreation; gardening and outdoor living; food and entertaining; building, design, and crafts.

Sunset is looking for thoroughly researched, well-written stories and Garden Guide items that describe home gardening

projects which can be successfully accomplished in a day or over a weekend or growing season.

Submission Procedures: Writers must submit a query letter to the editor in advance. The query letter should explain and outline the proposed story idea, and suggest an appropriate month or season and the intended edition. Snapshots showing gardens or plants may be submitted with the query letter.

Once an editor approves an idea for a Garden Guide item or story, the writer will be issued a Story Contract assigning an approximate word length and due date for the text. The contract specifies the terms of the agreement between the writer and Sunset Publishing Corporation.

Writers must have computer capabilities to submit stories on floppy disks (3½" or 5¼" inch) or to transmit text via modem or the Internet. The assigned text should be submitted with the resource material specified in the contract. (Floppy disks are not returnable.)

Following submission of the text, the writer may be asked to revise the manuscript for publication or to supply further information or answer questions posed by the editor.

Payment will be made upon acceptance of the text with submission of an invoice in the amount specified in the contract.

After acceptance, the text will then be processed by staff copy editors and fact checker. Writers will be credited with a byline if the manuscript is not substantially altered before publication in *Sunset* Magazine.

Word Length: One-page stories usually run from 450 to 500 words, depending on the number of color photographs or illustrations such as charts or drawings.

Items for *Sunset*'s Garden Guide currently run about 150 to 250 words.

Take-action Magazine: *Sunset* is not an armchair magazine. While each item or story ought to be interesting to read, it must also take a how-to approach so that readers can use the information to duplicate the activity in their own home gardens.

Climate Zones: In the West, the kinds of gardening people do, and the seasons in which they garden, are determined by the climate and topography of the area in which they live. The *Sunset Western Garden Book* identifies 24 different plant climate zones in the West, and it is to these zones (not USDA zones) to which stories in *Sunset* Magazine refer. These climate zones dictate different planting times, gardening seasons of varying lengths, and, in most cases, different plants that will grow in different zones. For this reason, *Sunset*'s Garden Guide items and many of the garden stories are zoned in regional editions.

Regional Editions: Garden Guide items are tailored to meet the home gardening needs of readers in *Sunset*'s seven regional editions: Northern California (San Francisco Bay Area); Southern California (including Los Angeles, Santa Barbara, Ventura, and western parts of Riverside and San Bernardino counties); San Diego County; Northwest (Oregon and Washington); and National (including Arizona, Colorado, Nevada, New Mexico, Utah, and other intermountain states).

Seasonality: *Sunset* times the publication of its garden stories to coincide with the periods during which plants are planted, in bloom, or ready for harvest.

Plant Availability: Every plant *Sunset* describes must be readily available in nurseries or from mail-order suppliers of plants or seeds. For plants not commonly available, be sure to list sources, including complete mailing addresses, telephone numbers, and prices for plants or seeds.

Accuracy: Every *Sunset* article must be correct. *Sunset* is proud of its reputation for accuracy and dependability. Writers are urged to verify their information by consulting with several expert sources such as botanists, horticulturists, Certified Nurserymen, extension agents, commercial growers, Master Gardeners, and landscape architects and designers. Writers are also urged to check botanical and common names for plants as listed in the *Sunset Western Garden Book* or other widely respected reference such as *Hortus Third*.

Style: Stories should be written using the active voice. The tone should be informative but friendly, intelligent but not intimidating. Write as if you were giving gardening guidance to a friend or family member visiting your backyard. Writers may want to address the reader in the familiar (you) form. Begin with an arresting lead that clearly establishes a reason for reading on.

Logical Order: Establish a logical order for topics, categories and listings: alphabetical (by common name), chronological (step-by-step technique), physical characteristics (plant size or flower color), sun to shade, etc.

Straight Facts: Basic gardening facts are essential: plant form and size; leaf color and shape; flower color, shape, size, and scent; fruit or vegetable size, flavor, and texture. Give clear directions for planting, fertilizing, harvesting, etc.

Variety: *Sunset* publishes Garden Guide items and stories that address a wide range of gardening subjects, including the following:

• **Plants:** Flowering plants (annuals, bulbs, perennials); landscape plants (deciduous and evergreen trees, shrubs, vines, ground covers, grasses); fruits (berries, citrus, grapes, nuts, pome and stone fruits); vegetables and herbs. Emphasis is on what's new, rediscovered, or otherwise noteworthy.

• **Gardens:** Borders (mixed and formal); containers (pots, hanging baskets, window boxes); country-style (informal or old-fashioned Western look); raised beds; small spaces (narrow yards, rooftops); specialty gardens (antique roses, cooks' gardens, herbs, native plants, rock gardens, wildflowers).

• **Landscaping:** Drought-tolerant landscapes; garden remodels; outdoor "rooms" (spaces defined by plants, decks); privacy screens using plants; steep-slope landscaping solutions; water features (ponds). Timeliness is important: for example, a story on landscaping in fire-prone areas of California might be appropriate for September when there is a greater chance of wildfires.

• **Indoor Gardening:** House plant care and culture, greenhouses, lighting techniques.

• **Tips & Techniques:** Soil preparation, planting, transplanting, propagation (cuttings, grafting), irrigation, mulching, fertilizing, harvesting, composting, pruning, plant disease and pest control using environmentally safe methods, lawn care, flower arrangement (fresh and dry). *Sunset* looks for new and better ways to solve familiar gardening problems.

• **Homemade Devices:** Tools and other devices that help gardeners achieve success while saving time and effort. These devices must be tested and their usefulness proven.

Photography: Writers are encouraged to submit the names of prospective sources of color photographs (35mm or medium-format transparencies preferred) to illustrate stories. However, *Sunset* will arrange for all photo submissions and/or assignments to photographers. Photo rates are available upon request from the Photography Editor.

Sunset Editorial Guidelines for Freelance Travel Writers

Sunset is looking for well-written stories and Travel Guide items that offer our readers reliably satisfying travel experiences that can be successfully accomplished in a day or weekend outing, or included as part of a vacation.

Submission Procedures: Writers must submit a query letter to the editor in advance. The query letter should explain and outline the proposed story idea, and suggest an appropriate month or season.

Once an editor approves an idea for a story or travel Guide item, the writer will be issued a Story Contract assigning an approximate word length and due date for the text. The contract specifies the terms of the agreement between the writer and Sunset Publishing Corporation.

Writers must have computer capabilities to submit stories on floppy disks (3½" or 5¼") or to transmit text via modem or the Internet. The assigned text should be submitted with the resource material specified in the contract. Floppy disks are not returnable.

Following submission of the text, the writer may be asked to revise the manuscript for publication, or to supply further information or answer questions posed by the editor.

Payment will be made upon acceptance of the text with submission of an invoice in the amount specified in the contract.

After acceptance, the text will then be processed by staff copy editors and fact checker. Writers will be credited with a byline if the manuscript is not substantially altered before publication in *Sunset Magazine*.

Word Length: One-page stories usually run from 450 to 500 words, depending on the number of color photographs or other illustrations such as maps.

Items for *Sunset*'s Travel Guide currently run from 250 to 350 words. Longer items generally deal with several related attractions or events, or treat one destination or activity in detail.

Regional Editions: Travel Guide items offer close-to-home outings for readers in *Sunset*'s seven regional editions: Northern California (San Francisco Bay Area); Southern California including Los Angeles, Santa Barbara, Ventura, and western parts of Riverside and San Bernardino counties); San Diego County; Northwest (Oregon, Washington, British Columbia); and National (including Arizona, Colorado, Nevada, New Mexico, Utah, and other intermountain states).

Take-action Magazine: *Sunset* is not an armchair magazine. While each Travel Guide item or story ought to be entertaining to read, it must also take a how-to approach so that readers can actually participate.

Accuracy & Readability: Every story or Travel Guide item must be correct, clear, and interesting. *Sunset* is proud of its reputation for accuracy and dependability.

Style: Stories should be written using the active voice. The tone should be informative but friendly, intelligent but not intimidating. Write as if you were giving travel guidance to a friend or family member. Writers may want to address the reader in the familiar (you) form ("You've probably never heard of a calf blabber, a chain-gang persuader, or a frozen Charlotte. Even if you have, you'll enjoy a stop at the Frontier Relic Museum.")

Sense of Place: Travel writers should strive to convey a sense of place: the characteristics that set a place apart and make it a worthwhile destination.

The writer's personal insight into a place or event can help the reader to more thoroughly enjoy a travel experience ("Upon arrival, honk your horn."); or to avoid an unpleasant one (crowds, sunburn, dangerous terrain, etc.).

Insight and local flavor also can be expressed through the judicious use of a quote or two from an expert source ("I've traveled the world, and always come back. There's a lot of hype about Malibu but also an intangible magic.")

Logical Order: Establish a logical order for topics, categories and listings: alphabetical, chronological, geographical (north to south, near to far, etc.). Begin with an arresting lead that clearly establishes a reason for reading on.

Straight Facts: Basic travel facts are essential—directions for getting to a destination, distances, addresses, dates, hours of operation, costs, and telephone numbers for further information.

Freshness: Look for news pegs and fresh angles on familiar destinations or events. Often a single destination offers multiple opportunities for readers to visit related attractions such as art galleries, specialty shops, or restaurants.

Variety: Look for activities that would appeal to a wide range of readers, from families to empty nesters. Here are some subjects regularly treated in *Sunset*'s stories and Travel Guide items:

• **Outdoor Recreation:** Bike tours; bird-watching spots;

camping and hiking in state and national parks; cruising; fishing; hiking; skiing (downhill and cross-country); walking or driving tours of historic districts, fruit- or wine-producing areas.

• **Indoor Adventures:** New museums and displays; art exhibits with unique Western themes; living history programs dealing with Western lore; hands-on science programs at institutions such as aquariums or planetariums; specialty shopping (Western art, crafts, antiques).

Special Events: Festivals that celebrate a region's unique social, cultural, or agricultural heritage (examples: Oktoberfest, jazz festival, strawberry festival).

• **Surprise Us:** Look for great weekend getaways, backroad drives, urban adventures, culinary discoveries (ethnic dining enclaves).

Photography: Writers are encouraged to submit the names of prospective sources of color photographs (35mm or medium-format transparencies preferred) to illustrate stories. However, *Sunset* will arrange for all photo submissions and/or assignments to photographers.

Categories: Nonfiction—Architecture—Cooking—Crafts—Family—Food/Drink—Gardening—Outdoors—Recreation—Reference—Regional—Travel—Western

Name: Editorial Services
Material: All
Address: 80 WILLOW RD
City/State/ZIP: MENLO PARK CA 94025
Telephone: 415-321-3600

Sunshine Magazine

SUNSHINE is a weekly color magazine published with the Sunday edition of the *Sun-Sentinel,* a Tribune Company newspaper which circulates throughout Broward and Palm Beach Counties in South Florida. Major cities in this area include Fort Lauderdale, Hollywood, Hallandale, Plantation, Coral Springs, Boca Raton, Pompano Beach and West Palm Beach. The circulation averages 260,000, reaching nearly 600,000 readers.

The magazine accepts the work of freelance writers, photographers and artists. Most of our current contributors are established in their fields. However, we are always seeking new contributors and fresh ideas which can result in publishable features.

WHAT DO WE BUY?

Generally, anything that would interest an intelligent adult reader living on South Florida's famous "Gold Coast." We live and work in one of the nation's fastest growing regions (we have more new people coming to live here then any other area of Florida; 30 percent have been here five years or less). Because of our sub-tropical climate and the affluence that tourism has brought to our area, *Sunshine* readers are "leisure active" consumers who spend a high percentage of their incomes in spare-time pursuits, which include boating (Fort Lauderdale is one of the world's yachting capitals) and shopping (people here do more shopping in a month than most regions in the country do in three).

For the half of our population that works, the Gold Coast offers opportunities as diverse as filmmaking and high technology. For example, the IBM Personal Computer is manufactured in Boca Raton—just one of 20 major high-tech installations in our area.

We like stories that shed light on what makes life in South Florida unique: Profiles, Florida and Caribbean lifestyles, guides (recent offerings have included guides to salad bars, happy hours, health spas, bakeries, and tropical bird shops), offbeat sports and personal essays. Major stories run an average of 2,000-3,000 words (occasionally 4,000 if the subject matter warrants it), but we're also in the market for shorter (1,000-1,500) personal essays and "think" pieces.

WHAT DO WE PAY?

All fees are negotiable, but as a general guide, our rates for accepted articles range from 20 to 25 cents per word up to $750, occasionally higher. Photo rates are also negotiable: Up to $200 for covers, up to $150 per page for inside color and up to $75 per page for inside black-and-white. We pay up to $500 for cover or doubletruck color illustrations, up to $400 per page for inside color, and up to $300 for inside black-and-white. Payment is made within 30 days of acceptance.

HOW TO BREAK IN

Send us an idea, or better yet, several ideas. Include a telephone number. We will contact you within four weeks (usually less) if we're interested. Articles or proposals that are totally unsuitable are returned with a form letter, usually within two weeks.

Each story idea should be outlined in 100-200 words in which you tell us what you intend to write about, and why you are qualified. If you wish, you may include the lead to the story, to give us a better idea of your approach and writing style. Include a summary of previous writing experience and publishing credits.

Categories: Nonfiction—Florida (people, places, unsolved mysteries, travel)—General Interest—Humor

Name: Mark Gauert, Editor
Material: All
Address: 200 E LAS OLAS BLVD
City/State/ZIP: FORT LAUDERDALE FL 33301
Telephone: 954-356-4685
Fax: 954-356-4624
E-mail: mgauert@tribune.com

Supervision

Supervision is a monthly magazine for supervisory and middle management personnel. Its primary objective is to provide informative articles which develop the attitudes, skills, personal and professional qualities of the supervisory staff, enabling them to use more of their potential to increase productivity, reduce operating costs and achieve personal and company goals.

CONTENT: *Supervision* usually contains five or six feature articles each month, plus several regular columns prepared by our contributing editors. Most of the articles are contributed by people with practical experience in business and industry. We will also use question-and-answer interviews with people in industry and in-depth third-person features about how foremen and supervisors are doing their jobs in innovative ways. No advertising is used in this publication.

NEEDS: We are interested in articles addressing the following: time management, planning, delegating authority and assigning responsibility, building morale, empowering their staff, goal setting, quality management, motivating staff, teamwork, discipline, safety/accident prevention, cost cutting and new innovative management concepts.

We can use articles that deal with human relations and communication, such as specific ways in which people in business and industry can deal with each other more effectively; ways the supervisor can aid in the development of an individual employee; specific methods of supervision that produce results such as improved morale, lowered turnover, reduced absenteeism; ways to improve the communication of facts and feelings both upward and downward. How product costs and product quality affect the company's competitive position; topics that will stimulate the supervisor to broaden his/her perspective, develop personally and thus make an increasing contribution to a company.

SUBMISSION OF ARTICLES: We work in advance. Therefore, articles may be retained over a year. NRB *buys all rights.* A signed release is required before publication. Finished articles should contain from 1,500 to 1,800 words. We pay 4 cents a word. Payment is made according to the release date of the issue in which the manuscript appears. A sample is mailed to the freelancer.

Manuscripts should be high quality typed (suitable for scanning—do not submit articles on low quality dot-matrix printers), double-spaced and on only one side of the paper. The *Associated Press Stylebook* is followed for editing. Please list the approximate number of words on each manuscript. The author should indicate address, current by-line containing background employment, company affiliation and educational degrees listing alma mater. Send a black-and-white glossy author photo to accompany credit line upon acceptance.

Your experience and your ideas are valuable. Through the pages of *Supervision*, your message may become helpful to thousands of supervisors.

Categories: Business—Careers—Cartoons—Money/Finance—Personnel—Relationships

Name: George Eckley, Editor
Material: All
Address: 320 VALLEY ST
City/State/ZIP: BURLINGTON IA 52601-5513
Telephone: 319-752-5415
Fax: 319-752-3421

SWANK

Erotic Fiction

All of the fiction currently used by SWANK is erotic in some sense – that is, both theme and content are sexual. Most of the stories (The Mysterious Stranger, The Bawdy Birthday Present) have been done before, so familiarity with previous tales of this type—in SWANK and elsewhere—is recommended. New angles are always welcome.

• Canadian restrictions: SWANK is distributed in Canada and the censors there practice their own strict standards regarding sexual material. To avoid problems, we generally shy away from material we know they'll object to or edit out any offensive references. Thus, we cannot consider stories about, or containing, the following: 1) S&M (including light bondage and mild humiliation); 2) Sex involving, or between, minors; 3) Unconscious, or dead, participants in sex; 4) Incest; 5) Bestiality.

Other Fiction

The magazine's format is currently flexible, and we will consider stories that are not strictly sexual in theme (humor, adventure, detective stories, etc.). However, these types of stories are much more likely to be considered if they portray some sexual element, or scene, within their content.

Nonfiction

1) **Sex-related**: Although dealing with sex and sexually related topics, these articles should be serious and well researched without being overwritten. Examples: "Sexaholics Anonymous," "Dream Programming," and "Voyeurism." Advice-type articles are also regularly featured. Examples: "How To Pick Up Girls At The Beach," and "How To Make The Man Shortage Work For You."

2) **Action-oriented**: We will consider non-sexual articles on topics dealing with action and adventure. The availability of photos to illustrate the articles is crucial to their acceptance—frequently, we will buy a package that includes both the article and transparencies. Recent features include such diverse topics as mercenaries, dangerous occupations and off-road racing. Automotive features run monthly.

3) **Interviews**: Although SWANK has not been running interviews lately, we will consider conversations with entertainment, sports and sex-industry celebrities.

Procedure

In most cases we respond to article queries within three weeks and manuscripts within five weeks. Due to the volume of material we receive, we discourage phone calls.

Terms

Payment is upon publication. You will be notified of the publication date after acceptance. A sample copy is available for $5.95 postpaid; please make checks or money orders payable to Swank Publications.

Categories: Fiction—Nonfiction—Adventure—Erotica—Horror—Men's Issues—Paranormal

Name: Paul Gambino, Editor
Material: All
Address: 210 RT 4 E STE 401
City/State/ZIP: PARAMUS NJ 07652
Telephone: 201-843-4004
Fax: 201-843-8636

Swim Magazine

Established 1984. *SWIM Magazine*, "the world's foremost authority on adult swimming," is an internationally recognized swimming magazine dedicated to adult fitness and competitive swimmers. *SWIM Magazine* has a circulation of over 45,000 subscribers and is the official magazine of United States Masters Swimming (USMS). Subscribers are about 50% male and 50% female. The average reader is a college-educated professional in his or her mid-30's to mid-40's; almost 17% of our readers have "terminal" (i.e., professional) degrees, such as M.D., Ph.D., etc. Swimmers subscribe to our magazine for entertainment, instruction and inspiration. Masters swimmers range in age from 19 to 103+. Articles must be well written and appeal to a broad audience. Query first.

SPECIFICS

Bimonthly. Pays approximately within one month after publication, generally 12 cents per word. Publishes ms. an average of four months after acceptance. Buys all rights. Byline given. Negotiates payment for artwork and photos. Photo credit given. Query first. Reports in two months on queries. Sample copy for $3.95 prepaid and 9"x12" SASE with $1.67 for postage.

EDITORIAL

Training Tips, Interview profiles, inspirational stories, new products, medical advice, dryland exercise, swim drills, nutrition, fitness, competition and exercise physiology make **SWIM Magazine** the #1 source worldwide of information for adults about the sport of swimming.

COPY

All submissions must include a brief background about the author. If possible, send disk as well (WordPerfect preferred). **SWIM Magazine** accepts freelance articles on a continuing basis. Articles range in length from 500-3,500 words. **SWIM Magazine** reserves the right to make any editorial changes.

Categories: Nonfiction—Diet—Health—Lifestyles—Physical Fitness—Recreation—Sports—Swimming

Name: Submissions Editor
Material: All
Address: PO BOX 2025
City/State/ZIP: SEDONA AZ 86339-2025
Telephone: 520-282-4799
Fax: 520-282-4697
E-mail: swimworld@aol.com

Swimming World

Established 1959. *Swimming World* magazine, acknowledged as "the Bible" of competitive swimming, is the foremost authority on all aspects of competitive swimming, an internationally recognized swimming magazine dedicated to adult fitness, and is the official magazine of United States Swimming (USS). Subscribers are about 55% female and 45% male. Though readers include top competitive swimmers in their teens and twenties, and coaches, technical directors and officials from around the world, the average reader is a 14-year-old American girl. Swimmers subscribe to our magazine for information, instruction and inspiration. Articles must be well written and appeal to at least one of the major segments of our readership. Query first.

SPECIFICS

Monthly. Pays approximately within one month after publication, generally 12 cents per word. Publishes ms an average of two months after acceptance. Buys all rights. Byline given. Negotiates payment for artwork and photos. Photo credit given. Query first. Reports in two months on queries. Sample copy for $2.95 prepaid and 9"x12" SASE with $1.67 for postage.

EDITORIAL

Training tips, meet results, insider information, Interview profiles, inspirational stories, new products, medical advice, dry-land exercise, swim drills, nutrition, fitness, competition and exercise physiology make *Swimming World* the #1 source worldwide of information for competitive swimmers. The "Junior Swimmer" section of each issue includes articles written by and for kids.

COPY

All submissions must include a brief background about the author. If possible, send disk as well (WordPerfect preferred). *Swimming World* accepts freelance articles on a continuing basis. Articles range in length from 500-3,500 words. *Swimming World* reserves the right to make any editorial changes.

Categories: Nonfiction—Children—Health—Physical Fitness—Recreation—Sports—Swimming—Teen—Young Adult

Name: Phillip Whitten, Editor-in-Chief
Material: All
Address: PO BOX 2025
City/State/ZIP: SEDONA AZ 86339-2025
Telephone: 520-282-4799
Fax: 520-282-4697
E-mail: swimworld@aol.com

Sycamore Review
Purdue University

1) The editors aim to publish the new writer alongside the established writer; in all cases we look for exceptional writing. Please send us only your very best work.

2) *Sycamore Review* accepts original poetry, short fiction (stories or novel excerpts), creative nonfiction (e.g., personal essays), short drama and translations. We generally do not accept genre pieces (conventional science fiction, romance, horror, etc.) or critical essays. All graphic artwork, interviews and book reviews in the magazine are solicited or staff work. Aside from translations, we do not publish material that has already appeared in another publication.

3) Poetry manuscripts should be typed single-spaced, one poem to a page. All other submissions should be typed double-spaced. We do accept simultaneous submissions, though we expect prompt notification if the work is accepted elsewhere.

4) *Sycamore Review* reads manuscripts from September 1 through April 30. Manuscripts received during the summer months will be returned if accompanied by a SASE.

5) As a general *rule*, *Sycamore Review* will not publish creative work by any student currently attending Purdue University. Former students of Purdue University should wait one (1) calendar year before submitting a manuscript to the magazine. (This rule does not apply to book reviews or otherwise solicited work.)

7) Purdue University acquires first-time North American rights to work published in *Sycamore Review*. After publication, all rights revert to the author.

8) The artist shall receive two (2) copies of the issue in which his or her work appears.

9) Subscriptions to the *Sycamore Review* are $10.00/year ($12.00 foreign) in U.S. funds for two issues/year (Winter/ Spring and Summer/Fall). A sample copy of the latest issue is available for $7.00. Back issues of volumes 1-7 of the magazine are available for $4.00 each; back issues of volume 8 and all subsequent volumes are $5.60 each. Please make checks payable to Purdue University. Indiana residents add 5% sales tax.

This document is subject to change without notice.

Thank you for your interest in our magazine.

The Editors

Categories: Fiction—Nonfiction—Arts—Drama—Interview—Literature—Men's Fiction—Photography—Poetry—Short Stories—Women's Fiction—Writing

Name: Poetry Editor
Material: Poetry
Name: Fiction Editor
Material: Fiction
Name: Editor-in-Chief
Material: All other submissions
Address: DEPT OF ENGLISH HEAVILON HALL
Address: PURDUE UNIVERSITY
City/State/ZIP: W LAFAYETTE IN 47907
Telephone: 765-494-3783
Fax: 765-494-3780
E-mail: Sycamore@expert.cc.purdue.edu
Internet: www.sla.purdue.edu/academic/engl/sycamore/

360 Degrees
Art & Literary Review

360 Degrees is a quarterly review containing artwork and literature from artists and writers across the nation. It was founded in 1993 by Vassar College and University of Iowa Writer's Workshop graduate Karen Kinnison. Its vision is to provide a forum for daring, quality creative talent.

Since 1993, the Review has received national exposure from the following listings: *Writer's Market, Novel & Short Story Writers Market, Poet's Market, Dust Books Small Press Directory and International Directory of Little Magazines & Small Presses, California Writer's Guide (William August & Co., Publishers), The Gila Queen's Guide to Markets, Ulrich's International Periodicals Directory, ArtScene, Artweek,* and *The American Directory of Writer's Guidelines*. The Review has been noted in *The Writer* (June 1994) and *Vassar Quarterly* (Summer 1994). One outstanding feature is its use of color artwork. Copies are kept at the Rare Book Library at the University of Wisconsin-Madison. ISSN #1085-1542

Sample recent issue $5.00
Yearly subscription $12.00
GUIDELINES

100% freelance written. Quarterly literary magazine covering the arts—literature and artwork. We are interested in writing and art which we feel contributes to civilization, that moves us forward. More like a museum than a magazine, we want to preserve the best from our times so readers in the future will seek us a rare source. Estab. 1993, Circ. 1,000. Pays on publication. Publishes ms. an average of 3 months after acceptance. Buys one-time rights and second serial (reprint) rights. Editorial lead time 6 months. Submit seasonal material 3 months in advance. Accepts simultaneous submissions. Reports in 2 weeks on queries; 1 month on mss. Pays with one copy.

Nonfiction: Book excerpts, essays, personal experience. No technical or religious submissions. Buys 2 mss./year. Send complete ms. Length: no minimum or maximum.

Photos: Send photos with submission. Reviews contact sheets, negatives, 3"x5" prints. Offers no additional payment for photos accepted with ms. Identification of subjects required. Buys one-time rights with secondary reprints rights.

Fiction: Experimental, historial, mainstream, novel excerpts, stories by children or young writers. No religious or erotica. Buys 4 mss./year. Send complete ms.

Poetry: Avant-garde, free verse, haiku, traditional, poetry by children or young writers. No light verse. Buys 40 poems/year.

Tip: For writers, write well. For artists, send clear photographs of artwork. The poetry department is most open to freelancers. Most of the poems we accept not only show mastery of words, but present new ideas. The mastery of language is something we expect from freelancers, but the content of the idea being presented is the selling point.

Categories: Fiction—Arts—General Interest—Poetry—Writing

Name: Karen Kinnison, Managing Editor
Material: All
Address: 980 BUSH ST STE 404
City/State/ZIP: SAN FRANCISCO CA 94109

Table Talk
Family Devotional Guide

Thanks for requesting writer's guidelines to *Table Talk*. This publication is a quarterly devotional book for families with children between kindergarten and sixth grade. The 13-week devotional section in each issue is preceded by several articles on parenting. *Table Talk*'s Sunday devotionals are correlated with the Sunday School curriculum published by WordAction Publishing. The devotionals are intended to help children make the connection between Sunday Bible lessons and daily Christian living, as well as assist families in developing a habit of family biblical study.

While the daily devotionals are assigned by the editors, we rely heavily on freelance submissions for the parenting articles. Articles may vary widely in content and style, and usually provide advice and amusement regarding parenting and family life.

Table Talk articles range from parenting advice, to anecdotes, to lists. All genres and styles of writing will be given consideration. Submissions may be humorous or serious.

The editors of *Table Talk* strive to keep variety a major component of the pre-devotional pages. No submissions relevant to parenting which are appropriate and consistent with Nazarene beliefs will be dismissed on the basis of alterity. Regarding the same goal, submissions which closely resemble the themes of recently published material will not be accepted.

The writers for *Table Talk* are responsible for providing all documentation regarding sources quoted or paraphrased. Articles omitting vital publication information for sources will be drastically altered, and possibly dropped. Writers are responsible for honesty regarding their work.

Articles for our publication should be approximately 1,500 words, and should be written for the average reader. Submissions to "Kid Talk" and "Humor at Home" should be no longer than two or three paragraphs. Keep complex and compound-complex sentences to a minimum. We value writers who can communicate effectively and efficiently, without unnecessary qualification and elaboration.

Humor At Home

"Humor At Home" is an occasional feature in *Table Talk*. Items for this feature should provide real-life humorous anecdotes about the actions of children and parents.

Kid Talk

"Kid Talk" is also an occasional feature in *Table Talk*. This section features true accounts of humorous instances regarding the funny things children say. Submissions must be concise, and must be amusing in print.

Payment

All freelance work which is accepted for publication is paid five cents per published word. Exceptions to this are "Humor At Home" and "Kid Talk," which, due to their brevity, are paid ten dollars per item.

Published manuscripts are purchased *only* with multi-use rights. Purchased manuscripts are not returned.

Categories: Children—Family—Humor—Parenting

Name: Bruce Nuffer, Editor
Name: Kathleen Johnson, Assistant Editor
Material: Any
Address: 6401 THE PASEO
City/State/ZIP: KANSAS CITY MO 64131
Telephone: 816-333-7000 ext. 2359
Fax: 816-333-4439

T'ai Chi

T'AI CHI is interested in articles on T'ai Chi Ch'uan, other internal martial arts and related topics such as qigong, Chinese Traditional Medicine (Acupuncture, Herbs, Acupressure, Tuina, Daoyin, etc.), and Chinese philosophy and culture.

Generally speaking, an article should take into account the special needs and desires of the readers of T'AI CHI. Many readers are beginners or about to begin. Many are serious students, and have studied and even taught for years.

More specifically, articles may be about a style, self-defense techniques, internal martial arts principles and philosophy, training methods, weapons, case histories of benefits, or new or unusual uses for T'ai Chi Ch'uan. Try to avoid profiles or biographies of teachers that focus just on their many skills and accomplishments. These usually try to please the teacher rather than the reader.

Interviews with teachers or personalities should focus on their unique or individual insights into T'ai Chi Ch'uan, internal martial arts, qigong, or Traditional Chinese Medicine, rather than on their personal achievement, although their background can be woven into the article. Do not begin the article with the biography of the teacher or a biography of the author. No infomercials, please.

New approaches to teaching, practice or the basic principles are almost always of interest as long as the article doesn't try to promote a particular teacher. If the article is interesting and useful, it will naturally reflect positively on the teacher or writer. When planning and writing the article, ask yourself: Is the material new or fresh? Is it useful? Is it interesting? Does it help people to solve problems?

An examination of past issues is one of your best guides to what we publish. A sample copy is $3.50.

Present the information clearly, fairly, and objectively. Quotations, anecdotes, examples, and parallel references help make an article more readable and interesting. Writing that is simple and direct is understood best.

If you want to discuss a story possibility first, please feel free to contact me by phone or with a note or by e-mail.

Please do not send articles that have been published or are simultaneously being sent to other publications, unless it specifies on the first page that it is a news release. Manuscripts should be typed, with a margin not more than 80 characters wide. Put a tentative title on the front page. Put the title abbreviated on each subsequent page with a page number. At the end of the article write "-30-" to indicate it is complete.

Include your name, address, and phone number on the first page and the best times to reach you by phone. Include biographical information.

Articles can be from 500 to 3,500 words long or more. Payment can range from $75.00 to $500.00, depending on the length and quality of the article. This includes payment for photos. Including good photos or other artwork does increase the amount of payment. Payment is for first North American serial rights only. Payment is usually within 30 days of publication.

If possible, include one or more 4"x6" or 5"x7" glossy black and white prints. Color photos can be used but may print a little dark. Indicate if you want them returned. The photos should have identification of the individuals in the photo written on a separate piece of paper sent with the photos or on a post-it on the photo. If the photo is of a posture, the name of the style and posture should be given. Don't write on the back of the photo. Model releases are required. Releases authorizing use of the photos should be dated and witnessed.

We can accept material that has been saved on a disk to Windows WordPerfect or Microsoft Word format or in ASCII text format. If you have a Mac, we can convert from a Mac Word format into Windows Word. But it should be on an IBM formatted disk otherwise we won't be able to read it. You can also send a file as an attachment to our e-mail address. But in any case, please send a hardcopy, too.

Editorial deadlines are: February 15, April 15, June 15, August 15, October 15, December 15.

Categories: Asian-American—Health—Martial Arts—Physical Fitness—Sports

Name: Submissions Editor
Material: All
Address: PO BOX 39938
City/State/ZIP: LOS ANGELES CA 90039
Telephone: 213-665-7773
Fax: 213-665-1627
E-mail: taichi@tai-chi.com
Internet: www.tai-chi.com

Talent Plus!

Publisher: Turquoise Butterfly Press
Format: 14-page quarterly newsletter. Established in 1998.
Focus: The goal of *Talent Plus!* is to (1) Publish young artists and writers [up till age 18] and (2) To teach young artists and writers how to get published, make money off their writing and to build a career. All work published will be from young people, except for the How-To and interview articles. (Interviews of up-

coming publishers, writers, artists, sculptures, teachers, photographers, etc..)

Submissions: Lead articles should be 900-1,500 words. All other articles and stories should be 100-900 words. Pays in copies. All material must be typed or neatly handwritten. *Include a word count!* Editor has the right to edit material. Photos or artwork may be sent with submission. Include research citations. Buys one-time rights. Reprints okay. Pays upon publication. Sample copy $4.50

Categories: Nonfiction—Interview—Writing—Young Adult

Name: Terri J. Andrews, Editor
Material: All
Address: PO BOX 1127
City/State/ZIP: ATHENS OH 45701-1127
Telephone: 614-664-3030

Tampa Review
University of Tampa Press

1. *Tampa Review* is the faculty-edited literary journal of The University of Tampa. We publish two issues a year, one in the Fall and one in the Spring. *Our editorial staff considers submissions between September and December for publication in the following year.* Manuscripts received prior to August will be returned unread. We maintain this policy so that works submitted to us are not held for an unduly long time.

2. We suggest you submit 3 to 6 poems and/or one or more prose manuscripts of up to 5,000 words. We do not print book-length poetry, and rarely publish excerpts from larger works of either poetry or prose.

3. Poetry may be submitted single-spaced. Clearly indicate any space breaks within stories, and stanza breaks in poetry, especially when they occur at the end of a page, so that these breaks will be obvious to our editors.

4. Please do not send us work which is also being submitted elsewhere. We do not consider simultaneous submissions. This policy saves our editors from reading work which is not actually available for first North American publication, and it saves authors the embarrassment of having to withdraw a manuscript.

5. The writer's name and complete address should appear on the first page of each manuscript. For multiple-page submissions, subsequent pages should be numbered and should include the author's name and short title at the top of each page. We also appreciate receiving a telephone number and/or e-mail address.

6. Fiction and nonfiction submissions should state a total word count at the top of the first page (upper right-hand corner). For poetry manuscripts, a line count is useful.

7. Translations must be submitted in original language as well as translated versions. Please also include a short biographical note on the translated author and the author's permission to translate.

8. A reporting time of approximately 12 weeks can be expected.

9. Our payment is ten dollars per page for both prose and poetry, payable upon publication, one free copy of the review in which the work(s) appears, and a 40% discount on additional copies.

Suggestion: It is sometimes helpful to get an idea of the kinds of work a magazine is publishing; sample copies are available for that purpose. *Tampa Review* sample copies are $5.00, including postage.

Categories: Fiction—Nonfiction—Poetry

Name: Poetry Editor
Name: Fiction Editor
Name: Nonfiction Editor
Material: As Appropriate
Address: UNIVERSITY OF TAMPA PRESS
Address: 401 W KENNEDY BLVD
City/State/ZIP: TAMPS FL 33606
Telephone: 813-253-6266

Teaching Tolerance

The semiannual magazine *Teaching Tolerance* is dedicated to helping pre-school, elementary, and secondary teachers promote tolerance and understanding between widely diverse groups of students. It includes articles, teaching ideas, and reviews of other resources available to educators. Our interpretation of "tolerance" follows the definition of *American Heritage Dictionary: The capacity for or the practice of recognizing and respecting the beliefs or practices of others.*

In general, we want lively, simple, concise writing. The writing style should be descriptive and reflective. Writers should show the strength of programs dealing successfully with diversity by employing clear descriptions of real scenes and interactions, and by using quotes from teachers and students. We cannot accept articles that employ jargon, rhetoric, or academic analysis. We ask that prospective writers study previous issues of the magazine before sending a query with ideas.

Features: 1,000 - 3,000 words. Should have a strong classroom focus, with national perspective where appropriate. Usually accompanied by sidebars of helpful information such as resources, how-to steps, short profiles. Writers are typically freelance journalists with knowledge of issues in education or educators with experience writing for national non-academic publications. Fees range from $500 to $3,000 depending on length and complexity. The freelance fee is paid **on acceptance**. If the story is unacceptable as submitted, we will assist in preparing a publishable manuscript, but sometimes, despite the best intentions of both author and editor, a manuscript will be judged unacceptable. In such instances, we will pay the writer's expenses but no freelance fee. A kill fee of $200 will be paid only if the story is accepted for publication and then not used.

Essays: 400-800 words. Personal reflection, description of school program, community-school program, classroom activity, how-to. Writers are typically teachers, parents or other educators. "Between the Lines" essays describe how literature can be used to teach tolerance. Fees range from $300-$800 upon publication.

Idea Exchange: 250-500 words. Brief descriptions of classroom lesson plans, special projects, or other school activities that promote tolerance. These are usually submitted by teachers, administrators or parents who have used the technique or program. Fee: $100 upon publication.

Student Writing: Poems and short essays dealing with diversity, tolerance and justice. Printed when appropriate to magazine content. Fee: $50 upon publication.

If you have any questions concerning submissions, please contact Elsie Williams, Departments Editor.
Categories: Education—Multicultural

Name: Submissions Editor
Material: All
Address: 400 WASHINGTON AVE
City/State/ZIP: MONTGOMERY AL 36104
Telephone: 334-264-0286
Fax: 334-264-3121

Technical Analysis of Stocks & Commodities

This is to acquaint you, as a *Technical Analysis* of Stocks & Commodities author or prospective author, with our needs and requirements. There are few hard and fast rules, and acceptance of a manuscript or program is not necessarily contingent on strict compliance with the guidelines set forth herein.

CONTENT AND TOPIC

We are looking for items with wide audience appeal. Computer trading utilities, charting methods and how-to tutorials are in highest demand, but anything of interest to most investors is also appropriate for submission.

First consideration for publication will be given to material, regardless of topic, that presents the subject in terms that are easily understandable by the novice trader. One of our prime considerations is to instruct, and we must do so in a manner that the lay person can comprehend. This by no means bars material of a complex nature, but the author must first establish the groundwork.

An article or trading example that takes the time to develop the whys as well as the hows will carry more weight in the selection process. For instance, an article that explains how the user can use a moving average might merit publication, but an article that first explained the purpose and function of a moving average would be given preference.

THEME BLOCKS

We have an editorial calendar with general areas that we attempt to cover in each issue. These include:

Classic Techniques: Definitive explanations of technical charting techniques or numerical methods.

Trading Techniques: Here we are looking for information that isn't normally covered in introductory articles and generally is only picked up through experience. Market quirks, floor smarts and rules of thumb are especially handy. Sometimes this is integrated with new technical analysis techniques, but usually these "tricks of the trade" aren't quantifiable. They are everyday ways of surviving in order to prosper.

New Technical Methods: Here we are looking for new ways to look at the markets or modifications to traditional techniques. Although many techniques tend to be computerized, this is not a necessity. Articles away from the beaten path are attention-getters. Spreading and hedging are particular favorites. Charting or computer programs to help the trader study or interpret market movements do enhance the value of the article.

Basics: There's always a need to explain the basics and a learn-by-example approach is best. Describe the use of a trading system or computer program to augment user application and analysis.

Reviews: New software or hardware on the market that can make the user's life easier; comparative reviews of books, articles, etc. We can supply the raw material if you let us know your availability and interests. **If you are a proven author and want to be considered to review software, let us know what computer setup you have.**

Using Statistics: How should traders use statistics productively? The best articles here are those describing quick-but-not-too-dirty ways of employing statistics when trading. Articles describing when and/or how to use statistical techniques are also welcome.

Artificial Intelligence: Includes neural networks, expert systems and hybrids and their applications to trading and technical analysis.

Real World: Describe how to use chart work and technical analysis in day-to-day trading of stocks or commodities. A blow-by-blow account of how a trade was made, including the trader's thought processes, is always well-received by our subscribers. Surveys, statistics or information accumulated from actual data also go here, the idea being to describe the trading arena as accurately as possible.

Psychology: Trading is a mental and emotional exercise, and articles in this theme block describe how traders can put themselves in the best frame of mind for trading, point out how to avoid common emotional traps, or describe the intuitive, personal aspects of being a trader who must deal with failures as well as successes.

Technical vs. Fundamental: This theme block is where we explore techniques, strategies, concepts and systems beyond the traditional technical approach. Is technical analysis bunk? Here's the place to describe why. Can you explain a wholly different, yet profitable approach to trading that encompasses anything from astrology to econometrics? This is the theme block where you can show how to mix trading methods or describe new trading approaches that show promise or are paying off already.

STYLE AND SUBMISSION REQUIREMENTS

We are not hypercritical of writing style, but accuracy is the keyword. Minor grammatical corrections will be made by the editorial staff. However, the completeness and accuracy of submitted material is extremely important.

We particularly expect documented features of trading systems to be positively confirmed. Computer programs must be thoroughly debugged and tested. **STOCKS & COMMODITIES** attempts to verify each program submitted, but there are many times when this is prevented by system configurations. Problems arising after publication will be directed to the author.

Articles, like computer programs, should be modular in form. Each paragraph should cover a single well-defined topic. The flow of logic should be easy to follow. If it is not easy for a novice to understand, then rewrite your article/paragraph/sentence so that it will be. This does not preclude articles on complicated topics but keep in mind that 13% of our readers are new to the field and need a lot of explanation.

All material—text and graphics—should be submitted on disk together with a hard copy. If submitting your article on disk is not possible, then the article should be typewritten and double-spaced. An article in this form would run from three to 10 pages, graphics not included. Each page of submitted material (article, program listing, figure or table) should include the author's name, address and telephone number to prevent loss of material.

We virtually insist that you include graphs or other illustrative graphics to clarify articles, all submitted on disk. (A list of acceptable computer file types is available. **We recommend 16-color .BMP, .PCX or TIF file formats for graphics. For article text, we prefer .DOC files.**) If not submitted on disk, send two copies of all graphs: one clean original and one copy marked with appropriate notes and labels. The graphs should be large enough to be read clearly when reduced to half their original size. All charts, graphs, tables, illustrations and computer listings should be in black ink and have complete and descriptive captions. If you are sending originals, keep copies for yourself.

Please include an author's biographic sketch for publication. One paragraph explaining your background is adequate. **STOCKS & COMMODITIES** magazine does not publish an author's address or phone number except when you request it or include it in your biography.

COPYRIGHTS

Every author must complete and return a Technical Analysis, Inc., copyright form with the following information: Author's name, address, telephone number and social security number. Your material must be an original work that has not been previously published and is not currently under consideration by any other publication.

Upon acceptance, Technical Analysis, Inc., acquires full copyright to the material, unless otherwise agreed to in writing. Certain rights to reuse the material are given to the author, so long as proper copyright notice in the name of Technical Analysis, Inc., is given.

ACKNOWLEDGMENT AND PUBLICATION

We try to acknowledge all material received within two to three weeks of receipt. Acceptance is determined later by the **STOCKS & COMMODITIES** editorial staff.

If the article is returned, we have declined it. If we keep it, we have conditionally accepted it for possible future publication. **Acceptance for possible future publication is not a firm guarantee to publish and should be interpreted to mean that the material will be given additional review.** All material that meets minimum acceptance requirements falls into this category. The author will be notified later as to the disposition of this material and whether additional work will be required by the author.

When an author has been advised that material will be published in a specific issue of the magazine, this is still not the final word. The intricacies of publishing often require that material be pulled from or added to a given issue at any time up to press time. This is dictated by such things as last-minute changes in advertising or new feature material that must be included because of its timely nature. To the best of our ability we will keep an author advised, which, on occasion, means an author may receive several subsequent notices of publication.

PAYMENT

Payment is made upon publication. Payment for articles is based on a flat rate per published page exclusive of advertising space, but including supplied art, tables, programs, etc. The rate paid is $3.00 per column inch (2-column format) or $2.00 per column inch (3-column format), with a $50 minimum. Art payment is assumed to be based on our normal reduced publication size. Whether it is actually reduced or not depends on final magazine layout.

Cartoons, short programs and special material running less than two-thirds of one page will be paid at a flat rate of $25 upon publication. We do not pay for letters published in the "Letters to STOCKS & COMMODITIES" column.

Payment is mailed along with a tearsheet or copy of the **STOCKS & COMMODITIES** issue in which the article appears. Authors wishing additional copies of the issue in which their material appears may order them from the main office (currently $3.50 per copy). Large quantity orders should be arranged prior to publication. Reprint rates are available for quantities of 100 or more.

A Premium page rate, calculated at 120% of the base rate, is payable as follows:

• For articles appearing under the heading "Anatomy of a Trade."

• For articles designated as the "lead" article in each issue. Premium rates are not compoundable—that is, if "Anatomy of a Trade" happens to be the lead story, payment will be made at base rate plus the 20% premium.

• To "Staff Writers" who are designated by the Editor and shall contribute a minimum of one story every two issues. A Staff Writer shall, in addition, have his or her name listed on the staff page. Technical Analysis, Inc., shall have first right of refusal of any material written for publication by a Staff Writer.

OTHER PUBLICATIONS/PRODUCTS

Computer programs, demos, simple study utilities and other programs may be included in our series of software products for traders. No cash payments are made for these, since they are considered as subscriber contributions for the benefit of all. The author of an accepted program will receive a free copy of the diskette on which the program appears.

Stand-alone diskettes are another major category of **STOCKS & COMMODITIES** products and programs, such as Technical Analysis Charts™. **STOCKS & COMMODITIES** pays royalties nearly double those of industry standards and a final agreement on royalties is the result of negotiation between the author and Technical Analysis, Inc.

IF AT FIRST YOU DON'T SUCCEED…

Don't get rejectionitis. If your story or program is rejected, it may be for any number of different reasons.

If your material has publishing potential but we feel it needs more work, or if the programming can be improved, we will let you know. Bear in mind that few **STOCKS & COMMODITIES** authors are professional writers who are accustomed to rejection slips, so we ask that you not be discouraged if your material is returned, but to consider us again in the future.

Categories: Money/Finance

Name: Thom Hartle, Editor
Material: All
Address: 4757 CALIFORNIA AVE SW
City/State/ZIP: SEATTLE WA 98126
Telephone: 206-938-0570
Fax: 206-938-1307
Internet: www.traders.com

Tequesta

Purpose of the Journal

To present articles about our region's past in a scholarly format that is informative and, when possible, illustrated with historic images.

Distribution

As of 5/31/97, 3,500 copies of the journal are printed, reaching an estimated readership of 7,700, not including users in libraries and at other institutions receiving the journal in their collections.

History

The Historical Association of Southern Florida began publication of the journal in 1941, and it has been published annually since its beginning. *Tequesta* has become one of the most authoritative journals on Florida's history.

Presentation Style

Articles should be suitable for academic audiences with interest in our region's history. The editors strive for variety and balance so that each issue contains at least one article of interest to each reader.

Style Authority

The *Chicago Manual of Style* should be consulted on matters of style as this is the guide used by the editors of the journal.

Webster's first choice is used when multiple spellings of a word are acceptable. Exceptions are made when the presentation form warrants.

Content

Articles should recall, retell and explore historic events, people, places and themes pertaining to southern Florida and the Caribbean. The journal covers Florida from about Lake Okeechobee on down, coast to coast, and all countries in the Caribbean. Articles are generally presented as annotated narratives in third person or first person, and must include citations from primary research material, such as historic records, diaries and other documents. Exceptions are made when material warrants. Footnotes are required; bibliographies are optional.

Photographs

Photographic illustration is helpful but not necessary in *Tequesta*. Authors are encouraged to identify available accompanying visual material whenever possible and provide copies of such images when submitting manuscripts. Original documents and photographs that must be returned to their owners will be copied by the historical Museum of Southern Florida and handled according to the highest level of curatorial standards. Materials will be returned via certified delivery systems after publication of the journal.

Submission of Articles

A typed manuscript is requested with accompanying computer disk copy of the article whenever possible (Preferred format is PC compatible 3.5" diskette, in Microsoft Word or WordPerfect; Macintosh is acceptable). Manuscripts are also accepted through e-mail. Photographs and other illustrative materials, if identified, should be submitted with the manuscript (copies acceptable). Scanned photographs and images may be sent electronically as well, but prints will be required upon acceptance of the article for production. Articles may be submitted at any time throughout the year and should be 2,500 to 6,000 words in length.

The editorial staff of *Tequesta* strives to respond to writers who have submitted manuscripts in a timely fashion. Writers are asked to call if a timely response has not been made. The first response back will generally be an indication of whether the material is of interest for the publication and subsequent correspondence will indicate whether any additional research or writing is requested. If acceptable, the article becomes part of the pool of material undergoing production steps to ready them for publication. Articles are pulled from the pool and assigned to specific issues on an ongoing basis. The Editors at the Historical Museum of Southern Florida maintain the right for flexibility in deciding publication dates as geographical, thematic and seasonal concerns are considered.

Payment to authors for articles used includes the Historical Museum of Southern Florida's most sincere appreciation and 10 copies of the journal.

Standards

The editorial staff of *Tequesta* strives for the highest level of accuracy and fairness possible when presenting the past. Standard journalistic and research practices and principles should be adhered to at all times. Please refer to the *Associated Press Stylebook and Libel Manual* and the *Chicago Manual of Style* for any questions or doubt.

The Historical Association of Southern Florida disclaims any responsibility for errors in factual material or statements of opinions expressed by contributors.

A Word to Contributors

You are the lifeblood of *Tequesta*. Your time, energy and thoughtfulness in submitting a contribution are sincerely appreciated as we strive to spread interest in and understanding of our region's rich past.

Thank you. The Editors, *Tequesta*

S-Z

Categories: Nonfiction—African-American—Arts—Asian-American—Biography—Civil War—Culture—Ethnic—Hispanic—History—Jewish Interests—Multicultural—Native American—Regional

Name: Rebecca Eads, Managing Editor
Name: Dr. Paul S. George, Editor
Material: Any
Address: 101 W FLAGLER ST
City/State/ZIP: MIAMI FL 33130
Telephone: 305-375-1492
Fax: 305-375-1609
E-mail: hasf@ix.netcom.com

Texas Connection

Texas Connection

Frequency: Monthly
Circulation: 20,000
Coverage: Arkansas, Kansas, Louisiana, Missouri, New Mexico, Oklahoma, Texas
Audience: Adults only
About TC: *Texas Connection* is in its twelfth year of publication and is distributed to over 4,000 adult bookstores, video stores, newsstands and convenience stores in 7 states. Cover and interior photography is soft-core.

Seeking: Fiction of interest sexually to singles and couples, with an emphasis on couples interacting with couples, preferably originating in a locale within the geographic region we are distributed in. We shy away from fiction involving extreme bondage or graphic anal depictions, as it prevents our inmate subscribers from receiving issues with that content.

A statement that you are over the age of 18, accompanied with your signature is required.

We will consider re-prints.

Always seeking investigative reports on activities related to the alternative lifestyle of swinging (mate swapping).

Pay: $50-200. Average for fiction. Other negotiable.
Sample copy: $12 including first class postage
Categories: Erotica—Lifestyles—Sexuality

Name: Alan Miles, Assistant Editor
Material: All
Address: 8170 S EASTERN AVE STE 4-501
City/State/ZIP: LAS VEGAS NV 89123
Telephone: 800-250-7562
Fax: 702-270-6119
E-mail: firstpub@vegasnet.net

Texas Gardener
The Magazine for Texas Gardeners, by Texas Gardeners®

TEXAS GARDENER is interested in articles containing practical, how-to information on gardening in **Texas**. Our readers want to know specific information on how to make gardening succeed in Texas' unique growing conditions. All articles must reflect this slant.

Our bimonthly magazine reaches over 30,000 home gardeners and covers vegetable and fruit production, flowers and ornamentals, landscape and trees, technique and features on gardeners.

We will accept both technical and feature articles. Technical articles should explain how to do some aspect of gardening (like graft pecans or plant bulbs) in a clear, easy-to-follow manner, and must be *accurate*. All technical articles should refer to experts in the field. Accompanying artwork such as photographs, illustrations or diagrams are essential.

Feature articles, including interviews or profiles of Texas gardeners, new gardening techniques or photo features should relate specifically to Texas. We will not publish general gardening essays. Personality profiles may be on hobby gardeners or professional horticulturists who are doing something unique.

In-depth articles should run 8 to 10 double-spaced type pages (approximately 1,400 to 1,750 words) though we encourage shorter, concise articles that run 4 to 6 typed pages (700 to 1,050 words). All articles are reviewed on speculation. Writers should submit a query and outline of a proposed article first, unless they wish to send a manuscript they have already completed. We accept articles on PC disks written in Microsoft Word for Windows or WordPerfect 5.0. Writers should include a list of areas of expertise and a writing sample or copy of published work.

Rights negotiable. We pay $25 for submission to Between Neighbors and $50 to $200 for feature articles. Payment is made upon publication and includes two copies of the issue in which the author's article appears. We respond to queries within 6 weeks. Please—no duplicate submissions.

We accept only high-quality color and clear black-and-white photographs. Slides are preferable, but prints, transparencies and contact sheets may be acceptable. Model releases and identification of subjects are required. Rights negotiable.

Categories: Nonfiction—Gardening (Texas)

Name: Chris S. Corby, Publisher, Editor
Name: Vivian D. Whatley, Managing Editor
Material: Any
Address: PO BOX 9005
City/State/ZIP: WACO TX 76714
Telephone: 817-772-1270
Fax: 817-772-8696
E-mail: suntex@calpha.com

Texas Parks & Wildlife

Texas Parks & Wildlife magazine, published monthly by the Texas Parks and Wildlife Department, is "dedicated to the conservation and enjoyment of Texas wildlife, parks, waters and all outdoors"

Readership and Editorial Focus

Our readership surveys indicate a majority of our readers are around 50 years old, well-educated and enjoy various outdoor activities. They are primarily interested in learning more about the outdoors and how to enjoy it. Many of them hunt and fish, and a considerable number visit state parks with some regularity.

We hope to satisfy this reader group while attracting more younger people by featuring more active pursuits, such as bicycling, canoeing, hiking and the like. Although our magazine has expanded its editorial offerings to include many of these "nonconsumptive" activities, we still need the more traditional hunting and fishing stories, especially those that help the reader find good hunting and fishing opportunities. We believe many of our readers, however, are armchair sportsmen who don't get to hunt and fish as much as they would like. Therefore, they are well-served by general stories that deal in the basics, including plenty of how-to material as well as dealing with the esthetic pleasures of their sport.

Manuscripts

Diskettes in 3.5" size, either Mac or DOS format, are appreciated. If you would like to send a manuscript via modem, call Mary-Love Bigony, 512-912-7002. Name and address should be on each page of your manuscript. Queries should be brief, a page or less, but should fully explain why you consider the subject worthwhile, and how you intend to cover it. Please be aware that your copy is subject to editing and fact checking. Manuscripts requiring less editing bring more compensation to the author. All manuscripts are accepted on speculation; even those we have "assigned."

The magazine is seasonal in content and contributors should keep this in mind. Most stories are scheduled from six months to a year in advance. All work submitted for an issue must be in our offices no later than 90 days prior to publication. Assigned stories have a 90-day deadline unless other arrangements are made. A story schedule is available upon request.

Regular feature stories should be from 800 to 2,000 words, depending on subject matter. With lengthy features it's helpful to list details such as locations, addresses, telephone numbers and the like in a sidebar.

Manuscripts for departments such as Woods & Waters and Places To Go should be limited to 1,000 words or fewer.

All stories of a biological or historical nature will be checked for accuracy by Texas Parks and Wildlife Department experts. An edited copy will be sent to the author prior to publication. When a copy is sent to you for review, make your marks only on the copy we send you; do not retype.

Payment is upon acceptance, up to $600; payment for photos is extra. Please include your social security number for processing payment. Photos submitted with a story are a definite plus. If photos are not included, please indicate where and how they may be obtained.

Editorial Style

In general, we prefer straight text style stories, with first-person used only when it is an "adventure" or personal account situation.

There are several other matters of style you should keep in mind:

• Always use lower case for names of animals, unless they are named after a person, such as Attwater's prairie chicken.

• Use "said," not "says" when quoting people.

• Use the correct name of animals, such as "white-tailed deer," not "whitetail deer," although secondary reference of "whitetails" is fine. When in doubt, check a reference such as the Mammals of Texas or a bird field guide for correct usages.

• Scientific names are not usually needed, unless you deem it important in distinguishing similar species.

• Spell out months, "October 1, 1992," and use "1990s" when talking about decades, not "1990's or 90s."

• Avoid anthropomorphisms such as mama, papa, his and hers, babies and other human forms of reference when writing about animals.

• Avoid and/or and etc., and be sparing in the use of parentheses.

• Capitalize a person's title when it precedes the name, lower case when it follows the name. Don't capitalize occupational titles such as biologist or game warden.

• Capitalize governmental agency names: Texas Parks and Wildlife Department, but do not capitalize on second reference or when standing alone (department, state). Use of TPWD in second reference is acceptable.

• Spell out numbers under 10. Numbers over 999 need a comma (9,000, not 9000).

• Avoid abbreviations.

• Use words instead of symbols for percent and degrees.

• Italicize the titles of periodical publications (those published on a regular basis: daily, weekly, monthly, quarterly, annually) such as newspapers and magazines. Use quotation marks around the title of a book.

• Form the possessive of a singular noun by adding an apostrophe and an s, even if the word ends in s: Texas's capital, the cactus's thorns, the boss's desk.

• Although the plural of deer is deer, most animal plurals require an "s" at the end: six turkeys, not six turkey; four does, not four doe.

• If you're writing about a place to go—state park, museum or the like—please include information such as hours of operation, admission charges, how to get there and a number to call for more information. Maps also are helpful.

• When you use a person's name in the text, please put a check mark over it to let us know you have verified spelling.

• You need not provide a formal bibliography, but include a list of sources used for writing the manuscript, unless such sources are quoted in the text.

• Include a brief writer biography to be placed at the end of your story: "Jim Ned Brown is a professor at Wotsamotta University and freelance writer living in Vidor."

There are several good style manuals on the market. Our style generally tracks the Associated Press version with few exceptions.

All manuscripts are submitted on speculation, even those formally assigned.

Photography and Artwork

A. Transparencies in any format, 35mm and larger, are acceptable. Photographers may submit duplicate transparencies for consideration, provided that originals can be furnished on request.

B. Each transparency must be labeled, stamped or marked with the photographer's name and address.

C. A caption or description of each transparency must be included with every submission. All transparencies will be returned if this is not done.

D. Properly exposed transparencies are preferred. One—half stop overexposed is better than any underexposure. Do not underexpose for deeper color saturation.

E. Make it your goal to submit transparencies that are as good or better than those you see in our magazine. Edit your photos carefully before submitting. More is not better. Submit no more than 80 transparencies per story. Use separate slide file pages for each story submission so slides can be reviewed and those selected can be placed in the respective story folder. Those rejected will be returned promptly.

Photographs of a location such as a state park should evoke a sense of place. Photos should show an intelligent selection of subject and time of day. No pictures of mounted animals, please.

Artwork to be published will be on assignment to illustrate a specific story. Contact the magazine art director for size and medium limitations. Payment to be determined.

We occasionally use previously published photos in departments such as the letters page. Payment for use of the photos will be one-half the original payment.

F. Photo payment schedule:
Front Cover—$250
Wraparound and gatefold—$350
Other covers—$200
Inside color—per individual picture
More than a full page—$165
Three-quarters to full page—$140
One-half to three-quarters of a page—$100
Less than one-half page—$65

S-Z

Black-and-white—$50 for all sizes

Payment is upon publication.

The magazine retains possession of color separations for all photos and art published. No original separations leave the magazine, but duplicates are available at cost. Occasionally, other publications request the use of *Texas Parks & Wildlife* separations. No freelance material will be released without permission from the contributor, but it will be the responsibility of the contributor to arrange for compensation from the requesting publication.

Texas Parks & Wildlife magazine will exercise care in the handling of all materials received, but the department will not be responsible for loss or damage. Color separator is responsible for the care of color photos and art while in his possession.

Categories: Nonfiction—Adventure—Boating—Camping—Conservation—Environment—Fishing—Hiking—Hunting—Outdoors—Regional—State Parks—Travel—Wildlife

Name: David Baxter, Editor
Material: All
Address: 3000 S INTERSTATE HIGHWAY 35E
City/State/ZIP: AUSTIN TX 78704
Telephone: 512-912-7000
Fax: 512-707-1913
E-mail: magazine@tpwd.state.tx.us

THEMA

All short stories and poems must relate to the premise specified for the target issue (see below).

Upcoming premises and deadlines for submission:

The Premise

Deadline for Submission (postmarked)

Don't call me Thelma! March 1, 1998

Magnolias in my briefcase July 1,1998

The premise must be an integral part of the plot, not necessarily the central theme but not merely incidental. Fewer than 20 double-spaced pages preferred. Indicate premise on title page. Because manuscripts are evaluated in blind review, do *not* put author's name on any page beyond page 1. *Include self-addressed, stamped envelope (SASE)*. Response time: 3 months after premise deadline.

Payment: short story, $25; short-short piece (up to 900 words), $10; poem, $10; artwork (black and white), $10.

Short Stories: All types welcome—both traditional and experimental

What we like: a carefully constructed plot; good character delineation; clever plot twists

What we don't like: bedroom/bathroom profanity, unless absolutely necessary for advancing the plot. Why we object to bedroom/bathroom profanity:

• It's boring! Writers should be more creative than to depend on the same tired and dubious language crutches to express surprise, disdain, shock, bemusement, anger, sadness, and other emotions.

• Such profanity, used in excess, often serves as a camouflage for a weak plot. If the plot is good, the story can be told much more effectively in nonscatologic language even though a character in the story may be sleazy.

• Stories of lasting quality rarely need it.

Poetry: All types of poetic form welcome. No more than three submissions per theme, please.

What we like: poems that are thoughtfully constructed and carefully distilled.

What we don't like: sexually explicit wording. Subtlety is more creative.

Sample copies of THEMA are available at $8.00 per copy. Subscription rate: $16.00 per year for three issues. Make check payable to "THEMA."

NOTE: Each issue is theme-related—a different theme for each issue. Writers are encouraged to send for a list of upcoming themes before submitting manuscripts. Include a SASE with your request.

Categories: Fiction—Cartoons—Literature—Poetry—Short Stories

Name: Virginia Howard, Editor
Material: Short Stories
Address: PO BOX 74109
City/State/ZIP: METAIRIE LA 70033-4109
Name: Gail Howard, Poetry Editor
Material: Poetry
Address: PO BOX 117
Address: 1959 N PEACEHAVEN RD
City/State/ZIP: WINSTON-SALEM NC 27106
Telephone: 504-887-1263 (Virginia)

Thoughts For All Seasons
The Magazine of Epigrams

The guidelines for writing epigrams published in Vol. 3 of TFAS (1989 issue) are still applicable, but here we would like to focus on the criteria used by our editors in evaluating material submitted for review:

1) Is the statement (or question) original, or have we heard it somewhere before?

2) If the stem of the statement (question) is an old saw, has the author put an interesting twist on it?

3) Is the statement (question) intelligible, or are we uncertain about the author's intentions?

4) Is the statement (question) succinct, or is it overly wordy?

5) Is the statement (question) funny, or is it preachy?

6) If it is not funny, is it a profound and original truth?

7) If the statement (question) is silly, is it at least a good play on words?

8) Is it a dancing thought, or a sinking thought?

9) Is it sour grapes, or is it wine?

10) Is it outrageous, or is merely tasteless?

Readers who are interested in a more technical analysis may wish to refer to "A Taxonomy of Epigrams" by M. P. Richard in the Autumn 1989 issue of *Verbatim: The Language Quarterly*.

Categories: Humor—Language—Literature—Poetry—Society—Writing

Name: Prof. Michel P. Richard, Editor
Material: All
Address: 478 NE 56TH ST
City/State/ZIP: MIAMI FL 33137
Telephone: 305-756-8800
Fax: 305-665-7352
E-mail: PRICHARD@umiami.ir.miami.edu

The Threepenny Review

1. At present *The Threepenny Review* is paying $200 per story or article, $100 per poem or Table Talk piece. In addition, each

writer gets a year's free subscription and may buy extra copies of the issue in which his or her item appears at a discounted rate ($3.00 each, including postage).

2. All manuscripts should be submitted with a stamped, self-addressed envelope.

3. All articles should be double-spaced, with at least one-inch margins. Critical articles should be about 1500 to 3000 words, stories and memoirs 4000 words or less, and poetry 100 lines or less. Exceptions are possible.

4. Xeroxes and computer-printed copies are acceptable (letter quality preferred to dot matrix). We will not, however, consider simultaneous submissions.

5. Critical articles that deal with books, theater, films, etc., should cite these occasions at the front of the article in the following form:

Theater Piece by Playwright.
Theater, City,
Season 19
Book Title
by Author's Name, Publisher, Year Published, Price (cloth) (paper).

Remember that *The Threepenny Review* is quarterly and national; therefore each "review" should actually be an essay, broader than the specific event it covers and of interest to people who cannot see the event.

6. Writers will be consulted on all significant editing done on their articles, and will have the opportunity to proofread galleys for typographical errors.

7. Response time for unsolicited manuscripts ranges from three weeks to two months.

8. It is recommended that those submitting work for the first time to *The Threepenny Review* take a look at a sample copy beforehand. Individual copies are available from the publisher for $6.00 each (cover price plus $2.00 postage/handling).

Categories: Fiction—Nonfiction—Arts—Book Reviews—Dance—Drama—Film/Video—General Interest—History—Literature—Music—Poetry—Politics—Short Stories—Essay—Personal Experience—Memoirs

Name: Wendy Lesser, Editor
Material: All
Address: P.O. BOX 9131
City/State/ZIP: BERKELEY, CA 94709
Telephone: 510-849-4545

Tikkun Magazine
A Bimonthly Jewish Critique of Politics, Culture & Society

Bimonthly magazine covering politics, culture and society. 95% freelance written. Established in 1986. Circulation 20,000. Publishes manuscripts an average of six months after acceptance. Byline given. Kill fee varies, buys first North American serial rights. Editorial lead time two months. Submit seasonal material four months in advance. Reports in six months. Sample copy for $8.00.

Nonfiction: Book excerpts, essays, general interest, historic/nostalgic, humor, opinion, personal experience, photo feature, religious, political analysis, media and cultural analysis. Prints 25 manuscripts/yr. Send complete manuscript. Length: 2,000 words maximum.

Photos: State availability of photos with submissions. Reviews contact sheets or prints. Negotiates payment individually. Buys onetime rights.

Fiction: Contact Thane Rosenbaum, fiction editor, 60 W 87th, NY, NY 10024. Ethnic, historical, humorous, novel excerpts, reli-

gious, romance, slice-of-life vignettes. Prints 6 manuscripts/yr.

Poetry: Avant-garde, free verse, Haiku, light verse traditional. Submit a maximum of five poems. Long poems cannot be considered. *Tikkun* does not pay for poetry.

Tips: Internships are available. Write to *Tikkun* for information. Enclose a résumé and a self-revealing letter. Read magazine as writer's guidelines.

Telephone Contact: Jodi Perelman, Assistant to the Editor

Categories: Fiction—Nonfiction—Culture—Economics—Education—Environment—Feminism—Government—Humor—Jewish Interests—Literature—Poetry—Politics—Psychology—Religion—Sexuality—Society—Spiritual—Writing

Name: Michael Lerner, Editor
Material: All
Name: Thane Rosenbaum, Fiction Editor
Material: Fiction (to address above)
Name: Josh Weiner, Assistant Poetry Editor
Material: Poetry
Address: 26 FELL ST
City/State/ZIP: SAN FRANCISCO CA 94102
Telephone: 415-575-1200
Fax: 415-575-1434
E-mail: Tikkun@ncgate.newcollege.edu

Time Magazine

Does not accept unsolicited submissions.

Timeline

TIMELINE is an illustrated magazine published bimonthly by the Ohio Historical Society. TIMELINE's editorial content embraces the fields of history, prehistory, and the natural sciences, and is directed towards readers located in the Midwest.

Each issue features lively, authoritative, and well-illustrated articles, photo essays, and occasional reviews, and special departments.

Since its inception in 1984, TIMELINE has received numerous local, state, and national awards. Among them are Printing and Publishing Executive's Gold Ink Award, American Association of Museums Award of Merit, Ohio Museums Association Award of Excellence, Ohioana Award for Editorial Excellence, Printing Association of America Award of Merit, and American Association for State and Local History Award of Merit.

TIMELINE is distributed to subscribers, to members of the Ohio Historical Society, and to public libraries throughout Ohio. Single copies may be obtained from the Ohio Historical Society or from selected retail outlets.

Manuscripts

The editors are accepting manuscripts of 1,500 to 6,000 words related to the history; prehistory; and natural history of Ohio and to the broader cultural and natural environments of which Ohio is a part. Articles with a regional or national focus also will be considered. Suitable topics include the traditional fields of political, economic, military, and social history; biography; the history of science and technology; archaeology and anthropology; architecture; the fine and decorative arts; and the natural sciences including botany, geology, zoology, ecology and paleontology.

In addition to full-length feature articles, shorter, more sharply focused vignettes of 500 to 1,000 words will be considered.

Both feature-length manuscripts and short submissions should be susceptible to high-quality black-and-white or color illustrations and will be evaluated, in part, on that basis. Authors are encouraged to include photographic prints, transparencies, or photocopies concurrently with submission of manuscripts and will be expected to supply the editors with suggestions for supplementary illustration.

Unless otherwise specified, the publishers will purchase one-time North American serial rights to both manuscripts and illustrations. Manuscript fees are negotiable and will be paid upon acceptance. Photographs and transparencies will be purchased separately. The editors reserve the right to edit all accepted manuscripts to conform to the style and usages of TIMELINE. For further information in this regard, please refer to the guidelines.

Manuscript Guidelines

- Articles are intended for the lay person, not the specialist.
- Writing style should be simple and direct. Vary the arrangements of sentence elements, paragraph length, and sentence length. Avoid one-sentence paragraphs.
- Avoid jargon and non-standard English. Limit use of technical terms to those necessary for clarity and accuracy.
- Although formal documentation will not be reproduced, manuscripts should be accompanied by a list of sources and suggestions for further reading. Limit internal documentation.
- Graphics should be accompanied by captions that do not duplicate textual information. Authors are expected to provide suggestions for illustrations.
- Avoid first-person narratives except in special cases where the first-person point-of-view is an essential element of the manuscript.
- Avoid extended direct quotations and parenthetical materials. TIMELINE does not accept fiction, fictionalizations, or poetry.
- Where questions of style or usage arise, refer to *The Chicago Manual of Style*.
- Manuscripts should be 1,500 to 6,000 words in length. Longer manuscripts will be considered if suitable for serialization.
- If unsure of a manuscript's suitability, authors are encouraged to submit outlines in advance.
- If your manuscript is prepared on an IBM-compatible, Apple II, or Macintosh computer system, please indicate this in your submission letter.

Illustrations

TIMELINE features photo essays related to the subject areas described. In addition, some freelance photographic contracts for article illustration may be offered from time to time. Photographers and illustrators are encouraged to submit portfolios to the editors for consideration. Proposals for photo essays should be submitted in advance. Appropriate model releases are required.

Categories: History

Name: Christopher S. Duckworth, Editor
Material: All
Address: 1982 VELMA AVE
City/State/ZIP: COLUMBUS OH 43211-2497
Telephone: 614-297-2360
Fax: 614-297-2367

Times News Service

Thank you for your interest in writing for the Times News Service, which serves *Army Times*, *Navy Times*, and *Air Force Times*, with a combined worldwide circulation of approximately 300,000.

We are always interested in receiving free-lance articles that are informative, helpful, entertaining and stimulating to a military audience. We prefer that you first send a query, describing your purpose and goal. If you have an idea with a military angle and aren't sure whether we would be interested, don" hesitate to write us.

WHAT WE WANT: We are looking for articles about military life, its problems and how to handle them, as wells as interesting things people are doing, on the job and in their leisure. Keep in mind that our readers come from all of the military services. For instance, a story can focus on an Army family, but may need to include families or sources from other services as well.

You do not have to be in the military, or part of a military family, to write for us. But the stories we publish reflect a detailed understanding of military life.

WHAT WE DON'T WANT: We don't publish fiction or poetry. We cannot use historical essays or unit histories. We don't want articles that have nothing to do with the military. They are our oudience, and it must affect their lives in one way or another

RIGHTS: We purchase only first rights (worldwide). This means that the story, or portions of it, must not have appeared previously in another publication. We will not consider reprinting articles that have been published elsewhere. You may, however, submit an article that has been rewritten extensively. This also means that we have the electronic rights. Most of our stories appear on our websites, and those rights are included inour "first rights."

Payment for articles is made upon acceptance. Remember that once we purchase an article, it might be several months before we publish it. You cannot resell the article to someone else until we have published it. When we do, the article will appear simultaneously on the electronic service Military City Online, a division of Army Times Publishing Co. Your acceptance of payment is acceptance of these conditions.

CATEGORIES OF ARTICLES: Our R&R section appears every week with a variety of features devoted to leisure activities for military people. Many of those features are written by freelancers. They fall into the following categories:

TRAVEL: We look for 700 words on places of distinct interest to military people. We want to give readers stories they can't find in a general-interest newspaper. Rather than an overall piece on the Outer Banks of North Carolina, for instance, we recently published one on scuba diving around sunken warships in the area.

We want our travel stories to focus on a single destination or attraction, but would like you to include a short sidebar covering "other things to see" in the area.

Payment for story and sidebar is $100. (Photos are bought separately; see below.)

PEOPLE: We are looking for members of the military community who have done something unusual. Examples of recent people we have featured are a Navy doctor who took leave to provide free care to the Cheyenne Indians; two civilian colleagues who put together a critical guide to Pentagon eateries; and a retired serviceman and his wife who have made a name for themselves with a newsletter on how to scrimp. These stories should be 600-700 words; we pay $75.

ON THE HOMEFRONT: This feature consists of an essay of about 750 words in which a member of the military community relates a personal experience that would interest other military members or their families. Homefront pieces must be about the writer's own experience. No fiction is accepted. Payment is $100.

PHOTOS: We pay for use of original photographs. Color slides or prints are acceptable. By original, we mean photos that you own either because you took them or because you bought the rights to them. We do not pay for photos bought at a souvenir stand, for example. Generally our payment is $35, but it can be negotiated.

SPECIAL SECTIONS: The Times News Service also publishes regular supplements to *Army Times*, *Navy Times*, and *Air Force Times*. Topics include careers after military service, travel, personal finance and education. Stories generally should include military people. Payment is $150 to $250, on acceptance, for completed articles of 800 to 1,200 words.

Categories: Adventure—Careers—Civil War—Entertainment—Film/Video—Military—Money and Finance—Nonfiction—TV/Radio—Travel

Name: Editor, R&R
Material: All except material for supplements
Name: Supplements Editor
Material: Material for supplements
Address: Times News Service
Army Times Publishing Co.
City/State/ZIP: Springfield, VA 22159
Telephone: 703-750-8125
Fax: 703-750-8781

Today's $85,000 Freelance Writer

We welcome new writers to join our team of columnists and contributors. Please read the following guidelines.

Today's $85,000 Freelance Writer is a bimonthly magazine for writers who want to start a freelance writing career or expand their existing freelance writing business and make a lucrative (or steady) living writing for downsized corporations, large and small businesses, ad agencies, manufacturers, home-based businesses, organizations, and other commercial markets.

Each issue of *Today's $85,000 Freelance Writer* helps our readers locate freelance work, secure clients, market their services, break into different types of industries and commercial markets, write better or new forms of commercial copy, and operate a successful freelance copywriting business.

Our most popular topics that we publish include: Commercial Copywriting Business Start-ups; Getting Clients; Second Profit Ventures; Commercial Copywriting Experiences; Marketing Your Services to Clients; How to Build a Successful Commercial Copywriting Business; How to Promote Yourself and Your Business; How to Write Various Types of Copy for Clients; and many other topics, such as Internet marketing.

Although the magazine's content and focus is primarily commercial copywriting, we will consider other writing-related articles, such as writing and publishing newsletters, setting up a workshop or seminar, working as a journalist or as an ad agency staff writer, etc.

We publish only nonfiction material, mostly how-to articles, feature articles, tips and professional advice, freelance writing experiences, interviews and profiles. Many of our articles are written in first-person, subjective point-of-view; however, for longer articles (1,000+ words) it's strongly recommended that you use quotes from professional people and sources to supplement your point(s) of view. Word length will be negotiated when you speak with Brian Konradt, the editor.

All contributors who write for *Today's $85,000 Freelance Writer* are experienced writers, either freelancers or staff writers, who have three or more years of professional (workforce) experience. Because we don't pay commercial rates, many of our writers contribute their articles as a way to promote their writing talents, receive national publicity for their business, and use the published article as clip for their portfolio or for reprints.

Our positions for columnists are currently filled—however, we are still accepting material from contributors.

At this time we are accepting queries, which should summarize the primary thrust or purpose of your article. We also recommend you submit an outline of the article so we can better understand its contents.

We pay contributors .5 cents per word, paid upon acceptance, and we pay our columnists .10 cents per word, paid upon acceptance, plus free ad space. All contributors receive two complimentary copies. Additional copies can also be requested, at no cost.

We offer first North American rights, give you a national byline, and include your photo and bio. with your article. We also publish contact info., if you wish for readers to contact you about your article.

We advise you to read an issue of *Today's $85,000 Freelance Writer* to see specifically the type of content, format and information we publish. Because our readers are busy writers and entrepreneurs, we try to provide articles with bullets, breaks, white space, and pull-outs that are easy and quick to read, rather than long-winded sentences and puddles of paragraphs. If your article is long, break it up into smaller blurbs or smaller supporting articles and use subheadings or capsules.

You may obtain an issue of *Today's $85,000 Freelance Writer* for $4.95 from your local bookstore or newsstand or by calling us at 1-800-797-9027 or sending check or money order (payable to BSK Communications and Associates) to the address below. If we do publish your work, we reimburse you for the price of an issue.

You can submit your article idea(s) either by e-mail or by mail. Always enclose a SASE if you want a response via snail mail. Otherwise, you can speak to Brian S. Konradt, editor, to discuss your article ideas. We try to respond to queries as quickly as possible, usually in 1-3 weeks.

If a specific issue was not addressed in these guidelines, please call.

Categories: Nonfiction—Business—Copywriting—Writing

Name: Brian Konradt, Editor
Material: All
Address: PO BOX 543
City/State/ZIP: ORADELL NJ 07649
Telephone: 201-262-3277

Today's Catholic Teacher
The Voice of Catholic Education

Today's Catholic Teacher is a nationally circulated magazine for K-8 educators concerned with private education in general and Catholic education in particular. Issued six times during the school year, it has a circulation of about 50,000 copies and an estimated total readership of about 200,000. Although that readership is primarily classroom teachers, *Today's Catholic Teacher* is read also by principals, supervisors, superintendents, boards of education, pastors, and parents.

Articles: *Today's Catholic Teacher* aims to be for Catholic educators a *source* of information not available elsewhere. Subject matter may be any topic of practical help, concern, or interest to educators in Catholic schools. Examples include:

• Developments in curriculum, testing, technology, school relationships, creative teaching, school and community needs, classroom management, and administration as it affects the classroom

• National issues and trends which are of concern to Catholic educators

• Suggestions on the teaching of curricular subjects, including all academic areas as well as religion

Audience: The focus of articles should span the interests of teachers from early childhood through junior high. Articles may be directed to just one age group yet have wider implications. Preference is given to material directed to teachers in grades 4 through 8.

Style: The desired magazine style is direct, concise, informative, and accurate. Writing should be enjoyable to read, informal rather than scholarly, lively, and free of educational jargon.

Length: Feature articles fall into three general categories: 600-800 words, 1,000-1,200 words, and 1,200-1,500 words.

Photographs: Prints, slides, or transparencies in color or black and white are helpful. Write identifying information on back or accompanying paper. Photos will not be returned unless requested.

Payment: Paid on publication, payment for features is generally $100 to $250, depending on length and quality of writing. Photos or other illustrations may increase payment.

Sample Issue: Send $3 for mailing and handling.

Contact: Query letters are encouraged. Write, call, fax, or e-mail the editor for editorial calendar, current editorial plans, and specifications for computer submissions.

Categories: Nonfiction—Education—Religion

Name: Mary C. Noschang, Editor
Material: All
Address: 330 PROGRESS RD
City/State/ZIP: DAYTON OH 45449
Telephone: 937-847-5900
Fax: 937-847-5910
E-mail: PeterLi1@connectinc.com

Today's Photographer International

Published six times per year. International distribution, subscriber and newsstand circulation

The focus of *Today's Photographer Magazine* editorial is to share the success stories that prove you can succeed with your camera. The intent is to encourage a reader's involvement in photography. Inspiration, instruction and information is at the very heart of *Today's Photographer Magazine.*

WHO MAY MAKE EDITORIAL SUBMISSIONS?

Today's Photographer publishes the work of IFPO (International Freelance Photographers Organization) members *only*. If you are not a member, you may participate by sending your *membership/subscription* either with your editorial submission or any time prior to sending your submission.

Today's Photographer does not pay for photos published in the bimonthly magazine. The opportunity to be published is one of the most important benefits of IFPO membership.

Photo submissions are also considered for use in IFPO advertising or other publications. Should your photo be selected for such purposes, you will be contacted and offered a fixed fee for publishing rights for a specified period of time. These fees range from $50 to $150.

WHAT MAKES A GOOD EDITORIAL SUBMISSION?

First you should have quality photos to illustrate your story. Then review recent issues of *Today's Photographer* for editorial content to see if your story "fits." Your submission should be an interesting and factual story about your activities as a photographer. We want those step by step experiences, how to make money, operate with clients, find assignments, gain recognition or how to do anything else successfully. Your story should appeal to photographers. If you are unsure, the following information may be helpful:

Feature articles: usually focus on how to make money or gain access to important events. If you have been published or accomplished anything else noteworthy, your story could be a feature.

"On Assignment" articles: are a forum for you to share your expertise in any aspect of photography and be recognized for your

knowledge and business savvy. Frequent topics include how to start or expand a business, protect your rights or copyrights, work with clients, and take advantage of opportunities.

Technical how-to tips: allow you to writhe about special uses of equipment, supplies or processes. Unusual ideas, practical techniques and "build your own" projects work well.

Maybe you have a story with a different slant—submit it. You may inspire us to expand our editorial range. Our readers share a special bond in their passion for succeeding as photographers...and making money. Our resolution is to support that effort in every issue and to make sure that *Today's Photographer International* "works" for you.

GENERAL SUBMISSION CHECKLIST:

• Name, 5-Digit Member Number, Address and Phone Number.

• A photo of yourself (preferably with your camera).

• A typed or clearly handwritten copy of your Article, letter or editorial.

• *Prints* or *transparencies* that illustrate your story (color or b&w) with captions and proper identification. Include an inventory list of your photos. All photos must be clearly marked on the back with the member's name, member number, address and phone number. All photos must be clearly identified by title or an inventory number.

• Include information about yourself such as awards or publishing accomplishments.

• List of camera equipment and accessories you use.

• Kinds of film and photo processing services you use.

• A properly self-address envelope with correct postage if you would like you submission returned. Submissions not accompanied by a return envelope will be held on file for future consideration.

Your best chance of being published is when your submission may be kept on file for further consideration in future issues. Entries will be returned *only* if properly self-addressed envelope with correct postage is included with your submission. Although extreme care will be exercised, *Today's Photographer* will not be responsible for any damage or lost submissions. Submission of your story and photos gives *Today's Photographer Magazine* one-time rights to publish your story and photos.

Categories: Photography

Name: Vonda Blackburn, Editor
Name: Ralph Bryant, Editorial Staff
Material: Any
Address: PO BOX 777
City/State/ZIP: LEWISVILLE NC 27023
Telephone: 910-945-9867
Fax: 910945-3711
Internet: www.aipress.com
Nota bene: Membership in IFPO required.

tomorrow Speculative Fiction

First of all, we are now an electronic magazine, not a print one.

We buy first World English-Language electronic print rights, only.

But all submissions must be snail mailed to the address below.

We take *any* kind of science fiction, fantasy or horror, up to about 30,000 words—*more in exceptional cases*. We will also look at novels, for serialization, but we encourage you to have a recognizable name; first novels are very difficult to sell us. Use your own judgement, but always include return postage.

We take poetry and cartoons. We pay $25 per cartoon, and on esthetic impulse for poetry. We commission almost all our nonfiction, which will almost always be short.

We pay at least four cents a word, with a $75 minimum. Novels are a flat $2,000. Payment is on publication.

On fiction, submit a hard copy. On nonfiction, query us with a brief outline of the idea and a sample of your writing style. In either case, we'll ask you for a diskette, if you have one, *after* we accept your work.

We normally turn manuscripts around very swiftly; 48 hours, or less, in most cases. If your manuscript takes what seems a long time, chances are (1) it got lost in the mail, or (2) you did not enclose a stamped self-addressed envelope, or a self-addressed envelope and IRC coupons. Category (2) manuscripts are held for a while, but after three months they get tossed.

Don't enclose a covering letter unless it's to tell us the manuscript is a reprint or simultaneous submission. We don't take reprints any more, and we don't read simultaneous submissions. Generally speaking, covering letters are useless. Synopses of the story are *actively* counterproductive. And don't tell us about other sales, or how much your mother liked your work. Don't enclose a bio. We don't publish authors; we publish their work. If we buy the story or article, we'll ask the author for particulars.

We also never read single-spaced manuscripts, or manuscripts folded-over and stuffed into small envelopes.

And that's it. The best of luck to you.

Categories: Fiction—Nonfiction—Fantasy—Hobbies—Science Fiction

Name: Algis Budrys, Publisher
Material: All
Address: PO BOX 6038
City/State/ZIP: EVANSTON IL 60204
Telephone: 847-864-3668
Fax: 847-864-2840
E-mail: ajbudrys@tomorrowsf.com (no submissions)
Internet: www.tomorrowsf.com

Toy Shop
The Indexed Toy Publication

Submissions

Unsolicited manuscripts are welcome, but should include a self-addressed, stamped envelope (SASE) with sufficient return postage.

Content

Toy Shop is published biweekly and includes feature stories and columns in alternating issues. Articles are of general interest to toy collectors, focusing mainly (but not exclusively) on toys of the 1940s-present. Stories should focus on the collectibility of specific toys or manufacturers' lines. Features should not be too narrow, but rather hit the highlights of particular types of toys, such as board games, play sets, farm toys, or construction sets. Smaller features may focus on more specific topics.

Features generally run around 1,500 words for a short piece to 2,000-3,500 words for a longer feature. All stories are subject to editing for clarity, conciseness, and space considerations.

Current values of toys and other pricing information should be incorporated into features or placed in an accompanying sidebar. Readers want to know not only the historical information about toys, but also what is available and how much it's worth.

Other ideas for stories may include histories of prominent toy companies; interviews with collectors of note; or features on particularly unique, unusual, or large toy collections.

Rights and Payment

Krause Publications purchases perpetual but non-exclusive rights to manuscripts, meaning that after our initial publication, the author is free to sell the work elsewhere, but Krause Publications retains the right to republish the material.

Authors must warrant that each contribution is original work that has not been in the public domain or previously published, unless noted otherwise, and that each is free of unauthorized extractions from other sources, copyrighted or otherwise.

Payment for articles appearing in *Toy Shop* is based on a per-story basis at the editor's discretion. Payment is upon publication, unless other arrangements have been agreed upon. Contact Editor Sharon Korbeck for specific rates.

Manuscript Format

Hard copy submitted must be typewritten with the author's name, address, and phone number at the top. Computer submissions should be on a DS/HD disk in ASCII (text) format with accompanying hard copy.

Style

We follow the basic journalistic style guidelines in *The Associated Press Stylebook*. Consult Strunk & White's *The Elements of Style* for additional considerations.

Photographs

Authors are encouraged to submit color or black-and-white photographs (slides, prints, or transparencies) to accompany their submissions. If desired, photo credits will be given, and photos will be returned upon publication.

Categories: Collectibles—Consumer—Hobbies (toy collecting)

Name: Sharon Korbeck, Editor
Material: All
Address: 700 E STATE ST
City/State/ZIP: IOLA WI 54990
Telephone: 715-445-2214
Fax: 715-445-4087

Traditional Quiltworks

Please refer to Chitra Publications.

Trailer Boats

EDITORIAL PROFILE: As the name implies, *Trailer Boats* is written for owners and prospective buyers of trailerable powerboats-generally under 30' with no more than an 8'6" beam (no sailboats). Most of our readers are seasoned boating veterans who use their boats and equipment frequently.

Regular features include reports and evaluations of products useful to trailerboaters, including boat tests on current-model cruisers, runabouts, skiboats, fishing boats, pontoon/deck boats, etc. Related topics such as maintenance, seamanship, towing, navigation, electronics, repairs, watersports, etc., are also regularly covered, often in either a technical or how-to format. Each issue also includes travel destinations and a high-performance (racing oriented) article.

SPECIFICS: Boat tests, comparisons, and product evaluations are generally staff written. Technical articles are always in demand, wherein experts in the field either write them or are consulted for accuracy. When consulting "experts" it is best to go to more than one source—our readers catch errors. How-to articles should be explained in simple, easy-to-follow terms, but should not be superficial in content. Travel articles on destinations in and around the continental U.S. and its Canadian and Mexican borders, as well as Alaska, are welcome.

We prefer a hands-on boating approach to travel pieces, rather than a simple travelogue. The boating theme must permeate the story.

We don't want redone news releases from local chambers of commerce. The high-performance story in each issue is generally presented as race coverage, a personality profile, or a how-to, although general-interest pieces on new developments run occasionally.

Fishing articles should center around the boat—its special design, equipment and accessories, etc.—more than on fishing techniques. How to install downriggers or how to choose the right electronics are examples. An occasional fishing oriented destination story is also acceptable.

SUBMISSIONS: Study the magazine first. (Sample copies are available for $1.25.) Then query. Please allow 4-6 weeks for a response. We prefer submissions on computer disk (WordPerfect 5.1 or ASCII), accompanied by a type written hard copy of the manuscript. We also accept transmissions via modem. We desire complete packages, including headline, subhead, photos (and/or artwork) and captions. Travel articles should also include a map of the area.

PHOTOGRAPHY: *Trailer Boats* is a visually oriented magazine that uses photos with virtually all stories. We want sharp—no dupes, please—color slides or medium-format transparencies. First-time travel articles are usually assigned after we've seen the quality of photos. Please identify all photos with a tag line or caption. Photos are usually included as part of the editorial package, but when submitted separately, we will negotiate price. That includes the cover. Technical and how-to articles often utilize 5"x7" or 8"x10" glossy B&W photos, but it's wise to verify with the editor first.

PAYMENT: We pay on acceptance except for departments, which are paid on publication. Payment ranges from $100 for short fill pieces, to between $300 and $700 for features, depending on length, nature of assignment and quality of product.

Categories: Nonfiction—Automobiles—Boating—Outdoors—Travel

Name: Mike Blake, Managing Editor
Name: Randy Scott, Editor
Material: Any
Address: 20700 BELSHAW AVE
City/State/ZIP: CARSON CA 90746-3510
Telephone: 310-537-6322

Transitions Abroad

Tourists are those who bring their homes with them wherever they go, and apply them to whatever they see…. Travelers leave home at home, bringing only themselves and a desire to see and hear and feel and take in and grow and learn.
—Gary Langer, *Transitions Abroad*, Vol.1, #1(1977)

Transitions Abroad, in its 20th year of publication, is the magazine for independent travelers of all ages who seek practical information on international travel that involves "growing and learning"—by living, studying, working, or vacationing alongside the people of the host country. The title "Transitions" is meant to suggest the changes in perception and understanding as well as in place which result from such cultural immersion travel.

Our readers—most of whom travel on a limited budget to increase their time abroad and their exposure to the culture—are interested in active involvement rather than in passive tourism. Contributors write from direct experience and supplement their material with sidebars containing contact names, addresses, etc. Readers seek the practical details they can use to plan their own adventures. The more usable information presented in a concise manner, the greater the likelihood of publication.

What We Are Looking For

Features (one or two per issue) and departments provide practical information and ideas ("nuts and bolts") on immersion travel, work, study, or living in another culture. Since *Transitions Abroad* assumes that all travel abroad involves active engagement and learning, articles should be written with this assumption in mind.

As a resource guide, our purpose is to facilitate educational and culturally sensitive, life-enriching travel-not to distract or entertain. Information should be fresh, timely, and "unique"-not readily available in guidebooks or from tourist offices. We cannot use descriptions of first-hand experience that merely evoke local color from an outside observer's perspective and do not involve direct engagement with the people and culture.

As the editors are unable to check sources, *current and accurate information is essential*. Writers should be sensitive to the age range of our readers-from high school students to senior citizens. The average age is 40. Most travel abroad at least once a year. Most are college graduates; more than half hold a graduate degree.

What We Do Not Want in Features or Departments

Sightseeing or "destination" pieces that focus on what to see rather than on the people and culture; personal travelogues or descriptions of unique personal experiences (unless readers can use the account in making their own travel plans); "consumer-oriented" articles that objectify the people of other countries or that emphasize what visitors can get from them rather than what they can learn from them.

FEATURES
Feature Articles (1 per issue)
Maximum length: 2,000 words. Average length: 1,000-1,500 words. We edit tightly. Manuscripts should be typewritten. The author's name and address should appear on at least the first page of the manuscript.

Sidebars
Sidebars include information not in the body of the article: relevant names and addresses, telephone numbers, costs, other options similar to the ones you are describing, etc. *Well-researched supporting material in sidebars greatly increases the likelihood of acceptance.*

DEPARTMENTS
Information Exchange (10 per issue)
Readers are encouraged to exchange *factual and current practical information* on work, study, living, or immersion travel abroad. *Be as brief as possible.* Material submitted for other departments or as features will sometimes be shortened for inclusion in Information Exchange. *500 words maximum.*

Travel Resources and Program Notes (35 per issue)
News of publications, services, new travel programs, deals on transportation and lodging, and other useful information for the independent traveler. *250 words maximum.*

Responsible Travel News

News, events, or resources on culturally and environmentally responsible travel. *250 words maximum.*

Ecologically Responsible Travel (1 per issue)

Information on how local communities abroad organize and profit from ecotourism, plus details on responsible tour organizers. *1,000 words maximum.*

Worldwide Travel Bargains (5 per issue)

Current information on good value for money options (not necessarily cheap), usually by travelers just back from a "discovery." Be specific about dates, contacts, etc. in the text. (No sidebars.) *1,000 words maximum.*

The Working Traveler (3 per issue)

Informative pieces on working around the world. *1,000 words maximum.*

Activity and Special Interest Holidays (5 per issue)

Ways to combine a vacation abroad with a rewarding activity, from language study to mountain hiking. *1,000 words maximum.*

Education Abroad (3 per issue)

Columns within this department (primarily for students and international educators) include: Study Abroad Adviser, Work Abroad Adviser, International Careers, and Third World Focus. Guest columnists are always welcome. *2,000 words maximum.*

The Independent Traveler, The Learning Traveler, Living Abroad

Columns in these departments are shorter versions of features: Practical information on immersion travel, work, study, or living abroad. *500 words maximum.*

SUBMISSION PROCEDURES

A **query letter** is suggested but not essential. All material is submitted on speculation. We purchase one-time rights only; rights revert to writers on publication. However, *we reserve the right to reprint published articles in part or whole.* We will consider reprinted material from publications outside our primary circulation area. Since ours is not the usual travel publication, writers may want to review a recent issue of *Transitions Abroad* for style and content.

If possible, submit manuscripts on diskette or via e-mail (always accompanied by a paper copy). We can use materials submitted on disks formatted for IBM-compatibles (Microsoft Word or ASCII is preferred).

Include *black-and-white photographs* with your manuscript when available (see below).

Include a *short biographical note* at the end of each submission.

Include your *name, address, and telephone numbers* (day and evening) on at least the first page of your manuscript and on the back of each photograph.

Initial response time to manuscripts is usually four weeks or less. We often request permission to hold a submission pending final decision shortly before publication. We record and file each submission and take great care with material "on hold" awaiting the appropriate issue. Unless you need your manuscript or photographs returned immediately, please do not telephone. We cannot provide status reports by phone.

Payment

Payment is on publication, normally $1.50-$2.00 per column inch (50-55 words), sometimes more for repeat contributors. For the most part, our contributors are not professional travel writers but people with information and ideas to share; we are much more interested in usable first-hand information than in polished prose.

We are always looking for experienced writers to become regular contributors or contributing editors. Fees for regular contributors are negotiable. Two copies of the issue in which your story appears will be included with payment. Photos submitted with manuscripts pay an additional $10 each ($25 each for independent submissions).

PHOTOGRAPHS

We seek only black-and-white glossy photographs depicting the people of other countries. We cannot use color prints or slides.

What specifically are we looking for? Our greatest ongoing need is for good cover photos: interesting and engaging close-ups of people of other countries in a "natural" setting. Photographers are encouraged to review a copy of the magazine prior to submission.

We use only people on the cover. For those issues with a geographical focus our cover photo clearly represents one of the countries of that region. The subjects should be seen in the context of their normal lives, not as interesting curiosities for tourists. They should not appear in pain or distress.

Cover photos also require a particular composition to allow room to overprint the masthead (top two inches) and cover blurbs (left two inches) on a full bleed without interfering with the central image of the photograph.

We encourage photographers to send us not just a stock list but photocopies of selected prints for possible cover use. With these on file, we can contact them and tell them which photographs we would like to receive.

All prints must be identified with a caption as well as the photographer's name and address on the back of the photo. We return all used and unused photos if an SASE is provided.

Payment for photographs used in the text is normally $25-$50, for cover photos normally $125-$150, one-time rights only. Photographers are encouraged to submit stock or photocopies of stock for file as potential covers.

Categories: Travel

Name: Clay Hubbs, Editor
Material: All
Address: PO BOX 1300
City/State/ZIP: AMHERST MA 01004-1300
Telephone: 413-256-3414
Fax: 413-256-0373
E-mail: trabroad@aol.com

Travel & Leisure

Travel & Leisure is published monthly and has a circulation of 900,000 subscribers, plus limited newsstand distribution. Our readers are sophisticated, active travelers who look to this magazine for help in planning both pleasure and business trips.

About 95 percent of the magazine is written by freelance writers on assignment. Every assignment is confirmed by a contract; we buy only first-time world rights, and request that the work not be published elsewhere until 90 days after it appears in *T&L*. We pay upon acceptance of the article. Neither editors nor contributors may accept free travel.

How to Proceed:

Look at several issues of the magazine and become familiar with the types of articles published in the various sections, and the two regional editions, whose page numbers carry letters that indicate the region - E (East), and W (West).

Please note that a place is not an idea, and that editors are looking for a compelling reason to assign an article: a specific angle, news that makes the subject fresh, a writer's enthusiasm for and familiarity with the topic.

Service information is important to every destination article: when to go, how to get there, where to stay, where to eat, what to see and do. The reader must be able to follow in the author's footsteps, and articles are scheduled with that in mind - i.e., before the season in question. We have a three-month lead time.

Please do not telephone us about story proposals; instead send a query letter that briefly outlines the ideas (no more than three at once) being proposed. And please enclose recent clips of your published work.

It is rare that we will assign a major color feature to a writer with whom we have not worked. The best sections to start with are departments in the front and back of the magazine and the regional editions.

Categories: Nonfiction—Consumer—Fashion—Food/Drink—Recreation—Lifestyles

Name: Nancy Novogrod, Editor-in-Chief
Material: All
Address: 1120 AVENUE OF THE AMERICAS
City/State/ZIP: NEW YORK, NY 10036
Telephone: 212-382-5600
Fax: 212-382-5877
E-mail: tlquery@amexpub.com
Internet: www.amexpub.com

Travel News

• *Travel News,* published by Travel Agents International, a franchiser of retail travel agencies, has a monthly circulation in excess of 170,000. Its audience is the American leisure traveler. Articles should be 500 to 1,000 words, written with a positive slant. The idea is to encourage travel. The average printed story is about 1,000 words.

• Copy is due 60 days in advance of an issue. If a story is running in the December issue, it must be in by Oct. 1.

• Please do not send photos without a written request from the editor. The publisher assumes no liability for unsolicited photos. If you have photos to go with a story, send a list of cutlines.

• Generally, the editor does not return manuscripts. Make sure you keep a copy.

• Pay for *Travel News* and *Cruise News* depends on story length, quality and prominence in the issue in which it runs. Following are the pay guidelines. Keep in mind that they are subject to change and editor's discretion:

Cover story or cover photo $50 to $75

Inside story or inside color photo $25 to $50

Feature story or feature photo $30 to $50

Short story or B&W photo $15 to $25

• The editor recommends that all prospective writers review a sample copy before sitting down to write. To get sample copy, send a 9"x12" SASE with three first-class stamps.

• Stories should be written in Associated Press style, approximately 60 characters per line. The editor accepts stories on 3.5" Macintosh or IBM (ASCII text) diskette, or in hard copy via mail or fax. Hard-copy submissions should be letter-quality printouts (no dot matrix, please). *E-mail submissions may be sent to the address below.*

• **Put your name, address, phone and social security number on page one, with your name and page number on following pages.** Staple your pages, making sure the staple does not penetrate the type.

• Queries are preferred over unsolicited manuscripts. Send queries with a No. 10 or 9"x12" SASE (No envelopes smaller than No. 10.) that can returned with the editor's comments.

• **At no time should a freelance writer represent himself or herself as a staff writer for *Travel News*.** Additionally, unless you are told in writing that you have been "assigned" a story, assume you are writing on speculation. Assignment letters include a description of the story, your pay and the deadline. Without prior written notification, writer's are responsible for all expenses, including (but not limited to) postage, phone charges, travel costs, etc.

• **Phone calls**—Writers who have an established track record

will be given a special phone number and told the best times to call. Writers working on speculation or writers who have submitted unsolicited material will receive a written response to all correspondence within 60 days. **Writers who have not written for *Travel News* before probably will not get their messages returned.** Faxes are wonderful. If you need a quick response, fax your detailed question and provide a return fax number (U.S. or Canada). Under most circumstances you will receive a response by fax within two business days.

• *Travel News* has one important editorial rule: **All stories should encourage the reader to take a trip that can be booked through a Travel Agents International office.** Stories that feature destinations packaged by a T.A.I. preferred supplier will receive 90 to 100 percent of the editorial space each issue. Except cruise stories, avoid naming travel suppliers...hotels, airlines, tour operators, etc.

• Don't quote Mark Twain, the Diary of Christopher Columbus or any other historical figure. This travel-writing device has become trite. Also avoid references to dolphins as "frolicking denizens of the deep." The only thing worse is to use your spouse's name in your lead..."My wife Martha and I just loved our trip to Mexico." And lastly,

• Avoid first-person stories unless your experience is vital to the action. Honestly, *Travel News* readers are not interested in stories that begin... "When I rushed through the metal detector...," "As I settled into my seat....," "I never thought I would take a cruise..." or "As the captain switched off the 'fasten seatbelts' sign." Professional writers understand the difference between reader-based and writer-based prose. Before sitting down to write for *Travel News*, ask yourself if you are writing your experience for posterity, or are you writing to an audience that needs to be grabbed by the throat and told "Hey, there's something really important here you should read!"

Travel News

Editing Checklist

The following criteria are used to evaluate stories. Three or more no's will make a story unacceptable.

• Is there an SAS return envelope or postcard? (This is a must!)

• Does the story feature a major destination?

• Does the manuscript promote a travel product commissionable to travel agents?

• If a travel supplier is mentioned, is it a T.A.I. Preferred Supplier? (It's best to avoid mentioning suppliers, unless you have received prior approval from the editor.) This does not apply to cruise stories. You may mention the ship and the line, but it must be a T.A.I. Preferred Cruise Line to be considered.

• Is the lead strong? Does it encourage travel?

• Are all verbs strong and active voice?

• Have adjectives been trimmed to a minimum?

• Do sentences follow subject-verb-object format?

• Is the story in inverted-pyramid style with the most important fact listed first and the least important listed last?

• Will the story fit into the established Editorial Calendar within the next four months?

• Is there a strong transition between one complete item and the next?

• Are paragraphs short; no more than 50 words?

• Is the manuscript in Associated Press style?

• Is the manuscript formatted according to the Writer's Guidelines?

• Is the story less than 1,200 words?

Categories: Travel—Travel Agents

Name: Submissions Editor
Material: All
Address: PO BOX 42008

City/State/ZIP: ST PETERSBURG FL 33742-4008
Fax: 813-894-6318
E-mail: mattw@gte.net

Travelers Guide for Aspen, Snowmass, and the Roaring Fork Valley

Please refer to *Aspen Magazine*.

Tree Care Industry

Feature Stories

Text should be approximately eight typewritten, double-spaced pages with 1-inch margins. This equates to about 160 lines of type or 2,400 words. If possible, the author should provide TCI with illustrations, including but not limited to: color/black & white photos, line drawings, graphs, diagrams or tables.

Standard payment for a feature story as described above will range from $200 to $350 or more, depending upon the expertise of the author, amount of editing needed and relevance of the story to the issue in which it is published.

Short Features

Text should be approximately six typewritten, double-spaced pages with 1-inch margins. This equates to about 120 lines of type or 1,800 words. If possible, the author should provide TCI with illustrations, including but not limited to: color/black & white photos, line drawings, graphs, diagrams or tables.

Standard payment for a short feature as described above is $200 to $250.

Management Exchange Column

Text should be approximately three typewritten, double-spaced pages with 1-inch margins. This equates to about 60 lines of type or 900 words. Articles may be longer, but should not exceed 120 lines of type or 1,800 words. If possible, the author should provide TCI with illustrations, including but not limited to: color/black & white photos, line drawings, graphs, diagrams or tables.

Management Exchange articles offer practical advice on finance, sales, accounting, personnel, regulations, advertising and other matters of interest to small business owners in the green industry.

Standard payment for a column as described above is $150.

From the Field Column

Text should be approximately two typewritten, double-spaced pages with 1-inch margins. This equates to about 40 lines of type or 600 words. The author may provide a photo. Though artwork is not required, a colorful photo will increase the author's chances of publication.

From the Field articles are interesting stories from an arborist to a nationwide audience. Generally these are incidents, tense moments, small triumphs or safety lessons learned that would be of interest to our readers.

Entries must be submitted by field workers and must bear the name of the worker and his or her employer or they will not be considered for publication.

The standard payment for a From the Field article is $100.

Arborist Innovations

Text should be approximately two typewritten, double-spaced pages with 1-inch margins. This equates to about 40 lines of type or 600 words. The author may provide a photo. Though artwork is not required, a colorful photo will increase the author's chances of publication.

Arborist Innovations may cover a variety of topics: a standard piece of tree care equipment or machinery adapted for a special purpose or a novel way to increase sales or customer sat-

isfaction that would be of specific interest to tree care professionals.

The standard payment for an Arborist Innovations article is $100.

TCI Editorial Policy

Original artwork will be returned only if requested.

TCI buys first and exclusive U.S. rights for the green industry. TCI reserves the right to edit articles for grammar, punctuation, length and content.

Articles and artwork are due on the second-to-last Monday of the month, two months prior. For instance, an article submitted for the December 1997 TCI is due no later than Monday, October 20.

Tips for Freelance Writers

TCI is the official publication of the National Arborist Association. As such, it is a journal for and about the tree care industry. It is not a general interest magazine sold at newsstands. Our primary audience is arborists working for commercial and residential tree care companies. We also serve the landscaping, golf course and turf industries.

Writers without an expertise in arboriculture or horticulture may find the business features published in "Management Exchange" to be closer to their interest and abilities. Be aware, however, that competition for this monthly slot is most keen. Generic sales, marketing or business articles are rarely accepted for this feature. Management Exchange articles should be geared toward service-oriented small businesses, and should specifically address challenges faced by companies in the green industry.

Other avenues for contributors include stories in your area on tree care projects of national significance, or local stories that may one day have a national significance. Examples of these types of stories would be: local efforts to restrict spraying; research at universities near you on disease-resistant elms; a profile on a company that would serve as the starting point for a larger, industry-wide article; 24 hours spent riding with a storm clean-up crew; the effect of utility deregulation on the line clearance industry; unique or innovative educational/technical programs; insect infestation challenges; construction projects that saved or made the best use of existing trees; aerial rescues; and new product ideas for the tree care industry.

All articles submitted to TCI will be read. We highly recommend, however, that writers query us with topics and story ideas beforehand. Send a 50 to 75 word summary outline of your idea. We are able to offer guidance on direction and sources, and will discourage you from writing an article that we are unlikely to publish.

Tips for Arborists Without Experience as Freelance Writers

A thorough article requires research. Usually, that means working the phone for facts, photos or quotes to accompany your article. Remember to verify names and titles. A great article with everyone's name spelled wrong is not a great article.

Your job is to explain a facet of tree care in a way that keeps the reader interested and the information memorable. Don't try to be so entertaining, however, that you leave out the important facts and supporting information. One way to accomplish this is to use examples from the industry to support your drier facts and figures.

Keep in mind, also, that a color magazine is a visual medium. A creative use of photos, charts, numbers and diagrams is often the best way to make your point.

A good magazine article has an introduction, a central point or points and a conclusion. Don't just stop when you have reached 1,500 words or when you run out of new things to say. A summary, concluding paragraph or a link back to the lead is needed.

The lead should catch the reader's attention immediately. If you can't think of a good lead, consider starting with your best quote or statistic. Following the lead, the opening paragraphs should inform the reader about where the article is headed and why it is worth his time to read it.

The body of the article should flow naturally from one point to another. Your article is not a series of disconnected points, so lead the reader from one to another with effective transition sentences. Sub-headlines may help you and the reader to organize the information presented in a clearer way.

Your conclusion should wrap up the article's points without restating them. You may wish to refer back to the lead, or suggest areas for further research. Draw conclusions based on the facts and opinions you have presented.

Once you have finished, put the article aside. Read it from start to finish a day later to see if it still makes sense. Is there anything you want to add or cut? Would a reader who is knowledgeable—but without your expertise—understand what you have written? Do you have enough sources?

Finally, get a second opinion. Let someone who hasn't spent hours researching and writing the article read it for style and clarity.

We encourage writers to submit stories on disk in PC format on Word or WordPerfect. We are also able to accept stories via E-mail.

Categories: Arboriculture—Business—Landscaping—Money/Finance

Name: Mark Garvin, Editor
Material: All
Address: PO BOX 1094
City/State/ZIP: AMHERST NH 03031-1094
Telephone: 603-673-3311
Fax: 603-672-2613
E-mail: 76142.463@compuserve.com

Troika Magazine

Dear Freelance writer,

It was a pleasure receiving your inquiry regarding editorial matter for our award-winning* magazine, TROIKA.

TROIKA is a magazine for men and women seeking a balanced lifestyle: personal achievement, family commitment, and community involvement. Our readership is highly educated, achievement-oriented, and upscale, in the 30s-50s age bracket. The magazine focuses on issues such as the arts, health, science, human interest, international, pro bono, business, leisure, ethics and personal finance.

We are currently seeking professional, freelance writers interested in writing, with creativity and humor, for this target audience.

Typically, our Editorial Calendar for the year has a number of articles unassigned, and we are always open to reviewing proposals for story ideas. Please be aware that we only purchase finished manuscripts.

We are especially interested in writers looking to develop a long term relationship with a magazine named by Hearst Magazine Enterprises as "one of the top launches of 1994". Our standard fees are $250 for a one page column (750-1,200 words), up to $1,000 for feature length articles (approx. 2,500 words), payable 30 days after publication.

We purchase first North American rights; accepted manuscripts should be submitted in hard copy and on 3½" diskette, ASCII format (if IBM compatible) or MacWord (Macintosh); or forwarded via e-mail.

Should you find the above of interest, please feel free to send queries.

Sincerely,
Celia Meadow
Editor
*Top 50 Launches of 1994; Samir Husni, *Guide to New Magazines* (Hearst) Ozzie Silver; Best New Magazine Design-Consumer; over 100,000 circulation. Ozzie Silver; Best Cover Design-Summer '94-Consumer; over 100,000 circ.; Print Magazine Regional Design Annual; Best Cover Design: Spring '94, Fall '94, Winter 94/95. Insider Report Profile: 1997 Writer's Market.
Categories: Nonfiction—General Interest—Lifestyles—Literature

Name: Submissions Editor
Material: All
Address: PO BOX 1006
City/State/ZIP: WESTON CT 06883
Telephone: 203-227-5377
Fax: 203-222-9332
E-mail: TROIKAMAG@aol.com

True Love

True Love is a women's magazine written by the readers. Each month, we print between ten and twelve stories, several poems, and features such as "How I Know I'm In Love" and "Here Comes The Bride." The best way to learn our editorial style is to read the magazine itself and study the range of possibilities.

We look for true stories that involve real people and real emotions. Our subject matter ranges from light romance to inspirational to current social concerns. Some aspect of love and romance will usually figure in, but it need not be the primary focus of the story, Characters will often face a conflict or solve a problem in their lives that can inspire *True Love* readers.

All stories should be written in the first person. Stories can range from 2,000 to 10,000 words. Holiday submissions should be sent six months ahead of time. Our current rate of pay is three cents a word, and payment is made on the last Friday of the month the story is published. *No byline is offered. We buy all rights* to every story, poem, and feature, including those with pictures.

Due to the amount of stories we receive, it may take up to nine months for us to respond. But don't let that discourage you- we are always on the lookout for a good story! Don't forget to include a phone number where you can be reached, in case we have any questions.

As for poetry, we accept love poems of up to twenty-four lines. The current rate is $2.00 per line. For information about any of our columns, please consult a current issue.

Thank you for your interest in *True Love.* Please don't hesitate to call us if you have any more questions.

Good luck, and we hope to be reading your *True Love* story soon!

The Editors
Categories: Fiction—Confession—Romance—Women's Fiction

Name: Michele Berman, Associate Editor
Name: Alison Way, Editor
Material: Any
Address: 233 PARK AVE S
City/State/ZIP: NEW YORK NY 10003

Telephone: 212-979-4895
Fax: 212-979-7342

True Romance

True Romance features first-person narratives written for average, high school educated women. She is juggling family and work responsibilities, but family comes first. After a long day, she wants to read compelling, realistic stories about other women and how they have overcome obstacles. Stories must be set in towns, cities, and neighborhoods where hardworking Americans live.

Emotionally charged stories with a strong emphasis on characterization and well-defined plots are preferred. Our suspenseful stories deal with romance, families, marital problems, tragedy, peril, mystery, and Americana. The plots and characters should reflect the average American's value and desires.

Do not send query letters. Send completed manuscripts. Seasonal materials should be sent six months in advance. Mark the outside of the envelope: Seasonal Material. We do not accept multiple submissions. We buy all rights of our published materials.

Typewritten and letter-quality inkjet or laser printer manuscripts are acceptable. A dot-matrix printer manuscript is only acceptable if it is letter-quality. Unfortunately, the editorial staff cannot critique each manuscript.

Tips: Writers should read three or four issues of *True Romance* before sending submissions. Do not talk down to our readers. Timely, first-person stories told by a sympathetic narrator are appreciated. Dramatic stories and stories featuring ethnic characters are always needed, but stay away from stereotypical plots and characteristics.

Greatest Needs: Stories 3,000 to 8,000 words.

Terms: We receive a vast number of submissions, and each one is given careful consideration; therefore, we ask for your patience in receiving replies. *True Romance* reports back to writers in eight to twelve months. The editor reads all stories. We pay three cents per word a month after publication. We repeat, do not send multiple submissions.

Columns: "That's My Child" pays $50 for photo and up to 50 words about your child. Only the parents of the child may submit his or her picture. "Loving Pets" pays $50 for photo and up to 50 words about your pets. Photos must be in focus and no other people should be in the picture. "Cupid's Corner" pays $100 for photo and up to 500 words about you and your spouse. "That Precious Moment" pays $50 for 1,000 words about a unique personal experience.

Poetry: Look at poetry published in three or four issues before submitting. Poetry should be no longer than twenty-four lines. Payment is $10 to $30.

Good luck with your writing,
The Editors

Categories: Confession—Inspirational—Romance—Rural America—Short Stories—Women's issues

Name: Pat Vitucci, Editor
Material: All
Address: 233 PARK AVE S
City/State/ZIP: NEW YORK NY 10003
Telephone: 212-979-4800
Fax: 212-979-7342

True West

Please refer to Western Publications.

Turtle

Please refer to Children's Better Health Institute

Twins® Magazine

TWINS, The Magazine for Parents of Multiples, is a bimonthly, international publication that provides informational and educational articles regarding parenting twins, triplets and more. Thank you for your interest: We look forward to reviewing your submission.

• TWINS magazine consists of four to six features and 10 departments per issue. Features are 1,100 to 1,300 words and departments are 750 to 950 words including sidebars and additional materials. Please limit your manuscripts to these lengths.

• Because our readers are very busy, articles must be written in an easy, conversational style. Please study our format before starting an article. To make articles more readable, please break up copy with subheads. TWINS conforms to AP style.

• All department articles must have a happy ending, as well as teach a lesson or provide a moral that parents of multiples can learn from.

• TWINS accepts queries for feature articles. For departments, we accept either queries or manuscripts sent on speculation. Submissions must tell stories that teach lessons about family life with multiples. Subjects of interest include perspectives on being or parenting multiples, as well as child-rearing, family and social issues.

• Please send queries by mail to the contact listed below, along with a resume and samples of your work. Please indicate if you are interested in us contacting you for feature assignments.

• When submitting assigned articles, please include a hard copy as well as the file saved on a 3.5" floppy disk. To insure our computers can read the file, save it as an ASCII or "text only" file. If you would like your disk back, please enclose a self-addressed, stamped envelope. Please also include your signed contract, an invoice and a snapshot of you for your author biography. We cannot publish an article without a signed contract and cannot pay a you without an invoice. The invoice must have your name, address, payment amount and social security number.

• Fees are negotiated prior to publication and payment is made within 30 days following publication. A contract is sent after assignment is made.

• A byline is supplied, and one complimentary copy of the magazine is sent to each contributor following publication.

• TWINS Magazine purchases first North American serial rights.

Categories: Family—Parenting

Name: Heather White, Assistant Editor
Material: All
Address: 5350 S ROSLYN ST STE 400
City/State/ZIP: ENGLEWOOD CO 80111
Telephone: 303-290-8928
Fax: 303-290-9025
E-mail: Twins@businessword.com

Two Rivers Review

The goal of *Two Rivers Review* is to present the audience with an experience in poetry which is both readable and astounding, including work by the well-established and astonishing newcomers. All forms, lengths and styles of poems are welcome: our only nonnegotiable demand is that the work display excellence.

Poets who wish to submit work to *Two Rivers Review* should follow these simple guidelines:

495 •

• Please submit no more than four poems per submission.
• All poems must be previously unpublished.
• All poems must be typed (clean copies are acceptable).
• Include an SASE with sufficient return postage.
• No e-mail submissions, please.

Payment is one copy of the issue in which your work is published.

If you are interested in writing either reviews or essays for *Two Rivers Review,* please inquire first.

Copies of the premiere issue (March, 1998) of *Two Rivers Review* can be purchased for $7.50. Subscriptions to *Two Rivers Review* (two issues, spring and fall) are available for $15. To order, send a check or money order to Anderie Poetry Press, TRR, P.O. Box 85, Easton, PA 18044.

Categories: Poetry

Name: Philip Memmer, Submissions Editor
Material: All
Address: 215 MCCARTNEY ST
City/State/ZIP: EASTON PA 18042
E-mail: tworiversreview@juno.com

U.S. Art

Circulation: 55,000 nationwide, primarily through a network of 900 galleries
Editorial mission: to reflect current events in the limited-edition-print market; to educate collectors and the trade about the market's practices and trends
Frequency: monthly
Writer qualifications: We are open to working with writers whose background is not arts-specific. We generally do not look for art critics but prefer general-assignment reporters who can present factual material with flair in a magazine format. We also are open to opinion pieces from experts (gallery owners, publishers, consultants, show promoters) within the industry.
Freelance submissions: Mss. considered but queries preferred. Unsolicited articles not accepted for publication are returned (in SASE only) within four months.
Features: We run an average of six per issue, 1,000-2,000 words each. These are most often: 1) roundups of painters whose shared background in limited-edition prints illustrates a point-that is, artists who share a geographical region, heritage or currently popular style; 2) related to a current news event or art exhibition; 3) educational on the topic of various print media buying/selling practices and services available to help collectors make intelligent purchases.
Artist profiles (two per issue) concentrate on current information such as new prints or artistic styles, upcoming shows, anecdotes and future plans.
Feature illustration: Color transparencies are preferred. (U.S.ART keeps these materials for a month or two, then returns them to the source.)
Departments are staff-written. We consider news items and black-and-white photos for the Inside Prints, Showtime and New Releases columns. Local Color briefly profiles artists whose focus is regional, with a sidebar exploring the region.
Writer fee: U.S.ART pays between $400 and $550 for feature articles within 30 days of acceptance. Publication lead time is three to four months for features, two months for departments. To obtain a sample issue, contact the circulation department at the address, phone or fax below.

Categories: Arts—Consumer

Name: Sara Gilbert, Managing Editor
Material: All
Address: 220 S 6TH ST STE 500

City/State/ZIP: MINNEAPOLIS MN 55402
Telephone: 612-339-7571
Fax: 612-339-5806

Underground Construction

Please refer to Oildom Publishing.
Categories: Underground Construction

Name: Robert Carpenter, Editorial Director
Material: All
Address: PO BOX 219368
City/State/ZIP: HOUSTON TX 77218-9368
Telephone: 281-558-6930
Fax: 281-558-7029
E-mail: www.undergroundinfo.com

Unique Opportunities®
The Physician's Resource

EDITORIAL PHILOSOPHY
Unique Opportunities is a national bimonthly magazine for physicians looking for their first or next practice opportunity. Its goal is to educate the reader about how to evaluate career opportunities, negotiate the benefits offered, plan career moves, and provide information on the legal and economic aspects of accepting a position.

AUDIENCE
Unique Opportunities is distributed to 80,000 physicians who are interested in new practice opportunities or who are in their final years of residency.

TYPES OF ARTICLES
Unique Opportunities publishes feature articles that cover the economic, business, and career-related issues of interest to physicians who would like to relocate. Feature articles range in length from 1,500 to 3,500 words. Previously run stories include:
• MAR/APR 1997, *The Practice Quest*-A guide to finding the right practice.
• NOV/DEC 1996, *Profit or Patient*-Is the quality of care suffering under managed care systems?
• SEP/OCT 1996, *From Employee to Owner*-A step-by-step guide to buying into a practice.
• MAY/JUN 1996, *Compensation Chaos*-An evaluation of the status of physician income.
• SEP/OCT 1995, *Spreading the Word*-Marketing can help your practice reach new heights.

FORMAT FOR SUBMISSIONS
Submit articles on a 3.5" diskette compatible with Microsoft Word or ASCII text files from either a Macintosh or MS-DOS computer. Articles may also be sent via e-mail. Typewritten articles may be accepted. Call for details.

PAYMENT
Unique Opportunities pays within 30 days of acceptance. Standard rate is $.50 a word plus expenses up to $50. (Any expenses incurred over $50 must be approved at the Louisville office.) Rights: first North American, exclusive for 90 days after publication. Will not consider duplicate submissions.

Categories: Nonfiction—Careers (physicians)

Name: Bett Coffman, Associate Editor
Material: All
Address: 455 S FOURTH AVE STE 1236
City/State/ZIP: LOUISVILLE KY 40202
Telephone: 502-589-8250
Fax: 502-587-0848
E-mail: UNOP@aol.com

The Upper Room

You can write for *The Upper Room*.

The meditations in each issue are written by people just like you, people who are listening to God and trying to live by what they hear. *The Upper Room* is built on a worldwide community of Christians who share their faith with one another.

The Upper Room is meant for an international, interdenominational audience. We want to encourage Christians in their personal life of prayer and discipleship. We seek to build on what unites us as believers and to link believers in prayer around the world.

Literally millions of people use the magazine each day. Your meditation will be sent around the world, to be translated into more than 40 languages and printed in over 60 editions. Those who read the day's meditation and pray the prayer join with others in over 80 countries around the world, reading the same passage of scripture and bringing the same concerns before God.

Have God's care and presence become real for you in your interactions with others? Has the Bible given you guidance and helped you see God at work? Has the meaning of scripture become personal for you as you reflected on it? Then you have something to share in a meditation.

Where do I begin?

You begin in your own relationship with God. Christians believe that God speaks to us and guides us as we study the Bible and pray. Good meditations are closely tied to scripture and show how it has shed light on a specific situation. Good meditations make the message of the Bible come alive.

Good devotional writing is first of all authentic. It connects real events of daily life with the ongoing activity of God. It comes across as the direct, honest statement of personal faith in Christ and how that faith grows. It is one believer sharing with another an insight or struggle about what it means to live faithfully.

Second, good devotional writing uses many sensory details—what color it was, how high it bounced, what it smelled like. The more sensory details the writing includes, the better. Though the events of daily life may seem too mundane to be the subject of devotional writing, actually they provide the richest store of sensory details. And when we connect God's activity to common objects and activities, each encounter with them can serve as a reminder of God's work.

Finally, good devotional writing is exploratory. It searches and considers and asks questions. It examines the faith without knowing in advance what all the answers will be. It is open to God's continuing self-revelation through scripture, people, and events. Good writing chronicles growth and change, seeing God behind both.

What goes in a meditation?

Each day's meditation includes a title, a suggested Bible reading, a scripture text, a personal witness or reflection on scripture, a prayer, a "thought for the day" (a pithy, summarizing statement), and a suggested subject for prayer during the day (usually tied to the content of the story). Including all of these elements, the meditation should be about 250 words long. Indicate what version of the Bible is quoted in the text, and give references for any scripture passages mentioned.

Use clear, simple words and develop one idea only. Think about how you can deepen the Christian commitment of readers and nurture their spiritual growth. Encourage readers to deeper engagement with the Bible.

Include your name, address, and social security number on each page you submit. Always give the original source of any materials you quote. Meditations containing quotes or other secondary material which cannot be verified will not be used.

What should *not* go in a meditation?

Previously published material cannot be used.

Hymns, poems, and word plays such as acrostics or homonyms make meditations unusable because the material in *The Upper Room* is translated into many languages. Translations cannot do justice to these forms.

Also, very familiar illustrations ("The Touch of the Master's Hand," stories like George Washington cutting down the cherry tree) have little impact and should not be used. Remember that your personal experience provides unique material—no one is exactly like you.

How do I get started writing a meditation?

When you find yourself in the middle of some situation thinking, "Why—that's how God is, too!" or, "That's like that story in the Bible...," that can become a meditation. Excellent ideas come from reading and meditating in scripture, looking for connections between it and daily life. When you see such a helpful connection, here's a simple formula for getting it to paper:

1. Retell the Bible teaching or summarize the passage briefly.

2. Describe the situation you link to the Bible passage, using a specific incident. Write down as many details of the real-life situation as you can. For example, if you write about an incident when people were talking, write down what each person said.

3. Tell how you can apply this spiritual truth in days to come.

After a few days, look carefully at what you have written. Decide which details best convey your message, and delete the others. Ask yourself whether this insight will be helpful to believers in other countries and other situations. If you feel that it will, add any elements that are necessary to *The Upper Room*'s format. Then you are ready to submit your meditation for consideration for possible use in *The Upper Room*.

When are the deadlines?

We continually need meditations, and you can submit a meditation at any time. However, seasonal material should reach us fifteen months before use date. Below are due dates and special emphases for the various issues.

Issue Due Date Special Emphases

January-February—August 1 of second year preceding. (For example, 1997 should reach us by Aug. 1, 1996.) New Year, Epiphany, Ash Wednesday

March-April—Oct. 1 of second year preceding. Lent, Palm Sunday, Maundy Thursday, Good Friday; Easter; World Day of Prayer

May-June—Dec. 1 of second year preceding. Festival of the Christian home, Ascension Day, Pentecost, Trinity Sunday.

July-August—Feb. 1 of preceding year. Creative uses of leisure.

September-October—April 1 of preceding year. World Communion Sunday; God and our daily work.

November-December—June 1 of preceding year. Bible Sunday, All Saints' Day, Thanksgiving, Advent, Christmas

When will I know if my meditation is going to be used?

If your work is being considered for use, we will send you a postcard, usually within six weeks after receiving your work. Later, if your meditation is chosen for publication, you will receive a copyright release card to sign and return to us. It may be as much as a year before a final decision is made; seasonal material may be held even longer. We are unable to give updates on the status of individual meditations. All published meditations are edited. We buy the right to translate your meditation for one-time use in our editions around the world, including electronic and software-driven formats. We pay $15 for each meditation, on publication.

Where do I send my meditation?

Meditations cannot be returned, so please keep copies of what you submit. Please send no more than three meditations at a time.

Categories: Religion

Name: Managing Editor
Material: All
Address: PO BOX 189
City/State/ZIP: NASHVILLE TN 37202-0189
Telephone: 615-340-7252
Fax: 615-340-7006
Internet: www.upperroom.org

U.S. Airways Attaché

ATTACHÉ, the in-flight magazine of US Airways, is published by Pace Communications, Inc., for the passengers who fly US Airways. The magazine's 441,000 monthly copies reach 2.3 million readers. Articles for the magazine are written by in-house staff, freelance writers, and contributing editors. An average of 70 percent of the editorial is written out of house.

ATTACHÉ's mission is to bring the best of the world to the business traveler. The heart of the magazine is superlatives-the best of any category.

What We're Looking For

We look for cleverly written, entertaining articles with a unique angle, particularly pieces that focus on "the best of" something.

ATTACHÉ is a heavily departmentalized magazine with a preferred format for most departments and some features. Please study sample copies, which are available for $5 each from Ellen Kerr at our address. Checks must be made payable to Pace Communications.

Queries should be concise. Writers must include a stamped, self-addressed envelope with all correspondence to ensure a reply/return of their materials. We try to report on queries within six weeks.

Articles should be delivered as a printout accompanied by a diskette containing a text-based file. Delivery via an online service or through an Internet account is preferable but should first be arranged through the assigning editor.

Payment for articles is upon acceptance and the return of a signed contract. Amount of pay depends on length of article and varies somewhat according to experience. Due to our international circulation, we buy first global serial rights for most articles.

The Magazine

ATTACHÉ publishes 3-6 main features and a variety of departmental articles.

Features

A 1,500-word feature called *The Insider's Guide to the World* anchors the main editorial well. This image-heavy piece appeals to the business traveler who wants to find the lesser-known restaurants, shops, and attractions in a different major business city each month. The writer should be a resident of or live close to the featured city.

Other features are also highly visual, focusing on some unusual or unique angle of travel, food, business, or other topic approved by an ATTACHÉ editor.

Departments

Most of the departments are handled by regular columnists, but submissions will be reviewed.

Passions includes several topics such as "Vices," "Food," "Golf," "Sporting," "Shelf Life," and "Things That Go."

Paragons features short lists of the best in a particular field or category, as well as 400-word pieces describing the best of something—for example, the best home tool, the best ice cream in Paris, and the best reading library. Each piece should lend itself to highly visual art.

Informed Sources are departments of expertise and first-person accounts. They include "How It Works," "Keys to the City," "Home Front," "Improvement," "To Market," and "Genius at Work."

Photography

ATTACHÉ works solely with professional photographers and stock houses. We discourage writers from sending their own photos or stock lists. Please do not send unsolicited selections of photography. We assume no responsibility for the safety or return of material that we do not expressly request to receive. Only assigned writers who are also published photographers should submit color transparencies with their articles.

Categories: General Interest

Name: Submissions Editor
Material: All
Address: 1301 CAROLINA ST
City/State/ZIP: GREENSBORO NC 27401
Telephone: 910-378-6065
Fax: 910-275-2864
E-mail: AttacheAir@aol.com

USA Outdoors

We really do not have writers guidelines, but here is a brief description of what we are looking for:

How-to articles (generic) on bass and walleye fishing. First rights only. Must be accompanied by two black and white photos. 1,200 to 1,600 words at 4½ cents per word including photos. We accept hard copy.

Categories: Nonfiction—Fishing

Name: Linda Brett, Editor
Material: All
Address: PO BOX 118228
City/State/ZIP: CARROLLTON TX 75011-8228
Telephone: 972-380-2656
Fax: 972-380-2621

Vacation Industry Review

Editorial Policy: *Vacation Industry Review* is a bimonthly trade magazine published by Interval International, a global vacation-exchange company. The readership of VIR consists of people who develop, finance, market, sell, and manage timeshare resorts and mixed-use projects such as hotels, resorts, and second-home communities with a vacation-ownership component; and suppliers of products and services to the vacation-ownership industry. Interval International operates The Quality Vacation Exchange Network, and resorts featured in VIR should be part of that network.

We assign practically every article in VIR. Most ideas originate with us, although we make some assignments based on detailed queries. We accept practically nothing "over the transom" because few such submissions meet our very specific and specialized needs. VIR is *not* a consumer travel magazine. The standard destination piece about your cruise down the Mississippi River or your hegira to Helsinki has no place here.

We want articles about the business aspects of the vacation-ownership industry: entrepreneurship, project financing, design and construction, marketing and sales, operations, management—

in short, anything that will help our readers plan, build, sell, and run a quality vacation-ownership property that satisfies the owners/guests and earns a profit for the developer, marketer, and management entity. We're also interested in owners associations at vacation-ownership resorts (but not residential condos).

Our destination pieces are trade-oriented, reporting the status of tourism and the development of vacation-ownership resorts in a city, region, or country. You can discuss things to see and do in the context of a resort located near an attraction, but the "news hook" should relate to some business aspect of the vacation-ownership industry. If you're going somewhere special, tell us before you leave and be prepared to do some research along the way to get our kind of story.

Articles in VIR typically range in length from 1,000 to 1,500 words. Queries should include a suggested length.

To Break In: By way of introduction, write a letter to tell us about yourself and enclose two or three (non-returnable) samples of published work that show you can meet our specialized needs.

Computer Requirements: All manuscripts must come to us in some electronic form. Please tell us at the outset about your delivery capabilities. We prefer e-mail. Also acceptable is a 3.5" IBM-compatible disk, double or high density, with files in Microsoft Word (preferred) or WordPerfect. If you work in any other word processing software, please convert your files for us to Word, WordPerfect, or text (ASCII).

Photo Requirements: We don't pay extra for photos, but we may require them as a condition of purchase. Our needs include portrait-type photos of people quoted in your article and, when relevant, a selection of captioned color photos of the properties and places about which you are writing. Try to obtain images that recognizably depict the article's locale; avoid the generic beach, golf, or ski shot that could have been taken anywhere.

Resort and destination photos must be in color (transparencies 35mm or larger, or prints 5"x7" or larger). We prefer people photos in color, though black-and-white prints are acceptable. Images must be esthetically effective and must reproduce well in print. We will reject photos that are grainy or poorly focused.

Rights and Payment: Unless otherwise specified, we buy all rights to original material, on a work-for-hire basis. When we accept an article, we will ask you to sign a letter of agreement that confirms your understanding of these terms.

Upon written request, we will allow you to reprint your material without compensation to us, providing that you require any subsequent user to identify this material as having been reproduced from *Vacation Industry Review.*

We pay on acceptance at the rate of 30 cents a word (calculated after editing), plus legitimate expenses such as long-distance phone calls (but not mileage). To get paid, please submit an invoice that identifies the assignment and includes the fee due, itemized expenses (including a copy of your phone bill and any other relevant receipts), the total amount due, and your social security number.

Categories: Outdoors—Recreation—Timeshare Resorts—Travel

Name: George Leposky, Editor
Material: All
Address: 6262 SUNSET DR PENTHOUSE ONE
City/State/ZIP: MIAMI FL 33143
Telephone: 305-666-1861 ext. 7022
Fax: 305-668-3408
E-mail: gleposky@interval-intl.com
Internet: www.interval-intl.com

Valley Parent Magazine

Please refer to Bay Area Publishing Group, Inc.

Variations

Thank you for expressing interest in contributing to *Penthouse Variations* magazine. Your unique lifestyles and liberated erotic experiences make up our entire publication.

Contributions to *Variations* should reflect good grammar and the kind of language you would be proud to use with a good friend.

Variations is proud of its reader-generated sections and less experienced writers should feel free to make submissions to the editor on this basis. Although we do not make payments for letter material, the staff makes necessary editorial corrections and letters are published supporting most of the featured stories. Unfortunately, we cannot reply to each letter personally with sexual advice or the date of publication.

You may feel your material is good enough to qualify to compete with other professional writers. If you are making a professional freelance submission to be published as one of our featured stories, be sure to clearly indicate this in a cover letter to the editor. We pay up to $400 for an accepted, fully-revised manuscript. We publish 3,000-word first person narratives of erotic experience, squarely focused within one of the pleasure categories, described as an earnest contribution to a couple's sexual lifestyle.

Manuscripts take six to eight weeks to be read. They are rejected usually because of the quality of the writing or because the category described is unsuitable or oversold to us. Thorough perusal of several issues will show you categories most often used, as well as our style and vocabulary.

We guarantee confidentiality of all material, both letters and articles, Your name will never appear in print. In fact, we choose pseudonyms in order to avoid any inclination toward the writers libeling themselves in choosing their own.

Good luck with your writing.
The Editors
Categories: Erotica

Name: Submissions Editor
Material: All
Address: 277 PARK AVE 4TH FLOOR
City/State/ZIP: NEW YORK NY 10172
Telephone: 212-702-6000

Veggie Life

Veggie Life is a full-color food, health and organic gardening magazine for people who are interested in growing and eating a seasonal, low fat, meatless diet for good health. Veggie Life focuses on the positive aspects of living a meatless, healthy life without actively condemning opposing views.

Our purpose is to encourage and educate our readers in the areas of meatless cuisine, organic gardening and safe and sensible use of natural herbal remedies and nutritional supplements for maintaining good nutrition and health. *Veggie Life* is an international publication, published six times a year primarily in the US and Canada-January, March, May, July September, and November.

GENERAL REQUIREMENTS

• All articles must be credible and authoritatively written. We're not interested in personal opinion (product/company bashing), dogma, or religious beliefs. Provide us with clear, concisely written information indicating your expertise in a particular topic, and you'll have our attention.

• All articles must be accompanied by pertinent reference material for fact verification. Reference information must include full names, phone numbers, and any other necessary information. No article will be considered without sufficient fact verification information.

• Queries are preferred to completed manuscripts. If possible, send us a couple of clips or copies of previously published work. Please, no phone queries. Allow six weeks for a response.

• Manuscripts should be submitted in a typed format with proper identification. Include a few sentences about yourself for your "author blurb." For Macintosh or PC users, you may include a digital copy of the manuscript on a 3½" disk, along with a hard copy of the file. For online writers, e-mail text to the address below.

• Payment rate is based upon a predetermined scale at the discretion of the publisher. Quality, level of expertise, research complexity, and professional background are major factors that are considered in the determination of payment (see following features for more information). Payment is made half upon acceptance of the completed manuscript, and half upon publication. EGW Publishing owns all rights to manuscripts and artwork published in *Veggie Life* magazine.

FOOD FEATURES

Food features include a 300 to 500 word article and 8 to 10 recipes with short introductions. Facts about the nutritional benefits of the ingredients are encouraged and information that can be highlighted in a sidebar format is also welcome. Please observe the *Veggie Life* recipe style and write your recipes in the same manner (See below).

We're looking for a wide variety of delicious, low fat, vegetarian recipes. Regional, ethnic, special occasion, and down-home cooking are our favorites, but we're open to your original ideas. We're always looking for scrumptious low fat desserts, snack foods, appetizers, kid foods, and new ways to take the fat and meat out of old favorites. Some of our meatless recipes may contain dairy and/or eggs, but vegan options are regularly included, as well as recipes to accommodate special health restrictions (i.e. wheat-free or lacto intolerance).

All recipes accepted for publication will undergo a nutritional analysis. With few exceptions, all of the recipes in *Veggie Life* must have 30% or less calories from fat, and never more than 10 grams of fat per serving; ideally less.

Payment scale and conditions: 25 to 30 cents per published word for feature text and sidebar information, plus 25 to 35 dollars per published recipe. Recipe scale is based on type and complexity of recipe.

FOOD DEPARTMENTS

Meal in Minutes—100 to 150 word introduction followed by three recipes for a quick and easy meal. Meals must be ready on the table in 60 minutes or less.

Cooking with Soy—150 to 200 word introduction followed by three to four eggless, dairy-free recipes made with a soy product-tofu, tempeh, miso, etc. Remakes of old favorites encouraged.

HEALTH & NUTRITION FEATURES

1,500-2,000 word features on topics related to natural health, nutrition, and fitness as they relate to a meatless diet. Gender specific and age specific (i.e., children, adolescents, seniors) topics are encouraged. We look for author expertise and credibility. Solid authority and reference information is crucial. Pays 35 cents per word (or more for professional, credentialed authors).

HEALTH DEPARTMENTS

Preventive/Healing Foods—1,000 word article followed by four or five recipes focusing on eating to improve health and prevent disease.

To Your Health—200-500 word shorts on the latest-breaking news in the area of natural health and nutrition.

GARDENING FEATURES

1,500 word gardening features clearly related to growing vegetables, fruits, herbs, or other edible plants organically. Example topics would be: focus on growing a particular type of edible plant, basic gardening techniques, chemical-free pest control, space-saving and container gardening. Photographs are a strong plus in considering gardening submissions. Although we do illustrate some features, professional-quality photos are preferred. Payment: 25-30 cents per word.

GARDENING DEPARTMENTS

Featured Herb—800-1,000 words with two to three recipes focusing on a particular herb covering: historic origins; locality; folklore; medicinal and culinary uses; how to grow, harvest and store the herb.

Blooming Gardens—800-1,000 word feature on growing organic ornamentals. Photos helpful.

The Tool Shed—500 words about purchasing and using a featured gardening tool or product.

Veggie Life Recipe Guide

RECIPE TITLE:

The recipe title should be descriptive and creative. Avoid personalizing the recipe like "Aunt Betty's Marmalade."

RECIPE INTRO:

Give two to three descriptive phrases about the recipe's taste, nutrition, and/or compatibility with other foods, etc. Our editors will take it from there.

INGREDIENTS:

The ingredients should be listed in the order in which the steps refer to them.

Preparation should follow whole units (i.e., 1 large onion, chopped; 1 16-oz can kidney beans, drained) and should precede prepared ingredients (i.e., 1/2 cup chopped onions; 1 cup cooked kidney beans).

Spell out measurements (i.e., tablespoon, ounce, quart).

Our definition of a low fat recipe is one that derives 30% or less of its total calories from fat and no more than 10 grams of fat per serving. All of our recipes undergo a nutritional analysis and will be tested for this criteria before they are accepted.

• Low fat cooking tips: Cut back on nuts, oils, butters, and eggs. Sauté vegetables in vegetable stock or water instead of oil. Use pan sprays instead of oils or margarines.

• In most recipes, substitute 2 egg whites for one whole egg.

• Use non or low fat dairy products

List ingredients in the easiest unit of measure (i.e. 1/4 cup, not 4 tablespoons)

When possible, use the entire unit (can, package, carrot, or apple) in the recipe.

Provide can and package sizes—(1 15-1/2 ounce can kidney beans).

If an ingredient is optional, follow the ingredient with the word "optional" in parenthesis.

INSTRUCTIONS:

Keep the steps simple. Be sure to note the size and type of mixing bowls, cookware, and bakewear used (*in a large skillet; 9x13-inch baking pan*).

Use phrases that create a picture of the procedure or result in the reader's mind (*Chill until syrupy; beat until frothy; mixture thickens to the consistency of sour cream*).

Name each ingredient as they are to be combined rather than saying, for example, "Add spices."

Try to foresee questions, problems, or doubts. For example, if you have developed a cake recipe and the batter is unusually thin, say so.

Instructions for preheating the oven generally should be the first step.

Give specific and descriptive cooking or baking times. For example, Bake 20 minutes, or until puffed and golden.

Number of Servings:

List how many cups, cookies, slices, etc. per recipe and/or state how many servings per recipe; most of our recipes serve 6.

SAMPLE RECIPE

Pasta Fagioli Soup

"Fagioli" is the Italian word for "bean"—and there's plenty more good things to be found in this hearty meal in a pot.

1 large onion, chopped
6 cups vegetable stock or water
2 cloves garlic, chopped
1 cup diced carrots
1 cup sliced celery
1 28-ounce can crushed tomatoes
1 teaspoon each, dried oregano and basil
1 15-ounce can cannelloni or navy beans, drained
4 ounces ziti or penne pasta
6 ounces prepared veggie or soy burgers, crumbled
Salt and pepper
Chopped parsley (optional)
Parmesan cheese (optional)

1. In a large pot over medium heat, cook onion in 1/2 cup vegetable stock or water until softened, about 4 minutes. Add garlic, carrots, celery, tomatoes, oregano, basil, beans, and remaining vegetable stock or water. Bring to a boil, reduce heat to low, and simmer, partially covered, until vegetables are tender, about 15 minutes.

2. Add ziti and cook until almost tender, 7 to 10 minutes. Stir in crumbled burgers, and salt and pepper to taste. Cook until heated through, about 3 minutes. Garnish with chopped parsley and Parmesan cheese, if desired.

Makes 6 servings.

Categories: Nonfiction—Consumer—Cooking—Diet—Gardening—Health—Herbs—Physical Fitness—Remedies

Name: Sharon Barela, Editor
Material: All
Address: 1041 SHARY CIRCLE
City/State/ZIP: CONCORD CA 94518
Fax: 510-671-0692
E-mail: VeggieEd@aol.com

Verses Magazine

Verses Magazine is a quarterly publication dedicated to publishing both new and experienced poets, essayists and short-story writers. *Verses* is designed as a learning, teaching and publishing tool for writers, students and teachers alike.

In each issue of *Verses* we include poetry, prose and short stories from authors all around the world. We will also include information on poetry competitions, awards programs, workshops, seminars, writing groups and other educational programs. We will publish book reviews, articles on copyright, publication, etc. A sample issue of *Verses* is only $6. A one-year (4 issue) subscription is only $21.00.

THE LAUREATES PROGRAM
QUARTERLY LITERARY COMPETITIONS
General Guidelines

The *Verses Magazine* competition, the **Laureates Program,** is running continuously. There are three (3) categories of competition: Poetry, Short Prose and Short Story. Each issue will feature a "Poet Laureate," "Prose Laureate," and "Short Story Laureate."

• Each quarter, a winner will be picked in each of the categories and awarded $50 plus one (1) complimentary copy of the issue of *Verses* in which he/she was published.

• In addition, the winners will receive a handsome, personalized "Laureate" award certificate.

• In consideration of publication, each published writer will receive one complimentary copy of *Verses*.

• All published contributors in the magazine can purchase additional copies of the magazine at $3 while supplies last.

Judging

Entries will be judged by the editorial staff appropriate to each genre, based upon content, style, clarity, meter, ability to hold the reader's interest, aesthetic appeal and subject matter. All decisions are final.

Poetry Competition

• There are no line-limits or style limitations for the *Laureates Program*.

• Selected, non-winning entries will be published in *Verses*.

Prose Competition

• Prose pieces arc limited to 575 words.

• Selected, non-winning prose will be published in *Verses* at the discretion of the editors.

Short Story Competition

• Short stories may range from 600 to 2,500 words.

• Selected, non-winning short stories will be published in *Verses* at the discretion of the editors.

Submission Procedures

• Please send entries with the entry form below. *Use a separate entry form for each of the three categories*, (i.e., do not send both prose and poetry on the same form).

• Be sure to put your name and address in the upper left-hand corner of each entry. Write the name of the contest below your name and address, (i.e., "Poet Laureate," "Prose Laureate," "Short Story Laureate"). Improperly addressed and/or labeled entries will be disqualified.

• Send only copies of your works, not originals. Entries cannot be returned.

• If you would like confirmation that your entry has been received, either send your submission certified mail, return receipt requested, or enclose a self-addressed, stamped post card, and we'll drop the post card in the mail when we receive your submission(s).

• Submit with the appropriate reading fees if necessary.

Reading Fees & Number of Allowable Submissions

• Lifetime Members of the National Authors Registry may submit an unlimited number of *Laureates Program* entries in any combination of categories.

• Regular NAR members and Associate Members may submit up to 10 entries per quarter.

• Subscribers to *Verses* may submit up to three (3) entries per quarter.

• Contestants who are neither subscribers nor members must submit a reading fee of $2 per entry with every entry.

• Entries submitted may be in any single category, or any combination of categories.

• The fourth and subsequent entries in a calendar quarter must be accompanied by a $2 reading fee per entry.

ARTICLE/BOOK/REVIEW/FILLER GUIDELINES

There are no reading or submission fees for articles, book reviews or fillers. We pay on publication at the rate of 2 cents per word for articles and book reviews. Other fillers, quotes and comics may be published at the editors' discretion. All published authors will receive as consideration, a complimentary copy of the issue of *Verses* containing his/her work. We do not pay kill fees.

Submission Guidelines

• Send copies and not originals. Your submissions cannot be returned.

• Send your submissions certified, return receipt requested, or, include two self-addressed, stamped post cards with your submission. We will drop the first post card in the mail upon receipt to confirm that we have, in fact, received your submission. We will return the second post card when your work has been accepted or rejected. Please do not call to inquire whether or not we have received your submissions. Please allow three to six months for notification of acceptance/rejection.

• Be sure to put your name and address in the upper left-hand corner of page 1 of each article/review. Write "Article," "Book Review," or "Filler" below your name and address. Improperly addressed and/or labeled submissions cannot be considered for publication.

This form may he reproduced.

VERSES LAUREATES ENTRY FORM

Please enter the attached poems/essays/stories in the *Laureates Program*. I grant *Cader Publishing, Ltd* permission to print all listed/attached entries in *Verses*. I understand that I will receive cash compensation only if I am a *Laureate* winner. If my non-winning entry(ies) are selected for publication, I will receive one (1) complimentary copy of *Verses*.

Name _____
*Age _____
Address _____
City _____
State, Zip _____

*If you are under age 21 and your work appears in the "Youthful Voices" section, your age will be published.

[ ] **Yes, include my name *and* full address in *Verses* if I am published.**

Check category of work submitted. One entry form required per category.

[ ] **POETRY** [ ] **PROSE** [ ] **SHORT STORY**

Check one of the following:
[ ] I am a subscriber to *Verses* [limit 3 entries]
[ ] I am an Assoc. NAR member [limit 10 entries]
[ ] I am a regular NAR member [limit 10 entries]
[ ] I am not a subscriber or member. I have enclosed $2.00 per entry as a reading fee.

I have read, understood and agreed to the guidelines for regular submission to VERSES.

Contestant's Signature
X _____

Parent or guardian must sign if author is under 18 years of age.

All entries must be accompanied with this form. The Verses Laureates Entry Form may be reproduced. Failure to submit entries with this form properly filled out will result in disqualification of entries.

Categories: Fiction—Literature—Poetry—Writing

Name: Sharon Derderian, Executive Editor
Material: Poetry, Prose, Short Stories, Articles
Address: 36915 RYAN RD STE WG
City/State/ZIP: STERLING HTS MI 48310
Telephone: 810-795-3635
Fax: 810-795-9875
Nota bene: Entry fees required under certain conditions.

VFW Magazine

VFW Magazine is published by the Veterans of Foreign Wars at national headquarters in Kansas City, Mo. VFW is the nation's 29th largest magazine in circulation. It is published monthly (the June and July issues are combined), and has a readership of some two million.

Subscription is largely through VFW membership, which is restricted to honorably discharged veterans who received an of-

ficially recognized campaign medal. Founded in 1899, the VFW is the oldest major veterans organization in America.

TOPICS

Recognition of veterans and military service is paramount at the VFW. Articles related to current foreign policy and defense along with all veterans issues are of prime interest. Topics pertaining to American armed forces abroad and international events affecting U.S. national security are particularly in demand.

Some national political and social issues also qualify for inclusion in the magazine, especially if covered by VFW resolutions. New resolutions are passed each August at the VFW national convention and priority goals are subsequently established, based on these formal issue positions.

And, of course, we are always looking for up-to-date stories on veterans' concerns. Insight into how recent legislation affects the average veteran is always welcome. Anything that contributes to a better understanding of how the Department of Veterans Affairs operates is useful to fellow veterans. Positive, upbeat stories on successful veterans who have made significant contributions to their communities make for good reading, too.

Also, interviews with prominent figures are of interest if professionally done. No first-person accounts or personality profiles accepted.

We *do not* accept poetry , fiction, reprints or book reviews.

MANUSCRIPTS

Manuscripts should be no longer than five double-spaced typewritten pages (or about 1,000 words), depending on the subject. Simultaneous submissions and reprints are not considered. Changes are often required to make copy conform to editorial requirements. Absolute accuracy is a must. If little-known facts or statistics and quotes are used, please cite a reference.

Quotes from relevant individuals are a must. Bibliographies are useful if the subject required extensive research and/or is open to dispute. If you work on a word processor, please use a 40 column format and letter-quality print. Submit manuscripts on 3½" diskette, and please include a hard copy. Most word processing software is translatable, however, it is advised to also send in ASCII format.

STYLE

Clarity and simplicity are the two cardinal virtues of good writing. Originality, concrete detail, short paragraphs and strong words are essential. Write in the active voice, and avoid flowery prose and military jargon. Please feel free to suggest descriptive decks (sub-titles) and use sub-heads in the body of the copy. Consult *The Associated Press Stylebook* for correct grammar and punctuation.

PHOTOGRAPHS

Photos of exceptional interest are considered for publication. Payment is arranged in advance. Captions must accompany photos, including a separate caption sheet. Pictures accompanying manuscripts are generally for one-time use only. Please send along all relevant sketches, maps, charts and photos. Sources of additional artwork are also most helpful. Color transparencies (35mm slides or 2¼"x2¼") are preferred. But we can always use color as well as black and white prints (5"x7" or 8"x10").

PAYMENT

Payment generally ranges up to $500 per article, depending on length and writing quality. Commissioned articles are negotiable. Payment is made upon acceptance, and entitles *VFW Magazine* to first North American serial rights. Kill fees are paid if the writer is working on assignment and the article is not published.

QUERIES

Do not query over the telephone. A one-page outline (theme, scope, organization) of the proposed article will save the author and editor valuable time and effort in determining the suitability of a piece for *VFW Magazine*. Articles are submitted on a speculative basis for first-time contributors unless commissioned. Topics that coincide with an anniversary should be submitted at least four months in advance.

Use the query letter to demonstrate your knowledge and writing ability. Send along published examples of your work. Familiarize yourself with *VFW Magazine* before writing full-length features.

BIOGRAPHIES

Finally, please enclose a brief biography describing your military service and expertise in the field in which you are writing. Three sentences is generally sufficient. If you are a VFW member, let us know.

VFW Magazine looks forward to receiving submissions from members and freelancers alike.

Categories: Nonfiction—Associations—History—Military—Public Policy

Name: Richard K. Kolb, Editor-in-Chief
Name: Tim Dyhouse, Senior Editor
Name: David M. Gosoroski, Staff Writer
Material: Any
Address: 406 W 34TH ST STE 523
City/State/ZIP: KANSAS CITY MO 64111
Telephone: 816-968-1167
Fax: 816-968-1169

Via

Via (formerly *Motorland*) is the magazine of the California State Automobile Association (AAA). It is published bimonthly and goes to almost 2.5 million members in northern and central California, Nevada, and Utah. It is primarily a service magazine, with articles on travel, events, leisure activities, and matters of interest to the motoring public—car care, insurance issues, consumer information, legislation, and transportation.

Although most of our content is staff-written, we do buy a few freelance articles each year, almost all of them on travel. The purpose of our travel stories is two-fold: first, to encourage members to use the free-with-membership services of the CSAA, such as maps, trip-planning, reservations for hotels, tours, car rental, air and train travel. Second, we also consider the magazine a service in itself, and giving our readers ideas about places to go is part of that service. Our emphasis is on close-to-home travel in our territory and nearby western states, although we do occasional stories on foreign travel.

Competition is very keen; we receive between 1,200 and 1,500 freelance queries and manuscripts each year, and can buy only 12 to 20 of these (in other words, a little over one percent of stories submitted). Because our small staff is perpetually occupied with writing and editing, it may take us a very long time to respond to queries. In fact, most of our freelance stories are purchased from, or assigned to, writers already known to us for excellent, accurate, and dependable work.

If you are still interested, here are some guidelines: We are always looking for excellent writing. We like our stories to be personal, original, and literary, not the usual dry guidebook recounting of where-and-what. We want to sense the magic and wonder—or even squalor—of a place, to know what it means to go there, to know how the visitor might be changed by the journey. We urge you to read our magazine to get a sense of what we're looking for. We also need the service details which will help our readers go, too.

At this time, we are not giving firm assignments for features to writers new to us—even if they have an impressive portfolio of clippings. We prefer to see a finished manuscript. You may, of course, query to see whether we'd consider a story on a certain subject.

Our articles are short—between 250 words for our travel columns and 1,500 words for a feature. We pay from $150 to $700, depending on the research required, length and quality of the writing. We illustrate our articles with freelance photography, and you're welcome to submit your finest color transparencies with your story. We pay separately for any photography published.

We are unhappy with writers who get their facts wrong. Because of our small staff, we don't have the facilities for extensive fact-checking. We are also unhappy with writers who do not send SASE's with their queries and manuscripts. Also, we do not buy stories from writers who do any kind of public relations work with travel, automotive, or other suppliers which might be covered in the magazine.

Thank you for your interest in *Via*.
Bruce Anderson, Editor
Categories: Nonfiction—Automobiles—Consumer—Travel

Name: Bruce Anderson, Editor
Material: All
Address: 150 VAN NESS AVENUE
City/State/ZIP: SAN FRANCISCO, CA 94102-5292
Telephone: 415-565-2451
Fax: 415-863-4726

Vietnam

Please refer to Cowles Enthusiast Media, Inc.

Virginia Quarterly Review

1. For results only, include a #10 SASE. You *will not* be notified otherwise.

2. No simultaneous submissions are accepted.

3. Submissions per envelope are limited to two stories or five poems.

4. Articles, essays, memoirs, and short stories are usually reviewed within three weeks, but, due to the large number of poems we receive, results for these may be delayed three months or longer.

The Emily Clark Balch awards for fiction and poetry are made annually for the best short story and best poem *published* in the *Virginia Quarterly Review* during the calendar year. There are no specific guidelines except that submissions be of reasonable length (fiction: 2,000-7,000 words; no length restrictions on poetry).

Categories: Fiction—Nonfiction—Literature—Poetry—Politics

Name: Submissions Editor
Material: All
Address: ONE W RANGE
City/State/ZIP: CHARLOTTESVILLE VA 22901
Telephone: 804-924-3124
Fax: 804-924-1397

Virtue
Helping Women Build Christ-like Character

So you want to write for *Virtue*...

First know who we are: *Virtue* brings insight and inspiration to Christian women who want their faith to lead their lives. Recognizing the common journey, *Virtue* walks alongside readers in the everydayness of *life*, leads them into a deeper relationship with God, celebrates the joys found in relationships with family and friends, affirms the many ways women express their faith in ministry; offers hope when the path becomes difficult and unclear and encourages each one to continue the journey toward being everything God created them to be.

Meet our reader

Sandwiched between new roles of caring for aging parents and parenting budding-adult children, the *Virtue* reader (a true baby boomer) sees life as a journey to continually strengthen her marriage and relationships with family and friends. The place called home is important to her, but she cares most about deepening her relationship with God. She wants to live out her faith and seeks self-improvement in every aspect of her life: spiritually emotionally and physically. That's why she spends time each day in devotions, looks for new ways to study Scripture, tunes into the latest books and music exploring or inspiring her to hold fast to her Christian convictions, and looks for models of how to develop Christ-like character.

How to meet her needs

Every issue of *Virtue* is carefully planned to feed readers' greatest appetites: tools and ideas fostering spiritual growth, inspiration and ways to enhance intimate relationships, practical help for staying fit in mind and body and spirit; and news readers can use on ways to create homes that serve Christ's purposes such as exercising hospitality and strengthening families.

Features we look for

Stories on growing spiritually and personally enhancing relationships (with husband, children, parents, siblings, friends, brothers and sisters in Christ and especially with God); creating the place we call home and keeping healthy and fit. Our standard article length is 1,000 to 1,300 words and we're also interested in sidebars with practical tips, further reading and other resources that complement your story.

Department material and guest columns we look for

• **Family Matters.** A mix of the latest news and practical help for strengthening your marriage, parenting young adult children and parenting your aging parents. Each short article should be no more than 300 words; packed with news, statistics (noting sources), practical tips or resources. Space is precious so we regard highly news readers can use, not just information.

• **One Woman's Journal.** One woman's story (in first-person) of a struggle and how God works in it or what she learns of herself and her faith in the process. No more than 1,200 words.

• **Virtue in Action.** A compendium of news and trends regarding how virtues, values and character are viewed or evidenced in our culture, world and selves. No more than 200-words per short article, packed with statistics, sources, practical tips and resources.

About your stories

For the best way of knowing what we look for, see what we've done. Write for a sample issue of the magazine. Send a 9"x12" SASE with $3.00 postage. Please note: We do not publish our editorial calendar.

How to submit your article

We prefer queries first, except for One Woman's Journal, Virtue in Action and Family Matters. Be sure to include:

• a clear statement of purpose, noting how you think this story benefits the Virtue reader

• a working title

• a tentative, detailed outline

• anticipated length

• your qualifications for writing the article

• your name, address, phone/fax/e-mail and social security number

Please allow at *least* eight weeks for a response as our full-time, 2-person staff reads every manuscript as soon as possible.

How we pay and rights we buy

Our payment range is 15 to 25 cents per printed word. Assigned articles are paid within eight weeks of acceptance. Unassigned articles are paid within eight weeks of publication. We buy

first rights, on-line rights and rights to reprint material in compilation form.

When and where we publish

The magazine is published every two months (January, March, May, July, September, and November) by Good Family Magazines, part of Cook Communications Ministries (formerly David C. Cook Publishing of Illinois), now in Colorado Springs, Colorado.

Meet the staff

The *Virtue* team includes editorial director Brad Lewis, editor Laura Barker, art director John Hamilton, associate editor Debbie Coldough, associate art director Colin Miller, editor-at-large Nancie Carmichael (based in Oregon and traveling nationwide) and editorial assistant Sherry Dixon-Leonard.

Categories: Inspirational—Spiritual—Women's Issues

Name: Debbie Coldough, Associate Editor
Material: All
Address: 4050 LEE VANCE VIEW
City/State/ZIP: COLORADO SPRINGS CO 80918

Vision

VISION is a monthly newsletter for Christian educators. Its goals are to inspire, inform and equip teachers and administrators for greater service to Christ in the educational arena. In the words of CEAI Director Forrest Turpen, "It is an extended faculty room," a place of refreshment, dialogue, encouragement and guidance.

Our Readers

Readers of **VISION** are members of CEAI and look to its pages for organizational news as well as general interest educational articles. Our audience is comprised of approximately 80% public school educators. The rest of our readers are teachers in private schools, college educators, concerned parents and school board members.

Our Writers

We need writers who are:

• committed to the goals of CEAI,

• up to date on trends in contemporary education,

• faithful to the teachings of Scripture, and

• able to integrate secular and spiritual insights.

Our Editorial Needs

We invite writers to submit the following types of manuscripts:

• feature articles between 800-1,000 words, dealing with specific issues of interest to Christian educators. These may be written as how-to articles, personal experience pieces, educational philosophy/methodology, or documented reports. Payment: first rights, $40; reprint rights, $30.

• mini-features between 400-500 words that: highlight a holiday or special event and its classroom relevance, describe a successful teaching technique, or update readers on newsworthy happenings in the educational world. Payment: $20.

• interviews of 500-8,000 words with outstanding Christian educators. Payment: $20-30.

• classroom resource reviews between 100-200 words. These may be on books, curriculum, videos, visual aids, games or other items related to teaching grades K-12. Payment: $5.

• Reports of CEAI meetings and chapter activities. Payment: one-time discount of 20% on book or tape purchase from CEAI.

When you submit manuscripts, remember:

• We have a very limited staff. As a result, we may take several months to respond. You are welcome to inquire on the status of your manuscript when it has been with us 8 weeks or longer.

• We cannot guarantee that your article will be accepted.

• We may ask you to rewrite the article once in order to improve its focus or to cut its length.

• We appreciate receiving professional looking manuscripts with pages numbered and appropriate headers, sources noted in conventional end note style. (computer diskettes of manuscripts written with WordPerfect appreciated)

• We need a two-sentence author bio with your article.

• We reserve the right to edit material for length or content.

• We have the right to reprint your article in other CEAI publications.

• We accept previously published articles, provided the author informs us of where the article has appeared and verifies ownership of reprint rights.

• You are welcome to query us with article ideas in order to avoid submitting material we cannot use (send a brief description of the article, detailing its main points).

• Seasonal material must be received at least 4 months in advance.

Resources for Writers

Barnhart, Helene Schellenberg. *How to Write & Sell the 8 Easiest Article Types.* Cincinnati, OH: Writer's Digest Books, 1985.

Cheney, Theodore A. Rees. *Writing Creative Nonfiction.* Berkeley, CA: Ten Speed Press, 1991.

Herr, Ethel. *Introduction to Christian Writing.* Wheaton, IL: Tyndale House Publishers, 1983.

Hudson, Bob & Shelly Townsend. *A Christian Writers Style Manual.* Grand Rapids, MI: Zondervan Publishing House, 1988.

Jacobi, Peter. *The Magazine Article: How to Think It, Plan It, Write It.* Cincinnati, OH: Writer's Digest Books, 1991.

Lindskoog, Kathryn. *Creative Writing: For People Who Can't Not Write.* Grand Rapids, MI: Zondervan Publishing House, 1985.

Strunk, William & E.B. White. The Elements of Style. New York: Macmillan Publishing Company, 1972.

Guidelines for *Vision* Reviews

Vision welcomes reviews of books, videos and other educational products of outstanding benefit to public school teachers and administrators in Grades K-12. It is not mandatory that all products reviewed be explicitly Christian in nature, but they should be harmonious with a Christian world view and the philosophy of CEAI.

The essentials for a successful *Vision* review are:

• **Brevity**. Limit reviews to 100-150 words. Failure to respect this length will probably result in rejection of your review.

• **Breadth of reader interest.** Preference will be given to product reviews of benefit to the largest number of readers.

• **Engaging style.** We are looking for reviews with a warm and personal rather than formal tone. Think of your review as a letter to a fellow educator in which you want to convey your enthusiasm for the book or product and convincing points about why your reader could profit from it as well.

• **Helpful information.** Be sure to include the complete title, author's name, publisher, publication date and price. Give a basic summary of the work's purpose and intended audience. If possible, include an outstanding quote from the work (limit to one sentence). Include brief background information about the work's author.

Please *do not* send reviews of books that you have not read in their entirety. We depend on you to judge the entire work for its soundness and usefulness. *Do* refer to *Vision's* editorial calendar for clues as to how relevant or appropriate a particular review might be to a given issue.

For help in learning to write reviews, study reviews in magazines and newspapers. *Instructor* magazine offers the type of reviews we prefer.

Guidelines for *Vision* News Items

We need news items about CEAI members (special honors, achievements and milestones) and chapter events. These should be from 100-300 words in length and written in newspaper style (pertinent facts first with details given in descending order of importance).

When submitting news items, please include copies for our files of newspaper clippings or other research material used in writing your story. Photos are also accepted (black and white preferred).

Vision is looking for a few good articles on the following topics:

Creative use of the classics in today's classroom—Why & how

Working with single parents

Making the most of classroom volunteers

Encouraging creativity in your classroom

Cultivating professional relationships without compromising your faith

Teaching students responsibility

Multicultural teaching—tested ideas

Combating materialism in the classroom

A balanced approach to environmental education

Students who suffer from school anxiety—Who they are & how they can be helped

Coping with an "impossible" administrator (practical how-to with illus.)

How effective is affective education? (pros & cons)

Turning TV into an educational ally

When your children resent your students (time management/ priorities)

Make way for grandparents: cross-generational education strategies

We're always looking for:

• creative holiday curriculum ideas,

• inspirational teaching success stories, and

• CEAI outstanding member profiles

Keep in mind that our articles need a distinctively Christian viewpoint. However, please avoid even the appearance of preaching and cut all religious jargon! We need writers who are able to present topics naturally and who portray issues of faith as an integrated part of teaching.

Categories: Nonfiction—Education—Religion

Name: Judy Turpen, Contributing Editor
Material: All
Address: PO BOX 41300
City/State/ZIP: PASADENA CA 91114
Telephone: 626-798-1124
Fax: 626-798-2346
E-mail: ceaieduca@aol.com

Visions

Please refer to Communications Publishing Group, Inc.

VISIONS-International Arts

How to Send & Submit Poems to Magazines

As an editor and active poet I've learned a lot about the mistakes you can make in submitting poems. It's important to know the simple courtesies that make an editor not feel like trashing your work or returning it unread. It pays to check what the requirements are. One source for this information is the *International Directory of Little Magazines and Small Presses*. Among the things it will tell you are: 1. If they accept unsolicited mss. 2. Are copies acceptable. 3. Are there certain times when they don't read mss. 4. What are the length and number limits. 5. Usually it will also tell the kind of work they're looking for, how long the response time is, and if there's any payment (some don't even give copies, a questionable policy in this editor's opinion).

Most editors appreciate a brief vita (1/2 a page or less) and don't want to see another submission from a rejected author within a year (unless asked).

Before selecting poems try to review a sample of the magazine to see what they like (a sample of *VISIONS-International* is only $4.00). Here are some of our own policies:

1. We like to see 3-6 poems (rarely more than three double-spaced pages each).

2. We don't accept old fashioned, sentimental stuff. On the other hand we don't like the obscure, ultra-modern, often emotionless pap published by some well known academic type journals. (We don't mind rhyme but it's hard to do well.)

3. We like to see vita but don't let it influence our judgement and a "big name" means nothing to us.

4. If you don't want us to make editorial comments on your poems tell us ahead of time. If we do it's a compliment (means it was worth the bother).

Also don't forget that if you're going to get published the magazines have to survive (believe it or not most editors are poor and their magazines don't make money), so subscribe to at least a couple (*VISIONS-International* is only $15.00 per year for 3 issues).

Good luck, B.R. Strahan

Categories: Arts—Poetry

Name: Bradley R. Strahan, Editor
Material: Poetry
Name: Kathleen Oettinger, Editor
Material: Art
Address: 1007 FICKLEN RD
City/State/ZIP: FREDERICKSBURG VA 22405

Vogue

Thank you for inquiring about *Vogue*'s writers' guidelines.

Articles for *Vogue* are written in an upbeat, engaging manner to appeal to a broad-based, well-educated audience. Ranging in length from 500 to 2,500 words, stories are informative and thoroughly researched. Payment depends on source, length, and use.

Writers are welcome to direct article ideas and writing samples for consideration to the appropriate editor listed on the masthead.

We appreciate your interest in *Vogue* and hope that this brief outline of Vogue's editorial standards is helpful.

The Editors

Categories: Culture—Fashion

Name: Laurie Jones, Managing Editor
Material: All
Address: 350 MADISON AVE
City/State/ZIP: NEW YORK NY 10017
Telephone: 212-880-6910
Fax: 212-880-8169
E-mail: Voguemail@aol.com

Vogue Knitting

We have several article categories:

Technical articles:

1 to 2 pages (more if the subject warrants the additional length). This should include charts, swatches or other visual ideas.

Knitting Around the World articles:

Specific information on areas throughout the world. If possible, we would like slides, photos or samples of regional works. Covering 2 or more pages.

Short Stories:

Knitting-related human interest anecdotal short stories or essays. 1 page in length with ideas for visuals accepted.

We ask that the articles be submitted on a disk in either Microsoft Word or WordPerfect for PC or Mac. A one page article is considered approximately 1,000 words.

Please send any ideas along with an outline and perhaps ideas for visuals.

Categories: Nonfiction—Crafts—Hobbies

Name: Patricia Malcolm, Editor-in-Chief
Material: All
Address: 161 AVENUE OF THE AMERICAS
City/State/ZIP: NEW YORK NY 10013
Telephone: 212-620-2500
Fax: 212-620-2731
Internet: www.vogueknitting.com

Voyageur
Northeast Wisconsin's Historical Review

Voyageur: Northeast Wisconsin's Historical Review is a nonprofit magazine about the history and prehistory of a seventeen-county region of Northeast Wisconsin. Its coverage area extends from the Lake Winnebago region northward to the Michigan border. *Voyageur* is cosponsored by the University of Wisconsin, Green Bay; St. Norbert College; and the Brown County Historical Society. It is published twice a year, each June and December. Submissions may focus on social, economic, intellectual, political, legal or other historical issues and themes.

Manuscripts are blind-reviewed by three readers and will be returned upon request. Authors will be notified within three months.

1. **Submissions.** *Voyageur* is produced on Macintosh computers using Microsoft Word 5.1. Authors are encouraged to submit their works on a DOS-based or Macintosh disk and specify the word processing program used. Authors should also submit at least one typed or computer-processed copy of their manuscripts.

Manuscripts should be no longer than 5,000 words, not including notes and tables. Only with the author's approval, longer manuscripts may be edited down or split in two as a two-part series. Please indicate word count on your manuscript.

2. **Style**. Use *Chicago Manual of Style* (14th ed.) guidelines for all manuscripts. Do not use in-text references, i.e., (Weston, 1972). In ordinary text, whole numbers from one through ninety-nine are spelled out. However, when normally spelled numbers cluster in a sentence or paragraph, use figures. Use % instead of percent in reference to statistics; for rounded percentages write the word. Underline or italicize names of cities when using newspaper names, i.e., *New York Times*.

3. **Heading Styles**. First-level headings should be typed in bold and justified left. Second-level headings should be indented and typed in bold italic. Third-level headings should be indented and typed in italic. Note this example:

Method

Sample. A random sample....

Sampling Techniques. These techniques are useful when...

4. **Tables**. Do not duplicate material in text and tables. Tables and figures are helpful when they aid the reader in clarifying complicated or voluminous information or data.

5. **Photographs/Images**. *Voyageur* strongly urges authors to submit images or photocopies of images that could be used with their texts.

6. **Abstract**. Please include an abstract of no more than 150 words.

7. **Deadlines**. Deadlines for manuscripts submitted to *Voyageur* are June 1st and January 1st of each year.

8. **Copyright**. The contents of *Voyageur* are protected by copyright in the name of the Brown County Historical Society. Permission is freely granted by *Voyageur* and the Society to authors to have their submissions published elsewhere at a later date if proper credit is given to *Voyageur Magazine*.

9. **Remuneration**. Because of *Voyageur's* limited budget and nonprofit status, it is not possible to pay authors at this time.

If your manuscript is accepted, please submit the final copy on a 3½" disk in WordPerfect or Microsoft Word for the IBM-compatible or in Microsoft Word 5.1 for the Macintosh. Please submit images to accompany the story and include appropriate captions on a separate piece of paper. Also indicate the source of your images on the same sheet. Finally, please write a 100-word biography and include a photograph of yourself (head shot).

Thank you for your time and effort.

Categories: Nonfiction—History—Regional

Name: Walter Herrscher, Book/Video Review Editor
Material: Book/Video Reviews
Name: Victoria Goff, Editor
Material: History of Northeast Wisconsin
Address: PO BOX 8085
City/State/ZIP: GREEN BAY WI 54308-8085
Telephone: 920-465-2446
Fax: 920-465-2890
E-mail: voyageur@gbms01.uwgb.edu

Walleye Report

Please refer to USA Outdoors.

WE

WE welcomes article proposals relating to or about people with disabilities (from MS, hearing and sight impairment to heart conditions, cancer and AIDS, as well as emotional and so-called mental disabilities). Manuscripts should be preferably stored on disc for transmission on approval, outlining the story idea accompanied by a number of relevant hard facts on the subject, potential sources of information with qualifications for the story and sample(s) of writing.

It is essential to understand that WE is a consumer lifestyle magazine.

A) Articles must be entertaining and informative.

B) *Dining Out* and *Travel* articles must include extensive Access Reports *detailing* the accessibility of recommended nearby hotels, restaurants, museums/galleries, places of interest.

Stories accompanied by photographs/illustrations or ideas and sources of strong visuals will be given priority.

Categories: Fiction—Nonfiction—Adventure—Animals—Architecture—Arts—Automobiles—Boating—Business—Careers—Children—Computers—Consumer—Culture—Dance—Disabilities—Education—Fishing—Gardening—Government—Health—Hunting—Internet—Lifestyles—Martial Arts—Men's Issues—Money/Finance—Music—New Age—Outdoors—Photography—Physical Fitness—Public Policy—Recreational—Regional—Relationships—Religion—Science—Senior Citizens—Sexuality—Spiritual—Sports—Theatre—Travel (foreign)

Name: Charles A. Riley II, Editor-in-Chief
Material: All
Address: 372 CENTRAL PARK W STE 6B
City/State/ZIP: NEW YORK NY 10023
Fax: 212-316-7641
E-mail: CHARLES@webmagazine.com

Weatherwise
The Magazine About the Weather

Weather is one of the common denominators of our lives. It helps shape our culture, character, conduct, and health. It frequents the pages of our history and can change its course. It colors our conversations, folklore, and literature; it rains on our parades, awes us with its power and beauty, frightens us and sometimes kills us.

Weatherwise magazine shares this force of nature with engaging features and breathtaking photography. *Weatherwise* articles are anecdotal, analytical, and illuminating. They take a creative look at everyday occurrences and are accurate, authoritative, and easily understood by a large, non-technical audience that includes teachers, students, farmers, and travel agents. A free sample issue is available to prospective authors upon request.

Generally—Please initiate your interest in writing for *Weatherwise* by sending a query letter to Doyle Rice, Managing Editor, at the address below. Your letter should outline the direction of the article, give an indication of your writing style and perspective, and list potential sources and illustration possibilities. We will consider research topics, but do not publish academic papers. Authors are expected to write (or rewrite) in a conversational, magazine style suitable for a popular audience. Don't save your best examples and anecdotes for the last page.

We get a lot of queries and manuscripts that are nothing more than a blow-by-blow account of the biggest storm ever to hit the writer's backyard. Please don't be the next. Also, we get a lot of queries from writers proposing broadbrush articles on the Greenhouse Effect, the Ozone Hole, or El Niño. These are certainly valid topics, but you won't be able to do them justice in 2,000 words. Look for the story within the story, and emphasize the human element. Tell us about the triumphs, failures, and other anecdotes of the people you meet while researching your article.

Be aware of the *Weatherwise* production schedule and submit your story ideas and photos accordingly. We begin planning an issue at least six months before the cover date (i.e. August/September in February). In other words, think hurricanes in January and blizzards in July. We try to respond to queries within two months. Unsolicited manuscripts may be held indefinitely without response.

Please remember that queries and manuscripts under consideration at *Weatherwise* should not be submitted to other publications concurrently. Formal acceptance of an article will be extended after receipt of your manuscript. Payments to established authors are at the discretion of the managing editor and are made upon publication. A copyright agreement must be signed and on file at the *Weatherwise* office before payment is made.

Manuscripts—Feature articles are relatively short (1,500 to 2,500 words) and well illustrated. Departments-including software, video, and book reviews; essays on topics ranging from folklore to personal experiences; and simple experiments and demonstrations-should be between 800 and 1,500 words. Short articles (200 to 500 words) about noteworthy people, events, or trends will also be considered. Where appropriate, include a list of sources, both published materials and personal interviews. Authors also should include a list of potential illustration sources if no illustrations are provided (see below).

Include your name and phone number on everything you submit. Also, include other ways we can contact you-a fax number or e-mail address. Manuscripts should include at least a three-inch right margin for editing purposes. On the first page, include a word count. Authors are encouraged to send manuscripts on disk with hard-copy back-up. Our preferred format is Microsoft Word 5.1 for Macintosh. We also can convert most DOS-formatted files and disks.

You will be contacted by an editor when a specific publication date for your article has been chosen. We make every effort to consult with authors on editorial changes and provide a typeset galley of the final edited version for your approval about six weeks prior to publication. You will receive three to five complimentary copies of the issue featuring your article.

Illustrations—Published articles are often chosen as much for the quality and impact of the photographs as for editorial excellence. Authors must at least provide sources, leads, or ideas on illustrating an article. We will gladly research photo leads or commission artwork for an author whose article is worthy of publication. On the other hand, photos are rarely accepted without supporting text, even if that's just a short but enlightening discussion of the circumstances under which the photos were taken. We maintain a file of stock weather photos and prefer photos of recent events or unique treatments of familiar sights. Great photos that stand alone may be considered for our annual Photo Contest with permission and a signed entry form from the photographer. We do not publish cartoons.

Photographs may be submitted as prints, slides, or electronic files. Color is preferred. Please provide captions on a separate sheet of paper. Do not write on the backs of photos. Other illustrations (i.e. maps, graphs, charts, tables, etc.) should be submitted as finished, camera-ready art or on disk with hardcopy back-up that need not be camera-ready. Many software formats are acceptable.

Please feel free to call our editorial office to discuss your ideas or ask questions.

Categories: Environment—Meteorology—Science

Name: Doyle Rice, Managing Editor
Material: Features
Name: Kimbra Cutlip, Assistant Editor
Material: News, Reviews, Short Features
Address: 1319 18TH ST NW
City/State/ZIP: WASHINGTON DC 20036-1802
Telephone: 202-296-6267 ext.223

Weems Concepts
Special Collections

The following are SPECIAL future collections and will be published as soon as they fill up. If you find something of interest here, and would like to submit your work, please address it to the name of the collection (i.e., Christmas Collection, What If...Collection, etc.). This will assure proper placement and eliminate lost submissions. No reading fee. Send poetry to 36 lines max (sometimes longer), short stories to 2,500 words max. All books 8½"x11" in size, on white paper with a colored cover, spiral bound. A $5 "Editor's Choice Award" given to my favorite poem and story in each collection. Prices listed below are for USA & Canada. Overseas, please add $2.00 for postage—*payable to WEEMS CONCEPTS*.

WEEMS CONCEPTS is always looking for small art illustrations to be used with poetry and short stories. Send B/W ink drawings—no color. Artists receive a copy of any publication their work appears in. If your art work is used as a cover, you receive a copy of the publication, plus $5.00.

The 3rd HEAVEN COLLECTION seeks poetry & short stories for this spiritual collection. Title not selected yet. Price is $8.00 per book. Deadline not set yet.

The FUNNY BONE COLLECTION wants to make everyone laugh. We all need laughter in our lives, and this is the book to do it. So make me laugh. Make us all laugh. A great book for a shut-in, or someone in need of cheering up. Price, $8.00 per book. Deadline not set yet.

Price & Deadline not set yet for the following.

The SAGE COLLECTION seeks wise sayings and words of wisdom included in poetry and stories. Tell us why "a bird in the hand is worth two in the bush" or "a stitch in time saves nine," etc.

HEROES COLLECTION, open for submissions about anyone (person or animal) you feel is deserving to be called a hero. I'd especially like to hear from the veterans that fought for our country. Let your voices be heard.

OUR TOWN is now accepting submissions. Tell us about your town, big towns, small towns, the place you grew up in, the towns you like to visit, your neighbors, block parties, the girl next door, etc.

CHANGES will be a collection about anything that makes a difference...fashion, hair styles, the Berlin Wall, watching your health, our country's leaders, the death of someone famous, etc. Anything you can think of that made a difference because of a change.

PICTURE THIS gives you a chance to poetically paint a picture (or write a very descriptive story) of anything that pleases you, (in good taste). No porno or sex. Let your words be the camera's eye that leads us through an imaginary album.

2ND NATIVE AMERICAN COLLECTION is open for submissions. You need not be native but research the subject and send your best. Bring honor to our Native Americans!

WHAT IF...asks the question. It's up to you to answer with your poetry & short stories. We could use some deep thinkers here. What if we lived on the ocean floor, or another planet? What if we were ruled by women? What if there was no hunger or hopelessness? What if there was no sickness or pain? What if animals could talk? What if everyone had a clone? (Would it be fun or a hindrance?) What if we were born with the wisdom of our parents? What if we were angels living in Heaven; or even on earth? What if we lived during biblical times? What if we lived in a land with giants? Etc.

COAST-TO-COAST COLLECTION seeks poetry and short stories about something that happened, or an interesting place visited, during your travels. Not limited to USA. It could be anywhere; but keep it on land.

DEAR HEAVENLY FATHER seeks prayers only. Not just for seasons, but prayers for everything (i.e., Grace, bedtime, healing, guidance, travel, prayers of thanks, prayers for world peace, prayers for the sick, etc.).

BROKEN HEART COLLECTION needs poetry & short stories. Remember those poems & stories you wrote when your love affair went sour? Dig them out and dust them off 'cause they could see the light of day here. Remember your first love in high school? It lasted 2 weeks and you cried for months when it was over. Or did you heal your broken heart by finding another right away? Let us feel the pain you felt, or are feeling. When all this comes together, it might help you to laugh and move on.

ABOVE THE MOUNTAIN TOPS seeks poetry & short stories on anything happening between mountain peaks and Heaven. Flying, hot air ballooning, star gazing, other planets, space travel, etc.

SOMETHING TO THINK ABOUT seeks poetry & short stories on any subject that really makes you think. Such as altering DNA for perfect babies, cloning a superhuman race that could go to war against us. If God gave each of us a soul when we were created, do clones have souls too? Could we become a nation of "old" people, if the younger generation died off due to AIDS, unknown viruses, war, and population control? Do doctors really know what is good for us? It makes one wonder when they tell us that a new drug is OK to use, and change their mind as more testing is done, and then take it off the market. Do you feel like a guinea pig?

ANIMALS IN MY LIFE wants poetry and short stories. Happy or sad, but no cruelty to animals.

MY HEART'S DESIRE seeks poetry & short stories on anything you really, really want, or would like to see happen. Could it be world peace, an end to sickness and hunger, a date with a famous person, to become a millionaire, to marry the person of your dreams, etc.?

HOW DOES YOUR GARDEN GROW? needs poetry & short stories about anything that grows in a garden or on a farm, or in a pot. Tell us about the beautiful flowers, the trees, the crops, the harvest, the planting, the pickers, the good times and the bad. The joy and the hard work. Moving from farm to farm looking for work. Entering your "prize..." at the fair. Even windowsill gardening, your greenhouse, a sun space, etc. How does nature play a hand in this? How about cats and plants? How about a giant "man eating" plant? Tell me about plants that complement each other, and those good for the environment. This is an interesting subject.

A MOMENT IN TIME—if you could stop time and make it stand still, what moment would you hold on to? Would it be the day he proposed? the day you were married? the day your child was born? the day a loved one died? the day you won $1,000,000? Fact or fiction, I need poetry and short stories.

SAILING, SAILING will need poetry & short stories on rivers, oceans, lakes, and seas. Rafting, cruises, rescue, sunken ships, fishing, rapids, falls, etc.

A POTPOURRI collection will pick up all the poetry I especially like; but have no place to use it. This collection will probably take some time to fill.

There will be a Mystery Short Story Contest and a Children's Story Contest; but details are not available at this time. Cash prizes—Entry Fee required.

NOTE: Since this list is updated from time to time, it is best to contact me before submitting to be sure the deadline has not passed.

Best of luck to you with your writing.

Categories: Fiction—Native American—Poetry—Short Stories

Name: Kay Weems, Editor/Publisher
Material: All
Address: HCR-13 BOX 21AA
City/State/ZIP: ARTEMAS PA 17211-9405
Telephone: 814-458-3102
Nota bene: Annual contests require entry fees.

Weight Watchers Magazine

Weight Watchers Magazine is the proven authority on motivating self-improvement, self-image, and healthy, active living with an emphasis on weight loss and weight maintenance. Nearly 85% of our 4.8 million readers are women, most between the ages of 30 and 60. Our readers are affluent, sophisticated, well-educated, professional, and interested in living healthy lives. Here's what the editors of *Weight Watchers* look for when assigning articles:

LEAD TIME

Articles are assigned anywhere from three to eight months prior to scheduled publication dates. And for food articles it's even longer—six months to a year.

STORY IDEAS

Those lead times require that our stories be seasonal, long-range, and forward-looking. A trend of today can be old news in six months—or in six days. Please keep that in mind when developing queries. We're looking for fresh, innovative stories that yield worthwhile information for our readers—the latest exercise alternatives, a suggestion of how they can reduce stress, nutritional information that may not be common knowledge, suggestions from experts on skin care, reassurance about their lifestyle or health concerns, etc. In general, we cover the following topics: fitness, nutrition, psychology, health clubs, spas, beauty, fashion, style, travel, and products for both the kitchen and an active lifestyle.

FOOD QUERIES

Weight Watchers strives to offer new ideas and information to help readers make informed meal-planning decisions for a healthier way of eating—with more starch, dietary fiber, and water, but less fat, sodium, sugar, and alcohol.

SUBMITTING QUERIES

All story ideas must be submitted in writing. Please enclose a paragraph or two about each idea, your resume, and some sample clips. Because *Weight Watchers* is a national magazine, writers should submit clips from other national publications. The volume of mail we receive dictates that we guarantee a response *only* if you include a self-addressed stamped envelope with your query. If an issue is requested, you must include a check made out to Weight Watchers Magazine for $1.95 and a self-addressed 9"x12" envelope. We'll get back to you, even if by form letter, within about eight weeks.

Categories: Diet—Fashion—Inspirational—Internet

Name: Senior Editor
Material: All Except Food Queries
Name: Food Editor
Material: Food Queries
Address: 2100 LAKESHORE DR
City/State/ZIP: BIRMINGHAM AL 35209
Telephone: 205-877-6066
Fax: 205-877-5790

S-Z

Western Outdoors

WESTERN OUTDOORS covers freshwater and saltwater fishing like no other outdoor magazine. We are the West's leading authority on fishing techniques, tackle and destinations, and all reports present the latest and most reliable information. Our writers demonstrate the highest journalistic integrity and credibility, and accept responsibility for the accuracy of their work.

We look for new and extraordinary ideas. They must pertain to fishing in the West, involving species found in the West such as salmon, steelhead, trout, largemouth, smallmouth and striped bass, or tuna, marlin, wahoo, yellowtail, halibut and other Pacific Ocean game fish. They must be authoritative, with facts and comments attributed to recognized authorities in their fields. Keep your writing style creative, fresh, contemporary and entertaining; work hard to hold your audience's attention from lead to finish.

Photography and Graphics: We want the highest quality photos and artwork with which to illustrate articles. Authors supply photos, plus maps and sketches for guiding our artists. Color transparencies—35mm and 2¼"x2¼"—are preferred over prints.

We Pay on Acceptance: Articles, including manuscript and photos, $400 up; mini-features, $300; cover photos, $250. We buy first North American serial rights for articles; photos, one-time use.

Basic Tips: Writers who are new to us should submit only one query at a time. Send queries via mail; no faxes or phone calls. E-mail is OK. Because **WESTERN OUTDOORS** is distinct from other magazines, simultaneous queries are discouraged. All contributions receive reasonable care, but **WESTERN OUTDOORS** and the publisher cannot be held responsible for unsolicited manuscripts, photos or artwork.

Submissions, including queries, should include an addressed envelope and sufficient postage for return. We reply in two or three weeks. Lousy stuff goes back the day it's received. Queries and other submissions are answered with a personal letter or note from the editor.

Final Tips: You can become a regular **WESTERN OUTDOORS** byliner by submitting professional quality packages of fine writing accompanied by excellent photography. Pros anticipate what is needed, and immediately provide whatever else we request. Furthermore, they meet deadlines!

OUTDOOR WRITER HANDICAP

Where do *you* rate in the Editors' Consensus?

1. **TOP OF THE LINE**

The "never miss" bunch. Proven track record of consistently top-quality writing and photo support. Always gives 110% effort, displaying resourcefulness, creativity and credibility.

2. **BEST OF THE REST**

Solid producers. Just off the top pace. Dependable for good to excellent copy and photos. Always worth considering.

3. **BACKSTRETCH FLASHES**

The "once in a while" gang. Spotty track record. Not consistent, but occasionally surprises with excellent editorial packages. Sometimes good writing is negated by poor photography, or vice versa.

4. **ONE-SHOTS**

Usually strong in one or two areas, but not dependable for general assignments. Proceed with caution.

5. **HICKS & HACKS**

"Grind-outers" with limited ability, and not likely to improve. Formula writers with little chance of graduating to a higher rating. Not worth a second look.

Burt Twilegar
Founding Publisher
1960-1992
Categories: Fishing

Name: Jack Brown, Editor
Material: All
Address: PO BOX 2027
City/State/ZIP: NEWPORT BEACH CA 92659-1027
Telephone: 714-546-4370
E-mail: WOUTDOORS@aol.com

Western Publications
Publishers of Western Americana Since 1953

TRUE WEST and OLD WEST magazines publish nonfiction articles on the history of the American West from prehistory to 1930. More recent topics may be used if they have a historical angle or retain the Old West flavor of trail dust and saddle leather.

Our readers are predominantly male, forty-five years of age or older, from rural areas and small towns. Nearly all have graduated from high school, and slightly more than half have attended college. They are knowledgeable about western history and ranching and want articles to be informative and entertaining.

We cover all states west of the Mississippi and all areas of western history—Native Americans, trappers, miners, cowboys, ranchers, farmers, pioneers, the military, ghost towns, lost mines, women, and minorities. Current, travel-oriented stories work well if they have a historical angle. We especially need good western humor and stories on lesser-known people and events. If widely-known topics are used, the article should include newly discovered information or take a fresh approach to the subject. We cannot use anything on western movies, television, or fiction.

Historical accuracy and strict adherence to the facts are essential. We much prefer material based on primary sources (archives, court records, documents, contemporary newspapers, and first person accounts) to those that rely mainly on secondary sources (published books, magazines, and journals). We occasionally use first person reminiscences, but proper names and dates must be accurate and double-checked by the author. We do not want dialogue unless it can be documented, and we do not use fictionalized treatments of historical subjects. Manuscripts other than first person recollections should be accompanied by a bibliographic list of sources.

We usually need from four to eight photos for each story, and we rely on writers to provide them. It is best to send photocopies of available photos with your manuscript. Let us know from whom the photos are available, the cost of prints, use fees, etc. When we accept your manuscript, we will let you know which photos we want to use. We will reimburse you for your photo expenses. If photos are unavailable for an especially good article, we will have it illustrated by an artist. Appropriate maps enhance our articles, and we appreciate receiving sketches for our artists to work from.

Nearly all our articles are written by freelance writers on speculation. A byline is always given, and photos and illustrations are credited. Writers are given an opportunity to proofread galleys before their articles go to press. We will consider unsolicited manuscripts, but it is best to query us in writing first. Manuscripts are processed in the order received, usually within six to eight weeks. We pay from three to five cents per word, on acceptance. Rate of pay depends entirely on the quality of the writing and the depth of the research. On publication of your article, we will return your photos and send two complimentary copies of the issue.

Your name, address, telephone number, social security number, and an approximate word count should appear on the first page of your manuscript, along with your byline exactly as you want it to appear. Maximum length is 4,500 words; ideal length to break in is about 2,500 words. We also take shorter pieces, especially humor, ranging from 300 to 1,500 words.

To judge our needs, consult our back issues; a 1953-1980 index is available for purchase. "Writing the Short Western Article," by John Joerschke, in *The Western Writer's Handbook*, James L. Collins, editor (Boulder, Colorado: Johnson Books, 1987), explains our approach in detail.

Categories: History—Native American—Travel—Western

Name: Marcus Huff, Editor
Material: All
Address: PO BOX 2107
City/State/ZIP: STILLWATER OK 74076
Telephone: 405-743-3370
E-mail: Western@cowboy.net

Western RV News

The goal of *Western RV News* is to further the RV lifestyle. Editorial is aimed at both newcomers and seasoned RVers, providing them with practical information on the proper use and care of their vehicles, unusual and exciting destinations to explore, unique uses of RVs and the latest news of the RV world.

Western RV News accepts for review material that pertains directly to the RV lifestyle. Articles must be well-written in an informative and interesting manner. Of particular interest are articles that depict interesting and/or unusual uses or adaptations of RVs.

Destination pieces preferably should be of less publicized locales and should include, usually in a sidebar, clear directions, if needed. Include information regarding nearby RV parks and facilities with addresses and telephone numbers. A length between 800-1,400 words is acceptable. Articles should be written from the third party point of view (avoid: I, we, they, you, etc.).

Technical articles must be thoroughly researched and accurately written in a clear and easily read style. Short fillers, humorous anecdotes, cartoons, and RV tips are also encouraged.

Photographs add much to a story. Black and white, color prints or slides are acceptable if of good quality. (We are moving to include some color photos in the near future, so keep this in mind also.) Photos on computer disk are also acceptable on 3.5 IBM-compatible, (check disk before sending to make sure it works). Include captions and releases. All photo material will be returned following publication.

If material has been published previously, indicate when and in what publication it appeared. If possible, include a copy.

In addition to hard copy, articles may be submitted on IBM-compatible, high density disks. *Make sure disks can be read and are not faulty!*

Responses are usually made within six weeks. Publication is normally within six months of submission. Editorial material is due before the first of the month prior to the month of publication. Payment is made upon publication. We pay $.08 per published word for first rights. Second rights are $.05 per *Western RV News* published word. Photos are $5.00 per published photo.

Western RV News is a monthly publication. Rather than adhering to a set editorial calendar, we are always looking for fresh, new material. In general, RV camping is the summer focus, "snowbirds" highlight the winter issues, and the RV show season is emphasized during the fall and spring.

Categories: Adventure—Lifestyles—Outdoors—Recreation—Recreational Vehicles—Senior Citizens

Name: Terie Snyder, Editor
Material: All
Address: 42070 SE LOCKSMITH LN
City/State/ZIP: SANDY OR 97055
Telephone: 503-668-5660
Fax: 503-668-6387

Whetstone

We are a journal of fiction and poetry published annually.

We seek submissions of up to seven poems and not more than 25 pages of fiction. We publish top-quality, non-formula stories and poetry that goes beyond description to provide a "Leap to the Universal."

Payment varies and includes two copies of the magazine, which is about 120 pages, perfect bound.

Published works are eligible for the $500 *Whetstone* Prize, awarded to the best story or group of poems in each issue.

We are open to both emerging, unpublished writers and well-published writers.

Categories: Fiction—Literature—Poetry—Short Stories

Name: Jean Tolle, Editor
Name: Marsha Portnoy, Editor
Name: Sandra Berris, Editor
Material: Any
Address: PO BOX 1266
City/State/ZIP: BARRINGTON IL 60011

Whispering Willow Mysteries

Pays 4 cents a word on publication. 80% free lance written. Publishes an average of 3 to 6 months after acceptance. We consider all quality mystery manuscripts. Send complete manuscript, length 500 to 5,000 words. Reports in eight to twelve weeks. Must be original, unpublished words.

Fiction: Mystery or Mystery/Suspense.

Cartoons: Single or double B/W panel with gag-line, pays $15.00 to $25.00.

Prose or Poetry: Limit 30 lines. Pays $10.00 to $35.00 (limit three submissions).

Manuscripts without proper return postage are discarded. Please advise if your manuscript is a simultaneous submission.

Editors reserve the right to edit stories as needed for acceptance of manuscript. Buys first North American serial rights or one-time rights.

Manuscript Requirements

Good, clear computer printouts are acceptable.

Include your name, address, and telephone number on upper left of first page. Place approximate word count on upper right side of your first page. Center the title of your story 10 spaces from top. Put your name on upper left and number consecutively in upper right beside story title on each page thereafter. Submit a neat, clean, and well organized manuscript.

Whispering Willow Publications
Annual Contests for Writers and Artists
DAGGER
Mystery competition
Deadline: March 10; Publication date: July Edition
$200.00 plus publication. Illustration of winning story will be on the cover of this edition book. $5.00 reading fee for each entry.
TRAVEL
Mystery Competition
Deadline: July 1; Publication date: October Edition
First place $200.00 plus publication and illustration of cover of book. Second place winner $150.00 plus publication. $5.00 reading fee for each entry. Story must happen someplace away from home.
BOOKMARK
Mystery Contest
Deadline: October 1; Publication date: January Edition
First place $200.00 plus publication and illustration of cover. Picture illustrating story will be on the limited edition bookmark

for the year. $5.00 reading fee for each entry.

SLEUTH

Mystery Competition

Deadline: December 31; Publication date: April Edition

First place $200.00 plus publication and illustration of their story on cover. Second place $150.00 plus publication. Third place $125.00 plus publication. $10.00 reading fee for each entry. Story about an amateur sleuth.

Categories: Fiction—Literature—Mystery—Short Stories

Name: Darlene Hoffman, Acquisitions Editor
Material: Mystery
Address: PO BOX 890294
City/State/ZIP: OKLAHOMA CITY OK 73189-0294
Telephone: 405-239-2531
Fax: 405-232-3848
E-mail: wwillows@telepath.com
Nota bene: Annual contests require reading fees.

Whole Life Times

Calling all freelancers!

Whole Life Times relies almost entirely on freelance material to fill its pages every month. We have only a few "regulars," so the field is wide open to all who wish to submit. To put it more bluntly: We depend on freelancers like you!

What kind of articles should I submit?

As a holistic publication, *Whole Life Times* is open to articles on a wide variety of topics. In general, we're looking for articles dealing with new approaches to: spiritual/metaphysical/personal growth; the environment; alternative politics and sociopolitical concerns; alternative lifestyles; health, nutrition and natural foods; conscious parenting; education; the latest developments in innovative healing methods; in short, anything that deals with a holistic lifestyle. The important word to remember when writing for WLT is *information*: We strive to provide leading edge editorial that is directly usable by our readers—information that the mainstream media often either ignores, abridges, or is unwilling to print.

In addition to our feature stories (length: 1,000 to 2,500 words), we also have a number of departments (length: 750 to 1,200 words) open to freelancers: Healing, Parenting, Finance, Food, Personal Growth, Relationships, Humor, Travel, Sexuality, Spirituality and Psychology. As you can see, our department headings are general enough to cover a wide scope of issues pertaining to the holistic lifestyle. However, we will happily create a new department if your article captures our interest but doesn't quite fit any of the above categories.

We occasionally do reprints from publications outside our distribution area. We occasionally print book excerpts. We generally prefer original pieces. We are not looking for promotional material, opinion pieces or poetry.

Another tip: keep in mind that WLT readers are more sophisticated than the average Joe or Joan when it comes to holistic and metaphysical issues—write your article with them in mind.

Manuscript Format

Typed submissions are best. If we decide to use your article, we will contact you about sending it either on Macintosh diskette format or via e-mail. Disk format is not a necessity for acceptance, however, so don't fret if you have not joined the computer age.

Notification of Acceptance or Rejection

Ah, the life of an editor—deadlines, deadlines and more deadlines. Every time we look up from our desks, it seems there's another deadline to meet. So, we set aside time to look at submissions during our precious yet limited "quiet time," that early time of the month just after we've completed the last issue. Sometimes we have no quiet time at all—so, unfortunately, our response rate to submissions is probably not as quick as you'd like it to be.

If we do not immediately love or use your article, we may set it aside for a rainy day. Some writers like it this way because it increases their chances of being published, and articles have been printed in this fashion. If you despise such ambiguity or are in a hurry because you want to submit it to other publications, be sure to make note of it on your submission.

No matter what, be sure to include a self-addressed, stamped envelope for notification of acceptance or rejection. Articles will not be returned unless specifically requested, so be sure to keep a duplicate. Please don't call to tell us how wonderful the subject of your article is and why we should print it—let your article speak for itself.

Query Letters

Some magazines like query letters—we're not one of them. Since we don't have luxuries like kill fees, we prefer to see completed manuscripts. If you are unsure whether your article is appropriate for our magazine, feel free to call with specific questions. If it falls into the categories described above, your treatment of the issue, the timeliness of the article and the quality of your writing are the main keys to getting published.

Of course, every rule has an exception. If you are a published writer and would like to send a query, along with writing samples, we will be happy to consider your idea.

Deadlines

Be sure to get your article to us by the first of the month if you want it to be considered for the following month's issue. That means sending your article in by July 1st if you wish consideration for the August issue, by August 1st for the September issue...you get the picture.

Pay

Aha, the big question! (As opposed to the big budget.) Many writers who are trying to build up their portfolios and/or are passionately committed to getting out information contribute their work to WLT. When this is possible, we are sincerely grateful.

Although we cannot pay for departments, we do offer compensation for professional, comprehensive, investigative features. Our first choice is the barter system. Do you have a book or a service you would like to advertise? Ads have a higher dollar value than we can offer, with the added bonus of possibly creating future revenue.

If you are a professional writer for whom financial recompense is the only alternative, we are able to pay $.05 per word for feature stories only. Occasionally we use reprints and for those we pay 50% of feature rate. We pay within 30 days of publication.

The writers we are most interested in are usually the ones who know they are worth more than we can pay (just as we know it), but who believe in what they/we are doing and want to participate anyway. Please don't think we are getting rich off the fruits of your labor. We are paying what we think we can afford at this point in time.

Since we acquire only first North American serial rights, you can make it more financially rewarding by reselling your article elsewhere, as long as WLT is given a reprint credit.

Please join *Whole Life Times* in our endeavor to make our world a healthier, happier place!

Categories: Nonfiction—Conservation—Consumer—Cooking—Culture—Diet—Ecology—Environment—Feminism—Food/Drink—General Interest—Government—Holistic Health—Humor—Inspirational—Interview—Lifestyles—Marriage—Men's Issues—Money/Finance—Multicultural—Music—New Age—Outdoors—Paranormal—Parenting—Philosophy—Physical Fitness—Politics—Psychology—Regional—Relationships—Sexuality—Spiritual—Sports—Technology—Travel—Women's Issues

Name: S.T. Alcantara, Associate Editor
Material: All
Address: PO BOX 1187
City/State/ZIP: MALIBU CA 90265
Telephone: 310-317-4200
Fax: 310-317-4206
E-mail: wholelifex@aol.com

Wholeness

Wholeness

SIZE: There is no minimum size but the maximum should be no more than two, single spaced, 8½"x11" pages (approx. 500-1,000 words).

FORMAT: Good quality, typed copy is needed—with or without a diskette. Articles can also be sent on 5¼" or 3½" IBM compatible diskettes using WordPerfect or ASCII format.

DEADLINE: *"Wholeness"* is distributed the Wednesday following the 15th of each month. If selected for publication in *"Wholeness,"* articles received/approved by the end of one month will appear in the following month's issue on a space available basis. Articles will be saved for future use if space is not immediately available.

PICTURES: A picture of the author is appreciated—these can be any size or type, but black and white or 35mm work best. Screened pictures (those ready for printing) are ideal.

TOPIC: We want the article to be on a particular topic, or thoughts/views held by the author—**not an advertisement for your business.** We feel it is best for the author to select the actual topic so it comes from the heart. We only require it be applicable to our audience (see AUDIENCE).

EDITING: *"Wholeness"* reserves the right to edit submitted articles.

REPRINTS: After appearing in *"Wholeness,"* your article can be reprinted in other publications. We would appreciate your including the following note at the beginning or ending of the article: "This article is a reprint, with permission, from the (month, year) issue of *"The Wholeness Paper."*

MISSION: *"The Wholeness Paper's"* mission statement is: To provide a network for people working on emotional, behavioral and spiritual growth. The desire is to make it possible to share aspirations, idealism, interests, information and values in order to increase personal growth and fulfillment.

AUDIENCE: People wanting to make personal behavior changes; Wholistic thinking people; Positive thinking people; People working on Spiritual growth; People in recovery (AA, ACA, Alanon, Over Eaters, other 12 step programs, etc.)

Categories: Cooking (natural)—Diet—Ecology—Environment—Holistic Health—Inspirational—Metaphysical—New Age—Spiritual

Name: Ellen Houghton, Owner/Publisher
Material: All
Address: 14701 WELLINGTON RD
City/State/ZIP: WAYZATA MN 55391-2446
Telephone: 612-404-9981
Fax: 612-404-9982

The Wild Foods Forum

The Wild Foods Forum is a bimonthly publication with articles on wild edible foods, rare or poisonous plants, book reviews, upcoming events, trip reports, forager feature stories, herbal folklore, and survival skills. Articles are accepted from a large pool of contributing writers. A few are regular, but most are occasional. Informative or unusual topics based on personal experiences are preferred.

Articles
• *Length:*
Recipes—25-50 words
Book Reviews—50-100 words
Trip Reports—100-200 words
Herbal Folklore—200-500 words
Informative or How-to Articles—500-1,200 words
• *Format:* Typed, single-spaced. Each page should contain author's name, address and phone number.
• *Subject: See topics* listed above. Articles should be seasonal and relate to what is available at that time of year.
• *Deadline:* Articles should be submitted at least 2 months before the publication date. If it is an article that would be better suited for another time period, it will be held until that time.

Art, Illustrations, Photography
• Original line drawings with captions and artist's name, address, and phone number.
• Color or black-and-white photos or slides are accepted. Identification, including scientific names, should accompany each photo or slide. Duplicates should be used for irreplaceable slides, photos, or artwork.
All art work and photos or slides will be returned to the contributing artist or photographer.

Payment
Contributing writers and artists receive a free subscription. Additional payments are not always possible and depend on the length, amount of research and uniqueness of the article.

Editing
All work is subject to editing, depending on space and the quality of writing. When possible, editing is reviewed with the author. Please indicate with your submission if you wish to be notified of editorial changes or if you feel strongly about keeping the article intact.

Categories: Nonfiction—Cooking—Diet—Food/Drink—Gardening—Health—Outdoors—Recreation

Name: Submissions Editor
Material: All
Address: PO BOX 61413
City/State/ZIP: VIRGINIA BEACH VA 23466-1413
Telephone: 757-421-3929
E-mail: wildfood@infi.net

Wild West

Please refer to Cowles Enthusiast Media, Inc.

Wildlife Art
The Art Journal of the Natural World

Wildlife Art magazine is the recognized journal about art and artists, both modern and historical, depicting wildlife and the natural world. As reader enthusiasm for this art genre grows, *Wildlife Art* magazine strives to present informative, thought-provoking features on wildlife and art topics, while providing a forum for news and events of the wildlife art industry. A secondary element of our editorial mission is to inform our readers about the state of the environment, as preservation of habitat is essential to the survival of wildlife subjects. Occasional theme issues (on sporting art, conservation, e.g.) provide special writing opportunities.

Founded in 1982, the magazine currently has nearly 20,000

S-Z

subscribers worldwide. An additional 25,000 copies of each issue are sold through newsstands, art shows, and galleries in the United States and Canada. Our audience consists of art collectors, wildlife art enthusiasts, publishers, galleries, and artists interested in the genres of wildlife and nature art.

TOPICS AND TYPES OF ARTICLES

Many of our features spotlight individual artists. These articles define artists' skills and techniques, share details of artists' personalities and experience, and provide insight into their art. We also publish authoritative and thematic pieces on art history or current art trends, and about groups of artists who share the same medium, location, style, nationality, etc. Read the current issue of the magazine, scan back issues, and refer to our annual editorial index to learn more about the range of subjects we cover, what we have addressed recently, typical topics and lengths of articles, and what things to avoid.

WRITING FOR WILDLIFE ART

Articles must be original, accurate, timely, educational, memorable, and entertaining to our readers. We are looking for dynamic, evocative art and articles that provide new treatments of familiar issues. *Good writing is essential.* We want to take our readers on a journey of words and images that reveals the thoughts, techniques, and styles of present-day and historical artists who depict nature.

You should be able to describe works of art with clarity and perception, and use insight to assess the place of the artists in the field—but we don't want academic criticism. We do want lively, knowledgeable writing that places art and artists in context and helps readers judge for themselves. Biographical highlights of an individual's life can play in, but shouldn't be overemphasized— the art should be at the core of the piece. The in-depth articles should examine what artists are trying to communicate and the techniques they employ to accomplish this end. When possible, include appropriate assessment and evaluation from recognized experts in the field.

You must query us to gain an assignment.

QUERY AND ASSIGNMENT PROCEDURE

The best way to query us is with a letter containing:

• A suggested title and topic heading for your article.

• A one- or two-paragraph outline of the story's content, structure, and topical peg, indicating its significance and why *Wildlife Art* magazine should publish it.

• Several sentences about why you are particularly qualified to write this article. Send photocopies of writing samples (writing samples will not be returned).

• Samples of the artist's/artists' work(s) in the form of photographs, slides, or transparencies - we must see the art to give proper consideration to the article idea. Without art we cannot proceed.

Mail your query to the Editor—if you elect to fax it, send your art samples via the mail. It usually takes a minimum of eight to ten weeks to hear from us. Writers receiving an assignment may be asked to sign a writer's agreement. Deadlines will be arranged when assignments are made, but the general editorial deadline is three months in advance of the publication month (e.g., April 1 for the July/August issue).

SUBMITTED ARTICLES

Articles must be typed on numbered pages. Final page of article should include a brief note about the writer (see samples in magazine), a courtesy line, if possible, and a listing of the captions for the accompanying artwork. We also require that you provide title suggestions, along with bold-out possibilities, and subheads when appropriate.

Do include a data disk (3½") for Macintosh using Microsoft Word, if possible. If using a DOS system, save in text format. Send a hard copy of the manuscript whether you send a disk or not. Include full contact information with each submission.

All manuscripts submitted to the magazine are subject to approval/acceptance.

Fundamentals that increase your article's chances of acceptance:

• A snappy, creative lead, a well-crafted structure, and a strong close

• Incorporation of specific examples, descriptive details, and quotations

• The ability to capture the artist's vision and to elicit anecdotes about experiences

• Verified accuracy, especially of quotations and proper names. Do your research thoroughly.

• Judicious sprinkling of expert opinions from gallery owners, collectors, museum curators, other artists, etc., to bolster the credibility of your evaluation. *(Wildlife Art* magazine may be able to assist you with contacts.)

• Assurance that you checked with the artist(s) about art availability (do not focus your article on one or two works without being certain that reproduction-quality transparencies or slides are available for possible use in the article).

• Use of the *Chicago Manual of Style* and the *American Heritage Dictionary* as authorities.

In all cases, articles are subject to editing by the magazine staff. In cases of dispute, we have the final word, but we like to negotiate an agreement acceptable to everyone. We do not guarantee publication of manuscripts even if they are accepted.

We ask all authors to send background materials and a source/ contact list with their articles to help us in checking facts. We may use this information to create a "Read More About It" sidebar, if warranted. Authors are responsible for obtaining any necessary permissions to quote from other publications and to reproduce copyrighted photographs or artwork. Enclose permission letters with submitted materials (see the *Chicago Manual of Style* for sample permission requests).

ARTWORK AND CAPTIONS

Do not send original art. Polaroids and snapshots are acceptable at the query phase, but are not considered reproduction quality. Slides or transparencies are generally the best means of showing art in its most favorable light - an essential consideration in an art publication.

Captions must accompany art submissions, including complete and accurate title, dimensions (height x width x depth), medium(s), and year completed. Be sure to code the slides or transparencies to the caption list and label all slides and transparencies with title, artist, "top," and "front." Artwork will be returned only if you ask to have it returned at the time of submittal and only if accompanied by a SASE with appropriate packaging and postage. Delays in requested returns can result from the review process and/or the production process.

RIGHTS AND REQUIREMENTS

All articles must be exclusive to *Wildlife Art* magazine in the form submitted, and the content must be original and essentially exclusive. A manuscript (or parts of a manuscript) that appeared in other, non-competing publications may be considered, but only if the author makes *Wildlife Art* magazine aware of this previous publication at the time of submittal. By submission, contributing artists, writers, and advertisers agree to indemnify and protect the publisher from any claim or action based on unauthorized use of any person's name, photography, or copyrighted material.

Wildlife Art magazine purchases rights to the article for a period of ninety (90) days from the date of publication and has the unlimited right to use the article for other purposes and to authorize reprints. If *Wildlife Art* magazine authorizes a reprint of the article, a fee of $100 will be paid to the writer for reprint rights. If *Wildlife Art* magazine is able to negotiate a "larger press run," or if the reprint is for special purposes, every effort will be made to obtain a larger fee. After ninety days, all rights to the article, except for use by *Wildlife Art* magazine for promotional, advertising, historical, anthological, or reprint purposes, revert to the writer. Any subsequent appearances of the article elsewhere must indicate the article first appeared in *Wildlife Art* magazine. If *Wildlife Art* magazine reprints the article in a separate magazine or book published by Pothole Publications, a flat $150 fee will be paid to the writer.

PAYMENT

Material submitted for publication is considered on speculation; we are not obligated to buy an article until we have read and approved it, even when we assign it. Payment is made upon acceptance. Should your story be accepted you will need to submit a formal invoice that includes your social security number. We do not usually pay a kill fee, although this can be negotiated at the time of assignment.

Basic phone expenses are reimbursed. Any other expenses (e.g., for travel) must be authorized prior to expenditure.

HOW TO REACH US

Writers on assignment for us with questions may call. Queries should be submitted in writing, either mailed, faxed, or e-mailed.

Categories: Animals—Arts—Collectibles—Environment

Name: Submissions Editor
Material: All
Address: 4725 HWY 7
Address: PO BOX 16246
City/State/ZIP: ST LOUIS PARK MN 55416-0246
Telephone: 612-927-9056
Fax: 612-927-9353
Internet: www.wildlifeart.com

The William and Mary Review
College of William and Mary

The William and Mary Review is published annually by the College of William and Mary. The *Review is* dedicated to publishing visual arts, fiction, nonfiction, poetry and innovative literary works by established artists and authors in addition to introducing those by new and vital talents.

When submitting, it is best to send no more than one or two fiction or nonfiction works, unless they are under 1,000 words; length should not exceed 7,000 words in any case. For poetry, five to eight poems is a good size selection. All work must be typed; visual arts must be submitted in color slide format. We do not acknowledge receipt of work, and decisions are usually reached within four months. Please note that staff members are not available during the summer months; all material received then will be considered beginning in September.

As the *Review* is published in April of each year, the deadline for each issue is January 15th. Back issues of the *Review* are available from the above address at $5.50 including postage. Direct all inquires to Fiction, Poetry, Nonfiction, Art or Managing Editors, whichever is most applicable.

PAST CONTRIBUTORS TO THE REVIEW INCLUDE

Douglas Crase, Amy Clampitt, Julie Agoos, W.S. Penn, Debbie Lee Wesselmann, John Allmann, Dana Gioia, W.D. Snodgrass, David Ignatow, Cornelius Eady, A.R. Ammons, Barnie K. Day, Paul Wood, Carolyn Harris, Geneva Beavers, Michael Mott, William Logan, Debora Greger, Ron Smith, David Acker, Jane Hirschfield, Judson Jerome, and Richard Kostelanetz.

Categories: Fiction—Nonfiction—Arts—Literature—Poetry—Short Stories

Name: Adriana X. Tatum, Editor

Material: All
Address: CAMPUS CENTER
Address: PO BOX 8795
City/State/ZIP: WILLIAMSBURG VA 23187
Telephone: 757-221-3290

WIN Informer

WHO WE ARE

The WIN INFORMER is a bimonthly publication of the Writers Information Network, *The Professional Association for Christian Writers*, organized in 1983 to provide a much needed link between writers, editors and other users of inspirational communication.

THE PURPOSE OF OUR MAGAZINE

1.) to further professional development in writing and marketing skills of Christian writers

2.) to provide a meeting ground of encouragement/fellowship for persons engaged in writing and speaking

3.) to furnish writers with up-to-date market information on religious book and magazine/periodical publishers

4.) to keep writers abreast of industry news and trends, and

5.) to share quality writing helps, tips, connections, and how-to advice.

WHAT WE PUBLISH

UP-TO-DATE MARKET INFORMATION

Anything that is newsworthy that will tell our writers what today's religious editors seek.

INDUSTRY NEWS AND TRENDS

If you learn a hot tip, spot a trend or see an announcement made in the religious periodicals you read, pass it on. If you can quote editors/publishers, agents or other industry insiders, all the better.

WRITING HELPS, CONNECTIONS, HOW-TO ADVICE and CHALLENGING ARTICLES

We will share short, pithy ideas of what is working for you, or the best suggestions that you've picked up at conferences. We like practical advice writers can put to work to advance their freelance writing/speaking career. We also consider devotional/inspirational material and quotes with "take-away value" from successful Christian authors.

WRITERS CLUBS/FELLOWSHIP GROUPS/AND CONFERENCE ANNOUNCEMENTS

We are happy to pass along news of events of interest to Christian writers and speakers. Send a press release. Our publication is read in all 50 states and 12 foreign countries. Our readers want to learn of happenings in their part of the world.

BOOK REVIEWS

Books of special writing/speaking interest to writers; books by any of our WIN members; books by name authors that show what is happening in our world; books by authors that writers and speakers should be reading for broader exposure to the thinking and successes of our day.

YOUR SUBMISSION

Manuscripts must most of all be "encouraging" to Christian writers. They should also be crisp, show vigor and vitality, and be "reader friendly". Queries not necessary. 50-300 words maximum length. We try to respond within two months. Payment varies, $20-$50 depending on length and quality, or often a one-year subscription to WIN. Accepts first rights *only*. Sample Copy $5.00. Send 9"x12" envelope with 4 stamps, and your check made payable to WIN.

Categories: Christian Interests—Inspirational—Religion—Writing

Name: Elaine Wright Colvin, Editor/Publisher

Material: All
Address: PO BOX 11337
City/State/ZIP: BAINBRIDGE ISLAND WA 98110
Telephone: 206-842-9103
Fax: 206-842-0536
E-mail: WritersInfoNetwork@juno.com

Wines & Vines
The Authoritative Voice of the Grape and Wine Industry Since 1919

Dear Writer:

Since 1919 *Wines & Vines* has been the Authoritative Voice of the Wine and Grape Industry. From prohibition to phylloxera we have covered it all—and our paid circulation reaches all 50 states and 40 foreign countries. Because we are intended for the trade, including growers, winemakers, winery owners, retailers, wholesalers, restaurateurs and serious amateurs, we do not accept "gee whiz" type articles on the "wonders of wine," the romance of the grape, etc.

All articles should be summated on typed pages and the cover page should include your name, address, phone and fax. We encourage you to send photos with your article but we cannot guarantee the return of unsolicited manuscripts and photos.

Our current rate for articles accepted for publication is $.10 per word and $10 per photo.

If you have any questions please call me.

Sincerely,

Philip E. Hiaring
Editor & Publisher

In 1919, *Wines & Vines* (originally named *California Grape Grower*) opened its doors. The premise for starting the industry's first magazine was to report on the new and growing wine and grape business. The wine industry was cut short at the end of that year because of the 19th Amendment to the U.S. Constitution. Prohibition had begun and would last 14 years.

Wines & Vines kept on printing and reporting, trying to keep an odd lot of vintners and winemakers together and aware of what was happening.

Wines & Vines and the industry survived and blossomed. From 1933, *Wines & Vines* became the information resource for the grape and wine industry.

At Repeal, the reborn industry was very short on winemakers. So *Wines & Vines emphasized* the technology of the times with valuable, scientific winemaking articles, much like the magazine of today. The winemaker in the 1930s would be amazed at the strides taken by today's industry. And, from the advent of stainless steel, temperature-controlled wine tanks and reverse osmosis to consumers and regulators and from vine diseases to market changes, *Wines & Vines* has covered it all. *Wines & Vines* has reported on the prosperous years and the not so prosperous years.

As the industry grows and changes, *Wines & Vines* has maintained its vigorous attention to covering the business of wine making.

We've been around a long time and we've changed to meet the demands of an ever-changing audience. We're enhancing our international coverage and expanding our attention to smaller wineries. We're reporting on changing attitudes of regulators and consumers and we're letting our audience know about the influx of markets of which, in 1919, no one would have ever dreamed.

But one thing that hasn't changed through the years: our vigilance and dedication to bringing the most up-to-date news and commentary to those in the business of making, selling and buying wine.

Wines & Vines Magazine

Wines & Vines magazine has been published every month since December, 1919. Issues include the latest industry news, editorial columns on politics, legal and regulatory opinions, the world wine market, health, vineyard management, a variety of pertinent articles, profiles of industry people and businesses and a calendar of upcoming events. Each month we also devote a portion of the magazine to one particular focus.

Our **January** issue focuses on the annual **WineTECH** trade show, sponsored by *Wines & Vines*. It has become a major U.S. wine industry trade show with increasing attendance each year. Included in this issue is a brief description of WineTECH exhibitors as well as a floor plan of the exhibit hall. Advertisers who do not exhibit at the show can still get exposure at WineTECH because our January issue is the official program and is distributed to all attendees.

In **February,** we focus on the **Vineyard:** An overview of last year's harvest; crop size; quality by regions and by states. Other editorial covers pest control, vineyard management and much more.

In **March** we zero in on **Wine Marketing.** We cover such things as electronic wine marketing, the top retail players and their markets, interviews with marketers, designers, those who create the new campaigns and those who pay for them.

April is our **Transportation** issue.

In **May** we focus on the **Export** and **Import** markets. This area of sales is expanding rapidly. Some new and innovative countries and exporting practices are unveiled.

June is the Annual Open Meeting of the Society for Enology and Viticulture (**ASEV**) and **Enology** issue. We supply our readers with extensive convention information and the most accurate floor plan available. Exhibitors are given an opportunity to tell our readers what they will be displaying at the show. This issue is given out at the convention so our advertisers are seen even if they can't attend.

July is the most comprehensive **Statistical** resource available from an industry publication. It contains charts, graphs, and editorial on everything from grape and wine production, per capita growth and consumption, acreage figures, export and import statistics, even the most up-to-date list of the 100 largest U.S. wineries.

August is devoted to **Merchandising.** The issue focuses on industry trends; wineries and how they merchandize, the retailers' perspective and the merchandisers' outlook.

September, our **State-of-the-art** issue, is just that. It covers the new, the innovative and the future, throughout the grape and wine industry.

October is set aside for what we term **Management.** It's a compilation of what is going on within the industry; how companies are being run; how problems are being tackled and solved. In this issue we focus on the business of wine.

November is primarily reserved for **Equipment, Supplies** and **Services.** In this big issue we list the suppliers, contact information and descriptions of new products and services.

In the **December** issue we look at Champagne. We visit wineries and cover the new and the not so new but always fun side of champagne.

Categories: Nonfiction—Agriculture—Business—Careers—Diet—Food/Drink—Government—Health—Interview

Name: Philip E. Hiaring, Editor and Publisher
Material: All
Address: 1800 LINCOLN AVE

City/State/ZIP: SAN RAFAEL CA 94901
Telephone: 415-453-9700
Fax: 415-453-2517
E-mail: geninfo@winesandvines.com
Internet: www.winesandvines.com

Wired

The purpose of *Wired* is to illuminate the roots, issues and possible destiny of the emerging digital culture. If you want to write for us, here are some things to keep in mind:

Amaze us.

We know a lot about digital computers and we are bored with them. Tell us something about them we've never heard before, in a way we've never seen before. If it challenges our assumptions, so much the better. *Wired* is a multimedia event on paper. Fiction, non-fiction, semi-fiction; essay, how-to, expose; picture story, profile, interview - all in one issue.

We seek young and new voices - voices that are passionate and involved.

Events drive the news of television and newspapers. *Ideas—*conceptual reporting—drive the news in *Wired*. It shouldn't matter too much if someone rereads your piece next month or next year. Poet Ezra Pound calls this kind of information "news that stays news."

It's rare. We'll go out of our way to find it and publish it.

If you care deeply about something that's inextricably tied to digital technologies, chances are we cover it. If the topic is just cresting the digital horizon, it's perfect.

Write it well - long, if the material demands. Take chances. Sweep, color, scene, and strong character anecdotes are imperative. If there's no conflict - moral, institutional, cultural - there's no story.

The piece must be definitive.

We are re-inventing paper as a communication tool for the digital era. Send us an example of what a re-invented magazine article would be like.

We don't want anything that duplicates what you can read elsewhere.

We print complaints.

How to review a product, book, or item: Write your review. Then write us a letter explaining why we should devote space to your item. Throw away your review and send us the letter.

Give it to us in digital, or analog form. We'd prefer you send it on Mac diskette, Word ready. Don't send us the only copy of anything. If it's a long piece, (over 7500 words) we'd prefer you first send an under-300 word synopsis of what it's about.

Thanks for your interest in *Wired*.

Categories: Fiction—Nonfiction—Computers—Electronics—Interview—Software—Technology—Communication—Lifestyles—Essay—Opinion—How-to—Interview—Profiles

Name: Patricia Reilly, Editorial Assistant
Material: All
Address: 520 THIRD ST., 4TH FLOOR
City/State/ZIP: SAN FRANCISCO, CA 94107-1815
Telephone: 415-276-5000
Fax: 415-276-5150
E-mail: submissions@wired.com
Internet: www.wired.com

Wisconsin Trails
The Magazine of Life in Wisconsin

Who We Are

Wisconsin Trails, a privately owned, bimonthly magazine, recently entered its fourth decade of publication. As the "Magazine of Life in Wisconsin," it features articles on Wisconsin people, history, nature, adventure, lifestyle, arts, theater, crafts, sports, recreation, and business. We're interested in the out-of-the-way (ever been to Blueberry Bog, known for its bluegills and blueberries?) and the popular (we find places like Door County and the Apostle Islands endlessly fascinating). Nearly eighty percent of our readers are Wisconsin residents, while most of the other twenty percent are frequent visitors here.

Subjects

Wisconsin Trails magazine gives readers experiences of all kinds. Some articles are meant to entertain, some to provoke readers' desires to participate in an adventure, others to educate or enlighten. It is important that you write in a style that lets the reader join you in the experience. If you're camping by a northwoods stream, we'd like to hear about the last thing you saw at night or the first thing you heard in the morning. What kind of creatures inhabit this place?

Tell us what sort of impact the area has on a person, what makes it special enough to send your friends there. If it's a piece on canoeing, biking, hiking, etc., we want a sense of the action. Not an hour by hour rundown, but a vital account of the experience, one that lets readers join you in the adventure. If you're writing about people, ethnic festivals, community events, we're interested in the spirit and interaction and what makes them unique and exciting.

Style

We always appreciate a moderate use of the verb "to be" and we welcome fresh, descriptive approaches.

Length

Varies from 1,000 to 2,000 words.

Contract and Payment

We buy first North American serial rights and expect original work. Payment varies from 20 to 25 cents a word—on publication.

Submissions

One-page written queries are preferred over manuscripts. We do not find telephone queries effective; instead, we prefer written materials we can share at editorial planning meetings.

We appreciate your interest in *Wisconsin Trails* and welcome you as a contributor.

Categories: Nonfiction—Adventure—Conservation—Culture—Ecology—Entertainment—Environment—Food/Drink—General Interest—History—Lifestyles—Outdoors—Recreation—Regional—Travel

Name: Kate Bast, Managing Editor
Material: All
Address: 6225 UNIVERSITY AVE
City/State/ZIP: MADISON WI 53705
Telephone: 608-231-2444
Fax: 6O8-231-1557
E-mail: wistrail@mailbag.com

With
The Magazine for Radical Christian Youth

With is published eight times a year for Mennonite Brethren and Mennonite Brethren youth, ages 15 to 18, in the U.S. and Canada. Each issue focuses on a theme such as peer pressure, peacemaking, or devotional life. A list of upcoming themes is available for a #10 SASE. *With* has a reputation for tackling tough social issues other Christian magazines won't touch.

WHAT WE NEED

FIRST-PERSON STORIES: (800 to 1,800 words): We like

to lead off with a Christian teen's first-person story of a life-changing experience. Such a story usually involves the teen's faith, and the lesson the teen learned must be one readers can apply in their lives. We sometimes use a how-to sidebar (100 to 600 words) with a personal experience article.

These stories are usually written on an as-told-to basis. You interview the teen then write his/her story in first-person. You receive an as-told-to byline unless you prefer not to. We also welcome stories from adults describing such experiences from their own teen years. We consider stories of any Christian youth, but give preference to stories of youth involved in Mennonite, Mennonite Brethren, or Church of the Brethren congregations.

We prefer a query on this kind of story. *Detailed guidelines for first-person stories available* for a #10 SASE. We pay $100 for first rights on first-person stories written on assignment and pay extra for photos. Usual rates for reprints.

HUMOR: (prose 100 to 1,500 words; poetry up to 50 lines): We're hungry for more well-written humor—fiction, nonfiction, light verse, or cartoons. When it comes to humor, it doesn't have to be religious, just wholesome. If your writing makes teens laugh, we want to hear from you.

REALISTIC FICTION: (800 to 2,000 words): Most issues include a short story with many of the same elements we look for in the first-person stories described above, except that fiction can be either first- or third-person. Fiction must have strong elements of conflict and change, and the message must be one readers can apply to their lives. We look for fiction that is believable and engages the readers' emotions. We're interested in occasional fiction with an "unreliable narrator."

HOW-TO ARTICLES: (800 to 1,500 words): Most issues include a how-to article with practical teaching on the issue's theme. Examples: "How to Help a Friend Who's Suffering" and "How Not to Be a Witless Witness." How-to articles need a strong opening hook (usually a true anecdote from the author's teen years), a clear step-by-step outline, anecdotes to illustrate at least most outline points, and a satisfying conclusion. To avoid sounding preachy, tell how you learned through your mistakes or from another's example. *Detailed how-to guidelines available* for a #10 SASE. We pay $75 for first rights on an assigned how-to. Query to receive an assignment.

SPECULATIVE FICTION: (500 to 1,800 words): We like parables, allegories, and fantasy that communicate spiritual truth with symbolism, but the symbolism must be clear. Subtle writing goes right by some of our younger readers.

POETRY: (up to 50 lines): We consider poetry of any style. While most poetry has a spiritual theme, we also use short nature poems (often seasonal), and light verse (just because it's funny). We look for strong sensory images, fresh insight or perspective, and language that pleases the ear. We use about six poems a year.

MEDITATIONS: (100 to 1,200 words): We use meditations that inspire wonder, awe, or reflection in the reader. These can be based on personal experience, a biblical event or symbol, or even a dream or imagined scene. We occasionally publish prayers (up to 200 words).

BOOK EXCERPTS: Send us the whole book (no novels, please) or photocopy an excerpt you think might work for *With*. If you own the copyright, we pay our usual rate. If the publisher owns it, we negotiate with the publisher.

PHOTOS, CARTOONS, ILLUSTRATIONS: Photographers' guidelines available for #10 SASE. For cartoons, see "HUMOR" above and check recent issues for samples. If you wish to illustrate on assignment, send samples of your work.

OUR WRITER-FRIENDLY APPROACH

Because we have a small circulation (about 6,000), we can't pay top dollar, yet we expect top-quality writing. So we try to make it worthwhile for good writers to work with us through favorable policies on rights, prompt replies and payments—in general, lots of TLC. Here are the specifics:

RIGHTS AND PAYMENT: We pay *on acceptance* 5 cents a word for *simultaneous* rights (unpublished manuscripts you are free to submit elsewhere simultaneously) and 3 cents a word for reprint rights. We pay $10 to $25 for poetry (one-time rights) depending on length and how it is used. We pay more for first rights to assigned work (see "First-Person" and "How-To" articles). We sometimes offer a 30%-50% kill fee for assigned articles. You get two author's copies upon publication.

REPLY TIME: We respond to most submissions within four to six weeks. If we want to hold a manuscript longer, we'll ask your permission.

SAMPLES: For a sample copy, send a self-addressed stamped 9"x12" envelope ($1.24 postage). For two issues, affix $1.93 postage. For three, $2.62.

SUBMISSIONS AND QUERIES: Make seasonal and theme-specific submissions at least 6 months before publication date. All manuscripts except poetry should be double-spaced. Type your name, address and phone in the upper left corner of the first page, and the approximate word count and rights offered in the upper right corner.

Queries should be no more than a page and a half, accompanied by published clips if you haven't written for us before. Include your phone number. Don't phone us with a query without prior invitation from an editor.

Categories: Fiction—Nonfiction—Cartoons—Christian Interests—Fantasy—Humor—Inspirational—Religion—Teen

Name: Submissions Editor
Material: All
Address: PO BOX 347
City/State/ZIP: NEWTON KS 67053
Telephone: 316-283-5100

Wolf Head Quarterly

Submissions: Prose submissions must not exceed 15 pages (3,750 words). Poetry submissions must not exceed 5 pages of material. We accept e-mail submissions. Insert your work into the e-mail itself or attach your file (PC compatible). Please include a short bio as well.

Deadlines: Autumn June 1st; Winter Sept. 1st; Spring Dec. 1st; Summer Mar. 1st

We are especially drawn toward works exploring the relationship between nature and ourselves. The subject may be personal or universal, but not strictly environmental.

Categories: Fiction—Nonfiction—Literature—Poetry—Short Stories—Writing

Name: W.H. Mitchell, Managing Editor
Material: All
Address: PO BOX 30057
City/State/ZIP: KANSAS CITY MO 64112
E-mail: whmitch@aol.com

Woman's Day

Every article submitted to *Woman's Day* should, of course, be well-written, well-researched and readable. Bear in mind that while you're as close to your subject as anyone, you cannot afford to let that cloud your critical vision. If you're bored with something, chances are we'll be comatose. Trust your instincts, do your homework and please do not submit anything in the hopes that a vigilant editor will catch, fix, revise, refine or rewrite it for you. Some additional points about writing for *Woman's Day*...

We, like everyone else, want articles based on new studies, new statistics, new theories and new insights, particularly if the subject you're writing about has already received considerable media coverage. Keep your material timely and authoritative and support any unusual theories, controversial opinions and debatable points with solid data and/or expert quotes. But be judicious: There is no need to cite an M.D. on the frequency of winter colds. Any authority you do quote—psychologist, educator, financial adviser or government official—should have a national reputation as an expert in his or her field. Seek out leading authorities, preferably those who have written a book or chaired a conference in their field of expertise. If no such expert exists, quote people who are well-known or affiliated with prestigious institutions. Identify experts as briefly as possible. Choose what's most relevant to your material.

Anyone who is prominently featured in a *Woman's Day* article should grant us exclusive rights to her or his story until publication. This is especially true for articles about ordinary people with an extraordinary story to tell, and it's your duty to alert your sources to that effect.

Once your manuscript has been accepted, you'll be asked to supply an electronic version. Please submit the material on a 3.5" diskette save to Xywrite, an IBM-compatible program or to an ASCII file. If you use a Macintosh, save the file to whatever software program you use. If you cannot submit a 3.5" diskette, a 5-1/4" diskette will be accepted. All diskettes will be returned. If your manuscript includes sidebars and boxes, save them to the same file rather than a separate one. Please type only one space between sentences and after all punctuation marks. Be sure that your diskette contains the most recent version of your manuscript (i.e., the electronic version should be exactly the same as the hardcopy version we accepted.) Although we prefer to work with diskettes, you may also send your manuscript via modem. Contact your editor to arrange for transmission.

Maureen McFadden, Senior Editor

Categories: Fiction—Nonfiction—Biography—Business—Careers—Children—Consumer—Cooking—Crafts—Family—Fashion—Food/Drink—Health—Hobbies—Money/Finance—Physical Fitness—Psychology—Relationships—Self-Help—Nutrition—Beauty—Home—Women's Issues—Education—Leisure Activities—Celebrities—Lifestyles

Name: Maureen McFadden, Senior Editor
Material: All
Address: 1633 BROADWAY
City/State/ZIP: NEW YORK, NY 10019
Telephone: 212-767-6492
Fax: 212-767-5600
E-mail: maureenmcf@aol.com

woman's touch

Woman's Touch
An Inspirational Magazine for Women

Woman's Touch is a bimonthly inspirational magazine for women published by the Women's Ministries Department, Division of Church Ministries, Assemblies of God. We are committed to providing help and inspiration for Christian women, strengthening family life, and reaching out in witness to others. *Woman's Touch* is the voice of Women's Ministries across the nation.

The editors of **Woman's Touch** would like strong, original articles written from the Christian's perspective and geared specifically for women.

Our greatest demand is for practical articles on women's relationships with various family members and peers, personal/spiritual growth, health and beauty, current issues in society, women and careers, crafts and humor.

We would also like to see feature articles written about women's Ministries groups or individuals. *We are not currently accepting articles on abortion, Mary and Martha, Christmas' loss of meaning, or personal life stories.*

In planning the magazine, the editorial staff follows these general themes:

JANUARY/FEBRUARY
MAIN THEME: *Personal Growth*
SECONDARY THEME: couple relationships and friendships, Valentine's Day, new year (starting over, becoming a better person, goal-setting, etc.), singleness, careers, health and beauty.

MARCH/APRIL
MAIN THEME: Personal Relationship with God—building character, daily walk, understanding God
SECONDARY THEMES: Easter, church, home, parent care/relationships, local evangelism

MAY/JUNE
MAIN THEME: Family—relationship with husband and children, Mother's Day
SECONDARY THEMES: working mothers; singleness and single parenting; step-parenting, parents dealing with loss of a child, teenagers, adoption

JULY/AUGUST
MAIN THEME: Country-patriotism; current issues facing women in America
SECONDARY THEMES: helping others (outreach), relationships with peers (friends, siblings, coworkers, etc.), prayer, vacations/moving

SEPTEMBER/OCTOBER
MAIN THEME: Education and Careers
SECONDARY THEMES: raising children-traditionally, as a working mother, as a single mother, home organization, personal friendships, school, the workplace, dealing with divorce

NOVEMBER/DECEMBER
MAIN THEME: Holidays-seasonal articles for Thanksgiving and Christmas
SECONDARY THEMES: relationships with extended family and in-laws, family evangelism, elderly, dealing with loss

ABOUT WRITING YOUR MANUSCRIPT
• We will consider manuscripts up to 1,000 words. Longer manuscripts would probably not be usable due to our limited space.

• Study our style and content to find what type of articles we use. For a sample copy of *Woman's Touch*, send a self-addressed manila envelope (9"x12") with 75¢ postage, or subscribe to the magazine.

• **Give the version of the Bible** you are using when you quote Scripture. Verify and identify other sources you have used. **Confirm all illustrations and references to Scripture, history, nature, animal life, science, etc.**

• Woman's Touch **does not accept fiction. We very rarely** use poetry.

ABOUT SUBMITTING YOUR MANUSCRIPT
• In the upper left-hand corner of your manuscript, place your **name, mailing address, city, state, ZIP code, telephone number and area code, and social security number,** which we

S-Z

will need if we purchase your manuscript. In the upper right-hand corner place the **approximate number of words of your manuscript, and printing rights offered (first rights, second rights, reprinted from...).** Also indicate if you have submitted the manuscript simultaneously to other publications.

• We would also like to know if your manuscript is on computer disk so we may request the disk if we do purchase your manuscript. A 3.5" DOS or Mac disk with your article in a Microsoft Word for Windows format is best. Our second preference is WordPerfect 5.0 or 5. 1. **Please indicate at the bottom of your cover letter if your article is available on disk and in what format,** even if it is not one mentioned above. You do not need to send the disk with your initial submission.

ABOUT YOUR MANUSCRIPT'S EVALUATION

• All manuscripts will be evaluated. **We prefer not to receive query letters.**

• We will endeavor to respond within 90 days of your submission.

• Payment will be made on publication of the manuscript. When the manuscript is printed, you will receive two complimentary copies of the issue in which it appears.

• Seasonal manuscripts to be evaluated should reach us I to 2 months prior to the holiday or season described. If your manuscript is chosen, it will be scheduled for the following year.

• The editors of *Woman's Touch* reserve the right to edit your manuscript for clarity and space.

Thank you for considering *Woman's Touch* for your manuscripts. God bless your writing ministry!

Categories: Nonfiction—Christian Interests—Inspirational—Women's Issues

Name: Submissions Editor
Material: All
Address: 1445 BOONVILLE AVE
City/State/ZIP: SPRINGFIELD MO 65802-1894
Telephone: 417-862-2781

Woman's World

If you can write for—and about—the average woman, we want to hear from you! *Woman's World*, a weekly magazine reaching women in the United States and Canada, publishes heart-tugging feature articles about ordinary women's real-life experiences.

Our magazine caters to a cross section of the female population—from women in their twenties to lively senior citizens, from homemakers to harried mothers juggling home and job. What we strive to do through our feature stories is provide our readers with a brief escape into someone else's life—to let them experience another woman's drama, turning point or happy ending.

Articles must be thoroughly researched, not only providing pertinent facts but also revealing the innermost thoughts and feelings of the women profiled. We seek to unfold a story that gets the reader involved with the subject and makes her care about the heroine.

To get to know *Woman's World*, read several issues from cover to cover; the magazine (which you can find at supermarket checkout counters) is your best guide. We suggest you carefully study our style and the types of stories we publish.

Woman's World pays approximately 50 cents a word for feature stories.

Our feature articles are divided into categories. A brief description of each is listed below. Keep in mind that some of the categories overlap and that a story may fit into more than one classification. Don't worry if you're not sure which category would suit a particular story or even if it doesn't fit an established category—we always have room for a compelling story.

Emergency!: Gripping, minute-by-minute accounts of heart-pounding dramas are told as they unfold, so the reader can feel as if she is an actual witness to the event. Written in the third person, dramatic quotes and splashes of colorful detail (but no gore!) should give the reader a vivid mental picture of what occurred. The focus is on a true story of a woman (or child) overcoming a life-threatening crisis, such as a disaster or a dangerous situation.

Examples: (1) A four-year-old girl calls 911 and saves her diabetic mother. (2) Three strangers appear as if by fate to save a woman's life. (3) When a teenager falls through the ice, a woman braves frigid water temperatures to save him. (4) When a sudden storm overturns their boat, a couple spends seven terrifying hours in the water until they're rescued. (5) While walking to school one morning, a teenager notices smoke billowing out of an apartment building. She heroically risks her life to save the 13 elderly people living there. (6) When a little boy wanders into the woods and gets lost, his dog saves his life by keeping him warm through the night until searchers find him. (7) When flood waters reach her doorstep, a grandmother risks her life to save her grandchild.

Happy Ending: These third-person stories may resemble those in other categories, but here the emphasis is on the joyous resolution, which comes almost as a surprise considering how bleak the situation appeared.

Examples: (1) After he finds his birth mother, a young man asks her to help him find his birth father. She does, and after they reunite, love blossoms again. They marry and live happily ever after. (2) A 40-year-old woman wants to have a baby but is told she's in the early stages of cervical cancer and must have a hysterectomy. By chance, she finds a woman who wants to give a baby up for adoption—two weeks after the surgery, she's holding a baby in her arms. (3) A handicapped man nobody really notices discovers a town full of friends after his bike is stolen. (4) After an on-again, off-again romance, a cop at last recognizes true love in his girlfriend as she helps him recover from a gunshot wound.

Helping Each Other: Heartwarming tales of good Samaritans who reach out to someone in need. These are third-person stories, told from a female point of view—either the good Samaritan, the person in need or someone (spouse, daughter, or the like) close to the story. Lots of emotion, vivid descriptions and strong quotes are needed. We need to know how grateful the recipients are, and how terrific the do-gooders are.

Examples: (1) When a young mom gives birth to triplets, 25 members of her church volunteer to change, feed and play with the babies. (2) When they learn a little boy needs a bone-marrow transplant, friends, neighbors and even caring strangers turn out in droves to become possible donors—and one is found. (3) A young man's dreams are shattered when his 20-year-old fiancee is diagnosed with terminal cancer. Friends and neighbors give the couple a wedding. The rings, gown, cake—even the reception—are all gifts to the couple, who can't believe so many people care. (4) When a four-year-old girl suddenly goes into kidney failure and isn't expected to live, the people in her hometown start a prayer chain. Almost as suddenly as she was stricken, the little girl recovers. Her doctors can't explain why—but everyone else knows it's a miracle. (5) A homeless family of six gets a fairy godmother when a woman reads a newspaper article about their plight. She moves them into her own home until they can get back on their feet.

Medical Miracle: A third-person retelling of a recovery, birth or the like that defied all odds or was made possible by a new medical procedure.

Examples: (1) Almost seven months into her pregnancy a woman suffers two heart attacks. An emergency angioplasty saves her and her unborn child. (2) When a brain aneurysm nearly kills a 22-year-old student, her doctors worry, is her identical twin in danger too? They find that she, too, has an aneurysm, and clamp it before it bursts. (3) After battling cystic fibrosis her whole life, a 29-year-old mom is told only a lung transplant can save her life. She's put on a transplant list, but when her condition worsens, her sister donates a lobe from one of her own lungs, giving her a second chance at life. (4) After trying for 10 years to have a baby, in vitro fertilization makes a couple's dream of conceiving come true. They feel triply blessed to learn they're having three babies, but when she goes into premature labor the woman fears for the lives of her unborn children. After delivering one baby, her doctors are able to stop her labor, giving the other two more time to grow. Sixteen days later, the other two are born. All are healthy.

My Guardian Angel: Told in either the first or third person, My Guardian Angel tells the story of a woman facing a crisis or situation she doesn't think she can overcome. At her darkest moment, help appears. It can be a good Samaritan in the form of a friend, family member or perfect stranger. Or fate can step in, leaving the woman with a strong feeling that someone is watching over her.

Examples: (1) Although she was never able to have a child, a woman loves her teenage nephew as her own. When he dies in a car accident, she thinks she'll never get over her grief. Then one day, she hears a bluebird chirping in her yard. She remembers that, as a young boy, her nephew promised that if he died before her, he'd come back as a bluebird and sing to her. Realizing that the love they shared could never die, her heart begins to heal. (2) A young mom is struggling to raise her two young children when her four-year-old is diagnosed with a brain tumor. She wonders how she'll cope with a sick child and pay the mounting hospital bills. Just when she feels she's all alone, a friend offers her a job that allows her to work from her daughter's hospital room. (3) After her abusive husband's beating leaves a woman visually impaired, she leaves him. But she feels worthless and alone until a service dog helps her reclaim her life and her happiness. (4) While in a coma, a young woman waits for death until she's "visited" by her deceased sister. Told it isn't her time to die, the young woman finds the will to live again and makes a full recovery. (5) A mother is heartbroken over her daughter's infertility. Desiring her child to know the happiness she's known as a mom, she prays that her daughter will have a baby. Miraculously, the daughter and son-in-law are soon blessed with an adopted baby. A few years later, knowing her daughter aches for another adopted baby, she prays again. It works! Sure that God hears her prayers, the mom asks once more for a blessing of a child for her daughter. This time—against all odds—the daughter finally conceives! (6) After years in an abusive marriage, a woman feels so trapped and alone she doesn't think there's a way out. But one night, a stranger in a parking lot sees the pain in her eyes and hands her a card with her name and phone number on it. Telling her she isn't alone, the stranger asks the woman to call if she needs to talk. She does, and the kind stranger becomes her lifeline, helping her find the strength to leave her abusive marriage and build a new life for herself and her children.

My Story: A first-person narrative that reveals one woman's thoughts and emotions as she comes to terms with a major life problem. We must be able to sympathize with the woman and her plight: Her hopes, fears and aspirations must be candidly exposed. On occasion a man's story is told, but only as it relates to his wife's, daughter's or girlfriend's situation. Sometimes a child's story is told. No matter what the age or gender of the subject, the story must be moving.

Examples: (1) When her baby girl tragically dies, a young mother's grief is so deep it tears her marriage apart. Just when all seems lost, she realizes she's pregnant. Although she could never forget her firstborn child, the new life growing inside her

helps her realize life must go on. Her heart and her marriage are healed. (2) When an 18-year-old girl is diagnosed with breast cancer and undergoes a mastectomy, she faces a mountain of fear. Afraid she'll feel like a victim for the rest of her life, she takes on the challenge of joining a mountain-climbing expedition to raise money for breast cancer research. The grueling 19,000-foot hike teaches her she's stronger than she realized. At the end of the climb she realizes she's no longer a victim but a survivor. (3) After living her whole life hiding the fact that she has AIDS, an 11-year-old girl wants to share her secret in the hopes that her teachers, friends and the kids at school will understand why she's often tired and sick. She bravely stands before her class and tells her story. To her great joy, she wins understanding and acceptance. (4) A young mother's life turns into a nightmare when, just days after giving birth, she experiences severe mood swings that have her laughing one minute and crying the next. Things go from bad to worse when she becomes obsessed with cleanliness and begins hallucinating. She's diagnosed with postpartum psychosis and is hospitalized. Medication, therapy and her desire to be a mother to her child help her reclaim her life. (5) When her teenage daughter is diagnosed with anorexia, a heartbroken mother is determined to make her well. But her loving intentions turn their home into a battleground. As her daughter withers away before her eyes, the mom realizes her daughter will only get better when and if she decides she wants to live. She lets go, and the daughter chooses life and makes a full recovery. (6) After battling her weight all her life, a wife and mother decides that being happy and healthy is more important than being thin. Once she stops hating her reflection in the mirror, she feels freer and happier than she imagined possible.

One Woman's Battle: (runs in the magazine as Courage, Triumph, Victory, Justice or Success) One Woman's Battle is a third-person account of how a woman meets a challenge, injustice, poverty or other setback. The cause she takes up can be her own or one taken up on behalf or in memory of a loved one. Whenever possible, the piece should have strong quotes reflecting both sides of the story, and some sort of resolution. Take care not to approach it like a newspaper account—we don't want a list of facts. If legal proceedings are part of the story, include them as a springboard that gives us insight into how the situation has affected the woman and her family. As with any *Woman's World* story, we need to share her experience.

Examples: (1) A teenager beseeches a high school to post-humously award an honorary diploma to her younger sister who, at the time of her death, was just a few credits short of graduation. (2) A woman sues her ex-husband on behalf of her young children because he's a deadbeat dad. (3) An emergency room nurse fights to get a law passed enabling doctors and nurses to notify the police when drivers responsible for DWI accidents are brought in for medical treatment. (4) A mom fights for anti-stalking laws after her teenage daughter is stalked. (5) Told she'll never walk again, a stroke victim refuses to give up hope for a complete recovery. With nothing but faith and her family's love to sustain her, she undergoes painful physical therapy for 10 years until, one day on the beach; she realizes she can wriggle her toes in the sand! Eventually she regains the use of her legs. (6) After her hairdresser gives her a bad perm, a woman sues the salon. (7) After she's told her pet pig must go, a woman fights her condominium association and wins the right to keep her beloved pet. (8) A woman whose little boy is diagnosed as learning disabled designs computer programs to help him—and winds up starting a successful business helping kids learn. (9) A woman left struggling after a layoff decides to become her own boss and launches her own construction business.

A Woman's Story: A third-person account of real, undying love—a moving piece about the bond that exists between a parent and child, a husband and wife or friends, or even a pet and owner. It can also be about the love that blossoms between a man and woman. The story should leave the reader with a warm, wonderful feeling. It has to be filled with tender, loving quotes and anecdotes.

Examples: (1) An 11-year-old is in a coma after a car accident and nothing can rouse him until his dog Rusty gives him a kiss, waking his young master. (2) Although she's never had a child of her own, a single woman keeps a promise to her dying friend and raises her teenage daughter. (3) When their stepdad is diagnosed with terminal cancer, the kids he selflessly helped raise return his love a hundred fold. Telling their mom to quit her job so she can spend all her time with Dad, they make sacrifices to pay the bills—moving back home to pay rent, getting second jobs to cover the mortgage payments. They cook meals, cut the grass and take care of repairs. He tearfully thanks them—but they tell him he's the one who deserves the thanks for giving them the fatherly love, understanding and guidance they needed growing up. (4) A grandma donates her kidney to her critically ill granddaughter and saves the little girl's life. (5) An adoptive mom finds her son's birth mother to fill an empty place in his heart. (6) A dying dad leaves his two-year-old daughter a legacy of love by writing her letters for her to open on all the important days of her life—the first day of school, her graduation, wedding, birthdays, days when she's feeling sad.

Woman's Best Friend: We run real-life stories in our pets column.

Examples: (1) A family's cat wakes a mom just in time for her to get help for her son, who was having seizures while the family slept. (2) An ailing cat receives a kidney transplant, and the owners adopt the donor cat, a stray who would have been euthanized at the shelter. (3) A family is heartbroken when their dog has a stroke. They can't bear to put her to sleep, so they give her lots of tender loving care, and against all odds, she walks again and makes a full recovery.

Send your story idea/synopsis typed and double-spaced, with the original newspaper clip, if any, along with a self-addressed, stamped envelope (SASE) and your name, address and day and evening phone numbers to the address below. Please be sure to include which category you think your article is appropriate for and write it on the envelope. Or fax to Features. Sorry, we can only return your submission if you provide an SASE.

Categories: Nonfiction—Business—Children—Consumer—Cooking—Crafts—Economics—Entertainment—Family—Fashion—Food/Drink—Gardening—Health—Hobbies—Marriage—Physical Fitness—Nutrition—How-to—Beauty—Home—Nature—Women's Issues

Name: Stephanie Saible, Editor-in-Chief
Material: All
Address: 270 SYLVAN AVE.
City/State/ZIP: ENGLEWOOD CLIFFS, NJ 07632
Telephone: 201-569-6699
Fax: 201-569-3584
E-mail: DearWW@aol.com

Women Alive!

We are especially interested in articles which encourage spiritual growth such as those on prayer, praise, and Bible reading.

Other topics of interest to our readers:

Living as a Christian in the workplace

Mothering—helps in discipline and in rearing spiritual children

Improving marriage

Discouragement—especially in ministry

Self-consciousness/shyness—relating to new people

Improve communication in family and marriage

Help with handling finances

Do retired women still have a place of service?

Temptations known only to the singles

Reinforcement techniques for single mothers

How can I reach the unsaved?

We are interested in articles which show Scripture applied to daily living. Most Christian women understand what they should do but need godly role models, so we prefer that you use examples of your obedience rather than your failures.

To receive a sample magazine please send $1.25 or a 9 x 12 envelope with four first-class stamps.

Editors of *Women Alive* evaluate a manuscript using the following criteria:

1. Can the focus of the article be supported by Scripture?

2. Does it meet our purpose of helping women who are intent on spiritual growth?

3. Is the focus maintained throughout the article?

4. Is it well developed and illustrated?

5. Does it have a unique approach to the subject?

6. Is it written in a natural style (avoiding triteness and clichés)?

7. Will it have impact?

8. Will the reader's interest be maintained throughout the article?

Women Alive pays from $15 to $30 for each article depending on length and quality of article. *Women Alive* purchases either first rights or reprints but with payment we purchase the right to allow the articles to be translated into other languages by nonprofit missionary organizations.

We look forward to receiving your articles!

Categories: Nonfiction—Christian Interests

Name: Aletha Hinthorn, Editor
Material: All
Address: PO BOX 4683
City/State/ZIP: OVERLAND PARK
Telephone: KS 66212
Fax: 913-649-8583

Women Artists News Book Review

Please refer to Midmarch Arts Press.

Categories: Arts—Literature—Poetry—Women Artists—Women's Issues

Name: Submissions Editor
Material: All
Address: 300 RIVERSIDE DR
City/State/ZIP: NEW YORK NY 10025

Women's Sports + Fitness

Thank you for your interest in *Women's Sports + Fitness* magazine. WS + F is dedicated to celebrating the lifestyle of active women through the spirit of sports and fitness. Our pages reflect this with articles that inform, entertain and inspire our readers, America's most active women.

NEWS + VIEWS (50-500 words), our front-of-book section, contains short, newsy articles on health. fitness, sports and nutrition. We are always interested in timely or offbeat information on accomplishments of well-known athletes or "firsts" for women in sports. We also review books, software and videos relevant to active women.

BEING THERE (700-1,000 words) articles provide first-person accounts of unusual or adventure events and trips. These should include a section of tips, providing phone numbers and information for readers interested in participating in such an event.

WINNING WAYS (700 words) profiles an amateur athlete who competes at a high level. These are women with full-time jobs, mothers and students—our readers—who manage to fit their athletics successfully into a full life.

The **HEALTH + FITNESS** section provides service information about training, health, nutrition and sports medicine topics, as well as equipment reviews.

• **TRAINING** columns (700-1,200 words) offer expert coaching on recommended training regimens for specific sports.

• **MINDING THE BODY** articles (700-1,200 words) contain the most progressive mind-body advice and the latest information on holistic issues for women.

• Our **NUTRITION** column (700-1,200 words) provides current nutrition news and recommendations for maximizing the benefits of exercise through diet.

• **REVIEWS** (1,000-1,200 words) provide well-tested and well-researched advice on the latest sports equipment for women. These are usually done in-house, but your suggestions are welcome.

FEATURES (1,000-2,000 words) include profiles of the pros, recreational athletes. amateurs and the athlete next door, health-, sports- and/or nutrition-related issues, adventure travel, and other topics relevant to today's active woman. We look for timely. well-written and thoughtful pieces. Remember the words should *inform, inspire* and *entertain*.

We close each issue with **OBSERVATIONS**. We look for well-written. humorous, provocative or insightful essays that will touch a responsive cord in active women.

Please submit queries with recent clips. Also, let us know why *Women's Sports + Fitness* readers would be interested in your story. We will send you a copy of a current issue if you enclose a check for $5.00 for postage and handling. Allow at least a month for a response.

Categories: Adventure—Diet—Outdoors—Sports—Travel

Name: Dagney Scott, Editor
Material: Features, Observations
Name: Heather Prouty, Associate Editor
Material: News + Views
Name: Jean Weiss, Senior Editor
Material: Columns
Address: 2025 PEARL ST
City/State/ZIP: BOULDER CO 80302
Telephone: 303-440-5111
Fax: 303-440-7253

Wonderful Ideas
For Teaching, Learning, and Enjoying Mathematics!

1. Manuscripts should focus on a successful teaching idea, lesson, strategy, project, problem, or program for teaching, learning, and enjoying mathematics. While the readers of WI cover a wide range of ages and abilities, we generally publish ideas geared to grades 2 through 8. We prefer hands-on, classroom-tested ideas.

2. Manuscripts should be typed and not more than 900 words in length. Manuscripts submitted on 3.5" Macintosh format (Microsoft Word preferred) are welcome and appreciated. If sending a disk, please also send a printout of your article.

3. There are different types of articles that appear in *Wonderful Ideas:*

• **Puzzlers:** double-sided, problem-solving cards to be passed out directly to students. Featured every month.

• **Kids' Corner:** monthly "brain teaser" problems for stu-

dents to solve. Each month, we include at least six problems and solutions.

• **Wonderful Materials:** occasional feature reviewing worthwhile math materials of many kinds, such as manipulatives, books, or games. In the past, reviews have included Fraction Bars® and NCTM's *Addenda Series*.

• **Make-It Math:** occasional feature showcasing a puzzle or activity that requires students to make something. Past Make-It Math articles have included tessellations, Tangrams, and Pentominoes.

• **Wonderful Ideas:** general category for all other activities, games, and lessons.

4. Manuscripts should include the following information: topics involved, appropriate grade levels, materials needed, type of activity, description of the idea, and extensions or variations. If appropriate, include discussion questions, student responses, or samples of student work. Also, include author's name, address, phone number, current position, and school name.

5. Oftentimes in WI, text is accompanied by a reproducible page featuring worksheets, charts, game boards, problems or other graphics. We encourage you to include graphics with your article. Graphics must be black and white. Photographs are not acceptable. Examples of student work are welcome.

6. We reserve the right to edit and rewrite articles without prior author approval.

7. Payment is rendered upon publication. Rates of pay are modest and vary according to the material sent. Authors receive one copy of the newsletter in which the material is published.

8. Manuscripts are normally evaluated within ten weeks of receipt.

9. If you have an idea, but dislike writing, we will be happy to talk to you about your idea. If it matches our needs, we will write it up for publication and credit you for the idea. However, no payment is offered.

10. All submissions must be original and not previously published.

11. Samples of previously published articles are available upon request.

WI is always pleased to receive manuscripts and to talk to teachers about their ideas. Please call us with any questions you might have.

Note: Payment is not provided for students and/or teachers who send in names and solutions for **Kids' Corner** Problem Solvers. In addition, payment is not provided for contest entries that are published.

Multiple authors share the standard pay.

Categories: Education—Mathematics

Name: Nancy Segal Janes, Publisher
Material: All
Address: PO BOX 64691
City/State/ZIP: BURLINGTON VT 05406-4691
Telephone: 973-376-9382
Fax: 973-376-9386
E-mail: nancy@wonderful.com

Remember: Editors change jobs and publishers change addresses. It is wise to invest in a phone call for the current information before submitting.

Woodall's Publications

Woodall Publications publishes several regional tabloids for RV owners, prospective RV owners, campers and others interested in the RV lifestyle. Our regional publications are:

WOODALL'S California Traveler, The RV Lifestyle Source for the Golden State
- California
- 12 issues per year
- Minimum monthly circulation: 25,000

WOODALL'S Camperways, The Mid-Atlantic RV Lifestyle Source
- Delaware, Maryland, New Jersey, New York, Pennsylvania and Virginia
- 12 issues per year
- Minimum monthly circulation: 30,000-38,000

WOODALL'S Camp-orama, The RVers Guide to Florida
- Florida
- 12 issues per year
- Minimum monthly circulation: 30,000-35,000

WOODALL'S RV Traveler (formerly Trails-a-Way). The RVers Guide to the Midwest and Heartland
- Illinois, Indiana, Michigan, Ohio and Wisconsin
- 12 issues per year
- Minimum monthly circulation 30,000-38,000

WOODALL'S Southern RV, the RV Lifestyle Source for the Southeast
- Georgia, Kentucky, North Carolina, South Carolina and Tennessee
- 12 issues per year
- Minimum monthly circulation: 28,000

WOODALL'S Carolina RV Traveler: The RV Lifestyle Source for the Carolinas
- North and South Carolina
- 12 issues per year
- Minimum monthly circulation: 10,000

WOODALL'S Northeast Outdoors, The RV Lifestyle Source for the Northeast
- Connecticut, Maine, Massachusetts, New Hampshire, New Jersey, New York, Rhode Island and Vermont
- 12 issues per year
- Minimum monthly circulation: 12,000

WOODALL'S Texas RV, The RVers Guide to Family Camping in Texas
- Texas
- 6 issues per year (bi-monthly)
- Minimum monthly circulation: 25,000-30,000

WOODALL'S Discover RVing, An Introduction to the Camping and RVing Lifestyle
- Distributed in the Midwest and Southeast; focus on potential RV buyers, noting how to get started RVing
- 1 issue per year; distributed in the spring

WOODALL'S Northeast Summers, The RV Traveler's Guide to Vacations in the Northeast
- Distributed in the Mid-Atlantic and Midwest; focus on summer RV traveling in the Northeast
- 1 issue per year; distributed in the winter

WOODALL'S Sunny Destinations, A Snowbird's Guide to Camping in the Sunbelt
- Distributed in the Mid-Atlantic and Midwest; focus on winter destinations such as Florida, southern Texas, Arizona, South Carolina, southern California
- 1 issue per year; distributed in the fall

READERSHIP

Our readers are owners or prospective owners of RVs. They are primarily interested in nonfiction articles about places to go and things to see and do in the respective geographic regions of each publication. We will review articles on the following topics:
- Specific destinations within the regions
- Regional activities such as fishing, festivals or special events
- Profiles of RV owners
- RV hints or technical information on RVing or camping
- Humorous or insightful camping trips
- Interesting or unusual campgrounds
- Opinion pieces on the RVing lifestyle
- RVing lifestyle pieces from the RV Man or RV Woman's perspective

SUBMISSIONS

Please send query letters. Queries by phone and unsolicited manuscripts are *not* encouraged. Each publication is produced by Woodall Publications at the address below. All queries, manuscripts and materials should be submitted to this location to the editor's attention.

The author's name, address, telephone number and social security number, word count, and rights offered should appear on the first page [of the manuscript]. If a submitted article has been previously published, the publication and date must be noted.

The author's name and story title should appear on subsequent pages, along with page numbers.

Each article should include a sidebar listing any sources, contacts or destinations mentioned, noting exact addresses, phone numbers, directions, admission prices, hours of operation and restrictions. Photos (*prints, not slides*) and/or illustrations should accompany stories. (Destination stories need accompanying photos.) Each photograph must include the author's name and the story name on the back.

We have the capability to copy manuscripts from 3½" computer floppy disks. We use Macintosh Microsoft Word software, and can read all versions up to and including MacWrite and WordPerfect for the Macintosh.

The publisher reserves the right to edit all copy. Payment will be made on the published word count.

For sample copies, send a 10"x13" SASE (four first class stamps) for each publication requested.

PAYMENT

Standard payment is $.10 per published word, $5 per published photo, for first North American rights, made upon publication. In the rare case that an article (not a query) be accepted for publication and then not used, we offer a kill fee of 50%.

We reserve reprint rights for accepted material with multi-regional applications, as well as Woodall Publications' Internet home page, for a period of one year. Generally, manuscripts previously published in non-RV/camping-related publications will be considered for one-time rights.

Payment for first rights to a column with possible reprint rights in other publications will be determined by the editor.

Payment, return of materials and a writer's copy are sent at the end of the month in which the article is published. Materials and tearsheets are returned under separate cover.

Categories: Nonfiction—Outdoors—Regional—RV—Travel

Name: Brent Peterson, Editor
Material: Recreational Vehicles
Address: 13975 W POLO TRAIL DR
City/State/ZIP: LAKE FOREST IL 60045
Telephone: 800-323-9076

Fax: 847-362-6844
E-mail: bpeterson@woodallpub.com
Internet: www.woodallpub.com

WoodenBoat

WoodenBoat is the bimonthly magazine for wooden boat owners, builders, and designers. Unlike any other periodical in our field, we are devoted exclusively to the design, building, care, preservation, and use of wooden boats, both commercial and pleasure, old and new, sail and power. We work to convey quality, integrity, and involvement in the creation and care of these craft, to entertain, to inform, to inspire, and to provide our varied readers with access to individuals who are deeply experienced in the world of wooden boats.

WoodenBoat publishes approximately 60 feature articles a year, from many parts of the world. Many are unsolicited, submitted by both amateur and professional writers. Our primary interest is to publish informative material, so writing style is secondary when we consider an article for publication. Obviously, our ideal manuscript is informative *and* smoothly written, but we're willing to do some work to help make it so.

We'll consider your ideas in all forms-from a short query to a detailed outline, from a rough draft to a finished manuscript. Our preference is to receive a detailed article proposal or outline, accompanied by a sampling of the slides, photos, or drawings that will be available for illustrations. We can then advise whether we would be likely to publish the proposed article, and we can occasionally make your job easier by suggesting information or illustration sources and by asking for certain details that would make the article more acceptable.

Since our magazine is published for professionals and amateurs, our featured articles usually explore subjects in great depth. To gain a better understanding of the type of article we tend to publish, take a careful look at a few recent back issues of the magazine. Please understand, however, that we welcome other ideas and approaches, and encourage you to share your thoughts on creative and innovative projects.

SOME OF OUR INTERESTS

If you've been reading *WoodenBoat* for long, you'll have noticed that although our interests are wide and varied, we like to present detailed, informative material. If you're writing an article about a boat builder, for example, we'll want to know (at least) these kinds of things:

• Some history of the builder or the boatyard.

• Names of any famous boats or types of boats developed there.

• Number of builders and carpenters employed, and number of apprentices, if any.

• Delivery schedules and costs for boats built.

• Design modification and/or drafting capabilities available at the yard.

• Specific design or drafting experience of the builder or draftsman.

• Lumber storage and drying facilities; capacity in board feet, and the quality of the facility.

• Primary types of lumber used in construction; e.g., red or white oak for keels and frames, fir or cedar for planking, and teak for decks and trim.

• Be specific with names of wood types; e.g. Philippine mahogany, Honduras mahogany, hard pine (Southern yellow, longleaf, etc.), or teak, etc. And, where possible, give the technical Latin name.

• Where does the builder get his lumber? What does he think about the availability of boat-building lumber?

• Types of fastenings used, such as wood screws, boat nails, copper rivets, etc.; and what metals, such as bronze, Monel,

wrought iron, galvanized steel, etc., are used.

• Types of glues used in the permanent joining of wood, such as resorcinol, epoxy, or older and more traditional glues.

• Types of bedding compounds; are they oil based, or are they the more modern two-part mixes like Thiokol (polysulfide) compounds?

• Special boat building techniques or suggestions.

• Types of finishes used; some builders finish entire boats with linseed oil, while others use oil-based paints and varnishes, and still others use epoxy- or polyurethane-based paints.

• Does the builder use wood preservatives? How does the builder build long life into his boat?

If you're writing about an amateur boat-building project, we'd like an article that explains how you figured out the tasks at hand and executed them correctly, rather than a litany of errors followed by an account of how you bailed yourself out.

The possibilities for how-to articles on individual projects are limitless-our readers like to learn how to make their own tools, spars, oars, rudders, tillers, grabrails, hatches, hanging lockers, hardware, and more. They're also interested in learning how to repair their own boats and in exploring not only the methods, but the economics, too.

We welcome general interest material on types of boats or on particular boats as long as substantial detail is available. This material could focus on the evolution and impact of the craft, as well as its construction. Other general interest material could include features on boatbuilding schools, cooperatives, the evaluation and analysis of products, materials, tools, books, and more.

We're interested in the use of wooden boats as well. We'll consider information about seamanship, rigs, and uses for types of boats (who's found the perfect pocket cruiser?). We do not publish fiction, or poetry, and our acceptance of cruising tales is rare; we just don't have the space.

NEWS MATERIAL

"On the Waterfront" is a column of news and comment published in each issue of *WoodenBoat* magazine. "Eclectic" best describes its contents, which run the gamut from straight news concerning all aspects of wooden boat construction and ownership to news about museums, magazines, books, organizations, events, maritime preservation and politics, interesting products, and people.

"On the Waterfront" is written by Peter H. Spectre, who obtains his information from various sources, including a number of correspondents around the world. Few of these correspondents are journalists; most are enthusiasts who enjoy sharing news about the goings-on in their area.

Since Peter writes the column himself, the best way to contribute to "On the Waterfront" is to send information only. There is no need for finished reports or polished articles; the "who, what, when, where, and why" is sufficient. You may submit notes, letters, news clippings, tear sheets, brochures-anything that clarifies the story. Comment—your opinion on matters pertaining to wooden boats and nautical subjects in general—is welcome but should be short, a paragraph or two at most. Our space is limited, so succinctness is an imperative. Photographs and line art are helpful but not necessary.

All material is credited to source, and contributions from both regular and occasional correspondents are acknowledged and paid for upon use. Payment is based on the form and complexity of the submission. For example, we pay $5 for a newspaper clipping; $10 to $15 for a newspaper clipping with a few words of comment from the contributor; $20 to $25 for a moderately detailed report. Long reports or letters that are quoted extensively in the column earn more. Photographs and line art are paid for at the rate of $15 apiece.

BOAT DESIGNS

We seek all manner of boat plans (traditional and radical) for our "Designs" column. If you would like to have your work considered for publication, please send reduced photocopies (8½"x11" or 11"x17") of the *complete* drawings, specifications, and designer's commentary to Mike O'Brien, Designs, here at *WoodenBoat*.

As we do not usually return unsolicited material, please do not send us your original drawings. Plans that we don't publish immediately will be placed in our files for future consideration.

WHAT TO SEND

Text

Most of our articles run from 1,000 to 4,000 words, and while we are not restricted by the same space requirements as most magazines, we do limit the size of certain types of articles. If in doubt, inquire. Whenever possible, please send text on disk. We can currently read or translate files in any ASCII program. Be sure your name and address are on your manuscript, your disk, and on each slide, photo, or drawing that you send us. All reasonable care is taken with contributions. Keep a copy of your manuscript, and a list of submitted material.

Photos

We like to see a sampling of photos or slides when you send us an article proposal, and when you send us a full manuscript, we'd like to see as large a selection of photos or slides as possible. We prefer slides.

When evaluating photographs, we consider how well a photograph tells the story, as well as its basic composition and design. If you're taking your own photos of a project, plan them carefully to be as clear and instructive as possible. Think picture-on-the-page when you look through the viewfinder. Shoot only what you want your readers to see-move the patio furniture, garbage cans, cars, and smiling relatives. If you're photographing the whole boat, be sure the bow doesn't get lopped off—or the top 6" of the sail. If you're shooting on the water, take care to keep the horizon straight so the boat and the ocean aren't going uphill. Many of the beautiful photos you see on the pages of *WoodenBoat* were taken by amateurs who paid attention to these kinds of details.

If you work with black-and-white film, we like good-quality, glossy prints, preferably 8"x10". Rich blacks, crisp whites, and good gradation of grays are essential to fine reproduction. Be sure to keep your negatives-in the case of poor-quality or very small prints, we require the loan of negatives for printing by our staff photographer. We cannot use photos printed on silk-finish paper.

If you have old photos that complement a historical article, we'd like to see them (or clear copies), even if the quality isn't top-notch. We know a retoucher who can work wonders with an airbrush to spruce up copies of antique photos.

Be sure your name and address are on each slide or photo. And please tell us the name and address of the person who took each photo so that we can give credit properly. Photographic material should be sent via certified or registered mail to minimize the risk of loss or damage in transit. If you would like any special precautions taken with the handling or return of your material, please make these arrangements with Betsy Powell, our editorial assistant.

If you don't have photos or drawings to illustrate your article, don't give up. We work with a number of talented photographers and illustrators who are happy to take assignments.

Your Biography

We would like to know about you. Tell us what you do, what current project you're involved in, what you plan for the near future that might be of interest to *WoodenBoat* readers—whatever you wouldn't mind seeing in print about yourself.

What Happens Next

It takes us a lot of time to consider all the material that comes into our office each day. We have a relatively small staff, and the task of reading each manuscript takes time if it is to be carefully considered. We will acknowledge receipt of your editorial submission soon after its arrival, but we ask for your patience until a decision can be made. Once accepted, articles may have a lengthy wait before being published. Because we are a hi-monthly, we must plan issues well in advance. We ask that you bear in mind the possibility of delays of up to eight months (if not more) before publication of some material.

When we've decided to publish your article, we'll ask you to sign a copyright statement. Copyright laws require that we obtain written permission from authors for the use of their material. This provides protection for you and grants us first North American serial rights only to your material.

PAYMENT

Payment for articles is made on publication. We will send you a check and a copy of the new issue as soon as it is available, and we will return all your material a couple of weeks later, when it comes back to us from the printer. The following are our usual rates:

Feature Text
$150-$200 per 1,000 words.

Photos	Color	B&W
Cover	$350	
Full page	$125	$75
¾ page	$100	$60
½ page	$ 75	$45
¼ page	$ 50	$30
Spot	$ 25	$15

Professional Drawings and Illustrations
Depending upon the size and complexity of the work, payment for drawings ranges from $50 to $400.

WHERE TO SEND IT ALL

Material directed to Peter Spectre or Mike O'Brien can be flagged with their names. Don't forget to put your name and address on each piece of material, and please enclose a return envelope with sufficient postage.

If you are inclined toward writing or reporting, and understand the objectives of *WoodenBoat*, we hope you'll share your ideas with us.

Matthew P. Murphy, Editor

Categories: Nonfiction—Boat Building—Seamanship

Name: Refer to Guidelines
Address: PO BOX 78
City/State/ZIP: BROOKLIN ME 04016
Telephone: 207-359-4651
Fax: 207-359-8920
E-mail: Wbeditor@woodenboat.com
Internet: www.woodenboat.com

The Worcester Review

The Worcester County Poetry Association, Inc. was founded in 1971 and incorporated as a non-profit organization in 1972. Over the years it has sponsored readings by nationally and internationally-known writers, providing a forum for local poets and students, and celebrating the rich literary history of Central Massachusetts.

The Association prints and distributes original poetry broadsides and publishes *The Worcester Review*, an annual literary magazine.

SUBMISSIONS

The Worcester Review invites submission of previously unpublished poetry, fiction, literary articles, photography, and graphic art.

Guidelines are as follows:

POETRY:

Submit 3-5 poems, typed on 8½"x11" paper. The author's name should appear in the upper left-hand corner of each page.

FICTION:

Submit 4,000 words maximum on 8½"x11" paper. Author's name should appear in the upper left-hand corner of each page. Pages must be numbered in sequence.

LITERARY ARTICLES:

Submit scholarly and critical articles (10 typed, double-spaced pages maximum using MLA guidelines) on 8½"x11" paper.

PHOTOGRAPHY:

Submit black and white glossy prints (minimum size 5"x7").

GRAPHIC ART:

Submit black and white graphic art on white paper (5"x7").

All submissions must be accompanied by a cover letter indicating author, materials submitted, and return address.

The Worcester Review reserves first publication rights for all submissions chosen for publication. Payment will be two copies upon publication plus a small honorarium.

Response time is six-12 months so multiple submissions are acceptable if you note that.

Categories: Fiction—Literature—Poetry

Name: Rodger Martin, Editor
Material: All
Address: 6 CHATHAM ST
City/State/ZIP: WORCESTER MA 01609
Telephone: 508-797-4770
Internet: www.geocities.com/paris/leftbank/6433

Working Mother Magazine

Writers' Guidelines for unsolicited articles and queries:

Thank you for your interest in *Working Mother*. The magazine is looking for articles (about 1,500 to 1,800 words in length) that help women in their task of juggling job, home and family. We like tightly focused pieces that sensibly solve or illuminate a problem unique to our readers. (The most successful queries are those that reflect a clearly thought-out working mother angle.) Topics that particularly interest us include: child rearing, home and money management, health, family relationships and job-related (work/family) issues. Pieces dealing with travel, food, beauty and fashion are usually staff-written.

If you submit a manuscript, it should be typewritten, double-spaced and accompanied by a self-addressed stamped envelope large enough to contain the manuscript. All submissions are made on speculation and at the author's risk. (The magazine will not be responsible for lost material.) We prefer receiving article proposals rather than completed works. Then, if we find the subject suitable, we can discuss the best way to handle the material.

All manuscripts and queries should be addressed to:
Editorial Department
Working Mother Magazine
The Editors

Categories: Nonfiction—Careers—Children—Cooking—Family—Fashion—Food/Drink—Marriage—Money/Finance—Parenting—Relationships—Travel—Humor—Nutrition—Women's Issues—Home—Beauty

Name: Judsen Culbreth, Editor-in-Chief
Material: All
Address: 135 W. 50TH ST.
City/State/ZIP: NEW YORK, NY 10020
Telephone: (212)445-6100
Fax: (212)445-6174
E-mail: jculbreth@womweb.com

Working Woman

Dear Writer,

Thank you for your interest in *Working Woman*. For the best idea of the kind of material we publish, we strongly encourage you to study several recent issues of the magazine. Thoroughly examine the voice and content of the magazine. *Working Woman* is a business and technology publication. We are concerned with the larger business picture. We are particularly interested in trend pieces that target a specific industry and demonstrate how it is affected by new technology, business practices or market situations. We do not publish straightforward profiles of successful executives or entrepreneurs.

The best sections through which to break into our magazine are Fast Forward and Workshop. Fast Forward pieces are usually 200 to 750 words. They are trend-oriented stories featuring new technology, business strategies, people or products and demographic data that are changing the face of their respective markets. The voice of this section is insider, edgy, and irreverent. Although the articles are short, they are heavily reported and must be tightly focused.

Workshop pieces are 750 to 1,500 words. These are service pieces focused on career and money management, office technology, management practices, and entrepreneurial and legal issues. Workshop serves as a guide for these topics but is not a collection of advice columns or how-to articles. The voice of workshop is knowledgeable and sophisticated without being overly technical.

Please take note of the subjects that we do NOT cover: kids, school, beauty, health, fitness, fashion, lifestyle, entertainment, home, books, food, sexual harassment. Don't be fooled by our name. Our readers are women, but our content is business and finance. Our readers are high level executives and entrepreneurs who are looking for newsworthy information about the changing marketplace and its effects on their businesses and careers.

Unsolicited manuscripts—in lieu of queries—are accepted but not encouraged.

Please include a SASE, (submissions without a SASE will not be returned) and clips of your previous work. We make every effort to respond to all queries within four to six weeks. Payment is upon publication.

Again we thank you for your interest in our publication and we look forward to seeing your query.

Categories: Nonfiction—Business—Careers—Economics—Women's Issues

Name: Editorial
Material: All
Address: 135 WEST 50TH STREET, 16TH FLOOR
City/State/ZIP: NY, NY 10020
Telephone: 212-551-9500
Fax: 212-599-4763

World War II

Please refer to Cowles Enthusiast Media, Inc.

World
The Journal of Life

The World is the bimonthly denominational magazine of the Unitarian Universalist Association of Congregations. Its purpose is to articulate Unitarian Universalist and other liberal religious values, purposes, aesthetics, and spirituality and to publicize UU activities, personalities, and history.

To be considered for publication in the **World**, an article must be directly relevant to Unitarian Universalism. In addition, many issues of the **World** have themes. Topics we plan to cover in the near future include cultural diversity; theology; leadership; and money and charitable giving. It's a good idea to read a few issues to become familiar with the **World** before submitting your work. To order an issue, send $4.00 to the address below.

We publish unsolicited manuscripts most often as "op ed" Commentaries, Among Ourselves news notes about UU activities, or letters to the editor. Occasionally, we publish unsolicited book reviews. Writers of these articles receive two copies of the issue in which they appear; there is no payment.

Materials or story ideas submitted by readers have served as the basis for feature articles, sidebars, and profiles; however, these kinds of articles are usually solicited from freelancers well in advance. If you would like to be considered for **World** feature assignments, send us your resume and one or two writing samples. Payment for features is negotiated when the article is assigned.

We receive many manuscripts; send us your best work. Manuscripts should be succinct, well-thought-out final drafts. We do not accept previously published material, fiction, or unsolicited poetry.

You may also send your article or query by e-mail, or you may submit your work on 3½" high-density disks. Most word processing programs are acceptable; limited formatting is preferable—do not insert carriage returns at the end of each line. **Include a hardcopy,** and let us know what program you used.

Thank you for considering the **World.** Every submission increases our understanding of Unitarian Universalism and thus represents a real contribution to our efforts.

Categories: Religion

Name: Submissions Editor
Material: All
Address: 25 BEACON ST
City/State/ZIP: BOSTON MA 02108
Telephone: 617-742-2100
E-mail: ahoffman@uua.org
Internet: www.uua.org

Worlds of Fantasy & Horror
(formerly Weird Tales®)

There are only three **Rules** for writing; all else is commentary.

RULE ONE: You must seize, then hold, your readers' and your editor's interest and attention, then repay the readers' time and the editor's money by having something to say and sharing it with them.

Rudyard Kipling wrote: "There are nine and sixty ways/ of constructing tribal lays,/ and every single one of them is right!" What follows is commentary not rules. These suggestions may help, but what's important is the result—selling an *interesting* story.

The archetypical plot consists of a *Situation* (the protagonist meets a problem), a *Complication* (the problem makes the protagonist do something about it in a series of actions/reactions of rising intensity), a *Climax* (the protagonist must solve the problem or be broken by it), a *Resolution* (the problem unwinds, the protagonist succeeds or fails), and an *Anticlimax* (leftovers are carted off or explained away). Most (not all) stories follow this pattern.

One of those nine and sixty ways to construct your story is based on suggestions from the science-fiction writer and teacher James Gunn:

• Begin with an idea: What would happen if...? and then work out the natural, believable consequences of that one central idea.

• Create a background, colorful enough to hold interest, but not one that will overwhelm the story. Remember background is just background; you are writing a story not a gazetteer.

• Select characters who will best dramatize the conflict you've plotted. Observe *real* people, and model your cast on them. Show them in action from the start; show their characters by what they say and do. You are writing a story not a set of résumés.

• Pick the best viewpoint for telling *this* story (almost always the most important decision made when writing fiction). Put the reader so firmly into that viewpoint that the reader as he reads, *is* that character. Do not pull the reader out of a viewpoint character to describe what he looks like or to present his biography. Get *on* with the *story.* If your protagonist's appearance is important to him, he'll stop by a mirror soon enough and thus *show* the reader that facet of character without your having to *tell* the reader about it; if it's not important, get on with the story

• Begin your story *where* and when things become *interesting.* Homer began the *Iliad* right in the middle of a war ("I sing of the anger of Achilles...") and Homer sings to us still! Backtrack to explanation or flashback only when it's so relevant to the story that the viewpoint character and the reader still *being* that character remember what happened before this story began. You'll be surprised how few flashbacks you *really* need!

• Write in scenes, dramatizing everything possible. In every scene, put your characters—and readers—firmly into the time and place of that scene. Appeal to the senses—go beyond how things look, go on to the sound and smell and *feel* of the setting. But don't overdo it; omit everything that doesn't advance the story.

• Don't lecture; exposition is all dead matter. Avoid clichés like the plague! Learning to avoid triteness in word and phrase *and* in ideas, plots, characters, and backgrounds is easily half of becoming a good writer.

Mark Twain wrote, in his famous essay, "Fenimore Cooper's Literary Offenses," that:

1. A tale shall accomplish something and arrive somewhere.

2. The episodes of a tale shall be necessary parts of the tale, and shall help to develop it.

3. The personages in a tale shall be alive, except in the case of corpses, and always the reader shall be able to tell the corpses from the others.

4. The personages in a tale, both dead and alive, shall exhibit a sufficient excuse for being there.

5. When the personages of a tale deal in conversation, the talk shall sound like human talk, and be talk such as human beings would be likely to talk in the given circumstances, and have a discoverable meaning, also a discoverable purpose, and a show of relevancy, and remain in the neighborhood of the subject in hand, and be interesting to the reader, and help out the tale, and stop when the people cannot think of anything more to say.

6. When the author describes the character of a personage in his tale, the conduct and conversation of that personage shall justify said description.

7. When a personage talks like an illustrated, gilt-edged, tree-calf, hand-tooled, seven-dollar Friendship's Offering in the beginning of a paragraph, he shall not talk like a Negro minstrel in the end of it.

8. Crass stupidities shall not be played upon the reader by either the author or the people in the tale.

9. The personages of a tale shall confine themselves to possibilities and let miracles alone; or, if they venture a miracle, the author must so plausibly set it forth as to make it look possible and reasonable.

10. The author shall make the reader feel a deep interest in the personages of his tale and in their fate; and shall make the reader love the good people in the tale and hate the bad ones.

11. The characters in a tale shall be so clearly defined that the reader can tell beforehand what each will do in a given emergency.

12. The author shall say what he is proposing to say, not merely come near it.

13. He shall use the right word, not its second cousin.

14. He shall eschew surplusage.

15. He shall not omit necessary details.

16. He shall avoid slovenliness of form.

17. He shall use good grammar.

18. He shall employ a simple, straightforward style.

Elsewhere, he wrote: "The difference between the right word and the almost-right word is the difference between the lightning and the lightning bug." Also: "Truth *is* stranger than fiction, because fiction is obliged to stick to possibilities. Truth isn't."

But all this is commentary not **Rules**.

RULE TWO: You must put your story into a format the editor can read, the copy-editor can edit, & the compositor can set into type.

Ursula Le Gum, in her *The Language of the Night*, writes: "Your story may begin in longhand on the backs of old shopping lists; but when it goes to an editor it should be typed, double-spaced, on one side of the paper only with generous margins - especially the left-hand one—and not too many grotty corrections per page.

"Your name and its name and the page number should be on the top [right corner] of every single page; and when you mail it to the editor it should have enclosed with it a stamped, self-addressed envelope."

Typed (or **machine-printed**) means just that. If you use ribbons, have a supply of new ones on hand; change to a new ribbon when you start the final draft of a story. The output must be *black*, not grey. But do not overink. The typesetter must follow copy to the letter. To do this, he must be able to read, without guessing, every letter on every page. Although your printer may have no end of fancy fonts, it's best to use a simple font that looks like the output of a typewriter like 12-point Courier type, which is ideal; the closer to that, the better. *Italic*, script, or ALL-CAPITAL-LETTER typefaces are Not Acceptable. Never change typefaces within your manuscript; if you want the editor to make such a change, say so in a penciled, marginal note. AVOID typefaces that confuse "i," "I," and "1," or the comma"," with the period"."

Double-spaced means leaving a full, blank line after every typed line; it does not mean putting extra space between words! On a typewriter set the line-feed control to advance the paper two full lines at a time; on a printer set the line spacing at 24 points. Either should give you three typed lines per vertical inch. Do *not* use the one-&-a-half-line setting some typewriters have; do *not* reduce the line spacing anywhere in the manuscript.

Indent every paragraph five spaces, *including dialog.* Leave extra space between paragraphs only where you want to mark a shift in scene or a lapse of time.

On one side of the paper, which should be white, 8.5"x11", 16 or 20 pound bond. Do *not* use any paper that claims to be erasable.

With generous margins, about an inch, all the way around. It's quite all right to put a small mark on the paper about an inch from the bottom to tell you where to stop typing. Margins much larger than one inch waste paper and postage. If you use a word processor check its manual, and then turn *off* the right-justification *and* the hyphenation; do *not* let it suppress "widows & orphans." Do *not* break words at the end of lines. Editors (all editors!) prefer ragged right margins with even spacing between words, and we prefer the same number of lines on every page but the first and the last.

And not too many grotty corrections per page. Neither editors nor compositors are grading for neat-ness; we don't demand letter-perfect-the-first-time typing. We *do* object to erasures. If you use a typewriter XXX-out or line out your deletions, and type or legibly hand-print any corrections above the place each is to be inserted. Lift-off correction tape or white, opaque correction fluid are acceptable but not necessary; cover-up correction tape is *never* acceptable. If you are using a word processor and printer you should make all corrections before you print the submission copy.

Identify your story. Type (or machine-print) your full real name, your social security number **and your address** (so we can send you money!) at the upper left-hand corner of the first page, an inch inside the top and left edges of the page. Your story's title (*your* responsibility; editors don't buy nameless stories) goes about a quarter of the way down the first page, with your name (or your pen name, if you use one) directly under that title. (Two suggestions: Avoid cutesy pen names; your own real name, especially an unusual one, is far better. But if a well-known writer has the same name as yours, change yours in some way such as spelling out your middle name instead of an initial, or the like.) Use paper clips, *not* staples, to hold manuscripts together.

Pages sometimes do go astray. Therefore, a glance at *any* page in the manuscript should reveal the story title, its author and the page number. So: type or print your last name (plus initials if your name is a common one), a word or two from the title, and the page number on the upper right-hand corner of every page, starting with page 2, like this:

XmasCarol/Dickens/pg 26, or **Cujo/S.King/7.** (If you use a separate title page, page numbering starts with the first page of text.)

And when you mail it to the editor, it should have enclosed with it a stamped, self-addressed envelope. Editors much prefer a new 9"x12", *non*-clasp envelope to carry the story to the editor with a second envelope of the same size, folded once, paper-clipped to the back of the manuscript. (The post office doesn't like clasps, those brass things that stick through holes in envelope flaps; editors don't like clasps; and clasp-envelopes cost more. So, please, use *non*-clasp envelopes!)

Please do not use envelopes larger than 9"x12". Address the return envelope to yourself. Both the outgoing and return envelopes should be addressed by typewriter (or machine-printer); if the envelope won't fit in the typewriter type addresses on labels.

Please *affix* U.S. postage stamps (foreign postage is useless to us, and you do us no favors by sending loose stamps!); do *not* use padded envelopes, binders, or stiffeners; do *not* make the editor stand in line at the post office to sign for registered or certified mail; your *only* protection against loss is to keep a good copy of anything you send out. Need U.S. postage? See next page.

The more standard your format, the less editors are distracted from what is really important: *the story itself*

To find out how long the story is, don't actually count the words. Instead, take an average-length, mid-paragraph line. Count the letters and spaces and punctuation in that line. Divide by six. Multiply by lines per page. Multiply by pages (correcting for partly blank pages at beginning and end). Put this "word" count in the upper right corner of the first page.

Call for *italics* by *underlining*; do *not* use an italic typeface in the manuscript itself. Distinguish between the hyphen, as in "mother-in-law" and the dash—typeset like this—but in your manuscript it should look like this — with a space before and a space after.

It's hard for an editor to take seriously an author who keeps mixing up *its* and *it's*, or *lie* and *lay* and their various tenses (*lying, laying, laid, lied, lain,* and *so on*).

Other words you should watch out for are *there/their/they're,*

S-Z

through/threw, were/we're, yoke/yolk, and *form/from* (we have trouble with that last pair ourselves). Spell-check programs do *not* catch errors like these; *you're* responsible for proofreading your manuscripts.

We say, "You must punctuate, paragraph, and indent carefully and correctly."

"How about in dialog?" you ask.

"Especially in dialog," we say. "If in doubt, you must look up how to do it properly. Note that when two or more *consecutive* paragraphs are spoken by the *same* speaker, all have quote marks at the beginning, but only the last has quote marks at the end.

"Also," we suddenly, excitedly expostulate unto thee, "when you're writing dialog, *do not* reach for substitutes for 'say' or 'said,' as we did in this paragraph, nor hang unnecessary adverbs on 'say.' Doing so will soon get silly; worse, it takes attention away from the story. And please notice how we punctuated and capitalized all through our conversation."

You look puzzled. "Can I identify the speaker without using 'said' or a synonym for 'said'?"

"You just did." We smile reassuringly. "Just don't overdo it. Identify the speaker often enough that the reader always knows who is speaking. Don't let pronouns run wild, as in: 'He saw him look at him.' Since 'deep blue sea can mean 'deep-blue sea' or 'deep, blue sea,' you must use commas or hyphens to tell the reader which."

Cover letter? No more than one page long, and only if you really want to; remember that editors don't buy cover letters; they buy stories. Don't distract an editor by telling him how good your story is, or spoil the suspense by giving a synopsis. Do not attach your bibliography or résumé; you may cite two or three earlier sales in the body of that one-page letter. Then get out of the way and let the story sell itself.

However, if the editor's seen the story before, a cover letter *is* necessary to remind her what she said about the story before and to tell her exactly what you've done about her suggestions. And you need a cover letter to explain anything unusual about the rights offered—for example, if the story is part of a novel to be published by [insert name] on [insert date]. Put your typed name and address, and your story's title on every cover letter. But if you don't *need* a cover letter and you're not sure what to put in one, then it's probably better to omit it.

If it's cheaper for you to send a disposable copy mark the manuscript "disposable" so the editor can throw it away if she doesn't buy it. You must still provide a business-letter-sized return envelope, what stationers call a number 10 envelope (NOT a postcard!), with letter-postage affixed, for the editor's reply.

If you are sending us stories from outside the U.S., remember that only U.S. stamps can be used for return postage. Since international postage is so expensive, we strongly recommend that you send a disposable manuscript (so marked) and a return envelope at least 10 by 22 centimeters in size, for the editor's reply. You can send International Postal Reply Coupons to pay for the return postage; each is worth about US$0.60 to us. To send a one-ounce (28 gram) letter to Canada costs us US$0.52; to an overseas address, US$1.00. Reply Coupons cost you a lot, but you can buy U.S. postage by sending a postal money order payable in U.S. funds, to cover the cost of 10 stamps or more, to Postmaster, Bridgeport PA 19405, U.S.A. (or to the Postmaster of any other U.S. city). Include your own address. Explain what stamps you want, and how many of each.

When a reply envelope is to be mailed in the U.S. for delivery to another country, put the name of that country at the *end* of the *last* line of the address.

Dot-matrix printing is acceptable only if one cannot tell at a glance that the print *is* dot-matrix. Do not use draft mode, nor seven- or nine-pin dot-matrix machines.

Submissions to us must be on paper in the format described above, *not* on disk and *not* by e-mail. Unless an editor announces otherwise, assume this is so for all publications. An editor who buys your story will want to know if you can supply it on disk and if so, which word processor and which kind of computer: PC, Apple, or Macintosh. Put these data on the manuscript's first page. (We use a PC, XyWrite®, and Ventura®.)

Manuscript format is not the place to be innovative; do not divert the editor's attention from the *story!* What editors buy is your choice of words (including punctuation!) and the order you put them on paper. Manuscript format, therefore, should be as invisible as possible.

RULE THREE: You must put your story before an editor who might buy it.

Parents, siblings, spouses, offspring, teachers, and friends don't count; neither do closets or desk drawers. You simply *must* send your story to editors (one editor at a time). Remember that editors do not reject people, nor do they predict careers. At worst, editors reject pieces of paper that you typed on; at best, editors send you money. The only opinion that really counts here is that of someone who might buy your story.

We call your attention to the chorus in the opening song of *The Music Man:* "But ya gotta know the territory!" Read your target publications. See what kind of stories they use; note what kinds of stories they do not use. Send for guidelines, always including a return envelope (with postage affixed) for the reply.

In the short-story market, it is almost always better to send a complete manuscript rather than a "would you like to see?" letter. If you fear that a particular market might not be open for submissions, write to the editor and ask if it's open now; and if it's not open, when will it be, with a post card (addressed to you, with postage affixed) for the editor's reply.

How does the "who might buy it" part of the Rule apply to *Worlds of Fantasy & Horror?* Please keep in mind our magazine's title. We almost never buy a story or a poem which has no fantasy content; we hardly ever buy science fiction which lacks fantasy elements.

But this leaves room for an extraordinary range of fiction—and poetry: Robert E. Howard's Conan the Cimmerian and modern swordplay-&-sorcery were born in *Weird Tales®,* and *WoF&H* continues that tradition. H.P Lovecraft's Cthulhu Mythos, Miskatonic University and all, are welcome to our pages, as are stories set in fantasy-worlds of your own invention. We're looking for the best in fantasy-based horror heroic fantasy and exotic mood pieces, plus the occasional "odd" story that won't fit anywhere else. We want to please our readers with superior writing and to surprise them with new ideas. To this end, we will *occasionally* publish a story in which the ominous, eldritch, and/or squamous horrors waiting to pounce turn out to be quite harmless. We almost never use material already published in the U.S.

A 10,000-word story—which takes up almost a quarter of an issue—is about the longest we can use. Most of what we buy is shorter than 8,000 words. We do not serialize novels. We have no minimum length. Short-short stories (less than 1,000 words or so) are very hard to write, but they are easy to sell.

WoF&H does use humor but the humor should touch on fantasy or horror themes. We find that humor works best when structured like other fiction, with high points and low tension and relief; building to a climax and (usually) a very quick anticlimax or none at all. Beware of trying to make every line screamingly funny.

Remember that printed fantasy stories (and science fiction, for that matter) are usually years even decades—ahead of movie and TV versions of the same themes. Especially beware of building a story *(any* kind of story) on current newspaper headlines, which may well be forgotten by the time the story could be printed. As an example: spousal and child abuse are real-life problems, yes—but they're perhaps too familiar to our readers to work as fiction just now.

To know *our* territory ("...ya gotta know the territory!"), look at what we published in *Weird Tales*® in the past and what we publish now in WoF&H. Then try to do even better. (Back issues of *Weird Tales*® and WoF&H are available from the address below: single copies, $5.00 each, including postage; four-issue subscriptions, $16.00 in the U.S. and its possessions; elsewhere, $6.00 and $22.00; all prices in U.S. dollars.)

We respond as fast as we can, and we write an individual letter for almost every rejection. In return, we expect that your submission is not now being seen by any other editor and we hope you will not get *too* upset if we tell you why *we* don't want to use it. Ours is only one opinion, but it *is* possible for us to be right, and our comments might help you to do better with your next story. Remember that we only reject pieces of paper that have been typed on; we do not and cannot reject you. We pay from 3¢ to 6¢ per word on acceptance.

Story elements we see too often:

• We don't object to corpses nor to tragic endings, but protagonists who exist only to wallow in woe and then succumb quietly to an undeserved doom really don't belong in WoF&H. Your protagonists must at least *try* to cope, and must try to change something, even if the outcome is tragic. Stories whose only point is that the world is a dreadful, dreadful place tell our readers what they already know; people read WoF&H to escape everyday futility not to be splattered with more.

• Mere description of a horror is not as effective as telling a *story* about people trying to cope with one, successfully or not. Believable, often sympathetic people make horror stories scary, while standard-issue, cardboard villains who come to a (usually predictable) bad end do not.

• The pseudo-Medieval never-never land, overrun with generic swords-persons, wizards, and dragons has been swordplayed (and ensorcelled) into the ground by now. But *your* imaginary-world setting, characters, and plot elements can be fresh, and new and *interesting*. Look at real histories; get a feel for just how complex the pre-industrial world was. Don't base your characters or your magic on a role-playing game; invent your own.

• Now there's nothing inherently wrong with stories about classical vampires, deals with the Devil, formalities of the Hereafter or people eating people (and vice versa); but our readers have already seen stories based on these ideas. If you wrap a story around an old, familiar idea, add something new and different! A story never surprises readers if all it does is reveal, as a "surprise" ending, that the protagonist is a vampire, or that he finally noticed he's been dead since page 2.

• Please remember that WoF&H is a *fiction* magazine; the Real Inside Truth About The Occult belongs elsewhere, as do real-life ghost sightings and anything about airborne crockery and/or alien abductions.

To sum up:

Most stories rejected by *any* fiction editor are rejected for one or more of these flaws:

• Lack of a clear consistent point of view.

• Too much exposition and too little narration, especially at the beginning.

• Failure to establish the characters' identity and setting, in both time and place, early in the story

• Characters so uninteresting, unpleasant, or unconvincing that the readers don't *care* whether or not those characters get eaten alive (or worse) on stage. Characters who don't even *try* to cope with their problems *(your* protagonists should *protag!)*.

• Plots that fail to resolve (tragically, happily or otherwise) problems or conflicts, but just present them. Plots with neither problems nor conflicts. Plots based on ideas so old and tired that the ending is obvious half-way down page 1. Plots that cheat readers by holding back information for a "surprise" ending.

• Writing so flowery and so filled with sesquipedalian prose that the basic story is lost under too many adjectives, adverbs, and not-quite-right words. Writing which *feels* as if the author were being paid by the word (well, you *are*, but don't let the reader know *that*). Writing too murky or opaque to decipher and decode. Writing so filled with errors in spelling, punctuation, and grammar that no editor wants to wade through the mess.

Things for you to read:

The Elements of Style by Strunk and White, third edition, published by Macmillan, is widely available from good bookstores in hard covers and soft. Absolutely essential. Get hold of a copy and you better believe it!

On Writing Science Fiction: The Editors Strike Back! by Scithers, Schweitzer and Ford—we wrote it, so of course we recommend it. Also: *Science Fiction Writer's Workshop I* by Barry B. Longyear. Both discuss fantasy as well as science fiction; you can order them from Owlswick Press, 123 Crooked Lane, King of Prussia PA 19406-2570, for $19.50 and $9.50, respectively, postpaid. (In Pennsylvania, please add 6% sales tax!)

Any good library should have copies of two different books with the same title: *The Craft of Fiction*, one by Percy Lubbock, the other by William Knott. The chapters on viewpoint in both books are outstanding.

Categories: Fiction—Fantasy—Horror

Name: Submissions Editor
Material: All
Address: 123 CROOKED LN
City/State/ZIP: KING OF PRUSSIA PA 19406-2570
Telephone: 610-275-4463
E-mail: owlswick@netaxs.com

WormWood Review
A Queer Literary/Arts Journal

The *WormWood Review* is a queer literary and arts journal of poetry, fiction, and artwork. As such, our mission is twofold: to publish work *on any theme by* gay, lesbian, bisexual, and transgendered poets and writers; and to publish work/literature *about* the g/l/b/t community. So, while work doesn't have to be "on theme," heterosexual love stories are the least apt to be accepted in this journal.

Our writing style tends toward modern/postmodern. Both the editor and the publisher have biases toward movements such as the beats and the dadas. However, the primary criteria are literary quality and innovation in form and language. Thus, rhyming/iambic pentameter poems do not do well with us. If you are unsure about what this means, we encourage you to buy a sample copy from us to see what we have used in the past, available for $3 (a 40% discount off the cover price).

We publish 2-3 issues per year. *WormWood* is 20-24 pp., 8½"x11" side stapled, with a circulation of 100 primarily in the Twin Cities area. As part of its circulation, however, *WormWood* solicits and has received favorable reviews in national small press and 'zine-related magazines, such as *FactSheet Five.*

You may submit 3-7 original pages of poetry or fiction up to 2,000 words (this means *no more than six pages!*). If you have a longer short story of a piece of a novel, you must submit it in excerpts or in serialized segments of roughly 2,000 words and each segment should be able to stand on its own as well as being part of a larger work. We have an *ongoing deadline.*

Please submit items with a 2-4 line biography and a SASE for reply and return of your work. We encourage you to submit the longer pieces, such as long poems and works of fiction, on computer disk as well as in hard copy. Computer disk submissions should be on IBM-formatted disks in MS Word, WordPerfect, Microsoft Works, or .txt files. It is better if the disk is *formatted in a pre-Windows '95 format.* We can also take work in Word or IBM-compatible programs for Macintosh, provided the disk is IBM-formatted.

For artwork, please submit camera-ready artwork of any size up to 8½"x11". For cover art, the dimensions should be no larger than 7"x7". We encourage you to send graphics on disk as well, and can work with them in the following formats:

*.pcx, *.tif, *.wmf, *.cgm, *.eps, or *.bmp. Bitmaps, or *.bmp, have the least professional resolution and come out very sketchy, but they do always work.

At the present time, contributors receive one copy of the issue in which they are published. Additional copies are available to contributors at $2.50 each. We regret that we are unable to pay you at the moment.

The **WormWood Review** accepts and encourages simultaneous submissions and previously published work. If your work has been previously published, you must have retained your subsequent reprint (also known as second serial) rights and you must give us the name and date of the previous publication(s). If your work is accepted elsewhere while it is under consideration here, please notify us as soon as possible.

If you live in or are visiting the Twin Cities area, we encourage you to attend the monthly **WormWood Review Reading and Open Mic,** held the third Tuesday of each month between 7 and 8:30 p.m. Please call us to confirm location.

Thanks for your interest in the *WormWood Review.*
Keep Writing!
Categories: Arts—Gay/Lesbian—Literature—Poetry—Short Stories

Name: Laura Winton, Editorial Director
Name: Scott Adam, Publisher/Managing Editor
Material: Any
Address: PO BOX 50003
City/State/ZIP: MINNEAPOLIS MN 55405-0003
Telephone: 612-377-6507

Writer's Digest ®

General Focus

Writer's Digest is a monthly handbook for writers who want to write better and sell more. Every word we publish must inform, instruct or inspire the freelancer. Our readers want specific ideas and tips that will help them succeed—and success to our readers means getting into print.

Yet, that doesn't mean that we don't have a little fun in WD. Our style is informal and personal. We try to entertain as well as instruct. We try to speak with the voice of a compassionate colleague, a friend as well as a teacher. And though we don't shy away from explaining the difficulties of getting published today, all of our articles share a certain optimism. WD is infused with a belief in anyone's potential to succeed as a writer.

You can best understand our philosophy by being intimately familiar with *Writer's Digest.* We are a monthly publication with a circulation of more than 200,000. Our readers are of all ages and are scattered throughout the US, Canada and several other countries. Each year we buy about 60-90 major articles and scores of shorter items; our annual *Writer's Yearbook* and associated publications use an additional 15-30 manuscripts.

To obtain sample issues of *Writer's Digest,* send $3.50 per copy ($3.70 in Ohio) to the Circulation Secretary at the address below. An index of each year's contents is published in the December issue.

How to Submit

Writer's Digest editors prefer queries over unsolicited manuscripts. Queries allow us to review your article ideas and to suggest how to tailor them for our audience before you begin writing. Queries also save you time and energy should we reject your idea.

Queries should include a thorough outline that introduces your article proposal and highlights each of the points you intend to make. Your query should discuss how the article will benefit our readers and why you are the appropriate writer to discuss the topic. Although we welcome the work of new writers, we respect success and believe the selling writer can instruct our reader better and establish more credibility than the writer with a good idea but no sales.

Please submit only one query at a time, and allow us 4-8 weeks to review your proposal; ideas that spark our interest are routed among the magazine's editors for review. Queries to *Writer's Digest* are also considered for *Writer's Yearbook* and associated publications. There is no need to query these publications separately.

If we like your proposal, we may either assign you to do the article or ask to see it on speculation ("on spec"). We often work on spec with authors who are new to us or whose article ideas are not as clearly developed as we would like. It's also possible that we'll ask to see a more detailed query before we make a decision.

In certain cases, we do prefer complete manuscripts. These include short items and poetry for The Writing Life department, Tip Sheet items, and Chronicle articles. We'll look at good-quality dot-matrix printed manuscripts, but we prefer letter quality. Each submission must include your name, address and daytime telephone number.

No simultaneous submissions, please.

Also, we do not use fiction or scripts; we do not buy newspaper clippings; and we handle book and software reviews in-house.

In your query, tell us if you can submit assigned work on disk or via modem. We do accept unsolicited electronic submissions.

Finally, we expect writers to double-check all facts included in their stories and to submit documentation to support the information included in their stories.

Photos and Artwork

Whenever possible, we want to *show* our readers how writers work, and we encourage you to suggest how your article can be enhanced with graphics. Past issues have included marked-up manuscript pages (to show how Joe Gores revises his work), photos of Hong Kong by Robert Ludlum (to show how he keeps a sense of his novels' settings), character sketches used by Clive Cussler, timesheets, book promotional materials, correspondence with editors, submission logs, and similar materials related to writing and the business of freelancing.

We use cartoons, but they must be well drawn to merit consideration here. A clever gagline alone won't do. Send finished cartoons only, in batches of ten or more. We prefer single panels, either with or without gaglines. The theme is the writing life-we want cartoons that deal with writers and the trials of writing and selling their work. Also, cartoons about writing from a historical standpoint (past works), language use, and other literary themes. Original artwork is returned after publication.

We do not accept unsolicited illustrations.

Payment and General Terms

For manuscripts, we usually pay 10-30¢ per word, on acceptance, for first North American serial rights, one-time use only. Poetry earns $25-$50, depending on length. Cartoons bring $50-$100. Contributor copies are sent to writers and artists whose work appears in that issue. (Should we want to reprint anything we've purchased from you, we will pay you 25% of the original purchase price for reprint rights for each use.)

What We Want—Long Stuff

Freelance submissions are accepted for all sections of the magazine, with the exception of our regular columns and bylined department sections.

How-to Articles are our mainstay: how to write better, market successfully, recycle and resell manuscripts, maintain records...and more. These articles present a common problem or goal, offer the appropriate solution, and give an example of how that solution has worked. Articles generally run 2,000-3,000 words, though cover stories often run longer. We also took for pieces that Can cover a topic completely in 1,000 words or fewer. Actual length will be discussed when the article is assigned.

Topics for features vary widely. Categories that we seek material for include writers' opportunities and money-making ideas; the business of writing; reference sources; writers' tools, equipment and supplies (however, we are not interested in material on word processing, which is covered by one of our columnists and seldom appears elsewhere in the magazine); writing discipline; language use; quizzes; personal experiences (but only if they teach a lesson or prove a point); marketing mechanics; and three types that will be covered more fully below: writing techniques, profiles/interviews and market reports.

In general, don't shy away from the word *I* in your articles. The first-person perspective is important to establishing your credibility. But don't overdo it. We want instructive articles, not "and then I wrote" essays. Round out your experiences with those of other writers and with information from editors, when appropriate.

We use a friendly, informal—but not lackadaisical or cutesy—style. We demand lively writing. Use anecdotes, examples, samples and quotes to strengthen the message of the article. We like lively headlines, and our articles are sprinkled with subheads at appropriate places to help readers locate particular sections when returning to the article. Writers who use lively headlines and subheads in their manuscripts demonstrate their familiarity with our style.

Writing Technique Articles. This brand of how-to article is most important to *Writers Digest*. These pieces highlight an often misunderstood or poorly utilized writing method and detail how to use it precisely, appropriately and successfully. We are always hungry for these articles. Examples include how to write an effective lead, how to use dialogue to establish character, how to brighten your prose, how to use suspense effectively.

Articles may cover fiction, nonfiction, poetry or scriptwriting techniques, but must be accessible to all writers and offer advice that can be applied directly or indirectly to all forms of writing. How a particular piece is structured depends on the complexity of the subject, but every piece will need to:

• Define the technique and its importance. Draw broad lines of application to other forms of writing.

• Outline how to use the technique. The best explanations break the technique down into distinct parts and deal with each part individually. When appropriate, use a step-by-step explanation.

• Give examples of its usage. A vital part of your article; give us more than you think necessary—and then add two more. Illustrate every point with examples—either from your own writing or from well-known works. On major points, readers can benefit from "right" and "wrong" or "before" and "after" examples, showing writing before the technique is applied or when it is used inappropriately, followed by the corrected version.

• If appropriate, give readers tips on incorporating the technique into their writing. For example, an article on using anecdotes gave tips on how to collect anecdotes to use.

As with all how-to articles, instruction is the key to making the article work. Analyze your own writing to determine what gives it power, what makes it successful. Then give our readers a thorough guide to using that technique powerfully and successfully, too.

Interviews and Profiles. Major interviews, using the Q&A format, should be with authors of stature—those currently in the news or on the bestseller lists. Length ranges from 2,500 to 4,000 words; we occasionally use longer pieces as the subject warrants.

Narrative-style profiles of major writers usually run 2,500-3,000 words. We also use short profiles (about 1,000 words or fewer) of lesser-known authors who can inspire and give advice to our readers.

Lively quotes, anecdotes and solid information are as essential for profiles and interviews as they are for other WD articles.

Even more essential is an understanding of the major elements of a WD interview or profile. These articles must be directed at the working writer; pieces rewritten from general interest magazines or book-review tabloids are not acceptable. For that reason, we require a detailed query for all interviews.

These are the major elements of a WD interview or profile (in order of importance):

• The writer's product. What the writer produces and why it is different and noteworthy; why it succeeds. (Writing samples often help, but they cannot tell the full story.) How the writer developed this trait and refined it. What the writer thinks of his work. What needs the writer thinks he is fulfilling. What brings power to his work. The conscious process of putting words on paper.

• Advice to other writers. What can other writers learn from the author and his work, his career? What problems can the writer steer readers around? What techniques can he instruct them in? What shortcuts can the writer suggest? What solutions to common problems can the writer recommend?

• The road to success. Failures and handicaps the writer has overcome, and how they were overcome. When the writer first realized he could succeed at the typewriter. The first break, and where it led. The rewards and the costs of success.

• How the writer works. Work habits, including number of hours per day and his or her timetable. The physical act of writing-does the writer use pencil, pen, typewriter or word processor? Where does the writer work? How does the writer discipline himself?

Photos and graphics are essential to the interview/profile, Photos should concentrate on the subject's face and upper body. We like a good selection of shots that show gestures and capture the character of the subject. We prefer shots in which the subject is looking directly into the camera-though not awkwardly so.

We also like to see a few middle-distance shots that show the subject in his/her work area, at the typewriter, or interacting with others who are pertinent to the story. If there's something special about the writer's environment, give, us a long shot of the writer in this atmosphere. Natural lighting is best—avoid shadows, etc. If you cannot provide these photos yourself, provide us with a source for them. Other graphics for profiles and features should give our readers a glimpse of the writer's work. Original drafts, revised manuscript pages, notes, outlines, journal pages and other materials help demonstrate the universality of the writing experience. For more information, see "Photos and Artwork" on page 2.

Market Reports highlight general article or book styles and offer instruction on how any writer might break into this lucrative area. Examples might be writing the true-life drama, or the as-told-to article or book. A market report may also identify a particular market, such as writing for trade publications or writing a cookbook, but the market most be large and diverse, we aren't interested in pieces that spotlight highly specialized markets that can embrace only a few writers. Paint with a large brush in market reports—we're more likely to publish an article on writing expertly about health and fitness than an article on writing for the health and fitness market. There's a difference. If you don't understand that difference, don't attempt to write market reports.

In writing the market report, you'll want to cover several essential elements. This isn't a formula—only a checklist. Remember, anecdotes, specific examples and quotes are important here, too.

• Establish the market. It must be current and have a growing need for manuscripts. Quote editors. Emphasize specific sales and payments, either your own or other writers'.

• Describe the market. Detail the differences from and similarities to other markets and types of writing. Give an idea of who's interested in these types of articles so readers will know if this is a market that appeals to them.

• Explain how to find ideas for the market. What kinds of topics and treatments does the market use most? Point out how writers can generate ideas that are salable. Provide tips on matching ideas to publications.

• Explain how to write for the market. Detail the process of turning ideas into salable stories. What are the special requirements of writing for this market or writing this type of article or book? Point out common pitfalls and how to avoid them.

What We Want—Short Stuff

The Writing Life. This section uses brief, lively items that are offbeat or on-the-mark glimpses of the traits, transgressions and follies peculiar to writers and their life. This section is always fun and light, but instructional tips that also entertain are welcome. Length is 50-500 words—and here, shorter is better. We don't buy jokes, but we do buy short bits of humor (anecdotes, ironies, quotes and puns). Submit items on separate sheets of paper, please.

Poetry. We seldom use more than two poems an issue, so competition is severe. And we have very definite needs. Poetry is used only in The Writing Life department, so short, light verse is preferred. Serious verse is acceptable, but stands less chance of acceptance. Whether it's light or serious, all poetry must focus on writers—their joys, despairs, strategies and relationships to the world. Length rarely exceeds 20 lines.

Tip Sheet. This department offers short (1,000 words, tops), instructional bits of information that help writers live, write and market more successfully. Topics include advice on manuscript problems, business concerns, language stumbling blocks and tax questions; suggestions on new ways to make money as a writer; useful "tricks of the trade"; reports on legal and business developments that affect writers; and explanations of more efficient office procedures.

Chronicle. These are first-person accounts of writing successes, failures, incidents, problems and insights. They should be, as the name suggests, open, honest accounts—told either humorously or dramatically—as if you were sharing a few pages of your journal. A narrative style and a message that all readers can share are musts. Length is 1,500 words maximum.

Categories: Writing

Name: Submissions Editor
Material: All
Address: 1507 DANA AVE
City/State/ZIP: CINCINNATI OH 45207
E-mail: writersdig@juno.com

Writer's Exchange

Writer's Exchange

Founded 1983. Editor Eugene Boone. Please put the editor's name on *all* submissions or other correspondence.

Periodical Needs: *Writer's Exchange* is a quarterly magazine focusing on the small press and its markets and featuring articles on writing and poetry, with a special emphasis on beginning writers and poets. Articles sought, especially reprints, on writing techniques, computer-related articles, essays on poetic techniques and forms (free verse, traditional, haiku, and other fixed-forms). He wants "poetry to 40 lines, any subject or style. I also consider short poems such as haiku, tanka, senryu, and other fixed forms. I like writing that is upbeat (or at least hopeful, positive, enlightening, or inspiring, including humorous poems about everyday life, writing, etc. I will *not* consider material that is anti-religious, racist or obscene."

WE is 36 pages, digest-sized, saddle-stitched, with a full-color cover. He accepts about half or more of the poetry received. Press run is 250. Subscription: $12. Sample postpaid: $3.

How to Submit: Submit 3-10 poems at a time, with SASE. "I prefer typed mss., one poem per page, readable. Poets should always proofread mss. before sending them out. Errors can cause rejection." Previously published poetry OK; no simultaneous submissions. Cover letter appreciated; list "prior credits, if any, and give other details of writing background, such as writing interests." Time between acceptance and publication is 4 months. Request status if mss. hasn't been published after 6 months. Also, please notify the editor of change of address: too many contributor's copies are being returned because the writer has moved and left no forwarding address.

E-mail submissions are *not* encouraged. Reports in 2 to 6 weeks. Acquires one-time rights. Staff reviews books about writing, poetry, working with computers, etc. Creative software and products for writers, poets and others are on our website through *Creative Computing!*, a link to Writer's Network. Freelance reviews, under 1,000 words, will also be considered. *Only* reviews for *Creative Computing!* (website) can be submitted by e-mail. There is no pay for reviews at CC! WRITER'S EXCHANGE pays one contributor's copy; extra copies available on request, with SASE.

Also Offers: They offer cash awards for quarterly contests sponsored through the magazine. Send SASE for current rules. The *New Markets* newsletter has become a column feature in WE in 1998 as a new Paying Small Press Markets column, added to the magazine.

The editor says he rejects on submissions, "if I feel it will benefit the poet in the long [run], never anything too harsh or overly discouraging."

Advice: His advice to poets: "Support the small press publications you read and enjoy. Without your support, these publications will cease to exist. The small press has given many talented poets their start. In essence, the small press is where poetry lives!"

Categories: Poetry—Writing

Name: Eugene Boone, Editor
Material: All
Address: PO BOX 2764
City/State/ZIP: SUMTER SC 29151
Telephone: 803-778-4097
E-mail: EBoone@aol.com
Internet: http://users.aol.com/writernet

Writers' Forum
University of Colorado-Colorado Springs

Founded in 1974, *Writers' Forum* is an independent, non-commercial, annual book-sized magazine (average pages 180-200) featuring contemporary American poetry and fiction with an emphasis upon Western American literature. The magazine has been ranked by *Writers' Digest* as first in the U.S.A. among university-sponsored non-paying fiction markets. Back issues $7.00. For current subscription send $10.00 check or money order to the address below.

We publish per volume 10-14 stories or novel-excerpts, 3,000-

8,500 words usual range, 25-35 poems (up to 5 poems by one author considered). We encourage submissions by accomplished writers in early-career status. We look for substantive, solidly crafted, imaginative work, verbally interesting, with subtle texture and strong voice. Mainstream is our stock-in-trade, but we will give a fair look to all fictional and poetic categories. We report in 6-8 weeks; inquire after 10 weeks. Manuscripts are read year-around, but best submission period is between July and November. We don't use printed rejection slips, and we comment on manuscripts of perceived merit. We pay in free copies. The magazine is copyrighted, with all rights returning to authors upon publication.

Send complete manuscript. If you do not wish to have your manuscript returned, enclose SASE with first-class stamp. We welcome a personal cover letter giving relevant biographical and career information. Indicate simultaneous submission.

Categories: Fiction—Poetry

Name: Submissions Editor
Material: All
Address: ENGLISH DEPT UCCS
Address: PO BOX 7150
City/State/ZIP: COLORADO SPRINGS CO 80933-7150
Telephone: 719-262-3302
Fax: 719-262-3582
E-mail: Kpellow@brain.uccs.edu

Writer's Gazette

Brenda Williamson, Publisher/Editor

This is a small press publication designed for writers, by writers, about writing. The format is 8½"x11" copyrighted newsletter published quarterly. Simultaneous, photocopied & previously published material is okay. New writers are always encouraged and regularly published. Even children are welcome to submit.

The forum, while the most part is on writing related topics, we also include a wide variety of poetry, stories & essays, to showcase some of our reader/writer's own work and styles. E-mail submissions are okay but remember to include your real name and mailing address.

Payments: At this time there is no pay except a tearsheet of your published manuscript. If your prefer to have a complete copy of the issue, please order as soon as possible because we sell out fast. Single issue is $4.00. As finances permit, we do from time to time pay one cent per word for nonfiction only.

NONFICTION—Must be writer related, but will accept a wide range of categories such as, the common how-to, computers, photography, bookkeeping, audio writing, advertising and the usual 'how I got published', plus more. 2,000 word maximum, but prefer under 800 words and especially like under 400 word topics.

FICTION—Any subject, theme, topic, etc. is welcomed. We like to see seasonal pieces 4 months prior to the season or holiday. **2,000 word maximum,** but you have a better shot at grabbing our attention with short-shorts under 800 words.

POETRY—Any style, subject or length. Prefer short verses of 24 lines or less.

FILLERS—Use artwork, cartoons & occasionally photos which are in conjunction with a story.

STAFF-WRITTEN DEPARTMENTS

The Book Report is generally aimed a approx. 6 books and an overview of each. Most books being geared at writing or showcasing a writer. If you have a **book** that has been published (self-published is okay) send one review copy, ordering information and any press information. You will receive one tearsheet of the published review. (Because of the sometimes overwhelming number of books received, we can not guarantee when or if your book will be reviewed.) No books are returned.

Market & Publication Listings—Each issue contains a list of potential markets or publications of interest. If you are looking for a writer, send a copy of your publication and guidelines to get a free listing. Generally, publications will not have a repeat listing for at least a year, allowing for as many different publications [as possible] to have a slot.

Contest Listings—Each issue has a list of current contests spanning from short range deadlines to at least 6 months away.

Sample copy $4.00. Subscriptions: 1 yr. $15.00; 2 yrs. $28.00; 3 yrs. $40.00.

Categories: Fiction—Nonfiction—Computers—Drama—General Interest—Horror—Inspirational—Literature—Mystery—Poetry—Short Stories—Writing

Name: Submissions Editor
Material: All
Address: TROUVERE COMPANY
Address: 899 WILLIAMSON TRAIL
City/State/ZIP: ECLECTIC AL 36024-6131

Writer's Guidelines & News
The Who, What, When
and Where Magazine For Writers

We consider ourselves "The Friend of the Writer" and so, as a friend, we are very flexible in our guideline policy. We will consider anything that is well-written and informative with a writing slant as long as it is done in a "friendly" and not a "preachy" manner.

As in the past, articles that help bridge the gap between writers and editors have the best chance of acceptance. Short interview articles with photos also receive a warm welcome here. Most of all, we look for "News" items about writers or the writing profession.

General interest, historical articles on writers/writing, how-to, profile pieces, personal experience, opinion, motivational, humor and fillers are always needed. Length: 700-1,500 wds. Pay varies from $5 to $25 plus one-year FREE subscription per article. Poetry, fillers and short pieces receive payment in copies. Payment upon publication. Buys first North American serial rights. No electronic or simultaneous submissions at this time. Best to send complete manuscript but written queries acceptable from published authors.

No phone queries or phone requests for guidelines or copies. SASEs only, please. Include a short, friendly biography and letter with your submission.

We are always seeking new and innovative writers with imagination and promise. In fact, we will "showcase" such talent whenever possible, both with fiction and nonfiction submissions.

Fiction pieces should be no more than 2,000 words and contain a writing slant of some sort, preferably with the protagonist being a writer. Have fun with it! Pays $10 plus one-year subscription.

TIPS: As is true for any market, read a copy of WG&N before submitting so you will know what we are all about. A sample copy is $3.00. One-year subscription is $18.00.

Categories: Fiction—Nonfiction—General Interest—How-To—Poetry—Writing

Name: Ned Burke, Editor
Material: All
Address: PO BOX 18566
City/State/ZIP: SARASOTA FL 18576
Telephone: 941-924-3201
Fax: 921-925-4468

X-RAY Magazine

Publishing, Workgroup & Multimedia Technology for Quark Users

Dear Writer:

Thank you for thinking of *X-RAY Magazine*. Following are some of our writer's guidelines:

X-RAY Magazine focus:

Publishing, workshop and multimedia technology for Quark users

Content:

64 pages, glossy

Each issue: Cover story and two lengthy features on a specific desktop publishing-related theme. Departments focus on: Quark tips and tricks, Scripting, General desktop publishing tips and tricks, QuarkXTension reviews, Troubleshooting conflicts, and XClamation Point—a place where writers/readers can wax philosophical about Quark, XTensions, the future of desktop publishing and much more.

Readers:

QuarkXPress users, graphic designers, book publishers, service bureaus and general desktop publishers

Tips for writers:

X-RAY welcomes submissions of topic ideas or completed articles. We will respond to all inquiries.

When writing for X-RAY, please keep the tone light, without being flippant. We strive to have information-packed articles, without sounding like a manual.

Sincerely,

Heather Speirs

Managing Editor

X-RAY Magazine

Categories: Nonfiction—Computers—Consumer—Desktop Publishing (using QuarkXpress)—Internet—Software

Name: Heather Spiers, Managing Editor
Material: All
Address: 2700 49TH ST 1ST FLOOR
City/State/ZIP: SAN FRANCISCO CA 94110
Telephone: 415-643-1855
Fax: 415-642-7422
E-mail: editor@xraymag.com
Internet: www.xraymag.com

Yachting

Overview

Yachting is edited for experienced, affluent boat owners—power and sail—who don't have the time or the inclination to read sub-standard stories. They love carefully crafted stories about places they've never been or a different spin on places they have,

meticulously reported pieces on issues that affect their yachting lives, personal accounts of yachting experiences from which they can learn, engaging profiles of people who share their passion for boats, insightful essays that evoke the history and traditions of the sport and compelling photographs of others enjoying the game as much as they do.

They love to know what to buy and how things work. They love to be surprised. They don't mind getting their hands dirty or saving a buck here and there, but they're not interested in learning how to make a masthead light out of a mayonnaise jar.

If you love what they love and can communicate like a pro (that means meeting deadlines, writing tight, being obsessively accurate and never misspelling a proper name), we'd love to hear from you. We prefer written queries. Send them to the appropriate editor in charge (see list below). Include a self-addressed, stamped envelope. Response time is about a month.

A few pointers: Don't bother sending us anything about sailboarding or hydroplane racing. Translation: Read the magazine. We have a great desire for good powerboat stories and we kill for great first-person stuff, especially when our readers can learn something from it. Don't bother us with queries about sailboat racing. We have the scene covered. Send your fiction and poetry to *The New Yorker.*

If you have an idea you want to pitch to us, make sure it is focused and well-evolved. For instance, don't send us a query for a piece on "Cruising the Virgin Islands." Propose a lead. Make us love it. Share your enthusiasm. It wouldn't hurt to send some clips with your query.

Boat reviews and technical articles on navigation, electronics, engines, materials, etc., are mostly written by experts we know. However, if you have expertise in these areas, we'd be happy to review a resume and sample manuscript—submitted on speculation.

Payments

Generally, we pay $300-$500 for short pieces (columns) and $750-$1000 or more for longer stories (features). We do have an appetite for very short items for our Cross Currents, Yacht Yard and Cruising Yachtsman sections. Payment for these usually is less than $100.

Photos

Most photographs in *Yachting* are shot on assignment by professionals we know. However, we would be happy to review your portfolio. We prefer 35mm Kodachrome 25. Kodachrome 64 is acceptable. Ektachrome should be avoided when possible. Larger-format chromes are acceptable. All must be properly exposed (preferable 1/2 stop under to anything overexposed), tack-sharp, and show sound composition and graphic sense. We can't be responsible for unsolicited material.

For photos we pay:

• Cover: $500

• Four-color inside $350/page; $200 1/2 page;

• Black and white $50 for spot art. Up to $250 for full page (rarely used).

For assignments we pay $400 a day against page rate (whichever is greatest). In most cases a cap is agreed upon beforehand. We pay all reasonable expenses (to be discussed beforehand).

Whom to query:

Charter and Cross Currents: Executive Editor Kenny Wooton

Cruising: Senior Editor Dennis Caprio

Gear, Electronics, How-to Technical, Boat Tests: Senior Editor Dennis Caprio/Senior Editor Peter Frederiksen

Custom yachts: Editor-in-Chief Charles Barthold

Photography:

Art Director: David Pollard

If in doubt: Executive Editor Kenny Wooton

If You Have an Assignment From Us

This is a guide written for the *Yachting* contributor or freelancer who has received an assignment from the magazine or is sending in an article on spec. All queries and copy submissions should follow these forms unless negotiated with the editor in charge beforehand.

Columns

These should contribute much toward defining the personality and authority of the magazine. They should inform, entertain and stimulate the reader to think beyond the surface of an issue, product, event, personality or how-to concept.

Whenever possible, columns should build upon, or launch from a news event, new product or emerging trend. They should have a narrow subject focus—not be "a column about sails" or "a column about depth sounders"—and should reveal the unique perspective of the writer.

They should be meticulously factual and the writer should indicate somewhere in the text that his point of view is based on experience or interviews with other experts in the field.

While *Yachting* hires columnists and contributors more for their expertise in a given field, we expect copy that is tight and reasonably polished. Word count is important. If we ask for 350 words, we expect 350, not 600.

The editing process often involves queries to authors and may sometimes include requests for rewrites. We may send unsatisfactory material back to the author for rewrites, more than once if necessary.

Columnists and contributors are expected to be our eyes and ears in the field. We expect them to provide briefs each month and keep us informed on developments in the field.

Features

Features are the heart of the magazine. They generally contain the greatest amount of space for copy and visual elements.

They should follow the classic feature model: they should have a beginning, preferably an anecdote involving someone using a boat or equipment that illuminates the "theme" or lead of the story which follows close behind; a middle that contains evidence to back up the lead; and an end that ties back into the lead.

Because we are a four-color magazine and visually driven, writers and EICs should work to obtain the best possible photos to accompany the story. Whenever possible, photos should illustrate the "theme" of the story, not just be a running shot of the boat and a shot of the interior. As with columns, writers should expect queries from editors and editors may request rewrites.

Feature Categories

Man And His Boat

Man and his boat stories in Yachting should combine elements of Peers, On Board and Design columns. Among the criteria for deciding to do one are that the boat should be newsworthy by *Yachting* standards (a custom or semi-custom yacht) and the human subject should be interesting (someone we would consider doing a Peers column on). These stories should address the subject's background, both personal and boating; how he arrived at the place in his life where can afford a custom or semi-custom yacht; what he learned from his previous boats and experiences and how that experience is reflected in the concept and execution of his new boat. We should go sailing or cruising with him and this experience should be addressed in the copy.

Art should include a sailing/running shot of the boat, at least one tight shot of the subject and interiors, photos of the specific touches achieved by the designer/builder at the behest of the owner—things that he included because of previous experiences or history with previous boats, details and a sail plan/accommodation plan of the boat. An old photo of a boat or the subject would be a nice touch.

Wild Card

Wild cards run the gamut of yachting topics. They should be visually oriented and entertaining to read. They should catch the reader by surprise and be the kind of story he must read right away and can't put down. They can bank off news items or trends.

Yachting History/Lore

These stories should tap into the vast well of yachting history and tradition. The stories can focus on individual boats, events, personalities, fine art and any other aspect of the sport. They should capture the romance of the sea. Whenever possible, we should take advantage of the considerable volume of great old photos of yachts steaming and under sail.

On Board

First and foremost, copy should reflect that we were "on board" whatever boat we're writing about, preferably in the lead and in the performance sections of the piece. This is our forum for "testing" new boats and the copy should contain details about construction, accommodations, systems, power, sailing/running performance, aesthetics, fit and finish, the manufacturer's stated "mission" for the boat and pricing. The pieces should follow general feature structure.

The writer should develop a lead, present it at the beginning of the story (not at the end in the form of a conclusion as some writers are inclined to do) and the rest of the piece should flow from it. They should concentrate on features of the boat that delight, surprise and disappoint us—things that make the writer—a yachtsman—want to talk about the boat.

Power tests should include performance data gathered by our writers. "Supplied by the company" has little credibility in the eyes of readers.

Sail tests should, when possible, include polar plots. While these are supplied by the company or designer, they provide useful theoretical performance information we cannot obtain independently.

The reader should also come away with some nugget of knowledge he didn't expect—something we take for granted. For instance, a phrase or sentence that provides additional perspective on woven roving or prop pitch.

Adventure

In these pieces, *Yachting* takes the reader to a place he's never been before or somewhere he has been, but we discover something he missed. These are our travel stories. They should have focused themes (i.e., not "Cruising the Caribbean") and they should be first person. The art package should include at least one shot of the boat that made the trip.

Cruising Yachtsman

Our readers also have a strong appetite for ports of call they normally visit once a season. These are not the adventure destinations but places he/she is apt to visit with the family. Much of the information should be about what to do ashore. Save the buoy and tidal info for the cruising guides. Instead, concentrate on the places to go during the stay plus any good tips you found during your trip.

Equipment Test

We are experts in the field and should use these pieces to help the reader cut through the maze of sales and promotional material he encounters at the boat shows. He should finish reading one of these stories having a good idea of how the items work and which one is best for his purpose. We don't have to rate the products the way Consumer Reports does, but we should draw conclusions that position the products in the marketplace.

Whenever possible, we should create a graph or table reflecting the results or some aspect of the results, of the tests. Whenever possible, the tests should be done on boats and should involve testers who are experienced in using the equipment. Manufacturer's instructions should always be followed.

Boat Owner's Buyer's Guide

A monthly column that analyzes one category of equipment. There are three elements to each month's column: an overview of the category and any significant changes that have been made; tips that will help the reader make an intelligent buying decision;

a grid of specs from top manufacturers.

Regattas/racing

These should have a feature structure and should convey a sense of drama and action. Ideally, we transport the reader onto the foredeck or behind the wheel. The reader should walk away with real insight into what made the winners successful, not the standard "good crew, good preparation, good..." For example: what equipment did the skipper buy beforehand to make his boat faster; what kind of sails does the boat have; any special tuning tips; crew prep. Be specific.

Custom Yachts

We have access to spectacular yachts that our readers don't. We should walk them through these vessels and write about their accommodations, systems, unique design solutions, execution and performance (when possible). As always, our tone should reflect our enthusiasm for the subject.

Categories: Boating

Name: Refer to Guidelines.
Address: 20 E ELM ST
City/State/ZIP: GREENWICH CT 06830
Telephone: 203-625-4480
Fax: 203-625-4481
E-mail: editor@yachtingnet.com
Internet: www.yachtingnet.com

The Yalobusha Review
The University of Mississippi

The Yalobusha Review, founded in 1995, is an annual journal of fiction, poetry, and nonfiction and is open to submissions from students, *writers* in the Oxford community, the region, and across the country. Its second issue in 1996 featured six short stories and 27 poems, including an introductory essay by Larry Brown and works by Cynthia Shearer, Theron Hopkins, and Alida Moore. It is published in April of each year by the University of Mississippi with an approximate distribution of 500 copies. Single issue copies are available for $7.00 including postage. Multiple-year subscriptions are available for $6.00 per year. Send checks made out to *The Yalobusha Review* to the address below.

Submission Guidelines:

• We are looking primarily for short fiction (up to 40 pages) and poetry, but other forms—longer stories, novellas, plays, nonfiction essays, etc.—will be considered if they are very good.

• There is no preferred or restricted subject matter or theme; we just want good stuff.

• There is no maximum word length, but the longer it is, the better it has to be.

• Submit a maximum of two short stories or six poems at one time.

• Submit only previously unpublished work.

• **The annual deadline for submitting is March 1.**

Submissions received by March 1 will be responded to by late March at the latest. Response time for submissions received after March 1 may be somewhat longer.

• We pay two contributor's copies on publication.

• Cover letters are optional. We will contact you if we need biographical information.

• You may submit by regular mail or by e-mail. If you submit by regular mail, please include a SASE. If you submit by e-mail, we will respond via e-mail. Electronic submissions may be sent as e-mail or as attached documents in any format.

Categories: Literature—Writing

Name: Fiction Editor
Name: Poetry Editor
Material: As Appropriate
Address: PO BOX 186
City/State/ZIP: UNIVERSITY MS 38677-0186
Telephone: 601-232-7103
E-mail: yalobush@olemiss.edu.
Internet: www.olemiss.edu/depts/english/pubs/yalobusha_review.com

---

Yankee

It is to your advantage to read several issues of the magazine before sending us a query or a manuscript. In general, these are the sorts of stories we are most likely to accept from freelancers who have not published with us before.

The New England Sampler: We have six pages of very short, usually humorous stories up front in every issue. Much is written by editors, but we occasionally accept a Sampler item from freelance writers. In no case are such items longer than 500 words, and in most cases they are much shorter. The subtitle of the section describes it best: "Strange occurrences, remarkable people, and curious information." Payment ranges from $50-$200.

Travel: We may purchase short stories about favorite inns, restaurants, tourist attractions, historical sites, or area of natural beauty in New England. Articles should not exceed 500 words, and you should query us first. Payment ranges from $25 to $250.

Food: We are always looking for suggestions for our "Great New England Cooks" series. We need about 500 words on the personality and cooking style of the individual cook plus at least eight of her or his best recipes, with lists of ingredients and complete instructions for preparing them. We will pay up to $800 for an accepted article. It also features "Recipes with a History," favorite family recipes that come with a story attached to them. Payment for these short articles is usually $50.

Humor: Must be based in New England, but no dialect stories. It's impossible to describe or predict what will strike us as funny, but bear in mind that we've been in business since 1935 and have heard every old Yankee story many times. Keep it under 1,000 words.

Fiction: Must be of the highest quality, between 1,000 and 3,000 words. We pay $1,000 or more. A New England setting or atmosphere is desirable, though it need not be explicit. Anything obviously outside of New England is unacceptable.

Poetry: We recommend a close study of the poems we published over the past year; 32 lines maximum preferred; previously unpublished poems only. We pay $50 per poem for all rights; $35 for first magazine rights.

I Remember: A personal anecdote recalling something that happened to you in the not-too-recent past in New England. Not general nostalgia - be specific, like "the day I poured detergent in the Tunnel of Love." No more than 500 words. We pay $200.

Book Review: We do not accept book reviews from freelancers.

Fillers: We do not use fillers.

Last Page: A 500 to 600 word personal or humorous essay that evokes a New England place or time of year and contains some kind of surprise. Competition is intense for this space - we pay $400.

Feature Articles: These are generally written by staff or well-established freelancers who have worked for us before. This is the most difficult kind of story for a first-timer to sell to us, but not without precedent. Study the magazine and query us first. Payment $800 and up.

Photographs: We generally assign photography to experienced professionals who have worked for us before. If you want to break in, show us your best work. We prefer 35mm 2 1/4", or 4" x 5" color transparencies. We do publish some amateur photos in our "Reader's Photo" department - they should be humorous or otherwise remarkable shots. No kids on toilets, please.

Rights, Deadlines, Etc.: We usually buy first magazine rights and pay on acceptance. If a story relates to a particular time of year (i.e., Christmas, baseball season, maple sugaring), we need it at least five months before that time of year, and earlier is still better, in order to get seasonal photographs. A year or more in advance is not too early. Unsolicited manuscripts, art, or photos submitted must be accompanied by a self-addressed envelope with appropriate postage. We do not assume responsibility for the return of unsolicited material, so if it's priceless or irreplaceable, don't send it! It is always a good idea to query us first and send clips of previous work. Allow 4 to 8 weeks for reply or return of manuscripts.

Categories: Fiction—Nonfiction—Cooking—Crafts—Food/Drink—Gardening—General Interest—History—Hobbies—Interview—Poetry—Travel—Essay—Nostalgia—Personal Experience—Home—Humor

Name: Judson D. Hale Sr., Managing Editor
Material: All
Address: P.O. BOX 520
City/State/ZIP: DUBLIN, NH 03444-0520
Telephone: 603-563-8111
Fax: 603-563-8252
E-mail: queries@yankeepub.com
Internet: www.newengland.com

YESTERDAY'S MAGAZETTE
The Original Magazine of Memories Since 1973

Yesterday's Magazette
The Original Magazine of Memories

Hello Friend!
Welcome to YESTERDAY'S MAGAZETTE—"The Original Magazine of Memories"!
Sit Back And Relax
Let us take you back to the Roaring 20s, the Thrifty 30s, those Fervent 40s, the Fabulous 50s and the Sexy 60s and 70s. We cover more than a half century of memories from Vaudeville to Elvis!
Remember...
Each issue will carry you back to a happier time, a happier place. Remember the Ice Man? Early Radio and TV? Mom in the kitchen cooking the holiday feast? Pop taking everyone out for a Sunday drive in his new car? Sis getting ready for the Prom? Families gathered on the front porch after supper just to talk or look at the stars? All these memories and more are found in each issue of *Yesterday's Magazette.*
Sharing Memories
That's what *Yesterday's Magazette* is all about. For more than two decades YM has recaptured that down-home honesty and goodness of the average American. Nothing fancy here...just plain folks relating their life experiences.
Everyone Has A Yesterday
Since 1973 YM's motto has been "Everyone Has A Yesterday" and everyone, regardless of age, has a cherished memory of general interest worth telling.
Our goal is to keep each individual's history...or at least a small part of it...for posterity.
Please join us in this noble endeavor by becoming an avid subscriber or advertiser.
Future generations will thank you!
Guidelines
YM is a bimonthly magazine of nostalgia. Our guidelines are

flexible but we prefer stories in the 500-1,000 word range set in the time frame of the 1920s to the 70s. Stories with photos have the best chance of acceptance here. Payment is $5-$25 for most major stories and contributors copies for short pieces and poetry.
We are always seeking new and innovative writers with imagination and promise. We will—and have!—altered our guidelines when we feel the submission warrants special consideration. (Surprise us! Make us laugh...make us cry.)
TIPS: We would like to see more 40s, 50s and 60s pieces. All writers are urged to send comments and opinions for review. When you write, do so as one friend to another.
YM Subscription Information
One year ($18.00); Two years ($27.00); Sample issue $3.00
Categories: Fiction—Nonfiction—Antiques—Biography—Cartoons—Collectibles—Family—General Interest—Nostalgia (20s-70s)—Poetry—Rural America—Senior Citizens

Name: Ned Burke, Editor
Material: All
Address: PO BOX 18566
City/State/ZIP: SARASOTA FL 18576
Telephone: 941-924-3201
Fax: 941-925-4468
E-mail: YMagazette@aol.com

YM

Thanks for you interest in *YM*.
We are a national magazine for young women, ages 15 to 24. Our readers are bright, enthusiastic and inquisitive. Our goal is to guide them-in effect, to be a second "best friend" through the many exciting, yet often rough, aspects of young adulthood.
Writers who are not familiar with the magazine or who have not read it recently are advised to go through back issues-your local library might have a selection, or send us a check (for $2.50 an issue) and we'll send them to you to learn more about how we are changing and what we publish. While most of the *YM*'s columns and all our fashion, beauty and lifestyle copy are staff written, we buy articles (up to 2,500 words for a major piece) on topics of interest to young women. In the past year, for example, we have tackled everything from interracial dating to sexual abuse and eating disorders.
All articles should be lively and informative (but not in academic tone), and any "expert" opinions (psychologists, authors and teachers) should be included as a supplement to the feelings and experiences of young women. Writers whose work has not appeared in *YM* should include tearsheets of published articles.
Payment varies according to the length and type of article, but writers who have few or no published articles will be asked to write on speculation (no guarantee of payment). Please query us in writing, we prefer that to telephone calls, faxes and unsolicited manuscripts (mark "Query" on the envelope). Allow four weeks for consideration. Seasonal material should be submitted at least eight weeks in advance. Work that is accepted is paid upon approval.
All queries should be accompanied by a self-addressed stamped envelope.
We do not publish fiction or poetry.
Again, thank you for your interest in *YM* and good luck!

Categories: Nonfiction—How-to—Interview—Personal Experience—Profiles—Women's Issues

Name: Christina Boyle, Senior Editor
Material: All
Address: 375 LEXINGTON AVENUE

City/State/ZIP: NEW YORK, NY 10017-5514
Telephone: 212-499-2000

YogaJournal
For Health and Conscious Living

The Yoga Journal

Yoga Journal covers a variety of fields and disciplines devoted to enhancing human health and consciousness, while maintaining our emphasis on the practice and philosophy of yoga. We define yoga broadly to encompass practices that aspire to union or communion with some higher power, greater truth, or deeper source of wisdom, as well as practices that tend to increase harmony of body, mind, and spirit.

In particular we welcome articles on the following themes:

1. Leaders, spokespersons, and visionaries who teach and exemplify a conscious, holistic lifestyle;

2. Spiritual disciplines, teachings, and leading practitioners and teachers, both Eastern and Western;

3. The practice of hatha yoga;

4. Applications of yoga to everyday life (e.g., relationships, social issues, livelihood, environment, etc.);

5. Hatha yoga anatomy and kinesiology and therapeutic yoga;

6. Transpersonal philosophy anal psychology and their application to everyday life situations and problems;

7. Natural healing, massage and bodywork, the martial arts, and exercise that is consonant with the practice of yoga.

8. Nutrition and diet, cooking, and natural skin and body care.

9. Relevant ideas, people, and events that broaden or deepen our understanding of ourselves, each other, and the world.

If you have an idea that does not fall into one of these categories, feel free to suggest it to us. We encourage a well-written query letter outlining your subject and describing its appeal. (Query before submitting an article, and please include a SASE (self-addressed, stamped envelope).

We encourage you to read an issue of *Yoga Journal* carefully before submitting a query. Please keep in mind our editorial department's three E's: Articles should be enlightening, educational, and entertaining. Please avoid New Age jargon and in-house buzz-words as much as possible. Features run approximately 3,000 to 5,000 words. Departments run 1,000 to 2,500 words. Centering runs about 750 words. We do not print unsolicited poetry or cartoons. We consider everything except a direct assignment to be submitted on a speculative basis. When an article has been assigned, we will send you a contract specifying terms, kill fee, and deadline.

Remember to indicate the availability of photos or artwork in your query letter or with your article. (Pertinent, high quality photos or illustrations can greatly enhance an article's desirability.)

Payment varies, depending on length, depth of research, etc. We pay within 90 days of final acceptance: $1,000 to $3,000 for features, $600 to $800 for departments, $25 to $150 for World of Yoga and Spectrum, and $250 to $300 for book reviews.

All manuscripts should be typed, double spaced, and clean. Include your name, address, phone number, and word count on the title page, and your name and page number on each subsequent page. Also include a concise, two-sentence tagline identifying yourself to our readers. Always keep a copy of your work, and include a SASE with your submission if you want it returned.

If possible, please also send your work on a computer floppy disk. We strongly prefer submissions in Microsoft Word 5.1 for Macintosh. However, we may also be able to translate files from the following applications (for Mac) ClarisWorks, FrameMaker, MacWrite, Macwrite II, MacWrite Pro, Nisus, Microsoft Works, RTF; Text, WordPerfect, WriteNow; (for PCs) Ami Pro, ClarisWorks, DCA-RFT, FrameMaker, Microsoft Word, Microsoft Works, MultiMate, OfficeWriter, Professional Write, RTF, Text, WordPerfect, WordPerfect Works, WordStar, XYWrite. Please do not send us files written in other applications.

We cannot be held responsible for loss or damage to unsolicited manuscripts or artwork. We do not accept unsolicited manuscripts by e-mail or fax. Make sure all photos are marked with a brief descriptive caption and the photographer's name and address.

Categories: Nonfiction—Alternate Lifestyles—Arts—Book Reviews—Conservation—Consumer—Cooking—Ecology—Entertainment—Food/Drink—Health—Inspirational—Interview—New Age—Physical Fitness—Psychology—Spiritual—Travel—Nutrition—How-to—Opinion—Philosophy—Nature

Name: Rick Fields, Editor-in-Chief
Material: All
Address: 2054 UNIVERSITY AVE.
City/State/ZIP: BERKELEY, CA 94704
Telephone: 510-841-9200
Internet: www.yogajournal.com

Your Church

Our Readers

Our readers are the decision makers in the church—pastors, board members, church administrators, treasurers. Our slant is that pastors and key lay leaders are good at what they do; they are dedicated Christians wanting to be good stewards of their church-business responsibilities, and they are eager for cutting-edge, down-to-earth advice from people who know what they're talking about. We don't patronize them or scold them. Instead, we provide for them the best of current thinking—material far beyond first-consideration thoughts almost anybody could produce after a little thought.

Our Subject Matter

The purpose of YOUR CHURCH magazine is to provide pastors and other church leaders the insight, information, and action initiatives they need to be effective Christian stewards of the church resources entrusted to them. YOUR CHURCH focuses particularly on the fields of church business administration, purchasing, and facilities management.

We've given YOUR CHURCH a narrow focus on the business administration side of church life. The articles are brief, factual, bare bones. We would never be accused of being too literary or artsy. Instead, we want to be a bottom-line, here's-the-facts kind of magazine. How-to articles form our editorial backbone—articles coming from real life, not just theory, from experience, not just what ought to be.

Whatever YOUR CHURCH prints needs to be information church leaders can put right to work. Brief examples help, as do checklists, points to consider, rules of thumb, short illustrations, and key ideas.

Our Writing Style

Content makes an article worthwhile; style makes it readable and interesting. While our businesslike style is hardly lyrical, it has to be clear, compelling, and concise. We must get the most use out of every column inch we devote to editorial copy.

We place many "road signs" in the text to give the reader the ability to scan and spot the essential information. *Road signs* are words such as: *Example, Reason,* Key, *First Step, Next, Problem, Advice, Impact, Opportunity,* and *Options.* Rather than writing "The reason for this is...," we write "Reason:."

We know that many pastors place administration near the bottom of their interest lists. Therefore, YOUR CHURCH must bend over backwards to provide lucid and compelling writing that draws readers into the subject matter. We want to produce such a well-written and useful magazine that readers will approach it with a sense of anticipation, considering it indispensable.

Have you read *The Elements of Style* by Strunk and White? We recommend this widely read little paperback as a guide for style.

• *Use action verbs.* Forms of the verb "to be"—is, was, were, etc.—make for dead writing. In every possible case, choose forceful verbs.

• *Use short sentences whenever possible.* Variety of length, of course, *contributes* to good style, but writers err more often with too many long sentences than short ones.

• *Always define your jargon.* Some technical terms simply have to be used, but assume your reader isn't among the initiated. Give the definition to necessary but obscure words. And avoid long words whenever possible.

• *Assume your reader bores easily.* Keep asking yourself, "What grabs my attention? An *illustration*? A fresh insight? A well-turned phrase? A solution to a difficult problem?" Keep the reader with you by introducing a constant stream of interesting material.

After writing your manuscript, go through it and see how many action verbs you have. Mark each noun you can taste, hear, see, smell, or feel. Good writers fill their prose with objects you can see in your mind's eye. Be as specific as possible. For instance, "crashing cymbal" is better than "a loud noise" for conjuring up an image.

Rewording and simplifying sentences always improves copy. Dig for fresh ideas and then polish your work. Find all unnecessary words and slash them out. Scores of phrases and words just sit there without contributing force to the sentence. The discipline of our kind of writing demands a readable, commanding, and fluent style.

YOUR CHURCH solicits most of its manuscripts. It does, however, receive unsolicited manuscripts that are typed. The full name, address, and phone number of the author should appear on the first page of the manuscript, with the last name appearing near the page number on each succeeding page. We prefer material on floppy disk in ASCII format, but please enclose an accompanying printout.

Categories: Religion—Church Business

Name: Submissions Editor
Material: All
Address: 465 GUNDERSEN DR
City/State/ZIP: CAROL STREAM IL 60188
Telephone: 630-260-6200
Fax: 630-260-0114
E-mail: YCEditor@aol.com

Your Health

YOUR HEALTH magazine invites professional health and medical writers to contribute both original and previously published material for consideration. Our editorial focus: consumer-oriented general health, fitness and medical stories and service articles (how-to), targeting any adult age group, but with an emphasis on women over 35. We've recently added more articles on natural health and healing.

The most important requirement in writing for YOUR HEALTH is to provide well-researched stories. Writers must include up-to-date statistics, cite from the latest studies conducted at respected research institutions and include quotes from recognized experts in the field both pro and con.

Examples of department topics are: Natural Health and Healing, Skin, Nutrition, Dieting, Fitness, In The Kitchen (cooking & recipes), Behavior, Controversies, Women's Health, Men's Health, Trends, Environment, New Products, Consumer Watch, Aging, Lifestyle, Parenting, First Person (personal experience with a health problem and its resolution—must include well-researched advice from experts), Diseases (Heart Disease, Cancer, Diabetes, Arthritis, etc.), Safety...the list is endless.

Articles for departments should be 1,000 - 1,500 words; longer feature articles, up to 2,500 words. If available, black and white glossy photos or color transparencies are appreciated.

Payment is upon publication and depends on length of article and whether photos are included. Please keep in mind that even though we are nationally distributed, our circulation is about 50,000.

Sincerely,
Susan Gregg
Editor

Categories: Diet—Health—Physical Fitness—Women's Issues

Name: Susan Gregg, Editor
Material: All
Address: 5401 NW BROKEN SOUND BLVD
City/State/ZIP: BOCA RATON FL 33487
Telephone: 561-989-1184
Fax: 561-998-0798
E-mail: Yhealth@aol.com

Your Money

Useful advice on saving, investing, spending-indeed all personal-finance topics-is the overriding editorial concept of *Your Money*. Although many of our readers are sophisticated investors, *Your Money* provides jargon-free financial-planning, personal-finance, and investment advice for people who may not be sophisticated either in finance or investments.

Your Money's goal is to encourage our readers to handle their money wisely, to make their nest eggs grow through sound investment, and to enjoy the rewards of their wise money management. Financial-planning topics include debt management, how to save, retirement planning, and funding a college education, among others. Investment topics exclude stocks and bonds, mutual funds, collectibles, Treasuries, and bank CDs. Enjoying the rewards of sound money management means spending wisely, so *Your Money* includes articles on travel bargains, how to get the best deal on a new car, and other, more consumer-oriented topics.

Most important, we want to give our readers very practical advice: recommendations they can put to use. If we think a particular investment area has strong potential, we recommend specific vehicles- stocks, for example- that will help our readers profit from our analysis. In any financial-planning story, we give readers step-by-step instructions on what to do and how to do it, so that even a newcomer to money management can proceed safely and profitably.

The typical *Your Money* reader is about 52 years old (although the age range is extremely wide, from early 20s through retirement). The male/female ratio is about 70/30; most readers are married and own their homes. Median household income is about $53,000, more than 70 percent are college-educated. Although many have much larger sums available for investment, we operate on the assumption that our readers have investable capital of $5,000 to $50,000.

Your Money is published on a bimonthly schedule beginning with the December/January issue. Articles are scheduled and assigned according to topical interest, commonly two to four months prior to publication. Articles must be thoroughly researched and professionally written. We ask writers to supply documentation: phone numbers of people interviewed, original sources of facts and figures, annual reports of recommended companies, etc. Sidebars, charts, tables, and graphs are frequently used, and these are expected from writers. Authors must be well-acquainted with the areas they discuss and should be prepared to render subjective and objective opinions about profit potential and risk.

Authors should use the experiences of real, everyday people to illustrate article concepts. As authors interview individuals for this purpose, they should also secure the interviewee's verbal permission to be photographed later by a *Your Money*-assigned photographer.

Categories: Nonfiction—Automobiles—Business—Collectibles—Consumer—Economics—Money/Finance—Travel—Retirement—Education—Investing, Institutional

Name: Dennis Fertig, Editor
Material: All
Address: 5705 N. LINCOLN AVE.
City/State/ZIP: CHICAGO, IL 60659
Telephone: 773-275-3590
Fax: 847-763-0200
E-mail: drogus@consumerdigest.com

Youth Update

Youth Update is a four-page monthly publication that aims to support the growth of teenagers in faith through the application of Catholic/Christian principles to topics of timely interest. Please send a query letter and/or an outline before submitting a finished article.

The Audience: *Youth Update* is for high-school-age teens who vary both in their religious education and in their reading ability. Write for a 15-year-old with a C+ average. Avoid glib phrases and cliches. Aim towards a more casual, conversational sound rather than an academic or erudite approach.

The Style: Since you are not the same age as the readership, steer clear of inferring that you are "with it" in any superficial sense. Second person plural is preferred. In other words, not "I" or "they" but "you." Articles should be filled with examples, anecdotes, references to the real world. Avoid citations from printed sources. Don't preach. Use inclusive language.

The Presentation: Try for 2,300 words; roughly seven double-spaced pages of elite type. Guide the reader by dividing the material with lively subheads. Draft an involving quiz, checklist, inventory or table that relates to your topic. Consult samples. When citing the Bible, please refer to the New American Bible as your translation.

Follow-up Questions: The *Youth Update* format requires the author to answer questions from advisors gathered by the editor and representing a cross-section of readers. These questions will be in response to the edited manuscript and need to be answered quickly. Answers are published in the same issue as the ms. and are no more than 150 words each.

Topics: In recent issues, *Youth Update* has dealt with drugs, the death penalty, Native American traditions, parents, the Church's social teachings, Lent and Advent, Jesus, Confirmation, the millennium and prayer.

Submission of Computer Files: St. Anthony Messenger Press can work with PC files from an IBM compatible system, and will accept either 5.25" or 3.5" high-density diskettes. Label the diskette noting the word processing program and the level of software used—Microsoft Word 7.0, WordPerfect 5.1, etc. Always enclose a printed copy. You can also attach your file to an e-mail message.

Payment and Identity: We pay 15 cents a published word following receipt of answers to the teenager's questions and the completion of a contractual agreement provided by us for rights to publish in both our print and our online editions. Please provide a short bio for inclusion in *Youth Update*.

Categories: Nonfiction—Christian Interests—Religion—Spiritual—Teen

Name: Carol Ann Morrow, Editor
Material: All
Address: 1615 REPUBLIC ST
City/State/ZIP: CINCINNATI OH 45210-1298
E-mail: CarolAnn@americancatholic.org
Internet: www.americancatholic.org

Zoetrope: All-Story

Zoetrope: All-Story, a literary magazine, seeks to provide a new forum for short fiction and to make short fiction more accessible to the public at large.

Zoetrope considers unsolicited submissions of short stories and one-act plays no longer than 7,000 words. Excerpts from larger works, screenplays, treatments and poetry will be returned unread.

Simultaneous submissions are accepted, and first serial rights are required. Please do not submit more than one story or one-act at a time for consideration.

Submissions accompanied by an SASE will receive a response within four months. We regret that we are unable to respond to submissions without an SASE.

Categories: Fiction

Name: Adrienne Brodeur, Editor-in-Chief
Name: Joanna Yas, Assistant Editor
Material: Any
Address: 260 FIFTH AVE STE 1200
City/State/ZIP: NEW YORK NY 10001
Telephone: 212-696-5720
Fax: 212-696-5845
E-mail: 219-3004@mcimail.com

ZYZZYVA

West Coast writers and artists only. This means currently living in AK, HI, WA, OR, or CA.

We pay on acceptance an honorarium of $50, plus two author's copies, for first North American serial rights (and *ZYZZYVA* anthology rights) only. We reserve the right to put your piece up on our Web page.

We do not commission work.

We are committed to reflecting the full range of talent in our neighborhood—many genres, many generations, many schools. We have published a wide range of poetry, fiction, and nonfiction. Take your best shot.

We do not do interviews, reviews, or criticism. We do translations, especially of Latin American and Asian writers.

Photographers and graphic artists: submit copies or slides only. Only of work originally done in black & white on paper. No photos of paintings or sculpture, please. Self-addressed stamped envelope required.

If you would like to volunteer to work on ad sales, circulation, distribution, or editorial, please send a cover note and resume.

If you would like a sample copy, send us a check for $5 ($4 off the cover price).

Categories: Fiction—Nonfiction—Book Reviews—General Interest—History—Literature—Multicultural—Short Stories—Nostalgia—Humor—Personal Experience

Name: Howard Junker, Editor
Material: All
Address: 41 SUTTER ST STE 1400
City/State/ZIP: SAN FRANCISCO CA 94104-4987
Telephone: 415-752-4393
Fax: 415-752-4391
E-mail: zyzzyvainc@aol.com
Internet: www.webdelsol.com/zyzzyva

S-Z

Book Publishers

Abbott, Langer & Associates

We do not have a formal set of guidelines for manuscripts. Initially, just the title and table of contents would help us decide whether to reject a manuscript or investigate further.

Categories: Nonfiction—Associations—Business—Computers—Reference—Security & Loss Prevention—Human Resources Management

Name: Dr. Steven Langer, President

Material: All
Address: 548 FIRST ST
City/State/ZIP: CRETE IL 60417
Telephone: 708-672-4200
Fax: 708-672-4674
E-mail: slanger@abbott-langer.com
Internet: www.abbott-langer.com

ASSISTING CHRISTIANS TO ACT
PUBLICATIONS

ACTA Publications
Assisting Christians To Act

1. If you are not familiar with our products, please request our current catalog. Read it carefully and see if your book or tape seems to fit. You might even want to order one or two items to get a feel for the kind of material we publish.

2. If you truly feel we would be the best publisher for you, then send a proposal with three parts:

　　a. A cover letter that explains your proposal and tells a little bit about yourself and why your proposed work fits our product line.

　　b. A table of contents for your proposed work.

　　c. One chapter of a book or one segment from a proposed tape. (We will *not* read entire manuscripts.)

3. Be sure to enclose a self-addressed, stamped envelope with your proposal, indicating whether you want the entire proposal returned or just our answer. Your proposal will *not* receive a response without this.

4. Upon our receipt of your proposal you will receive either an immediate rejection or a letter indicating that it has been received and when you can expect an answer (usually six weeks).

5. At the end of that time period, you will receive another letter either giving the reasons why we are not interested in your proposal or indicating that we are interested and asking for additional information or samples.

6. Upon our receipt of that requested material you will receive another letter indicating when you can expect a response.

7. At the end of that time period, we will contact you either with a final rejection or with an offer of a contract.

8. If a contract is signed, then a timetable will be set up for the completion and publication of your work.

9. We do not offer advances to any of our first-time authors.

10. We will accept proposals which have been sent to other publishers simultaneously. You must, however, indicate this on your initial proposal. If not, your proposal will be automatically rejected at the point this fact becomes known—no matter how far along we are in the process.

Categories: Religion

Name: Gregory F. Pierce, Acquisitions Editor
Material: All
Address: 4848 N CLARK ST
City/State/ZIP: CHICAGO IL 60640
Telephone: 773-271-1030
Fax: 773-271-7399
E-mail: acta@one.org

Addicus Books, Inc.

Addicus Books, Inc. is based in Omaha, Nebraska. An independent publisher, the business currently publishes five to ten nonfiction books a year. (We do not publish poetry or fiction.) Part of our focus is on regional books-those that will have a solid market in a region, but not necessarily nationally.

At the same time however, we are also interested in books that may have broader, national appeal. Our two recent titles, *Straight Talk About Breast Cancer* as well as *Prescription Drug Abuse: The Hidden Epidemic*, are examples.

We're seeking titles on: health, self-help, psychology, how-to, business, economics, Americana, true crime, books of regional interest-profiles, histories.

Submission Guidelines

We first prefer a one-page query letter, explaining the nature of your work, who your market is and information about your background. If we're interested in taking a closer look, we'll ask for a proposal.

Book Proposals Should Include:
- A one-page overview of the book
- A chapter-by-chapter outline
- Author's background/credentials
- Market/audience information
- Two or three sample chapters
- Number of photos or illustrations
- Target completion date
- Word count/number of pages

Audience/Market Information Should Include:
- Who Is the Audience?
- What is the market for your book and how many potential buyers?
- Who wants this book? Why do they want it? Why do they need it?
- Do you have specific marketing ideas in mind?

Does Your Book Help the Reader?
- How will this book benefit the buyer? How will it help them?
- What need does it fill for your target market?

What Makes Your Book Special?
- What makes your book different from other such books? (Are there other such books?*)
- Does your book have more information? Is it more comprehensive, easier to use?
- What advantages does it have over the competition?
- Why will people buy it instead of something else?

*Please do a database search for competing nonfiction titles through the Internet on Amazon.com (the largest on-line book store with more than one million titles). Report your findings in your proposal.

Marketing Niches/Special markets? (Please be thorough here.)
- List any special markets your book may have outside regular trade book channels (book stores). Could sales result from

your contacts-associations, organizations, corporations, groups, hospitals, treatment centers, workshops, seminars or speaking engagements?

• Which magazines or professional/trade journals may review your book or print articles by you which in turn promotes the book?

• Do you have specific ideas for marketing your book?

• How willing are you to be active in marketing your book?

True-Crime Submissions

We'd like a synopsis with a clear layout of the story line, how the plot unfolds. Also, give us a sense of the book's structure as well as its scope. Why does this book need to be written?

Note: we are seeking manuscripts that have good stories behind the crimes. Unfortunately, heinous crimes happen everyday, but that does not a book make. We're looking for twists and turns in the story behind the crime-a plot with rising action. And, we want the author to get us inside the minds of the main characters so we know what makes them tick. Characters' motivation must be established. As you can see, we're looking for many of the devices used in fiction. We also prefer fairly recent, high-profile cases.

We publish high-quality, trade paperbacks and do extensive promotion within the given region.

Submission of Text (for all genres)

All materials should be clearly printed, no more than 250-300 words per page. No dot matrix printouts, please.

Categories: Nonfiction—Business—Economics—Family—General Interest—Health Relationships—True Crime

Name: Acquisition Department
Material: All
Address: PO BOX 45327
City/State/ZIP: OMAHA NE 68145
Telephone: 402-330-7493
Fax: 402-330-7493
E-mail: Addicusbks@aol.com

Aegina Press

Aegina Press, Inc.
Book Publishers

Aegina Press will be considering new manuscripts for possible book publication in the following categories:

Fiction
Nonfiction
Children's Books
Poetry
Genre Fiction (Science Fiction, Fantasy, Horror, etc.)
Short Story Collections
General Nonfiction: Biographies, Essays, Histories, etc.

Manuscripts should be typed. A cover letter should accompany the manuscript, which states the approximate length to the nearest 5,000 words (not necessary for poetry). A brief synopsis of the manuscript and a listing of the author's publishing credits (if any) is helpful but not required.

Queries, sample chapters, synopses, and completed manuscripts are welcome. Allow 1-2 weeks for reply to queries, one month for reply to complete manuscripts.

Categories: Fiction—Nonfiction—Adventure—African-American—Asian-American—Children—Confession—Crime—Fantasy—General Interest—Horror—Juvenile—Literature—Men's Fiction—Mystery—Poetry—Romance—Science Fiction—Short Stories—Women's Fiction—Writing—Young Adult

Name: Ira Herman, Managing Editor
Material: All
Address: 1905 MADISON AVE
City/State/ZIP: HUNTINGTON WV 25704
Telephone: 304-429-7204
Fax: 304-429-7234

Aegis Publishing Group, Ltd.

We specialize in telecommunications books for non-technical end users such as small businesses (small office/home office) and entrepreneurs. We do not publish anything that does not fit this niche.

Categories: Nonfiction—Small Business—Telecommunications

Name: Robert Mastin, President
Material: All
Address: 796 AQUIDNECK AVE
City/State/ZIP: NEWPORT RI 02842
Telephone: 401-849-4200
Fax: 401-849-4231
E-mail: Aegis@aegisbooks.com
Internet: www.aegisbooks.com

African American Images

EDITORIAL POLICY

To expedite the processing of your manuscript, we have developed the following:

• We are not able to review incomplete manuscripts. You will receive a written response generally within ten (10) weeks.

• We do not publish poetry, essays, novels, autobiographies, or biographies.

• Typically, we do not publish religious materials nor those manuscripts exclusively addressing the Continent of Africa.

• Generally speaking, African American Images publishes books from an Africentric frame of reference that promote self-esteem, collective values, liberation, and skill development.

• We do not publish adult nonfiction. Our adult books, however, must provide solutions for African Americans.

• We do publish Juvenile fiction and nonfiction.

• We can provide illustrations for the publishable work.

• Once a manuscript is accepted for publishing, a rough draft should be submitted on a 3½" and 5¼" diskette, and a hardcopy should be included using WordPerfect 6.0 (DOS version).

• African American Images does not advance royalties.

HOUSE STYLE

In the event that our office agrees to publish your work and in order to expedite the production of your book, please incorporate the following format when typing the script.

• Two (2) manuscripts should be submitted. One should be typed single-space and printed in the style the author wants it to appear. The second manuscript should be typed double-spaced.

• Each chapter should be placed in a separate file. There should also be separate files for back matter (References, Bibliography, and Appendix) and separate files for front matter (Table of Contents, Introduction, and Preface).

• The manuscript's left and right margins should be 1" each.

• You may use whatever style would be most helpful in spelling, pronunciation and emphasis; consistency, however, is crucial.

• When using charts, please use WordPerfect's chart format.

• Use the spell check function to make sure all spelling is correct.

We appreciate your interest in our publishing services.

Categories: Nonfiction—African-American—Education—Ethnic—Family—Parenting—Relationships

Name: Acquisitions Editor
Material: All
Address: 1909 W 95 ST
City/State/ZIP: CHICAGO IL 60643
Telephone: 773-445-0322
Fax: 773-445-9844
E-mail: AAI@AfricanAmericanImages.com
Internet: www.AfricanAmericanImages.com

Agony In Black

Thank you for inquiring as to guidelines for submission for CFD Productions' line of titles. CFD Productions considers the following types of submissions:

• comic book and comic story scripts
• comic book and comic story art - pencils, inks prose fiction
• cover illustrations
• various illustrations
• other related types of submissions

For submissions, artists, writers and painters should send good photocopies with name, address and phone number included on each page of submission (stamped or written on back of pages). CFD recommends that creators look over our current titles to see if your work suits our needs.

If proposing a comic book series, please query with a brief synopsis and pertinent details: series length, page count current level of completion, etc. Include brief sample of artwork if applicable.

Writers and artists may also include a brief bio of previous publishing ventures.

Replies take 6-8 weeks.

GUIDELINES FOR SUBMISSION—COMIC BOOK TITLES

CFD Productions is currently accepting submissions for short stories for a line of upcoming anthologies dealing with the following:

"Classic" horror genres {i.e. mummies, werewolves, mad scientists, etc.} but with modern, up-to-date & cutting edge storylines.

Dark fantasy/science-fiction. No space-opera

"Modern" horror—i.e., Poppy Z. Brite, Jack Ketchum, John Shirley. Very disturbing stories that tend to cover new ground in the field.

Drama/General fiction—covering a wide array of subjects, genres.

To have work considered for any line, please refer to the following guidelines. As always, each work should avoid cliches and rehashings of older works.

1. Story concepts should be presented in the following format:

A) Synopsis only for initial submission—*not* full scripts.
B) Maximum 1 page synopsis per story.
C) Snail mail preferred.
D) Multiple submissions accepted.
E) Storylines should be based upon 4-12 pages in finished comic-book format. Twelve pages maximum.

2. Story restrictions:

A) Only genres listed—all stories should represent a cutting edge, modern, gut-wrenching tone in work.
B) No humor elements—no clichés please.
C) Mature Audience is the target—Adult only concepts will be considered but remember that they will be presented in illustrated form for a Mature Readers title.
D) Vampire stories will be among the last considered at present.

3. General Information

AGONY IN BLACK: A digest-sized anthology consisting mainly of prose fiction with single page & spot illustrations. Looking for prose submissions only of the hardest-hitting, most disturbing fiction. Accepts illustrations on a submission basis but more than likely all illustration jobs will be assigned in order to adequately match content.

4. Selection

CFD Productions President Joe Monks will be going through every submission himself. Submissions are open to all writers, professionals and newcomers alike. On the basis of synopsis alone, stories fitting the CFD Productions line of titles will be accepted for full-scripting and (where applicable) an artist will be assigned to the piece. (Artist writer teams are welcome—artists will be assigned only in the event the submitted script has no artist upon acceptance.)

5. Compensation

Varies upon publication, title and line. At time of acceptance standards contracts will be tendered and compensation will be negotiated.

IMPORTANT

Regardless of how much success any genre has shown in the past or present, the current comic book marketplace is a tumultuous and ever-changing area of publishing. As in life, in comics publishing there are absolutely no guarantees. Since most CFD Productions titles are based upon revenues, consider the following: If a book makes a substantial amount of money beyond printing costs, the contributors will make roughly 75%—80% of the title's net revenues. If a book does poorly or basically "breaks even" you're looking at doing it on spec., for the love of the craft, and for a whole load of contributor copies. (Well, some notoriety, too, but that doesn't come with any financial value, and it should be understood up front that such possibilities both good and bad are flip sides of the same coin. That's as honest as it can be told.)

This said, best of luck, we'll be looking forward to all submissions.

Categories: Fiction—Horror

Name: Pamela Hazelton, Editor
Material: All
Address: 360-A W MERRICK RD STE 350
City/State/ZIP: VALLEY STREAM NY 11580
E-mail: CFDPROD@aol.com

Allworth Press

Allworth Press publishes helpful guides for photographers, artists, graphic designers, writers, and other professionals in the arts. Our books have few illustrations, if any; and we do not publish full-color books.

If you are submitting a proposal that falls outside of these areas, please call and speak to the editor, Ted Gachot, to see if your project is one that Allworth might consider publishing.

We prefer to see a one or two page outline of a proposed book, even if the book has already been written. The outline should give a chapter by chapter summary of the book's contents. It should also indicate the author's background, the intended audience for the book, any books that might be considered competitive, and why this book will compete successfully with those books. If the book has been written, please include two sample chapters with the outline.

Categories: Nonfiction—Arts—Business—Crafts—Film/Video—Money/Finance—Music—Photography—Theatre—Writing—Graphic Design

Name: Ted Gachot, Editor
Material: All
Address: 10 E 23RD ST
City/State/ZIP: NEW YORK NY 10010
Telephone: 212-777-8395
Fax: 212-777-8261
E-mail: PUB@allworth.com
Internet: www.allworth.com

ALPHA BEAT PRESS

Alpha Beat Press
Chapbook Publishers

Alpha Beat Press has been publishing Beat Generation, post-Beat independent and other modern writings of known and lesser known writers since 1986. Now provides co-operative publishing for new and established writers.

We print quality chapbooks of approximately 30 to 50 pages. The poet pays production costs on a 100 copy press run. Author cost and other details available upon request.

The books go out to people in the small press who should see them—distributors, reviewers and other small press magazine poets and editors.

If you would like to publish your book, send a 30 to 50 page, single-spaced, preferably camera-ready and proof read manuscript, with bio notes for back cover and acknowledgements if needed. Artwork may also be included.

Co-operative publishing allows us to put a little money back into **Alpha Beat Press** and gives the poet who works with us exposure they normally wouldn't receive.

Your published chapbook will arrive within four weeks from the day we receive your order.

Thank you for considering **Alpha Beat Press**, we look forward to publishing you.

Sample: $6.00
Categories: Poetry

Name: Dave Christy, Editor/Publisher
Name: Ana Christy, Editor/Publisher
Material: Chapbooks
Address: 31 WATERLOO ST
City/State/ZIP: NEW HOPE PA 18938
Telephone: 215-862-0299
Nota bene: Author financing required.

Alyson Publications, Inc.

QUERY SUBMISSIONS

Alyson Publications is the leading publisher of books by, for, and about lesbians, gay men, and bisexuals from all economic and social segments of society and of all ages, from children to adults. In fiction and nonfiction format, Alyson books explore the political, legal, financial, medical, spiritual, social, and sexual aspects of gay, lesbian, and bisexual life and the contributions to and experiences in society of our community.

We are happy to consider book queries. We only consider solicited manuscripts. Please note the following before submitting a query:

INQUIRY: Please send a query letter detailing your novel's plot or your nonfiction idea. Give a summary of the book, a chapter outline if you have it, approximately how many words, and what qualifies you to write this particular book. We do NOT want to see sample chapters at this stage.

MANUSCRIPT: Unsolicited manuscripts will not be considered and will be returned if accompanied by appropriate SASE. They will be destroyed if *not* accompanied by appropriate SASE.

OTHER: Nonfiction should be written in a popular (i.e., non-academic) style. We do not consider individual short stories or poetry. At this time, we do not have a service referring individual short stories to any anthologies we will be publishing. We prefer manuscript length to be around 100,000 words. If you would like to see what Alyson has previously published, our books are available at all gay and lesbian bookstores as well as larger chains.

DECISION TIME: We try to give serious consideration to each query we receive. Each query mill be reviewed and a response sent to you within one month of its receipt. Please do not call to check on the status of your submission.

Categories: Fiction—Nonfiction—Children—Gay/Lesbian

Name: Acquisitions Editor
Material: All
Address: PO BOX 4371
City/State/ZIP: LOS ANGELES CA 90078-4371
Telephone: 213-871-1225
Fax: 213-467-6805
E-mail: alyson@advocate.com
Internet: www.advocate.com

American Correctional Association

ACA is a professional association whose members work in corrections or are affiliated with corrections. This includes involvement in all areas of prisons, jails, halfway houses, detention centers, community programs, probation, parole, and counseling. Our members interact with both adults and juveniles-males and females.

We are seeking practical books that will enable people working in the corrections profession to perform their jobs efficiently and humanely. We do not publish fiction, poetry, or biographical/autobiographical material. We do not publish materials from inmates or ex-inmates.

ACA accepts manuscript submissions on any relevant topic. We are eager to develop new titles and hope that you can join the growing number of authors who write for the American Correctional Association.

We publish books on corrections that concern a broad range

of topics. We are seeking authors for books on the following subjects and other areas:
- Correctional Careers
- Classification
- Community Partnerships
- Correctional Management
- Correctional Nursing
- Evaluation
- Job Training for Youthful Offenders
- Incarceration Alternatives
- Jails
- Juvenile Issues
- Megatrends in Crime and Punishment
- Offender Fees
- Ombudsman's Role
- Probation/Parole Issues
- Proven Rehabilitation Strategies
- Recidivism Reduction
- Security
- Training

Your ideas are welcome!

Submit to ACA

To submit your proposal, send us an outline and a summary plus two sample chapters of your proposed work. The outline should describe the contents and scope of each chapter and list any appendices or graphics.

The following Information must accompany your submission:
- Working title
- Anticipated manuscript length (i.e., number of words)
- Comparison of your book to others on the same or similar topic that explains how your treatment of the subject is unique
- Statement about the target audience for your book (e.g. administrators of juvenile agencies)
- Summary of your qualifications, along with a description of other materials you have written that would bolster your authority to handle the subject
- Your complete address and daytime and evening phone and fax numbers

Please note: even if you submit the full manuscript, the outline and other information is required for your submission to be complete.

Wheels in Motion

After we receive the requested material-the outline, summary, and sample chapters-we will review it to determine whether it meets our publishing mandate.

If the material is appropriate, the core management staff of the Association will carefully analyze the submission, which also will be sent out for peer review.

Next, we will determine whether the full manuscript will be reviewed. If so, you will be asked to submit two hard copies and a disk copy in WordPerfect format. You also will be asked to complete an author-history questionnaire.

If your manuscript elicits favorable reviews, you will receive a contract. Once we receive your signed contract and your completed manuscript, we may again send it out for review. Then, after receiving favorable reviews, the production phase will begin.

Categories: Nonfiction—Careers—Crime—Disabilities—Psychology—Reference—Senior Citizens—Corrections—Criminal Justice—Sociology

Name: Alice Fins, Publications Managing Editor
Material: Book submissions
Name: Gabrielle de Groot, Editor, *Corrections Today*
Material: Magazine submissions
Address: 4380 FORBES BLVD
City/State/ZIP: LANHAM MD 20706-4322

Telephone: 301-918-1800
Fax: 301-918-1886
E-mail: afins@aca.org
Internet: www.aca.org
Nota bene: No submissions by inmates/ex-inmates.

American History Press

Please refer to The Conservatory of American Letters.

American Literary Press

American Literary Press, Inc.
Noble House

Typed or laser printed, unbound 8.5"x11" pages, upper and lower case letters. Title page should include authors name, address, work and phone numbers with complete word count. Forwarding a 2-3 paragraph synopsis of your manuscript would be helpful to our staff. Please be aware that we will keep your work in our files for three months only.

Categories: Fiction—Adventure—Children—Cooking—Feminism—Health—History—Horror—Humor—Juvenile—New Age—Poetry—Religion—Romance—Science Fiction—Short Stories—Sports—Western—Women's Fiction—Young Adult

Name: Acquisitions Editor
Material: All
Address: 8019 BELAIR RD STE 10
City/State/ZIP: BALTIMORE MD 21236
Telephone: 410882-7700
Fax: 410-882-7703
E-mail: amerlit@erols.com

Anchorage Press

Guidelines for Submission of Play Manuscripts

Anchorage Press publishes plays for children and youth. It is respectfully suggested that prospective submissions be appropriate in subject, theme and language to universal norms for juveniles and adolescents: fantasy, fable, adventure, quest, journey, unfolding maturity, self discovery, etc. "Send-ups" of famous stories, while amusing to the adult possessing knowledge of the originals, are inappropriate to an audience probably unfamiliar with the material. Adaptations of books beloved by young people require proof of authorization to create a dramatic adaptation, and permission to submit for publication.

1.) Manuscripts must be typewritten.

2.) Submitted by mail—not handed to representatives at conferences.

3.) There must be at least *three distinct* productions, in three different locales, and by three different directors.

4.) No production directed by the playwright to be included in the requisite number.

5.) Proof of productions required—programs, reviews.

6.) If the work is an adaptation of a copyrighted work, the

above conditions must be adhered to.

Only such manuscripts in full conformity to the above requirements will be considered for publication. Several months are required to respond to a submission as we may consult a number of advisors and prospective producers.

Categories: Arts—Children—Drama—Theatre

Name: O. R. Corey, Editor
Material: Plays/Musicals for Children
Address: PO BOX 8067
City/State/ZIP: NEW ORLEANS LA 70182
Telephone: 504-283-8868

Archway Paperbacks
An Imprint of Simon & Schuster's Pocketbooks

Please refer to Pocketbooks.

Arden Press, Inc.

Arden Press publishes nonfiction books, including women's titles (women's history, biography, general guides), popular how-to books, directories, guides, and film titles. We sell primarily to bookstores and to public and academic libraries. Many of our titles are adopted as texts for college courses. We do *not* publish fiction, poetry, or personal memoirs.

We prefer to receive manuscript proposals rather than complete manuscripts. If we believe that your project might fit our publication profile, we will request the manuscript.

What To Include In Your Manuscript Proposal

1.) Tentative Title: A descriptive title for the purpose of identifying the particular manuscript.

2.) Scope/Purpose: Describe in one paragraph the intended purpose of the book, the scope of coverage, and primary and secondary audience.

3.) Outline: A preliminary outline should show all chapters and key subsections. The outline should be accompanied by written chapter summaries that explain the main theme and scope of each chapter.

4.) Methodology & Presentation: Summarize the search plan that is to be used in locating necessary data. List the types of sources to be consulted. Indicate the need for illustrations, maps, appendixes, indexes, etc.

5.) Sample Section: A sample chapter or section in preliminary form should be submitted to demonstrate the organization, content, writing style, and documentation to be used.

6.) Similar or Related Works: Identify books on the same topic or on similar or related topics. Explain the need for the proposed book and how it will fill a specific gap in coverage or take a unique approach to the subject.

Thank you for your interest in Arden Press.

Categories: Nonfiction—Biography—Film/Video—General Interest—History—Reference—Women's Issues—College Course Adoptions

Name: Susan Conley, Publisher/Editor
Material: All
Address: PO BOX 418
City/State/ZIP: DENVER CO 80201
Telephone: 303-697-6766
Fax: 303-697-3443

Ardsley House Publishers

We are a college-textbook publishing company, specializing in mathematics, music, and philosophy texts. We will consider manuscripts that concern other disciplines (especially those of history, dance and cinema studies), or combined disciplines.

Guidelines for manuscript submission include:
• At least two chapters of the work,
• A thorough prospectus,
• A detailed table of contents,
• Curriculum vitae.

Categories: College Textbooks—Dance—History—Music—Philosophy

Name: Acquisitions Editor
Material: All
Address: 320 CENTRAL PARK W
City/State/ZIP: NEW YORK NY 10025
Telephone: 212-496-7040
Fax: 212-496-7146

Art Direction Book Company, Inc.

Want to see a Table of Contents and a chapter; not an introduction. Please list your various positions.

Categories: Advertising Art

Name: Don Barron, Publisher
Material: Ad Art
Address: 456 GLENBROOK RD
City/State/ZIP: GLENBROOK CT 06906
Telephone: 203-353-1441
Fax: 203-353-1371

Arte Público Press
The University of Houston

Recovering the past, creating the future

Arte Público Press of the University of Houston publishes contemporary fiction, novels, short stories, poetry, and drama written by U.S. Hispanic authors: Mexican American, Puerto Ricans, Cuban Americans, etc.

Manuscripts are accepted in either English or Spanish, although the majority of the submissions published are in English.

Submissions are accepted typed, double-spaced and accompanied by a self-addressed, stamped envelope to return manuscripts that are not selected for publication.

Please note: Accepted manuscripts must be presented in IBM format (WordPerfect 5.1, 5.2 or Microsoft Word for Windows 1.0 or 2.0).

Piñata Books

Piñata Books is Arte Público Press' imprint for children's and young adult literature that seeks to authentically and realistically portray themes, characters and customs unique to U.S. Hispanic culture. Submissions and manuscript formalities are the same as for Arte Público Press.

Recovering the U.S. Hispanic Literary Heritage

Recovering the U.S. Hispanic Literary Heritage series publishes recovered literature written by Hispanics between the colonial period and 1960 in the geographic area that has become the United States.

For further details, contact the coordinator, Dr. Lynn Cortina, at the address below.

Categories: Fiction—Nonfiction—Hispanic—Juvenile—Literature—Multicultural—Women's Issues—Young Adult

Name: Nicolas Kanellos, Director
Material: All
Address: UNIVERSITY OF HOUSTON
City/State/ZIP: HOUSTON TX 77204-2090
Telephone: 713-743-2846
Fax: 713-743-3080
E-mail: mtristan@uh.edu

ATL Press
Science Technology Science Technology

1. We are interested in many science and non-fiction areas, including astronomy, biochemistry, biomedicine, biotechnology, chemistry, computers, earth science, foods, medicine, nutraceuticals, pharmaceuticals and polymers. We publish monographs, edited volumes and conference proceedings. However, ATL Press also welcomes submissions on other topics, including fiction titles. Our interests include non-book products, such as software, CDs, audiovisual materials, etc. Your submission will be particularly appealing to us, if it is unique or of special topical interest. Examples of such titles include leading edge research results, topics with broad public appeal, and areas of major scientific discoveries with notable impact on society.

2. Before you send us the completed manuscript or work, we prefer to receive an introductory letter that describes your proposed project, together with an outline, estimated length, expected completion date, nature (that is, line drawings, color, B&W photos, etc.) and number of any illustrations, and, if available, perhaps a few sample chapters (please include a SASE with your submission).

3. A very essential point to consider in your submission is the ultimate customer: who are your target readers, why should they be interested in your book, what makes your book unique, which other titles do you know of on your topic, and how does your book differ from these? A visit to one of the major bookstores or libraries in your neighborhood may help you answer some of these questions, if you look up the section that is most relevant to your topic.

4. Can you suggest individuals who can review and comment on your manuscript? If so, please provide a list with the relevant contact information.

5. Please tell us also about yourself: your educational background, professional credentials, any achievements, awards, etc. (a resume and a list of publications—if applicable—are acceptable).

6. We generally accept only manuscripts prepared with word processing software. Please indicate in your submission the word processor used, and the platform (PC or Mac). Detailed information on submitting camera-ready manuscripts is available upon request.

7. Last, and not least: if you have not embarked on this venture yet, be prepared to spend a substantial amount of time and effort. At the same time, it can be an extremely enjoyable undertaking. On our part, we work very closely with our authors to produce and market their projects.

Categories: Business—Computers—Juvenile—Science—Technology

Name: Paul Lucio
Material: All
Address: PO BOX 4563 T STN
City/State/ZIP: SHREWSBURY MA 01545
Internet: www.atlpress.com

ATHENEUM
BOOKS FOR YOUNG READERS

Atheneum Books for Young Readers
Simon & Schuster Children's Publishing Division

Atheneum publishes original hardcover trade books for children from pre-school age through young adult. Our list includes picture books, chapter books, mysteries, science fiction and fantasy, and middle grade young adult fiction and nonfiction. The style and subject matter of the books we publish is almost unlimited. We do not, however, publish textbooks, coloring or activity books, greeting cards, magazines or pamphlets or religious publications. Anne Schwartz Books is a new and highly selective line of books recently added to the Atheneum imprint. The lists of Charles Scribner's Sons Books for Young Readers have been folded into the Atheneum program.

General Submission Guidelines

Atheneum accepts **only** letters of inquiry describing your work, regardless of length or type (picture books, novels, nonfiction). Should the work seem to be in line with our current publishing needs, we will then request the complete picture book manuscripts or outlines and sample chapters of longer works.

With your submission, you may also wish to include a brief resume of your previous publishing credits.

Please allow twelve weeks for your material to be considered. Although it often takes less time, it can take even longer than we would like because of the many thousands of submissions we receive and because **every** submission is carefully considered.

Picture Book Submissions

Atheneum publishes 15-20 picture books each year. Do **not** include illustrations with your manuscript submission since a good book can be turned down because of poor or inappropriate illustrations. It is the prerogative of the publisher to choose illustrators. If you yourself are a professional artist, you might wish to send samples (no larger than 8½"x11") to our art director, Ann Bobco. Should you wish to show your portfolio when you are in the New York area, please contact Ethan Trask at (212) 698-2785. Drop-offs are accepted only on Thursdays at 10 a.m. and will be left at the reception desk for pick up at noon. **No** manuscripts will be read or considered at this time.

Questions frequently asked:

"What are you looking for?"

The most common answer each editor gives to this question is simply, "Nothing specific—just good writing." Atheneum puts less emphasis on particular trends, fads and gimmicks and more on quality of craftsmanship—fine writing and artwork. This and originality are the most important things we look for in a manuscript.

"Why did you turn my manuscript down?"

Although it is easy to understand a writer's desire for a critique of his work, the constant heavy influx of submissions makes it impossible to offer evaluations of work that has been declined. Form rejection letters are not meant as an insult, but simply are the only way publishers can handle the number of submissions received. A writer can expect feed-back on his work by taking one of the many excellent writing courses offered by local colleges and universities—some of them specifically geared to children's books. Another source of evaluation can be found in joining a local writers group. Such groups commonly critique members' work in progress. THE SUBJECT GUIDE TO BOOKS IN PRINT by R.R. Bowker Company also lists helpful books on writing for children and the Children's Book Council (568 BROADWAY, NEW YORK NY 10003) has a pamphlet on the subject available on request. But perhaps the simplest and cheapest way of finding out what publishers look for is to go to your local public or school library and read.

Categories: Children—Juvenile—Teen—Young Adult

Name: Jonathan J. Lanman, Editorial Director
Material: Any not assigned below
Name: Marcia Marshall, Executive Editor
Material: Science Fiction, Fantasy, All Nonfiction
Name: Anne Schwartz, Editorial Director
Material: Anne Schwartz Books
Name: Sarah Caguiat, Editor
Material: Any not assigned above
Name: Ana Cerro, Associate Editor
Material: Any not assigned above
Address: 1230 AVENUE OF THE AMERICAS
City/State/ZIP: NEW YORK NY 10020
Telephone: 212-698-2715
Fax: 212-698-2796

Avery Publishing Group, Inc.

Dear Potential Author:

Thank you for your letter inquiring about Avery Publishing Group. Avery is a publisher of non-fiction adult oriented books. We do not publish fiction, poetry or children's books.

When submitting a manuscript proposal for the first time, we ask that you send us the following items:

• Cover letter explaining the type of book you intend to write, its market, the need for such a book, and some background about yourself.

• Table of Contents outlining what material will be covered in your book.

• Preface which explains your overall approach.

We ask that you not send us a manuscript without a specific request from us. If you send us a manuscript without a request we are, in fact, less likely to review your work.

Should you have any further questions, you can contact our Garden City Park office.

Thank you very much for your interest in Avery Publishing Group.

Categories: Nonfiction—Business—Cooking—Diet—Health—Alternative Health—Money/Finance—New Age—Parenting—Reference—Romance

Name: Rudy Shur, Managing Editor
Material: All
Address: 120 OLD BROADWAY
City/State/ZIP: GARDEN CITY PARK NY 11040
Telephone: 516-741-2155

Avon
Books for Young Readers

AVON FLARE

Books for Young Adults. For ages 12 and up. Manuscript length should run between 35,000 and 45,000 words. General fiction (coming of age, family, peer stories), historical fiction, horror, suspense. Romance can be a plot element, but we are not interested in formula romance. No poetry, story collections, science fiction/fantasy, or nonfiction.

CAMELOT

Books for Middle Readers. For ages 8-12. Manuscript length should run between 20,000 and 35,000 words. General fiction (family, peer, school related stories), historical fiction, mystery/adventure, humor. Limited interest in science fiction/fantasy, or nonfiction.

PLEASE NOTE: We do not publish picture books, poetry or short stories.

We prefer to see complete manuscripts or sample chapters plus an outline. We are interested in writing style as well as plot, so it is difficult for us to evaluate from a query letter.

Handwritten and/or single-spaced manuscripts will not be read. Please *do not* send us the only copy of your manuscript.

For a copy of our catalogue, please send an 8"x11" SASE.

Categories: Fiction—Children—Fantasy—Horror—Juvenile—Teen—Young Adult

Name: Elise Howard, Executive Editor
Material: Any
Name: Stephanie Siegel, Assistant Editor
Material: Any
Name: Abigail McAden, Editorial Assistant
Material: Any
Address: 1350 AVENUE OF THE AMERICAS
City/State/ZIP: NEW YORK NY 10019
Telephone: 212-261-6800
Fax: 212-261-6895

Baen Books

Dear Author:

We publish only science fiction and fantasy. Writers familiar with what we have published in the past will know what sort of material we are most likely to publish in the future: powerful plots with solid scientific and philosophical underpinnings are the *sine qua non* for consideration for science fiction submissions. As for fantasy, any magical system must be both rigorously coherent and integral to the plot, and overall the work must at least strive for originality.

Those manuscripts which survive the "first cut" as outlined above are then judged primarily on plot and characterization. Style: simple is generally better; in our opinion good style, like good breeding, never calls attention to itself.

Payment rates: very competitive.

Preferred length: 80,000 - 110,000 words.

Standard manuscript format only: double-spaced, one side

of the page only, 1½" margins on all four sides of the page. We will consider photocopies if they are dark and clear. Letter quality dot matrix is acceptable. Manuscripts that are difficult to read probably won't be.

Submission procedures: Query letters not necessary. We prefer to see complete manuscripts, accompanied by synopsis. We prefer not to see simultaneous submissions. All submissions should be accompanied by a stamped return envelope. Submissions from outside the U.S. should be accompanied by sufficient International Reply Coupons. We do not accept electronic submissions.

Reporting time: Usually within six months.
Thank you for thinking of Baen Books.
The Editors
Categories: Fantasy—Science Fiction

Name: Acquisitions Editor
Material: All
Address: PO BOX 1403
City/State/ZIP: RIVERDALE NY 10471

Baker Book House Company
Baker, Revell, and Chosen Books

Preparing a Proposal

Book proposals are always welcomed by the editors of Baker, Revell, and Chosen Books. Indeed, we editors insist on seeing a proposal before examining a manuscript. So whether you wish to submit an idea for a manuscript or a finished manuscript, you must supply us first with a proposal.

There are good reasons for you to develop a proposal before writing most of the manuscript. This enables you to obtain from us guidelines for the project, which increases the likelihood that we will accept it for publication.

Should your book be intended, not for a more general Christian readership, but more specifically for pastors and others in Christian ministry, please request the brochure "Preparing a Proposal: Professional Books" and follow its guidelines, not those that follow in this brochure. Should your book be designed as a text for use in Christian colleges or evangelical seminaries, ask for the brochure "Preparing a Proposal: Academic Books."

Proposals for "trade books" consist of answers to several key questions, along with some supporting materials. First some questions for you to answer briefly.

Questions

1. What has motivated you to pursue this project?
2. What primary point(s) do you seek to make in this work?
3. For what specific audience(s) are you writing?
4. Have you presented this material in any other media or public forums? If so, describe the medium or forum and characterize audience response.
5. What additional evidence do you have that a readership exists for this material in book form?
6. If you have not already made this clear, explain the impact you want this book to have on the reader.
7. What title (and subtitle) do you now favor for this book? (Include several possibilities if no one title has yet risen to the top.)
8. What evangelical books now in print would your book compete with? What uniqueness and strengths set your book apart from the competition? If no competition exists, does this say anything, positive or negative, about the market for your book?
9. Is the manuscript complete? If not, when do you plan to finish it?

Other Material

1. An outline of the book (the table of contents), with paragraph summaries or brief outlines of each chapter.
2. An estimate of the length of each chapter and of the entire work (see table 1 below). Most trade books have a total of 125-225 printed pages.
3. An explanation of the kinds and quantity of illustrative material (such as photographs, line drawings, maps, charts, and tables) that need to be included. If you plan to provide any original artwork, please include a sample or two.
4. Preferably one or two chapters. This chapter should be drawn from the part of your book that represents its most important contribution. At least one sample chapter is essential if this is your first book.
5. Your resumé, which should include, in addition to standard items, the following:
    a. a complete bibliography of your published articles and books,
    b. a description of any public speaking that you do on a reasonably regular basis,
    c. your ecclesiastical connections, including any parachurch organizations in which you have been active, and
    d. any information that will demonstrate your qualifications to write the proposed volume.
6. For a first-time author: the names of any published writers with whom you are personally acquainted. You might want to include a letter of recommendation from one of them.

Pointers

Put your proposal in the most refined form you can. We will judge your ability to craft a well-written manuscript by the quality of your proposal.

If you prepare your proposal on a word-processor, do not send the proposal in electronic form; supply hard-copy only.

We naturally prefer that you submit your proposal to our company first. If you choose to submit it simultaneously to other publishers as well, we ask only that you say as much in your cover letter.

After evaluating your proposal, we will: (1) advise you to send it elsewhere, (2) suggest ways to revise it, (3) encourage you to proceed with the project, or (4) offer you a contract (*if* you are an experienced author and *if* we are totally committed to your book-idea.)

When we encourage you to complete the manuscript but offer no contract (option 3), this means that we accept the basic concept for your book as a valid one, find evidence in the proposal that you can write an acceptable manuscript, and will very likely publish the completed manuscript if it meets our standards.

Appendix: Estimating Length

When estimating the length of a project, use table 1. This table is based on these specifications: a typewritten page of 65 characters per line (on average) and 26 lines per page; and a typeset page of 11-point type, 23 picas per line, and 37 lines per page. As you count characters, include the notes and ignore the fact that, when typeset, they will appear in smaller type than regular text.

Table 1

Characters	Words	Typed Pages	Printed Pages
180,000	30,000	107	104
240,000	40,000	142	139
300,000	50,000	178	174
360,000	60,000	213	208
420,000	70,000	248	243

Categories: Fiction—Nonfiction—Christian Interests—Inspirational—Religion—Spiritual

Name: Ms. Jane Schrier, Asst. to Director of Publications
Material: *Baker Books* or *Fleming H. Revell*
Address: PO BOX 6287
City/State/ZIP: GRAND RAPIDS MI 49516-6287

Name: Acquisitions Editor
Material: Chosen Books
Address: 3985 BRADWATER ST
City/State/ZIP: FAIRFAX VA 22031
Telephone: (Baker) 616-676-9185
Fax: (Baker) 616-676-9573

Balcony Press

Balcony Press is interested in manuscripts on art, architecture and design topics with a preference for west coast or southwest subject matter. Books normally take a historic or cultural slant as opposed to technical, biographical or how-to.

Proposals should include the following:
• Book title and brief summary of the book's content.
• Proposed length of ms. and approximate quantity of illustrations, photos etc.
• Description of the audience for the book and any ideas you have for promoting it
• What is unusual about the book and what is the competition?
• Author bio or resume
• Suggested table of contents
• Sample chapter and introduction
In general:
• Authors are responsible for providing all illustrations and permissions to be used in the book
• No royalty advances or expenses are offered
• Royalties are 10% of net revenues from book sales
• Proposals will be responded to within 1 month
• Full ms. will be responded to in 3 months
Categories: Architecture—Arts

Name: Acquisitions Editor
Material: All
Address: 2690 LOCKSLEY PL
City/State/ZIP: LOS ANGELES CA 90039
E-mail: balconypress@earthlink.net

Barricade Books

Dear Writer:
We're sorry for this impersonal response to your query. However, we get so many letters it would be impossible to answer them all personally. We believe you would rather get a response-albeit in the way of a form letter-than none at all.

We publish virtually no fiction, so please do not submit novels. We don't publish poetry or children's books.

We do look for nonfiction, mostly of the controversial type. We look for books that we can promote with authors who can talk about their topics on radio and television and to the press.

If your material falls into any of these categories please send an outline and one or two chapters together with a stamped addressed envelope. We don't read submissions from disk. And please let us know if you want the material returned.

Sincerely,
Carole Stuart
Publisher

Categories: Nonfiction—African-American—Biography—Entertainment —Gay/Lesbian—Humor—Martial Arts—Regional—Relationships—Sexuality

Name: Carole Stuart, Publisher
Material: All
Name: Andrew Richter, Associate Editor
Material: All, especially regional
Address: 150 FIFTH AVE STE 700
City/State/ZIP: NEW YORK NY 10011
Telephone: 212-627-7000
Fax: 212-627-7028

Barron's Educational Series

1. For initial consideration of your project a brief outline is acceptable. The outline should include a table of contents or headings for the material that you plan to include; the market you are trying to reach with the book (i.e., children, ages 2-4, secondary school teachers, etc.); and a brief summary of the project.
2. Manuscripts for children's story books should be sent in their entirety.
3. It is not necessary to submit illustrations for a children's story book to be considered for publication.
4. If you will be providing the illustrations please include a sample.
5. When submitting a work of nonfiction please include a Table of Contents, two sample chapters, an overview of the project and author's credentials.
6. We will contact you if additional information or material is needed in order to properly evaluate your project. *Do not send additional material unless specifically requested to do so! It will be discarded!*
7. Complete evaluation of your project may take as long as ten months. We accept simultaneous submissions.
8. If you would like a catalog please submit a 9"x12" SASE.
9. Due to the large number of submissions we receive we can no longer track the status of individual projects.

Thank you for your adherence to the above guidelines.

Categories: Nonfiction—Animals—Business—Careers—Children—College—Cooking—Crafts—Diet—Education—Gardening—Health—Juvenile—Language—Parenting—Reference—Textbooks—Young Adult

Name: Grace Freedson, Managing Editor/Director of Acquisitions
Material: All
Address: 250 WIRELESS BLVD
City/State/ZIP: HAUPPAUGE NY 11788
Telephone: 516-434-3311
Fax: 516-434-3723

Baywood Publishing Company, Inc.

Baywood Publishing invites authors to forward proposals for publications in counseling, death & bereavement, psychology, gerontology, health policy, and technical communication. We welcome submissions in these areas from authors who desire to publish with a scholarly professional press. These guidelines are provided to expedite the submission process.

The Proposal Package
1. *Cover letter* introducing yourself, the title of your proposed publication, a concise description of the purpose and scope of the book, and an indication of whom the audience will be.
2. *Curriculum vita(e)* for each author(s)/editor(s) involved. This should include: Names, titles, addresses, and phone/fax

numbers.

3. List of contributors, if applicable. Please indicate the total number of contributors and provide their names, titles, addresses, and phone/fax numbers.

4. Table of Contents, to include chapter titles and paragraphs describing those chapters.

5. Introduction or Preface, and at least one chapter for the proposed publication.

6. The Primary Specialty and any areas of subspecialization for the author/editor.

7. Status of the manuscript: Is it in the idea stage? Is it less than 50% complete? More than 50% complete? Has any of the material been previously published?

8. Probable date that the manuscript will be completed.

9. Mechanical dimensions including: Number of typed double-spaced pages; number of charts; number of tables.

10. Potential markets. Describe the primary and any secondary professional and/or student markets for which this book is intended and the level of readership at which it is aimed.

11. Timeliness. Please try to estimate how long, in years, the content of the book will remain current and useful.

12. List of competing titles. Please include the author, title, publisher, year, pages, price of each competing publication.

13. Uniqueness. How does this book differ from competing titles? List any special or unique features your work contains.

BAYWOOD'S INSTRUCTIONS TO AUTHORS

Manuscript is to be submitted in triplicate (1 original and 2 copies). Retain one copy as manuscript will not be returned-original art work will be returned. Accompanying WordPerfect 5.1 disks if available should also be included with paper copy. Paginate consecutively starting with title page, include numbering of tables, figures, references, appendices, etc. An abstract of 100-125 words is required. The organization of the article should be clearly indicated by appropriate headings and subheadings.

The receipt of all manuscripts will be acknowledged by return mail. Authors should note that only **original articles** are accepted for publication. Submission of a manuscript represents certification on the part of the author(s) that neither the article submitted nor a version of it has been published or is being considered for publication elsewhere.

Copyright Agreement

The author's Warranty and Transfer of Copyright Agreement must be signed and received before an article is refereed and composition begins. A copyright agreement is required by law (Public Law 94-553) which states publishers must receive a signed copyright agreement for all manuscripts received.

The publisher grants permission to the author/s to use their articles in whole, or part, without further consent of the publisher. In reuse state journal name, volume, issue and date of original appearance. The use of this copyrighted material, by other than the author, is prohibited without expressed written permission of the publisher.

Title Page and Affiliation

The title page should include the complete title of the article, the author's name/s, degrees earned, and the academic or professional affiliation/s and location. If the title contains 45 or more letters, include a shortened version for the right-hand running head. If the study has been supported by a grant or institutional funding include it on the first page with an asterisk. All other acknowledgments appear at the end of the article preceding References. Supply a **complete address** for shipment of the reprints/proofs-this appears on the very last page of the article.

Reference Style

In Text—References are to be placed on separate numbered pages at the end of the article. A reference is a direction to, or consultation of books, periodicals, proceedings, etc., for information cited within text. When using a direct quote from a title, it is necessary to cite the exact page number [1, p.5]; it is plagiarism otherwise. Every reference is indicated numerically with each new reference listed in ascending order (no op. cit., ibid.). When a previously cited reference is used again, it keeps its original reference number. Reference numbers are to be enclosed in brackets, i.e., [1], when more than one [1,2] or [1-3].

In Listing—A compiled list of references which have been cited in text appear in **numerical sequence** at the end of the article. No op. cit. and ibid. are allowed. **Do not alphabetize.**

Journal/Periodical

1. Author's name: first and middle initials, surname, J. J. Jones

2. Title of referenced work: Instructions to Authors

3. *Editor's name: first and middle initial, surname (abbreviate word editor and place in parentheses after surname) T. A. Smith (ed.)

4. Title of journal/periodical: underlined/italics, *Journal of Publishing Specifications*

5. Volume number: underlined/italics, *3*

6. Issue number: 2

7. Pages: p. or pp. 1-4

8. Year of publication: 1992

SAMPLE: 1. J. J. Jones, Instructions to Authors, *Journal of Publishing Specifications,* *3*:2 pp. 1-4, 1992.

*It is not necessary to designate editor. Use this format only when applicable. J. J. Jones, Instructions to Authors, T. A. Smith (ed.), *Journal of Publishing Specifications,* *3*:2, pp. 1-4,1994.

Book

1. Author's name: first and middle initials, surnames: J. J. Jones and A. David

2. Chapter of book: Manuscript Preparation

3. Title of book: underlined/italics, *Publishing Specifications and Style Guide*

4. Editor: B. Olszewski (ed.)

5. Publisher: Baywood Publishing Co., Inc.

6. Location: Amityville, New York

7. Page/s: p.6, pp. 1-6

8. Year of publication: 1994

SAMPLE: J. J. Jones and A. David, Manuscript Preparation in *Publishing Specifications and Style Guide,* B. Olszewski (ed.), Baywood Publishing, Amityville, New York, pp. 1-6,1994.

Bibliography

A bibliography is an unnumbered, alphabetical list of publications relating to a given subject, author/s, and not necessarily cited within text. Baywood format is an alphabetized list of authors' last names, followed by a comma and initials. The balance of the entry is identical to the reference style above.

Footnotes

Footnotes are notes placed at the foot of the page where cited. They give information or commentary that, though related to the subject under discussion, would interrupt the flow of the narrative/discussion. They should be brief; **no more than four lines,** and not contain any full references. (Reference items belong at the end of the article.) Footnotes are numbered with superior Arabic numbers; no parentheses or brackets. Table footnotes are indicated with lower case italic letters; probability (p) is an exception which is indicated by an asterisk within the table. Source footnotes appear on the first page of the article, are indicated with an asterisk, and are limited to grants or funding from institutions. Other acknowledgments appear at end of article just prior to the references.

Display Material

Figures

All line art figures submitted must be original art in black ink on white paper and done to professional standards. Photographs should be black/white glossy prints with high contrast. Identify all figures on front with journal name, author name, fig-

Books

ure number, and top of figure (if necessary). Anticipate what your figures will look like on our 6"x9" page. The image area for vertical figures is 41/8"x6½" (horizontal size is 6¾"x3¾") which determines the maximum space your figures can occupy. Callouts (figure labeling) are 8 point size and this should be taken into consideration when art work must be reduced. Figures must be cited in text and numbered sequentially; **No** Figure 1.1, Figure 1.2, or Figure 1a, Figure 1b. Computer-generated copy of less than 300 DPI is not acceptable. SAMPLE: Figure 1. Figures are display material at Baywood Publishing.

Tables

Tables must be cited in text before next number one primary head and appear in ascending numerical order. Indicate table placement in text manuscript. Keep in mind our final page and image area size when planning tabular layout because anything larger will have to be reduced. Each table must have a descriptive title, an opening rule, a rule under the column heads, and a closing rule-no vertical rules. Do not abbreviate entries or column heads unless absolutely necessary. Table footnotes are lower case italic letters, excepting probability (p) which is indicated with an asterisk. Source appears as **Source:** Table titles are upper and lower case. SAMPLE: Table 1. Figures Are Display Material at Baywood Publishing

Scheduling

After acknowledged acceptance of manuscript by the editor and receipt of signed copyright warranty, the manuscript is sent to the publisher for production editing and composition. On completion of these phases, proofs are sent to the contributor and editor for careful proofreading and checking. Your article is **final page copy.** Do not add new material. Make revisions only where material was omitted by the typesetter or to mark typos. Answer all QA's and mark any corrections in ink color other than black, before returning Master Set to editor. All changes and additions may be vetoed at the discretion of the editor. It is mandatory that proofs be returned within 48 hours of receipt in order to keep the journal on schedule.

Authors may order reprints of their articles by completing the reprint order form enclosed with the proofs. All reprint orders must be prepaid.

Categories: Textbooks—Gerontology—Public Health—Death & Bereavement

Name: Acquisitions Editor
Material: All
Address: 26 AUSTIN AVE
Address: PO BOX 337
City/State/ZIP: AMITYVILLE NY 11701
Telephone: 516-691-1270
Fax: 516-691-1770
E-mail: baywood@baywood.com
Internet: www.baywood.com

Berkshire House Publishers

We specialize in a series of guides, the Great Destinations™ Series, about specific destinations around the U.S. that are of unusual charm and cultural importance—destinations such as Berkshire County, Santa Fe and Taos, Napa and Sonoma, the coast of Maine, the Adirondacks, the Chesapeake Bay area, the Hamptons on Long Island, Newport and Narragansett Bay in Rhode Island, the central coast of California, Aspen, the Gulf Coast of Florida, and the Texas Hill Country. Our greatest interest would be in writers who reside in U.S. destinations that are particularly attractive to upscale visitors. Writers must be willing to write in the Great Destinations format—comprising chapters on the history, lodging, dining, culture, recreation, shopping, etc., of each area.

We also specialize in books about our own region (the Berkshires in Western Massachusetts) and the various recreational activities that can be enjoyed here. We occasionally publish cookbooks that are related to New England and/or to country living/country inns in general. We have a line of books on Shaker crafts and artifacts, but we are not currently seeking to add to it. We offer books of historical interest in our American Classics™ series, notably books by Alice Morse Earle—*Home Life in Colonial Days* and *Child Life in Colonial Days*—but have no immediate plans to add to this series.

Categories: Nonfiction—Cooking—History—Travel

Name: Jean Rousseau, Publisher
Material: All
Name: Philip Rich, Managing Editor
Material: All
Address: 480 PLEASANT ST STE 5
City/State/ZIP: LEE MA 01238
Telephone: 413-243-0303
Fax: 413-243-4737
E-mail: Berkhouse@aol.com
Nota bene: Main emphasis at this time is travel.

Beyond Words Publishing

Inspire to Integrity
OUR DECLARED VALUES
We give to all of life as life has given us.
We honor all relationships.
Trust and stewardship are integral to fulfilling dreams.
Collaboration is essential to create miracles.
Creativity and aesthetics nourish the soul.
Unlimited thinking is fundamental.
Living your passion is vital.
Joy and humor open our hearts to growth.
It is important to remind ourselves of love.
Dear Prospective Author:

Thank you for your inquiry about our writers' guidelines. Our company's mission statement is *Inspire to Integrity*. Every book we publish must fulfill this mission. We generally publish in only a few areas:

- Photography
- Personal Growth
- Women's
- Spirituality
- Children's

We do *not* publish: adult fiction, poetry, autobiographies, or fiction stories by children. If your book does not fit our guidelines, please do not submit it. It may be helpful for you to research books that Beyond Words has previously published, so that you can determine whether or not your proposal fits with what we do best.

All manuscript submissions should include a query letter containing a description of your book idea and information about you as a potential author. With adult book proposals, you may also include an outline, as well as some sample chapters, if you wish.

As part of your proposal, we would like to tell us: 1) what similar books are already out there; 2) how have those books sold; 3) how is your book idea different from these; 4) additional markets your book could sell to, aside from retail bookstores; 5) why you are the best person to write this book; and 6) your ability and willingness to participate in regional and national publicity.

In the children's area, we are particularly interested in authors who can devote time to doing programs in schools to help promote and sell books. We prefer to see complete manuscripts. You may send sample illustrations to give us an idea of the artwork you have in mind. Black and white copies are fine, or a few color copies will give us enough of an idea. Please do not send any original artwork.

We receive close to 4,000 proposals a year and only publish 15-20 new books each year. We regret that we are not able to answer all the phone calls we receive regarding the status of proposals, since we receive so many manuscripts and inquiries each day. If you follow these guidelines, you will either receive a phone call from us (if we are interested in your proposal), or your proposal will be sent back with a letter (if we are not interested). It can take up to six months for a response and/or return of your work. We appreciate your patience and thank you for considering us as a possible publisher of your work.

Best wishes,
Submissions Department
Categories: Fiction—Nonfiction—African-American—Children—Christian Interests—Conservation—Culture—Ecology—Ethnic—Family—Feminism—General Interest—Juvenile—Men's Issues—Multicultural—Native American—New Age—Paranormal—Photography—Psychology—Publishing—Relationships—Religion—Self-Help—Spiritual—Teen—Television/Radio (tie-ins with network shows or specials)—Women's issues—Young Adult

Name: Michelle Boehm, Children's Director
Material: Children's/Young Adult
Name: Cynthia Black, Editor-in-Chief
Material: Adult
Address: 20827 NW CORNELL RD STE 500
City/State/ZIP: HILLSBORO OR 97124
Telephone: 503-531-8700
Fax: 503-531-8773

BkMk Press
University of Missouri-Kansas City

1. Send a sample of your work: approximately 10 pp. poetry; or 50 pp. prose.

2. Typed and paginated. Prose should be double-spaced.

3. Please include a cover letter indicating your name and address and the title of your submission.

4. Please also send a self addressed stamped envelope for our reply (with sufficient postage to return the manuscript, if applicable). Please indicate whether you want your manuscript returned or recycled.

5. BkMk publishes quality poetry, short fiction collections, and creative non-fiction essays. We do not currently publish novels or chapbooks.

6. We try to reply to your submission in two to six months.

Note: Do not send submissions via e-mail.

Categories: Fiction—Creative Nonfiction—Literature—Poetry—Regional—Short Stories

Name: Kelly Freeman, Managing Editor
Material: Poetry, Short Fiction, Creative Nonfiction
Address: UNIVERSITY HOUSE

Address: 5100 ROCKHILL RD
City/State/ZIP: KANSAS CITY MO 64110-2499
Telephone: 816-235-2558
Fax: 816-235-2611

Black Forest Press
Arbenteuer Books, Dichter Books, Kinder Books

Dear Author:

Black Forest Press is a self-publishing book publisher. What we do is of interest to authors who want to see their book in print but cannot get traditional publishing editors to read their manuscript. Black Forest Press is for authors who have considered the alternative to traditional or subsidy publishing and have decided to financially invest in their own work, maintaining 100% of their profit, and paying no book royalties to the publisher. That's right! All profits and book sale royalties belong 100% to the author...that's you. Self-publishing with the experts makes much better sense.

Most vanity/subsidy presses will charge an author thousands of dollars to publish his or her work. The break down is simple: production, printing and promotion equal MEGA-dollars. At Black Forest Press we've learned how to cut costs throughout the publishing process. This includes all phases of production and printing. Lastly, we suggest the best private book marketing companies to sell and promote an author's work, like Simone Book Promotions, The Advocate Media Group, Book World, or Black Forest Book Promotions (a company not owned by Black Forest Press). We simply coordinate the efforts of the marketing professionals and pass the savings on to each author.

Our process is very easy to understand. Initially an author sends his or her non-returnable manuscript, preferably a laser printed copy, and a 3½" computer disk with the manuscript in WordPerfect 6.0 or 6.1, or Microsoft Word 6.0. If the book has not been word processed on computer, we will charge the author to input the text into WordPerfect.

Secondly, we copy edit, line edit, and proofread the manuscript. WordPerfect galley prints are then sent to the author for changes and approval. When the galleys are returned, we typeset the text into Adobe PageMaker 6.0 or QuarkXpress 3.3; once again we proofread the text, making necessary typo or format changes. Then new galleys are printed and sent to the author for further perusal and approval. This is the last chance for an author to see his or her work before the bluelines (camera ready negatives) are made. An author can see his or her bluelines, but that takes more time and any new changes are additional charges.

Unlike most subsidy or vanity presses, Black Forest Press will provide you open and ongoing communication with production staff members working on your book. You'll be one telephone call away, eight hours a day, five days a week, from knowing how your book is maturing and progressing on schedule. This is a plus when an author self-publishes with guidance, direction, instruction, awareness and confidence.

After we receive the PageMaker or QuarkXpress typeset galleys from the author, we make requested or needed changes and send the book to the printer. Prior to the copy edit stages, an author is assigned an artist who will design the cover or dust jacket. Each author will see his or her cover design prior to Black Forest Press printing it. If an author desires his or her picture on the back cover, it will be necessary to send a black and white picture and a small personal biographical sketch. Any endorsements will be placed inside or on the back of the book cover; they must come from the author. An author can have a color portrait printed on the back cover instead of a black and white one, because all book covers are full color, unless specified otherwise by the author. Any special artwork requested, like metallic ink or embossed lettering, will be an additional charge. All these charges are totaled and a final figure is given to the author by Black Forest Press, and agreed upon in the formal written author contract.

As previously mentioned, the promotion of an author's book is not formally done by Black Forest Press. Although we do have a small marketing package we offer separately, as we do indexing, for an extra modest, reasonable fee. However, we do give authors choices of various book marketing companies that will package, distribute and sell their books.

Promotion is a separate cost, as was publishing (production and printing). When an author's book is printed, the majority of the books will be shipped directly to the promoter, or a specified amount to the author's residence with the remainder of the books, perhaps, going to the promoter's warehousing facility. Black Forest Press will not stock or warehouse books. We do, however, request a sample copy of an author's book for each contributing member of your production team. This should never exceed seven copies; two of those copies go into our archives.

The normal time to prepare a book for printing is 60 to 90 days. Much of that time depends on how long the author takes to review the galley copies and return them to Black Forest Press. On occasion, some extra requested author changes may also hold up the production schedule of the book, such time delays are not the responsibility of Black Forest Press.

Once the author's book goes to press, an author should allow four to six weeks for perfect bound books, or two to three months for hardback/case bound books, to be printed and packaged for shipment. Color page inserts are very expensive and are usually done in groups of four pictures. Full color books, especially children's books, will take about three months. This is fairly standard for any reputable quality printer. Printing overruns are additional charges, if an author requests, in writing, his or her desire to purchase the overruns. Overruns can be used by promoters to effectively market an author's book along with or inside of press kits or promo packages, etc. Black Forest Press provides each author with an additional 100 covers, for promotional purposes, at no extra cost.

Common sizes for books are 5½"x8½" and 8½"x11". Books which are 6"x9" or 4½"x6" are considered special cuts which cost the same as the next larger size. Printing runs of 1,000, 2,000 or 2,500 books are usual for an author. Remember: although the cost of printing more books goes up, the unit cost per book will decrease drastically. For example, 1,000 books may have a unit cost of $3.00 per copy, but 2,000 books may drop the price to $2.00 or less per book. The unit price goes down with larger printing runs. With full color insides, the prices may vary or increase.

Unless an author sells most of his or her books directly, without any middle men, distributors, wholesalers or libraries being involved in the sales process and/or taking a healthy percentage out of the actual sales price, then an author may possibly clear a respectable profit from printing 1,000 books. Otherwise, depending upon the cost of publishing, the retail price at which the book is sold, and third party percentages, an author should consider printing upwards of over 1,350 to break even or make a negligible profit. Serious profits begin with a minimum printing of 1,500 or 2,000, if the book is promoted properly and sells. The book's marketability should be discussed with the publisher and the promoter, early in the publishing process, if not ahead of time.

If you are interested in self-publishing with Black Forest Press please write us and let us know the specifics of your book. Only then can we give you a realistic cost for the publishing of your book. You'll find a copy of our Production Procedure Steps For Processing Author Manuscripts below. Read it carefully. You'll find it details the most important specifics of the Black Forest Press publishing process. If another publisher will not furnish you with similar detailed information, you better consider what they may be hiding from you, like hidden costs, or not so comprehensive work.

For authors who are serious about publishing with Black Forest Press, we will provide the names and telephone numbers of other Black Forest Press authors, upon request, prior to contract signing, for your convenience to call them and chat about their experiences and the published product they each received from Black Forest Press. Because we do the job right, we are proud of our publications, all of them.

Payments are made in two parts: One payment is to be made at the beginning of production; the second payment must be made just prior to press time. Personal blueline changes will result in an extra cost to the author who will be billed separately for his or her blueline changes. All payments should be a cashier's check or money order and made out to Black Forest Productions. No credit cards are accepted. Personal checks are accepted, however, Black Forest Press will wait until your check clears our bank before we begin production or printing work. When you receive our contract please have an attorney review it for approval. You'll feel better and not worry. An author's trust and cooperation is paramount to us. This process can't be made much easier.

We accept only good books worthy of being sold and read by the public. No obscene, racist, pornographic, sexist, overly violent, blasphemous or discriminating manuscripts will be accepted by Black Forest Press. The materials we accept are totally at our own discretion; decisions are made without prejudice or bias. We reserve the right to refuse work. Black Forest Press chooses only works of good taste, offensive to no one.

If an author has suffered permanent physical disabilities, is a United States Armed Forces veteran, or receives social security benefits a special 5% deduction of production costs will be given. However, Black Forest Press requests substantiating evidence or legal documentation for that claim. Keep claim submissions simple. Send no original documents or personal paperwork, only photocopies. This information must be presented to Black Forest Press prior to negotiating the contract or receiving the initial cost work-up. We will not be surprising you, so please extend us the same courtesy and don't surprise us.

Black Forest Press looks forward to hearing from you. We hope we can serve you in a timely, efficient, and friendly manner. Oh, yes! Prior to considering Black Forest Press as your publisher, we do suggest that you get at least two or three vanity/subsidy press quotes for publishing your book, you'll see the difference we make when the bucks hit the table. We'll show you where we can save you money and probably time.

Keep in mind, most vanity presses will only do a limited marketing or promotional campaign for your book; a book marketing company will cost extra, but it gets the job done correctly. You can judge for yourself what they do. Black Forest Press has no ownership in any of the book marketing companies herein mentioned, we can only direct you and give you our best advice. You'll know a good deal when you see it. For further information, call us or fax your questions. If you do not choose Black Forest Press to do your work, we wish you good fortune and success elsewhere, there are many decent, fair and honest publishers around. Good luck!

Black Forest Press's hours of operation are Monday through Friday, 8:00 a.m. to 5:00 p.m. Pacific Standard Time. No weekend or collect telephone calls are accepted. You can e-mail us at the address below.

Sincerely,

Dahk Knox, Ph.D., Ed.D.

Publisher

Black Forest Press Production Procedure Steps
For Processing Author Manuscripts

1. Black Forest Press (BFP) reviews manuscript for acceptance or rejection; the author is informed of decision.

2. BFP sends author a brochure, Information Letter/s, Book Pricing List and Production Procedure Steps.

3. BFP sends out a Manuscript Request Form for the book if it's interested in publishing it; BFP requests the author's biography, a book synopsis, a chapter outline of the book and a laser printed copy of the manuscript.

4. BFP starts an author file and determines preliminary publishing costs.

5. BFP informs Black Forest Book Promotions (BFBP) to prepare a marketing package for the prospective author.

6. BFP does a cost work up of final production costs (marketing and promotional costs are separate with BFBP)

7. After author's material is reviewed and accepted, BFP contacts the author with a publishing cost offer; if the author decides to publish with BFP, a publishing contract is filled out and sent to the author and an informal author publishing file is officially opened.

8. BFP assigns an ISBN to the author's book and retail pricing for its sale is determined and approved by the author; the author's color or black and white portrait is requested for use inside the book or on its cover for promotional purposes; the author receives a BFP Letter of Publishing Acceptance; a Personal Information Form is filled out for the author's official publishing file.

9. BFP requests the author to send a disk/s, identifying the Word Processing software used on the author's manuscript and the file name and system, IBM or Mac. Incompatible systems must be fully converted, by the author, before sending the disk/s to BFP for production processing.

10. The author's disk/s is then copied to the BFP computer and matched for an appropriate desktop publishing system selection; BFP begins the cover design and artwork.

11. BFP begins the content copy edit (red ink) and reviews the first pencil sketches of cover design artwork; BFP requests any author Prefaces, Forewords, Prologues, Epilogues, endorsements, etc.

12. The first line edit is done, then the first proof of the initial line edit; next, second line edit is done, then the second proof of the line edit and so forth, until all line edits are completed and ready for typesetting.

13. BFP begins typesetting the author's book: this is choosing appropriate fonts, setting-up an appealing aesthetic interior text design and planning the overall layout of the book, with or without pictures, graphs, charts, illustrations etc.; after this is completed, BFP send the author the first galley.

14. BFP reviews the ink proofs of the cover artwork and any internal illustrated pictures; their placement in the internal test is determined; BFP starts the Table of Contents.

15. BFP requests any outstanding author endorsements (if necessary); BFP sets-up back cover artwork and spine.

16. BFP begins the format edits, proofs are done after each format edit; all initial publisher Title Pages are reviewed for errors as is each section (Table of Contents, Disclaimer, Dedication and Acknowledgments); BFP begins any necessary indexing/glossaries and makes author changes from the returned first galley; BFP then sends the second galley to the author.

17. BFP adds and/or checks over glossaries or indexes (if included in book); BFP makes author changes to the returned second galley; third galleys are done only when determined necessary by BFP.

18. BFP adds logo, barcode, ISBN and pricing to the back cover and confirms index/glossary corrections.

19. BFP thoroughly checks cover artwork, making sure measurements and text/picture placements are correct, BFP sends BFBP a copy of the book's cover so appropriate advanced marketing strategies can begin.

20. BFP sends Authorization to Print Form to author; upon return receipt of this form, the book goes to press.

21. BFP completes blue lines; BFP sends out advance book information to appropriate data collection center/s.

22. BFP fills out Copyright Forms, sending two copies of the final published book to the Library of Congress.

23. BFBP schedules author's marketing package dates and determines marketing data recipients; BFBP sets-up promotional book sales bookkeeping program; a sample Marketing Plan Schedule may be mailed to author.

24. When approved by the author, BFBP sends the author the final twenty-four month Marketing Plan Schedule.

25. BFBP conducts the ongoing marketing/promotional campaign; BFBP sends the author quarterly reports on his or her book sales.

*Black Forest Book Promotions (BFBP)** is a separate company from **Black Forest Press (BFP)**. Please do not confuse the two companies as being one in the same company even though the two companies work together for the benefit of their authors. BFBP promotes books, while BFP only publishes books.

Categories: Fiction—Nonfiction—Adventure—Biography—Business—Careers—Children—Christian Interests—Civil War—College—Cooking—Culture—Disabilities—Drama—Education—Ethnic—Family—Fantasy—General Interest—Government—Health—Hispanic—History—Inspirational—Literature—Military—Multicultural—Mystery—Native American—Philosophy—Poetry—Politics—Psychology—Reference—Religion—Romance—Science Fiction—Short Stories—Society—Spiritual—Sports—Textbooks—Western—Writing

Name: Keith Pearson, Acquisitions Editor
Material: All
Address: 539 TELEGRAPH CANYON RD BOX 521
City/State/ZIP: CHULA VISTA CA 91910
Telephone: 619-656-8048
Fax: 619-482-8704
E-mail: BFP@flash.net
Internet: www.flash.net/~dbk
Nota bene: Self-publishing; requires author investment.

Black Iron Cookin' Company

• Cookbooks especially for men, with heavy emphasis on outdoor subjects. Macho stuff about huntin', fishin', growin' hair and kickin' the tires. Also, subjects other than cookbooks. Prefer the recipes in the cookbooks to be interspersed with 1-5 page short stories re the subject involved.

• Vary in size from 120 to 500 recipes.

• We would want the product, in final form, to be camera-ready...illustrated, clip art okay.

• We pay royalty equal to 10 percent of wholesale.

Categories: Animals—Cookbooks—Cooking—Fishing—Food/Drink—Hobbies—Hunting—Men's Issues—Native American—Recreation—Sexuality—Sports

Name: Bruce Carlson, President
Material: All
Address: 3544 BLAKESLEE ST

City/State/ZIP: WEVER IA 52658
Telephone: 319-372-7480
Fax: 319-372-7485
Nota bene: Camera-ready submissions required.

Bloomberg Press
Bloomberg Professional Library, Bloomberg Personal Bookshelf, Bloomberg Small Business

Bloomberg Professional Library Compact, action-oriented books for brokers, traders, portfolio managers, analysts, money managers, CEOs, CFOs, bankers, and other financial professionals, as well as for consultants, financial planners, and sophisticated investors worldwide. Subject areas include:
- investment intelligence
- portfolio management
- markets
- financial analytics
- economic analysis of use to traders and other financial professionals

Bloomberg Personal Bookshelf Concise, practical books for consumers, individual investors, and business people:
- managing personal wealth, tax strategies, estate planning, philanthropic planning
- investing
- choosing products and services, including financial planning help, insurance, health care, banking services, and real estate
- personal-finance reference, education, using personal computers for investment decisions, and on-line information
- other topics with a personal-finance angle, such as credit, taxes, and estate planning

Bloomberg Small Business (launched Spring, 1998) Step-by-step guides-books useful as tools-in the following areas, with a financial focus:
- starting, organizing, operating a small business
- obtaining capital, cash flow, debt and equity financing, securitization
- growth, succession, reorganization, risk management, selling a business, IPOs
- global markets
- getting competitively valuable data and information

We can give our authors worldwide exposure in a number of media, including but not limited to our own TV, radio, magazines, international news service, and THE BLOOMBERG (the company's proprietary global network of business-news and information terminals).

Bloomberg Press books are distributed to the trade by W. W. Norton & Company, Inc.

Categories: Investing—Institutional Investing—Personal Finance—Small Business—Small Business Finance—Professional Finance Books

Name: Editor, Bloomberg Personal Bookshelf
Material: Personal Finance, Investing
Name: Editor, Bloomberg Professional Library
Material: Professional Finance, Institutional Investing
Name: Editor, Bloomberg Small Business
Material: Small Business, Small Business Finance
Address: 100 BUSINESS PARK DR
Address: PO BOX 888
City/State/ZIP: PRINCETON NJ 08542-0888
Fax: 609-279-5967
E-mail: jkieling@bloomberg.com
Internet: www.bloomberg.com

Blue Mountain Arts, Inc.
Publishers of quality books, cards, calendars, and prints

Blue Mountain Arts is interested in reviewing poetry and writings that would be appropriate for greeting cards. We strongly suggest that you familiarize yourself with our products before submitting material.

1.) We like to receive *original*, sensitive poetry and prose on love, friendship, family, philosophies, and any other topic that one person might want to communicate or share with another person. Writings on special occasions (birthday, anniversary, graduation, etc.) as well as the challenges, difficulties, and aspirations of life are also considered. We welcome material for the following holidays: Christmas, Valentine's Day, Easter, Mother's Day, and Father's Day.

2.) Poetry should be about real emotions and feelings written from personal experience. We suggest that you have someone in mind (a friend, relative, etc.) as you write. The majority of the poetry we publish *does not rhyme*.

3.) We prefer that manuscripts be typewritten; one poem per page please. Your name should appear on every page. You may submit as many poems at one time as you wish.

4.) We do not wish to receive artwork, photography, novels, short stories, books (unless you are interested in having portions excerpted for greeting cards), or narrative poems.

5.) Your work need not be copyrighted prior to submission. However, to obtain a copyright, you may contact the Copyright Office (address: United States Copyright Office, Library of Congress, Washington, D.C. 20559).

6.) While we will always try to respond to your submission as quickly as possible, please allow 6 to 10 weeks for a reply. *Be sure to include your name, address, and telephone number with your submission, and please keep us informed of all telephone and address changes.*

7.) We pay $200 per poem for the world-wide, exclusive rights to publish it on a greeting card and other products, and $25 per poem for one-time use in a book. Publication procedures will be explained in detail prior to actually publishing any work.

8.) All manuscript submissions and questions concerning your work should be directed in writing to the address below. E-mail submissions are welcome. *Please do not telephone.*

Categories: Poetry

Name: Editorial Department
Material: All
Address: PO BOX 1007
City/State/ZIP: BOULDER CO 80306
E-mail: bma@rmi.net.

Blue Poppy Press, Inc.

Blue Poppy Press, Inc. publishes books on acupuncture and Chinese medicine primarily for professional practitioners. Most of what we publish is translated from Chinese sources. All our authors should be professional practitioners of acupuncture and Chinese medicine with not less than five (5) years clinical experience *and* be able to read modern medical Chinese.

We appreciate query letters first. If the project is interesting, we then ask to see the introduction and/or preface describing the purpose of the book and its target market, table of contents, one or two sample chapters, and the author's resume or curriculum vitae. If material has been taken from Chinese language sources, we require a copy of the source to check translational accuracy. We also require all our authors to use Nigel

Wiseman's Chinese-English Chinese medical terminology as it appears in *English-Chinese Chinese-English Dictionary of Chinese Medicine,* Hunan Science & Technology Press, Changsha, 1995.

Blue Poppy Press does not pay cash advances. Authors are compensated by royalties computed two times per year. Authors are responsible for all illustrations, diagrams, or photos. In general, we favor denotative over connotative translations by native English speakers.

Categories: Nonfiction—Health—Acupuncture—Chinese Medicine

Name: Bob Flaws, Editor
Material: All
Address: 1775 LINDEN AVE
City/State/ZIP: BOULDER CO 80304
Telephone: 303-447-8293
Fax: 803-447-0740
E-mail: BPPoppy@compuserve.com

Blue River Publishing, Inc.

Blue River Publishing loves to publish books that authors love to write. To determine your love we need a book proposal. Remember, if your proposed book does not fit our schedule or the subject matter does not match our area of interest or abilities, we'll let you know—and you'll still be steps ahead in finding a publisher with the enthusiasm and ability to successfully publish and market your book.

We publish only nonfiction but in a broad range: contemporary social issues, health, how-to, community development, youth leadership, biography (very limited), and some history of the Old West with a contemporary tie-in.

The proposal, including sample chapters, will probably range from 30-80 pages. To reflect your ability to research, organize and write a successful nonfiction book, and to determine the final size and market for your book, the proposal should consist of an introduction, a chapter-by-chapter outline and one or two sample chapters.

The introduction

The introduction will have three parts: the **Overview, Resources needed to complete the book,** and **About the author**.

Overview—In the first paragraph, describe your book with the single most exciting, compelling thing that you can say about the subject. This first paragraph may be the last thing you write while preparing the proposal.

In the second paragraph include the title, selling point, and length.

The title and subtitle must tell and *sell*. They must say what the book is and give book buyers an irresistible reason for purchasing it.

The book's selling point is crucial to its success. Give the essence of the book and why it will sell. Remember, until you become as successful and well-known as Stephen King or Carl Sagan, sales representatives will need to convince booksellers to take a chance on your book, and on the average, sales reps have less than 14 seconds to sell the book. You want to make sure the rep will have the *best* selling handle. Also, if you have a difficult time summarizing your book this way, it may indicate the you haven't really narrowed down your subject. A good selling point may begin: "(The title of the book) will be the first book to..."

The next sentence should read: "The complete manuscript will contain x pages and x illustrations (if it will have illustrations)." You will estimate these numbers as you write the outline. Most nonfiction runs 200-400 typewritten pages at 250 words per page or 50,000-100,000 words.

The third and succeeding paragraphs will list the book's other special features and should include elements such as tone, structure, anecdotes, checklists, exercises, sidebars, notable information resources, etc.

If you have a well-known authority who will write the introduction, mention the source here.

If the book will raise technical or legal questions, add a sentence about what you have done to answer them.

If the book is on a specialized subject, find an expert to verify it for you and mention who the person is. Publishers are extremely concerned about lawsuits, so if your book will present legal problems, give the name of the experienced literary attorney you hired to go over it.

Include information about any back matter—appendices, glossary, bibliography, notes, or an index—that will add to the book's value.

Then list the groups of readers waiting for your book, starting with the largest one. Be sure to include any information about large clubs or organizations that have members who would be interested in the book's subject. (For instance, a book on retirement might be marketed to large corporations and AARP.) If your book will have adoption potential, list the courses and teachers who said they will adopt it.

If relevant, describe any subsidiary rights possibilities: book clubs, movies, audio and videocassettes, foreign sales, electronic rights, etc.

If your book can be a series or lends itself to sequels, mention the other books. This might lead to a multi-book deal.

A list of what you will do to promote the book, and your experience and demand in doing that promotion, can also be an important part of the proposal. Create a marketing plan that you will carry out to promote the book. This list can't be too long. If the book lends itself, one of the best openers may be: "To coincide with the publication of the book, the author will present seminars (or lectures) in the following cities..." Follow this with a list of the major cities around the country you can get yourself to, and the number of copies you think you can sell at these events.

A list of books that will compete with and complement yours is important because the editor must have that information to make a decision on your manuscript. Make sure the list is as complete and accurate as you can make it. Many publishing decisions may be made on this information—the book, the publisher, and your success may depend on your openness in providing this information. Remember, if there is a negative, we must be aware of it to adapt a strategy to compensate. List the books that will compete with yours—title, author, publisher, year—and in a phrase or sentence, say what each book does and fails to do. End this list with a statement of how your book will be different or better than the competition. A list of books on the same subject that don't compete with yours will prove that there's interest in the subject.

Resources needed to complete the book—Starting on a new page, list any travel (and your ability to complete it) you will need to do, illustrations (and sources if you are providing them), permissions you will need (for quoting or reprinting), and, if not already mentioned, possible sources to provide the introduction. If the book will require updating, indicate when this will happen.

The last sentence should read: "The manuscript will be completed x months after contract approval."

About the author—Your bio is your opportunity to prove that you are qualified to write the book. One new page (most of us have led one-page lives), tell editors everything you want them to know about you in order of importance to the sale of the book.

This is also a good time to describe your personal sense of mission about the project.

The chapter-by-chapter outline

The chapter-by-chapter outline for most books starts with a page listing the chapters in the book and the page of the proposal the chapter outline is on. An exception will be for a collected bi-

Books

ography of notables for which you will list the people and what each chapter will cover.

Most books require no more than a page of outline for every chapter of the book. Give each chapter a sense of structure in one of two ways:

1. Start the outline with a sentence saying the chapter is divided into "x" parts, then write about each part, or

2. Divide the chapter into parts as you write it by using the following phrases:

The chapter beings with...

The next part of the chapter...

The chapter ends with...

Here are three tips to help ease your way through the outline:

1. Write about what will be in the chapter. Don't write about the subject. That's what the sample chapters are for.

2. Use "outline" verbs such as describe, explain, examine, discuss and analyze.

3. If appropriate for the type of book you are writing, create "hooks" for the beginning and end of every chapter to entice readers into the chapter and to encourage them to go on to the next one.

After you have written the outline, go back through and guess how long each part of the chapter will be. Add these numbers up to arrive at the length of the chapter.

If the book will have illustrations, add "photo" or "line art" after every person, event or instruction to be illustrated. If your illustrations come from various sources, make sure your "Resources..." section above includes all illustrations mentioned here. If you are working with an illustrator, enclose samples of their work, and include a statement indicating their ties to your project (i.e., if the illustrations are rejected, would you still provide the manuscript?).

Start each chapter outline on a new page that begins:

Chapter

Chapter title (___ pages, ___ photos ___ line drawings, charts, graphs, etc.)

After you have finished the outline, add up the number of pages and illustrations in the book. These are the numbers you will use in the Overview. These numbers will probably change in the course of writing the book, but being definite will help convince an editor that you have thought the project through, and will also give the publisher the information needed to determine the final format and printing requirements.

Sample chapters

Sample chapters show the editor how well you write and develop the ideas from your outline.

For most books, editors like to see two chapters or 40-50 pages of sample material. One might be an introductory chapter, the other a chapter representative of the rest of the book. If you're writing an inspirational story that should read like a novel and will have the greatest impact if the editor sees all of it, have the complete manuscript ready to submit if you can. If you send the complete manuscript, you can send a one-page synopsis instead of an outline with it.

First time book authors

If you have yet to write and publish a nonfiction book, you will need additional items in your book proposal. The first is samples of your previously published work, either from professional journals or mainstream magazines. It would also be wise to explain how much of the writing is original and how much was edited, rewritten, or co-written. The second is a statement of willingness, or desire, to work with a co-writer or a ghostwriter, and if you have another writer willing to work with you or if you desire the publisher to select one for you. Also, if you do not have a proven track record, do not assume that a publisher's expressed interest in your project is an agreement to publish your work.

The final contract will not become effective until an "acceptable" manuscript is completed, or the contract states otherwise. And if this is your first book and you have no previous published material, do not expect an advance.

Once you have proven that you can write a book, you will not need as elaborate a proposal as the one described above. However, most published book authors find the exercise very valuable in organizing and fleshing out their ideas for a book.

The specifics

• Standard format for sample chapters, single-space all other.

• Floppies (any size) okay if for PC. Indicate software used in cover letter.

• All books must clearly make an original contribution to the subject area and be representative of current trends in the subject area. Information must be accurate and the scholarship and research must be sound and verifiable. The reader must gain an insight or learn a very minimum of one new piece of information on every page.

• Double-check all facts obtained from primary or secondary sources; *Do not rely on the research of others*.

• Expect a reply from us within six weeks.

• Enjoy putting together your proposal. We look forward to the enjoyment of reading it.

Thank you for considering Blue River as your next publisher.

Categories: Nonfiction—Biography—Consumer—Crime—Culture—General Interest—Health—History—Native American—Regional (Colorado-Cheyenne Mountain)—Social Issues—Western

Name: Jim Scheetz, Editor
Material: All
Address: PO BOX 6786D
City/State/ZIP: COLORADO SPRINGS CO 80934-6786
Telephone: 719-634-3918
Fax: 719-634-7559
E-mail: AKA.Jim@worldnet.att.net

BLUE WATER

Blue Water Publishing, Inc.
Wild Flower Press, Swan • Raven & Co.

To Whom It May Concern:

Blue Water Publishing accepts only a few manuscripts per year; and those that are accepted must follow the following guidelines:

The work must deal with some aspect of the UFO/ET phenomena, spirituality, shamanism environmental issues, or a related area. The work must be factual, i.e., nonfiction. We do not do stories, fiction, novels, novellas. or poetry. The work must demonstrate high scholarship.

The work must demonstrate coherent thinking and novel insights, it must break new ground and be significantly different from other works on the market.

The work must be well organized, cleanly developed and in electronic form. Acceptable electronic forms are Macintosh 3.5" diskette, PC 3.5" diskette. Recommended software formats include Microsoft Word or WordPerfect 5.1. Writing style must be clear, interesting and effective. Spelling must be exact as specified in *Webster's Ninth Collegiate Dictionary*, and grammar must follow the *Chicago Manual of Style*. Submissions should include a chapter outline, some representative chapters and a cover letter about yourself and about why the book will be of interest to a wide audience. See *Non-Fiction Book Proposals Anybody Can Write* by Elizabeth Lyon.

Thank you for asking about our publishing your book. If it follows the above guidelines, we would like you to send a proposal to us for our review. Be aware, however, that our pipeline is full at the present time, and any publication would be off in the future. If you are interested in accelerating your book's potential publication schedule by investing in the publication of your book, inquire separately of us about that possibility.

Sincerely yours,
Pamela Meyer
Publisher

Categories: Nonfiction—Environment—Inspirational—Native American—New Age—Paranormal—Spiritual—UFO Experiences—UFO Research

Name: Brian Crissey, Publisher
Material: UFO/ET
Name: Pam Meyer, Publisher
Material: New Age
Name: Terese Sayers, Editor
Material: Environment
Address: PO BOX 190
City/State/ZIP: MILL SPRING NC 28756
Telephone: 704-894-8444
Fax: 704-894-8454
E-mail: BlueWaterP@aol.com

Bonus Books, Inc.
Precept Press

We publish primarily nonfiction trade books.

If you would like to submit a manuscript or proposal for our review, please follow these guidelines.

1. Because of the large volume of submissions we receive, if you don't include an SASE, you will not receive a reply.

2. If you are submitting a proposal, please include an outline or summary of your book and a few sample chapters.

3. Allow six to eight weeks for a response.

Thank you for the opportunity to consider your work.

Categories: Nonfiction—Business—Cooking—Games—Sports—Textbooks (Medical, Health)

Name: Assistant Editor
Material: All
Address: 160 E ILLINOIS ST
City/State/ZIP: CHICAGO IL 60611
Telephone: 312-467-0580
Fax: 312-467-9271
E-mail: Webmaster@bonus-books.com
Internet: www.bonus-books.com

Branden Publishing Company

Branden Publishing Company is always interested in publishing new books and finding new authors. If you wish to contact Branden regarding the publishing of your work, please mail your query (one or two paragraphs) with a self-addressed, stamped envelope to the address below; no other form accepted.

Due to the high volume of publishing requests, we will not accept phone calls, e-mails, or faxes.

Categories: Fiction—Nonfiction—African-American—Arts—Aviation—Biography—Business—Children—Civil War—Consumer—Culture—Disabilities—Drama—Education—Entertainment—Ethnic—Family—General Interest—Government—Health—History—Internet—Jewish Interests—Language—Law—Literature—Military—Multicultural—Poetry—Politics—Regional—Religion—Society—Sports—Teen—Textbooks—Theatre—True Crime—Western—Women's Issues—Young Adult

Name: Adolph Caso, Editor
Material: All
Address: 17 STATION ST
Address: BOX 843
City/State/ZIP: BROOKLINE VILLAGE MA 02147
E-mail: Branden@branden.com
Internet: www.branden.com

Brassey's, Inc.

With many of the publishing production functions rapidly becoming more automated, submission of a manuscript adhering to certain guidelines in format and style becomes increasingly important. A properly prepared manuscript (and attendant computer disk) and an attentive copy editor go a long way toward both simplifying and assisting the tasks of the long line of people involved in turning a project into a book. A manuscript goes through many stages before arriving in a bookstore in its final incarnation, each one of them an essential part of the publishing process. This short guide is intended to address some of the most common initial pitfalls that are encountered in the often complex transition from manuscript to printed word.

FINAL SUBMISSION

In order for a book to be judged acceptable for publication by the acquiring editor, the final draft manuscript must adhere to the following guidelines:

1.) The entire manuscript, including notes and bibliography, must be double-spaced and paginated consecutively (i.e., do not number each chapter individually). Submitted manuscript must be the original, not a photocopy. Do not white out mistakes or irregularities.

2.) Manuscript must be complete. Please include in this order: dedication, table of contents, list of illustrations, list of tables, foreword, preface, acknowledgments (if not part of preface), and introduction (if not part of text), manuscript text, appendix(es), notes section, bibliography, and your author's bio. (Numbered notes should always appear as a complete notes section in the back of the book—see also point 3 below). The industry-standard style guide, *The Chicago Manual of Style*, lists the proper sequence and accepted form(s) of these and other elements. Your editor or the production manager will discuss with you the proper submission of photos, art, captions, and/or map materials if applicable to the respective project.

3.) Your contract will call for a computer disk, so both the original printout and the disk must be submitted. Use a 3½" disk and WordPerfect 5.1 or faster. Set up chapters and other components as separate, easy-to-i dentify files in the master directory (e.g., CH1, CH2). Use only the base font. Where the manuscript calls for italics, simply underline. Do not use any other type distinctions. Do not use running heads. If your book has numbered notes, please *do not* use any of the "handy" features, which insert and automatically number and format footnotes, that your word-processing program may offer. Simply key in your notes in a separate endnotes section within its own file, just like a chapter. Asterisk footnotes should just be typed at the bottom of the respective manuscript page, but should be avoided if possible. Although it may not look as nice, the fewer typeface codes in the manuscript, the easier it will be to make it into a book. We will provide the design.

4.) If your text is subdivided under headings, please be consistent in their form, i.e., all main headings should look alike, all first-order subheadings should look alike, etc. Again, avoid boldface, italics, or other type distinctions.

HOUSE STYLE

In general, American punctuation and spelling are to be used, as is the serial comma. At Brassey's, we follow *The Chicago Manual of Style*, also known as the Chicago manual or Chicago style guide. We highly recommend authors refer to it as they develop their manuscript.

FACT CHECKING

Authors are ultimately responsible for the facts stated in their books. They are expected to use proper spelling of names of real people and places, newspapers and magazines, poems and songs, brand names and trademarks, as well as foreign words and phrases. The copy editor will attempt to verify these.

If the copy editor is unable to verify something, s/he will query the author ("AU: VERIFY SP."). Dates will be similarly checked. Moreover, the content of any quoted material that can be found in a library will be checked.

PERMISSIONS AND LIBEL

The copy editor will query anything that seems potentially libelous and will indicate any quoted material that may require permissions. This includes all song lyrics and poetry, and prose quotations longer than three hundred words. The author is responsible for obtaining any necessary permissions and informing the production manager of any additions to the copyright page as soon as possible after manuscript submission. See the Chicago manual for a more detailed explanation of the author's responsibilities in these areas. A sample permission request letter is illustrated below.

REQUEST FOR PERMISSION
From:

_____

DATE: _____

TO: PERMISSIONS DEPARTMENT

_____

_____

_____

Dear Copyright Holder:
I am currently preparing a book tentatively to be entitled

_____

Publication by Brassey's, Inc., McLean, VA is scheduled for Permission is requested to reprint in this book the following material:

_____

This request is for world rights to the first and all future editions, including revised editions, in all languages. Appropriate credit will, of course, be given. If you have specific credit line requirements, please note them below.

I would appreciate the name and address of any other publisher/individual who holds any rights to this material should I be required to secure this permission. Due to our tight production

schedule)   I   would   appreciate   a   response   by

Thank you for your cooperation and prompt reply.
Sincerely,

_____

Signature granting permission for above material; Date

_____

Credit Line:

_____

Categories: Nonfiction—Aviation—Biography—Civil War—Defense—Foreign Policy—Government—History—Intelligence—International Affairs—Military—Sports

Name: Don McKeon, Editorial Director
Material: All
Address: 22883 QUICKSILVER DR STE 100
City/State/ZIP: DULLES VA 20166
Telephone: 703-260-0602
Fax: 703-260-0701

Nota bene: Brassey's guidelines also includes a lengthy manuscript preparation/style guide. It deals with requirements for *final submissions*. Request a copy of this MANUSCRIPT PREPARATION AND STYLE GUIDE when submitting a proposal. You will need it if you are asked to submit a final manuscript.

BrickHouse Books, Inc.

BRICKHOUSE BOOKS, INC. (formerly New Poets Series, Inc.) was founded in 1970. The editor/director is Clarinda Harriss. **New Poets Series** (NPS), along with **Chestnut Hills Press** and **Stonewall Series**, is now a division of BrickHouse Books. BrickHouse Books brings out 64-112 page works, whether poetry, fiction, plays or artistic nonfiction. It looks for excellent, fresh, nontrendy, literate, intelligent material, any form, any style.

Provides 20 copies to the author, the sales proceeds going back into the corporation to finance the next volume (usual press run 1,000). It has been successful in its effort to provide writers with a national distribution; in fact, the press (under its original company name, **New Poets Series**, was named an Outstanding Small Press by the prestigious Pushcart Awards Committee, which judges some 5,000 small press publications annually.

The **New Poets Series** retains its original mission of publishing first books only (though prior publication in journals and anthologies is strongly encouraged). Poets who have previously had book-length mss published are not eligible for NPS. NPS remains Brick House Books' premier imprint. **Chestnut Hills Press** (CHP) publishes author-subsidized books—high quality work only, however. CHP has achieved a reputation for prestigious books, printing only the top 10% of mss CHP and NPS receive. CHP authors receive proceeds from sale of their books. NPS/CHP has recently published books by Patricia Adams, Nancy Carter, Richard Fein, Donald Menaker and Gerald George. As a sample we selected these lines by Nancy Adams from Carter/Adams' *SO CLOSE*:

My mother had a vanity.
It stood against the wall and flanking either side
were other mirrors, framed in ornate wood.
She searched her face.
What if the mirror lied?
I searched but never found that magic bond.
So, if you have a daughter
See and hear her. Be clear as glass,
translucent as a pond
for you may be her first and only mirror.

Stonewall Series publishes work with a gay, lesbian or bisexual perspective. In addition to full-length mss., Stonewall offers chapbook publication (30 pages of poetry or short fiction) to each annual winner of its chapbook competition. Rane Arroyo's THE NAKED THIEF is a recent Stonewall winner.

Send BrickHouse Books a 50-60 page ms., $10 reading fee and cover letter giving publication credits and bio. **Indicate if ms. is to be considered for BrickHouse (no thematic, formal, or prior-publication restrictions), New Poets Series, or Stonewall.** Simultaneous submissions OK. Editor sometimes comments briefly on rejections. Reports in 6 weeks to 12 months. Mss. are circulated to an editorial board of professional, publishing writers. Brick House is backlogged, but the best 10% of the submissions are automatically eligible for **Chestnut Hills Press** consideration, a subsidy arrangement. Send $5.00 and 7"x10" SASE for sample volume. To enter the **Stonewall Chapbook Competition,** send 20-30 poems with $20.00 entry/reading fee postmarked no later than August 15.

Categories: Fiction—Nonfiction—Feminism—Gay/Lesbian—General Interest—Literature—Poetry—Women's Fiction—Women's Issues—Writing

Name: Clarinda Harriss, Editor/Director
Material: All
Address: 541 PICCADILLY RD
City/State/ZIP: TOWSON MD 21204
Telephone: 410-828-0724
E-mail: harriss@towson.edu
Internet: www.saber.towson.edu.80/~harriss/!bhbwebs.ite/bhb.htm
Nota bene: Reading fee required.

Bright Mountain Books, Inc.
Historical Images

Bright Mountain Books, Inc., was founded in 1985 as a Southern Appalachian regional publisher. We have published manuscripts written by area writers, republished books originally self-published, and have secured reprint rights for regional out-of-print books. While our major emphasis is on nonfiction, we have published some creative nonfiction, i.e., fictionalized histories based on factual events. We have not published poetry, textbooks, novels, self-help manuals, religious texts, or family histories.

Once manuscripts are accepted for publication, the text must be available to us in a computer format compatible with our typesetting system. Our computers are IBM compatible and editing is done in WordPerfect, version 6.0 or earlier. An ASCII file will usually convert satisfactorily for review purposes if you have worked in a different word processing system.

If you already have your work on computer, please send a disk of the entire manuscript plus a printout of the first several pages. If the manuscript exists only in typed form, please do not send the entire manuscript; three sample chapters and an outline are sufficient. Photos or artwork should be submitted in the form of photocopies or computer printouts, not the originals.

Send your materials to the address below. We will acknowledge their receipt, but since our procedure is to have at least two readers evaluate each submitted manuscript, a process which can be as short as a day or two or take several weeks, please be patient during our evaluation. If we feel that yours is a book we have a definite interest in publishing, we will request the entire manuscript.

If we cannot consider publication, we will return your manuscript to you only if you supply an appropriate postage-paid envelope. We will be happy to recommend other publishing avenues for you to consider if we can do so.

Categories: Nonfiction—General Interest—Native American—Outdoors—Regional

Name: Cynthia F. Bright, Editor
Material: All
Address: 138 SPRINGSIDE RD
City/State/ZIP: ASHEVILLE NC 28803
Telephone: 704-681-1790
Fax: 704-681-1790

Bristol Publishing Enterprises
nitty gritty® cookbooks

Greetings:

We currently have no specific manuscript guidelines but are primarily interested in cookbooks.

Our Nitty Gritty cookbooks are 5¼"x8¼", bound on the short side, and include approximately 100 to 120 recipes. We are looking for authors with a proven history of success in the food industry: dietitians, professional chefs or bakers, teachers or others. Topics must be of interest to the mass market and must have an expected term of interest of at least 5 years.

Rather than submit an entire manuscript, we prefer that you send an initial proposal (an outline is also recommended), a resume and a sample of your published writing.

Sincerely,
Jennifer Newens
Managing Editor
Categories: Cookbooks—Cooking—Gardening

Name: Jennifer Newens, Managing Editor
Material: All
Address: PO BOX 1737
City/State/ZIP: SAN LEANDRO CA 94577
Telephone: 510-895-44691
Fax: 510-895-4459

Broadman & Holman Publishers

Broadman & Holman actively seeks to enlist both new and established authors to work with us in producing the finest books in Christian publishing. We have been publishing books since 1934, and we bring a commitment to traditional Christian values and beliefs to everything we do.

OPPORTUNITIES

Broadman & Holman publishes books for adults, youth, pastors, church staff, and lay ministers. We are currently accepting submissions in these general categories:

Bible Study Helps—Books in the Bible Study Helps Series help ministers and lay leaders communicate biblical truths to others.

Christian Living—Books in the Christian Living Series are designed for adults ages twenty-five and older. These books apply sound, biblical principles to issues and concerns that face Christians, enabling them to grow in their faith.

Inspirational—Books in the Inspirational Series are designed to inspire adults to grow in their Christian faith and relationships with others. Biographies, inspiring stories of faith and courage, and devotional books are included in this series.

Ministry—Books in the Ministry Series are designed to equip laypersons with ministry and relational skills.

Parenting/Leadership—Books in the Parenting/Leadership Series are designed for parents or adult leaders of children from birth through college. These books assist readers in dealing with children, teenagers, and college students as they face issues and develop as persons and Christians.

Practical Theology—Books in the Practical Theology Series are designed for adults, ages twenty-five and older. These books apply timeless truths from the Bible, Christian theology, and church history to real-life situations, enabling believers to understand their faith and communicate the gospel clearly.

Professional—Books in the Professional Series are designed to equip ministers for their work.

Youth/Juvenile—Books in the Youth/Juvenile Series are designed for older children through college students. These books introduce readers to a relationship with Christ in an age-appropriate manner; offer guidance as they face questions, issues, and decisions; and encourage them to grow in their Christian faith and share that faith with others.

Please Do Not Send:
• Poetry
• Articles or short stories
• Adult fiction or Juvenile fiction
• Tracts or Pamphlets
• Exposés of prominent persons or organizations
• Art books
• Children's picture books

GETTING OUR ATTENTION

One of the secrets to catching our attention is helping us see the marketability of your idea. The following questions are commonly asked by our editorial, sales, and marketing staffs as we consider products.

• What other books or articles have you published?

• Have you read other books in your subject category? What makes your idea unique? What features or reader benefits have you included to make your book attractive to potential customers?

• Is your topic timely?

• How can you help market your book? Do you lead conferences or speak frequently in public? Do you have access to radio or television? Are you a recognized authority in your field?

• Are there prominent people who could give endorsements for this book?

OUR PROPOSAL FORMAT

While Broadman & Holman accepts ideas in several forms, we prefer that you query first. If sample chapters are available, please include at least two with your submission. We ask that you use this format for your query:

I. **Content**

A. Premise: a one-paragraph description of what the book is about.

B. The manuscript:

1. Status (Is it complete? When do you expect to complete it?)

2. Special features (epigraphs, charts, illustrations, lists, index, bibliography, etc.)

3. Anticipated length

4. Outline

5. Competition. List other recent titles in your subject area and compare the features and benefits of your manuscript to each title.

II. **Audience**

A. Target audience: age, sex, special interests or needs

B. Motivation: Why will readers want to purchase this book?

III. **Author**

A. Background

B. Previous writing

C. Resumé: include address, phone number, birth date, and social security number

D. Opportunities you have to market and promote the book

IV. **Chapter synopsis: a one paragraph summary of the premise of each chapter.**

V. **Sample chapters (two)**

Broadman & Holman receives over fifteen hundred unsolicited trade book submissions each year. We try to respond within two months. If you haven't heard from us within that time, please feel free to ask about your submission.

GENERAL GUIDELINES
• Do not bind or staple your submission.
• If you're submitting to several publishers, please tell us.
• Be open to editorial guidance.
• Provide suggestions for charts, graphs, photographs, illustrations, or other features that would make your idea attractive to readers.
• Final proposal submissions and finished manuscripts must be available on computer disk.

A FINAL WORD

Thanks for thinking of Broadman & Holman Publishers. If you're as committed as we are to being a leader in Christian publishing, you may be the type of author we're looking for; we may be the kind of publisher you need. If you have an idea for a book that will meet needs and change lives, we want to hear from you. Please write to the address below.

We look forward to hearing from you!

Sincerely,

Broadman & Holman Editorial Staff

Categories: Nonfiction—Christian Interests—Family—Humor—Inspirational

Name: Acquisitions Editor
Material: All
Address: 127 9TH AVE N
City/State/ZIP: NASHVILLE TN 37234
Telephone: 615-251-3638

Brookline Books
Lumen Editions

The trade and professional lines of Brookline Books publish titles in education, disabilities, psychology, parenting, and other related topics. Our selection includes workbooks for teachers and students, scholarly texts for teachers and health professionals, and trade books for students, parents, and a general audience. Please call and request a catalogue to get a better sense of our selection.

We look for well-written, well-organized manuscripts with a clear and original focus. We primarily consider texts based on solid research or professional experience. Books based solely on personal (vs. professional) experience are considered only if they display exceptional writing quality, provide original insights, and do not attempt to offer advice on parenting, self-help or education. We do accept multiple submissions, with notification. We rarely accept a book without first seeing the entire manuscript, and never accept one without at least seeing several chapters.

Categories: Fiction—Nonfiction—Animals—Disabilities—Education—Hispanic—Jewish Interests—Literature—Parenting—Poetry—Psychology—Short Stories—Travel—Writing

Name: Sadi Ranson, Series Editor, Lumen

Material: Fiction, Literature, Writing
Name: Amy Yeager, Assistant to the Publisher
Material: Disabilities, Education, Psychology, Parenting
Address: PO BOX 1047
City/State/ZIP: CAMBRIDGE MA 02238
Telephone: 617-868-0360
Fax: 617-868-1772
E-mail: brooklinebks@delphi.com

Bryant & Dillon Publishers, Inc.

Nonfiction
Send the following:
• Cover Letter
• Overview or Outline
• Author's Information Sheet
• Three Sample Chapters
• Marketing Information
Must be on subjects of interest to African-Americans.
Fiction
Send the following:
• Cover Letter
• Overview or Outline
• Author's Information Sheet
• Three Sample Chapters
• Marketing Information
Main characters must be African-American/or African-American themes.

We are currently looking for the following nonfiction subjects:

Anything about African-American film, Biographies, Black History, Black Studies, Self Help, Women's issues, etc.

Please note: We do not publish poetry or children's books.

Categories: Fiction—Nonfiction—African-American—Biography—Business—Education—Entertainment—Ethnic—Film/Video—History—Romance—Women's Fiction—Women's Issues

Name: Acquisitions Editor
Material: All
Address: PO BOX 39
City/State/ZIP: ORANGE NJ 07050
Telephone: 973-763-1470
Fax: 973-763-2533

Bucknell University Press

Bucknell University Press publishes scholarly books in the humanities and social sciences for a scholarly audience. Our primary criteria are the originality and importance of the scholarship and the clarity of its presentation.

Please do not send us your manuscript unless we have asked for it. Send us a proposal explaining clearly what you have done. With it, send us a copy of your current *curriculum vitæ.* We will then respond to your proposal.

We expect that each scholarly work we publish will have an appropriate scholarly bibliography. We expect it to be included with the manuscript at the time of submission.

Associated University Presses, our publishers, use the latest edition of the University of *Chicago Manual of Style* in copyediting all manuscripts. *Manuscripts may be submitted to us in any recognized format, but once we have accepted a manuscript its author or editor must make whatever changes in it may be necessary to bring it into conformity with the Manual of Style.*

All manuscripts submitted to **Bucknell University Press** must be typewritten or printed by laser printer or other printer producing texts of similar quality; we will accept clear photocopies of such originals. *We will not print out manuscripts from diskettes.*

Categories: Nonfiction—Anthropology—Architecture—Arts—Biography—Culture—Dance—Drama—Feminism—Gay/Lesbian—Government—History—Language—Literature—Music—Philosophy—Psychology—Theatre—Travel

Name: Professor G. Clingham, Director
Material: All
Address: BUCKNELL UNIVERSITY PRESS
City/State/ZIP: LEWISBURG PA 17837
Telephone: 717-524-3674
Fax: 717-524-3797
E-mail: clingham@bucknell.edu

Calyx Books

CALYX Books is a nonprofit feminist publisher particularly interested in fine literature by women. We are committed to publishing work by women of color, working class women, lesbians, and other women whose voices need to be heard. We publish three to four books each year: novels, collections of short fiction, poetry, translations of writers (poetry and fiction), nonfiction works of exceptional literary merit, and special anthologies.

Follow the guidelines below for submitting manuscripts. If we are interested in the manuscript, after the initial review we will request the complete manuscript for further consideration.

ALL MANUSCRIPTS

All manuscripts should include page numbers, the manuscript title, and the author's name and address. Submit a resume, a biographical statement, and an SASE with the manuscript.

POETRY

In addition, submit **only up to 10 poems** (not to exceed 20 pages of poetry), a table of contents, and a one-page description (synopsis) of the book manuscript.

FICTION

In addition: for **novels,** submit **three chapters,** a table of contents (if appropriate), and a synopsis; for **short story manuscripts,** submit **three short stories,** a table of contents, and a synopsis.

TRANSLATIONS

In addition: follow the above guidelines for poetry and fiction and include the same parts of the manuscript in the original language as well as the English translations. Include biographical data on both the translator and the author. Include the information on who holds the English translation rights on the author's work. Include a letter showing permission to translate from the author or the author's estate by the translator. Include the address for the author or the author's estate and any appropriate information on the publisher of the original edition or editions of the author's work.

NONFICTION/ANTHOLOGIES

In addition: for **nonfiction,** submit **three chapters** or **sections,** a table of contents, and a synopsis; for **anthologies,** submit **three samples** of the work included, an introduction and/or synopsis, and a table of contents.

Manuscripts submitted that do not follow the guidelines above will not receive consideration. Allow six to nine months for response from the editorial board.

Categories: Fiction—Nonfiction—African-American—Asian-American—Feminism—Gay/Lesbian—General Interest—Hispanic—Literature—Multicultural—Native American—Poetry—Short Stories—Textbooks—Women's Fiction—Women's Issues

Name: Margarita Donnelly, Director
Material: Any

Name: Micki Reaman, Managing Editor
Material: Any
Address: PO BOX B
City/State/ZIP: CORVALLIS OR 97339
Telephone: 541-753-9384
Fax: 541-753-0515
E-mail: Calyx@proaxis.com

Carolrhoda Books
The Lerner Publishing Group, Inc.

Carolrhoda Books publishes high-quality fiction and nonfiction for children ages 4 to 12. We specialize in **nonfiction:** biographies, photo essays, nature and science books, beginning readers, and books published in series. We look for nonfiction that is interesting and entertaining as well as informative.

We publish only a few **picture books** each year. We like to see unique, honest stories that stay away from moralizing, unoriginal plots, religious themes, and anthropomorphic protagonists. We also publish some **fiction** for ages 7 to 10 and some **historical fiction** for ages 8 to 12.

In both fiction and nonfiction, we are especially interested in new ideas and fresh topics. We like to see multicultural themes. Make sure your writing **avoids racial and sexual stereotypes. We do not publish** alphabet books, textbooks, workbooks, songbooks, puzzles, plays, or religious material. The best way to familiarize yourself with our list is to study our catalog or find our books in the library. For a catalog, send a self-addressed 9"x12" envelope with three dollars in postage.

We prefer to see a completed manuscript, but we will accept an outline and sample chapters for longer biographies or fiction. Please include a cover letter outlining your project and listing any previous publications.

You do not need to send art with your submission as we generally commission our own artists, but if you are sending art samples, *do not send originals.*

We will notify you of our decision regarding your manuscript at the earliest possible time. Our response time is generally three months. Please do not expect a personal response from an editor, as time does not permit this. If you would like confirmation that your manuscript has been received, please send a self-addressed stamped postcard.

Thank you for your interest in Carolrhoda Books. **We look forward to hearing from you.**
Categories: Juvenile

Name: Rebecca Poole, Submissions Editor
Material: All
Address: 241 FIRST AVE N
City/State/ZIP: MINNEAPOLIS MN 55401
Telephone: 612-332-3344
Fax: 612-332-7615

Catbird Press

We prefer to receive submissions in the form of an outline or synopsis, sample text (10-20 pages), and a curriculum vitae. We do not accept query letters. We would also like to receive a cover letter that, in the case of nonfiction, looks at similar books in print and differentiates yours (we will immediately turn down any nonfiction proposal that does not do this), and that, in every case, discusses what makes your book special, whether it be style, viewpoint, vision, or a need that is met. The more concise, complete, and organized the information we receive, the faster and more intelligently we can respond. If you don't want your sample returned, a regular #10 SASE will do.

Please let us know whether or not you are sending a similar submission to other publishers, or if similar submissions are still outstanding, and if so how many. This is a courtesy that allows us to respond most quickly to those authors who have sent their submissions to Catbird alone. If you don't say one way or the other, we will assume yours is a multiple submission.

We respond quickly to submissions we reject because the book is clearly not appropriate to Catbird's list or because the quality is clearly not professional (this is about 90% of submissions we receive); there are some times of year, however, that we fall a month or two behind. If we are more interested in the submission, we might take longer to respond.

Catbird Press specializes in quality, imaginative prose humor (we call it "humor for grownups") and Central European literature in translation. The English-language fiction we are interested in has a comic (although sometimes darkly comic) vision, excellent writing, and a fresh, unique style (we really mean this).

We are not interested in wacky characters, plots, or writing, or in satirical attacks on contemporary society as a whole; we do not publish children's books or genre books, such as science fiction or thrillers; we do not publish humor mixed with how-to; and we are not interested in standard, plot-and-character-oriented realistic fiction (about 90% of what is being published in the U.S.).

With respect to nonfiction, we are especially interested in books about law and business, books about Central Europe, and nonfiction of general interest that takes a unique approach (again, we really mean it) and is especially well written.

We thank you for your interest in Catbird, and look forward to receiving your submission. But please be sure Catbird is right for you first; we don't want you to waste your money or our time. Like most publishers, we accept very few books "through the transom," and those books are of a first-rate, professional quality. And we are interested in acquiring authors, rather than one-time books.
Categories: Fiction—Humor—Law

Name: Mary Mazzara, Assistant to the Publisher
Material: All
Address: 16 WINDSOR RD
City/State/ZIP: NORTH HAVEN CT 06473-3015

CCC Publications

1. CCC Publications is currently interested in reviewing HUMOR—especially Humorous *How-to* and *Self Help.*

2. Our decision to publish a book is based on two criteria: the *quality of writing* and *marketability.* Both qualifications must be met before we will offer a contract.

3. For best results, send a query letter first, briefly explaining your book idea and your background (if it relates to the book). If we then solicit your ms. it has a much better chance of receiving priority in getting reviewed by an editor.

4. We prefer to see a *complete* manuscript—not chapter samples or outlines—submit photocopy or good quality computer printout.

5. Most of the books we do require some cartoon art or illustrations. Providing art or illustrations is the responsibility of the *author.* We will make an exception only in the case of an unusually well-written ms. If your book requires illustrations and you do not have them available at this time, include a list of your "proposed art" (short description and placement in the text).

6. As we receive approximately 200-300 submissions per month, our response time may be up to three months (shorter for query letters). Feel free after sixty days to inquire about the status of your submissions.

7. All manuscripts and correspondence that *do not* include a SASE receive *low* priority.

We thank you for your interest in CCC Publications and look forward to reviewing your manuscript for possible publication.

Editorial Department

Categories: Humor

Name: Cliff Carle, Editorial Director
Material: Humor
Address: 9725 LURLINE AVE
City/State/ZIP: CHATSWORTH CA 91311
Telephone: 818-718-0507

Celebrity Press
Celebrity Books, Dercum Audio, Everywhere Press
Hambleton-Hill Publishing Group, Inc.

Celebrity Press publishes trade-oriented non-fiction adult books about business, cooking and personal growth. In order for us to further consider a manuscript for publication, please send the following items:

1. A table of contents;

2. One to three sample chapters of your manuscript;

3. Information on the author: credentials, other published works, what the author is currently doing and planning to do to support the book; (1-2 pages max.)

4. Five or six specific markets for your book—who will buy the book and why;

5. A list of five to ten similar and/or competing books;

6. A concise, 1-2 page synopses of the work.

Thank you,

S.A. Jernigan

Production Administrator

Categories: Nonfiction—Business—Cooking—Inspirational—Relationships

Name: Dawson Church, Publisher
Material: All
Address: 3356 COFFEY LN
City/State/ZIP: SANTA ROSA CA 95403
Telephone: 707-541-3333
Fax: 707-542-5444
E-mail: jernigan@wco.com

Centerstream Publishing

Hello Writers,

We really don't have any formal guidelines. Since we only publish music history and music instructional books our guidelines are simple: Just send it in.

We use Macs and request a hard copy and disk if we decide to do the project.

Thanks for considering Centerstream Publishing.

Ron Middlebrook

Categories: Music History—Music

Name: Ron Middlebrook
Material: All
Address: PO BOX 17878
City/State/ZIP: ANAHEIM HILLS CA 92807
Telephone: 714-779-9390
Fax: 714-779-9390
E-mail: Centerstrm@aol.com

Century Press

The subsidy press with a world of difference.

What's the difference?

Ownership! We're owned by the Conservatory of American Letters, a non profit tax exempt literary educational foundation whose purpose is:

To conserve and make public literary works of exceptional merit without regard to commercial potential.

To encourage and develop literary talent.

To offer the reading public an alternative to modern mass marketing mediocrity.

Honesty!

We make it part of our policy to advise all writers *in writing* that few authors recover their investment in subsidy publishing. Having said that, we work as hard as we can to help them recover.

Absence of Hype!

We don't really believe that everyone who reads this has the *Great American Novel*. We do realize that there are many good reasons to publish books. It remains our opinion that the next best deal to a big advance from a big publishing house is to self publish. But for writers who don't want the responsibility of being their own editor, of promoting, shipping, marketing, warehousing, and all of the other work that goes with self publishing, the Century Press becomes the best deal out there.

There are lots of differences in our contract, here are perhaps the four biggest differences.

Guarantee of Longevity!

We guarantee to keep your book in print for a minimum of five years, and as long thereafter as sales total only $250.00 per year net to us. After that, remaindering is at our option, if we elect to remainder all rights are returned, plus all unsold books. Free! *This is an extremely important feature, as it often takes several years for any work to reach its potential.*

High payback!

Authors get royalties of 40% of the cover price, plus 40% bookstore discounts, making 80% of the cover price on all personal sales. Kind of like eating your cake and having it too. You make almost as much as self publishing without the responsibilities. *Big paybacks make it possible to recover sooner and move on to other literary projects.*

Your Contract!

If you don't like our often-used standard contract we invite you/your agent/attorney to draft one you do like.

Fast!

Books in hand within 90 days of completion of editorial work, less time galleys are in the hands of others for proofing. *Even faster when paperback option is exercised.*

And of course we offer all the other things, hardcovers, color dust jackets, bar codes, promotion...

When you're ready to take the next step. send us your manuscript with a letter telling us as much about yourself and your project/purpose as you can. You're likely to become an author. (A writer writes, an author has a book.)

We are accepting work in all subjects. Including poetry, fiction, cook books, how-to, specialized fields, local and family histories, biography, nature, you name it.

No reading fee, but do send SASE for correspondence and return of ms.

Simultaneous submissions OK, just tell us. We'll always surrender our contract for whatever we have invested in it at the time of surrender, plus $1.00. This, in case you find a better deal once we start. We do work with agents and encourage writers to use agents or attorneys.

The most important thing that can happen to a writer is the publication of a book. It is best if the book comes with a quarter million or more advance, but the absence of an advance doesn't change anything: The best thing that can happen to a writer is the publication of a book.

It doesn't matter how you do it, just do it!

Nothing can happen until you do!

While the Century Press is brand new, the publisher is not. The Conservatory of American Letters and Robert Olmsted have been publishing books sine 1969. Olmsted has over 225 titles to his credit (not subsidy). Additionally, the Conservatory acting as a fee based printer/partner has helped over 2,000 different titles to be created through its **Personal Publishing Program.**

Categories: Any subject considered.

Name: Robert W. Olmsted, Editor
Material: All
Address: PO BOX 298
City/State/ZIP: THOMASTON ME 04861
Telephone: 207-354-0998
Fax: 207-354-8953
E-mail: olrob@midcoast.com
Nota bene: Century Press is a subsidy publisher.

Charles River Press

Charles River Press is a new independent publishing house committed to bringing to readers true personal stories that illustrate and illuminate historical events and current issues. Launched in November, 1995 the press's focus is on narrative nonfiction in the areas of race relations, women, and multicultural history (especially African-American) from both the U.S. and global perspectives. We publish 3-5 titles per year.

We are especially interested in:
• memoirs,
• travel narratives,
• biographies,
• autobiographies,
• family histories,
• history that tells stories and focuses on individuals and/or small groups, and
• academic work, including dissertations, that can be adapted

for general audiences.

The quality of writing is a factor in all manuscript decisions.

We do not publish children's or young adult books, how-to, poetry, fiction, or any nonfiction other than that outlined above.

Submit a query with book outline, sample chapter, resumé including list of previously published work, and cover letter telling why you wrote (or want to write) the book and how it compares with other books on the subject. If you want feedback on whether we would he interested in a subject in principle, please send a one-page query letter. Response within one month.

Categories: Nonfiction—African-American—Asian-American—Biography—Ethnic—Feminism—Gay/Lesbian—Hispanic—History—Jewish Interests—Memoir—Multicultural—Native American—Regional—Travel—Women's Issues

Name: Lynn Whittaker, Editor-in-Chief
Material: All
Address: 427 OLD TOWN COURT
City/State/ZIP: ALEXANDRIA VA 22314-3544
E-mail: lpwcrp@aol.com
Nota bene: Two query types defined in last paragraph.

Charlesbridge Publishing
Talewinds

Charlesbridge publishes a unique variety of illustrated trade picture books and board books for children from 1 to 10 years old. In addition to our focus on appealing and educational nature and science titles, our list is strong in other nonfiction subjects and in multicultural books. The launching of our new imprint, Talewinds, marks our increased commitment to publishing quality fiction picture books with enduring themes.

Charlesbridge is currently open to unsolicited manuscripts. At this time, we do not publish chapter books, books with audio tapes, or CD-ROM products, and we are not looking for more alphabet books. We are considering all fiction submissions, but we're not looking for talking animals or stories with alliterative characters ("Murray the Manatee," "Rodrigo the Rabbit," etc.).

To become better acquainted with our publishing program, we encourage you to review some of our published books through a library or bookstore or to take a look at our Website. If you would like to request a catalog, please send a 9"x12" self-addressed, stamped envelope with $1.47 in postage.

Manuscripts should be submitted in their entirety. Please be sure that your name, address, and telephone number appear on at least the first page of your manuscript as well as in your cover letter. Be sure to list any previously published works or relevant writing experience in your cover letter.

Please submit only one or two manuscripts at a time. We make every effort to respond in four months, but cannot guarantee that we will be able to do so, due to the volume of submissions.

It is not necessary to copyright your work before submitting it for consideration. Copyright is understood upon creation of a work, and formal registration is completed by the publisher upon publication. Like most trade publishers, we pay royalties or a flat fee to the author in the event a manuscript is contracted.

For more information about Charlesbridge and other publishers, we recommend R. R. Bowker's *Literary Market Place* and the Children's Book Council's membership list. The latter may be obtained by sending a self-addressed, stamped envelope with $.78 postage and a $2.00 fee to Children's Book Council, 568 Broadway, Suite 404, New York, NY 10012.

Categories: Fiction—Nonfiction—Children—Environment—Juvenile—Multicultural—Picture Books

Name: Submissions Editor, Trade Editorial Department

Material: All
Address: 85 MAIN ST
City/State/ZIP: WATERTOWN MA 02172
Telephone: 617-926-0329
Fax: 617-926-5720
Internet: www.charlesbridge.com

Chelsea Green
Publishing Company

Chelsea Green is a small, independent publisher, located in Vermont. We specialize in authors and books exploring contemporary environmental issues—ecology, renewable energy, self-sufficiency, and sustainable ways of living. We look for books that are comprehensive, fluent, and practical.

We are not presently considering fiction and poetry.

We appreciate submissions that include:

• A brief proposal summarizing your idea, with a table of contents.

• A representative sample chapter. Please do not send a copy of the complete manuscript unless we request one.

• A description of your previous experiences as an author and your qualifications for completing the project you propose.

• A self-addressed, stamped business envelope for our response to your query, and a self-addressed, stamped mailer if you would like your materials returned. Please do not send original art work or irreplaceable documents as we cannot assume responsibility for these.

Please allow 4-6 weeks for a response.

Please let us know if you would like to see our current catalog, and if you would like to be on our mailing list to receive semi-annual announcements of new Chelsea Green titles.

Categories: Nonfiction—Ecology—Energy—Environment—Gardening

Name: The Editors
Material: All
Address: PO BOX 428
City/State/ZIP: WHITE RIVER JUNCTION VT 05001
Telephone: 802-295-6300
Fax: 802-295-6444
E-mail: jschley@sover.net

Chess Enterprises

Chess Enterprises *only* publishes books on the game of chess: instruction, game collections, analysis.

Categories: Nonfiction—Games—Chess

Name: Submissions Editor
Material: All
Address: 107 CROSSTREE RD
City/State/ZIP: MOON TOWNSHIP PA 15108-2607
Telephone: 412-262-2138
Fax: 412-262-2138
E-mail: Dudley@robert-morris.edu

Chestnut Hills Press

Chestnut Hills Press (CHP) is an author-financed subsidiary of BrickHouse Books/New Poets Series (NPS). Far from being a so-called vanity press, Chestnut Hills considers fewer than ten percent of the 1,000 manuscripts received annually by New Poet Series for possible publication; the sole criterion is excellence. CHP mss are those which NPS would have accepted for non-subsidized publication if funds remained to be allocated. Books published through Chestnut Hills are identical to other New Poets Series books. All are perfect bound, with glossy two-color covers. All NPS books, including those from Chestnut Hills, are distributed to a large group of libraries, universities and periodicals for review. CHP books receive the same library, Library of Congress, ISBN, and promotional listings as those brought out directly by NPS.

Using the highly selective Chestnut Hills Press alternative, the author pays the costs of design, typesetting, printing and shipping, while avoiding the problems of coordinating artist, designer, typesetter, printer and binder, and eliminating the awkwardness sometimes attendant upon self-publication. CHP takes care of all publishing details and, for all practical purposes, such as review copies and publicity, makes no distinction between the two logos. CHP has provided a satisfactory option for many talented professionals.

How to Submit

Chestnut Hills Press accepts book submissions year round. Send a full ms. consisting of about 55 pages of poetry. There is a $10.00 readers' fee for each submission.

Please refer to BrickHouse Books, Inc. for more information.

Categories: Fiction—Nonfiction—Feminism—Gay/Lesbian—General Interest—Literature—Poetry—Women's Fiction—Women's Issues—Writing

Name: Clarinda Harriss, Editor/Director
Material: All
Address: 541 PICCADILLY RD
City/State/ZIP: TOWSON MD 21204
Telephone: 410-828-0724
E-mail: harriss@towson.edu
Internet: www.saber.towson.edu.80/~harriss/ !bhbwebs.ite/bhb.htm
Nota bene: Reading fee and author financing required.

Chicago Review Press
Lawrence Hill Books

Chicago Review Press publishes 20-25 general nonfiction titles a year, most often in trade paperback. In addition to serious nonfiction and how-to books, we publish children's activity books, specialty cookbooks, some parenting books, and biographies. We also publish many regional titles, including various guidebooks for Chicago, as well as books on gardening. We do not publish fiction or poetry, and we are very reluctant to take on self-help books.

In 1987 Chicago Review Press purchased Independent Publishers Group (IPG), a marketing and distribution company that has grown to represent more than 200 publishers. Chicago Review Press titles are distributed by IPG.

If you would like to submit a book proposal, please write to us at the address below. Enclose a cover letter describing your book and your credentials. If you want to include a portion of your manuscript, please send no more than the table of contents and 1-2 sample chapters. Make certain that the author's name,

Books

address, and phone number appear on the first page of the manuscript. Also, please provide the following information:

Audience/Market For what audience is the book written? Are there possibilities for special sales of your book to organizations and institutions? If so, which ones?

Competition Indicate competing titles. How will your book be superior or different from them?

Manuscript Length and Electronic Submission What is the estimated length of the proposed manuscript, typed or printed double-spaced on 8½x11" paper? Can you submit the manuscript on computer disk? If so, what word processing program and version number will you use?

Date of Completion Indicate the date by which you expect to have a completed manuscript.

Because we receive more queries and manuscripts than we can process promptly, please allow eight to ten weeks for our response.

Simultaneous submissions are acceptable as long as they are so identified. Contact us immediately if your manuscript is accepted elsewhere for publication.

If you would like us to send you our current catalog, please send a 9"x12" SASE with postage valued at $3.00.

Categories: Nonfiction—African-American—Animals—Biography—Children—Cooking—Film/Video—Gardening—General Interest—Multicultural—Music—Outdoors—Parenting—Regional—Travel—Women's Issues—Young Adult

Name: Cynthia Sherry, Senior Editor
Material: All
Address: 814 N FRANKLIN ST
City/State/ZIP: CHICAGO IL 60610
Telephone: 312-337-0747
Fax: 312-337-5985

Christian Publications, Inc.
Horizon Books

OWNERSHIP AND DOCTRINAL POSITION OF THE PUBLISHING HOUSE

Christian Publications, Inc. (CPI) is the official publishing house of The Christian and Missionary Alliance church. CPI and its imprint, Horizon Books, adhere to the same evangelical doctrinal position as their sponsoring denomination. A copy of the leaflet, *Statement of Faith*, is available free of charge to all who request it.

BOOK SUBJECTS CONSIDERED

Christian Publications, Inc. publishes both for the denomination and for the general Christian public. To be considered, all manuscripts must be compatible with our doctrinal position.

• CPI will consider book manuscripts dealing with theology, the church, pastoral helps, Bible studies, the Christian home, devotional studies, Christian living and Alliance mission stories and educational materials.

• **The *Jaffray* Collection.** Of particular current interest are Alliance missionary biographies for The Jaffray Collection series.

• **The Global Family Series.** Manuscript submissions are invited for a new series featuring biographies of international Christian leaders within the denomination.

• **The Walk Around the World Series.** The Walk Around the World series features short stories from Alliance missionaries.

• **Horizon Books.** The Horizon books line includes youth books, adult fiction (limited acquisitions), Americana and other manuscripts dealing with a wide range of Christian subjects.

• Poetry, short stories and unsolicited fiction manuscripts

are not accepted.

• While other unsolicited, complete manuscripts will be considered, it is strongly recommended that the author first send a query letter along with a table of contents, a book summary and several sample chapters. If the publishing house is interested, it will request the rest.

PREPARATION OF MANUSCRIPTS

All submissions should meet the following standards:

• Close adherence to the *Chicago Manual of Style*, published by the University of Chicago.

• A photocopy of your manuscript on 8½"x11" white bond paper. It should have 1½" margins on all four sides.

• Do NOT try to format the manuscript into book-like appearance, headers, ornate chapter titles, special borders etc. This only complicates the typesetting process.

• Pages should be numbered consecutively from the beginning to the end of the manuscript rather than by chapters.

• The author should prepare a title page, preface, foreword, dedication and introduction if such are desired.

• If an index, bibliographies and appendices are to be included, the author should advise the editor when submitting the manuscript.

• The author is also responsible to obtain permission to use any copyrighted material.

• Please allow a minimum of four months for your manuscript to be evaluated by our review committee and editor.

• Upon acceptance, CPI prefers manuscripts on standard computer disks in a word processing format convertible to WordPerfect.

• Each chapter should be self-contained in an individual file.

FINANCIAL ARRANGEMENTS FOR BOOK MANUSCRIPTS

• Contract arrangements are made upon final acceptance of the book by the publisher.

• While a flat rate is paid for some books, most are contracted on a royalty basis.

• There is a financial advantage for authors when a contracted manuscript is accompanied by an IBM compatible disk.

BOOKLETS

• Christian Publications Inc. accepts shorter manuscripts to publish in booklet form.

• Topics include moral, social and doctrinal issues of interest to Christians.

• Submissions should be no more than 32 pages in length.

• Payment is by outright purchase.

NEWSPAPER ARTICLES FOR *PERSONALLY YOURS*

• *Personally Yours* is a direct-mail, mass-distribution evangelistic newspaper published six times per year. Current circulation exceeds 100,000. Sample copies mailed upon request.

• Due to the *ministry* orientation of *Personally Yours* no payment can be provided-the author's benefit is being published and having an evangelistic outreach ministry.

• CPI accepts evangelistic articles, utilizing personal experiences of changed lives, historical events and matters of current interest as vehicles to clearly proclaim the gospel.

• The target audience is the non-Christian; getting and holding attention is crucial.

• Christian cliche must be avoided.

• Specific help for the reader in experiencing repentance toward God and faith toward the Lord Jesus Christ is invaluable.

Categories: Christian Interests—Inspirational—Religion—Spiritual

Name: David Fessenden, Managing Editor
Material: All book queries/proposals
Name: Editor, *Personally Yours*
Material: Newspaper article manuscripts/queries

Address: 3825 HARTZDALE DR
City/State/ZIP: CAMP HILL PA 17011
Telephone: 717-761-7044
Fax: 717-761-7273
E-mail: editors@cpi-horizon.com
Internet: www.cpi-horizon.com

Clarity Press, Inc.

Political, social and minority issues viewed in the context of universally recognized human rights norms

Dear Writer:

Clarity's writer's guidelines are as follows:

Human rights issues only: visit Website for editorial purview. Please send query letter first, with brief bio, table of contents, synopsis and endorsements. SASE unnecessary; due to volume of queries, we will respond only if interested. Manuscript should be available on disk in Microsoft Word 6 for Macintosh.

Sincerely,
Diana G. Collier
Editorial Director

Categories: Nonfiction—African-American—Asian-American—Ethnic—Human Rights—Multicultural—Politics—Public Policy

Name: Diana G. Collier, Editorial Director
Material: All
Address: 3277 ROSWELL RD NE
City/State/ZIP: ATLANTA GA 30305
Telephone: 404-231-0649
Fax: 404-231-3899
E-mail: clarity@islandnet.com
Internet: www.bookmasters.com/clarity

Clover Park Press
Great Books About Life's Wonders and Wanderings

Clover Park Press, publisher of great books about life's wonders and wanderings, is seeking book-length manuscripts for its current publishing interests. We are looking for fresh ideas and superior writing in the following categories:

Non-Fiction in the areas of:

• California (history, natural history, travel, culture or the arts).

• Biography of extraordinary women.

• Acts of Courage (Please request further information before submitting in this category.)

• Nature, the environment or place.

• Other cultures.

• Travel, exploration, adventure.

• Scientific/medical discovery.

No fiction, poetry, children's, photography, true crime, diaries or journals, new age, or books about alcoholism or addiction.

Submission guidelines:

• Query with letter summary of one page; author's prior publications and background relevant to the subject; outline; and two strong sample chapters including the first chapter.

• Manuscript should have font between 10-12 pt, be paginated and secured with a clip (not stapled).

• If you have any questions, do inquire by mail, fax or e-mail (preferred) before sending submission. Because of our heavy volume of e-mail, begin your subject line with "A-Query." Do not fax or e-mail manuscript; send hard copy.

• No phone calls.

• Include your phone and fax numbers and e-mail address.

Categories: Nonfiction—Adventure—Biography—History—Multicultural—Regional (California)—Travel—Women's Issues

Name: Martha Grant, Acquisitions Editor
Material: All
Address: PO BOX 5067-A
City/State/ZIP: SANTA MONICA CA 90409
E-mail: cloverparkpr@loop.com
Internet: www.loop.com/~cloverparkpr

Commune-A-Key Publishing

Dear Writer,

Thank you for your inquiry about our publishing company. We are an independent publishing and seminars company launched in 1992 with the mission statement of "Communicating Keys to Growth and Empowerment." This company specializes in niches of growth and empowerment for health care workers, woman's issues, men's issues, recovery, personal growth, Native American, and wellness for the general audience, caregivers, and inspirational gift books.

We currently have 14 titles, and are publishing four more next season. We have national distribution, and can be found in bookstores across the country, New Zealand, Australia, Canada and the UK. We have an active direct mail program and catalog accounts department. We also promote our authors in our speaker's bureau.

Our Guidelines for submissions follows:

How to Submit: Send queries or proposals with synopsis, chapter outline, *and SASE* to above address. Reports on queries will be sent to you within 1 month. Please do not send manuscripts until requested.

For additional information send message e-mail, fax, call or write.

Thank you,
Caryn Summers,
Editor-in-Chief

Categories: Nonfiction—Diet—Feminism—Health—Inspirational—Men's issues—Native American—New Age—Nursing—Poetry—Psychology—Religion—Spiritual—Women's Issues

Name: Caryn Summers, Editor-in-Chief
Material: All
Address: PO BOX 58637
City/State/ZIP: SALT LAKE CITY UT 84158
Telephone: 801-581-9191
Fax: 801-581-9196
E-mail: caryn@lgcy.com

Remember: Editors change jobs and publishers change addresses. It is wise to invest in a phone call for the current information before submitting.

Books

COMPANION
★ P ★ R ★ E ★ S ★ S ★
Naked Cinema Books

Companion Press

Publishes: Trade paperback nonfiction only.

Number of books published per year: 6-8

Types of books published: *Cinema books only*—with a focus on sexuality in the movies. We are interested in receiving proposals for biographies, photo fan books, video guidebooks, quote books and other books that fit into this niche. Please keep in mind that our books are sold to the general reader, rather than the academic or scholar.

Book topics most interested in: adult/erotic, beefcake/cheesecake, bisexuality, censorship, drag/transgender, fetish, gay/lesbian, nudity, sexuality, sex symbols, sexual taboos and related movie topics.

Recent titles: *The Voyeur Video Guide, Coming of Age Movie & Video Guide,* and *Penis Puns, Jokes & One-liners-A Movie Quote Book.*

Upcoming titles: *The Films Of Joe Dallesandro, Hollywood Drag* and *The Nudist Video Guide.*

Unagented authors welcome: We work with *unagented authors only* and welcome first-time authors.

Payment: If we accept your manuscript for publication, we will offer you a contract stipulating the amount of royalties (usually ranging between 6-9% of the cover price of your book). Occasionally we also offer an outright purchase.

Advances: Advances of between $500-$1,000 are generally offered. Advance is paid when your completed manuscript is turned in, provided it is acceptable and not returned for revisions.

Publishing schedule: Books are generally published from 6-9 months after your finished manuscript is turned in.

How to submit a proposal: *Do not send your manuscript!* Send a query letter briefly describing the content of your book along with photocopies of sample photos and a few sample pages or chapters for style. Also send appropriate promotional data/information and describe your qualifications for writing this book. If we are interested, we will request the entire manuscript. We generally reply within 60 days.

Categories: Erotica—Film/Video—Gay/Lesbian—Sexuality

Name: Steve Stewart, Publisher
Material: All
Address: PO BOX 2575
City/State/ZIP: LAGUNA HILLS CA 92654
Telephone: 714-362-9726
Fax: 714-362-9726
E-mail: sstewart@companionpress.com
Internet: www.companionpress.com (Under Construction)
Nota bene: Unagented authors only.

The Conservatory Of American Letters
Royalty Book Publishing

The Conservatory of American Letters (CAL) is a nonprofit, tax-exempt, literary/educational foundation. CAL's purpose is:

To conserve and make public literary works of exceptional merit without regard to commercial potential.

To encourage and develop literary talent.

To provide the reading public with an alternative to modern mass marketing mediocrity.

To achieve this purpose, CAL solicits memberships at $24.00 per year. CAL constantly solicits donations from writers and others. CAL works at selling books it publishes and selling services to writers. All proceeds from all activities go to advance our purpose. In keeping with our purpose, we offer publishing under four different logos, under four different plans which are: **Dan River Press**, **Northwoods Press**, **American History Press**, and our **University-Press** Division. Each plan seeks as many excellent books as can be found and funded. Publishing under various logos differs, and the writer is urged to pay close attention to all details, and to order one or more sample books in the area of interest.

It is important for an author to understand that CAL is a last resort publisher, and should not even be considered until commercial potential is exhausted. Once considered, efforts to secure a commercial publisher should continue, using CAL and CAL publications as a stepping stone, as a tool.

CAL is a small unfinanced publisher with little effective distribution, promotion, or advertising. All books are accepted on an as-funds-become-available basis. This may mean that a book sits in line waiting for funding for several years. While awaiting funding, the author should continue to seek commercial publication. CAL will not be upset if the author finds a commercial house to take on the manuscript. In fact, we encourage it. In the past we have turned over contracts to larger houses for as little as $1.00 and two copies of the finished book.

As writers consider publication with CAL, they must realize that CAL is nonprofit, and is offered only non-profitable properties. It stands to reason that if your book is commercially valuable, you don't need CAL.

Dan River Press

If a manuscript is of high quality, CAL will try to determine the degree of commercial viability. A book with commercial potential will make funding easier, faster, surer. If it does not have even the least bit of commercial potential required to produce it, and CAL still believes the book to be excellent, CAL will fund the book from general revenues as funds become available. This is the way of most CAL acceptances, and writers should be prepared to wait for two years or more for publication. During this wait, the writer should continue to seek out a larger, more commercial publisher, as well as undertake the work of creating an audience for the work.

CAL will publish, by Dan River Press, under these 15 points. This is the basic contract so read it carefully. The part you actually sign says you agree to conditions as outlined here. So this is extremely important.

1. Book will be professionally typeset, with professional design and printing. All paperbacks will be perfect bound. If you have your manuscript on a disk that our system can read, it will cut costs.

2. Cover to be created by the author with advice and consent of the publisher.

3. Unlimited production in both hardcover and paperback. Initial press run of 1,000 copies is anticipated, unless prepublication activities show that 1,000 will not be a reasonable

press run. Hardcovers may or may not be produced, depending on apparent demand.

4. Publisher will keep book in print for two years, and as long thereafter as annual sales total $250.00 net to publisher. When sales fall below that level, continuing or remaindering shall be at the option of the publisher. Before remaindering, the books will be offered to the author. Once remaindered, no further royalties will be paid.

5. Books will normally sell for $11.95 in paperback and $39.95 in hardcover. Prices are subject to change.

6. Discounts on paperbacks are the same for all. We do not discount single copies, or hardcover books.

Terms

2-24 books-Discount equals the number of books ordered x 2%.

Maximum discount is 50% for 25 or more books.

Shipping is $2.75 for the first copy, plus $.60 each for the next 5, and $.25 each for all over 6.

We do have special terms for bookstores. For a copy of our special bookstore terms, send #10 SASE and request it.

7. An advance of $250 to $1,000 or more will be made against royalties of 10% of the first 2,500 copies sold, and 15% on all after that. The percentage is based on the amount received by the publisher. Royalties are paid annually in March for the prior year. Amounts below $25.00 are held on account until that level is reached.

8. Before acceptance the publisher may submit a questionnaire to the writer to help determine if the book can stand on its own commercial potential (immediate sales of at least $8,000 and continuing sales). If it appears unlikely, publication may be delayed until funds become available or other steps may be taken to raise the funds such as our Patron Publishing Program.

9. Authors will be given 10 paperback books. Shipping paid by author. Publisher will send review copies which seem to be in its interest.

10. Publisher will maintain a catalogue of books in print.

11. Publisher will assist author with appropriate and likely-to-be profitable publicity and promotion. We have a minimum promotion schedule. If you would like a copy, send #10 SASE and request it.

12. Books will be copyrighted in the name of the author. Library of Congress cataloging information will be sought where appropriate and possible. ISBN numbers will be assigned, bar codes will be obtained, and the book will be offered for listings in such appropriate places as *Books In Print, Small Press Books In Print,* etc.

13. All books will be released in paperback within 150 working days of receipt of signed contract and funding, less the days the book is in the hands of others for proofing. *Proof reading is 100% the responsibility of the author.* Errors in our typesetting are corrected free, but changes are billed at $36.00 per hour, $15.00 minimum. Any correction missed in the first proofing and caught in a subsequent one is agreed to be considered a change. Proofread your ms. carefully. Proofing after typesetting is very expensive.

14. Prepublication offers may be made to the author's mailing list. The flyer will be a simple announcement of the book, not employing any high pressure tactics. Author's input for creation of the flyer is sought.

15. While no guarantee of sales is possible, or implied, publisher agrees to do everything possible within the limits of good business practice to increase sales.

This program is no panacea. Publication due to G.E.R. (grim economic reality) may be quite slow. Once achieved, neither fame nor fortune will follow. This program is for the author who has a following.

Reading Donations

A donation for reading is requested. CAL suggests a donation of whatever your hourly earnings are, with a $7.00 per hour minimum, plus $7.00 administrative. We regret the reading fee, but it is necessary, as without it we receive more manuscripts than we can read. Because of the huge amount of paid manuscripts we receive, it may take as long as 90 days to get to your manuscript.

Dan River Press rejects most manuscripts. In 1995 there were about 80 manuscripts submitted to Dan River Press and only 1 was accepted and published. (8 others were accepted but could not be funded and 2 others are pending.)

The donation to cover a reader's time is not a fee for criticism. Editors will rarely comment on a rejected manuscript. However, CAL does offer literary criticism. Rates vary with each project. For more information, send #10 SASE and request it.

Northwoods Press

Northwoods Press publishes only poetry, and has designed this program for the poet with a modest following, or one ready and willing to create one. Interested poets should submit poetry manuscripts of high quality, and consisting of poems that have not been published before. As a conservatory, we are interested in conserving what may otherwise be lost. By our understanding, if it is published, it is already conserved.

15 Point Program

1. 1 & 2. Same as Dan River Press, above.

3. Initial press run usually anticipated to be 500 copies with poetry, unless prepublication activities and interest indicates that 500 copies would not be reasonable.

4. Publisher will keep book in print for two full years, and as long thereafter as poet keeps the book in at least 5 retail establishments, and gives at least two personal appearances per year. Burden of proof is with the poet When requirements are not met, remaindering will be at the option of the publisher. Before remaindering, books will be offered to the author. Once remaindered, no further royalties will be paid.

5. Books will be priced at $8.95 in paperback and $39.95 in hardcover. Hardcover books may or may not be produced, depending on apparent demand. Publisher has the right to change prices without notice.

6. 6. & 7 same as Dan River Press, above.

7. 8. Same as Dan River Press, above (except immediate sales of only $2,500).

9. 9—15 same as Dan River Press, above.

As with Dan River Press, a donation for reading is required.

We do offer to critique poetry. The critique will be by Robert Olmsted. It is not really a school, just Olmsted's opinion of a given poem or poems. The fee is $12.00 per two manuscript pages of poetry. Caution: Olmsted does not believe the critique is worth its cost if publication is the goal. It may help the on-going learning process that is being a poet. For book length works, fee must be arranged.

University Press Division

Our University Press Division is open to any college or high school teacher who can garner a prepaid or non-cancelable bookstore or school district order of 80 copies or more. Any subject is acceptable. Standard bookstore discounts are offered, and royalties are a flat 15% on the amount publisher receives. An advance of $250 - $1,000 will be paid against royalties.

American History Press

To Publish The Impossible Book! Because of the increasingly prohibitive costs, the traditional commercial publishing industry is being forced to reject all but the most highly commercial and saleable manuscripts, leaving thousands of excellent literary and important historical works unpublished, and lost to future generations.

In answer to this reality, we have developed a cost efficient

Books

approach to the publishing of important local histories, family histories, genealogies, etc. An approach that enables the important, well written work to appear in permanent book form.

An innovation drawn from need! Our approach is based on extreme simplification of the publishing process. Time consuming and costly elements like proof reading, editorial rewrites, and much that is simply cosmetic or unneeded are eliminated.

Nothing is sacrificed in the quality and appearance of the finished product. The completed book, usually produced in both hardcover and paperback, will make any author proud.

Author's Role

This answer to publishing the book with little commercial potential is only possible with significant involvement (not financial) from the author/historian.

Once a manuscript is accepted the author must:

A. Present a well typed manuscript on paper, or on a computer disk that our system can read.

B. Accept responsibility for all proof reading and copy editing.

C. Get written permission to reprint any previously published materials.

D. Secure a minimum prepaid, non-cancelable order from your local historical society, church, university book store, family members, or others for no fewer than 80 paperback copies. Bookstores, gift shops, museums, and others buying for resale get a 20% discount with no return privilege.

E. Continue to use your good influence to help us promote and distribute your book in your area of influence and the area represented by the book.

Author's Payment

American History Press offers its authors a minimum advance of $250 against royalties of 15% of the amount received by the publisher. Further, we guarantee the book to remain in print for at least 2 full years, and as long thereafter as sales total only $250 per year. On remaindering, books will be offered to the author. After remaindering, no further royalties will be paid.

The author will receive ten free paperback copies, plus standard bookstore discounts on any additional paperback copies. Hardcover copies are not eligible for discounts.

Copyright, LCCN, ISBN, & bar code are all provided where needed and possible.

Marketing and Promotion: In addition to "E" [above], we will use direct mail to individuals, library distributors, and any others who may be expected to respond favorably to your book.

COSTS AND CAVEATS

There is a reading fee of $50.00 per book manuscript. The reading fee is just that, a fee to pay a reader with YES authority. We are nonprofit, therefore, there are no profits from which to pay for the reading of manuscripts. Since there are no profits and we cannot get people to read for free, we must charge. The reading fee does not guarantee an acceptance, nor is it a fee for a critique, nor does it invite dialogue. It is not refundable. This reading fee is normally the only cost to the author/historian.

Charts, photographs, drawings, extensive footnotes, etc. can add significantly to the cost of production.

Color is expensive, but if the work is to be sold through bookstores and other retail outlets, a full color cover can often be quite profitable.

Anything which increases the cost of production (previously referred to), can cause the price of the book to increase or require a larger initial order, or both. Each book is considered individually as to exactly what is needed.

We will spend as much on advertising as sales justify, but in most cases, initial amounts will be small. Advertising by others is encouraged and may be eligible for expense sharing by the publisher.

Decorative dust jackets are not normally provided for our

hardcovers, but are possible.

To Sum Up Everything

If you've a well written local or regional history, family history, church history and if you can generate very modest support from others interested, American History Press will be proud to publish, promote, and distribute your book. In most cases a book can be ready within 100 days of the signing of the contract. Histories must be at least 80% factual.

First, submit your manuscript with the $50.00 reading fee. Your manuscript will be read by someone with YES authority, and you will be notified within 90 days (usually sooner) of acceptance or rejection.

If you garner an acceptance, we promise to work to make your publishing experience highly enjoyable, and profitable.

Patron Publishing Program

Our Patron Publishing Program is available to any author whose work is accepted. It is an easy plan to explain, a tough one to complete.

We offer a limited number of collector edition hardcovers, personally autographed by the author, for a high price. The funds received finance the regular production of the book.

CAL has done a number of these with such numbers as 100 copies for $59.00 each, 50 copies for $50.00 each, etc. If you have the following, it is a fast way of funding. Advances and royalties are paid. Seek full details once you get a letter of acceptance.

Personal Publishing

CAL also offers self-publishing services in which you personally become your own publisher. No acceptance is necessary, and while CAL is acting only as a printer, we do offer recommendations, advice, services, etc. that publishers offer. For example, we can get you an ISBN number, do LCCN and copyright filing, and obtain bar codes, etc.

For more information send #10 SASE and request it. Or you can call Debbie Benner at (207) 832-6665, Mon. - Fri. from 9-6 EST *only*, please. She'll be glad to help.

For information on any of our programs, you can write to the Conservatory. Address the Press or Division that you want. We'll be pleased to hear from you. All mail with SASE is answered promptly.

Categories: Fiction—Nonfiction—Adventure—Biography—Civil War—Conservation—Drama—Erotica—Fantasy—Fishing—History—Hunting—Literature—Men's Fiction—Mystery—Outdoors—Paranormal—Romance—Rural America—Science Fiction—Short Stories—Sports—Textbooks—Western—Writing

Name: Richard S. Danbury III, Senior Editor
Material: Fiction, Biography
Name: Robert W. Olmstead, Editor
Material: All other
Address: PO BOX 298
City/State/ZIP: THOMASTON ME 04861
Telephone: 207-354-0998
Fax: 207-354-8953
E-mail: olrob@midcoast.com
Nota bene: Reading fees required. Amount of author time/ financial resources required vary depending on the program selected.

Cornell Maritime Press, Inc.
Tidewater Publishers

Thank you for thinking of Cornell Maritime Press/Tidewater Publishers as a prospective publisher for your book. The topic of your proposed book must fall within our current areas of interest. As specialized publishers, we undertake only three kinds of projects:

    1. pragmatic works for the merchant marine,

    2. a few books for serious boaters (also of a practical nature), and

    3. regional works mostly confined to Maryland, the Delmarva Peninsula, and the Chesapeake Bay.

Our very particular publishing focus excludes personal narratives, adult fiction, and poetry. We publish only two children's books per year, and they also must have a regional element.

To determine our interest in your book, please submit to us the items listed below. These guidelines apply whether you are proposing a book for publication or have a completed manuscript.

1. A proposal letter describing the book that answers these questions:

    a. What is the book about?

    b. Who is its audience?

    c. How large is that audience and in what ways might the audience be reached?

    d. Are there any special marketing opportunities for the book of which you are aware?

    e. In what ways are you qualified to write the work?

    f. How does the proposed work differ from other books on the topic?

    g. How many pages do you anticipate will make up the final manuscript?

    h. What additional elements are to be included: illustrations (drawings, photographs, or other), appendices, bibliography, index?

    i. When do you think the manuscript will be ready for submission?

2. An outline or a detailed table of contents to indicate the breadth and depth of the work.

3. A sample chapter or two to demonstrate the basic qualities of your written work. Please be sure that the sample you submit is something with which you are completely satisfied. Do not send something that is incomplete, needs "polishing," or is not your best work.

All submissions must:

    1. Have consecutively numbered pages

    2. Not be stapled or bound in a folder

It is best not to send unique documents or artwork. In the preliminary stages, rough copies or photocopies of photographs or sketches will convey your intention quite adequately.

We look forward with interest to receiving your submission.

Categories: Nonfiction—Boating—Professional Maritime—Regional

Name: Charlotte Kurst, Managing Editor
Material: All
Address: PO BOX 456
City/State/ZIP: CENTREVILLE MD 21617
Telephone: 410-758-1075
Fax: 410-758-6849

Cottonwood Press, Inc.

Cottonwood Press is always looking for fresh material for our customers—English and language arts teachers, grades 5 - 12.

We like to use material that is clever, requiring thought and creativity from students—not mindless busy work. Many of our books have both ideas for teachers as well as ready-to-use activities designed for the teacher to photocopy and pass out to his or her students.

We are not interested in variations of the same old games and ideas you see everywhere. (If we see one more game on homonyms, for example, we may scream.) We also do not use word search (word find) puzzles. We love to use materials with a humorous, light-hearted, offbeat or down-to-earth approach, the kind of material that *real* teachers can use with *real* kids.

A careful look through our catalog will help you better understand our products. We strongly suggest that you also familiarize yourself with some of the activities in our books. It is impossible to write for Cottonwood Press without understanding how our books are different from similar products on the market.

We try to get a response to the author within two to four weeks after receiving a manuscript.

    Sincerely,

    Cheryl Thurston

    Editor

Categories: Education

Name: Acquisitions Editor
Material: All
Address: 305 W MAGNOLIA STE 398
City/State/ZIP: FORT COLLINS CO 80521
Telephone: 970-204-0715
Fax: 970-204-0761

Books

Cowles Creative Publishing, Inc.
NorthWord Press

As an imprint of Cowles Creative Publishing, NorthWord Press is a publisher whose primary commitment is to wildlife, habitat, and natural history topics of the world.

The following topics may be considered, but generally stand little chance of acceptance: "how-to" titles, collections of magazine stories or articles, journal memoirs, essays about travel, and manuscripts dealing with limited regional subject matter.

• We publish non-fiction wildlife and nature topics, including substantial species natural history information.

• Our books generally focus on the species with little human interaction; we do not publish stories involving animals in domestic situations.

• We do not publish these kinds of books: fantasy, adventure novel, rhyme/poetry, biography, memoir/journal, A-B-C or counting books.

• Our list does not include books about pets, or with talking animals or vegetation; or those which are otherwise anthropomorphic.

• We do not publish books with ecology or "green" themes. Nor do we particularly emphasize endangered species.

• Our children's list does not include "relationship" or growing-up stories.

Please include the following details when submitting a book proposal:

• Author background, credentials, writing experience

• Brief synopsis of the book being proposed

• Detailed outline or table of contents

• Sample chapters (generally 2 or 3 on hard copy)

• Samples of art, photos, or transparencies intended for use in the book (duplicate photos or transparencies only, please)

• Bibliography (if appropriate)

If the proposal is accepted, manuscripts should be submitted on 3½" floppy disks formatted in Macintosh or DOS word processing program. A hard copy (double spaced) should accompany the disk. Letter-quality is preferred, but easily readable dot matrix print is acceptable.

Proposals submitted to NorthWord Press are reviewed for style, content, appropriateness, conceptual integrity, author expertise, and marketability. Therefore, a rejection does not necessarily reflect any judgment regarding the literary merit of an author's work.

NorthWord uses a standard author contract, which may be modified upon mutual agreement by the author and publisher. Advances against royalties are negotiable, and royalties are paid semi-annually.

Categories: Nonfiction—Animals—Nature—Outdoors—Wildlife

Name: Submissions Editor
Material: All
Address: 5900 GREEN OAK DR
City/State/ZIP: MINNETONKA MN 55343
Telephone: 612-936-4700
Fax: 612-933-1456

Craftsman Book Company

REFERENCES THAT CRAFTSMAN BOOK COMPANY WOULD LIKE TO PUBLISH

Books on the following subjects would sell well to Craftsman customers. The book should be loaded with step-by-step instructions, illustrations, charts, reference data, diagrams, forms, pictures, samples, cost estimates, rules of thumb, man-hour estimates and examples that show how work should be done on the construction site or that solve actual problems in the builder's office. The book must cover the subject completely, become the owner's primary reference on the subject, and have a high utility-to-cost ratio. This list is by no means complete, and is subject to changing trends in the marketplace. Any reference manual that will help construction tradespersons, builders, remodelers, construction estimators or adjusters make a better living in their profession is a good candidate for publication by Craftsman Book Company.

* How to Estimate Sitework (or Concrete, Steel, Masonry, Roofing, HVAC, etc.)
* Man-hour Estimates for Commercial and Industrial Construction
* Cost Estimates for Commercial and Industrial Construction
* Estimating Remodeling and Renovation Costs (With Man-hour Estimates)
* Demolition Methods & Estimating (With Man-hour Estimates)
* How to Take-off Construction Material Quantities
* Estimating Building Losses and Damage Repair Costs (With Man-hours)
* Construction Estimating Programs for Construction Contractors
* Construction Scheduling, CPM and Project Control
* Set Up and Run Your Subcontracting Business
* How to Design and Build Homes and Apartments
* Legal Guide for Running a Construction Contracting Business
* How to Get the Insurance and Bonds You Need at the Right Price
* Field Supervision for Construction Contractors
* How to Get Lucrative Government Construction Projects
* How to Remodel and Renovate Commercial and Industrial Buildings
* Operating Excavation and Grading Equipment (all types)
* Start and Run an Excavation and Grading Contracting Business
* General Excavation Methods (Earth, Rock, Hauling, Placing, Banks)
* Concrete Formwork: Designing, Installing and Estimating
* Simplified Design of Reinforced Concrete for Builders
* Installing and Estimating Concrete Reinforcing Bars

* Modern Masonry (Block, Brick, Tile, Terrazzo—With Man-hour Estimates)
* Estimating and Erecting Structural Steel and Fabricated Metals
* Stair Building from Simple to Complex
* Modern Cabinet Making and Installation Manual
* The Complete Manual of Roof and Stair Layout
* Modern Carpentry in Commercial and Industrial Buildings
* How to Install and Replace Flooring: Hardwood, Resilient, Carpet, and Tile
* Painting and Decorating Commercial and Industrial Buildings
* Planning, Estimating, and Installing HVAC Systems (Gas, Oil and Electric)
* Commercial and Industrial Plumbing—Design and Installation
* Plumbing Repair and Renovation Manual (With Troubleshooting Guide)
* Air Conditioning Installation Manual (With Man-hour Estimates)
* Practical Guide to the Uniform Mechanical Code
* Plumber's Vest Pocket Reference Book
* Low Voltage Electrical Guide: Design, Installation, Estimating
* Electrical Wiring for Commercial and Industrial Buildings
* Electrician's Vest Pocket Reference Book
* Post & Beam House Construction
* Getting Financing to Develop Land
* Footing & Foundation Construction & Estimating
* The Right Markup for Your Business
* Computer Applications Tutorial for Contractors
* Steel Stud Framing Methods
* Sources of Financing for Construction
* Construction Estimating for Beginners
* How to Get Insurance Repair Work
* Specifications for Construction Plans

Categories: Business—Engineering—Construction—Reference

Name: Laurence Jacobs, Managing Editor
Material: Professional Building Books
Address: PO BOX 6500
City/State/ZIP: CARLSBAD CA 92009
Telephone: 760-438-7828
Fax: 760-438-0398
Internet: www.craftsman-book.com

Cross Cultural Publications, Inc.

Submit book proposal in summary, with table of contents and resumé of author. If we are interested we will invite the author for more details and completed manuscript.

Categories: Asian-American—Biography—Christian Interests—College—Conservation—Culture—Ecology—Economics—Education—Environment—Ethnic—Family—Feminism—General Interest—Government—History—Inspirational—Jewish Interests—Literature—Multicultural—Native American—New Age—Philosophy—Politics—Public Policy—Religion—Society—Spiritual—Women's Issues

Name: Acquisitions Editor
Material: All
Address: PO BOX 506
City/State/ZIP: NOTRE DAME IN 46556
Telephone: 219-273-6526
Fax: 219-273-5973

The Crossing Press

The Crossing Press is accepting book proposals in the following areas: Natural health; Spirituality; and Empowerment/self-help. We no longer publish fiction, poetry or calendars.

Please submit as much of the following information as possible in your book proposal. We find this information essential in evaluating the project for publication consideration.

Description of the book. Includes text content, style, number of manuscript pages, and how you envision the published book (physical attributes).

Definition of the market. Who is the intended audience? What need is this book fulfilling? What is the book designed to accomplish? How is the topic of increasing rather than declining or passing interest? How does it compare with other books on the market (please list)?

Outline and description of contents. Provide a few sentences about the purpose and contents of each chapter, giving specific details and examples as well as general statements. Explain the logic of the book's organization.

Introduction and sample chapters. If complete, please submit 1-2 sample chapters as well as an introduction to the manuscript.

Timetable. Is the manuscript complete? If not, provide a schedule for submitting sample chapters (if not already included), and the complete manuscript.

Author information. Include your resume, vita, or biography detailing your professional and educational background, including prior publications and publicity materials, and any other relevant information.

We look forward to reviewing your proposal.

Categories: Nonfiction—Cooking—Diet—Empowerment—Health—Natural Healing—New Age—Spiritual

Name: Jill Schettler, Acquisitions Editor
Material: All
Address: PO BOX 1048
City/State/ZIP: FREEDOM CA 95019
Telephone: 408-722-0711
E-mail: Crossing@aol.com

Dan River Press

Please refer to The Conservatory of American Letters.

David R. Godine, Publisher

Founded in 1970, David R. Godine, Inc., is a small publishing house located in Lincoln, Massachusetts, producing between twenty and thirty titles per year and maintaining an active reprint program. The company is independent (a rarity these days) and its list tends to reflect the individual tastes and interests of its president and founder, David Godine.

At Godine, quality has remained foremost. Our aim is to identify the best work and to produce it in the best possible way. All of our hardcover and softcover books are printed on acid-free paper. Many hardcovers are still bound in cloth. The list is deliberately eclectic and features works that many other publishers can't or won't support, books that won't necessarily become bestsellers but that still deserve publication. In a world of spin-offs and commercial "product," Godine's list stands apart by offering original fiction and nonfiction of the highest rank, rediscovered masterworks, translations of outstanding world literature, poetry, art, photography, and beautifully designed books for children.

Godine has recently launched two new series: **Imago Mundi**, a line of original books devoted to photography and the graphic arts; and **Verba Mundi**, featuring the most notable contemporary world literature in translation. Volumes in the **Imago Mundi** series, which has received praise from reviewers and booksellers alike, include *Jean Cocteau: The Mirror and the Mask* by Julie Saul and Arthur Leipzig's *Growing Up in New York*. **Verba Mundi** has so far published works by world-renowned authors Jose Donoso, Isaac Babel, and Dino Buzzati, and has introduced new voices such as Sylvie Germain (whose *Book of Nights* was named a Notable Book of the Year by the New York Times) and the acclaimed Swedish novelist Goran Tunstrom, author of *The Christmas Oratorio.*

Godine does not accept unsolicited manuscripts.

Categories: Fiction—Nonfiction—Architecture—Arts—Biography—Boating—Children—Cooking—Crime—Feminism—Food/Drink—Gardening—Gay/Lesbian—History—Jewish Interests—Juvenile—Literature—Men's Fiction—Mystery—Outdoors—Photography—Poetry—Religion—Rural America—Short Stories—Women's Fiction—Writing—Young Adult

Name: Editorial Department
Material: All
Address: PO BOX 9103
City/State/ZIP: LINCOLN MA 01773
Telephone: 617-259-0700
Fax: 617-259-9198

The Denali Press

The Denali Press publishes books on multiculturalism. We emphasize reference and scholarly books with a strong appeal to the library and institutional market. Selected titles include: *Hispanic Resource Directory; Refugee and Immigrant Resource Directory; Judaica Reference Sources;* and *Lives Between Cultures: A Study of Human Nature, Identity and Culture.*

The Denali Press would like to see queries, proposals, summaries, and outlines rather than full manuscripts. If the substance of the work cannot be fully communicated in this manner, a couple of chapters may be included. We encourage queries with full descriptions both of the proposed work and of the author's background and interests, since from them we may be able to identify ideas for books other than the one proposed. Specifically, proposals should discuss:

• the book's subject matter and approach

• the audience, i.e., the size of the market and how it can be reached

• how the book differs from similar books currently in print, and

• author qualifications

We are pleased to sponsor the American Library Association's The Denali Press Award. This award is presented to recognize achievement in creating reference works, outstanding in quality and significance, that provide information specifically about ethnic and minority groups in the United States.

Categories: Nonfiction—Academic—African-American—Asian-American—Biography—College—Culture—Economics—Environment—Ethnic—Government—Hispanic—History—Jewish Interests—Multicultural—Native American—Politics—Reference—Textbooks

Name: Sally Silvas-Ottumwa, Editorial Associate
Material: All
Address: PO BOX 021535
City/State/ZIP: JUNEAU AK 99802
Telephone: 907-586-6014
Fax: 907-463-6780
E-mail: denalipr@alaska.net

Denlinger's Publishers, Ltd.
Thelton Hall Books

Thelton Hall Books, an associate of Denlinger's Publishers, Ltd., is committed to publishing the genre known as The Memoir. We believe that it is an historical contribution to the oral tradition in Western literature. We also believe that it is best told in the author's own words, style and flavor of spelling and structure. We do as little as possible to change that. We are interested in preserving a small slice of history, not in presenting a literary masterpiece, although sometimes they do come along. When The Memoir is studied in the future, we feel the thoughts, feelings and inconsistencies of humanity will tell the real tale, not the revisionist historians.

Denlinger's is a company established in 1926, and we feel that the best of the past should be preserved, while we at Thelton Hall Books stand on the threshold of the 21st Century looking with excitement and anticipation at the challenge before us when we move "Forward into Light," the light of a new millennium.

Categories: Nonfiction—Feminism—History—Women's Issues

> **Name:** Thelma Spencer, CEO, Ozark Division
> **Material:** Memoirs
> **Address:** PO BOX 4769
> **City/State/ZIP:** SPRINGFIELD MO 65808-4769
> **Telephone:** 417-887-4521
> **Fax:** 417-887-4521

DIMI Press

DIMI Press is a small, independent publisher of books and cassettes. At present we have published 16 cassettes and nine books, but intend to publish many more (mostly books). Dick Lutz, President, was the 1988 President of the Northwest Association of Book Publishers. We welcome your query letter if you are a serious author with a book manuscript or well-conceived outline for a book you want to write.

At this time we are looking for the following type of nonfiction manuscripts:

Practical, hands-on instruction books of the 'how-to' variety. These should be designed to appeal to the lay reader and should help the reader solve a significant problem of his. It should speak to a problem that afflicts millions, e.g., headaches, arthritis, insomnia, depression, buying a used car, etc.

Writing should be clear, simple, and well-organized. Your initial contact with us should be a one or two page query letter accompanied by a SASE. Unsolicited manuscripts will not be read. Simultaneous submissions are fine.

A DIMI Press author should have some credentials in the field in which he/she writes. An advanced academic degree, books and/or articles on the general subject, or extensive personal experience are all considered credentials.

Authors, in their query letter, must address the marketing of the book. Who is going to buy this book? How can they he reached? The author must have the poise and ability to be a good interviewee on radio and TV. If the author has what it takes to put on seminars on the subject of the book that will certainly increase our interest in his/her manuscript. In other words, the author must be able to promote the book.

Royalties to the author will generally be 10% on net revenues. Advances are not given. (We are a small company and need all the cash possible for promotion.)

It is best that the title and subject of the book be of such general interest that it can be marketed through bookstores, libraries, and sold in other countries. Regional titles, fiction, po-

etry, and first-hand accounts are not desired. Children's books are not wanted. Books that require color illustrations are a no-no. We prefer previously published authors, but do not insist on this.

It is not necessary for you to spend a great deal of time cleaning up things like spelling, punctuation and grammar. Everything we publish is carefully edited. After the manuscript is accepted for publication, we would prefer that the author put it on either an IBM or a Macintosh disk. However, if this is difficult for him/her we can get it done ourselves. The manuscript being on a Macintosh disk will enable us to proceed with typesetting and page design immediately.

If we like your query letter (and we'll try to tell you in two weeks) we will ask to see the manuscript. The manuscript review may well take more than four weeks, but if we're reading the manuscript you can be sure that we are very serious about it.

DIMI Press feels that a book is a joint project of the author and the publisher and we need to have a good feeling about working with you. In other words, we're not looking for an adversarial relationship.

Categories: Nonfiction—How-to—Nature

> **Name:** Dick Lutz, President
> **Material:** All
> **Address:** 3820 OAK HOLLOW LN SE
> **City/State/ZIP:** SALEM OR 97302-4774
> **Telephone:** 503-364-7698
> **Fax:** 503-364-9727
> **E-mail:** dickbook@aol.com

Dorchester Publishing Co., Inc.
Leisure Books, Love Spell

THE FOLLOWING ARE THE *ONLY* CATEGORIES OF ORIGINAL FICTION WE ARE CURRENTLY ACQUIRING.

HISTORICAL ROMANCE—Sensual romances with strong plots and carefully thought out characterizations. Spunky heroine whose love for the hero never wavers; he's the only one she makes love with and she's as passionate as he, although he may have to instruct her in the ways of love, since she's almost invariably untouched before she falls in love with the hero. Hero is often arrogant, overbearing; heroine often can't stand him at first, but discovers that beneath the surface lies a tender, virile, and experienced lover. It helps if both the heroine and hero have a sense of humor—a certain amount of wit leavens the heavy-breathing passion. Hero and heroine are separated by emotional conflict or the twists and turns of the plot, but in the end they overcome the barriers between them and live happily ever after.

We *don't* want a heroine who sleeps around, or a hero who's sadistic, although if there's a villain or villainess, he or she can be as nasty as possible.

Historical background, details of costume, etc., should be accurate; however, we don't want endless descriptions of battles, the political climate of the period, or a treatise on contemporary social history. Our readers are much more interested in the trials, tribulations, and love life of the heroine than in how many men Napoleon lost at the Battle of Waterloo.

Historical Romances should be approximately 120,000 words.

FUTURISTIC ROMANCE—Futuristic Romances contain all the elements of Historical Romances—beautiful heroine, dashing hero, some conflict that separates them, a happy ending, etc.—but they are set in lavish lands on distant worlds.

Avoid science-fiction-type hardware, technology, etc.

Finished manuscripts should be 120,000 words.

TIME-TRAVEL ROMANCE—A modern-day hero or heroine goes back in time and falls in love. Traditional guidelines for

Historical Romances apply. The challenge here is to maintain credibility during the transition between the present and the past. The fun is seeing history and another way of life through the eyes of someone from our own time. The conflict and resolution of the romance arise from the fact that the hero and heroine are from different eras.

Beware of a lot of philosophizing about fate, the meaning of time, and how the past affects the present. No time machines please.

Finished manuscripts should be 120,000 words.

PARANORMAL ROMANCE—Either historical or contemporary romance with magic, witches, ghosts, vampires, etc., as a subsidiary element. Must have a happy ending.

Finished manuscripts should be 120,000 words.

OTHER CATEGORIES

WESTERNS—Exciting novels set in the Old West (before 1900 and west of the Mississippi River) with three-dimensional characters and strong plots. Historical accuracy is important, but should not eclipse the story. In addition to traditional heroes, Native Americans, women, African Americans, etc. are fine as protagonists.

Finished manuscripts should be 70,000 - 90,000 words.

HISTORICAL FICTION—Sweeping sagas set primarily in the Old West, containing all of the general elements of Westerns, but with a larger scope and greater cast of characters.

Finished manuscripts should be 90,000 to 115,000 words.

HORROR—Suspenseful, terrifying novels in a contemporary setting. Supernatural horrors (ghosts, vampires, demons, monsters, etc.) are strongly preferred, although psychological suspense and killers on the loose can work if well-handled and original. Please avoid science fiction.

Finished manuscripts should be 80,000 – 115,000 words.

TECHNOTHRILLERS—Action-filled, contemporary or near-future thrillers with emphasis on cutting-edge technology, frequently featuring advanced jets, submarines, weaponry, etc. Conflict should be on a large, usually international, scale.

Finished manuscripts should be 90,000 - 115,000 words.

GUIDELINES FOR SUBMITTING MATERIAL TO LEISURE BOOKS AND LOVE SPELL

Please query or submit synopsis and first three chapters *only*—no complete manuscripts unless specifically requested.

Synopsis, sample chapters (and manuscript if requested) must be typed, double-spaced. Word processors are okay, but letter quality only.

For a free catalogue of Leisure Books, please send a self-addressed, stamped envelope (#10) to the address below.

The best way to learn to write a Leisure or a Love Spell romance is to read a Leisure or a Love Spell romance.

Categories: Romance—Western

Name: Mira Son, Editorial Assistant
Material: Any
Name: Christopher Keeslar, Assistant Editor
Material: Any
Address: 276 FIFTH AVE STE 1008
City/State/ZIP: NEW YORK NY 10001
Telephone: 212-725-8811-
Fax: 212-532-1054

Duke Press

About the Company

Duke Communications International, publisher of Duke Press books, *Windows NT Magazine, NEWS/400,* and *Controller Magazine,* maintains its corporate headquarters in Loveland, Colorado, with regional sales offices in New York, Chicago, and San Francisco. Duke Communications currently employs about 100 people in Colorado, plus a staff of technical editors and reporters throughout the U.S. Duke Communications began publishing a newsletter, *NEWS 34/38,* in 1982 when founder and president David A. Duke, a former IBMer, recognized the need for information about the proliferating IBM midrange systems entering the market.

About Duke Press

In January 1991, the Duke Press division of Duke Communications published its first book for 3X/400 professionals. Currently, Duke Press maintains a list of about 50 titles in print, including reference books and textbooks. **Target audiences are AS/400 professionals, and Windows NT users, administrators, and developers.**

Duke Press strives to publish practical, easy-to-read books that present clear, complete explanations of underlying concepts needed by readers. Practitioners who can communicate their technological expertise in a down-to-earth manner are the mainstays of the Duke Press publishing tradition. Many of our authors are technical editors for or contributors to leading technology journals, as well as pioneers and entrepreneurs in their respective fields.

Check our Web site for new Windows NT and AS/400 books, as well as an online catalog of our entire product line.

How to Submit a Proposal

If you are interested in submitting a proposal to Duke Press, you should send us the following information about your project and yourself:

• An overview that describes the type of book, its approximate length, and any special features or accompanying materials (diskette, CD, and so forth)

• A description of the intended audience

• A content outline or proposed Table of Contents

• A sample chapter or several pages from a typical chapter

• An estimate of the length of time to complete the final manuscript

• Information about competing products and market potential

• Personal information about your background and writing experience, including such items as a resume, a list of previously published works, and a writing sample

• Personal information about your background and writing experience, including such items as a resume, a list of previously published works, and a writing sample

Categories: Nonfiction—Computers—IBM AS/400—Windows NT

Name: Mick Gusinde-Duffy, Acquisitions Editor
Material: Windows NT
Name: Dave Bernard, Publisher
Material: AS/400
Address: 221 E 29TH ST
City/State/ZIP: LOVELAND CO 80538
Telephone: 970-663-4700
Fax: 970-203-2756
E-mail: dbernard *or* **mduffy@dukepress.com**
Internet: www.dukepress.com

Dutton Children's Books
Penguin Putnam, Inc.

• Please include a self-addressed stamped envelope (SASE) to cover the full weight of all materials submitted or a business-sized SASE for a reply only.

• Please supply **a covering letter** with the following information:

• titles and publishers of any published children's books

• names of magazines and/or newspapers in which any work has appeared

• whether manuscript is simultaneous submission (will not disqualify)

• **Picture books** may be sent in their entirety. Unless author is also the illustrator, publishers usually select suitable illustrators for manuscripts chosen for publication. We do not require or encourage authors to seek out illustrators for materials they plan to submit.

• For **longer manuscripts,** please send synopsis and only first three chapters. Author's full name and address must appear on title page of manuscript. Last name should be typed on each page of manuscript.

• Authors who wish to confirm that Dutton has received their materials may include a "return receipt requested" (available at the post office) or a self-addressed stamped postcard with the work's title on it.

• We recommend that authors send their materials via first class or fourth class manuscript rate. Costly overnight letters draw no attention to manuscripts.

• Manuscripts are read as soon as possible and are returned to the author (if a SASE is enclosed) or discarded. Some are held for further consideration.

• Unfortunately, the volume of manuscripts makes it impossible for us to write a critique of every submission. We do, however, give all materials a fair and extensive reading.

• While we take reasonable care of all items we receive, we can assume no responsibility for loss of or damage to submissions. We discourage the submission of costly or irreplaceable items.

Categories: Fiction—Nonfiction—Adventure—Animals—Children—Literature—Middle Grade Fiction—Picture Books—Young Adult Novels

Name: Submissions Editor
Material: All
Address: 375 HUDSON ST
City/State/ZIP: NEW YORK NY 10014
Telephone: 212-366-2600

Eastern National

Serving America's National Parks and Other Public Trusts

Unsolicited materials not accepted.

All book ideas come from the national park level. It is suggested that authors approach the interpretive staffs of individual national parks with manuscript ideas.

Some freelance projects available. Authors are encouraged to send resume and writing samples.

Categories: Nonfiction—Associations—Civil War—Education—History

Name: Patti Plummer, Production Manager
Material: All

Address: 446 NORTH LN
City/State/ZIP: CONSHOHOCKEN PA 19428
Telephone: 610-832-0555
Fax: 610-832-0308
E-mail: EastNatl@ix.netcom.com

Emerald Ink Publishing

Dear Author,

Our submission guidelines are fairly simple.

We prefer electronic submission or on disk, PC readable (simply access our Website to begin communications, or send files). You should not send files larger than 300-400KB by attaching to e-mail. If files are larger, arrange transmission via ftp. Word, WordPerfect, text or ASCII files, .pdf or .rtf file formats are fine. However, if you wish to send us a manuscript, query first with a stamped, self-addressed envelope or include a return postage postcard.

We always answer inquiries.

Sincerely,

Chris Carson

Categories: Nonfiction—Business—Energy—Health—Inspirational

Name: Chris Carson, Owner
Material: Business, Energy
Name: Patrick Zale, Editor
Material: Health, Inspirational
Address: 7141 OFFICE CITY DR STE 200
City/State/ZIP: HOUSTON TX 77087
Telephone: 713-643-9945
Fax: 713-643-1986
E-mail: emerald@emeraldink.com
Internet: www.emeraldink.com

ETC Publications

Our guidelines are the *Chicago Manual of Style* (the book).

Categories: Nonfiction—Christian Interests—Education—Textbooks

Name: Acquisitions Editor
Material: All
Address: 700 E VEREDA DEL SUR
City/State/ZIP: PALM SPRINGS CA 92262
Telephone: 760-325-5352
Fax: 760-325-8844

Excalibur Publications

We publish books on military history, firearms history, antique arms and accessories, military personalities, tactics and strategy, history of battles. Query with an outline and three sample chapters. Royalty or flat fee.

Categories: Nonfiction—Antiques—Civil War—Collectibles—History—Military

Name: A.M. Petrillo, Editor
Material: All
Address: PO BOX 36
City/State/ZIP: LATHAM NY 12110-0036

Excelsior Cee Publishing

Publishes nonfiction, general interest books. Simultaneous

submissions accepted. Reports in one month.

Categories: Nonfiction—Family—Genealogy—General Interest—How-to—Inspirational—Writing

Name: Acquisitions Editor
Material: All
Address: POB 5861
City/State/ZIP: NORMAN OK 73070
Telephone: 405-329-3909
Fax: 405-329-6886

Faber & Faber, Inc.
Publishers

Dear Author,

Thank you for your recent inquiry concerning Faber and Faber's submission guidelines.

1. Faber and Faber publishes adult trade titles only, fiction and nonfiction. Currently we are not reviewing poetry, children's books, young adult titles, mass-market romances or mysteries, how-to books, photo/art books, or humor.

2. Submissions must be limited to a one- or two-page outline of the book's subject, the intended audience, and the author's credentials.

3. No SASE is required. If we feel that your proposal may fit our publishing needs, we will contact you and request to see more.

4. Because of staffing limitations, please do not call to check on your proposal. Such phone calls will not be returned.

For examples of recent titles published by Faber and Faber, please check your local bookstore. Fiction titles include *Leaning Towards Infinity* by Sue Woolfe and *Child out of Alcatraz* by Tara Ison. Nonfiction titles are *Hell with the Fire Out* by Arthur Quinn, *House on the Ocean, House on the Bay* by Felice Picano, and *The Light in the Skull* by Dr. Ronald Glasser.

By following these guidelines, you ensure the most efficient editorial consideration of your material.

Thank you for your cooperation.

Yours sincerely,

The Editorial Department

Categories: Fiction—Nonfiction—Cooking—Drama—Film/Video—Gay/Lesbian—History—Music—Science—Travel—Women's issues

Name: Dan Weaver, Senior Editor
Material: Any
Name: Valerie Cimino, Senior Editor
Material: Any
Address: 53 SHORE RD
City/State/ZIP: WINCHESTER MA 01890
Telephone: 617-721-1427
Fax: 617-729-2783

Fairleigh Dickinson University Press

Established in 1967, Fairleigh Dickinson University Press has published over 800 titles in a variety of scholarly fields, including literature, history, art, and the social sciences.

Authors wishing to submit work to FDU Press should write a query letter that describes the manuscript and the contribution it will make to its scholarly field. If the Director and Editorial Committee believe the project is suitable for us, we will ask that the manuscript be submitted. Because of the costs associated with evaluation, FDU Press requires that we be the only press considering the work during the time we have it under review.

Manuscripts considered for publication by FDU Press are subject to internal review and external evaluation by specialist readers. The identity of evaluators is kept confidential, unless they specifically permit us to reveal their names. Authors may suggest possible evaluators, but should note any previous connection they may have had to the project.

The editorial committee of FDU Press, composed of university faculty in a variety of disciplines, meets every two months to select manuscripts for publication.

The typical run for FDU Press is 500-1,000 copies. Time from delivery of the final manuscript to publication averages between 14-18 months.

FDU Press discourages submission of unrevised dissertations. It does not publish textbooks or original fiction, poetry, or plays. It does, however, publish scholarly editions of literary works, in English or in translation.

FDU Press welcomes inquiries about essay collections. It requires, however, that the majority of the material in a collection be previously unpublished; that the essays have a unifying and consistent theme; and that the editor provides a substantial scholarly introduction. The press holds festschrifts to the same standards we would any other collection of essays.

Decisions of the Editorial Committee of FDU Press are based on the scholarly merit and value of manuscripts under consideration. FDU does not require subsidies or subventions for publication. Where such support is available, it will be employed in a manner mutually acceptable to the author, the press, and the subsidizing organization or individual.

Manuscripts must be submitted in "hard" copy for evaluation. However, once a manuscript has been accepted for publication, the press is prepared to accommodate authors whose work is on disk. In some cases, this may speed publication. For manuscripts that present special typographical difficulties, FDU Press may require that authors provide camera-ready copy.

Books accepted for publication by the FDU Press Editorial Committee are published by Associated University Presses, 440 Forsgate Drive, Cranbury, NJ 08512, which has similar arrangements with the University of Delaware, Bucknell University, Lehigh University, and Susquahanna University. Only in exceptional cases will manuscripts rejected by one of the above mentioned presses be considered by one of the others.

For documentation, FDU Press books follow the *University of Chicago Stylebook, 14th edition.* MLA format is not accepted. Bibliographies are required. For spelling, the press follows *Webster's Third New International Dictionary* and the *Tenth New Collegiate Dictionary.* The press very strongly recommends that translations be provided for all foreign language extracts. As stated in the *Chicago Manual of Style,* the original language quotations should be retained only when the original language itself is of scholarly significance. For example, in a work of Racine, quotations from Racine's plays should be given in French, followed by English translations. Quotations from critical works on the plays, however, should be given in English translation only.

Fairleigh Dickinson University, founded in 1942, has campuses in Florham-Madison, NJ, Teaneck-Hackensack, NJ, and Wroxton, England.

Members of the Editorial Committee of FDU Press are: Patricia Bazan-Figueras, Walter Cummins, Bernard Dick, Kalman Goldstein, Martin Green, Samuel Raphalides, Irene Taviss-Thomson. Ex Officio members: Francis Mertz and Geoffrey Weinman.

A complete catalogue of FDU Press books is available.

Categories: Nonfiction—Drama—Ethnic—Feminism—Film/Video—History—Jewish Interests—Language—Literature—Philosophy—Poetry—Politics—Psychology—Public Policy—Western—Women's Issues

Books

Name: Harry Keyishian, Director
Material: All
Address: FAIRLEIGH DICKINSON UNIVERSITY
Address: 285 MADISON AVE (M010C)
City/State/ZIP: MADISON NJ 07940
Telephone: 973-443-8564
Fax: 973-443-8564
E-mail: fdupress@fdu.edu

Fairview Press
(formerly Deaconess Press)

Fairview Press publishes books related to family issues, however we do tend to have a wide definition of family issues: relationships, social issues, community issues, women's and men's issues, aging, grief and loss, parenting, growing-up issues, early childhood, and some physical health and workplace issues. We are also getting into children's picture books on family issues, values and virtues, problem-solving and coping skills, relationships, personal growth, cultural diversity, and special needs.

Submissions should include (described in more depth below):
• Cover letter
• Outline of book
• Marketing plan for the book

Cover letter:
• Give a summary of the book
• Tell us your vision of the book-How many pages? What size? Any interior illustration? How many parts or chapters?
• List and describe existing books that compete with your proposal. Why is yours different? What void do you fill in the market? Give us an angle.
• Tell us why you are qualified to write this book. List your previously published writing, including books or articles in journals, magazines, newspapers, or newsletters.
• Describe the market of the book-who would buy it?

Outline of the book
• Chapter-by-chapter outline; send sample chapters if available.

Marketing plan (sketch) for the book
• Are you marketable as the author of the book? Have you appeared on radio or TV? Do you lead seminars or guest-speak for events or conventions? Are you a self-promoter?
• Is there a time of year that would best accommodate the release of the book?
• Do you have contacts that would endorse or write a foreword for the book? (The bigger the name, the better!)

Categories: Nonfiction—Children—Disabilities—Educational—Family Issues—General Issues—Gift—Health—Humor—Institutional—Juvenile—Marriage—Men's Issues—Parenting—Psychology—Reference—Relationships—Senior Citizens—Sexuality—Society—Teen—Women's Issues—Young Adult

Name: Carla Green, First Reader
Material: All
Address: 2450 RIVERSIDE AVE
City/State/ZIP: MINNEAPOLIS MN 55454
Telephone: 612-672-4180
Fax: 612-672-4980

Falcon Publishing
FalconGuides, TwoDot, Skyhouse

About Falcon

Falcon Publishing is a fast-growing, mid-sized publisher specializing in outdoor guides, high-quality photographic gift books on regional or natural history themes, and general interest nonfiction books with Western Americana or environmental themes. We also publish books in partnership with state agencies and nonprofit organizations such as the Montana Historical Society and the Rocky Mountain Elk Foundation. We publish about sixty new titles a year and have more than three hundred titles currently in print. Before submitting your proposal, you may wish to send us a 9"x12" self addressed stamped envelope with a note requesting our latest catalog. This will give you a good idea of what we publish and may save time and confusion later.

We Publish:
Outdoor recreation guidebooks (FalconGuides):
• Birding
• Camping
• Fishing
• Hiking (regions and statewide)
• Mountain Biking (cities and statewide)
• Rock climbing
• Rockhounding
• Paddling
• Scenic Driving
• Touring/Historic Traveling
• Walking
• Wild Areas
How-to camping/wilderness/outdoor guides
Field guides (wildflowers, wildlife, etc.)
TwoDot Books (an imprint of Falcon): Western Americana, History, Biography
General non-fiction with Western/wilderness/Rocky Mountain regional themes
Large format photo gift books (coffee table books)
Some cookbooks (with outdoor or Rocky Mountain regional themes)
Some children's and young adult books (with environmental education themes)

We Don't Publish:
Fiction
Poetry
Picture books for small children
Coloring books
New Age texts
Religious texts
Self-help books
Scientific treatises

Submitting a Book Proposal to Falcon Publishing

Do not send us a complete manuscript. Instead, your proposal should include the following materials **only:**
• A letter explaining your proposal, its sales potential, and a description of its competition.
• A resume and/or list of publishing credits.
• An outline or annotated table of contents.
• One, or at most two, sample chapters.

• Sample copies of any illustrations or photographs. Do not send original materials (transparencies, original art, original copy of manuscript)!

The above materials should be organized, self-explanatory, and succinct. Address all queries to the Editorial Director.

Considering Your Book

Our primary criteria are accuracy, lively and readable prose, and a new angle on natural history, regional, or environmental topics. We will analyze your proposal for editorial value, marketability, and projected costs, as well as for how well it fits with our existing line and publishing plan.

We will respond to queries within eight to ten weeks of their receipt. If your proposal is a likely candidate for a Falcon book, one of our editors may contact you for further writing samples or other materials. Once again, *do not submit original materials*— clear and readable photocopies are acceptable and preferred.

What You Can Expect From Falcon

Should Falcon decide to publish your book, you will be contracted and paid on a negotiated royalty basis, although we occasionally pay a flat fee. Once we have a contract with an author, we will invest in every necessary resource to produce an attractive, high-quality product and market it effectively.

Thank you for considering Falcon as a possible publisher for your book.

Categories: Nonfiction—Cooking—Fishing—History—Outdoors—Recreation—Regional—Rural America—Travel—Western (nonfiction)

Name: Editorial Director
Material: All
Address: PO BOX 1718
City/State/ZIP: HELENA MT 59624
Telephone: 406-442-6597
Fax: 406-442-2995
E-mail: FalconBk@ix.netcom.com

Farrar, Straus & Giroux, Inc.
Books For Young Readers

Especially in the case of longer manuscripts, it is a good idea to send a letter of inquiry before submitting the entire manuscript.

Include a cover letter containing any pertinent information about yourself, your writing, your manuscript, etc.

Be sure that your name and address are on the manuscript itself as well as on the cover letter.

If you have illustrations, please send only two or three samples. Do NOT send original artwork.

The length of the story depends on the age of the reader for whom it is intended; there are no fixed lengths.

Do not expect an editor to give you specific comments. We receive far too many manuscripts for this to be possible.

We suggest familiarizing yourself with various children's publishers to get a sense of which company would be most receptive to your type of work. Most publishers will send their catalogue if you write a letter requesting it and provide a self-addressed, stamped manila envelope for it. Our catalogue requires a 9"x12" SASE with $0.96 postage.

The Literary Marketplace, published by R.R. Bowker, contains a list of all publishers; a list of children's book publishers can be obtained from the Children's Book Council, 568 BROADWAY, NEW YORK NY 10012.

Please note: Response time for queries is generally within eight weeks; for manuscripts, between one and three months.

Categories: Hardcover Fiction—Children—Young Adult

Name: Acquisitions Editor
Material: All
Address: 19 UNION SQUARE W
City/State/ZIP: NEW YORK NY 10003
Telephone: 212-741-6900

The Feminist Press
The City University of New York

The Feminist Press at The City University of New York offers alternatives in education and in literature. We are a non-profit, tax-exempt educational and publishing organization that works to eliminate gender stereotypes in books and schools and to provide literature with a broad vision of human potential. Through publications and projects, The Feminist Press at The City University of New York attempts to contribute to the rediscovery of the history of women in the United States and internationally and the emergence of a more humane society.

The publishing program includes:

• Reprints of important fiction and nonfiction works by women from the United States and around the world;

• The Cross-Cultural Memoir Series (please request separate guidelines about this series);

• Original nonfiction anthologies for use in the women's studies classroom;

• The Women and Music Series and the Women and Peace Series;

• Curricular materials;

• *Women's Studies* Quarterly (please request separate guidelines for submission);

• Nonsexist books for children ages 10 and up.

We do not publish original fiction, original poetry, drama, doctoral dissertations, or original literary criticism.

To submit a project, please send a proposal that includes a cover letter outlining the nature, scope, and intended audience of your work; the table of contents and up to thirty sample pages (typed double-spaced); and your resume. Please also indicate how you heard about The Feminist Press.

We retain material that is submitted without an SASE for three weeks only after it has been reviewed, if it is not accepted for publication.

If you have specific questions about our publication policy, we trust you will write to us again. We hope you will find our books interesting enough to order, and that you will also enjoy becoming one of our general supporters. All funds contributed to The Feminist Press at The City University of New York are tax-deductible.

Thank you for your interest in The Feminist Press.

Categories: Feminism—Gay/Lesbian—Literature—Memoir—Multicultural—Reprints—Textbooks—Women's Fiction—Women's Issues—Young Adult

Name: Sara Clough, Assistant Editor
Material: All
Address: 311 E 94TH ST
City/State/ZIP: NEW YORK NY 10128
Fax: 212-348-1241

Books

Fiesta City Publishers
ASCAP

Before submitting material send a *query letter*.

Query should include brief description of work to be submitted.

With music or song submissions 1.) a lead sheet or complete manuscript and 2.) a cassette must be included.

Fiesta City Publishers will consider unique, unusual and well-constructed material in the fields of fiction, nonfiction (how-to books especially) and music and/or songs.

Categories: Fiction—Nonfiction—How-to—Music—Songs

Name: Frank E. Cooke, President
Material: All
Address: PO BOX 5861
City/State/ZIP: SANTA BARBARA CA 93110
Telephone: 805-681-9199

Focal Press
Butterworth-Heinemann

Focal Press publishes textbooks and professional books in photography, broadcasting and communications, cinematography and videography, and theatre. The guidelines below stress the most important components of a proposal. The materials you send will, in part, depend on the nature and stage of your project, which may be anything from an idea to a completed manuscript

Please use our standard Book Proposal form, reproduced below, when preparing your submission. You may complete the form itself or simply use it to structure your presentation, but it is important that you answer every question. The more information you can provide, the better we will be able to assess your project

Please include the following information about your book project.

• Title

• A brief description of the book's aim, scope, reading level, and primary and secondary audiences.

• A table of contents or outline. Please include your thoughts about features such as bibliographies, forewords, and glossaries. Please describe the art that the book will require (line drawings, black-and-white photographs, tables, etc.).

• Market information including information on who will buy it, what avenues exist to reach these buyers, an appropriate price, and competing titles. If the project is a textbook, what specific courses would it be required or recommended for?

• The schedule for completion of the manuscript, including special schedule considerations such as sabbaticals or leaves-of-absence and conferences important to the book's marketing.

• Any particular project needs, such as an unusual trim size, four-color reproductions, unusual research, etc.

Please also include a current resume or curriculum vitae and a sample chapter or samples of your work published elsewhere on related subjects.

Please contact us if you have questions about our publishing program or about preparing a book proposal.

Thank you for your interest in Focal Press.

BOOK PROPOSAL FORM

Note to author: Please attach your current vita or biographical information. BE AS THOROUGH AS POSSIBLE ON ALL YOUR RESPONSES.

Author/Editor:

Affiliation/Address:

Telephone no.:

Fax no.:

Date form completed:

Title:

Subtitle:

Series:

Anticipated, realistic manuscript completion date:

Type of book:

Monograph Textbook Edited Volume Translation Conference Proceedings Handbook Other _____

Level of material:

Undergraduate Graduate Postgraduate Professional Practitioner Other _____

Manuscript specifications:

____ # double-spaced ms pages ____ # tables

____ # line drawings ____ # black & white photos

____ # color photographs

Can manuscript be prepared camera ready? Yes No

Brief description of work:

Marketing information:

1. Primary audience for the book:

Secondary audience:

2. Through what professional societies would it be best to reach the primary audience? Will this book meet industry or training needs? Describe:

3. Competitive books:

4. If a textbook, in what courses would your book be used?

5. What are this book's unique features? Why is your book needed?

Attach an outline or table of contents.

Major subheadings for each chapter will be helpful.

Attach additional information such as sample chapters.

Categories: Nonfiction—Audio—Broadcast—Communication Technology—Film/Video—Multimedia—Photography—Radio—Theatre

Name: Marie Lee, Senior Editor
Material: All
Name: Tammy Harvey, Associate Acquisitions Editor
Material: Photography, Theatre/Live Performance
Address: 313 WASHINGTON ST
City/State/ZIP: NEWTON MA 02158
Telephone: 617-928-2500
Fax: 617-928-2640
Internet: www.bh.com/focalpress

Franciscan University Press

We have prepared the following general description of Franciscan University Press's editorial program, standards, and review procedures for the purpose of clarity. If you are considering having Franciscan University Press publish your work, please read this document and feel free to talk with our director and me or editors.

Standards

The Press publishes material that is consistent with its mission as a Catholic and Franciscan university press-to foster and enhance the moral, spiritual, and intellectual development of its constituents. We exercise high standards with respect to literary quality (i.e., content, readability, and impact), as determined by the editors, and ultimately by the University's Publications Board.

Editorial Program

The Press publishes principally for the serious reader in the following areas of Catholic theology: apologetics; biblical studies; catechesis [teaching on faith (including Mariology) and morals and the application thereof]; Church history; and spirituality, including inspirational books and devotional guides. The Press also considers republication of "classics" currently out of print. Submissions are not invited in the hard sciences, mathematics, poetry, children's books, textbooks, or doctoral dissertations.

Review Procedures

Because we have more submissions than we can pursue, we do not seek reviews of manuscripts that are of little interest or are incompatible with our editorial program; these we reject out of hand as quickly as possible after they are received. By the same token, once we decide to pursue publication, our editors make every effort to find reviewers who will provide fair and constructively critical reviews. Thus we turn to people of standing in the field in question.

Peer review serves two functions: it helps to ensure that only work that meets a certain standard and is suitable for publication receives our imprint; and it provides help and advice for authors who want to ensure that their work realizes its best possibilities. We always secure at least two reviews beyond review by a Press editor of every manuscript under serious consideration. If a work crosses disciplinary boundaries, we seek reviews from scholars in the appropriate fields.

Recommendations for *revisions based on positive reviews* are made to the author(s) or editor(s) [henceforth, "the author"] of a given manuscript; it is expected that the author actively respond to these recommendations, after which the manuscript will again be reviewed. We work with authors as they work to develop their manuscripts when reviews are generally supportive. *A manuscript must be in relatively final form prior to presentation to the University's Publications Board.*

Publications Board

The Franciscan University of Steubenville Publications Board is composed of the University president and members of the University faculty and administration. Board members are appointed by the president and are charged with preserving the integrity of the Press's imprint. No work may be published by the Press without the approval of the Board.

In considering individual manuscripts or projects, the Board sees the following materials: a summary of reviews and the author's response; a curriculum vitae or biographical note on the author; a table of contents; and a brief statement on the general content (and argument) of the book. Dossiers on individual manuscripts are compiled, duplicated, and placed in the hands of members of the Board one week to ten days before each Board meeting to give Board members an opportunity to read and consider the materials carefully. Board members may ask for the opportunity to read all or part of any manuscript scheduled for presentation to the Board as a whole.

Board members also receive a list of manuscripts that have been rejected or withdrawn since the previous Board meeting, so that they may see what projects the Press editors have not chosen to pursue or have lost the opportunity to publish.

The Publications Board meets formally five times per year (Sept., Nov., Jan., March, and May). At each meeting, Press editors present manuscripts, the publication of which we have recommended to the Board. Board members may question the editors about the manuscripts and the Press's decision to pursue publication. The Board then decides, on the basis of the manuscript reviews and the Press's recommendations, whether to authorize publication of each work in question.

Procedures may vary somewhat, given the special needs of particular books or proposals, but the constants in the process are the Press's reliance upon reviews and the necessity of formal Board approval of publication.

Guidelines for Submitting a Manuscript

If after reviewing a copy of our *Editorial Program, Standards, and Review Procedures* you discover your manuscript fits our Editorial Program, please send the following items to the Press:

1. A brief autobiography of no more than one and one half pages, and a curriculum vitae if applicable

2. A copy of the table of contents (and later, if Press requests them, two typed copies of the manuscript)

3. An outline of the manuscript based on the table of contents, in addition to a summary of the manuscript

Also, please be sure to review our *Manuscript Format Requirements* if you anticipate our acceptance of your manuscript. Manuscripts reviewed and accepted for publication must be submitted on disk and adhere to Press's format requirements in order for our editors to begin working on them.

Manuscript Format Requirements
(for mss. accepted for publication)
Submit Manuscript:

• on disk (WordPerfect 5.1 or Microsoft Word 4.0 or higher)
• and two hard copies (photocopies or printouts)

Text Style/Format:

• generally follow *The Chicago Manual of Style* (e.g., lowercase personal pronouns for God); differ on some points (e.g., always uppercase Church in reference to the Catholic Church) [Call us if you have questions.]

Author is responsible for providing:

• all permissions in writing (originals) necessary for reproducing previously copyrighted materials
• title page
• table of contents
• any other preliminaries (dedication, epigraph, preface)
• all text matter
• tables, if any, on separate pages
• notes, or footnotes, created with auto-footnoting or on separate pages
• all end matter (appendixes, bibliography, etc.), except index
• all illustrations, and all permissions, in writing, necessary to reproduce them

Specific Guidelines for Submission to Press Editors for Editing Purposes:

• automatic double-space entire text (do not create any double-spaced sections using the return key)
• chapter titles and subtitles, type with initial capitals only
• do not separate chapters-i.e., at the end of each chapter, simply press the return key once and type the title of the next chapter
• in a manuscript of five or more chapters, create a separate document for each chapter
• after typing a period at the end of each sentence, type one space only
• no boldface
• no italics (if italics is desired, indicate by underlining the pertinent material)
• number pages with automatic numbering only-center numbers at the bottom of each page outside the text margin

Books

• tab indent each paragraph (do not use the space bar to indent)

• leave ragged right edge (do not justify text-the copyeditor will do so after all editing is complete)

• block quotations: indent with automatic indent only (do not use tabs or space bar)

• citing another author's work: supply complete information in parentheses following first quote or reference, including the name(s) of the author(s), editor(s), and/or translator(s), copyright year, name of publisher, edition (if applicable), the number(s) of page(s) quoted, and a *photocopy of the quoted material* for the editor's use.

Categories: Religion

Name: Celeste Gregory, Editor
Material: All
Address: FRANCISCAN UNIVERSITY PRESS
Address: FRANCISCAN UNIVERSITY OF STEUBENVILLE
City/State/ZIP: STEUBENVILLE OH 43952
Telephone: 614-283-6357
Fax: 614-283-6442
E-mail: FUSPRESS@aol.com

Front Row Experience

Perceptual-Motor Development Movement Education
We are only interested in "Movement Education" activities for pre-school to sixth grade teachers. Send a one-page letter of inquiry with proposal. If we are interested, we will request more information, sample activities, manuscript, etc. Do not send unsolicited manuscripts! Call us for more information.

Categories: Education—Movement Education—Physical Fitness

Name: Frank Alexander, Editor
Material: All
Address: 540 DISCOVERY BAY BLVD
City/State/ZIP: DISCOVERY BAY CA 94514
Telephone: 510-634-5710

Gem Guides Book Company

Gem Guides requests a book outline including Table of Contents and two or three sample chapters, along with examples of photos and illustrations that would accompany text. Please include information about the market for the book, how it is differentiated from competitive titles in print on the same topic, and your qualifications to produce a book on the subject.

Categories: Nonfiction—Bead Crafts—Crafts—Hobbies—Lapidary—Native American—Outdoors—Prospecting—Regional (West & Southwest)—Rocks & Minerals—Travel (West & Southwest)

Name: Kathy Mayerski, Editorial Assistant
Material: All
Address: 315 CLOVERLEAF DR STE F
City/State/ZIP: BALDWIN PARK CA 91706
Telephone: 626-855-1611-
Fax: 626-855-1610

The Globe Pequot Press

Thank you for your interest in The Globe Pequot *Press.* As you know, Globe Pequot is primarily a publisher of travel and outdoor recreation guides and would welcome your submission in any of these areas. We sometimes explore the areas of nature titles, selected cookbooks, business books, and how-to guides and would welcome selected submissions in these areas.

Although we do venture into new areas from time to time, we generally do not publish in the categories of fiction, poetry, children's stories, personal memoir or biography.

When submitting a book proposal please send the following:

1. A brief synopsis of the proposed work. The synopsis should include a definition of the book's projected target audience/market and an analysis of competing titles, if any. (The latter can be found by researching *Books in Print.)*

2. A table of contents or outline of the entire book.

3. A biographical statement of your credentials. This statement should explain why you are particularly qualified to undertake the proposed project.

I do wish you the best of luck in your writing ventures. Please allow six to eight weeks for a response to your proposal.

Again, thank you for your interest in Globe Pequot.

Categories: Nonfiction—Adventure—Boating—Business—Careers—Cooking (limited)—Economics—Family—Fishing—Gardening (limited)—History (limited)—Language—Outdoors—Recreation—Regional—Rural America—Sports—Travel

Name: Cindi D. Pietrzyk, Associate Editor
Material: All
Address: 6 BUSINESS PARK RD
Address: PO BOX 833
City/State/ZIP: OLD SAYBROOK CT 04475-0833
Telephone: 860-395-0440
Fax: 860-395-1418
E-mail: cpietrzyk@globe-pequot.com

GOLDEN WEST ☼ PUBLISHERS

Golden West Publishers

Golden West Publishers specializes in cookbooks and books about outdoor recreation (Southwest). Currently we are expanding our cookbook line and are interested in regional titles. We are creating a cookbook for each state as part of our Cooking Across America series and we also want to add regional titles of interest. We prefer buyouts as opposed to royalties. We require a query letter with sample Table of Contents and sample chapter, if possible.

Categories: Cooking—Cookbooks—Regional

Name: Hal Mitchell, Editor
Material: Cookbooks
Address: 4113 N LONGVIEW
City/State/ZIP: PHOENIX AZ 85014
Telephone: 602-265-4392
Fax: 602-279-6901

The Graduate Group

We look for manuscripts that will be helpful to high school, college and graduate students in their attempt to establish themselves in a career, manuscripts which alert students to opportunities and ways to become more effective.

Graduate Group books are distributed exclusively to career planning offices and libraries in the U.S. and abroad.

Authors are provided a liberal royalty.

Categories: Nonfiction—Business—Careers—College—Computers—Crime—Education—Environment—General Interest—Government—Health—Internet—Interview—Law—Law Enforcement—Military—Money/Finance—Nursing—Reference

Name: Robert Whitman, Vice President
Material: Any
Name: Mara Whitman, President
Material: Any
Address: PO BOX 370351
City/State/ZIP: WEST HARTFORD CT 06137-0351
Telephone: 860-233-2330

Great Quotations Publishing

Great Quotations seeks **original** material for the following general categories:
* Humor
* Inspiration
* Motivation
* Success
* Romance
* Tributes to mom/dad/grandma/grandpa, etc.

Generally speaking we *do not* currently publish:
* Children's books and others requiring multi-color illustration on the inside
* Novels and other such fiction, or text that is extremely narrative and detailed
* Manuscripts substantially consisting of poetry
* Highly controversial subject matter

Our books are often purchased on impulse. Therefore the material must be simple, concise and a light read. They are also physically small and short in length, and comprise five different formats:

Paperback Books 6"x4½", 168 pp., Retail $5.95
Comb Bound Books 4½"x6", 78 pp., Retail $7.95
Mini-Perpetual Calendars 4"x3¾", 365 pp., Retail $6.50
Large Perpetual Calendars 5½"x4½", 365 pp., Retail $8.95
Hard Cover Books 4"x5½", 64 pp., Retail $6.50

The ideal submission consists of a cover letter explaining the idea and a few sample pages of text. Include two SASEs for both a response and for the return of materials if such is desired. Submissions sent without a SASE are subject to disposal without consideration. We do not respond initially by phone.

We publish new books twice a year, in January and July. Submissions are usually reviewed approximately six months prior to publishing deadlines.

As an aside, we do not hire freelance readers/editors.

Thank you, and Good Luck!

The New Product Team at Great Quotations

Categories: African-American—Cartoons—Christian Interests—College—Comedy—Education—Entertainment—Ethnic—Family—General Interest—Humor—Inspirational—Lifestyles—Marriage—Parenting—Regional—Relationships—Romance—Senior Citizens—Spiritual—Women's Issues

Name: Patrick Caton, Senior Editor
Material: All
Address: 1967 QUINCY CT
City/State/ZIP: GLENDALE HEIGHTS IL 60139
Telephone: 630-582-2800
Fax: 630-582-2813

Gryphon House

GRYPHON HOUSE publishes books of active educational experiences for preschool children (ages 1 to 5). We *do not* publish paper and pencil activity books; activity books that involve cutting out patterns and pasting them on paper; ditto books, or books about microcomputers (or worse, television) and preschoolers. *We do not publish children's books at all.*

We are looking for books of creative, participatory learning experiences that have a common conceptual theme to tie them together. The hooks should be on subjects that teachers want to do on a daily basis in the classroom. If a book caters to a particular market in addition to teachers, that would be a plus.

BEFORE YOU SUBMIT YOUR BOOK

Research your competition. Find and review books similar to yours. You can find books in the library, *Books In Print* and teacher and school supply stores. How are they selling?

Identify your market. Is there a need for another book on your topic? Why? Describe specifically what your book does that others do not. What makes your book unique?

DESCRIBE THE BOOK

We prefer to receive a letter of inquiry rather than a manuscript. Include the proposed title, the purpose of the book, table of contents, introductory material, and a dozen or so pages of the actual activities.

Why is this a book which teachers already probably want to own? Is it one they will use every day?

Who has reviewed or tested your book? Classes or workshops you have led? Experts in the field? We are not terribly interested in knowing how your children, or teachers with whom you work have liked the material. We would, however, be most interested in knowing how the material was tested by teachers with whom you had no direct contact.

TELL US ABOUT YOURSELF

What is your background? Why did you write this book? How are
you qualified to write this book? Any previous publications? How will you be able to promote your book? Workshops at professional meetings? Active demonstrations at book stores and school supply stores? What else?

WHAT SHOULD YOU SEND US?

Please write a letter answering the questions above. Also include a copy of the table of contents and a dozen or so pages of activities.

If we accept a book for publication, our first choice is for it to be written on a personal computer with a word processing program. Our favorite computer would be one that is IBM compatible, and our favorite word processing program is Microsoft Word for Windows.

Categories: Nonfiction—Education—New Age—Paranormal—Parenting

Name: Kathy Charner, Editor-in-Chief
Material: All
Address: PO BOX 207
City/State/ZIP: BELTSVILLE MD 20704
Telephone: 301-595-9500
Fax: 301-595-0051-
E-mail: Kathy@ghbooks.com
Internet: www.ghbooks.com

Hancock House

Hancock House requires the following for reviewing prospective manuscripts:
• A brief (one or two page) synopsis of the proposed manuscript.
• An account of any miscellaneous support information, such as the writer's expertise, or any marketing advantage inherent to the manuscript.
• A sample of the writer's work, such as a chapter from the work in question.
• Enclose your phone number as well as address.
Hancock House Titles
Our titles are predominantly as follows:
Pacific Northwest history and biography, nature guides, and native culture; and international natural history, biological science, and conservation biology including aviculture and animal husbandry.
Manuscript Format
We require both a computer disc, DOS format, and a hard copy.
Categories: Nonfiction—Animals—Aviation—Biography—Birds—Conservation—Outdoors—Pacific Northwest

Name: Editor
Material: All
Address: 1431 HARRISON AVE
City/State/ZIP: BLAINE WA 98230
Telephone: 604-538-1114
Fax: 604-538-2262
E-mail: hancock@uniserve.com

Harlequin Historicals
An Imprint of Silhouette Books

Thank you for your interest in Harlequin Historicals.
The primary element of the Harlequin Historicals is romance. The story should focus on the characters and how their love for one another changes their lives forever. For this reason, it is important that you have an appealing and believable hero and heroine, and that their relationship is compelling. The conflicts your characters must face and overcome can be as varied as the setting, but there must be a dynamic spark between your hero and heroine that keeps your reader interested.
The overall tone of the stories may vary. Some will be more humorous and entertaining; some more adventurous; others more dramatic and emotional. It's up to you, however, there is no better way to determine what we are looking for than reading our books.
Time period and setting are the author's preference. *However, we are not looking for manuscripts set in the 20th century.* Period, place, and cultural events are vital to creating an historical feel. They should be well developed, authentic and enrich your story, but be sure to avoid travelogue descriptions. Your characters must make history come alive.
The length of a Harlequin Historical is generally 95,000 to 105,000 words, but we will also consider longer books.
If you are not published in the historical romance genre, please submit a complete manuscript. If you are published, you may send us a partial with a cover letter, a two-page synopsis and any pertinent information about your writing experience.
HARLEQUIN SUBMISSION GUIDELINES
This Tip sheet will give you some tips but no easy answers. *There is no "formula" to writing a publishable romance novel.*
With your query, please send a clearly written one or two page synopsis. The query letter should include a word count, and pertinent facts about yourself as a writer and your familiarity with the romance genre. The synopsis should discuss your characters, their conflicts, and the setting. A self-addressed stamped envelope will ensure a reply.
When you send us your project, please note the following:
1) We publish only romances! Please do not submit any other type of fiction or non-fiction.
2) All material should be the author's own original work.
3) When you send in a complete manuscript, please include a synopsis.
4) *Do not* submit your material bound. Secure with rubber bands. Cover sheets must have your complete name, address and phone number. Each page should be numbered sequentially, with your name and title in the upper left-hand corner.
5) All material *must* be typewritten. No disk submissions. A dot matrix copy material is acceptable, but it must be letter quality, and the pages *must* be separated.
6) All material will be evaluated in as timely a fashion as volume allows. Please do not call regarding the status of your manuscript. You will be notified by mail as soon as your work has been reviewed.
7) Do not send any material that is being considered by another publisher. "Multiple submissions" are not accepted.
Mark your submission "Historical."
Categories: Fiction—Romance—Women's Fiction

Name: Tracy Farrell
Name: Margaret O'Neill Marbury
Name: Karen Kosztolnyik
Name: Deborah Beaudry
Address: HARLEQUIN HISTORICALS
Address: 300 E 42ND ST 6TH FLOOR
City/State/ZIP: NEW YORK NY 10017
Telephone: 212-682-6080
Fax: 212-682-4539

Harvest House Publishers

Thank you for your interest in Harvest House Publishers. We are pleased to provide this information regarding our publishing objectives and marketing philosophy. **Read over it carefully before you submit your material. If your manuscript is not within our guidelines, then we suggest you contact other publishers.**
"Books That Help the Hurts of People"
1) Harvest House Publishers is a strong evangelical Christian publishing company which is progressive and eager to proclaim the Gospel of Jesus Christ, even though sometimes in only parts of a book. Our goal is to publish books which will encourage the faith of our readers and turn their attention to Jesus Christ as the answer to the problems and questions of life. The foundation of our publishing program is to publish books that "help the hurts of people" and nurture spiritual growth.
2) Harvest House also publishes study books, Bible-related material, topical, contemporary, and fiction works which have a

message to promote the Gospel.

3) We seek exceptional manuscripts which are original, relevant, well-written, and grounded in the teachings of Scripture.

Guidelines for Manuscript Submission

Many publishing houses are quite general in their line of publication, but we have specialty books that "help the hurts of people" and help men, women, and children grow spiritually strong. We publish books with a biblical emphasis and fiction with a Christian theme or message consistent with Scripture.

Harvest House Book Subjects

Adult fiction Counseling Marriage
Biblical study Cults Prayer
Bible study aids Devotions Stewardship
Bible study methods Discipling Theology
Bible teaching Ethics Witnessing
Christian education Evangelism Women
Christian living Family life
Contemporary issues Leadership

Harvest House does not publish poetry or short stories, cookbooks, sheet music, theses or dissertations, biographies, autobiographies, sermon collections, or booklets.

Instructions for submitting a manuscript:

1) Pages should be numbered consecutively throughout the manuscript-not by chapters.

2) All Scripture references in the manuscript must state the translation or paraphrase from which they were taken.

3) Footnotes must be complete with the author, name of the book, publisher, state where published, copyright date, and page number of quote. The author is responsible for obtaining permissions for copyrighted material that goes beyond the guidelines of "fair use."

4) We prefer that a query letter be sent-that is, one page telling what the manuscript is about, why you wrote it, who it is for (projected audience), and what the benefit will be for the reader. The table of contents and the first two or three chapters can also be sent at this stage. Please include an information sheet about yourself-your spiritual experience, qualifications for writing, educational background, and previous published works, if any.

5) If after receiving this material we are still interested, we will request the remainder of the manuscript for further review.

6) At this point a decision will be made. Once a manuscript satisfies our editorial requirements, we assume all costs of production and distribution. The author receives a royalty on each book sold, the rates being comparable with those paid by other publishers in our industry.

7) Please note that your manuscript will be disposed Of unless you include a SASE with sufficient postage for its return.

We normally respond within two to eight weeks. While each submission is given individual attention, we are unable to critique manuscripts. If you have not heard from us after eight weeks, feel free to write and inquire about the status of your submission. Send all manuscripts to:

Categories: Fiction—Nonfiction—Family—Inspirational—Marriage—Men's issues—Spiritual

Name: Manuscript Coordinator
Material: All
Address: 1075 ARROWSMITH
City/State/ZIP: EUGENE OR 97402
Telephone: 541-343-0123
Fax: 541-342-6410

Hay House, Inc.
Astro Room

Hay House publishes hardcover and trade paperback origi-

nals, and trade paperback reprints. Firm averages 12 titles a year. Receives approximately 1,200 submissions/year. 5% of books are from first-time authors. 25% from unagented writers. Pays standard royalty. Publishes books an average of 8 - 15 months after acceptance. Simultaneous submissions OK. Reports in 4 weeks on queries; 2 months on manuscripts. Free book catalog.

NONFICTION: Self-help, New Age, Sociology, Philosophy, Psychology, and Astrology. Subjects include social issues, current events, ecology, business and economics, foods and nutrition, education/environment, health/medicine, money/finance, nature, recreation, religion, and women's issues/studies. Hay House is interested in a variety of subjects as long as they have a positive self-help slant to them. No poetry, quotation books, children's books, or negative concepts that are not conducive to helping/healing ourselves, or our planet. Query, or submit outline/synopsis and sample chapters.

BEST SELLING NONFICTION TITLES: *You Can Heal Your Life*, by Louise L. Hay (metaphysics/self-help). *Losing Your Pounds of Pain*, by Doreen Virtue, Ph.D.; *As Someone Dies*, by Elizabeth A. Johnson.

TIPS: Our audience is concerned with our planet, the healing properties of love, and self-help principles. Hay House has noticed that our readers are interested in taking more control of their lives. If I were a writer trying to market a book today, I would research the market thoroughly to make sure that there weren't already too many books on the subject I was interested in writing about. Then I would make sure that I had a unique slant on my idea.

Categories: Nonfiction—Astrology—Cooking—Diet—Environment—Feminism—General Interest—Health—Inspirational—Marriage—Men's Issues—New Age—Philosophy—Psychology—Relationships—Self-help—Spiritual—Women's Issues

Name: Jill Kramer, Editorial Director
Material: All
Address: PO BOX 5100
City/State/ZIP: CARLSBAD CA 92018-5100
Telephone: 760-431-7695
Fax: 760-431-6948

Health Communications, Inc.

Health Communications, Inc.

Dear Prospective Author:

Thank you for your interest in Health Communications, Inc. For over two decades, we have enhanced our readers' lives through top-quality books promoting recovery, personal growth, and the enrichment of mind, body and soul. In that time, we have become one of the nation's leading life-issues publishers.

Seven of our over 30 national bestsellers have appeared on the *New York Times* bestsellers list: *Healing the Shame That Binds You* by John Bradshaw; *Adult Children of Alcoholics* by Janet G. Woititz; and five books in the *Chicken Soup for the Soul* series by Jack Canfield and Mark Victor Hansen—*Chicken Soup for the Soul, A 2nd Helping of Chicken So up for the Soul, A 3rd Serving of Chicken Soup for the Soul, Chicken Soup for the Woman's Soul* (co-authored by Jennifer Read Hawthorne and Marci Shimoff) and *Chicken Soup for the Soul at Work* (co-authored by Maida Rogerson, Martin Rutte and Tim Clauss).

Although we have been a forerunner in recovery publishing, we have grown in new directions. Today, recovery/addiction is only one of several categories that comprise our title base. In

Books

addition, we now publish in the following areas: self-help/psychology, health/wellness, soul/spirituality, inspiration, women's issues, relationships, and the family.

To continue our tradition of excellence in publishing, we seek high-caliber authors who produce original material that appeals to a broad readership. We are interested in nonfiction books that emphasize self-improvement, personal motivation, psychological health, overall wellness or mind/body/spirit integration. *We do not publish biographies, autobiographies, poetry, children's books or fiction of any kind.*

Most of our authors are established experts in their fields and, in some cases, already enjoy national recognition. Many of the authors we publish are professional speakers and consultants who conduct workshops, seminars, or training classes regionally or nationwide. Therefore, these authors are well prepared to promote their books successfully.

The publishing process at HCI begins with a book proposal, which is evaluated by our editorial department. To ensure that book proposals are evaluated on an equal basis and that all necessary information is provided, we require prospective authors to follow our submission guidelines in preparing their proposals. Material that does not conform to our guidelines is rejected.

SUBMISSION GUIDELINES

In order to consider publishing a book, we need a book proposal consisting of the elements outlined below. *Do not send a complete manuscript unless asked to do so.* All submissions are evaluated on the basis of content, author credentials and marketability. Submissions that do not conform to these guidelines are rejected.

I. AUTHOR INFORMATION

Send us your bio or curriculum vitae. Include information on professional credentials, current occupation, previously published works, any public speaking or promotional experience you have, and any television or radio appearances you have made.

II. MARKETING DATA

Supply detailed information on the marketability of your book, including:

Target Audience

Who is it? How big is it? How do you know it exists?

Competing Titles

What other books on the same or a similar topic have already been published? How popular are they?

Uniqueness Value

What makes your book interesting and different from others already on the market? Why would readers choose your book over others currently available?

Marketing Plan

How *do* you intend to promote the book? What marketing channels can you propose? Do you have access to any special avenues for marketing the book?

III. MANUSCRIPT SAMPLE

Please send no more or less than the following:

    A. Detailed outline of the book.

    B. Table of contents.

    C. Introduction.

    D. Two sample chapters.

In preparing the manuscript sample, please observe our format requirements (these also apply if you are asked to send a complete manuscript):

Spacing and Type Size: All text, tables and caption material must be double spaced. Use at least 12-point type.

Chapter and Section Titles: All words in these titles should be upper- and lowercase.

Spelling: Use the first spelling listed in the most recent edition of *Webster's New International Dictionary* or *Webster's Collegiate Dictionary.*

Punctuation and Style: Do not use the serial comma. In run-

ning text, numbers below 10 should be spelled out; all others should be written as numerals. Otherwise, refer to the most recent edition of *The Chicago Manual of Style.*

Pagination (applies to complete manuscript only): Pages should be numbered continuously throughout a manuscript, not chapter by chapter.

IV. SASE

Due to new postal regulations, we can no longer use a SASE to return parcels weighing 16 ounces or more. Therefore, we no longer return any submissions weighing 16 ounces or over—even if a SASE is included. *If your parcel weighs 16 ounces or more, neither your submission nor your SASE will be returned.*

We are not responsible for submissions that exceed the returnable weight limit. Include a cover letter containing your name, return address and daytime phone number with your proposal. The cover letter is for our records and will not be returned to you. Send book proposals to the address below.

You should allow a *minimum* of six to eight weeks for a response. During periods when we receive a large number of submissions, response time can be two to three times longer. We consider all book proposals in the order received. We will notify you of our decision by mail. *No phone calls, please.* Calling to check the status of your submission will not expedite consideration of your proposal.

Categories: Nonfiction—Family—Health—Inspirational—Men's Issues—Psychology—Relationships—Spiritual—Women's Issues

Name: Editorial Committee
Material: All
Address: 3201 SW 15TH ST
City/State/ZIP: DEERFIELD BEACH FL 33442
Telephone: 954-360-0909 x404
Fax: 954-360-0034

HEARTS & TUMMIES
COOKBOOK COMPANY
-a Dinky Division of Quixote Press

Hearts 'N Tummies Cookbook Company

• Regional cookbooks, fun cookbooks, special interest cookbooks, offbeat cookbooks and cookbooks particularly suitable for sale at farmers' markets and tourist traps.

• Vary in size from 120 to 500 recipes.

• We would want the product, in final form, to be camera-ready...illustrated, clip art okay.

Categories: Children—Cookbooks—Cooking—Fishing—Food/Drink—Gardening—Hunting—Native American—Outdoors—Regional—Sexuality

Name: Bruce Carlson, President
Material: All
Address: 3544 BLAKESLEE ST
City/State/ZIP: WEVER IA 52658
Telephone: 319-372-7480
Fax: 319-372-7485
Nota bene: Submissions must be camera-ready.

Heinemann
Boynton/Cook, Beeline

Thank you for your interest in Heinemann. We're pleased to send you our guidelines for submitting material for publication.

A Cover Letter

This should tell us something about you as the author behind the manuscript and should be as brief as possible—no more than one page. We receive many manuscripts—you'll want to make your work stand out among the others.

A Formal Proposal

This is a statement describing the purpose of the book, much like the preface to a text. It should offer specific details, including: the objectives and reasons for writing the book; what will make the book stand out among its competition; a comparison of the book to others in the market that resemble it; what you foresee the audience of the book to be; what you think the size of the market will be.

A Complete Table of Contents and Chapter Summaries

This should show all the chapter titles, with short descriptions of what is included in each.

Status of the Manuscript

How long will it take to complete the manuscript? How much is now written and in what draft is the material? How many pages will make up the manuscript? How many illustrations do you think will be included? Please give us the approximate number and type of photographs and line drawings.

Sample Chapters

Select two or three sample chapters that you think will give us a clear idea of the manuscript's content as a whole. These chapters should be an accurate example of how the book will read and should not be limited to the first two or three in the manuscript. For example, you might send in chapter one, which may provide and overview of the project, and one or two later chapters. Double-space all material and include sample of the line art and photocopies (not originals) of photographs or artwork.

Reviewers

You are welcome to suggest names of potential reviewers (along with their addresses and affiliations) whom you feel will give a thoughtful, thorough critique of your work. We may ask them and/or other reviewers of our own selection for written responses. Our policy is to submit the material to one or more reviewers who are actively involved in the field. Please keep in mind that it may take several weeks before the reviewers are able to give us their responses. Our reviewers are, like our authors, busy professionals, and their schedules may prevent them from responding as quickly as they'd like. We have a strict policy of keeping their identity unknown, unless they ask us to specifically reveal their names.

Resume

Although we weigh our decision most heavily on your proposal or manuscript, we also prefer to see a resume or curriculum vitae. We are open to previously unpublished authors.

Categories: Drama—Education—Gay/Lesbian—Multicultural—Parenting—Theatre—Writing

Name: Editorial Department
Material: All
Address: 361 HANOVER ST
City/State/ZIP: PORTSMOUTH NH 03801-3912
Telephone: 603-431-7894
Fax: 603-431-4971

Herbelin Publishing

Guidelines for story submissions:

Our guidelines are very informal. We are simply collecting original, unpublished, workplace-related stories of any size. The stories must be amusing, and our emphasis is on light-hearted humor. Short stories of 1,000 words or more can be fiction or nonfiction—anything that relates to work and is fun to read. For shorter stories, we prefer real-life situations, but are open to anything that is funny.

We pay $25 for stories of fewer than 250 words in length.

We pay $50 for stories from 250 to 999 words in length.

We pay $100 for stories 1,000 words and longer.

Several options are available for submitting stories. They can be submitted via the Internet, using the handy submission form located at our Internet site, by e-mail or by regular mail. Single-spaced, double-spaced or handwritten stories will be accepted, as we are interested in the content of the stories—not the format. Please include SASE for mail reply.

We mail the honorarium within 30 days of our acceptance of the story to the person and address specified by the submitter of the story, and retain all publishing and copy rights to the story. In the event a story is reprinted by another publisher, the original author will receive 50% of any royalties received by Herbelin Publishing.

Original authors retain biographical rights. That is, the original author may use his or her stories at any time in conjunction with any collection of his or her own works, without obtaining advance permission from Herbelin Publishing.

If the submitter offers first or second serial rights only, we will pay an honorarium of ½ of the above-stated amounts if we choose to publish the story.

Stories may sometimes be edited; we will pay according to the edited length of the story.

Selected stories will appear in the book, "It's All Happening at the Zoo!" which is a collection of workplace-related stories and anecdotes. First edition, July 1998; the book will grow with subsequent editions as new stories are added.

Steve Herbelin, editor

Categories: Nonfiction—Business—Humor—Short Stories

Name: Steve Herbelin, Editor
Material: All
Address: PO BOX 74
City/State/ZIP: RIVERBANK CA 95367
Telephone: 209-869-6389
Fax: 209-869-6389
E-mail: herbelin@netfeed.com
Internet: www.netfeed.com/~herbelin/stories.htm

Highsmith Press
Alleyside Press

Our primary interests are library reference and professional books, and instructional resources that aid teachers and librarians in serving youth from preschool through high school. These include reading activity books, storytelling aids, library skills and study guides. Until recently, we also published multicultural picture books for youth, but we are no longer accepting any new manuscripts of that type.

We welcome unsolicited manuscripts, and we seek to reach a decision on each submission or proposal within 60 days. The press has expanded its current list to 120 titles, and we intend to publish approximately 20 new titles a year for the next several years. You can find our most complete catalog, detailed author submission guidelines and a current list of the projects we are interested in publishing through the Internet. Our URL on the World Wide Web is shown below. We do not have any guidelines for photos, although we do consider photos submitted with manuscripts.

You may mail your proposal or manuscript to the address shown below. Please include 1) a cover letter summarizing the project, the potential market, information on the computer software you used to develop the project, 2) a current resume listing your qualifications, and 3) a self-addressed, stamped envelope for returning your manuscript. You can also send an inquiry by e-mail to the address shown below.

The specific terms we can offer authors and illustrators will vary with the nature of each project. However, we provide very competitive royalties and advances, and we emphasize quality design and high production standards. Please call us if you have any questions or concerns.

Categories: Nonfiction—Education—Multicultural—Reference

Name: Donald J. Sager, Publisher
Material: All
Address: PO BOX 800
City/State/ZIP: FORT ATKINSON WI 53538-0800
Telephone: 414-563-9571
Fax: 414-563-4801
E-mail: hpress@highsmith.com
Internet: www.highsmith.com

The Hoffman Press

Our guidelines are simple:
1. Send brief bio.
2. Send contents page.
3. Send two sample chapters, not the whole book.
4. Don't call us. If we are interested or not, we will advise you.

Categories: Nonfiction—Cooking—Food/Drink

Name: R.P. Hoffman, Publisher

Material: All
Address: PO BOX 2996
City/State/ZIP: SANTA ROSA CA 95405
Telephone: 707-538-5527
Fax: 707-538-7371

Holiday House, Inc.

Holiday house is a small independent publisher of **children's books only.** We specialize in quality trade hardcovers from picture books to young adult, both fiction and nonfiction, primarily targeting the school and library market.

We are now especially interested in acquiring picture books, short chapter books, both humorous and serious middle-grade novels, multicultural stories, historical fiction, fantasy for ages 8-12, and exciting nonfiction books for all ages. We are not currently seeking folktales or fairy tales, picture books for the preschool market, or books with a religious theme other than some limited Judaica.

We do accept unsolicited manuscripts and simultaneous submissions. However, we do request that if you are making multiple submissions, you state this in your cover letter.

If you do not include a SASE, your manuscript will be discarded. This policy is strictly enforced

We do not accept certified or registered mail.

Picture Books: Please send a complete manuscript. We do not respond to picture book queries. We do accept artwork with the text as long as they may be considered separately.

Novels: Please send a synopsis and the first three chapters.

Artwork: Please do not submit original artwork or slides; color photocopies or printed samples are preferred. Please send samples that can be kept on file.

Allow 8-10 weeks for a response. A manuscript under serious consideration may require more time. If 10 weeks have passed and you have not received an answer, follow up with a written query, including an SASE. No phone calls please.

Thank you for your interest in Holiday House.

Categories: Children

Name: Acquisitions Editor
Material: All
Address: 425 MADISON AVE
City/State/ZIP: NEW YORK NY 10017
Telephone: 212-688-0085

Horizon Books

Please refer to Christian Publications, Inc.

Howell's House, Inc.
The Compass Press, Whalesback Books

We have no formal, written guidelines. Instead, we ask for a query letter giving a synopsis and description of the work and the qualifications and experience of the author. If we think we might be interested, we will request more information or samples. Ultimately, we will need sample chapters or the entire ms. on 3½" disk formatted in WordPerfect 6.0. Any necessary permissions will be the responsibility of the author.

Thank you for your interest.

Categories: Fiction—Nonfiction—Biography—General Interest—Government—History—Literature—Military—Politics—Public Policy—Science

Name: Acquisitions Editor

Material: All
Address: PO BOX 9546
City/State/ZIP: WASHINGTON DC 20016
Telephone: 202-333-2182
Fax: 202-333-2184

Humanics Publishing Group
Humanics Trade, Humanics Learning

Thank you for considering Humanics as your potential publisher. In order to submit a manuscript to us, please observe the following guidelines and requirements.

A brief summary of the work is as good as the whole manuscript for us to consider it for publication. Please include a resume or curriculum vitae.

A brief discussion of possible marketing and/or targeting strategies for the work: institutional sales, timeliness and topicality, professional acquaintances and organizations available for review, workshops, ideas for publicity, personal plans for promotion, etc.

Full address and telephone number, and preferably the author's name and book title on each page of the manuscript.

Please bear in mind that the review process is a long one. Please write with inquiries about the status of your manuscript. *No phone inquiries.*

Good luck with your proposal and thank you for your interest in Humanics.

Categories: Humanics Trade: Nonfiction—Business—Culture—Education—Ethnic—Feminism—Inspirational—Multicultural—New Age—Paranormal—Religion—Spiritual—**Humanics Learning:** Nonfiction—Children—Crafts—Education—Environment—Parenting—Reference

Name: W. Arthur Bligh, Acquisitions Editor
Material: Learning
Name: Geoffrey Select, Acquisitions Editor
Material: Trade
Address: PO BOX 7400
City/State/ZIP: ATLANTA GA 30357
Fax: 404-874-1976
E-mail: humanics@mindspring.com

Hunter House Publishers
Books for Health, Family and Community

The guidelines below are in two parts: (a) the subject areas we publish in and the kind of books we do; and (1) the kind of proposals we like to see. They reflect our tag line, which is Books for health, family and community, although sometimes it is difficult to keep a clear separation between these three areas.

SUBJECT AREAS
Health and wellness, especially women's health
Our health books focus on emerging or current health issues that may be inadequately covered for the general population. We look for comprehensive, balanced and up-to-date information presented in a clear and accessible manner. The book should describe causes, symptoms, medical theories, current and possible treatments, complementary and alternative therapies, successful strategies for coping, prevention, and so on. Illustrations, sidebars, reading lists, and resource sections that provide additional information or enhance the content are desirable. We specialize in women's health, with sublists on cancer; pregnancy & childbirth; women's health reference; and women's health as a women's issue. We are currently interested in books about aging and complementary therapies. At the top of our health list are

Menopause Without Medicine; Women's Cancers; Running on Empty: The Complete Guide to Chronic Fatigue Syndrome (CFIDS); and *The Women's Health Products Handbook.*

Family: Personal growth, lifestyles, relationships, sexuality
Personal growth topics that we are currently interested in are sexuality; partner and family relationships; and changing, evolutionary lifestyles. Successful titles provide step-by-step aids or a program to help readers understand and approach new perspectives on family issues or dynamics, celebrate their sexuality, and establish healthy, fulfilling lives that incorporate a planetary perspective. Examples include: *Sexual Healing: How Good Loving is Good for You and Your Relationship; Helping Your Child Through Your Divorce;* and *The Pleasure Prescription—A New Way to Well-being.*

Violence prevention and intervention, social justice
We have a small but growing line of books and workbooks, often done in collaboration with nonprofits, which address community issues such as violence prevention, access for people with disabilities, and human rights. They should include clear reviews and explanations, new activities and exercises, provocative insights, and practical theory. Examples are: *Violent No More: Helping Men End Domestic Abuse; Helping Teens Stop Violence: A Practical Guide for Counselors, Educators, and Parents; Computer Resources for People With Disabilities;* and *The Amnesty International Handbook.*

Resources for counselors and educators
Resources for educators are generally specialized curricula that address violence prevention and social justice issues, including *The Uprooted: Refugees and the United States; Human Rights for Children;* and *Making the Peace: A Violence Prevention Curriculum for Young People.*

Books for counselors and helping professionals tend to offer information in new and underexplored fields, such as trauma and crisis in children. Titles include *Trauma in the Lives of Children: Crisis and Stress Management Techniques for Counselors and Other Professionals.*

We are also looking for additions to our Growth and Recovery Workbooks series. These materials are for professional or supervised use with young children who have experienced trauma, abuse, or other critical life events. It is important that they have accompanying guides for the professionals who will use them. Titles include *No More Hurt* and *Someone I Love Died.*

Audience
Our health and family books are meant to appeal to both the general reading public and health care and mental health professionals. They should be written clearly to the general reader, but include enough background explanation, theory, and resources so that they are good references for professionals. This comprehensive approach also ensures that readers can trust the authors as authorities on the topic. It is important that author have credentials and experience within the field. If you do not have this background, it is important that you have a co-author who does. It also helps if a reputable and well-known expert contributes a foreword or the introduction.

Our social issues books should be accessible to lay readers but should speak clearly to the specialized groups involved with the subject on a professional, volunteer, or community basis. Again, we look for credentialed authors with experience and a resource network in their field.

It is crucial that the authors of educational or professional books have credentials and experience within the specific areas they address. We look for a need for information within these areas, and networks through which we can reach the professionals who will use these materials. Endorsements and a preface or foreword from noted individuals within the field are important and helpful.

We do not publish fiction or illustrated books for children.

Books

PREPARING A BOOK PROPOSAL FOR US

A good non-fiction book proposal is made up of the following components: an overview; a chapter-by-chapter outline; about the author(s); and marketing considerations.

The Overview should be a two- to three-page summary of the work: the content, and your presentation and approach. It should include the following:

1. The subject hook, which creates interest in the book, including the title, subtitle, the book's angle on the current market, and approximate length of the book.

2. An anecdote or example that illustrates your theme and its significance.

3. Discussion of the book's other essential ingredients—illustrations, exercises, etc.

4. A foreword, preface, or endorsements for the book written by authorities or celebrities.

The final page of your proposal should discuss the markets for your work, your experience and credibility as an author, and any other information that makes the book unique. Our editors and salespeople must understand why your book should be written. Specify the audience your book will address (women, professionals, tradespeople). Include marketing or promotional ideas you have for getting the book known to your audience. Lastly, list current books that compete with and complement yours.

The Chapter-by-chapter Outline is a 3-6 page outline, including all chapter titles and itemized lists of the major topics or contents of each chapter. Significant illustrations, appendices, and recommended reading should be listed. Work from a table of contents. You should have enough chapters to break up the topic in digestible pieces for the reader, but not so many that the material is scattered. Most books flow from an overall organizing subject or theme—the subject "hook" we ask for in the overview. For example, a book on breast cancer can be organized according to risks and detection, operations and choices involved, and recovery processes. After you complete your table of contents, go on to outline each chapter. Make a brief listing of topics which will be discussed in each chapter, or summarize each chapter in a paragraph.

About the Author: your credentials as evidence you are qualified to write on the subject, and any experience or training that qualifies you especially well for this project. A resume or short biography that includes other publishing experience and media experience is helpful. The more you can tell us about yourself, the more we understand your proposal as a whole.

Marketing and Promotion Information: We look for authors who are positive about and have access to publicity. Explain what you will do to help promote the book. Describe your speaking, mass media, TV, radio, or promotional experience and include a plan of how your work can be promoted. Do you lecture, do seminars, tour, or travel for training and business; do you belong to active organizations and have strong networks; do you teach classes or write a newspaper column; are you prepared to market your materials?

The Review Process

If we are interested in pursuing your project further, we will request sample chapters. Please send only two to three sample chapters—not the whole manuscript. Each chapter should have one concept, subject, skill, or technique. Use main headings and subheads so a reader can know at a glance where the chapter is going.

In a chapter that explains a process or teaches a technique, explain the process step-by-step in exactly the order a reader should follow to understand the process. The general and most important concepts come first, while the exceptions and special considerations come last. Any background information can be explained first or in a separate chapter.

To effectively teach an individual step of a process or technique, follow this sequence: state the rule or instruction first. Be clear and to the point. Then give an example of how someone else did this step. Finally, provide an exercise for the reader to perform. This gives the reader three ways to learn the technique: intellectually by precept, emotionally by example, and experientially by doing.

Sending Us Your Manuscript

After you have done your marketing research and written your chapter outlines, consider whether Hunter House is the right publisher for you. We do not publish fiction, autobiography, or general children's books, so those types of works get returned right away. If you do have what we are looking for, then send it on. Proposals received without an SASE that are not accepted for publication will not be returned or responded to.

We do accept simultaneous submissions and look for computer printouts of good quality, or e-mail. Please inform us if a manuscript is available on computer disk (IBM format is preferable).

Categories: Nonfiction—Diet—Disabilities—Family—General Interest—Growth & Recovery—Health—Inspirational—Lifestyles—Men's issues—Multicultural—New Age—Psychology—Relationships—Self-Help—Sexuality—Spiritual—Teen—Violence Prevention—Women's Issues—Writing

Name: Kiran Rana, Publisher
Material: Any
Name: Dana Weissman, Editorial Coordinator
Material: Any
Address: PO BOX 2914
City/State/ZIP: ALAMEDA CA 94501
Telephone: 800-266-5592
Fax: 510-865-4295
E-mail: editorial@hunterhouse.com
Internet: www.hunterhouse.com

ICS Press

ICS Press is part of the Institute for Contemporary Studies (ICS), a nonprofit, nonpartisan public policy research organization founded in 1974. To fulfill its mission of promoting self-governing and entrepreneurial ways of life around the world, ICS sponsors a variety of work on a wide range of issues, including those in the key areas of entrepreneurship, education, governance and leadership, social policy, and international development.

ICS Press is dedicated to the publication of serious, innovative books that will further understanding of these issues among scholars, policy makers, and the wider community of citizens. The Press has published more than a hundred scholarly books, which include the writings of eight Nobel laureates and have been influential in setting the nation's policy agenda.

The Press welcomes your inquiries and will be happy to review your proposal.

To propose a work for publication by ICS Press, please submit the following documents, in hard copy only:

• A two- to three-page overview of the manuscript (a narrative summary, outline, or detailed table of contents)

• One to three sample chapters, together with scholarly apparatus (if appropriate) for that portion of text

• Brief (one paragraph or less) description of the proposed book's audience/market and appeal

• The author's résumé or curriculum vitae

Categories: Nonfiction—Business—College—Crime—Economics—Education—Environment—Government—Politics—Public Policy—Textbooks

Name: Editor, Acquisitions and Development
Material: All

Address: 720 MARKET ST 4TH FLOOR
City/State/ZIP: SAN FRANCISCO CA 94102
Telephone: 415-981-5353
Fax: 415-986-4878
Internet: www.icspress.com

Ideals Children's Books

Ideals Children's Books accepts *submissions only from agented authors and members of the Society of Children's Book Writers and Illustrators (SCBWI).* Authors who have previously published books may also submit with a list of writing credits. Please become familiar with our publications and the children's market before you submit material.

Accepted Material

We publish fiction and non-fiction picture books for preschool and beginning readers. Book lengths generally are 24, 32, or 48 pages, and vary from 600-2,000 words. We prefer to see the entire manuscript rather than a query letter. Reply time is three to six months. *Please include a self-addressed, stamped envelope (SASE) for a response.*

Preparing Your Manuscript

1. Manuscripts should be typewritten, double-spaced, with at least 1 1/2-inch margins, on white, non-erasable paper. Good photocopies are also acceptable.

2. Document all quotes, statistical information, and unusual facts. Provide photocopies of sources if possible.

3. Simultaneous submissions of book-length manuscripts are acceptable, but please identify them as such in your cover letter.

4. Send manuscripts to the attention of the Copy Editor at the address given below.

5. Include a self-addressed envelope *stamped with appropriate postage* for the return of your manuscript in case it does not suit our editorial needs. Manuscripts which are not accompanied by the appropriate SASE will *not* be returned. If you desire only a reply, just include a standard SASE. If no SASE is included, *no response will be sent.*

Payments and copyrights are determined by contract.

If your manuscript is accepted, Ideals Children's Books retains the right to edit your material as we deem necessary.

Categories: Fiction—Nonfiction—Children's
Name: Copy Editor
Material: All
Address: 1501 COUNTY HOSPITAL ROAD
City/State/ZIP: NASHVILLE. TN 37218
Telephone: 615-254-2480
Fax: 615-254-2405

Ide House

Please refer to Publishers Associates.

IDG Books Worldwide, Inc.
Computer Publishing Group (CPG)

Thank you for your interest in CPG. We welcome your interest and suggest the following guidelines for submission of your manuscript proposal. We are always open to considering new ideas and approaches, particularly due to the constantly evolving areas of information technology for which we publish. We expect that the ways in which people learn to use that technology must evolve also, as should the books which they read.

The Computer Publishing Group Advantage

Our attitude and style have made us the most popular networking publisher. We allow authors to have voice and presence, although we do ask that authors follow guidelines when writing manuscripts in order to make the process more efficient for all involved, thus speeding books to market. The quality and consistency for which we strive in our titles are enabled by the streamlined editorial processes we have designed.

Submitting Your Proposal

Your submission should consist of a cover letter introducing the project, an overview of the book, a detailed Table of Contents and outline with chapter abstracts, marketing information you may have about the topic or category of products, observations you have noted regarding competitive titles, and a brief biography of yourself. Use headers or footers on each page of your submission and include your name, the project title, and page numbers.

The Cover Letter

The purpose of the cover letter is to introduce yourself and your proposal. The cover letter is a summary of the entire proposal and should highlight salient features of the manuscript you intend to write.

The Overview

The overview section describes your vision for the book. This part of the proposal is important, as it gives us an idea of your intended scope and your understanding of the subject. The overview should include a brief description of the title product or products, as well as a description of how you intend to present the material on these products. Is the book to be a tutorial that guides readers step by step through task-oriented instruction? Is the book to be a comprehensive handbook that details everything the user needs to know in order to operate the product? Is the book filled with tips, techniques, or shortcuts for getting the most out of the product? What is the target audience of the book? System administrators? Developers? End-users?

The overview should also explain why there is a need for a book on this topic. There may already be competing titles; if so, tell us how your book is different, why your approach is better, and what features you intend to include that will differentiate it from the others. Keep in mind that we don't make books that are a rehash of manuals; we prefer that our books bring added value to the reader by providing either inside tips, a unique learning approach to the package, relevant software utilities, and so on. If you do intend to include electronic material on disk, or would like to recommend Novell products for the disk, please do so in a separate section and discuss why it adds value.

Parts, Chapter Summaries, and Outline

We would like to see a detailed outline/table of contents in your proposal with a narrative description of the parts and chapters you intend to include. We may receive more than one proposal on a particular topic; each of these could very well have similar outlines that delineate features of the product and how to use them. How *you* propose to discuss those features is what distinguishes your idea from others. We want to see your method of organization and how you plan the content to unfold. You are creating a scenario, not just a proposal, and are telling us how and why you are presenting information to the reader. Why is it you want to make a certain point at a particular time? What will the reader get out of your method of presentation?

Also include an approximate page count for each section. A page estimation can help us determine how deeply you intend to cover each topic. One manuscript page equals approximately one and one-third book pages.

About the Topic or Product

You should also provide information on the topic or product you intend to write about. Is it a new product? A revision? A category of products? Include any information you have on the installed base and trends towards growing interest in the topic or product. If you have read or heard estimates on product distribution, please quote your sources.

Books

Also include any marketing material you may have about the product or category of products you'll be writing about. If you are a consultant, for example, you may have information about the planned use of a particular product on a wide scale. When writing about new software especially, this kind of data could help us determine whether we want to do such a book.

A book is a large investment on our part in time and money. We market our books extensively, and that's why we want as much information as possible on your topic or product. It's possible that you won't be able to tell us more than we already know, but information you provide can be used by sales and marketing to maximize the selling of your book.

Competing titles

We want you to produce a "best of class" book. You should be familiar with other titles in the subject area you are writing on, if there are any. Knowing how other writers present information, as well as their relative strengths and weaknesses can benefit you in your planning.

Author biography

Please provide any information about yourself that we can use to promote you as an "Expert Author." Include any previous writing experience you have and books you have published, as well as pertinent positions you have held, software you have written, and so on.

For More Information

If you need more information on how to submit a manuscript proposal, contact our Acquisitions Editor.

Categories: Nonfiction—Computers—Internet

Name: Acquisitions Editorial Assistant
Material: All
Address: 919 E HILLSDALE BLVD STE 400
City/State/ZIP: FOSTER CITY CA 94404-2112
Telephone: 650-655-3000
Fax: 650-655-3299
Internet: www.idgbooks.com

Impact Publishers®

If you are a professional in the human services who's been working on—or at least thinking seriously about—a book manuscript, and wondering how to connect with the right publisher, this may help.

Impact Publishers, Incorporated

Impact is a small, family-owned and operated publishing firm which has been publishing self-help by qualified human services professionals since 1970. Impact produces up to six new books each year, and has about 40 currently active titles in its catalog. Our purpose is to make the best human services expertise available to the widest possible audience. We are recognized both in the book trade and among human service professionals as an outstanding publisher of self-help materials.

Impact's door is always open to qualified new authors. We invite your written inquiries, and ask that you follow the guidelines presented in this flyer.

Author-Publisher Relations

• We believe an author-publisher relationship should be collaborative, not adversarial.

• The author's job—and it is hard work—is to prepare the best possible manuscript on a subject of interest to a definable audience.

• The publisher's job—it's not easy either—is to help the author "polish" that work for the marketplace, to produce it attractively and appropriately for its audiences, and to place it in the hands of as many buyers as possible through effective marketing.

• Impact, like all legitimate publishers, pays royalties to au-

thors; we do not ask authors to subsidize their books. A modest advance and a royalty of 10 to 15 percent of sales receipts are typical.

• Active authors (those who do workshops, make public and professional presentations, write articles, get media exposure) almost always have the most successful books.

• You need not have a literary agent. We're happy to work with your agent if you have one, but we frequently contract directly with authors.

• If you're writing now, keep your audience in mind, and remember that writing self—help is like talking to clients, but it's not the same. In a book, you must spell everything out clearly, simply, and completely. You won't be there for your readers to ask questions.

Subject Fields and Author Qualifications

Impact Publishers, Inc. publishes only popular psychology and self-help materials written in "everyday language" by *professionals with advanced degrees and significant experience in the human services*. The Impact list is focused in five fields:

• Personal Growth (e.g., emotional development, self-esteem, self-expression, coping with change, individuality, life choices...)

• Relationships (e.g., intimacy, love, marriage, divorce, on-the-job, getting along with others...)

• Families (e.g., children's emotional development and self-esteem, parenting, prevention of sexual assault, child behavior management...)

• Communities (e.g., small groups, leadership, community life, non-competitive games...)

• Health (e.g., stress management, smoking, hearing loss, depression, mental health...)

The Impact Publishers catalog will give you more information about the type of books of interest to us. It will help you determine if your manuscript is likely to fit our list.

Manuscript Submission Procedures

We look at all submitted material.

Your chances of hearing from us promptly are greatly enhanced by the inclusion of a self-addressed stamped envelope.

We love to see initial inquiries which look like this:

1. a brief *letter of introduction*, telling us:
    a. what your book is about,
    b. the audience to whom you've addressed it,
    c. why you're the right person to have written it,
    d. why Impact is the right house to publish it, and
    e. why it's outstanding enough to have a chance when 50,000 other books will be published that year.

2. An *annotated table of contents* (with a paragraph summarizing each chapter)

3. A couple of *sample chapters*

4. A *short resume or curriculum vita* (we don't need your lists of publications in refereed journals and/or presentations at professional meetings—yet).

It'll take us a few weeks (from four to twelve, on average) to respond. Please don't telephone. If you want to be sure we got the manuscript, include a simple response device (postcard, or check-off letter & SASE) with your submission.

Impact's publisher (psychologist Robert E. Alberti, Ph.D.) has written a book for writers of the kinds of books we publish. It's called *Your Perfect Write: The Manual for Self-Help Writers*. Manuscripts which are prepared and submitted in accordance with the guidelines in the book have a much better chance of success here (and elsewhere, so we're told).

Criteria for Manuscript Selection

Since its founding in 1970, Impact Publishers has elected to publish only books which serve human development. A manuscript we select for publication will exhibit a strong combination of the following characteristics:

• it will present a message we believe in.

• it will be a work which, in our opinion, needs to be published.

• it will present practical ideas which an individual, family, group, organization, or community may use to improve its well being in one or more of the following realms: emotional, intellectual, interpersonal/social, physical, political.

• it will fit well into the Impact Publishers catalog of books.

• it will honor the principles set forth in the Universal Declaration of Human Rights (although it need not be a work devoted to human rights per se).

• it will be written in non-academic readable style. We're fond of the saying, "The language of truth is unadorned, and always simple."

• it will be written by person(s) whom we believe to be qualified to speak with authority on the subject.

• it will be more likely to present an integrative perspective than one which reflects a single school of thought regarding human behavior.

• it will be marketable within our means. We have an assertive and effective marketing program which emphasizes publicity, direct mail, limited advertising, and energetic author activity. We do not send authors on extensive personal appearance tours.

• it will have promise of selling enough copies—at a fair price—to pay its own way.

Categories: Nonfiction—Family—Health—Human Services—Relationships—Self-Help

Name: Acquisitions Editor
Material: All
Address: PO BOX 1094
City/State/ZIP: SAN LUIS OBISPO CA 93406
Telephone: 805-543-5911
Fax: 805-461-0554
E-mail: BooksWithImpact@compuserve.com

In Print Publishing
Experiences Through Sight & Sound

In Print publishes nonfiction books for a general sophisticated audience.

In these most difficult times of change the manuscript must be able to leave a reader with a positive message of HOPE or have impact for timely issues.

In Print does consider some metaphysical books but we will not consider any personal journey to awakening or any channeled material. Our editorial staff will only consider *how-to* books and other general manuscripts in the metaphysical genre.

At the present time there is no reading fee.

Submit letters of query or submissions with synopsis, three chapters and a bio of the author. In Print will respond in eight to ten weeks.

I wish you every bit of success in finding a publisher for your work. GOOD LUCK

Sincerely,
Tomi Keitlen
Publisher

Categories: Nonfiction—Biography—Business—Cartoons—Dance (Video)—Disabilities—Film/Video—General Interest—Health—History—Inspirational—Money/Finance—Native American—New Age—Politics—Relationships—Spiritual

Name: Tomi Keitlen, Publisher
Material: General Interest—Eclectic
Address: 6770 W HWY 89 & 46
City/State/ZIP: SEDONA AZ 86336
Telephone: 520-282-4589

Fax: 520-282-4631

Innisfree Press
A Call to the Deep Heart's Core

STEP 1: Send us your proposal.

It is our policy to review proposals before we review completed manuscripts. Please send the following information:

• proposed working title

• why you want to create this book who the intended audience is and what your work offers that audience

• what the potential competition is and what your work offers that is unique

• brief overall description of your book

• chapter outline and synopsis of each chapter

• one chapter of your manuscript or

• a short sample of similar writing style

• significant illustration or appendices that would be needed

• anticipated length

• anticipated completion date

• information regarding your computer and word-processing format (would you be able to send us the manuscript on a disk?)

• your credentials for writing this book

• brief summary of your previous publications

If we invite you to submit a manuscript, we require 2 typed copies. It will take approximately 6 weeks to make our final evaluations for editorial, financial, scheduling, and marketing feasibility.

STEP 2: Sign the contract.

Contract: If your proposal fits our catalog, we will issue our standard royalty contract; royalties are paid quarterly. Please note that no work will begin on your project until all contracts have been signed.

Permissions: If your work involves previously copyrighted material, it is *your* responsibility to write the copyright owners for permission. All permission fees will be paid in advance by Innisfree Press but will be deducted from your future royalties. We will be happy to discuss with you problems/alternatives regarding copyrighted material.

STEP 3: Join our pre-press team.

The process of getting your book into print normally takes 12 months, and during that time you become an integral part of our team. You will be given a proposed production schedule and asked for your full cooperation.

Substantive Editing (20 weeks): We will be collaborating very closely with you during this developmental editing phase to work through mutually-agreed-upon structural and content revisions.

Copyediting (10 weeks): We will need your complete manuscript on a computer disk, along with a hardcopy printout, before we can begin the copyediting phase. You will be asked to check and approve the final copyedited version before we go to typeset.

Cover Design: We will be producing cover art for your book during the editing phases so that it will be ready in time for ad-

Books

vance promotions and catalogs

Typesetting, Proofs, and Corrections (10 weeks): You will have an opportunity to correct typeset page proofs, which will also be mailed simultaneously to advance reviewers who have agreed to "blurb" the book. You will also see copies of the final pages before we go to press. However, the options for author changes (other than to correct typesetting errors) are extremely limited at this final stage.

Printing/Shipping (12 weeks): It is important to us that we honor our promised release dates, so we allow a generous amount of time for printing and shipping to circumvent any delays that might be beyond our control. We print our books within the United States and endeavor to use ecologically-sound materials.

STEP 4: Join our marketing team.

Innisfree Press is distributed to trade bookstores through Consortium Book Sales and Distribution. We will be working closely with you to send press releases, flyers, catalogs, announcements, and sales kits to the media and key contacts. We also exhibit at major book conventions, present new titles twice a year at New York sales conferences, and endeavor to set up appearances that coincide with your travel schedule. In addition, we have a quarterly newsletter that we send to a growing mailing list of interested buyers, supporters, and reviewers.

Acquaint yourself with Innisfree Press.

All Innisfree Press (formerly LuraMedia) titles include a spiritual dimension. We are particularly interested in these topics:

Spiritual Perspective
• of everyday living
• of feminine development
• of relationships and sexuality
• of aging

Spiritual Study
• a new look at Scripture
• a new look at faith

Spiritual Nourishment
• through prayers and meditations
• through parables, fables, and story
• through the arts and creativity

Spiritual Action
• in the home and family
• in the workplace
• in the local and global community

Our audience includes:
• therapists
• educators
• ministers
• artists, writers, musicians
• women's groups
• support groups
• church groups
• college classes
• individuals interested in personal growth

Innisfree Press Highlights
Bestsellers:
• *Circle Of Stones* (Judith Duerk)-over 165,000 sold
• *Just A Sister Away* (Renita J. Weems)-over 75,000 sold
• *Guerrillas Of Grace* (Ted Loder)-over 55,000 sold

Award-Winning Books: Top finalists in the Publishers Marketing Association Benjamin Franklin Awards competition have included:
• *The Bridge To Wholeness* (Jean B. Raffa)
• *It All Begins With Hope* (Ronna F. Jevne)

Award-Winning Artwork: Many of our books feature artwork from award-winning watercolorist Sara Steele.

Categories: Nonfiction—Relationships—Spirituality—Women's Issues

Name: Acquisitions Editor

Material: All
Address: 136 ROUMFORT RD
City/State/ZIP: PHILADELPHIA PA 19119
Telephone: 215-247-4085
Fax: 215-247-2343
E-mail: InnisfreeP@aol.com

Intercontinental Publishing
New Amsterdam Publishing, Inc.

TO: WHOM IT MAY CONCERN
FROM: H.G. (Dutch) Smittenaar, Publisher
REF: WRITER'S GUIDELINES

In order to be considered, please submit the following:
1. Synopsis (about 2 pages maximum) of your book.
2. At least one (1), but no more than 3 *sample* chapters.
Additional suggestions:

Additional material may, or may not be requested, but final manuscript should be on disk in either WordPerfect 5.1 or ASCII. Text should contain *no codes* other than Tab [TAB], Underline [UND][und] to indicate italics and [RETURN]. *Do not* load any (unnecessary) parameters at beginning of manuscript, or repeat a lot of "macros" throughout text. *Do not* paginate, and do NOT add "headers" and/or "footers."

Material should be original and above all, should be *entertaining*. Use proper English and grammar. Do not use slang, vulgarisms or contractions (I'll, you'd, we're, etc.) in narrative and/or descriptive text unless book is written in the *first* person.

For *spoken* text (i.e. text within quotation marks ("/") almost anything goes, but Publisher frowns on the gratuitous use of vulgarisms, unless it is clearly a characteristic of the person (or character) speaking (being quoted).

We (me, myself and I) are a very small publisher and we will respond to *all* inquiries as soon as possible, but are not bound by a specific time frame. We *only* publish books in the spring of each year, therefore only submissions made (*and* accepted) *before* the 4th of July, will be published the next spring.

Our books are manufactured in the United States and distributed by Independent Publishers Group (IPG) in Chicago.

Thank You and Good Luck!

Categories: Mystery

Name: H.G. Smittenaar, Publisher
Material: All
Address: 6451 STEEPLE CHASE LN
City/State/ZIP: MANASSAS VA 20111-2611
Telephone: 703-369-4992
Fax: 703-670-7825
E-mail: icpub@worldnet.att.net

Intercultural
P R E S S

Intercultural Press

The Intercultural Press publishes books which focus on cross-cultural interaction-the interaction of people who come from different cultural backgrounds. These books are directed at readers who (1) have administrative, training, or other responsibilities relative to programs and operations which involve cross-cultural interaction, (2) are engaged themselves in cross-cultural interaction, or (3) are teachers, researchers, or students of cross-cultural interaction. This focus includes multiculturalism and diversity in the U.S. as well as international cross-cultural relations.

The Intercultural Press would like to see queries or proposals. A query is a one-page letter briefly describing the prospective submission. It enables us to give you a quick indication of whether or not we would like to see a formal proposal.

Alternatively, you may begin by submitting a proposal, which should consist of three parts.

1. A two- or three-page prospectus (a) describing the subject and content of the book, (b) defining the potential audience or market for the book, (c) differentiating the proposed book from similar books currently in print, and (d) stating your qualifications for writing or editing the book.

2. An outline or tentative table of contents.

3. Your resumé.

Some areas in which we have particular interest at the present time are as follows:

1. Analyses of intercultural communication and cross-cultural adaptation from both a general perspective and relative to specific other countries and cultures. Included here is our InterAct Series, each volume of which focuses on interaction between Americans and the people of another country (example:

With Respect to the Japanese: A Guide for Americans) or between people of different cultural backgrounds in the U.S. [Refer to the separate general guidelines for the InterAct Series below.]

2. Basic conceptual works that provide a framework for comprehending intercultural issues aimed at the general reader or which may be adopted as textbooks at the college level (example: *American Cultural Patterns: A Cross-Cultural Perspective).*

3. Materials for international cross-cultural training or diversity training of any kind, including self-assessments, simulations, videos and activities; for example, *Developing Intercultural Awareness* and *Global Winners* (activities), *Barnga* (simulation), and *Cold Water* (video). The written materials may be full-length books or shorter pieces for inclusion in a volume in an Intercultural Press series.

Some of the subjects we are particularly interested in-all from an intercultural perspective-are business operations and negotiations; education; counseling and health care; multicultural education; and diversity in work, educational, and other settings.

Many of our titles have a strong practical orientation and are cast in a how-to format (example: *Survival Kit for Overseas Living),* offer special guidelines on cross-cultural adaptation (example: *Moving Your Family Overseas),* or focus on a subject in a way that allows the reader to extract practical guidelines for dealing with cross-cultural relationships (example: *The Art of Crossing Cultures).* We also publish books which provide basic conceptual or theoretical models and frameworks that can be applied in practice (example: *Understanding Cultural Differences).*

Guidelines for Writing a Volume in the
Intercultural Press InterAct Series

The purpose of an InterAct is to provide readers with a succinct guide to interacting with people from a specific other culture. It does so by examining the nature of the two cultures, identifying the differences between them, and laying out the implications of these differences for cross-cultural interaction. The theories on which this analysis is most often based are derived from the works of Edward T. Hall (see our publication *Understanding Cultural Differences* for a useful summary of his ideas) and from Edward C. Stewart and Milton J. Bennett's *American Cultural Patterns.* But an InterAct is not an academic or theoretical treatise.

InterActs are designed for people who are involved in cross-cultural interactions: business executives, professional people of all sorts, managers and administrators of international organizations, foreign service and technical assistance personnel, educators and students (including those who study abroad), international volunteers, and others.

In the examination of each of the cultures (the "target" culture and the United States), emphasis is on the target culture and on the contrast between the two cultures. An InterAct attempts to capture the particular mindset or worldview of each culture as it is manifest in its assumptions, values, patterns of behavior, ways of thinking, and styles of communication. An InterAct addresses what actually happens, and why, when people of two cultures come together, and it makes specific recommendations for managing interactions with people of the other culture most effectively.

Dialogues, anecdotes and stories of actual encounters or misunderstandings are often effective ways to get the message across or to bring out cultural contrasts. A discussion of the language and characteristic phrases and idioms can also help illuminate the subject. We want the readers to be able to spot differences in perception, behavior, communicative style, and patterns of thinking and respond to them in ways that are comfortable and productive. There are frequently two or three fundamental traits in any given culture which are especially characteristic of and central to an understanding of it. Examining these with some care lends particular substance and richness to an InterAct.

Special attention is usually given to conducting business in the target culture—establishing contact, negotiating agreements, developing positive relationships, and managing the workplace (although the author may also focus on other kinds of organizational or institutional settings where cultural encounters occur).

Sources from which information is derived or quoted should be cited, and a short bibliography and/or resource list included. InterActs usually range from thirty to forty thousand words, but they may run longer if the author feels the subject warrants a more lengthy treatment. This is especially true when the InterAct involves a region or a large country.

We suggest you use one or more of the published InterActs as models, but we do not expect InterActs to slavishly imitate each other. We suggest, therefore, that you let the InterAct concept evolve in whatever direction you feel best captures the essence of the interactive process between the cultures and best realizes the overall aim of the InterAct series.

To the degree that the InterAct can be written so as to be of interest to both cultures, all the better. In most of the InterActs we publish, however, the emphasis is on their usefulness to the American and, when the contrast is with a non-Western culture, to the Western European reader as well.

Benjamin Broome, in the preface to his Greek InterAct *(Exploring the Greek Mosaic),* has insightfully captured the challenge faced by the InterAct author:

Making generalizations about Greeks is not an easy task. I am sure that many Greek readers will disagree with some of the statements I have made about their culture. The difficulty of describing cultural patterns in a manner that does not distort reality is one that challenges any writer who dares to enter a world that is not his or her own. Generalizations are inherently misleading, yet without them the human mind cannot survive the onslaught of incoming stimuli that results from new experiences. This creates a dilemma about how best to present observations and hypotheses about other cultures.

My own response to this issue is not a simple one, but it allows me to seek general cultural patterns while avoiding putting individuals into preconceived molds or stereotypes. The key lies in learning what it is that people in the society consider *appropriate* and *acceptable.* In those cases when I am talking with some-

Books

one who does not exhibit a particular cultural attitude or behavior, he or she may nevertheless consider it appropriate and acceptable for others to do so. If several people are surprised by a conclusion that I have formed about the culture, then it is likely that I am mistaken. If there is general consensus, however, that such an attitude or behavior is appropriate and acceptable within the society, then I can be more confident in making a statement about cultural characteristics. I believe it is best to view culture as a vast reservoir of values, attitudes, and communication patterns that exist within a society, and from which its people obtain the nourishment that shapes their own worldview and their understanding of what is appropriate behavior.

Note: The Intercultural Press is now developing an InterAct Series on cultural diversity in the United States. In this series we are looking for manuscripts which analyze and provide practical guidelines for interaction among U.S. culture groups. We are particularly interested in books focusing on relationships between a single ethnic minority or identifiable nonethnic culture group and the majority culture. We would be willing to consider, however, proposals for books that examine intercultural relations in the United States from other perspectives, for example, *between* minority cultures.

An InterAct with a domestic focus will, of course, vary from one with an international focus. While we expect significant attention to be given to work and workplace issues, for instance, there is less of a "doing business in" emphasis. The analysis falls wholly within the domain of multiculturalism (interethnic/intergroup relations) in the United States. It examines contrasting values, communication styles, mindsets and traditional behaviors and covers such issues as prejudice, stereotyping, and status differences in the educational and work settings.

Categories: Nonfiction—African-American—Asian-American—Business—College—Culture—Education—Ethnic—Film/Video—Intercultural Communication—Multicultural—Textbooks

Name: Judy Carl-Hendrick, Managing Editor
Material: All
Address: PO BOX 700
City/State/ZIP: YARMOUTH ME 04096
Telephone: 207-846-5168
Fax: 207-846-5181
E-mail: interculturalpress@internetmci.com

International Foundation of Employee Benefit Plans

How To Submit Your Ideas for Publication
1. Send your proposal

Please send proposals to the Publications Department. We make our initial decisions based on brief outlines. If you are interested in writing a book, please submit a one-to-four page typed outline. Indicate the nature and scope of each chapter as well as significant appendixes. Also tell us:
• Your proposed title
• Anticipated length of manuscript
• Titles of any previous books or articles
• Briefly why your treatment of the subject will be unique
• Briefly where/how you will collect and verify the factual information that you will be including
• Briefly why you are particularly qualified to write a book on this subject.

Be sure to include your complete address and telephone number.

2. What happens next?

You may anticipate our initial response to your proposal within one month. We will tell you if we feel that the proposed book is appropriate for our audience. If we are potentially interested in publishing the book, we will send you an autobiographical questionnaire that will help us in preparing future promotional material. At that time, we may request samples of your previous work.

Next, we will begin our formal review process. One step of the process is to submit the proposal to our Executive Committee for final approval. We will inform you of their decision as soon as possible after their review.

3. Sign a book agreement

Our basic agreement gives the author a standard royalty from our net receipts (after discounts and refunds) from all of our sales of the book. There is also a standard royalty paid for each copy of the work distributed without charge (excluding those distributed for advertising/promotional purposes and the copies provided to the author).

We will also require you to sign a copyright transfer agreement that will enable us to disseminate the work to the fullest extent.

4. What about the manuscript?

A completion date for the final version of your manuscript will be specified in your contract. Failure to meet this deadline could result in delays in publication or production.

Please submit your manuscript on diskette along with the hard copy. The diskette must be a 3.5" high density disk. If using a word processing system other than WordPerfect, use an IBM format and save the document as text.

After the book agreement has been signed, we will send a more detailed list of suggestions for submitting your manuscript.

5. Work with us

We will keep you informed of the schedule for publication of your book. An editor assigned to the project will keep you informed of our progress, give you suggestions for possible improvements, clear any major revisions with you, and seek your input for possible ideas for marketing and promotion of the book.

Learn about the Foundation

Since 1954 the International Foundation of Employee Benefit Plans has been recognized as the foremost educational association in the employee benefits field. The International Foundation is a nonprofit organization offering educational programs, publications, information services, the Certified Employee Benefit Specialist (CEBS) Program and a student intern program.

The International Foundation continuously examines the latest issues and trends in the employee benefits field, and publishes in-depth reports, studies, survey results, periodicals and books for both the benefits professional and the general consumer.

Categories: Nonfiction—Employee Benefits

Name: Dee Birschel, Senior Director of Publications
Material: All
Address: PO BOX 69
City/State/ZIP: BROOKFIELD WI 53008-0069
Telephone: 414-786-6710 x8240
Fax: 414-786-2990
E-mail: books@ifebp.org
Internet: www.ifebp.org

Ivan R. Dee, Inc.
Publisher

If you wish to inquire about our interest in a book manuscript you have prepared or are preparing, please send a query letter along with a brief description of the work, if possible a listing of contents or chapters, and at least two sample chapters. If you simply have an idea for a book, write us about it in detail.

Ordinarily you will hear from us within thirty days—sooner

if the manuscript is clearly not for us, occasionally later if the work presents a difficult publishing decision.

We are publishers of serious nonfiction, in both hardcover and paperback, in history, politics, literature, biography, and theatre.

Categories: Nonfiction—Biography—History—Literature—Politics—Theatre

Name: Ivan R. Dee, President
Material: All
Address: 1332 N HALSTED ST
City/State/ZIP: CHICAGO IL 60622
Telephone: 312-787-6262
Fax: 312-787-6269

Jason Aronson, Inc.
Judaica

Dear Jason Aronson Author:

We are pleased to be sending you the enclosed Guidelines for Authors. They were developed to help you prepare your manuscript for publication. Please follow them carefully to ensure that your submission will not be rejected for technical problems.

Attached are instructions on:
- General Format
- Front Matter
- Tables and Illustrations
- Permissions
- Index
- Footnotes and References
- Guidelines for Disk Usage
- Manuscript Checklist
- Submission
- Sample Footnotes and References

If you follow the guidelines and your manuscript is accepted, please be patient. The evaluation process takes several weeks to several months. Once this process is completed, the production department will contact you and begin the task of guiding you and your manuscript to publication.

Sincerely,
Steven Palmé
Director of Editorial Production
Manuscript Preparation
General Format

The following basic guidelines are essential to the preparation and acceptance of your manuscript. Please follow them carefully. If they are not followed you may submit a manuscript with problems that will cause the production department to reject it and you will have to reformat and resubmit your book.

1. It is necessary to double-space everything, including footnotes, references and bibliographies, and quoted material. A manuscript that does not follow this most basic format will be rejected immediately and without question.

2. Number Pages Consecutively. In the upper right-hand corner, number pages *consecutively* from start to finish. Do not number pages by chapter or section.

3. Do not staple or bind your pages. Simply rubber-band them securely.

4. Submit a disk with your manuscript whenever possible. A disk will make the process of publishing your manuscript much less error-prone when the pages are being typeset. Note: if you do submit a disk, see the instructions included in this packet for electronic submissions.

5. Style. If you have questions about style, refer to the Chicago Manual of Style (14th ed.). It is our House Style Manual and what our copyeditors will be using when they edit your manuscript.

6. Photocopied Material. If you are including photocopied material from other sources, make sure these copies are clean and readable. Paste or tape them securely to 8-1/2x11 sheets of paper.

Front Matter

Front matter is all material that appears in a book before the text proper. It is submitted to the publisher at the same time as the text.

Essential front matter includes:

1. A Title Page with your name written *exactly* as you wish it to appear on the book, and the complete working title and subtitle (if any).

2. A complete and detailed Table of Contents.

3. A List of Contributors: If you are preparing a contributed book (with chapters written by different authors), you must include a list of contributors along with a one-sentence bio.

Optional front matter that you may want to include:

Dedication, list of illustrations, list of tables, preface, acknowledgments (which may be part of your preface), and introduction.

If you wish to include any of these elements in your finished book, they must be submitted with the completed manuscript.

Tables and Illustrations

Tables and illustrations must be discussed and approved by the publisher before the completed manuscript is accepted. They will be added at a later date only at the publisher's discretion. Tables and illustrations should always enhance or increase understanding of, not duplicate, the text.

1. **Type tables double-spaced** on sheets of paper separate from the text and number them individually for each chapter (chapter number, then table number within chapter-for example, Table 2-1, Table 2-2, and Table 3-1).

2. **"Illustrations" includes:** charts, graphs, and photographs. They should be numbered consecutively using Arabic numbers, throughout the chapter, (e.g. Figure 7-1, Figure 7-2, Figure 7-3, and Figure 9-1).

3. **Illustrations must be camera-ready.**

4. **Photographs** should be black-and-white glossies and **Drawings** must be black and white.

5. **Be sure to indicate the *exact* placement of tables and illustrations in the text.** We will be unable to use them if you do not.

6. **Identify each illustration** on the back by figure and page number, and your name, either written or attached with an adhesive label.

7. **Hebrew text:** Hebrew is included only by prior agreement with the publisher. If it is incorporated into the text itself; it must be typed. Handwritten Hebrew will not be accepted. Long passages or sections are treated as illustrations and it is the responsibility of the author to supply camera ready copy. **Remember, if the publisher agrees to allow Hebrew in the text it is entirely your responsibility to see that it is correct.**

Permissions

Do You Need Permission?

This is a critical part of preparing your manuscript. If you have quoted material from other sources, especially to use as an epigraph for a chapter or for the entire book, you must determine whether or not permission is needed. Below are a few simple rules for determining whether or not you will need permission for material, and what you must do to obtain it.

Bear in mind that you are held *personally responsible* for violations of copyright law if you do not obtain permission for material, and we reserve the right to place on hold or even cancel publication if you fail to obtain permission for material taken from other sources.

1. **You must obtain *written* permission** from the copyright owner for reproducing or reprinting any illustrations, tables,

Books

charts, long verbatim quotations, or paraphrasing from another publication.

2. **The normal guidelines for permission requests** are material exceeding 150 words from a journal or 350 words from a book.

3. **Epigraphs, poetry and song lyrics** *always* **need permission.**

4. **Obtain permission for anything questionable in your text.** If permission is not obtained the publisher has a right to put your book on hold.

5. **When writing to the original publisher for permission,** include a copy of the excerpt(s) you want to reprint, and where and when the material was printed originally. Use the form letter included in this packet when writing for permission. Put the letter on your own letterhead.

Only written permission is considered valid.

Obtaining Permission

Once you have determined that you need permission for material, you must obtain it from the publisher. Here are some more detailed guidelines on how to go about securing permission to reprint material.

Be aware that it often takes weeks or months to obtain permission, so begin this process as early as possible.

1. Request permissions well in advance of the completion of your manuscript. It is advisable to ask for permission for each quotation as soon as the decision to use it is made. You may find that you will have to write more than one letter before you can locate the copyright holder, or permission for some item may be refused, so that you will have to substitute other material. *Early clearance of permissions is critical so that publication of your book will not be delayed*

2. Keep a list of what your are requesting permission for, the publisher or author you are requesting it from, and whether or not you have obtained it. Submit this checklist to your Production Editor when one has been assigned to you.

3. If you do not receive a reply to your request within three or four weeks, send a follow-up letter. Send all copies of correspondence to us when you submit your final manuscript.

4. It is common for major publishers to send their own form for completion and signature rather than returning the request form you sent them. Simply supply whatever information is called for on their form, sign the form, and return it to the publisher.

5. If a publisher is able to grant U.S. and Canadian rights only (often Canadian and/or world rights are controlled by a foreign publisher), the publisher will advise you to whom you must write for additional rights. Simply send another request form to the foreign publisher. It is necessary for you to obtain world rights.

6. Permission fees are the responsibility of the author.

7. If a publisher specifies a charge for granting permission to reproduce certain material, payment is normally due on publication. Usually, a publisher requests a flat fee as payment for permission. Occasionally, the fee may be based on a pro-rata share of your royalties. We prefer to avoid a royalty arrangement in making permissions payments. In such a case, write to the publisher again with the request for a flat fee.

8. When submitting your manuscript for publication, send us your completed permissions file, including the copies of your permissions requests and your Permissions Checklist. If you have not yet received full clearance on some permissions requests, include a careful documentation on the status of those permissions.

[Author's Letterhead]

Date:

[Addressee]

I am writing to request permission to reprint the following material from your publication:

[Author, title, date of publication]

[Pages on which material appears or other identifying information]

This material is to appear as originally published [or with changes or deletions as noted on the reverse side of this letter] in the following work, which Jason Aronson Inc. is currently preparing for publication:

[Author or editor, title, approx. no. pages]

This book is scheduled to be published in [month, year] in clothbound form.

[Additional remarks, if needed]

I am requesting nonexclusive world rights to use this material as part of my work in all languages and for all editions.

If you are the copyright holder, I would like to have your permission to reprint the material described above in my book. Unless you request otherwise, I shall use the conventional scholarly form of acknowledgment, including author and title, publisher's name, and date.

If you are not the copyright holder, or if for world rights I need additional permission from another source, please so indicate.

Thank you for your consideration of this request. A duplicate copy of this letter is enclosed for your convenience.

Yours sincerely,

The above request is approved on the conditions specified below and on the understanding that full credit will be given to the source.

Approved by:_____ Date:_____

Index

Compilation of an index completed by Jason Aronson Inc. is the author's financial responsibility. Our production department will hire an experienced freelancer for the job, with the cost to be deducted from royalties.

Authors sometimes request to create their own index.

Our policy regarding author-created indexes is as follows:

Author-created indexes will be evaluated by the same standards that we use to evaluate indexes created by professional indexers. If the index does not meet our standards, we will not use it. If it is rejected, the author cannot resubmit. We will simply proceed by hiring a professional indexer if your index is rejected.

We are aware, as you may be, that there are computer programs that create indexes. *The quality of indexes that are computer generated are not acceptable to us for publication, nor are indexes produced by a nonprofessional indexer.*

The cost for the index is initially paid for by the house (most indexes range between $400 and $800) and this figure is then deducted from the book's future royalty earnings.

Footnotes and References

1. Be sure to double-space all footnotes and references.

2. It is our policy to use footnotes, and not endnotes or chapter notes, in our text.

3. Number footnotes consecutively for each chapter with superscript Arabic numbers, unless there is only one footnote per chapter, in which case an asterisk can be used.

4. When chapters in a book have footnotes, each chapter should begin with footnote 1 (superscript).

5. References are listed in alphabetical order by the last name of the first author of the work.

6. When an author has repeated listings, the author name is replaced by a 3-em dash in the second and subsequent entries, with no period following the 3-em dash.

7. For the format and style of footnotes and bibliographical references, please refer to the *Chicago Manual of Style* (14th ed.).

Note: If you do not format your footnotes and references according to the above guidelines, you will simply be required to rewrite them once the manuscript is copyedited. To avoid delays in publication, it is in your best interest to prepare footnotes and references as outlined above.

Guidelines for Disk Usage

The following guidelines should be followed for manuscripts prepared on disks.

1. Provide two double-spaced printouts of disk in hard manuscript form.

2. Shut off automatic hyphenation.

3. Do not use carriage returns in the main text.

4. All new paragraphs should have an indent.

5. Disks should be clearly labeled with author's name, book name, and the name and version number of the software used to create it (i.e., WP 5.1, MS Word 6.0, etc.).

6. Files should be in original word processing format, not ASCII.

7. File names should be simple and organized, for example, chapter1, chapter2, or, in an edited work, authors' names (for example, Smith, Jones, Roberts).

8. Supply table of contents and indicate disk file names for each chapter on copy of contents.

9. .Zip files are perfectly acceptable. However, do not send UU-encoded or other types of encoded files as they are prone to corruption and other decoding problems.

Checking the Manuscript

Just before you send us the manuscript, check it against this list. It will save you time, correspondence, and probably money later on. Remember, what you submit is considered the completed manuscript. **Any additions or deletions after this point are at the discretion of Jason Aronson Inc. and the Production Editor.**

1. Read the final typescript carefully. Check the organization of your material and look for any typing errors or omissions.

2. Be sure that all pages are accounted for, are in proper sequence, and that all inserts have been numbered and their position noted in the text.

3. Check the presence and numbering of all tables, illustrations, and footnotes with great care. A mistake here may involve considerable time and money.

4. Check all cross-references. Numbered sequences like tables and illustrations should be referred to by number, but a cross reference to another page of the manuscript should read "see page 000". *The correct page numbers for cross-references in the finished manuscript are entirely the responsibility of the author.* If a manuscript page number is used, the fact that it must later be changed to a book page may escape everyone's notice. Because each line containing a page cross-reference must be reset after the book is paged is a costly and time-consuming procedure, we urge you to hold page cross-references to the absolute minimum necessary.

Submission

Make two photocopies of your original manuscript. Send us the original and one duplicate. If you intend to submit a disk, include it with your manuscript at this time.

Categories: Nonfiction—Jewish Interests—Judaica—Religion

Name: Arthur Kurzweil, Publisher
Material: All
Address: 230 LIVINGSTON ST
City/State/ZIP: NORTHVALE NJ 07647
Telephone: 201-767-4093
Fax: 201-767-4330

Jason Aronson, Inc.
Psychotherapy

We are pleased to be sending you the enclosed Manuscript Preparation Guidelines, designed to help you prepare your manuscript for publication. Please take a few minutes and read the guidelines carefully (they really are a help!) to ensure that your submission will not be returned for technical reasons. We look forward to launching your book into production, but we cannot begin to tackle our jobs until you have finished yours. Attached are instructions on:

- General Format
- Front Matter
- Tables and Illustrations
- Permissions
- Index
- Footnotes
- References
- Disk Usage
- Manuscript Checklist
- Submission

Once the final manuscript has been received, you can expect that the Production Editor assigned to your book will call to introduce him- or herself, advise you of the manuscript's status, clear up anything that may be unclear, and relate the next steps in the process.

This comes with our thanks in advance for your cooperation. Questions? Problems?

Call one of our production editors:

Bob ext.28 Elaine ext.38 Judy ext.37

Manuscript Preparation

General Format

The following basic guidelines are essential to the preparation and acceptance of your manuscript. Please follow them carefully. If they are not followed you may submit a manuscript with problems that will cause the Publisher to reject it and you will have to reformat and resubmit your book.

- **Type and print on one side of 8½"x11" paper.** This includes every page of the manuscript. Leave 1" margins on all four sides. Small corrections to the typed text can be inserted above a line. *A manuscript that does not follow this most basic format will be rejected.*

- **It is *imperative* that you double-space everything,** including footnotes, references/bibliographies, and quoted material.

- **Number pages consecutively from start to finish.** Number pages *consecutively,* either in the upper right-hand corner or bottom center. If large corrections or additions are needed, type on a separate sheet of paper and identify the new page with the page number of the preceding page plus a letter (e.g., 29A). *Do not number pages by chapter or section.*

- **Do not staple or bind your pages.** Simply rubber-band them securely.

- **Submit a disk with your manuscript whenever possible.** A disk will make the process of publishing your manuscript much less error-prone when the pages are typeset. *Note:* If you do submit a disk, see the instructions under "Disk Usage."

- **Style:** If you have questions about style, refer to *The Chicago Manual of Style* (14th ed.). It is our house style manual and is used by our copy editors when editing your manuscript.

- **Photocopied material:** If you are including photocopied material from other sources, be sure the copies are clean, readable, and *double-spaced.*

Front Matter

Front matter is all material that appears in a book before the text proper. *It is submitted to the publisher at the same time as the text.* Essential front matter includes:

- **Title Page**—with your name written *exactly* as you wish it to appear in the book, along with the complete working title and subtitle (if any).

- **Table of Contents:** This is a necessary item to help us evaluate your manuscript for content and completeness. It is also a required element for Library of Congress filing.

• **List of Contributors:** If you are preparing a contributed book (with chapters written by different authors), you must include a list of contributors along with a short professional biography on each individual.

Optional front matter that you may want to include:

Dedication, List of Illustrations, List of Tables, Preface, Foreword, Acknowledgments (which may be part of your Preface), and Introduction.

Again, if you wish to include any of these elements in your finished book, they must be submitted with the completed manuscript.

Tables and Illustrations

Tables and illustrations should be discussed with the publisher before the completed manuscript is accepted.

• **Type tables double-spaced,** on 8½"x11" paper, separate from the text, and number them individually for each chapter (i.e., chapter number, then table number within chapter-for example, Table 2-1, Table 2-2, Table 3-1, etc.).

• **Illustrations include:** charts, graphs, and photographs. They should be numbered consecutively throughout the chapter using Arabic numbers (e.g., Figure 7-1, Table 7-1, etc.) and cited in the same manner in the text. All illustrations must be camera-ready artwork. Photographs should be black and white glossies; all drawings should be black and white. *Remember*: the quality of the illustrations will be reflected in the final product.

• Be sure to indicate the **exact placement** of tables and illustrations in the text. **Identify each illustration** by figure and page number.

References

• References must be complete and accurate. When making **citations within the text,** place the author's last name and the date of publication in parentheses. No comma is used between the name and the date.

• With a **string of references in parentheses,** the sources must be in alphabetical order. If there are multiple references for one author, they must be in chronological order within that author's name. If two references are by the same author in the same year, a and b for example, only then are they separated by a comma, with no space between.

• A direct quotation in the text, regardless of length, must be followed by a *page no.* reference.

• **Every source** given in the text **must be listed in the reference (bibliography) section** at the end of the book, or, in the case of a contributed book, at the end of each chapter. References are listed alphabetically by authors' last names, followed by first initial (and sometimes second initial). Check that authors' names are spelled correctly. The following data *must be included* for each entry:

- author's last name, first initial (second initial)
- date of publication
- title of chapter or journal article
- full name of book or journal

The following additional data must be included *for a book*:

- volume or edition number, if any
- editor(s) and/or translator(s), if any
- place of publication followed by a colon and full name of the publisher;

for a journal:

- volume number followed by a colon and inclusive page numbers for the article.

Disk Usage

The following guidelines should be followed for manuscripts prepared on disks:

• Disks should be clearly labeled with author's name, book title, and hardware/software used (e.g., PC or Mac/WP 5.1, Word 6.0, etc.).

• File names should be simple and organized (e.g., contents, foreword, chapter 1, chapter 2, refs), or, in an edited work, authors' names (e.g., Doe, Smith, Jones).

• Files should be in word processing format, not ASCII.

• Shut off automatic hyphenation.

• Do not use carriage returns in the main text.

• All paragraphs should be indented.

• Send disk in a protective envelope.

Checking the Manuscript

Just prior to your sending us the manuscript, check the following list. It will save you time and correspondence, and help prevent delays in the schedule. Remember, what you submit is considered the completed manuscript. **Any additions or deletions after this point are at the discretion of Jason Aronson Inc. and the Production Editor.**

• **Read the final manuscript carefully.** Check for organization, typos, and consistency.

• **Be sure that all pages are accounted for,** are in the proper sequence, and that all inserts have been numbered and their position noted in the text.

• **Check the presence and numbering of all tables, illustrations, and footnotes** with great care. A mistake here may involve considerable time and money later on.

• **Check all cross-references.** Numbered sequences like tables and illustrations should be referred to by number, but a cross reference to another page of the manuscript should read "see page 000." *This is extremely important, since the cross-referenced page will change from manuscript to final proof*

Submission

Make two photocopies of your original manuscript. *Send us the original and one duplicate.* **Include your disk** with the manuscript at this time.

Categories: Psychoanalysis—Psychology—Psychotherapy—Relationships—Sexuality

Name: Michael Moskowitz, Ph.D., Publisher
Material: All
Address: 230 LIVINGSTON ST
City/State/ZIP: NORTHVALE NJ 07647
Telephone: 201-767-4093
Fax: 201-767-4330
E-mail: 73232.37@compuserve.com

Jewish Lights Publishing

Jewish Lights publishes books for people of all faiths and all backgrounds who yearn for books that attract, engage, educate, and spiritually inspire. Our authors are at the forefront of spiritual thought and deal with the quest for the self and for meaning in life by drawing on the Jewish wisdom tradition. Our books cover topics including history, spirituality, life cycle, children's, self-help, recovery, theology and philosophy. We do *not* publish autobiography, biography, fiction, *haggadot*, poetry, or cookbooks. At this point we plan to do only one book for children annually, and that one will be for younger children (ages 4-10).

Because of the tremendous number of manuscript submissions we receive, we cannot correspond individually with authors until we receive a proposal of what they would like to submit for publication. A proposal includes:

1. A cover letter
2. A table of contents
3. Two sample chapters (do not send the entire book)

If your project is a short children's picture book, you may send the entire text. Send the material to the Submissions Editor at Jewish Lights at the address below.

After sending us your material, please allow approximately three months for a reply. We are very sorry that this process is slow, but it is the only way we can ensure that all material receives proper consideration.

Thank you for considering Jewish Lights Publishing.

Categories: Nonfiction—Business—Children's Picture Books—Ecology—Healing/Recovering—History—Inspirational—Jewish Interests—Life Cycle—Mysticism—Philosophy—Reference—Spirituality—Theology—Travel—Women's Issues

Name: Submissions Editor
Material: All
Address: PO BOX 237
Address: SUNSET FARM OFFICES RTE 4
City/State/ZIP: WOODSTOCK VT 05091
Telephone: 802-457-4000
Fax: 802-457-4004
E-mail: everyone@longhillpartners.com

JIST Works, Inc.
Park Avenue Books

When JIST Works was incorporated in 1981, we were primarily a job search training firm. The company broke ground by training counselors to teach people to conduct their own job searches, then moved into publishing information on self-directed job search skills. Over the years, our publishing operation has grown dramatically to include text and trade books, assessment devices, reference materials, curricula, workbooks, videos, and software packages. Although the company is beginning to move into the consumer market, the lion's share of our sales are to institutions. Professional career counselors in schools, government agencies, colleges, and universities are our primary audience. We currently support two imprints: JIST Works and Park Avenue Productions.

Our Market

JIST books are job search and career development materials. These include assessment devices, workbooks, teacher's guides, curricula, video, and software designed to help students and people of all ages (and the professionals who work with them):

- Assess skills & interests
- Explore & choose jobs & careers
- Find good jobs faster & succeed on the job

Recent titles have explored using the Internet in the job search, preparing superior resumes, negotiating a good salary, and finding career satisfaction.

Park Avenue books address business success skills, education, and life skills. Recent titles have focused in meeting management, adults returning to school, organizing your life, and juggling the roles of worker and parent.

Submissions

Please do not send unsolicited complete manuscripts.

The single best action you can take before submitting material is to study our catalog. Does your idea fit our list? Does it compete with a recently published title? Does it aim at our target audience?

For a copy of our catalog, contact us using the address below.

Your Book Proposal

Briefly explain what you want to write (or have written), and why. Tell us (in no more than two pages) your premise for the book, what makes it unique, and why it is appropriate for our market. Don't forget to include your full name, mailing address, a phone number where you can be reached during business hours, and a complete list of what you have sent. Your submission package should also include:

- **Your vitae or resume:** What qualifies you to write this book? List your previous publications, your expertise in the field, your professional background, your degrees, affiliations, and any associations to which you belong. Also tell us how you can help market the book.
- **A market survey:** Identify the market; tell us what else has been published in the field, and what makes your proposal different. In other words, who will buy your book, and why?
- **A book outline:** This is the meat of your submission, and should include:
  1. A detailed Table of Contents (if the book has been written).
  2. Brief chapter synopses that detail chapter contents, what problems or questions are addressed, and what answers are given.
  3. A detailed outline of the major topics, and how you plan to cover them.
- **The Introduction:** What questions the book answers and why it is worth reading.
- **A sample chapter:** Send a good representation of your writing (not necessarily the first chapter), so we can see how you handle your material.
- **A list of the art/graphics** that will be included in the final manuscript.

Manuscript Specifications

Include your name and the title of the manuscript at the top of each page, with the page number.

Style

Refer to *The Chicago Manual of Style*, 14th Edition, for references, notes, and style usage. We also use *Merriam Webster's Collegiate Dictionary*, Tenth Edition.

Avoid sexist language. We don't use *he/she* or *s/he*; instead, we prefer to alternate between he and she and "his or her" when necessary.

Be aware of gender and race equity. Show women and minorities in nontraditional roles and in positions of leadership.

Avoid academic or technical lingo. Use a conversational tone, with natural language. For example, we discourage phrases such as *utilize* (for use); *in the event that* (if); *with reference to* (about).

Do not use the "editorial we." If you are a single author, refer to yourself as "I." If you have a co-author, use "we." And never refer to yourself in the third person—i.e., "the author of this book observed…"

We do not intentionally publish works containing obscenities or material that is offensive to groups or classes of people.

We generally respond to proposals within eight weeks. If you have not heard from us within that time, you may write or call to inquire about the status of your manuscript.

If we decide not to pursue your project, we will return your materials in the SASE you provide, with a note explaining why.

If we like your proposal, we will contact you with any changes required, negotiate a contract, answer your questions, and set up a timetable for project completion.

Completed Manuscripts

If we ask for a complete manuscript, we prefer a hard copy of the manuscript *and* the entire work on an IBM-compatible 3.5" disk in Word or WordPerfect. We are a Windows™ environment. Your manuscript should include:

- **All front matter:** A title page, acknowledgements, and dedication if necessary, and a complete Table of Contents.
- **All artwork:** Illustrations, tables, and graphics.
- **Permissions:** Material from another source requires proof of permission. Examples are poems, song lyrics, artwork, tables, and excerpts from fiction and creative prose works.

The best rule of thumb for permissions is this: When in doubt, secure them, **in writing.**

- **Complete references:** Follow *The Chicago Manual of Style*, and include for each citation of a book the author, title, city of

Books

publication, publisher, and date:

Farr, J. Michael. *The Very Quick Job Search.* 2nd ed. Indianapolis: JIST Works, 1996.

For journal articles, include the author, article, journal, volume number, date, and page numbers:

Hall, Sara. "How to Publish Your Book." *American Journal of Bookselling* 24 (1996): 124-126.

Miscellaneous

Number all manuscript pages.

Use endnotes following each chapter, rather than footnotes. Again, follow *The Chicago Manual of Style.*

Mark headings in your manuscript with tags, such as H1 for a level 1 head, H2, and so on.

Please do not refer to specific page numbers within your text for reference, as these will change when the manuscript is typeset.

Thank you for your interest in JIST Works, Inc.

Categories: Nonfiction—Business—Careers—Interview—Reference—Retirement (Business/Careers)

Name: Acquisitions Editor
Material: All
Address: 720 N PARK AVE
City/State/ZIP: INDIANAPOLIS IN 46202-3490
Telephone: 317-264-3720
Fax: 317-264-3709

John Daniel *&* Company
P U B L I S H E R S

John Daniel & Company
A division of Daniel & Daniel Publishers, Inc.

About the press.

John Daniel and Company is a small press publisher of belles lettres. We publish only four titles a year, with print runs averaging 1,000-2,000. Our books are distributed to the trade by various book wholesalers, including Bookpeople, Sunbelt Publications, Ingram Book Company, and Baker and Taylor. In addition to trade sales, we rely heavily on direct-mail sales from our yearly catalog and from announcements we send out for each book we publish.

Editorial focus.

"Belles lettres" is a fuzzy term that allows us a lot of leeway, but it does exclude children's books, genre fiction, cookbooks, photography books, how-to books, and a number of other categories that are better published by the major-league publishing establishment. "Belles lettres," for us, means stylish and elegant writing; beyond that definition I should mention that we are particularly interested in essays, literary memoirs, and short fiction dealing with social issues. We publish only one poetry title a year. For economic reasons almost all our books are under 200 pages long.

Royalties.

We do not pay advances, and our royalties are based on 10 percent of the net receipts (cover price minus discount allowed to the customer).

Submission requirements.

To submit material, send synopsis plus 50 sample pages. Allow six to eight weeks for response. Manuscripts received without SASE will be discarded. We do not accept submissions in the form of disks, e-mail, fax, or phone calls.

Some free advice.

We receive over five thousand unsolicited manuscripts and query letters a year. We publish four manuscripts a year, of which fewer than half were received unsolicited. Obviously the odds are not with you. For this reason we encourage you to send out multiple submissions and we do not expect you to tie up your chances while waiting for our response.

Categories: Fiction—Nonfiction—Essays—Literature—Memoir—Poetry—Short Stories

Name: John Daniel, Publisher
Material: All
Address: PO BOX 21922
City/State/ZIP: SANTA BARBARA CA 93121
Telephone: 805-962-1780
Fax: 805-962-8835
E-mail: dandd@silcom.com

John Muir Publications
JMP Travel, JMP Wellness

Thank you for considering John Muir Publications for your book proposal. We are looking for unique book ideas in two subject areas: Travel and Alternative Health. Please include the following in your submission:

1) *Cover letter*—start with a one or two page cover letter that states the following:

a) Summarize the topic of your proposed book and state its title.

b) Briefly state why such a book would be in demand by book buyers. Include appropriate statistics and statements of general trends.

c) State why you would be a successful author for such a book. Include applicable experience, education, and other materials previously published.

d) Describe other books currently available that would be competition for your proposed book. Evaluate their strengths and weaknesses.

e) Provide a more elaborate description of the contents of your proposed book. Include estimated word count, types of photographs and illustrations that you think it would require and where they could be obtained.

f) Briefly outline how you think your book could be most effectively promoted.

2) *Outline and sample chapter*-Provide a detailed outline of your book idea and include a sample chapter.

3) *News articles and photographs*-Include photocopies of any news articles or similar materials that demonstrate a public interest in your topic. Include photographs or illustrations (where appropriate) that will help bring the topic to life as we review your proposal.

NOTE: Make certain that the title (or working title) of your book appears on all materials that you send us.

Finally, remember to be patient and allow us enough time to carefully review your proposal. This can take two to four months.

Categories: Nonfiction—Health—Travel Guidebooks

Name: Cassandra Conyers, Acquisitions Editor
Material: All
Address: PO BOX 613

City/State/ZIP: SANTA FE NM 87504
Telephone: 505-982-4078
Fax: 505-988-1680

Johnston Associates International
(JASI)

JASI publishes nonfiction trade-format books. The following guidelines are designed to assist you in submitting a book proposal:

Submission Guidelines

Your proposal should consist of seven sections:

1. Important and unique features of the topic

Explain what your book is about and why it is needed. Also describe the unique features of your book and anything that makes it different from all other books of the same topic.

2. Market

Describe the audience for your book. Who are the most likely readers to buy your book? Why should they buy it, keep it or talk about it?

3. Competition

List the books that directly compete with the project you are proposing. How do they compare with your book subject in length, scope, format and visual appeal? Explain why they are not adequate to meet the need you have identified. If no such book is available for the market you're addressing, cite any books that seem even remotely comparable and explain the difference between your approach and theirs.

4. Outline or annotated table of contents

The outline of your book should be similar to a table of contents. It should include chapter titles and subheads, if any. For each chapter, include a paragraph of about 100 words summarizing the chapter's contents.

5. Publishing details

Give an estimate of how long your book will be. Do you plan to have photographs or illustrations? Maps? How many? How long will you need to complete the manuscript?

6. Author background

Please include a resume or information sheet detailing your background and areas of expertise and/or interest, including prior publications.

7. Promotion

How will you help promote your book? Do you have databases, lists of contacts?

Additional Tips

If you submit to other publishers simultaneously, please let us know.

Be sure to include phone and fax numbers and an e-mail address (if you have one) where you may be reached.

Allow 4 weeks for initial response.

Please include sample chapters. If you don't have these, the outline will suffice.

Thank you for thinking of JASI!

Categories: Nonfiction—General Interest—Outdoors—Recreation—Regional—Senior Citizens—Travel

Name: Ann Schuessler, Publisher
Material: All
Address: PO BOX 313

City/State/ZIP: MEDINA WA 98039
Telephone: 425-454-3490
Fax: 425-462-1335
E-mail: JasiBooks@aol.com

Judson Press

Judson Press is a ministry of the Board of Educational Ministries, American Baptist Churches in the USA. For more information, call and ask for the editorial department.

Before you complete your manuscript and submit a proposal to Judson Press or another publisher, there are several preliminary steps you need to take. It is essential that you consider your content, identify your audience, and seek publishers who publish resources for that market.

Consider the Content

What do you have to say? Does your material constitute a book, or did you write articles that you can submit to outlets other than book publishers? A publisher will more likely be interested if your book is in some way *unique and compelling*. Think about whether what you want to say has already been said, and make sure that your material is well organized and clearly written.

Identify Your Audience

The next step in seeking publication is to think about the persons whom you wish to reach-your audience. Who will be most interested in what you have to say? What are their needs? What characteristics, knowledge level, and demographic traits will your readers have in common? If your book is not clearly targeted to a specific audience, publishers will not be able to market it effectively. The entire content of your book should be focused on and directed to the audience you have identified.

Find the Right Publisher

After you have identified your audience, the next step is to find a publisher who has had success in marketing books to that audience. You will avoid needless misuse of your own resources of time and money by becoming knowledgeable about publishers' niches in the marketplace. Often the best way to find such information (and to ascertain your competition) is to visit several religious bookstores to see which publishers are publishing books in your particular area of interest. Public libraries have various resources available (such as *The Writer's Market* and *The Literary Marketplace)* that contain basic information about most publishers in this country.

Submit Your Proposal

Judson Press publishes only Christian nonfiction in these areas:

• practical Christian resources for pastors and laity on such topics as: church life, community, discipleship, drama, education, evangelism, family, games and crafts, how-to, leadership, marriage, ministry, parenting, renewal, self-help, seniors, social and world justice, spirituality, theology, women's issues, and worship

• specific church administration resources

• devotional materials

• African-American church resources

• sermon resources

• Christian nurture and growth materials

• Baptist heritage and identity materials

• seasonal resources (including dramas)

Judson Press accepts unsolicited manuscript proposals according to the following guidelines:

1. Please do not send an entire manuscript; Judson Press accepts proposals only.

2. Your proposal should include the following:

    • table of contents of your book

    • estimated length of the material

    • the audience for whom you are writing

    • your qualifications (resumé, pertinent biographical

Books

information, education)

 • an outline of your book as well as a summary of chapters, the introduction, and/or one or two sample chapters

 • expected completion date, if the manuscript is not already complete

3. Review of unsolicited proposals takes eight to twelve weeks on average.

4. If the editorial review results in continued interest in your work, you will be invited to submit the entire manuscript for further review.

Know the Basics

If your manuscript is approved for publication, you will be offered a contract. This contract turns over to the publisher all rights to the manuscript, and, in turn, the publisher agrees to pay all costs of editing, designing, manufacturing, promoting, selling, and distributing the book. Judson Press requires that all manuscripts under contract for publication be submitted on computer disk and be accompanied by a double-spaced hard copy. At this point in the process you would be provided with a packet of information detailing your responsibilities and the steps in the publishing process.

Categories: Nonfiction—African-American—Christian Interests—Family—Inspirational—Multicultural—Religion—Senior Citizens—Spiritual—Women's Issues

Name: Acquisitions Editor
Material: All
Address: PO BOX 851
City/State/ZIP: VALLEY FORGE PA 19482-0851
Telephone: 610-768-2118
Fax: 610-768-2441

Kali Press
Little Kali Press

Mission Statement

There are two divisions which accept queries and manuscript submissions:

Kali Press currently has five titles published which focus on specialized areas of natural health care topics. Kali Press is interested in endemic cultures nonfiction works with emphasis on spiritual breakthroughs and/or teachings.

Little Kali Press is interested in children's literature in picture book or reader format. Little Kali Press is especially responsive to books with a spiritual message, or with an inspirational view of children's lives and affairs.

Submission Guidelines

Queries must precede submissions. The query must include the following: A synopsis or outline of the manuscript; a description of figures, captions, photos or illustrations together with a number count. Full manuscripts will be requested and further instructions will be provided upon approval of the book concept.

Categories: Nonfiction—Children—Education—Environment—Health—Parenting

Name: Cynthia Olsen, Managing Director

Material: All
Address: PO BOX 2169
City/State/ZIP: PAGOSA SPRINGS CO 81147
Telephone: 970-264-5200
Fax: 970-264-5202
E-mail: Kalipres@rmi.net

Kids Books By Kids
A Beyond Words Publishing Series

Dear Kid Writer,

Thanks for your interest in sending your book idea to Beyond Words Publishing. We do publish books written by kids like you in our "Kids Books By Kids" series. We only publish *nonfiction* book ideas by kids—no fiction stories or poetry.

So far, we've published three "Kids Books By Kids": ***Better Than A Lemonade Stand***, written by a 15-year-old, describes 50 small business ideas for kids; ***100 Excuses For Kids***, co-written by 10 and 11-year-old best friends, gives excuses for everything from escaping vegetables to avoiding chores; and ***Girls Know Best*** was written by 38 girls, ages 7-16, and gives advice and activities for girls. We are looking for unusual, practical, *nonfiction* book ideas for kids. If you can look at any of these three books (at a bookstore or library), they'll give you a better idea of what we're looking for.

When you send us your book idea, here's what we'd like you to include: 1 page about you, 1 page summarizing your book idea, 2-3 pages of writing from your book, 1 self-addressed stamped envelope (we call it a "SASE") so we can send back your story if we decide not to publish it. Also include 1 page of "market research" about your book idea. "Market research" is when you go to the library or a big bookstore and see if there are any other books like yours. If there are, tell us why yours is different and better. Also, tell us *who* you think will buy your book and *why*. Can you think of any places besides bookstores that will buy it?

It may take us a while to read and return your book idea, because we get so many every day. It can take up to six months. Thank you for being patient.

Thank you for thinking of us. By following these guidelines, it really helps us to see if your book idea is right for us.

We can't wait to see what you send us!
Submissions Department
Beyond Words Publishing, Inc.
Categories: Nonfiction—Kids

Name: Michelle Boehm, Children's Director
Material: Nonfiction by kids
Address: 20827 NW CORNWELL RD STE 500
City/State/ZIP: HILLSBORO OR 97124
Telephone: 503-531-8700
Fax: 503-531-8773

Kodansha America

To whom it may concern:

Kodansha America is interested in submissions for nonfiction titles relating to international, cross-cultural, human interest, and contemporary affairs, for a general trade audience.

Submissions (proposals, outlines, sample chapters, etc.) should be addressed to the Editorial Department.

Sincerely,
The Editorial Department
Kodansha America, Inc.

Categories: Nonfiction—Adventure—African-American—Animals—Asian-American—Biography—Civil War—Cooking—Culture—Fishing—Food/Drink—History—Internet—Jewish Interests—Sports—Women's Issues

Name: Editorial Department
Material: All
Address: 113 FIFTH AVE
City/State/ZIP: NEW YORK NY 10025
Telephone: 212-727-6460
Fax: 212-727-9177

Kregel Publications

Our Mission Statement

As an evangelical Christian publisher, we seek to provide—with integrity and excellence—trusted, biblically based resources that challenge and encourage individuals in their Christian life and service.

Books published present a conservative, evangelical faith and uphold the following primary doctrines: the verbal and plenary inspiration of the Bible as God's Word, inerrant in the original writings; one God existing in three person: Father, Son, and Holy Spirit; the deity of Jesus Christ; His virgin birth; vicarious death, bodily resurrection, and personal return; the Holy Spirit who regenerates and indwells all believers.

Our Priorities

Kregel Publications is interested in books that will meet the spiritual needs of general readers as well as the professional needs of pastors, missionaries, teachers, and Christian leaders. in addition to reprints of classic works, we publish new material in the areas of Christian education and ministry, Bible commentaries and reference, contemporary issues, and devotional books. We also publish a limited number of titles in the genre of biblical/historical fiction. We do not publish school curriculum, poetry, cartoons, cookbooks, or games. Reading levels should be appropriate for the target audience.

Your Query Letter

Rather than sending a complete manuscript, please address a query letter to the address below. The query letter should contain the following information: a summary of your proposed book, its target audience, and an assessment of its uniqueness in comparison to other books currently available in the same subject area. Please include a brief description of your own qualifications to write on this subject and educational background. Enclose an outline or table contents of the book and two sample chapters. In response to your query letter, we may request a complete manuscript.

Our Procedure

Your manuscript will be reviewed by qualified readers and our editorial staff. Based upon their favorable response, your manuscript will be recommended to our Editorial Committee. They will evaluate your manuscript based upon the reviewers' evaluations, its quality of writing, timeliness, and consistency with the mission of Kregel Publications. Please allow six to eight weeks for us to complete this process. You will be notified of the committee's decision. Should we decide to publish your work, a contract will be sent to you that clearly sets forth the legal agreement to publish, promote, and distribute your book.

Categories: Biblical Studies—Devotional—Pastoral Studies—Religion—Religious/Theological

Name: Dennis Hillman, Senior Editor
Material: All
Address: PO BOX 2607
City/State/ZIP: GRAND RAPIDS MI 49501
Telephone: 616-451-4775

Kroshka Books
Nova Science Publishers, Inc.

Nova Science Publishers, Inc. was founded in 1985. We presently have three main divisions:
• Nova Science Books;
• Nova Science Journals;
• and Kroshka Books
Both Nova Science Divisions are scholarly oriented with authors from throughout the world. Kroshka Books is a trade line. The company now publishes about 175 books per year and 30 journals.

INVITATION TO AUTHORS

Our company invites authors from all countries to submit their proposals for books and journals. A response time of 30-45 days is strived for. Contact should be made with the Editor-in-Chief by e-mail, letter, or fax or by voice contact. An outline or table of contents and sample chapters if available are desirable. Final manuscripts are expected on computer diskette with rare exceptions permitted. Publication time can be from 3-18 months depending upon schedules and the manuscript status.

SPECIALIZED SUBJECTS

Our company is interested in all fields of human endeavor and knowledge. However, in recent years about 60% of the list is in social sciences with heavy representations in economics and political science.

Categories: Fiction—Nonfiction—Adventure—African-American—Asian-American—Biography—Business—Christian Interests—Civil War—College—Computers—Conservation—Cooking—Diet—Disabilities—Ecology—Economics—Education—Energy—Environment—Ethnic—Family—Feminism—Government—Health—History—Inspirational—Internet—Law—Lifestyles—Literature—Multicultural—Mystery—Native American—New Age—Paranormal—Parenting—Philosophy—Physical Fitness—Poetry—Politics—Psychology—Public Policy—Reference—Regional—Relationships—Religion—Rural America—Science—Science Fiction—Society—Spiritual—Sports—Technology—Textbooks—Women's issues

Name: Frank Columbus, President
Material: All
Address: 6080 JERICHO TURNPIKE STE 207
City/State/ZIP: COMMACK NY 11725
Telephone: 516-499-3103
Fax: 516-499-3146
E-mail: NovaScience@earthlink.net

Kumarian Press

Mission Statement
Kumarian Press is dedicated to publishing and distributing books and other media that will have a positive social and eco-

Books

nomic impact on the lives of people living in "Third World" conditions, no matter where they live.

The diverse books that you will find in our catalog are for students, teachers, professionals, policy makers, practitioners, researchers, non-governmental organizations and all those interested in a world that works. Please take the time to look through our list. Write to us with your comments and ideas. We would love to hear from you so that we can continue to publish books that increase our readers' awareness regarding global and local issues by offering visionary analysis and pointers to solutions. A number of our authors are available for speaking engagements. Write to us if you are interested in contacting them.

Kumarian Press is looking for manuscripts in the following areas:

- International Development and Global Issues
- Non-governmental Organizations (NGOs)
- Women/Gender in Development
- Peace and Conflict Resolution
- International Relations
- Environmental Sustainability
- Globalization and Economics
- International Health

Please include in your proposal:
- a cover letter that explains the concept of the book;
- a description of the intended readership;
- a description of how your book is different from the other books currently available;
- a c.v. or resume;
- a detailed table of contents. Please include a chapter-by-chapter written description, setting out the scope of each chapter and the contribution it will make to the book's argument;
- a sample chapter or two.

Please do not send the complete manuscript.

Categories: Nonfiction—Ecology—Economics—Environment—Government—Politics—Society—Women's Issues

Name: Linda Beyus, Acquisitions Editor
Material: All
Address: 14 OAKWOOD AVE
City/State/ZIP: W HARTFORD CT 06119-2127
Telephone: 860-233-5895
Fax: 860-233-6072

Latin American Literary Review Press

The Latin American Literary Review Press is a non-profit publishing house dedicated to bringing the fiction and poetry of Latin American, Spanish, Brazilian and Portuguese authors to the English-speaking public.

- Publications focus on works that were originally written in Spanish or Portuguese and translated into English.
- Manuscripts are considered for publication only after the translations have been completed and received by us in their entirety.
- Unsolicited manuscripts are considered.

Categories: Fiction—Hispanic—Jewish Interests—Literature—Poetry—Short Stories—Women's Fiction

Name: Yvette E. Miller, Editor
Name: Kathlean M. Ballew, Assistant Editor
Material: Any
Address: 121 EDGEWOOD AVE
City/State/ZIP: PITTSBURGH PA 15218
Telephone: 412-371-9023
Fax: 412-371-9025
E-mail: LALRP@aol.com

Legacy Press
An Imprint of Rainbow Publishers

Our objective:

We publish growth and development books for the evangelical Christian—from a non-denominational viewpoint—that may be marketed primarily through Christian bookstores.

These books may include but are not limited to:
- Devotionals
- Activity ideas for church groups
- Study guides
- Books that encourage or promote Christian values
- Books that teach the Bible

We will not publish:
- Academic work of a scholarly nature
- Poetry
- Fiction
- Curricula

The kinds of writers we are looking for:
- Have accepted Jesus as Savior and are dedicated to serving Him and leading others to Him
- Relate well to the needs of the evangelical Christian market
- Are active participants in a Bible-believing church
- Write creatively, either published or unpublished

To submit your proposal:
- Send a query, synopsis or the entire manuscript for our evaluation
- Enclose a resume or statement explaining your qualifications for writing the book
- Explain the audience for your book and how your book differs from those already on the market
- We normally respond in two to eight weeks.

After evaluating your proposal/manuscript we will do one of the following:
- Suggest you contact another publisher
- Request a contents summary and sample chapters
- Ask for revisions and resubmittal
- Seek expanded material from you
- Offer you a contract. We issue both royalty and full-rights contracts, depending on the type of book.

Categories: Nonfiction—Christian Interests—Inspirational—Religion—Spiritual

Name: Christy Allen, Editor
Material: All
Address: PO BOX 261129
City/State/ZIP: SAN DIEGO CA 92196
Telephone: 619-271-7600

Lehigh University Press
The World of Academic Publishing

The Lehigh University Press is a conduit for nonfiction works of scholarly interest not appropriate for the popular market. Less constrained by demands for profit than a commercial publisher, LUP bases its selection criteria on a manuscript's contribution to the world of ideas. The Press does not publish fiction, poetry, or textbooks.

Our Ever Widening Publication List

Established in 1985 and initially publishing in areas of Lehigh's established strengths in technology and society and eighteenth century studies, LUP today is moving beyond these areas in pursuing its mission to provide high quality monographs for the academic community.

The Press's increasingly wide-ranging publication list includes titles on local, national, and international history; foreign affairs, biography, film, politics, philosophy, and works for bibliographical reference.

Goals

The director and editorial board have recently made the commitment to publish an increasing amount of primary source material. Titles in our current catalogue include a memoir of the holocaust, an immigrant woman's frontier diary, and the autobiography of a noted scientist. Forthcoming publications will expand the list.

How We Work

Lehigh University Press is an affiliate of Associated University Presses, Cranbury, NJ. LUP's director acquires manuscripts through submission, has them reviewed, and gives his recommendation to the editorial board, which makes the final decision to publish. Approved manuscripts are forwarded to Associated University Presses, which handles the entire production and distribution process.

Inquiries are Encouraged

The Press welcomes for submission any manuscript (or synopsis and sample text of an unfinished manuscript) which is nonfiction, intellectually substantive, and whose format conforms to *The Chicago Manual of Style*, 14th ed. A current resume should accompany all submissions.

The Road to Publication

All manuscripts must be read by one or more scholarly reviewers, and it is rare that some degree of revision is not called for. Once favorably reviewed and revised, a manuscript must be approved by the editorial board, composed of Lehigh faculty members, which meets two or three times a year. To shorten a journey that extensive revision could make lengthy, it is wise to submit as polished a manuscript as possible. A clearly conceived, sharply focused, thoroughly researched, logically organized, fully documented, and crisply written manuscript sets the author well on the road to publication.

One Last Note

A very important point that scholars seeking to publish dissertations must remember is that dissertations and monographs address rather different audiences. Significant revision or reorganization is usually necessary before a dissertation can make the transition from research piece to scholarly publication.

For information or assistance please write or call Dr. Philip A. Metzger, Director, at the addresses given below.

INSTRUCTIONS FOR PREPARATION AND REVISION OF MANUSCRIPTS

1. We use *The Chicago Manual of Style* (University of Chicago Press), 14th edition, in copyediting all manuscripts. We strongly suggest that all authors consult the sections of the *Manual* dealing with notes and bibliographies. We very much prefer the use of endnotes for documentation of works in the humanities. This is the second method of documentation discussed in Chapter 15 of the *Manual*. We will reluctantly accept the author-date method discussed in Chapter 16. We cannot accept manuscripts prepared using the MLA style sheet.

2. A bibliography is essential for nearly all the books we publish. Please consult the appropriate sections of *The Chicago Manual of Style* for guidelines.

3. For spelling we use *Webster's Third New International* unabridged and *Webster's Ninth New Collegiate* dictionaries, using the first spelling given for each word.

4. All manuscript copy must be double-spaced, including all notes and back matter.

5. Volume editors must edit each paper for sense and grammar, checking lists of references and other apparatus for uniformity of style. Quotations should be taken from the same standard sources throughout. See *The Chicago Manual of Style* 2.179-82 for other volume editor responsibilities.

Manuscript Information Sheet

Author _____

Current Position _____

Title of Book _____

1. Has any part of this manuscript been published previously? If so, where? _____

2. Is this work a doctoral dissertation? _____ From what University? _____

Date _____ If so, has it been revised? _____ How?

3. Please list any previous publications. _____

4. Is the manuscript under consideration by any other publisher? (Please list) _____

5. How long is the manuscript? _____
Number of chapters or sections? _____

6. Please supply an abstract (ca. 500 words).

7. Has this manuscript been previously considered by another Associated Universities Presses member? _____ These include:

BALCH INSTITUTE PRESS
BUCKNELL UNIVERSITY PRESS
CORNING MUSEUM OF GLASS PRESS
UNIVERSITY OF DELAWARE PRESS
FAIRLEIGH DICKINSON UNIVERSITY PRESS
FOLGER SHAKESPEARE LIBRARY
LEHIGH UNIVERSITY PRESS
MORAVIAN MUSIC FOUNDATION PRESS
UNIVERSITY OF SCRANTON PRESS
SUSQUEHANNA UNIVERSITY PRESS
VIRGINIA CENTER FOR THE CREATIVE ARTS
WESTERN RESERVE HISTORICAL SOCIETY

Categories: Academic—Architecture—Arts—Asian-American—Business—Civil War—Comedy—Culture—Dance—Drama—Economics—Engineering—Film/Video—Government—History—Language—Literature—Philosophy—Politics—Psychology—Public Policy—Reference—Religion—Science—Society—Technology—Theatre—Women's Issues—Writing

Name: Dr. Philip H. Metzger, Director, LUP
Material: All
Address: 30 LIBRARY DR
City/State/ZIP: BETHLEHEM PA 18015-3067
Telephone: 610-758-3933
Fax: 610-974-2823
E-mail: inlup@lehigh.edu
Internet: www.lehigh.edu

Lerner Publications
The Lerner Publishing Group

What types of manuscripts are we looking for?

Before sending your manuscripts to us, you might find it helpful to take a look at our catalog and at some of the books our company publishes. Primarily, we publish educational books for children, ages 7-18. Our nonfiction books cover a variety of subjects: social issues, history, biography, science and technology, geography, the environment, sports, entertainment, the arts, and crafts and activities.

In general, no matter what the topic, we are looking for manuscripts that are well researched, well organized, and written clearly and simply with fresh, engaging language.

Note: We do not publish textbooks, workbooks, songbooks, puzzles, plays, religious material, fiction for adults, picture books (for the very young), or alphabet books.

HOW TO SUBMIT

Along with a brief letter of introduction and your resume or a biographical sketch, submit your proposal, an outline, and 1-2 sample chapters-or a complete manuscript-to our editorial department. If you are writing a query letter to clarify whether or not your idea would suit our needs, we prefer to see an outline along with the query.

If any of the material in your manuscript is drawn from published sources, be sure to include a complete bibliography.

Manuscripts may be sent on paper or diskette (preferably 3½").

The length of your manuscript should be no more than 100 double-spaced type-written pages. Many of our manuscripts fall in the range of 30 to 50 pages.

You need not submit artwork (illustrations, slides, photographs, etc.) with your manuscript. In most cases, we commission our own artists or photographers to illustrate the books we publish. If, however, you are an author-illustrator or you have a particular artist in mind, you may wish to enclose sample artwork for our consideration. If you are an author-photographer or have located sources for photographs and illustrations for your work, you may submit sample photocopies or prints if you wish. Keep the originals and supply a self-addressed, stamped envelope in the event we cannot use your illustrations.

NOTES ON STEREOTYPES

We avoid publishing works containing stereotypes of race, religion, and nationality. We are averse to the use of gender stereotypes (e.g., strong, aggressive, unemotional males; weak, submissive, emotional females) and to the use of sexist language. Words such as mankind, men, and salesman should be replaced with nonsexist words such as humankind, people, and salesperson when they apply to both genders.

SUGGESTED READING

Aspiring writers of books for young people might find it worthwhile to spend some time in public libraries to find out what is happening in the world of children's literature today. You might find it helpful to read *School Library Journal, Booklist, Bulletin for the Center for Children's Books, Cricket, The Horn Book Magazine, Publishers Weekly* and other magazines dealing with children's literature. In addition, several books offer information and suggestions on writing books for children. Three that are especially helpful are: *Writing Illustrating and Editing Children's Books,* by Jean Poindexter Colby; *Writing Books for Children,* by Jane Yolen; and *Nonfiction for Children,* by Ellen E. M. Roberts.

HOW LONG BEFORE YOU HEAR FROM US?

After you have submitted your manuscript to us, please be patient. We receive hundreds of manuscripts each year, and it takes time for us to give all of them careful consideration. We will notify you of our decision regarding your manuscript as soon as possible. Be assured, however, that we do read and evaluate each manuscript that comes to us.

We realize that many authors desire editorial suggestions concerning their work. Unfortunately, time does not permit us to prepare written evaluations of all the unsolicited manuscripts we receive each year.

Thank you for your interest in Lerner Publications, and good luck! We are always glad to consider the works of talented new authors, and we hope to hear from you soon.

Categories: Juvenile

Name: Jennifer Martin, Submissions Editor
Material: All
Address: 241 FIRST AVE N
City/State/ZIP: MINNEAPOLIS MN 55401
Telephone: 612-332-3344
Fax: 612-332-7615

Liberal Arts Press

Please refer to Publishers Associates.

The Liberal Press

Please refer to Publishers Associates.

Lifetime Books, Inc.
Fell Publishers, Compact Books

We were established in 1943 in New York City as Fell Publishers, relocating to Hollywood, FL in 1984. We renamed to Lifetime Books in 1991. Our two imprints are Fell Publishers and Compact Books. In addition to the 20 annual titles published, we distribute books to the trade for 7 publishers. Our books are marketed to the book trade through National Book Network.

Lifetime Books, distributed by the nation's third largest distributor, National Book Network, has door-to-door sales reps, telemarketers and direct mailers in the US, representing us in all fifty states. Our books are sold primarily to bookstores, libraries and special markets. Our international reps force spans across the globe, securing sales and foreign rights for our titles.

We will consider publishing your book or distributing an existing book. We welcome your submission.

In reviewing manuscript proposals we prefer not to receive the entire manuscript right away. It becomes an unnecessary expense on your part. Rather, we would first like to receive an outline of your book. Submit, for example, a list of sample chapters—convince us your book is different or better than the competition in this field. Send us an extensive author biography—tell us how you will be able to push promotions and sales of your book. Lastly, send us a sample chapter and an introduction synopsis of the book.

Do not phone us or visit our office to solicit a response to your proposal. Careful consideration of your proposal may take months.

We publish both trade hardcover and paperback, ranging from 200 to 300 pages (45,000 to 60,000 words). If we accept your proposal we will need the manuscript provided to us on a WordPerfect 5.1 disk. Our turnaround time from acceptance to publication is approximately six to eight months, with an average first print run of 5,000 - 20,000 books. We generally do not pay an advance—but will consider it in special circumstances.

We accept submissions from best-selling professionals or first-time authors. Some of our more prestigious authors include the best-selling Og Mandino, Irving Wallace, Walter B. Gibson, Robert L. Shook, Alan Truscott, Jane Roberts and Lillian Roth.

The genres or subject matters we prefer are: self-help, business, how-to, health, reference, cookbooks, inspirational and spirituality (but not on a specific religion). We especially like books containing information people need to have or find interesting.

Sensational biographies or tabloid-oriented manuscripts will always receive our full attention. We prefer not to consider works of fiction, poetry, children's, or games.

We are looking to discover something truly unique or special about your book or your credentials, so make it easy for us and tell us up front just what exactly it is that you are proposing to us. Please include relevant samples of artwork (photos, illustrations, etc.) as well.

Nonfiction books will be given strong consideration. You should consult the library, bookstore or publishers' catalogs and compare your idea with their product. Look at Bowker's *Books In Print* or *Forthcoming Titles*. Ask yourself: Is my book really different, better or new and improved? If the answer is "yes" send it to us.

Thank you for considering Lifetime Books, Inc.

Categories: Nonfiction—Business—College—Cooking—Diet—Entertainment—Health—Hobbies—Inspirational—Jewish Interests—New Age—Sexuality

Name: Brian Feinblum, Senior Editor
Material: All
Address: 2131 HOLLYWOOD BLVD
City/State/ZIP: HOLLYWOOD FL 33020
Telephone: 954-925-5242
Fax: 954-925-5244
E-mail: LIFETIME@SHADOW.NET

LionHearted Publishing, Inc.

Romance writers are invited to submit previously unpublished single title historical and contemporary romance novels.

LionHearted does not find romantic: Horror, gore, rape, degradation, sexual depravity, and gratuitous graphic violence. Manuscripts under 65,000 words may be returned without review. We are a new publisher of romance and strongly recommend that authors have read the types of books we publish.

HISTORICAL ROMANCE—**Historical accuracy is important! Be able to document your sources!**

Classic Historical romances, any time period (approx. 100,000 to 150,000 words)

Regency romances (approx. 65,000 to 100,000 words) with Spice* or with love scene

Western, Indian, Colonial American romances (approx. 90,000 to 105,000 words)

Time-Travel romances (Historical or forward to Contemporary or Future) (approx. 90,000 to 105,000 words)

CONTEMPORARY ROMANCE—**Do not submit category, series, saga, anthologies, or young adult.**

Contemporary, Action-Adventure, Humor romances (approx. 70,000 to 125,000 words)

Suspense, Intrigue, Mystery romances (approx. 70,000 to 90,000 words)

Futuristic, Technology, Sci-Fi romances (approx. 90,000 to 105,000 words) *must be 51% a romance*

Paranormal, Ghost, Fantasy romances (approx. 90,000 to 105,000 words) *no vampire or horror please*

Our editors prefer expanded plots and more character depth. The hero's and heroine's goals and/or ruling passions should be revealed early and preferably be in conflict with each other. The hero and heroine should meet early and not be separated for long periods of time. They can be any age, and physical attributes are not as important as fully developed and clearly defined personalities. Motivation and personality should be revealed through dialogue, actions and narrative. Create a likeable heroine, and a hero readers will fall in love with by the end of the book. Humor is always welcome.

Three major reasons for LH editors rejecting a manuscript are:

1. lack of conflict
2. underdeveloped characters
3. too many points of view

Make sure your story is a romance! Romance novels always have a happy ending. Limit point of view to the heroine and hero. Our editors like the main story focus to be the *relationship* conflict. Sexual tension should not be confused with conflict, but both are vital. If without love scenes there should still be sexual tension. Love scenes can be light to heavy sensual. If love scenes are present, they should advance the story or characters and tastefully establish emotional intimacy rather than focus on the mechanics.

Master the techniques and skills of good writing. Present a professional image. Self-edit to the best of your ability. Check spelling, grammar, punctuation, sentence structure and use proper submission format.

Be a master storyteller. If you first create your unique and memorable characters they will help you develop and expand your plot with lots of lively dialogue, sexual tension, and conflict. Our editors prefer that some external conflict is introduced by the end of the first chapter, and want to see both internal and external conflict in the work. External is defined as beyond the hero's or heroine's control and could prevent them from having a happy ending together. Use all five senses and bring the reader into the adventure and setting. Write from your heart the romance you would love to read and readers will love it, too. Have fun!

Romance Submission Guidelines

COVER LETTER Address submissions to address below. PLEASE include in your cover letter the following: 1) whether the MS is contemporary or historical, 2) the sub-genre of romance, or if you are attempting some new blend, 3) word count, 4) a paragraph thumbnail sketch of the storyline, and 5) your phone, fax and e-mail addresses. *Always include a #10 SASE for editor's comments.*

SYNOPSIS A synopsis must be included with every submission. It should be a double-spaced, clear, concise rendering of the complete storyline, approx. 1-5 pages.

FORMAT Typewritten. Title page must include the author's real name, address and phone number, the title and word count. Indicate if a pseudonym will be used. In the upper left hand corner include the author's last name and the first *major* word in the title, e.g., Mitchell/Gone; Woodiwiss/Flame. Chapters should start a third to halfway down a page which leaves room for editor's comments.

AGENTS Unsolicited and non-agent manuscripts are welcome. All manuscripts are evaluated equally at LionHearted. The contract is standard for all authors.

SUBMISSIONS Manuscripts must have a cover letter and a synopsis. From overseas, or if an unusual genre blend, a query and synopsis and/or partial is acceptable. Turnaround approx. 4-12 weeks. Simultaneous submissions are discouraged.

PAYMENT LionHearted is not a vanity or subsidy press. There is a partial guarantee advance paid that is market competitive or above. In addition to alternative distribution channels, LionHearted does store distribution on a national level. No author is required to promote or sell their book, although most know the wisdom of promotion and enjoy book signings, etc. No author monies are withheld due to reserve against returns. 10% royalty checks with computer statements commence approx. 60-90 days after release.

COPYRIGHT Copyright is in the author's name.

WE RECOMMEND:

1) Use two or three rubber bands in both directions to secure your pages.

2) Include a #10 SASE for editor's personal comments and critique even if you include a large return envelope.

3) For ease in handling we prefer return envelopes to be the red/white/blue Priority Mail envelopes, which are free from any post office. Self-address and attach return postage (*if metered, postage* MUST be without a date).

Categories: Romance (only over 65,000 words)

Name: Acquisitions Editor
Material: All
Address: PO BOX 618
City/State/ZIP: ZEPHYR COVE NV 89448
Telephone: 702-588-1388
Fax: 702-588-1386
E-mail: admin@lionhearted.com
Internet: www.lionhearted.com

Llewellyn Publications
New Worlds of Mind and Spirit

ABOUT LLEWELLYN PUBLICATIONS

Thank you for your interest in Llewellyn Publications. We always welcome new writers in what we consider the most fascinating and rewarding area of publishing: *The New Age*. Llewellyn is the oldest and one of the largest publishers specializing in the New Age Sciences.

To save you time and effort, we have prepared these guidelines. They will tell both what we are looking for in subject matter and the information we need to consider a manuscript for publication. **Please read the guidelines *carefully* before submitting any material.**

Llewellyn's New Age areas include the following:

• **Self-Improvement.** Creative visualization, hypnosis and self-hypnosis; subliminal reprogramming; psychic and magical uses of color, music, sound, amulets; some types of magic with the object of better living, health and longevity, recovery, success, happiness, or luck.

• **Self-Development**. Meditation, healing, personal programming, guided imagery, active imagination, regression and memory recall, some types of yoga and martial arts, high magick and the development of psychic abilities.

• **Self-Awareness.** Dream recall, past life memory, personality analysis, mythology, consciousness exploration and occult anatomy (chakras, psychic energies, etc.).

• **Spiritual Science.** Techniques for spiritual growth, prayer, mantra, adoration and worship, and the esoteric side of religious and ritual drama.

• **Men's and Women's Studies.** New issues and approaches to gender-related spiritual, psychic, and physical concerns and needs.

• **Certain Types of Alternative Technologies.** Emphasis on small-scale intensive farming and gardening, organic gardening, herb gardening and preparation, and use of herbs.

• **Crafts.** Construction of magical and psychotronic tools and instruments, healing, lunar-related activities, and especially moon gardening, fishing, and personal cycles, alternative energy sources, home brewing, wine making, and cookbooks.

• **Alternative Health and Healing.** Diet and nutrition, cookbooks, seasonal recipes, inner body awareness, longevity, massage and movement, visualization, and use of sound.

• **Nature Religions and Lifestyles.** Certain aspects of mythology and folklore, solar and lunar related festivals, Paganism, Wicca, rituals, meditations, Earth energies, and ecology.

• **Spiritist and Mystery Religions.** Voudoun, Macumba, Huna, Shamanism, Candomble, techniques of trance, drumming, and the use of masks.

• **Divination.** Tarot, I Ching, runes, dowsing, geomancy, numerology, cards, palmistry, graphology, and body language.

• **FATE Presents.** "Unexplained phenomenon," including UFOs, "monsters," hauntings, poltergeists, mysterious places, alternative science, and unfamiliar practices. Emphasis on new approaches (including "traditional" occult concepts, proof of survival, true mystical experiences) to understanding phenomenon.

• **Tantra.** Sex-magick, bio-energies, body awareness, Tai Chi, martial arts, the "esoteric" side of dance, Goddess worship, sensual enhancement, and relationships.

• **Fiction.** Topics reflecting true "occult" principles: astrology, parapsychology, mythology, archetypal psychology, Witchcraft/Wicca, Pagan lifestyles, Zen. Our fiction is meant to be educational and entertaining. We do not want "supernatural horror."

In addition to books, we publish calendars, datebooks, almanacs, magazines, card deck kits, and audio and video cassettes.

Our emphasis is always on the practical: how it works, how to do it, and self-help material. We aim our products at a general audience and do not assume our readers possess previous specialist knowledge. We do not publish "about" books, collections of aphorisms or poetry, or "famous people" books. We are *not* academic or scholarly publishers.

We prefer books that have strong mail-order potential as well as general bookstore appeal, and we actively promote our publications, via mail order and direct mail.

PREPARING YOUR MANUSCRIPT FOR SUBMISSION

Seeing your book in print is every writer's dream, the reward for a long, arduous creative effort. We understand and respect that. But we ask that you keep in mind that publishing is a business, and authors should regard potential publishers as they would any other professional contact. That is, be prepared, well-informed, and realistic. We encourage you to use your library and any good bookstore for "How to Get Published" guides.

Llewellyn accepts entire manuscripts for submission or proposals (cover letter, outline, and sample chapters). In either case, we ask you to observe some simple submission rules.

In your cover letter, inform us if you are currently working with a literary agent, or have the intention of doing so, providing us with the agent's name, address, and phone number. Also, if this is a multiple submission, inform us of the number of current submissions.

Date and sign all correspondence.

Specifications. On the manuscript itself, consistent page format is a very important consideration. We require the following specifications:

Use a standard, easy-to-read typestyle—Times, Courier, Palatino—in 11 or 12 point type. We cannot accept handwritten manuscripts or manuscripts set in script type or all capitals. Your margin should be ragged right, and use tabs to create paragraph indents.

Do not add an extra line space between paragraphs.

Paginate the manuscript consecutively from beginning to end. Do not paginate chapters separately. Format your running heads to include the manuscript title, chapter number/name, and the page number. Date your manuscript cover page.

We prefer letter quality, laser printed pages, but we will accept *high-quality* dot matrix printouts.

Provide an accurate character or word count for each chapter, and a total page count.

Disk Submission. In addition to a printed copy of the manuscript, we usually require a computer disk copy. We prefer 3.5" disks in a format compatible with our own. Our first choice is a Macintosh disk in QuarkXPress or Microsoft Word, but MacWrite is also acceptable.

If you work in any other word-processing or page layout software, please save your files as "text only." Likewise, if you are using IBM or an IBM clone, we prefer Microsoft Word, also saved as text only.

Saving text only will remove your formatting codes, eliminating many production problems later. However, our editors do benefit from seeing formatting on your hard copy, for bold headings, etc. Therefore, we recommend that you output the hard copy with the formatting codes, *then* save the text only. (If you would like to keep a record of your formatting, please make an additional copy of the files before the final save.) Formatting should be the only difference between the hard copy and the disk: *the texts of both must match exactly!*

Break the manuscript up into small, manageable files, e.g., one chapter per file.

Label your disk(s) clearly with the following information:
1. Title of manuscript
2. Author's name
3. Date (disks *must* be dated)
4. Software used to create files

Later in the acquisitions process, we may ask you to do revisions on your manuscript. In that case, we require that you submit a complete, revised hard copy and disk, dated and labeled as a "Revised Version."

Contents. There are certain text elements and supplements that have either proven useful to our readers or that are required by libraries. They include the following.

• A table of contents, complete and consistent with your text.

• An index or a list of terms you wish included in an index. (An index is almost always required for library acquisitions.)

• A glossary, if you believe it will benefit the reader.

• A bibliography, annotated if appropriate.

Also in regard to content, we cannot, of course, accept writing that reflects sexist, racist, or intolerant attitudes.

Permissions. If your text includes quotations or data from other published sources, *you* are responsible for determining fair use or public domain status, or for obtaining, *in writing*, all required permission grants.

At the time of manuscript submission, you must include a complete list of excerpts or quotations for which you intend to seek permission to use. When you do apply to the copyright holder for permission grants, you may use the form below. The signed permission grants should be returned directly to you, and you are responsible for presenting Llewellyn with complete documentation within 180 days of signing your Publishing Agreement.

Start your permissions process as soon as possible, and be prepared to pursue your applications. Granting other authors permission to use their materials is not a high priority for most publishers. Response times vary greatly. Keep in mind, too, that you may be refused permission, that the paper trail may be longer than expected, etc.

Copyright law does include the doctrine of "fair use," which allows limited use of copyrighted materials without a formal permission grant. Fair use is based on the principle of "amount and substantiality"—how much of the original work has been copied and how is it being used? There are no hard and fast rules: fair use usually applies if the quote is brief, is taken from a lengthy narrative, and is used only as an illustrative point in the borrowing work.

Llewellyn uses a rule of thumb of 200 words total quoted from a 300-page book or 50 words total from a periodical as fair use. Note that fair use applies only to prose-it rarely covers poetry or music. For more information on copyright law, we recommend *Kirsch's Handbook of Publishing Law*, by Jonathan Kirsch (1st edition, 1995, Acrobat Books, Los Angeles, CA) and *The Copyright Handbook: How to Protect and Use Written Works*, by

Stephen Fishman (2nd edition, 1994, Nolo Press, Berkeley, CA). Your library should also have resources on copyright law, and there are useful websites at http://www.patents.com/copyright.sht and http://gopher.uconn.edu/~bxb95001.

When your manuscript is being prepared for committee discussion, it is reviewed for copyright and citation issues. Any questions or outstanding issues will be returned to you, and you may edit, delete, or apply for permission grants to resolve those issues.

In addition to permission grants. Llewellyn also requires proper attribution and documentation. When citing an outside source in your text-footnotes, endnotes, daggers, etc.—include the complete title of the cited source, its author(s), the publisher, the date and city of publication, and the page number. At the end of your text, all cited materials should be listed in a bibliography, in alphabetical order according to the author's last name. For more information on citation and documentation, we recommend the *Chicago Manual of Style*, 14th edition, The University of Chicago Press.

Illustrations. If there are specific illustrations or diagrams that supplement your text, you may send us sketches, which we will then redo. We do not recommend that you hire your own illustrator. If your sketches are on their own sheets, note their intended locations in the text and include any instructions to the Art Department.

If you are sending photographs to be used as illustrations, they must be professional quality, high contrast, black and white or color prints. Indicate clearly where they belong in the text. We reserve the right to reject or reshoot.

If you are using illustrations or photographs from other published sources, you must obtain permission. Photographs of museum pieces, even very old and famous ones, are not "public domain," as there is an issue of photographic rights involved. As in the case of text quotations, you are responsible for obtaining all art clearances. If your book is art-intensive, you must include all signed art releases or grants with your submission package, as our decision to contract may rest on the available artwork.

If you have created diagrams in any electronic drawing program (e.g., Adobe Illustrator or CorelDraw), please call the Acquisition Department before sending your submission.

Please include postage if you would like your artwork returned. We accept no responsibility for lost materials.

PROMOTING AND MARKETING YOUR BOOK

"Publishing" involves much more than merely printing a book and waiting for orders. The success of any book's sales involves publicity and promotion, and it is vital that you work with us in this regard.

When it is advantageous, we arrange author interviews and advertise appropriately. We also regularly use other marketing and media outlets. Many authors find it worthwhile to hire an independent publicity agent to work with our Publicity Department in scheduling bookstore signings, TV and radio interviews, and promotional bookings. If you already give lectures, workshops, and book signings, or participate in conferences, please let us know as soon as possible, so that we can coordinate sales and promotions.

Our sales program is international, with distributors in Australia, Britain, Canada, Mexico, Continental Europe, India, New Zealand, and elsewhere. We have arrangements with French, German, Italian and Spanish language publishers who market foreign language editions of many of our publications. We also publish original works in Spanish.

Our own *New Worlds* publication is also an opportunity to promote you and your book. As an author, you may provide short articles about different aspects of your book's subject, or you may respond to readers' questions and letters (which we solicit and forward to you). This all helps expand interest in the subject

Books

matter and the sales of your book. Our Marketing Department will contact you and send guidelines for *New Worlds*.

In addition, trade catalogs are produced three times a year to match the buying and promotional patterns of the book industry.

AUTHOR QUESTIONNAIRE

About the author. This information will be used for publicity and promotional tools, as well as in the front matter of your book. Please do not provide any information you would not like to see in print!

In 100-250 words, tell us about yourself.

• Who are you and what is interesting about you?

• What are your credentials?

• Why should the reader respect your expertise in the subject area of the book?

What strengths do you possess that we can use in promoting your book? Experience in media interviews? Lectures and workshop programs? Acknowledged expertise in the subject matter? Willingness to travel? Please list the following specifics:

• Membership in any significant organizations or associations, including offices held and dates, that may be help us develop promotional material or establish your "value" to the media.

• Any significant periodicals in which your work (especially work related to the subject area of this book) has been published.

• Media or broadcast interview programs (or types of programs) that you believe will be particularly interested in this book (including names of personal contacts).

• Organizations (or even types of organizations, such as church study groups) you believe will want to use this book (in bulk purchases) as program resource material (with names of contacts if known).

• Recognized authorities on the book's subject matter whom you believe might be willing to read galleys and write comments for publication, including cover and advertising "blurbs" and reviews. Please include addresses, if known, and indicate whether the person is known to you personally.

• Bookstores or other pertinent sales organizations where you are known and that may be responsive to personal promotional opportunities (book signings, lectures, workshops).

About the book. In 300-500 words tell us "Why You (the consumer) Should Read This Book." In answering, consider the following:

• What will this book do for the reader in practical, immediate terms?

• What makes this product *unique?*

Also list the major points of value about this book. Think in terms of the points you wish us to emphasize in developing advertising and promotional copy, including back cover copy.

• What do you believe distinguishes this book from comparable titles?

• Develop some advertising blurbs. You are the author; you know the book better than anyone else. How will the book be sold? What will motivate people to buy it?

• Describe the audience, including age group, to whom this book is directed, and why you believe this audience will be responsive to your book.

• Other than through trade or specialty bookstores, how do you believe this audience can best be reached?

Finally, tell us about your other publications or works-in-progress.

• List any previously published works, sequentially, with title, publisher, year.

• List any works that are forthcoming, with title, publisher, and anticipated publication year. List any books you are now working on or planning.

PERMISSIONS REQUEST

Date:

To:

From:

I am writing to request permission to reproduce the following:

Title:

Author:

Edition and year of publication:

Excerpt(s), as indicated on the attached page(s):

For use in my work:

Tentative Title:

Author:

Publisher: TBD

Est. Print Run: 5,000—20,000

Est. Retail Price: TBD

Rights Requested: Worldwide

Will you kindly give the author permission to reproduce the material indicated above in all editions and reprints of the work and any and all derivations thereof? Full credit will be given in whatever form you specify.

For your convenience, a release form is provided below. In signing, you warrant that you are the sole owner of the rights granted herein, and that the work does not infringe upon the copyright or other rights of anyone.

IRREVOCABLE PERMISSION IS HEREBY GRANTED FOR USE OF THE MATERIAL AS STIPULATED.

Form of copyright acknowledgment:

Authorized signature: Date:

Categories: Fiction—Nonfiction—Cooking—Diet—Fantasy—Gardening—Health—Inspirational—New Age—Paranormal—Psychology—Religion—Spiritual

Name: Nancy Mostad, Acquisitions Manager
Material: All
Address: PO BOX 64383
City/State/ZIP: ST PAUL MN 55164-0383
Telephone: 612-291-1970
Fax: 612-291-1908-
E-mail: lwlpc@llewellyn.com
Internet: www.llewellyn.com

Lodestar Books

Lodestar Books publishes picture books, photo essays, and fiction and nonfiction for children and young adults ages 8-10, 10-14, and 12 up.

Because of the large number of submissions we receive, we are no longer accepting unsolicited manuscripts. If you wish to query us, please send a one-page letter/synopsis.

As a rule, publishers select a suitable illustrator unless the author does his/her own illustrations. You are welcome to send samples of artwork, but please do not send original artwork.

If you are submitting photographs, please send duplicate slides, film transparencies, or several photo prints. Do not send contact sheets.

Categories: Juvenile

Name: Virginia Buckley, Editorial Director
Material: All
Address: 375 HUDSON ST
City/State/ZIP: NEW YORK NY 10014
Telephone: 212-366-2627
Fax: 212-366-2011

Remember: Editors change jobs and publishers change addresses. It is wise to invest in a phone call for the current information before submitting.

Love Inspired
Steeple Hill

Thank you for your interest in Love Inspired. This series of contemporary, inspirational love stories portrays Christian characters facing the many challenges of life, faith and love in today's world.

Compelling and thoughtfully developed, Love Inspired stories lift readers' spirits and gladden their hearts.

Drama, humor and even a touch of mystery all have a place in this series. Subplots are welcome and should further the story's main focus or intertwine in a meaningful way. Secondary characters (children, family, friends, neighbors, fellow church members, etc.) may all contribute to a substantial and satisfying story.

These wholesome tales of romance include strong family values and high moral standards. While there is no premarital sex between characters, a vivid, exciting romance that is presented with a mature perspective is essential.

Although the element of faith must clearly be present, it should be well integrated into the characterizations and plot. The conflict between the main characters should be an emotional one, arising naturally from the well developed personalities you've created.

Suitable stories should also impart an important lesson about the powers of trust and faith.

Manuscript length is 75,000 to 80,000 words.

Submission:

Submit material by contacting us with a query letter, or by sending a partial manuscript (the first three chapters and an outline of no more than five pages, double-spaced). We are not accepting unsolicited, complete manuscripts at this time. We do not accept partials or manuscripts on disk.

The cover letter for all submissions should indicate: if the project is completed, complete word length and the author's previous publishing experience, if any. Queries should include a synopsis of the story that gives a clear idea of the characters and plot and should be no more than two single-spaced pages.

Secure manuscripts with rubber bands only. Please include your complete name, address and phone number on all correspondence and on cover sheets to manuscripts.

Please include a SASE for our reply to any correspondence.

Categories: Fiction—Inspirational—Romance—Women's fiction

Name: Anne Canadeo, Editor
Material: All
Address: STEEPLE HILL
Address: 300 E 42ND ST
City/State/ZIP: NEW YORK NY 10017

Lumen Editions

All manuscripts submitted to Lumen Editions should be typed. We do not publish genre writing, i.e., science fiction, fantasy, horror, romance. We look for intelligent fiction and nonfiction that is original and that is, most importantly, memorable and evocative of the senses. We do accept multiple submissions, but writers should note in their cover letter that the book is under consideration at other houses. It is suggested that before submitting any manuscript to Lumen, that you telephone and request a catalogue to get a sense of what we do publish. For a catalogue, please send an SASE with two first class stamps.

Categories: Fiction—Nonfiction—Hispanic—Jewish Interests—Literature—Travel—Writing

Name: Sadi Ranson, Series Editor
Material: All
Address: PO BOX 1047
City/State/ZIP: CAMBRIDGE MA 02238
Telephone: 617-868-0360
Fax: 617-868-1772
E-mail: brooklinebks@delphi.com

Lyons & Burford, Publishers

Lyons & Burford welcomes all book proposals that fit our publishing profile—books on outdoor leisure sports, natural history, camping, fishing and the like—whether of a practical or literary nature. Proposals should include a full contents and a representative sample of the text and illustrations. We need to see hard copy rather than electronic submissions.

Bear in mind that our list is expanding al the time and many proposals that may not seem to fit what we have published in the past may in fact be of interest. If you have any question about whether a book is right for us, drop us a note (with SASE please) and we will be glad to respond.

Categories: Nonfiction—Animals—Arts—Cooking—Crafts—Food/Drink—Games—Gardening—General Interest—History—Natural History—Outdoors—Physical Fitness—Recreation—Rural America—Sports

Name: Lilly Golden, Editor
Material: All
Address: 31 W 21ST ST
City/State/ZIP: NEW YORK NY 10010
Telephone: 212-620-9580
Fax: 212-929-1836

MacMurray & Beck

MacMurray & Beck is an independent publisher located in Denver, Colorado. The company has distinguished itself from other small presses by publishing new nonfiction with original approaches. Their strong and diverse list of nonfiction includes health-related titles as well as books for the armchair scientist. Dr. O.T. Bonnett, M.D., examines the relationship between health and personal intent, covering both how we become sick and what the mechanisms are for healing ourselves in his book, *Why Healing Happens*. Dr. Bonnett also wrote *Confessions Of a Healer*, which investigates the specific mechanisms of individual illnesses and the sources of chronic pain. In *The Planetary Mind*, astrophysicist Arne A. Wyller, Ph.D., explores the possibility that there is an unrecognized, organized force behind the evolution of the universe.

MacMurray & Beck has also made a name for itself as a publisher of commercial fiction of notable literary quality. We published *St. Burl's Obituary* by Daniel Akst, a finalist for both this year's PEN/Faulkner Award and the 1996 Los Angeles Times Book Prize for First Fiction. *Stygo* by Laura Hendrie was a PEN/Hemingway finalist in 1994 and winner of the Rosenthal Foundation Award from the Academy of Arts and Letters in 1995. Other titles include Rick Collignon's *The Journal of Antonio Montoya* and *Perdido*, Cathryn Alpert's *Rocket City*, recently released in paperback by Vintage. The company's reputation is based on the core of talented, unrepresented new writers it continues to introduce.

Many of MacMurray & Beck's novels have been included in the Barnes & Noble Discover Program.

MacMurray & Beck is the winner of design awards from the Rocky Mountain Book Publishers Association as well as the Art Directors Club of Denver. Their books are available through bookstores nationwide and the following wholesalers: Baker & Taylor, Bookpeople, Bookazine, and Ingram. Or, direct through MacMurray & Beck at the address below.

Submission Guidelines

• MacMurray & Beck is a general trade publisher of personal nonfiction and reflective, literary novels with contemporary settings.

• We do not publish historical fiction or genre fiction of any type.

• We do not publish self-help books or children's books. Nor do we publish poetry.

• The nonfiction titles we choose to handle are, we believe, both surprising and challenging in perspective. We are most interested in manuscripts that reflect carefully and emotionally on the ways we live our lives, on the things that happen to us, on what we know and believe. Our editors are also drawn to works that contemplate the roles that geography, culture, family, and tradition play in all our efforts to define ourselves. We search for works that are free of the modern habit of accepting the world without thought.

• If you believe from the above that your work would fit tightly into our list, we'd be happy to take a look at it.

• Please send a one-page synopsis, a table of contents (for nonfiction), and fifty sample pages (including all or part of the first chapter).

Categories: Fiction—Nonfiction—Biography—Ethnic—Feminism—Literature—Multicultural—Women's Fiction

Name: Acquisitions Editor
Material: All
Address: 1649 DOWNING ST
City/State/ZIP: DENVER CO 80218
Telephone: 303-832-2152
Fax: 303-832-2158
E-mail: Koffler@macmurraybeck.com
Internet: www.macmurraybeck.com

Mage Publishers

Mage Publishers publishes high-quality English-language books about Persian culture, including: cookbooks, translations of literature, history, children's tales, biography and autobiography, architectural studies, and books on music and poetry.

Only books relating to Persian culture are considered by the editors; submissions not falling within these boundaries are returned unread.

Authors interested in submitting work for consideration should send a letter outlining their work and a brief biographical statement. We will usually respond to your letter within 2-4 weeks.

Categories: Fiction—Nonfiction—Architecture—Cooking—Culture—Ethnic—Gardening—History—Literature—Multicultural—Music—Short Stories

Name: Amin Sepehri
Material: All
Address: 1032 29TH ST NW

City/State/ZIP: WASHINGTON DC 20007
Telephone: 202-342-1642
Fax: 202-342-9269
E-mail: Mage1@access.digex.net

Margaret K. McElderry Books
An Imprint of Simon & Schuster
Children's Publishing Division

Margaret K. McElderry Books publishes original hardcover trade books for children from pre-school age through young adult. The list includes picture books, easy-to-read books, fiction and nonfiction for eight to twelve-year-olds, poetry, science fiction, fantasy and young adult fiction and nonfiction. The style and subject matter of the books we publish is almost unlimited. We do not publish textbooks, coloring and activity books, greeting cards, magazines and pamphlets or religious publications.

General Submission Guidelines

Margaret K. McElderry Books is not currently evaluating unsolicited manuscripts. You may send a query letter. The letter should *briefly* describe the nature of the book. You may also include a very brief resumé of your previous publishing credits. Query letters may be addressed to Margaret K. McElderry, Vice President and Publisher.

If we ask to see your manuscript

We do not consider submissions sent on computer disk. If you would like to insure the safe arrival of your manuscript, please enclose a self-addressed, stamped postcard which we will date and send back to you.

Please note: Margaret K. McElderry Books publishes a limited number of picture books each year. It is the prerogative of the publisher to choose illustrators and the art director regularly interviews professional artists for this purpose.

Categories: Children's Trade—Young Adult Trade

Name: Margaret K. McElderry,
 Vice President and Publisher
Material: Query Letters
Address: 1230 6TH AVE
City/State/ZIP: NEW YORK NY 10020

Markowski International Publishers, Success Publishers

Established in 1976. Publishes trade paperback originals. Publishes 10 titles/year. Receives 1,000+ submissions/year. 50% of books from first time authors; 100% from unagented authors. Average print order for a first book is 5,000-50,000. Pays on royalty basis. Publishes book 1 year or less from acceptance. Accepts simultaneous submissions. Reports within 2 months. Books catalog and ms. guidelines for #10 SASE with 2 first-class stamps.

Nonfiction: Primary focus on personal development, self-help, sales and marketing, leadership training, network marketing, entrepreneurship, motivation and success topics. We are interested in how-to, motivational and instructional books of short to medium length that will serve recognized and emerging needs of focus topics. Query or submit outline, table of contents, and entire ms.

Recent Nonfiction Title: REJECT ME-I LOVE IT! by John Fuhrman.

Tips: We're intensifying our search for best-selling manuscripts. We're looking for authors who are dedicated to their message and want to make a difference in the world. We especially like to work with authors who speak and consult.

Categories: Business—Entrepreneurship—Inspirational—Money/Finance—Opportunity—Pop Psychology—Self-Help—Success

Name: Marjorie L. Markowski, Editor-in-Chief
Material: All
Address: ONE OAKGLADE CIRCLE STE 222
City/State/ZIP: HUMMELSTOWN PA 17036
Telephone: 717-566-0468
Fax: 717-566-6423

Masquerade Books

Thank you for inquiring about our company. Masquerade Books publishes 10 titles per month, as well as a bimonthly erotic journal, *Masquerade*.

The imprints are as follows:

MASQUERADE: Straight erotica, usually with an SM bent. Classic Victorian titles, Paul Little, Titian Beresford, Amarantha Knight.

BADBOY: Erotica for gay men. Authors include John Preston, Aaron Travis, Larry Townsend.

ROSEBUD: Erotica for lesbians. Authors include Valentina Cilescu, Lindsay Welsh and the *Leatherwomen* series. This imprint is only open to women writers.

HARD CANDY: Literary works by gay men and women with a strong emphasis on sexuality and sexual themes. Authors include Lars Eighner, Felice Picano and Chea Villanueva.

RHINOCEROS: Pansexual literary works with a strong emphasis on sexuality and sexual themes. Authors include Philip José Farmer, Grant Antrews and Sara Adamson/Laura Antoniou (Marketplace Trilogy).

We are not buying poetry.

Our basic guidelines are as follows:

• Both novels and short story collections are accepted, though we *strongly* prefer the former.

• Short story collections should contain no more than 30% previously published material.

• Accepted manuscripts are approximately 60,000 words.

• Hard copy or electronic submission are both acceptable.

• There are content boundaries as well, so please keep characters and relationships legal: no one under eighteen, no familial relationships etc. If you require more clarification on this point, please contact us.

• Submission packages should contain the following: a cover letter, including prior publishing and/or writing experience, an outline and two sample chapters, and an SASE.

Categories: Fiction—Erotica

Name: Richard Kasak
Material: All
Address: 801 SECOND AVE
City/State/ZIP: NEW YORK NY 10017
Fax: 212-986-7355
E-mail: MasqBks@aol.com

Masters Press
Spalding Sports Library

Welcome to Masters Press!

As a new Masters Press author, you'll be joining such illustrious names as Isiah Thomas, Dusty Baker, Chuck Daly, Tom Flores, Del Harris, Dick Vitale and many others who have previously published books with our press. Masters Press has been publishing quality sports instructional and informational books since 1986. We expect to continue this tradition by acquiring titles written by qualified authors, such as yourself, on a variety of different topics and issues. We consider ourselves to be in partnership with our authors to create books that both writer and publisher can look upon with pride. In order for us to achieve this goal, it is imperative that you have a clear idea of exactly what is involved in the publishing process here at Masters Press.

Because Masters Press produces a variety of publications each month, we have established a set of standards for authors to follow in order to bring out the best qualities in both themselves and their manuscripts. It is important that we adhere to a certain semblance of priority and order to ensure that Masters Press books are accurate, high-quality, and are moved through production as efficiently as possible.

The *Masters Press Author's Guide* has been prepared to provide a guideline for authors and to provide a comprehensive explanation of the production process. Even experienced authors should find this booklet interesting and informative.

Because of the wide variety of sports books we produce, the information in this booklet is somewhat general in nature. When and where it is appropriate, authors will receive more detailed information from the editor assigned to work with them on their book.

THE REVIEW PROCESS

With most sports books, it is impossible for any one editor to be completely knowledgeable about the field and to make appropriate value judgments about the content, the quality of the outlines and manuscripts, the artwork, etc. In most cases, it is up to the author to make sure that the information presented in the manuscript is as accurate as possible.

Usually, manuscripts are sent to the director before the author is offered a book contract, as this allows the director a chance to determine if the manuscript is appropriate to the publisher's book line and customer base. The director shares the manuscript review process with a staff made up of the managing editor, editorial assistants, and sales and marketing personnel. Reviews vary in thoroughness depending upon the nature of the manuscript, from superficially scanning the work for general information, to an in-depth examination of the grammar, illustrations and diagrams. Depending on the nature of the manuscript, it may be subjected to many rounds of such reviews before the publisher contacts the author to discuss the work and a possible contract. Reviewing a manuscript can last anywhere from a few weeks to up to a year, so the author needs to be patient with the publisher. As long as the publisher has the manuscript, the likelihood of it being accepted as a book remains good.

Once the review process of the manuscript is complete, the director will contact the author to discuss the work and set up a book contract. Once the contract negotiations are settled, and the author and publisher have signed copies of the agreement, the author will be assigned to a book editor, and production on the book will begin.

COPYRIGHTS AND PERMISSIONS

Permission to use copyrighted material in a manuscript or book must be provided, in writing, to both the author and the publisher by the party whose copyrighted work is being considered for the manuscript. Copyright is often a confusing problem for authors, often due to ignorance of the copyright laws. Here, we will attempt to clarify those laws. For more detailed information or to research recent updates to the copyright laws, the author should check with the local library.

First of all, it is important to determine what is copyrighted, and what may or may not be used in a publication without obtaining permission. In a nutshell, the only published material that is NOT under copyright protection is material originally published by the U.S. government (such as the Constitution of the United States), material considered to be in the public domain from the date of publication (most libraries keep track of public domain material), and copyrighted material which, due to the expiration of time parameters, is no longer protected by copyright laws. Authors may feel free to use as much of these types of materials as they wish without restriction, although common courtesy de-

Books

mands that they at least give credit to the source in their footnotes. For all other materials, written permission must be obtained from the source before information from these materials can be included in a manuscript, including text, artwork, photographs, etc.

Unpublished work is also protected by copyright laws. Under the Copyright Act of 1976 (title 17 of the United States Code), a work is protected by copyright from the time it is created in a fixed form. In other words, when a work is written down or otherwise set into tangible form, it is automatically copyrighted in the author's or artist's name. Only the author, or individuals deriving their rights from the author, can claim copyright ownership. A manuscript sent to a publisher by an author, for example, is already copyrighted in the author's name, so the publisher cannot reproduce material from the manuscript without direct permission of the author. Drawings and photographs are also automatically copyrighted under the name of the illustrator or photographer who produced them.

However, under a copyright law that defines the category "Works Made For Hire," if a work is made for hire - such as an employee producing something requested by his or her employer - the employer and not the employee is considered to be the author, and thus holds the copyright. The employer can be a firm, an organization, or an individual. (See Section 101 of the copyright law for a complete statutory definition.)

Let's examine some copyright concerns in which many authors have personal interest:

Time Parameters: Under the old copyright laws, material published before 1906 was considered to be in the public domain. After 1906, copyright protection was granted for a period of 28 years, and ONE renewal for an additional, similar period was permitted. Therefore, the maximum term of copyright protection granted to a book published in 1910, for example, would be *56* years if the copyright was renewed. Copyright protection for that book would expire in either 1938 or 1966, depending on whether or not the copyright was renewed. However, if the book was revised to a respectable extent, it could be copyrighted in a new edition as if it were a new, original book. There are a number of medical books dating back to the 1890s that are still under copyright protection because they are still in print and have been revised sufficiently to give each new revision its own copyright protection.

The current copyright law, from 1976, states that material published after January 1978 carries a copyright for the life of the author plus 50 years, or 75 years after publication, or 100 years after creation, whichever period is shortest. For example.

Joe Author published a book in 1979. Joe Author was 35 years old at the time of the creation of the book, and we can assume that he will not live to be 135 years old. The 100-year period is ruled out. The second longest period is 75 years after publication, or the year 2054. So, the book's copyright protection expires in 2054.

Suppose that at age 40, in 1984, Joe Author died. Add fifty years to 1984, which would be the year 2034. The law states that copyright protection is granted for the period that is the shortest in duration. So, since Joe Author died in 1984, copyright protection of his book expires in 2034. If Joe Author lived past 2004, however, the copyright protection would expire in 2054 because this period is shorter than the year of the author's death plus 50 years.

Time of Creation: This has to do with the precise time that the work was complete, not to the actual publication date. If an author wrote a book in 1990 but didn't attempt to get it published until 1992, under the maximum period provided for copyright protection, the year of creation would be 1990 plus 100 years. Of course, this provision is rarely used.

Amount of Material Requiring Permission: Sometimes it is difficult to determine if permission needs to be obtained for use of an occasional quote in quotation marks or an actual excerption of a large body of work. There's no strict definition regarding when permission is needed. Primarily, it depends on the length of the quote, its importance, and how closely it is tied to the rest of the work. Permission for use should always be obtained for the following:

1. All quotations of 200 words or more from any one source. This covers either one single quotation or a number of different ones that, totaled, add up to more than 199 words.

2. All quotations of 30 words or more from any newspaper, magazine, periodical, or journal.

3. All artwork required from a source other than the author, even with minor modifications, including photos, hand drawings, halftones, line drawings, computer graphics, tables, schematics, etc.

Trademarks: Permission is not necessary to cite a particular trademark, but it is important for authors to acknowledge logos that are registered as trademarks or trade names. For example, names like PageMaker and Macintosh are trade names for products that have been granted protection under copyright or patent laws. All trademarks should be followed with the designation ® or ™. Initials like IBM do not need to be denoted by these symbols as they represent a firm rather than a product.

Obtaining Permissions: It is the author's responsibility to obtain permission and to submit them, in writing, with the complete manuscript when it is sent to the publisher. Usually, obtaining permissions is not difficult, particularly where manufacturers are concerned because they see it as a form of free advertising. Sometimes a manufacturer will also provide authors with free artwork when approached about having its products featured in a book.

On occasion, a copyright holder will request a permissions fee when an author asks to use material from a journal, periodical, or book. These fees are the responsibility of the author and are paid upon publication of the author's book. Authors who are asked to pay permission fees should seriously consider whether or not the material in question is worth the fee requested.

A sample permission letter appears below, which authors can copy for their own use. Authors should keep the following things in mind when requesting permission of use:

1. When requesting permission from a book publisher, the author should address the letter to the person in charge of handling rights and permissions. For a comprehensive list of publisher addresses and phone numbers, authors should consult the *Literary Market Place,* a directory produced annually that can be found in most public libraries. In magazines and periodicals, the front matter of the issue, usually found in the masthead, should contain a complete list of the staff and their titles, as well as the name and address of the publisher. When requesting permission from a manufacturer, authors should write to either the public relations department or the marketing department of the firm. Complete names and addresses for manufacturers can be found in several directories available at the library.

2. If the amount of work that the author wants to include in a manuscript is too large to fit into the body of the permission letter, the author should provide photocopies with the permission letter of everything being considered for use in the manuscript.

3. If a copyright holder requires a permissions fee, and the author feels that the fee is not appropriate to the manuscript's needs or budget, the author should try to find an alternate source for the material needed for the manuscript. Permissions fees are not required unless the material is actually used and the book is published, so the author has no obligation to pay the copyright holder.

4. If a copyright holder requests a copy of the book once it is complete, it can be arranged between the author and the pub-

lisher at no charge to the author.

SAMPLE PERMISSION LETTER

\<Name and address of publisher, company or copyright holder\>

Dear \<Copyright holder\>,

I am preparing a book tentatively called \<title\>, to be submitted to Masters Press for publishing. I would like permission to use, in this and future editions, the following material:

I would also like permission for worldwide rights in all languages. Full credit will be given in the finished book. If you would like a copy of the book once it is published, please let me know. For your convenience, a release statement is given below. A duplicate of this letter is attached, and if you would sign both copies and return the original to me, I would be very grateful.

Sincerely,

Permission is hereby granted for the use of the described materials as outlined above.

_____

Signature

_____

Title (if applicable)

_____

Date

5. The author should request worldwide rights in all languages from the copyright holder, in case the book is translated in a foreign language. If this is not possible, then the author should ask for worldwide English language rights. Rights can also be specified as North American or domestic US rights. If book contents only have North American rights, for example, the publisher cannot sell the book beyond North American geographical borders, so the book cannot be sold in South America or overseas. Obtaining worldwide rights should not be difficult unless the author is dealing with a foreign company or publisher.

6. It is a good idea for the author to request rights for the first and all subsequent editions of the book, as this prevents having to request permissions again when the book is scheduled for a revision.

ILLUSTRATIONS

Illustrations are very important to the content of sports books because they help the reader bridge the gap between text and reality. For example, it is much easier to understand an inbound play by looking at a diagram rather than reading about it. The logic becomes more clear when the reader can refer to a drawing of the play. Good illustrations are also an important selling point of a sports book. Well-illustrated books are more appealing to impulse shoppers, and more user-friendly to readers who dislike the idea of reading through pages of text.

An author's illustrations do not necessarily have to be of perfect reproducible quality unless photographs are used. Pencil sketches can be reproduced into finished art in the Masters Press art department, for example. If an author does not have the technical resources to produce print-ready art, the publisher can usually produce the artwork as long as the author is very clear as to the details and overall desired appearance of the illustrations.

Planning the illustrative content of a book is just as important as creating the text. Also, when creating a manuscript, it is important that the author make certain that the placement of each illustration is clearly marked in the text.

Photographs: All photographs must be of good quality and display their images clearly. Photos that are cloudy, badly exposed, cluttered, or out of date do nothing to enhance the overall quality of the book. Photographs usually come from a wide variety of sources: manufacturers, advertising agencies, professional photographers, other publishers, amateur photographers, or the authors themselves.

Masters Press, at this point, prefers to use black-and-white glossy photos that are unmarred and devoid of greasy marks or smudges. Most Masters Press books are done in one color, and black-and-white photos are better for this format than color photos. Black-and-white photos are easier to reproduce than color photos, and it is much easier for a computer technician to scan them for insertion into the text. If the photos have already been taken in color, we can use them, but it may affect the quality of the reproduction in the finished product. The author should refrain from marking on the photo or cropping it (trimming it to size), and should make certain that the surface does not become marred or creased by paper clips, mounting anchors, etc. If only part of the photo is to be used as an illustration, the author needs to indicate which part of the photo the publisher should use, either by writing on the border or on the back of the photo. The author should not mark on the picture itself. It is also important for the author to label the back of the photograph with its figure designation. *(Figure 2-1, Figure 2-2, etc.)*

Photo placement is a very time-consuming task. It is very important that the author turn in any photographs as early as possible. Please understand that we are a publishing company that produces between 30 to 40 books per year. Unfortunately, our schedule limits the amount of time available to work on projects. Turning photos in two weeks before the book goes to press will not only delay the publication of your book but also the publication of other books as well.

Photograph Sources: Often, an author will spot the "perfect" photograph in a magazine or other publication. In most cases, the photograph was probably produced by a source other than the publisher, and permission for its use must be obtained if the author wishes to use it. Usually, the source of the photo is printed as a credit line beneath the photo or the photo's caption. The author can contact the original publisher to get information about the photo source, so permissions can be obtained.

As mentioned before, it is important for the author to obtain a black-and-white glossy copy of the desired photograph. This can be requested when the author contacts the source for permission to use the photo. (See the section, COPYRIGHTS AND PERMISSIONS.)

If for some reason the source gives permission for the author to use the photo, but cannot supply an original photo, it is possible for the author to submit the tear sheet or publication page containing the picture to the publisher. The author must keep in mind, however, that the quality of the artwork reproduced from the tear sheet or original page will be inferior to an actual photograph, or even the original page.

Some authors take their own photos, which is fine as long as the photos submitted with the manuscript to the publisher are of good reproductive quality. The author should have a professional studio develop the negatives to ensure the highest quality possible.

Line Drawings: Line drawings include all artwork that is not photographic, including stick figures, graphs, diagrams, etc. Masters Press has an art department capable of producing a wide variety of illustration types, including technical drawings, computer graphics, and complex freehand drawings. If an author submits a rough pencil sketch of an illustration, the art department can usually reproduce it as print-ready artwork. While authors are not expected to be professional artists or draftspersons, it is important that the submitted illustrations be as accurate as possible. Authors must make certain that all information displayed in the illustrations is accurate and will not confuse the reader.

Art Preparation: Masters Press prefers that each drawing be prepared on a separate piece of 8½"x11" bond paper. If the author wants the illustration to have a caption, the caption should be included on the same page as the drawing. The drawings should be labeled clearly enough to be easily understood by the staff artists and editors. Graphs and charts should be consistent in appearance with the other illustrations or graphs. It should also be possible for the artist to reproduce each illustration on a single book page. Two-page spreads of tables or illustrations can be difficult to reproduce and confusing to the reader.

If an illustration is created using a computer program or other printed documentation, the author should submit both a hard copy of the illustration (on paper), and a copy stored on floppy disk.

For both drawings and photographs requiring permission, the author needs to make sure that the signed permission letter is included with the artwork being submitted to the publisher. The author also needs to make sure that a credit line is included that is appropriate to the art being submitted.

MANUSCRIPT PREPARATION

Once the author's manuscript arrives at Masters Press and the contract is negotiated and signed, the production and technical staff begins to create a design for the book. Book design includes typeface selection, trim size, cover design, order and sequence of headings, indentations, artwork placement, equation placement, etc. The author can make this process easier by keeping the format of the manuscript as neat and simple as possible. The manuscript should be created following these guidelines:

1. All manuscripts should be presented to the publisher on paper and on a 3.5" disk.

2. Illustration captions should be provided in a caption list, in addition to on the illustrations themselves, so the layout artists can use them as a reference for keeping track of illustrations.

3. Where credit must be included for a particular illustration, that line should be added in parentheses at the end of the caption. If the illustration source is a company or firm, the full name should be used rather than abbreviations.

4. All tables should be treated like artwork and kept separate from the text. The author should place the table on a separate sheet of paper and indicate in the text where the table should appear.

5. If a table comes from a source other than the author, and permission has been received to use it, the credit should be cited in the caption, labeling it as "source."

6. Photo placement should be indicated in the text. A simple line such as "Place photo 1 here" is sufficient. Make sure the markings on the backs of the photos match the markings in the text.

7. The author is expected to write the front matter for the book. The front matter consists of the author biography page, the preface, the acknowledgment page, and the table of contents. The author biography should include a brief biographical description of the author, highlighting professional training and accomplishments. The preface should inform the reader what the book is about and what is to be gained by reading it. The acknowledgment page is not necessary, but should be included if the author feels in debt to someone for help with the book's contents, or wishes to acknowledge someone's support. A dedication can be substituted for the acknowledgment page, or the book can contain both if the author wishes it.

8. The author should produce three copies of the manuscript, one to be sent to the publisher and two to keep on file in case something happens to the publisher's copy. The publisher's copy should be as complete as possible, and should include a 3.5" disk containing the manuscript. Text, illustrations, tables, front matter, appendices, floppy disks, etc., should all be included in the shipment to the publisher. The pages should NOT be stapled together; a bindery clip or a rubber band is better. When shipping, United Parcel Service is preferable to the U.S. Postal service, as packages are easier to trace through UPS. Finished artwork and other hard-to-replace items should be insured.

THE PRODUCTION PROCESS

Once a manuscript is accepted by a publisher and contracts are finalized, an editor is assigned to the manuscript to guide it through book production. The author will work with the editor for the next few weeks to troubleshoot the book's content.

First, the editor will establish a working schedule for the book to ensure that it is published by a predetermined date. Once this schedule is established, the author needs to work with the editor to ensure that deadlines are met. A delay of a few days on the author's end could result in weeks of delays on the publisher's end. If the author anticipates any delays, the editor needs to be alerted immediately.

Sketches sent to the publisher to be processed into illustrations will be assigned to an artist or group of artists. Once the illustrations are complete, copies of these will also be sent to the author for checking and corrections. The author should check to make sure that the illustrations match the text content, and make any corrections that are necessary. Corrections should be drawn directly onto the illustrations with a red pen and sent back to the project manager. An artist will also be assigned to design the book's cover, and the author may be asked to examine back-cover copy written for the book.

It is very important for the author to double-check all information in the manuscript for accuracy. Though the individuals assigned to work on the manuscript are knowledgeable of sports, they may not be experts in the field being discussed. Ultimately, the author bears full responsibility for the veracity and accuracy of the book's content. Errors that appear in finished books are often the result of the author's assumption that the information was written down correctly the first time. It is extremely easy to make errors while writing a manuscript, so the author should not take for granted that the information in the manuscript is 100 percent correct or that someone will catch all the content errors.

If there are many errors or inconsistencies in the content of the manuscript, the editor may ask the author to rewrite portions of it. The editor is not a ghost writer, and cannot be expected to rewrite the book for the author, so the author is responsible for any weaknesses in the text. However, if any rewriting is requested, the author should not take such a request personally, as the editor is there to help the author make the prose flow as correctly and logically as possible. The author should keep in mind that if the editor cannot understand the intent or meaning of a sentence, then the reader will not be able to understand it either.

The editor will closely examine and read the manuscript for errors, awkward sentences, style consistency, etc. After this first edit, the editor will send the author a hard copy of the corrected manuscript. The author should carefully look over this manuscript. If the author wishes to make changes in the text, he should do so at this stage. Once the book is typeset, changes become difficult. The author should mark any changes directly on the hard copy and mail it back to the editor. Please do not send a disk with changes or only the pages that have changes. Unless there are no changes, the author should send back the complete manuscript.

Once the editor has received the author's corrections, the corrections will be made and the manuscript will be sent through typesetting, producing what is known as a galley proof. The galley contains all of the text, artwork, captions, page numbers, etc., that will appear in the finished book, set in the layout style selected by the editor. The author will receive a copy of the galley once it is complete, in order to check it. The copy quality of the galley may not be the best, as the galleys are simply rough drafts to allow the editors to check for accuracy in composition. Artwork, text, equations, etc., may not appear in the galley as they will in the finished book. However, the author needs to keep in mind that once a book is typeset, further changes and revisions become very expensive and time-consuming.

Further revisions or corrections should have been made in the corrected version of the manuscript that the author returned to the editor. The purpose of the galley is to catch blatant errors or typos. Any changes in content at this point are considered to be the author's alterations: If an author's changes exceed the time allotted for this kind of correction, the publisher may charge the excess time against future royalties. Therefore, any changes in content should be made in the first corrected manuscript copy sent to the author. When looking through a galley, the author needs to check for errors in punctuation, illustration arrangements, etc. If the author has doubts about any of the content, changes or revisions can be documented while the author researches the area, and corrections can be included in the book's second printing.

Once the galleys have been proofread and final changes have been made, the book is sent to a printer to be printed and bound. The book arrives at the printer either stored on disk or on opti-copy boards, depending on the type of book and the amount of paste-up work required for the book. The author will receive a copy of the book as it was sent to the printer. If he finds an error in this copy, he should notify the editor immediately. At the same time the book is being printed, the sales and marketing department begins to work on press releases, flyers, magazine ads, and direct mail ads designed to sell the book to book stores, libraries, sporting goods stores, etc. The author can also suggest companies or individuals that should receive materials about the book.

Categories: Nonfiction—Biography—Diet—Health—Sports

Name: Holly Kondras, Managing Editor
Material: All
Address: 2647 WATERFRONT PKWY E DR STE 100
City/State/ZIP: INDIANAPOLIS IN 46214
Telephone: 317-298-5706-
Fax: 317-298-5604

Mayhaven Publishing
Interesting Books for Interesting People

When Considering a Manuscript for Mayhaven or our Co-op option (Wild Rose): For *each* manuscript we require one hard copy of the completed work, and a $25.00 Reading Fee.

ACCEPTING A MANUSCRIPT IS BASED ON A NUMBER OF FACTORS:
The subject
The slant
Writing style
Marketing Considerations
Our Schedule

If the manuscript is a nonfiction work, we require the author's credentials and a summary of the research.

Children's books have special considerations in regard to number of pages and the type of artwork required.

If a manuscript is accepted, we offer the appropriate Mayhaven or Wild Rose Agreement.

Thank you for your interest in Mayhaven/Wild Rose Publishing

Categories: Fiction—Nonfiction—African-American—Animals—Asian-American—Associations—Biography—Business—Cartoons—Children—Civil War—Comedy—Computers—Confession—Cooking—Crime—Disabilities—Entertainment—Family—Food/Drink—General Interest—History—Horror—Humor—Lifestyles—Literature—Mystery—Native American—Paranormal—Poetry—Reference—Regional—Relationships—Romance—Rural America—Science Fiction—Senior Citizens—Short Stories—Teen—True Crime—Western—Writing—Young Adult

Name: Tonya Abbott, Assistant to the Editor
Material: All
Address: PO BOX 557
City/State/ZIP: MAHOMET IL 61853
Telephone: 217-586-4493

Fax: 217-586-6330
E-mail: IBFIPONE@aol.com
Nota bene: Requires reading fee.

McBooks Press

A small but growing outfit around since 1980, McBooks Press has established focuses on vegetarianism and parenting, sports and regional upstate New York topics; we have recently embarked (!) on the publication of some historical nautical fiction. We are not closed to other subjects, but before we would take on something very far outside these realms, we would have to be convinced of its potential for success. Although McBooks has published poetry in the past, we are not looking at any more or at new fiction.

If you have something you think we should see, it's best to send a brief description of the proposed project, an outline and one or two sample chapters rather than an entire manuscript. We operate with a full plate, few hands and limited resources, so well-thought-out proposals of manageable size are most welcome.

Categories: Nonfiction—Diet—Family—Health—Parenting—Regional—Sports—Vegetarian

Name: S.K. List, Editorial Director
Material: All
Address: 908 STEAM MILL RD
City/State/ZIP: ITHACA NY 14850
Telephone: 607-272-2114
Fax: 607-273-6068
E-mail: alex908@aol.com

McFarland & Company, Inc.
Publishers

McFarland is what has traditionally been known as a scholarly and reference publisher (no fiction, poetry, etc.). Our market has seen more libraries (of all kinds, including academic, public, corporate, etc.) than bookstores, though direct-mail sales to individuals are prominent in our overall marketing picture, particularly in certain specialty lines. We publish around 130 books a year and that's headed upward.

We welcome nonfiction manuscripts on a wide range of subjects, not limited to the following: performing arts (especially film, television, and radio), pop culture, history, women's studies, black studies, sports, chess, art, music, international studies, librarianship, criminal justice, environmental studies (especially chemical sensitivity), and literature. Reference books are one of our specialties.

We do *not* publish fiction, poetry, children's books, inspirational works, cookbooks, diet or self-help books, religious or political tracts, exposés, stories of personal triumph over adversity, or occult or New Age works.

What We Need to See

Authors may contact us with a query letter, a full proposal, or even (if the manuscript is complete and you're confident it could fit in among the books we've already published) a finished manuscript with cover letter. In a query letter you should describe the

Books

manuscript, tell us how far along you are, estimate its final length (in either word count or double-spaced typescript pages), and tell us what is unique about the manuscript (or about you!).

We answer most queries within a few days; if we're interested we'll invite you to send either the complete manuscript or a full proposal, consisting usually of the following elements: an outline or table of contents, estimates of length and completion date, a preface or introduction, comments on how the book differs from any competing works on the same topic, a summary of what you might offer in the way of photographs or other illustrations, and some samples of the manuscript (1-2 chapters or the equivalent, plus representative pages of any special parts).

How to Present the Work

The most important thing is that it be typed and submitted on paper rather than disk (though if we accept the manuscript we will later be interested in your disks for possible use in typesetting). Manuscripts must have pages numbered consecutively, and we prefer that they not be bound in any way. Valuable documents or photographs need not be sent at the proposal stage, though photocopies of them are helpful.

Because of the nature of manuscripts and of reading, we prefer to operate via old-fashioned mail (or UPS) as opposed to phone, fax, or e-mail. We won't summarily turn you down if you come to us through electronic means, but (a) you won't get a faster reply that way, and (b) a proper, easy-to-deal-with copy makes a better impression. Please do not send copies to two or more of our editorial staff.

Be sure to put your name and return address on your cover letter, and on the top page of the proposal or manuscript.

What to Expect from Us

We usually respond to proposals quickly—within two to three weeks. Our decisions are based largely on the freshness of the topic, how well it fits in with our list, how thoroughly and authoritatively you cover it, the quality of the research and writing, and the likely marketability of the book.

When we do accept a book, publication cannot occur immediately. Because we can handle only a certain number of books in a year, and publication entails time-consuming processes (editing, design, typesetting, proofreading, promotion, printing and binding, and so forth), as well as considerable advance planning, a manuscript generally must reach us complete in every way no later than midsummer in order to be a candidate for publication in the following calendar year.

Categories: African-American—Asian-American—Civil War—Environment—Film/Video—History—Multicultural—Scholarly & Reference—Sports—Televison/Radio—Theatre

Name: Robert Franklin, President
Name: Steve Wilson, Editor
Name: Virginia Tobiassen, Editor
Material: Any
Address: UPS: 960 HWY 88 W
Address: PO BOX 611
City/State/ZIP: JEFFERSON NC 28640
Telephone: 910-246-4460
Fax: 910-246-5018
E-mail: mcfarland@skybest.com

Meadowbrook Press

Meadowbrook Press has been in business since 1975 and has grown to become one of the leading publishers in the Midwest. Our books are sold nationally through bookstores and other retail outlets. We specialize in pregnancy, baby care, child care, humorous poetry anthologies for children, party planning, children's activities, children's literature, humor, and quotation collections (plus an occasional cooking title). We will consider any adult nonfiction book proposal that has significant potential. We do not publish autobiographical works. **We are primarily a nonfiction press. We do not consider unsolicited children's picture books or novels.** Our children's short story and poetry collections have very specific guidelines. Send an SASE for the appropriate guidelines before you begin writing. Without reading our guidelines, your chances of acceptance are slim to none.

We take great pride in our ability to edit, design, and promote books so that they achieve their full commercial potential. Four of our books have sold more than a million copies, three books have been *New York Times* best-sellers, two have been #1 bestsellers, and over twenty have been on B. Dalton's and Waldenbooks' best-seller lists.

Guidelines for Submitting Manuscripts to Meadowbrook Press

1. Summarize your manuscript in a cover letter. (What is it about? How is it organized? Does it have or require illustrations, charts, graphs, or photographs?)

2. Tell us why your book will sell. (Why do you think there is a need for this book? How large is the market? What is the precise market? What potential secondary distribution channels-outside of bookstores-exist?)

3. State the competition and why your book is better. Share any knowledge of the sales history of competing books.

4. Tell us what qualifies you to write this book. Also, if you have any promotional experience, or would be willing to promote the book, say so.

5. Please state your publishing history, if any. State what books you have written, when, and by whom they were published. Please include sales figures for your books.

6. Be neat! Typos and sloppiness have a negative impact.

7. After you have submitted your work, please allow four months for a response.

Categories: Nonfiction—Baby Care—Child Care—Humor—Poetry—Pregnancy—Quotation Collections—Short Stories

Name: Submissions Editor
Material: All
Address: 5451 SMETANA DR
City/State/ZIP: MINNETONKA MN 55343
Telephone: 612-930-1100
Fax: 612-930-1940

Medical Physics Publishing
Cogito Books

We are a small, nonprofit publishing company designed to publish books by and for medical physicists. We only publish books written by authors working in the fields of medical physics, diagnostic radiology, oncology, and related areas.

Medical Physics Publishing welcomes manuscript proposals for technical books written by professionals working in medical physics, mammography, radiation oncology, diagnostic radiology, and related areas. We are not able to accept general trade manuscripts.

Elizabeth A. Seaman
Managing Editor
Categories: Diagnostic Radiology—Mammography—Medical Physics—Radiation Oncology—Related Technical Medical

Areas

Name: Acquisitions Editor
Material: All
Address: 4513 VERNON BLVD
City/State/ZIP: MADISON WI 53705
Telephone: 608-262-4021
Fax: 608-265-2121
E-mail: mpp@medicalphysics.org
Internet: www.medicalphysics.org

Metamorphous Press

Dear Writer:

Thank you for inquiring about our manuscript guidelines for new works. Since we receive from 2,500-3,000 unsolicited submissions each year, we ask that you first submit a query letter with an outline of your work, and a sufficient sample of your writing style for our acquisitions staff to determine if your work fits within our editorial policy. From there, we can decide whether we need to request a complete manuscript for further review.

We cannot be responsible for returning manuscripts due to the large quantity we receive. We encourage you to submit your work for consideration at this time:

• it may be considered (budget allowing) for publication by Metamorphous Press,

• we may offer subsidy publishing,

• or we can assist you with the details of self-publishing.

In any case, we are always excited about being involved in projects that can make a positive difference.

Thank you for your interest in Metamorphous Press.

Sincerely,

Nancy Wyatt-Kelsey

Acquisitions Editor

Categories: Nonfiction—Business—Education—Enneagram—Ericksonian Hypnosis—Health—N.L.P.—Personal Development—Psychology—Self-Help—Sexuality

Name: Nancy Wyatt—Kelsey, Acquisitions Editor
Material: All
Address: PO BOX 10616
City/State/ZIP: PORTLAND OR 97296-0616
Telephone: 503-228-4972
Fax: 503-223-9117
E-mail: metabooks@metamodels.com

Mid-List Press

Guidelines for novelists: Since 1990, Mid-List Press has sponsored the **First Series Award for the Novel** for writers who have never published a novel. (Writers who have yet to publish a novel may only submit manuscripts through the First Series.) The award includes publication and an advance of $1,000.00. Previous winners include David F. Weiss for *The Mensch* (1996), Roy Shepard for *The Latest Epistle of Jim* (1995), John Prendergast

for *Jump* (1994), Kristen Staby Rembold for *Felicity* (1993), William Sutherland for *News from Fort Cod* (1992), and Hugh Gross for *Same Bed, Different Dreams* (1990). There are no genre restrictions, but manuscripts must be at least 50,000 words in length. Submissions are accepted between October 1 and February 1. To receive the 1998 guidelines and an entry form, send a self-addressed, stamped #10 business envelope to the address below.

Previously published novelists should query first with a representative sample from the manuscript.

Guidelines for writers of short fiction: Since 1995, Mid-List Press has sponsored the **First Series Award for Short Fiction** for writers who have never published a book of short fiction. (Writers who have yet to publish a collection of short stories and/or novellas may only submit manuscripts through the First Series.) The award includes publication and an advance of $1,000.00. Previous winners include Bill Oliver for *Women & Children First* (1996) and Leslee Becker for *The Sincere Cafe* (1995). Manuscripts must be at least 50,000 words in length. Submissions are accepted between April 1 and July 1. To receive guidelines and an entry form, send a self-addressed, stamped #10 business envelope to the address below.

Writers who have previously published a collection of short fiction should query first. The query should include at least one story or novella.

Guidelines for writers of creative nonfiction and general nonfiction: Since 1996, Mid-List Press has sponsored the **First Series Award for Creative Nonfiction** for writers who have never published a book of creative nonfiction (either a collection of essays or a single book-length work). The award includes publication and an advance of $1,000. The 1996 winner was Daniel Minock for *Thistle Journal*. Manuscripts must be at least 50,000 words in length. Submissions are accepted between April 1 and July 1. To receive guidelines and an entry form, send a self-addressed, stamped #10 business envelope to the address below.

Writers who have previously published a book of creative nonfiction should query first. The query should include at least one essay or sample chapter.

Writers who wish to submit a general nonfiction manuscript should query first. The query should include a proposal, synopsis, and at least one sample chapter.

Guidelines for poets: Since 1990, Mid-List Press has sponsored the **First Series Award for Poetry** for poets who have never published a book of poetry. (Poets who have yet to publish a book of poetry may only submit manuscripts through the First Series; a chapbook is not considered a book of poetry.) The award includes publication and an advance of $500.00. Previous winners include Dina Ben-Lev for *Broken Helix* (1996), Neva Hacker for *My World, My Fingerhold, My Bygod Apple* (1995), Jeff Worley for *The Only Time There Is* (1994), Douglas Gray for *Words on the Moon* (1993), Neil Shepard for *Scavenging the Country for a Heartbeat* (1992), Stephen Behrendt for *Instruments of the Bones* (1991), J.E. Sorrell for *On the Other Side of the River* (1991), and Mary Logue for *Discriminating Evidence* (1990). Manuscripts must be at least 60 pages in length, single-spaced, and numbered. Submissions are accepted between October 1 and February 1. To receive the 1998 guidelines and an entry form, send a self-addressed, stamped #10 business envelope to the address below.

Poets who have previously published a book of poetry should query first. The query should include a representative sample from the collection.

At this time Mid-List Press does not consider children's books, young adult fiction, or photographic essay material.

Categories: Fiction—Nonfiction—Literature—Poetry—Short Stories

Name: Lane Stiles, Senior Editor
Material: All

Address: 4324 12th AVE S
City/State/ZIP: MINNEAPOLIS MN 55407-3218
Telephone: 612-822-3733
E-mail: midlist@concentric.net

Midmarch Arts Press

Midmarch Arts Press publishes from two to four books a year and an annual magazine, *Women Artists News Book Review.* Our books are mostly on the arts and poetry with a focus on women artists. It is a feminist press that is neither sexist, racist, or homophobic. We seek to represent the widest possible range of feminist perspective in our books and reviews and essays in our periodical.

• Include name, address and telephone number on all manuscripts and pictures.

• Include a brief biographical note for author's blurb.

• Submit computer disk and hard copy.

• Reviews or essays for the Book Review should be 1,200 to 1,800 words.

• Provide photographs if possible.

• Book manuscripts should be queried before submission.

• Subjects: Our focus is on art, women artists, literature and poetry, and women's issues.

• Style: Avoid wordiness. Art doesn't have to be the best thing since Da Vinci to be worth writing and reading about. Gushing praise, rhetorical clichés, and overblown jargon are not interesting to read. Personal, social, historical, political, and artistic particulars are interesting—that is, information and explication.

Categories: Arts—Literature—Poetry—Women Artists—Women's Issues

Name: Acquisitions Editor
Material: All
Address: 300 RIVERSIDE DR
City/State/ZIP: NEW YORK NY 10025
Telephone: 212-666-6990
Fax: 212-865-5509

Milkweed Editions

Mission statement: Milkweed Editions publishes with the intention of making a humane impact on society, in the belief that literature is a transformative art uniquely able to convey the essential experiences of the human heart and spirit. To that end, Milkweed Editions publishes distinctive voices of literary merit in handsomely designed, visually dynamic books, exploring the ethical, cultural, and esthetic issues that free societies need continually to address.

All Submissions must be typed or computer-printed. Please indicate if you want us simply to recycle the manuscript—in this event, submit your manuscript with a self-addressed, stamped envelope for our reply.

For notification of the safe arrival of your manuscript, please include a stamped, self-addressed postcard. Send a photocopy of your manuscript, not the original. Our review process can take from one to six months. Milkweed books are available at most fine bookstores. You can write to us for a catalog; enclose $1.50 for postage.

FICTION GUIDELINES

Milkweed Editions is looking for fiction manuscripts of high literary quality that embody humane values and contribute to cultural understanding. Our recently published fiction titles include *All American Dream Dolls* by David Haynes (1997), *The Tree of Red Stars* by Tessa Bridal (1997), *The Empress of One* by Faith Sullivan (1996), *Live at Five* by David Haynes (1996), *The Children Bob Moses Led* by William Heath (1995), *Swimming in the Congo* by Margaret Meyers (1995), and *Somebody Else's Mama* by David Haynes (1995).

We welcome submissions from writers who have previously published a book of fiction (novel, short stories, or novellas) or a minimum of three short stories (or novellas) in nationally distributed commercial or literary journals. Novels, novellas, and collections of short stories are welcome, as are translations. Your fiction manuscript must be 150-400 pages.

NONFICTION GUIDELINES

Milkweed is focusing its nonfiction publishing on a program called *The World As Home: Literature about the Natural World* and is actively seeking book-length literary essays and essay collections about the physical and natural world, as well as book-length works about community—that is, about living well and harmoniously in place, whether that is rural, urban, or suburban. Recently published titles in Milkweed's *The World As Home* publishing program are *Grass Roots: The Universe of Home* by Paul Gruchow (1995) and *Homestead* by Annick Smith (1995).

As part of that publishing program, Milkweed is continuing its *Literature for a Land Ethic* series of literary books about specific endangered places by regionally committed writers. *Literature for a Land Ethic* supports writers, educators, and activists in defining and evolving the role of literature in furthering our culture's environmental knowledge and in articulating the possibilities for a sustainable future. Milkweed recently published *Boundary Waters: The Grace of the Wild* by Paul Gruchow (1997) and *Testimony: Writers of the West Speak On Behalf of Utah Wilderness,* compiled by Stephen Trimble and Terry Tempest Williams (1996) as part of this series.

We welcome submissions from writers who have previously published a book of nonfiction (this can be a collection of essays) or a minimum of two essays in nationally distributed commercial or literary journals. Collections of essays are welcome, as are translations. Your nonfiction manuscript must be 150-300 pages.

CHILDREN'S LITERATURE GUIDELINES

Milkweed Editions is looking for high-quality novels for readers aged 8-13 for its children's book publishing program, Milkweeds for Young Readers.

At this age, readers are ready for well-written books that range widely in subject matter, from fantasy to fiction grounded in history to books about everyday life. Manuscripts should be of high literary quality, embody humane values, and contribute to cultural understanding. Our recently published children's titles include *The Monkey Thief* by Aileen Kilgore Henderson (1997), *The Gumma Wars* and *Business As Usual* by David Haynes (1997), *Behind the Bedroom Wall* by Laura E. Williams (1996), *The Boy with Paper Wings* by Susan Lowell (1995), and *Summer of the Bonepile Monster* by Aileen Kilgore Henderson (1995).

We are especially interested in fiction set in the contemporary world and in fiction that explores our relationship to the natural world.

We welcome submissions from writers who have previously published a book of fiction or nonfiction for children or adults, or a minimum of three short stories or pieces of nonfiction in nationally distributed commercial or literary journals. Translations are welcome. Please note that we do not publish children's picture books, poetry, or collections of stories. Your children's manuscript must be 90-200 pages.

POETRY GUIDELINES

Milkweed Editions is looking for poetry manuscripts of high literary quality that embody humane values and contribute to cultural understanding. Milkweed usually reads poetry manuscripts in January and June of each year. Our next reading period will be June, 1998. Recently published poetry titles include *Eating Bread and Honey* by Pattiann Rogers (1997), *Night Out: Poems about Hotels, Motels, Restaurants, and Bars,* edited by

Kurt Brown and Laure-Anne Bosselaar (1997), *Invisible Horses* by Patricia Goedicke (1996), *The Long Experience of Love* by Jim Moore (1995), *The Phoenix Gone, The Terrace Empty* by Marilyn Chin (1994) and *Firekeeper* by Pattiann Rogers (1994). Although poetry manuscripts are not limited in subject matter, we are particularly interested in poetry about the natural world as part of our publishing program, *The World As Home: Literature about the Natural World.*

We welcome submissions from writers who have previously published a book of poetry or a minimum of six poems in nationally distributed commercial or literary journals. Translations are welcome, as are bilingual books. We encourage simultaneous submissions. Your poetry manuscript must be 90-200 pages.

Thank you for your interest in Milkweed Editions, and good luck in your writing endeavors.

Categories: Fiction—Nonfiction—Children—Conservation—Culture—Ecology—Environment—General Interest—Literature—Multicultural—Poetry—Science

Name: Elisabeth Fitz, First Reader
Material: All
Address: 430 FIRST AVE N STE 400
City/State/ZIP: MINNEAPOLIS MN 55401
Telephone: 612-332-3192
Fax: 612-332-6248
Internet: www.milkweed.org

Minstrel Books
An Imprint of Simon & Schuster's Pocketbooks

Please refer to Pocketbooks

Mitchell Lane Publishers

We have no published guidelines; we accept queries and sample chapters on multicultural nonfiction, primarily biographies of role models for children and young adults. We also hire freelance writers by assignment.

Categories: Nonfiction—Biography—Children—Hispanic—Multicultural

Name: Barbara Mitchell, Publisher
Material: All
Address: 17 MATTHEW BATHON CT
City/State/ZIP: ELKTON MD 21921
Telephone: 410-392-5036
Fax: 410-392-4781

Momentum Books Ltd.

Please submit an outline and three chapters.
Categories: Nonfiction—Cooking—Food/Drink—Great Lakes—Michigan—Military—Women's Issues

Name: Franklin Fox, Acquisitions Editor
Material: All
Address: 6964 CROOKS RD STE 1

City/State/ZIP: TROY MI 48098
Telephone: 248-828-3666
Fax: 248-828-0142
E-mail: Momentumbooks@glis.net

Monument Press

Please refer to Publishers Associates.

Motorbooks International
Bicycle Books, Crestline

Motorbooks International is the largest distributor of automotive and aviation/military books in the world. We also publish more than 100 books a year.

Motorbooks International books usually cover the following subjects:

Automotive (cars, trucks,), motorcycles, farm tractors, bicycles, railroads and trains, boats, aviation (planes, jets, etc.), and military vehicles and hardware.

These topics can be covered in a variety of ways, including, but not limited to:

Histories, photo books (color or black-and-white), how-to guides, restoration guides, racing histories, directories, and biographies.

Motorbooks titles are usually heavily illustrated:

A 16-page book will commonly contain 150-200 photos, and some photo histories contain up to 500 photos.

Prospective authors should submit a written proposal consisting of a cover letter and an outline or synopsis of each project.

In a cover letter, tell us a little about your own background and why you're qualified to write the book you're proposing. The proposal should include a description of the book (several paragraphs covering the scope of the subject, projected word and photo count, etc., an outline is helpful), as well as a sample table of contents. If you're an unpublished author, we are likely to want at least one sample chapter as well.

If the book will rely heavily on photography, samples will help tremendously. If it's archival photography, good quality photocopies will suffice. If it's current color photography, we prefer transparencies 35mm or larger-duplicates are satisfactory for a proposal. If it's current black and white (as in a how-to book), sample prints or high-quality photocopies will be helpful.

Also helpful is your best estimate on the size of the market for the book-who is most likely to buy it, and how many such people there are. To the extent you're able, support your estimate with information such as how many machines were manufactured, the number and circulation of any enthusiast magazines or newsletters that cover the manufacturer or activity, the estimated turnout at shows featuring the machines.

When you send your proposal, please allow 6-8 weeks for us to consider it.

We may pass it around for several people to look over, and ultimately will bring it up for discussion at several meetings in which we consider proposals. Send it to the address below.

If your proposal is accepted, we will offer you a contract:

• MBI pays royalties from a book's net revenue. Royalty advances are usually split, with half paid upon signature of the contract and half paid upon acceptance of the book.

• Books must be submitted on computer disk, preferably from Macintosh computers, but disks from IBM-compatible PCs are also acceptable. We use Microsoft Word, but other word processing software is acceptable.

• MBI has a brief stylebook and uses the *American Heritage Dictionary* and the *Chicago Manual of Style* as its guides.

• Depending on the book, the photography can be either historical or new.

• For color books, we prefer transparencies, either 35mm slides or a larger format. We are able to use color prints if they're of high-quality.

• For black-and-white books, we work with prints-no negatives-preferably at least 5"x7" in size.

• Photo fees are negotiable, and rates will vary according to factors such as the number of shots provided for a single book, and whether the photo(s) is shot specifically for a book or cover.

Categories: Automobiles—Aviation—Boating—Collectibles—Military

Name: Book Proposal Desk
Material: All
Address: 729 Prospect Ave
City/State/ZIP: Osceola, WI 54020
Telephone: 715-294-3345-
Fax: 715-294-4448

Mountain Press Publishing Company

Mountain Press publishes nonfiction trade books for general audiences, primarily adults. We will consider proposals for projects in natural history (including field guides for birds, wildlife, plants, etc.) western or frontier history; non-technical earth science and ecology; and some horse-related topics. Mountain Press is perhaps best known for its state-by-state series on Roadside Geology and Roadside History; extended guidelines are available for these.

Other than reprints of the works of Will James, we do not publish fiction or poetry.

STANDARDS. We accept only well-written, responsibly researched manuscripts. Your composition must engage the reader with lively, colorful prose. The sources you rely on must be thoroughly documented and not infringe on any existing copyrights. Double-space everything—text, notes, bibliography, everything. You are responsible for supplying all photographs, maps, and other graphics your book may need.

STYLE. We urge authors to follow the tenets set forth in *The Chicago Manual of Style* (14th edition) and Strunk & White's *The Elements of Style.*

EQUIPMENT. Prepare your manuscript on a computer using a Macintosh, Windows, or MS-DOS compatible word-processing program. We will not accept camera-ready copy. Do not send your disk until we ask for it.

PROPOSALS. Submit a cover letter addressed to the Editorial Department with your proposal telling us who you are, what your manuscript is about, who your target audience is, and why you think Mountain Press should publish your work. Include an outline or table of contents, a sample of the manuscript (one or two chapters), a core bibliography, and photocopied examples of the artwork you plan to use. Normally we can respond to your proposal within one month. Please call first if you have any questions.

WEBSITE. For more information about Mountain Press, we encourage you to visit our Website.

Categories: Nonfiction—Biography—Ecology—Field Guides—Geology—History—Native American—Nature—Outdoors—Regional

Name: Acquisitions Editor
Material: All
Address: PO BOX 2399
City/State/ZIP: MISSOULA MT 59806
Telephone: 406-728-1900

Fax: 406-728-1635
E-mail: mtnpress@montana.com
Internet: www.montana.com/mtnpress

Mountaineers Books

The Mountaineers, founded in 1906, is a non-profit outdoor activity and conservation club based in Seattle, Washington. The club is now the third largest organization in the United States, with 12,000 members and four branches throughout Washington state.

Background

The Mountaineers has sponsored both mountain-climbing expeditions and hiking outings in many parts of the world, as well as presenting regular classes and year-round outdoor activities in the Pacific Northwest. Club members enjoy a scheduled program of hiking, mountain climbing, ski-touring, snowshoeing, bicycling, camping, kayaking and canoeing, nature study, sailing, and adventure travel. The club's Conservation Division supports both regional and national environmental causes through educational activities, sponsoring legislation, and presenting informational programs. All club activities and programs are led by skilled, experienced volunteers, who are dedicated to promoting safe and responsible enjoyment and preservation of the outdoors.

The Mountaineers Books, an active, non-profit publishing program of the club, produces guidebooks, instructional texts, historical works, adventure narratives, natural history guides, and works on environmental conservation. More than 300 titles from The Mountaineers are now in print. All of the books published are aimed at fulfilling the club's mission—to explore, study, preserve and enjoy the natural beauty of the outdoors—and, by extension, addressing the needs and concerns of like-minded outdoor enthusiasts throughout the world.

The authors of books published by The Mountaineers come from all over the world. Some are professional writers, others are just people who want to share their specialized knowledge of some aspect of outdooring. If you have a book project in mind that would fit our line, we would be delighted to hear from you. Information on making a proposal to us follows.

Submitting Proposed Books To The Mountaineers
Subject matter

The Mountaineers publishes nonfiction material on the outdoors. This includes non-competitive, non-motorized, self-propelled sports such as mountain climbing, hiking, walking, skiing, bicycling, canoeing, kayaking, snowshoeing, and adventure travel. We also publish works on environmental and conservation subjects, narratives of mountaineering expeditions and adventure travel, outdoor guidebooks (not general tourist guides) to specific areas, nature field guides, natural history, mountaineering history, safety/first aid, and books on techniques of the above sports. If you plan to submit an adventure narrative, please request information about the Barbara Savage *Miles From Nowhere* Memorial Award.

We *do not* publish fiction, general tourist guides, or guides dealing with hunting, fishing, snowmobiling, RV travel, horseback riding, or team sports.

Our procedures

The Mountaineers is a non-profit outdoor activity club which publishes books via a paid staff. Everything we publish must first be approved by our volunteer board. If a project is rejected, that answer comes fairly swiftly; however, if we choose to publish something the review and approval process can take up to three months. Not until a project is approved is any commitment made to an author.

Submissions

If you are in doubt as to our possible interest in a project, please send a query letter and SASE. If you feel your proposal or manuscript fits the above subject matter, then we need to see the following, as a minimum:

• A statement that explains the proposed project's purpose, focus, scope, and significance, including a brief summary of the text

• A detailed chapter/subject outline

• At least ten pages of introductory material and a complete table of contents

• At least two sample chapters (not necessarily the first in the book) or trip write-ups, written in the style and length of the proposed book

• Information on the number and type of any photos, artwork, maps, or other illustrations proposed, along with samples (or good photocopies) of each type

• Information on the author's background and credentials to do this particular project

• Samples of other previously published writings by this author, if any

• Data on the size and scope of the intended market/audience of the project

• Information on any competitive books now in print (list and comment on specific titles) and how the proposed book is different and better than each.

Mechanics

We will accept dot-matrix submissions if printed with a dark ribbon. *Do not* send disks.

Do not submit original manuscript materials; send only legible photocopies. When sending original art or photos, use UPS or Registered Mail to prevent loss in shipping.

Be sure your name and address appear on all submitted materials—not just the outside envelope!

All submissions are acknowledged upon receipt, or returned promptly if not appropriate to our line.

The Mountaineers Books are distributed nationally and internationally.

If you have something you think would fit in our line of books, we'd be happy to have a look and respond. Send query letters, manuscripts, and/or proposals.

Categories: Conservation—Hiking—Outdoors

Name: Acquisitions Editor
Material: All
Address: 1001 SW KLICKITAT WAY STE 201
City/State/ZIP: SEATTLE WA 98134
Telephone: 206-223-6303
Fax: 206-223-6306
E-mail: mbooks@mountaineers.org
Internet: www.mountaineers.org

Mustang Publishing

Mustang Publishing Company, Inc.

We welcome book proposals on almost any nonfiction topic. We prefer to see an outline and a few sample chapters. We try to respond in 2-3 weeks. Please—*no* phone calls regarding book ideas/proposals, and *no* submissions by fax or e-mail.

Categories: Nonfiction—Careers—College—Consumer—Culture—Entertainment—Family—Food/Drink—Games—General Interest—Hobbies—Humor—Lifestyles—Parenting—Recreation—Reference—Sports—Travel

Name: Rollin Riggs, President
Material: All
Address: PO BOX 3004
City/State/ZIP: MEMPHIS TN 38173-0004
Telephone: 901-521-1406
Fax: 901-521-1412
E-mail: MustangPub@aol.com

The Nature Conservancy's Habitat Series
Soundprints

The Nature Conservancy's Habitat Series introduces children to animals and their unique habitats. Each book tells an interesting story that communicates facts about the animals habitat, what they eat, how they live, and unique or interesting characteristics of the animal.

The Nature Conservancy's Collection focuses on ecosystems around the world. Stories should illustrate the special ways in which the animals are adapted to live in their environments, as well as characteristics that might set them apart from similar species. All of these facts are incorporated into an engaging storyline, highlighting a specific animal that children can learn about and relate to.

General information:

• Animals should be realistic, not anthropomorphic. Animals in the stories should exhibit natural behaviors as they move about and interact with other animals within the habitat.

• Target reading level is preschool through second grade.

• Finished stories should be approximately 1,000 words long.

• Each book also contains a passage about the geographic area being introduced. Authors are responsible for submitting this with the final manuscript.

In addition to editing by Soundprints, The Nature Conservancy Habitat Series stories are subject to the review and approval of The Nature Conservancy and should be based on good, solid research. All elements of each story should be supportable by current references. For an example of a Habitat Series storybook, please see the following:

Cactus Cafe by Kathleen Weidner Zoehfeld
Canopy Crossing by Ann Whitehead Nagda
Categories: Fiction—Animals—Children

Name: Cassia Farkas, Editor
Name: Diane Hinze Kanzler, Graphic Designer
Material: Any
Address: 353 MAIN AVE
City/State/ZIP: NORWALK CT 06851
Telephone: 203-846-2274
Fax: 203-846-1776
E-mail: sndprnts@ix.netcom.com

Naturegraph Publishers

Please approach us first with a query letter, outline of your work, and a sample chapter or two of your manuscript.

Your query letter should tell us what is unique about your book, your qualifications to write it, how it compares and contrasts with similar books on the same subject, why there is a need for your book, and how you can help us to make it a marketing success. We will acknowledge receipt of your proposal immediately.

If we are interested in your proposal, we will send you an author questionnaire to fill out and request to see the rest of your work. Authors whose work is accepted for publication will receive a contract specifying author responsibilities, royalties, expected

Books

publication date, etc.

Proposals submitted to us for consideration by our reviewing committee should belong to one of the following general categories: natural history, Native Americans, outdoor subjects, and natural crafts. Look at our catalog on our website or write to request our free catalog to get an idea of the types of books we publish.

Thank you for considering Naturegraph Publishers.

Categories: Nonfiction—Native Americans—Nature—Outdoors

Name: Barbara Brown, Editor
Material: All
Address: 3543 INDIAN CREEK RD
Address: PO BOX 1075
City/State/ZIP: HAPPY CAMP CA 96039
Telephone: 916-493-5353
Fax: 916-493-5240
E-mail: Naturgraph@aol.com
Internet: http://members.aol.com/Naturgraph

Naval Institute Press
Bluejacket Books

Joint and general military subjects; naval biography; naval history; oceanography; navigation; military law; naval science textbooks; seapower; shipbuilding; professional guides; nautical arts and lore; technical guides. Limited military fiction.

Submissions require a minimum of two sample chapters, chapter outline, list of sources used, and authors biography. Include a cover letter.

All submissions must be typed, unbound, and accompanied by a cover letter. Only photocopies of artwork and photographs should be sent, not originals. Do not send disks with your submission. No manuscripts in binders!

Receipt of your manuscript will be acknowledged. Evaluation may take as long as twelve weeks.

Thank you for your interest in the Naval Press Institute.

Categories: Fiction—Nonfiction—Aviation—Boating—History—Military—Reference

Name: Jean Tyson, Acquisitions Coordinator
Material: All
Address: 118 MARYLAND AVE
City/State/ZIP: ANNAPOLIS MD 21402-5035
Telephone: 410-295-4004
Fax: 410-269-7940

New Poets Series
BrickHouse Books, Inc.

New Poets Series (NPS) publishes first books by uniquely promising poets who have not yet brought out a collection of their work. Now a division of BrickHouse Books, Inc., NPS was incorporated in 1973 by Clarinda Harriss, who remains as editor/director. Well-known poets Josephine Jacobsen and Ogden Nash helped support NPS in its early years.

NPS publishes books of the highest quality. An editing staff of outstanding publishing/teaching poets reviews all submissions with extreme care, for, of the approximately 1,000 mss. NPS receives annually, not more than six can be published each year. The result of this intensive scrutiny is that NPS poets can be numbered among the finest of their generation.

How to Submit

New Poets Series accepts book submissions year round. Send a full ms. consisting of about 55 pages of poetry. There is a $10.00 readers fee for each submission.

[Please refer to BrickHouse Books, Inc. for more information.]

Categories: Poetry

Name: Clarinda Harriss, Editor and Director
Material: All
Address: 541 PICCADILLY RD
City/State/ZIP: TOWSON MD 21204
Telephone: 410-828-0724
E-mail: harriss@towson.edu
Internet: www.towson.edu/~harriss/!bhbwebsite/bhb.htm
Nota bene: Reading fee required.

New Rivers Press

Call for Submissions

Although the Southeast Asian American community has a long history and a rapidly growing population, there are few books that feature the poetry, fiction, and creative nonfiction of the established and emerging authors of this community.

We are soliciting fiction, creative nonfiction, and poetry created by Southeast Asian Americans, for a literary anthology of previously unpublished work. By Southeast Asian Americans we mean residents of the United States with Bruneian, Burmese (Myanmar), Cambodian, Filipino, Hmong, Indonesian, Laotian, Malaysian, Singaporean, Thai, or Vietnamese heritage, including recent immigrants as well as second, third, fourth, etc., generation writers. Subject matter is not limited. The work may, for instance, explore such ideas as community, memory, locations, genders, the subject of the artist and language—and may do so in creative writing that celebrates, records, preserves, explores, questions, problematizes, invents, and defines—and would do so for an audience who may be both familiar and unfamiliar with Southeast Asian Americans.

The co-editors for this anthology are:

Shirley Lim
Department of English
University of California—Santa Barbara
Santa Barbara, CA 93106
Cheng Lok Chua
English Department, M.S. #98
California State University, Fresno
5245 North Backer Avenue
Fresno, CA 93740-8001

Guidelines

• All submissions must be typed/word-processed.

• Submit three copies (original plus two photocopies) of each piece.

• We will not be able to return your work.

• Send a stamped, self-addressed envelope (SASE) for notification of results.

• Author's name, address, and phone number must appear at the top of the first page, and author's name and page number should appear on each following page.

• Include a brief resume (no more than two pages) with mention of author's Southeast Asian heritage.

• Authors should keep us informed of any address changes.

• Only previously unpublished work will be considered.

Categories: Fiction—Poetry—Regional

Name: Jim Cihlar, Managing Editor
Material: All
Address: 420 N FIFTH ST STE 910
City/State/ZIP: MINNEAPOLIS MN 55401
Telephone: 612-339-7114
Fax: 612-339-9047
E-mail: newrivpr@mtn.org

New Victoria Publishers
Quality Lesbian Books Since 1976

In 1860 women's rights activist Emily Faithful founded Victoria Press, an all-woman print shop in London, England. Her tradition was revived in New England in 1975 with the establishment of New Victoria Printers and, in 1976, New Victoria Publishers, a non-profit feminist literary and cultural organization publishing the finest in lesbian feminist fiction and nonfiction.

We are primarily interested in well-crafted fiction in all genres featuring lesbians or strong female protagonists. The following ingredients should be present:

• Clear narrative story line.

• Well-drawn, intelligent, introspective characters.

• Accurate background locations or atmosphere.

• Issues pertinent to the lesbian community whether emotional, societal, or political.

• Humor and/or eroticism.

We are especially interested in lesbian or feminist mysteries, ideally with a character or characters who can evolve through a series of books. Mysteries should involve a complex plot, accurate legal/procedural detail, and protagonists with full emotional lives.

We prefer science/speculative fiction or fantasy with amazon adventure themes and/or detailed, well-crafted alternative realities, complete with appropriately original language and culture.

We are also interested in well-researched nonfiction on women, lesbian-feminist herstory, or biography of interest to a general as well as academic audience.

We advise you to look through our catalog to see our past editorial decisions as well as what we are currently marketing. Our books average 80-90,000 words, or 200-250 single-spaced pages.

Please send your enquiry to us with:

• A brief outline or synopsis highlighting key issues in the story, why you wrote it, and any target audience you have in mind.

• Several sample chapters or approximately 50-75 pages.

We prefer single submissions (ms. sent to one publisher only), so please let us know if you have submitted your manuscript to or are under contract with another publisher.

A partial List of New Victoria Authors: Sarah Dreher (*The Stoner McTavish Mysteries*); Lesléa Newman (*Secrets, In Every Laugh a Tear, Saturday is Pattyday, Every Womans Dream*); Kate Allen (*Tell Me What You Like, Give My Secrets Back, I Knew You Would Call*); J.M. Redmann (*Death by the Riverside, Deaths of Jocasta, Chris Anne Wolfe, Shadows of Agar, Fires of Agar*); Cris Newport (*Sparks Might Fly*); Jane Meyerding (*Everywhere House*); Lesa Luders (*Lady God*); Morgan Grey & Julia Penelope (*Found Goddesses*); Claudia McKay (*Promise of the Rose Stone, The Kali Connection*); ReBecca Béguin (*Runway at Eland Springs, In Unlikely Places, Hers Was the Sky*)

Categories: Fiction—Nonfiction—Feminism—Gay/Lesbian—Mystery—Romance

Name: Acquisitions Editor
Material: All
Address: PO BOX 27
City/State/ZIP: NORWICH VT 05055
Telephone: 802-649-5297
Fax: 802-649-5297

New View Publications, Inc.

The path to happiness and success in today's chaotic world is paved with many obstacles. At New View, our mission is to help people overcome these obstacles and realize their fullest potential. Over-worked teachers, troubled teens, concerned parents, stressed-out managers, and other ordinary people going through tough times—all have used the practical, easy-to-grasp concepts in our books to solve their problems and change their lives for the better.

New View will consider for publication any book-length manuscript that is consistent with the mission statement outlined above. While we prefer to review completed manuscripts, we will consider works in progress if accompanied by a proposal, outline, sample chapter, bibliography, and resumé.

Submissions should be typeset to conform to the following specifications: text formatted in a legible font (e.g., Times 12-point), pages numbered clearly. All graphics, charts, tables, and notes should be labeled as such and attached separately. Any style of citation (e.g., footnotes, endnotes, author-date, etc.) is acceptable but it should be observed consistently throughout. For all other matters of style, please consult the most recent edition of *The Chicago Manual of Style*. We also accept electronic submissions at our e-mail address. These must be formatted either as rich-text files (RTF) or portable document files (PDF).

Categories: Nonfiction—Education—Parenting—Psychology—Relationships

Name: Trevor Hoyt, Managing Editor
Material: All
Address: PO BOX 3021
City/State/ZIP: CHAPEL HILL NC 27515
Telephone: 919-942-8491
Fax: 919-942-3760
E-mail: NView@aol.com

Nicolas-Hays, Inc.

Please refer to Samuel Weiser, Inc.

Nolo Press

The Nolo Editorial Process:
A Disclosure Sheet for Prospective Authors
Nolo Press is not a typical trade publishing company. That

may be one reason you'll want to work with us, and we think our different way of doing things is a big plus. To begin with, we don't have writer's guidelines. Instead, we offer this disclosure.

Nolo Press was founded in 1971 by two former legal aid lawyers who wanted to bring law to ordinary people. Today, we're the country's foremost publisher of law and consumer books and software for non-lawyers. Nolo Press has nearly 120 titles, with subjects ranging from divorce, writing a will or trust, forming and running a small business, and personal finance, debts and bankruptcy, to landlord-tenant relations, buying and selling real estate, employment rights, working as an independent contractor, copyrights, trademarks and patents, going to court and immigrating to the U.S. To find out more about us, visit our web site.

Before you sign a contract with Nolo, understand that our editorial process entails a great deal of hard work on your part (and ours). We think that spelling out this expectation in advance is a must.

In some publishing houses, the only editing a manuscript receives is a quick check for egregious errors of grammar or syntax. It may also be sent out for cursory review by a few people knowledgeable about the subject. Editors spend their time hunting for potential best-sellers, negotiating contracts and (we hear) going out for expensive lunches.

Nolo editors do precious little of these things. Instead, we edit each manuscript line by line, draft after draft, until it meets the Nolo standard of quality. It is, we can proudly but honestly say, a tougher standard than other trade publishers use; Nolo's reputation is built on well-written, complete, easy to use law books.

Our dedication to getting it right means that much will be expected of you. We insist that every legal process or topic covered be explained clearly, concisely and above all accurately. Every time you give a chapter to an editor, it will come back to you covered with substantive suggestions and questions as well as basic editing changes to your writing. You will almost certainly have to reorganize and rewrite whole chapters.

A typical manuscript goes through at least five drafts, and usually two editors work on it. Almost no one, no matter how knowledgeable or gifted a writer, ever gets a Nolo book out in less than a year.

The process will almost surely try your patience. For example, if you tell readers to "Enter your name" on a form, your editor will remind you that many people don't know what name to use, and ask you to head off this problem with detailed instructions.

One of the reasons we work so hard on new books is that we build books to last. Unlike most publishers, we expect to revise books regularly and keep them in print indefinitely. We publicize and promote our back list constantly.

Nolo takes on only about half a dozen new book projects a year. That means all our eggs are in very few baskets. We need to stick to deadlines as best as we possibly can; we can't afford to tie up editors for much longer. If a manuscript falls seriously behind schedule because its quality is poor or you miss deadlines, we may have to cancel the contract.

If the process sounds grueling, well, it can be at times. But it's the only way the Nolo editors (each of whom is also a Nolo author) have found to produce books that really work for our readers. And most of our authors agree; many of them have stuck around the place for years, making all or part of their living from writing Nolo books.

If you're still interested in sending us a proposal, we'd be happy to review it. At a minimum, we need an outline and sample chapter (something other than the Introduction, please), along with a bit of background information about yourself.

Categories: Nonfiction—Business—Consumer—Law—Money/Finance—Reference

Name: Acquisitions Editor

Material: All
Address: 950 PARKER ST
City/State/ZIP: BERKELEY CA 94710
Telephone: 510-549-1976
Fax: 510-548-5902
E-mail: cs@nolo.com
Internet: www.nolo.com

Northwoods Press

Please refer to The Conservatory of American Letters.

Nova Press

We publish only books and software for, or closely related to, test preparation for college entrance exams: LSAT, GRE, SAT, GMAT, MCAT.

Categories: Nonfiction—College—Education

Name: Acquisitions Editor
Material: All
Address: 11659 MAYFIELD AVE STE 1
City/State/ZIP: LOS ANGELES CA 90049
Telephone: 310-207-4078
Fax: 310-571-0908
E-mail: NovaPress@aol.com

NTC/Contemporary Publishing Company

NTC/Contemporary Publishing Company is a commercial nonfiction publishing company that publishes over 100 titles per year in the categories of sports, health, parenting, self-help, how-to, business, careers, quilting, and crafts.

Your proposal, which should be no more than 30 pages in length, should include:

1. A cover letter briefly describing your book and the market you are trying to reach.

2. A proposed table of contents

3. A chapter outline and summary

4. A sample chapter, typed and double-spaced

5. Photocopied samples of the photos, line drawings, or other artwork needed to illustrate your manuscript

6. A brief market summary which answers the following questions: Who will read my book? Which existing titles compete with my book? How does my book differ from the other titles in its category?

7. Your qualifications as an author and/or a list of recent publications

Please allow 2-3 weeks for our reply. *Because of the large number of proposals we receive, proposals sent without an enclosed SASE will not receive a reply.*

Categories: Nonfiction—Business—Careers—Cooking—Crafts—Gardening—Humor—Martial Arts—Money/Finance—NewAge—Paranormal—Parenting—Relationships—Spiritual—Sports—Travel

Name: Acquisitions Editor
Material: All
Address: 4255 W TOUHY AVE
City/State/ZIP: LINCOLNWOOD IL 60646
Telephone: 847-679-5500
Fax: 847-679-2494

Orchises Press

Orchises Press is a small literary and general publisher located outside of Washington, D. C. It publishes five to eight books a year and has a list of fifty titles, many of them original poetry, a love of the editor, Roger Lathbury. Unlike many other presses, small and large, Orchises reads unsolicited manuscripts and tries to publish books on their merit, both literary and commercial. It prides itself on the attractiveness of its volumes, both paperback and hardcover.

MANUSCRIPT SUBMISSION GUIDELINES

Orchises is one of the few publishers that reads unsolicited freelance submissions. If a manuscript is presented in a reasonable manner, well look at it. "Reasonable" means:

1. Typed, preferably double-spaced. Photocopies are OK; they're indistinguishable from laser print anyhow.

2. A return envelope is enclosed-a self-addressed stamped envelope large enough to accommodate the manuscript if you want the manuscript returned, a size 10 or 6 3/4 envelope if a response is all that's needed. While understanding that such is not the fate writers most want, Orchises recycles all unreturnable manuscripts. In general, mail with no materials for a response will not receive a response nor will it be retained pending the arrival of a forgotten envelope.

3. A phone number is helpful for those rare occasions when we accept.

OTHER REMARKS

1. Orchises does not publish original fiction.

2. If you submit poetry, you may be interested to know that in one year Orchises receives 200-300 poetry manuscripts or queries accompanied by poems. Two or three such may be accepted; one year four were, another none was. Usually poetry Orchises publishes has appeared previously in magazines of national repute, e.g., *American Poetry Review, The Atlantic Monthly, Harpers, The New Republic, The New Yorker, Poetry*—as well as respected literary magazines (e.g., *The Paris Review, Shenandoah, The Southern Review*). These places build audiences. Of course, publication in those magazines is not an absolute criterion. All readers, I expect, have read poems in those venues that are quite fine but also others that seem less good than poems in less prominent places. The only way to judge is to read; well read.

3. Reporting times vary but usually are within 1 month. Longer means closer.

4. The volume of submissions makes it impossible to provide commentary.

With thanks and good wishes,
Roger Lathbury
Orchises Press
Categories: Poetry—Textbooks

Name: Acquisitions Editor
Material: All
Address: PO BOX 20602
City/State/ZIP: ALEXANDRIA VA 22320-1602
E-mail: rlathbur@osf1.gmu.edu

Orion House
UFO Research Library

Orion House is interested in book manuscripts of any length dealing with UFOs or other unexplained phenomenon. Publishes 4-6 titles per year. Responds in 30 days. Standard royalty contract available. Submit complete manuscript or query with outline. Submissions may also be made on 3.5" disk (PC or Mac).

Categories: New Age

Name: Bob Canino, Publisher
Material: UFOs, Unexplained Mysteries
Address: 1807 COLD SPRINGS RD
City/State/ZIP: LIVERPOOL NY 13090
Telephone: 315-451-0667
Fax: 315-461-9066
E-mail: RobertC130@aol.com

Osborne/McGraw-Hill

How to Prepare Your Manuscript Proposal

The following guidelines outline the major areas that you should cover in your proposal. Please be as complete as possible, as it will help us make a decision more quickly. Also, feel free to add relevant information even if we haven't specifically asked for it below. The most important elements are (a) why we should publish this book, (b) what specific skills do you bring to this book/topic, and (c) why will this book sell better than other similar books (or if there is no competition, what are the market conditions that make you believe that this is a book worth publishing.)

Your proposal should include the following information:

• Brief description of the book.

• Brief description of the product or technology.

• Audience: Who is the major audience for your book; for whom is your book intended? At what level is your book written; what technical background will the reader of your book need?

• Outstanding features: List what you consider to be the outstanding or unique features of your work.

• Outline: Provide a detailed outline of your book. This will give reviewers an idea of what topics you are including and how your material is organized. Your outline should include part titles, chapter headings, subheadings, and appendixes, with explanations as necessary. It should also include your estimate of the length in manuscript pages of each chapter.

• Competition: List the existing books, if any, with which yours will compete and discuss specifically their strengths and weaknesses. Spell out how your work will be similar to and different from competing books.

• The Market: Mention any factors that might have an impact (positive or negative) on the market for your work. How is the market changing? If your work focuses on particular hardware or software, and you have sales figures for the product, include these.

• Schedule: What is your timetable for completing your book? What portion of the material is now complete? When do you expect to have a complete manuscript?

• Size: What do you estimate to be the size of the complete book? (Double-spaced typewritten pages normally reduce by about one-third when set into type: for example, 300 typewritten pages equal approximately 200 printed pages).

• Resume: Include a copy of your vita, or a paragraph or two of relevant biographical information. Please include a list of hardware and software for which you have expertise.

• Writing Sample: Please include a magazine article or the introduction or chapter of the book, or other writing samples.

You may send your proposal directly to members of our Acquisitions Team either through regular mail or e-mail.

Categories: Computers—Internet

Name: Megg Bonar, Acquisitions Editor
Material: Internet, Applications
Name: Joanne Cuthbertson, Acquisitions Editor
Material: Internet, Applications
Name: Wendy Rinaldi, Acquisitions Editor;
Material: Programming, Networking

Books

Name: Scott Rogers, Editor-in-Chief
Material: ORACLE
Address: 2600 TENTH ST
City/State/ZIP: BERKELEY CA 94710
Telephone: 510-549-6600/800-227-0900
Fax: 510-549-6603
E-mail: mbonar@mcgraw-hill.com; jcuthber@mcgraw-hill.com; wrinaldi@mcgraw-hill.com; srogers@mcgraw-hill.com
Internet: www.mcgraw-hill.com

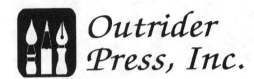

Outrider Press, Inc.
Feminist Writers Guild

[Editor's note: The guidelines below describe the requirements for entering the 1998 Literary Anthology/Contest. They are printed here to provide general information about the Outrider Press competition. The theme for the 1999 contest will be *Feathers, Fins & Fur: ANIMAL STORIES*. The following changes to the 1998 guidelines apply to the 1999 contest:

Writers should send a SASE to request full 1999 guidelines and contest entry form(s).]

1998 Literary Anthology/Contest Guidelines

Planned publication date: mid-1998. Diverse writings by feminists of all ages, genders and orientations on the theme of *FREEDOM'S JUST ANOTHER WORD...*(tentative title), poetry and fiction on various concepts of freedom. What does it mean to live in a free society w/freedom of speech and movement? What is the role of the artist in a democracy? How do we see the face of freedom in the 21st century? How are our basic civil rights changing here and elsewhere?

• Yearnings for freedoms not yet gained; artistic/spiritual/economic/sexual expression freedoms;

• Dependence on dogma, materialism, our notions of security; and

• Personal limitations on freedom caused by others expectations, dysfunctional family backgrounds.

All accepted poetry and fiction submissions will be published in the anthology, with $100 cash prizes for best in each category as determined by independent judges; also a $50 cash prize from Outrider Press for the best entry submitted by a member of the Feminist Writers Guild (FWG). Each published contributor will receive a complimentary copy of the anthology. Reading/entry fees *for each category* are $16, reduced to $11 each for FWG members. Annual FWG membership fee of $22 includes six 12-page newsletters each year. Newsletters contain a calendar of upcoming arts events; member news; women's health news; book reviews; notices of upcoming FWG Open Mikes and formal readings; and pages of Manuscripts Wanted, listing periodicals, anthologies and contests seeking writers submissions. An entry form for the *1998 FREEDOM'S JUST ANOTHER WORD...* Contest (available w/SASE) must be completed and accompany *each entry category*.

POETRY: Up to four poems per author, with each poem not more than one page in length (single spacing okay for poetry). READING FEE FOR FOUR POEMS: $16/$11 FWG MEMBER.

FICTION: 1,750 word limit per entry; excerpts from longer works permitted. READING FEE PER STORY: $16/$11. MAXI-MUM TWO ENTRIES PER PERSON: $32/$22 FWG MEMBER.

CASH PRIZES
$100-Poetry • $100-Fiction
$50-Best FWG Submission-Sponsored by Outrider Press
Writers should send *two* copies of each manuscript PLUS disk as follows:

• HARD COPY—Double-spaced manuscript on one side, on 8.5"x11" unlined white paper. Single-spacing okay for poetry. Only LaserJet, inkjet or letter-quality dot matrix acceptable; PLUS: Four-sentence bio; PLUS:

• ELECTRONIC—Provide ms. and bio on 3.5" IBM disk, using WordPerfect 5.0, 5.1, 5.2 or 6.0 for DOS, Rich-Text-Format (.rtf), MS Word 7.0—no ASCII, no centering, bold, italics codes; only tabs for paragraph indents. Specify word-processing program on label, along with author's name and phone number. No Mac. Disks can be converted quickly and inexpensively at Kinkos or comparable computer support center.

• Include name, address, and phone/fax numbers (w/area code) on first sheet of fiction; each sheet of poetry.

• Include a stamped, self-addressed #10 (business size) envelope. Items selected for publication will not be returned. Include a stamped, self-addressed postcard if you wish to have receipt of ms. confirmed.

Categories: Fiction—Animals—Feminism—Gay/Lesbian—Humor—Poetry—Short Stories—Women's Fiction—Women's Issues

Name: Whitney Scott, Senior Editor
Material: All
Address: 1004 E STEGER RD STE C-3
City/State/ZIP: CRETE IL 60417
Telephone: 708-672-6630
Fax: 708-672-5820
E-mail: Outrider@aol.com
Nota bene: Reading fee required.

Owl Creek Press

Owl Creek Press is pleased to announce that a prize of $750, as an advance against royalties, will be awarded to the winner of the annual Owl Creek Poetry Prize. This is in addition to the annual Green Lake Chapbook Prize for poetry, which offers a $500 prize. Owl Creek Press has awarded publication to the winners of these two prizes for more than ten years and is now offering a cash award in addition to publication. Previous winners have included Harry Humes, Hark Rubin, Angela Ball, Michael Cadnum, Suzanne Paola, Art Homer, Bea Opengart, Sue Ellen Thompson, Joseph Duemer, Mary Swander, David Baker, Walter Pavlich, Judy Longley, Julie Fay, Jan Minich, John Morgan, Lawrence Russ, Kevin Clark, Carol Frost, Michael Cole, Francine Witte, Stuart Bartow, Jon Davis and Carolyne Wright.

The deadlines and entry fees for each contest are listed below. Deadlines are applied by postmark date. An acknowledgments page noting any previous magazine or anthology publication of poems included in the manuscript is encouraged, but previous publication is not a requirement of entry. Any combination of published and unpublished poems is acceptable as long as the work has not previously appeared in book form (except anthologies). Simultaneous submission to other contests is acceptable as long as Owl Creek Press receives immediate notice of any other acceptance of publication. All manuscripts will be judged on literary artistic achievement and multiple entries are acceptable. Each entry is judged individually by the editors of Owl Creek Press and poets are encouraged to read the work of previously selected authors as a sampling of the variety of poetic achievement which has been selected.

	Green Lake Chapbook Prize	Owl Creek Poetry Prize
Length:	under 40 pages	over 50 pages
Entry fee:	$10	$15
Deadline:	August 15	February 15
Categories:	Fiction—Poetry	

Name: Acquisitions Editor
Material: All
Address: 2693 SW CAMANO DR
City/State/ZIP: CAMANO ISLAND WA 98292
Nota bene: Contest entry fee required.

Pacific View Press

Dear Author,

We apologize for this form letter, but we receive many queries, and cannot personally respond to those which are not within our area of publication interest.

We are a small press focusing on the Pacific Rim and its unique, growing interplay of economic and cultural forces. We publish titles in three series:

Contemporary Affairs, on Pacific Rim topics only, including guides for Asia-related international business;

Books for a Multicultural *Society;* nonfiction on Asia and Asian-American themes, primarily for children [see guidelines below];

Traditional Chinese Medicine, primarily texts, for practitioners.

We do not publish travel books or travelogues, autobiographies or biographies, photojournalism, literature or fiction.

If you feel your project fits our publishing interests, you are welcome to submit a proposal, accompanied by a sample chapter, and an outline or table of contents. Please include autobiographical information. We prefer not to receive manuscripts. We do not accept typewritten material. You may wish to request a current catalog first.

If we are interested in your proposal we will respond within 6 weeks, after your proposal has been evaluated by our editorial committee. Your material is assumed to be copyrighted and will be kept confidential.

Thank you for your interest, and good luck.

Regards,

Pacific View Press

Guidelines for Children's Book Authors and Artists

Our children's books focus on hardcover illustrated nonfiction for readers aged eight to twelve. We look for titles on aspects of the history and culture of the countries and peoples of the Pacific Rim, especially China, presented in an engaging, informative and respectful manner. We are interested in books that all children will enjoy reading and using, and that parents and teachers will want to buy. Our titles are available nationally through quality trade bookstores, museum stores, multicultural specialty catalogs, and the leading library and trade distributors. Recent titles have included *Kneeling Carabao and Dancing Giants: Celebrating Filipino Festivals,* and *Made in China: Ideas and Inventions from Ancient China.*

We welcome proposals from persons with expertise, either academic or personal, in their area of interest. While we do accept proposals from previously unpublished authors, we would expect submitters to have considerable experience presenting their interests to children in classroom or other public settings, and to have skill in writing for children.

We do not publish folk tales, literature translations, fiction, or picture stories, or photo-picture books. At this time we are not considering natural history or biographies.

Our finished books are usually 48 pages, 8½"x11", with full-color illustration throughout.

You are welcome to submit proposals, accompanied by a sample chapter or unit and an outline for the entire book. Please include autobiographical information. We would prefer not to receive completed manuscripts.

If we are interested in your proposal we will respond within 6 weeks, after your proposal has been evaluated by our editorial committee. Our contracts with authors are fairly standard for small publishers and cover finances, time frames and obligations of both author and publisher. We pay royalties based on net sales, with a small advance against royalties paid upon acceptance of the final manuscript.

Categories: Nonfiction—Asia—Asian-Americans—Children—Contemporary Affairs—Multicultural

Name: Acquisitions Editor
Material: All
Address: PO BOX 2657
City/State/ZIP: BERKELEY CA 94702
Telephone: 510-849-4213

Palace Corbie
Merrimack Books

DESCRIPTION: *Palace Corbie* is an annual anthology of fiction and poetry published in trade paperback format (with a full color cover). The length of successive volumes has been increasing, and the newest (#7) is 330 pages long. The press run has been around 1,000 copies recently. The first four volumes have sold out. Retail prices on remaining volumes are $10.95 for #5, $9.95 for #6, and $12.95 for #7 [checks payable to Merrimack Books].

SITUATION: Reading right now for fiction and poetry. Volumes will be published when enough work is received to fill them.

FICTION: *Technical.* Submissions in non-standard manuscript format will be rejected out of hand. Disposable manuscripts are encouraged (SASEs are still needed with these, of course). Word limit is strictly enforced. 2,000-10,000 words only, none longer or shorter. Any fiction sent that is outside this range will not be read. No electronic submissions. A disk will be requested if your material is accepted, however. *Topical.* Any subject or theme is theoretically acceptable. No firm genre restrictions.

I am looking for good stories that cause an emotional reaction in the reader. I prefer psychological work to gore or "supernatural." There are no taboos here. *Style.* I know writers hate to read this same advice over and again, but if you want to know what kind of material I accept, read a recent volume of *Palace Corbie.* Barring that, note some of the authors whose fiction I have published recently: Steve Rasnic Tem, Bentley Little, Brian Hodge, Yvonne Navarro, Douglas Clegg, JN Williamson, Edward Lee, Gemma Files, Elizabeth Engstrom, Wayne Allen Sallee, Elizabeth Massie, Norman Partridge, Michael A. Arnzen, Lucy Taylor, John Maclay, Mark Rich, Sue Storm, and Michael Hemmingson. Other writers whose work I admire and would like to publish but *have not so far* include Patrick McGrath, Poppy Z. Brite, Kathe Koja, Tanith Lee, Peter Straub, Clive Barker, Thomas M. Disch, David J. Schow, etc. This might give you some idea of what I seek.

POETRY: *Technical.* Submissions in non-standard manuscript format will be rejected out of hand. Disposable manuscripts are encouraged (SASE are still needed with these, of course). There is no line or word limit for poetry. No electronic submissions. A disk will be requested if your material is accepted, however. *Topical.* Any subject or theme is theoretically acceptable. There are no taboos. *Style.* This is a tough one for poetry. I will

Books

almost never accept rhyming poetry simply because I do not like it (not contemporary rhyming poetry, anyway).

Free and blank verse are the best bets. To figure out what I am looking for you can either buy a copy of *Palace Corbie,* read some of my poetry (after all, I probably do like the kind of material I write, wouldn't you think?), or refer to the following lists. Some poets I have published: John Grey, Richard L. Levesque, James S. Dorr, William F. Nolan, Cesslie Ladehoff, Charlee Jacob, William Kopecky, Holly Day, Denise Dumars, Wayne Allen Sallee, and Karen Verba. Contemporary poets I most admire but have not published include Yevgeny Yevtushenko, Philip Levine, Diane Wakoski, Pablo Neruda, Guiseppe Ungaretti, Octavio Paz, Sylvia Plath, and Patti Smith (yes, I am aware that some of these people are dead).

Poetry is difficult to place with *Palace Corbie* because I have diverse tastes (poems have to hit me just right in order for me to accept them for publication) and because I am a poetry snob.

RIGHTS RETAINED BY MERRIMACK BOOKS: One time, non-exclusive (print media) publication rights.

PAYMENT: *Unsolicited.* Fiction: Flat $20.00 payment on acceptance plus one copy of the publication. Poetry: Flat $5.00 payment on acceptance plus one copy of the publication. *Solicited.* Negotiated.

Categories: Fiction—Horror—Literature—Poetry—Short Stories

Name: Acquisitions Editor
Material: All
Address: PO BOX 83514
City/State/ZIP: LINCOLN NE 68501-3514
E-mail: we45927@navix.net (Queries only, please)
Internet: www.para-net.com/~palace_corbie

Paladin Press
Sycamore Island Books

Paladin Press primarily publishes original nonfiction manuscripts on military science, self-defense, personal privacy, espionage, police science, action careers, guerilla warfare, and other action topics. Submissions may be outlines with 1-3 sample chapters or complete manuscripts. Allow 1 month from receipt for a reply. Paladin also produces videos on the above topics.

Categories: Nonfiction—Adventure—Crime—History—Martial Arts—Military—Money/Finance—Outdoors—Personal Freedom—Weaponry

Name: Editorial Department
Material: All
Address: PO BOX 1307
City/State/ZIP: BOULDER CO 80306
Telephone: 303-443-7250
Fax: 303-442-8741
E-mail: clubed@rmii.com

Paradigm Publications

Dear Writer,
Paradigm Publications will review submissions appropriate to both professional and lay markets interested in Acupuncture, Chinese Medicine and other Complementary Medical topics. However, regardless of the intended readership, we seek mss that are rooted either in known primary sources or documented clinical experience. Translators must follow published translational standards, preferably those we publish, or present a suitable peer-reviewable gloss. Clinical claims require appropriate documentation.

Please write prior to submission to discuss the suitability, extent and format of your mss. Our web site will give prospective authors a useful review of our interests.

Sincerely,
Robert L. Felt
Paradigm Publications
Categories: Acupuncture—Chinese Language—Chinese Medicine—Complementary Medicine—Diet—Health—Herbal Medicine—Martial Arts—Multicultural—Philosophy—Textbooks

Name: Robert L. Felt, Publisher
Material: All
Address: 44 LINDEN ST
City/State/ZIP: BROOKLINE MA 02146
Telephone: 617-738-4664
Fax: 617-738-4620
E-mail: bob@paradigm-pubs.com
Internet: www.paradigm-pubs.com

Park Avenue Productions

Please refer to JIST Works, Inc.

Pelican Publishing Company

Submissions Policy: Pelican Publishing Company does not accept unsolicited manuscripts. All writers should send us a query letter and SASE, describing the project briefly and concisely. Multiple (or "simultaneous") queries are not considered.

A query letter should discuss the following: the book's content, its anticipated length (in double-spaced pages, not in words), its intended audience, the author's writing and professional background, and any promotional ideas and contacts the author may have. If the author has previously been published by another firm, please specify why a change is being sought. A formal synopsis, chapter outline and or one or two sample chapters may be sent with a query letter, but these are not required. Never send the original copy of any material.

Be advised that we have certain expectations in the length of a proposed manuscript. Most young children's books are 32 illustrated pages when published; their manuscripts cover about 7 pages when typed continuously. Proposed books for middle readers (ages 8 and up) should be at least 150 pages. Adult books should be more than this. For cookbooks, we require at least 200 proposed recipes.

If necessary, brief children's books (for readers under nine) may be submitted in their entirety. Photocopies of any accompanying artwork are welcome, but again, *never* send any original artwork.

We will respond as promptly as possible (usually one month), letting you know whether or not we feel the project is worth pursuing further. If we feel that it is worthy of consideration, we will request a partial or full manuscript. Following this procedure ensures the most expeditious treatment of all inquiries.

We do not require that writers contacting us have a literary agent representing them.

A phone call to the editor or secretary or an in-person drop off of unrequested material does not automatically imply that a project has been solicited. For this and other obvious reasons, we discourage phone inquiries and in-person drop offs. If an author we have requested additional material from is unclear as to what were asking for, a phone call to clarify the matter is acceptable.

Solicited manuscripts are carefully scrutinized by the editor(s). On occasion, they may be examined by our sales and/or promotions departments to gauge their marketability. They are then passed on to the publisher for preliminary and final consideration. The submissions are reported on as soon as possible, but this process may take up to three months (12 weeks). If acceptance is recommended, the author(s) will be asked to sign a contract with Pelican Publishing Company.

If the three-month period for solicited manuscripts passes without the author being informed of a decision, a polite note of reminder from the author is not out of order. Phone calls on the status of manuscripts are very strongly discouraged. Never badger the editor for an instant decision or make demands or threats; this can only hurt the author's chances of acceptance. Authors who feel unsatisfied with our procedures or the amount of time being taken to reach a decision are free to request the manuscripts return at any time.

Pelican Publishing requires exclusive submission for all solicited manuscripts during the 12-week period mentioned above. This is for obvious reasons. We can only give full attention to those manuscripts which we are likely to be able to publish if accepted by us.

We also ask that authors who have solicited works under consideration please refrain from sending us other works or proposals during this time unless they are specifically requested to do so. Agreement on our part to look at a particular work does not imply blanket authorization to send unrelated materials and doing so could hurt, rather than help, an author. Materials related to the requested submission, such as favorable newspaper clippings, endorsements by qualified professionals in the field the author is writing about, or other amended data may be sent and added to the material already on file.

Use careful judgment in selecting these items and be certain that they enhance the material and its chances of being accepted. Sending in later data that refutes or calls into question points made in the earlier submission may cast doubts on the whole project's veracity and damage its chances of acceptance. Always be certain to refer to the work's title, the author name under which it was submitted, and the date the original query was mailed.

Materials will not be returned unless they are accompanied by sufficient postage. Policies regarding SASEs apply to all submissions from foreign countries, including Canada. Return postage must be in stamps, checks on U.S. banks, or International Money Orders in U.S. money.

We require all submissions, including outlines, resumes, sample chapters, etc., be neatly typed. If corrections are made, they should be "whited-out" as inconspicuously as possible. Submissions with numerous misspellings, typographical errors, and handwritten corrections reflect unfavorably on the author and may contribute heavily toward a rejection.

Writers are cautioned not to rely on editors to clean up after them or interpret unclear information, regardless of how good they think their material may be. A sloppy submission is often indicative of worse problems—the type editors and publishers prefer not to deal with.

Handwritten submissions and/or queries, unless neatly printed in the absence of a typewriter, do not make favorable impressions on editors and could jeopardize your chances of acceptance. For those using computers, we strongly advise you to send us your submissions in letter quality or near-letter-quality type—not dot matrix. Electronic submissions (disks) are not accepted. These would only be needed once a contract was signed. Never send disks, videotapes, or audio tapes without inquiring beforehand.

Authors should avoid undue "hyping" of their work. Materials submitted with author projections of it being a "blockbuster" or "the next *Gone With the Wind*" rarely live up to these pretensions. The publisher and editor(s) are professionals who can make up their own minds on the quality and potential of a proposal without the "self-hype." Comments and/or reviews from qualified professionals or publications, as stated earlier, can be desirable in many cases. Likewise for rejection letters from other publishing companies that acknowledge a project's potential value and which base their rejections on other factors unrelated to quality of author workmanship.

We look for clarity and conciseness of expression and presentation in a synopsis/outline and we ask to see those that will most likely yield proposals fitting our list and that we feel we can market successfully. We turn down thousands of adequate proposals every year just because they have no clear "hooks" or well-defined audiences.

The author should present a strong case as to why we should take on the book and who would buy it. Saying that "all children would love it" is very vague, but saying "libraries and schools in Tennessee would like this" is more informative.

All work submitted to us must be in good taste, nonlibelous, and consistent with the level of quality we have established for our company. Although many of our titles are specialized, they are **all** suitable for general readership and are free of gratuitous, off-color words, phrases, or references.

If an author seeking to publish an illustrated work plans to use artwork copyrighted by an author, illustrator, publication, or syndicate, permission must be obtained *in writing* from that source. Permission in writing must also be obtained by any author seeking to use quotes or other materials from previously copyrighted publications. We will not publish illustrations or portions of another copyrighted work without written authorization to do so.

Authors seeking to have previously published books reprinted must have, *in writing* from their previous publisher, a signed letter transferring all rights (including copyright) to them. This is required under the 1978 Copyright Law and must be adhered to in all such cases.

Under the revisions contained in the 1978 Copyright Law, a work is *automatically* copyrighted at the time of creation. If we agree to accept the work for publication, we will apply for the copyright in the author's name on publication.

TYPES OF BOOK PUBLISHED: Hardcover and trade paperback originals (90%) and reprints (10%) including hardcover, trade paperback and mass market. We publish an average of 50 to 60 titles a year and have about 800 currently in print.

Specialties are art/architecture books, cooking/cookbooks, motivational, travel guides, history (especially Louisiana/regional), nonfiction, children's books (illustrated and otherwise), inspirational and religious, humor, social commentary, folklore, and textbooks. A *very limited* number of fictional works are accepted for publication, but we will consider fiction if well written and/or timely.

We seek writers on the cutting edge of ideas who do not write in cliches, or take the old, tired, unimaginative way of foul language and sex scenes to pad a poor writing effort. We strongly urge writers to be aware of ideas gaining currency. We believe ideas have consequences. One of the consequences is that they lead to best-selling books.

We do publish a limited number of posters, cards, giftware, and similar works of art. Consideration of submission of this type is based on consistency with other motifs we are marketing at the present time.

Finally, we would ask you to study Pelican's books and lists. Our latest catalog is available for free on request, and a look through it will help you understand where our interests lie. We have been called "innovative" by the *New York Times*. We will consider almost any well-written work by an author who understands promotion.

PAYMENT POLICY: Pelican pays its authors a royalty based on sales. The rate depends on the type of material and the format.

All terms are specified in the contract all authors publishing under our imprint(s) are required to sign. No book will be published by Pelican without a signed contract.

All guidelines listed above are subject to revision at any time by Pelican Publishing Company and its editorial board.

Categories: Fiction—Nonfiction—African-American—Architecture—Arts—Asian-American—Biography—Boating—Business—Cartoons—Children—Civil War—Cooking—Ethnic—Family—Hispanic—History—Humor—Inspirational—Jewish Interests—Multicultural—Music—Native American—Outdoors—Regional—Religion—Sports—Textbooks—Travel—Western

Name: Acquisitions Editor
Material: All
Address: PO BOX 3110
City/State/ZIP: GRETNA LA 70054-3110

Pennycorner Press

Pennycorner Press is dedicated to publishing works in any media that promote or support inclusive communities. Works produced or published by Pennycorner emphasize expanding personal choice and freedom, and reducing institutional constraints and limits on human possibility.

Pennycorner projects have included how-to solutions for independent living, ideas for including children with special needs in regular classrooms, and documenting the human cost of institutionalization. We are interested in projects that contribute to professional training as well as those that directly empower individuals and families.

Because Pennycorner works in both print and film, we look for projects that can be collateralized into another media; i.e., a book title that could be made into an accompanying film; a film that could give rise to a newsletter, etc.

Categories: Disabilities—Education—Health

Name: G.M. Greider, Development
Material: All
Address: PO BOX 8
City/State/ZIP: GILMAN CT 06336
Telephone: 860-873-2545
Fax: 860-873-1311
E-mail: ggreider@pennycorner.com

> **Remember: Editors change jobs and publishers change addresses. It is wise to invest in a phone call for the current information before submitting.**

THE PERMANENT PRESS
SECOND CHANCE PRESS

The Permanent Press
Second Chance Press

Dear Writer:

We are looking for material of a high literary quality; material that is original and stimulating with an authentic point of view and a unique voice.

If you are interested in submitting a manuscript, we would prefer a short synopsis, and the first chapter. We will get back to you as soon as possible.

Please note that we publish novel-length fiction, and occasionally nonfiction. We no longer publish cookbooks, children's stories, story collections, novellas, or poetry.

The above criteria is used for both *Second Chance Press* and *The Permanent Press*. Books submitted for reprint by *Second Chance Press* must be at least twenty years old.

Sincerely,
Judith Shepard
Editor and Co-Publisher
Categories: Fiction

Name: Acquisitions Editor
Material: All
Address: 4170 NOYAC RD
City/State/ZIP: SAG HARBOR NY 11963
Telephone: 516-725-1101

Perron Press

Dear Writer:

Thank you for inquiring about our manuscript guidelines for new

works. Since we receive increasing numbers of unsolicited submissions, we ask that you first submit a query letter with an outline of your work, and a sufficient sample of your writing style for our staff to determine if your work fits within our editorial policy. From there, we can decide whether we need to request a complete manuscript for further review.

We cannot be responsible for returning manuscripts due to the large quantity we receive. We encourage you to submit your work for consideration at this time:

• it may be considered (budget allowing) for publication by Perron Press,

• we may offer subsidy publishing,

• or we can assist you with the details of self-publishing.

In any case, we are always excited about being involved in projects that can make a positive difference.

Thank you for your interest in Perron Press.

Sincerely,
David Balding
Publisher
Categories: Nonfiction—Education—Psychology—Relationships

Name: Kelley Lee, Acquisitions Editor
Material: All
Address: PO BOX 10826
City/State/ZIP: PORTLAND OR 97296-0826
Telephone: 503-228-4972
Fax: 503-223-9117
E-mail: perron@metamodels.com
Nota bene: Subsidy and self-publishing options.

Perspective Press
The Infertility and Adoption Publisher

Since 1982 we've been providing everything that's anything related to:
- reproductive health education
- adoption information and education
- choices for treating impaired fertility
- the emotional impact of infertility
- lifestyle alternatives and family building avenues beyond infertility:
  - childfree living
  - adoption
- collaborative reproduction (donor insemination, surrogacy, donor ova, donor embryo, gestational carrier)
- parenting after infertility and/or in adoption through...
- books, articles and fact sheets for adults and for children on adoption and infertility
- workshops for consumers and for medical, mental health counseling and allied professionals on infertility and reproductive health, adoption and alternative family building

WRITER'S GUIDELINES
perspective, n. the relationship of aspects of a subject to each other and to the whole. Point of view.

Perspectives Press is a small publisher focusing narrowly on infertility issues and alternatives, and on adoption and closely related child welfare issues such as interim (foster) care or psychological services. Our purpose is to promote understanding of these issues and to educate and sensitize those personally experiencing these life situations, professionals who work with such clients, and the public at large. We invite authors whose philosophy concerning these issues agrees with ours to follow our process for submitting manuscripts for consideration, beginning with a query letter.

OUR POINT OF VIEW Regarding infertility and alternatives, Perspectives Press takes the position that we live in the best and worst of times to be infertile. Though research daily provides new treatment options, it has become increasingly difficult for couples to know when to stop treatment, and alternatives are becoming more and more complex: infant adoption is a shrinking alternative, surrogate parenting is in legal limbo, donor insemination's traditional secrecy is being questioned, some technical alternatives provide for as many as five "parents" for a single child, and rising costs of testing and treatment and family building alternatives stifle the dreams of many families.

We believe in and actively promote adoption as a positive option for family planning and family building. We do not accept the philosophy that adoption should be eliminated, nor are we accepting of the absolutist idea that any one form of adoption is the appropriate approach. We agree that adoption is a service designed first to benefit children, not adults, and that every adoption should be child-centered. But we believe that it is incumbent upon professionals working in this arena to treat birth families and prospective adopters with respect and sensitivity and with objective regard for their needs, which will vary widely, as each set of birth parents and each set of adopters is unique.

We believe that children deserve the permanency of family as quickly as possible after the disruption of a birth family. We believe that any societal institution, including adoption, must meet the needs of a current society, and to that end we are open to discussion and debate of a variety of approaches to and issues in adoption. Perspectives works actively to promote understanding between adoptees, adoptive parents, and birth parents.

We feel that it is important that manuscripts respect the variety of feelings of and the decisions made by those who are members of the adoption triad and that they be written using realistic and neutral adoption language.

OUR EDITORIAL POLICIES Perspectives Press titles are never duplicative. We seek out and publish materials that are currently unavailable through other sources. Furthermore, because our company is small and our list of titles is kept short, we will not consider manuscripts that seriously overlap or compete with titles already on our list. After over ten years in business, we know our own subject matter and its audience very well, but we also know our limitations!

We are not a general publisher. Please do not ask us to consider stretching our focus beyond infertility- or adoption-related issues or to change our stated decisions about what topics and genres we will consider as described here.

Manuscripts outside our specific field are returned unread if SASE is supplied. When submitting (see adult-specific and children's-specific query/submission information which follows) we respectfully request that you *not* use registered, certified or other signature-required mail to send a manuscript to our post office box address. This necessitates a long and irritating wait in a post office line during "rush hour" or a trip back later in the day!

OUR AUTHORS While we do consider manuscripts from writers who are not personally or professionally involved in our field, we are more inclined to accept a manuscript submitted by an infertile person, an adoptee, a birth parent, an adoptive parent, or a professional working with these clients. Because we work most frequently with never-before-published authors, we make it a policy not to offer a contract based simply on a proposal.

At a minimum we require a completed first draft. Authors are oriented before a contract is signed so that they have realistic expectations about the realities and complexities of marketing in our niche.

We expect our authors to be closely involved in an ongoing way in their own title's promotion and in the full line of books from Perspectives Press, seeking opportunities to speak and write on the issue, distributing our catalog broadly, etc.

OUR NEEDS *For adults* we are looking for nonfiction in the form of decision-making materials, books dealing with issue-related parenting concerns, books to share with others to help explain infertility or adoption issues, special programming or training manuals. Our audience is made up of both consumers and professionals in our field.

We are not an academic publisher and are disinclined toward research-oriented materials, though we are favorable toward research-based perspectives presented in consumer style. We insist that the books we publish be written in an open, engaging, and user-friendly style, free of jargon.

Manuscripts must be book length—a minimum of 40,000 words. We will not consider pamphlets or singly submitted essays, short stories, or poems.

Because in general first person, autobiographical, and jour-

Books

nal-style books in this field have not sold well (no matter what size the publisher) we are not accepting "our infertility experience" or "how we got our child" or "the story of my search" manuscripts. The exception would be books in which the personal materials are included only to provide anecdotal color in a manuscript whose larger purpose is to offer decision-making materials or advice on developing coping skills.

We are not currently publishing novels or other adult fiction. We are a secular publisher and do not publish books rooted in a specific religious view.

Writers of adult material should **schedule a reading** by querying first with a proposal packet before sending a completed manuscript. [A reply] will follow within two weeks. (Unsolicited manuscripts arriving without having scheduled a reading will usually be returned unread.) Your proposal should fully describe your topic and should include an outline and/or a table of contents. Tell us the number of typed, double-spaced pages in the full manuscript and the approximate word count.

Your query should mention similarly-themed books both in and out of print and discuss how your book would differ from and be superior to them. Also include a careful description of your book's potential audience, including a researched estimate of the realistic size of that audience and a marketing proposal discussing how you think your audience could best be located and reached out to. Tell us about yourself and your qualifications for writing your proposed book. If we are interested in your concept we will give you a date for sending the full manuscript for a scheduled reading. We will respond within two months of the scheduled reading date.

Our *children's books* are primarily fiction and nonfiction manuscripts appropriate for preschoolers and elementary aged youngsters. We encourage authors to familiarize themselves with Piagetan theories about children's cognitive development before trying to write for a particular audience. We see far too many manuscripts which really deal with parent's issues rather than children's. We will read nonfiction, but not fiction, for middle schoolers and young adults.

We encourage writers to carefully examine materials that are already available for children about the issues which we address and to avoid developing materials which compete with or overlap well regarded books already in print from any publisher. Unless you are an author/illustrator submitting your own artwork, we would prefer that you *not* find your own illustrator before submitting your manuscript. We ask you to recall that because this market is narrow, it is important to make such materials as inclusive as possible. We are not likely to accept, for example, international adoption stories which are country-specific. Make stories racially and ethnically inclusive, remember that some adoptees join their families as infants and some at an older age, keep in mind that not all adoptive parents adopt for reasons of infertility and that many are single parents, and speak respectfully of birth parents.

Currently there are glaring gaps in the children's market for single parent adoption-built families and families built by donor insemination, donor embryo and all forms of surrogacy. We are looking hard for manuscripts to fill these gaps.

Because our children's publication program is currently under re-evaluation, writers of children's picture books, too, should **query first before submitting**. Your submission packet should include your writing resume and pertinent information about your personal or professional connections to the filed about which you are writing. It should include information which indicates that you have familiarized yourself thoroughly enough with available materials in the field to understand how and why your book fills a heretofore empty niche. We will reply within two months.

I look forward to hearing from you!

Pat Johnston, Publisher

Categories: Nonfiction—Children—Family—Health—Infertility and Adoption—Parenting—Psychology

Name: Acquisitions Editor
Material: All
Address: PO BOX 90318
City/State/ZIP: INDIANAPOLIS IN 46290-0318
E-mail: ppress@iquest.net
Internet: www.perspectivespress.com
Nota bene: Manuscript reading/evaluation must be scheduled.

Phi Delta Kappa
Educational Foundation

The Special Publications department of Phi Delta Kappa is an activity of the Phi Delta Kappa Educational Foundation.

When Dr. George H. Reavis made possible the establishment of the Foundation, he articulated a vision of the Foundations work:

The purpose of the Phi Delta Kappa Educational Foundation is to contribute to a better understanding of 1) the nature of the educative process, and 2) the relation of education to human welfare.

Dr. Reavis viewed this purpose in a larger sense as shaping public policy through understanding:

In our democracy public policy is determined by popular will, and popular will is based upon popular understanding. Our governmental (and educational) policy can be no better in the long run than our popular understanding.

This statement of purpose and its rationale laid a foundation for the role of Special Publications within the Foundation. Since the establishment of the Foundation in 1966, Special Publications has acquired and published a variety of works designed to enhance the professional literature of education. Those works are brought to print either as Foundation monographs, which are books of various lengths, or as Fastbacks.

Following are guidelines for writers who wish to develop a manuscript for one of these forms.

Fastbacks®

The PDK fastbacks were initiated in 1972 as a continuing series of short, authoritative publications for educators at all levels. Since the series was created, more than 7 million copies of the fastbacks have been disseminated. Today, the fastbacks are published in two annual sets of eight titles. These sets are released in the fall and spring.

The fastbacks often have been described as "sophisticated primers." Each one focuses on a specific, often fairly narrow topic. Many, if not most, are oriented to the practitioner, such as an elementary classroom teacher, an instructional specialist, a principal, a school superintendent, or a university professor. A few are more theoretical. Several focus on exemplary programs or profile specific schools.

In short, the topic range is as broad as the profession. Indeed, this is specifically done in order to mirror the broad membership base of Phi Delta Kappa.

Manuscript length: 10,000 words

Honorarium: $500

Short Monographs

Like the fastbacks, PDK's short monographs are narrowly focused and practical in character. Good examples in this range are titles such as *Planning for Disaster, Responding to Adolescent Suicide,* and the nine volumes of the Elementary Principal series.

Manuscript length: 20,000 - 30,000 words

Honorarium: $1,000 - $2,000

Books

Books published by the PDK Educational Foundation, like the fastbacks and short monographs, reflect a broad range of professional interests and topics. Some are sweeping in scope; a good example is John I. Goodlad's classic *What Schools Are For.* Others focus more narrowly, such as Kenneth Chuska's *Improving Classroom Questions* and Carol Hillman's *Before the School Bell Rings.* Some concentrate on current issues, such as John F. Jenning's four-volume series, *National Issues in Education.* Still others are basic resources, an example being the third edition of A *Digest of Supreme Court Decisions Affecting Education.*

Manuscript length: 40,000 - 70,000 words

Honorarium: $3,000 - $5,000

Of course, the best way to understand the scope and character of PDK Special Publications is to peruse the product catalogue and to read a few of the books, monographs, and fastbacks.

Guidelines for Submissions

1. Initially, a query letter is preferred. This letter should succinctly state the purpose and audience for the publication, a proposed manuscript length, and a suggested writing timeline. The editor responds to queries usually within two weeks.

2. A prospective author should be prepared to submit a well-developed, annotated outline. For longer works, the editor may request a sample chapter. The editor responds to such proposals usually within two months, often sooner.

3. In most instances, an author-publisher agreement (contract) is issued on the basis of a proposal. In some cases, however, submission of the full manuscript will be required prior to the issuance of a contract to publish.

4. The editor will assist the author in developing a successful manuscript. However, despite the best intentions of both author and editor, sometimes a manuscript will be judged unacceptable. Authors should be aware that PDK editors reserve the right to edit extensively and, on occasion, to rewrite poorly written materials. But substantive changes are not made without the author's permission.

5. Authors are advised to avoid education jargon. Simple, straight-forward prose that makes ample use of examples, anecdotes, and case studies is preferred. Any citations must be complete and the PDK style is based on the *Chicago Manual of Style.*

6. Tables, charts, and graphs should be used only when they are necessary to understand the text. Large figures are discouraged, particularly for the fastbacks which are printed in a small format.

7. Photographs may be submitted with a manuscript. Clear, 5"x7" (or larger) black-and-white prints are preferred. All photos must include captions. A model release must be provided for all persons who can be identified in a photograph.

8. Manuscripts must be submitted on standard size paper using a type that can be electronically scanned. Authors may submit their work on computer disk; however, a hard copy also must be provided.

9. PDK purchases all rights by contract. Payment is made in the form of a one-time honorarium, which is paid about one month prior to publication. Special Publications does not pay royalties.

10. The editor reserves the right to select the manner of publication—for example, whether to bring out a book in a paperback or hardback form—and how the work will be promoted. Costs of production, promotion, and dissemination are borne by PDK.

Categories: Nonfiction—Education

Name: Donovan R. Walling, Editor of Special Publications

Material: All

Address: PO BOX 789

City/State/ZIP: BLOOMINGTON IN 47402-0789

Telephone: 812-339-1156

Fax: 812-339-0018

E-mail: Headquarters@pdkintl.org

Internet: www.pdkintl.org

Philomel Books
A division of The Putnam & Grosset Group

Picture Books

We accept full picture book manuscripts for review. Art should not be sent until specifically requested.

Fiction

(middle—grade, chapter books, young adult)

Please send a query letter before submitting fiction. Please include a synopsis and one to three sample chapters. Your query letter and sample chapters will be circulated among the editors and the entire work will be requested upon interest.

Nonfiction

Please send a query letter before submitting nonfiction. Please include a synopsis and one or two sample chapters, as well as a table of contents. Your query letter and sample chapters will be circulated among the editors and the entire work will be requested upon interest.

If you would like to receive a catalog, you must send a 9"x12" envelope with the appropriate postage.

Categories: Fiction—Nonfiction—Children—Fantasy—History—Juvenile—Multicultural—Mystery—Poetry—Regional—Young Adult

Name: Patricia Gauch, Editorial Director

Material: Any

Name: Michael Green, Editor

Material: Any

Address: 200 MADISON AVE

City/State/ZIP: NEW YORK NY 10016

Telephone: 212-951-8700

PICCADILLY BOOKS

Piccadilly Books
HealthWise Publications

Piccadilly Books specializes in the publication of books within two general subject categories (1) Theater & Entertainment and (2) Nutrition and Health.

THEATER AND ENTERTAINMENT

In this category we are looking for nonfiction, how-to, and activity topics suitable for children and adults. We have a strong interest in family entertainment—magic, clowning, puppetry, etc. Comedy skits, games, unique fun activities and any business topics related to these subjects are also of interest. Samples of the type of titles we publish are:

Books

- Creative Clowning
- Ventriloquism Made Easy
- Clown Magic
- Tricks and Stunts to Fool Your Friends
- Humorous Dialogs
- The Birthday Party Business

NUTRITION AND HEALTH

Books in this category are published under our imprint name HealthWise Publications. We are interested in nonfiction books on any aspect of health, diet, exercise, and bodywork. Must be written from a holistic or natural health viewpoint. Samples of the type of titles we publish are:

- *The Detox Book*
- *The Healing Crisis*
- *The Healing Power of Rebounding*

We do not accept children's picture books, novels, or any subject outside those described above. Material from unagented and first-time authors are welcomed and encouraged.

Submissions should consist of a query letter and sample chapters of your manuscript. You may submit a full manuscript if it is completed along with a cover letter describing the contents of the manuscript. We do not return manuscripts or sample chapters, if rejected they are discarded. We review all submissions within a few days of their arrival and send responses as soon as we have made a decision. The most promising submissions take several weeks to thoroughly evaluate. Please allow up to two months for a response.

All manuscripts should include the title, your name, and your address on the first page. Following pages should be numbered consecutively.

Computer printout submissions are acceptable. Letter quality printouts are highly preferred over dot-matrix. Hand written manuscripts are not acceptable.

Be sure to obtain permission to use any quotation, illustration, or other copyrighted material. Contact the house which published the material and get their written permission.

Categories: Nonfiction—Comedy—Diet—Entertainment—Health—Humor—Theatre

Name: Submissions Department
Material: All
Address: PO BOX 25203
City/State/ZIP: COLORADO SPRINGS CO 80936
Telephone: 719-550-9887

Picton Press
Cricketfield Press, Penobscot Press

Our guidelines for submissions, in our categories of *history* and *genealogy*:

Picton Press publishes top quality scholarly works in these two fields, with emphasis on the 17th and 18th centuries. Manuscripts to be submitted should show:

- 17th or 18th century subjects preferred; 19th century acceptable
- highest quality technical expertise
- comprehensive grasp of the subject matter
- new subject matter or a new approach to well-established subject matter

We will publish works with relatively limited markets, and even books which are unlikely to break even, so long as they demonstrate the items above. On a common-sense basis we give priority to works which are camera-ready and/or require only limited editing.

Categories: History—Genealogy

Name: Acquisitions Editor
Material: All
Address: PO BOX 250
City/State/ZIP: ROCKPORT ME 04856-0250
Telephone: 207-236-6565
Fax: 207-236-6713
E-mail: Picton@midcoast.com

Pilot Books

To: Authors who wish to present work to Pilot Books
From: The Publisher

Pilot Books, founded in 1959, concentrates on books on small and home-based business, franchising, budget travel, how-to, career and personal guides and senior citizen interests. Our usual publication is an 80 to 120 page book containing "how-to" information in a concise format.

We welcome material from authors new to us. Unsolicited material should fit one or more of our specific areas of interest and we require at least a brief outline and sample chapter for review. Enclose a self-addressed, stamped envelope, and if you wish to have your manuscript returned to you after our decision, please so indicate.

We value the opportunity to review new possibilities for publication, and accordingly, we give each submission our prompt attention and response.

Categories: Nonfiction—Business—Careers—Fishing—General Interest—Lifestyles—Recreation—Reference—Senior Citizens—Travel

Name: Acquisitions Editor
Material: All
Address: PO BOX 2102
Address: 127 STERLING AVE
City/State/ZIP: GREENPORT NY 11944
Telephone: 516-477-1094
Fax: 516-477-0978
E-mail: Feedback@pilotbooks.com
Internet: www.pilotbooks.com

Players Press, Inc.

Players Press, Inc. is continually looking for new works to publish. Send a clearly typed copy of your play, musical, or performing arts book to the address below.

Remember to enclose the following:

1. Two stamped, self-addressed #10 envelopes for correspondence.

2. A copy of the flyer and program with production dates on it. **No manuscript will be considered unless it has been produced.** (Produced means: one professional production, or two amateur productions, or one award-winning amateur production. *A reading is not considered a production.*)

4. A brief biography and/or resume of the writer.

5. Reviews, when available.

6. If accepted for publication, the script must be made available on computer disk. We prefer Macintosh in either Microsoft Word or PageMaker. Please advise.

Our editors will try to read your work and return it to you within 90 days.

Categories: Crafts—Crime—Drama—Entertainment—Fashion—Film/Video—Television/Radio—Textbooks—Theatre—Writing

Name: Robert W. Gordon, Vice President, Editorial
Material: All
Address: PO BOX 1132
City/State/ZIP: STUDIO CITY CA 91614-0132

Plenum Publishing

We are interested in proposals for trade nonfiction books only. Our editor should be sent:
- A resumé on the author(s)
- A table of contents
- Marketing ideas
- Sample chapter(s)

Please—no telephone calls relating to proposals or submissions.

Categories: Nonfiction—Archaeology—Crime—Engineering—Health (not how-to)—Mathematics—Politics—Psychology—Science—Society—Technology—True Crime

Name: Linda Greenspan Regan, Executive Editor
Material: All
Address: 233 SPRING ST
City/State/ZIP: NEW YORK NY 10013
Telephone: 212-620-8000

Pocket Books
Simon & Schuster

General Information

Our **Archway Paperbacks** imprint is for young adults, ages 12-16. These books are an average of 160 pages or 35,000 words.

Our **Minstrel Books** imprint is for middle grade readers, ages 7-11. These books are an average of 96 pages or 6,000 to 10,000 words.

We publish juvenile fiction with a current setting, school and animal stories, and popular biographies. We do not publish picture books.

Currently we are very successful with mass market oriented suspense/thrillers and romantic sagas or comedies for the young adult and scary/funny stories for the middle grade reader.

You may find it helpful to familiarize yourself with some of the titles we have recently published. Your local library or bookstore should have a selection of our titles in their Young Adult and Intermediate or Middle Grade sections.

Guidelines

Please send us a proposal first. Include in your proposal:
1) a brief cover letter introducing your work
2) *a very detailed outline* of the *entire* book
3) (optional) a few sample chapters.

If we are interested in seeing more of your manuscript, we will contact you.

You need not send your manuscript through priority mail; third or first class mail is fine, as submissions are not read on a daily basis. Please note that it is also unnecessary to send your manuscript in a heavily padded envelope.

Submissions will be answered within 3-4 weeks.

Thank you for your interest in Archway Paperbacks and Minstrel Books. We look forward to hearing from you.

Categories: Fiction—Nonfiction—Adventure—Animals—Biography—Children—Comedy—Fantasy—Horror—Humor—Juvenile—Mystery—Teen—Young Adult

Name: Patricia MacDonald, Vice President and Editorial Director
Material: All
Address: 1230 AVENUE OF THE AMERICAS
City/State/ZIP: NEW YORK NY 10020
Telephone: 212-698-7268
Fax: 212-698-7337

PREP PUBLISHING

PREP Publishing

Established in 1994, PREP Publishing is the publishing division of a company, PREP, Inc., founded in 1981 by graduates of Harvard Business School and Yale University. The parent company is a diversified writing/editing organization and is the country's largest resume writing organization.

The company's first title was published in 1995: *Second Time Around* is a mystery/romance and literary fiction by Southern writer Patty Sleem. *Library Journal* described Patty Sleem's second book, *Back In Time,* as "an engrossing look at the discrimination faced by female ministers."

In 1996 PREP Publishing launched its line of career titles with the publication of *Resumes and Cover Letters That Have Worked for Military Professionals,* a how-to guide to resume and cover letter preparation for veterans and military professionals leaving active duty. Praised by the highly respected *Booklist* as "A guide that significantly translates Veterans' experience into viable repertoires of achievement," that 256-page book contains resumes and cover letters of "real people" who used those resumes and cover letters to transition into civilian jobs. The second title in PREP's line of career titles was *Resumes and Cover Letters That Have Worked,* a 272-page how-to book containing more than 100 resumes and cover letters of "civilians" with special sections devoted to Experienced Professionals, People Changing Careers, and Recent College Graduates.

PREP's publishing interests include mysteries and other fiction and nonfiction, including biographies of famous people, business books, self-help and how-to books, and career titles. We are also developing a line of Christian fiction. Our mission is to publish quality materials, both for children and adults, that enrich people's lives and help them optimize their human experience.

PREP Publishing is listed in *Literary Marketplace* and our titles are listed in *Books in Print* and in *Forthcoming Books in Print.* PREP Publishing is a member of the American Booksellers Association, Southeast Booksellers Association, Publishers Association of the South, Publishers Marketing Association, the Christian Booksellers Association, and the Council of Literary Magazines and Small Presses. Our titles are distributed by Seven Hills Book Distributors and by Ingram Book Company, Baker & Taylor Books, Quality Books, Unique Books, and others.

There are two ways to make submissions to PREP Publishing.

1. One way is to send a cover letter and synopsis of your book. Published authors may prefer this query-first method. Address cover-letter-and-synopsis submissions to Frances Sweeney at the address below. **Limit your total submission to three pages! Try to sell us on your concept; if we are interested, we will get in touch with you.**

2. The other way to make a submission to PREP is to send your complete manuscript with a non-refundable reading fee of one hundred dollars payable to PREP. Because of the volume of

mail received, it has become impossible for our existing staff to read all the manuscripts which authors wish to submit to us and we now employ outside readers to evaluate the book's suitability for publication and write a written "Reader's Report" which the author gets a copy of. Pre-published authors or published authors writing in a new genre may find this professional evaluation helpful.

If you wish to submit your complete manuscript, please send a hard copy (not an electronic submission) of the entire manuscript along with a check for $100 to PREP and an SASE with sufficient postage for the manuscript's return to you. Our readers are professional editors, "book doctors," and respected librarians, and our turn-around time is two weeks. Please bear in mind that our professional readers do try to identify the areas in plot, characterization, etc. which need to be "fixed" if it is the reader's opinion that author revisions are necessary. Address such submissions to Janet Abernethy at the address below.

Once a manuscript is selected for publication, payment to authors is through a royalty schedule based on final sales. Once a manuscript is accepted, publication usually takes 18 months.

Thank you for your interest in PREP Publishing.

Categories: Fiction—Nonfiction—Adventure—Biography—Business—Careers—Christian Interests—Crime—Family—Humor—Inspirational—Literature—Military—Mystery—Relationships—Religion—Romance—Spiritual—Women's Issues—Writing—Young Adult

> **Name: Anne McKinney, Editor-in-Chief**
> **Material: All**
> **Address: 110½ HAY ST**
> **City/State/ZIP: FAYETTEVILLE NC 28305**
> **Telephone: 910-483-8049**
> **Fax: 910-483-2439**
> **Nota bene: Complete manuscript submissions require a reading fee.**

Prima Publishing

PRIMA PUBLISHING, founded in 1984, publishes hardcovers and trade paperbacks in nonfiction categories including popular culture, current affairs and international events, travel, business, careers, legal topics, sports, cooking, health, lifestyle, self-help, and music. Prima also produces a line of computer books geared towards business, professional, and recreational uses, and a line of video/computer game clue books. Prima is among the fastest-growing of the independent publishers and maintains a solid backlist.

The following Prima titles reflect the varied interests of the company: *Churchill on Leadership* by Steven F. Hayward, *The Wave 3 Way to Building Your Downline* by Richard Poe, *Positive Discipline A-Z* by Jane Nelsen, Lynn Lott, and H. Stephen Glenn, *The Wealthy Barber* by David Chilton, *Encyclopedia of Natural Medicine* by Michael Murry, N. D. and Joseph Pizzorno, N.D.

Please include the following when sending a proposal to Prima Publishing:

1. **Brief explanation of the book.** What is the manuscript about, and why would someone buy it? Like the short text written on the back cover of a book, the explanation should describe the contents of the book while also enticing the reader to know more about it. The overview is also an opportunity for the author to display his or her unique writing style. To prepare for an overview, it may be a worthwhile practice to read the back covers of several books in a local bookstore, noting the way the publisher tries to catch and hold the reader's interest.

2. **Detailed table of contents and chapter outlines.** Breaking the manuscript down into individual chapters, write a para-

graph discussing the information in each chapter.

3. **Sample chapter.** The editor will need to see your best chapter in order to evaluate your writing.

4. **Anticipated market for the book.** Who is the target audience? Publishers are looking for profitable books, and especially if it is a new area for Prima, we need to know the size of the market and the likelihood of reaching it. What makes your book unique from others already on the market? How will you promote the book? Will it have appeal outside the usual trade bookstore channels? are there books currently on the bestseller lists that reach the same type of market?

5. **Competition for the book.** Are there other books currently on the market that address the same or similar subjects? How and why is your book different? Does your proposed book fill a niche presently open? Identify the competition but tell us how your book will surpass that competition because of the added material or new slant it offers.

6. **Author's Qualifications.** What makes you the right person to write this book? Tell us about your career experience and educational credentials as well as your experience in the area of your subject and with the media, for example, speaking and teaching experience. Also of interest is your publishing history and why you came to write this book. Do you have periodical, journal, or book writing experience?

Prima does not publish original fiction, personal narrative, or poetry.

If you are a first-time author, the book should be completed before the proposal is sent. Please do not send a manuscript unless specifically requested.

For help in preparing a proposal, refer to Prim's *The Writer's Guide to Book Editors, Publishers, and Literary Agents* by Jeff Herman.

Please allow four to six weeks for an answer.

Categories: Nonfiction—Business—Careers—Sports—Cooking—Health—Lifestyle—Self-Help—Computers

> **Name: Acquisition Editor**
> **Material: All**
> **Address: P.O. BOX 1260**
> **City/State/ZIP: ROCKLIN, CA 95677**
> **Telephone: 916-632-4400**
> **Fax: 916-632-4405**

PROMPT® Publications
Howard W. Sams & Company

Welcome to PROMPT Publications and Howard W. Sams & Company.

For over 50 years, Howard W. Sams & Company has been the nation's leading technical publisher. Since its inception in 1946, Howard W. Sams has seen its product offerings expand and diversify. Today, Howard W. Sams boasts the most complete lineup of technical documentation, services, and publications found anywhere.

1995 marked an historic period for Howard W. Sams as it was acquired by Bell Atlantic Directory Graphics, a member of the Bell Atlantic family based in Valley Forge, PA. Directory Graphics provides complete graphics services, database design, typesetting, pagination, and state-of-the-art electronic database publishing, multimedia, and CD-ROM applications for Bell Atlantic and other Yellow Pages and catalog publishers. While the acquisition has had the most profound effect on Howard W. Sams' catalog division, it brings increased potential and expansion opportunities to all elements of the business. This includes preliminary plans to make PROMPT Publications books available online via the Internet.

Created in 1991, PROMPT Publications has grown to become one of the top technical imprints in the nation and one of Howard W. Sams' brightest stars. PROMPT Publications concentrates its efforts on producing technical books designed for both the novice and the experienced electronics technician. Each PROMPT book provides a clear understanding of the principles involved in the installation, maintenance, and performance of electronic devices that have become such a large part of our everyday lives.

Because PROMPT Publications produces a variety of publications each month, we have established a set of standards for authors to follow in order to bring out the best qualities in both themselves and their manuscripts. It is important that we adhere to a certain semblance of priority and order to ensure that PROMPT books are accurate and high-quality, and are moved through production as efficiently as possible.

The *PROMPT Publications Authors Guide* has been prepared to provide a guideline for authors and to provide a comprehensive explanation of the production process. Terms such as *opticopy boards* and *galley proofs* are discussed, along with suggestions for artwork preparation and methods for obtaining permissions. Even experienced authors should find this booklet interesting and informative.

Because of the wide variety of technical books we produce, the information in this booklet is somewhat general in nature. When and where it is appropriate, authors will receive more detailed information from the book editor or project manager assigned to work with them on their book.

THE REVIEW PROCESS

With most technical books, it is impossible for any one editor to be completely knowledgeable about the field and to make appropriate value judgments about the content, the quality of the outlines and manuscripts, the artwork, etc. In most cases, it is up to the author to make sure that the information presented in the manuscript is as accurate as possible. Most authors have their material examined by a colleague or an outside evaluator before submitting it to a publisher. The publisher may also commission outside evaluators to review the material. These reviewers are usually people who are knowledgeable about a particular subject in the manuscript, and whose observations are meant to be constructive and informative to the editor.

Usually, book proposals are sent to the acquisitions editor first, rather than a complete manuscript. A proposal typically consists of a short outline describing the book and its contents, a profile of the author, and perhaps a copy of the Table of Contents. If the editor is interested in seeing a manuscript, the author will be contacted and a date will be set for manuscript completion and shipment, for review by the editor. Before the author is offered a book contract, the editor will determine if the manuscript is appropriate to the publisher's book line and customer base.

The acquisitions editor shares the manuscript review process with a staff made up of project managers, editorial assistants, sales and marketing personnel, and qualified technicians. Reviews vary in thoroughness depending upon the nature of the manuscript, from superficially scanning the work for general information, to an in-depth examination of the grammar, equations, and schematics. Depending on the nature of the manuscript, it may be subjected to many rounds of such reviews before the publisher contacts the author to discuss the work and a possible contract. Reviewing a manuscript can last anywhere from a few weeks to up to a year, so the author needs to be patient with the publisher. As long as the publisher has the manuscript, the likelihood of it being accepted as a book remains good.

The review process is not intended to attack or to find fault with the manuscript, but to highlight the areas that perhaps may need revision or clarification. Plus, the review process is valuable in pinpointing possible errors that slipped by the author due to over-concentration or unintentional neglect. Even the most obvious errors can be overlooked if the author becomes too accustomed to reading through the manuscript. The mind tends to skip over information that it's used to seeing, or often fails to notice when information is entered into the wrong place. However, this is not something for the author to be overly concerned about until contracts have been negotiated and production has begun on the book. The editors will carefully examine the book for errors and give the author an opportunity to make sure they are corrected.

In addition to the content of the manuscript, reviewers also carefully examine the writing style and the sophistication level of the prose. It is the intention of PROMPT Publications to produce books that are useful and reader-friendly to not only the experienced and professional technician, but also to the beginning student and the average electronics hobbyist.

Therefore, in order to ensure that our books communicate properly to our audience, we ask that authors write their manuscripts in a style that is conversational and easy to follow; rather than dry and overly technical. Readers often lack the experience and knowledge of the technical writer; and for this reason it is important for the author to write in a manner that is both simple and concise, taking care to emphasize and reinforce important points through example and light redundancy.

In other words, authors should keep explanations simple, brief, and to-the-point, and repeat them as necessary to drive the point home. Also, though the very nature of technical books demands that equations be used, it is important to note that even among professional technicians, a book filled with equations will not sell as well as a book that keeps the math to a minimum. Therefore, it's best to use equations only if they are absolutely necessary to the subject matter of the book.

Once the review process of the manuscript is complete, the acquisitions editor will contact the author to discuss the work and set up a book contract. Once the contract negotiations are settled, and the author and publisher have signed copies of the agreement, the author will be assigned to a book editor or project manager, and production on the book will begin.

COPYRIGHTS AND PERMISSIONS

Permission to use copyrighted material in a manuscript or book must be provided, in writing, to both the author and the publisher by the party whose copyrighted work is being considered for the manuscript. Copyright is often a confusing problem for authors, often due to ignorance of the copyright laws. Here, we will attempt to clarify those laws. For more detailed information or to research recent updates to the copyright laws, the author should check with the local library.

First of all, it is important to determine what is copyrighted, and what may or may not be used in a publication without obtaining permission. In a nutshell, the only published material that is NOT under copyright protection is material originally published by the U.S. government (such as the Constitution of the United States), material considered to be in the public domain from the date of publication (most libraries keep track of public domain material), and copyrighted material which, due to the expiration of time parameters, is no longer protected by copyright laws. Authors may feel free to use as much of these types of materials as they wish without restriction, although common courtesy demands that they at least give credit to the source in their footnotes. For all other materials, written permission must be obtained from the source before information from these materials can be included in a manuscript, including text, artwork, photographs, etc.

Unpublished work is also protected by copyright laws. Under the Copyright Act of 1976 (title 17 of the United States Code), a work is protected by copyright from the time it is created in a fixed form. In other words, when a work is written down or otherwise set into tangible form, it is automatically copyrighted in the author's or artist's name. Only the author, or individuals deriving their rights from the author, can claim copyright ownership. A manuscript sent to a publisher by an author, for example, is already copyrighted in the author's name, so the publisher cannot reproduce material from the manuscript without the direct permission of the author. Drawings and photographs are also automatically copyrighted under the name of the illustrator or photographer who produced them.

However, under a copyright law that defines the category "Works Made For Hire," if a work is made for hire—such as an employee producing something requested by his or her employer—the employer (NOT the employee) is considered to be the author, and thus holds the copyright. The employer can be a firm, an organization, or an individual. (See Section 101 of the copyright law for a complete statutory definition.)

Time Parameters: Under the old copyright laws, material published before 1906 was considered to be in the public domain. After 1906, copyright protection was granted for a period of 28 years, and ONE renewal for an additional, similar period was permitted. Therefore, the maximum term of copyright protection granted to a book published in 1910, for example, would be 56 years if the copyright was renewed. Copyright protection for that book would expire in either 1938 or 1966, depending on whether or not the copyright was renewed. However, if the book was revised to a respectable extent, it could be copyrighted in a new edition as if it were a new, original book. There are a number of medical books dating back to the 1890s that are still under copyright protection because they are still in print and have been revised sufficiently to give each new revision its own copyright protection.

The current copyright law, from 1976, states that material published after January 1978 carries a copyright for the life of the author plus 50 years, or 75 years after publication, or 100 years after creation, whichever period is shortest. For example:

Joe Author published a book in 1979. Joe Author was 35 years old at the time of the creation of the book, and we can assume that he will not live to be 135 years old. The 100-year period is ruled out. The second longest period is 75 years after publication, or the year 2054. So, the book's copyright protection expires in 2054.

Suppose that at age 40, in 1984, Joe Author died. Add fifty years to 1984, which would be the year 2034. The law states that copyright protection is granted for the period that is the shortest in duration. So, since Joe Author died in 1984, copyright protection of his book expires in 2034. If Joe Author lived until 2004, however, the copyright protection would expire in 2054 because this period is shorter than the year of the author's death plus 50 years.

Time of Creation: This has to do with the precise time that the work was complete, not to the actual publication date. If an author wrote a book in 1990 but didn't attempt to get it published until 1992, under the maximum period provided for copyright protection, the year of creation would be 1990 plus 100 years. Of course, this provision is rarely used.

Amount of Material Requiring Permission: Sometimes it is difficult to determine if permission needs to be obtained for use of an occasional quote in quotation marks or an actual excerption of a large body of work. There's no strict definition regarding when permission is needed. Primarily, it depends on the length of the quote, its importance, and how closely it is tied to the rest of the work. If a quotation is more than one sentence

long, then permission for its use in a manuscript should be obtained. Permission for use also should always be obtained for the following:

1. All quotations of 200 words or more from any one source. This covers either one single quotation or a number of different ones that, totaled, add up to more than 199 words.

2. All quotations of 30 words or more from any newspaper, magazine, periodical, or journal.

3. All artwork required from a source other than the author; even with minor modifications, including photos, hand drawings, halftones, line drawings, computer graphics, tables, schematics, etc.

Trademarks: Permission is not necessary to cite a particular trademark, but it is important for authors to acknowledge logos that are registered as trademarks or trade names. For example, names like PageMaker and Macintosh are trade names for products that have been granted protection under copyright or patent laws. All trademarks should be followed with the designation ® or ™. Initials like IBM do not need to be denoted by these symbols as they represent a firm rather than a product.

Obtaining Permissions: It is the author's responsibility to obtain permissions and to submit them, in writing, with the complete manuscript when it is sent to the publisher. Usually, obtaining permissions is not difficult, particularly where manufacturers are concerned because they see it as a form of free advertising. Sometimes a manufacturer will also provide authors with free artwork when approached about having their products featured in a book.

On occasion, a copyright holder will request a permission fee when an author asks to use material from a journal, periodical, or book. These fees are the responsibility of the author and are paid upon publication of the author's book. Authors who are asked to pay permission fees should seriously consider whether or not the material in question is worth the fee requested.

A sample permission letter appears below, which authors can copy for their own use. Authors should keep the following things in mind when requesting permission of use:

1. When requesting permission from a book publisher, the author should address the letter to the person in charge of handling rights and permissions. For a comprehensive list of publisher addresses and phone numbers, authors should consult the *Literary Market Place*, a directory produced once a year that can be found in most public libraries. In magazines and periodicals, the front matter of the issue, usually found in the masthead, should contain a complete list of the staff and their titles, as well as the name and address of the publisher. When requesting permission from a manufacturer, authors should write to either the public relations department or the marketing department of the firm. Complete names and addresses for manufacturers can be found in several directories available at the library.

2. If the amount of work that the author wants to include in a manuscript is too large to fit into the body of the permission letter, the author should provide photocopies with the permission letter of everything being considered for use in the manuscript.

3. If a copyright holder requires a permission fee, and the author feels that the fee is not appropriate to the manuscript needs or budget, the author should try to find an alternate source for the material needed for the manuscript. Permission fees are not required unless the material is actually used and the book is published, so the author has no obligation to pay the copyright holder.

SAMPLE PERMISSION LETTER

<Name and address of publisher, company or copyright holder>

Dear <Copyright holder>,

I am preparing a book tentatively called <title>, to be submitted to Howard W. Sams & Co. and PROMPT Publications for publishing. I would like permission to use, in this and future editions, the following material:

I would also like permission for worldwide rights in all languages. Full credit will be given in the finished book. If you would like a copy of the book once it is published, please let me know. For your convenience, a release statement is given below. A duplicate of this letter is attached, and if you would sign both copies and return the original to me, I would be very grateful.

Sincerely,

Permission is hereby granted for the use of the described materials as outlined above.

_____

Signature

_____

Title (if applicable)

_____

Date

4. If a copyright holder requests a copy of the book once it is complete, it can be arranged between the author and the publisher at no charge to the author.

5. The author should request worldwide rights in all languages from the copyright holder, in case the book is translated in a foreign language. If this is not possible, then the author should ask for worldwide English language rights. Rights can also be specified as North American or domestic US rights. If book contents only have North American rights, for example, the publisher cannot sell the book beyond North American geographical borders, so the book cannot be sold in South America or overseas. Obtaining worldwide rights should not be difficult unless the author is dealing with a foreign company or publisher.

6. It is a good idea for the author to request rights for the first and all subsequent editions of the book, as this prevents having to request permissions again when the book is scheduled for a revision.

ILLUSTRATIONS

Illustrations are very important to the content of a technical book because they help the reader bridge the gap between text and reality. For example, it is much easier to understand the function of a circuit by looking at a diagram rather than reading about it. The logic becomes clearer when the reader can refer to a schematic of the circuit. For more effectiveness, a close-up photograph of the components would complete the panorama and the overall impression on the reader. Good illustrations are also an important selling point of a technical book. Well-illustrated books are more appealing to impulse shoppers, and more user-friendly to readers who dislike the idea of reading through pages of text.

It is the responsibility of the author to obtain illustrations for manuscripts. Though illustrations are important, the author must be careful not to overload the book with illustrations. Too many illustrations can break up the text in a finished book and make it difficult for the reader to follow the author's train of thought. Illustrations should, therefore, be kept to a minimum in relation to the amount of text, and should only be used to clarify a point or an explanation that cannot be easily conveyed by text alone.

An author's illustrations do not necessarily have to be of perfect reproducible quality unless photographs are used. Pencil sketches of circuits can be reproduced into finished CAD art in the PROMPT Publications technical art department, for example. If an author does not have the technical resources to produce print-ready art, the publisher can usually produce the artwork as long as the author is very clear as to the details and overall desired appearance of the illustrations.

Planning the illustrative content of a technical book is just as important as creating the text. Also, when creating a manuscript, it is important that the author make certain that each illustration is clearly referred to in the text. PROMPT Publications uses a system whereby each illustration is designated by the chapter

and unit number separated by a hyphen. For example, *Figure 7-8* is the eighth illustration of Chapter 7. Table and figure illustrations are usually kept separate by their own set of designations. For example, Chapter 2 might contain both *Figure 2-1* and *Table 2-1*. CAD drawings, schematics, photographs, line drawings, etc., all fall under the *Figure* designation.

Photographs: All photographs must be of good quality and display their images clearly. Photos that are cloudy, badly exposed, cluttered, or out of date do nothing to enhance the dialog and overall quality of the book. Photographs usually come from a wide variety of sources: manufacturers, advertising agencies, professional photographers, other publishers, amateur photographers, or the authors themselves.

PROMPT Publications, at this point, prefers to use black-and-white glossy photos that are unmarred and devoid of greasy marks or smudges. Most PROMPT books are done in one or two colors, and black-and-white photos are better for this format than color photos. Black-and-white photos are easier to reproduce than color photos, and it is much easier for a computer technician to scan them for insertion into the text.

If the only photos the author has are color, then the author should have black-and-white prints made from the color negative. The author should refrain from marking on the photo or cropping it (trimming it to size), and should make certain that the surface does not become marred or creased by paper clips, mounting anchors, etc.

If only part of the photo is to be used as an illustration, the author needs to indicate which part of the photo the publisher should use, either by writing on the border or on the back of the photo. The author should not mark on the picture itself. It is also important for the author to label the back of the photograph with its figure designation. *(Figure 2-1, Figure 2-2, etc.)*

Photograph Sources: Often, an author will spot the "perfect" photograph in a magazine or other publication. In most cases, the photograph was probably produced by a source other than the publisher, and permission for its use must be obtained if the author wishes to use it. Usually, the source of the photo is printed as a credit line beneath the photo or the photo's caption. The author can contact the original publisher to get information about the photo source, so permissions can be obtained.

As mentioned before, it is important for the author to obtain a black-and-white glossy copy of the desired photograph. This can be requested when the author contacts the source for permission to use the photo. (See the section, COPYRIGHTS AND PERMISSIONS.)

If for some reason the source gives permission for the author to use the photo but cannot supply an original photo, it is possible for the author to submit the tear sheet or publication page containing the picture to the publisher. The author must keep in mind, however, that the quality of the artwork reproduced from the tear sheet or original page will be inferior to the actual photograph or even the original page. If the subject of the photograph is a product, then it might be possible to obtain a good quality glossy photo from the manufacturer.

Some authors take their own photos, which is fine as long as the photos submitted with the manuscript to the publisher are of good reproductive quality. The author should have a professional studio develop the negatives to ensure the highest quality possible.

Line Drawings: Line drawings include all artwork that is not photographic, including stick figures, graphs, CAD drawings, schematics, etc. PROMPT Publications has an art department capable of producing a wide variety of illustrations, including technical drawings, computer graphics, and complex freehand drawings. If an author submits a rough pencil sketch of an illustration, the art department can usually reproduce it as print-ready artwork. While authors are not expected to be professional artists or draftspeople, it is important that the submitted illustrations be as accurate as possible. Physical characteristics such as length, scale, direction, dimensions, etc., are vital to technical illustrations and must be conveyed accurately. Forward and reverse logic gates, for example, can easily be mixed up and misdrawn. The logic of a circuit drawing can be destroyed if a vector sign is drawn in the wrong direction, an inverter symbol is omitted, or a junction is not noted. Authors must make certain that the information displayed in an illustration is accurate and will not confuse the reader.

Art Preparation: PROMPT Publications prefers that each drawing be prepared on a separate piece of 8½"x11" bond paper. Any specific instructions regarding scale or ganging should be circled so they will not be misinterpreted as labels. If the author wants the illustration to have a caption, the caption should be included on the same page as the drawing. The drawings should be labeled clearly enough to be easily understood by the staff artists and editors. Graphs and charts should be drawn on graph paper and should be consistent in appearance with the other illustrations or graphs. It should also be possible for the artist to reproduce each illustration on a single book page. Two-page spreads of tables or schematic illustrations can be difficult to reproduce and confusing to the reader.

If an illustration is created using a computer program or other printed documentation, the author should submit BOTH a hard copy of the illustration (on paper), and a copy stored on floppy disk or sent via e-mail.

For both drawings and photographs requiring permission, the author needs to make sure that the signed permission letter is included with the artwork being submitted to the publisher. The author also needs to make sure that a credit line is included that is appropriate to the art being submitted.

COVER DESIGN

In many ways, the cover is one of the most important parts of a finished book. The design and overall appearance of the cover often determines the eventual success or failure of the book. Appealing, informative covers, even for technical books, tend to stand out from bookshelves and attract potential readers, while bland, vague covers usually deter readers.

At PROMPT Publications, an author isn't required to submit a cover design with a manuscript. The author can supply illustrations or photographs, a brief author biography, a self-portrait (photo), and perhaps some back cover copy for the book; but for the most part, the cover design is up to the PROMPT Publications marketing and art departments. The author can request a review copy of the cover; in which case a full-color copy will be sent to the author, which the author can keep.

Sometimes the author will be called upon to help proofread the cover; but this is very rare. If there is some concern about the back cover copy, for example, the author may be mailed or faxed a black-and-white copy of the cover for review. The author would then mark any necessary changes on the cover and return it to PROMPT Publications. As stated before, this rarely occurs.

MANUSCRIPT PREPARATION

Once the author's manuscript arrives at PROMPT Publications and the contract is negotiated and signed, the production and technical staff immediately begins to create a design for the book. Book design includes typeface selection, trim size, cover design, order and sequence of headings, indentations, artwork placement, equation placement, etc. The author can make this process easier by keeping the format of the manuscript as neat and simple as possible. The manuscript should be created following these guidelines:

1. All manuscripts, even if stored in a computerized format, should be presented to the publisher in hardcopy form (on paper). A floppy disk containing a copy of the manuscript should also be sent to the publisher; or sent via e-mail.

2. All manuscripts should be printed on 8½"x11" white bond 20 lb. paper. Please do not use erasable bond or color paper. Make sure the printing is clear and dark.

3. All type should be double-spaced so that the copy editor has room to make corrections and add proofreaders marks. The type should also be flushed left rather than justified.

4. Illustration captions should be provided in a caption list (in addition to on the illustrations themselves) so the layout artists can use it as a reference for keeping track of illustrations.

5. Where credit must be included for a particular illustration, a line containing source information should be added in parentheses at the end of the caption. If the illustration source is a company or firm, the full name should be used rather than abbreviations.

6. All tables should be treated like artwork and kept separate from the text. The author should place a table on a separate sheet of paper and indicate where in the text the table should appear.

7. If a table comes from a source other than the author, and permission has been received to use it, the credit should be cited in the caption, labeling it as "source."

8. All illustrations and tables should be specifically referred to in the text, as *Table 2-1 or Figure 2-1*, etc. The author should refrain from using references like "to the table below" or "to the following table."

9. When using equations or mathematical symbols, care is required when using symbols not normally found on the keyboard or in a program. Also, it is important for the author to exercise care when using superscript and subscript placements. A wrong placement could result in an entire chapter of equations being wrong. Authors should consult the *Chicago Manual of Style* as a guide for mathematical symbols and placements. The author also needs to be aware that the use of difficult symbols such as uppercase sigmas or fractions need to be minimized or simplified so as to minimize the difficulty of setting such type. For example:

$(a + b)$ could be simplified to $(a + b)/(c - d)$
$(c - d)$

For important symbols which do not appear on the keyboard or in a program, the author should write them in the manuscript legibly with a dark pen, and identify the symbol the first time it appears on each page. For example, t = tau. The author should also italicize the symbols that need it.

10. The author is expected to write the front matter for the book. The front matter consists of the author biography page, the preface, the acknowledgment page, and the table of contents. The author biography should include a brief biographical description of the author, highlighting professional training and accomplishments. The preface should inform the reader what the book is about and what is to be gained by reading it. The acknowledgment page is not necessary, but should be included if the author feels in debt to someone for help with the book's contents, or wishes to acknowledge someone's support. A dedication can be substituted for the acknowledgment page, or the book can contain both if the author wishes it.

11. The author is not expected to supply the index for the book, but can write a glossary and appendices if they are needed or desired in the finished book. A bibliography should also be supplied, and should be as concise and accurate as possible.

12. The author should produce three copies of the manuscript, one to be sent to the publisher and two to keep on file in case something happens to the publisher's copy. The publisher's copy should be as complete as possible, and should include a floppy disk containing the manuscript, if it was written on a computer. Text, illustrations, tables, front matter; appendices, floppy disks, etc., should all be included in the shipment to the publisher. The pages should NOT be stapled together; a bindery clip or a rubber band is better. When shipping, United Parcel Service is pref-

erable to the U.S. Postal Service, as packages are easier to trace through UPS. Finished artwork and other hard-to-replace items should be insured.

THE PRODUCTION PROCESS

Once a manuscript is accepted by a publisher and contracts are finalized, an editor or project manager is assigned to the manuscript to guide it through book production. The author will work with the project manager for the next few months to troubleshoot the book's content.

First, the project manager will establish a working schedule or production calendar for the book to ensure that it is published by a predetermined date. Once this schedule is established, the author needs to work with the project manager to ensure that deadlines are met. A delay of a few days on the author's end could result in weeks of delays on the publisher's end, which is detrimental to many electronics books due to the short shelf life of some electronic information. If the author anticipates any delays, the project manager needs to be alerted immediately.

Second, the project manager will closely examine and proofread the manuscript for errors, awkward sentences, style consistency, etc. The project manager will proofread the hard copy and load the computer files containing the manuscript into a network. After the project manager has examined the manuscript, two or three editorial assistants will be assigned to proofread the manuscript as well. Once all of the editors have completed their proofreading, their changes will be included in the manuscript files stored in the computer network. The corrected manuscript will then be printed out and sent to the author so that the author will have a chance to double-check it and make further corrections or additions. Once the author has completed the corrections, the corrected pages need to be sent back to the project manager within the time frame stipulated.

Sketches sent to the publisher to be processed into illustrations will be assigned to an artist or group of artists. Once the illustrations are complete, copies of these will also be sent to the author for checking and corrections. The author should check to make sure that the illustrations match the text content, and make any corrections that are necessary. Corrections should be drawn directly onto the illustrations with a red pen and sent back to the project manager. An artist will also be assigned to design the book's cover, and the author may be asked to examine back-cover copy written for the book.

It is very important for the author to double-check all information in the manuscript for accuracy. Though the individuals assigned to work on the manuscript are technically proficient, they may not be experts in the field being discussed. Ultimately, the author bears full responsibility for the veracity and accuracy of the book's content, including mathematical calculations. Errors that appear in finished books are often the result of the author's assumption that the information was written down correctly the first time. It is extremely easy to make errors while writing a manuscript, so the author should not take for granted that the information in the manuscript is 100% correct or that someone will catch all the content and calculation errors.

If there are many errors or inconsistencies in the content of the manuscript, the project manager may ask the author to rewrite portions of it. The editor is not a ghost writer and cannot be expected to rewrite the book for the author, so the author is responsible for any weaknesses in the content or "prose." However, if any rewriting is requested, the author should not take such a request personally, as the editor is there to help the author make the prose flow as correctly and logically as possible. The author should keep in mind that if the editor cannot understand the intent or meaning of a sentence, then the reader will not be able to understand it either.

Once the project manager has received the author's changes, the corrections will be made and the manuscript will be sent

through typesetting, producing what is known as a galley proof The galley contains all of the text, artwork, captions, page numbers, etc., that will appear in the finished book, set in the layout style selected by the project manager. The author can request a copy of the galley once it is complete, in order to check it. The copy quality of the galley may not be the best, as the galleys are simply rough drafts to allow the editors to check for accuracy in composition. Artwork, text, equations, etc., may not appear in the galley as they will in the finished book. However, the author needs to keep in mind that once a book is typeset, further changes and revisions become very time-consuming and expensive. Further revisions or corrections should have been made in the corrected version of the manuscript that the author returned to the project manager.

The purpose of the galley is to catch blatant errors or typos. When looking though a galley, the author needs to check for errors in punctuation, illustration arrangements, etc. Any changes in content at this point are considered to be the author's alterations. If an author's changes exceed the time allotted for this kind of correction, the publisher may charge the excess time against future royalties. Therefore, any changes in content should be made in the first corrected manuscript copy sent to the author. If the author has any doubts about the content, changes or revisions can be documented while the author researches the area, and corrections can be included in the book's second printing.

Once the galleys have been proofread and final changes have been made, the book is sent to a printer to be printed and bound. The book arrives at the printer either stored on floppy disk or laid out on opticopy boards, depending on the type of book, the expense of printing it, and the amount of paste-up work required for the book. At the same time, the sales and marketing department begins to work on press releases, flyers, magazine ads, and direct-mail ads designed to sell the book to book stores, libraries, electronics stores and distributors, technical schools, etc. The author can also suggest companies or individuals that should receive information about the book.

MARKETING

PROMPT Publications uses a variety of marketing tools to make a new book available to book distributors and readers. While trade and electronics representatives work to get the book to nationwide distributors and bookstores, the PROMPT marketing department advertises the book through press releases, flyers, magazine ads, direct-mail ads, catalogs, telemarketing, trade shows, Web sites, and other means.

The purpose of marketing is to make the book available to as many interested buyers as possible. PROMPT also sends galleys to editors of publishing and electronics periodicals for book reviews. Authors can sometimes find reviews of their books in such magazines as *Popular Electronics, Electronic Servicing & Technology,* or *Publishers Weekly,* to name a few.

While the author isn't expected to help PROMPT market the book, the author is welcome to contact the marketing director with suggestions of people or companies that might be interested in the book. The author can send a list of interested parties to the marketing director, so these parties can have materials sent to them about the book and how to order it. Also, for authors who often go on lecture or workshop tours, PROMPT can supply flyers, catalogs, and other materials for the author to help make the book available to members of the audience.

If the author has any ideas about how to market the book, the marketing director will be more than happy to follow up on any suggestions received.

BOOK REVISIONS

Because many aspects in the electronics field undergo frequent changes, electronics and technology books tend to require many revisions, sometimes as many as one per year. For example, if an author produces a book about computer repair, changes and

Books

updates may be required often to keep up with the constant innovations or obsolescence in computer technology. The author may need to delete information that has become obsolete, add new information to compensate for new advances, rewrite introductions and conclusions to acknowledge the new technological advances, etc. An editor may contact the author about book revisions, or the author can contact the publisher about a revision once there is enough information or material to warrant one.

To revise a book, an author does not need to completely rewrite the current edition of the book. Most of the material from the original book will be used, so the author only needs to concentrate on those areas that need changes. To prepare a revision, the author needs to provide the publisher rewritten text and new illustrations with copies of the original pages to show the publisher where the new information should be inserted, and what needs to be deleted from the original pages. If new material is to be inserted between old, this should be indicated on the original page copies.

All cross-references to other chapters or pages should also be checked for consistency. The author needs to make certain that all figure references are updated as well. Permissions letters also need to be reviewed just in case illustrations or other sources need to be renewed for the revised edition. Copies of the updated source permissions need to be enclosed with the review changes.

Revisions should not be confused with corrections, though an author can make corrections while the book is being revised. Once the first edition of the book has been produced and distributed, if the author notices any errors that were not caught before the book went to print, the author can alert the publisher to the errors and supply corrections so that the publisher can include the corrections in the book's second printing. Second printings usually occur within eight months to a year after the first printing. A corrected printing is not necessarily a revised edition, since the main content or essence of the book is unchanged.

The author should contact the publisher regarding questions about revisions or corrections to the book.

Categories: Nonfiction—Electronics—Technology—Television/Radio

Name: Candace Drake Hall, Managing Editor
Material: All
Address: 2647 WATERFRONT PKWY E DR
City/State/ZIP: INDIANAPOLIS IN 46214-2041
Telephone: 800-428-7267
Fax: 317-298-5604
Internet: www.hwsams.com

PSI Research
Oasis Press, Hellgate Press

These guidelines were created to help answer your questions about submitting book proposals to us.

Established in 1975, The Oasis Press was the first publishing imprint of PSI Research. Our objective was to give the people who own and manage businesses—especially small businesses—the information and tools they need to make sound business decisions and operate their companies successfully.

Oasis Press is known for the *Starting and Operating* series which has sold over 2 million copies and includes an edition for each of the 50 states, plus the District of Columbia. Also we offer more than 60 additional book titles to round out our Successful Business Library line. Some of our recently published titles include *Location Location Location: How to Select The Best Site For Your Business*, *Profit Power: 101 Pointers To Give Your Small Business A Competitive Advantage*, *Target Smart: Database*

Marketing for the Small Business, *InstaCorp-Incorporate in Any State Book & Software*, and *Which Business? Help in Selecting Your New Venture*.

The Oasis Press book is a how-to, step-by-step guide designed for business owners and managers. The textual information focuses on solutions-oriented action plans or procedures for starting a business or operating one more efficiently. To appeal to our audience of busy lay people, the writing needs to be friendly and concise, not technical or academic.

Oasis Press books include checklists, worksheets, charts, and sample documents to build on points in the text. Through our page design, we try to make the information in our books quickly accessible to busy readers. Many of our 8½"x11" paperbacks, which are generally priced at $19.95 to $24.95 retail, are also released in expanded binder editions priced at $39.95 to $49.95. These editions are bound in 3-ring binder workbooks and usually feature extra sections that the paperbacks do not include.

Binder editions and binder/software sets are distributed through a number of business associations, direct mail organizations, and catalogs, including PSI Research's own mail order catalog, *Tools for Business Success*. Our own in-house telemarketing sales force actively promotes our publications also.

Many of the books are accompanied by software. We don't require authors to submit software for their books. Software that compliments your book may be developed by The Oasis Press.

The Oasis Press publishes an average of 15 titles per year. We receive approximately 150 to 200 submissions annually. Sixty percent of these come from first-time authors. Ninety percent come from unagented authors.

We are interested in any books that will supplement or complement our present Successful Business Library titles (please review our current booklist). We are especially interested in books that will address new laws, regulations, or concerns that businesses will face in the future.

Hellgate Press is a new imprint that will enable us to diversify our publishing. Hellgate Press is named after the historic Hellgate Canyon on the Rogue River which was the first river in the US to be designated as a wild and scenic river. We are looking for books that personify the adventure of the canyon: subjects that include outdoor recreation, adventure travel, history and military history. Books for the Hellgate Press do not have to be based in the Pacific Northwest.

Our books are distributed nationwide to independent and chain booksellers and retailers, as well as discount houses, libraries, and book clubs. Major booksellers include Waldenbooks, Barnes and Noble, and B. Dalton Bookseller. Publishers Group West is our main book distributor, and our books are also available through Baker & Taylor, Midwest Library Services, The Bookhouse, Blackwell North America, Ingram, and Quality Books.

May 30th and November 30th are our two yearly cutoff dates for reviewing proposals. All book proposals we have received by May 30th will be reviewed in June, and we will inform each author about our decision in July. Similarly, all book proposals we have received by November 30th will be evaluated in December, and we'll inform each author of our decision in January. If our review schedule creates an unusual problem for you, please send a fax describing the situation to our acquisitions department.

If you want to know if The Oasis Press would consider publishing your topic before you submit your complete proposal, please don't call to describe the book over the phone. Instead, send us a brief letter describing your book, an outline or synopsis, a proposed table of contents, a sample chapter, and a one-page writing sample. We'll carefully review this material and respond with a letter.

If we want to further consider your proposal, we will request the following information:

- Your complete manuscript. If not complete, we will need to review at least two chapters.

- A list of your proposed worksheets, forms, and checklists.
- Your completed Editorial Fact Sheet. (We will forward a blank fact sheet for you to complete if we wish to publish your book.)

Once we have accepted your complete manuscript, we will ask our distributor to put it on their annual schedule to announce its publication for a given month within the next year.

We pay an author a royalty of 10% on the net cash we receive on all sales, except wholesale sales. It is not our policy to pay advances. Once the book is in the marketplace generating sales, you will receive monthly sales status reports. Monthly royalty payments begin 120 days after receipt of your first sales report.

Your book has a better chance of acceptance if you take the time to explain why our readership will buy and use your book, who your potential audience is, and what competition your book faces in the bookstores. Much of the success of any book depends largely on how well recognized the author is and how adept at promotion. Please list ways you will promote your book.

Simultaneous submissions are acceptable.

Categories: Nonfiction—Business—History—Military

Name: Emmett Ramey, President
Material: All
Address: 300 N VALLEY DR
City/State/ZIP: GRANTS PASS OR 97526
Telephone: 541-479-9464
Fax: 541-476-1479
E-mail: psi4@magick.net

Publishers Associates
The Liberal Press, Ide House, Monument Press, Tangelwuld Press, Scholars Books, Liberal Arts Press

1. Unsolicited manuscripts will be returned if not preceded with a letter of inquiry containing:
   - a cover letter stating that it is not a simultaneous submission
   - a synopsis
   - a tentative table of contents
2. All works submitted must be nonfiction.
3. Footnoting must follow this format:
   - Author's first, middle, last name(s), *Title*; *subtitle(s)*, (City, State/Province: Publisher's full nomenclature, date), volume number (if any), pages cited.
4. Bibliography must include:
   - Author's first, middle, last name(s), *Title*; *subtitle(s)*, (City, State/Province: Publisher's full nomenclature, date), volume number (if any), pages cited.
   - be in alphabetic order using the author's last name
5. All content must be gender free of references unless work is about one particular gender. We do not publish sexist materials.
6. All publications must reflect liberal thinking in all areas.
7. The publisher has the right to edit grammar, spelling, and syntax. The publisher will not edit or change the author's style.

The presses of Publishers Associates (The Galaxy Group, The Liberal Press, Liberal Arts Press, Minuteman Press, Monument Press, Nichole Graphics, Stardate 2000, Tangelwüld Press) publish only liberal history, liberal politics, gay/lesbian/feminist/minority studies (history, social condition, etc.), and liberation theology. We do not contract for biographies, poetry, autobiographies, conservative or doctrinal works.

Publishers Associates will direct the manuscript to the Press that would be most likely to contract for it. All contracts are issued by the contracting press, not by the consortium Publishers Associates as a whole/unit.

Categories: Feminism—Gay/Lesbian—History—Politics—Sexuality—Women's Issues

Name: Rick Donovon, Sr. Vice President, Manuscripts
Material: Gay/Lesbian
Name: Geoffrey Stryker, Sr. Vice President, Manuscripts
Material: Politics (liberal)
Name: Mary Markal, Sr. Vice President, Manuscripts
Material: Women
Address: PO BOX 140361
City/State/ZIP: IRVING TX 75014-0361
Telephone: 972-686-5332
Fax: 972-686-5332
Internet: www.idehouse.com

Quill Driver Books/
Word Dancer Press, Inc

We publish nonfiction books only and if you have one that has a large, identifiable and reachable audience, we'd like to hear from you. We do not publish poetry, children's books or fiction.

We prefer to receive a query letter along with a book proposal. Please submit to us by snail mail. We consider simultaneous submissions. Naturally, if we are interested, we will contact you, however, if you wish to hear from us in the event we are not interested, please enclose an SASE. Keep in mind that every publisher turns down projects for reasons that have nothing to do with the merit or publishability of the book. Even if we aren't interested, we encourage you to keep trying with other publishers.

We suggest you read the workshop by Michael Larsen on how to write a nonfiction book proposal in QDB's *The Portable Writers' Conference: Your Guide to Getting and Staying Published*, edited by Stephen Blake Mettee and available at libraries and bookstores, and follow Larsen's instructions in preparing your book proposal. While this isn't absolutely necessary, a properly prepared book proposal will increase your chances with us as well as with other publishers. It will also help you think your project through completely.

Recent titles we have published include *The Longest Trek: My Tour of the Galaxy* by Grace Lee Whitney (aka Yeoman Janice Rand) and *The Pediatrician's New Baby Owner's Manual*, by Horst D. Weinberg, M.D.

We are particularly interested in seeing proposals that fit the following three areas:

The Best Half of Life ™ series

The Best Half of Life books are practical, upbeat, encouraging works that enhance the lives of people in their 50s and over. These titles help the reader to improve and to better enjoy his or her life. We want sound, well-thought-out, positive, focused writing. No personal *How-I-Survived* (*-Cancer, -Caring for a Spouse Afflicted with Alzheimer's*, etc.) essays. The book must offer something distinctly helpful to the reader. Books with the greatest chance of being published as a part of The Best Half of Life series will have life-changing potential.

Text should be for the popular market rather than the academic market. The inclusion of checklists, sidebars, real-life anecdotes, exercises and similar elements is encouraged.

Subjects may include the whole gamut of human experience, from cooking to creativity, sex to careers, recreation to finances. A recent Best Half of Life book is: *The Memory Manual: 10 Simple Things You Can Do to Improve Your Memory After 50*, by Betty Fielding.

Writing

We are always interested in seeing proposals on books for writers. Here the credentials of the author are very important. If you have never published a novel, it is doubtful that we would be interested in a book from you on how to write a novel.

There are quite a number of everything-an-author-needs-to-know-about-writing books out there. Try to focus your project to a specific aspect of writing or getting published. This focus is shown in our title *Feminine Wiles: Creative Techniques for Writing Women's Feature Stories that Sell* by Donna Elizabeth Boetig.

California

We try to publish one or two regional California titles each year. Titles with a narrow focus, yet a broad appeal have the best chance of catching our interest. Examples are our *Black Bart Boulevardier Bandit* by George Hoeper, about the 1880s stagecoach robber ; *California's Geographic Names* by David Durham, California's definitive gazetteer and *From Mud-Flat Cove to Gold to Statehood: California 1840-1850* by Irving Stone. Titles may be on the history or the recreation of California, or on any other subject distinctive to the state. The availability of illustrations is often a necessity.

Thanks for your interest, we look forward to hearing from you.

Categories: Nonfiction—Aging—Biography—Californiana—Celebrities—Directories—Fund-raising—Health—History, Western—How-to—Lifestyles—Reference—Regional—Self-help—Senior Citizens—True Crime—Western—Writing

Name: Stephen Blake Mettee
Material: All
Address: 8386 NORTH MADSEN
City/State/ZIP: CLOVIS, CA 93611
Telephone: 559-322-5917
Fax: 559-322-5917

QUIXOTE PRESS
PUBLICATIONS

Quixote Press

• Regional humor and folklore. Region could be state or larger area.

• Also kid stuff, designed to be read by an adult to a child.

• Nothing scholarly or academic.

• Contact us before finishing the manuscript.

• Minimum profanity or sex.

• Of particular interest are products suitable for sale in gift shops and at farmers markets. Tourist areas important to us.

• We would want the product, in final form, to be camera-ready...illustrated, clip art okay.

• We pay royalty equal to 10 percent of wholesale.

Categories: Nonfiction—Animals—Children—Comedy—

Food/Drink—Gardening—History—Hunting—Outdoors—Regional—Rural America—Sexuality

Name: Bruce Carlson, President
Material: All
Address: 3544 BLAKESLEE ST
City/State/ZIP: WEVER IA 52658
Telephone: 319-372-7480
Fax: 319-372-7480

Rainbow Books
Books for Children's Ministries

Our objective:

We publish helpful how-to books, activity books and "teaching tips" for leaders of children in both the church and home settings. Generally, our children's ministries products are reproducible books issued in series for various ages and grade levels. All are Bible-based and at least 64 pages.

We specifically seek:

• Classroom resources for Christian educators, such as crafts, activities and worksheets, bulletin boards and games

• Proposals for our *52 Ways* series. Each book contains 52 amplified hints, tips, ideas or lessons on a specific topic for Christian educators.

• Manuscripts or queries for other "teacher help" books. All materials must be designed to help Christian educators lead ministries to children.

• Additional proposals for books that encourage or teach children about the Christian life

We will not publish:

• Poetry

• Picture books

• Fiction

• Symbolic stories

• Books that require four-color illustrations

The kinds of writers we are looking for:

• Have accepted Jesus as Savior and are dedicated to serving Him and leading others to Him

• Relate well to children and teachers

• Have hands-on experience working with children

• Are active participants in a Bible-believing church

• Write creatively, either published or unpublished

To submit your proposal:

• Send a query, synopsis or the entire manuscript for our evaluation.

• Enclose a resume or statement explaining your qualifications for writing the book.

• Explain the audience for your book and how your book differs from those already on the market.

• We normally respond in two to eight weeks.

• If your proposal includes crafts, be prepared to send the completed crafts, if requested.

After evaluating your proposal/manuscript we will do one of the following:

• Suggest you contact another publisher

• Request a contents summary and sample chapters (including sample crafts, if applicable)

• Ask for revisions and resubmittal

• Seek expanded material from you

• Offer you a contract
Categories: Nonfiction—Children—Christian Interests—Crafts—Education—Games—Inspirational

Name: Christy Allen, Editor
Material: All
Address: PO BOX 261129
City/State/ZIP: SAN DIEGO CA 92196
Telephone: 619-271-7600

Richard C. Owen Publishers, Inc.

BOOKS FOR YOUNG LEARNERS

Richard C. Owen Publishers, Inc. seeks brief, bright, fresh stories with charm, magic, meaning, and appeal for five, six, and seven year old children that they can read by themselves. We want stories that interest, inform, entertain, and inspire children.

We are interested in publishing a variety of themes in different styles and genres.

Fiction: includes original, realistic, contemporary stories, as well as tall tales, legends, myths, and folktales of all cultures.

Nonfiction: fascinating subjects presented as a story in language accessible to five-, six- and seven-year olds. No dry facts, or encyclopedia type pieces, please.

Structure: well-developed stories with captivating beginnings, clear and energetic middles, that end with a fresh, humorous, or unexpected twist or flourish. Length: between **45** and **100** words is best.

Storyline: fresh, strong, focused [i.e. one theme], lively, and interesting to today's children.

Characters: vivid, believable, and child-appealing, whom children can relate to, identify with, and care about. Animals in stories must act authentically and not be humanized or "cute."

Sentences: complete and grammatically correct.

Language: a mix of both natural and book language. If dialog is used it must sound natural and realistic.

Please do not submit:

Holiday or religious themes

Lessons, morals, vocabulary lists, or language skills

Manuscripts that stereotype or demean individuals or groups, or present violence, or hopelessness

Stories with talking, humanized, personified animals or objects

Stories that have been previously published, unoriginal, or imitative stories or characters

List stories

BOOKS FOR OLDER LEARNERS

Richard C. Owen Publishers, Inc. seeks brief, easy to read, high-interest manuscripts that will fascinate, inspire, entertain and inform eight, nine, and ten year old children in the third, fourth, and fifth grades.

We want short, strong, snappy, exciting pieces that will capture a child's imagination and hold a child's interest.

Please write clearly and simply, yet with richness, and style about topics, and events that have meaning for this age group. We want tight, concise, well-structured, and well-developed strong pieces in different genres about a variety of themes.

All submissions should have the brevity, economy of words, and the vitality, freshness, energy, and impact of high quality magazine or newspaper articles.

We will publish prose and poetry, fiction and nonfiction in a variety of styles, and formats.

We seek: adventure, action, mysteries, humor, science, science-fiction, journals, diaries, photo essays current trends, sports, music, how-to, letters, nature and the environment, careers, technology, geography, architecture, travel, myths and legends, and wordless pieces.

Word length: 100—500 words is best.
Our response time is 4—8 months.
Submission procedures:

1. Manuscripts should include your name, phone number, and the page number on each page.

2. Include a short cover letter with your name, address, and the manuscript title.

3. Send photocopies, no originals please.

Requests for revisions do not in any way imply, suggest, or guarantee acceptance or publication of a manuscript.

Categories: Fiction—Nonfiction—Adventure—African-American—Animals—Asian-American—Children—Environment—Humor—Juvenile

Name: Janice Boland, Director of Children's Books
Material: All
Address: PO BOX 585
City/State/ZIP: KATONAH NY 10536
Telephone: 914-232-3903
Fax: 914-232-3977

Rising Tide Press

Our Publishing Philosophy

Rising Tide Press is a lesbian-owned and operated publishing company committed to publishing books by, for, and about lesbians and their lives. We are not only committed to readers, but also to lesbian writers who need nurturing and support, whether or not their manuscripts are accepted for publication. Through quality writing, the press aims to entertain, educate, and empower readers, whether they are women-loving-women or heterosexual. It is our intention to promote lesbian culture, community, and civil rights, nationwide, through the printed word.

In addition, RTP will seek to provide readers with images of lesbians aspiring to be more than their prescribed roles dictate. The novels selected for publication will aim to portray women from all walks of life, (regardless of class, ethnicity, religion or race), women who are strong, not just victims, women who can and do aspire to be more, and not just settle, women who will fight injustice with courage. Hopefully, our novels will provide new ideas for creating change in a heterosexist and homophobic society. Finally, we hope our books will encourage lesbians to respect and love themselves more, and at the same time, convey this love and respect of self to the society at large. It is our belief that this philosophy can best be actualized through fine writing that entertains, as well as educates the reader. Books, even lesbian books, can be fun, as well as liberating.

Rising Tide Press is primarily interested in publishing quality lesbian fiction: romance, mystery/suspense, action/adventure, and fantasy/sci-fi. We will also consider nonfiction if it is unique and has a focus that has not been published elsewhere. In addition, both fiction and nonfiction books for children of lesbians will be considered. We are not interested in poetry, or biographies. Sorry!

NOVEL WRITING TIPS

1. THE PLOT

• Outline your story to give it boundaries and structure.

• Be sure your plot is not predictable.

• Find a new and creative way to tell common, or not so common stories.

• Does your story contain sufficient sources of tension and conflict?

2. CHARACTERS

• Find creative ways to introduce your characters.

• Create characters that readers will either love or hate.

• Create characters that are real and alive, that think and feel, that have strengths and flaws.

• What do your characters look like? If necessary, cut out pictures from magazines that you feel represent your characters. Refer to this picture gallery when writing.

3. KEEPING THE READER'S ATTENTION

• Begin the story in the middle of some action and dialogue.

• Many writers have good beginnings and terrific endings, but they let their story sag in the middle. Keep the reader's attention throughout by pacing the action and tension.

4. SEXUAL TENSION

If you are writing a story that contains some romance, build up and graduate the sexual tension. Characters should not jump into bed immediately. Elaborate on the forces driving the characters toward each other.

5. RESEARCH

• Write about things that you know about.

• Make sure you do your homework when writing about unfamiliar subjects. Ignorance and misinformation will dramatically affect the credibility of your novel.

6. GRAMMAR/PUNCTUATION

If you want to get past the first reader on our editorial board, carefully proof your ms. for errors in spelling, punctuation and grammar.

7. STYLE

• Be creative in the way you begin your sentences. Don't begin each sentence in the same way.

• Dialog: Try to make your characters' voices sound different from each other. Use descriptive phrases to show how the characters sound, look, and behave, as they speak.

• Do not put anything into your story that doesn't directly relate to the story.

• Use active, rather than passive tenses, and vivid action verbs whenever possible.

• Be creative in the linking of events in your story by using clear and interesting transitional phrases.

• Avoid the use of cliches.

• Use narration judiciously. It is better to let the story unfold before the reader through action and dialogue, rather than omniscient author narration.

• Remember, less is more!

Manuscript Submission Guidelines

If you are a writer with a manuscript, please use the following guidelines when submitting it to Rising Tide Press:

• One page synopsis of plot
• One page autobiography
• An outline of the plot
• Entire novel (unstapled, easy to read print, and proofread)
• No multiple submissions of same manuscript to several publishers simultaneously, please.
• If you are under contract with another publisher, please indicate this in your cover letter.

New writers welcome!

Categories: Fiction—Nonfiction—Feminism—Gay/Lesbian—Mystery—Romance—Science Fiction—Women's Fiction

Name: Lee Boojamra, Senior Editor
Material: Genre Fiction
Name: Alice Frier, Senior Editor
Material: Nonfiction
Address: 65161 E EMERALD DR
City/State/ZIP: TUCSON AZ 85739
Telephone: 516-427-1289
E-mail: RTPress@aol.com

Rockbridge Publishing Company

Rockbridge Publishes books about the Civil War and travel guides to Virginia and nearby areas. We do not publish any fiction. We are especially interested in adding annotated first-hand accounts of Civil War events, biographies of Confederate generals, and ghost stories related to the war, regardless of their location.

We prefer a query with a table of contents, a bibliography and three sample chapters and a cover letter that tells us what your book is about, what other books on the same topic are currently available, why your book is different (why will someone buy your book instead of another on the topic), and what makes you the right person to write on this topic. Be concise, but be complete.

Submissions should be printed in no less than 11-point type, left justified (ragged right) and every page numbered. Do not submit "camera ready" pages or leave space for photographs, maps or other support material. A separate sheet with suggestions for illustrations may be helpful, but is not necessary.

We will notify you by postcard when your materials are received.

Categories: Nonfiction—Civil War—Travel Guides (Virginia Area)

Name: Acquisitions Editor
Material: All
Address: PO BOX 351
City/State/ZIP: BERRYVILLE VA 22611
Telephone: 540-955-3980
Fax: 540-955-4126
E-mail: ewpub@visuallink.com

Rutledge Hill Press

In your submission letter please include such information as why you have written (or want to write) the work, what the market for your manuscript is, what it will contribute to potential readers, and what makes it *unique*. We are particularly interested in how you see it relating to similar or competing works already in print.

Send a synopsis of no more than three pages, an outline or table of contents, and two or three chapters (30 to 40 pages). This will let us see how well you arrange your thoughts and evaluate your writing style and writing skills.

In the case of reference works or cookbooks, include enough material to illustrate the scope and purpose of the work in detail.

All correspondence will be handled by mail. You will receive a response concerning your submission within five to seven weeks. If you would like a copy of our current book catalog, please mail us a self-addressed, stamped 9"x12" envelope.

Rutledge Hill Press will not accept manuscripts delivered in person. All materials must be mailed.

Rutledge Hill Press will *not* review the following:

• Autobiographies
• Children's books or short stories
• Educational and/or academic materials, including psychology and self-help
• Fictional materials
• Poetry
• Religious materials

Categories: Nonfiction—African-American—Biography—Civil War—Cooking—Entertainment—Film/Video—Food/Drink—History—Humor—Inspirational—Outdoors—Quilts—Sports—Travel—Women's Issues

Name: Mike Towle, Executive Editor
Material: All
Address: 211 SEVENTH AVE N
City/State/ZIP: NASHVILLE TN 37219
Telephone: 615-244-2700 ext. 169
Fax: 615-244-2978

St. Bede's Publications

We are a small Roman Catholic publishing company owned and operated by a monastery of Benedictine nuns. Our major interests are in the areas of monastic sources and spirituality and patristics. Most of our books are in the areas of theology and philosophy, prayer and spirituality. We do not publish fiction and only rarely do we publish poetry.

Please do not send your entire manuscript unless requested. We prefer to receive an inquiry first, at which time you may submit a summary of your book, table of contents and a few sample chapters. If we are interested, we will request the full manuscript. Faxed proposals will *not* be considered.

Manuscripts should be formatted with at least 1½" margins on all four sides. Please use the same typewriter or printer font for the entire manuscript. All pages should be numbered consecutively. The first line of each paragraph should be indented one-half inch. Sketches, photographs and other art that is to be included must be submitted with the manuscript. Authors should submit a short biographical sketch and a précis of their book. If we accept the manuscript for publication, we will require two copies.

We prefer the University of *Chicago Manual of Style*, but any major style manual is acceptable as long as the manuscript is consistent. If your manuscript is accepted, we can accept, along with the hard copy, computer disks in IBM-compatible format. The computer files must be exactly the same as the printed copy.

If your manuscript is accepted, the final copy must be in perfect condition before it goes into production. Any alterations made in the text after page proofs will be charged against author royalties.

Categories: Nonfiction—Catholic—Christian Interests—Religion—Spiritual

Name: Sr. Scholastica Crilly, O.S.B., Editor
Material: All
Address: PO BOX 545
City/State/ZIP: PETERSHAM MA 01366-0545
E-mail: scrilly@stbedes.org
Internet: www.stbedes.org

SAMUEL WEISER, INC.
Box 612 • York Beach, Maine • 03910-0612

Samuel Weiser, Inc.

Thank you for your inquiry about our manuscript reviewing policy. For many years, our firm has been happy to look at any unsolicited manuscripts we receive. The following information should be of help when deciding where to send your manuscript for review.

1. Samuel Weiser is a specialty publisher. Our books include such subjects as: Alchemy, Alternative Health, Astral Projection, Astrology, Kabbalah, Celtic Mythology, Magic, Mysticism, Psychology, Numerology, Tarot and Taoism among others. We do not publish poetry, fiction, novels, children's books or mass market (mainstream) titles. If you feel that your work fits our field, feel free to send a copy of the original for review.

2. Contents and Appearance:

(a) We look at completed manuscripts only (no computer disks).

(b) Proposal letters may be sent. They must clearly state the contents of the manuscript. Evaluation will not be made on proposal letters or sample chapters. They only give us an idea if we might be interested in seeing the completed work.

(c) If you send a complete manuscript it should include: table of contents, preface (if you have one), introduction, dedication (if you have one), list of illustrations or figures, footnotes, bibliography. Footnotes (if necessary to the text) should be handled by the author. Permissions are also handled by the author (see below).

(d) Footnotes: If you are referencing other published works in your manuscript, you must supply complete footnote data. Before considering the manuscript complete, have you supplied the complete author, title, publisher, city of publication, year of publication and page numbers for the books that are cited in your text?

(e) Permissions: If you quote material from other published sources, you may need to seek permission to quote that material prior to using it. Obtaining permission is the responsibility of the author and any permission fees are paid by the author. If you have questions about how to handle permissions requests, you might consult the CHICAGO MANUAL OF STYLE, published by the University of Chicago Press, usually available at your library.

(f) Illustrations: If you are using illustrations in your text, please submit copies along with captions or legends that explain what the illustrations are. You should also indicate where the illustrations belong in your text. If you are using a previously published illustration, you must obtain permission before using it in your book.

3. Evaluation:

(a) We review all manuscripts.

(b) We do not acknowledge receipt of unsolicited manuscripts. Send either UPS or request a return receipt from your local Post Office.

(c) Evaluation can take anywhere from 4 to 12 weeks (possibly longer) depending on number of submissions. We are a small house with a small staff.

(d) Please do not phone to see if we've received your work or to check on the progress of it. If it has been longer than 12 weeks and you haven't heard from us, drop us a line.

(e) If we are seriously considering your work, it will be evaluated in the following areas:

(1) Can we market this material effectively? Being able to reach the right market for your work is very important. If we can't reach the market you need, we won't be able to sell the book for you.

(2) Do we have another manuscript under contract that would compete with this book?

(3) Is the material interesting enough to warrant the necessary sales?

(4) Do we want to increase our list in this subject category?

4. How to submit:

(a) Please supply a dated cover letter.

(b) Your name and address should be clearly written on both the letter and title page of the manuscript. We cannot return the manuscript to you if we don't have the proper information.

Categories: Health—Martial Arts—Native American—New Age—Psychology—Religion—Spiritual

Name: Eliot Stearnes, Editor

Material: All
Address: PO BOX 612
City/State/ZIP: YORK BEACH ME 03910
Telephone: 207-363-4393
Fax: 207-363-5799
E-mail: weiserbooks@worldnet.att.net

Scarecrow Press, Inc.

The following guidelines are for submitting a book proposal to Scarecrow Press.

1. Please provide a tentative descriptive title.

2. Tell us the subject matter, scope, and intended purpose of your manuscript. If you have the completed manuscript, you may send it to us but be sure to keep a copy yourself. If you do not yet have a manuscript, please send us the Introduction, Table of Contents, and chapter summaries. A completed sample chapter that shows us your writing style, organizational techniques, and documentation would also be helpful. If your proposed book is a bibliography, we would like to see sample annotated entries.

3. Describe the research methods you will use and potential sources of data.

4. Please indicate whether the book will require photographs, illustrations, maps, appendix, index, etc.

5. When would you estimate the work will be completed? What length do you envisage for it?

6. What audience do you see for your work? What other books exist in this same subject area?

7. Has any part of your book been published previously and if so, where? If it is a doctoral dissertation, what changes are you proposing to prepare it for monograph publication?

8. Do you have written permissions to use material that may be copyrighted (illustrations, lengthy quotations from scholarly works, or *any* quotations from fiction or poetry)?

9. Please send us your c.v.

10. Please indicate how you will submit your manuscript if it is accepted: camera-ready or double-spaced manuscript pages. If you would be submitting double-spaced manuscript pages, it is preferable that you be able to submit a diskette containing the ms. as well.

Categories: Nonfiction—Reference—Library Science

Name: Amanda Irwin, Assistant Editor
Material: All
Address: 4720 BOSTON WAY
City/State/ZIP: LANHAM MD 20706
Telephone: 301-459-3366
Fax: 301-459-2118

Schirmer Books

Schirmer Books
An Imprint of Macmillan, Inc.

GUIDELINES FOR WRITING A MANUSCRIPT PROPOSAL

A. *The Book*:

1. Brief Description

In one or two paragraphs, describe the work, including its rationale, approach, and pedagogy. "This book is…It does…Its distinguishing features are…"

2. Outline

A detailed outline of the book should be prepared, including the chapters being submitted for review. This gives us an idea of how the material fits together, and how the remaining chapters will be developed. It should include chapter headings and sub-headings, with explanations as necessary.

3. Outstanding features

List briefly what you consider to be the outstanding, distinctive, or unique features of the work.

4. Apparatus

a. Will the book include photographs, line drawings, musical examples, cases, questions, problems, glossaries, bibliography, references, appendices, etc.?

b. If the book is a text, do you plan to provide supplemental material to accompany it? (Teacher's manual, study guide, solutions, answers, workbook, anthology, or other material.)

5. Competition

a. Consider the existing books in this field and discuss specifically their strengths and weaknesses. Spell out how your book will be similar to, as well as different from, competing works.

b. Consider what aspects of topical coverage are similar to or different from the competition. What topics have been left out of competing books and what topics have been left out of yours?

c. Please discuss each competing book in a separate paragraph. The above information will provide the reviewers and the publisher with a frame of reference for evaluating your material. Remember, you are writing for reviewers and not for publication, so be as frank as possible regarding your competition. Give credit where credit is due, and show how you can do it better.

B. *Market Considerations*:

1. The Primary Market

a. What is the major market for the book? (Text, scholarly/professional, reference, trade?)

b. If this is a *text*, for what course is the book intended? Is the book a core text or a supplement? What type of student takes this course? What is the level? (Major or non-major; freshman, senior, graduate?) Do you offer this course yourself? If so, how many times have you given it? Is your text class-tested?

c. If the market is scholarly/professional, reference, or trade, how may it best be reached? (Direct mail, relevant journals, professional associations, libraries, book or music stores?) For what type of reader is your book intended?

2. Other Markets

Please list secondary markets where your book may be of interest. (Other course titles, related fields, subsidiary audiences, etc.) If you have done any market research of your own, we would appreciate receiving a brief summary of your findings.

C. *Status of the Work*:

1. Do you have a timetable for completing the book?

a. What portion or percentage of the material is now complete?

b. When do you expect to have a complete manuscript?

2. What do you estimate to be the size of the completed book?

Double-spaced typewritten pages normally reduce about 1/3 when set in type; e.g., 300 typewritten pages make about 200 printed pages. There are about 450 words on a printed page.

a. Approximately how many photographs do you plan to include?

b. Approximately how many line drawings (charts, graphs, diagrams, etc.) will you need?

c. Do you intend to include music examples? If so, how many single lines of music do you estimate will be included? How much of it do you anticipate can be reproduced from existing sources, and how much will need to be newly autographed?

d. Do you plan to include material requiring permission (text, music, lyrics, illustrations)? To what extent? Have you started the permissions request process?

3. Do you plan to class-test the material in your own or other sections of the course? (Any material distributed to students should be protected by copyright notice on the material.)

Sample Chapters

Select one or two chapters of the manuscript that are an integral part of the book. They should be those you consider to be the best-written ones, and do not have to be in sequence. For example, you might submit chapters 3, 7 and 14 of a 20-chapter book, so long as these chapters represent the content and reflect your writing style and pedagogy in the best possible light. It is also advisable to submit any chapter that is innovative or unique.

Sample chapters should contain rough sketches, charts, handwritten musical examples or photocopy reproductions, and descriptions of photographs to be included. The material need not be in final form. In your preparation, emphasis should be on readability.

Reviews

We will, of course, obtain the best available reviewers to consider your work. We would like to include some whose opinions you would consider particularly important. For this purpose, please provide the names, addresses, and phone numbers (if available) of three or four whom you feel would be competent to review your material and whose opinion you would find valuable. We will try to use some of these along with some of our own selection.

Naturally, we do not reveal the names of reviewers without their permission.

Categories: Music

Name: Acquisitions Editor
Material: All
Address: 1633 BROADWAY
City/State/ZIP: NEW YORK NY 10019
Telephone: 212-654-8414
Fax: 212-654-4745

Scholars Books

Please refer to Publishers Associates.

Serendipity Systems
Books-on-disks™, Bookware™

Serendipity Systems publishes fiction and reference works related to literature, writing, and publishing.

We are only interested in seeing works which can take advantage of computer-enhanced features such as hypertext or multimedia. Except in rare cases, we do not publish works which are straight prose (no hypertext or multimedia.) We can NOT use manuscripts on paper. We may be able to use Macintosh files if they have been saved as ASCII under System 7 or higher, however, we only publish IBM PC-compatible disks. Royalties for books published under the BOOKS-ON-DISKS™ imprint are thirty-three percent of the retail or wholesale sales, less shipping. No advance is offered. Serendipity Systems only contracts for the electronic rights; all on-paper, movie, and similar rights are retained by the author. Publications will be featured at our BOOKWARE Internet site.

We do not want to see:
• romance novels
• religious tracts
• sword and sorcery fantasy
• occult works
• anything "new age"
• political diatribes
• imitations of Stephen King or Tom Clancy
• "Penthouse Forum" quality materials
• children's literature (pre-teenage)
• nonfiction works not related to literature, writing, or publishing

We are interested in seeing:
• hypertext novels
• mixed-media works
• new computer-enhanced genres
• interactive fiction
• experimental works
• reference works on literature, writing, and publishing
• Windows-compatible works
• manuscripts written in HTML

Submissions should:
• be on IBM PC-compatible disks (160K, 5.25" to 1.44MB, 3.5"; 100MB ZIP disks)
• be in ASCII (unless the author has already added hypertext/multimedia features)
• have margins of 1 and less than 80 (WordPerfect users note this!)
• include the complete manuscript
• include a cover letter describing the work and the author's qualifications
• send the complete manuscript by postal mail; send ONLY queries by e-mail

Check our internet site for the latest guidelines information, plus a book catalog, sample chapters, free books, writers' manuscript help, and a large collection of reference material for writers, readers, and publishers.

BOOKS-ON-DISK is a trademark of Books on Tape, Inc.

Categories: Fiction—Nonfiction—Internet—Literature—Writing

Name: Acquisitions Editor
Material: All
Address: PO BOX 140
City/State/ZIP: SAN SIMEON CA 93452
E-mail: bookware@thegrid.net

Sierra Club Books

Dear Writer,

The following list describes briefly the items we like to receive with submissions if they apply to your work and if you have them available:

1. Table of contents
2. Précis: overview of the plot, theme, and events of the book in summary
3. Sample chapter
4. Book specifications (if this is a previously published work): number of pages, type size, page format, etc.
5. Outline
6. Samples of any illustrations or photos if appropriate
We appreciate your interest in Sierra Club Books.
Categories: Nonfiction—Environment

Name: Editorial Department
Material: All
Address: 85 2ND STREET
City/State/Zip: SAN FRANCISCO, CA 94105
Telephone: 415- 291-1600
Fax: 415- 291-1602

Silhouette Books

Thank you for your interest in Silhouette Books. We do not accept unsolicited complete or partial manuscripts, but ask instead that you submit a query letter.

Please indicate what Silhouette series you think your project is appropriate for, if it is completed, what you think makes it special, and previous publishing experience (if any). Also include a synopsis of your story that gives a clear idea of both your plot and characters and is no more than two single-spaced pages. A self-addressed stamped envelope (SASE) will ensure a reply.

Should your manuscript be requested, please note the following information:

1. We publish only category romances! Please do not submit any other type of fiction or nonfiction. Your manuscript should take place in the present and be told in the third person, primarily from the heroine's point of view. However, the hero's perspective may be used to enhance tension, plot or character development.

2. All material should be the author's own original work. Stories that contain scenes or plot lines that bear a striking resemblance to previously published work are in breach of copyright law and are not acceptable.

3. No disk submissions. Computer-generated material is acceptable, but must be letter quality, and pages must be separated. Any material received on computer reams will be returned without evaluation.

4. Do not submit your material bound in binders, boxes or containers of any kind. Secure material by rubber bands. Cover sheets must have your complete name, address and phone number. Each page should be numbered sequentially thereafter. Please type your name and title in the upper left-hand corner of each page. If we ask to see your manuscript, please include a complete synopsis.

5. All material will be evaluated in as timely a fashion as volume allows. Please do not call regarding the status of your manuscript. You will be notified by mail as soon as your work has been reviewed.

6. Do not send any material that is being considered by another publisher. "Multiple submissions" are not acceptable. A literary agent is not required in order to submit.

7. This sheet is designed as a guide to aid you in understanding our requirements and standards. However, there is no better way to determine what we are looking for than reading our books.
Categories: Fiction—Romance—Women's Fiction

Name: Refer to guidelines.
Address: 300 E 42ND ST 6TH FLOOR

City/State/ZIP: NEW YORK NY 10017
Telephone: 212-682-6080
Fax: 212-682-4539

Silhouette Desire®
An Imprint of Silhouette Books

55,000 – 60,000 words
Senior Editor: Lucia Macro
Sensual, believable, compelling, these books are written for today's woman. Innocent or experienced, the heroine is someone we identify with; the hero irresistible. The conflict should be an emotional one, springing naturally from the unique characters you've chosen. The focus is on the developing relationship, set in a believable plot. The characters don't have to be married to make love, but lovemaking is never taken lightly. Secondary characters and subplots must blend with the core story. Innovative new directions in storytelling and fresh approaches to classic romantic plots are welcome.

Silhouette Intimate Moments®
An Imprint of Silhouette Books

80,000 – 85,000 words
Senior Editor & Editorial Coordinator: Leslie Wainger
Believable characters swept into a world of larger-than-life romance, such is the magic of Silhouette Intimate Moments. These books offer you the freedom to combine the universally appealing elements of a category romance with the flash and excitement of mainstream fiction. Adventure, suspense, melodrama, glamour—let your imagination be your guide as you blend old and new to create a novel with emotional depth and tantalizing complexity, a novel that explores new directions in romantic fiction, a novel that is quintessentially Intimate Moments.

Silhouette Romance™
An Imprint of Silhouette Books

53,000 – 58,000 words
Senior Editor: Melissa Senate
Silhouette Romance requires talented authors able to portray modern relationships in the context of romantic love. Although the hero and heroine don't actually make love unless married, sexual tension is a vitally important element. Writers are encouraged to try new twists and creative approaches to this winning formula. Our ultimate goal is to give readers a romance with heightened emotional impact—books that make them laugh or cry, books that touch their hearts.

Silhouette Special Edition®
An Imprint of Silhouette Books

75,000 – 80,000 words
Senior Editor: Tara Gavin
Sophisticated, substantial, and packed with emotion, Special Edition demands writers eager to probe characters deeply, to explore issues that heighten the drama of living and loving, to create compelling romantic plots. Whether the sensuality is sizzling or subtle, whether the plot is wildly innovative or satisfyingly traditional, the novel's emotional vividness, its depth and dimension, should clearly label it a very special contemporary romance. Subplots are welcome, but must further or parallel the developing romantic relationship in a meaningful way.

Silhouette Yours Truly
An Imprint of Silhouette Books

(formerly known as "The Written Word")

Yours Truly—Silhouette's new line of short, sassy contemporary romance novels about unexpectedly meeting, dating...and marrying Mr. Right.

How does the heroine unexpectedly meet Mr. Right? Through a form of written communication, such as a personal ad, an invitation to a wedding, or a misdirected Dear John letter—just to name a few fun and intriguing examples. Hook readers in the snappiest way possible—in the first few pages. **How does she date him?** Date him? Considering the compelling romantic conflict standing in their way, they're too busy letting the emotional and romantic tension develop. Plus she just might—she just might—date other men—for humorous touches that teach her who she really belongs with—the hero. **How does she marry him?** *That* depends on the page-turning plot. And in **Yours Truly** novels, only a satisfying, happy ending is required—marriage isn't.

Yours Truly: Love—when you least expect it.

Word Count: 50,000. **Tone:** Category romance that is very contemporary, fast-paced, fun, flirtatious, entertaining, upbeat. **Level of Sensuality:** Sexy, but no requirements. **Examples of movies that capture the tone and type of stories:** Sleepless in Seattle, Four Weddings and a Funeral, Married to the Mob, Crossing Delancey. **Absolute No-No:** Paranormal elements (Yours Truly novels are an entertaining reflection of real life.) **Absolute Must:** Hero and heroine meet, directly or indirectly, through a form of written communication. **Submission info:** Yours Truly is actively seeking submissions from unpublished and published authors. (Silhouette & Harlequin authors: submit to your respective editors.) Send a query or a partial (with a full synopsis) or a complete manuscript with a cover letter and manuscript-sized SASE to:

Name: Leslie Wainger, Senior Editor, or to any member of the editorial staff.
Address: See Silhouette Books, above.

Simon & Schuster

Please refer to Atheneum Books for Young Readers, Margaret K. McElderry Books, Pocketbooks, Archway Paperbacks, Minstrel Books, and the magazines published by Cobblestone Publishing, Inc.: *Calliope, Faces, Odyssey,* and *Cobblestone.*

Smithsonian Oceanic Collection
Smithsonian's Backyard
Soundprints

The Smithsonian Oceanic Collection and Smithsonian's Backyard introduce children to animals and their unique behaviors. Each book tells an interesting story that communicates facts about the animal's habitat, what they eat, how they live, and unique or interesting characteristics of the animal.

The Smithsonian Oceanic Collection focuses on marine wildlife. Stories should illustrate the special ways in which the animals are adapted to live in their environments, as well as characteristics that might set them apart from other marine wildlife. All of these facts are incorporated into an engaging storyline, highlighting a specific animal that children can learn about and relate to.

Smithsonian's Backyard includes wild animals that children might be exposed to on a regular basis, such as squirrels, rab-

bits, and birds (not pets!). Stories should answer the kinds of questions that children often raise about these animals: What do they eat? Where do they sleep? Etc. These facts should be communicated through an exciting and engaging storyline, highlighting a specific animal. Each story takes place in a yard of a specific house on a specific street.

General information:

• Animals should be realistic, not anthropomorphic. Animals in the stories should exhibit natural behaviors as they move about and interact with other animals within the habitat.

• Target reading level is preschool through second grade.

• Finished stories should be approximately 800 words long.

In addition to editing by Soundprints, Smithsonian Oceanic Collection and Smithsonian's Backyard stories are subject to the review and approval of the Smithsonian Institution and should be based on good, solid research. All elements of each story should be supportable by current references. For an example of a Smithsonian Oceanic Collection and Smithsonian's Backyard storybook, please see the following:

Dolphin's First Day by Kathleen Weidner Zoehfeld
Screech Owl at Midnight Hollow by C. Drew Lamm
Categories: Fiction—Animals—Children

Name: Cassia Farkas, Editor
Material: Any
Name: Diane Hinze Kanzler, Graphic Designer
Address: 353 MAIN AVE
City/State/ZIP: NORWALK CT 06851
Telephone: 203-846-2274
Fax: 203-846-1776
E-mail: sndprnts@ix.netcom.com

Smithsonian Odyssey

The Smithsonian Odyssey follows four children, Emma, Kevin, Lucy, and Tomas, as they explore the Smithsonian Institution's museums and exhibits. In each story, one of the children becomes engrossed in an exhibit and is carried away by his or her imagination to the time of the actual event that is depicted. The story should be an accurate explanation of the historical event or phenomenon. At the same time, it should incorporate an adventure involving the main character and his or her involvement in the event.

General information:

• Subjects of the stories must be represented by an existing exhibit at one of the Smithsonian Institution's museums.

• Target reading level is 2nd through 5th grade.

• Finished stories should be approximately 1,500-2,000 words long.

• Transitions from the present to the past should be smooth and viable.

• All four children should be incorporated into the story, with one of the children highlighted.

In addition to editing by Soundprints, Smithsonian Odyssey stories are subject to the review and approval of the Smithsonian Institution and should be based on good, solid research. All elements of each story should be supportable by current references.

For an example of a Smithsonian Odyssey book, please see the following:

One Giant Leap by Dana Meachan Rau
Categories: Fiction—Adventure—Children—History

Name: Cassia Farkas, Editor
Material: Any
Name: Diane Hinze Kanzler, Graphic Designer
Address: 353 MAIN AVE
City/State/ZIP: NORWALK CT 06851

Telephone: 203-846-2274
Fax: 203-846-1776
E-mail: sndprnts@ix.netcom.com

SpanPress, Inc.

SpanPress, Span Universitaria, Havahthar

Building a Bridge Between Cultures
Language: Spanish
Format: Double-space, typed
Illustrations: SpanPress provides (suggestions/written specifications welcome)
Market: Educational (Supplemental)
Grade Levels: Pre-school, K, 1-4 (Nothing higher than 6th)
Themes*: a)Concerns/experiences/reflections of Hispanic-American children and their families in the United States. b)Nonfiction, content area based.
SASE: Not required, but helpful in expediting review.
*We prefer pedagogically valid series, adaptable to developing strong teacher support material.
Categories: Fiction—Nonfiction—Adventure—Children—Educational (Hispanic-American Experiences)—Ethnic—Family—Hispanic—Young Adult

Name: Barbara A. Teuten, Director, Editorial Services
Material: Hispanic-American experiences in USA
Address: 5722 S FLAMINGO RS STE 277
City/State/ZIP: COOPER CITY FL 33330
Telephone: 305-592-7913
Fax: 305-477-5632
Nota bene: We publish in Spanish, with translations &/or illustrations done in-house.

Spinsters Ink

Spinsters Ink is primarily interested in full-length novels and nonfiction works that deal with significant issues in women's lives from a feminist perspective: books that not only name crucial issues in women's lives, but—more important—encourage change and growth. We are particularly interested in creative works by women writing from the periphery: fat women, Jewish women, lesbians, old women, women examining classism, women of color, women with disabilities, women who are writing books that help make the best in our lives possible. We want well-told stories that exhibit fine writing, are lively and engaging, and treat our lives with the honesty and complexity they deserve. The main characters and/or narrators must be women.

Submission requirements and procedures:

If you wish us to read your manuscript, first send a query letter, including a *synopsis* of the work, for our review. If we want to review the work in greater depth, we will send you a letter asking for two to five chapters (depending on length-should not exceed 50 pages or five chapters) of the work itself. Include a self-addressed, stamped postcard which we will return to you, letting you know that we received the material. Also, include a self-addressed, stamped envelope in which we'll respond to you when we've finished reading your materials. If the preliminary work looks suitable to us, we will ask you to send us the entire manuscript.

Please do not send anything—neither the query materials or the manuscript itself—by certified mail or return receipt requested.

Do allow at least three months to review your manuscript. Depending on our workload and availability of staff, we will get to your submission as quickly as possible and give it the thorough attention it deserves.

At the top of each manuscript page should be written the chapter number, the page number, and your last name.

If you have submitted your work to other publishers, please do us the courtesy of informing us of this and notifying us immediately if another publisher begins to give the manuscript serious consideration. We have no intention of "competing" with our publishing colleagues, so please don't put us in this position.

If you are offered a contract:

If you are offered a contract, we will go through it in detail with you. We can recommend reading resources to help you understand publishing contracts, and we encourage you to check with an attorney if you desire.

Spinsters Ink pays for all production costs of the books we publish. Because we are a small press, we cannot afford to pay advances or provide travel allowances for promoting your book. However, we do extensive publicity both prior to and after publication. Your royalties are a percentage of the sales of the books and of the sale of subsidiary rights, such as foreign translations and television rights.

When your contract is signed, we will determine a publication schedule for your book. This includes editing, text design, cover design, proofreading, and marketing. Generally, a book is published about 12 to 18 months after the contract is signed.

Call us with any questions you may have.

Categories: Fiction—Nonfiction—Feminism—Gay/Lesbian—Mystery—Women's Fiction—Women's Issues

Name: Acquisitions Editor
Material: All
Address: 32 E FIRST ST
City/State/ZIP: DULUTH MN 55802
Telephone: 218-727-3222
Fax: 218-727-3119
E-mail: spinsters@aol.com

Sta-Kris, Inc.

Thoughtful Books

Sta-Kris, Inc. publishes nonfiction/fiction adult-level gift books that 1.) portray universal feelings, truths, and values, or 2.) have a special occasion theme, plus small format compilations of statements about professions, issues, attitudes etc.

Our audiences tend to be women ranging in age from their 20s on up. They generally are well read, in touch with themselves and interested in others. They exhibit a great capacity for listening to and sharing with other people.

Sta-Kris, Inc. is an independent publisher who supports the marketing of their books with great energy and knowledge of the market place. Our publicist won the 1993 LMP's Publicist of the Year.

Submissions: Query with bio, list of credits, and complete manuscript accompanied by SASE.

If you have any questions please contact Kathy.
Categories: Nonfiction—Family—Relationships

Name: Kathy Wagoner, President
Material: All
Address: PO BOX 1131
City/State/ZIP: MARSHALLTOWN IA 50158
Telephone: 515-753-4139
Fax: 515-753-0985

Staplegun Press
Poetry, Rants, Images and Anything Else That Burns

We actively support the unpublished schizophrenic.

• Submit up to 5 poems, with name and address on every page.

• If you do not enclose a SASE, all your stuff is going straight to the waste bin, no matter *how* good it is…. Must have sufficient postage for work to be returned.

• Any style, any subject matter (but here's a hint: we *hate* religious poetry, love poetry and nature poetry). We want urban decay, focused rage and stuff that'll make our ears bleed.

Categories: Poetry

Name: Submissions Editor
Material: All
Address: PO BOX 190184
City/State/ZIP: BIRMINGHAM AL 35219
Telephone: 205-933-4025
E-mail: staplegunp@aol.com

Stonewall Series
Brickhouse Books, Inc.

In 1992, New Poets Series/Chestnut Hill Press (NPS/CHP) inaugurated a new division, The Stonewall Series, dedicated to publishing poetry and short fiction written from a gay, lesbian, or bisexual perspective. Its first two volumes are Jan-Mitchell Sherrill's *Friend of the Groom* and Joel Zizik's *Hypoglycemia and the Need to Practice It.*

Stonewall sponsors an annual chapbook contest in addition to bringing out book-length mss. Chapbook entries between 20 and 28 pages are solicited with an entry fee of $20.00 (to defray judges' stipends and production costs, as well as to contribute to the book-length publication's costs); the postmark deadline is August 15, with the winner announced early in the winter.

The winning chapbook is published and distributed nationally by NPS/CHP/Stonewall. Honorable mentions are publicized, and all entrants become eligible to submit a full book-length ms. to Stonewall at a later date, with the customary $10.00 fee waived.

How to Submit

Stonewall Series accepts book submissions year round. Send a full ms. consisting of about 55 pages of poetry. There is a $10.00 readers' fee for each submission.

Categories: Gay/Lesbian—Poetry

Name: Clarinda Harriss, Editor/Director
Material: All
Address: 541 PICCADILLY RD
City/State/ZIP: TOWSON MD 21204
Telephone: 410-828-0724

E-mail: harriss@towson.edu
Internet: www.saber.towson.edu.80/~harriss/!bhbwebs.ite/bhb.htm
Nota bene: Reader's fee required with submission.

Storey Communications, Inc.
Storey Publishing, Garden Way Publishing

The mission of Storey Communications is to serve our customers by publishing practical information that encourages personal independence in harmony with the environment. We seek to do this in a positive atmosphere that promotes editorial quality, team spirit, and profitability. The books we select to carry out this mission include titles on gardening, small-scale farming, building, cooking, crafts, part-time businesses, home improvement, woodworking, animals, nature, kids, and country living.

We are always pleased to review new proposals, which we try to process expeditiously. We offer both work-for-hire and standard royalty contracts. If you have ideas for a book on any of the subjects in our line, and if you are intrigued by the philosophy expressed in our mission statement, we hope you will think of Storey Communications/Garden Way Publishing.

Book proposal packages should include the following:

• A letter of introduction

• A one-paragraph description of your book idea

• A brief statement explaining why you think your book is needed and describing the potential readers of your book

• A list of recent books (if any) that are similar to your own, with an explanation of how yours will be different

• A paragraph about yourself and your credentials for writing the book you are proposing (you may also wish to enclose your resume)

• A table of contents, including a brief description of each chapter

• Some of your thoughts about the length, general appearance, and illustrative requirements of the book

• A sample of your writing, if available

Categories: Nonfiction—Agriculture—Animals—Architecture—Arts—Cooking—Crafts—Gardening—Hobbies—How-to

Name: Gwen Steege, Editorial Director
Material: All
Address: SCHOOLHOUSE RD
City/State/ZIP: POWNAL VT 05261
Telephone: 802-823-5200
Fax: 802-823-5819

Tangelwuld Press

Please refer to Publishers Associates.

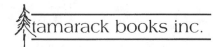

Tamarack Books, Inc.
Classics of the Fur Trade

Thank you for your interest in Tamarack Books. We are a traditional publishing house which specializes in nonfiction western Americana: particularly history and travel, and other topics concerning the West. We do *not* do fiction, poetry, inspirational, family histories, etc.

To submit a manuscript for publishing consideration, send

us a short proposal and two to three sample chapters of your book. The proposal should tell us the main theme of the book, an outline, your sources of information, and your marketing research. Also, tell us why *you* are qualified to write this book. The sample chapters should be in standard manuscript format. Send only copies of photographs or drawings; do not send originals. Always include an SASE for our response. We will not respond if we don't have this envelope.

We do not read manuscripts which have been printed with a dot matrix printer. That is simply too tough on our old editors' eyes! We also prefer that all manuscripts being considered for publication be available on disk (Word, WP, Mac, etc.) when we accept them for publication. We don't want the disk now, but if the manuscript goes into production, a disk speeds the process up.

We have a large number of manuscripts submitted to us. Because of that, we ask that you do not telephone regarding your manuscript until after three months. Normally, we try to complete the review process within six to eight weeks, and will contact you as soon as we can.

Please be aware that Tamarack publishes only three to five books annually, and we receive over 300 manuscripts per year. To increase your chance of acceptance, we recommend the following:

1. Make sure that your manuscript topic is similar to what we already publish. Match your manuscript to the publisher.

2. Make sure that you have researched the market for your book, and then tell us about your research. What are you planning to do for marketing?

3. Belong to a professional writing organization and read the writer's magazines monthly. Learn not only the craft of writing, but the business of writing.

4. Submit your materials in a professional manner.

5. Don't call the editor.

Please read this over carefully, and pick up the publishing hints that we have liberally sprinkled throughout!

Good Luck!

Categories: Nonfiction—History—Regional—Western

Name: Acquisitions Editor
Material: All
Address: PO BOX 190313
City/State/ZIP: BOISE ID 83719-0313
Telephone: 208-387-2656
Fax: 208-387-2650
E-mail: tamarack@cyberhighway.net

Technical Books for the Layperson, Inc.

Technical Books for the Layperson (TBL) is a publisher of books by consumers for consumers. This means that the perspective of the text is that of an uninformed but reasonably intelligent reader. We try to avoid the extremes of excessive jargon or over-simplification.

We promise our readers that we will ask all the "stupid" questions—those questions that elicit sneers from sales people. We also want our writers to be as comprehensive as possible about what information and products are currently available (thus saving the consumer a good bit of time). We want our writers to peel away "sales speak" and tell the reader what is left that is important.

In other words, we want to create an informed consumer from someone who knows nothing about any of our areas. We want the consumer to be able to talk to experts and judge the quality of the advice gotten. And we want the text to be fairly informal,

imitating the way consumers talk to one another.

To maximize royalties for our authors, we at TBL keep our overhead as low as possible, let each author handle the marketing of his or her own book(s), and accept only camera-ready manuscripts. Consequently, we recommend to potential authors that they send their manuscripts to more conventional publishers first so as to have a basis for comparison to what we offer.

Hints on Finding a Conventional Publisher
(These are *not* guidelines for submitting to TBL.)
Choosing publishers

Rather than mass mail to everyone, go through your own books and pick out the ones that look the way you want yours to look. Note the names of the publishers of those books. Then pick out the books that are of the same type as yours (nonfiction in a specific area) and make note of the names of those publishers.

If you don't have many books, use your library or bookstore to find books you like and those that are in your area. Usually, the address of the publisher is listed on the copyright page in the front of the book. It you can't find it, your library will have a copy of *Literary Market Place* which will have the mailing address you need.

Submitting the manuscript

Include a complete table of contents, the first chapter of the book and a *prospectus* in which you describe your book and its marketing potential. This means identify the readers you expect for your book, identify other, similar, books already on the market for these readers and say how your book differs from these other books.

We recommend submitting to all the publishers on your list to see who is interested. At some point the publisher might ask you not to submit to others until they have made a decision. Whereas you may only sign with one publisher, you do have the right to make multiple submissions. You can reassure the interested publisher that you won't sign with another publisher without first checking with them.

Evaluating the responses

An *advance* means just that: the publisher advances you some money against your future royalties. You won't start receiving royalties until the advance is paid back.

Royalties generally run 5-10% of the retail—list—price (but you don't earn anything on copies of your book that are given away). For your general information, publishers only make, at most, 35-40% of the list price of the book (this is what the distributor pays the publishers about 3 months after taking the books).

Usually, royalties are paid once a year. You get a statement of how many books were sold at what price and you get the agreed percentage of that total.

Submitting to TBL

Basically our authors work very hard on behalf of their books. Consequently, your initial query to us can be very brief. We don't need you to take the time telling us about marketing and such. We are interested that your book fits our "how to" style,.guiding a completely naive reader through your technical terrain.

TBL pays for the printing of your book, distribution, and passive advertising (reprinting our "catalogue" to include your book). Until book sales cover these initial costs, the author pays advertising expenses but bills TBL for reimbursement. You send out review copies and determine who should get them, for example. We will work with you to help minimize expense and maximize exposure; your own cleverness and stamina will ultimately determine sales. Because you are in charge of marketing your book, there is no preset quota from us of how much your book has to earn to stay in print.

Your book does not have to address a large audience nor will we drop it so long as the information remains current. We print in very small runs (1,000 copies and under) as we assess demand.

This means that your book won't take up a lot of storage space or become obsolete while you are finding receptive audiences. We also support annual revisions to keep the information as timely as possible.

When you are ready to show us your work, just send the first chapter and table of contents to us. We will tell you our thoughts and you can decide whether to continue the dialogue.

The most frequent problem we have with manuscript submissions is the fact that most of them have been written by experts. Whereas we value their expertise, we find that experts don't think like naive consumers. We do have at hand very outspoken consumers who are willing to work closely with an author to make a manuscript consumer-friendly. This arrangement doesn't suit everyone, of course. Our primary goal is clarity.

Your camera ready copy should be between 200-300 pages (including the front pages and index). The text on each page should be contained in a 4½"x7" block, including header, footer and page number. We have a standard size to keep printing costs low.

Above all, please send only photocopies of your manuscript and make sure your name and address are on the manuscript. Never include cut-and-pasted pages—only photocopies of such pages. We are not able to return any of your material, nor do we need a self addressed stamped envelope to reply to you. Please, no telephone inquiries about manuscripts submitted. We are unable to return those calls.

Good luck!

Categories: Nonfiction (All categories are appropriate.)

Name: Acquisitions Editor
Material: All
Address: PO BOX 391
City/State/ZIP: LAKE GROVE NY 11755
Telephone: 540-877-1477
Nota bene: Camera-ready submissions required.

Temple University Press

Temple University Press invites inquiries and proposals that include a project overview, a tentative table of contents, and the author/editor's resume. Proposals might also include sample chapters or writing samples, but they are not required for an initial inquiry. Prospective authors are encouraged to contact the Editor-in-Chief by phone, e-mail or letter before sending completed manuscripts. Temple University Press has no specific guidelines for proposals, but editors prefer to see double-spaced copy with no justification on the right margin and unbound pages.

Categories: Nonfiction—African-American—Animals—Asian-American—Biography—Culture—Dance—Disabilities—Drama—Ecology—Education—Ethnic—Family—Feminism—Film/Video—Gay/Lesbian—General Interest—Health—Hispanic—History—Jewish Interests—Law—Literature—Multicultural—Music—Politics—Psychology—Public Policy—Regional—Religion—Sexuality—Sports—Television/Radio—Theatre—Women's Issues

Name: Janet M. Francendese, Editor-in-Chief
Material: General Interest, History, Film and Media, Art and Photography, Ethnic Studies, Cultural Studies
Name: Doris B. Braendel, Senior Acquisitions Editor
Material: Latino/Latin American Studies, Law, Anthropology, Political Science
Name: Michael Ames, Senior Acquisitions Editor
Material: Sociology, Public Policy, Psychology, Health and Science
Address: UNIVERSITY SERVICES 083-42
Address: 1601 N BROAD ST

City/State/ZIP: PHILADELPHIA PA 19122-6099
Telephone: 215-204-8787
Fax: 215-204-4719
E-mail: tempress@astro.ocis.temple,edu

Ten Speed Press
Celestial Arts, Tricycle Press

If you wish to submit a book proposal to us, please include:
• a cover letter detailing the work as a whole-including any and all information that you think we should have in order to make a decision about your project. In particular, be sure to tell us who your target audience is, and why.
• a chapter-by-chapter outline of the entire work.
• one or two sample chapters-whatever you consider to be enough material to give us a sense of the work as a whole. It is not necessary to send the entire manuscript.
• A brief bio, or a note as to who you are and why you are the right person to write this book. Needn't be a formal resume.

Be prepared to wait about six to eight weeks for a reply.

Do familiarize yourself with our house and our list before submitting your manuscript, and provide a rationale for why we are the best house for this work. If you're not sure which publisher would be best for your proposal, there are resources available to help you clarify your decision. A particularly good one is *The American Directory of Writer's Guidelines*, available at most libraries and bookstores.

Thank you for your interest in Ten Speed Press/Celestial Arts, and we look forward to reading your proposal soon.

Categories: Nonfiction—Agriculture—Animals—Business—Careers—Children—College—Cooking—Crafts—Diet—Food/Drink—Gardening—General Interest—Humor—Interview—Juvenile—Money/Finance—Outdoors—Recreation—reference—Regional—Travel

Name: Acquisitions Editor
Material: All
Address: PO BOX 7123
City/State/ZIP: BERKELEY CA 94707

Texas A&M University Press

Overview of the Publishing Process
ACQUISITION/SUBMISSION
The Press has established a respected list in several disciplines and will continue to build on those strengths by publishing books in the following fields: regional, military, and business history; natural history and related nature subjects; economics; agriculture; nautical archaeology; literature of Texas and the American West, including some works of short fiction and creative nonfiction; Texas art and photography; and women's, Borderlands, regional, and environmental studies.

If your manuscript or book idea seems to fit in one of these categories, or if you think it is on a subject the Press might wish to explore, your first step is to send a letter to the Press to describe the book you are writing or have written and the audience for which it is intended. With the letter, provide a table of contents, with a short synopsis of each chapter, as well as the introduction and another sample chapter if they are available.

We will respond to your query promptly to let you know if

your book is a candidate for full consideration by the Press. If it is, we will invite submission of the full work, which should include an indication of illustrative materials that will be available. Do not send original photographs or art work at that time.

The manuscript will be evaluated first by the Press staff. If it seems appropriate to our list, we will then send it to outside reviewers-specialists in the field-who usually remain anonymous to the author. The outside readers will be asked to provide specific recommendations for revision of the manuscript, if such are necessary, as well as general comments on its overall potential. The review process may take several weeks. To speed the process you may offer a second copy of the manuscript.

We will provide copies of the readers' reports, and you will be given the opportunity to respond to them. If extensive revisions are recommended by the readers, we may ask that you make those revisions before we continue with the review process. If the manuscript receives favorable reviews and does not need revision, or if recommended revisions are satisfactorily handled, the manuscript will be brought before the Faculty Advisory Committee, which meets monthly, for their approval to publish. Once the manuscript is approved, the Press staff prepare a preliminary estimate of its publishing costs and then offer a contract.

When the manuscript has been approved by the Faculty Advisory Committee and revised to the Press's satisfaction, and the contract has been signed, submit three copies of the final revised manuscript and a disk containing the files of the manuscript, as well as all illustrative material and copies of all permissions. The manuscript should be submitted as flat, loose sheets-unfolded, unbound, and unstapled-in a box. A more detailed description of how to prepare the final manuscript, on paper and on disk, and illustrations is included later in this guide.

Publishers normally divide the year into two publishing seasons: spring/summer (February through July) and fall/winter (August through January). We must work well ahead-sometimes as much as two to four seasons-and take many factors into account before deciding which season would be the appropriate time to publish a particular book. Because of these complexities and the unique requirements of every book, there is no rule of thumb to determine how long after acceptance a manuscript can be put into production and, ultimately, be offered for sale. Be assured, though, that we make every effort to produce every book that bears our imprint in a timely manner.

COPYEDITING

The manuscript will be edited by a copy editor, and the author will review the edited manuscript. When the house editor has resolved all editorial issues with the author and prepared a manuscript "package" of the book's parts, the manuscript is ready to be designed. This process of copyediting, review, and resolution normally takes three to four months. More time is required for large or difficult books.

DESIGN AND PRODUCTION

A book designer will specify type and layout for the book and design a dust jacket. Although the specifications and jacket design are ultimately the designer's and the Press's prerogative, authors are welcome to make suggestions to their editors.

The manuscript will be typeset, and the author will then proofread the typeset pages and prepare an index within the time agreed to in the contract.

The Press staff will check all subsequent proofs. After the book is printed and the bindery ships the finished books, the author will be sent the number of complimentary copies stipulated in the contract. The entire production process, from design through shipment of the books, normally takes six to eight months. More time is needed for books that are large, very complex, or heavily illustrated.

MARKETING

Near the time a fully executed contract is returned to the Press offices, the author will receive an author information form from the marketing department.

Authors should give the items on that questionnaire prompt and careful attention. Detailed responses on this form not only help the marketing staff as they prepare promotion plans but also serve as a reference for the house editor and the Library of Congress.

Books are promoted through advertising, publicity, direct mail, exhibits, on-line, classroom adoption, and trade sales programs, supported by national and international sales representation. Books are also entered in appropriate award competitions.

POST-PUBLICATION

Authors should contact the Press's order department if they wish to buy copies of their book (Phone Orders: 800-826-8911, FAX: 409-847-8752). Press authors receive a 40 percent discount on any book that TAMU Press publishes (excluding limited editions).

Physical Preparation of the Manuscript

Manuscripts submitted to Texas A&M University Press should be prepared according to the guidelines given here. Even if the book is to be typeset from the author's diskettes, three hard (paper) copies of the manuscript are needed.

THE HARD COPY

• All elements of the manuscript (including indented quotations often or more lines, epigraphs, captions, notes, and bibliography) should be typed or printed double-spaced.

• All pages should be printed or typed with ten-pitch (i.e., pica) type if possible, and word-processed manuscripts should be printed with a letter-quality or near-letter-quality printer.

• Turn off the right-justification and proportional letter spacing features on word processors and printers before printing a manuscript; it is difficult to make an accurate character count of the manuscript when lines have been justified.

• Late corrections may be made on the final copy by neatly writing them above the line in which they should be inserted. Longer revisions may be inserted as separate pages. Pages that have been corrected and reprinted using a word processor should be matched carefully to the preceding and following pages to be sure the newly printed page does not drop or duplicate any lines. To match such pages, it may be necessary to insert a temporary hard page code.

COMPUTER DISKS

The Press prefers that all manuscripts be submitted on disk. The Press can accept either 5¼" or 3½" disks and can work with the following IBM-compatible word processor formats: Microsoft Word, MultiMate, NotaBene, PFS:Write, Sprint, Wang PC (IWP), WordPerfect, WordStar, XyWrite. Acceptable Apple Macintosh formats include Microsoft Word, WordPerfect, and MacWrite II. "Text only" or "generic" files are also acceptable. If you use some other word processor, you should check with your editor to determine compatibility.

The following general guidelines are excerpted from a brochure produced by the Association of American University Presses.

• Prepare your manuscript on the same system-both hardware and software-from start to finish.

• Name files sequentially: chap01, chap02, etc. A list of file names submitted with your disks is helpful.

• Front matter, bibliography, and other apparatus should be in separate files. (In other words, do not put an entire manuscript in one file.)

• Notes should be grouped together in one or more separate files-not at the bottoms of pages or at the ends of chapters. If your word-processing software has the capability to do on-page (embedded) footnotes, please do not use it. Instead, use superscript callouts for note numbering. The notes should all be together, in a separate file or files, grouped and numbered by chapter, double-spaced and paragraph-indented, with no extra spaces between notes.

• Keep formatting to a minimum. Most if not all formatting must be removed before typesetting can begin, and this can be time-consuming or even unfeasible if it cannot be accomplished on a global basis. If you do use any formatting, make certain you are consistent.

• The hard copy of the manuscript and computer files must match exactly.

PARTS OF A MANUSCRIPT

Front Matter

The completed manuscript should contain a title page, dedication (if desired), book epigraph (if desired), table of contents, lists of any illustrations or tables, and a preface, acknowledgments, introduction, or foreword, if desired. Authors should note the differences between a preface, introduction, and foreword. In the preface the author gives details about the writing of the book; it may include brief acknowledgments. An introduction, as the name implies, introduces the subject of the book and background for that subject. A foreword is written by someone other than the author of the book. It provides another viewpoint and should attest to the book's value in the field.

Text

The text consists of all material through the end of the last chapter, epilogue, or postscript. If you use chapter epigraphs, keep them brief, citing only the author of the words quoted and perhaps the title of the work in which they appeared. Epigraphs should not be documented with endnotes or footnotes.

Back Matter

Back matter comprises the notes, bibliography, and any appendixes or glossary that will appear at the end of the book. In a manuscript, as opposed to a finished book, the last pages are usually tables and captions.

Page Numbers and Running Heads

Pages should be numbered consecutively through the manuscript, not by chapters. It is not necessary to add a running head (a top-of-the-page label such as chapter title or author's name) to the page number.

Elements to Be Aware of when Preparing a Manuscript

RIGHTS AND PERMISSIONS

Authors who are in the process of writing book manuscripts should take care to see that their work does not violate copyright laws.

If any substantial part of your work has been previously published, you will need to show evidence that you have the right to allow us to republish it. Such evidence should be presented to the Press when the manuscript is submitted for consideration.

The term fair use in the copyright law designates the way in which copyrighted material may be quoted without permission. In general, authors may quote without permission up to five hundred words in order to illustrate a point, substantiate a position, clarify an argument, or fulfill some such scholarly need. Letters of permission should be submitted with the manuscript.

Always obtain written permission to use:

• Any copyrighted material that is an entity itself, such as a map, a table, photograph, chapter of a book, article in a journal or newspaper, short story, poem, essay, or chart. Permission should be obtained from the author or copyright holder as well as the publisher.

• A private letter (the letter writer, not the recipient, holds the rights.)

• More than one line of a short poem or one stanza of a long poem.

• Music or words to a song.

• A reproduction of a work of art such as a painting or statue. The authority to grant permission to reproduce works of art may be held by the museum in which the art is located, by the artist, or by a private owner. Permission should be obtained at the time reproduction is made.

Signed releases should also be obtained from the subjects of interviews. U.S. government publications, uncopyrighted publications, and publications for which the copyright has expired may be used without requesting permission. Copyright duration under U.S. law is summarized here:

WORKS	COPYRIGHT TERM

Created or Published after 1978 Lifetime of author + 50 years

Anonymous, or made for hire 75 years from publication or 100 years from creation, whichever is sooner

Copyrighted between 1950 and 1978 28 years from original copyright date; may be renewed for 47 years more (for a total of 75 years); renewal is automatic for books published between 1964 and 1978

Copyrighted before 1950 and renewed 75 years from original copyright date

Copyrighted before 1950 and not renewed Expired

Works created before 1978 but not copyrighted or published Considered to be copyrighted as of January, 1978, except that copyright will not expire before December 31, 2002

To find out whether a copyright has been renewed, authors should consult the Catalog of Copyright Entries of the U.S. Copyright Office for the year in which the renewal should have been made (i.e., twenty-eight years after the original copyright date). It is best to send permissions requests to the rights holder in duplicate so that one copy can be retained by the rights holder and the signed copy returned to the author, who should make an additional copy for the Press.

The author is responsible for any fees assessed by rights holders and for supplying any complimentary copies of the book requested by the rights holders as a condition of granting permission.

A form that may be used to request permission or to gain use of material under different conditions is reproduced below.

When in doubt about using copyrighted material, authors should consult a Press editor.

INCLUSIVE LANGUAGE

The language and tone of books published by Texas A&M University Press should not be offensive to persons of any race, ethnic origin, religion, physical or mental condition, or gender and should be as inclusive as possible.

Editors employed by the Press will ensure that the accepted terms for designating racial or ethnic origin are used, except in direct quotations where historical accuracy requires special usage. Racial, ethnic, and gender stereotypes should not be used, except when clearly attributed to a source in a scholarly work and then only when such usage furthers the scholarly purpose of the work. Words derived from proper names should be capitalized; others should be lowercased. Two-word designations that indicate national origin are not hyphenated.

Inclusive language omits words that imply exclusion of either gender. Although it may be a historical fact that all the members of a city council were men, the word councilmen suggests the assumption that there could be no women on the council. On the other hand, it would never be inaccurate to say that there were x council members making decisions, etc., and that phrase avoids gender-biased implications.

Because there are suitable, neutral synonyms for most gender-based words in common usage, we discourage the use of such awkward constructions as "he or she" or compounds ending with the suffix "-person." Texas A&M University Press advocates the use of neutral synonyms and the third-person plural to eliminate language that is gender-based.

For example, the sentence

A group of influential businessmen was behind the decision.

is gender-specific. A good way to recast it would be:

Books

Influential members of the business community were behind the decision.

Language that creates imagery based on gender should be avoided. The example below illustrates how gender-based language can be replaced.

The sea beckoned men to explore her.

The sea beckoned, inviting explorers.

To avoid the possibility of heavy editing later on, authors who have questions about inclusive language may want to contact the copyediting department at the Press while they are still drafting the manuscript.

HOUSE STYLE

In general, Texas A&M University Press follows the style guidelines of the *Chicago Manual of Style* and the spelling conventions of *Webster's Third New International Dictionary* or *Webster's New Collegiate Dictionary.* Dictionaries differ on preferred spellings, so the Press follows Webster's in order to have a standard source when questions arise.

On some points Texas A&M University Press house style will differ from that described in the *Chicago Manual.* For example, we use American-style dates, with commas before and after the year, rather than the inverted European style:

October 6, 1966, NOT 6 October 1966

April, 1977, NOT April 1977

TAMUP house style also differs from that of the *Chicago Manual* in the writing of inclusive numbers. Because inclusive numbers are most often found in the index, detailed rules are listed in the indexing subsection of this guide, under Design and Production.

A variant on usual house style exists for military history titles, and authors writing in this field may request a copy of the special style sheet from a Press editor.

An author using a specialized style guide for a particular field should notify the Press editor of this and discuss the decision before submitting the manuscript for copyediting.

MULTI-AUTHOR VOLUMES

The compiler or editor of a volume consisting of symposium papers or other unpublished papers by various authors must submit written permission to publish from each of those authors at the time the manuscript is submitted for consideration. The compiler of a manuscript containing any previously published articles must have written permission from both the author of the article and from the original publisher. This written permission must be provided when the manuscript is submitted for consideration. If the original publisher or author of an article refuses permission or charges a fee beyond the amount the compiler wishes to pay, the content of the book will change. The problems that would arise if permission were not requested early on need not be spelled out.

The volume editor should see that the manuscript is submitted in a form that is internally consistent and follows the guidelines in this manual.

Photocopies of journal or newspaper articles should not be submitted as part of the manuscript. All components of the manuscript should be typewritten or printed with the same equipment.

Documentation should be consistent; if one article has footnotes, another has endnotes, and another has author-date citations and a reference list, one system should be selected and the rest of the articles in the volume be revised to conform to that style.

See the section of this guide on manuscript apparatus for more specific details on style for notes, bibliographies, display,. and so forth.

Manuscript Apparatus

NOTES

For most scholarly works in the humanities and social sciences, endnotes have become the standard form of documenta-

tion. In some circumstances, however, footnotes may be used instead. Authors should talk with Press editors before putting documentation in footnote style.

In books that have a bibliography, the notes need contain only author's name, title of article and journal (plus volume and issue number) or book, and relevant page numbers. Books that have notes but no bibliography (typically, an anthology or volume of essays) will generally have chapter endnotes, which will contain full publication information at first citation.

BIBLIOGRAPHIES

The bibliography should be as concise and easy to use as the content of the manuscript allows. Division of the bibliography into numerous sections for magazine articles, books, newspapers, and archival materials may be unnecessary and make the bibliography difficult to use. Make sure each subdivision is absolutely necessary and logical.

Bibliographies that list not only those works cited in the notes but also those which are of major significance in the field should be discussed with and approved by the Press editor responsible for development of that manuscript.

Double-space bibliographies, listing entries in alphabetical order (by section, if sections are used), starting each entry flush left, and indenting runover lines. When two or more works by one author are listed, replace the author's name with five hyphens on the second and subsequent entries.

For multi-author works, invert only the first name, and separate the author's names with semicolons.

ILLUSTRATIONS

In most cases authors are responsible for obtaining any photographs or drawings to be used in their books, securing written permission to use these materials, and paying any usage fees. Illustrations may add considerably to the cost of manufacturing a book, so their use should be discussed with the editors before the author has incurred the costs of obtaining them. Illustrations of any kind (including maps) should contribute significantly to the text; they should not be mere decoration. The Press will determine, in consultation with the author, the final number and selection of illustrations used.

Author-furnished illustrations received by the Press will be logged in and placed in our vault. They will be returned to the author about one year after the book is published, unless the Press is requested to return them sooner. The Press will exercise due caution when working with illustrations but is not responsible for loss or damage.

Permissions and Credit

After obtaining written agreements to use material owned by institutions or individuals other than yourself, submit the illustrations, double-spaced captions with the appropriate credit lines, and copies of letters granting permission to reproduce illustrations in your book and in its promotion.

Photographs

Photographs should be submitted as glossy black-and-white prints of at least 5"X7" for best reproduction. Consult the editor regarding the suitability of other sizes. Photocopied items do not reproduce well and should not be submitted as book illustrations.

Photographs should be submitted for color reproduction only with the approval of the editor. If color transparencies or slides are submitted for color reproduction, a color print should be submitted with them to show color quality. Color prints should not be submitted for illustrations to be produced in black and white. A glossy, black-and-white reproduction of a color print or transparency made in a professional photo-processing lab (which has been instructed to provide camera-quality copy) is usually acceptable, however.

Drawings and Diagrams

All line art should be professionally drawn. Clean, clear drawings or photographic prints of the original drawings should be proportional to the book page and no more than 50 percent larger than the approximate page size. Consult with the Press before committing to graphs or diagrams of a certain size.

Black sans-serif lettering is preferable. It should be large enough to be legible after reduction to book page size. Lines should be black and heavy enough to hold up in reduction.

A tissue overlay may be used to protect the surface of the finished drawing.

Maps

Authors are responsible for supplying professional-quality maps to be used in their books, unless special arrangements are made and agreed to in writing by the director or acquiring editor. Maps are protected under copyright laws and cannot simply be copied and reprinted from other books.

Before proposing to use a map, authors must ask themselves if the map is necessary, what it adds to the words in the text, what the clearest way of presenting the information is, if the map will look good on the printed page, and if the quality of a particular map is good enough for use in a book.

A map may be for purposes of reference, showing point locations, or it may be thematic, with information conveyed by means of shading, to show, for example, areas of low annual rainfall.

To compile a base map for use by a professional cartographer, find a map of the area needed. Trace a sketch map from the base map, eliminating any irrelevant detail while adding any details from individual research or from other maps. Like drawings, maps should be no more than 50 percent larger than they will appear on the book page.

Press editors will assist authors in determining the number of maps needed and can provide the names of qualified cartographers.

In making arrangements with cartographers, authors should keep in mind that all maps should be prepared as one-piece, black-and-white camera-ready art (Velox or photographic prints) suitable for reduction. Photocopies of the finished maps to be supplied should be submitted to the Press before an author fully commits to a final rendering. Final approval must await the copy editor's checking of the map against the text.

Map Materials

BASE: Use heavy, smooth white graphic board. Avoid Mylar, which may cast shadows when photographed by the printer.

GRAPHICS: U.S. Geographical Survey standards should normally be used in designating features. Lines should be even and black and thick enough to hold in reduction. Roman type is used for labeling cities, town, and mountain, and italic type is used for bodies of water. Compass north designation and graphic scale in miles (with metric equivalent) should be given.

TYPE: Use calligraphy or typeset lettering in Times Roman or Century serif face, or Optima, Helvetica, or Univers sanserif face. Maps or map labels generated by computer must be reviewed by the Press for legibility and output capabilities.

SHADING: Use Zip-a-Tone patterns, tightly burnished to minimize shadows. Overlays for multiple exposures are strongly discouraged and can be used only with the prior approval of the Press staff.

COMPUTER GENERATED MAPS: Many people are using computers to generate maps and using patterns from the computer. Please show samples to your editor (for referral to the design and production departments) before producing final copy. When the final manuscript is submitted, font files used on the maps should be included on the disk.

NUMBERING ILLUSTRATIONS

Never write on the front of photographs. Number them (and drawings) on the back, preferably with a soft grease pencil or a stick-on label. Ballpoint pen or pencil can leave a visible line on the photograph's emulsion, and ink can permanently damage the front of a photograph stacked underneath. Paper clips can also

damage photographs. Maps should be numbered on the front, outside the text area.

CAPTIONS

Write a caption for each illustration, putting any required credit line at the end. Captions should be numbered and typed double-spaced on a separate sheet of paper; captions should not be written on the illustrations themselves or attached to them. If an illustration is keyed to a particular page in the manuscript, indicate that page number on the caption sheet or an accompanying illustration identification list.

TABLES

• Separate the tables from the text, placing them with other text apparatus at the back of the manuscript.

• Tables should be numbered sequentially throughout the text unless (1) the manuscript is a compilation of essays, or (2) the manuscript is a reference work with figures and tables numbered to indicate chapter (e.g., Table 2.3, Fig. 3.1). In the text discussion, refer to each table by number, not by position.

• Each table should have a title of reasonable length.

• When preparing tables, keep in mind the size of a normal vertical book page. Tables that would require quarter-turns (sideways placement) should be avoided.

• Horizontal lines may be used to separate the table title from column heads and table text from table notes. Do not use vertical lines.

• Footnotes to a table should be called out by italic letters rather than by Arabic numerals.

• If the table is taken from a published source, the author must have the original author's and publisher's written permission to use it. Under the table text, above any footnotes, indicate the source of the table using standard bibliographical information.

• If tables are to be provided on disks with the manuscript, please consult with the editor, who will check with Design and Production on specific guidelines.

Copyediting

University presses can bring forth a high-quality book in ten to twelve months. More complicated books may take longer. The time required to actually produce the book begins when the manuscript is assigned to a copy editor.

A manuscript is a candidate for assignment to a copy editor when all materials are in house-two final, complete manuscript copies; all illustrations; and all permissions documents. At this time the tentative season of publication may be designated.

The copy editor will edit the manuscript for style, grammar, spelling, punctuation, and general integrity of text. Manuscripts edited on disk will show queries as footnotes on the edited printout and will usually also include a comparison printout showing changes made. Queries will be written on tabs attached to the margin of manuscripts not submitted on disk. At this stage, the editor may also select the illustrations to be used from those submitted. The editor also compares map text to manuscript text. If there are discrepancies, corrections may be needed on the map, and the authors should keep their cartographers aware of this possibility.

Discussion about the title of the book may not occur until the manuscript-editing stage. The editor may relay to the author suggestions for a new title or subtitle. Although the title of a book is ultimately the publisher's decision, we do everything possible to make sure that authors approve of the final titles of their books.

When copyediting is complete, the editor will draft some text to be used on the dust jacket flaps or on the back cover of a paperbound book. The editor then sends the edited manuscript and this draft of dust jacket or cover copy to the author for approval.

At this point, authors should read through the manuscript carefully, page by page, and answer all queries. Responses may be written at the point of the query, or check marks placed there to indicate concurrence with the editor's comment. If a response requires more space, the author may attach an additional query tab or page and write responses there.

The review of edited copy by authors represents the last opportunity to make changes in the text. Corrections to proofs are expensive and time consuming and may not be made unless the unaltered material would compromise the integrity of the book. Alterations required for this reason may be charged to the author.

Editors responsible for volumes of essays will likely be asked to send photocopies of the copyedited essays to the authors. The volume editor must be sure to convey the importance of retaining consistency, making sure that all changes are final, and meeting the deadline. Essays not returned by the deadline should be considered approved by the author.

The edited copy should be returned to the Press by the date requested. A missed deadline anytime during the copyediting and production phase can delay a book's publication and cause a host of related problems. Deadlines missed by a significant amount, such as a week or two, may translate into a publication delay of many weeks or even months.

The Press prefers that manuscripts be shipped by a private carrier whose shipping fee includes insurance and tracing services if the package is lost. Manuscripts sent by U.S. mail should go first class and be insured for fifty dollars.

The editor reviews the author's responses to queries, consulting with the author on any final points, and then submits the manuscript to the design and production departments.

Design and Production
DESIGN
Authors are invited to convey to the editor any ideas about their book's design or dust jacket. The editor will pass this information along to the designer, but the decision on all elements of design, including the dust jacket, belongs to the Press and the designers it employs.

PROOFREADING
After the manuscript has been designed and typeset, the author will receive proofs. The Press usually sends galley proofs (long sheets of unpaged type) to authors only when the book is very heavily illustrated. Most authors will receive only page proofs. These are facsimiles of the made-up pages.

Proofreading is the author's responsibility; page proofs will not necessarily be read by the editor or production staff. Most authors will receive two sets of page proof plus the edited manuscript. The first set of pages is to be proofread and marked for correction. The second set is to be marked up in preparation for indexing.

To proofread typeset text, compare it word for word to the edited manuscript. Pay close attention to the lines that contain an error; errors found in the same general vicinity are often missed. Also pay careful attention to display type; it is easy to pore carefully through ten-point text type and overlook typos in the large display type. Repeated or missing lines of manuscript text and substitution of one word for another can escape a careless proofreader.

Proofs must be marked clearly so that the editor and compositor know exactly what corrections are needed.

Make a small slash mark in the line of type that needs a correction, and in the margin place the appropriate proofreading symbol. If more than one alteration is needed in a line, the correction symbols in the margin should appear in the proper order, from left to right, separated by a vertical or diagonal line.

Use regular lead pencil to indicate typographic errors—those errors which differ from the edited manuscript. The compositor is obliged to follow the manuscript letter for letter, so any mistakes in proof that are copied from the manuscript should not be considered compositor's errors.

Use a colored pencil to indicate editorial errors or author's alterations. Such changes are expensive, both in time and money, and new errors could be introduced when the change is made. Pagination must not be affected in making a change, as the index must be prepared from this set of paginated proof.

If an author alteration is deemed necessary, however, make the altered line approximately the same length as the original line.

As specified in the contract, compositor's errors will be corrected without expense to you, but you will be charged for author alterations that exceed the percentage of the total typesetting cost specified in your contract. Correction of editorial errors will not be charged to you.

INDEXING
Indexing may not be the most enjoyable aspect of producing a book, but it is one of the most important for scholarly works. An inadequate or error-ridden index may lock the door to an otherwise valuable resource.

If the Press determines that an index will be needed for a particular book, it is the author's responsibility to provide one within the time allotted, typically a couple of weeks. Authors are strongly encouraged to prepare their own indexes and review indexing procedures well in advance. If the author chooses not to do so, the Press can hire a freelance indexer at the author's expense. If a freelancer prepares the index, there is rarely enough time for the author to review the product.

Although many authors now produce manuscripts on word processors, the software programs that include an "indexing" feature will still require the author's expertise in analyzing the text for main entries, subentries, and cross-references. Without a special program designed specifically for indexing complex material, a considerable amount of manual alphabetizing and editing will also be needed for the index sorted by computer.

The finished index should be typed or printed on 8½"x11" paper. Double-space the entire index, including subentries. If possible, a disk should be sent in addition to the printout.

Form
Texas A&M University Press follows closely the style recommendations of the *Chicago Manual of Style*. The Press will lend authors an offprint of the *Chicago Manual*'s chapter on indexing. By following its guidelines, authors can be confident that their indexes will be acceptable in form.

Follow the example in the *Chicago Manual* that uses run-in subentries. Authors should consult their editors before deciding to prepare an index that may require a more elaborate breakdown of entries.

Content
In general, an index should be more than a proper-name list. It should include substantive entries (e.g., alcoholism; customs; dress; political parties) and conceptual entries (e.g., authority; imperialism; manifest destiny; natural law). Only in rare circumstances are separate indexes (e.g., for subjects as opposed to persons) advisable.

Alphabetizing
• Use the letter-by-letter system of alphabetizing described in the *Chicago Manual.*

Main
• Start main entries with a lowercase letter unless the entry is a proper name.
• Reverse the order of words in a main entry to place a descriptive adjective or phrase after it. If there are no subentries and the reversal places the beginning of the description in the reversed position, separate the entry from the page numbers with commas:

Subentries
• If subentries are used or if the descriptive phrase comes after the main entry, separate the main entry from the suben-

tries or descriptive phrase with a colon:

• Use the run-in style for subentries unless instructed to do otherwise.

Page Numbers

• Use italics for page numbers that refer to illustration legends or caption. Place a note to that effect at the beginning of the index.

• Use no more than ten page numbers after a main entry. If more page numbers are required, break the entry down into subentries.

• Never use ff. after page numbers.

• Texas A&M University Press follows a style for inclusive numbers that is somewhat different from that suggested by the *Chicago Manual.* In preparing an index, please follow the style summarized here:

Use *all digits* if:

a) the first number is under 100:

3-10 32-37 97-129

b) the second number ends in 00-09:

704-705 997-1102 1002-1003 1895-1902

c) the second number goes into the next hundred or more:

996-1138 1697-1721 2,000-2,500

For all other inclusive numbers, use only the *last two digits* of the second number of the pair:

107-23 321-25 1304-29 1536-38

Authors who have read their proofs and prepared a satisfactory index have completed their work on the book. The editor will transfer all appropriate corrections to the master proofs and copyedit the index. After the compositors have set corrections and the index, the editor will proofread them.

The Press will send the author a finished dust jacket as soon as it is printed. The author will also receive one complimentary advance copy of the book; the remainder of the author's allotment of complimentary copies will be mailed after the main shipment of books has arrived at the Press.

If you have further questions about publishing with Texas A&M University Press, feel free to call or write and we will be glad to help in any way we can.

Permission to Use material

I am presently preparing a book to be entitled

_____

I would like to include the following material:

_____

I request your permission to include this material in the original and all subsequent editions of my book and in all foreign-language translations published by the Texas A&M University Press or its licensees, and in publicity, promotion, and advertising for this book.

Please indicate your agreement by signing and returning this letter.

Thank you for your cooperation.

Sincerely yours,

AGREED TO AND ACCEPTED:

By: Date _____

Unless otherwise specified, the credit line will acknowledge the granting agency and/or collection by name only. Please provide the name as you wish it to appear:

_____

Categories: Nonfiction—Agriculture—Anthropology—Archaeology—Architecture (Texas)—Business—Culture—Economics—Eastern Europe—Folklore—Geography—Hispanic—History (Texas)—Military—Multicultural—Native American—Natural Science—Regional (Southwestern Borderlands)—Social Sciences—Women's Issues

Name: Diane L. Vance, Editorial Assistant
Material: All

Address: DRAWER C
City/State/ZIP: COLLEGE STATION TX 77843-4354
Telephone: 409-845-1436
Fax: 409-847-8752
E-mail: dlv@tampress.tamu.edu

Third Side Press

KIND OF THINGS WE ARE LOOKING FOR

• Third Side Press publishes books by women in two basic categories: lesbian literary fiction and women's health.

• We define *lesbian fiction* to mean fiction that is written by a lesbian and that has at least one lesbian as a primary character. We are looking for well-crafted, contemporary novels. We are particularly swayed by creative use of language and innovative ways of looking at the world. Also, we are particularly interested in plots that involve women in their communities (however they define them).

• We are particularly interested in manuscripts that focus on diseases (lupus, chronic fatigue syndrome, ovarian cancer, etc.) and ways of dealing with them. We are also particularly interested in manuscripts that focus on, or at least include information specifically for, lesbians.

THINGS WE ARE *NOT* LOOKING FOR

• We do not publish poetry.

• We do not publish collections of short stories by individual authors.

• We occasionally publish anthologies of short stories, but those are developed by their editors. Therefore, we do not consider individual short stories for publication.

• We rarely publish novels with plots that focus on "coming out."

• We rarely publish mysteries.

TIPS

• **ALL WRITERS:** Please read or at least look at a few of our books to get a feel for what we do, before you send us a manuscript.

• **FICTION WRITERS:** We prefer completed manuscripts, but will read a sample chapter if you let us know that it's from a completed novel manuscript. Please include a plot synopsis.

• **NONFICTION WRITERS:** Please query first. After that, if you do not have a completed manuscript, please provide at least an outline and two sample chapters.

• **POETS:** Please do not send manuscripts to Third Side Press.

MANUSCRIPT PREPARATION

1. If you have any doubt about whether your manuscript (fiction or nonfiction) fits our basic categories, send a query letter first.

2. For initial reading purposes, a typed (or computer-printed) copy is required. Please make sure the type is large enough to read (not smaller than the type on this page, for example). Some form of binding (comb binding or vitabinding, for example) is recommended but not required.

3. Ultimately, manuscripts accepted for publication must be provided on computer diskette (IBM-compatible or high-density Mac format).

4. Please include a resume, vita, or other form of biographical information to let us get a sense of who you are.

5. Send a self addressed, stamped postcard if you want immediate acknowledgment that your manuscript has been received.

6. Please do not send manuscripts by e-mail.

MISSION STATEMENT

At Third Side Press, we believe in taking risks by publishing ideas that need to get out into the world, thereby strengthening the ties among humans and making better understandings possible. Our goal is to help readers look at their lives through a new

Books

lens, from a third side, focusing on what is good in themselves and considering what is possible.

Categories: Fiction—Nonfiction—Feminism—Lesbian—Health—Literature—Psychology—Women's Fiction—Women's issues

Name: Midge Stocker, Editor and publisher
Material: All
Address: 2250 W FARRAGUT
City/State/ZIP: CHICAGO IL 60625-1863
Telephone: 773-271-3029
Fax: 773-271-0459
E-mail: Third Side@aol.com

Thomas Jefferson University Press
New Odyssey Press, New Odyssey Review

TJUP publishes scholarly works in the humanities. Our series include Sixteenth Century Essays and Studies, Mediterranean Studies, and the Bethsaida Excavations Project. We have also published trade titles such as *Naked Heart: A Soldier's Journey to the Front*, a memoir of a private's experience in WWII and *Hurley and the Bone*, a children's book. Obviously, our interests are wide and varied. Please query before sending a manuscript.

New Odyssey Press Editorial Statement
New Odyssey Press selects for publication only the best creative and critical works in poetry (including work in translation), works worthy of leading the American poetic tradition into the next millennium with vision, sincerity, and integrity. Series and serials include the T. S. Eliot Prize for Poetry and *New Odyssey Review*

Submission Guidelines
Please take a look at our books or the *New Odyssey Review* to get a feel for what we publish. Our readers are intelligent and educated, but they're not necessarily professional academics.

Manuscripts may be either single or double spaced, typed or computer printed (laser-printed materials preferred). Always include a cover letter. If your manuscript is over 200 pages, please query first and include an excerpt from the manuscript.

Response time varies, but you should usually hear something from us within a month. We often prefer to communicate via e-mail, so please include your e-mail address, if available.

Don't hesitate to contact New Odyssey Press for more information.

Categories: Literature—Poetry

Name: Timothy Rolands, Poetry Editor
Material: All
Address: 100 E NORMAL ST MC111L
City/State/ZIP: KIRKSVILLE MO 63501-4221
Telephone: 816-785-7299
Fax: 816-785-4181
E-mail: newodyssey@tjup.truman.edu

Thomas Nelson Reference Publishing

We welcome proposals for reference books that promise to serve readers well. We want to review a book proposal before receiving a completed manuscript. Reviewing and making initial

publishing decisions on the basis of a proposal, rather than a completed manuscript, is almost always in the best interests of both the author and the publisher. Even if you have completed a manuscript you wish us to review, **please prepare and submit a proposal first.** Write the proposal as well as you can; in deciding whether or not to pursue publication, we will consider not only the merits of your proposal, but also the quality of your writing.

Do the following in your proposal:

1. State the books purpose and scope. Usually one paragraph is sufficient. The purpose statement should identify what your proposed work enables readers to do; and the statement of scope should identify your works range or depth of treatment. Keep in mind that we publish almost exclusively for the lay and general audience. We rarely publish works primarily for an academic audience. However, we do publish works that have special value for ministers and other church leaders when those works are also clearly useable by lay and general readers.

2. Describe the primary audience of the book and any secondary audiences. For us, the formula to publishing success requires books to have both merit and marketability. To determine marketability, we need to know who are the target buyers and who are the secondary ones.

Think carefully about who would benefit the most from what your work offers. Think about the situations in which your work would be used and what it assumes the target reader will already know, be able to do, and desire.

Sometimes the primary audience may be truly general. For example, the primary audience for a desktop or collegiate dictionary of American English includes all truly literate Americans—all who want help with words they find in their reading or use in their writing or speaking. But often the primary audience of a book is smaller. For example, the primary audience of our academically oriented *Word Biblical Commentary* differs greatly from the primary audience of our *Communicators Commentary*, which aims at helping preachers and teachers move from the biblical text to their contemporary listeners.

Describe your works primary and secondary audience(s) as realistically and precisely as you can.

3. Demonstrate the need for the book by analyzing the books already on the market with which it will compete. Research all books on the market that are at all similar to the work you propose. Identify and list in a comparative table the features and benefits to the reader for each; then list the features and benefits of your work. Indicate how your book will surpass what is now available. If no other books do what you propose to do, explain why that is the case. *Do not overlook the importance of this step.* Your proposal is your attempt to make a strong case for our publishing your work, and we need you to show us that you know what is already available and why the target audience for your work would buy it over another book.

4. Summarize the main points of each chapter with an annotated Table of Contents. Two to five sentences per chapter is usually enough. State concisely what each chapter does, as well as how each chapter benefits the reader. Some reference books are not, of course, divided into chapters. For such a work, treat each major section as a chapter.

5. Provide two or three complete chapters (or representative samples of major sections if the work is not organized in chapters). Provide an introductory chapter that sets the task of the rest of the book, the chapter you believe provides the most helpful or distinctive information, and a chapter that summarizes and concludes the work. For works not divided into chapters, provide a full introduction and representative samples of each major section. For these representative samplings, include a group of continuous pages that shows all the features of that section.

6. Estimate the length of the complete manuscript (in double-spaced pages and in total words) and the date by which

you could complete it.

7. Describe the kinds and quantity of non-text material to be included in the work. Such items include photographs, line art, charts, tables, graphs, and maps. Indicate which you can provide and which you expect the publisher to provide. Keep in mind that properly illustrating a book enhances its value greatly but that such illustrations usually also raise the cost of its production. Be judicious in specifying non-text material that will not be provided in camera-ready form. (For example, photographs are not camera ready, while line drawings are.)

8. Identify authorities in the subject field of your work who you believe will endorse or contribute a Foreword to your work. Especially if you are a new author, the marketability of your work increases at least partly to the extent to which you can solicit good endorsements. At the proposal stage, we must have only a list of potential endorsers. Depending on the work and the extent to which you are known as an author, we may agree to publish your work contingent on your getting enough satisfactory endorsements.

9. Indicate if you are submitting this proposal to other publishers at the same time. We prefer that you propose your work only to us; however, if you have proposed it to other publishers also, please tell us.

10. Provide information about you—the contents of a resume or vita (although not necessarily that formal), along with an emphasis on the education and/or experience that qualifies you as somewhat of an authority on the topic your work covers.

11. Allow us twelve weeks after receipt of your proposal before you call to ask about its review. We will acknowledge receipt of your proposal by letter.

Categories: Reference—Religion

Name: Mark Roberts, Acquisitions Editor
Material: All
Address: 501 NELSON PL
Address: [PO BOX 141000]
City/State/ZIP: NASHVILLE TN 37214[-1000]
Telephone: 615-889-9000
Fax: 615-391-5225

Tia Chucha Press

Dear Author:

Thank you for your interest in Tia Chucha Press. Ours is a culturally diverse, performance-oriented publishing house of emerging socially-engaged poetry. There are no restrictions as to style or content—poetry that "knocks us off our feet" is what we are looking for.

Our annual deadline is June 30. Please send a complete manuscript, your best work (no fillers please). The submission should be single-spaced, typed or on a letter quality printer, and no more than one poem per page (although a poem can go on for several pages). We need more than 50 pages preferably 60 to 100 pages). We publish only in English, but will look at bilingual editions if they are powerful in both languages.

The editors decide in the fall which books to publish for the following year. The process is competitive. We receive about 100 manuscripts a year; we can only publish two to four books a year. Still, it's worth trying.

Good luck in all your writing efforts.
The Editors
Categories: Poetry

Name: Editors
Material: Poetry manuscripts
Address: PO BOX 476969
City/State/ZIP: CHICAGO IL 60647

Telephone: 773-907-2189
Fax: 773-907-2184
E-mail: Guild@charlie.cns.iit.edu

Timson Edwards Publishing
The Leaping Frog Press

An Overview of the Submission Process For Our Annual Anthology

The Wild Wood Reader was created as a bedside book filled with a whimsical collection of short fiction written by contemporary writers for today's leisure and casual reader.

It was also intended to become a collection of books that could be looked upon as and for, a reference of an author's early work, as done by the new writers of our society. Magazines and most paper backs books are generally not kept for very long, we hope that these books will.

There are many things that a small publisher wants and needs to see from an author sending in their manuscript for consideration. None of it, for the most part, hinges or is based on, whether or not that writer has ever been published.

Good writing for the most part begins with a terrific idea, story line, plot and characters. Like ingredients in a meal, if you take exotic herbs, spices, meats, vegetables and you mix the right amounts, cook them and present them properly you have a wonderful meal. The, same goes for something healthy and not so exotic, done right and you still have a wonderful meal. Now you take the two examples above and do just one thing wrong and your guest will not be pleased.

The same theory applies to stories, and it is more basic than cooking. If you do not present it professionally, it is not going to be seen much less read by anyone except the mail room clerk. Especially if you are sending something that is unsolicited. *Always query first and use the KIS approach, keep it simple.*

This does not mean that everything written has got to be deep, thought provoking prose with Ph.D. college level words. There are many good stories that are light and flow and are entertaining on many levels. Good work and professional presentations go hand in hand with acceptance and publishing. There is no good reason, with the exception of an incredible story idea and or plot, for an editor or publisher to subject themselves to bad grammar, punctuation and syntax. Even with the few exceptions, there are markets for this stream of conscience style of writing and you should do your research to find them and query etc.

Nobody likes to do someone else's work. This includes editors. Time after time I've heard it said that this writer should have had their story read by someone else. It is difficult, sometimes, to read your own work objectively. That is why we have editors who refine, with subtle changes, the writing to coincide with their idea of how it should read. They are not paid to rewrite material other than perhaps their own.

Nobody likes to see their work changed in any way. Folks! the publisher and editor are paying you for your writing, usually, and they will want to make sure that it is to their liking. They will want to see their influence, because it is their book or magazine. Later if you do not like what they did to the story, it is then up to you to accept it and move on or decline the use. Create valid arguments for keeping something in the story. Either way, it becomes sort of a chess game, it is still your story, plot and characters which ever way it is published or refined.

Books

Build yourself a small group of peers that have the same goals, to network and read each other's materials. Make it a point to show the work by committee, in order to read and critique each one's work prior to sending it in. A critical review or reading by someone you know is easier to handle than by an editor in the form of a rejection slip.

There are several things involved when there is a presentation of material to make, to anyone. They are not in any specific order, however, each one weighs heavily on the other and it makes for a better looking package.

Your Stationery:

As any business person will attest, like clothing at a function, your letterhead should be well designed if not simple and printed on good paper. There is a big difference between the good, white 24 lb. (weight of the ream) 100% rag paper and the decorative parchment and embellished variety. Save the pretty and embellished papers for greeting cards, personal invitations and fliers; it will not function well as a good business to business tool.

Your Treatment of the Manuscript:

Binding the pages of your manuscript is every bit as important as your selection of stationery. Stapled, folded and clipped pages have their own unique way of making themselves obtrusive and annoying. Those methods of binding will not make for easy page turning or efficient interoffice mail. Some editors like loose pages, again follow the guidelines.

Use plastic comb binding and good solid undecorated, though titled covers for your manuscripts. There is nothing worse than trying to meet deadlines with a pile of work in front of you, and fearing the disassembly of a manuscript. Don't leave the handling of your work to chance and rely on other peoples' consideration and respect for your body of work.

We (and that means just us because all presses are different) want our submissions to have a cover page which outlines the word count (800 minimum to 4,200 maximum for us) name, address, phone number, social security number for payment, 50 words about the story and the total number of pages. The story should have headers with your last name, title, page number. Double-spaced lines printed by laser, ink jet or a 24-pin dot matrix printer set on high quality.

Packaging:

The care and packaging of your work will help the handler realize that you care about the handling. It tells them please be careful, this is precious and should be handled with care. If using paper envelopes, use board inserts.

Shipping Method:

If you skimp on the methods, and try to get the cheapest price and service then likewise it shows that you don't care about the contents. Everyone knows that the post office will not handle things as well if first class is not indicated nor is it paid for. Printed matter is not the way to go, printed matter is just that to them: printed matter and easily replaced.

Return Methods and Packaging:

Make it just as easy for someone to return your materials neat and easy. Make all packaging materials re-useable. Always include air bills, international reply coupons or postage, do not make that person get up and do your work.

Summary:

The above briefs and ideas are just the small suggestions I can offer, it is all encompassed under marketing and presentations. Whether you are presenting a cake or a manuscript, the fanfare with which it is done will have a direct effect on the product and the presenter.

All of these items will no doubt serve to affect the editor's perception of you as a professional writer and business person overall, particularly with regard to responsibility to your writing and delivery of future stories. Anything you do to your material will reflect your work habits and professionalism.

Future Submission Opportunities:

I will share some of the future projects that I intend to pursue and hopefully move on to publish. The areas that most concern me are family, photography and music. The story possibilities are always endless, but I'm looking for material that has a long shelf life, with exposure to different values and cultures.

When sending me a manuscript, think along the lines that it should be a classic and that many years from now, someone will talk about it, and feel that many of those issues still apply. Read the classics and anything else you can get your hands on. Reading good work exposes you to good technique and helps embellish your own thinking and style. I know we hardly have the time to even read many of the instructional materials out there. But, think of the classics as just a classroom tutorial and reread them with a researcher's mindset, not entertainment.

I want this sort of writing because it would be nice to stay in print and on the shelves for many years. Have the works become a sort of must read for anyone at any level. Eventually each anthology will have its own theme and find its own audience. For now the books will be loosely constructed of a wide choice in the subject matter and many voices, albeit in harmony.

All books will come under the title or imprint, *The Wild Wood Reader,* with the appropriate subtitles or headings that follow for each region of the country. Southeast, Northeast, Northwest, Southwest; Anthology of New and Emerging Writers.

Personal Comments:

Thank you for taking the time to read this through, I hope that it is useful and inspirational to you for your future works. I know that if you put these things in practice you will better your odds of being read and published.

What I have attempted here is to give you a general overview of what you will discover and my experiences with presenting material to a buyer. In essence, you are selling and they are buying. Spruce it up before sending it out, but don't overdo it.

About the Press

The Leaping Frog Press was formed and is dedicated to helping new and emerging writers find their inner voice and their audience. With future regional editions forthcoming, it is the perfect vehicle to help those new writers become known in their own backyards first [before] moving on to greater and greener pastures.

If you know of someone that is interested in subscribing to these small, limited, collector's editions please have them contact me.

Thank your for your time.

Sincerely,

Alejandro "Alex" Gonzalez

Publisher & Editorial Director

Categories: Fiction—Culture—Family—Gay/Lesbian—General Interest—Hispanic—Inspirational—Lifestyles—Literature—Marriage—Photography—Relationships—Romance—Rural America—Short Stories—Society

Name: Alejandro Gonzalez-Cerda, Publisher/Editorial Director
Material: All
Address: PO BOX 44-0735 (AD)
City/State/ZIP: MIAMI FL 33144-0735
Fax: 305-668-0636

Tower Publishing

Tower specializes in legal and professional business publications. Submittals should take the form of a listing of chapters offered and at least three sample chapters. The market should be business or legal.

Categories: Business—Law—Reference

Name: Acquisitions Editor
Material: All
Address: 588 SACO RD
City/State/ZIP: STANDISH ME 04084
Telephone: 207-642-8400
Fax: 207-642-5463

Unity Books
Unity House

Unity Books is a department of Unity School of Christianity, a non-denominational religious organization. Unity's teachings are based on metaphysical interpretation of scriptures with an emphasis on practical application, and the demonstration of the spiritual Truth of life as taught by Jesus Christ. If you would like further information about Unity's teachings and beliefs, please contact Customer Service at the address below, or call 1-800-669-0282, 7:30-4:30 CST, Monday through Thursday.

WHAT WE'RE LOOKING FOR

We publish metaphysical Christian books based on Unity principles, as well as inspirational books on metaphysics and practical spirituality. All manuscripts must reflect a spiritual foundation and express the Unity philosophy, practical Christianity, universal principles, and/or metaphysics. We're looking for proposals (not complete manuscripts).

In reviewing proposals, one of the first things we consider is whether or not the subject would be appropriate for a person on a path of enlightenment and wholeness. The subject should be dealt with in such a way as to inform and uplift the reader, give hope, and assist with practical advice on meeting life's challenges creatively and positively. Emphasis should be on practical application of spiritual principles in everyday living. The following will give you an idea of a few of our editorial interests:

Fiction: Metaphysical fiction for adults and adolescents, children's stories (5-12 years) based on Unity principles*

Nonfiction: Bible interpretation, biblical studies, children's issues (5-12 years), comparative religion, Eastern thought, family, finances, holistic health, humor, inspiration, leadership, meditation, marriage, mythology, philosophy, parenting, personal experience, prayer, psychology, recovery, renewal, spirituality, teens, and young adult issues

Some of our current titles and authors include: *Finding Yourself in Transition* by Robert Brumet; *The Quest* and *Adventures on the Quest* by Mary-Alice and Richard Jafolla; *Spiritual Economics* by Eric Butterworth.

WHAT SHOULD I INCLUDE IN MY PROPOSAL?

When sending a proposal, we would like to receive the following:

• A brief cover letter introducing yourself and a brief biographical resume describing your writing, education, and religious background.

• A summary highlighting your proposal and its compelling, unique features—include suggested sales and publicity strategies.

• A project outline and/or table of contents.

• One to three sample chapters.

• Date your manuscript will be finished.

Please do not submit an entire manuscript at this stage. If we receive a manuscript in a form other than we have described above, we will not begin to evaluate the manuscript until we have received the aforementioned items. When we receive your proposal, we will review it and make our decision within eight weeks.

WHEN WE ASK FOR YOUR MANUSCRIPT

If we decide that your proposal will fit within the Unity Books guidelines, we may request additional materials. If done on a computer-driven printer, your manuscript must be of laser quality. If we decide to publish your manuscript, we will ask to receive an IBM-compatible computer disc using a version of WordPerfect. The same guidelines apply to typewritten manuscripts. If we publish your manuscript we do have the capability to scan your manuscript into our system.

We prefer that manuscripts be between 40,000 and 75,000 words in length. The pages should be numbered consecutively throughout the manuscript, with your book title at the top of each page.

If you quote an individual source more than casually (roughly more than 200 words in 200 pages of manuscript—less than this will usually constitute "fair use"), then you must seek formal permission from the publisher of your source. Furthermore, this guideline is not a legal guarantee of fair use nor a protection that we are offering as the publisher. Receiving permission to quote copyrighted material is your responsibility, and you are responsible for paying any fees (usually minimal) for this. Your manuscript draft will not be considered final until we have received a copy of each permission for our files.

All quotes must be verified by sending us a photocopy of the page on which the quote appears as well as a photocopy of the work's title and copyright page. If we cannot verify your quote, then we cannot use it. Please be sure all quoted material is quoted exactly.

If in your text you are referring to facts or statistics that are not easily verifiable with a good encyclopedia, world almanac, or unabridged dictionary, we would strongly appreciate your sending us a copy of your source reference. This will help us assure that your book will be accurate.

We prefer to have Bible quotations conform to the New Revised Standard Version, but we will accept other translations if their version better makes your textual point. Please identify which version you are using.

We do not solicit artwork or graphic design. However, if your manuscript requires specific photographs that you can furnish, we will be happy to consider them.

IF WE PUBLISH YOUR MANUSCRIPT

If accepted, expect publication in 12-18 months. Payment contracts vary for the individual author. Copyrights are registered in the author's name.

*Due to the large quantity of our current projects we are not accepting submissions for the **WEE WISDOM**® children's book line at this time. Please feel free to contact our offices in the future regarding the status of children's manuscript submissions.

Thank you for your interest in publishing through Unity. If you have further questions regarding book publishing, please feel free to contact this office.

Categories: Fiction—Nonfiction—New Age—Religion—Spiritual—New Thought/Metaphysical

Name: Raymond Teague, Associate Editor
Material: All
Address: 1901 NW BLUE PKWY
City/State/ZIP: UNITY VILLAGE MO 64086
Telephone: 816-524-3550 ext. 3190
Fax: 816-251-3552
Internet: www.unityworldhq.org

University Editions, Inc.
Book Publishers

University Editions will be considering new manuscripts for possible book publication in the following categories:

Fiction
Nonfiction
Children's Books
Poetry
Genre Fiction (Science Fiction, Fantasy, Horror, etc.)
Short Story Collections
General Nonfiction: Biographies, Essays, Histories, etc.

Manuscripts should be typed. A cover letter should accompany the manuscript, which states the approximate length to the nearest 5,000 words (not necessary for poetry). A brief synopsis of the manuscript and a listing of the author's publishing credits (if any) is helpful but not required.

Queries, sample chapters, synopses, and completed manuscripts are welcome. Allow 1-2 weeks for reply to queries, one month for reply to complete manuscripts.

Categories: Fiction—Nonfiction—Adventure—African-American—Asian-American—Children—Confession—Crime—Fantasy—General Interest—Horror—Juvenile—Literature—Men's Fiction—Mystery—Poetry—Romance—Science Fiction—Short Stories—Women's Fiction—Writing—Young Adult

Name: Ira Herman, Managing Editor
Material: All
Address: 1905 MADISON AVE
City/State/ZIP: HUNTINGTON WV 25704
Telephone: 304-429-7204
Fax: 304-429-7234

University of Maine Press

The University of Maine Press publishes scholarly books and original writing which focus on the intellectual concerns of the Maine region. Although the Press occasionally publishes works of regional fiction, and works of nonfiction which are outside its area of focus, the Press is primarily interested in publishing scholarly studies in the sciences, social sciences and humanities.

An author who is considering the University of Maine Press should send a letter of inquiry, a synopsis, and—if appropriate—a few representative chapters or sections from the manuscript of the proposed book. The entire manuscript should not be sent to the Press with the initial inquiry.

Since proposals for books need to be considered by the Director of the Press, the Board of Directors and outside expert readers, a thorough consideration of the initial manuscript material may take several months. The Director of the Press will make every attempt to expedite this process. Correspondence about the status of a proposal should be sent to the Diirector of the Press at the address below.

All manuscript material should be presented in a typewriter typeface, to facilitate reading and annotation. Manuscript material in obvious need of basic copy-editing will not be considered by the Press. In general, authors should prepare manuscript material by following the guidelines in *The Chicago Manual of Style* or a comparable standard style manual in the author's discipline.

Categories: Nonfiction—Agriculture—Arts—Biography—Civil War—History—Regional

Name: Michael Alpert, Director
Material: All
Address: 5717 CORBETT HALL RM 444
City/State/ZIP: ORONO ME 04469
Telephone: 207-581-1408

University of Nebraska Press
Bison Books

Mission of the University of Nebraska Press

The University of Nebraska Press, founded in 1941, seeks to encourage, develop, publish, and disseminate research, literature, and the publishing arts. The Press is the largest academic publisher in the Great Plains and a major publisher of books about that region. It is the state's largest repository of the knowledge, arts, and skills of publishing and advises the University and the people of Nebraska about book publishing. Reporting to the Vice-Chancellor for Research and having a faculty advisory board, the Press maintains scholarly standards and fosters innovations guided by refereed evaluations.

What Is the University of Nebraska Press?

The University of Nebraska Press is the second largest state university press in the nation (following only the University of California Press) in terms of titles published, and is among the top ten university presses in the nation in terms of annual sales volume.

The Press is the largest and most diversified university press between Chicago and California, and seeks to serve as the publisher for that enormous region. We proudly publish excellent writers and scholars, including those of our own university system, and foster projects on the culture and history of the state and of the entire West. As the population and influence of the West increase, we intend to keep pace, providing our university, state, and region with a publishing program equal to the energies, needs and intelligence of the area.

We currently have influential programs in Native American studies, the history of the American West, literary and cultural studies, music, and psychology. We are among the leading scholarly publishers of books in translation. We have recently inaugurated successful lists in natural science, photography, sports history, and agricultural policy and planning. Catalogs describing our new books are available, as are specialty catalogs for several of our publishing programs.

We have initiated programs in nonprint publishing, including cassettes, CD-ROM, and on-demand databases, and have an electronic media department that not only produces materials in the current technologies but is actively researching state-of-the-art technological developments to assess their likely opportunities and impact on scholarly publishing.

How to Choose a Publisher

The most important work an aspiring author must do is read. The writer who does not read will seldom become an author. An author must read for two reasons: first, to be sure that what he or she writes is genuinely new; and second, to know which publishers are interested in different kinds of books.

Publishers tend to specialize. Some concentrate on gardening, some on children's books, some on religion, computers, or stamp collecting. Look in a large library and look for recent books like the one you are writing. Write to those publishers that best match your needs. Don't waste time, energy, and postage on publishers that have never shown any interest in the kind of book that interests you. Some guidebooks, available in the reference books section of public and university libraries, that may help in this search are *LMP (Literary Market Place)*, an annual published by R. R. Bowker, *The American Directory of Writer's Guidelines*, published by Quill Driver Books, and *Writers Market*, an annual published by Writer's Digest Books.

Remember that publishers look upon publishing as a profession. They will want you to behave professionally. Very few amateurs can tolerate the stress and effort required to be a published author.

What Does the University of Nebraska Press Publish?

We publish books and scholarly journals only, and have no programs in contemporary fiction or poetry. On occasion, we reprint previously published fiction of established reputation and we have several programs to publish literary works in translation. But we cannot undertake original fiction, regardless of topic, children's books, or the work of living poets. Our mission, defined by the University through the Press Advisory Board of faculty members working in concert with the Press, is to find, evaluate, and publish in the best fashion possible, serious works of nonfiction.

How Do I Approach a Publisher?

We prefer to see prospectuses prior to inviting completed manuscripts. Such prospectuses should include the following: an outline, with a paragraph describing each chapter; a cover letter describing the length and focus of the manuscript; and a copy of the author's *curriculum vitae* or resume.

We receive more than 1,000 inquiries each year. Although we are delighted to find so much interest in our press, we can only invite submission of a small fraction of these projects, and then publish an even smaller fraction of the manuscripts actually invited. Literary translations are especially competitive.

When we receive an invited manuscript an acknowledgment of receipt is immediately sent, and we evaluate the work promptly to determine whether it would fit our list. If we think it may be appropriate, we send it to two experts in the field for their comments. If both readers endorse publication, we take the manuscript and readers' reports to our faculty committee and request approval to publish. The entire review process usually takes four to six months, and can be longer if the expert readers counsel significant changes.

We are becoming increasingly adept at using computer disks. Nevertheless, we prefer to see printed pages for any prospectus or invited manuscript. All pages should be prepared in conformity with the *Chicago Manual of Style*, 14th edition.

A guide to manuscript preparation is available from our receptionist, or by mail upon request.

What If I Write Fiction, Poetry, or Children's Books?

Again, be sure to read dozens if not hundreds of books to understand what other people are reading and writing.

If you want to publish a book of fiction or poetry or a book for children, you must be prepared for a difficult challenge. These are the most competitive areas of publishing, with thousands of authors vying for attention.

Publishers of fiction and poetry prefer authors who have published their work in journals. Most poets and fiction writers have begun publishing in literary magazines. When they have established a reputation they can collect their poems and stories into books.

Spend time in a large library looking at literary journals like *Prairie Schooner, Iowa Review, Chicago Review, and TriQuarterly*. Find a journal that you like and which you believe will like you. Look for its editorial policy and rules for submission.

Where Can I Go for Help?

For addresses of literary journals see *International Directory of little Magazines and Small Presses*. For addresses of book publishers see *Literary Market Place*.

Should you try to find an agent? Probably not until you have already published several works in different places.

What if the publisher asks for money? Be cautious and learn as much as you can about the publisher and its reputation, as you would in buying any product or service. Be sure you understand what is being offered for the money.

Should I Publish Myself?

Many of the most famous and beloved writers in American literature published their works themselves. These writers include Walt Whitman, Marianne Moore, Ezra Pound, John Neihardt, Edgar Allan Poe, and Upton Sinclair.

Family stories and family histories are best published by the authors themselves. It is very difficult to sell books you publish yourself, but you can give books to people whose affection and attention matters to you.

To publish yourself you need to find a printer you trust. Look in the phone book to find a list of printers, then call them to see whether they can print and bind books. If they do, visit their offices and see samples of their work. Check different printers to find the best quality at the best price.

There are several guides to publishing books yourself, also, there are professional consultants who offer assistance with the process (see section 64 in *LMP*). Additionally there are a number of guidebooks to the individual parts of book publishing (production, marketing, publicity, etc.). Large public libraries and writers' workshops may be able to suggest appropriate and useful cities.

Can the University of Nebraska Press Help Me?

Even if we can't publish your book (we, too, must specialize) we can offer some help to citizens of Nebraska. If you receive an offer from a publisher, we will be happy to discuss the offer with you. If you have questions about publishing jargon, we can try to explain it.

If you have a specific question or would like to make an appointment, please call. To place an order for our books, we encourage readers whenever possible to patronize a local bookstore—they are indispensable links in the chain from authors to readers. If necessary, our Customer Service department can be reached at (402) 472-3584.

Preparing Your Manuscript

We at Nebraska want to publish your work as expertly and expeditiously as possible. Because each ms. is unique, we cannot present the instructions herein as complete or exhaustive. Keeping in constant contact with your acquisitions editor throughout the ms.-writing and -revision process will help eliminate duplicate or unproductive effort on everyone's part and will ensure that we can help and advise you at each step.

The Manuscript

Keep formatting to a minimum, but follow these general guidelines. All parts of the ms., *without exception*, should be double spaced in 12-point (10-cpi) Courier for ease in copyediting and proofreading. Margins all around should be set to 1", with ragged-right margins and with chapter openings dropped 2" from the top of the page. Automatic hyphenation should be turned off. Use underlining instead of italics, and do not set text or heads in full caps. Add extra space between paragraphs only where you wish a space break in the book to indicate a change of subject. Number the pages of the ms. straight through from beginning to end (do not start over from 1 in each chapter). The numbering of notes, however, should begin with 1 in each chapter; notes should be collected at the end of text, before the bibliography. Tables,

Books

figures, and other illustrations should be on unnumbered pages at the end of the manuscript. (If yours is a contributed volume, ask your editor about special preparation.) Your editor will supply you with a ms. checklist and a review memo to which you should refer before undertaking revision of your manuscript. Please fill out and sign the checklist and return it with the final version of your ms.

Since we use your ms. disk for typesetting, it is critical that the disk and hard copy you submit be identical. *Print the hard copy directly from the floppy disk that you submit with the ms.* Complete the Disk Information Sheet and keep it with the disk. The version of your ms. submitted should be the original, not a photocopy.

Illustrations

We must have in hand all artwork (illustrations, maps, graphs, tables, etc.), complete captions, and any necessary permissions before we can undertake the copyediting of your ms.. Please read the section on permissions if your ms. contains illustrations. Number the illustrations with a gummed label on the back (never write directly on photos, front or back).

Obtaining complete permissions for illustrations remains the responsibility of the author. Start early, since it can take several months to secure permissions.

Photographs

Black-and-white, high-contrast glossies are necessary for sharp reproduction. If at all possible, please provide 8"x10" photographs. All photographs must be accompanied by letters of permission from your source, unless, of course, you took the photograph yourself. Please read the section on Permissions carefully if your ms. has photographs.

Drawings and figures

Keep the lines small and light. Extraneous details and great variation in shading and lettering (size, weight) will make the drawing or figure difficult to reproduce. The original should be sharp and legible, on high quality paper, in order to accept the reduction necessary for it to fit within the finished book page area. Please read the Permissions section carefully if your ms. has drawings or figures that you have not created yourself for this ms..

Graphs

Although software abounds that enables authors to create their own graphs, at the ms. stage no one can know what the design of the final book will be. For that reason, in general we prefer to generate graphs ourselves. This enables our typesetters to generate high quality graphs in a typeface compatible with the text design. Please provide all data points for graphs, whether you or someone else has generated them.

Maps

If you photographically reproduce a map (such as a historical map), follow the quality guidelines for photographs. Treat such maps as photographs in terms of permissions, as well. If you would like to generate your own maps or engage your own freelancer to prepare them, you must send samples to your editor, who will confer with the managing editor and the production manager about usability. Do not place type on your base map; place names should be printed on an overlay. In many cases we can engage a freelance cartographer to provide finished maps for your book. In that case, please provide a double-spaced list of all place names to be included on the map. Use upper- and lowercase as appropriate. This text should also be on your ms. disk.

List of illustrations and caption copy

The final version of your ms. should be accompanied by two separate lists on unnumbered pages: one list with brief descriptions of all illustrations, and a list of full captions that will accompany the actual illustrations in the finished book. Both the illustrations and captions lists should present the illustrations in the order in which they are to appear in the book.

Captions for images that you do not own yourself should include the credit line as stipulated in the permission letter from the owner (see the section on Permissions).

Permissions

Permissions are probably the least understood aspect of the entire publishing process.

Nonetheless, attention to permissions is essential for the timely publication of your ms. Please identify to your editor any parts of your ms. that are not your own words or images or that you have published elsewhere. He or she can then help you determine if your use constitutes fair use or if you should seek permission from the rights holder. We do not recommend that you seek permission without advice from your editor, since unnecessarily requesting permission jeopardizes the concept of fair use and can ultimately defeat it.

Do seek permission as soon as you have established with your editor that you must do so for certain materials. When requesting permission, specify the working title of your ms., the publisher as the University of Nebraska Press (nonprofit), and the estimated season of publication (many permissions expire within 24 months of request). It is most helpful for us if permissions allow for nonexclusive electronic distribution, as well as for printed editions.

Permissions for illustrations must specify by negative number or by description each illustration for which permission is granted. You should request that all letters of permission be sent directly to you: please send us photocopies and retain the originals for your own records. We also need for our files photocopies of any statements defining conditions of use so that we can process stipulations for gratis copies of your book.

Fair and unfair use

Previously published written material requires permission if it is still in copyright (in general, if it was published fewer than 75 years ago) and if your use exceeds fair use. Under current copyright law, fair use is determined not by word count but by the nature of the copyrighted work, the purpose of its use and the amount used, and the effect of its use on the value of the original work. Most quotation in scholarly books constitutes fair use, although stanzas of poetry, letters, diary entries, and other such items that constitute complete entities in themselves usually require permission.

Note that unpublished documents not your own (e.g., unpublished letters) require permission (see section on Manuscript materials).

Manuscript materials

Fair use does not apply to manuscript materials: permission is always required for unpublished writings. If the material is held by an archives permission is often required from the holder of the literary rights (i.e., the author or the author's heir) as well as from the archives. For letters, the writer rather than the recipient holds the literary rights.

Illustrations

Obtaining permissions for illustrations is time-consuming and can be expensive. Permission for illustrations, like that for manuscript material, is based on two separate and distinct legal theories; ownership of the photo, painting, etc., and ownership of the copyright. In other words, there are two forms of legal protection against unauthorized publication of a photo or piece of art: one is extended to the owner (libraries, archives, or other institutions) of the item, and the other is extended to the holder of the copyright (if there is one), normally the photographer or artist or that person's heir.

That a photograph (or other item of visual art) carries no copyright notice does not necessarily mean that it is in the public domain. It is your responsibility to ascertain its status from the institution holding it. The institution in turn will alert you if further permission is required from an owner of publishing rights.

Permission is required for the use of certain materials held by agencies of the federal government such as the National Archives and the Library of Congress. Again, if you are uncertain about whether you need to request permission, check with your editor or the managing editor.

Your own previously published material

If more than a page or two of your ms. substantially duplicates material you have published elsewhere, you must obtain permission from the copyright holder (usually the original publisher) for its use. Some scholarly journals specify in their publishing agreements that the author holds all further publishing rights. If that is the case, please send us a photocopy of the agreement or other correspondence indicating that and identify the full bibliographic information on the earlier publication so that we can credit the source appropriately.

Before You Send Us the Final Manuscript

We would like to publish your work in the most expeditious and successful fashion possible. However, the success of our effort depends in large part on your delivery of an accurate, complete, and meticulously prepared ms. Please ensure that we receive in one package everything you want to appear in your book; all text, including acknowledgments and a dedication if appropriate, and all artwork. All necessary letters of permission and conditions-of-use statements should accompany the ms. The computer disk you send should contain the final version of your ms, and you should print the final hard copy from that disk. Before you send in the final draft of your ms, we also urge you to do the following:

Ensure that the title page has your name spelled exactly as you wish it to appear in your book.

Verify the contents page against the chapter titles on the chapter opening pages.

Verify all direct quotations and all source citations and bibliographic entries.

Check credit lines against corresponding letters of permission to ensure that you have met any obligations for specific wording.

Double-check the lists of illustrations, maps, tables, etc., against the caption copy and against the artwork or tables themselves to ensure they correspond.

Final checklist

Along with your final ms. draft, we should have on file the following:

• computer disk with all text files (and graphics files as appropriate), preferably in PC/IBM format
• Disk Information Sheet
• Previously Published Work form
• University of Nebraska Press Author Checklist
• letters of permission for all artwork, all previously published text, and all ms. materials not your own (except those identified by the Press as falling under fair use definitions)

Categories: Nonfiction—African-American—Agriculture—Arts—Biography—Civil War—Conservation—Culture—Ecology—Environment—Ethnic—Feminism—Film/Video—Government—Hispanic—History—Jewish Interests—Language—Literature—Military—Music—Native American—Philosophy—Politics—Psychology—Public Policy—Regional—Rural America—Sports—Western—Women's Fiction—Women's Issues

Name: Humanities Editor
Name: History Editor
Name: Native American Studies Editor
Material: As appropriate
Address: 312 N 14TH ST
City/State/ZIP: LINCOLN NE 68588-0484
Telephone: 402-472-3581
Fax: 402-472-0308

E-mail: press@unlinfo.unl.edu

University of Nevada Press

The University of Nevada Press is a public service division of the University and Community College System of Nevada. Its mission is to make a contribution to the State of Nevada, as well as to the national and international scholarly communities, by publishing books in the humanities, sciences, and social sciences that deal with the history, literature, natural history and resources, environment, economy, politics, anthropology, ethnic groups and cultures of Nevada and the West; the Basque people of Europe and the Americas; Native Americans; gambling and commercial gaming; and contemporary affairs.

In addition to books of general and scholarly interest, the Press publishes seven distinguished series of books: the Basque Series; the Wilbur S. Shepperson Series in History and the Humanities; the Western Literature Series; the Max C. Fleischmann Series in Great Basin Natural History; the Vintage West Reprint Series; the Gambling Studies Series; and the Ethnonationalism in Comparative Perspective Series. The Press also publishes original fiction, poetry, and creative nonfiction; photography books on regional topics; and books on regional themes for a general audience.

INITIAL REVIEW

We ask authors interested in submitting their work to the University of Nevada Press to send us first a manuscript proposal, which should consist of a table of contents; a summary or chapter outline of the manuscript; information about its length, number and type of illustrations (if any are planned), and any special components, such as footnotes, bibliography, appendices, tables, glossaries, etc.; information about the book's intended audience and any competing works already in publication; and a representative sample section of the text, consisting of a chapter or two, or in the case of short fiction or poetry, a couple of sample stories or a half dozen or so sample poems. A brief vita of the author should accompany this material.

Once we have reviewed the proposal, we shall, if the project seems suited for our publishing program, invite the author to submit the entire manuscript for formal consideration.

FORMAL REVIEW

When we invite an author to submit a full manuscript for our consideration, we ask for two clean paper copies of the entire manuscript, including all notes, bibliography, appendices, and any other components.

If the book is to include illustrations, please send *only* photocopies at this time.

If the manuscript exists on an electronic disk, we do not need to have access to the disk during the review process. If the manuscript exists only on paper, please provide us with two clear photocopies.

Do not bind the manuscript or enclose it in a binder. Double-space everything (all text, quotations, footnotes, bibliography, figure captions, tables, lists, appendices, etc.). Number the pages consecutively from the beginning to the end of the manuscript. Long quotations (10 lines or more) should be indented an extra five spaces. Use paragraph indents if the quotations were indented in the original. Notes should be placed at the end of the manuscript (not at the bottoms of the pages or ends of the chapters).

Photographs, figures, charts, graphs, tables, etc., should be on separate pages, not on pages with text.

Authors of manuscripts that contain illustrations or large amounts of quoted material and editors of anthologies will be responsible, if the Press makes a publishing commitment, for obtaining all necessary permissions to reprint and for paying any related fees.

Authors of poetry and fiction should include information about any previous publication of this material, including date of first publication and titles of venue.

If the Press makes a publishing offer, the author is required to provide two paper copies of the final draft of the manuscript (which incorporates all revisions recommended by the Press's editors and outside readers) and a disk containing the manuscript formatted to the Press's specifications.

Helpful reference book: *Chicago Manual of Style,* available at most libraries and books stores.

MANUSCRIPT EVALUATION PROCESS

The review process consists of several stages. Manuscripts are read first by an in-house editor. If they appear suited for our publishing program, they are evaluated by readers from outside the house who are recognized authorities in the subject matter of the manuscript or, in the case of literary work, by distinguished critics or writers in the genre of the manuscript (usually both). After two favorable outside evaluations, the manuscript is presented to the Press's Editorial Board, which consists of eight representatives from the campuses of the University and Community College System of Nevada and the Desert Research Institute, which controls the Press's imprint. Only after Board approval is the Press able to make a publishing commitment.

Publication takes place after negotiation and acceptance of a formal contract between the Press and the author or his/her agent. In most cases, the author receives a royalty on book sales, the amount of which is negotiated at the time the contract is offered.

Categories: Fiction—Nonfiction—Biography—Ecology—Environment—Ethnic—General Interest—History—Literature—Native American—Poetry—Politics—Regional—Science

Name: Margaret Dalrymple, Assistant Director and Editor-in-Chief
Material: All
Address: MS 166
City/State/ZIP: RENO NV 89557-0076
Telephone: 702-784-6573
Fax: 702-784-6200

University of North Texas Press

The University of North Texas Press was established in August 1987, and its first books were published in 1989. We publish approximately 16 to 20 books a year, with more than 140 books currently in print. Our books are distributed and marketed nationally and internationally through a university press consortium.

The University of North Texas Press is dedicated to producing the highest quality scholarly, academic and general interest books for the Dallas-Fort Worth-Denton metroplex, state, national and international communities as part of an outreach activity. As a part of the largest and most comprehensive research university in North Texas, UNT Press holds to the philosophy that university presses should be on the cutting edge of publishing and thus is not averse to the different and unusual in its publishing agenda.

We are committed to serving *all* peoples by publishing stories of their cultures and their experiences that have been overlooked. We seek to nurture the development of writers by publishing first books and by publishing poetry. We strive to advance understanding and appreciation of the historical, intellectual, scientific and cultural milieu through our publications. Through sales, advertisements, and reviews of UNT Press books nationally and internationally, we strive to enhance and support the University of North Texas as an academic presence in education and community life.

Publishing Emphasis

The University of North Texas Press is the publisher of the Texas Folklore Society Publications, thus we place an emphasis on folklore in our publishing. We also publish series on War and the Southwest, the Vassar Miller Prize in Poetry, Texas Writers' Series of critical biographies, Western Life Series, Practical Guide Series. We place emphasis on multicultural topics, women's issues, history, Texana and Western Americana.

Please note that manuscripts for the Vassar Miller Prize in Poetry should be sent, along with the entry fee, directly to the editor of the series: Scott Cairns, English Department, Old Dominion University, Norfolk, VA 23529.

Procedures

The decision-making process at UNT Press is like other university presses. If we feel your proposal fits with our publishing list and publishing schedule, we will ask for a complete manuscript, which will then be evaluated by at least two expert readers. These confidential reports are taken to the UNT Press Editorial Board, which has the final say on whether or not we will publish the book. Both the readers and the Editorial Board may have suggestions on revising and improving the manuscript. Sometimes their approval may be contingent on whether or not these changes are made.

The review process can take several weeks or months, depending upon the time necessary to receive and compile reports from the readers and the Editorial Board. Once the Editorial Board recommends publication, we will send you a contract for your consideration. Once the contract is signed by both parties, the publication process will usually be from nine months to a year.

Publication Process

UNT Press books are all printed on acid-free paper, according to the American National Standard for Permanence of paper for printed library materials. Many of our books are sent to the printer in electronic form, with design and typesetting done on computer, both by in-house and by outside designers and typesetters.

Editing is done by both in-house and freelance editors, with the author being given an opportunity to check the edited manuscript, answer questions asked by the editor and offer input on changes made. The author also sees the book in page proofs, for the final chance to correct typographical errors and other problems that may arise. If the book is to be indexed, it will be done at this time.

Once the book goes to the printer, it usually takes around 40 working days for a hardback book and around 35 working days for a paperback book to be printed, bound, wrapped and shipped to the warehouse for distribution to bookstores.

Marketing

You will be sent an author biography form to fill out which will help in marketing your book. You are encouraged to become actively involved in the marketing. It is our experience that the most successful books are the ones in which the author has been particularly aggressive in seeking out markets for the books, arranging speaking engagements with appropriate groups, arranging book signings and other venues offering opportunities for book sales. Contacting your sources for book reviews is another effective marketing tool.

We will have your book at most of the major conferences and will consider taking them to other meetings you notify us about.

Since we consider our backlist books the backbone of our publishing house, we actively promote the backlist titles and seek course adoptions for the books. Your book will be kept in print as long as demand justifies.

We have sales representatives throughout the United States, including Hawaii and Alaska. We have representation in Canada, Europe, Latin America, Asia, Australia, New Zealand, and the Pacific Islands.

We are part of a university press consortium that actively markets our books to major bookstore and library accounts and to national and regional distributors, as well as to individuals, through both extensive mailing lists and professional sales representation.

The Final Manuscript

Manuscripts submitted should be prepared according to the guidelines given here. Even if the book is to be typeset from diskettes provided by the author, one hard (paper) copy of the manuscript is needed.

Hard Copy:
- Once a contract is signed, we need two hard copies of the ms.
- Word-processed manuscripts printed with letter-quality or near letter-quality printer. No dot matrix.
- No right-justification or proportional interspacing on word-processed manuscripts.
- Number pages consecutively through the manuscript; DO NOT begin renumbering with each chapter.
- Include photocopies, with captions, of any photographs or illustrations. (If you have already signed a contract with us, at this point we need original photos or duplicate prints.)

Computer Disks:
- These are not necessary until after a decision to publish the book has been made. (At that time, we will also need actual photographs and art work submitted with disks and hard copy.)
- Use the same hardware and software systems from start to finish.
- Keep formatting and fonts to a minimum. Most of it must be removed before typesetting.
- Once you have printed out the hard copy, do not make further changes on the computer disks.
- Name files sequentially ("A. Front matter," "B. Ch 1," "C. Ch 2," etc.) Submit a list of file names with disks. Do not put an entire manuscript in a single document.
- Front matter (title page, dedication, book epigraph, table of contents, lists of illustrations or tables, preface, acknowledgments, introduction, and foreword) and back matter (notes, bibliography, appendixes, index, and/or glossary) should be in separate files.
- Use endnotes at the end of chapters rather than footnotes at the bottom of the page.
- Double-space endnotes and bibliography.
- Do not put two spaces after periods like you do in a typewritten document. This causes formatting problems. Do not put two spaces after colons, or anywhere else in the manuscript.
- Do not double-space between paragraphs.
- Use tabs, not spaces, to indent paragraphs.

Style Manual:

In general, the University of North Texas Press follows the *Chicago Manual of Style*. However, we like to remain flexible to the needs of each manuscript, so alternate styles are open for discussion.

Categories: Nonfiction—Crime—Film/Video—General Interest—History—How-to—Military—Multicultural—Regional (Southwestern)—True Crime—Women's Issues

Name: Acquisitions Editor
Material: All

Address: PO BOX 311336
City/State/ZIP: DENTON TX 76203-1336
Telephone: 940-565-2142
Fax: 940-565-4590

University of Oklahoma Press

The University of Oklahoma Press is dedicated to the publication of outstanding scholarly works by national and international scholars. The major editorial goal of the Press is to maintain its position as a preeminent publisher of books about the West and the American Indian while expanding its program in other scholarly disciplines, including archaeology, classical studies, energy studies, language and literature, natural sciences, political science, and women's studies.

Series currently published by the Press include:
- American Exploration and Travel Series
- American Indian Literature and Critical Studies Series
- Animal Natural History Series
- Bruce Alonzo Goff Series in Creative Architecture
- Centers of Civilization Series
- Civilization of the American Indian Series
- Congressional Studies Series
- D'Arcy McNickle Center Bibliographies in American Indian History
- Gilcrease-Oklahoma Series on Western Art and Artists
- Julian J. Rothbaum Distinguished Lecture Series
- Legal History of North America
- Oklahoma Museum of Natural History Publications
- Oklahoma Project for Discourse and Theory
- Oklahoma Series in Classical Culture
- Oklahoma Western Biographies
- Variorum Chaucer
- Western Frontier Library

HOW TO SUBMIT A MANUSCRIPT PROPOSAL

Our decision to publish a book is based chiefly upon its contribution to knowledge in fields compatible with our list, sound scholarship, clear writing style, and financial feasibility.

Manuscripts and manuscript proposals are often solicited by the Press. For unsolicited inquiries we prefer to receive:

1. a letter of inquiry, directed to the Editor-in-Chief or the appropriate Acquisitions Editor, that briefly describes the manuscript, its approximate length, including number and kinds of illustrations, its purpose, and its relationship to other books in its field

2. the author's qualifications to write such a book;

3. the contents; and

4. a sample chapter.

When we have evaluated your proposal, we will contact you. If we wish to pursue the project, we will ask to see the complete manuscript. Unless we are told otherwise, we assume that, while we are considering the manuscript for publication, no other publisher has it under consideration.

Manuscripts that pass initial in-house scrutiny are evaluated by experts in the subject area and are then considered by an in-house Editorial Committee. Authors of those manuscripts not recommended for publication are informed immediately. Those manuscripts still under consideration are either presented to the Press's Faculty Advisory Board or returned to the author for revision and later submission. When resubmitted, the manuscript

Books

again goes to the Editorial Committee; if approved, it is presented to the Faculty Advisory Board. If the Board approves publication, a contract is drawn up between the author and the Press. An in-house decision to publish a book is usually made in three to six months, depending on the length and complexity of the manuscript and the availability of readers.

HOW TO PREPARE A MANUSCRIPT

Following the acceptance and contracting of a manuscript for publication, the Press requests the submission of two typed copies and, if available, IBM-compatible disks with the name of software indicated, along with all illustrative materials in the form in which they will be reproduced and permission to reproduce them.

All materials should be typed double-spaced, including elements such as extended quotations, the notes, the bibliography, and illustration legends. The notes, the bibliography, and the legends should each be typed separate from the text. All materials should be prepared in accordance with *The Chicago Manual of Style*, 14th edition. (Exceptions to the style recommended by the *Chicago Manual* may be made in consultation with the Press, if other manuals are used consistently.) Observing the following guidelines will greatly facilitate the movement of your manuscript through editing and production.

A. In preparing your manuscript, follow these rules:

1. Computer printouts should be run out from letter-quality printers. Italics should be indicated by the use of underlining. Submit the original and one high-quality copy.

2. Maintain consistent 1-to 1½" margins on all sides. Leave at least 3" at the top of the first page of a chapter.

3. Do not strike over mistyped letters.

4. Number all manuscript pages consecutively with Arabic numerals in the upper right-hand corner.

5. Set off direct quotations of more than eight to ten typed lines from the text by indenting from each margin, using no opening or closing quotation marks. Shorter quotations should be run into the text, with quotation marks used.

6. Double-space tables and source information. Type the source information beneath the table. Double space titles above tables.

7. Double-space legends for maps, tables, and other illustrations. Mark placement of these elements by numbers in the left margins of the manuscript (as: Table 1). Type the legends for the different kinds of illustrations separately, including the numbers if the illustrations are numbered. Also prepare lists of plates, figures, maps, and tables to follow the Contents page in the front matter.

8. Do not use pins, tape, or staples. Do not use pens or colored pencils on any part of the manuscript. For minor additions or corrections, print legibly with a sharpened number-2 pencil; for major changes, type insert on separate page, label with previous page number and A, indicate insertion on text page (as: see 134A), and place insert after text page.

9. Follow a simple, consistent pattern for indicating headings and subheadings. Type all headings in capital and lower-case letters, never all in capitals. No terminal periods are necessary for heads.

B. In preparing an electronic manuscript, please also observe the following guidelines from the Association of American University Presses' booklet, "Preparing Your Electronic Manuscript":

1. Prepare your manuscript on the same system—both hardware and software—from start to finish.

2. Name files sequentially: title.01fm, title.02chapl, titleo3.chap2, etc. A list of file names submitted with your disks is helpful.

3. Front matter, bibliography, and other apparatus should be in separate files.

4. Notes should be grouped together in one or more separate files following the text, not at the bottoms of pages or at the ends of chapters, unless you are instructed otherwise. If your word processing software has the capability to do on-page footnotes, please do not use it. The notes should be all together, in a separate file or files, grouped and numbered by chapter, double-spaced, with no extra spaces between notes.

5. Keep all formatting to a minimum. Book designers will determine treatment of elements, and most if not all formatting must be removed before typesetting can begin, which can be time-consuming and costly. If you do use any formatting, make certain you are consistent. The best solution might be to print out your hard copy with the formatting you intend, then delete all formatting from your disks before sending them to the publisher.

6. Once you have printed out the final manuscript (hard copy), do not make any further corrections to the computer files. Any further changes should be made on the hard copy in a contrasting color of ink.

7. Do not put "soft" hyphens at the ends of lines; i.e., do not break words. In fact, it's best to turn off the automatic hyphenation feature on your word processing software. The only hyphens in your manuscript should be in hyphenated compound words.

8. Do not use running heads.

9. Do not put any extra spaces between paragraphs or between notes or bibliographical entries, or before and after an extract. Introduce extra vertical space only where extra space is to appear in the book to indicate a semantic break.

10. Use the tab key, not the space bar, to indent paragraphs, and the indent key, not the tab key or the space bar, to indent extracts and epigraphs. Make sure that the size of the indent is consistent throughout the manuscript. Use the tab key for columns.

11. Use one space after colons, and one space after periods at the ends of sentences. If you are so accustomed to using two that you find it impossible to use one consistently, then use two, consistently.

12. Type everything paragraph style. Even if you can hang-indent with your word processing system, do not do so.

13. Use two hyphens for a dash, with no space before, between, or after the hyphens.

14. Your word processor's codes for superscripts may be used.

15. When several words in a row are to be underlined, issue the underlining command at the beginning of the first word and turn it off at the end of the last word; do not issue separate underlining commands for each word.

16. Hard carriage returns should be used only at the ends of paragraphs and at the ends of items in lists and lines of poetry.

17. Never use letters for numbers, or vice versa; i.e., don't type the lowercase "l" for the number one or the letter "O" for zero.

18. If there are tables in your manuscript, make certain you have an accurate printout of them so the typesetter can easily follow the format. Use tabs, not hard spaces, to define columns, and avoid tables with more than ten columns.

19. If your manuscript has accented letters or special characters that are not available on your computer, provide a list of them and indicate how you have manually marked them.

20. In printing out materials, use a standard font with ten characters per inch. Do not use variable spacing, and do not justify right-hand margins. Print out manuscript using a 300 dpi or better laser printer.

21. Never use paper clips on computer disks.

C. In matters of punctuation and style, consult *The Chicago Manual of Style*, 14th edition. Please note especially the following:

1. Place commas and final periods inside quotation marks. Other punctuation marks go outside unless they are a part of the

quotation.

2. Use three spaced periods (ellipses) to show an intentional omission within a sentence. To show an omission at the end of a sentence, use three spaced periods in addition to the sentence's terminal punctuation.

3. Use a comma before the final conjunction in a series.

4. Type hyphens and dashes without spacing before and after these punctuation marks. Type two hyphens to indicate a dash.

5. Avoid the use of sexist, racist, or other biased language; when in doubt about the former, consult *The Handbook of Nonsexist Writing*, 2d edition, by Casey Miller and Kate Swift.

6. It is University of Oklahoma Press preferred style to use "American Indian" rather than "Native American."

7. Note that an author's preface is concerned with the assembling of the book. It may include reasons for undertaking the work, the method of research, acknowledgments (unless these are sufficiently lengthy to merit a separate section), and, sometimes, a reference to permissions granted. An author's introduction provides a context and background for the subject of the book, and may be placed in the front matter or at the beginning of the text depending on how closely it is related to the text.

8. In documentation, use one of the note systems described in *The Chicago Manual of Style*, 14th edition, aiming for the minimal information needed to distinguish sources. The University of Oklahoma Press prefers that place and date of publication and name of publisher be omitted in all notes, including first references to works, with complete citations listed in the bibliography. Bibliographical entries should include names of publishers. The bibliography should be arranged so that the readers will find a source easily where only the author and (possibly) short title are cited in a note.

HOW TO SUBMIT ILLUSTRATIONS AND MAPS FOR YOUR MANUSCRIPT

1. Choose photographs carefully, bearing in mind that they are almost always reduced somewhat in the finished book, and also that they are almost never improved in the printing. Look for good contrast and clear focus. We recognize, however, that sometimes it may be necessary to use historical photographs of lesser quality.

2. Avoid using illustrations from books. They will not reproduce well. If you have found a significant photograph or painting in a book, look for a credit line that will tell you where the original is and obtain a glossy print from that source.

3. Never write on the backs of photographs if doing so can be avoided. To identify a photograph, tape a written or typed identification on white paper to the photo with Scotch Magic Transparent tape or attach a gummed flap that will show when the illustration is photographed for reproduction. If you must write on the back of a photograph, use a number-2B or softer pencil with a light pressure and write as close as possible to the edge of the image.

4. Indicate "top" at the top of all illustrations, including all base maps and map overlays. Cropping is best done by the designer, though any concerns you may have about cropping can be conveyed in writing to the editor.

5. Never use paper clips on photographs.

6. We do not routinely publish in color, as the cost can be prohibitive. If color is used, however, transparencies are preferable for color illustrations, and the best sizes are 4"x5" or 2"x2". Printed color photographs from a book or magazine are nearly impossible to reproduce satisfactorily and should be avoided. If you are printing your own color photographs or having a professional photographer print them, be sure to include a gray scale or color bar in the edge of each photograph. Converting color prints to black and white is generally unsatisfactory, but you may often be successful in converting color slides to acceptable black-and-white prints.

7. If you are preparing original graphics for your book, it is best to consult with your editor before you begin, demonstrating your ideas with preliminary sketches. Lettering is best done by having type set and pasted onto your finished drawing. Please consult with your editor before having type set so that an appropriate typeface can be chosen. Bear in mind that names should be spelled the same on maps and in charts as they are in the text. Always give your editor the original artwork, not photographs.

8. Unless you are a trained cartographer, the best solution to providing maps is to make very clean, accurate drawings with pencil and hire a professional to draw the finished maps under your supervision. Be sure that everything is correctly located and correctly spelled before the cartographer begins. Free-lance artists and cartographers can be found around colleges, architecture studios, and so forth, and in all but the smallest towns. If you have further questions, please contact the Production Department of the University of Oklahoma Press.

HOW TO OBTAIN PERMISSIONS FOR QUOTES AND ILLUSTRATIONS

Written permission should be secured for illustrations and for quotations that do not fall under the doctrine of "fair use." Both the length of the quoted material in proportion to the whole and the purpose of the use should be taken into account in judging whether a use is fair. Uses such as criticism, comment, news reporting, teaching, scholarship, and research are generally acceptable, while more commercial uses may not be. Permission is needed to quote "even a snippet" of poetry. If you have questions regarding fair use, consult the Copyright Act of 1976 and *The Chicago Manual of Style*, 14th edition.

Permission must also be secured for the use of illustrations owned or copyrighted by others.

Write for Permissions as soon as you have a contract that is based on a complete manuscript. The model of a permission request letter below can be modified to suit individual circumstances. Provide your editor with photocopies of the permissions and keep the originals for your records. If a permission agreement requires specific wording in acknowledgment, this should be followed to the letter.

All copyrighted materials require acknowledgment in the notes, the legends, or elsewhere in the book.

SAMPLE PERMISSION REQUEST LETTER

[Author's letterhead]

Reference:

Date:

[Addressee]

I am writing to request permission to reprint the following material [or reproduce the following illustration] from your publication:

[Author, title, date of publication]

[Pages on which material appears or other identifying information.]

This material is to appear as originally published [or with changes or deletions as noted on the reverse side of this letter] in the following work, which the University of Oklahoma Press is currently preparing for publication:

[Author or editor, title, approx. no. pages]

I am requesting nonexclusive world rights to use this material as part of my work in all languages and for all editions.

If you are the copyright holder, may I have your permission to reprint the material described above in my book? Unless you request otherwise, I shall use the conventional scholarly form of acknowledgment, including author and title, publisher's name, and date.

If you are not the copyright holder, or if for world rights I need additional permission from another source, will you kindly so indicate?

Thank you for your consideration of this request. A duplicate copy of this letter is enclosed for your convenience.

Yours sincerely,

The above request is approved on the conditions specified below and on the understanding that full credit will be given to the source.

Approved by: _____ Date: _____

Categories: Nonfiction—Archaeology—Biography—Civil War—Classical Studies—Ethnic—History—Legal History—Literature—Native American—Natural History—Political Science—Regional—Western

Name: John Drayton, Editor-in-Chief
Material: History of the American West
Name: Kimberly Wiar, Senior Editor
Material: Classical Studies, Political Science, Natural History
Name: Randolph Lewis, Acquisitions Editor
Material: Native American studies
Address: 1005 ASP AVENUE
City/State/ZIP: NORMAN OK 73019-6051
Telephone: 405-325-5111
Fax: 405-325-4000
Internet: www.ou.edu

Mississippi

University Press of Mississippi

Please send a cover letter, table of contents, sample chapter and author's resume before submitting a manuscript.

Instructions for the Preparation of a Manuscript

1. The manuscript should be prepared on a 3.5" computer diskette, according to the AAUP guidelines "Preparing Your Electronic Manuscript," reproduced below. Submit both a diskette and a hard copy of the manuscript. Do not bind the manuscript in any way; submit it as loose sheets in a box or envelope. The author should take the precaution of retaining a copy of the original manuscript and diskette.

2. The manuscript must be typed, double-spaced, including block quotations (prose quotations of 10 lines or more), poetry, notes, and bibliography. Manuscripts should be numbered consecutively from the first page through the back matter.

3. The manuscript should be prepared according to the Modern Language Association's style of intext documentation and works cited, restricting footnotes to explanatory notes. You should try to type all notes as endnotes, rather than as footnotes: that is, the notes should not appear on page bottoms but should be typed together in one section and placed at the end of the text and preceding the bibliography. The notes should be double-spaced. Number notes consecutively by chapter, beginning anew with number 1 in each chapter.

4. The author should go over the final copy of the manuscript carefully to check for consistency in spelling, capitalization, etc.

5. If the manuscript includes illustrations, photocopies with captions should be submitted with the manuscript, with an indication as to where they are to be placed. If the manuscript is accepted for publication, the press will advise on the form in which illustrations are to be submitted.

6. Seeking permissions for material used in the manuscript is the responsibility of the author/editor. The press will advise on material for which permission is needed and on how to seek it, and this should be discussed with the in-house editor at the earliest stages of manuscript preparation.

7. For more information, see *The Chicago Manual of Style* (University of Chicago Press). We generally follow the guidelines of this manual.

Editorial Program

Scholarly and trade titles in American literature, history, and culture; southern studies; Afro-American, women's and American studies; social sciences; popular culture; folklife; art and architecture; natural sciences; reference; other liberal arts.

Preparing Your Electronic Manuscript
*AAUP Guidelines**
The Journey of an Electronic Manuscript

The injunctions in these instructions may seem unreasonable or excessive to you, but there are good reasons for them, the best reason being the timely, economical production of your book. To demonstrate why we're asking you to follow these procedures, we'll give you an idea of what happens to your book during the editing and typesetting process. This is the journey an electronic manuscript makes at a typical publishing house.

At some point during the review process, the acquisitions editor may indicate to the author that the publisher would prefer the manuscript be on disk if it is accepted for publication. If the manuscript already is on disk, the editor will inquire about the hardware and software used in its preparation.

When the manuscript is accepted for publication, many presses send a questionnaire to the author asking for more formal information on hardware and software. Most editors routinely request a sample disk. If the editor is not familiar with the author's system, a sample disk will be required.

Editing

While the author is finishing the final revisions on the manuscript, the press uses the author's sample disk to verify that the disks will be usable by the typesetters and to determine how much work will be involved in any conversions or clean-up.

When the author's revisions are complete, the manuscript will go either directly to the copyeditor (at some publishing houses) or to the compositor or production department (at other publishing houses) for converting the files and inserting the press's codes for formatting extracts, different levels of headings, and soon. In addition, the compositor or editor will clean up any problems the author may have introduced in his or her work on the files, deleting unnecessary boldface commands, lowercasing chapter titles that are typed in all capital letters, deleting any soft hyphens, making sure the author has not used the letter I when he or she was supposed to use the number 1, and so forth.

How long this work takes depends entirely on how carefully the author prepared his or her disks and manuscript.

The manuscript is then edited. Some publishing houses edit electronic manuscripts on-screen using either in-house or freelance editors. Others find editing the hard copy most useful, letting the compositor, author, or an editor make final editing changes on the disks.

Presses also differ in the style of printout they send to the author for review of the copyediting. The press may send the actual copyedited manuscript. When the manuscript is edited on-screen, the editor will use a software program to prepare a printout that shows all the deletions, insertions, and changes in somewhat the same way a conventionally edited manuscript would. This printout is then sent to the author for review, along with a clean printout of the final edited manuscript if the changes are extensive enough for the printout showing the changes to be difficult to read.

After the author has reviewed the editing and indicated on the hard copy any final changes he or she would like to make in the manuscript, the copyeditor, compositor, or author will enter those changes on the disks and make a final mechanical check of the manuscript before giving it to the production department for typesetting.

Production

The designer prepares sample pages and specifications for the typesetter. Some designers use the author's files on their computers with page layout software to create these sample pages. With the sample pages the typesetter can verify that the output from the coded disks matches the design specifications.

Meanwhile, the compositor converts the editorially correct files into the language that will he read by the typesetter's computer. The conversion software reads the formatting codes and commands and converts them to the more complicated commands that tell the typesetting equipment what typeface, type size, and so forth to use.

The typesetter mails finished sets of proof to the publisher, who sends proof to the author. The importance of proofreading is unchanged. Alterations in proof are still expensive and undesirable.

The same electronic files originally prepared by the author have been used to run the typesetting equipment, helping to assure that the final book is as close as possible to what the author intended.

If the author has carefully prepared the disks according to the guidelines given here, the production of the finished book may be accomplished more expeditiously and thus less expensively, ensuring the most timely publication of the hook at the lowest possible price.

Tips on Preparing Your Electronic Manuscript

If you have prepared your manuscript on a computer, submitting it to your publisher on disks can save valuable time and effort if you follow the guidelines suggested here.

• Prepare your manuscript on the same system-both hardware and software—from start to finish. On the disks themselves, note the type of computer and the word processing program you have used.

• Create a new file for each chapter or other major subdivision of the hook. Front matter, bibliography, and other apparatus should be in separate files. DO NOT put the entire manuscript into one enormous file, which may be impossible for the publisher to convert.

• Name files sequentially: chap01, chap02, etc. Include a list of the file names with the disks.

• Most presses prefer to receive the notes grouped together in one or more separate files-not at the bottoms of pages or at the ends of chapters, unless you are instructed otherwise.

• Eliminate all formatting that is not essential to your manuscript. Do not use right-hand justification or font changes other than for underlining. Although most word processors now incorporate desktop publishing functions that enable you to produce an elaborate or fancy printout, remember that the typeset book will look quite different from your manuscript hard copy. Your publisher is interested in using your disks only to avoid re-keying the manuscript, and in general, the plainer the printout, the easier it will he to edit and design your book.

• Do not use running heads. Do number your manuscript consecutively from beginning to end.

• The manuscript (hard copy) and the disk that you send to the publisher must be identical. Thus, once you have printed out the final manuscript, do not make any further corrections to the computer files. If you make additional notations on the hard copy, do so in a bright-colored ink and be sure to let your publisher know that there are additions that will need to be entered on the disk.

• Do not put "soft" hyphens at the ends of lines; i.e., do not break words. In fact, it's best to turn off the automatic hyphenation feature on your word processing software. The only hyphens that should occur in your manuscript should be in hyphenated compound words.

• Double-space the entire manuscript, including notes, ex-

tracts, and bibliography. But do not put any extra spaces between paragraphs or between notes or bibliographical entries, or to set off an extract. Introduce extra vertical space only where extra space is to appear in the book to indicate a change of topic or abrupt break in the discussion.

• Use the tab key, not the space bar, your word processor's paragraphs.

• Use one space after colons, one after periods at the ends of sentences. If you are so accustomed to using two that you find it impossible to use one consistently, then use two consistently. In short, be consistent in your practice.

• When typing extracts, epigraphs, etc., use whatever commands your word processor has for changing the left margin. Do not insert extra spaces between words to achieve the effect of an indentation.

• Align all poetry passages so that they appear on manuscript hard copy exactly as you want them to appear in the printed book.

• Use two hyphens for a dash, with no space before, between, or after the hyphens. Use six hyphens to indicate the repetition of an author's name in a bibliography.

• Your word processor's codes for superscripts may be used.

• Caps and lowercase—not all caps—should be used for all subheads, chapter titles, and other elements of your manuscript that will eventually be display type. Never use all caps for authors' names in bibliographies or notes. Words typed all caps must be re-keyboarded, and errors can easily be introduced in this way.

• When several words in a row should be underlined, issue the underlining command at the beginning of the first word and turn it off at the end of the last word; do not issue separate underlining commands for each word.

• Hard returns (starting a new line by using the Enter key) should be used where you want a new line to appear in the printed book. Thus, they should never occur within a paragraph. but only at the ends of paragraphs and at the ends of items in lists and lines of poetry.

• Never use letters for numbers-or vice versa; i.e., don't type the lowercase "ell" for the number one or the letter "oh" for zero.

• If there are tables in your manuscript, make certain you have an accurate printout of them so the typesetter can easily follow the format. Use tabs, not hard spaces, to define columns, and avoid tables with more than 10 columns.

• If your manuscript has accented letters or special characters that are not available on your computer, provide a list of them and indicate how you have marked them on the hard copy and indicated them on disk. If possible, bring those special characters to your editor's attention in advance; many presses have devised coding systems for unusual characters and can supply you with a list.

*AAUP: The Association of American University Presses, Inc., 584 Broadway, New York NY 10012

Categories: Fiction—Nonfiction—African-American—Architecture—Arts—Asian-American—Biography—Civil War—College—Culture—Disabilities—Ethnic—Feminism—Film/Video—Gardening—General Interest—Health—History—Literature—Music—Native American—Photography—Reference—Regional—Scholarly—Textbooks—Theatre

Name: Seetha Srinivasan, Editor-in-Chief
Material: Scholarly Books
Name: JoAnne Prichard, Executive Editor
Material: Trade Books
Address: 3825 RIDGEWOOD RD
City/State/ZIP: JACKSON MS 39211-6492
Telephone: 601-982-6205
Fax: 601-982-6217
E-mail: press@ihl.state.ms.us

University Press

Please refer to The Conservatory of American Letters.

Valiant Press

Valiant Press, Inc.

Dear Author:

Thank you for your interest in Valiant Press, Inc. Our objective is to publish high quality nonfiction books about Florida subjects. This may include history, literature, travel, recreation, and biography. We prefer Florida authors, but will consider non-residents.

In an effort to help us assess your manuscript or book idea, we suggest the following guidelines:

1. Cover letter-brief with address, phone number

2. Book proposal-a description of the book with proposed title, author's name, a one or two sentence description, an estimate of the length either in words or pages, and the number and nature of any illustrations or photographs that are available

3. Intended audience or market—can include statistics, names of mailing lists, special interest groups, similar or competing books and how your book is different

4. Author's qualifications—should include occupational experience related to the book subject, writing experience (published books, articles, stories), awards, grants, professional affiliations, any experience in public speaking, radio or television appearances

5. Outline of book—should include a brief description of each chapter in two to ten pages

6. Two or three sample chapters/(if available)—should represent either the main theme or conclusion of the book

All of this information is optional. However, the more we know about your idea, the better able we are to give it thorough consideration.

We hope this is helpful and look forward to hearing from you.

Sincerely,

Charity Johnson

President

Categories: Regional—Florida Nonfiction

Name: Charity Johnson, President
Material: All
Address: PO BOX 330568
City/State/ZIP: MIAMI FL 33233
Telephone: 305-665-1889
Fax: 305-665-1889 (call first)

VOYAGEUR

Voyageur Press
Town Square Books
Where Good Books Are Second Nature

In 1992, Voyageur Press celebrated twenty years of excellence in publishing. While we've changed since 1972, our commit-

ment to producing beautiful, quality books and calendars has not. Today, we publish books on a variety of topics including natural history, wildlife, travel, hunting/fishing, how-to photography, titles of regional interest, calendars, and children's books related to these topics. Our extensive backlist demonstrates our versatility and success in producing substantive books.

Though we are known for producing quality, coffee-table-style books, we currently publish titles in most every format and welcome proposals of all types. We take pride in publishing books that include both exceptional four-color photography and informative, entertaining text.

Our authors include well-known authorities such as wolf expert L. David Mech, as well as relative newcomers to publishing such as sports attorney Ron Simon. Other established Voyageur Press authors include Les, Fran, Craig and Nadine Blacklock, Erwin and Peggy Bauer, Connie Toops, Boyd Norton, Chris Dorsey, and Rick Sammon. We take pride in the fact that many of our authors have published a number of books with us.

What should I include in my proposal?

• Brief cover letter introducing yourself and your writing experiences

• Summary (250 words) highlighting your proposal and its compellingly unique features

• Project outline and/or table of contents, including any appendices

• Brief biographical resume detailing your qualifications

• Sales and publicity strategies

• Reasons why you want to publish your work with Voyageur Press

• Date your manuscript will be finished

Please do not submit an entire manuscript at this stage.

If you intend to send artwork of any sort, please call us to obtain an Artwork Submissions Guideline and Liability Release Form. If we receive artwork without this form, we will immediately return the materials without considering them for publication.

When we receive your proposal

We will review your work and make our decision within two months. If it appears that your work is a good fit for Voyageur Press, we will request additional materials and ask that you complete our author questionnaire. After reviewing these materials, we will fill out a feasibility analysis, which investigates such basics as our cost of producing the book and our ability to market your work successfully and competitively. Please keep in mind that we'll base our final decision on your outline and summary, the information on the author questionnaire, your writing sample(s) and photography (if applicable), and our feasibility analysis. Each step plays an equally important role in the acquisitions process.

Since each proposal is unique, the decision process varies. While this is often the most anxious time for you, we ask that you please have patience as we evaluate your proposal.

If at any point in the process we decide not to publish your work, everything you've submitted will be returned to you via the U.S. Postal Service or United Parcel Service.

Please keep in mind

The acquisitions process is the first in a series of steps that can sometimes take more than a year. We publish new titles each year and since most of our books take at least twelve months to produce, we schedule our new titles approximately two seasons in advance.

If we do publish your work, we will ask that you submit text to us on IBM-compatible computer disks (along with two hard copies) and the originals of any artwork.

Thank you for your interest in Voyageur Press.

We look forward to receiving your proposal.

Categories: Agriculture—Animals—Automobiles—Aviation—Collectibles—Native American—Regional—Travel

Name: Michael Dregni, Editorial Director
Material: All
Address: 123 N 2ND ST
City/State/ZIP: STILLWATER MN 55082
Telephone: 612-430-2210
Fax: 612-430-2211
E-mail: books@voyageurpress.com

Warner Books
Warner Aspect

Due to the volume of submissions we receive, our policy is not to accept anything unsolicited, so we generally request that authors seek an agent. For our subject requirements, we are specifically interested in EPIC fantasy and science fiction for adults. Otherwise, the standard book proposal format applies: We prefer to receive a cover letter with the whole manuscript and a synopsis but are happy to review at least 3 chapters and a synopsis. We strongly encourage including a self addressed, stamped return package. When we are reviewing submissions, we are looking at both the plot and subject of the project as well as the author's writing ability and style.

Jaime Levine
Editorial Assistant
Categories: Fantasy—Science Fiction

Name: Betsy Mitchell, Editor-in-Chief
Material: Any
Name: Jaime Levine, Editorial Assistant
Material: Any
Address: 1271 AVENUE OF THE AMERICAS
City/State/ZIP: NEW YORK NY 10020
Telephone: 212-522-5113
Fax: 212-522-7990

Washington State University Press

What Do We Publish?

The WSU Press primarily publishes books dealing with the natural history, prehistory, history, politics, and culture of the northern West, particularly the states of Washington, Idaho, Montana, Oregon, and Alaska, and the province of British Columbia, although many of our books deal with people, events, and themes in the broader American and Canadian West. The WSU Press accepts manuscripts of history, anthropology/archaeology; biography, personal essays, and a wide variety of other genres. We do not encourage submissions of literary criticism, poetry, or fiction. Please request a copy of the WSU Press catalog if you are unsure whether or not your manuscript is appropriate and would like to see examples of our recent titles.

Your Initial Contact with the Press

Please do not submit complete manuscripts on initial inquiry. A letter describing your manuscript, a table of contents or chapter outline, and a sample chapter is all that is necessary upon the initial inquiry. If your proposed book will include illustrations, please send high-quality photocopies of a few of these at this stage.

Our Decision-making Process

If your initial inquiry seems like a promising proposal that fits the scope of the WSU Press publications program, we will ask you to submit an entire manuscript. The staff will review the manuscript, and if we believe it has publication potential, we will send it to confidential outside reviewers qualified to address the merits of your topic.

If the outside reviews are favorable, we then will take your manuscript, along with the outside reports and staff analysis, to our editorial board for a final recommendation on whether or not to publish. The length of the review process varies from manuscript to manuscript, but normally a review can be completed in four to six months.

Submitting Your Manuscript:
The Hard Copy

• All manuscripts must be completed on computer equipment. Only on rare occasions will typewritten and/or handwritten manuscripts be considered for publication.

• Everything—including notes, bibliography, long quotations, captions, etc.-must be double-spaced. Do not add extra space between paragraphs unless you wish to introduce a space break in the book to indicate a change of subject. If introducing such a space break, please insert asterisks-centered on the page—to indicate a subject change.

• If your work includes endnotes, a complete citation of a work must be given the first time it appears in each chapter. In other words, do not give a full citation in chapter one, and then an abbreviated citation the next time the citation occurs a few chapters later.

• With very few exceptions, citations should be ganged at the end of a paragraph. In other words, do not enter note numbers or several sentences in a paragraph; rather, use only one note number at the end of a paragraph, and include a more extensive citation that notes all the pertinent materials used for that paragraph.

• Be sure that your pages are numbered (this can be done by hand) consecutively from page one to the end. Do not start over on page one with each chapter.

• For a dash, use two hyphens with no space before, after, or between.

• Use caps and lower case—not full caps—for all chapter titles, subheads, and other elements that will be set as display type. Never use full caps for authors' names in bibliographies or notes.

• Never use letters for numbers, or vice versa; i.e., don't type the lowercase letter "ell" for the number one, or the letter "oh" for zero.

• Use one space after periods. Use one space after colons. If you are so accustomed to using two spaces that you find it impossible to use one consistently, then use two, consistently. In short, be consistent in your practice.

• Include acknowledgments and a dedication if you wish to have them in your book.

• We do not have a uniform style sheet because we publish in a number of disciplines. We want your manuscript to conform to the norms of your discipline. If your work includes endnotes and/or a bibliography, we do, however, ask that your citation style be consistent throughout. Generally, we encourage you to follow *The Chicago Manual of Style*, 14th edition.

Submitting Your Manuscript:
The Electronic Version

• Most Important: Once you have printed the final manuscript (hard copy), do not make any further changes in the computer files. In other words, the manuscript and the disk must be identical.

• Do not submit computer disks at the time you submit your manuscript for review. Should your manuscript pass the review

Books

process, we will then ask you to submit disks.

• We prefer that manuscripts be completed on WordPerfect, Microsoft Word, or another well-known word processing application software. If you are using an unusual software, please check with the Press before submitting your disk.

• Label each disk with file name(s), software used, and software version.

• Submit files on 3½" floppy disks. We do not accept 5¼" disks.

• Prepare your manuscript on the same system-both hardware and software-from start to finish.

• Chapters, notes, front matter, bibliography, etc., should all be kept in separate files. Please submit a list of file names with the disks. Name files sequentially, such as Chapt 1, Chapt 2.

• Notes must be placed together in one or more separate files, not at the bottoms of pages or at the ends of chapters. If your word processing software has the capability to do on-page footnotes, do not use it.

• Keep all formatting (typeface changes, spacing, etc.) to a minimum. Although most word processors now incorporate desktop publishing functions that enable you to produce an elaborate printout, ignore the urge to do so. The simpler the printout, the easier it will be to edit and design your book

• Do not use running headers or footers.

• Do not put "soft" hyphens at the ends of lines; i.e., do not break words. It is best to turn off the automatic hyphenation feature on your word processing software.

• Do not use right-hand justification.

• Use the tab key, not the space bar, to indent paragraphs, and make sure the length of the indentation is consistent throughout the manuscript.

• When keyboarding extracts and other features indented from the left margin, do not insert hard spaces in the manuscript (i.e., do not tab, type a line, hit "enter," and tab for the next line). Instead, simply add a return before and after the quotation; software commands allowing you to indent the whole passage at once should not be used.

• Your word processor's codes for superscripts may be used.

• Hard returns (starting a new line by using the "enter" key) should be used only where you want a new line to appear in the printed book. Thus, they should never occur within a paragraph, but only at the ends of paragraphs.

• If your manuscript has accented letters or special characters that are not available on your computer, provide a list of them and mark them by hand in the manuscript.

• If there are tables in your manuscript, make certain you have an accurate printout of them so the typesetter can easily follow the format. Use single tabs (not hard spaces or multiple tabs or spaces), to define columns, and avoid tables with more than ten columns.

Photographs, Maps, and Illustrations

Authors are responsible for obtaining illustrations for their work, including obtaining the rights to have illustrations published. The WSU Press can provide assistance in map design. For example, we can note special features that might not appear on standard maps, and we can delete features that are unnecessary for your book. However, authors must provide a "base map" that accurately depicts the area you want to show. This map is then scanned electronically by the Press prior to making a final map for the book. If the "base map" is not the author's own, or in the public domain, the author must obtain the rights to the map—including, if necessary, the rights to publish an altered map if WSU Press makes changes. Obtaining illustration reproductions and publication rights involves expenses and a considerable amount of time. Authors should anticipate both the expenses and the search and reproduction time required. Not having illustration reproductions or publication rights to those illustrations can dramatically slow the publication process.

When requesting photos, ask for 5"x7" or 8"x10" black and white glossies. Specify that they are to be used in a book and ask for the best copy obtainable.

If you intend to prepare maps or other artwork yourself, or hire it done, let us know so we can supply you with instructions that will ensure the usability of your art.

Number each photo, map, or illustration with a label on the back (never write directly on photos with pencil or pen). Type a separate list of captions, keyed to the number on each illustration (do not attach captions to the illustrations). The captions should include an acknowledgment of the source of the illustration (libraries and other repositories will usually provide specific instructions for how a photo or illustration is to be credited). If particular wording is not specified, use "courtesy of ...." Authors must provide both a hard copy and a disk copy of all captions.

Permissions

Authors are responsible for obtaining permission to use previously published written material and illustrations. Further, if more than a page or two of your manuscript substantially duplicates material you have published elsewhere, you must obtain permission from the copyright holder (usually the original publisher) for its use. Please send us copies of your letters of permission so we can ensure that special requirements-for example, that the grantor be provided a complimentary copy of the book-are fulfilled.

The Author's Contract

Once the editorial board recommends publication, we will draft a contract for your consideration. Royalty provisions and some other contract terms vary depending on the kind of book and its estimated market.

Categories: Nonfiction—History—Native American—Regional

Name: Keith Petersen, Acquisitions Editor
Material: All
Address: PO BOX 645910
City/State/ZIP: PULLMAN WA 99164-5910
Telephone: 509-335-3518
Fax: 509-335-8568
E-mail: pkeithc@wsu.edu
Internet: www.wsu.edu

Weidner & Sons Publishing
Delaware Estuary Press, Medlaw Books, Tycooly USA, Perspectives in Psychotherapy

We get hundreds of letters and manuscripts from authors wishing to have us consider publishing their book. Many ask for a list of our publications and our guidelines for manuscript submissions. We suggest the following:

• Always include a return envelope of sufficient size and with sufficient postage to cover a response or return of your manuscript. We will not, indeed *cannot*, respond to any inquiries that do not come accompanied by postage. The number of inquiries and submissions would soon bankrupt us for return postage!

• We are an academic textbook and reference book publisher. We do not publish fiction, children's books, elementary or high school texts, short stories, novels, or poetry.

• Include a few chapters, an outline, and your credentials. The latter is important to establish your authority in the subject area. It is not necessary that you include a resume; however, if you are on the faculty of a college or university and your manuscript could be used as a text in your course, it helps us to evaluate its potential sales. (That's why we're in business.)

• Rather than requesting a catalog of our publications, go to our "Booklist" where all our publications are listed.

• Let us know what word processing program (if any) was used to create your manuscript. We prefer Word or WordPerfect 6.0 but can work from others. When in doubt, save as an ASCII text file. Submissions can be made on disk, but also include two printed copies. We do not have the time or resources to load every disk and print out several copies for our editors to evaluate.

• You can contact us here at our e-mail address.

• Where possible, send us your e-mail address, as well as your snail mail, FAX, and telephone numbers.

Categories: Nonfiction—Ecology—Economics—Education—Environment—Medicine—Natural History—Nursing—Ornithology—Psychology—Psychotherapy—Reference—Textbooks

Name: Submissions Editor
Material: All
Address: PO BOX 2178
City/State/ZIP: RIVERTON NJ 08077
Telephone: 609-486-1755
Fax: 609-486-7583
E-mail: weidner@waterw.com
Internet: www.waterw.com/~weidner

White-Boucke Publishing

Here are some guidelines:
• nonfiction only
• send summary, TOC, a few sample chapters and intended length
• September is cutoff for following year
• reply time varies from two weeks to six months
• no advances paid (royalties only)
• if we accept your manuscript and it needs extensive editing, you pay the editor
• if we accept your manuscript, we'll require it eventually be submitted on IBM-compatible diskette

Thanks and good luck with your book!

Laurie Boucke
White-Boucke Publishing

Categories: Nonfiction—Humor—Parenting—Reference—Travel

Name: Laurie Boucke, Vice President
Material: All
Address: PO BOX 400
City/State/ZIP: LAFAYETTE CO 80026
Telephone: 303-604-0661
E-mail: LaurieB@compuserve.com

White Mane Publishing Company, Inc.
Burd Street, Ragged Edge, WM Kids

To follow through on your idea for a book, all we ask for in the way of particulars is a one to two page proposal. The proposal should include:

1) a chapter outline indicating the approximate length of the book and the number of illustrations you would like to use;

2) as realistic as possible a time table for completion of the manuscript;

3) a sample dust jacket paragraph that would provide an idea of how you would describe the book to prospective buyers;

4) a biographical paragraph about yourself stressing your qualifications to write the book (again, think in terms of the dust jacket, how you would describe yourself to a potential buyer in a bookstore);

5) your marketing ideas to help us determine the marketing potential of your manuscript;

6) your evening telephone number if we needed to discuss your proposal.

We are definitely interested in your proposal. However, we need to be able to consider it in our standard format to make sure we don't overlook important details.

Thank you for your interest in White Mane Publishing Company, and its various imprints. We look forward to receiving your proposal and will reply to it promptly.

Harold E. Collier
Business Manager
Categories: Biography—Children—Civil War—Military

Name: Acquisitions Editor
Material: All
Address: PO BOX 152
City/State/ZIP: 63 W BURD ST
Telephone: SHIPPENSBURG PA 17257
Fax: 717-532-2237
E-mail: 717-532-7704

White Pine Press
Springhouse Editions

Dear Writer,

Thank you for your interest in publishing your work with White Pine Press. As a nonprofit literary publisher, our goal is to enrich our heritage by publishing works by writers and translators which might be overlooked by commercial publishing houses. We publish fiction, nonfiction and poetry. Along with our general titles, we have established four distinct series. We receive in excess of one thousand submissions each year and publish eight to ten books per year. We do not publish romance novels, science fiction, "how-to" or "self-help" books, or children's literature.

It generally takes between three and six months for unsolicited material to be read by our editorial staff. Please do not telephone us to check on the manuscript. If you want to know if your manuscript has reached us, please include a self-addressed, stamped postcard marked "Manuscript received by White Pine Press" and we will return it to you upon receipt of the manuscript.

Series

Our Secret Weavers Series brings the voices of Latin American women to an English-speaking audience. The Human Rights Series is dedicated to discussing and revealing human rights issues from around the world. Our Dispatches Series presents fine fiction from around the world and our New American Voice Series, established in 1996, consists of first novels by American writers.

Fiction/Nonfiction

Please submit a query letter, along with a synopsis, several sample chapters, a brief biographical note and a list of previous publications.

American Poetry

We are not presently accepting unsolicited poetry manuscripts except as entries for the White Pine Press Poetry Prize competition. This award, given once each year, consists of a cash prize and publication by the press. The final judge is a poet of national stature. Previous judges have included David St. John, Mekeel McBride and Maurice Kenny. Please send an SASE for guidelines for this competition.

Poetry in Translation

Please send a query letter and a representative sample of the work, along with biographical information and publication credentials of the author.

Categories: Fiction—Nonfiction—Hispanic—Literature—Native American—Short Stories—Women's Fiction

Name: Elaine LaMattina
Material: Fiction
Name: Dennis Maloney
Material: Nonfiction
Address: 10 VILLAGE SQUARE
City/State/ZIP: FREDONIA NY 14063
Telephone: 716-672-5743
Fax: 716-672-4724
E-mail: pine@net.bluemoon.net

Wilder Publishing Center
Amherst H. Wilder Foundation

How to Write a Book for the Wilder Publishing Center

You've helped a lot of people. Maybe you set up a neighborhood bank, put a violence-torn community on a peaceful track, led a community development initiative, or mastered the art of nonprofit management. Perhaps you've written about your work in professional journals and other texts. You may be training and teaching. People frequently turn to you for your professional expertise, and you've decided its time to share that expertise with a larger audience. Wilder Publishing Center may be the place for you to do just that.

What We're Looking for

Wilder Publishing Center is looking for book proposals from experts in community issues, nonprofit management and organizational development, and human services.

We want manuscripts that identify "best practice" and make it easy to understand. We feel our publications are successful if the reader can pick one up and put it to work immediately. Thus our publications emphasize practical experience and step-by-step directions. To date, we've used three formats, although we are open to others:

• Workbooks that explain a process and provide worksheets to guide the reader through that process.

• Research reports and literature reviews that sift through many studies to distill basic trends useful for community organizers and policy makers.

• Curricula that human services professionals can easily follow and adapt for their programs.

Our publications are used by nonprofit managers, community organizers, grassroots groups, policy makers, consultants, trainers, funders, and human service professionals. We seek proposals that appeal to one or more of these audiences.

How to Submit Your Proposal

Do not send a computer disk. You need not send an entire manuscript.

Your proposal should specify the following:

• *Audience*—who you see as the users of your information.

• *Objective*—one paragraph that describes the impact your book will make on its readers.

• *Market-types* of organizations most likely to purchase the book, and your estimate of the number of such organizations.

• *Competing* publications—competing or similar titles, if any; be sure to describe how your book will differ from them.

• *Contents*, including:

• A chapter outline with paragraphs or lists of all topics to be covered in each chapter.

• A sample worksheet, if worksheets are to be part of the book. Appendix headings, partial bibliography, and headings for other back matter.

• A description of any illustrations you feel are necessary.

• Sample chapter(s). This is optional. You may enclose a sample chapter if you've already written one, or save yourself the postage by waiting for us to respond to your detailed outline.

• *Process*—a brief description of the sources you will use as you write.

• *Author qualifications*—a brief description of yourself, relevant experience, any previous publications, and why you are qualified to write this book.

We encourage you to look through our publications brochure *before* sending us a proposal. Better still, get a hold of our books and review them first.

When to Expect an Answer

Within two months of receiving your proposal, we will respond telling you either:

We are not interested in the proposal, or we have an interest in the proposal, but need more time to study it.

If we have an interest in the proposal, the actual decision to publish may take another two to three months. During this time we will evaluate the manuscript for its fit with our mission, niche, existing publications, and marketing capacities; its uniqueness, contribution to the field, and impact on readers; and your qualifications as an author and expert. We may also send the proposal for peer review, ask for writing samples, request sample chapters (or a complete manuscript if available), and speak with you about timelines, funding, and other information as appropriate.

What Happens When We Accept Your Book

If we're interested in publishing the book, we work with you to develop a contract we're both happy with. In some cases, we are able to raise funds to pay for the writing of the book, in which case we prefer to purchase the manuscript outright. In others, we are able to work out a royalty agreement. Once you deliver the manuscript, expect rigorous editing and revision; your manuscript will be reviewed by a minimum of three outside experts and often many more. The amount of time it takes to produce the book varies with the scope and size of the work. Once the book is printed, it will be promoted a minimum of four times each year through direct mail.

About the Wilder Publishing Center

Based in St. Paul, Minnesota, the Wilder Publishing Center is a part of the Amherst H. Wilder Foundation, one of the oldest and largest nonprofit human service agencies in North America. Our first book, *Strategic Planning Workbook for Nonprofit Organizations*, has become a classic. Among our other titles are *Collaboration Handbook: Creating, Sustaining, and Enjoying the Journey* and *Preventing Violence in Rural America: A Review of What Works*.

Categories: Nonfiction—Nonprofit Management—Community Building

Name: Acquisitions Editor
Material: All
Address: WILDER PUBLISHING CENTER
Address: 919 LAFOND AVE
City/State/ZIP: ST PAUL MN 55104
Telephone: 612-659-6013
Internet: www.wilder.org

Woman in the Moon Publications

Our Founding and Mission

Woman in the Moon Publications was founded in Compton, California, on April 12, 1979, when the sole owner/publisher, Dr. SDiane Bogus, was seeking publication for a poetry collection entitled *Woman in the Moon*. A nationally known African-American poet/writer, Dr. Bogus holds a Ph.D. in American Literature and Composition from Miami University in Ohio and a Ph.D. in Parapsychology from the American International University in Hawaii. In addition to her position as publisher of Woman in the Moon Publications, Dr. Bogus is a professor at DeAnza College in the San Francisco Bay area.

Feminism has changed the ideological view of women on Planet Earth, and so too, the face of the proverbial "man in the moon," hence our logo of a "woman in the moon."

Today, Woman in the Moon's mission is symbolic of its logo, the moon itself, a symbol of nocturnal peace, luminescence, female power, psychic ability, and compassionate love. We see ourselves as humanists in service to the New Age. We wish to bring people and ideas together as well as help usher in the Age of Peace, serving as a conduit for the arts and the human potential. Woman in the Moon is particularly open to works that help others by inspiration, encouragement and enlightenment. An author looking to publish under the Woman in the Moon imprint must convey peace and understanding.

We Publish Books On
Narrative Poetry

Written to trace personal, spiritual journeys or fictional sojourns, such as "The Rhyme of the Ancient Mariner," or "The Raven," or "Casey at the Bat." We also like collections based on a single theme. 48-64 pages including introduction and preface.

Self-Help/How-To Prose

We like topics on health and healing: physical, mental, spiritual, psychic and personal relationships, dreams, race, business, money, sex, learning a new skill, and the art of writing. 64-300 pages including introduction and preface.

Nonfiction

Informational reference, autobiography/biography, women's issues, cookbooks, ethnic, cultural traditions, memoirs, family history. 64-300 pages.

Fiction

Prefer themes on psychic phenomena, angels, life after death, astral projection, and New Age topics. 64-300 pages.

Children's Books

Poetry, inspirational stories.

Manuscript Submission Procedure

Following your telephone or letter query, you will be invited to submit your manuscript for evaluation as to possible publication by Woman in the Moon publisher, Dr. SDiane Adamz-Bogus. Woman in the Moon has a reading fee, which must be submitted with the manuscript, to have an editor assigned to read and evaluate it.

Manuscripts must be as editorially polished as you, the author, can produce. Occasionally, due to our prior publishing and budget commitments, urgency of topic or seasonal timing, we may ask the prospective author to co-pay specific pre-publication costs, if necessary to expedite the process. These expenses are only addressed after an editor has evaluated your work and the publisher has informed you that we desire to publish it. Do not let these requirements deter you from querying us about submission of your manuscript. Rough works can hide great writing! Let Woman in the Moon be the judge. Let us read and evaluate your manuscript and give our recommendation as to publishing.

Once your editor has been assigned, she or he will notify you of receipt of your manuscript and contact you within four to six weeks with a complete evaluation report of your manuscript. A copy is sent to Dr. Adamz-Bogus' desk at the same time one is sent to you. If your work is recommended for publication by Woman in the Moon, the publisher will read the manuscript personally. If she concurs with the advice, you will hear directly from the publisher with her comments and opinions of your work; she'll provide contractual information, including editorial, production, design, book credentials, promotions, marketing, or costs. However, we are not a subsidy publisher. We have another division for alternative publishing.

If your manuscript is rejected for any reason, the two- to three-page evaluation report from your assigned editor will tell you specifically why it has been rejected, what can be done to improve it and you will be given recommendations to professional editorial services and other sources. We want you to accomplish your goal: becoming a published author. If Woman in the Moon cannot publish your manuscript, we want you to know the options open to you. You are welcome to resubmit the same manuscript to Woman in the Moon after it has been reworked (a reading fee will still apply), and to expedite a second evaluation report, you should mention this is a resubmission so the same editor can be re-assigned if possible.

Books

Submission Instructions

1. Type or word-process manuscript, double-space with your legal name, address and telephone number (single-space this information) in the upper left corner of the first page and on subsequent pages. Page numbers should be on upper right corner of each page.

2. Entitle the manuscript and include pseudonym (if any) for your byline on the cover page.

3. Submit two (2) copies of the manuscript.

4. Attach a cover letter outlining your manuscript and tell us about yourself: any qualifications or experience pertaining to writing the enclosed manuscript.

5. Include the reading fee to expedite processing.

Woman in the Moon accepts manuscripts for consideration January 1 to April 30. Reading fee is $50.00, after April 30, $100.00.

Categories: Fiction—Nonfiction—Children—Inspirational—Poetry—Self-help/How-to Prose—Narrative Poetry

Name: Acquisitions Editor

Material: All

Address: 1409 THE ALAMEDA

City/State/ZIP: SAN JOSE CA 408-279-6636

Telephone: 408-279-6626

Fax: 408-279-6636

E-mail: womaninmoon@earthlink.com

Nota bene: Reading fee required. Possible other author financial involvement required.

Woodbine House
Publishers of the Special-Needs Collection

Woodbine House welcomes submissions from all writers-agented and unagented, previously published and unpublished. We will gladly consider book-length, nonfiction manuscripts on almost any subject related to disabilities, but **we do not publish and will not consider fiction, poetry, and personal accounts.**

We favor books that are one of a kind, but will also consider books that take fresh slants on old subjects. Regardless of a book's subject, we are always impressed by authors who 1) can write with clarity, authority, and style; and 2) can demonstrate that their book has a clearly defined market that they know how to reach.

To submit a proposal, please send a query letter. If you would like to submit more than a query letter, you can send the following information:

1. The table of contents;

2. 2-3 sample chapters;

3. An annotated list of books in print on the subject, explaining how your book differs from the competition;

4. A list of potential markets, including specific organizations, book clubs, and groups of individuals that would buy your book;

5. A short biographical note describing your qualifications to write this book;

6. Estimated length and completion date.

Manuscripts should be typed. Photocopies and computer printouts are acceptable, as are simultaneous submissions, if so marked. Allow 3-6 weeks for a response.

Categories: Disabilities

Name: Susan Stokes, Editor
Material: All
Address: 6510 BELLS MILL RD
City/State/ZIP: BETHESDA MD 20817
Telephone: 301-897-3570
Fax: 301-897-5838

Word Dancer Press

Please refer to Quill Driver Books/Word Dancer Press, Inc.

World Leisure Corporation

TO: WRITERS
FROM: CHARLES LEOCHA, WORLD LEISURE
RE: SUBMISSION GUIDELINES

Here are the submission guidelines you requested. We are publishing sports travel, family travel, gift/self-help books and some children's books.

Before any submissions will be considered please prepare:

• an introduction explaining why someone should read the materials you are presenting

• an annotated table of contents outlining each chapter of your proposed book

• at least one sample chapter so I can see your writing style

If I feel your book will fit into our coming book lists I will contact you. Do not send queries.

Send a SASE if you wish to have your manuscript returned. Otherwise I will return your cover letter with my notes to you.

Sincerely, Charles Leocha, Publisher

Categories: Nonfiction—Children—Relationships—Sports—Travel

Name: Charles Leocha, Publisher
Material: All
Address: 177 PARIS ST
City/State/ZIP: BOSTON MA 02128
Telephone: 617-569-1966
Fax: 617-561-7654
E-mail: WLEISURE@aol.com

YMAA Publication Center

The proposed work should address some aspect of Chinese culture—martial arts, Qigong (Chi Kung), medicine, etc. No children's stories, please.

For fastest response, please use the following guidelines:

• Send a brief summary of each chapter and one complete sample chapter. Include sample photos or drawings, if available (photocopies or facsimiles acceptable).

• Include a one page (maximum) author biography. Relate salient experience and qualifications.

• Include a one page (maximum) cover letter. State your intention for writing the book, the proposed audience, and describe the unique, compelling features of the book.

• Letter quality computer printouts acceptable.

Categories: Nonfiction—Health—Martial Arts

Name: Andrew Murray, Acquisitions Editor
Material: Chinese Martial Arts, Chinese Healing Arts
Address: 38 HYDE PARK AVE
City/State/ZIP: JAMAICA PLAIN MA 02130
Telephone: 617-524-9235
Fax: 617-524-4184
E-mail: ymaa@aol.com

ZondervanPublishingHouse

Zondervan Publishing House

The Book Group editorial staff is unable to take query calls or answer query letters from authors and agents. To be considered by our review editors, both previously published books and manuscripts must be submitted to the address shown below.

• Although every proposal is reviewed, we cannot acknowledge any submission or return any material that does not include a self-addressed, stamped envelope.

• Responses are generally sent within three months.

• We are unable to acknowledge receipt of your submission or give status reports.

• We cannot be responsible for original copies of manuscripts, photos, artwork, etc. Do not send these materials.

Thank you for your understanding about these necessary policies in regard to the thousands of proposals we receive each year.

Zondervan is a nondenominational religious publisher that publishes primarily for the Protestant evangelical market, so we look for books written from that perspective. We publish both general books and academic and professional books. As a division of HarperCollinsPublishers, Zondervan maintains its editorial independence and its evangelical integrity while having an avenue into the general marketplace.

Trade books include general nonfiction, biographies, autobiographies, self-help books, some fiction, books for children and youth, books for ministry to children and youth, and devotional books. **Academic and professional books** include college and seminary textbooks (such as books on biblical studies, theology, church history, and the humanities); books on such subjects as preaching, counseling, discipleship, worship, and church renewal for pastors, professionals, and lay leaders in ministry; theological and biblical reference books; and a variety of books written from a Wesleyan perspective, as well as Bible study resources and references for the lay audience. For separate academic and professional guidelines, write to Manuscript Review at the address listed below.

Zondervan *does not review* booklets, sermons, dissertations; four-color children's storybooks; game, puzzle, or craft books (except for children); art books, cookbooks, charts; books of quotation or poetry; short story collections, plays, or romances; Sunday school curriculum, high school textbooks, coloring books, tracts, or books on tape. (We only produce tapes for books we have previously published in printed form.)

Submissions should include:

1. A cover letter

2. An outline and a sample chapter or two*

3. A one-paragraph synopsis of each of the other chapters*

*If you are submitting a previously published book, please send a copy of the book in lieu of a manuscript

In your cover letter, please answer these questions:

1. What is the book's subject matter and approach?

2. For whom is the book written?

3. What distinguishes your book from others on the subject?

4. What need or purpose does your book fulfill that the others do not?

5. What are your qualifications for writing this book?

6. Why is your book appropriate for Zondervan?

Audio cassettes, computer disks, or video tapes in lieu of typed manuscripts are not acceptable. Proposals should be submitted in this format:

1. Unbound and without staples, paste-up, or anything that will interfere with photocopying should multiple copies be necessary for committee review

2. Consecutively numbered throughout

Clean photocopies are acceptable. It is helpful for your name and address to be on each document.

Although Zondervan does do extensive editing on many manuscripts, we do not have the staff for re-writing, so-called "ghost-writing," or to serve as co-authors. You may want to contact local universities or colleges, writers guilds, or editorial services for help.

Categories: Fiction—Nonfiction—Adventure—African-American—Biography—Children—Christian Interests—Family—Marriage—Parenting—Relationships—Spiritual—Women's issues

Name: Diane Bloem, Review editor
Material: All
Address: 5300 PATTERSON AVE SE
City/State/ZIP: GRAND RAPIDS, MICHIGAN 49530
Telephone: 616-698-6900
Fax: 616-698-3454
E-mail: zph.editorial@zph.com

Books

Topic Index

This index provides the names of publishers interested in seeing material on or relating to the topics listed. Periodical publishers are *italicized,* book publishers are set in Roman type.

-A-

Academic

The Denali Press, *Journal of Modern Literature,* Lehigh University Press

Acting

Dramatics

Activism, social

Country Connections

Acupuncture

Blue Poppy Press, Paradigm Publications

Adoption

Perspective Press

Adventure

Acorn, Adventure Journal, Aegina Press, *Amelia Press, American Fitness,* American Literary Press, *Belletrist Review, Bike,* Black Forest Press, *Boys' Life, Bugle, California Explorer, Canoe & Kayak,* Century Press, Clover Park Press, The Conservatory of American Letters, *Creative With Words Publications, Crusader, Dagger of the Mind,* Dutton Children's Books, *FATE, Georgia Journal,* The Globe Pequot Press, *Gold and Treasure Hunter, Happy Times Monthly, HeartLand Boating, Heartland USA, Home Times, House, Home & Garden, Iconoclast, INK Literary Review, INsider, It's Your Choice,* Kodansha America, Kroshka Books, *Marlin, Men's Journal,* Minstrel Books, *My Le!gacy, National Enquirer, Nostalgia, Oatmeal & Poetry, On the Scene, Outdoor Life, Paddler,* Paladin Press, Pocket Books, *Potpourri, Power and Light,* PREP Publishing, *R-A-D-A-R, Radiance, Recreation News,* Richard C. Owen Publishers, *Rider, Rising Star Publishers, Skiing,* Smithsonian Odyssey, *Snow Country,* SpanPress, *Specialty Travel Index, Sports Afield, Swank, Texas Parks & Wildlife, Times News Service,* University Editions, *WE, Western RV News, Wisconsin Trails, Women's Sports & Fitness,* Zondervan Publishing House

Advertising Art

Art Direction Book Company

Aesthetics

Dermascope

African-American

Aegina Press, *Affaire de Coeur,* African American Images, *Amelia Press, Arkansas Review,* Barricade Books, Beyond Words Publishing, *Birth Gazette, Black Child, Black Lace, Blackfire, BLK,* Branden Publishing Company, Bryant & Dillon Publishers, Calyx Books, *Calyx Journal, Career Focus, Careers & the disABLED, Carolina Quarterly, Centennial Review,* Century Press, Charles River Press, *Chicago Review Press, Circle K,* Clarity Press, *Communications Publishing Group,* The Denali Press, *EEO BiMonthly, Emerge, Equal Opportunity Publications, Essence, Feminist Studies, First Opportunity, Headway, HealthQuest, Home Times,* Intercultural Press, *It's Your Choice,* Judson Press, Kodansha America, Kroshka Books, *Kuumba,* Mayhaven Publishing, McFarland & Company, *Message, Minority Engineer, Mother Jones, Obsidian II, Oracle Story & Letters, Papyrus,* Pelican Publishing Company, *Power and Light, Radiance,* Richard C. Owen Publishers, *Rising Star Publishers,* Rutledge Hill Press, *South Florida History, Spirit, Successful Black Parenting,* Temple University Press, *Tequesta,* University Editions, University of Nebraska Press, University Press of Mississippi, *WD-Workforce Diversity, Woman Engineer,* Zondervan Publishing House*! ain*

Aging

Quill Driver Books/Word Dancer Press

Agriculture

Alabama Living, The American Cottage Gardener, Centennial Review, Environment, Feed-Lot, Futurific, Georgia Journal, Pennsylvania Farmer, Small Farm Today, Storey Communications, Ten Speed Press, Texas A&M University Press, University of Maine Press, University of Nebraska Press, Voyageur Press, *Wines & Vines*

Airlines

ASU Travel Guide

Aliens/UFO/ET

Planetary Connections

Alternate Lifestyles

American Fitness, National Enquirer, Natural Health, The Yoga Journal

American History

Cobblestone

American Sovereignty

American Survival Guide

Animal Protection

Animal People

Animal Rights

Animals' Agenda

Animals

American Hunter, American Kennel Club Gazette, Animal People, Animals, Back Home in Kentucky, Barron's Educational Series, *Birds & Blooms*, Black Iron Cookin' Company, *Boys' Life, Boys' Quest*, Brookline Books, *Bugle, Cat Fancy, CATsumer Report*, Chicago Review Press, *Country Connections*, Cowles Creative Publishing, *Crayola Kids, Creative With Words Publications, Defenders, DogGone*, Dutton Children's Books, *E, Environment, Florida Wildlife, Girls' Life, Good Dog!, GRIT*, Hancock House, *Happy Times Monthly, Heartland USA, Hopscotch for Girls, House,Home & Garden*, Kodansha America, Lumen Editions, *Lutheran Digest*, Lyons & Burford Publishers!lain, Mayhaven Publishing, Minstrel Books, *Mushing, My Legacy, National Enquirer*, The Nature Conservancy's Habitat Series, *Northeast Equine Journal, Oatmeal & Poetry, On the Scene, Outdoor Life*, Outrider Press, *PanGaia, Planetary Connections*, Pocket Books, Quixote Press, *R-A-D-A-R, Ranger Rick, Reptile & Amphibian*, Richard C. Owen Publishers, Smithsonian Oceanic Collection/Smithsonian's Backyard, Storey Communications, Temple University Press, Ten Speed Press, Voyageur Press, *WE, Wildlife Art*

Anthropology

Bucknell University Press, *Natural History*, Texas A&M University Press

Antiques

Amelia Press, Antique Trader Weekly, Back Home in Kentucky, Collecting Toys, Collectors News, Colonial Homes, Country America, Country Living, Early American Homes, Echoes, Excalibur Publications, *Georgia Journal, House, Home & Garden, Mountain Living, Nineteenth Century, Pennsylvania Heritage, Yesterday's Magazette*

Arboriculture

Tree Care Industry

Archaeology

Archaeology, Plenum Publishing, *Smithsonian Magazine*, Texas A&M University Press, University of Oklahoma Press

Archery, primitive

Backwoodsman

Architecture

Back Home in Kentucky, Balcony Press, Bucknell University Press, *Centennial Review, Charleston, Christianity and the Arts, Colonial Homes*, David R. Godine, *Early American Homes, Echoes, Futurific, Home Improver, House, Home & Garden, Joiners' Quarterly*, Lehigh University Press, Mage Publishers, *Metropolis, Mountain Living, Nineteenth Century*, Pelican Publishing Company, *Pennsylvania Heritage*, Storey Communications, *Sunset*, Texas A&M University Press, University Press of Mississippi, *WE*

Art, B/W

Maelstrom

Arts

Afterimage, Allworth Press, *Amelia Press, American Indian Art, American Scholar, American Legion*, Anchorage Press, *Arkansas Review, Artist's, Art Papers, Art Times, Avenues, Back Home in Kentucky*, Balcony Press, *Bleach, Boston Review*, Branden Publishing Company, Bucknell University Press, *Career Focus, Carefree Enterprise, Centennial Review*, Century Press, *Charleston, Chiron Review, Christianity and the*

Arts, Chrysalis Reader, Clockwatch Review, Communications Publishing Group, Cream City Review, Critique, Cross & Quill, Curriculum Vitae, David R. Godine, *Decorative Artist's Workbook, Early American Homes, Evergreen Chronicles, FIBERARTS, Harper's Magazine, Heaven Bone, Home Times, Hope, House, Home & Garden, Iconoclast, Illinois Entertainer, INK Literary Review, INsider, IRIS, Kaleidoscope, Kalliope, Kenyon Review, Kite Lines, Ladies' Home Journal, Left Curve*, Lehigh University Press, *Letter Arts Review, Life, Liquid Ohio, Long Island Update*, Lyons & Burford Publishers, *Mail Call Journal, ME, Meat Whistle Quarterly, Metropolis*, Midmarch Arts Press, *Mountain Living, National Enquirer, Nimrod, Northwest Review, Owen Wister Review, Papyrus, Passages North*, Pelican Publishing Company, *Pennsylvania Heritage, Planetary Connections, Potomac Review, Potpourri, Radiance, Rag Mag, Redbook, Response, Rhino, River Styx, Rosebud, Sandlapper, Shuttle Spindle & Dyepot, Silver Web, Small Press Creative Explosion, Smithsonian Magazine, Snake Nation Review, Southern Humanities Review, South Florida History, Southwest Review, Spectacle, Stage Directions*, Storey Communications, *Sycamore Review, Tequesta, 360 Degrees, The Threepenny Review*, University of Maine Press, University of Nebraska Press, University Press of Mississippi, *U.S. Art, Visions-International, WE, Wildlife Art, William and Mary Review, Women Artists News Book Review, WormWood Review, The Yoga Journal*

Asia

Pacific View Press

Asian-American

Aegina Press, *Amelia Press, Asian Pacific American Journal, Birth Gazette*, Calyx Books, *Calyx Journal, Careers & the disABLED*, Century Press, Charles River Press, *Circle K*, Clarity Press, Cross Cultural Publications, The Denali Press, *Equal Opportunity Publications*, Intercultural Press, *It's Your Choice, Journal of Asian Martial Arts*, Kodansha America, Kroshka Books, Lehigh University Press, *Manoa*, Mayhaven Publishing, McFarland & Company, *Minority Engineer, MoonRabbit Review, Mother Jones*, Pacific View Press!, Pelican Publishing Company, *Power and Light*, Richard C. Owen Publishers, *South Florida History, T'ai Chi*, Temple University Press, *Tequesta*, University Editions, University Press of Mississippi, *WD-Workforce Diversity, Woman Engineer*

Associations

Abbott, Langer & Associates, The American Cottage Gardener, Career Focus, Careers & the disABLED, Circle K, Commercial Investment Real Estate Journal, Communications Publishing Group, Cross & Quill, DECA Dimensions, Equal Opportunity Publications, Eastern National, *Florida Hotel & Motel Journal, Hope, Kiwanis, Lion*, Mayhaven Publishing, *Midwest Motorist, Minority Engineer, Muzzle Blasts, National Parks, Optometric Economics, Paddler, Planetary Connections, Shuttle Spindle & Dyepot, VFW, WD-Workforce Diversity, Woman Engineer*

Astrology

Hay House, *National Enquirer*

Audio

Audio Amateur Corporation, Focal Press, *Popular Mechanics*

Automobiles

American Woman Motorscene, Automobile Quarterly, Av-

enues, Better Homes and Gardens, Boys' Life, British Car, Car & Driver Century Press, *Consumers Digest, Futurific, Heartland USA, INsider, Midwest Motorist,* Motorbooks International, *Popular Mechanics, Popular Science, Rider, Trailer Boats, Via,* Voyageur Press, *WE, Your Money*

Aviation

Balloon Life, Boys' Life, Branden Publishing Company, Brassey's, *Cowles Enthusiast Media, Futurific,* Hancock House, *Heartland USA,* Motorbooks International, *Mountain Pilot,* Naval Institute Press, *Popular Mechanics, Popular Science, Professional Pilot,* Voyageur Press

-B-

Baby Care

Meadowbrook Press

Basketball

Slam

Bead Crafts

Gem Guides Book Company

Beat Generation

Plain Jane

Beauty

Cosmopolitan, Bride's, Fitness, Glamour, Ladies' Home Journal, Modern Bride, Nails, Natural Health, New Woman, Parents, Redbook, Shape Magazine, The Star, Woman's Day, Woman's World, Working Mother

Biblical Studies

Kregel Publications

Biking

Bicycling, Big World, Bike, Sports Afield

Biography

Acorn, Amelia Press, Arden Press, *Avenues, Back Home in Kentucky,* Barricade Books, Black Forest Press, Blue River Publishing, Bonus Books, Branden Publishing Company, Brassey's, Bryant & Dillon Publishers, Bucknell University Press, *Centennial Review,* Century Press, Charles River Press, Chicago Review Press, *Christian Living,* Clover Park Press, The Conservatory of American Letters, *Crone Chronicles,* Cross Cultural Publications, David R. Godine, The Denali Press, *Early American Homes, Georgia Journal,* Hancock House, *Heartland USA,* Howell's House, *Iconoclast, INK Literary Review,* In Print Publishing, Ivan R. Dee, *Kalliope,* Kodansha America, Kroshka Books, *Ladies' Home Journal, Life, Light of Consciousness, Lilith, Literary Sketches,* MacMurray & Beck, *Mail Call Journal,* Masters Press, Mayhaven Publishing, Minstrel Books, Mitchell Lane Publishers, Mountain Press Publishing Company, *National Enquirer, Northeast Corridor, Oatmeal & Poetry, Oracle Story & Letters,* Pelican Publishing Company, *Pennsylvania Heritage,* Pocket Books, *Potpourri,* PREP Publishing, Quill Driver Books/Word Dancer Press, *Radiance, Redbook, Rising Star Publishers, Rosebud,* Rutledge Hill Press, *Senior, South Florida History, Spectacle, The Star,* Temple University Press,

Tequesta, University of Maine Press, University of Nebraska Press, University of Nevada Press, University of Oklahoma Press, University Press of Mississippi, White Mane Publishing Company, *Woman's Day, Yesterday's Magazette,* Zondervan Publishing House

Biology

Reptile & Amphibian

Birds

Hancock House

Blacksmithery

Anvil

Boat building

WoodenBoat

Boating

Canoe & Kayak, Cornell Maritime Press, David R. Godine, *Florida Wildlife,* The Globe Pequot Press, *HeartLand Boating, Heartland USA, Houseboat, Marlin,* Motorbooks International, Naval Institute Press, *Nor'Westing, Paddler,* Pelican Publishing Company, *Pontoon & Deck Boat, Popular Mechanics, Power & Motoryacht, Sailing Magazine, Sailing World, SEA, Sport Fishing, Sports Afield, Texas Parks & Wildlife, Trailer Boats, WE, Yachting*

Book Reviews

Audubon, Byte, Chelsea, Cosmopolitan, Glamour, Gothic Journal, Kinesis, Maelstrom, Modern Bride, Mid-American Review, Natural Health, New Mexico, Outdoor Life, Parenting Magazine, Pleiades, Redbook, Southern Living, The Star, The Threepenny Review, The Yoga Journal, ZYZZYVA

Books, kids

Kids Books by Kids

Border Issues

BorderLines

Bowling

Bowling

Boys

Crusader

Bridal

Elegant Bride, Signature Bride

Broadcasting

Focal Press

Buckskinning

Backwoodsman

Business

Abbott, Langer & Associates, Addicus Books, Allworth Press, *American Brewer, American Business Review, American Demographics, American Legion, American Salesman, Area*

Topics

Development, Attain, ATL Press, Avery Publishing Group, Barron's Educational Series, Black Forest Press, Bonus Books, Branden Publishing Company, Bryant & Dillon Publishers, *Business97, Business Start-Ups, Career Focus*, Celebrity Press, *Circle K, Colorado Business*, Communications Publishing Group, *Complete Woman, Construction Marketing Today, Corporate Legal Times*, Craftsman Book Company, *DECA Dimensions, Drum Business*, Emerald Ink Publishing, *Entrepreneur, Financial Freedom Report Quarterly, Florida Hotel & Motel Journal, Food Channel, Futurific, Harper's Magazine*, The Globe Pequot Press, The Graduate Group, *Group IV Communications, Happy Times Monthly*, Herbelin Publishing, *High Technology Careers, Home Business News, Home Furnishings Executive, Home Times*, Humanics Publishing Group, ICS Press, *ID Systems, Independent Business, Industry Week*, In Print Publishing, Intercultural Press, Jewish Lights Publishing, JIST Works, Kids Books by Kids, Kroshka Books, Lehigh University Press, Lifetime Books, *Managed Care*, Markowski International Publishers, Mayhaven Publishing, *Mentor & Protégé*, Metamorphous Press, Nolo Press, NTC/Contemporary Publishing, *Oregon Business*, Pelican Publishing Company, *Permanent Buildings & Foundations*, Pilot Books, *Playboy, Podiatry Management, Popular Mechanics*, PREP Publishing, *Presentations*, Prima Publishing, PSI Research, *Redbook, Self Employed Professional, Skin, Spare Time, Spilled Candy, Spirit, Supervision*, Ten Speed Press, Texas A&M University Press, *Today's $85,000 Freelance Writer*, Tower Publishing, *Tree Care Industry, WE, Wines & Vines, Woman's Day, Woman's World, Working Woman, Your Money*

Business Opportunities

Spare Time

-C-

Californiana

Fithian Press, Quill Driver Books/Word Dancer Press

Calligraphy

Letter Arts Review

Camping

American Hunter, Big World, Sports Afield, Texas Parks & Wildlife, Woodall Publications, Woodall's California RV Traveler, Woodall's Camp-orama, Woodall's Carolina RV Traveler, Woodall's Discover RVing, Woodall's Northeast Outdoors, Woodall's RV Traveler, Woodall's Southern RV

Career Planning

Vision

Careers

American Careers, American Correctional Association, *American Salesman*, Barron's Educational Series, Black Forest Press, *Boys' Life, Career Focus, Careers & the disABLED, Centennial Review, Christian Living, Circle K*, Communications Publishing Group, *Complete Woman, Cosmopolitan, Cross & Quill, DECA Dimensions, Dramatics, EEO BiMonthly*, Equal Opportunity Publications, *Glamour*, The Globe Pequot Press, The Graduate Group, *Happy Times Monthly, High Technology Careers, Home Times, INsider*, JIST Works, *Mademoiselle, Mature Years, Men's Health*,

Mentor & Protégé, Minority Engineer, Modern Maturity, Mustang Publishing Company, NTC/Contemporary Publishing, *Pilot Books*, Prima Publishing, PREP Publishing, *Radiance, SciTech Magazine, Spare Time, Spilled Candy, Succeed, Supervision*, Ten Speed Press, *Times News Service, Unique Opportunities*, WD-Workforce Diversity, *WE, Wines & Vines, Woman Engineer, Woman's Day, Working Mother, Working Woman*

Caribbean

Hot Calaloo

Cartoons

Amelia Press, American Legion, *Birth Gazette, Boys' Life, Boys' Quest, Cartoonist and Comic Artist Magazine, Comedy, Curriculum Vitae, Family Digest*, Great Quotations Publishing, *Happy Times Monthly, Heartland USA, Home Times, Hopscotch for Girls, Iconoclast*, In Print Publishing, *Light, Liquid Ohio, Lutheran Digest, Maelstrom*, Mayhaven Publishing, *MEDIPHORS, New Writer's, Oatmeal & Poetry*, Pelican Publishing Company, *Power and Light, Protooner, R-A-D-A-R, Radiance, Response, Slick Times, Small Press Creative Explosion, Spare Time, Sports Afield, Supervision, Thema, With, Yesterday's Magazette*

Catholic Church

Catholic Digest, Family Digest, Montana Catholic, St. Anthony Messenger, St. Bede's Publications

Cattle Feeding

Feed-Lot

Celebrities

Avenues, Cosmopolitan, Ladies' Home Journal, Life, National Enquirer, New Choices, Penthouse, Quill Driver Books/Word Dancer Press, *Redbook, The Star, Woman's Day*

Chess

Chess Enterprises

Child Care

Family Circle, Meadowbrook Press

Childbirth

Midwifery Today

Children

Aegina Press, Alyson Publications, *American Fitness, American Legion*, American Literary Press, Anchorage Press, Atheneum Books for Young Readers, *Atlanta Parent, Attain*, Avon, *Babybug*, Barron's Educational Series, Beyond Words Publishing, *Black Child*, Black Forest Press, *Boys' Life, Boys' Quest*, Branden Publishing Company, *Calliope, Cat Fancy*, Charlesbridge Publishing, Chicago Review Press, *Child, Circle K, Club Connection, Cobblestone, Creative With Words Publications, Cricket*, David R. Godine, *Dinosaurus, Dollar Stretcher*, Dutton Children's Books, *Faces*, Fairview Press, *Family Life*, Farrar, Straus & Giroux, *Girls' Life, GRIT, Guideposts For Kids, Happy Times Monthly*, Hearts 'n Tummies Cookbook Company, *Highlights for Children, Hopscotch for Girls, House, Home & Garden*, Holiday House, Humanics Publishing Group, *It's Your Choice, Journal of Christian Nursing*, Kali Press, Kids Books by Kids, *Ladies' Home Jour-*

nal, *Ladybug*, *L.A. Parent*, *Long Island Parenting News*, *Lutheran Digest*, *Mama's Little Helper Newsletter*, Margaret K. McElderry Books, Mayhaven Publishing, Milkweed Editions, Minstrel Books, Mitchell Lane Publishers, *My Legacy*, The Nature Conservancy's Habitat Series, *New Moon*, *Odyssey*, *On the Scene*, Pacific Currents, Pacific View Press, *Pack-O-Fun*, *Parent & Child*, *ParentGuide News*, *Parenting Magazine*, *Parents*, *Parents' Press*, Pelican Publishing Company, Perspective Press, Philomel Books, Pocket Books, *Pockets*, *Potluck Children's Literary*, *Potomac Review*, *Power and Light*, Quixote Press, *R-A-D-A-R*, *Radiance*, Rainbow Books, *Ranger Rick*, *Redbook*, Richard C. Owen Publishers, *Rising Star Publishers*, Smithsonian Oceanic Collection/Smithsonian's Backyard, Smithsonian Odyssey, SpanPress, *Spider*, *Sports Illustrated for Kids*, *Stone Soup*, *Swimming World*, *Table Talk*, Ten Speed Press, University Editions, *WE*, White Mane Publishing Company, Woman in the Moon Publications, *Woman's Day*, *Woman's World*, *Working Mother*, World Leisure Corporation, Zondervan Publishing House

Children's Books

Crayola Kids, Ideals Children's Books, Jewish Lights Publishing

Chinese Language/Medicine

Paradigm Publications

Christian Interests

Alive!, *Attain*, Baker Book House Company, Beyond Words Publishing, Black Forest Press, Broadman & Holman Publishers, *Catholic Near East*, Century Press, *Christianity Today*, *Christian Living*, *Christian New Age Quarterly*, *Christian Parenting Today*, Christian Publications, *Christian Social Action*, *Chronicles*, *Club Connection*, *Cornerstone*, Cross Cultural Publications, *Cross & Quill*, *Crusader*, *Discipleship Journal*, ETC Publications, *Evangel*, *Family Digest*, *First Things*, Great Quotations Publishing, *GRIT*, *Guideposts For Kids*, *Home Times*, *Insight*, *Journal of Adventist Education*, *Journal of Christian Nursing*, Judson Press, Kroshka Books, Legacy Press, *Liguorian*, *Lookout*, *Lutheran Digest*, *Mature Years*, *Message*, *My Legacy*, *Oblates*, *Oracle Story & Letters*, *Plain Truth*, *Power and Light*, PREP Publishing, *R-A-D-A-R*, Rainbow Books, *Rising Star Publishers*, *Seek*, St. Bede's Publications, *WIN Informer*, *With*, *Woman's Touch*, *Women Alive!*, *Youth Update*, Zondervan Publishing House

Christianity, evangelical

Moody

Church Business

Your Church

Civil Liberties/Rights

Nation

Civil War, American

Back Home in Kentucky, Black Forest Press, Branden Publishing Company, Brassey's, *Columbiad*, The Conservatory of American Letters, *Cowles Enthusiast Media*, Eastern National, Excalibur Publications, *Georgia Journal*, *Heartland USA*, Kodansha America, Kroshka Books, Lehigh University Press, *Mail Call Journal*, Mayhaven Publishing, McFarland & Company, *Military Images*, *My Legacy*, Pelican Publishing Company, *Pennsylvania Heritage*, Rockbridge

Publishing Company, Rutledge Hill Press, *Tequesta*, *Times News Service*, University of Maine Press, University of Nebraska Press, University of Oklahoma Press, University Press of Mississippi, White Mane Publishing Company

Classical Studies

University of Oklahoma Press

Clip Art

Library Imagination Paper

Coal Mining

Coal People

Collectibles

Antique Trader Weekly, *Back Home ih Kentucky*, Century Press, *Collecting Toys*, *Collector Editions*, *Collectors News*, *Country America*, *Country Living*, *Early American Homes*, *Echoes*, Excalibur Publications, *GRIT*, *House, Home & Garden*, Kalmbach Publishing Company, *Martha Stewart Living*, Motorbooks International, *Nineteenth Century*, *Senior*, *Toy Shop*, Voyageur Press, *Wildlife Art*, *Yesterday's Magazette*, *Your Money*

College

Amelia Press, Ardsley House Publishers, *Attain*, Barron's Educational Series, Black Forest Press, *Career Focus*, *Careers & the disABLED*, *Centennial Review*, Century Press, *Change*, *Circle K*, *Communications Publishing Group*, Cross Cultural Publications, The Denali Press, *Equal Opportunity Publications*, Great Quotations Publishing, The Graduate Group, ICS Press, *INsider*, Intercultural Press, Kroshka Books, Lifetime Books, *Liquid Ohio*, *Minority Engineer*, Mustang Publishing Company, Nova Press, *Oregon Quarterly*, *Playgirl*, *Pulp*, *Response*, Ten Speed Press, University Press of Mississippi, *WD-Workforce Diversity*, *Woman Engineer*

College Course Adoptions

Arden Press

Comedy

Amelia Press, *Atlanta Singles*, *Attain*, *Bleach*, Century Press, *Circle*, *Comedy*, Creative With Words Publications, *Crusader*, Great Quotations Publishing, *Happy Times Monthly*, Lehigh University Press, *Light*, Mayhaven Publishing, Minstrel Books, *Nostalgia*, *On the Scene*, *PanGaia*, Piccadilly Books, *Planetary Connections*, Pocket Books, *Protooner*, Quixote Press, *Rising Star Publishers*, *Slick Times*, *Small Press Creative Explosion*, *Spy*

Comic Books/Comics

Small Press Creative Explosion

Commentary, social

Lynx Eye

Communication

Managing Office Technology, *Wired*

Communication, intercultural

Intercultural Press

Topics

Communication Technology

Focal Press

Community Building

Wilder Publishing Center

Complementary Medicine

Paradigm Publications

Computers

Abbott, Langer & Associates, ATL Press, *Better Homes and Gardens, Boys' Life, Byte, Career Focus*, Century Press, *Circle K, ComputorEdge, Communications Publishing Group, Computing Today, Consumers Digest*, Duke Press, *FBI Law Enforcement Bulletin, Futurific*, The Graduate Group, *Gray Areas, High Technology Careers, House, Home & Garden*, IDG Books Worldwide, *INsider*, Kroshka Books, *Long Island Update, Managing Office Technology*, Mayhaven Publishing, *MICROpendium*, Osborne/McGraw-Hill, *PC World, Popular Electronics, Popular Mechanics, Popular Science, Presentations*, Prima Publishing, *SciTech Magazine, WE, Wired, Writer's Gazette, X-Ray*

Community Service

American Legion Magazine

Confession

Aegina Press, *Lutheran Digest*, Mayhaven Publishing, *Oracle Story & Letters, Playgirl, Rising Star Publishers, True Love, True Romance*, University Editions

Conservation

Audubon, Beyond Words Publishing, *BorderLines, Boys' Life, Bugle, Christian Living*, The Conservatory of American Letters, *Country Living*, Cross Cultural Publications, *Defenders, E, Florida Wildlife*, Hancock House, *Heartland USA, INsider*, Kroshka Books, *Lutheran Digest, Marlin*, Milkweed Editions, Mountaineers Books, *Mountain Living, National Parks, Natural Health, Outdoor Life, Paddler, PanGaia, Ranger Rick, Reptile & Amphibian, Safari, Sierra, Smithsonian Magazine, South Florida History, Sport Fishing, Sports Afield, Texas Parks & Wildlife*, University of Nebraska Press, *Whole Life Times, Wisconsin Trails, The Yoga Journal*

Conservative Issues

Home Times

Construction

Craftsman Book Company, *Permanent Buildings & Foundations, SouthWest Contractor*

Construction, underground

Oildom Publishing, Underground Construction

Consumer

Alabama Living, American Demographics, American Fitness, American Health, Arthritis Today, Automobile Quarterly, Avenues, Bicycling, BlueRidge Country, Blue River Publishing, Branden Publishing Company, *Byte, Canoe & Kayak, Career Focus, Carefree Enterprise, Child, Communications Publishing Group, Consumers Digest, Country Woman, Dol-*

lar Stretcher, E, FATE, Fitness, Florida Keys, Gibbons-Humms Guide to the Florida Keys & Key West, Guns & Ammo, Home Improver, INsider, Ladies' Home Journal, Long Island Update, Lutheran Digest, Marlin, Men's Fitness, Message, Metropolis, Midwest Motorist, Modern Bride, Moderna, Mustang Publishing Company, *National Geographic Traveler, Natural Health*, Nolo Press, *North Dakota Horizons, Oklahoma Today, Outdoor Life, Parenting Magazine, Playgirl, Popular Mechanics, Radiance, Rosebud, Sneeze the !Day!, Snow Country, Sports Afield, The Star, Toy Shop, Travel & Leisure, U.S. Art, Veggie Life, Via, WE, Whole Life Times, Woman's Day, Woman's World, X-Ray, The Yoga Journal, Your Money*

Contemporary Affairs

Pacific View Press

Cookbooks

Black Iron Cookin' Company, Bristol Publishing Enterprises, Century Press, Golden West Publishers, Hearts 'n Tummies Cookbook Company

Cooking

American Literary Press, *Atlanta Singles, Attain*, Avery Publishing Group, *Back Home in Kentucky*, Barron's Educational Series, *Better Homes and Gardens*, Berkshire House Publishers, Black Forest Press, Black Iron Cookin' Company, Bonus Books, Bristol Publishing Enterprises, *Carefree Enterprise*, Celebrity Press, Chicago Review Press, *Cooking Light, Country America, Country Living, Country Woman*, Crossing Press, David R. Godine, Faber & Faber, Falcon Publishing, *Fast and Healthy Magazine, Girls' Life, Glamour*, The Globe Pequot Press, Golden West Publishers, *GRIT, Happy Times Monthly*, Hay House, *Health*, Hearts 'n Tummies Cookbook Company, The Hoffman Press, *Home Times, House, Home & Garden, Kitchen Garden*, Kodansha America, Kroshka Books, *Ladies' Home Journal, L.A. Parent*, Lifetime Books, Llewellyn Publications, Lyons & Burford Publishers, Mage Publishers, *Martha Stewart Living*, Mayhaven Publishing, *Modern Maturity*, Momentum Books, *Mountain Living, Natural Health, New Choices*, NTC/Contemporary Publishing, *Outdoor Life, Pack-O-Fun*, Pelican Publishing Company, *Prevention Magazine*, Prima Publishing, *Radiance, Redbook*, Rutledge !Hill Press, *Sandlapper, Shape Magazine, Southern Living, The Star*, Storey Communications, *Sunset*, Ten Speed Press, *Veggie Life, Whole Life Times, Wild Foods Forum, Woman's Day, Woman's World, Working Mother, Yankee, The Yoga Journal*

Cooking, natural

Wholeness

Copywriting

Today's $85,000 Freelance Writer

Corrections

American Correctional Association

Crafts

Allworth Press, *American Woodworker, Art Times, Back Home in Kentucky, Backwoodsman*, Barron's Educational Series, *Boys' Life, Cat Fancy*, Chitra Publications, *Country America, Country Living, Country Woman*, Crayola Kids, *Decorative Artist's Workbook, FIBERARTS*, Gem Guides Book Company,

Girls' Life, GRIT, Handcraft Illustrated, House, Home & Garden, Humanics Publishing Group, Ladies' Home Journal, Ladybug, L.A. Parent, Lyons & Burford Publishers, Martha Stewart Living, Modern Bride, NTC/Contemporary Publishing, Outdoor Life, Pack-O-Fun, Players Press, Popular Mechanics, Power and Light, Radiance, Rainbow Books, Ranger Rick, Shuttle Spindle & Dyepot, Storey Communications, Sunset, Ten Speed Press, Vogue Knitting, Woman's Day, Woman's World, Yankee

Crime

Aegina Press, Alfred Hitchcock Mystery Magazine, American Correctional Association, Attain, Belletrist Review, Blue River Publishing, City Primeval, Dagger of the Mind, David R. Godine, FBI Law Enforcement Bulletin, Good Housekeeping, The Graduate Group, Harper's Magazine, Heartland USA, ICS Press, It's Your Choice, Mayhaven Publishing, My Legacy, Paladin Press, Players Press, Plenum Publishing, PREP Publishing, Redbook, Rising Star Publishers, Sleuthhound memorandum, University Editions, University of North Texas Press !in

Criminal Justice

American Correctional Association

Criticism, literary

minnesota review, Southern Humanities Review

Critique, cultural

Left Curve

Culture

Above the Bridge, Afterimage, Aloha, Amelia Press, American Demographics, American Visions, Arkansas Review, Art Times, Belletrist Review, Beyond Words Publishing, Black Forest Press, Blue River Publishing, BorderLines, Branden Publishing Company, Bucknell University Press, Career Focus, Centennial Review, Century Press, Christianity and the Arts, Chronicles, Cimarron Review, Circle, Circle K, Commonweal, Communications Publishing Group, Country Connections, Creative With Words Publications, Crone Chronicles, Cross Cultural Publications, Curriculum Vitae, East Bay Monthly, Eye, Faces, FATE, Feminist Studies, First Things, Girlfriends, Gray Areas, Home Times, Humanics Publishing Group, Hurricane Alice, Iconoclast, Illinois Entertainer, INK Literary Review, INsider, Intercultural Press, It's Your Choice, Journal of Asian Martial Arts, Kodansha America, Left Curve, Lehigh University Press, Mage Publishers, Magical Blend, Metropolis, Milkweed Editions, minnesota review, Mountain Living, Mustang Publishing Company, My Legacy, new renaissance, Nimrod, Nineteenth Century, Oatmeal & Poetry, Obsidian II, Oracle Story & Letters, Oregon Quarterly, PanGaia, Pennsylvania Heritage, Plain Jane, Planetary Connections, Playboy, Potomac Review, Potpourri, Radiance, Rising Star Publishers, Sandlapper, San Francisco, Shuttle Spindle & Dyepot, Smithsonian Magazine, Snake Nation Review, South Florida History, Southwest Review, Spy, Temple University Press, Stage Directions, Tequesta, Texas A&M University Press, Tikkun, Timson Edwards Publishing, University of Nebraska Press, University Press of Mississippi, Vogue, WE, Whole Life Times, Wisconsin Trails

Culture, Foreign Countries

Intercultural Press

Culture, Persian

Mage Publishers

Custom Homes

Log Home Living

-D-

Dance

Amelia Press, Ardsley House Publishers, Art Times, Bucknell University Press, Century Press, Christianity and the Arts, In Print Publishing, Lehigh University Press, PanGaia, Radiance, Temple University Press, The Threepenny Review, WE

Death & Bereavement

Baywood Publishing Company

Defense

Brassey's

Desktop Publishing

X-Ray

Development

BorderLines

Devotional

Kregel Publications, Secret Place

Diagnostic Radiology

Medical Physics Publishing

Diamonds

Diamond Insight

Diet

American Fitness, Aspen, Avery Publishing Group, Barron's Educational Series, Birth Gazette, Career Focus, Century Press, Commune-A-Key Publishing, Communications Publishing Group, Cooking Light, Country Connections, Crossing Press, Diabetes Self-Management, Fitness, Good Housekeeping, Hay House, Health, HealthQuest, Home Times, House, Home & Garden, Hunter House Publishers, It's Your Choice, Kroshka Books, Lifetime Books, Llewellyn Publications, Lutheran Digest, Masters Press, McBooks Press, Muscle & Fitness, National Enquirer, Natural Living Today, New Times, Paradigm Publications, ParentGuide News, Piccadilly Books, Planetary Connections, Playgirl, Radiance, Senior, Shape Magazine, Swim, Ten Speed Press, The Star, Veggie Life, Weight Watchers Magazine, Whole Life Times, Wholeness, Wild Foods Forum, Wines & Vines, Women's Sports & Fitness, Your Health

Directories

Quill Driver Books/Word Dancer Press,

Disabilities

Accent on Living, Adolescence, American Correctional Association, *Attain*, Black Forest Press, Branden Publishing Company, Brookline Books, *Careers & the disABLED*, *Christian Living*, *Circle K*, The Denali Press, *Dialogue*, *Equal Opportunity Publications*, Fairview Press, *Heartland USA*, *Hope*, Hunter House Publishers, In Print Publishing, *Journal of Christian Nursing*, *Kaleidoscope*, Kroshka Books, Lumen Editions, Mayhaven Publishing, *Minority Engineer*, *Newswaves*, *Oracle Story & Letters*, Pennycorner Press, *Radiance*, *Ragged Edge*, *Rising Star Publishers*, !2Temple University Press, University Press of Mississippi, *WD-Workforce Diversity*, *WE*, Woodbine House, *Woman Engineer*

Draft Animals

Rural Heritage

Drama

Amelia Press, Anchorage Press, *Art Times*, Black Forest Press, Branden Publishing Company, Bucknell University Press, *Carolina Quarterly*, *Centennial Review*, Century Press, *Christianity and the Arts*, The Conservatory of American Letters, *Dramatics*, Faber & Faber, Fairleigh Dickinson University Press, *Fourteen Hills*, Heinemann, *Iconoclast*, *Illinois Entertainer*, *INK Literary Review*, *Kenyon Review*, Lehigh University Press, *Lilith*, *Nimrod*, *Northeast Corridor*, *Obsidian II*, Players Press, *Pleiades*, *Rockford Review*, *Rosebud*, *Stage Directions*, *Sycamore Review*, Temple University Press, *The Threepenny Review*, *Writer's Gazette*

Dreams

Dream Network

-E-

Eastern Europe

Texas A&M University Press

Eating Disorders

American Fitness

Ecology

Audubon, Beyond Words Publishing, *BorderLines*, *Boys' Life*, *Bugle*, *California Wild*, *Centennial Review*, Century Press, Chelsea Green Publishing Company, *Christian Living*, *Country Connections*, *Creation Spirituality Network*, Cross Cultural Publications, *Dollar Stretcher*, *E*, *Eclectic Rainbows*, *Environment*, *Florida Wildlife*, *Georgia Journal*, *Girls' Life*, *Heartland USA*, Jewish Lights Publishing, Kroshka Books, Kumarian Press, *Magical Blend*, Milkweed Editions, *Mountain Living*, Mountain Press Publishing Company, *Nation*, *National Geographic Traveler*, *Natural Health*, *New Times*, *Pack-O-Fun*, *Outdoor Life*, *PanGaia*, *Planetary Connections*, *Potomac Review*, *Reptile & Amphibian*, *Sierra*, *Smithsonian Magazine*, *Sports Afield*, Temple University Press, University of Nebraska Press, University of Nevada Press, Weidner & Sons Publishing, *Whole Life Times*, *Wholeness*, *Wisconsin Trails*, *The Yoga Journal*

Economics

Addicus Books, *American Salesman*, *Attain*, *BorderLines*, *Boston Review*, *Career Focus*, *Centennial Review*, Century Press, *Communications Publishing Group*, Cross Cultural Publications, The Denali Press, *Freeman*, *Futurific*, The Globe Pequot Press, *Home Times*, ICS Press, *INsider*, Kroshka

Books, Kumarian Press, Lehigh University Press, *Mother Jones*, *National Geographic Traveler*, Texas A&M University Press, *Tikkun*, Weidner & Sons Publishing, *Woman's World*, *Working Woman*, *Your Money*

Education

African American Images, *American Careers*, *The American Cottage Gardener*, *American Legion*, *Attain*, Barron's Educational Series, *Birth Gazette*, Black Forest Press, *BorderLines*, *Boys' Life*, Branden Publishing Company, Brookline Books, Bryant & Dillon Publishers, *Career Focus*, *Careers & the disABLED*, *Careers and Majors*, *Centennial Review*, Century Press, *Change*, *Christian Home & School*, *Chronicles*, *Circle K*, *College Bound*, *Communications Publishing Group*, *Computing Today*, Cottonwood Press, *Creative With Words Publications*, Cross Cultural Publications, *Cross & Quill*, *DECA Dimensions*, *Dinosaurus*, *Dollar Stretcher*, Eastern National, *Educational Leadership*, *Education in Focus*, *Electron*, *Equal Opportunity Publications*, *Et Cetera*, ETC Publications, *First Things*, *Florida Leader for College Students*, *Freeman*, Front Row Experience, *Futurific*, The Graduate Group, Great Quotations Publishing, Gryphon House, Heinemann, Highsmith Press, *Home Education*, *Home Times*, *Hope*, Humanics Publishing Group, ICS Press, *Instructor*, Intercultural Press, *It's Your Choice*, *Journal of Adventist Education*, *Journal of Christian Nursing*, Kali Press, Kroshka Books, *Ladies' Home Journal*, *L.A. Parent*, *Library Imagination Paper*, Lumen Editions, *Mail Call Journal*, *Mentor & Protégé*, Metamorphous Press, *Mercury*, *Minority Engineer*, *National Enquirer*, *National Geographic Traveler*, *Natural Health*, New View Publications, Nova Press, *Oracle Story & Letters*, *Oregon Quarterly*, *Pack-O-Fun*, *Parent & Child*, *ParentGuide News*, *Parenting Magazine*, *Pennsylvania Heritage*, Pennycorner Press, Perron Press, Phi Delta Kappa Educational Foundation, *Planetary Connections*, *Potpourri*, *Presentations*, *Radiance*, Rainbow Books, *Reader's Digest*, *Rising Star Publishers*, *Shuttle Spindle & Dyepot*, *Sleuthhound memorandum*, *The Star*, *Student Leader*, *Succeed*, *Teaching Tolerance*, Temple University Press, *Tikkun*, *Today's Catholic Teacher*, *Vision*, *WD-Workforce Diversity*, *WE*, Weidner & Sons Publishing, *Woman Engineer*, *Woman's Day*, *Wonderful Ideas*, *Your Money*

Education, exceptional child

Adolescence

Education, higher

First Opportunity

Education, movement

Front Row Experience

Education, theatre

Dramatics

Education, vocational

Spare Time

Educational

Fairview Press

Educational, Hispanic-American

SpanPress

Electronics

Boys' Life, Centennial Review, Consumers Digest, Electron, Electronic Servicing & Technology, Electronics Now, Futurific, High Technology Careers, House, Home & Garden, Illinois Entertainer, Popular Electronics, Popular Mechanics, Popular Science, Prompt Publications, *Wired*

Emergency Services

Fire Chief

Employee Benefits

Employee Benefits Digest, Employee Benefits Journal, International Foundation of Employee Benefit Plans

Empowerment

Crossing Press

Energy

Alabama Living, Chelsea Green Publishing Company, Emerald Ink Publishing, *Environment, Futurific,* Kroshka Books, *Magical Blend*

Engineering

Ad Astra, Career Focus, Careers & the disABLED, Centennial Review, Communications Publishing Group, Craftsman Book Company, *Equal Opportunity Publications, Futurific, High Technology Careers, Joiners' Quarterly,* Lehigh University Press, *Minority Engineer,* Plenum Publishing, *Popular Mechanics, Progressive Engineer, Radio World WD-Workforce Diversity, Woman Engineer*

Engineering, industrial

IIE Solutions, Industrial Management

Enneagram

Metamorphous Press

Entertainment

Amelia Press, Art Times, Atlanta Singles, Avenues, Barricade Books, *Bleach, Boxoffice, Boys' Life,* Branden Publishing Company, Bryant & Dillon Publishers, *Café Eighties, Career Focus, Comedy, Communications Publishing Group, Cosmopolitan, Country America, Country Living, Dogwood Tales, Dramatics, Eclectic Rainbows, Eye, FATE, Girlfriends, Girls' Life, Glamour, Gold and Treasure Hunter,* Great Quotations Publishing, *Happy Times Monthly, Home Times, House, Home & Garden, Illinois Entertainer, INsider, Jam Rag, Lacunae, Ladies' Home Journal,* Lifetime Books, *Long Island Update, Mademoiselle, Mail Call Journal, Martha Stewart Living,* Mayhaven Publishing, *Mountain Living,* Mustang Publishing Company, *National Enquirer,! Nocturnal Ecstasy, Penthouse,* Piccadilly Books, *Playboy,* Players Press, *Playgirl, Radiance, Redbook,* Rutledge Hill Press, *Sandlapper, Sci Fi Invasion!, Senior, Spy, Times News Service, Wisconsin Trails, Woman's World, The Yoga Journal*

Entrepreneurship

Markowski International Publishers

Environment

American Forests, Audubon, Better Homes and Gardens, Blue Water Publishing, *BorderLines, Boys' Life, Bugle, California*

Explorer, California Wild, Carefree Enterprise, Century Press, Charlesbridge Publishing, Chelsea Green Publishing Company, *Christian Living, Chronicles, Country Connections,* Cross Cultural Publications, *Defenders,* The Denali Press, *Dollar Stretcher, E, Eclectic Rainbows, Environment, Erosion Control, Florida Wildlife, Flower and Garden Magazine, Georgia Journal, Girls' Life,* The Graduate Group, *Happy Times Monthly,* Hay House, *Heartland USA,* Humanics Publishing Group, ICS Press, *INsider, It's Your Choice, Joiners' Quarterly,* Kali Press, Kroshka Books, Kumarian Press, McFarland & Company, *Metropolis,* Milkweed Editions, *Mother Jones, Mountain Living, MSW Management, Nation, National Parks, Natural History, NEBRASKAland, New Times, Oatmeal & Poetry, Pacific Currents, Paddler, PanGaia, Planetary Connections, Popular Mechanics, Popular Science, Potomac Review, Radiance, Ranger Rick, Remediation Management,* Richard C. Owen Publishers, *Sandlapper, Sierra,* Sierra Club Books, *Sports Afield, Texas Parks & Wildlife, Tikkun,* University of Nebraska Press, University of Nevada Press, *Weatherwise,* Weidner & Sons Publishing, *Whole Life Times, Wholeness, Wildlife Art, Wisconsin Trails*

Environmental Science & Policy

Environment

Equestrian

Northeast Equine Journal

Ergonomics

IIE Solutions

Ericksonian Hypnosis

Metamorphous Press

Erotica

Amelia Press, Belletrist Review, Companion Press, The Conservatory of American Letters, *In Touch/Indulge, Libido,* Masquerade Books, *Nocturnal Ecstasy, Paramour, Penthouse, Plain Jane, Playgirl, Radiance, Rosebud, Sensual Aspirations, Swank, Texas Connection, Variations*

Esoteric

Planetary Connections

Essay

AIM, Cosmopolitan, Harper's Magazine, John Daniel & Company, *Lynx Eye, Massachusetts Review, Mississippi Review, New Choices, New England Review, Outdoor Life, OutLoud and Proud!, River Styx, Senior Living, Southwest Review, The Threepenny Review, Wired, Yankee*

Essay, critical

Critical Review

Essay, literary

Higginsville Reader

Essay,

Flying Horse

Essay, personal

Pleiades

Topics

Essay, review

Critical Review

Ethics

It's Your Choice, Journal of Information Ethics

Ethnic

African American Images, *Amelia Press, American Demographics, American Visions, Belletrist Review,* Beyond Words Publishing, *Black Child,* Black Forest Press, *BorderLines,* Branden Publishing Company, Bryant & Dillon Publishers, *Career Focus, Careers & the disABLED,* Charles River Press, *Child of Colors, Christian Living,* Clarity Press, *Communications Publishing Group,* Cross Cultural Publications, The Denali Press, *Equal Opportunity Publications,* Fairleigh Dickinson University Press, Great Quotations Publishing, *HealthQuest, Highlander, The Hellenic Calendar, Hot Calaloo,* Humanics Publishing Group, *INK Literary Review,* Intercultural Press, *Interrace,* Kroshka Books, MacMurray & Beck, Mage Publishersin, *Minority Engineer, MoonRabbit Review, My Legacy, Oatmeal & Poetry,* Obsidian II, *Oracle Story & Letters, PanGaia, Papyrus,* Pelican Publishing Company, *Pennsylvania Heritage, Planetary Connections, Radiance, Response, Rising Star Publishers, South Florida History,* SpanPress, *Spirit,* Temple University Press, *Tequesta,* University of Nebraska Press, University of Nevada Press, University of Oklahoma Press, University Press of Mississippi, *WD-Workforce Diversity, Woman Engineer*

-F-

Facilities Planning

IIE Solutions

Family

Above the Bridge, Addicus Books, African American Images, *Amelia Press, American Legion, Atlanta Parent, Attain, Better Homes and Gardens,* Beyond Words Publishing, *Birds & Blooms, Birth Gazette, Black Child,* Black Forest Press, Branden Publishing Company, *Bride's, Canoe & Kayak, Carefree Enterprise, Challenges, Christian Home & School, Christian Living, Computing Today, Country Living, Country Woman, Creative With Words Publications,* Cross Cultural Publications, *Crusader, Dollar Stretcher, Dovetail,* Excelsior Cee Publishing, Fairview Press, *Family Circle, FamilyFun, Family Digest, Fan,* The Globe Pequot Press, *Gold and Treasure Hunter, Good Housekeeping,* Great Quotations Publishing, *GRIT,! Happy Times Monthly,* Harvest House Publishers, *Health,* Health Communications, *Home Times, Hope, House, Home & Garden,* Hunter House Publishers, Impact Publishers, *It's Your Choice, Journal of Christian Nursing,* Judson Press, Kroshka Books, *Ladies' Home Journal, L.A. Parent,* Liguorian, *Long Island Parenting News, Lookout, Lutheran Digest, Masonia Roundup,* Mayhaven Publishing, McBooks Press, *Modern Bride, Mother Is Me,* Mustang Publishing Company, *My Legacy, Natural Health, New Woman, Oatmeal & Poetry, On the Scene, Over the Back Fence, PanGaia, Parent & Child, ParentGuide News, Parenting Magazine, Parents,* Pelican Publishing Company, Perspective Press, *Power and Light,* PREP Publishing, *Radiance, Reunions, Rosebud,* SpanPress, *St. Anthony Messenger,* Sta-Kris, *The Star, Sunset, Table Talk,* Temple University Press, Timson Edwards Publishing, *tomorrow SPECULATIVE FIC-*

TION, Twins, Woman's Day, Woman's World, Working Mother, Yesterday's Magazette, Zondervan Publishing House

Family and Marital Therapy

Family Therapy

Fantasy

Acorn, Aegina Press, *Amelia Press,* Asimov's Science Fiction, Avon, Baen Books, Black Forest Press, The Conservatory of American Letters, Dagger *of the Mind, Dreams of Decadence,* Eternity Press, *Hadrosaur Tales, INK Literary Review, Ladybug,* Llewellyn Publications, *Magazine of Fantasy & Science Fiction, Magazine of Speculative Poetry, Marion Zimmer Bradley's Fantasy, Medusa's Hairdo,* Minstrel Books, *My Legacy, Nocturnal Ecstasy, Oatmeal & Poetry, PanGaia,* Philomel Books, *Playgirl,* Pocket Books, *Ranger Rick, Riverside Quarterly, Rosebud, Scavenger's Newsletter,* University Editions, Warner Books, *With, Worlds of Fantasy and Horror*

Farriery

ANVIL

Fashion

Cosmopolitan, Fitness, Girls' Life, Glamour, House, Home & Garden, Ladies' Home Journal, Mademoiselle, Men's Health, Modern Bride, Moderna, National Enquirer, Natural Health, Parents, Penthouse, Playboy, Players Press, *Playgirl, Radiance, Redbook, Shape Magazine, Shuttle Spindle & Dyepot, The Star, Travel & Leisure, Vogue, Weight Watchers Magazine, Woman's Day, Woman's World, Working Mother*

Feminism

Amelia Press, American Literary Press, Beyond Words Publishing, *BorderLines,* BrickHouse Books, Bucknell University Press, Calyx Books, *Calyx Journal, Centennial Review,* Charles River Press, Chestnut Hills Press, Commune-A-Key Publishing, *Country Connections, Crone Chronicles,* Cross Cultural Publications, David R. Godine, Denlinger's Publishers, Fairleigh Dickinson University Press, Feminist Press, *Feminist Studies, Frontiers, Girlfriends,* Hay House, *House, Home & Garden,* Humanics Publishing Group, *Hurricane Alice, INsider, Iris, It's Your Choice, Journal of Christian Nursing,* Kroshka Books, *L.A. Parent, Libido, Liquid Ohio,* MacMurray & Beck, *Magical Blend, minnesota review, Mom Guess What Newspaper, Mother Is Me, Ms., Nation, New Moon, New Times,* New Victoria Publishers, Outrider Press, *Playgirl,* Publishers Associates, *Radiance, Response,* Rising Tide Press, *Rosebud, SageWoman,* Spinsters Ink, *Spirit,* Stonewall Series, Temple University Press, Third Side Press, *Tikkun,* University of Nebraska Press, University Press of Mississippi, *Whole Life Times*

Fiction

Above the Bridge, Acorn, Aegina Press, *Affaire de Coeur,* Agony in Black, *AIM, Alaska Quarterly Review, Alfred Hitchcock Mystery Magazine, Alive!,* Alyson Publications, *Amelia Press,* American Literary Press, *Americas Review, Antioch Review, Arkansas Review,* Arte Público Press, *Artful Dodge, Asimov's Science Fiction,* Avon, *Babybug,* Baker Book House Company, *Belletrist Review, Bellingham Review, Bellowing Ark,* Beyond Words Publishing, BkMk Press, Black Forest Press, *Black Mountain Review, Boston Review, Boys'*

Life, Boys' Quest, Branden Publishing Company, BrickHouse Books, *Bridge,* Brookline Booksplain, Bryant & Dillon Publishers, *Buffalo Spree, Bugle, Café Eighties,* Calyx Books, *Calyx Journal, Carolina Quarterly,* Catbird Press, *Cat Fancy,* Century Press, Charlesbridge Publishing, *Chattahoochee Review, Chelsea,* Chestnut Hills Press, Chicago Review Press, *Christianity and the arts, Chrysalis Reader, Cimarron Review, Circle, City Primeval, Clockwatch Review, Coal People,* The Conservatory of American Letters, *Cosmopolitan, Cream City Review, Creative With Words Publications, Cricket, Crusader, Curriculum Vitae, CutBank, Dagger of the Mind,* David R. Godine, *Dogwood Tales, Downstate Story, Dreams of Decadence,* Dutton Children's Books, *Entre Nous, Essence,* Eternity Press, *Evangel,* Faber & Faber, *Fan, Farmer's Market,* Fiesta City Publishers, Fithian Press, *Flying Horse, Fractal, George & Mertie's Place, Girls' Life, Glimmer Train Stories, Gold and Treasure Hunter, Good Housekeeping, Green Hills Literary Lantern, Green Mountains Review, Greensboro Review, GRIT, Guideposts For Kids, Hadrosaur Tales,* Harlequin Historicals, *Harper's Magazine,* Harvest House Publishers, *Hawaii Review, Hayden's Ferry Review, Heaven Bone, Higginsville Reader, Home Times, Hopscotch for Girls,* Howell's House, *Hurricane Alice, Iconoclast,* Ideals Children's Books, *Iliad Press, INK Literary Review, In Touch/Indulge, Iris, It's Your Choice,* John Daniel & Company, *Kalliope, Kenyon Review, Kinesis,* Kroshka Books, *Lacunae, Ladies' Home Journal, Ladybug,* Latin American Literary Review Press, , *Light, Light of Consciousness, Lilith, Liquid Ohio, Literal Latté, Literary Review,* Llewellyn Publications, Lumen Editions, *MacGuffin,* MacMurray & Beck, *Maelstrom, Magazine of Fantasy & Science Fiction,* Mage Publishers, *Mail Call Journal, Manoa, Marion Zimmer Bradley's Fantasy,* Masquerade Books , Massachusetts Review, Maverick Press, Mayhaven Publishing, *Meat Whistle Quarterly, MEDIPHORS, Medusa's Hairdo, Mid-American Review,* Mid-List Press, Milkweed Editions, *minnesota review,* Minstrel Books, *Mississippi Review, My Legacy,* The Nature Conservancy's Habitat Series, Naval Institute Press, *NEBO, Nebraska Review, New England Review, New Letters, New Millennium Writings, New Moon, new renaissance,* New Rivers Press, New Victoria Publishers, *New Writer's, Nightshade Press, Nimrod, Nocturnal Ecstasy, North American Review, Northeast Corridor, Northwest Review, Northwoods Journal, Oatmeal & Poetry, Obsidian II, Office Number One, Ohio Writer, On the Scene, Options, Oracle Story & Letters, Other Voices,* Outrider Press, *Outside: Speculative and Dark Fiction, Owen Wister Review,* Owl Creek Press, *Pacific Coast Journal,* Palace Corbie, *PanGaia, Pangolin Papers, Papyrus, Passager, Passages North, Pearl,* Pelican Publishing Company, *Penthouse, Peregrine,* Permanent Press, *Phic Shun,* Philomel Books, *Phoebe, Planetary Connections, Playgirl, Pleiades, Ploughshares,* Pocket Books, *Potato Eyes Literary Arts Journal, Potomac Review, Potpourri, Power and Light, Prairie Schooner,* PREP Publishing, *Press, Primavera, Quarterly West, R-A-D-A-R, Radiance, Ranger Rick, Redbook, Response, Rhino,* Richard C. Owen Publishers, *Rising Star Publishers,* Rising Tide Press, *River Styx, Rockford Review, Rosebud, Scavenger's Newsletter, Seek, Sensual Aspirations,* Serendipity Systems, Silhouette Books, *Silver Web, Skylark, Sleuthhound memorandum, Slipslream,* Smithsonian Oceanic Collection/Smithsonian's Backyard, Smithsonian Odyssey, *Snake Nation Review, Southern California Anthology, Southern Humanities Review, Southern Review, Southwest Review,* SpanPress, *Special Collections, Spider,* Spinsters Ink, *Sports Afield,* St. Anthony Messenger, *The Star, Stoneflower Literary Journal,* Stonewall Series, *Story, Straight, Sun, Swank, Sycamore Review, Tampa Review, Thema,* Third Side Press,

360 Degrees, The Threepenny Review, Tikkun, Timson Edwards Publishing, *tomorrow SPECULATIVE FICTION, True Love,* Unity Books, University Editions, University of Nevada Press, University Press of Mississippi , *Verses, Virginia Quarterly Review, WE,* Weems Concepts, *Whetstone,* Whispering Willow Mysteries, White Pine Press, *William and Mary Review, Wired, With, Wolf Head Quarterly,* Woman in the Moon Publications, *Woman's Day, Worcester Review, Worlds of Fantasy and Horror, Writers' Forum, Writer's Gazette, Writer's Guidelines & News, Yankee, Yesterday's Magazette, Zoetrope,* Zondervan Publishing House, *ZYZZYVA*

Fiction, middle grade

Dutton Children's Books

Fiction, speculative

Silver Web

Fiction, sudden

Maverick Press

Field Guides

Mountain Press Publishing Company

Film Exhibition/Distribution

Boxoffice

Film/Video

Afterimage, Allworth Press, *Amelia Press,* Arden Press, *Art Times, Bleach, Boxoffice,* Bryant & Dillon Publishers, Chicago Review Press, *Christianity and the arts, Cineaste,* Companion Press, *Dramatics, Eye,* Faber & Faber, Fairleigh Dickinson University Press, *Film Comment, Film Quarterly,* Focal Press, *Girls' Life, Gray Areas, Home Times, Illinois Entertainer,* In Print Publishing, *INsider,* Intercultural Press, Lehigh University Press, *Lilith, Mademoiselle,* McFarland & Company, *minnesota review, Mother Jones, MovieMaker, new renaissance,* Players Press, *Planetary Connections, Playgirl, Radiance, Real People,* Rutledge Hill Press, *Sci Fi Invasion!, Spectacle,* Temple University Press, *Times News Service, The Threepenny Review,* University of Nebraska Press, University of North Texas Press, University Press of Mississippi

Finance, personal/professional

Bloomberg Press, *Mother Jones*

Fine Arts

Heaven Bone

Firearms

American Hunter, American Rifleman, Guns & Ammo,

Fire-related

Firehouse

Fire Services

Fire Chief

Fishing

American Hunter, Bass West, Black Iron Cookin' Company, *Boys' Life,* Carefree Enterprise, *Champion Bass,* The Conservatory of American Letters, *Dakota Outdoors,* Falcon

Publishing, *Field & Stream, Fly Fisherman, Flyfisher, Fly Fishing in Salt Waters,* The Globe Pequot Press, *Happy Times Monthly,* Hearts 'n Tummies Cookbook Company, *Heartland USA, Houseboat, Knives Illustrated,* Kodansha America, *Marlin, Mountain Living, NEBRASKAland, Outdoor Life, Paddler,* Pilot Books, *Pontoon & Deck Boat, Sport Fishing, Sports Afield, Texas Parks & Wildlife, USA Outdoors, WE, Western Outdoors*

Fishing, bass

Florida Wildlife

Fishing, salt water

Salt Water Sportsman

Fitness

American Health, Children's Better Health Institute, *Fitness Management*

Florida

Sunshine, Valiant Press

Folklore

Creative With Words Publications, Parenting Magazine, Texas A&M University Press

Food/Drink

American Brewer, American Demographics, American Fitness, Black Iron Cookin' Company, *Carefree Enterprise, Cooking Light, Country Living,* David R. Godine, *Fast and Healthy Magazine, Fitness, Food Channel, Fresh Cut, Girls' Life, Glamour, Health,* Hearts 'n Tummies Cookbook Company, The Hoffman Press, *House, Home & Garden, INsider, Kinesis,* Kodansha America, *Ladies' Home Journal,* Lyons & Burford Publishers, *Magazine of La Cucina Italiana, Martha Stewart Living,* Mayhaven Publishing, *Modern Maturity,* Momentum Books, Mustang Publishing Company, *National Geographic Traveler, Natural Health, New Choices, Penthouse, Prevention Magazine,* Quixote Pressplain, *Radiance, Redbook,* Rutledge Hill Press, *Shape Magazine, Southern Living, The Star, Sunset,* Ten Speed Press, *Travel & Leisure, Whole Life Times, Wild Foods Forum, Wines & Vines, Wisconsin Trails, Woman's Day, Woman's World, Working Mother, Yankee, The Yoga Journal*

Foreign Policy

Brassey's

Freedom, personal

Paladin Press

Fund-raising

Quill Driver Books/Word Dancer Press

Fur Trade

Backwoodsman

-G-

Games

Attain, Bonus Books, *Boys' Life, Card Player, Cat Fancy,*

Chess Enterprises, *Collecting Toys, Happy Times Monthly,* Lyons & Burford Publishers, Mustang Publishing Company, *Power and Light,* Rainbow Books, *Ranger Rick, Sports Illustrated for Kids*

Gardening

The American Cottage Gardener, American Gardener, Aspen, Barron's Educational Series, *Better Homes and Gardens, Birds & Blooms, Bride's,* Bristol Publishing Enterprises, Chelsea Green Publishing Company, Chicago Review Press, *Country Living, Creative With Words Publications,* David R. Godine, *Early American Homes, Fine Gardening, Flower and Garden Magazine, Georgia Journal,* The Globe Pequot Press, *GreenPrints, GRIT, Happy Times Monthly,* Hearts 'n Tummies Cookbook Company, *Heartland USA, Home Improver, Home Times, Horticulture, House, Home & Garden, Kitchen Garden, Ladies' Home Journal,* Llewellyn Publications, *Lutheran Digest,* Lyons & Burford Publishers, Mage Publishers, *Martha Stewart Living, Mountain Living, Natural Health,* NTC/Contemporary Publishing, *On the Scene, PanGaia,* Quixote Press, *Radiance, Sandlapper, Senior, Southern Living,* Storey Communications, *Sunset,* Ten Speed Press, *Texas Gardener,* University Press of Mississippi, *Veggie Life, WE, Wild Foods Forum, Woman's World, Yankee*

Gay/Lesbian

Alyson Publications, *Amelia Press,* Barricade Books, *Black Lace, Blackfire, BLK,* BrickHouse Books, Bucknell University Press, Calyx Books, *Calyx Journal, Carolina Quarterly,* Charles River Press, Chestnut Hills Press, *Chiron Review,* Companion Press, David R. Godine, Eternity Press, *Evergreen Chronicles,* Faber & Faber, Feminist Press, *Feminist Studies, Fourteen Hills, Frontiers, Girlfriends,* Heinemann, *Hurricane Alice, In Touch/Indulge, INK Literary Review, Iris, It's Your Choice, Kuumba, Libido, minnesota review, Mom Guess What Newspaper, New Times,* New Victoria Publishers, *Nocturnal Ecstasy, Options, Out & About,* Outrider Press, Publishers Associates, *Radiance, Response,* Rising Tide Press, Spinsters Ink, *Spirit,* Stonewall Series, Temple University Press, Timson Edwards Publishing, *WormWood Review*

Genealogy

Excelsior Cee Publishing, Picton Press

General Interest

Acorn, Addicus Books, Aegina Press, *Alabama Living, Amelia Press, American Hunter, American Legion, American Scholar,* Arden Press, *Atlanta Singles, Attain, Baltimore Magazine, Belletrist Review,* Beyond Words Publishing, Black Forest Press, *BlueRidge Country,* Blue River Publishing, *Boston Review, Boys' Life,* Branden Publishing Company, BrickHouse Books, Bright Mountain Books, Calyx Books, *Calyx Journal, Carefree Enterprise,* Century Press, *Charleston,* Chestnut Hills Press, Chicago Review Press, *Circle K, City Primeval, Comedy, Complete Woman, Consumers Digest, Country America, Creative Nonfiction,* Cross Cultural Publications, *Eclectic Rainbows, Elks, Emerge, Essence, Et Cetera,* Excelsior Cee Publishing, *Eye,* Fairview Press, *Family Circle, Fan, FATE, First Things,* Fithian Press, *Futurific, George & Mertie's Place, Girls' Life, Good Housekeeping,* The Graduate Group, Great Quotations Publishing, *GRIT, Happy Times Monthly,* Hay House, *Heartland USA, HerbalGram, Highways, Home Times, Hope,* Howell's House, Hunter House Publishers, *Iconoclast,* In Print Publishing, *INK Literary Review, INsider,* Johnston Associates International, *Journal of*

Christian Nursing, Kenyon Review, Liguorian, Liquid Ohio, Long Island Update, Lutheran Digest, Lyons & Burford Publishers, *Masonia Roundup, Massage,* Mayhaven Publishing, *Men's Journal, Metropolis,* Milkweed Editions, *Milwaukee, Modern Bride, Mother Jones,* Mustang Publishing Company, *new renaissance, Nineteenth Century, On the Scene, Oracle Story & Letters, Over the Back Fence, Parade, Passages North,* Pilot Books, *Playboy, Popular Science, Pulp, Radiance, Reader's Digest, Real People, Rising Star Publishers, Rosebud, Rotarian, Sandlapper, San Francisco, Senior Living, Shuttle Spindle & Dyepot, Sports Illustrated for Kids,* Stonewall Series, *Sunshine,* Temple University Press, Ten Speed Press, *360 Degrees, The Threepenny Review,* Timson Edwards Publishing, *TROIKA,* University Editions, University of Nevada Press, University Press of Mississippi, University of North Texas Press, *U. S. Airways Attaché, Whole Life Times, Wisconsin Trails, Writer's Gazette, Yankee, Yesterday's Magazette, ZYZZYVA*

Geography

Texas A&M University Press

Geology

Mountain Press Publishing Company

Gerontology

Baywood Publishing Company

Gift

Fairview Press

Girls

Club Connection

Golf

Golf Digest, Golfer, Golf Journal

Good Deeds/News

Happy Times Monthly

Goth Scene

Nocturnal Ecstasy

Government

Black Forest Press, *BorderLines,* Branden Publishing Company, Brassey's, Bucknell University Press, *California Journal, Career Focus, Centennial Review,* Century Press, *Chronicles, Communications Publishing Group,* Cross Cultural Publications, The Denali Press, *FBI Law Enforcement Bulletin, Fire Chief, First Things, Freeman, Government Executive,* The Graduate Group, *Home Times,* Howell's House, ICS Press, *INsider, It's Your Choice,* Kroshka Books, Kumarian Press, Lehigh University Press, *Long Term View, Mother Jones, National Enquirer, Oracle Story & Letters, Penthouse, Politically Correct, Presentations, Rising Star Publishers, The Star, Tikkun,* University of Nebraska Press, *WE, Whole Life Times, Wines & Vines*

Government, Cover-up

Planetary Connections

Graphic Design

Allworth Press, *Critique*

Great Lakes

Momentum Books

Growth & Recovery

Hunter House Publishers

-H-

Habitat

Florida Wildlife

Haiku

Modern Haiku

Healing, natural

Crossing Press

Healing & Recovery

Jewish Lights Publishing, *Light of Consciousness*

Health

Addicus Books, *Alive!, American Demographics, American Fitness, American Health for Women,* American Literary Press, *American Medical News, American Legion, Arthritis Today, Aspen, Attain,* Avery Publishing Group, Barron's Educational Series, *Better Homes and Gardens, Bicycling, Birth Gazette,* Black Forest Press, Blue Poppy Press, Blue River Publishing, *BorderLines, Boys' Life,* Branden Publishing Company, *Career Focus, Careers & the disABLED, Carefree Enterprise, Cat Fancy, Challenges,* Children's Better Health Institute, Commune-A-Key Publishing, *Communications Publishing Group, Consumers Digest, Continuum, Cooking Light, Cosmopolitan, Crone Chronicles,* Crossing Press, *Dermascope, Diabetes Self-Management, Dialogue,* Emerald Ink Publishing, *Equal Opportunity Publications, Essence,* Fairview Press, *Family Circle, Family Safety and Health, Fast and Healthy Magazine, Fitness, Glamour, Golfer, Good Housekeeping,* The Graduate Group, Hay House, Health Communications, *HealthQuest, HerbalGram, Home Times, House, Home & Garden,* Hunter House Publishers, Impact Publishers, In Print Publishing, *It's Your Choice,* John Muir Publications, *Journal of Asian Martial Arts, Journal of Christian Nursing,* Kali Press, Kroshka Books, *Ladies' Home Journal, L.A. Parent,* Lifetime Books, Llewellyn Publications, *Long Island Update, Lutheran Digest, Magical Blend, Managed Care, Massage,* Masters Press, *Mature Years,* McBooks Press, *Medical Device & Diagnostic Industry, MEDIPHORS, Men's Fitness, Men's Health,* Metamorphous Press, *Minority Engineer, Modern Bride, Moderna, Modern Maturity, Mountain Living, Muscle & Fitness, National Enquirer, National Geographic Traveler, Natural Health, Natural Living Today, New Choices, New Times, New Woman, On the Scene, Optometric Economics, Outdoor Life, Pacific Currents, PanGaia,* Paradigm Publications, *Parent & Child, ParentGuide News, Parenting Magazine, Parents,* Pennycorner Press, Perspective Press, Piccadilly Books, *Planetary Connections,* Plenum Publishing, *Podiatry Management, Prevention Magazine,* Prima Publishing, *Prime Health & Fitness, Psychology Today,* Quill Driver Books/Word Dancer Press, *Radiance, Reader's Digest, Redbook, Runner's World,* Samuel Weiser, *Senior, Senior Living, Shape Magazine, Sneeze the Day!, Spare Time, Spirit, The Star, Swim,*

Topics

Swimming World, T'ai Chi, Temple University Press, Third Side Press, University Press of Mississippi, *Veggie Life, WD-Workforce Diversity, WE, Wild Foods Forum, Wines & Vines, Woman Engineer, Woman's World,* YMAA Publication Center, *The Yoga Journal, Your Health*

Health, alternative

Avery Publishing Group

Health Care Marketing

Strategic Health Care Marketing

Health, mental

Adolescence, Challenges

Health, public

Baywood Publishing Company

Herbal Medicine

HerbalGram, Paradigm Publications

Herbs

HerbalGram, Veggie Life

Heritage, Scottish

Highlander

Herpetology

Reptile & Amphibian

High Technology Careers

High Technology Careers

Hiking

Mountaineers Books, *Sports Afield, Texas Parks & Wildlife, Travelers Guide for Aspen*

Hispanic

Amelia Press, Americas Review, Arte Público Press, *Birth Gazette,* Black Forest Press, *BorderLines,* Brookline Books, Calyx Books, *Calyx Journal, Career Focus, Careers & the disABLED,* Charles River Press, *Communications Publishing Group,* The Denali Press, *EEO BiMonthly, Equal Opportunity Publications, First Opportunity, Frontiers, Latin American Literary Review Press,* Lumen Editions, *Minority Engineer,* Mitchell Lane Publishers, *Moderna,* Pelican Publishing Company, *South Florida History,* SpanPress, Temple University Press, *Tequesta,* Texas A&M University Press, Timson Edwards! Publishing, University of Nebraska Press, *WD-Workforce Diversity,* White Pine Press, *Woman Engineer*

History

Acorn, Adventure Journal, Amelia Press, American Fitness, American Literary Press, *American Scholar,* Arden Press, *Arkansas Review, Audubon, Back Home in Kentucky, Backwoodsman,* Berkshire House Publishers, Black Forest Press, Blue River Publishing, *Boys' Life,* Branden Publishing Company, Brassey's, Bryant & Dillon Publishers, Bucknell University Press, *Bugle, Calliope, Car & Driver, Cascades East, Cat Fancy, Centennial Review,* Century Press, Charles River Press, Clover Park Press, The Conservatory of American Letters, *Cowles Enthusiast! Media, Creative With Words*

Publications, Cross Cultural Publications, David R. Godine, The Denali Press, Denlinger's Publishers, *Early American Homes,* Eastern National, *East Texas Historical Journal, Elks,* Excalibur Publications, Faber & Faber, Fairleigh Dickinson University Press, Falcon Publishing, *Fan, Feminist Studies, Florida Wildlife, Flower and Garden Magazine, Freeman, Frontiers, Gateway Heritage,* The Globe Pequot Press, *Gold and Treasure Hunter, GRIT, Guns & Ammo, Highlander, Historic Traveler, Home Times,* Howell's House, In Print Publishing, Ivan R. Dee, Jewish Lights Publishing, *Journal o!f Asian Martial Arts, Journal of Christian Nursing,* Kodansha America, Kroshka Books, Lehigh University Press, Lyons & Burford Publishers, Mage Publishers, *Magical Blend, Mail Call Journal,* Mayhaven Publishing, McFarland & Company, *Michigan Historical Review, Military Images, Montana Western History, Mountain Living,* Mountain Press Publishing Company, *Muzzle Blasts,* Naval Institute Press, *Oklahoma Today, Oracle Story & Letters, Outdoor Life, Overland Journal, Over the Back Fence,* Paladin Press, *PanGaia,* Pelican Publishing Company, *Pennsylvania, Pennsylvania Heritage,* Philomel Books, Picton Press, PSI Research, Publishers Associates, Quill Driver Books/Word Dancer Press, Quixote Press, *Radiance, Renaissance, Rising Star Publishers, Russian !Life,* Rutledge Hill Press, *Sailing Magazine, Sandlapper, Senior Living, Smithsonian Magazine,* Smithsonian Odyssey, *South Florida History, Southern Humanities Review, Spectacle,* Tamarack Books, Temple University Press, *Tequesta,* Texas A&M University Press, *The Threepenny Review, Timeline, True West,* University of Maine Press, University of Nebraska Press, University of Nevada Press, University of Oklahoma Press, University Press of Mississippi, University of North Texas Press, *VFW, Voyageur,* Washington State University Press, *Western Publications, Wisconsin Trails, Yankee, ZYZZYVA*

History, legal

University of Oklahoma Press

History, music

Centerstream Publishing

History, natural

Lyons & Burford Publishers, *Natural History,* University of Oklahoma Press, Weidner & Sons Publishing

History, Western

Montana, Montana Western History, Quill Driver Books/Word Dancer Press

Hobbies

The American Cottage Gardener, American Demographics, American Kennel Club Gazette, American Woodworker, Ardsley House Publishers, *Birds & Blooms,* Black Iron Cookin' Company, *Boys' Life, Backwoodsman, Collecting Toys, Collectors News, Decorative Artist's Workbook, FineScale Modeler,* Gem Guides Book Company, *Gold and Treasure Hunter, Guns & Ammo, Handcraft Illustrated, Happy Times Monthly, HeartLand Boating, Home Times, House, Home & Garden,* Kalmbach Publishing Company, *Kite Lines, Ladies' Home Journal,* Lifetime Books, *Linn's Stamp News, Lutheran Digest, Mail Call Journal, Martha Stewart Living, Model Railroader, Modern Bride,* Mustang Publishing Company, *Muzzle Blasts, Nor'Westing, Oracle Story & Letters, Outdoor Life, Popular Electronics, Popular Mechanics, Popular Woodworking, Radiance, Ranger Rick, Rising Star Pub-*

lishers, *Sandlapper, Senior, Shuttle Spindle & Dyepot,* Storey Communications, *Toy Shop, Vogue Knitting, Woman's Day, Woman's World, Yankee*

Holistic Health

Natural Health, Planetary Connections, Whole Life Times, Wholeness

Home

American Fitness, Bride's Magazine, Cosmopolitan, Country Living, Flower & Garden, Martha Stewart Living, Modern Bride, Natural Health, New Choices, Popular Mechanics, Southern Living, Woman's Day, Woman's World, Working Mother, Yankee

Home Furnishings

Home Furnishings Executive

Home Improvement

Home Improver

Homeschooling

Home Education

Horror

Aegina Press, Agony in Black, *Amelia Press,* American Literary Press, Avon, *Dagger of the Mind,* Eternity Press, *Fractal, Lacunae, Magazine of Fantasy & Science Fiction, Magazine of Speculative Poetry,* Mayhaven Publishing, *Medusa's Hairdo,* Minstrel Books, *Nocturnal Ecstasy,* Office Number One, *Oracle Story & Letters,* Palace Corbie, *Outside: Speculative and Dark Fiction,* Pocket Books, *Rising Star Publishers, Scavenger's Newsletter, Swank, tomorrow SPECULATIVE FICTION,* University Editions, *Worlds of Fantasy and Horror, Writer's Gazette*

Hotel/Motel Management

Florida Hotel & Motel Journal

How-to

American Hunter, Bicycling, Cat Fancy, Consumers Digest, Cosmopolitan, DIMI Press, Excelsior Cee Publishing, Fiesta City Publishers, *Flower and Garden Magazine, Glamour, Ladies' Home Journal, Modern Bride, National Enquirer, Natural Health, Outdoor Life, Popular Mechanics,* Quill Driver Books/Word Dancer Press, *Ranger Rick, Shape Magazine,* SignCraft, *Sports Afield, Sports Illustrated for Kids, The Star,* Storey Communications, University of North Texas Press, *Wired,* Woman in the Moon Publications, *Woman's World, Writer's Guidelines & News, The Yoga Journal, YM*

Human Insight

Hope, Radiance

Human Interest

Good Housekeeping, Hope, Life, National Enquirer, Reader's Digest, The Star

Humanities

Harper's Magazine, Southern Humanities Review

Human Resources Management

Abbott, Langer & Associates

Human Rights

Clarity Press

Human Services

Impact Publishers

Human Spirit

Hope

Humor

Acorn, Alive!, Amelia Press, American Fitness, American Hunter, American Literary Press, *Annals of Improbable Research, Attain, Avenues,* Barricade Books, *Belletrist Review, Bicycling, Birth Gazette, Bleach, Boys' Life,* Broadman & Holman Publishers, *Bugle, Café Eighties, Car & Driver,* Catbird Press, *Cat Fancy,* CCC Publications, *Circle, Comedy, Cosmopolitan, Creative With Words Publications, Dogwood Tales, Door,* Fairview Press, *Funny Times, Good Housekeeping,* Great Quotations Publishing, *Happy Times Monthly, Harper's Magazine,* Herbelin Publishing, *Home Times, Iconoclast, INK Literary Review, Journal of Christian Nursing, Light, Lutheran Digest, Maelstrom,* Mayhaven Publishing, Meadowbrook Press, *MEDIPHORS,* !Minstrel Books, Mustang Publishing Company, NTC/Contemporary Publishing, *Oatmeal & Poetry,* Office Number One, *On the Scene, Oracle Story & Letters,* Outrider Press, *PanGaia, Parenting Magazine,* Pelican Publishing Company, *Penthouse,* Piccadilly Books, *Planetary Connections, Playboy,* Pocket Books, *Power and Light,* PREP Publishing, *Protooner, Reader's Digest,* Richard C. Owen Publishers, *Rising Star Publishers, Rosebud,* Rutledge Hill Press, *Sandlapper, Senior Living, Sensual Aspirations,* Small Press Creative Explosion, *Spectacle, Sports Afield, Sports Illustrated for Kids, Spy, Sunshine, Table Talk,* Ten Speed Press, *Thoughts for All Seasons, Tikkun,* White-Boucke Publishing, *Whole Life Times, With, Working Mother, Yankee, ZYZZYVA*

Hunting

American Hunter, Black Iron Cookin' Company, *Bugle,* The Conservatory of American Letters, *Dakota Outdoors, Field & Stream, Guns & Ammo,* Hearts 'n Tummies Cookbook Company, *Heartland USA, Knives Illustrated, NEBRASKAland, Outdoor Life, Pennsylvania Game News, Petersen's Bowhunting,* Quixote Press, *Safari, Sports Afield, Texas Parks & Wildlife, WE*

Hypnosis, Ericksonian

Metamorphous Press

-I-

IBM AS/400

Duke Press

Infertility

Perspective Press

Information Science

Journal of Information Ethics

Information, suppressed

Planetary Connections

Inspirational

Amelia Press, American Fitness, Angels on Earth, Attain, Baker Book House Company, Black Forest Press, Blue Water Publishing, Broadman & Holman Publishers, *Carefree Enterprise,* Celebrity Press, *Challenges,* Christian Publications, *Club Connection,* Commune-A-Key Publishing, *Complete Woman, Crone Chronicles,* Cross Cultural Publications, *Discipleship Journal,* Emerald Ink Publishing, *Evangel,* Excelsior Cee Publishing, *Family Digest, Fan, Good Housekeeping,* Great Quotations Publishing, *GRIT, Gryphon Publications, Guideposts, Happy Times Monthly,* Harvest House Publishers, *Hay House, Heartland USA,* Health Communications, *Home Times,* Humanics Publishing Group, Hunter House Publishers, In Print Publishing, *INK Literary Review, It's Your Choice,* Jewish Lights Publishing, *Journal of Christian Nursing,* Judson Press, Kroshka Books, Legacy Press, *Lessons on Life,* Lifetime Books, Llewellyn Publications, *Lutheran Digest, Magical Blend, Mail Call Journal,* Markowski International Publishers, *Men's Fitness, Message, My Legacy, Natural Health, New Times, Oatmeal & Poetry, Oblates, On the Scene, Oracle Story & Letters, PanGaia,* Pelican Publishing Company, *Plain Truth, Planetary Connections,* PREP Publishing, *R-A-D-A-R, Radiance,* Rainbow Books, *Reader's Digest, Rising Star Publishers,* Rutledge Hill Press, *Science of Mind, Seek, Senior Living, Spirit, Sports Illustrated for Kids, St. Anthony Messenger,* Timson Edwards Publishing, *True Romance, Virtue, Weight Watchers Magazine, Whole Life Times, Wholeness, WIN Informer, With, Woman's Touch, Writer's Gazette, The Yoga Journal*

Intelligence, military

Brassey's

Interfaith

Christian New Age Quarterly

Interior Decorating

Colonial Homes, Cosmopolitan, Country Living, Ladies' Home Journal

International Affairs

Brassey's, *Harper's Magazine*

Internet

Annals of Improbable Research, Branden Publishing Company, *Career Focus, Communications Publishing Group, Computing Today, Cross & Quill, EEO BiMonthly, Eye, Futurific,* The Graduate Group, *Gray Areas,* IDG Books Worldwide, *INsider, Journal of Information Ethics,* Kodansha America, Kroshka Books, Osborne/McGraw-Hill, *Planetary Connections, Presentations, Radiance, Radio World, SciTech Magazine,* Serendipity Systems, *WE, Weight Watchers Magazine, X-Ray*

Interview

Amelia Press, American Fitness, Annals of Improbable Research, Audubon, Bleach, Café Eighties, Carolina Quarterly, Circle, Crone Chronicles, Eclectic Rainbows, Girls' Life, The Graduate Group, *Home Times, Iconoclast, Illinois Entertainer, INsider, Inside Sports,* JIST Works, *Journal of Christian Nursing,* Kodansha America, *Lacunae, Magical Blend, Mother Jones, New Choices, new renaissance, New Times, Northeast Corridor, Obsidian II, Outdoor Life, Penthouse, Play-*

boy, Playgirl, Quarterly West, Reader's Digest, River Styx, Sandlapper, Shape Magazine, Southern Review, Southwest Review, Spectacle, Spilled Candy, Sports Illustrated for Kids, St. Anthony Messenger, Stoneflower Literary Journal, Sun, Sycamore Review, Talent Plus!, Ten Speed Press, Whole Life Times, Wines & Vines, Wired, Yankee, The Yoga Journal, YM

Inventions

Planetary Connections

Investing, Institutional

Bloomberg Press, *Your Money*

Issues, social

Blue River Publishing, *Christian Social Action*

-J-

Jewelry

Diamond Insight

Jewish Children

Shofar

Jewish Interests

Amelia Press, Branden Publishing Company, Brookline Books, Century Press, Charles River Press, *Circle K,* Cross Cultural Publications, David R. Godine, The Denali Press, Fairleigh Dickinson University Press, *First Things,* Fithian Press, *Home Times,* Jason Aronson, *Jewish Action, Jewish Currents,* Jewish Lights Publishing, *Jewish News of Western Massachusetts,* Kodansha America, *Latin Americn Literary Review Press,* Lifetime Books, *Lilith,* Lumen Editions, *Na'amat Woman,* Pelican Publishing Company, *Power and Light, Response, South Florida History,* Temple University Press, *Tequesta, Tikkun,* University of Nebraska Press

Judaica

Jason Aronson

Justice

Fellowship

Juvenile

Aegina Press, American Literary Press, Arte Público Press, Atheneum Books for Young Readers, ATL Press, Avon, Barron's Educational Series, Beyond Words Publishing, *Boys' Life, Calliope,* Carolrhoda Books, Charlesbridge Publishing, *Cobblestone, Creative With Words Publications, Crusader,* David R. Godine, *Faces,* Fairview Press, *It's Your Choice,* Lerner Publications, Lodestar Books, Minstrel Books, *Odyssey, Oracle Story & Letters,* Philomel Books, Pocket Books, *Potluck Children's Literary, Power and Light, Pulp,* Richard C. Owen Publishers, *Rising Star Publishers,* Ten Speed Press, University Editions

-K-

Kayaking

Canoe & Kayak, Sea Kayaker

Kites

Kite Lines

-L-

Labor

BorderLines

Landscaping

Flower and Garden Magazine, Tree Care Industry

Language

Amelia Press, Barron's Educational Series, Branden Publishing Company, Bucknell University Press, *Centennial Review, Cross & Quill, Et Cetera*, Fairleigh Dickinson University Press, The Globe Pequot Press, *INK Literary Review, Kenyon Review*, Lehigh University Press, *Literary Sketches, Nimrod, Obsidian II, Oracle Story & Letters, Rhino, Rising Star Publishers, Rosebud, Thoughts for All Seasons*, University of Nebraska Press

Lapidary

Gem Guides Book Company

Latino Issues

BorderLines

Law

American Hunter, Boston Review, Branden Publishing Company, *Career Focus, Catbird Press, Centennial Review*, Century Press, *Communications Publishing Group, Consumers Digest, Corporate Legal Times, FBI Law Enforcement Bulletin, First Things*, The Graduate Group, *Gray Areas, INsider*, Kroshka Books, *Long Term View*, Nolo Press, Temple University Press, Tower Publishing

Law Enforcement

Attain, BorderLines, Career Focus, Chief of Police, Communications Publishing Group, FBI Law Enforcement Bulletin, The Graduate Group, *Law and Order, Police Times*

Leadership

Circle K

Leisure Activities

Kalmbach Publishing Company, *Woman's Day*

Lesbian

Third Side Press

Lettering

Letter Arts Review

Libraries

American Libraries

Library Science

Journal of Information Ethics, Scarecrow Press

Life Cycle

Jewish Lights Publishing

Lifestyles

Amelia Press, American Demographics, Birth Gazette, Bleach, Career Focus, Carefree Enterprise, Charleston, Circle K, Communications Publishing Group, Country America, Country Woman, Cosmopolitan, Crone Chronicles, Dialogue, East Bay Monthly, Eye, Florida Keys, Glamour, Gold and Treasure Hunter, Good Housekeeping, Good Times, Great Quotations Publishing, *Happy Times Monthly, Highways, Home Improver, Houseboat*, Hunter House Publishers, *Illinois Entertainer, It's Your Choice*, Kroshka Books, *Lilith, Long Island Parenting News, Long Island Update, Mademoiselle, Magical Blend*, Mayhaven Publishing, *Mid-Atlantic Country, Moderna, Mom Guess What Newspaper, Mountain Living*, Mustang Publishing Company, *Natural Living Today, New Home Life, new renaissance, New Times, On the Scene, Orange Coast, Paddler, Penthouse, Pilot Books, Planetary Connections, Playgirl, Pontoon & Deck Boat*, Prima Publishing, *Pulp*, Quill Driver Books/Word Dancer Press, *Radiance, Sandlapper, San Francisco, Singles, Snow Country, Snowshoer, South Florida History, Swim, Texas Connection*, Timson Edwards Publishing, *Travel & Leisure, Troika, WE, Western RV News, Whole Life Times, Wired, Wisconsin Trails, Woman's Day*, Woodall Publications, *Woodall's California RV Traveler, Woodall's Camp-orama, Woodall's Carolina RV Traveler, Woodall's Discover RVing, Woodall's Northeast Outdoors, Woodall's RV Traveler, Woodall's Southern RV*

Literature

Aegina Press, *Amelia Press, American Scholar, Antioch Review, Arkansas Review, Art Times*, Arte Público Press, *Babybug, Belletrist Review, Bellowing Ark*, BkMk Press, *Black Forest Press, Black Mountain Review, Bleach, Boston Review*, Branden Publishing Company, BrickHouse Books, *Bridge*, Brookline Books, Bucknell University Press, Calyx Books, *Calyx Journal, Carolina Quarterly, Centennial Review*, Century Press, *Chattahoochee Review, Chelsea*, Chestnut Hills Press, Chicago Review Press, *Chiron Review, Christianity and the Arts, Chronicles, Chrysalis Reader, Cimarron Review, Circle, City Primeval, Clockwatch Review, Commonweal*, The Conservatory of American Letters, *Cream City Review, Creative Nonfiction, Cricket*, Cross Cultural Publications, *Cross & Quill, Curriculum Vitae*, David R. Godine, Dutton Children's Booksin, *Ellery Queen's Mystery Magazine, Entre Nous, Et Cetera, Evergreen Chronicles*, Fairleigh Dickinson University Press, *Fan, Farmer's Market*, Feminist Press, *Feminist Studies, Fourteen Hills, Fractal, Glimmer Train Stories, Gothic Journal, Green Mountains Review, Hadrosaur Tales, Harper's Magazine, Hollins Critic, Home Times*, Howell's House, *Hurricane Alice, Iconoclast, Iliad Press, INK Literary Review*, Ivan R. Dee, John Daniel & Company, *Journal of Modern Literature, Kaleidoscope, Kalliope, Kenyon Review, Kinesis*, Kroshka Books, Latin American Literary Review Press, *Left Curve*, Lehigh University Press, *Libido, Light, Literal Latté, Literary Magazine Review, Literary Review, Literary Sketches*, Lumen Editions, *MacGuffin*, MacMurray & Beck, Mage Publishers, *Mail Call Journal, Manoa*, Mayhaven Publishing, *Meat Whistle Quarterly, MEDIPHORS, Medusa's Hairdo*, Mid-List Press, Midmarch Arts Press, Milkweed Editions, *minnesota review, MoonRabbit Review, Nebraska Review, New England Review, New Letters, New Millennium Writings, New Writer's, Nightshade Press, Nimrod, Nite Writer's International Literary Arts*

Topics

Journal, Nocturnal Ecstasy, Northeast Corridor, Northwest Review, Northwoods Journal, Obsidian II, Ohio Writer, Oracle Story & Letters, Owen Wister Review, Palace Corbie, *Pangolin Papers, Papyrus, Passages North, Pearl, Phoebe, Plain Jane, Planetary Connections, Pleiades, Ploughshares, Potato Eyes Literary Arts Journal, Potluck Children's Literary, Potomac Review, Potpourri,* PREP Publishing, *Press, Quarterly West, Radiance, Rag Mag, Response, Rhino, Rising Star Publishers, RiverSedge, River Styx, Rosebud,* Serendipity Systems, *Sleuthhound memorandum, Slipstream, Southern Humanities Review, Southern Review, Southwest Review, Spectacle,* Stonewall Series, *Story, Sun, Sycamore Review,* Temple University Press, *Thema,* Third Side Press, Thomas Jefferson University Press, *Thoughts for All Seasons, The Threepenny Review, Tikkun,* Timson Edwards Publishing, *Troika,* University Editions, University of Nebraska Press, University of Nevada Press, University of Oklahoma Press, University Press of Mississippi, *Verses, Virginia Quarterly Review, Whetstone, Whispering Willow Mysteries,* White Pine Press, *William and Mary !Review, Wolf Head Quarterly, Women Artists News Book Review, Worcester Review, WormWood Review, Writer's Gazette, ZYZZYVA*

Livestock

Rural Heritage

Llamas

Llamas

Logistics

IIE Solutions

-M-

Mammography

Medical Physics Publishing

Management

Corporate Legal Times, Managing Office Technology, Podiatry Management, Self Employed Professional

Maquiladora

Borderlines

Maritime, professional

Cornell Maritime Press

Marketing

American Demographics, Critique, Self Employed Professional, Spare Time

Marketing Communications

Critique

Marriage

Atlanta Singles, Attain, Bride's, Challenges, Christian Home & School, Complete Woman, Country Living, Dollar Stretcher, Elegant Bride, Fairview Press, *Family Digest, Good Housekeeping,* Great Quotations Publishing, *Happy Times Monthly,* Harvest House Publishers, Hay House, *Health, Home Times, It's Your Choice, Ladies' Home Journal, Lutheran Digest,*

Modern Bride, New Woman, On the Scene, ParentGuide News, Parenting Magazine, Parents, Radiance, Redbook, Timson Edwards Publishing, *Whole Life Times, Woman's World, Working Mother,* Zondervan Publishing House

Martial Arts

Barricade Books, *Black Belt, Heartland USA, Journal of Asian Martial Arts, Karate/Kung Fu Illustrated, Martial Arts Training,* NTC/Contemporary Publishing, Paladin Press, Paradigm Publications, Samuel Weiser, *T'ai Chi, WE,* YMAA Publication Center

Mathematics

Plenum Publishing, *Wonderful Ideas*

Medical

SciTech Magazine

Medical Devices

Medical Device & Diagnostic Industry

Medical, physics/technical

Medical Physics Publishing

Medicinal Plants

HerbalGram

Medicine

American Fitness, American Medical News, Health, Ladies' Home Journal, MEDIPHORS, *Modern Maturity, National Enquirer, Prevention Magazine, Reader's Digest, Shape Magazine,* Weidner & Sons Publishing

Medicine, Chinese

Blue Poppy Press

Memoirs

Charles River Press, Feminist Press, *Harper's Magazine,* John Daniel & Company, *Massachusetts Review, Passager, The Threepenny Review*

Men's Fiction

Aegina Press, *Amelia Press, Carolina Quarterly,* Century Press, *City Primeval,* The Conservatory of American Letters, David R. Godine, *Dogwood Tales, In Touch/Indulge, INK Literary Review, Libido, Obsidian II, Oracle Story & Letters, Rising Star Publishers, Rosebud, Sycamore Review,* University Editions

Men's Issues

Amelia Press, Atlanta Singles, Beyond Words Publishing, *Big Apple Parent's Paper,* Black Iron Cookin' Company, *Carolina Quarterly,* Century Press, *Christian Living,* Commune-A-Key Publishing, *Esquire,* Fairview Press, *Happy Times Monthly,* Harvest House Publishers, Hay House, *Heartland USA,* Health Communications, *Home Times,* Hunter House Publishers, *INsider, Libido, Magical Blend, Men's Journal, Mom Guess What Newspaper, Muscle & Fitness, New Times, Oracle Story & Letters, Prime Health & Fitness, Rising Star Publishers, Rosebud, Swank, WE, Whole Life Times*

Mentoring

Mentor & Protégé

Metalworking

NOMMA Fabricator

Metaphysical

Natural Health, Spirit, Wholeness

Meteorology

Weatherwise

Mexico

BorderLines

Michigan

Momentum Books

Midwifery/Midwives

Birth Gazette, Midwifery Today

Military

American Legion, Army Magazine, Black Forest Press, Branden Publishing Company, Brassey's, Century Press, *Cowles Enthusiast Media*, Excalibur Publications, *Futurific*, The Graduate Group, *Heartland USA*, Howell's House, *Journal of Asian Martial Arts, Mail Call Journal, Marine Corps Gazette, Military Images*, Momentum Books, Motorbooks International, Naval Institute Press, *Navy Times, Oracle Story & Letters*, Paladin Press, *Parameters, Popular Mechanics*, PREP Publishing, PSI Research, *Rising Star Publishers,* !Texas A&M University Press, University of Nebraska Press, University of North Texas Press, *Times News Service, VFW*, White Mane Publishing Company

Money/Finance

Allworth Press, *American Salesman*, Avery Publishing Group, *Career Focus, Communications Publishing Group, Consumers Digest, Cosmopolitan, Dollar Stretcher, Drum Business, EEO BiMonthly, Family Circle, Financial Freedom Report Quarterly, Futurific, Girls' Life*, The Graduate Group, *Home Business News, Home Times, House, Home & Garden*, In Print Publishing, *Lutheran Digest*, Markowski International Publishers, *Modern Bride, Modern Maturity, National Geographic Traveler, New Choices*, Nolo Press, NTC/Contemporary Publishing, Paladin Press, *Playboy, Redbook, Self Employed Professional, Spare Time, Supervision, Technical Analysis of Stocks & Commodities*, Ten Speed Press, *Times News Service, Tree Care Industry, WE, Whole Life Times, Woman's Day, Working Mother, Your Money*

Montana

Montana Catholic

Morality

American Legion, It's Your Choice

Motorcycles/Motorcycling

American Motorcyclist, Rider

Movie Reviews

Kinesis

Multicultural

AIM, Amelia Press, Arkansas Review, Art Times, Arte Público

Press, Beyond Words Publishing, Black Forest Press, *BorderLines*, Branden Publishing Company, Calyx Books, *Calyx Journal, Career Focus, Careers & the disABLED, Carolina Quarterly, Centennial Review*, Charlesbridge Publishing, Charles River Press, Chicago Review Press, *Child of Colors, Christian Living, Circle K*, Clarity Press, Clover Park Press, *Communications Publishing Group*, Cross Cultural Publications, *Curriculum Vitae*, The Denali Press, *Equal Opportunity Publications, Faces*, Feminist Press, *Frontiers*, Heinemann, Highsmith Press, Hunter House Publishers, Humanics Publishing Group, *Hurricane Alice, INK Literary Review*, Intercultural Press, *Interrace, Iris, Journal of Christian Nursing*, Judson Press, *Kenyon Review*, Kroshka Books, MacMurray & Beck, Mage Publishers, *Magical Blend, Manoa*, McFarland & Company, Milkweed Editions, *minnesota review, Minority Engineer*, Mitchell Lane Publishers, *new renaissance, Obsidian II*, Pacific View Press, *PanGaia*, Paradigm Publications, Pelican Publishing Company, *Pennsylvania Heritage*, Philomel Books, *Planetary Connections, Potpourri, Power and Light, Radiance, Ranger Rick, River Styx, South Florida History, Southwest Review, Spectacle, Spirit, Teaching Tolerance*, Temple University Press, *Tequesta*, Texas A&M University Press, University of North Texas Press, *WD-Workforce Diversity, Whole Life Times, Woman Engineer, ZYZZYVA*

Topics

Multimedia

Focal Press

Music

Allworth Press, *Amelia Press*, Ardsley House Publishers, *Arkansas Review, Art Times, Bleach*, Bucknell University Press, *Café Eighties*, Centerstream Publishing, Century Press, Chicago Review Press, *Christianity and the Arts, Circle, Clockwatch Review, Curriculum Vitae*, Faber & Faber, Fiesta City Publishers, *Girls' Life, Gray Areas, Guitar Player, Heartland USA, Illinois Entertainer, INsider, Jam Rag, Journal of Christian Nursing, Lacunae, Lilith*, Mage Publishers, *Mississippi Rag, Modern Drummer, new renaissance, Nocturnal Ecstasy, On the Scene, PanGaia*, Pelican Publishing Company, *Planetary Connections, Playboy, Rosebud*, Schirmer Books, *Senior, Small! Press Creative Explosion, Southern Humanities Review, Spy*, Temple University Press, *The Threepenny Review*, University of Nebraska Press, University Press of Mississippi, *WE, Whole Life Times*

Music, country

Country America

Mystery

Aegina Press, *Alfred Hitchcock Mystery Magazine, Amelia Press, Belletrist Review*, Black Forest Press, Century Press, The Conservatory of American Letters, David R. Godine, *Dogwood Tales, Ellery Queen's Mystery Magazine, Gothic Journal*, Intercontinental Publishing, Kroshka Books, *Lacunae*, Mayhaven Publishing, Minstrel Books, *Murderous Intent Mystery, My Legacy*, New Victoria Publishers, *Oatmeal & Poetry*, Philomel Books, Pocket Books, *Power and Light*, PREP Publishing, Rising Tide Press, *Rosebud, Sleuthhound memorandum*, Spinsters Ink, University Editions, *Whispering Willow Mysteries, Writer's Gazette*

Mysticism

Jewish Lights Publishing

-N-

Narrative, dramatic/human interest

Good Housekeeping

Narrative, poetry

Woman in the Moon Publications

Native American

Amelia Press, American Indian Art, Backwoodsman, Beyond Words Publishing, *Birth Gazette,* Black Forest Press, Black Iron Cookin' Company, Blue River Publishing, Blue Water Publishing, *BorderLines,* Bright Mountain Books, *Calyx Books, Calyx Journal, Career Focus, Careers & the disABLED, Carolina Quarterly,* Century Press, Charles River Press, *Cimarron Review, Circle K,* Commune-A-Key Publishing, *Communications Publishing Group,* Cross Cultural Publications, The Denali Press, *Eclectic Rainbows, Equal Opportunity Publications, Florida Wildlife,* !Gem Guides Book Company, *Good Red Road,* Hearts 'n Tummies Cookbook Company, In Print Publishing, Kroshka Books, *Light of Consciousness, Magical Blend,* Mayhaven Publishing, *Minority Engineer,* Mountain Press Publishing Company, *My Legacy,* Naturegraph Publishers, *New Times, Oklahoma Today, On the Scene, PanGaia,* Pelican Publishing Company, *Pennsylvania Heritage, Planetary Connections, Rosebud,* Samuel Weiser, *South Florida History, Special Collections, Tequesta,* Texas A&M University Press, *True West,* University of Nebraska Press, University of Nevada Press, University of Oklahoma Press, *University Press of Mississippi,* Voyageur Press, Washington State University Press, *WD-Workforce Diversity, Weems Concepts, Western Publications,* White Pine Press, *Woman Engineer*

Natural Science

Texas A&M University Press

Nature

Century Press, *Country Living,* Cowles Creative Publishing, *Creative With Words Publications,* DIMI Press, Mountain Press Publishing Company, *Natural Health,* Naturegraph Publishers, *Outdoor Life, Ranger Rick, Smithsonian Magazine, Woman's World, The Yoga Journal*

Needlework

Crochet World

News

Emerge, Life, Newsweek, Redbook, The Star, Time

New Age

Amelia Press, American Literary Press, *Attain,* Avery Publishing Group, Beyond Words Publishing, Blue Water Publishing, Century Press, *Christian New Age Quarterly,* Commune-A-Key Publishing, *Crone Chronicles,* Cross Cultural Publications, Crossing Press, *Eclectic Rainbows, Evolving Woman, Futurific,* Gryphon House, Hay House, Humanics Publishing Group, Hunter House Publishers, In Print Publishing, *Intuition, It's Your Choice,* Kroshka Books, Lifetime Books, *Light of Consciousness,* Llewellyn Publication, *Magical Blend, My Legacy, National Enquirer, Natural Health, New Millennium Writings, New Times,* NTC/Contemporary

Publishing, *On the Scene,* Orion House, *PanGaia, Planetary Connections, Radiance, Rosebud,* Samuel Weiser, *Spirit, WE, Whole Life Times, Wholeness, The Yoga Journal*

New Thought/Metaphysical

Unity Books

New Thought/Spiritual

Science of Mind

N.L.P.

Metamorphous Press

Nonfiction

Abbott, Langer & Associates, *Above the Bridge, Acorn,* Addicus Books, *Ad Astra, Adolescence,* Aegina Press, Aegis Publishing Group, African American Images, *Afterimage, AIM, Alaska Quarterly Review, Alive!,* Allworth Press, Alyson Publications, *Amelia Press, American Careers,* American Correctional Association, *The American Cottage Gardener, American Demographics, American Fitness, American Hunter, American Indian Art, American Legion, American Motorcyclist, American Scholar, American Survival Guide, Angels on Earth, Antioch Review, Antique Trader Weekly, Archaeology,* Arden Press, *Arkansas Review,* Arte Público Press, *Arthritis Today, Aspen, Atlanta Parent, Atlanta Singles, Audubon, Automobile Quarterly, Avenues,* Avery Publishing Group, *Babybug, Back Home in Kentucky,* Baker Book House Company, *Balloon Life, Baltimore Magazine,* Barricade Books, *Barron's Educational Series, Bellingham Review,* Berkshire House Publishers, *Better Homes and Gardens,* Beyond Words Publishing, *Bicycling, Big World, Bike, Birth Gazette, Black Child,* Black Forest Press, *Black Mountain Review,* Blue Poppy Press, Blue River Publishing, Blue Water Publishing, *BlueRidge Country,* Bonus Books, *BorderLines, Boston Review, Boxoffice, Boys' Life, Boys' Quest,* Branden Publishing Company, Brassey's, BrickHouse Books, *Bride's,* Bright Mountain Books, Broadman & Holman Publishers, Brookline Books, Bryant & Dillon Publishers, Bucknell University Press, *Buffalo Spree, Bugle, Byte, Café Eighties, California Explorer,* Calyx Books, *Calyx Journal, Camperways, Canoe & Kayak, Car & Driver, Career Focus, Careers & the disABLED, Carefree Enterprise, Carolina Quarterly, Cascades East, Cat Fancy, CATsumer Report,* Celebrity Press, *Centennial Review,* Century Press, *Challenges,* Charlesbridge Publishing, Charles River Press, *Charleston, Chattahoochee Review, Chelsea,* Chelsea Green Publishing Company, Chess Enterprises, Chestnut Hills Press, Chicago Review Press, *Child of Colors, Children's Better Health Institute, Christian Living, Christian New Age Quarterly, Christianity and the Arts, Chrysalis Reader, Cimarron Review, Circle, Circle K,* Clarity Press, Clover Park Press, *Club Connection, Coal People, Colonial Homes, Collectors News, Common Boundary, Commonweal,* Commune-A-Key Publishing, The Conservatory of American Letters, *Consumers Digest, Cooking Light,* Cornell Maritime Press, *Corporate Legal Times, Cosmopolitan, Country America, Country Living,* Cowles Creative Publishing, *Crayola Kids, Cream City Review, Creation Spirituality Network, Creative Nonfiction, Cricket, Crone Chronicles,* Crossing Press, *Cross & Quill, Crusader, Curriculum Vitae, CutBank, Dagger of the Mind,* David R. Godine, The Denali Press, Denlinger's Publishers, DIMI Press, *Discipleship Journal, Discover, Divorced Parents X-Change,* Duke Press, Eastern National, *East Texas Historical Journal, Echoes, Eclectic Rainbows, Educational*

Topics

Nonviolence

Fellowship

Northwest

Nor'Westing

Nostalgia

American Fitness, Car & Driver, Outdoor Life, Senior Living, Sports Afield, Yankee, Yesterday's Magazette, ZYZZYVA

Nursing

Birth Gazette, Career Focus, Commune-A-Key Publishing, *Communications Publishing Group, Continuum,* The Graduate Group, *Journal of Christian Nursing, Midwifery Today,* Weidner & Sons Publishing

Nutrition

American Fitness, Aspen, Avery Publishing Group, *Bicycling,* Barron's Educational Series, *Birth Gazette, Career Focus,* Century Press, Commune-A-Key Publishing, *Communications Publishing Group, Cooking Light, Cosmopolitan, Country Connections,* Crossing Press, *Diabetes Self-Management, Fitness, Good Housekeeping,* Hay House, *Health, HealthQuest, Home Times, House, Home & Garden,* Hunter House Publishers, *It's Your Choice,* Kroshka Books, *Ladies' Home Journal,* Lifetime Books, Llewellyn Publications, *Lutheran Digest,* Masters Press, *Men's Fitness,* McBooks Press, *Men's Health, Muscle & Fitness, Natural Health, Natural Living Today, New Times,* Paradigm Publications, *ParentGuide News,* Piccadilly Books, *Planetary Connections, Playgirl, Prevention Magazine, Radiance, Senior, Shape Magazine, Southern Living, The Star, Swim,* Ten Speed Press, *Veggie Life, Weight Watchers Magazine, Whole Life Times, Wholeness, Wild Foods Forum, Wines & Vines, Woman's Day, Woman's World, Women's Sports & Fitness, Working Mother, The Yoga Journal, Your Health*

-O-

Office

Managing Office Technology

Opinion

Cosmopolitan, Guns & Ammo, Newsweek, OutLoud and Proud!, Reader's Digest, Wired, The Yoga Journal

Opportunity

Markowski International Publishers

Optometry/Eyecare

Optometric Economics

Ornithology

Weidner & Sons Publishing

Outdoors

Above the Bridge, Acorn, Adventure Journal, Amelia Press, American Hunter, Aspen, Balloon Life, Big World, Boys' Life, BlueRidge Country, Bright Mountain Books, *Bugle, California Explorer, Canoe & Kayak, Carefree Enterprise, Cascades East,* Chicago Review Press, The Conservatory of American

Letters, Cowles Creative Publishing, *Creative With Words Publications,* David R. Godine, *DogGone,* Falcon Publishing, *Field & Stream, Florida Wildlife,* Gem Guides Book Company, *Georgia Journal, Girls' Life,* The Globe Pequot Press, *Gold and Treasure Hunter, Guns & Ammo,* Hancock House, *Happy Times Monthly, HeartLand Boating, Heartland USA,* Hearts 'n Tummies Cookbook Company, *Highways, Inside Texas Running, INsider,* Johnston Associates International, *Knives Illustrated, Lutheran Digest,* Lyons & Burford Publishers, *Marlin, MidWest Streams & Trails,* Mountaineers Books, Mountain Press Publishing Company, *National Parks,* Naturegraph Publishers, *NEBRASKAland, New Home Life, Nightshade Press, Nor'Westing, Northwest Regional, Outdoor Life, Paddler,* Paladin Press, *PanGaia,* Pelican Publishing Company, *Petersen's Bowhunting, Popular Mechanics, Potato Eyes Literary Arts Journal, Power & Motoryacht,* Quixote Press, *Ranger Rick,* Rutledge Hill Press, *Safari, Sailing Magazine, Sailing World, Sandlapper, Ski Tripper, Skiing, Snow Country, Snowshoer, Sports Afield, Sun Valley, Sunset,* Ten Speed Press, *Texas Parks & Wildlife, Trailer Boats, Vacation Industry Review, WE, Western RV News, Whole Life Times, Wild Foods Forum, Wisconsin Trails, Women's Sports & Fitness,* Woodall Publications, *Woodall's California RV Traveler, Woodall's Camp-orama, Woodall's Carolina RV Traveler, Woodall's Discover RVing, Woodall's Northeast Outdoors, Woodall's RV Traveler, Woodall's Southern RV*

-P-

Pacific Northwest

Hancock House

Paddlesports

Paddler

Pagan

PanGaia

Painting

ME

Paranormal

Attain, Beyond Words Publishing, Blue Water Publishing, *Circle,* The Conservatory of American Letters, *Crone Chronicles, Dagger of the Mind, Eye, FATE, Gate, Gnosis,* Gryphon House, Humanics Publishing Group, Kroshka Books, Llewellyn Publications, Mayhaven Publishing, *New Times,* NTC/Contemporary Publishing, *Office Number One, Planetary Connections, Skeptical Inquirer, Swank, Whole Life Times*

Parenting

African American Images, Avery Publishing Group, *BaBY,* Barron's Educational Series, *Bay Area Publishing Group, Better Homes and Gardens, Big Apple Parent's Paper, Black Child, Bride's,* Brookline Books, Chicago Review Press, *Child, Christian Parenting Today, Dovetail,* Fairview Press, *Family Digest, Family Life,* Great Quotations Publishing, Gryphon House, *Happy Times Monthly,* Heinemann, *Home Times,* Humanics Publishing Group, *It's Your Choice,* Kali Press, Kroshka Books, *Ladies' Home Journal, L.A. Parent, Lessons on Life, Liguorian, Living With Teenagers, Long! Island Parenting News,* Lumen Editions, *Lutheran Digest,*

Mama's Little Helper Newsletter, McBooks Press, *Mother Is Me*, Mustang Publishing Company, New View Publications, NTC/Contemporary Publishing, *On the Scene, PanGaia, Parent & Child, ParentGuide News, Parenting Magazine, ParentLife, Parents' Press, Parent.TEEN*, Perspective Press, *Radiance, Redbook, San Francisco Peninsula Parenting, The Star, Success Connection, Successful Black Parenting, Table Talk, Twins*, White-Boucke Publishing, *Whole Life Times, Working Mother*, Zondervan Publishing House

Pastoral Studies

Kregel Publications

Peace

Fellowship

Pennsylvania

Pennsylvania Heritage

Personal Development

Cosmopolitan, Quill Driver Books/Word Dancer Press, Metamorphous Press

Personal Experience

American Fitness, American Hunter, Angels on Earth, Baby Magazine, Cat Fancy, Cosmopolitan, Family Circle, Modern Bride, Natural Health, Outdoor Life, Parenting Magazine, Reader's Digest, Senior Living, The Threepenny Review, Yankee, YM, ZYZZYVA

Personnel

Supervision

Pets

American Kennel Club Gazette, Cat Fancy, House, Home & Garden

Philosophy

Amelia Press, Ardsley House Publishers, Black Forest Press, Bucknell University Press, *Centennial Review*, Century Press, *Chrysalis Reader, Circle, Crone Chronicles*, Cross Cultural Publications, *Curriculum Vitae, Eclectic Rainbows*, Fairleigh Dickinson University Press, *First Things, Freeman, Gnosis, Happy Times Monthly*, Hay House, *Home Times, It's Your Choice*, Jewish Lights Publishing, *Journal of Information Ethics*, Kroshka Books, Lehigh University Press, *Magical Blend, minnesota review, Natural Health, New Millennium Writings, Nimrod, Office Number One, Oracle Story & Letters, PanGaia, Parabola*, Paradigm Publications, *!Planetary Connections, Radiance, Response, Rising Star Publishers, Southern Humanities Review*, University of Nebraska Press, *Whole Life Times, The Yoga Journal*

Photography

Adventure Journal, Afterimage, Allworth Press, *Amelia Press*, Beyond Words Publishing, *Bleach, Bugle*, David R. Godine, Focal Press, *Happy Times Monthly, Iris, Libido, Liquid Ohio, MEDIPHORS, Military Images, National Geographic Traveler, Nimrod, Outdoor Life, Pennsylvania Heritage, Popular Mechanics, Popular Science, Rag Mag, Sandlapper, Sun, Sycamore Review*, Timson Edwards Publishing, *Today's Photographer International*, University Press of Mississippi, *WE*

Physical Fitness

American Fitness, American Health, Attain, Bicycling, Better Homes and Gardens, Carefree Enterprise, Consumers Digest, Cooking Light, Cosmopolitan, Fitness, Front Row Experience, *Glamour, Golf Digest, Golfer, Happy Times Monthly, Health, Inside Texas Running, Journal of Asian Martial Arts, Journal of Christian Nursing*, Kroshka Books, Lyons & Burford Publishers, *Mademoiselle, Men's Fitness, Men's Health, Men's Journal, Muscle & Fitness, Modern Bride, National Enquirer, Natural Health, New Choices, New Home Life, New Woman, Outdoor Life, Paddler, Parenting Magazine, Parents, Prevention Magazine, Prime Health & Fitness, Radiance, Reader's Digest, Runner's World, Senior Living, Shape Magazine, Snowshoer, The Star, Swim, Swimming World, T'ai Chi, Veggie Life, WE, Weight Watchers Magazine, Whole Life Times, Wom!an_92s Day, Woman's World, The Yoga Journal, Your Health*

Physical Science

Odyssey, Popular Science,

Physicians, careers

Unique Opportunities

Picture Books

Charlesbridge Publishing, Dutton Children's Books

Plays

1812, Ranger Rick

Playscripts

Dramatics

Podiatry

Podiatry Management

Poetry

Above the Bridge, Acorn, Aegina Press, *Alaska Quarterly Review*, Alpha Beat Press, *Amelia Press*, American Literary Press, *The American Poetry Review, Americas Review, Antioch Review, Arkansas Review, Artful Dodge, Art Times, Babybug, Baltimore Review, Bellingham Review, Bellowing Ark, Beloit Poetry Journal, Birmingham Poetry Review*, BkMk Press, Black Forest Press, *Black Mountain Review*, Blue Mountain Arts, *Boston Review*, Branden Publishing Company, BrickHouse Books, *Bridge*, Brookline Books, *Buffalo Spree, Café Eighties*, Calyx Books, *Calyx Journal, Carolina Quarterly, Cat Fancy, Centennial Review*, Century Press, *Chattahoochee Review, Chelsea*, Chestnut Hills Press, Chicago Review Press, *Chiron Review, Christian Living, Christianity and the Arts, Chronicles, Chrysalis Reader, Cimarron Review, Circle, Clockwatch Review*, Commune-A-Key Publishing, *Country Connections, Cream City Review, Creative With Words Publications, Cricket, Crone Chronicles, Cross & Quill, Curriculum Vitae, CutBank, Dagger of the Mind*, David R. Godine, *Dreams of Decadence, Eclectic Rainbows, 1812, Entre Nous*, Eternity Press, *Evergreen Chronicles*, Fairleigh Dickinson University Press, *Fan, Farmer's Market, Field, Flying Horse, Fourteen Hills, Fractal, George & Mertie's Place, Georgia Journal, Girls' Life, Green Hills Literary Lantern, Green Mountains Review, Greensboro Review, GRIT, Hadrosaur Tales, Harper's Magazine, Hawaii Review, Hayden's Ferry Review, Heaven Bone, Higginsville Reader,*

Hollins Critic, Iconoclast, Iliad Press, INK Literary Review, Iris, John Daniel & Company, Kalliope, Kenyon Review, Kinesis, Kroshka Books, Ladybug, Latin American Literary Review Press, Ledge, Left Curve, Lessons on Life, Light, Light of Consciousness, Lilith, Liquid Ohio, Literal Latté, Literary Review, Lucidity Poetry Journal, Lumen Editions, Lynx Eye, MacGuffin, Maelstrom, Magazine of Speculative Poetry, Mail Call Journal, Manoa, Massachusetts Review, Mature Years, Maverick Press, Mayhaven Publishing, ME, Meadowbrook Press, Meat Whistle Quarterly, MEDIPHORS, Medusa's Hairdo, Mid-American Review, Mid-List Press, Midmarch Arts Press, MidWest Poetry Review, Milkweed Editions, Mind Fire, minnesota review, Mississippi Review, Modern Haiku, MoonRabbit Review, Nation, NEBO, Nebraska Review, Nedge, New England Review, New Letters, New Millennium Writings, New Odyssey Review, New Poets Series, new renaissance, New Rivers Press, New Writer's, Nightshade Press, Nimrod, Nocturnal Ecstasy, Northeast Corridor, Northwest Review, Northwoods Journal, Nostalgia, Oatmeal & Poetry, Oblates, Obsidian II, Office Number One, Ohio Writer, Omnific, Orchises Press, Outrider Press, Owl Creek Press, Pacific Coast Journal, Palace Corbie, PanGaia, Parnassus Literary Journal, Passager, Passages North, Pearl, Peregrine, Philomel Books, Phoebe, Pleiades, Ploughshares, Poem, Poet's Paper, Poetic Realm, Poetry, Poetry Motel, Potato Eyes Literary Arts Journal, Potluck Children's Literary, Potomac Review, Potpourri, Prairie Schooner, Press, Primavera, Quarterly West, Radiance, Rag Mag, Rhino, Rising Star Publishers, RiverSedge, River Styx, Rockford Review, Rosebud, Science of Mind, Senior Living, Sensual Aspirations, Silver Web, Skylark, Slipstream, Snake Nation Review, Southern California Anthology, Southern Humanities Review, Southern Review, Southwest Review, Special Collections, Spider, Spirit, Staplegun Press, Stoneflower Literary Journal, Stonewall Series, Sun, Sycamore Review, Tampa Review, Thema, Thomas Jefferson University Press, Thoughts for All Seasons, 360 Degrees, The Threepenny Review, Tia Chucha Press, Tikkun, Two Rivers Review, University Editions, University of Nevada Press, Verses, Virginia Quarterly Review, Visions International, Weems Concepts, Whetstone, William and Mary Review, Wolf Head Quarterly, Women Artists News Book Review, Woman in the Moon Publications, Worcester Review, WormWood Review, Writer's Exchange, Writers' Forum, Writer's Gazette, Yankee, Yesterday's Magazette

Poker

Card Player

Political Science

University of Oklahoma Press

Politics

Amelia Press, American Hunter, American Legion, Black Forest Press, *BorderLines, Boston Review,* Branden Publishing Company, *California Journal, Centennial Review, Chronicles,* Clarity Press, *Commonweal,* Cross Cultural Publications, *Curriculum Vitae,* The Denali Press, *E,* Fairleigh Dickinson University Press, *First Things, Futurific, George & Mertie's Place, Girlfriends, Harper's Magazine, Headway,* Howell's House, ICS Press, In Print Publishing, *INsider, It's Your Choice,* Ivan R. Dee, *Jam Rag,* Kroshka Books, Kumarian Press, *Left Curve,* !Lehigh University Press, *Long Term View, minnesota review, Mother Jones, Nation, National Review, new renaissance, Oracle Story & Letters, Planetary Connections, Playboy,* Plenum Publishing, *Politically Correct, Radiance,* Rising Star Publishers, *Slick Times, Spy,*

Temple University Press, *The Threepenny Review, Tikkun,* University of Nebraska Press, University of Nevada Press, *Virginia Quarterly Review, Whole Life Times*

Politics, progressive

Country Connections

Pregnancy

American Fitness, Meadowbrook Press

Printing, methods

Small Press Creative Explosion

Produce & Processing

Fresh Cut

Production & Inventory Control

IIE Solutions

Profiles

Fitness, Good Housekeeping, Guns & Ammo, Inside Sports, New Choices, Penthouse, Playboy, Reader's Digest, Shape Magazine, SignCraft, Sports Illustrated for Kids, St. Anthony Messenger, Stoneflower Literary Journal, Wired, YM

Prospecting

Gem Guides Book Company

Psychoanalysis

Jason Aronson

Psychology

Adolescence, Amelia Press, American Correctional Association, *Angels on Earth, Attain,* Beyond Words Publishing, Black Forest Press, Brookline Books, Bucknell University Press, *Centennial Review,* Century Press, *Challenges, Common Boundary,* Commune-A-Key Publishing, *Crone Chronicles, Eclectic Rainbows, Et Cetera, Evolving Woman, Eye,* Fairleigh Dickinson University Press, Fairview Press, *Fitness, Glamour,* Hay House, *Health,* Health Communications, Hunter House Publishers, *It's Your Choice,* Jason Aronson, *Journal of Christian Nursing,* Kroshka Books, *Ladies' Home Journal,* Lehigh University Press, Lumen Editions, Llewellyn Publications, *Magical Blend,* Markowski International Publishers, *Men's Fitness,* Metamorphous Press, *Modern Bride, Modern Maturity, Natural Health, New Times,* New View Publications, *New Woman, Oracle Story & Letters, Parenting Magazine,* Perron Press, Perspective Press, Plenum Publishing, *Prime Health & Fitness, Psychology Today, Radiance, Redbook, Rising Star Publishers,* Samuel Weiser, *Spectacle, The Star,* Temple University Press, Third Side Press, *Tikkun,* University of Nebraska Press, Weidner & Sons Publishing, *Whole Life Times, Woman's Day, The Yoga Journal*

Psychology, pop

Markowski International Publishers

Psychotherapy

Jason Aronson, Weidner & Sons Publishing

Public Policy

American Forests, Boston Review, Bugle, California Jour-

nal, Centennial Review, Christian Social Action, Clarity Press, Commonweal, Critical Review, Cross Cultural Publications, The Denali Press, Fairleigh Dickinson University Press, *First Things, Futurific, Home Times,* Howell's House, ICS Press, *INsider, It's Your Choice, Journal of Information Ethics,* Kroshka Books, Lehigh University Press, *minnesota review, Nation, National Review, Oracle Story & Letters, Parameters, Planetary Connections, Politically Correct,* Rising Star Publishers, Temple University Press, University of Nebraska Press, *VFW, WE, Public Relations, Library Imagination Paper*

Publishing

Beyond Words Publishing

Puzzles

Crayola Kids, SciTech Magazine, Spider

-Q-

Quilts/Quilting

Chitra Publications, Rutledge Hill Press

Quotations, collection

Meadowbrook Press

-R-

Radiation Oncology

Medical Physics Publishing

Radio

Focal Press

Real Estate

Commercial Investment Real Estate Journal, Country Living, Financial Freedom Report Quarterly

Recovery

Challenges

Recreation

Adventure Journal, American Demographics, American Fitness, American Hunter, Avenues, Bicycling, Bike, Black Iron Cookin' Company, *Bowling, Bugle, Canoe & Kayak, Car & Driver, Carefree Enterprise, Cascades East, Christian Living, DogGone,* Falcon Publishing, *Fitness, Florida Wildlife,* The Globe Pequot Press, *Gold and Treasure Hunter, Golf Digest, Guns & Ammo, Happy Times Monthly, HeartLand Boating, Heartland USA, Highways, Home Times, Houseboat, Inside Sports, Inside Texas Running,* Johnston Associates International, *Kite Lines, Lutheran Digest,* Lyons & Burford Publishers, *Mail Call Journal, Marlin, Men's Health, Mid-Atlantic Country, MidWest Streams & Trails, Mushing,* Mustang Publishing Company, *National Geographic Traveler, NEBRASKAland, New Choices, New Home Life, Nor'Westing, On the Scene, Outdoor Life, Pack-O-Fun, Paddler, Penthouse,* Pilot Books, *Playboy, Pontoon & Deck Boat, Popular Mechanics, Radiance, Recreation News, Runner's World, RV West, Sailing Magazine, Sandlapper, SEA, Senior Living, Shape Magazine, Ski Tripper, Snow Country, Snowshoer, Sports Afield, Sports Illustrated for Kids, Sun*

Valley, Sunset, Swim, Swimming World, Ten Speed Press, *Travel & Leisure, Vacation Industry Review, WE, Western RV News, Wild Foods Forum, Wisconsin Trails*

Recreational Vehicles

Camping Today, Coast to Coast, Consumers Digest, Highways, RV West, Woodall Publications, *Woodall's California RV Traveler, Woodall's Camp-orama, Woodall's Carolina RV Traveler, Woodall's Discover RVing, Woodall's Northeast Outdoors, Woodall's RV Traveler, Woodall's Southern RV*

Reference

Abbott, Langer & Associates, Affaire de Coeur, Amelia Press, American Correctional Association, Arden Press, Avery Publishing Group, Barron's Educational Series, Black Forest Press, *California Journal,* Century Press, *Consumers Digest,* Craftsman Book Company, The Denali Press, Fairview Press, *Gibbons-Humms Guide,* The Graduate Group, Highsmith Press, Humanics Publishing Group, Jewish Lights Publishing, JIST Works, Kroshka Books, Lehigh University! Press, *Mail Call Journal,* Mayhaven Publishing, Mustang Publishing Company, Naval Institute Press, *Nelson Reference Publishing,* Nolo Press, *Obsidian II,* Pilot Books, Quill Driver Books/Word Dancer Press, *Radiance, Reptile & Amphibian,* Scarecrow Press, *Shuttle Spindle & Dyepot, Sunset,* Ten Speed Press, Tower Publishing, University Press of Mississippi, Weidner & Sons Publishing, White-Boucke Publishing

Regional

Above the Bridge, Alabama Living, Amelia Press, American Demographics, Arkansas Review, Avenues, Back Home in Kentucky, Baltimore Magazine, Barricade Books, BkMk Press, *BlueRidge Country,* Blue River Publishing, *BorderLines,* Branden Publishing Company, Bright Mountain Books, *Cascades East,* Charles River Press, *Charleston,* Chicago Review Press, *Chronicles,* Clover Park Press, *Commonweal,* Cornell Maritime Press, Falcon Publishing, *Florida Hotel & Motel Journal, Gateway Heritage,* Gem Guides Book Company, *Georgia Journal,* The Globe Pequot Press, Golden West Publishers, Great! Quotations Publishing, Hearts 'n Tummies Cookbook Company, *Inside Texas Running, INsider,* Johnston Associates International, Kroshka Books, *L.A. Parent, Lansing City Limits, Long Island Update,* Mayhaven Publishing, McBooks Press, *Mid-Atlantic Country, MidWest Streams & Trails, Mississippi Review, Montana Catholic, Montana, Montana: Magazine of Western History,* Mountain Press Publishing Company, *National Geographic Traveler,* Naturegraph Publishers, *NEBRASKAland, New Mexico,* New Rivers Press, *Nevada, North Dakota Horizons, Northwest Regional, Oklahoma Today, Ohio, Orange Coast, Oregon Business, Oregon Quarterly, Outdoor Life, Over the Back Fence, Paddler,* Pelican Publishing Company, *Pennsylvania, Pennsylvania Heritage,* Philomel Books, *Pittsburgh, Potomac Review, Progressive Engineer,* Quill Driver Books/Word Dancer Press, Quixote Press, *Sandlapper, San Francisco, Seattle, Ski Tripper, Skylark, South Florida History, Southern Living, Spotlight, Sunset, Sun Valley,* Tamarack Books, Temple University Press, Ten Speed Press, *Tequesta,* Texas A&M University Press, *Texas Parks & Wildlife,* Thomas Nelson Reference Publishing, University of Maine Press, University of Nebraska Press, University of Nevada Press, University of North Texas Press, University of Oklahoma Press, University Press of Mississippi, Valiant Press, *Voyageur,* Voyageur Press, Washington State University Press, *WE, Whole Life Times, Wisconsin Trails,* Woodall Publications, *Woodall's California RV Trav-*

Topics

eler, Woodall's Carol!ina RV Traveler, Woodall's Northeast Outdoors, Woodall's Southern RV

Regional, city

Chicago, FOCUS Kansas City, San Francisco, Seattle

Relationships

African American Images, *Alive!, Attain,* Barricade Books, Beyond Words Publishing, *Bride's,* Celebrity Press, *Challenges, Christian Living, Complete Woman, Cosmopolitan, Creative With Words Publications, Crone Chronicles, Dovetail, Eclectic Rainbows, Essence,* Fairview Press, *Family Circle, Fan, Fitness, Girls' Life, Glamour, Happy Times Monthly,* Hay House, *Health,* Health Communications, *Home Times,* Hunter House Publishers, Impact Publishers, Innisfree Press, In Print Publishing, *INsider, It's Your Choice,* Jason Aronson, *Journal of Christian Nursing,* Kroshka Books, *Ladies' Home Journal, Libido, Liguorian, Lutheran Digest, Mademoiselle, Magical Blend,* Mayhaven Publishing, *Men's Health, Modern Bride, Modern Maturity, Mom Guess What Newspaper, National Enquirer, Natural Living Today, New Choices,* New View Publications, *New Woman,* NTC/Contemporary Publishing, *On the Scene, PanGaia, Parent & Child, Parenting Magazine, Parents,* Perron Press, *Planetary Connections,* PREP Publishing, *Prime Health & Fitness, Radiance,* Sta-Kris, *Supervision,* Timson Edwards Publishing, *WE, Whole Life Times, Woman's Day, Working Mother,* World Leisure Corporation, Zondervan Publishing House

Religion

ACTA Publications, *American Legion,* American Literary Press, *Angels on Earth, Attain,* Baker Book House Company, Beyond Words Publishing, Black Forest Press, Branden Publishing Company, *Catholic Near East,* Century Press, *Christian New Age Quarterly,* Christian Publications, *Christian Social Action, Christianity and the Arts, Christianity Today, Common Boundary, Creation Spirituality Network, Crone Chronicles,* Cross Cultural Publications, *Cross & Quill, Crusader,* David R. Godine, *Door, Dovetail, Family Digest, First Things,* Franciscan University Press, *Gnosis,* Great Quotations Publishing, *Gryphon Publications, Guideposts, Home Times,* Humanics Publishing Group, *Insight, It's Your Choice,* Jason Aronson, Jewish Lights Publishing, *Journal of Christian Nursing,* Judson Press, Kregel Publications, Kroshka Books, Legacy Press, Lehigh University Press, *Light of Consciousness, Liguorian,* Llewellyn Publications, *Lutheran Digest, Magical Blend, Mature Years, Message, Montana Catholic, Moody, Natural Health, Nelson Reference Publishing, New Times, Nostalgia, Oblates, PanGaia, Parabola,* Pelican Publishing Company, *Plain Truth, Planetary Connections, Pockets, Power and Light, Preacher's,* PREP Publishing, *Presbyterians Today, Response, SageWoman,* Samuel Weiser, *Science of Mind, Seek, Signs of the Times, Standard, Secret Place,* St. Anthony Messenger, St. Bede's Publications, *Straight,* Temple University Press, Thomas Nelson Reference Publishing, *Tikkun, Today's Catholic Teacher,* Unity Books, *Upper Room, Vision, WE, WIN Informer, With, World, Your Church, Youth Update*

Religious, theological

Kregel Publications

Remedies

Veggie Life

Remodeling

Home Improver

Rental Property

Financial Freedom Report Quarterly

Reprints

Feminist Press

Retirement

JIST Works, *Modern Maturity, New Choices, Parents,* Quill Driver Books/Word Dancer Press, *Senior Living, Your Money*

Reviews

Carolina Quarterly, Dagger of the Mind, Heaven Bone

Reviews, music

Kinesis

Rock Climbing

Rock & Ice

Rocks & Minerals

Gem Guides Book Company

Romance

Aegina Press, *Affaire de Coeur, Amelia Press,* American Literary Press, *Atlanta Singles,* Avery Publishing Group, Black Forest Press, Bryant & Dillon Publishers, The Conservatory of American Letters, *Cosmopolitan, Dogwood Tales,* Dorchester Publishing Company, Eternity Press, *Gothic Journal,* Great Quotations Publishing, *Happy Times Monthly,* Harlequin Historicals, *INK Literary Review,* LionHearted Publishing, Love Inspired, Mayhaven Publishing, *Modern Romances,* New Victoria Publishers, *On the Scene, Oracle Story & Letters, Playgirl,* PREP Publishing, *!Radiance, Rising Star Publishers,* Rising Tide Press, Silhouette Books, Silhouette Desire, Silhouette Intimate Moments, Silhouette Romance, Silhouette Special Edition, Silhouette Yours Truly, Timson Edwards Publishing, *True Love, True Romance,* University Editions

Rotary News

Rotarian

Rugby Football

Rugby

Rural America

Acorn, Alabama Living, Amelia Press, The American Cottage Gardener, Back Home in Kentucky, The Conservatory of American Letters, *Country America, Country Woman,* David R. Godine, *Elks,* Falcon Publishing, The Globe Pequot Press, *GRIT, Heartland USA, Home Times,* Kroshka Books, *Lutheran Digest,* Lyons & Burford Publishers, Mayhaven Publishing, *Montana Catholic, My Legacy, North Dakota Horizons, Oatmeal & Poetry, Over the Back Fence, Pennsylvania Heritage,* Quixote Press, *Rosebud, Rural Heritage, Sandlapper,* Timson Edwards Publishing, *True Romance,* University of Nebraska Press, *Yesterday's Magazette*

-S-

Sailing

Sailing World

Sales

American Salesman

Satire

Car & Driver, Office Number One, Rockford Review, Spy

Sawmills

Southern Lumberman

Scholarly

Frontiers, McFarland & Company, University Press of Mississippi

Scholarly & Reference

McFarland & Company

Science

Ad Astra, Analog Science Fiction and Fact, Annals of Improbable Research, Archaeology, ATL Press, *Boys' Life, Bugle, California Wild*, Century Press, *Circle, Dagger of the Mind, Dinosaurus, E, Elks, Environment, Eye*, Faber & Faber, *Futurific, Harper's Magazine, High Technology Careers, Home Times*, Howell's House, Kroshka Books, Lehigh University Press, *Magical Blend, Men's Fitness, Mercury*, Milkweed Editions, *National Enquirer, Natural History, Odyssey, PanGaia, Planetary Connections, Playboy*, Plenum Publishing, *Popular Electronics, Popular Mechanics, Popular Science, Psychology Today, Ranger Rick, Reptile & Amphibian, SciTech Magazine, Skeptical Inquirer, Smithsonian Magazine*, University of Nevada Press, *WE, Weatherwise*

Science Fiction

Absolute Magnitude, Acorn, Aegina Press, *Amelia Press*, American Literary Press, *Analog Science Fiction and Fact, Asimov's Science Fiction*, Baen Books, Black Forest Press, *Boys' Life*, Century Press, *Circle*, The Conservatory of American Letters, *Dagger of the Mind*, Eternity Press, *Fractal, Hadrosaur Tales*, Kroshka Books, *Magazine of Fantasy & Science Fiction*, Mayhaven Publishing, *Medusa's Hairdo, Millennium Science Fiction & Fantasy, My Legacy, New Millennium Writings, Nocturnal Ecstasy, Outside: Speculative and Dark Fiction, Pacific Coast Journal, PanGaia, Ranger Rick*, Rising Tide Press, *Riverside Quarterly, Rosebud, Scavenger's Newsletter, Sci Fi Invasion!, Snake Nation Review, tomorrow SPECULATIVE FICTION*, University Editions, Warner Books

Science Fiction/Fantasy, erotic

Circlet Press

Sciences, Educational

Adolescence

Sciences, Social

Adolescence, Texas A&M University Press

Seamanship

WoodenBoat

Security & Loss Prevention

Abbott, Langer & Associates

Self Employment

Success Connection

Self-help

Angels on Earth, Beyond Words Publishing, *Challenges, Cosmopolitan*, Quill Driver Books/Word Dancer Press, *Essence*, Hay House, *Health, Hope*, Hunter House Publishers, Impact Publishers, *Ladies' Home Journal*, Markowski International Publishers, *Men's Fitness*, Metamorphous Press, *Modern Bride, National Enquirer, Natural Health, New Woman*, Prima Publishing, Quill Driver Books/Word Dancer Press, Woman in the Moon Publications, *Woman's Day*

Self Reliance

American Survival Guide

Selling/Marketing

Spare Time

Senior Citizens

Alive!, Amelia Press, American Correctional Association, *American Fitness*, Century Press, *Continuum, Creative With Words Publications, Crone Chronicles, DogGone*, Fairview Press, *Gold and Treasure Hunter, Good Times*, Great Quotations Publishing, *GRIT, Happy Times Monthly, Highways, Home Times, It's Your Choice*, Johnston Associates International, Judson Press, *Liguorian, Lutheran Digest, Mature Years*, Mayhaven Publishing, *Modern Maturity, My Legacy*, Pilot Books, Quill Driver Books/Word Dancer Press, *RV West, Senior Living, Senior World Newsmagazine, WE, Western RV News, Yesterday's Magazette*

Sermons

Attain

Sexuality

Amelia Press, Atlanta Singles, Barricade Books, *Birth Gazette*, Black Iron Cookin' Company, Companion Press, *Complete Woman, Cosmopolitan, Crone Chronicles*, Fairview Press, *Fitness, Girlfriends*, Hearts 'n Tummies Cookbook Company, Hunter House Publishers, *INsider, It's Your Choice*, Jason Aronson, *Ladies' Home Journal, Libido*, Lifetime Books, *Mademoiselle, Men's Fitness*, Metamorphous Press, *Mom Guess What Newspaper, National Enquirer, Natural Living Today, Nocturnal Ecstasy, Options, PanGaia, Penthouse, Playboy, Playgirl, Prime Health & Fitness*, Publishers Associates, Quixote Press, *Radiance, Redbook, Response, Snake Nation Review*, Temple University Press, *Texas Connection, Tikkun, WE, Whole Life Times*

Shelter/Homes

Log Home Living

Shooting

American Rifleman, Guns & Ammo

Short Stories

Acorn, Aegina Press, *AIM, Alfred Hitchcock Mystery Magazine, Alive!, Amelia Press*, American Literary Press, *Arkansas Review, Art Times, Babybug, Baltimore Review, Belletrist Review*, BkMk Press, Black Forest Press, *Bleach, Boston Review, Boys' Life*, Brookline Books, *Buffalo Spree, Bugle, Café Eighties*, Calyx Books, *Calyx Journal, Carolina Quarterly, Cat Fancy*, Century Press, *Chattahoochee Review, Chelsea*, Chicago Review Press, *Cimarron Review, Circle*, Circlet Press, *Clockwatch Review*, The Conservatory of American Letters, *Cream City Review, Creative With Words Publications, Cricket, Curriculum Vitae, CutBank*, David R. Godine, *Dogwood Tales, Downstate Story, Eclectic Rainbows, 1812, Ellery Queen's Mystery Magazine*, Eternity Press, *Fan, Farmer's Market, Flying Horse, Fourteen Hills, Fractal, Glimmer Train Stories, Good Housekeeping, Happy Times Monthly*, Herbelin Publishing, *Higginsville Reader, Home Times, House, Home & Garden, Hurricane Alice, Iconoclast, INK Literary Review, Iris, It's Your Choice*, John Daniel & Company, *Kenyon Review, Kinesis, Ladybug*, Latin American Literary Review Press, *Libido, Light, Literary Review*, Lumen Editions, *Lynx Eye, MacGuffin*, Mage Publishers, *Mail Call Journal, Manoa, Maverick Press*, Mayhaven Publishing, Meadowbrook Press, *MEDIPHORS, Medusa's Hairdo*, Mid-List Press, *minnesota review, My Legacy, Nebraska Review, New Letters, New Millennium Writings, new renaissance*, Nightshade Press, *North American Review, Northeast Corridor, Oatmeal & Poetry, Obsidian II, Office Number One, Ohio Writer, On the Scene, Oracle Story & Letters*, Outrider Press, *Paddler,* Palace Corbie, *PanGaia, Pangolin Papers, Papyrus, Passages North, Pearl, Playgirl, Potato Eyes Literary Arts Journal, Potluck Children's Literary, Potomac Review, Potpourri, Power and Light, Press, Quarterly West, R-A-D-A-R, Radiance, Rhino, Rising Star Publishers, RiverSedge, River Styx, Rosebud, Seek, Sensual Aspirations, Skylark, Sleuthhound memorandum, Slipstream, Small Press Creative Explosion, Southern Humanities Review, Southern Review, Special Collections*, St. Anthony Messenger, *Story, Sun, Sycamore Review, Thema, The Threepenny Review*, Timson Edwards Publishing, *True Romance*, University Editions, *Weems Concepts, Whetstone, Whispering Willow Mysteries*, White Pine Press, *William and Mary Review, Wolf Head Quarterly, WormWood Review, Writer's Gazette, ZYZZYVA*

Singles

On the Scene

Site and Facility Planning

Area Development

Skin Care

Skin

Small Business

Aegis Publishing Group, Bloomberg Press

Small Business, operating

Business97, Group IV Communications

Small Business, finance

Bloomberg Press

Society

Amelia Press, American Legion, Angels on Earth, Atlanta

Singles, Attain, Black Forest Press, Branden Publishing Company, *Centennial Review, Christian Living*, Cross Cultural Publications, *Eye*, Fairview Press, *Futurific, Glamour, Gray Areas, Harper's Magazine, Illinois Entertainer, INsider, It's Your Choice, Jam Rag*, Kroshka Books, Kumarian Press, *Ladies' Home Journal*, Lehigh University Press, *Penthouse*, Plenum Publishing, *Radiance, Reader's Digest, Redbook, Response, Smithsonian Magazine, Thoughts for All Seasons, Tikkun*, Timson Edwards Publishing

Sociology

American Correctional Association

Software

Byte, Wired, X-Ray

Songs

Fiesta City Publishers

Sovereignty, American

American Survival Guide

Space

Ad Astra

Special Interest, German

German Life

Spiritual

Alive!, Attain, Baker Book House Company, Beyond Words Publishing, Black Forest Press, Blue Water Publishing, *Challenges, Christian Living, Christian New Age Quarterly*, Christian Publications, *Chrysalis Reader, Common Boundary*, Commune-A-Key Publishing, *Creation Spirituality Network, Crone Chronicles*, Cross Cultural Publications, Crossing Press, *Discipleship Journal, Eclectic Rainbows, Evolving Woman, FATE, First Things*, Great Quotations Publishing, Harvest House Publishers, Hay House, Health Communications, *Home Times*, Humanics Publishing Group, *Hunter House Publishers*, In Print Publishing, *It's Your Choice, Journal of Christian Nursing*, Judson Press, Kroshka Books, Legacy Press, *Light of Consciousness, Liguorian*, Kali Press, Llewellyn Publications, *Lutheran Digest, Mademoiselle, Magical Blend, Mature Years, Message, My Legacy, Natural Health, New Millennium Writings, New Times, Nocturnal Ecstasy*, NTC/Contemporary Publishing, *PanGaia, Parabola, Planetary Connections*, PREP Publishing, *Radiance, SageWoman*, Samuel Weiser, *Science of Mind*, St. Bede's Publications, *Tikkun*, Unity Books, *Virtue, WE, Whole Life Times, Wholeness, The Yoga Journal, Youth Update*, Zondervan Publishing House

Spirituality

Innisfree Press, Jewish Lights Publishing

Sports

Adventure Journal, Amelia Press, American Fitness, American Hunter, American Kennel Club Gazette, American Literary Press, *Attain, Balloon Life, Bicycling*, Black Forest Press, Black Iron Cookin' Company, Bonus Books, *Bowling, Boys' Life*, Branden Publishing Company, Brassey's, *Bugle, California Explorer, Canoe & Kayak, Car & Driver*, Century Press, The Conservatory of American Letters, *Crusader, Elks,*

Fan, Fitness, Girls' Life, The Globe Pequot Press, *Golf Digest, Golfer, Golf Journal, Guns & Ammo, Heartland USA, Hockey Player, Home Times, Inside Texas Running, INsider, Inside Sports, International Sports Journal, Journal of Asian Martial Arts,* !Kodansha America, Kroshka Books, Lyons & Burford Publishers, *Marlin,* Masters Press, McBooks Press, McFarland & Company, *Men's Health, Men's Journal,* Mustang Publishing Company, *National Geographic Traveler, New Choices, Northeast Equine Journal,* NTC/Contemporary Publishing, *Outdoor Life, Paddler,* Pelican Publishing Company, *Penthouse, Petersen's Bowhunting, Playboy,* Prima Publishing, *Radiance, Recreation News, Rock & Ice, Rugby, Runner's World,* Rutledge Hill Press, *Sailing Magazine, Sailing World, Sandlapper, SEA, Sea Kayaker, Senior Living, Shape Magazine, Ski Tripper, Skiing, Snow Country, Snowshoer, Sports Afield, Sports Illustrated for Kids, Sun Valley, Swim, Swimming World, T'ai !Chi,* Temple University Press, University of Nebraska Press, *WE, Whole Life Times, Women's Sports & Fitness,* World Leisure Corporation

Sports Officiating

Referee

Stamp Collecting

Linn's Stamp News

State Parks

Texas Parks & Wildlife

Student Service

Circle K

Studies, Family

Adolescence

Success

Markowski International Publishers

Survival

American Survival Guide

Sustainable Building

Joiners' Quarterly

Swimming

Swim, Swimming World

-T-

Taxes

New Choices, Spare Time

Technology

Ad Astra, ATL Press, *Bicycling, Boys' Life, Bugle, Byte, Career Focus, Careers & the disABLED, Centennial Review, Communications Publishing Group, Compressed Air, Electronic Servicing & Technology, Equal Opportunity Publications, Eye, FBI Law Enforcement Bulletin, Fresh Cut, Futurific, Girls' Life, Heartland USA, High Technology Careers, IIE Solutions, Illinois Entertainer, Industrial Management, INsider, Joiners' Quarterly, Journal of Information Eth-*

ics, Kroshka Books, Lehigh University Press, *Magical Blend, Minority Engineer, PC World, Planetary Connections, Playboy,* Plenum Publishing, *Popular Mechanics, Popular Science, Presentations, Progressive Engineer,* Prompt Publications, *SciTech Magazine, Self Employed Professional, Smithsonian Magazine, WD-Workforce Diversity, Whole Life Times, Wired, Woman Engineer*

Teen

Atheneum Books for Young Readers, *Attain,* Avon, Beyond Words Publishing, Branden Publishing Company, *Creative With Words Publications, DECA Dimensions,* Fairview Press, *First Opportunity, Florida Leader for High School Students, Happy Times Monthly, Home Times,* Hunter House Publishers, *Insight, It's Your Choice,* Mayhaven Publishing, Minstrel Books, *New Moon, Pulp, Oracle Story & Letters,* Oxendine Publishing, *Parent.TEEN,* Pocket Books, *Politically Correct, Potluck Children's Literary, Power and Light, Rising Star Publishers, Straight, Swimming World, With, Youth Update*

Telecommunications

Aegis Publishing Group, *Popular Mechanics*

Television/Radio

Amelia Press, Beyond Words Publishing, *Eye, Film Quarterly, Futurific, Home Times, Illinois Entertainer, Mademoiselle,* McFarland & Company, *new renaissance,* Players Press, *Playgirl,* Prompt Publications, *Radiance, Radio World, Real People, Sci Fi Invasion!, Senior, Spectacle,* Temple University Press, *Times News Service*

Texas Restaurants

Food & Service

Textbooks

Barron's Educational Series, Baywood Publishing Company, Black Forest Press, Bonus Books, Branden Publishing Company, Calyx Books, *Calyx Journal,* The Conservatory of American Letters, ETC Publications, Feminist Press, ICS Press, Intercultural Press, Kroshka Books, *Northwoods Journal, Oracle Story & Letters,* Orchises Press, Paradigm Publications, Pelican Publishing Company, Players Press, *Rising Star Publishers,* University Press of Mississippi, Weidner & Sons Publishing

Textbooks, college

Ardsley House Publishers

Theatre

Allworth Press, *Amelia Press,* Anchorage Press, *Art Times,* Branden Publishing Company, Bucknell University Press, *Centennial Review,* Focal Press, Heinemann, *Illinois Entertainer, INK Literary Review, INsider,* Ivan R. Dee, Lehigh University Press, McFarland & Company, *new renaissance, North American Review, Obsidian II,* Piccadilly Books, Players Press, *Radiance, Rosebud, Senior, Stage Directions,* Temple University Press, University Press of Mississippi, *WE*

Theology

Jewish Lights Publishing, Kregel Publications

Therapy, marital

Family Therapy

Timber Framing

Joiners' Quarterly

Time Management

Success Connection

Timeshare Resorts

Vacation Industry Review

Tourist Guide

Gibbons-Humms Guide to the Florida Keys & Key West

Toy Collecting

Toy Shop

Translations

Chelsea, Mid-American Review

Travel

Above the Bridge, Ad Astra, Adventure Journal, Alive!, Aloha, Amelia Press, American Fitness, ASU Travel Guide, Atlanta Singles, Avenues, Back Home in Kentucky, Better Homes and Gardens, Berkshire House Publishers, *Bicycling, Big World, Bleach, BlueRidge Country,* Brookline Books, Bucknell University Press, *California Explorer, Camperways, Carefree Enterprise,* Charles River Press, Chicago Review Press, Clover Park Press, *Coast to Coast, Colonial Homes, Consumers Digest, Cooking Light, Cosmopolitan, Country America, Country Living, Creative With Words Publications, Curriculum Vitae,* The Denali Press, *DogGone, Eclectic Rainbows, Educated Traveler, Endless Vacation,* Faber & Faber, Falcon Publishing, *Florida Wildlife,* Gem Guides Book Company, *Girls' Life, Glamour,* The Globe Pequot Press, *Gold and Treasure Hunter, Golfer, HeartLand Boating, Highways, Historic Traveler, Home Times, House, Home & Garden, INsider, International Railway Traveler,* Jewish Lights Publishing, Johnston Associates International, *Ladies' Home Journal,* Lumen Editions, *Martha Stewart Living, Mature Years, Men's Health, Men's Journal, Mid-Atlantic Country, Midwest Motorist, MidWest Streams & Trails, Modern Bride, Modern Maturity, Mountain Living,* Mustang Publishing Company, *National Geographic Traveler, Naturally, NEBRASKAland, Nevada, New Choices, New Home Life, New Mexico, New Millennium Writings, Newsday, North American Review, North Dakota Horizons, Northwest Regional,* NTC/Contemporary Publishing, *Oklahoma Today, Oracle Story & Letters, Out & About, Outdoor Life, Over the Back Fence, Pacific Currents, Paddler,* Pelican Publishing Company, Pilot Books, *Potpourri, Power & Motoryacht, Prime Health & Fitness, Rail Classics, Recreation News, Rising Star Publishers,* Rockbridge Publishing Company, *Russian Life,* Rutledge Hill Press, *RV West, Sandlapper, SEA, Senior, Shape Magazine, Sierra, Ski Tripper, Sleuthhound memorandum, Smithsonian Magazine, Southern Living, Specialty Travel Index, Spectacle, Sunset, Sunshine,* Ten Speed Press, *Texas Parks & Wildlife, Times News Service, Trailer Boats, Transitions Abroad, Travel News, Travelers Guide for Aspen, Snowmass, and the Roaring Fork Valley, True West, Vacation Industry Review, Via,* Voyageur Press, *WE, Western Publications,* White-Boucke Publishing, *Whole Life Times, Wisconsin Trails, Woman's Day, Women's Sports & Fitness, Working Mother, Woodall Publications, Woodall's California RV Traveler, Woodall's Camporama, Woodall's Carolina RV Traveler, Woodall's Discover RVing, Woodall's Northeast Outdoors, Woodall's RV Traveler, Woodall's Southern RV,* World Leisure Corporation, *Yankee,*

The Yoga Journal, Your Money

Travel Agents

Travel News

Travel Guidebooks

John Muir Publications

Travel, rail

International Railway Traveler

Travel, specialty

Specialty Travel Index

Treasure Hunting

Lost Treasure

True Crime

Addicus Books, Branden Publishing Company, Century Press, *It's Your Choice,* Mayhaven Publishing, *Oracle Story & Letters,* Plenum Publishing, Quill Driver Books/Word Dancer Press, *Rising Star Publishers, Sleuthhound memorandum,* University of North Texas Press

-U-

UFO Experiences/Research

Blue Water Publishing, *National Enquirer, Planetary Connections*

Underground

Nocturnal Ecstasy

Urban Decay

Staplegun Press

-V-

Vampires

Nocturnal Ecstasy

Vegetarian

McBooks Press

Veterinary

Anvil

Violence Prevention

Hunter House Publishers

-W-

Warehousing

IIE Solutions

Weaponry

Paladin Press